Date Due

BRODART, CO. Cat. No. 23-233-003 Printed in U.S.A.

The Abstract Primer Of Thoroughbred Racing

Separating Myth From Fact to Identify the Genuine Gems & Dandies 1946-2003

Presented to

____

Date

____

By

____

The Abstract Primer Of Thoroughbred Racing

Separating Myth From Fact to Identify the Genuine Gems & Dandies 1946-2003

The Abstract Primer Of Thoroughbred Racing

Separating Myth From Fact to Identify the Genuine Gems & Dandies 1946-2003

By Richard Sowers

OLD SPORT PUBLISHING COMPANY

Library of Congress Catalog Card Number: 2004103815

ISBN: 0-975-4392-0-0

Sowers, Richard, 1950 -
The abstract primer of thoroughbred racing: separating myth from fact to identify the genuine gems & dandies 1946-2003 / by Richard Sowers.
1. Horse racing—United States—History 2. Horse racing—United States—Records 3. Sports—United States—History 4. Sports—United States—Reference 5. Sports—United States—Records I. Title

Book and cover design: Galerie Graphics

Printed in the United States of America

10 9 8 7 6 5 4 3 2 1

OLD SPORT PUBLISHING COMPANY
P. O. Box 2757
Stockbridge, Ga. 30281
770-914-2237
770-914-9261 (fax)
www.oldsportpublishing.com

Photo Credits

COVER PHOTOS:

Front, clockwise from top left: Citation with Eddie Arcaro aboard, *courtesy of Bob Coglianese Photo's, Inc.;* Secretariat, *courtesy of Bob Coglianese Photo's, Inc.;* Bill Winfrey (left) and Alfred G. Vanderbilt, *courtesy of Santa Anita Park;* Forego, *courtesy of Galerie Graphics;* Elle Seule and her foal, Ashraakat, *courtesy of Shadwell Farm;* Shadwell Farm winter wonderland, *courtesy of Shadwell Farm;* 1990 Kentucky Derby, *courtesy of Churchill Downs;* Kent Desormeaux wins the 2000 Kentucky Derby aboard Fusaichi Pegasus, *Four Footed Fotos, Inc., courtesy of Churchill Downs;* Oaklawn Park racing action, *courtesy of Oaklawn Park;* (center) Pat Day celebrates his victory in the 1998 Breeders' Cup Classic on Awesome Again, *Michael J. Marten photo courtesy of the National Thoroughbred Racing Association.* **Front Flap Background:** Lady's Secret, ridden by Pat Day, *courtesy of Santa Anita Park.* **Back Flap Background:** Cigar, with Jerry Bailey aboard, *courtesy of Gulfstream Park.* **End Pages Photo:** *Courtesy of Oaklawn Park.*

OPENING PHOTOS:

Page 3: *Photo courtesy of Oaklawn Park*
Action from a race at Oaklawn Park typifies the beauty of thoroughbred racing.

Page 4: *Photo courtesy of Oaklawn Park*
Few horsemen or horseplayers fail to get goose bumps when a tight pack of horses, as in this race at Oaklawn Park, turn for home.

Pages 6 & 7: *Bill Straus photo courtesy of Keeneland Association*
A tightly bunched field competes on the turf at beautiful Keeneland Race Course.

Page 10 (Top): *Photo courtesy of Shadwell Farm*
While Desirable munches on Kentucky blue grass at Shadwell Farm, her foal poses for the camera.

Page 10 (Bottom): *Photo courtesy of Oaklawn Park*
One of the most exciting moments in sports: The starting gate opens, and a field is sent on its way.

Page 13 (Top): *Bill Straus photo courtesy of Keeneland Association*
Prospective buyers inspect a thoroughbred in Keeneland's well-manicured barn area during one of the track's many sales.

Page 13 (Bottom): *Kinetic Corporation photo courtesy of Churchill Downs*
Sunday Silence, with Pat Valenzuela in the saddle, reached the wire first in America's favorite horse race, the Kentucky Derby, in 1989.

Page 14: *Equi-Photo, Inc. courtesy of Gulfstream Park*
A huge crowd surrounds the palm-lined paddock and walking ring before a race at

ELAND

FERDINAND

Dedication

This book is dedicated to the memory of Ferdinand (pictured winning the 1986 Kentucky Derby under Bill Shoemaker) and Exceller—and all departed friends and heroes of the animal kingdom who have enriched our lives—and the hope that no future great is a victim of the same cruel fate.

The Abstract Primer Of Thoroughbred Racing

Separating Myth From Fact to Identify the Genuine Gems & Dandies 1946-2003

Table of Contents

10
CHURCHILL DOWNS

SUNDAY, MARCH 16
IS THE FINAL DAY AT
GULFSTREAM PARK ...
RACE 11

PREFACE

My fascination with thoroughbred racing initially was manifested while watching a humbly bred but highly regarded colt lag far behind in a field of 15 throughout most of the Kentucky Derby.

The pace—23 4/5 seconds for the first quarter-mile, 47 3/5 seconds for the half-mile, and 1:11 2/5 for six furlongs—set by a colt named Globemaster wasn't particularly taxing. Because my knowledge of the sport at that point virtually was limited to the name of the colt who trailed by some 17 lengths, all I knew with a half-mile remaining was that he was a hopelessly beaten 11th. Little did I realize that those relatively slow fractions made that colt's improbable stretch run, when he rallied from sixth place—more than seven lengths in arrears with a quarter-mile remaining—to post a three-quarter-length victory even more remarkable.

That may or may not have been the first horse race I ever saw, but it was decidedly the first I cared about.

Despite the limitations presented by the antiquated black-and-white Zenith via which I viewed the 1961 Kentucky Derby, Carry Back's stunning triumph made an indelible impression: I fell in love not only with Carry Back, but with thoroughbred racing.

Almost from the moment Carry Back strolled proudly into the winner's circle with Johnny Sellers on his back, I began trying to learn everything I could about this colorful and exciting sport—a daunting task for a youngster on a very modest allowance who grew up in states that still don't have parimutuel wagering.

Two decades later, when I landed a dream job for anyone who loves thoroughbred racing—covering the sport for *The Courier-Journal* in Louisville, home of the Kentucky Derby—I realized that reading every word I could get my hands on about thoroughbred racing for 20 years still left me considerably lacking in the knowledge I needed and craved about the sport. Such information, it should be noted, was readily available about most other sports for which I shared a similar passion.

Because reading—and understanding—the fine print in the *Daily Racing Form* often seems like hieroglyphics to the novice, it's easy enough to find books and seminars that explain handicapping, or rating, the competitors in a given race.

What's far more difficult to find is the necessary information to determine how Carry Back, Sellers—or any other human or equine participant in thoroughbred racing—ranks against the greats of the past or present. It's easy enough to learn that Carry Back, for example, won 21 times and finished in the money in 43 of his 62 starts or that Susan's Girl won 29 of her 63 starts and finished in the money on 25 other occasions.

Because of the irrefutable variations in the classes of races in which each competed, however, that information doesn't begin to reveal whether Carry Back and Susan's Girl established their records and reputations against inferior competition or beat the very best opponents the sport had to offer.

That is the primary mission of this book—to define and distinguish what our equine and human heroes accomplished only when they competed at the sport's highest levels.

Many armchair analysts contend that it's pointless to compare legendary athletes from different eras. Wilt Chamberlain never played against Michael Jordan, nor Johnny Unitas against Brett Favre, nor Ben Hogan against Tiger Woods, nor Walter Johnson against Roger Clemens. So no one actually knows—or ever will—who truly was the greatest in any particular sport.

Yet it's virtually impossible to visit a grandstand, tavern, or in-laws' family room without overhearing—or participating in—such debates, whether it's Joe Louis vs. Muhammad Ali or Secretariat vs. Citation.

It's easy enough to argue that Citation won 32 of 45 races, Secretariat 16 of 21, and that each finished out of the money only once. But it's very difficult to separate top-of-the-line achievements for the ages from lesser accomplishments when most thoroughbred rankings and statistics include the results of more than 60,000 races held annually in North America.

In the case of Secretariat and Citation, fabled Triple Crown winners who were born 25 years apart—or for any such argument about thoroughbred racing—that task is even more arduous.

If, for example, information about major-league baseball was presented in the same manner in which that about thoroughbred racing normally is, Pete Rose's record for career hits would be 4,683 instead of 4,256, because the base hits he collected in the minor leagues certainly would be included. And, if baseball followed thoroughbred racing's practice of including all races in its statistical data without separating major events from minor ones, we'd all be aware that Rose collected 485 more hits than Hank Aaron. That Aaron launched 595 more home runs than Rose, however, quite probably would be overlooked.

Further muddying thoroughbred racing's conventional statistics is that many include the deeds of horses, jockeys, trainers, sires, etc., in, among other locales, England, Ireland, France, Germany, Italy, and Dubai—but not Japan, Hong Kong, or South America—in addition to North America. Once again, if baseball followed a similar principal, Sadaharu Oh, whose 868 home runs all came across the Pacific, would be recognized as major-league baseball's career leader in home runs instead of Aaron.

Because of these notable inconsistencies, myth often substitutes for fact in thoroughbred racing lore, both for newcomers and hardboots who have been around the sport since Seabiscuit.

"I think we have a tendency to throw around the word 'great' a little too prematurely and sometimes create paper All-Americas," said noted trainer Wayne Lukas, one of thoroughbred racing's most astute observers.

There is obviously some value for both horsemen and horseplayers to have the often unwieldy totals from more than 60,000 races in North America and perhaps that many more from selected locales around the world lumped together.

But this book enlightens both newcomers to thoroughbred racing and seasoned horsemen and horseplayers by arming them with data that is easier to understand and far more meaningful in separating myth from fact. By identifying and cataloguing the achievements of race horses, jockeys, trainers, owners, stallions, dams, broodmare sires, and sire lines *only in major North American races from 1946-2003,* this book gives aficionados and novices alike who wish to engage in the Secretariat vs. Citation debate—or any other involving thoroughbred racing since World War II—more *significant* ammunition than ever before to support an argument, or ample reason to throw in the towel.

Further, winning those top-of-the-line, prestigious events for the ages long has been the ultimate dream of virtually all of thoroughbred racing's human participants.

"I love to win," jockey Pat Day said long before he reached the Hall of Fame. "Every winner is a good winner, but some are better than others—like the Lady's Secret races. Any time you win a major fixture, it's a thrill."

While winning a stakes race, the most noteworthy of thoroughbred racing's four basic classifications of events, long has been considered a superior achievement for both human and equine participants, only a minute portion of the more than 2,500 of those run each year in North America truly define greatness for the ages. For the purposes of this book, major races are defined as the 110 most prestigious in any calendar year, and both an explanation of how those races were selected and a complete listing of those events appear in the opening chapter. Although there is nothing necessarily magical about the number 110, careful study of the conditions and results of hundreds of stakes races each year from 1946-2003 revealed 110 to be the nearest round number to separate the events that should define truly historic achievements from those that are merely noteworthy accomplishments.

Benoit & Associates, Inc., photo courtesy of Del Mar Thoroughbred Club

An overflow crowd watched from the Del Mar infield as Dare and Go, with Alex Solis in the saddle, thundered home three-and-one-half lengths in front of Cigar in the $1 million Pacific Classic in 1996, a defeat that ended Cigar's 16-race winning streak.

For example, Citation and Cigar were widely acclaimed for capturing a modern "record" 16 consecutive races—unquestionably a notable feat by two of history's greatest thoroughbreds.

When the New York Yankees' Joe DiMaggio hit safely in 56 straight games in 1941, however, all 56 games were against *major-league* competition. Citation and Cigar both counted 10 major races in their 16-race streaks, and when that "record" was tied by a Louisiana-bred filly, Hallowed Dreams, none of her races were against anything remotely resembling major competition. For the record, the streaks of Cigar and Citation trail only the 12 consecutive major races, as defined by this book, won by Buckpasser as the longest such strings since World War II. If baseball's records were compiled in the same manner as thoroughbred racing's, Rose would have been advised to leave the Cincinnati Reds and visit the Cape Cod Summer League to bat against amateur pitchers for several weeks in 1978 instead of allowing the Atlanta Braves to end his chase of DiMaggio's milestone at 44 games. And Ted Williams would not be acclaimed as the last to hit .400: Hundreds of high school players do it every year.

This book further recognizes that greatness isn't necessarily defined by wealth and proposes that it is a far truer measure of the ability of both equine and human stars to win eight major races worth $500,000 each in a calendar year than one $4 million event, although the monetary value would be the same.

As Lukas said, "The bottom line in racing is winning consistently. Do you get the batting title by hitting one home run in the World Series or for hitting all season?"

Therefore, although each chapter lists the achievements of participants in the three recognized American classics—the Kentucky Derby, Preakness Stakes, and Belmont Stakes—as well as the Breeders' Cup races, it rates each major race equally in defining the accomplishments of both human and equine participants both for simplicity and to reward consistent excellence instead of "one home run in the World Series."

And, in comparing the achievements of both human and equine stars in thoroughbred racing from different eras, it is foolish to use money as a criteria. For example, the 111 most prestigious races in 1946 (the Beldame Handicap was split into two divisions) had total purses of $4,528,500. The purse for the 2003 Breeders' Cup Classic/Powered by Dodge *alone* was $4 million.

So while it's easy to assume that a race such as the Santa Anita Handicap, for instance, is more prestigious than the Santa Monica Handicap, another major event at Santa Anita, rating all major races equally, as this book does, prevents such distortions as the one that has occurred in recent years on the list of leading sires: Five times in the eight-year period from 1994-2001, the sire of the Breeders' Cup Classic winner led the money list.

Further distorting an accurate picture of thoroughbred racing in North America is a longtime rule that allowed horses who made at least one start in North America to be listed among the earnings leaders. A filly could earn $3 million in France, for example, then finish last in a U.S. race, yet suddenly appear atop the list of America's earnings leaders. Worse yet is the case of Dubai Millennium, who won the 2000 Dubai World Cup, now the world's richest race with a purse of $6 million, and spent most of the season atop the list of North American money winners. Dubai Millennium, who never ran on this continent, was no doubt a superior race horse, but Dubai is on the Persian Gulf and adjacent to Saudi Arabia, not Santa Anita.

And, although horses and horsemen based outside North America, particularly from Europe, have earned many notable victories in the United States and Canada, in painting a true picture of major North American racing since World War II, it would be as pointless to include the achievements of participants in events staged outside this continent as it would be to add Woods's victories in Europe or Asia to his Professional Golfers' Association Tour total or to recognize Oh, instead of Aaron, as major-league baseball's all-time home-run king.

So what's abstract about this book is simply that it presents the achievements of both human and equine participants based solely on their performances in major North American races. By separating the wheat from the chaff to emphasize quality rather than sometimes misleading quantities, the information presented in this book is easier for both novices and longtime observers of the sport to comprehend and use—and paints more meaningful portraits of the accomplishments of human and equine participants.

Even skeptics who don't wholeheartedly agree with this innovative method of judging thoroughbred racing achievements should find this book makes the task of differentiating between the ordinary and extraordinary infinitely easier than any other and serves as an invaluable reference tool.

When I wrote *The Complete Statistical History of Stock-Car Racing: Records, Streaks, Oddities, and Trivia,* which was published in 2000, it was intended to give fans of that sport the type of tangible data to support their arguments that fans of baseball, football, basketball, golf, and other sports have employed to debate the relative merits of Jordan vs. Chamberlain or Woods vs. Hogan in grandstands, taverns, and family rooms throughout America.

Richard Petty, stock-car racing's "King," said that aforementioned book "should be the bible for our sport."

Although it would be pretentious to make a similar claim about this book, I sincerely believe it provides the captivating information I for so long have craved—data that both longtime observers and newcomers to thoroughbred racing will find extraordinarily relevant and useful.

Further, I hope it will help build a following of avid fans, not merely ardent handicappers, among those who are being introduced to the sport, serve as an indispensable reference source, and offer fresh insight on the best and brightest human and equine achievements in the magnificent "Sport of Kings" since World War II.

Glossary of Terms and Definitions

Modern Era: This book covers the years 1946-2003 and frequently refers to that period as the "modern era," although, unlike such sports as baseball and stock-car racing, thoroughbred racing has no officially defined "modern era."

But there is no clearer demarcation line in separating the way things were from the way things are in thoroughbred racing than 1946. The two leading racing centers in North America during the entire "modern" era have been New York and Southern California. World War II shut down virtually all of California racing during 1942 and '43 and most of it in '44. While racing continued in the East, it was hampered by transportation problems that prevented many competitors from being able to travel to major races away from their home bases. Count Fleet's victory in the 1943 Kentucky Derby, for example, is widely known as the "Street Car Derby" because wartime restrictions prevented Churchill Downs from selling tickets to out-of-town fans. Then, from January 1, 1945, until May 9 of that year, thoroughbred racing was suspended in the United States at the request of the federal government. That effectively lopped many of the most important events of 1945 off the racing calendar and pushed others back. Hoop Jr.'s victory in the 1945 Kentucky Derby, for example, came on June 9.

The Kentucky Derby, America's most celebrated horse race, became firmly entrenched on the first Saturday in May in 1946—the inaugural year of the modern era—and many of the events that have come to define major-league thoroughbred racing in North America didn't exist until after World War II. Further, examining the records of the participants in major thoroughbred races since World War II clearly demonstrates that two changes often cited by longtime observers and participants as among the sport's most significant—frequent travel to major races by both human and equine participants to locations far from their home bases and year-round racing—have been quite common throughout the modern era.

Unofficial: The records and achievements defined in this book are, of course, unofficial. Essentially, however, until Equibase was formed less than 15 years ago, all thoroughbred racing records were unofficial, although the *Daily Racing Form* widely was considered the sport's ultimate authority. "There isn't anything that says the *Racing Form* is official," the late Keene Daingerfield, a Kentucky State Racing Commission steward and one of the most respected officials in the sport's history, said in the early '80s. "But because of (the absence of) anything better, historically we have relied on the *Racing Form* as official."

Clarifying the Totals: Defining 110 races as major for 58 years seemingly would result in a total of 6,380 races. Yet this book recognizes 6,461 major races during the modern era. That's because on 81 occasions—such as the 1946 Beldame Handicap—a major race was split into two divisions, including a record six times in 1972, because an extraordinarily large number of horses were entered. No major North American race has been split into two divisions since the 1991 Hollywood Derby, but the reason for inclusion of those that were split from 1946-91 is simple: If selecting any year's 110 most prestigious races before the campaign began, no one could have anticipated or predicted which, if any, would be split into more than one division. And it would be patently unfair to Louisiana Downs, for example, to remove the Super Derby from major status in 1991 to accommodate split divisions of the Hollywood Derby.

After a record 23 horses went postward in the 100th renewal of the Kentucky Derby in 1974, Churchill Downs limited the number of starters in subsequent Derbies to 20 to prevent the possible occurrence of two runnings of the Kentucky Derby on the same day. Likewise, the Breeders' Cup, which began in 1984, never has allowed more than 14 starters in order to prevent having to split its races into more than one division.

And, while there have been 6,461 major races during the modern era, this book credits 6,475 victories, 6,464 runner-up finishes, and 6,463 third-place showings. That's because those 6,461 major races have included 14 dead heats for first, 18 for second (including a triple dead heat), 26 for third, four two-horse fields, and walkovers in which Citation and Spectacular Bid struck such fear into the connections of their would-be opponents that no one chose to challenge them.

Win, Place, and Show: Because jockeys compete in considerably *more* major races than other human participants and because the careers of most race horses are so brief that they compete in considerably *fewer,* their feats are rated on the basis of victories, second-, and third-place finishes. Those of owners, trainers, stallions, etc., are rated only on victories in major races.

Conflicting Information: This may be the only reference book that will state clearly: It might include some mistakes. Because of conflicting information, such basic facts as the particular spelling of a horse's name, for example, may be listed in certain sources as Spend a Buck and in others as Spend A Buck. And, in many instances, the only people who could verify a particular fact died years ago. Further, the first names of some of the jockeys, trainers, and owners who have had significant accomplishments in major races may be lost to history. Despite those caveats, every effort has been made to make this the most accurate reference book about thoroughbred racing—and the most thorough volume of first names of jockeys, trainers, and owners.

Clarifying Terms: If this book credits John Doe with 40 wins as a trainer or jockey, for example, it is referring only to *major North American victories from 1946-2003* as defined by this book. No one is disputing that Bill Shoemaker, for instance, was aboard 8,833 winners during his career in the saddle. His victory total in this book is merely his number of modern major North American victories, and it would be redundant to repeat modern, major, and North American on each occasion.

Trainers of Record: While it's easy enough today to determine who trained the winner of a race, that hasn't always been the case. Because many trainers have entered horses in major races at more than one track on the same day, they obviously have had to trust an assistant or rival trainer to saddle one of those horses. Some—but not all—states listed the person who actually saddled the horse, rather than the trainer of record, as the winning trainer during varying portions of the modern era. In the cases in which those situations were able to be determined, the trainer of record, rather than the credited winning trainer, is listed as the winning trainer in this book.

Ownership Listings: Every attempt has been made to credit the correct owner or owners, in the case of partnerships, at the time any particular race was held as the winning owners. In many cases, particularly those of horses owned in partnership, horses have been owned by multiple partners, with not all of them necessarily listed as the winning owners. In other cases, people have become partners in horses who won major races without announcing their participation in ownership until long after races had been held—or in some cases, not at all. Every effort was made to credit the proper winning owners at the time that each race occurred, but a completely accurate listing is virtually impossible.

Disputed Parentage: In certain instances, a major winner's sire or dam's sire might have been in question because the dam was bred to different stallions in the same season. In each case, the first stallion listed, presumably the first cover, is used as the sire or dam's sire.

Identical Names: Seventeen horses—Blue Moon, Dispute, Don Rickles, Drama Critic, Festin, Grand Canyon, Include, Kamehameha, Red Cross, Roving Minstrel, Stephanotis, Tahitian King, True North, Vaudeville, Willa on the Move, Wistful, and Yonder—with in-the-money finishes in major races during the modern era share the exact same name with other horses who also posted top-three finishes in major races from 1946-2003. When those 34 horses are mentioned, the year the horse was born often is included in parenthesis beside the horse's name to avoid confusion. Thus, Don Rickles (1957), who finished third in the 1960 Travers Stakes, is not to be confused with Don Rickles (1981), who was second in both the 1983 Hopeful Stakes and the 1984 Tropical Park Derby. And neither is to be confused with the comedian for whom they were named.

Note Dates: In other cases, it will be helpful to note the dates of achievements of certain horses with the same name. Grand Slam, who was born in 1995, won two major races for two-year-olds in 1997, and sired two major winners in 2003, obviously isn't the same Grand Slam who was born in 1933 and sired Piet, winner of the 1947 Arlington Futurity and 1950 Whitney Stakes.

Correctly Labeling Certain Imports: Horses imported to North America who share the same name with one already registered by The Jockey Club generally have the roman numeral II added to their names. Nijinsky II, who in 1970 became the only horse since 1935 to win the English Triple Crown, was known as Nijinsky before he was imported to Kentucky's Claiborne Farm for an outstanding career at stud. There presumably was another Nijinsky already registered, but his achievements weren't worthy of inclusion in this book. Regardless, the roman numeral has been retained in all mentions of Nijinsky II's name. Similarly, Tiger was a prominent sire in the early part of the modern era. He was not the sire of Nor II, winner of the 1972 San Luis Rey Handicap, however. Nor II, who was bred in England, was sired by a Tiger who presumably wasn't imported to North America and therefore was not designated Tiger II. To avoid confusion, however, the latter is designated Tiger II in this book.

What No. 1 Seasons, Etc., Mean: Citations of No. 1 seasons, top-two seasons, top-25 seasons, etc., refer not to conventional listings for leaders for horses, jockeys, stallions, etc.—earnings or otherwise—but only as defined in the parameters of this book.

Standings—Not Rankings: Standings for any given category, such as the standings for trainers' victories from 1946-2003, are just that: standings, not ratings. For example, a National Football League team that has a 6-1 record seven games into a season would be listed in the standings ahead of a team that has a 5-2 record. Conversely, a college football team with a 5-2 record well may be *ranked* ahead of a team with a 6-1 record based on the *opinions* of voters about the accomplishments of the two teams. Although this book questions the results of the voting for numerous championships and other acclaim lavished on the participants in thoroughbred racing during the modern era, it does not unequivocally state that because a participant in a particular category finished ahead of another participant in the standings necessarily means that the former participant's particular achievements were greater. If a horse wins six prestigious events in a given year, for example, yet was denied a championship that was awarded to a rival who won five major races, further examination may reveal that the former's six prestigious victories came in events that possibly ranked between 80th and 110th and the latter's five triumphs came in races that possibly ranked among the top 40 in prestige—or included a victory or two in stakes that barely missed inclusion among the 110 most prestigious. So while the standings for victories—or in-the-money finishes for race horses and jockeys—in major races indeed may be the most important criteria for rating participants in thoroughbred racing, it is by no means the only one.

Major Races

Photo courtesy of Churchill Downs

There is no more famous—or breathtaking—view in thoroughbred racing than the cavalry charge around the first turn in the Kentucky Derby. With the fabled twin spires of Churchill Downs in the background, Houston led the field at that point in the 1989 Kentucky Derby. But the lasting fame that comes with a triumph in the Run for the Roses went to Sunday Silence (in fifth place in light cap on the rail). Easy Goer (in sixth place in dark silks on the outside) finished second to Sunday Silence in both the Derby and the Preakness, then reversed the order of finish in the Belmont Stakes.

I: Major Races

Class Distinctions

As Samuel Langhorne Clemens said, "There are lies, damn lies, and statistics."

In few sports is that more evident than in thoroughbred racing, thanks to an inherent flaw: Few, if any, sports consistently present attractions with a greater variation in class.

Thoroughbred racing has four basic categories of races:

• Maiden, for those who have never won a race;

• Claiming, in which every starter is for sale to any licensed owner or trainer at a designated price;

• Allowance, in which all starters are subject to strict conditions that may include such restrictions as no more than two triumphs at a mile or more since Halloween;

• Stakes, in which owners put up fees that range from modest to extraordinary to enter and/or have their horses actually start such races, which are enhanced by "added" money from the track.

Further complicating those categories are wide ranges from the top to the bottom of each and other restrictions that make them difficult to rate.

Horses who advance from the claiming ranks to win stakes races, such as John Henry or dual classic winner Charismatic, usually are heralded for their rags-to-riches achievements.

In many cases, such acclaim is justified. But the difference between the competitors in a $3,500 claimer for state-bred maidens at Podunk Downs and those racing for a $1 million tag at Santa Anita is at least as significant as it is among the participants in the NCAA basketball tournament's Final Four and half a dozen overweight, middle-aged businessmen visiting the local YMCA for a game of three-on-three during their lunch break.

While winning a stakes race—the highest of the four basic classifications—long has been considered a major achievement for horses and horsemen, even that status is far less than authoritative. For example, is the winner of a $30,000 stakes actually superior to that of an allowance race worth more than twice as much?

A typical nine-race Saturday card at a thoroughbred track may present a couple of maiden races, three claiming races, three allowance races, and a stakes race. If football did the same, there would be a couple of Pop Warner games, three high school, three college, and a National Football League game on the same field on the same day.

Yet thoroughbred racing lumps the statistics for all of those races, roughly 60,000 per year in North America, together for the purpose of ranking both human and equine participants. Joe Blow could lead all jockeys in victories, for example, simply by capturing nothing but low-level claiming races, or the Black Stallion could go down in history as a memorable sire because he produced 75 stakes winners—even if none of them won a major race, or even a second stakes race.

Determining Major Events

Seven criteria were used to select the 110 most prestigious races—those designated major—in any given year:

• Purse;

• Grading of the race by the American Graded Stakes Committee;

• When the race was held;

• Where the race was held;

• Tradition;

• Accomplishments of the entire field during the previous five runnings of a particular race;

• Other accomplishments of the winners in the previous five runnings of a particular race.

The most important criteria during most of the modern era was a race's purse. Owners and trainers with horses they believe capable of winning big-money races are going to enter those horses in events with lucrative purses. That was true before the modern era, and it was as true in 2003 as it was in 1946.

In recent years, the most important criteria has been the ratings of the American Graded Stakes Committee, founded in 1973 as the North American Graded Stakes Committee, which divides stakes races into four classifications. In order of importance, they are Grade I, Grade II, Grade III, and ungraded. Because the American Graded Stakes Committee didn't begin classifying races until 1973, that obviously was not a criteria from 1946-72, and that committee's ratings weren't nearly as important in 1973 as in 2003. The *Daily Racing Form,* for example, didn't bother to include the grading for stakes races in its charts until 1979, and it took years for the concept of graded stakes to be accepted widely by horsemen, horseplayers, and media.

Those gradings have gained considerable prestige in recent years, however, and they now often eclipse purse as a reason for horsemen to select particular races for their charges. The label "Grade I winner" or "graded stakes winner" often attaches such prestige that it outweighs money—at least in the short term. Grade I or graded stakes winners whom owners envision as future breeding stock—which includes all but geldings—indeed may earn their owners more money in the long run via higher stud fees and sale prices both for the animal itself and its offspring.

Although the input of the American Graded Stakes Committee has evolved from non-existent to the most important criteria in determining the 110 major races in a given year, a significant difference remains between this book's criteria for designation as a major race and those that are designated Grade I or graded stakes races. To make accurate comparisons of the achievements of both human and equine participants in 1946, 2003, and all years in between, the number of races defined as major should be the same each year. Further analysis revealed that to include a sampling of the significant tests in each division that more often than not had an effect on determining championships and legendary careers, the nearest round figure to use as a yearly measure of major status was 110 races. Again, that is not necessarily a magic number. But analysis of hundreds of races each year yielded the conclusion that simply including 100 events omitted too many significant races, and stretching the total to as many as 125 both allowed too many questionable events and somewhat diluted the achievements.

Further, both the number of races designated as Grade I and the total of graded stakes has fluctuated considerably since their inception in 1973. In 1973, there were 327 graded stakes races, including 62 Grade I events. By 2003, there were 487 graded stakes races, with 101 awarded Grade I status. Whether the quality of North American racing has improved to the point that, just 30 years after the inception of graded races, an additional 49 percent of events are worthy of that acclaim and an additional 63 percent are important enough to receive the ultimate designation, is, of course, highly questionable.

Even supporters of those considerable increases would not deny that it was infinitely easier for a jockey to capture 15 Grade I events in 2003 (15 percent of the total) than in 1973 (24 percent).

When and where a race is held sometimes plays a key role in determining its prestige. If the Kentucky Derby, which has been contested at one-and-one-quarter miles throughout the modern era, suddenly is moved from the first Saturday in May to the first Saturday in January without a change in distance, the cavalry charge that usually numbers nearly 20 three-year-olds might be fortunate to draw more participants than the Wimbledon men's singles final. And countless races have benefitted, or been hurt, by significant changes in their dates. Using where a race is held as a criteria may seem to give preferential treatment to such major racing centers as New York and Southern California. In a manner of speaking, that's true, but only in a practical sense. If owners or trainers stabled at Belmont Park or Santa Anita can compete in a $200,000 race without leaving the grounds, logic dictates that they're not going to ship their horses 1,500 miles away to race unless the purse is significantly higher or they don't believe their horses are as capable of winning against the tougher competition that probably exists at their home track.

The role tradition plays in the selection process is similar: If Backwater Park decides to hold a stakes for three-year-olds on the same day as Saratoga's $1 million Travers Stakes, which has been among America's most important races since its inception in 1864, it had better be prepared for a second-string field or strongly consider making its event a $3 million race.

The accomplishments of the entire field during the previous five runnings—if the race is that old—are more significant than simply the accomplishments of the winner. A major benefit of this book is that it eliminates the padding of records of horses and horsemen who often competed against inferior competition. And since the majority of major winners capture only one such race, the depth of the field becomes far more important because it answers one of the most significant questions in testing a horse's mettle: Who did he beat?

By weighing the field for the previous five years, with the most recent year being the most important and the race of five years earlier being the least, a pattern often emerges that shows whether a race is gaining or losing favor among horsemen with the best stock. It also helps prevent knee-jerk reactions that would penalize races that, in track parlance, "come up weak," knowing that even the Santa Anita Handicaps and the Preakness Stakes of the world are going draw better fields in some years than in others.

Likewise, it's unquestionably possible that in certain instances a race not listed among the 110 most prestigious in a given year attracted a far stronger field than had been expected, perhaps a couple of champions and several other major winners who made that year's edition one of the 30 or 60 strongest fields of the season. But like events that "come up weak," those that prove to be exceptionally strong in a given year despite no reasonable expectations based on their purse, grading, or history are all but impossible to predict.

Therefore, the above factors combine to make the selection of those 110 races per season *most likely* to meet this criteria: If an owner or trainer wants to enter his best horse or horses against the toughest competition that North America has to offer, these are the 110 races that, before the year starts, are most likely to offer that ultimate test based on past results and the race's announced purse and grading.

Many races, of course, are restricted. Some are restricted

Photo courtesy of Gulfstream Park

Gulfstream Park, just a few furlongs from high-rise hotels and condominiums that overlook the Atlantic Ocean in Hallandale, Fla., has emerged as the East Coast's premier haven for handicappers who love racing in the winter without the handicaps of winter weather.

by age or sex; others are limited to horses bred only in a particular state, usually the one in which the race is being contested, and some exclude horses who have achieved certain accomplishments in a particular time frame.

Only those races that are restricted because of either age or sex were eligible for consideration among the 110 most prestigious. While it may be folly to expect a two-year-old to compete against older horses, the inclusion of such races as New York's Champagne Stakes, long one of America's most prestigious tests for juveniles, is justified because horsemen know they are likely to face top-of-the-line two-year-olds. The same could be said for the Breeders' Cup Distaff, perhaps America's ultimate test for fillies and mares, who generally fare much better when competing against their own sex than when racing against males. And the inclusion of such races recognizes that they are, like the NCAA Final Four and the Wimbledon's women's draw, major events, even if the NCAA champions or the Wimbledon women's winner are unlikely to beat the National Basketball Association champions or Wimbledon men's titlist once in 100 attempts.

By the same token, races restricted to horses bred in a single state or country, such as Santa Anita's Santa Catalina Stakes, an event that ranked among America's richest in the early part of the modern era but was limited to California-breds, are not included. Neither are match races, which by definition are restricted to two participants.

Significant Trends

No effort was made to include "X" number of races for a particular division, such as two-year-old fillies, three-year-olds, or older horses on the grass. In fact, there have been significant trends in the categories of races that have gained in stature during the 58-year modern era. Among them:

• Grass racing was almost non-existent in this country until the modern era. Only 11 races on the turf are included from 1946-52 and none for fillies and mares on the grass until 1966, yet 30 grass races were included in 2003. Quite simply, horses whose pedigrees and confirmation indicate they have a preference for grass now can conduct major campaigns without having to set foot on the dirt. In the early part of the modern era, an owner or trainer with a top-flight turf horse had only three choices: Run the horse for pocket change on the grass, ship him to Europe, or run on the dirt even if that surface was not to his horse's liking.

• Comparatively, which may surprise many horsemen, prestigious races for two-year-olds were far rarer in 2003 than in 1946. The 1946 campaign included 24 races for two-year-olds, including 10 restricted to fillies, one to colts and geldings, and another to colts and fillies. Because two-year-olds now generally start their careers much later in the season than they did in the early part of the modern era and make far fewer starts, it is an accurate reflection of the times that the 2003 calendar included just 14 races for juveniles, with seven of them limited to fillies and one to colts and geldings.

• More prestigious races for fillies and mares have been added in recent years at the expense of races for three-year-olds and older horses.

• Major events for sprinters, hardly existent during much of the modern era, have grown considerably in recent years.

For the record, the major races from 1984-2003 were selected using the above criteria before those seasons began. The major events from 1946-83 were selected in retrospect based on the aforementioned criteria, with only the purse and the grading for a race in 1977, for example, being included in the data used to select that season's events. A race's grading for the upcoming year and its purse are the only two criteria in which a race can be judged in advance, since it's impossible to predict, for example, who'll compete in the 2004 Breeders' Cup Juvenile Fillies in December of 2003 or January of 2004. But horsemen know well in advance that the race will be a Grade I event with a purse of $1 million.

While there are certain to be arguments about which races were or were not included among the 110 used in a given year, unlike the American Graded Stakes Committee's criteria, there are *exactly* 110 races that are more prestigious than others in a given year, just as there are 10 or 210 most prestigious races. The trick, of course, is to determine *which* races to include, and it's unlikely that even someone with Solomon's wisdom would be infallible. The most difficult period to narrow the field to 110 races was the late '70s and early '80s, when purses for stakes races experienced their most explosive growth in the modern era and a host of new big-money events joined the fray. Conversely, the highest number of Grade I events was from 1984-89—at least 112 each year, including an all-time high of 122 in 1988.

And it's a pretty safe bet that if 100 people spend several years studying the conditions and fields of modern North American stakes races, they'd agree on all but a handful of the 110 races chosen in any given year. It's an equally safe assumption that no two would have exactly the same 110 on his or her list.

One of the primary faults in creating myths about the achievements of both human and equine stars in thoroughbred racing is placing too much importance on the history of particular races. That a race may be ranked among the 110 most prestigious in 1993 or 2003 doesn't mean it would have ranked among the top 510 in prestige in 1953 or 1983. Many of today's most prestigious events did not exist in 1946, and there has been a constant evolution of races falling in and out of favor with the owners and trainers of North America's premier horses.

There are a number of ways a race falls out of favor and is dropped from the list of the most prestigious events. Many races that once were included among the 110 most prestigious have suffered significant reductions in purses or failed to increase their purses to meet those being offered by other races. Some races have been hurt by changing the date or the location, including those in which a track that offered several prestigious events went out of business and had its races absorbed by another track, which then relegated them to second-class status compared to the prestigious events it already offered. Many tracks, of course, have gone out of business, their prestigious races dying along with them. And even tracks that temporarily have gone out of business often have seen their races suffer a loss in prestige when they reopened. And, in some cases, local horsemen's groups argued vociferously that a track's one or two prestige events were siphoning too many funds to out-of-town horses and horsemen. The track responded by greatly reducing the purse of its signature event or abandoning it.

Further, certain events that probably would have been included on a particular year's list were not held for whatever reason, most recently the 2001 Futurity Stakes, Matron Stakes, and Ruffian Handicap at Belmont Park, which were canceled in the wake of the attacks on the nearby World Trade Center on September 11, 2001.

Other events that once were included among the 110 most prestigious, of course, still carry considerable prestige, simply not enough to crack the top 110.

A reflection of this evolution is that, while 101 races were accorded Grade I status in 2003, more than 150 different events have carried that designation since the inception of grading races in North America began in 1973. Since the time period for this book is nearly twice as long, considerably more races have made the list of the most prestigious events during the past 58 years.

As noted earlier, representation among the most prestigious races has been a continuing evolution. Many horses could have won six or seven events that carried major status in their era that no longer do today, which unfairly penalizes that competitor and his connections when they are evaluated for inclusion in the Hall of Fame or other lofty acclaim. Conversely, a horse of 50 years ago could have won six or seven races that now are included on the list of most prestigious races or are Grade I events that were comparatively minor at the time, unfairly rewarding that competitor and his or her connections when being evaluated.

A further indication of how much the major events in North America have changed during the modern era is that only four were rated among the top 110 every year with no change in the race's name or conditions: age or ages included, sex or sexes included, distance, track, and track surface. They are the Kentucky Derby, the Preakness Stakes, the Travers Stakes, and the Alabama Stakes.

The 6,461 races included in this book were held at 39 different tracks in 15 states and Canada. More were held in New York, a total of 2,288 (35.4 percent), than any other state. New York's Belmont Park has held more major races (1,145) during the modern era than any other track, including a single-season record of 34 in 1995, when the Breeders' Cup made its second of three appearances in Elmont, N.Y. California is a strong second with 1,719 races (26.6 percent), and Santa Anita's 809 races rank second to Belmont Park. Florida, Illinois, Kentucky, and New Jersey rank third through sixth, respectively, each with between six and seven percent of the major races held in North America during the modern era.

Major North American Races 1946-2003

Arkansas

Oaklawn Park

Race	Conditions	Distance	Years Included
Apple Blossom Handicap (a)	f&m 4&up	8.5f	1977-2003
Arkansas Derby (b)	3	9f	1959-2003
Fantasy Stakes (c)	3f	8.5f	1973-93
Oaklawn Handicap (d)	4&up	9f	1965-83, 1989-2003

(a) Eight furlongs and 70 yards from 1977-79.
(b) Run in two divisions in 1960.
(c) Eight furlongs and 70 yards in 1973.
(d) For 3-year-olds & up from 1965-76; 8.5 furlongs from 1965-83.

California

Bay Meadows

Race	Conditions	Distance	Years Included
Bay Meadows Handicap (a)	3&upT	9f	1978-83
California Derby (b)	3	9f	1946, 1948, 1960, 1963
William P. Kyne Handicap	3&up	9f	1954-55
William P. Kyne Memorial Handicap	3&up	9f	1957

(a) Run on the dirt in 1980.
(b) 8.5 furlongs in 1946 and 1948.

Golden Gate Fields

Race	Conditions	Distance	Years Included
California Derby (a)	3	9f	1961, 1964-89
Golden Gate Handicap (b)	3&up	9.5f	1947-53

(a) 8.5 furlongs from 1976-81.
(b) 10 furlongs from 1947-50 and in 1952; nine furlongs in 1951.

Hollywood Park

Race	Conditions	Distance	Years Included
American Handicap (a)	3&upT	9f	1946-48, 1950-65, 1970-78
Beverly Hills Handicap (b)	f&m 3&upT	10f	1970-76, 1995-2002
Breeders' Cup Classic	3&up	10f	1984, 1987, 1997
Breeders' Cup Distaff (c)	f&m 3&up	9f	1984, 1987, 1997
Breeders' Cup Juvenile (d)	2c&g	8.5f	1984, 1987, 1997
Breeders' Cup Juvenile Fillies (e)	2f	8.5f	1984, 1987, 1997
Breeders' Cup Mile	3&upT	8f	1984, 1987, 1997
Breeders' Cup Sprint	3&up	6f	1984, 1987, 1997
Breeders' Cup Turf	3&upT	12f	1984, 1987, 1997
Californian Stakes (f)	3&up	9f	1954-99
Century Handicap (g)	3&upT	9f	1968-85
Charles Whittingham Handicap	3&upT	10f	1999-2003
Cinema Handicap (h)	3T	9f	1946-48, '50-66, '69-73, '75-78
Crown Royal Hollywood Derby	3T	9f	1995-97
Early Times Hollywood Derby	3T	9f	1998-2000
Ford Pinto Inv. Turf Handicap	3&upT	12f	1971
Gamely Breeders' Cup Handicap	f&m 3&upT	9f	1998-2003
Gamely Handicap	f&m 3&upT	9f	1979-80, 1986-97
Hollywood Derby (i)	3T	10f	1946-47, 1959-94, 2001-03
Hollywood Futurity (j)	2	8.5f	1981-2003
Hollywood Gold Cup	3&up	10f	1946-48, 1950-98, 2001-03
Hollywood Invitational Handicap (k)	3&upT	10f	1972-88
Hollywood Juvenile Champ. (l)	2	6f	1959-80
Hollywood Oaks (m)	3f	9f	1946-48, '50-52, '62-79, '84-98
Hollywood Park Inv. Turf Handicap	3&upT	12f	1969-70
Hollywood Starlet Stakes (n)	2f	8.5f	1981-83, 1988-2003
Hollywood Turf Cup (o)	3&upT	12f	1981-2003
Hollywood Turf Handicap	3&upT	10f	1989-98
Inglewood Handicap (p)	3&up	9f	1946-48, 1950-52, 1956-64, '71
John Henry Handicap	3&upT	9f	1986-90
Los Angeles Handicap	3&up	7f	1957-64
Matriarch Stakes (q)	f&m 3&upT	8f	1981-83, 1992-2003
Milady Breeders' Cup Handicap	f&m 3&up	8.5f	1996-2003
Milady Handicap	f&m 3&up	8.5f	1991-95
Miller High Life Inglewood Handicap	3&up	9f	1972
Sempra Energy Hollywood Gold Cup	3&up	10f	1999-2000
Shoemaker Breeders' Cup Mile	3&upT	8f	2000-03
Starlet Stakes (r)	2	6f	1946-48, 1950-58
Sunset Handicap (s)	3&upT	12f	1946-48, 1950-91
Swaps Stakes (t)	3	9f	1974-2002
Triple Bend Breeders' Cup Handicap	3&up	7f	2003
Vanity Handicap (u)	f&m 3&up	9f	1946-48, 1950-2003
Westerner Handicap	3	10f	1948
Westerner Stakes (v)	3	10f	1950-58
Will Rogers Handicap (w)	3	6f	1946-48, 1950-51
Will Rogers Stakes	3c&g	6f	1952

(a) Run in two divisions in 1975; run on the dirt from 1946-48 and from 1950-65; 8.5 furlongs in 1946; 10 furlongs from 1950-54.
(b) 11 furlongs from 1970-75; nine furlongs in 1976, 1995, and 1996.
(c) 10 furlongs in 1984 and 1987.
(d) Eight furlongs in 1984 and 1987.
(e) Eight furlongs in 1984 and 1987.
(f) 8.5 furlongs from 1954-79; eight furlongs in 1984 and 1985.
(g) 11 furlongs from 1969-80.
(h) Run in two divisions in 1961 and 1963; run on the dirt from 1946-48 and from 1950-66; 8.5 furlongs from 1946-48 and from 1951-56; eight furlongs in 1950.
(i) Run in two divisions from 1981-87 and in 1991; run on the dirt in 1946, 1947, from 1959-72, and from 1976-80; 12 furlongs from 1973-75; nine furlongs from 1976-94 and in 2001 and 2002.
(j) Eight furlongs from 1985-90.
(k) 12 furlongs from 1972-87.
(l) Run in two divisions from 1962-64 and in 1977.
(m) Eight furlongs in 1946, 1948, and 1950; seven furlongs in 1947; 8.5 furlongs in 1951 and 1952.
(n) Eight furlongs from 1988-90.
(o) Run in two divisions in 1982; 11 furlongs from 1982-84.
(p) Seven furlongs in 1946 and 1947; six furlongs in 1948; 8.5 furlongs in 1951, 1952, and from 1956-64.
(q) Run in two divisions in 1982; nine furlongs from 1981-83, from 1992-94, and from 1999-2002; 10 furlongs from 1995-98.
(r) 8.5 furlongs in 1950.
(s) Run in two divisions in 1975; run on the dirt from 1946-48 and from 1950-66; 13 furlongs from 1946-48 and from 1951-66; nine furlongs in 1950; 16 furlongs in 1969, 1970, and 1972.
(t) 10 furlongs from 1974-94.
(u) Run in two divisions in 1959; 8.5 furlongs from 1946-48 and from 1951-53; 10 furlongs in 1986 and 1987.
(v) Nine furlongs in 1950.
(w) Seven furlongs in 1946 and 1947.

Santa Anita

Race	Conditions	Distance	Years Included
American Handicap	3&up	9f	1949
Ancient Title Breeders' Cup Handicap	3&up	6f	2001-03
Bessemer Trust BC Juvenile	2c&g	8.5f	2003
Breeders' Cup Classic	3&up	10f	1986, 1993
Breeders' Cup Classic/by Dodge	3&up	10f	2003
Breeders' Cup Distaff (a)	f&m 3&up	9f	1986, 1993, 2003
Breeders' Cup Filly and Mare Turf	f&m 3&upT	10f	2003
Breeders' Cup Juvenile	2c&g	8.5f	1986, 1993
Breeders' Cup Juvenile Fillies	2f	8.5f	1986, 1993, 2003
Breeders' Cup Mile	3&upT	8f	1986, 1993
Breeders' Cup Sprint	3&up	6f	1986, 1993, 2003
Breeders' Cup Turf	3&upT	12f	1986, 1993
Champions Invitational Handicap	3&up	10f	1976
Charles H. Strub Stakes (b)	4	10f	1963-93
Cinema Handicap	3	8.5f	1949
Clement L. Hirsch Mem. Turf Ch.	3&upT	10f	2000-03
Hollywood Gold Cup	3&up	10f	1949
Hollywood Oaks	3f	8f	1949
Inglewood Handicap	3&up	8.5f	1949
John Deere Breeders' Cup Turf	3&upT	12f	2003
La Brea Stakes	3f	7f	1998-2003
La Canada Stakes	4f	9f	1976-91
Las Virgenes Stakes	3f	8f	1995-2003
Malibu Stakes (c)	3	7f	1968-69, 1971-74, 1995-2003
National Championship Inv. 'Cap	3&up	10f	1975
NetJets Breeders' Cup Mile	3&upT	8f	2003
Norfolk Stakes (d)	2	8f	1970-2000
Oak Leaf Stakes (e)	2f	8f	1969-2001
Oak Tree Stakes	3&upT	12f	1969-70
Oak Tree Invitational Stakes (f)	3&upT	10f	1971-95
Oak Tree Turf Championship	3&upT	10f	1996-1999
San Antonio Handicap (g)	4&up	9f	1946-67, 1984-2001
San Antonio Stakes	4&up	9f	1968-83
San Carlos Handicap (h)	4&up	7f	1946-49, '51-52, '58-64, '01-03
San Felipe Handicap (i)	3	8.5f	1952-90
San Felipe Stakes (j)	3	8.5f	1946-51, 1991-2001
San Fernando Stakes (k)	4	9f	1952, 1960-69, 1971-91
San Juan Capistrano Handicap (l)	4&upT	a14f	1946, 1949-2003
San Luis Rey Handicap (m)	4&upT	12f	1956-57, 1963-73
San Luis Rey Stakes (n)	4&upT	12f	1974-96
San Pasqual Handicap	3&up	8.5f	1946-51
Santa Anita Derby (o)	3	9f	1946-2003
Santa Anita Handicap (p)	4&up	10f	1946-2003
Santa Anita Maturity	4	10f	1948-62
Santa Anita Oaks	3f	8.5f	1986-2003
Santa Barbara Handicap (q)	f&m 4&upT	10f	1966-95
Santa Margarita Handicap (r)	f&m 4&up	9f	1946-2003
Santa Maria Handicap	f&m 4&up	8.5f	1972-74, 1993-2003
Santa Monica Handicap	f&m 4&up	7f	1997-2003
Santa Susana Stakes (s)	3f	8.5f	1946-51, 1964-72, 1978-85
San Vicente Handicap (t)	3	8.5f	1946-48
Starlet Stakes	2	6f	1949
Strub Stakes (u)	4	9f	1994-2003
Sunset Handicap	3&up	13f	1949
Vanity Handicap	f&m 3&up	8.5f	1949
Westerner Stakes	3	10f	1949
Will Rogers Handicap	3	6f	1949
Yellow Ribbon Stakes	f&m 3&upT	10f	1977-2003

(a) 10 furlongs in 1986.
(b) Nine furlongs in 1970.

(c) Run in two divisions in 1972; for 4-year-olds in 1968, 1969, and from 1971-73.
(d) Run in two divisions in 1980; 8.5 furlongs from 1970-96.
(e) 8.5 furlongs from 1969-96.
(f) 12 furlongs from 1971-94.
(g) For 3-year-olds and up from 1946-62.
(h) Run on both January 1 and December 31, 1949; for 3-year-olds and up from 1946-49 and in 1951, 1952, and from 1958-60.
(i) Run in two divisions in 1968 and 1970.
(j) For 3-year-old colts and geldings from 1946-51; six furlongs in 1946; seven furlongs from 1947-51.
(k) Run in two divisions in 1964, 1975, and 1977; 8.5 furlongs in 1952.
(l) Run in two divisions in 1964; run on the dirt in 1946 and from 1949-53; for 3-year-olds and up in 1946 and from 1949-67; 12 furlongs in 1946, 1949, and 1954; 14 furlongs from 1950-53.
(m) Run in two divisions from 1966-68 and in 1970.
(n) Run on the dirt in 1975.
(o) 10 furlongs in 1947.
(p) For 3-year-olds and up from 1946-68.
(q) Run in two divisions in 1967 and 1968; run on the dirt in 1973, 1977, and 1982; about 10 furlongs in 1968.
(r) Run in two divisions in 1964; for fillies and mares 3 years old and up from 1946-59; 8.5 furlongs from 1946-48, in 1953, and 1954.
(s) Six furlongs in 1946; seven furlongs from 1947-51.
(t) Eight furlongs in 1946.
(u) 10 furlongs from 1994-97.

Del Mar

Del Mar Debutante Stakes (a)	2f	7f	1951-83, 2001-2003
Del Mar Derby (b)	3	9f	1949-51
Del Mar Futurity (c)	2	7f	1949-83, 1986-2003
Del Mar Handicap (d)	3&up	a10f	1946-56, 1970-80
Del Mar Oaks	3fT	9f	1997-2003
Eddie Read Handicap	3&upT	9f	1981-83, 1991-2003
John C. Mabee Handicap	f&m 3&upT	9f	2003
John C. Mabee Ramona Handicap	f&m 3&upT	9f	2002
Pacific Classic	3&up	10f	1991-2003
Ramona Handicap	f&m 3&upT	9f	1974-83, 1993-2001
Vinery Del Mar Debutante Stakes	2f	7f	1999-2000

(a) Six furlongs from 1951-73; eight furlongs from 1974-83.
(b) 8.5 furlongs in 1949.
(c) Run in two divisions in 1971; run on the grass from 1971-73; six furlongs from 1949-70; about 7.5 furlongs from 1971-73; eight furlongs from 1974-83 and from 1986-92.
(d) Run in two divisions in 1972; run on the grass from 1970-75; 8.5 furlongs from 1946-48; nine furlongs from 1949-56; 11 furlongs in 1970, 1971, and from 1973-75; 10 furlongs in 1972.

Tanforan

California Derby	3	9f	1954-56, 1958-59, 1962

Canada

Long Branch

Canadian Championship Stakes (a)	3&up	9.5f	1954-55

(a) Nine furlongs in 1954.

Woodbine

Arlington Million	3&upT	10f	1988
Breeders' Cup Classic	3&up	10f	1996
Breeders' Cup Distaff	f&m 3&up	9f	1996
Breeders' Cup Juvenile	2c&g	8.5f	1996
Breeders' Cup Juvenile Fillies	2f	8.5f	1996
Breeders' Cup Mile	3&upT	8f	1996
Breeders' Cup Sprint	3&up	6f	1996
Breeders' Cup Turf	3&upT	12f	1996
Canadian Championship Stakes (a)	3&upT	13f	1956-65
Canadian Int. Championship (b)	3&upT	12f	1966-80, 1996-98
Molson Export Million	3	9f	1992-95
Rothmans International Stakes (c)	3&upT	12f	1981-95
Woodbine Mile	3&upT	8f	1997-98
Woodbine Million	3	9f	1996

(a) Run on the dirt in 1956 and 1957.
(b) 13 furlongs from 1966-80.
(c) 13 furlongs from 1981-86.

Delaware

Delaware Park

Delaware Handicap	f&m 3&up	10f	1955-82, 1986-90
Delaware Oaks	3f	9f	1946-62
New Castle Handicap (a)	f&m 3&up	10f	1946-54

(a) 8.5 furlongs from 1946-50.

Florida

Calder

Tropical Park Derby (a)	3	9f	1984-89

(a) 8.5 furlongs in 1984 and 1985.

Gulfstream Park

Breeders' Cup Classic	3&up	10f	1989, 1992, 1999
Breeders' Cup Distaff	f&m 3&up	9f	1989, 1992, 1999
Breeders' Cup Filly and Mare Turf	f&m 3&upT	11f	1999
Breeders' Cup Juvenile	2c&g	8.5f	1989, 1992, 1999
Breeders' Cup Juvenile Fillies	2f	8.5f	1989, 1992, 1999
Breeders' Cup Mile	3&upT	8f	1989, 1992, 1999
Breeders' Cup Sprint	3&up	6f	1989, 1992, 1999
Breeders' Cup Turf	3&upT	12f	1989, 1992, 1999
Donn Handicap (a)	3&up	9f	1961-77, 1991-2003
Florida Derby (b)	3	9f	1952-2003
Fountain of Youth Stakes (c)	3	8.5f	1972-74, 1984-89, 1996-2003
Gulfstream Handicap	4&up	10f	1946
Gulfstream Park Breeders' Cup 'Cap	3&upT	11f	1999-2003
Gulfstream Park Handicap	3&up	10f	1947-2003
Hutcheson Stakes	3	7f	1984-88
Pan American Handicap (d)	3&upT	12f	1965-83

(a) Run on the grass from 1961-64; 12 furlongs from 1961-64; seven furlongs in 1976.
(b) Run in two divisions in 1977.
(c) Run in two divisions in 1986.
(d) Run in two divisions in 1983; run on the dirt in 1975.

Hialeah

Black Helen Handicap (a)	f&m 3&up	9f	1946-73
Bougainvillea Handicap (b)	3&upT	9.5f	1946, 1949-51, 1962
Bougainvillea Turf Handicap	3&upT	9.5f	1954-61
Everglades Stakes	3	9f	1953-69, 1984-87
Flamingo Stakes (c)	3	9f	1946-89, 1992-93
Hialeah Turf Cup (d)	3&upT	12f	1959-89
Hialeah Turf Handicap	3&upT	12f	1954-58
McLennan Handicap	3&up	9f	1946-61
Miami Beach Handicap (e)	3&upT	12f	1946-48, 1953
Seminole Handicap	3&up	9f	1962-67
Widener Handicap	3&up	10f	1946-87, 1989

(a) For fillies and mares 4 years old and up in 1963.
(b) 8.5 furlongs in 1946.
(c) Run in two divisions in 1952.
(d) Run in two divisions in 1976.
(e) 10 furlongs in 1946.

Tropical Park

Tropical Handicap	3&up	9f	1954-58
Tropical Park Handicap	3&up	9f	1953, 1959-62

Illinois

Arlington Park

American Derby (a)	3T	9.5f	1958-85, 1987, 1990-94
Arlington Invitational Challenge Cup	3&up	10f	1990
Arlington Classic (b)	3	9f	1946-70, 1978-87, 1990-92
Arlington Classic Inv. Handicap	3&up	10f	1977
Arlington Futurity	2	6f	1946-61
Arlington Handicap (c)	3&upT	10f	1946-62, 1964-67, 1973-84
Arlington Lassie Stakes (d)	2f	6.5f	1946-62
Arlington Matron Handicap (e)	f&m 3&up	9f	1946-51, 1953-63
Arlington Matron Stakes	3f	8f	1952
Arlington Million	3&upT	10f	1981, 1989-97, 2000-03
Arlington Park Handicap (f)	3&up	12f	1963, 1972
Arlington-Washington Futurity (g)	2c&g	8f	1962-69, '71-84, '86-87, '90-94
Arlington-Wash. Lassie Stakes (h)	2f	8f	1963-69, '72-84, '86-87, '90-94
Bessemer Trust BC Juvenile	2c&g	9f	2002
Beverly D. Stakes	f&m 3&upT	9.5f	1992-97, 2000-03
Breeders' Cup Classic	3&up	10f	2002
Breeders' Cup Distaff	f&m 3&up	9f	2002
Breeders' Cup Filly and Mare Turf	f&m 3&upT	10f	2002
Budweiser-Arlington Million	3&upT	10f	1984-87
Budweiser Million	3&upT	10f	1982-83
John Deere Breeders' Cup Turf	3&upT	12f	2002
Long John Silver's BC Juvenile Fillies	2f	9f	2002
Matron Handicap	f&m 3&up	9f	1964-65
NAPA Breeders' Cup Sprint	3&up	6f	2002
NetJets Breeders' Cup Mile	3&upT	8f	2002
Pontiac Grand Prix Stakes (i)	3	8.5f	1971-73
Princess Pat Stakes	2f	6f	1958-60
Secretariat Stakes (j)	3T	10f	1974-83, 1986, 1991-97, '00-03
Stars and Stripes Handicap (k)	3&up	9f	1946-53, 1969-70
Washington Park Futurity (l)	2	6.5	1958-61
Washington Park Handicap (m)	3&up	8f	1958-71

(a) Run on the dirt from 1958-69, from 1977-85, and in 1987, 1990, and 1991; nine furlongs from 1958-61, from 1966-74, and in 1976; 10 furlongs from 1962-65, from 1977-85, and in 1987, 1990, and in 1991; 8.5 furlongs in 1975.
(b) 10 furlongs from 1946-51 and in 1978 and 1979; eight furlongs from 1952-70.
(c) Run on the dirt from 1946-1953, from 1965-67, and in 1975; 9.5 furlongs from 1953-62, in 1964, and from 1973-76; nine furlongs in 1952 and 1965; eight furlongs in 1966 and 1967; 12 furlongs from 1977-83.
(d) Six furlongs from 1946-61.
(e) Eight furlongs from 1946-51 and from 1953-57.
(f) Eight furlongs in 1963.
(g) Run in two divisions in 1967 and 1971; for 2-year-olds from 1962-69; seven furlongs

from 1962-69 and from 1979-84; six furlongs from 1971-73; 6.5 furlongs from 1974-78.
(h) Run in two divisions in 1972; 6.5 furlongs from 1963-69; six furlongs from 1972-79; seven furlongs from 1980-84 and in 1986 and 1987.
(i) Eight furlongs in 1971 and 1972.
(j) Run on the dirt in 1977; 8.5 furlongs in 1974 and 1977; nine furlongs in 1975 and 1976; 12 furlongs from 1978-83.
(k) Run on the grass from 1950-53 and in 1969.
(l) Six furlongs in 1958.
(m) Nine furlongs in 1959, 1963, and 1964.

Hawthorne

Arlington Handicap	3&upT	10f	1985
Arlington-Washington Futurity	2c&g	6.5f	1985
Arlington-Washington Lassie Stakes	2f	6.5f	1985
Hawthorne Gold Cup	3&up	10f	1946-77, 1980-83

Sportsman's Park

Hawthorne Gold Cup	3&up	9f	1979
Illinois Derby	3	9f	1966-69, 1972-89

Washington Park

American Derby (a)	3T	9.5f	1946-57
Princess Pat Stakes	2f	6f	1946-57
Stars and Stripes Handicap (b)	3&upT	9f	1958-59
Washington Park Futurity	2	6f	1946-57
Washington Park Handicap (c)	3&up	8f	1946-57

(a) Run on the dirt from 1946-54; 10 furlongs from 1946-51; nine furlongs from 1952-54.
(b) Run on the dirt in 1958; for 3-year-olds in 1958.
(c) 10 furlongs from 1946-50.

Kentucky

Churchill Downs

Breeders' Cup Classic	3&up	10f	1988, 1991, 1994, 1998, 2000
Breeders' Cup Distaff	f&m 3&up	9f	1988, 1991, 1994, 1998, 2000
Breeders' Cup Filly and Mare Turf	f&m 3&upT	11f	2000
Breeders' Cup Juvenile	2c&g	8.5f	1988, 1991, 1994, 1998, 2000
Breeders' Cup Juvenile Fillies	2f	8.5f	1988, 1991, 1994, 1998, 2000
Breeders' Cup Mile	3&upT	8f	1988, 1991, 1994, 1998, 2000
Breeders' Cup Sprint	3&up	6f	1988, 1991, 1994, 1998, 2000
Breeders' Cup Turf	3&upT	12f	1988, 1991, 1994, 1998, 2000
Early Times Turf Classic	3&upT	9f	1996-99
Humana Distaff Handicap	f&m 3&up	7f	2002-03
Kentucky Derby	3	10f	1946-2003
Kentucky Jockey Club Stakes	2	8f	1946-70
Kentucky Oaks (a)	3f	9f	1946-2003
Stephen Foster Handicap	3&up	9f	2002-03
Woodford Reserve Turf Classic	3&upT	9f	2000-03

(a) Run in two divisions in 1959; 8.5 furlongs from 1946-81.

Keeneland

Alcibiades Stakes (a)	2f	8.5f	1952-56, 1966-83, 1988
Ashland Stakes (b)	3f	8.5f	1975-77, 1988-2003
Blue Grass Stakes (c)	3	9f	1946-96
Breeders' Futurity (d)	2	8.5f	1946-85, 1988
Darley Alcibiades Stakes	2f	8.5f	2003
Lane's End Breeders' Futurity	2	8.5f	1998-2003
Overbrook Spinster Stakes	f&m 3&up	9f	2001-03
Queen Elizabeth II Challenge Cup	3fT	9f	1996-2003
Shadwell Keeneland Turf Mile	3&upT	8f	2002
Shadwell Turf Mile	3&upT	8f	2003
Spinster Stakes (e)	f&m 3&up	9f	1956-95
Three Chimneys Spinster Stakes	f&m 3&up	9f	1996-2000
Toyota Blue Grass Stakes	3	9f	1997-2003
Walmac Int. Alcibiades Stakes	2f	8.5f	1998-2002

(a) Seven furlongs from 1952-55; seven furlongs and 184 feet in 1956 and from 1966-80.
(b) Seven furlongs and 184 feet from 1975-77.
(c) Run in two divisions in 1951.
(d) Six furlongs from 1946-49; seven furlongs from 1950-55; seven furlongs and 184 feet from 1956-80.
(e) For fillies and mares 3, 4, and 5 years old from 1956-63.

Turfway Park/Latonia

Gallery Furniture.com Stakes	3	9f	1999
Jim Beam Stakes (a)	3	9f	1984-98
Jim Beam Spiral Stakes	3	8.5f	1983
Turfway Spiral Stakes	3	9f	2000-01

(a) 8.5 furlongs from 1984-87.

Louisiana

Fair Grounds

Louisiana Derby	3	9f	1946-85, 1999
New Orleans Handicap (a)	4&up	10f	1946-82

(a) For 3-year-olds and up in from 1946-78; 8.5 furlongs from 1946-53; nine furlongs from 1954-77.

Louisiana Downs

Golden Harvest Handicap (a)	f&m 3&upT	11f	1979-83
Isle of Capri Casino Super Derby	3	10f	1996
Louisiana Downs Handicap (b)	3&upT	11f	1979-83
Super Derby (c)	3	9f	1980-95, 1997-2003

(a) Run in two divisions in 1980 and 1982; run on the dirt in 1979; 10 furlongs in 1979.
(b) Run in two divisions from 1980-82; run on the dirt in 1979; 10 furlongs in 1979.
(c) 10 furlongs from 1980-95 and from 1997-2001.

Maryland

Bowie

John B. Campbell Handicap (a)	3&up	10f	1959-76, 1978
John B. Campbell Memorial 'Cap (b)	3&up	8.5f	1954-58

(a) Run in two divisions in 1970, 1972, and 1973; 8.5 furlongs from 1959-73.
(b) Nine furlongs in 1954.

Laurel

Budweiser International Stakes (a)	3&upT	8f	1987-93
Frank J. De Francis Memorial Dash	3&up	6f	1995-2003
Laurel Futurity (b)	2	8.5f	1972-78, 1980-89
Pimlico Futurity	2	8.5f	1966
Pimlico-Laurel Futurity	2	8.5f	1967-71
Selima Stakes (c)	2f	8.5f	1946-78, 1980-89
Washington D.C. International (d)	3&upT	10f	1952-86, 1994

(a) 10 furlongs from 1987-92.
(b) Run on the grass in 1987 and 1988.
(c) Run on the grass in 1987 and 1988.
(d) about 12 furlongs from 1952-58; 12 furlongs from 1959-85.

Pimlico

Black-Eyed Susan Stakes (a)	3f	9f	1951-52
Dixie Handicap (b)	3&upT	12f	1946-57, 1962-71
Laurel Futurity	2	8.5f	1979
Marguerite Stakes	2f	8.5f	1946-51
Pimlico Futurity (c)	2	8.5f	1946-65
Pimlico Oaks (d)	3f	8.5f	1946-49
Pimlico Special (e)	4&up	9.5f	1946-58, 1990-2001, 2003
Preakness Stakes	3	9.5f	1946-2003
Selima Stakes	2f	8.5f	1979

(a) 8.5 furlongs in 1951.
(b) Run in two divisions in 1965; run on the dirt from 1946-54; 9.5 furlongs from 1946-52; nine furlongs in 1953 and 1954; 11 furlongs from 1955-57.
(c) For 2-year-old colts and fillies from 1956-58.
(d) Nine furlongs in 1948.
(e) For 3-year-olds and up from 1946-53 and from 1955-57; for 3-year-olds in 1954; for 2-year-olds and up in 1958.

Massachusetts

Suffolk Downs

Massachusetts Handicap	3&up	9f	1946-73

(a) Run on the grass in 1970 and 1971; 10 furlongs from 1948-69; 12 furlongs in 1970; about 12 furlongs in 1971.

Michigan

Detroit

Michigan Mile	3&up	8f	1953-56, 1958
Michigan Mile and One-Eighth (a)	3&up	9f	1965-78
Michigan Mile and One-Sixteenth	3&up	8.5f	1957, 1959-64

(a) Run in two divisions in 1972.

New Jersey

Atlantic City

Caesars International Handicap	3&upT	9.5f	1990-97
Jersey Derby	3	9f	1977, 1984
United Nations Handicap	3&upT	9.5f	1953-89

Garden State Park

Garden State Stakes (a)	2	8.5f	1946-72
Gardenia Stakes	2f	8.5f	1955-72
Jersey Derby (b)	3	9f	1960-76, 1985-92
Trenton Handicap (c)	3&up	10f	1946-63
Vineland Handicap (d)	f&m 3&up	9f	1946-65

(a) Six furlongs in 1946, 1947, and from 1949-52; five furlongs in 1948.
(b) 10 furlongs from 1985-90.
(c) Nine furlongs from 1946-53.
(d) 8.5 furlongs from 1946-53.

Meadowlands

Buick Meadowlands Cup Handicap	3&up	9f	1996, 1998
Buick Pegasus Handicap	3	9f	1997-99
Meadowlands Cup (a)	3&up	9f	1977-83, 1986-95
Meadowlands Cup Handicap	3&up	9f	1999
Pegasus Breeders' Cup Handicap	3	9f	1996
Pegasus Handicap (b)	3	8.5f	1981-83, 1990-95
Young America Stakes (c)	2T	8.5f	1977-91

(a) 10 furlongs from 1977-83 and from 1986-89.
(b) Nine furlongs from 1981-83 and from 1990-94.
(c) Run on the dirt from 1977-90.

Monmouth Park

Amory L. Haskell Handicap (a)	3&up	9f	1967-80
Buick Haskell Invitational Handicap	3	9f	1996-98
Haskell Invitational Handicap	3	9f	1981-1995, 1999-2003
Molly Pitcher Handicap	f&m 3&up	8.5f	1946-58, 1967, 1970
Monmouth Invitational Handicap	3	9f	1968-80
Monmouth Handicap (b)	3&up	9f	1946-66, 1981-85
Monmouth Oaks (c)	3f	9f	1950-71
Philip H. Iselin Handicap (d)	3&up	9f	1986-2002
Sapling Stakes (e)	2	6f	1946-47, 1950-80, 1984-85
Sorority Stakes	2f	6f	1960-85
United Nations Handicap	3&upT	11f	2001-03

(a) 10 furlongs from 1967-78.
(b) 10 furlongs from 1946-66.
(c) 8.5 furlongs from 1950-52.
(d) 8.5 furlongs in 1996 and 1997.
(e) Run in two divisions in 1952.

New York

Jamaica

Brooklyn Handicap	3&up	9.5f	1956, 1958-59
Comely Handicap (a)	f&m 3&up	8.5f	1946-53
Demoiselle Stakes (b)	2f	8.5f	1946-53
Display Handicap	3&up	16.5f	1956-58
Dwyer Handicap	3	9.5f	1956, 1958-59
Excelsior Handicap	3&up	8.5f	1946-55
Firenze Handicap (c)	f&m 3&up	9f	1948-56
Frizette Stakes (d)	2f	8.5f	1946-48, 1952-58
Gallant Fox Handicap (e)	3&up	13f	1946-58
Gotham Stakes (f)	3	8.5f	1953-57, 1959
Grey Lag Handicap (g)	3&up	9f	1946-47, 1949-53, 1956-59
Remsen Handicap (h)	2	8.5f	1946-47, 1949-50, 1952-53
Remsen Stakes (i)	2	8.5f	1948, 1954-58
Roamer Handicap	3	9.5f	1946-47, 1952, 1954-58
Saranac Handicap	3	8.5f	1948-53, 1955
Westchester Handicap (j)	3&up	9f	1946-53
Withers Stakes	3	8.5f	1956
Wood Memorial Stakes (k)	3	9f	1946-59

(a) Run in two divisions in 1953.
(b) Six furlongs in 1946 and 1947.
(c) 8.5 furlongs from 1948-50.
(d) Six furlongs in 1946, 1947, 1952, and 1953; five furlongs in 1948.
(e) 9.5 furlongs from 1948-53.
(f) Run in two divisions in 1953.
(g) 8.5 furlongs in 1949 and 1950.
(h) Six furlongs in 1950.
(i) For 2-year-old colts from 1954-56; for 2-year-old colts and geldings in 1957; Five furlongs in 1948.
(j) 9.5 furlongs from 1946-50.
(k) Run in two divisions in 1947; for 3-year-old colts and fillies in 1954; 8.5 furlongs from 1946-51.

Saratoga

Alabama Stakes	3f	10f	1946-2003
Ballerina Handicap	f&m 3&up	7f	1998-2003
Ballerina Stakes	f&m 3&up	7f	1997
Delaware Handicap	f&m 3&up	10f	1983-85
Diana Handicap (a)	f&m 3&upT	9f	1956-59, 2003
Forego Handicap (b)	3&up	7f	2001-03
Go for Wand Handicap	f&m 3&up	9f	1998-2003
Go for Wand Stakes	f&m 3&up	9f	1994-97
Hopeful Stakes (c)	2	7f	1946-2003
Jim Dandy Stakes	3	9f	1984-2003
John A. Morris Handicap	f&m 3&up	10f	1996-97
King's Bishop Stakes	3	7f	1999-2003
Personal Ensign Handicap	f&m 3&up	10f	1998-2003
Sanford Stakes (d)	2	6f	1963-68, 1970-71
Saratoga Special	2	6f	1947-51, 1959-68
Spinaway Stakes (e)	2f	7f	1946-76, 1990-2003
Sword Dancer Invitational Handicap	3&upT	12f	1994-2003
Sword Dancer Handicap	3&upT	12f	1992-93
Test Stakes	3f	7f	1994-95, 1997-2003
Travers Stakes	3	10f	1946-2003
Whitney Handicap (f)	3&up	9f	1954, 1960-61, '75-77, '81-2003
Whitney Stakes (g)	3&up	9f	1946-53, '55-59, '62-74, '78-80

(a) Run on the dirt from 1956-59.
(b) 6.5 furlongs in 2001 and 2002.
(c) Run in two divisions in 1974 and 1975; 6.5 furlongs from 1946-93.
(d) 5.5 furlongs from 1963-68.
(e) Six furlongs from 1946-76 and from 1990-93.
(f) For 4-year-olds and up in 1960 and 1961; 10 furlongs in 1954.
(g) For 4-year-olds and up from 1957-59 and from 1962-69; 10 furlongs from 1946-53.

Aqueduct

Acorn Stakes (a)	3f	8f	1960-67, 1969-75
Aqueduct Handicap (b)	3&up	9f	1946-55, 1959-60, 1966
Aqueduct Stakes	3&up	9f	1962-65, 1967-68
Astoria Stakes	2f	5.5f	1947-52
Astarita Stakes	2f	6f	1946-47, 1951
Beldame Handicap (c)	f&m 3&up	9f	1946-55, 1959
Beldame Stakes	f&m 3&up	9f	1962-68
Belmont Stakes	3	12f	1963-67
Bowling Green Handicap	3&upT	13f	1965-67
Breeders' Cup Classic	3&up	10f	1985
Breeders' Cup Distaff	f&m 3&up	10f	1985
Breeders' Cup Juvenile	2c&g	8f	1985
Breeders' Cup Juvenile Fillies	2f	8f	1985
Breeders' Cup Mile	3&upT	8f	1985
Breeders' Cup Sprint	3&up	6f	1985
Breeders' Cup Turf	3&upT	12f	1985
Brooklyn Handicap (d)	3&up	11f	1946-55, 1960-74, 1976, '91-93
Carter Handicap (e)	3&up	7f	1970-71, '75-78, '89-93, '97-03
Champagne Stakes	2	8f	1959, 1961, 1963-67
Cigar Mile Handicap	3&up	8f	1997-2003
Coaching Club American Oaks	3f	10f	1963-67
Cowdin Stakes (f)	2	7f	1946-55, 1959, 1963-67
Delta Air Lines Top Flight Handicap	f&m 3&up	9f	1996
Demoiselle Stakes (g)	2f	9f	1963-64, 1974-78, 1988-90
Discovery Handicap	3	9f	1946-53
Display Handicap	3&up	16f	1959-68
Dwyer Handicap (h)	3	9f	1960-74, 1976
Dwyer Stakes	3	10f	1946-55
Fall Highweight Handicap	3&up	6f	1998
Frizette Stakes	2f	8f	1959-61, 1963-67
Futurity Stakes	2	6.5f	1959-60, 1962-67
Gallant Fox Handicap (i)	3&up	13f	1959-68
Gazelle Handicap	3f	9f	1965-68
Gazelle Stakes	3f	8.5f	1946-55
Gotham Stakes (j)	3	8f	1960-73, 1983-97
Grey Lag Handicap (k)	3&up	10f	1960-75
Hempstead Handicap	f&m 3&up	9f	1973-74
Jerome Handicap	3	8f	1960, 1962-67, 1972, 1974
Jockey Club Gold Cup	3&up	16f	1959-61, 1963-67, 1969-74
Ladies Handicap (l)	f&m 3&up	10f	1959, 1961-80, 1984-90
Lawrence Realization Stakes	3	13f	1959, 1961, 1963-67
Manhattan Handicap (m)	3&up	13f	1959, 1961, 1963-67
Man o' War Handicap (n)	3&upT	13f	1959, 1961
Man o' War Stakes (o)	3&upT	11f	1963-67, 1987
Maskette Handicap	f&m 3&up	8f	1959
Matron Stakes	2f	6f	1960, 1962-68
Metropolitan Handicap	3&up	8f	1960-67, 1969, 1975
Mother Goose Stakes	3f	9f	1963-67, 1969, 1975
NYRA Mile Handicap	3&up	8f	1990-92, 1994-96
Queens County Handicap	3&up	8.5f	1947-54
Remsen Stakes (p)	2	9f	1959-62, 1974-2000
Roamer Handicap	3	9.5f	1959-64
Suburban Handicap (q)	3&up	9.5f	1960-74, 1976
Top Flight Handicap (r)	f&m 3&up	8f	1961-92, 1994-95
Tremont Stakes	2c&g	5.5f	1946-50
Turf Classic	3&upT	12f	1977, 1979-83, 1986
Vagrancy Handicap (s)	f&m 3&up	7f	1948, 1953-54
Vosburgh Handicap	3&up	7f	1965-74, 1976-77
Vosburgh Stakes	3&up	7f	1979-83, 1985-86, 1988-89
Withers Stakes	3	8f	1960-71, 1975
Wood Memorial Stakes (t)	3	9f	1960-2003
Woodward Stakes	3&up	10f	1959-60, 1962-67

(a) Run in two divisions in 1970 and 1974.
(b) 8.5 furlongs from 1946-55; eight furlongs in 1959 and 1960.
(c) Run in two divisions in 1946, 1947, and 1952.
(d) 10 furlongs from 1946-55, from 1960-71, and in 1976; 9.5 furlongs from 1972-74.
(e) Carter Handicap at Aqueduct also is included from 1947-55 and from 1960-67; run in two divisions in 1977 and 1978.
(f) Run in two divisions in 1963; 6.5 furlongs from 1946-55.
(g) Eight furlongs in 1963, 1964, and 1974.
(h) 10 furlongs from 1960-74.
(i) 14 furlongs in 1960.
(j) Eight furlongs and 70 yards in 1984.
(k) Nine furlongs from 1960-68 and in 1970 and 1971; seven furlongs in 1969.
(l) 10.5 furlongs in 1959, 1961, and 1962; 12 furlongs in 1963 and 1964.
(m) 10.5 furlongs in 1961; 12 furlongs in 1963 and 1964.
(n) Run in two divisions in 1959; 12 furlongs in 1959.
(o) 13 furlongs from 1963-67.
(p) Eight furlongs from 1959-62.
(q) 10 furlongs from 1960-74.
(r) Nine furlongs from 1961-92.
(s) 8.5 furlongs in 1948.
(t) Run in two divisions in 1974 and 1983.

Belmont Park

Race	Conditions	Distance	Years
Acorn Stakes (a)	3f	8f	1946-59, 1968, 1976-2003
Aqueduct Handicap	3&up	9f	1961
Astoria Stakes	2f	5.5f	1946
Beldame Handicap	f&m 3&up	9f	1956-58
Beldame Stakes (b)	f&m 3&up	9f	1960-61, 1969-2003
Belmont Stakes (c)	3	12f	1946-62, 1968-2003
Bessemer Trust BC Juvenile	2c&g	8.5f	2001
Bowling Green Handicap (d)	3&upT	11f	1958-61, 1968-83
Breeders' Cup Classic	3&up	10f	1990, 1995, 2001
Breeders' Cup Distaff	f&m 3&up	9f	1990, 1995, 2001
Breeders' Cup Filly and Mare Turf	f&m 3&upT	10f	2001
Breeders' Cup Juvenile	2c&g	8.5f	1990, 1995
Breeders' Cup Juvenile Fillies	2f	8.5f	1990, 1995, 2001
Breeders' Cup Mile	3&upT	8f	1990, 1995, 2001
Breeders' Cup Sprint	3&up	6f	1990, 1995
Breeders' Cup Turf	3&upT	12f	1990, 1995, 2001
Brooklyn Handicap (e)	3&up	9f	1957, 1975, 1977-90, 1994-2001
Carter Handicap	3&up	7f	1946, '56-59, '68-69, '72-74, '94-96
Champagne Stakes (f)	2	8.5f	1957-58, '60, '62, '68-95, '99-03
Coaching Club American Oaks (g)	3f	12f	1946-62, 1968-2003
Cowdin Stakes (h)	2	7f	1956-58, '60-62, '68-71, '86-90
Dwyer Handicap (i)	3	9f	1957, 1975, 1977-78
Dwyer Stakes (j)	3	8.5f	1979-95
Early Times Manhattan Handicap	3&upT	10f	1994-96
Fall Highweight Handicap (k)	3&up	6f	1946-58, 1975-76
Flower Bowl Invitational Handicap	f&m 3&upT	10f	1994-2001
Flower Bowl Invitational Stakes	f&m 3&upT	10f	2002-03
Flower Bowl Handicap	f&m 3&upT	10f	1979-83, 1988-93
Frizette Stakes (l)	2f	8.5f	1962, 1968-2003
Futurity Stakes (m)	2	8f	1946-58, '61, 1968-2000, '02-03
Garden City Breeders' Cup Handicap	3fT	9f	1999-2002
Garden City Breeders' Cup Stakes	3fT	9f	2003
Gazelle Handicap (n)	3f	9f	1956-58, 1969-75, 1993-2003
Go for Wand Stakes	f&m 3&up	8f	1992-93
Hempstead Handicap (o)	f&m 3&up	8.5f	1975-77, 1991-2001
Jerome Handicap	3	8f	1946-59, '61, '68-71, '73, '75-98
Jockey Club Gold Cup (p)	3&up	10f	1946-58, 1962, 1968, 1975-2003
Ladies Handicap	f&m 3&up	12f	1946-58, 1960
Lawrence Realization Stakes (q)	3T	12f	1946-58, 1960, 1962, 1968-70
Manhattan Handicap (r)	3&upT	10f	1946-58, 60, 62, 68-74, 76, 97-03
Man o' War Stakes (s)	3&upT	11f	1960, 1962, 1968-86, 1988-2003
Marlboro Cup Handicap (t)	3&up	10f	1973-87
Maskette Handicap (u)	f&m 3&up	8f	1954-58, 1973-79
Maskette Stakes	f&m 3&up	8f	1980-91
Matron Stakes (v)	2f	8f	1946-59, '61, 1969-2000, '02-03
Metropolitan Handicap	3&up	8f	1946-59, 1968, 1970-74, '76-03
Moet Champagne Stakes	2	8.5f	1996-98
Mother Goose Stakes (w)	3f	9f	1957-62, 1968, 1970-74, '76-03
Nassau County Handicap	3&up	9f	1991-93
New York Handicap (x)	3&up	9f	1946-53
Ogden Phipps Handicap	f&m 3&up	8.5f	2002-03
Penske Auto Center BC Sprint	3&up	6f	2001
Peter Pan Stakes	3	9f	1986-95
Prioress Stakes	3f	6f	2001-03
Roseben Handicap (y)	3&up	7f	1946-50, 1954-55
Ruffian Handicap (z)	f&m 3&up	8.5f	1977-2000, 2002-03
Ruffian Stakes	f&m 3&up	10f	1976
Sheepshead Bay Handicap	f&m 3&upT	10f	1978-79
Shuvee Handicap (aa)	f&m 3&up	8f	1992-96
Suburban Handicap (bb)	3&up	10f	1946-59, 1975, 1977-2003
Swift Stakes	3	7f	1946-47, 1950
Sword Dancer Handicap	3&upT	12f	1983, 1988-91
Sword Dancer Stakes	3&upT	12f	1980-82
Top Flight Handicap (cc)	f&m 3&up	9f	1946-60, 1993
Turf Classic	3&upT	12f	1978, 1984-85, 1987-2003
Vosburgh Handicap (dd)	3&up	7f	1946-53, 1975, 1978
Vosburgh Stakes (ee)	3&up	6.5f	1984, 1987, 1990-2003
Withers Stakes (ff)	3	8f	1946-55, '57-59, '72-74, '76, '84-90
Woodward Handicap (gg)	3&up	9f	1976-77, 1988-90
Woodward Stakes (hh)	3&up	9f	1954-58, '61, '68-75, '78-87, '91-03

(a) Run in two divisions in 1951.
(b) 10 furlongs from 1977-89.
(c) For 3-year-old colts and fillies from 1946-56.
(d) 12 furlongs in 1960, 1961, and from 1968-76; 10 furlongs in 1977.
(e) 9.5 furlongs in 1957; 10 furlongs in 1975; 12 furlongs from 1977-90.
(f) Champagne Stakes at Belmont Park also is included from 1946-55; run in two divisions in 1973; eight furlongs from 1946-55, in 1957, 1958, 1960, 1962, from 1968-83, and from 1985-94; nine furlongs in 1984.
(g) 11 furlongs from 1946-58; 10 furlongs from 1959-62, from 1968-70, and from 1990-97.
(h) 6.5 furlongs in 1956 and 1957.
(i) 9.5 furlongs in 1957.
(j) Nine furlongs from 1979-94.
(k) Run in two divisions in 1976; for 2-year-olds and up from 1946-58.
(l) Seven furlongs from 1982-93.
(m) For 2-year-old colts and fillies from 1946-58; 6.5 furlongs from 1946-58, in 1961, and from 1968-75; seven furlongs from 1976-93.
(n) 8.5 furlongs from 1956-58.
(o) Nine furlongs from 1975-77 and from 1991-94.
(p) For colts, horses, fillies and mares 3 years old and up from 1946-52 and in 1954 and 1955; 16 furlongs from 1946-58, in 1962, 1968, and 1975; 12 furlongs from 1976-89.
(q) Run on the dirt from 1946-58 and in 1960, 1962, 1968, and 1969; 13 furlongs from 1946-58 and in 1960, 1962, 1968, and 1969.
(r) Run in two divisions in 1971 and 1972; run on the dirt from 1946-58 and in 1960, 1968, and 1969; 12 furlongs from 1946-58 and in 1960, 1962, 1968, and 1969; 11 furlongs from 1970-74 and in 1976.
(s) 12 furlongs in 1960, 1962, and from 1968-77; 10 furlongs in 1997.
(t) Nine furlongs in 1973, 1974, and from 1978-80.
(u) Run in two divisions in 1976.
(v) Six furlongs from 1946-1959, in 1961, and from 1969-71; seven furlongs from 1972-93.
(w) 8.5 furlongs in 1957 and 1958.
(x) 18 furlongs from 1946-50.
(y) Six furlongs from 1946-50.
(z) Nine furlongs from 1977-89.
(aa) 8.5 furlongs from 1992-94.
(bb) 12 furlongs in 1975.
(cc) 8.5 furlongs from 1946-60.
(dd) For 2-year-olds and up from 1946-53.
(ee) Seven furlongs in 1984, 1987, and from 1990-2002.
(ff) For 3-year-old colts and fillies from 1946-55.
(gg) 10 furlongs in 1988 and 1989.
(hh) Eight furlongs in 1954; 10 furlongs from 1956-58, in 1961, from 1968-71, and from 1978-80; 12 furlongs from 1972-75.

Ohio

Thistledown

Race	Conditions	Distance	Years
Ohio Derby (a)	3	9f	1953-58, 1963-80, 1984-98

(a) 8.5 furlongs in 1963 and 1964.

Pennsylvania

Philadelphia Park/Keystone

Race	Conditions	Distance	Years
Pennsylvania Derby	3	9f	1979-91

Washington

Longacres

Race	Conditions	Distance	Years
Longacres Mile	3&up	8f	1946-50, 1978-80

Legend

Conditions: (2, 3, 4, 3&up, 4&up) age or ages; (f) fillies; (f&m) fillies and mares; (c&g) colts and geldings; (T) turf or grass.

Distance: (f) furlongs. One furlong is 220 yards or one eighth of a mile.

Note: The conditions for any particular race are only for the last year that particular race was included among the 110 most prestigious. Changes in conditions during the years that any particular race was included are listed in the footnotes.

Photo courtesy of Thistledown

Among Skip Away's 14 victories—more than any colt since the retirement of Spectacular Bid in 1980 or by any thoroughbred since John Henry's retirement four years later—in major races was a three-and-one-half-length romp in the 1996 Ohio Derby with Jose Santos in the saddle. Skip Away not only romped to victory in the Ohio Derby, but to his first of three consecutive championship seasons that culminated in Horse of the Year acclaim in 1998.

Race Horses

II: Race Horses

No Comparing Apples to Oranges

In chronicling the achievements of the best race horses of the modern era, it's significant to categorize them.

Secretariat, for instance, accomplished nothing on the track as a four-year-old compared to the other Triple Crown winners of the modern era—Assault, Citation, Seattle Slew, and Affirmed—for the most basic reason: He never raced.

As great as Secretariat was during his two-year career, like so many others before and since, he was rushed to the breeding shed before he even reached maturity.

"Horses are not really mature until late in their four-year-old year," said Dr. Gary Lavin, a noted Kentucky veterinarian. "Consider the three-year-old sort of a college athlete and your two-year-old as a high school athlete, and you'll see they're very immature."

Perhaps the most significant tool necessary to make valid comparisons of the achievements of equine athletes—and one that is employed in this chapter—is rarely used: separating them by sex. Some sources may separate the achievements of males and distaffers, but to make relevant comparisons, those achievements should be divided into three sexes: colts, who become horses at age five; fillies, who are designated mares at age five, and geldings, males who have suffered the "unkindest cut of all" and have no breeding value.

Because of an 11-month gestation period, a mare rarely, if ever, produces more than one foal per year. So it is far more common for top-flight fillies, including major winners, to continue their racing careers for a year or two or three longer than their male counterparts. Superior fillies and mares well may be kept on the track as long as they can win, or simply stay competitive at the top level, because they figure to earn more in purse money than the resulting maximum of one foal per year could produce.

Because their male counterparts usually were bred to 40 or so mares during much of the modern era—a figure that crept above the century mark for many stallions during the '90s and into the 21st Century—simple math shows that a one-time major winner who can command a more-than-reasonable initial stud fee of $10,000 who is bred to 100 mares will earn $1 million. Should that same colt capture six races worth $250,000, each with the winner receiving his normal 60 percent of the purse, he'd fall $100,000 short of that target. Further consider that 2001 Horse of the Year Point Given's initial stud fee was $125,000, and there is little wonder why colts far less accomplished than Secretariat and Point Given are rushed to stud at the earliest opportunity.

While the owners of Kelso and John Henry no doubt regretted that those legendary geldings had no ancillary value, they, like most geldings, weren't necessarily the most fashionably bred animals in the barn. And since most colts who become geldings do so before they ever step on the race track—and virtually all before their three-year-old campaigns begin—there is little indication which of those modestly bred animals, in time, will become superior race horses. Many geldings are victims of that fate because of behavioral problems, so it's not surprising that they aren't necessarily stars of the show as two- or three-year-olds. And, since they're not headed to the breeding shed, it's no surprise that they frequently dominate the ranks of older horses.

Forego, for example, never won a major race until he was a four-year-old, when the gelding began a string of three consecutive Horse of the Year campaigns. Yet Heliodoro Gustines, who earned 15 major victories aboard Forego, doesn't consider him the best mount of his career.

"I liked Stage Door Johnny better than Forego," Gustines said of the 1968 Belmont Stakes winner, who didn't compete past age three. "Stage Door Johnny never had the chance to prove himself. When he won the Belmont, he still didn't know how to run."

So, with only a few exceptions, this chapter will compare the achievements of superior race horses only to others of the same sex. Further, it is as foolish to compare a colt who excelled at sprint races on dirt as a three-year-old with a six-year-old mare whose specialty was mile-and-one-half grass races as it is the taste of a fine Cabernet and a frosty mug of beer. They're both great in their own way, so this chapter's primary focus won't include equine-equivalent discussions that compare the merits of a Winesap to Florida orange juice.

"You can't compare horses year to year," said standout jockey Jacinto Vasquez. "You can't compare a Joe Louis or a Muhammad Ali."

While it's easy to agree with Vasquez that it may be pointless to say that Kelso was superior to Forego, Citation to Secretariat, or Susan's Girl to Lady's Secret—or vice versa in any of those cases—this book hopes to give horsemen and horseplayers more ammunition than ever to argue the merits of their favorites or, in many cases, to agree that their arguments lack merit.

Colts and Horses

Two-Year-Olds: A Real Battlefield

Since today's two-year-olds generally make far fewer starts than they did half a century ago, it's not surprising that they're often judged on the basis of one or two fantastic performances rather than a series of superior ones.

Shortly after he syndicated Devil's Bag after his championship two-year-old campaign in 1983, Claiborne Farm's Seth Hancock said, "He and Seattle Slew are the best two-year-olds I've ever seen. I'd have to put him above Secretariat. I think that's a widely shared opinion."

Yet neither Devil's Bag nor Seattle Slew is among the 28 colts who won three or more major races as juveniles. Neither is Native Dancer nor Favorite Trick, who, along with Secretariat, are the only modern two-year-old colts to earn Horse of the Year acclaim.

Thirty-eight of the 50 two-year-olds who won at least three major races in the modern era were crowned juvenile champions, and another six lost that acclaim to rivals who accomplished that same feat. A sign of the changing times, however, is that four of the six occasions in which two-year-olds with three or more major victories lost championships to a rival without that distinction came from 1983-1992. The only earlier exceptions were Laffango, who lost the 1952 juvenile title to Native Dancer, and Carry Back, whose bid for 1960 two-year-old honors was trumped by Hail to Reason.

The only two-year-old colt to capture five major events was the underrated Battlefield, who won the 1950 Sapling Stakes, Saratoga Special, Hopeful Stakes, Tremont Stakes, and Futurity Stakes. Battlefield eventually earned five more major victories and ranks among the most accomplished horses who haven't been enshrined in the National Museum of Racing and Hall of Fame in Saratoga Springs, N.Y.

Ten more two-year-old colts captured four races, including Triple Crown winners Secretariat and Affirmed, dual classic winner Riva Ridge, and Preakness winner Hasty Road. The only other colt to capture four races at two, then subsequently earn multiple major victories, was Buckpasser. Three of the other five, Blue Peter, Sadair, and Vitriolic, never won another significant race, and Bold Lad and Jewel's Reward added only one more major triumph apiece.

It long has been suggested that owners and trainers with good two-year-olds in the barn are among the least likely candidates for suicide, but superstar status as a juvenile obviously isn't necessarily a guarantee of future success.

"Sometimes when a horse turns from two to three, his ability changes," trainer Stanley Rieser said.

Added the late Lucien Laurin, who trained both Secretariat and Riva Ridge: "Even Riva Ridge wasn't as good a three-year-old as he was a two-year-old."

There are many reasons that some stellar two-year-olds accomplish little afterward, including injuries, the strain of continuous top-level competition at an early age, late-blooming horses of greater ability muscling their way into the picture, or the desire of owners to rush their charges to stallion duty before their reputations are diminished. Regardless, it's clear that for every Secretariat or Buckpasser who becomes a great three-year-old, there are plenty of accomplished two-year-olds who never enhance their reputations afterward.

In fact, of the 17 colts who won exactly three major races at two, only First Landing, Carry Back, Top Knight, Foolish Pleasure, Spectacular Bid, Swale, and Chief's Crown posted multiple major victories thereafter. Of the other 10, only Laffango and Never Bend won major events again, meaning that eight of the 17 never did.

And, as former Churchill Downs President Lynn Stone pointed out, "There are a lot of colts who don't do much as two-year-olds who blossom as three-year-olds."

Three-Year-Olds: Classic Heroes

Casual followers of thoroughbred racing usually are amazed to learn that the Kentucky Derby winner isn't the best horse in America. He eventually *might* be, but the first Saturday in May of a sophomore campaign is simply too early in the career of a race horse to expect even the greatest of Kentucky Derby winners to beat the best older horses in training, particularly at one-and-one-quarter miles.

Yet because of the classics, the three-year-olds are the sport's glamour division, the horses who attract the attention of even the most casual followers of racing, those whose only contact with the sport is watching the Derby, and perhaps the Preakness and Belmont Stakes, on television once a year.

"Not wanting to win the Derby'd be like playing the entire baseball season and saying you're not interested in the World Series or playing the entire football season and saying you don't care about the Super Bowl," said Wayne Lukas, who has trained four winners of the Run for the Roses.

To win at a mile and a quarter against the best of his generation on the first Saturday in May requires an almost error-free foundation from the colt's first training session as a two-year-old until the final strides of Churchill Downs's punishing 1,234.5-foot stretch.

"That's a graveyard through the stretch. It always has been," said trainer Smiley Adams.

"Something happens in a horse's mind that happens in any athlete's mind when they turn for home and see that expan-

Keeneland-Cook photo courtesy of Keeneland Association

Dual classic winner Nashua—and jockey Eddie Arcaro—were such a respected combination that rival jockeys knew it was wise to pay close attention to the 1955 Horse of the Year.

sive stretch run," said the late Eddie Gregson, who trained 1982 Derby winner Gato Del Sol. "They know where the wire is. Horses can brave it out for a mile and an eighth, but a lot start backing up by then."

A standout three-year-old virtually is guaranteed lasting fame. Five in the modern era captured all three classics—Assault, Citation, Secretariat, Seattle Slew, and Affirmed—and all, of course, are Hall of Famers. So are 24 of the other 35 modern colts who won five or more major races as three-year-olds, and only one of those 35 failed to win a classic, earn a championship, or a berth in the Hall of Fame.

Broad Brush was a five-time winner in 1986, when Snow Chief was selected the champion sophomore male on the strength of his victories in the Preakness and three other major races. It's difficult to argue that Snow Chief wasn't a proper choice, and the classic winners who won at least five major events who were denied three-year-old titles and haven't been enshrined in the Hall of Fame also lost championships to very formidable competition. Candy Spots, whose six 1963 victories included the Preakness, lost the title to Chateaugay, whose four triumphs included two classics. Ponder, whose five 1949 victories included the Kentucky Derby, was bypassed for the championship in favor of Capot, whose four victories included two classics. And Quadrangle won four races in addition to the Belmont Stakes in 1964 but lost the championship to dual classic winner Northern Dancer, also a five-time winner.

Seven other three-year-olds who won five or more races as sophomores are not in the Hall of Fame, although two of them, 1996 champion Skip Away and Point Given, whose six major victories in 2001 included both the Preakness and Belmont, are not yet eligible. The other five who aren't in the Hall of Fame were champions at three, and Key to the Mint is the only member of the group who wasn't a classic winner.

The aforementioned four classic-winning champion sophomores who haven't been voted into the Hall of Fame are headed by Forward Pass, a six-time winner in 1968 who won both the Derby and the Preakness, yet is better known for having won the former on the disqualification of Dancer's Image some two years after the fact because of a failed drug test. Thunder Gulch, who won both the Derby and the Belmont in 1995; 1962 Belmont winner Jaipur, and 1980 Belmont winner Temperence Hill also won five major races in championship seasons at three but haven't earned Hall of Fame plaques.

The 24 modern-era colts who captured five or more races at three, then later were enshrined in the Hall of Fame, naturally reads like a "Who's Who" of thoroughbred racing, including Triple Crown winners Citation, who claimed eight victories at three, Secretariat (7), Assault (7), Affirmed (6), and Seattle Slew (5).

Three colts won nine major events at three, including dual classic winners Native Dancer in 1953 and Damascus in 1967. Even more remarkable may have been the other to accomplish that feat, Buckpasser, since he missed the 1966 classics because of an injury. The only other colt among those 24 Hall of Famers to win five times at three without competing in a classic was Dr. Fager, who was trained by John Nerud, not a fan of trying sophomores at 10 furlongs the first week in May.

"The Derby is a great publicity gimmick," Nerud once said, "but it has ruined more horses than any two races put together."

Joining Citation with eight victories at three was dual classic winner Nashua, who lost the 1955 Kentucky Derby to Swaps in the first of the great three-year-old rivalries of the modern era.

Swaps, a five-time winner at three, and Nashua were among six pairs of modern three-year-old duos to accomplish five or more victories in the same year. The other cosmic convergences of greatness were Round Table (7) and Bold Ruler (5) in 1957, Northern Dancer and Quadrangle in 1964,

Photo courtesy of Santa Anita Park

Victories like this 10-length annihilation of Johnny's Image in the 1979 Charles H. Strub Stakes at Santa Anita enabled Affirmed, with Laffit Pincay Jr. in the saddle, to become the only Triple Crown winner in the modern era to capture Horse of the Year honors as a four-year-old.

Damascus and Dr. Fager in 1968, Affirmed (6) and Alydar (6) in 1978, and Easy Goer (7) and Sunday Silence (6) in 1989.

While Alydar is one of three of those 24 Hall of Fame colts, joining Round Table and Holy Bull, each a seven-time major winner at three, who tried yet failed to earn a classic victory, he is the only horse in history to finish second in all three. And, awarding four points for a major victory, two for a runner-up effort, and one for a third-place finish, only one horse has entered the Kentucky Derby starting gate since World War II who was more accomplished than Alydar, who had earned 28 points: Affirmed, who had 30. So the accomplishments of those colts who excelled at three despite the presence of another superstar—such as Sunday Silence, who won the Derby and Preakness and finished second in the Belmont to Derby and Preakness runner-up Easy Goer—shouldn't be minimized.

"They're really great horses—champions. They remind me of Affirmed and Alydar," jockey Angel Cordero said of Sunday Silence and Easy Goer, although he never rode either colt.

"Some people were questioning whether these two horses were really great. I think they answered that," Charlie Whittingham, Sunday Silence's trainer, said after his colt edged Easy Goer in the Breeders' Cup Classic in their final meeting. "He's the best I've ever had."

Added Pat Day, the only jockey ever to ride Easy Goer, who lost three of his four clashes with Sunday Silence: "This is the best horse I've ever ridden. It's a marvelous rivalry. It's been great for racing."

The same could be said, of course, for Affirmed vs. Alydar or Swaps vs. Nashua.

The other five colts in that elite group of 35 who deserve mention among the sport's all-time greats include four seven-time winners as sophomores: dual classic winners Carry Back and Spectacular Bid, Belmont winner Arts and Letters, and Preakness winner Hill Prince, as well as Tim Tam, who won the Derby and Preakness, then suffered a career-ending injury in the Belmont during a five-victory 1958 campaign.

Conventional wisdom long has held that it's virtually impossible for a three-year-old to be selected Horse of the Year without passing the ultimate test: beating older horses in major competition. Indeed, only four three-year-olds have been selected Horse of the Year in the modern era without beating their elders in a major race: Triple Crown winners Seattle Slew (1977) and Affirmed (1978) and dual classic winners Charismatic (1999) and Point Given (2001).

There indeed are few truer signs of greatness than a three-year-old who repeatedly defeats his elders in major races. Only Sword Dancer managed that feat four times, winning the Metropolitan and Monmouth Handicaps, Woodward Stakes, and Jockey Club Gold Cup during his 1959 Horse of the Year campaign. Of the seven colts who accomplished that feat three times, six were champions that season: Buckpasser, Damascus, Key to the Mint, Manila, Round Table, and Secretariat. The only exception was Easy Goer, who is in the Hall of Fame, as are all but Key to the Mint and Manila, the 1986 turf champion as a three-year-old.

Cordero called Manila "the best grass horse I ever rode. If my life depended on riding two horses, I'd pick Seattle Slew and him."

Although Secretariat was the only Triple Crown winner to beat his elders three times, Citation and Assault each managed that feat twice. Affirmed and Seattle Slew not only failed to beat their elders in a major race, but neither captured a significant event as a sophomore after the grueling Triple Crown campaign.

So who was the best three-year-old colt of the modern era? Opinions, of course, vary.

"Secretariat was head and shoulders above any of them. He was the best," said Ron Turcotte, Secretariat's regular rider.

"Secretariat was a great horse, but Citation would have grabbed him by the head and made him run the other way," said Eddie Arcaro, the regular jockey aboard Citation.

The following chart includes all 174 classic races of the modern era, with four points awarded for a victory, two for a second-place finish, and one for a third-place showing, with most victories and/or second-place finishes, when applicable, used to settle tiebreakers.

Classic-Placed Runners 1946-2003

	W	P	S
1. Affirmed, Assault, Citation, Seattle Slew, Secretariat	3	0	0
6. Capot, Chateaugay, Forward Pass, Majestic Prince, Middleground, Nashua, Native Dancer, Needles, Real Quiet, Silver Charm, Sunday Silence, Tim Tam (10)	2	1	0
18. Bold Forbes, Charismatic, Damascus, Funny Cide, Northern Dancer, Pleasant Colony, Risen Star, Spectacular Bid, Thunder Gulch (9)	2	0	1
27. Alysheba, Canonero II, Carry Back, Hansel, Kauai King, Little Current, Point Given, Riva Ridge, Swale, Tabasco Cat, War Emblem	2	0	0
38. Arts and Letters, Bet Twice, Easy Goer, Foolish Pleasure, Genuine Risk, Go for Gin, Sword Dancer, Victory Gallop (8)	1	2	0
46. Blue Man, Candy Spots, Fabius, Ferdinand, Phalanx, Tom Rolfe (7)	1	1	1
52. Avatar, Bally Ache, Counterpoint, Empire Maker, Fusaichi Pegasus, Gallant Man, Gato Del Sol, Hasty Road, Hill Prince, Iron Liege, Ponder, Prairie Bayou, Strike the Gold, Summer Squall, Unbridled, Venetian Way	1	1	0
67. Cannonade	1	0	2
68. Alydar (6)	0	3	0
69. Amberoid, Bold Ruler, Caveat, Celtic Ash, Editor's Note, Elocutionist, Faultless, Hail to All, High Echelon, Master Derby, Monarchos, One Count, Pine Bluff, Proud Clarion, Royal Orbit, Timber Country, Winning Colors	1	0	1
86. Golden Act, Jim French, Run Dusty Run (5)	0	2	1
89. Aloma's Ruler, A.P. Indy, Bee Bee Bee, Bold, Cavan, Coastal, Codex, Colonial Affair, Commendable, Conquistador Cielo, Creme Fraiche, Count Turf, Danzig Connection, Dark Star, Decidedly, Deputed Testamony, Determine, Dust Commander, Gate Dancer, Go and Go, Greek Money, Grindstone, High Gun, Hill Gail, Jaipur, Jet Pilot, Lemon Drop Kid, Lil E. Tee, Louis Quatorze, Lucky Debonair, Pass Catcher, Personality, Quadrangle, Red Bullet, Sarava, Sea Hero, Sherluck, Snow Chief, Spend A Buck, Stage Door Johnny, Summing, Sunny's Halo, Swaps, Tank's Prospect, Temperence Hill, Tomy Lee, Touch Gold	1	0	0
136. Aptitude, A.P. Valentine, Dapper Dan, Desert Wine, Globemaster, Jamie K., Lincoln Road, Menifee, My Dad George, No Le Hace, Sham, Skip Away, Stephan's Odyssey	0	2	0
149. Chief's Crown, Free House, Palestinian (4)	0	1	2
152. Advocator, Brian's Time, Captain Bodgit, Casual Lies, Crozier, Cryptoclearance, Hill Rise, Inside Tract, Never Bend, Proud Citizen, Ridan, Roman Line, Strodes Creek, The Scoundrel, Victoria Park	0	1	1
167. Mane Minister (3)	0	0	3
168. Admiral's Voyage, Alydeed, Bagdad, Barbs Delight, Battlefield, Best Pal, Better Self, Bold Arrangement, Bold Ego, Blazing Count, Buffle, Career Boy, Cavonnier, Cherokee Run, Coaltown, Coax Me Chad, Cool Reception, Corporate Report, Correlation, Eastern Fleet, Fisherman, Forty Niner, Francie's Hat, General Assembly, Highland Blade, Honest Pleasure, Hudson County, In Reality, Invisible Ink, Iron Constitution, Jampol, Johns Treasure, Jolly Johu, Kingpost, Kissin Kris, Laser Light, Lights Up, Linkage, Lord Boswell, Magic Weisner, McKenzie Bridge, Medaglia d'Oro, My Memoirs, Midway Road, Natchez, Neapolitan Way, Needles N Pens, Oliver's Twist, On Trust, Out of the Way, Pine Circle, Play On, Play the Red, Roman Brother, Royal Mustang, Rumbo, Ruritania, Saratoga, Slew O' Gold, Spy Song, Star Standard, Stupendous, Sub Fleet, Tejano Run, Ten Most Wanted, Thirty Six Red, Tide Rips, Twice a Prince, Vision and Verse, Vulcan's Forge, Woodchopper	0	1	0
236. Believe It, Bold Reason, Broad Brush, Congaree, Diabolo, Dike, Hampden, Hasseyampa, Impeachment, Mr. Trouble, Our Native, Royal Bay Gem, Sanhedrin, Wild Gale (2)	0	0	2
249. Agitate, Alerted, Armageddon, At the Threshold, Avies Copy, Awe Inspiring, Badge, Barberstown, Baron de Vaux, Bass Clef, Battle Morn, Blue Skyer, Blumin Affair, Bovard, Cable, Call Me Prince, Cat Thief, Choker, Citadeed, Classic Cat, Cloudy Dawn, Colonel Moran, Come On Red, Concern, Crimson Satan, Cut Away, Dance Floor, Darby Creek Road, Disperse, Dooly, Dunce, El Bakan, Escadru, Eternal Prince, Fight Over, First Family, First Landing, Flamingo, Gentleman James, Gone Fishin', Great Contractor, Guadalcanal, Gulch, High Honors, Hold Your Peace, Illuminate, Indian Charlie, Invigorator, Jaklin Klugman, Jay Ray, Key to the Mint, Le Voyageur, Limelight, Mister Frisky, Morning Bob, My Flag, My Gallant, My Request, Naskra, Noble Impulse, Nodouble, No Regrets, Noureddin, Paristo, Partez, Peace Rules, Perfect Drift, Pleasant Tap, Portersville, Prince of Thieves, Reinvested, Rockhill Native, Rock Point, Round Table, Ruhe, Screen King, Scrimshaw, Silent Screen, Summer Tan, Sunday Break, Tailspin, Thomas Jo, Traffic Judge, T.V. Commercial, Unshaded (1)	0	0	1

Four-Year-Olds: A Loaded Gun

It's quite possible that no four-year-old colt ever enjoyed a better campaign than Gun Bow did in 1964. His eight major victories included three at Santa Anita, two at Aqueduct, and one each at Gulfstream Park, Arlington Park, and Saratoga. He also finished second in four major races, two each in New York and Maryland, and third in one in New Jersey and another in New York.

Awarding four points for a major victory, two for a runner-up effort, and one for a third-place showing, Gun Bow's 42 points are the highest single-season total in the modern era for any thoroughbred of any age or sex.

Yet he failed to win a championship, falling to seven-year-old gelding Kelso, who won his fifth consecutive Horse of the Year title. Kelso won the Aqueduct Stakes, Jockey Club Gold Cup, and Washington D.C. International and had three runner-up efforts in major races that season.

Gun Bow and Kelso split their four 1964 meetings. Gun Bow won the Brooklyn Handicap, and Kelso was fifth, while Gun Bow captured the Woodward Stakes, with Kelso finishing second. Gun Bow finished second to Kelso in the Washington D.C. International and third to Kelso's second in the Monmouth Handicap.

At least Gun Bow is enshrined in the Hall of Fame, as is Coaltown, a seven-time winner during his Horse of the Year campaign in 1949. Hillsdale won all seven of his major victories as a four-year-old in 1959, including seven-furlong sprints and mile-and-a-quarter races at both Santa Anita and Hollywood Park and the one-mile Aqueduct Handicap. While it's difficult to argue with the choice of Round Table, a five-time winner in 1959, as champion older horse, Hillsdale was beaten for the sprint championship by Intentionally, whose two major victories came in the Withers Stakes and Jerome Handicap, both one-mile tests for three-year-olds.

In Excess, a five-time winner in 1991, probably could sympathize. Black Tie Affair made the Breeders' Cup Classic his second major victory of the year and earned Horse of the Year honors, while In Excess's hopes were compromised by his poor finish in the Breeders' Cup Mile in his first start on grass. The only other colts to win five races at four and be denied both championship and Hall of Fame acclaim are Crimson Satan and Droll Role.

The rest are notable Hall of Famers: six-time four-year-old winners Tom Fool, Round Table, Dr. Fager, Affirmed, Spectacular Bid, and Alysheba, as well as Swaps and Nashua, who each won five times at four. Unlike Hillsdale, however, all of those already had established their reputations. All except Alysheba and Tom Fool also won at least five races as three-year-olds, and Tom Fool was a juvenile champion and Alysheba a dual classic winner and three-year-old champion.

Photo courtesy of Bob Coglianese Photo's, Inc.

Cigar, with Jerry Bailey aboard, capped his Horse of the Year campaign in 1995 by capturing the Breeders' Cup Classic at Belmont Park.

Five-Year-Olds: A Victorious Cigar

Ten five-year-old horses, the age at which unaltered males no longer are considered colts, won five or more races. Not surprisingly, only two of them had enjoyed previous five-victory campaigns yet still remained in training at five. Round Table, a five-time victor in 1959, was selected the handicap champion, and Skip Away, a six-time winner in 1998, was named Horse of the Year.

So, of course, was Cigar, whose eight victories in 1995 were the most ever by a five-year-old.

Exceller, a six-time winner at five, had no such luck. He lost Horse of the Year honors to Affirmed, whose six victories included the Triple Crown. Exceller won both the Hollywood Gold Cup and the Jockey Club Gold Cup, beating Seattle Slew by a nose, with Affirmed fifth in the latter. Seattle Slew beat Exceller by four lengths, however, in the Woodward Stakes to earn champion older male acclaim despite posting only one other major victory, the Marlboro Cup Handicap. Exceller also won four major turf races, two at Santa Anita and two at Hollywood Park, but lost that title to Mac Diarmida, who won three times on grass and didn't race against Exceller.

At least Exceller, Noor, Round Table, and Stymie are in the Hall of Fame. Among the horses who won exactly five times at five, including Bald Eagle, Prove It, Social Outcast, and 1993 Horse of the Year Kotashaan, only Noor, Round Table, and Stymie can make that claim.

Six-Year-Olds and Up: Stymied

Believe it or not, there have been horses who have enjoyed success on the track rather than at stud at advanced ages.

While Stymie is the only horse with four victories at six, three others posted three-win campaigns at seven: Cougar II, Niarkos, and Noble Dancer II.

It should be noted, however, that of the six horses who captured major races at eight—Mashkour, Niarkos, Olhaverry, Primordial II, Redattore, and Yumbel—only Redattore had tasted major success before seven. Olhaverry's victory in the 1948 San Pasqual Handicap is the only major triumph by a nine-year-old horse, and Stymie is the only member of this group in the Hall of Fame.

Sprinters: A Short Fuse

For a number of reasons, including less margin for error at shorter distances and fewer opportunities, few sprinters have made an indelible mark on the sport by posting significant victory totals in sprints, defined in this book as races shorter than one mile.

And those who have sometimes have gone unnoticed. If sprints for two-year-olds are excluded, only one modern thoroughbred has captured four major sprint races. Lite the Fuse won both the Carter Handicap and the Frank J. De Francis Memorial Dash in 1995, then repeated that feat a year later, but he was not honored as the champion sprinter on either occasion.

Only two other colts captured three major sprint races beyond their two-year-old campaigns, Artax and Rippey.

Battlefield won five major sprints and Blue Peter four, but all were against fellow two-year-olds. Olympia, Guillotine, and Dr. Fager also won three major sprints if their one sprint success at two is included, while Foolish Pleasure, Gulch, and To Market each earned a pair of sprint triumphs at two, then added another later.

Hasty Road, Bold Lad, Buckpasser, and Affirmed each won three sprints as two-year-olds, but none won a major test at less than a mile after he turned three.

Milers: Call the Doctor

Although many breeders long have contended that milers make the best sires, major races at one mile are far more common in Europe than in North America. Mile races, such as New York's Metropolitan Handicap, often are among the year's most intriguing because they frequently match the best sprinters and the best horses at longer distances.

Only one modern-era colt has won four major races at one mile, fittingly enough Dr. Fager, who generally is considered the best miler ever. And Dr. Fager added another triumph at one-and-one-sixteenth miles. Native Dancer, Traffic Judge, Clem, Carry Back, Buckpasser, and Lure each won three times at one mile, and Carry Back and Native Dancer each added a victory at one-and-one-sixteenth miles. Stymie won twice at one mile and twice at one-and-one-sixteenth.

Capot, Fisherman, and Intentionally each won twice at one mile with another victory at one-and-one-sixteenth miles.

Those who won twice at one-and-one-sixteenth miles with one victory at a mile are Secretariat, Spectacular Bid, Riva Ridge, Bertrando, Bet Twice, Chief's Crown, In Reality, Linda's Chief, River Special, and Roving Boy. Affirmed, Crimson Satan, Fali Time, and My Request each won three times at one-and-one-sixteenth miles, but never without the additional 110 yards.

Mile-and-a-Quarter: Knights of the Round Table

The classic distance in American racing long has been considered one-and-one-quarter miles. It's a distance that requires both endurance and, because major races at 10 furlongs more often than not are contested at testing early fractions, considerable speed.

Such races as the Kentucky Derby, when three-year-olds are asked to try that distance for the first time, and the Santa Anita Handicap, which for many years was the world's richest race, have been contested at one-and-one-quarter miles throughout the modern era, as has the Breeders' Cup Classic, now the defining American test, since its inception in 1984.

"A mile and a quarter is a different game," trainer Frank LaBoccetta said before he saddled previously unbeaten Air Forbes Won to a seventh-place finish in the 1982 Kentucky Derby.

Sixty-five of the 85 modern thoroughbreds who have won three or more times at 10 furlongs or its comparable distance, a mile and three sixteenths (the length of the Preakness), are entire males.

Seventeen of the 22 modern thoroughbreds who won five or more times at the classic American distance—or nine-and-one-half furlongs—are colts. Befitting the spotlight that shines brightest on 10-furlong races, only Helioscope, Mongo, Ponder, and One Hitter among those 17 failed to win a championship.

Round Table captured 11 such races, although five of those were at one-and-three-sixteenths miles. Assault won nine, with four in the latter category, and Alysheba earned eight such victories, with seven of them actually at one-and-one-quarter miles, more than any other colt. Skip Away won six 10-furlong races and Affirmed and Spectacular Bid five apiece, and each of those immortals also captured a mile-and-three-sixteenths event. One of Spectacular Bid's 10-furlong victories produced the largest winning margin of the modern era—a mile-and-a-quarter plus the distance to the barn, since no one opted to challenge him in the 1980 Woodward Stakes.

Ponder and Sword Dancer each won five 10-furlong majors, and Carry Back, Cigar, Coaltown, Damascus, Helioscope, Nashua, and One Hitter won four each, with each capturing one at nine-and-a-half furlongs for good measure. Citation and Mongo each won three times at 10 furlongs and twice more at a mile-and-three-sixteenths.

Four major triumphs at one-and-one-quarter miles don't necessarily offer the same guarantee of lasting recognition. Only five of the nine entire males who captured four races at the classic American distance—Noor, Gun Bow, Buckpasser, Nodouble, and Tiznow—were champions, with that honor eluding Beau Purple, Mr. Right, Rejected, and West Coast Scout. Those who earned four victories either at one-and-one-quarter or one-and-three-sixteenths miles include champions Tom Fool, Swaps, Dedicate, Bold Ruler, Manila, Sunday Silence, and Real Quiet, as well as Fervent, Sailor, and Devil His Due.

Distance: A Great Divide

A good indication that, as Dr. Lavin said, most horses don't reach maturity until late in their four-year-old campaigns is the performance of colts and horses in long-distance races, defined by this book as those at one-and-one-half miles or longer.

"The dividing line between a mile and a quarter and a mile and a half is even greater than between a mile and an eighth and a mile and a quarter," said the late Eddie Gregson.

Both entire males who won six times at distances of one-and-one-half miles or more, Cougar II and Exceller, enjoyed their greatest success after their status had changed from colt to horse upon reaching their fifth birthdays. The same could be same said for those who won four distance races: Czar Alexander, Erins Isle, George Royal, Kotashaan, Niarkos, Noble Dancer II, and Stymie.

Endurance hasn't necessarily ensured enduring fame, either. Only Exceller and Stymie are in the Hall of Fame among that group, and only three of the 23 colts and horses who won exactly three times at distances of 12 or more furlongs are in the Hall of Fame: Nashua, Gallant Man, and Secretariat.

Grass: Cougar II Top Cat

Grass, rather than dirt, is the dominant surface in most of the world, particularly the major racing centers of Europe, Japan, and Hong Kong.

Since grass racing was virtually non-existent in North America until after World War II and because more than 90 percent of North American races still are contested on dirt, it's no surprise that colts and horses who dominate on the turf aren't accorded the same respect as their counterparts on dirt, who become household names among racing fans via their exploits centered on their paths toward the Triple Crown and remain in the public consciousness thereafter.

For those who don't believe that grass campaigners are the Rodney Daingerfields of thoroughbred racing, consider that of the 45 colts and horses who have won three or more grass races, only two are enshrined in the Hall of Fame, Round Table and Exceller.

Cougar II leads entire males with seven grass victories, followed by Round Table and Noble Dancer II with six apiece. Those with five are Exceller, Bien Bien, Kotashaan, Majesty's Prince, Manila, and Sandpit.

Versatile: But Unappreciated

Virtually all horses have a preference for a particular racing surface, dirt or grass. There have been numerous examples of horses whose primary achievements were on the dirt winning a major race or two on the grass and vice versa.

Amazingly, however, one of the rarest accomplishments in thoroughbred annals—three or more major victories on each surface—is among the least appreciated.

Only four campaigners in the modern era have accomplished that feat, including three entire males. Round Table won 13 major races on dirt and another six on grass on his way to the Hall of Fame. Cougar II won seven times on the grass and three times on the dirt, and Mongo captured four dirt and three grass victories, but neither has been enshrined in the Hall of Fame.

You've Got to Carry That Weight

"I don't understand handicapping," said the late Fred W. Hooper, one of thoroughbred racing's most successful owners. "It's the only sport in the world where you get penalized for being good."

Indeed, the National Football League never required Johnny Unitas to pass lefthanded, and the National Basketball Association didn't make Michael Jordan wear 25-pound ankle weights.

In order to ensure competitive events, however, thoroughbred racing long has required its biggest stars to carry more weight than their opponents in handicap races in order to equalize the competition and generate interest at the betting windows.

The old adage that enough weight can stop a train indeed has proved to be true on many occasions, with the age-old question facing any superstar being: How much weight is too much?

Even Hooper agreed that the system has merit when trying to compare stars of one era with those of another.

"I've always believed that horses prove themselves in handicap races," he said.

"When you win, you have to pay the price. You have to pick up weight," said Bud Delp, trainer of Spectacular Bid. "Weight is a great equalizer."

Many major races, of course, are contested at equal weights. Colts and geldings competing in the Triple Crown races carry 126 pounds—far more than most ever carry again in their lives. Fillies who compete in the classics are assigned 121 pounds and generally receive similar weight allowances when competing against colts that vary according to distance and the time of year a race is held.

While many pretenders to greatness do find their imposts enough to stop a train, 20 modern thoroughbreds—16 colts and four geldings—have won three or more races while carrying 127 or more pounds and therefore carry considerable, er, weight in any debate about the best handicap horses of the modern era.

Leading the way among colts is Round Table, who won nine times while carrying 127 or more pounds. Dr. Fager accomplished that feat seven times; Stymie, Coaltown, and Gun Bow earned five such victories apiece; Tom Fool, Nashua, Swaps, and Bold Ruler each had four, and Assault, Buckpasser, Damascus, Cougar II, Affirmed, Spectacular Bid, and Skip Away posted three each.

All are in the Hall of Fame except Skip Away and Cougar II. Skip Away, the only colt or horse to accomplish the feat since Spectacular Bid's Horse of the Year campaign in 1980, is not yet eligible.

Round Table actually carried at least 129 pounds in each of those aforementioned nine victories, and his eight triumphs with imposts of 130 or more pounds lead all colts in that category. Only three entire males carried 131 pounds to victory on three or more occasions: Dr. Fager (5), Round Table (4), and Bold Ruler (3), and that trio carried at least 132 in each of those assignments. And perhaps Dr. Fager and Bold Ruler never learned just how much weight was required to stop them: Each won three times with an impost of 135 or more pounds.

Runaways: Successful Bid

One way thoroughbreds stamp an indelible mark on the memory is not just by winning, but by destroying the competition. Sixty-five modern thoroughbreds have captured three or more races by margins of four or more lengths. Of the 31 who achieved that feat on four or more occasions, 30 were champions or Hall of Famers.

Posting the most such victories among colts was Spectacular Bid, whose eight runaway romps inspired Delp to call him "the best horse ever to look through a bridle."

Dr. Fager and Round Table destroyed their competition by four or more lengths on six occasions. Affirmed, Citation,

Coaltown, Damascus, Easy Goer, Secretariat, and Gun Bow each posted five such triumphs, and Alydar, Cigar, Hill Prince, Holy Bull, Native Dancer, Riva Ridge, Seattle Slew, and Skip Away recorded four apiece.

Spectacular Bid won six races by five or more lengths, one more than Dr. Fager and Secretariat, while Dr. Fager won five races by six or more lengths, one more than Damascus.

Seven colts blew away their competition by seven or more lengths on three occasions: Damascus, Dr. Fager, Gun Bow, Riva Ridge, Spectacular Bid, and, although their memorable races against each other were anything but runaways, Affirmed and Alydar.

Alydar, Dr. Fager, and Gun Bow were the only colts who won three races by eight or more lengths, and Alydar and Gun Bow each bested rivals by double-figure margins on each occasion.

Photo courtesy of Santa Anita Park

Bill Shoemaker guiding Spectacular Bid to the winner's circle was a familiar sight to thoroughbred racing fans during Bid's 1980 Horse of the Year campaign. Spectacular Bid opened his unbeaten campaign with four victories at Santa Anita, including major scores in the Charles H. Strub Stakes, the San Fernando Stakes, and the Santa Anita Handicap, the latter two on off tracks.

The largest winning margin in a major race in the modern era—ignoring the walkover victories by Citation and Spectacular Bid—was Secretariat's 31-length romp in the 1973 Belmont Stakes, an incredible feat, yet one that was predictable in one sense. Belmont Stakes competitors have yet to try running a mile and a half, a distance for which few thoroughbreds are suited and a distance few Belmont participants will run again after the second Saturday in June. That added distance also means that those who are ill-equipped to handle it may tire noticeably with more than a quarter of a mile—or even farther—remaining and are going to fall much farther behind the winner than in virtually any other North American race.

In addition to Secretariat's record runaway, 11 other Belmont winners have devastated their rivals by at least seven lengths in the modern era, more than any other race: Risen Star (14 3/4) in 1988, Conquistador Cielo (14) in 1982, Bet Twice (14) in 1987, Point Given (12 1/4) in 2001, Nashua (9) in 1955, Go and Go (8 1/4) in 1990, Citation (8) in 1948, Gallant Man (8) in 1957, Easy Goer (8) in 1989, Riva Ridge (7) in 1972, and Little Current (7) in 1974.

Quite simply, most three-year-olds are ill-equipped to carry 126 pounds one-and-one-half miles in early June and, until they try that mission, it's difficult to forecast which Belmont Stakes competitors truly will become distance specialists. None of the 17 modern thoroughbreds who captured four or more major North American stakes at one-and-one-half miles or longer even competed in the Belmont, and only six of the 29 others who won exactly three races at 12 furlongs or longer were Belmont Stakes winners: Counterpoint, High Gun, Nashua, Gallant Man, Secretariat, and Creme Fraiche. Further, only one thoroughbred since World War II has lost the Belmont Stakes, yet eventually captured three or more major races at the Belmont distance or longer: Chompion.

Conversely, of the 85 modern thoroughbreds who have won three or more major races at either one-and-one-quarter or one-and-three sixteenths miles, nine won both the Derby and the Preakness (Assault, Citation, Carry Back, Seattle Slew, Affirmed, Alysheba, Spectacular Bid, Sunday Silence, and Real Quiet). Four others won the Derby (Ponder, Swaps, Riva Ridge, and Ferdinand), and five more won the Preakness (Native Dancer, Nashua, Bold Ruler, Damascus, and Snow Chief). So 18 of the 85 won either the Derby or the Preakness, and 13 others who won three major stakes at those distances ran in either the Derby, Preakness, or both, yet failed to win either, making those classics—or virtually any other major North American stakes races—far less susceptible to Secretariat's 31-length romp or the 11 other modern Belmont triumphs by seven or more lengths.

As the following chart shows, however, Secretariat's 31-length romp was no fluke. The chart lists the record for the largest winning margin for every distance at which major races have been contested in the modern era both on dirt and grass. Only Secretariat holds the record at two distances, with his six-and-one-half length runaway in the 1973 Canadian International Championship the most onesided romp in a 13-furlong grass race.

Largest Winning Margins in Major North American Races 1946-2003

Distance	Winner	Race	Track	Time	Age	Weight	Margin
5f	Blue Peter	1948 Garden State Stakes	Garden State Park	:58 4/5	2	122	4 1/2
5.5f	King Emperor	1968 Sanford Stakes	Saratoga	1:03 2/5	2	115	5
6f	Ruffian	1974 Spinaway Stakes	Saratoga	1:08 3/5	2	120	12 3/4
6.5f	Hail to Reason	1960 Hopeful Stakes	Saratoga	1:16	2	122	10
7f	Truly Bound	1980 Arlington-Washington Lassie Stakes	Arlington Park	1:25 1/5	2	119	11
7f & 184ft	Optimistic Gal	1975 Alcibiades Stakes	Keeneland	1:28	2	119	21
a7fT	MacArthur Park	1971 Del Mar Futurity	Del Mar	1:29	2	119	10
8f	Althea	1982 Del Mar Debutante Stakes	Del Mar	1:36	2	119	15
8fT	Miesque	1988 Breeders' Cup Mile	Churchill Downs	1:38 3/5	4	123	4
8f & 70yd	Bear Hunt	1984 Gotham Stakes	Aqueduct	1:40 2/5	3	114	4 3/4
8.5f	Flanders	1994 Frizette Stakes	Belmont Park	1:43 3/5	2	119	21
8.5fT	Capades	1980 Selima Stakes	Laurel	1:44 3/5	2	119	3 1/4
9f	Western Playboy	1989 Pennsylvania Derby	Philadelphia Park	1:47 3/5	3	122	17
9fT	Tranquility Lake	1999 Gamely Breeders' Cup Handicap	Hollywood Park	1:46	4	119	5 1/2
9.5f	Funny Cide	2003 Preakness Stakes	Pimlico	1:55 3/5	3	126	9 3/4
9.5fT	England's Legend	2001 Beverly D. Stakes	Arlington Park	1:56 3/5	4	123	7 3/4
a10f	Ancient Title	1977 Del Mar Handicap	Del Mar	1:55 2/5	7	123	5
a10fT	Princessnesian	1968 Santa Barbara Handicap	Santa Anita	2:00 4/5	4	124	8
10f	Damascus	1967 Travers Stakes	Saratoga	2:01 3/5	3	126	22
10fT	Dahlia's Dreamer	1994 Flower Bowl Invitational Handicap	Belmont Park	2:05 2/5	5	112	13
10.5f	Tempted	1961 Ladies Handicap	Aqueduct	2:09	4	128	2 3/4
11f	Chief Honcho	1992 Brooklyn Handicap	Aqueduct	2:16 4/5	5	117	5 1/2
11fT	Hill Circus	1972 Beverly Hills Handicap	Hollywood Park	2:13 1/5	4	115	10
12f	Secretariat	1973 Belmont Stakes	Belmont Park	2:24	3	126	31
12fT	Erins Isle	1983 Hollywood Invitational Handicap	Hollywood Park	2:25 4/5	5	127	12
a12fT	Master Boing	1956 Washington D.C. International	Laurel	2:39	3	122	5
13f	School Tie	1946 Lawrence Realization Stakes	Belmont Park	2:43 3/5	3	110	25
13fT	Secretariat	1973 Canadian International Championship	Woodbine	2:41 4/5	3	117	6 1/2
a14T	Fly Till Dawn	1992 San Juan Capistrano Handicap	Santa Anita	2:46 2/5	6	121	7
14f	Don Poggio	1960 Gallant Fox Handicap	Jamaica	2:55 4/5	4	126	7
16f	Autobiography	1972 Jockey Club Gold Cup	Aqueduct	3:21 2/5	4	124	15
16fT	Petrone	1969 Sunset Handicap	Hollywood Park	3:18	5	124	3 1/2
16.5f	Midafternoon	1956 Display Handicap	Jamaica	3:29 3/5	4	126	5 1/2
18f	Miss Grillo	1948 New York Handicap	Belmont Park	3:53 3/5	6	120	5

Consistency: The Fab Five

No fewer than 126 modern thoroughbreds have managed to record a major victory in three consecutive seasons. Surprisingly enough, considering their residual value at stud, 78 of those have been colts and horses.

Only five of those, however, have shown such brilliance as juveniles that they also were allowed to become major winners as three-, four-, and five-year-olds. And that distinction has eluded all but one colt born since 1958, Free House, who won major races at two, three, four, and five from 1996-99 to join Better Self, My Request, Round Table, and Carry Back as the fifth colt in the modern era to earn a major victory in four consecutive campaigns.

All but five of those 78 colts indeed started their strings of winning campaigns before the age of five, with Olhaverry the latest bloomer, scoring a major victory in three consecutive campaigns from 1946-48 at ages seven, eight, and nine.

Round Table is one of two modern-era colts who can claim three consecutive campaigns with four or more victories, which he accomplished as a three-, four-, and five-year-old. Affirmed earned four or more triumphs as a two-, three-, and four-year-old.

Only five other colts or horses had three consecutive seasons with three or more victories, with Carry Back, Buckpasser, and Spectacular Bid beginning that accomplishment at two. Skip Away started his run of three-plus victory seasons as a three-year-old and Cougar II at five.

Just nine other colts strung together three consecutive multiple-victory seasons: Stymie, Battlefield, One Hitter, Nashua, Mongo, Riva Ridge, Foolish Pleasure, Gulch, and Devil His Due.

Awarding four points for a victory, two for a runner-up finish, and one for a third-place showing in major races, Skip Away is the only modern thoroughbred to rank as the overall leader three times. Skip Away posted five wins, two seconds, and two thirds in 1996 (26 points); three victories, five seconds, and one third in 1997 (23), and six triumphs and a third-place finish (25) as Horse of the Year in 1998. Skip Away's 76 points, earned via 14 victories, eight runner-up finishes, and four third-place showings, rank second among modern colts. Round Table, who led the points list in both 1957 (33) and '58 (30), leads all modern colts with 19 victories, 25 two-top finishes, 29 in-the-money efforts, and 92 points. Only two other colts led the points list more than once. Nashua's 34 points led the list in 1955, and his 22 points shared that honor with Swaps a year later. Alysheba's 19 points shared the 1987 leadership with Gone West, and his 26 led the list in '88.

Horses for Courses

While it's easier to explain a thoroughbred's preference for grass or dirt—and certainly for a particular distance—many have demonstrated quite specific preferences for one dirt surface, perhaps a hard, fast track, or grass surface, perhaps a soft, yielding course, over another on a consistent basis.

Take Churchill Downs, for example. Cannonade won all three of his starts in Louisville and gained lasting fame as the winner of the 100th Kentucky Derby in 1974. That was his only major victory in 25 career starts, and he won only four of 22 races away from Churchill Downs.

"Some horses come in here and don't handle this track," said longtime Churchill Downs trainer Ronnie Warren. "They run bad, then leave, and do all right."

Skip Away, for instance, captured 14 major victories, more than any colt born later than 1976, and recorded 26 top-three finishes in major races. In his two starts at Churchill Downs, however, he finished 12th in the 1996 Kentucky Derby and sixth in the 1998 Breeders' Cup Classic.

Unlike Cannonade, some colts have been able to fashion careers with three or more major victories—yet claimed all of those victories at the same track.

Most notable among them is Fit to Fight, whose four major victories all came at Belmont Park. Belmont Park also was the only site of a major victory for three-time winners Ogygian, Waquoit, Albert the Great, and 1982 Horse of the Year Conquistador Cielo.

Dean Carl, Flag Raiser, and Munden Point all enjoyed three-victory careers without winning anywhere but Aqueduct. California-based colts who proved to be horses for courses were Colorado King and Y Flash, three-time winners at Hollywood Park, and three-time Santa Anita victors Intent and Terrang. Yorky earned all three of his major victories at Hialeah, and Diplomatic Jet is the only colt who scored all three of his major victories on the same turf course, Belmont Park's.

Tough Luck

You'll probably never hear the names All Hands or Royal Gunner in discussions about history's greatest thoroughbreds. Nor should you.

Yet they rank as the two most accomplished colts who never won a major race in the modern era. All Hands accumulated 15 points via five runner-up efforts and another five third-place showings. Incredibly, All Hands lost to a different winner in each of those 10 defeats. His five runner-up efforts came at the hands of Toby's Brother in the Breeders' Futurity, to Oil Wick in the Kentucky Jockey Club Stakes, and to Progressing in the Pimlico Futurity as a two-year-old in 1959; to Moslem Chief in the 1960 Everglades Stakes, and to Kelso by a mere neck—All Hands's closest taste to a major victory—in the 1961 Metropolitan Handicap. All Hands's third-place efforts came against Weatherwise in the 1959 Futurity Stakes and in the 1961 McLennan (Yorky), New Orleans (Greek Star), John B. Campbell (Conestoga), and Grey Lag (Mail Order) Handicaps.

Royal Gunner posted six runner-up efforts and two third-place showings without tasting victory. Three of those eight losses came at the hands of Tom Rolfe, including Royal Gunner's closest call, a loss by a neck in the 1965 Arlington Classic.

Geldings

Two-Year-Olds: Pal's the Best

For those who don't think geldings are late bloomers, consider that 50 two-year-olds have won three or more major races in the modern era. But the only gelding who can claim that distinction is Best Pal, who captured the Del Mar Futurity, Norfolk Stakes, and Hollywood Futurity in 1990.

Three-Year-Olds: Just Four Scores in Classics

Further proof that geldings don't rise to the top until they're older horses: Forty-seven three-year-olds have won five or more major events, and none of them have been geldings.

And just four of the 174 modern-era classic races—the Kentucky Derby, Preakness Stakes, and Belmont Stakes—have been won by geldings. Creme Fraiche captured the 1985 Belmont Stakes, which excluded geldings from participation until 1957; Prairie Bayou won the 1993 Preakness Stakes, and Funny Cide became the first dual classic winner among geldings when he captured the 2003 Derby and Preakness.

Likewise, only two sophomore geldings have managed to beat their elders at least twice in major competition, a feat accomplished 42 times by modern colts and fillies. Kelso won the Hawthorne Gold Cup and Jockey Club Gold Cup on his way to the first of five consecutive Horse of the Year titles in 1960, and Johnny D. captured the Washington D.C. International and the Turf Classic in 1977, when he was named the champion male on grass.

Four-Year-Olds: The Cream Begins to Rise

Geldings, at least the best of them, begin rising to the top by age four. Only three of them managed five or more victories as four-year-olds, but they are unquestionably the three best geldings of the modern era and perhaps of all time. Forego earned eight victories in 1974 on his way to the first of three consecutive Horse of the Year titles, Kelso six in 1961, and John Henry five in 1979.

Five-Year-Olds: Bowl Game for Forego

Two geldings have captured five major victories at five: Forego during his 1975 Horse of the Year campaign and Bowl Game, who was named turf champion after earning five victories on the grass in 1979.

Six-Year-Olds and Up: John Henry's Signature

No modern thoroughbred ever excelled so late in his career as did John Henry, who captured four victories and earned his second Horse of the Year title as a nine-year-old in 1984.

Only three other modern thoroughbreds managed to cap-

Photo courtesy of Santa Anita Park

John Henry, under Chris McCarron in a race at Santa Anita, was the most accomplished North American campaigner since World War II on grass, at distances of one-and-one-half miles or longer, and as a nine-year-old, earning his second Horse of the Year crown at that age in 1984.

ture major victories at the age of nine, including John's Call, who won twice at nine in 2000. Despite John Henry's brilliance, one reason it is difficult to compare the achievements of geldings and those horses who are headed to the breeding shed is because the latter don't get the chance to set records for longevity.

"He's the best horse I've ever ridden. There's no question about it," Chris McCarron said after he guided Alysheba to a 1988 Breeders' Cup Classic victory that clinched Horse of the Year honors for his mount.

Instructively, McCarron was also the regular rider aboard John Henry during his 1984 Horse of the Year campaign.

Four of the seven thoroughbreds who have enjoyed three-victory campaigns as seven-year-olds—Find, Kelso, Yankee Affair, and With Anticipation—also are geldings, and geldings who won a major race at eight include Air Pilot, Autocrat, Biggs, John Henry, Kelso, Native Diver, Punch Line, Sir Bear, and Affirmed Success.

Sprinters: Forego Without Equal

Forego is the only gelding who has managed three major sprint victories.

Milers: Kelso Has a Pal

No modern gelding can claim three major victories at one mile, although both Kelso and Best Pal earned two victories at one mile and another at one-and-one-sixteenth miles. Telly's Pop won a major race at one mile and two more with the extra 110 yards added, and although Find never won at a mile, he did win three times at one-and-one-sixteenth miles.

Mile-and-One-Quarter: No Asterisks for Kelso

The most accomplished mile-and-a-quarter campaigner—no asterisks for nine-and-half furlongs necessary—was five-time Horse of the Year Kelso, who had eight triumphs at 10 furlongs.

Armed and Forego had seven and six wins at a mile-and-a-quarter, respectively, and each had another at nine-and-a-half furlongs. Best Pal won five times at 10 furlongs, Bardstown and John Henry four, and Royal Glint three, with the latter also winning twice at one-and-three-sixteenths miles.

The only other geldings with three victories at the classic American distance were Native Diver, Creme Fraiche, and Ancient Title, whose triumphs actually included the 1977 Del Mar Handicap at about 10 furlongs.

John Henry Goes the Distance

The classic distance in Europe is one-and-one-half miles. By American racing standards, that's a marathon, and the greatest distance horses—those who consistently excelled at 12 furlongs or more—have been geldings.

Seven of the 17 with four or more victories at 12 furlongs or longer, six of the eight with five or more such triumphs, and all three with seven or more have been geldings.

The greatest distance performer of the modern era has been John Henry, who scored an incredible 14 long-distance victories, twice as many as runners-up Kelso and Fort Marcy. A measure of just how impressive John Henry's successful journeys at 12 furlongs or more actually is: Only seven other modern thoroughbreds have more *total* major victories.

Bowl Game, Cedar Key, and Quicken Tree each won five times at long distances and Forego four, which makes him the only modern thoroughbred with three or more victories in both sprints and long-distance races.

Splendor on the Grass for Big Bad John

Even more phenomenal than John Henry's 14 long-distance triumphs is his record of 16 major victories on grass. Only Round Table and fellow geldings Kelso and Forego earned more total major victories.

Fort Marcy is the only other gelding to earn Hall of Fame recognition via his splendor on the grass, a surface on which he posted eight victories. Bowl Game, with six victories, and Cedar Key and With Anticipation, each with five, also rank among the best turf campaigners of the modern era.

Versatile: A Rags-to Riches Saga

Among the many one-of-a-kind accomplishments that John Henry posted during his rags-to-riches career in which he once was sold for $1,100 and earned nearly $7 million was that, in addition to his 16 major victories on grass, he also posted three on dirt. The only gelding to win three or more on each surface won both the Jockey Club Gold Cup and Santa Anita Handicap in 1981—the two richest dirt races of the year for older horses—then became the first of only two two-time winners in the history of the Big 'Cap a year later.

Forego: Beast of Burden

Not only are geldings deprived of a career at stud, but the great ones have to continue to prove their mettle by carrying heavy loads.

Four geldings won three or more major races under imposts of 127 or more pounds, and three of them rank as the greatest weight carriers of the modern era.

Forego achieved that distinction a record 15 times, Kelso 12, and Armed 10. John Henry was the only other gelding to achieve that distinction, winning four times with an impost of 128 pounds or heavier. Kelso won a dozen times and Armed 10 carrying that much weight and, in fact, Kelso carried 130 or more pounds to victory 10 times, and Armed did it on seven occasions. Kelso won five races carrying 131 or more pounds and four in which his impost was 133 or higher.

But the greatest weight carrier of the modern era undoubtedly was Forego. He won 14 times with an impost of 129 or more pounds, 11 times with at least 130 on his back, and also holds the records for major victories carrying at least 131 (10), 132 (8), 133 (7), and 134 (5) or more pounds.

Runaways: Kelso Is King

Perhaps because of their considerable weight imposts, only three modern-era geldings destroyed their opposition by four or more lengths more than three times.

Kelso, who trails only Forego among modern weight carriers, humiliated his opposition by four or more lengths a record 11 times, while Roman Brother and Native Diver each managed that feat on four occasions.

Kelso also hammered his opponents by five or more lengths on seven occasions and by six lengths or more three times, both without equal among geldings.

Consistency, Thy Name Is Kelso

It isn't surprising that half of the 14 modern thoroughbreds who have posted major victories in four or more consecutive seasons are geldings. And only three of those, Kelso, Cedar Key, and Fort Marcy, began their streaks at age three.

Kelso won at least one race in a record six consecutive seasons from 1960-65. Native Diver and John Henry each won five years in a row beginning at four and five years old, respectively. Forego and Ancient Title join Cedar Key and Fort Marcy as geldings who won in four consecutive years, with each beginning his string as a four-year-old.

Kelso also is the only modern campaigner to enjoy five straight multiple-victory seasons, which he managed in his Horse of the Year campaigns from 1960-64. Forego posted multiple victories in four consecutive seasons beginning at age four, and in the first three of those, his Horse of the Year campaigns from 1974-76, he actually won at least four times. No other gelding has put together even three straight seasons with three or more victories, and John Henry and Best Pal are the only other geldings who have had three consecutive multiple-victory campaigns, with Best Pal starting his streak as a two-year-old and John Henry at five.

Not surprisingly, Kelso, Forego, and John Henry rank as the three most accomplished modern thoroughbreds in terms of points accumulated in major races. Kelso posted 24 victories, 34 top-two finishes, and 35 in-the-money efforts, all records, for 117 points. Forego and John Henry each had 19 victories and seven second-place efforts, but Forego's five third-place showings, one more than John Henry, give him 95 total points to John Henry's 94.

Forego led the points list in both 1974 (26) and '75 (23), while John Henry's 28 points led the list in 1981, and his 19 shared the leadership with At the Threshold in 1984.

Horses for Courses: 'Diver' Ruled Hollywood

Only one modern thoroughbred has managed a Hall of Fame career with all of his major victories coming on the same track. Although Native Diver finished in the money in major competition at Santa Anita six times, all six of the celebrated California gelding's major victories came at Hollywood Park.

Winter's Tale's four major triumphs all came at Belmont Park and Stardust Mel's three at Santa Anita. Two geldings achieved considerable success as horses for courses by winning three times on Belmont Park's turf course, Solar Splendor and Val's Prince.

Tough Luck for Tick Tock

No winless gelding was blessed with as much success—or less luck—than Tick Tock, who had six second-place finishes and four third-place efforts in major stakes without a victory on his resume. And all 10 losses were to different horses.

Tick Tock finished second to Noorsaga in the 1955 Cowdin Stakes, to Oh Johnny in the 1956 Travers Stakes, to Reneged in the 1956 Jerome Handicap, to Promised Land in the 1957 Pimlico Special, to Bold Ruler in the 1958 Carter Handicap, and to Jimmer in the 1959 Carter Handicap. Three of those losses, to Noorsaga, to Jimmer, and to Oh Johnny, were by less than one length. Tick Tock finished third to Greek Spy in the 1957 Massachusetts Handicap, to Portersville in the 1957 Brooklyn Handicap, to Kingmaker in the 1957 Whitney Stakes, and to Hillsdale in the 1959 Aqueduct Handicap.

Fillies and Mares

Two-Year-Olds: La Prevoyante Follows Numbered Footsteps

While Battlefield is the only male who won five major races at two, two fillies accomplished that feat. Numbered Account won the Spinaway Stakes, Matron Stakes, Frizette Stakes, Selima Stakes, and Gardenia Stakes in 1971, and La Prevoyante triumphed in the same five events a year later.

Such stunning success for two-year-old fillies, however, is even less of a harbinger of future greatness than it is for colts. Numbered Account added only one more major victory, and La Prevoyante is one of nine fillies among the 21 who won three or more major races at two who never again won a major stakes.

Bed o' Roses, Cicada, Meadow Star, and Optimistic Gal each won four times at two, then earned subsequent multiple victories, but four-time winners Flanders, Moccasin, and Queen of the Stage never won major stakes again.

Four of the 11 fillies who won three times as juveniles—Forward Gal, Idun, Miss Oceana, and Althea—subsequently added multiple triumphs, while Dearly Precious, First Flight, and Lakeville Miss each added one more major victory.

Winning three major races at two virtually has assured fillies of championship acclaim, however. Seventeen of the 21 have been so honored, and all four who failed to earn that title were beaten by fellow winners of three or more races.

Stunning success as a two-year-old filly hasn't necessarily ensured immortality, however. Only three of those illustrious 21 are in the Hall of Fame: Bed o' Roses, Cicada, and La Prevoyante, who is the only modern-era Hall of Famer who never won a major race after his or her juvenile season.

Three-Year-Olds: Bold, But Not Genuine

Winning six or more major races at three hasn't provided the same level of immortality for fillies as it has for colts.

That feat has been accomplished only four times, by seven-time winners Bold 'n Determined in 1980 and Serena's Song in 1995 and by six-time winners But Why Not in 1947 and Next Move in 1950.

Bold 'n Determined was the only member of that group who was denied a championship. That honor went to 1980 Kentucky Derby winner Genuine Risk, who was the first filly to win a classic in the modern era, a feat also accomplished eight years later in the same race by Winning Colors.

Yet Bold 'n Determined and Serena's Song are the only members of that quartet of fillies who won six or more times as sophomores who have been elected to the Hall of Fame.

Six of the eight fillies who won exactly five major races at three have been elected to the Hall of Fame—Dark Mirage, Davona Dale, Go for Wand, Real Delight, Shuvee, and Susan's Girl. Five of those six immortals were champions at three, the lone exception being Shuvee, who lost the title to Gallant Bloom despite capturing New York's Triple Tiara—which then consisted of the Acorn Stakes, Mother Goose Stakes, and Coaching Club American Oaks—Saratoga's Alabama Stakes, and defeating her elders in the Ladies Handicap.

The pair whom Hall voters have overlooked have strong credentials for inclusion. Open Mind is the only filly to win New York's Triple Tiara for sophomore distaffers as well as the Kentucky Oaks and Alabama Stakes, arguably America's five most important races for three-year-old fillies. The other was Optimistic Gal, the only modern filly with at least three major victories at two and five as a sophomore, although she didn't win a championship either time, losing the 1976 three-year-old filly title to Revidere after losing juvenile honors to Dearly Precious a year earlier.

Further, beating their elders three times in a season has not been a similar ticket to stardom for fillies as it has been for colts.

That has been accomplished just three times, by Next Move, Cum Laude Laurie in 1977, and Lady's Secret in 1985.

Photo courtesy of Santa Anita Park

Among the many accomplishments of champion filly Serena's Song was that she was one of only five fillies since World War II who posted three consecutive multiple-victory seasons in major stakes and her record-tying 18 top-two finishes in major events.

Cum Laude Laurie lost the title to Our Mims and Lady's Secret to Triple Tiara winner Mom's Command. A year later, Lady's Secret became the third of four fillies in the modern era to earn Horse of the Year acclaim, joining Moccasin, who shared the title as a two-year-old in 1965; 1983 Horse of the Year All Along, and 2002 honoree Azeri. And, unlike Cum Laude Laurie, Our Mims, Mom's Command, Next Move, and Moccasin, Lady's Secret is most certainly in the Hall of Fame.

"This a superstar—the best filly ever to race," her owner, the late Gene Klein, said after Lady's Secret clinched Horse of the Year honors by winning the 1986 Breeders' Cup Distaff by five lengths at Santa Anita. "She has done extraordinary things on the track."

But Lady's Secret never accomplished what transpired in the Breeders' Cup in 1987 across Greater Los Angeles at Hollywood Park. Very Subtle captured the Breeders' Cup Sprint and Miesque the Breeders' Cup Mile, both beating older males in major competition as three-year-old fillies.

Before Very Subtle and Miesque turned the trick on the same day, that had been accomplished just seven times in the modern era. Siama won the 1950 Monmouth Handicap, Parading Lady the 1952 Vosburgh Handicap, Misty Morn the 1955 Gallant Fox Handicap, Dahlia the 1973 Washington D.C. International, Nobiliary the 1975 Washington D.C. International, April Run the 1981 Turf Classic, and River Memories the 1987 Rothmans International Stakes. Those victories helped earn championships for Misty Morn, April Run, and Miesque.

Miesque, who won the same race a year later in her only other North American start, repeated as the distaff turf champion in 1988. Dahlia won the same honor in 1974, and they are the only members of that elite group enshrined in the Hall of Fame.

But three-year-old fillies beating males in major competition is such a rare feat that, after Very Subtle and Miesque accomplished that on the same day in 1987, it didn't happen again until Six Perfections captured the 2003 NetJets Breeders' Cup Mile at Santa Anita.

Four-Year-Olds: Lady Has No Peer

"To say she's one in a million would be an understatement," Pat Day said after he dismounted from Lady's Secret in the wake of her romp in the 1986 Breeders' Cup Distaff. "She's a real work of art."

Among four-year-old fillies, Lady's Secret, a seven-time winner in 1986, certainly had no peer. The only other four-year-old fillies to win as many as five times in the modern era were Susan's Girl in 1973 and Azeri in 2002.

"What Secretariat, Seabiscuit, and John Henry had, she has," said Lukas, Lady's Secret's trainer. "It's that intangible you can't put your finger on—the heart, the will, the competitiveness. (Hall of Fame trainer) Woody Stephens says Lady's Secret is the greatest filly of all time. She deserves to be in the archives, the history books."

Photo courtesy of Santa Anita Park

After Pat Day guided Lady's Secret to a two-and-a-half-length triumph in the Breeders' Cup Distaff at Santa Anita that clinched 1986 Horse of the Year honors for the four-year-old filly, her trainer, Wayne Lukas, said she "deserves to be in the archives, the history books."

Five-Year-Olds: McAnally's Secret

If there is a secret to winning major races with five-year-old mares—and there well may be—ask Ron McAnally.

The only mare to win six races at five was Argentine-bred Bayakoa in 1989. McAnally, who trained Bayakoa, almost duplicated that feat in 1992, when he saddled Paseana, another Argentine-bred, to victories in five major stakes.

The only other time a five-year-old mare has earned five major victories in the modern era was 2000, when trainer Eduardo Inda managed that feat with Riboletta. Inda, a longtime assistant to McAnally, threw a slight curveball, however: Riboletta wasn't bred in Argentina, but across the continent in Brazil.

Six-Year-Olds and Up: The Old Brown Mare

Successful mares, like their male counterparts, obviously are being targeted for the breeding shed. Of the six who have accomplished three-victory campaigns at six, three had enjoyed better seasons at an earlier age: Bayakoa, Paseana, and Susan's Girl. Dulcia and Typecast had not won major races before their three-victory seasons at six, and Old Hat didn't win in prestigious company until she was five.

Likewise, My Celeste, the only two-time winner at age seven, hadn't won before, and Brown Bess, whose victory in the 1990 Santa Barbara Handicap is the only major score for an eight-year-old mare, earned her only other major victory at seven.

Sprinters: Flight Leader

Fillies from Ta Wee to Honorable Miss to Very Subtle have scored notable success against colts in major sprint races.

But none of them have been able to compile as many as three victories in major sprints after reaching age three. First Flight managed four such triumphs, but three of them came during her two-year-old campaign, and Optimistic Gal earned two of her three sprint victories at two.

Bewitch, Queen of the Stage, and Dearly Precious all won three sprints during their championship campaigns at two, but none of them managed a major sprint victory afterward.

Milers: Another Bold Achievement

No fewer than 41 fillies and mares have captured three or more major races at one mile or at one-and-one-sixteenth miles, and all but 11 of that group are champions or Hall of Famers.

While Dr. Fager is the only colt to win five or more major events at one mile or a sixteenth longer, eight distaffers have accomplished that feat. Leading the way is Bold 'n Determined, who won four times at a mile and another two with an extra half a furlong. Sharp Cat won three times at each of those distances, and although Serena's Song won only once at one mile, she added five more victories at one-and-one-sixteenth miles.

But Why Not and Heavenly Cause each had two victories at one mile and another three with the extra 110 yards, Honeymoon and Idun each captured four at a one-and-one-sixteenth miles and another at a mile, and Bed o' Roses triumphed five times at eight-and-a-half furlongs.

Also with four victories at some combination of one mile and one-and-one-sixteenth miles are Miss Oceana, Althea, Azeri, Cicada, Excellent Meeting, Inside Information, Lithe, Surfside, Susan's Girl, Paseana, and You. Fourteen of those 19 are either champions or Hall of Fame members, with the only exceptions being Sharp Cat, Lithe, Miss Oceana, Excellent Meeting, and You.

Mile-and-a-Quarter: No Four Score

Although major races for fillies and mares are often shorter than those for their male counterparts, it's still somewhat surprising that no distaffer has captured more than three major races at one-and-one-quarter miles.

Six of the nine who won three—Lady's Secret, Life's Magic, Straight Deal (1962), Late Bloomer, Shuvee, and Susan's Girl—were champions, an honor that eluded Busanda, Love Sign, and Nastique. Two others won two races at 10 furlongs and another at one-and-three-sixteenths miles, Kostroma and champion Possibly Perfect.

Distance: A Royal Flush

Fillies and mares who win consistently at one-and-one-half miles or more are almost as rare as drawing the right five cards for a royal flush. In fact, the number is the same.

Dahlia won four times at 12 furlongs or more, and All Along, April Run, Drumtop, and Typecast each won three long-distance events. Only Drumtop wasn't voted a champion among that group.

Grass: Flawless and Perfect

With even fewer big-money races than their male counterparts, it's no surprise that fillies and mares whose preferred racing surface is grass often are omitted from discussions about the sport's all-time greats.

Flawlessly and Possibly Perfect were two of the premier distaffers of the '90s, and their five grass victories apiece are the most among females. Dahlia, Sangue, and Astra each won four times on the turf, and Sangue is one of only two of the 18 distaffers who won three or more grass races who also earned a major victory on the dirt, capturing the 1982 Vanity Handicap. Waya, a three-time winner on the grass, also won twice on the dirt, capturing both the Top Flight Handicap and the Beldame Stakes in 1979.

Inside Information on Runaways

Six modern distaffers have managed to humiliate their foes with romps of four lengths or more on five occasions: Bayakoa, Dark Mirage, Heavenly Prize, Inside Information, Lady's Secret, and Optimistic Gal. The latter, whose name keeps popping up everywhere but on a Hall of Fame plaque, is the only campaigner of either sex to accomplish that feat four or more times without netting a championship or Hall of Fame recognition.

Distaffers who accomplished victories of four or more lengths four times were Beautiful Pleasure, Meadow Star, Sky Beauty, Desert Vixen, and Sightseek.

Heavenly Prize and Inside Information, stablemates in the '90s, are the only fillies to humble their opponents by five or more lengths five times, and the former is the only distaffer with five triumphs of six or more lengths. Heavenly Prize also won three major races by seven or more lengths. That feat has been matched by Desert Vixen, Inside Information, and the ill-fated Ruffian, who scored three times by eight or more lengths.

The only filly to win three or more races by nine or more lengths earned three victories by 11 or more—the only modern thoroughbred who can make that claim. Inside Information scored by 11 lengths in the 1994 Acorn Stakes, captured the 1995 Ruffian Handicap by the same margin, then capped her career in style with a 13 1/2-length romp in the Breeders' Cup Distaff later that fall.

The latter race earned Inside Information a championship, but her overlooked achievements have yet to earn her a spot in the Hall of Fame.

Shuvee Was Miss Consistency

Only two modern fillies have managed to string together four consecutive seasons with at least one major triumph, Bed o' Roses and Shuvee, and both started their streaks as two-year-olds.

All four of Shuvee's campaigns included at least two victories, a record for a distaffer. The only other fillies who have put together three consecutive multiple-victory seasons are Straight Deal (1962), Sharp Cat, and Serena's Song, with each beginning her streak as a juvenile.

The all-time points leader among females was not Shuvee, however, but Susan's Girl, whose 13 victories, 24 top-three finishes, and 68 points are records for distaffers. Susan's Girl's 18 top-two finishes share that distinction with Paseana and Serena's Song.

Real Tough Luck

Leading the way among hard-luck fillies is Real Connection, who posted five runner-up finishes and two third-place efforts, all in California in the mid-'90s, without a victory.

Four of her five runner-up efforts came by less than one length, including two losses to Donna Viola—by a nose in the 1996 Gamely Handicap and by half a length in the 1996 Yellow Ribbon Stakes. Real Connection finished only three-quarters of a length behind Escena in the 1997 Ramona Handicap and a head behind Twice the Vice in the 1997 Vanity Handicap.

Beating the Boys: Gallorette's Forte

Although it's unlikely to expect the women's NCAA basketball champions to beat the men's champions or the women's Olympic 100-meter gold medalist to defeat her male counterpart—even once in 50 tries—fillies and mares *are* capable of beating males in thoroughbred racing.

"I have always felt that outstanding fillies could compete with colts, regardless of age," said trainer John Veitch. "If you come up in a weak year—and Genuine Risk ran in a weak year—and you've got a great filly . . . "

When Genuine Risk captured the 1980 Kentucky Derby to become the first filly in 65 years to win the Run for the Roses, it was probably the most celebrated victory by a distaffer in the modern era. That was the only time she conquered colts in major competition, however.

Four Footed Fotos, Inc., photo by Terry Jones, courtesy of Churchill Downs

Winning Colors, with Gary Stevens in the irons, edged Forty Niner (1A) by a neck in the 1988 Kentucky Derby to become only the third filly in history to capture the Run for the Roses.

Distaffers generally carry less weight when competing against males regardless of age or distance. Genuine Risk, for example, carried 121 pounds in the Derby, five fewer than her male counterparts. Yet it's still quite an accomplishment for a distaffer to defeat males, and only 28 modern fillies and mares have managed that feat more than once in major competition.

Leading the way is Gallorette, who beat males to win the 1946 Metropolitan and Brooklyn Handicaps as a four-year-old, captured the 1947 Queens County Handicap, and won both the Carter Handicap and the Whitney Stakes in 1948.

Dahlia accomplished the feat four times, and April Run, Typecast, Drumtop, and All Along three each, the latter on her way to the 1983 Horse of the Year crown. Drumtop is the only member of that group who is neither a champion nor a member of the Hall of Fame.

Fillies who twice defeated colts in major races in the modern era include champions Althea, Bridal Flower, Estrapade, First Flight, Miesque, Miss Alleged, My Juliet, Royal Heroine, Serena's Song, Shuvee, Silver Spoon, Tosmah, Waya, and Winning Colors, who in 1988 became the third filly to win the Kentucky Derby. Also beating colts twice in major competition in the modern era were A Gleam, Honeymoon, Honorable Miss, June Darling, Lithe, Miss Grillo, Miz Clementine, and Summer Guest.

Fillies for Courses, Particularly Belmont Park

Three of the five fillies who earned four or more major victories without winning at more than one track accomplished that feat at Belmont Park—Turnback the Alarm (5), Berlo (4), and First Flight (4). The other fillies in their company are Take Charge Lady, who captured all four of her major triumphs at Keeneland, and Astra, who claimed all four of her major scores on Hollywood Park's turf course.

Happyanunoit earned all three of her major victories on Hollywood Park's grass course.

Colts, Horses, Geldings, Fillies, and Mares

Great Times for Swaps, Secretariat, And Even Bienamado

Winning against the best competition—and doing it repeatedly—may be the best way to judge the feats of thoroughbreds, but it is by no means the only one.

If there was no significance, for example, why would anyone bother to time the races?

The following chart includes the record for every distance in major races that have been contested in North America, on both grass and dirt, since World War II. The chart includes the fastest victorious times recorded at that distance for each division that has competed in major stakes at that distance and the 10 fastest times for the popular distances of six furlongs, seven furlongs, one mile, one-and-one-eighth miles, one-and-one-quarter miles, one-and-one-half miles, and one-and-one-half miles on the turf.

Note that 14 names appear more than once, and five of the six who are listed more than twice are legendary Hall of Famers: Swaps (4), Kelso (4), Secretariat (3), Affirmed (3), and John Henry (3). Such recognition has escaped the other member of that august group, First Flight, the only filly whose name appears three times.

Swaps ran both the fastest one-and-one-sixteenth miles (1:39) and the fastest one-and-five-eighths miles (2:38 1/5) in winning the 1956 Inglewood and Sunset Handicaps, respectively. His clocking of 1:40 2/5 in the 1955 Californian Stakes was the fastest mile-and-one-sixteenth by a three-year-old, and his time of 1:58 3/5 in the 1956 Hollywood Gold Cup was one of the 10 fastest times for 10 furlongs.

J.C. Skeets Meaders photo courtesy of Keeneland Association

Kelso, who is being paraded before a packed house at Keeneland Race Course, not only won 24 major North American stakes—more than any other thoroughbred since World War II—and earned five consecutive Horse of the Year awards from 1960-64, but his eye-popping clockings, particularly at distances of more than one-and-one-half miles, remain among the fastest in history.

Kelso ran the fastest one-and-five-eighths-mile race by a three-year-old (2:40 4/5) in winning the 1960 Lawrence Realization Stakes, the fastest two miles (3:19 1/5) in the 1964 Jockey Club Gold Cup, the fastest two miles by a three-year-old (3:19 2/5) in the 1960 Jockey Club Gold Cup, and one of the 10 fastest mile-and-one-half grass races (2:23 4/5) in capturing the 1964 Washington D.C. International.

Secretariat's three appearances on the list are the fastest 12 furlongs on dirt (2:24) in the 1973 Belmont Stakes, a 1:45 2/5 clocking for nine furlongs in the 1973 Marlboro Cup Handicap that has been equaled only once, and the disputed *Daily Racing Form* clocking of 1:53 2/5 for the 1973 Preakness, which equals the fastest mile-and-three-sixteenths by a three-year-old.

"To me, he was always No. 1. He was the greatest of them all," trainer Lucien Laurin said of Secretariat. "Nobody'll be a Secretariat. You don't make miracles overnight."

Affirmed's 1:21 3/5 clocking in the 1977 Futurity Stakes equals the fastest seven furlongs for a two-year-old, and his victories in the 1979 Hollywood Gold Cup (1:58 2/5) and Santa Anita Handicap (1:58 3/5) are among the 10 fastest mile-and-a-quarter clockings. John Henry's 2:23 clocking in the 1980 San Luis Rey Stakes equals the fastest 12 furlongs on the grass by a thoroughbred four or older, and his clockings of 2:23 2/5 in both the 1980 and '81 Oak Tree Invitational Stakes are among the seven fastest recorded at that distance.

First Flight, a brilliant sprinter, ran the fastest five-and-one-half (1:04 3/5) and six-and-one-half furlongs (1:15 1/5) by a two-year-old filly in the 1946 Astoria and Futurity Stakes, respectively. Her 1:08 3/5 clocking in the 1946 Matron Stakes also equals the fastest six furlongs by a two-year filly.

Those who appear twice on the chart are Ruffian, the only filly other than First Flight with multiple mentions, Artax, Dr. Fager, Greinton, Easy Goer, Spectacular Bid, Noor, and Bienamado.

Bienamado joins Swaps and Secretariat as one of three who had *the* fastest clockings in two categories. Bienamado's time in the 2001 San Juan Capistrano Handicap was 2:42 4/5, the fastest clocking for the distance of about one-and-three-quarter miles on the grass. Despite that effort and his subsequent 1:57 for 10 furlongs—the fastest mile and a quarter on either surface—in winning the Charles Whittingham Handicap on the grass, he was not among the finalists for turf championship honors.

Fastest Winning Times in Major North American Races 1946-2003

Five Furlongs

Division	Winner	Race	Track	Time	Age	Weight	Margin
2	Blue Peter	1948 Garden State Stakes	Garden State Park	:58 4/5	2	122	4 1/2
2f	Our Fleet	1948 Frizette Stakes	Jamaica	1:01	2	115	1/4

Five and One-Half Furlongs

Division	Winner	Race	Track	Time	Age	Weight	Margin
2	King Emperor	1968 Sanford Stakes	Saratoga	1:03 2/5	2	115	5
2f	First Flight	1946 Astoria Stakes	Belmont Park	1:04 3/5	2	119	3 1/4

Six Furlongs

Division	Winner	Race	Track	Time	Age	Weight	Margin
4&up	Kona Gold	2000 Breeders' Cup Sprint	Churchill Downs	1:07 3/5	6	126	1/2
4&up	Swept Overboard	2001 Ancient Title Breeders' Cup Handicap	Santa Anita	1:07 3/5	4	116	2 1/2
4&up	Artax	1999 Breeders' Cup Sprint	Gulfstream Park	1:07 4/5	4	126	1/2
4&up	Richter Scale	2000 Frank J. De Francis Memorial Dash	Laurel	1:07 4/5	6	123	1 3/4
3	Cajun Beat	2003 Breeders' Cup Sprint	Santa Anita	1:07 4/5	3	123	2 1/4
4&up	Elmhurst	1997 Breeders' Cup Sprint	Hollywood Park	1:08	7	126	1/2
4&up	Avanzado	2003 Ancient Title Breeders' Cup Handicap	Santa Anita	1:08	6	116	1/2
4&up	Up Beat	1949 Roseben Handicap	Belmont Park	1:08 1/5	4	120	3/4
2	Fleet Allied	1968 Del Mar Futurity	Del Mar	1:08 1/5	2	116	2 3/4
2	George Lewis	1969 Del Mar Futurity	Del Mar	1:08 1/5	2	116	6
4&up	Thirty Slews	1992 Breeders' Cup Sprint	Gulfstream Park	1:08 1/5	5	126	neck
3f	Xtra Heat	2001 Prioress Stakes	Belmont Park	1:08 1/5	3	121	neck
f&m 4&up	Kalookan Queen	2002 Ancient Title Breeders' Cup Handicap	Santa Anita	1:08 1/5	6	116	1/2
2f	First Flight	1946 Matron Stakes	Belmont Park	1:08 3/5	2	123	2 1/4
2f	Romanita	1956 Matron Stakes	Belmont Park	1:08 3/5	2	119	nose
2f	Atomic Wings	1969 Del Mar Debutante Stakes	Del Mar	1:08 3/5	2	113	1 1/4
2f	Ruffian	1974 Spinaway Stakes	Saratoga	1:08 3/5	2	120	12 3/4

Six and One-Half Furlongs

Division	Winner	Race	Track	Time	Age	Weight	Margin
2	Native Dancer	1952 Futurity Stakes	Belmont Park	1:14 2/5	2	122	2 1/4
3	Ghostzapper	2003 Vosburgh Stakes	Belmont Park	1:14 3/5	3	123	6 1/2
2f	First Flight	1946 Futurity Stakes	Belmont Park	1:15 1/5	2	123	1 3/4
4&up	Delaware Township	2001 Forego Handicap	Saratoga	1:15 2/5	5	116	1 1/4

Seven Furlongs

Division	Winner	Race	Track	Time	Age	Weight	Margin
4&up	Artax	1999 Carter Handicap	Aqueduct	1:20	4	114	3 1/4
4&up	Dr. Fager	1968 Vosburgh Handicap	Aqueduct	1:20 1/5	4	139	6
4&up	King's Bishop	1973 Carter Handicap	Belmont Park	1:20 2/5	4	114	5 1/2
4&up	Left Bank	2001 Vosburgh Stakes	Belmont Park	1:20 3/5	4	126	1/2
4&up	Porterhouse	1957 Los Angeles Handicap	Hollywood Park	1:20 4/5	6	123	5
4&up	Finnegan	1960 Los Angeles Handicap	Hollywood Park	1:20 4/5	4	113	1 1/2
4&up	Doc Jocoy	1963 Los Angeles Handicap	Hollywood Park	1:20 4/5	4	117	1/2
4&up	Lite the Fuse	1996 Carter Handicap	Belmont Park	1:20 4/5	5	121	head
3f	Lady Tak	2003 Test Stakes	Saratoga	1:20 4/5	3	122	4 1/2
4&up	Bolero	1951 San Carlos Handicap	Santa Anita	1:21	5	121	4
4&up	Hillsdale	1959 Los Angeles Handicap	Hollywood Park	1:21	4	121	2 3/4
4&up	Kfar Tov	1972 Malibu Stakes	Santa Anita	1:21	4	115	nose
3	Affiliate	1977 Vosburgh Handicap	Aqueduct	1:21	3	114	3 1/2
4&up	Dr. Patches	1978 Vosburgh Handicap	Belmont Park	1:21	4	117	3/4
3	General Assembly	1979 Vosburgh Stakes	Aqueduct	1:21	3	123	2
3	A Phenomenon	1983 Vosburgh Stakes	Aqueduct	1:21	3	123	1 3/4
4&up	Sewickley	1990 Vosburgh Stakes	Belmont Park	1:21	5	126	4 1/2
f&m 4&up	Exotic Wood	1998 Santa Monica Handicap	Santa Anita	1:21	6	121	3
4&up	Wild Rush	1998 Carter Handicap	Aqueduct	1:21	4	117	neck
3	Forestry	1999 King's Bishop Stakes	Saratoga	1:21	3	121	2 1/2
2	Iron Ruler	1967 Cowdin Stakes	Aqueduct	1:21 3/5	2	117	3
2	Affirmed	1977 Futurity Stakes	Belmont Park	1:21 3/5	2	122	nose
2	Forest Camp	1999 Del Mar Futurity	Del Mar	1:21 3/5	2	116	5 1/2
2f	Halfbridled	2003 Del Mar Debutante Stakes	Del Mar	1:22 1/5	2	116	1/2

Seven Furlongs and 184 Feet

Division	Winner	Race	Track	Time	Age	Weight	Margin
2	Hard Work	1969 Breeders' Futurity	Keeneland	1:25 3/5	2	122	4
3f	Sun and Snow	1975 Ashland Stakes	Keeneland	1:26 3/5	3	116	head
2f	Leallah	1956 Alcibiades Stakes	Keeneland	1:27	2	119	2 1/2
2f	Patelin	1970 Alcibiades Stakes	Keeneland	1:27	2	119	nose
2f	Coraggioso	1972 Alcibiades Stakes	Keeneland	1:27	2	119	2 1/2

About Seven Furlongs (Turf)

Division	Winner	Race	Track	Time	Age	Weight	Margin
2	Groshawk	1972 Del Mar Futurity	Del Mar	1:28 3/5	2	119	1 1/4

One Mile

Division	Winner	Race	Track	Time	Age	Weight	Margin
4&up	Dr. Fager	1968 Washington Park Handicap	Arlington Park	1:32 1/5	4	134	10
3	Buckpasser	1966 Arlington Classic	Arlington Park	1:32 3/5	3	125	1 3/4
4&up	Bold Bidder	1966 Washington Park Handicap	Arlington Park	1:32 3/5	4	120	3 1/2
4&up	Greinton	1985 Californian Stakes	Hollywood Park	1:32 3/5	4	119	2 3/4
3	Easy Goer	1989 Gotham Stakes	Aqueduct	1:32 4/5	3	123	13
4&up	Quiet American	1990 NYRA Mile Handicap	Aqueduct	1:32 4/5	4	116	4 3/4
3	Honour and Glory	1996 Metropolitan Handicap	Belmont Park	1:32 4/5	3	110	1
3	Conquistador Cielo	1982 Metropolitan Handicap	Belmont Park	1:33	3	111	7 1/4
2	Grand Canyon	1989 Hollywood Futurity	Hollywood Park	1:33	2	121	6 1/2
4&up	Langfuhr	1997 Metropolitan Handicap	Belmont Park	1:33	5	122	neck
4&up	Congaree	2002 Cigar Mile Handicap	Aqueduct	1:33	4	119	5 1/2
f&m 4&up	Lady's Secret	1986 Maskette Stakes	Belmont Park	1:33 3/5	4	125	7
3f	Pearl Necklace	1977 Maskette Handicap	Belmont Park	1:33 4/5	3	123	3/4
2f	Althea	1982 Del Mar Futurity	Del Mar	1:34 4/5	2	117	6 1/2

One Mile (Turf)

Division	Winner	Race	Track	Time	Age	Weight	Margin
4&up	Val Royal	2001 Breeders' Cup Mile	Belmont Park	1:32	5	126	1 3/4
f&m 4&up	Royal Heroine	1984 Breeders' Cup Mile	Hollywood Park	1:32 3/5	4	123	1 1/2
3f	Miesque	1987 Breeders' Cup Mile	Hollywood Park	1:32 4/5	3	120	3 1/2
3	Lure	1992 Breeders' Cup Mile	Gulfstream Park	1:32 4/5	3	122	3

One Mile and 70 Yards

Division	Winner	Race	Track	Time	Age	Weight	Margin
3	Bear Hunt	1984 Gotham Stakes	Aqueduct	1:40 2/5	3	114	4 3/4
f&m 4&up	Hail Hilarious	1977 Apple Blossom Handicap	Oaklawn Park	1:41 2/5	4	121	1 1/4
3f	Knitted Gloves	1973 Fantasy Stakes	Oaklawn Park	1:42 3/5	3	121	1 1/2

One and One-Sixteenth Miles

Division	Winner	Race	Track	Time	Age	Weight	Margin
4&up	Swaps	1956 Inglewood Handicap	Hollywood Park	1:39	4	130	2 3/4
f&m 4&up	Mossflower	1998 Hempstead Handicap	Belmont Park	1:39 4/5	4	114	12
3	Swaps	1955 Californian Stakes	Hollywood Park	1:40 2/5	3	115	1 1/4
2	Grand Slam	1997 Moet Champagne Stakes	Belmont Park	1:40 2/5	2	122	3/4
3f	Bold 'n Determined	1980 Santa Susana Stakes	Santa Anita	1:41 1/5	3	115	1/2
3f	My Darling One	1984 Fantasy Stakes	Oaklawn Park	1:41 1/5	3	121	3/4
2f	Tempera	2001 Breeders' Cup Juvenile Fillies	Belmont Park	1:41 2/5	2	119	1 1/2

One and One-Sixteenth Miles (Turf)

Division	Winner	Race	Track	Time	Age	Weight	Margin
3	Glossary	1974 Secretariat Stakes	Arlington Park	1:42 4/5	3	114	1 1/2
2	Maston	1991 Young America Stakes	Meadowlands	1:43 2/5	2	115	1/2
2f	Capades	1988 Selima Stakes	Laurel	1:44 3/5	2	119	3 1/4
4&up	Cat Bridge	1946 Bougainvillea Handicap	Hialeah	1:46	4	110	2

One and One-Eighth Miles

Division	Winner	Race	Track	Time	Age	Weight	Margin
3	Secretariat	1973 Marlboro Cup Handicap	Belmont Park	1:45 2/5	3	124	3 1/2
3	Forty One Carats	1999 Pegasus Handicap	Meadowlands	1:45 2/5	3	120	nose
4&up	Forego	1975 Woodward Stakes	Belmont Park	1:45 4/5	5	135	1 1/4
4&up	Seattle Slew	1978 Marlboro Cup Handicap	Belmont Park	1:45 4/5	4	128	3
4&up	Spectacular Bid	1980 Californian Stakes	Hollywood Park	1:45 4/5	4	130	4 1/4
3f	Go for Wand	1990 Beldame Stakes	Belmont Park	1:45 4/5	3	119	4 1/2
4&up	Dispersal	1990 Woodward Handicap	Belmont Park	1:45 4/5	4	123	1 1/4
3	Free House	1997 Swaps Stakes	Hollywood Park	1:45 4/5	3	122	3 1/2
4&up	Precisionist	1986 Woodward Stakes	Belmont Park	1:46	5	126	4 3/4
f&m 4&up	Inside Information	1995 Breeders' Cup Distaff	Belmont Park	1:46	4	123	13 1/2
3	K.J.'s Appeal	1998 Buick Meadowlands Cup	Meadowlands	1:46	3	112	1 1/4
f&m 4&up	Riboletta	2000 Beldame Stakes	Belmont Park	1:46	5	123	2
2	Believe It	1977 Remsen Stakes	Aqueduct	1:47 4/5	2	122	2
2f	Storm Flag Flying	2002 Long John Silver's Breeders' Cup Juvenile Fillies	Arlington Park	1:49 3/5	2	119	1/2

One and One-Eighth Miles (Turf)

Division	Winner	Race	Track	Time	Age	Weight	Margin
f&m 4&up	Toussaud	1993 Gamely Handicap	Hollywood Park	1:45	4	116	1
3f	Memories of Silver	1996 Queen Elizabeth II Challenge Cup	Keeneland	1:45 4/5	3	121	1/2
3	Super Quercus	1999 Early Times Hollywood Derby	Hollywood Park	1:45 4/5	3	122	2
4&up	Special Ring	2003 Eddie Read Handicap	Del Mar	1:45 4/5	6	117	5

One and Three-Sixteenth Miles

Division	Winner	Race	Track	Time	Age	Weight	Margin
4&up	Riva Ridge	1973 Brooklyn Handicap	Aqueduct	1:52 2/5	4	127	head
4&up	Farma Way	1991 Pimlico Special	Pimlico	1:52 2/5	4	119	3
3	Secretariat	1973 Preakness Stakes	Pimlico	1:53 2/5	3	126	2 1/2
3	Tank's Prospect	1985 Preakness Stakes	Pimlico	1:53 2/5	3	126	nose
3	Louis Quatorze	1996 Preakness Stakes	Pimlico	1:53 2/5	3	126	3 1/4
3f	Bridal Flower	1956 Roamer Handicap	Jamaica	1:57 2/5	3	118	1/2

One and Three-Sixteenth Miles (Turf)

Division	Winner	Race	Track	Time	Age	Weight	Margin
4&up	Steinlen	1990 Caesars International Handicap	Atlantic City	1:52	7	124	3 3/4
3	Manila	1986 United Nations Handicap	Atlantic City	1:52 3/5	3	114	1 1/4
f&m 4&up	Kostroma	1992 Beverly D. Stakes	Arlington Park	1:54	6	123	1 1/2

About One and One-Quarter Miles (Turf)

Division	Winner	Race	Track	Time	Age	Weight	Margin
4&up	Ancient Title	1977 Del Mar Handicap	Del Mar	1:55 2/5	7	123	5
f&m 4&up	Princessnesian	1968 Santa Barbara Handicap	Santa Anita	2:00 4/5	4	124	8

One and One-Quarter Miles

Division	Winner	Race	Track	Time	Age	Weight	Margin
4&up	Spectacular Bid	1980 Charles H. Strub Stakes	Santa Anita	1:57 4/5	4	126	3 1/4
4&up	Noor	1950 Golden Gate Handicap	Golden Gate Fields	1:58 1/5	5	127	3
3	Quack	1972 Hollywood Gold Cup	Hollywood Park	1:58 1/5	3	115	5 1/2
4&up	In Excess	1991 Suburban Handicap	Belmont Park	1:58 1/5	4	119	1
4&up	Affirmed	1979 Hollywood Gold Cup	Hollywood Park	1:58 2/5	4	132	3/4
4&up	Greinton	1985 Hollywood Gold Cup	Hollywood Park	1:58 2/5	4	120	1 3/4
4&up	Swaps	1956 Hollywood Gold Cup	Hollywood Park	1:58 3/5	4	130	2
3	Round Table	1957 Hollywood Gold Cup	Hollywood Park	1:58 3/5	3	109	3 1/2
3	J.O. Tobin	1977 Swaps Stakes	Hollywood Park	1:58 3/5	3	120	8
4&up	Affirmed	1979 Santa Anita Handicap	Santa Anita	1:58 3/5	4	128	4 1/2
4&up	Turkoman	1986 Widener Handicap	Hialeah	1:58 3/5	4	121	1/2
f&m 4&up	Coup de Fusil	1987 Delaware Handicap	Delaware Park	1:59 4/5	4	114	4
3f	Lite Light	1991 Coaching Club American Oaks	Belmont Park	2:00 2/5	3	121	7
3f	Ajina	1997 Coaching Club American Oaks	Belmont Park	2:00 2/5	3	121	2 1/4

One and One-Quarter Miles (Turf)

Division	Winner	Race	Track	Time	Age	Weight	Margin
4&up	Bienamado	2001 Charles Whittingham Handicap	Santa Anita	1:57	5	124	1 1/2
f&m 4&up	Bequest	1991 Santa Barbara Handicap	Santa Anita	1:57 2/5	5	117	2
3f	Plenty of Grace	1990 Yellow Ribbon Stakes	Santa Anita	1:58 2/5	3	119	1
3	Hawk Attack	1995 Secretariat Stakes	Arlington Park	2:00	3	120	head

One and Five-Sixteenths Miles

Division	Winner	Race	Track	Time	Age	Weight	Margin
f&m 4&up	Tempted	1959 Ladies Handicap	Aqueduct	2:09	4	128	2 3/4
4&up	Nickel Boy	1961 Manhattan Handicap	Aqueduct	2:10	6	113	2
3f	Royal Patrice	1962 Ladies Handicap	Aqueduct	2:10 3/5	3	114	1

One and Three-Eighths Miles

Division	Winner	Race	Track	Time	Age	Weight	Margin
3f	Next Move	1950 Coaching Club American Oaks	Belmont Park	2:15 4/5	3	121	1
4&up	Chief Honcho	1992 Brooklyn Handicap	Aqueduct	2:16 4/5	4	117	5 1/2
3	Living Vicariously	1993 Brooklyn Handicap	Aqueduct	2:17 4/5	5	111	2 1/2

One and Three-Eighths Miles (Turf)

Division	Winner	Race	Track	Time	Age	Weight	Margin
4&up	Yagli	1999 Gulfstream Park Breeders' Cup Handicap	Gulfstream Park	2:10 3/5	6	121	3/4
f&m 4&up	Manta	1971 Beverly Hills Handicap	Hollywood Park	2:12 3/5	5	127	3 1/2
3	Prince Spellbound	1982 Hollywood Turf Cup	Hollywood Park	2:14	3	122	3
3f	Blush With Pride	1982 Golden Harvest Handicap	Louisiana Downs	2:15 2/5	3	113	3 1/4

About One and One-Half Miles (Turf)

Division	Winner	Race	Track	Time	Age	Weight	Margin
4&up	Sailor's Guide	1958 Washington D.C. International	Laurel	2:33 1/5	6	126	3 1/2
3	Master Boing	1956 Washington D.C. International	Laurel	2:39	3	122	5

One and One-Half Miles

Division	Winner	Race	Track	Time	Age	Weight	Margin
3	Secretariat	1973 Belmont Stakes	Belmont Park	2:24	3	126	31
4&up	Prove Out	1973 Woodward Stakes	Belmont Park	2:25 4/5	4	126	4 1/2
3	Nasty and Bold	1978 Brooklyn Handicap	Belmont Park	2:26	3	112	3/4
4&up	Hechizado	1981 Brooklyn Handicap	Belmont Park	2:26	5	116	4
3	Easy Goer	1989 Belmont Stakes	Belmont Park	2:26	3	126	8
3	A.P. Indy	1992 Belmont Stakes	Belmont Park	2:26	3	126	3/4
3	Slew O' Gold	1983 Jockey Club Gold Cup	Belmont Park	2:26 1/5	3	121	3
3	Point Given	2001 Belmont Stakes	Belmont Park	2:26 2/5	3	126	12 1/4
4&up	Little Missouri	1986 Brooklyn Handicap	Belmont Park	2:26 2/5	4	109	3
3	Risen Star	1988 Belmont Stakes	Belmont Park	2:26 2/5	3	126	14 3/4
3f	Magazine	1973 Coaching Club American Oaks	Belmont Park	2:27 4/5	3	121	1 1/2
3f	Ruffian	1975 Coaching Club American Oaks	Belmont Park	2:27 4/5	3	121	2 3/4
f&m 4&up	Marta	1956 Ladies Handicap	Belmont Park	2:29 4/5	4	116	1 3/4

One and One-Half Miles (Turf)

Division	Winner	Race	Track	Time	Age	Weight	Margin
3	Hawkster	1989 Oak Tree Invitational Stakes	Santa Anita	2:22 4/5	3	121	4
4&up	Fiddle Isle	1970 San Luis Rey Handicap	Santa Anita	2:23	5	124	nose
4&up	John Henry	1980 San Luis Rey Stakes	Santa Anita	2:23	5	126	1 1/2
4&up	Awad	1997 Sword Dancer Invitational Handicap	Saratoga	2:23 1/5	7	117	2
4&up	Czar Alexander	1969 Oak Tree Stakes	Santa Anita	2:23 2/5	4	126	1 1/2
4&up	John Henry	1980 Oak Tree Invitational Stakes	Santa Anita	2:23 2/5	5	126	1 1/2
4&up	John Henry	1981 Oak Tree Invitational Stakes	Santa Anita	2:23 2/5	6	126	neck
4&up	Filago	1991 Oak Tree Invitational Stakes	Santa Anita	2:23 3/5	4	126	3/4
4&up	Kelso	1964 Washington D.C. International	Laurel	2:23 4/5	7	126	4 1/2
4&up	Fleet Host	1967 San Luis Rey Handicap	Santa Anita	2:23 4/5	4	119	4
4&up	Rial	1990 Oak Tree Invitational Stakes	Santa Anita	2:23 4/5	5	126	1 1/4
4&up	Kotashaan	1993 San Luis Rey Stakes	Santa Anita	2:23 4/5	5	124	1 1/4
f&m 4&up	Drumtop	1971 Bowling Green Handicap	Belmont Park	2:25 2/5	5	124	3/4
3f	Nobiliary	1975 Washington D.C. International	Laurel	2:31 1/5	3	117	3/4
3f	April Run	1981 Turf Classic	Aqueduct	2:31 1/5	3	118	3/4

One and Five-Eighths Miles

Division	Winner	Race	Track	Time	Age	Weight	Margin
4&up	Swaps	1956 Sunset Handicap	Hollywood Park	2:38 1/5	4	130	4 1/4
3	Kelso	1960 Lawrence Realization Stakes	Belmont Park	2:40 4/5	3	120	4 1/2
3f	Bed o' Roses	1950 Lawrence Realization Stakes	Belmont Park	2:42 3/5	3	107	4 1/2

One and Five-Eighths Miles (Turf)

Division	Winner	Race	Track	Time	Age	Weight	Margin
4&up	Moontrip	1966 Bowling Green Handicap	Aqueduct	2:38 4/5	5	112	head
f&m 4&up	Dahlia	1974 Canadian International Championship	Woodbine	2:40	4	123	1
3	Mac Diarmida	1978 Canadian International Championship	Woodbine	2:41 1/5	3	118	1 1/2

About One and Three-Quarter Miles (Turf)

Division	Winner	Race	Track	Time	Age	Weight	Margin
4&up	Bienamado	2001 San Juan Capistrano Handicap	Santa Anita	2:42 4/5	5	122	1/2

One and Three-Quarter Miles

Division	Winner	Race	Track	Time	Age	Weight	Margin
4&up	Noor	1950 San Juan Capistrano Handicap	Santa Anita	2:52 4/5	5	117	nose

Two Miles

Division	Winner	Race	Track	Time	Age	Weight	Margin
4&up	Kelso	1964 Jockey Club Gold Cup	Aqueduct	3:19 1/5	7	124	5 1/2
3	Kelso	1960 Jockey Club Gold Cup	Aqueduct	3:19 2/5	3	119	3 1/2
f&m 4&up	Shuvee	1971 Jockey Club Gold Cup	Aqueduct	3:20 2/5	5	121	7

Two Miles (Turf)

Division	Winner	Race	Track	Time	Age	Weight	Margin
4&up	Petrone	1969 Sunset Handicap	Hollywood Park	3:18	5	124	3 1/2
f&m 4&up	Typecast	1972 Sunset Handicap	Hollywood Park	3:20 3/5	6	120	head

Two and One-Sixteenth Miles

Division	Winner	Race	Track	Time	Age	Weight	Margin
4&up	Midafternoon	1956 Display Handicap	Jamaica	3:29 3/5	4	126	5 1/2

Two and One-Quarter Miles

Division	Winner	Race	Track	Time	Age	Weight	Margin
4&up	Rico Monte	1947 New York Handicap	Belmont Park	3:48 2/5	5	126	nose
f&m 4&up	Miss Grillo	1948 New York Handicap	Belmont Park	3:53 3/5	6	120	5

Best of Their Generation

In the neighborhood of 35,000 thoroughbreds are foaled every year in North America and many more around the world. As the best and the brightest of each group begin earning impressive victories, they often are referred to as "the best of their generation," those born in a particular year. On numerous occasions, that acclaim is premature and, in most, strictly a matter of opinion. The following chart shows the most successful North American campaigners foaled in each year based on their records (four points for a victory, two for a runner-up effort, and one for a third-place showing) in major races during the modern era. In the cases of those foaled before 1944, only their records after 1945 are included. And, although Olhaverry, who was born in 1939, and 1940 foals War Knight and Adroit are included, no gelding born before 1941 or mare foaled prior to 1940 captured a major race during the modern era. Further, the records of Funny Cide, who captured the 2003 Kentucky Derby and Preakness Stakes, and others who are still in training remain a work in progress. And late bloomers from generations who still are campaigning eventually could replace those listed as a particular generation's most successful major campaigners.

Foaling Year	Colt/Horse	Record	Gelding	Record	Filly/Mare	Record
1939	Olhaverry	3-2-1/17				
1940	War Knight	1-0-0/4			Adroit	1-0-0/4
1941	Stymie	11-12-5/73	Armed	10-5-4/54	Canina	1-1-2/8
1942	Talon	2-5-3/21	Coincidence	3-0-1/13	Gallorette	6-6-8/44
1943	Assault	12-1-3/53	Stud Poker	2-1-2/12	Honeymoon	6-5-3/37
1944	Phalanx	5-5-5/35	Royal Governor	4-1-4/22	But Why Not	8-4-2/42
1945	Citation	12-5-0/58	Three Rings	5-3-3/29	Bewitch	6-5-2/36
1946	One Hitter	6-5-5/39	Moonrush	2-1-2/12	Lithe	4-3-3/25
1947	Hill Prince	9-3-2/44	Picador	1-2-0/8	Bed o' Roses	8-6-5/49
1948	Battlefield	10-6-1/53	Ruhe	1-3-4/14	Kiss Me Kate	6-2-4/32
1949	Tom Fool	9-4-1/45	Smoke Screen	1-2-3/11	Real Delight	6-0-0/24
1950	Native Dancer	12-1-0/50	Find	8-9-12/62	Grecian Queen	5-3-3/29
1951	Fisherman	7-6-3/43	St. Vincent	2-0-3/11	Parlo	6-2-0/28
1952	Nashua	15-3-0/66	Bardstown	6-2-0/28	High Voltage	6-0-3/27
1953	Needles	6-1-2/28	How Now	2-2-2/14	Dotted Line	3-5-4/26
1954	Round Table	19-6-4/92	General Arthur	2-0-0/8	Bayou	4-1-0/18
1955	Bald Eagle	8-4-3/43	Talent Show	1-5-11/25	Idun	6-2-1/29
1956	Sword Dancer	9-5-2/48	Polylad	3-4-2/22	Royal Native	6-3-1/31
1957	T.V. Lark	8-4-1/41	Kelso	24-10-1/117	Berlo	4-0-1/17
1958	Carry Back	14-5-7/73	Parka	1-3-2/12	Bowl of Flowers	5-1-2/24
1959	Crimson Satan	7-6-3/43	Native Diver	6-2-5/33	Cicada	8-4-3/43
1960	Gun Bow	11-5-3/57	Cedar Key	5-1-0/22	Smart Deb	3-2-5/21
1961	Hill Rise	6-3-5/35	Roman Brother	7-6-4/44	Tosmah	5-1-2/24
1962	Tom Rolfe	5-3-2/28	Just About	1-2-0/8	Straight Deal	7-4-4/40
1963	Buckpasser	16-3-1/71	Quicken Tree	6-5-3/37	Lady Pitt	2-5-2/20
1964	Damascus	13-5-3/65	Fort Marcy	8-8-7/55	Gamely	5-5-2/32
1965	Nodouble	8-7-2/48	Big Shot II	2-0-0/8	Gay Matelda	2-6-3/23
1966	Cougar II	10-5-12/62	Red Reality	1-3-3/13	Shuvee	12-2-3/55
1967	Judgable	4-1-1/19	Loud	1-6-5/21	Cathy Honey	2-4-2/18
1968	Droll Role	5-3-2/28	Delay	1-1-0/6	Forward Gal	5-0-4/24
1969	Riva Ridge	10-1-1/43	Cruiser II	2-0-0/8	Susan's Girl	13-5-6/68
1970	Secretariat	11-3-1/51	Forego	19-7-5/95	La Prevoyante	5-1-0/22
1971	Stonewalk	2-4-1/17	Stardust Mel	3-2-1/17	Chris Evert	3-2-1/17
1972	Foolish Pleasure	8-2-2/38	Improviser	2-4-1/17	Ruffian	5-0-0/20
1973	Exceller	7-3-3/37	Life's Hope	4-2-2/22	Optimistic Gal	9-5-1/47
1974	Seattle Slew	8-1-0/34	Bowl Game	7-2-2/34	Waya	5-2-2/26
1975	Affirmed	16-4-0/72	John Henry	19-7-4/94	Lakeville Miss	4-3-0/22
1976	Spectacular Bid	16-1-1/67	Winter's Tale	4-2-0/20	It's In the Air	6-3-4/34
1977	Temperence Hill	7-2-1/33	Rockhill Native	3-1-2/16	Bold 'n Determined	9-1-0/38
1978	Erins Isle	5-3-2/28	Lord Darnley	2-2-0/12	Sangue	5-2-2/26
1979	Majesty's Prince	5-2-7/31	Prince Spellbound	2-4-3/19	Heatherten	3-2-1/17
1980	Slew O' Gold	7-4-0/36	Both Ends Burning	2-2-2/14	Princess Rooney	5-1-0/22
1981	Precisionist	6-6-2/38	Birdie's Legend	1-1-1/7	Life's Magic	5-9-5/43
1982	Chief's Crown	7-2-3/35	Creme Fraiche	7-6-8/48	Lady's Secret	10-3-2/48
1983	Broad Brush	7-1-5/35	Great Communicator	4-5-1/27	Family Style	3-3-4/22
1984	Alysheba	9-5-2/48	Chart the Stars, J.T.'s Pet	1-0-0/4	Bayakoa	9-2-0/40
1985	Forty Niner	5-4-0/28	Kingpost	1-1-1/7	Goodbye Halo	4-4-2/26
1986	Easy Goer	10-4-1/49	Music Merci	2-2-2/14	Open Mind	7-1-2/32
1987	In Excess	5-1-3/25	Solar Splendor	3-2-1/17	Paseana	9-9-1/55
1988	Strike the Gold	4-5-3/29	Best Pal	10-5-2/52	Flawlessly	5-3-2/28
1989	Devil His Due	7-10-3/51	Majestic Sweep, Tri to Watch	1-1-0/6	Turnback the Alarm	5-1-2/24
1990	Cigar	11-2-1/49	Prairie Bayou	3-1-0/14	Sky Beauty	9-1-2/40
1991	Holy Bull	8-0-0/32	Dramatic Gold	2-2-4/16	Heavenly Prize	7-3-3/37
1992	Gentlemen	5-3-2/28	Val's Prince	3-3-1/19	Serena's Song	11-7-2/60
1993	Skip Away	14-8-4/76	Sir Bear	3-2-7/23	Escena	4-5-1/27
1994	Free House	7-2-3/35	Affirmed Success	3-3-3/21	Sharp Cat	8-3-0/38
1995	Real Quiet	5-3-0/26	With Anticipation	5-3-1/27	Beautiful Pleasure	6-5-0/34
1996	Lemon Drop Kid	7-2-1/33	General Challenge	4-2-0/20	Silverbulletday	6-1-0/26
1997	Tiznow	4-3-1/23	Sarafan	1-2-1/9	Surfside	4-2-2/22
1998	Point Given	7-2-0/32	Balto Star	3-1-1/15	Azeri	8-0-0/32
1999	Medaglia d'Oro	5-5-0/30	Gygistar, Perfect Drift	1-0-1/5	You	5-6-1/33
2000	Empire Maker	3-2-0/16	Funny Cide	2-1-2/12	Elloluv	2-3-0/14
2001	Action This Day	1-0-0/4			Halfbridled	2-0-0/8
	Birdstone, Cuvee					
	Eurosilver, Lion Heart					
	Silver Wagon					
	Siphonizer					

Upsets That Would Make Their Namesake Proud

Because of the high quality of competition in major races, rank outsiders don't win at a particularly impressive rate.

That upsets are significant in thoroughbred lore, however, is indisputable. The term wasn't used to define an underdog's victory over a heavy favorite in any sport until Man o' War suffered the only loss of his career in the 1919 Sanford Stakes—to Upset, whose name subsequently became ingrained in sports terminology.

The following chart shows the biggest upset in major races in each year from 1946-2003 and all instances in which the winner was at least a 49-1 shot, therefore paying $100 or more.

Only 51 times, once in roughly 127 of the 6,461 major races held in the modern era, has a 50-1 or longer shot won. Only nine times—once in every 718 races—has a 100-1 or longer shot emerged victorious. And only in the greatest win payoff in a major race in the modern era, when Great Normand ($364.80) captured the 1990 Meadowlands Cup Handicap, has a horse won at longer odds than 150-1.

Sixteen of the longshot winners on the chart were multiple winners and, surprisingly enough, two of them had captured major races before their memorable upsets. Sherluck's victory in the 1961 Belmont Stakes paid $132.10, and Temperence Hill's triumph in the same race 19 years later rewarded his backers with a payoff of $108.80 for a $2 bet. Those payoffs were surprisingly large because Sherluck and Temperence Hill already had demonstrated their class by winning the Blue Grass Stakes and the Arkansas Derby, respectively.

Rash Statement, whose victory in the 1960 Delaware Oaks returned $90.40, had finished third in both the Princess Pat and Matron Stakes at two and was third in the Coaching Club American Oaks, her last start before her Delaware Oaks triumph. Judgable had finished third in the San Fernando Stakes in his last start before the 1971 Charles H. Strub Stakes, in which his victory was worth $80.60 at the betting window. And Spain, who rewarded her backers with a payoff of $113.80 for her victory in the 2000 Breeders' Cup Distaff, had finished second in the Vinery Del Mar Debutante Stakes and third in the Oak Leaf Stakes as a two-year-old, then scored runner-up finishes in the Las Virgenes and Three Chimneys Spinster Stakes, the latter her final start before the Breeders' Cup Distaff, at three.

Temperence Hill also proved to be the only longshot winner on the chart who ended the season as a champion. He followed his victories in the Arkansas Derby and Belmont Stakes with scores in the Travers Stakes, Super Derby, and Jockey Club Gold Cup to earn the three-year-old championship, then won both the Oaklawn and Suburban Handicaps a year later.

Bold Bidder hadn't finished in the money in a major race before his victory in the 1965 Jerome Handicap, which was worth $164.20 at the mutuel windows. But a year later he shared the handicap championship by virtue of victories in the Charles H. Strub Stakes, the Monmouth and Washington Park Handicaps, and the Hawthorne Gold Cup.

Biggest Upsets in Major North American Races 1946-2003

Year	Race (Track)	Winner	Paid
1946	American Derby (Washington Park)	Eternal Reward	$205.60
1947	San Carlos Handicap (Santa Anita)	Texas Sandman	111.90
1948	Hollywood Oaks (Hollywood Park)	Flying Rhythm	167.80
1949	Vanity Handicap (Santa Anita)	Silver Drift	85.50
1950	Vineland Handicap (Garden State Park)	Almahmoud	103.00
1951	Astarita Stakes (Aqueduct)	Place Card	246.60
1952	Trenton Handicap (Garden State Park)	Ken	131.60
1953	Saranac Handicap (Jamaica)	First Aid	134.40
1954	Black Helen Handicap (Hialeah)	Gainsboro Girl	98.90
1955	Selima Stakes (Laurel)	Levee	96.20
1956	San Felipe Handicap (Santa Anita)	Social Climber	111.20
1956	Hialeah Turf Handicap (Hialeah)	Guardian II	178.80
1957	William P. Kyne Memorial 'Cap (Bay Meadows)	Pibe Carlitos	70.00
1958	Princess Pat Stakes (Arlington Park)	Battle Heart	94.80
1959	Wood Memorial Stakes (Jamaica)	Manassa Mauler	129.50
1960	Delaware Oaks (Delaware Park)	Rash Statement	90.40
1961	Vanity Handicap (Hollywood Park)	Perizade	180.60
1961	Belmont Stakes (Belmont Park)	Sherluck	132.10
1961	Bowling Green Handicap (Belmont Park)	Dead Center	114.60
1962	Hollywood Derby (Hollywood Park)	Drill Site	88.00
1963	Delaware Handicap (Delaware Park)	Waltz Song	148.60
1964	San Luis Rey Handicap (Santa Anita)	Inclusive	205.40
1965	Jerome Handicap (Aqueduct)	Bold Bidder	164.20
1965	Washington Park Handicap (Arlington Park)	Take Over	152.20
1965	Pimlico Futurity (Pimlico)	Spring Double	112.40
1966	Florida Derby (Gulfstream Park)	Williamston Kid	183.60
1967	Michigan Mile and One-Eighth (Detroit)	Estreno II	250.60
1967	Jerome Handicap (Aqueduct)	High Tribute	158.40
1967	Massachusetts Handicap (Suffolk Downs)	Good Knight	115.20
1968	Widener Handicap (Hialeah)	Sette Bello	100.00
1969	Widener Handicap (Hialeah)	Yumbel	94.40
1970	Dwyer Handicap (Aqueduct)	Judgable	80.60
1971	San Luis Rey Handicap (Santa Anita)	Try Sheep	110.40
1971	Charles H. Strub Stakes (Santa Anita)	War Heim	100.00
1972	John B. Campbell Handicap (Bowie)	Boone the Great	81.20
1973	Louisiana Derby (Fair Grounds)	Leo's Pisces	109.80
1974	Metropolitan Handicap (Belmont Park)	Arbees Boy	$122.00
1975	San Antonio Stakes (Santa Anita)	Cheriepe	72.00
1976	Ohio Derby (Thistledown)	Return of a Native	184.00
1977	Del Mar Futurity (Del Mar)	Go West Young Man	144.80
1978	Ohio Derby (Thistledown)	Special Honor	203.20
1978	Del Mar Handicap (Del Mar)	Palton	141.60
1978	Frizette Stakes (Belmont Park)	Golferette	131.60
1979	Champagne Stakes (Belmont Park)	Joanie's Chief	72.60
1980	Belmont Stakes (Belmont Park)	Temperence Hill	108.80
1981	La Canada Stakes (Santa Anita)	Summer Siren	111.20
1982	California Derby (Golden Gate Fields)	Rockwall	83.60
1983	Florida Derby (Gulfstream Park)	Croeso	172.00
1983	Fantasy Stakes (Oaklawn Park)	Brindy Brindy	120.20
1984	Breeders' Cup Turf (Hollywood Park)	Lashkari	108.80
1985	Turf Classic (Belmont Park)	Noble Fighter	113.40
1986	Hollywood Derby (Hollywood Park)	Spellbound	176.00
1987	Hollywood Oaks (Hollywood Park)	Perchance to Dream	74.00
1988	Flower Bowl Handicap (Belmont Park)	Gaily Gaily	157.80
1989	Santa Anita Handicap (Santa Anita)	Martial Law	103.60
1990	Meadowlands Cup (Meadowlands)	Great Normand	364.80
1990	Yellow Ribbon Stakes (Santa Anita)	Plenty of Grace	114.00
1991	Pennsylvania Derby (Philadelphia Park)	Valley Crossing	158.60
1992	Molson Export Million (Woodbine)	Benburb	65.50
1993	Breeders' Cup Classic (Santa Anita)	Arcangues	269.20
1993	Arkansas Derby (Oaklawn Park)	Rockamundo	218.00
1994	Breeders' Cup Distaff (Churchill Downs)	One Dreamer	96.20
1995	Alabama Stakes (Saratoga)	Pretty Discreet	87.50
1996	Fountain of Youth Stakes (Gulfstream Park)	Built for Pleasure	288.20
1997	Eddie Read Handicap (Del Mar)	Expelled	49.80
1998	Las Virgenes Stakes (Santa Anita)	Keeper Hill	111.20
1999	Br. Cup Juvenile Fillies (Gulfstream Park)	Cash Run	67.00
2000	Breeders' Cup Distaff (Churchill Downs)	Spain	113.80
2001	Metropolitan Handicap (Belmont Park)	Exciting Story	115.50
2001	Acorn Stakes (Belmont Park)	Forest Secrets	102.50
2002	Belmont Stakes (Belmont Park)	Sarava	142.50
2003	Arkansas Derby (Oaklawn Park)	Sir Cherokee	113.20

Photo courtesy of Churchill Downs

Chris McCarron paid little attention to a driving Giant's Causeway (14) on the outside as he guided Tiznow home in front by a neck in the 2000 Breeders' Cup Classic at Churchill Downs. A year later, the California-bred Tiznow won the Breeders' Cup Classic at Belmont Park to become the only two-time winner of America's richest horse race.

Breeders' Cup

Few sportsmen had more legitimate reasons to boast than the late John Galbreath. He saw two of his Darby Dan Farm runners, Chateaugay and Proud Clarion, win the Kentucky Derby and another, Roberto, capture the Epsom Derby. Roberto was named for Hall of Fame outfielder Roberto Clemente of the Pittsburgh Pirates, who won three World Series titles under Galbreath's stewardship.

So it's a quite a testimony to the importance of the Breeders' Cup that Galbreath considered Proud Truth's victory in the second Breeders' Cup Classic in 1985 his ultimate sporting accomplishment.

"When Maz hit that ball over the grandstand and we beat the damn Yankees, everybody went crazy. You couldn't write a storybook like that," Galbreath said of Bill Mazeroski's ninth-inning home run that gave the Pirates a 10-9 victory over the New York Yankees in the seventh game of the 1960 World Series. "But that didn't compare with winning (the Breeders' Cup Classic). Nothing—and I mean nothing—compares with winning this."

Since its inception in 1984, the Breeders' Cup, held annually in late October or early November before packed houses at different tracks and now featuring eight races worth a total of $14 million on the same day, undoubtedly has been the best single-day racing program anywhere in the world.

Five thoroughbreds have managed back-to-back Breeders' Cup victories: Miesque in the 1987 and '88 Mile, Bayakoa in the 1989 and '90 Distaff, Lure in the '92 and '93 Mile, Tiznow in the 2000 and 2001 Classic, and High Chaparral in the 2002 and 2003 John Deere Turf, winning the latter in a thrilling dead heat with Johar. Da Hoss won the Mile in 1996 and again in 1998.

Heavenly Prize and Breeders' Cup winners Alysheba and Kona Gold hold the special distinction of three in-the-money finishes in Breeders' Cup competition. Alysheba finished third in the 1986 Juvenile, second in the '87 Classic, and clinched Horse of the Year honors when he crossed the wire first in virtual darkness in the 1988 Classic at Churchill Downs. Kona Gold took the same third-to-first route in the Sprint from 1998-2000. Heavenly Prize was third in the 1993 Juvenile Fillies, then finished second in the Distaff in both 1994 and '95.

The Breeders' Cup, now collectively known as the World Thoroughbred Championships, was intended from the outset to be the sport's season-ending championship showdown. That it has become just that is indisputable.

A closer look, however, reveals that, in a considerable number of cases, the other 364 days of the year have been deemed irrelevant by Eclipse Award voters.

Of the 146 times the winners have crossed the finish line in the 145 Breeders' Cup races (including High Chaparral's dead heat with Johar), that was the victor's first major North American victory on 65 occasions. On 79 occasions, that was the winner's first major North American victory of the season, and on 52 occasions that was the first, last, and only major North American victory of the winner's career. Further, 102 of the 290 second- and third-place finishers hadn't previously posted an in-the-money finish in a major North American race, 114 hadn't done so that year, and 68 were accomplishing that feat for the only time.

There are two obvious reasons why so many competitors who have spent the entire year out of the spotlight have risen to the occasion in the Breeders' Cup:

• Most of the two-year-olds competing in the Juvenile and Juvenile Fillies have only a few races under their belts;

• The Breeders' Cup draws a large number of European invaders.

And while no one questions that the Breeders' Cup is the single most important day on thoroughbred racing's calendar, it is still somewhat mystifying that 39 Breeders' Cup winners have earned Eclipse Awards as North American champions without another major victory on this continent during the entire year.

But nine winners of the Juvenile have been voted champions, including in a six row and seven of the last eight through 2003, without another major North American victory to their credit the entire year. That same scenario has happened six times in the Juvenile Fillies, including both 2000 and 2001. Eight winners of the Sprint were crowned champions with no other major North American victories that season, and 14 grass champions have been crowned whose only major victory of the year on this side of the pond came in the Breeders' Cup. Two Distaff winners also earned championship honors without a second major triumph on their championship season resumes.

Awarding championships based on one race ignores such factors as track bias or preference and probably encourages owners and trainers to send their highly capable charges against lesser competition or perhaps avoid the track entirely to point for a particular day in the sun.

"I'm convinced that races like the Kentucky Derby are won by pointing all of your strategy in that direction and not worrying about all the races leading to it," the late Eddie Gregson said a few days after saddling 1982 Kentucky Derby winner Gato Del Sol.

The same obviously could be said for Breeders' Cup races.

"Horses aren't like sports cars," said trainer Wayne Lukas. "You can't just tune the carburetor and adjust them. They're fragile."

And the championship voting sometimes penalizes horses who have enjoyed otherwise banner seasons competing in major races who, like all athletes, simply have an off day. After all, even Tiger Woods occasionally shoots an 81.

"Every horse has bad days now and then," said Bert Firestone, one of the sport's most prominent owners during the '70s and '80s. "Every great athlete has off days. Secretariat had one in the Wood Memorial just before the Derby."

The following chart includes all 145 Breeders' Cup races, with four points awarded for a victory, two for a second-place finish, and one for a third-place showing, with most victories and/or second-place finishes, when applicable, used to settle tiebreakers.

Breeders' Cup-Placed Runners 1984-2003

	W	P	S
1. Bayakoa, Da Hoss, High Chaparral, Lure, Miesque, Tiznow (8)	2	0	0
7. Alysheba, Kona Gold (7)	1	1	1
9. Banks Hill, Lady's Secret, Life's Magic, Paseana, Safely Kept, Smile, Spain, Spinning World, Steinlen, Theatrical (6)	1	1	0
19. Black Tie Affair, Buck's Boy, Cardmania, Cat Thief, Cigar, Cozzene, Dance Smartly, Escena, Gilded Time, Islington, Lit de Justice, Open Mind, Outstandingly, Precisionist, Unbridled	1	0	1
34. Heavenly Prize (5)	0	2	1
35. Action This Day, Adoration, Ajina, Alphabet Soup, Anees, Answer Lively, A.P. Indy, Arazi, Arcangues, Artax, Awesome Again, Azeri, Barathea, Beautiful Pleasure, Boston Harbor, Brave Raj, Brocco, Cajun Beat, Caressing, Cash Run, Capote, Cherokee Run, Chief Bearhart, Chief's Crown, Concern, Countess Diana, Dancing Spree, Daylami, Desert Stormer, Domedriver, Eillo, Elmhurst, Eliza, Epitome, Fantastic Light, Favorite Trick, Ferdinand, Flanders, Fly So Free, Fraise, Great Communicator, Go for Wand, Gulch, Halfbridled, Hollywood Wildcat, Inside Information, In the Wings, Is It True, Jewel Princess, Johannesburg, Johar, Kalanisi, Kotashaan, Lashkari, Last Tycoon, Macho Uno, Manila, Meadow Star, Miss Alleged, My Flag, Northern Spur, One Dreamer, Opening Verse, Orientate, Pebbles, Perfect Sting, Personal Ensign, Phone Chatter, Pilsudski, Pleasantly Perfect, Pleasant Stage, Princess Rooney, Prized, Proud Truth, Reraise, Rhythm, Ridgewood Pearl, Royal Academy, Royal Heroine, Sacahuista, Sheikh Albadou, Silic, Silverbulletday, Six Perfections, Skip Away, Skywalker, Soaring Softly, Squirtle Squirt, Starine, Storm Flag Flying, Storm Song, Success Express, Sunday Silence, Tasso, Tempera, Thirty Slews, Tikkanen, Timber Country, Twilight Ridge, Unbridled Elaine, Unbridled's Song, Val Royal, Very Subtle, Vindication, Volponi, War Chant, Wild Again	1	0	0
142. Banshee Breeze, Bertrando, Easy Goer, Itsallgreektome, Meafara, Medaglia d'Oro, Pleasant Tap, Serena's Song, Versailles Treaty (4)	0	2	0
151. Gate Dancer, Imperial Gesture, Paradise Creek, Surfside, Tabasco Cat, Turkoman (3)	0	1	1
157. Acceptable, All Along, Al Mamoon, Aly's Alley, Ashado, Bien Bien, Bluesthestandard, Blumin Affair, Borgia, Budroyale, Cara Rafaela, Career Collection, Chief Seattle, Chilukki, Clabber Girl, Colonial Waters, Commemorate, Composure, Coretta, Darby Shuffle, Dawson's Legacy, Dayjur, Deputy Commander, Dusty Heart, Educated Risk, Elloluv, Eltish, Excellent Meeting, Family Style, Farda Amiga, Fastness, Forbidden Apple, Fran's Valentine, Freedom Cry, Geri, Giant's Causeway, Gorgeous, Grand Canyon, Grand Slam, Groovy, Hatoof, Hawksley Hill, Hennessy, Hesabull, Honest Lady, Ibn Bey, It'sal'lknownfact, Jeanne Jones, Johann Quatz, Kafwain, L'Ancresse, L'Carriere, La Spia, Louis Quatorze, Love That Jazz, Milan, Minister Eric, Mr. Greeley, North East Bound, Palace Music, Paying Dues, Pine Tree Lane, Platinum Tiara, Play the King, Point Given, Private Treasure, Qualify, Quiet Resolve, Regal Classic, Repent, Rock of Gibraltar, Royal Anthem, Sabona, Sakhee, Sardula, Seeking the Gold, Sharp Cat, Show Dancer, Sierra Roberta, Silver Charm, Singspiel, Ski Paradise, Sky Classic, Slew O' Gold, Soviet Problem, Spook Express, Star Choice, Storm Cat, Strawberry Road II, Sunshine Forever, Sweet Roberta, Take Me Out, Tank's Prospect, Tappiano, Thunderello, Touch of the Blues, Tout Charmant, Trempolino, Tuzla, Twilight Agenda, Val Des Bois, Winning Colors, With Anticipation, With Approval, Xtra Heat, Yagli	0	1	0
263. Bet on Sunshine, Heritage of Gold, Quest for Fame, Swain (2)	0	0	2
267. Adored, Afleet, Albert the Great, Bach, Bedside Promise, Bella Bellucci, Big Jag, Blushing John, Boots 'n Jackie, Brief Truce, Brought to Mind, Caller One, Cadillac Women, Captain Steve, Carnegie, Catella, Century City, Chapel Royal, Crafty C.T., Critical Factor, Dansili, Decorated Hero, Different, Dispersal, Docksider, Dontstop Themusic, Dramatic Gold, Dream Team, Dowty, Dushyantor, Dynever, Editor's Note, El Senor, Estrapade, Exclusive Enough, Falbrav, Falcon Flight, Fighting Fit, Fine Spirit, Flag Down, Fourstars Allstar, Fred Astaire, Golden Attraction, Golden Missile, Goodbye Halo, Good Journey, Got Koko, High Yield, Hold That Tiger, Honour and Glory, Indian Skimmer, John's Call, Jolypha, Judge Angelucci, Keeper Hill, Kissin Kris, Labeeb, Lakeway, Lea Lucinda, Lost Mountain, Luazur, Magical Maiden, Milwaukee Brew, Most Welcome, Miss Dominique, Mourjane, Mt. Livermore, Nationalore, Ordway, Oueee Bebe, Primaly, Priolo, Raami, Re Toss, River Special, Robyn Dancer, Rubiano, Same Old Wish, Santa Catarina, Saros Brig, Sayyedati, Scat Dancer, Shadeed, Shake You Down, She's a Devil Due, Simply Majestic, Siphonic, Slavic, Snappy Landing, Sonic Lady, Spend A Buck, Spring Oak, Star Lift, Star of Cozzene, Steal a Kiss, Stella Madrid, Stormy Blues, Street Cry, Tagel, Tejano, Tejano Run, Thirty Six Red, Three Ring, Timboroa, Two Item Limit, Unaccounted For, Unfinished Symph, Valay Maid, Victory U.S.A., Village Star II, Waquoit, Yesterday, Zomaradah (1)	0	0	1

The following charts show the champions, co-champions, and points leaders in major races for each division in thoroughbred racing from 1946-2003. Prior to the inception of the Eclipse Awards in 1971, more than one entity awarded championships. In those cases, more than one champion is listed. In other cases, champions were not selected in all categories. Those are left blank. Points leaders are awarded on the basis of four points for a major victory, two for a runner-up finish, and one for a third-place showing, with victories serving as the first tiebreaker and runner-up finishes as the second. Points listed in the sprint and turf categories are not necessarily the horse's total points for that season. Only races of less than one mile are included in the sprint totals, and only grass races are included in the turf totals. Further note that in some cases prior to the inception of the Eclipse Awards, a three-year-old is listed as champion older horse or distaffer. Those actually were called handicap champions prior to 1971, and the records for any three-year-olds who were named handicap champions from 1946-70 include only those races in which he or she competed against his or her elders in the Older Male and Older Female listings. Champions are denoted by an asterisk, and three-year-olds awarded championships as handicap horses are denoted by a plus sign.

Juvenile, Sophomore, and Sprint Champions & Points Leaders 1946-2003

Year	2-Year-Old Filly	Record	2-Year-Old Male	Record	3-Year-Old Filly	Record	3-Year-Old Male	Record	Sprinter	Record
1946	* First Flight	3-0-0/12	* Double Jay	2-0-0/8	* Bridal Flower	4-1-2/20	* Assault	7-1-3/33	Enfilade	1-1-0/6
			* Education	2-1-0/10					Flood Town	1-1-0/6
			Jet Pilot	2-1-2/12						
1947	* Bewitch	3-0-1/13	* Citation	2-1-0/10	* But Why Not	6-2-0/28	* Phalanx	4-3-4/26	* Polynesian	0-0-0/0
									Owners Choice	2-0-0/8
									Rippey	2-0-0/8
1948	* Myrtle Charm	2-1-0/10	* Blue Peter	4-0-0/16	* Miss Request	2-1-0/10	* Citation	8-0-0/32	* Coaltown	0-0-0/0
					Scattered	2-1-1/11			Rippey	1-2-0/8
1949	* Bed o' Roses	4-1-1/19	* Hill Prince	1-0-0/4	* Two Lea	0-0-0/0	* Capot	4-1-2/20	* Delegate	0-0-0/0
			* Oil Capitol	2-0-0/8	* Wistful	3-0-0/12	Ponder	5-1-0/22	* Royal Governor	1-0-0/4
									Autocrat	1-0-0/4
									Better Self	1-0-0/4
									Blue Dart	1-0-0/4
									Gaffery	1-0-0/4
									Loser Weeper	1-0-0/4
									Manyunk	1-0-0/4
									Olympia	1-0-0/4
									Up Beat	1-0-0/4
1950	* Aunt Jinny	2-1-0/10	* Battlefield	5-0-0/20	* Next Move	6-3-0/30	* Hill Prince	7-2-2/34	* Sheilas Reward	0-1-0/2
									Arise	1-0-0/4
									Ferd	1-0-0/4
									Guillotine	1-0-0/4
									Olympia	1-0-0/4
									Special Touch	1-0-0/4
									Tea-Maker	1-0-0/4
									Your Host	1-0-0/4
1951	* Rose Jet	3-1-2/16	* Tom Fool	1-1-0/6	* Kiss Me Kate	4-1-3/21	* Counterpoint	3-1-1/15	* Sheilas Reward	0-0-0/0
			Cousin	2-0-0/8			Battlefield	3-3-0/18	Gold Note	1-1-0/6
									Ruth Lily	1-1-0/6
1952	* Sweet Patootie	2-0-0/8	* Native Dancer	2-0-0/8	* Real Delight	5-0-0/20	* One Count	3-2-1/17	* Tea-Maker	0-2-0/4
	Fulvous	2-0-0/8	Laffango	3-0-0/12					To Market	1-0-1/5
1953	* Evening Out	2-0-0/8	* Hasty Road	4-0-0/16	* Grecian Queen	4-1-1/19	* Native Dancer	9-1-0/38	* Tom Fool	1-0-0/4
	Queen Hopeful	2-2-1/13	* Porterhouse	1-0-0/4					Home-Made	1-0-0/4
									Indian Land	1-0-0/4
									Kaster	1-0-0/4
1954	* High Voltage	2-0-1/9	* Nashua	2-1-0/10	* Parlo	4-0-0/16	* High Gun	4-1-3/21	* White Skies	2-0-0/8
	Myrtle's Jet	2-1-1/11	Summer Tan	2-2-0/12			Fisherman	4-5-1/27		
1955	* Doubledogdare	2-1-0/10	* Nail	3-0-0/12	* Misty Morn	3-2-1/17	* Nashua	8-1-0/34	* Berseem	0-0-0/0
	* Nasrina	2-0-1/9	* Needles	2-0-1/9	High Voltage	4-0-1/17			Bobby Brocato	1-0-0/4
									Red Hannigan	1-0-0/4
									Sailor	1-0-0/4
1956	* Leallah	2-0-0/8	* Barbizon	1-0-0/4	* Doubledogdare	1-1-1/7	* Needles	4-1-0/18	* Decathlon	0-0-0/0
	* Romanita	1-1-2/8	King Hairan	2-0-0/8	Levee	3-1-2/16			Impromptu	1-0-0/4
									Red Hannigan	1-0-0/4
1957	* Idun	3-0-0/12	* Jewel's Reward	4-0-0/16	* Bayou	4-1-0/18	* Bold Ruler	5-2-2/26	* Decathlon	0-0-0/0
			* Nadir	1-1-0/6			Round Table	7-1-3/33	Itobe	1-0-0/4
									Porterhouse	1-0-0/4
									Portersville	1-0-0/4
1958	* Quill	2-0-1/9	* First Landing	3-1-0/14	* Idun	2-1-1/11	* Tim Tam	5-1-0/22	* Bold Ruler	1-0-0/4
	Rich Tradition	2-1-1/11			A Glitter	2-1-1/11			Bull Strength	1-0-0/4
									How Now	1-0-0/4
									Seaneen	1-0-0/4
1959	* My Dear Girl	2-1-0/10	* Warfare	3-0-2/14	* Royal Native	2-0-0/8	* Sword Dancer	6-4-0/32	* Intentionally	0-0-0/0
					* Silver Spoon	2-1-1/11			Hillsdale	2-0-0/8
					High Bid	2-1-1/11				
1960	* Bowl of Flowers	2-0-0/8	* Hail to Reason	2-0-0/8	* Berlo	4-0-1/17	* Kelso	4-0-0/16	Clandestine	1-1-0/6
	Good Move	2-0-2/10	Carry Back	3-0-1/13			T.V. Lark	4-0-1/17		
1961	* Cicada	4-0-0/16	* Crimson Satan	2-0-0/8	* Bowl of Flowers	3-1-2/16	* Carry Back	7-1-2/32	T.V. Lark	1-1-0/6
			* Ridan	2-0-0/8						
			Jaipur	2-3-0/14						
1962	* Affectionately	2-0-2/10	* Never Bend	3-1-2/16	* Cicada	4-3-2/24	* Jaipur	5-2-0/24	Four-and-Twenty	1-0-0/4
	* Smart Deb	2-1-1/11							Merry Ruler	1-0-0/4
									Winonly	1-0-0/4
1963	* Castle Forbes	2-0-2/10	* Hurry to Market	1-0-0/4	* Lamb Chop	3-2-2/18	* Chateaugay	4-1-2/20	Admiral's Voyage	1-0-0/4
	* Tosmah	1-0-0/4	* Raise a Native	0-0-0/0			Candy Spots	6-1-1/27	Crozier	1-0-0/4
			Duel	2-1-0/10					Doc Jocoy	1-0-0/4

Year	2-Year-Old Filly	Record	2-Year-Old Male	Record	3-Year-Old Filly	Record	3-Year-Old Male	Record	Sprinter	Record
1964	* Queen Empress	2-1-2/12	* Bold Lad	4-0-0/16	* Tosmah	3-1-0/14	* Northern Dancer	5-0-1/21	Cyrano	1-1-0/6
			Sadair	4-1-1/19			Quadrangle	5-1-4/26		
1965	* Moccasin	4-0-0/16	* Buckpasser	4-1-0/18	* What A Treat	3-2-0/16	* Tom Rolfe	3-1-1/15	* Affectionately	0-0-0/0
							Hail to All	3-2-3/19	R. Thomas	1-0-0/4
									Viking Spirit	1-0-0/4
1966	* Mira Femme	1-0-0/4	* Successor	2-2-1/13	* Lady Pitt	2-3-1/15	* Buckpasser	9-0-0/36	* Impressive	0-0-0/0
	* Regal Gleam	2-0-1/9							Davis II	1-1-0/6
1967	* Queen of the Stage	4-0-0/16	* Vitriolic	4-3-0/22	* Furl Sail	2-1-1/11	* Damascus	9-2-1/41	* Dr. Fager	1-0-0/4
					* Gamely	1-1-1/7			Tumiga	1-0-0/4
					Quillo Queen	2-2-0/12				
1968	* Gallant Bloom	2-1-0/10	* Top Knight	3-0-1/13	* Dark Mirage	5-0-0/20	* Forward Pass	6-2-0/28	* Dr. Fager	1-0-0/4
	* Process Shot	1-1-0/6	King Emperor	3-1-1/15			* Stage Door Johnny	2-0-0/8	Damascus	1-0-0/4
									In Reality	1-0-0/4
1969	* Fast Attack	1-0-0/4	* Silent Screen	3-0-0/12	* Gallant Bloom	3-0-0/12	* Arts and Letters	7-4-0/36	* Ta Wee	1-0-0/4
	* Tudor Queen	1-0-0/4			Shuvee	5-0-2/22			Bushido	1-0-0/4
	Belle Noire	1-1-0/6							First Mate	1-0-0/4
									Promise	1-0-0/4
1970	* Forward Gal	3-0-1/13	* Hoist the Flag	1-0-0/4	* Fanfreluche	1-1-1/7	* Personality	4-0-0/16	* Ta Wee	0-0-0/0
	June Darling	3-1-0/14	Limit to Reason	2-2-0/12	* Office Queen	1-0-2/6			Best Turn	1-1-0/6
					Cathy Honey	2-3-0/14				
1971	* Numbered Account	5-0-0/20	* Riva Ridge	4-0-0/16	* Turkish Trousers	2-0-0/8	* Canonero II	2-0-0/8	* Ack Ack	0-0-0/0
					Forward Gal	2-0-3/11	Jim French	2-3-3/17	Duck Dance	1-0-0/4
									King of Cricket	1-0-0/4
									Native Royalty	1-0-0/4
1972	* La Prevoyante	5-0-0/20	* Secretariat	4-1-0/18	* Susan's Girl	5-1-2/24	* Key to the Mint	5-1-1/23	* Chou Croute	0-0-0/0
									Kfar Tov	1-0-0/4
									Leematt	1-0-0/4
									Triple Bend	1-0-0/4
									Wing Out	1-0-0/4
1973	* Talking Picture	2-0-1/9	* Protagonist	2-1-0/10	* Desert Vixen	3-0-0/12	* Secretariat	7-2-1/33	* Shecky Greene	0-0-0/0
									Aljamin	1-0-0/4
									Bicker	1-0-0/4
									King's Bishop	1-0-0/4
1974	* Ruffian	2-0-0/8	* Foolish Pleasure	3-0-0/12	* Chris Evert	3-1-1/15	* Little Current	2-2-0/12	* Forego	2-0-0/8
							Agitate	3-0-2/14		
1975	* Dearly Precious	3-0-0/12	* Honest Pleasure	3-0-0/12	* Ruffian	3-0-0/12	* Wajima	3-3-0/18	* Gallant Bob	0-0-0/0
	Optimistic Gal	4-2-0/20							No Bias	1-1-0/6
1976	* Sensational	2-1-1/11	* Seattle Slew	1-0-0/4	* Revidere	2-1-1/11	* Bold Forbes	3-0-2/14	* My Juliet	1-0-0/4
			Royal Ski	2-1-0/10	Optimistic Gal	5-3-1/27	Honest Pleasure	4-2-2/22	Honorable Miss	1-1-0/6
1977	* Lakeville Miss	3-1-0/14	* Affirmed	4-1-0/18	* Our Mims	4-1-1/19	* Seattle Slew	5-0-0/20	* What a Summer	0-0-0/0
									Affiliate	1-0-0/4
									Gentle King	1-0-0/4
									Quiet Little Table	1-0-0/4
									Sound of Summer	1-0-0/4
									Soy Numero Uno	1-0-0/4
1978	* Candy Eclair	1-0-0/4	* Spectacular Bid	3-0-0/12	* Tempest Queen	2-0-4/12	* Affirmed	6-2-0/28	* Dr. Patches	1-0-0/4
	* It's In the Air	2-1-0/10					Alydar	6-3-0/30	* J.O. Tobin	0-0-0/4
									Jaipur's Gem	1-0-0/4
									Pumpkin Moonshine	1-0-0/4
1979	* Smart Angle	3-0-0/12	* Rockhill Native	2-1-0/10	* Davona Dale	5-1-0/22	* Spectacular Bid	7-1-1/31	* Star de Naskra	0-0-0/0
			Gold Stage	1-3-2/12					General Assembly	1-0-0/4
1980	* Heavenly Cause	2-1-0/10	* Lord Avie	2-3-0/14	* Genuine Risk	2-3-1/15	* Temperence Hill	5-1-0/22	* Plugged Nickle	1-0-0/4
					Bold 'n Determined	7-1-0/30				
1981	* Before Dawn	1-1-0/6	* Deputy Minister	2-0-0/8	* Wayward Lass	2-0-2/10	* Pleasant Colony	4-1-1/19	* Guilty Conscience	1-0-0/4
	Apalachee Honey	2-0-0/8	Timely Writer	2-0-1/9	Heavenly Cause	3-1-0/14				
	Skillful Joy	2-0-0/8								
1982	* Landaluce	2-0-0/8	* Roving Boy	3-0-0/12	* Christmas Past	2-1-1/11	* Conquistador Cielo	3-0-1/13	* Gold Beauty	0-1-0/2
			Copelan	3-0-0/12	Blush With Pride	3-1-1/15			Engine One	1-0-0/4
1983	* Althea	3-1-0/14	* Devil's Bag	2-0-0/8	* Hearlight No. One	1-1-0/6	* Slew O' Gold	3-3-0/18	* Chinook Pass	0-0-0/0
	Miss Oceana	3-1-0/14	Swale	3-0-1/13	High Schemes	1-1-0/6	Play Fellow	4-1-0/18	A Phenomenon	1-0-0/4
					Princess Rooney	1-1-0/6				
					Spit Curl	1-1-0/6				
1984	* Outstandingly	1-0-0/4	* Chief's Crown	3-1-0/14	* Life's Magic	3-3-1/19	* Swale	4-0-1/17	* Eillo	1-0-0/4
	Tiltalating	1-4-0/12					At the Threshold	4-1-1/19	Swale	1-0-0/4
									Track Barron	1-0-0/4
1985	* Family Style	2-2-0/12	* Tasso	2-0-0/8	* Mom's Command	4-0-0/16	* Spend A Buck	3-1-0/14	* Precisionist	1-0-0/4
							Creme Fraiche	4-4-2/26	Another Reef	1-0-0/4
									Banner Bob	1-0-0/4
1986	* Brave Raj	1-0-0/4	* Capote	2-0-1/9	* Tiffany Lass	2-0-0/8	* Snow Chief	4-0-0/16	* Smile	1-0-0/4
	Sacahuista	1-2-0/8	Gulch	2-1-0/10	Life at the Top	2-2-3/15	Broad Brush	5-0-2/22	King's Swan	1-0-0/4
									Papal Power	1-0-0/4
1987	* Epitome	1-0-0/4	* Forty Niner	2-0-0/8	* Sacahuista	2-1-1/11	* Alysheba	3-3-1/19	* Groovy	1-1-0/6
	Lost Kitty	1-1-0/6	Tejano	3-0-2/14	Fiesta Gal	2-1-1/11	Gone West	3-3-1/19		
1988	* Open Mind	2-1-0/10	* Easy Goer	2-1-0/10	* Winning Colors	3-2-1/17	* Risen Star	2-0-1/9	* Gulch	1-1-0/6
			Fast Play	2-1-1/11			Seeking the Gold	3-5-0/22		
1989	* Go for Wand	1-1-0/6	* Rhythm	1-1-0/6	* Open Mind	5-0-2/22	* Sunday Silence	6-2-0/28	* Safely Kept	0-1-0/2
	Stella Madrid	2-1-0/10	Grand Canyon	2-1-0/10			Easy Goer	7-3-0/34	Dancing Spree	1-0-0/4
									On the Line	1-0-0/4
									Sewickley	1-0-0/4
1990	* Meadow Star	4-0-0/16	* Fly So Free	2-0-0/8	* Go for Wand	5-1-0/22	* Unbridled	3-2-1/17	* Housebuster	0-0-0/0
			Best Pal	3-0-0/12			Summer Squall	4-1-0/18	Sewickley	1-0-1/5
1991	* Pleasant Stage	2-0-0/8	* Arazi	1-0-0/4	* Dance Smartly	1-0-0/4	* Hansel	3-1-2/16	* Housebuster	2-0-0/8
			Bertrando	2-1-0/10	Lite Light	4-1-0/18	Olympio	3-2-0/16		
1992	* Eliza	2-0-0/8	* Gilded Time	2-0-0/8	* Saratoga Dew	1-1-0/6	* A.P. Indy	4-0-1/17	* Rubiano	2-0-1/9
			River Special	3-0-1/13	Prospectors Delite	2-0-1/9				
					Turnback the Alarm	2-0-1/9				
1993	* Phone Chatter	2-0-0/8	* Dehere	2-1-0/10	* Hollywood Wildcat	2-0-0/8	* Prairie Bayou	3-1-0/14	* Cardmania	1-0-0/4
					Sky Beauty	4-0-0/16			Alydeed	1-0-0/4
									Birdonthewire	1-0-0/4
1994	* Flanders	4-0-0/16	* Timber Country	2-0-1/9	* Heavenly Prize	3-1-1/15	* Holy Bull	7-0-0/28	* Cherokee Run	1-0-2/6
					Lakeway	3-2-0/16				

Year	2-Year-Old Filly	Record	2-Year-Old Male	Record	3-Year-Old Filly	Record	3-Year-Old Male	Record	Sprinter	Record
1995	* Golden Attraction	3-0-1/13	* Maria's Mon	2-0-1/9	* Serena's Song	7-1-0/30	* Thunder Gulch	5-0-1/21	* Not Surprising	1-0-0/4
									Lite the Fuse	2-0-0/8
1996	* Storm Song	2-1-0/10	* Boston Harbor	1-0-0/4	* Yanks Music	4-1-0/18	* Skip Away	5-2-2/26	* Lit de Justice	1-0-0/4
			Ordway	1-1-1/7					Lite the Fuse	2-0-1/9
1997	* Countess Diana	2-0-0/8	* Favorite Trick	2-0-0/8	* Ajina	3-2-1/17	* Silver Charm	2-4-0/16	* Smoke Glacken	1-0-0/4
			Grand Slam	2-0-0/8	Sharp Cat	4-2-0/20	Free House	3-1-3/17	Pearl City	1-0-1/5
			Souvenir Copy	2-0-0/8						
1998	* Silverbulletday	2-0-0/8	* Answer Lively	1-1-0/6	* Banshee Breeze	3-2-2/18	* Real Quiet	2-3-0/14	* Reraise	1-0-0/4
	Excellent Meeting	2-1-0/10	Lemon Drop Kid	1-1-0/6			Victory Gallop	2-4-0/16	Affirmed Success	1-1-0/6
			Tactical Cat	1-1-0/6						
1999	* Chilukki	2-1-0/10	* Anees	1-0-1/5	* Silverbulletday	4-1-0/18	* Charismatic	2-0-1/9	* Artax	3-0-0/12
	Surfside	2-1-1/11	Greenwood Lake	2-1-0/10			Cat Thief	2-3-3/17		
2000	* Caressing	1-0-0/4	* Macho Uno	1-0-1/5	* Surfside	2-1-0/10	* Tiznow	2-2-0/12	* Kona Gold	1-0-0/4
	Raging Fever	2-0-0/8	Flame Thrower	2-0-0/8	Spain	2-2-1/13	Fusaichi Pegasus	3-1-0/14	Dream Supreme	2-0-0/8
2001	* Tempera	1-0-1/5	* Johannesburg	1-0-0/4	* Xtra Heat	1-2-1/9	* Point Given	6-0-0/24	* Squirtle Squirt	2-1-0/10
	Habibti	2-0-0/8	Officer	2-0-1/9	Exogenous	2-2-1/13				
			Siphonic	2-0-1/9						
2002	* Storm Flag Flying	3-0-0/12	* Vindication	1-0-0/4	* Farda Amiga	2-1-0/10	* War Emblem	3-0-0/12	* Orientate	2-0-0/8
			Sky Mesa	2-0-0/8	You	4-2-1/21	Medaglia d'Oro	2-3-0/14		
			Toccet	2-0-0/8						
2003	* Halfbridled	2-0-0/8	* Action This Day	1-0-0/4	* Bird Town	2-2-0/12	* Funny Cide	2-1-2/12	* Aldebaran	2-1-0/10
			Chapel Royal	0-2-1/5			Empire Maker	3-2-0/16		

Handicap and Turf Champions & Points Leaders 1946-2003

Year	Older Female	Record	Older Male	Record	Turf Female	Record	Turf Male	Record	Horse of the Year	Record
1946	* Gallorette	3-0-1/13	* Armed	4-2-0/20	Milcave	0-1-0/2	Cat Bridge	1-0-0/4	* Assault	7-1-3/33
			Stymie	5-5-1/31	Moon Maiden	0-1-0/2	Frere Jacques	1-0-0/4		
1947	* + But Why Not	2-1-0/10	* Armed	6-0-1/25			Tel O'Sullivan	1-0-0/4	* Armed	6-0-1/25
	Elpis	3-1-2/16							But Why Not	6-2-0/28
1948	* Conniver	4-1-0/18	* + Citation	2-0-0/8			Stud Poker	1-0-0/4	* Citation	8-0-0/32
			* Shannon II	2-0-1/9						
			Stymie	2-3-2/16						
1949	* Bewitch	1-1-0/6	* Coaltown	7-1-0/30			Frere Jacques	1-0-0/4	* Capot	4-1-2/20
	But Why Not	2-2-1/13							* Coaltown	7-1-0/30
1950	* Two Lea	1-1-1/7	* Noor	5-3-1/27			Chicle II	1-0-0/4	* Hill Prince	7-2-2/34
	Red Camelia	2-0-0/8					Inseparable	1-0-0/4		
1951	* Bed o' Roses	2-2-3/15	* Citation	2-0-0/8	Aegina	0-0-1/1	Chicle II	1-0-0/4	* Counterpoint	3-1-1/15
			* + Hill Prince	1-1-0/6			Royal Governor	1-0-0/4	County Delight	3-2-6/22
			County Delight	3-2-6/22						
1952	* Next Move	2-1-0/10	* Crafty Admiral	3-2-1/17			Royal Mustang	1-0-0/4	* Native Dancer	2-0-0/8
	* Real Delight	1-0-0/4	To Market	4-1-2/20			Wilwyn	1-0-0/4	* One Count	3-2-1/17
									Real Delight	5-0-0/20
1953	* Sickle's Image	1-0-0/4	* Tom Fool	6-0-0/24			* Iceberg II	1-1-2/8	* Tom Fool	6-0-0/24
	Atalanta	2-2-0/12							Native Dancer	9-1-0/38
1954	* Lavender Hill	2-1-1/11	* Native Dancer	1-0-0/4	Banassa	0-1-0/2	* Stan	1-0-0/4	* Native Dancer	1-0-0/4
	* + Parlo	2-0-0/8	Rejected	3-4-0/20			Picador	1-1-0/6	Fisherman	4-5-1/27
1955	* + Misty Morn	2-1-0/10	* High Gun	2-2-0/12			* St. Vincent	2-0-0/8	* Nashua	8-1-0/34
	* Parlo	2-0-0/8	Social Outcast	5-2-3/27						
1956	* Blue Sparkler	1-0-0/4	* Swaps	5-1-0/22	Manotick	0-1-0/2	* Career Boy	1-0-0/4	* Swaps	5-1-0/22
	Searching	3-0-1/13	Nashua	5-1-0/22			Mister Gus	1-1-1/7	Nashua	5-1-0/22
1957	* Pucker Up	3-2-0/16	* Dedicate	3-2-1/17			* Round Table	2-0-0/8	* Bold Ruler	5-2-2/26
									* Dedicate	3-2-1/17
									Round Table	7-1-3/33
1958	* Bornastar	2-0-0/8	* Round Table	6-3-0/30			* Round Table	1-1-0/6	* Round Table	6-3-0/30
	Endine	2-1-0/10					Clem	1-1-0/6		
1959	* Tempted	3-1-2/16	* Round Table	5-2-1/25			* Round Table	3-0-0/12	* Sword Dancer	6-4-0/32
			* + Sword Dancer	4-1-0/18					Hillsdale	7-3-0/34
			Hillsdale	7-3-0-34						
1960	* Royal Native	4-2-1/21	* Bald Eagle	5-2-2/26			Amerigo	2-0-1/9	* Kelso	4-0-0/16
									Bald Eagle	5-2-2/26
1961	* Airmans Guide	2-0-0/8	* Kelso	6-1-0/26	Geechee Lou	0-0-1/1	* T.V. Lark	1-0-0/4	* Kelso	6-1-0/26
							Wolfram	2-2-0/12	Carry Back	7-1-2/32
1962	* Primonetta	1-0-0/4	* Kelso	2-4-0/16			El Bandido	2-0-1/9	* Kelso	2-4-0/16
	Seven Thirty	2-0-0/8	Carry Back	3-4-3/23					Jaipur	5-2-0/24
1963	* Cicada	0-1-1/3	* Kelso	8-2-0/36			* Mongo	2-0-0/8	* Kelso	8-2-0/36
	Oil Royalty	2-0-0/8					The Axe II	3-0-0/12		
1964	* Old Hat	2-1-0/10	* Kelso	3-3-0/18	Canebora	0-1-0/2	Cedar Key	2-0-0/8	* Kelso	3-3-0/18
	* + Tosmah	2-1-0/10	Gun Bow	8-4-2/42			Will I Rule	2-0-0/8	Gun Bow	8-4-2/42
1965	* Affectionately	1-0-1/5	* Roman Brother	3-2-2/18	Desert Love	0-0-1/1	* Parka	1-0-0/4	* Moccasin	4-0-0/16
	* Old Hat	3-0-1/13	Hill Rise	3-2-3/19			Or et Argent	2-1-2/12	* Roman Brother	3-2-2/18
									Hail to All	3-2-3/19
									Hill Rise	3-2-3/19
1966	* Open Fire	2-0-0/8	* Bold Bidder	4-0-2/18	Straight Deal	1-0-0/4	* Assagai	2-0-1/9	* Buckpasser	9-0-0/36
	* Summer Scandal	2-0-1/9	* + Buckpasser	3-0-0/12						
	Straight Deal	2-2-1/13								
1967	* Straight Deal	3-2-2/18	* Buckpasser	3-2-1/17	April Dawn	1-0-0/4	* Fort Marcy	1-1-1/7	* Damascus	9-2-1/41
			* + Damascus	3-1-0/14	Ormea	1-0-0/4	War Censor	3-0-0/12		
1968	* Gamely	3-2-0/16	* Dr. Fager	6-1-0/26	Amerigo's Fancy	1-0-0/4	* Dr. Fager	1-0-0/4	* Dr. Fager	6-1-0/26
					Princessnesian	1-0-0/4	* Fort Marcy	1-1-2/8	Forward Pass	6-2-0/28
							Irish Rebellion	1-3-0/10		
1969	* + Gallant Bloom	1-0-0/4	* + Arts and Letters	3-0-0/12	Pink Pigeon	1-0-2/6	* Hawaii	3-1-0/14	* Arts and Letters	7-4-0/36
	* Gamely	1-2-1/9	* Nodouble	4-6-0/28			Czar Alexander	3-1-1/15		
	Amerigo Lady	2-2-1/13								
1970	* Shuvee	3-0-0/12	* Fort Marcy	5-2-1/25	Drumtop	1-4-1/13	* Fort Marcy	5-2-1/25	* Fort Marcy	5-2-1/25
			* Nodouble	1-0-1/5					* Personality	4-0-0/16

Year	Older Female	Record	Older Male	Record	Turf Female	Record	Turf Male	Record	Horse of the Year	Record
1971	* Shuvee	2-1-1/11	* Ack Ack	4-0-0/16	Manta	2-0-1/9	* Run the Gantlet	3-0-0/12	* Ack Ack	4-0-0/16
	Manta	3-2-2/18	Cougar II	4-2-2/22			Champion	3-1-2/16	Cougar II	4-2-2/22
1972	* Typecast	3-3-2/20	* Autobiography	2-3-1/15	Typecast	3-1-1/15	* Cougar II	2-1-1/11	* Secretariat	4-1-0/18
			Droll Role	5-2-1/25			Droll Role	2-1-1/11	Droll Role	5-2-1/25
1973	* Susan's Girl	5-0-2/22	* Riva Ridge	2-1-0/10	Dahlia	1-0-0/4	* Secretariat	2-0-0/8	* Secretariat	7-2-1/33
			Cougar II	3-0-6/18	Le Cle	1-0-0/4	Life Cycle	1-4-2/14		
					Summer Guest	1-0-0/4				
1974	* Desert Vixen	1-2-0/8	* Forego	8-1-2/36	* Dahlia	2-0-1/9	Big Whippendeal	2-1-0/10	* Forego	8-1-2/36
	Tallahto	3-0-2/14								
1975	* Susan's Girl	3-2-2/18	* Forego	5-1-1/23	La Zanzara	2-0-1/9	* Snow Knight	2-0-0/8	* Forego	5-1-1/23
							Barclay Joy	2-0-0/8		
							Cruiser II	2-0-0/8		
							Intrepid Hero	2-0-0/8		
1976	* Proud Delta	3-1-0/14	* Forego	4-1-1/19	Stravina	1-1-0/6	* Youth	2-0-0/8	* Forego	4-1-1/19
							Caucasus	2-1-1/11	Optimistic Gal	5-3-1/27
1977	* Cascapedia	1-1-2/8	* Forego	2-2-0/12	Dancing Femme	1-0-0/4	* Johnny D.	2-0-2/10	* Seattle Slew	5-0-0/20
	Mississippi Mud	0-4-1/9	Crystal Water	4-0-2/18	Star Ball	1-0-0/4	Hunza Dancer	2-1-0/10		
1978	* Late Bloomer	4-0-0/16	* Seattle Slew	2-1-0/10	Waya	2-1-1/11	* Mac Diarmida	3-0-1/13	* Affirmed	6-2-0/28
			Exceller	6-1-0/26			Exceller	4-0-0/16	Alydar	6-3-0/30
1979	* Waya	2-1-1/11	* Affirmed	6-1-0/26	* Trillion	0-4-0/8	* Bowl Game	5-0-1/21	* Affirmed	6-1-0/26
					Country Queen	2-1-0/10			Spectacular Bid	7-1-1/31
1980	* Glorious Song	3-2-0/16	* Spectacular Bid	6-0-0/24	* Just A Game II	1-1-0/6	* John Henry	5-2-1/25	* Spectacular Bid	6-0-0/24
									Bold 'n Determined	7-1-0/30
1981	* Relaxing	2-0-1/9	* John Henry	7-0-0/28	* De La Rose	1-1-0/6	* John Henry	5-0-0/20	* John Henry	7-0-0/28
	Queen to Conquer	2-1-0/10			Queen to Conquer	2-1-0/10				
1982	* Track Robbery	2-2-0/12	* Lehmi Gold	4-1-0/18	* April Run	2-0-0/8	* Perrault	2-0-2/10	* Conquistador Cielo	3-0-1/13
			It's the One	3-2-3/19	Castilla	2-0-0/8	Lemhi Gold	2-1-0/10	It's the One	3-2-3/19
							Naskra's Breeze	2-1-0/10		
1983	* Ambassador of Luck	1-0-0/4	* Bates Motel	3-1-1/15	* All Along	3-0-0/12	* John Henry	1-2-0/8	* All Along	3-0-0/12
	Sangue	4-0-1/17	Erins Isle	3-1-2/16	Sangue	4-0-0/16	Erins Isle	3-1-2/16	Play Fellow	4-1-0/18
1984	* Princess Rooney	3-0-0/12	* Slew O' Gold	4-1-0/18	* Royal Heroine	1-1-0/6	* John Henry	4-1-1/19	* John Henry	4-1-1/19
	Heatherten	3-0-1/13	John Henry	4-1-1/19					At the Threshold	4-1-1/19
1985	* Life's Magic	1-2-3/11	* Vanlandingham	3-1-3/17	* Pebbles	1-0-0/4	* Cozzene	1-0-0/4	* Spend A Buck	3-1-0/14
			Greinton	2-5-0/18	Estrapade	1-1-0/6	Prince True	2-0-0/8	Creme Fraiche	4-4-2/26
1986	* Lady's Secret	7-2-2/34	* Turkoman	2-2-0/12	* Estrapade	2-2-1/13	* Manila	3-0-0/12	* Lady's Secret	7-7-2/34
			Dahar	2-3-0/14			Dahar	2-3-0/14		
1987	* North Sider	3-1-0/14	* Ferdinand	2-2-1/13	* Miesque	1-0-0/4	* Theatrical	4-0-1/17	* Ferdinand	2-2-1/13
			Theatrical	4-0-1/17	Northern Aspen	1-1-0/6			Alysheba	3-3-1/19
					Reloy	1-1-0/6			Gone West	3-3-1/19
					River Memories	1-1-0/6				
1988	* Personal Ensign	4-0-0/16	* Alysheba	6-1-0/26	* Miesque	1-0-0/4	* Sunshine Forever	3-2-1/17	* Alysheba	6-1-0/26
					Pen Bal Lady	2-0-0/8	Great Communicator	3-2-1/17		
1989	* Bayakoa	6-0-0/24	* Blushing John	1-1-1/7	* Brown Bess	1-0-0/4	* Steinlen	2-1-0/10	* Sunday Silence	6-2-0/28
			Yankee Affair	3-2-1/17	Fitzwilliam Place	1-0-0/4	Yankee Affair	3-2-1/17	Easy Goer	7-3-0/34
					No Review	1-0-0/4				
					River Memories	1-0-0/4				
1990	* Bayakoa	3-1-0/14	* Criminal Type	5-1-0/22	* Laugh and Be Merry	1-0-0/4	* Itsallgreektome	2-1-0/10	* Criminal Type	5-1-0/22
	Gorgeous	3-2-0/16			Petite Ile	1-1-0/6			Go for Wand	5-1-0/22
1991	* Queena	2-0-0/8	* Black Tie Affair	2-1-0/10	* Miss Alleged	2-0-0/8	* Tight Spot	2-0-0/8	* Black Tie Affair	2-1-0/10
	Fit to Scout	1-3-1/11	In Excess	5-0-1/21			Exbourne	2-0-0/8	In Excess	5-0-1/21
							Solar Splendor	2-0-0/8		
1992	* Paseana	5-1-0/22	* Pleasant Tap	2-4-0/16	* Flawlessly	1-1-1/7	* Sky Classic	2-2-0/12	* A.P. Indy	4-0-1/17
					Kostroma	2-0-1/9	Fraise	2-2-0/12	Paseana	5-1-0/22
1993	* Paseana	3-4-0/20	* Bertrando	2-4-1/17	* Flawlessly	3-0-0/12	* Kotashaan	5-0-0/20	* Kotashaan	5-0-0/20
			Kotashaan	5-0-0/20						
1994	* Sky Beauty	4-0-0/16	* The Wicked North	3-0-0/12	* Hatoof	1-1-0/6	* Paradise Creek	3-0-1/13	* Holy Bull	7-0-0/28
			Devil His Due	2-6-1/21	Flawlessly	1-1-1/7				
1995	* Inside Information	4-0-0/16	* Cigar	8-0-0/32	* Possibly Perfect	3-1-0/14	* Northern Spur	2-0-1/9	* Cigar	8-0-0/32
							Sandpit	2-3-0/14		
1996	* Jewel Princess	2-1-1/11	* Cigar	2-2-1/13	* Wandesta	1-1-0/6	* Singspiel	1-1-0/6	* Cigar	2-2-1/13
	Serena's Song	2-5-2/20	Wekiva Springs	3-2-0/16	Windsharp	1-2-0/8	Diplomatic Jet	3-1-0/14	Skip Away	5-2-2/26
1997	* Hidden Lake	3-0-1/13	* Skip Away	3-5-1/23	* Ryafan	3-0-0/12	* Chief Bearhart	2-0-0/8	* Favorite Trick	2-0-0/8
							Marlin	2-0-2/10	Skip Away	3-5-1/23
1998	* Escena	3-1-0/14	* Skip Away	6-0-1/26	* Fiji	2-0-1/9	* Buck's Boy	2-1-1/11	* Skip Away	6-0-1/26
					Squeak	2-0-1/9				
1999	* Beautiful Pleasure	3-2-0/16	* Victory Gallop	1-0-0/4	* Soaring Softly	2-0-0/8	* Daylami	1-0-0/4	* Charismatic	2-0-1/9
			Behrens	3-3-0/18	Perfect Sting	2-0-0/8	Val's Prince	2-1-0/10	Silverbulletday	4-1-0/18
2000	* Riboletta	5-0-0/20	* Lemon Drop Kid	4-0-1/17	* Perfect Sting	1-0-0/4	* Kalanisi	1-0-0/4	* Tiznow	2-2-0/12
					Happyanunoit	1-2-1/9	Manndar	2-1-0/10	Riboletta	5-0-0/20
					Tout Charmant	1-2-1/9				
2001	* Gourmet Girl	2-0-0/8	* Tiznow	2-1-1/11	* Banks Hill	1-0-0/4	* Fantastic Light	1-0-0/4	* Point Given	6-0-0/24
	Lazy Slusan	2-1-1/11	Albert the Great	2-4-1/17	Janet	2-0-0/8	With Anticipation	2-1-0/10		
2002	* Azeri	5-0-0/20	* Left Bank	1-0-0/4	* Golden Apples	2-2-0/12	* High Chaparral	1-0-0/4	* Azeri	5-0-0/20
			With Anticipation	3-2-0/16			With Anticipation	3-2-0/16	You	4-2-1/21
2003	* Azeri	3-0-0/12	* Mineshaft	4-1-0/18	* Islington	1-0-0/4	* High Chapparal	1-0-0/4	* Mineshaft	4-1-0/18
	Sightseek	4-2-0/20			Heat Haze	2-1-1/11	Storming Home	2-0-0/8	Sightseek	4-2-0/20
							Sulamani	2-0-0/8		

The following chart lists every thoroughbred who earned at least eight points, with four points awarded for a victory, two for a runner-up finish, and one for a third-place showing, in the 6,461 major races held in North America from 1946-2003. Victories are used as the first tiebreaker and runner-up finishes as the second tiebreaker.

Following that chart are charts that show the annual points leaders, which is followed by an alphabetical listing of all thoroughbreds who posted in-the-money finishes—and their records in those events—in major North American races from 1946-2003 with the year each was born in parenthesis.

Leaders Among Thoroughbreds Who Posted In-the-Money Finishes In Major North American Races From 1946-2003

	W	P	S
1. Kelso (117)	24	10	1
2. Forego (95)	19	7	5
3. John Henry (94)	19	7	4
4. Round Table (92)	19	6	4
5. Skip Away (76)	14	8	4
6. Carry Back	14	5	7
7. Stymie (73)	11	12	5
8. Affirmed (72)	16	4	0
9. Buckpasser (71)	16	3	1
10. Susan's Girl (68)	13	5	6
11. Spectacular Bid (67)	16	1	1
12. Nashua (66)	15	3	0
13. Damascus (65)	13	5	3
14. Cougar II	10	5	12
15. Find (62)	8	9	12
16. Serena's Song (60)	11	7	2
17. Citation (58)	12	5	0
18. Gun Bow (57)	11	5	3
19. Shuvee	12	2	3
20. Paseana	9	9	1
21. Fort Marcy (55)	8	8	7
22. Armed (54)	10	5	4
23. Dr. Fager	12	2	1
24. Assault	12	1	3
25. Battlefield	10	6	1
26. Ancient Title (53)	9	6	5
27. Best Pal (52)	10	5	2
28. Secretariat	11	3	1
29. Devil His Due (51)	7	10	3
30. Native Dancer (50)	12	1	0
31. Cigar	11	2	1
32. Easy Goer	10	4	1
33. Alydar	8	8	1
34. Bed o' Roses (49)	8	6	5
35. Lady's Secret	10	3	2
36. Alysheba, Sword Dancer	9	5	2
38. Nodouble	8	7	2
39. Creme Fraiche (48)	7	6	8
40. Optimistic Gal (47)	9	5	1
41. Next Move	8	6	2
42. Social Outcast (46)	8	4	6
43. Tom Fool (45)	9	4	1
44. Bold Ruler, Hill Prince	9	3	2
46. Roman Brother	7	6	4
47. Gallorette (44)	6	6	8
48. Riva Ridge	10	1	1
49. Coaltown	9	3	1
50. Bald Eagle, Cicada	8	4	3
52. Crimson Satan, Fisherman	7	6	3
54. Life's Magic (43)	5	9	5
55. Swaps	10	1	0
56. But Why Not	8	4	2
57. First Landing (42)	6	8	2
58. T.V. Lark (41)	8	4	1
59. Bayakoa	9	2	0
60. Sky Beauty	9	1	2
61. Arts and Letters	8	4	0
62. Straight Deal (40)	7	4	4
63. Gulch	6	6	3
64. One Hitter (39)	6	5	5
65. Bold 'n Determined	9	1	0
66. Sharp Cat	8	3	0
67. Foolish Pleasure	8	2	2
68. Jaipur	7	5	0
69. Precisionist (38)	6	6	2
70. Exceller, Heavenly Prize	7	3	3
72. Honeymoon, Quicken Tree	6	5	3
74. Summer Tan (37)	5	8	1
75. Prove It	8	2	0
76. Ponder	8	1	2
77. Mongo, Slew O' Gold	7	4	0
79. In Reality	6	6	0
80. Bewitch (36)	6	5	2
81. Candy Spots, Hillsdale	7	3	1
83. Chief's Crown, Free House	7	2	3
85. Broad Brush	7	1	5
86. Oil Capitol, Traffic Judge	6	5	1
88. Hill Rise, My Request	6	3	5
90. Tompion	5	7	1
91. Behrens	5	6	3
92. Phalanx (35)	5	5	5
93. Seattle Slew	8	1	0
94. Sunday Silence	7	3	0
95. Bowl Game, Honest Pleasure	7	2	2
97. Beautiful Pleasure	6	5	0
98. It's In the Air (34)	6	3	4
99. Lemon Drop Kid, Temperence Hill	7	2	1
101. Gallant Man	6	4	1
102. Crafty Admiral, Dedicate, High Gun	6	3	3
105. Native Diver	6	2	5
106. Bertrando, Rejected, You	5	6	1
109. Sandpit	5	5	3
110. Admiral's Voyage (33)	4	6	5
111. Azeri, Holy Bull	8	0	0
113. Point Given	7	2	0
114. Open Mind	7	1	2
115. Olympia	6	4	0
116. Key to the Mint	6	3	2
117. Kiss Me Kate, Quadrangle	6	2	4
119. Promised Land	6	1	6
120. Bien Bien	5	6	0
121. Banshee Breeze, Better Self, Gamely, Ridan	5	5	2
125. Desert Wine	4	8	0
126. Alerted (32)	3	7	6
127. Snow Chief	7	0	3
128. Cosmic Bomb, Royal Native	6	3	1
130. Noble Dancer II	6	2	3
131. Intentionally, Miss Oceana	5	5	1
133. Summer Guest	5	4	3
134. Majesty's Prince	5	2	7
135. True Knight	4	7	1
136. Mister Gus	4	6	3
137. Chompion (31)	4	3	9
138. Swale	7	0	2
139. Medaglia d'Oro	5	5	0
140. Crozier	4	6	2
141. Double Jay (30)	4	5	4
142. Forward Pass, Idun	6	2	1
144. Congaree	6	1	3
145. Flying Paster	5	4	1
146. Bet Twice, Bridal Flower, Grecian Queen, Three Rings	5	3	3
150. Bally Ache, Golden Act, Strike the Gold	4	5	3
153. County Delight	4	3	7
154. Amerigo, On Trust (29)	2	8	5
156. Bardstown, Go for Wand, Parlo	6	2	0
159. Capot, Crystal Water, Mark-Ye-Well, Needles, To Market	6	1	2
164. Forty Niner, Gorgeous, Majestic Light	5	4	0
167. Donor, Droll Role, Erins Isle, Flawlessly, Gentlemen, Tom Rolfe	5	3	2
173. Clem	5	2	4
174. Silver Charm	4	5	2
175. Amerigo Lady (28)	4	4	4
176. Hasty Road, Meadow Star, Thunder Gulch	6	1	1
179. High Voltage	6	0	3
180. Noor, Old Hat, West Coast Scout, With Anticipation	5	3	1
184. Arise	5	2	3
185. Escena, Great Communicator, Tiller, Vulcan's Forge	4	5	1
189. Awad, Never Bend, Royal Vale	4	4	3
192. Cat Thief, Cryptoclearance, Ferdinand (27)	3	5	5
195. Ack Ack, Gallant Bloom, Silverbulletday	6	1	0
198. Real Quiet, Royal Glint	5	3	0
200. Helioscope, Sangue, Searching, Waya	5	2	2
204. Tempted	5	1	4
205. Glorious Song	4	5	0
206. Affluent, Goodbye Halo, Lights Up	4	4	2
209. Tizna	4	3	4
210. Dotted Line, Olden Times	3	5	4
212. Big Spruce (26)	2	7	4
213. Four-and-Twenty, Inside Information, Numbered Account	6	0	1
216. Master Derby, Quill, Straight Face	5	2	1
219. Ace Admiral, In Excess	5	1	3
221. Fervent, Fiddle Isle, Quack, Smart, Swoon's Son	4	4	1
226. Great Circle, Lithe	4	3	3
228. Iron Ruler, Stop the Music	2	7	3
230. Eddie Schmidt	2	6	5
231. Talent Show (25)	1	5	11
232. Personal Ensign, Real Delight	6	0	0
234. Althea, Heavenly Cause, Interco, Lite Light, Summer Squall	5	2	0
239. Bowl of Flowers, Faultless, Tosmah, Turnback the Alarm	5	1	2
243. Forward Gal	5	0	4
244. Bold Hour, Smarten	4	4	0
246. Determine, Steinlen, Super Moment	4	3	2
249. Jewel Princess, Oh Johnny, Solidarity	4	2	4
252. Seeking the Gold	3	6	0
253. Aldebaran, Greek Ship, Manta	3	5	2
256. Elpis, Keeper Hill, Palestinian	3	4	4
259. Ambiopoise, Concern	3	3	6
261. Sir Bear	3	2	8
262. Spain (24)	2	6	4
263. Counterpoint, Jewel's Reward, Pleasant Colony, Skip Trial, Top Knight, War Censor	5	1	1
269. Bryan G., Linda's Chief, State Dinner, Tiznow	4	3	1
273. A Gleam, Miss Grillo	4	2	3
275. Albert the Great, Convenience, Drumtop	3	5	1
278. Miss Cavandish, Mr. Consistency, Typecast	3	4	3
281. Manotick, Tudor Era	3	3	5
283. Run Dusty Run	2	7	1

284. Gay Matelda, Valley Crossing (23)	2	6	3
286. Cedar Key, Criminal Type, Davona Dale, La Prevoyante, Possibly Perfect, Princess Rooney, Tim Tam, Vertex	5	1	0
294. Bold Bidder	5	0	2
295. Dispute (1990), Lakeville Miss, Take Charge Lady, Vitrolic	4	3	0
299. Executioner, Fly So Free, Hansel, Life's Hope, Mr. Right, Niarkos, Sea Cadet, Surfside, Theatrical	4	2	2
308. Marlin, Royal Governor	4	1	4
310. Greinton	3	5	0
311. Polylad, Rare Treat, Rippey	3	4	2
314. Bagdad, Dike, Family Style, Hail to All, Intent, It's the One, Love Sign, Mecke	3	3	4
322. Gate Dancer	2	4	6
323. Garwol (22)	1	5	8
324. A.P. Indy, Beau Purple, Bold Lad, Mom's Command, Northern Dancer, Plugged Nickle, Sailor	5	0	1
331. Artax, Chicle II, Conniver, Czar Alexander, Denon, Formal Gold, Lite the Fuse, Our Mims, Paradise Creek, Scan, Spend A Buck, Tomy Lee, Track Barron, Unconscious	4	2	1
345. Busanda, Captain Steve, My Flag	4	1	3
348. Dahar, Farma Way, Golden Apples, Happyanunoit, Lord Avie	3	4	1
353. Affirmed Success, Bobby Brocato, Estrapade, Pretense, Sensational	3	3	3
358. Smart Deb	3	2	5
359. Balzac, Globemaster, Mount Marcy	2	6	1
362. Gato Del Sol, My Celeste, Talon	2	5	3
364. Loud, Third Brother (21)	1	6	5
366. Dark Mirage, Kotashaan, Manila, Riboletta, Ruffian, Run the Gantlet, Spartan Valor	5	0	0
373. Atalanta, Desert Vixen, General Challenge, Java Gold, Sightseek, Twice the Vice, What A Treat, Winter's Tale	4	2	0
381. Chateaugay, Excellent Meeting, Levee, Silver Spoon, Warhead	4	1	2
386. Loser Weeper	4	0	4
387. Avatar, General Assembly, Proud Truth, Steeple Jill, Victory Gallop, Wajima	3	4	0
393. Funny Fellow, Highland Blade, Lamb Chop, Triple Bend	3	3	2
397. Castle Forbes, Porterhouse, Sunglow, Verbatim, Wistful (1946)	3	2	4
402. Dewan, Terrang	3	1	6
404. Lady Pitt, Pleasant Tap, Tranquility Lake, Versailles Treaty	2	5	2
408. Advocator	2	4	4
409. Clear Dawn (20)	1	5	6
410. At the Threshold, Diplomat Way, Judgable, Marquetry, Sadair, Sherluck	4	1	1
416. Pistols and Roses, Polish Navy	4	0	3
418. Flying Continental, Gone West, Harlan's Holiday, Lido Palace, Middleground, Rico Monte, Sacahuista, Stephan's Odyssey, Terry's Secret, Val's Prince, Wekiva Springs	3	3	1
429. Caucasus, Firm Policy, Gaffery, La Zanzara, Tejano, Text, Unbridled	3	2	3
436. Louis Quatorze, Poker Night, Tout Charmant, Turkoman	2	5	1
440. Amberoid, Artismo, Autocrat, Chief Honcho, Dunce, Iron Liege, Nickel Boy, Prince Spellbound, Queen Hopeful	2	4	3
449. Nadir	2	3	5
450. Colonial Waters (19)	1	7	1
451. Astra, Bayou, Coronado's Quest, Fit to Fight, Housebuster, Island Whirl, Late Bloomer, Lemhi Gold, Lucky Debonair, Lure, Mineshaft, Noble Nashua, Play Fellow, Yanks Music	4	1	0
465. Dahlia, George Royal	4	0	2
467. Afternoon Deelites, Midafternoon, Sky Classic, Stupendous	3	3	0
471. Carolyn A., Colonial Affair, Cyrano, Doc Jocoy, El Senor, First Aid, Fraise, High Yield, How, Lakeway, Miss Request, On-and-On, One Count, Silver Series, Social Climber, Successor	3	2	2
487. Beau Prince, Cum Laude Laurie	3	0	6
489. Cosmic Missile, Country Queen, Grafitti, Harmonica	2	5	0
493. Cathy Honey, Fleet Bird, Invigorator, Rising Market	2	4	2
497. Jim French, Piet, Sturdy One	2	3	4
500. Knightly Manner (18)	1	4	6
501. Berlo, Bug Brush, First Flight, Go West Young Man, Manistique, Moccasin, Timely Writer	4	0	1
508. Ajina, Chris Evert, Dancing Spree, Don Poggio, Doubledogdare, Gourmet Girl, Heatherten, King Pellinore, King's Bishop, Lucky Lucky Lucky, Misty Morn, Olhaverry, Primonetta, Princessnesian, Pucker Up, Solar Splendor, Stardust Mel, Sunshine Forever, Thinking Cap, Track Robbery, Winning Colors, Yankee Affair	3	2	1
530. Handsome Boy, Our Native, Silent Screen, Sultry Song, Vanlandingham, Yorky	3	1	3
536. Bastonera II, Dr. Carter, Educated Risk, Improviser, Itsallgreektome, Manassa Mauler, Mr. Brick, Stonewalk, Tentam	2	4	1
545. Amber Pass, Gentleman James, Tomisue's Delight, Tronado	2	3	3
549. Adile, Buffalo Lark, Great Contractor (17)	2	2	5
552. Blue Peter, Came Home, Dearly Precious, Flanders, Laffango, Personality, Proper Reality, Queen of the Stage, Turkish Trousers	4	0	0
561. Chief Bearhart, Duel, Empire Maker, Endine, Fran's Valentine, Intrepid Hero, Marta, Olympio, Politely, Proud Delta	3	2	0
571. Astray, Clear Mandate, Coastal, Copelan, Festin (1987), Frisk Me Now, Jet Pilot, King Emperor, Lost Code, Lost Mountain, Make Sail, Perrault, Rockhill Native, Rose Jet, Sickle's Image, Soy Numero Uno, Timber Country, Waquoit, Your Host	3	1	2
590. La Corredora, Plion	3	0	4
592. Career Boy, Carr de Naskra, Dr. Patches, For the Moment, Never Bow	2	4	0
597. Armageddon, Chieftan, Dare and Go, Defensive Play, Marshua, Mogambo, Pearl Necklace, Seaneen, Tabasco Cat, Urbane, Whodunit, Wise Margin	2	3	2
609. Dramatic Gold, Golden Don	2	2	4
611. B. Major, Cara Rafeala, Exploded	1	5	2
614. Arbees Boy, Cold Command, Sunrise County	1	4	4
617. Tick Tock (16)	0	6	4
618. Balto Star, Bates Motel, Beat Hollow, Big Effort, Blue Man, Blush With Pride, Bornastar, Christmas Past, Cochise, Eliza, Exotic Wood, Finnegan, Freetex, Holding Pattern, Inseparable, Nasr El Arab, North Sider, Oil Royalty, One For All, Princess Turia, Queen to Conquer, Rubiano, Tap Shoes, Tinners Way, Two Lea, Vigors, Western Playboy	3	1	1
645. Affectionately, Hidden Lake, Moontrip, Pia Star, Pine Bluff	3	0	3
650. Autobiography, Da Hoss, Decidedly, Fast Play, Frankly Perfect, Genuine Risk, George Navonod, Geri, Grand Slam, Menifee, Reviewer, Royal Owl, Snow Sporting, Sub Fleet, Tasso	2	3	1
665. Hawkster, Imbros, Life at the Top, Mrs. Warren, Prince Blessed, Sensitivo, T.V. Commercial	2	2	3
672. Diabolo, Different, The Bart	2	1	5
675. Selari, Shy Guy, Sunrise Flight	1	4	3
678. All Hands (15)	0	5	5
679. All Along, April Run, Big Whippendeal, Delta, Diplomatic Jet, Dixie Union, Dulcia, Evening Out, Fusaichi Pegasus, Hatchet Man, Hawaii, Hill Gail, Hollywood Wildcat, June Darling, Left Bank, Majestic Prince, Nastique, Prairie Bayou, Raging Fever, River Keen, Round View, Summing, Twice Worthy, Unbridled's Song	3	1	0
703. Agitate, Bold Forbes, Bold Reason, Fast Hilarious, Gold and Myrrh, Jolie's Halo, Nail, Native Royalty, Prized, Sea Hero, Star of Cozzene, Stella Madrid, Tallahto, The Axe II, Warfare	3	0	2
717. Coup de Fusil, Deputy Commander, Elloluv, Go for Gin, Kennedy Road, Lotowhite, Miz Clementine, Native Charger, Quillo Queen, Sardula	2	3	0
727. Admiral Vic, Believe It, Both Ends Burning, Camargo, Cherokee Run, Cohoes, Cox's Ridge, Danzig Connection, Earshot, Exclusive Native, Gleaming, How Now, Jameela, John William, Light Hearted, London Company, Malicious, Music Merci, No Le Hace, Reneged, Rhythm, Roo Art, Tamarona	2	2	2
750. Ack's Secret, A Glitter, Al Hattab, Group Plan, Ruken, Wandesta	2	1	4
756. Rash Statement	2	0	6
757. Corn off the Cob	1	5	0
758. Life Cycle, The Very One	1	4	2
760. De Roche, Nostalgia's Star, Ruhe	1	3	4
763. Royal Gunner	0	6	2
764. Honeys Alibi, Top Crowd (14)	0	5	4
766. Arrogate, Awesome Again, B. Thoughtful, Coincidence, Colorado King, Conquistador Cielo, Favorite Trick, Flag Raiser, Going Abroad, Golden Attraction, High Echelon, Ibero, Jet Action, Kostroma, Mac Diarmida, Munden Point, Nell K., Quiet Little Table, River Special, Spruce Needles, Summer Scandal, Sunny's Halo, Telly's Pop, Temperate Sil, Triplicate, Y Flash	3	0	1
792. Adjudicating, Affiliate, Afleet, Aptitude, Assagai, Aunt Jinny, Avigaition, Cutlass Reality, Dotted Swiss, Drin, Exogenous, Favorable Turn, George Lewis, Habibti, Habitony, Imperial Gesture, Kona Gold, My Dad George, Outer Space, Pleasant Stage, Private Account, Renew, Siphon, Slew City Slew, Terlingua, Venetian Way, Will I Rule, Will's Way, With Pleasure, Yagli	2	2	1
822. Brian's Time, Editor's Note, Heritage of Gold, Mi Selecto, Or et Argent, Romanita, Tri Jet, Victory Speech, War Heim	2	1	3
831. Czaravich	2	0	5
832. Doonesbury, Hail to Patsy, Irish Rebellion, Joe Jones, Kissin Kris, Lemon Twist, Properantes, Ring Twice	1	4	1
840. Dance Spell, Dinner Gong, Figonero, Fit to Scout, Gold Stage, Hanalei Bay, Hitchcock, Personal Flag, Red Reality, Stepfather, Wing Out	1	3	3
851. Lets Dance	1	2	5
852. Flag Down, Guadalcanal (13)	0	4	5
854. Bienamado, Codex, Dean Carl, Errard King, Fali Time, Fly Till Dawn, Grantor, Guillotine, Home-Made, Jersey Girl, King Glorious, Kingmaker, Knockdown, Langfuhr, Ogygian, Perfect Sting, Pet Bully, Prove Out, Roving Boy, Ryafan, Siama, Smart Angle, Storm Flag Flying, Subordination, The Wicked North, War Emblem, Windy's Daughter, Wise Times, Zoffany	3	0	0
883. Atoll, Bird Town, Brocco, Castilla, Composure, Correlation, Fastness, Flute, Graeme Hall, Groshawk, Hitting Away, Honorable Miss, Hypnotic, Irish Jay, Jostle, King of the Castle, Ladies Din, Legion, Lil E. Tee, Limit to Reason, Little Current, Lord Darnley, Manndar, Miss Alleged, Out of the Way, Patelin, Pay Tribute, Phil D., Riley, Ruth Lily, Silver Buck, Skillful Joy, Soul of the Matter, Special Team, Spicy Living, Windsharp, Wolfram	2	2	0
920. Adored, Alpride, Big Stretch, Bonnie Beryl, Buck's Boy, Captain Bodgit, Deceit, Dontstop Themusic, Funny Cide, Galaxy Libra, Hall of Fame, Jaklin Klugman, Judge Angelucci, Judger, Landlocked, Lavender Hill, Lazy Lode, Miner's Mark, Moonrush, Morning Bob, Mr. Leader, My Portrait, Northern Spur, Obeah, Outing Class, Papal Power, Plankton, Queen Empress, Rampart, Real Cash, Rich Tradition, Scattered, Storm Song, Stud Poker, Tank's Prospect, Tona, Wavering Monarch	2	1	2
957. Cloudy Dawn, Coraggioso, Milwaukee Brew, Platan, Sir Gaylord, Tempest Queen	2	0	4
963. Amoret, Bag of Tunes, Budroyale, Charon, Corporate Report, Shirley Jones, Tiltalating, Win	1	4	0
971. Beau Brummel, Fabius, Lt. Stevens, Parka, Pine Circle, Pipette, Romeo, Traffic, Twilight Agenda, Victoria Park, Water Bank	1	3	2
982. Buffle, Hasseyampa, Pattee Canyon, Poleax, Prides Profile	1	2	4
987. Real Connection	0	5	2
988. Paper Tiger	0	4	4
989. Double Discount (12)	0	3	6
990. Airmans Guide, Allie's Pal, Alphabatim, Answer, Antespend, Beau's Eagle, Bicker, Biggs, Black Tie Affair, Bushido, Cerise Reine, Cetewayo, Curious Clover, Deputy Minister, Drumbeat, Event of the Year, Explosive Red, Fairway Phantom, Fiesta Gal, Fleet Host, Flying Fury, Frere Jacques, Fowda, Furl Sail, Heat Haze, High Bid, J.O.	2	1	1

Tobin, Kalookan Queen, Labeeb, Lalun, Lazy Slusan, Mercedes Won, Miss Huntington, Missile Belle, Monarchos, Myrtle's Jet, Nijinsky's Secret, Noble Bronze, On the Sly, Owners Choice, Parading Lady, Pardala, Pavot, Peace Rules, Pen Bal Lady, Prince True, Quita Dude, Real Good Deal, Redattore, Restless Wind, Revidere, River Bay, Sabette, Secret Status, Shine Again, Silver Ending, Skywalker, Smile, Some Romance, Spinney, Starine, Star Maggie, Starrer, Super Diamond, Taisez Vous, Thirty Six Red, Traffic Mark, Twist the Axe, Umbrella Fella, Unaccounted For, Upper Case, Voodoo Dancer, Wine List, You and I

1,064. Be Faithful, Bounding Basque, Cadiz, Ecton Park, Level Lea, Memories of Silver, Nasty and Bold, Portersville, Rivlia, St. Vincent, Viking Spirit 2 0 3

1,075. Drama Critic (1974), Eternal Reward, Get Around, Groovy, Helmsman, Hot Dust, Jay Ray, Joanie's Chief, Laser Light, Mahout, Missionary Ridge, Natchez, Ordway, Outdoors, Pass Catcher, Saratoga, Star Reward, Star Standard, Street Cry, Sunshine Nell, The Pruner, Try Something New 1 3 1

1,097. Alma North, Capeador, Day Court, Ferd, O'Hara, Royal Orbit, Saidam, Smoke Screen, Wallenda, West by West 1 2 3

1,107. Iceberg II (11) 1 1 5

1,108. Alphabet Soup, Annihilate 'Em, A Phenomenon, Badger Land, Baffle, Battle Joined, Bellesoeur, Best Turn, Blue Norther, Bold, Bold Reasoning, Caesar's Wish, Canonero II, Chilukki, Clear Choice, Cover Up, Cupecoy's Joy, Dehere, Dubassoff, Education, Exchange, Farda Amiga, Federal Hill, Flying Chevron, Fulvous, Gainsboro Girl, Gen. Duke, Golden Ballet, Grand Canyon, Greek Game, Greek Star, Greenwood Lake, Hal's Hope, He's a Smoothie, Hubble Bubble, Hunza Dancer, Is It True, Johar, Kirby Lane, MacArthur Park, Mac's Sparkler, Mighty Appealing, My Dear Girl, My Juliet, Myrtle Charm, Naskra's Breeze, Natashka, Northernette, Old Trieste, Our Betters, Petrone, Profit Key, Protagonist, Pulpit, Race the Wild Wind, Resaca, River Memories, Roanoke, Royal Anthem, Royal Heroine, Royal Ski, Senure, Skimming, Sky Mesa, Squirtle Squirt, Stub, Swift Ruler, Tates Creek, Technology, Ten Most Wanted, Terra Firma, The Carpenter, Tunerup, Vaudeville (1991), Virginia Rapids, White Heart, Wickerr, Yankee Valor, Yorktown 2 1 0

1,186. A Letter to Harry, Annie-Lu-San, Awe Inspiring, Banner Bob, Blessing Angelica, Correspondent, Favorecidian, Finder's Fee, First Balcony, Frankly, Good Move, Heavenly Body, Hill Circus, Hold Your Peace, Johnny D., Mameluke, Miche, Pinjara, Prince Dantan, Relaxing, Sewickley, Sharp Gary, Snow Goose, Spoken Fur, Stop Traffic, Taken Aback, Tenacious, Very Subtle, Wayward Lass 2 0 2

1,215. Admiral Vee, Artfully, Bolshoi Boy, Chevron Flight, Dear Doctor, Hillsborough, Itsabet, Lady Tak, Lil's Lad, Mustard Plaster, One-Eyed King, Protanto, Royal Mustang, Ruritania, Sham, Twogundan 1 3 0

1,231. Chevation, Clabber Girl, Darn That Alarm, Donut King, Eastern Fleet, Flutterby, Forever Silver, Golden Gloves, Hampden, Harem Lady, Honour and Glory, Impressive, Jampol, Kiri's Clown, Load the Cannons, Mahan, Mahogany Hall, Mighty Fair, Peeping Tom, Pellicle, Prize Spot, Quinta, Red Shoes, Roman Line, Rough'n Tumble, Sea Orbit, Silver Supreme, Single Empire, Sing Sing, Spring Double, Switch On, Treacherous 1 2 2

1,263. Close By, Master Dennis, Office Queen, Raisela, Re Toss, Step Nicely 1 1 4

1,269. King Cugat, Lot O' Gold 0 5 0

1,271. Indian Maid, Noureddin, Open Sesame, Pluck, Thunder Puddles 0 4 2

1,276. Going Away (10) 0 3 4

1,277. Agincourt, Air Pilot, Amble In, Bad 'n Big, Beau Genius, Blue Ruler, Brought to Mind, Charismatic, Corn Husker, Crewman, Desert Love, Donna Viola, Dream Supreme, Dust Commander, El Bandido, Elocutionist, Esops Foibles, Eternal Prince, Fiji, Fleet Renee, Francis S., Gigantic, Gilded Time, Go and Go, Golden Pheasant, Great Neck, Historian, Instrument Landing, Janet, Jay Fox, John's Call, Kilijaro, Land Girl, Lord at War, Maria's Mon, Mi Preferido, Nasrina, Officer, On the Line, Opening Verse, Peaks and Valleys, Physician, Political Ambition, Prospectors Delite, Quaze Quilt, Queens Court Queen, Quilche, Radar Ahead, Red Hannigan, Regal Gleam, Risen Star, Salmagundi, Schossberg, Seven Thirty, Shannon II, Siphonic, Slewpy, Solar Salute, Squeak, Stephen Got Even, Sun and Snow, Super Quercus, Talking Picture, Toccet, Turn-to, Vicar, White Star Line, Wild Rush, Winonly, Wise Ship, Wolfie's Rascal, Yonder (1987), Yvonand 2 0 1

1,350. Abe's Hope, A Dragon Killer, A Kiss For Luck, Aloma's Ruler, Batonnier, Before Dawn, Blue Banner, Brave Lad, Burning Dream, Captain's Gig, Caveat, Chanlea, Choker, Cornish Prince, First Fiddle, Flat Fleet Feet, Forbidden Apple, Goyamo, Grand Flotilla, Grenzen, Harmonizing, Honey Mark, Jeanne Jones, Jean's Joe, Johns Joy, Kaster, Krislin, Linkage, Middle Brother, Misty Flight, More Than Ready, Nearly On Time, Night Invader, Pass the Glass, Pleasant Breeze, Polynesian, Precocity, Rico Reta, Roi Danzig, Roman Candle, Royal Patrice, Sarafan, Shared Interest, Strike Your Colors, Tea-Maker, The Bagel Prince, Thelma Berger, Tide Rips, True North (1966), Tumiga, Tunex, Volponi, Xtra Heat 1 2 1

1,403. Angle Light, Aptostar, Be Fleet, Cannonade, Carotene, Colosal, Curandero, Earl of Barking, El Basco, Gold Capitol, Good Counsel, Halory Hunter, Indulto, Inside Tract, Let Me Linger, Mandy's Gold, No Score, Reason to Hail, Royal Bay Gem, Trusting 1 1 3

1,423. Discipline, Maharajah, Sea O Erin 1 0 5

1,426. Barbs Delight, Combat Boots, Dictar, Happy Princess, Mississippi Mud, Primal, Rumbo, Trillion 0 4 1

1,434. Crafty C.T., Tenacle 0 3 3

1,436. Tejano Run (9) 0 2 5

1,437. Amen II, American Comet, Apalachee Honey, As Indicated, Banker's Lady, Barclay Joy, Bemo, Big Shot II, Black Sheep, Bolero, Bring Out the Band, Brown Bess, Bubbley, Candalita, Capote, Chief of Chiefs, Clev Er Tell, Countess Diana, Cousin, Critical Eye, Cruiser II, Cyane, Daryl's Joy, Daylami, Delaware Township, Deputed Testamony, Devil's Bag, Diazo, Eleven Stitches, El Mono, Estreno II, Exbourne, Fabulous Notion, Fantastic Light, Fast Count, Flame Thrower, Flower Bowl, Forever Whirl, Four Winds, Future Quest, General Arthur, Gladwin, Good Behaving, Good Blood, Greek Song, Gushing Oil, Hail to Reason, Halfbridled, Hidden Light, High Chaparral, High Hat, Honor Glide, Hurry Up Blue, Influent, Irgun, Island Fashion, Jovial, Kauai King, King Hairan, Landaluce, Leallah, Listening, Lucie Manet, Marfa, Mash One, Mat Boy, May Reward, Mehmet, Miesque, Miss Musket, Missy's Mirage, Mister Jive, Mizzen Mast, Native Street, Noble Noor, Oil Painting, Old Pueblo, Open Call, Open Fire, Opening Bid, Orientate, Pappa's All, Pedigree, Phone Chatter, Polar Expedition, Priceless Gem, Primordial II, Prince Noor, Private Terms, Providential II, Queena, Quick Reward, Rainbow Dancer, Raintrap, Red Camelia, Reflected Glory, Repetoire, Richter Scale, Rio Bravo, Roman Patrol, Rose Bower, Royal Serenade, Scuffleburg, Sensitive Prince, Shecky Greene, Silic, Sisterhood, Smoke Glacken, Snow Knight, Soaring Softly, Southjet, Souvenir Copy, Spearfish, Special Touch, Stage Door Johnny, Stalwart, Stan, Staunchness, Storming Home, Strategic Maneuver, Sulamani, Sweet Folly, Sweet Patootie, Swept Overboard, Swing Till Dawn, Talkin Man, Taylor's Special, Terlago, The Wonder, Thunder Rumble, Tiffany Lass, Tight Spot, Tikkanen, Time for a Change, Touch Gold, Trackmaster, Tutankhamen, Twist Afleet, U Time, Variety Road, Vent du Nord, Vertee, Whirl Some, White Skies, Yes You Will, Youth 2 0 0

1,582. Adonis, All Blue, Al Mamoon, Ambassador of Luck, Answer Lively, A.P. Valentine, Banquet Table, Blen Host, Bureaucracy, Cabildo, Caline, Canadiana, Capades, Cat's Cradle, Clandestine, Classic Crown, Colonel Power, Commissary, Creme dela Creme, De La Rose, Demons Begone, Divine Comedy, Dreams Gallore, Dublino, Easy Now, E. Dubai, El Baba, El Loco, Evening Kris, Fantastic Look, First Albert, Flaunt, Fleet Khal, Fleet Nasrullah, Furlough, Glitter Woman, Halo America, Head Man, Hitex, Honest Lady, Imaginary Lady, Indian Land, Irish Actor, Is Proud, I Will, Jabneh, Jim's Orbit, Just About, Kfar Tov, Missile, Mister Black, Mitterand, More Sun, Navy Page, New Policy, Noble Sel, Nothirdchance, Odyle, Oink, One On the Aisle, Outofthebox, Pacific Princess, Picador, Prime Timber, Prince John, Princelet, Princess Lygia, Quiet American, Quiet Step, Runup the Colors, Sabona, Say Blue, Sea Saga, Seaward, Sharpsburg, Sheilas Reward, Sirde, Sky Gem, Spence Bay, Storm Tower, Tumble Wind, Tuzla, Wanda, What a Summer, Wise Exchange 1 2 0

1,667. Abbe Sting, Aldiza, Athenia, Bass Clef, Blitey, Bupers, Buy the Firm, Canina, Cascapedia, Cavonnier, Cherokee Colony, City Zip, Cozzene, Decorated, Devilkin, Flame Tree, Flying Pidgeon, Funloving, General Staff, Gold Note, Hemet Squaw, Herbalist, Joe Price, Lily White, Lively One, Lord Rebeau, Manteau, My Gallant, Pearl City, Pleasant Variety, Prince Thou Art, Puerto Madero, Riot in Paris, Riskaverse, Riverina, R. Thomas, Sharp Dance, Spanish Fern, Spinning Top, Star de Naskra, Star Envoy, Sugar and Spice, Sun Bahram, Table Mate, Texas Sandman, The Liberal Member, Theory, Twixt, Valdez, Valiant Nature, Volcanic, Warbucks, Weber City Miss, Well Decorated, Willa on the Move (1985), Wooden Phone 1 1 2

1,723. Arab Actress, Catinca, Impromptu, Kudos, Quest for Fame 1 0 4

1,728. Candi's Gold, Caterman, Lincoln Road, Prince Majestic, Rossi Gold, Shoop 0 4 0

1,734. Battle Morn, Bet Big, Craftiness, Fathers Image, Happy Go Lucky, Impasse, Iron Constitution, Make Change, Steal a Kiss, Striking, Terentia, Touch of the Blues, Vulcania, Windy Sands 0 3 2

1,748. Dollar Bill, Dottie's Doll, Hydrologist, Muse, Woodlawn (8) 0 2 4

1946

	W	P	S
1. Assault (33)	7	1	3
2. Stymie (31)	5	5	1
3. Armed	4	2	0
4. Bridal Flower (20)	4	1	2
5. Honeymoon (17)	3	2	1
6. Gallorette (13)	3	0	1
7. First Flight	3	0	0
8. Hypnotic	2	2	0
9. Bonnie Beryl, Jet Pilot (12)	2	1	2
11. Pavot	2	1	1
12. Mahout (11)	1	3	1
13. Education	2	1	0
14. Hampden (10)	1	2	2
15. Donor, Historian, Triplicate (9)	2	0	1

1947

	W	P	S
1. But Why Not (28)	6	2	0
2. Phalanx (26)	4	3	4
3. Armed (25)	6	0	1
4. Stymie (24)	4	3	2
5. Cosmic Bomb (23)	4	3	1
6. Faultless (17)	4	0	1
7. Assault	4	0	0
8. Elpis	3	1	2
9. On Trust (16)	2	3	2
10. Rico Monte	3	1	0
11. Cosmic Missile	1	5	0
12. Gallorette (14)	1	3	4
13. Bewitch	3	0	1
14. Talon (13)	0	5	3
15. Bellesoeur, Citation, Cover Up, Fervent, Yankee Valor (10)	2	1	0

1948

	W	P	S
1. Citation (32)	8	0	0
2. Conniver	4	1	0
3. Better Self (18)	2	4	2
4. Gallorette (17)	2	3	3
5. Blue Peter	4	0	0
6. Stymie (16)	2	3	2
7. Coaltown	2	2	0
8. Double Jay (12)	1	2	4
9. Drumbeat, Fervent, Scattered, Stud Poker (11)	2	1	1
13. Miss Request, Myrtle Charm	2	1	0
15. Rampart (10)	2	0	2

1949

	W	P	S
1. Coaltown (30)	7	1	0
2. Ponder (22)	5	1	0
3. Capot (20)	4	1	2
4. Bed o' Roses (19)	4	1	1
5. Olympia	4	1	0
6. Three Rings (18)	3	2	2
7. Vulcan's Forge (17)	2	4	1
8. Ace Admiral (14)	3	1	0
9. But Why Not	2	2	1
10. Dinner Gong (13)	1	3	3
11. Wistful	3	0	0
12. Gaffery, Lithe (12)	2	1	2
14. Allie's Pal, My Request (11)	2	1	1

1950

	W	P	S
1. Hill Prince (34)	7	2	2
2. Next Move (30)	6	3	0
3. Noor (27)	5	3	1
4. Battlefield (20)	5	0	0
5. Chicle II (17)	3	2	1
6. Greek Ship (16)	3	2	0
7. Ponder	3	0	2
8. Middleground	2	3	0
9. Great Circle (14)	2	2	2
10. Siama	3	0	0
11. Sunglow (12)	2	2	0
12. Arise, Big Stretch (11)	2	1	1
14. Aunt Jinny	2	1	0
15. Loser Weeper, Your Host (10)	2	0	2

1951

	W	P	S
1. County Delight (22)	3	2	6
2. Kiss Me Kate (21)	4	1	3
3. Battlefield (18)	3	3	0
4. Rose Jet (16)	3	1	2
5. Counterpoint	3	1	1
6. Bed o' Roses (15)	2	2	3
7. Bryan G. (14)	3	1	0
8. Busanda (13)	3	0	1
9. One Hitter	2	2	0
10. Alerted (12)	2	1	2
11. How, Moonrush (11)	2	1	1
13. Cochise, Palestinian, Ruth Lily (10)	2	1	0

1952

	W	P	S
1. Real Delight	5	0	0
2. To Market (20)	4	1	2
3. Crafty Admiral, One Count (17)	3	2	1
5. Spartan Valor	4	0	0
6. Intent (16)	2	3	2
7. Blue Man, Mark-Ye-Well	3	1	1
9. Tom Fool (15)	2	3	1
10. One Hitter (14)	2	1	4
11. Alerted (13)	1	3	3
12. A Gleam, Laffango	3	0	0
14. Battlefield (12)	2	2	0
15. Next Move (10)	2	1	0

1953

	W	P	S
1. Native Dancer (38)	9	1	0
2. Tom Fool (24)	6	0	0
3. Royal Vale (21)	4	2	1
4. Grecian Queen (19)	4	1	1
5. Hasty Road	4	0	0
6. Crafty Admiral (16)	3	1	2
7. Queen Hopeful (13)	2	2	1
8. Atalanta	2	2	0
9. Fleet Bird (12)	1	3	2
10. Oil Capitol (11)	2	1	1
11. Artismo	2	1	0
12. La Corredora	2	0	2
13. Cold Command (10)	1	2	2
14. First Aid, Level Lea, My Celeste (9)	2	0	1

1954

	W	P	S
1. Fisherman (27)	4	5	1
2. High Gun (21)	4	1	3
3. Rejected (20)	3	4	0
4. Parlo (16)	4	0	0
5. Determine (15)	3	1	1
6. Pet Bully	3	0	0
7. Find, Helioscope, Summer Tan (12)	2	2	0
10. Imbros, Lavender Hill, Myrtle's Jet (11)	2	1	1
13. Correlation, Delta, Nashua, Straight Face, Wise Margin (10)	2	1	0

1955

	W	P	S
1. Nashua (34)	8	1	0
2. Social Outcast (27)	5	2	3
3. Traffic Judge (23)	4	3	1
4. Swaps (20)	5	0	0
5. High Voltage	4	0	1
6. Misty Morn (17)	3	2	1
7. Helioscope (14)	3	0	2
8. Manotick (13)	2	1	3
9. Nail, Sailor	3	0	0
11. High Gun (12)	2	2	0
12. Thinking Cap (11)	2	1	1
13. Doubledogdare, Lalun, Swoon's Son (10)	2	1	0

1956

	W	P	S
1. Nashua, Swaps	5	1	0
3. Mister Gus (22)	3	4	2
4. Needles	4	1	0
5. Midafternoon	3	3	0
6. Summer Tan (18)	2	5	0
7. Levee	3	1	2
8. Find (16)	1	3	6
9. Dedicate (15)	3	1	1
10. Searching	3	0	1
11. Oh Johnny (13)	2	1	3
12. Career Boy, Social Climber (12)	2	2	0
14. Princess Turia	2	1	1
15. Bobby Brocato (11)	2	0	3

1957

	W	P	S
1. Round Table (33)	7	1	3
2. Bold Ruler (26)	5	2	2
3. Gallant Man (20)	3	4	0
4. Find (19)	3	1	5
5. Bayou (18)	4	1	0
6. Dedicate (17)	3	2	1
7. Jewel's Reward	4	0	0
8. Pucker Up	3	2	0
9. Promised Land (16)	3	1	2
10. Bardstown (14)	3	1	0
11. Iron Liege (13)	1	3	3
12. Idun, Kingmaker (12)	3	0	0
14. Spinney (11)	2	1	1
15. Gen. Duke (10)	2	1	0

1958

	W	P	S
1. Round Table (30)	6	3	0
2. Tim Tam (22)	5	1	0
3. Clem (19)	3	2	3
4. Warhead	3	1	1
5. Promised Land (15)	3	0	3
6. Bold Ruler, First Landing (14)	3	1	0
8. Gallant Man	3	0	1
9. Seaneen (13)	2	2	1
10. Intentionally (12)	2	2	0
11. A Glitter, Idun, Rich Tradition, Tomy Lee	2	1	1
15. Eddie Schmidt (11)	1	2	3

1959

	W	P	S
1. Hillsdale (34)	7	3	0
2. Sword Dancer (32)	6	4	0
3. Round Table (25)	5	2	1
4. Bald Eagle (17)	3	2	1
5. Tempted	3	1	2
6. Amerigo (16)	0	7	2
7. Warfare (14)	3	0	2
8. Dunce (13)	2	2	1
9. Bug Brush, Vertex	3	0	0
11. Tudor Era (12)	2	0	4
12. High Bid, Intentionally, Silver Spoon	2	1	1
15. Tompion (11)	1	3	1

1960

	W	P	S
1. Bald Eagle (26)	5	2	2
2. Royal Native, T.V. Lark (21)	4	2	1
4. Bally Ache (19)	4	1	1
5. First Landing (18)	2	5	0
6. Berlo (17)	4	0	1
7. Kelso	4	0	0
8. Tompion	3	2	0
9. On-and-On (16)	3	1	2
10. Sword Dancer (15)	3	1	1
11. Bagdad, John William (14)	2	2	2
13. Carry Back	3	0	1
14. Dotted Swiss	2	2	1
15. Amerigo (13)	2	1	3

1961

	W	P	S
1. Carry Back (32)	7	1	2
2. Kelso (26)	6	1	0
3. Sherluck (18)	4	1	0
4. Cicada	4	0	0
5. Bowl of Flowers (16)	3	1	2
6. Globemaster	2	3	1
7. Prince Blessed (15)	2	2	3
8. Prove It, T.V. Lark	3	1	0
10. Jaipur (14)	2	3	0
11. Primonetta	2	2	1
12. Ambiopoise (13)	2	1	3
13. Four-and-Twenty	3	0	0
14. Wolfram (12)	2	2	0
15. Beau Prince (11)	2	0	3

1962

	W	P	S
1. Jaipur	5	2	0
2. Cicada (24)	4	3	2
3. Carry Back (23)	3	4	3
4. Prove It	5	1	0
5. Ridan (22)	3	4	2
6. Admiral's Voyage (19)	2	4	3
7. Beau Purple (17)	4	0	1
8. Never Bend	3	1	2
9. Kelso (16)	2	4	0
10. Olden Times (14)	2	2	2
11. Four-and-Twenty	3	0	1
12. Firm Policy (13)	2	1	3
13. Sensitivo (12)	2	1	2
14. Smart Deb (11)	2	1	1
15. Affectionately, Doc Jocoy (10)	2	0	2

1963

	W	P	S
1. Kelso (36)	8	2	0
2. Crimson Satan (31)	5	5	1
3. Candy Spots (27)	6	1	1
4. Chateaugay (20)	4	1	2
5. Lamb Chop (18)	3	2	2
6. B. Major (14)	1	4	2
7. Dean Carl, The Axe II	3	0	0
9. Mongo, Spicy Living (12)	2	2	0
11. Get Around, Never Bend (11)	1	3	1
13. Duel	2	1	0
14. Castle Forbes	2	0	2
15. Traffic (10)	1	2	2

1964

	W	P	S
1. Gun Bow (42)	8	4	2
2. Quadrangle (26)	5	1	4
3. Northern Dancer (21)	5	0	1
4. Miss Cavandish	3	4	0
5. Roman Brother (20)	3	3	2
6. Sadair (19)	4	1	1
7. Kelso (18)	3	3	0
8. Bold Lad	4	0	0
9. Mongo (16)	3	2	0
10. Tosmah (14)	3	1	0
11. Colorado King, Going Abroad	3	0	1
13. Mr. Consistency (13)	2	2	1
14. Hill Rise, Queen Empress (12)	2	1	2

1965

	W	P	S
1. Hail to All, Hill Rise (19)	3	2	3
3. Buckpasser	4	1	0
4. Roman Brother (18)	3	2	2
5. Moccasin	4	0	0
6. What A Treat	3	2	0
7. Steeple Jill (16)	2	4	0
8. Gun Bow, Tom Rolfe (15)	3	1	1
10. Lucky Debonair (14)	3	1	0
11. Old Hat (13)	3	0	1
12. Flag Raiser	3	0	0
13. Or et Argent (12)	2	1	2
14. Terry's Secret	2	1	0
15. George Royal, Pia Star (10)	2	0	2

1966

	W	P	S
1. Buckpasser (36)	9	0	0
2. Bold Bidder (18)	4	0	2
3. Lady Pitt (15)	2	3	1
4. Straight Deal, Successor (13)	2	2	1
6. Bold Hour	2	2	0
7. Tronado	2	1	2
8. Selari	1	3	2
9. Buffle (12)	1	2	4
10. Amberoid (11)	2	1	1
11. Stupendous	1	3	0
12. O'Hara (10)	1	2	2
13. Assagai, Moontrip, Regal Gleam, Summer Scandal (9)	2	0	1

1967

	W	P	S
1. Damascus (41)	9	2	1
2. Vitriolic (22)	4	3	0
3. Dr. Fager	5	0	1
4. Pretense (21)	3	3	3
5. Straight Deal (18)	3	2	2
6. Buckpasser (17)	3	2	1
7. Queen of the Stage	4	0	0
8. Handsome Boy	3	1	2
9. In Reality (16)	2	4	0
10. Niarkos (13)	3	0	1
11. War Censor	3	0	0
12. Quillo Queen	2	2	0
13. Gay Matelda (12)	1	3	2
14. Furl Sail, T.V. Commercial (11)	2	1	1

1968

	W	P	S
1. Forward Pass (28)	6	2	0
2. Dr. Fager (26)	6	1	0
3. Damascus (24)	4	3	2
4. Dark Mirage (20)	5	0	0
5. Quicken Tree (17)	3	2	1
6. Gamely (16)	3	2	0
7. King Emperor, Nodouble (15)	3	1	1
9. Funny Fellow (14)	2	2	2
10. Top Knight	3	0	1
11. Iron Ruler (13)	1	4	1
12. In Reality	3	0	0
13. Bold Hour, Out of the Way, Politely, Princessnesian (12)	2	2	0

1969

	W	P	S
1. Arts and Letters (36)	7	4	0
2. Nodouble (28)	4	6	0
3. Shuvee (22)	5	0	2
4. Dike (16)	2	2	4
5. Czar Alexander (15)	3	1	1
6. Hawaii, Majestic Prince (14)	3	1	0
8. Amerigo Lady	2	2	1
9. Hail to Patsy (13)	1	4	1
10. Gallant Bloom, Silent Screen	3	0	0
12. King of the Castle	2	2	0
13. Al Hattab, Verbatim (12)	2	1	2
15. Jay Ray (11)	1	3	1

1970

	W	P	S
1. Fort Marcy (25)	5	2	1
2. Fiddle Isle (22)	4	3	0
3. Personality (16)	4	0	0
4. June Darling	3	1	0
5. Cathy Honey	2	3	0
6. Corn off the Cob (14)	1	5	0
7. Forward Gal	3	0	1
8. My Dad George	2	2	1
9. Drumtop (13)	1	4	1
10. Shuvee	3	0	0
11. Limit to Reason, Patelin	2	2	0
13. Loud (12)	1	4	0
14. Missile Belle (11)	2	1	1
15. Best Turn, Judgable, Quicken Tree, Snow Sporting (10)	2	1	0

1971

	W	P	S
1. Cougar II (22)	4	2	2
2. Numbered Account (20)	5	0	0
3. Manta (18)	3	2	2
4. Jim French (17)	2	3	3
5. Ack Ack, Riva Ridge	4	0	0
7. Chompion (16)	3	1	2
8. Bold Reason (14)	3	0	2
9. Run the Gantlet (12)	3	0	0
10. Shuvee, Twist the Axe	2	1	1
12. Forward Gal (11)	2	0	3
13. Deceit, Drumtop, MacArthur Park, Twice Worthy, Unconscious, West Coast Scout (10)	2	1	0

1972

	W	P	S
1. Droll Role (25)	5	2	1
2. Susan's Girl (24)	5	1	2
3. Key to the Mint (23)	5	1	1
4. La Prevoyante	5	0	0
5. Typecast (20)	3	3	2
6. Secretariat	4	1	0
7. Cougar II (18)	3	2	2
8. Riva Ridge (17)	4	0	1
9. Triple Bend (16)	3	2	0
10. Autobiography (15)	2	3	1
11. Quack (14)	2	3	0
12. Freetex	3	0	0
13. King's Bishop, No Le Hace	2	2	0
15. Summer Guest (12)	2	1	2

1973

	W	P	S
1. Secretariat (33)	7	2	1
2. Susan's Girl (22)	5	0	2
3. Linda's Chief (19)	4	1	1
4. Cougar II (18)	3	0	6
5. Our Native	3	1	2
6. Big Spruce (16)	1	5	2
7. Summer Guest	2	3	0
8. Life Cycle (14)	1	4	2
9. Tentam (13)	2	2	1
10. Desert Vixen (12)	3	0	0
11. Light Hearted	2	1	1
12. Convenience	1	3	1
13. Golden Don (11)	1	2	3
14. Kennedy Road, Protagonist, Riva Ridge, West Coast Scout (10)	2	1	0

1974

	W	P	S
1. Forego (36)	8	1	2
2. Ancient Title, True Knight (18)	3	3	0
4. Chris Evert (15)	3	1	1
5. Agitate, Tallahto (14)	3	0	2
7. Foolish Pleasure	3	0	0
8. Little Current, Stonewalk	2	2	0
10. Tizna (12)	2	1	2
11. Judger (11)	2	1	1
12. Big Whippendeal	2	1	0
13. Prince Dantan	2	0	2
14. Poker Night	1	3	0
15. Big Spruce (10)	1	2	2

1975

	W	P	S
1. Forego (23)	5	1	1
2. Optimistic Gal (20)	4	2	0
3. Royal Glint	4	1	0
4. Wajima	3	3	0
5. Susan's Girl (18)	3	2	2
6. Foolish Pleasure (17)	3	2	1
7. Ancient Title (15)	3	0	3
8. Dulcia (14)	3	1	0
9. Gold and Myrrh, Master Derby, Stardust Mel	3	0	1
12. Tizna (13)	2	2	1
13. Dearly Precious, Honest Pleasure, Ruffian (12)	3	0	0

1976

	W	P	S
1. Optimistic Gal (27)	5	3	1
2. Honest Pleasure (22)	4	2	2
3. Forego (19)	4	1	1
4. King Pellinore, Majestic Light, Proud Delta	3	1	0
7. Bold Forbes (14)	3	0	2
8. Bastonera II (13)	2	2	1
9. Caucasus, Life's Hope, Revidere, Sensational (11)	2	1	1
13. Crystal Water, Hatchet Man Master Derby, Royal Ski (10)	2	1	0

1977

	W	P	S
1. Seattle Slew (20)	5	0	0
2. Our Mims (19)	4	1	1
3. Affirmed	4	1	0
4. Crystal Water (18)	4	0	2
5. Alydar (16)	2	4	0
6. Run Dusty Run (15)	0	7	1
7. Lakeville Miss	3	1	0
8. Cum Laude Laurie	3	0	2
9. Majestic Light (14)	2	3	0
10. Affiliate (13)	2	2	1
11. Forego (12)	2	2	0
12. Silver Series	2	1	1
13. Properantes (11)	1	3	1
14. Hunza Dancer, Stub (10)	2	1	0

1978

	W	P	S
1. Alydar (30)	6	3	0
2. Affirmed (28)	6	2	0
3. Exceller (26)	6	1	0
4. Late Bloomer (16)	4	0	0
5. Noble Dancer II (15)	3	1	1
6. Mac Diarmida (13)	3	0	1
7. Spectacular Bid	3	0	0
8. Tempest Queen (12)	2	0	4
9. Bowl Game, Terlingua, Waya	2	1	1
12. Tiller (11)	1	3	1
13. Flying Paster, It's In the Air, Life's Hope Northernette, Seattle Slew, Taisez Vous (10)	2	1	0

1979

	W	P	S
1. Spectacular Bid (31)	7	1	1
2. Affirmed (26)	6	1	0
3. Smarten (24)	4	4	0
4. Bowl Game	5	1	1
5. Golden Act (23)	4	3	1
6. Davona Dale (22)	5	1	0
7. It's In the Air (17)	3	2	1
8. Coastal (16)	3	1	2
9. Noble Dancer II, Waya (15)	3	1	1
11. State Dinner (13)	3	0	1
12. Smart Angle	3	0	0
13. Country Queen, General Assembly, Tiller (12)	2	2	0

1980

	W	P	S
1. Bold 'n Determined (30)	7	1	0
2. John Henry (27)	5	3	1
3. Spectacular Bid (24)	6	0	0
4. Temperence Hill (22)	5	1	0
5. Glorious Song (16)	3	2	0
6. Genuine Risk (15)	2	3	1
7. Lord Avie (14)	2	3	0
8. Go West Young Man, Plugged Nickle (13)	3	0	1
10. Codex, Winter's Tale	3	0	0
12. Jaklin Klugman (12)	2	1	2
13. Love Sign	2	1	1
14. Balzac (11)	0	5	1
15. Heavenly Cause (10)	2	1	0

1981

	W	P	S
1. John Henry (28)	7	0	0
2. Pleasant Colony (19)	4	1	1
3. Noble Nashua (16)	4	0	0
4. Heavenly Cause, Summing (14)	3	1	0
6. Galaxy Libra, Super Moment (12)	2	1	2
8. Temperence Hill (11)	2	1	1
9. Queen to Conquer	2	1	0
10. Wayward Lass	2	0	2
11. Glorious Song (10)	1	3	0
12. Relaxing, Timely Writer	2	0	1
14. Amber Pass (9)	1	2	1
15. Apalachee Honey, Deputy Minister, Eleven Stitches, Providential II, Skillful Joy, Stalwart (8)	2	0	0

1982

	W	P	S
1. It's the One (19)	3	2	3
2. Lemhi Gold (18)	4	1	0
3. Perrault (16)	3	1	2
4. Blush With Pride (15)	3	1	1
5. Conquistador Cielo (13)	3	0	1
6. Copelan, Roving Boy	3	0	0
8. Erins Isle, Silver Buck, Track Robbery (12)	2	2	1
11. Christmas Past (11)	2	1	1
12. Cupecoy's Joy, Naskra's Breeze	2	1	0
14. John Henry, The Bart (10)	2	0	2

1983

	W	P	S
1. Play Fellow	4	1	0
2. Slew O' Gold (18)	3	3	0
3. Sangue (17)	4	0	1
4. Erins Isle (16)	3	1	2
5. Bates Motel, Highland Blade (15)	3	1	1
7. Althea, Miss Oceana (14)	3	1	0
9. Sunny's Halo, Swale	3	0	1
11. Majesty's Prince	2	0	5
12. Life's Magic (13)	1	4	1
13. All Along	3	0	0
14. Desert Wine (12)	1	4	0
15. Avigaition (11)	2	1	1

1984

	W	P	S
1. At the Threshold, John Henry	4	1	1
3. Life's Magic (19)	3	3	1
4. Slew O' Gold, Interco (18)	4	1	0
6. Swale	4	0	1
7. Miss Oceana (17)	2	4	1
8. Chief's Crown, Desert Wine (14)	3	1	0
10. Heatherten (13)	3	0	1
11. Fit to Fight, Princess Rooney	3	0	0
13. Track Barron	2	2	0
14. Adored, Gate Dancer, Morning Bob (12)	2	1	2

1985

	W	P	S
1. Creme Fraiche (26)	4	4	2
2. Chief's Crown (21)	4	1	3
3. Greinton (18)	2	5	0
4. Vanlandingham (17)	3	1	3
5. Mom's Command	4	0	0
6. Precisionist, Proud Truth (16)	3	2	0
8. Stephan's Odyssey (15)	2	3	1
9. Fran's Valentine, Lady's Secret, Spend A Buck (14)	3	1	0
12. Skip Trial (13)	3	0	1
13. Family Style (12)	2	2	0
14. Life's Magic (11)	1	2	3
15. Banner Bob (10)	2	0	2

1986

	W	P	S
1. Lady's Secret (34)	7	2	2
2. Broad Brush (22)	5	0	2
3. Snow Chief (16)	4	0	0
4. Life at the Top (15)	2	2	3
5. Dahar	2	3	0
6. Precisionist (14)	2	2	2
7. Estrapade, Roo Art (13)	2	2	1
9. Manila, Wise Times	3	0	0
11. Turkoman	2	2	0
12. Danzig Connection (12)	2	1	2
13. Mogambo (11)	1	3	1
14. Badger Land, Clear Choice, Gulch (10)	2	1	0

1987

	W	P	S
1. Alysheba, Gone West (19)	3	3	1
3. Theatrical	4	0	1
4. Cryptoclearance (17)	2	3	3
5. Bet Twice	3	2	0
6. Lost Code (16)	3	1	2
7. Java Gold, North Sider	3	1	0
9. Tejano	3	0	2
10. Creme Fraiche, Gulch (14)	2	2	2
12. Ferdinand	2	2	1
13. Broad Brush (13)	2	1	3
14. Fiesta Gal, Sacahuista (11)	2	1	1

1988

	W	P	S
1. Alysheba (26)	6	1	0
2. Seeking the Gold (22)	3	5	0
3. Forty Niner (20)	3	4	0
4. Great Communicator, Sunshine Forever, Winning Colors (17)	3	2	1
7. Personal Ensign (16)	4	0	0
8. Goodbye Halo	3	1	1
9. Gulch (15)	2	3	1
10. Brian's Time (13)	2	1	3
11. Waquoit (12)	2	1	2
12. Fast Play (11)	2	1	1
13. Easy Goer, Open Mind, Pen Bal Lady (10)	2	1	0

1989

	W	P	S
1. Easy Goer (34)	7	3	0
2. Sunday Silence (28)	6	2	0
3. Bayakoa (24)	6	0	0
4. Open Mind (22)	5	0	2
5. Yankee Affair (17)	3	2	1
6. Western Playboy (14)	3	1	0
7. Frankly Perfect, Gorgeous (12)	2	2	0
9. Slew City Slew	2	1	1
10. Goodbye Halo (11)	1	3	1
11. Adjudicating, El Senor, Grand Canyon, Nasr El Arab, Steinlen (10)	2	1	0

1990

	W	P	S
1. Criminal Type, Go for Wand (22)	5	1	0
3. Summer Squall (18)	4	1	0
4. Unbridled (17)	3	2	1
5. Meadow Star	4	0	0
6. Gorgeous (16)	3	2	0
7. Bayakoa (14)	3	1	0
8. Flying Continental (13)	3	0	1
9. Best Pal	3	0	0
10. Real Cash (12)	2	1	2
11. Thirty Six Red (11)	2	1	1
12. Housebuster, Itsallgreektome, Profit Key, Silver Ending (10)	2	1	0

1991

	W	P	S
1. In Excess (21)	5	0	1
2. Farma Way (19)	3	3	1
3. Lite Light (18)	4	1	0
4. Olympio	3	2	0
5. Festin, Hansel (16)	3	1	2
7. Lost Mountain	3	1	0
8. Strike the Gold (14)	2	2	2
9. Scan (13)	2	2	1
10. Best Pal	2	2	0
11. Fly So Free	2	1	2
12. Corporate Report (12)	1	4	0
13. Fit to Scout (11)	1	3	1
14. Bertrando, Black Tie Affair, Meadow Star (10)	2	1	0

1992

	W	P	S
1. Paseana (22)	5	1	0
2. A.P. Indy (17)	4	0	1
3. Pleasant Tap (16)	2	4	0
4. Sea Cadet	3	1	0
5. Strike the Gold (14)	2	3	0
6. River Special, Sultry Song (13)	3	0	1
8. Best Pal	3	0	0
9. Fraise, Sky Classic (12)	2	2	0
11. Devil His Due (11)	2	1	1
12. Bien Bien, Lil E. Tee, Technology	2	1	0
15. Versailles Treaty (10)	1	2	2

1993

	W	P	S
1. Kotashaan	5	0	0
2. Paseana (20)	3	4	0
3. Devil His Due	3	2	1
4. Bertrando (17)	2	4	1
5. Sky Beauty	4	0	0
6. Dispute (16)	3	2	0
7. Prairie Bayou (14)	3	1	0
8. Turnback the Alarm (13)	3	0	1
9. Flawlessly, Star of Cozzene	3	0	0
11. Miner's Mark (12)	2	1	2
12. Explosive Red	2	1	1
13. Kissin Kris (11)	1	3	1
14. Dehere	2	1	0
15. Bien Bien (10)	1	3	0

1994

	W	P	S
1. Holy Bull (28)	7	0	0
2. Devil His Due (21)	2	6	1
3. Concern (17)	2	3	3
4. Flanders, Sky Beauty	4	0	0
6. Lakeway (16)	3	2	0
7. Heavenly Prize	3	1	1
8. Tabasco Cat (15)	2	3	1
9. Paradise Creek (13)	3	0	1
10. The Wicked North	3	0	0
11. Bien Bien (12)	2	2	0
12. Serena's Song, Vaudeville	2	1	0
14. Go for Gin (10)	1	3	0
15. Colonial Affair, Inside Information, Timber Country (9)	2	0	1

1995

	W	P	S
1. Cigar (32)	8	0	0
2. Serena's Song (30)	7	1	0
3. Thunder Gulch (21)	5	0	1
4. Inside Information	4	0	0
5. Heavenly Prize (16)	3	2	0
6. Possibly Perfect	3	1	0
7. Sandpit (14)	2	3	0
8. Golden Attraction (13)	3	0	1
9. You and I (11)	2	1	1
10. Afternoon Deelites, Awad, Lite the Fuse	2	1	0
13. Mecke (10)	1	2	2
14. Alpride, Maria's Mon, Northern Spur (9)	2	0	1

1996

	W	P	S
1. Skip Away (26)	5	2	2
2. Serena's Song (20)	2	5	2
3. Yanks Music (18)	4	1	0
4. Wekiva Springs (16)	3	2	0
5. Louis Quatorze (15)	2	3	1
6. Diplomatic Jet, Twice the Vice	3	1	0
8. My Flag (14)	3	0	2
9. Cigar (13)	2	2	1
11. Editor's Note, Marlin (12)	2	1	2
13. Antespend, Jewel Princess, Lite the Fuse, Mecke (11)	2	1	1

1997

	W	P	S
1. Skip Away (23)	3	5	1
2. Sharp Cat (20)	4	2	0
3. Formal Gold (19)	4	1	1
4. Gentlemen	4	0	1
5. Ajina	3	2	1
6. Free House (17)	3	1	3
7. Silver Charm (16)	2	4	0
8. Hidden Lake	3	0	1
9. Jewel Princess (13)	2	1	3
10. Ryafan	3	0	0
11. Deputy Commander	2	2	0
12. Captain Bodgit (12)	2	1	2
13. Clear Mandate (11)	2	1	1
14. Pulpit	2	1	0
15. Marlin (10)	2	0	2

1998

	W	P	S
1. Skip Away (25)	6	0	1
2. Banshee Breeze (18)	3	2	2
3. Keeper Hill (17)	2	4	1
4. Victory Gallop (16)	2	4	0
5. Coronado's Quest, Escena	3	1	0
7. Real Quiet (14)	2	3	0
8. Jersey Girl (12)	3	0	0
9. Buck's Boy	2	1	1
10. Gentlemen (11)	1	3	1
11. Excellent Meeting, Exotic Wood (10)	2	1	0
13. Fiji, Squeak	2	0	1
15. Sir Bear (9)	1	1	3

1999

	W	P	S
1. Silverbulletday	4	1	0
2. Behrens (18)	3	3	0
3. Cat Thief (17)	2	3	3
4. Beautiful Pleasure (16)	3	2	0
5. Menifee (15)	2	3	1
6. Banshee Breeze (14)	2	3	0
7. Artax (12)	3	0	0
8. Surfside (11)	2	1	1
9. Chilukki, Free House, General Challenge, Greenwood Lake, Lemon Drop Kid, River Keen, Val's Prince (10)	2	1	0

2000

	W	P	S
1. Riboletta (20)	5	0	0
2. Lemon Drop Kid (17)	4	0	1
3. Fusaichi Pegasus (14)	3	1	0
4. Spain (13)	2	2	1
5. Beautiful Pleasure, Tiznow (12)	2	2	0
7. Heritage of Gold, Secret Status (11)	2	1	1
9. General Challenge, High Yield, Jostle, Manndar, Surfside	2	1	0
14. Behrens (10)	1	2	2
15. John's Call (9)	2	0	1

2001

	W	P	S
1. Point Given (24)	6	0	0
2. Albert the Great (17)	2	4	1
3. Exogenous (13)	2	2	1
4. Flute	2	2	0
5. Affluent (12)	2	1	2
6. Lazy Slusan, Monarchos, Tiznow	2	1	1
9. Congaree (11)	2	0	3
10. Golden Ballet, Left Bank, Lido Palace, Senure, Squirtle Squirt, With Anticipation (10)	2	1	0

2002

	W	P	S
1. You (21)	4	2	1
2. Azeri (20)	5	0	0
3. With Anticipation (16)	3	2	0
4. Beat Hollow (15)	3	1	1
5. Medaglia d'Oro (14)	2	3	0
6. Came Home, Storm Flag Flying, War Emblem	3	0	0
9. Denon, Golden Apples (12)	2	2	0
11. Harlan's Holiday (11)	2	1	1
12. Astra, Farda Amiga, Take Charge Lady	2	1	0
15. Affluent (10)	1	3	0

2003

	W	P	S
1. Sightseek (20)	4	2	0
2. Mineshaft (18)	4	1	0
3. Empire Maker, Medaglia d'Oro (16)	3	2	0
5. Aldebaran (15)	3	1	1
6. Congaree (14)	3	1	0
7. Azeri	3	0	0
8. Bird Town	2	2	0
9. Funny Cide (12)	2	1	2
10. Heat Haze, Peace Rules (11)	2	1	1
12. Tates Creek, Ten Most Wanted	2	1	0
14. Spoken Fur	2	0	2
15. Elloluv, Lady Tak (10)	1	3	0

Photo courtesy of Churchill Downs

Perhaps the most dramatic stretch run in Kentucky Derby history came in 1987, when Alysheba (left under Chris McCarron) clipped heels, stumbled, and nearly fell to his knees just inside the three-sixteenths pole before he rallied to beat Bet Twice (right) by three-quarters of a length. The victory helped propel Alysheba to a championship season as a three-year-old, and he earned Horse of the Year acclaim a year later.

Race Horses' RESUMES

Horses With In-the-Money Finishes In Major North American Races 1946-2003

ABBE STING (1948)
At 3: 2nd American Derby
At 4: 3rd Hawthorne Gold Cup
At 5: Won Stars and Stripes Handicap
At 6: 3rd Bougainvillea Turf Handicap

ABBY GIRL (1997)
At 2: 2nd Oak Leaf Stakes
3rd Hollywood Starlet Stakes

ABE'S HOPE (1963)
At 3: Won Blue Grass Stakes
2nd Flamingo Stakes
Illinois Derby
3rd Everglades Stakes

ABLE MONEY (1980)
At 3: Won Mother Goose Stakes

ABLOOM (1984)
At 4: 3rd Vanity Handicap

ABOVE PERFECTION (1988)
At 3: 2nd Prioress Stakes

ABSTRACT (1946)
At 4: 3rd Pimlico Special

ACADEMIC (1985)
At 4: 3rd San Juan Capistrano Handicap

ACAROID (1978)
At 4: 2nd United Nations Handicap
At 5: Won United Nations Handicap

ACCELERATOR (1994)
At 2: 3rd Remsen Stakes
At 3: 2nd Wood Memorial Stakes
At 4: 3rd Metropolitan Handicap

ACCEPTABLE (1994)
At 2: 2nd Breeders' Cup Juvenile
At 3: 2nd Toyota Blue Grass Stakes

ACCIPITER (1971)
At 3: Won Withers Stakes

ACCLIMATIZATION (1968)
At 4: Won United Nations Handicap

ACCORDANT (1960)
At 3: 2nd Jerome Handicap

ACE ADMIRAL (1945)
At 2: 3rd Cowdin Stakes
Pimlico Futurity
At 3: Won Travers Stakes
Lawrence Realization Stakes
3rd Saranac Handicap
At 4: Won Inglewood Handicap
Sunset Handicap
Santa Anita Maturity
2nd Hollywood Gold Cup

ACK ACK (1966)
At 3: Won Withers Stakes
Arlington Classic
2nd Jersey Derby
At 5: Won Hollywood Gold Cup
San Antonio Stakes
Santa Anita Handicap
American Handicap

ACK'S SECRET (1976)
At 4: 2nd Yellow Ribbon Stakes
At 5: 3rd Santa Margarita Handicap
Yellow Ribbon Stakes
Santa Barbara Handicap
At 6: Won Santa Barbara Handicap
Santa Margarita Handicap
3rd Golden Harvest Handicap

ACTION THIS DAY (2001)
At 2: Won Bessemer Trust Breeders' Cup Juv.

ACT OF MAGIC (1983)
At 2: 2nd Sorority Stakes

ACTOR II (1961)
At 6: 2nd Oaklawn Handicap

ADEL (1995)
At 3: 2nd Del Mar Oaks

ADEPT (1979)
At 4: Won Top Flight Handicap
At 5: 3rd Top Flight Handicap

ADILE (1946)
At 3: Won Alabama Stakes
2nd Coaching Club American Oaks
Delaware Oaks
3rd Acorn Stakes
Gazelle Stakes
Ladies Handicap
At 4: Won New Castle Handicap
3rd Jockey Club Gold Cup
Whitney Stakes

ADJUDICATING (1987)
At 2: Won Cowdin Stakes
Champagne Stakes
2nd Futurity Stakes
At 3: 2nd Arlington Classic
3rd American Derby

ADMETUS (1970)
At 4: Won Washington D.C. International

ADMIRABLY (1962)
At 2: Won Del Mar Debutante Stakes

ADMIRAL DRAKE (1947)
At 5: Won American Handicap
3rd Inglewood Handicap

ADMIRAL LEA (1946)
At 2: 3rd Washington Park Futurity
At 3: 2nd Arlington Classic
3rd Santa Anita Derby
San Felipe Stakes

ADMIRAL PORTER (1951)
At 3: 3rd Blue Grass Stakes

ADMIRALS PRIDE (1947)
At 3: 3rd Swift Stakes

ADMIRAL'S SHIELD (1967)
At 2: 3rd Kentucky Jockey Club Stakes
At 3: 3rd Arkansas Derby

ADMIRAL'S VOYAGE (1959)
At 2: 3rd Arlington Futurity
At 3: Won Louisiana Derby
Wood Memorial Stakes
2nd Santa Anita Derby
Jersey Derby
Belmont Stakes
Hollywood Derby
3rd San Felipe Handicap
Florida Derby
Arlington Classic
At 4: Won Carter Handicap
2nd Massachusetts Handicap
American Handicap
At 5: Won San Carlos Handicap
3rd Los Angeles Handicap

ADMIRALTY (1992)
At 4: 3rd Brooklyn Handicap

ADMIRAL VEE (1952)
At 5: 2nd Brooklyn Handicap
At 6: Won Gallant Fox Handicap
2nd Grey Lag Handicap
Whitney Stakes

ADMIRAL VIC (1960)
At 3: Won Hawthorne Gold Cup
2nd Arlington Classic
Roamer Handicap
At 4: Won Seminole Handicap
3rd Widener Handicap
Gulfstream Park Handicap

ADMIRED (1946)
At 3: 3rd Pimlico Oaks

ADMIRING (1962)
At 2: Won Arlington-Washington Lassie Stakes
2nd Matron Stakes
At 3: 3rd Santa Susana Stakes

ADMISE (1992)
At 4: Won Oak Tree Turf Championship

ADONIS (1996)
At 3: Won Wood Memorial Stakes
2nd Cigar Mile Handicap
At 4: 2nd Gulfstream Park Handicap

ADORATION (1999)
At 4: Won Breeders' Cup Distaff

ADORED (1980)
At 4: Won Delaware Handicap
Santa Margarita Handicap
2nd Vanity Handicap
3rd Ruffian Handicap
Breeders' Cup Distaff

ADORYDAR (1990)
At 3: 2nd Fantasy Stakes
3rd Hollywood Oaks

A DRAGON KILLER (1955)
At 2: 3rd Sapling Stakes
At 3: Won Arlington Classic
2nd Ohio Derby
At 4: 2nd McLennan Handicap

ADRIATICO (1971)
At 7: 2nd Widener Handicap

ADROGUE (1940)
At 6: 2nd Del Mar Handicap

ADROIT (1940)
At 6: Won Black Helen Handicap

ADVANCE GUARD (1966)
At 5: Won Inglewood Handicap

ADVANCE MAN (1979)
At 3: Won San Felipe Handicap

ADVANCING STAR (1993)
At 2: 2nd Hollywood Starlet Stakes
At 5: 3rd Santa Monica Handicap

ADVOCATE TRAINING (1986)
At 3: 3rd Arkansas Derby

ADVOCATOR (1963)
At 2: Won Cowdin Stakes
3rd Champagne Stakes
At 3: 2nd Wood Memorial Stakes
Kentucky Derby
3rd Belmont Stakes
American Derby
At 4: Won Seminole Handicap
At 5: 2nd Metropolitan Handicap
United Nations Handicap
3rd Man o' War Stakes

AEGEAN (1948)
At 3: 3rd Santa Anita Derby

AEGINA (1947)
At 3: 2nd Coaching Club American Oaks
Arlington Handicap
At 4: 3rd Bougainvillea Handicap

AENEAS (1999)
At 4: 2nd Gulfstream Park Handicap

AEROFLINT (1958)
At 4: 2nd Tropical Park Handicap

AEROLITE (1950)
At 2: 2nd Arlington Lassie Stakes
Matron Stakes
3rd Alcibiades Stakes

AEROPOLIS (1959)
At 3: Won Arkansas Derby

AESTHETE (1949)
At 2: 3rd Arlington Lassie Stakes
At 3: 2nd Gazelle Stakes
At 4: 3rd Vagrancy Handicap

AESTHETIC (1956)
At 3: 2nd Spinster Stakes
3rd Kentucky Oaks

AFFECTIONATELY (1960)
At 2: Won Sorority Stakes
Spinaway Stakes
3rd Matron Stakes
Frizette Stakes
At 5: Won Top Flight Handicap
3rd Metropolitan Handicap

AFFILIATE (1974)
At 3: Won Monmouth Invitational Handicap
Vosburgh Handicap
2nd Hollywood Derby
Swaps Stakes
3rd Jerome Handicap

AFFIRMED (1975)
At 2: Won Hollywood Juvenile Championship
Hopeful Stakes
Futurity Stakes
Laurel Futurity
2nd Champagne Stakes
At 3: Won San Felipe Handicap
Santa Anita Derby
Hollywood Derby
Kentucky Derby
Preakness Stakes
Belmont Stakes
2nd Travers Stakes
Marlboro Cup Handicap
At 4: Won Californian Stakes
Hollywood Gold Cup
Woodward Stakes
Jockey Club Gold Cup
Charles H. Strub Stakes
Santa Anita Handicap
2nd San Fernando Stakes

AFFIRMED CLASSIC (1986)
At 2: 2nd Alcibiades Stakes
At 3: 3rd Fantasy Stakes
At 4: 3rd Apple Blossom Handicap

AFFIRMED SUCCESS (1994)
At 3: 3rd Jim Dandy Stakes
At 4: Won Vosburgh Stakes
2nd Frank J. De Francis Memorial Dash
Cigar Mile Handicap
At 5: Won Cigar Mile Handicap
2nd Carter Handicap
At 6: 3rd Carter Handicap
Cigar Mile Handicap
At 8: Won Carter Handicap

AFFLUENT (1998)
At 3: Won Queen Elizabeth II Challenge Cup
La Brea Stakes
2nd Del Mar Oaks
3rd Las Virgenes Stakes
Santa Anita Oaks
At 4: Won John C. Mabee Ramona Handicap
2nd Apple Blossom Handicap
Milady Breeders' Cup Handicap
Vanity Handicap
At 5: Won Santa Monica Handicap

AFIFA (1974)
At 4: Won Vanity Handicap

AFLEET (1984)
At 3: Won Jerome Handicap
Pennsylvania Derby
2nd Meadowlands Cup
At 4: 2nd Metropolitan Handicap
3rd Breeders' Cup Sprint

AFRICAN DANCER (1992)
At 5: 2nd San Juan Capistrano Handicap

AFTERNOON DEELITES (1992)
At 2: Won Hollywood Futurity
At 3: Won San Felipe Stakes
Malibu Stakes
2nd Santa Anita Derby
At 4: 2nd Strub Stakes
Metropolitan Handicap

AGAIN II (1948)
At 5: 2nd Monmouth Handicap

AGAINST THE SNOW (1970)
At 5: 3rd American Handicap
Del Mar Handicap

AGGADAN (1999)
At 4: 2nd Vosburgh Stakes

AGGRESSIVELY (1967)
At 3: 2nd Dwyer Handicap
3rd Santa Anita Derby

AGINCOURT (1989)
At 2: Won Futurity Stakes
At 3: Won Dwyer Stakes
3rd Pegasus Handicap

AGITATE (1971)
At 3: Won California Derby
Swaps Stakes
Hollywood Derby
3rd Santa Anita Derby
Kentucky Derby

A GLEAM (1949)
At 2: Won Princess Pat Stakes
3rd Matron Stakes
At 3: Won Hollywood Oaks
Cinema Handicap
Westerner Stakes
At 4: 2nd Vanity Handicap
American Handicap
3rd Santa Margarita Handicap
Hollywood Gold Cup

A GLITTER (1955)
At 2: 3rd Selima Stakes
At 3: Won Coaching Club American Oaks
Monmouth Oaks
2nd Beldame Handicap
3rd Vineland Handicap
At 4: 3rd Black Helen Handicap
Vineland Handicap

AGUILA (1980)
At 2: 3rd Norfolk Stakes

AHOY (1960)
At 4: Won Carter Handicap

AHOY MATE (1974)
At 2: 2nd Sapling Stakes

A HUEVO (1996)
At 7: Won Frank J. De Francis Memorial Dash

AIMING HIGH (1953)
At 2: 3rd Spinaway Stakes

AIM N FIRE (1960)
At 2: 2nd Saratoga Special

AIR DISPLAY (1983)
At 3: 2nd Hollywood Derby
At 4: 3rd United Nations Handicap

AIR FORBES WON (1979)
At 3: Won Wood Memorial Stakes
2nd Pennsylvania Derby

AIRMANS GUIDE (1957)
At 3: 2nd Acorn Stakes
3rd Kentucky Oaks
At 4: Won Delaware Handicap
Beldame Stakes

AIR PILOT (1954)
At 5: Won Massachusetts Handicap
3rd Gulfstream Park Handicap
At 8: Won Massachusetts Handicap

AIR RATE (1943)
At 3: Won San Vicente Handicap

AIR RIGHTS (1964)
At 3: 2nd Jersey Derby

AIR WONDER (1954)
At 3: 3rd Ohio Derby

AJINA (1994)
At 3: Won Mother Goose Stakes
Coaching Club American Oaks
Breeders' Cup Distaff
2nd Alabama Stakes
Beldame Stakes
3rd Acorn Stakes

A.J. JETT (1992)
At 2: 3rd Hollywood Futurity

AKBAR KHAN (1952)
At 4: 2nd Dixie Handicap
At 5: Won Dixie Handicap
3rd John B. Campbell Mem. Handicap

AKIMBO (1947)
At 3: 3rd Cinema Handicap

A KISS FOR LUCK (1979)
At 2: 2nd Oak Leaf Stakes
3rd Del Mar Debutante Stakes
At 4: Won Vanity Handicap
2nd Maskette Stakes

AKITA (1975)
At 2: 3rd Matron Stakes

AKSAR (1987)
At 4: 3rd San Juan Capistrano Handicap

AKUREYRI (1978)
At 2: 3rd Remsen Stakes
At 3: 2nd Florida Derby

ALABAMA BOUND (1960)
At 2: 2nd Hopeful Stakes

ALABAMA NANA (1981)
At 4: 3rd Ladies Handicap

ALABLUE (1945)
At 3: 2nd Acorn Stakes
Alabama Stakes
At 4: 3rd Santa Margarita Handicap

ALADANCER (1968)
At 4: 3rd Top Flight Handicap

ALADEAR (1943)
At 3: 2nd Beldame Handicap

A LADY FROM DIXIE (1995)
At 4: 3rd Three Chimneys Spinster Stakes

ALAIRNE (1945)
At 3: 3rd Travers Stakes

ALAMOND (1943)
At 3: 2nd Lawrence Realization Stakes

ALANESIAN (1954)
At 2: Won Spinaway Stakes
At 4: 2nd Maskette Handicap

ALANNAN (1996)
At 5: 3rd Metropolitan Handicap
Forego Handicap

ALA RAM (1963)
At 4: 3rd Santa Anita Handicap
At 5: 3rd Santa Anita Handicap

ALATE (1949)
At 2: 2nd Starlet Stakes
At 3: 2nd Cinema Handicap
Will Rogers Stakes

ALBERT THE GREAT (1997)
At 3: Won Jockey Club Gold Cup
2nd Travers Stakes
At 4: Won Brooklyn Handicap
Suburban Handicap
2nd Donn Handicap
Pimlico Special
Whitney Handicap
Woodward Stakes
3rd Breeders' Cup Classic

AL DAVELLE (1956)
At 3: Won Arkansas Derby

ALDEBARAN (1998)
At 3: 3rd Hollywood Derby
At 4: 2nd Metropolitan Handicap
Forego Handicap
Vosburgh Stakes
Cigar Mile Handicap
At 5: Won San Carlos Handicap
Metropolitan Handicap
Forego Handicap
2nd Carter Handicap
3rd Stephen Foster Handicap

ALDERMAN (1947)
At 4: Won Sunset Handicap
3rd Del Mar Handicap

ALDERSHOT (1958)
At 5: 2nd Hollywood Gold Cup
3rd Inglewood Handicap

AL DESIMA (1997)
At 4: 3rd Yellow Ribbon Stakes

ALDIZA (1994)
At 2: 3rd Frizette Stakes
At 3: 2nd Test Stakes
At 4: Won Go for Wand Handicap
3rd Three Chimneys Spinster Stakes

ALERTED (1948)
At 3: Won Discovery Handicap
Jerome Handicap
2nd Dwyer Stakes
3rd Preakness Stakes
Lawrence Realization Stakes
At 4: Won Dixie Handicap
2nd Gulfstream Park Handicap
Gallant Fox Handicap
Trenton Handicap
3rd McLennan Handicap
Grey Lag Handicap
Westchester Handicap
At 5: 2nd Widener Handicap
Manhattan Handicap
Jockey Club Gold Cup
3rd Pimlico Special

ALERT PRINCESS (1966)
At 2: 2nd Sorority Stakes

A LETTER TO HARRY (1974)
At 3: 3rd Louisiana Derby
At 4: Won Michigan Mile and One-Eighth
At 5: Won New Orleans Handicap
3rd Oaklawn Handicap

ALEXINE (1996)
At 4: 3rd Ramona Handicap

ALEXIS (1942)
At 4: 2nd Vosburgh Handicap

ALEX THE GREAT (1989)
At 5: Won Sword Dancer Handicap
3rd San Juan Capistrano Handicap

ALEZAINA (1999)
At 3: 3rd Del Mar Oaks

ALFOXIE (1945)
At 2: 2nd Selima Stakes
At 3: 3rd Black Helen Handicap

ALGASIR (1946)
At 2: Won Cowdin Stakes

ALGENIB (1987)
At 4: 2nd Arlington Million

ALHAMBRA (1955)
At 2: 2nd Washington Park Futurity
3rd Futurity Stakes

AL HATTAB (1966)
At 2: 3rd Sapling Stakes
At 3: Won Jersey Derby
Monmouth Invitational Handicap
2nd Wood Memorial Stakes
3rd Everglades Stakes
Florida Derby
At 4: 3rd Gulfstream Park Handicap

ALIAS SMITH (1973)
At 4: 3rd United Nations Handicap

ALIBI BLUE (1955)
At 3: 3rd California Derby

ALICE SPRINGS (1990)
At 5: 2nd Beverly D. Stakes
3rd Caesars International Handicap

ALIDON (1951)
At 4: Won American Handicap
2nd Hollywood Gold Cup
3rd Sunset Handicap

ALINES PET (1951)
At 2: 2nd Spinaway Stakes

ALI OOP (1974)
At 2: Won Sapling Stakes

ALI'S GEM (1950)
At 3: Won Cinema Handicap

ALI'S THEME (1963)
At 3: 3rd Hollywood Oaks
At 4: 3rd Vanity Handicap

ALIWAR (1955)
At 3: 2nd San Felipe Handicap
3rd Santa Anita Derby

ALJAMIN (1970)
At 3: Won Vosburgh Handicap
3rd Monmouth Invitational Handicap
Michigan Mile and One-Eighth

ALLADIER (1949)
At 2: Won Breeders' Futurity
2nd Kentucky Jockey Club Stakes

ALL ALONG (1979)
At 4: Won Turf Classic
Washington D.C. International
Rothmans International Stakes
At 5: 2nd Breeders' Cup Turf

ALLAMERICAN BERTIE (1999)
At 3: 2nd Alabama Stakes

ALL BLUE (1947)
At 3: 2nd American Derby
At 4: Won San Antonio Handicap
2nd Inglewood Handicap

ALLELUIA (1975)
At 6: 2nd Golden Harvest Handicap

ALLEN ADAIR (1961)
At 3: 2nd Blue Grass Stakes

ALLEY FIGHTER (1965)
At 3: Won Santa Anita Derby
2nd San Felipe Handicap

ALLEZ MILORD (1983)
At 4: Won Oak Tree Invitational Stakes

ALL FIRED UP (1981)
At 2: Won Arlington-Washington Futurity

ALL FOOLS DAY (1960)
At 3: 3rd Louisiana Derby

ALL HANDS (1957)
At 2: 2nd Breeders' Futurity
Kentucky Jockey Club Stakes
Pimlico Futurity
3rd Futurity Stakes
At 3: 2nd Everglades Stakes
At 4: 2nd Metropolitan Handicap
3rd McLennan Handicap
New Orleans Handicap
John B. Campbell Handicap
Grey Lag Handicap

ALLIED (1951)
At 3: 2nd Westerner Stakes
At 5: 3rd San Luis Rey Handicap

ALLIED FORCES (1993)
At 3: Won Pegasus Breeders' Cup Handicap

ALLIE'S PAL (1945)
At 5: 3rd Molly Pitcher Handicap

ALLIE'S SERENADE (1965)
At 3: Won Santa Susana Stakes

ALL RAINBOWS (1973)
At 3: 3rd Fantasy Stakes

ALL THE BOYS (1997)
At 6: 2nd San Juan Capistrano Handicap

ALL THEE POWER (1985)
At 3: Won California Derby

ALL THE MORE (1973)
At 5: 3rd Oaklawn Handicap
At 6: 2nd Hawthorne Gold Cup

ALLTHEWAY BERTIE (1992)
At 2: 3rd Arlington-Washington Lassie Stakes

ALMAHMOUD (1947)
At 3: Won Vineland Handicap

ALMA MATER (1943)
At 3: 3rd Alabama Stakes

AL MAMOON (1981)
At 4: 2nd San Antonio Handicap
Breeders' Cup Mile
At 6: Won John Henry Handicap

ALMA NORTH (1968)
At 3: 2nd Monmouth Oaks
Alabama Stakes
3rd Gazelle Handicap
Spinster Stakes
Monmouth Invitational Handicap
At 4: Won Black Helen Handicap

ALMOST GROWN (1972)
At 4: Won Hawthorne Gold Cup

ALMUTAWAKEL (1995)
At 4: 2nd Woodward Stakes
3rd Jockey Club Gold Cup
At 5: 2nd Oaklawn Handicap

ALOHA HAWAII (1980)
At 2: 3rd Hopeful Stakes

ALOHA MOOD (1971)
At 3: Won San Felipe Handicap
2nd Santa Anita Derby

ALOMA'S RULER (1979)
At 3: Won Preakness Stakes
2nd Haskell Invitational Handicap
Travers Stakes
3rd Suburban Handicap

ALONDRA II (1961)
At 5: 2nd Black Helen Handicap

ALPHABATIM (1981)
At 3: Won Hollywood Turf Cup
At 5: Won Hollywood Turf Cup
2nd Hollywood Gold Cup
3rd San Luis Rey Stakes

ALPHABET (1961)
At 3: 3rd Withers Stakes

ALPHABET SOUP (1991)
At 5: Won San Antonio Handicap
Breeders' Cup Classic
At 6: 2nd San Antonio Handicap

ALPINE LASS (1972)
At 2: Won Matron Stakes
2nd Demoiselle Stakes

ALPRIDE (1991)
At 4: Won Beverly Hills Handicap
Yellow Ribbon Stakes
3rd Beverly D. Stakes
At 5: 2nd Ramona Handicap
3rd Beverly D. Stakes

ALRENIE (1944)
At 3: 3rd Acorn Stakes

ALSAB'S DAY (1946)
At 2: Won Marguerite Stakes
2nd Arlington Lassie Stakes
3rd Princess Pat Stakes

ALSAY (1953)
At 3: 2nd Everglades Stakes

ALSPAL (1952)
At 2: 3rd Arlington Lassie Stakes

ALTHEA (1981)
At 2: Won Del Mar Futurity
Del Mar Debutante Stakes
Hollywood Starlet Stakes
2nd Oak Leaf Stakes
At 3: Won Arkansas Derby
Santa Susana Stakes
2nd Fantasy Stakes

ALVARADA (1973)
At 3: 2nd Ashland Stakes

ALVO CERTO (1993)
At 6: 3rd Charles Whittingham Handicap

ALWAYS A CINCH (1978)
At 3: Won California Derby

ALWAYS A CLASSIC (1993)
At 4: Won Early Times Turf Classic
3rd Manhattan Handicap

ALWAYS GALLANT (1974)
At 5: Won Longacres Mile

ALWAYS SILVER (1989)
At 3: 3rd Ohio Derby

ALWUHUSH (1985)
At 4: 3rd Man o' War Stakes
At 5: 2nd Turf Classic
3rd Caesars International Handicap

ALYDAR (1975)
At 2: Won Sapling Stakes
Champagne Stakes
2nd Hopeful Stakes
Futurity Stakes
Laurel Futurity
Remsen Stakes
At 3: Won Flamingo Stakes
Florida Derby
Blue Grass Stakes
Arlington Classic
Travers Stakes
Whitney Stakes
2nd Kentucky Derby
Preakness Stakes
Belmont Stakes
At 4: 2nd Oaklawn Handicap
3rd Suburban Handicap

ALYDAR'S BEST (1982)
At 3: 2nd Yellow Ribbon Stakes

ALYDEED (1989)
At 3: 2nd Preakness Stakes
At 4: Won Carter Handicap
3rd Metropolitan Handicap

ALY'S ALLEY (1996)
At 2: 2nd Breeders' Cup Juvenile
At 4: 2nd Sword Dancer Invitational Handicap

ALYSBELLE (1989)
At 3: 3rd Hollywood Oaks
At 5: 3rd Santa Maria Handicap

ALYSHEBA (1984)
At 2: 2nd Hollywood Futurity
3rd Breeders' Cup Juvenile
At 3: Won Kentucky Derby
Preakness Stakes
Super Derby
2nd San Felipe Handicap
Haskell Invitational Handicap
Breeders' Cup Classic
3rd Blue Grass Stakes
At 4: Won Charles H. Strub Stakes
Santa Anita Handicap
Philip H. Iselin Handicap
Woodward Handicap
Meadowlands Cup
Breeders' Cup Classic
2nd Hollywood Gold Cup

ALYWOW (1991)
At 3: 2nd Flower Bowl Invitational Handicap
Rothmans International Stakes

ALYZIG (1997)
At 5: 2nd San Carlos Handicap

A MAGIC SPRAY (1979)
At 3: 3rd Pennsylvania Derby

AMARULLAH (1954)
At 2: 2nd Cowdin Stakes
3rd Futurity Stakes
Garden State Stakes

AMASTAR (1961)
At 2: 2nd Hopeful Stakes

AMATHOS (1991)
At 2: 3rd Champagne Stakes

AM AWAY (1956)
At 3: 3rd Arkansas Derby

AMAZER (1975)
At 3: Won Yellow Ribbon Stakes
3rd Canadian International Championship

AMBASSADOR OF LUCK (1979)
At 2: 2nd Selima Stakes
At 3: 2nd Maskette Stakes
At 4: Won Maskette Stakes

AMBEHAVING (1954)
At 2: Won Remsen Stakes
3rd Pimlico Futurity
At 3: 3rd Roamer Handicap

AMBER EVER (1978)
At 3: 2nd Ramona Handicap

AMBER HAWK (1968)
At 5: 2nd John B. Campbell Handicap

AMBER MORN (1956)
At 4: Won Bowling Green Handicap
2nd Manhattan Handicap

AMBEROID (1963)
At 2: 3rd Pimlico Futurity
Garden State Stakes
At 3: Won Wood Memorial Stakes
Belmont Stakes
2nd Travers Stakes
3rd Preakness Stakes
At 4: 2nd Gulfstream Park Handicap
Grey Lag Handicap
Amory L. Haskell Handicap

AMBER PASS (1977)
At 3: Won Dwyer Stakes
2nd Swaps Stakes
3rd Monmouth Invitational Handicap
Travers Stakes
At 4: Won Monmouth Handicap
2nd Woodward Stakes
Marlboro Cup Handicap
3rd Metropolitan Handicap

AMBER'S FOLLY (1952)
At 3: 2nd Everglades Stakes

AMBIENT (1952)
At 3: 3rd Everglades Stakes

AMBIOPOISE (1958)
At 2: 2nd Saratoga Special
Garden State Stakes
3rd Remsen Stakes
At 3: Won Gotham Stakes
Jersey Derby
2nd Lawrence Realization Stakes
3rd Wood Memorial Stakes
Travers Stakes
Trenton Handicap
At 4: Won Grey Lag Handicap
3rd Widener Handicap
Massachusetts Handicap

AMBIVALENT (1993)
At 4: 3rd Strub Stakes

AMBLE IN (1943)
At 3: Won Longacres Mile
At 5: Won Longacres Mile
At 6: 3rd Inglewood Handicap

AMBULANCE (1954)
At 3: 2nd Mother Goose Stakes

AM CAPABLE (1980)
At 3: 3rd Maskette Stakes

AMEN II (1970)
At 3: Won Cinema Handicap
Hollywood Derby

AMENT (1953)
At 2: 2nd Alcibiades Stakes

AMERICAN CHAMP (1994)
At 4: 2nd Fall Highweight Handicap

AMERICAN CHANCE (1989)
At 3: Won Jersey Derby
3rd Meadowlands Cup
At 5: 2nd Vosburgh Stakes

AMERICAN COMET (1956)
At 5: Won San Antonio Handicap
Michigan Mile and One-Sixteenth

AMERICAN GIRL (1968)
At 2: 3rd Norfolk Stakes

AMERICAN HISTORY (1972)
At 4: 2nd Whitney Handicap
At 5: 2nd Whitney Handicap
3rd Brooklyn Handicap

AMERICAN SYSTEM (1999)
At 3: 3rd Malibu Stakes

AMERICAN TIGER (1965)
At 3: 3rd Hollywood Derby

AMERICA'S FRIEND (1986)
At 3: 3rd Flamingo Stakes

AMERIGO (1955)
At 4: 2nd Gulfstream Park Handicap
Californian Stakes
Inglewood Handicap
Monmouth Handicap
Trenton Handicap
Whitney Stakes
Man o' War Handicap
3rd Los Angeles Handicap
Brooklyn Handicap
At 5: Won Hialeah Turf Cup
San Juan Capistrano Handicap
2nd Gulfstream Park Handicap
3rd Santa Anita Handicap
John B. Campbell Handicap
Bougainvillea Turf Handicap

AMERIGO LADY (1964)
At 3: Won Hollywood Oaks
3rd Spinster Stakes
At 4: Won Top Flight Handicap
2nd Ladies Handicap

Santa Barbara Handicap
3rd Beldame Stakes
Santa Margarita Handicap
At 5: Won Black Helen Handicap
Top Flight Handicap
2nd Beldame Stakes
Ladies Handicap
3rd Vanity Handicap

AMERIGO'S FANCY (1962)
At 6: Won Santa Barbara Handicap

AMERIQUE (1994)
At 4: Won San Juan Capistrano Handicap

AMERIVAN (1962)
At 3: Won Kentucky Oaks

AMERRICO (1972)
At 4: 3rd Carter Handicap

AMIGA (1947)
At 2: 3rd Princess Pat Stakes

AMORET (1952)
At 4: 2nd Arlington Matron Handicap
Beldame Handicap
Vineland Handicap
At 5: Won Black Helen Handicap
At 6: 2nd Black Helen Handicap

AMPOSE (1961)
At 4: Won Gulfstream Park Handicap
3rd Monmouth Handicap
Arlington Handicap

AMRI-AN (1958)
At 2: Won Del Mar Debutante Stakes

AN ACT (1973)
At 3: Won Santa Anita Derby

ANCESTOR (1949)
At 3: Won Discovery Handicap

ANCIENT FABLES (1973)
At 3: 3rd Mother Goose Stakes

ANCIENT TITLE (1970)
At 3: 2nd San Felipe Handicap
At 4: Won Malibu Stakes
San Fernando Stakes
Charles H. Strub Stakes
2nd Californian Stakes
Hollywood Gold Cup
Santa Anita Handicap
At 5: Won Californian Stakes
Hollywood Gold Cup
Whitney Handicap
3rd Marlboro Cup Handicap
San Antonio Stakes
American Handicap
At 6: Won Californian Stakes
2nd Santa Anita Handicap
At 7: Won Del Mar Handicap
San Antonio Stakes
3rd Californian Stakes
Oak Tree Invitational Stakes
At 8: 2nd San Antonio Stakes

ANDESTINE (1990)
At 4: Won Milady Handicap

ANDOVER WAY (1978)
At 4: Won Top Flight Handicap
2nd Apple Blossom Handicap

ANDRE (1949)
At 4: 3rd Trenton Handicap
At 5: 3rd Widener Handicap

ANDREW ALAN (1955)
At 3: 3rd Canadian Championship Stakes

ANDROCLES (1947)
At 2: 2nd Champagne Stakes

ANECDOTE (1944)
At 5: 2nd Bougainvillea Handicap

ANEES (1997)
At 2: Won Breeders' Cup Juvenile

3rd Norfolk Stakes
At 3: 3rd San Felipe Stakes

AN EMPRESS (1983)
At 3: 2nd Hollywood Oaks
3rd Santa Anita Oaks

ANET (1994)
At 3: 2nd Ohio Derby
Buick Haskell Invitational Handicap
Buick Pegasus Handicap

ANGEL IN MY HEART (1992)
At 3: 2nd Yellow Ribbon Stakes
Matriarch Stakes

ANGEL ISLAND (1976)
At 2: Won Alcibiades Stakes
2nd Arlington-Washington Lassie Stakes

ANGEL SPEED (1958)
At 2: 2nd Gardenia Stakes

ANGLE LIGHT (1970)
At 2: 2nd Garden State Stakes
3rd Laurel Futurity
At 3: Won Wood Memorial Stakes
3rd Flamingo Stakes
Louisiana Derby

ANH DUONG (1989)
At 2: Won Matron Stakes
3rd Frizette Stakes

ANIFA (1976)
At 4: Won Turf Classic

ANILINE (1961)
At 3: 3rd Washington D.C. International
At 5: 2nd Washington D.C. International

ANISADO (1954)
At 5: 3rd Man o' War Handicap

ANKA GERMANIA (1982)
At 6: Won Sword Dancer Handicap

ANKLET (1994)
At 3: 2nd Ashland Stakes

ANNAPOLIS JOHN (1983)
At 3: 3rd Flamingo Stakes

ANNE'S PRETENDER (1972)
At 5: Won Century Handicap
2nd American Handicap
3rd Hollywood Invitational Handicap

ANNIE ALMA (1958)
At 2: 3rd Del Mar Debutante Stakes

ANNIE-LU-SAN (1953)
At 4: Won Vanity Handicap
At 5: Won Vanity Handicap
3rd Maskette Handicap
Ladies Handicap

ANNIHILATE 'EM (1970)
At 2: Won Breeders' Futurity
At 3: Won Travers Stakes
2nd Monmouth Invitational Handicap

ANNOCONNOR (1984)
At 4: Won Vanity Handicap
At 5: 3rd Santa Barbara Handicap

ANNSIE PIE (1956)
At 2: 3rd Selima Stakes

ANNUAL REUNION (1987)
At 2: 2nd Hollywood Starlet Stakes
At 4: 3rd Santa Barbara Handicap

ANONO (1970)
At 4: 2nd Manhattan Handicap

ANOTHER NELL (1965)
At 3: Won Gazelle Handicap
2nd Acorn Stakes

ANOTHER REEF (1982)
At 3: Won Vosburgh Stakes

2nd Withers Stakes
3rd Illinois Derby

ANOTHER REVIEW (1988)
At 3: 3rd Gotham Stakes
At 4: Won Californian Stakes
3rd Hollywood Gold Cup

ANOTHER WORLD (1951)
At 3: 2nd Vineland Handicap
At 5: 3rd Molly Pitcher Handicap

ANSHAN (1987)
At 3: 3rd Hollywood Derby
At 4: 2nd San Antonio Handicap
Californian Stakes

ANSWER (1973)
At 2: Won Oak Leaf Stakes
3rd Alcibiades Stakes
At 3: Won Hollywood Oaks
2nd Fantasy Stakes

ANSWER LIVELY (1996)
At 2: Won Breeders' Cup Juvenile
2nd Lane's End Breeders' Futurity
At 3: 2nd Louisiana Derby

ANTAGONISM (1947)
At 3: 2nd Comely Handicap
3rd Alabama Stakes
At 4: Won Black Helen Handicap

ANTAHKARANA (1996)
At 2: 2nd Oak Leaf Stakes

ANTESPEND (1993)
At 3: Won Las Virgenes Stakes
Santa Anita Oaks
2nd Hollywood Oaks
3rd Queen Elizabeth II Challenge Cup

ANTI LIB (1978)
At 4: 2nd Top Flight Handicap
3rd Maskette Stakes

ANTIQUA (1985)
At 2: Won Laurel Futurity

ANTIQUE GOLD (1977)
At 2: 2nd Sapling Stakes

ANYOLDTIME (1948)
At 3: 3rd Flamingo Stakes

ANY TIME GIRL (1974)
At 2: Won Oak Leaf Stakes

AONBARR (1938)
At 8: 3rd Monmouth Handicap

AORANGI (1952)
At 8: 3rd San Juan Capistrano Handicap

APALACHEE HONEY (1979)
At 2: Won Sorority Stakes
Alcibiades Stakes

APATONTHEBACK (1958)
At 2: Won Sorority Stakes
3rd Arlington Lassie Stakes

A.P. FIVE HUNDRED (1999)
At 3: 3rd Super Derby

A PHENOMENON (1980)
At 3: Won Jerome Handicap
Vosburgh Stakes
At 4: 2nd Metropolitan Handicap

A.P. INDY (1989)
At 2: Won Hollywood Futurity
At 3: Won Santa Anita Derby
Peter Pan Stakes
Belmont Stakes
Breeders' Cup Classic
3rd Jockey Club Gold Cup

APPASSIONATO (1973)
At 3: 2nd Monmouth Invitational Handicap
Jockey Club Gold Cup

APPEALING PLEASURE (1986)
At 3: 2nd Tropical Park Derby

APPLEBY GARDENS (2000)
At 2: 3rd Frizette Stakes

APPLE OF KENT (1996)
At 5: 3rd Hempstead Handicap

APPLE TREE (1989)
At 4: Won Turf Classic

APPLE VALLEY (1950)
At 4: Won Santa Anita Maturity

APPROACH THE BENCH (1988)
At 6: Won Eddie Read Handicap
3rd Oak Tree Invitational Stakes

APRIL AXE (1975)
At 3: 2nd Secretariat Stakes
3rd American Handicap

APRIL DAWN (1963)
At 4: Won Santa Barbara Handicap

APRIL RUN (1978)
At 3: Won Turf Classic
2nd Washington D.C. International
At 4: Won Turf Classic
Washington D.C. International

APRIL SKIES (1957)
At 4: 2nd John B. Campbell Handicap
Carter Handicap

APTITUDE (1997)
At 3: 2nd Kentucky Derby
Belmont Stakes
3rd Wood Memorial Stakes
At 4: Won Hollywood Gold Cup
Jockey Club Gold Cup

APTOS HONEY (1943)
At 3: 2nd Hollywood Oaks

APTOSTAR (1985)
At 3: Won Acorn Stakes
2nd Coaching Club American Oaks
3rd Mother Goose Stakes
At 4: 3rd Top Flight Handicap
Maskette Stakes

A.P. VALENTINE (1998)
At 2: Won Champagne Stakes
At 3: 2nd Preakness Stakes
Belmont Stakes

AQUA BELLE (1968)
At 3: 3rd Ladies Handicap

ARAB ACTRESS (1950)
At 3: 3rd Kentucky Oaks
Monmouth Oaks
Comely Handicap
Vineland Handicap
At 5: Won Arlington Matron Handicap

ARABIAN DANCER (1979)
At 2: 2nd Matron Stakes

ARABIAN LIGHT (1998)
At 2: Won Lane's End Breeders' Futurity
3rd Del Mar Futurity

ARAZI (1989)
At 2: Won Breeders' Cup Juvenile

ARBEES BOY (1970)
At 3: 2nd Dwyer Handicap
3rd Ohio Derby
At 4: Won Metropolitan Handicap
2nd Marlboro Cup Handicap
Woodward Stakes
3rd Brooklyn Handicap
At 5: 2nd Suburban Handicap
3rd Donn Handicap
Whitney Handicap

ARBITRAGE (1958)
At 5: Won Sunset Handicap

ARCADES AMBRO (1977)
At 2: 3rd Del Mar Debutante Stakes
Oak Leaf Stakes

ARCANGUES (1988)
At 5: Won Breeders' Cup Classic

ARCH (1995)
At 3: Won Super Derby

ARCHERS BAY (1995)
At 4: 2nd Gulfstream Park Handicap

ARCHIE SPEARS (1968)
At 4: 3rd John B. Campbell Handicap

ARCHITECT (1976)
At 3: 3rd Hawthorne Gold Cup

ARCTARUS (1968)
At 2: 2nd Champagne Stakes

ARDELL C. (1962)
At 3: 2nd Santa Susana Stakes

ARDIENTE (1975)
At 4: Won Del Mar Handicap
2nd Sunset Handicap

AREWEHAVINGFUNYET (1983)
At 2: Won Oak Leaf Stakes

ARGUMENT (1977)
At 3: Won Washington D.C. International

ARGYLE LAKE (1986)
At 7: 3rd Carter Handicap

ARISE (1946)
At 2: 3rd Tremont Stakes
At 3: Won Travers Stakes
2nd Jerome Handicap
3rd Saranac Handicap
At 4: Won Fall Highweight Handicap
Excelsior Handicap
2nd Widener Handicap
3rd Grey Lag Handicap
At 5: Won Carter Handicap
Monmouth Handicap

ARI'S MONA (1947)
At 3: Won Kentucky Oaks

ARKSRONI (1962)
At 3: Won Cinema Handicap
2nd Hollywood Derby

ARMAGEDDON (1949)
At 2: Won Champagne Stakes
At 3: Won Withers Stakes
2nd Arlington Classic
Travers Stakes
3rd Belmont Stakes
Flamingo Stakes
At 4: 2nd Stars and Stripes Handicap

ARMED (1941)
At 5: Won Widener Handicap
Dixie Handicap
Suburban Handicap
Washington Park Handicap
2nd McLennan Handicap
Arlington Handicap
At 6: Won McLennan Handicap
Widener Handicap
Gulfstream Park Handicap
Stars and Stripes Handicap
Arlington Handicap
Washington Park Handicap
3rd Pimlico Special
At 7: 2nd Gulfstream Park Handicap
3rd McLennan Handicap
At 8: 2nd Stars and Stripes Handicap
Washington Park Handicap
3rd Gulfstream Park Handicap
Arlington Handicap

ARMED FOR PEACE (1987)
At 2: 3rd Remsen Stakes

ARMORIAL (1955)
At 2: 2nd Spinaway Stakes
3rd Matron Stakes

AROUND THE HORN (1966)
At 3: 3rd Hollywood Oaks

AROUND THE ROSES (1963)
At 3: 2nd Acorn Stakes

ARP (1989)
At 3: 2nd San Felipe Stakes

ARRESTED DREAMS (1996)
At 2: 2nd Matron Stakes

ARROGATE (1951)
At 2: Won Starlet Stakes
At 4: Won Del Mar Handicap
3rd William P. Kyne Handicap
At 5: Won Del Mar Handicap

ARROVENTE (1991)
At 2: 2nd Remsen Stakes

ARROZ (1949)
At 2: 3rd Del Mar Futurity
At 3: 2nd Westerner Stakes
3rd Santa Anita Derby

ARTAX (1995)
At 2: 2nd Hollywood Futurity
At 3: Won San Felipe Stakes
2nd Malibu Stakes
3rd Santa Anita Derby
At 4: Won Carter Handicap
Vosburgh Stakes
Breeders' Cup Sprint

ARTFULLY (1973)
At 2: 2nd Frizette Stakes
Selima Stakes
Demoiselle Stakes
At 3: Won Maskette Handicap

ARTICHOKE (1981)
At 2: 3rd Norfolk Stakes

ARTILLERIST (1982)
At 3: 2nd Tropical Park Derby

ARTILLERY (1943)
At 4: Won Inglewood Handicap

ARTISMO (1951)
At 2: Won Sapling Stakes
Hopeful Stakes
2nd Futurity Stakes
At 3: 3rd Roamer Handicap
At 4: 2nd McLennan Handicap
Roseben Handicap
Metropolitan Handicap
3rd Carter Handicap
At 5: 3rd Carter Handicap

ARTISTS PROOF (1967)
At 3: 3rd Kentucky Oaks

ART MARKET (1958)
At 3: 3rd United Nations Handicap

ARTS AND LETTERS (1966)
At 3: Won Everglades Stakes
Blue Grass Stakes
Belmont Stakes
Travers Stakes
Metropolitan Handicap
Woodward Stakes
Jockey Club Gold Cup
2nd Flamingo Stakes
Florida Derby
Kentucky Derby
Preakness Stakes
At 4: Won Grey Lag Handicap

A RUN (1978)
At 3: 2nd Louisiana Derby

AS DE COPAS (1973)
At 5: 3rd Oak Tree Invitational Stakes
Bay Meadows Handicap

ASHADO (2001)
At 2: Won Spinaway Stakes
2nd Breeders' Cup Juvenile Fillies
3rd Frizette Stakes

ASHBORO (1993)
At 4: 2nd Ballerina Stakes

ASHUA (1967)
At 2: 3rd Sorority Stakes

ASIDERO (1996)
At 4: 3rd Clement L. Hirsch Mem. Turf Champ.

AS INDICATED (1990)
At 3: Won Gotham Stakes
At 4: Won Pimlico Special

ASK FATHER (1961)
At 4: 3rd Sunset Handicap
At 5: 3rd San Luis Rey Handicap

ASK ME (1979)
At 3: 3rd Hollywood Derby
At 4: 3rd Eddie Read Handicap

ASK THE FARE (1964)
At 3: Won Louisiana Derby
2nd Arkansas Derby
3rd Everglades Stakes

ASPRO (1978)
At 4: 3rd New Orleans Handicap

ASSAGAI (1963)
At 3: Won United Nations Handicap
Man o' War Stakes
3rd Washington D.C. International
At 4: 2nd Bowling Green Handicap
United Nations Handicap

ASSAGAI JR. (1970)
At 2: Won Sapling Stakes

ASSAULT (1943)
At 3: Won Wood Memorial Stakes
Kentucky Derby
Preakness Stakes
Belmont Stakes
Dwyer Stakes
Pimlico Special
Westchester Handicap
2nd Roamer Handicap
3rd Discovery Handicap
Manhattan Handicap
Gallant Fox Handicap
At 4: Won Grey Lag Handicap
Dixie Handicap
Suburban Handicap
Brooklyn Handicap
At 6: Won Brooklyn Handicap

ASSEMBLYMAN (1954)
At 3: 2nd Lawrence Realization Stakes

ASTAS FOXY LADY (1991)
At 2: 2nd Spinaway Stakes
Matron Stakes

ASTERISCA (1974)
At 2: 2nd Del Mar Debutante Stakes

ASTRA (1996)
At 4: Won Gamely Breeders' Cup Handicap
At 5: Won Beverly Hills Handicap
At 6: Won Gamely Breeders' Cup Handicap
Beverly Hills Handicap
2nd Beverly D. Stakes

ASTRAY (1969)
At 4: 3rd Bowling Green Handicap
At 5: Won San Luis Rey Stakes
San Juan Capistrano Handicap
3rd Bowling Green Handicap
At 6: Won Century Handicap
2nd San Juan Capistrano Handicap

ASTRIOUS (1978)
At 2: Won Oak Leaf Stakes

ASTRO (1948)
At 3: 2nd Kentucky Oaks

ATALANTA (1948)
At 2: Won Spinaway Stakes
Matron Stakes
At 5: Won Black Helen Handicap
Beldame Handicap
2nd Molly Pitcher Handicap
Vagrancy Handicap

AT ARMS LENGTH (1968)
At 3: 3rd Kentucky Oaks

ATHENE (1943)
At 3: 2nd Vineland Handicap
3rd Arlington Matron Handicap

ATHENIA (1943)
At 3: Won Ladies Handicap
2nd Kentucky Oaks
3rd Jerome Handicap
New York Handicap

ATHENIAN (1951)
At 2: 2nd Washington Park Futurity

A THOUSAND STARS (1975)
At 5: 2nd Ramona Handicap

ATOLL (1956)
At 2: Won Remsen Stakes
2nd Cowdin Stakes
At 3: Won Gotham Stakes
2nd Jerome Handicap

ATOMIC WINGS (1967)
At 2: Won Del Mar Debutante Stakes
3rd Del Mar Futurity

AT THE THRESHOLD (1981)
At 3: Won Jim Beam Stakes
Arlington Classic
Ohio Derby
American Derby
2nd Pennsylvania Derby
3rd Kentucky Derby

ATTICUS (1992)
At 5: Won Oaklawn Handicap

AUBE INDIENNE (1990)
At 4: Won Yellow Ribbon Stakes
2nd Matriarch Stakes

AUDACIOUS MAN (1946)
At 2: 2nd Starlet Stakes

AUDITING (1948)
At 4: 2nd Dixie Handicap
3rd Gallant Fox Handicap
Queens County Handicap

AUNT ANNE (1995)
At 2: 3rd Spinaway Stakes

AUNTIE MAME (1994)
At 3: 2nd Queen Elizabeth II Challenge Cup
At 4: Won Flower Bowl Invitational Handicap

AUNT JIN (1972)
At 2: Won Selima Stakes
At 3: 2nd Alabama Stakes

AUNT JINNY (1948)
At 2: Won Demoiselle Stakes
Selima Stakes
2nd Marguerite Stakes
At 3: 2nd Arlington Matron Handicap
3rd Alabama Stakes

AU POINT (1980)
At 3: Won Dwyer Stakes

AURIETTE (1992)
At 4: Won Gamely Handicap

AUSTIN MITTLER (1972)
At 4: 3rd Californian Stakes

AUSTRALIAN ACE (1948)
At 3: 2nd Westerner Stakes

AUTOBIOGRAPHY (1968)
At 4: Won Jockey Club Gold Cup
San Fernando Stakes
2nd Brooklyn Handicap
Woodward Stakes
Malibu Stakes
3rd Michigan Mile and One-Eighth

AUTOCRAT (1941)
At 5: 2nd San Antonio Handicap
3rd American Handicap
At 6: 3rd Golden Gate Handicap
At 7: Won San Carlos Handicap
2nd San Pasqual Handicap
American Handicap
At 8: Won San Carlos Handicap
2nd San Antonio Handicap
3rd San Pasqual Handicap

AUTRY (1970)
At 2: 2nd Norfolk Stakes

AVANZADO (1997)
At 6: Won Ancient Title Breeders' Cup Handicap

AVATAR (1972)
At 3: Won Santa Anita Derby
Belmont Stakes
2nd Kentucky Derby
At 4: Won San Luis Rey Stakes
2nd Hollywood Gold Cup
Del Mar Handicap
San Fernando Stakes

AVE VALEQUE (1965)
At 2: 2nd Arlington-Washington Lassie Stakes

AVIES COPY (1984)
At 3: Won Jersey Derby
3rd Kentucky Derby
Arlington Classic

AVIES GAL (1985)
At 3: 3rd Acorn Stakes

AVIE'S SHADOW (1990)
At 3: 2nd Ashland Stakes

AVIGAITION (1979)
At 3: 2nd Yellow Ribbon Stakes
At 4: Won La Canada Stakes
Santa Barbara Handicap
2nd Santa Margarita Handicap
3rd Golden Harvest Handicap

AVILION (1974)
At 2: 2nd Alcibiades Stakes

AWAD (1990)
At 3: Won Secretariat Stakes
At 5: Won Early Times Manhattan Handicap
Arlington Million
2nd Sword Dancer Invitational Handicap
At 6: 2nd Arlington Million
Turf Classic
3rd San Juan Capistrano Handicap
Hollywood Turf Handicap
At 7: Won Sword Dancer Invitational Handicap
2nd Hollywood Turf Cup
3rd Man o' War Stakes

AWAKEN (1973)
At 2: 3rd Del Mar Debutante Stakes
Oak Leaf Stakes

AWAY AWAY (1948)
At 2: Won Cowdin Stakes

AWE INSPIRING (1986)
At 3: Won Flamingo Stakes
Jersey Derby
3rd Kentucky Derby
Super Derby

AWESOME AGAIN (1994)
At 3: Won Jim Dandy Stakes
3rd Travers Stakes
At 4: Won Whitney Handicap
Breeders' Cup Classic

AWESOME HUMOR (2000)
At 2: Won Spinaway Stakes
At 3: 2nd Alabama Stakes

AWFUL SMART (1996)
At 3: 2nd Test Stakes
3rd Gazelle Handicap

A WILD RIDE (1987)
At 4: Won Hempstead Handicap

A WILD RIDE *(Continued)*
3rd La Canada Stakes
Santa Margarita Handicap

AYRTON S (1993)
At 2: 3rd Hollywood Futurity

AZERI (1998)
At 4: Won Santa Margarita Handicap
Apple Blossom Handicap
Milady Breeders' Cup Handicap
Vanity Handicap
Breeders' Cup Distaff
At 5: Won Apple Blossom Handicap
Milady Breeders' Cup Handicap
Vanity Handicap

AZTEC HILL (1990)
At 3: Won Fantasy Stakes

AZTEC RED (1980)
At 3: 3rd Wood Memorial Stakes
Illinois Derby

AZURE'S ORPHAN (1957)
At 2: Won Del Mar Futurity

AZURE TE (1962)
At 2: 2nd Hollywood Juvenile Championship
Del Mar Futurity

BA BA BEE (1975)
At 3: 2nd Fantasy Stakes

BABA KARAM (1984)
At 4: 2nd Hollywood Invitational Handicap

BABINGTON (1959)
At 6: 2nd Hollywood Gold Cup
Pan American Handicap

BABU (1954)
At 5: Won Brooklyn Handicap

BABY COMET (1947)
At 2: Won Astoria Stakes
2nd Arlington Lassie Stakes

BACH (1997)
At 4: 3rd Breeders' Cup Mile

BACHELOR BEAU (1983)
At 3: Won Blue Grass Stakes
3rd Jim Beam Stakes

BACK BAY BARRISTER (1981)
At 2: 3rd Breeders' Futurity
At 3: 3rd Withers Stakes

BACKBONE (1955)
At 4: 2nd John B. Campbell Handicap

BACK TALK (1945)
At 3: 3rd Kentucky Oaks

BACUCO (1966)
At 4: 3rd Washington D.C. International
At 5: 3rd San Luis Rey Handicap

BADGE (1996)
At 3: 3rd Preakness Stakes

BADGER GOLD (1996)
At 3: 3rd Jim Dandy Stakes

BADGER LAND (1983)
At 3: Won Everglades Stakes
Flamingo Stakes
2nd Florida Derby

BAD 'N BIG (1974)
At 3: Won Cinema Handicap
At 4: Won Longacres Mile
At 5: 3rd Longacres Mile

BAFFLE (1965)
At 2: Won Del Mar Futurity
At 5: Won Californian Stakes
2nd American Handicap

BAG (1989)
At 2: 3rd Norfolk Stakes

BAGDAD (1956)
At 2: 3rd Del Mar Futurity
At 3: Won Hollywood Derby
2nd Belmont Stakes
3rd Withers Stakes
At 4: Won San Antonio Handicap
Inglewood Handicap
2nd Santa Anita Maturity
Hollywood Gold Cup
3rd Californian Stakes
American Handicap

BAG OF TUNES (1970)
At 2: 2nd Alcibiades Stakes
At 3: Won Kentucky Oaks
2nd Coaching Club American Oaks
Alabama Stakes
Gazelle Handicap

BAGSHOT (1994)
At 4: 2nd Santa Anita Handicap
3rd Strub Stakes

BAHR (1995)
At 3: 3rd Flower Bowl Invitational Handicap

BAILJUMPER (1974)
At 3: Won Dwyer Handicap

BAILLAMONT (1982)
At 3: 3rd Man o' War Stakes

BAIL OUT BECKY (1992)
At 4: 2nd Beverly Hills Handicap

BAITMAN (1961)
At 5: 3rd Massachusetts Handicap

BALBOA NATIVE (1980)
At 2: 3rd Del Mar Futurity
At 3: Won Louisiana Derby

BALCONY'S BABE (1968)
At 3: 3rd Hollywood Oaks

BALD EAGLE (1955)
At 4: Won Suburban Handicap
Gallant Fox Handicap
Washington D.C. International
2nd Aqueduct Handicap
Manhattan Handicap
3rd Massachusetts Handicap
At 5: Won Widener Handicap
Gulfstream Park Handicap
Metropolitan Handicap
Aqueduct Handicap
Washington D.C. International
2nd McLennan Handicap
Man o' War Stakes
3rd Woodward Stakes
Jockey Club Gold Cup

BALDPATE (1958)
At 3: 2nd Dwyer Handicap

BALDSKI'S STAR (1984)
At 3: Won Tropical Park Derby

BALISIAN BEAUTY (1995)
At 2: 3rd Oak Leaf Stakes

BALLERINA (1950)
At 2: 2nd Demoiselle Stakes
At 4: Won Maskette Handicap

BALLET KHAL (1954)
At 4: 2nd Vanity Handicap

BALLINDAGGIN (1985)
At 3: 3rd Pennsylvania Derby

BALLY ACHE (1957)
At 2: 2nd Arlington Futurity
Sapling Stakes
Washington Park Futurity
Garden State Stakes
3rd Cowdin Stakes
Champagne Stakes
At 3: Won Flamingo Stakes
Florida Derby
Preakness Stakes
Jersey Derby
2nd Kentucky Derby
3rd United Nations Handicap

BALLYMOSS (1954)
At 4: 3rd Washington D.C. International

BAL MUSETTE (1958)
At 2: 2nd Pimlico Futurity

BALTIMORE COUNTY (1978)
At 4: 2nd Brooklyn Handicap
Bowling Green Handicap

BALTO STAR (1998)
At 3: Won Turfway Spiral Stakes
Arkansas Derby
At 4: 2nd Man o' War Stakes
At 5: Won United Nations Handicap
3rd Turf Classic

BALUSTRADE (1965)
At 3: Won Monmouth Invitational Handicap

BALZAC (1975)
At 2: Won Norfolk Stakes
At 3: 2nd Santa Anita Derby
At 4: Won Oak Tree Invitational Stakes
At 5: 2nd Hollywood Gold Cup
Century Handicap
Hollywood Invitational Handicap
Sunset Handicap
Oak Tree Invitational Stakes
3rd Del Mar Handicap

BANASSA (1950)
At 4: 2nd Washington D.C. International

BAND IS PASSING (1996)
At 4: 3rd Gulfstream Park BC Handicap
At 6: 2nd Gulfstream Park BC Handicap

BANGBOROUGH (1952)
At 3: 3rd Gotham Stakes

BANKER'S GOLD (1994)
At 4: 2nd Carter Handicap
Metropolitan Handicap

BANKER'S LADY (1985)
At 3: Won Ladies Handicap
At 4: Won Top Flight Handicap

BANKS HILL (1998)
At 3: Won Breeders' Cup Filly and Mare Turf
At 4: 2nd Breeders' Cup Filly and Mare Turf
3rd Yellow Ribbon Stakes

BANNER BOB (1982)
At 3: Won Hutcheson Stakes
Jim Beam Stakes
3rd Tropical Park Derby
Blue Grass Stakes

BANNER GALA (1978)
At 3: 2nd Alabama Stakes
3rd Mother Goose Stakes
Coaching Club American Oaks

BANQUET TABLE (1974)
At 2: Won Hopeful Stakes
2nd Futurity Stakes
Breeders' Futurity

BANSHEE BREEZE (1995)
At 3: Won Coaching Club of American Oaks
Alabama Stakes
Three Chimneys Spinster Stakes
2nd Kentucky Oaks
Breeders' Cup Distaff
3rd Ashland Stakes
Mother Goose Stakes
At 4: Won Apple Blossom Handicap
Go for Wand Handicap
2nd Personal Ensign Handicap
Three Chimneys Spinster Stakes
Breeders' Cup Distaff

BANSHEE WINDS (1990)
At 2: 2nd Arlington-Washington Lassie Stakes

BARAKA (1961)
At 2: 2nd Matron Stakes

BARATHEA (1990)
At 4: Won Breeders' Cup Mile

BARBARON (1960)
At 5: 3rd Pan American Handicap

BARBERSTOWN (1980)
At 3: 3rd Belmont Stakes

BARBIZON (1954)
At 2: Won Garden State Stakes

BARBIZON STREAK (1968)
At 3: 2nd Arkansas Derby

BARBS DELIGHT (1964)
At 3: 2nd Kentucky Derby
3rd Arkansas Derby
At 4: 2nd Oaklawn Handicap
John B. Campbell Handicap
At 5: 2nd John B. Campbell Handicap

BARCAS (1971)
At 4: Won Bowling Green Handicap
2nd Hialeah Turf Cup
Widener Handicap

BARCLAY JOY (1970)
At 5: Won Hollywood Invitational Handicap
Sunset Handicap

BARDSTOWN (1952)
At 4: Won Trenton Handicap
At 5: Won Tropical Handicap
Widener Handicap
Gulfstream Park Handicap
2nd McLennan Handicap
At 6: 2nd Trenton Handicap
At 7: Won Tropical Park Handicap

BARELY EVEN (1969)
At 2: 3rd Frizette Stakes
At 3: 2nd Kentucky Oaks
3rd Spinster Stakes

BARELY ONCE (1966)
At 4: 3rd Donn Handicap

BARE NECESSITIES (1999)
At 4: 3rd Vanity Handicap

BAROMETER (1965)
At 5: Won Suburban Handicap

BARON DE VAUX (1987)
At 3: 2nd Haskell Invitational Handicap
3rd Belmont Stakes

BARRERA (1973)
At 4: 2nd Carter Handicap

BAR TENDER (1983)
At 2: 2nd Arlington-Washington Futurity

BARTER TOWN (1995)
At 4: 3rd Pacific Classic

BASIE (1981)
At 4: Won Delaware Handicap
2nd Ladies Handicap

BASQUEIAN (1991)
At 6: 3rd Cigar Mile Handicap

BASSANIO (1950)
At 4: Won Michigan Mile
2nd Suburban Handicap

BASS CLEF (1958)
At 3: Won Louisiana Derby
3rd Arkansas Derby
Kentucky Derby
At 4: 2nd Hawthorne Gold Cup

BASTOGNE (1944)
At 2: 3rd Pimlico Futurity

BASTONERA II (1971)
At 5: Won Ladies Handicap
Beverly Hills Handicap
2nd Vanity Handicap
Ruffian Stakes
3rd Beldame Stakes
At 6: 2nd Vanity Handicap
Santa Margarita Handicap

BATES MOTEL (1979)
At 4: Won Monmouth Handicap
San Antonio Stakes
Santa Anita Handicap
2nd Woodward Stakes
3rd Marlboro Cup Handicap

BATONNIER (1975)
At 3: Won Illinois Derby
2nd Ohio Derby
Swaps Stakes
3rd Louisiana Derby

BATTER UP (1959)
At 2: Won Sorority Stakes

BATTEUR (1960)
At 4: Won Santa Margarita Handicap
At 6: 3rd Santa Margarita Handicap

BATTLEFIELD (1948)
At 2: Won Sapling Stakes
Saratoga Special
Hopeful Stakes
Tremont Stakes
Futurity Stakes
At 3: Won Withers Stakes
Dwyer Stakes
Travers Stakes
2nd Belmont Stakes
Arlington Classic
Discovery Handicap
At 4: Won New York Handicap
Westchester Handicap
2nd Metropolitan Handicap
Grey Lag Handicap
At 5: 2nd Gulfstream Park Handicap
3rd Widener Handicap

BATTLE HEART (1956)
At 2: Won Princess Pat Stakes

BATTLE JOINED (1959)
At 2: Won Saratoga Special
2nd Sapling Stakes
At 3: Won Lawrence Realization Stakes

BATTLE MORN (1948)
At 2: 2nd Hopeful Stakes
Champagne Stakes
3rd Saratoga Special
At 3: 2nd Wood Memorial Stakes
3rd Belmont Stakes

BATTLE NECK (1955)
At 5: 3rd Massachusetts Handicap

BATTY (1985)
At 2: Won Remsen Stakes

B.A. VALENTINE (1993)
At 5: 2nd Flower Bowl Invitational Handicap

BAYAKOA (1984)
At 5: Won Santa Margarita Handicap
Apple Blossom Handicap
Vanity Handicap
Ruffian Handicap
Spinster Stakes
Breeders' Cup Distaff
At 6: Won Santa Margarita Handicap
Spinster Stakes
Breeders' Cup Distaff
2nd Apple Blossom Handicap
At 7: 2nd Santa Margarita Handicap

BAYBROOK (1949)
At 2: 3rd Cowdin Stakes

BAY MONSTER (1999)
At 3: 3rd Arkansas Derby

BAYOU (1954)
At 3: Won Acorn Stakes
Delaware Oaks
Gazelle Handicap
Maskette Handicap
2nd Coaching Club American Oaks

BAY STREET STAR (1991)
At 3: 3rd Dwyer Stakes
Super Derby

BEACHCOMBER (1950)
At 3: 2nd Saranac Handicap

BEAL STREET BLUES (1990)
At 2: 3rd Frizette Stakes

BEAM RIDER (1953)
At 4: 2nd Grey Lag Handicap
Gallant Fox Handicap
Santa Anita Maturity

BEAN BAG (1981)
At 3: 3rd Hollywood Derby

BEANIR (1951)
At 2: 3rd Arlington Lassie Stakes

BEAR HUNT (1981)
At 3: Won Gotham Stakes
3rd Wood Memorial Stakes

BEAT HOLLOW (1997)
At 5: Won Woodford Reserve Turf Classic
Manhattan Handicap
Arlington Million
2nd Eddie Read Handicap
3rd Shadwell Keeneland Turf Mile

BEAU BRUMMEL (1966)
At 2: Won Garden State Stakes
2nd Champagne Stakes
3rd Cowdin Stakes
At 3: 3rd Flamingo Stakes
At 4: 2nd Widener Handicap
Donn Handicap

BEAU BUSHER (1952)
At 3: 2nd San Felipe Handicap

BEAUCHEF (1943)
At 5: Won Massachusetts Handicap
3rd Jockey Club Gold Cup

BEAU DIABLE (1953)
At 5: 2nd Manhattan Handicap
At 6: Won Display Handicap
At 7: 3rd Display Handicap

BEAU FOND (1953)
At 2: Won Champagne Stakes

BEAU GENIUS (1985)
At 5: Won Arlington Invitational Challenge Cup
Philip H. Iselin Handicap
3rd Meadowlands Cup

BEAU GROTON (1971)
At 2: 2nd Arlington-Washington Futurity
At 3: 3rd Louisiana Derby

BEAU JULIAN (1969)
At 3: 3rd Illinois Derby

BEAU MARKER (1965)
At 4: Won Massachusetts Handicap

BEAU PRINCE (1958)
At 2: 3rd Arlington Futurity
At 3: Won American Derby
Travers Stakes
3rd Florida Derby
Dwyer Handicap
Jerome Handicap
At 4: Won Michigan Mile and One-Sixteenth
3rd John B. Campbell Handicap
Grey Lag Handicap

BEAU PURPLE (1957)
At 5: Won Suburban Handicap
Brooklyn Handicap
Hawthorne Gold Cup
Man o' War Stakes
3rd Monmouth Handicap
At 6: Won Widener Handicap

BEAUPY (1962)
At 4: 2nd Grey Lag Handicap

BEAU RIT (1978)
At 3: 3rd Louisiana Derby

BEAU'S EAGLE (1976)
At 3: Won California Derby
2nd Santa Anita Derby
At 4: Won San Antonio Stakes
3rd Santa Anita Handicap

BEAU SHAM (1975)
At 3: 3rd American Derby

BEAU SULTAN (1988)
At 3: 3rd Man o' War Stakes

BEAU TALENT (1973)
At 2: 3rd Futurity Stakes
At 3: 2nd San Felipe Handicap

BEAUTIFUL DAY (1961)
At 2: 2nd Frizette Stakes
3rd Matron Stakes
At 3: 2nd Alabama Stakes

BEAUTIFUL MELODY (1986)
At 4: 3rd Gamely Handicap

BEAUTIFUL NOISE (1996)
At 5: 3rd Gamely Breeders' Cup Handicap

BEAUTIFUL PLEASURE (1995)
At 2: Won Matron Stakes
At 4: Won Personal Ensign Handicap
Beldame Stakes
Breeders' Cup Distaff
2nd Hempstead Handicap
Go for Wand Stakes
At 5: Won Hempstead Handicap
Personal Ensign Handicap
2nd Go for Wand Handicap
Beldame Stakes
At 6: 2nd Personal Ensign Handicap

BEAUTILLION (1953)
At 2: 3rd Matron Stakes
At 4: 3rd Vanity Handicap

BEAUTY HOUR (1976)
At 2: 2nd Del Mar Debutante Stakes

BE CAUTIOUS (1957)
At 4: Won Black Helen Handicap

BED O' ROSES (1947)
At 2: Won Matron Stakes
Selima Stakes
Marguerite Stakes
Demoiselle Stakes
2nd Astoria Stakes
3rd Arlington Lassie Stakes
At 3: Won Lawrence Realization Stakes
2nd Gazelle Stakes
Arlington Classic
Travers Stakes
At 4: Won Vineland Handicap
Comely Handicap
2nd Beldame Handicap
Ladies Handicap
3rd Santa Margarita Handicap
Westchester Handicap
Santa Anita Maturity
At 5: Won Santa Margarita Handicap
3rd San Antonio Handicap

BEDSIDE PROMISE (1982)
At 4: 3rd Breeders' Cup Sprint
At 5: Won San Antonio Handicap

BEE ANN MAC (1944)
At 2: Won Selima Stakes
At 3: 3rd Alabama Stakes

BEE A SCOUT (1978)
At 2: 3rd Oak Leaf Stakes
At 3: 2nd Santa Susana Stakes

BEE BEE BEE (1969)
At 3: Won Preakness Stakes

BEEKEEPER (1960)
At 2: 2nd Del Mar Futurity

BE FAITHFUL (1942)
At 4: Won Vanity Handicap
3rd Santa Margarita Handicap
At 5: Won Hawthorne Gold Cup
3rd Santa Margarita Handicap
Top Flight Handicap

BE FEARLESS (1942)
At 5: 2nd Del Mar Handicap

BE FLEET (1947)
At 4: Won San Juan Capistrano Handicap
3rd Inglewood Handicap
Hollywood Gold Cup
At 5: 2nd San Juan Capistrano Handicap
3rd Santa Anita Handicap

BEFORE DAWN (1979)
At 2: Won Matron Stakes
2nd Champagne Stakes
At 3: 2nd Kentucky Oaks
3rd Fantasy Stakes

BE GENTLE (2001)
At 2: Won Darley Alcibiades Stakes
2nd Spinaway Stakes

BEHAVING DEBY (1961)
At 2: 3rd Sorority Stakes

BEHISTOUN (1963)
At 3: Won Washington D.C. International

BEHRAM (1970)
At 2: 3rd Spinaway Stakes

BEHRENS (1994)
At 3: Won Buick Pegasus Handicap
2nd Travers Stakes
At 4: 3rd Gulfstream Park Handicap
At 5: Won Gulfstream Park Handicap
Oaklawn Handicap
Suburban Handicap
2nd Donn Handicap
Whitney Handicap
Jockey Club Gold Cup
At 6: Won Gulfstream Park Handicap
2nd Suburban Handicap
Woodward Stakes
3rd Donn Handicap
Whitney Handicap

BEJA (1967)
At 3: 2nd Hollywood Oaks
At 4: 2nd Santa Margarita Handicap

BEL BOLIDE (1978)
At 5: 2nd Eddie Read Handicap

BELIEVE IT (1975)
At 2: Won Remsen Stakes
2nd Young America Stakes
At 3: Won Wood Memorial Stakes
2nd Florida Derby
3rd Kentucky Derby
Preakness Stakes

BELIEVE THE QUEEN (1980)
At 4: Won Monmouth Handicap

BELLA BELLUCCI (1999)
At 2: 3rd Breeders' Cup Juvenile Fillies
At 3: 3rd Acorn Stakes
Gazelle Handicap
At 4: 3rd Santa Margarita Handicap

BELLA CHIARRA (1995)
At 4: 3rd Vanity Handicap

BELLADORA (1976)
At 2: 3rd Demoiselle Stakes

BELLA FIGURA (1949)
At 2: 3rd Princess Pat Stakes
At 3: 2nd Arlington Matron Stakes
At 4: 3rd Arlington Matron Handicap

BELLEAU CHIEF (1955)
At 4: 3rd Washington Park Handicap

BELLE GESTE (1968)
At 4: 2nd Canadian International Championship

BELLE JOLIE (1945)
At 3: 2nd Hollywood Oaks
Cinema Handicap

BELLE NOIRE (1967)
At 2: Won Alcibiades Stakes
2nd Arlington-Washington Lassie Stakes

BELLE OF COZZENE (1992)
At 4: 3rd Three Chimneys Spinster Stakes

BELLE'S FLAG (1993)
At 6: 2nd Santa Monica Handicap
3rd Santa Maria Handicap

BELLESOEUR (1945)
At 2: Won Spinaway Stakes
Astarita Stakes
2nd Demoiselle Stakes

BELL HOP (1955)
At 4: Won Bowling Green Handicap

BELLO (1981)
At 3: 2nd Everglades Stakes

BELLO CIELO (1992)
At 3: 3rd Hollywood Oaks

BEL'S STARLET (1987)
At 2: 2nd Oak Leaf Stakes
At 6: 3rd Gamely Handicap

BELTERRA (1999)
At 3: 3rd Ashland Stakes

BEMISSED (1980)
At 2: Won Selima Stakes
At 3: 3rd Kentucky Oaks

BEMO (1970)
At 3: Won American Derby
At 7: Won United Nations Handicap

BE MY HONEY (1955)
At 2: 3rd Del Mar Debutante Stakes

BE MY NATIVE (1979)
At 3: 2nd Budweiser Million

BEN A. JONES (1953)
At 3: 2nd Arlington Classic

BENBURB (1989)
At 3: Won Molson Export Million

BENCHMARK (1991)
At 6: 3rd Californian Stakes

BENEFICIAL (1990)
At 4: 3rd Washington D.C. International

BEN FAB (1977)
At 3: 3rd Canadian Int. Championship
At 4: 2nd United Nations Handicap

BEN LEWIS (1944)
At 3: 3rd Fall Highweight Handicap

BEN LOMOND (1954)
At 2: 2nd Sapling Stakes

BEQUA (1976)
At 2: 3rd Arlington-Washington Lassie Stakes

BEQUEST (1986)
At 5: Won Santa Barbara Handicap

BERENJENAL (1960)
At 5: 2nd Jockey Club Gold Cup

BERKLEY FITZ (1989)
At 3: 3rd Peter Pan Stakes

BERKLEY PRINCE (1966)
At 3: Won Ohio Derby

BERLO (1957)
At 3: Won Mother Goose Stakes
Coaching Club American Oaks
Beldame Stakes
Ladies Handicap
3rd Delaware Oaks

BERNBURGOO (1953)
At 5: 3rd John B. Campbell Memorial Handicap

BERNWOOD (1948)
At 2: 2nd Washington Park Futurity
Kentucky Jockey Club Stakes
At 3: 3rd American Derby
At 5: 3rd Del Mar Handicap

BERRY BUSH (1977)
At 5: 2nd Matriarch Stakes

BERSEEM (1950)
At 2: 3rd Kentucky Jockey Club Stakes

BERSID (1978)
At 3: 3rd Matriarch Stakes

BERTRANDO (1989)
At 2: Won Del Mar Futurity
Norfolk Stakes
2nd Breeders' Cup Juvenile
At 3: Won San Felipe Handicap
2nd Santa Anita Derby
At 4: Won Pacific Classic
Woodward Stakes
2nd Charles H. Strub Stakes
Metropolitan Handicap
Hollywood Gold Cup
Breeders' Cup Classic
3rd Philip H. Iselin Handicap

BERT'S TRYST (1969)
At 3: 2nd Hollywood Oaks

BESSARABIAN (1982)
At 3: 2nd Coaching Club American Oaks

BEST BEE (1973)
At 2: 2nd Breeders' Futurity

BEST DECORATED (1989)
At 3: 3rd Gotham Stakes

BEST FRIEND STRO (1995)
At 3: 3rd Coaching Club American Oaks

BEST OF IT (1971)
At 3: 2nd Withers Stakes
Jerome Handicap

BEST OF LUCK (1996)
At 3: 2nd Wood Memorial Stakes

BEST PAL (1988)
At 2: Won Del Mar Futurity
Norfolk Stakes
Hollywood Futurity
At 3: Won Swaps Stakes
Pacific Classic
2nd Santa Anita Derby
Kentucky Derby
At 4: Won Charles H. Strub Stakes
Santa Anita Handicap
Oaklawn Handicap
At 5: Won Hollywood Gold Cup
2nd Hollywood Turf Handicap
3rd Oaklawn Handicap
Pacific Classic
At 6: 2nd Pacific Classic
At 7: Won San Antonio Handicap
2nd Santa Anita Handicap

BEST PERSON (1974)
At 3: 3rd Arkansas Derby

BEST TURN (1966)
At 4: Won John B. Campbell Handicap
Vosburgh Handicap
2nd Carter Handicap

BEST YEARS (1951)
At 2: 2nd Champagne Stakes
3rd Futurity Stakes

BE SURE (1946)
At 2: 3rd Frizette Stakes

BET BIG (1980)
At 2: 2nd Young America Stakes
At 3: 2nd Arlington Classic
Haskell Invitational Handicap

At 4: 3rd Monmouth Handicap
Woodward Stakes

BETH'S SONG (1982)
At 5: 2nd Top Flight Handicap

BET ON SUNSHINE (1992)
At 5: 3rd Breeders' Cup Sprint
At 8: 3rd Breeders' Cup Sprint

BETSY BE GOOD (1969)
At 3: 3rd Alabama Stakes

BETTER ARBITOR (1971)
At 3: Won Jersey Derby
2nd Ohio Derby
3rd Monmouth Invitational Handicap

BETTER BEE (1954)
At 4: 3rd Pimlico Special

BETTER SEA (1963)
At 3: Won Arkansas Derby

BETTER SELF (1945)
At 2: Won Saratoga Special
2nd Pimlico Futurity
At 3: Won Discovery Handicap
Westchester Handicap
2nd Belmont Stakes
Dwyer Stakes
Saranac Handicap
Travers Stakes
3rd Withers Stakes
Wood Memorial Stakes
At 4: Won Carter Handicap
At 5: Won Gallant Fox Handicap

BETTER THAN HONOUR (1996)
At 3: 2nd Acorn Stakes
3rd Mother Goose Stakes

BET TWICE (1984)
At 2: Won Arlington-Washington Futurity
Laurel Futurity
3rd Champagne Stakes
At 3: Won Fountain of Youth Stakes
Belmont Stakes
Haskell Invitational Handicap
2nd Kentucky Derby
Preakness Stakes
At 4: 2nd Philip H. Iselin Handicap
3rd Suburban Handicap
United Nations Handicap

BEVO (1997)
At 2: Won Futurity Stakes

BEWITCH (1945)
At 2: Won Washington Park Futurity
Arlington Lassie Stakes
Princess Pat Stakes
3rd Futurity Stakes
At 4: Won Vineland Handicap
2nd Arlington Matron Stakes
At 5: Won Black Helen Handicap
2nd Vanity Handicap
3rd Vineland Handicap
At 6: Won Vanity Handicap
2nd Santa Margarita Handicap
American Handicap
Hollywood Gold Cup

BEYOND (1953)
At 3: Won Acorn Stakes

BEYOND PERFECTION (1988)
At 2: 3rd Oak Leaf Stakes

BF'S OWN (1962)
At 5: 3rd Oaklawn Handicap

B. GOLDEN (1963)
At 3: 3rd Illinois Derby

BICARB (1950)
At 4: 2nd Gallant Fox Handicap
3rd Jockey Club Gold Cup
Manhattan Handicap

BICKER (1969)
At 3: 2nd Hollywood Derby

3rd Oak Tree Invitational Stakes
At 4: Won Malibu Stakes
San Fernando Stakes

BIC'S GOLD (1977)
At 3: 3rd Santa Anita Derby

BIDDY JANE (1950)
At 2: 2nd Princess Pat Stakes

BIENAMADO (1996)
At 4: Won Hollywood Turf Cup
At 5: Won San Juan Capistrano Handicap
Charles Whittingham Handicap

BIEN BIEN (1989)
At 3: Won Swaps Stakes
Hollywood Turf Cup
2nd Hollywood Derby
At 4: Won Hollywood Turf Handicap
2nd San Luis Rey Stakes
San Juan Capistrano Handicap
Breeders' Cup Turf
At 5: Won San Luis Rey Stakes
San Juan Capistrano Handicap
2nd Santa Anita Handicap
Hollywood Turf Handicap

BIEN NICOLE (1998)
At 5: 2nd Beverly D. Stakes

BIG ADVANCE (1966)
At 2: Won Sorority Stakes
At 3: 3rd Acorn Stakes

BIG BAMBU (1997)
At 3: 2nd Test Stakes

BIG BAND (1970)
At 5: 2nd Californian Stakes
Hollywood Gold Cup
American Handicap

BIG BIZ (1957)
At 2: 3rd Sapling Stakes

BIG BRIGADE (1961)
At 5: 2nd Oaklawn Handicap

BIG CREST (1951)
At 3: 2nd Everglades Stakes
3rd Florida Derby

BIG DIAL (1945)
At 3: 2nd Flamingo Stakes

BIG EARL (1986)
At 3: 2nd Super Derby

BIG EE (1997)
At 4: 3rd Vosburgh Stakes

BIG EFFORT (1955)
At 3: Won Acorn Stakes
Delaware Oaks
At 4: Won Top Flight Handicap
2nd Grey Lag Handicap
3rd Ladies Handicap

BIGFORK (1956)
At 6: 3rd Donn Handicap

BIG FRIGHT (1955)
At 2: 3rd Frizette Stakes

BIGGS (1960)
At 7: Won Californian Stakes
2nd San Juan Capistrano Handicap
3rd Hollywood Gold Cup
At 8: Won San Luis Rey Handicap

BIG IF (1945)
At 2: Won Remsen Handicap

BIG JAG (1993)
At 6: 3rd Breeders' Cup Sprint

BIG JOHN TAYLOR (1974)
At 4: 3rd Carter Handicap

BIG LATCH (1971)
At 3: 2nd Blue Grass Stakes

BIG MO (1949)
At 3: Won Delaware Oaks
3rd Kentucky Oaks

BIG NOISE (1949)
At 2: Won Del Mar Futurity
3rd Starlet Stakes

BIG PETE (1961)
At 2: 2nd Sapling Stakes

BIG PISTOL (1981)
At 3: Won Haskell Invitational Handicap
3rd Super Derby

BIG PLAY (1983)
At 3: 2nd San Felipe Handicap

BIG RAFF (1960)
At 4: 3rd San Fernando Stakes

BIG ROCK CANDY (1962)
At 4: 3rd Aqueduct Handicap
At 6: 2nd Massachusetts Handicap

BIG SHOT II (1965)
At 6: Won Century Handicap
Manhattan Handicap

BIG SMOKY (1958)
At 2: 3rd Hollywood Juvenile Championship

BIG SPRUCE (1969)
At 4: Won San Luis Rey Handicap
2nd Charles H. Strub Stakes
Manhattan Handicap
Canadian International Championship
Washington D.C. International
San Juan Capistrano Handicap
3rd San Antonio Stakes
Man o' War Stakes
At 5: Won Marlboro Cup Handicap
2nd Canadian International Championship
San Luis Rey Stakes
3rd Santa Anita Handicap
San Juan Capistrano Handicap

BIG STANLEY (1986)
At 3: Won Tropical Park Derby
3rd Florida Derby

BIG STORY (1944)
At 4: 2nd Fall Highweight Handicap

BIG STRETCH (1948)
At 2: Won Breeders' Futurity
Pimlico Futurity
2nd Futurity Stakes
3rd Hopeful Stakes
At 3: 3rd Travers Stakes

BIG WHIPPENDEAL (1970)
At 3: Won Illinois Derby
At 4: Won Hialeah Turf Cup
Century Handicap
2nd Sunset Handicap

BILLER (1964)
At 3: 2nd Florida Derby

BILL E. SHEARS (1985)
At 2: 2nd Hopeful Stakes
At 4: 2nd Philip H. Iselin Handicap

BILLINGS (1945)
At 3: Won Hawthorne Gold Cup
2nd Blue Grass Stakes

BILL MONROE (1978)
At 3: 3rd Hawthorne Gold Cup

BILL'S SKY BOY (1953)
At 3: 3rd Dwyer Handicap
Travers Stakes
At 5: 3rd Monmouth Handicap
At 6: 3rd Widener Handicap

BILLY BALL (1980)
At 3: 3rd California Derby

BILLY COME LATELY (1970)
At 4: 2nd Brooklyn Handicap
3rd Hawthorne Gold Cup

BILLY JANE (1976)
At 4: Won Apple Blossom Handicap

BILOXI INDIAN (1981)
At 3: 2nd Ohio Derby
3rd Pennsylvania Derby

BIMLETTE (1944)
At 2: Won Frizette Stakes

BIMONT (1943)
At 4: 3rd Miami Beach Handicap

BIO (1986)
At 2: 2nd Futurity Stakes
3rd Breeders' Futurity

BIRDIE'S LEGEND (1981)
At 3: Won Jersey Derby
2nd Haskell Invitational Handicap
3rd Illinois Derby

BIRDONTHEWIRE (1989)
At 4: Won Vosburgh Stakes

BIRDSTONE (2001)
At 2: Won Champagne Stakes

BIRD TOWN (2000)
At 3: Won Kentucky Oaks
Acorn Stakes
2nd Test Stakes
Beldame Stakes

BISHOP'S CHOICE (1976)
At 3: 3rd Blue Grass Stakes

BISTRO GARDEN (1988)
At 3: 2nd Hollywood Derby

BIT O' FATE (1947)
At 3: 3rd Saranac Handicap
Discovery Handicap

BIT OF PUDDIN (1991)
At 3: 2nd Gotham Stakes

BITTERROOK (1978)
At 3: 3rd Illinois Derby

BIXA (1968)
At 3: 3rd Arkansas Derby

BLACK BEARD (1959)
At 3: Won Jerome Handicap

BLACK CASH (1995)
At 4: 3rd Philip H. Iselin Handicap

BLACK DAD (1962)
At 2: 3rd Kentucky Jockey Club Stakes

BLACK DARTER (1958)
At 3: 2nd Acorn Stakes

BLACK DOUGLAS (1948)
At 4: 3rd Santa Anita Maturity

BLACK HILLS (1956)
At 2: 3rd Pimlico Futurity

BLACK METAL (1951)
At 3: 2nd Flamingo Stakes

BLACK MONDAY (1986)
At 5: Won Sunset Handicap

BLACK MOUNTAIN (1961)
At 2: 2nd Futurity Stakes

BLACK PEPPER (1942)
At 4: 3rd Bougainvillea Handicap

BLACK SHEEP (1959)
At 3: Won Cinema Handicap
American Derby

BLACK SWAN (1941)
At 5: 3rd Carter Handicap

BLACK THUMPER (1957)
At 4: 3rd Monmouth Handicap

Aqueduct Handicap
Gallant Fox Handicap

BLACK TIE AFFAIR (1986)
At 4: 3rd Breeders' Cup Sprint
At 5: Won Philip H. Iselin Handicap
Breeders' Cup Classic
2nd Carter Handicap

BLADE OF THE BALL (1985)
At 3: 2nd Swaps Stakes

BLADE PROSPECTOR (1995)
At 6: 2nd San Carlos Handicap

BLANCO (1984)
At 3: 2nd Illinois Derby
3rd California Derby

BLANK CHECK (1957)
At 3: 3rd Hollywood Derby

BLANQUETTE II (1964)
At 5: Won Hialeah Turf Cup

BLASTING CHARGE (1964)
At 3: 3rd Dwyer Handicap

BLAZE (1950)
At 3: 2nd Everglades Stakes
Florida Derby

BLAZING COUNT (1952)
At 3: 2nd Belmont Stakes

BLAZING FURY (1998)
At 3: 3rd Hollywood Turf Cup
At 4: 2nd Turf Classic

BLAZING SWORD (1994)
At 3: 2nd Fountain of Youth Stakes
3rd Super Derby
Crown Royal Hollywood Derby

BLEACHERITE (1961)
At 2: 3rd Breeders' Futurity
Kentucky Jockey Club Stakes

BLEN HOST (1953)
At 2: Won Del Mar Futurity
2nd Starlet Stakes
At 3: 2nd Cinema Handicap

BLESSING ANGELICA (1968)
At 3: Won Delaware Handicap
At 4: Won Delaware Handicap
At 5: 3rd Black Helen Handicap
Hempstead Handicap

BLITEY (1976)
At 3: Won Maskette Stakes
2nd Ruffian Handicap
At 4: 3rd Top Flight Handicap
Delaware Handicap

BLONDEINAMOTEL (1986)
At 3: 2nd Ashland Stakes
3rd Kentucky Oaks

BLOWIN' WIND (1976)
At 2: 3rd Del Mar Debutante Stakes

BLOW UP II (1966)
At 4: 2nd Beverly Hills Handicap

BLUE BANNER (1952)
At 2: 2nd Matron Stakes
At 3: 2nd Alabama Stakes
At 4: Won Firenze Handicap
3rd Diana Handicap

BLUEBILITY (1954)
At 2: 2nd Alcibiades Stakes
3rd Princess Pat Stakes

BLUE BORDER (1944)
At 2: Won Hopeful Stakes
At 4: 3rd Fall Highweight Handicap

BLUE BUCKAROO (1983)
At 3: 3rd Illinois Derby

BLUE BURNER (1999)
- At 3: 2nd Florida Derby
- 3rd Fountain of Youth Stakes

BLUE BUTTERFLY (1949)
- At 6: Won Santa Margarita Handicap

BLUE CASE (1949)
- At 2: Won Spinaway Stakes

BLUE CHIP DAN (1970)
- At 3: 2nd Pontiac Grand Prix Stakes

BLUE CHOIR (1951)
- At 4: Won United Nations Handicap
- At 5: 3rd Hialeah Turf Handicap
- At 6: 3rd Hialeah Turf Handicap
- Dixie Handicap

BLUE CROONER (1957)
- At 2: 2nd Gardenia Stakes

BLUE DART (1946)
- At 3: Won Will Rogers Handicap
- 3rd Cinema Handicap

BLUE GRASS (1944)
- At 3: Won Kentucky Oaks

BLUE HILLS (1946)
- At 3: 2nd Lawrence Realization Stakes

BLUE LEM (1952)
- At 3: 2nd Florida Derby

BLUE MAN (1949)
- At 3: Won Flamingo Stakes
- Preakness Stakes
- Dwyer Stakes
- 2nd Belmont Stakes
- 3rd Kentucky Derby

BLUE MOON (1950)
- At 4: 3rd Top Flight Handicap

BLUE MOON (1997)
- At 3: 2nd Queen Elizabeth II Challenge Cup

BLUE NORTHER (1961)
- At 2: 2nd Gardenia Stakes
- At 3: Won Santa Susana Stakes
- Kentucky Oaks

BLUE PETER (1946)
- At 2: Won Garden State Stakes
- Saratoga Special
- Hopeful Stakes
- Futurity Stakes

BLUEPRINT (1995)
- At 6: 3rd San Juan Capistrano Handicap

BLUE READING (1947)
- At 3: 3rd Del Mar Derby
- San Felipe Stakes
- At 4: Won Del Mar Handicap
- 3rd San Carlos Handicap

BLUE RINGS (1947)
- At 2: 2nd Del Mar Futurity

BLUER THAN BLUE (1977)
- At 2: 3rd Sorority Stakes

BLUE RULER (1952)
- At 2: Won Starlet Stakes
- Del Mar Futurity
- At 3: 3rd Santa Anita Derby

BLUE SERENADE (1959)
- At 3: 2nd California Derby

BLUE SKYER (1963)
- At 3: Won Louisiana Derby
- 3rd Flamingo Stakes
- Kentucky Derby

BLUE SPARKLER (1952)
- At 3: 2nd Monmouth Oaks
- At 4: Won Molly Pitcher Handicap

BLUE SPRUCE (1954)
- At 3: 3rd San Felipe Handicap

BLUE STELLER (1998)
- At 4: 3rd Clement L. Hirsch Mem. Turf Champ.

BLUESTHESTANDARD (1997)
- At 6: 2nd Breeders' Cup Sprint
- 3rd Ancient Title Breeders' Cup Handicap

BLUES TRAVELLER (1990)
- At 4: 3rd Hollywood Turf Handicap
- At 5: 2nd Early Times Manhattan Handicap

BLUE THANKS (1946)
- At 4: 2nd New Orleans Handicap

BLUE TIGER (1943)
- At 6: Won Longacres Mile

BLUE TRUMPETER (1949)
- At 5: 3rd Del Mar Handicap

BLUE VIC (1954)
- At 2: Won Del Mar Debutante Stakes

BLUE VIOLIN (1951)
- At 3: 3rd Kentucky Oaks

BLUE VOLT (1949)
- At 7: Won San Luis Rey Handicap
- 3rd Sunset Handicap

BLUE YONDER (1943)
- At 4: 3rd Massachusetts Handicap

BLUMIN AFFAIR (1991)
- At 2: 2nd Breeders' Cup Juvenile
- At 3: 2nd Arkansas Derby
- 3rd Kentucky Derby
- At 4: 3rd Pacific Classic

BLUNT REMARK (1943)
- At 3: 2nd Swift Stakes

BLUSHING JOHN (1985)
- At 4: Won Hollywood Gold Cup
- 2nd Californian Stakes
- 3rd Breeders' Cup Classic

BLUSHING K.D. (1994)
- At 3: Won Kentucky Oaks

BLUSH WITH PRIDE (1979)
- At 3: Won Santa Susana Stakes
- Kentucky Oaks
- Golden Harvest Handicap
- 2nd Spinster Stakes
- 3rd Mother Goose Stakes

B. MAJOR (1960)
- At 3: Won Everglades Stakes
- 2nd American Derby
- Lawrence Realization Stakes
- Arlington Park Handicap
- Gallant Fox Handicap
- 3rd Arlington Classic
- Washington Park Handicap
- At 4: 2nd San Fernando Stakes

BOATMAN (1996)
- At 4: 2nd Manhattan Handicap
- Clement L. Hirsch Mem. Turf Champ.

BOB BACK (1981)
- At 4: 2nd Man o' War Stakes

BOBBY BROCATO (1951)
- At 3: 2nd Louisiana Derby
- At 4: Won Carter Handicap
- 2nd Del Mar Handicap
- William P. Kyne Handicap
- At 5: Won Santa Anita Handicap
- San Juan Capistrano Handicap
- 3rd San Antonio Handicap
- Inglewood Handicap
- American Handicap

BOB MANN (1942)
- At 4: 3rd McLennan Handicap

BODY BEND (1973)
- At 2: 3rd Del Mar Futurity

BOLD (1948)
- At 2: 2nd Pimlico Futurity
- At 3: Won Preakness Stakes
- Saranac Handicap

BOLD AND BRAVE (1963)
- At 3: Won Jerome Handicap
- 2nd Florida Derby

BOLD AND GOLD (1978)
- At 2: Won Del Mar Futurity

BOLD ARRANGEMENT (1983)
- At 3: 2nd Kentucky Derby
- 3rd Blue Grass Stakes
- Hollywood Derby

BOLD BABY (1972)
- At 4: 3rd Vanity Handicap

BOLD BAZOOKA (1953)
- At 2: Won Starlet Stakes

BOLD BIDDER (1962)
- At 3: Won Jerome Handicap
- At 4: Won Monmouth Handicap
- Washington Park Handicap
- Hawthorne Gold Cup
- Charles H. Strub Stakes
- 3rd San Fernando Stakes
- San Antonio Handicap

BOLD BRYN (1986)
- At 2: 2nd Norfolk Stakes

BOLD CHAPEAU (1972)
- At 3: 2nd Arkansas Derby

BOLD COMMANDER (1960)
- At 4: 2nd New Orleans Handicap

BOLD EGO (1978)
- At 2: 3rd Hollywood Juvenile Championship
- At 3: Won Arkansas Derby
- 2nd Preakness Stakes

BOLD EXPERIENCE (1960)
- At 2: Won Sorority Stakes

BOLD FAVORITE (1965)
- At 3: Won Illinois Derby

BOLD FORBES (1973)
- At 3: Won Wood Memorial Stakes
- Kentucky Derby
- Belmont Stakes
- 3rd Preakness Stakes
- Vosburgh Handicap

BOLD GALLANT (1945)
- At 2: Won Kentucky Jockey Club Stakes

BOLD HOUR (1964)
- At 2: Won Hopeful Stakes
- Futurity Stakes
- 2nd Saratoga Special
- Garden State Stakes
- At 4: Won Grey Lag Handicap
- Amory L. Haskell Handicap
- 2nd Widener Handicap
- Suburban Handicap

BOLD JOEY (1968)
- At 2: 3rd Del Mar Futurity

BOLD LAD (1962)
- At 2: Won Sapling Stakes
- Hopeful Stakes
- Futurity Stakes
- Champagne Stakes
- At 3: 3rd Wood Memorial Stakes
- At 4: Won Metropolitan Handicap

BOLD LIZ (1970)
- At 2: Won Hollywood Juvenile Championship

BOLD MEMORY (1970)
- At 2: 3rd Sorority Stakes

BOLD MIDWAY (1984)
- At 5: 2nd Gulfstream Park Handicap

BOLD MONARCH (1964)
At 3: 3rd Flamingo Stakes

BOLD 'N DETERMINED (1977)
At 2: Won Oak Leaf Stakes
At 3: Won Santa Susana Stakes
Fantasy Stakes
Kentucky Oaks
Acorn Stakes
Coaching Club American Oaks
Maskette Stakes
Spinster Stakes
2nd Mother Goose Stakes
At 4: Won Apple Blossom Handicap

BOLDNESIAN (1963)
At 3: Won Santa Anita Derby

BOLD 'N RULLING (1977)
At 3: 2nd Arkansas Derby
3rd California Derby

BOLD REASON (1968)
At 3: Won Hollywood Derby
Travers Stakes
American Derby
3rd Kentucky Derby
Belmont Stakes

BOLD REASONING (1968)
At 3: Won Withers Stakes
Jersey Derby
At 4: 2nd Metropolitan Handicap

BOLD RENDEZVOUS (1975)
At 3: 3rd Kentucky Oaks

BOLD ROLL (1972)
At 4: 3rd Arlington Handicap

BOLD RUCKUS (1976)
At 3: 2nd Ohio Derby

BOLD RULER (1954)
At 2: Won Futurity Stakes
At 3: Won Flamingo Stakes
Wood Memorial Stakes
Preakness Stakes
Jerome Handicap
Trenton Handicap
2nd Everglades Stakes
Florida Derby
3rd Belmont Stakes
Woodward Stakes
At 4: Won Carter Handicap
Suburban Handicap
Monmouth Handicap
2nd Metropolitan Handicap

BOLD RUN (1979)
At 4: 2nd Louisiana Downs Handicap

BOLD RURITANA (1990)
At 5: 3rd Yellow Ribbon Stakes

BOLD SECOND (1985)
At 2: 2nd Del Mar Futurity
3rd Norfolk Stakes

BOLD SOUTHERNER (1981)
At 3: 2nd Jim Beam Stakes

BOLD STYLE (1979)
At 3: 3rd Arkansas Derby
At 4: Won Oaklawn Handicap
2nd Whitney Handicap

BOLD SULTAN (1961)
At 2: 3rd Sapling Stakes

BOLD TACTICS (1963)
At 4: 2nd Arlington Handicap
3rd Washington Park Handicap

BOLD TIM (1960)
At 2: 3rd Saratoga Special

BOLD T. JAY (1981)
At 2: 2nd Hollywood Futurity

BOLD TROPIC (1975)
At 5: 3rd Oak Tree Invitational Stakes
At 6: 2nd Century Handicap

BOLD WINDY (1989)
At 4: 2nd Milady Handicap

BOLERO (1946)
At 3: Won Del Mar Derby
At 5: Won San Carlos Handicap

BOLINGOVER (1947)
At 2: 2nd Kentucky Jockey Club Stakes

BOL 'N JAC (1963)
At 3: 2nd Display Handicap
At 4: 3rd Gallant Fox Handicap

BOLSHOI BOY (1983)
At 3: Won Illinois Derby
2nd Flamingo Stakes
Blue Grass Stakes
Ohio Derby

BOLTING HOLME (1982)
At 2: 3rd Remsen Stakes

BOMBAY DUCK (1972)
At 2: 2nd Remsen Stakes
3rd Sapling Stakes
Laurel Futurity
At 3: 2nd Wood Memorial Stakes
3rd Jersey Derby

BONAPARTISTE (1994)
At 4: 2nd Eddie Read Handicap
Oak Tree Turf Championship
At 5: 3rd Oak Tree Turf Championship
At 7: 2nd Hollywood Turf Cup

BONAPAW (1996)
At 6: Won Vosburgh Stakes

BONETERO (1961)
At 5: 3rd New Orleans Handicap

BONJOUR (1960)
At 2: 2nd Sapling Stakes
At 3: 2nd Gotham Stakes
Wood Memorial Stakes
At 4: 3rd Grey Lag Handicap

BONNE ILE (1981)
At 5: Won Yellow Ribbon Stakes

BONNIE AND GAY (1968)
At 2: Won Matron Stakes
2nd Alcibiades Stakes

BONNIE BERYL (1943)
At 3: Won Delaware Oaks
Comely Handicap
2nd Acorn Stakes
3rd Coaching Club American Oaks
Gazelle Stakes

BONNIE'S GIRL (1960)
At 3: 2nd Kentucky Oaks

BONUS MONEY (1991)
At 4: 3rd Donn Handicap

BOOKKEEPER (1987)
At 2: 2nd Demoiselle Stakes

BOOKLET (1999)
At 3: Won Fountain of Youth Stakes
2nd Toyota Blue Grass Stakes

BOOK OF KINGS (1974)
At 6: 3rd New Orleans Handicap

BOONE THE GREAT (1968)
At 4: Won John B. Campbell Handicap

BOOT ALL (1948)
At 3: 2nd Gazelle Stakes

BOOTS 'N JACKIE (1990)
At 2: 3rd Breeders' Cup Juvenile Fillies

BORDEAUX BOB (1983)
At 4: Won Philip H. Iselin Handicap
2nd Brooklyn Handicap
3rd Suburban Handicap

BORDELAISE (1995)
At 5: 2nd Santa Margarita Handicap
Milady Breeders' Cup Handicap
3rd Apple Blossom Handicap

BORGIA (1994)
At 3: 2nd Breeders' Cup Turf

BORNASTAR (1953)
At 4: Won Spinster Stakes
2nd Arlington Matron Handicap
At 5: Won Vineland Handicap
Spinster Stakes
At 6: 3rd Maskette Handicap

BORN MIGHTY (1953)
At 3: Won Ohio Derby

BORN RICH (1953)
At 5: Won Santa Margarita Handicap
At 6: 3rd Arlington Matron Handicap

BOSTON COMMON (1999)
At 3: 2nd King's Bishop Stakes

BOSTON HARBOR (1994)
At 2: Won Breeders' Cup Juvenile

BOSWELL LADY (1945)
At 2: 2nd Arlington Lassie Stakes
Princess Pat Stakes
At 3: 3rd Hollywood Oaks

BOTH ENDS BURNING (1980)
At 4: Won Oak Tree Invitational Stakes
3rd Hollywood Turf Cup
At 5: Won Hollywood Invitational Handicap
2nd Century Handicap
Oak Tree Invitational Stakes
At 6: 3rd Hollywood Invitational Handicap

BOTTLE BRUSH (1970)
At 2: 3rd Hollywood Juvenile Championship
Norfolk Stakes
Del Mar Futurity

BOTTLED WATER (1978)
At 4: 3rd Turf Classic

BOTTLE TOP (1981)
At 2: 3rd Arlington-Washington Lassie Stakes

BOUCCANEER (1995)
At 4: 3rd Eddie Read Handicap

BOUND (1984)
At 3: 3rd Acorn Stakes

BOUNDING BASQUE (1980)
At 3: Won Wood Memorial Stakes
3rd Pegasus Handicap
Jockey Club Gold Cup
At 4: 3rd Jockey Club Gold Cup
At 5: Won Brooklyn Handicap

BOUNDING HOME (1941)
At 5: 2nd Grey Lag Handicap

BOUNDING MAIN (1959)
At 4: Won Arlington Park Handicap

BOUNDLESSLY (1990)
At 2: 2nd Arlington-Washington Futurity
At 3: 2nd Ohio Derby

BOURBON BELLE (1995)
At 4: 2nd Ballerina Handicap
At 5: 3rd Ballerina Handicap

BOURBON PRINCE (1957)
At 2: 3rd Hopeful Stakes
At 3: 3rd Everglades Stakes
At 4: Won Tropical Park Handicap
3rd Widener Handicap

BOVARD (1945)
At 3: Won Louisiana Derby
3rd Preakness Stakes

BOWL GAME (1974)
At 4: Won Gulfstream Park Handicap
Pan American Handicap

	2nd	Hollywood Invitational Handicap
	3rd	Bowling Green Handicap
At 5:	Won	Hialeah Turf Cup
		Arlington Handicap
		Man o' War Stakes
		Turf Classic
		Washington D.C. International
	2nd	Brooklyn Handicap
	3rd	Bowling Green Handicap

BOWL OF FLOWERS (1958)

At 2:	Won	Gardenia Stakes
		Frizette Stakes
At 3:	Won	Acorn Stakes
		Coaching Club American Oaks
		Spinster Stakes
	2nd	Mother Goose Stakes
	3rd	Alabama Stakes
		Roamer Handicap

BOWMAN MILL (1998)

At 5:	2nd	Hollywood Turf Cup

BOWMAN'S BAND (1998)

At 4:	2nd	Oaklawn Handicap
		Philip H. Iselin Handicap

BOX THE COMPASS (1967)

At 2:	Won	Sorority Stakes

BOYS NITE OUT (1978)

At 4:	2nd	New Orleans Handicap

BRABANCON (1944)

At 2:	3rd	Cowdin Stakes
At 3:	2nd	Withers Stakes
		Flamingo Stakes
	3rd	Swift Stakes
		Dwyer Stakes

BRAC DRIFTER (1995)

At 2:	2nd	Spinaway Stakes
	3rd	Frizette Stakes

BRACH'S HILARIOUS (1974)

At 3:	3rd	American Derby

BRADLEY'S COPY (1978)

At 4:	3rd	Golden Harvest Handicap

BRAHMS (1997)

At 3:	Won	Early Times Hollywood Derby
At 4:	3rd	Woodford Reserve Turf Classic
		Shoemaker Breeders' Cup Mile

BRAMALEA (1959)

At 3:	Won	Coaching Club American Oaks
	2nd	Delaware Oaks
	3rd	Delaware Handicap

BRANCUSI (2000)

At 3:	2nd	Toyota Blue Grass Stakes

BRASS SCALE (1991)

At 3:	Won	Pegasus Handicap

BRAVE DEED (1995)

At 3:	2nd	Test Stakes
	3rd	Acorn Stakes

BRAVE EMPEROR (1967)

At 2:	2nd	Champagne Stakes
	3rd	Pimlico-Laurel Futurity

BRAVE LAD (1961)

At 4:	Won	Display Handicap
	2nd	Gallant Fox Handicap
		Canadian Championship Stakes
	3rd	Jockey Club Gold Cup

BRAVE RAJ (1984)

At 2:	Won	Breeders' Cup Juvenile Fillies

BRAZANY (1990)

At 3:	3rd	Secretariat Stakes

BRAZE AND BOLD (1975)

At 5:	3rd	Oaklawn Handicap

BREAK OF DAY (1948)

At 3:	2nd	Black-Eyed Susan Stakes

BREAKSPEAR (1961)

At 2:	2nd	Pimlico Futurity

BREAK UP THE GAME (1971)

At 5:	3rd	United Nations Handicap

BRENDA BEAUTY (1969)

At 2:	Won	Sorority Stakes

BRENT'S PRINCE (1972)

At 3:	Won	Ohio Derby

BRENT'S TRANS AM (1977)

At 2:	3rd	Arlington-Washington Futurity
At 3:	3rd	Louisiana Derby

BRE'R RABBIT (1960)

At 3:	3rd	Cinema Handicap

BREVITO (1984)

At 2:	3rd	Del Mar Futurity

BRIAN'S TIME (1985)

At 3:	Won	Florida Derby
		Jim Dandy Stakes
	2nd	Preakness Stakes
	3rd	Jim Beam Stakes
		Belmont Stakes
		Travers Stakes

BRIARTIC CHIEF (1986)

At 3:	3rd	California Derby

BRICK DOOR (1969)

At 3:	2nd	Pontiac Grand Prix Stakes

BRIDAL FLOWER (1943)

At 3:	Won	Gazelle Stakes
		New Castle Handicap
		Beldame Handicap
		Roamer Handicap
	2nd	Alabama Stakes
	3rd	Comely Handicap
		Pimlico Special
At 4:	Won	Westchester Handicap
	2nd	Vosburgh Handicap
		Arlington Handicap
	3rd	New Castle Handicap

BRIDGEWORK (1955)

At 2:	3rd	Spinaway Stakes

BRIEF TRUCE (1989)

At 3:	3rd	Breeders' Cup Mile

BRIGHT AGAIN (1987)

At 3:	2nd	Jim Beam Stakes

BRIGHT BARON (1980)

At 2:	3rd	Breeders' Futurity

BRIGHT CANDLES (1987)

At 3:	2nd	Santa Anita Oaks
	3rd	Kentucky Oaks

BRIGHT CROCUS (1980)

At 3:	2nd	Kentucky Oaks

BRIGHTEST STAR (1952)

At 4:	3rd	Ladies Handicap
		Display Handicap

BRIGHT HOLLY (1958)

At 2:	2nd	Princess Pat Stakes

BRIGHT SONG (1944)

At 2:	2nd	Spinaway Stakes

BRIGHT SUN (1967)

At 2:	3rd	Spinaway Stakes

BRILLIANT NATIVE (1969)

At 2:	3rd	Breeders' Futurity

BRINDY BRINDY (1980)

At 3:	Won	Fantasy Stakes

BRING OUT THE BAND (1974)

At 2:	Won	Demoiselle Stakes
At 3:	Won	Acorn Stakes

BRISK N' BRIGHT (1951)

At 5:	3rd	Del Mar Handicap

BRITISH ROMAN (1957)

At 5:	3rd	San Antonio Handicap

BROAD BRUSH (1983)

At 3:	Won	Jim Beam Stakes
		Wood Memorial Stakes
		Ohio Derby
		Pennsylvania Derby
		Meadowlands Cup
	3rd	Kentucky Derby
		Preakness Stakes
At 4:	Won	Santa Anita Handicap
		Suburban Handicap
	2nd	San Fernando Stakes
	3rd	Charles H. Strub Stakes
		Metropolitan Handicap
		Whitney Handicap

BROAD SHADOWS (1965)

At 2:	2nd	Del Mar Futurity
	3rd	Hollywood Juvenile Championship

BROADWAY (1959)

At 2:	2nd	Selima Stakes

BROADWAY FLYER (1991)

At 5:	Won	Sword Dancer Invitational Handicap

BROADWAY FORLI (1974)

At 3:	Won	Jerome Handicap
	2nd	Vosburgh Handicap

BROCCO (1991)

At 2:	Won	Breeders' Cup Juvenile
	2nd	Hollywood Futurity
At 3:	Won	Santa Anita Derby
	2nd	San Felipe Stakes

BROKEN VOW (1997)

At 4:	Won	Philip H. Iselin Handicap
	3rd	Gulfstream Park Handicap

BRONZE BABU (1958)

At 5:	2nd	Hialeah Turf Cup
	3rd	Canadian Championship Stakes

BRONZERULLAH (1958)

At 2:	Won	Saratoga Special
	2nd	Hopeful Stakes
	3rd	Champagne Stakes

BROOKLYN NICK (1995)

At 2:	3rd	Remsen Stakes

BROOKSICKLE (1952)

At 3:	2nd	Cinema Handicap

BROOM DANCE (1979)

At 3:	Won	Alabama Stakes
At 4:	2nd	Top Flight Handicap
	3rd	Delaware Handicap

BROTHER (1980)

At 3:	3rd	American Derby

BROTHER BROWN (1990)

At 4:	3rd	Oaklawn Handicap

BROTHER TEX (1952)

At 2:	Won	Breeders' Futurity

BROUGHT TO MIND (1987)

At 4:	Won	Milady Handicap
		Vanity Handicap
	3rd	Breeders' Cup Distaff

BROWN BERRY (1960)

At 2:	Won	Del Mar Debutante Stakes

BROWN BESS (1982)

At 7:	Won	Yellow Ribbon Stakes
At 8:	Won	Santa Barbara Handicap

BROWNIAN (1944)

At 4:	2nd	Arlington Matron Handicap
At 5:	2nd	Black Helen Handicap

BROWN MOGUL (1943)

At 4:	2nd	Metropolitan Handicap

BROWN MOGUL *(Continued)*
3rd New Orleans Handicap
Roseben Handicap

BRUCE'S MILL (1991)
At 3: 2nd Molson Export Million
3rd Meadowlands Cup Handicap

BRUHO (1986)
At 2: 2nd Del Mar Futurity

BRUISER (1983)
At 3: 3rd Hollywood Derby
At 4: 3rd San Antonio Handicap

BRUNSWICK (1989)
At 4: Won Whitney Handicap
3rd Jockey Club Gold Cup

BRUSH BURN (1949)
At 4: 2nd United Nations Handicap
3rd Arlington Handicap
At 5: 2nd Arlington Handicap
3rd Washington D.C. International

BRUTALLY FRANK (1994)
At 6: Won Carter Handicap

BRYAN G. (1947)
At 4: Won Aqueduct Handicap
Westchester Handicap
Pimlico Special
2nd Vosburgh Handicap
At 5: Won Aqueduct Handicap
2nd San Carlos Handicap
3rd San Juan Capistrano Handicap
At 6: 2nd Excelsior Handicap

B. THOUGHTFUL (1975)
At 2: Won Oak Leaf Stakes
At 3: Won Hollywood Oaks
3rd Ramona Handicap
At 4: Won La Canada Stakes

BUBBLEWIN (1972)
At 2: Won Del Mar Debutante Stakes

BUBBLEY (1950)
At 3: Won Kentucky Oaks
At 4: Won Vanity Handicap

BUCHANETTE (1979)
At 3: 2nd Bay Meadows Handicap

BUCKAROO (1975)
At 3: 2nd Dwyer Handicap
Whitney Stakes

BUCKFINDER (1974)
At 4: 2nd Metropolitan Handicap

BUCKHAR (1988)
At 5: Won Budweiser International Stakes

BUCKLE DOWN BEN (1998)
At 2: 3rd Remsen Stakes

BUCK'N GEE (1950)
At 3: 2nd Ohio Derby

BUCKPASSER (1963)
At 2: Won Sapling Stakes
Hopeful Stakes
Arlington-Washington Futurity
Champagne Stakes
2nd Futurity Stakes
At 3: Won Everglades Stakes
Flamingo Stakes
Arlington Classic
American Derby
Travers Stakes
Lawrence Realization Stakes
Brooklyn Handicap
Woodward Stakes
Jockey Club Gold Cup
At 4: Won Metropolitan Handicap
Suburban Handicap
San Fernando Stakes
2nd Brooklyn Handicap
Woodward Stakes
3rd Bowling Green Handicap

BUCKPOINT (1976)
At 4: 2nd Canadian International Championship
At 5: 3rd Pan American Handicap
Hialeah Turf Cup

BUCK RUN (1966)
At 2: 3rd Saratoga Special

BUCK'S BID (1971)
At 3: 2nd Louisiana Derby
3rd Florida Derby

BUCK'S BOY (1993)
At 5: Won Turf Classic
Breeders' Cup Turf
2nd Man o' War Stakes
3rd Manhattan Handicap
At 6: 3rd Breeders' Cup Turf

BUCK THE SYSTEM (1969)
At 2: 3rd Sanford Stakes

BUCK TROUT (1996)
At 2: Won Norfolk Stakes

BUDDHA (1999)
At 3: Won Wood Memorial Stakes

BUDDY (1954)
At 2: 3rd Washington Park Futurity

BUDDY GIL (2000)
At 3: Won Santa Anita Derby

BUDROYALE (1993)
At 6: 2nd Californian Stakes
Sempra Energy Hollywood Gold Cup
Breeders' Cup Classic
At 7: Won San Antonio Handicap
2nd Santa Anita Handicap

BUFFALO LARK (1970)
At 3: 3rd American Derby
At 4: Won Arlington Handicap
2nd Hawthorne Gold Cup
At 5: Won Pan American Handicap
2nd Hawthorne Gold Cup
3rd Gulfstream Park Handicap
Arlington Handicap
Hialeah Turf Cup
Oak Tree Invitational Stakes

BUFFLE (1963)
At 3: Won Suburban Handicap
2nd Belmont Stakes
Brooklyn Handicap
3rd Wood Memorial Stakes
Dwyer Handicap
Travers Stakes
Woodward Stakes

BUFFYTHECENTERFOLD (2000)
At 3: 3rd La Brea Stakes

BUG BRUSH (1955)
At 3: Won Kentucky Oaks
At 4: Won Santa Margarita Handicap
San Antonio Handicap
Inglewood Handicap
At 5: 3rd Top Flight Handicap

BUGGED (1965)
At 2: Won Garden State Stakes

BUG JUICE (1943)
At 5: 2nd Miami Beach Handicap
3rd Widener Handicap
Monmouth Handicap
At 6: 3rd Queens County Handicap

BUGLEDRUMS (1948)
At 2: 2nd Arlington Futurity

BUILT FOR PLEASURE (1993)
At 3: Won Fountain of Youth Stakes

BULLET BLADE (1983)
At 2: 3rd Hopeful Stakes

BULL INTHE HEATHER (1990)
At 3: Won Florida Derby
2nd Flamingo Stakes

BULL REIGH (1938)
At 8: 3rd San Pasqual Handicap

BULL STRENGTH (1954)
At 4: Won Fall Highweight Handicap

BULVERDE (1948)
At 3: 2nd Louisiana Derby

BUNDLER (1971)
At 2: Won Frizette Stakes

BUNNY'S BABE (1952)
At 2: 3rd Cowdin Stakes

BUNTING (1991)
At 3: 2nd Ashland Stakes

BUOY (1985)
At 3: 3rd Fountain of Youth Stakes

BUPERS (1961)
At 2: Won Futurity Stakes
2nd Cowdin Stakes
3rd Champagne Stakes
Pimlico Futurity

BURD ALANE (1967)
At 3: 3rd Flamingo Stakes

BUREAUCRACY (1954)
At 3: Won Dwyer Handicap
2nd Travers Stakes
Jerome Handicap

BURMA CHARM (1954)
At 2: 3rd Sapling Stakes

BURNING DREAM (1942)
At 4: 3rd Brooklyn Handicap
At 5: Won American Handicap
2nd Hollywood Gold Cup
Sunset Handicap

BURNING ON (1968)
At 5: 3rd John B. Campbell Handicap

BURNING ROMA (1998)
At 2: Won Futurity Stakes
At 3: 3rd Haskell Invitational Handicap
At 4: 3rd Carter Handicap

BURNT HILLS (1987)
At 3: 2nd Wood Memorial Stakes
3rd Gotham Stakes

BURRA SAHIB (1943)
At 3: Won Will Rogers Handicap

BURYYOURBELIEF (1984)
At 3: Won Kentucky Oaks
2nd Santa Anita Oaks

BUSANDA (1947)
At 2: 3rd Selima Stakes
At 3: Won Alabama Stakes
2nd Delaware Oaks
3rd Coaching Club American Oaks
At 4: Won Top Flight Handicap
New Castle Handicap
Suburban Handicap
3rd Manhattan Handicap

BUSHEL-N-PECK (1958)
At 3: Won Cinema Handicap
3rd Hollywood Derby

BUSHER'S BEAUTY (1958)
At 2: 3rd Breeders' Futurity

BUSH FLEET (1969)
At 5: 3rd Pan American Handicap

BUSHIDO (1966)
At 2: 3rd Hopeful Stakes
At 3: Won Grey Lag Handicap
At 4: 2nd John B. Campbell Handicap
At 5: Won John B. Campbell Handicap

BUSHONGO (1971)
At 3: Won Flamingo Stakes

BUTTEVANT (1951)
At 3: 2nd Withers Stakes

BUT WHY NOT (1944)
At 3: Won Pimlico Oaks
Acorn Stakes
Alabama Stakes
Arlington Matron Stakes
Beldame Handicap
Arlington Classic
2nd Ladies Handicap
Dwyer Stakes
At 5: Won Firenze Handicap
Top Flight Handicap
2nd Comely Handicap
Suburban Handicap
3rd Metropolitan Handicap
At 6: 3rd Santa Margarita Handicap

BUY THE FIRM (1986)
At 4: 2nd Ladies Handicap
3rd Beldame Stakes
At 5: Won Top Flight Handicap
3rd Hempstead Handicap

BUY THE SPORT (2000)
At 3: Won Gazelle Handicap
3rd Beldame Stakes

BUZFUZ (1942)
At 4: 3rd Fall Highweight Handicap
At 6: 3rd Roseben Handicap

BUZKASHI (1967)
At 5: Won American Handicap

BUZZAROUND (1943)
At 3: 3rd Kentucky Oaks

BUZZ MY BELL (1981)
At 2: 2nd Selima Stakes
3rd Matron Stakes

BY JEEPERS (1951)
At 2: 2nd Remsen Handicap

BY LAND BY SEA (1984)
At 4: Won Apple Blossom Handicap
2nd La Canada Stakes

BYMEABOND (1942)
At 5: 2nd Longacres Mile
Golden Gate Handicap

BYNODERM (1973)
At 3: 3rd Cinema Handicap

BYWAYOFCHICAGO (1974)
At 4: Won Bay Meadows Handicap

BY ZEUS (1950)
At 3: 3rd Dwyer Stakes
At 4: Won San Juan Capistrano Handicap
2nd Santa Anita Maturity

CABILDO (1963)
At 4: Won New Orleans Handicap
At 5: 2nd New Orleans Handicap
Hawthorne Gold Cup

CABIN (1967)
At 6: 3rd Santa Anita Handicap

CABLE (1943)
At 3: 3rd Belmont Stakes

CACOETHES (1986)
At 4: Won Turf Classic

CACTUS ROAD (1977)
At 3: 3rd Hollywood Derby
Super Derby

CAD (1978)
At 5: 2nd Hawthorne Gold Cup

CADILLACING (1984)
At 4: 3rd Top Flight Handicap

CADILLAC WOMEN (1989)
At 2: 2nd Arlington-Washington Lassie Stakes
3rd Breeders' Cup Juvenile Fillies

CADIZ (1956)
At 6: Won Californian Stakes
3rd Hollywood Gold Cup
Washington Park Handicap
At 7: Won Hollywood Gold Cup
3rd Sunset Handicap

CAESAR (1986)
At 3: 3rd Ohio Derby

CAESAR'S WISH (1975)
At 2: Won Demoiselle Stakes
At 3: Won Mother Goose Stakes
2nd Coaching Club American Oaks

CAFFE LATTE (1996)
At 3: 2nd Yellow Ribbon Stakes
At 4: Won Ramona Handicap

CAGNEY (1997)
At 4: 3rd Clement L. Hirsch Mem. Turf Champ.
At 6: 3rd Charles Whittingham Handicap

CAHILL ROAD (1988)
At 3: Won Wood Memorial Stakes

CAJUN (1949)
At 2: Won Pimlico Futurity

CAJUN BEAT (2000)
At 3: Won Breeders' Cup Sprint

CALAIS II (1955)
At 4: 3rd Canadian Championship Stakes

CALANDRITO (1965)
At 4: Won Michigan Mile and One-Eighth

CALIFORNIA KID (1954)
At 2: 2nd Washington Park Futurity

CALINE (1976)
At 2: 2nd Oak Leaf Stakes
At 3: Won Santa Susana Stakes
2nd Fantasy Stakes

CALL BELL (1945)
At 3: 2nd San Vicente Handicap
Santa Anita Derby

CALL CARD (1957)
At 4: 2nd Arlington Matron Handicap

CALLER I.D. (1989)
At 2: Won Arlington-Washington Futurity
3rd Hopeful Stakes

CALLER ONE (1997)
At 3: 2nd Malibu Stakes
At 4: 3rd Penske Auto Center BC Sprint

CALL ME MR. VAIN (1994)
At 5: 2nd Philip H. Iselin Handicap

CALL ME PRINCE (1965)
At 3: Won Withers Stakes
3rd Belmont Stakes

CALL NOW (1992)
At 2: 2nd Oak Leaf Stakes

CALL OVER (1947)
At 4: Won Trenton Handicap
3rd Pimlico Special

CALTECH (1986)
At 3: Won Budweiser International Stakes

CAMARADO (1975)
At 4: 3rd Gamely Handicap

CAMARGO (1944)
At 2: 2nd Marguerite Stakes
At 3: Won Delaware Oaks
2nd Vineland Handicap
3rd Arlington Matron Handicap
Beldame Handicap
At 4: Won Molly Pitcher Handicap

CAM AXE (1970)
At 2: 2nd Frizette Stakes

CAME HOME (1999)
At 2: Won Hopeful Stakes
At 3: Won Santa Anita Derby
Swaps Stakes
Pacific Classic

CAMPAGNARDE (1987)
At 5: 3rd Yellow Ribbon Stakes

CAMPION KID (1965)
At 3: 3rd Ohio Derby

CAMPSIE FELLS (2000)
At 3: 3rd Garden City Breeders' Cup Handicap

CANADEL (1963)
At 4: 2nd Canadian International Championship

CANADIANA (1950)
At 3: 2nd Gazelle Handicap
Comely Handicap
At 4: Won Vagrancy Handicap

CANADIAN B. (1961)
At 3: 3rd San Fernando Stakes

CANADIAN FACTOR (1980)
At 4: 2nd Suburban Handicap
3rd Marlboro Cup Handicap

CANDALITA (1962)
At 2: Won Spinaway Stakes
Matron Stakes

CANDI'S GOLD (1984)
At 3: 2nd Swaps Stakes
Super Derby
At 4: 2nd San Fernando Stakes
Charles H. Strub Stakes

CANDLE WOOD (1949)
At 2: Won Garden State Stakes

CANDYEAN (1962)
At 2: 2nd Del Mar Debutante Stakes

CANDY ECLAIR (1976)
At 2: Won Selima Stakes

CANDY KANE (1945)
At 3: 3rd Santa Susana Stakes

CANDY RIDE (1999)
At 4: Won Pacific Classic

CANDY SPOTS (1960)
At 2: Won Arlington-Washington Futurity
At 3: Won Santa Anita Derby
Florida Derby
Preakness Stakes
Jersey Derby
American Derby
Arlington Classic
2nd Belmont Stakes
3rd Kentucky Derby
At 5: 2nd San Antonio Handicap
Santa Anita Handicap

CANEBORA (1960)
At 4: 2nd Canadian Championship Stakes

CANINA (1941)
At 5: Won Santa Margarita Handicap
2nd Inglewood Handicap
3rd Del Mar Handicap
At 7: 3rd Vanity Handicap

CANNONADE (1971)
At 2: 3rd Champagne Stakes
At 3: Won Kentucky Derby
2nd Florida Derby
3rd Preakness Stakes
Belmont Stakes

CANONERO II (1968)
At 3: Won Kentucky Derby
Preakness Stakes
At 4: 2nd Carter Handicap

CAN TRUST (1955)
At 2: 2nd Breeders' Futurity
Kentucky Jockey Club Stakes

CANVASSER (1972)
At 3: 3rd Ohio Derby

CAPADES (1986)
At 2: Won Selima Stakes
At 3: 2nd Flower Bowl Handicap
At 4: 2nd Caesars International Handicap

CAPEADOR (1950)
At 4: Won Tropical Handicap
3rd New Orleans Handicap
Excelsior Handicap
Dixie Handicap
At 5: 2nd Widener Handicap
Hialeah Turf Handicap

CAPELET (1954)
At 2: Won Frizette Stakes

CAPE TOWN (1995)
At 3: Won Florida Derby
3rd Toyota Blue Grass Stakes

CAPICHI (1980)
At 3: 2nd Santa Susana Stakes

CAPITAL IDEA (1973)
At 4: 2nd Amory L. Haskell Handicap

CAPITOL SOUTH (1981)
At 2: Won Hopeful Stakes

CAPONOSTRO (1990)
At 2: 3rd Futurity Stakes

CAPOT (1946)
At 2: Won Champagne Stakes
Pimlico Futurity
At 3: Won Preakness Stakes
Belmont Stakes
Jerome Handicap
Pimlico Special
2nd Kentucky Derby
3rd Wood Memorial Stakes
Grey Lag Handicap

CAPOTE (1984)
At 2: Won Norfolk Stakes
Breeders' Cup Juvenile

CAPOTE BELLE (1993)
At 4: 3rd Frank J. De Francis Memorial Dash

CAPS AND BELLS (1958)
At 2: 2nd Arlington Lassie Stakes

CAPTAIN BODGIT (1994)
At 3: Won Florida Derby
Wood Memorial Stakes
2nd Kentucky Derby
3rd Fountain of Youth Stakes
Preakness Stakes

CAPTAIN CEE JAY (1970)
At 5: 2nd Hollywood Invitational Handicap
Sunset Handicap

CAPTAIN PHIL (1974)
At 5: 3rd Louisiana Downs Handicap

CAPTAIN'S GIG (1965)
At 2: Won Futurity Stakes
3rd Champagne Stakes
At 3: 2nd Jersey Derby
Jerome Handicap

CAPTAIN SQUIRE (1999)
At 4: 2nd Ancient Title Breeders' Cup Handicap

CAPTAIN STEVE (1997)
At 2: Won Lane's End Breeders' Futurity
Hollywood Futurity
3rd Del Mar Futurity
At 3: Won Swaps Stakes
2nd Haskell Invitational Handicap
3rd Santa Anita Derby
Breeders' Cup Classic
At 4: Won Donn Handicap

CAPTAIN VALID (1984)
At 2: 3rd Futurity Stakes

CAPT. DON (1975)
At 3: 2nd California Derby
At 4: 3rd Bay Meadows Handicap

CARA RAFAELA (1993)
At 2: Won Hollywood Starlet Stakes
2nd Matron Stakes
Breeders' Cup Juvenile Fillies
At 3: 2nd Las Virgenes Stakes
Santa Anita Oaks
Ashland Stakes
3rd Kentucky Oaks
Mother Goose Stakes

CARDINAL GEORGE (1972)
At 2: 3rd Hopeful Stakes

CARDMANIA (1986)
At 7: Won Breeders' Cup Sprint
At 8: 3rd Breeders' Cup Sprint

CARD TABLE (1970)
At 3: 3rd Cinema Handicap

CAREER BOY (1953)
At 2: 2nd Hopeful Stakes
Garden State Stakes
At 3: Won Gotham Stakes
United Nations Handicap
2nd Blue Grass Stakes
Belmont Stakes

CAREER COLLECTION (1995)
At 2: 2nd Breeders' Cup Juvenile Fillies
Hollywood Starlet Stakes

CARELESS JOHN (1957)
At 3: 2nd Jerome Handicap

CARESSING (1998)
At 2: Won Breeders' Cup Juvenile Fillies

CAR GAL (1988)
At 3: 3rd Coaching Club American Oaks

CARIELLOR (1981)
At 4: 3rd Oak Tree Invitational Stakes

CARMELITA GIBBS (1973)
At 3: 3rd Kentucky Oaks

CARNEGIE (1991)
At 4: 3rd Breeders' Cup Turf

CARNEY'S POINT (1969)
At 5: 3rd Canadian International Championship
At 6: 3rd Canadian International Championship

CARO BAMBINO (1975)
At 5: 3rd Californian Stakes
Hollywood Gold Cup

CAROLINA COMMAND (1978)
At 2: 3rd Selima Stakes

CAROLINA QUEEN (1948)
At 2: Won Marguerite Stakes

CAROLYN A. (1944)
At 2: Won Demoiselle Stakes
2nd Frizette Stakes
At 3: Won Louisiana Derby
2nd Wood Memorial Stakes
At 4: Won Firenze Handicap
3rd Comely Handicap
New Orleans Handicap

CAROTENE (1983)
At 3: 3rd Yellow Ribbon Stakes
At 4: Won Yellow Ribbon Stakes
At 5: 2nd Santa Barbara Handicap
3rd San Juan Capistrano Handicap
Sword Dancer Handicap

CARPENTER'S RULE (1962)
At 5: 3rd Michigan Mile and One-Eighth

CARRARA MARBLE (1945)
At 2: 2nd Breeders' Futurity

CARR DE NASKRA (1981)
At 3: Won Jim Dandy Stakes
Travers Stakes
2nd Marlboro Cup Handicap
At 4: 2nd Suburban Handicap
Whitney Handicap
Monmouth Handicap

CARRIELLE (1995)
At 2: 3rd Matron Stakes

CARRIER X. (1955)
At 3: Won San Felipe Handicap

CARRY A TUNE (1979)
At 3: 3rd Santa Susana Stakes

CARRY BACK (1958)
At 2: Won Cowdin Stakes
Garden State Stakes
Remsen Stakes
3rd Sapling Stakes
At 3: Won Everglades Stakes
Flamingo Stakes
Florida Derby
Kentucky Derby
Preakness Stakes
Jerome Handicap
Trenton Handicap
2nd Wood Memorial Stakes
3rd Lawrence Realization Stakes
Woodward Stakes
At 4: Won Metropolitan Handicap
Monmouth Handicap
Whitney Stakes
2nd Seminole Handicap
Widener Handicap
Grey Lag Handicap
Trenton Handicap
3rd New Orleans Handicap
Gulfstream Park Handicap
Washington D.C. International
At 5: Won Trenton Handicap
3rd United Nations Handicap

CARRY THE NEWS (1950)
At 5: 3rd Arlington Matron Handicap

CARSON HOLLOW (1999)
At 3: Won Prioress Stakes
2nd Test Stakes

CARTERET (1958)
At 6: Won Hialeah Turf Cup
3rd Arlington Handicap

CARVIN II (1962)
At 3: 2nd Washington D.C. International

CASA CAMARA (1944)
At 4: 3rd Vagrancy Handicap

CASCANUEZ (1948)
At 7: Won Bougainvillea Turf Handicap

CASCAPEDIA (1973)
At 4: Won Vanity Handicap
2nd Hollywood Gold Cup
3rd Ruffian Handicap
Del Mar Handicap

CASE GOODS (1951)
At 2: 2nd Frizette Stakes
3rd Demoiselle Stakes

CASEMATE (1947)
At 2: 2nd Garden State Stakes
At 4: Won Metropolitan Handicap

CASEY TIBBS (1994)
At 3: 2nd Secretariat Stakes

CASH DEAL (1998)
At 2: 3rd Walmac International Alcibiades Stakes

CASHIER'S DREAM (1999)
At 2: Won Spinaway Stakes
2nd Frizette Stakes

CASH RUN (1997)
At 2: Won Breeders' Cup Juvenile Fillies
3rd Walmac International Alcibiades Stakes

CASSALERIA (1979)
At 2: 2nd Hollywood Futurity
At 3: 3rd San Felipe Handicap
California Derby
Swaps Stakes

CASSIE RED (1967)
At 3: 3rd Florida Derby

CASSIS (1939)
At 7: Won Fall Highweight Handicap

CASTILLA (1979)
At 3: Won Yellow Ribbon Stakes
Matriarch Stakes
At 4: 2nd Ramona Handicap
Matriarch Stakes

CASTLE FORBES (1961)
At 2: Won Sorority Stakes
Gardenia Stakes
3rd Arlington-Washington Lassie Stakes
Frizette Stakes
At 3: Won Acorn Stakes
2nd Coaching Club American Oaks
Monmouth Oaks
3rd Alabama Stakes
Beldame Stakes

CASTLE ROYALE (1978)
At 4: 2nd Hialeah Turf Cup

CAST PARTY (1980)
At 2: Won Laurel Futurity

CASUAL (1979)
At 2: 3rd Alcibiades Stakes

CASUAL FRIEND (1954)
At 4: 2nd Display Handicap

CASUAL LIES (1989)
At 2: 3rd Hollywood Futurity
At 3: 2nd Kentucky Derby
3rd Santa Anita Derby
Preakness Stakes

CASUAL LOOK (2000)
At 3: 3rd Queen Elizabeth II Challenge Cup

CATALAN (1974)
At 3: 3rd Wood Memorial Stakes

CATANE (1982)
At 3: 3rd Hollywood Derby

CATAPULT (1957)
At 2: 3rd Pimlico Futurity

CATATONIC (1982)
At 5: 3rd Delaware Handicap

CAT BRIDGE (1942)
At 4: Won Bougainvillea Handicap
3rd Gulfstream Handicap

CATELLA (1996)
At 4: 3rd Breeders' Cup Filly and Mare Turf

CATERMAN (1976)
At 5: 2nd Hollywood Gold Cup
Hollywood Invitational Handicap
Sunset Handicap
At 6: 2nd Hollywood Turf Cup

CAT GIRL (1978)
At 4: 3rd Vanity Handicap

CATHERINE'S BET (1975)
At 4: 2nd Ladies Handicap

CATHY HONEY (1967)
At 3: Won Acorn Stakes
Ladies Handicap
2nd Santa Susana Stakes
Mother Goose Stakes
Coaching Club American Oaks
At 4: 2nd Top Flight Handicap
3rd Beldame Stakes
Delaware Handicap

CATHY'S REJECT (1974)
At 3: 2nd California Derby

CATIENUS (1994)
At 5: 2nd Suburban Handicap
3rd Whitney Handicap

CATINCA (1995)
At 3: 3rd Test Stakes
At 4: Won Ruffian Handicap
3rd Hempstead Handicap
Ballerina Handicap
Beldame Stakes

CATMOUSAM ROAD (1969)
At 2: 3rd Gardenia Stakes

CAT'S AT HOME (1997)
At 5: Won Philip H. Iselin Handicap

CAT'S CRADLE (1992)
At 3: Won Acorn Stakes
2nd Las Virgenes Stakes
At 5: 2nd Santa Maria Handicap

CAT THIEF (1996)
At 2: Won Lane's End Breeders' Futurity
3rd Breeders' Cup Juvenile
At 3: Won Swaps Stakes
Breeders' Cup Classic
2nd Fountain of Youth Stakes
Toyota Blue Grass Stakes
Haskell Invitational Handicap
3rd Florida Derby
Kentucky Derby
Malibu Stakes
At 4: 2nd San Antonio Handicap
Whitney Handicap
3rd Oaklawn Handicap

CAUCASUS (1972)
At 4: Won Sunset Handicap
Manhattan Handicap
2nd Hollywood Invitational Handicap
3rd American Handicap
At 5: Won San Luis Rey Stakes
2nd Hollywood Invitational Handicap
3rd Hollywood Gold Cup
San Juan Capistrano Handicap

CAVALANCHE (1959)
At 2: 3rd Saratoga Special

CAVAMORE (1965)
At 4: Won San Fernando Stakes
3rd Charles H. Strub Stakes

CAVAN (1955)
At 3: Won Belmont Stakes

CAVEAT (1980)
At 2: 2nd Breeders' Futurity
At 3: Won Belmont Stakes
2nd Arkansas Derby
3rd Kentucky Derby

CAVONNIER (1993)
At 2: 3rd Del Mar Futurity
At 3: Won Santa Anita Derby
2nd Kentucky Derby
3rd San Felipe Stakes

CAVORT (1952)
At 3: 2nd Roamer Handicap
Gallant Fox Handicap
At 5: 2nd Manhattan Handicap

CEDAR KEY (1960)
At 3: Won Dixie Handicap
At 4: Won San Juan Capistrano Handicap
Donn Handicap
At 5: Won San Luis Rey Handicap
At 6: Won San Luis Rey Handicap
2nd Pan American Handicap

CEE'S TIZZY (1987)
At 3: 3rd Super Derby

CEFIS (1985)
At 3: Won Pennsylvania Derby
3rd Flamingo Stakes
Jersey Derby

CELLIST (1970)
At 3: 2nd Hollywood Oaks

CELLYAR (1956)
At 3: 3rd Vanity Handicap

CELTIC ARMS (1991)
At 4: 2nd Caesars International Handicap
3rd Turf Classic

CELTIC ASH (1957)
At 3: Won Belmont Stakes
3rd Preakness Stakes
Jersey Derby

CELTIC MELODY (1998)
At 4: Won Humana Distaff Handicap

CENTENNIAL PRIDE (1974)
At 4: 3rd San Fernando Stakes

CENTRAL PARIS (1969)
At 2: 2nd Breeders' Futurity

CENTURY (1963)
At 2: Won Del Mar Debutante Stakes

CENTURY CITY (1999)
At 4: 3rd NetJets Breeders' Cup Mile

CENTURY'S ENVOY (1971)
At 2: Won Hollywood Juvenile Championship
At 4: 2nd San Fernando Stakes
3rd Californian Stakes

CERISE REINE (1950)
At 3: Won Delaware Oaks
2nd Kentucky Oaks
At 4: Won Santa Margarita Handicap
3rd Santa Anita Maturity

CERTAIN (1996)
At 3: Won Arkansas Derby
3rd Fountain of Youth Stakes

CERTAIN ROMAN (1973)
At 3: 2nd Blue Grass Stakes

C'EST L'AMOUR (1997)
At 3: 2nd Acorn Stakes

CETEWAYO (1994)
At 4: Won Sword Dancer Invitational Handicap
2nd Turf Classic
At 7: 3rd Turf Classic
At 8: Won Gulfstream Park BC Handicap

CHAIN BRACELET (1977)
At 4: Won Top Flight Handicap

CHAINS (1945)
At 4: Won Dixie Handicap
2nd Trenton Handicap
3rd New York Handicap

CHALK FACE (1971)
At 2: 2nd Oak Leaf Stakes

CHALLE ANNE (1945)
At 3: Won Kentucky Oaks
3rd Coaching Club American Oaks

CHALLENGE ME (1941)
At 5: 2nd Washington Park Handicap
At 6: 3rd Arlington Handicap

CHALLENGE MY DUTY (1987)
At 3: 2nd Pennsylvania Derby

CHALLTACK (1949)
At 2: 2nd Del Mar Futurity

CHALVEDELE (1957)
At 3: 2nd Mother Goose Stakes

CHAMPAGNE CHARLIE (1970)
At 3: 2nd Gotham Stakes

CHAMPAGNEFORASHLEY (1987)
At 3: 3rd Wood Memorial Stakes

CHAMPAGNE GLOW (1988)
At 2: 2nd Frizette Stakes

CHAMPION LODGE (1997)
At 6: 3rd San Juan Capistrano Handicap

CHAMROUSSE (1999)
At 3: 2nd Mother Goose Stakes

CHANCE DANCER (1975)
At 3: 2nd San Felipe Handicap

CHANGE FORA DOLLAR (1992)
At 2: 2nd Frizette Stakes
At 3: 3rd Coaching Club American Oaks

CHANLEA (1950)
At 2: 2nd Del Mar Futurity
3rd Starlet Stakes
At 3: Won San Anita Derby
2nd San Felipe Handicap

CHAPEL OF DREAMS (1984)
At 4: 2nd Gamely Handicap

CHAPEL ROYAL (2001)
At 2: 2nd Hopeful Stakes
Champagne Stakes
3rd Bessemer Trust Breeders' Cup Juvenile

CHAPOSA SPRINGS (1992)
At 3: Won Test Stakes
2nd Top Flight Handicap

CHARACTER (1988)
At 3: 3rd Arlington Classic

CHARGERETTE (1969)
At 2: 3rd Del Mar Debutante Stakes
At 3: 3rd Santa Susana Stakes

CHARGER'S KIN (1962)
At 2: Won Hollywood Juvenile Championship
At 3: 3rd Santa Anita Derby
Cinema Handicap

CHARGER'S STAR (1970)
At 5: 3rd Ramona Handicap
At 6: 3rd Santa Margarita Handicap
At 7: 3rd Santa Barbara Handicap

CHARISMATIC (1996)
At 3: Won Kentucky Derby
Preakness Stakes
3rd Belmont Stakes

CHARLATAN III (1985)
At 5: 3rd Californian Stakes

CHARLES ELLIOTT (1964)
At 6: 2nd Amory L. Haskell Handicap

CHARLESTON RAG (1982)
At 2: Won Frizette Stakes

CHARLIE BARLEY (1986)
At 3: 2nd Hollywood Derby
3rd Rothmans International Stakes

CHARLIE JR. (1966)
At 4: Won Oaklawn Handicap

CHARLIE MCADAM (1949)
At 3: Won Flamingo Stakes

CHARMING DUKE (1982)
At 3: Won Hollywood Derby

CHARMING ROOK (1981)
At 3: 3rd Blue Grass Stakes

CHARMING STORY (1974)
At 3: 3rd Beldame Stakes
Ladies Handicap

CHARON (1987)
At 3: Won Coaching Club American Oaks
2nd Ashland Stakes
Mother Goose Stakes
Alabama Stakes
At 4: 2nd Apple Blossom Handicap

CHART THE STARS (1984)
At 3: Won San Felipe Handicap

CHATEAUGAY (1960)
At 3: Won Blue Grass Stakes
Kentucky Derby
Belmont Stakes
Jerome Handicap
2nd Preakness Stakes
3rd Dwyer Handicap
Travers Stakes

CHAUFFEUR (1969)
At 2: 2nd Sapling Stakes

CHEAP SHADES (1989)
At 2: 3rd Remsen Stakes

CHEAPSKATE (1983)
At 3: 2nd Super Derby
3rd Arlington Classic

CHECK BYE (1963)
At 4: 3rd Santa Barbara Handicap

CHEERY KNIGHT (1990)
At 3: 2nd Molson Export Million

CHELSEA BARRACKS (1996)
At 4: 3rd San Juan Capistrano Handicap

CHELSEY FLOWER (1991)
At 5: Won Flower Bowl Invitational Handicap

CHENIN BLANC (1986)
At 6: 2nd Caesars International Handicap

CHERIEPE (1970)
At 5: Won San Antonio Stakes

CHEROKEE COLONY (1985)
At 2: 2nd Young America Stakes
At 3: Won Flamingo Stakes
3rd Wood Memorial Stakes
At 4: 3rd San Antonio Handicap

CHEROKEE FROLIC (1978)
At 2: 3rd Sorority Stakes

CHEROKEE MISS (1957)
At 2: 3rd Del Mar Debutante Stakes

CHEROKEE ROSE (1951)
At 3: Won Coaching Club American Oaks

CHEROKEE RUN (1990)
At 3: Won Dwyer Stakes
2nd Preakness Stakes
At 4: Won Breeders' Cup Sprint
2nd Metropolitan Handicap
3rd Carter Handicap
Vosburgh Stakes

CHERRY FIZZ (1950)
At 3: 3rd Alabama Stakes

CHERRY LAUREL (1959)
At 2: 2nd Arlington Lassie Stakes

CHERRY SUNDAE (1967)
At 2: 2nd Frizette Stakes

CHESTER HOUSE (1995)
At 5: Won Arlington Million
2nd Eddie Read Handicap

CHEVAL VOLANT (1987)
At 2: Won Hollywood Starlet Stakes

CHEVATION (1951)
At 3: 3rd Travers Stakes
At 4: 2nd United Nations Handicap
3rd Whitney Stakes
At 5: Won Dixie Handicap
2nd Bougainvillea Turf Handicap

CHEVRON FLIGHT (1969)
At 2: Won Sapling Stakes
2nd Arlington-Washington Futurity
Futurity Stakes
Champagne Stakes

CHIAROSCURO (1978)
At 2: 2nd Norfolk Stakes

CHICHA (1958)
At 2: 2nd Del Mar Debutante Stakes

CHICLE II (1945)
At 5: Won Gulfstream Park Handicap
Trenton Handicap
Bougainvillea Handicap
2nd Gallant Fox Handicap
Pimlico Special
3rd Westchester Handicap
At 6: Won Bougainvillea Handicap

CHIC SHIRINE (1984)
At 3: 3rd Mother Goose Stakes

CHIEF BEARHART (1993)
At 3: 2nd Canadian International Championship
At 4: Won Canadian International Championship
Breeders' Cup Turf
At 5: Won Manhattan Handicap
2nd Canadian International Championship

CHIEF FANELLI (1950)
At 2: 3rd Sapling Stakes

CHIEF HAWK EAR (1968)
At 7: 3rd Hollywood Invitational Handicap

CHIEF HONCHO (1987)
At 3: Won Jim Dandy Stakes
At 4: 2nd Suburban Handicap
Whitney Handicap
Jockey Club Gold Cup
Brooklyn Handicap
3rd Gulfstream Park Handicap
Philip H. Iselin Handicap
At 5: Won Brooklyn Handicap
3rd Whitney Handicap

CHIEF OF CHIEFS (1957)
At 4: Won Carter Handicap
Washington Park Handicap

CHIEF OF DIXIELAND (1975)
At 3: 2nd Arkansas Derby
Arlington Classic

CHIEF PLANNER (2000)
At 2: 3rd Del Mar Futurity

CHIEF'S CROWN (1982)
At 2: Won Hopeful Stakes
Norfolk Stakes
Breeders' Cup Juvenile
2nd Futurity Stakes
At 3: Won Flamingo Stakes
Blue Grass Stakes
Travers Stakes
Marlboro Cup Handicap
2nd Preakness Stakes
3rd Kentucky Derby
Belmont Stakes
Woodward Stakes

CHIEF SEATTLE (1997)
At 2: 2nd Champagne Stakes
Breeders' Cup Juvenile

CHIEFTAN (1961)
At 2: Won Cowdin Stakes
2nd Arlington-Washington Futurity
At 4: Won Arlington Handicap
2nd Metropolitan Handicap
Washington Park Handicap
3rd Carter Handicap
United Nations Handicap

CHILE CHATTE (1993)
At 2: 3rd Hollywood Starlet Stakes
At 4: 2nd Milady Breeders' Cup Handicap

CHILLING THOUGHT (1979)
At 2: 2nd Alcibiades Stakes
3rd Frizette Stakes
Selima Stakes

CHILUKKI (1997)
At 2: Won Vinery Del Mar Debutante Stakes
Oak Leaf Stakes
2nd Breeders' Cup Juvenile Fillies

CHIMES BAND (1991)
At 3: 3rd Jim Beam Stakes

CHIMICHURRI (2000)
At 3: 2nd Prioress Stakes

CHINCHILLA (1958)
At 2: 3rd Saratoga Special
Hopeful Stakes

CHISELLING (1999)
At 3: Won Secretariat Stakes

CHOCTAW RIDGE (1989)
At 3: 3rd Flamingo Stakes

CHOKER (1960)
At 3: 3rd Belmont Stakes
At 5: Won Gallant Fox Handicap
2nd Vosburgh Handicap
Display Handicap

CHOMPION (1965)
At 3: Won Travers Stakes
2nd Monmouth Invitational Handicap
3rd Dwyer Handicap
Lawrence Realization Stakes
Jockey Club Gold Cup
Gallant Fox Handicap
At 4: 2nd Manhattan Handicap
3rd Massachusetts Handicap
Suburban Handicap
Amory L. Haskell Handicap
At 6: Won Pan American Handicap
Dixie Handicap
Massachusetts Handicap
2nd Manhattan Handicap
3rd United Nations Handicap
Washington D.C. International

CHOOSE A PARTNER (1980)
At 3: 3rd Fantasy Stakes

CHORUS KHAL (1951)
At 2: 2nd Princess Pat Stakes

CHORWON (1993)
At 6: 3rd Sword Dancer Invitational Handicap

CHOU CROUTE (1968)
At 3: Won Spinster Stakes
At 4: 2nd Spinster Stakes
3rd Beldame Stakes

CHRISAWAY (1968)
At 4: Won Del Mar Handicap

CHRIS EVERT (1971)
At 2: 2nd Frizette Stakes
At 3: Won Acorn Stakes
Mother Goose Stakes
Coaching Club American Oaks
2nd Alabama Stakes
3rd Travers Stakes

CHRISTIECAT (1987)
At 4: 3rd Flower Bowl Handicap
At 5: Won Flower Bowl Handicap

CHRISTINE'S OUTLAW (2000)
At 3: 3rd Arkansas Derby

CHRISTMAS PAST (1979)
At 3: Won Coaching Club American Oaks
Ruffian Handicap
2nd Mother Goose Stakes
3rd Jockey Club Gold Cup
At 4: Won Gulfstream Park Handicap

CHRISTOFORO (1971)
At 3: 3rd Jersey Derby

CHUMMING (1980)
At 2: 2nd Remsen Stakes
At 3: 2nd Flamingo Stakes

CICADA (1959)
At 2: Won Spinaway Stakes
Matron Stakes
Frizette Stakes
Gardenia Stakes
At 3: Won Kentucky Oaks
Acorn Stakes
Mother Goose Stakes
Beldame Stakes
2nd Coaching Club American Oaks
Delaware Handicap
Florida Derby
3rd Delaware Oaks
Alabama Stakes
At 4: 2nd Delaware Handicap
3rd Top Flight Handicap

CICERO'S COURT (1969)
At 4: 2nd San Luis Rey Handicap

CIGAR (1990)
At 4: Won NYRA Mile Handicap
At 5: Won Donn Handicap
Gulfstream Park Handicap
Oaklawn Handicap
Pimlico Special
Hollywood Gold Cup
Woodward Stakes
Jockey Club Gold Cup
Breeders' Cup Classic
At 6: Won Donn Handicap
Woodward Stakes
2nd Pacific Classic
Jockey Club Gold Cup
3rd Breeders' Cup Classic

CINDY'S HERO (1998)
At 2: Won Vinery Del Mar Debutante Stakes
3rd Oak Leaf Stakes

CINNAMON SUGAR (1991)
At 3: 2nd Acorn Stakes
Mother Goose Stakes
Gazelle Handicap

CIRCLE HOME (1972)
At 2: 3rd Remsen Stakes

CIRCLE OF LIFE (1997)
At 2: Won Spinaway Stakes
3rd Matron Stakes
At 3: 3rd Ashland Stakes

CIRCLE OF LIGHT (1993)
At 4: 3rd Brooklyn Handicap

CIRCUS PRINCE (1983)
At 5: 3rd Sunset Handicap
Oak Tree Invitational Stakes

CIRO (1997)
At 3: Won Secretariat Stakes

CISK (1974)
At 3: 3rd Illinois Derby

CITADEED (1992)
At 3: Won Peter Pan Stakes
3rd Belmont Stakes
Haskell Invitational Handicap

CITATION (1945)
At 2: Won Pimlico Futurity
Futurity Stakes
2nd Washington Park Futurity
At 3: Won Flamingo Stakes
Kentucky Derby
Preakness Stakes
Belmont Stakes
American Derby
Jockey Club Gold Cup
Stars and Stripes Handicap
Pimlico Special
At 5: 2nd San Antonio Handicap
Santa Anita Handicap
San Juan Capistrano Handicap
Golden Gate Handicap
At 6: Won American Handicap
Hollywood Gold Cup

CITIDANCER (1987)
At 3: 2nd Jerome Handicap

CITY BAND (1994)
At 2: Won Oak Leaf Stakes
2nd Hollywood Starlet Stakes

CITY GIRL (1971)
At 2: Won Alcibiades Stakes

CITY LINE (1960)
At 3: Won Louisiana Derby

CITY ZIP (1998)
At 2: Won Hopeful Stakes
2nd Futurity Stakes
At 3: 3rd Fountain of Youth Stakes
King's Bishop Stakes

CIVET (1953)
At 4: 3rd Display Handicap
At 5: Won Display Handicap
3rd Jockey Club Gold Cup

CIVIC GUARD (1957)
At 4: 2nd Donn Handicap
3rd Hialeah Turf Cup

CIVIC PRIDE (1956)
At 3: 3rd Cinema Handicap
At 4: 3rd San Fernando Stakes

CLABBER GIRL (1983)
At 4: 2nd Ruffian Handicap
Breeders' Cup Distaff
3rd Vanity Handicap
At 5: Won Top Flight Handicap
3rd Santa Margarita Handicap

CLAIRE MARINE (1985)
At 4: 2nd Gamely Handicap

CLANDESTINE (1955)
At 3: 2nd Withers Stakes
At 5: Won San Carlos Handicap
2nd Los Angeles Handicap

CLARET (1988)
At 4: 3rd Pacific Classic

CLARK COTTAGE (1988)
At 2: 3rd Matron Stakes

CLASH BY NIGHT (1993)
At 3: 3rd Ohio Derby

CLASSIC ACCOUNT (1985)
At 3: 3rd Illinois Derby

CLASSIC CAT (1995)
At 3: Won Ohio Derby
2nd Super Derby
3rd Preakness Stakes

CLASSIC CROWN (1985)
At 2: Won Frizette Stakes
At 3: 2nd Ruffian Handicap
Beldame Stakes

CLASSIC FAME (1986)
At 4: 2nd John Henry Handicap
At 6: 2nd Hollywood Turf Handicap

CLASSIC GO GO (1978)
At 3: 3rd Pennsylvania Derby

CLASS PLAY (1981)
At 3: Won Coaching Club American Oaks
3rd Alabama Stakes

CLASSY CARA (1997)
At 3: 3rd Santa Anita Oaks
Kentucky Oaks

CLASSY CATHY (1983)
At 3: Won Alabama Stakes
3rd Beldame Stakes

CLASSY MIRAGE (1990)
At 4: 3rd Beldame Stakes

CLASSY SURGEON (1973)
At 3: 2nd California Derby

CLEAN BILL (1973)
At 3: 3rd Jerome Handicap

CLEAR CHOICE (1983)
At 3: Won Swaps Stakes

CLEAR CHOICE *(Continued)*
Withers Stakes
2nd Peter Pan Stakes

CLEAR COPY (1971)
At 3: 2nd Acorn Stakes

CLEAR DAWN (1951)
At 2: 3rd Princess Pat Stakes
Matron Stakes
Selima Stakes
At 3: 2nd Monmouth Oaks
Vagrancy Handicap
3rd Beldame Handicap
At 4: 2nd Molly Pitcher Handicap
Arlington Matron Handicap
Beldame Handicap
3rd Delaware Handicap
Maskette Handicap
At 5: Won Black Helen Handicap

CLEAR MANDATE (1992)
At 4: Won Shuvee Handicap
3rd Beldame Stakes
At 5: Won John A. Morris Handicap
Three Chimneys Spinster Stakes
2nd Ruffian Handicap
3rd Go for Wand Stakes

CLEAR ROAD (1957)
At 3: 2nd Alabama Stakes

CLEM (1954)
At 3: Won Withers Stakes
Arlington Classic
3rd Gotham Stakes
At 4: Won Washington Park Handicap
Woodward Stakes
United Nations Handicap
2nd Suburban Handicap
Arlington Handicap
3rd Metropolitan Handicap
Massachusetts Handicap
Manhattan Handicap

CLEMANNA'S ROSE (1981)
At 6: 3rd Top Flight Handicap

CLEOFOSTA (1953)
At 3: 3rd California Derby

CLEONE (1989)
At 4: 3rd Budweiser International Stakes

CLEVER ALLEMONT (1982)
At 3: 3rd Arlington Classic

CLEVER PILOT (1994)
At 2: 2nd Oak Leaf Stakes

CLEVER SONG (1982)
At 4: 2nd John Henry Handicap

CLEV ER TELL (1974)
At 3: Won Louisiana Derby
Arkansas Derby

CLEVER TREVOR (1986)
At 3: 2nd Arkansas Derby
Travers Stakes

CLEVER TRICK (1976)
At 2: 3rd Laurel Futurity
At 3: 2nd Illinois Derby

CLIMBER (1967)
At 3: Won Ohio Derby

CLIQUOT (1996)
At 3: 3rd Wood Memorial Stakes

CLOSE ATTENTION (1966)
At 5: 3rd Massachusetts Handicap

CLOSE BY (1961)
At 2: 3rd Hollywood Juvenile Championship
At 3: Won Cinema Handicap
2nd Hollywood Derby
3rd Arlington Classic
American Derby
Michigan Mile and One-Sixteenth

CLOSED DOOR (1949)
At 5: Won United Nations Handicap
2nd Monmouth Handicap

CLOSED ESCROW (1993)
At 6: 3rd Santa Monica Handicap

CLOUDLAND (1967)
At 2: 3rd Alcibiades Stakes

CLOUDY DAWN (1969)
At 3: Won Dwyer Handicap
Arlington Park Handicap
3rd Belmont Stakes
Monmouth Invitational Handicap
At 4: 3rd Suburban Handicap
Hawthorne Gold Cup

CLOVER LANE (1967)
At 2: Won Arlington-Washington Lassie Stakes

COALTOWN (1945)
At 3: Won Blue Grass Stakes
Jerome Handicap
2nd Withers Stakes
Kentucky Derby
At 4: Won McLennan Handicap
Widener Handicap
Gulfstream Park Handicap
Gallant Fox Handicap
Stars and Stripes Handicap
Arlington Park Handicap
Washington Park Handicap
2nd Pimlico Special
At 5: 3rd McLennan Handicap

COALTOWN CAT (1967)
At 3: 3rd American Derby

COASTAL (1976)
At 3: Won Belmont Stakes
Dwyer Stakes
Monmouth Invitational Handicap
2nd Woodward Stakes
3rd Marlboro Cup Handicap
Jockey Club Gold Cup

COAX KID (2000)
At 2: 3rd Hollywood Futurity

COAX ME CHAD (1981)
At 3: 2nd Kentucky Derby

COAX ME MATT (1980)
At 2: 2nd Arlington-Washington Futurity

COBRA CLASSIC (1987)
At 5: 3rd San Antonio Handicap

COBUL (1956)
At 3: 2nd Acorn Stakes

COCHISE (1946)
At 4: Won Massachusetts Handicap
3rd Metropolitan Handicap
At 5: Won Grey Lag Handicap
Arlington Handicap
2nd Whitney Stakes

COCKEY MISS (1965)
At 2: 2nd Sorority Stakes

CODEX (1977)
At 3: Won Santa Anita Derby
Hollywood Derby
Preakness Stakes

CODIFIED (1990)
At 3: 3rd Swaps Stakes

COEUR DE LION (1984)
At 5: 3rd Hialeah Turf Cup

COGENCY (1978)
At 2: 3rd Norfolk Stakes

COHASSET TRIBE (1969)
At 2: Won Sanford Stakes

COHOES (1954)
At 2: 2nd Pimlico Futurity
3rd Hopeful Stakes
At 3: 2nd Withers Stakes
At 4: Won Brooklyn Handicap
Whitney Stakes
3rd Fall Highweight Handicap

CO HOST (1972)
At 5: 2nd Metropolitan Handicap

COINCIDENCE (1942)
At 4: Won Vosburgh Handicap
Aqueduct Handicap
At 5: Won Excelsior Handicap
3rd Grey Lag Handicap

COINED SILVER (1974)
At 3: Won Florida Derby

COJAK (1973)
At 3: 2nd Jersey Derby
Ohio Derby

COLD COMFORT (1967)
At 2: Won Matron Stakes
At 3: 2nd Acorn Stakes
3rd Beldame Stakes

COLD COMMAND (1949)
At 2: 2nd Cowdin Stakes
At 3: 2nd Blue Grass Stakes
At 4: Won Westchester Handicap
2nd Gallant Fox Handicap
Dixie Handicap
3rd Vosburgh Handicap
Suburban Handicap
At 5: 3rd Queens County Handicap
Brooklyn Handicap

COLD ROLL (1944)
At 3: 2nd Hollywood Oaks

COLFAX MAID (1958)
At 2: Won Arlington Lassie Stakes

COLLECT CALL (1998)
At 3: 3rd Kentucky Oaks
At 4: 3rd Milady Breeders' Cup Handicap
Vanity Handicap

COLLECT THE CASH (1997)
At 3: Won Queen Elizabeth II Challenge Cup

COLLINS (1984)
At 2: Won Selima Stakes
2nd Frizette Stakes

COLONEAST (1954)
At 5: 3rd Manhattan Handicap

COLONEL MACK (1952)
At 2: 2nd Starlet Stakes
Del Mar Futurity

COLONEL MORAN (1977)
At 3: 2nd Wood Memorial Stakes
Ohio Derby
3rd Preakness Stakes

COLONEL O'F (1944)
At 2: 2nd Cowdin Stakes
3rd Arlington Futurity
At 3: 3rd Travers Stakes

COLONEL POWER (1972)
At 2: 2nd Arlington-Washington Futurity
At 3: Won Illinois Derby
2nd Louisiana Derby

COLONIAL AFFAIR (1990)
At 3: Won Belmont Stakes
2nd Peter Pan Stakes
Jockey Club Gold Cup
3rd Jim Dandy Stakes
At 4: Won Whitney Handicap
Jockey Club Gold Cup
3rd Woodward Stakes

COLONIAL MINSTREL (1994)
At 4: 3rd Hempstead Handicap

COLONIAL WATERS (1985)
At 3: 3rd Ashland Stakes
At 4: 2nd Top Flight Handicap

Delaware Handicap
Ruffian Handicap
Beldame Stakes
At 5: Won Ladies Handicap
2nd Beldame Stakes
Breeders' Cup Distaff
At 6: 2nd Top Flight Handicap

COLONY LIGHT (1989)
At 3: 2nd Peter Pan Stakes
Jerome Handicap

COLORADO DANCER (1986)
At 3: 3rd Yellow Ribbon Stakes

COLORADO KING (1959)
At 5: Won American Handicap
Hollywood Gold Cup
Sunset Handicap
3rd Californian Stakes

COLOSAL (1943)
At 5: Won Vosburgh Handicap
2nd Metropolitan Handicap
3rd Suburban Handicap
At 6: 3rd Vosburgh Handicap
At 7: 3rd Stars and Stripes Handicap

COLOUR CHART (1987)
At 5: 3rd Santa Margarita Handicap

COLSTAR (1996)
At 4: Won Flower Bowl Invitational Handicap

COMBAT BOOTS (1948)
At 4: 2nd Monmouth Handicap
Manhattan Handicap
3rd New York Handicap
At 5: 2nd Whitney Stakes
Aqueduct Handicap

COMBAT READY (1969)
At 4: Won New Orleans Handicap

COMBUSTION II (1953)
At 5: 3rd United Nations Handicap

COMEDY ACT (1979)
At 4: 3rd Santa Barbara Handicap
At 5: Won Santa Barbara Handicap

COMEDY COURT (1985)
At 3: 3rd Hollywood Oaks

COME ON II (1961)
At 5: 3rd Hawthorne Gold Cup

COMEONMOM (1996)
At 2: Won Remsen Stakes

COME ON RED (1953)
At 3: 3rd Kentucky Derby

COME RAIN OR SHINE (1977)
At 5: 2nd Pan American Handicap

COMIC (1959)
At 3: 3rd Lawrence Realization Stakes

COMIC STRIP (1995)
At 3: 3rd Buick Pegasus Handicap

COMMEMORATE (1981)
At 3: 2nd Breeders' Cup Sprint
3rd San Felipe Handicap

COMMENDABLE (1997)
At 3: Won Belmont Stakes
2nd Super Derby
3rd Travers Stakes

COMMENDATION (1954)
At 3: 2nd Fall Highweight Handicap

COMMISSARY (1966)
At 3: 2nd Hollywood Oaks
At 4: Won Vanity Handicap
2nd Santa Margarita Handicap

COMMITISIZE (1995)
At 2: 3rd Del Mar Futurity

COMMONER (1969)
At 4: 3rd San Fernando Stakes

COMPELLING SOUND (1988)
At 3: 3rd San Felipe Stakes
Swaps Stakes

COMPLIANCE (1945)
At 3: Won Alabama Stakes
3rd Gazelle Stakes

COMPOSER (1992)
At 3: Won Jim Dandy Stakes

COMPOSURE (2000)
At 2: 2nd Long John Silver's BC Juvenile Fillies
Hollywood Starlet Stakes
At 3: Won Las Virgenes Stakes
Santa Anita Oaks

COMPTROLLER (1977)
At 3: 3rd Dwyer Stakes

COMTAL (1966)
At 4: 3rd Charles H. Strub Stakes
San Antonio Stakes
At 5: 2nd Hollywood Gold Cup

COMTESSE DE LOIR (1971)
At 4: 2nd Canadian International Championship
Washington D.C. International

CONCERN (1991)
At 3: Won Arkansas Derby
Breeders' Cup Classic
2nd Ohio Derby
Travers Stakes
Super Derby
3rd Preakness Stakes
Haskell Invitational Handicap
Molson Export Million
At 4: Won Californian Stakes
3rd Oaklawn Handicap
Pimlico Special
Meadowlands Cup Handicap

CONCERT (1982)
At 3: 3rd Withers Stakes

CONCERTO (1994)
At 3: Won Jim Beam Stakes

CONCORDE BOUND (1981)
At 3: 3rd Jerome Handicap

CONCORDE'S REVENGE (1989)
At 2: 3rd Young America Stakes

CONCORDIAN (1942)
At 4: Won McLennan Handicap
2nd Widener Handicap
At 5: 3rd Gulfstream Park Handicap

CONESTOGA (1957)
At 4: Won John B. Campbell Handicap
2nd Grey Lag Handicap

CONFEDERATE YANKEE (1971)
At 3: 2nd California Derby
At 4: 2nd Charles H. Strub Stakes
3rd San Fernando Stakes

CONFESSIONAL (1996)
At 2: Won Frizette Stakes

CONFORT ZONE (1973)
At 3: 2nd Kentucky Oaks
3rd Ashland Stakes

CONGAREE (1998)
At 3: Won Wood Memorial Stakes
Swaps Stakes
3rd Kentucky Derby
Preakness Stakes
Jim Dandy Stakes
At 4: Won Cigar Mile Handicap
At 5: Won Carter Handicap
Hollywood Gold Cup
Cigar Mile Handicap
2nd Santa Anita Handicap

CONGELEUR (1985)
At 3: 2nd Pennsylvania Derby

CONGRATS (2000)
At 3: 3rd Jim Dandy Stakes

CONNIVER (1944)
At 4: Won Vagrancy Handicap
Beldame Handicap
Comely Handicap
Brooklyn Handicap
2nd Aqueduct Handicap
At 5: 2nd Queens County Handicap
3rd Firenze Handicap

CONQUISTADOR CIELO (1979)
At 3: Won Belmont Stakes
Dwyer Stakes
Metropolitan Handicap
3rd Travers Stakes

CONQUISTADORESS (1992)
At 3: 2nd Ashland Stakes

CONQUISTAROSE (1984)
At 2: Won Young America Stakes
2nd Arlington-Washington Futurity

CONTE DI SAVOYA (1989)
At 3: 2nd Blue Grass Stakes

CONTEST (1944)
At 5: 2nd Dixie Handicap

CONTESTED BID (1989)
At 3: 3rd Budweiser International Stakes

CONTESTED COLORS (1986)
At 3: 2nd Dwyer Stakes

CONTINENTAL RED (1996)
At 6: 3rd San Juan Capistrano Handicap

CONTINUING (1979)
At 3: 3rd Secretariat Stakes

CONTINUOUS COUNT (1968)
At 7: 3rd John B. Campbell Handicap

CONTINUOUSLY (1999)
At 4: Won Hollywood Turf Cup

CONTRATODOS (1964)
At 6: 3rd Del Mar Handicap

CONTREDANCE (1982)
At 2: Won Arlington-Washington Lassie Stakes
3rd Matron Stakes

CONVENIENCE (1968)
At 3: 2nd Hollywood Oaks
At 4: Won Vanity Handicap
2nd Santa Margarita Handicap
At 5: Won Vanity Handicap
2nd Maskette Handicap
Santa Maria Handicap
Santa Margarita Handicap
3rd Beverly Hills Handicap
At 6: Won Santa Maria Handicap

CONVENIENTLY (1976)
At 4: 2nd Vanity Handicap

CONVERSION (1947)
At 3: 3rd Golden Gate Handicap

CONVEX (1962)
At 4: Won Seminole Handicap

CONVEYOR (1988)
At 6: Won Meadowlands Cup

COOKIE PUDDIN (1976)
At 3: 3rd Golden Harvest Handicap

COOL (1981)
At 4: 3rd United Nations Handicap

COOL HAND (1967)
At 3: Won San Felipe Handicap

COOL MOON (1968)
At 2: 3rd Hopeful Stakes

COOL PRINCE (1960)
At 3: 3rd Florida Derby
At 5: Won Pan American Handicap

COOL RECEPTION (1964)
At 3: 2nd Belmont Stakes

COPELAN (1980)
At 2: Won Hopeful Stakes
Futurity Stakes
Champagne Stakes
At 3: 2nd Florida Derby
3rd Blue Grass Stakes
Jerome Handicap

COPERNICA (1972)
At 2: 2nd Matron Stakes
Frizette Stakes

COPPER MEL (1972)
At 5: 3rd Sunset Handicap

COPPER STUDENT (1960)
At 2: 2nd Hollywood Juvenile Championship

COPTE (1970)
At 4: 2nd Jockey Club Gold Cup

COPY CHIEF (1960)
At 2: 2nd Breeders' Futurity
Kentucky Jockey Club Stakes

CORAGGIOSO (1970)
At 2: Won Alcibiades Stakes
3rd Matron Stakes
At 3: 3rd Kentucky Oaks
Spinster Stakes
At 4: Won Ladies Handicap
3rd Spinster Stakes

CORBY (1990)
At 3: Won San Felipe Stakes

CORDIALLY (1962)
At 2: 3rd Demoiselle Stakes
At 3: Won Mother Goose Stakes
2nd Vineland Handicap

CORETTA (1994)
At 5: 2nd Flower Bowl Invitational Handicap
Breeders' Cup Filly and Mare Turf

CORKER (1993)
At 3: 3rd Santa Anita Derby

CORMORANT (1974)
At 3: Won Jersey Derby
2nd Ohio Derby

CORN HUSKER (1953)
At 4: Won Santa Anita Handicap
San Juan Capistrano Handicap
3rd Los Angeles Handicap

CORNISH KNIGHT (1944)
At 3: 3rd Wood Memorial Stakes
Jerome Handicap

CORNISH PRINCE (1962)
At 2: Won Sanford Stakes
2nd Saratoga Special
At 3: 2nd Jerome Handicap
3rd Travers Stakes

CORN OFF THE COB (1967)
At 3: Won Arlington Classic
2nd Flamingo Stakes
Florida Derby
Blue Grass Stakes
Jersey Derby
Hollywood Derby

CORNWALL (1947)
At 2: Won Garden State Stakes
2nd Remsen Handicap

CORONADO'S QUEST (1995)
At 2: Won Remsen Stakes
At 3: Won Wood Memorial Stakes
Buick Haskell Invitational Handicap
Travers Stakes
2nd Fountain of Youth Stakes

CORPORATE REPORT (1988)
At 3: Won Travers Stakes
2nd Arkansas Derby
Preakness Stakes
Swaps Stakes
Haskell Invitational Handicap

CORRELATION (1951)
At 2: 2nd Garden State Stakes
At 3: Won Wood Memorial Stakes
Florida Derby
2nd Preakness Stakes

CORRESPONDENT (1950)
At 3: Won Blue Grass Stakes
3rd Santa Anita Derby
At 4: Won Hollywood Gold Cup
At 5: 3rd San Antonio Handicap

COSINE (1997)
At 2: 3rd Hollywood Futurity

COSMAH (1953)
At 2: 2nd Gardenia Stakes
3rd Frizette Stakes
At 3: 2nd Gazelle Handicap

COSMIC BOMB (1944)
At 2: Won Arlington Futurity
Cowdin Stakes
At 3: Won Discovery Handicap
Lawrence Realization Stakes
Roamer Handicap
Trenton Handicap
2nd American Derby
Jerome Handicap
Pimlico Special
3rd Arlington Classic

COSMIC MISSILE (1944)
At 2: Won Marguerite Stakes
At 3: Won Gazelle Stakes
2nd Kentucky Oaks
Pimlico Oaks
Coaching Club American Oaks
Delaware Oaks
Alabama Stakes

COSMIC TIGER (1983)
At 2: 3rd Selima Stakes

COSMIC TIP (1960)
At 3: Won Arkansas Derby

COSMOPOLITE (1946)
At 3: 3rd Hollywood Oaks

COSTLY DREAM (1971)
At 4: 3rd Spinster Stakes

COSTLY SHOES (1985)
At 3: 3rd Fantasy Stakes

COUGAR II (1966)
At 4: 2nd Del Mar Handicap
3rd Manhattan Handicap
Oak Tree Stakes
At 5: Won Californian Stakes
Ford Pinto Invitational Turf Handicap
Oak Tree Invitational Stakes
San Juan Capistrano Handicap
2nd Santa Anita Handicap
Sunset Handicap
3rd Woodward Stakes
Century Handicap
At 6: Won Californian Stakes
Century Handicap
Oak Tree Invitational Stakes
2nd Santa Anita Handicap
San Juan Capistrano Handicap
3rd San Antonio Stakes
Hollywood Invitational Handicap
At 7: Won Santa Anita Handicap
Century Handicap
Sunset Handicap
3rd Hollywood Gold Cup
Marlboro Cup Handicap
Woodward Stakes
Hollywood Invitational Handicap
San Luis Rey Handicap
San Juan Capistrano Handicap

COUNT-A-BIT (1946)
At 4: 2nd Gulfstream Park Handicap

COUNT AMBER (1957)
At 3: 2nd Withers Stakes
Travers Stakes
3rd Gotham Stakes

COUNT BUD (1961)
At 2: 2nd Saratoga Special
Cowdin Stakes
3rd Hopeful Stakes
Futurity Stakes

COUNT CAIN (1950)
At 2: 2nd Pimlico Futurity
At 4: 2nd Tropical Handicap
Excelsior Handicap

COUNT CHIC (1953)
At 3: 2nd San Felipe Handicap
Florida Derby
At 4: 3rd William P. Kyne Memorial Handicap

COUNTERATE (1957)
At 3: 3rd Roamer Handicap

COUNTER CALL (1958)
At 2: 2nd Frizette Stakes
At 4: 2nd Top Flight Handicap

COUNTERFEIT MONEY (1981)
At 3: 2nd Fountain of Youth Stakes

COUNTERMAND (1953)
At 2: 3rd Pimlico Futurity
At 3: 3rd Jerome Handicap

COUNTERPOINT (1948)
At 3: Won Belmont Stakes
Lawrence Realization Stakes
Jockey Club Gold Cup
2nd Preakness Stakes
3rd Blue Grass Stakes
At 4: Won San Fernando Stakes
Whitney Stakes

COUNTESS DIANA (1995)
At 2: Won Spinaway Stakes
Breeders' Cup Juvenile Fillies

COUNTESS FAGER (1974)
At 4: 2nd Santa Barbara Handicap

COUNTESS FLEET (1951)
At 4: Won Vanity Handicap
3rd Beldame Handicap
Ladies Handicap

COUNTESS JANE (1950)
At 2: 3rd Astoria Stakes

COUNT FLAME (1949)
At 3: 3rd Flamingo Stakes
Saranac Handicap

COUNT OF HONOR (1953)
At 3: Won Westerner Stakes

COUNTRY BE GOLD (1997)
At 4: 3rd Jockey Club Gold Cup

COUNTRY CAT (1992)
At 3: 2nd Acorn Stakes

COUNTRY COZ (1950)
At 2: 3rd Champagne Stakes

COUNTRY DAY (1987)
At 3: 2nd Peter Pan Stakes

COUNTRY GARDEN (1995)
At 5: 3rd Beverly D. Stakes

COUNTRY HIDEAWAY (1996)
At 4: 2nd Ballerina Handicap
3rd Ruffian Handicap
At 5: 2nd Ballerina Handicap

COUNTRY PINE (1980)
At 3: 2nd Wood Memorial Stakes

COUNTRY QUEEN (1975)
At 3: 2nd Hollywood Oaks
Ramona Handicap
At 4: Won Ramona Handicap
Yellow Ribbon Stakes
2nd Vanity Handicap
Gamely Handicap
At 5: 2nd Gamely Handicap

COUNT THE TIME (1989)
At 2: 2nd Arlington-Washington Futurity
At 3: 2nd Super Derby

COUNT TURF (1948)
At 3: Won Kentucky Derby
At 5: 3rd Massachusetts Handicap
Queens County Handicap

COUNTY CLARE (1950)
At 2: 3rd Pimlico Futurity

COUNTY DELIGHT (1947)
At 4: Won Dixie Handicap
Gallant Fox Handicap
Manhattan Handicap
2nd Westchester Handicap
Pimlico Special
3rd Widener Handicap
Grey Lag Handicap
Suburban Handicap
Brooklyn Handicap
Arlington Handicap
Washington Park Handicap
At 5: Won Queens County Handicap
2nd Brooklyn Handicap
3rd Monmouth Handicap

COUP DE FUSIL (1982)
At 4: 2nd Beldame Stakes
Ladies Handicap
At 5: Won Delaware Handicap
Ruffian Handicap
2nd Beldame Stakes

COUP LANDING (1965)
At 6: 3rd Vosburgh Handicap

COUPLE O'QUID (1963)
At 2: 2nd Del Mar Futurity

COURAGEOUSLY (1964)
At 4: 3rd Santa Barbara Handicap

COURSING (1963)
At 2: Won Del Mar Futurity

COURTEOUS MAJESTY (1980)
At 4: 3rd Gulfstream Park Handicap

COURT FOOL (1965)
At 4: 3rd Hollywood Park Inv. Turf Handicap

COURT OPEN (1974)
At 4: 3rd Pan American Handicap

COURT RECESS (1965)
At 4: Won Gulfstream Park Handicap

COURT ROAD (1966)
At 3: 3rd Hollywood Derby

COURT RULING (1970)
At 4: Won Hollywood Invitational Handicap
3rd Century Handicap

COURT TOWER (1960)
At 2: 3rd Hollywood Juvenile Championship

COUSIN (1949)
At 2: Won Saratoga Special
Hopeful Stakes

COVER GAL (1997)
At 3: 2nd La Brea Stakes

COVER UP (1943)
At 4: Won Hollywood Gold Cup
Sunset Handicap
2nd American Handicap

COX'S RIDGE (1974)
At 3: 3rd Jockey Club Gold Cup

At 4: Won Metropolitan Handicap
Oaklawn Handicap
3rd Californian Stakes
At 5: 2nd Whitney Stakes
Amory L. Haskell Handicap

COXWOLD (1988)
At 4: 3rd Beldame Stakes

COZZENE (1980)
At 4: 2nd United Nations Handicap
3rd Man o' War Stakes
Breeders' Cup Mile
At 5: Won Breeders' Cup Mile

COZZENE'S PRINCE (1987)
At 3: 3rd Rothmans International Stakes
At 6: 2nd Rothmans International Stakes

CRAB GRASS (1972)
At 5: 2nd Maskette Handicap

CRAELIUS (1979)
At 3: 2nd Oak Tree Invitational Stakes
At 4: Won Sunset Handicap

CRAFTINESS (1955)
At 2: 2nd Gardenia Stakes
At 3: 3rd Coaching Club American Oaks
Monmouth Oaks
At 6: 2nd Beldame Stakes
Ladies Handicap

CRAFTY ACTOR (1959)
At 2: 3rd Breeders' Futurity

CRAFTY ADMIRAL (1948)
At 4: Won Gulfstream Park Handicap
Brooklyn Handicap
Washington Park Handicap
2nd Suburban Handicap
Carter Handicap
3rd Jockey Club Gold Cup
At 5: Won McLennan Handicap
Gulfstream Park Handicap
New York Handicap
2nd Westchester Handicap
3rd Tropical Park Handicap
Dixie Handicap

CRAFTY C.T. (1998)
At 3: 2nd Santa Anita Derby
At 4: 2nd Ancient Title Breeders' Cup Handicap
3rd Metropolitan Handicap
NAPA Breeders' Cup Sprint
Cigar Mile Handicap
At 5: 2nd San Carlos Handicap

CRAFTY DUDE (1989)
At 6: 2nd Frank J. De Francis Memorial Dash

CRAFTY FRIEND (1993)
At 2: 3rd Remsen Stakes
At 4: 3rd Pacific Classic
At 6: 2nd Metropolitan Handicap

CRAFTY KHALE (1969)
At 4: 2nd Massachusetts Handicap
At 5: 2nd Man o' War Stakes

CRAFTY PROSPECTOR (1979)
At 4: 2nd Gulfstream Park Handicap

CRAFTY SKIPPER (1956)
At 2: Won Cowdin Stakes

CRAIGSTEEL (1995)
At 5: 2nd Turf Classic

CRANBERRY SAUCE (1957)
At 4: 2nd Tropical Park Handicap

CRARY (1991)
At 2: 2nd Champagne Stakes

CRASH DIVE (1950)
At 4: Won Aqueduct Handicap

CRATER FIRE (1982)
At 2: Won Breeders' Futurity

CRAZY ENSIGN (1996)
At 6: 3rd Beverly Hills Handicap
At 7: 3rd Yellow Ribbon Stakes

CRAZY KID (1958)
At 4: 2nd Los Angeles Handicap
At 5: 2nd Los Angeles Handicap

CREAKING BOARD (1990)
At 2: Won Hollywood Starlet Stakes

CREATOR (1986)
At 4: 3rd Budweiser International Stakes

CREME DELA CREME (1963)
At 3: Won Jersey Derby
2nd Withers Stakes
Arlington Classic

CREME FRAICHE (1982)
At 3: Won Belmont Stakes
American Derby
Jerome Handicap
Super Derby
2nd Hutcheson Stakes
Everglades Stakes
Louisiana Derby
Jersey Derby
3rd Haskell Invitational Handicap
Jockey Club Gold Cup
At 4: Won Jockey Club Gold Cup
3rd Suburban Handicap
Brooklyn Handicap
At 5: Won Jockey Club Gold Cup
Meadowlands Cup
2nd Widener Handicap
Gulfstream Park Handicap
3rd Hialeah Turf Cup
Woodward Stakes
At 6: 3rd Gulfstream Park Handicap
Brooklyn Handicap

CREST OF THE WAVE (1976)
At 2: Won Futurity Stakes
3rd Champagne Stakes
At 3: 3rd California Derby

CREWMAN (1960)
At 2: Won Garden State Stakes
At 3: Won Travers Stakes
3rd Gotham Stakes

CRIMINAL TYPE (1985)
At 5: Won San Antonio Handicap
Pimlico Special
Metropolitan Handicap
Hollywood Gold Cup
Whitney Handicap
2nd Santa Anita Handicap

CRIMSON CLEM (1968)
At 3: 2nd Cinema Handicap
3rd California Derby

CRIMSON FALCON (1970)
At 2: 3rd Breeders' Futurity
At 4: 2nd Oaklawn Handicap

CRIMSON FURY (1958)
At 2: Won Kentucky Jockey Club Stakes

CRIMSON SATAN (1959)
At 2: Won Garden State Stakes
Pimlico Futurity
At 3: 2nd Arlington Handicap
3rd Jersey Derby
Belmont Stakes
At 4: Won Massachusetts Handicap
Michigan Mile and One-Sixteenth
Washington Park Handicap
San Fernando Stakes
Charles H. Strub Stakes
2nd Santa Anita Handicap
John B. Campbell Handicap
Grey Lag Handicap
Aqueduct Stakes
San Antonio Handicap
3rd Woodward Stakes

CRIMSON SLEW (1984)
At 4: 3rd San Antonio Handicap

CRISSET (1951)
At 4: 2nd Black Helen Handicap
3rd Vineland Handicap

CRITICAL EYE (1997)
At 3: Won Gazelle Handicap
At 4: Won Hempstead Handicap

CRITICAL FACTOR (1994)
At 2: 3rd Breeders' Cup Juvenile Fillies

CRITIKOLA (1995)
At 6: 3rd Santa Maria Handicap
Santa Margarita Handicap

CROESO (1980)
At 3: Won Florida Derby

CROQUIS (1976)
At 3: 3rd Coaching Club American Oaks
At 4: 2nd Delaware Handicap

CROSSTIE (1970)
At 2: 2nd Arlington-Washington Lassie Stakes

CROW (1973)
At 4: 3rd Turf Classic

CROWDUS (1960)
At 3: 3rd American Derby

CROWN (1955)
At 2: 2nd Selima Stakes

CROWN ATTORNEY (1993)
At 4: 3rd Woodbine Mile

CROWNED (1987)
At 3: 2nd Coaching Club American Oaks

CROWNED KING (2000)
At 3: 3rd Super Derby

CROZIER (1958)
At 2: Won Washington Park Futurity
2nd Arlington Futurity
At 3: 2nd Flamingo Stakes
Florida Derby
Kentucky Derby
Jersey Derby
3rd Preakness Stakes
Arlington Classic
At 4: Won Aqueduct Stakes
2nd Whitney Stakes
At 5: Won Santa Anita Handicap
San Carlos Handicap

CRUISER II (1969)
At 6: Won Sunset Handicap
Del Mar Handicap

CRUSADER SWORD (1985)
At 2: Won Hopeful Stakes
3rd Futurity Stakes

CRUSADING (1968)
At 5: 2nd San Antonio Stakes

CRYPTOCLEARANCE (1984)
At 3: Won Everglades Stakes
Florida Derby
2nd Flamingo Stakes
Belmont Stakes
Travers Stakes
3rd Preakness Stakes
Jim Dandy Stakes
Meadowlands Cup
At 4: 2nd Gulfstream Park Handicap
At 5: Won Widener Handicap
2nd Jockey Club Gold Cup
3rd Gulfstream Park Handicap
Whitney Handicap

CRYPTO STAR (1994)
At 3: Won Arkansas Derby
At 4: 3rd Whitney Handicap

CRYSTAL WATER (1973)
At 3: Won San Felipe Handicap
Hollywood Derby
2nd Swaps Stakes
At 4: Won Californian Stakes
Hollywood Gold Cup
Santa Anita Handicap
Oak Tree Invitational Stakes
3rd Marlboro Cup Handicap
San Fernando Stakes

CUDDLES (1988)
At 2: Won Hollywood Starlet Stakes

CULLENDALE (1982)
At 2: 3rd Breeders' Futurity

CUM LAUDE (1941)
At 5: 2nd Longacres Mile

CUM LAUDE LAURIE (1974)
At 3: Won Ruffian Handicap
Beldame Stakes
Spinster Stakes
3rd Mother Goose Stakes
Alabama Stakes
At 4: 3rd Delaware Handicap
Beldame Stakes
Ladies Handicap
Apple Blossom Handicap

CUNNING PLAY (1999)
At 2: 3rd Walmac International Alcibiades Stakes

CUNNING TRICK (1973)
At 4: Won Arlington Handicap

CUORE (1946)
At 5: 2nd Bougainvillea Handicap
At 6: 2nd Stars and Stripes Handicap

CUPECOY'S JOY (1979)
At 3: Won Acorn Stakes
Mother Goose Stakes
2nd Coaching Club American Oaks

CUPID (1961)
At 4: 2nd Carter Handicap
At 5: 2nd Santa Anita Handicap

CUP MAN (1952)
At 3: 3rd Flamingo Stakes

CURANDERO (1946)
At 2: 3rd Hopeful Stakes
At 3: 3rd Discovery Handicap
At 4: 2nd Hawthorne Gold Cup
3rd Washington Park Handicap
At 5: Won Washington Park Handicap

CURE THE BLUES (1978)
At 2: Won Laurel Futurity
At 3: 3rd Wood Memorial Stakes

CURIOUS CLOVER (1960)
At 3: 3rd Hollywood Oaks
At 4: Won Santa Margarita Handicap
2nd Vanity Handicap
At 5: Won Santa Margarita Handicap

CURRENT HOPE (1980)
At 3: Won Flamingo Stakes

CURTICE (1947)
At 2: Won Washington Park Futurity

CURULE (1997)
At 3: 2nd Jim Dandy Stakes

CUT AWAY (1979)
At 3: 3rd Preakness Stakes

CUT CLASS (1972)
At 2: Won Oak Leaf Stakes
3rd Del Mar Debutante Stakes

CUTLASS REALITY (1982)
At 2: 2nd Laurel Futurity
At 3: 2nd Dwyer Stakes
At 4: 3rd Vosburgh Stakes
At 6: Won Californian Stakes
Hollywood Gold Cup

CUT THE COMEDY (1967)
At 4: 2nd Carter Handicap

CUVEE (2001)
At 2: Won Futurity Stakes

CUZWUZWRONG (1974)
At 3: Won California Derby

CYANE (1959)
At 2: Won Futurity Stakes
At 3: Won Dwyer Handicap

CYCLOTRON (1948)
At 4: 2nd Hollywood Gold Cup
3rd Vosburgh Handicap
At 6: 3rd Santa Anita Handicap

CYRANO (1959)
At 3: 3rd Withers Stakes
At 4: Won Metropolitan Handicap
Brooklyn Handicap
At 5: Won Los Angeles Handicap
2nd San Carlos Handicap
San Antonio Handicap
3rd Santa Anita Handicap

CZAR ALEXANDER (1965)
At 3: Won Man o' War Stakes
2nd Washington D.C. International
At 4: Won Dixie Handicap
Bowling Green Handicap
Oak Tree Stakes
2nd Hialeah Turf Cup
3rd Washington D.C. International

CZARAVICH (1976)
At 3: Won Jerome Handicap
3rd Wood Memorial Stakes
Woodward Stakes
Man o' War Stakes
At 4: Won Metropolitan Handicap
3rd Suburban Handicap
Whitney Stakes

CZARINA (1956)
At 3: 3rd Coaching Club American Oaks

DA BULL (1992)
At 6: 2nd San Antonio Handicap

D'ACCORD (1979)
At 2: Won Breeders' Futurity

DADDY R. (1959)
At 2: 2nd Remsen Stakes

DAHAR (1981)
At 4: Won Century Handicap
2nd Hollywood Invitational Handicap
3rd San Luis Rey Stakes
At 5: Won San Luis Rey Stakes
San Juan Capistrano Handicap
2nd Hollywood Invitational Handicap
Hollywood Turf Cup
Sunset Handicap

DAHLIA (1970)
At 3: Won Washington D.C. International
At 4: Won Man o' War Stakes
Canadian International Championship
3rd Washington D.C. International
At 6: Won Hollywood Invitational Handicap
3rd Century Handicap

DAHLIA'S DREAMER (1989)
At 4: 2nd Flower Bowl Handicap
At 5: Won Flower Bowl Invitational Handicap

DA HOSS (1992)
At 3: 2nd Gotham Stakes
Swaps Stakes
Pegasus Handicap
3rd Crown Royal Hollywood Derby
At 4: Won Breeders' Cup Mile
At 6: Won Breeders' Cup Mile

DAIJIN (1992)
At 3: 3rd Test Stakes

DAIQUARI (1946)
At 3: 2nd Travers Stakes

DAISY MILLER (1977)
At 2: 2nd Sorority Stakes

DALE'S DELIGHT (1954)

At 3:	3rd	Kentucky Oaks

DALHART (1990)

At 2:	2nd	Remsen Stakes

DAMASCUS (1964)

At 3:	Won	Wood Memorial Stakes
		Preakness Stakes
		Belmont Stakes
		Dwyer Handicap
		American Derby
		Travers Stakes
		Aqueduct Stakes
		Woodward Stakes
		Jockey Club Gold Cup
	2nd	Gotham Stakes
		Washington D.C. International
	3rd	Kentucky Derby
At 4:	Won	Brooklyn Handicap
		Aqueduct Stakes
		Malibu Stakes
		San Fernando Stakes
	2nd	Michigan Mile and One-Eighth
		Woodward Stakes
		Charles H. Strub Stakes
	3rd	Suburban Handicap
		Amory L. Haskell Handicap

DAMASCUS DRAMA (1984)

At 2:	2nd	Young America Stakes

DAMELO II (1961)

At 5:	Won	Display Handicap

DAME MYSTERIEUSE (1978)

At 3:	2nd	Acorn Stakes

DAMISTER (1982)

At 4:	2nd	Turf Classic

DANADA GIFT (1945)

At 4:	2nd	Santa Margarita Handicap
	3rd	Arlington Matron Handicap

DANAHONEY (1969)

At 2:	3rd	Arlington-Washington Futurity

DANCE ALL NIGHT (1956)

At 2:	2nd	Frizette Stakes

DANCEALOT (1971)

At 2:	Won	Selima Stakes
	2nd	Matron Stakes

DANCE COLONY (1987)

At 2:	3rd	Frizette Stakes

DANCE DESIGN (1993)

At 4:	3rd	Beverly D. Stakes

DANCE FLOOR (1989)

At 2:	2nd	Hollywood Futurity
At 3:	2nd	Florida Derby
	3rd	Kentucky Derby
		Travers Stakes

DANCE FOR VANNY (1990)

At 3:	3rd	Santa Anita Oaks

DANCE NUMBER (1979)

At 4:	Won	Beldame Stakes
	2nd	Spinster Stakes
	3rd	Top Flight Handicap

DANCE OF LIFE (1983)

At 2:	3rd	Remsen Stakes
At 3:	Won	Man o' War Stakes
	2nd	Washington D.C. International

DANCE PARTNER (1969)

At 2:	2nd	Sorority Stakes

DANCERS COUNTESS (1972)

At 3:	3rd	Fantasy Stakes

DANCER'S IMAGE (1965)

At 3:	Won	Wood Memorial Stakes

DANCE SMARTLY (1988)

At 2:	3rd	Breeders' Cup Juvenile Fillies
At 3:	Won	Breeders' Cup Distaff
At 4:	3rd	Beverly D. Stakes

DANCE SPELL (1973)

At 2:	2nd	Champagne Stakes
		Remsen Stakes
	3rd	Laurel Futurity
At 3:	Won	Jerome Handicap
	2nd	Woodward Handicap
	3rd	Dwyer Handicap
		Travers Stakes

DANCE TEACHER (1985)

At 4:	Won	Ladies Handicap

DANCETHRUTHEDAWN (1998)

At 4:	Won	Go for Wand Handicap
	3rd	Personal Ensign Handicap

DANCING FEMME (1973)

At 4:	Won	Ramona Handicap

DANCING FRED (1993)

At 3:	3rd	Secretariat Stakes

DANCING GUN (1972)

At 4:	Won	Whitney Handicap
	3rd	Michigan Mile and One-Eighth
		Charles H. Strub Stakes
At 5:	3rd	Whitney Handicap

DANCINGINMYDREAMS (1998)

At 2:	2nd	Matron Stakes

DANCING MASTER (1975)

At 5:	2nd	Hialeah Turf Cup

DANCING PAPA (1970)

At 4:	2nd	Charles H. Strub Stakes
	3rd	Malibu Stakes
		San Antonio Stakes
At 6:	2nd	San Antonio Stakes

DANCING PIRATE (1983)

At 3:	3rd	San Felipe Handicap

DANCING PRETENSE (1985)

At 5:	2nd	Carter Handicap

DANCING SPREE (1985)

At 4:	Won	Suburban Handicap
		Breeders' Cup Sprint
	3rd	Metropolitan Handicap
At 5:	Won	Carter Handicap
	2nd	Whitney Handicap
		NYRA Mile Handicap

DANDY K. (1961)

At 3:	3rd	Florida Derby

DANEBO (1979)

At 5:	3rd	San Antonio Handicap

DANGER AHEAD (1946)

At 2:	3rd	Astoria Stakes
At 4:	Won	Molly Pitcher Handicap

DANGER'S HOUR (1982)

At 4:	3rd	Turf Classic

DAN HORN (1972)

At 6:	3rd	United Nations Handicap

DANISH (1991)

At 3:	3rd	Flower Bowl Invitational Handicap
At 4:	2nd	Flower Bowl Invitational Handicap

DANNY'S KEYS (1983)

At 2:	2nd	Sapling Stakes
		Hopeful Stakes

DANSIL (1986)

At 3:	Won	Arkansas Derby

DANSILI (1996)

At 4:	3rd	Breeders' Cup Mile

DANZIG CONNECTION (1983)

At 2:	2nd	Young America Stakes
At 3:	Won	Peter Pan Stakes
		Belmont Stakes
	2nd	Travers Stakes
	3rd	Haskell Invitational Handicap
		Jockey Club Gold Cup

DANZIG'S BEAUTY (1987)

At 3:	2nd	Acorn Stakes

DAPPER DAN (1962)

At 3:	2nd	Gotham Stakes
		Kentucky Derby
		Preakness Stakes
At 4:	3rd	Carter Handicap

DAPPER DELEGATE (1962)

At 3:	Won	Louisiana Derby

DARBY CREEK ROAD (1975)

At 2:	3rd	Champagne Stakes
At 3:	2nd	Wood Memorial Stakes
		Jerome Handicap
	3rd	Belmont Stakes
		Dwyer Handicap

DARBY D-DAY (1943)

At 3:	2nd	California Derby
	3rd	San Vicente Handicap
		San Felipe Stakes

DARBY FAIR (1983)

At 2:	3rd	Norfolk Stakes

DARBY'S DAUGHTER (1986)

At 2:	2nd	Demoiselle Stakes
At 3:	2nd	Yellow Ribbon Stakes

DARBY SHUFFLE (1986)

At 2:	2nd	Selima Stakes
		Breeders' Cup Juvenile Fillies

DARE AND GO (1991)

At 3:	2nd	Secretariat Stakes
		Hollywood Derby
		Hollywood Turf Cup
At 4:	Won	Strub Stakes
	3rd	Santa Anita Handicap
At 5:	Won	Pacific Classic
	3rd	San Antonio Handicap

DARING GENERAL (1996)

At 2:	2nd	Del Mar Futurity
	3rd	Norfolk Stakes

DARK COUNT (1949)

At 4:	3rd	Excelsior Handicap

DARK MIRAGE (1965)

At 3:	Won	Kentucky Oaks
		Acorn Stakes
		Mother Goose Stakes
		Coaching Club American Oaks
		Monmouth Oaks

DARK PETER (1948)

At 6:	3rd	Fall Highweight Handicap

DARK STAR (1950)

At 2:	3rd	Futurity Stakes
At 3:	Won	Kentucky Derby

DARK VENUS (1944)

At 2:	3rd	Astoria Stakes

DARK VINTAGE (1956)

At 2:	Won	Arlington Lassie Stakes
	2nd	Princess Pat Stakes

DARLING ADELLE (1954)

At 2:	2nd	Del Mar Debutante Stakes

DARLING JUNE (1957)

At 2:	Won	Del Mar Debutante Stakes

DARLING MY DARLING (1997)

At 2:	2nd	Matron Stakes
		Frizette Stakes

DARN THAT ALARM (1981)

At 3:	Won	Fountain of Youth Stakes
	2nd	Dwyer Stakes
	3rd	Hutcheson Stakes
		Florida Derby
At 5:	2nd	Widener Handicap

DAROS (1989)

At 3:	3rd	Oak Tree Invitational Stakes

DARRYLL (1963)
At 2: 3rd Selima Stakes

D'ARTAGNAN (1967)
At 3: Won Cinema Handicap

DART BY (1945)
At 5: 3rd New Orleans Handicap

DARYL'S JOY (1966)
At 4: Won Del Mar Handicap
Oak Tree Stakes

DASHBOARD DRUMMER (2001)
At 2: 3rd Champagne Stakes

DASH OF HOPE (1981)
At 2: 3rd Sorority Stakes

DASH O'PLEASURE (1978)
At 2: 2nd Futurity Stakes

DAVE'S FRIEND (1975)
At 3: 2nd Monmouth Invitational Handicap
At 4: 3rd Vosburgh Stakes

DAVID (1996)
At 4: 3rd Sempra Energy Hollywood Gold Cup

DAVID COPPERFIELD (1997)
At 3: 2nd Early Times Hollywood Derby

DAVIS II (1960)
At 6: Won Carter Handicap
2nd Vosburgh Handicap

DAVONA DALE (1976)
At 3: Won Fantasy Stakes
Kentucky Oaks
Acorn Stakes
Mother Goose Stakes
Coaching Club American Oaks
2nd Alabama Stakes

DAWN GLORY (1964)
At 3: 3rd Wood Memorial Stakes

DAWN QUIXOTE (1987)
At 2: 3rd Futurity Stakes

DAWSON'S LEGACY (1995)
At 2: 2nd Breeders' Cup Juvenile

DAY COURT (1955)
At 3: 3rd Dwyer Handicap
At 4: Won Hawthorne Gold Cup
2nd Massachusetts Handicap
Sunset Handicap
3rd Grey Lag Handicap
At 5: 3rd New Orleans Handicap

DAYDREAMING (2001)
At 2: 3rd Spinaway Stakes

DAYJUR (1987)
At 3: 2nd Breeders' Cup Sprint

DAYLAMI (1994)
At 4: Won Man o' War Stakes
At 5: Won Breeders' Cup Turf

DAYTIME PRINCESS (1984)
At 2: 3rd Matron Stakes

DAZZLE ME JOLIE (1988)
At 3: 3rd Acorn Stakes

DAZZLING FALLS (1992)
At 3: Won Arkansas Derby
2nd Ohio Derby

D.B. CARM (1969)
At 2: Won Del Mar Futurity
2nd Norfolk Stakes

DEAD AHEAD (1959)
At 3: Won Roamer Handicap

DEAD CENTER (1957)
At 4: Won Bowling Green Handicap

DEAL PRICE (1982)
At 3: 3rd Hollywood Oaks

DEAN CARL (1960)
At 3: Won Lawrence Realization Stakes
Roamer Handicap
Display Handicap

DEAR DOCTOR (1987)
At 4: 2nd Man o' War Stakes
Turf Classic
At 5: Won Arlington Million
2nd Man o' War Stakes

DEARLY LOVED (1986)
At 3: 2nd Alabama Stakes

DEARLY PRECIOUS (1973)
At 2: Won Sorority Stakes
Spinaway Stakes
Arlington-Washington Lassie Stakes
At 3: Won Acorn Stakes

DEAUVILLE (1964)
At 3: 3rd California Derby

DEBBIE LORRAINE (1956)
At 2: 3rd Arlington Lassie Stakes

DEBBY DEB (1969)
At 2: 3rd Spinaway Stakes

DEBBYSMAN (1960)
At 3: Won Gotham Stakes

DEBBY'S TURN (1974)
At 2: 3rd Selima Stakes

DEBONAIR JOE (1999)
At 3: Won Malibu Stakes

DEB'S CHARM (2001)
At 2: 3rd Darley Alcibiades Stakes

DEB'S DARLING (1966)
At 4: 3rd Molly Pitcher Handicap

DEBUTANT'S HALO (1988)
At 2: Won Demoiselle Stakes

DECADRACHM (1979)
At 4: 3rd Sunset Handicap

DECARCHY (1997)
At 6: 2nd Eddie Read Handicap

DECATHLON (1953)
At 2: 2nd Sapling Stakes

DECEIT (1968)
At 2: 3rd Sorority Stakes
Spinaway Stakes
At 3: Won Acorn Stakes
Mother Goose Stakes
2nd Delaware Handicap

DECIDEDLY (1959)
At 3: Won Kentucky Derby
2nd Everglades Stakes
Blue Grass Stakes
At 4: Won Monmouth Handicap
2nd Michigan Mile and One-Sixteenth
3rd Grey Lag Handicap

DECIMAL (1952)
At 4: 2nd Fall Highweight Handicap

DECK HAND (1963)
At 4: 2nd Dixie Handicap

DECLINE AND FALL (1957)
At 5: 2nd Black Helen Handicap

DECORATED (1950)
At 2: 2nd Starlet Stakes
3rd Del Mar Futurity
At 3: Won San Felipe Handicap
At 4: 3rd San Antonio Handicap

DECORATED HERO (1992)
At 5: 3rd Breeders' Cup Mile

DEDICATE (1952)
At 3: 3rd Woodward Stakes
At 4: Won Brooklyn Handicap
Whitney Stakes
Hawthorne Gold Cup
2nd Suburban Handicap
3rd Gallant Fox Handicap
At 5: Won John B. Campbell Mem. Handicap
Monmouth Handicap
Woodward Stakes
2nd Carter Handicap
Metropolitan Handicap
3rd Suburban Handicap

DEDICATION (1999)
At 4: 3rd Matriarch Stakes

DEDIMOUD (1959)
At 3: 3rd Jerome Handicap

DEELITEFUL IRVING (1998)
At 5: 2nd Turf Classic

DEEMSTER (1957)
At 3: 3rd Arkansas Derby

DEEP SILVER (1983)
At 2: 2nd Arlington-Washington Lassie Stakes

DEER RUN (1997)
At 5: 2nd Frank J. De Francis Memorial Dash

DEFACTO (1993)
At 3: 3rd Pegasus Breeders' Cup Handicap

DEFENSIVE PLAY (1987)
At 3: Won Man o' War Stakes
At 4: Won Charles H. Strub Stakes
At 5: 2nd Californian Stakes
Pacific Classic
Oak Tree Invitational Stakes
3rd Santa Anita Handicap
Suburban Handicap

DEGENERATE GAL (1985)
At 6: Won Apple Blossom Handicap

DEGENERATE JON (1977)
At 2: 2nd Breeders' Futurity

DEHERE (1991)
At 2: Won Hopeful Stakes
Champagne Stakes
2nd Futurity Stakes

DE LA ROSE (1978)
At 3: Won Hollywood Derby
2nd Kentucky Oaks
Flower Bowl Handicap

DELAWARE CHIEF (1967)
At 3: 2nd Gotham Stakes
Withers Stakes
3rd Wood Memorial Stakes

DELAWARE TOWNSHIP (1996)
At 5: Won Forego Handicap
Frank J. De Francis Memorial Dash

DELAY (1968)
At 5: Won John B. Campbell Handicap
At 6: 2nd John B. Campbell Handicap

DELEGANT (1984)
At 6: Won San Juan Capistrano Handicap

DELEGATE (1944)
At 2: 3rd Washington Park Futurity
At 5: 2nd Westchester Handicap
At 6: 2nd Fall Highweight Handicap
3rd Excelsior Handicap

DELHI MAID (1960)
At 3: Won Hollywood Oaks

DELICATE CURE (1991)
At 2: 3rd Arlington-Washington Futurity

DELICATE VINE (1984)
At 2: Won Arlington-Washington Lassie Stakes
3rd Oak Leaf Stakes

DELIGHTER (1985)
At 3: Won Yellow Ribbon Stakes
3rd Rothmans International Stakes

DELIRIUM (1961)
At 2: Won Sanford Stakes

DEL MAR DENNIS (1990)
At 4: 3rd Hollywood Gold Cup

DELNITA (1955)
At 2: 2nd Arlington Lassie Stakes
3rd Princess Pat Stakes

DELTA (1952)
At 2: Won Arlington Lassie Stakes
Princess Pat Stakes
2nd Arlington Futurity
At 4: Won Arlington Matron Handicap

DELTA FLAG (1975)
At 3: Won Monmouth Invitational Handicap

DELTA FORM (1996)
At 6: 3rd Turf Classic
Hollywood Turf Cup

DELTA JUDGE (1960)
At 2: Won Sapling Stakes
2nd Pimlico Futurity
At 4: 3rd Whitney Stakes

DELTA LADY (1991)
At 2: 3rd Spinaway Stakes

DELTA TRACE (1981)
At 3: Won Illinois Derby

DE LUXE (1946)
At 4: 3rd Aqueduct Handicap

DEMOBILIZE (1956)
At 2: 3rd Washington Park Futurity
Cowdin Stakes
At 3: 2nd American Derby

DEMON ACQUIRE (1994)
At 3: 3rd Las Virgenes Stakes

DEMONS BEGONE (1984)
At 2: 2nd Futurity Stakes
Champagne Stakes
At 3: Won Arkansas Derby

DENODADO (1960)
At 3: Won San Felipe Handicap

DENON (1998)
At 3: Won Hollywood Derby
At 4: Won Charles Whittingham Handicap
Turf Classic
2nd United Nations Handicap
Sword Dancer Invitational Handicap
At 5: Won Manhattan Handicap
3rd Man o' War Stakes

DENTRIFICE (1947)
At 2: 3rd Astoria Stakes

DENVER EXPRESS (1982)
At 3: 2nd Fantasy Stakes

DEPENDABILITY (1962)
At 3: 3rd Gotham Stakes

DEPLOY VENTURE (1996)
At 4: 3rd Charles Whittingham Handicap

DEPOSIT TICKET (1988)
At 2: Won Hopeful Stakes
2nd Futurity Stakes

DEPUTATION (1989)
At 4: 2nd Hempstead Handicap

DEPUTED TESTAMONY (1980)
At 3: Won Preakness Stakes
Haskell Invitational Handicap

DEPUTY COMMANDER (1994)
At 3: Won Travers Stakes
Super Derby
2nd Swaps Stakes
Breeders' Cup Classic
At 4: 2nd Californian Stakes

DEPUTY DIAMOND (1995)
At 3: 2nd Jim Dandy Stakes
At 4: 2nd Brooklyn Handicap

DEPUTY GOVERNOR (1984)
At 4: Won John Henry Handicap

DEPUTY MINISTER (1979)
At 2: Won Laurel Futurity
Young America Stakes
At 4: 2nd Meadowlands Cup
3rd Vosburgh Stakes

DE ROCHE (1986)
At 3: Won Jerome Handicap
At 4: 2nd Oaklawn Handicap
Suburban Handicap
Jockey Club Gold Cup
3rd Pimlico Special
Brooklyn Handicap
Philip H. Iselin Handicap
At 5: 3rd Brooklyn Handicap

DERRICK (1956)
At 2: 3rd Breeders' Futurity
Remsen Stakes
At 5: 2nd Gulfstream Park Handicap

DESERT CHIEF III (1956)
At 8: 3rd San Juan Capistrano Handicap

DESERT FORCE (1989)
At 3: 2nd Arlington Classic
3rd Arkansas Derby

DESERT HERO (1996)
At 3: 3rd Santa Anita Derby

DESERT LAW (1964)
At 4: 3rd Vanity Handicap
At 5: Won Vanity Handicap
2nd Santa Barbara Handicap

DESERT LOVE (1962)
At 3: Won Santa Susana Stakes
3rd Dixie Handicap
At 5: Won Vanity Handicap

DESERT MIRAGE (1992)
At 2: 2nd Norfolk Stakes

DESERT STORMER (1990)
At 5: Won Breeders' Cup Sprint

DESERT VIXEN (1970)
At 3: Won Alabama Stakes
Gazelle Handicap
Beldame Stakes
At 4: Won Beldame Stakes
2nd Spinster Stakes
Washington D.C. International

DESERT WINE (1980)
At 2: 2nd Del Mar Futurity
Norfolk Stakes
Hollywood Futurity
At 3: Won San Felipe Handicap
2nd Blue Grass Stakes
Kentucky Derby
Preakness Stakes
Jerome Handicap
At 4: Won Californian Stakes
Hollywood Gold Cup
Charles H. Strub Stakes
2nd San Fernando Stakes

DESIGNATED DANCER (1988)
At 3: 3rd Alabama Stakes

DESIREE (1973)
At 4: Won Santa Barbara Handicap

DESSERT (2000)
At 3: Won Del Mar Oaks

DESTRO (1963)
At 3: Won Ladies Handicap

DESTROYER (1971)
At 3: Won Santa Anita Derby

DETECTIVE (1947)
At 2: 3rd Tremont Stakes

DETERMINE (1951)
At 3: Won San Felipe Handicap
Santa Anita Derby
Kentucky Derby
2nd Californian Stakes
3rd Westerner Stakes
At 4: Won Santa Anita Maturity
2nd San Juan Capistrano Handicap
Californian Stakes
3rd Hollywood Gold Cup

DETERMINED KING (1971)
At 3: Won American Derby

DEUCES OVER SEVEN (1977)
At 3: 3rd Golden Harvest Handicap

DEVIL DIAMOND (1990)
At 2: 3rd Norfolk Stakes

DEVIL HIS DUE (1989)
At 3: Won Gotham Stakes
Wood Memorial Stakes
2nd Travers Stakes
3rd Jim Dandy Stakes
At 4: Won Gulfstream Park Handicap
Pimlico Special
Suburban Handicap
2nd Philip H. Iselin Handicap
Woodward Stakes
3rd Whitney Handicap
At 5: Won Brooklyn Handicap
Suburban Handicap
2nd Oaklawn Handicap
Pimlico Special
Whitney Handicap
Woodward Stakes
Jockey Club Gold Cup
NYRA Mile Handicap
3rd Metropolitan Handicap
At 6: 2nd Pimlico Special

DEVILKIN (1949)
At 3: Won Comely Handicap
3rd Monmouth Oaks
At 4: 2nd New Castle Handicap
3rd Monmouth Handicap

DEVIL'S BAG (1981)
At 2: Won Laurel Futurity
Champagne Stakes

DEVIL'S CUP (1993)
At 3: 3rd Crown Royal Hollywood Derby

DEVIL'S HONOR (1993)
At 2: 3rd Champagne Stakes
At 3: 3rd Isle of Capri Casino Super Derby

DEVIL'S PRIDE (1995)
At 2: 3rd Futurity Stakes

DEVIOUS COURSE (1992)
At 3: 3rd Gotham Stakes
At 5: Won Cigar Mile Handicap

DEVONWOOD (1994)
At 4: 2nd Manhattan Handicap

DEVOTED BRASS (1990)
At 3: Won Swaps Stakes
3rd San Felipe Stakes

DEWAN (1965)
At 3: Won San Felipe Handicap
2nd Hollywood Derby
3rd Santa Anita Derby
Jerome Handicap
At 4: 3rd San Fernando Stakes
Whitney Stakes
At 5: Won Brooklyn Handicap
San Antonio Stakes
3rd Metropolitan Handicap
Whitney Stakes

DEWAN KEYS (1975)
At 5: 3rd Meadowlands Cup

DEW LINE (1979)
At 3: 2nd American Derby
Secretariat Stakes
3rd Arlington Classic
At 5: 3rd Brooklyn Handicap

DHARAN (1946)
At 3: 3rd Del Mar Derby
At 4: 2nd Inglewood Handicap
American Handicap

DHAUSLI (1977)
At 6: 3rd Pan American Handicap

DIABLO (1987)
At 4: 3rd NYRA Mile Handicap

DIABOLO (1972)
At 2: Won Del Mar Futurity
2nd Norfolk Stakes
At 3: Won California Derby
3rd San Felipe Handicap
Santa Anita Derby
Kentucky Derby
Preakness Stakes
Swaps Stakes

DIACHRONY (1981)
At 2: 2nd Del Mar Debutante Stakes

DIAGRAMATIC (1973)
At 5: 2nd American Handicap
Sunset Handicap

DIAMOND BLACK (1969)
At 6: 3rd New Orleans Handicap

DIAMOND DONNIE (1986)
At 3: 2nd Gotham Stakes

DIAMOND LANE (1947)
At 3: 3rd Kentucky Oaks

DIAMOND ON THE RUN (1995)
At 2: 2nd Matron Stakes
Frizette Stakes

DIANES HALO (1991)
At 3: 2nd Santa Anita Oaks
3rd Kentucky Oaks

DIATOME (1962)
At 3: Won Washington D.C. International

DIAZO (1990)
At 3: Won Pegasus Handicap
At 4: Won Strub Stakes

DICE DANCER (1995)
At 3: 2nd Wood Memorial Stakes

DICTAR (1950)
At 3: 2nd Travers Stakes
Discovery Handicap
Lawrence Realization Stakes
Grey Lag Handicap
3rd Ohio Derby

DIDINA (1992)
At 4: 3rd Gamely Handicap

DIFFERENT (1992)
At 4: Won Beverly Hills Handicap
Three Chimneys Spinster Stakes
3rd Breeders' Cup Distaff
At 5: 2nd Beverly Hills Handicap
3rd Apple Blossom Handicap
Gamely Handicap
Ramona Handicap
At 6: 3rd Vanity Handicap

DIG FOR IT (1995)
At 6: 3rd Pacific Classic

DIGNITAS (1965)
At 4: Won Charles H. Strub Stakes
2nd San Fernando Stakes
3rd Malibu Stakes

DIGRESS (1985)
At 2: 3rd Cowdin Stakes
At 3: Won Tropical Park Derby

DIHELA (1966)
At 2: 3rd Frizette Stakes

DIKE (1966)
At 2: Won Breeders' Futurity
2nd Pimlico-Laurel Futurity
At 3: Won Gotham Stakes
Wood Memorial Stakes
2nd Travers Stakes
Suburban Handicap
3rd Kentucky Derby
Belmont Stakes
American Derby
Brooklyn Handicap

DILIGENCE (1993)
At 2: 2nd Champagne Stakes
At 3: 2nd NYRA Mile Handicap
3rd Jerome Handicap

DIMAGGIO (1972)
At 2: Won Hollywood Juvenile Championship
3rd Del Mar Futurity

DIMITROVA (2000)
At 3: Won Flower Bowl Invitational Stakes
2nd Garden City Breeders' Cup Handicap

DINARD (1988)
At 3: Won Santa Anita Derby
At 4: 2nd Charles H. Strub Stakes

DINEWISELY (1949)
At 3: 2nd Black-Eyed Susan Stakes
Delaware Oaks
Black Helen Handicap

DINGLE BAY (1959)
At 3: Won Hollywood Oaks
At 4: 3rd Vanity Handicap

DINNER GONG (1945)
At 4: Won San Antonio Handicap
2nd San Carlos Handicap
Santa Anita Handicap
San Juan Capistrano Handicap
3rd American Handicap
Sunset Handicap
Santa Anita Maturity

DINNER PARTY (1940)
At 6: 2nd Massachusetts Handicap
3rd Miami Beach Handicap

DIN'S DANCER (1985)
At 3: 2nd Jerome Handicap
3rd Jim Dandy Stakes

DIORAMA (1977)
At 2: 2nd Alcibiades Stakes

DIPLOMATIC AGENT (1968)
At 4: 3rd Malibu Stakes

DIPLOMATIC JET (1992)
At 4: Won Early Times Manhattan Handicap
Man o' War Stakes
Turf Classic
2nd Caesars International Handicap

DIPLOMAT WAY (1964)
At 2: Won Arlington-Washington Futurity
At 3: Won Blue Grass Stakes
2nd Louisiana Derby
3rd Arlington Classic
At 4: Won New Orleans Handicap
Oaklawn Handicap

DIPLOMETTE (1982)
At 2: 2nd Selima Stakes
At 3: 3rd Acorn Stakes

DISASTROUS NIGHT (1981)
At 2: 2nd Young America Stakes

DISCIPLINARIAN (1964)
At 2: 3rd Sapling Stakes

DISCIPLINE (1962)
At 2: Won Demoiselle Stakes
3rd Selima Stakes
Gardenia Stakes

At 3: 3rd Alabama Stakes
Gazelle Handicap
At 4: 3rd Delaware Handicap

DISCORAMA (1978)
At 3: 3rd Alabama Stakes
At 4: 3rd Top Flight Handicap

DISCOVER (1988)
At 2: 3rd Arlington-Washington Futurity
At 3: 2nd American Derby

DISCOVERED (1979)
At 4: 2nd Hialeah Turf Cup

DISCREET (1948)
At 3: Won Black-Eyed Susan Stakes

DISDAINFUL (1955)
At 2: 2nd Del Mar Futurity

DISPERSAL (1986)
At 3: 2nd Blue Grass Stakes
3rd Breeders' Cup Sprint
At 4: Won Woodward Handicap

DISPERSE (1957)
At 3: 3rd Belmont Stakes

DISPUTE (1951)
At 3: 3rd Vagrancy Handicap

DISPUTE (1990)
At 3: Won Kentucky Oaks
Gazelle Handicap
Beldame Stakes
2nd Mother Goose Stakes
Ruffian Handicap
At 4: Won Spinster Stakes
2nd Ruffian Handicap

DISTANT RYDER (1981)
At 3: Won California Derby

DISTINCT HONOR (1976)
At 2: 2nd Demoiselle Stakes

DISTINCTIVE MOON (1979)
At 2: 2nd Sorority Stakes

DISTORTED HUMOR (1993)
At 3: 2nd Jerome Handicap
At 4: 3rd Philip H. Iselin Handicap
At 5: 3rd Cigar Mile Handicap

DISTRAY (1966)
At 3: 3rd Dwyer Handicap
Travers Stakes

DIVIDE AND RULE (1966)
At 5: 2nd American Handicap
3rd Ford Pinto Invitational Turf Handicap

DIVINE COMEDY (1957)
At 3: Won Roamer Handicap
At 4: 2nd Brooklyn Handicap
Woodward Stakes

DIVINE GRACE (1971)
At 2: Won Oak Leaf Stakes
3rd Del Mar Debutante Stakes

DIVING BOARD (1951)
At 4: 2nd Whitney Stakes
3rd Trenton Handicap

DIVULGE (1982)
At 4: 2nd Budweiser-Arlington Million

DIXIE BRASS (1989)
At 3: Won Metropolitan Handicap
2nd Jim Dandy Stakes
3rd Jerome Handicap

DIXIE DOT COM (1995)
At 3: 2nd Early Times Hollywood Derby
At 6: 2nd Pacific Classic

DIXIE FLAG (1994)
At 3: 2nd Acorn Stakes

DIXIE FLYER (1947)
At 4: 3rd Vineland Handicap
At 5: Won Molly Pitcher Handicap

DIXIELAND BAND (1980)
At 3: Won Pennsylvania Derby

DIXIELAND BRASS (1986)
At 3: Won Fountain of Youth Stakes

DIXIELAND HEAT (1990)
At 3: 3rd Blue Grass Stakes

DIXIE PEARL (1992)
At 4: 3rd Yellow Ribbon Stakes

DIXIE UNION (1997)
At 2: Won Norfolk Stakes
2nd Del Mar Futurity
At 3: Won Haskell Invitational Handicap
Malibu Stakes

DIXIE VALOR (1951)
At 2: 2nd Del Mar Debutante Stakes

DIXIE WIND (1967)
At 2: 3rd Arlington-Washington Lassie Stakes

DOC JOCOY (1959)
At 2: 2nd Hollywood Juvenile Championship
At 3: Won San Felipe Handicap
California Derby
3rd Cinema Handicap
Hollywood Derby
At 4: Won Los Angeles Handicap
At 5: 2nd Santa Anita Handicap

DOCKSIDER (1995)
At 4: 3rd Breeders' Cup Mile

DOC MARCUS (1970)
At 2: 2nd Hollywood Juvenile Championship

DOC'S T.V. (1966)
At 4: Won Washington Park Handicap

DOCTOR BROCATO (1962)
At 3: 2nd Louisiana Derby

DODODURA (1945)
At 4: 3rd New Castle Handicap

DOGOON (1952)
At 2: 3rd Washington Park Futurity

DOGTOOTH VIOLET (1970)
At 4: 3rd Vanity Handicap
Beverly Hills Handicap

DO IT AGAIN DAN (1982)
At 2: 3rd Sapling Stakes
At 3: 3rd Hutcheson Stakes
Fountain of Youth Stakes
Florida Derby

DO IT WITH STYLE (1988)
At 3: Won Ashland Stakes

DOLLAR BILL (1998)
At 2: 2nd Lane's End Breeders' Futurity
At 3: 3rd Toyota Blue Grass Stakes
Travers Stakes
At 4: 2nd Stephen Foster Handicap
3rd Oaklawn Handicap
At 5: 3rd Suburban Handicap

DOM ALARIC (1974)
At 4: 2nd Canadian International Championship
At 5: 2nd United Nations Handicap
3rd Hollywood Invitational Handicap

DOM D'ALBIGNAC (1977)
At 5: 2nd Louisiana Downs Handicap

DOMEDRIVER (1998)
At 4: Won NetJets Breeders' Cup Mile

DOMESTIC DISPUTE (2000)
At 2: 2nd Hollywood Futurity

DOMINANT DANCER (1987)
At 2: Won Oak Leaf Stakes

DOMINANT RULER (1975)
At 2: 3rd Sapling Stakes

DOMINION DAY II (1964)
At 4: 3rd Canadian International Championship

DOMQUIL (1950)
At 4: 3rd Whitney Handicap

DOMYNSKY (1980)
At 6: 3rd Hialeah Turf Cup

DON B. (1965)
At 3: 2nd San Felipe Handicap
Santa Anita Derby
California Derby

DONNAJACK (1951)
At 2: 3rd Arlington Futurity

DONNA VIOLA (1992)
At 4: Won Yellow Ribbon Stakes
At 5: Won Gamely Handicap
3rd Beverly Hills Handicap

DONOR (1944)
At 2: Won Sapling Stakes
Champagne Stakes
3rd Remsen Handicap
At 3: Won Jerome Handicap
3rd Westchester Handicap
At 4: 2nd Manhattan Handicap
New York Handicap
At 5: Won Manhattan Handicap
New York Handicap
2nd Whitney Stakes

DON PEPPINO (1943)
At 3: 2nd Cinema Handicap

DON POGGIO (1956)
At 4: Won Manhattan Handicap
Gallant Fox Handicap
2nd Jockey Club Gold Cup
At 5: Won Monmouth Handicap
2nd McLennan Handicap
3rd Gulfstream Park Handicap

DON REBELDE (1949)
At 4: 2nd San Antonio Handicap
San Juan Capistrano Handicap

DON RICKLES (1957)
At 3: 3rd Travers Stakes

DON RICKLES (1981)
At 2: 2nd Hopeful Stakes
At 3: 2nd Tropical Park Derby

DON ROBERTO (1977)
At 5: 2nd Sunset Handicap
3rd United Nations Handicap
Arlington Handicap
Louisiana Downs Handicap

DON'S CHOICE (1982)
At 3: 2nd Jim Dandy Stakes

DON SEBASTIAN (1974)
At 3: 2nd Monmouth Invitational Handicap

DONSON (1962)
At 2: 2nd Hollywood Juvenile Championship

DON'T ALIBI (1956)
At 5: Won San Juan Capistrano Handicap

DON'T BLAME RIO (1993)
At 5: 3rd Santa Anita Handicap

DON'T READ MY LIPS (1991)
At 4: 3rd Gamely Handicap

DON'T SAY HALO (1982)
At 3: 3rd Swaps Stakes

DON'T STOP ME (1967)
At 3: 2nd Arkansas Derby

DONTSTOP THEMUSIC (1980)
At 5: Won Vanity Handicap
Spinster Stakes
3rd Breeders' Cup Distaff
At 6: 2nd Vanity Handicap
3rd Santa Margarita Handicap

DONUT KING (1959)
At 2: Won Champagne Stakes
2nd Garden State Stakes
3rd Del Mar Futurity
At 3: 3rd Wood Memorial Stakes
At 4: 2nd Hawthorne Gold Cup

DOOLIN POINT (1960)
At 3: 3rd San Felipe Handicap

DOOLY (1947)
At 3: 3rd Preakness Stakes

DOONESBURY (1977)
At 2: 2nd Hollywood Juvenile Championship
Del Mar Futurity
At 3: 2nd California Derby
At 4: Won San Fernando Stakes
2nd San Antonio Stakes
3rd Charles H. Strub Stakes

DORCARO (1978)
At 3: 2nd Swaps Stakes
At 4: 2nd Charles H. Strub Stakes

DO-REIGH-ME (1941)
At 5: Won Gulfstream Handicap

DOROTHY BROWN (1943)
At 3: 3rd Pimlico Oaks

DORRENO (1969)
At 2: 2nd Del Mar Futurity

DOT ED'S BLUESKY (1966)
At 3: 2nd Monmouth Invitational Handicap
At 6: 3rd Donn Handicap

DO TELL GEORGE (1973)
At 5: 2nd Meadowlands Cup

DOTHAN (1968)
At 2: 3rd Kentucky Jockey Club Stakes

DOTTED LINE (1953)
At 3: Won Delaware Oaks
2nd Alabama Stakes
Ladies Handicap
3rd Monmouth Oaks
Gazelle Handicap
At 4: Won Vineland Handicap
At 5: 2nd Delaware Handicap
Ladies Handicap
Jockey Club Gold Cup
3rd Beldame Handicap
At 6: Won Man o' War Handicap
3rd Display Handicap

DOTTED SWISS (1956)
At 4: Won Hollywood Gold Cup
Sunset Handicap
2nd Washington Park Handicap
Woodward Stakes
3rd Los Angeles Handicap

DOTTIE'S DOLL (1973)
At 2: 3rd Demoiselle Stakes
At 4: 2nd Ladies Handicap
3rd Delaware Handicap
At 5: 2nd Delaware Handicap
3rd Top Flight Handicap
Vanity Handicap

DOUBLE BED (1983)
At 5: Won Hialeah Turf Cup

DOUBLE BRANDY (1946)
At 3: 3rd Jerome Handicap
At 4: 2nd Dixie Handicap
Brooklyn Handicap

DOUBLE DELTA (1966)
At 3: 2nd Kentucky Oaks
At 5: Won Beldame Stakes

DOUBLE DISCOUNT (1973)
At 3: 2nd Santa Anita Derby
3rd San Felipe Handicap

DOUBLE DISCOUNT *(Continued)*
Hollywood Derby
Swaps Stakes
At 4: 2nd San Fernando Stakes
San Antonio Stakes
3rd Charles H. Strub Stakes
At 5: 3rd San Antonio Stakes
At 7: 3rd San Antonio Stakes

DOUBLEDOGDARE (1953)
At 2: Won Matron Stakes
Alcibiades Stakes
2nd Spinaway Stakes
At 3: Won Spinster Stakes
2nd Kentucky Oaks
3rd Arlington Classic

DOUBLE ENTRY (1967)
At 5: 2nd Pan American Handicap
Hialeah Turf Cup

DOUBLE FEINT (1983)
At 3: 2nd Hollywood Derby

DOUBLE F.F. (1942)
At 4: 3rd Vanity Handicap
At 5: 2nd Santa Margarita Handicap

DOUBLE HONOR (1995)
At 2: 3rd Norfolk Stakes

DOUBLE JAY (1944)
At 2: Won Garden State Stakes
Kentucky Jockey Club Stakes
At 3: 2nd Discovery Handicap
Roamer Handicap
Trenton Handicap
At 4: Won Trenton Handicap
2nd San Antonio Handicap
Excelsior Handicap
3rd Santa Anita Handicap
Aqueduct Handicap
Massachusetts Handicap
Santa Anita Maturity
At 5: Won American Handicap

DOUBLE LEA (1958)
At 3: 3rd Cinema Handicap

DOUBLE PARK (1994)
At 3: 3rd Santa Anita Oaks

DOUBLE QUICK (1986)
At 2: 3rd Norfolk Stakes

DOUBLE RIPPLE (1965)
At 4: 2nd Delaware Handicap
At 5: Won Molly Pitcher Handicap

DOUBLE SONIC (1978)
At 3: 3rd Flamingo Stakes
American Derby
At 4: 3rd Gulfstream Park Handicap

DOUBLE SPEED (1951)
At 2: Won Del Mar Futurity

DOUBLE WEDGE (1985)
At 5: Won Gamely Handicap
3rd Santa Barbara Handicap

DOUBLE YOU LOU (1972)
At 2: 2nd Oak Leaf Stakes

DOUBLE YOUR FUN (1970)
At 2: Won Arlington-Washington Lassie Stakes

DOUBLY CLEAR (1982)
At 2: Won Sapling Stakes

DOWERY (1981)
At 4: 2nd Maskette Stakes
3rd Spinster Stakes

DOWN THE AISLE (1993)
At 4: 2nd Canadian International Championship
3rd Early Times Turf Classic
At 7: 3rd Brooklyn Handicap

DOWNTOWN DAVEY (1986)
At 2: 3rd Laurel Futurity

DOWTY (1992)
At 5: 3rd Breeders' Cup Classic

D'PARROT (1987)
At 3: 3rd Jerome Handicap

DRACHMA (1984)
At 2: 3rd Remsen Stakes

DRAFT CARD (1965)
At 3: 2nd Lawrence Realization Stakes

DRAG RACE (1987)
At 2: Won Del Mar Futurity

DRAGSET (1971)
At 5: 3rd Oaklawn Handicap
At 6: 3rd Arlington Classic Invitational Handicap
Oaklawn Handicap

DRAMA CRITIC (1974)
At 2: 3rd Arlington-Washington Lassie Stakes
At 4: Won Ramona Handicap
2nd Vanity Handicap
La Canada Stakes
Yellow Ribbon Stakes

DRAMA CRITIC (1996)
At 4: 3rd Man o' War Stakes

DRAMATIC DESIRE (1981)
At 4: 3rd Suburban Handicap

DRAMATIC GOLD (1991)
At 3: Won Molson Export Million
2nd Swaps Stakes
3rd Pacific Classic
Breeders' Cup Classic
At 4: 2nd Strub Stakes
3rd NYRA Mile Handicap
At 5: Won Buick Meadowlands Cup Handicap
At 8: 3rd San Antonio Handicap

DRAPEAU TRICOLORE (1985)
At 4: 2nd Brooklyn Handicap

DR. BRENDLER (1998)
At 5: 3rd Manhattan Handicap

DR. CARRINGTON (1985)
At 4: 3rd Carter Handicap

DR. CARTER (1981)
At 2: Won Remsen Stakes
2nd Champagne Stakes
3rd Young America Stakes
At 3: 2nd Flamingo Stakes
Florida Derby
At 4: Won Gulfstream Park Handicap
2nd Widener Handicap

DR. CATON (1993)
At 3: 2nd Buick Haskell Invitational Handicap

DR. DAN EYES (1983)
At 3: 2nd Tropical Park Derby

DR. DEATH (1985)
At 3: 3rd Hollywood Derby

DREAM DEAL (1986)
At 3: 3rd Alabama Stakes

DREAM'N BE LUCKY (1973)
At 3: 3rd Ohio Derby

DREAM PATH (1965)
At 2: 2nd Spinaway Stakes

DREAMS GALLORE (1996)
At 3: Won Mother Goose Stakes
2nd Kentucky Oaks
Coaching Club American Oaks

DREAM SUPREME (1997)
At 3: Won Test Stakes
Ballerina Handicap
At 4: 3rd Ballerina Handicap

DREAM TEAM (1985)
At 2: Won Oak Leaf Stakes
3rd Breeders' Cup Juvenile Fillies

DREAM WELL (1995)
At 4: 2nd Turf Classic

DREAMY MIMI (1986)
At 2: 3rd Matron Stakes
At 5: Won Top Flight Handicap

DRESS TO THRILL (1999)
At 3: Won Matriarch Stakes

DRESS UP (1957)
At 4: 2nd Inglewood Handicap
American Handicap
Sunset Handicap
3rd Manhattan Handicap

DR. FAGER (1964)
At 2: Won Cowdin Stakes
2nd Champagne Stakes
At 3: Won Gotham Stakes
Withers Stakes
Arlington Classic
Hawthorne Gold Cup
Vosburgh Handicap
3rd Woodward Stakes
At 4: Won Californian Stakes
Suburban Handicap
Washington Park Handicap
Vosburgh Handicap
Whitney Stakes
United Nations Handicap
2nd Brooklyn Handicap

DR. FONG (1995)
At 4: 2nd Strub Stakes

DRIFTING MAID (1947)
At 5: 3rd Black Helen Handicap

DRILL SITE (1959)
At 3: Won Hollywood Derby
At 5: 2nd Sunset Handicap

DRIN (1963)
At 3: Won Cinema Handicap
2nd Hollywood Derby
3rd California Derby
At 4: Won Charles H. Strub Stakes
2nd San Antonio Handicap

DR. KACY (1959)
At 4: Won American Handicap
3rd Charles H. Strub Stakes
San Luis Rey Handicap

DR. KIERNAN (1989)
At 4: 3rd Sword Dancer Handicap
Man o' War Stakes

DR. OLE NELSON (1946)
At 4: Won Hawthorne Gold Cup
At 6: 2nd Hawthorne Gold Cup

DROLLERY (1970)
At 5: 2nd Bowling Green Handicap
3rd Man o' War Stakes
At 6: 2nd Bowling Green Handicap

DROLL ROLE (1968)
At 2: 3rd Pimlico-Laurel Futurity
At 3: 2nd Gotham Stakes
At 4: Won Grey Lag Handicap
Hawthorne Gold Cup
Massachusetts Handicap
Canadian International Championship
Washington D.C. International
2nd Hollywood Gold Cup
Manhattan Handicap
3rd Man o' War Stakes

DROP ME A NOTE (1976)
At 2: 3rd Selima Stakes

DROP YOUR DRAWERS (1979)
At 3: 2nd Illinois Derby
Arlington Classic
3rd Super Derby

DR. PATCHES (1974)
At 4: Won Vosburgh Handicap
Meadowlands Cup
At 5: 2nd Metropolitan Handicap

At 6: 2nd Vosburgh Stakes
Whitney Stakes
Meadowlands Cup

DR. ROOT (1987)
At 4: Won Sword Dancer Handicap

DRUMBEAT (1945)
At 3: Won Cinema Handicap
Sunset Handicap
2nd Westerner Handicap
3rd Santa Anita Derby

DRUM FIRE (1969)
At 2: 3rd Pimlico-Laurel Futurity

DRUMTOP (1966)
At 4: Won Canadian International Championship
2nd Santa Barbara Handicap
Hialeah Turf Cup
Bowling Green Handicap
Massachusetts Handicap
3rd Man o' War Stakes
At 5: Won Hialeah Turf Cup
Bowling Green Handicap
2nd Century Handicap

DR. VALERIE (1975)
At 3: 3rd Flamingo Stakes
Florida Derby

DRY BEAN (1990)
At 3: 3rd Haskell Invitational Handicap

DUBASSOFF (1969)
At 3: Won American Derby
2nd United Nations Handicap
At 4: Won Arlington Handicap

DUBLINO (1999)
At 3: Won Del Mar Oaks
At 4: 2nd Gamely Breeders' Cup Handicap
John C. Mabee Handicap

DUC DE FLANAGAN (1970)
At 3: 3rd Dwyer Handicap

DUC DE THOR (1960)
At 2: 2nd Remsen Stakes

DUCHESS KHALED (1961)
At 3: 3rd Hollywood Oaks

DUCK DANCE (1967)
At 4: Won Vosburgh Handicap

DUDA (1991)
At 4: Won Matriarch Stakes
3rd Flower Bowl Invitational Handicap

DUE DILIGENCE (1972)
At 4: Won Carter Handicap

DUEL (1961)
At 2: Won Saratoga Special
Breeders' Futurity
2nd Kentucky Jockey Club Stakes
At 4: Won Charles H. Strub Stakes
2nd San Juan Capistrano Handicap

DUE TO THE KING (1987)
At 2: 3rd Norfolk Stakes

DUGAN KNIGHT (1981)
At 3: 3rd Arlington Classic

DUKE FANELLI (1949)
At 2: 3rd Garden State Stakes

DUKE'S LEA (1951)
At 3: 2nd Santa Anita Derby
California Derby
At 4: 2nd Washington Park Handicap

DUKE TOM (1970)
At 5: 3rd Pan American Handicap

DULAT (1948)
At 5: 2nd Miami Beach Handicap
3rd Gulfstream Park Handicap

DULATUREE (1959)
At 2: 3rd Selima Stakes

DULCIA (1969)
At 6: Won Vanity Handicap
Ramona Handicap
National Championship Inv. Handicap
2nd Beverly Hills Handicap

DUMPTY'S DREAM (1969)
At 3: 2nd Santa Susana Stakes

DUMPTYS LADY (1966)
At 3: Won Santa Susana Stakes

DUNCAN JUNCTION (1964)
At 3: 2nd Hollywood Derby

DUNCE (1956)
At 2: 2nd Arlington Futurity
3rd Futurity Stakes
At 3: Won Arlington Classic
American Derby
2nd Blue Grass Stakes
Washington Park Handicap
3rd Preakness Stakes
At 4: 2nd Bowling Green Handicap
3rd Carter Handicap

DUNDE MARMALADE (1968)
At 2: 3rd Sanford Stakes

DUNDERHEAD (1963)
At 4: 2nd Manhattan Handicap

DUNFEE (1961)
At 2: Won Cowdin Stakes
3rd Arlington-Washington Futurity

DUPAGE LADY (1960)
At 3: 3rd Ladies Handicap
At 4: 2nd Ladies Handicap

DUSHYANTOR (1993)
At 5: 3rd Sword Dancer Invitational Handicap
Breeders' Cup Turf

DUSKY DAMION (1957)
At 7: 3rd San Juan Capistrano Handicap
San Luis Rey Handicap

DUST COMMANDER (1967)
At 3: Won Blue Grass Stakes
Kentucky Derby
3rd Monmouth Invitational Handicap

DUSTY COUNTY (1972)
At 3: 3rd California Derby
Cinema Handicap

DUSTY HEART (1982)
At 2: 2nd Breeders' Cup Juvenile Fillies

DUSTY LEGS (1945)
At 2: 3rd Astarita Stakes

DUSTY'S DARBY (1982)
At 2: 2nd Arlington-Washington Futurity

DUTCHESS PEG (1947)
At 2: Won Arlington Lassie Stakes
2nd Princess Pat Stakes

DUTCH LANE (1948)
At 5: 3rd Fall Highweight Handicap
At 6: 2nd Fall Highweight Handicap

DUTY DANCE (1982)
At 4: 2nd Man o' War Stakes

D'WILDCAT (1998)
At 4: Won Frank J. De Francis Memorial Dash

DYNAFORMER (1985)
At 3: Won Jersey Derby

DYNAMIC STAR (1983)
At 3: 2nd Acorn Stakes
Mother Goose Stakes

DYNASTIC (1968)
At 3: 2nd Flamingo Stakes
3rd Blue Grass Stakes

DYNEVER (2000)
At 3: 3rd Breeders' Cup Classic / by Dodge

EAGER EXCHANGE (1969)
At 3: 2nd Gotham Stakes

EAGLE ADMIRAL (1957)
At 3: 3rd Santa Anita Derby

EAGLESHAM (1966)
At 4: 3rd Pan American Handicap

EAGLETAR (1974)
At 2: 3rd Arlington-Washington Futurity

EAGLETON (1996)
At 2: 2nd Norfolk Stakes

EARL OF BARKING (1990)
At 2: 3rd Hollywood Futurity
At 3: 2nd American Derby
3rd Hollywood Derby
At 5: Won Hollywood Turf Handicap
3rd Hollywood Turf Cup

EARLY FLYER (1998)
At 3: 2nd Frank J. De Francis Memorial Dash

EARLY PIONEER (1995)
At 5: Won Sempra Energy Hollywood Gold Cup

EARSHOT (1943)
At 3: Won Acorn Stakes
2nd Pimlico Oaks
Louisiana Derby
3rd Vineland Handicap
At 4: Won New Orleans Handicap
3rd Trenton Handicap

EASTERN ECHO (1988)
At 2: Won Futurity Stakes

EASTERN FLEET (1968)
At 3: Won Florida Derby
2nd Wood Memorial Stakes
Preakness Stakes
3rd Ohio Derby
At 4: 3rd Amory L. Haskell Handicap

EASTERN PAGEANT (1971)
At 4: 3rd Oaklawn Handicap

EASTERN PRINCESS (1958)
At 2: 3rd Selima Stakes

EASY ERN (1970)
At 3: 2nd California Derby

EASY GOER (1986)
At 2: Won Cowdin Stakes
Champagne Stakes
2nd Breeders' Cup Juvenile
At 3: Won Gotham Stakes
Wood Memorial Stakes
Belmont Stakes
Whitney Handicap
Travers Stakes
Woodward Handicap
Jockey Club Gold Cup
2nd Kentucky Derby
Preakness Stakes
Breeders' Cup Classic
At 4: Won Suburban Handicap
3rd Metropolitan Handicap

EASY GRADES (1999)
At 3: 2nd Santa Anita Derby

EASY LIME (1962)
At 3: 2nd Cinema Handicap
3rd Hollywood Derby

EASY N DIRTY (1983)
At 4: 3rd Jockey Club Gold Cup
At 5: 3rd Jockey Club Gold Cup
At 6: 3rd Suburban Handicap

EASY NOW (1989)
At 3: Won Go for Wand Stakes
2nd Mother Goose Stakes
Coaching Club American Oaks

EASY SPUR (1956)
At 3: Won Florida Derby
2nd Hawthorne Gold Cup

EATONTOWN (1946)
At 3: 2nd Saranac Handicap
At 7: 3rd Carter Handicap

EBONY PEARL (1955)
At 3: 3rd Louisiana Derby

ECOLE ETAGE (1970)
At 4: 2nd Amory L. Haskell Handicap
3rd John B. Campbell Handicap

ECSTATIC RIDE (1989)
At 3: 3rd Blue Grass Stakes

ECTON PARK (1996)
At 3: Won Jim Dandy Stakes
Super Derby
3rd Louisiana Derby
Arkansas Derby
At 4: 3rd Pacific Classic

EDDIE SCHMIDT (1953)
At 4: Won Gallant Fox Handicap
2nd William P. Kyne Memorial Handicap
Inglewood Handicap
Sunset Handicap
At 5: Won Inglewood Handicap
2nd Hollywood Gold Cup
Sunset Handicap
3rd American Handicap
Trenton Handicap
San Juan Capistrano Handicap
At 6: 3rd San Carlos Handicap
At 7: 2nd Californian Stakes
3rd Hollywood Gold Cup

EDIE'S SISTER (1953)
At 2: 3rd Del Mar Debutante Stakes

EDITORIALIST (1958)
At 3: 2nd Arlington Classic
American Derby

EDITOR'S NOTE (1993)
At 2: 3rd Breeders' Cup Juvenile
At 3: Won Belmont Stakes
Isle of Capri Casino Super Derby
2nd Florida Derby
3rd Blue Grass Stakes
Preakness Stakes

ED'S PRIDE (1949)
At 2: 2nd Breeders' Futurity

E. DUBAI (1998)
At 3: 2nd Travers Stakes
Super Derby
At 4: Won Suburban Handicap

EDUCATED RISK (1990)
At 2: Won Frizette Stakes
2nd Matron Stakes
Breeders' Cup Juvenile Fillies
At 3: 2nd Acorn Stakes
At 4: Won Top Flight Handicap
2nd Beldame Stakes
3rd Ruffian Handicap

EDUCATION (1944)
At 2: Won Washington Park Futurity
Breeders' Futurity
2nd Kentucky Jockey Club Stakes

EEQUALSMCSQUARED (1989)
At 5: 2nd Donn Handicap

EFFERVESCING (1973)
At 3: 3rd Canadian International Championship
At 4: 3rd Century Handicap
At 5: Won American Handicap
3rd Sunset Handicap

EGGY (1968)
At 2: Won Gardenia Stakes

EGO TWIST (1963)
At 3: 2nd Santa Susana Stakes

EIDOLON (1959)
At 3: 3rd Arkansas Derby

EIFFEL BLUE (1953)
At 3: 2nd Withers Stakes

EIFFEL TOWER (1943)
At 3: 3rd Cinema Handicap
Hollywood Derby

EIGHT BALL (1959)
At 2: 3rd Washington Park Futurity

EILLO (1980)
At 4: Won Breeders' Cup Sprint

EJEMPLO (1966)
At 5: 2nd Suburban Handicap

EKABA (1954)
At 3: 3rd American Derby
Michigan Mile and One-Sixteenth
At 4: 3rd Hawthorne Gold Cup
At 5: 2nd Bougainvillea Turf Handicap
Hialeah Turf Cup

ELA ATHENA (1996)
At 4: 2nd Man o' War Stakes
3rd Turf Classic
At 5: 3rd Man o' War Stakes

ELABORADO (1971)
At 5: 2nd San Juan Capistrano Handicap

ELABORATE (1995)
At 5: 3rd San Antonio Handicap

ELADIO (1963)
At 3: 2nd Arkansas Derby
Ohio Derby

EL ANGELO (1992)
At 5: 2nd Eddie Read Handicap

ELATED GUY (1989)
At 3: 2nd Molson Export Million

EL BABA (1979)
At 3: Won Louisiana Derby
2nd Arkansas Derby
Super Derby

EL BAKAN (1990)
At 3: 3rd Preakness Stakes

EL BANDIDO (1957)
At 5: Won Arlington Handicap
Canadian Championship Stakes
3rd Dixie Handicap

EL BASCO (1982)
At 3: Won Withers Stakes
2nd Pennsylvania Derby
3rd Gotham Stakes
Jersey Derby
Jerome Handicap

EL BORA (1960)
At 5: 3rd Oaklawn Handicap

EL BOTIJA (1970)
At 5: 3rd Century Handicap

ELBUTTE (1946)
At 3: 2nd Del Mar Derby

EL CAJON (1955)
At 3: 3rd Cinema Handicap

EL CHAMA (1951)
At 4: Won Washington D.C. International
At 5: 2nd Hialeah Turf Handicap

EL CORREDOR (1997)
At 3: Won Cigar Mile Handicap

EL CUBANASO (1980)
At 2: 3rd Young America Stakes
Champagne Stakes

ELECTRIC BLUE (1983)
At 2: 2nd Hollywood Futurity

ELECTRIC SOCIETY (1991)
At 5: 3rd Flower Bowl Invitational Handicap

ELECT THE RULER (1966)
At 3: Won San Felipe Handicap

ELEGANT HEIR (1965)
At 7: 3rd Oaklawn Handicap

ELEPHANT WALK (1966)
At 5: 3rd Manhattan Handicap

ELEVEN KEYS (1960)
At 3: 2nd Spinster Stakes

ELEVEN STITCHES (1977)
At 4: Won Californian Stakes
Hollywood Gold Cup

EL FANTASTICO (1975)
At 3: 2nd Cinema Handicap

ELITE MERCEDES (1997)
At 3: 2nd Turfway Spiral Stakes
3rd Fountain of Youth Stakes

ELIXIR (1948)
At 5: 3rd Aqueduct Handicap
At 6: Won McLennan Handicap

ELIZA (1990)
At 2: Won Arlington-Washington Lassie Stakes
Breeders' Cup Juvenile Fillies
At 3: Won Santa Anita Oaks
2nd Kentucky Oaks
3rd Santa Anita Derby

ELJAY (1949)
At 4: 2nd Michigan Mile

ELLIE MILOVE (1977)
At 2: 2nd Arlington-Washington Lassie Stakes

EL LOBO (1941)
At 6: Won San Antonio Handicap
2nd San Carlos Handicap

EL LOCO (1957)
At 5: Won Hialeah Turf Cup
2nd Bougainvillea Handicap
At 6: 2nd Donn Handicap

ELLOLUV (2000)
At 2: Won Hollywood Starlet Stakes
At 3: Won Ashland Stakes
2nd Las Virgenes Stakes
Santa Anita Oaks
Breeders' Cup Distaff

ELMHURST (1990)
At 7: Won Breeders' Cup Sprint

EL MONO (1944)
At 4: Won McLennan Handicap
Widener Handicap

ELOCUTIONIST (1973)
At 3: Won Arkansas Derby
Preakness Stakes
3rd Kentucky Derby

ELOQUENT (1976)
At 3: 2nd Acorn Stakes
Mother Goose Stakes

ELPIS (1942)
At 4: 3rd Molly Pitcher Handicap
At 5: Won New Castle Handicap
Comely Handicap
Molly Pitcher Handicap
2nd Massachusetts Handicap
3rd Beldame Handicap
Aqueduct Handicap
At 6: 2nd Santa Margarita Handicap
Vineland Handicap
New Castle Handicap
3rd Trenton Handicap

EL PITIRRE (1972)
At 2: Won Remsen Stakes

EL PORTUGUES (1973)
At 3: 2nd Withers Stakes

EL PRADO ROB (2001)
At 2: 3rd Futurity Stakes

EL REY (1968)
At 6: 2nd San Juan Capistrano Handicap

EL SENOR (1984)
At 4: 2nd Rothmans International Stakes
At 5: Won Hialeah Turf Cup
Sword Dancer Handicap
2nd Turf Classic
At 6: Won Sword Dancer Handicap
3rd Breeders' Cup Turf
At 7: 3rd Sword Dancer Handicap

EL TARTA (1971)
At 4: 3rd Hollywood Gold Cup

ELTISH (1992)
At 2: 2nd Breeders' Cup Juvenile
At 4: 2nd Philip H. Iselin Handicap

ELUSIVE (1979)
At 4: 2nd La Canada Stakes

ELVA'S KING (1967)
At 3: 2nd Louisiana Derby

EL ZAG (1957)
At 3: 3rd Arkansas Derby

EMANATING (1996)
At 3: 3rd Test Stakes

EMARDEE (1950)
At 4: 3rd Black Helen Handicap

EMINENCY (1978)
At 4: Won Oaklawn Handicap
At 5: 2nd Oaklawn Handicap

EMPIRE MAKER (2000)
At 3: Won Florida Derby
Wood Memorial Stakes
Belmont Stakes
2nd Kentucky Derby
Jim Dandy Stakes

ENCHANTED EVE (1949)
At 3: 2nd Alabama Stakes
Comely Handicap
3rd Ladies Handicap

ENCHANTING (1961)
At 2: 3rd Selima Stakes

ENCINO (1977)
At 2: 3rd Hollywood Juvenile Championship

ENCOLURE (1982)
At 3: 2nd Arkansas Derby
Ohio Derby
Super Derby

ENDEAR (1982)
At 4: 2nd Delaware Handicap
Spinster Stakes
3rd Maskette Stakes
Ruffian Handicap

ENDINE (1954)
At 4: Won Delaware Handicap
Ladies Handicap
2nd Diana Handicap
At 5: Won Delaware Handicap
2nd Top Flight Handicap

ENDOW (1986)
At 3: Won California Derby
3rd Illinois Derby
Swaps Stakes

ENDOWMENT (1949)
At 4: 2nd Sunset Handicap

END SWEEP (1991)
At 3: 3rd Jerome Handicap

ENDS WELL (1981)
At 4: Won United Nations Handicap
At 5: 2nd Whitney Handicap

ENDYMION (1959)
At 2: 3rd Pimlico Futurity
At 4: Won New Orleans Handicap

ENFILADE (1943)
At 3: Won Santa Susana Stakes
2nd Will Rogers Handicap

ENGINE ONE (1978)
At 4: Won Vosburgh Stakes

ENGLAND EXPECTS (1990)
At 2: 3rd Hopeful Stakes

ENGLAND'S LEGEND (1997)
At 4: Won Beverly D. Stakes
2nd Flower Bowl Invitational Handicap
At 5: 3rd Beverly D. Stakes

ENGLISH MUFFIN (1964)
At 3: 2nd Ohio Derby

ENJOY (1999)
At 4: 2nd Milady Breeders' Cup Handicap

ENJOY THE MOMENT (1995)
At 5: 3rd Santa Monica Handicap

ENNOBLED (1946)
At 5: Won Gulfstream Park Handicap

ENSIGN RAY (1993)
At 3: 2nd Jim Beam Stakes

ENSIGN RHYTHM (1983)
At 3: Won Fountain of Youth Stakes

ENTRUST (1946)
At 2: 3rd Saratoga Special

EPICENTRE (1999)
At 4: 3rd Hollywood Turf Cup

EPIC HONOR (1996)
At 3: 3rd Gallery Furniture.com Stakes

EPIC JOURNEY (1968)
At 3: 3rd Dwyer Handicap

EPITOME (1985)
At 2: Won Breeders' Cup Juvenile Fillies

EQUAL CHANGE (1972)
At 3: 2nd Coaching Club American Oaks

EQUALIZE (1982)
At 6: Won United Nations Handicap
2nd Arlington Million
At 7: 3rd Hollywood Turf Handicap

EQUANIMITY (1975)
At 3: Won Fantasy Stakes
2nd Santa Susana Stakes

EQUIFUN (1956)
At 5: 3rd Arlington Matron Handicap

ERADICATE (1985)
At 5: 2nd Oak Tree Invitational Stakes

ERICA'S SMILE (1999)
At 3: 3rd La Brea Stakes

ERIC'S CHAMP (1971)
At 3: 3rd Fountain of Youth Stakes

ERINS ISLE (1978)
At 4: Won Californian Stakes
Sunset Handicap
2nd Hollywood Gold Cup
Sword Dancer Stakes
At 5: Won Hollywood Invitational Handicap
San Luis Rey Stakes
San Juan Capistrano Handicap
2nd Man o' War Stakes
3rd Sword Dancer Handicap
Turf Classic

ERINSOUTHERMAN (2000)
At 2: 3rd Champagne Stakes

ERIN'S WORD (1977)
At 3: 2nd Coaching Club American Oaks
3rd Mother Goose Stakes

ERRARD KING (1951)
At 2: Won Pimlico Futurity
At 3: Won Arlington Classic
American Derby

ERRULLAH (1967)
At 5: 2nd Oaklawn Handicap

ERWIN BOY (1971)
At 5: Won Bowling Green Handicap
3rd Whitney Handicap

ESCADRU (1945)
At 2: 2nd Champagne Stakes
Remsen Handicap
At 3: 3rd Belmont Stakes

ESCENA (1993)
At 3: 2nd Kentucky Oaks
Mother Goose Stakes
Alabama Stakes
Gazelle Handicap
At 4: Won Ramona Handicap
3rd Breeders' Cup Distaff
At 5: Won Apple Blossom Handicap
Vanity Handicap
Breeders' Cup Distaff
2nd Go for Wand Handicap

ESOPS FOIBLES (1975)
At 2: 3rd Hollywood Juvenile Championship
At 3: Won Louisiana Derby
Arkansas Derby

ESPEA (1953)
At 4: Won Bougainvillea Turf Handicap

ESPIRIT DU NORD (1980)
At 4: 3rd Rothmans International Stakes

ESQUIMAU PIE (1965)
At 2: 3rd Del Mar Debutante Stakes

ESSENCE OF DUBAI (1999)
At 3: Won Super Derby
3rd Jim Dandy Stakes

ESTACION (1953)
At 5: Won Arlington Matron Handicap

ESTAMBUL II (1963)
At 6: 3rd San Antonio Stakes

ESTIMATOR DAVE (1967)
At 3: 3rd Jerome Handicap

ESTRAPADE (1980)
At 4: 3rd Yellow Ribbon Stakes
At 5: Won Yellow Ribbon Stakes
2nd San Juan Capistrano Handicap
3rd Vanity Handicap
At 6: Won Budweiser-Arlington Million
Oak Tree Invitational Stakes
2nd Santa Barbara Handicap
Gamely Handicap
3rd Breeders' Cup Turf

ESTRENO II (1961)
At 6: Won Michigan Mile and One-Eighth
At 7: Won Pan American Handicap

ETERNAL DREAM (1946)
At 2: 2nd Remsen Stakes

ETERNAL FLAG (1946)
At 2: Won Astoria Stakes

ETERNAL FLIGHT (1987)
At 2: 3rd Hopeful Stakes

ETERNAL MOON (1949)
At 2: Won Cowdin Stakes
3rd Champagne Stakes

ETERNAL PRINCE (1982)
At 3: Won Gotham Stakes
Wood Memorial Stakes
3rd Preakness Stakes

ETERNAL REWARD (1943)
At 3: Won American Derby
3rd Hawthorne Gold Cup
At 4: 2nd McLennan Handicap
At 5: 2nd Stars and Stripes Handicap
Washington Park Handicap

ETERNAL WAR (1944)
At 2: 3rd Tremont Stakes

ETERNAL WORLD (1946)
At 2: Won Remsen Stakes

ETERNITY STAR (1988)
At 3: Won Hollywood Derby

ETOILE DU MATIN (1979)
At 4: 3rd La Canada Stakes

ETONIAN (1954)
At 2: 3rd Arlington Futurity

ETONY (1965)
At 3: 3rd Arkansas Derby
At 5: Won New Orleans Handicap
3rd Hawthorne Gold Cup

EUGENE'S THIRD SON (2000)
At 3: 2nd Arkansas Derby

EUGENIA II (1952)
At 4: Won Canadian Championship Stakes

EUPHROSYNE (1976)
At 4: 3rd Flower Bowl Handicap
At 5: 3rd Flower Bowl Handicap

EURASIA (1956)
At 6: Won Bougainvillea Handicap
2nd Hialeah Turf Cup

EURASIAN (1962)
At 3: 3rd Everglades Stakes

EURO EMPIRE (1998)
At 2: 2nd Oak Leaf Stakes
3rd Vinery Del Mar Debutante Stakes

EUROSILVER (2001)
At 2: Won Lane's End Breeders' Futurity

EUSTACE (1973)
At 2: Won Hopeful Stakes
3rd Sapling Stakes

EVANESCENT (1987)
At 6: 2nd Arlington Million

EVANSTEP (1945)
At 5: 3rd Arlington Matron Handicap

EVANSVILLE SLEW (1992)
At 2: Won Arlington-Washington Futurity

EVASIVE ACTION (1967)
At 2: Won Kentucky Jockey Club Stakes

EVENING ATTIRE (1998)
At 4: Won Jockey Club Gold Cup
At 5: 3rd Whitney Handicap
Jockey Club Gold Cup

EVENING KRIS (1985)
At 3: Won Jerome Handicap
2nd Dwyer Stakes
Jim Dandy Stakes

EVENING OUT (1951)
At 2: Won Spinaway Stakes
Matron Stakes
At 3: Won Monmouth Oaks
2nd Gazelle Handicap

EVENING TIME (1954)
At 3: 2nd Monmouth Oaks
Gazelle Handicap

EVENT OF THE YEAR (1995)
At 3: Won Jim Beam Stakes
3rd Malibu Stakes
At 4: Won Strub Stakes
2nd Santa Anita Handicap

EVER BEST (1952)
At 2: 3rd Remsen Stakes

EVERTON II (1969)
At 5: 2nd Grey Lag Handicap

EXBOURNE (1986)
At 5: Won Hollywood Turf Handicap
Caesars International Handicap

EXCEEDINGLY (1963)
At 4: 3rd John B. Campbell Handicap

EXCELLENT MEETING (1996)
At 2: Won Oak Leaf Stakes
Hollywood Starlet Stakes
2nd Breeders' Cup Juvenile Fillies
At 3: Won Las Virgenes Stakes
Santa Anita Oaks
At 4: 3rd Milady Breeders' Cup Handicap
Vanity Handicap

EXCELLENT TIPPER (1988)
At 3: 2nd Jerome Handicap

EXCELLER (1973)
At 4: Won Canadian International Championship
2nd Man o' War Stakes
3rd Washington D.C. International
At 5: Won Hollywood Gold Cup
Jockey Club Gold Cup
Hollywood Invitational Handicap
Sunset Handicap
Oak Tree Invitational Stakes
San Juan Capistrano Handicap
2nd Woodward Stakes
At 6: 2nd San Juan Capistrano Handicap
3rd Santa Anita Handicap
Century Handicap

EXCHANGE (1988)
At 5: Won Santa Barbara Handicap
At 6: Won Matriarch Stakes
2nd Vanity Handicap

EXCITING STORY (1997)
At 2: 3rd Hopeful Stakes
At 4: Won Metropolitan Handicap

EXCLUSIVE ENOUGH (1984)
At 3: 3rd Breeders' Cup Sprint

EXCLUSIVE NATIVE (1965)
At 2: Won Sanford Stakes
2nd Saratoga Special
Arlington-Washington Futurity
3rd Hopeful Stakes
Futurity Stakes
At 3: Won Arlington Classic

EXCLUSIVE ONE (1979)
At 3: 3rd Pegasus Handicap

EXCLUSIVE PRALINE (1991)
At 3: Won Ohio Derby

EXECUTIONER (1968)
At 2: Won Sanford Stakes
2nd Garden State Stakes
3rd Cowdin Stakes
At 3: Won Flamingo Stakes
2nd Florida Derby
3rd Wood Memorial Stakes
At 4: Won Gulfstream Park Handicap
Metropolitan Handicap

EXECUTION'S REASON (1977)
At 2: Won Arlington-Washington Futurity

EXECUTIVE COUNSEL (1977)
At 2: 3rd Del Mar Futurity

EXECUTIVE PRIDE (1981)
At 3: 2nd Hollywood Derby
At 4: 3rd Arlington Handicap

EXERENE (1974)
At 2: 2nd Spinaway Stakes

EXETERA (1993)
At 2: 3rd Norfolk Stakes

EXHIBITIONIST (1963)
At 3: 2nd San Felipe Handicap
Dwyer Handicap
3rd Santa Anita Derby

EXILE KING (1980)
At 3: 3rd Arkansas Derby

EXOGENOUS (1998)
At 3: Won Gazelle Handicap
Beldame Stakes
2nd Coaching Club American Oaks
Alabama Stakes
3rd Mother Goose Stakes

EXOTICO (1966)
At 6: 3rd Manhattan Handicap

EXOTIC WOOD (1992)
At 4: Won Go for Wand Stakes
At 5: 3rd Milady Breeders' Cup Handicap
At 6: Won Santa Monica Handicap
Santa Maria Handicap
2nd Santa Margarita Handicap

EXPELLED (1992)
At 5: Won Eddie Read Handicap

EXPENSIVE DECISION (1986)
At 3: 3rd Gotham Stakes

EXPLODED (1977)
At 4: 2nd Charles H. Strub Stakes
San Juan Capistrano Handicap
3rd Santa Anita Handicap
At 5: Won Hollywood Invitational Handicap
2nd San Luis Rey Stakes
San Juan Capistrano Handicap
3rd Sunset Handicap
At 6: 2nd Hollywood Invitational Handicap

EXPLOIT (1996)
At 3: 2nd San Felipe Stakes

EXPLOSIVE DANCER (1982)
At 6: 3rd Hialeah Turf Cup

EXPLOSIVE RED (1990)
At 3: Won American Derby
Hollywood Derby
2nd Secretariat Stakes
3rd Hollywood Turf Cup

EXPRESSIVE DANCE (1978)
At 2: 2nd Alcibiades Stakes
At 3: 3rd Acorn Stakes

EXPRESS TOUR (1998)
At 4: 3rd Woodward Stakes

EXTENDED APPLAUSE (1996)
At 2: 2nd Spinaway Stakes
Walmac International Alcibiades Stakes

EXTRA CHECK (1999)
At 3: 3rd Secretariat Stakes

EXTRAVAGANT (1975)
At 2: Won Del Mar Debutante Stakes

EXUBERANT (1976)
At 2: 2nd Hopeful Stakes
Arlington-Washington Futurity
3rd Hollywood Juvenile Championship

EYE DAZZLER (2001)
At 2: 3rd Matron Stakes

EYE OF THE STORM (1975)
At 2: 3rd Selima Stakes

EZGO (1954)
At 4: 2nd New Orleans Handicap

FABEROSE (1949)
At 2: 2nd Selima Stakes

FABIUS (1953)
At 3: Won Preakness Stakes
2nd Kentucky Derby
Ohio Derby
3rd Flamingo Stakes
Belmont Stakes
At 4: 2nd Gulfstream Park Handicap

FABULIST (1951)
At 4: 2nd Aqueduct Handicap

FABULOUSLY FAST (1994)
At 2: 3rd Spinaway Stakes
Matron Stakes
At 3: Won Test Stakes

FABULOUS NOTION (1980)
At 2: Won Hollywood Starlet Stakes
At 3: Won Santa Susana Stakes

FABULOUS VEGAS (1952)
At 3: 2nd Westerner Stakes
3rd California Derby

FACE THE FACTS (1961)
At 3: 2nd Santa Susana Stakes
Mother Goose Stakes
3rd Acorn Stakes

FACT FINDER (1979)
At 6: Won Santa Barbara Handicap

FACTS OF LOVE (1991)
At 2: 2nd Frizette Stakes

FADEYEV (1991)
At 3: 3rd Hollywood Derby

FAHIM (1993)
At 4: 2nd Sword Dancer Invitational Handicap

FAHRIS (1994)
At 5: 3rd Turf Classic

FAIR ADVANTAGE (1976)
At 2: 2nd Matron Stakes

FAIR ANN (1941)
At 5: 2nd Molly Pitcher Handicap

FAIRLY RANSOM (2000)
At 3: 2nd Hollywood Derby

FAIR MAGGIE (1957)
At 2: 2nd Del Mar Debutante Stakes

FAIR MOLLY (1952)
At 2: Won Del Mar Debutante Stakes

FAIR TRUCKLE (1943)
At 5: 3rd Inglewood Handicap

FAIRWAY FABLE (1971)
At 2: 2nd Alcibiades Stakes
At 3: 3rd Fantasy Stakes

FAIRWAY FLYER (1969)
At 2: 3rd Selima Stakes
At 3: 3rd Kentucky Oaks
At 5: 3rd Hempstead Handicap

FAIRWAY FUN (1962)
At 3: 3rd Spinster Stakes

FAIRWAY PHANTOM (1978)
At 2: Won Breeders' Futurity
3rd Arlington-Washington Futurity
At 3: Won Arlington Classic
2nd American Derby

FAIS DO DO (1947)
At 2: 2nd Matron Stakes
3rd Spinaway Stakes
Marguerite Stakes

FAITHFUL LEADER (1967)
At 3: 2nd California Derby

FALBRAV (1998)
At 5: 3rd John Deere Breeders' Cup Turf

FALCON FLIGHT (1996)
At 4: 2nd Woodford Reserve Turf Classic
At 6: 3rd John Deere Breeders' Cup Turf

FALIRAKI (1973)
At 4: 2nd Santa Anita Handicap

FALI TIME (1981)
At 2: Won Norfolk Stakes
Hollywood Futurity
At 3: Won San Felipe Handicap

FALKENBURG (1995)
At 5: 3rd Frank J. De Francis Memorial Dash

FALL ASPEN (1976)
At 2: Won Matron Stakes

FAME AND POWER (1969)
At 3: Won Illinois Derby
3rd Louisiana Derby

FAMED PRINCE (1966)
At 4: 2nd Washington Park Handicap

FAMILY ENTERPRIZE (1990)
At 2: Won Spinaway Stakes
3rd Matron Stakes

FAMILY FUN (1965)
At 2: 2nd Breeders' Futurity
3rd Cowdin Stakes
Garden State Stakes

FAMILY STYLE (1983)
At 2: Won Arlington-Washington Lassie Stakes
Frizette Stakes
2nd Matron Stakes
Breeders' Cup Juvenile Fillies
At 3: 3rd Arkansas Derby
Kentucky Oaks
Mother Goose Stakes
Hollywood Oaks
At 4: Won La Canada Stakes
2nd Apple Blossom Handicap

FAMOUS DIGGER (1994)
At 3: Won Del Mar Oaks

FAMOUS TALE (1970)
At 2: 3rd Selima Stakes

FANCY AS (1998)
At 4: 3rd Strub Stakes

FANCY NASKRA (1978)
At 2: Won Sorority Stakes

FANCY 'N FABULOUS (1991)
At 3: 3rd Hollywood Oaks

FANFRELUCHE (1967)
At 3: Won Alabama Stakes
2nd Spinster Stakes
3rd Gazelle Handicap

FANMORE (1988)
At 6: 2nd Hollywood Gold Cup
Arlington Million

FANTASTIC LIGHT (1996)
At 4: Won Man o' War Stakes
At 5: Won Breeders' Cup Turf

FANTASTIC LOOK (1986)
At 2: 2nd Hollywood Starlet Stakes
At 3: Won Fantasy Stakes
At 4: 2nd Vanity Handicap

FANTASY 'N REALITY (1976)
At 3: 3rd Florida Derby

FAPPIANO (1977)
At 3: 2nd Jerome Handicap
At 4: Won Metropolitan Handicap

FARA'S TEAM (1985)
At 3: 2nd Fantasy Stakes

FARDA AMIGA (1999)
At 3: Won Kentucky Oaks
Alabama Stakes
2nd Breeders' Cup Distaff

FAREWELL LETTER (1977)
At 3: 3rd Coaching Club American Oaks

FAREWELL PARTY (1968)
At 3: 2nd Dwyer Handicap
At 4: 2nd Grey Lag Handicap

FAR FLYING (1980)
At 3: 3rd Mother Goose Stakes

FARMA WAY (1987)
At 2: 2nd Hollywood Futurity
At 4: Won San Antonio Handicap
Santa Anita Handicap
Pimlico Special
2nd Hollywood Gold Cup
Philip H. Iselin Handicap
Woodward Stakes
3rd Nassau County Handicap

FARNESIO (1974)
At 4: 2nd Del Mar Handicap

FAR OUT BEAST (1987)
At 6: Won Flower Bowl Handicap

FAR TO REACH (1966)
At 5: 3rd Inglewood Handicap

FASCINATING GIRL (1972)
At 4: Won Santa Margarita Handicap
2nd La Canada Stakes

FASCINATOR (1951)
At 3: Won Kentucky Oaks
3rd Gazelle Handicap

FASHION VERDICT (1960)
At 2: 2nd Sorority Stakes
Matron Stakes

FAST ACCOUNT (1982)
At 3: 2nd Santa Anita Derby
At 4: 3rd San Fernando Stakes
Charles H. Strub Stakes

FAST ATTACK (1967)
At 2: Won Gardenia Stakes
At 3: 3rd Acorn Stakes

FAST COUNT (1963)
At 3: Won Massachusetts Handicap
At 5: Won Display Handicap

FAST CURE (1989)
At 4: 3rd San Luis Rey Stakes

FAST DISH (1965)
At 2: Won Del Mar Debutante Stakes

FASTER THAN SOUND (1984)
At 3: 2nd Jim Beam Stakes
3rd Hutcheson Stakes

FAST FELLOW (1968)
At 2: Won Hollywood Juvenile Championship
At 3: 3rd San Felipe Handicap

FAST FORWARD (1984)
At 3: 2nd American Derby

FAST GOLD (1979)
At 3: Won Pegasus Handicap

FAST HILARIOUS (1966)
At 3: Won American Derby
3rd Arlington Classic
At 4: Won Michigan Mile and One-Eighth
3rd Carter Handicap
At 5: Won Gulfstream Park Handicap

FAST LUCK (1960)
At 2: 3rd Arlington Lassie Stakes

FASTNESS (1990)
At 4: 2nd Eddie Read Handicap
At 5: Won Eddie Read Handicap
2nd Breeders' Cup Mile
At 6: Won Eddie Read Handicap

FAST PAPPA (1971)
At 2: 2nd Del Mar Futurity

FAST PLAY (1986)
At 2: Won Breeders' Futurity
Remsen Stakes
2nd Hopeful Stakes
3rd Futurity Stakes
At 3: 2nd Jim Dandy Stakes
Jerome Handicap

FATHER HOGAN (1973)
At 3: 3rd Marlboro Cup Handicap
At 4: 2nd Meadowlands Cup
At 5: 2nd Brooklyn Handicap
3rd Whitney Stakes
Amory L. Haskell Handicap

FATHERS IMAGE (1963)
At 2: 2nd Arlington-Washington Futurity
Cowdin Stakes
Pimlico Futurity
At 3: 3rd Withers Stakes
Jersey Derby

FAULT FREE (1951)
At 3: Won Westerner Stakes
2nd Cinema Handicap

FAULTLESS (1944)
At 3: Won Withers Stakes
Flamingo Stakes
Blue Grass Stakes
Preakness Stakes
3rd Kentucky Derby
At 4: Won Gallant Fox Handicap
At 5: 2nd McLennan Handicap
3rd Widener Handicap

FAULTLESS ENSIGN (1986)
At 3: 3rd Jersey Derby

FAUVE (1959)
At 3: 2nd Jerome Handicap

FAVORABLE TURN (1964)
At 2: Won Saratoga Special
At 3: 2nd Dwyer Handicap
3rd American Derby
At 4: Won Donn Handicap
2nd Widener Handicap

FAVORECIDIAN (1967)
At 5: Won John B. Campbell Handicap
Michigan Mile and One-Eighth
3rd Vosburgh Handicap
At 6: 3rd John B. Campbell Handicap

FAVORITE FUNTIME (1997)
At 5: Won Santa Maria Handicap

FAVORITE TRICK (1995)
At 2: Won Hopeful Stakes
Breeders' Cup Juvenile
At 3: Won Jim Dandy Stakes
3rd Arkansas Derby

FAVORITO (1943)
At 3: 2nd San Vicente Handicap

FEASIBILITY STUDY (1992)
At 5: 2nd Three Chimneys Spinster Stakes

FEATHER BOX (1993)
At 3: 3rd Gotham Stakes

FEATHER RIDGE (1986)
At 3: 2nd Jim Beam Stakes

FEDERAL FUNDS (1989)
At 5: 3rd Suburban Handicap
At 6: 3rd Suburban Handicap

FEDERAL HILL (1954)
At 2: Won Kentucky Jockey Club Stakes
2nd Garden State Stakes
At 3: Won Louisiana Derby

FEDERAL JUDGE (1954)
At 3: 3rd Louisiana Derby

FEDERAL TRIAL (1995)
At 4: 2nd Manhattan Handicap
3rd Man o' War Stakes

FEEL THE BEAT (1985)
At 5: 2nd Maskette Stakes

FELANE (1970)
At 2: 3rd Arlington-Washington Lassie Stakes

FELONIOUSLY (1969)
At 3: 2nd Louisiana Derby

FERD (1947)
At 3: Won Swift Stakes
3rd Withers Stakes
Wood Memorial Stakes
At 4: 2nd Excelsior Handicap
Grey Lag Handicap
3rd Fall Highweight Handicap

FERDINAND (1983)
At 2: 3rd Hollywood Futurity
At 3: Won Kentucky Derby
2nd Preakness Stakes
3rd Santa Anita Derby
Belmont Stakes
At 4: Won Hollywood Gold Cup
Breeders' Cup Classic
2nd Charles H. Strub Stakes
Santa Anita Handicap
3rd John Henry Handicap
At 5: 2nd San Antonio Handicap
Santa Anita Handicap
3rd Hollywood Gold Cup

FERLY (1968)
At 5: 3rd Ladies Handicap

FERRARA (1991)
At 2: 3rd Del Mar Futurity
Norfolk Stakes

FERRARI (1994)
At 4: 3rd Hollywood Turf Cup

FERROUS (1973)
At 2: 2nd Hopeful Stakes

FERVENT (1944)
At 2: 2nd Pimlico Futurity
At 3: Won American Derby
Pimlico Special
2nd Arlington Classic
At 4: Won Dixie Handicap
Washington Park Handicap
2nd Gallant Fox Handicap
3rd Arlington Handicap
At 6: 2nd Washington Park Handicap

FESTIN (1952)
At 5: 3rd American Handicap

FESTIN (1987)
At 4: Won Oaklawn Handicap
Nassau County Handicap
Jockey Club Gold Cup
2nd Santa Anita Handicap
3rd San Antonio Handicap
Woodward Stakes

FESTIVAL KING (1956)
At 3: 3rd Louisiana Derby

FESTIVE MOOD (1969)
At 2: 2nd Pimlico-Laurel Futurity
At 7: Won John B. Campbell Handicap
3rd Champions Invitational Handicap

FEVERISH (1995)
At 6: 2nd Santa Maria Handicap
3rd Milady Breeders' Cup Handicap

FIA (1974)
At 3: 3rd Coaching Club American Oaks

FICTION (1984)
At 4: 2nd San Juan Capistrano Handicap

FIDDLE ISLE (1965)
At 3: 3rd Sunset Handicap
At 4: 2nd Oak Tree Stakes
At 5: Won Hollywood Park Inv. Turf Handicap
American Handicap
San Luis Rey Handicap
San Juan Capistrano Handicap
2nd Santa Anita Handicap
United Nations Handicap
Oak Tree Stakes

FIDELES (1953)
At 2: 3rd Princess Pat Stakes

FIELD CAT (1977)
At 5: 3rd Sword Dancer Stakes
At 6: Won Pan American Handicap

FIELD MASTER (1964)
At 3: 3rd San Felipe Handicap
At 6: 3rd Santa Anita Handicap

FIELD OF HONOR (1954)
At 3: 3rd Travers Stakes

FIESTA GAL (1984)
At 3: Won Mother Goose Stakes
Coaching Club American Oaks
2nd Acorn Stakes
3rd Alabama Stakes

FIESTA LADY (1982)
At 2: Won Matron Stakes

FIESTA LIBRE (1971)
At 3: 2nd Coaching Club American Oaks
3rd Acorn Stakes
Alabama Stakes

FIESTERO (1975)
At 5: 2nd San Juan Capistrano Handicap
At 6: 3rd San Luis Rey Stakes

FIFTH DIVISION (1980)
At 2: 3rd Hollywood Futurity
At 3: 2nd Hollywood Derby
3rd San Felipe Handicap

FIFTH MARINE (1973)
At 3: Won American Derby

FIFTH QUESTION (1980)
At 3: 2nd Fantasy Stakes

FIGARO BOB (1959)
At 2: Won Remsen Stakes

FIGHT FOR LOVE (1990)
At 2: 2nd Futurity Stakes

FIGHTING FALCON (1996)
At 3: 3rd Early Times Hollywood Derby

FIGHTING FIT (1979)
At 5: 3rd Breeders' Cup Sprint

FIGHTING FRANK (1943)
At 4: 2nd Roseben Handicap
3rd San Carlos Handicap

FIGHTING STEP (1942)
At 4: Won Excelsior Handicap
3rd Grey Lag Handicap

FIGHTIN INDIAN (1956)
At 3: 3rd Santa Anita Derby

FIGHT OVER (1981)
At 3: 3rd Louisiana Derby
Preakness Stakes

FIGONERO (1965)
At 4: Won Hollywood Gold Cup
3rd Michigan Mile and One-Eighth
At 5: 2nd Californian Stakes
Michigan Mile and One-Eighth
At 6: 3rd American Handicap
At 7: 2nd Michigan Mile and One-Eighth
3rd Miller High Life Inglewood Handicap

FIJI (1994)
At 4: Won Gamely Breeders' Cup Handicap
Yellow Ribbon Stakes
3rd Ramona Handicap

FILAGO (1987)
At 4: Won Oak Tree Invitational Stakes

FILLYPASSER (1966)
At 2: 3rd Spinaway Stakes

FILM MAKER (2000)
At 3: Won Queen Elizabeth II Challenge Cup

FINALISTA (1969)
At 3: Won Cinema Handicap
3rd Hollywood Derby

FINAL ROUND (2000)
At 2: 3rd Walmac International Alcibiades Stakes
At 3: 3rd Acorn Stakes
Mother Goose Stakes

FINAL RULING (1960)
At 2: 3rd Hopeful Stakes

FINANCE WORLD (1964)
At 4: 3rd San Luis Rey Handicap

FINANCIAL GENIUS (1978)
At 2: 3rd Young America Stakes

FIND (1950)
At 3: Won Ohio Derby
Grey Lag Handicap
At 4: Won Excelsior Handicap
Queens County Handicap
2nd Massachusetts Handicap
Brooklyn Handicap
At 6: Won New Orleans Handicap
2nd Grey Lag Handicap
Massachusetts Handicap
United Nations Handicap
3rd Gulfstream Park Handicap
Metropolitan Handicap
Brooklyn Handicap
Hawthorne Gold Cup
Trenton Handicap
Pimlico Special
At 7: Won Inglewood Handicap
American Handicap
Sunset Handicap
2nd Washington Park Handicap
3rd Californian Stakes
Hollywood Gold Cup
Hawthorne Gold Cup
Canadian Championship Stakes
United Nations Handicap
At 8: 2nd John B. Campbell Memorial Handicap
At 9: 2nd American Handicap
Hollywood Gold Cup
3rd Sunset Handicap

FINDER'S CHOICE (1985)
At 8: 3rd Caesars International Handicap

FINDER'S FEE (1997)
At 2: Won Matron Stakes
At 3: Won Acorn Stakes
3rd Mother Goose Stakes
Test Stakes

FINE PROSPECT (1976)
At 2: 2nd Sorority Stakes

FINE SPIRIT (1982)
At 2: 3rd Breeders' Cup Juvenile Fillies

FINE TUNING (1970)
At 2: 3rd Frizette Stakes
Gardenia Stakes

FINLANDIA (1954)
At 2: 3rd Remsen Stakes

FINNEGAN (1956)
At 2: 2nd Starlet Stakes
At 3: Won San Felipe Handicap
California Derby
At 4: Won Los Angeles Handicap
3rd San Carlos Handicap

FIO RITO (1975)
At 6: Won Whitney Handicap

FIRCROFT (2000)
At 2: 3rd Matron Stakes
At 3: 2nd Coaching Club American Oaks

FIRE MAKER (1986)
At 2: 2nd Remsen Stakes
3rd Cowdin Stakes
At 3: Won Withers Stakes

FIRE POINT (1945)
At 3: 3rd New York Handicap

FIRERY ENSIGN (1985)
At 2: Won Young America Stakes

FIRE THE GROOM (1987)
At 4: 3rd Gamely Handicap
Yellow Ribbon Stakes

FIRM POLICY (1959)
At 2: 2nd Frizette Stakes
At 3: Won Monmouth Oaks
Alabama Stakes
2nd Mother Goose Stakes
3rd Coaching Club American Oaks
Beldame Stakes
Spinster Stakes
At 4: Won Top Flight Handicap

FIRM STANCE (1988)
At 4: Won Top Flight Handicap

FIRST ADVANCE (1979)
At 4: 3rd Ramona Handicap

FIRST AID (1950)
At 3: Won Saranac Handicap
Aqueduct Handicap
3rd Jerome Handicap
At 4: 2nd Roseben Handicap
Carter Handicap
At 5: Won Whitney Stakes
3rd Roseben Handicap

FIRST ALBERT (1977)
At 3: Won Swaps Stakes
2nd Travers Stakes
Super Derby

FIRST AMBASSADOR (1974)
At 2: 3rd Sapling Stakes

FIRST APPROACH (1978)
At 5: Won Flower Bowl Handicap

FIRST BACK (1971)
At 4: Won San Fernando Stakes
2nd San Antonio Stakes

FIRST BALCONY (1957)
At 4: Won Californian Stakes
San Carlos Handicap
3rd Los Angeles Handicap
Inglewood Handicap

FIRST CABIN (1952)
At 3: 3rd Florida Derby

FIRST FAMILY (1962)
At 3: 3rd Belmont Stakes
At 4: Won Gulfstream Park Handicap

FIRST FIDDLE (1939)
At 7: Won San Antonio Handicap
2nd San Carlos Handicap
Santa Anita Handicap
3rd Metropolitan Handicap

FIRST FLIGHT (1944)
At 2: Won Futurity Stakes
Astoria Stakes
Matron Stakes
At 4: Won Fall Highweight Handicap
3rd Vosburgh Handicap

FIRST GLANCE (1947)
At 6: Won Excelsior Handicap
3rd San Antonio Handicap
Santa Anita Handicap

FIRST LANDING (1956)
At 2: Won Hopeful Stakes
Champagne Stakes
Garden State Stakes
2nd Futurity Stakes
At 3: Won Everglades Stakes
2nd Wood Memorial Stakes
Roamer Handicap
3rd Flamingo Stakes
Kentucky Derby
At 4: Won Santa Anita Maturity
Monmouth Handicap
2nd San Antonio Handicap
Grey Lag Handicap
Metropolitan Handicap
Suburban Handicap
San Fernando Stakes

FIRST LIEUTENANT (1997)
At 4: 2nd Philip H. Iselin Handicap

FIRST MATE (1965)
At 4: Won Malibu Stakes

FIRST MINISTER (1956)
At 2: 2nd Hopeful Stakes

FIRST NIGHTER (1945)
At 4: Won Massachusetts Handicap
At 5: 3rd New York Handicap

FIRST NORMAN (1982)
At 2: 2nd Hollywood Futurity

FIRST PAGE (1943)
At 3: Won Kentucky Oaks

FIRST REPEATER (1948)
At 2: 3rd Washington Park Futurity

FIRST RETURN (1973)
At 3: 3rd California Derby

FISHERMAN (1951)
At 2: Won Cowdin Stakes
Champagne Stakes
At 3: Won Gotham Stakes
Travers Stakes
Lawrence Realization Stakes
Washington D.C. International
2nd Wood Memorial Stakes
Belmont Stakes
Jerome Handicap
Jockey Club Gold Cup
Whitney Handicap
3rd Pimlico Special
At 4: Won Excelsior Handicap
2nd John B. Campbell Memorial Handicap
At 5: 3rd John B. Campbell Memorial Handicap
Grey Lag Handicap

FISH HOUSE (1964)
At 2: 2nd Gardenia Stakes
At 3: Won Santa Susana Stakes

FISH NET (1965)
At 3: 2nd Santa Susana Stakes

FIT FOR A QUEEN (1986)
At 6: 2nd Apple Blossom Handicap

FIT TO FIGHT (1979)
At 3: Won Jerome Handicap
At 4: 2nd Vosburgh Stakes
At 5: Won Metropolitan Handicap
Suburban Handicap
Brooklyn Handicap

FIT TO LEAD (1990)
At 3: 2nd Hollywood Oaks

FIT TO SCOUT (1987)
At 3: 3rd Santa Anita Oaks
Fantasy Stakes
At 4: Won La Canada Stakes
2nd Hempstead Handicap
Vanity Handicap
Maskette Stakes
3rd Apple Blossom Handicap

FITZWILLIAM PLACE (1984)
At 5: Won Gamely Handicap

FIVE STAR DAY (1996)
At 3: 2nd King's Bishop Stakes

FIVE STAR FLIGHT (1978)
At 3: Won Haskell Invitational Handicap

FIVE STAR GENERAL (1975)
At 5: 2nd New Orleans Handicap

FLAG (1960)
At 5: Won Dixie Handicap
At 6: 2nd Bowling Green Handicap

FLAGBIRD (1991)
At 5: 2nd Gamely Handicap
3rd Beverly Hills Handicap

FLAG DOWN (1990)
At 4: 2nd Man o' War Stakes
3rd Jockey Club Gold Cup
At 6: 2nd Early Times Manhattan Handicap
3rd Sword Dancer Invitational Handicap
At 7: 2nd Manhattan Handicap
Turf Classic
3rd Caesars International Handicap
Breeders' Cup Turf
Hollywood Turf Cup

FLAG OFFICER (1974)
At 3: Won Illinois Derby
3rd Secretariat Stakes

FLAG RAISER (1962)
At 3: Won Gotham Stakes
Wood Memorial Stakes
Withers Stakes
At 4: 3rd Vosburgh Handicap

FLAGS FLYING (1948)
At 2: 2nd Princess Pat Stakes

FLAMA ARDIENTE (1972)
At 3: 2nd Spinster Stakes

FLAME THROWER (1998)
At 2: Won Del Mar Futurity
Norfolk Stakes

FLAME TREE (1963)
At 2: Won Sanford Stakes
2nd Saratoga Special
3rd Hollywood Juvenile Championship
Arlington-Washington Futurity

FLAMINGO (1955)
At 3: 3rd Blue Grass Stakes
Belmont Stakes

FLAMING PAGE (1959)
At 3: 2nd Kentucky Oaks

FLANDERS (1992)
At 2: Won Spinaway Stakes
Matron Stakes
Frizette Stakes
Breeders' Cup Juvenile Fillies

FLAREBACK (1942)
At 4: 3rd Manhattan Handicap

FLASH CLIMBER (1962)
At 3: 2nd Arkansas Derby
3rd Louisiana Derby

FLASHCO (1944)
At 3: 3rd Roamer Handicap
At 4: Won Santa Anita Maturity

FLASHY N SMART (1993)
At 4: 3rd Ballerina Stakes

FLASHY RUNNER (1985)
At 2: 3rd Matron Stakes

FLAT FLEET FEET (1993)
At 2: 2nd Spinaway Stakes
3rd Frizette Stakes
At 3: Won Delta Air Lines Top Flight Handicap
At 4: 2nd Go for Wand Stakes

FLAUNT (1949)
At 3: 2nd Discovery Handicap
At 4: Won Queens County Handicap
2nd New York Handicap

FLAUNTER (1975)
At 4: Won Golden Harvest Handicap

FLAWLESSLY (1988)
At 2: 3rd Frizette Stakes
At 3: 2nd Yellow Ribbon Stakes
At 4: Won Matriarch Stakes
2nd Yellow Ribbon Stakes
At 5: Won Ramona Handicap
Beverly D. Stakes
Matriarch Stakes
At 6: Won Ramona Handicap
2nd Beverly D. Stakes
3rd Gamely Handicap

FLAWLY (1997)
At 3: 2nd Garden City Breeders' Cup Handicap

FLEET ALLIED (1966)
At 2: Won Del Mar Futurity
3rd Hollywood Juvenile Championship
At 3: 2nd California Derby

FLEET BIRD (1949)
At 4: Won Golden Gate Handicap
2nd Hollywood Gold Cup
Del Mar Handicap
Santa Anita Maturity
3rd American Handicap
Sunset Handicap
At 5: Won Sunset Handicap
2nd William P. Kyne Handicap

FLEET DRAGOON (1974)
At 2: Won Hollywood Juvenile Championship

FLEET GAR (1975)
At 4: 2nd Pan American Handicap

FLEET GREEK (1957)
At 2: 3rd Remsen Stakes

FLEET HOST (1963)
At 3: Won Hollywood Derby
3rd Cinema Handicap
At 4: Won San Luis Rey Handicap
2nd San Fernando Stakes

FLEETING STAR (1946)
At 2: 2nd Kentucky Jockey Club Stakes
3rd Breeders' Futurity

FLEET KHAL (1950)
At 3: Won Vanity Handicap
2nd Westerner Stakes
At 4: 2nd Del Mar Handicap

FLEET KIRSCH (1966)
At 2: Won Hollywood Juvenile Championship
2nd Del Mar Futurity

FLEET LADY (1994)
At 4: 2nd Milady Breeders' Cup Handicap

FLEET NASRULLAH (1955)
At 2: 2nd Starlet Stakes
At 5: Won Californian Stakes
2nd Santa Anita Handicap

FLEET PATH (1952)
At 2: 2nd Kentucky Jockey Club Stakes

FLEET PEACH (1971)
At 2: Won Del Mar Debutante Stakes

FLEET RENEE (1998)
At 3: Won Ashland Stakes
Mother Goose Stakes
3rd Gazelle Handicap

FLEET RINGS (1947)
At 4: 2nd Vanity Handicap

FLEET ROSE (1949)
At 3: 3rd Delaware Oaks

FLEETSTREET DANCER (1998)
At 5: 3rd Pacific Classic

FLEET SURPRISE (1966)
At 5: 3rd Californian Stakes

FLEET TEMPO (1977)
At 3: 2nd Bay Meadows Handicap

FLEET VELVET (1972)
At 2: 3rd Norfolk Stakes
At 3: Won San Felipe Handicap

FLEET VICTRESS (1972)
At 4: 3rd Maskette Handicap
At 5: 3rd Hempstead Handicap

FLIGHT HISTORY (1953)
At 4: 2nd Los Angeles Handicap

FLIGHT TO GLORY (1970)
At 2: 2nd Hopeful Stakes

FLIPPERS (1981)
At 2: 2nd Alcibiades Stakes

FLIP SAL (1971)
At 3: Won Wood Memorial Stakes

FLIP'S PLEASURE (1980)
At 5: Won Top Flight Handicap

FLIRTATIOUS (1950)
At 2: Won Spinaway Stakes

FLITABOUT (1945)
At 3: 2nd Coaching Club American Oaks

FLITALONG (1976)
At 4: Won Pan American Handicap

FLITCH (1992)
At 3: 2nd Arkansas Derby

FLIT-TO (1963)
At 4: Won United Nations Handicap
2nd San Luis Rey Handicap
At 5: 3rd Hialeah Turf Cup

FLOATING RESERVE (1982)
At 3: 2nd Blue Grass Stakes

FLOOD TOWN (1942)
At 4: Won Carter Handicap
2nd Roseben Handicap

FLORIANO (1979)
At 4: 3rd Bay Meadows Handicap

FLORIDA STATE (1962)
At 2: 2nd Kentucky Jockey Club Stakes
3rd Breeders' Futurity

FLOWER BOWL (1952)
At 4: Won Delaware Handicap
Ladies Handicap

FLOW LINE (1957)
At 3: Won San Felipe Handicap

FLUORESCENT LIGHT (1974)
At 4: 2nd Arlington Handicap

FLUORESEE (1958)
At 4: 3rd Arlington Matron Handicap

FLUSH (1970)
At 3: 3rd Gotham Stakes

FLUTE (1998)
At 3: Won Kentucky Oaks
Alabama Stakes
2nd Santa Anita Oaks
Beldame Stakes

FLUTTERBY (1958)
At 3: Won San Felipe Handicap
2nd California Derby
Blue Grass Stakes
3rd Santa Anita Derby
American Derby

FLYAMANITA (1948)
At 2: Won Princess Pat Stakes

FLYING CHEVRON (1992)
At 3: Won Pegasus Handicap
NYRA Mile Handicap
At 4: 2nd Carter Handicap

FLYING CONTINENTAL (1986)
At 3: 2nd San Felipe Handicap
Santa Anita Derby
California Derby
At 4: Won San Fernando Stakes
Charles H. Strub Stakes
Jockey Club Gold Cup
3rd Santa Anita Handicap

FLYING DAD (1976)
At 3: 3rd Secretariat Stakes

FLYING DISC (1946)
At 2: 3rd Champagne Stakes

FLYING FLAGS (1984)
At 3: 2nd California Derby

FLYING FURY (1952)
At 2: Won Champagne Stakes
2nd Pimlico Futurity
3rd Garden State Stakes
At 4: Won Manhattan Handicap

FLYING GRANVILLE (1984)
At 2: 3rd Hopeful Stakes

FLYING IN THE LANE (1991)
At 3: 3rd Santa Anita Oaks

FLYING JOHNNIE (1959)
At 3: 2nd Dwyer Handicap

FLYING JULIA (1983)
At 5: Won Santa Margarita Handicap
At 6: 2nd Vanity Handicap

FLYING KATUNA (1984)
At 2: 3rd Frizette Stakes

FLYING MISSEL (1945)
At 4: 2nd Jockey Club Gold Cup
3rd Suburban Handicap
Brooklyn Handicap

FLYING NASHUA (1978)
At 3: 3rd San Felipe Handicap

FLYING PARTNER (1979)
At 2: 3rd Hollywood Starlet Stakes
At 3: Won Fantasy Stakes
3rd Kentucky Oaks
Coaching Club American Oaks

FLYING PASTER (1976)
At 2: Won Del Mar Futurity
Norfolk Stakes
2nd Hollywood Juvenile Championship
At 3: Won Santa Anita Derby
Hollywood Derby
3rd San Felipe Handicap
At 4: 2nd San Fernando Stakes
Charles H. Strub Stakes
Santa Anita Handicap
At 5: Won San Antonio Stakes

FLYING PIDGEON (1981)
At 4: 2nd Hialeah Turf Cup
3rd Budweiser-Arlington Million
At 5: Won Hollywood Invitational Handicap
3rd Sunset Handicap

FLYING RHYTHM (1945)
At 3: Won Hollywood Oaks

FLYING SENSATION (1991)
At 2: 3rd Hollywood Futurity

FLYING TARGET (1977)
At 5: Won Arlington Handicap

FLY SO FREE (1988)
At 2: Won Champagne Stakes
Breeders' Cup Juvenile
At 3: Won Florida Derby
Jim Dandy Stakes
2nd Blue Grass Stakes
3rd Dwyer Stakes
Travers Stakes
At 4: 2nd Pimlico Special

FLY TILL DAWN (1986)
At 4: Won Budweiser International Stakes
At 6: Won San Luis Rey Stakes
San Juan Capistrano Handicap

FLY WHEEL (1950)
At 3: 2nd Trenton Handicap
3rd Gotham Stakes
Saranac Handicap

FOLK ART (1982)
At 2: Won Oak Leaf Stakes

FOLLOW THRU (1960)
At 4: 2nd San Juan Capistrano Handicap

FOND EMBRACE (1946)
At 2: 3rd Selima Stakes

FONDLY REMEMBERED (1990)
At 4: 2nd Yellow Ribbon Stakes

FONZ'S (1999)
At 2: 2nd Hollywood Futurity
At 3: 3rd Swaps Stakes

FOOLISH MISS (1966)
At 2: 3rd Alcibiades Stakes

FOOLISH PLEASURE (1972)
At 2: Won Sapling Stakes
Hopeful Stakes
Champagne Stakes
At 3: Won Flamingo Stakes
Wood Memorial Stakes
Kentucky Derby
2nd Preakness Stakes
Belmont Stakes
3rd Florida Derby
At 4: Won Donn Handicap
Suburban Handicap
3rd Brooklyn Handicap

FOOLISH TANNER (1978)
At 2: 2nd Remsen Stakes

FOOL'S PLAY (1960)
At 2: Won Selima Stakes
2nd Frizette Stakes

FOOTING (1991)
At 2: 3rd Frizette Stakes

FORAGE (1969)
At 5: 2nd San Antonio Stakes

FOR ALL SEASONS (1990)
At 4: 2nd Shuvee Handicap

FORAY VINA (1946)
At 2: 2nd Tremont Stakes

FORBIDDEN APPLE (1995)
At 6: Won Manhattan Handicap
2nd Breeders' Cup Mile
At 7: 2nd Manhattan Handicap
3rd Arlington Million

FOR CERTAIN DOC (1982)
At 2: Won Champagne Stakes

FORCETEN (1972)
At 3: Won Swaps Stakes

FORCING BID (1991)
At 4: 2nd Go for Wand Stakes

FOREFOOT (1963)
At 2: 3rd Spinaway Stakes

FOREGO (1970)
At 3: 2nd Florida Derby
Jerome Handicap
3rd Withers Stakes
At 4: Won Donn Handicap
Widener Handicap
Gulfstream Park Handicap
Carter Handicap
Brooklyn Handicap
Woodward Stakes
Vosburgh Handicap
Jockey Club Gold Cup
2nd Metropolitan Handicap
3rd Suburban Handicap
Marlboro Cup Handicap
At 5: Won Widener Handicap
Carter Handicap
Brooklyn Handicap
Suburban Handicap
Woodward Stakes
2nd Marlboro Cup Handicap
3rd Metropolitan Handicap
At 6: Won Metropolitan Handicap
Brooklyn Handicap
Woodward Handicap
Marlboro Cup Handicap
2nd Suburban Handicap
3rd Amory L. Haskell Handicap
At 7: Won Metropolitan Handicap
Woodward Handicap
2nd Suburban Handicap
Brooklyn Handicap

FORELOCK (1949)
At 3: Won Will Rogers Stakes

FORESTA (1986)
At 4: 2nd Flower Bowl Handicap

FOREST CAMP (1997)
At 2: Won Del Mar Futurity
2nd Norfolk Stakes

FORESTED (1992)
At 3: 3rd Mother Goose Stakes

FORESTRY (1996)
At 3: Won King's Bishop Stakes
3rd Haskell Invitational Handicap

FOREST SECRETS (1998)
At 3: Won Acorn Stakes

FOREVER CASTING (1975)
At 2: Won Young America Stakes
3rd Arlington-Washington Futurity

FOREVER PARTNERS (2000)
At 2: 2nd Spinaway Stakes

FOREVER SILVER (1985)
At 4: Won Brooklyn Handicap
2nd Suburban Handicap
Whitney Handicap
3rd Woodward Handicap
Jockey Club Gold Cup

FOREVER WHIRL (1990)
At 3: Won Flamingo Stakes
Ohio Derby

FOR EXAMPLE (1951)
At 2: 3rd Del Mar Futurity

FORGOTTEN DREAMS (1964)
At 2: Won Hollywood Juvenile Championship

FOR HALO (1981)
At 3: 2nd Hutcheson Stakes

FORLITANO (1981)
At 6: 2nd Sunset Handicap
Hollywood Turf Cup

FORMAL DINNER (1988)
At 2: 2nd Cowdin Stakes
3rd Norfolk Stakes

FORMAL GOLD (1993)
At 3: 2nd Buick Meadowlands Cup Handicap
At 4: Won Donn Handicap
Brooklyn Handicap
Philip H. Iselin Handicap
Woodward Stakes
2nd Whitney Handicap
3rd Suburban Handicap

FOR NO REASON (1968)
At 3: 3rd Monmouth Oaks

FOR ONCE'N MY LIFE (1980)
At 2: Won Arlington-Washington Lassie Stakes
2nd Sorority Stakes

FORT DRUM (1964)
At 4: 3rd Aqueduct Stakes
Whitney Stakes

FOR THE MOMENT (1974)
At 2: Won Futurity Stakes
2nd Champagne Stakes
Laurel Futurity
At 3: Won Blue Grass Stakes
2nd Florida Derby
Santa Anita Derby

FOR THE ROAD (1959)
At 4: 2nd Carter Handicap

FORT MARCY (1964)
At 3: Won Washington D.C. International
2nd Man o' War Stakes
3rd United Nations Handicap
At 4: Won Sunset Handicap
2nd Grey Lag Handicap
Man o' War Stakes
3rd United Nations Handicap
Washington D.C. International
At 5: Won Hollywood Park Inv. Turf Handicap
2nd San Juan Capistrano Handicap
3rd United Nations Handicap
Man o' War Stakes
At 6: Won Dixie Handicap
Bowling Green Handicap
United Nations Handicap
Man o' War Stakes
Washington D.C. International
2nd Century Handicap
Hollywood Park Inv. Turf Handicap
3rd San Juan Capistrano Handicap
At 7: 2nd Bowling Green Handicap
Ford Pinto Invitational Turf Handicap
3rd Hialeah Turf Cup

FORTNIGHTLY (1980)
At 3: Won Secretariat Stakes

FORT PREVEL (1974)
At 3: 3rd Florida Derby
Flamingo Stakes

FORTUNATE ISLE (1959)
At 3: 3rd Kentucky Oaks
Monmouth Oaks

FORTUNATE MOMENT (1984)
At 3: Won American Derby

FORTUNE'S WHEEL (1988)
At 3: 3rd Turf Classic

FORTUNE TELLER (1950)
At 2: 2nd Del Mar Debutante Stakes

FORTUNEWAY (1953)
At 2: 3rd Starlet Stakes
Del Mar Futurity

FORTY KINGS (1983)
At 3: 3rd Ohio Derby

FORTY NINER (1985)
At 2: Won Futurity Stakes
Champagne Stakes
At 3: Won Fountain of Youth Stakes
Haskell Invitational Handicap
Travers Stakes
2nd Hutcheson Stakes
Florida Derby
Kentucky Derby
Woodward Handicap

FORTY NINER DAYS (1987)
At 4: 2nd Caesars International Handicap

FORTY ONE CARATS (1996)
At 3: Won Pegasus Handicap

FORUM (1967)
At 2: Won Garden State Stakes

FORWARD GAL (1968)
At 2: Won Sorority Stakes
Spinaway Stakes
Frizette Stakes
3rd Gardenia Stakes
At 3: Won Monmouth Oaks
Gazelle Handicap
3rd Acorn Stakes
Mother Goose Stakes
Alabama Stakes

FORWARD PASS (1965)
At 2: 3rd Sanford Stakes
At 3: Won Everglades Stakes
Florida Derby
Blue Grass Stakes
Kentucky Derby
Preakness Stakes
American Derby
2nd Belmont Stakes
Travers Stakes

FORZANDO II (1981)
At 4: Won Metropolitan Handicap

FOSCARINI (1981)
At 3: Won Hollywood Derby

FOUND PEARL HARBOR (1980)
At 3: 2nd Louisiana Derby

FOUR-AND-TWENTY (1958)
At 3: Won Santa Anita Derby
Cinema Handicap
Hollywood Derby
At 4: Won San Fernando Stakes
Santa Anita Maturity
San Carlos Handicap
3rd Santa Anita Handicap

FOUR BASES (1979)
At 5: 2nd Hialeah Turf Cup

FOURDRINIER (1976)
At 3: 2nd Beldame Stakes

FOUR LANE (1957)
At 3: 3rd Jerome Handicap

FOURSTARS ALLSTAR (1988)
At 5: 3rd Breeders' Cup Mile
At 6: 2nd Caesars International Handicap

FOURTH ROUND (1966)
At 2: Won Del Mar Debutante Stakes

FOUR WINDS (1944)
At 2: Won Arlington Lassie Stakes
At 4: Won Arlington Matron Handicap

FOWDA (1988)
At 3: Won Hollywood Oaks
At 4: Won Spinster Stakes
2nd Vanity Handicap
3rd Milady Handicap

FOXIE GREEN (1947)
At 3: 3rd Hollywood Oaks

FOX TIME (1947)
At 2: Won Tremont Stakes

FOXTRAIL (1990)
At 3: 3rd Arkansas Derby

FOXY DEEN (1982)
At 3: 2nd Kentucky Oaks
3rd Coaching Club American Oaks
Alabama Stakes

FOXY JULIANA (1975)
At 2: 2nd Del Mar Debutante Stakes

FRAISE (1988)
At 4: Won Sword Dancer Handicap
Breeders' Cup Turf
2nd Turf Classic
Hollywood Turf Cup
At 5: Won Hollywood Turf Cup
3rd San Juan Capistrano Handicap
At 6: 3rd Man o' War Stakes

FRANC ARGUMENT (1986)
At 5: 2nd Flower Bowl Handicap

FRANCIE'S HAT (1965)
At 3: 2nd Kentucky Derby
3rd Blue Grass Stakes

FRANCIS S. (1957)
At 3: Won Wood Memorial Stakes
Dwyer Handicap
3rd Withers Stakes

FRANCIS U. (1963)
At 2: 2nd Breeders' Futurity
At 4: Won Donn Handicap

FRANJICA (1992)
At 5: 2nd Yellow Ribbon Stakes

FRANKLY (1945)
At 3: Won Del Mar Handicap
At 5: Won Del Mar Handicap
3rd Inglewood Handicap
American Handicap

FRANKLY PERFECT (1985)
At 3: 2nd Budweiser International Stakes
At 4: Won San Luis Rey Stakes
Hollywood Turf Cup
2nd San Antonio Handicap
Sunset Handicap
At 5: 3rd San Luis Rey Stakes

FRANK'S FLOWER (1954)
At 2: 3rd Arlington Lassie Stakes

FRAN LA FEMME (1961)
At 3: 2nd Hollywood Oaks

FRANMARI (1973)
At 3: 2nd Hollywood Oaks

FRAN'S VALENTINE (1982)
At 3: Won Santa Susana Stakes
Kentucky Oaks
Hollywood Oaks
2nd Alabama Stakes
At 4: 2nd Breeders' Cup Distaff

FRAU ALTIVA (1982)
At 5: 3rd Santa Margarita Handicap
Gamely Handicap

FRED ASTAIRE (1983)
At 3: 3rd Breeders' Cup Mile

FRED BEAR CLAW (1994)
At 5: 3rd Pimlico Special

FREE AMERICA (1945)
At 2: 3rd Washington Park Futurity
At 3: 2nd American Derby
3rd Jerome Handicap

FREE AT LAST (1987)
At 5: 3rd Santa Barbara Handicap

FREEDOM CRY (1991)
At 4: 2nd Breeders' Cup Turf

FREE HOUSE (1994)
At 2: Won Norfolk Stakes
At 3: Won San Felipe Stakes
Santa Anita Derby
Swaps Stakes
2nd Preakness Stakes
3rd Kentucky Derby
Belmont Stakes
Buick Haskell Invitational Handicap
At 4: Won Pacific Classic
At 5: Won San Antonio Handicap
Santa Anita Handicap
2nd Pimlico Special

FREE JOURNEY (1973)
At 2: Won Demoiselle Stakes
2nd Arlington-Washington Lassie Stakes
3rd Selima Stakes

FREE OF LOVE (1998)
At 3: 2nd Jim Dandy Stakes

FREEPORT FLIGHT (1994)
At 3: 2nd Hollywood Oaks
At 4: 3rd Beverly Hills Handicap

FREE SPIRIT'S JOY (1988)
At 3: Won Super Derby

FREETEX (1969)
At 2: 2nd Garden State Stakes
At 3: Won Gotham Stakes
Ohio Derby
Monmouth Invitational Handicap
At 4: 3rd Gulfstream Park Handicap

FREEZING DOCK (1988)
At 3: 2nd Arlington Classic

FRENCH ADMIRAL (1947)
At 2: 2nd Breeders' Futurity

FRENCH BRAIDS (1995)
At 3: 3rd Gazelle Handicap

FRENCH CHARMER (1978)
At 4: 3rd Ramona Handicap

FRENCH COLONIAL (1975)
At 5: Won Man o' War Stakes

FRENCH DEPUTY (1992)
At 3: Won Jerome Handicap

FRENCH GLORY (1986)
At 4: Won Rothmans International Stakes

FRENCHPARK (1990)
At 4: Won Hollywood Turf Cup

FRENCH SASSAFRAS (1978)
At 3: 2nd Hollywood Derby

FRENDSWOOD (1948)
At 2: 2nd Starlet Stakes

FRENETICO (1964)
At 4: Won Canadian International Championship
At 6: 3rd Canadian International Championship
At 7: 2nd Canadian International Championship

FRERE JACQUES (1942)
At 4: Won Miami Beach Handicap
At 5: 2nd Miami Beach Handicap
At 6: 3rd Miami Beach Handicap
At 7: Won Bougainvillea Handicap

FRESH PEPPER (1970)
At 2: Won Oak Leaf Stakes

FRESNO STAR (1971)
At 2: 2nd Del Mar Debutante Stakes

FRIAR ROACH (1956)
At 3: 2nd Cinema Handicap

FRIAR TUCK (1945)
At 4: 3rd Bougainvillea Handicap

FRIENDLY BEAUTY (1992)
At 3: 2nd Alabama Stakes

FRIENDLY BEE (1971)
At 3: 2nd Wood Memorial Stakes

FRIMANAHA (1957)
At 4: Won Vineland Handicap
At 6: 3rd Santa Margarita Handicap

FRISK ME NOW (1994)
At 3: Won Ohio Derby
3rd Florida Derby
Buick Pegasus Handicap
At 4: Won Suburban Handicap
2nd Oaklawn Handicap
At 5: Won Philip H. Iselin Handicap

FROLIC (1992)
At 4: 3rd Go for Wand Stakes
John A. Morris Handicap

FROSTY DAWN (1951)
At 4: 3rd Vanity Handicap

FROSTY MR. (1953)
At 3: 3rd Louisiana Derby

FROSTY THE SNOWMAN (1985)
At 4: 2nd Hialeah Turf Cup

FROZEN DELIGHT (1968)
At 2: 3rd Futurity Stakes

FULCRUM (1955)
At 2: Won Breeders' Futurity

FULL COURAGE (1983)
At 4: 3rd Brooklyn Handicap

FULL FLIGHT (1951)
At 3: 2nd Lawrence Realization Stakes
3rd Jerome Handicap
At 6: 2nd New Orleans Handicap

FULL OF FUN (1962)
At 6: 3rd Metropolitan Handicap

FULL OUT (1973)
At 2: Won Sapling Stakes
At 3: 3rd Withers Stakes
At 4: 3rd Carter Handicap
Metropolitan Handicap

FULL REGALIA (1959)
At 3: 3rd California Derby

FULVOUS (1950)
At 2: Won Arlington Lassie Stakes
Princess Pat Stakes
At 3: 2nd Arlington Matron Handicap

FUNALON (1972)
At 2: 3rd Demoiselle Stakes
At 3: 2nd Kentucky Oaks
3rd Alabama Stakes

FUN HOUSE (1958)
At 4: 2nd Vanity Handicap

FUNISTRADA (1983)
At 2: 2nd Frizette Stakes
At 4: 3rd Maskette Stakes

FUNLOVING (1958)
At 3: Won Mother Goose Stakes
2nd Coaching Club American Oaks
3rd Delaware Oaks
Monmouth Oaks

FUNNY BONE (1957)
At 4: 2nd Top Flight Handicap

FUNNY CAT (1972)
At 2: 2nd Alcibiades Stakes
Selima Stakes
At 3: 3rd Kentucky Oaks

FUNNY CIDE (2000)
At 3: Won Kentucky Derby
Preakness Stakes
2nd Wood Memorial Stakes
3rd Belmont Stakes
Haskell Invitational Handicap

FUNNY FELLOW (1965)
At 3: Won Lawrence Realization Stakes
Gallant Fox Handicap
2nd Ohio Derby
Jockey Club Gold Cup
3rd Monmouth Invitational Handicap
Travers Stakes
At 4: Won Donn Handicap
2nd Widener Handicap

FURIOUSLY (1989)
At 3: Won Jerome Handicap

FURLOUGH (1994)
At 4: 2nd Ruffian Handicap
At 5: Won Ballerina Handicap
2nd Ruffian Handicap

FURL SAIL (1964)
At 3: Won Acorn Stakes
Mother Goose Stakes
2nd Spinster Stakes
3rd Kentucky Oaks

FURYVAN (1955)
At 3: 3rd San Felipe Handicap

FUSAICHI PEGASUS (1997)
At 3: Won San Felipe Stakes
Wood Memorial Stakes
Kentucky Derby
2nd Preakness Stakes

FUSSY GIRL (1970)
At 3: 2nd Fantasy Stakes

FUTURAL (1996)
At 5: 3rd Hollywood Gold Cup

FUTURE PRETENSE (1990)
At 3: 2nd Coaching Club American Oaks
Alabama Stakes

FUTURE QUEST (1993)
At 2: Won Del Mar Futurity
Norfolk Stakes

FUTURE STORM (1990)
At 3: 2nd Swaps Stakes

FUZZBUSTER (1976)
At 2: 3rd Hopeful Stakes

FUZZY (1982)
At 4: 3rd Whitney Handicap

GAB BAG (1972)
At 3: 2nd Secretariat Stakes

GAELIC DANCER (1966)
At 4: 3rd Grey Lag Handicap

GAFFERY (1946)
At 2: Won Selima Stakes
3rd Spinaway Stakes
At 3: Won Santa Susana Stakes
Ladies Handicap
2nd Acorn Stakes
3rd Alabama Stakes
Comely Handicap
At 4: 2nd Santa Margarita Handicap

GAGE LINE (1966)
At 6: Won Oaklawn Handicap
At 7: 3rd Oaklawn Handicap

GAILY GAILY (1983)
At 5: Won Flower Bowl Handicap
At 7: 3rd Flower Bowl Handicap

GAIN (1976)
At 3: 3rd Canadian International Championship

GAINSBORO GIRL (1950)
At 4: Won Black Helen Handicap
New Castle Handicap
At 5: 2nd Top Flight Handicap

GALA HARRY (1973)
At 5: 3rd John B. Campbell Handicap

GALA HOST (1962)
At 3: 3rd Hollywood Oaks

GALANT VERT (1980)
At 4: 2nd Hollywood Invitational Handicap

GALA PERFORMANCE (1964)
At 3: 2nd Wood Memorial Stakes

GALARULLAH (1955)
At 3: 2nd Kentucky Oaks

GALA SPINAWAY (1988)
At 3: 2nd Pennsylvania Derby

GALAXY LIBRA (1976)
At 5: Won Sunset Handicap
Man o' War Stakes
2nd Turf Classic
3rd Hollywood Invitational Handicap
Washington D.C. International

GALDAR (1951)
At 2: Won Remsen Handicap
3rd Cowdin Stakes
At 3: 2nd Gotham Stakes

GAL IN A RUCKUS (1992)
At 3: Won Kentucky Oaks

GALLA DAMION (1943)
At 3: Won San Felipe Stakes

GALLANT BEST (1976)
At 3: 3rd Jerome Handicap

GALLANT BLOOM (1966)
At 2: Won Matron Stakes
Gardenia Stakes
2nd Frizette Stakes
At 3: Won Monmouth Oaks
Gazelle Handicap
Spinster Stakes
At 4: Won Santa Margarita Handicap

GALLANT BOB (1972)
At 5: 3rd Carter Handicap

GALLANT GENTLEMAN (1979)
At 4: 3rd Hawthorne Gold Cup

GALLANT LAD (1962)
At 3: 2nd Withers Stakes
3rd Florida Derby

GALLANT MAN (1954)
At 3: Won Belmont Stakes
Travers Stakes
Jockey Club Gold Cup
2nd Wood Memorial Stakes
Kentucky Derby
Woodward Stakes
Trenton Handicap
At 4: Won Metropolitan Handicap
Hollywood Gold Cup
Sunset Handicap
3rd Carter Handicap

GALLANT MOMENT (1964)
At 3: 3rd Jersey Derby

GALLANT ROMEO (1961)
At 4: 3rd Washington Park Handicap
At 5: Won Vosburgh Handicap

GALLANT TRIAL (1972)
At 3: 3rd Acorn Stakes

GALLATIA (1961)
At 2: 3rd Spinaway Stakes

GALLOPING GAL (2001)
At 2: 2nd Darley Alcibiades Stakes

GALLORETTE (1942)
At 4: Won Beldame Handicap
Metropolitan Handicap
Brooklyn Handicap
3rd Massachusetts Handicap
At 5: Won Queens County Handicap
2nd Beldame Handicap
Whitney Stakes
Aqueduct Handicap
3rd Ladies Handicap
Metropolitan Handicap
Carter Handicap
Monmouth Handicap
At 6: Won Carter Handicap
Whitney Stakes
2nd Firenze Handicap
Ladies Handicap
Brooklyn Handicap
3rd Top Flight Handicap
Beldame Handicap
Gallant Fox Handicap

GALLUP POLL (1963)
At 3: 2nd Man o' War Stakes

GALUNPE (1983)
At 5: 3rd Santa Barbara Handicap
Gamely Handicap
At 6: 2nd Santa Barbara Handicap

GAME (1958)
At 5: 2nd Santa Anita Handicap
3rd San Antonio Handicap

GAME GENE (1950)
At 2: 2nd Sapling Stakes

GAMELY (1964)
At 3: Won Alabama Stakes
2nd Hollywood Oaks
3rd Beldame Stakes
At 4: Won Vanity Handicap
Beldame Stakes
Santa Margarita Handicap
2nd Santa Barbara Handicap
Californian Stakes
At 5: Won Beldame Stakes
2nd Vanity Handicap
Santa Anita Handicap
3rd Santa Barbara Handicap

GANDER (1996)
At 4: 2nd Jockey Club Gold Cup
3rd Woodward Stakes
At 5: 3rd Donn Handicap
Whitney Handicap
At 6: 2nd Woodward Stakes

GANDHARVA (1952)
At 2: Won Spinaway Stakes
3rd Alcibiades Stakes

GANDRIA (1996)
At 3: 3rd Alabama Stakes

GANGWAY (1945)
At 5: 3rd Gulfstream Park Handicap
At 6: Won McLennan Handicap

GANNET (1954)
At 2: 2nd Hopeful Stakes

GARBU (1994)
At 5: 2nd Early Times Turf Classic

GARDEN GAL (1988)
At 2: 2nd Spinaway Stakes
Oak Leaf Stakes
3rd Hollywood Starlet Stakes
At 3: 2nd Santa Anita Oaks

GARDEN VERSE (1972)
At 4: 2nd Hempstead Handicap

GARIBI (1978)
At 4: 2nd Louisiana Downs Handicap

GARLAND OF ROSES (1969)
At 5: 2nd Bowling Green Handicap

GARTHORN (1980)
At 6: Won Metropolitan Handicap

GARWOL (1958)
At 2: Won Pimlico Futurity
2nd Champagne Stakes
3rd Futurity Stakes
Cowdin Stakes
At 3: 2nd Jerome Handicap
At 4: 2nd Brooklyn Handicap
Santa Anita Maturity
3rd Suburban Handicap
Whitney Stakes
At 5: 3rd Suburban Handicap
Aqueduct Stakes
Manhattan Handicap
Jockey Club Gold Cup
At 6: 2nd Gulfstream Park Handicap

GASH (1991)
At 3: 3rd Peter Pan Stakes

GASPARILLA (1945)
At 3: 3rd Queens County Handicap

GASTRONOMICAL (1993)
At 2: 3rd Oak Leaf Stakes

GATE DANCER (1981)
At 3: Won Preakness Stakes
Super Derby
2nd San Felipe Handicap
3rd Arkansas Derby
Breeders' Cup Classic
At 4: 2nd Marlboro Cup Handicap
Jockey Club Gold Cup
Breeders' Cup Classic
3rd San Fernando Stakes
Charles H. Strub Stakes
Santa Anita Handicap
At 5: 3rd Widener Handicap

GATO DEL SOL (1979)
At 2: Won Del Mar Futurity
3rd Norfolk Stakes
At 3: Won Kentucky Derby
2nd San Felipe Handicap
Blue Grass Stakes
Belmont Stakes
At 5: 2nd Oak Tree Invitational Stakes
San Luis Rey Stakes
3rd Budweiser-Arlington Million
Santa Anita Handicap

GATORS N BEARS (2000)
At 3: 3rd Frank J. De Francis Memorial Dash

GAVIOLA (1997)
At 3: Won Garden City Breeders' Cup Handicap

GAY CAVALIER (1948)
At 2: 2nd Del Mar Futurity

GAY GRECQUE (1949)
At 3: 3rd Alabama Stakes
At 4: 2nd Comely Handicap
At 5: 3rd Maskette Handicap

GAY JITTERBUG (1973)
At 3: 3rd Louisiana Derby
At 4: 3rd Pan American Handicap

GAY LANDING (1958)
At 3: 3rd California Derby

GAY LIFE (1953)
At 4: 2nd Ladies Handicap
3rd Black Helen Handicap
Beldame Handicap
At 5: 3rd Black Helen Handicap

GAY MATELDA (1965)
At 2: Won Gardenia Stakes
2nd Matron Stakes
Frizette Stakes
Selima Stakes
3rd Sorority Stakes
Spinaway Stakes
At 3: Won Alabama Stakes
2nd Coaching Club American Oaks
Gazelle Handicap
3rd Acorn Stakes
At 4: 2nd Black Helen Handicap

GAY MOOD (1946)
At 2: 2nd Frizette Stakes

GAY MOONBEAM (1943)
At 3: 3rd Flamingo Stakes

GAY REVOKE (1958)
At 7: Won Oaklawn Handicap

GAY RIGHTS (1985)
At 3: 3rd Peter Pan Stakes
Dwyer Stakes

GAY SAILORETTE (1964)
At 3: 2nd Kentucky Oaks

GAY SERENADE (1960)
At 2: 2nd Selima Stakes

GAY STYLE (1970)
At 5: Won Santa Barbara Handicap
3rd Santa Margarita Handicap

GAY WARRIOR (1953)
At 3: 3rd Fall Highweight Handicap
At 4: 3rd Fall Highweight Handicap

GEECHEE LOU (1956)
At 3: 3rd Mother Goose Stakes
At 4: 3rd Delaware Handicap
At 5: 3rd Santa Margarita Handicap
Man o' War Handicap

GEEVILLA (1981)
At 2: 3rd Alcibiades Stakes

GEM MASTER (1984)
At 3: 2nd Arlington Classic
3rd American Derby

GEN. DUKE (1954)
At 3: Won Everglades Stakes
Florida Derby
2nd Flamingo Stakes

GENERAL ARTHUR (1954)
At 5: Won Bougainvillea Turf Handicap
At 7: Won Donn Handicap

GENERAL ASSEMBLY (1976)
At 2: Won Hopeful Stakes
2nd Champagne Stakes
Laurel Futurity
At 3: Won Travers Stakes
Vosburgh Stakes
2nd Kentucky Derby
Marlboro Cup Handicap

GENERAL CHALLENGE (1996)
At 3: Won Santa Anita Derby
Pacific Classic
2nd Swaps Stakes
At 4: Won Strub Stakes
Santa Anita Handicap
2nd Sempra Energy Hollywood Gold Cup

GENERAL MEETING (1988)
At 2: 2nd Hollywood Futurity

GENERAL PRACTITIONER (1980)
At 3: Won Illinois Derby
3rd Flamingo Stakes

GENERAL STAFF (1948)
At 2: 3rd Pimlico Futurity
At 3: 3rd Vosburgh Handicap
At 4: Won Pimlico Special
2nd New York Handicap

GENEROUS PORTION (1968)
At 2: Won Del Mar Debutante Stakes
At 3: 2nd Santa Susana Stakes

GENEROUS ROSI (1995)
At 6: 2nd Jockey Club Gold Cup

GENTLE KING (1973)
At 2: 3rd Hopeful Stakes
At 4: Won Carter Handicap

GENTLEMAN JAMES (1964)
At 2: Won Breeders' Futurity
2nd Kentucky Jockey Club Stakes
At 3: 2nd Everglades Stakes
Lawrence Realization Stakes
3rd Blue Grass Stakes
Illinois Derby
Belmont Stakes
At 4: Won Gulfstream Park Handicap

GENTLEMEN (1992)
At 5: Won San Antonio Handicap
Pimlico Special
Hollywood Gold Cup
Pacific Classic
3rd Santa Anita Handicap
At 6: Won San Antonio Handicap
2nd Pacific Classic
Woodward Stakes
Jockey Club Gold Cup
3rd Hollywood Gold Cup

GENTLE SMOKE (1969)
At 3: Won Fountain of Youth Stakes
3rd Florida Derby
At 4: 3rd Donn Handicap

GENUINE RISK (1977)
At 3: Won Ruffian Handicap
Kentucky Derby
2nd Maskette Stakes
Preakness Stakes
Belmont Stakes
3rd Wood Memorial Stakes

GEORGE AUGUSTUS (1987)
At 6: 3rd Turf Classic

GEORGE BARTON (1957)
At 6: 2nd Metropolitan Handicap

GEORGE LEWIS (1967)
At 2: Won Del Mar Futurity
At 3: Won California Derby
2nd San Felipe Handicap
Santa Anita Derby
3rd Arlington Classic

GEORGE NAVONOD (1972)
At 2: Won Norfolk Stakes
2nd Del Mar Futurity
3rd Hollywood Juvenile Championship
At 3: 2nd San Felipe Handicap
California Derby
At 4: Won Charles H. Strub Stakes

GEORGE ROYAL (1961)
At 4: Won San Juan Capistrano Handicap
Canadian Championship Stakes
3rd San Antonio Handicap
Santa Anita Handicap
At 5: Won San Juan Capistrano Handicap
Canadian International Championship

GEORGIAN (1952)
At 2: Won Washington Park Futurity

GERALDINE'S STORY (1979)
At 4: 3rd Matriarch Stakes

GERI (1992)
At 4: Won Oaklawn Handicap
2nd Hollywood Gold Cup
3rd Pimlico Special
At 5: Won Woodbine Mile
2nd Caesars International Handicap
Breeders' Cup Mile

GERVAZY (1987)
At 4: 2nd Nassau County Handicap
3rd Carter Handicap
Metropolitan Handicap

GET AROUND (1960)
At 3: Won Withers Stakes
2nd Blue Grass Stakes
Jersey Derby
Hollywood Derby
3rd Roamer Handicap

GET THE AXE (1974)
At 2: 3rd Breeders' Futurity

GHAZI (1989)
At 3: Won Secretariat Stakes
2nd Rothmans International Stakes

GHOSTLY MOVES (1992)
At 3: 3rd Pegasus Handicap

GHOST RUN (1945)
At 2: Won Demoiselle Stakes
3rd Matron Stakes

GHOSTZAPPER (2000)
At 3: Won Vosburgh Stakes
3rd King's Bishop Stakes

GIANT GENTLEMAN (1998)
At 3: 2nd Malibu Stakes
At 4: 2nd Strub Stakes

GIANT GUY (1957)
At 3: 3rd California Derby

GIANT'S CAUSEWAY (1997)
At 3: 2nd Breeders' Cup Classic

GIBOULEE (1974)
At 3: 2nd Flamingo Stakes

GIDEON (1950)
At 2: 2nd Garden State Stakes

GIGANTIC (1951)
At 3: Won Louisiana Derby
At 4: Won San Antonio Handicap
3rd San Juan Capistrano Handicap

GIGGLING GIRL (1974)
At 5: 3rd Yellow Ribbon Stakes

GILD (1986)
At 2: 3rd Demoiselle Stakes

GILDED TIME (1990)
At 2: Won Arlington-Washington Futurity
Breeders' Cup Juvenile
At 3: 3rd Breeders' Cup Sprint

GIMME GLORY (1991)
At 2: 2nd Arlington-Washington Futurity

GINGER BRINK (1980)
At 3: Won Hollywood Derby

GINGER FIZZ (1962)
At 4: 2nd United Nations Handicap
At 5: 3rd Pan American Handicap

GIN-ROB (1965)
At 2: 2nd Arlington-Washington Futurity
Kentucky Jockey Club Stakes
3rd Pimlico-Laurel Futurity

GIRL IN LOVE (1973)
At 3: Won Mother Goose Stakes

GLADWIN (1966)
At 4: Won Amory L. Haskell Handicap
Hawthorne Gold Cup

GLAMOUR (1953)
At 2: 2nd Matron Stakes

GLASSY DIP (1973)
At 3: 2nd Louisiana Derby

GLEAMING (1968)
At 3: 2nd Manhattan Handicap
Man o' War Stakes
3rd Canadian International Championship
At 4: Won Hialeah Turf Cup
3rd Pan American Handicap
At 5: Won Hialeah Turf Cup

GLEAMING LIGHT (1966)
At 3: Won Dwyer Handicap

GLEEFULLY (1996)
At 3: 3rd Santa Anita Oaks

GLENARIS (1974)
At 2: 3rd Oak Leaf Stakes
At 3: Won Hollywood Oaks

GLENARY (1967)
At 3: 2nd Kentucky Oaks

GLIDING WINGS (1953)
At 2: 2nd Del Mar Futurity

GLITMAN (1994)
At 3: 2nd Jim Dandy Stakes

GLITTERMAN (1985)
At 5: 3rd Vosburgh Stakes

GLITTER WOMAN (1994)
At 3: Won Ashland Stakes
At 4: 2nd Apple Blossom Handicap
Hempstead Handicap

GLOBALIZE (1997)
At 3: Won Turfway Spiral Stakes

GLOBEMASTER (1958)
At 2: 2nd Futurity Stakes
Cowdin Stakes
At 3: Won Wood Memorial Stakes
Arlington Classic
2nd Gotham Stakes
Preakness Stakes
Belmont Stakes
3rd Jersey Derby
At 4: 2nd John B. Campbell Handicap

GLOK (1994)
At 3: 3rd Secretariat Stakes

GLORIOUS SONG (1976)
At 4: Won Top Flight Handicap
La Canada Stakes
Santa Margarita Handicap

GLORIOUS SONG *(Continued)*
2nd Amory L. Haskell Handicap
Marlboro Cup Handicap
At 5: Won Spinster Stakes
2nd Beldame Stakes
Santa Margarita Handicap
Matriarch Stakes

GLOSSARY (1971)
At 3: Won Secretariat Stakes

GLOW (1983)
At 3: 2nd Arlington Classic
Secretariat Stakes
3rd Everglades Stakes
Pennsylvania Derby

GO AND GO (1987)
At 2: Won Laurel Futurity
At 3: Won Belmont Stakes
At 4: 3rd San Fernando Stakes

GODDESS (1949)
At 2: 2nd Astoria Stakes

GOFF'S GAY (1961)
At 3: 3rd Arkansas Derby

GO FOR GIN (1991)
At 2: Won Remsen Stakes
At 3: Won Kentucky Derby
2nd Wood Memorial Stakes
Preakness Stakes
Belmont Stakes

GO FOR GLAMOUR (2000)
At 3: 3rd Santa Anita Oaks

GO FOR LOVE (1971)
At 2: 3rd Sapling Stakes

GO FORTH (1975)
At 3: 3rd Blue Grass Stakes

GO FOR WAND (1987)
At 2: Won Breeders' Cup Juvenile Fillies
2nd Frizette Stakes
At 3: Won Ashland Stakes
Mother Goose Stakes
Alabama Stakes
Maskette Stakes
Beldame Stakes
2nd Kentucky Oaks

GO GO WINDY (1965)
At 2: 2nd Gardenia Stakes

GOING ABROAD (1960)
At 4: Won Michigan Mile and One-Sixteenth
Manhattan Handicap
Hawthorne Gold Cup
3rd Washington Park Handicap

GOING AWAY (1946)
At 3: 2nd Massachusetts Handicap
3rd Dwyer Stakes
At 4: 2nd New York Handicap
Bougainvillea Handicap
3rd Widener Handicap
Dixie Handicap
At 6: 3rd Stars and Stripes Handicap

GOING STRAIGHT (1968)
At 4: Won Donn Handicap

GOING WITH ME (1943)
At 3: 3rd Will Rogers Handicap

GOLD AND MYRRH (1971)
At 3: 3rd Blue Grass Stakes
At 4: Won Gulfstream Park Handicap
Grey Lag Handicap
Metropolitan Handicap
3rd Widener Handicap

GOLD AND STEEL (1992)
At 4: 3rd Eddie Read Handicap

GOLD BEAUTY (1979)
At 3: 2nd Vosburgh Stakes

GOLD BOX (1952)
At 2: 3rd Champagne Stakes

GOLD CAPITOL (1948)
At 2: Won Starlet Stakes
3rd Del Mar Futurity
At 3: 3rd Will Rogers Handicap
Cinema Handicap
At 4: 2nd Santa Anita Maturity

GOLD DIGGER (1962)
At 2: 3rd Matron Stakes
At 3: 2nd Kentucky Oaks

GOLD DOLLAR (1999)
At 3: 2nd Jim Dandy Stakes

GOLDEN ACT (1976)
At 2: 2nd Norfolk Stakes
At 3: Won Louisiana Derby
Arkansas Derby
Secretariat Stakes
Canadian International Championship
2nd California Derby
Preakness Stakes
Belmont Stakes
3rd Kentucky Derby
At 4: 2nd Turf Classic
3rd Century Handicap
Man o' War Stakes

GOLDEN APPLES (1998)
At 3: Won Del Mar Oaks
2nd Queen Elizabeth II Challenge Cup
3rd Matriarch Stakes
At 4: Won Beverly D. Stakes
Yellow Ribbon Stakes
2nd John C. Mabee Ramona Handicap
Matriarch Stakes
At 5: 2nd John C. Mabee Handicap

GOLDEN ARCHES (1994)
At 3: 2nd Del Mar Oaks
3rd Queen Elizabeth II Challenge Cup

GOLDEN ATTRACTION (1993)
At 2: Won Spinaway Stakes
Matron Stakes
Frizette Stakes
3rd Breeders' Cup Juvenile Fillies

GOLDEN BALLET (1998)
At 3: Won Las Virgenes Stakes
Santa Anita Oaks
2nd Ashland Stakes

GOLDEN BEAR (1953)
At 2: 3rd Arlington Futurity

GOLDEN BRI (1992)
At 3: Won Coaching Club American Oaks
2nd Mother Goose Stakes
3rd Gazelle Handicap

GOLDEN CURRA (1960)
At 2: 3rd Del Mar Debutante Stakes

GOLDEN DERBY (1978)
At 3: 2nd Arlington Classic
3rd Blue Grass Stakes

GOLDEN DON (1970)
At 3: Won Michigan Mile and One-Eighth
2nd American Derby
Hawthorne Gold Cup
3rd Pontiac Grand Prix Stakes
Illinois Derby
Canadian International Championship
At 4: Won Manhattan Handicap
3rd Gulfstream Park Handicap

GOLDEN GLOVES (1949)
At 3: Won Saranac Handicap
3rd Dwyer Stakes
At 4: 2nd Brooklyn Handicap
At 5: 2nd Dixie Handicap
At 6: 3rd Excelsior Handicap

GOLDEN KLAIR (1990)
At 4: 2nd Milady Handicap
3rd Vanity Handicap

GOLDEN LARCH (1991)
At 4: 3rd Woodward Stakes
At 5: 3rd Woodward Stakes

GOLDEN LOUIS (1961)
At 2: 3rd Sanford Stakes

GOLDEN MISSILE (1995)
At 4: 3rd Breeders' Cup Classic
At 5: Won Pimlico Special
2nd Donn Handicap

GOLDEN NOTES (1954)
At 4: 2nd Los Angeles Handicap

GOLDEN OR (1966)
At 5: 2nd Black Helen Handicap

GOLDEN PHEASANT (1986)
At 4: Won John Henry Handicap
Arlington Million
At 6: 3rd Arlington Million

GOLDEN POST (1990)
At 6: 3rd Oak Tree Turf Championship

GOLDEN REEF (1987)
At 2: 2nd Matron Stakes

GOLDEN RULER (1961)
At 2: Won Arlington-Washington Futurity

GOLDEN TENT (1989)
At 9: 3rd Fall Highweight Handicap

GOLDEN TICKET (1998)
At 2: 3rd Hollywood Futurity

GOLDEN TREAT (1989)
At 3: Won Santa Anita Oaks
2nd Fantasy Stakes

GOLDEN TREND (1948)
At 5: 3rd Michigan Mile

GOLD FEVER (1993)
At 3: Won NYRA Mile Handicap

GOLD FINERY (1954)
At 3: 3rd Mother Goose Stakes

GOLD FLEECE (1988)
At 5: 2nd Gamely Handicap

GOLD FROM THE WEST (1996)
At 3: 3rd Ashland Stakes

GOLDIAN (1969)
At 2: 2nd Oak Leaf Stakes

GOLDIKO (1977)
At 4: Won Louisiana Downs Handicap
3rd Hollywood Turf Cup

GOLD MOVER (1998)
At 4: 2nd Humana Distaff Handicap
At 5: 2nd Humana Distaff Handicap
3rd Ballerina Handicap

GOLD N DELICIOUS (1993)
At 3: 2nd Coaching Club American Oaks

GOLD NOTE (1948)
At 3: Won Will Rogers Handicap
2nd San Felipe Stakes
3rd Westerner Stakes
At 4: 3rd San Carlos Handicap

GOLD NUGGET (1995)
At 5: 3rd Eddie Read Handicap

GOLD ON GREEN (1984)
At 2: 3rd Norfolk Stakes

GOLD STAGE (1977)
At 2: Won Breeders' Futurity
2nd Hopeful Stakes
Laurel Futurity
Young America Stakes
3rd Sapling Stakes
Futurity Stakes
At 3: 3rd Blue Grass Stakes

GOLD TRIBUTE (1994)
At 2: 2nd Del Mar Futurity
3rd Moet Champagne Stakes

GOLF ACE (1953)
At 3: 2nd Flamingo Stakes
Wood Memorial Stakes

GOLFERETTE (1976)
At 2: Won Frizette Stakes

GO LIGHTLY (1952)
At 3: Won Gotham Stakes

GO LINE (1975)
At 2: 3rd Arlington-Washington Lassie Stakes

GONE FISHIN' (1955)
At 3: 3rd Preakness Stakes

GONE WEST (1984)
At 3: Won Gotham Stakes
Withers Stakes
Dwyer Stakes
2nd Hutcheson Stakes
Wood Memorial Stakes
Peter Pan Stakes
3rd Fountain of Youth Stakes

GONQUIN (1975)
At 2: Won Breeders' Futurity
2nd Arlington-Washington Futurity

GOOD AND TOUGH (1995)
At 4: 2nd Frank J. De Francis Memorial Dash

GOOD BEHAVING (1968)
At 3: Won Gotham Stakes
Wood Memorial Stakes

GOOD BLOOD (1942)
At 4: Won Arlington Matron Handicap
Vineland Handicap

GOODBYE HALO (1985)
At 3: Won Kentucky Oaks
Mother Goose Stakes
Coaching Club American Oaks
2nd Santa Anita Oaks
3rd Breeders' Cup Distaff
At 4: Won La Canada Stakes
2nd Santa Margarita Handicap
Apple Blossom Handicap
Spinster Stakes
3rd Vanity Handicap

GOOD CALL (1950)
At 2: 2nd Alcibiades Stakes
At 4: 2nd Washington Park Handicap

GOOD COUNSEL (1968)
At 3: 3rd Travers Stakes
At 4: Won Widener Handicap
2nd Hawthorne Gold Cup
3rd San Fernando Stakes
Charles H. Strub Stakes

GOOD EXCUSE (1943)
At 3: 3rd Hollywood Oaks
At 4: 2nd Vanity Handicap
At 6: 3rd Vanity Handicap

GOOD INVESTMENT (1965)
At 3: 3rd Arlington Classic

GOOD JOURNEY (1996)
At 6: 3rd NetJets Breeders' Cup Mile

GOOD KNIGHT (1962)
At 5: Won Massachusetts Handicap
3rd Amory L. Haskell Handicap

GOOD LORD (1971)
At 7: 3rd Oak Tree Invitational Stakes
At 8: 3rd San Luis Rey Stakes

GOOD LOSER (1948)
At 2: 3rd Starlet Stakes

GOOD MANNERS (1966)
At 5: 2nd San Antonio Stakes

GOOD MOVE (1958)
At 2: Won Spinaway Stakes
Selima Stakes
3rd Matron Stakes
Frizette Stakes

GOOD POTENTIAL (1988)
At 2: 2nd Arlington-Washington Lassie Stakes
3rd Spinaway Stakes

GOOD REPORT (1970)
At 6: 3rd Del Mar Handicap

GOOFALIK (1987)
At 4: 3rd Caesars International Handicap
Budweiser International Stakes

GOOFED (1960)
At 3: Won Ladies Handicap

GOOGOPLEX (1977)
At 2: 2nd Remsen Stakes
3rd Hopeful Stakes
Champagne Stakes

GOOSE KHAL (1949)
At 4: Won Del Mar Handicap
3rd Golden Gate Handicap

GORDIE H. (1975)
At 3: 3rd Arlington Classic

GORGEOUS (1986)
At 3: Won Ashland Stakes
Hollywood Oaks
2nd Mother Goose Stakes
Breeders' Cup Distaff
At 4: Won La Canada Stakes
Apple Blossom Handicap
Vanity Handicap
2nd Santa Margarita Handicap
Spinster Stakes

GORGEOUS REDED (1948)
At 3: 2nd Acorn Stakes

GOT KOKO (1999)
At 3: Won La Brea Stakes
At 4: 3rd Breeders' Cup Distaff

GO TO THE BANK (1972)
At 3: 3rd American Derby

GOT TO FLY (1988)
At 2: 3rd Del Mar Futurity

GOURMET GIRL (1995)
At 3: 2nd La Brea Stakes
At 4: Won Milady Breeders' Cup Handicap
At 5: 2nd Ruffian Handicap
3rd Santa Maria Handicap
At 6: Won Apple Blossom Handicap
Vanity Handicap

GOVERNMENT CORNER (1982)
At 3: 3rd Jim Dandy Stakes
Super Derby

GOVERNOR MAX (1969)
At 2: Won Arlington-Washington Futurity
2nd Hopeful Stakes

GOVERNORS PARTY (1965)
At 5: 3rd Hollywood Park Inv. Turf Handicap

GO WEST YOUNG MAN (1975)
At 2: Won Del Mar Futurity
At 5: Won Hollywood Gold Cup
Del Mar Handicap
Century Handicap
3rd Hollywood Invitational Handicap

GOYALA (1961)
At 2: 3rd Del Mar Debutante Stakes

GOYAMO (1951)
At 2: 2nd Kentucky Jockey Club Stakes
3rd Garden State Stakes
At 3: Won Blue Grass Stakes
2nd Florida Derby

GRAB IT (1967)
At 2: 3rd Matron Stakes

GRAB THE PRIZE (1992)
At 5: 3rd Santa Monica Handicap

GRACE BORN (1964)
At 4: 2nd Manhattan Handicap
3rd Woodward Stakes

GRAEME HALL (1997)
At 2: 2nd Lane's End Breeders' Futurity
At 3: Won Arkansas Derby
Jim Dandy Stakes
At 4: 2nd Cigar Mile Handicap

GRAF (1987)
At 3: 3rd Dwyer Stakes

GRAFITTI (1968)
At 3: 2nd Kentucky Oaks
Mother Goose Stakes
Coaching Club American Oaks
At 4: Won Ladies Handicap
2nd Black Helen Handicap
Delaware Handicap
At 5: Won Black Helen Handicap

GRAMMARIAN (1998)
At 4: 2nd Hollywood Turf Cup

GRANACUS (1985)
At 3: Won Blue Grass Stakes
3rd Tropical Park Derby

GRANBID (1968)
At 2: 2nd Kentucky Jockey Club Stakes

GRAND ADMIRAL (1944)
At 2: 2nd Hopeful Stakes

GRAND CANYON (1953)
At 4: 2nd Canadian Championship Stakes

GRAND CANYON (1987)
At 2: Won Norfolk Stakes
Hollywood Futurity
2nd Breeders' Cup Juvenile

GRAND DEED (1996)
At 2: 3rd Walmac International Alcibiades Stakes

GRAND FLOTILLA (1987)
At 7: Won Hollywood Turf Handicap
2nd San Juan Capistrano Handicap
Oak Tree Invitational Stakes
3rd San Luis Rey Stakes

GRAND GIRLFRIEND (1988)
At 3: 2nd Hollywood Oaks

GRANDMA JOSIE (1949)
At 4: 3rd Molly Pitcher Handicap

GRANDPAW (1952)
At 2: 2nd Champagne Stakes
Remsen Stakes
At 3: 3rd Travers Stakes

GRANDPERE (1945)
At 2: 2nd Starlet Stakes

GRAND PREMIERE (1964)
At 3: 3rd Louisiana Derby

GRAND ROL (1984)
At 2: 3rd Laurel Futurity

GRAND SLAM (1995)
At 2: Won Futurity Stakes
Moet Champagne Stakes
At 3: 2nd Swaps Stakes
Jerome Handicap
Breeders' Cup Sprint
3rd Buick Haskell Invitational Handicap

GRAND STAND (1960)
At 3: 3rd Ohio Derby

GRAND VIZIER (1984)
At 4: 3rd San Fernando Stakes

GRANJA REINA (1980)
At 2: 3rd Del Mar Debutante Stakes
Oak Leaf Stakes

GRANTOR (1948)
At 3: Won Westerner Stakes

GRANTOR *(Continued)*
Del Mar Derby
At 4: Won Del Mar Handicap

GRAUSTARK (1963)
At 3: 2nd Blue Grass Stakes

GRAVELINES (1972)
At 5: Won Pan American Handicap

GRAY CASHMERE (1989)
At 4: 2nd Spinster Stakes

GRAY MIRAGE (1969)
At 4: 3rd Santa Barbara Handicap

GRAY PET (1960)
At 3: 2nd Everglades Stakes

GRAY PHANTOM (1953)
At 4: 2nd Tropical Handicap

GREAT ABOVE (1972)
At 3: 3rd Jerome Handicap
At 5: 3rd Vosburgh Handicap

GREAT BEAR LAKE (1969)
At 3: 3rd Arkansas Derby
Jerome Handicap

GREAT CAREER (1968)
At 3: 3rd Del Mar Handicap

GREAT CIRCLE (1947)
At 2: 2nd Starlet Stakes
At 3: Won Cinema Handicap
Del Mar Derby
2nd Westerner Stakes
San Felipe Stakes
3rd Santa Anita Derby
Sunset Handicap
At 4: Won Santa Anita Maturity
3rd Excelsior Handicap
At 5: Won Sunset Handicap

GREAT COHOES (1965)
At 4: 2nd Stars and Stripes Handicap

GREAT COMMUNICATOR (1983)
At 4: 2nd Hollywood Invitational Handicap
Budweiser International Stakes
At 5: Won San Juan Capistrano Handicap
Breeders' Cup Turf
Hollywood Turf Cup
2nd San Luis Rey Stakes
Oak Tree Invitational Stakes
3rd Hollywood Invitational Handicap
At 6: Won Hollywood Turf Handicap
2nd San Luis Rey Stakes

GREAT CONTRACTOR (1973)
At 3: Won Jockey Club Gold Cup
2nd Florida Derby
3rd Belmont Stakes
At 4: Won Brooklyn Handicap
2nd Jockey Club Gold Cup
3rd Woodward Handicap
At 5: 3rd Suburban Handicap
Brooklyn Handicap
Jockey Club Gold Cup

GREAT DREAM (1946)
At 5: 3rd Vanity Handicap

GREAT ERA (1964)
At 2: 2nd Spinaway Stakes
Matron Stakes

GREATEST (1950)
At 5: Won Michigan Mile

GREAT MYSTERY (1967)
At 3: Won Jerome Handicap
At 4: 3rd Oaklawn Handicap

GREAT NAVIGATOR (1990)
At 2: Won Hopeful Stakes

GREAT NECK (1976)
At 4: Won Canadian International Championship
At 5: Won Bowling Green Handicap
3rd Man o' War Stakes

GREAT NORMAND (1985)
At 5: Won Meadowlands Cup

GREAT NOTION (2000)
At 3: 2nd King's Bishop Stakes

GREAT POWER (1964)
At 2: Won Sapling Stakes
2nd Hopeful Stakes

GREAT SHUFFLE (1946)
At 3: 3rd Louisiana Derby

GREAT SOUND (1976)
At 3: 3rd Hialeah Turf Cup

GRECIAN FLIGHT (1984)
At 3: Won Acorn Stakes
2nd Mother Goose Stakes

GRECIAN PRINCESS (1961)
At 3: Won Louisiana Derby

GRECIAN QUEEN (1950)
At 2: Won Demoiselle Stakes
2nd Spinaway Stakes
3rd Matron Stakes
Frizette Stakes
At 3: Won Coaching Club American Oaks
Gazelle Handicap
Monmouth Oaks
New Castle Handicap
2nd Alabama Stakes
3rd Delaware Oaks
At 4: 2nd Maskette Handicap

GRECO II (1969)
At 5: Won Sunset Handicap

GREEK ANSWER (1972)
At 2: Won Arlington-Washington Futurity
2nd Hopeful Stakes

GREEK COSTUME (1988)
At 3: Won Jersey Derby

GREEK FORM (1960)
At 4: 3rd Canadian Championship Stakes

GREEK GAME (1954)
At 2: Won Arlington Futurity
Washington Park Futurity
2nd Futurity Stakes

GREEK JAB (1963)
At 4: 2nd Hialeah Turf Cup

GREEK LOVELINESS (1970)
At 2: 3rd Arlington-Washington Lassie Stakes

GREEK MONEY (1959)
At 3: Won Preakness Stakes
At 4: 3rd Michigan Mile and One-Sixteenth

GREEK SHIP (1947)
At 3: Won Louisiana Derby
Metropolitan Handicap
Monmouth Handicap
2nd Jerome Handicap
Lawrence Realization Stakes
At 4: 3rd Gallant Fox Handicap
At 5: 2nd Widener Handicap
New Orleans Handicap
Excelsior Handicap
3rd Trenton Handicap

GREEK SONG (1947)
At 3: Won Dwyer Stakes
Arlington Classic

GREEK SPY (1953)
At 4: Won Massachusetts Handicap
3rd Metropolitan Handicap

GREEK STAR (1955)
At 4: Won Trenton Handicap
At 5: 2nd Brooklyn Handicap
At 6: Won New Orleans Handicap

GREEN GAMBADOS (1971)
At 2: 2nd Champagne Stakes
At 3: Won Fountain of Youth Stakes

GREEN GLADE (1964)
At 4: 3rd Black Helen Handicap

GREEN HORNET (1959)
At 3: 3rd Louisiana Derby
At 5: Won New Orleans Handicap

GREEN JEWEL (1994)
At 4: 3rd Matriarch Stakes
At 5: 3rd Gamely Breeders' Cup Handicap

GREEN ROOM (1970)
At 6: 2nd Pan American Handicap

GREEN TICKET (1959)
At 2: 2nd Arlington Futurity
Pimlico Futurity
3rd Sapling Stakes
At 3: 2nd Withers Stakes

GREENWOOD LAKE (1997)
At 2: Won Champagne Stakes
Remsen Stakes
2nd Futurity Stakes

GREINTON (1981)
At 4: Won Californian Stakes
Hollywood Gold Cup
2nd San Fernando Stakes
Charles H. Strub Stakes
Santa Anita Handicap
Sunset Handicap
Budweiser-Arlington Million
At 5: Won Santa Anita Handicap

GRENZEN (1975)
At 2: 2nd Oak Leaf Stakes
At 3: Won Santa Susana Stakes
2nd Kentucky Oaks
3rd Hollywood Oaks

GREY EAGLE (1957)
At 4: 2nd Hollywood Gold Cup
3rd San Antonio Handicap
Santa Anita Maturity
Santa Anita Handicap

GREY FLIGHT (1945)
At 2: 2nd Astarita Stakes
Frizette Stakes
3rd Astoria Stakes
Spinaway Stakes

GREY MEMO (1997)
At 4: 3rd San Carlos Handicap
At 5: 3rd San Carlos Handicap
At 6: 3rd San Carlos Handicap

GREY MONARCH (1955)
At 3: 2nd Travers Stakes
Roamer Handicap
3rd Florida Derby

GREY MOON RUNNER (1974)
At 2: 2nd Hollywood Juvenile Championship

GREY WHIZ (1965)
At 4: 3rd Canadian International Championship

GRINDSTONE (1993)
At 3: Won Kentucky Derby
2nd Arkansas Derby

GRISE MINE (1981)
At 3: 2nd Yellow Ribbon Stakes

GRITTIE SANDIE (1996)
At 5: 3rd United Nations Handicap

GROOM'S RECKONING (1988)
At 2: 2nd Young America Stakes
3rd Futurity Stakes

GROOVY (1983)
At 2: 2nd Futurity Stakes
Champagne Stakes
At 3: 3rd Wood Memorial Stakes
At 4: Won Vosburgh Stakes
2nd Breeders' Cup Sprint

GROSHAWK (1970)
At 2: Won Norfolk Stakes

Del Mar Futurity
At 3: 2nd Hollywood Derby
Oak Tree Invitational Stakes

GROTON HIGH (1976)
At 2: 2nd Sapling Stakes

GROUND CONTROL (1962)
At 3: Won Acorn Stakes

GROUP PLAN (1970)
At 4: Won Hawthorne Gold Cup
3rd Woodward Stakes
Jockey Club Gold Cup
At 5: Won Jockey Club Gold Cup
2nd Whitney Handicap
3rd Woodward Stakes
Hawthorne Gold Cup

GROVER B. (1949)
At 5: Won New Orleans Handicap

G.R. PETERSEN (1949)
At 5: 2nd Aqueduct Handicap

GUADALCANAL (1958)
At 2: 3rd Garden State Stakes
At 3: 2nd Travers Stakes
3rd Belmont Stakes
At 4: 2nd Aqueduct Stakes
Jockey Club Gold Cup
3rd Woodward Stakes
At 5: 2nd Jockey Club Gold Cup
3rd Monmouth Handicap
Man o' War Stakes

GUADERY (1983)
At 2: 3rd Frizette Stakes

GUARDIAN II (1950)
At 3: 2nd Dwyer Stakes
3rd Travers Stakes
At 6: Won Hialeah Turf Handicap

GUARD RAIL (1953)
At 2: 2nd Arlington Lassie Stakes
Princess Pat Stakes

GUARDS UP (1972)
At 3: Won Jerome Handicap

GUEST ROOM (1965)
At 3: 2nd Mother Goose Stakes
3rd Monmouth Oaks
At 4: 2nd Santa Margarita Handicap

GUIDED TOUR (1996)
At 5: Won San Antonio Handicap

GUIDE LINE (1955)
At 2: Won Selima Stakes

GUILLAMOU CITY (1997)
At 3: 3rd Secretariat Stakes

GUILLOTINE (1947)
At 2: Won Futurity Stakes
At 3: Won Carter Handicap
At 4: Won Fall Highweight Handicap

GUILTON MADERO (1952)
At 3: Won Cinema Handicap

GUILTY CONSCIENCE (1976)
At 5: Won Vosburgh Stakes

GUITAR PLAYER (1968)
At 5: 3rd New Orleans Handicap

GUIZA (1987)
At 5: 2nd Gamely Handicap
At 6: 3rd Santa Margarita Handicap
Vanity Handicap

GULCH (1984)
At 2: Won Hopeful Stakes
Futurity Stakes
2nd Norfolk Stakes
At 3: Won Wood Memorial Stakes
Metropolitan Handicap
2nd Whitney Handicap
Woodward Stakes

3rd Gotham Stakes
Belmont Stakes
At 4: Won Metropolitan Handicap
Breeders' Cup Sprint
2nd Californian Stakes
Whitney Handicap
Vosburgh Stakes
3rd Philip H. Iselin Handicap

GUMBOY (1981)
At 2: 3rd Del Mar Futurity

GUMMO (1962)
At 2: 3rd Hollywood Juvenile Championship

GUN BOW (1960)
At 4: Won Gulfstream Park Handicap
Brooklyn Handicap
Washington Park Handicap
Woodward Stakes
San Fernando Stakes
Charles H. Strub Stakes
San Antonio Handicap
Whitney Stakes
2nd John B. Campbell Handicap
Aqueduct Stakes
Man o' War Stakes
Washington D.C. International
3rd Carter Handicap
Monmouth Handicap
At 5: Won Donn Handicap
Metropolitan Handicap
San Antonio Handicap
2nd Massachusetts Handicap
3rd Gulfstream Park Handicap

GUN FIGHT (1994)
At 2: 3rd Hopeful Stakes

GUNFLINT (1963)
At 2: 2nd Garden State Stakes

GUN TUNE (1969)
At 3: 2nd Illinois Derby
3rd Pontiac Grand Prix Stakes

GUSHING OIL (1949)
At 3: Won Louisiana Derby
Blue Grass Stakes

GUSHING WIND (1959)
At 4: 3rd John B. Campbell Handicap

GUSTY O'SHAY (1971)
At 2: Won Hopeful Stakes

GYGISTAR (1999)
At 3: Won King's Bishop Stakes
At 4: 3rd Forego Handicap

HABAR (1987)
At 2: 2nd Selima Stakes

HABIBTI (1999)
At 2: Won Del Mar Debutante Stakes
Hollywood Starlet Stakes
At 3: 2nd Las Virgenes Stakes
Santa Anita Oaks
3rd Kentucky Oaks

HABITONY (1974)
At 2: Won Norfolk Stakes
2nd Del Mar Futurity
At 3: Won Santa Anita Derby
2nd San Felipe Handicap
3rd Hollywood Derby

HADASSAH (1949)
At 3: 3rd Gazelle Stakes

HADN'T ORTER (1949)
At 2: 2nd Arlington Lassie Stakes

HADRIAN (1943)
At 3: 3rd Swift Stakes

HAGLEY (1967)
At 2: 2nd Hopeful Stakes
At 3: Won Withers Stakes

HAIL A CAB (1983)
At 5: Won Spinster Stakes
3rd Apple Blossom Handicap

HAIL ATLANTIS (1987)
At 3: Won Santa Anita Oaks

HAIL BOLD KING (1981)
At 2: 2nd Laurel Futurity
3rd Futurity Stakes
Remsen Stakes
At 3: 2nd Jockey Club Gold Cup
At 4: 3rd San Antonio Handicap

HAIL HILARIOUS (1973)
At 4: Won Apple Blossom Handicap
2nd La Canada Stakes

HAIL THE GREY (1967)
At 4: 3rd Beverly Hills Handicap
At 5: Won Santa Barbara Handicap

HAIL THE PIRATES (1970)
At 6: Won Gulfstream Park Handicap
3rd Widener Handicap

HAIL TO ALL (1962)
At 2: 2nd Pimlico Futurity
3rd Garden State Stakes
At 3: Won Jersey Derby
Belmont Stakes
Travers Stakes
2nd Florida Derby
Wood Memorial Stakes
3rd Flamingo Stakes
Preakness Stakes
Dwyer Handicap

HAIL TO PATSY (1966)
At 3: Won Kentucky Oaks
2nd Acorn Stakes
Mother Goose Stakes
Coaching Club American Oaks
Monmouth Oaks
3rd Alabama Stakes

HAIL TO REASON (1958)
At 2: Won Sapling Stakes
Hopeful Stakes

HAIL TO ROME (1980)
At 3: 3rd Jim Beam Spiral Stakes

HAJJI'S TREASURE (1982)
At 3: Won California Derby

HALFBRIDLED (2001)
At 2: Won Del Mar Debutante Stakes
Breeders' Cup Juvenile Fillies

HALF HIGH (1973)
At 5: 3rd Carter Handicap

HALF ICED (1979)
At 3: Won Secretariat Stakes

HALL OF FAME (1948)
At 3: Won Arlington Classic
American Derby
3rd Blue Grass Stakes
Jerome Handicap
At 4: 2nd Aqueduct Handicap

HALO (1969)
At 3: 3rd Jersey Derby
Dwyer Handicap
At 5: Won United Nations Handicap

HALO AMERICA (1990)
At 5: 2nd Apple Blossom Handicap
At 6: 2nd Apple Blossom Handicap
At 7: Won Apple Blossom Handicap

HALO HANSOM (1986)
At 3: 2nd Jersey Derby

HALORY HUNTER (1995)
At 2: 2nd Remsen Stakes
3rd Moet Champagne Stakes
At 3: Won Toyota Blue Grass Stakes
3rd Fountain of Youth Stakes
Florida Derby

HALO'S IMAGE (1991)
At 3: 3rd Florida Derby

HALO'S STRIDE (1998)
At 3: 2nd Turfway Spiral Stakes

HALO SUNSHINE (1993)
At 3: 3rd Arkansas Derby

HALSGAL (1944)
At 3: 3rd Delaware Oaks
At 4: 3rd Molly Pitcher Handicap

HAL'S HOPE (1997)
At 3: Won Florida Derby
2nd Fountain of Youth Stakes
At 5: Won Gulfstream Park Handicap

HAL'S PAL (1993)
At 5: 2nd Buick Meadowlands Cup Handicap

HALT (1946)
At 3: Won Blue Grass Stakes

HAMPDEN (1943)
At 3: Won Withers Stakes
2nd Wood Memorial Stakes
San Felipe Stakes
3rd Kentucky Derby
Preakness Stakes

HANALEI BAY (1967)
At 3: Won Hollywood Derby
3rd California Derby
Cinema Handicap
At 4: 2nd Malibu Stakes
San Fernando Stakes
Charles H. Strub Stakes
3rd San Antonio Stakes

HANDLEBARS (1944)
At 3: 2nd Will Rogers Handicap

HANDSOME BOY (1963)
At 3: 3rd Gotham Stakes
At 4: Won Amory L. Haskell Handicap
Brooklyn Handicap
Washington Park Handicap
2nd Jockey Club Gold Cup
3rd Grey Lag Handicap
Man o' War Stakes

HANDSOME TEDDY (1949)
At 3: 2nd Florida Derby

HANG TEN (1973)
At 2: Won Remsen Stakes

HANK H. (1943)
At 4: Won Longacres Mile
2nd San Antonio Handicap
At 5: 3rd Longacres Mile

HANNAH'S HILL (1954)
At 5: 2nd Canadian Championship Stakes

HANNIBAL (1949)
At 2: 3rd Hopeful Stakes

HANSEL (1988)
At 2: Won Arlington-Washington Futurity
2nd Hopeful Stakes
At 3: Won Jim Beam Stakes
Preakness Stakes
Belmont Stakes
2nd Travers Stakes
3rd Florida Derby
Haskell Invitational Handicap

HANUMAN HIGHWAY (1995)
At 3: 2nd Arkansas Derby
At 4: 3rd Strub Stakes

HAP (1996)
At 5: 2nd Arlington Million
At 6: 3rd Woodford Reserve Turf Classic

HAPPYANUNOIT (1995)
At 4: Won Matriarch Stakes
2nd Ramona Handicap
At 5: Won Beverly Hills Handicap
2nd Gamely Breeders' Cup Handicap
Beverly D. Stakes
3rd Matriarch Stakes
At 6: Won Gamely Breeders' Cup Handicap
2nd Beverly Hills Handicap

HAPPYASALARK TOMAS (1985)
At 3: 2nd Super Derby

HAPPY BRIDE (1978)
At 5: 2nd Santa Barbara Handicap

HAPPY GO LUCKY (1949)
At 2: 3rd Washington Park Futurity
At 3: 2nd Louisiana Derby
At 4: 2nd New Orleans Handicap
3rd Santa Anita Maturity
At 7: 2nd New Orleans Handicap

HAPPY INTELLECTUAL (1966)
At 3: 3rd Illinois Derby

HAPPY ISSUE (1940)
At 6: 2nd Santa Margarita Handicap
At 8: 3rd Arlington Matron Handicap

HAPPY JAZZ BAND (1988)
At 2: 2nd Champagne Stakes
At 3: 3rd Wood Memorial Stakes

HAPPY MOOD (1951)
At 3: Won Acorn Stakes

HAPPY PRINCESS (1952)
At 4: 2nd Maskette Handicap
Firenze Handicap
At 6: 3rd Top Flight Handicap
At 7: 2nd Black Helen Handicap
At 8: 2nd Black Helen Handicap

HAPPY WAY (1967)
At 4: Won Manhattan Handicap

HARBOR SPRINGS (1973)
At 2: Won Breeders' Futurity

HARBOUR CLUB (1987)
At 5: 2nd Shuvee Handicap
Hempstead Handicap

HARCALL (1955)
At 3: 2nd Santa Anita Derby

HARD ROCK MAN (1959)
At 4: 2nd Canadian Championship Stakes

HARDSHIP (1977)
At 2: 3rd Frizette Stakes

HARD WORK (1967)
At 2: Won Breeders' Futurity
2nd Kentucky Jockey Club Stakes
3rd Sapling Stakes

HAREM LADY (1964)
At 3: 2nd Ladies Handicap
At 4: 3rd Manhattan Handicap
At 5: Won Manhattan Handicap
2nd Top Flight Handicap
3rd Jockey Club Gold Cup

HARE RAISING (1953)
At 6: 3rd New Orleans Handicap

HARHAM'S SIZZLER (1979)
At 3: 2nd Hawthorne Gold Cup

HARLAN (1989)
At 5: Won Vosburgh Stakes

HARLAN'S HOLIDAY (1999)
At 2: 2nd Lane's End Breeders' Futurity
At 3: Won Florida Derby
Toyota Blue Grass Stakes
2nd Fountain of Youth Stakes
3rd Jockey Club Gold Cup
At 4: Won Donn Handicap
2nd Hollywood Gold Cup

HARLEY TUNE (1994)
At 2: 3rd Futurity Stakes

HARMONICA (1944)
At 3: Won Coaching Club American Oaks
2nd Acorn Stakes
Gazelle Stakes
At 4: Won Suburban Handicap
2nd Vagrancy Handicap
Beldame Handicap
Massachusetts Handicap

HARMONIZING (1954)
At 6: Won Man o' War Stakes
2nd Washington D.C. International
At 7: 2nd Man o' War Handicap
At 8: 3rd Canadian Championship Stakes

HARMONY LODGE (1998)
At 3: 3rd Prioress Stakes
At 5: Won Ballerina Handicap

HARPIE (1957)
At 5: 3rd American Handicap
At 6: 3rd Californian Stakes

HARRY H. (1961)
At 2: 3rd Del Mar Futurity

HARRY'S LOVE (1975)
At 4: 3rd Californian Stakes

HARVARD MAN (1972)
At 2: 2nd Champagne Stakes

HARVEST GIRL (1974)
At 3: 3rd Maskette Handicap

HASSEYAMPA (1951)
At 3: 2nd Blue Grass Stakes
Pimlico Special
3rd Kentucky Derby
Preakness Stakes
Hawthorne Gold Cup
At 4: Won Hawthorne Gold Cup
At 5: 3rd Michigan Mile

HASSI'S IMAGE (1969)
At 3: 2nd Arkansas Derby

HASTEN TO ADD (1990)
At 5: 3rd Rothmans International Stakes

HASTY DOLL (1955)
At 2: Won Princess Pat Stakes
3rd Arlington Lassie Stakes
At 3: 3rd Kentucky Oaks

HASTY FLYER (1971)
At 2: 2nd Laurel Futurity
At 3: 2nd Flamingo Stakes

HASTY HITTER (1966)
At 3: 2nd Santa Susana Stakes

HASTY MATELDA (1961)
At 2: Won Matron Stakes
2nd Spinaway Stakes

HASTY REQUEST (1948)
At 2: 3rd Arlington Lassie Stakes

HASTY ROAD (1951)
At 2: Won Arlington Futurity
Washington Park Futurity
Breeders' Futurity
Kentucky Jockey Club Stakes
At 3: Won Preakness Stakes
2nd Kentucky Derby
3rd American Derby
At 4: Won Widener Handicap

HATCHET MAN (1971)
At 3: Won Dwyer Handicap
At 5: Won Widener Handicap
Amory L. Haskell Handicap
2nd New Orleans Handicap

HAT FULL (1971)
At 4: 2nd Widener Handicap

HATIM (1981)
At 5: Won San Antonio Handicap
3rd Santa Anita Handicap

HATOOF (1989)
At 5: Won Beverly D. Stakes
2nd Breeders' Cup Turf

HATTIESBURG (1998)
At 4: 3rd Humana Distaff Handicap

HAUNTING (1988)
At 4: 2nd Top Flight Handicap

HAWAII (1964)
At 5: Won Stars and Stripes Handicap
United Nations Handicap
Man o' War Stakes
2nd Washington D.C. International

HAWAIIAN RULER (1966)
At 2: 3rd Kentucky Jockey Club Stakes

HAWK ATTACK (1992)
At 3: Won Secretariat Stakes

HAWKSLEY HILL (1993)
At 5: 2nd Breeders' Cup Mile
3rd Early Times Turf Classic
Eddie Read Handicap
At 6: 3rd Early Times Turf Classic

HAWKSTER (1986)
At 2: Won Norfolk Stakes
3rd Hollywood Futurity
At 3: Won Oak Tree Invitational Stakes
At 4: 2nd San Luis Rey Stakes
Hollywood Turf Handicap
3rd Charles H. Strub Stakes
San Juan Capistrano Handicap

HAYSEED (1946)
At 3: 2nd San Felipe Stakes

HAZEL R. (1977)
At 2: 2nd Del Mar Debutante Stakes
Oak Leaf Stakes

HEAD EAST (1992)
At 4: 3rd Ruffian Handicap

HEADER CARD (1979)
At 2: Won Oak Leaf Stakes
2nd Hollywood Starlet Stakes
3rd Hollywood Futurity

HEAD MAN (1953)
At 2: 2nd Champagne Stakes
Futurity Stakes
At 3: Won Wood Memorial Stakes

HEAD OF THE RIVER (1969)
At 2: 3rd Champagne Stakes
At 3: 3rd Wood Memorial Stakes

HEAD SPY (1973)
At 2: 3rd Arlington-Washington Lassie Stakes

HEARTLAND (1965)
At 3: 2nd Alabama Stakes

HEARTLIGHT NO. ONE (1980)
At 3: Won Ruffian Handicap
2nd Beldame Stakes

HEART OF JOY (1987)
At 6: 2nd Ramona Handicap

HEARTS OF LETTUCE (1970)
At 3: 2nd Ohio Derby

HEAT HAZE (1999)
At 4: Won Beverly D. Stakes
Matriarch Stakes
2nd Diana Handicap
3rd Flower Bowl Invitational Stakes

HEATHERTEN (1979)
At 5: Won Ruffian Handicap
Ladies Handicap
Apple Blossom Handicap
3rd Spinster Stakes
At 6: 2nd Apple Blossom Handicap
Delaware Handicap

HEAVENLY ADE (1976)
At 4: Won Delaware Handicap

HEAVENLY BODY (1957)
At 2: Won Princess Pat Stakes
Matron Stakes
3rd Arlington Lassie Stakes
Gardenia Stakes

HEAVENLY CAUSE (1978)
At 2: Won Frizette Stakes
Selima Stakes
2nd Matron Stakes
At 3: Won Fantasy Stakes
Kentucky Oaks
Acorn Stakes
2nd Mother Goose Stakes

HEAVENLY PRIZE (1991)
At 2: Won Frizette Stakes
3rd Breeders' Cup Juvenile Fillies
At 3: Won Alabama Stakes
Gazelle Handicap
Beldame Stakes
2nd Breeders' Cup Distaff
3rd Test Stakes
At 4: Won Apple Blossom Handicap
Hempstead Handicap
Go for Wand Stakes
2nd Beldame Stakes
Breeders' Cup Distaff
At 5: 3rd Donn Handicap

HEAVYWEIGHT CHAMP (1999)
At 2: 3rd Champagne Stakes

HECHIZADO (1976)
At 5: Won Brooklyn Handicap

HEDEVAR (1962)
At 4: 2nd Metropolitan Handicap
Arlington Handicap

HEDONIST (1995)
At 3: Won Santa Anita Oaks

HEIR TO THE LINE (1971)
At 3: 3rd Jerome Handicap

HEISANATIVE (1969)
At 2: 2nd Arlington-Washington Futurity

HE JR. (1963)
At 3: 3rd Arlington Classic

HELEN JENNINGS (1965)
At 5: 3rd Delaware Handicap
At 6: 2nd Ladies Handicap

HELIANTHUS (1951)
At 4: 2nd Tropical Handicap

HELIO RISE (1968)
At 4: 2nd New Orleans Handicap

HELIOSCOPE (1951)
At 3: Won Pimlico Special
Trenton Handicap
2nd Roamer Handicap
Arlington Classic
At 4: Won Massachusetts Handicap
Suburban Handicap
Monmouth Handicap
3rd John B. Campbell Memorial Handicap
Washington Park Handicap

HELLENIC HERO (1958)
At 4: 3rd Gallant Fox Handicap
At 5: 3rd Arlington Park Handicap

HELLO (1994)
At 3: 3rd Santa Anita Derby

HELLO CHICAGO (1991)
At 3: 2nd Pegasus Handicap

HELMSMAN (1992)
At 3: 2nd Crown Royal Hollywood Derby
At 4: Won Strub Stakes
2nd Californian Stakes
3rd Hollywood Gold Cup
At 5: 2nd Woodbine Mile

HELOISE (1971)
At 4: 2nd Top Flight Handicap

HELP ON WAY (1963)
At 3: 3rd Coaching Club American Oaks

HEM AND HAW (1961)
At 2: 3rd Demoiselle Stakes

HEMET SQUAW (1944)
At 2: 3rd Starlet Stakes
At 3: 3rd Hollywood Oaks
At 4: Won Vanity Handicap
2nd Del Mar Handicap

HENNESSY (1993)
At 2: Won Hopeful Stakes
2nd Breeders' Cup Juvenile

HEN PARTY (1952)
At 2: 2nd Princess Pat Stakes
Frizette Stakes
At 3: 2nd Delaware Oaks
3rd Acorn Stakes

HENRIJAN (1957)
At 3: 2nd California Derby

HERAT (1982)
At 3: 2nd Hollywood Derby
At 4: 2nd Santa Anita Handicap

HERBALIST (1967)
At 3: Won Arkansas Derby
3rd Louisiana Derby
At 4: 3rd New Orleans Handicap
At 6: 2nd Oaklawn Handicap

HERB WATER (1977)
At 4: 3rd Woodward Stakes

HERE AND THERE (1954)
At 3: Won Alabama Stakes
3rd Acorn Stakes

HERE'S HOPING (1947)
At 2: Won Princess Pat Stakes

HERITAGE OF GOLD (1995)
At 4: 3rd Go for Wand Handicap
Breeders' Cup Distaff
At 5: Won Apple Blossom Handicap
Go for Wand Handicap
2nd Personal Ensign Handicap
3rd Breeders' Cup Distaff

HERNANDO (1990)
At 5: 2nd Turf Classic

HERONSLEA (1962)
At 5: 3rd Massachusetts Handicap

HEROSHOGALA (1957)
At 3: 2nd Hawthorne Gold Cup
3rd American Derby
At 4: 2nd Hawthorne Gold Cup
At 6: 3rd Widener Handicap

HERO'S HONOR (1980)
At 4: Won United Nations Handicap

HERO'S TRIBUTE (1998)
At 5: Won Gulfstream Park Handicap
2nd Donn Handicap

HERSCHELWALKER (1979)
At 2: 2nd Futurity Stakes

HESABULL (1993)
At 3: 2nd Malibu Stakes
3rd Swaps Stakes
At 4: 2nd Californian Stakes
Breeders' Cup Sprint

HE'S A PISTOL (1958)
At 2: Won Breeders' Futurity
2nd Sapling Stakes

HE'S A SMOOTHIE (1963)
At 4: Won Canadian International Championship
2nd Display Handicap
At 5: Won Hialeah Turf Cup

HE'S DEWAN (1975)
At 2: 2nd Hollywood Juvenile Championship

HE'S TAILOR MADE (1987)
At 2: 3rd Young America Stakes

HEUTEL (1949)
At 7: 2nd Tropical Handicap

HEY BABE (1976)
At 4: 2nd Flower Bowl Handicap

HEY GOOD LOOKIN (1966)
At 2: 2nd Sanford Stakes
Saratoga Special

HEY HEY J.P. (1974)
At 2: 3rd Norfolk Stakes
Remsen Stakes
At 3: 3rd Jersey Derby

HEY RUBE (1970)
At 4: 3rd Amory L. Haskell Handicap
At 5: 2nd Oaklawn Handicap
3rd Michigan Mile and One-Eighth

HIBERNIAN (1965)
At 4: Won Pan American Handicap
3rd Hialeah Turf Cup

HICKMAN CREEK (1989)
At 3: 3rd San Felipe Stakes

HICKORY HILL (1950)
At 5: 3rd Canadian Championship Stakes

HIDDEN LAKE (1993)
At 3: 3rd Las Virgenes Stakes
Santa Anita Oaks
At 4: Won Hempstead Handicap
Go for Wand Stakes
Beldame Stakes
3rd Santa Margarita Handicap

HIDDEN LIGHT (1983)
At 3: Won Santa Anita Oaks
Hollywood Oaks

HIDDEN TALENT (1956)
At 3: Won Kentucky Oaks

HIERARCH (1949)
At 2: 3rd Arlington Futurity

HIGH ALEXANDER (1981)
At 3: Won American Derby

HIGH BID (1956)
At 3: Won Alabama Stakes
Vineland Handicap
2nd Ladies Handicap
3rd Beldame Handicap

HIGHBINDER (1968)
At 3: 2nd Withers Stakes
At 5: 2nd Vosburgh Handicap

HIGH BRITE (1984)
At 3: 2nd Withers Stakes
At 4: 3rd Vosburgh Stakes

HIGH CHAPARREL (1999)
At 3: Won John Deere Breeders' Cup Turf
At 4: Won John Deere Breeders' Cup Turf

HIGH COUNSEL (1978)
At 2: Won Norfolk Stakes
At 3: 2nd Hollywood Derby
At 4: 3rd San Antonio Stakes

HIGH ECHELON (1967)
At 2: Won Futurity Stakes
Pimlico-Laurel Futurity
At 3: Won Belmont Stakes
3rd Kentucky Derby

HIGH GUN (1951)
At 3: Won Belmont Stakes
Dwyer Stakes
Jockey Club Gold Cup
Manhattan Handicap
2nd American Derby
3rd Wood Memorial Stakes
Withers Stakes
Arlington Classic
At 4: Won Metropolitan Handicap
Brooklyn Handicap
2nd Suburban Handicap
Monmouth Handicap

HIGH HAT (1964)
At 4: Won Dixie Handicap
Bowling Green Handicap

HIGH HEAVEN (1979)
At 5: 2nd Santa Margarita Handicap

HIGH HEELED HOPE (1994)
At 2: 3rd Hollywood Starlet Stakes
At 3: 2nd Las Virgenes Stakes

HIGH HONORS (1980)
At 3: 3rd Wood Memorial Stakes
Preakness Stakes

HIGHLAND BLADE (1978)
At 3: 2nd Wood Memorial Stakes
Belmont Stakes
3rd Suburban Handicap
At 5: Won Brooklyn Handicap
Marlboro Cup Handicap
Pan American Handicap
2nd Jockey Club Gold Cup
3rd Suburban Handicap

HIGHLAND PARK (1980)
At 2: Won Breeders' Futurity
3rd Arlington-Washington Futurity

HIGH PHEASANT (1975)
At 2: 3rd Oak Leaf Stakes

HIGH QUOTIENT (1967)
At 3: 3rd Ohio Derby

HIGH SCHEMES (1980)
At 3: Won Coaching Club American Oaks
2nd Mother Goose Stakes

HIGH SCUD (1949)
At 4: 2nd Golden Gate Handicap
3rd Brooklyn Handicap
At 5: 2nd American Handicap
3rd Californian Stakes

HIGH STAKES PLAYER (1992)
At 3: 3rd Malibu Stakes

HIGH STEEL (1972)
At 2: 2nd Futurity Stakes
At 3: 2nd American Derby

HIGH TREND (1944)
At 5: 3rd Carter Handicap

HIGH TRIBUTE (1964)
At 3: Won Jerome Handicap
At 4: 3rd New Orleans Handicap

HIGH VOLTAGE (1952)
At 2: Won Selima Stakes
Matron Stakes
3rd Spinaway Stakes
At 3: Won Acorn Stakes
Coaching Club American Oaks
Delaware Oaks
Vineland Handicap
3rd Gazelle Stakes
At 4: 3rd Black Helen Handicap

HIGH WIRE ACT (1996)
At 3: 3rd San Felipe Stakes

HIGH YIELD (1997)
At 2: Won Hopeful Stakes
2nd Hollywood Futurity
3rd Champagne Stakes
Breeders' Cup Juvenile
At 3: Won Fountain of Youth Stakes
Toyota Blue Grass Stakes
2nd Florida Derby

HI JAC JET (1987)
At 2: 3rd Cowdin Stakes

HILCO SCAMPER (1983)
At 2: Won Sapling Stakes

HILLBIZON (1977)
At 3: 3rd Ohio Derby

HILL CIRCUS (1968)
At 4: Won Beverly Hills Handicap
Del Mar Handicap
3rd Ladies Handicap
At 5: 3rd Santa Maria Handicap

HILL CLOWN (1963)
At 3: 3rd San Felipe Handicap
At 4: Won Sunset Handicap
3rd San Luis Rey Handicap

HILL COUNTRY (1955)
At 2: Won Kentucky Jockey Club Stakes

HILL GAIL (1949)
At 2: Won Arlington Futurity
2nd Washington Park Futurity
At 3: Won Santa Anita Derby
Kentucky Derby

HILL PASS (1989)
At 5: 3rd San Antonio Handicap

HILL PRINCE (1947)
At 2: Won Cowdin Stakes
At 3: Won Withers Stakes
Wood Memorial Stakes
Preakness Stakes
American Derby
Jerome Handicap
Jockey Club Gold Cup
Sunset Handicap
2nd Kentucky Derby
Dwyer Stakes
3rd Suburban Handicap
Hollywood Gold Cup
At 4: Won New York Handicap
2nd Jockey Club Gold Cup

HILL RISE (1961)
At 3: Won San Felipe Handicap
Santa Anita Derby
2nd Kentucky Derby
3rd Preakness Stakes
Travers Stakes
At 4: Won Santa Anita Handicap
San Fernando Stakes
Man o' War Stakes
2nd Manhattan Handicap
United Nations Handicap
3rd American Derby
Hollywood Gold Cup
San Juan Capistrano Handicap
At 5: Won San Antonio Handicap

HILL RUN (1966)
At 5: 3rd San Juan Capistrano Handicap
At 6: 2nd San Luis Rey Handicap

HILLSBOROUGH (1957)
At 4: Won Display Handicap
2nd Gallant Fox Handicap
Jockey Club Gold Cup
At 5: 2nd New Orleans Handicap

HILLSDALE (1955)
At 3: 3rd Westerner Stakes
At 4: Won San Carlos Handicap
Los Angeles Handicap
Californian Stakes
American Handicap
Hollywood Gold Cup
Aqueduct Handicap
Santa Anita Maturity
2nd San Antonio Handicap
Santa Anita Handicap
Woodward Stakes

HILL SHINE (1964)
At 4: 2nd Century Handicap

HILLYER COURT (1942)
At 4: Won New Orleans Handicap

HIMALAYAN (1976)
At 3: 2nd Kentucky Oaks

HI Q. (1966)
At 5: Won Vanity Handicap
2nd Santa Barbara Handicap

HIRAM JR. (1949)
At 3: 3rd Louisiana Derby

HI RATED (1960)
At 3: 2nd Hollywood Oaks
At 4: 2nd Santa Margarita Handicap

HIS DUCHESS (1950)
At 2: 2nd Selima Stakes

HIS MAJESTY (1968)
At 4: 2nd Widener Handicap

HISTORIAN (1941)
At 5: Won Arlington Handicap
Sunset Handicap
3rd Hollywood Gold Cup

HITCHCOCK (1966)
At 4: 2nd San Luis Rey Handicap
3rd Suburban Handicap
Bowling Green Handicap
At 6: Won Suburban Handicap
2nd Massachusetts Handicap
Amory L. Haskell Handicap
3rd Hawthorne Gold Cup

HITEX (1949)
At 3: Won Fall Highweight Handicap
2nd Dwyer Stakes
Saranac Handicap

HITTING AWAY (1958)
At 3: Won Withers Stakes
Dwyer Handicap
2nd Roamer Handicap
At 4: 2nd Carter Handicap

HODGES BAY (1985)
At 4: Won Rothmans International Stakes
At 5: 3rd Sword Dancer Handicap

HOEDOWN'S DAY (1978)
At 3: 2nd California Derby
3rd Santa Anita Derby

HO HO (1961)
At 4: 2nd Delaware Handicap

HOIST AWAY (1956)
At 3: 3rd Dwyer Handicap

HOIST THE FLAG (1968)
At 2: Won Cowdin Stakes

HOIST THE SILVER (1975)
At 3: 3rd California Derby

HOLANDES II (1953)
At 4: 2nd Santa Anita Handicap

HOLDING PATTERN (1971)
At 2: Won Champagne Stakes
3rd Norfolk Stakes
At 3: Won Monmouth Invitational Handicap
Travers Stakes
At 4: 2nd Donn Handicap

HOLD THAT TIGER (2000)
At 2: 3rd Bessemer Trust Breeders' Cup Juvenile
At 3: 2nd Woodward Stakes

HOLD YOUR PEACE (1969)
At 2: Won Arlington-Washington Futurity
3rd Futurity Stakes
At 3: Won Flamingo Stakes
3rd Kentucky Derby

HOLD YOUR TRICKS (1975)
At 5: 2nd Oaklawn Handicap

HOLIDAY DANCER (1980)
At 4: 3rd Apple Blossom Handicap

HOLIDAY LADY (2000)
At 3: 3rd Ashland Stakes

HOLIDAY THUNDER (1998)
At 2: 3rd Lane's End Breeders' Futurity

HOLLYWOOD GLITTER (1984)
At 4: Won La Canada Stakes
2nd Santa Margarita Handicap

HOLLYWOOD STORY (2001)
At 2: Won Hollywood Starlet Stakes
2nd Del Mar Debutante Stakes

HOLLYWOOD WILDCAT (1990)
At 3: Won Hollywood Oaks
Breeders' Cup Distaff
At 4: Won Gamely Handicap
2nd Ramona Handicap

HOLME ON TOP (1981)
At 2: 2nd Arlington-Washington Futurity

HOLY BULL (1991)
At 2: Won Futurity Stakes
At 3: Won Florida Derby
Blue Grass Stakes
Metropolitan Handicap
Dwyer Stakes
Haskell Invitational Handicap
Travers Stakes
Woodward Stakes

HOME AT LAST (1987)
At 3: Won Super Derby
2nd American Derby
3rd Arlington Classic

HOMEBUILDER (1984)
At 3: 3rd Jim Beam Stakes
Ohio Derby
Pennsylvania Derby
At 5: 3rd Oaklawn Handicap

HOME JEROME (1970)
At 6: 3rd Donn Handicap

HOME-MADE (1950)
At 2: Won Astoria Stakes
At 3: Won Vagrancy Handicap
Comely Handicap

HOMESTAKE (1951)
At 2: 3rd Breeders' Futurity

HOMETOWN QUEEN (1984)
At 3: 2nd Kentucky Oaks
3rd Fantasy Stakes

HONEST AND TRUE (1977)
At 3: 3rd Fantasy Stakes
Kentucky Oaks

HONEST LADY (1996)
At 4: Won Santa Monica Handicap
2nd Metropolitan Handicap
Breeders' Cup Sprint

HONESTOUS (1969)
At 3: 2nd Gazelle Handicap

HONEST PLEASURE (1973)
At 2: Won Champagne Stakes
Laurel Futurity
Arlington-Washington Futurity
At 3: Won Flamingo Stakes
Florida Derby
Blue Grass Stakes
Travers Stakes
2nd Kentucky Derby
Marlboro Cup Handicap
3rd Monmouth Invitational Handicap
Woodward Handicap

HONEY BUNNY (1960)
At 2: 2nd Arlington Lassie Stakes
3rd Hollywood Juvenile Championship

HONEY DEAR (1958)
At 2: 2nd Spinaway Stakes
3rd Sorority Stakes
At 4: 3rd Top Flight Handicap

HONEY FOX (1978)
At 4: Won Ramona Handicap

HONEY JAR (1975)
At 2: 3rd Del Mar Debutante Stakes

HONEY MARK (1972)
At 3: Won American Derby
2nd Blue Grass Stakes
Jersey Derby
3rd Louisiana Derby

HONEYMOON (1943)
At 3: Won Hollywood Oaks
Cinema Handicap
Hollywood Derby
2nd Santa Susana Stakes
Hollywood Gold Cup
3rd Santa Anita Derby
At 4: Won Vanity Handicap
2nd Washington Park Handicap
3rd Hollywood Gold Cup
At 5: Won Vineland Handicap
Top Flight Handicap
3rd Ladies Handicap
At 6: 2nd Vanity Handicap
Del Mar Handicap

HONEYS ALIBI (1952)
At 3: 3rd Ohio Derby
At 4: 2nd San Antonio Handicap
Sunset Handicap
Del Mar Handicap
Manhattan Handicap
3rd Santa Anita Handicap
Santa Anita Maturity
San Juan Capistrano Handicap
At 5: 2nd San Antonio Handicap

HONEY'S GAL (1947)
At 3: 3rd Acorn Stakes
Monmouth Oaks

HONEYS GEM (1955)
At 4: 2nd Vanity Handicap
Arlington Matron Handicap
At 5: 3rd Vanity Handicap

HONKY STAR (1971)
At 2: 2nd Sorority Stakes

HONORABLE MISS (1970)
At 5: Won Fall Highweight Handicap
2nd Maskette Handicap
At 6: Won Fall Highweight Handicap
2nd Carter Handicap

HONOR GLIDE (1994)
At 3: Won Secretariat Stakes
At 5: Won Sword Dancer Invitational Handicap

HONORIFICO (1994)
At 5: 3rd Cigar Mile Handicap

HONOR IN WAR (1999)
At 4: Won Woodford Reserve Turf Classic
2nd Shadwell Turf Mile

HONOUR AND GLORY (1993)
At 2: 3rd Futurity Stakes
At 3: Won Metropolitan Handicap
2nd Santa Anita Derby
Vosburgh Stakes
3rd Breeders' Cup Sprint

HOOK AND LADDER (1997)
At 4: 3rd Carter Handicap

HOOKEDONTHEFEELIN (1996)
At 3: Won La Brea Stakes

HOOLIE (1992)
At 3: Won Dwyer Stakes

HOOP BAND (1953)
At 4: 2nd American Handicap
At 5: 3rd Tropical Handicap
Widener Handicap
Bougainvillea Turf Handicap

HOOP BOUND (1957)
At 6: 3rd New Orleans Handicap

HOOPLAH (1965)
At 3: Won Hollywood Oaks

HOORAY HOORAY (1972)
At 3: 2nd Gazelle Handicap

HOPEFUL WORD (1981)
At 6: 2nd San Antonio Handicap
3rd Santa Anita Handicap

HOPE IS ETERNAL (1956)
At 3: 3rd Acorn Stakes

HOPE OF GLORY (1972)
At 2: Won Alcibiades Stakes
At 5: 3rd Santa Margarita Handicap

HORMONE (1944)
At 3: 2nd San Vicente Handicap

HORSETRADER-ED (1949)
At 3: 3rd Cinema Handicap

HOSIERY (1971)
At 2: 3rd Champagne Stakes
At 3: 3rd Withers Stakes

HOSO (1972)
At 3: Won Fantasy Stakes

HOSTAGE (1979)
At 3: Won Arkansas Derby

HOT BRUSH (1994)
At 4: 3rd Pimlico Special

HOT DEBATE (1982)
At 2: 2nd Remsen Stakes

HOT DUST (1960)
At 3: 2nd Travers Stakes
At 4: 3rd Hialeah Turf Cup
At 5: Won Hialeah Turf Cup
2nd Widener Handicap
Bowling Green Handicap

HOT JAWS (1990)
At 5: 3rd Frank J. De Francis Memorial Dash

HOT N NASTY (1972)
At 2: Won Arlington-Washington Lassie Stakes
2nd Sorority Stakes

HOT NOVEL (1986)
At 3: 2nd Acorn Stakes

HOT WELLS (1995)
At 3: 3rd Ohio Derby

HOUR REGARDS (1950)
At 2: Won Del Mar Futurity

HOUSA DANCER (1993)
At 5: 2nd Vanity Handicap

HOUSEBUSTER (1987)
At 3: Won Withers Stakes
Jerome Handicap
2nd Metropolitan Handicap
At 4: Won Carter Handicap
Vosburgh Stakes

HOUSE OF FORTUNE (2001)
At 2: 3rd Hollywood Starlet Stakes

HOUSE PARTY (2000)
At 3: Won Prioress Stakes
3rd Test Stakes

HOW (1948)
At 3: Won Kentucky Oaks
Coaching Club American Oaks
2nd Top Flight Handicap
3rd New Castle Handicap
At 4: Won Ladies Handicap
At 5: 2nd Tropical Park Handicap
3rd Ladies Handicap

HOW CLEVER (1980)
At 2: 3rd Arlington-Washington Lassie Stakes

HOW NOW (1953)
At 5: Won Los Angeles Handicap
American Handicap
2nd Inglewood Handicap
At 6: 3rd Inglewood Handicap
At 7: 3rd San Antonio Handicap
At 8: 2nd San Antonio Handicap

HUBBLE BUBBLE (1944)
At 2: 2nd Princess Pat Stakes
At 3: Won Santa Susana Stakes
San Vicente Handicap

HUDSON COUNTY (1971)
At 3: 2nd Kentucky Derby
3rd Wood Memorial Stakes

HULA CHIEF (1971)
At 2: 3rd Arlington-Washington Futurity

HULL DOWN (1948)
At 3: 3rd Dwyer Stakes
At 4: 3rd Dixie Handicap

HUNKA PAPA (1972)
At 3: 3rd Dwyer Handicap

HUNNEMANNIA (1967)
At 3: 2nd Alabama Stakes

HUNSTON (1978)
At 4: 2nd Flower Bowl Handicap

HUNTER'S SUN (1945)
At 3: 3rd California Derby

HUNZA DANCER (1972)
At 5: Won Bowling Green Handicap
American Handicap
2nd Sunset Handicap

HUR POWER (1980)
At 3: 3rd Hollywood Derby

HURRICANE BERTIE (1995)
At 4: 3rd Ballerina Handicap

HURRY TO MARKET (1961)
At 2: Won Garden State Stakes

HURRY UP BLUE (1977)
At 3: Won American Derby
At 4: Won Gulfstream Park Handicap

HUSBAND (1990)
At 3: Won Rothmans International Stakes

HUSHABY BABY (1949)
At 3: Won Gazelle Stakes

HUSH DEAR (1978)
At 4: 3rd Flower Bowl Handicap

HUSTLIN GREEK (1969)
At 4: 2nd New Orleans Handicap

HYDROLOGIST (1966)
At 3: 3rd Monmouth Invitational Handicap
Jerome Handicap
At 4: 2nd Whitney Stakes
Woodward Stakes
3rd Brooklyn Handicap
Jockey Club Gold Cup

HY FROST (1963)
At 5: 3rd Oaklawn Handicap

HYMIENT (1955)
At 5: 2nd Michigan Mile and One-Sixteenth

HY-NAT (1958)
At 4: 3rd Display Handicap

HYPERBOREAN (1980)
At 3: Won Swaps Stakes
2nd Pegasus Handicap
3rd Travers Stakes

HYPHASIS (1947)
At 3: 3rd Carter Handicap

HYPNOTIC (1943)
At 3: Won Coaching Club American Oaks
Alabama Stakes
2nd Gazelle Stakes
Comely Handicap

HYPOCRITE II (1944)
At 6: 2nd Monmouth Handicap
3rd Brooklyn Handicap

I AIN'T BLUFFING (1994)
At 4: Won Milady Breeders' Cup Handicap

IAMARELIC (1948)
At 2: 3rd Cowdin Stakes
Garden State Stakes

I APPEAL (1951)
At 4: 2nd Fall Highweight Handicap

I BELIEVE IN YOU (1998)
At 2: Won Hollywood Starlet Stakes

IBERO (1987)
At 5: Won San Antonio Handicap
NYRA Mile Handicap
3rd Californian Stakes
At 6: Won Metropolitan Handicap

IBN BEY (1984)
At 6: 2nd Breeders' Cup Classic

ICARIAN (1951)
At 4: Won Aqueduct Handicap
3rd Manhattan Handicap

ICEBERG II (1948)
At 5: Won United Nations Handicap
2nd Washington D.C. International
3rd Miami Beach Handicap
Stars and Stripes Handicap
At 6: 3rd Tropical Handicap
At 7: 3rd Bougainvillea Turf Handicap
Hialeah Turf Handicap

ICECAPADE (1969)
At 3: 2nd Withers Stakes

ICECOLDBEERATREDS (2000)
At 2: Won Del Mar Futurity
2nd Champagne Stakes

ICE PRINCESS (1978)
At 3: 3rd Santa Susana Stakes

ICY GROOM (1983)
At 3: 2nd Santa Anita Derby

ICY TIME (1980)
At 2: 2nd Selima Stakes

IDA DELIA (1974)
At 4: Won Ladies Handicap
2nd Maskette Handicap
At 5: 3rd Santa Margarita Handicap

IDUN (1955)
At 2: Won Matron Stakes
Gardenia Stakes
Frizette Stakes
At 3: Won Mother Goose Stakes
Gazelle Handicap
2nd Delaware Oaks
3rd Roamer Handicap
At 4: Won Maskette Handicap
2nd Beldame Handicap

IDYLL (1977)
At 2: 3rd Norfolk Stakes
At 4: 3rd San Fernando Stakes

IF WINTER COMES (1978)
At 5: 2nd Flower Bowl Handicap

IFYOUCOULDSEEMENOW (1988)
At 3: 3rd Santa Anita Oaks

I GOING (1973)
At 3: 3rd Hollywood Oaks

ILE DE FRANCE (1999)
At 3: 3rd Santa Anita Oaks

ILLUMINATE (1979)
At 3: 3rd Belmont Stakes

ILLUSIONED (1998)
At 3: 2nd King's Bishop Stakes

ILLUSIONIST (1952)
At 4: Won Tropical Handicap
At 5: 2nd Massachusetts Handicap

I LOVE SILVER (1998)
At 3: 2nd San Felipe Stakes
3rd Santa Anita Derby
Ancient Title Breeders' Cup Handicap
Malibu Stakes

ILUSORIA (1998)
At 2: 3rd Matron Stakes

IMACOMIN (1946)
At 3: 2nd Pimlico Oaks
Vineland Handicap

IMACORNISHPRINCE (1973)
At 2: 2nd Hollywood Juvenile Championship
Norfolk Stakes

IMAGE OF GREATNESS (1982)
At 3: Won San Felipe Handicap
2nd Jim Beam Stakes

IMAGE OF REALITY (1976)
At 4: 3rd Vanity Handicap
Gamely Handicap

IMAGINARY LADY (1986)
At 3: Won Santa Anita Oaks
2nd Fantasy Stakes
Kentucky Oaks

IMAH (1990)
At 4: 3rd Top Flight Handicap

I'MA HELL RAISER (1977)
At 3: 2nd Arlington Classic

I'M A PLEASURE (1971)
At 2: 2nd Selima Stakes
3rd Frizette Stakes

IMBIBE (1986)
At 3: Won Peter Pan Stakes
2nd Withers Stakes

IMBROS (1950)
At 3: 3rd Cinema Handicap
Westerner Stakes
At 4: Won William P. Kyne Handicap
Californian Stakes
2nd Santa Anita Handicap
3rd American Handicap
At 5: 2nd San Antonio Handicap

I'M INFLUENTIAL (1986)
At 3: 3rd Jerome Handicap

IMPASSE (1950)
At 4: 2nd Roseben Handicap
John B. Campbell Memorial Handicap
3rd Woodward Stakes
At 5: 2nd Arlington Handicap
3rd Tropical Handicap

IMPEACHMENT (1997)
At 3: 3rd Arkansas Derby
Kentucky Derby
Preakness Stakes

IMPECUNIOUS (1970)
At 3: Won Arkansas Derby
3rd Blue Grass Stakes

IMPERIAL DILEMMA (1977)
At 4: 3rd Gulfstream Park Handicap

IMPERIAL GESTURE (1999)
At 2: 2nd Oak Leaf Stakes
Breeders' Cup Juvenile Fillies
At 3: Won Gazelle Handicap
Beldame Stakes
3rd Breeders' Cup Distaff

IMPERIAL RIDGE (1990)
At 2: 2nd Norfolk Stakes

IMPERIOUS SPIRIT (1983)
At 3: 2nd California Derby

IMPETUOSITY (1968)
At 3: Won Blue Grass Stakes

IMPORTANT BUSINESS (1982)
At 3: Won Illinois Derby
3rd Dwyer Stakes
At 4: 3rd Gulfstream Park Handicap

IMPRESSIVE (1963)
At 2: Won Saratoga Special
2nd Hopeful Stakes
3rd Sanford Stakes
At 3: 2nd Gotham Stakes
At 4: 3rd Metropolitan Handicap

IMPRESSIVE STYLE (1969)
At 2: Won Del Mar Debutante Stakes

IMPROMPTU (1952)
At 2: 3rd Arlington Futurity
Sapling Stakes
At 3: 3rd Arlington Classic
Jerome Handicap
At 4: Won Fall Highweight Handicap

IMPROVISER (1972)
At 4: Won Pan American Handicap
2nd Arlington Handicap
United Nations Handicap
Canadian International Championship
At 5: Won Hialeah Turf Cup
2nd Bowling Green Handicap
At 6: 3rd Arlington Handicap

IMPRUDENCE II (1944)
At 4: 2nd Molly Pitcher Handicap

I'M SPLENDID (1983)
At 2: Won Selima Stakes

I'M SWEETS (1983)
At 2: 3rd Matron Stakes

INCA QUEEN (1968)
At 3: 3rd Coaching Club American Oaks
At 4: Won Top Flight Handicap
At 5: 2nd Hempstead Handicap

INCA ROCA (1973)
At 3: 2nd Flamingo Stakes
3rd Blue Grass Stakes
At 4: 2nd New Orleans Handicap
At 5: 3rd New Orleans Handicap

INCINERATE (1990)
At 5: 3rd Ruffian Handicap

INCLINE (1943)
At 5: 3rd Gulfstream Park Handicap
Dixie Handicap

INCLUDE (1947)
At 3: 3rd Delaware Oaks

INCLUDE (1997)
At 4: Won Pimlico Special
3rd Suburban Handicap

INCLUSIVE (1960)
At 4: Won San Luis Rey Handicap

IN CONTENTION (1993)
At 3: 2nd Wood Memorial Stakes

INCREDIBLE EASE (1976)
At 3: Won Louisiana Downs Handicap
2nd Pennsylvania Derby
3rd Louisiana Derby

INCUBATOR (1976)
At 3: 3rd Pennsylvania Derby

INDIA DIVINA (1994)
At 5: Won Santa Maria Handicap
3rd Santa Margarita Handicap

INDIAN (1969)
At 3: 3rd San Felipe Handicap

INDIAN BLOOD (1959)
At 2: 3rd Hollywood Juvenile Championship
At 3: 2nd Cinema Handicap

INDIAN CHARLIE (1995)
At 3: Won Santa Anita Derby
3rd Kentucky Derby

INDIAN EMERALD (1966)
At 2: 2nd Kentucky Jockey Club Stakes

INDIAN EXPRESS (2000)
At 3: 2nd Santa Anita Derby

INDIAN HEMP (1949)
At 4: 3rd Washington Park Handicap
Hawthorne Gold Cup

INDIAN LAND (1949)
At 3: 2nd San Felipe Handicap
At 4: Won Vosburgh Handicap
2nd Queens County Handicap

INDIAN LEGEND (1951)
At 2: Won Frizette Stakes

INDIAN LEI (1980)
At 4: 2nd Widener Handicap

INDIAN MAID (1956)
At 3: 2nd Kentucky Oaks
Monmouth Oaks
3rd Delaware Oaks
At 4: 2nd Spinster Stakes
Santa Margarita Handicap
At 5: 3rd Black Helen Handicap

INDIAN SKIMMER (1984)
At 4: 3rd Breeders' Cup Turf

INDIAN SUNLITE (1963)
At 3: 2nd Monmouth Oaks
At 4: 3rd Molly Pitcher Handicap

INDULTO (1963)
At 2: 3rd Hopeful Stakes
Futurity Stakes
At 3: Won Withers Stakes
2nd Jersey Derby
At 4: 3rd Carter Handicap

INDY DANCER (2000)
At 3: 3rd Florida Derby

INDY FIVE HUNDRED (2000)
At 3: Won Garden City Breeders' Cup Handicap

INDY GROOVE (2000)
At 2: 3rd Del Mar Debutante Stakes

INDY VIDUAL (1994)
At 4: 3rd Man o' War Stakes

IN EARNEST (1943)
At 3: 3rd Blue Grass Stakes

IN EXCESS (1987)
At 4: Won San Fernando Stakes
Metropolitan Handicap
Suburban Handicap
Whitney Handicap
Woodward Stakes
3rd Charles H. Strub Stakes
At 5: 2nd San Antonio Handicap
3rd Carter Handicap
Metropolitan Handicap

IN EXCESSIVE BULL (1994)
At 2: 3rd Hollywood Futurity

INFAMY (1984)
At 4: Won Rothmans International Stakes

INFANTRY (1953)
At 4: 2nd San Luis Rey Handicap
3rd San Juan Capistrano Handicap
At 6: 3rd San Juan Capistrano Handicap

INFINIDAD (1982)
At 5: Won Vanity Handicap

INFINITE (1980)
At 3: 3rd Yellow Ribbon Stakes

INFLUENT (1991)
At 6: Won Caesars International Handicap
Man o' War Stakes

INFO (1964)
At 4: 3rd Washington Park Handicap

INFORMATIVE (1969)
At 2: 3rd Matron Stakes

INFURIATOR (1970)
At 4: 2nd Whitney Stakes

IN HER GLORY (1990)
At 3: 3rd Acorn Stakes
Gazelle Handicap

INHERITANCE (1945)
At 2: Won Matron Stakes
2nd Spinaway Stakes

IN HOT PURSUIT (1971)
At 2: 3rd Sorority Stakes

INKERMAN (1975)
At 4: 3rd Sunset Handicap
At 5: Won Sunset Handicap

INNUENDO (1974)
At 5: 3rd Vanity Handicap

IN REALITY (1964)
At 2: Won Pimlico Futurity
2nd Sapling Stakes
Cowdin Stakes
At 3: Won Florida Derby
Jersey Derby
2nd Flamingo Stakes
Preakness Stakes
American Derby
Jerome Handicap
At 4: Won John B. Campbell Handicap
Carter Handicap
Metropolitan Handicap

INROC (1943)
At 4: Won Roseben Handicap
2nd Carter Handicap

INSEPARABLE (1945)
At 2: Won Tremont Stakes
At 5: Won Washington Park Handicap
Stars and Stripes Handicap
3rd Arlington Handicap
At 6: 2nd Trenton Handicap

INSIDE INFORMATION (1991)
At 3: Won Ashland Stakes
Acorn Stakes
3rd Mother Goose Stakes
At 4: Won Shuvee Handicap
Ruffian Handicap
Spinster Stakes
Breeders' Cup Distaff

INSIDE TRACT (1954)
At 3: 2nd Belmont Stakes
3rd Preakness Stakes
At 4: Won Jockey Club Gold Cup
3rd Brooklyn Handicap
Whitney Stakes

INSTANT FRIENDSHIP (1993)
At 4: 2nd Jockey Club Gold Cup

INSTRUMENT LANDING (1976)
At 2: Won Remsen Stakes
3rd Young America Stakes
At 3: Won Wood Memorial Stakes

INSUBORDINATION (1967)
At 2: Won Hollywood Juvenile Championship
2nd Arlington-Washington Futurity
3rd Cowdin Stakes

INTEGRA (1984)
At 4: 3rd Spinster Stakes

INTENCION (1949)
At 5: 3rd Gulfstream Park Handicap

INTENSITIVO (1966)
At 5: 3rd Washington Park Handicap

INTENSIVE (1958)
At 2: 2nd Washington Park Futurity

INTENSIVE COMMAND (1985)
At 3: 2nd Tropical Park Derby
Blue Grass Stakes
3rd Ohio Derby

INTENT (1948)
At 3: 3rd Wood Memorial Stakes
At 4: Won San Juan Capistrano Handicap
Santa Anita Maturity
2nd San Antonio Handicap
Santa Anita Handicap
Golden Gate Handicap
3rd American Handicap
San Fernando Stakes
At 5: Won San Juan Capistrano Handicap
3rd Metropolitan Handicap

INTENTION (1980)
At 3: 3rd Pennsylvania Derby
Dwyer Stakes

INTENTIONALLY (1956)
At 2: Won Futurity Stakes
Pimlico Futurity
2nd Sapling Stakes
Champagne Stakes
At 3: Won Withers Stakes
Jerome Handicap
2nd Gotham Stakes
3rd Arlington Classic
At 4: 2nd Aqueduct Handicap
At 5: 2nd Trenton Handicap
At 6: Won Seminole Handicap

INTERCEPTED (1959)
At 4: Won Hialeah Turf Cup
At 5: 2nd Hawthorne Gold Cup

INTERCO (1980)
At 3: Won Bay Meadows Handicap
2nd Hollywood Derby
At 4: Won Century Handicap
San Fernando Stakes
Santa Anita Handicap
San Luis Rey Stakes
2nd Californian Stakes

INTERPRETATION (1948)
At 3: 2nd Santa Anita Derby

IN THE POCKET (1960)
At 2: 2nd Garden State Stakes

IN THE WINGS (1986)
At 4: Won Breeders' Cup Turf

INTREPID HERO (1972)
At 3: Won Hollywood Derby
Secretariat Stakes
2nd Monmouth Invitational Handicap
At 4: Won United Nations Handicap
2nd Amory L. Haskell Handicap

INVIGORATING (1976)
At 4: 2nd Golden Harvest Handicap

INVIGORATOR (1950)
At 2: Won Cowdin Stakes
2nd Champagne Stakes
At 3: 2nd Withers Stakes
Gotham Stakes
3rd Wood Memorial Stakes
Kentucky Derby
At 4: Won Brooklyn Handicap
2nd Queens County Handicap

INVINCIBLE YOU (1970)
At 6: 3rd Hialeah Turf Cup

INVISIBLE INK (1998)
At 3: 2nd Kentucky Derby
3rd Florida Derby

INVITED GUEST (1984)
At 4: 2nd Apple Blossom Handicap
At 5: 3rd Apple Blossom Handicap

INYUREYE (1949)
At 2: 3rd Pimlico Futurity

I OWE (1961)
At 3: 3rd Louisiana Derby
At 6: 2nd New Orleans Handicap

IRENE'S ANGEL (1946)
At 3: 2nd Longacres Mile

IRGUN (1991)
At 3: Won Gotham Stakes
Wood Memorial Stakes

IRISEN (1944)
At 5: 3rd Molly Pitcher Handicap

IRISH ACTOR (1986)
At 2: Won Young America Stakes
At 3: 2nd Flamingo Stakes
Peter Pan Stakes

IRISH ARRIVAL (1978)
At 2: 2nd Oak Leaf Stakes

IRISH BALL (1968)
At 3: 2nd Washington D.C. International

IRISH BRUSH (1952)
At 2: 3rd Breeders' Futurity

IRISH CASTLE (1967)
At 2: Won Hopeful Stakes
3rd Futurity Stakes

IRISH COUNTY (1964)
At 2: 2nd Frizette Stakes

IRISH DUDE (1965)
At 3: 3rd Hawthorne Gold Cup

IRISHER (1954)
At 3: 2nd Westerner Stakes

IRISH FIGHTER (1982)
At 3: 3rd Louisiana Derby
Arkansas Derby

IRISH HEART (1978)
At 4: 3rd Hawthorne Gold Cup

IRISH JAY (1957)
At 2: Won Spinaway Stakes
2nd Matron Stakes
Frizette Stakes
At 3: Won Acorn Stakes

IRISH LANCER (1957)
At 2: Won Saratoga Special
At 3: 2nd Dwyer Handicap

IRISH MARTINI (1979)
At 2: Won Futurity Stakes

IRISH PRIZE (1996)
At 5: Won Shoemaker Breeders' Cup Mile

IRISH REBELLION (1964)
At 3: 3rd Lawrence Realization Stakes
At 4: Won Pan American Handicap
2nd Hialeah Turf Cup
Dixie Handicap
Bowling Green Handicap
At 5: 2nd Pan American Handicap

IRISH RULER (1963)
At 2: 3rd Saratoga Special

IRISH SONNET (1971)
At 2: Won Sorority Stakes

IRISH SUN (1946)
At 2: 3rd Garden State Stakes

IRISH SUR (1982)
At 3: Won Tropical Park Derby
2nd Florida Derby
3rd Everglades Stakes

IRISH SWAP (1987)
At 5: 2nd NYRA Mile Handicap
At 6: 2nd Donn Handicap

IRISH TOWER (1977)
At 4: 2nd Metropolitan Handicap

IRISH WARRIOR (1998)
At 5: 3rd Eddie Read Handicap
Clement L. Hirsch Mem. Turf Champ.

IRON BIT (1973)
At 2: 2nd Hopeful Stakes

IRON CONSTITUTION (1974)
At 3: 2nd Preakness Stakes
Jersey Derby
Cinema Handicap
3rd Dwyer Handicap
Monmouth Invitational Handicap

IRON EYES (1983)
At 4: 2nd Californian Stakes

IRON LIEGE (1954)
At 3: Won Kentucky Derby
2nd Preakness Stakes
Arlington Classic
American Derby
3rd Everglades Stakes
Flamingo Stakes
Florida Derby
At 4: Won McLennan Handicap
2nd Widener Handicap

IRON MAIDEN (1941)
At 6: Won Del Mar Handicap
At 7: 2nd Vanity Handicap

IRON PEG (1960)
At 4: Won Suburban Handicap

IRON RULER (1965)
At 2: Won Cowdin Stakes
2nd Champagne Stakes
Garden State Stakes
3rd Sapling Stakes
At 3: Won Jerome Handicap
2nd Flamingo Stakes
Florida Derby
Wood Memorial Stakes
Arlington Classic
3rd Jersey Derby
At 4: 2nd Carter Handicap
3rd John B. Campbell Handicap

IRRADIATE (1966)
At 2: 2nd Matron Stakes

IRVING'S BABY (1997)
At 4: 3rd Personal Ensign Handicap

IRVKUP (1961)
At 3: Won Jerome Handicap
2nd Roamer Handicap

ISAFLORIDIAN (1968)
At 2: 2nd Frizette Stakes
3rd Selima Stakes

ISASMOOTHIE (1950)
At 2: Won Pimlico Futurity

ISAYSO (1979)
At 6: 2nd Ruffian Handicap
Beldame Stakes

ISHKOODAH (1961)
At 2: 2nd Breeders' Futurity
3rd Garden State Stakes

ISIGNY (1945)
At 4: 2nd New Orleans Handicap

ISITINGOOD (1991)
At 6: 2nd Oaklawn Handicap

IS IT TRUE (1986)
At 2: Won Breeders' Cup Juvenile
2nd Champagne Stakes
At 3: Won Jim Dandy Stakes

ISLAND CHARM (1977)
At 4: 3rd Maskette Stakes

ISLAND FASHION (2000)
At 3: Won Alabama Stakes
La Brea Stakes

ISLAND JAMBOREE (1986)
At 5: 2nd Gamely Handicap

ISLAND KISS (1975)
At 2: 3rd Demoiselle Stakes
At 4: 3rd Top Flight Handicap
La Canada Stakes
Santa Barbara Handicap

ISLAND KITTY (1976)
At 2: 3rd Matron Stakes

ISLAND QUEEN (1952)
At 4: 2nd Santa Margarita Handicap

ISLAND SULTAN (1975)
At 5: 2nd Longacres Mile

ISLAND WHIRL (1978)
At 3: Won Super Derby
At 4: Won Woodward Stakes
At 5: Won Hollywood Gold Cup
Whitney Handicap
2nd Monmouth Handicap

ISLE OF GREECE (1962)
At 3: 3rd San Felipe Handicap
At 4: Won San Fernando Stakes
2nd Charles H. Strub Stakes

ISLINGTON (1999)
At 3: 3rd Breeders' Cup Filly and Mare Turf
At 4: Won Breeders' Cup Filly and Mare Turf

ISOGRADE (1949)
At 2: 3rd Astoria Stakes

IS OURS (1961)
At 2: 2nd Selima Stakes

IS PROUD (1950)
At 2: Won Matron Stakes
2nd Astoria Stakes
At 4: 2nd Vanity Handicap

ISSUES N' ANSWERS (1980)
At 2: 2nd Del Mar Debutante Stakes
3rd Alcibiades Stakes

IS SVEIKATAS (1992)
At 3: 3rd Wood Memorial Stakes
Ohio Derby

ISTAN (1945)
At 4: 2nd Roseben Handicap

ISWAS (1948)
At 2: Won Garden State Stakes

IS YOUR PLEASURE (1981)
At 3: Won Jerome Handicap

ITAKA (1990)
At 3: 2nd Gotham Stakes
3rd Peter Pan Stakes

ITOBE (1953)
At 4: Won Fall Highweight Handicap

ITSABET (1945)
At 2: Won Garden State Stakes
2nd Sapling Stakes
At 3: 2nd Santa Susana Stakes
Pimlico Oaks

IT'S ACEDEMIC (1984)
At 5: 2nd Woodward Handicap

ITSALLGREEKTOME (1987)
At 3: Won Hollywood Derby
Hollywood Turf Cup
2nd Breeders' Cup Mile
At 4: 2nd Hollywood Turf Handicap
Breeders' Cup Turf
Hollywood Turf Cup
3rd Hollywood Gold Cup

IT'SAL'LKNOWNFACT (1990)
At 2: 2nd Breeders' Cup Juvenile

ITSAMAZA (1975)
At 2: 3rd Frizette Stakes

IT'S FREEZING (1972)
At 4: 2nd Vosburgh Handicap
At 6: 3rd Woodward Stakes

IT'S IN THE AIR (1976)
At 2: Won Arlington-Washington Lassie Stakes
Oak Leaf Stakes
2nd Frizette Stakes
At 3: Won Alabama Stakes
Vanity Handicap
Ruffian Handicap
2nd Hollywood Oaks
Maskette Stakes
3rd Santa Susana Stakes
At 4: Won Vanity Handicap
3rd Ruffian Handicap
Beldame Stakes
La Canada Stakes

IT'S THE ONE (1978)
At 4: Won New Orleans Handicap
San Fernando Stakes
Charles H. Strub Stakes
2nd Californian Stakes
Suburban Handicap
3rd Hollywood Gold Cup
Santa Anita Handicap
Hollywood Turf Cup
At 5: 2nd Santa Anita Handicap
3rd San Antonio Stakes

IT'S TRUE (1976)
At 4: Won Louisiana Downs Handicap

IVANJICA (1972)
At 4: 3rd Washington D.C. International

IVOR'S IMAGE (1983)
At 4: 3rd Santa Barbara Handicap

IVORY HUNTER (1974)
At 6: 3rd Jockey Club Gold Cup
Hialeah Turf Cup

IVORY WAND (1973)
At 3: 2nd Spinster Stakes
At 4: 3rd Spinster Stakes

I WILL (1944)
At 2: 2nd Futurity Stakes
At 3: Won Wood Memorial Stakes
2nd Swift Stakes

IZ A SAROS (1985)
At 3: 3rd Swaps Stakes

IZVESTIA (1987)
At 3: 3rd Jockey Club Gold Cup

JABNEH (1952)
At 5: Won Hialeah Turf Handicap
2nd Dixie Handicap
At 6: 2nd Hialeah Turf Handicap

JACINTO (1962)
At 3: Won San Felipe Handicap
2nd Santa Anita Derby

JACK FLASH (1994)
At 3: 2nd Jim Beam Stakes

JACKIE WACKIE (1988)
At 3: Won Secretariat Stakes
3rd American Derby

JACK KETCH (1954)
At 4: Won Canadian Championship Stakes

JACKKNIFE (1973)
At 2: Won Hopeful Stakes
Futurity Stakes

JACK OF CLUBS (1983)
At 6: 3rd Brooklyn Handicap

JACK'S JILL (1942)
At 4: Won Hawthorne Gold Cup
2nd Arlington Matron Handicap

JACK S.L. (1940)
At 7: 2nd New Orleans Handicap
At 8: 2nd New Orleans Handicap

JACK SLADE (1980)
At 3: 2nd Secretariat Stakes
At 4: 2nd Rothmans International Stakes

JACKSONPORT (1989)
At 4: 3rd Brooklyn Handicap

JACODEMA (1948)
At 3: 3rd Acorn Stakes
Coaching Club American Oaks
Delaware Oaks

JACODY (1990)
At 3: 3rd Spinster Stakes

JACQUE L'HEUREUX (1982)
At 3: 3rd Ohio Derby
Pennsylvania Derby

JACQUE'S TIP (1980)
At 3: 2nd Pennsylvania Derby

JADE FLUSH (1991)
At 4: 2nd Spinster Stakes

JADE HUNTER (1984)
At 4: Won Gulfstream Park Handicap

JAGGERY JOHN (1991)
At 3: 3rd Secretariat Stakes

JAIPUR (1959)
At 2: Won Hopeful Stakes
Cowdin Stakes
2nd Saratoga Special
Futurity Stakes
Champagne Stakes
At 3: Won Gotham Stakes
Withers Stakes
Jersey Derby
Belmont Stakes
Travers Stakes
2nd Roamer Handicap
Woodward Stakes

JAIPUR'S GEM (1973)
At 5: Won Carter Handicap

JAKLIN KLUGMAN (1977)
At 3: Won California Derby
Jerome Handicap
2nd Vosburgh Stakes
3rd Kentucky Derby
Marlboro Cup Handicap

JALOUSIE II (1959)
At 5: 2nd Santa Margarita Handicap
3rd Vanity Handicap
At 6: Won Vanity Handicap

JAMAICAN RUM (1998)
At 3: 2nd Arkansas Derby
3rd San Felipe Stakes
Swaps Stakes

JAMEELA (1976)
At 4: 2nd Apple Blossom Handicap
At 5: Won Maskette Stakes
2nd Beldame Stakes
3rd Ruffian Handicap
At 6: Won Delaware Handicap
3rd Apple Blossom Handicap

JAMES SESSION (1951)
At 2: 2nd Del Mar Futurity
3rd Starlet Stakes
At 4: 3rd Santa Anita Maturity

JAMIE K. (1950)
At 2: 3rd Sapling Stakes
At 3: 2nd Preakness Stakes
Belmont Stakes
3rd Florida Derby
At 4: 3rd Metropolitan Handicap

JAMPOL (1949)
At 2: 2nd Flamingo Stakes
Preakness Stakes
At 4: Won Manhattan Handicap
3rd New York Handicap
Westchester Handicap

JAM-TOOTIN (1959)
At 3: 3rd American Derby

JANET (1997)
At 4: Won Ramona Handicap
Yellow Ribbon Stakes
At 5: 3rd John C. Mabee Ramona Handicap

JATSKI (1974)
At 3: Won Travers Stakes

JAVA GOLD (1984)
At 2: Won Remsen Stakes
2nd Cowdin Stakes
At 3: Won Whitney Handicap
Travers Stakes
Marlboro Cup Handicap
2nd Jockey Club Gold Cup

JAVAMINE (1973)
At 3: 2nd Alabama Stakes

JAYCEAN (1975)
At 2: 3rd Breeders' Futurity

JAY FOX (1958)
At 4: Won Gulfstream Park Handicap
Donn Handicap
At 5: 3rd Gulfstream Park Handicap

JAY RAY (1966)
At 3: Won California Derby
2nd Louisiana Derby
Hollywood Derby
Dwyer Handicap
3rd Preakness Stakes

JAZZ BABY (1946)
At 3: 2nd Gazelle Stakes
3rd Coaching Club American Oaks
At 4: 3rd New Castle Handicap

JAZZ BEAT (1999)
At 3: 2nd Secretariat Stakes

JAZZ CLUB (1995)
At 4: 2nd Meadowlands Cup Handicap

JAZZING AROUND (1984)
At 2: 3rd Arlington-Washington Futurity

JAZZ QUEEN (1959)
At 2: 2nd Matron Stakes
3rd Spinaway Stakes
Frizette Stakes
At 5: 3rd Santa Margarita Handicap

JEAN BAPTISTE (1953)
At 2: 3rd Hopeful Stakes
At 3: 2nd Gotham Stakes

JEANENES LARK (1968)
At 2: 2nd Norfolk Stakes

JEANNE JONES (1985)
At 2: 2nd Breeders' Cup Juvenile Fillies
At 3: Won Fantasy Stakes
2nd Kentucky Oaks
3rd Santa Anita Oaks

JEAN-PIERRE (1964)
At 5: 3rd Dixie Handicap
Bowling Green Handicap

JEAN'S JOE (1952)
At 3: Won San Felipe Handicap
2nd Santa Anita Derby
Blue Grass Stakes
3rd Westerner Stakes

JEFFOREE (1987)
At 3: 2nd Hollywood Oaks

JELLY BEAN HOLIDAY (1980)
At 2: Won Alcibiades Stakes

JENKINS FERRY (1980)
At 4: 2nd San Juan Capistrano Handicap

JENNIE LEE (1948)
At 4: 3rd Vanity Handicap

JERSEY GIRL (1995)
At 3: Won Acorn Stakes
Mother Goose Stakes
Test Stakes

JESSE F (1991)
At 3: 3rd Gotham Stakes

JESSI JESSI (1984)
At 6: 3rd Ladies Handicap

JESS M (1995)
At 2: 3rd Hopeful Stakes

JESTER (1955)
At 2: Won Futurity Stakes
3rd Cowdin Stakes
At 3: 3rd Jerome Handicap

JET ACTION (1951)
At 3: Won Withers Stakes
Roamer Handicap
At 4: Won Washington Park Handicap
At 5: 3rd Woodward Stakes

JET COLONEL (1954)
At 2: 2nd Arlington Futurity
3rd Kentucky Jockey Club Stakes

JET GIRL (1952)
At 5: 2nd Black Helen Handicap

JETIN EXCESS (1998)
At 2: 2nd Hollywood Starlet Stakes

JET MASTER (1949)
At 4: 2nd Fall Highweight Handicap

JET PILOT (1944)
At 2: Won Pimlico Futurity
Tremont Stakes
2nd Arlington Futurity
3rd Champagne Stakes
Futurity Stakes
At 3: Won Kentucky Derby

JET'S CHARM (1954)
At 2: 2nd Matron Stakes

JET'S DATE (1949)
At 2: 3rd Futurity Stakes

JET'S KINGDOM (1965)
At 3: 3rd Illinois Derby

JETT-JETT (1944)
At 2: 2nd Washington Park Futurity

JEUNE HOMME (1990)
At 3: 2nd Hollywood Derby

JEWEL PRINCESS (1992)
At 4: Won Vanity Handicap
Breeders' Cup Distaff
2nd Milady Breeders' Cup Handicap
3rd Santa Margarita Handicap
At 5: Won Santa Maria Handicap
Santa Margarita Handicap
2nd Apple Blossom Handicap
3rd Hempstead Handicap
Vanity Handicap
Beldame Stakes

JEWEL'S REWARD (1955)
At 2: Won Washington Park Futurity
Cowdin Stakes
Champagne Stakes
Pimlico Futurity
At 3: Won Wood Memorial Stakes
2nd Flamingo Stakes
At 4: 3rd Santa Anita Maturity

JIG'S HAVEN (1983)
At 3: 2nd Fountain of Youth Stakes

JILBAB (1999)
At 3: Won Coaching Club American Oaks

JIM AND TONIC (1994)
At 4: 2nd Woodbine Mile

JIM FRENCH (1968)
At 2: 3rd Champagne Stakes
At 3: Won Santa Anita Derby
Dwyer Handicap
2nd Kentucky Derby
Belmont Stakes

Hollywood Derby
3rd Flamingo Stakes
Florida Derby
Preakness Stakes

JIM J. (1964)
At 3: 2nd Vosburgh Handicap
3rd Jerome Handicap
At 4: 3rd Vosburgh Handicap

JIMMER (1955)
At 2: 3rd Hopeful Stakes
At 4: Won Carter Handicap
2nd Metropolitan Handicap

JIMMINY BAXTER (1950)
At 2: 2nd Breeders' Futurity

JIMMY Z (1997)
At 4: 3rd Strub Stakes

JIM'S ALIBHI (1967)
At 3: Won Louisiana Derby

JIM'S ORBIT (1985)
At 2: 2nd Arlington-Washington Futurity
At 3: Won Ohio Derby
2nd Illinois Derby

JIM WHITE (1965)
At 2: Won Hollywood Juvenile Championship

JOACHIM (1973)
At 3: Won Secretariat Stakes

JOANIE'S CHIEF (1977)
At 2: Won Champagne Stakes
3rd Young America Stakes
At 4: 2nd Monmouth Handicap
At 5: 2nd Widener Handicap
Gulfstream Park Handicap

JOBSTOWN (1944)
At 3: 3rd Louisiana Derby

JOCKO'S WALK (1954)
At 3: 2nd Display Handicap
3rd Lawrence Realization Stakes
At 4: 3rd Gallant Fox Handicap
Display Handicap

JOE BEAR (2000)
At 3: 2nd Secretariat Stakes

JOE FRAZIER (1967)
At 4: 2nd New Orleans Handicap

JOE JONES (1950)
At 4: Won John B. Campbell Memorial Handicap
2nd Woodward Stakes
At 5: 2nd Santa Anita Handicap
Excelsior Handicap
3rd Metropolitan Handicap
At 6: 2nd John B. Campbell Memorial Handicap

JOE PRICE (1954)
At 2: 3rd Starlet Stakes
At 3: Won San Felipe Handicap
2nd Cinema Handicap
3rd Westerner Stakes

JOE'S TAMMIE (1985)
At 2: Won Arlington-Washington Lassie Stakes

JOE WHO (1993)
At 6: Won Eddie Read Handicap

JOEY BOB (1968)
At 4: 3rd Michigan Mile and One-Eighth

JOEY FRANCO (1999)
At 4: Won Triple Bend Breeders' Cup Handicap

JOGGING (1967)
At 6: 2nd Arlington Handicap

JOHANNESBURG (1999)
At 2: Won Bessemer Trust Breeders' Cup Juvenile

JOHANN QUATZ (1989)
At 4: 3rd Arlington Million
At 5: 2nd Breeders' Cup Mile
3rd Eddie Read Handicap

JOHAR (1999)
At 3: Won Hollywood Derby
At 4: Won John Deere Breeders' Cup Turf
2nd Clement L. Hirsch Mem. Turf Champ.

JOHN BRUCE (1956)
At 2: 3rd Kentucky Jockey Club Stakes

JOHN HENRY (1975)
At 4: 2nd Bay Meadows Handicap
At 5: Won Hialeah Turf Cup
Hollywood Invitational Handicap
Oak Tree Invitational Stakes
San Luis Rey Stakes
San Juan Capistrano Handicap
2nd Jockey Club Gold Cup
Bowling Green Handicap
Sword Dancer Stakes
3rd Turf Classic
At 6: Won Jockey Club Gold Cup
Santa Anita Handicap
Hollywood Invitational Handicap
Sword Dancer Stakes
Arlington Million
Oak Tree Invitational Stakes
San Luis Rey Stakes
At 7: Won Santa Anita Handicap
Oak Tree Invitational Stakes
3rd Meadowlands Cup
San Luis Rey Stakes
At 8: Won Hollywood Turf Cup
2nd Budweiser Million
Oak Tree Invitational Stakes
At 9: Won Hollywood Invitational Handicap
Sunset Handicap
Budweiser-Arlington Million
Turf Classic
2nd Hollywood Gold Cup
3rd San Luis Rey Stakes

JOHNICA (1981)
At 5: 2nd Santa Margarita Handicap

JOHNLEE N' HAROLD (1978)
At 3: 2nd Santa Anita Derby

JOHNNY APPLESEED (1973)
At 3: Won Louisiana Derby
3rd Flamingo Stakes

JOHNNY D. (1974)
At 3: Won Washington D.C. International
Turf Classic
3rd Man o' War Stakes
Canadian International Championship

JOHNNY DANCE (1978)
At 3: 2nd Pegasus Handicap
3rd Rothmans International Stakes
At 4: 2nd Bowling Green Handicap

JOHNNY DIMICK (1944)
At 2: 3rd Hopeful Stakes

JOHNNY'S IMAGE (1975)
At 4: Won Hollywood Invitational Handicap
2nd Charles H. Strub Stakes
3rd New Orleans Handicap

JOHN'S CALL (1991)
At 9: Won Sword Dancer Invitational Handicap
Turf Classic
3rd Breeders' Cup Turf

JOHN'S GOLD (1979)
At 3: 2nd Dwyer Stakes
Jerome Handicap
At 4: 3rd Metropolitan Handicap

JOHNS JOY (1946)
At 2: Won Kentucky Jockey Club Stakes
2nd Breeders' Futurity
At 3: 2nd Blue Grass Stakes
3rd American Derby

JOHN'S PRIDE (1944)
At 2: 2nd Breeders' Futurity
At 3: 3rd Blue Grass Stakes

JOHNS TREASURE (1983)
At 3: 2nd Belmont Stakes
Dwyer Stakes
At 4: 3rd Widener Handicap

JOHN WILLIAM (1957)
At 3: Won Gotham Stakes
Withers Stakes
2nd Santa Anita Derby
Arlington Classic
3rd San Felipe Handicap
Wood Memorial Stakes

JOLIE'S HALO (1987)
At 4: Won Donn Handicap
Gulfstream Park Handicap
3rd Oaklawn Handicap
Pimlico Special
At 5: Won Philip H. Iselin Handicap

JOLLY JET (1963)
At 3: 2nd American Derby

JOLLY JOHU (1971)
At 3: 2nd Belmont Stakes
At 4: Won John B. Campbell Handicap
At 5: 3rd John B. Campbell Handicap

JOLYPHA (1989)
At 3: 3rd Breeders' Cup Classic

JONTILLA (1967)
At 4: Won Amory L. Haskell Handicap

JOSE BINN (1976)
At 2: Won Arlington-Washington Futurity

JOSTLE (1997)
At 3: Won Coaching Club American Oaks
Alabama Stakes
2nd Mother Goose Stakes
At 4: 2nd Hempstead Handicap

JOTA (1983)
At 3: 3rd Swaps Stakes

JOTA JOTA (1954)
At 2: 2nd Spinaway Stakes

J.O. TOBIN (1974)
At 3: Won Swaps Stakes
At 4: Won Californian Stakes
2nd San Fernando Stakes
3rd Charles H. Strub Stakes

JOURNALIST (1961)
At 2: Won Kentucky Jockey Club Stakes
At 3: 3rd Everglades Stakes

JOURNEY AT SEA (1979)
At 3: Won Swaps Stakes
3rd Santa Anita Derby
At 5: 2nd Santa Anita Handicap

JOVIAL (1987)
At 3: Won Swaps Stakes
At 6: Won Oaklawn Handicap

JOVIAL JOVE (1953)
At 2: Won Breeders' Futurity
2nd Kentucky Jockey Club Stakes

JOYEAUX DANSEUR (1993)
At 5: Won Early Times Turf Classic

J.P. BROTHER (1977)
At 2: Won Hopeful Stakes

J.R.'S PET (1971)
At 3: Won Arkansas Derby

J.T.'S PET (1984)
At 3: Won Jim Beam Stakes

JUANRO (1958)
At 4: 2nd San Antonio Handicap
San Juan Capistrano Handicap
At 5: 2nd San Juan Capistrano Handicap

JUDGABLE (1967)
At 3: Won Dwyer Handicap
Whitney Stakes
2nd Travers Stakes
At 4: Won Donn Handicap
Grey Lag Handicap
3rd Michigan Mile and One-Eighth

JUDGE (1955)
At 3: 3rd Stars and Stripes Handicap

JUDGE ANGELUCCI (1983)
At 4: Won Californian Stakes
2nd Hollywood Gold Cup
3rd Breeders' Cup Classic
At 5: Won San Antonio Handicap
3rd Californian Stakes

JUDGER (1971)
At 2: 3rd Futurity Stakes
At 3: Won Florida Derby
Blue Grass Stakes
2nd Fountain of Youth Stakes
3rd Flamingo Stakes

JUDGE'S CASE (1997)
At 6: 3rd Pimlico Special

JUDY-RAE (1944)
At 3: 3rd Santa Susana Stakes

JUDY RULLAH (1953)
At 2: Won Arlington Lassie Stakes

JUKE JOINT (1970)
At 2: 2nd Sorority Stakes

JULES (1994)
At 2: 2nd Remsen Stakes

JULIE'S DANCER (1976)
At 3: 3rd Illinois Derby

JULIET'S PRIDE (1981)
At 2: 2nd Del Mar Futurity

JUMBO (1948)
At 2: 3rd Arlington Futurity
At 3: 2nd Withers Stakes

JUMPING HILL (1972)
At 6: 3rd Santa Anita Handicap
At 7: Won Widener Handicap
2nd Gulfstream Park Handicap

JUMP START (1999)
At 2: 2nd Champagne Stakes

JUMRON (1992)
At 3: 3rd Santa Anita Derby

JUNCTION (1975)
At 2: 3rd Young America Stakes
At 3: Won Dwyer Handicap

JUNE BRIDE (1946)
At 3: Won Hollywood Oaks
2nd Santa Susana Stakes

JUNE DARLING (1968)
At 2: Won Del Mar Futurity
Norfolk Stakes
Oak Leaf Stakes
2nd Del Mar Debutante Stakes

JUNE FETE (1951)
At 3: 3rd Monmouth Oaks

JUNGLE COVE (1966)
At 4: 2nd Canadian International Championship
3rd Dixie Handicap
Massachusetts Handicap

JUNGLE PRINCESS (1970)
At 3: 3rd Hollywood Oaks

JUNGLE ROAD (1964)
At 4: 2nd Santa Anita Handicap
San Juan Capistrano Handicap

JUNGLE TOUGH (1978)
At 3: 3rd Secretariat Stakes

JUPITER ISLAND (1979)
At 6: 3rd Washington D.C. International
At 7: 3rd San Juan Capistrano Handicap

JUPITER LIGHT (1943)
At 3: 3rd Beldame Handicap

JUST ABOUT (1962)
At 4: Won New Orleans Handicap
2nd Donn Handicap
John B. Campbell Handicap

JUST A GAME II (1976)
At 4: Won Flower Bowl Handicap
2nd Man o' War Stakes

JUSTAKISS (1963)
At 3: 3rd Monmouth Oaks

JUSTA LITTLE ONE (1979)
At 2: 3rd Arlington-Washington Lassie Stakes

JUST CALL ME CARL (1995)
At 5: 2nd Frank J. De Francis Memorial Dash

JUST FANCY THAT (1961)
At 3: 3rd Mother Goose Stakes

JUST JAVA (1991)
At 5: 3rd Santa Anita Handicap

JUST KIDDING (1964)
At 2: 2nd Sorority Stakes

JUST LISTEN (1996)
At 7: 2nd Gulfstream Park BC Handicap

JUSTSAYNO (1985)
At 2: 2nd Matron Stakes
3rd Frizette Stakes

JUST THE TIME (1972)
At 2: Won Futurity Stakes

JUST WHY (1946)
At 3: 2nd Hollywood Oaks
Westerner Stakes

JUTLAND (1953)
At 4: 3rd Carter Handicap

JUVENILE JOHN (1965)
At 4: Won John B. Campbell Handicap

KABEMA (1959)
At 2: 2nd Del Mar Debutante Stakes

KAFWAIN (2000)
At 2: 2nd Del Mar Futurity
Bessemer Trust Breeders' Cup Juvenile
At 3: 3rd Santa Anita Derby

KAHL KABEE (1964)
At 3: 2nd California Derby

KAHOOLAWE (1966)
At 2: 2nd Arlington-Washington Lassie Stakes

KAIETEUR (1999)
At 4: 2nd Arlington Million

KAI KAI (1944)
At 2: 3rd Princess Pat Stakes
Astorita Stakes

KALANISI (1996)
At 4: Won Breeders' Cup Turf

KALDOUNEVEES (1991)
At 4: 2nd Man o' War Stakes

KALITA MELODY (1988)
At 6: 2nd Santa Margarita Handicap

KALOOKAN QUEEN (1996)
At 3: 3rd La Brea Stakes
At 4: 2nd Santa Monica Handicap
At 6: Won Santa Monica Handicap
Ancient Title Breeders' Cup Handicap

KALYPSO KATIE (1997)
At 4: 3rd Beverly Hills Handicap

KAMARAAN II (1971)
At 5: 3rd Manhattan Handicap

KAMEHAMEHA (1950)
At 2: 3rd Arlington Futurity

KAMEHAMEHA (1975)
At 3: Won Cinema Handicap

KAMIKAZE RICK (1982)
At 3: 3rd Beldame Stakes

KAMSACK (1999)
At 2: 2nd Del Mar Futurity

KANKAM (1975)
At 5: 3rd Santa Margarita Handicap

KAN REASON (1978)
At 2: 3rd Laurel Futurity

KARABAS (1965)
At 4: Won Washington D.C. International

KARLA'S ENOUGH (1977)
At 4: 3rd Apple Blossom Handicap

KARMANI (1985)
At 6: 2nd Sword Dancer Handicap

KARTAJANA (1987)
At 4: 3rd Arlington Million
Oak Tree Invitational Stakes

KASTER (1949)
At 4: Won Fall Highweight Handicap
At 5: 3rd United Nations Handicap
At 6: 2nd Bougainvillea Turf Handicap
Dixie Handicap

KATHY H. (1956)
At 3: 3rd Kentucky Oaks

KATONKA (1972)
At 4: 2nd Santa Barbara Handicap

KAUAI KING (1963)
At 3: Won Kentucky Derby
Preakness Stakes

KAYE'S COMMANDER (1971)
At 3: 3rd Kentucky Oaks

KAY GIBSON (1943)
At 3: 3rd Beldame Handicap

KAZZIA (1999)
At 3: Won Flower Bowl Invitational Stakes

KEENATION (1957)
At 3: 3rd Flamingo Stakes

KEEPER HILL (1995)
At 3: Won Las Virgenes Stakes
Kentucky Oaks
2nd Santa Anita Oaks
Mother Goose Stakes
Coaching Club American Oaks
Gazelle Handicap
3rd Breeders' Cup Distaff
At 4: Won Three Chimneys Spinster Stakes
3rd Beverly Hills Handicap
Personal Ensign Handicap
Ruffian Handicap

KELLY (1986)
At 3: 2nd Hollywood Oaks
At 4: 3rd La Canada Stakes
Vanity Handicap

KELLY KIP (1994)
At 4: Won Frank J. De Francis Memorial Dash

KELSO (1957)
At 3: Won Jerome Handicap
Lawrence Realization Stakes
Hawthorne Gold Cup
Jockey Club Gold Cup
At 4: Won Metropolitan Handicap
Suburban Handicap
Brooklyn Handicap
Woodward Stakes
Jockey Club Gold Cup
Whitney Handicap
2nd Washington D.C. International
At 5: Won Woodward Stakes
Jockey Club Gold Cup
2nd Suburban Handicap

Monmouth Handicap
Man o' War Stakes
Washington D.C. International
At 6: Won Seminole Handicap
Gulfstream Park Handicap
John B. Campbell Handicap
Suburban Handicap
Aqueduct Stakes
Woodward Stakes
Jockey Club Gold Cup
Whitney Stakes
2nd Widener Handicap
Washington D.C. International
At 7: Won Aqueduct Stakes
Jockey Club Gold Cup
Washington D.C. International
2nd Suburban Handicap
Monmouth Handicap
Woodward Stakes
At 8: Won Whitney Stakes
3rd Brooklyn Handicap

KEN (1948)
At 4: Won Trenton Handicap
At 5: 3rd McLennan Handicap

KENDOR (1943)
At 3: 3rd Louisiana Derby

KENNEDY ROAD (1968)
At 4: 2nd Californian Stakes
Miller High Life Inglewood Handicap
At 5: Won Hollywood Gold Cup
San Antonio Stakes
2nd Santa Anita Handicap

KENTUCKIAN (1969)
At 3: 2nd California Derby
At 4: Won American Handicap
3rd Oak Tree Invitational Stakes

KENTUCKY JUG (1961)
At 4: 2nd Dixie Handicap
At 5: Won Hialeah Turf Cup

KENTUCKY PRIDE (1955)
At 3: 2nd Everglades Stakes

KENTUCKY SHERRY (1965)
At 3: Won Louisiana Derby

KERRY'S TIME (1966)
At 4: 2nd Stars and Stripes Handicap

KESSEM POWER (1992)
At 6: 3rd San Juan Capistrano Handicap

KEY CONTENDER (1988)
At 7: Won Suburban Handicap
2nd Brooklyn Handicap

KEY DANCER (1981)
At 3: 3rd Beldame Stakes
Ladies Handicap

KEY HUNTER (1994)
At 3: 3rd Coaching Club American Oaks

KEYNOTE (1944)
At 2: Won Astarita Stakes

KEY OF LUCK (1991)
At 5: 2nd Pimlico Special

KEY PHRASE (1991)
At 4: 3rd Santa Maria Handicap

KEY TO CONTENT (1977)
At 4: Won United Nations Handicap
2nd Bowling Green Handicap

KEY TO THE MINT (1969)
At 2: 2nd Cowdin Stakes
3rd Garden State Stakes
At 3: Won Withers Stakes
Travers Stakes
Brooklyn Handicap
Whitney Stakes
Woodward Stakes
2nd Jockey Club Gold Cup
3rd Preakness Stakes
At 4: Won Suburban Handicap
2nd Metropolitan Handicap

KEY TO THE MOON (1981)
At 3: 2nd Jersey Derby
At 4: 2nd Gulfstream Park Handicap

KFAR TOV (1968)
At 2: 2nd Hollywood Juvenile Championship
Del Mar Futurity
At 4: Won Malibu Stakes

KHAL IRELAND (1960)
At 6: Won Vanity Handicap

KHALITA (1956)
At 2: Won Del Mar Debutante Stakes

KHARIYDA (1984)
At 3: 3rd Yellow Ribbon Stakes

KHORAZ (1990)
At 6: 2nd Oak Tree Turf Championship

KHYBER KING (1973)
At 2: 2nd Arlington-Washington Futurity

KICKEN KRIS (2000)
At 3: Won Secretariat Stakes
3rd Hollywood Derby

KID RUSSELL (1986)
At 6: 2nd Carter Handicap

KILIJARO (1976)
At 4: Won Yellow Ribbon Stakes
At 5: Won Matriarch Stakes
3rd Californian Stakes

KILLER DILLER (1987)
At 4: 3rd Suburban Handicap
Whitney Handicap

KILTS N KAPERS (1967)
At 3: Won Monmouth Oaks
3rd Coaching Club American Oaks

KIMBERLITE PIPE (1996)
At 3: Won Louisiana Derby

KING CRIMSON (1994)
At 3: 3rd San Felipe Stakes

KING CUGAT (1997)
At 3: 2nd Secretariat Stakes
At 4: 2nd Woodford Reserve Turf Classic
Manhattan Handicap
Sword Dancer Invitational Handicap
Turf Classic

KINGDOM FOUND (1990)
At 4: 2nd Californian Stakes
At 7: 3rd San Antonio Handicap

KING DORSETT (1942)
At 4: 2nd Excelsior Handicap
Carter Handicap
3rd New Orleans Handicap
Aqueduct Handicap

KING EMPEROR (1966)
At 2: Won Sanford Stakes
Cowdin Stakes
Pimlico-Laurel Futurity
2nd Arlington-Washington Futurity
3rd Champagne Stakes
At 3: 3rd Grey Lag Handicap

KING GLORIOUS (1986)
At 2: Won Hollywood Futurity
At 3: Won Ohio Derby
Haskell Invitational Handicap

KING GO GO (1975)
At 6: 2nd Santa Anita Handicap
3rd San Antonio Stakes

KING GRAIL (1953)
At 6: 2nd Bowling Green Handicap
At 7: 2nd Arlington Handicap

KING HAIRAN (1954)
At 2: Won Sapling Stakes
Hopeful Stakes

KING LOMA (1966)
At 3: 3rd California Derby

KINGMAKER (1953)
At 4: Won New Orleans Handicap
Grey Lag Handicap
Whitney Stakes

KING MAPLE (1951)
At 3: 2nd Canadian Championship Stakes

KING MUTESA (1988)
At 3: 2nd Gotham Stakes
3rd Jerome Handicap

KING OF CORNISH (1969)
At 2: 3rd Sapling Stakes

KING OF CRICKET (1967)
At 4: Won Malibu Stakes

KING OF KENTUCKY (1958)
At 3: 3rd Louisiana Derby

KING OF THE CASTLE (1966)
At 3: Won Louisiana Derby
Illinois Derby
2nd Arkansas Derby
Arlington Classic

KING OF THE HEAP (1993)
At 3: Won Malibu Stakes

KING O' TURF (1956)
At 3: 3rd Hollywood Derby
At 4: Won San Fernando Stakes
2nd San Juan Capistrano Handicap

KING PELLINORE (1972)
At 4: Won Champions Invitational Handicap
American Handicap
Oak Tree Invitational Stakes
2nd Sunset Handicap
At 5: 2nd San Luis Rey Stakes
3rd Santa Anita Handicap

KING PIN (1950)
At 2: 3rd Washington Park Futurity

KINGPOST (1985)
At 2: 3rd Young America Stakes
At 3: Won Jim Beam Stakes
2nd Belmont Stakes

KING'S BISHOP (1969)
At 3: Won Pontiac Grand Prix Stakes
Michigan Mile and One-Eighth
2nd Monmouth Invitational Handicap
American Derby
At 4: Won Carter Handicap
3rd Metropolitan Handicap

KING'S CANASTA (1955)
At 3: 2nd California Derby

KING'S EDGE (1970)
At 2: 2nd Del Mar Debutante Stakes

KINGS FAVOR (1963)
At 4: 3rd Charles H. Strub Stakes

KINGS ISLAND (1981)
At 4: Won Sunset Handicap
3rd Hollywood Gold Cup

KING'S PALACE (1964)
At 4: 3rd Massachusetts Handicap

KING'S SWAN (1980)
At 6: Won Vosburgh Stakes
At 7: 2nd Metropolitan Handicap
At 8: 3rd Whitney Handicap

KING'S THEATRE (1991)
At 4: 3rd Sword Dancer Invitational Handicap

KING TOOTS (1960)
At 3: 2nd Flamingo Stakes

KIN RUN (1971)
At 3: 3rd Dwyer Handicap

KIRBY LANE (1973)
At 3: 2nd Fall Highweight Handicap
At 4: Won San Fernando Stakes
Charles H. Strub Stakes

KIRI'S CLOWN (1989)
At 5: 2nd Sword Dancer Invitational Handicap
At 6: Won Sword Dancer Invitational Handicap
3rd Early Times Manhattan Handicap
At 7: 2nd Sword Dancer Invitational Handicap
3rd Early Times Manhattan Handicap

KIRRARY (1970)
At 3: 2nd Cinema Handicap
3rd Hollywood Derby
Oak Tree Invitational Stakes
At 5: 3rd Sunset Handicap

KISS A NATIVE (1997)
At 5: 2nd Donn Handicap

KISSING BELLE (1958)
At 4: 3rd Vanity Handicap

KISSIN' GEORGE (1963)
At 5: 2nd Vosburgh Handicap

KISSIN KRIS (1990)
At 3: Won Haskell Invitational Handicap
2nd Arkansas Derby
Belmont Stakes
Travers Stakes
3rd Breeders' Cup Classic
At 5: 2nd Suburban Handicap

KISSIN SAINT (2000)
At 3: 3rd Wood Memorial Stakes

KISS ME KATE (1948)
At 3: Won Acorn Stakes
Delaware Oaks
Gazelle Stakes
Alabama Stakes
2nd Coaching Club American Oaks
3rd Beldame Handicap
Ladies Handicap
Jockey Club Gold Cup
At 4: Won New Castle Handicap
2nd Vineland Handicap
3rd Firenze Handicap
At 5: Won Firenze Handicap

KITCHEN POLICE (1943)
At 3: 3rd Jerome Handicap

KIT'S DOUBLE (1973)
At 6: 2nd Apple Blossom Handicap
3rd Beldame Stakes

KITTYLUCK (1973)
At 4: 2nd Apple Blossom Handicap
At 5: Won Santa Barbara Handicap

KITWOOD (1989)
At 3: 3rd Hollywood Derby

K.J.'S APPEAL (1994)
At 4: Won Buick Meadowlands Cup Handicap

KLARION (1952)
At 3: 3rd United Nations Handicap

KLASSY KIM (1991)
At 4: 3rd Santa Margarita Handicap

KLEN KLITSO (1973)
At 3: 3rd Arkansas Derby

KLING KLING (1967)
At 3: Won Lawrence Realization Stakes
At 5: 2nd Bowling Green Handicap

KNIGHT IN ARMOR (1967)
At 4: 3rd Grey Lag Handicap
Metropolitan Handicap

KNIGHTLY DAWN (1970)
At 3: Won Jersey Derby

KNIGHTLY MANNER (1961)
At 3: 2nd Santa Anita Derby
Travers Stakes
3rd Lawrence Realization Stakes
Man o' War Stakes
At 4: 2nd John B. Campbell Handicap
Man o' War Stakes
3rd Manhattan Handicap
Hialeah Turf Cup
At 5: Won Dixie Handicap
3rd Man o' War Stakes
Bowling Green Handicap

KNIGHTLY SPORT (1972)
At 2: 2nd Hopeful Stakes

KNIGHT OF THE ROAD (1967)
At 3: 2nd Jerome Handicap

KNIGHTS CHOICE (1976)
At 2: 3rd Norfolk Stakes

KNITTED GLOVES (1970)
At 3: Won Fantasy Stakes

KNOCKADOON (1992)
At 3: 2nd Wood Memorial Stakes

KNOCKDOWN (1943)
At 3: Won Santa Anita Derby
At 5: Won Excelsior Handicap
Queens County Handicap

KNOT HOLE (1949)
At 2: 2nd Matron Stakes
Marguerite Stakes
3rd Selima Stakes

KNOW HEIGHTS (1989)
At 4: 2nd Hollywood Turf Cup

KODIACK (1974)
At 3: 2nd Arkansas Derby

KOHEN WITHA K. (1985)
At 2: 3rd Laurel Futurity

KOLUCTOO BAY (1977)
At 2: Won Young America Stakes
At 3: 2nd Flamingo Stakes

KONA GOLD (1994)
At 4: 3rd Breeders' Cup Sprint
At 5: 2nd Breeders' Cup Sprint
At 6: Won Breeders' Cup Sprint
At 7: Won San Carlos Handicap
2nd Ancient Title Breeders' Cup Handicap

K ONE KING (1996)
At 3: 2nd Gallery Furniture.com Stakes
At 4: Won Oaklawn Handicap

KOOL ARRIVAL (1986)
At 3: 3rd Santa Anita Oaks

KOOL KAT KATIE (1994)
At 4: 2nd Gamely Breeders' Cup Handicap

KOOTENAI (1958)
At 4: Won Arlington Matron Handicap

K.O. PUNCH (1995)
At 2: 2nd Hopeful Stakes
Futurity Stakes

KOSTROMA (1986)
At 5: Won Yellow Ribbon Stakes
At 6: Won Santa Barbara Handicap
Beverly D. Stakes
3rd Matriarch Stakes

KOTASHAAN (1988)
At 5: Won San Luis Rey Stakes
San Juan Capistrano Handicap
Eddie Read Handicap
Oak Tree Invitational Stakes
Breeders' Cup Turf

KRISLIN (1969)
At 4: 3rd Maskette Handicap
At 5: Won Delaware Handicap
2nd Top Flight Handicap
Hempstead Handicap

KUDOS (1997)
At 5: Won Oaklawn Handicap
3rd Santa Anita Handicap
At 6: 3rd Santa Anita Handicap
Oaklawn Handicap
Hollywood Gold Cup

KUMARI CONTINENT (1997)
At 3: 2nd Santa Anita Oaks

KY. COLONEL (1946)
At 3: 2nd American Derby

KY. FRONT (1962)
At 2: 3rd Del Mar Futurity

KYLE'S OUR MAN (1988)
At 2: 3rd Remsen Stakes
At 3: Won Gotham Stakes

KY. PIONEER (1961)
At 4: 3rd Display Handicap

LABEEB (1992)
At 3: Won Crown Royal Hollywood Derby
At 5: 2nd Early Times Turf Classic
At 6: Won Woodbine Mile
3rd Breeders' Cup Mile

LA BONZO (1976)
At 5: 2nd Apple Blossom Handicap

LA BRISA (1969)
At 2: 2nd Alcibiades Stakes

LACHESIS (1972)
At 4: 2nd Fall Highweight Handicap

LA CORREDORA (1949)
At 3: Won Monmouth Oaks
3rd Beldame Handicap
At 4: Won Ladies Handicap
Comely Handicap
3rd Firenze Handicap
Beldame Handicap
At 5: 3rd Top Flight Handicap

LAC OUIMET (1983)
At 3: Won Jim Dandy Stakes

LACQUARIA (1996)
At 2: 2nd Hollywood Starlet Stakes

LADIES DIN (1995)
At 4: 2nd Eddie Read Handicap
At 5: Won Eddie Read Handicap
2nd Shoemaker Breeders' Cup Mile
At 7: Won Shoemaker Breeders' Cup Mile

LADIGA (1969)
At 3: 3rd Ohio Derby

LADY AFFIRMED (1991)
At 4: 2nd Gamely Handicap

LADY AFT (1962)
At 2: 2nd Demoiselle Stakes

LADY BLESSINGTON (1988)
At 5: 3rd Flower Bowl Handicap

LADY COVER UP (1951)
At 2: Won Del Mar Debutante Stakes

LADY D'ACCORD (1987)
At 4: 3rd Ruffian Handicap
Beldame Stakes
At 5: 3rd Top Flight Handicap

LADY DORIMAR (1946)
At 2: 2nd Spinaway Stakes
Selima Stakes
Demoiselle Stakes
At 3: 3rd Kentucky Oaks

LADY IN SILVER (1986)
At 3: 2nd Arlington Million

LADY LISTER (1986)
At 2: 3rd Oak Leaf Stakes

LADY LOVE (1970)
At 3: 2nd Mother Goose Stakes
3rd Coaching Club American Oaks
At 4: Won Top Flight Handicap

LADY MELESI (1997)
At 4: 2nd Milady Breeders' Cup Handicap

LADY NORCLIFFE (1980)
At 3: 2nd Alabama Stakes
3rd Coaching Club American Oaks
At 4: 2nd Top Flight Handicap

LADY OAKLEY (1977)
At 4: 2nd Top Flight Handicap

LADY OF PROMISE (1977)
At 4: 3rd Delaware Handicap

LADY PITT (1963)
At 2: 2nd Frizette Stakes
Gardenia Stakes
At 3: Won Mother Goose Stakes
Coaching Club American Oaks
2nd Kentucky Oaks
Alabama Stakes
Gazelle Handicap
3rd Beldame Stakes
At 5: 3rd Santa Barbara Handicap

LADY'S ACE (1944)
At 3: 2nd Louisiana Derby

LADY SHIRL (1987)
At 4: Won Flower Bowl Handicap

LADY'S SECRET (1982)
At 3: Won Maskette Stakes
Ruffian Handicap
Beldame Stakes
2nd Breeders' Cup Distaff
At 4: Won La Canada Stakes
Santa Margarita Handicap
Whitney Handicap
Maskette Stakes
Ruffian Handicap
Beldame Stakes
Breeders' Cup Distaff
2nd Apple Blossom Handicap
Woodward Stakes
3rd Metropolitan Handicap
Philip H. Iselin Handicap

LADY SWORDS (1953)
At 3: 3rd Coaching Club American Oaks
Spinster Stakes
At 4: 3rd Arlington Matron Handicap

LADY TAK (2000)
At 3: Won Test Stakes
2nd Ashland Stakes
Acorn Stakes
Gazelle Handicap

LADY TRAMP (1965)
At 2: Won Alcibiades Stakes
At 3: 3rd Kentucky Oaks

LADY T.V. (1974)
At 2: 2nd Oak Leaf Stakes

LADY VI-E (1967)
At 3: Won Kentucky Oaks

LAFFANGO (1950)
At 2: Won Sapling Stakes
Champagne Stakes
Garden State Stakes
At 3: Won Gotham Stakes

LA FUERZA (1957)
At 2: Won Selima Stakes

LAGER (1994)
At 6: 2nd Brooklyn Handicap
3rd Suburban Handicap

LAHINT (1991)
At 3: 2nd Peter Pan Stakes

LAILANI (1998)
At 3: Won Flower Bowl Invitational Handicap

LAKE GEORGE (1992)
At 3: 3rd San Felipe Stakes

LAKEVILLE MISS (1975)
At 2: Won Matron Stakes
Frizette Stakes
Selima Stakes
2nd Demoiselle Stakes
At 3: Won Coaching Club American Oaks
2nd Acorn Stakes
Mother Goose Stakes

LAKEWAY (1991)
At 3: Won Santa Anita Oaks
Mother Goose Stakes
Hollywood Oaks
2nd Kentucky Oaks
Alabama Stakes
At 4: 3rd Beldame Stakes
Breeders' Cup Distaff

LAK NAK (1960)
At 3: 2nd California Derby

LA KOUMIA (1982)
At 3: 3rd Yellow Ribbon Stakes
Hollywood Derby
At 4: Won Gamely Handicap

L'ALEZANE (1975)
At 2: Won Alcibiades Stakes
2nd Selima Stakes

LALUN (1952)
At 2: 3rd Matron Stakes
At 3: Won Kentucky Oaks
Beldame Handicap
2nd Coaching Club American Oaks

LAMB CHOP (1960)
At 3: Won Coaching Club American Oaks
Monmouth Oaks
Spinster Stakes
2nd Alabama Stakes
Beldame Stakes
3rd Acorn Stakes
Mother Goose Stakes
At 4: 2nd San Fernando Stakes

LAMBENT (1946)
At 5: 3rd Gulfstream Park Handicap

LANCASTRIAN (1962)
At 3: 3rd Dixie Handicap

L'ANCRESSE (2000)
At 3: 2nd Breeders' Cup Filly and Mare Turf

LANDALUCE (1980)
At 2: Won Del Mar Debutante Stakes
Oak Leaf Stakes

LAND GIRL (1972)
At 2: Won Demoiselle Stakes
At 3: Won Gazelle Handicap
At 4: 3rd Maskette Handicap

LANDING PLOT (1983)
At 3: 3rd Withers Stakes

LANDLOCKED (1950)
At 2: Won Sapling Stakes
At 3: 2nd American Derby
3rd Discovery Handicap
Jerome Handicap
At 4: Won Widener Handicap

LANDMARK (1949)
At 2: 2nd Astarita Stakes
3rd Matron Stakes

LAND OF EIRE (1975)
At 6: Won Widener Handicap

LANDRESSE (1978)
At 4: 2nd Santa Barbara Handicap

LAND RUSH (1987)
At 3: 2nd Blue Grass Stakes

LANDSCAPER (1972)
At 6: Won Century Handicap

LANDSEAIR (1949)
At 2: Won Sapling Stakes

LANDSEER (1999)
At 3: Won Shadwell Keeneland Turf Mile

LANGFUHR (1992)
At 4: Won Vosburgh Stakes
At 5: Won Carter Handicap
Metropolitan Handicap

LANVIN (1957)
At 3: 3rd Brooklyn Handicap

LANYON (1967)
At 2: 3rd Breeders' Futurity

LAP FULL (1950)
At 2: Won Del Mar Debutante Stakes
At 4: 3rd Vanity Handicap

LA PLUME (1955)
At 4: 2nd Vanity Handicap

LA PREVOYANTE (1970)
At 2: Won Spinaway Stakes
Matron Stakes
Frizette Stakes
Selima Stakes
Gardenia Stakes
At 3: 2nd Kentucky Oaks

LARAMIE MOON (1987)
At 5: 2nd Santa Margarita Handicap

LARAMIE TRAIL (1972)
At 3: 2nd Withers Stakes

LARKS MUSIC (1951)
At 2: 2nd Starlet Stakes

LARKY DAY (1941)
At 6: 3rd Brooklyn Handicap

LARRIKIN (1972)
At 3: 2nd Cinema Handicap
3rd Secretariat Stakes
At 4: 2nd Charles H. Strub Stakes
3rd San Fernando Stakes

LARRY ELLIS (1948)
At 5: 2nd Massachusetts Handicap

LARRY THE LEGEND (1992)
At 3: Won Santa Anita Derby

LASER LIGHT (1979)
At 2: Won Remsen Stakes
2nd Laurel Futurity
Young America Stakes
At 3: 2nd Kentucky Derby
3rd Wood Memorial Stakes

LASHKARI (1981)
At 3: Won Breeders' Cup Turf

LA SPIA (1989)
At 2: 2nd Breeders' Cup Juvenile Fillies
3rd Oak Leaf Stakes

LASSIGNY (1991)
At 4: Won Rothmans International Stakes

LASTING APPROVAL (1994)
At 3: 2nd Crown Royal Hollywood Derby
At 4: 2nd Early Times Turf Classic

LASTING PEACE (1943)
At 4: 2nd Vanity Handicap

LAST OF THE LINE (1967)
At 3: Won Hollywood Oaks
At 4: 3rd Santa Margarita Handicap

LAST TYCOON (1983)
At 3: Won Breeders' Cup Mile

LAST WAVE (1950)
At 4: 2nd Santa Margarita Handicap

LATE ACT (1979)
At 4: Won Louisiana Downs Handicap
3rd Arlington Handicap

LATE BLOOMER (1974)
At 4: Won Delaware Handicap
Ruffian Handicap
Beldame Stakes
Sheepshead Bay Handicap
At 5: 2nd Sheepshead Bay Handicap

LATIN AMERICAN (1988)
At 5: Won Californian Stakes

L'ATTRAYANTE (1980)
At 3: 2nd Yellow Ribbon Stakes
At 4: 2nd Santa Barbara Handicap

LATOUR (1998)
At 3: 3rd Ashland Stakes

LAUGH AND BE MERRY (1985)
At 5: Won Flower Bowl Handicap

LAUGHING BREEZE (1960)
At 3: 3rd Spinster Stakes

LAUGHING BRIDGE (1972)
At 2: 2nd Spinaway Stakes

LAUGHING GULL (1979)
At 2: 3rd Sorority Stakes

LAUNCH A PEGASUS (1982)
At 5: Won Widener Handicap

LAUREL MAE (1959)
At 2: 3rd Sorority Stakes

LAURIES DANCER (1968)
At 3: Won Alabama Stakes

LAVENDER HILL (1949)
At 5: Won Arlington Matron Handicap
Ladies Handicap
2nd Black Helen Handicap
3rd New Castle Handicap
At 6: 3rd Black Helen Handicap

LAWLESS (1953)
At 3: 3rd Withers Stakes

LAWLESS MISS (1943)
At 4: 3rd Molly Pitcher Handicap

LAW ME (1978)
At 3: 2nd Blue Grass Stakes

LAW OF THE SEA (1992)
At 2: 3rd Hopeful Stakes

LAW TALK (1980)
At 3: 3rd Florida Derby

LAWYER TALK (1984)
At 4: 3rd Delaware Handicap

LAY DOWN (1984)
At 6: 3rd Gulfstream Park Handicap

LA ZANZARA (1970)
At 4: Won Beverly Hills Handicap
2nd Vanity Handicap
Santa Barbara Handicap
3rd Ramona Handicap
At 5: Won Beverly Hills Handicap
San Juan Capistrano Handicap
3rd Vanity Handicap
Santa Barbara Handicap

LAZER SHOW (1983)
At 2: Won Sorority Stakes

LAZ'S JOY (1983)
At 2: 3rd Oak Leaf Stakes

LAZY LODE (1994)
At 4: Won Hollywood Turf Cup
3rd Turf Classic
At 5: Won Hollywood Turf Cup
2nd Oak Tree Turf Championship
At 6: 3rd Hollywood Turf Cup

LAZY SLUSAN (1995)
At 6: Won Santa Margarita Handicap
Milady Breeders' Cup Handicap
2nd Vanity Handicap
3rd Apple Blossom Handicap

L'CARRIERE (1991)
At 4: 2nd Whitney Handicap
Breeders' Cup Classic
At 5: 2nd Woodward Stakes
3rd Suburban Handicap

LEADING HOME (1946)
At 5: 2nd New Castle Handicap
3rd Top Flight Handicap
Molly Pitcher Handicap

LEADING LIGHT (1995)
At 7: 2nd Santa Monica Handicap

LEADING PROSPECT (1986)
At 2: 3rd Hopeful Stakes

LEA LANE (1952)
At 2: 2nd Arlington Lassie Stakes
Alcibiades Stakes
At 3: 2nd Kentucky Oaks

LEA LARK (1945)
At 2: 3rd Arlington Lassie Stakes
At 3: 3rd Pimlico Oaks

LEALLAH (1954)
At 2: Won Arlington Lassie Stakes
Alcibiades Stakes

LEA LUCINDA (1986)
At 2: 3rd Breeders' Cup Juvenile Fillies
At 3: 3rd Hollywood Oaks

LEA MOON (1955)
At 3: 3rd Mother Goose Stakes

LEAP TIDE (1952)
At 5: 2nd Bougainvillea Turf Handicap

LEARIVA (1987)
At 4: Won Budweiser International Stakes

LEATHER BUTTON (1955)
At 2: Won Arlington Futurity

LEBKUCHEN (1954)
At 2: Won Selima Stakes

LE CLE (1969)
At 4: Won Beverly Hills Handicap

LE COU COU (1980)
At 3: 2nd American Derby

LE CYPRIOTE (1972)
At 5: 2nd Pan American Handicap

LE DANSEUR (1979)
At 3: 3rd Flamingo Stakes

LEECOO (1981)
At 5: 3rd Top Flight Handicap
Delaware Handicap

LEEMATT (1968)
At 4: Won Carter Handicap

LEFT BANK (1997)
At 4: Won Vosburgh Stakes
Cigar Mile Handicap
2nd Forego Handicap
At 5: Won Whitney Handicap

LEGENDAIRE (1973)
At 4: 3rd American Handicap

LEGER CAT (1986)
At 6: 3rd Eddie Read Handicap
At 7: 2nd Eddie Read Handicap
3rd Hollywood Turf Handicap

LEGION (1970)
At 6: Won Hialeah Turf Cup
2nd Gulfstream Park Handicap
At 7: Won Donn Handicap
2nd Gulfstream Park Handicap

LE GLORIEUX (1984)
At 3: Won Budweiser International Stakes
2nd Man o' War Stakes

LEISURELY KIN (1961)
At 2: Won Del Mar Debutante Stakes
3rd Hollywood Juvenile Championship

LEIX (1957)
At 4: 3rd Bowling Green Handicap

LEJOLI (1979)
At 2: 3rd Hopeful Stakes
At 3: 3rd Haskell Invitational Handicap

LE L'ARGENT (1982)
At 3: 2nd Acorn Stakes
Mother Goose Stakes

LE MARMOT (1976)
At 3: 3rd Washington D.C. International

LEMHI GOLD (1978)
At 4: Won Marlboro Cup Handicap
Jockey Club Gold Cup
Sword Dancer Stakes
San Juan Capistrano Handicap
2nd Hollywood Invitational Handicap

L'EMIGRANT (1980)
At 3: 3rd Man o' War Stakes

LEMON DROP KID (1996)
At 2: Won Futurity Stakes
2nd Moet Champagne Stakes
At 3: Won Belmont Stakes
Travers Stakes
2nd Jim Dandy Stakes
At 4: Won Brooklyn Handicap
Suburban Handicap
Whitney Handicap
Woodward Stakes
3rd Pimlico Special

LEMON TWIST (1960)
At 3: Won Ohio Derby
2nd Louisiana Derby
Arkansas Derby
3rd Blue Grass Stakes
At 4: 2nd Washington Park Handicap
At 5: 2nd Hawthorne Gold Cup

L'ENJOLEUR (1972)
At 2: Won Laurel Futurity

LEO CASTELLI (1984)
At 3: Won Peter Pan Stakes
2nd Blue Grass Stakes
3rd Flamingo Stakes

LEONOTIS (1973)
At 6: Won Bay Meadows Handicap

LEO'S PISCES (1970)
At 3: Won Louisiana Derby

LE PAILLARD (1994)
At 5: 2nd San Juan Capistrano Handicap

LEROY S. (1981)
At 3: Won Wood Memorial Stakes

LES ABEILLES (1948)
At 2: 2nd Spinaway Stakes

LES ASPRES (1976)
At 6: 3rd Bay Meadows Handicap

LET (1995)
At 3: 2nd Ashland Stakes

LETHAL INSTRUMENT (1996)
At 5: 2nd San Antonio Handicap

LETHALS LADY (1998)
At 3: 2nd Matriarch Stakes

LET ME LINGER (1972)
At 3: Won Maskette Handicap
3rd Coaching Club American Oaks
Gazelle Handicap
At 4: 2nd Top Flight Handicap
3rd Hempstead Handicap

LETMENOW (1941)
At 5: 2nd Black Helen Handicap
At 6: 2nd Hawthorne Gold Cup
3rd Vineland Handicap

LETS BE ALERT (1991)
At 3: 2nd Spinster Stakes

LET'S BE GAY (1966)
At 2: 3rd Gardenia Stakes

LETS DANCE (1942)
At 4: 2nd Aqueduct Handicap
3rd Excelsior Handicap
Westchester Handicap
At 5: Won San Pasqual Handicap
2nd Grey Lag Handicap
3rd Widener Handicap
Excelsior Handicap
Sunset Handicap

LETS DONT FIGHT (1979)
At 2: Won Arlington-Washington Futurity
2nd Breeders' Futurity

LET'S ELOPE (1987)
At 6: 3rd Ramona Handicap
Beverly D. Stakes
Oak Tree Invitational Stakes

LEVEE (1953)
At 2: Won Selima Stakes
At 3: Won Coaching Club American Oaks
Monmouth Oaks
Beldame Handicap
2nd Delaware Oaks
3rd Acorn Stakes
Alabama Stakes

LEVELIX (1956)
At 2: 3rd Matron Stakes

LEVEL LEA (1950)
At 3: Won Discovery Handicap
Jockey Club Gold Cup
3rd Lawrence Realization Stakes
At 4: 3rd Monmouth Handicap
Aqueduct Handicap

LE VOYAGEUR (1986)
At 3: 3rd Belmont Stakes

LEXINGTON LAUGH (1973)
At 2: 2nd Del Mar Futurity

LEXINGTON PARK (1967)
At 6: 2nd John B. Campbell Handicap

L'HERMINE (1989)
At 5: 3rd Sword Dancer Invitational Handicap

L'HEUREUX (1973)
At 3: 2nd Cinema Handicap
Champions Invitational Handicap
3rd Secretariat Stakes
Oak Tree Invitational Stakes

LIBERTY GOLD (1994)
At 5: 3rd Metropolitan Handicap

LIBERTY RULER (1955)
At 3: 3rd Everglades Stakes

LIBERTY SUN (1953)
At 2: 2nd Pimlico Futurity
At 3: Won Everglades Stakes

LIDO ISLE (1980)
At 4: 3rd Santa Barbara Handicap

LIDO PALACE (1997)
At 4: Won Whitney Handicap
Woodward Stakes
2nd Suburban Handicap
At 5: Won Woodward Stakes
2nd Suburban Handicap
Jockey Club Gold Cup
3rd Whitney Handicap

LIEUTENANT'S LARK (1982)
At 4: Won Washington D.C. International
3rd United Nations Handicap

LIFE AT THE TOP (1983)
At 3: Won Mother Goose Stakes
Ladies Handicap
2nd Kentucky Oaks
Coaching Club American Oaks
3rd Acorn Stakes
Alabama Stakes
Spinster Stakes

LIFE CYCLE (1969)
At 4: Won Hollywood Invitational Handicap
2nd Hialeah Turf Cup
Pan American Handicap
American Handicap
Sunset Handicap
3rd Century Handicap
Del Mar Handicap

LIFE IS DELICIOUS (1990)
At 4: 3rd Go for Wand Stakes

LIFE'S HOPE (1973)
At 3: Won Illinois Derby
Jersey Derby
2nd Hollywood Derby
3rd Santa Anita Derby
At 5: Won New Orleans Handicap
Amory L. Haskell Handicap
2nd Michigan Mile and One-Eighth
At 6: 3rd San Antonio Stakes

LIFE'S MAGIC (1981)
At 2: Won Oak Leaf Stakes
2nd Norfolk Stakes
Arlington-Washington Lassie Stakes
Frizette Stakes
Hollywood Starlet Stakes
3rd Hollywood Futurity
At 3: Won Mother Goose Stakes
Alabama Stakes
Beldame Stakes
2nd Acorn Stakes
Coaching Club American Oaks
Breeders' Cup Distaff
3rd Santa Susana Stakes
At 4: Won Breeders' Cup Distaff
2nd Brooklyn Handicap
Spinster Stakes
3rd La Canada Stakes
Apple Blossom Handicap
Delaware Handicap

LIGHT BROOM (1948)
At 4: 3rd New Orleans Handicap

LIGHT HEARTED (1969)
At 3: 2nd Alabama Stakes
3rd Gazelle Handicap
At 4: Won Hempstead Handicap
Maskette Handicap
2nd Spinster Stakes
3rd Delaware Handicap

LIGHTNING MANDATE (1971)
At 4: 2nd San Fernando Stakes
At 5: Won San Antonio Stakes
3rd Santa Anita Handicap

LIGHTNING ORPHAN (1964)
At 2: Won Kentucky Jockey Club Stakes
3rd Arlington-Washington Futurity
At 3: 2nd Arlington Classic

LIGHT 'N LOVELY (1954)
At 2: 2nd Gardenia Stakes
Frizette Stakes

LIGHT SABRE (1984)
At 3: 3rd Hollywood Derby

LIGHT SPIRITS (1981)
At 3: 3rd Jersey Derby

LIGHTS UP (1947)
At 2: Won Remsen Handicap
At 3: Won Travers Stakes
2nd Belmont Stakes
Saranac Handicap
3rd Dwyer Stakes
At 4: 2nd Massachusetts Handicap
Queens County Handicap
3rd Metropolitan Handicap

At 5: Won Golden Gate Handicap
At 6: Won Sunset Handicap

LIGHT TALK (1958)
At 3: Won Arkansas Derby

LIKE A CHARM (1964)
At 2: Won Sorority Stakes

LIKE A HERO (1999)
At 3: 2nd Swaps Stakes
3rd Haskell Invitational Handicap

LIKELY EXCHANGE (1974)
At 4: 3rd Spinster Stakes
At 5: Won Delaware Handicap
At 6: 3rd Spinster Stakes

LIL E. TEE (1989)
At 3: Won Jim Beam Stakes
Kentucky Derby
2nd Arkansas Derby
At 4: 2nd Oaklawn Handicap

LI'L FELLA (1955)
At 2: 2nd Sapling Stakes
At 4: 3rd United Nations Handicap

LIL'S BAG (1966)
At 2: Won Alcibiades Stakes

LIL'S LAD (1995)
At 2: 2nd Moet Champagne Stakes
At 3: Won Fountain of Youth Stakes
2nd Florida Derby
Toyota Blue Grass Stakes

LILY WHITE (1949)
At 3: Won Alabama Stakes
2nd Coaching Club American Oaks
3rd Acorn Stakes
Vineland Handicap

LIMEHOUSE (2001)
At 2: 2nd Lane's End Breeders' Futurity

LIMELIGHT (1951)
At 3: 3rd Belmont Stakes

LIMIT OUT (1995)
At 3: Won Jerome Handicap
2nd Buick Pegasus Handicap

LIMIT TO REASON (1968)
At 2: Won Champagne Stakes
Pimlico-Laurel Futurity
2nd Futurity Stakes
Cowdin Stakes

LINCOLN CENTER (1959)
At 3: 2nd Alabama Stakes
3rd Vineland Handicap

LINCOLN ROAD (1955)
At 3: 2nd Florida Derby
Kentucky Derby
Preakness Stakes
Stars and Stripes Handicap

LINDA'S CHIEF (1970)
At 3: Won San Felipe Handicap
California Derby
Withers Stakes
Pontiac Grand Prix Stakes
2nd Santa Anita Derby
3rd Jerome Handicap
At 4: 2nd Malibu Stakes
San Fernando Stakes

LINE CITY (1968)
At 2: Won Kentucky Jockey Club Stakes

LINITA (1957)
At 5: Won Vanity Handicap

LINK (1988)
At 2: 3rd Hopeful Stakes

LINKAGE (1979)
At 3: Won Blue Grass Stakes
2nd Louisiana Derby
Preakness Stakes
At 4: 3rd Monmouth Handicap

LINKATARIAT (1991)
At 2: 3rd Remsen Stakes

LINK RIVER (1990)
At 4: 2nd Go for Wand Stakes

LINMOLD (1956)
At 4: Won Santa Anita Handicap
3rd Santa Anita Maturity

LINNLEUR (1978)
At 3: 3rd Florida Derby

LION CAVERN (1989)
At 4: 3rd Vosburgh Stakes

LION HEART (2001)
At 2: Won Hollywood Futurity

LISMORE KNIGHT (2000)
At 3: 3rd Secretariat Stakes

LIST (1968)
At 3: 2nd Louisiana Derby
At 6: 3rd Michigan Mile and One-Eighth

LISTADO (1964)
At 5: Won Oaklawn Handicap

LISTCAPADE (1979)
At 4: 3rd Oaklawn Handicap

LISTENING (1993)
At 3: Won Hollywood Oaks
At 4: Won Milady Breeders' Cup Handicap

LIT DE JUSTICE (1990)
At 5: 3rd Breeders' Cup Sprint
At 6: Won Breeders' Cup Sprint

LITE APPROVAL (1993)
At 3: 2nd Pegasus Breeders' Cup Handicap

LITE LIGHT (1988)
At 2: Won Oak Leaf Stakes
2nd Hollywood Starlet Stakes
At 3: Won Santa Anita Oaks
Fantasy Stakes
Kentucky Oaks
Coaching Club American Oaks
2nd Mother Goose Stakes

LITE THE FUSE (1991)
At 4: Won Carter Handicap
Frank J. De Francis Memorial Dash
2nd Metropolitan Handicap
At 5: Won Carter Handicap
Frank J. De Francis Memorial Dash
2nd Metropolitan Handicap
3rd Vosburgh Stakes

LITHAN (1978)
At 4: 3rd Hollywood Turf Cup
At 5: 3rd Century Handicap

LITHE (1946)
At 2: Won Demoiselle Stakes
3rd Matron Stakes
At 3: Won Arlington Matron Handicap
Comely Handicap
2nd Vosburgh Handicap
3rd Vineland Handicap
Washington Park Handicap
At 4: Won Arlington Matron Handicap
2nd Top Flight Handicap
Vineland Handicap

LITTLE BIDDY COMET (1982)
At 3: 3rd Fantasy Stakes

LITTLE BIG CHIEF (1970)
At 2: 2nd Sapling Stakes

LITTLEBITLIVELY (1994)
At 5: 2nd Oaklawn Handicap

LITTLE BONNY (1977)
At 4: Won Pan American Handicap

LITTLE BRIANNE (1985)
At 6: Won Santa Margarita Handicap

LITTLE BUCKLES (1991)
At 4: 2nd Hempstead Handicap
3rd Go for Wand Stakes

LITTLE CURRENT (1971)
At 3: Won Preakness Stakes
Belmont Stakes
2nd Monmouth Invitational Handicap
Travers Stakes

LITTLE FITZ (1955)
At 5: Won Michigan Mile and One-Sixteenth

LITTLE GRAY PET (1962)
At 3: 3rd Ohio Derby

LITTLE HERMIT (1954)
At 3: 2nd Dwyer Handicap

LITTLE KID (1956)
At 2: 2nd Arlington Lassie Stakes

LITTLE LOOK (1981)
At 5: 3rd John Henry Handicap

LITTLE MISSOURI (1982)
At 4: Won Brooklyn Handicap
3rd Meadowlands Cup

LITTLE PACHE (1953)
At 4: 3rd Delaware Handicap

LITTLE REB (1975)
At 2: 2nd Hollywood Juvenile Championship
At 4: 3rd San Fernando Stakes

LITTLE REQUEST (1950)
At 2: Won Starlet Stakes

LITTLE ROLLO (1943)
At 4: 3rd Longacres Mile

LITTLE TUMBLER (1958)
At 2: Won Futurity Stakes
2nd Matron Stakes
3rd Spinaway Stakes

LITTLE TYTUS (1956)
At 3: 3rd American Derby

LIVEINTHESUNSHINE (1975)
At 4: 3rd Arlington Handicap

LIVELY KING (1977)
At 3: Won Pennsylvania Derby

LIVELY ONE (1985)
At 3: Won Swaps Stakes
2nd Santa Anita Derby
3rd Super Derby
At 4: 3rd Californian Stakes

LIVE THE DREAM (1986)
At 3: Won Hollywood Derby
At 4: 2nd Sunset Handicap
3rd Hollywood Turf Cup

LIVING VICARIOUSLY (1990)
At 3: Won Brooklyn Handicap

LIYOUN (1988)
At 7: 3rd San Juan Capistrano Handicap

LOACH (1988)
At 5: 2nd Carter Handicap

LOAD THE CANNONS (1980)
At 3: 3rd Oak Tree Invitational Stakes
At 4: Won San Juan Capistrano Handicap
2nd Sunset Handicap
Charles H. Strub Stakes
3rd Hollywood Invitational Handicap

LOBSANG II (1976)
At 5: Won Hialeah Turf Cup
2nd Pan American Handicap

LOCKTON (1984)
At 3: 2nd Hollywood Derby

LOCUST BAYOU (1981)
At 3: 3rd Haskell Invitational Handicap

LOFTY PEAK (1952)
At 5: 2nd Suburban Handicap

LOGICAL (1972)
At 5: 2nd Donn Handicap

LOKOYA (2001)
At 2: 2nd Matron Stakes

LOMA MALAD (1978)
At 2: Won Hollywood Juvenile Championship

LONDON COMPANY (1970)
At 3: Won Manhattan Handicap
At 4: Won Pan American Handicap
2nd United Nations Handicap
3rd Hollywood Invitational Handicap
Man o' War Stakes
At 5: 2nd Pan American Handicap

LONDON JET (1964)
At 5: 3rd Californian Stakes

LONE BID (1995)
At 3: 3rd Early Times Hollywood Derby

LONE EAGLE (1946)
At 5: 2nd Suburban Handicap
3rd Whitney Stakes
At 6: Won Manhattan Handicap

LONELY GIRL (1987)
At 3: 2nd Fantasy Stakes

LONE STAR SKY (2000)
At 2: 2nd Lane's End Breeders' Futurity

LONETREE (1970)
At 5: 3rd Fall Highweight Handicap
Vosburgh Handicap

LONG MICK (1981)
At 6: 2nd Hialeah Turf Cup
3rd San Luis Rey Stakes

LONNY'S SECRET (1966)
At 3: 2nd San Felipe Handicap
3rd Santa Anita Derby

LOOIE CAPOTE (1989)
At 2: 2nd Hollywood Starlet Stakes
At 4: 2nd Apple Blossom Handicap
Top Flight Handicap
At 5: 3rd Shuvee Handicap

LOOKINFORTHEBIGONE (1984)
At 3: 2nd Arkansas Derby

LOOKOUT SON (1944)
At 2: 2nd Sapling Stakes

LOOKS LIKE RAIN (1978)
At 2: 2nd Del Mar Futurity

LOPAR (1955)
At 2: 2nd Frizette Stakes
At 3: 2nd Mother Goose Stakes
3rd Acorn Stakes
Alabama Stakes

LOQUACIOUS DON (1969)
At 2: Won Cowdin Stakes
3rd Hopeful Stakes

LORD ALLISON (1983)
At 2: 2nd Norfolk Stakes

LORD AT WAR (1980)
At 5: Won San Antonio Handicap
Santa Anita Handicap
3rd Californian Stakes

LORD AVIE (1978)
At 2: Won Champagne Stakes
Young America Stakes
2nd Sapling Stakes
Hopeful Stakes
Arlington-Washington Futurity
At 3: Won Florida Derby
2nd Haskell Invitational Handicap
3rd Travers Stakes

LORD BOSWELL (1943)
At 3: Won Blue Grass Stakes
2nd Preakness Stakes
3rd Dwyer Stakes

LORD DARNLEY (1978)
At 4: Won Widener Handicap
Gulfstream Park Handicap
At 5: 2nd Widener Handicap
At 6: 2nd Gulfstream Park Handicap

LORD GALLANT (1977)
At 3: 3rd Florida Derby
At 4: 2nd Hawthorne Gold Cup

LORD GRILLO (1994)
At 3: Won Malibu Stakes

LORD HENHAM (1972)
At 4: Won Hialeah Turf Cup

LORD JAIN (1992)
At 5: 2nd Oak Tree Turf Championship

LORD LISTER (1979)
At 3: 3rd Jerome Handicap

LORD PRIAM (1949)
At 2: 2nd Garden State Stakes
Pimlico Futurity

LORD PUTNAM (1948)
At 2: 3rd Sapling Stakes

LORD REBEAU (1971)
At 4: Won New Orleans Handicap
At 5: 2nd Brooklyn Handicap
3rd Metropolitan Handicap
Suburban Handicap

LORD TRENDY (1978)
At 3: 3rd Hollywood Derby

LORD VANCOUVER (1968)
At 4: 3rd Canadian Int. Championship
At 5: Won Pan American Handicap

LORENZONI (1986)
At 2: 2nd Breeders' Futurity

LORIDALE (1948)
At 3: 2nd Saranac Handicap

LORI-EL (1954)
At 3: Won Kentucky Oaks

LOSER WEEPER (1945)
At 3: 3rd Dwyer Stakes
Discovery Handicap
At 4: Won Vosburgh Handicap
Metropolitan Handicap
At 5: Won Dixie Handicap
Suburban Handicap
3rd Gallant Fox Handicap
Massachusetts Handicap

LOST CODE (1984)
At 3: Won Illinois Derby
Ohio Derby
Arlington Classic
2nd Pennsylvania Derby
3rd Haskell Invitational Handicap
Philip H. Iselin Handicap

LOST KITTY (1985)
At 2: Won Del Mar Futurity
2nd Oak Leaf Stakes

LOST MESSAGE (1962)
At 5: 3rd Santa Margarita Handicap

LOST MOUNTAIN (1988)
At 2: 3rd Breeders' Cup Juvenile
At 3: Won Peter Pan Stakes
Dwyer Stakes
Haskell Invitational Handicap
2nd Wood Memorial Stakes
At 4: 3rd Brooklyn Handicap

LOTKA (1983)
At 3: Won Acorn Stakes
2nd Fantasy Stakes
3rd Coaching Club American Oaks

LOT O' GOLD (1976)
At 2: 2nd Breeders' Futurity
At 3: 2nd Florida Derby
Blue Grass Stakes
At 4: 2nd Widener Handicap
Gulfstream Park Handicap

LOT O'HONEY (1950)
At 2: 3rd Spinaway Stakes

LOT O LUCK (1947)
At 2: 2nd Pimlico Futurity

LOTOWHITE (1947)
At 3: Won Grey Lag Handicap
2nd Flamingo Stakes
At 4: Won Excelsior Handicap
2nd New Orleans Handicap
Santa Anita Maturity

LOTTA DANCING (1991)
At 4: 3rd Top Flight Handicap

LOTUS POOL (1987)
At 5: 3rd Caesars International Handicap

LOU-BRE (1941)
At 5: Won San Pasqual Handicap
3rd San Carlos Handicap

LOUD (1967)
At 3: Won Travers Stakes
2nd Lawrence Realization Stakes
Jockey Club Gold Cup
Manhattan Handicap
Man o' War Stakes
At 4: 3rd Jockey Club Gold Cup
At 5: 3rd Grey Lag Handicap
Whitney Stakes
At 6: 2nd Grey Lag Handicap
Jockey Club Gold Cup
3rd Massachusetts Handicap
At 8: 3rd Suburban Handicap

LOUISADOR (1964)
At 2: 2nd Del Mar Debutante Stakes

LOUIS CYPHRE (1986)
At 5: 3rd San Antonio Handicap

LOUIS D'OR (1955)
At 2: 2nd Hopeful Stakes

LOUIS LE GRAND (1982)
At 5: 2nd San Luis Rey Stakes
Oak Tree Invitational Stakes

LOUIS QUATORZE (1993)
At 2: 2nd Hopeful Stakes
Futurity Stakes
At 3: Won Preakness Stakes
Jim Dandy Stakes
2nd Blue Grass Stakes
Travers Stakes
Breeders' Cup Classic
3rd Jockey Club Gold Cup

LOUJAC (1945)
At 3: 3rd Arlington Classic

LOUKAHI (1961)
At 2: 2nd Del Mar Debutante Stakes
At 3: Won Hollywood Oaks

LOVE AT NOON (1998)
At 3: 3rd La Brea Stakes

LOVED (1967)
At 2: 3rd Oak Leaf Stakes
At 3: 3rd Hollywood Oaks

LOVEJOY (1961)
At 2: 2nd Demoiselle Stakes

LOVELLON (1996)
At 5: Won Santa Maria Handicap

LOVE LOCK (1995)
At 2: Won Hollywood Starlet Stakes
2nd Oak Leaf Stakes

LOVELY GYPSY (1963)
At 2: 3rd Sorority Stakes

LOVER JOHN (1971)
At 2: Won Arlington-Washington Futurity

LOVER'S QUARREL (1966)
At 3: 3rd Santa Susana Stakes

LOVE SIGN (1977)
At 3: Won Alabama Stakes
Beldame Stakes
2nd Spinster Stakes
3rd Maskette Stakes
At 4: Won Beldame Stakes
2nd Maskette Stakes
Ruffian Handicap
At 5: 3rd Delaware Handicap
Ruffian Handicap
Beldame Stakes

LOVE SMITTEN (1981)
At 4: 2nd Santa Barbara Handicap
At 5: Won Apple Blossom Handicap

LOVE STREET (1977)
At 2: Won Sorority Stakes

LOVE THAT JAZZ (1994)
At 2: 2nd Breeders' Cup Juvenile Fillies

LOVE THAT MAC (1982)
At 4: 2nd Metropolitan Handicap
Vosburgh Stakes

LOVE THAT RED (1996)
At 3: Won Malibu Stakes

LOVE YOU BY HEART (1985)
At 3: 2nd Flower Bowl Handicap

LOVE YOU SO (1966)
At 2: 3rd Del Mar Debutante Stakes

LOVLIER LINDA (1980)
At 4: 3rd La Canada Stakes
At 5: Won Santa Margarita Handicap

LOVONSITE (1943)
At 3: 3rd Santa Susana Stakes

LOYAL LEGION (1944)
At 4: Won Manhattan Handicap
2nd Whitney Stakes

LOYAL SON (1958)
At 3: 2nd Louisiana Derby
Arkansas Derby
At 5: 2nd New Orleans Handicap

LT. FLAG (1981)
At 3: 2nd Gotham Stakes

LT. STEVENS (1961)
At 3: 2nd Arlington Classic
American Derby
Jerome Handicap
At 4: Won John B. Campbell Handicap
3rd Donn Handicap
Grey Lag Handicap

LUAZUR (1989)
At 4: 2nd Oak Tree Invitational Stakes
3rd Breeders' Cup Turf

LUCAYAN INDIAN (1995)
At 4: 3rd San Juan Capistrano Handicap

LUCAYAN PRINCE (1993)
At 4: 2nd Cigar Mile Handicap

LUCIE MANET (1973)
At 4: Won La Canada Stakes
Santa Margarita Handicap

LUCI TEE (1967)
At 3: 3rd Acorn Stakes

LUCKY DEBONAIR (1962)
At 3: Won Santa Anita Derby
Blue Grass Stakes
Kentucky Derby

LUCKY DEBONAIR *(Continued)*

	2nd	San Felipe Handicap
At 4:	Won	Santa Anita Handicap

LUCKY DRAW (1941)

At 5:	Won	Monmouth Handicap
	2nd	Westchester Handicap

LUCKY G.L. (1953)

At 3:	2nd	California Derby
At 4:	3rd	Santa Anita Maturity

LUCKY LAVENDER GAL (1992)

At 3:	3rd	Acorn Stakes

LUCKY LUCKY LUCKY (1981)

At 2:	Won	Matron Stakes
		Alcibiades Stakes
	3rd	Frizette Stakes
At 3:	Won	Kentucky Oaks
	2nd	Alabama Stakes
		Spinster Stakes
	3rd	Hollywood Oaks

LUCKY MEL (1954)

At 2:	Won	Starlet Stakes

LUCKY MIKE (1970)

At 2:	2nd	Del Mar Futurity

LUCKY MISTAKE (1954)

At 2:	3rd	Matron Stakes

LUCKY ROBERTO (1996)

At 2:	Won	Hopeful Stakes

LUCKY SPELL (1971)

At 3:	2nd	Hollywood Oaks

LUCRATIVE (1950)

At 4:	3rd	San Juan Capistrano Handicap

LUCRETIA BORI (1965)

At 2:	3rd	Arlington-Washington Lassie Stakes

LUCY'S AXE (1976)

At 2:	2nd	Remsen Stakes

LUFITKUS (1996)

At 4:	2nd	Strub Stakes

LUGE II (1986)

At 2:	Won	Laurel Futurity

LUNA ELEGANTE (1986)

At 5:	2nd	Milady Handicap
	3rd	Vanity Handicap

LUNAR SOVEREIGN (1999)

At 4:	Won	Man o' War Stakes
	3rd	United Nations Handicap

LUNAR SPOOK (1990)

At 3:	Won	Ashland Stakes

LU RAVI (1995)

At 3:	2nd	Alabama Stakes
At 5:	2nd	Apple Blossom Handicap
At 6:	2nd	Apple Blossom Handicap

LURE (1989)

At 3:	Won	Gotham Stakes
		Breeders' Cup Mile
At 4:	Won	Breeders' Cup Mile
	2nd	Caesars International Handicap
At 5:	Won	Caesars International Handicap

LURLINE B. (1945)

At 4:	Won	Santa Margarita Handicap

LURULLAH (1957)

At 2:	3rd	Arlington Futurity
		Washington Park Futurity
At 3:	3rd	Louisiana Derby
		Blue Grass Stakes

LUSH SOLDIER (1999)

At 3:	3rd	Queen Elizabeth II Challenge Cup

LUSTY LATIN (1999)

At 3:	3rd	Santa Ania Derby

LUTHIER ENCHANTEUR (1987)

At 5:	2nd	Eddie Read Handicap

LUTHIER FEVER (1991)

At 5:	2nd	Santa Anita Handicap

LUTHIER'S LAUNCH (1986)

At 4:	2nd	La Canada Stakes
	3rd	Santa Margarita Handicap
		Spinster Stakes

LUV ME LUV ME NOT (1989)

At 3:	Won	Kentucky Oaks
	3rd	Ashland Stakes
At 4:	3rd	Apple Blossom Handicap

LUXURY (1972)

At 3:	2nd	Fantasy Stakes

LUZ DEL SOL (1964)

At 6:	3rd	Santa Barbara Handicap

LYNCHUS (1951)

At 3:	2nd	Travers Stakes
At 5:	2nd	San Luis Rey Handicap

LYNN DAVIS (1974)

At 3:	2nd	Dwyer Handicap

LYNNE'S ORPHAN (1966)

At 2:	3rd	Arlington-Washington Lassie Stakes

LYPHARD'S WISH (1976)

At 4:	Won	United Nations Handicap
	3rd	Bowling Green Handicap
		Arlington Handicap

LYVETTE (1963)

At 2:	2nd	Matron Stakes

MACARTHUR PARK (1969)

At 2:	Won	Norfolk Stakes
		Del Mar Futurity
	2nd	Hollywood Juvenile Championship

MACAW (1999)

At 4:	2nd	Sword Dancer Invitational Handicap

MAC BEA (1950)

At 2:	3rd	Selima Stakes

MACBETH (1945)

At 2:	2nd	Garden State Stakes

MAC DIARMIDA (1975)

At 3:	Won	Secretariat Stakes
		Canadian International Championship
		Washington D.C. International
	3rd	Man o' War Stakes

MACHO UNO (1998)

At 2:	Won	Breeders' Cup Juvenile
	3rd	Hopeful Stakes
At 4:	3rd	Suburban Handicap

MACKIE (1993)

At 3:	3rd	Ashland Stakes

MACKINAW (1945)

At 2:	Won	Astoria Stakes
At 3:	2nd	Delaware Oaks

MAC'S SPARKLER (1962)

At 5:	Won	Black Helen Handicap
		Beldame Stakes
	2nd	Top Flight Handicap

MADAME L'ENJOLEUR (1990)

At 2:	3rd	Oak Leaf Stakes
		Hollywood Starlet Stakes

MADAME PANDIT (1993)

At 5:	2nd	Santa Monica Handicap

MADAM GAY (1978)

At 3:	3rd	Arlington Million

MADAM JET (1952)

At 2:	2nd	Del Mar Debutante Stakes

MADEMOISELLE FORLI (1979)

At 3:	2nd	Ruffian Handicap
		Beldame Stakes
	3rd	Alabama Stakes
At 5:	2nd	Delaware Handicap

MADEMOISELLE IVOR (1978)

At 4:	2nd	Golden Harvest Handicap

MADISON'S CHARM (1996)

At 3:	3rd	Acorn Stakes

MADJARISTAN (1986)

At 5:	3rd	Eddie Read Handicap

MAFOSTA (1942)

At 6:	2nd	Inglewood Handicap

MAGAZINE (1970)

At 3:	Won	Coaching Club American Oaks

MAGICAL ALLURE (1995)

At 3:	Won	La Brea Stakes
At 4:	2nd	Santa Margarita Handicap

MAGICAL MAIDEN (1989)

At 2:	Won	Hollywood Starlet Stakes
At 3:	2nd	Santa Anita Oaks
	3rd	Breeders' Cup Distaff

MAGIC FOREST (1954)

At 2:	Won	Gardenia Stakes
	3rd	Spinaway Stakes

MAGIC LAMP (1950)

At 3:	2nd	Gotham Stakes

MAGIC MISSION (1998)

At 4:	3rd	Matriarch Stakes

MAGIC STORM (1999)

At 2:	3rd	Spinaway Stakes

MAGIC WEISNER (1999)

At 3:	2nd	Preakness Stakes
		Haskell Invitational Handicap

MAGNIFICENT LINDY (1982)

At 3:	2nd	Hollywood Oaks
At 4:	Won	Vanity Handicap

MAHAN (1951)

At 6:	Won	Washington D.C. International
At 7:	2nd	Bougainvillea Turf Handicap
		Canadian Championship Stakes
At 8:	3rd	Bougainvillea Turf Handicap
		Hialeah Turf Cup

MAHARAJAH (1951)

At 3:	Won	Everglades Stakes
	3rd	Flamingo Stakes
At 4:	3rd	Gulfstream Park Handicap
		Dixie Handicap
At 5:	3rd	Dixie Handicap
At 6:	3rd	Bougainvillea Turf Handicap

MAHARETTA (1944)

At 3:	2nd	Santa Susana Stakes

MAHMOUDESS (1942)

At 4:	Won	Molly Pitcher Handicap
	3rd	New Castle Handicap

MAHOGANY HALL (1991)

At 3:	3rd	Blue Grass Stakes
At 4:	3rd	Gulfstream Park Handicap
At 5:	Won	Whitney Handicap
	2nd	Brooklyn Handicap
		Suburban Handicap

MAHOUT (1943)

At 3:	Won	Jerome Handicap
	2nd	Travers Stakes
		Discovery Handicap
		Whitney Stakes
	3rd	Lawrence Realization Stakes

MAIDEN TOWER (2000)

At 3:	2nd	Queen Elizabeth II Challenge Cup

MAIL ORDER (1956)

At 4:	2nd	Carter Handicap
At 5:	Won	Grey Lag Handicap

MAINLANDER (1952)
At 3: 3rd Dwyer Stakes

MAIN SWAP (1960)
At 2: Won Gardenia Stakes

MAINTAIN (1962)
At 5: 2nd Santa Margarita Handicap
Santa Barbara Handicap

MAIRZY DOATES (1976)
At 3: 3rd Alabama Stakes
At 5: 2nd Santa Barbara Handicap

MAJESTIC LIGHT (1973)
At 3: Won Swaps Stakes
Monmouth Invitational Handicap
Cinema Handicap
2nd American Derby
At 4: Won Amory L. Haskell Handicap
Man o' War Stakes
2nd Canadian International Championship
Washington D.C. International
Turf Classic

MAJESTIC PRINCE (1966)
At 3: Won Santa Anita Derby
Kentucky Derby
Preakness Stakes
2nd Belmont Stakes

MAJESTIC SHORE (1981)
At 3: 2nd California Derby
3rd Swaps Stakes
At 4: 3rd Century Handicap

MAJESTIC SWEEP (1989)
At 3: Won Ohio Derby
2nd Jersey Derby

MAJESTY'S PRINCE (1979)
At 2: 3rd Laurel Futurity
At 3: Won Rothmans International Stakes
2nd Washington D.C. International
Hollywood Turf Cup
At 4: Won Sword Dancer Handicap
Man o' War Stakes
3rd Bowling Green Handicap
United Nations Handicap
Washington D.C. International
Rothmans International Stakes
San Luis Rey Stakes
At 5: Won Man o' War Stakes
Rothmans International Stakes
3rd Turf Classic

MAJORIEN (1994)
At 5: 2nd Charles Whittingham Handicap

MAJOR IMPACT (1989)
At 4: 3rd Charles H. Strub Stakes
Santa Anita Handicap
Hollywood Gold Cup

MAJOR SPORT (1977)
At 5: 3rd Californian Stakes

MAKE CHANGE (1985)
At 3: 2nd Mother Goose Stakes
Alabama Stakes
Ladies Handicap
3rd Coaching Club American Oaks
Ruffian Handicap

MAKE ME LAUGH (1968)
At 2: 2nd Selima Stakes
3rd Matron Stakes
Frizette Stakes

MAKE MONEY (1961)
At 5: 2nd Californian Stakes
At 6: 2nd Californian Stakes

MAKE SAIL (1957)
At 3: Won Kentucky Oaks
Alabama Stakes
2nd Vineland Handicap
3rd Mother Goose Stakes
Beldame Stakes
At 4: Won Top Flight Handicap

MAKE THE MOST (1985)
At 4: 2nd Meadowlands Cup Handicap

MAKOR (1966)
At 3: 3rd Cinema Handicap
At 5: 2nd Del Mar Handicap

MALAYSIA (1957)
At 2: 3rd Breeders' Futurity

MALEK (1993)
At 5: Won Santa Anita Handicap
At 6: 2nd San Antonio Handicap
3rd Sempra Energy Hollywood Gold Cup

MALHOA (1961)
At 5: 2nd Top Flight Handicap
At 6: 2nd Delaware Handicap
3rd Black Helen Handicap
Top Flight Handicap

MALICIOUS (1961)
At 2: Won Hollywood Juvenile Championship
At 3: 2nd Dwyer Handicap
At 4: Won Aqueduct Stakes
2nd Whitney Stakes
3rd Woodward Stakes
At 5: 3rd Whitney Stakes

MALTHUS (1992)
At 3: 2nd Jim Dandy Stakes
3rd Travers Stakes

MAMA MUCCI (1992)
At 2: 3rd Oak Leaf Stakes

MAMELUKE (1948)
At 2: 3rd Kentucky Jockey Club Stakes
At 3: Won Blue Grass Stakes
At 4: Won Metropolitan Handicap
3rd Suburban Handicap

MAMSELLE BEBETTE (1990)
At 4: 2nd Apple Blossom Handicap

MAN ALRIGHT (1988)
At 3: 2nd Peter Pan Stakes

MANANAN MCLIR (1999)
At 3: 2nd Hollywood Derby

MANASSA MAULER (1956)
At 3: Won Wood Memorial Stakes
2nd Withers Stakes
At 4: Won Trenton Handicap
2nd Monmouth Handicap
Gallant Fox Handicap
Display Handicap
3rd Whitney Handicap

MANASSAS (1953)
At 4: Won Arlington Handicap
At 6: 2nd Arlington Handicap

MANASTASH RIDGE (1986)
At 3: 3rd Withers Stakes

MANDINGO (1948)
At 3: 2nd Jerome Handicap
3rd Saranac Handicap
At 4: 2nd Whitney Stakes
At 6: 3rd Suburban Handicap

MANDY'S GOLD (1998)
At 4: Won Ruffian Handicap
2nd Beldame Stakes
3rd Ballerina Handicap
At 5: 3rd Apple Blossom Handicap
Ogden Phipps Handicap

MANE MINISTER (1988)
At 3: 3rd Kentucky Derby
Preakness Stakes
Belmont Stakes

MAN FROM WICKLOW (1997)
At 5: 3rd Man o' War Stakes
At 6: Won Gulfstream Park Breeders' Cup Handicap

MANGONEO (1942)
At 5: 3rd Queens County Handicap

MANHATTAN'S WOODY (1984)
At 3: 2nd Tropical Park Derby

MANICHES (1979)
At 2: 2nd Arlington-Washington Lassie Stakes

MANIHIKI (1953)
At 2: 2nd Selima Stakes
3rd Gardenia Stakes

MANILA (1983)
At 3: Won United Nations Handicap
Turf Classic
Breeders' Cup Turf
At 4: Won United Nations Handicap
Budweiser-Arlington Million

MANISTIQUE (1995)
At 3: Won Hollywood Oaks
3rd Alabama Stakes
At 4: Won Santa Margarita Handicap
Vanity Handicap
At 5: Won Santa Maria Handicap

MANNDAR (1996)
At 3: 2nd Early Times Hollywood Derby
At 4: Won Woodford Reserve Turf Classic
Manhattan Handicap
2nd Arlington Million

MAN OF THE MOMENT (1968)
At 2: Won Breeders' Futurity

MAN O' GLORY (1942)
At 4: 3rd Trenton Handicap

MANOTICK (1952)
At 3: Won Gazelle Stakes
Ladies Handicap
2nd Vineland Handicap
3rd Coaching Club American Oaks
Monmouth Oaks
Molly Pitcher Handicap
At 4: 2nd Delaware Handicap
San Juan Capistrano Handicap
3rd Firenze Handicap
Vineland Handicap
At 5: Won Molly Pitcher Handicap

MANTA (1966)
At 4: 2nd Ladies Handicap
At 5: Won Santa Margarita Handicap
Beverly Hills Handicap
Santa Barbara Handicap
2nd Vanity Handicap
Inglewood Handicap
3rd Hollywood Gold Cup
Oak Tree Invitational Stakes
At 6: 2nd Beverly Hills Handicap
Santa Barbara Handicap

MANTEAU (1954)
At 3: Won Ohio Derby
3rd Blue Grass Stakes
Arlington Classic
At 4: 2nd Tropical Handicap

MANYUNK (1945)
At 4: Won San Carlos Handicap
At 6: 2nd San Pasqual Handicap

MAPLEJINSKY (1985)
At 3: Won Alabama Stakes

MARBELLA (1954)
At 3: 3rd Delaware Oaks

MARCADOR (1949)
At 3: 2nd Jerome Handicap
3rd San Felipe Handicap
American Derby
Discovery Handicap
Lawrence Realization Stakes

MARCHIO (1960)
At 6: 2nd Dixie Handicap

MARCH MAGIC (1997)
At 2: 3rd Frizette Stakes
At 4: 3rd Go for Wand Handicap

MARFA (1980)
At 3: Won Santa Anita Derby
Jim Beam Spiral Stakes

MARGARETTA (1955)
At 2: 2nd Princess Pat Stakes

MARIACHE II (1970)
At 4: 3rd San Fernando Stakes

MARIAH'S STORM (1991)
At 2: Won Arlington-Washington Lassie Stakes
At 4: 3rd Spinster Stakes

MARIA'S MON (1993)
At 2: Won Futurity Stakes
Champagne Stakes
3rd Hopeful Stakes

MARIMBULA (1978)
At 5: Won Santa Margarita Handicap

MARINE VICTORY (1943)
At 3: 3rd Wood Memorial Stakes

MARINO MARINI (2000)
At 3: 2nd Malibu Stakes

MARI'S SHEBA (1992)
At 3: 3rd Santa Anita Oaks

MARKED GAME (1949)
At 5: 3rd Canadian Championship Stakes

MARKED TREE (1990)
At 3: 3rd Wood Memorial Stakes

MARKET BASKET (1954)
At 2: 3rd Del Mar Debutante Stakes
At 3: 3rd Monmouth Oaks
At 4: 2nd Santa Margarita Handicap

MARKING TIME (1963)
At 3: Won Acorn Stakes
2nd Mother Goose Stakes

MARK'S PLACE (1972)
At 5: 2nd Californian Stakes

MARK'S PUZZLE (1952)
At 3: 3rd Jockey Club Gold Cup

MARK'S RICKEY (1953)
At 2: 2nd Arlington Futurity

MARK-YE-ROYAL (1962)
At 3: 3rd Arkansas Derby

MARK-YE-WELL (1949)
At 3: Won Arlington Classic
American Derby
Lawrence Realization Stakes
2nd Jockey Club Gold Cup
3rd Jerome Handicap
At 4: Won Santa Anita Maturity
Santa Anita Handicap
At 5: Won San Antonio Handicap
At 6: 3rd Arlington Handicap

MARLEY VALE (1996)
At 2: 3rd Matron Stakes
At 3: Won Test Stakes
2nd Ashland Stakes

MARLIN (1993)
At 3: Won Secretariat Stakes
Crown Royal Hollywood Derby
2nd Hollywood Turf Cup
3rd Man o' War Stakes
Turf Classic
At 4: Won San Juan Capistrano Handicap
Arlington Million
3rd Hollywood Turf Handicap
Eddie Read Handicap

MARL LEE ANN (1979)
At 2: 2nd Del Mar Debutante Stakes

MARLOW ROAD (1955)
At 4: 2nd Man o' War Handicap

MARQUETRY (1987)
At 4: Won Hollywood Gold Cup
3rd Californian Stakes
At 5: Won Eddie Read Handicap
2nd Hollywood Gold Cup
At 6: Won San Antonio Handicap
Meadowlands Cup

MARSHUA (1962)
At 2: Won Selima Stakes
2nd Spinaway Stakes
Gardenia Stakes
3rd Frizette Stakes
At 3: Won Coaching Club American Oaks
2nd Acorn Stakes
3rd Monmouth Oaks

MARSHY DELL (1948)
At 2: 2nd Astoria Stakes

MARTA (1947)
At 4: Won Molly Pitcher Handicap
Ladies Handicap
At 5: 2nd Beldame Handicap
Ladies Handicap
At 6: Won Top Flight Handicap

MARTIAL LAW (1985)
At 4: Won Santa Anita Handicap

MARTINI II (1954)
At 5: Won Canadian Championship Stakes
At 6: 3rd Arlington Handicap

MARTINS RULLAH (1955)
At 3: Won Lawrence Realization Stakes
3rd Wood Memorial Stakes

MARTYR (1951)
At 3: Won Jerome Handicap

MARYLAND MOON (1989)
At 4: 2nd Budweiser International Stakes

MARYLEBONE (2001)
At 2: Won Matron Stakes

MARY MACHREE (1951)
At 5: Won Vanity Handicap

MASAKE (1988)
At 3: 3rd Hollywood Oaks

MASHKOUR (1983)
At 7: 2nd Hollywood Turf Cup
At 8: Won San Juan Capistrano Handicap
3rd San Luis Rey Stakes

MASH ONE (1994)
At 5: Won Oak Tree Turf Championship
At 6: Won Clement L. Hirsch Mem. Turf Champ.

MASHTEEN (1975)
At 3: 3rd Santa Susana Stakes

MASS MARKET (1997)
At 3: 3rd Super Derby

MASS O'GOLD (1948)
At 4: 2nd McLennan Handicap

MASTER BID (1943)
At 3: Won Swift Stakes

MASTER BOING (1953)
At 3: Won Washington D.C. International
At 5: 3rd Bowling Green Handicap

MASTER BOLD (1965)
At 3: 3rd Everglades Stakes

MASTER DENNIS (1960)
At 2: 2nd Champagne Stakes
3rd Pimlico Futurity
At 3: 3rd Lawrence Realization Stakes
Gallant Fox Handicap
Display Handicap
At 4: Won Arlington Handicap

MASTER DERBY (1972)
At 2: 2nd Breeders' Futurity
At 3: Won Louisiana Derby
Blue Grass Stakes
Preakness Stakes
3rd Belmont Stakes
At 4: Won New Orleans Handicap
Oaklawn Handicap
2nd Metropolitan Handicap

MASTER FIDDLE (1949)
At 2: 3rd Sapling Stakes
At 3: Won Wood Memorial Stakes
2nd Flamingo Stakes

MASTERFUL ADVOCATE (1984)
At 2: 3rd Hollywood Futurity
At 3: 2nd Santa Anita Derby

MASTER HAND (1966)
At 5: 2nd Californian Stakes

MASTER MUSIC (1971)
At 3: 3rd Swaps Stakes

MASTER PALYNCH (1956)
At 2: 3rd Arlington Futurity
At 3: Won Louisiana Derby
3rd Florida Derby

MASTER RIBOT (1969)
At 2: 2nd Del Mar Futurity

MASTERS DREAM (1978)
At 2: 3rd Arlington-Washington Lassie Stakes
Alcibiades Stakes

MASTER SPEAKER (1985)
At 4: 3rd Meadowlands Cup

MASTON (1989)
At 2: Won Young America Stakes

MATAGORDA (1950)
At 3: Won Louisiana Derby

MAT BOY (1979)
At 5: Won Widener Handicap
Gulfstream Park Handicap

MATCH II (1958)
At 4: Won Washington D.C. International

MATCHING GIFT (1978)
At 2: 2nd Laurel Futurity

MATCH THE HATCH (1976)
At 4: 2nd United Nations Handicap
At 5: 2nd Man o' War Stakes
3rd Bowling Green Handicap

MATERCO (1987)
At 2: 3rd Oak Leaf Stakes

MATIARA (1992)
At 4: Won Ramona Handicap

MATTHEW T. PARKER (1982)
At 2: 2nd Norfolk Stakes

MATTY G (1993)
At 2: Won Hollywood Futurity

MAUDLIN (1978)
At 3: 2nd Jerome Handicap
3rd Pegasus Handicap
At 4: 3rd Vosburgh Stakes

MAUD MULLER (1971)
At 3: Won Gazelle Handicap
2nd Mother Goose Stakes
3rd Coaching Club American Oaks

MAXINE N. (1974)
At 2: 3rd Del Mar Debutante Stakes

MAXZENE (1993)
At 4: 2nd Beverly D. Stakes
Flower Bowl Invitational Handicap
Matriarch Stakes

MAYAKOVSKY (1999)
At 2: 2nd Hopeful Stakes

MAY DAY EIGHTY (1979)
At 4: Won Delaware Handicap

MAY I INQUIRE (1989)
At 3: 3rd American Derby

MAY REWARD (1945)
At 3: Won California Derby
San Felipe Stakes

MAZZA (1952)
At 3: 3rd Kentucky Oaks

MCCRACKEN (1978)
At 2: 3rd Futurity Stakes

MCKENZIE BRIDGE (1973)
At 3: 2nd Belmont Stakes

MEADOW FLIGHT (1991)
At 3: 2nd Haskell Invitational Handicap

MEADOWLAKE (1983)
At 2: Won Arlington-Washington Futurity

MEADOW MONSTER (1991)
At 5: 2nd Frank J. De Francis Memorial Dash

MEADOW STAR (1988)
At 2: Won Matron Stakes
Spinaway Stakes
Frizette Stakes
Breeders' Cup Juvenile Fillies
At 3: Won Acorn Stakes
Mother Goose Stakes
2nd Coaching Club American Oaks
At 4: 3rd Spinster Stakes

MEAFARA (1989)
At 3: 2nd Breeders' Cup Sprint
At 4: 2nd Breeders' Cup Sprint

MEAN MARTHA (1978)
At 3: Won Golden Harvest Handicap

MEANT WELL (1955)
At 2: 3rd Gardenia Stakes

MECKE (1992)
At 3: Won Super Derby
2nd Secretariat Stakes
Rothmans International Stakes
3rd Florida Derby
Jim Beam Stakes
At 4: Won Early Times Turf Classic
Arlington Million
2nd Man o' War Stakes
3rd Canadian International Championship
At 5: 3rd Donn Handicap

MEDAGLIA D'ORO (1999)
At 3: Won Jim Dandy Stakes
Travers Stakes
2nd Wood Memorial Stakes
Belmont Stakes
Breeders' Cup Classic
At 4: Won Strub Stakes
Oaklawn Handicap
Whitney Handicap
2nd Pacific Classic
Breeders' Cup Classic / Dodge

ME DARLIN ANNA B. (1981)
At 2: 3rd Selima Stakes

MEDIA (1972)
At 3: 2nd Travers Stakes
3rd Wood Memorial Stakes

MEDIEVAL MAN (1974)
At 2: 3rd Laurel Futurity

MEDIEVEL HERO (1996)
At 2: 3rd Futurity Stakes

MEETING (1953)
At 5: Won Hialeah Turf Handicap
2nd Gulfstream Park Handicap

MEGAHERTZ (1999)
At 3: 2nd Del Mar Oaks
At 4: Won John C. Mabee Handicap
3rd Gamely Breeders' Cup Handicap

MEHMET (1978)
At 4: Won Monmouth Handicap
Meadowlands Cup

MELANION (1959)
At 2: 3rd Remsen Stakes

MEL LEAVITT (1951)
At 3: 3rd Gotham Stakes

MELLOW FELLOW (1995)
At 7: 3rd Ancient Title Breeders' Cup Handicap

MEMO (1987)
At 6: 3rd Californian Stakes

MEMORIES OF SILVER (1993)
At 3: Won Queen Elizabeth II Challenge Cup
3rd Matriarch Stakes
At 4: Won Beverly D. Stakes
3rd Flower Bowl Invitational Handicap
Yellow Ribbon Stakes

MENIFEE (1996)
At 3: Won Toyota Blue Grass Stakes
Haskell Invitational Handicap
2nd Kentucky Derby
Preakness Stakes
Super Derby
3rd Travers Stakes

MERCEDES WON (1986)
At 2: Won Hopeful Stakes
At 3: Won Florida Derby
2nd Fountain of Youth Stakes
3rd Jim Beam Stakes

MERCENARY (1945)
At 5: 3rd Del Mar Handicap

MERCY DEE (1971)
At 4: 3rd Beverly Hills Handicap

MERITUS (1967)
At 2: Won Spinaway Stakes

MERRY FELLOW (1971)
At 2: 2nd Norfolk Stakes

MERRY HILL (1956)
At 2: Won Frizette Stakes

MERRY LADY III (1972)
At 6: 3rd Santa Margarita Handicap

MERRYMAN (1950)
At 3: 2nd Santa Anita Derby

MERRY RULER (1958)
At 3: 3rd Gotham Stakes
At 4: Won Carter Handicap
2nd Metropolitan Handicap

MERRY TOP II (1956)
At 5: 2nd Hialeah Turf Cup
3rd Donn Handicap

MESSENGER OF SONG (1972)
At 4: Won San Fernando Stakes
3rd San Antonio Stakes

METAMORPHOSE (1988)
At 4: Won Gamely Handicap

METATRON (1999)
At 2: 3rd Del Mar Futurity
Lane's End Breeders' Futurity

METEOR DANCER (1974)
At 3: 3rd Fantasy Stakes

METHDIOXYA (1972)
At 3: 3rd Illinois Derby
At 4: 2nd Michigan Mile and One-Eighth

MIA AMORE (1972)
At 3: 3rd Hollywood Oaks

MIAMI SUN (1974)
At 3: 3rd San Felipe Handicap

MIATUSCHKA (1988)
At 5: 3rd Yellow Ribbon Stakes

MICARLO (1956)
At 6: 3rd San Carlos Handicap

MICHE (1945)
At 4: 3rd San Carlos Handicap
At 5: Won Inglewood Handicap
At 6: 3rd Stars and Stripes Handicap
At 7: Won Santa Anita Handicap

MICHELLE CAN PASS (1988)
At 5: 2nd Meadowlands Cup
Brooklyn Handicap

MICHIGAN III (1944)
At 5: 3rd Massachusetts Handicap

MICHIGAN AVENUE (1963)
At 3: Won Illinois Derby

MI CIELO (1990)
At 3: 3rd Jerome Handicap

MICKERAY (1991)
At 4: 3rd Philip H. Iselin Handicap

MICKEY MCGUIRE (1967)
At 4: 3rd Charles H. Strub Stakes

MIDAFTERNOON (1952)
At 4: Won Metropolitan Handicap
Massachusetts Handicap
Display Handicap
2nd Brooklyn Handicap
Gallant Fox Handicap
Pimlico Special

MIDAS EYES (2000)
At 3: 2nd Cigar Mile Handicap
3rd Malibu Stakes

MIDDLE BROTHER (1956)
At 3: Won Lawrence Realization Stakes
2nd Dwyer Handicap
Travers Stakes
3rd Roamer Handicap

MIDDLEGROUND (1947)
At 2: Won Hopeful Stakes
3rd Arlington Futurity
At 3: Won Kentucky Derby
Belmont Stakes
2nd Withers Stakes
Wood Memorial Stakes
Preakness Stakes

MIDDLESEX DRIVE (1995)
At 4: 3rd Manhattan Handicap

MIDNIGHT COUSINS (1983)
At 4: 3rd Man o' War Stakes

MIDNIGHT CRY (2000)
At 2: 3rd Spinaway Stakes

MIDNIGHT LINE (1995)
At 4: 2nd Gamely Breeders' Cup Handicap

MIDNIGHT SUN (1956)
At 3: 2nd Washington D.C. International

MIDWAY CAT (2000)
At 3: 3rd Fountain of Youth Stakes

MIDWAY ROAD (2000)
At 3: 2nd Preakness Stakes

MIELLEUX (1952)
At 4: 2nd Gulfstream Park Handicap
3rd Massachusetts Handicap
Monmouth Handicap

MIESQUE (1984)
At 3: Won Breeders' Cup Mile
At 4: Won Breeders' Cup Mile

MIGHT (1966)
At 4: 2nd Charles H. Strub Stakes

MIGHT AND MAIN (1960)
At 3: 2nd San Felipe Handicap

MIGHTY ADVERSARY (1981)
At 3: Won Santa Anita Derby

MIGHTY APPEALING (1982)
At 2: Won Laurel Futurity
Remsen Stakes
2nd Champagne Stakes

MIGHTY AVANTI (1990)
At 3: 3rd Ohio Derby

MIGHTY FAIR (1958)
At 3: Won Ladies Handicap
2nd Delaware Oaks
Alabama Stakes
3rd Mother Goose Stakes
Coaching Club American Oaks

MIGHTY FENNEC (1959)
At 3: 2nd Arlington Classic

MIGHTY MAGEE (1992)
At 2: 3rd Remsen Stakes

MIGHTY RETURN (1977)
At 3: 2nd Illinois Derby

MIGHTY STORY (1943)
At 3: Won Discovery Handicap
3rd Arlington Classic
At 4: 3rd Stars and Stripes Handicap

MIGRATING MOON (1990)
At 4: 2nd Gulfstream Park Handicap

MIKE FOGARTY (1975)
At 5: 3rd Bay Meadows Handicap
At 6: 3rd Eddie Read Handicap

MIKE'S RED (1962)
At 5: Won Oaklawn Handicap
3rd New Orleans Handicap

MILAN (1998)
At 3: 2nd Breeders' Cup Turf

MILCAVE (1940)
At 6: 2nd Miami Beach Handicap
3rd Black Helen Handicap

MILES TYSON (1968)
At 4: 3rd Californian Stakes

MILINGO (1979)
At 2: Won Arlington-Washington Lassie Stakes

MILITARY (1994)
At 4: Won Oak Tree Turf Championship

MILITARY PLUME (1959)
At 3: 3rd Travers Stakes

MIL KILATES (1993)
At 4: 3rd Ruffian Handicap

MILK PACT (1944)
At 2: 3rd Sapling Stakes

MILLENCOLIN (1997)
At 2: 3rd Lane's End Breeders' Futurity
At 3: 3rd King's Bishop Stakes

MILLENNIUM WIND (1998)
At 2: 2nd Hollywood Futurity
At 3: Won Toyota Blue Grass Stakes

MILLIE'S QUEST (1997)
At 3: 3rd Garden City Breeders' Cup Handicap

MILLIONS (1996)
At 2: 2nd Remsen Stakes

MILLKOM (1991)
At 4: Won Man o' War Stakes

MILL NATIVE (1984)
At 4: Won Arlington Million

MILLY K. (1955)
At 4: 2nd Santa Margarita Handicap

MILWAUKEE AVENUE (1973)
At 4: 2nd Hawthorne Gold Cup

MILWAUKEE BREW (1997)
At 3: 3rd Haskell Invitational Handicap
At 5: Won Santa Anita Handicap
3rd Hollywood Gold Cup
Pacific Classic
Breeders' Cup Classic
At 6: Won Santa Anita Handicap

MI-MARIGOLD (1950)
At 3: Won Vineland Handicap

MIMI MINE (1950)
At 2: 3rd Princess Pat Stakes

MINERAL ICE (1988)
At 2: 3rd Cowdin Stakes

MINER'S MARK (1990)
At 3: Won Jim Dandy Stakes
Jockey Club Gold Cup
2nd Dwyer Stakes
3rd Jim Beam Stakes
Travers Stakes

MINESHAFT (1999)
At 4: Won Pimlico Special
Suburban Handicap
Woodward Stakes
Jockey Club Gold Cup
2nd Stephen Foster Handicap

MING YELLOW (1950)
At 3: 3rd Coaching Club American Oaks
At 4: 2nd Ladies Handicap

MINING (1984)
At 4: Won Vosburgh Stakes

MINISTER ERIC (2001)
At 2: 2nd Del Mar Futurity
Bessemer Trust Breeders' Cup Juvenile

MINNESOTA GUS (1974)
At 3: 3rd Cinema Handicap

MINOR DETAILS (1997)
At 4: 3rd Ramona Handicap

MINORITY DATER (1991)
At 2: 3rd Arlington-Washington Lassie Stakes

MINSTREL BOY (1943)
At 5: 2nd Longacres Mile

MINSTREL MISS (1967)
At 2: 2nd Del Mar Debutante Stakes
At 6: 2nd Vanity Handicap
3rd Santa Margarita Handicap

MINSTREL'S LASSIE (1985)
At 2: Won Selima Stakes

MINTAGE (1979)
At 4: 3rd Flower Bowl Handicap

MINT COOLER (1984)
At 3: 2nd Coaching Club American Oaks

MI PREFERIDO (1985)
At 3: Won San Felipe Handicap
3rd Santa Anita Derby
At 4: Won San Fernando Stakes

MIRACLE HILL (1964)
At 5: Won New Orleans Handicap

MIRACLE WOOD (1983)
At 2: 3rd Laurel Futurity
At 3: 2nd Jim Beam Stakes

MIRA FEMME (1964)
At 2: Won Arlington-Washington Lassie Stakes
At 3: 2nd Santa Susana Stakes

MIRLIVAM (1968)
At 4: 2nd Del Mar Handicap

MI SELECTO (1985)
At 4: Won Meadowlands Cup Handicap
3rd Widener Handicap
Philip H. Iselin Handicap
At 5: Won Gulfstream Park Handicap
2nd Brooklyn Handicap
3rd Whitney Handicap

MISGIVINGS (1975)
At 2: 2nd Frizette Stakes

MISREPRESENTATION (1975)
At 2: 2nd Norfolk Stakes

MISS ALLEGED (1987)
At 4: Won Breeders' Cup Turf
Hollywood Turf Cup
At 5: 2nd Santa Barbara Handicap
San Juan Capistrano Handicap

MISS ARLETTE (1952)
At 4: 2nd Black Helen Handicap

MISS BAJA (1975)
At 3: 3rd Fantasy Stakes
At 4: Won Apple Blossom Handicap
3rd Spinster Stakes
At 5: 3rd Apple Blossom Handicap

MISS BLUE GEM (1956)
At 3: 2nd Alabama Stakes

MISS BONIFACE (1985)
At 2: 3rd Selima Stakes

MISS BRIO (1984)
At 5: Won Maskette Stakes

MISS CAVANDISH (1961)
At 2: 3rd Gardenia Stakes
At 3: Won Coaching Club American Oaks
Monmouth Oaks
Alabama Stakes
2nd Kentucky Oaks
Delaware Handicap
Beldame Stakes
Spinster Stakes
At 4: 3rd Delaware Handicap
Matron Handicap

MISS CIGARETTE (1974)
At 2: 3rd Sorority Stakes

MISS COX'S HAT (1987)
At 2: 3rd Matron Stakes

MISS DAN II (1967)
At 3: 2nd Washington D.C. International

MISS DELICE (1982)
At 2: 3rd Arlington-Washington Lassie Stakes

MISS DICKEY (1962)
At 4: 3rd Ladies Handicap

MISS DOMINIQUE (1989)
At 5: 3rd Spinster Stakes
Breeders' Cup Distaff

MISS DOREEN (1942)
At 6: Won Santa Margarita Handicap

MISS GOLDEN CIRCLE (1992)
At 3: 2nd Test Stakes
Gazelle Handicap
At 4: 3rd Delta Air Lines Top Flight Handicap

MISS GRILLO (1942)
At 5: Won Black Helen Handicap
2nd Top Flight Handicap
Beldame Handicap
3rd Gallant Fox Handicap
At 6: Won New Castle Handicap
New York Handicap
3rd Santa Margarita Handicap
At 7: Won San Juan Capistrano Handicap
3rd Santa Anita Handicap

MISS HOUDINI (2000)
At 2: Won Del Mar Debutante Stakes

MISS HUNTINGTON (1977)
At 4: 2nd La Canada Stakes
At 5: Won Golden Harvest Handicap
At 6: Won Apple Blossom Handicap
3rd Spinster Stakes

MISSILE (1954)
At 2: Won Pimlico Futurity
2nd Breeders' Futurity
Remsen Stakes

MISSILE BELLE (1967)
At 3: Won Coaching Club American Oaks
Gazelle Handicap
2nd Acorn Stakes
3rd Mother Goose Stakes

MISSILERY (1960)
At 3: 2nd Cinema Handicap

MISSIONARY RIDGE (1987)
At 4: 2nd Oak Tree Invitational Stakes
At 5: Won Pacific Classic
At 6: 2nd Californian Stakes
Pacific Classic
3rd Donn Handicap

MISS IRON SMOKE (1989)
At 2: Won Spinaway Stakes
2nd Matron Stakes

MISSISSIPPI MUD (1973)
At 4: 2nd Hempstead Handicap
Delaware Handicap
Ruffian Handicap
Spinster Stakes
3rd Top Flight Handicap

MISS JENNIFER LYNN (1996)
At 2: 3rd Spinaway Stakes

MISS J.G. (1955)
At 4: 2nd Vineland Handicap

MISS JOANNE (1950)
At 4: 2nd Molly Pitcher Handicap

MISS JOSH (1986)
At 5: Won Gamely Handicap

MISS KIMO (1944)
At 2: 2nd Astoria Stakes
At 3: Won Vineland Handicap

MISS LADY BUG (1969)
At 2: 2nd Del Mar Debutante Stakes
3rd Oak Leaf Stakes

MISS LINDA (1997)
At 4: Won Overbrook Spinster Stakes
At 5: 3rd Apple Blossom Handicap
At 6: 3rd Personal Ensign Handicap
Overbrook Spinster Stakes

MISS LODI (1999)
At 4: 3rd Humana Distaff Handicap

MISS MARCELLA (1958)
At 5: 3rd Black Helen Handicap

MISS MOMMY (1945)
At 2: 2nd Marguerite Stakes
3rd Selima Stakes
At 4: 3rd Black Helen Handicap

MISS MOONA (1963)
At 4: Won Santa Margarita Handicap

MISS MUSKET (1971)
At 3: Won Fantasy Stakes
Hollywood Oaks

MISS OCEANA (1981)
At 2: Won Arlington-Washington Lassie Stakes
Selima Stakes
Frizette Stakes
2nd Matron Stakes
At 3: Won Acorn Stakes
Maskette Stakes
2nd Kentucky Oaks
Mother Goose Stakes
Ruffian Handicap
Beldame Stakes
3rd Coaching Club American Oaks

MISSOURI GENT (1964)
At 5: 2nd Oaklawn Handicap

MISS REQUEST (1945)
At 3: Won Delaware Oaks
Ladies Handicap
2nd Comely Handicap
At 4: Won Beldame Handicap
2nd Ladies Handicap
3rd Jockey Club Gold Cup
New Orleans Handicap

MISS RIBOT (1965)
At 3: 2nd Kentucky Oaks
3rd Santa Susana Stakes
Alabama Stakes
At 4: 2nd Spinster Stakes

MISS RINCON (1962)
At 4: 2nd Santa Barbara Handicap
At 5: 3rd Santa Barbara Handicap

MISS SPIN (1963)
At 4: 3rd Delaware Handicap

MISS TODD (1953)
At 2: Won Del Mar Debutante Stakes
At 4: 2nd Vanity Handicap
3rd Santa Margarita Handicap

MISS TOKYO (1972)
At 4: 3rd Beverly Hills Handicap
Ramona Handicap

MISS TOSHIBA (1972)
At 4: Won Vanity Handicap
2nd Beverly Hills Handicap

MISS TRAFFIC (1948)
At 3: 2nd Hollywood Oaks
At 5: 2nd Beldame Handicap

MISS UNNAMEABLE (1984)
At 5: 3rd Flower Bowl Handicap

MISS UPPITY (1956)
At 2: 3rd Del Mar Debutante Stakes

MISS WEESIE (1950)
At 5: 2nd Maskette Handicap

MISS WINESHINE (1997)
At 2: 3rd Spinaway Stakes

MISSY'S MIRAGE (1988)
At 4: Won Shuvee Handicap
Hempstead Handicap

MISTAURIAN (1986)
At 4: 3rd Maskette Stakes
Ruffian Handicap

MISTER ACPEN (1998)
At 5: 2nd Charles Whittingham Handicap

MISTER BLACK (1949)
At 5: 2nd Hawthorne Gold Cup
At 6: Won Gulfstream Park Handicap
2nd Hawthorne Gold Cup

MISTER BREA (1974)
At 5: 2nd Suburban Handicap

MISTER FRISKY (1987)
At 3: Won Santa Anita Derby
3rd Preakness Stakes

MISTER GUS (1951)
At 4: Won William P. Kyne Handicap
2nd American Handicap
Pimlico Special
3rd Californian Stakes
At 5: Won San Antonio Handicap
Woodward Stakes
Arlington Handicap
2nd Inglewood Handicap
American Handicap
Hollywood Gold Cup
Washington D.C. International
3rd Californian Stakes
United Nations Handicap

MISTER JIVE (1954)
At 2: Won Cowdin Stakes
At 3: Won Gotham Stakes

MISTER MODESTY (1985)
At 2: 2nd Laurel Futurity

MISTER ROUGE (1977)
At 4: 3rd Louisiana Downs Handicap

MISTER S.M. (1984)
At 3: 3rd Withers Stakes

MISTER WONDERFUL II (1983)
At 6: 3rd Budweiser International Stakes

MISTY (1952)
At 2: 3rd Selima Stakes

MISTY FLIGHT (1955)
At 2: Won Remsen Stakes
2nd Champagne Stakes
Futurity Stakes
At 3: 3rd Withers Stakes

MISTY GALLORE (1976)
At 4: 2nd Top Flight Handicap
Ruffian Handicap
Beldame Stakes

MISTY MORN (1952)
At 3: Won Monmouth Oaks
Molly Pitcher Handicap
Gallant Fox Handicap
2nd Ladies Handicap
Saranac Handicap
3rd Alabama Stakes

MISTY RUN (1964)
At 4: 3rd Michigan Mile and One-Eighth

MITEY LIVELY (1977)
At 3: 2nd Kentucky Oaks
Acorn Stakes

MITEY PRINCE (1965)
At 5: Won John B. Campbell Handicap

MITTERAND (1981)
At 3: 2nd Hollywood Oaks
At 4: Won La Canada Stakes
2nd Santa Margarita Handicap

MITYME (1944)
At 2: 3rd Garden State Stakes

MIZ CLEMENTINE (1951)
At 2: 2nd Arlington Lassie Stakes
At 3: Won Cinema Handicap
California Derby
At 4: 2nd Santa Margarita Handicap
Santa Anita Maturity

MIZZEN MAST (1998)
At 3: Won Malibu Stakes
At 4: Won Strub Stakes

MOCCASIN (1963)
At 2: Won Spinaway Stakes
Matron Stakes
Selima Stakes
Gardenia Stakes
At 3: 3rd Acorn Stakes

MOCHILA (1979)
At 4: 2nd Ruffian Handicap
3rd Beldame Stakes

MOCOPO (1946)
At 4: 3rd San Juan Capistrano Handicap
Santa Anita Maturity
At 5: 2nd Sunset Handicap
3rd San Juan Capistrano Handicap

MODEL CADET (1946)
At 2: Won Washington Park Futurity

MODEL FOOL (1963)
At 4: 2nd John B. Campbell Handicap
At 5: Won Century Handicap

MODEL TEN (1979)
At 2: 3rd Oak Leaf Stakes

MODERN WORLD (1952)
At 2: 3rd Starlet Stakes

MODUS VIVENDI (1971)
At 3: 2nd Ramona Handicap
3rd Hollywood Oaks

MO EXCEPTION (1981)
At 4: 2nd Metropolitan Handicap

MOGAMBO (1983)
At 2: Won Champagne Stakes
3rd Young America Stakes
At 3: Won Gotham Stakes
2nd Wood Memorial Stakes
Jersey Derby
Jerome Handicap
3rd Florida Derby

MOLLY BALLENTINE (1972)
At 2: Won Frizette Stakes

MOMENT OF HOPE (1983)
At 3: 2nd Jim Dandy Stakes
3rd Jerome Handicap
At 4: 2nd Vosburgh Stakes

MOMENT TO BUY (1981)
At 3: Won Hollywood Oaks

MOMENTUM (1998)
At 4: 2nd Hollywood Gold Cup
Pacific Classic

MOM'S COMMAND (1982)
At 2: Won Selima Stakes
3rd Frizette Stakes
At 3: Won Acorn Stakes
Mother Goose Stakes
Coaching Club American Oaks
Alabama Stakes

MOMSFURRARI (1984)
At 3: 2nd Everglades Stakes

MOMUS (1952)
At 4: 3rd Tropical Handicap

MONARCHOS (1998)
At 3: Won Florida Derby
Kentucky Derby
2nd Wood Memorial Stakes
3rd Belmont Stakes

MONARCHY (1957)
At 2: Won Arlington Lassie Stakes

MONETARY PRINCIPLE (1970)
At 5: 2nd Grey Lag Handicap
Brooklyn Handicap

MONEY BROKER (1950)
At 3: Won Florida Derby
2nd Louisiana Derby
3rd Blue Grass Stakes

MONEY LENDER (1971)
At 2: Won Norfolk Stakes
At 3: 2nd San Felipe Handicap
3rd California Derby

MONEY MOVERS (1986)
At 2: 3rd Selima Stakes

MONEY TO BURN (1962)
At 2: 2nd Frizette Stakes

MONGO (1959)
At 3: Won Trenton Handicap
United Nations Handicap
At 4: Won Washington D.C. International
United Nations Handicap
2nd Monmouth Handicap
Trenton Handicap
At 5: Won Widener Handicap
John B. Campbell Handicap
Monmouth Handicap
2nd Grey Lag Handicap
Whitney Stakes

MONGOOSE (1998)
At 3: 3rd Turfway Spiral Stakes
At 4: Won Donn Handicap
2nd Gulfstream Park Handicap

MONGO QUEEN (1976)
At 2: Won Sorority Stakes

MONITOR (1964)
At 2: 2nd Breeders' Futurity
3rd Kentucky Jockey Club Stakes
At 3: Won Arkansas Derby

MONK'S HOOD (1956)
At 2: 3rd Starlet Stakes
At 3: 2nd California Derby

MON MIEL (1970)
At 4: 2nd Beverly Hills Handicap

MONSOON (1942)
At 5: Won Santa Margarita Handicap

MONTMARTRE (1970)
At 4: 3rd Oak Tree Invitational Stakes
At 5: Won American Handicap
3rd San Luis Rey Stakes

MONTREAL RED (1992)
At 2: Won Futurity Stakes
2nd Hopeful Stakes

MONTSERRAT (1988)
At 4: 3rd Sword Dancer Handicap

MONTUBIO (1985)
At 5: Won Brooklyn Handicap
3rd Suburban Handicap

MOON GLORY (1955)
At 3: 2nd Spinster Stakes

MOONLIGHT CHARGER (1995)
At 6: 3rd San Antonio Handicap

MOON MAIDEN (1938)
At 8: 2nd Bougainvillea Handicap

MOONRUSH (1946)
At 5: Won San Pasqual Handicap
Santa Anita Handicap
2nd Aqueduct Handicap
3rd Golden Gate Handicap
At 6: 3rd Del Mar Handicap

MOONSIGHT (1951)
At 3: 2nd Alabama Stakes

MOONSPLASH (1968)
At 2: 3rd Hollywood Juvenile Championship

MOONTEE (1973)
At 3: 3rd Alabama Stakes

MOONTRIP (1961)
At 5: Won Manhattan Handicap
Bowling Green Handicap
3rd Gallant Fox Handicap
At 6: Won Grey Lag Handicap
3rd Manhattan Handicap
San Luis Rey Handicap

MOONY (1956)
At 3: 2nd Everglades Stakes

MORE GLORY (1953)
At 3: 3rd Santa Anita Derby

MORE SCENTS (1964)
At 4: 2nd Aqueduct Stakes

MORE SO (1975)
At 4: 2nd Ramona Handicap

MORE SUN (1947)
At 2: Won Saratoga Special
At 3: 2nd Vosburgh Handicap
At 4: 2nd Carter Handicap

MORE THAN READY (1997)
At 2: 3rd Futurity Stakes
At 3: Won King's Bishop Stakes
2nd Toyota Blue Grass Stakes
Vosburgh Stakes

MORGAISE (1965)
At 3: 2nd Hollywood Oaks

MORGANA (1991)
At 4: 2nd Ramona Handicap
3rd Santa Barbara Handicap

MORNING BOB (1981)
At 3: Won Tropical Park Derby
Pennsylvania Derby
2nd Withers Stakes
3rd Belmont Stakes
Travers Stakes

MORNING CAST (1961)
At 3: 2nd Ohio Derby

MORNING FROLIC (1975)
At 5: 2nd Pan American Handicap

MORO (1979)
At 5: 3rd Metropolitan Handicap

MOSLEM CHIEF (1957)
At 3: Won Everglades Stakes

MOSSFLOWER (1994)
At 4: Won Hempstead Handicap
At 5: 3rd Flower Bowl Invitational Handicap

MOSS VALE (1961)
At 4: Won Hawthorne Gold Cup

MOST HOST (1964)
At 4: Won Charles H. Strub Stakes
2nd San Fernando Stakes

MOST WELCOME (1984)
At 4: 3rd Turf Classic
At 5: 3rd Breeders' Cup Mile

MOTAVATO (1978)
At 4: 3rd Budweiser Million

MOTHER (1944)
At 3: 3rd Kentucky Oaks
Gazelle Stakes
At 5: 3rd Beldame Handicap

MOTIVITY (1978)
At 2: 2nd Hollywood Juvenile Championship

MOT JUSTE (1998)
At 4: 3rd Flower Bowl Invitational Stakes

MOTLEY (1984)
At 3: 3rd Budweiser International Stakes

MOUNTAIN BEAR (1981)
At 5: Won Santa Barbara Handicap
2nd San Juan Capistrano Handicap

MOUNTAIN GLORY (1956)
At 5: 2nd Vanity Handicap

MOUNTAIN TOP (1995)
At 4: 3rd Vosburgh Stakes

MOUNT MARCY (1945)
At 3: Won Saranac Handicap
2nd Wood Memorial Stakes
Discovery Handicap
Jerome Handicap
At 4: 3rd Aqueduct Handicap
At 5: 2nd Queens County Handicap
At 6: Won New Orleans Handicap
2nd McLennan Handicap
Gulfstream Park Handicap

MOUNT STERLING (1973)
At 4: 3rd Widener Handicap

MOURJANE (1980)
At 5: 3rd Breeders' Cup Turf

MOVE ABROAD (1971)
At 4: 2nd Santa Barbara Handicap

MR. AL L. (1952)
At 3: 2nd Gotham Stakes

MR. AMERICA (1958)
At 2: 2nd Del Mar Futurity
At 3: 2nd Cinema Handicap

MR. BOB W. (1953)
At 3: 2nd Louisiana Derby

MR. BRICK (1961)
At 2: Won Sapling Stakes
At 3: Won Withers Stakes
2nd Everglades Stakes
Flamingo Stakes
Wood Memorial Stakes
Jersey Derby
3rd Gotham Stakes

MR. BROGANN (1965)
At 2: Won Kentucky Jockey Club Stakes
At 4: 3rd Widener Handicap

MR. B'S SISTER (1962)
At 2: 3rd Arlington-Washington Lassie Stakes

MR. BUSHER (1946)
At 2: Won Arlington Futurity

MR. CLASSIC (1983)
At 2: 2nd Remsen Stakes
3rd Futurity Stakes
Champagne Stakes
At 3: 3rd Hutcheson Stakes

MR. CLINCH (1966)
At 3: 2nd Ohio Derby

MR. COCKATOO (1969)
At 5: 3rd American Handicap

MR. COINCIDENCE (1966)
At 3: 3rd Blue Grass Stakes

MR. COLD STORAGE (1960)
At 2: Won Saratoga Special

MR. CONSISTENCY (1958)
At 3: Won California Derby
3rd Blue Grass Stakes
At 4: 2nd Californian Stakes
Sunset Handicap
3rd American Handicap
At 6: Won Santa Anita Handicap
San Juan Capistrano Handicap
2nd Californian Stakes
San Luis Rey Handicap
3rd Inglewood Handicap

MR. FIRST (1951)
At 4: 2nd Trenton Handicap
At 5: 2nd Monmouth Handicap
At 6: 2nd Widener Handicap

MR. FRECKLES (1998)
At 2: 3rd Norfolk Stakes

MR. GOOD (1950)
At 2: Won Arlington Futurity
2nd Washington Park Futurity

MR. GREELEY (1992)
At 3: 2nd Jerome Handicap
Breeders' Cup Sprint

MR. GROUSH (1994)
At 3: 3rd Ohio Derby

MR. ICONOCLAST (1975)
At 5: 3rd Louisiana Downs Handicap

MR. JOE F. (1966)
At 3: 2nd Santa Anita Derby
3rd San Felipe Handicap

MR. LEADER (1966)
At 2: 2nd Breeders' Futurity
3rd Pimlico-Laurel Futurity
At 3: Won Jerome Handicap
At 4: Won Stars and Stripes Handicap
3rd United Nations Handicap

MR. LUCKY PHOENIX (1970)
At 5: Won Michigan Mile and One-Eighth

MR. MOONLIGHT (1961)
At 3: Won Gotham Stakes

MR. MUD (1977)
At 3: 3rd Swaps Stakes

MR. MUSTARD (1951)
At 3: 2nd San Felipe Handicap

MR. NICKERSON (1986)
At 3: 3rd Vosburgh Stakes

MR. PAK (1962)
At 3: 3rd Blue Grass Stakes
American Derby

MR. PARADISE (1950)
At 2: Won Washington Park Futurity
2nd Arlington Futurity

MR. PAUL B. (1969)
At 2: 3rd Cowdin Stakes

MR. POW WOW (1968)
At 3: 2nd Pontiac Grand Prix Stakes
American Derby
At 4: 2nd Donn Handicap

MR. PROSECUTOR (1951)
At 2: 2nd Arlington Futurity

MR. PROSPECTOR (1970)
At 4: 2nd Carter Handicap

MR. PURPLE (1992)
At 2: 3rd Arlington-Washington Futurity
At 4: Won Santa Anita Handicap
3rd Strub Stakes
Californian Stakes

MR. REDOY (1974)
At 4: Won Charles H. Strub Stakes
2nd Santa Anita Handicap

MR. RIGHT (1963)
At 3: Won Dixie Handicap
At 4: 3rd Brooklyn Handicap
At 5: Won Santa Anita Handicap
Woodward Stakes
2nd Amory L. Haskell Handicap
3rd Brooklyn Handicap
At 6: Won Suburban Handicap
2nd Michigan Mile and One-Eighth

MR. ROSS (1995)
At 6: 2nd Oaklawn Handicap

MR. SAM S. (1954)
At 2: 2nd Del Mar Futurity

MRS. CORNWALLIS (1969)
At 2: Won Alcibiades Stakes

MRS. E.B. (1955)
At 2: 2nd Del Mar Debutante Stakes

MRS. FUDDY (1947)
At 3: Won Hollywood Oaks
2nd Del Mar Derby

MR. SINATRA (1994)
At 4: 3rd Brooklyn Handicap

MRS. JO JO (1966)
At 3: 3rd Kentucky Oaks

MR. SPIFFY (1983)
At 2: 3rd Sapling Stakes

MRS. RABBIT (1945)
At 3: Won Santa Susana Stakes

MRS. REVERE (1981)
At 4: 3rd Maskette Stakes

MR. STEU (1957)
At 6: 2nd Dixie Handicap

MR. SULLIVAN (1952)
At 3: 3rd Cinema Handicap

MRS. WARREN (1974)
At 2: Won Spinaway Stakes
Matron Stakes
3rd Frizette Stakes
At 3: 2nd Ashland Stakes
Mother Goose Stakes
3rd Kentucky Oaks
Acorn Stakes

MR. TROUBLE (1947)
At 2: 3rd Hopeful Stakes
At 3: Won Blue Grass Stakes
3rd Kentucky Derby
Belmont Stakes

MR. TURF (1949)
At 2: 3rd Saratoga Special

MR. WASHINGTON (1964)
At 4: 3rd Carter Handicap

MS. ELOISE (1983)
At 4: Won Top Flight Handicap
At 5: 2nd Delaware Handicap

MS. GOLD POLE (1986)
At 2: 3rd Frizette Stakes

MS LOUISETT (1999)
At 2: 3rd Oak Leaf Stakes

MS. MARGI (1984)
At 3: 2nd Spinster Stakes

MT. LIVERMORE (1981)
At 4: 3rd Breeders' Cup Sprint

MT. SASSAFRAS (1992)
At 3: 3rd Molson Export Million
At 4: 3rd Buick Meadowlands Cup Handicap
At 5: Won Gulfstream Park Handicap

MUCHO HOSSO (1948)
At 3: Won Cinema Handicap
2nd Del Mar Derby

MUD ROUTE (1994)
At 4: Won Californian Stakes
2nd Strub Stakes

MUGZY'S RULLAH (1982)
At 2: 3rd Hopeful Stakes
Futurity Stakes

MUHTARRAM (1989)
At 5: 3rd Arlington Million

MULA GULA (1996)
At 4: 3rd Arlington Million

MULTIPLE CHOICE (1998)
At 4: 3rd Forego Handicap

MUNCH (1955)
At 3: 2nd Gazelle Handicap
Arlington Matron Handicap

MUNCHAUSEN (1952)
At 3: 3rd Blue Grass Stakes

MUNDEN POINT (1962)
At 3: Won Lawrence Realization Stakes
At 4: Won Gallant Fox Handicap
3rd Display Handicap
At 5: Won Manhattan Handicap

MUSE (1964)
At 3: 2nd Coaching Club American Oaks
3rd Mother Goose Stakes
Alabama Stakes
Ladies Handicap
At 4: 2nd Display Handicap
3rd Top Flight Handicap

MUSICAL CHIMES (2000)
At 3: 2nd Yellow Ribbon Stakes
Matriarch Stakes

MUSICAL LADY (1944)
At 2: 2nd Arlington Lassie Stakes

MUSICAL LARK (1983)
At 2: Won Matron Stakes

MUSIC KHAL (1962)
At 2: 3rd Del Mar Debutante Stakes

MUSIC LEADER (1979)
At 2: 3rd Arlington-Washington Futurity

MUSIC MERCI (1986)
At 2: Won Del Mar Futurity
2nd Hollywood Futurity
At 3: Won Illinois Derby
2nd Haskell Invitational Handicap
3rd San Felipe Handicap
Santa Anita Derby

MUSIC PROSPECTOR (1987)
At 3: 2nd Pegasus Handicap
3rd San Felipe Handicap

MUSTARD PLASTER (1959)
At 5: Won Californian Stakes
2nd Inglewood Handicap
American Handicap
Hollywood Gold Cup

MUTINEER (1977)
At 3: 2nd Pennsylvania Derby

MUTTERING (1979)
At 3: Won Santa Anita Derby
2nd Pegasus Handicap

MY BIG BOY (1983)
At 5: 2nd Turf Classic
3rd Man o' War Stakes
At 6: 2nd Man o' War Stakes
3rd Sword Dancer Handicap
Turf Classic

MY BLUE SKY (1952)
At 2: 2nd Spinaway Stakes

MY BOY ADAM (1987)
At 4: 2nd Charles H. Strub Stakes

MY CARD (1961)
At 2: Won Selima Stakes

MY CELESTE (1946)
At 2: 2nd Marguerite Stakes
At 3: 3rd Delaware Oaks
At 4: 2nd Molly Pitcher Handicap
Ladies Handicap
At 5: 2nd Molly Pitcher Handicap
At 6: 2nd Molly Pitcher Handicap
3rd New Castle Handicap
At 7: Won Molly Pitcher Handicap
Monmouth Handicap
3rd New Castle Handicap

MY DAD GEORGE (1967)
At 3: Won Flamingo Stakes
Florida Derby
2nd Kentucky Derby
Preakness Stakes
3rd Amory L. Haskell Handicap

MY DARLING ONE (1981)
At 3: Won Fantasy Stakes
3rd Kentucky Oaks

MY DEAR GIRL (1957)
At 2: Won Gardenia Stakes
Frizette Stakes
2nd Arlington Lassie Stakes

MY EMMA (1945)
At 4: 2nd Molly Pitcher Handicap

MY FLAG (1993)
At 2: Won Breeders' Cup Juvenile Fillies
2nd Frizette Stakes
3rd Matron Stakes
At 3: Won Ashland Stakes
Coaching Club American Oaks
Gazelle Handicap
3rd Belmont Stakes
Alabama Stakes

MY FRIEND GUS (1972)
At 3: 3rd Arkansas Derby
Monmouth Invitational Handicap

MY GALLANT (1970)
At 3: Won Blue Grass Stakes
2nd Flamingo Stakes
3rd Fountain of Youth Stakes
Belmont Stakes

MY HABITONY (1980)
At 3: 2nd Santa Anita Derby
Swaps Stakes
3rd Super Derby

MYKAWA (1983)
At 3: 2nd Fountain of Youth Stakes

MY JULIET (1972)
At 3: 2nd Ashland Stakes
At 4: Won Vosburgh Handicap
At 5: Won Michigan Mile and One-Eighth

MY MEMOIRS (1989)
At 3: 2nd Belmont Stakes

MY NIGHT OUT (1953)
At 4: Won Michigan Mile and One-Sixteenth
At 5: 3rd Michigan Mile

MY OLD FRIEND (1969)
At 5: 2nd Del Mar Handicap

MY PORTRAIT (1958)
At 2: 3rd Princess Pat Stakes
At 3: Won Kentucky Oaks
Monmouth Oaks
3rd Vineland Handicap
At 5: 2nd Vineland Handicap

MY PRINCE CHARMING (1983)
At 3: Won Fountain of Youth Stakes

MYRAKALU (1988)
At 6: 3rd Santa Anita Handicap

MY REQUEST (1945)
At 2: Won Cowdin Stakes
3rd Hopeful Stakes
Champagne Stakes
Remsen Handicap
At 3: Won Wood Memorial Stakes
Dwyer Stakes
3rd Kentucky Derby
At 4: Won New Orleans Handicap
Excelsior Handicap
2nd Manhattan Handicap
3rd Whitney Stakes
At 5: Won Brooklyn Handicap
2nd Suburban Handicap
Massachusetts Handicap

MYRTLE CHARM (1946)
At 2: Won Spinaway Stakes
Matron Stakes
2nd Futurity Stakes

MYRTLE'S JET (1952)
At 2: Won Alcibiades Stakes
Frizette Stakes
2nd Selima Stakes
3rd Princess Pat Stakes

MYSTERY MOOD (1972)
At 2: 3rd Arlington-Washington Lassie Stakes
Frizette Stakes

MYSTICAL MOOD (1979)
At 2: 2nd Frizette Stakes
3rd Matron Stakes

MYSTIC EYE (1954)
At 4: 2nd San Antonio Handicap
3rd San Carlos Handicap

MYSTIC HAWK (1989)
At 2: 3rd Arlington-Washington Lassie Stakes

MZ. ZILL BEAR (1989)
At 5: 2nd Gamely Handicap

NADIR (1955)
At 2: Won Garden State Stakes
2nd Cowdin Stakes
At 3: Won American Derby
2nd Woodward Stakes
3rd Arlington Classic
Washington Park Handicap
At 4: 2nd Widener Handicap
3rd Tropical Park Handicap
McLennan Handicap
Carter Handicap

NAEVUS (1980)
At 3: 2nd San Felipe Handicap
3rd Santa Anita Derby

NAIDNI DIAM (1963)
At 3: 3rd Kentucky Oaks

NAIL (1953)
At 2: Won Pimlico Futurity
Futurity Stakes
Remsen Stakes
At 3: 3rd Everglades Stakes
Gotham Stakes

NAIVE (1970)
At 2: 2nd Selima Stakes

NAJRAN (1999)
At 4: 2nd Forego Handicap

NAKED SKY (1977)
At 3: 2nd Florida Derby

NALA (1955)
At 2: 2nd Pimlico Futurity

NALEE (1960)
At 2: 2nd Spinaway Stakes
3rd Sorority Stakes
Gardenia Stakes
At 3: 2nd Acorn Stakes

NALEES PIN (1988)
At 3: 3rd Fantasy Stakes
Mother Goose Stakes

NAMON (1956)
At 2: Won Breeders' Futurity

NANCE'S LAD (1952)
At 3: 2nd Withers Stakes
3rd Saranac Handicap
Roamer Handicap

NANCY CHERE (1976)
At 4: 3rd Golden Harvest Handicap

NANCY HUANG (1979)
At 3: 2nd Acorn Stakes

NANCY JR. (1964)
At 3: Won Kentucky Oaks

NANNERL (1987)
At 5: 3rd Ruffian Handicap
At 6: 2nd Go for Wand Stakes

NANTUA (1954)
At 2: 3rd Alcibiades Stakes

NANTWICE (1969)
At 5: 3rd Del Mar Handicap

NANY (1980)
At 4: 3rd Maskette Stakes

NANY'S SWEEP (1996)
At 5: Won Santa Monica Handicap

NAROLA (1959)
At 2: 2nd Gardenia Stakes

NARVA (1956)
At 4: 3rd Santa Margarita Handicap

NASCO (1955)
At 3: 2nd Dwyer Handicap

NASHARCO (1962)
At 3: 3rd California Derby

NASHMEEL (1984)
At 3: 2nd Yellow Ribbon Stakes

NASHUA (1952)
At 2: Won Hopeful Stakes
Futurity Stakes
2nd Cowdin Stakes
At 3: Won Flamingo Stakes
Florida Derby
Wood Memorial Stakes
Belmont Stakes

Preakness Stakes
Dwyer Stakes
Arlington Classic
Jockey Club Gold Cup
2nd Kentucky Derby
At 4: Won Widener Handicap
Grey Lag Handicap
Suburban Handicap
Monmouth Handicap
Jockey Club Gold Cup
2nd Woodward Stakes

NASHUA BLUE (1958)
At 2: 3rd Del Mar Futurity
At 3: 3rd Withers Stakes

NASHVILLE (1954)
At 2: 2nd Starlet Stakes

NASKRA (1967)
At 3: 3rd Blue Grass Stakes
Belmont Stakes
Lawrence Realization Stakes
At 5: 3rd Suburban Handicap

NASKRA COLORS (1992)
At 5: 3rd Three Chimneys Spinster Stakes

NASKRA'S BREEZE (1977)
At 5: Won United Nations Handicap
Man o' War Stakes
2nd Turf Classic

NASOMO (1956)
At 3: 3rd Lawrence Realization Stakes
At 6: 2nd Donn Handicap

NASOPHAR (1946)
At 3: Won Delaware Oaks

NASR EL ARAB (1985)
At 3: Won Oak Tree Invitational Stakes
3rd Hollywood Turf Cup
At 4: Won Charles H. Strub Stakes
San Juan Capistrano Handicap
2nd Hollywood Turf Handicap

NASRINA (1953)
At 2: Won Gardenia Stakes
Frizette Stakes
3rd Selima Stakes

NASSIPOUR (1980)
At 5: Won Rothmans International Stakes

NASTIQUE (1984)
At 3: Won Ladies Handicap
At 4: Won Delaware Handicap
2nd Yellow Ribbon Stakes
At 5: Won Delaware Handicap

NASTURTIUM (1956)
At 2: 3rd Princess Pat Stakes

NASTY AND BOLD (1975)
At 2: 3rd Futurity Stakes
At 3: Won American Derby
Brooklyn Handicap
3rd Travers Stakes
Marlboro Cup Handicap

NASTY STORM (1998)
At 2: 2nd Spinaway Stakes
Walmac International Alcibiades Stakes
At 3: 3rd Test Stakes

NATALMA (1957)
At 2: 3rd Spinaway Stakes

NATASHKA (1963)
At 3: Won Monmouth Oaks
Alabama Stakes
At 4: 2nd Vanity Handicap

NATCHEZ (1943)
At 3: Won Travers Stakes
2nd Withers Stakes
Belmont Stakes
At 4: 2nd Suburban Handicap
At 5: 3rd Whitney Stakes

NATEGO (1957)
At 4: 2nd Michigan Mile and One-Sixteenth

NATIONAL (1961)
At 3: Won Ohio Derby
2nd Withers Stakes
3rd Jersey Derby

NATIONALORE (1995)
At 2: 3rd Breeders' Cup Juvenile
Hollywood Futurity

NATIVE ADMIRAL (1969)
At 3: 2nd Fountain of Youth Stakes

NATIVE BOUNDARY (1988)
At 3: 2nd Hollywood Derby

NATIVE CHARGER (1962)
At 2: 2nd Sapling Stakes
Hopeful Stakes
Futurity Stakes
At 3: Won Flamingo Stakes
Florida Derby

NATIVE COURIER (1975)
At 4: 2nd Man o' War Stakes
3rd Turf Classic

NATIVE DANCER (1950)
At 2: Won Hopeful Stakes
Futurity Stakes
At 3: Won Gotham Stakes
Wood Memorial Stakes
Preakness Stakes
Withers Stakes
Belmont Stakes
Dwyer Stakes
Arlington Classic
Travers Stakes
American Derby
2nd Kentucky Derby
At 4: Won Metropolitan Handicap

NATIVE DESERT (1993)
At 8: 2nd Eddie Read Handicap

NATIVE DIVER (1959)
At 4: Won Inglewood Handicap
2nd San Fernando Stakes
3rd San Carlos Handicap
At 5: Won Inglewood Handicap
3rd Hollywood Gold Cup
San Carlos Handicap
At 6: Won American Handicap
Hollywood Gold Cup
At 7: Won Hollywood Gold Cup
3rd Santa Anita Handicap
At 8: Won Hollywood Gold Cup
2nd Santa Anita Handicap
3rd San Antonio Handicap

NATIVE FANCY (1978)
At 2: 3rd Del Mar Debutante Stakes

NATIVE HONEY (1964)
At 2: Won Del Mar Debutante Stakes

NATIVE PLUNDER (1978)
At 4: 3rd La Canada Stakes

NATIVE ROYALTY (1967)
At 3: Won Gotham Stakes
At 4: Won Carter Handicap
Michigan Mile and One-Eighth
At 5: 3rd Carter Handicap
Massachusetts Handicap

NATIVE STALWART (1985)
At 2: 3rd Arlington-Washington Futurity

NATIVE STREET (1963)
At 2: Won Sorority Stakes
At 3: Won Kentucky Oaks

NATIVE UPROAR (1977)
At 3: 2nd Louisiana Derby

NATURAL (1945)
At 4: 2nd Sunset Handicap

NATURAL BID (1957)
At 4: 3rd Carter Handicap

NATURALIST (1962)
At 3: 2nd Everglades Stakes

NATURAL SOUND (1970)
At 2: Won Arlington-Washington Lassie Stakes

NATURE II (1963)
At 6: 3rd Black Helen Handicap

NAVAJO (1970)
At 3: 2nd Louisiana Derby

NAVAJO PRINCESS (1974)
At 5: 3rd Apple Blossom Handicap

NAVARONE (1988)
At 4: Won Oak Tree Invitational Stakes

NAVIRE (1989)
At 5: 2nd San Luis Rey Stakes

NAVY CHIEF (1947)
At 2: 2nd Hopeful Stakes
Tremont Stakes
3rd Saratoga Special
At 3: 3rd Jerome Handicap

NAVY PAGE (1950)
At 3: Won Jerome Handicap
2nd Vosburgh Handicap
Pimlico Special

NEAPOLITAN WAY (1971)
At 3: 2nd Preakness Stakes

NEARCTIC (1954)
At 4: Won Michigan Mile

NEARLY ON TIME (1974)
At 3: Won Whitney Handicap
2nd Florida Derby
3rd Suburban Handicap
At 4: 2nd Suburban Handicap

NEARWAY (1945)
At 4: 3rd Excelsior Handicap

NEDIYM (1985)
At 4: 2nd Sword Dancer Handicap

NEEDLE HIM (1963)
At 4: 3rd Dixie Handicap

NEEDLES (1953)
At 2: Won Sapling Stakes
Hopeful Stakes
3rd Garden State Stakes
At 3: Won Flamingo Stakes
Florida Derby
Kentucky Derby
Belmont Stakes
2nd Preakness Stakes
At 4: 3rd Gulfstream Park Handicap

NEEDLES N PENS (1967)
At 3: 2nd Belmont Stakes
3rd Dwyer Handicap

NEEDLES STITCH (1964)
At 5: 3rd Pan American Handicap

NEGOTIATOR (1974)
At 2: 2nd Matron Stakes

NEKE (1962)
At 2: Won Hollywood Juvenile Championship

NELL K. (1946)
At 3: Won Acorn Stakes
Gazelle Stakes
At 4: Won Top Flight Handicap
3rd Firenze Handicap

NELL'S BRIQUETTE (1978)
At 3: Won Santa Susana Stakes
2nd Fantasy Stakes

NEPOTISM (1943)
At 4: 3rd Vanity Handicap

NEUROLOGO (1965)
At 5: 2nd Hollywood Gold Cup

NEVADA BATTLER (1960)
At 4: Won San Fernando Stakes

NEVADA BIN (1961)
At 2: Won Hollywood Juvenile Championship

NEVADA P.J. (1961)
At 2: 2nd Hollywood Juvenile Championship

NEVER BEND (1960)
At 2: Won Futurity Stakes
Cowdin Stakes
Champagne Stakes
2nd Arlington-Washington Futurity
3rd Sapling Stakes
Garden State Stakes
At 3: Won Flamingo Stakes
2nd Kentucky Derby
Woodward Stakes
United Nations Handicap
3rd Preakness Stakes

NEVER BOW (1966)
At 4: Won Widener Handicap
2nd Grey Lag Handicap
At 5: Won Brooklyn Handicap
2nd John B. Campbell Handicap
Grey Lag Handicap
Amory L. Haskell Handicap

NEVER CONFUSE (1966)
At 2: 2nd Cowdin Stakes
3rd Futurity Stakes

NEVER GIVE IN (1957)
At 3: 2nd Wood Memorial Stakes
At 4: 2nd Widener Handicap

NEVER OUT (1999)
At 2: 2nd Walmac International Alcibiades Stakes

NEVER WINK (1966)
At 6: 2nd John B. Campbell Handicap

NEW ACT (1962)
At 2: 2nd Sanford Stakes

NEW COLLECTION (1973)
At 3: 2nd Arkansas Derby
3rd Illinois Derby

NEW COMMANDER (1957)
At 3: 2nd Gotham Stakes

NEW DISCOVERY (1979)
At 2: 3rd Champagne Stakes
At 3: 2nd Flamingo Stakes

NEW POLICY (1957)
At 3: Won Cinema Handicap
2nd American Derby
At 4: 2nd Los Angeles Handicap

NEW PROSPECT (1969)
At 4: 3rd Charles H. Strub Stakes

NEW REGENT (1977)
At 2: 3rd Laurel Futurity

NEW ROUND (1968)
At 2: 2nd Pimlico-Laurel Futurity

NEWSBEAT (1941)
At 7: 3rd Longacres Mile

NEWTON'S LAW (1990)
At 3: 3rd American Derby

NEXT MOVE (1947)
At 2: 2nd Demoiselle Stakes
At 3: Won Coaching Club American Oaks
Delaware Oaks
Gazelle Stakes
Beldame Handicap
Ladies Handicap
Vanity Handicap
2nd Acorn Stakes
Alabama Stakes
Sunset Handicap
At 4: 2nd Santa Anita Handicap
3rd Firenze Handicap
San Antonio Handicap
At 5: Won Firenze Handicap
Beldame Handicap
2nd Santa Margarita Handicap

NIAGARA (1968)
At 3: Won Cinema Handicap

NIARKOS (1960)
At 6: 2nd Jockey Club Gold Cup
3rd Manhattan Handicap
At 7: Won Gallant Fox Handicap
San Juan Capistrano Handicap
San Luis Rey Handicap
3rd Sunset Handicap
At 8: Won San Juan Capistrano Handicap
At 9: 2nd Century Handicap

NICE GUY (1955)
At 3: Won California Derby

NICKEL BACK (1982)
At 2: 2nd Breeders' Futurity

NICKEL BOY (1955)
At 4: 2nd Display Handicap
At 5: Won Display Handicap
2nd Sunset Handicap
3rd Gallant Fox Handicap
At 6: Won Manhattan Handicap
2nd Suburban Handicap
3rd Massachusetts Handicap
At 7: 2nd Display Handicap
3rd Jockey Club Gold Cup

NICK'S FOLLY (1971)
At 3: 3rd Arkansas Derby

NICOSIA (1972)
At 3: Won Hollywood Oaks

NIGHT IN RENO (1994)
At 2: 2nd Futurity Stakes

NIGHT INVADER (1966)
At 2: 2nd Sapling Stakes
3rd Arlington-Washington Futurity
At 3: Won Washington Park Handicap
2nd American Derby

NIGHT PATROL (1996)
At 6: 2nd Charles Whittingham Handicap

NIJINSKY'S PASSION (1995)
At 3: 3rd Santa Anita Oaks

NIJINSKY'S SECRET (1978)
At 5: Won Hialeah Turf Cup
3rd Budweiser Million
At 6: Won Hialeah Turf Cup
2nd Arlington Handicap

NILUFER (1949)
At 3: 3rd Beldame Handicap

NIMMER (1956)
At 3: 3rd Travers Stakes

NINE KEYS (1990)
At 4: Won Apple Blossom Handicap

NINES WILD (1989)
At 3: 2nd Haskell Invitational Handicap
Pegasus Handicap
3rd NYRA Mile Handicap

NIRGAL LAD (1951)
At 2: 3rd Pimlico Futurity

NITEANGE (1974)
At 4: 3rd Meadowlands Cup
At 7: 2nd Meadowlands Cup

NITE OF FUN (1986)
At 3: 2nd Coaching Club American Oaks
3rd Mother Goose Stakes

NO BIAS (1970)
At 5: Won Vosburgh Handicap
2nd Fall Highweight Handicap

NOBILIARY (1972)
At 3: Won Washington D.C. International

NOBLE AND NICE (1986)
At 5: 2nd Santa Barbara Handicap

NOBLE BRONZE (1975)
At 2: Won Hollywood Juvenile Championship
3rd Norfolk Stakes
At 3: Won California Derby
2nd Bay Meadows Handicap

NOBLE DANCER II (1972)
At 5: 3rd Bowling Green Handicap
At 6: Won Hialeah Turf Cup
United Nations Handicap
San Luis Rey Stakes
2nd San Juan Capistrano Handicap
3rd Hollywood Invitational Handicap
At 7: Won Pan American Handicap
United Nations Handicap
San Luis Rey Stakes
2nd Hialeah Turf Cup
3rd San Juan Capistrano Handicap

NOBLE FIGHTER (1982)
At 3: Won Turf Classic

NOBLE HERO (1945)
At 3: 2nd Lawrence Realization Stakes

NOBLE HOME (1980)
At 3: 2nd Jim Beam Spiral Stakes

NOBLE IMPULSE (1946)
At 2: 2nd Garden State Stakes
At 3: 3rd Preakness Stakes
At 4: 2nd Carter Handicap

NOBLE JAY (1959)
At 3: 3rd Dwyer Handicap

NOBLE MINSTREL (1984)
At 3: 3rd Hollywood Derby

NOBLE NASHUA (1978)
At 2: 2nd Champagne Stakes
At 3: Won Dwyer Stakes
Swaps Stakes
Jerome Handicap
Marlboro Cup Handicap

NOBLE NOOR (1957)
At 2: Won Hollywood Juvenile Championship
At 3: Won California Derby

NOBLE SEL (1956)
At 4: Won Bougainvillea Turf Handicap
2nd New Orleans Handicap
Canadian Championship Stakes

NO BODY ELSE'S (1980)
At 2: 3rd Selima Stakes

NO CHOICE (1983)
At 4: 3rd Ladies Handicap

NODOUBLE (1965)
At 3: Won Arkansas Derby
Michigan Mile and One-Eighth
Hawthorne Gold Cup
2nd American Derby
3rd Preakness Stakes
At 4: Won Californian Stakes
Brooklyn Handicap
Hawthorne Gold Cup
Santa Anita Handicap
2nd Gulfstream Park Handicap
Metropolitan Handicap
Hollywood Gold Cup
Woodward Stakes
Jockey Club Gold Cup
Charles H. Strub Stakes
At 5: Won Metropolitan Handicap
3rd Californian Stakes

NO DUPLICATE (1973)
At 3: 3rd Coaching Club American Oaks

NOHOLME II (1956)
At 5: 2nd Bougainvillea Turf Handicap

NOHOLME ATOLL (1966)
At 4: 3rd San Luis Rey Handicap

NOHOLME JR. (1966)
At 3: Won Cinema Handicap

NO LE HACE (1969)
At 3: Won Louisiana Derby
Arkansas Derby
2nd Kentucky Derby
Preakness Stakes

NO MATTER WHAT (1997)
At 3: Won Del Mar Oaks

NO MORE FLOWERS (1984)
At 3: 2nd Fountain of Youth Stakes
Florida Derby

NONNIE JO (1951)
At 5: Won Michigan Mile

NO NO BILLY (1967)
At 4: 2nd Washington Park Handicap
At 5: 3rd New Orleans Handicap

NO NO-NOS (1975)
At 2: 3rd Alcibiades Stakes

NONPRODUCITIVEASSET (1990)
At 4: 2nd Strub Stakes

NONSUCH BAY (1999)
At 3: Won Mother Goose Stakes
At 4: 3rd Go for Wand Handicap

NOON TIME SPENDER (1975)
At 2: 2nd Sapling Stakes
At 3: 2nd Flamingo Stakes

NOOR (1945)
At 5: Won Santa Anita Handicap
San Juan Capistrano Handicap
Golden Gate Handicap
American Handicap
Hollywood Gold Cup
2nd Jockey Club Gold Cup
San Pasqual Handicap
Manhattan Handicap
3rd San Antonio Handicap

NOORAN (1952)
At 5: 2nd Santa Margarita Handicap
At 6: 3rd Santa Margarita Handicap

NOORSAGA (1953)
At 2: Won Cowdin Stakes
3rd Remsen Stakes

NOORS IMAGE (1953)
At 2: 2nd Frizette Stakes

NOR II (1967)
At 5: Won San Luis Rey Handicap
3rd San Juan Capistrano Handicap

NORDICAN INCH (1996)
At 3: 2nd Garden City Breeders' Cup Handicap

NO REGRETS (1953)
At 3: Won California Derby
3rd Preakness Stakes

NO REPRIEVE (1960)
At 2: 3rd Breeders' Futurity

NO REVIEW (1985)
At 3: 3rd Yellow Ribbon Stakes
At 4: Won Santa Barbara Handicap
3rd Santa Margarita Handicap

NORMANDY GREY (1969)
At 2: 3rd Del Mar Futurity

NO ROBBERY (1960)
At 3: Won Wood Memorial Stakes

NORQUESTER (1986)
At 4: 2nd Meadowlands Cup

NORTH BROADWAY (1970)
At 2: 2nd Gardenia Stakes
At 3: 3rd Mother Goose Stakes

NORTH EAST BOUND (1996)
At 4: 2nd Breeders' Cup Mile

NORTHERN AFLEET (1993)
At 3: 3rd Malibu Stakes
At 4: 3rd Metropolitan Handicap

NORTHERN ASPEN (1982)
At 5: Won Gamely Handicap
2nd Santa Barbara Handicap

NORTHERN DANCER (1961)
At 3: Won Flamingo Stakes
Florida Derby
Blue Grass Stakes
Kentucky Derby
Preakness Stakes
3rd Belmont Stakes

NORTHERN DEAMON (1962)
At 5: 3rd Hialeah Turf Cup

NORTHERN EMERALD (1990)
At 5: Won Flower Bowl Invitational Handicap

NORTHERN ENSIGN (1992)
At 2: 2nd Futurity Stakes

NORTHERNETTE (1974)
At 4: Won Top Flight Handicap
Apple Blossom Handicap
2nd Spinster Stakes

NORTHERN MAJESTY (1979)
At 3: 3rd American Derby

NORTHERN QUEST (1995)
At 5: 2nd Hollywood Turf Cup

NORTHERN SEA (1974)
At 2: 2nd Frizette Stakes
Selima Stakes

NORTHERN SPUR (1991)
At 4: Won Oak Tree Invitational Stakes
Breeders' Cup Turf
3rd Eddie Read Handicap
At 5: 2nd Hollywood Turf Handicap
3rd Caesars International Handicap

NORTHERN STAR (1948)
At 2: 2nd Saratoga Special
At 4: Won Carter Handicap

NORTHERN TREND (1988)
At 5: 3rd Meadowlands Cup

NORTHFIELDS (1968)
At 3: Won Louisiana Derby
2nd Monmouth Invitational Handicap
3rd American Derby

NORTH FLIGHT (1966)
At 3: 2nd United Nations Handicap
Man o' War Stakes
At 4: 3rd John B. Campbell Handicap
At 5: 3rd Dixie Handicap

NORTH POLE II (1956)
At 4: 3rd Hialeah Turf Cup
Bowling Green Handicap
At 5: 3rd Bougainvillea Turf Handicap

NORTH SIDER (1982)
At 4: 3rd La Canada Stakes
At 5: Won Santa Margarita Handicap
Apple Blossom Handicap
Maskette Stakes
2nd Vanity Handicap

NORTH SOUTH GAL (1959)
At 3: Won Delaware Oaks

NORWICK (1979)
At 5: 3rd San Juan Capistrano Handicap

NO SCORE (1949)
At 2: Won Marguerite Stakes
3rd Demoiselle Stakes
At 3: 2nd Monmouth Oaks
At 4: 3rd Black Helen Handicap
Top Flight Handicap

NOSTALGIA (1974)
At 2: 2nd Remsen Stakes

NOSTALGIA'S STAR (1982)
At 3: 2nd Illinois Derby
3rd San Felipe Handicap
Santa Anita Derby
California Derby
At 4: Won Charles H. Strub Stakes
2nd San Fernando Stakes
3rd San Antonio Handicap
At 5: 2nd Marlboro Cup Handicap

NOTABLE II (1955)
At 6: 3rd San Juan Capistrano Handicap
At 7: 3rd Sunset Handicap

NOTABLE CAREER (1998)
At 2: Won Oak Leaf Stakes
2nd Vinery Del Mar Debutante Stakes

NOTATION (1986)
At 3: 2nd Illinois Derby

NOTEBOOK (1985)
At 3: 2nd Fountain of Youth Stakes
3rd Hutcheson Stakes
Florida Derby

NOTHING FLAT (1999)
At 3: 3rd Travers Stakes

NOTHIRDCHANCE (1948)
At 3: Won Acorn Stakes
2nd Comely Handicap
At 5: 2nd Ladies Handicap

NOTI (1960)
At 2: Won Hollywood Juvenile Championship

NOTORIOUS ROGUE (2001)
At 2: 3rd Hopeful Stakes

NOT SURPRISING (1990)
At 5: Won Vosburgh Stakes

NO TURNING (1973)
At 4: 3rd Arlington Handicap
At 5: 3rd Century Handicap

NOUREDDIN (1955)
At 3: 2nd Louisiana Derby
Wood Memorial Stakes
3rd Kentucky Derby
At 4: 2nd Stars and Stripes Handicap
United Nations Handicap
3rd Arlington Handicap

NOVEL NOTION (1975)
At 5: 3rd Pan American Handicap

NOVEMBER SNOW (1989)
At 3: Won Alabama Stakes
At 4: 3rd Go for Wand Stakes

NOW DANCE (1989)
At 3: 3rd Fantasy Stakes

NOWORK ALL PLAY (1988)
At 3: 3rd Blue Grass Stakes

NUBILE (1959)
At 4: 3rd Arlington Matron Handicap
At 5: 3rd Matron Handicap

NUCLEAR POWER (1953)
At 2: 3rd Washington Park Futurity

NUIT D'AMOUR (1977)
At 2: 3rd Matron Stakes

NULLIFY (1948)
At 2: 3rd Champagne Stakes
Tremont Stakes
At 3: 3rd Withers Stakes

NUMBERED ACCOUNT (1969)
At 2: Won Spinaway Stakes
Matron Stakes
Frizette Stakes
Selima Stakes
Gardenia Stakes
At 3: Won Spinster Stakes
3rd Delaware Handicap

NUNYA (1955)
At 2: 3rd Breeders' Futurity

NURSE O'WAR (1949)
At 2: 2nd Del Mar Debutante Stakes

NYCROS (1960)
At 3: 3rd Washington D.C. International

OAK DANDY (1958)
At 2: 3rd Washington Park Futurity

O'ALISON (1951)
At 2: Won Demoiselle Stakes
At 3: 3rd Delaware Oaks

OATH (1994)
At 2: Won Spinaway Stakes

OATS (1948)
At 3: 3rd Del Mar Derby

OBEAH (1965)
At 2: 3rd Frizette Stakes
At 4: Won Delaware Handicap
3rd Ladies Handicap
At 5: Won Delaware Handicap
2nd Beldame Stakes

OBEROD (1944)
At 2: 3rd Marguerite Stakes
At 3: 3rd Pimlico Oaks

OBEY (1959)
At 2: 2nd Washington Park Futurity
Cowdin Stakes
3rd Garden State Stakes

OBRAZTSOVY (1975)
At 5: 3rd Sunset Handicap
At 6: Won San Juan Capistrano Handicap
2nd San Luis Rey Stakes

OBSESSION (1958)
At 4: 3rd San Fernando Stakes

OCCASIONALY MONDAY (1977)
At 4: 2nd Louisiana Downs Handicap

OCCHI VERDI (1995)
At 3: 3rd Las Virgenes Stakes

OCEAN BAR (1965)
At 4: 2nd Grey Lag Handicap
At 5: 3rd Vosburgh Handicap

OCEAN DRIVE (1946)
At 2: 2nd Washington Park Futurity
At 3: 2nd Withers Stakes

OCEAN SOUND (1999)
At 3: 3rd Toyota Blue Grass Stakes

OCEAN VIEW (1993)
At 2: 2nd Oak Leaf Stakes
At 3: 3rd Hollywood Oaks

ODE (1986)
At 4: 2nd Budweiser International Stakes
3rd Man o' War Stakes

ODYLE (1993)
At 2: 2nd Norfolk Stakes
Hollywood Futurity
At 3: Won San Felipe Stakes

OFF (1964)
At 5: 3rd Sunset Handicap

OFFBEAT (1989)
At 2: 2nd Remsen Stakes
At 4: 2nd Gulfstream Park Handicap

OFFICE QUEEN (1967)
At 2: 2nd Selima Stakes
3rd Gardenia Stakes
At 3: Won Mother Goose Stakes
3rd Monmouth Oaks
Alabama Stakes
At 4: 3rd Top Flight Handicap

OFFICER (1999)
At 2: Won Del Mar Futurity
Champagne Stakes
3rd Hollywood Futurity

OFFICER'S BALL (1981)
At 2: Won Sorority Stakes

OFFLEE WILD (2000)
At 3: 3rd Toyota Blue Grass Stakes

OGYGIAN (1983)
At 2: Won Futurity Stakes
At 3: Won Dwyer Stakes
Jerome Handicap

O'HAPPY DAY (1980)
At 2: 2nd Hollywood Starlet Stakes
At 3: 3rd Santa Susana Stakes

O'HARA (1962)
At 2: 3rd Saratoga Special
At 4: Won Sunset Handicap
2nd Hollywood Gold Cup
Manhattan Handicap
3rd Jockey Club Gold Cup
San Luis Rey Handicap

OH JOHNNY (1953)
At 3: Won Withers Stakes
Travers Stakes
2nd Dwyer Handicap
3rd Wood Memorial Stakes
Lawrence Realization Stakes
Roamer Handicap
At 4: Won Display Handicap
At 5: Won Grey Lag Handicap
2nd McLennan Handicap
3rd New Orleans Handicap

OH LEO (1949)
At 2: Won Washington Park Futurity
2nd Arlington Futurity

OH WHAT A WINDFALL (1996)
At 2: Won Matron Stakes
At 3: 2nd Mother Goose Stakes

OIL CAPITOL (1947)
At 2: Won Breeders' Futurity
Pimlico Futurity
At 3: Won Flamingo Stakes
2nd Blue Grass Stakes
At 4: 2nd Arlington Handicap
Washington Park Handicap
At 5: Won New Orleans Handicap
2nd Arlington Handicap
At 6: Won Widener Handicap
Arlington Handicap
2nd McLennan Handicap
3rd New Orleans Handicap

OILFIELD (1973)
At 4: 2nd Hialeah Turf Cup

OIL PAINTING (1951)
At 2: Won Alcibiades Stakes
At 4: Won Maskette Handicap

OIL POWER (1966)
At 3: Won Lawrence Realization Stakes
2nd Jerome Handicap

OIL ROYALTY (1958)
At 4: 2nd Santa Margarita Handicap
3rd Ladies Handicap
At 5: Won Beldame Stakes
Vineland Handicap
At 6: Won Top Flight Handicap

OIL WICK (1957)
At 2: Won Kentucky Jockey Club Stakes

OINK (1957)
At 4: Won United Nations Handicap
2nd Santa Anita Handicap
Arlington Handicap

OKAVANGO (1970)
At 5: 2nd San Luis Rey Stakes
3rd Santa Anita Handicap

OKUBO (1978)
At 3: 3rd California Derby

OLD BAG (1963)
At 2: 3rd Kentucky Jockey Club Stakes

OLD COIN (1960)
At 6: 3rd Oaklawn Handicap

OLD DUDLEY (1964)
At 5: 3rd Oaklawn Handicap

OLD ENGLISH (1940)
At 6: 3rd San Juan Capistrano Handicap

OLDEN TIMES (1958)
At 3: 2nd San Felipe Handicap
At 4: Won San Antonio Handicap
San Juan Capistrano Handicap
2nd Santa Anita Handicap
San Fernando Stakes
3rd Californian Stakes
Santa Anita Maturity
At 5: 2nd San Carlos Handicap
At 6: Won Metropolitan Handicap
2nd Brooklyn Handicap
3rd Suburban Handicap
Hawthorne Gold Cup

OLD GOAT (1973)
At 2: 2nd Alcibiades Stakes

OLD HAT (1959)
At 4: 2nd Black Helen Handicap
At 5: Won Delaware Handicap
Spinster Stakes
2nd Matron Handicap
At 6: Won Black Helen Handicap
Matron Handicap
Michigan Mile and One-Eighth
3rd Top Flight Handicap
At 7: 2nd Spinster Stakes

OLDIE (1961)
At 2: 2nd Del Mar Futurity

OLD IRONSIDES (1949)
At 2: 2nd Saratoga Special

OLD KENTUCK (1941)
At 5: 3rd Stars and Stripes Handicap

OLD MOSE (1962)
At 2: 3rd Hollywood Juvenile Championship

OLD PUEBLO (1955)
At 2: Won Starlet Stakes
Del Mar Futurity

OLD ROCKPORT (1946)
At 3: Won Santa Anita Derby

OLD STORIES (1985)
At 2: 2nd Remsen Stakes

OLD TOPPER (1995)
At 2: 2nd Del Mar Futurity
At 3: 3rd Swaps Stakes

OLD TRIESTE (1995)
At 2: 2nd Norfolk Stakes
At 3: Won Swaps Stakes
At 4: Won Californian Stakes

OLE BOB BOWERS (1963)
At 5: 3rd San Luis Rey Handicap

OLE FOLS (1956)
At 4: 2nd San Carlos Handicap
At 5: 3rd San Carlos Handicap
At 6: 2nd San Carlos Handicap

OLE LIZ (1963)
At 2: 2nd Arlington-Washington Lassie Stakes

OLHAVERRY (1939)
At 7: Won Del Mar Handicap
2nd American Handicap
At 8: Won Santa Anita Handicap
2nd San Pasqual Handicap
At 9: Won San Pasqual Handicap
3rd Hollywood Gold Cup

OLIGARCHY (1954)
At 3: 2nd Hialeah Turf Handicap
At 4: Won Widener Handicap
3rd Gulfstream Park Handicap

OLIVER'S TWIST (1992)
At 3: 2nd Preakness Stakes

OLMODAVER (1999)
At 4: 2nd Strub Stakes

OLYMPIA (1946)
At 2: Won Breeders' Futurity
2nd Arlington Futurity
Cowdin Stakes
At 3: Won Withers Stakes
Flamingo Stakes
Wood Memorial Stakes
San Felipe Stakes
2nd Santa Anita Derby
At 4: Won Roseben Handicap
2nd Excelsior Handicap

OLYMPIAD KING (1960)
At 3: 3rd California Derby
Cinema Handicap
Hollywood Derby
Hollywood Gold Cup

OLYMPIC (1949)
At 4: Won Trenton Handicap
3rd Grey Lag Handicap

OLYMPIC CHARMER (1996)
At 3: 2nd La Brea Stakes

OLYMPIO (1988)
At 3: Won Arkansas Derby
American Derby
Hollywood Derby
2nd Secretariat Stakes
Super Derby

OMMADON (1998)
At 2: 2nd Remsen Stakes

ONANDAGA (1966)
At 4: 2nd Sunset Handicap
At 6: 3rd Bowling Green Handicap

ON-AND-ON (1956)
At 3: 2nd Arlington Classic
At 4: Won Tropical Park Handicap
McLennan Handicap
Brooklyn Handicap
2nd Widener Handicap
3rd Gulfstream Park Handicap
Hawthorne Gold Cup

ON A SOAPBOX (1996)
At 3: Won Coaching Club American Oaks

ONCE WILD (1985)
At 3: Won Withers Stakes
At 4: 2nd Vosburgh Stakes

ONE BOLD STROKE (1995)
At 3: 2nd Ohio Derby

ONE COUNT (1949)
At 3: Won Belmont Stakes
Travers Stakes
Jockey Club Gold Cup
2nd Withers Stakes
Lawrence Realization Stakes
3rd Preakness Stakes
At 4: 3rd Gallant Fox Handicap

ONE DREAMER (1988)
At 6: Won Breeders' Cup Distaff

ONE-EYED KING (1954)
At 3: 2nd Blue Grass Stakes
At 4: 2nd Massachusetts Handicap
Bowling Green Handicap
At 6: Won Arlington Handicap

ONE FOR ALL (1966)
At 3: 2nd Canadian International Championship
At 4: Won Pan American Handicap
Sunset Handicap
At 5: Won Canadian International Championship
3rd Pan American Handicap

ONE HITTER (1946)
At 3: 2nd Dwyer Stakes
Discovery Handicap
3rd Withers Stakes
At 4: Won Manhattan Handicap
Pimlico Special
At 5: Won Massachusetts Handicap
Whitney Stakes
2nd New York Handicap
Manhattan Handicap
At 6: Won Suburban Handicap
Monmouth Handicap
2nd Pimlico Special
3rd Metropolitan Handicap
Massachusetts Handicap
Whitney Stakes
Manhattan Handicap

ONE MAGIC MOMENT (1983)
At 3: 2nd Everglades Stakes

ONE MORE CHORUS (1966)
At 2: 2nd Hollywood Juvenile Championship

ONE MORE JUMP (1973)
At 4: 2nd Widener Handicap

ONE OF A KLEIN (1986)
At 2: Won Oak Leaf Stakes
3rd Hollywood Starlet Stakes

ONE ON THE AISLE (1972)
At 3: 2nd Man o' War Stakes
At 4: Won San Juan Capistrano Handicap
2nd Hialeah Turf Cup

ONE RICH LADY (1994)
At 4: 3rd Personal Ensign Handicap

ONE SUM (1974)
At 3: 2nd Hollywood Oaks
At 4: 2nd Top Flight Handicap

ONE WAY LOVE (1995)
At 5: 3rd Vosburgh Stakes

ONGOING MISTER (1985)
At 3: 3rd California Derby

ONION (1969)
At 4: Won Whitney Stakes
2nd Carter Handicap

ON MY HONOR (1960)
At 3: Won California Derby

ON MY WAY II (1970)
At 5: 3rd Washington D.C. International
At 6: 2nd Washington D.C. International

ON TARGET (1992)
At 2: Won Del Mar Futurity
3rd Champagne Stakes
At 3: 3rd Arkansas Derby

ON THE HALF (1943)
At 3: 3rd Swift Stakes

ON THE LINE (1984)
At 4: Won San Fernando Stakes
3rd Charles H. Strub Stakes
At 5: Won Carter Handicap

ON THE MARK (1947)
At 3: 3rd Blue Grass Stakes
At 4: 2nd Dixie Handicap

ON THE SAUCE (1981)
At 3: 3rd Gotham Stakes

ON THE SLY (1973)
At 3: 2nd Wood Memorial Stakes
At 4: Won Jockey Club Gold Cup
Hawthorne Gold Cup
3rd Michigan Mile and One-Eighth

ON TO ROYALTY (1985)
At 3: 2nd Ashland Stakes

ON TRUST (1944)
At 3: Won Santa Anita Derby
Will Rogers Handicap

2nd Preakness Stakes
Hollywood Derby
Cinema Handicap
3rd San Vicente Handicap
San Felipe Stakes
At 4: 2nd Santa Anita Handicap
Hollywood Gold Cup
Sunset Handicap
Santa Anita Maturity
3rd San Antonio Handicap
American Handicap
At 5: 2nd San Pasqual Handicap
At 6: 3rd Golden Gate Handicap

ON YOUR OWN (1951)
At 3: Won Gazelle Handicap

OPEN CALL (1978)
At 3: Won Rothmans International Stakes
At 4: Won Bowling Green Handicap

OPEN FIRE (1961)
At 5: Won Delaware Handicap
Spinster Stakes

OPENING BID (1967)
At 2: Won Oak Leaf Stakes
At 3: Won Santa Susana Stakes

OPENING VERSE (1986)
At 4: Won Oaklawn Handicap
3rd Hollywood Gold Cup
At 5: Won Breeders' Cup Mile

OPEN MIND (1986)
At 2: Won Breeders' Cup Juvenile Fillies
Demoiselle Stakes
2nd Frizette Stakes
At 3: Won Kentucky Oaks
Acorn Stakes
Mother Goose Stakes
Coaching Club American Oaks
Alabama Stakes
3rd Ruffian Handicap
Breeders' Cup Distaff

OPEN ROAD (1965)
At 4: 3rd Manhattan Handicap

OPEN SESAME (1951)
At 3: 2nd Coaching Club American Oaks
Delaware Oaks
Beldame Handicap
3rd Alabama Stakes
At 4: 2nd Delaware Handicap
At 5: 3rd Delaware Handicap

OPEN VIEW (1956)
At 3: 2nd Flamingo Stakes
3rd Gotham Stakes

OPS SMILE (1992)
At 5: Won Manhattan Handicap
3rd Turf Classic

OPTIMISTIC GAL (1973)
At 2: Won Matron Stakes
Frizette Stakes
Alcibiades Stakes
Selima Stakes
2nd Sorority Stakes
Spinaway Stakes
At 3: Won Ashland Stakes
Kentucky Oaks
Alabama Stakes
Delaware Handicap
Spinster Stakes
2nd Acorn Stakes
Mother Goose Stakes
Coaching Club American Oaks
3rd Ruffian Stakes

ORATION (1945)
At 3: 2nd California Derby

ORBITER (1961)
At 5: 2nd Canadian International Championship

ORBIT'S REVENGE (1989)
At 3: 3rd Super Derby

ORDERS (1971)

At 3:	2nd	American Derby
At 4:	3rd	Carter Handicap

ORDWAY (1994)

At 2:	Won	Moet Champagne Stakes
	2nd	Hopeful Stakes
	3rd	Breeders' Cup Juvenile
At 3:	2nd	Gotham Stakes
At 4:	2nd	Suburban Handicap

OR ET ARGENT (1961)

At 3:	3rd	California Derby
At 4:	Won	Bowling Green Handicap
		Dixie Handicap
	2nd	Charles H. Strub Stakes
	3rd	Man o' War Stakes
		San Luis Rey Handicap

ORIENTATE (1998)

At 4:	Won	Forego Handicap
		NAPA Breeders' Cup Sprint

ORMEA (1961)

At 5:	2nd	Vanity Handicap
At 6:	Won	Santa Barbara Handicap

ORNAMENTO (1960)

At 2:	Won	Breeders' Futurity
	3rd	Remsen Stakes

ORNERY ODIS (1978)

At 3:	3rd	Haskell Invitational Handicap

OTHELLO (1993)

At 2:	2nd	Del Mar Futurity

OTOMANO II (1965)

At 5:	3rd	New Orleans Handicap

OUEEE BEBE (1984)

At 3:	3rd	Breeders' Cup Distaff

OUIJA (1947)

At 3:	2nd	Monmouth Oaks
At 4:	3rd	Black Helen Handicap

OUIJA BOARD (1957)

At 3:	2nd	Roamer Handicap

OUR BETTERS (1952)

At 4:	Won	Santa Margarita Handicap
	2nd	Vanity Handicap
At 5:	Won	Santa Margarita Handicap

OUR CASEY'S BOY (1981)

At 2:	3rd	Champagne Stakes

OUR CHERI AMOUR (1968)

At 3:	Won	Coaching Club American Oaks
	2nd	Gazelle Handicap

OUR DAD (1956)

At 3:	3rd	Wood Memorial Stakes

OUR DARLING (1979)

At 3:	3rd	Spinster Stakes

OUR EMBLEM (1991)

At 4:	2nd	Carter Handicap
	3rd	Metropolitan Handicap
		Vosburgh Stakes

OUR ESCAPADE (1979)

At 3:	3rd	Florida Derby

OUR FIRST DELIGHT (1972)

At 4:	3rd	La Canada Stakes

OUR FLEET (1946)

At 2:	Won	Frizette Stakes

OUR HOPE (1957)

At 4:	2nd	Massachusetts Handicap
		Monmouth Handicap
		Whitney Handicap

OUR JEEP (1957)

At 4:	Won	Canadian Championship Stakes
At 5:	2nd	Canadian Championship Stakes

OUR MADAM LUCKY (1968)

At 2:	3rd	Oak Leaf Stakes

OUR MICHAEL (1963)

At 2:	2nd	Champagne Stakes
	3rd	Sapling Stakes
		Cowdin Stakes
At 3:	3rd	Jerome Handicap
At 4:	2nd	Carter Handicap

OUR MIMS (1974)

At 2:	2nd	Demoiselle Stakes
At 3:	Won	Fantasy Stakes
		Coaching Club American Oaks
		Alabama Stakes
		Delaware Handicap
	2nd	Kentucky Oaks
	3rd	Ashland Stakes

OUR NATIVE (1970)

At 3:	Won	Flamingo Stakes
		Ohio Derby
		Monmouth Invitational Handicap
	2nd	Blue Grass Stakes
	3rd	Kentucky Derby
		Preakness Stakes
At 4:	3rd	Grey Lag Handicap

OUR PAPPA JOE (1967)

At 5:	3rd	Arlington Park Handicap

OUR REQUEST (1946)

At 2:	3rd	Kentucky Jockey Club Stakes

OUR TALISMAN (1972)

At 2:	3rd	Hopeful Stakes

OUTDOORS (1969)

At 5:	2nd	Pan American Handicap
		Hialeah Turf Cup
		Hollywood Invitational Handicap
At 6:	Won	Hialeah Turf Cup
	3rd	Jockey Club Gold Cup

OUTER SPACE (1954)

At 3:	Won	Mother Goose Stakes
	2nd	Top Flight Handicap
	3rd	Alabama Stakes
At 4:	Won	Beldame Handicap
	2nd	Top Flight Handicap

OUTING CLASS (1960)

At 2:	Won	Hopeful Stakes
	2nd	Futurity Stakes
	3rd	Champagne Stakes
At 3:	Won	Dwyer Handicap
	3rd	Jerome Handicap

OUTLAND (1946)

At 5:	3rd	Massachusetts Handicap

OUT OF HOCK (1979)

At 2:	2nd	Hopeful Stakes

OUT OF PLACE (1987)

At 5:	2nd	Donn Handicap
		Philip H. Iselin Handicap
		Whitney Handicap
	3rd	Woodward Stakes

OUT OF SYNC (1998)

At 2:	2nd	Frizette Stakes

OUTOFTHEBOX (1998)

At 3:	Won	Super Derby
	2nd	Fountain of Youth Stakes
		Florida Derby

OUT OF THE EAST (1970)

At 3:	3rd	San Felipe Handicap
		Santa Anita Derby
At 5:	2nd	Santa Anita Handicap

OUT OF THE WAY (1965)

At 3:	Won	Jersey Derby
		Massachusetts Handicap
	2nd	Preakness Stakes
		Dwyer Handicap

OUTSTANDINGLY (1982)

At 2:	Won	Breeders' Cup Juvenile Fillies
At 4:	3rd	Vanity Handicap
		Breeders' Cup Distaff

OUT THE WINDOW (1964)

At 3:	Won	Ohio Derby
At 5:	2nd	Washington Park Handicap
	3rd	Donn Handicap

OUT TO LUNCH (1971)

At 3:	2nd	Fantasy Stakes

OVER ALL (1985)

At 2:	Won	Matron Stakes

OVERBURY (1991)

At 3:	Won	American Derby

OVERSKATE (1975)

At 4:	Won	Bowling Green Handicap
	3rd	United Nations Handicap

OVER THE COUNTER (1964)

At 6:	3rd	Sunset Handicap
At 7:	Won	Sunset Handicap
At 8:	2nd	Sunset Handicap

OWNERS CHOICE (1944)

At 3:	Won	Swift Stakes
		San Felipe Stakes
	3rd	Wood Memorial Stakes
At 4:	2nd	Roseben Handicap

PACIFICBOUNTY (1994)

At 3:	3rd	Arkansas Derby
At 4:	3rd	Pacific Classic

PACIFIC PRINCESS (1973)

At 2:	2nd	Matron Stakes
At 3:	2nd	Maskette Handicap
At 4:	Won	Hempstead Handicap

PACIFIC SQUALL (1989)

At 3:	Won	Hollywood Oaks
	3rd	Alabama Stakes

PACKER CAPTAIN (1972)

At 2:	Won	Breeders' Futurity
At 4:	2nd	Donn Handicap
	3rd	Gulfstream Park Handicap

PACK TRIP (1960)

At 2:	3rd	Futurity Stakes

PAC MANIA (1980)

At 3:	3rd	Hollywood Derby

PADDLEDUCK (1945)

At 4:	2nd	Top Flight Handicap
		New Castle Handicap

PADUA (1982)

At 3:	Won	Swaps Stakes

PAGE SEVEN (1955)

At 2:	3rd	Kentucky Jockey Club Stakes

PAIL OF WATER (1946)

At 2:	Won	Arlington Lassie Stakes
	2nd	Astoria Stakes

PAINTED WAGON (1973)

At 4:	2nd	Del Mar Handicap
At 6:	2nd	San Antonio Stakes
	3rd	Santa Anita Handicap

PAINT KING (1976)

At 3:	3rd	Swaps Stakes
At 4:	2nd	Californian Stakes

PAIRO (1963)

At 4:	3rd	Display Handicap

PAIR OF DEUCES (1978)

At 4:	Won	Louisiana Downs Handicap
	3rd	Marlboro Cup Handicap
At 6:	3rd	Sunset Handicap

PALACE LINE (1989)

At 3:	3rd	Jersey Derby

PALACE MUSIC (1981)

At 5:	Won	John Henry Handicap
	2nd	Breeders' Cup Mile
	3rd	Washington D.C. International

PALE PURPLE (1978)
- At 4: Won Matriarch Stakes

PALESTINIAN (1946)
- At 3: 2nd Wood Memorial Stakes
- Preakness Stakes
- 3rd Kentucky Derby
- Belmont Stakes
- Arlington Classic
- At 4: Won Westchester Handicap
- 2nd Hollywood Gold Cup
- 3rd Trenton Handicap
- At 5: Won Brooklyn Handicap
- Golden Gate Handicap
- 2nd Gallant Fox Handicap

PALIKARAKI (1978)
- At 5: Won Arlington Handicap
- 2nd Sunset Handicap
- 3rd Hollywood Turf Cup

PALLISIMA (1969)
- At 3: Won Hollywood Oaks
- At 4: 2nd Beverly Hills Handicap

PALM TREE (1951)
- At 3: 2nd Dwyer Stakes

PALTON (1973)
- At 5: Won Del Mar Handicap

PAMELA KAY (1983)
- At 2: 3rd Arlington-Washington Lassie Stakes

PAMPERED JABNEH (1970)
- At 6: 3rd Pan American Handicap

PAMPERED STAR (1987)
- At 3: 3rd Hollywood Oaks
- Alabama Stakes

PAMS EGO (1960)
- At 2: Won Frizette Stakes

PANCHO VILLA (1982)
- At 3: 2nd Gotham Stakes
- Jerome Handicap
- Vosburgh Stakes

PANICUM REPENS (1967)
- At 5: 3rd Gulfstream Park Handicap

PANORAMIC (1987)
- At 4: 2nd Rothmans International Stakes

PAOLINI (1997)
- At 6: 2nd Arlington Million

PAOLUCCIO (1962)
- At 4: 2nd Monmouth Handicap
- 3rd Suburban Handicap
- Dixie Handicap

PAPA KOO (1981)
- At 3: 3rd Tropical Park Derby

PAPAL POWER (1983)
- At 2: Won Hopeful Stakes
- 2nd Laurel Futurity
- 3rd Arlington-Washington Futurity
- At 3: Won Hutcheson Stakes
- 3rd Fountain of Youth Stakes

PAPA REDBIRD (1945)
- At 2: 3rd Kentucky Jockey Club Stakes
- At 3: Won Arlington Classic

PAPERBOY (1940)
- At 6: 2nd Sunset Handicap
- 3rd San Antonio Handicap

PAPER MONEY (1987)
- At 3: 3rd Coaching Club American Oaks

PAPER TIGER (1951)
- At 3: 3rd Dwyer Stakes
- At 4: 2nd Brooklyn Handicap
- Woodward Stakes
- Manhattan Handicap
- Canadian Championship Stakes
- 3rd Aqueduct Handicap
- At 5: 3rd Whitney Stakes
- Manhattan Handicap

PAPOOSE (1949)
- At 2: 2nd Demoiselle Stakes
- At 3: 3rd Fall Highweight Handicap

PAPPA RICCIO (1980)
- At 2: 2nd Champagne Stakes

PAPPA'S ALL (1958)
- At 2: Won Hollywood Juvenile Championship
- Arlington Futurity

PAPPA STEVE (1965)
- At 2: 3rd Saratoga Special

PARADE GROUND (1995)
- At 3: 3rd Wood Memorial Stakes
- Canadian International Championship

PARADE MARSHAL (1983)
- At 3: 3rd Peter Pan Stakes

PARADIES (1980)
- At 4: 2nd Maskette Stakes

PARADING LADY (1949)
- At 3: Won Acorn Stakes
- Vosburgh Handicap
- 3rd Black-Eyed Susan Stakes
- At 4: 2nd Firenze Handicap

PARADISE (1979)
- At 3: 3rd Rothmans International Stakes

PARADISE CREEK (1989)
- At 3: Won Hollywood Derby
- 2nd Secretariat Stakes
- Breeders' Cup Mile
- At 5: Won Early Times Manhattan Handicap
- Arlington Million
- Washington D.C. International
- 3rd Breeders' Cup Turf

PARADISE FOUND (1987)
- At 3: 3rd Peter Pan Stakes
- Jim Dandy Stakes

PARADOR (1952)
- At 2: 3rd Kentucky Jockey Club Stakes
- At 3: 3rd American Derby

PARAJE (1966)
- At 5: 2nd Jockey Club Gold Cup

PARDALA (1953)
- At 4: Won Diana Handicap
- 2nd Vineland Handicap
- At 5: Won Black Helen Handicap
- 3rd Molly Pitcher Handicap

PARDAO (1958)
- At 5: Won San Juan Capistrano Handicap

PAR EXCELLANCE (1977)
- At 2: 2nd Selima Stakes

PARFAITEMENT (1980)
- At 3: 2nd Wood Memorial Stakes
- 3rd Haskell Invitational Handicap

PAR FLITE (1981)
- At 3: 2nd Arlington Classic
- 3rd American Derby

PARIDA (1965)
- At 3: 3rd Mother Goose Stakes

PARIS PIKE (1957)
- At 4: 2nd Santa Margarita Handicap

PARIS PRINCE (1980)
- At 3: Won California Derby
- At 4: 3rd San Fernando Stakes

PARISTO (1978)
- At 3: Won Illinois Derby
- 3rd Preakness Stakes

PARKA (1958)
- At 5: 3rd Donn Handicap
- Dixie Handicap
- At 6: 2nd Donn Handicap
- Arlington Handicap

- United Nations Handicap
- At 7: Won United Nations Handicap

PARK DANDY (1950)
- At 5: Won Canadian Championship Stakes

PARLAY ME (1985)
- At 2: 2nd Champagne Stakes
- At 3: 2nd Jerome Handicap

PARLIAMENT (1946)
- At 2: 3rd Cowdin Stakes

PARLO (1951)
- At 2: 2nd Demoiselle Stakes
- At 3: Won Delaware Oaks
- Alabama Stakes
- Beldame Handicap
- Firenze Handicap
- At 4: Won Top Flight Handicap
- Delaware Handicap
- At 5: 2nd Top Flight Handicap

PARNASSUS (1950)
- At 4: Won Bougainvillea Turf Handicap
- 3rd Hialeah Turf Handicap

PARNELL (1968)
- At 4: 2nd Washington D.C. International

PAROCHIAL (1984)
- At 3: 3rd Super Derby

PARSEC (1977)
- At 2: Won Hollywood Juvenile Championship

PARTEZ (1978)
- At 2: 3rd Norfolk Stakes
- At 3: 3rd Kentucky Derby

PARTNER'S HERO (1994)
- At 4: 3rd Frank J. De Francis Memorial Dash

PASEANA (1987)
- At 5: Won Santa Margarita Handicap
- Apple Blossom Handicap
- Milady Handicap
- Vanity Handicap
- Breeders' Cup Distaff
- 2nd Spinster Stakes
- At 6: Won Apple Blossom Handicap
- Milady Handicap
- Spinster Stakes
- 2nd Santa Maria Handicap
- Santa Margarita Handicap
- Vanity Handicap
- Breeders' Cup Distaff
- At 7: Won Santa Margarita Handicap
- 2nd Santa Maria Handicap
- At 8: 2nd Santa Maria Handicap
- Santa Margarita Handicap
- Milady Handicap
- 3rd Apple Blossom Handicap

PASS A GLANCE (1971)
- At 4: 2nd Hempstead Handicap
- Delaware Handicap
- Ladies Handicap
- 3rd Beldame Stakes

PASS CATCHER (1968)
- At 2: 2nd Sapling Stakes
- Hopeful Stakes
- At 3: Won Belmont Stakes
- 2nd Jersey Derby
- 3rd Amory L. Haskell Handicap

PASSEMBUD (1951)
- At 2: 3rd Sapling Stakes

PASSEMSON (1947)
- At 3: 3rd Travers Stakes

PASSINETTI (1996)
- At 7: Won San Juan Capistrano Handicap

PASSING BASE (1980)
- At 3: 2nd Illinois Derby
- 3rd Arlington Classic

PASSING SHOT (1999)
- At 4: Won Personal Ensign Handicap
- 3rd Ruffian Handicap

PASSING VICE (1990)
At 2: 2nd Hollywood Starlet Stakes

PASSING ZONE (1977)
At 4: 2nd Sword Dancer Stakes

PASS THE GLASS (1971)
At 4: Won American Handicap
2nd Sunset Handicap
At 5: 2nd Century Handicap
3rd Hollywood Invitational Handicap

PASS THE LINE (1981)
At 4: Won Arlington Handicap
3rd Hialeah Turf Cup

PASS THE TAB (1978)
At 3: 2nd Illinois Derby

PASS THE WORD (1962)
At 3: 2nd Travers Stakes

PAST FORGETTING (1978)
At 4: 3rd Santa Margarita Handicap

PATCH (1948)
At 2: Won Del Mar Futurity
2nd Tremont Stakes

PATCHES (1987)
At 3: Won Hollywood Oaks

PATELIN (1968)
At 2: Won Alcibiades Stakes
Selima Stakes
2nd Spinaway Stakes
Matron Stakes

PATMIBOY (1944)
At 2: 3rd Kentucky Jockey Club Stakes

PATMIGAL (1947)
At 3: 3rd Santa Susana Stakes

PAT N JAC (1992)
At 3: 2nd Peter Pan Stakes
3rd Jim Dandy Stakes

PATROL (1999)
At 4: 3rd Woodford Reserve Turf Classic

PATROL WOMAN (1959)
At 5: 2nd Black Helen Handicap

PATTEE CANYON (1965)
At 3: 3rd Gazelle Handicap
Spinster Stakes
At 4: 3rd Delaware Handicap
At 5: Won Beverly Hills Handicap
2nd Black Helen Handicap
Vanity Handicap
3rd Spinster Stakes

PATTERN STEP (1985)
At 3: Won Hollywood Oaks

PAVOT (1942)
At 4: Won Jockey Club Gold Cup
Massachusetts Handicap
2nd Manhattan Handicap
3rd Roseben Handicap

PAX IN BELLO (1980)
At 2: Won Remsen Stakes
2nd Laurel Futurity
3rd Futurity Stakes

PAYANT (1984)
At 5: 3rd San Luis Rey Stakes
Hollywood Gold Cup

PAYING DUES (1992)
At 4: 2nd Breeders' Cup Sprint

PAY SECTION (1952)
At 3: 2nd California Derby

PAY THE BUTLER (1984)
At 4: 2nd Man o' War Stakes
At 5: 2nd Oak Tree Invitational Stakes
3rd John Henry Handicap

PAY TRIBUTE (1972)
At 4: Won Hollywood Gold Cup
2nd Californian Stakes
At 5: Won Meadowlands Cup
2nd Arlington Classic Invitational Handicap

PEACE (1985)
At 4: Won John Henry Handicap

PEACE CORPS (1966)
At 5: 2nd Whitney Stakes
At 6: 3rd Metropolitan Handicap

PEACE ISLE (1956)
At 5: 3rd Jockey Club Gold Cup

PEACE RULES (2000)
At 3: Won Toyota Blue Grass Stakes
Haskell Invitational Handicap
2nd Travers Stakes
3rd Kentucky Derby

PEAKS AND VALLEYS (1992)
At 3: Won Molson Export Million
Meadowlands Cup
At 4: 3rd Whitney Handicap

PEARL CITY (1994)
At 2: 2nd Spinaway Stakes
At 3: Won Ballerina Stakes
3rd Test Stakes
Gazelle Handicap

PEARLIE GOLD (1985)
At 2: 3rd Arlington-Washington Lassie Stakes

PEARL NECKLACE (1974)
At 4: Won Maskette Handicap
2nd Ruffian Handicap
Beldame Stakes
3rd Sheepshead Bay Handicap
At 5: Won Flower Bowl Handicap
2nd Top Flight Handicap
3rd Maskette Stakes

PEAT MOSS (1975)
At 6: 2nd Jockey Club Gold Cup
3rd Brooklyn Handicap
Meadowlands Cup
Sword Dancer Stakes

PEBBLES (1981)
At 4: Won Breeders' Cup Turf

PEDIGREE (1946)
At 3: Won Westerner Stakes
Cinema Handicap

PEEKSILL (1999)
At 3: 3rd Florida Derby

PEEPING TOM (1997)
At 3: 2nd Cigar Mile Handicap
At 4: Won Carter Handicap
2nd Metropolitan Handicap
At 6: 3rd Carter Handicap
Metropolitan Handicap

PEGEEN (1951)
At 2: 2nd Alcibiades Stakes

PELEGRIN (1961)
At 3: 3rd Cinema Handicap
At 4: 2nd San Fernando Stakes
3rd Charles H. Strub Stakes

PELLICLE (1943)
At 3: Won Louisiana Derby
2nd Blue Grass Stakes
American Derby
At 5: 3rd Stars and Stripes Handicap
At 7: 3rd Bougainvillea Handicap

PELLINORE (1966)
At 2: 3rd Del Mar Futurity

PELOUSE (1951)
At 4: 2nd Michigan Mile

PEN BAL LADY (1984)
At 3: 3rd Hollywood Oaks
At 4: Won Santa Barbara Handicap
Gamely Handicap
2nd Vanity Handicap

PENNINE WALK (1982)
At 4: 3rd Budweiser-Arlington Million

PENNON (1945)
At 2: 3rd Breeders' Futurity

PENNY FLIGHT (1970)
At 4: 2nd Santa Margarita Handicap
3rd Top Flight Handicap

PENNY'S RESHOOT (1991)
At 3: 2nd Test Stakes

PENTATONIC (1995)
At 5: 2nd Hempstead Handicap
3rd Personal Ensign Handicap
Beldame Stakes

PENUMBRA (1955)
At 4: 3rd Santa Margarita Handicap

PEPPER PATCH (1957)
At 5: Won Top Flight Handicap

PEPPERWOOD (1964)
At 2: Won Gardenia Stakes
3rd Frizette Stakes
At 3: 3rd Acorn Stakes
Coaching Club American Oaks

PEPPY ADDY (1972)
At 5: 3rd Amory L. Haskell Handicap

PERCEIVE ARROGANCE (1985)
At 4: 2nd Charles H. Strub Stakes
3rd San Fernando Stakes

PERCHANCE TO DREAM (1984)
At 3: Won Hollywood Oaks

PERCIPIENT (1981)
At 4: 2nd La Canada Stakes
3rd Santa Margarita Handicap

PERCUTANT (1991)
At 6: 3rd Arlington Million

PERE TIME (1943)
At 3: 2nd Hollywood Derby
At 4: 3rd San Antonio Handicap
Santa Anita Handicap

PERFECT ARC (1992)
At 4: 2nd Beverly D. Stakes

PERFECT BAHRAM (1943)
At 3: 3rd Withers Stakes

PERFECT CAT (1997)
At 4: 2nd Brooklyn Handicap

PERFECT DRIFT (1999)
At 3: 3rd Kentucky Derby
At 4: Won Stephen Foster Handicap

PERFECTLY PROUD (1988)
At 3: 3rd Hollywood Derby

PERFECT MOON (2001)
At 2: 3rd Del Mar Futurity

PERFECT PLAYER (1981)
At 3: 3rd Ohio Derby

PERFECT SIX (1996)
At 2: 3rd Hollywood Starlet Stakes

PERFECT SKY (1962)
At 3: Won California Derby

PERFECT SOUL (1998)
At 5: Won Shadwell Turf Mile

PERFECT SPY (1985)
At 3: Won Hutcheson Stakes
3rd Gotham Stakes
Withers Stakes

PERFECT STING (1996)
At 3: Won Garden City Breeders' Cup Handicap
Queen Elizabeth II Challenge Cup
At 4: Won Breeders' Cup Filly and Mare Turf

PERFECT TAN (1965)
At 3: 3rd Florida Derby

PERFORMING ART (1961)
At 3: 3rd Hollywood Derby

PERIZADE (1956)
At 5: Won Vanity Handicap

PERMIAN (1951)
At 2: 2nd Sapling Stakes

PERRAULT (1977)
At 5: Won Hollywood Gold Cup
Budweiser Million
San Luis Rey Stakes
2nd Santa Anita Handicap
3rd Eddie Read Handicap
San Juan Capistrano Handicap

PERRIS (1961)
At 2: Won Del Mar Futurity

PERSEVERED (1984)
At 2: 2nd Hopeful Stakes

PERSIAN GOLD (1957)
At 3: Won Arkansas Derby

PERSIANLUX (1996)
At 5: 2nd San Juan Capistrano Handicap

PERSIAN TIARA (1980)
At 4: 2nd Washington D.C. International

PERSISTENT (1981)
At 2: 3rd Oak Leaf Stakes

PERSONABLE LADY (1981)
At 3: 2nd Santa Susana Stakes
3rd Fantasy Stakes

PERSONAL BUSINESS (1986)
At 4: 2nd Ruffian Handicap

PERSONAL ENSIGN (1984)
At 2: Won Frizette Stakes
At 3: Won Beldame Stakes
At 4: Won Whitney Handicap
Maskette Stakes
Beldame Stakes
Breeders' Cup Distaff

PERSONAL FLAG (1983)
At 3: 2nd Haskell Invitational Handicap
3rd Dwyer Stakes
Travers Stakes
Woodward Stakes
At 5: Won Suburban Handicap
2nd Brooklyn Handicap
Jockey Club Gold Cup

PERSONAL HOPE (1990)
At 3: Won Santa Anita Derby
2nd San Felipe Stakes

PERSONALITY (1967)
At 3: Won Wood Memorial Stakes
Preakness Stakes
Jersey Derby
Woodward Stakes

PERSONAL LEGEND (2000)
At 3: 3rd Del Mar Oaks

PERSONAL MERIT (1991)
At 3: 2nd Meadowlands Cup

PERTUISANE (1999)
At 3: 3rd Garden City Breeders' Cup Handicap
At 4: 3rd Diana Handicap

PESTER (1953)
At 2: 3rd Breeders' Futurity

PET BULLY (1948)
At 6: Won Fall Highweight Handicap
Washington Park Handicap
Woodward Stakes

PETER PIPER (1963)
At 5: 3rd John B. Campbell Handicap
Grey Lag Handicap

PETER PUMPKIN (1962)
At 3: 3rd Hawthorne Gold Cup

PETE'S FOLLY (1953)
At 4: 2nd Michigan Mile and One-Sixteenth
At 6: 2nd New Orleans Handicap

PETESKI (1990)
At 3: Won Molson Export Million
3rd Super Derby

PETEY COTTER (1946)
At 3: 2nd Louisiana Derby

PETIONVILLE (1992)
At 3: Won Ohio Derby
3rd Swaps Stakes

PETIT DUC (1964)
At 4: 2nd Canadian International Championship

PETITE ILE (1986)
At 4: Won Sunset Handicap
2nd Yellow Ribbon Stakes

PETITE ROUGE (1961)
At 2: Won Spinaway Stakes
2nd Sorority Stakes

PETIT POUCET (1992)
At 3: 3rd Secretariat Stakes
At 4: 2nd Early Times Turf Classic

PETROGRAD (1969)
At 4: 3rd Carter Handicap

PETRONE (1964)
At 5: Won Sunset Handicap
San Juan Capistrano Handicap
2nd San Luis Rey Handicap

PETRON'S LOVE (1975)
At 4: 2nd La Canada Stakes
Santa Barbara Handicap
At 5: 2nd Santa Barbara Handicap

PETTICOAT (1961)
At 4: 3rd Santa Margarita Handicap
At 5: 3rd Santa Barbara Handicap

PEU A PEU (1998)
At 4: 2nd Beverly Hills Handicap

PHALANX (1944)
At 2: Won Remsen Handicap
2nd Champagne Stakes
At 3: Won Wood Memorial Stakes
Belmont Stakes
Dwyer Stakes
Jockey Club Gold Cup
2nd Kentucky Derby
Travers Stakes
Lawrence Realization Stakes
3rd Preakness Stakes
American Derby
Discovery Handicap
New York Handicap
At 4: 2nd Jockey Club Gold Cup
3rd Westchester Handicap

PHANTOM JET (1984)
At 2: 3rd Cowdin Stakes
At 3: 3rd Everglades Stakes

PHANTOM ON TOUR (1994)
At 3: 2nd Arkansas Derby
At 4: 3rd Oaklawn Handicap

PHILATELY (1962)
At 2: 3rd Champagne Stakes

PHIL D. (1948)
At 3: Won San Felipe Stakes
2nd Blue Grass Stakes
At 4: Won San Antonio Handicap
2nd San Fernando Stakes

PHONE CHATTER (1991)
At 2: Won Oak Leaf Stakes
Breeders' Cup Juvenile Fillies

PHYSICIAN (1957)
At 4: 3rd Michigan Mile and One-Sixteenth
At 5: Won Santa Anita Handicap
At 6: Won San Antonio Handicap

PIANO JIM (1955)
At 3: Won Travers Stakes
2nd Jerome Handicap

PIA STAR (1961)
At 4: Won Suburban Handicap
Brooklyn Handicap
3rd Vosburgh Handicap
Whitney Stakes
At 5: Won Widener Handicap
3rd Seminole Handicap

PIAVE (1957)
At 8: 2nd Seminole Handicap

PIBE CARLITOS (1953)
At 4: Won William P. Kyne Memorial Handicap

PICADOR (1947)
At 4: 2nd Hawthorne Gold Cup
At 7: Won Hialeah Turf Handicap
2nd Bougainvillea Turf Handicap

PICK UP THE PHONE (1989)
At 3: 2nd Flamingo Stakes

PICO TENERIFFE (1996)
At 2: 3rd Frizette Stakes
At 4: 3rd Flower Bowl Invitational Handicap

PICTURE CARD (1945)
At 2: 3rd Sapling Stakes
Garden State Stakes

PICTURESQUE (1976)
At 2: 2nd Futurity Stakes
3rd Remsen Stakes
At 3: 3rd Ohio Derby

PICTURE TUBE (1973)
At 2: 3rd Frizette Stakes

PICTUS (1948)
At 2: 3rd Remsen Handicap

PIED A'TIERRE (1981)
At 2: 3rd Laurel Futurity

PIEDMONT LASS (1950)
At 2: 2nd Frizette Stakes

PIERPONTELLA (1957)
At 2: 2nd Princess Pat Stakes

PIET (1945)
At 2: Won Arlington Futurity
At 5: Won Whitney Stakes
2nd Metropolitan Handicap
Grey Lag Handicap
3rd Vosburgh Handicap
Queens County Handicap
At 6: 2nd Metropolitan Handicap
3rd Queens County Handicap
Carter Handicap

PIGREENY (1945)
At 3: 3rd Alabama Stakes

PIKE PLACE DANCER (1993)
At 3: Won Kentucky Oaks

PILASTER (1944)
At 5: 3rd Dixie Handicap
At 6: Won New York Handicap
At 8: 3rd Widener Handicap

PILLANLEBUN (1961)
At 5: Won Pan American Handicap
2nd Hialeah Turf Cup
At 7: 3rd Pan American Handicap

PILLARING (1988)
At 2: 2nd Del Mar Futurity
Norfolk Stakes

PILLASTER (1983)
At 2: Won Remsen Stakes
At 3: 3rd Man o' War Stakes

PILLOW TALK (1954)
At 3: 2nd Kentucky Oaks
Delaware Oaks

PILOT (1956)
At 2: 2nd Kentucky Jockey Club Stakes
Breeders' Futurity

PILSUDSKI (1992)
At 4: Won Breeders' Cup Turf

PINEAFF (1996)
At 3: 3rd Super Derby

PINEBLOOM (1945)
At 2: 2nd Arlington Futurity

PINE BLUFF (1989)
At 2: Won Remsen Stakes
3rd Futurity Stakes
Champagne Stakes
At 3: Won Arkansas Derby
Preakness Stakes
3rd Belmont Stakes

PINE CIRCLE (1981)
At 3: 2nd Arkansas Derby
Belmont Stakes
Travers Stakes
At 4: Won Widener Handicap
3rd Gulfstream Park Handicap
Brooklyn Handicap

PINEING PATTY (1992)
At 3: 2nd Super Derby

PINE TREE LANE (1982)
At 4: 2nd Breeders' Cup Sprint

PINETUM (1951)
At 2: 3rd Washington Park Futurity
Kentucky Jockey Club Stakes

PINJARA (1965)
At 4: Won Century Handicap
At 5: 3rd Century Handicap
American Handicap
At 6: Won Del Mar Handicap

PINK PIGEON (1964)
At 5: Won Santa Barbara Handicap
3rd Century Handicap
Oak Tree Stakes

PINK VELVET (1954)
At 3: 3rd Gazelle Handicap
Maskette Handicap

PINNACLE (1964)
At 2: 3rd Futurity Stakes

PIN PULLER (1979)
At 4: 2nd Pan American Handicap

PINTOR (1949)
At 3: 3rd Wood Memorial Stakes

PINTOR LEA (1953)
At 3: 3rd Florida Derby

PIPER PIPER (1987)
At 3: 3rd Ashland Stakes

PIPER'S SON (1958)
At 2: 2nd Washington Park Handicap
3rd Hawthorne Gold Cup

PIPETTE (1944)
At 2: Won Spinaway Stakes
2nd Demoiselle Stakes
Matron Stakes
3rd Frizette Stakes
At 3: 2nd Fall Highweight Handicap
At 5: 3rd Roseben Handicap

PIQUE (1941)
At 5: 2nd New Orleans Handicap

PIRATE COVE (1959)
At 4: 2nd Inglewood Handicap
Charles H. Strub Stakes
3rd San Fernando Stakes

PIRATE'S GLOW (1982)
At 2: 2nd Oak Leaf Stakes

PIRATE'S REVENGE (1991)
At 4: Won Milady Handicap

PISTOLS AND ROSES (1989)
At 3: Won Flamingo Stakes
Blue Grass Stakes
3rd Florida Derby
At 4: Won Donn Handicap
3rd Gulfstream Park Handicap
Pimlico Special
At 5: Won Donn Handicap

PIT BOSS (1953)
At 4: 3rd Inglewood Handicap

PIT BUNNY (1966)
At 3: 2nd Alabama Stakes
Gazelle Handicap

PIXIE ERIN (1959)
At 4: Won Santa Margarita Handicap
2nd Vanity Handicap

PIXY GAL II (1962)
At 5: 2nd Santa Barbara Handicap

PLACE CARD (1949)
At 2: Won Astarita Stakes

PLACID FUND (1992)
At 4: 3rd Carter Handicap

PLAINS AND SIMPLE (1975)
At 4: 3rd Delaware Handicap

PLANCHETTE (1954)
At 2: 3rd Selima Stakes

PLANKTON (1976)
At 2: Won Demoiselle Stakes
At 3: 2nd Coaching Club American Oaks
3rd Acorn Stakes
Mother Goose Stakes
At 4: Won Ladies Handicap

PLAQUE (1961)
At 5: 2nd San Luis Rey Handicap
San Juan Capistrano Handicap

PLATAN (1950)
At 2: 3rd Hopeful Stakes
Cowdin Stakes
At 3: Won Lawrence Realization Stakes
3rd Jockey Club Gold Cup
At 5: Won Arlington Handicap
3rd Michigan Mile

PLATINUM TIARA (1998)
At 2: 2nd Breeders' Cup Juvenile Fillies

PLAY FELLOW (1980)
At 3: Won Blue Grass Stakes
Arlington Classic
American Derby
Travers Stakes
2nd Super Derby

PLAY ON (1981)
At 3: Won Withers Stakes
2nd Preakness Stakes

PLAY TAG (1945)
At 3: 3rd Alabama Stakes

PLAY THE FIELD (1969)
At 5: 3rd Widener Handicap

PLAY THE KING (1983)
At 5: 2nd Breeders' Cup Sprint

PLAY THE RED (1973)
At 2: 3rd Remsen Stakes
At 3: 2nd Preakness Stakes
3rd American Derby

PLAY TIME (1958)
At 3: 2nd Kentucky Oaks

PLEASANT BREEZE (1995)
At 4: Won Meadowlands Cup Handicap
At 5: 2nd Pimlico Special
At 6: 2nd Gulfstream Park Handicap
3rd Pimlico Special

PLEASANT COLONY (1978)
At 2: Won Remsen Stakes
At 3: Won Wood Memorial Stakes
Kentucky Derby
Preakness Stakes
Woodward Stakes
2nd Travers Stakes
3rd Belmont Stakes

PLEASANTLY PERFECT (1998)
At 5: Won Breeders' Cup Classic / Dodge

PLEASANTNESS (1965)
At 2: 3rd Gardenia Stakes

PLEASANT STAGE (1989)
At 2: Won Oak Leaf Stakes
Breeders' Cup Juvenile Fillies
At 3: 2nd Kentucky Oaks
Acorn Stakes
3rd Coaching Club American Oaks

PLEASANT TAP (1987)
At 3: 3rd Kentucky Derby
At 4: 2nd Breeders' Cup Sprint
3rd Santa Anita Handicap
At 5: Won Suburban Handicap
Jockey Club Gold Cup
2nd Metropolitan Handicap
Nassau County Handicap
Woodward Stakes
Breeders' Cup Classic

PLEASANT VARIETY (1984)
At 5: 2nd San Juan Capistrano Handicap
3rd Sunset Handicap
Hollywood Turf Cup
At 7: Won San Luis Rey Stakes

PLEASANT VIRGINIAN (1984)
At 4: 3rd Meadowlands Cup

PLEASURE SEEKER (1966)
At 4: Won Hollywood Gold Cup
2nd Brooklyn Handicap
3rd Michigan Mile and One-Eighth

PLEDGE CARD (1984)
At 2: 2nd Laurel Futurity
At 3: 2nd Dwyer Stakes
Jim Dandy Stakes
3rd Swaps Stakes

PLENTY OF GRACE (1987)
At 3: Won Yellow Ribbon Stakes
At 5: 3rd Flower Bowl Handicap

PLENTY OF LIGHT (1997)
At 3: Won Three Chimneys Spinster Stakes
2nd Gazelle Handicap

PLENTY OF SUGAR (1991)
At 3: 2nd Coaching Club American Oaks

PLENTY OLD (1967)
At 3: 2nd San Felipe Handicap

PLENTY O'TOOLE (1977)
At 5: 3rd Santa Barbara Handicap

PLION (1955)
At 2: Won Sapling Stakes
At 3: Won Blue Grass Stakes
3rd Ohio Derby
Lawrence Realization Stakes
At 4: Won Whitney Stakes
3rd Michigan Mile and One-Sixteenth
Suburban Handicap

PLOTTER (1953)
At 4: Won Top Flight Handicap
2nd Beldame Handicap

PLUCK (1961)
At 4: 2nd Aqueduct Stakes
At 5: 2nd Massachusetts Handicap

Suburban Handicap
Aqueduct Handicap
3rd Monmouth Handicap
Brooklyn Handicap

PLUCKY LUCKY (1965)
At 4: 2nd Vosburgh Handicap

PLUCKY PAN (1964)
At 4: 2nd Delaware Handicap

PLUCKY ROMAN (1954)
At 4: Won Top Flight Handicap

PLUGGED NICKLE (1977)
At 2: Won Laurel Futurity
Remsen Stakes
At 3: Won Florida Derby
Wood Memorial Stakes
Vosburgh Stakes
3rd Jerome Handicap

PLUNDER (1946)
At 3: 2nd Alabama Stakes
Beldame Handicap

PLUNK (1970)
At 4: Won American Handicap
2nd Suburban Handicap

PLYMOUTH (1967)
At 3: 3rd Travers Stakes

POCHO'S DREAM GIRL (1994)
At 4: 3rd Beldame Stakes

POCKET PARK (1973)
At 4: Won San Fernando Stakes

POCKET ZIPPER (1978)
At 3: Won American Derby

POCOSABA (1957)
At 6: Won Black Helen Handicap

POINT DU JOUR (1961)
At 3: Won Roamer Handicap
At 4: 3rd Seminole Handicap

POINTER (1956)
At 4: 2nd Tropical Park Handicap

POINT GIVEN (1998)
At 2: Won Hollywood Futurity
2nd Champagne Stakes
Breeders' Cup Juvenile
At 3: Won San Felipe Stakes
Santa Anita Derby
Preakness Stakes
Belmont Stakes
Haskell Invitational Handicap
Travers Stakes

POINTMENOW (1964)
At 3: 2nd Illinois Derby
3rd Hawthorne Gold Cup

POKACHIEF (1969)
At 2: 3rd Arlington-Washington Futurity

POKER (1963)
At 3: 3rd Lawrence Realization Stakes
At 4: Won Bowling Green Handicap
2nd San Luis Rey Handicap

POKER NIGHT (1970)
At 3: Won Top Flight Handicap
2nd Acorn Stakes
Beldame Stakes
3rd Gazelle Handicap
At 4: Won Hempstead Handicap
2nd Maskette Handicap
Beldame Stakes
Ladies Handicap

POLAIRE (1996)
At 4: 3rd Beverly Hills Handicap
Yellow Ribbon Stakes

POLAMBY (1955)
At 3: 2nd Acorn Stakes
At 4: 2nd Delaware Handicap
Diana Handicap

POLAR EXPEDITION (1991)
At 2: Won Arlington-Washington Futurity
At 3: Won Jim Beam Stakes

POLAR SEA (1960)
At 6: Won San Luis Rey Handicap

POLAR TRAFFIC (1966)
At 3: 3rd Ohio Derby

POLEAX (1965)
At 2: 2nd Hollywood Juvenile Championship
3rd Del Mar Futurity
At 3: Won Hollywood Derby
3rd San Felipe Handicap
American Derby
At 4: 2nd Hollywood Park Inv. Turf Handicap
3rd Hollywood Gold Cup

POLE POSITION (1976)
At 3: Won San Felipe Handicap
At 4: 2nd Hawthorne Gold Cup

POLEY (1979)
At 4: 2nd Hollywood Gold Cup
3rd Californian Stakes
At 5: Won San Antonio Handicap

POLISH MINER (1997)
At 2: 3rd Remsen Stakes

POLISH NAVY (1984)
At 2: Won Cowdin Stakes
Champagne Stakes
At 3: Won Jim Dandy Stakes
Woodward Stakes
3rd Dwyer Stakes
Travers Stakes
Marlboro Cup Handicap

POLITELY (1963)
At 4: Won Molly Pitcher Handicap
At 5: Won Delaware Handicap
Ladies Handicap
2nd Beldame Stakes
Spinster Stakes

POLITICAL AMBITION (1984)
At 3: Won Hollywood Derby
3rd Hollywood Turf Cup
At 4: Won Hollywood Invitational Handicap

POLIZONTE (1960)
At 5: 2nd San Luis Rey Handicap

POLLEN (1962)
At 4: 2nd Santa Margarita Handicap
Vanity Handicap

POLLUTION (1966)
At 3: 3rd Lawrence Realization Stakes

POLLY PIPER (1968)
At 4: 2nd Top Flight Handicap

POLLY'S JET (1953)
At 2: 3rd Sapling Stakes
Futurity Stakes

POLY HI (1955)
At 2: Won Arlington Lassie Stakes
2nd Matron Stakes

POLYLAD (1956)
At 3: Won Roamer Handicap
2nd Lawrence Realization Stakes
At 4: 2nd Massachusetts Handicap
3rd Manhattan Handicap
At 5: Won Massachusetts Handicap
Gallant Fox Handicap
2nd Display Handicap
At 6: 2nd Massachusetts Handicap
3rd Brooklyn Handicap

POLYLADY (1959)
At 2: 2nd Sorority Stakes

POLYNESIAN (1942)
At 4: Won Roseben Handicap
2nd Trenton Handicap
3rd Vosburgh Handicap
At 5: 2nd Excelsior Handicap

POMONA (1993)
At 5: 3rd Yellow Ribbon Stakes

POMPEII (1997)
At 4: Won Personal Ensign Handicap
2nd Go for Wand Handicap

PONDER (1946)
At 3: Won Kentucky Derby
Arlington Classic
American Derby
Lawrence Realization Stakes
Jockey Club Gold Cup
2nd Belmont Stakes
At 4: Won San Antonio Handicap
Arlington Handicap
Santa Anita Maturity
3rd San Pasqual Handicap
Manhattan Handicap

PONTE VECCHIO (1970)
At 4: Won Maskette Handicap

PONTIFEX (1967)
At 2: 3rd Hopeful Stakes

PONTIVY (1959)
At 2: 2nd Spinaway Stakes
3rd Matron Stakes

POOL COURT (1975)
At 5: Won New Orleans Handicap

POONA II (1951)
At 4: Won Santa Anita Handicap

POOR BUT HONEST (1990)
At 5: 2nd Philip H. Iselin Handicap
Meadowlands Cup

POP CORN (1954)
At 5: 3rd Bowling Green Handicap

POPPY POPOWICH (1975)
At 3: 3rd Swaps Stakes

POR PROPHET (1957)
At 3: 2nd Arkansas Derby

PORT DIGGER (1965)
At 3: 3rd Louisiana Derby

PORTENTOUS (1970)
At 3: Won Oak Tree Invitational Stakes
At 4: 2nd Century Handicap

PORTERHOUSE (1951)
At 2: Won Futurity Stakes
At 4: 3rd Santa Anita Handicap
At 5: Won Californian Stakes
3rd Hollywood Gold Cup
At 6: Won Los Angeles Handicap
2nd Hollywood Gold Cup
3rd Sunset Handicap
At 7: 2nd San Carlos Handicap
3rd Santa Anita Handicap

PORTERSVILLE (1952)
At 3: 3rd Louisiana Derby
Withers Stakes
Belmont Stakes
At 5: Won Carter Handicap
Brooklyn Handicap

PORT WINE (1963)
At 2: Won Hollywood Juvenile Championship

PORVENIR II (1954)
At 8: 3rd Bougainvillea Handicap
Hialeah Turf Cup
At 9: 3rd Hialeah Turf Cup

POSADAS (1951)
At 6: Won San Luis Rey Handicap

POSSE (2000)
At 3: 3rd Vosburgh Stakes

POSSIBLY PERFECT (1990)
At 3: Won Yellow Ribbon Stakes
At 4: Won Santa Barbara Handicap
At 5: Won Gamely Handicap

POSSIBLY PERFECT *(Continued)*
Ramona Handicap
Beverly D. Stakes
2nd Beverly Hills Handicap

POSTAGE (1963)
At 3: 2nd California Derby

POST CARD (1947)
At 4: 2nd Monmouth Handicap
3rd Aqueduct Handicap
Trenton Handicap

POST IT (1992)
At 3: 3rd Ashland Stakes

POSTWARD (1957)
At 2: 2nd Selima Stakes

POTEEN (1994)
At 4: 3rd Woodbine Mile

POTENTIATE (1980)
At 3: 2nd Dwyer Stakes

POT O' LUCK (1942)
At 5: 2nd Gulfstream Park Handicap

POTRIDEE (1989)
At 5: Won Vanity Handicap
3rd Beverly D. Stakes

POURQUOI PAS (1992)
At 4: 3rd Ramona Handicap

POWDER BOWL (1992)
At 4: 2nd Flower Bowl Invitational Handicap

POWERFUL PUNCH (1989)
At 7: 3rd Gulfstream Park Handicap

POWER LUNCH (1987)
At 3: 3rd Arkansas Derby

POWER OF DESTINY (1961)
At 5: 3rd Grey Lag Handicap

POWER PLAY (1992)
At 5: 3rd John A. Morris Handicap

POWER TO STRIKE (1960)
At 3: 3rd Kentucky Oaks

POWIS CASTLE (1991)
At 3: 2nd Jim Beam Stakes

PRACER (1990)
At 4: 2nd Santa Barbara Handicap

PRACTICANTE (1966)
At 5: 3rd Bowling Green Handicap
Man o' War Stakes
At 6: Won San Juan Capistrano Handicap

PRAIRIE BAYOU (1990)
At 3: Won Jim Beam Stakes
Blue Grass Stakes
Preakness Stakes
2nd Kentucky Derby

PRAISE JAY (1964)
At 5: Won San Antonio Stakes

PRANKE (1984)
At 5: Won Sunset Handicap

PRAVIANA (1994)
At 4: 3rd Santa Margarita Handicap

PRAYERS'N PROMISES (1978)
At 2: Won Matron Stakes
3rd Frizette Stakes

PREACH (1989)
At 2: Won Frizette Stakes
3rd Spinaway Stakes

PRECIOUS STONE (1950)
At 3: 3rd American Derby
At 4: 2nd Michigan Mile

PRECISIONIST (1981)
At 3: Won Swaps Stakes
2nd Santa Anita Derby
Super Derby
At 4: Won San Fernando Stakes
Charles H. Strub Stakes
Breeders' Cup Sprint
2nd Californian Stakes
Hollywood Gold Cup
At 5: Won Californian Stakes
Woodward Stakes
2nd Philip H. Iselin Handicap
Marlboro Cup Handicap
3rd Hollywood Gold Cup
Breeders' Cup Classic

PRECOCITY (1994)
At 3: 2nd Super Derby
At 4: Won Oaklawn Handicap
2nd Pimlico Special
At 5: 3rd Oaklawn Handicap

PREDICTABLE (1967)
At 2: Won Selima Stakes
At 3: 2nd Gazelle Handicap

PREDICTED GLORY (1992)
At 3: 2nd Hollywood Oaks

PREEMPTIVE (1977)
At 2: 2nd Arlington-Washington Futurity

PREFONTAINE (1974)
At 4: 2nd Carter Handicap

PREGO (1959)
At 3: Won Flamingo Stakes
3rd Everglades Stakes

PREMIERE CREATION (1997)
At 3: 3rd Del Mar Oaks

PREMIER PROPERTY (1996)
At 2: 3rd Hollywood Futurity

PREMISE (1963)
At 2: 3rd Del Mar Debutante Stakes

PRENDASE (1951)
At 4: 2nd Washington D.C. International

PRENUP (1991)
At 2: 3rd Futurity Stakes
At 3: Won Jerome Handicap

PRENUPCIAL (1956)
At 5: 3rd Washington D.C. International

PRESS CARD (1990)
At 2: 3rd Champagne Stakes
At 3: 2nd Pegasus Handicap

PRESTIGIOUS LADY (1978)
At 2: 2nd Del Mar Debutante Stakes

PRETAL (1944)
At 5: 2nd Inglewood Handicap
3rd Hollywood Gold Cup

PRETENSE (1963)
At 4: Won Santa Anita Handicap
Gulfstream Park Handicap
San Antonio Handicap
2nd Hollywood Gold Cup
Washington Park Handicap
Sunset Handicap
3rd Californian Stakes
San Fernando Stakes
San Juan Capistrano Handicap

PRETKO (1963)
At 4: 3rd Canadian International Championship

PRETTY DISCREET (1992)
At 2: 3rd Matron Stakes
Frizette Stakes
At 3: Won Alabama Stakes

PRETTY PATTERN (1948)
At 3: 2nd Monmouth Oaks

PRETTY WILD (2000)
At 2: 2nd Hopeful Stakes
Futurity Stakes

PREVARICATOR (1943)
At 5: 2nd Del Mar Handicap
3rd San Carlos Handicap
At 6: 3rd Del Mar Handicap

PRICELESS GEM (1963)
At 2: Won Futurity Stakes
Frizette Stakes

PRIDE OF BURKAAN (1990)
At 5: 2nd Gulfstream Park Handicap

PRIDE PREVAILS (1990)
At 3: 3rd Flamingo Stakes

PRIDES PROFILE (1963)
At 2: 3rd Arlington-Washington Lassie Stakes
Gardenia Stakes
At 3: Won Gazelle Handicap
2nd Coaching Club American Oaks
3rd Mother Goose Stakes
Alabama Stakes
At 5: 2nd Black Helen Handicap

PRIMAL (1985)
At 3: 2nd Arkansas Derby
Ohio Derby
3rd Haskell Invitational Handicap
At 6: 2nd Gulfstream Park Handicap
Oaklawn Handicap

PRIMALY (1995)
At 2: 3rd Breeders' Cup Juvenile Fillies

PRIMATE (1949)
At 2: 2nd Futurity Stakes
At 3: 3rd Withers Stakes

PRIMERICA (1998)
At 5: 3rd Triple Bend Breeders' Cup Handicap

PRIME TIMBER (1996)
At 2: 2nd Hollywood Futurity
At 3: Won San Felipe Stakes
2nd Santa Anita Derby

PRIMITIVE HALL (1989)
At 6: 2nd Donn Handicap

PRIMITIVE PLEASURE (1980)
At 2: 3rd Laurel Futurity
Remsen Stakes

PRIMONETTA (1958)
At 3: Won Delaware Oaks
Alabama Stakes
2nd Monmouth Oaks
Spinster Stakes
3rd Beldame Stakes
At 4: Won Spinster Stakes

PRIMORDIAL II (1957)
At 7: Won Display Handicap
At 8: Won Widener Handicap

PRINCE ASTRO (1969)
At 4: Won Oaklawn Handicap

PRINCE BLESSED (1957)
At 4: Won American Handicap
Hollywood Gold Cup
2nd Santa Anita Maturity
San Juan Capistrano Handicap
3rd Sunset Handicap
San Fernando Stakes
Arlington Handicap

PRINCE BOBBY B. (1983)
At 3: 3rd California Derby

PRINCE CORTAULD (1950)
At 6: 3rd Washington D.C. International

PRINCE DALE (1959)
At 3: 2nd Arkansas Derby

PRINCE DANTAN (1970)
At 4: Won San Antonio Stakes
Santa Anita Handicap

3rd Vosburgh Handicap
Charles H. Strub Stakes

PRINCE DAVELLE (1961)
At 3: Won Arkansas Derby

PRINCE EVERETT (1987)
At 2: 2nd Young America Stakes

PRINCE HILL (1951)
At 3: 3rd John B. Campbell Memorial Handicap

PRINCE JOHN (1953)
At 2: Won Garden State Stakes
2nd Washington Park Futurity
Remsen Stakes

PRINCE KHALED (1954)
At 2: 3rd Del Mar Futurity

PRINCELET (1978)
At 3: Won Meadowlands Cup
At 4: 2nd Brooklyn Handicap
San Fernando Stakes

PRINCELY NATIVE (1971)
At 4: 3rd San Fernando Stakes

PRINCELY PROOF (1983)
At 5: 3rd Flower Bowl Handicap

PRINCE MAJESTIC (1974)
At 4: 2nd Oaklawn Handicap
At 5: 2nd Louisiana Downs Handicap
New Orleans Handicap
At 7: 2nd New Orleans Handicap

PRINCE MORVI (1952)
At 4: 2nd Canadian Championship Stakes

PRINCE NOOR (1952)
At 2: Won Kentucky Jockey Club Stakes
At 3: Won Everglades Stakes

PRINCE OF GREINE (1953)
At 4: 3rd San Luis Rey Handicap

PRINCE OF REASON (1971)
At 2: 2nd Champagne Stakes
3rd Hopeful Stakes
Laurel Futurity

PRINCE OF THIEVES (1993)
At 3: 2nd Swaps Stakes
3rd Kentucky Derby

PRINCE O'PILSEN (1960)
At 5: 3rd Bowling Green Handicap

PRINCE PABLO (1965)
At 3: Won San Felipe Handicap

PRINCE REAPER (1961)
At 4: 3rd Oaklawn Handicap

PRINCE SAIM (1963)
At 2: Won Garden State Stakes

PRINCE SPELLBOUND (1979)
At 3: Won Hollywood Turf Cup
2nd Santa Anita Derby
Hollywood Derby
At 4: Won Eddie Read Handicap
2nd Californian Stakes
San Luis Rey Stakes
3rd Hollywood Gold Cup
San Fernando Stakes
Hollywood Invitational Handicap

PRINCESS ARLE (1960)
At 4: Won Black Helen Handicap

PRINCESS DOUBLEDAY (1970)
At 2: 2nd Spinaway Stakes

PRINCESS KARENDA (1977)
At 4: Won Santa Margarita Handicap
2nd Vanity Handicap

PRINCESS LEEYAN (1958)
At 2: 2nd Sorority Stakes

PRINCESS LYGIA (1949)
At 2: Won Arlington Lassie Stakes
2nd Princess Pat Stakes
At 3: 2nd Hollywood Oaks

PRINCESS MITTERAND (1991)
At 2: 2nd Hollywood Starlet Stakes

PRINCESSNESIAN (1964)
At 3: 3rd Hollywood Oaks
At 4: Won Santa Barbara Handicap
Hollywood Gold Cup
2nd Vanity Handicap
Santa Margarita Handicap
At 5: Won Santa Margarita Handicap

PRINCESS ROONEY (1980)
At 2: Won Frizette Stakes
At 3: Won Kentucky Oaks
2nd Acorn Stakes
At 4: Won Vanity Handicap
Spinster Stakes
Breeders' Cup Distaff

PRINCESS TURIA (1953)
At 3: Won Kentucky Oaks
Acorn Stakes
2nd Coaching Club American Oaks
3rd Delaware Oaks
At 4: Won Delaware Handicap

PRINCESS V. (2000)
At 3: 3rd Prioress Stakes

PRINCE THOU ART (1972)
At 3: Won Florida Derby
2nd Flamingo Stakes
3rd Blue Grass Stakes
Travers Stakes

PRINCE TRUE (1981)
At 3: 2nd Swaps Stakes
3rd Santa Anita Derby
At 4: Won San Luis Rey Stakes
San Juan Capistrano Handicap

PRINCE VALIANT (1977)
At 3: Won Louisiana Derby
At 4: 3rd Widener Handicap

PRINCE WILLY (1954)
At 5: 3rd Man o' War Handicap

PRINCIPE (1965)
At 3: 2nd Gallant Fox Handicap

PRINTEMPS (1997)
At 4: 3rd Overbrook Spinster Stakes
At 5: 3rd Santa Maria Handicap
Santa Margarita Handicap
Overbrook Spinster Stakes

PRIOLO (1987)
At 3: 3rd Breeders' Cup Mile

PRIORITY (1976)
At 2: 2nd Del Mar Futurity

PRISMATICAL (1978)
At 3: Won Alabama Stakes

PRIVACY (1951)
At 3: 3rd Lawrence Realization Stakes

PRIVATE ACCOUNT (1976)
At 3: 2nd Dwyer Stakes
Arlington Classic
3rd Travers Stakes
At 4: Won Widener Handicap
Gulfstream Park Handicap

PRIVATE EMBLEM (1999)
At 3: Won Arkansas Derby

PRIVATE MAN (1988)
At 3: Won Ohio Derby
3rd Jersey Derby

PRIVATE PERSUASION (1991)
At 4: Won Vanity Handicap
3rd Milady Handicap

PRIVATE SCHOOL (1987)
At 3: Won Ohio Derby

PRIVATE STATUS (1991)
At 3: 3rd Ashland Stakes

PRIVATE TERMS (1985)
At 3: Won Gotham Stakes
Wood Memorial Stakes

PRIVATE THOUGHTS (1973)
At 4: Won Arlington Classic Invitational Handicap
2nd Marlboro Cup Handicap

PRIVATE TREASURE (1988)
At 2: 2nd Breeders' Cup Juvenile Fillies
Demoiselle Stakes
At 3: 2nd Ashland Stakes

PRIVILEGED (1962)
At 2: 2nd Arlington-Washington Lassie Stakes

PRIZED (1986)
At 3: Won Swaps Stakes
Breeders' Cup Turf
3rd Tropical Park Derby
At 4: Won San Luis Rey Stakes
At 5: 3rd Hollywood Turf Handicap

PRIZE GIVING (1993)
At 5: 3rd Hollywood Turf Handicap

PRIZE HOST (1955)
At 5: Won American Handicap
3rd Inglewood Handicap
Hollywood Gold Cup

PRIZE SILVER (1967)
At 2: 3rd Garden State Stakes

PRIZE SPOT (1976)
At 3: Won Hollywood Oaks
2nd Yellow Ribbon Stakes
3rd Kentucky Oaks
Ramona Handicap
At 4: 2nd La Canada Stakes

P.R. MAN (1974)
At 2: 3rd Hopeful Stakes

PRO BIDDER (1968)
At 4: 2nd John B. Campbell Handicap

PROBLEM SOLVER (1965)
At 3: 2nd Louisiana Derby

PROCESS SHOT (1966)
At 2: Won Arlington-Washington Lassie Stakes
2nd Selima Stakes

PROCIDA (1981)
At 3: Won Hollywood Derby

PROCTOR (1977)
At 2: 3rd Remsen Stakes
At 3: 2nd Secretariat Stakes

PRODANA NEVIESTA (1960)
At 3: 3rd Alabama Stakes

PROFIT KEY (1987)
At 3: Won Peter Pan Stakes
Dwyer Stakes
2nd Withers Stakes

PROFIT OPTION (1995)
At 7: 3rd Gulfstream Park Breeders' Cup Handicap

PROGRESSING (1957)
At 2: Won Pimlico Futurity
2nd Remsen Stakes

PROLIJO (1962)
At 4: 2nd Whitney Stakes

PROMINENT LADY (1958)
At 2: 3rd Gardenia Stakes

PROMISE (1965)
At 4: Won Carter Handicap
3rd Metropolitan Handicap

PROMISED CITY (1972)
At 3: Won Arkansas Derby
At 4: 3rd New Orleans Handicap

PROMISED LAND (1954)
At 3: Won Lawrence Realization Stakes
Roamer Handicap
Pimlico Special
2nd Gotham Stakes
3rd Wood Memorial Stakes
Gallant Fox Handicap
At 4: Won John B. Campbell Memorial Handicap
Massachusetts Handicap
San Juan Capistrano Handicap
3rd San Antonio Handicap
Grey Lag Handicap
Santa Anita Maturity
At 6: 3rd Trenton Handicap

PROMPT HERO (1956)
At 4: 3rd Canadian Championship Stakes
At 5: 3rd Canadian Championship Stakes

PROPERANTES (1973)
At 4: Won San Juan Capistrano Handicap
2nd San Fernando Stakes
Charles H. Strub Stakes
Century Handicap
3rd San Antonio Stakes
At 5: 2nd San Luis Rey Stakes

PROPER BOSTONIAN (1970)
At 5: 2nd Amory L. Haskell Handicap

PROPER EVIDENCE (1985)
At 4: 2nd Maskette Stakes

PROPER GAMBLE (1999)
At 3: 3rd Prioress Stakes

PROPER PROOF (1965)
At 3: Won California Derby
3rd San Felipe Handicap

PROPER REALITY (1985)
At 3: Won Arkansas Derby
Illinois Derby
At 4: Won Metropolitan Handicap
Philip H. Iselin Handicap

PROPHETS THUMB (1946)
At 3: Won Discovery Handicap
3rd Lawrence Realization Stakes

PROPONENT (1972)
At 5: 3rd Hialeah Turf Cup

PROSPECT BAY (1992)
At 4: 3rd Frank J. De Francis Memorial Dash

PROSPECTORS DELITE (1989)
At 3: Won Ashland Stakes
Acorn Stakes
3rd Kentucky Oaks

PROSPEROUS BID (1995)
At 3: 3rd San Felipe Stakes

PRO STYLE (1986)
At 3: 3rd Peter Pan Stakes

PROTAGONIST (1971)
At 2: Won Champagne Stakes
Laurel Futurity
2nd Futurity Stakes

PROTANTO (1967)
At 2: 2nd Garden State Stakes
At 4: Won Whitney Stakes
2nd Metropolitan Handicap
Brooklyn Handicap

PROUD AND BOLD (1970)
At 4: 3rd Donn Handicap
At 5: Won Donn Handicap
2nd Gulfstream Park Handicap

PROUD APPEAL (1978)
At 3: Won Blue Grass Stakes

PROUD ARION (1974)
At 4: 2nd Bowling Green Handicap

PROUD BIRDIE (1973)
At 3: 3rd Florida Derby
At 4: Won Marlboro Cup Handicap

PROUD CITIZEN (1999)
At 3: 2nd Kentucky Derby
3rd Preakness Stakes

PROUD CLARION (1964)
At 3: Won Kentucky Derby
2nd Blue Grass Stakes
3rd Preakness Stakes

PROUD CLARIONESS (1981)
At 3: 3rd Acorn Stakes

PROUD DELTA (1972)
At 4: Won Top Flight Handicap
Hempstead Handicap
Beldame Stakes
2nd Ladies Handicap
At 5: 2nd Top Flight Handicap

PROUDEST DUKE (1984)
At 3: 2nd Jersey Derby
Ohio Derby

PROUDEST ROMAN (1968)
At 2: Won Hopeful Stakes

PROUDEST ROMEO (1990)
At 3: 2nd Jim Beam Stakes

PROUD LOU (1979)
At 2: Won Frizette Stakes

PROUD SHOT (1990)
At 4: 3rd Philip H. Iselin Handicap

PROUD TRUTH (1982)
At 3: Won Fountain of Youth Stakes
Florida Derby
Breeders' Cup Classic
2nd Flamingo Stakes
Wood Memorial Stakes
At 4: 2nd Gulfstream Park Handicap
Suburban Handicap

PROVANTE (1971)
At 2: Won Breeders' Futurity

PROVE IT (1957)
At 4: Won San Fernando Stakes
Santa Anita Maturity
Santa Anita Handicap
2nd Californian Stakes
At 5: Won Inglewood Handicap
American Handicap
Hollywood Gold Cup
Sunset Handicap
Washington Park Handicap
2nd Californian Stakes

PROVE OUT (1969)
At 4: Won Woodward Stakes
Jockey Club Gold Cup
At 5: Won Grey Lag Handicap

PROVERB (1943)
At 3: 2nd Delaware Oaks
At 4: 2nd Molly Pitcher Handicap

PROVIDENTIAL II (1977)
At 4: Won Washington D.C. International
Hollywood Turf Cup

PROVINS (1988)
At 4: 2nd San Luis Rey Stakes

PROVISO (1964)
At 2: 3rd Champagne Stakes
Pimlico Futurity
Garden State Stakes

PROVOCATIVE (1946)
At 2: 3rd Arlington Futurity

PROWESS (1973)
At 2: 3rd Matron Stakes

PRUDY'S BOY (1949)
At 2: Won Starlet Stakes

PRUNEPLUM (1974)
At 3: 3rd Ohio Derby

PSYCHED (1983)
At 5: 2nd Top Flight Handicap

PUBLICATION (1999)
At 4: 2nd Triple Bend Breeders' Cup Handicap

PUBLIC PURSE (1994)
At 5: 2nd Hollywood Turf Cup

PUCKER UP (1953)
At 3: 3rd Maskette Handicap
At 4: Won Arlington Matron Handicap
Beldame Handicap
Washington Park Handicap
2nd Delaware Handicap
Spinster Stakes

PUERTO MADERO (1994)
At 4: 2nd Hollywood Gold Cup
At 5: Won Donn Handicap
3rd Californian Stakes
At 6: 3rd Santa Anita Handicap

PUKKA PRINCESS (1978)
At 4: 2nd Monmouth Handicap

PULPIT (1994)
At 3: Won Fountain of Youth Stakes
Toyota Blue Grass Stakes
2nd Florida Derby

PUMPKIN MOONSHINE (1974)
At 4: Won Carter Handicap

PUNCH LINE (1990)
At 4: 2nd Carter Handicap
3rd NYRA Mile Handicap
At 8: Won Fall Highweight Handicap

PUNKIN VINE (1951)
At 4: 3rd Monmouth Handicap

PURDUE KING (1985)
At 2: 2nd Norfolk Stakes
Hollywood Futurity
3rd Del Mar Futurity
At 3: 2nd San Felipe Handicap

PURE RUMOR (1989)
At 4: 2nd Suburban Handicap

PUR SANG (1948)
At 2: Won Kentucky Jockey Club Stakes

PUTNEY (1950)
At 2: 2nd Remsen Handicap

PUTOUT (1949)
At 2: 2nd Champagne Stakes

PUTTING (1983)
At 5: 2nd Sunset Handicap
Hollywood Turf Cup

PUYALLUP (1959)
At 5: 3rd San Juan Capistrano Handicap

PUZZLEMENT (1999)
At 4: 3rd Donn Handicap
Gulfstream Park Handicap
Woodward Stakes

PVT. SMILES (1970)
At 3: 2nd Jersey Derby

PYLADES (1953)
At 4: 3rd Grey Lag Handicap

PYRAMID PEAK (1992)
At 3: 2nd Haskell Invitational Handicap
Travers Stakes

PYRENEES (1952)
At 2: 3rd Hopeful Stakes

QUACK (1969)
At 3: Won California Derby
Hollywood Gold Cup
2nd San Felipe Handicap

Santa Anita Derby
Cinema Handicap
At 4: Won Californian Stakes
2nd Hollywood Gold Cup
At 5: Won Californian Stakes
3rd San Luis Rey Stakes

QUADRANGLE (1961)
At 2: Won Pimlico Futurity
At 3: Won Wood Memorial Stakes
Belmont Stakes
Dwyer Handicap
Travers Stakes
Lawrence Realization Stakes
2nd Metropolitan Handicap
3rd Flamingo Stakes
Jerome Handicap
Woodward Stakes
Jockey Club Gold Cup
At 4: 2nd Californian Stakes

QUADRAPHONIC SOUND (1998)
At 3: 3rd Super Derby

QUADRATIC (1975)
At 2: 3rd Remsen Stakes
At 3: 2nd Louisiana Derby

QUALIFY (1984)
At 2: Won Del Mar Futurity
2nd Breeders' Cup Juvenile

QUALITY T.V. (1977)
At 4: 3rd United Nations Handicap

QUARANTINE (1944)
At 2: 2nd Astorita Stakes
3rd Matron Stakes
Selima Stakes

QUARREL OVER (1980)
At 2: 2nd Alcibiades Stakes

QUAZE (1957)
At 3: 2nd Kentucky Oaks

QUAZE QUILT (1971)
At 3: Won Kentucky Oaks
Alabama Stakes
3rd Mother Goose Stakes

QUEENA (1986)
At 5: Won Maskette Stakes
Ruffian Handicap

QUEEN ALEXANDRA (1982)
At 5: 3rd Apple Blossom Handicap

QUEEN AMERICA (1956)
At 6: Won Santa Margarita Handicap

QUEEN EMPRESS (1962)
At 2: Won Frizette Stakes
Gardenia Stakes
2nd Selima Stakes
3rd Sorority Stakes
Spinaway Stakes

QUEEN HOPEFUL (1951)
At 2: Won Arlington Lassie Stakes
Princess Pat Stakes
2nd Matron Stakes
Selima Stakes
3rd Alcibiades Stakes
At 3: 2nd Kentucky Oaks
3rd Vineland Handicap
At 5: 2nd Spinster Stakes
3rd Arlington Matron Handicap

QUEEN LOUIE (1968)
At 4: 3rd Black Helen Handicap

QUEEN OF MONEY (1994)
At 3: 2nd Santa Anita Oaks

QUEEN OF SONG (1979)
At 4: 3rd Apple Blossom Handicap

QUEEN OF THE STAGE (1965)
At 2: Won Sorority Stakes
Spinaway Stakes
Matron Stakes
Frizette Stakes

QUEEN OF TRIUMPH (1989)
At 3: 3rd Mother Goose Stakes

QUEENS COURT QUEEN (1989)
At 3: 3rd Santa Anita Oaks
At 6: Won Santa Maria Handicap
Santa Margarita Handicap

QUEEN'S DOUBLE (1966)
At 2: Won Spinaway Stakes
3rd Matron Stakes
Selima Stakes

QUEEN'S HUSTLER (1969)
At 3: 2nd Oak Tree Invitational Stakes
At 4: Won San Juan Capistrano Handicap

QUEEN'S WORD (1996)
At 3: 2nd Gazelle Handicap

QUEEN TO BE (1973)
At 2: Won Del Mar Debutante Stakes
2nd Oak Leaf Stakes

QUEEN TO CONQUER (1976)
At 4: Won Ramona Handicap
3rd Yellow Ribbon Stakes
At 5: Won Ramona Handicap
Yellow Ribbon Stakes
2nd Hollywood Turf Cup

QUEEN TUTTA (1992)
At 4: 2nd Delta Air Lines Top Flight Handicap

QUEST (1999)
At 4: 2nd Jockey Club Gold Cup

QUEST FOR FAME (1987)
At 4: 3rd Breeders' Cup Turf
Hollywood Turf Cup
At 5: Won Hollywood Turf Handicap
3rd San Luis Rey Stakes
Breeders' Cup Turf

QUESTION TIME (1951)
At 3: 3rd Acorn Stakes

QUICK CARD (1973)
At 4: 2nd United Nations Handicap

QUICK CURE (1971)
At 2: 3rd Alcibiades Stakes

QUICKEN TREE (1963)
At 4: Won Display Handicap
2nd Gallant Fox Handicap
Charles H. Strub Stakes
At 5: Won Manhattan Handicap
Jockey Club Gold Cup
San Luis Rey Handicap
2nd San Antonio Handicap
Sunset Handicap
3rd Hollywood Gold Cup
At 6: 3rd Santa Anita Handicap
San Luis Rey Handicap
At 7: Won Santa Anita Handicap
San Juan Capistrano Handicap
2nd San Luis Rey Handicap

QUICK ICE (1978)
At 2: 3rd Breeders' Futurity

QUICK MISCHIEF (1986)
At 4: Won Ruffian Handicap
At 6: 2nd Ruffian Handicap

QUICK REWARD (1942)
At 4: Won Inglewood Handicap
American Handicap

QUICK TURNOVER (1975)
At 4: 2nd Del Mar Handicap

QUIET AMERICAN (1986)
At 4: Won NYRA Mile Handicap
2nd Charles H. Strub Stakes
Woodward Handicap

QUIET CROSSING (1976)
At 3: 3rd Dwyer Stakes

QUIET LITTLE TABLE (1973)
At 3: Won Dwyer Handicap
At 4: Won Carter Handicap
Suburban Handicap
At 5: 3rd Metropolitan Handicap

QUIET RESOLVE (1995)
At 5: 2nd Breeders' Cup Turf

QUIET STEP (1949)
At 3: Won Roamer Handicap
2nd Queens County Handicap
At 5: 2nd Widener Handicap

QUILCHE (1964)
At 5: 3rd Stars and Stripes Handicap
At 6: Won Century Handicap
San Luis Rey Handicap

QUILL (1956)
At 2: Won Matron Stakes
Gardenia Stakes
3rd Spinaway Stakes
At 3: Won Acorn Stakes
Mother Goose Stakes
2nd Coaching Club American Oaks
At 4: Won Delaware Handicap
2nd Top Flight Handicap

QUILLO MAID (1951)
At 4: 2nd Vanity Handicap

QUILLO QUEEN (1964)
At 2: 2nd Selima Stakes
At 3: Won Coaching Club American Oaks
Monmouth Oaks
2nd Acorn Stakes
Mother Goose Stakes

QUINPOOL (1990)
At 3: 3rd Kentucky Oaks

QUINTA (1963)
At 2: 2nd Sapling Stakes
At 4: Won John B. Campbell Handicap
2nd Seminole Handicap
3rd Donn Handicap
Gulfstream Park Handicap

QUINTAS VICKI (1973)
At 2: 3rd Spinaway Stakes

QUIP (1975)
At 4: 3rd Charles H. Strub Stakes

QUITA DUDE (1960)
At 3: Won Cinema Handicap
At 4: 2nd Los Angeles Handicap
3rd San Antonio Handicap
At 5: Won Grey Lag Handicap

RAAMI (1981)
At 3: 2nd Hollywood Turf Cup
3rd Oak Tree Invitational Stakes
Breeders' Cup Turf

RABIES (1943)
At 4: 3rd Vosburgh Handicap

RABLERO (1958)
At 4: 3rd Inglewood Handicap
Arlington Handicap
At 5: 2nd San Luis Rey Handicap
3rd San Juan Capistrano Handicap

RACE THE WILD WIND (1989)
At 3: Won Fantasy Stakes
2nd Hollywood Oaks
At 4: Won Santa Maria Handicap

RACETRACKER (1953)
At 6: 2nd Michigan Mile and One-Sixteenth

RACING FOOL (1952)
At 3: Won Blue Grass Stakes

RACING IS FUN (1979)
At 2: 2nd Norfolk Stakes
At 3: Won Hollywood Derby

RACING ROOM (1964)
At 4: 2nd Hollywood Gold Cup
Washington Park Handicap
At 5: 2nd San Antonio Stakes

RACING STAR (1982)
At 5: 2nd United Nations Handicap

RADAR AHEAD (1975)
At 3: Won Swaps Stakes
3rd Hollywood Derby
At 4: Won San Fernando Stakes

RAFFIE'S MAJESTY (1995)
At 3: 3rd Jim Dandy Stakes
Travers Stakes

RAFTY (1952)
At 6: Won Bowling Green Handicap
At 8: 2nd Hialeah Turf Cup

RAGING FEVER (1998)
At 2: Won Matron Stakes
Frizette Stakes
At 4: Won Ogden Phipps Handicap
2nd Ballerina Handicap

RAHY DOLLY (2001)
At 2: 2nd Hollywood Starlet Stakes

RAINBOW BLUES (1993)
At 3: 2nd Crown Royal Hollywood Derby

RAINBOW CONNECTION (1978)
At 2: 2nd Selima Stakes
At 3: 2nd Rothmans International Stakes
At 4: 2nd La Canada Stakes

RAINBOW CORNER (1989)
At 4: 3rd Eddie Read Handicap

RAINBOW DANCER (1991)
At 6: Won Hollywood Turf Handicap
Oak Tree Turf Championship

RAINTRAP (1990)
At 4: Won Rothmans International Stakes
At 6: Won San Juan Capistrano Handicap

RAINY PRINCESS (1975)
At 2: 2nd Arlington-Washington Lassie Stakes

RAISE A MAN (1977)
At 3: Won San Felipe Handicap
At 4: 2nd San Fernando Stakes

RAISE A Q (1982)
At 2: 2nd Sorority Stakes

RAISE D'ETRE (1964)
At 4: 3rd Ladies Handicap

RAISELA (1971)
At 2: 3rd Spinaway Stakes
Matron Stakes
At 3: 2nd Gazelle Handicap
3rd Acorn Stakes
At 4: Won Hempstead Handicap
3rd Delaware Handicap

RAISE YOUR GLASS (1968)
At 2: 2nd Sanford Stakes
3rd Sapling Stakes

RAISE YOUR SKIRTS (1972)
At 4: Won La Canada Stakes

RAJAB (1973)
At 4: 3rd San Fernando Stakes

RAJA BABA (1968)
At 2: 3rd Breeders' Futurity

RAJA'S DELIGHT (1978)
At 2: Won Del Mar Debutante Stakes

RAJA'S REVENGE (1983)
At 3: 2nd Hutcheson Stakes

RAJA'S SHARK (1981)
At 3: 2nd Wood Memorial Stakes
3rd Pennsylvania Derby

Jim Dandy Stakes
Vosburgh Stakes

RAMAHORN (1972)
At 2: 3rd Champagne Stakes
At 3: 3rd Withers Stakes

RAMANT (1961)
At 4: 2nd Sunset Handicap

RAMBLIN GUY (1991)
At 2: 2nd Del Mar Futurity
Norfolk Stakes

RAM O' WAR (1950)
At 5: 3rd McLennan Handicap

RAMPAGE (1983)
At 3: Won Arkansas Derby

RAMPART (1942)
At 5: 2nd New Castle Handicap
At 6: Won Black Helen Handicap
Gulfstream Park Handicap
3rd Vineland Handicap
New Castle Handicap

RAMPART ROAD (1986)
At 3: 3rd Dwyer Stakes

RANDAROO (2000)
At 3: 2nd La Brea Stakes

RANKIN (1977)
At 5: 3rd Century Handicap

RARE BEAUTY (1997)
At 2: 2nd Walmac International Alcibiades Stakes

RARE EXCHANGE (1960)
At 2: 3rd Spinaway Stakes

RARE PERFUME (1947)
At 2: 3rd Demoiselle Stakes

RARE RICE (1956)
At 3: 3rd Everglades Stakes

RARE TREAT (1952)
At 3: Won Firenze Handicap
At 4: Won Vineland Handicap
At 5: Won Ladies Handicap
2nd Molly Pitcher Handicap
Maskette Handicap
3rd Diana Handicap
At 6: 2nd Molly Pitcher Handicap
Vineland Handicap
3rd Diana Handicap

RASCAL LASS (1982)
At 3: Won Fantasy Stakes
2nd Santa Susana Stakes
3rd Kentucky Oaks

RASH PRINCE (1960)
At 2: 3rd Arlington-Washington Futurity

RASH STATEMENT (1957)
At 2: 3rd Princess Pat Stakes
Matron Stakes
At 3: Won Delaware Oaks
Spinster Stakes
3rd Coaching Club American Oaks
Monmouth Oaks
Alabama Stakes
At 4: 3rd Top Flight Handicap

RASTAFERIAN (1969)
At 5: 2nd Michigan Mile and One-Eighth
3rd New Orleans Handicap

RATINGS (1988)
At 4: 2nd Flower Bowl Handicap

RATTLE DANCER (1959)
At 2: Won Hollywood Juvenile Championship

RAVINELLA (1985)
At 4: 3rd Gamely Handicap

RAYKOUR (1985)
At 3: 2nd Hollywood Derby

RAYMOND EARL (1975)
At 3: 2nd Blue Grass Stakes
Illinois Derby

RAY'S FAIRY GOLD (1956)
At 3: 2nd Kentucky Oaks

RAY'S WORD (1977)
At 3: Won Illinois Derby

RAZEEN (1987)
At 4: 3rd Sunset Handicap

REAL BROTHER (1950)
At 3: 3rd Withers Stakes

REAL CASH (1987)
At 3: Won San Felipe Handicap
American Derby
2nd Arkansas Derby
3rd Jersey Derby
Ohio Derby

REAL CONNECTION (1991)
At 5: 2nd Yellow Ribbon Stakes
3rd Santa Maria Handicap
At 6: 2nd Gamely Handicap
Vanity Handicap
Ramona Handicap
At 7: 2nd Matriarch Stakes
3rd Milady Breeders' Cup Handicap

REAL COZZY (1998)
At 3: 2nd Kentucky Oaks
Mother Goose Stakes
3rd Acorn Stakes

REAL DELIGHT (1949)
At 3: Won Kentucky Oaks
Black-Eyed Susan Stakes
Coaching Club American Oaks
Arlington Matron Stakes
Beldame Handicap
At 4: Won Arlington Matron Handicap

REAL FOREST (1983)
At 3: 3rd Tropical Park Derby

REAL GOOD DEAL (1961)
At 3: Won California Derby
Hollywood Derby
2nd Cinema Handicap
3rd San Felipe Handicap

REALITY ROAD (1992)
At 3: 2nd Dwyer Stakes

REALLY HAPPY (1994)
At 3: 3rd Hollywood Oaks

REALLY POLISH (1995)
At 3: 3rd Kentucky Oaks

REAL PRIZE (1978)
At 3: 2nd Coaching Club American Oaks

REAL QUIET (1995)
At 2: Won Hollywood Futurity
At 3: Won Kentucky Derby
Preakness Stakes
2nd San Felipe Stakes
Santa Anita Derby
Belmont Stakes
At 4: Won Pimlico Special
Sempra Energy Hollywood Gold Cup

REAL SWEET DEAL (1962)
At 2: 3rd Del Mar Debutante Stakes

REAL TWISTER (1979)
At 2: 2nd Remsen Stakes
3rd Young America Stakes

REAP (1980)
At 3: 3rd Secretariat Stakes

REAPING RIGHT (1953)
At 3: Won Louisiana Derby
3rd Blue Grass Stakes

RE-ARMED (1947)
At 2: 2nd Washington Park Futurity

REASON TO HAIL (1964)
At 3: Won California Derby
2nd Travers Stakes
3rd Florida Derby
Gotham Stakes
Withers Stakes

RECCE (1942)
At 4: 3rd Top Flight Handicap

RECESS (1949)
At 2: 3rd Spinaway Stakes

RECITE (1956)
At 2: 2nd Spinaway Stakes

RECORD DASH (1962)
At 3: 3rd Withers Stakes

RECUSANT (1978)
At 4: Won Hawthorne Gold Cup

RED ATTACK (1982)
At 3: 2nd Arlington Classic
American Derby

REDATTORE (1995)
At 6: Won Eddie Read Handicap
3rd Arlington Million
At 7: 2nd Shoemaker Breeders' Cup Mile
3rd Eddie Read Handicap
At 8: Won Shoemaker Breeders' Cup Mile

RED BISHOP (1988)
At 7: Won San Juan Capistrano Handicap

RED BULLET (1997)
At 3: Won Preakness Stakes
2nd Wood Memorial Stakes
At 4: 3rd Cigar Mile Handicap

REDCALL (1990)
At 4: 2nd Washington D.C. International

RED CAMELIA (1946)
At 4: Won Firenze Handicap
New Orleans Handicap

RED CROSS (1947)
At 2: 2nd Arlington Lassie Stakes
3rd Princess Pat Stakes

RED CROSS (1972)
At 3: 3rd Ashland Stakes

RED GAR (1959)
At 5: 2nd Carter Handicap

RED HANNIGAN (1951)
At 3: 3rd Louisiana Derby
At 4: Won Roseben Handicap
At 5: Won Carter Handicap

RED ORANGE (1969)
At 4: 3rd Hialeah Turf Cup

RED REALITY (1966)
At 3: 2nd Lawrence Realization Stakes
At 4: 2nd Hawthorne Gold Cup
At 5: 3rd Manhattan Handicap
At 6: 3rd United Nations Handicap
At 7: Won Del Mar Handicap
2nd Bowling Green Handicap
3rd Arlington Handicap

RED SENSATION (1974)
At 2: 3rd Hollywood Juvenile Championship

RED SHOES (1943)
At 3: Won Pimlico Oaks
2nd Coaching Club American Oaks
3rd Delaware Oaks
At 5: 2nd Top Flight Handicap
3rd Firenze Handicap

REDTOP III (1969)
At 5: Won Del Mar Handicap

REEF SEARCHER (1977)
At 5: 2nd Oaklawn Handicap

REFINADO TOM (1993)
At 5: 3rd San Antonio Handicap

REFLECTED GLORY (1964)
At 3: Won Everglades Stakes
Flamingo Stakes

REFUTE (1957)
At 3: 2nd Monmouth Oaks

REGAL (1947)
At 4: 3rd Comely Handicap

REGAL AND ROYAL (1975)
At 2: 3rd Hopeful Stakes

REGALBERTO (1978)
At 2: 2nd Norfolk Stakes
At 4: 3rd Oak Tree Invitational Stakes

REGAL CLASSIC (1985)
At 2: 2nd Breeders' Cup Juvenile
3rd Hollywood Futurity
At 3: 3rd Blue Grass Stakes

REGAL DISCOVERY (1992)
At 3: 2nd Molson Export Million

REGAL DREAMER (1983)
At 2: 2nd Breeders' Futurity
At 3: 3rd Fountain of Youth Stakes

REGAL GLEAM (1964)
At 2: Won Frizette Stakes
Selima Stakes
3rd Matron Stakes

REGAL WINE (1967)
At 2: 3rd Del Mar Debutante Stakes

REGENCY (1990)
At 3: 3rd Rothmans International Stakes
At 4: 3rd Hollywood Turf Cup

REGION (1989)
At 5: 2nd San Antonio Handicap

REGISTER (1953)
At 2: Won Spinaway Stakes

REHABILITATE (1963)
At 3: 2nd Sunset Handicap
3rd Blue Grass Stakes
Hollywood Derby

REIGH BELLE (1945)
At 3: 2nd Kentucky Oaks

REIGN ROAD (1988)
At 2: 3rd Hollywood Futurity
At 4: 3rd Charles H. Strub Stakes
At 5: 3rd San Antonio Handicap

REINE DE ROMANCE (1998)
At 3: 3rd Del Mar Oaks

REINE MATHILDE (1981)
At 3: 3rd Hollywood Derby

REINVESTED (1979)
At 3: Won Super Derby
3rd Kentucky Derby
Dwyer Stakes

REINZI (1955)
At 5: 2nd Trenton Handicap
At 6: 3rd Whitney Handicap

REJECTED (1950)
At 3: Won Westerner Stakes
2nd Cinema Handicap
At 4: Won Santa Anita Handicap
American Handicap
Hawthorne Gold Cup
2nd San Antonio Handicap
Hollywood Gold Cup
Sunset Handicap
San Juan Capistrano Handicap
At 5: Won Hollywood Gold Cup
2nd Sunset Handicap
3rd American Handicap

RELAUNCH (1976)
At 4: 2nd Del Mar Handicap
San Antonio Stakes
San Luis Rey Stakes
3rd San Fernando Stakes

RELAXING (1976)
At 4: 3rd Santa Barbara Handicap
At 5: Won Delaware Handicap
Ruffian Handicap
3rd Jockey Club Gold Cup

RELENT (1971)
At 5: Won Fall Highweight Handicap

RELIC (1945)
At 2: Won Hopeful Stakes
2nd Saratoga Special

RELLIM S.W. (1955)
At 2: 2nd Arlington Futurity

RELOY (1983)
At 4: Won Santa Barbara Handicap
2nd Gamely Handicap

REMOLACHA (1949)
At 2: 3rd Del Mar Debutante Stakes

RENEGED (1953)
At 3: Won Jerome Handicap
2nd Roamer Handicap
At 4: Won Manhattan Handicap
3rd Jockey Club Gold Cup
At 5: 2nd Fall Highweight Handicap
3rd Woodward Stakes

RENEW (1947)
At 3: 3rd Gazelle Stakes
At 4: Won Firenze Handicap
At 5: Won Top Flight Handicap
2nd New Castle Handicap
Beldame Handicap

REPEATING (1961)
At 4: Won Monmouth Handicap

REPELUZ (1945)
At 6: 2nd San Juan Capistrano Handicap
3rd San Pasqual Handicap

REPENT (1999)
At 2: 2nd Bessemer Trust Breeders' Cup Juvenile
At 3: 2nd Travers Stakes

REPETOIRE (1948)
At 2: Won Remsen Handicap
At 3: Won Wood Memorial Stakes

REPLANT (1974)
At 2: 2nd Norfolk Stakes
At 4: 2nd Californian Stakes

REPLY PAID (1942)
At 4: 2nd Suburban Handicap
Gulfstream Handicap
3rd Widener Handicap

REPOISE (1967)
At 2: 2nd Matron Stakes
3rd Frizette Stakes

REPRIMAND (1950)
At 2: 2nd Cowdin Stakes

REQUETE (1999)
At 4: 2nd Woodford Reserve Turf Classic
Manhattan Handicap

RERAISE (1995)
At 3: Won Breeders' Cup Sprint

RESACA (1956)
At 2: 2nd Gardenia Stakes
At 3: Won Coaching Club American Oaks
Delaware Oaks

RESILIENT (1950)
At 4: Won Canadian Championship Stakes

RESOLVER (1974)
At 2: 3rd Matron Stakes
Alcibiades Stakes

RESORT (1997)
At 3: 2nd Coaching Club American Oaks
3rd Gazelle Handicap

RESOUND (1972)
At 6: 2nd John B. Campbell Handicap

RESTLESS CON (1987)
At 3: Won Haskell Invitational Handicap
2nd Ohio Derby

RESTLESS JET (1970)
At 3: 3rd Florida Derby

RESTLESS RESTLESS (1973)
At 2: Won Hollywood Juvenile Championship

RESTLESS TORNADO (1966)
At 3: 3rd Mother Goose Stakes

RESTLESS WIND (1956)
At 2: Won Arlington Futurity
Washington Park Futurity
3rd Sapling Stakes
At 4: 2nd John B. Campbell Handicap

RESTORED HOPE (1991)
At 4: 3rd Shuvee Handicap
At 5: 3rd Shuvee Handicap
Hempstead Handicap

REST YOUR CASE (1969)
At 2: Won Hopeful Stakes

RE TOSS (1987)
At 5: 2nd Milady Handicap
3rd Vanity Handicap
At 6: Won Vanity Handicap
3rd Milady Handicap
Breeders' Cup Distaff
At 7: 3rd Apple Blossom Handicap

RETURN OF A NATIVE (1973)
At 3: Won Ohio Derby

RETURN TO REALITY (1969)
At 4: 3rd United Nations Handicap

REVASSER (1989)
At 4: 3rd Santa Barbara Handicap

REVEILLE (1946)
At 3: 3rd Flamingo Stakes

REVERSE (1962)
At 3: 2nd Jersey Derby

REVIDERE (1973)
At 3: Won Coaching Club American Oaks
Ruffian Stakes
2nd Beldame Stakes
3rd Jockey Club Gold Cup

REVIEWER (1966)
At 2: Won Sapling Stakes
Saratoga Special
2nd Hopeful Stakes
At 3: 2nd Gotham Stakes
3rd Wood Memorial Stakes
At 4: 2nd Metropolitan Handicap

REVIVE (1986)
At 2: 3rd Young America Stakes

REVOLT (1951)
At 2: 2nd Breeders' Futurity
At 3: 3rd Everglades Stakes

REXSON'S HOPE (1981)
At 3: 3rd Everglades Stakes
Flamingo Stakes

RHIANA (1997)
At 6: 3rd Santa Maria Handicap

RHODES BULL (1946)
At 3: 2nd Cinema Handicap
3rd Westerner Handicap

RHODIE (1962)
At 2: 2nd Sorority Stakes

RHOMAN RULE (1982)
At 2: 3rd Laurel Futurity
At 3: Won Everglades Stakes
3rd Wood Memorial Stakes

RHUBARB (1964)
At 2: 3rd Sorority Stakes

RHYTHM (1987)
At 2: Won Breeders' Cup Juvenile
2nd Champagne Stakes
At 3: Won Travers Stakes
2nd Dwyer Stakes
3rd Haskell Invitational Handicap
Woodward Handicap

RIAL (1985)
At 5: Won Oak Tree Invitational Stakes

RIBBON (1977)
At 3: Won Golden Harvest Handicap

RIBOFILIO (1966)
At 4: 3rd Stars and Stripes Handicap

RIBOLETTA (1995)
At 5: Won Santa Margarita Handicap
Milady Breeders' Cup Handicap
Vanity Handicap
Ruffian Handicap
Beldame Stakes

RIBOT'S FLING (1962)
At 3: 2nd Dixie Handicap
3rd Canadian Championship Stakes
At 4: 3rd Hialeah Turf Cup

RICCI TAVI (1953)
At 2: 3rd Champagne Stakes
At 6: 2nd Tropical Park Handicap

RICH AND READY (1976)
At 6: Won Louisiana Downs Handicap

RICHLY BLENDED (1998)
At 3: 3rd Wood Memorial Stakes

RICHMAN (1988)
At 3: 2nd Jim Beam Stakes
Ohio Derby
3rd Arkansas Derby

RICHMOND JAC (1942)
At 4: 2nd Stars and Stripes Handicap

RICHTER SCALE (1994)
At 3: Won Jerome Handicap
At 6: Won Frank J. De Francis Memorial Dash

RICH TRADITION (1956)
At 2: Won Spinaway Stakes
Selima Stakes
2nd Matron Stakes
3rd Frizette Stakes
At 3: 3rd Alabama Stakes

RICO MONTE (1942)
At 4: 2nd New York Handicap
Gallant Fox Handicap
3rd Jockey Club Gold Cup
At 5: Won Whitney Stakes
Manhattan Handicap
New York Handicap
2nd Dixie Handicap

RICO RETA (1952)
At 3: Won Alabama Stakes
At 4: 2nd Molly Pitcher Handicap
Diana Handicap
3rd Top Flight Handicap

RICO ROMANCE (1952)
At 3: 3rd Delaware Oaks

RICO TESIO (1956)
At 2: 2nd Remsen Stakes
Pimlico Futurity

RIDAN (1959)
At 2: Won Arlington Futurity
Washington Park Futurity
At 3: Won Florida Derby
Blue Grass Stakes
Arlington Classic
2nd Flamingo Stakes
Preakness Stakes
American Derby
Travers Stakes
3rd Kentucky Derby
Aqueduct Stakes
At 4: 2nd Seminole Handicap

RIDE SALLY (1982)
At 4: Won Top Flight Handicap

RIDE THE RAILS (1991)
At 3: 2nd Florida Derby

RIDGEWOOD PEARL (1992)
At 3: Won Breeders' Cup Mile

RIFLERY (1988)
At 3: 3rd Pennsylvania Derby

RIGHT CON (1982)
At 2: 3rd Hollywood Futurity
At 4: Won San Fernando Stakes
2nd San Antonio Handicap

RIGHT MIND (1971)
At 5: 2nd John B. Campbell Handicap

RIGHT PROUD (1960)
At 2: Won Pimlico Futurity

RILEY (1953)
At 3: Won Dwyer Handicap
Lawrence Realization Stakes
2nd Jockey Club Gold Cup
At 4: 2nd Whitney Stakes

RINCONCITO (1966)
At 6: 3rd San Luis Rey Handicap

RINGASKIDDY (1996)
At 6: Won San Juan Capistrano Handicap

RINGERMAN (1986)
At 2: 2nd Laurel Futurity

RING FOR NURSE (1967)
At 2: Won Sapling Stakes

RING OF LIGHT (1975)
At 5: 3rd Brooklyn Handicap
At 6: 2nd Suburban Handicap
3rd Whitney Handicap
Monmouth Handicap

RING PROUD (1979)
At 2: 3rd Del Mar Futurity

RINGS A CHIME (1997)
At 3: Won Ashland Stakes
2nd Kentucky Oaks
3rd Las Virgenes Stakes

RING TWICE (1963)
At 3: 2nd Lawrence Realization Stakes
At 4: Won Widener Handicap
2nd Suburban Handicap
Aqueduct Stakes
Whitney Stakes
At 5: 3rd Donn Handicap

RIO BRAVO (1966)
At 5: Won New Orleans Handicap
Oaklawn Handicap

RIOT IN PARIS (1971)
At 5: Won Del Mar Handicap
2nd American Handicap
3rd Hollywood Gold Cup
Sunset Handicap

RIPARIUS (1952)
At 2: 3rd Del Mar Futurity

RIPON (1973)
At 5: Won John B. Campbell Handicap

RIPPEY (1943)
At 3: 2nd Jerome Handicap
At 4: Won Fall Highweight Handicap

		Carter Handicap
At 5:	Won	Roseben Handicap
	2nd	San Carlos Handicap
		Carter Handicap
	3rd	Metropolitan Handicap
At 6:	2nd	Carter Handicap
	3rd	San Carlos Handicap

RISE JIM (1976)

At 5:	2nd	Vosburgh Stakes

RISEN STAR (1985)

At 3:	Won	Preakness Stakes
		Belmont Stakes
	3rd	Kentucky Derby

RISING MARKET (1964)

At 3:	Won	San Felipe Handicap
At 4:	Won	Malibu Stakes
	2nd	San Antonio Handicap
	3rd	Californian Stakes
At 5:	2nd	Californian Stakes
		Vosburgh Handicap
	3rd	Washington Park Handicap
At 6:	2nd	San Antonio Stakes

RISKAVERSE (1999)

At 2:	3rd	Frizette Stakes
At 3:	Won	Queen Elizabeth II Challenge Cup
	2nd	Garden City Breeders' Cup Handicap
At 4:	3rd	Beverly D. Stakes

RISKOLATER (1944)

At 3:	2nd	Blue Grass Stakes
	3rd	Flamingo Stakes
At 4:	2nd	McLennan Handicap

RISOLATER (1943)

At 3:	2nd	Ladies Handicap
	3rd	Roamer Handicap
At 4:	2nd	Comely Handicap

RISQUE ROUGE (1949)

At 3:	3rd	Roamer Handicap

RI TUX (1963)

At 2:	2nd	Hollywood Juvenile Championship
	3rd	Del Mar Futurity

RIVALERO (1976)

At 3:	2nd	Louisiana Derby
At 4:	3rd	Widener Handicap
At 7:	3rd	Widener Handicap
		Gulfstream Park Handicap

RIVA RIDGE (1969)

At 2:	Won	Futurity Stakes
		Champagne Stakes
		Pimlico-Laurel Futurity
		Garden State Stakes
At 3:	Won	Blue Grass Stakes
		Kentucky Derby
		Belmont Stakes
		Hollywood Derby
	3rd	Jockey Club Gold Cup
At 4:	Won	Massachusetts Handicap
		Brooklyn Handicap
	2nd	Marlboro Cup Handicap

RIVER BAY (1993)

At 4:	Won	Hollywood Turf Cup
At 5:	2nd	Hollywood Turf Handicap
	3rd	Oak Tree Turf Championship
At 6:	Won	Charles Whittingham Handicap

RIVER FLYER (1991)

At 3:	Won	Hollywood Derby

RIVERINA (1951)

At 3:	Won	Acorn Stakes
	2nd	Firenze Handicap
	3rd	Coaching Club American Oaks
		Ladies Handicap

RIVER KEEN (1992)

At 5:	Won	Californian Stakes
At 7:	Won	Woodward Stakes
		Jockey Club Gold Cup
	2nd	Pacific Classic

RIVERLANE (1945)

At 3:	3rd	Louisiana Derby
At 4:	2nd	Aqueduct Handicap

RIVER MAJESTY (1989)

At 5:	3rd	Early Times Manhattan Handicap

RIVER MASTER (1986)

At 3:	3rd	Hollywood Derby

RIVER MEMORIES (1984)

At 3:	Won	Rothmans International Stakes
	2nd	Turf Classic
At 5:	Won	Flower Bowl Handicap

RIVER RHYTHM (1987)

At 8:	2nd	San Luis Rey Stakes

RIVERSIDE SAM (1973)

At 2:	2nd	Sapling Stakes

RIVER SPECIAL (1990)

At 2:	Won	Del Mar Futurity
		Norfolk Stakes
		Hollywood Futurity
	3rd	Breeders' Cup Juvenile

RIVER TRAFFIC (1988)

At 3:	3rd	Hollywood Derby
At 4:	3rd	Hollywood Turf Handicap

RIVER WARDEN (1986)

At 5:	2nd	San Juan Capistrano Handicap

RIVET (1964)

At 4:	2nd	San Luis Rey Handicap
	3rd	Century Handicap
		San Juan Capistrano Handicap
At 5:	3rd	San Juan Capistrano Handicap

RIVLIA (1982)

At 5:	Won	Hollywood Invitational Handicap
	3rd	San Juan Capistrano Handicap
		Sunset Handicap
		Oak Tree Invitational Stakes
At 6:	Won	San Luis Rey Stakes

RIXDAL (1963)

At 5:	2nd	Donn Handicap

RIZE (1996)

At 4:	Won	Philip H. Iselin Handicap
At 6:	3rd	Donn Handicap

ROAD HOUSE (1957)

At 4:	2nd	New Orleans Handicap

ROAD PRINCESS (1974)

At 2:	3rd	Demoiselle Stakes
At 3:	Won	Mother Goose Stakes
	2nd	Coaching Club American Oaks

ROAD TO ROMANCE (1961)

At 3:	3rd	Kentucky Oaks

ROAMIN RACHEL (1990)

At 3:	3rd	Ashland Stakes

ROANOKE (1987)

At 2:	Won	Young America Stakes
	2nd	Remsen Stakes
At 4:	Won	Californian Stakes

ROAR (1993)

At 3:	Won	Jim Beam Stakes

ROBA BELLA (1969)

At 4:	2nd	Ladies Handicap
	3rd	Top Flight Handicap

ROBALEA (1975)

At 2:	2nd	Alcibiades Stakes

ROBERT'S FLAG (1962)

At 4:	3rd	Pan American Handicap

ROBIN'S BUG (1967)

At 3:	2nd	American Derby

ROBSPHERE (1977)

At 5:	Won	Pan American Handicap
	3rd	Hialeah Turf Cup

ROBYN DANCER (1987)

At 2:	2nd	Laurel Futurity
At 4:	3rd	Breeders' Cup Sprint

ROCKAMUNDO (1990)

At 2:	3rd	Arlington-Washington Futurity
At 3:	Won	Arkansas Derby

ROCK BATH (1968)

At 5:	3rd	Sunset Handicap

ROCKCASTLE (1952)

At 5:	3rd	Monmouth Handicap

ROCKET POCKET (1970)

At 2:	2nd	Breeders' Futurity

ROCKHILL NATIVE (1977)

At 2:	Won	Sapling Stakes
		Futurity Stakes
	2nd	Champagne Stakes
At 3:	Won	Blue Grass Stakes
	3rd	Flamingo Stakes
		Belmont Stakes

ROCK OF AGES (1972)

At 3:	2nd	Santa Anita Derby

ROCK OF GIBRALTAR (1999)

At 3:	2nd	NetJets Breeders' Cup Mile

ROCK POINT (1986)

At 3:	2nd	Wood Memorial Stakes
	3rd	Preakness Stakes

ROCK SOFTLY (1978)

At 4:	3rd	San Fernando Stakes
		Charles H. Strub Stakes

ROCKWALL (1979)

At 3:	Won	California Derby

ROCKY LINK (1960)

At 2:	Won	Remsen Stakes
	3rd	Cowdin Stakes
At 4:	2nd	Charles H. Strub Stakes

ROCKY ROYALE (1956)

At 4:	Won	Canadian Championship Stakes

ROCKY TRIP (1972)

At 4:	3rd	Spinster Stakes

ROGUES WALK (1992)

At 3:	3rd	Alabama Stakes

ROI DANZIG (1986)

At 3:	Won	Dwyer Stakes
	2nd	Ohio Derby
		Pennsylvania Derby
	3rd	Jim Dandy Stakes

ROI NORMAND (1983)

At 5:	Won	Sunset Handicap

ROKEBY (1989)

At 3:	3rd	Wood Memorial Stakes

ROKEBY ROSE (1977)

At 4:	Won	Flower Bowl Handicap

ROLLICKING (1967)

At 2:	2nd	Sapling Stakes

ROLLIN WITH NOLAN (1997)

At 3:	3rd	Turfway Spiral Stakes

ROMAN BATH (1947)

At 2:	Won	Kentucky Jockey Club Stakes
	3rd	Breeders' Futurity

ROMAN BATTLE (1953)

At 4:	3rd	Hialeah Turf Handicap
At 5:	3rd	Hialeah Turf Handicap

ROMAN BROTHER (1961)

At 2:	Won	Champagne Stakes
	2nd	Garden State Stakes
At 3:	Won	Everglades Stakes
		Jersey Derby
		American Derby
	2nd	Belmont Stakes
		Lawrence Realization Stakes
		Jockey Club Gold Cup
	3rd	Wood Memorial Stakes
		Dwyer Handicap

ROMAN BROTHER *(Continued)*
At 4: Won Woodward Stakes
Manhattan Handicap
Jockey Club Gold Cup
2nd Brooklyn Handicap
Michigan Mile and One-Eighth
3rd Aqueduct Stakes
Washington D.C. International

ROMAN CANDLE (1944)
At 5: Won Black Helen Handicap
At 6: 2nd Black Helen Handicap
Firenze Handicap
3rd Top Flight Handicap

ROMAN FAN (1953)
At 2: 3rd Kentucky Jockey Club Stakes

ROMAN GODDESS (1961)
At 3: 3rd Santa Susana Stakes

ROMAN IN (1945)
At 4: 3rd Golden Gate Handicap

ROMANITA (1954)
At 2: Won Matron Stakes
2nd Princess Pat Stakes
3rd Gardenia Stakes
Frizette Stakes
At 3: Won Monmouth Oaks
3rd Vineland Handicap

ROMAN LINE (1959)
At 2: Won Breeders' Futurity
At 3: 2nd Louisiana Derby
Kentucky Derby
3rd Blue Grass Stakes
Preakness Stakes

ROMAN MISS (1948)
At 3: 2nd Black Helen Handicap
At 4: Won Black Helen Handicap

ROMAN OBLISK (1976)
At 2: 3rd Del Mar Futurity

ROMANO GUCCI (1993)
At 3: Won Gotham Stakes
3rd Wood Memorial Stakes

ROMANOV (1994)
At 3: 3rd Canadian International Championship

ROMAN PATROL (1952)
At 2: Won Remsen Stakes
At 3: Won Louisiana Derby

ROMAN SCOUT (1967)
At 3: 2nd Monmouth Invitational Handicap

ROMARIN (1990)
At 5: 2nd Eddie Read Handicap

ROMEO (1973)
At 3: 2nd Travers Stakes
Secretariat Stakes
3rd Hawthorne Gold Cup
At 4: 2nd Oaklawn Handicap
3rd Hawthorne Gold Cup
At 5: Won Arlington Handicap

RONDA (1996)
At 3: 3rd Garden City Breeders' Cup Handicap

RONDEAU (1969)
At 2: 2nd Spinaway Stakes
3rd Sorority Stakes

RONNIE'S ACE (1958)
At 3: 2nd Santa Anita Derby

ROO ART (1982)
At 3: 3rd Jim Beam Stakes
At 4: Won Suburban Handicap
Philip H. Iselin Handicap
2nd Charles H. Strub Stakes
Brooklyn Handicap
3rd Marlboro Cup Handicap

ROOKWOOD (1946)
At 3: Won Louisiana Derby

ROONEY'S SHIELD (1966)
At 3: 2nd Gotham Stakes
3rd Withers Stakes
Jersey Derby

ROOTENTOOTENWOOTEN (1987)
At 2: Won Demoiselle Stakes

ROSA BLANCA (1941)
At 5: 3rd Ladies Handicap

ROSACAW (1947)
At 3: 3rd Longacres Mile

ROSALIE MAE WYNN (1970)
At 2: 3rd Del Mar Debutante Stakes

ROSE BEAM (1945)
At 4: 2nd Santa Anita Maturity
3rd San Juan Capistrano Handicap

ROSEBERRY (1961)
At 3: 3rd Ohio Derby

ROSE BOWER (1958)
At 2: Won Princess Pat Stakes
Matron Stakes

ROSEDALE (1983)
At 4: Won San Juan Capistrano Handicap

ROSE DIAMOND (1986)
At 3: 3rd Coaching Club American Oaks

ROSE FERN (1948)
At 2: 3rd Demoiselle Stakes
Selima Stakes

ROSE JET (1949)
At 2: Won Matron Stakes
Selima Stakes
Demoiselle Stakes
2nd Spinaway Stakes
3rd Astarita Stakes
Marguerite Stakes

ROSEMARY B. (1951)
At 3: 3rd Arlington Matron Handicap
At 4: Won Black Helen Handicap

ROSEMONT BOW (1968)
At 2: 2nd Gardenia Stakes

ROSE'S CANTINA (1984)
At 5: 3rd Beldame Stakes

ROSE TRELLIS (1955)
At 2: Won Hopeful Stakes
3rd Champagne Stakes
Garden State Stakes
Remsen Stakes

ROSEWOOD (1954)
At 4: 3rd Arlington Matron Handicap
At 5: Won Black Helen Handicap

ROSSI GOLD (1976)
At 4: 2nd Arlington Handicap
Louisiana Downs Handicap
At 6: 2nd Arlington Handicap
At 7: 2nd Arlington Handicap

ROUGH'N TUMBLE (1948)
At 2: 2nd Garden State Stakes
Remsen Handicap
3rd Futurity Stakes
At 3: Won Santa Anita Derby
3rd San Felipe Stakes

ROUND ROCK (1960)
At 3: 3rd Santa Anita Derby

ROUND ROSE (1971)
At 2: 3rd Oak Leaf Stakes

ROUND TABLE (1954)
At 2: Won Breeders' Futurity
At 3: Won Blue Grass Stakes
Cinema Handicap
Westerner Stakes
American Derby
Hollywood Gold Cup
Hawthorne Gold Cup
United Nations Handicap
2nd Californian Stakes
3rd Santa Anita Derby
Kentucky Derby
Trenton Handicap
At 4: Won San Antonio Handicap
Santa Anita Handicap
Gulfstream Park Handicap
Hawthorne Gold Cup
Santa Anita Maturity
Arlington Handicap
2nd Californian Stakes
Washington Park Handicap
United Nations Handicap
At 5: Won Washington Park Handicap
Manhattan Handicap
Stars and Stripes Handicap
Arlington Handicap
United Nations Handicap
2nd San Carlos Handicap
Jockey Club Gold Cup
3rd Woodward Stakes

ROUND VIEW (1943)
At 3: Won Flamingo Stakes
At 4: Won Monmouth Handicap
At 6: Won Whitney Stakes
2nd Monmouth Handicap

ROVING BOY (1980)
At 2: Won Del Mar Futurity
Norfolk Stakes
Hollywood Futurity

ROVING MINSTREL (1958)
At 2: Won Champagne Stakes

ROVING MINSTREL (1981)
At 3: 2nd Hollywood Derby

ROXELANA (1997)
At 3: 3rd Acorn Stakes

ROYAL ACADEMY (1987)
At 3: Won Breeders' Cup Mile

ROYAL AND REGAL (1970)
At 3: Won Florida Derby

ROYAL ANTHEM (1995)
At 3: Won Canadian International Championship
At 4: 2nd Breeders' Cup Turf
At 5: Won Gulfstream Park BC Handicap

ROYAL ASCOT (1960)
At 3: 3rd Flamingo Stakes
At 4: 2nd Hialeah Turf Cup

ROYAL ATTACK (1959)
At 3: Won Santa Anita Derby
2nd San Felipe Handicap

ROYAL BAY GEM (1950)
At 3: Won Everglades Stakes
2nd Flamingo Stakes
3rd Preakness Stakes
Belmont Stakes
At 4: 3rd McLennan Handicap

ROYAL BLOOD (1945)
At 2: 2nd Cowdin Stakes
3rd Arlington Futurity
Tremont Stakes
At 4: 2nd Fall Highweight Handicap

ROYAL CAP (1965)
At 2: 3rd Arlington-Washington Futurity

ROYAL CHARIOT (1990)
At 5: Won Hollywood Turf Cup
3rd Oak Tree Invitational Stakes

ROYAL COINAGE (1952)
At 2: Won Sapling Stakes
3rd Futurity Stakes

ROYAL CONNECTIONS (1969)
At 2: 3rd Del Mar Futurity

ROYAL CRISIS (1967)
At 2: 2nd Sorority Stakes

ROYAL DERBY II (1969)
At 7: 2nd Oak Tree Invitational Stakes

ROYAL DYNASTY (1966)
At 4: 3rd San Luis Rey Handicap

ROYAL EXCHANGE (1965)
At 4: 3rd Carter Handicap

ROYAL GEM (1999)
At 3: 3rd Hollywood Derby

ROYAL GLINT (1970)
At 4: 2nd Arlington Handicap
At 5: Won Amory L. Haskell Handicap
Arlington Handicap
Hawthorne Gold Cup
United Nations Handicap
2nd National Championship Inv. Handicap
At 6: Won Santa Anita Handicap
2nd Oaklawn Handicap

ROYAL GOVERNOR (1944)
At 5: Won Fall Highweight Handicap
Grey Lag Handicap
3rd Westchester Handicap
At 6: Won Widener Handicap
2nd McLennan Handicap
3rd Fall Highweight Handicap
Roseben Handicap
At 7: Won Stars and Stripes Handicap
At 9: 3rd United Nations Handicap

ROYAL GUNNER (1962)
At 2: 2nd Champagne Stakes
Garden State Stakes
3rd Arlington-Washington Futurity
Cowdin Stakes
At 3: 2nd Arlington Classic
American Derby
Woodward Stakes
At 4: 2nd Woodward Stakes

ROYAL HARMONY (1964)
At 7: 2nd Michigan Mile and One-Eighth
Hawthorne Gold Cup
3rd Brooklyn Handicap

ROYAL HEROINE (1980)
At 3: Won Hollywood Derby
At 4: Won Breeders' Cup Mile
2nd Budweiser-Arlington Million

ROYAL INDY (1994)
At 3: Won Gazelle Handicap

ROYAL KNIGHT (1970)
At 4: Won Oaklawn Handicap

ROYAL LIVING (1955)
At 4: Won San Juan Capistrano Handicap
2nd Santa Anita Maturity
3rd Santa Anita Handicap

ROYALLY CHOSEN (1998)
At 3: 2nd La Brea Stakes

ROYAL MALABAR (1964)
At 3: Won Illinois Derby
3rd Ohio Derby
At 4: 3rd Dixie Handicap

ROYAL MINK (1948)
At 3: 3rd Hollywood Oaks

ROYAL MOUNTAIN INN (1989)
At 5: Won Man o' War Stakes

ROYAL MUSTANG (1948)
At 2: 2nd Breeders' Futurity
At 3: 2nd Blue Grass Stakes
Kentucky Derby
At 4: Won Stars and Stripes Handicap

ROYAL NATIVE (1956)
At 3: Won Monmouth Oaks
Spinster Stakes
At 4: Won Black Helen Handicap
Top Flight Handicap
Arlington Matron Handicap
Vineland Handicap
2nd Delaware Handicap
Beldame Stakes
3rd Spinster Stakes
At 5: 2nd Delaware Handicap

ROYAL NOTE (1952)
At 2: Won Arlington Futurity
2nd Sapling Stakes

ROYAL ORBIT (1956)
At 2: 2nd Del Mar Futurity
At 3: Won Preakness Stakes
2nd Santa Anita Derby
3rd San Felipe Handicap
California Derby
Belmont Stakes

ROYAL OWL (1969)
At 2: Won Hollywood Juvenile Championship
At 3: 3rd Santa Anita Derby
At 4: Won Charles H. Strub Stakes
2nd Californian Stakes
Malibu Stakes
San Fernando Stakes

ROYAL PATRICE (1959)
At 3: Won Ladies Handicap
2nd Monmouth Oaks
Spinster Stakes
3rd Mother Goose Stakes

ROYAL REACH (1986)
At 5: 2nd San Luis Rey Stakes

ROYAL REGATTA (1979)
At 7: 3rd Santa Barbara Handicap

ROYAL SERENADE (1948)
At 5: Won American Handicap
Hollywood Gold Cup

ROYAL SHUCK (1961)
At 3: 2nd Arkansas Derby
3rd Blue Grass Stakes

ROYAL SIGNAL (1967)
At 3: Won Acorn Stakes

ROYAL SKI (1974)
At 2: Won Laurel Futurity
Remsen Stakes
2nd Arlington-Washington Futurity

ROYAL STING (1953)
At 2: Won Kentucky Jockey Club Stakes

ROYAL SUITE (1977)
At 2: 2nd Matron Stakes
Frizette Stakes

ROYAL TOUCH (1985)
At 5: 2nd Santa Barbara Handicap
3rd Yellow Ribbon Stakes

ROYAL TRACE (1965)
At 2: 2nd Hopeful Stakes
3rd Arlington-Washington Futurity

ROYAL TREASURER (1983)
At 3: 3rd Rothmans International Stakes

ROYAL UNION (1955)
At 3: Won Louisiana Derby

ROYAL VALE (1948)
At 5: Won Gallant Fox Handicap
Dixie Handicap
Massachusetts Handicap
Miami Beach Handicap
2nd Metropolitan Handicap
Suburban Handicap
3rd Manhattan Handicap
At 6: 2nd Hialeah Turf Handicap
United Nations Handicap
3rd Massachusetts Handicap
Carter Handicap

ROZA ROBATA (1995)
At 5: 3rd Hempstead Handicap
Go for Wand Handicap
Three Chimneys Spinster Stakes

R. THOMAS (1961)
At 4: Won Vosburgh Handicap
At 5: 2nd New Orleans Handicap
At 6: 3rd Arlington Handicap
Vosburgh Handicap

R. TOM CAN (1971)
At 3: 3rd Manhattan Handicap
At 4: 3rd United Nations Handicap

RUBE THE GREAT (1971)
At 3: Won Wood Memorial Stakes
2nd Dwyer Handicap
At 4: 3rd Charles H. Strub Stakes

RUBIANO (1987)
At 4: Won NYRA Mile Handicap
2nd Metropolitan Handicap
At 5: Won Carter Handicap
Vosburgh Stakes
3rd Breeders' Cup Sprint

RUBY'S RECEPTION (2000)
At 2: 2nd Walmac International Alcibiades Stakes

RUBY TIGER (1987)
At 5: 2nd Beverly D. Stakes

RUDDY (1948)
At 2: 2nd Matron Stakes
At 3: Won Monmouth Oaks

RUDOMA (1959)
At 2: Won Arlington Lassie Stakes

RUE DE PALM (1987)
At 2: 2nd Del Mar Futurity

RUFFIAN (1972)
At 2: Won Sorority Stakes
Spinaway Stakes
At 3: Won Acorn Stakes
Mother Goose Stakes
Coaching Club American Oaks

RUFFINAL (1968)
At 2: 3rd Garden State Stakes

RUFFLED FEATHERS (1964)
At 3: Won Man o' War Stakes
At 4: 3rd Bowling Green Handicap
At 5: 2nd Bowling Green Handicap

RUGGLES FERRY (1972)
At 2: 3rd Breeders' Futurity
At 3: 2nd Illinois Derby

RUHE (1948)
At 3: Won Blue Grass Stakes
3rd Kentucky Derby
Arlington Classic
Hawthorne Gold Cup
At 4: 2nd Washington D.C. International
3rd Arlington Handicap
At 5: 2nd Washington Park Handicap
At 6: 2nd Gulfstream Park Handicap

RUHLMANN (1985)
At 5: Won Santa Anita Handicap
2nd Pimlico Special
3rd San Antonio Handicap

RUKEN (1964)
At 2: Won Del Mar Futurity
At 3: Won Santa Anita Derby
2nd San Felipe Handicap
3rd Hollywood Derby
At 4: 3rd Malibu Stakes
San Fernando Stakes
Charles H. Strub Stakes

RULE BY REASON (1967)
At 6: 3rd Whitney Stakes

RULER'S BLADE (1974)
At 3: 3rd California Derby

RULE THE RIDGE (1973)
At 2: 3rd Arlington-Washington Futurity

RULING ANGEL (1984)
At 2: 2nd Selima Stakes
3rd Arlington-Washington Lassie Stakes

RULLAH RED (1958)
At 4: 3rd Carter Handicap
Metropolitan Handicap

RUMBO (1977)
At 2: 2nd Norfolk Stakes
At 3: 2nd Santa Anita Derby
Hollywood Derby
Kentucky Derby
3rd San Felipe Handicap

RUNAWAY GROOM (1979)
At 3: Won Travers Stakes

RUNAWAY STREAM (1987)
At 3: 3rd Pegasus Handicap

RUN COME SEE (1984)
At 3: 3rd Coaching Club American Oaks

RUN DUSTY RUN (1974)
At 2: Won Breeders' Futurity
Arlington-Washington Futurity
At 3: 2nd Louisiana Derby
Blue Grass Stakes
Kentucky Derby
Belmont Stakes
American Derby
Travers Stakes
Secretariat Stakes
3rd Preakness Stakes

RUN FOR NURSE (1957)
At 2: 3rd Kentucky Jockey Club Stakes
At 4: 3rd Washington Park Handicap
Hawthorne Gold Cup
At 5: 3rd Michigan Mile and One-Sixteenth

RUN MAN RUN (1995)
At 3: Won Malibu Stakes

RUNNING FLAME (1992)
At 4: Won Hollywood Turf Cup

RUNNING SEAS (1948)
At 3: 3rd Louisiana Derby

RUNNING STAG (1994)
At 4: 3rd Woodward Stakes
At 5: Won Brooklyn Handicap

RUN'N PRINCE (1974)
At 3: 3rd Longacres Mile

RUNSPASTUM (1997)
At 5: 3rd Philip H. Iselin Handicap

RUN THE GANTLET (1968)
At 2: Won Garden State Stakes
At 3: Won United Nations Handicap
Man o' War Stakes
Washington D.C. International
At 4: Won Bowling Green Handicap

RUN TURN (1987)
At 3: 3rd Florida Derby

RUNUP THE COLORS (1994)
At 3: Won Alabama Stakes
At 4: 2nd Ballerina Handicap
Three Chimneys Spinster Stakes

RURITANIA (1969)
At 3: Won Manhattan Handicap
2nd Belmont Stakes
Dwyer Handicap
Man o' War Stakes

RUSH DATE (1966)
At 3: 2nd Illinois Derby

RUSHING MAN (1972)
At 4: 3rd Fall Highweight Handicap

RUSTIC BILLY (1951)
At 3: 2nd Ohio Derby

RUTHIE'S NATIVE (1974)
At 3: Won Florida Derby

RUTH LILY (1948)
At 3: Won Santa Susana Stakes
Hollywood Oaks
2nd Will Rogers Handicap
At 5: 2nd Santa Margarita Handicap

RUWENZORI (1956)
At 2: 3rd Gardenia Stakes

RYAFAN (1994)
At 3: Won Queen Elizabeth II Challenge Cup
Yellow Ribbon Stakes
Matriarch Stakes

RYTINA (1943)
At 3: 3rd Acorn Stakes
At 4: Won Top Flight Handicap
2nd Black Helen Handicap

SAARLAND (1999)
At 4: 2nd Metropolitan Handicap

SABER MOUNTAIN (1963)
At 3: Won San Felipe Handicap
2nd Santa Anita Derby

SABETTE (1950)
At 3: Won Alabama Stakes
2nd Coaching Club American Oaks
Monmouth Handicap
3rd Gazelle Handicap

SABIN (1980)
At 3: 3rd Alabama Stakes
At 4: Won Yellow Ribbon Stakes

SABONA (1982)
At 7: Won Californian Stakes
2nd Hollywood Gold Cup
Breeders' Cup Mile

SACAHUISTA (1984)
At 2: Won Oak Leaf Stakes
2nd Arlington-Washington Lassie Stakes
Del Mar Futurity
At 3: Won Spinster Stakes
Breeders' Cup Distaff
2nd Hollywood Oaks
3rd Ruffian Handicap

SACRAMENTO (1962)
At 6: 2nd Gulfstream Park Handicap

SADAIR (1962)
At 2: Won Saratoga Special
Arlington-Washington Futurity
Garden State Stakes
Pimlico Futurity
2nd Cowdin Stakes
3rd Sapling Stakes

SADJIYD (1984)
At 3: 2nd Rothmans International Stakes

SADO (1967)
At 4: 2nd Oaklawn Handicap

SAFE (1976)
At 3: Won Spinster Stakes

SAFELY (1948)
At 2: 2nd Cowdin Stakes

SAFELY KEPT (1986)
At 3: 2nd Breeders' Cup Sprint
At 4: Won Breeders' Cup Sprint

SAFE PLAY (1978)
At 2: 2nd Arlington-Washington Lassie Stakes
At 3: 3rd Spinster Stakes
At 4: Won La Canada Stakes

SAFE REWARD (1943)
At 3: 3rd California Derby

SAFE SWAP (1958)
At 2: 2nd Kentucky Jockey Club Stakes

SAGGY (1945)
At 2: 2nd Tremont Stakes
At 3: 3rd Flamingo Stakes

SAIDAM (1959)
At 4: 2nd Suburban Handicap
Whitney Stakes
3rd Carter Handicap
At 5: Won Grey Lag Handicap
3rd Metropolitan Handicap
Aqueduct Stakes

SAILOR (1952)
At 3: Won Roamer Handicap
Fall Highweight Handicap
Pimlico Special
At 4: Won Gulfstream Park Handicap
John B. Campbell Memorial Handicap
3rd Widener Handicap

SAILOR'S GUIDE (1952)
At 6: Won Washington D.C. International

SAILORS MATE (1967)
At 2: 2nd Oak Leaf Stakes

SAILORS NIGHT OUT (1970)
At 2: 3rd Arlington-Washington Futurity

SAIL TO ROME (1974)
At 2: 3rd Champagne Stakes

SAINT BALLADO (1989)
At 3: Won Arlington Classic

SAINTLY PROSPECTOR (1990)
At 3: 2nd Super Derby

SAINT'S HONOR (1996)
At 4: 3rd Strub Stakes

SAKHEE (1997)
At 4: 2nd Breeders' Cup Classic

SALATOM (1957)
At 2: 2nd Del Mar Futurity

SALE DAY (1965)
At 3: Won Spinster Stakes
At 4: 3rd Spinster Stakes

SALEM (1968)
At 2: Won Futurity Stakes
At 3: 3rd Withers Stakes

SALEM DRIVE (1982)
At 6: 2nd Hialeah Turf Cup
At 7: 2nd United Nations Handicap

SALERNO (1965)
At 3: 2nd Withers Stakes

SALLARINA (1966)
At 4: Won Santa Barbara Handicap

SALLY LEE (1955)
At 2: Won Del Mar Debutante Stakes

SALLY SHIP (1960)
At 3: Won Kentucky Oaks

SALMAGUNDI (1945)
At 3: Won San Vicente Handicap
Santa Anita Derby
3rd San Felipe Stakes

SALT LAKE (1989)
At 2: Won Hopeful Stakes
At 3: 3rd Vosburgh Stakes

SALT SPRING (1979)
At 5: 3rd Vanity Handicap
At 6: 2nd Vanity Handicap
3rd Santa Barbara Handicap

SALUD (1977)
At 2: Won Alcibiades Stakes

SALZBURG (1975)
At 4: 2nd Golden Harvest Handicap

SAME OLD WISH (1990)
At 6: 3rd Breeders' Cup Mile

SAMMYREN (1962)
At 3: 3rd Lawrence Realization Stakes

SAND DEVIL (1964)
At 2: 2nd Del Mar Futurity
At 3: 3rd Santa Anita Derby

SANDPIT (1989)
At 5: Won Oak Tree Invitational Stakes
At 6: Won San Luis Rey Stakes
Caesars International Handicap
2nd Hollywood Turf Handicap
Arlington Million
Oak Tree Invitational Stakes
At 7: Won Hollywood Turf Handicap
Caesars International Handicap
3rd Arlington Million
At 8: 2nd Santa Anita Handicap
Arlington Million
3rd Hollywood Gold Cup
Oak Tree Turf Championship

SANDTOP (1949)
At 3: 3rd Florida Derby

SANDY BLUE (1970)
At 3: Won Hollywood Oaks

SANEDTKI (1974)
At 5: Won Santa Margarita Handicap

SANGUE (1978)
At 4: Won Vanity Handicap
2nd Ramona Handicap
Matriarch Stakes
3rd Yellow Ribbon Stakes
At 5: Won Ramona Handicap
Golden Harvest Handicap
Yellow Ribbon Stakes
Matriarch Stakes
3rd Vanity Handicap

SANHEDRIN (1974)
At 3: 2nd Wood Memorial Stakes
3rd Kentucky Derby
Belmont Stakes

SAN JUAN HILL (1975)
At 4: Won Oaklawn Handicap

SAN ROQUE (1965)
At 4: 2nd New Orleans Handicap
Amory L. Haskell Handicap

SANS CRITIQUE (1974)
At 5: 2nd Delaware Handicap

SANS SUPPLEMENT (1974)
At 2: Won Alcibiades Stakes

SANTA CATARINA (2000)
At 2: 2nd Del Mar Debutante Stakes
Frizette Stakes
3rd Long John Silver's BC Juvenile Fillies
At 3: 2nd Kentucky Oaks

SANTANGELO (1984)
At 6: 3rd Hollywood Turf Handicap

SANTARIA (1995)
At 3: 2nd Acorn Stakes

SANTORIN II (1970)
At 4: 3rd Hialeah Turf Cup

SANTO'S JOE (1977)
At 6: 3rd Pan American Handicap

SAPOSE SPEED (1968)
At 2: 2nd Oak Leaf Stakes
At 3: 3rd Santa Susana Stakes

SARAFAN (1997)
At 5: Won Eddie Read Handicap
2nd Arlington Million
Clement L. Hirsch Mem. Turf Champ.
3rd United Nations Handicap

SARATOGA (1952)
At 2: 3rd Pimlico Futurity
At 3: Won Saranac Handicap
2nd Flamingo Stakes
Preakness Stakes
Dwyer Stakes

SARATOGA DEW (1989)
At 3: Won Beldame Stakes
2nd Alabama Stakes

SARATOGA PASSAGE (1985)
At 2: Won Norfolk Stakes
At 4: 3rd Oak Tree Invitational Stakes
At 5: 3rd Oak Tree Invitational Stakes

SARAVA (1999)
At 3: Won Belmont Stakes

SARCASTIC (1957)
At 2: 3rd Selima Stakes
Frizette Stakes
At 3: 2nd Coaching Club American Oaks
Delaware Oaks

SARDAUCKAR (1996)
At 7: 3rd Gulfstream Park Breeders' Cup Handicap

SARDULA (1991)
At 2: Won Hollywood Starlet Stakes
2nd Oak Leaf Stakes
Breeders' Cup Juvenile Fillies
At 3: Won Kentucky Oaks
2nd Hollywood Oaks

SARI'S DREAMER (1979)
At 5: 3rd Californian Stakes
Hollywood Gold Cup

SARI'S HEROINE (1983)
At 4: 3rd La Canada Stakes

SARI'S SONG (1961)
At 2: Won Arlington-Washington Lassie Stakes

SAROS BRIG (1984)
At 2: 3rd Breeders' Cup Juvenile Fillies

SARSAR (1972)
At 3: Won Withers Stakes
3rd Hempstead Handicap

SASSY HOUND (1997)
At 5: 3rd Frank J. De Francis Memorial Dash

SATAN'S CHARGER (1980)
At 2: 2nd Futurity Stakes

SATINA (1956)
At 2: 2nd Del Mar Debutante Stakes

SATIN RIBERA (1977)
At 3: 2nd Fantasy Stakes

SAUCE BOAT (1975)
At 2: Won Arlington-Washington Futurity

SAVAII (1959)
At 2: 3rd Del Mar Debutante Stakes
At 6: 3rd Vanity Handicap

SAVANNAH DANCER (1982)
At 3: 2nd Hollywood Derby

SAVANNAH'S HONOR (1985)
At 4: 3rd La Canada Stakes

SAVEDBYTHELIGHT (2000)
At 3: 3rd Coaching Club American Oaks

SAVE WILD LIFE (1977)
At 4: 3rd Vanity Handicap

SAVINIO (1990)
At 5: 3rd Hollywood Turf Handicap

SAXONY (1948)
At 3: 2nd Lawrence Realization Stakes

SAY BLUE (1944)
At 2: Won Princess Pat Stakes
2nd Selima Stakes
At 3: 2nd Arlington Matron Handicap

SAY FLORIDA SANDY (1994)
At 7: 2nd Carter Handicap

SAYYEDATI (1990)
At 5: 3rd Breeders' Cup Mile

SCAMPERING (1953)
At 3: Won Gazelle Handicap

SCAN (1988)
At 2: Won Cowdin Stakes
Remsen Stakes
At 3: Won Jerome Handicap
Pegasus Handicap
2nd San Felipe Stakes
Meadowlands Cup
3rd Peter Pan Stakes

SCANTLING (1970)
At 4: 2nd American Handicap
3rd Sunset Handicap
United Nations Handicap

SCAT DANCER (1983)
At 2: 3rd Breeders' Cup Juvenile

SCATMANDU (1995)
At 3: 3rd Jerome Handicap

SCATTERED (1945)
At 2: 3rd Marguerite Stakes
At 3: Won Pimlico Oaks
Coaching Club American Oaks
2nd Gazelle Stakes
3rd Delaware Oaks

SCENT (1950)
At 3: 2nd Jerome Handicap

SCEREE (1961)
At 3: Won Mother Goose Stakes
2nd Acorn Stakes
3rd Coaching Club American Oaks

SCHEMATIC (1982)
At 2: 3rd Sorority Stakes

SCHILLER (1982)
At 5: 3rd Hollywood Invitational Handicap

SCHISM (1984)
At 3: 3rd Tropical Park Derby

SCIMITAR (1950)
At 5: Won Tropical Handicap

SCHOOL TIE (1943)
At 3: Won Lawrence Realization Stakes
3rd Travers Stakes

SCHOSSBERG (1990)
At 3: Won Jerome Handicap
3rd Pegasus Handicap
At 5: Won Philip H. Iselin Handicap

SCHWAY BABY SWAY (1990)
At 4: 3rd Hempstead Handicap

SCORE A BIRDIE (1991)
At 6: 2nd Vosburgh Stakes

SCORE QUICK (1992)
At 3: 2nd Malibu Stakes

SCORE TWENTY FOUR (1977)
At 5: Won San Antonio Stakes

SCORPION (1998)
At 2: 3rd Futurity Stakes
At 3: Won Jim Dandy Stakes

SCOTCH SECRET (1944)
At 4: 3rd Hawthorne Gold Cup

SCOTLAND (1956)
At 3: 3rd Blue Grass Stakes

SCOTTISH MELODY (1972)
At 2: 3rd Spinaway Stakes

SCOTTISH RIFLE (1969)
At 4: 3rd Washington D.C. International

SCOTT'S SCOUNDREL (1992)
At 3: 3rd Super Derby
At 4: 3rd Oaklawn Handicap

SCRATCH PAD (1997)
At 2: Won Walmac International Alcibiades Stakes

SCREEN KING (1976)
At 3: 2nd Wood Memorial Stakes
3rd Preakness Stakes

SCREEN PROSPECT (1987)
At 4: 2nd Spinster Stakes
3rd Maskette Stakes

SCRIMSHAW (2000)
At 3: 3rd Preakness Stakes

SCRIPT (1950)
At 3: 2nd Delaware Oaks

SCRIPT OHIO (1982)
At 2: Won Young America Stakes

SCRUPLES (1980)
At 4: 3rd Hollywood Turf Cup

SCRUTINY (1973)
At 2: 3rd Breeders' Futurity

SCUDAN (1989)
At 3: 3rd Haskell Invitational Handicap

SCUFFLEBURG (1989)
At 3: Won Pegasus Handicap
At 5: Won Gulfstream Park Handicap

SCYTHIAN GOLD (1975)
At 5: 3rd United Nations Handicap

SEA BASQUE (1984)
At 2: 2nd Matron Stakes

SEA BREEZER (1992)
At 2: 2nd Spinaway Stakes

SEA CADET (1988)
At 3: Won San Felipe Stakes
2nd Pegasus Handicap
3rd Santa Anita Derby
Meadowlands Cup
At 4: Won Donn Handicap
Gulfstream Park Handicap
Meadowlands Cup
2nd Oaklawn Handicap

SEA CASTLE (1963)
At 7: 2nd John B. Campbell Handicap

SEA CHIMES (1976)
At 5: 3rd Arlington Handicap

SEA EAGLE (1962)
At 3: 2nd Hollywood Oaks

SEAFES (1962)
At 2: 2nd Breeders' Futurity

SEA GARDEN (1947)
At 3: 2nd Hollywood Oaks
3rd Santa Susana Stakes

SEA HERO (1990)
At 2: Won Champagne Stakes
At 3: Won Kentucky Derby
Travers Stakes
3rd Molson Export Million
At 4: 3rd Brooklyn Handicap

SEANEEN (1954)
At 3: 3rd Cinema Handicap
At 4: Won San Carlos Handicap
Californian Stakes
2nd American Handicap
Santa Anita Maturity
3rd Hollywood Gold Cup
At 5: 2nd Los Angeles Handicap

SEA O ERIN (1951)
At 3: 3rd Ohio Derby
At 4: Won New Orleans Handicap
3rd Hawthorne Gold Cup
At 5: 3rd McLennan Handicap
New Orleans Handicap
Washington Park Handicap

SEA ORBIT (1956)
At 4: 2nd Inglewood Handicap
At 5: Won Inglewood Handicap

3rd Californian Stakes
American Handicap
At 6: 2nd Inglewood Handicap

SEARCHING (1952)
At 3: 2nd Firenze Handicap
At 4: Won Top Flight Handicap
Diana Handicap
Maskette Handicap
3rd Beldame Handicap
At 5: 2nd Diana Handicap
3rd Spinster Stakes
At 6: Won Molly Pitcher Handicap
Diana Handicap

SEA SAGA (1968)
At 3: Won Ladies Handicap
2nd Acorn Stakes
At 4: 2nd Ladies Handicap

SEASIDE ATTRACTION (1987)
At 3: Won Kentucky Oaks
3rd Acorn Stakes

SEA TREK (1985)
At 3: 3rd Arkansas Derby

SEATTLE DAWN (1986)
At 4: Won Delaware Handicap

SEATTLE METEOR (1986)
At 2: 2nd Matron Stakes
3rd Alcibiades Stakes

SEATTLE SANGUE (1985)
At 2: 2nd Selima Stakes

SEATTLE SLEET (1990)
At 2: 3rd Del Mar Futurity

SEATTLE SLEW (1974)
At 2: Won Champagne Stakes
At 3: Won Flamingo Stakes
Wood Memorial Stakes
Kentucky Derby
Preakness Stakes
Belmont Stakes
At 4: Won Marlboro Cup Handicap
Woodward Stakes
2nd Jockey Club Gold Cup

SEATTLE SMOOTH (1985)
At 4: 2nd La Canada Stakes

SEATTLE SONG (1981)
At 3: Won Washington D.C. International

SEAWARD (1945)
At 5: 2nd Trenton Handicap
Stars and Stripes Handicap
At 6: Won Hawthorne Gold Cup

SEBA (1999)
At 3: 3rd Mother Goose Stakes

SECOND AVENUE (1947)
At 6: Won Michigan Mile

SECOND BAR (1969)
At 3: 2nd Jersey Derby
At 4: 2nd Donn Handicap

SECRETARIAT (1970)
At 2: Won Hopeful Stakes
Futurity Stakes
Laurel Futurity
Garden State Stakes
2nd Champagne Stakes
At 3: Won Gotham Stakes
Kentucky Derby
Preakness Stakes
Belmont Stakes
Marlboro Cup Handicap
Man o' War Stakes
Canadian International Championship
2nd Whitney Stakes
Woodward Stakes
3rd Wood Memorial Stakes

SECRET HELLO (1987)
At 4: 3rd Donn Handicap

SECRET MEETING (1950)
At 3: Won Acorn Stakes

SECRET ODDS (1990)
At 2: 2nd Champagne Stakes

SECRETO DE ESTADO (1993)
At 3: 3rd Jim Dandy Stakes

SECRET OF MECCA (1998)
At 5: 3rd Santa Monica Handicap

SECRET PRINCE (1981)
At 2: 2nd Remsen Stakes

SECRET PROMISE (1964)
At 3: 2nd Monmouth Oaks

SECRET RETREAT (1968)
At 2: 3rd Alcibiades Stakes

SECRET SLEW (1986)
At 4: 3rd San Fernando Stakes

SECRET STATUS (1997)
At 3: Won Kentucky Oaks
Mother Goose Stakes
2nd Alabama Stakes
3rd Coaching Club American Oaks

SECRET VERDICT (1966)
At 3: 3rd Coaching Club American Oaks

SEEKING IT ALL (1998)
At 2: 3rd Spinaway Stakes

SEEKING THE GOLD (1985)
At 3: Won Peter Pan Stakes
Dwyer Stakes
Super Derby
2nd Gotham Stakes
Wood Memorial Stakes
Haskell Invitational Handicap
Travers Stakes
Breeders' Cup Classic
At 4: 2nd Metropolitan Handicap

SEE-TEE-SEE (1943)
At 4: 3rd Inglewood Handicap
At 5: 2nd Golden Gate Handicap

SEE THE JAGUAR (1970)
At 3: 3rd Travers Stakes

SEE YOU SOON (1994)
At 3: 3rd Del Mar Oaks
At 4: Won Ramona Handicap

SEFA'S BEAUTY (1979)
At 4: 2nd Apple Blossom Handicap
At 6: Won Apple Blossom Handicap
At 7: 3rd Apple Blossom Handicap

SELARI (1962)
At 3: 2nd Lawrence Realization Stakes
3rd Jersey Derby
At 4: Won Grey Lag Handicap
2nd Seminole Handicap
Widener Handicap
Gulfstream Park Handicap
3rd Donn Handicap
Michigan Mile and One-Eighth

SELECTOR (1947)
At 2: 2nd Cowdin Stakes
3rd Remsen Handicap

SELF FEEDER (1994)
At 6: 2nd Charles Whittingham Handicap

SELINSGROVE (1952)
At 3: 2nd Ohio Derby

SELLOUT (1971)
At 3: Won Louisiana Derby

SELOUS SCOUT (1980)
At 5: Won Hialeah Turf Cup
3rd Widener Handicap

SEMILLANT (1965)
At 5: Won Massachusetts Handicap

SENATOR TO BE (1987)
At 3: 2nd Jim Dandy Stakes
At 4: 2nd Vosburgh Stakes

SENOR PETE (1987)
At 2: Won Futurity Stakes
3rd Champagne Stakes
At 3: 2nd Gotham Stakes

SENOR TOMAS (1989)
At 3: Won Super Derby

SENSATIONAL (1974)
At 2: Won Frizette Stakes
Selima Stakes
2nd Sorority Stakes
3rd Spinaway Stakes
At 3: Won Ladies Handicap
2nd Alabama Stakes
At 4: 2nd Santa Margarita Handicap
3rd Maskette Handicap
Santa Barbara Handicap

SENSITIVE MUSIC (1969)
At 3: 2nd Blue Grass Stakes

SENSITIVE PRINCE (1975)
At 3: Won Jerome Handicap
At 4: Won Gulfstream Park Handicap

SENSITIVO (1957)
At 5: Won Gallant Fox Handicap
Display Handicap
2nd Manhattan Handicap
3rd Hawthorne Gold Cup
Trenton Handicap
At 6: 2nd Gulfstream Park Handicap
3rd Seminole Handicap

SENURE (1996)
At 5: Won United Nations Handicap
Clement L. Hirsch Mem. Turf Champ.
2nd Charles Whittingham Handicap

SEPTEMBER (1946)
At 4: 2nd Beldame Handicap
3rd Comely Handicap

SEPTIEME CIEL (1987)
At 3: 2nd Hollywood Derby

SEQUENCE (1946)
At 2: Won Princess Pat Stakes

SEQUOIA (1955)
At 2: Won Spinaway Stakes

SERENA'S SONG (1992)
At 2: Won Oak Leaf Stakes
Hollywood Starlet Stakes
2nd Breeders' Cup Juvenile Fillies
At 3: Won Las Virgenes Stakes
Santa Anita Oaks
Jim Beam Stakes
Mother Goose Stakes
Haskell Invitational Handicap
Gazelle Handicap
Beldame Stakes
2nd Coaching Club American Oaks
At 4: Won Santa Maria Handicap
Hempstead Handicap
2nd Vanity Handicap
Whitney Handicap
Ruffian Handicap
Beldame Stakes
Breeders' Cup Distaff
3rd Apple Blossom Handicap
Philip H. Iselin Handicap

SERENE QUEEN (1964)
At 4: 2nd Top Flight Handicap

SERENITA (1997)
At 3: 3rd La Brea Stakes
At 4: 2nd Santa Monica Handicap

SERIOUS SPENDER (1991)
At 3: 3rd Pegasus Handicap

SERRA LAKE (1997)
At 4: Won Go for Wand Handicap

SERRANT (1988)
At 5: 2nd Man o' War Stakes

SETAREH (1997)
At 4: 3rd Vanity Handicap

SET STYLE (1983)
At 4: 2nd Suburban Handicap

SETTE BELLO (1962)
At 6: Won Widener Handicap
3rd Gulfstream Park Handicap

SETTLEMENT (1997)
At 2: 2nd Hopeful Stakes

SEVEN CORNERS (1956)
At 3: 3rd Jerome Handicap

SEVENGREENPAIRS (1989)
At 3: 3rd Swaps Stakes

SEVEN THIRTY (1958)
At 3: 3rd Acorn Stakes
At 4: Won Black Helen Handicap
Delaware Handicap

SEWICKLEY (1985)
At 4: Won Vosburgh Stakes
At 5: Won Vosburgh Stakes
3rd Carter Handicap
NYRA Mile Handicap

SEZYOU (1978)
At 2: 2nd Young America Stakes
3rd Champagne Stakes

SGT. SPENCE (1943)
At 3: 2nd Arlington Classic

SHABBY CHIC (1996)
At 3: 3rd Yellow Ribbon Stakes

SHACKLETON (1946)
At 3: Won Dwyer Stakes

SHADEED (1982)
At 3: 3rd Breeders' Cup Mile

SHADY TUNE (1950)
At 4: Won Molly Pitcher Handicap

SHAGBARK (1975)
At 7: 2nd Century Handicap

SHAKE THE YOKE (1993)
At 3: 2nd Queen Elizabeth II Challenge Cup

SHAKE YOU DOWN (1998)
At 5: 2nd Frank J. De Francis Memorial Dash
3rd Breeders' Cup Sprint

SHAM (1970)
At 3: Won Santa Anita Derby
2nd Wood Memorial Stakes
Kentucky Derby
Preakness Stakes

SHAMGO (1976)
At 3: 2nd Swaps Stakes
3rd Hollywood Derby

SHAMMY DAVIS (1994)
At 3: 3rd Jim Beam Stakes

SHAM SAY (1985)
At 3: Won Ruffian Handicap
3rd Maskette Stakes
Beldame Stakes

SHANNON II (1941)
At 7: Won Hollywood Gold Cup
Golden Gate Handicap
3rd Sunset Handicap

SHAN PAC (1954)
At 3: 2nd Louisiana Derby
Ohio Derby

SHAPELY SCRAPPER (1991)
At 2: 2nd Arlington-Washington Lassie Stakes

SHARAN (1995)
At 5: 3rd Shoemaker Breeders' Cup Mile

SHARDARI (1982)
At 4: 2nd Rothmans International Stakes

SHARED INTEREST (1988)
At 5: Won Ruffian Handicap
2nd Shuvee Handicap
Beldame Stakes
3rd Top Flight Handicap

SHARE THE FANTASY (1980)
At 2: 2nd Matron Stakes

SHARM A SHEIKH (1972)
At 2: 2nd Arlington-Washington Lassie Stakes

SHARP CAT (1994)
At 2: Won Matron Stakes
Hollywood Starlet Stakes
2nd Frizette Stakes
At 3: Won Las Virgenes Stakes
Santa Anita Oaks
Acorn Stakes
Hollywood Oaks
2nd Mother Goose Stakes
Breeders' Cup Distaff
At 4: Won Ruffian Handicap
Beldame Stakes

SHARP COUNT (1959)
At 2: 3rd Kentucky Jockey Club Stakes

SHARP DANCE (1986)
At 3: 3rd Spinster Stakes
At 5: Won Beldame Stakes
2nd Ruffian Handicap
3rd Top Flight Handicap

SHARP GARY (1971)
At 3: Won Illinois Derby
3rd Wood Memorial Stakes
Ohio Derby
At 5: Won Michigan Mile and One-Eighth

SHARP PERFORMANCE (1998)
At 3: 3rd Secretariat Stakes

SHARPSBURG (1953)
At 5: 2nd Pimlico Special
Monmouth Handicap
At 6: Won McLennan Handicap

SHARROOD (1983)
At 4: 2nd Budweiser-Arlington Million

SHAWI (1973)
At 4: Won Top Flight Handicap

SHAWKLIT WON (1984)
At 3: 2nd Gotham Stakes
3rd Wood Memorial Stakes
Peter Pan Stakes

SHAWNEE SQUAW (1948)
At 2: Won Arlington Lassie Stakes

SHE CAN (1987)
At 3: 2nd Top Flight Handicap

SHECKY GREENE (1970)
At 2: Won Arlington-Washington Futurity
At 3: Won Fountain of Youth Stakes

SHEET ANCHOR (1961)
At 4: 3rd Gallant Fox Handicap

SHEIKH ALBADOU (1988)
At 3: Won Breeders' Cup Sprint
At 4: 2nd Vosburgh Stakes

SHEIK OF BAGDAD (1966)
At 3: 3rd Arkansas Derby

SHEILAS REWARD (1947)
At 3: 2nd Swift Stakes
At 4: Won Queens County Handicap
2nd Brooklyn Handicap

SHELTER BAY (1966)
At 4: Won Manhattan Handicap

SHENOW (1965)
At 2: Won Arlington-Washington Lassie Stakes

SHEPHERD'S FIELD (1991)
At 2: Won Norfolk Stakes

SHERLUCK (1958)
At 2: 3rd Pimlico Futurity
At 3: Won Blue Grass Stakes
Belmont Stakes
Lawrence Realization Stakes
Roamer Handicap
2nd Everglades Stakes

SHE'S A DEVIL DUE (1998)
At 2: Won Walmac International Alcibiades Stakes
3rd Breeders' Cup Juvenile Fillies

SHE'S A LIVELY ONE (1992)
At 2: 2nd Arlington-Washington Lassie Stakes

SHE'S CLASSY (1997)
At 2: 2nd Hollywood Starlet Stakes
3rd Vinery Del Mar Debutante Stakes

SHE'S GOT THE BEAT (1999)
At 4: 2nd Go for Wand Handicap

SHIFTY SHEIK (1979)
At 5: 2nd Woodward Stakes

SHIMATOREE (1979)
At 3: 2nd Wood Memorial Stakes

SHIM MALONE (1944)
At 5: Won San Pasqual Handicap

SHIMMER (1945)
At 2: 3rd Demoiselle Stakes

SHIMMERING GOLD (1963)
At 2: 2nd Sorority Stakes
3rd Matron Stakes

SHINE AGAIN (1997)
At 4: Won Ballerina Handicap
At 5: Won Ballerina Handicap
3rd Ruffian Handicap
At 6: 2nd Ballerina Handicap

SHINING LIGHT (1992)
At 2: Won Arlington-Washington Lassie Stakes

SHIP LEAVE (1966)
At 4: 3rd Widener Handicap

SHIPROCK (1991)
At 3: 3rd Wood Memorial Stakes

SHIRES ENDE (1995)
At 3: 2nd Queen Elizabeth II Challenge Cup

SHIRLEY HEIGHTS (1964)
At 2: 3rd Spinaway Stakes

SHIRLEY JONES (1956)
At 5: Won Arlington Matron Handicap
2nd Vineland Handicap
At 6: 2nd Arlington Matron Handicap
Beldame Stakes
Vineland Handicap

SHISHKABOB (1978)
At 3: Won Louisiana Downs Handicap
At 5: 3rd Louisiana Downs Handicap

SHOCKER T. (1982)
At 4: Won Delaware Handicap

SHOERULLAH (1954)
At 4: 2nd Michigan Mile

SHOOP (1991)
At 5: 2nd Hempstead Handicap
Go for Wand Stakes
John A. Morris Handicap
At 6: 2nd John A. Morris Handicap

SHOOTING DUCK (1979)
At 2: 3rd Breeders' Futurity

SHOOTING PARTY (1998)
At 3: 2nd Garden City Breeders' Cup Handicap

SHOP TILL YOU DROP (1999)
At 3: 3rd Coaching Club American Oaks

SHORT JACKET (1958)
At 2: Won Del Mar Futurity

SHOT GUN SCOTT (1987)
At 3: 2nd Travers Stakes

SHOTSILK (1945)
At 3: Won Black Helen Handicap

SHOW DANCER (1982)
At 5: 2nd Breeders' Cup Mile

SHOW ME FIRST (1951)
At 3: 3rd California Derby

SHOW OFF (1966)
At 2: 2nd Spinaway Stakes
Alcibiades Stakes

SHUDANZ (1988)
At 3: 3rd Ohio Derby

SHUT EYE (1966)
At 5: 3rd Carter Handicap

SHUTTLE JET (1981)
At 2: 2nd Futurity Stakes

SHUVEE (1966)
At 2: Won Frizette Stakes
Selima Stakes
2nd Gardenia Stakes
At 3: Won Acorn Stakes
Mother Goose Stakes
Coaching Club American Oaks
Alabama Stakes
Ladies Handicap
3rd Gazelle Handicap
Beldame Stakes
At 4: Won Top Flight Handicap
Beldame Stakes
Jockey Club Gold Cup
At 5: Won Top Flight Handicap
Jockey Club Gold Cup
2nd Beldame Stakes
3rd Whitney Stakes

SHY BIM (1948)
At 3: 3rd Monmouth Oaks

SHY GUY (1945)
At 2: Won Breeders' Futurity
2nd Kentucky Jockey Club Stakes
At 3: 2nd Louisiana Derby
Arlington Classic
3rd Blue Grass Stakes
Lawrence Realization Stakes
At 4: 2nd Widener Handicap
3rd McLennan Handicap

SHY KATIE (1945)
At 2: 3rd Princess Pat Stakes

SHY TOM (1986)
At 3: 3rd Haskell Invitational Handicap
Travers Stakes
At 4: 2nd Man o' War Stakes

SHYWING (1982)
At 4: 2nd La Canada Stakes

SIAMA (1947)
At 3: Won Acorn Stakes
Monmouth Handicap
Comely Handicap

SIBERIAN SUMMER (1989)
At 4: Won Charles H. Strub Stakes

SIC EM JUDGE (1968)
At 3: 3rd Jerome Handicap

SICILY (1942)
At 4: Won Top Flight Handicap

SICKLE'S IMAGE (1948)
At 3: Won Arlington Matron Stakes
2nd Santa Susana Stakes
3rd Kentucky Oaks
At 4: Won Vineland Handicap
3rd Washington Park Handicap
At 5: Won Washington Park Handicap

SICKLE'S SOUND (1950)
At 3: 3rd Gotham Stakes

SICY D'ALSACE (1995)
At 3: Won Del Mar Oaks

SIDLUCK (1959)
At 3: 3rd Gotham Stakes

SIERRA DIABLO (1992)
At 2: 2nd Champagne Stakes

SIERRA FOX (1941)
At 6: 3rd Del Mar Handicap

SIERRA ROBERTA (1986)
At 3: 2nd Breeders' Cup Turf

SIERRA VIRGEN (1995)
At 3: 3rd Queen Elizabeth II Challenge Cup

SIGHTSEEK (1999)
At 4: Won Humana Distaff Handicap
Ogden Phipps Handicap
Go for Wand Handicap
Beldame Stakes
2nd Santa Monica Handicap
Santa Margarita Handicap

SIGNAL (1948)
At 3: 2nd Delaware Oaks

SIGNAL TAP (1991)
At 4: 3rd Man o' War Stakes

SILENT ACCOUNT (1983)
At 2: 2nd Selima Stakes

SILENT BEAUTY (1968)
At 3: Won Kentucky Oaks

SILENT CAL (1975)
At 4: 3rd Gulfstream Park Handicap
Amory L. Haskell Handicap
At 5: 3rd Gulfstream Park Handicap
Metropolitan Handicap

SILENT ESKIMO (1995)
At 4: 3rd Apple Blossom Handicap

SILENT FOX (1980)
At 4: 3rd Charles H. Strub Stakes

SILENT KING (1981)
At 3: 2nd Louisiana Derby
Blue Grass Stakes

SILENT SCREEN (1967)
At 2: Won Arlington-Washington Futurity
Cowdin Stakes
Champagne Stakes
At 3: 2nd Wood Memorial Stakes
3rd Gotham Stakes
Preakness Stakes
Jersey Derby

SILENT TURN (1984)
At 2: 3rd Selima Stakes
At 3: 3rd Beldame Stakes

SILIC (1995)
At 4: Won Breeders' Cup Mile
At 5: Won Shoemaker Breeders' Cup Mile

SILK HAT (1961)
At 5: 3rd Sunset Handicap

SILK'S LADY (1984)
At 2: 2nd Oak Leaf Stakes

SILKY FEATHER (1990)
At 3: 2nd Gazelle Handicap
3rd Mother Goose Stakes
Coaching Club American Oaks
Alabama Stakes

SILKY SULLIVAN (1955)

At 3: Won Santa Anita Derby

SILLERY (1988)

At 3: 2nd Budweiser International Stakes
At 4: 2nd Budweiser International Stakes

SILVANO (1996)

At 5: Won Arlington Million
2nd Man o' War Stakes

SILVER BRIGHT (1963)

At 2: Won Arlington-Washington Lassie Stakes

SILVER BUCK (1978)

At 4: Won Suburban Handicap
Whitney Handicap
2nd Metropolitan Handicap
Woodward Stakes

SILVERBULLETDAY (1996)

At 2: Won Walmac International Alcibiades Stakes
Breeders' Cup Juvenile Fillies
At 3: Won Ashland Stakes
Kentucky Oaks
Alabama Stakes
Gazelle Handicap
2nd Beldame Stakes

SILVER CHARM (1994)

At 2: Won Del Mar Futurity
At 3: Won Kentucky Derby
Preakness Stakes
2nd San Felipe Stakes
Santa Anita Derby
Belmont Stakes
Malibu Stakes
At 4: Won Strub Stakes
2nd Breeders' Cup Classic
At 5: 3rd Donn Handicap
Santa Anita Handicap

SILVER CIRCUS (1985)

At 3: Won Hollywood Derby
At 4: 3rd Charles H. Strub Stakes

SILVER COMET (1983)

At 4: 2nd Philip H. Iselin Handicap

SILVER CREST (1946)

At 2: 3rd Marguerite Stakes

SILVER DRIFT (1945)

At 4: Won Vanity Handicap

SILVER EAGLE (1974)

At 5: 3rd Oak Tree Invitational Stakes
At 6: 3rd San Luis Rey Stakes

SILVERED (1987)

At 3: Won Fantasy Stakes
At 5: 3rd Gamely Handicap

SILVER ENDING (1987)

At 2: 3rd Hollywood Futurity
At 3: Won Arkansas Derby
Pegasus Handicap
2nd Swaps Stakes

SILVER EXPRESS (1978)

At 3: 3rd Dwyer Stakes

SILVER FLORIN (1971)

At 3: 2nd Arkansas Derby

SILVER FOX (1991)

At 4: 3rd Whitney Handicap

SILVER GOBLIN (1991)

At 3: 3rd Arkansas Derby
At 4: 2nd Oaklawn Handicap

SILVER MAIDEN (1995)

At 2: Won Frizette Stakes

SILVER MUSIC (1991)

At 3: Won Swaps Stakes

SILVER NITRATE (1975)

At 3: 3rd Illinois Derby

SILVER OF SILVER (1990)

At 2: Won Remsen Stakes
At 3: 3rd Dwyer Stakes

SILVER SERIES (1974)

At 3: Won Ohio Derby
American Derby
2nd Woodward Handicap
3rd Travers Stakes
At 4: Won Widener Handicap
2nd New Orleans Handicap
3rd Gulfstream Park Handicap

SILVER SPOON (1956)

At 3: Won Santa Anita Derby
Cinema Handicap
2nd Delaware Oaks
3rd Monmouth Oaks
At 4: Won Vanity Handicap
Santa Margarita Handicap
3rd Arlington Matron Handicap

SILVER SUNSETS (1986)

At 2: 3rd Remsen Stakes

SILVER SUPREME (1978)

At 4: Won Brooklyn Handicap
2nd Marlboro Cup Handicap
Jockey Club Gold Cup
3rd Woodward Stakes
At 5: 3rd Brooklyn Handicap

SILVER SURVIVOR (1986)

At 4: 3rd Oaklawn Handicap

SILVER TRUE (1964)

At 2: Won Spinaway Stakes

SILVER WAGON (2001)

At 2: Won Hopeful Stakes

SILVER WIZARD (1990)

At 6: 3rd San Luis Rey Stakes

SILVEYVILLE (1978)

At 3: Won Hollywood Derby

SILWALL (1961)

At 3: 3rd Monmouth Oaks

SIMMY (1952)

At 2: 2nd Washington Park Futurity
Garden State Stakes
At 3: 3rd Wood Memorial Stakes

SIMONSEZ (1948)

At 3: 2nd Golden Gate Handicap

SIMPLY MAJESTIC (1984)

At 3: Won California Derby
At 4: 3rd Breeders' Cup Mile
At 5: 3rd United Nations Handicap

SINGH (1972)

At 3: Won Jersey Derby

SINGING RAIN (1965)

At 2: 3rd Selima Stakes
At 3: 2nd Monmouth Oaks
At 5: 2nd Top Flight Handicap

SINGING SURF (1966)

At 2: 2nd Del Mar Debutante Stakes

SINGING SUSAN (1980)

At 2: Won Sorority Stakes

SINGLE AGENT (1968)

At 4: 2nd American Handicap

SINGLE DAWN (1987)

At 2: 2nd Norfolk Stakes
3rd Del Mar Futurity

SINGLE EMPIRE (1994)

At 5: Won San Juan Capistrano Handicap
2nd Man o' War Stakes
3rd Hollywood Turf Cup
At 6: 2nd San Juan Capistrano Handicap
3rd Sword Dancer Invitational Handicap

SINGLETON (1974)

At 5: 3rd Widener Handicap

SING SING (1978)

At 3: Won Secretariat Stakes
3rd Jerome Handicap
At 5: 2nd Suburban Handicap
Brooklyn Handicap
3rd Woodward Stakes

SINGSPIEL (1992)

At 4: Won Canadian International Championship
2nd Breeders' Cup Turf

SINGULAR (1975)

At 3: 3rd Cinema Handicap

SINGULARITY (1977)

At 4: 3rd San Juan Capistrano Handicap

SINKING SPRING (1964)

At 5: 3rd Santa Margarita Handicap

SINK NOT SUNK (1955)

At 5: 3rd Michigan Mile and One-Sixteenth

SINTESIS (1959)

At 5: 3rd Santa Margarita Handicap

SINTRILLIUM (1978)

At 5: 3rd Santa Margarita Handicap
At 7: 2nd Top Flight Handicap
3rd Ruffian Handicap

SIPHON (1991)

At 5: Won Hollywood Gold Cup
3rd Pacific Classic
At 6: Won Santa Anita Handicap
2nd Hollywood Gold Cup
Pacific Classic

SIPHONIC (1999)

At 2: Won Lane's End Breeders' Futurity
Hollywood Futurity
3rd Bessemer Trust Breeders' Cup Juvenile

SIPHONIZER (2001)

At 2: Won Del Mar Futurity

SIR BEAR (1993)

At 5: Won Cigar Mile Handicap
2nd Brooklyn Handicap
3rd Donn Handicap
Suburban Handicap
Buick Meadowlands Cup Handicap
At 6: Won Metropolitan Handicap
3rd Gulfstream Park Handicap
Brooklyn Handicap
At 7: 2nd Philip H. Iselin Handicap
3rd Metropolitan Handicap
At 8: Won Gulfstream Park Handicap
3rd Philip H. Iselin Handicap
At 9: 3rd Gulfstream Park Handicap

SIR BEAUFORT (1987)

At 6: Won Santa Anita Handicap
2nd San Antonio Handicap

SIR CHEROKEE (2000)

At 3: Won Arkansas Derby

SIR DANCER (1978)

At 2: Won Norfolk Stakes
3rd Del Mar Futurity

SIRDE (1941)

At 5: Won San Carlos Handicap
2nd San Pasqual Handicap
Metropolitan Handicap

SIR GAYLORD (1959)

At 2: Won Sapling Stakes
3rd Hopeful Stakes
Futurity Stakes
Cowdin Stakes
Champagne Stakes
At 3: Won Everglades Stakes

SIR HARRY LEWIS (1984)

At 3: 3rd Rothmans International Stakes

SIRIBBI (1972)

At 3: 2nd Swaps Stakes
3rd Hollywood Derby

SIR IVOR (1965)
At 3: Won Washington D.C. International

SIR IVOR AGAIN (1976)
At 3: 3rd Flamingo Stakes

SIRLAD (1974)
At 5: Won Sunset Handicap
2nd Hollywood Gold Cup

SIR LISTER (1973)
At 3: 2nd Dwyer Handicap

SIR MANGO (1950)
At 3: 2nd Arlington Classic
At 4: 3rd Arlington Handicap

SIR RIBOT (1959)
At 3: 3rd Santa Anita Derby

SIR RICHARD LEWIS (1987)
At 2: 2nd Hopeful Stakes
At 3: 3rd Travers Stakes

SIR ROBBY (1955)
At 3: Won Withers Stakes

SIR RULER (1955)
At 2: 3rd Arlington Futurity

SIR SIR (1974)
At 3: 3rd Florida Derby

SIR TIFF (1995)
At 3: 3rd Super Derby

SIR TRIBAL (1951)
At 5: 3rd Arlington Handicap

SIR WIGGLE (1967)
At 3: 3rd San Felipe Handicap

SIR WILLIAM (1954)
At 3: Won Santa Anita Derby
2nd San Felipe Handicap

SIR WINZALOT (1964)
At 2: 2nd Sanford Stakes

SISSY'S TIME (1977)
At 2: Won Arlington-Washington Lassie Stakes

SISTER ACT (1995)
At 4: Won Hempstead Handicap
2nd Apple Blossom Handicap

SISTER ANTOINE (1957)
At 3: 3rd Acorn Stakes
At 4: Won Santa Margarita Handicap

SISTER GIRL BLUES (1999)
At 4: 2nd Vanity Handicap

SISTERHOOD (1975)
At 4: Won Gamely Handicap
At 5: Won Santa Barbara Handicap

SIX CROWNS (1976)
At 3: 3rd Ladies Handicap

SIX FIFTEEN (1950)
At 4: 3rd Sunset Handicap

SIX PERFECTIONS (2000)
At 3: Won NetJets Breeders' Cup Mile

SIXY SAINT (1994)
At 4: 2nd Beverly Hills Handicap

SKI DANCER (1992)
At 2: 3rd Hollywood Starlet Stakes
At 5: 2nd Santa Monica Handicap

SKI GOGGLE (1980)
At 3: Won Acorn Stakes

SKILLFUL JOY (1979)
At 2: Won Del Mar Debutante Stakes
Hollywood Starlet Stakes
At 3: 2nd Santa Susana Stakes
Fantasy Stakes

SKIMBLE (1989)
At 4: 3rd Matriarch Stakes
At 5: 3rd Ramona Handicap

SKIMMING (1996)
At 4: Won Pacific Classic
At 5: Won Pacific Classic
2nd Hollywood Gold Cup

SKI PARADISE (1990)
At 3: 2nd Breeders' Cup Mile

SKIP AWAY (1993)
At 2: 2nd Remsen Stakes
At 3: Won Blue Grass Stakes
Ohio Derby
Buick Haskell Invitational Handicap
Woodbine Million
Jockey Club Gold Cup
2nd Preakness Stakes
Belmont Stakes
3rd Florida Derby
Travers Stakes
At 4: Won Suburban Handicap
Jockey Club Gold Cup
Breeders' Cup Classic
2nd Donn Handicap
Gulfstream Park Handicap
Pimlico Special
Philip H. Iselin Handicap
Woodward Stakes
3rd Whitney Handicap
At 5: Won Donn Handicap
Gulfstream Park Handicap
Pimlico Special
Hollywood Gold Cup
Philip H. Iselin Handicap
Woodward Stakes
3rd Jockey Club Gold Cup

SKIP OUT FRONT (1982)
At 5: 2nd John Henry Handicap
At 6: 3rd Hollywood Invitational Handicap

SKIPPER BILL (1950)
At 6: 2nd Michigan Mile

SKIPPING (1997)
At 5: 3rd Charles Whittingham Handicap

SKIP TRIAL (1982)
At 3: Won Ohio Derby
Haskell Invitational Handicap
Pennsylvania Derby
3rd Travers Stakes
At 4: Won Gulfstream Park Handicap
2nd Meadowlands Cup
At 5: Won Gulfstream Park Handicap

SKOOKUM (1965)
At 4: 2nd Malibu Stakes

SKY BEAUTY (1990)
At 2: Won Matron Stakes
3rd Spinaway Stakes
At 3: Won Acorn Stakes
Mother Goose Stakes
Coaching Club American Oaks
Alabama Stakes
At 4: Won Shuvee Handicap
Hempstead Handicap
Go for Wand Stakes
Ruffian Handicap
At 5: 2nd Shuvee Handicap
3rd Hempstead Handicap

SKY CLASSIC (1987)
At 3: 2nd Rothmans International Stakes
At 4: Won Rothmans International Stakes
At 5: Won Caesars International Handicap
Turf Classic
2nd Arlington Million
Breeders' Cup Turf

SKY CLIPPER (1957)
At 2: Won Sapling Stakes

SKY GEM (1960)
At 2: Won Kentucky Jockey Club Stakes
At 3: 2nd Santa Anita Derby
Cinema Handicap

SKY GUY (1963)
At 3: 3rd Florida Derby
At 4: 2nd Donn Handicap

SKY JACK (1996)
At 6: Won Hollywood Gold Cup

SKYLIGHTER (1943)
At 5: 3rd Carter Handicap

SKY MESA (2000)
At 2: Won Hopeful Stakes
Lane's End Breeders' Futurity
At 3: 2nd Haskell Invitational Handicap

SKY MIRACLE (1946)
At 3: Won Trenton Handicap

SKY SHIP (1949)
At 3: Won Florida Derby

SKYWALKER (1982)
At 3: Won Santa Anita Derby
2nd San Felipe Handicap
At 4: Won Breeders' Cup Classic
3rd Californian Stakes

SKY WONDER (1960)
At 3: 2nd Florida Derby
Withers Stakes
3rd Jersey Derby

SLAM BANG (1946)
At 2: 2nd Pimlico Futurity

SLAVIC (1987)
At 2: 2nd Cowdin Stakes
3rd Breeders' Cup Juvenile
At 3: 2nd Florida Derby

SLEDGE (1959)
At 7: 3rd Californian Stakes

SLEEK AND FLEET (1970)
At 2: 3rd Oak Leaf Stakes

SLEEP EASY (1992)
At 3: Won Hollywood Oaks
At 4: 2nd Santa Margarita Handicap

SLEPT THRU IT (1988)
At 2: 3rd Demoiselle Stakes

SLEWBOP (1985)
At 3: 2nd California Derby

SLEW CITY SLEW (1984)
At 4: 2nd Meadowlands Cup
At 5: Won Gulfstream Park Handicap
Oaklawn Handicap
2nd Widener Handicap
3rd Meadowlands Cup

SLEW GIN FIZZ (1991)
At 2: 2nd Hopeful Stakes

SLEW OF DAMASCUS (1988)
At 6: Won Hollywood Gold Cup
3rd Californian Stakes
At 7: 2nd San Antonio Handicap

SLEW O' GOLD (1980)
At 3: Won Wood Memorial Stakes
Woodward Stakes
Jockey Club Gold Cup
2nd Belmont Stakes
Travers Stakes
Marlboro Cup Handicap
At 4: Won Whitney Handicap
Woodward Stakes
Marlboro Cup Handicap
Jockey Club Gold Cup
2nd Breeders' Cup Classic

SLEWPY (1980)
At 2: Won Young America Stakes
At 3: Won Meadowlands Cup
3rd Louisiana Derby

SLEW'S GHOST (1989)
At 2: 2nd Hopeful Stakes

SLEW THE COUP (1981)
At 3: 2nd Jim Dandy Stakes
3rd Dwyer Stakes

SLEW THE DRAGON (1982)
At 3: Won Hollywood Derby

SLEW VALLEY (1997)
At 4: 2nd Sword Dancer Invitational Handicap
At 6: 2nd Man o' War Stakes
3rd Sword Dancer Invitational Handicap

SLICK HORN (1990)
At 5: 3rd Brooklyn Handicap

SLIDE OUT FRONT (1988)
At 4: 3rd Apple Blossom Handicap

SLIDER (1998)
At 5: 2nd Oaklawn Handicap

SLIGO BAY (1998)
At 3: 2nd Hollywood Derby
At 4: Won Hollywood Turf Cup

SLIM (1950)
At 3: 3rd Florida Derby

SLIPPED DISC (1960)
At 2: Won Del Mar Futurity
2nd Hollywood Juvenile Championship

SLUMBER SONG (1945)
At 2: Won Frizette Stakes

SLY BIRD (1965)
At 3: 3rd Display Handicap

SLYSTITCH (1962)
At 3: 3rd Jerome Handicap
At 4: 3rd Widener Handicap

SMALL FAVOR (1951)
At 2: Won Selima Stakes
3rd Frizette Stakes

SMART (1959)
At 3: 2nd Lawrence Realization Stakes
At 4: Won Manhattan Handicap
2nd Display Handicap
3rd Trenton Handicap
At 5: Won Massachusetts Handicap
Gallant Fox Handicap
2nd Display Handicap
At 6: Won Massachusetts Handicap
2nd Suburban Handicap

SMART ANGLE (1977)
At 2: Won Matron Stakes
Frizette Stakes
Selima Stakes

SMART BARBARA (1950)
At 2: 3rd Del Mar Debutante Stakes

SMART DEB (1960)
At 2: Won Arlington Lassie Stakes
Matron Stakes
2nd Gardenia Stakes
3rd Selima Stakes
At 3: Won Arlington Matron Handicap
2nd Mother Goose Stakes
3rd Coaching Club American Oaks
Monmouth Oaks
Beldame Stakes
At 4: 3rd Top Flight Handicap

SMARTEN (1976)
At 3: Won Illinois Derby
Pennsylvania Derby
Ohio Derby
American Derby
2nd Arkansas Derby
Travers Stakes
Secretariat Stakes
Meadowlands Cup

SMART N SLICK (1981)
At 2: 3rd Arlington-Washington Futurity

SMART STRIKE (1992)
At 4: Won Philip H. Iselin Handicap

SMASHER (1974)
At 3: Won San Felipe Handicap

SMASHING GAIL (1958)
At 4: 3rd Black Helen Handicap

SMILE (1982)
At 3: Won Arlington Classic
2nd Breeders' Cup Sprint
3rd American Derby
At 4: Won Breeders' Cup Sprint

SMILEY'S DREAM (1974)
At 4: 2nd Longacres Mile

SMILING JACK (1969)
At 3: Won Jersey Derby

SMILIN SINGIN SAM (1991)
At 3: 3rd Ohio Derby

SMITHFIELD (1993)
At 3: 2nd San Felipe Stakes

SMOKE GLACKEN (1994)
At 2: Won Hopeful Stakes
At 3: Won Frank J. De Francis Memorial Dash

SMOKE SCREEN (1949)
At 2: 3rd Breeders' Futurity
Kentucky Jockey Club Stakes
At 3: 3rd Blue Grass Stakes
At 4: Won New Orleans Handicap
2nd Hawthorne Gold Cup
At 5: 2nd New Orleans Handicap

SMOKE VEIL (1954)
At 2: 2nd Selima Stakes

SMOKIN MEL (1994)
At 3: Won Gotham Stakes
3rd Wood Memorial Stakes
Jerome Handicap

SMOK'N FROLIC (1999)
At 2: 2nd Spinaway Stakes

SMOOTH CHARMER (1992)
At 4: 2nd Shuvee Handicap

SMOOTH DANCER (1970)
At 4: Won New Orleans Handicap

SMOOTH PERFORMANCE (1988)
At 3: 2nd Dwyer Stakes

SMOOTH PLAYER (1996)
At 3: 2nd Del Mar Oaks

SMOOTH RUNNER (1991)
At 5: 2nd Eddie Read Handicap

SNAP APPLE (1972)
At 3: 2nd Hollywood Oaks

SNAPPY KING (1959)
At 2: 2nd Del Mar Futurity

SNAPPY LANDING (1989)
At 2: 2nd Champagne Stakes
3rd Breeders' Cup Juvenile

SNEAK (1946)
At 3: 2nd Flamingo Stakes

SNEAKY QUIET (1992)
At 3: 3rd Kentucky Oaks

SNOOP (1953)
At 2: 2nd Del Mar Debutante Stakes

SNOOZE (1972)
At 4: 2nd Maskette Handicap

SNOWBERG (1995)
At 2: 3rd Hollywood Starlet Stakes
At 5: 2nd Santa Maria Handicap
3rd Santa Margarita Handicap

SNOW BOOTS (1942)
At 4: 3rd Santa Anita Handicap

SNOW CHIEF (1983)
At 2: Won Norfolk Stakes
Hollywood Futurity
At 3: Won Florida Derby
Santa Anita Derby
Preakness Stakes
Jersey Derby
At 4: Won Charles H. Strub Stakes
3rd San Fernando Stakes
Gulfstream Park Handicap
Californian Stakes

SNOW DANCE (1998)
At 3: 3rd Queen Elizabeth II Challenge Cup

SNOW DOLL (1972)
At 2: 3rd Alcibiades Stakes

SNOW FORT (1960)
At 3: 3rd Arkansas Derby

SNOW GOOSE (1944)
At 3: Won Beldame Handicap
Ladies Handicap
3rd Coaching Club American Oaks
Lawrence Realization Stakes

SNOW KNIGHT (1971)
At 4: Won Man o' War Stakes
Canadian International Championship

SNOW PLOW (1979)
At 2: Won Selima Stakes

SNOW POLINA (1995)
At 5: Won Beverly D. Stakes
2nd Flower Bowl Invitational Handicap

SNOW RIDGE (1998)
At 4: Won San Carlos Handicap

SNOW SPORTING (1966)
At 4: Won Gulfstream Park Handicap
Charles H. Strub Stakes
2nd Pan American Handicap
At 5: 2nd Donn Handicap
Pan American Handicap
3rd Gulfstream Park Handicap

SNOW WHITE (1954)
At 3: 2nd Alabama Stakes
3rd Ladies Handicap

SNUCK IN (1997)
At 3: 2nd Arkansas Derby

SNURGE (1987)
At 5: Won Rothmans International Stakes

SOARING SOFTLY (1995)
At 4: Won Flower Bowl Invitational Handicap
Breeders' Cup Filly and Mare Turf

SOCIAL CHARTER (1995)
At 4: 3rd Suburban Handicap

SOCIAL CLIMBER (1953)
At 3: Won San Felipe Handicap
Cinema Handicap
2nd Santa Anita Derby
Westerner Stakes
At 4: Won Californian Stakes
3rd San Antonio Handicap
At 5: 3rd Inglewood Handicap

SOCIAL OUTCAST (1950)
At 2: Won Remsen Handicap
At 3: 3rd San Felipe Handicap
At 4: Won Whitney Handicap
Gallant Fox Handicap
3rd Michigan Mile
Trenton Handicap
At 5: Won McLennan Handicap
John B. Campbell Memorial Handicap
Sunset Handicap
Manhattan Handicap
Trenton Handicap
2nd Massachusetts Handicap
Carter Handicap
3rd Widener Handicap
Pimlico Special
Washington D.C. International

SOCIAL OUTCAST *(Continued)*
At 6: 2nd McLennan Handicap
Widener Handicap

SOCIETY II (1965)
At 4: 2nd Sunset Handicap

SOCIETY SELECTION (2001)
At 2: Won Frizette Stakes

SOFT MACHINE (1985)
At 5: 3rd Sunset Handicap

SOLABAR (1960)
At 3: 2nd Arlington Matron Handicap

SOLAR ECHO (2000)
At 3: 2nd Del Mar Oaks

SOLAR HALO (1981)
At 3: 2nd Ladies Handicap

SOLAR SALUTE (1969)
At 2: 3rd Norfolk Stakes
At 3: Won San Felipe Handicap
Santa Anita Derby

SOLAR SPLENDOR (1987)
At 4: Won Man o' War Stakes
Turf Classic
At 5: Won Man o' War Stakes
3rd Turf Classic
At 6: 2nd Turf Classic
At 7: 2nd Early Times Manhattan Handicap

SOLICITING (1982)
At 2: 3rd Selima Stakes

SOLIDARITY (1945)
At 2: 3rd Starlet Stakes
At 3: Won Westerner Handicap
2nd San Felipe Stakes
3rd San Vicente Handicap
Will Rogers Handicap
Cinema Handicap
At 4: Won Golden Gate Handicap
Hollywood Gold Cup
2nd American Handicap
At 5: Won San Pasqual Handicap

SOLID MISS (1952)
At 4: 3rd Vanity Handicap

SOLID RAE (1952)
At 2: 3rd Del Mar Debutante Stakes
At 4: 3rd Santa Margarita Handicap

SOLID SON (1953)
At 5: 3rd San Juan Capistrano Handicap

SOLID THOUGHT (1957)
At 4: 3rd Vanity Handicap

SOME FOR ALL (1981)
At 4: 3rd Top Flight Handicap

SOME KINDA FLIRT (1980)
At 2: 2nd Arlington-Washington Lassie Stakes

SOME ROMANCE (1986)
At 2: Won Matron Stakes
Frizette Stakes
At 3: 2nd Santa Anita Oaks
3rd Ashland Stakes

SOMETHINGFABULOUS (1972)
At 3: 3rd Flamingo Stakes

SOMETHING LUCKY (1984)
At 3: 3rd Santa Anita Derby

SOMETHINGREGAL (1972)
At 3: 2nd Acorn Stakes

SOMETHING SUPER (1970)
At 5: 3rd Top Flight Handicap

SOMETIME THING (1952)
At 3: 2nd Acorn Stakes

SON ANGE (1968)
At 3: Won Pontiac Grand Prix Stakes

SONDRIO (1981)
At 5: Won Hialeah Turf Cup

SON EXCELLENCE (1967)
At 3: 2nd Ohio Derby

SONGANDAPRAYER (1998)
At 3: Won Fountain of Youth Stakes
2nd Toyota Blue Grass Stakes

SONGMAN (1958)
At 3: 2nd Cinema Handicap

SONG OF GLORY (1959)
At 2: 3rd Arlington Lassie Stakes

SONG SPARROW (1967)
At 2: 2nd Alcibiades Stakes

SONIC (1948)
At 4: 3rd Excelsior Handicap

SONIC LADY (1983)
At 4: 3rd Breeders' Cup Mile

SONJA'S FAITH (1994)
At 4: 2nd Ramona Handicap
Yellow Ribbon Stakes

SONKISSER (1973)
At 3: Won Withers Stakes
3rd Wood Memorial Stakes

SON OF ROCKET (1998)
At 3: 3rd Arkansas Derby

SOPHISTICATED GIRL (1980)
At 2: 2nd Oak Leaf Stakes

SORCERESS (1952)
At 2: 3rd Frizette Stakes
At 5: 3rd Top Flight Handicap

SORRY ABOUT THAT (1985)
At 3: 2nd Flamingo Stakes

SORRY LOOKIN (1975)
At 3: 3rd Jerome Handicap
Vosburgh Handicap
At 4: 2nd Widener Handicap
3rd Metropolitan Handicap

SOTO (2000)
At 3: 2nd Super Derby

SOUL OF THE MATTER (1991)
At 3: Won San Felipe Stakes
Super Derby
At 4: 2nd Pacific Classic
At 5: 2nd San Antonio Handicap

SOUND OF CANNONS (1987)
At 3: Won Arlington Classic

SOUND OFF (1968)
At 3: 3rd Gotham Stakes

SOUND OF SUMMER (1974)
At 3: Won Ashland Stakes

SOUTHERN APPEAL (1983)
At 2: Won Laurel Futurity

SOUTHERN HALO (1983)
At 3: 2nd Swaps Stakes
Super Derby

SOUTHERN IMAGE (2000)
At 3: Won Malibu Stakes

SOUTHERN SIGN (1988)
At 2: Won Young America Stakes

SOUTHERN TRUCE (1988)
At 5: Won Santa Margarita Handicap
3rd Santa Maria Handicap

SOUTHJET (1983)
At 3: Won Secretariat Stakes
Rothmans International Stakes

SOUVENIR COPY (1995)
At 2: Won Del Mar Futurity
Norfolk Stakes

SOVEREIGN DON (1983)
At 2: 3rd Futurity Stakes

SOVEREIGN KITTY (1991)
At 2: 3rd Matron Stakes
At 3: 3rd Acorn Stakes
Coaching Club American Oaks
Alabama Stakes
Gazelle Handicap

SOVIET PROBLEM (1990)
At 4: 2nd Breeders' Cup Sprint

SOVIET SOJOURN (1989)
At 2: 2nd Oak Leaf Stakes
3rd Hollywood Starlet Stakes

SOY EMPEROR (1979)
At 3: 3rd Illinois Derby

SOY NUMERO UNO (1973)
At 2: Won Futurity Stakes
At 3: 2nd Jerome Handicap
3rd Fall Highweight Handicap
At 4: Won Carter Handicap
Oaklawn Handicap
3rd New Orleans Handicap

SPACELINK (1997)
At 3: 3rd Swaps Stakes

SPAIN (1997)
At 2: 2nd Vinery Del Mar Debutante Stakes
3rd Oak Leaf Stakes
At 3: Won Breeders' Cup Distaff
La Brea Stakes
2nd Las Virgenes Stakes
Three Chimneys Spinster Stakes
3rd Alabama Stakes
At 4: 2nd Santa Margarita Handicap
Breeders' Cup Distaff
3rd Beldame Stakes
At 5: 2nd Santa Margarita Handicap
3rd Santa Monica Handicap

SPANISH CREAM (1948)
At 3: 3rd Gazelle Stakes
At 5: Won Santa Margarita Handicap
3rd Vanity Handicap

SPANISH DRUMS (1979)
At 3: Won Pennsylvania Derby

SPANISH FERN (1995)
At 4: Won Yellow Ribbon Stakes
3rd Ramona Handicap
Matriarch Stakes
At 5: 2nd Yellow Ribbon Stakes

SPANISH RIDDLE (1969)
At 3: 2nd Florida Derby

SPANISH WAY (1975)
At 2: 3rd Del Mar Futurity

SPARKALARK (1970)
At 2: Won Sorority Stakes

SPARKLING JOHNNY (1962)
At 3: Won Everglades Stakes
2nd Flamingo Stakes

SPARK OF LIFE (1975)
At 4: Won Ladies Handicap
2nd Spinster Stakes

SPARK PLUG (1959)
At 2: Won Del Mar Debutante Stakes

SPAR MAID (1955)
At 3: 2nd Coaching Club American Oaks
Monmouth Oaks
Alabama Stakes
At 4: 3rd Diana Handicap

SPARTAN EMPEROR (1976)
At 2: 3rd Sapling Stakes

SPARTAN VALOR (1948)
At 4: Won McLennan Handicap
Widener Handicap
Excelsior Handicap
Gallant Fox Handicap
At 5: Won Tropical Park Handicap

SPATS (1945)
At 2: 2nd Astoria Stakes

SPEAKING OF TIME (1996)
At 4: 2nd Vanity Handicap

SPEARFISH (1963)
At 3: Won Santa Susana Stakes
Hollywood Oaks

SPECIAL HAPPENING (1987)
At 2: 3rd Hollywood Starlet Stakes

SPECIAL HONOR (1975)
At 3: Won Ohio Derby
3rd Arkansas Derby
Monmouth Invitational Handicap

SPECIAL PRICE (1989)
At 6: 2nd San Juan Capistrano Handicap

SPECIAL RING (1997)
At 6: Won Eddie Read Handicap
2nd Shoemaker Breeders' Cup Mile

SPECIAL TEAM (1971)
At 2: Won Arlington-Washington Lassie Stakes
2nd Spinaway Stakes
At 3: Won Acorn Stakes
2nd Kentucky Oaks

SPECIAL TOUCH (1947)
At 3: Won Santa Susana Stakes
At 4: Won Santa Margarita Handicap

SPECIAL WARMTH (1974)
At 2: Won Arlington-Washington Lassie Stakes

SPECTACULAR BID (1976)
At 2: Won Champagne Stakes
Young America Stakes
Laurel Futurity
At 3: Won Florida Derby
Flamingo Stakes
Blue Grass Stakes
Kentucky Derby
Preakness Stakes
Marlboro Cup Handicap
Meadowlands Cup
2nd Jockey Club Gold Cup
3rd Belmont Stakes
At 4: Won Californian Stakes
Amory L. Haskell Handicap
Woodward Stakes
San Fernando Stakes
Charles H. Strub Stakes
Santa Anita Handicap

SPECTACULAR LOVE (1982)
At 2: Won Futurity Stakes

SPECTACULAR TIDE (1989)
At 4: Won Sword Dancer Handicap

SPECULATION (1945)
At 3: Won Will Rogers Handicap

SPEED DIALER (1989)
At 2: Won Arlington-Washington Lassie Stakes

SPEEDRATIC (1985)
At 4: 2nd San Fernando Stakes

SPEED ROUSER (1952)
At 3: 2nd Louisiana Derby
At 5: 3rd New Orleans Handicap

SPEEDY SHANNON (1983)
At 3: 2nd Illinois Derby

SPELLBOUND (1983)
At 3: Won Hollywood Derby

SPENCE BAY (1975)
At 6: Won Century Handicap

2nd Oak Tree Invitational Stakes
At 7: 2nd Eddie Read Handicap

SPEND A BUCK (1982)
At 2: Won Arlington-Washington Futurity
2nd Young America Stakes
3rd Breeders' Cup Juvenile
At 3: Won Kentucky Derby
Jersey Derby
Monmouth Handicap
2nd Haskell Invitational Handicap

SPENDER (1981)
At 2: 2nd Breeders' Futurity

SPHERE (1970)
At 2: 2nd Oak Leaf Stakes

SPICY LIVING (1960)
At 3: Won Acorn Stakes
Mother Goose Stakes
2nd Coaching Club American Oaks
Monmouth Oaks

SPIFFY LAREE (1976)
At 2: 3rd Oak Leaf Stakes

SPINDRIFT (1995)
At 5: 3rd Manhattan Handicap

SPINELESSJELLYFISH (1996)
At 6: 3rd Shoemaker Breeders' Cup Mile

SPINNEY (1953)
At 4: Won Canadian Championship Stakes
Santa Anita Maturity
2nd San Juan Capistrano Handicap
3rd Santa Anita Handicap

SPINNING (1987)
At 5: 3rd Man o' War Stakes

SPINNING AROUND (1964)
At 3: 2nd Santa Susana Stakes

SPINNING ROUND (1989)
At 3: 2nd Ashland Stakes

SPINNING TOP (1950)
At 4: Won Vineland Handicap
2nd Top Flight Handicap
3rd Firenze Handicap
At 5: 3rd Top Flight Handicap

SPINNING WORLD (1993)
At 3: 2nd Breeders' Cup Mile
At 4: Won Breeders' Cup Mile

SPIRIT ROCK (1969)
At 6: 2nd John B. Campbell Handicap

SPIT CURL (1980)
At 3: Won Alabama Stakes
2nd Coaching Club American Oaks

SPLASH (1945)
At 4: 3rd Monmouth Handicap

SPLENDID SPRUCE (1978)
At 3: Won Santa Anita Derby
2nd San Felipe Handicap

SPLENDORED (1954)
At 2: Won Princess Pat Stakes
2nd Arlington Lassie Stakes

SPLURGER (1986)
At 4: 2nd San Fernando Stakes

SPOKEN FUR (2000)
At 3: Won Mother Goose Stakes
Coaching Club American Oaks
3rd Alabama Stakes
Gazelle Handicap

SPOOK EXPRESS (1994)
At 7: 2nd Breeders' Cup Filly and Mare Turf
3rd Beverly D. Stakes

SPOON BAIT (1962)
At 6: 2nd Whitney Stakes

SPOONFUL OF HONEY (1979)
At 3: 3rd Louisiana Derby

SPORTFUL (1977)
At 2: 2nd Futurity Stakes

SPORTING LASS (1969)
At 2: Won Oak Leaf Stakes

SPORTIN' LIFE (1978)
At 3: 2nd Pennsylvania Derby

SPORT PAGE (1946)
At 2: 2nd Saratoga Special
Hopeful Stakes
3rd Futurity Stakes

SPORTS EDITOR (1971)
At 3: 3rd Illinois Derby

SPORTS VIEW (1987)
At 3: 3rd Pennsylvania Derby
At 4: 2nd Donn Handicap

SPOTTED BULL (1946)
At 3: 3rd Will Rogers Handicap

SPOTTED KID (1968)
At 3: 2nd Ohio Derby

SPOT T.V. (1967)
At 7: 3rd Arlington Handicap

SPOUT (1972)
At 2: 2nd Del Mar Debutante Stakes
At 3: Won Alabama Stakes

SPRING BROKER (1957)
At 3: Won Arkansas Derby

SPRING DOUBLE (1963)
At 2: Won Pimlico Futurity
2nd Sanford Stakes
At 6: 2nd Massachusetts Handicap
3rd New Orleans Handicap
At 7: 3rd John B. Campbell Handicap

SPRING IS HERE (1972)
At 2: 3rd Matron Stakes
At 4: 3rd Top Flight Handicap

SPRING LOOSE (1981)
At 2: 3rd Hollywood Starlet Stakes

SPRING MEADOW (1999)
At 3: 2nd Prioress Stakes
La Brea Stakes
3rd Test Stakes

SPRING OAK (1998)
At 3: 3rd Breeders' Cup Filly and Mare Turf

SPRINK (1978)
At 4: 2nd Man o' War Stakes
At 5: 2nd Bowling Green Handicap

SPRUCE BOUQUET (1977)
At 4: Won Hawthorne Gold Cup

SPRUCE NEEDLES (1977)
At 3: Won Arlington Classic
Secretariat Stakes
3rd American Derby
At 4: Won Arlington Handicap

SPUR ON (1948)
At 6: Won Michigan Mile
3rd Washington Park Handicap
At 7: 3rd New Orleans Handicap

SPUTNIK (1956)
At 3: 2nd Louisiana Derby
Arkansas Derby

SPY DEFENSE (1950)
At 2: 2nd Kentucky Jockey Club Stakes
3rd Breeders' Futurity
At 3: 3rd Louisiana Derby

SPY SONG (1943)
At 3: 2nd Kentucky Derby
Hawthorne Gold Cup
At 5: 2nd Vosburgh Handicap

SQUADRON E. (1963)
At 3: 3rd Ohio Derby

SQUANDER (1974)
At 2: Won Sorority Stakes

SQUAN SONG (1981)
At 5: 2nd Top Flight Handicap

SQUARE CUT (1989)
At 4: 2nd Sword Dancer Handicap
At 6: 3rd San Luis Rey Stakes

SQUARED AWAY (1947)
At 4: 2nd Fall Highweight Handicap
At 6: 2nd Carter Handicap

SQUEAK (1994)
At 4: Won Beverly Hills Handicap
Matriarch Stakes
3rd Gamely Breeders' Cup Handicap

SQUILL (1985)
At 3: 3rd Budweiser International Stakes

SQUIRTLE SQUIRT (1998)
At 3: Won King's Bishop Stakes
Penske Auto Center Breeders' Cup Sprint
2nd Vosburgh Stakes

SR. DIPLOMAT (1971)
At 3: 2nd Illinois Derby
3rd American Derby

STACEY D'ETTE (1969)
At 3: 3rd Acorn Stakes

STACKED PACK (1984)
At 3: 2nd Jerome Handicap
At 4: 3rd Metropolitan Handicap

STAGE DOOR BETTY (1971)
At 3: 2nd Acorn Stakes
3rd Gazelle Handicap

STAGE DOOR JOHNNY (1965)
At 3: Won Belmont Stakes
Dwyer Handicap

STAGE GLITTER (1945)
At 3: 2nd Will Rogers Handicap

STAGE KID (1944)
At 3: 3rd Withers Stakes

STAGING POST (1998)
At 4: 2nd San Juan Capistrano Handicap

STALCREEK (1990)
At 3: 2nd Santa Anita Oaks
3rd Fantasy Stakes
At 4: 3rd Santa Margarita Handicap

STALWARS (1985)
At 3: 2nd Jim Beam Stakes
At 4: 2nd Oaklawn Handicap

STALWART (1979)
At 2: Won Norfolk Stakes
Hollywood Futurity

STALWART CHARGER (1987)
At 3: 3rd Swaps Stakes

STALWART MEMBER (1993)
At 4: 2nd Carter Handicap

ST. AMOUR II (1953)
At 5: Won Tropical Handicap

STAN (1950)
At 4: Won Arlington Handicap
At 5: Won Hialeah Turf Handicap

STANCHARRY (1978)
At 3: Won San Felipe Handicap
3rd Swaps Stakes

STANDARD EQUIPMENT (1990)
At 2: 2nd Spinaway Stakes
Frizette Stakes

STANDIFORD (1989)
At 3: 2nd American Derby

STANISLAS (1962)
At 4: Won Michigan Mile and One-Eighth
At 5: 2nd Widener Handicap

STAR BALL (1972)
At 5: Won Yellow Ribbon Stakes

STAR BOUT (1945)
At 2: 3rd Saratoga Special

STAR CAMPAIGNER (1991)
At 3: 3rd American Derby

STAR CHOICE (1979)
At 4: Won Metropolitan Handicap
At 5: 2nd Breeders' Cup Mile
3rd Arlington Handicap

STAR DE LADY ANN (1993)
At 3: Won Acorn Stakes

STAR DE NASKRA (1975)
At 2: 3rd Laurel Futurity
At 3: 2nd American Derby
3rd Ohio Derby
At 4: Won Whitney Stakes

STARDUST MEL (1971)
At 3: 2nd Swaps Stakes
Hollywood Derby
At 4: Won San Fernando Stakes
Charles H. Strub Stakes
Santa Anita Handicap
3rd San Juan Capistrano Handicap

STAR-ENFIN (1949)
At 2: Won Astoria Stakes

STAR ENVOY (1968)
At 4: Won Manhattan Handicap
3rd Hialeah Turf Cup
Century Handicap
At 5: 2nd United Nations Handicap

STAR FIDDLE (1946)
At 2: Won Starlet Stakes

STAR GALLANT (1979)
At 3: Won Illinois Derby
2nd Florida Derby
3rd Metropolitan Handicap

STARINE (1997)
At 4: Won Matriarch Stakes
3rd Flower Bowl Invitational Handicap
At 5: Won Breeders' Cup Filly and Mare Turf
2nd Gamely Breeders' Cup Handicap

STAR LIFT (1984)
At 5: 3rd Breeders' Cup Turf

STAR MAGGIE (1960)
At 2: 2nd Del Mar Debutante Stakes
At 4: Won Vanity Handicap
3rd Vineland Handicap
At 5: Won Spinster Stakes

STAR OF BROADWAY (1995)
At 3: 2nd Las Virgenes Stakes

STAR OF COZZENE (1988)
At 3: 3rd Breeders' Cup Mile
At 5: Won Caesars International Handicap
Arlington Million
Man o' War Stakes
At 6: 3rd Caesars International Handicap

STAR OF ERIN II (1974)
At 4: 2nd Oak Tree Invitational Stakes

STAR OF KUWAIT (1968)
At 4: 2nd Malibu Stakes

STAR PASTURES (1978)
At 3: 2nd Yellow Ribbon Stakes
At 4: 3rd Matriarch Stakes

STAR PERFORMANCE (1993)
At 5: 2nd San Juan Capistrano Handicap

STAR PILOT (1943)
At 3: 2nd Santa Anita Derby

STAR RECRUIT (1989)
At 2: 3rd Del Mar Futurity
At 3: 3rd Arlington Classic
At 4: 2nd Santa Anita Handicap

STARRER (1998)
At 3: 2nd Overbrook Spinster Stakes
At 4: 3rd Vanity Handicap
At 5: Won Santa Maria Handicap
Santa Margarita Handicap

STAR REWARD (1944)
At 4: Won New Orleans Handicap
2nd Arlington Handicap
At 5: 2nd Arlington Handicap
San Carlos Handicap
3rd Stars and Stripes Handicap

STAR ROVER (1952)
At 3: 2nd Jerome Handicap

STARRY DREAMER (1994)
At 3: 2nd Gazelle Handicap

STAR SPANGLED (1974)
At 4: 2nd Century Handicap
At 5: 2nd Century Handicap
Hollywood Invitational Handicap

STAR STANDARD (1992)
At 3: 2nd Belmont Stakes
Woodward Stakes
3rd Jockey Club Gold Cup
At 4: Won Pimlico Special
2nd Gulfstream Park Handicap

STARTAC (1998)
At 3: Won Secretariat Stakes

STATE DINNER (1975)
At 4: Won Metropolitan Handicap
Suburban Handicap
Century Handicap
3rd Brooklyn Handicap
At 5: Won Whitney Stakes
2nd Metropolitan Handicap
Suburban Handicap
Brooklyn Handicap

STATELY DON (1984)
At 3: Won Hollywood Derby

STAUNCH AVENGER (1968)
At 2: Won Sapling Stakes
At 3: 3rd Pontiac Grand Prix Stakes

STAUNCHNESS (1962)
At 3: Won Dwyer Handicap
At 4: Won Whitney Stakes

ST. AVERIL (2001)
At 2: 2nd Hollywood Futurity

STAYSAIL (1955)
At 2: 3rd Pimlico Futurity

STEADY GROWTH (1976)
At 3: Won Arlington Classic
2nd Monmouth Invitational Handicap

STEADY POWER (1984)
At 5: 2nd Rothmans International Stakes

STEAL A DANCE (1968)
At 3: 2nd San Felipe Handicap

STEAL A KISS (1983)
At 2: 3rd Breeders' Cup Juvenile Fillies
At 3: 2nd Maskette Stakes
Ruffian Handicap
3rd Ladies Handicap
At 4: 2nd Delaware Handicap

STEEL BLUE (1947)
At 3: 2nd Discovery Handicap
Aqueduct Handicap

STEEL VIKING (1960)
At 4: 3rd Massachusetts Handicap

STEEPLE JILL (1961)
At 3: Won Ladies Handicap
At 4: Won Delaware Handicap
Vineland Handicap
2nd Black Helen Handicap
Top Flight Handicap
Beldame Stakes
Ladies Handicap

STEEP PULSE (1969)
At 3: 3rd Washington D.C. International

STEINLEN (1983)
At 5: 2nd John Henry Handicap
Breeders' Cup Mile
At 6: Won Arlington Million
Breeders' Cup Mile
2nd John Henry Handicap
At 7: Won Hollywood Turf Handicap
Caesars International Handicap
3rd John Henry Handicap
Arlington Million

STELLA MADRID (1987)
At 2: Won Matron Stakes
Frizette Stakes
3rd Breeders' Cup Juvenile Fillies
At 3: Won Acorn Stakes
3rd Mother Goose Stakes

STEN (1975)
At 5: Won Bowling Green Handicap
3rd Sword Dancer Stakes

STEPFATHER (1944)
At 2: 2nd Starlet Stakes
At 3: 2nd Wood Memorial Stakes
3rd Hollywood Derby
Cinema Handicap
At 4: Won American Handicap
3rd Golden Gate Handicap
At 5: 2nd Golden Gate Handicap

STEPHANIE BRYN (1980)
At 2: 3rd Hollywood Starlet Stakes

STEPHANOTIS (1953)
At 4: 3rd Washington D.C. International
At 5: Won Bougainvillea Turf Handicap

STEPHANOTIS (1993)
At 3: 3rd Woodbine Million
At 4: 2nd Brooklyn Handicap

STEPHAN'S ODYSSEY (1982)
At 2: Won Hollywood Futurity
At 3: Won Dwyer Stakes
Jim Dandy Stakes
2nd Fountain of Youth Stakes
Kentucky Derby
Belmont Stakes
3rd Flamingo Stakes

STEPHEN GOT EVEN (1996)
At 3: Won Gallery Furniture.com Stakes
3rd Woodward Stakes
At 4: Won Donn Handicap

STEP NICELY (1970)
At 2: 3rd Champagne Stakes
Garden State Stakes
At 3: Won Jerome Handicap
3rd Jersey Derby
At 5: 2nd Vosburgh Handicap
3rd Grey Lag Handicap

STEPPING HIGH (1969)
At 2: 2nd Matron Stakes
3rd Alcibiades Stakes

STEVE'S FRIEND (1974)
At 3: Won Hollywood Derby
3rd Santa Anita Derby

STITCH AGAIN (1940)
At 7: 2nd Santa Anita Handicap

STOCKS UP (1986)
At 2: Won Hollywood Starlet Stakes
2nd Oak Leaf Stakes

STOKOSKY (1996)
At 5: 3rd Gulfstream Park Breeders' Cup Handicap

STOLE (1946)
At 2: 2nd Princess Pat Stakes
Matron Stakes
3rd Arlington Lassie Stakes
Demoiselle Stakes

STOLEN GOLD (1994)
At 2: 2nd Hollywood Futurity
At 3: 3rd Toyota Blue Grass Stakes

STOLEN HOUR (1953)
At 4: 3rd Molly Pitcher Handicap

STONE AGE (1946)
At 2: 2nd Champagne Stakes

STONE MANOR (1977)
At 3: Won Ohio Derby
3rd Arlington Classic

STONEWALK (1971)
At 3: Won Ohio Derby
Jerome Handicap
2nd Jersey Derby
Secretariat Stakes
At 4: 2nd Michigan Mile and One-Eighth
United Nations Handicap
3rd Amory L. Haskell Handicap

STOP 'M COLD (1978)
At 4: 3rd Louisiana Downs Handicap

STOP THE FIGHTING (1983)
At 5: 3rd John Henry Handicap

STOP THE MUSIC (1970)
At 2: Won Champagne Stakes
2nd Futurity Stakes
Laurel Futurity
3rd Hopeful Stakes
At 3: Won Dwyer Handicap
2nd Withers Stakes
Travers Stakes
At 4: 2nd Vosburgh Handicap
3rd Whitney Stakes
At 5: 2nd Carter Handicap
Metropolitan Handicap
3rd Brooklyn Handicap

STOP TRAFFIC (1993)
At 3: 3rd Acorn Stakes
At 5: Won Ballerina Handicap
3rd Ruffian Handicap
At 6: Won Santa Monica Handicap

STORM AND SUNSHINE (1983)
At 2: 3rd Sorority Stakes

STORM CAT (1983)
At 2: Won Young America Stakes
2nd Breeders' Cup Juvenile

STORM FLAG FLYING (2000)
At 2: Won Matron Stakes
Frizette Stakes
Long John Silver's BC Juvenile Fillies

STORMIN FEVER (1994)
At 4: 2nd Philip H. Iselin Handicap
Vosburgh Stakes
At 5: 2nd Vosburgh Stakes

STORMING HOME (1998)
At 5: Won Charles Whittingham Handicap
Clement L. Hirsch Mem. Turf Champ.

STORM PUNCH (1995)
At 4: 3rd Frank J. De Francis Memorial Dash

STORM SONG (1994)
At 2: Won Frizette Stakes
Breeders' Cup Juvenile Fillies
2nd Matron Stakes
At 3: 3rd Ashland Stakes
Kentucky Oaks

STORM TOWER (1990)
At 3: Won Wood Memorial Stakes
2nd Florida Derby
Haskell Invitational Handicap

STORM TROOPER (1993)
At 5: Won Hollywood Turf Handicap

STORMY BLUES (1992)
At 2: 2nd Matron Stakes
3rd Spinaway Stakes
Breeders' Cup Juvenile Fillies

STORMY CLOUD (1946)
At 5: 3rd Sunset Handicap
At 6: 2nd Inglewood Handicap
Sunset Handicap
Del Mar Handicap

STORMY PICK (1998)
At 2: Won Spinaway Stakes

STRAIGHT DEAL (1962)
At 3: Won Hollywood Oaks
Ladies Handicap
3rd Beldame Stakes
At 4: Won Santa Margarita Handicap
Santa Barbara Handicap
2nd Beldame Stakes
Ladies Handicap
3rd Top Flight Handicap
At 5: Won Top Flight Handicap
Delaware Handicap
Spinster Stakes
2nd Black Helen Handicap
Molly Pitcher Handicap
3rd Aqueduct Stakes
Whitney Stakes

STRAIGHT FACE (1950)
At 2: Won Breeders' Futurity
Kentucky Jockey Club Stakes
At 3: Won Flamingo Stakes
2nd Blue Grass Stakes
At 4: Won Dixie Handicap
Suburban Handicap
2nd Metropolitan Handicap
At 5: 3rd Brooklyn Handicap

STRAIGHT MAN (1996)
At 3: 2nd Malibu Stakes

STRANGLEHOLD (1949)
At 3: 3rd Westerner Stakes
At 5: Won Del Mar Handicap

STRATEGIC MANEUVER (1991)
At 2: Won Spinaway Stakes
Matron Stakes

STRATMAT (1954)
At 6: 3rd Tropical Park Handicap

STRAVINA (1971)
At 5: Won Santa Barbara Handicap
2nd Ramona Handicap

STRAWBERRY LANDING (1973)
At 3: 3rd Jersey Derby

STRAWBERRY ROAD II (1979)
At 5: 3rd Washington D.C. International
At 6: 2nd Breeders' Cup Turf
3rd Turf Classic
At 7: 2nd San Luis Rey Stakes

STREAKING (1948)
At 2: 3rd Breeders' Futurity

STREAM ACROSS (1972)
At 2: 3rd Sorority Stakes

STREAMER (1963)
At 4: 3rd Santa Margarita Handicap

STREET BALLET (1977)
At 2: 3rd Selima Stakes
At 3: 2nd Santa Susana Stakes

STREET CRY (1998)
At 2: 2nd Del Mar Futurity
Norfolk Stakes
3rd Breeders' Cup Juvenile
At 4: Won Stephen Foster Handicap
2nd Whitney Handicap

STREET DANCER (1967)
At 5: 3rd Vanity Handicap
Santa Maria Handicap
Santa Barbara Handicap

STRETCHAPOINT (1966)
At 2: 2nd Garden State Stakes

STRIKE (1948)
At 3: 3rd Black-Eyed Susan Stakes

STRIKE ME LUCKY (1972)
At 5: Won Gulfstream Park Handicap
2nd Michigan Mile and One-Eighth

STRIKE THE GOLD (1988)
At 3: Won Blue Grass Stakes
Kentucky Derby
2nd Florida Derby
Belmont Stakes
3rd Jim Dandy Stakes
Jockey Club Gold Cup
At 4: Won Pimlico Special
Nassau County Handicap
2nd Gulfstream Park Handicap
Suburban Handicap
Jockey Club Gold Cup
At 5: 3rd Nassau County Handicap

STRIKE THE MAIN (1976)
At 3: 2nd Flamingo Stakes
3rd Arkansas Derby

STRIKE YOUR COLORS (1976)
At 2: Won Breeders' Futurity
2nd Futurity Stakes
Young America Stakes
3rd Arlington-Washington Futurity

STRIKING (1947)
At 2: 2nd Spinaway Stakes
Selima Stakes
Marguerite Stakes
3rd Pimlico Futurity
Matron Stakes

STRODES CREEK (1991)
At 3: 2nd Kentucky Derby
3rd Santa Anita Derby
Belmont Stakes

STROLLING ALONG (1990)
At 2: Won Futurity Stakes
2nd Hopeful Stakes
At 3: 3rd Gotham Stakes

STROLLING BELLE (1996)
At 3: 2nd Alabama Stakes
3rd Coaching Club American Oaks

STRONG ALLY (1992)
At 2: 3rd Norfolk Stakes

STRONG BAY (1955)
At 2: 3rd Del Mar Futurity
At 3: Won Westerner Stakes
2nd Cinema Handicap

STRONG HOPE (2000)
At 3: Won Jim Dandy Stakes
3rd Travers Stakes

STRONG PERFORMANCE (1983)
At 3: Won Tropical Park Derby

STRONG RULER (1955)
At 2: 3rd Starlet Stakes
Washington Park Futurity

STRONG STRONG (1966)
At 2: Won Arlington-Washington Futurity
At 4: 3rd Washington Park Handicap

STRUT THE STAGE (1998)
At 3: 2nd Secretariat Stakes
At 4: 3rd Manhattan Handicap

STUB (1975)
At 2: Won Sorority Stakes
Arlington-Washington Lassie Stakes
2nd Matron Stakes

STUD POKER (1943)
At 4: 3rd Hawthorne Gold Cup
At 5: Won Arlington Handicap
Miami Beach Handicap
2nd Widener Handicap
3rd Washington Park Handicap

STUKA (1990)
At 2: 2nd Hollywood Futurity
At 4: Won Santa Anita Handicap
3rd Strub Stakes

STUMPING (1970)
At 6: 3rd Woodward Handicap

STUNTS (1945)
At 4: 3rd Manhattan Handicap

STUPENDOUS (1963)
At 3: Won Gotham Stakes
2nd Everglades Stakes
Louisiana Derby
Preakness Stakes
At 4: Won Arlington Handicap
Whitney Stakes

STURDY ONE (1947)
At 2: 3rd Starlet Stakes
Del Mar Futurity
At 3: 2nd Santa Anita Derby
At 4: Won Inglewood Handicap
2nd Del Mar Handicap
3rd American Handicap
At 5: Won Inglewood Handicap
2nd American Handicap
3rd Hollywood Gold Cup

STUTZ BLACKHAWK (1977)
At 3: 3rd Illinois Derby
Pennsylvania Derby

ST. VINCENT (1951)
At 4: Won San Juan Capistrano Handicap
Dixie Handicap
At 6: 3rd Arlington Handicap
At 7: 3rd Sunset Handicap
Arlington Handicap

STYLISH STAR (1986)
At 4: 2nd Gamely Handicap

STYLISH TALENT (1996)
At 2: 3rd Oak Leaf Stakes

STYLISH WINNER (1984)
At 5: 3rd Santa Anita Handicap
At 6: 2nd San Antonio Handicap
Californian Stakes

STYMIE (1941)
At 5: Won Grey Lag Handicap
Whitney Stakes
Manhattan Handicap
New York Handicap
Gallant Fox Handicap
2nd Jockey Club Gold Cup
Dixie Handicap
Brooklyn Handicap
Monmouth Handicap
Pimlico Special
3rd Suburban Handicap
At 6: Won Metropolitan Handicap
Massachusetts Handicap
Aqueduct Handicap
Gallant Fox Handicap
2nd Queens County Handicap
Brooklyn Handicap
Manhattan Handicap
3rd Jockey Club Gold Cup
Whitney Stakes
At 7: Won Metropolitan Handicap
Aqueduct Handicap
2nd Dixie Handicap
Suburban Handicap
Queens County Handicap
3rd Excelsior Handicap
Brooklyn Handicap
At 8: 2nd New York Handicap

SUAVE PROSPECT (1992)
At 3: 2nd Florida Derby
Blue Grass Stakes

SUBAHDAR (1950)
At 4: 2nd Manhattan Handicap
Trenton Handicap
3rd Gallant Fox Handicap
At 5: 3rd Suburban Handicap
At 6: 3rd Suburban Handicap

SUB FLEET (1949)
At 2: Won Kentucky Jockey Club Stakes
At 3: 2nd Kentucky Derby
American Derby
3rd Arlington Classic
At 4: Won Hawthorne Gold Cup
2nd Arlington Handicap

SUBORDINATED DEBT (1988)
At 2: 2nd Remsen Stakes
3rd Champagne Stakes
Young America Stakes
At 3: 2nd Jersey Derby

SUBORDINATION (1994)
At 3: Won Crown Royal Hollywood Derby
At 4: Won Brooklyn Handicap
Eddie Read Handicap

SUBPET (1965)
At 2: Won Sapling Stakes
At 3: 3rd Flamingo Stakes

SUBTLE POWER (1997)
At 4: Won Gulfstream Park Breeders' Cup Handicap

SUCCESS EXPRESS (1985)
At 2: Won Breeders' Cup Juvenile
3rd Hopeful Stakes

SUCCESSFUL APPEAL (1996)
At 3: 3rd King's Bishop Stakes

SUCCESSOR (1964)
At 2: Won Champagne Stakes
Garden State Stakes
2nd Futurity Stakes
Pimlico Futurity
3rd Cowdin Stakes
At 3: Won Lawrence Realization Stakes
3rd Jockey Club Gold Cup

SUCH A RUSH (1971)
At 2: Won Del Mar Futurity
2nd Hollywood Juvenile Championship

SUDAN (1947)
At 4: 2nd San Antonio Handicap
3rd Santa Anita Handicap
New York Handicap

SUDANES (1973)
At 6: 3rd Del Mar Handicap

SUDDEN HUSH (1990)
At 2: 2nd Del Mar Futurity

SUE BABE (1978)
At 2: 2nd Sorority Stakes

SUFIE (1949)
At 3: 2nd Acorn Stakes
3rd Coaching Club American Oaks

SUGAR AND SPICE (1977)
At 3: Won Mother Goose Stakes
2nd Ladies Handicap
3rd Acorn Stakes
Alabama Stakes

SUGAR PLUM TIME (1972)
At 4: Won Maskette Handicap
3rd Ladies Handicap

SUITI (1959)
At 4: 2nd Ladies Handicap

SU KA WA (1959)
At 2: Won Kentucky Jockey Club Stakes
2nd Hopeful Stakes

SULAMANI (1999)
At 4: Won Arlington Million
Turf Classic

SULEIMAN (1947)
At 2: 2nd Saratoga Special
3rd Cowdin Stakes
Garden State Stakes

SULLIVAN (1944)
At 3: 3rd Will Rogers Handicap

SULLIVAN'S BUD (1958)
At 2: 2nd Hollywood Juvenile Championship

SULTRY SONG (1988)
At 3: 2nd NYRA Mile Handicap
3rd Secretariat Stakes
Pegasus Handicap
At 4: Won Hollywood Gold Cup
Whitney Handicap
Woodward Stakes
3rd Nassau County Handicap

SUMAYR (1982)
At 3: 2nd Rothmans International Stakes

SUMMER ADVOCATE (1977)
At 4: 2nd Arlington Handicap
3rd Louisiana Downs Handicap
At 5: 3rd Monmouth Handicap

SUMMER AIR (1967)
At 4: 2nd Vosburgh Handicap

SUMMER COLONY (1998)
At 4: Won Personal Ensign Handicap
3rd Beldame Stakes

SUMMER FESTIVAL (1970)
At 3: 3rd Alabama Stakes

SUMMER FLING (1975)
At 3: 2nd Alabama Stakes

SUMMER GUEST (1969)
At 3: Won Coaching Club American Oaks
Alabama Stakes
2nd Beldame Stakes
3rd Mother Goose Stakes
Woodward Stakes
At 4: Won Grey Lag Handicap
Bowling Green Handicap
2nd Black Helen Handicap
Top Flight Handicap
Delaware Handicap
At 5: Won Spinster Stakes
3rd Delaware Handicap

SUMMER SCANDAL (1962)
At 3: Won Monmouth Oaks
At 4: Won Top Flight Handicap
Beldame Stakes
3rd Spinster Stakes

SUMMER SIREN (1977)
At 4: Won La Canada Stakes

SUMMER SOLSTICE (1952)
At 4: Won Bougainvillea Turf Handicap

SUMMER SORROW (1965)
At 5: 3rd Beverly Hills Handicap

SUMMER SQUALL (1987)
At 2: Won Hopeful Stakes
At 3: Won Jim Beam Stakes
Blue Grass Stakes
Preakness Stakes
Pennsylvania Derby
2nd Kentucky Derby
At 4: 2nd Pimlico Special

SUMMER STORY (1953)
At 5: 3rd Vanity Handicap

SUMMER TAN (1952)
At 2: Won Cowdin Stakes
Garden State Stakes
2nd Hopeful Stakes
Futurity Stakes
At 3: 2nd Wood Memorial Stakes
3rd Kentucky Derby
At 4: Won Gallant Fox Handicap
Pimlico Special
2nd Whitney Stakes

Washington Park Handicap
Hawthorne Gold Cup
Trenton Handicap
Arlington Handicap
At 5: Won McLennan Handicap

SUMMERTIME PROMISE (1972)
At 2: 3rd Selima Stakes
At 4: 2nd Santa Margarita Handicap
At 5: 3rd Apple Blossom Handicap

SUMMER WIND DANCER (2000)
At 2: 3rd Hollywood Starlet Stakes

SUMMING (1978)
At 3: Won Pennsylvania Derby
Belmont Stakes
Pegasus Handicap
2nd Super Derby

SUMPTIOUS (1983)
At 3: Won Arlington Classic
2nd Pennsylvania Derby

SUM UP (1962)
At 3: 3rd Arlington Classic

SUN AND SNOW (1972)
At 3: Won Ashland Stakes
Kentucky Oaks
3rd Mother Goose Stakes

SUN BAHRAM (1946)
At 2: 3rd Pimlico Futurity
At 3: Won Saranac Handicap
3rd Travers Stakes
At 4: 2nd Whitney Stakes

SUN CATCHER (1977)
At 3: 3rd Arkansas Derby
At 4: Won New Orleans Handicap
2nd Oaklawn Handicap

SUNDAY BREAK (1999)
At 3: 3rd Wood Memorial Stakes
Belmont Stakes

SUNDAY EVENING (1947)
At 2: Won Spinaway Stakes

SUNDAY SILENCE (1986)
At 3: Won San Felipe Handicap
Santa Anita Derby
Kentucky Derby
Preakness Stakes
Super Derby
Breeders' Cup Classic
2nd Belmont Stakes
Swaps Stakes
At 4: Won Californian Stakes
2nd Hollywood Gold Cup

SUNGARI (1948)
At 2: Won Astoria Stakes
3rd Matron Stakes

SUNGLOW (1947)
At 2: 3rd Champagne Stakes
Kentucky Jockey Club Stakes
At 3: Won Saranac Handicap
Discovery Handicap
2nd Louisiana Derby
Westchester Handicap
At 4: Won Widener Handicap
3rd McLennan Handicap
At 6: 3rd Washington D.C. International

SUN HEROD (1942)
At 6: 2nd Hawthorne Gold Cup
At 7: 2nd Hawthorne Gold Cup

SUN MASTER (1981)
At 6: 3rd Vosburgh Stakes

SUNNINGDALE (1953)
At 4: 3rd Tropical Handicap

SUNNY BAY (1975)
At 2: 2nd Sorority Stakes

SUNNY DALE (1948)
At 5: 2nd Black Helen Handicap

SUNNY SAL (1967)
At 2: 2nd Gardenia Stakes

SUNNY SERVE (1987)
At 3: 3rd Withers Stakes

SUNNY'S HALO (1980)
At 3: Won Arkansas Derby
Kentucky Derby
Super Derby
3rd Whitney Handicap

SUNNY SONGSTER (1975)
At 2: 2nd Breeders' Futurity

SUNNY SOUTH (1970)
At 2: 2nd Arlington-Washington Futurity

SUNNY SUNRISE (1987)
At 5: 3rd Donn Handicap
Gulfstream Park Handicap

SUNNY TIM (1967)
At 4: 3rd Widener Handicap

SUNRISE COUNTY (1959)
At 3: 2nd Gotham Stakes
Wood Memorial Stakes
3rd Flamingo Stakes
At 4: Won Grey Lag Handicap
2nd Brooklyn Handicap
3rd Metropolitan Handicap
Massachusetts Handicap
Whitney Stakes
At 5: 2nd Massachusetts Handicap

SUNRISE FLIGHT (1959)
At 3: 2nd Gallant Fox Handicap
3rd Roamer Handicap
At 4: Won Gallant Fox Handicap
At 5: 2nd Widener Handicap
Manhattan Handicap
Gallant Fox Handicap
3rd Seminole Handicap
Brooklyn Handicap

SUNSHACK (1991)
At 6: 2nd San Juan Capistrano Handicap
Hollywood Turf Handicap

SUNSHINE CAKE (1958)
At 4: 2nd Dixie Handicap

SUNSHINE FOREVER (1985)
At 3: Won Man o' War Stakes
Turf Classic
Budweiser International Stakes
2nd Sword Dancer Handicap
Breeders' Cup Turf
3rd Arlington Million

SUNSHINE JIMMY (1987)
At 3: 2nd Vosburgh Stakes
At 4: 3rd Vosburgh Stakes

SUNSHINE NELL (1948)
At 5: 2nd Top Flight Handicap
Vineland Handicap
3rd Comely Handicap
At 6: Won Top Flight Handicap
2nd New Castle Handicap

SUNSHINE STREET (1995)
At 5: Won San Juan Capistrano Handicap

SUN STATE (1947)
At 3: 3rd Westerner Stakes

SUNSTRUCK (1960)
At 5: Won Seminole Handicap

SUN WARRIOR (1950)
At 2: 2nd Sapling Stakes

SUPAH BLITZ (2000)
At 3: 2nd Fountain of Youth Stakes

SUPAH GEM (1990)
At 4: Won Santa Maria Handicap

SUPER AVIE (1985)
At 3: 2nd Hollywood Oaks

SUPERBITY (1977)
At 3: Won Flamingo Stakes
2nd Monmouth Invitational Handicap

SUPER BOY (1973)
At 4: 3rd Meadowlands Cup

SUPER CHOLO (1987)
At 2: 3rd Laurel Futurity

SUPER COOK (1984)
At 3: 3rd Kentucky Oaks

SUPER DIAMOND (1980)
At 6: Won Hollywood Gold Cup
2nd Californian Stakes
At 8: 3rd Santa Anita Handicap
At 9: Won San Antonio Handicap

SUPER HIT (1976)
At 3: 2nd American Derby

SUPER MAY (1986)
At 5: 2nd Sunset Handicap

SUPER MOMENT (1977)
At 3: Won Bay Meadows Handicap
2nd Blue Grass Stakes
At 4: Won Charles H. Strub Stakes
Bay Meadows Handicap
2nd Eddie Read Handicap
3rd Hollywood Gold Cup
Century Handicap
At 5: Won Bay Meadows Handicap
2nd San Antonio Stakes

SUPER QUERCUS (1996)
At 3: Won Early Times Hollywood Derby
At 5: Won Hollywood Turf Cup
3rd Eddie Read Handicap

SUPER SAIL (1968)
At 5: 2nd Gulfstream Park Handicap

SUPER STAFF (1988)
At 4: Won Yellow Ribbon Stakes
2nd Matriarch Stakes

SUPER SUNRISE (1979)
At 4: 2nd Bay Meadows Handicap

SUPER VALLEY (1942)
At 4: 3rd Longacres Mile

SUPPLE (1953)
At 2: Won Princess Pat Stakes
3rd Alcibiades Stakes

SUPREME ENDEAVOR (1964)
At 2: 3rd Del Mar Debutante Stakes

SUPREMO (1992)
At 2: Won Norfolk Stakes
2nd Del Mar Futurity

SURERA (1973)
At 5: 3rd Yellow Ribbon Stakes
At 6: 2nd Santa Margarita Handicap

SURFSIDE (1997)
At 2: Won Frizette Stakes
Hollywood Starlet Stakes
2nd Spinaway Stakes
3rd Breeders' Cup Juvenile Fillies
At 3: Won Las Virgenes Stakes
Santa Anita Oaks
2nd Breeders' Cup Distaff
At 4: 3rd Santa Monica Handicap

SUROSA (1942)
At 4: 2nd Top Flight Handicap
New Castle Handicap

SURVIVE (1987)
At 3: 3rd Top Flight Handicap

SUSAN'S GENT (1961)
At 2: 3rd Cowdin Stakes

SUSAN'S GIRL (1969)
At 2: 2nd Frizette Stakes
Gardenia Stakes
At 3: Won Santa Susana Stakes
Kentucky Oaks
Acorn Stakes
Gazelle Handicap
Beldame Stakes
2nd Mother Goose Stakes
3rd Coaching Club American Oaks
Hollywood Oaks
At 4: Won Delaware Handicap
Spinster Stakes
Santa Maria Handicap
Santa Margarita Handicap
Santa Barbara Handicap
3rd Vanity Handicap
Beldame Stakes
At 6: Won Delaware Handicap
Beldame Stakes
Spinster Stakes
2nd Vanity Handicap
Santa Margarita Handicap
3rd Maskette Handicap
Ladies Handicap

SUSCEPTIBLE (1969)
At 2: 2nd Selima Stakes

SUSPICIOUS (1960)
At 4: 3rd Donn Handicap
At 5: 2nd Arlington Handicap
3rd New Orleans Handicap

SUTEKI (1964)
At 4: 3rd San Antonio Handicap

SWAIN (1992)
At 4: 3rd Breeders' Cup Turf
At 6: 3rd Breeders' Cup Classic

SWALE (1981)
At 2: Won Futurity Stakes
Young America Stakes
Breeders' Futurity
3rd Hopeful Stakes
At 3: Won Hutcheson Stakes
Florida Derby
Kentucky Derby
Belmont Stakes
3rd Fountain of Youth Stakes

SWAPS (1952)
At 3: Won Santa Anita Derby
Kentucky Derby
Westerner Stakes
American Derby
Californian Stakes
At 4: Won Inglewood Handicap
American Handicap
Hollywood Gold Cup
Sunset Handicap
Washington Park Handicap
2nd Californian Stakes

SWARMING BEE (1967)
At 2: 2nd Del Mar Futurity

SWEEPING STORY (1996)
At 3: 3rd Kentucky Oaks

SWEEPING VIEW (1975)
At 2: 3rd Sorority Stakes

SWEET ALLIANCE (1974)
At 3: Won Kentucky Oaks
2nd Fantasy Stakes

SWEET AND READY (1995)
At 3: 2nd Hollywood Oaks

SWEET AS HONEY (1951)
At 2: 3rd Del Mar Debutante Stakes

SWEET CAPRICE (1943)
At 4: 3rd Black Helen Handicap

SWEET CHARIOT (1952)
At 3: 3rd Lawrence Realization Stakes

SWEET DIANE (1980)
At 4: Won La Canada Stakes

SWEET DREAM (1945)
At 3: Won Gazelle Stakes

SWEETEST ROMAN (1977)
At 2: 3rd Alcibiades Stakes

SWEET FOLLY (1964)
At 3: Won Gazelle Handicap
Ladies Handicap

SWEET LIFE (1996)
At 4: 2nd Beverly Hills Handicap

SWEET LUDY (1996)
At 3: 3rd Del Mar Oaks

SWEET MISSUS (1980)
At 4: Won Top Flight Handicap

SWEET MIST (1967)
At 2: 3rd Selima Stakes
At 3: 2nd Monmouth Oaks

SWEET OLD GIRL (1972)
At 2: 3rd Oak Leaf Stakes
At 3: 2nd Mother Goose Stakes

SWEET PATOOTIE (1950)
At 2: Won Frizette Stakes
Alcibiades Stakes

SWEET RETURN (2000)
At 3: Won Hollywood Derby

SWEET REVENGE (1978)
At 2: Won Alcibiades Stakes
2nd Frizette Stakes
3rd Matron Stakes

SWEET ROBERTA (1987)
At 2: Won Selima Stakes
2nd Breeders' Cup Juvenile Fillies

SWEET TALK (1948)
At 3: 3rd Santa Susana Stakes

SWEET TOOTH (1965)
At 2: 2nd Alcibiades Stakes

SWEET WILLIAM (1957)
At 4: 3rd Metropolitan Handicap

SWEPT OVERBOARD (1997)
At 4: Won Ancient Title Breeders' Cup Handicap
At 5: Won Metropolitan Handicap

SWIFT COURIER (1970)
At 2: 3rd Sapling Stakes
Futurity Stakes

SWIFT LADY (1963)
At 2: 2nd Spinaway Stakes
Selima Stakes
3rd Frizette Stakes

SWIFT RULER (1962)
At 3: Won Arkansas Derby
2nd Blue Grass Stakes
At 4: Won Oaklawn Handicap

SWIFT SAVAGE (1967)
At 4: 3rd Malibu Stakes

SWIFT SWORD (1951)
At 2: 3rd Remsen Handicap

SWINGING MOOD (1963)
At 3: 3rd Gazelle Handicap

SWING TILL DAWN (1979)
At 4: Won Widener Handicap
Charles H. Strub Stakes

SWINGTIME (1972)
At 5: 2nd Santa Barbara Handicap
Yellow Ribbon Stakes
3rd Vanity Handicap
Ramona Handicap

SWINK (1983)
At 4: Won Sunset Handicap
At 5: 3rd San Luis Rey Stakes

SWIRLING ABBEY (1954)
At 2: Won Del Mar Futurity
At 3: 2nd Santa Anita Derby

SWISS CHEESE (1964)
At 2: Won Matron Stakes
At 3: 3rd Monmouth Oaks
Gazelle Handicap
At 6: 3rd Top Flight Handicap

SWISS YODELER (1994)
At 2: Won Hollywood Futurity
3rd Del Mar Futurity
Norfolk Stakes
At 3: 3rd Malibu Stakes

SWITCHEROO (1977)
At 5: 3rd Widener Handicap

SWITCH ON (1951)
At 5: Won McLennan Handicap
2nd Metropolitan Handicap
Carter Handicap
At 6: 3rd McLennan Handicap
Widener Handicap

SWITCH PARTNERS (1976)
At 3: 2nd San Felipe Handicap
Hollywood Derby
3rd Santa Anita Derby

SWOON (1978)
At 7: 3rd San Juan Capistrano Handicap
Hollywood Invitational Handicap

SWOONALONG (1961)
At 4: 2nd Matron Handicap
Spinster Stakes

SWOON'S FLOWER (1967)
At 4: Won Black Helen Handicap
3rd Vanity Handicap

SWOON'S SON (1953)
At 2: Won Arlington Futurity
Washington Park Futurity
2nd Breeders' Futurity
At 3: Won Arlington Classic
American Derby
At 4: 2nd Hawthorne Gold Cup
Arlington Handicap
3rd Washington Park Handicap
At 5: 2nd Hawthorne Gold Cup

SWORD DANCER (1956)
At 2: 3rd Garden State Stakes
At 3: Won Belmont Stakes
Travers Stakes
Metropolitan Handicap
Monmouth Handicap
Woodward Stakes
Jockey Club Gold Cup
2nd Florida Derby
Kentucky Derby
Preakness Stakes
Brooklyn Handicap
At 4: Won Grey Lag Handicap
Suburban Handicap
Woodward Stakes
2nd United Nations Handicap
3rd Man o' War Stakes

SYBIL BRAND (1956)
At 3: 3rd Vanity Handicap

SYLVAN PLACE (1972)
At 3: 2nd Florida Derby
Ohio Derby

SYNCOPATE (1975)
At 4: 2nd Californian Stakes
3rd Vosburgh Stakes

SYRIAN SEA (1965)
At 2: Won Selima Stakes
3rd Matron Stakes
At 3: 3rd Coaching Club American Oaks

TABASCO CAT (1991)
At 2: 3rd Breeders' Cup Juvenile
At 3: Won Preakness Stakes
Belmont Stakes
2nd Santa Anita Derby
Jim Dandy Stakes
Breeders' Cup Classic
3rd Travers Stakes

TABLE HANDS (1977)
At 2: Won Del Mar Debutante Stakes
At 3: 3rd Santa Susana Stakes

TABLE MATE (1959)
At 3: 3rd Hollywood Oaks
At 4: Won Vanity Handicap
2nd Santa Margarita Handicap
3rd Delaware Handicap

TABLE THE RUMOR (1974)
At 4: 3rd La Canada Stakes

TACKING (1956)
At 3: 3rd Spinster Stakes

TACTICAL CAT (1996)
At 2: Won Hollywood Futurity
2nd Hopeful Stakes

TACTILE (1986)
At 3: Won Beldame Stakes

TAGEL (1986)
At 2: 3rd Breeders' Cup Juvenile

TAHITI (1950)
At 5: 3rd Fall Highweight Handicap

TAHITIAN KING (1950)
At 2: 2nd Futurity Stakes
At 3: 2nd Wood Memorial Stakes

TAHITIAN KING (1976)
At 5: 2nd Bay Meadows Handicap

TAHKODHA HILLS (1997)
At 3: 3rd Florida Derby

TAILSPIN (1944)
At 3: 3rd Belmont Stakes

TAIPAN (1963)
At 3: 3rd Arkansas Derby

TAISEZ VOUS (1974)
At 3: 3rd Hollywood Oaks
At 4: Won La Canada Stakes
Santa Margarita Handicap
2nd Apple Blossom Handicap

TAKE BY STORM (1971)
At 2: 2nd Hopeful Stakes

TAKE CHARGE LADY (1999)
At 2: Won Walmac International Alcibiades Stakes
At 3: Won Ashland Stakes
Overbrook Spinster Stakes
2nd Gazelle Handicap
At 4: Won Overbrook Spinster Stakes
2nd Apple Blossom Handicap
Ogden Phipps Handicap

TAKE ME OUT (1988)
At 2: 2nd Breeders' Cup Juvenile
At 5: 2nd Vosburgh Stakes

TAKEN ABACK (1966)
At 4: Won Black Helen Handicap
Spinster Stakes
3rd Ladies Handicap
At 5: 3rd Black Helen Handicap

TAKE OFF (1969)
At 5: Won Bowling Green Handicap

TAKE OVER (1961)
At 4: Won Washington Park Handicap
3rd Michigan Mile and One-Eighth

TAKE THE CAKE (1999)
At 3: 2nd Ashland Stakes
Kentucky Oaks

TAKE WING (1938)
At 8: 3rd Arlington Handicap
Washington Park Handicap

TAKING RISKS (1990)
At 4: Won Philip H. Iselin Handicap

TALAKENO (1980)
At 7: 3rd Turf Classic

TALENT SHOW (1955)
At 3: 2nd Arlington Classic
3rd Flamingo Stakes
American Derby
At 4: 2nd Suburban Handicap
3rd John B. Campbell Handicap
Metropolitan Handicap
Monmouth Handicap
Trenton Handicap
At 5: Won Massachusetts Handicap
2nd Whitney Handicap
3rd Widener Handicap
Metropolitan Handicap
Monmouth Handicap
Washington Park Handicap
At 6: 2nd Washington Park Handicap
3rd Suburban Handicap
At 7: 2nd Michigan Mile and One-Sixteenth

TALE OF THE CAT (1994)
At 3: 3rd Vosburgh Stakes
At 4: 2nd Whitney Handicap
3rd Vosburgh Stakes

TALINUM (1984)
At 2: 2nd Remsen Stakes
At 3: Won Flamingo Stakes
3rd Florida Derby

TALI'SLUCKYBUSRIDE (1999)
At 2: Won Oak Leaf Stakes
3rd Hollywood Starlet Stakes
At 3: 3rd Las Virgenes Stakes

TALKATIVE TURN (1971)
At 3: 3rd Secretariat Stakes

TALKING PICTURE (1971)
At 2: Won Spinaway Stakes
Matron Stakes
3rd Selima Stakes

TALKING POINT (1947)
At 3: 2nd Santa Susana Stakes

TALKIN MAN (1992)
At 3: Won Gotham Stakes
Wood Memorial Stakes

TALK'S CHEAP (1996)
At 3: 3rd Pegasus Handicap
At 4: 3rd Philip H. Iselin Handicap

TALLAHTO (1970)
At 4: Won Vanity Handicap
Santa Barbara Handicap
Oak Tree Invitational Stakes
3rd Santa Maria Handicap
Santa Margarita Handicap

TALL CHIEF II (1952)
At 6: 2nd San Juan Capistrano Handicap
At 7: 2nd San Juan Capistrano Handicap

TALLOIRES (1990)
At 5: 2nd Hollywood Turf Cup
At 6: 3rd Hollywood Turf Cup

TALL POPPY (1983)
At 4: 3rd Spinster Stakes

TALLY HO THE FOX (1975)
At 2: 3rd Hollywood Juvenile Championship

TALON (1942)
At 5: 2nd Jockey Club Gold Cup
Widener Handicap
Monmouth Handicap
New York Handicap
Gallant Fox Handicap
3rd Dixie Handicap
Suburban Handicap
Manhattan Handicap
At 6: Won San Antonio Handicap
Santa Anita Handicap

TAMARONA (1959)
At 2: Won Selima Stakes
3rd Gardenia Stakes

TAMARONA *(Continued)*
At 3: Won Vineland Handicap
2nd Acorn Stakes
At 4: 2nd Top Flight Handicap
3rd Vineland Handicap

TAMPA TROUBLE (1965)
At 2: 3rd Breeders' Futurity
At 6: 2nd San Luis Rey Handicap

TAMPOY (1975)
At 2: 2nd Del Mar Futurity
At 3: 3rd San Felipe Handicap

TANEB (1963)
At 6: Won San Luis Rey Handicap
2nd Dixie Handicap

TANGO CHARLIE (1989)
At 3: 3rd Secretariat Stakes

TANISTAIR (1962)
At 2: 3rd Sanford Stakes

TANKS BRIGADE (1980)
At 3: 2nd California Derby
3rd Swaps Stakes

TANK'S PROSPECT (1982)
At 2: 2nd Breeders' Cup Juvenile
3rd Champagne Stakes
Young America Stakes
At 3: Won Arkansas Derby
Preakness Stakes

TANTALIZING (1979)
At 4: Won Bowling Green Handicap

TAPPIANO (1984)
At 2: Won Matron Stakes
2nd Breeders' Cup Juvenile Fillies

TAP SHOES (1978)
At 2: Won Hopeful Stakes
Futurity Stakes
At 3: Won Flamingo Stakes
2nd Dwyer Stakes
At 4: 3rd Whitney Handicap

TAP TO MUSIC (1995)
At 3: Won Gazelle Handicap

TAP YOUR TOES (1985)
At 2: 2nd Frizette Stakes

TARBOOSH (1969)
At 2: 2nd Sanford Stakes
At 3: 3rd Fountain of Youth Stakes
Flamingo Stakes

TARNISHED LADY (1999)
At 3: 2nd Coaching Club American Oaks

TASK (1945)
At 2: Won Sapling Stakes

TASSO (1983)
At 2: Won Breeders' Futurity
Breeders' Cup Juvenile
At 3: 2nd Gotham Stakes
Withers Stakes
3rd Jersey Derby
At 4: 2nd Hollywood Gold Cup

TATAO (1960)
At 6: 3rd Canadian International Championship

TATES CREEK (1998)
At 5: Won Gamely Breeders' Cup Handicap
Yellow Ribbon Stakes
2nd John C. Mabee Handicap

TATOI (1967)
At 3: 3rd Withers Stakes

TAVISTOCK (1944)
At 2: 2nd Remsen Handicap

TA WEE (1966)
At 3: Won Vosburgh Handicap

TAX DODGE (1981)
At 5: 3rd Gamely Handicap

TAYLOR'S SPECIAL (1981)
At 3: Won Louisiana Derby
Blue Grass Stakes

TEACATION (1957)
At 3: Won Monmouth Oaks
At 4: 2nd Black Helen Handicap

TEACHER'S ART (1964)
At 2: Won Alcibiades Stakes
2nd Arlington-Washington Lassie Stakes

TEA-MAKER (1943)
At 6: 3rd Fall Highweight Handicap
At 7: Won Vosburgh Handicap
At 9: 2nd Fall Highweight Handicap
Vosburgh Handicap

TEA OLIVE (1944)
At 2: 3rd Spinaway Stakes

TECHNOLOGY (1989)
At 3: Won Florida Derby
Haskell Invitational Handicap
2nd Ohio Derby

TEDDY'S COURAGE (1973)
At 3: 2nd Hawthorne Gold Cup

TEDS JEEP (1950)
At 2: 3rd Remsen Handicap

TEJANO (1985)
At 2: Won Arlington-Washington Futurity
Cowdin Stakes
Hollywood Futurity
3rd Champagne Stakes
Breeders' Cup Juvenile
At 3: 2nd Withers Stakes
Peter Pan Stakes
3rd San Felipe Handicap

TEJANO RUN (1992)
At 2: 3rd Breeders' Cup Juvenile
At 3: 2nd Jim Beam Stakes
Kentucky Derby
3rd Blue Grass Stakes
At 5: 3rd Gulfstream Park Handicap
Oaklawn Handicap
Pimlico Special

TELEFONICO (1971)
At 4: 3rd Bowling Green Handicap

TELEPROMPTER (1980)
At 5: Won Budweiser-Arlington Million

TELERAN (1954)
At 3: 2nd Acorn Stakes

TELETHON (1960)
At 2: 3rd Kentucky Jockey Club Stakes

TELEVISION STUDIO (1978)
At 3: 2nd Secretariat Stakes
3rd Arlington Classic

TELFERNER (1974)
At 2: Won Del Mar Debutante Stakes

TELL (1966)
At 3: Won Hollywood Derby
2nd Cinema Handicap

TELL ME ALL (1973)
At 3: 3rd Acorn Stakes

TELLY'S POP (1973)
At 2: Won Del Mar Futurity
Norfolk Stakes
3rd Hollywood Juvenile Championship
At 3: Won California Derby

TEL O'SULLIVAN (1943)
At 4: Won Miami Beach Handicap

TEMPER (1960)
At 5: 2nd Donn Handicap

TEMPERA (1999)
At 2: Won Breeders' Cup Juvenile Fillies
3rd Del Mar Debutante Stakes

TEMPERATE SIL (1984)
At 2: Won Hollywood Futurity
At 3: Won Santa Anita Derby
Swaps Stakes
3rd San Felipe Handicap

TEMPERENCE HILL (1977)
At 3: Won Arkansas Derby
Belmont Stakes
Travers Stakes
Super Derby
Jockey Club Gold Cup
2nd Dwyer Stakes
At 4: Won Suburban Handicap
Oaklawn Handicap
2nd Californian Stakes
3rd Marlboro Cup Handicap

TEMPEST QUEEN (1975)
At 3: Won Acorn Stakes
Spinster Stakes
3rd Mother Goose Stakes
Coaching Club American Oaks
Alabama Stakes
Ruffian Handicap

TEMPESTUOUS (1957)
At 3: Won Hollywood Derby
2nd Cinema Handicap

TEMPLAR HILL (1984)
At 3: 3rd Jersey Derby
Jerome Handicap

TEMPTED (1955)
At 3: Won Alabama Stakes
Maskette Handicap
3rd Delaware Oaks
Gazelle Handicap
At 4: Won Diana Handicap
Beldame Handicap
Ladies Handicap
2nd Maskette Handicap
3rd Top Flight Handicap
Delaware Handicap

TENACIOUS (1954)
At 3: 3rd Withers Stakes
Dwyer Handicap
At 4: Won New Orleans Handicap
At 5: Won New Orleans Handicap

TENACIOUS JR. (1967)
At 3: 2nd Arlington Classic

TENACLE (1960)
At 3: 2nd Dwyer Handicap
3rd Everglades Stakes
At 5: 2nd New Orleans Handicap
Monmouth Handicap
3rd Massachusetts Handicap
Suburban Handicap

TENDER HEART II (1976)
At 5: 2nd Louisiana Downs Handicap

TENDER SIZE (1956)
At 3: Won Vanity Handicap

TEN MOST WANTED (2000)
At 3: Won Travers Stakes
Super Derby
2nd Belmont Stakes

TENPINS (1998)
At 4: 3rd Stephen Foster Handicap

TENSKI (1995)
At 3: Won Queen Elizabeth II Challenge Cup

TENTAM (1969)
At 3: 2nd Travers Stakes
Jerome Handicap
At 4: Won Metropolitan Handicap
United Nations Handicap
2nd Amory L. Haskell Handicap
Man o' War Stakes
3rd Brooklyn Handicap

TENZING II (1963)
At 4: 2nd Michigan Mile and One-Eighth

TEPEE RINGS (1967)
At 2: 2nd Futurity Stakes

TERENTIA (1962)
At 3: 2nd Monmouth Oaks
Alabama Stakes
Gazelle Handicap
3rd Kentucky Oaks
Coaching Club American Oaks

TERETE (1972)
At 3: Won Cinema Handicap
2nd Hollywood Derby

TERLAGO (1967)
At 3: Won San Felipe Handicap
Santa Anita Derby

TERLINGUA (1976)
At 2: Won Hollywood Juvenile Championship
Del Mar Debutante Stakes
2nd Alcibiades Stakes
3rd Frizette Stakes
At 3: 2nd Santa Susana Stakes

TERPSICHORIST (1975)
At 4: Won Sheepshead Bay Handicap
3rd Flower Bowl Handicap

TERRA FIRMA (1955)
At 2: 2nd Garden State Stakes
At 3: Won Ohio Derby
Stars and Stripes Handicap

TERRANG (1953)
At 3: Won Santa Anita Derby
3rd San Felipe Handicap
Cinema Handicap
Westerner Stakes
At 4: Won San Antonio Handicap
At 5: 2nd Santa Anita Handicap
3rd Californian Stakes
At 6: Won Santa Anita Handicap
3rd San Antonio Handicap
Hollywood Gold Cup

TERRE FROIDE (1977)
At 5: 2nd Golden Harvest Handicap

TERRIBLE TERRI T. (1981)
At 2: 2nd Sorority Stakes

TERRI HI (1962)
At 3: Won Ohio Derby

TERRY'S MAN (1946)
At 3: 2nd Will Rogers Handicap

TERRY'S SECRET (1962)
At 2: Won Del Mar Futurity
At 3: Won Hollywood Derby
Sunset Handicap
2nd California Derby
At 4: 2nd San Fernando Stakes
San Antonio Handicap
3rd Charles H. Strub Stakes

TESSA (1951)
At 4: 3rd Santa Margarita Handicap

TESTAFLY (1994)
At 4: 3rd Philip H. Iselin Handicap

TETON HOLIDAY (1963)
At 2: 2nd Del Mar Debutante Stakes

TETRACK (1967)
At 5: 3rd Del Mar Handicap

TE VEGA (1965)
At 3: Won Ohio Derby
2nd Arkansas Derby

TEXAS SANDMAN (1941)
At 6: Won San Carlos Handicap
2nd Inglewood Handicap
3rd San Pasqual Handicap
American Handicap

TEXIAN (1986)
At 2: 3rd Del Mar Futurity

TEXT (1974)
At 3: Won Secretariat Stakes
3rd Swaps Stakes
At 4: Won San Fernando Stakes
2nd Hollywood Gold Cup
Charles H. Strub Stakes
3rd San Luis Rey Stakes
At 5: Won Amory L. Haskell Handicap
3rd Hollywood Gold Cup

THANKS AGAIN (1947)
At 2: Won Starlet Stakes

THANKS TO TONY (1977)
At 3: Won Monmouth Invitational Handicap

THAT LUCKY DAY (1956)
At 2: 3rd Hopeful Stakes

THAT'S A NICE (1974)
At 4: 2nd Hialeah Turf Cup
Pan American Handicap

THAT'S AN OUTRAGE (2001)
At 2: 3rd Hollywood Futurity

THAXTER (1950)
At 3: 3rd Everglades Stakes

THE ADMIRAL (1946)
At 2: Won Tremont Stakes

THEATRICAL (1982)
At 4: 2nd Oak Tree Invitational Stakes
Breeders' Cup Turf
3rd Hollywood Turf Cup
At 5: Won Hialeah Turf Cup
Turf Classic
Man o' War Stakes
Breeders' Cup Turf
3rd Budweiser-Arlington Million

THE AXE II (1958)
At 4: 3rd San Juan Capistrano Handicap
Man o' War Stakes
At 5: Won Canadian Championship Stakes
Man o' War Stakes
San Luis Rey Handicap

THE BAGEL PRINCE (1972)
At 2: Won Hopeful Stakes
2nd Hollywood Juvenile Championship
Sapling Stakes
3rd Arlington-Washington Futurity

THE BARKING SHARK (1993)
At 3: 2nd Isle of Capri Casino Super Derby
At 4: 2nd Strub Stakes

THE BARON (1960)
At 3: 2nd Ohio Derby

THE BART (1976)
At 5: 2nd Arlington Million
3rd Sunset Handicap
Oak Tree Invitational Stakes
Bay Meadows Handicap
At 6: Won Hialeah Turf Cup
Century Handicap
3rd Pan American Handicap
Hollywood Invitational Handicap

THE BOSS (1986)
At 2: 2nd Young America Stakes

THE CAPTAIN (1979)
At 2: 2nd Del Mar Futurity

THE CARPENTER (1977)
At 2: Won Del Mar Futurity
Norfolk Stakes
At 3: 2nd San Felipe Handicap

THE COOL VIRGINIAN (1976)
At 4: 3rd Amory L. Haskell Handicap

THE DEPUTY (1997)
At 3: Won Santa Anita Derby
2nd San Felipe Stakes

THE DIVER (1947)
At 2: 2nd Arlington Futurity
3rd Futurity Stakes

THE DUDE (1943)
At 3: Won Arlington Classic
3rd American Derby

THE FAT LADY (1946)
At 3: 2nd Kentucky Oaks

THE FIELD (1967)
At 4: 3rd Santa Anita Handicap

THE GAY GREEK (1971)
At 2: 3rd Del Mar Futurity

THE GOON (1953)
At 2: 3rd Cowdin Stakes

THE GROOM IS RED (1996)
At 2: Won Moet Champagne Stakes

THE HAGUE (1979)
At 3: Won Hollywood Turf Cup
2nd Hollywood Derby

THE HEIR (1966)
At 2: 3rd Breeders' Futurity

THEIA (1973)
At 4: 3rd Yellow Ribbon Stakes

THE IBEX (1960)
At 4: 3rd Manhattan Handicap

THE LIBERAL MEMBER (1975)
At 3: 3rd Secretariat Stakes
At 4: Won Brooklyn Handicap
3rd Whitney Stakes
At 6: 2nd Brooklyn Handicap

THELMA BERGER (1947)
At 4: Won Beldame Handicap
2nd Firenze Handicap
At 5: 2nd Firenze Handicap
3rd Comely Handicap

THE MATER (1946)
At 4: 2nd New Castle Handicap

THE MEDIC (1984)
At 3: 2nd Hollywood Derby

THE MESSANGER (1977)
At 3: 3rd Secretariat Stakes
Louisiana Downs Handicap

THE NAME'S JIMMY (1989)
At 3: Won American Derby

THE NOBLE PLAYER (1980)
At 5: 2nd Arlington Handicap

THEORETICALLY (1997)
At 3: 2nd Del Mar Oaks
3rd Queen Elizabeth II Challenge Cup

THEORY (1947)
At 2: Won Champagne Stakes
2nd Futurity Stakes
At 3: 3rd Flamingo Stakes
Lawrence Realization Stakes

THE PIE HOST (1969)
At 3: 3rd California Derby

THE PRUNER (1967)
At 3: Won American Derby
At 4: 2nd Gulfstream Park Handicap
Hialeah Turf Cup
Massachusetts Handicap
3rd Donn Handicap

THERMAL ENERGY (1973)
At 2: 3rd Norfolk Stakes

THESAURUS (1994)
At 6: 2nd Gulfstream Park Breeders' Cup Handicap

THE SCOUNDREL (1961)
At 3: 2nd Florida Derby
Preakness Stakes
3rd Kentucky Derby

THE SEARCHER (1954)
At 4: 3rd Los Angeles Handicap

THE SEVEN SEAS (1996)
At 5: 2nd Beverly D. Stakes

THE SHOE (1955)
At 3: Won Cinema Handicap
2nd Westerner Stakes

THE SILVER MOVE (1994)
At 2: Won Remsen Stakes

THE TIN MAN (1998)
At 4: Won Clement L. Hirsch Mem. Turf Champ.
At 5: 2nd United Nations Handicap

THE TRADER MAN (1976)
At 4: 3rd Hawthorne Gold Cup

THE VERY ONE (1975)
At 4: 2nd Flower Bowl Handicap
At 5: 2nd Santa Margarita Handicap
Washington D.C. International
3rd San Juan Capistrano Handicap
At 6: Won Santa Barbara Handicap
2nd Hialeah Turf Cup
3rd Turf Classic

THE VID (1990)
At 5: 3rd Arlington Million

THE WARRIOR (1953)
At 3: 2nd American Derby

THE WEB II (1945)
At 3: 3rd Westerner Handicap

THE WEDDING GUEST (1981)
At 3: 3rd Jim Beam Stakes

THE WICKED NORTH (1989)
At 5: Won San Antonio Handicap
Oaklawn Handicap
Californian Stakes

THE WONDER (1978)
At 5: Won Californian Stakes
Century Handicap

THINGS CHANGE (1996)
At 2: Won Spinaway Stakes
2nd Frizette Stakes

THIN ICE (1954)
At 2: 3rd Cowdin Stakes

THINKING CAP (1952)
At 2: Won Pimlico Futurity
At 3: Won Travers Stakes
Lawrence Realization Stakes
2nd Jockey Club Gold Cup
3rd Gallant Fox Handicap
At 4: 2nd Display Handicap

THINK SNOW (1975)
At 3: 2nd Hollywood Derby
3rd Santa Anita Derby

THIRD AND LEX (1976)
At 3: 3rd Arlington Classic

THIRD BROTHER (1953)
At 3: Won Roamer Handicap
2nd Lawrence Realization Stakes
3rd Jockey Club Gold Cup
At 4: 2nd John B. Campbell Memorial Handicap
Monmouth Handicap
Jockey Club Gold Cup
Washington D.C. International
3rd Manhattan Handicap
Pimlico Special
At 5: 2nd Brooklyn Handicap
3rd McLennan Handicap
Suburban Handicap

THIRTY EIGHT GO GO (1985)
At 3: 3rd Ladies Handicap
At 4: 3rd Delaware Handicap
At 5: 3rd Delaware Handicap

THIRTY EIGHT PACES (1978)
At 4: 2nd Meadowlands Cup
3rd Oaklawn Handicap

THIRTY FLAGS (1980)
At 3: 3rd Acorn Stakes

THIRTY FLIGHTS (1958)
At 3: 3rd Everglades Stakes

THIRTY ONE JEWELS (1971)
At 2: 2nd Arlington-Washington Lassie Stakes

THIRTY SIX RED (1987)
At 3: Won Gotham Stakes
Wood Memorial Stakes
2nd Belmont Stakes
3rd Breeders' Cup Classic

THIRTY SLEWS (1987)
At 5: Won Breeders' Cup Sprint

THOMAS JO (1995)
At 3: 3rd Belmont Stakes

THONG (1964)
At 2: 2nd Alcibiades Stakes
3rd Selima Stakes

THREE CARRSWOLD (1965)
At 3: 2nd Illinois Derby

THREE ENGINES (1985)
At 2: 3rd Remsen Stakes

THREE PEAT (1989)
At 3: 2nd Dwyer Stakes

THREE RING (1996)
At 2: 3rd Breeders' Cup Juvenile Fillies
At 3: Won Acorn Stakes

THREE RINGS (1945)
At 4: Won Queens County Handicap
Monmouth Handicap
Westchester Handicap
2nd Gulfstream Park Handicap
Grey Lag Handicap
3rd Gallant Fox Handicap
Trenton Handicap
At 5: Won McLennan Handicap
Queens County Handicap
3rd Monmouth Handicap
At 6: 2nd Widener Handicap

THRILL SHOW (1983)
At 3: Won Hollywood Derby

THROUGH FLIGHT (1988)
At 2: Won Arlington-Washington Lassie Stakes

THUMBSUCKER (1979)
At 5: 3rd Whitney Handicap

THUNDER DAYS (1999)
At 2: 3rd Hopeful Stakes
At 3: 3rd King's Bishop Stakes

THUNDERELLO (1999)
At 3: 2nd NAPA Breeders' Cup Sprint

THUNDER GULCH (1992)
At 2: Won Remsen Stakes
2nd Hollywood Futurity
At 3: Won Florida Derby
Kentucky Derby
Belmont Stakes
Swaps Stakes
Travers Stakes
3rd Preakness Stakes

THUNDERING FORCE (1983)
At 2: 3rd Breeders' Futurity

THUNDER PUDDLES (1979)
At 3: 2nd Rothmans International Stakes
3rd Man o' War Stakes
Washington D.C. International
At 4: 2nd Sword Dancer Handicap
Turf Classic
Rothmans International Stakes

THUNDER RUMBLE (1989)
At 3: Won Jim Dandy Stakes
Travers Stakes

THURLOE SQUARE (1969)
At 3: 3rd Blue Grass Stakes

THWARTED (1943)
At 8: 3rd New Orleans Handicap

TIBALDO (1960)
At 4: Won Michigan Mile and One-Sixteenth
3rd Gallant Fox Handicap
At 5: 2nd Grey Lag Handicap

TICKETED (1979)
At 3: 3rd Matriarch Stakes

TICK TOCK (1953)
At 2: 2nd Cowdin Stakes
At 3: 2nd Travers Stakes
Jerome Handicap
At 4: 2nd Pimlico Special
3rd Massachusetts Handicap
Brooklyn Handicap
Whitney Stakes
At 5: 2nd Carter Handicap
At 6: 2nd Carter Handicap
3rd Aqueduct Handicap

TIDE RIPS (1944)
At 3: 2nd Belmont Stakes
At 4: Won Monmouth Handicap
2nd Trenton Handicap
3rd Manhattan Handicap

TIFFANY ICE (1982)
At 2: 2nd Hopeful Stakes

TIFFANY LASS (1983)
At 3: Won Fantasy Stakes
Kentucky Oaks

TIGER HUNT (2001)
At 2: 2nd Lane's End Breeders' Futurity

TIGER SKIN (1950)
At 2: 2nd Hopeful Stakes

TIGER TALK (1993)
At 3: 2nd Gotham Stakes

TIGHT SPOT (1987)
At 4: Won Eddie Read Handicap
Arlington Million

TIJIYR (1996)
At 5: 3rd Manhattan Handicap

TIKKANEN (1991)
At 3: Won Turf Classic
Breeders' Cup Turf

TIL FORBID (1988)
At 3: 2nd Alabama Stakes
3rd Ashland Stakes
Kentucky Oaks
Spinster Stakes

TILLER (1974)
At 4: Won Bowling Green Handicap
2nd Man o' War Stakes
Turf Classic
Washington D.C. International
3rd Hialeah Turf Cup
At 5: Won San Antonio Stakes
San Juan Capistrano Handicap
2nd Santa Anita Handicap
San Luis Rey Stakes
At 6: Won Sword Dancer Stakes

TILTALATING (1982)
At 2: Won Sorority Stakes
2nd Sapling Stakes
Arlington-Washington Lassie Stakes
Matron Stakes
Frizette Stakes

TILT THE BALANCE (1975)
At 4: 2nd Longacres Mile
At 5: 3rd Longacres Mile

TIMARIDA (1992)
At 4: Won Beverly D. Stakes

TIMBER COUNTRY (1992)
At 2: Won Champagne Stakes
Breeders' Cup Juvenile
3rd Del Mar Futurity
At 3: Won Preakness Stakes
2nd San Felipe Stakes
3rd Kentucky Derby

TIMBOROA (1996)
At 5: Won Turf Classic
3rd Charles Whittingham Handicap
Breeders' Cup Turf

TIME BANDIT (1996)
At 2: 3rd Hopeful Stakes

TIME CALL (1974)
At 3: 2nd Illinois Derby

TIME FOR A CHANGE (1981)
At 3: Won Everglades Stakes
Flamingo Stakes

TIME FOR BED (1961)
At 3: 3rd Spinster Stakes

TIMELESS EVENT (1978)
At 2: 3rd Sapling Stakes

TIMELESS MOMENT (1970)
At 3: 3rd Vosburgh Handicap
At 4: 3rd Carter Handicap
Metropolitan Handicap

TIMELESS NATIVE (1980)
At 4: 2nd Vosburgh Stakes

TIMELY ASSERTION (1984)
At 3: Won Santa Anita Oaks

TIMELY REWARD (1948)
At 3: 2nd Flamingo Stakes

TIMELY TIP (1951)
At 3: Won Ohio Derby

TIMELY WARNING (1985)
At 6: Won Brooklyn Handicap

TIMELY WRITER (1979)
At 2: Won Hopeful Stakes
Champagne Stakes
3rd Futurity Stakes
At 3: Won Flamingo Stakes
Florida Derby

TIMERA (1978)
At 3: 3rd Golden Harvest Handicap

TIMES ROMAN (1959)
At 2: 2nd Breeders' Futurity
Kentucky Jockey Club Stakes

TIMES TWO (1958)
At 2: 2nd Selima Stakes
At 3: 3rd Kentucky Oaks
Spinster Stakes

TIME TESTED (1962)
At 2: 3rd Hopeful Stakes
At 4: 2nd Carter Handicap
3rd Arlington Handicap

TIME TO EXPLODE (1979)
At 4: 2nd San Antonio Stakes

TIME TO LEAVE (1965)
At 2: 2nd Del Mar Debutante Stakes

TIM TAM (1955)
At 3: Won Everglades Stakes
Flamingo Stakes
Florida Derby
Kentucky Derby
Preakness Stakes
2nd Belmont Stakes

TIM THE TIGER (1976)
At 2: Won Sapling Stakes

TINAJERO (1968)
At 3: Won Jerome Handicap
2nd Woodward Stakes

TINNERS WAY (1990)
At 4: Won Pacific Classic
At 5: Won Pacific Classic
2nd Hollywood Gold Cup
3rd Californian Stakes
At 6: Won Californian Stakes

TINSLEY (1963)
At 2: Won Breeders' Futurity
2nd Kentucky Jockey Club Stakes

TINSLEY'S IMAGE (1971)
At 2: 3rd Hollywood Juvenile Championship

TIO CIRO (1947)
At 5: 2nd Massachusetts Handicap

TIO VIEJO (1962)
At 4: 3rd Gulfstream Park Handicap
Metropolitan Handicap

TIPICALLY IRISH (1993)
At 2: Won Oak Leaf Stakes

TIPPING TIME (1966)
At 3: Won Hollywood Oaks
At 4: 3rd Vanity Handicap
Santa Margarita Handicap
At 5: 3rd Santa Barbara Handicap

TISAB (1971)
At 2: Won Sapling Stakes

TITLE (1967)
At 2: 2nd Spinaway Stakes

TIZNA (1969)
At 5: Won Santa Margarita Handicap
Ramona Handicap
2nd Santa Maria Handicap
3rd Beldame Stakes
Santa Barbara Handicap
At 6: Won Ladies Handicap
Santa Margarita Handicap
2nd Beldame Stakes
Ramona Handicap
3rd National Championship Inv. Handicap
At 7: 3rd Santa Barbara Handicap

TIZNOW (1997)
At 3: Won Super Derby
Breeders' Cup Classic
2nd Swaps Stakes
Pacific Classic
At 4: Won Santa Anita Handicap
Breeders' Cup Classic
2nd Strub Stakes
3rd Woodward Stakes

TIZON (1977)
At 3: 2nd American Derby

TOASTED (1967)
At 2: 2nd Breeders' Futurity
Pimlico-Laurel Futurity
3rd Champagne Stakes

TOBIN BRONZE (1962)
At 5: 3rd Washington D.C. International
At 6: 2nd San Luis Rey Handicap

TOBIN'S ROSE (1977)
At 4: 3rd La Canada Stakes

TOBY B. (1953)
At 3: Won Blue Grass Stakes
2nd Ohio Derby
American Derby

TOBY'S BROTHER (1957)
At 2: Won Breeders' Futurity

TOCCET (2000)
At 2: Won Champagne Stakes
Hollywood Futurity
At 3: 3rd Cigar Mile Handicap

TOCOLI (1947)
At 5: 3rd Aqueduct Handicap

TODA UNA DAMA (1993)
At 5: Won Santa Margarita Handicap
2nd Santa Maria Handicap
3rd Apple Blossom Handicap

TODAY'N TOMORROW (1973)
At 4: Won Sunset Handicap

TOGA TOGA TOGA (1992)
At 5: Won Santa Monica Handicap

TOLLWAY (1958)
At 6: 3rd New Orleans Handicap

TOLOMEO (1980)
At 3: Won Budweiser Million

TOLUENE (1956)
At 2: 2nd Selima Stakes
At 3: 2nd Mother Goose Stakes

TO MARKET (1948)
At 2: Won Arlington Futurity
Washington Park Futurity
At 4: Won San Carlos Handicap
Massachusetts Handicap
Arlington Handicap
Hawthorne Gold Cup
2nd Washington Park Handicap
3rd Carter Handicap
Brooklyn Handicap

TOM CAT (1960)
At 6: 3rd San Juan Capistrano Handicap

TOM FOOL (1949)
At 2: Won Futurity Stakes
2nd Hopeful Stakes
At 3: Won Jerome Handicap
Grey Lag Handicap
2nd Wood Memorial Stakes
Roamer Handicap
Westchester Handicap
3rd Travers Stakes
At 4: Won Metropolitan Handicap
Suburban Handicap
Carter Handicap
Brooklyn Handicap
Whitney Stakes
Pimlico Special

TOMISUE'S DELIGHT (1994)
At 3: Won Ruffian Handicap
2nd Kentucky Oaks
Coaching Club American Oaks
3rd Mother Goose Stakes
Alabama Stakes
At 4: Won Personal Ensign Handicap
2nd Beldame Stakes
3rd Go for Wand Handicap

TOMORROWS CAT (1995)
At 3: Won Buick Pegasus Handicap

TOMORROW'S CHILD (1985)
At 2: 2nd Arlington-Washington Lassie Stakes
3rd Oak Leaf Stakes

TOMPION (1957)
At 2: Won Hopeful Stakes
2nd Hollywood Juvenile Championship
Saratoga Special
Champagne Stakes
3rd Garden State Stakes
At 3: Won Santa Anita Derby
Blue Grass Stakes
Travers Stakes
2nd Jersey Derby
Lawrence Realization Stakes
At 4: Won Aqueduct Handicap
2nd San Fernando Stakes
United Nations Handicap

TOM ROLFE (1962)
At 2: Won Cowdin Stakes
3rd Futurity Stakes
At 3: Won Preakness Stakes
Arlington Classic
American Derby
2nd Belmont Stakes
3rd Kentucky Derby
At 4: Won Aqueduct Handicap
2nd Washington Park Handicap
Michigan Mile and One-Eighth

TOM TULLE (1970)
At 4: Won Michigan Mile and One-Eighth

TOMY LEE (1956)
At 2: Won Starlet Stakes
Del Mar Futurity
2nd Garden State Stakes
3rd Champagne Stakes
At 3: Won Blue Grass Stakes
Kentucky Derby
2nd San Felipe Handicap

TONA (1960)
At 3: Won Alabama Stakes
At 4: Won Vineland Handicap
2nd Top Flight Handicap
3rd Black Helen Handicap
Ladies Handicap

TONGA (1949)
At 2: Won Del Mar Debutante Stakes
At 3: 3rd Hollywood Oaks

TONKA WAKHAN (1977)
At 2: 3rd Breeders' Futurity

TONY GRAFF (1957)
At 3: Won Louisiana Derby
2nd Arkansas Derby

TONZARUN (1978)
At 5: 2nd Pan American Handicap
3rd Hialeah Turf Cup
At 6: 2nd Century Handicap
3rd Hialeah Turf Cup

TOO ANGRI (1965)
At 3: 3rd Hollywood Oaks

TOO CHIC (1979)
At 3: Won Maskette Stakes
2nd Alabama Stakes

TOO MANY SWEETS (1976)
At 2: 3rd Alcibiades Stakes

TOONDER (1971)
At 4: 2nd Century Handicap

TOONERVILLE (1971)
At 5: 2nd Widener Handicap
3rd Hialeah Turf Cup

TOO SCARLET (1998)
At 4: 3rd Go for Wand Handicap

TOOTH AND NAIL (1957)
At 3: 3rd Lawrence Realization Stakes

TOP ACCOUNT (1992)
At 3: 3rd Jerome Handicap
At 4: 3rd NYRA Mile Handicap

TOP AVENGER (1978)
At 3: 2nd Arkansas Derby

TOP BID (1964)
At 2: 3rd Sanford Stakes
Saratoga Special
Hopeful Stakes

TOP COMMAND (1971)
At 4: Won Oak Tree Invitational Stakes
At 5: 3rd San Luis Rey Stakes

TOP CORSAGE (1983)
At 3: Won Spinster Stakes
2nd Yellow Ribbon Stakes

TOP CROWD (1971)
At 3: 3rd Hollywood Derby
At 4: 2nd American Handicap
Del Mar Handicap
Oak Tree Invitational Stakes
3rd Sunset Handicap
At 5: 2nd San Luis Rey Stakes
3rd San Juan Capistrano Handicap
At 6: 2nd San Juan Capistrano Handicap
3rd San Luis Rey Stakes

TOP GALLANT (1960)
At 3: 3rd Wood Memorial Stakes

Withers Stakes
At 4: Won Seminole Handicap

TOPICOUNT (1985)
At 3: 2nd Acorn Stakes

TOP KNIGHT (1966)
At 2: Won Hopeful Stakes
Futurity Stakes
Champagne Stakes
3rd Garden State Stakes
At 3: Won Flamingo Stakes
Florida Derby
2nd Everglades Stakes

TOP OFFICIAL (1995)
At 6: 3rd Brooklyn Handicap

TOP RUNG (1991)
At 4: 2nd Vanity Handicap
At 5: 3rd Vanity Handicap
At 6: 2nd Santa Margarita Handicap
3rd Santa Maria Handicap

TOP'S BOY (1944)
At 5: Won Del Mar Handicap
At 6: 2nd Del Mar Handicap

TOP SECRET (1993)
At 3: 2nd Three Chimneys Spinster Stakes
3rd Gazelle Handicap

TOP THE MARKET (1967)
At 3: 2nd Cinema Handicap

TOP TURRETT (1946)
At 2: 3rd Starlet Stakes

TORRID SAND (1996)
At 3: 2nd Arkansas Derby

TOSMAH (1961)
At 2: Won Frizette Stakes
At 3: Won Matron Handicap
Beldame Stakes
Arlington Classic
2nd Vineland Handicap
At 4: 3rd Vineland Handicap
At 5: Won John B. Campbell Handicap
3rd Black Helen Handicap

TOSSOFTHECOIN (1990)
At 3: 2nd Wood Memorial Stakes
At 5: 2nd Californian Stakes
3rd San Antonio Handicap
Hollywood Gold Cup

TOTAL DEPARTURE (1980)
At 2: Won Arlington-Washington Futurity

TOTAL LIMIT (1999)
At 3: 2nd Malibu Stakes

TOTAL PLEASURE (1978)
At 2: 2nd Breeders' Futurity

TOTAL TRAFFIC (1954)
At 5: Won Michigan Mile and One-Sixteenth

TO THE QUICK (1974)
At 3: 2nd Jerome Handicap

TOTIE FIELDS (1973)
At 2: 3rd Sorority Stakes

TOTO (1948)
At 4: 3rd Santa Margarita Handicap

TOT OF RUM (1986)
At 5: 3rd Rothmans International Stakes

TOUCH GOLD (1994)
At 3: Won Belmont Stakes
Buick Haskell Invitational Handicap

TOUCH OF THE BLUES (1997)
At 4: 2nd Shoemaker Breeders' Cup Mile
At 5: 2nd Shadwell Keeneland Turf Mile
At 6: 2nd NetJets Breeders' Cup Mile
3rd Shoemaker Breeders' Cup Mile
Shadwell Turf Mile

TOUCH TONE (1998)
At 3: 2nd Haskell Invitational Handicap

TOUGH CRITIC (1979)
At 4: 3rd Metropolitan Handicap

TOULORE (1962)
At 4: 3rd United Nations Handicap

TOUR D'OR (1982)
At 8: 2nd Gulfstream Park Handicap

TOURNEY (1990)
At 2: 3rd Arlington-Washington Lassie Stakes

TOURNURE (1953)
At 3: Won Alabama Stakes
3rd Kentucky Oaks

TOUSSAUD (1989)
At 4: Won Gamely Handicap
2nd Matriarch Stakes

TOUT CHARMANT (1996)
At 3: Won Del Mar Oaks
2nd Las Virgenes Stakes
Santa Anita Oaks
Queen Elizabeth II Challenge Cup
At 4: Won Matriarch Stakes
2nd Ramona Handicap
Breeders' Cup Filly and Mare Turf
3rd Gamely Breeders' Cup Handicap

TOWER EAST (1968)
At 4: 3rd Malibu Stakes

TOWZIE TYKE (1966)
At 6: 3rd John B. Campbell Handicap

TRACEMARK (1999)
At 4: 3rd Strub Stakes

TRACK BARRON (1981)
At 3: Won Dwyer Stakes
Vosburgh Stakes
2nd Jerome Handicap
Whitney Handicap
At 4: Won Whitney Handicap
Woodward Stakes
3rd Metropolitan Handicap

TRACKMASTER (1952)
At 3: Won California Derby
At 4: Won Santa Anita Maturity

TRACK REWARD (1975)
At 3: 3rd Wood Memorial Stakes

TRACK ROBBERY (1976)
At 5: Won Vanity Handicap
3rd Ramona Handicap
At 6: Won Spinster Stakes
Apple Blossom Handicap
2nd Vanity Handicap
Santa Margarita Handicap

TRADITIONALLY (1997)
At 4: Won Oaklawn Handicap

TRAFALGER (1994)
At 3: 2nd Jerome Handicap

TRAFFIC (1961)
At 2: Won Hopeful Stakes
2nd Sanford Stakes
Champagne Stakes
3rd Saratoga Special
Cowdin Stakes
At 3: 2nd Gotham Stakes

TRAFFIC BEAT (1965)
At 3: 3rd California Derby

TRAFFIC COP (1969)
At 4: 3rd Grey Lag Handicap

TRAFFIC JUDGE (1952)
At 2: 2nd Breeders' Futurity
At 3: Won Withers Stakes
Ohio Derby
Jerome Handicap
Woodward Stakes

2nd Arlington Classic
Travers Stakes
American Derby
3rd Preakness Stakes
At 4: 2nd Santa Anita Maturity
At 5: Won Metropolitan Handicap
Suburban Handicap

TRAFFIC MARK (1966)
At 2: Won Kentucky Jockey Club Stakes
At 3: Won Arkansas Derby
2nd Blue Grass Stakes
At 4: 3rd Oaklawn Handicap

TRAGNIEW (1963)
At 3: Won California Derby
2nd Cinema Handicap

TRAIL CITY (1993)
At 3: 2nd Secretariat Stakes

TRAINING TABLE (1971)
At 2: 2nd Breeders' Futurity

TRAIN ROBBERY (1987)
At 5: 2nd Go for Wand Stakes

TRAITOR (1994)
At 2: Won Futurity Stakes
2nd Moet Champagne Stakes

TRANQUIL (1954)
At 2: 2nd Kentucky Jockey Club Stakes
3rd Breeders' Futurity

TRANQUILITY LAKE (1995)
At 3: 3rd Del Mar Oaks
La Brea Stakes
At 4: Won Gamely Breeders' Cup Handicap
2nd Beverly Hills Handicap
At 5: Won Yellow Ribbon Stakes
2nd Matriarch Stakes
At 6: 2nd Gamely Breeders' Cup Handicap
Ramona Handicap
Yellow Ribbon Stakes

TRANSCENDENTAL (1998)
At 4: 2nd Ogden Phipps Handicap
Go for Wand Handicap
Personal Ensign Handicap

TRANSFLUENT (1946)
At 2: 3rd Remsen Stakes

TRANS-WAY (1957)
At 5: Won Tropical Park Handicap

TRAPP MOUNTAIN (1986)
At 2: Won Futurity Stakes
3rd Champagne Stakes

TRAVELLING MUSIC (1978)
At 2: Won Sapling Stakes

TRAVEL ORB (1962)
At 4: Won Californian Stakes
3rd Hollywood Gold Cup

TRAVERTINE (1951)
At 3: 2nd San Felipe Handicap
3rd Santa Anita Derby

TREACHEROUS (1964)
At 3: 2nd Alabama Stakes
Gazelle Handicap
At 4: Won Black Helen Handicap
3rd Delaware Handicap
At 5: 3rd Top Flight Handicap

TREACHERY (1960)
At 5: 2nd Santa Margarita Handicap
At 6: 2nd Delaware Handicap

TREASURER (1992)
At 3: 3rd Peter Pan Stakes

TREEKSTER (1989)
At 3: 2nd Swaps Stakes
3rd Jim Beam Stakes

TREE OF KNOWLEDGE (1970)
At 4: Won Hollywood Gold Cup

TREMPOLINO (1984)
At 3: 2nd Breeders' Cup Turf

TRENTONIAN (1952)
At 3: 3rd San Felipe Handicap

TREVITA (1977)
At 5: Won Flower Bowl Handicap
At 6: 2nd United Nations Handicap

TRIANGULAR (1967)
At 5: 3rd Manhattan Handicap
At 6: 3rd Manhattan Handicap

TRIBE (1950)
At 3: 3rd Flamingo Stakes

TRIBULATION (1990)
At 3: 2nd Yellow Ribbon Stakes

TRIBUNAL (1997)
At 4: 3rd Santa Anita Handicap

TRICKY CODE (1991)
At 2: 3rd Oak Leaf Stakes

TRICKY CREEK (1986)
At 3: 3rd Blue Grass Stakes
Pennsylvania Derby
At 4: 2nd Philip H. Iselin Handicap

TRICKY SQUAW (1983)
At 4: 2nd Ladies Handicap

TRI FOR SIZE (1981)
At 5: 2nd Hialeah Turf Cup

TRIGONOMETRY (1951)
At 4: 3rd Del Mar Handicap

TRI JET (1969)
At 3: 3rd American Derby
At 4: Won Hawthorne Gold Cup
2nd Michigan Mile and One-Eighth
3rd Californian Stakes
Malibu Stakes
At 5: Won Whitney Stakes

TRILLION (1974)
At 4: 3rd Turf Classic
At 5: 2nd Canadian International Championship
Turf Classic
Oak Tree Invitational Stakes
Washington D.C. International

TRIM COLONY (1983)
At 2: 2nd Oak Leaf Stakes

TRIPLE BEND (1968)
At 3: 2nd California Derby
3rd Hollywood Derby
Cinema Handicap
At 4: Won Vosburgh Handicap
San Fernando Stakes
Santa Anita Handicap
2nd Charles H. Strub Stakes
San Antonio Stakes

TRIPLE BROOK (1962)
At 5: 2nd Beldame Stakes

TRIPLE BUCK (1986)
At 3: 3rd Fountain of Youth Stakes
Wood Memorial Stakes

TRIPLE CROWN (1971)
At 3: 2nd Wood Memorial Stakes
3rd San Felipe Handicap

TRIPLE JAY (1953)
At 3: 2nd Monmouth Oaks

TRIPLE STRIKE (1986)
At 3: 3rd Acorn Stakes

TRIPLICATE (1941)
At 5: Won San Juan Capistrano Handicap
Hollywood Gold Cup
3rd Sunset Handicap
At 6: Won Golden Gate Handicap

TRIPOLI SHORES (1983)
At 3: 3rd Secretariat Stakes

TRIPPI (1997)
At 3: Won Vosburgh Stakes

TRIPTYCH (1982)
At 3: 3rd Rothmans International Stakes

TRISHYDE (1989)
At 3: 3rd Hollywood Turf Cup
At 4: 2nd Santa Barbara Handicap

TRITEAMTRI (1985)
At 4: 2nd Santa Anita Handicap
At 5: 2nd Arlington Invitational Challenge Cup

TRITIUM (1950)
At 2: Won Selima Stakes
3rd Demoiselle Stakes
At 3: 3rd Acorn Stakes

TRITOMA (1956)
At 4: 2nd Vanity Handicap
At 5: 3rd Delaware Handicap
Ladies Handicap
At 6: 3rd Santa Margarita Handicap

TRI TO WATCH (1989)
At 2: Won Champagne Stakes
2nd Futurity Stakes

TRIUMPHANT (1969)
At 4: Won Donn Handicap
3rd Widener Handicap

TRIUMPH AT DAWN (1990)
At 4: 2nd Top Flight Handicap

TROILUS (1956)
At 3: Won Flamingo Stakes

TROJAN BRONZE (1971)
At 4: Won San Luis Rey Stakes

TRONADO (1960)
At 5: 2nd Gulfstream Park Handicap
American Handicap
3rd Californian Stakes
At 6: Won Donn Handicap
Arlington Handicap
2nd Hawthorne Gold Cup
3rd John B. Campbell Handicap
Washington Park Handicap

TROOPER SEVEN (1976)
At 4: Won Longacres Mile

TROPICAL BLOSSOM (1998)
At 5: 3rd Milady Breeders' Cup Handicap

TROPICAL SEA (1944)
At 3: 3rd Santa Anita Derby

TROPIC KING II (1963)
At 6: 2nd Donn Handicap
Whitney Stakes
3rd Gulfstream Park Handicap

TROPICOOL (1993)
At 2: Won Remsen Stakes

TROPIC RULER (1979)
At 2: 2nd Arlington-Washington Futurity

TROUBADOUR II (1957)
At 4: 2nd Manhattan Handicap

TRUCKLE FEATURE (2000)
At 2: 3rd Futurity Stakes
Lane's End Breeders' Futurity

TRUE AND BLUE (1985)
At 4: 2nd Carter Handicap

TRUE KNIGHT (1969)
At 3: Won Jerome Handicap
2nd Wood Memorial Stakes
Ohio Derby
3rd Travers Stakes
At 4: 2nd Brooklyn Handicap
Suburban Handicap
At 5: Won John B. Campbell Handicap
Amory L. Haskell Handicap
Suburban Handicap

TRUE KNIGHT *(Continued)*
2nd Donn Handicap
Gulfstream Park Handicap
Widener Handicap

TRUE NORTH (1940)
At 6: 2nd Fall Highweight Handicap

TRUE NORTH (1966)
At 2: 2nd Futurity Stakes
At 4: 2nd Vosburgh Handicap
At 5: Won Widener Handicap
3rd John B. Campbell Handicap

TRUE STATEMENT (1974)
At 4: 2nd Gulfstream Park Handicap
3rd Michigan Mile and One-Eighth

TRULUCK (1995)
At 3: 3rd Jim Beam Stakes

TRULY BOUND (1978)
At 2: Won Arlington-Washington Lassie Stakes
At 3: 2nd Spinster Stakes

TRUMPETER SWAN (1971)
At 5: 2nd Manhattan Handicap
3rd Bowling Green Handicap

TRUPAN (1967)
At 7: 2nd New Orleans Handicap

TRUSTING (1948)
At 5: Won San Antonio Handicap
2nd Santa Anita Handicap
3rd San Juan Capistrano Handicap
At 6: 3rd William P. Kyne Handicap
Hollywood Gold Cup

TRUST N LUCK (2000)
At 3: Won Fountain of Youth Stakes
2nd Florida Derby

TRY CASH (1958)
At 4: 2nd Washington Park Handicap

TRYMENOW (1942)
At 4: 3rd Dixie Handicap
Whitney Stakes

TRY SHEEP (1966)
At 6: Won San Luis Rey Handicap
2nd San Juan Capistrano Handicap

TRY SOMETHING NEW (1979)
At 4: Won Spinster Stakes
2nd Delaware Handicap
Vanity Handicap
3rd Ruffian Handicap
At 5: 2nd Apple Blossom Handicap

TSARBABY (1985)
At 2: 2nd Futurity Stakes
Cowdin Stakes
At 3: 2nd Jersey Derby

TSUNAMI SLEW (1981)
At 3: 3rd California Derby

TUC DE GREAT (1962)
At 3: 2nd Dwyer Handicap

TUDOR ERA (1953)
At 4: 2nd United Nations Handicap
At 5: 2nd Washington D.C. International
At 6: Won Hialeah Turf Cup
Man o' War Handicap
3rd Hawthorne Gold Cup
Jockey Club Gold Cup
Stars and Stripes Handicap
Washington D.C. International
At 7: Won New Orleans Handicap
2nd Bougainvillea Turf Handicap
3rd McLennan Handicap

TUDOR FAME (1962)
At 4: 2nd San Luis Rey Handicap

TUDORICH (1957)
At 4: Won Arlington Handicap

TUDOR QUEEN (1967)
At 2: Won Frizette Stakes

TUDOR REWARD (1967)
At 4: 2nd Dixie Handicap

TUDOR TAMBOURINE (1973)
At 4: Won New Orleans Handicap

TUDOR WAY (1956)
At 5: Won Gulfstream Park Handicap

TUMBLE WIND (1964)
At 2: 2nd Hollywood Juvenile Championship
At 3: Won Hollywood Derby
2nd Santa Anita Derby

TUMIGA (1964)
At 3: Won Carter Handicap
2nd Withers Stakes
3rd Travers Stakes
At 4: 2nd Carter Handicap

TUNERUP (1976)
At 4: Won Meadowlands Cup
Hawthorne Gold Cup
At 5: 2nd Widener Handicap

TUNEX (1966)
At 5: Won Metropolitan Handicap
3rd Suburban Handicap
At 6: 2nd Whitney Stakes
Vosburgh Handicap

TUOSIX (1951)
At 2: 2nd Cowdin Stakes

TURBINE (1942)
At 4: Won Trenton Handicap

TURBO JET II (1960)
At 4: Won Man o' War Stakes
2nd Dixie Handicap
3rd United Nations Handicap

TURF (1944)
At 2: 3rd Breeders' Futurity

TURIN (1955)
At 5: 3rd Sunset Handicap

TURKISH TROUSERS (1968)
At 3: Won Santa Susana Stakes
Hollywood Oaks
At 4: Won Santa Maria Handicap
Santa Margarita Handicap

TURKOMAN (1982)
At 3: 2nd California Derby
Swaps Stakes
Travers Stakes
3rd Breeders' Cup Classic
At 4: Won Widener Handicap
Marlboro Cup Handicap
2nd Jockey Club Gold Cup
Breeders' Cup Classic

TURK PASSER (1990)
At 5: Won Turf Classic

TURK'S DELIGHT (1951)
At 5: 2nd Santa Anita Handicap

TURKSTAND (1990)
At 2: 2nd Oak Leaf Stakes

TURN AND DANCE (1983)
At 3: 3rd Fantasy Stakes

TURNBACK THE ALARM (1989)
At 2: 2nd Spinaway Stakes
At 3: Won Mother Goose Stakes
Coaching Club American Oaks
3rd Acorn Stakes
At 4: Won Shuvee Handicap
Hempstead Handicap
Go for Wand Stakes
3rd Ruffian Handicap

TURN'N TURN ABOUT (1967)
At 3: 3rd Santa Susana Stakes

TURN OF COIN (1974)
At 2: 2nd Hopeful Stakes

TURN-TO (1951)
At 2: Won Garden State Stakes
3rd Hopeful Stakes
At 3: Won Flamingo Stakes

TURTLE BOW (1999)
At 3: 2nd Flower Bowl Invitational Stakes

TUTANKHAMEN (1958)
At 4: Won Manhattan Handicap
At 5: Won Donn Handicap

TUXEDO JUNCTION (1993)
At 5: 3rd Santa Maria Handicap

TUZADO (1948)
At 3: 2nd Cinema Handicap

TUZIA (1994)
At 4: 2nd Personal Ensign Handicap

TUZLA (1994)
At 5: Won Ramona Handicap
2nd Breeders' Cup Mile
Matriarch Stakes

T.V. COMMERCIAL (1965)
At 2: Won Arlington-Washington Futurity
Breeders' Futurity
2nd Pimlico-Laurel Futurity
3rd Kentucky Jockey Club Stakes
At 3: 2nd Blue Grass Stakes
3rd Kentucky Derby
At 5: 3rd Hollywood Gold Cup

T.V. LARK (1957)
At 2: Won Arlington Futurity
At 3: Won Arlington Classic
American Derby
Washington Park Handicap
United Nations Handicap
2nd San Felipe Handicap
Hollywood Derby
3rd Cinema Handicap
At 4: Won Los Angeles Handicap
Hawthorne Gold Cup
Washington D.C. International
2nd San Carlos Handicap
At 5: 2nd United Nations Handicap

T.V.'S PRINCESS (1964)
At 2: 3rd Alcibiades Stakes

T.V. TERESE (1973)
At 2: 2nd Del Mar Debutante Stakes

T.V. VIXEN (1973)
At 3: Won Fantasy Stakes
2nd Delaware Handicap

TWEEDSIDE (1998)
At 3: Won Coaching Club American Oaks

TWENTYONE GUNS (1955)
At 5: 2nd American Handicap

TWICE A PRINCE (1970)
At 3: 2nd Fountain of Youth Stakes
Belmont Stakes
3rd Jockey Club Gold Cup

TWICE AS GAY (1961)
At 3: 3rd Roamer Handicap

TWICE THE VICE (1991)
At 5: Won Santa Margarita Handicap
Apple Blossom Handicap
Milady Breeders' Cup Handicap
2nd Santa Maria Handicap
At 6: Won Vanity Handicap
2nd Hempstead Handicap

TWICE WORTHY (1967)
At 3: Won Monmouth Invitational Handicap
At 4: Won Suburban Handicap
Hawthorne Gold Cup
2nd United Nations Handicap

TWILIGHT AGENDA (1986)
At 5: Won Meadowlands Cup
2nd Pacific Classic
Breeders' Cup Classic

Age	Place	Race
At 6:	2nd	Santa Anita Handicap
	3rd	Oaklawn Handicap
		Pimlico Special
TWILIGHT RIDGE (1983)		
At 2:	Won	Breeders' Cup Juvenile Fillies
At 3:	2nd	Santa Anita Oaks
TWINING (1991)		
At 3:	Won	Peter Pan Stakes
	2nd	Dwyer Stakes
TWIN'S TORNADO (1979)		
At 4:	2nd	Century Handicap
TWIN TIME (1968)		
At 3:	2nd	Jerome Handicap
TWIST AFLEET (1991)		
At 3:	Won	Test Stakes
At 4:	Won	Top Flight Handicap
TWIST THE AXE (1968)		
At 3:	Won	Arkansas Derby
		Ohio Derby
	2nd	Blue Grass Stakes
	3rd	Jersey Derby
TWIXT (1969)		
At 5:	2nd	Delaware Handicap
	3rd	Maskette Handicap
		Ladies Handicap
At 6:	Won	Top Flight Handicap
TWO ALTAZANO (1991)		
At 3:	Won	Coaching Club American Oaks
TWO AND TWENTY (1946)		
At 4:	Won	Longacres Mile
TWOGUNDAN (1966)		
At 4:	Won	Donn Handicap
	2nd	Gulfstream Park Handicap
		Woodward Stakes
At 5:	2nd	Widener Handicap
TWO ITEM LIMIT (1998)		
At 3:	2nd	Las Virgenes Stakes
		Gazelle Handicap
	3rd	Alabama Stakes
		Breeders' Cup Distaff
At 4:	3rd	Ogden Phipps Handicap
TWO LEA (1946)		
At 4:	Won	Santa Margarita Handicap
	2nd	Santa Anita Maturity
	3rd	Santa Anita Handicap
At 6:	Won	Vanity Handicap
		Hollywood Gold Cup
TWO RAINBOWS (1948)		
At 2:	3rd	Astoria Stakes
		Marguerite Stakes
TWO STARS (1952)		
At 3:	2nd	Gazelle Stakes
TWO TIMING LASS (1971)		
At 2:	3rd	Arlington-Washington Lassie Stakes
TYPECAST (1966)		
At 5:	2nd	Beverly Hills Handicap
	3rd	Sunset Handicap
At 6:	Won	Hollywood Invitational Handicap
		Sunset Handicap
		Man o' War Stakes
	2nd	Vanity Handicap
		Santa Maria Handicap
		Manhattan Handicap
	3rd	Santa Margarita Handicap
		Beverly Hills Handicap
TYRANT (1966)		
At 3:	2nd	Withers Stakes
At 4:	Won	Carter Handicap
U CAN DO IT (1993)		
At 5:	3rd	Ballerina Handicap
UDAIPUR (1957)		
At 2:	2nd	Futurity Stakes
	3rd	Saratoga Special
ULISES (1991)		
At 3:	2nd	Jerome Handicap
	3rd	Jim Dandy Stakes
ULLA BRITTA (1968)		
At 2:	3rd	Del Mar Debutante Stakes
UMBRELLA FELLA (1962)		
At 2:	Won	Breeders' Futurity
		Kentucky Jockey Club Stakes
	2nd	Arlington-Washington Futurity
	3rd	Pimlico Futurity
UNACCOUNTED FOR (1991)		
At 3:	Won	Jim Dandy Stakes
At 4:	Won	Whitney Handicap
	2nd	Jockey Club Gold Cup
	3rd	Breeders' Cup Classic
UNANIME (1967)		
At 5:	Won	Pan American Handicap
UNBRIDLED (1987)		
At 3:	Won	Florida Derby
		Kentucky Derby
		Breeders' Cup Classic
	2nd	Preakness Stakes
		Super Derby
	3rd	Blue Grass Stakes
At 4:	3rd	Pacific Classic
		Breeders' Cup Classic
UNBRIDLED ELAINE (1998)		
At 3:	Won	Breeders' Cup Distaff
UNBRIDLED JET (1996)		
At 3:	2nd	Pegasus Handicap
UNBRIDLED LASSIE (1998)		
At 3:	3rd	Coaching Club American Oaks
UNBRIDLED'S SONG (1993)		
At 2:	Won	Breeders' Cup Juvenile
At 3:	Won	Florida Derby
		Wood Memorial Stakes
	2nd	Fountain of Youth Stakes
UNCLE FUDGE (1976)		
At 2:	3rd	Breeders' Futurity
UNCLE JEFF (1979)		
At 3:	3rd	Hollywood Derby
UNCLE MILTIE (1948)		
At 2:	Won	Champagne Stakes
	2nd	Sapling Stakes
UNCONSCIOUS (1968)		
At 3:	Won	San Felipe Handicap
		California Derby
	2nd	Santa Anita Derby
At 4:	Won	Charles H. Strub Stakes
		San Antonio Stakes
	2nd	Century Handicap
	3rd	Santa Anita Handicap
UNCOOL (1975)		
At 5:	Won	Oaklawn Handicap
At 6:	3rd	Oaklawn Handicap
UNDERSTANDING (1963)		
At 3:	2nd	Jerome Handicap
At 4:	2nd	Massachusetts Handicap
	3rd	Seminole Handicap
		Widener Handicap
UNFINISHED SYMPH (1991)		
At 3:	3rd	Breeders' Cup Mile
UN FINO VINO (1997)		
At 2:	2nd	Remsen Stakes
UNION CITY (1990)		
At 3:	2nd	Santa Anita Derby
UNITE'S BIG RED (1994)		
At 5:	3rd	Gulfstream Park Breeders' Cup Handicap
UNITY HALL (1968)		
At 2:	2nd	Sorority Stakes
UNKNOWN LADY (1979)		
At 4:	2nd	Golden Harvest Handicap
UNLAWFUL BEHAVIOR (1990)		
At 5:	2nd	Ruffian Handicap
UNRULED (1993)		
At 5:	2nd	Donn Handicap
		Gulfstream Park Handicap
UNSHADED (1997)		
At 3:	Won	Travers Stakes
	3rd	Belmont Stakes
		Jim Dandy Stakes
UNTIL SUNDOWN (1998)		
At 3:	2nd	Swaps Stakes
UP ABOVE (1970)		
At 2:	2nd	Matron Stakes
UP BEAT (1945)		
At 4:	Won	Roseben Handicap
UP OARS (1962)		
At 3:	3rd	Acorn Stakes
		Mother Goose Stakes
UPON MY SOUL (1988)		
At 3:	2nd	Jim Dandy Stakes
UPPER CASE (1969)		
At 3:	Won	Florida Derby
		Wood Memorial Stakes
	2nd	Flamingo Stakes
	3rd	Gotham Stakes
UPPERCUT (1959)		
At 5:	3rd	John B. Campbell Handicap
UPPER NILE (1974)		
At 4:	Won	Suburban Handicap
	2nd	United Nations Handicap
UP SCOPE (1958)		
At 3:	2nd	Withers Stakes
UPSWEPT (1959)		
At 3:	3rd	Acorn Stakes
UP THE APALACHEE (1984)		
At 3:	Won	Alabama Stakes
	2nd	Fantasy Stakes
UP TO JULIET (1973)		
At 4:	2nd	Ramona Handicap
	3rd	La Canada Stakes
UPTOWN SWELL (1982)		
At 4:	2nd	United Nations Handicap
	3rd	Oak Tree Invitational Stakes
URBANE (1992)		
At 2:	2nd	Hollywood Starlet Stakes
At 3:	Won	Ashland Stakes
	2nd	Santa Anita Oaks
		Kentucky Oaks
	3rd	Las Virgenes Stakes
At 4:	Won	John A. Morris Handicap
	3rd	Milady Breeders' Cup Handicap
URGENT MESSAGE (1968)		
At 4:	Won	New Orleans Handicap
	2nd	Gulfstream Park Handicap
	3rd	Widener Handicap
URGENT REQUEST (1990)		
At 5:	Won	Santa Anita Handicap
USELESS (1944)		
At 2:	2nd	Tremont Stakes
U TIME (1944)		
At 2:	Won	Starlet Stakes
At 3:	Won	Hollywood Oaks
VADIM (1970)		
At 7:	2nd	Arlington Handicap
VAGABONDA (1971)		
At 5:	Won	Ramona Handicap
VAGUELY FAMILIAR (1970)		
At 2:	2nd	Arlington-Washington Lassie Stakes
	3rd	Alcibiades Stakes

VALADIUM (1948)
At 3: 2nd Vineland Handicap
At 4: 2nd Top Flight Handicap
3rd Molly Pitcher Handicap

VALAY MAID (1987)
At 3: 3rd Breeders' Cup Distaff

VALDALI (1986)
At 4: 2nd San Juan Capistrano Handicap

VAL DANSEUR (1980)
At 5: 3rd Sunset Handicap

VAL DES BOIS (1986)
At 5: 2nd Eddie Read Handicap
Breeders' Cup Mile

VALDEZ (1976)
At 3: Won Swaps Stakes
2nd Jerome Handicap
3rd Meadowlands Cup
At 4: 3rd Charles H. Strub Stakes

VALIANT HALORY (1997)
At 3: 2nd King's Bishop Stakes

VALIANT LARK (1980)
At 5: 3rd Monmouth Handicap

VALIANT MAN (1960)
At 5: Won New Orleans Handicap

VALIANT NATURE (1991)
At 2: Won Hollywood Futurity
At 3: 2nd Blue Grass Stakes
3rd San Felipe Stakes
Swaps Stakes

VALIANT SKOAL (1960)
At 2: 2nd Cowdin Stakes

VALID APPEAL (1972)
At 2: 3rd Futurity Stakes
At 3: Won Dwyer Handicap
2nd Jerome Handicap

VALID PROSPECT (1984)
At 3: 3rd Illinois Derby

VALID VIDEO (2000)
At 3: Won King's Bishop Stakes

VALID WAGER (1992)
At 2: 2nd Arlington-Washington Futurity

VALLEY CROSSING (1988)
At 3: Won Pennsylvania Derby
At 4: 2nd Meadowlands Cup
Brooklyn Handicap
3rd Philip H. Iselin Handicap
At 5: Won Philip H. Iselin Handicap
2nd Pimlico Special
Nassau County Handicap
3rd Woodward Stakes
At 6: 2nd Suburban Handicap
Philip H. Iselin Handicap
3rd Pimlico Special

VALLEY VICTORY (1983)
At 3: Won Coaching Club American Oaks
2nd Alabama Stakes

VALQUEST (1947)
At 3: Won Westerner Stakes
3rd Cinema Handicap

VAL ROYAL (1996)
At 5: Won Breeders' Cup Mile

VAL'S PRINCE (1992)
At 5: Won Turf Classic
2nd Man o' War Stakes
3rd Sword Dancer Invitational Handicap
At 6: 2nd Sword Dancer Invitational Handicap
At 7: Won Man o' War Stakes
Turf Classic
2nd Sword Dancer Invitational Handicap

VALUE PLUS (2001)
At 2: 2nd Futurity Stakes

VAN CROSBY (1950)
At 2: 3rd Garden State Stakes
At 3: 3rd Arlington Classic

VANLANDINGHAM (1981)
At 4: Won Suburban Handicap
Jockey Club Gold Cup
Washington D.C. International
2nd Woodward Stakes
3rd Whitney Handicap
Marlboro Cup Handicap
Hollywood Turf Cup

VANSLAM (1941)
At 5: 3rd Inglewood Handicap

VAPOR WHIRL (1958)
At 2: 2nd Remsen Stakes
At 4: 3rd Tropical Park Handicap

VARIETY QUEEN (1976)
At 3: 3rd Hollywood Oaks

VARIETY ROAD (1983)
At 3: Won San Felipe Handicap
At 4: Won San Fernando Stakes

VAUDEVILLE (1945)
At 2: 2nd Matron Stakes

VAUDEVILLE (1991)
At 3: Won American Derby
Secretariat Stakes
2nd Turf Classic

V-BOY (1943)
At 5: 3rd San Pasqual Handicap

VEGAS VIC (1968)
At 3: 2nd Oak Tree Invitational Stakes
3rd Santa Anita Derby

VEILED DESIRE (1969)
At 4: 2nd Santa Barbara Handicap

VENCEDOR (1974)
At 4: 2nd Carter Handicap

VENETIAN WAY (1957)
At 2: Won Washington Park Futurity
At 3: Won Kentucky Derby
2nd Florida Derby
Belmont Stakes
3rd Arlington Classic

VENT DU NORD (1965)
At 4: Won Canadian International Championship
At 5: Won Hialeah Turf Cup

VERBASLE (1988)
At 2: 2nd Matron Stakes

VERBATIM (1965)
At 3: Won Gotham Stakes
3rd Wood Memorial Stakes
Withers Stakes
At 4: Won Amory L. Haskell Handicap
Whitney Stakes
2nd Brooklyn Handicap
3rd Woodward Stakes
Hawthorne Gold Cup
At 5: 2nd Suburban Handicap

VERGENNES (1995)
At 3: Won Early Times Hollywood Derby

VERNON CASTLE (1983)
At 3: Won California Derby

VERRUMA (1996)
At 6: 2nd Santa Maria Handicap

VERSAILLES TREATY (1988)
At 3: Won Alabama Stakes
2nd Acorn Stakes
Beldame Stakes
Breeders' Cup Distaff
At 4: Won Ruffian Handicap
2nd Beldame Stakes
Breeders' Cup Distaff
3rd Shuvee Handicap
Hempstead Handicap

VERTEE (1969)
At 4: Won Widener Handicap
John B. Campbell Handicap

VERTEX (1954)
At 3: 2nd Roamer Handicap
At 4: Won Pimlico Special
Trenton Handicap
At 5: Won Gulfstream Park Handicap
John B. Campbell Handicap
Grey Lag Handicap

VERTIGO II (1941)
At 7: 2nd Monmouth Handicap

VERY SPECIAL LADY (1976)
At 3: 3rd Fantasy Stakes

VERY SUBTLE (1984)
At 3: Won Fantasy Stakes
Breeders' Cup Sprint
3rd Santa Anita Oaks
At 4: 3rd La Canada Stakes

VESTRIS (1979)
At 3: 3rd Acorn Stakes

VIA BORGHESE (1989)
At 4: 2nd Beverly D. Stakes

VICAR (1996)
At 3: Won Fountain of Youth Stakes
Florida Derby
3rd Toyota Blue Grass Stakes

VIC'S MAGIC (1973)
At 5: 3rd Del Mar Handicap

VICTOR COOLEY (1993)
At 3: 2nd Woodbine Million
At 4: Won Vosburgh Stakes

VICTORIAN ERA (1962)
At 3: 2nd Ohio Derby

VICTORIAN PRINCE (1970)
At 6: Won Arlington Handicap

VICTORIA PARK (1957)
At 2: Won Remsen Stakes
At 3: 2nd Flamingo Stakes
Blue Grass Stakes
Preakness Stakes
3rd Florida Derby
Kentucky Derby

VICTORIOUS (1980)
At 2: 2nd Hopeful Stakes

VICTORIOUS JOY (1981)
At 2: 3rd Del Mar Debutante Stakes

VICTORY GALLOP (1995)
At 3: Won Arkansas Derby
Belmont Stakes
2nd Kentucky Derby
Preakness Stakes
Buick Haskell Invitational Handicap
Travers Stakes
At 4: Won Whitney Handicap

VICTORY MORN (1955)
At 3: Won Dwyer Handicap
2nd American Derby

VICTORY RIDE (1998)
At 3: Won Test Stakes
2nd Acorn Stakes

VICTORY SPEECH (1993)
At 3: Won Swaps Stakes
2nd Ohio Derby
3rd Fountain of Youth Stakes
Jim Beam Stakes
Buick Haskell Invitational Handicap
At 4: Won Strub Stakes

VICTORY STRIPES (1994)
At 5: 2nd Santa Maria Handicap
3rd Milady Breeders' Cup Handicap

VICTORY U.S.A. (2001)
At 2: 2nd Frizette Stakes
3rd Del Mar Debutante Stakes
Breeders' Cup Juvenile Fillies

VICTORY ZONE (1979)
At 3: Won Hollywood Derby
At 4: 3rd San Juan Capistrano Handicap
At 5: 3rd Century Handicap

VIDEOGENIC (1982)
At 3: Won Ladies Handicap

VIDEO RANGER (1987)
At 3: 2nd Santa Anita Derby
Jersey Derby

VIELLE VIGNE (1987)
At 4: 2nd La Canada Stakes
3rd Milady Handicap

VIETMINE (1970)
At 3: 3rd California Derby

VIEWPOISE (1968)
At 3: 2nd Spinster Stakes
At 4: 2nd Arlington Park Handicap
Michigan Mile and One-Eighth

VIF (1965)
At 4: 2nd Hawthorne Gold Cup
At 5: 2nd New Orleans Handicap
Oaklawn Handicap

VIGORS (1973)
At 4: Won Hollywood Invitational Handicap
2nd Oak Tree Invitational Stakes
At 5: Won San Antonio Stakes
Santa Anita Handicap
3rd Hollywood Gold Cup

VIKING SPIRIT (1960)
At 4: 3rd American Handicap
Sunset Handicap
At 5: Won Carter Handicap
Californian Stakes
3rd John B. Campbell Handicap

VILLADOR (1974)
At 4: 3rd Widener Handicap

VILLAGE IDIOT (1955)
At 4: 3rd Whitney Stakes

VILLAGE STAR II (1983)
At 4: 3rd Breeders' Cup Turf

VILZAK (1983)
At 4: Won Hollywood Turf Cup

VINDICATION (2000)
At 2: Won Bessemer Trust Breeders' Cup Juvenile

VIOLADO (1982)
At 3: Won Louisiana Derby

VIOLONOR (1968)
At 4: 2nd Hollywood Invitational Handicap
3rd Sunset Handicap

VIRGINIA RAPIDS (1990)
At 3: Won Peter Pan Stakes
2nd Jim Dandy Stakes
At 4: Won Carter Handicap

VIRGINIE (1994)
At 5: Won Beverly Hills Handicap

VISIBLE (1974)
At 2: Won Del Mar Futurity

VISION (1979)
At 5: 2nd Brooklyn Handicap

VISION AND VERSE (1996)
At 3: 2nd Belmont Stakes
Travers Stakes
3rd Meadowlands Cup Handicap
At 4: 3rd Jockey Club Gold Cup

VISUALIZER (1970)
At 4: 3rd Oaklawn Handicap

VITAL FORCE (1957)
At 2: 2nd Hopeful Stakes
Cowdin Stakes

VITERBO (1976)
At 4: 2nd Golden Harvest Handicap

VITRIOLIC (1965)
At 2: Won Saratoga Special
Arlington-Washington Futurity
Champagne Stakes
Pimlico-Laurel Futurity
2nd Sanford Stakes
Futurity Stakes
Cowdin Stakes

VIVA MAXI (1982)
At 2: 3rd Norfolk Stakes
Arlington-Washington Futurity

VIVANO (1989)
At 2: 2nd Frizette Stakes
3rd Matron Stakes
At 4: 3rd Shuvee Handicap
Beldame Stakes

VIVID ANGEL (1995)
At 2: Won Oak Leaf Stakes

VIXEN FIXIT (1949)
At 5: 2nd Arlington Matron Handicap

VIZ (1991)
At 2: 3rd Hollywood Starlet Stakes

VODIKA (1970)
At 3: 2nd Arkansas Derby

VODKA TIME (1972)
At 4: 3rd Delaware Handicap

VOGUE FOLKS (1977)
At 2: 3rd Arlington-Washington Lassie Stakes

VOLCANIC (1945)
At 3: 3rd American Derby
At 4: Won Hawthorne Gold Cup
At 5: 3rd Hawthorne Gold Cup
At 6: 2nd Stars and Stripes Handicap

VOLER (1970)
At 3: 3rd Acorn Stakes

VOLOCHINE (1991)
At 3: 3rd Rothmans International Stakes

VOLPONI (1998)
At 4: Won Breeders' Cup Classic
3rd Sword Dancer Invitational Handicap
At 5: 2nd Suburban Handicap
Whitney Handicap

VOLUNTARIO III (1961)
At 6: 2nd Pan American Handicap

VOODOO (1998)
At 4: 2nd Carter Handicap
3rd Vosburgh Stakes

VOODOO DANCER (1998)
At 3: Won Garden City Breeders' Cup Handicap
At 4: 2nd Yellow Ribbon Stakes
3rd Gamely Breeders' Cup Handicap
At 5: Won Diana Handicap

VULCANIA (1948)
At 2: 2nd Demoiselle Stakes
Selima Stakes
At 3: 2nd Alabama Stakes
3rd Acorn Stakes
Discovery Handicap

VULCAN'S FORGE (1945)
At 2: Won Champagne Stakes
At 3: Won Withers Stakes
2nd Preakness Stakes
At 4: Won Santa Anita Handicap
Suburban Handicap
2nd Excelsior Handicap
Gallant Fox Handicap
Metropolitan Handicap
Brooklyn Handicap
3rd Hawthorne Gold Cup

VYING VICTOR (1989)
At 3: 2nd Jim Beam Stakes
3rd Molson Export Million

WAGE RAISE (1971)
At 2: 3rd Breeders' Futurity

WAGON LIMIT (1994)
At 3: 3rd Jockey Club Gold Cup
At 4: Won Jockey Club Gold Cup

WAIKIKI (1953)
At 2: 3rd Arlington Lassie Stakes

WAITRYST (1989)
At 5: 3rd Santa Barbara Handicap

WAJIMA (1972)
At 2: 2nd Laurel Futurity
At 3: Won Monmouth Invitational Handicap
Travers Stakes
Marlboro Cup Handicap
2nd Dwyer Handicap
Woodward Stakes
Jockey Club Gold Cup

WAKEFIELD MISS (1968)
At 5: Won Ladies Handicap

WAKI AMERICAN (1996)
At 2: 3rd Del Mar Futurity

WALESA (1988)
At 2: 2nd Arlington-Washington Futurity

WALKING STICK (1966)
At 3: 3rd Louisiana Derby

WALK IN THE SNOW (1999)
At 3: 2nd Super Derby

WALK MY LADY (1965)
At 2: 3rd Alcibiades Stakes

WALK THAT WALK (1996)
At 3: 3rd Swaps Stakes

WALLENDA (1990)
At 3: Won Super Derby
2nd Blue Grass Stakes
3rd Florida Derby
At 4: 2nd Brooklyn Handicap
3rd Donn Handicap
Gulfstream Park Handicap

WALL STREET DANCER (1986)
At 6: 2nd Sword Dancer Handicap
3rd San Juan Capistrano Handicap

WALTZ (1956)
At 3: Won Dwyer Handicap
At 4: 3rd Suburban Handicap
Brooklyn Handicap

WALTZ SONG (1958)
At 4: 2nd Ladies Handicap
At 5: Won Delaware Handicap
At 6: 3rd Delaware Handicap

WALZERKOENIGIN (1999)
At 4: 2nd Flower Bowl Invitational Stakes

WANDA (1969)
At 3: Won Mother Goose Stakes
2nd Acorn Stakes
Coaching Club American Oaks

WANDERING WAYS (1947)
At 7: 3rd Santa Margarita Handicap

WANDERKIN (1983)
At 5: 2nd United Nations Handicap

WANDER MOM (1998)
At 3: 3rd Garden City Breeders' Cup Handicap

WANDESTA (1991)
At 3: 3rd Matriarch Stakes
At 4: Won Santa Barbara Handicap
3rd Beverly Hills Handicap
Vanity Handicap
Matriarch Stakes

WANDESTA *(Continued)*
At 5: Won Matriarch Stakes
2nd San Luis Rey Stakes

WANNABE GRAND (1996)
At 3: 3rd Queen Elizabeth II Challenge Cup

WAQUOIT (1983)
At 4: Won Brooklyn Handicap
At 5: Won Brooklyn Handicap
Jockey Club Gold Cup
2nd Suburban Handicap
3rd Woodward Handicap
Breeders' Cup Classic

WAR (1984)
At 3: Won Blue Grass Stakes

WAR AGE (1949)
At 2: 2nd Sapling Stakes

WARBUCKS (1970)
At 3: 3rd Arkansas Derby
Blue Grass Stakes
At 5: Won Oaklawn Handicap
2nd New Orleans Handicap

WAR CENSOR (1963)
At 2: Won Kentucky Jockey Club Stakes
At 3: Won Ohio Derby
At 4: Won Hialeah Turf Cup
Pan American Handicap
Dixie Handicap
At 7: 2nd Dixie Handicap
3rd Hialeah Turf Cup

WAR CHANT (1997)
At 3: Won Breeders' Cup Mile
2nd Santa Anita Derby

WARCOS (1949)
At 3: 3rd Will Rogers Stakes

WARCRAFT (1987)
At 3: 2nd San Felipe Handicap
3rd Santa Anita Derby
At 4: 2nd San Fernando Stakes

WAR DATE (1942)
At 4: 2nd Beldame Handicap
At 5: 3rd Comely Handicap

WARDLAW (1973)
At 3: 2nd Illinois Derby

WAR DOINGS (1951)
At 2: 2nd Pimlico Futurity

WAR EMBLEM (1999)
At 3: Won Kentucky Derby
Preakness Stakes
Haskell Invitational Handicap

WAR FAME (1976)
At 4: Won Golden Harvest Handicap

WAR FAN (1944)
At 2: 3rd Arlington Lassie Stakes

WARFARE (1957)
At 2: Won Cowdin Stakes
Champagne Stakes
Garden State Stakes
3rd Hollywood Juvenile Championship
Del Mar Futurity

WARFEVER (1975)
At 4: 3rd Sheepshead Bay Handicap
Pan American Handicap

WARFIE (1986)
At 3: 3rd Ladies Handicap
At 4: 2nd Delaware Handicap

WARHEAD (1955)
At 3: Won Jerome Handicap
Roamer Handicap
Manhattan Handicap
2nd Lawrence Realization Stakes
3rd Travers Stakes
At 5: Won Whitney Handicap
3rd Aqueduct Handicap

WAR HEIM (1967)
At 4: Won Charles H. Strub Stakes
3rd San Fernando Stakes
At 5: Won Miller High Life Inglewood Handicap
2nd Del Mar Handicap
3rd Hollywood Gold Cup
At 7: 3rd Hollywood Gold Cup

WAR KING (1947)
At 4: Won Vosburgh Handicap

WAR KNIGHT (1940)
At 6: Won Santa Anita Handicap

WARLIKE (1957)
At 2: 2nd Spinaway Stakes

WAR OF ROSES (1951)
At 5: 3rd Bougainvillea Turf Handicap

WAR PIPER (1951)
At 2: 2nd Hopeful Stakes
3rd Champagne Stakes

WARREN G. (1955)
At 3: 2nd Blue Grass Stakes

WAR SPUN (1943)
At 3: Won California Derby

WAR TALK (1947)
At 4: 3rd Arlington Matron Handicap

WAR TROPHY (1942)
At 6: 2nd Westchester Handicap
At 7: 3rd San Antonio Handicap

WAR TRYST (1951)
At 3: 3rd Cinema Handicap

WAR VALOR (1941)
At 5: 2nd San Juan Capistrano Handicap

WASHOE COUNTY (1974)
At 2: 3rd Del Mar Futurity

WATCHING YOU (2000)
At 3: 3rd Las Virgenes Stakes

WATCH YOUR STEP (1956)
At 2: Won Sapling Stakes

WATER BANK (1979)
At 3: 2nd California Derby
At 4: Won Hawthorne Gold Cup
2nd San Fernando Stakes
3rd Meadowlands Cup
Charles H. Strub Stakes
At 5: 2nd San Antonio Handicap

WATER MALONE (1974)
At 4: 2nd Ladies Handicap

WATERMILL (1945)
At 2: 3rd Frizette Stakes
At 3: Won Acorn Stakes

WATERWAY DRIVE (1978)
At 3: 3rd Hollywood Derby

WAVERING GIRL (1987)
At 2: 3rd Selima Stakes

WAVERING MONARCH (1979)
At 3: Won Haskell Invitational Handicap
3rd Blue Grass Stakes
At 4: Won San Fernando Stakes
2nd Charles H. Strub Stakes
3rd Santa Anita Handicap

WAVY WAVES (1974)
At 2: 2nd Arlington-Washington Lassie Stakes

WAYA (1974)
At 4: Won Man o' War Stakes
Turf Classic
2nd Sheepshead Bay Handicap
3rd Washington D.C. International
At 5: Won Top Flight Handicap
Beldame Stakes
Santa Barbara Handicap
2nd Bowling Green Handicap
3rd Ruffian Handicap

WAYAR (1983)
At 3: 3rd Jim Dandy Stakes

WAYWARD LASS (1978)
At 3: Won Mother Goose Stakes
Coaching Club American Oaks
3rd Fantasy Stakes
Kentucky Oaks

WAYWARD PIRATE (1982)
At 2: 3rd Oak Leaf Stakes

WEALTHY (1994)
At 2: 3rd Oak Leaf Stakes

WEATHER TAMER (1976)
At 3: 3rd American Derby

WEATHERWISE (1957)
At 2: Won Futurity Stakes
At 3: 3rd Dwyer Handicap

WEBER CITY MISS (1977)
At 3: 2nd Alabama Stakes
3rd Ladies Handicap
At 4: 3rd Top Flight Handicap
At 5: Won Beldame Stakes

WEDGE SHOT (1971)
At 2: Won Futurity Stakes
2nd Sapling Stakes

WEDLOCK (1956)
At 3: Won Kentucky Oaks

WEE ADMIRAL (1943)
At 3: 2nd Flamingo Stakes

WEEKEND IN SEATTLE (1993)
At 3: 3rd Coaching Club American Oaks

WEEKEND MONEY (1996)
At 2: 3rd Moet Champagne Stakes

WEEKEND SQUALL (1996)
At 3: 3rd Las Virgenes Stakes

WEEKEND SURPRISE (1980)
At 2: 3rd Matron Stakes
Frizette Stakes
At 4: 2nd La Canada Stakes
3rd Delaware Handicap
Santa Margarita Handicap

WEKIVA SPRINGS (1991)
At 4: 2nd NYRA Mile Handicap
3rd Strub Stakes
At 5: Won Gulfstream Park Handicap
Brooklyn Handicap
Suburban Handicap
2nd Donn Handicap
Oaklawn Handicap

WELDY (1959)
At 2: Won Del Mar Futurity

WELL CHOSEN (1995)
At 3: Won Ashland Stakes

WELL DECORATED (1978)
At 2: Won Arlington-Washington Futurity
3rd Hopeful Stakes
At 3: 2nd Flamingo Stakes
3rd Vosburgh Stakes

WELL MANNERED (1967)
At 4: Won Washington Park Handicap

WELL SELECTED (1984)
At 3: Won Hutcheson Stakes

WELSH TERM (1979)
At 4: 2nd Washington D.C. International

WE'RE HOPING (1958)
At 3: 2nd Hollywood Derby
3rd Cinema Handicap

WEST BY WEST (1989)
At 2: 3rd Arlington-Washington Futurity
At 3: 2nd Wood Memorial Stakes
At 4: Won Nassau County Handicap

	2nd	Whitney Handicap
	3rd	Suburban Handicap
At 5:	3rd	Whitney Handicap

WEST COAST NATIVE (1979)
At 3: 2nd Swaps Stakes

WEST COAST SCOUT (1968)
At 3: Won Monmouth Invitational Handicap
Woodward Stakes
2nd Travers Stakes
At 4: Won Amory L. Haskell Handicap
2nd Suburban Handicap
3rd Brooklyn Handicap
At 5: Won Gulfstream Park Handicap
Amory L. Haskell Handicap
2nd Widener Handicap

WESTERLY BREEZE (2000)
At 2: Won Walmac International Alcibiades Stakes

WESTERN (1978)
At 7: 2nd San Luis Rey Stakes

WESTERN BORDERS (1994)
At 4: 3rd Carter Handicap
At 5: 3rd Carter Handicap

WESTERN DREAMER (1993)
At 2: 3rd Spinaway Stakes

WESTERN ECHO (1992)
At 2: 2nd Remsen Stakes

WESTERN EXPRESSION (1996)
At 4: 2nd Carter Handicap

WESTERN JUSTICE (1998)
At 2: 3rd Frizette Stakes

WESTERN LARLA (1992)
At 3: 3rd Dwyer Stakes

WESTERN PLAYBOY (1986)
At 3: Won Jim Beam Stakes
Blue Grass Stakes
Pennsylvania Derby
2nd Florida Derby
At 4: 3rd Arlington Invitational Challenge Cup

WESTERN PRIDE (1998)
At 4: 2nd Santa Anita Handicap
At 5: 2nd Pimlico Special

WESTERN WARRIOR (1959)
At 5: Won United Nations Handicap

WESTERN WELCOME (1967)
At 3: 3rd Hollywood Derby

WESTERN WIND (1974)
At 2: 3rd Futurity Stakes
At 3: 3rd Blue Grass Stakes

WESTERN WINTER (1992)
At 5: 2nd Metropolitan Handicap
3rd Carter Handicap

WESTMINSTER (1941)
At 6: 3rd McLennan Handicap

WESTWARD (1970)
At 3: 3rd Fantasy Stakes

WESTWARD HO (1952)
At 3: 2nd Lawrence Realization Stakes

WHADJATHINK (1988)
At 3: Won Arlington Classic

WHANG BANG (1947)
At 3: 2nd Longacres Mile

WHATA BRAINSTORM (1997)
At 4: 2nd Gulfstream Park Breeders' Cup Handicap

WHAT A DREAM (1966)
At 4: 2nd Molly Pitcher Handicap
Delaware Handicap
3rd Black Helen Handicap

WHAT A PLEASURE (1965)
At 2: Won Hopeful Stakes
2nd Sapling Stakes
At 3: 3rd Gotham Stakes

WHAT A SUMMER (1973)
At 4: Won Maskette Handicap
2nd Beldame Stakes
At 5: 2nd Vosburgh Handicap

WHAT A TREAT (1962)
At 3: Won Alabama Stakes
Gazelle Handicap
Beldame Stakes
2nd Mother Goose Stakes
Coaching Club American Oaks
At 4: Won Black Helen Handicap

WHATSYOURPLEASURE (1973)
At 2: 2nd Laurel Futurity
3rd Hopeful Stakes
Champagne Stakes

WHAT WILL BE (1970)
At 3: 2nd Illinois Derby

WHEATLY HALL (1983)
At 3: 2nd Arkansas Derby

WHEELAWAY (1997)
At 3: 3rd Toyota Blue Grass Stakes

WHIRLA LEA (1949)
At 3: 2nd Kentucky Oaks
3rd Arlington Matron Stakes

WHIRLING BAT (1948)
At 3: Won Louisiana Derby

WHIRLING FOX (1945)
At 2: 2nd Hopeful Stakes
Futurity Stakes

WHIRL SOME (1945)
At 2: Won Selima Stakes
Marguerite Stakes

WHISK (1968)
At 2: 2nd Breeders' Futurity

WHISPER FLEET (1976)
At 2: 2nd Selima Stakes
3rd Sorority Stakes

WHISPER JET (1963)
At 4: 2nd Hawthorne Gold Cup

WHITE CROSS (1952)
At 3: 3rd Firenze Handicap

WHITE HEART (1995)
At 5: Won Charles Whittingham Handicap
At 6: Won Woodford Reserve Turf Classic
2nd Clement L. Hirsch Mem. Turf Champ.

WHITE SKIES (1949)
At 5: Won Roseben Handicap
Carter Handicap

WHITE STAR LINE (1975)
At 3: Won Kentucky Oaks
Alabama Stakes
3rd Acorn Stakes

WHITE XMASS (1966)
At 2: 3rd Sorority Stakes

WHITLEY (1955)
At 2: 2nd Remsen Stakes
At 4: 3rd Gallant Fox Handicap
At 5: 3rd Grey Lag Handicap

WHITMORE'S CONN (1998)
At 5: Won Sword Dancer Invitational Handicap

WHITNEY TOWER (1991)
At 2: 3rd Hopeful Stakes

WHIT'S PRIDE (1961)
At 3: 2nd Louisiana Derby

WHODUNIT (1955)
At 3: 2nd Gallant Fox Handicap
At 4: Won Sunset Handicap
2nd Gallant Fox Handicap
At 6: Won Sunset Handicap
2nd Aqueduct Handicap
3rd Hollywood Gold Cup
Display Handicap

WHO LOVES ALEYNA (1999)
At 2: 2nd Del Mar Debutante Stakes

WHOOPDDOO (1998)
At 2: 3rd Hollywood Starlet Stakes

WHOOP UP (1980)
At 5: 3rd Vosburgh Stakes

WHO'S AHEAD (1957)
At 3: 3rd Ladies Handicap

WHOSE DOUBT (1984)
At 5: 2nd Ladies Handicap

WHO'S FOR DINNER (1979)
At 5: Won Arlington Handicap
3rd United Nations Handicap
At 6: 2nd United Nations Handicap

WHY CHANGE (1993)
At 3: Won Jerome Handicap

WHY GO ON DREAMING (1987)
At 2: 3rd Demoiselle Stakes

WHY NOT NOW (1947)
At 4: 3rd Dixie Handicap
Monmouth Handicap
At 5: 3rd Gulfstream Park Handicap

WHYWHYWHY (2000)
At 2: Won Futurity Stakes

WICKERR (1975)
At 5: 2nd Louisiana Downs Handicap
At 6: Won Eddie Read Handicap
At 7: Won Eddie Read Handicap

WIDE COUNTRY (1988)
At 4: 3rd Go for Wand Stakes

WIGGLE II (1955)
At 4: Won Arlington Matron Handicap
At 5: 3rd Vineland Handicap

WIG OUT (1967)
At 2: 2nd Cowdin Stakes

WILBUR CLARK (1964)
At 2: 2nd Arlington-Washington Futurity
3rd Hollywood Juvenile Championship

WILD AGAIN (1980)
At 4: Won Breeders' Cup Classic
3rd Suburban Handicap

WILD APPLAUSE (1981)
At 3: 3rd Mother Goose Stakes

WILDERNESS SONG (1988)
At 3: Won Spinster Stakes

WILDER THAN EVER (1988)
At 3: 3rd Jim Beam Stakes

WILD ESCAPADE (1992)
At 2: Won Hopeful Stakes
3rd Futurity Stakes

WILD EVENT (1993)
At 6: Won Early Times Turf Classic
2nd Gulfstream Park Breeders' Cup Handicap

WILD FOR TRACI (1988)
At 2: 3rd Arlington-Washington Lassie Stakes

WILD GALE (1990)
At 2: 3rd Remsen Stakes
At 3: 3rd Kentucky Derby
Belmont Stakes

WILD HORSES (1999)
At 3: 2nd Arkansas Derby

WILD RUSH (1994)
At 3: 3rd Swaps Stakes
At 4: Won Carter Handicap
Metropolitan Handicap

WILD SNITCH (2000)
At 2: 2nd Matron Stakes

WILD SPIRIT (1999)
At 4: Won Ruffian Handicap
2nd Personal Ensign Handicap

WILD SYN (1992)
At 3: Won Blue Grass Stakes

WILD WONDER (1994)
At 3: 3rd Gotham Stakes

WILLAMETTE (1954)
At 3: Won Coaching Club American Oaks

WILLA ON THE MOVE (1985)
At 3: Won Ashland Stakes
2nd Spinster Stakes
3rd Kentucky Oaks
Alabama Stakes

WILLA ON THE MOVE (1999)
At 3: 2nd Acorn Stakes

WILL HALL (1963)
At 3: 3rd Santa Susana Stakes

WILL HAYS (1968)
At 3: 3rd Louisiana Derby

WILLIAMSTON KID (1963)
At 3: Won Florida Derby
3rd Louisiana Derby

WILLIAMSTOWN (1990)
At 3: 2nd Jerome Handicap

WILL I RULE (1960)
At 3: 2nd Manhattan Handicap
Man o' War Stakes
At 4: Won Canadian Championship Stakes
Dixie Handicap
3rd Display Handicap

WILLOW HOUR (1978)
At 3: Won Travers Stakes
3rd Super Derby

WILLOWICK (1967)
At 3: 3rd San Felipe Handicap
At 4: Won San Fernando Stakes

WILLOWY MOOD (1982)
At 3: 3rd Mother Goose Stakes

WILL'S WAY (1993)
At 3: Won Travers Stakes
2nd Jim Dandy Stakes
At 4: Won Whitney Handicap
2nd Suburban Handicap
3rd Woodward Stakes

WIL RAD (1961)
At 2: 2nd Hollywood Juvenile Championship
At 3: 2nd San Felipe Handicap
California Derby
3rd Santa Anita Derby

WILWYN (1948)
At 4: Won Washington D.C. International

WIN (1980)
At 4: 2nd Man o' War Stakes
Turf Classic
At 5: Won Man o' War Stakes
2nd Turf Classic
Hollywood Turf Cup

WINDFIELDS (1943)
At 3: 2nd Dwyer Stakes

WIND FLYER (1981)
At 3: 2nd Illinois Derby

WINDJAMMER (1969)
At 2: Won Breeders' Futurity

WIND'N SAND (1969)
At 2: 2nd Hollywood Juvenile Championship

WINDSHARP (1991)
At 5: Won San Luis Rey Stakes
2nd San Juan Capistrano Handicap
Matriarch Stakes
At 6: Won Beverly Hills Handicap

WINDS OF THOUGHT (1970)
At 6: Won Century Handicap

WINDSOR CASTLE (1998)
At 2: Won Remsen Stakes

WINDSOR LADY (1961)
At 2: Won Demoiselle Stakes
At 4: 3rd Black Helen Handicap

WINDTEX (1969)
At 4: 3rd Amory L. Haskell Handicap
Pan American Handicap

WINDUNDERMYWINGS (1989)
At 3: 3rd Dwyer Stakes

WIN DUSTY WIN (1984)
At 2: 3rd Young America Stakes

WINDWARD PASSAGE (1999)
At 3: 3rd Arkansas Derby

WINDY CITY II (1949)
At 3: Won San Felipe Handicap
2nd Santa Anita Derby

WINDY KATE (1963)
At 3: 2nd Hollywood Oaks

WINDY SANDS (1957)
At 5: 2nd American Handicap
Hollywood Gold Cup
Sunset Handicap
3rd Los Angeles Handicap
Manhattan Handicap

WINDY'S DAUGHTER (1970)
At 2: Won Del Mar Debutante Stakes
At 3: Won Acorn Stakes
Mother Goose Stakes

WINDY TIDE (1967)
At 2: 3rd Hollywood Juvenile Championship
Arlington-Washington Futurity

WINE LIST (1946)
At 3: Won Aqueduct Handicap
3rd Blue Grass Stakes
At 4: Won Aqueduct Handicap
2nd Roseben Handicap

WIN-EM-ALL (1960)
At 4: 3rd San Fernando Stakes
Charles H. Strub Stakes

WINGED MERCURY (1954)
At 3: 3rd Jerome Handicap

WINGED VICTORY (1990)
At 6: 3rd Early Times Turf Classic

WING OUT (1968)
At 3: 3rd Hawthorne Gold Cup
At 4: Won Malibu Stakes
3rd Del Mar Handicap
At 5: 2nd Century Handicap
Hollywood Invitational Handicap
Del Mar Handicap
3rd American Handicap

WINGS OF JOVE (1980)
At 2: Won Matron Stakes
3rd Sorority Stakes

WINGS O' MORN (1950)
At 3: 2nd Acorn Stakes

WINNERS LAUGH (1986)
At 2: 2nd Cowdin Stakes

WINNIES CHOICE (1966)
At 2: 3rd Sanford Stakes

WINNING COLORS (1985)
At 3: Won Santa Anita Oaks
Santa Anita Derby
Kentucky Derby
2nd Maskette Stakes
Breeders' Cup Distaff
3rd Preakness Stakes

WINNING PACT (1991)
At 2: Won Del Mar Futurity

WINNING STRIDE (1949)
At 5: 3rd Molly Pitcher Handicap

WINNING TACK (1980)
At 2: 2nd Frizette Stakes

WINONLY (1957)
At 5: Won Los Angeles Handicap
At 6: Won Californian Stakes
3rd Los Angeles Handicap

WINSOME WINNER (1956)
At 2: Won Kentucky Jockey Club Stakes
2nd Washington Park Futurity

WINTER'S TALE (1976)
At 4: Won Suburban Handicap
Brooklyn Handicap
Marlboro Cup Handicap
At 5: 2nd Whitney Handicap
At 6: 2nd Whitney Handicap
At 7: Won Suburban Handicap

WINTER TREASURE (1983)
At 4: 2nd La Canada Stakes
Santa Margarita Handicap

WIORNO (1988)
At 4: 3rd Rothmans International Stakes

WIRE US (1958)
At 3: 3rd San Felipe Handicap

WISCONSIN BOY (1947)
At 2: Won Arlington Futurity
3rd Washington Park Futurity

WISE DUSTY (1991)
At 6: 2nd Frank J. De Francis Memorial Dash

WISE EXCHANGE (1965)
At 3: Won Flamingo Stakes
2nd Everglades Stakes
Gotham Stakes

WISE MARGIN (1950)
At 4: Won Gulfstream Park Handicap
Massachusetts Handicap
2nd McLennan Handicap
At 5: 2nd New Orleans Handicap
Gulfstream Park Handicap
3rd Massachusetts Handicap
At 6: 3rd Canadian Championship Stakes

WISE PHILIP (1973)
At 5: 2nd Amory L. Haskell Handicap

WISE SHIP (1957)
At 4: Won Man o' War Handicap
At 5: Won Dixie Handicap
3rd United Nations Handicap

WISE TIMES (1983)
At 3: Won Haskell Invitational Handicap
Travers Stakes
Super Derby

WISHING WELL (1975)
At 5: Won Gamely Handicap
3rd Ramona Handicap

WISH N WAIT (1959)
At 3: 2nd Hollywood Oaks

WISING UP (1982)
At 3: 3rd Santa Susana Stakes

WISLA (1983)
At 4: 2nd Maskette Stakes

WISTERIA (1948)
At 2: 3rd Spinaway Stakes
At 3: 2nd Acorn Stakes

WISTFUL (1946)
At 3: Won Kentucky Oaks
Pimlico Oaks
Coaching Club American Oaks
At 4: 2nd Arlington Matron Handicap
3rd Beldame Handicap
Ladies Handicap
Vanity Handicap
At 6: 2nd Vanity Handicap
3rd Sunset Handicap

WISTFUL (1977)
At 4: 2nd Delaware Handicap

WITCH SIR (1942)
At 4: Won Stars and Stripes Handicap

WITHALLPROBABILITY (1988)
At 3: 2nd Fantasy Stakes
Kentucky Oaks

WITH ANTICIPATION (1995)
At 5: 3rd Gulfstream Park Handicap
At 6: Won Sword Dancer Invitational Handicap
Man o' War Stakes
2nd United Nations Handicap
At 7: Won United Nations Handicap
Sword Dancer Invitational Handicap
Man o' War Stakes
2nd Woodford Reserve Turf Classic
John Deere Breeders' Cup Turf

WITH APPROVAL (1986)
At 4: 2nd Sword Dancer Handicap
Arlington Million
Breeders' Cup Turf
3rd Turf Classic

WITH EVIDENCE (1967)
At 2: 2nd Hollywood Juvenile Championship

WITH HONOR (1944)
At 2: 3rd Demoiselle Stakes

WITHIN HAIL (1971)
At 3: 2nd Oak Tree Invitational Stakes

WITHOUT FEATHERS (1984)
At 3: 2nd Alabama Stakes

WITH PLEASURE (1943)
At 4: Won Vosburgh Handicap
2nd Stars and Stripes Handicap
Westchester Handicap
3rd Washington Park Handicap
At 5: Won Inglewood Handicap

W.L. SICKLE (1944)
At 3: 2nd Santa Anita Derby

WOLFGANG (1964)
At 2: 3rd Del Mar Futurity

WOLFIE'S RASCAL (1979)
At 2: 3rd Remsen Stakes
At 3: Won Arlington Classic
American Derby

WOLFRAM (1956)
At 5: Won Bougainvillea Turf Handicap
Hialeah Turf Cup
2nd Bowling Green Handicap
Canadian Championship Stakes

WOLVER HEIGHTS (1978)
At 5: 2nd San Juan Capistrano Handicap

WONDER AGAIN (1999)
At 3: Won Garden City Breeders' Cup Handicap

WONDERS DELIGHT (1986)
At 2: Won Alcibiades Stakes

WONDERTROSS (1996)
At 2: 3rd Remsen Stakes
At 3: 2nd Florida Derby

WONDRING (1947)
At 3: 2nd Kentucky Oaks

WOODCHOPPER (1978)
At 3: Won Louisiana Derby
2nd Kentucky Derby
3rd Arkansas Derby

WOODEN NICKEL (1958)
At 2: 3rd Kentucky Jockey Club Stakes

WOODEN PHONE (1997)
At 3: 3rd Malibu Stakes
At 4: Won Strub Stakes
2nd Santa Anita Handicap
3rd Oaklawn Handicap

WOODFORD (1963)
At 2: 3rd Breeders' Futurity

WOODLAND PINES (1969)
At 3: 3rd Cinema Handicap
At 5: 3rd Californian Stakes

WOODLAWN (1954)
At 3: 3rd Coaching Club American Oaks
At 4: 3rd Delaware Handicap
Spinster Stakes
At 6: 2nd Arlington Matron Handicap
Ladies Handicap
3rd Black Helen Handicap

WOOZEM (1964)
At 2: 3rd Arlington-Washington Lassie Stakes
Gardenia Stakes

WORDEN II (1949)
At 4: Won Washington D.C. International

WORLD APPEAL (1980)
At 3: Won Pegasus Handicap
At 4: 2nd Monmouth Handicap
3rd Widener Handicap

WORLDLY MANNER (1996)
At 2: Won Del Mar Futurity

WORLDLY WAYS (1994)
At 4: 3rd Californian Stakes

WORLD TRADE (1944)
At 2: 2nd Garden State Stakes

WORSHIPER (1956)
At 3: 2nd Hollywood Derby

WORTHY PIPER (1976)
At 3: 3rd Monmouth Invitational Handicap

WUSTENCHEF (1965)
At 7: 3rd American Handicap

WYLFA (1981)
At 6: 2nd San Juan Capistrano Handicap

XMAS BOX (1974)
At 4: 3rd San Juan Capistrano Handicap

XTRA HEAT (1998)
At 3: Won Prioress Stakes
2nd Test Stakes
Breeders' Cup Sprint
3rd Frank J. De Francis Memorial Dash

YAGLI (1993)
At 5: 2nd Breeders' Cup Turf
Hollywood Turf Cup
At 6: Won Gulfstream Park Breeders' Cup Handicap
Manhattan Handicap
At 7: 3rd Woodford Reserve Turf Classic

YAMANIN (1972)
At 5: Won Widener Handicap
3rd Donn Handicap
Gulfstream Park Handicap

YANKEE AFFAIR (1982)
At 7: Won United Nations Handicap
Man o' War Stakes
Turf Classic
2nd Budweiser International Stakes
Hollywood Turf Cup
3rd Arlington Million

YANKEE VALOR (1944)
At 3: Won Hollywood Derby
Cinema Handicap
2nd San Felipe Stakes

YANKEE VICTOR (1996)
At 4: Won Metropolitan Handicap

YANKS MUSIC (1993)
At 3: Won Mother Goose Stakes
Alabama Stakes
Ruffian Handicap
Beldame Stakes
2nd Acorn Stakes

YARROW BRAE (1995)
At 3: 2nd Jim Beam Stakes

YASHGAN (1981)
At 4: Won Oak Tree Invitational Stakes
2nd Washington D.C. International

YASHMAK (1994)
At 3: Won Flower Bowl Invitational Handicap

YASOU MINER (1989)
At 2: 2nd Young America Stakes

YEARLY TOUR (1991)
At 4: 2nd Santa Barbara Handicap
3rd Ramona Handicap

YE-CATS (1961)
At 2: 2nd Arlington-Washington Lassie Stakes

YELL (2000)
At 3: 2nd Mother Goose Stakes
3rd Kentucky Oaks

YENDA (1991)
At 3: 3rd Turf Classic

YES IT'S TRUE (1996)
At 2: 2nd Futurity Stakes
3rd Lane's End Breeders' Futurity
At 3: Won Frank J. De Francis Memorial Dash

YES PLEASE (1959)
At 6: 2nd Vanity Handicap
3rd Ladies Handicap

YESTERDAY (2000)
At 3: 3rd Breeders' Cup Filly and Mare Turf

YES YOU WILL (1956)
At 4: Won John B. Campbell Handicap
Carter Handicap

Y FLASH (1960)
At 2: Won Hollywood Juvenile Championship
3rd Del Mar Futurity
At 3: Won Cinema Handicap
Hollywood Derby

YILDIZ (1948)
At 3: Won Flamingo Stakes
2nd Travers Stakes

YING AND YANG (1955)
At 4: 3rd Californian Stakes
American Handicap

YNEZ QUEEN (1966)
At 3: 3rd Hollywood Oaks

YOGI (1947)
At 3: 3rd Louisiana Derby

YOKAMA (1993)
At 4: 3rd Matriarch Stakes

YOLO LADY (1995)
At 3: 3rd Hollywood Oaks
At 4: 2nd Milady Breeders' Cup Handicap
Vanity Handicap

YONAGUSKA (1998)
At 2: Won Hopeful Stakes
3rd Champagne Stakes

YONCALLA (1946)
At 4: 3rd Black Helen Handicap

YONDER (1963)
At 3: 2nd Gallant Fox Handicap
At 4: 2nd Metropolitan Handicap
3rd Suburban Handicap

YONDER (1987)
At 2: Won Remsen Stakes
At 3: Won Jersey Derby
3rd Jim Beam Stakes

YORKTOWN (1957)
At 3: 2nd Louisiana Derby
At 5: Won New Orleans Handicap
John B. Campbell Handicap

YORKVILLE (1964)
At 2: Won Sanford Stakes
3rd Breeders' Futurity
John B. Campbell Handicap

YORKY (1957)
At 4: Won McLennan Handicap
Widener Handicap
3rd Tropical Park Handicap
Brooklyn Handicap
At 5: Won Widener Handicap
2nd Gulfstream Park Handicap
3rd Seminole Handicap

YOSI BOY (1976)
At 5: 2nd Gulfstream Park Handicap
3rd New Orleans Handicap

YOU (1999)
At 2: Won Frizette Stakes
2nd Hollywood Starlet Stakes
At 3: Won Las Virgenes Stakes
Santa Anita Oaks
Acorn Stakes
Test Stakes
2nd Ruffian Handicap
Overbrook Spinster Stakes
3rd Alabama Stakes
At 4: 2nd Santa Maria Handicap
Ruffian Handicap
Overbrook Spinster Stakes

YOU AND I (1991)
At 4: Won Metropolitan Handicap
Brooklyn Handicap
2nd Vosburgh Stakes
3rd Carter Handicap

YOU'D BE SURPRISED (1989)
At 4: Won Top Flight Handicap
3rd Hempstead Handicap
At 5: 2nd Hempstead Handicap

YOUNG BOB (1975)
At 4: Won Hawthorne Gold Cup
2nd Arlington Handicap

YOUNG PETER (1944)
At 3: Won Travers Stakes

YOUR ALIBHAI (1958)
At 5: 3rd American Handicap
At 6: 3rd Dixie Handicap
At 7: 2nd Hialeah Turf Cup
3rd Widener Handicap

YOUR BILL (1958)
At 3: 3rd Flamingo Stakes

YOU'RE NO BARGAIN (1984)
At 3: 3rd Arkansas Derby

YOUR HOST (1947)
At 2: Won Del Mar Futurity
At 3: Won San Felipe Stakes
Santa Anita Derby
3rd Arlington Classic
American Derby
At 4: 2nd San Carlos Handicap

YOUR PLACE OR MINE (1974)
At 3: 2nd Acorn Stakes

YOUTH (1973)
At 3: Won Canadian International Championship
Washington D.C. International

YUMBEL (1961)
At 8: Won Widener Handicap

YVONAND (1976)
At 4: Won Arlington Handicap
Louisiana Downs Handicap
3rd Washington D.C. International

ZABALETA (1983)
At 3: 3rd Gotham Stakes

ZABEG (1957)
At 3: 3rd Washington D.C. International

ZALATAIA (1979)
At 4: Won Oak Tree Invitational Stakes
2nd Hollywood Turf Cup

ZARANI SIDI ANNA (1990)
At 4: 3rd Milady Handicap

ZARB'S MAGIC (1993)
At 3: Won Arkansas Derby

ZAVATA (2000)
At 2: 3rd Hopeful Stakes

ZEBADIAH (1958)
At 2: 2nd Breeders' Futurity

ZEERULER (1988)
At 3: 3rd Super Derby

ZENDA (1999)
At 3: 2nd Queen Elizabeth II Challenge Cup

ZENODA (1945)
At 2: Won Starlet Stakes

ZENTSOV STREET (1997)
At 3: 3rd Early Times Hollywood Derby

ZEV'S JOY (1955)
At 4: Won Vanity Handicap

ZIPPERSUP (1994)
At 2: 2nd Norfolk Stakes

ZOFFANY (1980)
At 5: Won Hollywood Turf Cup
At 6: Won Sunset Handicap
At 7: Won San Luis Rey Stakes

ZOFTIG (1997)
At 3: 2nd Ashland Stakes

ZOGRAFOS (1968)
At 7: 2nd Arlington Handicap
At 8: 2nd Hialeah Turf Cup

ZOMAN (1987)
At 5: Won Budweiser International Stakes

ZOMARADAH (1995)
At 4: 3rd Breeders' Cup Filly and Mare Turf

ZOONAQUA (1990)
At 2: Won Oak Leaf Stakes
At 4: 3rd Yellow Ribbon Stakes

ZUCCHERO (1948)
At 4: 3rd Washington D.C. International

ZULU TOM (1969)
At 3: 3rd Withers Stakes

ZURICH (1989)
At 2: 2nd Del Mar Futurity
Norfolk Stakes

ZVETLANA (1978)
At 4: 2nd Delaware Handicap

Photo courtesy of Santa Anita Park

Gary Stevens, the only jockey who has been named one of the 50 "most beautiful people" by People *magazine, has captured eight classic races, including the 1997 Kentucky Derby and Preakness Stakes aboard Silver Charm.*

Jockeys

III: Jockeys

The Shoe Fits

The late Red Smith, perhaps history's most revered sports-writer, often said that, pound for pound, jockeys are the world's best athletes.

In few of the some 60,000 races held in North America annually do horses carry as many as 126 pounds—and imposts of 10 or 15 fewer are far more common—so the pool of men small enough to succeed in the saddle is obviously a minute portion of the population.

"I have no weight problems whatsoever," said Hall of Fame jockey Pat Day, who tips the scales at about 100 pounds. "It's a godsend for me. I eat everything I want. I'm about the most fortunate rider I know of in that respect. I thank the Lord every night."

Day and the late Bill Shoemaker, who, as strange as this sounds, was small *for a jockey,* not only are two of only four North American riders in history with more than 8,000 total triumphs, but they are perhaps the only modern jockeys who have enjoyed tremendous long-term success without having to count every calorie and fat gram.

"It's a very, very sacrificing life," said Bill Gavidia, who won the 1974 Kentucky Oaks aboard Quaze Quilt. "There are about 2,000 riders in the United States. How many are making money? About 400? A lot of jockeys can't pay the rent. There are a lot of riders who spend four hours a day in the hot box to lose six or seven pounds."

In no other sport are athletes forced to retire because they add 10—or even fewer—pounds of muscle to bodies that, in the case of Laffit Pincay Jr., for example, would make Evander Holyfield look like the 98-pound weak-lings in the old Charles Atlas advertisements.

Photo courtesy of Santa Anita Park

Among the most successful combinations California racing has ever known were trainer Mesh Tenney (far left) and owner Rex Ellsworth (far right), beside his wife, Nola. Among their top major winners were Swaps, Prove It, and Candy Spots, who generally entered the winner's circle with Bill Shoemaker (second from left) in the saddle.

"Jockeys are better today. Physically, they help the horse more. When I was a kid, Eddie Arcaro and Johnny Longden were the top jockeys. Johnny, Eddie, and a few of their contemporaries could ride in any era because they were outstanding riders," Shoemaker, who never expected to join that elite group, said during his final year in the saddle. "I figured if I could ride for five years, I'd be doing pretty good."

That's because jockeys must manhandle thoroughbreds who weigh as much as 10 times more than they do at speeds of nearly 40 mph with only a helmet for protection. In few sports do a higher percentage of participants suffer disabling injuries.

"This is a profession you can't be afraid in," Gavidia said. "They used to tell me, 'If you want to be a jockey, then fall.' After the first spill, you'll know if you're in the right business. That's part of the game. In this profession, if you start feeling afraid or something, you'd better quit."

This chapter identifies the elite riders of the modern era—awarding four points for victories, two for runner-up finishes, and one for third-place efforts in major races. Most elite riders claim the same secret to success.

"Good horses make good jockeys," said Hall of Fame rider Don Brumfield.

"A great horse can make any-body look good," added the legendary Angel Cordero.

"The secret is getting on the best stock. The name of the game is being on the fastest horse. You can't win a Cadillac race in a Volkswagen, but you can win a

Volkswagen race in a Cadillac. You could take the top 20 riders in the country, and whoever had the best horse would win," Day said.

"When you have a rider like Angel Cordero, you don't have to tell him much: Just get on the horse, and stay awake," Hunter Farm owner Dennis Diaz said after Cordero guided Spend A Buck to an overpowering victory in the 1985 Kentucky Derby. "Don't give Angel an inch. He'll steal a race."

To get mounts on the best horses in major races, however, Cordero and the rest of the elite jockeys had to win consistently on the longest shots in the cheapest claiming races to demonstrate to owners and trainers of the best horses that they indeed were worthy of every rider's dream—winning prestigious events.

"When you get a chance to ride a (standout) horse, it makes the frustrations of being a jockey so much easier to take. It brings the fun back into race riding," said Darrel McHargue, who earned 39 major victories.

And, according to Day, those elite jockeys also share another common trait.

"I hate losing—period," he said. "I truly enjoy winning. I have the innate ability to sense when a horse is doing his best, to know how much horse I have left. It becomes a situation where everything clicks. The more I win, the more confident I ride, and the more the horse responds. You don't think (31-1 shot) Wild Again would have beaten Slew O' Gold and Gate Dancer (in the inaugural Breeders' Cup Classic in 1984) if I hadn't ridden him with so much confidence, do you?"

Head of the Class

Twenty riders in the modern era have enjoyed No. 1 seasons, and 18 of those are enshrined in the Hall of Fame. The cream of the crop, listed in order they appear in the rankings for their achievements in modern major races:

Bill Shoemaker doesn't hold every modern record for major-league accomplishments as a race rider. If it hadn't been for two injuries that many observers thought would end his career in the late '60s, however, he just might. Shoemaker suffered a broken right femur in 1968 that sidelined him for 13 months. His comeback abruptly ended on April 30, 1969, when his mount, Poona's Day, fell on him in the paddock at Hollywood Park, crushing Shoemaker's pelvis and rupturing his bladder.

"I thought about quitting then, but I never did," Shoemaker said during his farewell tour in 1990.

Shoemaker not only returned after those injuries, but he returned to the top. He posted three consecutive No. 1 seasons from 1970-72 and again from 1975-77, matching a feat he first accomplished from 1961-63.

Shoemaker's remarkable records include the most No. 1 (14), top-two (18), top-three (25), top-four (26), top-five (27), top-six (29), top-seven (31), top-eight (32), and top-nine (35) seasons. He also holds all records for most seasons in the top 10 through the top 25, including 37 top-16, 38 top-18, and 39 top-23 campaigns. Shoemaker captured at least one major race 34 years in a row (1950-83), posted multiple victories in 31 consecutive seasons (1953-83), and enjoyed a record-tying nine straight campaigns with nine or more victories (1974-82). Shoemaker also holds the records for double-figure (38), 20-point (36), 30-point (30), 40-point (27), 50-point (24), 60-point (15), 70-point (11), and 90-point seasons (4). Shoemaker is the only rider to post back-to-back 90-point seasons, and he did it twice, in 1958 and '59 and again in 1966 and '67.

Photo courtesy of Santa Anita Park

Few, if any, jockeys have demonstrated the amazing consistency of Chris McCarron, who earned at least five major victories 19 years in a row from 1983-2001. Included in those triumphs were victories aboard Paseana in the Santa Margarita Handicap in 1992 and '94. Although retired from race riding, McCarron is still a regular visitor to the winner's circle at Santa Anita as the track's general manager.

Further, Shoemaker is the only modern rider with back-to-back campaigns of 17 or more victories (1966-67) and the only rider to reach 19 victories twice, which he managed in both 1958 and '67. Shoemaker's 11 victories, 19 top-two finishes, and 25 in-the-money efforts in the classics—the Kentucky Derby, Preakness, and Belmont Stakes—are modern records, and he is one of two modern-era jockeys to rank as the leading classic rider on five occasions.

Of all of Shoemaker's many records, the most impressive

well may be his 357 victories, 602 top-two finishes, and 771 in-the-money efforts in major races for a total of 2,087 points—more than 700 ahead of his nearest rival.

"It's just amazing he could ride 40 years, considering the danger and all," jockey Herson Sanchez said of Shoemaker. "Anybody who's ever ridden a horse has heard of Willie Shoemaker. He's what we strive to be. He's like Babe Ruth. He's an idol."

Laffit Pincay Jr.'s most famous accomplishment, of course, is that he's the only jockey in history with more than 9,000 total victories—a record 9,530 in a 39-year career that ended when he suffered a broken neck in a 2003 spill. In a career that combined brilliance and productive longevity like few others, however, it is by no means his only singular achievement. Included in the achievements in which Pincay has no peer are 24 consecutive top-12 seasons (1967-90), 28 successive years (1967-94) in the top 16, and 29 straight in the top 23 (1967-95). His 25 straight top-15 campaigns (1967-91) equal yet another record. Pincay's records also include 27 straight seasons with three or more victories (1967-93), 24 consecutive 20-point campaigns (1967-90), and 28 double-figure seasons in a row (1967-94). Pincay's 30 consecutive seasons with at least one victory (1966-95) and 28 years in a row with multiple victories (1967-94) rank second, as do his 17 top-four seasons and 33 top-23 seasons. Pincay also won a classic a record-equaling three years in a row from 1982-84, is one of only four jockeys to rank as the leading classic rider in consecutive campaigns (1983-84), and ranks fourth with six No. 1 seasons.

Photo courtesy of Churchill Downs

"When you have a rider like Angel Cordero, you don't have to tell him much: Just get on the horse, and stay awake," Hunter Farm owner Dennis Diaz said after he watched Cordero earn his third Kentucky Derby victory, an overpowering, wire-to-wire triumph aboard Hunter Farm's Spend A Buck in 1985.

Through 2001, **Chris McCarron** had posted 24 top-13 seasons in a row and 23 consecutive years with four or more victories, all of them top-eight campaigns. He also had active 19-year strings of top-seven seasons, five-plus victory campaigns, and 30 or more points. All of the aforementioned are records, and his back-to-back seasons as the leading classic rider in 1986 and '87 share another mark. Further, McCarron's 24 consecutive seasons with three or more victories and 23 straight 20-point campaigns through 2001 both rank second, as do his nineteen 40-point, 20 top-six, and 22 top-seven seasons. McCarron, whose five seasons as the No. 1 rider are bettered by only four others, accomplished enough in 2002 to earn his 25th straight top-18 season, a streak only Pincay has exceeded. McCarron's assault on the record books, however, ended with his abrupt retirement in June of 2002.

Through 2003, **Jerry Bailey** had posted nine consecutive top-two seasons and 14 straight top-six seasons, feats bettered by only one rider. Bailey also claimed one of the most remarkable riding feats in history in 1997, winning 15 major races—on 15 *different* horses. But no rider has matched what Bailey managed from 1997-2003: seven consecutive No. 1 seasons and all of them with 80 or more points. Both streaks are more than twice as long as any other rider has managed. Bailey also won at least 12 races and earned 70 or more points nine campaigns in a row from 1995-2003, 13-plus victories seven straight years from 1997-2003, and 16 or more triumphs three successive seasons from 1998-2000—all records. Only three riders have won a Breeders' Cup race in four consecutive years, and Bailey is the only one to accomplish that twice, from 1993-96 and from 1998-2003, when he recorded six consecutive campaigns with a victory on racing's richest day. In 2003, Bailey unquestionably enjoyed the greatest year that any modern jockey—in fact, perhaps any athlete—has ever had. His 149-point campaign included 28 victories, 43 two-top placings, and 50 in-the-money finishes and obliterated the existing marks, some by nearly 50 percent. Perhaps it's a testimony to Bailey's amazingly consistent brilliance—or an indictment as to just how far thoroughbred racing has fallen from the sporting public's consciousness in the 27 years since Steve Cauthen was named *Sports Illustrated's* Sportsman of the Year and Man of the Year by *The Sporting News*—that Bailey's $23-million-plus campaign, roughly the equivalent of batting .450 and blasting 90 home runs, netted him a total of zero votes in The Associated

Press's Male Athlete of the Year poll. Although Bailey's feats at the turn of the century rank as the greatest seven-year stretch for any modern jockey, his longevity also has been notable: His 14 consecutive 40-point and 12 straight 50-point seasons through 2003 both rank second, only one rider has bettered his 14 consecutive seasons with at least six victories, and his 19 top-13 campaigns rank eighth.

Angel Cordero finished among the top 14 jockeys a record 25 consecutive seasons from 1967-91, and the double-figure point total he posted in each of those years is bettered by just one rival, as are his 16 straight 30-point seasons (1976-91). That Cordero enjoyed both amazing longevity and dominance is perhaps best illustrated by his 25 consecutive seasons with multiple victories (1967-91) and his three campaigns in a row (1987-89) with 13 or more triumphs. Each ranks among the top three such feats. Cordero also ranks among the top three in top-five (16) and top-eight (22) seasons and in the top five in top-two (8), top-four (13), and top-six (18) campaigns.

Photo courtesy of Thistledown

Few riders can match Pat Day's resume in major races. Only Bill Shoemaker and Eddie Arcaro have exceeded Day's nine victories and 22 in-the-money finishes in the classics since World War II. Although Jerry Bailey has exceeded Day's 12 Breeders' Cup triumphs, no one can match Day's 40 in-the-money finishes on racing's richest day.

Perhaps if the modern era had begun a decade or so earlier, all the jockeys' records would belong to **Eddie Arcaro.** His 10 modern-era classic victories, including the Triple Crown aboard Citation in 1948, rank second. But Arcaro won seven classics prior to the modern era, including a Triple Crown sweep aboard Whirlaway in 1941. Yet what the Master accomplished in the 16 seasons from 1946 through his retirement after the 1961 campaign was nothing short of magnificent. Arcaro is the only jockey to finish in the top six 16 years in a row, and all of those 16 campaigns actually were top-three seasons, including 11 consecutive years in the top two (1946-56). No one else has managed to finish in the top three more than nine years in a row. Arcaro enjoyed eight No. 1 seasons in the modern era, including three in a row from 1950-52 and again from 1954-56. Arcaro's 16 straight 40-point seasons and 13 consecutive 50-point campaigns (1946-58) are records, as are his 16 years in a row with seven or more victories and his nine straight campaigns (1950-58) with 11 or more triumphs. The Master captured 18 victories in both 1950 and '55 and is one of only two riders to reach that plateau twice.

Through 2003, **Pat Day** had logged 22 consecutive top-13 seasons and 21 in a row with 20 or more points, both among the top five such feats. So are his sixteen 40-point seasons, 16 top-six campaigns, and seven consecutive years (1986-92) with seven or more victories. Day also won a classic a record-tying three years in a row (1994-96); posted nine classic victories, a total exceeded by only two riders in the modern era, and ranks as the all-time leading jockey in the Breeders' Cup. Although Bailey has earned 14 triumphs to Day's 12, Day's 17 runner-up efforts and 11 third-place showings give him a 93-82 edge over Bailey.

Among the host of categories in which **Jorge Velasquez** ranks in the top five are 22 consecutive years with multiple victories and double-figure point totals (1967-88), 16 straight seasons with three or more triumphs (1973-88), 19 consecutive top-12 seasons (1968-86), and 25 top-25 campaigns, including 23 in a row from 1966-88.

Despite a brief retirement in 2000 and a leave of absence to portray legendary jockey George Woolf in the 2003 hit movie *Seabiscuit,* **Gary Stevens** had recorded 19 consecutive seasons with multiple victories and top-18 finishes through 2003. From 1985-99, Stevens won at least three races every year, and his 14 consecutive seasons with at least 30 points from 1986-99 have been bettered by just three jockeys. All of the aforementioned feats rank in the top 10, as do Stevens's ten 50-point seasons, five consecutive 50-point campaigns (1994-98), five top-two, seven top-three, eight top-four, 10 top-five, 16 top-eight, and 17 top-12 campaigns. Stevens has been the leading classic rider on three occasions and is one of only six jockeys with an 18-victory season, which he recorded in 1995.

Braulio Baeza finished among the top three jockeys in seven consecutive seasons (1963-69), a feat exceeded by only two riders, and won at least 16 times in back-to-back campaigns (1967-68), an achievement bettered by only one jockey. He also ranked among the top two jockeys from 1965-69, posted 13 top-eight finishes in succession (1961-73), and won at least nine races five years in a row (1965-69), all of which rank among the top six such achievements. So do his four consecutive 60-point (1965-68), three straight 70-point (1966-68), and two 80-point seasons in a row (1967-68). Baeza posted at least one victory and finished in the top 15 from 1960-76, which ranks among the top 10 such achievements, as do his 13 consecutive years with four or more victories (1961-73), eight consecutive campaigns with six or more wins (1962-69), and four seasons in a row with 10 or more triumphs (1965-68).

Through the 2002 campaign, **Eddie Delahoussaye's** last in the saddle, he had won a race in 26 consecutive seasons, a streak bettered by only two jockeys, and posted 25 consecutive double-figure and top-18 campaigns, streaks exceeded by only one. While longevity was Delahoussaye's forte, his 12 top-eight campaigns and 19 top-12 seasons also rank among the top 11, and his 22 years in a row (1978-99) with multiple victories are exceeded by only four others. Delahoussaye also was the leading rider in the Breeders' Cup a record-tying three times and shares the record of back-to-back years (1992-93) with a pair of Breeders' Cup wins.

Photo courtesy of Churchill Downs

Laffit Pincay Jr. won more races than any rider in history. His favorite among those 9,530 triumphs was his only Kentucky Derby victory, aboard Swale in 1984.

Only two jockeys had longer streaks of seasons with double-figure victory totals than the four straight **Eric Guerin** recorded from 1951-54, and just three had longer streaks of 11 or more triumphs, which he enjoyed in the latter three campaigns. Guerin finished in the top four seven years in a row from 1949-55, posted 11 consecutive top-10 seasons from 1948-58, and won at least four races every year from 1948-56. All of those feats rank among the top 10, as do his six successive top-three seasons (1950-55), eight consecutive 40-point campaigns (1949-56), and five straight 50-point seasons (1951-55).

Only five riders have bettered **Manny Ycaza's** three No. 1 and six top-two seasons, and just four have put together longer streaks of consecutive campaigns with six or more victories than the eight in a row Ycaza fashioned from 1959-66. Ycaza also recorded five straight top-four seasons (1962-66), eight in a row among the top six (1959-66), and 12 consecutive top-11 campaigns (1958-69). Those rank among the top 10 such achievements, as do his nine top-four, 10 top-six, and five 60-point seasons.

Mike Smith's 23 major victories in 1994 are second only to the 28 Jerry Bailey posted in 2003 and four more than any other modern rider has accomplished in a single campaign. Smith's 101 points, aided by three runner-up efforts and three third-place showings, also mark one of only two occasions a modern rider has reached the century mark. Smith also won at least one Breeders' Cup race four consecutive years (1992-95), including a record-equaling two wins in consecutive years (1994-95). His five consecutive years with nine or more victories and 50-point seasons (1993-97), three consecutive seasons with double-figure victory totals (1993-95), and back-to-back campaigns with 13 or more wins (1993-94) all rank among the top six such achievements. Smith, however, is hardly a one-year, or even a five-year, wonder. His 11 consecutive top-13 seasons (1990-2000) rank in a 14th-place tie on the all-time list.

Among the many categories in which **Ted Atkinson** ranks in the top 10 are eight consecutive top-five seasons (1948-55), 11 top-eight campaigns in a row (1946-56), six years in succession with seven or more victories and top-four finishes (1948-53), three consecutive top-three seasons (1948-50), and back-to-back double-figure victory campaigns (1948-49).

Bill Hartack won 19 races in 1957, one of only four modern riders to attain that plateau, and only Shoemaker can equal his five years as the leading jockey in the classics. Hartack's 17 consecutive years (1954-70) with at least one triumph and back-to-back seasons with double-figure victory totals (1956-57) rank among the top 10 such feats.

Steve Brooks ranks among the top 20 in top-three seasons (2) and in the top 30 in top-24 campaigns (14).

Ron Turcotte, whose career ended because of a riding injury that left him paralyzed, is the only modern jockey to earn multiple classic victories in consecutive seasons, winning the Kentucky Derby and Belmont Stakes aboard Riva Ridge in 1972 and sweeping the Triple Crown on Secretariat a year later. In each of those seasons, Turcotte earned 11 or more victories and 60 or more points to rank in the top 10 in both categories. So does his streak of three consecutive top-three campaigns (1971-73).

Two Who Should Be Hall of Famers

Only two jockeys in the modern era have finished a season ranked first for their performances in major races who haven't been enshrined in the Hall of Fame—**Eddie Maple** (1983) and **Jose Santos** (1990). Why Maple and Santos, who rank 12th and 16th, respectively, in the modern-era standings haven't merited inclusion is a mystery.

Among the categories in which Maple ranks no worse than seventh are the 20 consecutive seasons in which he posted double-figure point totals and ranked in the top 21 (1971-90), 20 top-16 campaigns, and 23 top-21 seasons. Maple's 19 consecutive years with at least one victory (1971-89), 18 straight seasons with multiple victories (1972-89), and 17 top-13 campaigns also rank among the top 10. Maple also enjoyed nine consecutive top-10 seasons (1980-88), 10 years in a row with three or more victories (1980-89), twelve 20-point seasons, seven top-six seasons, and eight top-seven campaigns, all of which rank among the top 15.

Santos earned at least 10 victories and 70 points in both 1989 and '90—streaks bettered by only seven and six riders, respectively—and finished in the top three in both seasons. Only 13 riders have bettered his 15 consecutive top-20 campaigns (1985-99), and Santos's 10 years with 30 points or more, six 40-point seasons, and four 50-point seasons all rank in the top 15, as do his five consecutive campaigns with seven or more victories (1986-90).

18 More Immortals

Another 18 modern riders have been inducted into the Hall of Fame. Some of their achievements in prestige events haven't necessarily been as glittering as a Hall of Fame resume might suggest. And, although performances in major races are the best measurement of a jockey's career, they are by no means the only ones.

Whether the winner's share of the purse is $2,000 or $2 million, any horseplayer or horseman expects jockeys to give their best efforts on all occasions. Some of the following Hall of Fame riders made a significant impact other than in major events. Russell Baze, for example, was the perennial leader in total victories and winning percentage through most of the '90s and into the 21st Century, leading the nation in the latter category for the ninth year in a row in 2003, but he rarely ventures away from Northern California for big-money events.

Johnny Longden, who won the 1943 Triple Crown aboard Count Fleet, and Jimmy Stout, who earned three Belmont Stakes victories in the late '30s, are among those whose careers—and perhaps best seasons—predate the modern era. Steve Cauthen, Sandy Hawley, and Avelino Gomez were stars in Europe, Canada, and the Caribbean, respectively, in addition to their feats in the United States. Like Turcotte, Sam Boulmetis saw his career end prematurely because of a paralyzing injury and, with the possible exceptions of sled-dog racer Susan Butcher and dragster Shirley Muldowney, Julie Krone undoubtedly has carved the best career in sports history for a female athlete who had to compete against men.

So these are true Hall of Fame riders, presented in the order of their ranking in the modern-era standings:

Among the categories in which **Jacinto Vasquez** ranks in the top 11 are double-figure seasons (21), top-15 campaigns (17), and top-19 seasons (22). He was the leading classic rider in both 1975 and '80, when he captured the Kentucky Derby aboard Foolish Pleasure and Genuine Risk, respectively. . . .

Photo courtesy of Churchill Downs

For a brief moment, Jerry Bailey was on top of the racing world when he took Sea Hero, adorned with a blanket of roses, to the winner's circle after the 1993 Kentucky Derby. Bailey enjoyed a much longer tenure atop the racing world from 1997-2003: seven consecutive seasons as the No. 1 rider in major races, a streak more than twice as long as any other modern jockey.

Among the categories in which **Johnny Longden** ranks among the top 10 are 20 consecutive top-23 seasons (1946-65) and 17 straight years (1946-62) with at least one victory. Longden finished among the top 17 riders in 13 consecutive seasons (1946-58), among the top five on five occasions, in the top eight 10 times, and in the top 10 on 11 occasions, all of which rank among the top 15 such accomplishments. . . . **John Rotz** finished among the top seven jockeys eight times, among the top 10 on 11 occasions, and in the top 13 in 13 seasons, each of which ranks among the top 15 such feats. Rotz also posted six straight seasons (1961-66) among the top eight, a feat bettered by only 14 riders. Rotz was the leading classic rider in 1962, when he won the Preakness aboard Greek Money, and shared that honor in 1970, when he captured the Belmont under High Echelon. . . . **Bobby Ussery** won at least one race in 17 consecutive years (1955-71), posted 11 consecutive 20-point seasons (1957-67), and 15 straight top-23 campaigns (1955-69), all of which rank in the top 15. . . . **Conn McCreary's** six seasons in a row (1951-56) with 20 or more points and finishes of 12th or better both rank among the top 25 such achievements. . . . **Sandy Hawley** enjoyed three straight years (1975-77) with six or more victories, back-to-back top-three campaigns (1976-77), and four top-six seasons, all of which rank among the top 25. . . . **Walter Blum** posted three consecutive top-five seasons from 1964-66, an accomplishment bettered by only 14 modern riders. . . . **Sam Boulmetis** earned at least one victory in 17 consecutive seasons (1950-66), a streak bettered by only nine riders, and his eight consecutive campaigns (1954-61) with at least two victories and a top-16 finish both rank among the top 27. . . . Among the most notable top-50 achievements for **Ralph Neves** are nine consecutive years (1946-54) with at least one victory, eight top-19 seasons, and three consecutive campaigns (1949-51) with at least three triumphs. . . . **Don Brumfield,** the leading classic rider in 1966 by virtue of his Kentucky Derby and Preakness scores aboard Kauai King, also ranks among the top 50 with 10 top-22 seasons. . . . **Earlie Fires** ranks among the top 52 in both top-25 (11) and top-22 seasons (8). . . . **Jack Westrope** was aboard at least three major winners in four consecutive campaigns (1946-49), which ranks in a 36th-place tie in that category. . . . Among the categories in which **Johnny Adams**—the leading classic jockey in 1954, when he won the Preakness aboard Hasty Road—ranks in the top 50 are five top-13 seasons, eight top-19 campaigns, and six consecutive top-24 seasons (1951-56). . . . **Julie Krone,** whose victory aboard Colonial Affair in the 1993 Belmont Stakes is the only classic win by a female rider, posted six straight top-17 seasons (1991-96) to rank among the top 40 in that category. Krone came out of retirement to claim her first major victory in six years in 2002, then won a career-high five major stakes a year later, when she captured the Breeders' Cup Juvenile Fillies aboard Halfbridled to become the only female jockey to earn a Breeders' Cup triumph. . . . **Steve Cauthen** won the 1978 Triple Crown aboard Affirmed, and only 14 riders have more consecutive seasons with eight or more victories than Cauthen's back-to-back 1977 and '78 campaigns. . . . **Jimmy Stout's** highest ranking is a 55th-place tie for his four consecutive seasons (1946-49) with multiple victories. . . . **Avelino Gomez's** highest ranking is an 89th-place tie for his three top-20 campaigns. . . . **Russell Baze's** highest ranking is a tie for 111th for his pair of top 21-seasons.

Photo courtesy of Thistledown

No jockey has approached the immediate impact in major races made by Steve Cauthen, who earned eight victories and finished in the top three on 16 occasions in 1977. That remarkable season, in which Cauthen became the first rider to earn $6 million, earned him acclaim as Sportsman of the Year by *Sports Illustrated* and Man of the Year by *The Sporting News*. It also earned him a ride aboard Affirmed, whom Cauthen guided to the 1978 Triple Crown.

Another Dandy Baker's Dozen

Another 13 riders have accumulated 300 or more career points and rank among the top 37 in the modern era, yet haven't been elected to the Hall of Fame. Seven of them—Kent Desormeaux, Corey Nakatani, Alex Solis, Craig Perret, Pat Valenzuela, Jorge Chavez, and John Velazquez—were still active at the beginning of 2004. Nakatani, Don Pierce, Hedley Woodhouse, Fernando Toro, and Velazquez are the only modern riders with 300-point careers who don't have classic victories on their resumes. Listed in the order they rank in the modern-era standings, with various career highlights that rank among the top 20 such achievements:

Through 2003, **Kent Desormeaux** had posted 14 consecutive top-19 seasons, including seven in the top six; nine straight seasons with five or more triumphs (1992-2000); nine 30-point, six 40-point, and four 50-point campaigns, and twice had been the leading classic rider. Included was a three-year stretch (1992-94) in which he won at least eight races and finished among the top four each season. . . . **Corey Nakatani** posted six consecutive seasons (1993-98) with five or more victories, including back-to-back campaigns with at least 11 in 1995 and '96. He ranked among the top seven riders five straight years (1994-98), the top five in four consecutive seasons (1995-98), and among the top 13 nine seasons in a row through 2001. Nakatani also earned a Breeders' Cup triumph in four consecutive years (1996-99), one of only three jockeys to accomplish that feat. . . . **Alex Solis** enjoyed his 15th top-15 campaign, eighth consecutive 30-point season, and seventh top-10 finish in a row in 2003. . . . **Don Pierce** had 19 double-figure seasons, including 13 in a row (1968-80), and 11 campaigns with 20 or more points. He ranked among the top 21 riders 17 times, finished in the top 11 on 10 occasions, and enjoyed eight top-eight campaigns. . . . **Craig Perret** has posted 17 top-24 seasons and 16 double-figure campaigns, and he was the leading classic rider in 1990, when he guided Unbridled to victory in the Kentucky Derby. . . . **Hedley Woodhouse** finished among the top four jockeys three times and among the top six on six occasions, including four times in a row from 1953-56. He also posted nine consecutive seasons in the top 13 (1949-57) and had four campaigns with 40 or more points. . . . **Pat Valenzuela,** whose seven-victory 2003 campaign enabled him to finish a career-best fourth in the standings, is one of only four jockeys to win two Breeders' Cup races two years in a row (1991 and '92). Valenzuela also was the leading classic jockey in 1989, when he won the Derby and Preakness aboard Sunday Silence, and posted 14 consecutive seasons in the top 23 (1980-93). . . . **Ismael Valenzuela** won two or more races and finished among the top 22 riders in 13 consecutive seasons (1956-68). He won at least three races nine years in a row (1956-64), posted six seasons in the top seven and nine in the top nine, and was the leading classic jockey in both 1958 and '68. . . . **Bill Boland's** eight top-seven seasons included six in a row from 1954-59. He enjoyed 12 seasons in the top 13, 14 among the top 18 riders, and was the leading classic jockey in 1950, when he piloted Middleground to victory in the Kentucky Derby and Belmont Stakes. . . . **Jorge Chavez** finished among the top 12 riders in eight consecutive campaigns through 2002, when he recorded his fourth straight 40-point season. . . . **Johnny Sellers** finished third in the overall rankings in both 1961, when he guided Carry Back to victories in the Kentucky Derby and Preakness, and again in 1962. Sellers won seven or more races three years in a row (1960-62) and enjoyed three top-three seasons. . . . **Fernando Toro** finished among the top 25 jockeys 17 times and among the top 20 on 15 occasions. . . . The 2003 campaign marked the sixth in which **John Velazquez** had finished among the top seven jockeys.

No One Made a Better First Impression Than Cauthen

It's no secret that most jockeys labor in bullrings far removed from the sport's spotlight before they get their shot at the big time. And even the hottest jockeys who move their tacks to major racing centers usually have to scrap for mounts aboard 40-1 shots—or worse—in the cheapest races before they get the opportunities of a lifetime.

Perhaps the best illustration of that is provided by the following chart, which lists the top "rookies" in major North American races from 1947-2003. For the purpose of this discussion, a jockey's "rookie" season is the first in which he earns a top-three finish in a major race.

The chart lists the highest-finishing rookie, or rookies, in each season from 1947-2003 based on four points for a victory in a major race, two for a second-place finish, and one for a third-place effort, with wins serving as the first tiebreaker and runner-up finishes as the second.

Note that only 10 "rookies" have posted seasons with 20 or more points, including just three since 1977—Walter Guerra, Gary Stevens, and Mike Smith. Further note that being the hottest new kid on the block is no guarantee of future greatness. Only seven of these jockeys have been elected to the Hall of Fame: Bill Hartack, Manny Ycaza, Braulio Baeza, Steve Cauthen, Russell Baze, Stevens, and Smith.

No modern jockey's immediate impact has approached that of Cauthen, who won eight races and earned 41 points—both rookie records—in 1977. Cauthen, then 17, became the first jockey to earn $6 million in a season, which is now pocket change for Jerry Bailey, and was named Sportsman of the Year by *Sports Illustrated* and Man of the Year by *The Sporting News,* the only jockey ever to be honored in that fashion by either publication.

Top 'Rookies' in Major North American Races 1947-2003

Year	Jockey	W-P-S/Pts
1947	Willie Garner, Charles Givens, Charlie Ralls	1-1-1/7
1948	David Gorman	2-2-0/12
1949	Gordon Glisson	3-5-4/26
1950	Joe Culmone	2-4-1/17
1951	Bennie Green	2-1-1/11
1952	James Hardinbrook	2-0-1/9
1953	Jorge Contreras	2-1-3/13
1954	Bill Hartack	5-1-0/22
1955	Angel Valenzuela	4-3-5/27
1956	Larry Gilligan	1-1-1/7
1957	Bill Harmatz	2-3-5/19
1958	Manny Ycaza	3-2-6/22
1959	Don Pierce	2-2-0/12
1960	Braulio Baeza	1-3-3/13
1961	Heliodoro Gustines	1-3-2/12
1962	Leroy Moyers	2-0-0/8
1963	Jerry Lambert, W.D. Lucas, Buck Thornburg	1-0-0/4
1964	Fernando Alvarez	2-3-2/16
1965	Mike Venezia	2-3-1/15
1966	B. Moreira	2-2-3/15
1967	Joe Lopez, A.R. Valenzuela	1-0-1/5
1968	Jean Cruguet	1-2-8/16
1969	Michael Hole	1-1-0/6
1970	Bobby Woodhouse	4-1-0/18
1971	Martin Fromin	1-3-0/10
1972	Victor Tejada	4-3-3/25
1973	Angel Santiago	2-3-6/20
1974	Darrel McHargue, Daryl Montoya	2-1-1/11
1975	Bryan Fann	1-1-2/8
1976	Roger Velez	2-0-2/10
1977	Steve Cauthen	8-1-7/41
1978	Ronnie Hirdes	1-1-1/7
1979	John Oldham	2-1-0/10
1980	Eric Beitia	2-0-0/8
1981	David Ashcroft, Russell Baze, Ray Danjean	1-0-1/5
1982	Walter Guerra	4-4-2/26
1983	Walter Swinburn	3-0-0/12
1984	Jose Valdivieso	2-0-0/8
1985	Gary Stevens	3-4-4/24
1986	Chris DeCarlo, Julio Pezua	1-0-0/4
1987	Luis Ortega	1-1-0/6
1988	Shane Romero	1-1-0/6
1989	Amir Cedeno	1-0-1/5
1990	Mike Smith	3-5-2/24
1991	Shane Sellers	1-2-3/11
1992	Fabio Arguello	1-1-1/7
1993	Abdiel Toribio	2-0-0/8
1994	Frankie Dettori, Mark Johnston	1-0-0/4
1995	Fernando Valenzuela	0-2-1/5
1996	Charles Lopez	1-0-0/4
1997	Eddie King	1-0-3/7
1998	Elibar Coa	1-0-1/5
1999	Stewart Elliott	0-1-0/2
2000	Shaun Bridgmohan	1-1-0/6
2001	Javier Castellano	2-2-0/12
2002	Pat Smullen, Cornelio Velasquez	1-1-0/6
2003	Ray Ganpath	1-0-0/4

The following chart shows every jockey who posted an in-the-money finish in the 6,461 major races held in North America from 1946-2003. Four points are awarded for a victory, two for a runner-up finish, and one for a third-place showing. Victories are used as the first tiebreaker and runner-up finishes as the second tiebreaker.

Following that chart are charts that give the same information for the 174 classic races held from 1946-2003, the 145 Breeders' Cup races staged from 1984-2003, and the annual points leaders, which are followed by an alphabetical listing of jockeys' victories in major North American races from 1946-2003, with their mounts in those events in parenthesis.

Jockeys' Standings for In-the-Money Finishes In Major North American Races From 1946-2003

	W	P	S
1. Bill Shoemaker (2,087)	357	245	169
2. Laffit Pincay Jr. (1,355)	220	157	161
3. Chris McCarron (1,307)	196	195	133
4. Jerry Bailey (1,241)	211	139	119
5. Angel Cordero (1,169)	161	172	181
6. Eddie Arcaro (1,161)	204	124	97
7. Pat Day (1,071)	166	145	117
8. Jorge Velasquez (891)	134	119	117
9. Gary Stevens (880)	132	120	112
10. Braulio Baeza (832)	135	111	70
11. Eddie Delahoussaye (824)	121	119	102
12. Eddie Maple (654)	91	101	88
13. Eric Guerin (648)	102	73	94
14. Jacinto Vasquez (604)	90	77	90
15. Manny Ycaza (603)	99	72	63
16. Jose Santos (596)	86	87	78
17. Mike Smith (592)	99	71	54
18. Ted Atkinson (532)	81	70	68
19. Kent Desormeaux (530)	86	63	60
20. Bill Hartack (525)	90	51	63
21. Corey Nakatani (510)	76	66	74
22. Alex Solis (494)	69	65	88
23. Johnny Longden (493)	78	64	53
24. John Rotz (445)	66	62	57
25. Don Pierce (443)	57	74	67
26. Bobby Ussery (425)	61	57	67
27. Craig Perret (410)	56	60	66
28. Hedley Woodhouse (403)	53	64	63
29. Pat Valenzuela (402)	60	55	52
30. Ismael Valenzuela (400)	58	57	54
31. Bill Boland (389)	52	63	55
32. Jorge Chavez (353)	50	53	47
33. Steve Brooks (337)	50	49	39
34. Johnny Sellers (330)	51	42	42
35. Fernando Toro (329)	41	53	59
36. Ron Turcotte (327)	55	33	41
37. John Velazquez (305)	42	42	53
38. Darrel McHargue	39	50	30
39. Jean Cruguet (286)	39	39	52
40. Conn McCreary (283)	33	56	39
41. Sandy Hawley (271)	37	43	37
42. Walter Blum (254)	34	44	30
43. Doug Dodson (249)	42	27	27
44. Sam Boulmetis (247)	39	29	33
45. Ray Broussard	38	26	41
46. Shane Sellers (245)	36	33	35
47. Edgar Prado (239)	35	40	19
48. Robbie Davis (237)	29	37	47
49. Randy Romero (234)	35	31	32
50. Eddie Belmonte (232)	35	34	24
51. Chris Antley (229)	31	33	39
52. David Flores (226)	29	41	28
53. Ralph Neves (223)	31	28	43
54. Jean-Luc Samyn	32	32	25
55. Larry Adams (217)	27	36	37
56. Heliodoro Gustines (209)	32	27	27
57. Ovie Scurlock (202)	32	23	28
58. Don Brumfield (197)	27	26	37
59. Jeffery Fell	28	31	20
60. Ruben Hernandez (194)	27	28	30
61. Kenny Church (191)	27	32	19
62. Ray York (187)	24	31	29
63. Jerry Lambert (186)	30	23	20
64. Richard Migliore (183)	18	28	55
65. Don MacBeth (180)	24	27	30
66. Henry E. Moreno (179)	26	26	23
67. Earlie Fires (177)	21	34	25
68. Julie Krone (176)	22	29	30
69. Jack Westrope	22	31	22
70. Herb McCauley (172)	20	33	26
71. Johnny Adams (165)	21	30	21

	W	P	S
72. Pete Anderson (160)	21	23	30
73. David Gorman (159)	23	20	27
74. Jimmy Nichols (155)	18	30	23
75. Warren Mehrtens (154)	23	20	22
76. Bill Harmatz	22	15	33
77. Marco Castaneda (151)	15	34	23
78. Howard Grant (144)	17	28	20
79. Eldon Nelson (140)	24	13	18
80. Paul Bailey (131)	17	23	17
81. Mike Venezia (130)	14	21	32
82. Cash Asmussen (124)	19	19	10
83. Victor Espinoza	15	20	12
84. Jimmy Combest (112)	13	20	20
85. John Ruane (111)	15	20	11
86. Job Dean Jessop (110)	15	16	18
87. Ray Sibille (107)	16	14	15
88. Steve Cauthen (106)	17	11	16
89. David Erb (105)	15	16	13
90. Garrett Gomez (103)	13	18	15
91. Carlos Marquez (98)	14	12	18
92. Angel Valenzuela	12	13	20
93. Alex Maese (94)	10	20	14
94. Fernando Alvarez (90)	11	14	18
95. Chuck Baltazar (88)	11	14	16
96. Jorge Tejeira (87)	13	13	9
97. Robby Albarado (84)	12	10	16
98. Nick Shuk	11	15	8
99. Basil James (82)	9	15	16
100. Garth Patterson	13	9	10
101. Miguel Rivera	12	9	14
102. Alvaro Pineda (80)	7	13	26
103. Herb Hinojosa	10	13	13
104. Angel Santiago (79)	10	11	17
105. Sam Maple (78)	13	9	8
106. Corey Black (77)	10	12	13
107. Walter Guerra (76)	11	9	14
108. Jimmy Stout	14	5	8
109. Gordon Glisson (74)	7	14	18
110. Tommy Barrow (73)	10	11	11
111. Bobby Woodhouse	12	7	10
112. Joe Culmone (72)	8	16	8
113. Jack Leonard (71)	7	13	17
114. Bobby Permane (70)	10	9	12
115. John Lively	9	11	11
116. John Heckmann (69)	7	14	13
117. Larry Snyder (68)	7	11	18
118. John Gilbert	9	10	11
119. David Whited	8	11	13
120. Joe Bravo (67)	6	18	7
121. Peter Moreno	8	11	12
122. Vince Bracciale Jr. (66)	7	13	12
123. Michael Hole (65)	11	6	9
124. Eddie Burns (64)	12	3	10
125. Frank Olivares (63)	9	6	15
126. Mickey Solomone (62)	6	12	14
127. Bobby Baird (61)	8	6	17
128. Ruperto Donoso (60)	8	9	10
129. Arnold Kirkland (57)	5	10	17
130. Logan Batchellor (56)	7	9	10
131. Wayne Chambers (55)	7	9	9
132. Bill Mahorney (54)	5	12	10
133. Bennie Green	8	4	13
134. Larry Gilligan	7	4	17
135. Kenny Knapp (53)	4	12	13
136. Leroy Moyers (52)	8	7	6
137. Avelino Gomez (51)	6	10	7
138. Buck Thornburg	9	4	5
139. Rudy Campas (49)	5	9	11
140. Charlie Burr	6	9	6
141. Nick Combest (48)	5	8	12
142. Robin Platts	7	4	11

	W	P	S
143. Brice Blanc	6	9	5
144. Gregg McCarron (47)	6	6	11
145. Chris Rogers	5	10	6
146. George Taniguchi	5	8	10
147. Mike Luzzi (46)	5	7	12
148. Louis Cook (45)	7	5	7
149. Gene St. Leon	6	6	7
150. Daryl Montoya	5	9	5
151. Bill Passmore (43)	5	3	17
152. Jesse Davidson	7	6	2
153. William Cook (42)	6	5	8
154. Russell Baze (41)	6	5	7
155. Mel Peterson	5	7	6
156. Javier Castellano, Francisco Mena (40)	5	5	10
158. Mark Guidry	5	4	11
159. George Hettinger (39)	3	11	5
160. August Catalano	5	7	4
161. Pat Eddery (38)	5	5	8
162. Abelardo DeLara	7	2	5
163. Tony DeSpirito (37)	2	11	7
164. Calvin Borel	5	4	8
165. Larry Melancon	3	8	8
166. Rafael Meza	3	6	12
167. Wayne Harris (36)	2	10	8
168. Terry Lipham, George Martens, Mike Miceli	5	5	5
171. Robert Martin	5	4	7
172. Tony Graell	4	6	7
173. Nick Wall	3	9	5
174. Rick Wilson	3	5	13
175. Rene Douglas, Glen Lasswell	2	10	7
177. Merlin Volzke (35)	2	9	9
178. Willie Garner	5	5	4
179. Frank Lovato	4	6	6
180. Bill Gavidia (34)	2	10	6
181. John Choquette, Michael Kinane, Mike Manganello, Newbold Pierson	5	4	5
185. Jose Valdivia Jr.	4	6	5
186. Julio Espinoza	4	5	7
187. H.B. Wilson (33)	2	8	9
188. Julio Garcia	6	2	4
189. Herberto Castillo	5	3	6
190. Larry Saumell	3	7	6
191. Goncalino Almeida (32)	2	7	10
192. Danny Gargan	5	5	1
193. Ronald Baldwin	5	3	5
194. Albert Snider	4	6	3
195. Conn Errico	4	5	5
196. Manuel Gonzalez	4	4	7
197. William Carstens (31)	3	7	5
198. Tony Skoronski	5	3	4
199. Roger Velez	5	2	6
200. Donald Miller Jr.	2	7	8
201. Aaron Gryder (30)	2	6	10
202. Ronnie Franklin	6	1	3
203. Phil Rubbicco, Walter Swinburn	5	4	1
205. Thomas May	4	6	1
206. Keith Stuart	4	5	3
207. Gerland Gallitano (29)	4	3	7
208. Ronald Ardoin	3	4	8
209. Eibar Coa (28)	2	5	10
210. Jack Kaenel, Porter Roberts	5	2	3
212. Ernest Cardone, Victor Tejada	4	4	3
214. Ira Hanford	4	2	7
215. Shaun Bridgmohan, Rudy Rosales	3	5	5
217. Sidney Cole	3	4	7
218. Rogelio Trejos (27)	1	6	11
219. Jose Velez Jr.	4	4	2
220. Cornelio Velasquez	4	3	4
221. Lawrence Hansman, William Lester	3	5	4
223. Sandino Hernandez (26)	3	4	6

	W	P	S
224. John LeBlanc	5	2	1
225. Frank Chojnacki	5	1	3
226. Carroll Bierman	3	5	3
227. Carlos Barrera, Earl Knapp	3	4	5
229. Robert Nono (25)	2	3	11
230. Yves St. Martin	4	3	2
231. Calvin Stone	3	5	2
232. Herbert Lindberg	3	3	6
233. Ronald Campbell	3	4	4
234. Bryan Fann	2	6	4
235. Willie Martinez, Mike Sorrentino	2	5	6
237. Frank Lovato Jr. (24)	1	6	8
238. Fred Smith	5	0	3
239. Gerald Porch, Ronnie Nash, Ferrill Zufelt	4	3	1
242. Freddie Head	4	2	3
243. Frank Iannelli	3	4	3
244. Julio Pezua	2	5	5
245. Dave Kassen (23)	2	7	1
246. Lester Piggott	5	0	2
247. Alain Lequeux, Angel Rivera	4	2	2
249. Billie Fisk	3	4	2
250. Tommy Lee	3	3	4
251. Mike Basile	2	6	2
252. Robert Bernhardt	2	5	4
253. Rudy Turcotte (22)	2	4	6
254. Juvenal Diaz, Michael Morgan	4	2	1
256. Jack Skelly	3	4	1
257. Al Popara	3	3	3
258. Tony Black	3	2	5
259. Jorge Contreras	3	1	7
260. Jess Higley	2	5	3
261. Steve Valdez (21)	1	7	3
262. Benny Feliciano	3	3	2
263. Frankie Dettori	3	2	4
264. Gary Stahlbaum	2	5	2
265. Don Scurlock	2	3	6
266. Wigberto Ramos (20)	1	6	4
267. Carlos Lopez	4	0	3
268. Joe Renick, Miguel Yanez	2	2	7
270. Jimmy Lynch	2	3	5
271. Dean Hall (19)	1	5	5
272. Joe Imparato, Danny Wright	3	2	2
274. Carson Kirk	3	1	4
275. Euclid LeBlanc, Bobby Mundorf, Albert Schmidt	2	4	2
278. Walter Litzenberg	2	3	4
279. Mike Gonzalez (18)	1	6	2
280. Abigail Fuller	4	0	1
281. Stanley Small, Benjamin Strange	3	2	1
283. Keith Allen	3	1	3
284. Don Lewis	2	4	1
285. Martin Pedroza	2	3	3
286. Jose Amy, Tony Diaz (17)	1	5	3
288. Noel Richardson	4	0	0
289. Ramon Perez	3	2	0
290. Tommy Chapman, Jack Kurtz, John Oldham	3	1	2
293. Phil Grimm, Ronnie Hirdes, Wayne Wright	2	3	2
296. Danny Velasquez	2	2	4
297. Shelby Clark	1	4	4
298. Billy Phelps (16)	0	5	6
299. Ray Mikkonen	3	1	1
300. Eddie King	3	0	3
301. Robert Campbell	2	3	1
302. Gary Baze, B. Moreira	2	2	3
304. Hal Keene	1	4	3
305. Doug Richard (15)	1	3	5
306. John Giovanni	3	0	2
307. Tony D'Amico	2	3	0
308. Britt Layton	2	2	2
309. Tony Rini, Denis Tierney	2	1	4
311. Tyler Baze, Dave Penna	1	4	2
313. Karl Korte	1	3	4
314. Kenny Black (14)	1	2	6
315. Lester Balaski, Ramon Dominguez, Claude Erickson, Robert Stevenson	2	2	1
319. Frank Moon, Willie Skuse	2	1	3
321. Carlos Gonzalez	1	4	1
322. John Burton	1	3	3
323. Mario Valenzuela (13)	0	5	3
324. John Murtagh	3	0	0
325. Kerwin Clark, Greg Smith, Larry Spraker	2	2	0
328. Martinez Heath	2	1	2
329. Martin Fromin, Senon Trevino	1	4	0
331. Don Howard	1	3	2
332. Jamie Arellano, Andrea Seefeldt (12)	1	2	4
334. David Hidalgo, Ricardo Lopez, Lonnie Meche, John Nazareth	2	1	1
338. Gary Boulanger, F. Fernandez, Albert Gilbert, Benny Sorensen	1	3	1

Photo courtesy of Bob Coglianese Photo's, Inc.

In the 16 years Eddie Arcaro competed after World War II, he never failed to finish among the top three jockeys in major races, including eight No. 1 seasons. One reason was such mounts as 1948 Triple Crown winner Citation, led by Hall of Fame trainer Jimmy Jones.

	W	P	S
342. Dennis Carr, Gene Pederson, Francisco Torres, Octavio Vergara	1	2	3
346. Bill Pearson	1	1	5
347. Don Seymour	0	5	1
348. Heriberto Arroyo, Patrick Johnson, Don Pettinger, E. Rodriguez (11)	0	4	3
352. John Delahoussaye, Robert Gallimore, Donnie Meche, Paul Miller, William Peake, Henry Pratt, Fernando Valdizan	2	1	0
359. Eric Beitia, Bobby Breen, Glen Brogan, Ray Cochrane, Ramon Encinas, Charles LeBlanc, Nick Santagata	2	0	2
366. Jack Robertson, T. Williams	1	3	0
368. Bill Nemeti, Santiago Soto	1	1	4
370. John Ralph Adams, Nick Jemas	0	4	2
372. Jeff Anderson, Darrell Madden	0	3	4
374. Constantino Hernandez (10)	0	1	8
375. Gustavo Avila, J. Deforge, Jose Ferrer, James Hardinbrook, Chris Lamance, Pete McLean, Patrick Milligan, Mary Russ	2	0	1
383. Fabio Arguello, Tim Doocy, Donald Holmes, Willie Parnell, Smokey Saunders	1	2	1
388. Roger Cox, George Gibb, Charles Givens, Richard Grubb, Darrell Haire, Olivier Peslier	1	1	3
394. James Miranda (9)	0	3	3
395. Curt Bourque, L. Hildebrandt, Joey Judice, Robert Kotenko, J. Sanchez, Abdiel Toribio, Jose Valdivieso, Robert Yanez	2	0	0
403. Raymond Adair, Anthony Agnello, Robert Dever, Charles O'Brien, Richard Quinn, Raul Ramirez, Andreas Suborics, Robert Thibeau	1	2	0
411. Kelly Castaneda, Kieren Fallon, Willie Lee Johnson, Carlos Marquez Jr., Kenneth Scawthorn, Hubert Trent, Angelo Trosclair	1	1	2
418. Tommy Wallis (8)	0	4	0
419. William Bailey, Perry Compton, Paul Frey, Roberto Gonzalez, Paul Kallai, Bobby Lester, Bobby Mitchell, P. Paquet, S. Perez, Beloin Pulido, Charlie Ralls, John Ramirez, Brian Swatuk, Owen Webster	1	1	1
433. William McKeever, Mark Sellers	1	0	3

	W	P	S
435. Willie Balzaretti, Joe Baze, Willie Carson, Jon Court, Jim McKnight, Emile Ramsammy	0	3	1
441. Menotti Aristone, Todd Kabel, Kenny Skinner, Robert Summers, Don Wagner, Duke Wellington	0	2	3
447. Stanley Spencer, Raul Sterling (7)	0	1	5
449. Leslie Ahrens, R. Bustamante, M.A. Buxton, Javier Canessa, John Covalli, Richard DePass, Ricky Frazier, Adalberto Lopez, Jack Martin, Sheridan Mellon, Gerald Mosse, Luis Ortega, Shane Romero, S. Roberts, Pat Smullen, Louis Spindler, Terry Thompson, Roy Yaka	1	1	0
467. Roy Lumm, Richard McLaughlin, Rocco Sisto, Bernard Walt, Jack Yother	1	0	2
472. Dean Butler, J.C. DeSaint, J. Engle, Bruce Poyadou	0	3	0
476. Norman Cox	0	2	2
477. Frank Alvarado	0	1	4
478. Doug Thomas (6)	0	0	6
479. Irving Anderson, David Ashcroft, Frank Bone, Amir Cedeno, Jack Chestnut, Charles Corbett, Ray Danjean, Melvin Duhon, Alonzo Guajardo, Tony Ives, Mark Johnston, Larry Kunitake, Raymond Layton, Sidney LeJeune, Joe Lopez, Andy LoTurco, S. McComb, Clarence Meaux, James W. Moseley, Raul Rojas, C. Smirke, A.R. Valenzuela, Charles Woods Jr.	1	0	1
502. Carlos Astorga, Donna Barton, Arlin Bassett, Harrel Bolin, Charlie Cooke, John Craigmyle, George Cusimano, Bobby Jennings, Fernando Valenzuela	0	2	1
511. Matt Garcia, Paul Glidewell, Enrique Jurado, Art Madrid Jr., Clarence Picou, Bill Zakoor	0	1	3
517. Richard Lawless (5)	0	0	5
518. Sherman Armstrong, C.J. Baker, R.L. Barnett, D. Beckon, Caesar Bisono, David Borden, N. Brennan, Kelly Broussard, Victor Centeno, G. Chancelier, C.M. Clark, Herb Clark, Robert Cotton, Eugene Curry, Chris DeCarlo, Richard Dos Ramos, Richard Evans, Ray Ganpath, Robert Gilbert, Ken Godkins, Richard Griffiths, Reginald Heather, Robert Howard, Lester Hulet, Patrick Husbands, Charlie Hussey, Joe Johnson, D. Jones, Ken Jones, Eric Legrix, John Long, Charles Lopez, W.D. Lucas, D. MacAndrew, Gerard Melancon, Eddie Mercer, Gerardo Mora, Alan Munro, David Nied, Donnie Padgett, F. Pannell, Maurice Philliperon, Joe Phillippi, William Pyers, W.W. Rice, Karen Rogers, Randy Schacht, Eugene Sipus, Joe Steiner, Thierry Thulliez, Heriberto Valdivieso, B.J. Walker Jr., B. Wall, E. Walsh, Paul Ward, Danny Winick, Marcel Zuniga	1	0	0
575. John Beebe, Ralph Borgemenke, James Breckons, Jack Fieselman, Ron Hansen, Rosemary Homeister Jr., G. Intellisano Jr., Odin Londono, Henry Manifold, Mario Pino, Jimmy Powell, Weston Soirez, Oswaldo Torres	0	2	0
588. Albert Bodiou, Michael Caffarella, Dale Cordova, William Downs, Ronnie Ferraro, Otto Grohs, Melvin Holland, Thierry Jarnet, Gordon Lanoway, G.R. Martin, N. Nasibov, Oswaldo Rosado, Alfredo Smith Jr.	0	1	2
601. Raul Cespedes, Robert Gaffglione, Lonnie Ray, Grant Zufelt (4)	0	0	4
605. Dominique Boeuf, Kenneth Bourque, Mike Carrozzella, Antonio Castanon, Howard Craig, Oliver Cutshaw, James Del Vecchio, Lawrence Duffy, Warren Ferguson, Billy Fox, Marty Freed, Carl Gambardella, George Glassner, Earl Gross, Alan Hill, Kirk LeBlanc, Filiberto Leon, J. Li Causi, Glynn Louviere, Dale Lynch, William Marsh, Bill Mayorga, Thomas Meyers, Freddie Miller, Victor Molina, Enrique Munoz, Grady Overton, E.J. Perrodin, E. Plesa, Larry Reynolds, Joe Rocco, Marlon St. Julien, N. Sellwood, Robyn Smith, Noel Turcotte, Robert Wholey Jr., Albert Widman, S. Williams, W.B. Williams	0	1	1
644. Jon Kunitake, Alan Patterson, Ignacio Puglisi (3)	0	0	3
647. Richard Adkins, Barry Alberts, Joe Alleman, Mary Ann Alligood, Jose Alvarez, Inocencio Ayarza, John Baboolal, A. Badel, Glynn Bernis, Omar Berrio, C.H. Borden, D. Boston, J.P. Bowlds, George Burns, Nestor Capitaine, Norman Cartwright, Arthur Chambers, Weldon Cloninger, Robert Corle, Bobby Craig, W. Crews, Richard Culberson, H. Dalton, Albert Delgado, Travis Dunkelberger, L.J. Durousseau, Stewart Elliott, Isaias Enriquez, J. Fabre, Ron Fairholm, Tony Farina, A.J. Fernandez, Alex Fernandez, Bud Giacomelli, Rogelio Gomez, A.E. Gutierez, William Hanka, Richard Hughes, Michael Hunter, E. Jenkins, Dean Kutz,	0	1	0

Jockey	W	P	S
C. Lalanne, Corey Lanerie, Wendell Leeling, Louis Leon, Gunther Lindberg, Larry Loughry, Oscar Mancilla, W. Mann, C.L. Martin, C. McKee, R. McPhee, Randall Meier, John Melendez, Nelson Menard, Larry Munster, Declan Murphy, L. Murray, Vincenzo Nodarse, J. Preston, R. Ranum, J. Regalbuto, Darby Rice, L. Richardson, Jack Robinson, J.A. Rodriguez, Jesus Rodriguez, Arturo Romero, Jimmy Ruybali, Mark Salvaggio, L.P. Sasso, Frank Saumell, Vernon Sayler, Al Scotti, A. Selderidge, Craig Silva, J. Sivewright, G.L. Smith, Eddie Snell, Christophe Soumillon, George South, Allen Stacy, Terry Stanton, Scott Stevens, Charles Swain, A. Tavares, Jim Terry, Mario Torres, J. Truman, Douglas Valiente, E. Van Hook, C.A. Vergara, Arthur Wolfe, J. Walford			
741. Harold Allgaier, Dale Beckner, Paul Bohenko, Terry Bove, James Bruin, Raul Caballero, Frank Costa, Joseph Deegan, Hugo Dittfach, Jimmy Edwards, Juan Gonzalez, Greg Hutton, Michael Lee, Tommy Luther, Thomas Malley, Michael McCarthy, Esteban Medina, G. Moore, Paul Nicolo, Rene Riera Jr., Tommy Turner, Mickey Walls (2)	0	0	2
763. A. Anderson, J. Anderson, J. Aragon, Jack Arterburn, Eduardo Asenjo, Paul Atkinson, Steve Bahen, R. Barnes, T. Bates, Robert Bauer, J. Bev, Raymond Bianco, Jack Bradley, Scobie Breasley, J. Breen, Richard Bruno, Frank Callico, Adam Campola, Paul Capalbo, W.H. Carr, Gary Carter, Fred Castillo, Jesus Castonen, Wayne Catalano, Felix Chavez, B. Civitello, G. Cohen, Glenn Corbett, S. Cosentino, William Cox, Alphonso Coy, James Craswell, Thomas Cruz, J.L. Cushing, Danny David, Carlos Delgadillo, Tony Dominguez, Eddie Donnally, Jorge Duarte, Wendell Eads, Ronnie Ebanks, Jose Espinoza, Jorge Estrada, Anthony Ferrainuolo, J. Fitzsimmons, Robert Ford, William Fox, A. Francesco, Basil Frazier, Daniel French, M. Garcia, Efrain Garza, E. Gifford, P. Gifford, W. Gilbert, Sal Gonzalez, Tommy Greer, Larry Grubb, David Guillory, Guy Guinard, L.H. Gurkas, Steve Hamilton, Carlos Hernandez, Albert Herrera, Darryll Holland, R. Hutchinson, Tex Jasperson, James Johnson, Sean Jones, Horabio Karamanos, E.D. Keller, Kempton Knott, Thomas Kupfer, D. Lamb, W. Lane, R. LeBlanc, Rick Lindsay, M. Lopez, Victor Lopez, James Louzon, Anthony Lovato, Sebastian Madrid, Bert Martin, Edward Martin, Felipe Martinez, Jose Martinez Jr., J. Mattioli, Mike McDowell, D.L. McKee, Bobby McRoberts, W.A. Miller, J.W. Mills, Raphael Mojica Jr., E. Monacelli, Willie Mongol, A. Monteiro, Henri Mora, Diane Nelson, Paul Nicol Jr., Johnny Nied Jr., Edward Nunez, Eliezer Ortiz, John Pagano, J. Parenti, Nunzio Pariso, Barry Pearl, Eric Perner, Joe Petersen, Nick Petro, E. Phelps, Hector Pilar, Julian Pimentel, Martin Ramirez, Octavio Ramirez, John Reid, Chandra Rennie, Layton Risley, Michael Roberts, W. Rodriguez, G. Roser, Emile Roy, M. Rujano, James Ruggeri, G.P. Ryan, Steven Rydowski, Oscar Sanchez, Mitch Shirota, Carlos Silva, Robert Smith, J. Sneller, Abner Sorrows Jr., Joseph Spinale, Eugene Stallings, Donald Stover, Lane Suire, Yutaka Take, F. Truschka, A. Turcotte, J.L. Vargas, Jorge Vasquez, Harry Vega, R. Verdi, Charles Wahler, Henry Wajda, H. Walker, D. Ward, Dan Weiler, W. Williamson, Bud Zollinger (1)	0	0	1

Classic-Placed Jockeys 1946-2003

Jockey	W	P	S
1. Bill Shoemaker (66)	11	8	6
2. Eddie Arcaro (62)	10	8	6
3. Pat Day (59)	9	10	3
4. Gary Stevens (47)	8	4	7
5. Bill Hartack (44)	9	3	2
6. Chris McCarron	6	6	4
7. Angel Cordero (40)	6	4	8
8. Laffit Pincay Jr. (35)	4	8	3
9. Jerry Bailey	6	3	4
10. Braulio Baeza (34)	4	8	2
11. Eddie Delahoussaye (28)	5	3	2
12. Ron Turcotte (27)	6	1	1
13. Eric Guerin (25)	4	3	3
14. Ismael Valenzuela	4	4	0
15. Jorge Velasquez (24)	2	4	8
16. Kent Desormeaux (22)	3	4	2
17. Craig Perret (20)	2	4	4
18. Jacinto Vasquez (19)	2	5	1
19. Bill Boland, Jose Santos, Johnny Sellers (18)	3	2	2
22. Chris Antley, Jean Cruguet (17)	3	1	3
24. Eddie Maple	2	2	4
25. Alex Solis	1	4	4
26. Manny Ycaza (16)	1	3	6
27. Ted Atkinson (15)	2	1	5
28. Warren Mehrtens	3	1	0
29. John Rotz (14)	2	2	2
30. Victor Espinoza, Conn McCreary, Bobby Ussery	2	2	1
33. Mike Smith (13)	1	3	3
34. Steve Cauthen	3	0	0
35. Doug Dodson (12)	1	2	4
36. Darrel McHargue (11)	1	2	3
37. David Erb, Pat Valenzuela	2	1	0
39. Don Brumfield (10)	2	0	2
40. Ronnie Franklin, Miguel Rivera	2	0	1
42. Gustavo Avila	2	0	0
43. Steve Brooks	1	2	0
44. Sandy Hawley (8)	0	3	2
45. John Lively, Eldon Nelson (7)	1	1	1
47. Johnny Adams, Julie Krone, Henry E. Moreno	1	1	0
50. Eddie Belmonte	1	0	2
51. Earlie Fires	0	2	2
52. Jimmy Combest (6)	0	1	4
53. Pete Anderson, Jorge Chavez, Bill Harmatz, Edgar Prado, Ray York	1	0	1
58. Shane Sellers (5)	0	1	3
59. Walter Blum, Ruperto Donoso, Rene Douglas, David Gorman, Heliodoro Gustines, Ruben Hernandez, Jack Kaenel, Michael Kinane, Mike Manganello, George Martens, Donald Miller Jr.	1	0	0
70. Ray Broussard, Johnny Longden, Chris Rogers, Phil Rubbicco	0	2	0
74. Don MacBeth	0	1	2
75. Sam Boulmetis (4)	0	0	4
76. Robby Albarado, Paul Bailey, Hedley Woodhouse	0	1	1
79. Arnold Kirkland (3)	0	0	3
80. Raymond Adair, Fernando Alvarez, Herberto Castillo, Robbie Davis, Albert Delgado, Tony DeSpirito, Benny Feliciano, F. Fernandez, Charles Givens, George Hettinger, Herb Hinojosa, Dave Kassen, Kenny Knapp, Herb McCauley, Mike Miceli, Richard Migliore, Newbold Pierson, Jean-Luc Samyn, L.P. Sasso, Nick Shuk, John Velazquez, Mike Venezia	0	1	0
102. Larry Adams, Job Dean Jessop, Ralph Neves (2)	0	0	2
105. David Ashcroft, Vince Bracciale Jr., Ronald Baldwin, David Flores, Garrett Gomez, Howard Grant, Mike Luzzi, Jimmy Lynch, Carlos Marquez, Robert Martin, William McKeever, Jimmy Nichols, John Oldham, Al Popara, Randy Romero, Smokey Saunders, Mickey Solomone, Fernando Toro, Octavio Vergara (1)	0	0	1

Breeders' Cup-Placed Jockeys 1984-2003

Jockey	W	P	S
1. Pat Day (93)	12	17	11
2. Jerry Bailey (82)	14	8	10
3. Gary Stevens (72)	8	15	10
4. Chris McCarron (67)	9	12	7
5. Mike Smith (55)	10	6	3
6. Laffit Pincay Jr. (45)	7	4	9
7. Corey Nakatani (41)	5	7	7
8. Eddie Delahoussaye (40)	7	3	6
9. Angel Cordero (37)	4	7	7
10. Jose Santos (36)	7	2	4
11. Pat Valenzuela (31)	7	0	3
12. Alex Solis (30)	3	7	4
13. John Velazquez (22)	4	1	4
14. Craig Perret	4	2	1
15. Michael Kinane (21)	3	3	3
16. Frankie Dettori	3	2	4
17. Kent Desormeaux (20)	2	3	6
18. Jorge Velasquez (19)	2	5	1
19. Shane Sellers (18)	2	3	4
20. Pat Eddery (17)	2	3	3
21. Randy Romero	3	0	1
22. Jorge Chavez, David Flores (13)	2	2	1
24. Bill Shoemaker	1	2	2
25. Edgar Prado (10)	0	4	2
26. Walter Guerra, Freddie Head	2	0	1
28. Julie Krone (9)	1	2	1
29. John Murtagh, Yves St. Martin	2	0	0
31. Victor Espinoza	1	2	0
32. Cash Asmussen, Kieren Fallon (8)	1	1	2
34. Olivier Peslier, Walter Swinburn, Jacinto Vasquez (7)	1	1	1
37. Fernando Toro, Jose Valdivia Jr. (6)	1	0	2
39. Eric Legrix, Don MacBeth, Lester Piggott, Ray Sibille, Thierry Thulliez, Cornelio Velasquez (4)	1	0	0
45. Marco Castaneda, Garrett Gomez, Thierry Jarnet (3)	0	1	1
48. Donna Barton, Willie Carson, Steve Cauthen, Jean Cruguet, Tony D'Amico, Todd Kabel, Darrel McHargue, Jim McKnight, Dave Penna, Richard Quinn, Don Seymour, Jose Velez Jr. (2)	0	1	0
60. Gary Baze, Calvin Borel, Gary Carter, Perry Compton, Mark Guidry, Sandy Hawley, Darryll Holland, Michael Lee, Mike Luzzi, Richard Migliore, Michael Roberts, Jean-Luc Samyn, Santiago Soto, Gary Stahlbaum (1)	0	0	1

1946

	W	P	S
1. Eddie Arcaro (69)	12	7	7
2. Basil James (46)	7	6	6
3. Job Dean Jessop (42)	7	5	4
4. Warren Mehrtens (36)	6	3	6
5. Ted Atkinson (34)	5	5	4
6. Abelardo DeLara	7	1	3
7. Doug Dodson (33)	5	5	3
8. Johnny Longden (27)	2	6	7
9. Eric Guerin (24)	2	5	6
10. Jack Westrope (22)	4	3	0

1947

	W	P	S
1. Eddie Arcaro (75)	11	13	5
2. Doug Dodson (71)	16	1	5
3. Johnny Longden (46)	8	6	2
4. Job Dean Jessop (37)	5	5	7
5. Ovie Scurlock	7	3	2
6. Ruperto Donoso (36)	5	5	6
7. Jack Westrope (30)	3	6	6
8. Warren Mehrtens	6	2	1
9. Ted Atkinson (29)	4	3	7
10. Conn McCreary (27)	4	4	3

1948

	W	P	S
1. Ted Atkinson (73)	14	6	5
2. Eddie Arcaro (68)	14	4	4
3. Johnny Longden (37)	5	5	7
4. Conn McCreary (36)	2	11	6
5. Warren Mehrtens (33)	4	6	5
6. Doug Dodson (32)	5	4	4
7. Jack Westrope (28)	4	4	4
8. Newbold Pierson (27)	4	4	3
9. Bobby Permane (25)	4	3	3
10. Eric Guerin (24)	5	1	2

1949

	W	P	S
1. Steve Brooks (71)	14	7	1
2. Eddie Arcaro (64)	7	12	12
3. Ted Atkinson (58)	11	4	6
4. Eric Guerin (45)	9	3	3
5. David Gorman (35)	7	2	3
6. Ovie Scurlock, Hedley Woodhouse (33)	4	6	5
8. Johnny Longden (27)	4	5	1
9. Gordon Glisson (26)	3	5	4
10. Doug Dodson (25)	4	3	3

1950

	W	P	S
1. Eddie Arcaro (96)	18	9	6
2. Ted Atkinson	8	5	6
3. Eric Guerin (48)	6	8	8
4. Hedley Woodhouse (40)	8	3	2
5. Johnny Longden (39)	8	3	1
6. Steve Brooks (36)	4	7	6
7. Ovie Scurlock (32)	6	2	4
8. Doug Dodson (31)	4	5	5
9. Nick Combest (30)	5	3	4
10. Bill Boland (24)	4	4	0

1951

	W	P	S
1. Eddie Arcaro (88)	14	13	6
2. Eric Guerin (61)	10	5	11
3. Bill Shoemaker (53)	10	4	5
4. Ted Atkinson (47)	7	8	3
5. Ovie Scurlock (43)	8	3	5
6. David Gorman (29)	4	2	9
7. Steve Brooks (28)	5	3	2
8. Warren Mehrtens	5	2	2
9. Hedley Woodhouse (26)	3	4	6
10. Conn McCreary (24)	4	4	0

1952

	W	P	S
1. Eddie Arcaro (81)	16	5	7
2. Ted Atkinson (64)	9	9	10
3. Eric Guerin (59)	11	6	3
4. David Gorman (38)	7	3	4
5. Bill Boland (32)	5	4	4
6. Conn McCreary (29)	4	6	1
7. Henry E. Moreno (28)	6	1	2
8. Ray York (27)	3	6	3
9. Jimmy Stout (22)	4	1	4
10. Bennie Green (20)	3	1	6

1953

	W	P	S
1. Eric Guerin (77)	16	4	5
2. Eddie Arcaro (66)	11	9	4
3. Ted Atkinson (43)	10	1	1
4. Conn McCreary (37)	4	7	7
5. Hedley Woodhouse (36)	3	10	4
6. David Gorman (29)	2	7	7
7. Bill Shoemaker (28)	4	4	4
8. Johnny Adams, Johnny Longden, Jack Westrope (23)	4	3	1

1954

	W	P	S
1. Eddie Arcaro (78)	14	8	6
2. Eric Guerin (59)	11	3	9
3. Bill Shoemaker (45)	8	6	1
4. Hedley Woodhouse (40)	4	9	6
5. Ted Atkinson (35)	3	9	5
6. Bill Boland (28)	2	8	4
7. Ray York (27)	5	2	3
8. Johnny Longden (25)	4	3	3
9. Sam Boulmetis	5	0	4
10. Conn McCreary (24)	3	3	6

1955

	W	P	S
1. Eddie Arcaro (96)	18	9	6
2. Eric Guerin (54)	8	6	10
3. Hedley Woodhouse (49)	9	5	3
4. Ted Atkinson (33)	3	6	9
5. Johnny Longden (32)	6	2	4
6. Bill Shoemaker (29)	6	2	1
7. Bill Boland (28)	4	3	6
8. Angel Valenzuela	4	3	5
9. Paul Bailey (27)	3	5	5
10. Ray York (25)	4	4	1

1956

	W	P	S
1. Eddie Arcaro (68)	13	6	4
2. Bill Hartack (60)	10	7	6
3. Bill Shoemaker (44)	8	4	4
4. Bill Boland	7	6	3
5. Eric Guerin (43)	4	11	5
6. Hedley Woodhouse (42)	6	4	10
7. David Erb (37)	7	4	1
8. Ted Atkinson (35)	5	4	7
9. Ismael Valenzuela (32)	4	7	2
10. Johnny Longden (30)	5	4	2

1957

	W	P	S
1. Bill Hartack (91)	19	6	3
2. Bill Shoemaker (81)	15	9	3
3. Eddie Arcaro (72)	13	8	4
4. Bobby Ussery (35)	7	1	5
5. Ralph Neves (34)	5	3	8
6. Bill Boland (26)	3	6	2
7. Ismael Valenzuela (24)	4	3	2
8. Eldon Nelson (22)	4	1	4
9. Hedley Woodhouse	3	4	1
10. Eric Guerin (21)	2	4	5

1958

	W	P	S
1. Bill Shoemaker (93)	19	6	5
2. Eddie Arcaro (64)	12	5	6
3. Ismael Valenzuela (43)	6	7	5
4. Bill Hartack (42)	8	3	4
5. Bill Boland (34)	3	8	6
6. Eric Guerin (31)	4	4	7
7. Bobby Ussery (29)	4	5	3
8. Bill Harmatz (26)	5	2	2
9. John Ruane (23)	4	2	3
10. Sam Boulmetis (22)	3	4	2

1959

	W	P	S
1. Bill Shoemaker (90)	15	12	6
2. Manny Ycaza (57)	12	3	3
3. Eddie Arcaro (49)	8	5	7
4. Tommy Barrow	7	3	0
5. Sam Boulmetis (34)	5	5	4
6. Bill Hartack (33)	3	7	7
7. Bill Boland	3	4	7
8. Bobby Ussery (27)	2	7	5
9. Henry E. Moreno (23)	3	4	3
10. Paul Bailey (21)	2	6	1

1960

	W	P	S
1. Manny Ycaza	10	7	6
2. Bill Hartack (60)	10	6	8
3. Eddie Arcaro (59)	11	4	7
4. Bill Shoemaker (58)	8	11	4
5. Bobby Ussery (39)	7	4	3
6. Johnny Sellers (38)	7	4	2
7. Eric Guerin (37)	6	4	5
8. Ismael Valenzuela (29)	3	7	3
9. Sam Boulmetis (26)	3	4	6
10. Ray Broussard (22)	3	2	6

1961

	W	P	S
1. Bill Shoemaker (70)	12	8	6
2. Eddie Arcaro (68)	12	7	6
3. Johnny Sellers (57)	10	6	5
4. Johnny Longden (46)	9	3	4
5. John Rotz (40)	6	5	6
6. Manny Ycaza	6	6	2
7. Bobby Ussery (38)	5	6	6
8. Braulio Baeza	4	2	4
9. Ismael Valenzuela (24)	3	4	4
10. Bill Hartack (20)	4	1	2

1962

	W	P	S
1. Bill Shoemaker (87)	16	9	5
2. Manny Ycaza (64)	10	8	8
3. Johnny Sellers	7	7	7
4. Braulio Baeza (49)	6	8	9
5. Ismael Valenzuela (39)	5	7	5
6. Johnny Longden	7	0	1
7. John Rotz (29)	4	5	3
8. Bobby Ussery (26)	3	4	6
9. Bill Harmatz (25)	5	0	5
10. Larry Adams (23)	4	1	5

1963

	W	P	S
1. Bill Shoemaker (73)	11	12	5
2. Ismael Valenzuela (63)	11	6	7
3. Braulio Baeza (61)	9	10	5
4. Manny Ycaza (44)	7	7	2
5. Bobby Ussery (43)	7	4	7
6. Herb Hinojosa (36)	6	5	2
7. John Rotz (35)	6	3	5
8. Bill Hartack (31)	5	3	5
9. Jimmy Combest (21)	3	3	3
10. Larry Adams (19)	3	1	5

1964

	W	P	S
1. Manny Ycaza (76)	14	10	10
2. Bill Shoemaker (70)	14	8	8
3. Braulio Baeza (39)	6	3	9
4. Walter Blum (37)	4	9	3
5. Howard Grant (36)	6	6	0
6. Ismael Valenzuela (35)	4	5	9
7. Bill Hartack, John Rotz (32)	5	4	4
9. Wayne Chambers (28)	4	4	4
10. Ray Broussard (23)	5	0	3

1965

	W	P	S
1. Braulio Baeza (61)	10	8	5
2. Bill Shoemaker (45)	7	6	5
3. Johnny Sellers (44)	7	5	6
4. Manny Ycaza (40)	6	4	8
5. Walter Blum	8	2	3
6. Bobby Ussery	7	3	5
7. Larry Adams (39)	5	7	5
8. John Rotz (31)	5	5	1
9. Don Pierce (27)	4	4	3
10. Kenny Church (23)	4	2	3

1966

	W	P	S
1. Bill Shoemaker (93)	17	11	3
2. Braulio Baeza (77)	13	9	7
3. John Rotz (51)	9	5	5
4. Manny Ycaza (41)	6	7	3
5. Walter Blum (39)	5	8	3
6. Don Pierce (27)	4	3	5
7. Larry Adams (25)	3	4	5
8. Don Brumfield (21)	4	1	3
9. Johnny Sellers	3	2	4
10. Bobby Ussery (20)	2	3	6

1967

	W	P	S
1. Bill Shoemaker (93)	19	6	5
2. Braulio Baeza (82)	16	8	2
3. Laffit Pincay Jr. (41)	7	5	3
4. Eddie Belmonte (37)	6	3	7
5. Bobby Ussery	5	5	5
6. Angel Cordero (35)	3	7	9
7. Bill Boland (31)	5	4	3
8. Earlie Fires (30)	5	5	0
9. Johnny Sellers (24)	4	4	0
10. Jerry Lambert (20)	3	3	2

1968

	W	P	S
1. Braulio Baeza (87)	17	7	5
2. Manny Ycaza (64)	11	8	4
3. John Rotz (47)	6	9	5
4. Laffit Pincay Jr. (40)	6	6	4
5. Angel Cordero (39)	3	13	1
6. Eddie Belmonte (38)	6	6	2
7. Ismael Valenzuela (30)	5	3	4
8. Jorge Velasquez (29)	5	2	5
9. Jerry Lambert (28)	6	1	2
10. Heliodoro Gustines (18)	4	0	2

1969

	W	P	S
1. Manny Ycaza (60)	10	7	6
2. Braulio Baeza (57)	9	8	5
3. Eddie Belmonte	7	7	3
4. Jorge Velasquez (45)	7	6	5
5. John Rotz (41)	8	3	3
6. Laffit Pincay Jr. (32)	5	5	2
7. Bill Shoemaker (28)	4	5	2
8. Bill Hartack (27)	5	2	3
9. Don Pierce (25)	5	2	1
10. Jesse Davidson (22)	5	0	2

1970

	W	P	S
1. Bill Shoemaker (54)	7	11	4
2. Laffit Pincay Jr. (53)	9	5	7
3. Jorge Velasquez (46)	7	7	4
4. Angel Cordero (41)	3	12	5
5. Eddie Belmonte (39)	7	4	3
6. John Rotz	5	3	5
7. Jacinto Vasquez (31)	2	8	7
8. Braulio Baeza (29)	4	5	3
9. Ron Turcotte (28)	6	1	2
10. Jerry Lambert (26)	5	3	0

1971

	W	P	S
1. Bill Shoemaker (73)	15	4	5
2. Laffit Pincay Jr. (56)	10	5	6
3. Ron Turcotte	8	1	2
4. Braulio Baeza (36)	4	9	2
5. Bobby Woodhouse (32)	6	3	2
6. Jacinto Vasquez	5	2	3
7. Jorge Velasquez	4	4	3
8. Angel Cordero (27)	2	6	7
9. John Rotz (25)	4	3	3
10. Chuck Baltazar (22)	5	0	2

1972

	W	P	S
1. Bill Shoemaker (72)	14	6	4
2. Ron Turcotte (71)	13	7	5
3. Laffit Pincay Jr.	8	7	4
4. Angel Cordero (50)	8	5	8
5. Braulio Baeza (39)	7	4	3
6. Eddie Maple (38)	5	6	6
7. Victor Tejada	4	3	3
8. Don Pierce (25)	3	4	5
9. Eddie Belmonte (23)	3	5	1
10. Jerry Lambert (22)	4	2	2

1973

	W	P	S
1. Ron Turcotte (61)	11	6	5
2. Braulio Baeza	11	5	2
3. Laffit Pincay Jr. (56)	9	7	6
4. Jorge Velasquez (49)	9	3	7
5. Jacinto Vasquez (47)	8	5	5
6. Angel Cordero (39)	6	4	7
7. Don Pierce	5	4	3
8. Bill Shoemaker (31)	5	3	5
9. Angel Santiago (20)	2	3	6
10. John Rotz (19)	1	5	5

Four Footed Fotos courtesy of Churchill Downs

Among Jerry Bailey's most noteworthy feats in the saddle are a record 14 victories in Breeders' Cup races, including a triumph aboard Black Tie Affair in the 1991 Classic that earned Horse of the Year acclaim for his mount.

1974

	W	P	S
1. Laffit Pincay Jr. (77)	15	6	5
2. Angel Cordero (60)	10	7	6
3. Bill Shoemaker (53)	9	7	3
4. Jorge Velasquez (48)	7	7	6
5. Heliodoro Gustines	9	1	4
6. Miguel Rivera (42)	8	3	4
7. Jacinto Vasquez (39)	7	3	5
8. Don Pierce (37)	4	7	7
9. Fernando Toro (33)	4	6	5
10. Ron Turcotte (24)	4	3	2

1975

	W	P	S
1. Bill Shoemaker (68)	13	4	8
2. Jacinto Vasquez (62)	11	7	4
3. Braulio Baeza (57)	9	9	3
4. Laffit Pincay Jr. (42)	7	3	8
5. Darrel McHargue (38)	7	4	2
6. Don Pierce (36)	5	7	2
7. Jean Cruguet (31)	2	9	5
8. Sandy Hawley (28)	3	6	4
9. Heliodoro Gustines (26)	5	2	2
10. Jorge Tejeira (24)	5	1	2

1976

	W	P	S
1. Bill Shoemaker (65)	13	5	3
2. Angel Cordero (50)	6	7	12
3. Sandy Hawley (49)	10	3	3
4. Eddie Maple (46)	7	6	6
5. Braulio Baeza (44)	8	6	0
6. Darrel McHargue (38)	5	7	4
7. Fernando Toro (37)	5	5	7
8. Jorge Velasquez (33)	6	3	3
9. Laffit Pincay Jr. (32)	5	6	0
10. Jean Cruguet (27)	4	4	3

1977

	W	P	S
1. Bill Shoemaker (54)	9	8	2
2. Angel Cordero (53)	8	6	9
3. Sandy Hawley (46)	7	6	6
4. Laffit Pincay Jr. (42)	7	3	8
5. Steve Cauthen (41)	8	1	7
6. Jean Cruguet	8	3	2
7. Eddie Maple (40)	5	7	6
8. Darrel McHargue (38)	5	7	4
9. Jorge Velasquez (36)	4	5	10
10. Ruben Hernandez (23)	4	2	3

1978

	W	P	S
1. Jorge Velasquez (82)	16	6	6
2. Darrel McHargue (62)	9	10	6
3. Angel Cordero (57)	8	8	9
4. Steve Cauthen (54)	9	6	6
5. Bill Shoemaker (51)	9	5	5
6. Jeffery Fell (42)	7	6	2
7. Eddie Delahoussaye (32)	5	6	0
8. Ruben Hernandez (30)	3	7	4
9. Eddie Maple (29)	4	4	5
10. Don Pierce (28)	5	3	2

1979

	W	P	S
1. Laffit Pincay Jr. (68)	10	10	8
2. Jorge Velasquez (64)	12	6	4
3. Bill Shoemaker (60)	9	10	4
4. Angel Cordero (47)	7	8	3
5. Sandy Hawley (45)	7	5	7
6. Chris McCarron (41)	6	5	7
7. Sam Maple (37)	7	4	1
8. Jacinto Vasquez (36)	6	5	2
9. Jeffery Fell (32)	3	7	6
10. Darrel McHargue (29)	3	8	1

1980

	W	P	S
1. Laffit Pincay Jr. (59)	8	8	11
2. Bill Shoemaker (53)	11	1	7
3. Eddie Delahoussaye (49)	10	4	1
4. Jeffery Fell	7	2	7
5. Jacinto Vasquez	6	5	5
6. Chris McCarron	5	8	3
7. Jorge Velasquez (39)	5	7	5
8. Angel Cordero (37)	3	10	5
9. Ruben Hernandez (33)	6	4	1
10. Eddie Maple (29)	5	3	3

1981

	W	P	S
1. Bill Shoemaker (57)	9	8	5
2. Laffit Pincay Jr. (56)	11	5	2
3. Chris McCarron (46)	7	8	2
4. Jorge Velasquez (45)	7	6	5
5. Angel Cordero (40)	5	5	10
6. Eddie Maple (38)	6	5	4
7. Cash Asmussen (34)	6	4	2
8. Jeffery Fell (28)	4	6	0
9. Darrel McHargue (25)	3	5	3
10. Ruben Hernandez (24)	4	2	4

1982

	W	P	S
1. Laffit Pincay Jr. (63)	11	6	7
2. Eddie Delahoussaye	11	7	2
3. Bill Shoemaker (60)	9	9	6
4. Angel Cordero (56)	7	10	8
5. Jorge Velasquez (42)	5	7	8
6. Eddie Maple (34)	4	7	4
7. Jeffery Fell (32)	6	4	0
8. Chris McCarron	4	4	3
9. Ruben Hernandez (27)	4	2	7
10. Ray Sibille (26)	5	2	2

1983

	W	P	S
1. Eddie Maple (61)	12	3	7
2. Laffit Pincay Jr. (58)	9	6	10
3. Chris McCarron (57)	6	16	1
4. Angel Cordero (50)	8	6	6
5. Jorge Velasquez (43)	8	3	5
6. Pat Day (42)	6	8	2
7. Eddie Delahoussaye (41)	7	5	3
8. Jacinto Vasquez (40)	7	4	4
9. Bill Shoemaker (37)	7	3	3
10. Terry Lipham (20)	4	1	2

1984

	W	P	S
1. Laffit Pincay Jr. (70)	13	5	8
2. Angel Cordero (62)	7	13	8
3. Eddie Maple (51)	8	7	5
4. Chris McCarron (50)	9	4	6
5. Eddie Delahoussaye (47)	7	7	5
6. Pat Day (41)	6	7	3
7. Jorge Velasquez (37)	3	9	7
8. Don MacBeth (31)	6	2	3
9. Jerry Bailey (25)	6	0	1
10. Pat Valenzuela (24)	5	2	0

1985

	W	P	S
1. Laffit Pincay Jr. (77)	13	9	7
2. Jorge Velasquez (62)	9	10	6
3. Chris McCarron (61)	10	10	1
4. Don MacBeth (51)	9	4	7
5. Angel Cordero (46)	8	3	8
6. Eddie Maple (40)	4	10	4
7. Pat Day (28)	3	5	6
8. Jacinto Vasquez	4	2	5
9. Bill Shoemaker (25)	3	4	5
10. Jean-Luc Samyn (22)	5	0	2

1986

	W	P	S
1. Chris McCarron (66)	11	6	10
2. Pat Day (59)	10	7	5
3. Bill Shoemaker (55)	8	8	7
4. Gary Stevens (51)	6	10	7
5. Jose Santos (44)	8	4	4
6. Laffit Pincay Jr. (43)	6	7	5
7. Randy Romero (42)	8	4	2
8. Jorge Velasquez (37)	4	8	5
9. Eddie Maple (34)	3	8	6
10. Angel Cordero (32)	4	6	4

1987

	W	P	S
1. Angel Cordero (85)	14	10	9
2. Pat Day (67)	13	5	5
3. Laffit Pincay Jr. (52)	7	8	8
4. Jose Santos (51)	8	7	5
5. Chris McCarron (48)	9	4	4
6. Bill Shoemaker (36)	6	4	4
7. Gary Stevens (35)	4	9	1
8. Randy Romero (34)	6	2	6
9. Craig Perret (33)	6	4	1
10. Eddie Maple (27)	4	4	3

1988

	W	P	S
1. Chris McCarron	16	2	4
2. Angel Cordero (72)	13	5	10
3. Gary Stevens (59)	8	12	3
4. Pat Day (55)	8	10	3
5. Jose Santos	7	8	6
6. Randy Romero (50)	6	10	6
7. Laffit Pincay Jr. (38)	5	5	8
8. Eddie Delahoussaye (34)	7	1	4
9. Bill Shoemaker (29)	2	8	5
10. Eddie Maple (25)	4	2	5

1989

	W	P	S
1. Pat Day (78)	13	11	4
2. Angel Cordero (76)	14	6	8
3. Jose Santos (73)	10	11	11
4. Chris McCarron	8	4	6
5. Laffit Pincay Jr. (46)	7	7	4
6. Eddie Delahoussaye (45)	7	7	3
7. Pat Valenzuela (41)	8	4	1
8. Gary Stevens (32)	3	7	6
9. Jacinto Vasquez (29)	4	5	3
10. Craig Perret (27)	4	3	5

1990

	W	P	S
1. Jose Santos (79)	14	8	7
2. Gary Stevens	11	5	3
3. Craig Perret (57)	7	11	7
4. Jerry Bailey (44)	7	5	6
5. Pat Day (42)	9	2	2
6. Chris McCarron (38)	5	5	8
7. Angel Cordero (36)	3	6	12
8. Eddie Delahoussaye (35)	5	7	1
9. Pat Valenzuela (27)	4	4	3
10. Randy Romero (25)	5	2	1

1991

	W	P	S
1. Eddie Delahoussaye (72)	13	6	8
2. Chris McCarron (66)	7	17	4
3. Gary Stevens (60)	10	5	10
4. Jerry Bailey (48)	7	7	6
5. Pat Day (44)	7	5	6
6. Craig Perret (42)	7	3	8
7. Angel Cordero (38)	6	5	4
8. Jose Santos (37)	6	5	3
9. Pat Valenzuela (36)	8	1	2
10. Mike Smith (31)	4	6	3

1992

	W	P	S
1. Chris McCarron (77)	14	9	3
2. Jerry Bailey (60)	11	5	6
3. Pat Day (58)	10	6	6
4. Kent Desormeaux (56)	11	3	6
5. Pat Valenzuela (44)	6	7	6
6. Eddie Delahoussaye (43)	6	7	5
7. Mike Smith (35)	4	7	5
8. Chris Antley (34)	4	5	8
9. Gary Stevens (32)	3	6	8
10. Herb McCauley (31)	5	4	3

1993

	W	P	S
1. Chris McCarron (96)	15	15	6
2. Mike Smith (70)	13	6	6
3. Jerry Bailey (60)	9	9	6
4. Kent Desormeaux (51)	8	6	7
5. Eddie Delahoussaye	7	5	3
6. Gary Stevens (41)	5	6	9
7. Laffit Pincay Jr. (35)	7	3	1
8. Jose Santos (34)	6	4	2
9. Herb McCauley (30)	4	6	2
10. Corey Nakatani (27)	5	1	5

1994

	W	P	S
1. Mike Smith (101)	23	3	3
2. Pat Day (70)	13	6	6
3. Kent Desormeaux (59)	11	6	3
4. Chris McCarron (58)	6	11	12
5. Gary Stevens	8	7	4
6. Jerry Bailey (50)	6	9	8
7. Corey Nakatani	6	5	6
8. Jose Santos (40)	6	4	8
9. Eddie Delahoussaye (35)	3	9	5
10. Craig Perret (21)	1	7	3

1995

	W	P	S
1. Gary Stevens (88)	18	6	4
2. Jerry Bailey (84)	14	12	4
3. Corey Nakatani (79)	12	11	9
4. Mike Smith (54)	10	3	8
5. Pat Day (52)	8	8	4
6. Chris McCarron (47)	5	10	7
7. Kent Desormeaux (36)	6	4	4
8. Robbie Davis (32)	6	2	4
9. Eddie Delahoussaye (30)	3	6	6
10. Julie Krone (28)	3	8	0

1996

	W	P	S
1. Chris McCarron (77)	11	11	11
2. Jerry Bailey (74)	12	9	8
3. Corey Nakatani (58)	11	5	4
4. Mike Smith (56)	9	6	8
5. Gary Stevens (53)	5	12	9
6. Pat Day (42)	4	10	6
7. John Velazquez (39)	8	3	1
8. Shane Sellers	5	4	5
9. Jose Santos (33)	3	9	3
10. Alex Solis (31)	4	2	11

1997

	W	P	S
1. Jerry Bailey (83)	15	5	13
2. Gary Stevens (73)	12	9	7
3. Mike Smith (64)	9	12	4
4. Alex Solis (62)	10	7	8
5. Corey Nakatani (55)	7	10	7
6. Pat Day (50)	7	6	10
7. Chris McCarron (49)	5	10	9
8. Shane Sellers (45)	7	7	3
9. Kent Desormeaux (44)	8	3	6
10. Jorge Chavez (23)	4	2	3

1998

	W	P	S
1. Jerry Bailey (91)	16	11	5
2. Gary Stevens (69)	12	7	7
3. Kent Desormeaux (62)	11	6	6
4. Corey Nakatani (61)	9	9	7
5. Chris McCarron (59)	7	13	5
6. Pat Day (40)	6	2	12
7. John Velazquez (38)	6	5	4
8. Shane Sellers (33)	6	2	5
9. Alex Solis (31)	3	6	7
10. Mike Smith (29)	6	2	1

1999

	W	P	S
1. Jerry Bailey (89)	17	7	7
2. Jorge Chavez (77)	15	8	1
3. Pat Day (66)	9	11	8
4. David Flores (56)	9	9	2
5. Alex Solis (42)	5	9	4
6. Kent Desormeaux (39)	6	4	7
7. Chris McCarron	5	6	5
8. Shane Sellers,	5	4	9
Gary Stevens (37)			
10. Chris Antley (31)	6	2	3

2000

	W	P	S
1. Jerry Bailey (81)	16	5	7
2. Pat Day (65)	11	9	3
3. Chris McCarron (55)	9	8	3
4. Corey Nakatani (54)	9	4	10
5. Shane Sellers (50)	8	6	6
6. Kent Desormeaux (47)	7	7	5
7. Jorge Chavez (41)	5	7	7
8. Victor Espinoza (34)	5	6	2
9. Edgar Prado (33)	4	6	5
10. Alex Solis (31)	4	5	5

2001

	W	P	S
1. Jerry Bailey (85)	13	13	7
2. Gary Stevens (56)	11	3	6
3. Chris McCarron (52)	10	4	4
4. Jorge Chavez (47)	4	12	7
5. Victor Espinoza	6	6	5
6. John Velazquez (41)	6	5	7
7. Edgar Prado	6	5	4
8. Eddie Delahoussaye (38)	3	11	4
9. Alex Solis (35)	5	5	5
10. Corey Nakatani (34)	4	6	6

2002

	W	P	S
1. Jerry Bailey (82)	14	8	10
2. Edgar Prado (66)	11	9	4
3. John Velazquez (59)	10	6	7
4. Mike Smith (49)	10	4	1
5. Jorge Chavez (46)	8	5	4
6. Kent Desormeaux (38)	6	5	4
7. Pat Day	6	5	2
8. Alex Solis (36)	6	4	4
9. Pat Valenzuela (35)	4	6	7
10. Victor Espinoza (27)	3	6	3

2003

	W	P	S
1. Jerry Bailey (149)	28	15	7
2. Edgar Prado (69)	11	11	3
3. Alex Solis (46)	6	6	10
4. Pat Valenzuela (44)	7	7	2
5. John Velazquez (42)	4	10	6
6. Robby Albarado	5	4	4
7. Jose Santos (32)	4	4	8
8. Gary Stevens (29)	4	3	7
9. Pat Day	5	2	3
10. David Flores (27)	4	5	1

Jockeys' Resumes

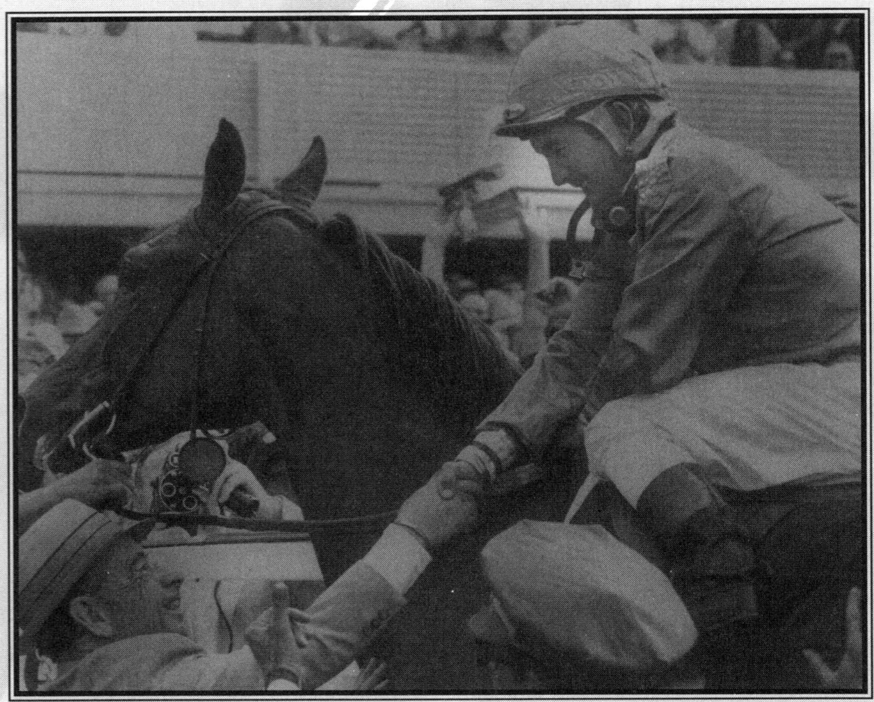

Photo courtesy of Del Mar Thoroughbred Club

Johnny Longden, who won 6,032 races, was the first to congratulate Bill Shoemaker on his record-breaking 6,033rd triumph aboard Dares J on September 7, 1970, at Del Mar. Shoemaker retired with a record 8,833 victories, which subsequently was exceeded by Laffit Pincay Jr., but no modern rider has approached Shoemaker's 357 triumphs in major races.

Jockeys' Victories In Major North American Races 1946-2003

RAYMOND ADAIR

1951: Blue Grass Stakes (Mameluke)

JOHNNY ADAMS

1946: Washington Park Futurity (Education)
Santa Anita Handicap (War Knight)
Excelsior Handicap (Fighting Step)
1947: Hopeful Stakes (Relic)
Coaching Club American Oaks (Harmonica)
1948: Hollywood Gold Cup (Shannon II)
1949: San Juan Capistrano Handicap (Miss Grillo)
1951: Kentucky Jockey Club Stakes (Sub Fleet)
Santa Susana Stakes (Ruth Lily)
1953: Breeders' Futurity (Hasty Road)
Kentucky Jockey Club Stakes (Hasty Road)
Arlington Lassie Stakes (Queen Hopeful)
Princess Pat Stakes (Queen Hopeful)
1954: Kentucky Jockey Club Stakes (Prince Noor)
Preakness Stakes (Hasty Road)
1955: Everglades Stakes (Prince Noor)
Widener Handicap (Hasty Road)
Gulfstream Park Handicap (Mister Black)
Hialeah Turf Handicap (Stan)
Arlington Handicap (Platan)
1956: Bougainvillea Turf Handicap (Summer Solstice)

LARRY ADAMS

1960: John B. Campbell Handicap (Yes You Will)
Carter Handicap (Yes You Will)
1961: Grey Lag Handicap (Mail Order)
1962: Black Helen Handicap (Seven Thirty)
Delaware Handicap (Seven Thirty)
Flamingo Stakes (Prego)
Jersey Derby (Jaipur)
1963: Sapling Stakes (Mr. Brick)
Gotham Stakes (Debbysman)
Gallant Fox Handicap (Sunrise Flight)
1964: Mother Goose Stakes (Sceree)
1965: Spinaway Stakes (Moccasin)
Matron Stakes (Moccasin)
Selima Stakes (Moccasin)
Gardenia Stakes (Moccasin)
Vosburgh Handicap (R. Thomas)
1966: United Nations Handicap (Assagai)
Man o' War Stakes (Assagai)
Bowling Green Handicap (Moontrip)
1969: Dwyer Handicap (Gleaming Light)
Grey Lag Handicap (Bushido)
1970: Vosburgh Handicap (Best Turn)
1971: Monmouth Invitational Handicap (West Coast Scout)
1973: Gulfstream Park Handicap (West Coast Scout)
Amory L. Haskell Handicap (West Coast Scout)
Illinois Derby (Big Whippendeal)
1974: New Orleans Handicap (Smooth Dancer)

ANTHONY AGNELLO

1972: John B. Campbell Handicap (Boone the Great)

LESLIE AHRENS

1977: Illinois Derby (Flag Officer)

ROBBY ALBARADO

1998: Early Times Turf Classic (Joyeaux Danseur)
Three Chimneys Spinster Stakes (Banshee Breeze)
1999: Louisiana Derby (Kimberlite Pipe)
Mother Goose Stakes (Dreams Gallore)
Hollywood Futurity (Captain Steve)
2000: Arkansas Derby (Graeme Hall)
2002: Walmac Int. Alcibiades Stakes (Westerly Breeze)
2003: Pimlico Special (Mineshaft)
Suburban Handicap (Mineshaft)
Woodward Stakes (Mineshaft)
Jockey Club Gold Cup (Mineshaft)
Ashland Stakes (Elloluv)

KEITH ALLEN

1984: Illinois Derby (Delta Trace)
1985: Hutcheson Stakes (Banner Bob)
Jim Beam Stakes (Banner Bob)

GONCALINO ALMEIDA

1995: Hollywood Turf Handicap (Earl of Barking)
1998: Santa Margarita Handicap (Toda Una Dama)

FERNANDO ALVAREZ

1964: Jersey Derby (Roman Brother)
American Derby (Roman Brother)
1966: Del Mar Futurity (Ruken)
1967: Santa Anita Derby (Ruken)
Display Handicap (Quicken Tree)
1969: Charles H. Strub Stakes (Dignitas)
1970: Santa Anita Handicap (Quicken Tree)
San Juan Capistrano Handicap (Quicken Tree)
1971: Oak Leaf Stakes (Sporting Lass)
San Luis Rey Handicap (Try Sheep)
1975: Ladies Handicap (Tizna)

JOSE AMY

1976: Carter Handicap (Due Diligence)

IRVING ANDERSON

1946: Arlington Lassie Stakes (Four Winds)

PETE ANDERSON

1951: Louisiana Derby (Whirling Bat)
1954: Breeders' Futurity (Brother Tex)
1956: Pimlico Futurity (Missile)
1957: Top Flight Handicap (Plotter)
1958: Acorn Stakes (Big Effort)
Delaware Oaks (Big Effort)
Belmont Stakes (Cavan)
Massachusetts Handicap (Promised Land)
1959: Hialeah Turf Cup (Tudor Era)
1960: Bowling Green Handicap (Amber Morn)
1964: Ohio Derby (National)
1966: Monmouth Handicap (Bold Bidder)
Washington Park Handicap (Bold Bidder)
Hawthorne Gold Cup (Bold Bidder)
Gotham Stakes (Stupendous)
1967: Arlington-Washington Futurity (T.V. Commercial)
1969: Amory L. Haskell Handicap (Verbatim)
Whitney Stakes (Verbatim)
Pan American Handicap (Hibernian)
1970: Coaching Club American Oaks (Missile Belle)
Gazelle Handicap (Missile Belle)

CHRIS ANTLEY

1985: Sorority Stakes (Lazer Show)
1987: Philip H. Iselin Handicap (Bordeaux Bob)
1988: Gotham Stakes (Private Terms)
Wood Memorial Stakes (Private Terms)
1990: Carter Handicap (Dancing Spree)
Woodward Handicap (Dispersal)
1991: Blue Grass Stakes (Strike the Gold)
Kentucky Derby (Strike the Gold)
1992: Mother Goose Stakes (Turnback the Alarm)
Coaching Club American Oaks (Turnback the Alarm)
Alabama Stakes (November Snow)
Futurity Stakes (Strolling Along)
1993: Shuvee Handicap (Turnback the Alarm)
Hempstead Handicap (Turnback the Alarm)
Go for Wand Stakes (Turnback the Alarm)
Philip H. Iselin Handicap (Valley Crossing)
1994: Santa Anita Handicap (Stuka)
Swaps Stakes (Silver Music)
Hollywood Derby (River Flyer)
1995: Acorn Stakes (Cat's Cradle)
Milady Handicap (Pirate's Revenge)
1996: Las Virgenes Stakes (Antespend)
Santa Anita Oaks (Antespend)
San Antonio Handicap (Alphabet Soup)
1997: Woodbine Mile (Geri)
1999: Kentucky Derby (Charismatic)
Preakness Stakes (Charismatic)
Woodward Stakes (River Keen)
Jockey Club Gold Cup (River Keen)
Eddie Read Handicap (Joe Who)
King's Bishop Stakes (Forestry)

EDDIE ARCARO

1946: Futurity Stakes (First Flight)
Matron Stakes (First Flight)
Pimlico Special (Assault)
Westchester Handicap (Assault)
Demoiselle Stakes (Carolyn A.)
Marguerite Stakes (Cosmic Missile)
Acorn Stakes (Earshot)
Top Flight Handicap (Sicily)
Withers Stakes (Hampden)
Blue Grass Stakes (Lord Boswell)
Jerome Handicap (Mahout)
Jockey Club Gold Cup (Pavot)
1947: Dixie Handicap (Assault)
Suburban Handicap (Assault)
Brooklyn Handicap (Assault)
Manhattan Handicap (Rico Monte)
New York Handicap (Rico Monte)
Saratoga Special (Better Self)
Cowdin Stakes (My Request)
Astoria Stakes (Mackinaw)
Beldame Handicap (But Why Not)
Wood Memorial Stakes (Phalanx)
Wood Memorial Stakes (I Will)
1948: Kentucky Derby (Citation)
Preakness Stakes (Citation)
Belmont Stakes (Citation)
American Derby (Citation)
Stars and Stripes Handicap (Citation)
Jockey Club Gold Cup (Citation)
Pimlico Special (Citation)
San Antonio Handicap (Talon)
Santa Anita Handicap (Talon)
Frizette Stakes (Our Fleet)
Acorn Stakes (Watermill)
Saranac Handicap (Mount Marcy)
San Felipe Stakes (May Reward)
Fall Highweight Handicap (First Flight)
1949: Withers Stakes (Olympia)
Wood Memorial Stakes (Olympia)
Cowdin Stakes (Hill Prince)
Alabama Stakes (Adile)
Beldame Handicap (Miss Request)
Saranac Handicap (Sun Bahram)
Suburban Handicap (Vulcan's Forge)
1950: Withers Stakes (Hill Prince)
Wood Memorial Stakes (Hill Prince)
Preakness Stakes (Hill Prince)
American Derby (Hill Prince)
Jerome Handicap (Hill Prince)
Jockey Club Gold Cup (Hill Prince)
Sunset Handicap (Hill Prince)
Sapling Stakes (Battlefield)
Saratoga Special (Battlefield)
Tremont Stakes (Battlefield)
Futurity Stakes (Battlefield)
Santa Susana Stakes (Special Touch)
Monmouth Oaks (Siama)
Swift Stakes (Ferd)
Saranac Handicap (Sunglow)
Roseben Handicap (Olympia)
Massachusetts Handicap (Cochise)
Longacres Mile (Two and Twenty)
1951: Withers Stakes (Battlefield)
Dwyer Stakes (Battlefield)
Travers Stakes (Battlefield)
Kentucky Oaks (How)
Coaching Club American Oaks (How)
Preakness Stakes (Bold)
Saranac Handicap (Bold)
Astoria Stakes (Star-Enfin)
Alabama Stakes (Kiss Me Kate)
Santa Anita Derby (Rough'n Tumble)
San Carlos Handicap (Bolero)
Excelsior Handicap (Lotowhite)
New York Handicap (Hill Prince)
Stars and Stripes Handicap (Royal Governor)
1952: Kentucky Oaks (Real Delight)
Black-Eyed Susan Stakes (Real Delight)
Coaching Club American Oaks (Real Delight)
Arlington Matron Stakes (Real Delight)
Beldame Handicap (Real Delight)
Arlington Classic (Mark-Ye-Well)
American Derby (Mark-Ye-Well)
Lawrence Realization Stakes (Mark-Ye-Well)
Washington Park Futurity (Mr. Paradise)
Belmont Stakes (One Count)
San Felipe Handicap (Windy City II)
Kentucky Derby (Hill Gail)
Fall Highweight Handicap (Hitex)
San Carlos Handicap (To Market)
New York Handicap (Battlefield)
Santa Anita Maturity (Intent)
1953: Arlington Futurity (Hasty Road)
Washington Park Futurity (Hasty Road)
Santa Anita Handicap (Mark-Ye-Well)
Santa Anita Maturity (Mark-Ye-Well)
Kentucky Oaks (Bubbley)
Arlington Matron Handicap (Real Delight)
Santa Anita Derby (Chanlea)
Blue Grass Stakes (Correspondent)
American Derby (Native Dancer)
San Juan Capistrano Handicap (Intent)
New York Handicap (Crafty Admiral)
1954: Hopeful Stakes (Nashua)
Futurity Stakes (Nashua)
Selima Stakes (High Voltage)
Matron Stakes (High Voltage)
Jockey Club Gold Cup (High Gun)
Manhattan Handicap (High Gun)
Arlington Futurity (Royal Note)
Monmouth Oaks (Evening Out)
Alabama Stakes (Parlo)
Top Flight Handicap (Sunshine Nell)
Blue Grass Stakes (Goyamo)
San Antonio Handicap (Mark-Ye-Well)
Brooklyn Handicap (Invigorator)
Washington D.C. International (Fisherman)
1955: Flamingo Stakes (Nashua)
Florida Derby (Nashua)
Preakness Stakes (Nashua)
Belmont Stakes (Nashua)
Dwyer Stakes (Nashua)
Arlington Classic (Nashua)
Jockey Club Gold Cup (Nashua)
Withers Stakes (Traffic Judge)
Ohio Derby (Traffic Judge)
Jerome Handicap (Traffic Judge)
Woodward Stakes (Traffic Judge)
Acorn Stakes (High Voltage)
Delaware Oaks (High Voltage)
Vineland Handicap (High Voltage)
Champagne Stakes (Beau Fond)
Matron Stakes (Doubledogdare)
Monmouth Oaks (Misty Morn)
Brooklyn Handicap (High Gun)
1956: Widener Handicap (Nashua)
Suburban Handicap (Nashua)
Monmouth Handicap (Nashua)
Jockey Club Gold Cup (Nashua)
Sapling Stakes (King Hairan)
Hopeful Stakes (King Hairan)
Futurity Stakes (Bold Ruler)
Santa Margarita Handicap (Our Betters)
Wood Memorial Stakes (Head Man)
Westerner Stakes (Count of Honor)
American Derby (Swoon's Son)
Brooklyn Handicap (Dedicate)
Display Handicap (Midafternoon)
1957: Flamingo Stakes (Bold Ruler)
Wood Memorial Stakes (Bold Ruler)
Preakness Stakes (Bold Ruler)
Jerome Handicap (Bold Ruler)
Trenton Handicap (Bold Ruler)
Starlet Stakes (Old Pueblo)
Del Mar Futurity (Old Pueblo)
Metropolitan Handicap (Traffic Judge)
Suburban Handicap (Traffic Judge)
Remsen Stakes (Misty Flight)
Gazelle Handicap (Bayou)
Monmouth Handicap (Dedicate)
San Juan Capistrano Handicap (Corn Husker)
1958: Hopeful Stakes (First Landing)
Champagne Stakes (First Landing)
Garden State Stakes (First Landing)
Jerome Handicap (Warhead)
Roamer Handicap (Warhead)
Manhattan Handicap (Warhead)
Carter Handicap (Bold Ruler)
Suburban Handicap (Bold Ruler)
Monmouth Handicap (Bold Ruler)
Kentucky Oaks (Bug Brush)
Wood Memorial Stakes (Jewel's Reward)
Fall Highweight Handicap (Bull Strength)
1959: Woodward Stakes (Sword Dancer)
Jockey Club Gold Cup (Sword Dancer)
Saratoga Special (Irish Lancer)
Futurity Stakes (Weatherwise)
Spinaway Stakes (Irish Jay)
Everglades Stakes (First Landing)
Gotham Stakes (Atoll)
Lawrence Realization Stakes (Middle Brother)
1960: Jerome Handicap (Kelso)
Lawrence Realization Stakes (Kelso)
Hawthorne Gold Cup (Kelso)
Jockey Club Gold Cup (Kelso)
Grey Lag Handicap (Sword Dancer)
Suburban Handicap (Sword Dancer)
Woodward Stakes (Sword Dancer)
Monmouth Handicap (First Landing)
Santa Anita Maturity (First Landing)
Frizette Stakes (Bowl of Flowers)
Santa Margarita Handicap (Silver Spoon)
1961: Metropolitan Handicap (Kelso)
Suburban Handicap (Kelso)
Brooklyn Handicap (Kelso)
Woodward Stakes (Kelso)
Jockey Club Gold Cup (Kelso)
Whitney Handicap (Kelso)
Acorn Stakes (Bowl of Flowers)
Coaching Club American Oaks (Bowl of Flowers)
Spinster Stakes (Bowl of Flowers)
Hopeful Stakes (Jaipur)
Cowdin Stakes (Jaipur)
Massachusetts Handicap (Polylad)

RONALD ARDOIN

1980: New Orleans Handicap (Pool Court)
1981: Louisiana Downs Handicap (Shishkabob)
1996: Arkansas Derby (Zarb's Magic)

JAMIE ARELLANO

1973: Jersey Derby (Knightly Dawn)

FABIO ARGUELLO

1992: Kentucky Oaks (Luv Me Luv Me Not)

SHERMAN ARMSTRONG

1952: Alcibiades Stakes (Sweet Patootie)

DAVID ASHCROFT

1981: Illinois Derby (Paristo)

CASH ASMUSSEN

1979: Beldame Stakes (Waya)
1980: Ladies Handicap (Plankton)
Vosburgh Stakes (Plugged Nickle)
1981: Mother Goose Stakes (Wayward Lass)
Coaching Club American Oaks (Wayward Lass)
Dwyer Stakes (Noble Nashua)
Jerome Handicap (Noble Nashua)
Monmouth Handicap (Amber Pass)
Vosburgh Stakes (Guilty Conscience)
1982: Turf Classic (April Run)
Washington D.C. International (April Run)
1984: Hollywood Derby (Procida)
Washington D.C. International (Seattle Song)
1987: Laurel Futurity (Antiqua)
1988: Arlington Million (Mill Native)
1992: Arlington Million (Dear Doctor)
1993: Rothmans International Stakes (Husband)
1994: Turf Classic (Tikkanen)
1997: Breeders' Cup Mile (Spinning World)

TED ATKINSON

1946: Vosburgh Handicap (Coincidence)
Aqueduct Handicap (Coincidence)
Ladies Handicap (Athenia)
Travers Stakes (Natchez)
Lawrence Realization Stakes (School Tie)
1947: Beldame Handicap (Snow Goose)
Ladies Handicap (Snow Goose)
Top Flight Handicap (Rytina)
Excelsior Handicap (Coincidence)
1948: Pimlico Futurity (Capot)
Champagne Stakes (Capot)
Vagrancy Handicap (Conniver)
Brooklyn Handicap (Conniver)
Travers Stakes (Ace Admiral)
Lawrence Realization Stakes (Ace Admiral)
Remsen Stakes (Eternal World)
Cowdin Stakes (Algasir)
Astoria Stakes (Eternal Flag)
Matron Stakes (Myrtle Charm)
Alabama Stakes (Compliance)
Ladies Handicap (Miss Request)
Dwyer Stakes (My Request)
Manhattan Handicap (Loyal Legion)
1949: Preakness Stakes (Capot)
Belmont Stakes (Capot)
Jerome Handicap (Capot)
Pimlico Special (Capot)
McLennan Handicap (Coaltown)
Widener Handicap (Coaltown)
Futurity Stakes (Guillotine)
Spinaway Stakes (Sunday Evening)

Flamingo Stakes (Olympia)
Queens County Handicap (Three Rings)
Aqueduct Handicap (Wine List)
1950: Breeders' Futurity (Big Stretch)
Pimlico Futurity (Big Stretch)
Manhattan Handicap (One Hitter)
Pimlico Special (One Hitter)
Acorn Stakes (Siama)
Carter Handicap (Guillotine)
Brooklyn Handicap (My Request)
Aqueduct Handicap (Wine List)
1951: Arlington Classic (Hall of Fame)
American Derby (Hall of Fame)
Massachusetts Handicap (One Hitter)
Whitney Stakes (One Hitter)
Futurity Stakes (Tom Fool)
Monmouth Oaks (Ruddy)
Fall Highweight Handicap (Guillotine)
1952: Jerome Handicap (Tom Fool)
Grey Lag Handicap (Tom Fool)
Suburban Handicap (One Hitter)
Monmouth Handicap (One Hitter)
Frizette Stakes (Sweet Patootie)
Alabama Stakes (Lily White)
Santa Anita Derby (Hill Gail)
Discovery Handicap (Ancestor)
Carter Handicap (Northern Star)
1953: Metropolitan Handicap (Tom Fool)
Suburban Handicap (Tom Fool)
Carter Handicap (Tom Fool)
Brooklyn Handicap (Tom Fool)
Whitney Stakes (Tom Fool)
Pimlico Special (Tom Fool)
Frizette Stakes (Indian Legend)
New Castle Handicap (Grecian Queen)
Flamingo Stakes (Straight Face)
Vosburgh Handicap (Indian Land)
1954: Firenze Handicap (Parlo)
Everglades Stakes (Maharajah)
Suburban Handicap (Straight Face)
1955: Spinaway Stakes (Register)
Coaching Club American Oaks (High Voltage)
Wood Memorial Stakes (Nashua)
1956: Dwyer Handicap (Riley)
Lawrence Realization Stakes (Riley)
Tropical Handicap (Illusionist)
Grey Lag Handicap (Nashua)
Manhattan Handicap (Flying Fury)
1957: Carter Handicap (Portersville)
1958: Gallant Fox Handicap (Admiral Vee)

GUSTAVO AVILA

1971: Kentucky Derby (Canonero II)
Preakness Stakes (Canonero II)

BRAULIO BAEZA

1960: Washington Park Futurity (Crozier)
1961: Blue Grass Stakes (Sherluck)
Belmont Stakes (Sherluck)
Lawrence Realization Stakes (Sherluck)
Kentucky Oaks (My Portrait)
1962: Kentucky Jockey Club Stakes (Sky Gem)
Gardenia Stakes (Main Swap)
Wood Memorial Stakes (Admiral's Voyage)
Jerome Handicap (Black Beard)
Aqueduct Stakes (Crozier)
Manhattan Handicap (Tutankhamen)
1963: Blue Grass Stakes (Chateaugay)
Kentucky Derby (Chateaugay)
Belmont Stakes (Chateaugay)
Jerome Handicap (Chateaugay)
Santa Anita Handicap (Crozier)
San Carlos Handicap (Crozier)
Sanford Stakes (Delirium)
Saratoga Special (Duel)
Withers Stakes (Get Around)
1964: Sapling Stakes (Bold Lad)
Hopeful Stakes (Bold Lad)
Futurity Stakes (Bold Lad)
Champagne Stakes (Bold Lad)
Spinaway Stakes (Candalita)
San Carlos Handicap (Admiral's Voyage)
1965: Sapling Stakes (Buckpasser)
Hopeful Stakes (Buckpasser)
Arlington-Washington Futurity (Buckpasser)
Champagne Stakes (Buckpasser)
Woodward Stakes (Roman Brother)
Manhattan Handicap (Roman Brother)
Jockey Club Gold Cup (Roman Brother)
Saratoga Special (Impressive)
Mother Goose Stakes (Cordially)
Display Handicap (Brave Lad)
1966: Arlington Classic (Buckpasser)
American Derby (Buckpasser)
Travers Stakes (Buckpasser)
Lawrence Realization Stakes (Buckpasser)
Brooklyn Handicap (Buckpasser)
Woodward Stakes (Buckpasser)
Jockey Club Gold Cup (Buckpasser)
Champagne Stakes (Successor)
Garden State Stakes (Successor)
Spinster Stakes (Open Fire)
Ladies Handicap (Destro)
Jerome Handicap (Bold and Brave)
Metropolitan Handicap (Bold Lad)
1967: Sorority Stakes (Queen of the Stage)
Spinaway Stakes (Queen of the Stage)
Matron Stakes (Queen of the Stage)
Frizette Stakes (Queen of the Stage)
Withers Stakes (Dr. Fager)
Arlington Classic (Dr. Fager)
Hawthorne Gold Cup (Dr. Fager)
Vosburgh Handicap (Dr. Fager)
Saratoga Special (Vitriolic)
Champagne Stakes (Vitriolic)
Pimlico-Laurel Futurity (Vitriolic)
Metropolitan Handicap (Buckpasser)
Suburban Handicap (Buckpasser)
San Fernando Stakes (Buckpasser)
Hopeful Stakes (What a Pleasure)
Lawrence Realization Stakes (Successor)
1968: Californian Stakes (Dr. Fager)
Suburban Handicap (Dr. Fager)
Washington Park Handicap (Dr. Fager)
Vosburgh Handicap (Dr. Fager)
Whitney Stakes (Dr. Fager)
United Nations Handicap (Dr. Fager)
Sapling Stakes (Reviewer)
Saratoga Special (Reviewer)
Sanford Stakes (King Emperor)
Cowdin Stakes (King Emperor)
Lawrence Realization Stakes (Funny Fellow)
Gallant Fox Handicap (Funny Fellow)
Garden State Stakes (Beau Brummel)
Sorority Stakes (Big Advance)
Spinaway Stakes (Queen's Double)
Aqueduct Stakes (Damascus)
Hialeah Turf Cup (He's a Smoothie)
1969: Belmont Stakes (Arts and Letters)
Travers Stakes (Arts and Letters)
Woodward Stakes (Arts and Letters)
Jockey Club Gold Cup (Arts and Letters)
Hopeful Stakes (Irish Castle)
Monmouth Oaks (Gallant Bloom)
Illinois Derby (King of the Castle)
Arlington Classic (Ack Ack)
Donn Handicap (Funny Fellow)
1970: Black Helen Handicap (Taken Aback)
Top Flight Handicap (Shuvee)
American Derby (The Pruner)
Grey Lag Handicap (Arts and Letters)
1971: Matron Stakes (Numbered Account)
Frizette Stakes (Numbered Account)
Selima Stakes (Numbered Account)
Gardenia Stakes (Numbered Account)
1972: Withers Stakes (Key to the Mint)
Travers Stakes (Key to the Mint)
Brooklyn Handicap (Key to the Mint)
Whitney Stakes (Key to the Mint)
Woodward Stakes (Key to the Mint)
Canadian International Championship (Droll Role)
Washington D.C. International (Droll Role)
1973: San Felipe Handicap (Linda's Chief)
California Derby (Linda's Chief)
Pontiac Grand Prix Stakes (Linda's Chief)
Sorority Stakes (Irish Sonnet)
Acorn Stakes (Windy's Daughter)
Spinster Stakes (Susan's Girl)
Fountain of Youth Stakes (Shecky Greene)
Donn Handicap (Triumphant)
Suburban Handicap (Key to the Mint)
Hawthorne Gold Cup (Tri Jet)
Del Mar Handicap (Red Reality)
1974: Hopeful Stakes (Foolish Pleasure)
1975: Monmouth Invitational Handicap (Wajima)
Travers Stakes (Wajima)
Marlboro Cup Handicap (Wajima)
Champagne Stakes (Honest Pleasure)
Laurel Futurity (Honest Pleasure)
Matron Stakes (Optimistic Gal)
Frizette Stakes (Optimistic Gal)
Beldame Stakes (Susan's Girl)
Florida Derby (Prince Thou Art)
1976: Flamingo Stakes (Honest Pleasure)
Florida Derby (Honest Pleasure)
Blue Grass Stakes (Honest Pleasure)
Ashland Stakes (Optimistic Gal)
Kentucky Oaks (Optimistic Gal)
Withers Stakes (Sonkisser)
Donn Handicap (Foolish Pleasure)
Gulfstream Park Handicap (Hail the Pirates)

JERRY BAILEY

1977: Gulfstream Park Handicap (Strike Me Lucky)
Pan American Handicap (Gravelines)
1980: Delaware Handicap (Heavenly Ade)
1982: Hopeful Stakes (Copelan)
Futurity Stakes (Copelan)
Champagne Stakes (Copelan)
Jerome Handicap (Fit to Fight)
1983: Hopeful Stakes (Capitol South)
Dwyer Stakes (Au Point)
1984: Metropolitan Handicap (Fit to Fight)
Suburban Handicap (Fit to Fight)
Brooklyn Handicap (Fit to Fight)
Everglades Stakes (Time for a Change)
Flamingo Stakes (Time for a Change)
United Nations Handicap (Hero's Honor)
1986: Acorn Stakes (Lotka)
Travers Stakes (Wise Times)
1988: Arkansas Derby (Proper Reality)
Illinois Derby (Proper Reality)
Gulfstream Park Handicap (Jade Hunter)
Jerome Handicap (Evening Kris)
1989: Metropolitan Handicap (Proper Reality)
Philip H. Iselin Handicap (Proper Reality)
Withers Stakes (Fire Maker)
Maskette Stakes (Miss Brio)
Demoiselle Stakes (Rootentootenwooten)
1990: Cowdin Stakes (Scan)
Remsen Stakes (Scan)
Gulfstream Park Handicap (Mi Selecto)
Top Flight Handicap (Dreamy Mimi)
Jersey Derby (Yonder)
Futurity Stakes (Eastern Echo)
Super Derby (Home at Last)
1991: Jim Beam Stakes (Hansel)
Preakness Stakes (Hansel)
Belmont Stakes (Hansel)
Acorn Stakes (Meadow Star)
Mother Goose Stakes (Meadow Star)
Arlington-Washington Futurity (Caller I.D.)
Breeders' Cup Classic (Black Tie Affair)
1992: Hollywood Gold Cup (Sultry Song)
Whitney Handicap (Sultry Song)
Woodward Stakes (Sultry Song)
Florida Derby (Technology)
Haskell Invitational Handicap (Technology)
Arkansas Derby (Pine Bluff)
Sword Dancer Handicap (Fraise)
Go for Wand Stakes (Easy Now)
Jerome Handicap (Furiously)
Champagne Stakes (Sea Hero)
Frizette Stakes (Educated Risk)
1993: Kentucky Oaks (Dispute)
Gazelle Handicap (Dispute)
Beldame Stakes (Dispute)
Kentucky Derby (Sea Hero)
Travers Stakes (Sea Hero)
Top Flight Handicap (You'd Be Surprised)
Jerome Handicap (Schossberg)
Breeders' Cup Classic (Arcangues)
Remsen Stakes (Go for Gin)
1994: Gotham Stakes (Irgun)
Test Stakes (Twist Afleet)
Jerome Handicap (Prenup)
Vosburgh Stakes (Harlan)
Breeders' Cup Classic (Concern)
NYRA Mile Handicap (Cigar)
1995: Donn Handicap (Cigar)
Gulfstream Park Handicap (Cigar)
Oaklawn Handicap (Cigar)
Pimlico Special (Cigar)
Hollywood Gold Cup (Cigar)
Woodward Stakes (Cigar)
Jockey Club Gold Cup (Cigar)
Breeders' Cup Classic (Cigar)
Suburban Handicap (Key Contender)
Test Stakes (Chaposa Springs)
Jim Dandy Stakes (Composer)
Super Derby (Mecke)
Breeders' Cup Juvenile Fillies (My Flag)
Matriarch Stakes (Duda)
1996: Ashland Stakes (My Flag)
Coaching Club American Oaks (My Flag)
Gazelle Handicap (My Flag)

JERRY BAILEY *(Continued)*

Donn Handicap (Cigar)
Woodward Stakes (Cigar)
Gulfstream Park Handicap (Wekiva Springs)
Oaklawn Handicap (Geri)
Kentucky Derby (Grindstone)
Hempstead Handicap (Serena's Song)
Swaps Stakes (Victory Speech)
Matron Stakes (Sharp Cat)
Breeders' Cup Juvenile (Boston Harbor)
1997: Strub Stakes (Victory Speech)
Gulfstream Park Handicap (Mt. Sassafras)
Early Times Turf Classic (Always a Classic)
Brooklyn Handicap (Formal Gold)
Test Stakes (Fabulously Fast)
Whitney Handicap (Will's Way)
Alabama Stakes (Runup the Colors)
Beverly D. Stakes (Memories of Silver)
Ruffian Handicap (Tomisue's Delight)
Buick Pegasus Handicap (Behrens)
Matron Stakes (Beautiful Pleasure)
Man o' War Stakes (Influent)
Jockey Club Gold Cup (Skip Away)
Frizette Stakes (Silver Maiden)
Crown Royal Hollywood Derby (Subordination)
1998: Donn Handicap (Skip Away)
Gulfstream Park Handicap (Skip Away)
Pimlico Special (Skip Away)
Hollywood Gold Cup (Skip Away)
Philip H. Iselin Handicap (Skip Away)
Woodward Stakes (Skip Away)
Apple Blossom Handicap (Escena)
Vanity Handicap (Escena)
Coaching Club American Oaks (Banshee Breeze)
Alabama Stakes (Banshee Breeze)
Fountain of Youth Stakes (Lil's Lad)
Metropolitan Handicap (Wild Rush)
Man o' War Stakes (Daylami)
Frizette Stakes (Confessional)
Breeders' Cup Juvenile (Answer Lively)
Cigar Mile Handicap (Sir Bear)
1999: Ashland Stakes (Silverbulletday)
Alabama Stakes (Silverbulletday)
Gazelle Handicap (Silverbulletday)
Gulfstream Park Breeders' Cup Handicap (Yagli)
Manhattan Handicap (Yagli)
Apple Blossom Handicap (Banshee Breeze)
Go for Wand Handicap (Banshee Breeze)
Flower Bowl Invitational Handicap (Soaring Softly)
Breeders' Cup Filly and Mare Turf (Soaring Softly)
Acorn Stakes (Three Ring)
Sempra Energy Hollywood Gold Cup (Real Quiet)
Frank J. De Francis Memorial Dash (Yes It's True)
Coaching Club American Oaks (On a Soapbox)
Whitney Handicap (Victory Gallop)
Hopeful Stakes (High Yield)
Ruffian Handicap (Catinca)
Breeders' Cup Juvenile Fillies (Cash Run)
2000: Matron Stakes (Raging Fever)
Frizette Stakes (Raging Fever)
Gulfstream Park BC Handicap (Royal Anthem)
San Juan Capistrano Handicap (Sunshine Street)
Preakness Stakes (Red Bullet)
Jim Dandy Stakes (Graeme Hall)
Beverly D. Stakes (Snow Polina)
Arlington Million (Chester House)
Hopeful Stakes (Yonaguska)
Garden City Breeders' Cup Handicap (Gaviola)
Del Mar Futurity (Flame Thrower)
Man o' War Stakes (Fantastic Light)
Vosburgh Stakes (Trippi)
Breeders' Cup Filly and Mare Turf (Perfect Sting)
Breeders' Cup Juvenile (Macho Uno)
Cigar Mile Handicap (El Corredor)
2001: Whitney Handicap (Lido Palace)
Woodward Stakes (Lido Palace)
King's Bishop Stakes (Squirtle Squirt)
Penske Auto Center BC Sprint (Squirtle Squirt)
Forego Handicap (Delaware Township)
Frank J. De Francis Mem. Dash (Delaware Township)
Donn Handicap (Captain Steve)
Kentucky Oaks (Flute)
Pimlico Special (Include)
Jim Dandy Stakes (Scorpion)
Flower Bowl Invitational Handicap (Lailani)
Jockey Club Gold Cup (Aptitude)
Hollywood Futurity (Siphonic)
2002: Las Virgenes Stakes (You)
Santa Anita Oaks (You)
Acorn Stakes (You)
Test Stakes (You)
Jim Dandy Stakes (Medaglia d'Oro)
Travers Stakes (Medaglia d'Oro)
Forego Handicap (Orientate)
NAPA Breeders' Cup Sprint (Orientate)
Stephen Foster Handicap (Street Cry)
Mother Goose Stakes (Nonsuch Bay)
Go for Wand Handicap (Dancethruthedawn)
Arlington Million (Beat Hollow)
Beldame Stakes (Imperial Gesture)
Cigar Mile Handicap (Congaree)
2003: Humana Distaff Handicap (Sightseek)
Ogden Phipps Handicap (Sightseek)
Go for Wand Handicap (Sightseek)
Beldame Stakes (Sightseek)
Florida Derby (Empire Maker)
Wood Memorial Stakes (Empire Maker)
Belmont Stakes (Empire Maker)
Strub Stakes (Medaglia d'Oro)
Oaklawn Handicap (Medaglia d'Oro)
Whitney Handicap (Medaglia d'Oro)
Las Virgenes Stakes (Composure)
Santa Anita Oaks (Composure)
Mother Goose Stakes (Spoken Fur)
Coaching Club American Oaks (Spoken Fur)
Metropolitan Handicap (Aldebaran)
Forego Handicap (Aldebaran)
Hollywood Gold Cup (Congaree)
Cigar Mile Handicap (Congaree)
Gulfstream Park BC 'Cap (Man From Wicklow)
Manhattan Handicap (Denon)
Test Stakes (Lady Tak)
Hopeful Stakes (Silver Wagon)
Ruffian Handicap (Wild Spirit)
Futurity Stakes (Cuvee)
Flower Bowl Invitational Stakes (Dimitrova)
Turf Classic (Sulamani)
Champagne Stakes (Birdstone)
NetJets Breeders' Cup Mile (Six Perfections)

PAUL BAILEY

1951: Washington Park Futurity (Oh Leo)
1952: Stars and Stripes Handicap (Royal Mustang)
1953: Louisiana Derby (Matagorda)
1954: New Orleans Handicap (Grover B.)
Michigan Mile (Spur On)
1955: Travers Stakes (Thinking Cap)
Lawrence Realization Stakes (Thinking Cap)
Roseben Handicap (Red Hannigan)
1956: Carter Handicap (Red Hannigan)
1957: Futurity Stakes (Jester)
Ladies Handicap (Rare Treat)
1958: Matron Stakes (Quill)
Gardenia Stakes (Quill)
1959: Mother Goose Stakes (Quill)
Delaware Handicap (Endine)
1960: Dwyer Handicap (Francis S.)
1961: Ladies Handicap (Mighty Fair)

WILLIAM BAILEY

1947: San Antonio Handicap (El Lobo)

BOBBY BAIRD

1948: Arlington Classic (Papa Redbird)
Arlington Handicap (Stud Poker)
1952: Will Rogers Stakes (Forelock)
1956: Louisiana Derby (Reaping Right)
Blue Grass Stakes (Toby B.)
1962: Arkansas Derby (Aeropolis)
1963: Louisiana Derby (City Line)
1969: Oaklawn Handicap (Listado)

C.J. BAKER

1980: Pennsylvania Derby (Lively King)

LESTER BALASKI

1946: Starlet Stakes (U Time)
1947: Hollywood Oaks (U Time)

RONALD BALDWIN

1953: Stars and Stripes Handicap (Abbe Sting)
1959: Arkansas Derby (Al Davelle)
1961: Louisiana Derby (Bass Clef)
1965: Hawthorne Gold Cup (Moss Vale)
1970: Louisiana Derby (Jim's Alibhi)

CHUCK BALTAZAR

1968: Arlington-Washington Lassie Stakes (Process Shot)
John B. Campbell Handicap (In Reality)
1970: John B. Campbell Handicap (Best Turn)
Canadian International Championship (Drumtop)
1971: Hialeah Turf Cup (Drumtop)
Bowling Green Handicap (Drumtop)
Spinaway Stakes (Numbered Account)
Wood Memorial Stakes (Good Behaving)
Pontiac Grand Prix Stakes (Son Ange)
1972: Gotham Stakes (Freetex)
1974: Fountain of Youth Stakes (Green Gambados)

R.L. BARNETT

1959: Arlington Matron Handicap (Wiggle II)

CARLOS BARRERA

1972: Gulfstream Park Handicap (Executioner)
United Nations Handicap (Acclimatization)
1974: Jersey Derby (Better Arbitor)

TOMMY BARROW

1950: Kentucky Jockey Club Stakes (Pur Sang)
1955: Michigan Mile (Greatest)
1959: San Carlos Handicap (Hillsdale)
Los Angeles Handicap (Hillsdale)
Californian Stakes (Hillsdale)
American Handicap (Hillsdale)
Hollywood Gold Cup (Hillsdale)
Aqueduct Handicap (Hillsdale)
Santa Anita Maturity (Hillsdale)
1965: John B. Campbell Handicap (Lt. Stevens)

MIKE BASILE

1948: Black Helen Handicap (Rampart)
Gulfstream Park Handicap (Rampart)

LOGAN BATCHELLOR

1949: Black Helen Handicap (Roman Candle)
1951: McLennan Handicap (Gangway)
1953: Molly Pitcher Handicap (My Celeste)
Monmouth Handicap (My Celeste)
1956: Remsen Stakes (Ambehaving)
Black Helen Handicap (Clear Dawn)
Delaware Handicap (Flower Bowl)

GARY BAZE

1980: Longacres Mile (Trooper Seven)
1987: Californian Stakes (Judge Angelucci)

RUSSELL BAZE

1981: California Derby (Always A Cinch)
1982: Bay Meadows Handicap (Super Moment)
1984: Oak Tree Invitational Stakes (Both Ends Burning)
1989: Oak Tree Invitational Stakes (Hawkster)
1990: Oak Leaf Stakes (Lite Light)
1998: Jim Beam Stakes (Event of the Year)

TYLER BAZE

2003: Ancient Title Breeders' Cup Handicap (Avanzado)

D. BECKON

1981: Frizette Stakes (Proud Lou)

ERIC BEITIA

1980: Arlington Handicap (Yvonand)
Louisiana Downs Handicap (Yvonand)

EDDIE BELMONTE

1966: Manhattan Handicap (Moontrip)
1967: Brooklyn Handicap (Handsome Boy)
Washington Park Handicap (Handsome Boy)
Garden State Stakes (Bugged)
Selima Stakes (Syrian Sea)
Gallant Fox Handicap (Niarkos)
Whitney Stakes (Stupendous)
1968: Pimlico-Laurel Futurity (King Emperor)
Matron Stakes (Gallant Bloom)
Flamingo Stakes (Wise Exchange)
Jersey Derby (Out of the Way)
Donn Handicap (Favorable Turn)
Bowling Green Handicap (High Hat)
1969: Californian Stakes (Nodouble)
Brooklyn Handicap (Nodouble)
Hawthorne Gold Cup (Nodouble)
Santa Anita Handicap (Nodouble)
San Felipe Handicap (Elect the Ruler)
Manhattan Handicap (Harem Lady)
San Fernando Stakes (Cavamore)
1970: Wood Memorial Stakes (Personality)
Preakness Stakes (Personality)
Jersey Derby (Personality)
Woodward Stakes (Personality)
Spinster Stakes (Taken Aback)
Arlington Classic (Corn off the Cob)
Widener Handicap (Never Bow)
1971: Jerome Handicap (Tinajero)
San Fernando Stakes (Willowick)
1972: Delaware Handicap (Blessing Angelica)
Metropolitan Handicap (Executioner)

San Fernando Stakes (Autobiography)
1973: Cinema Handicap (Amen II)
Hollywood Derby (Amen II)
Mother Goose Stakes (Windy's Daughter)

ROBERT BERNHARDT
1949: Dwyer Stakes (Shackleton)
1951: Black Helen Handicap (Antagonism)

CARROLL BIERMAN
1949: American Handicap (Double Jay)
1951: Breeders' Futurity (Alladier)
1953: Michigan Mile (Second Avenue)

CAESAR BISONO
1993: Gotham Stakes (As Indicated)

COREY BLACK
1987: Vanity Handicap (Infinidad)
1988: Vanity Handicap (Annoconnor)
1989: Gamely Handicap (Fitzwilliam Place)
1990: San Fernando Stakes (Flying Continental)
Charles H. Strub Stakes (Flying Continental)
Jockey Club Gold Cup (Flying Continental)
Sunset Handicap (Petite Ile)
1993: Hollywood Gold Cup (Best Pal)
1994: Hollywood Turf Cup (Frenchpark)
1999: Santa Monica Handicap (Stop Traffic)

KENNY BLACK
1984: California Derby (Distant Ryder)

TONY BLACK
1976: Vosburgh Handicap (My Juliet)
1977: Michigan Mile and One-Eighth (My Juliet)
1978: Selima Stakes (Candy Eclair)

BRICE BLANC
1997: Del Mar Oaks (Famous Digger)
1999: Matriarch Stakes (Happyanunoit)
2000: Beverly Hills Handicap (Happyanunoit)
Ramona Handicap (Caffe Latte)
2001: Gamely Breeders' Cup Handicap (Happyanunoit)
2003: San Juan Capistrano Handicap (Passinetti)

WALTER BLUM
1954: Alcibiades Stakes (Myrtle's Jet)
Frizette Stakes (Myrtle's Jet)
Molly Pitcher Handicap (Shady Tune)
1960: Monmouth Oaks (Teacation)
1964: Brooklyn Handicap (Gun Bow)
Washington Park Handicap (Gun Bow)
Woodward Stakes (Gun Bow)
Whitney Stakes (Gun Bow)
1965: Donn Handicap (Gun Bow)
Metropolitan Handicap (Gun Bow)
Futurity Stakes (Priceless Gem)
Frizette Stakes (Priceless Gem)
Bowling Green Handicap (Or et Argent)
Dixie Handicap (Or et Argent)
Top Flight Handicap (Affectionately)
United Nations Handicap (Parka)
1966: Mother Goose Stakes (Lady Pitt)
Coaching Club American Oaks (Lady Pitt)
Beldame Stakes (Summer Scandal)
Santa Anita Derby (Boldnesian)
San Fernando Stakes (Isle of Greece)
1967: Del Mar Futurity (Baffle)
California Derby (Reason to Hail)
1969: Garden State Stakes (Forum)
1971: Louisiana Derby (Northfields)
Belmont Stakes (Pass Catcher)
Donn Handicap (Judgable)
1972: Fountain of Youth Stakes (Gentle Smoke)
1973: Sapling Stakes (Tisab)
Florida Derby (Royal and Regal)
Pan American Handicap (Lord Vancouver)
1975: Gulfstream Park Handicap (Gold and Myrrh)
Grey Lag Handicap (Gold and Myrrh)
Metropolitan Handicap (Gold and Myrrh)

BILL BOLAND
1950: Kentucky Derby (Middleground)
Belmont Stakes (Middleground)
Kentucky Oaks (Ari's Mona)
Gallant Fox Handicap (Better Self)
1952: Massachusetts Handicap (To Market)
Arlington Handicap (To Market)
Hawthorne Gold Cup (To Market)
Top Flight Handicap (Renew)
Comely Handicap (Devilkin)
1953: Futurity Stakes (Porterhouse)
Jockey Club Gold Cup (Level Lea)
Miami Beach Handicap (Royal Vale)
1954: Acorn Stakes (Riverina)
Gazelle Handicap (On Your Own)
1955: Gardenia Stakes (Nasrina)
Frizette Stakes (Nasrina)
Alabama Stakes (Rico Reta)
San Felipe Handicap (Jean's Joe)
1956: Metropolitan Handicap (Midafternoon)
Massachusetts Handicap (Midafternoon)
Whitney Stakes (Dedicate)
Hawthorne Gold Cup (Dedicate)
Spinaway Stakes (Alanesian)
Firenze Handicap (Blue Banner)
San Antonio Handicap (Mister Gus)
1957: Selima Stakes (Guide Line)
Dwyer Handicap (Bureaucracy)
John B. Campbell Memorial Handicap (Dedicate)
1958: Spinaway Stakes (Rich Tradition)
Selima Stakes (Rich Tradition)
Grey Lag Handicap (Oh Johnny)
1959: Cinema Handicap (Silver Spoon)
Santa Anita Handicap (Terrang)
Man o' War Handicap (Dotted Line)
1960: San Felipe Handicap (Flow Line)
1962: Suburban Handicap (Beau Purple)
Brooklyn Handicap (Beau Purple)
Hawthorne Gold Cup (Beau Purple)
Man o' War Stakes (Beau Purple)
1963: Widener Handicap (Beau Purple)
Black Helen Handicap (Pocosaba)
1965: Seminole Handicap (Sunstruck)
1966: Wood Memorial Stakes (Amberoid)
Belmont Stakes (Amberoid)
Hialeah Turf Cup (Kentucky Jug)
1967: Black Helen Handicap (Mac's Sparkler)
Beldame Stakes (Mac's Sparkler)
Molly Pitcher Handicap (Politely)
Widener Handicap (Ring Twice)
Bowling Green Handicap (Poker)
1968: Withers Stakes (Call Me Prince)
Amory L. Haskell Handicap (Bold Hour)

FRANK BONE
1950: Marguerite Stakes (Carolina Queen)

DAVID BORDEN
1978: Carter Handicap (Pumpkin Moonshine)

CALVIN BOREL
1991: Super Derby (Free Spirit's Joy)
1993: Arkansas Derby (Rockamundo)
1997: Apple Blossom Handicap (Halo America)
2000: Oaklawn Handicap (K One King)
2001: Apple Blossom Handicap (Gourmet Girl)

GARY BOULANGER
1996: Fountain of Youth Stakes (Built for Pleasure)

SAM BOULMETIS
1950: Trenton Handicap (Chicle II)
Westchester Handicap (Palestinian)
1951: Brooklyn Handicap (Palestinian)
Monmouth Handicap (Arise)
1952: Flamingo Stakes (Charlie McAdam)
1953: Pimlico Futurity (Errard King)
1954: Arlington Classic (Errard King)
American Derby (Errard King)
Pimlico Special (Helioscope)
Trenton Handicap (Helioscope)
McLennan Handicap (Elixir)
1955: Massachusetts Handicap (Helioscope)
Suburban Handicap (Helioscope)
Monmouth Handicap (Helioscope)
Molly Pitcher Handicap (Misty Morn)
1956: Alcibiades Stakes (Leallah)
United Nations Handicap (Career Boy)
1957: New Orleans Handicap (Kingmaker)
Washington D.C. International (Mahan)
1958: Pimlico Special (Vertex)
Trenton Handicap (Vertex)
Widener Handicap (Oligarchy)
1959: Gulfstream Park Handicap (Vertex)
John B. Campbell Handicap (Vertex)
Grey Lag Handicap (Vertex)
Selima Stakes (La Fuerza)
Dwyer Handicap (Waltz)
1960: Manhattan Handicap (Don Poggio)
Gallant Fox Handicap (Don Poggio)
Gotham Stakes (John William)
1961: Monmouth Handicap (Don Poggio)
Canadian Championship Stakes (Our Jeep)
1962: Tropical Park Handicap (Trans-Way)
1963: Frizette Stakes (Tosmah)
1964: Matron Handicap (Tosmah)
Beldame Stakes (Tosmah)
Arlington Classic (Tosmah)
1965: Lawrence Realization Stakes (Munden Point)
1966: John B. Campbell Handicap (Tosmah)

CURT BOURQUE
1993: Arlington-Washington Futurity (Polar Expedition)
1994: Jim Beam Stakes (Polar Expedition)

VINCE BRACCIALE JR.
1974: Spinaway Stakes (Ruffian)
1976: Amory L. Haskell Handicap (Hatchet Man)
1980: Remsen Stakes (Pleasant Colony)
1984: Man o' War Stakes (Majesty's Prince)
1985: Selima Stakes (I'm Splendid)
1986: Jim Beam Stakes (Broad Brush)
Wood Memorial Stakes (Broad Brush)

JOE BRAVO
1997: Donn Handicap (Formal Gold)
Ballerina Stakes (Pearl City)
1998: Buick Pegasus Handicap (Tomorrows Cat)
Remsen Stakes (Comeonmom)
1999: Futurity Stakes (Bevo)
2003: King's Bishop Stakes (Valid Video)

BOBBY BREEN
1973: Louisiana Derby (Leo's Pisces)
1978: Ohio Derby (Special Honor)

N. BRENNAN
1949: Vanity Handicap (Silver Drift)

SHAUN BRIDGMOHAN
2000: Carter Handicap (Brutally Frank)
2001: Carter Handicap (Peeping Tom)
2002: Jockey Club Gold Cup (Evening Attire)

GLEN BROGAN
1973: Malibu Stakes (Bicker)
San Fernando Stakes (Bicker)

STEVE BROOKS
1946: Breeders' Futurity (Education)
1947: Breeders' Futurity (Shy Guy)
1948: Arlington Matron Handicap (Four Winds)
New Orleans Handicap (Star Reward)
1949: Kentucky Derby (Ponder)
Arlington Classic (Ponder)
American Derby (Ponder)
Jockey Club Gold Cup (Ponder)
Lawrence Realization Stakes (Ponder)
Gallant Fox Handicap (Coaltown)
Stars and Stripes Handicap (Coaltown)
Arlington Handicap (Coaltown)
Washington Park Handicap (Coaltown)
Pimlico Oaks (Wistful)
Coaching Club American Oaks (Wistful)
Champagne Stakes (Theory)
Arlington Lassie Stakes (Dutchess Peg)
Vineland Handicap (Bewitch)
1950: San Antonio Handicap (Ponder)
Arlington Handicap (Ponder)
Santa Anita Maturity (Ponder)
Santa Margarita Handicap (Two Lea)
1951: American Handicap (Citation)
Hollywood Gold Cup (Citation)
Arlington Futurity (Hill Gail)
Princess Pat Stakes (A Gleam)
Vanity Handicap (Bewitch)
1952: Arlington Lassie Stakes (Fulvous)
Blue Grass Stakes (Gushing Oil)
1953: Hawthorne Gold Cup (Sub Fleet)
1954: Arlington Lassie Stakes (Delta)
Princess Pat Stakes (Delta)
Starlet Stakes (Blue Ruler)
1955: Alcibiades Stakes (Doubledogdare)
1956: Breeders' Futurity (Round Table)
Arlington Matron Handicap (Delta)
1958: Kentucky Jockey Club Stakes (Winsome Winner)
1959: Tropical Park Handicap (Bardstown)
Widener Handicap (Bardstown)
Arlington Lassie Stakes (Monarchy)
1960: Tropical Park Handicap (On-and-On)
McLennan Handicap (On-and-On)
Arlington Lassie Stakes (Colfax Maid)
1961: American Derby (Beau Prince)
Travers Stakes (Beau Prince)
1962: Widener Handicap (Yorky)

STEVE BROOKS *(Continued)*

Michigan Mile and One-Sixteenth (Beau Prince)
1964: Seminole Handicap (Top Gallant)
1965: Hialeah Turf Cup (Hot Dust)
1967: John B. Campbell Handicap (Quinta)

KELLY BROUSSARD

1964: Louisiana Derby (Grecian Princess)

RAY BROUSSARD

1955: Selima Stakes (Levee)
Carter Handicap (Bobby Brocato)
1956: Beldame Handicap (Levee)
1958: Frizette Stakes (Merry Hill)
New Orleans Handicap (Tenacious)
1959: Louisiana Derby (Master Palynch)
Wood Memorial Stakes (Manassa Mauler)
New Orleans Handicap (Tenacious)
1960: Futurity Stakes (Little Tumbler)
Sorority Stakes (Apatontheback)
Massachusetts Handicap (Talent Show)
1961: Monmouth Oaks (My Portrait)
New Orleans Handicap (Greek Star)
1962: Arlington Handicap (El Bandido)
Canadian Championship Stakes (El Bandido)
Sapling Stakes (Delta Judge)
Louisiana Derby (Admiral's Voyage)
1963: Cowdin Stakes (Dunfee)
Carter Handicap (Admiral's Voyage)
1964: Michigan Mile and One-Sixteenth (Going Abroad)
Manhattan Handicap (Going Abroad)
Hawthorne Gold Cup (Going Abroad)
New Orleans Handicap (Green Hornet)
Hialeah Turf Cup (Carteret)
1965: Coaching Club American Oaks (Marshua)
1966: Kentucky Jockey Club Stakes (Lightning Orphan)
Louisiana Derby (Blue Skyer)
Seminole Handicap (Convex)
1967: Sapling Stakes (Subpet)
1968: Dixie Handicap (High Hat)
1969: Monmouth Invitational Handicap (Al Hattab)
1970: Flamingo Stakes (My Dad George)
Florida Derby (My Dad George)
1975: Delaware Handicap (Susan's Girl)
1977: Louisiana Derby (Clev Er Tell)
Arkansas Derby (Clev Er Tell)
Carter Handicap (Soy Numero Uno)
Oaklawn Handicap (Soy Numero Uno)

DON BRUMFIELD

1964: Spinster Stakes (Old Hat)
Arlington Handicap (Master Dennis)
1965: Black Helen Handicap (Old Hat)
1966: Kentucky Derby (Kauai King)
Preakness Stakes (Kauai King)
Kentucky Oaks (Native Street)
Jersey Derby (Creme dela Creme)
1968: Everglades Stakes (Forward Pass)
Florida Derby (Forward Pass)
Alcibiades Stakes (Lil's Bag)
1969: Breeders' Futurity (Hard Work)
1970: Breeders' Futurity (Man of the Moment)
Kentucky Jockey Club Stakes (Line City)
1972: Breeders' Futurity (Annihilate 'Em)
Alcibiades Stakes (Coraggioso)
1974: Breeders' Futurity (Packer Captain)
1976: Demoiselle Stakes (Bring Out the Band)
1977: Fantasy Stakes (Our Mims)
Acorn Stakes (Bring Out the Band)
United Nations Handicap (Bemo)
1978: Apple Blossom Handicap (Northernette)
1979: Breeders' Futurity (Gold Stage)
Oaklawn Handicap (San Juan Hill)
1980: Flower Bowl Handicap (Just A Game II)
1982: Alcibiades Stakes (Jelly Bean Holiday)
La Canada Stakes (Safe Play)
Louisiana Derby (El Baba)

EDDIE BURNS

1959: Del Mar Futurity (Azure's Orphan)
1960: Hollywood Gold Cup (Dotted Swiss)
Sunset Handicap (Dotted Swiss)
1961: Cinema Handicap (Bushel-n-Peck)
Californian Stakes (First Balcony)
1962: Hollywood Juvenile Championship (Noti)
Santa Anita Derby (Royal Attack)
1963: Cinema Handicap (Y Flash)
Hollywood Derby (Y Flash)
Hollywood Gold Cup (Cadiz)
1964: Hollywood Oaks (Loukahi)
1965: California Derby (Perfect Sky)

CHARLIE BURR

1959: Black Helen Handicap (Rosewood)
1960: Delaware Oaks (Rash Statement)
1961: Vineland Handicap (Frimanaha)
1962: Trenton Handicap (Mongo)
United Nations Handicap (Mongo)
1964: Arkansas Derby (Prince Davelle)

JOHN BURTON

1953: Vanity Handicap (Fleet Khal)

R. BUSTAMANTE

1955: Washington D.C. International (El Chama)

M.A. BUXTON

1946: Molly Pitcher Handicap (Mahmoudess)

RUDY CAMPAS

1962: Hollywood Juvenile Championship (Y Flash)
1963: San Felipe Handicap (Denodado)
1964: San Luis Rey Handicap (Inclusive)
1966: Del Mar Debutante Stakes (Native Honey)
1973: American Handicap (Kentuckian)

ROBERT CAMPBELL

1946: American Derby (Eternal Reward)
Stars and Stripes Handicap (Witch Sir)

RONALD CAMPBELL

1965: Ohio Derby (Terri Hi)
1967: Donn Handicap (Francis U.)
1971: Michigan Mile and One-Eighth (Native Royalty)

JAVIER CANESSA

1973: John B. Campbell Handicap (Delay)

ERNEST CARDONE

1966: Dwyer Handicap (Mr. Right)
Whitney Stakes (Staunchness)
1967: Coaching Club American Oaks (Quillo Queen)
Monmouth Oaks (Quillo Queen)

DENNIS CARR

1989: Jerome Handicap (De Roche)

WILLIAM CARSTENS

1956: Kentucky Jockey Club Stakes (Federal Hill)
1957: Louisiana Derby (Federal Hill)
1960: Kentucky Jockey Club Stakes (Crimson Fury)

KELLY CASTANEDA

1978: John B. Campbell Handicap (Ripon)

MARCO CASTANEDA

1973: Black Helen Handicap (Grafitti)
1974: Futurity Stakes (Just the Time)
Arlington-Washington Futurity (Greek Answer)
Louisiana Derby (Sellout)
1975: Bowling Green Handicap (Barcas)
1976: Louisiana Derby (Johnny Appleseed)
Hollywood Gold Cup (Pay Tribute)
1977: Del Mar Debutante Stakes (Extravagant)
Secretariat Stakes (Text)
1978: California Derby (Noble Bronze)
1981: Ramona Handicap (Queen to Conquer)
Yellow Ribbon Stakes (Queen to Conquer)
La Canada Stakes (Summer Siren)
1982: Ramona Handicap (Honey Fox)
Hollywood Turf Cup (Prince Spellbound)

JAVIER CASTELLANO

2001: Gazelle Handicap (Exogenous)
Beldame Stakes (Exogenous)
2003: Secretariat Stakes (Kicken Kris)
Vosburgh Stakes (Ghostzapper)
Lane's End Breeders' Futurity (Eurosilver)

HERBERTO CASTILLO

1992: Flamingo Stakes (Pistols and Roses)
1993: Donn Handicap (Pistols and Roses)
1994: Donn Handicap (Pistols and Roses)
1999: Matron Stakes (Finder's Fee)
2000: Metropolitan Handicap (Yankee Victor)

AUGUST CATALANO

1953: Saranac Handicap (First Aid)
Aqueduct Handicap (First Aid)
Fall Highweight Handicap (Kaster)
1954: Black Helen Handicap (Gainsboro Girl)
New Castle Handicap (Gainsboro Girl)

STEVE CAUTHEN

1977: Hopeful Stakes (Affirmed)
Futurity Stakes (Affirmed)
Laurel Futurity (Affirmed)
Washington D.C. International (Johnny D.)
Turf Classic (Johnny D.)
Arlington-Washington Futurity (Sauce Boat)
Whitney Handicap (Nearly On Time)
San Fernando Stakes (Pocket Park)
1978: San Felipe Handicap (Affirmed)
Hollywood Derby (Affirmed)
Kentucky Derby (Affirmed)
Preakness Stakes (Affirmed)
Belmont Stakes (Affirmed)
Hialeah Turf Cup (Noble Dancer II)
United Nations Handicap (Noble Dancer II)
San Luis Rey Stakes (Noble Dancer II)
Californian Stakes (J.O. Tobin)

AMIR CEDENO

1989: California Derby (Endow)

VICTOR CENTENO

1977: Santa Barbara Handicap (Desiree)

WAYNE CHAMBERS

1960: Louisiana Derby (Tony Graff)
1963: Washington D.C. International (Mongo)
United Nations Handicap (Mongo)
1964: Widener Handicap (Mongo)
Monmouth Handicap (Mongo)
Selima Stakes (Marshua)
Vineland Handicap (Tona)

G. CHANCELIER

1956: Washington D.C. International (Master Boing)

TOMMY CHAPMAN

1978: Cinema Handicap (Kamehameha)
1979: California Derby (Beau's Eagle)
1984: Hollywood Oaks (Moment to Buy)

JORGE CHAVEZ

1991: Futurity Stakes (Agincourt)
1992: Dwyer Stakes (Agincourt)
1994: Hopeful Stakes (Wild Escapade)
Flower Bowl Inv. Handicap (Dahlia's Dreamer)
1995: Metropolitan Handicap (You and I)
Brooklyn Handicap (You and I)
Remsen Stakes (Tropicool)
1996: Early Times Manhattan Handicap (Diplomatic Jet)
Man o' War Stakes (Diplomatic Jet)
Turf Classic (Diplomatic Jet)
Travers Stakes (Will's Way)
Vosburgh Stakes (Langfuhr)
1997: Carter Handicap (Langfuhr)
Metropolitan Handicap (Langfuhr)
Vosburgh Stakes (Victor Cooley)
Cigar Mile Handicap (Devious Course)
1998: Vosburgh Stakes (Affirmed Success)
Fall Highweight Handicap (Punch Line)
1999: Gulfstream Park Handicap (Behrens)
Oaklawn Handicap (Behrens)
Suburban Handicap (Behrens)
Carter Handicap (Artax)
Vosburgh Stakes (Artax)
Breeders' Cup Sprint (Artax)
Personal Ensign Handicap (Beautiful Pleasure)
Beldame Stakes (Beautiful Pleasure)
Breeders' Cup Distaff (Beautiful Pleasure)
Man o' War Stakes (Val's Prince)
Turf Classic (Val's Prince)
Wood Memorial Stakes (Adonis)
Meadowlands Cup Handicap (Pleasant Breeze)
Pegasus Handicap (Forty One Carats)
Cigar Mile Handicap (Affirmed Success)
2000: Hempstead Handicap (Beautiful Pleasure)
Personal Ensign Handicap (Beautiful Pleasure)
Gulfstream Park Handicap (Behrens)
Champagne Stakes (A.P. Valentine)
Jockey Club Gold Cup (Albert the Great)
2001: Florida Derby (Monarchos)
Kentucky Derby (Monarchos)
Brooklyn Handicap (Albert the Great)
Suburban Handicap (Albert the Great)
2002: Champagne Stakes (Toccet)
Hollywood Futurity (Toccet)
Fountain of Youth Stakes (Booklet)
Metropolitan Handicap (Swept Overboard)
Woodward Stakes (Lido Palace)
Super Derby (Essence of Dubai)
Flower Bowl Invitational Stakes (Kazzia)
Frank J. De Francis Memorial Dash (D'Wildcat)

JACK CHESTNUT

1949: Arlington Futurity (Wisconsin Boy)

FRANK CHOJNACKI

1946: California Derby (War Spun)
1948: Will Rogers Handicap (Speculation)
1949: Starlet Stakes (Thanks Again)
Del Mar Futurity (Your Host)
1951: Cinema Handicap (Mucho Hosso)

JOHN CHOQUETTE

1955: Sapling Stakes (Needles)
Hopeful Stakes (Needles)
1956: Ohio Derby (Born Mighty)
1957: Coaching Club American Oaks (Willamette)
Molly Pitcher Handicap (Manotick)

KENNY CHURCH

1949: Breeders' Futurity (Oil Capitol)
1950: Washington Park Handicap (Inseparable)
Stars and Stripes Handicap (Inseparable)
Remsen Handicap (Repetoire)
Flamingo Stakes (Oil Capitol)
1951: Arlington Lassie Stakes (Princess Lygia)
New Orleans Handicap (Mount Marcy)
1952: Black Helen Handicap (Roman Miss)
New Orleans Handicap (Oil Capitol)
1953: McLennan Handicap (Crafty Admiral)
Gulfstream Park Handicap (Crafty Admiral)
1954: Tropical Handicap (Capeador)
1955: New Orleans Handicap (Sea O Erin)
1957: Spinster Stakes (Bornastar)
Ohio Derby (Manteau)
1958: Vineland Handicap (Bornastar)
Spinster Stakes (Bornastar)
Princess Pat Stakes (Battle Heart)
1960: Canadian Championship Stakes (Rocky Royale)
1963: Kentucky Jockey Club Stakes (Journalist)
1964: Santa Anita Handicap (Mr. Consistency)
San Juan Capistrano Handicap (Mr. Consistency)
Santa Margarita Handicap (Curious Clover)
1965: Carter Handicap (Viking Spirit)
Californian Stakes (Viking Spirit)
Del Mar Futurity (Coursing)
Santa Margarita Handicap (Curious Clover)

C.M. CLARK

1959: Canadian Championship Stakes (Martini II)

HERB CLARK

1961: Kentucky Jockey Club Stakes (Su Ka Wa)

KERWIN CLARK

1981: Hawthorne Gold Cup (Spruce Bouquet)
1989: Pennsylvania Derby (Western Playboy)

SHELBY CLARK

1946: Arlington Futurity (Cosmic Bomb)

EIBAR COA

1998: Brooklyn Handicap (Subordination)
2001: Gulfstream Park Handicap (Sir Bear)

RAY COCHRANE

1988: Rothmans International Stakes (Infamy)
1990: Turf Classic (Cacoethes)

SIDNEY COLE

1953: Queens County Handicap (Flaunt)
1954: Monmouth Handicap (Bassanio)
1955: Gallant Fox Handicap (Misty Morn)

JIMMY COMBEST

1948: Kentucky Jockey Club Stakes (Johns Joy)
1953: Everglades Stakes (Royal Bay Gem)
1958: Breeders' Futurity (Namon)
Arlington Matron Handicap (Estacion)
Arlington Classic (A Dragon Killer)
1960: Arkansas Derby (Persian Gold)
1963: Acorn Stakes (Spicy Living)
Mother Goose Stakes (Spicy Living)
Matron Stakes (Hasty Matelda)
1964: Gotham Stakes (Mr. Moonlight)
Roamer Handicap (Point du Jour)
1967: New Orleans Handicap (Cabildo)
1968: Louisiana Derby (Kentucky Sherry)

NICK COMBEST

1950: Dixie Handicap (Loser Weeper)
Suburban Handicap (Loser Weeper)
Beldame Handicap (Next Move)
Lawrence Realization Stakes (Bed o' Roses)
Whitney Stakes (Piet)

PERRY COMPTON

1994: Arlington-Washington Futurity (Evansville Slew)

JORGE CONTRERAS

1953: Manhattan Handicap (Jampol)
United Nations Handicap (Iceberg II)
1954: Withers Stakes (Jet Action)

LOUIS COOK

1956: Michigan Mile (Nonnie Jo)
1957: Kentucky Jockey Club Stakes (Hill Country)
Kentucky Oaks (Lori-El)
1958: Ohio Derby (Terra Firma)
Stars and Stripes Handicap (Terra Firma)
1959: Arlington Classic (Dunce)
American Derby (Dunce)

WILLIAM COOK

1948: Black Helen Handicap (Shotsilk)
1953: Washington Park Handicap (Sickle's Image)
1955: Black Helen Handicap (Rosemary B.)
Arlington Matron Handicap (Arab Actress)
1961: Breeders' Futurity (Roman Line)
1963: Garden State Stakes (Hurry to Market)

CHARLES CORBETT

1946: Will Rogers Handicap (Burra Sahib)

ANGEL CORDERO

1967: Sanford Stakes (Exclusive Native)
Top Flight Handicap (Straight Deal)
Grey Lag Handicap (Moontrip)
1968: Delaware Handicap (Politely)
Ladies Handicap (Politely)
Pan American Handicap (Irish Rebellion)
1969: Suburban Handicap (Mr. Right)
Oak Tree Stakes (Czar Alexander)
San Luis Rey Handicap (Taneb)
1970: Ladies Handicap (Cathy Honey)
Gotham Stakes (Native Royalty)
Suburban Handicap (Barometer)
1971: Santa Anita Derby (Jim French)
Dwyer Handicap (Jim French)
1972: Sorority Stakes (Sparkalark)
Jerome Handicap (True Knight)
Widener Handicap (Good Counsel)
Michigan Mile and One-Eighth (Favorecidian)
Jockey Club Gold Cup (Autobiography)
San Antonio Stakes (Unconscious)
Hialeah Turf Cup (Gleaming)
Man o' War Stakes (Typecast)
1973: Coaching Club American Oaks (Magazine)
Ladies Handicap (Wakefield Miss)
Blue Grass Stakes (My Gallant)
Jerome Handicap (Step Nicely)
Vosburgh Handicap (Aljamin)
Hialeah Turf Cup (Gleaming)
1974: John B. Campbell Handicap (True Knight)
Suburban Handicap (True Knight)
Hopeful Stakes (The Bagel Prince)
Matron Stakes (Alpine Lass)
Gazelle Handicap (Maud Muller)
Delaware Handicap (Krislin)
Wood Memorial Stakes (Flip Sal)
Kentucky Derby (Cannonade)
Jerome Handicap (Stonewalk)
Pan American Handicap (London Company)
1975: Jersey Derby (Singh)
Secretariat Stakes (Intrepid Hero)
1976: Wood Memorial Stakes (Bold Forbes)
Kentucky Derby (Bold Forbes)
Belmont Stakes (Bold Forbes)
Sorority Stakes (Squander)
Ladies Handicap (Bastonera II)
San Antonio Stakes (Lightning Mandate)
1977: Ruffian Handicap (Cum Laude Laurie)
Beldame Stakes (Cum Laude Laurie)
Spinster Stakes (Cum Laude Laurie)
Blue Grass Stakes (For the Moment)
Dwyer Handicap (Bailjumper)
Brooklyn Handicap (Great Contractor)
Meadowlands Cup (Pay Tribute)
Canadian International Championship (Exceller)
1978: Marlboro Cup Handicap (Seattle Slew)
Woodward Stakes (Seattle Slew)
Vosburgh Handicap (Dr. Patches)
Meadowlands Cup (Dr. Patches)
Man o' War Stakes (Waya)
Turf Classic (Waya)
Arlington-Washington Futurity (Jose Binn)
Widener Handicap (Silver Series)
1979: Top Flight Handicap (Waya)
Santa Barbara Handicap (Waya)
San Antonio Stakes (Tiller)
San Juan Capistrano Handicap (Tiller)
Oak Leaf Stakes (Bold 'n Determined)
Maskette Stakes (Blitey)
Wood Memorial Stakes (Instrument Landing)
1980: Matron Stakes (Prayers'n Promises)
Preakness Stakes (Codex)
United Nations Handicap (Lyphard's Wish)
1981: Delaware Handicap (Relaxing)
Ruffian Handicap (Relaxing)
Metropolitan Handicap (Fappiano)
Woodward Stakes (Pleasant Colony)
Bowling Green Handicap (Great Neck)
1982: Young America Stakes (Slewpy)
Beldame Stakes (Weber City Miss)
Wood Memorial Stakes (Air Forbes Won)
Arlington Classic (Wolfie's Rascal)
Brooklyn Handicap (Silver Supreme)
Woodward Stakes (Island Whirl)
Sunset Handicap (Erins Isle)
1983: Jerome Handicap (A Phenomenon)
Vosburgh Stakes (A Phenomenon)
Woodward Stakes (Slew O' Gold)
Jockey Club Gold Cup (Slew O' Gold)
Matron Stakes (Lucky Lucky Lucky)
Beldame Stakes (Dance Number)
Meadowlands Cup (Slewpy)
United Nations Handicap (Acaroid)
1984: Whitney Handicap (Slew O' Gold)
Woodward Stakes (Slew O' Gold)
Marlboro Cup Handicap (Slew O' Gold)
Jockey Club Gold Cup (Slew O' Gold)
Preakness Stakes (Gate Dancer)
Kentucky Oaks (Lucky Lucky Lucky)
Vosburgh Stakes (Track Barron)
1985: Whitney Handicap (Track Barron)
Woodward Stakes (Track Barron)
Kentucky Derby (Spend A Buck)
Vanity Handicap (Dontstop Themusic)
Travers Stakes (Chief's Crown)
Champagne Stakes (Mogambo)
Breeders' Cup Distaff (Life's Magic)
Remsen Stakes (Pillaster)
1986: Hopeful Stakes (Gulch)
Futurity Stakes (Gulch)
Pennsylvania Derby (Broad Brush)
Meadowlands Cup (Broad Brush)
1987: Santa Margarita Handicap (North Sider)
Apple Blossom Handicap (North Sider)
Maskette Stakes (North Sider)
Santa Anita Handicap (Broad Brush)
Suburban Handicap (Broad Brush)
Mother Goose Stakes (Fiesta Gal)
Coaching Club American Oaks (Fiesta Gal)
Delaware Handicap (Coup de Fusil)
Ruffian Handicap (Coup de Fusil)
Flamingo Stakes (Talinum)
Budweiser-Arlington Million (Manila)
Matron Stakes (Over All)
Vosburgh Stakes (Groovy)
Frizette Stakes (Classic Crown)
1988: Man o' War Stakes (Sunshine Forever)
Turf Classic (Sunshine Forever)
Budweiser International Stakes (Sunshine Forever)
Breeders' Futurity (Fast Play)
Remsen Stakes (Fast Play)
Breeders' Cup Juvenile Fillies (Open Mind)
Demoiselle Stakes (Open Mind)
Jim Dandy Stakes (Brian's Time)
Alabama Stakes (Maplejinsky)
Futurity Stakes (Trapp Mountain)
Selima Stakes (Capades)
Breeders' Cup Sprint (Gulch)
Ladies Handicap (Banker's Lady)
1989: Kentucky Oaks (Open Mind)
Acorn Stakes (Open Mind)
Mother Goose Stakes (Open Mind)
Coaching Club American Oaks (Open Mind)
Alabama Stakes (Open Mind)
Gulfstream Park Handicap (Slew City Slew)
Oaklawn Handicap (Slew City Slew)
Suburban Handicap (Dancing Spree)
Breeders' Cup Sprint (Dancing Spree)
Matron Stakes (Stella Madrid)
Frizette Stakes (Stella Madrid)
Top Flight Handicap (Banker's Lady)
Peter Pan Stakes (Imbibe)
Hollywood Futurity (Grand Canyon)
1990: Acorn Stakes (Stella Madrid)
Sword Dancer Handicap (El Senor)
Vosburgh Stakes (Sewickley)

ANGEL CORDERO *(Continued)*

1991: Maskette Stakes (Queena)
Ruffian Handicap (Queena)
Gotham Stakes (Kyle's Our Man)
Alabama Stakes (Versailles Treaty)
Matron Stakes (Anh Duong)
Champagne Stakes (Tri to Watch)

ROBERT COTTON

1990: Delaware Handicap (Seattle Dawn)

JOHN COVALLI

1952: Santa Anita Handicap (Miche)

ROGER COX

1982: Arlington Handicap (Flying Target)

JEAN CRUGUET

1968: Travers Stakes (Chompion)
1969: Everglades Stakes (Arts and Letters)
Metropolitan Handicap (Arts and Letters)
Lawrence Realization Stakes (Oil Power)
1970: Cowdin Stakes (Hoist the Flag)
Pimlico-Laurel Futurity (Limit to Reason)
Lawrence Realization Stakes (Kling Kling)
Massachusetts Handicap (Semillant)
1974: Manhattan Handicap (Golden Don)
1975: Hopeful Stakes (Jackknife)
Alabama Stakes (Spout)
1976: Hopeful Stakes (Banquet Table)
Champagne Stakes (Seattle Slew)
Mother Goose Stakes (Girl in Love)
Pan American Handicap (Improviser)
1977: Flamingo Stakes (Seattle Slew)
Wood Memorial Stakes (Seattle Slew)
Kentucky Derby (Seattle Slew)
Preakness Stakes (Seattle Slew)
Belmont Stakes (Seattle Slew)
Bowling Green Handicap (Hunza Dancer)
American Handicap (Hunza Dancer)
Mother Goose Stakes (Road Princess)
1978: Secretariat Stakes (Mac Diarmida)
Canadian Int. Championship (Mac Diarmida)
Washington D.C. International (Mac Diarmida)
Futurity Stakes (Crest of the Wave)
1979: Ladies Handicap (Spark of Life)
Jerome Handicap (Czaravich)
1983: Alabama Stakes (Spit Curl)
Blue Grass Stakes (Play Fellow)
1984: Wood Memorial Stakes (Leroy S.)
Dwyer Stakes (Track Barron)
Coaching Club American Oaks (Class Play)
1985: Delaware Handicap (Basie)
1986: Tropical Park Derby (Strong Performance)
Matron Stakes (Tappiano)
1989: Rothmans International Stakes (Hodges Bay)
1993: Budweiser International Stakes (Buckhar)

JOE CULMONE

1950: Garden State Stakes (Iswas)
Monmouth Handicap (Greek Ship)
1951: Trenton Handicap (Call Over)
1955: Gotham Stakes (Go Lightly)
Tropical Handicap (Scimitar)
1959: Monmouth Oaks (Royal Native)
1960: Trenton Handicap (Manassa Mauler)
1965: Garden State Stakes (Prince Saim)

EUGENE CURRY

1960: Arkansas Derby (Spring Broker)

TONY D'AMICO

2001: Walmac Int. Alcibiades Stakes (Take Charge Lady)
2002: Ashland Stakes (Take Charge Lady)

RAY DANJEAN

1981: Hopeful Stakes (Timely Writer)

JESSE DAVIDSON

1968: Frizette Stakes (Shuvee)
1969: Acorn Stakes (Shuvee)
Mother Goose Stakes (Shuvee)
Coaching Club American Oaks (Shuvee)
Alabama Stakes (Shuvee)
Ladies Handicap (Shuvee)
1985: Laurel Futurity (Southern Appeal)

ROBBIE DAVIS

1985: Ladies Handicap (Videogenic)
1986: Washington D.C. International (Lieutenant's Lark)
1987: Gotham Stakes (Gone West)
Top Flight Handicap (Ms. Eloise)
Ladies Handicap (Nastique)
1988: Acorn Stakes (Aptostar)
Hopeful Stakes (Mercedes Won)
1990: Gamely Handicap (Double Wedge)
1992: Secretariat Stakes (Ghazi)
1993: Ruffian Handicap (Shared Interest)
Brooklyn Handicap (Living Vicariously)
1994: Pimlico Special (As Indicated)
Rothmans International Stakes (Raintrap)
1995: Futurity Stakes (Maria's Mon)
Champagne Stakes (Maria's Mon)
Pegasus Handicap (Flying Chevron)
NYRA Mile Handicap (Flying Chevron)
Dwyer Stakes (Hoolie)
Vosburgh Stakes (Not Surprising)
1996: Arlington Million (Mecke)
Queen Eliz. II Challenge Cup (Memories of Silver)
Flower Bowl Invitational Handicap (Chelsey Flower)
1997: Manhattan Handicap (Ops Smile)
1998: Wood Memorial Stakes (Coronado's Quest)
Hempstead Handicap (Mossflower)
Hopeful Stakes (Lucky Roberto)
Jockey Club Gold Cup (Wagon Limit)
2000: Remsen Stakes (Windsor Castle)
2001: United Nations Handicap (Senure)

PAT DAY

1976: Maskette Handicap (Artfully)
Jockey Club Gold Cup (Great Contractor)
1977: Jerome Handicap (Broadway Forli)
1980: Golden Harvest Handicap (Ribbon)
Ohio Derby (Stone Manor)
1982: Oaklawn Handicap (Eminency)
1983: Arlington Classic (Play Fellow)
American Derby (Play Fellow)
Travers Stakes (Play Fellow)
Spinster Stakes (Try Something New)
Secretariat Stakes (Fortnightly)
Oaklawn Handicap (Bold Style)
1984: Jim Beam Stakes (At the Threshold)
Arlington Classic (At the Threshold)
American Derby (At the Threshold)
Arlington-Washington Lassie Stakes (Contredance)
Blue Grass Stakes (Taylor's Special)
Breeders' Cup Classic (Wild Again)
1985: Apple Blossom Handicap (Sefa's Beauty)
Preakness Stakes (Tank's Prospect)
Jockey Club Gold Cup (Vanlandingham)
1986: Whitney Handicap (Lady's Secret)
Maskette Stakes (Lady's Secret)
Ruffian Handicap (Lady's Secret)
Beldame Stakes (Lady's Secret)
Breeders' Cup Distaff (Lady's Secret)
Arkansas Derby (Rampage)
Peter Pan Stakes (Danzig Connection)
Suburban Handicap (Roo Art)
Man o' War Stakes (Dance of Life)
Remsen Stakes (Java Gold)
1987: Hialeah Turf Cup (Theatrical)
Turf Classic (Theatrical)
Man o' War Stakes (Theatrical)
Breeders' Cup Turf (Theatrical)
Whitney Handicap (Java Gold)
Travers Stakes (Java Gold)
Marlboro Cup Handicap (Java Gold)
Jim Beam Stakes (J.T.'s Pet)
Arkansas Derby (Demons Begone)
Metropolitan Handicap (Gulch)
Jim Dandy Stakes (Polish Navy)
Breeders' Cup Juvenile Fillies (Epitome)
Hollywood Turf Cup (Vilzak)
1988: Peter Pan Stakes (Seeking the Gold)
Dwyer Stakes (Seeking the Gold)
Super Derby (Seeking the Gold)
Cowdin Stakes (Easy Goer)
Champagne Stakes (Easy Goer)
Suburban Handicap (Personal Flag)
Kentucky Oaks (Goodbye Halo)
Withers Stakes (Once Wild)
1989: Gotham Stakes (Easy Goer)
Wood Memorial Stakes (Easy Goer)
Belmont Stakes (Easy Goer)
Whitney Handicap (Easy Goer)
Travers Stakes (Easy Goer)
Woodward Handicap (Easy Goer)
Jockey Club Gold Cup (Easy Goer)
La Canada Stakes (Goodbye Halo)
Jim Beam Stakes (Western Playboy)
Hollywood Gold Cup (Blushing John)
United Nations Handicap (Yankee Affair)
Hopeful Stakes (Summer Squall)
Flower Bowl Handicap (River Memories)
1990: Jim Beam Stakes (Summer Squall)
Blue Grass Stakes (Summer Squall)
Preakness Stakes (Summer Squall)
Pennsylvania Derby (Summer Squall)
Florida Derby (Unbridled)
Breeders' Cup Classic (Unbridled)
Suburban Handicap (Easy Goer)
Arlington Classic (Sound of Cannons)
Arlington-Washington Futurity (Hansel)
1991: Apple Blossom Handicap (Degenerate Gal)
Philip H. Iselin Handicap (Black Tie Affair)
Secretariat Stakes (Jackie Wackie)
Arlington-Washington Lassie Stakes (Speed Dialer)
Spinster Stakes (Wilderness Song)
Rothmans International Stakes (Sky Classic)
Breeders' Cup Distaff (Dance Smartly)
1992: Jim Beam Stakes (Lil E. Tee)
Kentucky Derby (Lil E. Tee)
Caesars International Handicap (Sky Classic)
Turf Classic (Sky Classic)
Top Flight Handicap (Firm Stance)
Acorn Stakes (Prospectors Delite)
Jersey Derby (American Chance)
American Derby (The Name's Jimmy)
Spinaway Stakes (Family Enterprize)
Hollywood Derby (Paradise Creek)
1993: Dwyer Stakes (Cherokee Run)
1994: Spinaway Stakes (Flanders)
Matron Stakes (Flanders)
Frizette Stakes (Flanders)
Breeders' Cup Juvenile Fillies (Flanders)
Early Times Manhattan Handicap (Paradise Creek)
Arlington Million (Paradise Creek)
Washington D.C. International (Paradise Creek)
Preakness Stakes (Tabasco Cat)
Belmont Stakes (Tabasco Cat)
Champagne Stakes (Timber Country)
Breeders' Cup Juvenile (Timber Country)
Beldame Stakes (Heavenly Prize)
Spinster Stakes (Dispute)
1995: Apple Blossom Handicap (Heavenly Prize)
Hempstead Handicap (Heavenly Prize)
Go for Wand Stakes (Heavenly Prize)
Preakness Stakes (Timber Country)
Ohio Derby (Petionville)
Whitney Handicap (Unaccounted For)
Secretariat Stakes (Hawk Attack)
Rothmans International Stakes (Lassigny)
1996: Preakness Stakes (Louis Quatorze)
Jim Dandy Stakes (Louis Quatorze)
Early Times Turf Classic (Mecke)
Pimlico Special (Star Standard)
1997: Hopeful Stakes (Favorite Trick)
Breeders' Cup Juvenile (Favorite Trick)
Arkansas Derby (Crypto Star)
Ramona Handicap (Escena)
Sword Dancer Invitational Handicap (Awad)
Gazelle Handicap (Royal Indy)
Three Chimneys Spinster Stakes (Clear Mandate)
1998: Whitney Handicap (Awesome Again)
Breeders' Cup Classic (Awesome Again)
Jim Dandy Stakes (Favorite Trick)
Personal Ensign Handicap (Tomisue's Delight)
Gazelle Handicap (Tap to Music)
Lane's End Breeders' Futurity (Cat Thief)
1999: Toyota Blue Grass Stakes (Menifee)
Haskell Invitational Handicap (Menifee)
Garden City Breeders' Cup Handicap (Perfect Sting)
Queen Elizabeth II Challenge Cup (Perfect Sting)
Swaps Stakes (Cat Thief)
Breeders' Cup Classic (Cat Thief)
Frizette Stakes (Surfside)
Hollywood Starlet Stakes (Surfside)
Hempstead Handicap (Sister Act)
2000: Las Virgenes Stakes (Surfside)
Santa Anita Oaks (Surfside)
Fountain of Youth Stakes (High Yield)
Toyota Blue Grass Stakes (High Yield)
Kentucky Oaks (Secret Status)
Mother Goose Stakes (Secret Status)
Test Stakes (Dream Supreme)
Ballerina Handicap (Dream Supreme)
Belmont Stakes (Commendable)
King's Bishop Stakes (More Than Ready)
Early Times Hollywood Derby (Brahms)
2001: Sword Dancer Inv. Handicap (With Anticipation)
Man o' War Stakes (With Anticipation)
Gulfstream Park BC Handicap (Subtle Power)
Oaklawn Handicap (Traditionally)
Breeders' Cup Distaff (Unbridled Elaine)
2002: United Nations Handicap (With Anticipation)
Sword Dancer Inv. Handicap (With Anticipation)

Man o' War Stakes (With Anticipation)
Wood Memorial Stakes (Buddha)
Alabama Stakes (Farda Amiga)
Spinaway Stakes (Awesome Humor)
2003: Travers Stakes (Ten Most Wanted)
Super Derby (Ten Most Wanted)
Stephen Foster Handicap (Perfect Drift)
Gazelle Handicap (Buy the Sport)
Garden City BC Handicap (Indy Five Hundred)

CHRIS DeCARLO
1986: Haskell Invitational Handicap (Wise Times)

J. DEFORGE
1965: Washington D.C. International (Diatome)
1966: Washington D.C. International (Behistoun)

EDDIE DELAHOUSSAYE
1977: Young America Stakes (Forever Casting)
1978: Arlington-Washington Lassie Stakes (It's In the Air)
Oak Leaf Stakes (It's In the Air)
Breeders' Futurity (Strike Your Colors)
Alcibiades Stakes (Angel Island)
Michigan Mile and One-Eighth (A Letter to Harry)
1979: Arlington-Washington Futurity (Execution's Reason)
New Orleans Handicap (A Letter to Harry)
1980: Santa Susana Stakes (Bold 'n Determined)
Fantasy Stakes (Bold 'n Determined)
Kentucky Oaks (Bold 'n Determined)
Acorn Stakes (Bold 'n Determined)
Coaching Club American Oaks (Bold 'n Determined)
Maskette Stakes (Bold 'n Determined)
Spinster Stakes (Bold 'n Determined)
Hollywood Gold Cup (Go West Young Man)
Del Mar Handicap (Go West Young Man)
Hollywood Derby (Codex)
1981: Del Mar Futurity (Gato Del Sol)
Apple Blossom Handicap (Bold 'n Determined)
1982: Del Mar Futurity (Roving Boy)
Norfolk Stakes (Roving Boy)
Hollywood Futurity (Roving Boy)
Monmouth Handicap (Mehmet)
Meadowlands Cup (Mehmet)
Hialeah Turf Cup (The Bart)
Century Handicap (The Bart)
Apple Blossom Handicap (Track Robbery)
Kentucky Derby (Gato Del Sol)
Hollywood Derby (Victory Zone)
Eddie Read Handicap (Wickerr)
1983: La Canada Stakes (Avigaition)
Santa Barbara Handicap (Avigaition)
Arkansas Derby (Sunny's Halo)
Kentucky Derby (Sunny's Halo)
Hollywood Gold Cup (Island Whirl)
Whitney Handicap (Island Whirl)
San Fernando Stakes (Wavering Monarch)
1984: Vanity Handicap (Princess Rooney)
Spinster Stakes (Princess Rooney)
Breeders' Cup Distaff (Princess Rooney)
Californian Stakes (Desert Wine)
Hollywood Gold Cup (Desert Wine)
Charles H. Strub Stakes (Desert Wine)
Santa Anita Derby (Mighty Adversary)
1985: La Canada Stakes (Mitterand)
Hollywood Inv. Handicap (Both Ends Burning)
Hollywood Turf Cup (Zoffany)
1986: California Derby (Vernon Castle)
Sunset Handicap (Zoffany)
1987: San Felipe Handicap (Chart the Stars)
San Luis Rey Stakes (Zoffany)
Hollywood Derby (Political Ambition)
1988: Santa Barbara Handicap (Pen Bal Lady)
Gamely Handicap (Pen Bal Lady)
Preakness Stakes (Risen Star)
Belmont Stakes (Risen Star)
San Antonio Handicap (Judge Angelucci)
John Henry Handicap (Deputy Governor)
Hollywood Invitational Handicap (Political Ambition)
1989: Ashland Stakes (Gorgeous)
Hollywood Oaks (Gorgeous)
Swaps Stakes (Prized)
Breeders' Cup Turf (Prized)
San Luis Rey Stakes (Frankly Perfect)
Santa Barbara Handicap (No Review)
Oak Leaf Stakes (Dominant Dancer)
1990: La Canada Stakes (Gorgeous)
Apple Blossom Handicap (Gorgeous)
Vanity Handicap (Gorgeous)
San Luis Rey Stakes (Prized)
Pegasus Handicap (Silver Ending)
1991: Oaklawn Handicap (Festin)
Nassau County Handicap (Festin)
Jockey Club Gold Cup (Festin)
Arkansas Derby (Olympio)
American Derby (Olympio)
Hollywood Derby (Olympio)
Oak Leaf Stakes (Pleasant Stage)
Breeders' Cup Juvenile Fillies (Pleasant Stage)
Santa Barbara Handicap (Bequest)
Californian Stakes (Roanoke)
Hollywood Oaks (Fowda)
Hollywood Derby (Eternity Star)
Hollywood Futurity (A.P. Indy)
1992: Santa Anita Derby (A.P. Indy)
Peter Pan Stakes (A.P. Indy)
Belmont Stakes (A.P. Indy)
Breeders' Cup Classic (A.P. Indy)
Suburban Handicap (Pleasant Tap)
Breeders' Cup Sprint (Thirty Slews)
1993: Hollywood Oaks (Hollywood Wildcat)
Breeders' Cup Distaff (Hollywood Wildcat)
San Antonio Handicap (Marquetry)
Oaklawn Handicap (Jovial)
Vanity Handicap (Re Toss)
Breeders' Cup Sprint (Cardmania)
Hollywood Starlet Stakes (Sardula)
1994: Kentucky Oaks (Sardula)
Gamely Handicap (Hollywood Wildcat)
Pacific Classic (Tinners Way)
1995: Ashland Stakes (Urbane)
Pacific Classic (Tinners Way)
Crown Royal Hollywood Derby (Labeeb)
1996: Santa Anita Handicap (Mr. Purple)
San Luis Rey Stakes (Windsharp)
Californian Stakes (Tinners Way)
1997: San Juan Capistrano Handicap (Marlin)
Oak Leaf Stakes (Vivid Angel)
Malibu Stakes (Lord Grillo)
1998: San Juan Capistrano Handicap (Amerique)
Norfolk Stakes (Buck Trout)
1999: Milady Breeders' Cup Handicap (Gourmet Girl)
Gamely Breeders' Cup Handicap (Tranquility Lake)
2000: Yellow Ribbon Stakes (Tranquility Lake)
2001: Queen Elizabeth II Challenge Cup (Affluent)
La Brea Stakes (Affluent)
Ancient Title BC Handicap (Swept Overboard)
2002: Oaklawn Handicap (Kudos)
San Juan Capistrano Handicap (Ringaskiddy)
John C. Mabee Ramona Handicap (Affluent)

JOHN DELAHOUSSAYE
1949: Louisiana Derby (Rookwood)
1957: Breeders' Futurity (Fulcrum)

ABELARDO DeLARA
1946: Gazelle Stakes (Bridal Flower)
New Castle Handicap (Bridal Flower)
Beldame Handicap (Bridal Flower)
Roamer Handicap (Bridal Flower)
Hopeful Stakes (Blue Border)
Frizette Stakes (Bimlette)
Selima Stakes (Bee Ann Mac)

RICHARD DePASS
1980: Illinois Derby (Ray's Word)

KENT DESORMEAUX
1989: Selima Stakes (Sweet Roberta)
1990: San Juan Capistrano Handicap (Delegant)
1991: Yellow Ribbon Stakes (Kostroma)
1992: Charles H. Strub Stakes (Best Pal)
Santa Anita Handicap (Best Pal)
Oaklawn Handicap (Best Pal)
Santa Barbara Handicap (Kostroma)
Beverly D. Stakes (Kostroma)
Santa Anita Oaks (Golden Treat)
Californian Stakes (Another Review)
Hollywood Oaks (Pacific Squall)
Pacific Classic (Missionary Ridge)
Norfolk Stakes (River Special)
Yellow Ribbon Stakes (Super Staff)
1993: San Luis Rey Stakes (Kotashaan)
San Juan Capistrano Handicap (Kotashaan)
Eddie Read Handicap (Kotashaan)
Oak Tree Invitational Stakes (Kotashaan)
Breeders' Cup Turf (Kotashaan)
Santa Maria Handicap (Race the Wild Wind)
Gamely Handicap (Toussaud)
Meadowlands Cup (Marquetry)
1994: San Antonio Handicap (The Wicked North)
Oaklawn Handicap (The Wicked North)
Californian Stakes (The Wicked North)
Santa Anita Oaks (Lakeway)
Mother Goose Stakes (Lakeway)
Hollywood Oaks (Lakeway)
San Felipe Stakes (Soul of the Matter)
Super Derby (Soul of the Matter)
Santa Barbara Handicap (Possibly Perfect)
Yellow Ribbon Stakes (Aube Indienne)
Hollywood Futurity (Afternoon Deelites)
1995: San Felipe Stakes (Afternoon Deelites)
Malibu Stakes (Afternoon Deelites)
Del Mar Futurity (Future Quest)
Norfolk Stakes (Future Quest)
Gamely Handicap (Possibly Perfect)
Breeders' Cup Sprint (Desert Stormer)
1996: Gamely Handicap (Auriette)
Buick Meadowlands Cup Handicap (Dramatic Gold)
Norfolk Stakes (Free House)
Oak Tree Turf Championship (Admise)
Malibu Stakes (King of the Heap)
1997: Santa Anita Derby (Free House)
Swaps Stakes (Free House)
Philip H. Iselin Handicap (Formal Gold)
Woodward Stakes (Formal Gold)
Californian Stakes (River Keen)
Vanity Handicap (Twice the Vice)
Hollywood Starlet Stakes (Love Lock)
Hollywood Futurity (Real Quiet)
1998: Kentucky Derby (Real Quiet)
Preakness Stakes (Real Quiet)
Gamely Breeders' Cup Handicap (Fiji)
Yellow Ribbon Stakes (Fiji)
Oak Leaf Stakes (Excellent Meeting)
Hollywood Starlet Stakes (Excellent Meeting)
Santa Anita Oaks (Hedonist)
Carter Handicap (Wild Rush)
Hollywood Turf Handicap (Storm Trooper)
Del Mar Futurity (Worldly Manner)
Woodbine Mile (Labeeb)
1999: Las Virgenes Stakes (Excellent Meeting)
Santa Anita Oaks (Excellent Meeting)
Donn Handicap (Puerto Madero)
Arkansas Derby (Certain)
San Juan Capistrano Handicap (Single Empire)
Three Chimneys Spinster Stakes (Keeper Hill)
2000: San Felipe Stakes (Fusaichi Pegasus)
Wood Memorial Stakes (Fusaichi Pegasus)
Kentucky Derby (Fusaichi Pegasus)
Pimlico Special (Golden Missile)
Charles Whittingham Handicap (White Heart)
Gamely Breeders' Cup Handicap (Astra)
Eddie Read Handicap (Ladies Din)
2001: Santa Monica Handicap (Nany's Sweep)
Beverly Hills Handicap (Astra)
Malibu Stakes (Mizzen Mast)
2002: Gamely Breeders' Cup Handicap (Astra)
Beverly Hills Handicap (Astra)
Strub Stakes (Mizzen Mast)
Santa Anita Handicap (Milwaukee Brew)
Secretariat Stakes (Chiselling)
Del Mar Oaks (Dublino)
2003: La Brea Stakes (Island Fashion)

TONY DeSPIRITO
1954: Kentucky Oaks (Fascinator)
1955: Metropolitan Handicap (High Gun)

FRANKIE DETTORI
1994: Breeders' Cup Mile (Barathea)
1999: Breeders' Cup Turf (Daylami)
2001: Breeders' Cup Turf (Fantastic Light)

ROBERT DEVER
1959: Kentucky Jockey Club Stakes (Oil Wick)

JUVENAL DIAZ
1985: Illinois Derby (Important Business)
Arlington Handicap (Pass the Line)
Arlington-Washington Futurity (Meadowlake)
1994: Arlington-Washington Lassie Stakes (Shining Light)

TONY DIAZ
1975: Hollywood Invitational Handicap (Barclay Joy)

DOUG DODSON
1946: Widener Handicap (Armed)
Dixie Handicap (Armed)
Suburban Handicap (Armed)
Washington Park Handicap (Armed)
Vineland Handicap (Good Blood)
1947: McLennan Handicap (Armed)
Widener Handicap (Armed)
Gulfstream Park Handicap (Armed)
Stars and Stripes Handicap (Armed)
Arlington Handicap (Armed)

DOUG DODSON *(Continued)*
Washington Park Handicap (Armed)
Washington Park Futurity (Bewitch)
Arlington Lassie Stakes (Bewitch)
Princess Pat Stakes (Bewitch)
Withers Stakes (Faultless)
Blue Grass Stakes (Faultless)
Preakness Stakes (Faultless)
Pimlico Futurity (Citation)
Selima Stakes (Whirl Some)
Marguerite Stakes (Whirl Some)
American Derby (Fervent)
1948: Vineland Handicap (Honeymoon)
Top Flight Handicap (Honeymoon)
Beldame Handicap (Conniver)
Withers Stakes (Vulcan's Forge)
Wood Memorial Stakes (My Request)
1949: Acorn Stakes (Nell K.)
Gazelle Stakes (Nell K.)
Princess Pat Stakes (Here's Hoping)
Bougainvillea Handicap (Frere Jacques)
1950: Fall Highweight Handicap (Arise)
Excelsior Handicap (Arise)
Blue Grass Stakes (Mr. Trouble)
Discovery Handicap (Sunglow)
1951: Widener Handicap (Sunglow)
1952: Arlington Futurity (Mr. Good)
1953: Delaware Oaks (Cerise Reine)
1954: Pimlico Futurity (Thinking Cap)
Remsen Stakes (Roman Patrol)
1955: Breeders' Futurity (Jovial Jove)
Louisiana Derby (Roman Patrol)
1957: Arlington Handicap (Manassas)

RAMON DOMINGUEZ
2001: Philip H. Iselin Handicap (Broken Vow)
2003: Frank J. De Francis Memorial Dash (A Huevo)

RUPERTO DONOSO
1946: Cowdin Stakes (Cosmic Bomb)
Remsen Handicap (Phalanx)
1947: Belmont Stakes (Phalanx)
Dwyer Stakes (Phalanx)
Jockey Club Gold Cup (Phalanx)
Demoiselle Stakes (Ghost Run)
Whitney Stakes (Rico Monte)
1948: Massachusetts Handicap (Beauchef)

TIM DOOCY
1990: Haskell Invitational Handicap (Restless Con)

RICHARD DOS RAMOS
1992: Molson Export Million (Benburb)

RENE DOUGLAS
1989: Budweiser International Stakes (Caltech)
1996: Belmont Stakes (Editor's Note)

MELVIN DUHON
1946: Arlington Classic (The Dude)

PAT EDDERY
1983: Budweiser Million (Tolomeo)
1985: Breeders' Cup Turf (Pebbles)
1990: Man o' War Stakes (Defensive Play)
Rothmans International Stakes (French Glory)
1991: Breeders' Cup Sprint (Sheikh Albadou)

RAMON ENCINAS
1979: Brooklyn Handicap (The Liberal Member)
1980: Pan American Handicap (Flitalong)

DAVID ERB
1952: Princess Pat Stakes (Fulvous)
1955: Arlington Futurity (Swoon's Son)
Washington Park Futurity (Swoon's Son)
Arlington Lassie Stakes (Judy Rullah)
Californian Stakes (Swaps)
1956: Flamingo Stakes (Needles)
Florida Derby (Needles)
Kentucky Derby (Needles)
Belmont Stakes (Needles)
Gallant Fox Handicap (Summer Tan)
Pimlico Special (Summer Tan)
Arlington Classic (Swoon's Son)
1957: McLennan Handicap (Summer Tan)
1958: Black Helen Handicap (Pardala)
Blue Grass Stakes (Plion)

CLAUDE ERICKSON
1949: New Orleans Handicap (My Request)
Excelsior Handicap (My Request)

CONN ERRICO
1949: Travers Stakes (Arise)
1950: Louisiana Derby (Greek Ship)
1952: Gulfstream Park Handicap (Crafty Admiral)
Manhattan Handicap (Lone Eagle)

JULIO ESPINOZA
1973: Fantasy Stakes (Knitted Gloves)
1979: Alcibiades Stakes (Salud)
1980: Secretariat Stakes (Spruce Needles)
1981: Arlington Handicap (Spruce Needles)

VICTOR ESPINOZA
2000: Breeders' Cup Distaff (Spain)
La Brea Stakes (Spain)
Sempra Energy Hollywood Gold Cup (Early Pioneer)
Del Mar Oaks (No Matter What)
Norfolk Stakes (Flame Thrower)
2001: Del Mar Futurity (Officer)
Champagne Stakes (Officer)
Del Mar Debutante Stakes (Habibti)
Hollywood Starlet Stakes (Habibti)
Wood Memorial Stakes (Congaree)
Milady Breeders' Cup Handicap (Lazy Slusan)
2002: Kentucky Derby (War Emblem)
Preakness Stakes (War Emblem)
Haskell Invitational Handicap (War Emblem)
2003: Malibu Stakes (Southern Image)

RICHARD EVANS
1983: Arlington-Washington Futurity (All Fired Up)

KIEREN FALLON
2003: Breeders' Cup Filly and Mare Turf (Islington)

BRYAN FANN
1975: Michigan Mile and One-Eighth (Mr. Lucky Phoenix)
1977: Arlington Handicap (Cunning Trick)

BENNY FELICIANO
1967: Carter Handicap (Tumiga)
1975: Ohio Derby (Brent's Prince)
John B. Campbell Handicap (Jolly Johu)

JEFFERY FELL
1978: Sapling Stakes (Tim the Tiger)
Remsen Stakes (Instrument Landing)
Frizette Stakes (Golferette)
Top Flight Handicap (Northernette)
Dwyer Handicap (Junction)
Arlington Classic (Alydar)
Bowling Green Handicap (Tiller)
1979: Alabama Stakes (It's In the Air)
Widener Handicap (Jumping Hill)
Whitney Stakes (Star de Naskra)
1980: Suburban Handicap (Winter's Tale)
Brooklyn Handicap (Winter's Tale)
Marlboro Cup Handicap (Winter's Tale)
Widener Handicap (Private Account)
Gulfstream Park Handicap (Private Account)
Mother Goose Stakes (Sugar and Spice)
Bowling Green Handicap (Sten)
1981: Champagne Stakes (Timely Writer)
Flower Bowl Handicap (Rokeby Rose)
Wood Memorial Stakes (Pleasant Colony)
Blue Grass Stakes (Proud Appeal)
1982: Flamingo Stakes (Timely Writer)
Florida Derby (Timely Writer)
Remsen Stakes (Pax in Bello)
Frizette Stakes (Princess Rooney)
Arkansas Derby (Hostage)
Travers Stakes (Runaway Groom)
1983: Suburban Handicap (Winter's Tale)

F. FERNANDEZ
1952: Sapling Stakes (Landlocked)

JOSE FERRER
2000: Philip H. Iselin Handicap (Rize)
Spinaway Stakes (Stormy Pick)

EARLIE FIRES
1966: Gulfstream Park Handicap (First Family)
1967: Hialeah Turf Cup (War Censor)
Pan American Handicap (War Censor)
Dixie Handicap (War Censor)
Florida Derby (In Reality)
Jersey Derby (In Reality)
1968: Breeders' Futurity (Dike)
Widener Handicap (Sette Bello)
1970: Donn Handicap (Twogundan)
1972: Santa Barbara Handicap (Hail the Grey)
1973: Alcibiades Stakes (City Girl)
1976: Hialeah Turf Cup (Legion)
1978: Arlington Handicap (Romeo)
1979: Arlington-Washington Lassie Stakes (Sissy's Time)
Spinster Stakes (Safe)
1981: Widener Handicap (Land of Eire)
1982: Arlington-Washington Futurity (Total Departure)
1986: Alabama Stakes (Classy Cathy)
1987: American Derby (Fortunate Moment)
1989: Florida Derby (Mercedes Won)
1992: Ohio Derby (Majestic Sweep)

BILLIE FISK
1951: Arlington Matron Handicap (Sickle's Image)
1952: Vineland Handicap (Sickle's Image)
1955: Hawthorne Gold Cup (Hasseyampa)

DAVID FLORES
1991: Hollywood Gold Cup (Marquetry)
1992: Eddie Read Handicap (Marquetry)
1996: Hollywood Gold Cup (Siphon)
Del Mar Futurity (Silver Charm)
1997: Santa Anita Handicap (Siphon)
San Felipe Stakes (Free House)
1998: Las Virgenes Stakes (Keeper Hill)
Kentucky Oaks (Keeper Hill)
Eddie Read Handicap (Subordination)
1999: Vinery Del Mar Debutante Stakes (Chilukki)
Oak Leaf Stakes (Chilukki)
San Felipe Stakes (Prime Timber)
Del Mar Oaks (Tout Charmant)
Pacific Classic (General Challenge)
Ramona Handicap (Tuzla)
Del Mar Futurity (Forest Camp)
Oak Tree Turf Championship (Mash One)
La Brea Stakes (Hookedonthefeelin)
2000: Oak Leaf Stakes (Notable Career)
Clement L. Hirsch Mem. Turf Champ. (Mash One)
2001: Ramona Handicap (Janet)
Yellow Ribbon Stakes (Janet)
Santa Margarita Handicap (Lazy Slusan)
Breeders' Cup Juvenile Fillies (Tempera)
2002: Del Mar Futurity (Icecoldbeeratreds)
2003: Woodford Reserve Turf Classic (Honor in War)
Eddie Read Handicap (Special Ring)
Arlington Million (Sulamani)
Bessemer Trust BC Juvenile (Action This Day)

RONNIE FRANKLIN
1978: Laurel Futurity (Spectacular Bid)
1979: Florida Derby (Spectacular Bid)
Flamingo Stakes (Spectacular Bid)
Blue Grass Stakes (Spectacular Bid)
Kentucky Derby (Spectacular Bid)
Preakness Stakes (Spectacular Bid)

RICKY FRAZIER
1981: Golden Harvest Handicap (Mean Martha)

PAUL FREY
1963: California Derby (On My Honor)

MARTIN FROMIN
1971: Sapling Stakes (Chevron Flight)

ABIGAIL FULLER
1985: Acorn Stakes (Mom's Command)
Mother Goose Stakes (Mom's Command)
Coaching Club American Oaks (Mom's Command)
Alabama Stakes (Mom's Command)

ROBERT GALLIMORE
1965: Matron Handicap (Old Hat)
Michigan Mile and One-Eighth (Old Hat)

GERLAND GALLITANO
1974: Illinois Derby (Sharp Gary)
1980: American Derby (Hurry Up Blue)
1982: Louisiana Downs Handicap (Pair of Deuces)
1984: American Derby (High Alexander)

RAY GANPATH
2003: Frizette Stakes (Society Selection)

JULIO GARCIA
1984: Sapling Stakes (Doubly Clear)
1991: La Canada Stakes (Fit to Scout)
Santa Margarita Handicap (Little Brianne)
1996: Oak Leaf Stakes (City Band)
1997: Santa Monica Handicap (Toga Toga Toga)
Eddie Read Handicap (Expelled)

DANNY GARGAN
1964: Michigan Mile and One-Sixteenth (Tibaldo)
1966: Michigan Mile and One-Eighth (Stanislas)
1968: Arlington-Washington Futurity (Strong Strong)
1973: Kentucky Oaks (Bag of Tunes)
1975: Oaklawn Handicap (Warbucks)

WILLIE GARNER
1947: Hawthorne Gold Cup (Be Faithful)
1948: Breeders' Futurity (Olympia)
Demoiselle Stakes (Lithe)
Kentucky Oaks (Challe Anne)
1949: San Felipe Stakes (Olympia)

BILL GAVIDIA
1974: Kentucky Oaks (Quaze Quilt)
1976: Alcibiades Stakes (Sans Supplement)

GEORGE GIBB
1960: Bougainvillea Turf Handicap (Noble Sel)

ALBERT GILBERT
1980: Turf Classic (Anifa)

JOHN GILBERT
1946: Garden State Stakes (Double Jay)
Kentucky Jockey Club Stakes (Double Jay)
Pimlico Futurity (Jet Pilot)
San Carlos Handicap (Sirde)
1947: San Pasqual Handicap (Lets Dance)
1948: Trenton Handicap (Double Jay)
1949: Molly Pitcher Handicap (Allie's Pal)
Santa Anita Maturity (Ace Admiral)
1950: New Castle Handicap (Adile)

ROBERT GILBERT
1961: John B. Campbell Handicap (Conestoga)

LARRY GILLIGAN
1956: San Felipe Handicap (Social Climber)
1961: Donn Handicap (General Arthur)
United Nations Handicap (Oink)
1962: Gulfstream Park Handicap (Jay Fox)
Donn Handicap (Jay Fox)
1964: Hollywood Juvenile Championship (Neke)
1980: Norfolk Stakes (High Counsel)

JOHN GIOVANNI
1969: Ohio Derby (Berkley Prince)
John B. Campbell Handicap (Juvenile John)
1971: Amory L. Haskell Handicap (Jontilla)

CHARLES GIVENS
1947: Remsen Handicap (Big If)

GORDON GLISSON
1949: Saratoga Special (More Sun)
Kentucky Oaks (Wistful)
Santa Anita Derby (Old Rockport)
1951: Del Mar Debutante Stakes (Tonga)
1952: American Handicap (Admiral Drake)
1955: Hollywood Gold Cup (Rejected)
1957: San Felipe Handicap (Joe Price)

KEN GODKINS
1953: Vineland Handicap (Mi-Marigold)

AVELINO GOMEZ
1951: Washington Park Handicap (Curandero)
Hawthorne Gold Cup (Seaward)
1962: Arlington Classic (Ridan)
Roamer Handicap (Dead Ahead)
1963: Futurity Stakes (Bupers)
1969: Frizette Stakes (Tudor Queen)

GARRETT GOMEZ
1994: Arkansas Derby (Concern)
1995: Arkansas Derby (Dazzling Falls)
1997: Secretariat Stakes (Honor Glide)
1999: Santa Maria Handicap (India Divina)
Lane's End Breeders' Futurity (Captain Steve)
Malibu Stakes (Love That Red)
2000: San Antonio Handicap (Budroyale)
Pacific Classic (Skimming)
Vinery Del Mar Debutante Stakes (Cindy's Hero)
Three Chimneys Spinster Stakes (Plenty of Light)
2001: Del Mar Oaks (Golden Apples)
Pacific Classic (Skimming)
2002: Charles Whittingham Handicap (Denon)

CARLOS GONZALEZ
1998: Oaklawn Handicap (Precocity)

MANUEL GONZALEZ
1947: Delaware Oaks (Camargo)
1959: Gardenia Stakes (My Dear Girl)
Frizette Stakes (My Dear Girl)
Washington Park Futurity (Venetian Way)

MIKE GONZALEZ
1980: Louisiana Derby (Prince Valiant)

ROBERTO GONZALEZ
1979: Bay Meadows Handicap (Leonotis)

DAVID GORMAN
1948: Discovery Handicap (Better Self)
Westchester Handicap (Better Self)
1949: Firenze Handicap (But Why Not)
Top Flight Handicap (But Why Not)
Hopeful Stakes (Middleground)
Discovery Handicap (Prophets Thumb)
Santa Anita Handicap (Vulcan's Forge)
Carter Handicap (Better Self)
Brooklyn Handicap (Assault)
1951: Belmont Stakes (Counterpoint)
Lawrence Realization Stakes (Counterpoint)
Jockey Club Gold Cup (Counterpoint)
Metropolitan Handicap (Casemate)
1952: San Fernando Stakes (Counterpoint)
Whitney Stakes (Counterpoint)
Cowdin Stakes (Invigorator)
Spinaway Stakes (Flirtatious)
Wood Memorial Stakes (Master Fiddle)
Jockey Club Gold Cup (One Count)
Queens County Handicap (County Delight)
1953: Hopeful Stakes (Artismo)
Firenze Handicap (Kiss Me Kate)
1956: Delaware Oaks (Dotted Line)

TONY GRAELL
1983: Mother Goose Stakes (Able Money)
Maskette Stakes (Ambassador of Luck)
Pegasus Handicap (World Appeal)
1985: Brooklyn Handicap (Bounding Basque)

HOWARD GRANT
1958: Top Flight Handicap (Plucky Roman)
Washington D.C. International (Sailor's Guide)
1959: McLennan Handicap (Sharpsburg)
1961: Delaware Handicap (Airmans Guide)
Beldame Stakes (Airmans Guide)
Arlington Matron Handicap (Shirley Jones)
1962: Ladies Handicap (Royal Patrice)
1963: Monmouth Oaks (Lamb Chop)
Vineland Handicap (Oil Royalty)
1964: Coaching Club American Oaks (Miss Cavandish)
Monmouth Oaks (Miss Cavandish)
Alabama Stakes (Miss Cavandish)
Top Flight Handicap (Oil Royalty)
Carter Handicap (Ahoy)
Man o' War Stakes (Turbo Jet II)
1967: Spinster Stakes (Straight Deal)
1977: Yellow Ribbon Stakes (Star Ball)

BENNIE GREEN
1951: Acorn Stakes (Nothirdchance)
Firenze Handicap (Renew)
1952: Breeders' Futurity (Straight Face)
Kentucky Jockey Club Stakes (Straight Face)
Aqueduct Handicap (Bryan G.)
1953: Discovery Handicap (Level Lea)
1954: Dixie Handicap (Straight Face)
Canadian Championship Stakes (Resilient)

RICHARD GRIFFITHS
1958: California Derby (Nice Guy)

PHIL GRIMM
1969: Arkansas Derby (Traffic Mark)
1970: Jerome Handicap (Great Mystery)

RICHARD GRUBB
1968: Gulfstream Park Handicap (Gentleman James)

AARON GRYDER
1992: Hopeful Stakes (Great Navigator)
Super Derby (Senor Tomas)

ALONZO GUAJARDO
1981: New Orleans Handicap (Sun Catcher)

ERIC GUERIN
1946: Tremont Stakes (Jet Pilot)
Alabama Stakes (Hypnotic)
1947: Alabama Stakes (But Why Not)
Kentucky Derby (Jet Pilot)
1948: Saratoga Special (Blue Peter)
Hopeful Stakes (Blue Peter)
Futurity Stakes (Blue Peter)
Comely Handicap (Conniver)
Roseben Handicap (Rippey)
1949: Matron Stakes (Bed o' Roses)
Selima Stakes (Bed o' Roses)
Marguerite Stakes (Bed o' Roses)
Demoiselle Stakes (Bed o' Roses)
Tremont Stakes (Fox Time)
Ladies Handicap (Gaffery)
Fall Highweight Handicap (Royal Governor)
Vosburgh Handicap (Loser Weeper)
San Carlos Handicap (Manyunk)
1950: Coaching Club American Oaks (Next Move)
Delaware Oaks (Next Move)
Gazelle Stakes (Next Move)
Ladies Handicap (Next Move)
Vanity Handicap (Next Move)
Hopeful Stakes (Battlefield)
1951: Saratoga Special (Cousin)
Hopeful Stakes (Cousin)
Top Flight Handicap (Busanda)
New Castle Handicap (Busanda)
Vineland Handicap (Bed o' Roses)
Comely Handicap (Bed o' Roses)
Gallant Fox Handicap (County Delight)
Manhattan Handicap (County Delight)
Selima Stakes (Rose Jet)
Carter Handicap (Arise)
1952: Hopeful Stakes (Native Dancer)
Futurity Stakes (Native Dancer)
Firenze Handicap (Next Move)
Beldame Handicap (Next Move)
Brooklyn Handicap (Crafty Admiral)
Washington Park Handicap (Crafty Admiral)
Remsen Handicap (Social Outcast)
Astoria Stakes (Home-Made)
Demoiselle Stakes (Grecian Queen)
Travers Stakes (One Count)
San Juan Capistrano Handicap (Intent)
1953: Gotham Stakes (Native Dancer)
Wood Memorial Stakes (Native Dancer)
Preakness Stakes (Native Dancer)
Withers Stakes (Native Dancer)
Belmont Stakes (Native Dancer)
Dwyer Stakes (Native Dancer)
Arlington Classic (Native Dancer)
Travers Stakes (Native Dancer)
Coaching Club American Oaks (Grecian Queen)
Gazelle Handicap (Grecian Queen)
Vagrancy Handicap (Home-Made)
Comely Handicap (Home-Made)
Ohio Derby (Find)
Grey Lag Handicap (Find)
Santa Margarita Handicap (Spanish Cream)
Excelsior Handicap (First Glance)
1954: Cowdin Stakes (Summer Tan)
Garden State Stakes (Summer Tan)
Belmont Stakes (High Gun)
Dwyer Stakes (High Gun)
Excelsior Handicap (Find)
Queens County Handicap (Find)
Beldame Handicap (Parlo)
Metropolitan Handicap (Native Dancer)
Whitney Handicap (Social Outcast)
Aqueduct Handicap (Crash Dive)
Hawthorne Gold Cup (Rejected)
1955: McLennan Handicap (Social Outcast)
John B. Campbell Mem. Handicap (Social Outcast)
Sunset Handicap (Social Outcast)
Manhattan Handicap (Social Outcast)
Trenton Handicap (Social Outcast)
Top Flight Handicap (Parlo)
Delaware Handicap (Parlo)
Cowdin Stakes (Noorsaga)
1956: Matron Stakes (Romanita)
Alabama Stakes (Tournure)
Gotham Stakes (Career Boy)
New Orleans Handicap (Find)
1957: Arlington Lassie Stakes (Poly Hi)
Massachusetts Handicap (Greek Spy)
1958: Sapling Stakes (Watch Your Step)
Withers Stakes (Sir Robby)
Dwyer Handicap (Victory Morn)
Bowling Green Handicap (Rafty)
1959: Remsen Stakes (Victoria Park)
Maskette Handicap (Idun)
Display Handicap (Beau Diable)
1960: Mother Goose Stakes (Berlo)

ERIC GUERIN *(Continued)*
Coaching Club American Oaks (Berlo)
Beldame Stakes (Berlo)
Ladies Handicap (Berlo)
Spinaway Stakes (Good Move)
Selima Stakes (Good Move)
1963: Travers Stakes (Crewman)
1968: Spinster Stakes (Sale Day)
1971: Blue Grass Stakes (Impetuousity)

WALTER GUERRA
1982: New Orleans Handicap (It's the One)
San Fernando Stakes (It's the One)
Charles H. Strub Stakes (It's the One)
San Juan Capistrano Handicap (Lemhi Gold)
1984: Breeders' Cup Juvenile Fillies (Outstandingly)
Jersey Derby (Birdie's Legend)
1985: Futurity Stakes (Ogygian)
Breeders' Cup Mile (Cozzene)
1986: Dwyer Stakes (Ogygian)
Jerome Handicap (Ogygian)
Top Flight Handicap (Ride Sally)

MARK GUIDRY
2000: Walmac Int. Alcibiades Stakes (She's a Devil Due)
2001: Turfway Spiral Stakes (Balto Star)
Arkansas Derby (Balto Star)
2002: Humana Distaff Handicap (Celtic Melody)
Queen Elizabeth II Challenge Cup (Riskaverse)

HELIODORO GUSTINES
1961: Man o' War Handicap (Wise Ship)
1962: Dixie Handicap (Wise Ship)
1963: Coaching Club American Oaks (Lamb Chop)
1964: United Nations Handicap (Western Warrior)
1967: Gazelle Handicap (Sweet Folly)
Ladies Handicap (Sweet Folly)
1968: Belmont Stakes (Stage Door Johnny)
Dwyer Handicap (Stage Door Johnny)
Black Helen Handicap (Treacherous)
Woodward Stakes (Mr. Right)
1970: Ohio Derby (Climber)
Amory L. Haskell Handicap (Gladwin)
1971: Manhattan Handicap (Happy Way)
1972: Pan American Handicap (Unanime)
1973: Dwyer Handicap (Stop the Music)
1974: Donn Handicap (Forego)
Gulfstream Park Handicap (Forego)
Widener Handicap (Forego)
Carter Handicap (Forego)
Brooklyn Handicap (Forego)
Woodward Stakes (Forego)
Vosburgh Handicap (Forego)
Jockey Club Gold Cup (Forego)
Alabama Stakes (Quaze Quilt)
1975: Widener Handicap (Forego)
Carter Handicap (Forego)
Brooklyn Handicap (Forego)
Suburban Handicap (Forego)
Woodward Stakes (Forego)
1976: Metropolitan Handicap (Forego)
Brooklyn Handicap (Forego)
Widener Handicap (Hatchet Man)

DARRELL HAIRE
1980: Arkansas Derby (Temperence Hill)

DEAN HALL
1980: Del Mar Futurity (Bold And Gold)

IRA HANFORD
1948: New Castle Handicap (Miss Grillo)
1952: Monmouth Oaks (La Corredora)
1953: Ladies Handicap (La Corredora)
Comely Handicap (La Corredora)

LAWRENCE HANSMAN
1947: New Castle Handicap (Elpis)
Comely Handicap (Elpis)
1960: Breeders' Futurity (He's a Pistol)

JAMES HARDINBROOK
1952: Acorn Stakes (Parading Lady)
Vosburgh Handicap (Parading Lady)

BILL HARMATZ
1957: Hawthorne Gold Cup (Round Table)
Santa Anita Maturity (Spinney)
1958: Los Angeles Handicap (How Now)
American Handicap (How Now)
Beldame Handicap (Outer Space)
San Carlos Handicap (Seaneen)
Santa Anita Maturity (Round Table)
1959: Sapling Stakes (Sky Clipper)
San Felipe Handicap (Finnegan)
Preakness Stakes (Royal Orbit)
1960: American Handicap (Prize Host)
1961: Santa Margarita Handicap (Sister Antoine)
San Antonio Handicap (American Comet)
1962: San Felipe Handicap (Doc Jocoy)
California Derby (Doc Jocoy)
Vineland Handicap (Tamarona)
Los Angeles Handicap (Winonly)
Californian Stakes (Cadiz)
1963: Los Angeles Handicap (Doc Jocoy)
1966: Californian Stakes (Travel Orb)
1967: Californian Stakes (Biggs)
1968: Charles H. Strub Stakes (Most Host)

WAYNE HARRIS
1968: Vanity Handicap (Gamely)
1970: Vanity Handicap (Commissary)

BILL HARTACK
1954: Fall Highweight Handicap (Pet Bully)
Washington Park Handicap (Pet Bully)
Woodward Stakes (Pet Bully)
Roamer Handicap (Jet Action)
United Nations Handicap (Closed Door)
1955: Princess Pat Stakes (Supple)
United Nations Handicap (Blue Choir)
1956: Arlington Futurity (Greek Game)
Washington Park Futurity (Greek Game)
Gulfstream Park Handicap (Sailor)
John B. Campbell Memorial Handicap (Sailor)
Garden State Stakes (Barbizon)
Arlington Lassie Stakes (Leallah)
Kentucky Oaks (Princess Turia)
Everglades Stakes (Liberty Sun)
Preakness Stakes (Fabius)
Trenton Handicap (Bardstown)
1957: Matron Stakes (Idun)
Gardenia Stakes (Idun)
Frizette Stakes (Idun)
Tropical Handicap (Bardstown)
Widener Handicap (Bardstown)
Gulfstream Park Handicap (Bardstown)
Washington Park Futurity (Jewel's Reward)
Cowdin Stakes (Jewel's Reward)
Everglades Stakes (Gen. Duke)
Florida Derby (Gen. Duke)
Garden State Stakes (Nadir)
Princess Pat Stakes (Hasty Doll)
Delaware Oaks (Bayou)
Black Helen Handicap (Amoret)
Delaware Handicap (Princess Turia)
Kentucky Derby (Iron Liege)
Woodward Stakes (Dedicate)
Pimlico Special (Promised Land)
Hialeah Turf Handicap (Jabneh)
1958: Everglades Stakes (Tim Tam)
Flamingo Stakes (Tim Tam)
Florida Derby (Tim Tam)
Mother Goose Stakes (Idun)
Gazelle Handicap (Idun)
Diana Handicap (Searching)
McLennan Handicap (Iron Liege)
Bougainvillea Turf Handicap (Stephanotis)
1959: Spinster Stakes (Royal Native)
Florida Derby (Easy Spur)
Man o' War Handicap (Tudor Era)
1960: Black Helen Handicap (Royal Native)
Top Flight Handicap (Royal Native)
Arlington Matron Handicap (Royal Native)
Vineland Handicap (Royal Native)
Hialeah Turf Cup (Amerigo)
San Juan Capistrano Handicap (Amerigo)
Cowdin Stakes (Carry Back)
Kentucky Derby (Venetian Way)
Belmont Stakes (Celtic Ash)
Travers Stakes (Tompion)
1961: Arlington Futurity (Ridan)
Washington Park Futurity (Ridan)
Arlington Lassie Stakes (Rudoma)
Gulfstream Park Handicap (Tudor Way)
1962: Kentucky Derby (Decidedly)
Bougainvillea Handicap (Eurasia)
1963: Cowdin Stakes (Chieftan)
Pimlico Futurity (Quadrangle)
Sorority Stakes (Castle Forbes)
Demoiselle Stakes (Windsor Lady)
Arlington Matron Handicap (Smart Deb)
1964: Blue Grass Stakes (Northern Dancer)
Kentucky Derby (Northern Dancer)
Preakness Stakes (Northern Dancer)
Arlington-Washington Lassie Stakes (Admiring)
Wood Memorial Stakes (Quadrangle)
1965: Del Mar Debutante Stakes (Century)
Spinster Stakes (Star Maggie)
Cinema Handicap (Arksroni)
Pan American Handicap (Cool Prince)
1966: San Luis Rey Handicap (Polar Sea)
1967: Hollywood Juvenile Championship (Jim White)
1968: Manhattan Handicap (Quicken Tree)
Jockey Club Gold Cup (Quicken Tree)
Hollywood Derby (Poleax)
1969: Santa Anita Derby (Majestic Prince)
Kentucky Derby (Majestic Prince)
Preakness Stakes (Majestic Prince)
Del Mar Futurity (George Lewis)
Dixie Handicap (Czar Alexander)
1970: California Derby (George Lewis)
1972: Dwyer Handicap (Cloudy Dawn)
Arlington Park Handicap (Cloudy Dawn)

SANDY HAWLEY
1971: Alabama Stakes (Lauries Dancer)
1974: Laurel Futurity (L'Enjoleur)
1975: Hollywood Juvenile Championship (Restless Restless)
Whitney Handicap (Ancient Title)
Washington D.C. International (Nobiliary)
1976: Swaps Stakes (Majestic Light)
Monmouth Invitational Handicap (Majestic Light)
Cinema Handicap (Majestic Light)
Canadian International Championship (Youth)
Washington D.C. International (Youth)
Ramona Handicap (Vagabonda)
Illinois Derby (Life's Hope)
Californian Stakes (Ancient Title)
United Nations Handicap (Intrepid Hero)
San Juan Capistrano Handicap (One On the Aisle)
1977: Amory L. Haskell Handicap (Majestic Light)
Man o' War Stakes (Majestic Light)
Hollywood Juvenile Championship (Noble Bronze)
Vanity Handicap (Cascapedia)
San Felipe Handicap (Smasher)
Charles H. Strub Stakes (Kirby Lane)
San Antonio Stakes (Ancient Title)
1979: Louisiana Derby (Golden Act)
Arkansas Derby (Golden Act)
Secretariat Stakes (Golden Act)
Canadian International Championship (Golden Act)
Hollywood Oaks (Prize Spot)
San Felipe Handicap (Pole Position)
Hollywood Invitational Handicap (Johnny's Image)
1981: Californian Stakes (Eleven Stitches)
Hollywood Gold Cup (Eleven Stitches)
San Fernando Stakes (Doonesbury)
1983: Norfolk Stakes (Fali Time)
Hollywood Futurity (Fali Time)
Santa Margarita Handicap (Marimbula)
1984: San Felipe Handicap (Fali Time)
1986: Spinster Stakes (Top Corsage)

FREDDIE HEAD
1983: Oak Tree Invitational Stakes (Zalataia)
1987: Selima Stakes (Minstrel's Lassie)
Breeders' Cup Mile (Miesque)
1988: Breeders' Cup Mile (Miesque)

MARTINEZ HEATH
1968: Michigan Mile and One-Eighth (Nodouble)
Hawthorne Gold Cup (Nodouble)

REGINALD HEATHER
1952: Sunset Handicap (Great Circle)

JOHN HECKMANN
1954: Widener Handicap (Landlocked)
1955: Kentucky Jockey Club Stakes (Royal Sting)
1956: Princess Pat Stakes (Splendored)
Spinster Stakes (Doubledogdare)
1958: Arlington Lassie Stakes (Dark Vintage)
Louisiana Derby (Royal Union)
1965: Louisiana Derby (Dapper Delegate)

RUBEN HERNANDEZ
1976: Jerome Handicap (Dance Spell)
Fall Highweight Handicap (Relent)
1977: Matron Stakes (Lakeville Miss)
Frizette Stakes (Lakeville Miss)
Selima Stakes (Lakeville Miss)
Hollywood Derby (Steve's Friend)
1978: Demoiselle Stakes (Plankton)
Coaching Club American Oaks (Lakeville Miss)
Maskette Handicap (Pearl Necklace)

1979: Belmont Stakes (Coastal)
Dwyer Stakes (Coastal)
Monmouth Invitational Handicap (Coastal)
Champagne Stakes (Joanie's Chief)
1980: Hopeful Stakes (Tap Shoes)
Futurity Stakes (Tap Shoes)
Alabama Stakes (Love Sign)
Beldame Stakes (Love Sign)
Whitney Stakes (State Dinner)
Sword Dancer Stakes (Tiller)
1981: Top Flight Handicap (Chain Bracelet)
Flamingo Stakes (Tap Shoes)
Brooklyn Handicap (Hechizado)
Marlboro Cup Handicap (Noble Nashua)
1982: Maskette Stakes (Too Chic)
Flower Bowl Handicap (Trevita)
American Derby (Wolfie's Rascal)
Vosburgh Stakes (Engine One)

SANDINO HERNANDEZ
1961: Arlington Handicap (Tudorich)
1965: Widener Handicap (Primordial II)
1969: Hialeah Turf Cup (Blanquette II)

GEORGE HETTINGER
1950: Top Flight Handicap (Nell K.)
Travers Stakes (Lights Up)
1951: Black-Eyed Susan Stakes (Discreet)

DAVID HIDALGO
1967: Man o' War Stakes (Ruffled Feathers)
1968: Pan American Handicap (Estreno II)

JESS HIGLEY
1946: Hawthorne Gold Cup (Jack's Jill)
1953: Alabama Stakes (Sabette)

L. HILDEBRANDT
1946: Flamingo Stakes (Round View)
1947: Monmouth Handicap (Round View)

HERB HINOJOSA
1959: Michigan Mile and One-Sixteenth (Total Traffic)
1961: Gallant Fox Handicap (Polylad)
1963: Massachusetts Handicap (Crimson Satan)
Michigan Mile and One-Sixteenth (Crimson Satan)
Washington Park Handicap (Crimson Satan)
San Fernando Stakes (Crimson Satan)
Charles H. Strub Stakes (Crimson Satan)
Arlington-Washington Futurity (Golden Ruler)
1965: Pimlico Futurity (Spring Double)
1976: John B. Campbell Handicap (Festive Mood)

RONNIE HIRDES
1978: Illinois Derby (Batonnier)
1982: Hawthorne Gold Cup (Recusant)

MICHAEL HOLE
1969: Jersey Derby (Al Hattab)
1971: Monmouth Oaks (Forward Gal)
Gazelle Handicap (Forward Gal)
Pan American Handicap (Chompion)
Dixie Handicap (Chompion)
1972: Monmouth Invitational Handicap (Freetex)
1974: Marlboro Cup Handicap (Big Spruce)
1975: Sorority Stakes (Dearly Precious)
Spinaway Stakes (Dearly Precious)
Arlington-Washington Lassie Stakes (Dearly Precious)
Oak Leaf Stakes (Answer)

DONALD HOLMES
1967: Louisiana Derby (Ask the Fare)

DON HOWARD
1990: Fantasy Stakes (Silvered)

ROBERT HOWARD
1972: Del Mar Handicap (Chrisaway)

LESTER HULET
1981: Whitney Handicap (Fio Rito)

PATRICK HUSBANDS
2001: Metropolitan Handicap (Exciting Story)

CHARLIE HUSSEY
1984: Arlington-Washington Futurity (Spend A Buck)

FRANK IANNELLI
1970: Sorority Stakes (Forward Gal)
Spinaway Stakes (Forward Gal)
1972: Jersey Derby (Smiling Jack)

JOE IMPARATO
1972: Sapling Stakes (Assagai Jr.)
1976: Maskette Handicap (Sugar Plum Time)
1979: Hopeful Stakes (J.P. Brother)

TONY IVES
1985: Budweiser-Arlington Million (Teleprompter)

BASIL JAMES
1946: Whitney Stakes (Stymie)
Manhattan Handicap (Stymie)
New York Handicap (Stymie)
Gallant Fox Handicap (Stymie)
Discovery Handicap (Mighty Story)
Fall Highweight Handicap (Cassis)
Hollywood Gold Cup (Triplicate)
1947: Metropolitan Handicap (Stymie)
1955: Dixie Handicap (St. Vincent)

JOB DEAN JESSOP
1946: Beldame Handicap (Gallorette)
Metropolitan Handicap (Gallorette)
Brooklyn Handicap (Gallorette)
Sapling Stakes (Donor)
Champagne Stakes (Donor)
Swift Stakes (Master Bid)
San Juan Capistrano Handicap (Triplicate)
1947: Arlington Futurity (Piet)
Tremont Stakes (Inseparable)
Matron Stakes (Inheritance)
Jerome Handicap (Donor)
Queens County Handicap (Gallorette)
1948: Carter Handicap (Gallorette)
1949: Dixie Handicap (Chains)
1951: Blue Grass Stakes (Ruhe)

JOE JOHNSON
1990: Arlington-Washington Lassie Stakes (Through Flight)

WILLIE LEE JOHNSON
1946: New Orleans Handicap (Hillyer Court)

MARK JOHNSTON
1994: Philip H. Iselin Handicap (Taking Risks)

D. JONES
1949: Longacres Mile (Blue Tiger)

KEN JONES
1983: Fantasy Stakes (Brindy Brindy)

JOEY JUDICE
1983: Bay Meadows Handicap (Interco)
1985: California Derby (Hajji's Treasure)

JACK KAENEL
1981: Selima Stakes (Snow Plow)
1982: Delaware Handicap (Jameela)
Preakness Stakes (Aloma's Ruler)
1989: Yellow Ribbon Stakes (Brown Bess)
1990: Santa Barbara Handicap (Brown Bess)

PAUL KALLAI
1970: John B. Campbell Handicap (Mitey Prince)

DAVE KASSEN
1966: Ohio Derby (War Censor)
1969: Kentucky Oaks (Hail to Patsy)

HAL KEENE
1958: Molly Pitcher Handicap (Searching)

MICHAEL KINANE
1990: Belmont Stakes (Go and Go)
2000: Secretariat Stakes (Ciro)
2001: Bessemer Trust BC Juvenile (Johannesburg)
2002: John Deere Breeders' Cup Turf (High Chaparral)
2003: John Deere Breeders' Cup Turf (High Chaparral)

EDDIE KING
1997: Ohio Derby (Frisk Me Now)
1998: Suburban Handicap (Frisk Me Now)
1999: Philip H. Iselin Handicap (Frisk Me Now)

CARSON KIRK
1946: Pimlico Oaks (Red Shoes)
1948: Selima Stakes (Gaffery)
Molly Pitcher Handicap (Camargo)

ARNOLD KIRKLAND
1946: Santa Susana Stakes (Enfilade)
Massachusetts Handicap (Pavot)

1947: Champagne Stakes (Vulcan's Forge)
1948: Whitney Stakes (Gallorette)
1951: Astarita Stakes (Place Card)

EARL KNAPP
1949: Pimlico Futurity (Oil Capitol)
1957: Michigan Mile and One-Sixteenth (My Night Out)
1961: Michigan Mile and One-Sixteenth (American Comet)

KENNY KNAPP
1965: Gulfstream Park Handicap (Ampose)
1966: Vosburgh Handicap (Gallant Romeo)
1971: Kentucky Oaks (Silent Beauty)
Beldame Stakes (Double Delta)

KARL KORTE
1967: Massachusetts Handicap (Good Knight)

ROBERT KOTENKO
1971: Spinster Stakes (Chou Croute)
1973: Hopeful Stakes (Gusty O'Shay)

JULIE KRONE
1988: Flower Bowl Handicap (Gaily Gaily)
1991: Top Flight Handicap (Buy the Firm)
Frizette Stakes (Preach)
1992: Arlington Classic (Saint Ballado)
Pegasus Handicap (Scuffleburg)
Vosburgh Stakes (Rubiano)
1993: Belmont Stakes (Colonial Affair)
Sword Dancer Handicap (Spectacular Tide)
1994: Man o' War Stakes (Royal Mountain Inn)
1995: Frank J. De Francis Memorial Dash (Lite the Fuse)
Molson Export Million (Peaks and Valleys)
Meadowlands Cup (Peaks and Valleys)
1996: Carter Handicap (Lite the Fuse)
Frank J. De Francis Memorial Dash (Lite the Fuse)
Gotham Stakes (Romano Gucci)
Shuvee Handicap (Clear Mandate)
2002: Malibu Stakes (Debonair Joe)
2003: Del Mar Debutante Stakes (Halfbridled)
Breeders' Cup Juvenile Fillies (Halfbridled)
Pacific Classic (Candy Ride)
Del Mar Futurity (Siphonizer)
Hollywood Derby (Sweet Return)

LARRY KUNITAKE
1965: Washington Park Handicap (Take Over)

JACK KURTZ
1971: Coaching Club American Oaks (Our Cheri Amour)
1976: Laurel Futurity (Royal Ski)
Remsen Stakes (Royal Ski)

CHRIS LAMANCE
1983: Hawthorne Gold Cup (Water Bank)
Eddie Read Handicap (Prince Spellbound)

JERRY LAMBERT
1963: Del Mar Debutante Stakes (Leisurely Kin)
1964: Inglewood Handicap (Native Diver)
1965: American Handicap (Native Diver)
Hollywood Gold Cup (Native Diver)
1966: Hollywood Derby (Fleet Host)
Hollywood Gold Cup (Native Diver)
1967: Del Mar Debutante Stakes (Fast Dish)
Vanity Handicap (Desert Love)
Hollywood Gold Cup (Native Diver)
1968: Del Mar Futurity (Fleet Allied)
Del Mar Debutante Stakes (Fourth Round)
Santa Barbara Handicap (Amerigo's Fancy)
San Felipe Handicap (Dewan)
San Luis Rey Handicap (Biggs)
San Luis Rey Handicap (Quicken Tree)
1969: Malibu Stakes (First Mate)
1970: Century Handicap (Quilche)
San Luis Rey Handicap (Quilche)
Hollywood Oaks (Last of the Line)
San Felipe Handicap (Cool Hand)
Californian Stakes (Baffle)
1971: Sunset Handicap (Over the Counter)
1972: Oak Leaf Stakes (Fresh Pepper)
Vanity Handicap (Convenience)
Malibu Stakes (Kfar Tov)
Hollywood Invitational Handicap (Typecast)
1973: Hollywood Juvenile Championship (Century's Envoy)
Norfolk Stakes (Money Lender)
1976: San Fernando Stakes (Messenger of Song)
1977: Hollywood Invitational Handicap (Vigors)

GLEN LASSWELL

1951: Starlet Stakes (Prudy's Boy)
1952: Pimlico Special (General Staff)

BRITT LAYTON

1947: Santa Susana Stakes (Hubble Bubble)
San Vicente Handicap (Hubble Bubble)

RAYMOND LAYTON

1946: Kentucky Oaks (First Page)

CHARLES LeBLANC

1948: Delaware Oaks (Miss Request)
Firenze Handicap (Carolyn A.)

EUCLID LeBLANC

1952: Del Mar Futurity (Hour Regards)
1953: Starlet Stakes (Arrogate)

JOHN LeBLANC

1972: Spinaway Stakes (La Prevoyante)
Matron Stakes (La Prevoyante)
Frizette Stakes (La Prevoyante)
Selima Stakes (La Prevoyante)
Gardenia Stakes (La Prevoyante)

TOMMY LEE

1963: Dixie Handicap (Cedar Key)
1965: Dixie Handicap (Flag)
1966: Dixie Handicap (Knightly Manner)

ERIC LEGRIX

1991: Breeders' Cup Turf (Miss Alleged)

SIDNEY LeJEUNE

1963: Ohio Derby (Lemon Twist)

JACK LEONARD

1959: Massachusetts Handicap (Air Pilot)
Bougainvillea Turf Handicap (General Arthur)
1961: Carter Handicap (Chief of Chiefs)
1962: Pimlico Futurity (Right Proud)
1963: Cinema Handicap (Quita Dude)
Californian Stakes (Winonly)
1964: Californian Stakes (Mustard Plaster)

ALAIN LEQUEUX

1980: Yellow Ribbon Stakes (Kilijaro)
1981: Washington D.C. International (Providential II)
Hollywood Turf Cup (Providential II)
1985: Turf Classic (Noble Fighter)

BOBBY LESTER

1993: Arlington-Washington Lassie Stakes (Mariah's Storm)

WILLIAM LESTER

1957: Mother Goose Stakes (Outer Space)
1958: Tropical Handicap (St. Amour II)
1959: Trenton Handicap (Greek Star)

DON LEWIS

1955: California Derby (Trackmaster)
1956: Del Mar Futurity (Swirling Abbey)

HERBERT LINDBERG

1947: Inglewood Handicap (Artillery)
1949: Comely Handicap (Lithe)
1950: Molly Pitcher Handicap (Danger Ahead)

TERRY LIPHAM

1980: Oak Leaf Stakes (Astrious)
1983: Monmouth Handicap (Bates Motel)
San Antonio Stakes (Bates Motel)
Santa Anita Handicap (Bates Motel)
California Derby (Paris Prince)

WALTER LITZENBERG

1949: Santa Susana Stakes (Gaffery)
Santa Margarita Handicap (Lurline B.)

JOHN LIVELY

1976: Arkansas Derby (Elocutionist)
Preakness Stakes (Elocutionist)
1979: Golden Harvest Handicap (Flaunter)
1980: Breeders' Futurity (Fairway Phantom)
Apple Blossom Handicap (Billy Jane)
1981: Arlington-Washington Futurity (Lets Dont Fight)
Arkansas Derby (Bold Ego)
Arlington Classic (Fairway Phantom)
1982: Breeders' Futurity (Highland Park)

JOHN LONG

1975: Dwyer Handicap (Valid Appeal)

JOHNNY LONGDEN

1946: Santa Margarita Handicap (Canina)
San Antonio Handicap (First Fiddle)
1947: Santa Anita Derby (On Trust)
Will Rogers Handicap (On Trust)
Swift Stakes (Owners Choice)
San Felipe Stakes (Owners Choice)
Kentucky Oaks (Blue Grass)
Roseben Handicap (Inroc)
American Handicap (Burning Dream)
Golden Gate Handicap (Triplicate)
1948: San Vicente Handicap (Salmagundi)
Santa Anita Derby (Salmagundi)
Santa Margarita Handicap (Miss Doreen)
California Derby (May Reward)
Westerner Handicap (Solidarity)
1949: Westerner Stakes (Pedigree)
Cinema Handicap (Pedigree)
Hollywood Oaks (June Bride)
Sunset Handicap (Ace Admiral)
1950: Santa Anita Handicap (Noor)
San Juan Capistrano Handicap (Noor)
Golden Gate Handicap (Noor)
American Handicap (Noor)
Hollywood Gold Cup (Noor)
Santa Anita Derby (Your Host)
San Felipe Stakes (Your Host)
Del Mar Futurity (Patch)
1951: Santa Anita Handicap (Moonrush)
San Juan Capistrano Handicap (Be Fleet)
1952: Starlet Stakes (Little Request)
Del Mar Handicap (Grantor)
1953: American Handicap (Royal Serenade)
Hollywood Gold Cup (Royal Serenade)
San Felipe Handicap (Decorated)
Golden Gate Handicap (Fleet Bird)
1954: William P. Kyne Handicap (Imbros)
Californian Stakes (Imbros)
California Derby (Miz Clementine)
Hollywood Gold Cup (Correspondent)
1955: Santa Margarita Handicap (Blue Butterfly)
Vanity Handicap (Countess Fleet)
Santa Anita Derby (Swaps)
American Handicap (Alidon)
Del Mar Handicap (Arrogate)
San Juan Capistrano Handicap (St. Vincent)
1956: Starlet Stakes (Lucky Mel)
Selima Stakes (Lebkuchen)
California Derby (No Regrets)
Santa Anita Handicap (Bobby Brocato)
Del Mar Handicap (Arrogate)
1957: Santa Margarita Handicap (Our Betters)
Los Angeles Handicap (Porterhouse)
1958: Californian Stakes (Seaneen)
1959: California Derby (Finnegan)
1960: Vanity Handicap (Silver Spoon)
Californian Stakes (Fleet Nasrullah)
1961: Santa Anita Derby (Four-and-Twenty)
Cinema Handicap (Four-and-Twenty)
Hollywood Derby (Four-and-Twenty)
Los Angeles Handicap (T.V. Lark)
Hawthorne Gold Cup (T.V. Lark)
Washington D.C. International (T.V. Lark)
American Handicap (Prince Blessed)
Hollywood Gold Cup (Prince Blessed)
San Felipe Handicap (Flutterby)
1962: San Fernando Stakes (Four-and-Twenty)
Santa Anita Maturity (Four-and-Twenty)
San Carlos Handicap (Four-and-Twenty)
Cinema Handicap (Black Sheep)
American Derby (Black Sheep)
Hollywood Oaks (Dingle Bay)
Vanity Handicap (Linita)
1964: California Derby (Real Good Deal)
Hollywood Derby (Real Good Deal)
1965: San Juan Capistrano Handicap (George Royal)
Canadian Championship Stakes (George Royal)
Vanity Handicap (Jalousie II)
1966: San Juan Capistrano Handicap (George Royal)

ADALBERTO LOPEZ

1994: American Derby (Vaudeville)

CARLOS LOPEZ

1975: Jerome Handicap (Guards Up)
1980: Monmouth Invitational Handicap (Thanks to Tony)
1981: Gulfstream Park Handicap (Hurry Up Blue)
1990: Meadowlands Cup (Great Normand)

CHARLES LOPEZ

1996: Jerome Handicap (Why Change)

JOE LOPEZ

1967: Oaklawn Handicap (Mike's Red)

RICARDO LOPEZ

1990: Arlington Invitational Challenge Cup (Beau Genius)
Philip H. Iselin Handicap (Beau Genius)

ANDY LoTURCO

1946: Louisiana Derby (Pellicle)

FRANK LOVATO

1957: Hopeful Stakes (Rose Trellis)
1966: Delaware Handicap (Open Fire)
1970: Gardenia Stakes (Eggy)
1972: Black Helen Handicap (Alma North)

FRANK LOVATO JR.

1982: Selima Stakes (Bemissed)

W.D. LUCAS

1963: Breeders' Futurity (Duel)

ROY LUMM

1955: San Antonio Handicap (Gigantic)

MIKE LUZZI

1991: Brooklyn Handicap (Timely Warning)
1995: Sword Dancer Invitational Handicap (Kiri's Clown)
1998: Malibu Stakes (Run Man Run)
2001: Hempstead Handicap (Critical Eye)
2002: Coaching Club American Oaks (Jilbab)

JIMMY LYNCH

1949: Delaware Oaks (Nasophar)
1962: Breeders' Futurity (Ornamento)

D. MacANDREW

1948: Miami Beach Handicap (Stud Poker)

DON MacBETH

1974: Flamingo Stakes (Bushongo)
1980: Dwyer Stakes (Amber Pass)
1981: Laurel Futurity (Deputy Minister)
Young America Stakes (Deputy Minister)
Suburban Handicap (Temperence Hill)
1982: Suburban Handicap (Silver Buck)
Whitney Handicap (Silver Buck)
Secretariat Stakes (Half Iced)
1984: Hopeful Stakes (Chief's Crown)
Breeders' Cup Juvenile (Chief's Crown)
Norfolk Stakes (Chief's Crown)
Frizette Stakes (Charleston Rag)
Gotham Stakes (Bear Hunt)
Jerome Handicap (Is Your Pleasure)
1985: Flamingo Stakes (Chief's Crown)
Blue Grass Stakes (Chief's Crown)
Marlboro Cup Handicap (Chief's Crown)
Suburban Handicap (Vanlandingham)
Washington D.C. International (Vanlandingham)
Widener Handicap (Pine Circle)
Metropolitan Handicap (Forzando II)
Hopeful Stakes (Papal Power)
Matron Stakes (Musical Lark)
1986: Hutcheson Stakes (Papal Power)

ALEX MAESE

1958: Inglewood Handicap (Eddie Schmidt)
1959: Arlington Futurity (T.V. Lark)
1960: Del Mar Debutante Stakes (Amri-An)
1961: Vanity Handicap (Perizade)
1962: San Antonio Handicap (Olden Times)
1963: Del Mar Futurity (Perris)
1964: Del Mar Futurity (Terry's Secret)
1965: Hollywood Derby (Terry's Secret)
Sunset Handicap (Terry's Secret)
1966: Hollywood Juvenile Champ. (Forgotten Dreams)

BILL MAHORNEY

1970: Del Mar Futurity (June Darling)
Norfolk Stakes (June Darling)
Oak Leaf Stakes (June Darling)
Santa Barbara Handicap (Sallarina)
1974: Hollywood Invitational Handicap (Court Ruling)

MIKE MANGANELLO

1968: Ohio Derby (Te Vega)
1970: Blue Grass Stakes (Dust Commander)
Kentucky Derby (Dust Commander)
1973: Breeders' Futurity (Provante)
Michigan Mile and One-Eighth (Golden Don)

EDDIE MAPLE

1971: Florida Derby (Eastern Fleet)
1972: Grey Lag Handicap (Droll Role)
Hawthorne Gold Cup (Droll Role)
Massachusetts Handicap (Droll Role)
Pontiac Grand Prix Stakes (King's Bishop)
Michigan Mile and One-Eighth (King's Bishop)
1973: Carter Handicap (King's Bishop)
Canadian International Championship (Secretariat)
1974: Top Flight Handicap (Lady Love)
Ladies Handicap (Coraggioso)
Metropolitan Handicap (Arbees Boy)
1975: Breeders' Futurity (Harbor Springs)
Hempstead Handicap (Raisela)
1976: Spinaway Stakes (Mrs. Warren)
Matron Stakes (Mrs. Warren)
Alabama Stakes (Optimistic Gal)
Delaware Handicap (Optimistic Gal)
Futurity Stakes (For the Moment)
Dwyer Handicap (Quiet Little Table)
Suburban Handicap (Foolish Pleasure)
1977: Carter Handicap (Quiet Little Table)
Suburban Handicap (Quiet Little Table)
Sapling Stakes (Alydar)
Remsen Stakes (Believe It)
Hempstead Handicap (Pacific Princess)
1978: Metropolitan Handicap (Cox's Ridge)
Oaklawn Handicap (Cox's Ridge)
Kentucky Oaks (White Star Line)
Wood Memorial Stakes (Believe It)
1979: Apple Blossom Handicap (Miss Baja)
Sheepshead Bay Handicap (Terpsichorist)
1980: Belmont Stakes (Temperence Hill)
Travers Stakes (Temperence Hill)
Super Derby (Temperence Hill)
Jockey Club Gold Cup (Temperence Hill)
Louisiana Downs Handicap (It's True)
1981: Remsen Stakes (Laser Light)
Alabama Stakes (Prismatical)
Travers Stakes (Willow Hour)
Hollywood Derby (De La Rose)
Oaklawn Handicap (Temperence Hill)
Pan American Handicap (Little Bonny)
1982: Dwyer Stakes (Conquistador Cielo)
Metropolitan Handicap (Conquistador Cielo)
Arlington-Washington Lassie St. (For Once'n My Life)
Rothmans International Stakes (Majesty's Prince)
1983: Futurity Stakes (Swale)
Young America Stakes (Swale)
Breeders' Futurity (Swale)
Arlington-Washington Lassie Stakes (Miss Oceana)
Selima Stakes (Miss Oceana)
Frizette Stakes (Miss Oceana)
Laurel Futurity (Devil's Bag)
Champagne Stakes (Devil's Bag)
Sword Dancer Handicap (Majesty's Prince)
Man o' War Stakes (Majesty's Prince)
Wood Memorial Stakes (Slew O' Gold)
Louisiana Downs Handicap (Late Act)
1984: Acorn Stakes (Miss Oceana)
Maskette Stakes (Miss Oceana)
Young America Stakes (Script Ohio)
Hollywood Futurity (Stephan's Odyssey)
Tropical Park Derby (Morning Bob)
Hutcheson Stakes (Swale)
Jim Dandy Stakes (Carr de Naskra)
Yellow Ribbon Stakes (Sabin)
1985: Belmont Stakes (Creme Fraiche)
American Derby (Creme Fraiche)
Jerome Handicap (Creme Fraiche)
Super Derby (Creme Fraiche)
1986: Jim Dandy Stakes (Lac Ouimet)
Super Derby (Wise Times)
Young America Stakes (Conquistarose)
1987: Withers Stakes (Gone West)
Dwyer Stakes (Gone West)
Futurity Stakes (Forty Niner)
Champagne Stakes (Forty Niner)
1988: Fountain of Youth Stakes (Forty Niner)
Tropical Park Derby (Digress)
Delaware Handicap (Nastique)
Young America Stakes (Irish Actor)
1989: Dwyer Stakes (Roi Danzig)
Delaware Handicap (Nastique)
Remsen Stakes (Yonder)
1992: Shuvee Handicap (Missy's Mirage)
Hempstead Handicap (Missy's Mirage)
Matron Stakes (Sky Beauty)
1993: Peter Pan Stakes (Virginia Rapids)
1995: Early Times Manhattan Handicap (Awad)
Arlington Million (Awad)
Peter Pan Stakes (Citadeed)

SAM MAPLE

1976: Arlington-Washington Lassie Stakes (Special Warmth)
Secretariat Stakes (Joachim)
Michigan Mile and One-Eighth (Sharp Gary)
1977: Travers Stakes (Jatski)
1979: Illinois Derby (Smarten)
Pennsylvania Derby (Smarten)
Ohio Derby (Smarten)
American Derby (Smarten)
Matron Stakes (Smart Angle)
Frizette Stakes (Smart Angle)
Selima Stakes (Smart Angle)
1984: Louisiana Derby (Taylor's Special)
Apple Blossom Handicap (Heatherten)

CARLOS MARQUEZ

1967: Michigan Mile and One-Eighth (Estreno II)
1969: Louisiana Derby (King of the Castle)
Michigan Mile and One-Eighth (Calandrito)
1970: Mother Goose Stakes (Office Queen)
Michigan Mile and One-Eighth (Fast Hilarious)
1971: Arlington-Washington Futurity (Hold Your Peace)
Kentucky Jockey Club Stakes (Traffic Mark)
Black Helen Handicap (Swoon's Flower)
Ladies Handicap (Sea Saga)
1972: Arlington-Washington Futurity (Shecky Greene)
Flamingo Stakes (Hold Your Peace)
Suburban Handicap (Hitchcock)
1974: Selima Stakes (Aunt Jin)
1975: New Orleans Handicap (Lord Rebeau)

CARLOS MARQUEZ JR.

1997: Jim Beam Stakes (Concerto)

GEORGE MARTENS

1981: Pennsylvania Derby (Summing)
Belmont Stakes (Summing)
Pegasus Handicap (Summing)
United Nations Handicap (Key To Content)
1986: Selima Stakes (Collins)

JACK MARTIN

1948: Hollywood Oaks (Flying Rhythm)

ROBERT MARTIN

1947: Sapling Stakes (Task)
1948: Marguerite Stakes (Alsab's Day)
1949: New Castle Handicap (Allie's Pal)
1950: New York Handicap (Pilaster)
1957: Bougainvillea Turf Handicap (Espea)

WILLIE MARTINEZ

1994: Ohio Derby (Exclusive Praline)
1999: Walmac International Alcibiades Stakes (Scratch Pad)

THOMAS MAY

1946: Spinaway Stakes (Pipette)
1947: Spinaway Stakes (Bellesoeur)
Astarita Stakes (Bellesoeur)
Travers Stakes (Young Peter)

CHRIS McCARRON

1977: Kentucky Oaks (Sweet Alliance)
1978: Louisiana Derby (Esops Foibles)
Arkansas Derby (Esops Foibles)
New Orleans Handicap (Life's Hope)
1979: Del Mar Futurity (The Carpenter)
Norfolk Stakes (The Carpenter)
Metropolitan Handicap (State Dinner)
Century Handicap (State Dinner)
Del Mar Handicap (Ardiente)
Oak Tree Invitational Stakes (Balzac)
1980: La Canada Stakes (Glorious Song)
Santa Margarita Handicap (Glorious Song)
California Derby (Jaklin Klugman)
Jerome Handicap (Jaklin Klugman)
Del Mar Debutante Stakes (Raja's Delight)
1981: Norfolk Stakes (Stalwart)
Hollywood Futurity (Stalwart)
Del Mar Debutante Stakes (Skillful Joy)
Hollywood Starlet Stakes (Skillful Joy)
Florida Derby (Lord Avie)
San Antonio Stakes (Flying Paster)
Eddie Read Handicap (Wickerr)
1982: Jockey Club Gold Cup (Lemhi Gold)
Sword Dancer Stakes (Lemhi Gold)
San Felipe Handicap (Advance Man)
Swaps Stakes (Journey at Sea)
1983: Oak Leaf Stakes (Life's Magic)
Acorn Stakes (Ski Goggle)
Vanity Handicap (A Kiss For Luck)
San Felipe Handicap (Desert Wine)
Sunset Handicap (Craelius)
Hollywood Turf Cup (John Henry)
1984: Hollywood Invitational Handicap (John Henry)
Sunset Handicap (John Henry)
Budweiser-Arlington Million (John Henry)
Turf Classic (John Henry)
Swaps Stakes (Precisionist)
Fantasy Stakes (My Darling One)
Santa Barbara Handicap (Comedy Act)
Hollywood Turf Cup (Alphabatim)
San Antonio Handicap (Poley)
1985: San Fernando Stakes (Precisionist)
Charles H. Strub Stakes (Precisionist)
Breeders' Cup Sprint (Precisionist)
San Luis Rey Stakes (Prince True)
San Juan Capistrano Handicap (Prince True)
Santa Margarita Handicap (Lovlier Linda)
Century Handicap (Dahar)
Hollywood Oaks (Fran's Valentine)
Young America Stakes (Storm Cat)
Oak Tree Invitational Stakes (Yashgan)
1986: Woodward Stakes (Precisionist)
Californian Stakes (Precisionist)
La Canada Stakes (Lady's Secret)
San Felipe Handicap (Variety Road)
Widener Handicap (Turkoman)
Santa Barbara Handicap (Mountain Bear)
Apple Blossom Handicap (Love Smitten)
Belmont Stakes (Danzig Connection)
Vanity Handicap (Magnificent Lindy)
Swaps Stakes (Clear Choice)
Oak Leaf Stakes (Sacahuista)
1987: Kentucky Derby (Alysheba)
Preakness Stakes (Alysheba)
Super Derby (Alysheba)
Fantasy Stakes (Very Subtle)
Hollywood Invitational Handicap (Rivlia)
Brooklyn Handicap (Waquoit)
Rothmans International Stakes (River Memories)
Oak Leaf Stakes (Dream Team)
Oak Tree Invitational Stakes (Allez Milord)
1988: Charles H. Strub Stakes (Alysheba)
Santa Anita Handicap (Alysheba)
Philip H. Iselin Handicap (Alysheba)
Woodward Handicap (Alysheba)
Meadowlands Cup (Alysheba)
Breeders' Cup Classic (Alysheba)
San Felipe Handicap (Mi Preferido)
San Luis Rey Stakes (Rivlia)
Ashland Stakes (Willa on the Move)
Californian Stakes (Cutlass Reality)
Hollywood Oaks (Pattern Step)
Travers Stakes (Forty Niner)
Del Mar Futurity (Music Merci)
Oak Leaf Stakes (One of a Klein)
Yellow Ribbon Stakes (Delighter)
Hollywood Futurity (King Glorious)
1989: Ohio Derby (King Glorious)
Haskell Invitational Handicap (King Glorious)
San Fernando Stakes (Mi Preferido)
Fantasy Stakes (Fantastic Look)
Californian Stakes (Sabona)
Norfolk Stakes (Grand Canyon)
Breeders' Cup Classic (Sunday Silence)
Hollywood Turf Cup (Frankly Perfect)
1990: Santa Margarita Handicap (Bayakoa)
Oaklawn Handicap (Opening Verse)
Kentucky Oaks (Seaside Attraction)
John Henry Handicap (Golden Pheasant)
NYRA Mile Handicap (Quiet American)
1991: San Felipe Stakes (Sea Cadet)
Santa Anita Derby (Dinard)
San Juan Capistrano Handicap (Mashkour)
Caesars International Handicap (Exbourne)
Travers Stakes (Corporate Report)
Meadowlands Cup (Twilight Agenda)
Hollywood Turf Cup (Miss Alleged)
1992: Santa Margarita Handicap (Paseana)
Apple Blossom Handicap (Paseana)
Milady Handicap (Paseana)
Vanity Handicap (Paseana)
Breeders' Cup Distaff (Paseana)
Swaps Stakes (Bien Bien)
Hollywood Turf Cup (Bien Bien)
Arlington-Washington Futurity (Gilded Time)
Breeders' Cup Juvenile (Gilded Time)
Fantasy Stakes (Race the Wild Wind)
Preakness Stakes (Pine Bluff)
Del Mar Futurity (River Special)
Oak Leaf Stakes (Zoonaqua)
Matriarch Stakes (Flawlessly)
1993: Apple Blossom Handicap (Paseana)

CHRIS McCARRON *(Continued)*
Milady Handicap (Paseana)
Spinster Stakes (Paseana)
Ramona Handicap (Flawlessly)
Beverly D. Stakes (Flawlessly)
Matriarch Stakes (Flawlessly)
Jim Dandy Stakes (Miner's Mark)
Jockey Club Gold Cup (Miner's Mark)
Hopeful Stakes (Dehere)
Champagne Stakes (Dehere)
San Felipe Stakes (Corby)
Jim Beam Stakes (Prairie Bayou)
Hollywood Turf Handicap (Bien Bien)
Norfolk Stakes (Shepherd's Field)
Hollywood Turf Cup (Fraise)
1994: San Luis Rey Stakes (Bien Bien)
San Juan Capistrano Handicap (Bien Bien)
Santa Margarita Handicap (Paseana)
Kentucky Derby (Go for Gin)
Milady Handicap (Andestine)
Ramona Handicap (Flawlessly)
1995: Oak Tree Invitational Stakes (Northern Spur)
Breeders' Cup Turf (Northern Spur)
Beverly Hills Handicap (Alpride)
Yellow Ribbon Stakes (Alpride)
San Antonio Handicap (Best Pal)
1996: Santa Margarita Handicap (Twice the Vice)
Apple Blossom Handicap (Twice the Vice)
Milady Breeders' Cup Handicap (Twice the Vice)
Beverly Hills Handicap (Different)
Three Chimneys Spinster Stakes (Different)
Strub Stakes (Helmsman)
Santa Anita Derby (Cavonnier)
Hollywood Oaks (Listening)
Go for Wand Stakes (Exotic Wood)
Breeders' Cup Classic (Alphabet Soup)
Hollywood Turf Cup (Running Flame)
1997: Belmont Stakes (Touch Gold)
Buick Haskell Invitational Handicap (Touch Gold)
Travers Stakes (Deputy Commander)
Super Derby (Deputy Commander)
Del Mar Futurity (Souvenir Copy)
1998: Santa Monica Handicap (Exotic Wood)
Santa Maria Handicap (Exotic Wood)
San Felipe Stakes (Artax)
Milady Breeders' Cup Handicap (I Ain't Bluffing)
Californian Stakes (Mud Route)
Swaps Stakes (Old Trieste)
Pacific Classic (Free House)
1999: San Antonio Handicap (Free House)
Santa Anita Handicap (Free House)
Californian Stakes (Old Trieste)
Vanity Handicap (Manistique)
Yellow Ribbon Stakes (Spanish Fern)
2000: Milady Breeders' Cup Handicap (Riboletta)
Vanity Handicap (Riboletta)
Ruffian Handicap (Riboletta)
Beldame Stakes (Riboletta)
Super Derby (Tiznow)
Breeders' Cup Classic (Tiznow)
Santa Anita Derby (The Deputy)
Matriarch Stakes (Tout Charmant)
Hollywood Turf Cup (Bienamado)
2001: Las Virgenes Stakes (Golden Ballet)
Santa Anita Oaks (Golden Ballet)
San Juan Capistrano Handicap (Bienamado)
Charles Whittingham Handicap (Bienamado)
Santa Anita Handicap (Tiznow)
Breeders' Cup Classic (Tiznow)
Acorn Stakes (Forest Secrets)
Hopeful Stakes (Came Home)
Lane's End Breeders' Futurity (Siphonic)
Hollywood Derby (Denon)
2002: Santa Anita Derby (Came Home)
Kentucky Oaks (Farda Amiga)

GREGG McCARRON
1977: Jockey Club Gold Cup (On the Sly)
Hawthorne Gold Cup (On the Sly)
1982: Alabama Stakes (Broom Dance)
1983: Wood Memorial Stakes (Bounding Basque)
1984: Selima Stakes (Mom's Command)
Pennsylvania Derby (Morning Bob)

HERB McCAULEY
1982: Matron Stakes (Wings of Jove)
1983: Haskell Invitational Handicap (Deputed Testamony)
1987: Blue Grass Stakes (War)
1989: Hialeah Turf Cup (El Senor)
Sword Dancer Handicap (El Senor)
1990: Flower Bowl Handicap (Laugh and Be Merry)
Yellow Ribbon Stakes (Plenty of Grace)
1991: Man o' War Stakes (Solar Splendor)
Turf Classic (Solar Splendor)
Young America Stakes (Maston)
1992: Jim Dandy Stakes (Thunder Rumble)
Travers Stakes (Thunder Rumble)
Gotham Stakes (Devil His Due)
Man o' War Stakes (Solar Splendor)
Beldame Stakes (Saratoga Dew)
1993: Gulfstream Park Handicap (Devil His Due)
Pimlico Special (Devil His Due)
Suburban Handicap (Devil His Due)
Super Derby (Wallenda)
1995: Kentucky Oaks (Gal in a Ruckus)

S. McCOMB
1967: Canadian Int. Championship (He's a Smoothie)

CONN McCREARY
1946: Monmouth Handicap (Lucky Draw)
Miami Beach Handicap (Frere Jacques)
1947: Massachusetts Handicap (Stymie)
Gallant Fox Handicap (Stymie)
Aqueduct Handicap (Stymie)
Black Helen Handicap (Miss Grillo)
1948: Metropolitan Handicap (Stymie)
New York Handicap (Miss Grillo)
1949: Blue Grass Stakes (Halt)
1951: Cowdin Stakes (Eternal Moon)
Molly Pitcher Handicap (Marta)
Ladies Handicap (Marta)
Kentucky Derby (Count Turf)
1952: Flamingo Stakes (Blue Man)
Preakness Stakes (Blue Man)
Dwyer Stakes (Blue Man)
Matron Stakes (Is Proud)
1953: Widener Handicap (Oil Capitol)
Arlington Handicap (Oil Capitol)
Top Flight Handicap (Marta)
Lawrence Realization Stakes (Platan)
1954: Washington Park Futurity (Georgian)
Arlington Matron Handicap (Lavender Hill)
John B. Campbell Memorial Handicap (Joe Jones)
1956: Top Flight Handicap (Searching)
Diana Handicap (Searching)
Maskette Handicap (Searching)
Acorn Stakes (Beyond)
Fall Highweight Handicap (Impromptu)
1957: Withers Stakes (Clem)
Arlington Classic (Clem)
1958: Jockey Club Gold Cup (Inside Tract)
1959: Brooklyn Handicap (Babu)

DARREL McHARGUE
1974: Arlington-Washington Lassie Stakes (Hot n Nasty)
Arkansas Derby (J.R.'s Pet)
1975: Louisiana Derby (Master Derby)
Blue Grass Stakes (Master Derby)
Preakness Stakes (Master Derby)
Alcibiades Stakes (Optimistic Gal)
Selima Stakes (Optimistic Gal)
Arlington-Washington Futurity (Honest Pleasure)
Del Mar Debutante Stakes (Queen to Be)
1976: Breeders' Futurity (Run Dusty Run)
Arlington-Washington Futurity (Run Dusty Run)
New Orleans Handicap (Master Derby)
Oaklawn Handicap (Master Derby)
Hollywood Oaks (Answer)
1977: Oak Leaf Stakes (B. Thoughtful)
Santa Margarita Handicap (Lucie Manet)
Ramona Handicap (Dancing Femme)
Del Mar Handicap (Ancient Title)
San Juan Capistrano Handicap (Properantes)
1978: Hollywood Juvenile Championship (Terlingua)
Del Mar Debutante Stakes (Terlingua)
San Antonio Stakes (Vigors)
Santa Anita Handicap (Vigors)
Hopeful Stakes (General Assembly)
Santa Susana Stakes (Grenzen)
Ramona Handicap (Drama Critic)
Swaps Stakes (Radar Ahead)
Charles H. Strub Stakes (Mr. Redoy)
1979: Longacres Mile (Always Gallant)
San Fernando Stakes (Radar Ahead)
Sunset Handicap (Sirlad)
1980: Hialeah Turf Cup (John Henry)
Hollywood Invitational Handicap (John Henry)
San Luis Rey Stakes (John Henry)
San Juan Capistrano Handicap (John Henry)
1981: Breeders' Futurity (D'Accord)
Oak Leaf Stakes (Header Card)
Santa Anita Derby (Splendid Spruce)
1984: Hollywood Derby (Foscarini)

WILLIAM McKEEVER
1968: Arkansas Derby (Nodouble)

RICHARD McLAUGHLIN
1954: Louisiana Derby (Gigantic)

PETE McLEAN
1951: Wood Memorial Stakes (Repetoire)
1953: Selima Stakes (Small Favor)

CLARENCE MEAUX
1961: Washington Park Handicap (Chief of Chiefs)

DONNIE MECHE
2001: Spinaway Stakes (Cashier's Dream)
2002: Arkansas Derby (Private Emblem)

LONNIE MECHE
1997: Kentucky Oaks (Blushing K.D.)
2001: Super Derby (Outofthebox)

WARREN MEHRTENS
1946: Wood Memorial Stakes (Assault)
Kentucky Derby (Assault)
Preakness Stakes (Assault)
Belmont Stakes (Assault)
Dwyer Stakes (Assault)
Carter Handicap (Flood Town)
1947: Pimlico Oaks (But Why Not)
Acorn Stakes (But Why Not)
Arlington Matron Handicap (But Why Not)
Arlington Classic (But Why Not)
Grey Lag Handicap (Assault)
Westchester Handicap (Bridal Flower)
1948: Pimlico Oaks (Scattered)
Coaching Club American Oaks (Scattered)
Arlington Lassie Stakes (Pail of Water)
Suburban Handicap (Harmonica)
1949: Manhattan Handicap (Donor)
New York Handicap (Donor)
1951: Acorn Stakes (Kiss Me Kate)
Delaware Oaks (Kiss Me Kate)
Gazelle Stakes (Kiss Me Kate)
Spinaway Stakes (Blue Case)
Flamingo Stakes (Yildiz)

GERARD MELANCON
2002: Vosburgh Stakes (Bonapaw)

LARRY MELANCON
1972: Arlington-Washington Lassie St. (Double Your Fun)
1986: Blue Grass Stakes (Bachelor Beau)
2001: San Antonio Handicap (Guided Tour)

SHERIDAN MELLON
1963: Delaware Handicap (Waltz Song)

FRANCISCO MENA
1975: Del Mar Futurity (Telly's Pop)
Norfolk Stakes (Telly's Pop)
1976: California Derby (Telly's Pop)
1978: Century Handicap (Landscaper)
1980: Swaps Stakes (First Albert)

EDDIE MERCER
1952: Washington D.C. International (Wilwyn)

RAFAEL MEZA
1986: San Fernando Stakes (Right Con)
Metropolitan Handicap (Garthorn)
1990: Oak Tree Invitational Stakes (Rial)

MIKE MICELI
1969: Sapling Stakes (Ring For Nurse)
Gulfstream Park Handicap (Court Recess)
1973: Champagne Stakes (Holding Pattern)
1974: Monmouth Invitational Handicap (Holding Pattern)
Travers Stakes (Holding Pattern)

RICHARD MIGLIORE
1985: Gotham Stakes (Eternal Prince)
Wood Memorial Stakes (Eternal Prince)
Man o' War Stakes (Win)
1986: Illinois Derby (Bolshoi Boy)
1989: Beldame Stakes (Tactile)
1991: Flower Bowl Handicap (Lady Shirl)
1996: Pegasus Breeders' Cup Handicap (Allied Forces)
Remsen Stakes (The Silver Move)
1997: Hempstead Handicap (Hidden Lake)
Go for Wand Stakes (Hidden Lake)
Beldame Stakes (Hidden Lake)
1998: Queen Elizabeth II Challenge Cup (Tenski)

2000: Frank J. De Francis Memorial Dash (Richter Scale)
2001: Personal Ensign Handicap (Pompeii)
Overbrook Spinster Stakes (Miss Linda)
2002: Carter Handicap (Affirmed Success)
2003: Ballerina Handicap (Harmony Lodge)
Man o' War Stakes (Lunar Sovereign)

RAY MIKKONEN

1955: Firenze Handicap (Rare Treat)
1956: Vineland Handicap (Rare Treat)
Hialeah Turf Handicap (Guardian II)

DONALD MILLER JR.

1983: Preakness Stakes (Deputed Testamony)
1984: Monmouth Handicap (Believe the Queen)

PAUL MILLER

1946: Astoria Stakes (First Flight)
Coaching Club American Oaks (Hypnotic)

PATRICK MILLIGAN

1950: Firenze Handicap (Red Camelia)
New Orleans Handicap (Red Camelia)

BOBBY MITCHELL

1952: Pimlico Futurity (Isasmoothie)

DARYL MONTOYA

1974: Spinster Stakes (Summer Guest)
American Derby (Determined King)
1975: Hialeah Turf Cup (Outdoors)
1977: Carter Handicap (Gentle King)
1984: Breeders' Futurity (Crater Fire)

FRANK MOON

1947: Molly Pitcher Handicap (Elpis)
New Orleans Handicap (Earshot)

GERARDO MORA

1971: Alcibiades Stakes (Mrs. Cornwallis)

B. MOREIRA

1966: Donn Handicap (Tronado)
Arlington Handicap (Tronado)

HENRY E. MORENO

1952: Hollywood Oaks (A Gleam)
Cinema Handicap (A Gleam)
Westerner Stakes (A Gleam)
Vanity Handicap (Two Lea)
Hollywood Gold Cup (Two Lea)
Del Mar Debutante Stakes (Lap Full)
1953: Garden State Stakes (Turn-to)
Kentucky Derby (Dark Star)
1954: Champagne Stakes (Flying Fury)
Coaching Club American Oaks (Cherokee Rose)
Flamingo Stakes (Turn-to)
1955: Kentucky Oaks (Lalun)
Beldame Handicap (Lalun)
Blue Grass Stakes (Racing Fool)
1956: Acorn Stakes (Princess Turia)
1957: Santa Anita Derby (Sir William)
1959: Alabama Stakes (High Bid)
Vineland Handicap (High Bid)
Hawthorne Gold Cup (Day Court)
1960: Champagne Stakes (Roving Minstrel)
1962: Inglewood Handicap (Prove It)
American Handicap (Prove It)
Hollywood Gold Cup (Prove It)
1964: Metropolitan Handicap (Olden Times)
1978: Fantasy Stakes (Equanimity)
Del Mar Handicap (Palton)

PETER MORENO

1954: Acorn Stakes (Happy Mood)
1957: Del Mar Debutante Stakes (Sally Lee)
1960: Hollywood Derby (Tempestuous)
1962: Del Mar Debutante Stakes (Brown Berry)
1963: Santa Margarita Handicap (Pixie Erin)
Sunset Handicap (Arbitrage)
San Luis Rey Handicap (The Axe II)
1964: Hollywood Juvenile Championship (Charger's Kin)

MICHAEL MORGAN

1976: Hawthorne Gold Cup (Almost Grown)
1980: Arlington Classic (Spruce Needles)
1981: Sorority Stakes (Apalachee Honey)
1985: United Nations Handicap (Ends Well)

JAMES W. MOSELEY

1972: Ohio Derby (Freetex)

GERALD MOSSE

1988: Hialeah Turf Cup (Double Bed)

LEROY MOYERS

1962: Delaware Oaks (North South Gal)
Massachusetts Handicap (Air Pilot)
1966: New Orleans Handicap (Just About)
1968: New Orleans Handicap (Diplomat Way)
Oaklawn Handicap (Diplomat Way)
1969: Massachusetts Handicap (Beau Marker)
1970: Delaware Handicap (Obeah)
1973: New Orleans Handicap (Combat Ready)

BOBBY MUNDORF

1961: California Derby (Mr. Consistency)
1963: Arkansas Derby (Cosmic Tip)

ALAN MUNRO

1992: Budweiser International Stakes (Zoman)

JOHN MURTAGH

1995: Breeders' Cup Mile (Ridgewood Pearl)
1996: Beverly D. Stakes (Timarida)
2000: Breeders' Cup Turf (Kalanisi)

COREY NAKATANI

1990: Hollywood Derby (Itsallgreektome)
Hollywood Turf Cup (Itsallgreektome)
1991: Santa Anita Oaks (Lite Light)
Fantasy Stakes (Lite Light)
Kentucky Oaks (Lite Light)
Coaching Club American Oaks (Lite Light)
Sunset Handicap (Black Monday)
1992: Hollywood Starlet Stakes (Creaking Board)
1993: Charles H. Strub Stakes (Siberian Summer)
Santa Margarita Handicap (Southern Truce)
Del Mar Futurity (Winning Pact)
Hollywood Derby (Explosive Red)
Yellow Ribbon Stakes (Possibly Perfect)
1994: Oak Leaf Stakes (Serena's Song)
Hollywood Starlet Stakes (Serena's Song)
Santa Maria Handicap (Supah Gem)
Eddie Read Handicap (Approach the Bench)
Molson Export Million (Dramatic Gold)
Oak Tree Invitational Stakes (Sandpit)
1995: Las Virgenes Stakes (Serena's Song)
Santa Anita Oaks (Serena's Song)
Jim Beam Stakes (Serena's Song)
Santa Maria Handicap (Queens Court Queen)
Santa Margarita Handicap (Queens Court Queen)
San Luis Rey Stakes (Sandpit)
Caesars International Handicap (Sandpit)
Ramona Handicap (Possibly Perfect)
Beverly D. Stakes (Possibly Perfect)
Santa Barbara Handicap (Wandesta)
Hollywood Oaks (Sleep Easy)
Hollywood Starlet Stakes (Cara Rafaela)
1996: Hollywood Turf Handicap (Sandpit)
Caesars International Handicap (Sandpit)
Vanity Handicap (Jewel Princess)
Breeders' Cup Distaff (Jewel Princess)
San Felipe Stakes (Odyle)
Kentucky Oaks (Pike Place Dancer)
Ramona Handicap (Matiara)
Eddie Read Handicap (Fastness)
Breeders' Cup Sprint (Lit de Justice)
Matriarch Stakes (Wandesta)
Hollywood Starlet Stakes (Sharp Cat)
1997: Santa Maria Handicap (Jewel Princess)
Santa Margarita Handicap (Jewel Princess)
Las Virgenes Stakes (Sharp Cat)
Santa Anita Oaks (Sharp Cat)
Beverly Hills Handicap (Windsharp)
Flower Bowl Invitational Handicap (Yashmak)
Breeders' Cup Sprint (Elmhurst)
1998: Ruffian Handicap (Sharp Cat)
Beldame Stakes (Sharp Cat)
Ramona Handicap (See You Soon)
Del Mar Oaks (Sicy D'Alsace)
Super Derby (Arch)
Oak Tree Turf Championship (Military)
Moet Champagne Stakes (The Groom Is Red)
Breeders' Cup Sprint (Reraise)
Hollywood Turf Cup (Lazy Lode)
1999: Strub Stakes (Event of the Year)
Breeders' Cup Mile (Silic)
2000: Strub Stakes (General Challenge)
Santa Anita Handicap (General Challenge)
Woodford Reserve Turf Classic (Manndar)
Manhattan Handicap (Manndar)
Santa Monica Handicap (Honest Lady)
Santa Maria Handicap (Manistique)
Santa Margarita Handicap (Riboletta)
Shoemaker Breeders' Cup Mile (Silic)
Swaps Stakes (Captain Steve)
2001: Strub Stakes (Wooden Phone)
Manhattan Handicap (Forbidden Apple)
Beverly D. Stakes (England's Legend)
Garden City BC Handicap (Voodoo Dancer)
2002: Eddie Read Handicap (Sarafan)
2003: Diana Handicap (Voodoo Dancer)
Del Mar Oaks (Dessert)

RONNIE NASH

1947: Louisiana Derby (Carolyn A.)
1952: Selima Stakes (Tritium)
New Castle Handicap (Kiss Me Kate)
Florida Derby (Sky Ship)

JOHN NAZARETH

1964: Breeders' Futurity (Umbrella Fella)
Kentucky Jockey Club Stakes (Umbrella Fella)

ELDON NELSON

1950: Arlington Matron Handicap (Lithe)
1954: Arlington Handicap (Stan)
1957: Alabama Stakes (Here and There)
Fall Highweight Handicap (Itobe)
Dixie Handicap (Akbar Khan)
Brooklyn Handicap (Portersville)
1958: Delaware Handicap (Endine)
Ladies Handicap (Endine)
1959: Diana Handicap (Tempted)
Beldame Handicap (Tempted)
Ladies Handicap (Tempted)
Roamer Handicap (Polylad)
1962: Dwyer Handicap (Cyane)
1963: Manhattan Handicap (Smart)
1964: Massachusetts Handicap (Smart)
Gallant Fox Handicap (Smart)
1965: Cowdin Stakes (Advocator)
Jerome Handicap (Bold Bidder)
Massachusetts Handicap (Smart)
1970: Molly Pitcher Handicap (Double Ripple)
1971: John B. Campbell Handicap (Bushido)
1972: Preakness Stakes (Bee Bee Bee)
1973: Hempstead Handicap (Light Hearted)
Maskette Handicap (Light Hearted)

BILL NEMETI

1981: Meadowlands Cup (Princelet)

RALPH NEVES

1946: San Felipe Stakes (Galla Damion)
1947: Starlet Stakes (Zenoda)
Santa Margarita Handicap (Monsoon)
1948: Vanity Handicap (Hemet Squaw)
1949: Golden Gate Handicap (Solidarity)
Hollywood Gold Cup (Solidarity)
San Pasqual Handicap (Shim Malone)
Del Mar Handicap (Top's Boy)
1950: Cinema Handicap (Great Circle)
Del Mar Derby (Great Circle)
Starlet Stakes (Gold Capitol)
San Pasqual Handicap (Solidarity)
1951: Del Mar Futurity (Big Noise)
Hollywood Oaks (Ruth Lily)
Inglewood Handicap (Sturdy One)
1952: Golden Gate Handicap (Lights Up)
Inglewood Handicap (Sturdy One)
1953: Westerner Stakes (Rejected)
1954: Westerner Stakes (Fault Free)
Sunset Handicap (Fleet Bird)
1956: Santa Anita Maturity (Trackmaster)
1957: Inglewood Handicap (Find)
American Handicap (Find)
Sunset Handicap (Find)
Blue Grass Stakes (Round Table)
Santa Anita Handicap (Corn Husker)
1959: San Juan Capistrano Handicap (Royal Living)
1960: Del Mar Futurity (Short Jacket)
Los Angeles Handicap (Finnegan)
1962: Hollywood Derby (Drill Site)
1963: Inglewood Handicap (Native Diver)

JIMMY NICHOLS

1949: San Carlos Handicap (Autocrat)
1951: Dixie Handicap (County Delight)
Aqueduct Handicap (Bryan G.)
1953: Remsen Handicap (Galdar)
Demoiselle Stakes (O'Alison)
Acorn Stakes (Secret Meeting)
1956: Frizette Stakes (Capelet)
1962: New Orleans Handicap (Yorktown)

JIMMY NICHOLS *(Continued)*
John B. Campbell Handicap (Yorktown)
1963: New Orleans Handicap (Endymion)
Arlington Park Handicap (Bounding Main)
1965: Breeders' Futurity (Tinsley)
Arlington-Washington Lassie Stakes (Silver Bright)
1966: Breeders' Futurity (Gentleman James)
1967: Arkansas Derby (Monitor)
1970: Arkansas Derby (Herbalist)
1974: Alcibiades Stakes (Hope of Glory)
1975: Hopeful Stakes (Eustace)

DAVID NIED
1978: Monmouth Invitational Handicap (Delta Flag)

ROBERT NONO
1961: Arkansas Derby (Light Talk)
1968: Illinois Derby (Bold Favorite)

CHARLES O'BRIEN
1954: Vagrancy Handicap (Canadiana)

JOHN OLDHAM
1979: Sapling Stakes (Rockhill Native)
Futurity Stakes (Rockhill Native)
1980: Blue Grass Stakes (Rockhill Native)

FRANK OLIVARES
1975: Sunset Handicap (Cruiser II)
Del Mar Handicap (Cruiser II)
1976: Hollywood Juvenile Championship (Fleet Dragoon)
1977: Del Mar Futurity (Go West Young Man)
Breeders' Futurity (Gonquin)
1980: Norfolk Stakes (Sir Dancer)
1983: Florida Derby (Croeso)
1988: Santa Margarita Handicap (Flying Julia)
1989: Del Mar Futurity (Drag Race)

LUIS ORTEGA
1987: California Derby (Simply Majestic)

DONNIE PADGETT
1947: Garden State Stakes (Itsabet)

F. PANNELL
1952: Sapling Stakes (Laffango)

P. PAQUET
1981: Turf Classic (April Run)

WILLIE PARNELL
1947: Del Mar Handicap (Iron Maiden)

BILL PASSMORE
1972: John B. Campbell Handicap (Favorecidian)
1973: American Derby (Bemo)
1975: Top Flight Handicap (Twixt)
1982: Sorority Stakes (Singing Susan)
1983: Pennsylvania Derby (Dixieland Band)

GARTH PATTERSON
1965: Monmouth Oaks (Summer Scandal)
1966: Top Flight Handicap (Summer Scandal)
1970: Acorn Stakes (Royal Signal)
Monmouth Oaks (Kilts N Kapers)
1971: Arkansas Derby (Twist the Axe)
1972: Top Flight Handicap (Inca Queen)
1975: Ashland Stakes (Sun and Snow)
Kentucky Oaks (Sun and Snow)
American Derby (Honey Mark)
1976: Ohio Derby (Return of a Native)
1977: Widener Handicap (Yamanin)
1984: Ohio Derby (At the Threshold)
Haskell Invitational Handicap (Big Pistol)

WILLIAM PEAKE
1958: Display Handicap (Civet)
1960: Michigan Mile and One-Sixteenth (Little Fitz)

BILL PEARSON
1951: Del Mar Handicap (Blue Reading)

GENE PEDERSON
1948: American Handicap (Stepfather)

MARTIN PEDROZA
1989: Santa Anita Handicap (Martial Law)
1991: Spinaway Stakes (Miss Iron Smoke)

DAVE PENNA
1995: Philip H. Iselin Handicap (Schossberg)

RAMON PEREZ
1977: Arlington Classic Inv. Handicap (Private Thoughts)
1995: Carter Handicap (Lite the Fuse)
Flower Bowl Inv. Handicap (Northern Emerald)

S. PEREZ
1949: Whitney Stakes (Round View)

BOBBY PERMANE
1946: Santa Anita Derby (Knockdown)
San Pasqual Handicap (Lou-Bre)
1947: Hollywood Gold Cup (Cover Up)
Sunset Handicap (Cover Up)
1948: Tremont Stakes (The Admiral)
Santa Susana Stakes (Mrs. Rabbit)
Gazelle Stakes (Sweet Dream)
Aqueduct Handicap (Stymie)
1950: Alabama Stakes (Busanda)
1952: Trenton Handicap (Ken)

CRAIG PERRET
1968: Gazelle Handicap (Another Nell)
1970: Pan American Handicap (One For All)
1971: Arlington-Washington Futurity (Governor Max)
Gulfstream Park Handicap (Fast Hilarious)
1974: Michigan Mile and One-Eighth (Tom Tulle)
1975: Amory L. Haskell Handicap (Royal Glint)
1976: Spinster Stakes (Optimistic Gal)
Travers Stakes (Honest Pleasure)
1977: Florida Derby (Ruthie's Native)
Vosburgh Handicap (Affiliate)
1978: Amory L. Haskell Handicap (Life's Hope)
1980: Sapling Stakes (Travelling Music)
1981: Haskell Invitational Handicap (Five Star Flight)
1983: Sorority Stakes (Officer's Ball)
Widener Handicap (Swing Till Dawn)
1984: Breeders' Cup Sprint (Eillo)
1986: Arlington-Washington Futurity (Bet Twice)
Laurel Futurity (Bet Twice)
Hialeah Turf Cup (Sondrio)
1987: Fountain of Youth Stakes (Bet Twice)
Belmont Stakes (Bet Twice)
Haskell Invitational Handicap (Bet Twice)
Tropical Park Derby (Baldski's Star)
Acorn Stakes (Grecian Flight)
Arlington-Washington Lassie Stakes (Joe's Tammie)
1988: Jersey Derby (Dynaformer)
Sword Dancer Handicap (Anka Germania)
1989: Flamingo Stakes (Awe Inspiring)
Jersey Derby (Awe Inspiring)
Laurel Futurity (Go and Go)
Breeders' Cup Juvenile (Rhythm)
1990: Withers Stakes (Housebuster)
Jerome Handicap (Housebuster)
Kentucky Derby (Unbridled)
Coaching Club American Oaks (Charon)
Travers Stakes (Rhythm)
Breeders' Cup Sprint (Safely Kept)
Demoiselle Stakes (Debutant's Halo)
1991: Peter Pan Stakes (Lost Mountain)
Dwyer Stakes (Lost Mountain)
Haskell Invitational Handicap (Lost Mountain)
Carter Handicap (Housebuster)
Vosburgh Stakes (Housebuster)
Wood Memorial Stakes (Cahill Road)
Remsen Stakes (Pine Bluff)
1992: Pimlico Special (Strike the Gold)
Nassau County Handicap (Strike the Gold)
Ashland Stakes (Prospectors Delite)
1993: Carter Handicap (Alydeed)
Molson Export Million (Peteski)
1994: Gulfstream Park Handicap (Scuffleburg)
1996: Frizette Stakes (Storm Song)
Breeders' Cup Juvenile Fillies (Storm Song)
Philip H. Iselin Handicap (Smart Strike)
Hopeful Stakes (Smoke Glacken)
1997: Frank J. De Francis Memorial Dash (Smoke Glacken)

OLIVIER PESLIER
2001: Breeders' Cup Filly and Mare Turf (Banks Hill)

MEL PETERSON
1946: Del Mar Handicap (Olhaverry)
1947: San Carlos Handicap (Texas Sandman)
Santa Anita Handicap (Olhaverry)
1948: San Pasqual Handicap (Olhaverry)
Hawthorne Gold Cup (Billings)

JULIO PEZUA
1986: Fountain of Youth Stakes (Ensign Rhythm)
1992: Metropolitan Handicap (Dixie Brass)

MAURICE PHILLIPERON
1974: Washington D.C. International (Admetus)

JOE PHILLIPPI
1953: Del Mar Futurity (Double Speed)

DON PIERCE
1959: Hollywood Juvenile Championship (Noble Noor)
Del Mar Debutante Stakes (Darling June)
1960: Santa Anita Handicap (Linmold)
1961: Display Handicap (Hillsborough)
1962: Hopeful Stakes (Outing Class)
Top Flight Handicap (Pepper Patch)
Santa Anita Handicap (Physician)
1963: San Antonio Handicap (Physician)
1964: San Felipe Handicap (Hill Rise)
Santa Anita Derby (Hill Rise)
Sanford Stakes (Cornish Prince)
1965: Santa Anita Handicap (Hill Rise)
San Fernando Stakes (Hill Rise)
Santa Susana Stakes (Desert Love)
Acorn Stakes (Ground Control)
1966: Santa Susana Stakes (Spearfish)
Hollywood Oaks (Spearfish)
California Derby (Tragniew)
Sunset Handicap (O'Hara)
1968: Hollywood Gold Cup (Princessnesian)
1969: Del Mar Debutante Stakes (Atomic Wings)
Hollywood Oaks (Tipping Time)
Santa Margarita Handicap (Princessnesian)
Santa Barbara Handicap (Pink Pigeon)
Hollywood Derby (Tell)
1970: Santa Susana Stakes (Opening Bid)
1971: Del Mar Debutante Stakes (Impressive Style)
1972: San Fernando Stakes (Triple Bend)
Santa Anita Handicap (Triple Bend)
Hollywood Gold Cup (Quack)
1973: Del Mar Debutante Stakes (Fleet Peach)
Hollywood Oaks (Sandy Blue)
Californian Stakes (Quack)
San Antonio Stakes (Kennedy Road)
San Luis Rey Handicap (Big Spruce)
1974: Norfolk Stakes (George Navonod)
Beverly Hills Handicap (La Zanzara)
San Felipe Handicap (Aloha Mood)
Californian Stakes (Quack)
1975: Beverly Hills Handicap (La Zanzara)
San Juan Capistrano Handicap (La Zanzara)
Santa Margarita Handicap (Tizna)
Swaps Stakes (Forceten)
Hollywood Derby (Intrepid Hero)
1977: Apple Blossom Handicap (Hail Hilarious)
1978: Del Mar Futurity (Flying Paster)
Norfolk Stakes (Flying Paster)
La Canada Stakes (Taisez Vous)
Santa Margarita Handicap (Taisez Vous)
Hollywood Oaks (B. Thoughtful)
1979: Santa Anita Derby (Flying Paster)
Hollywood Derby (Flying Paster)
La Canada Stakes (B. Thoughtful)
1980: San Antonio Stakes (Beau's Eagle)
1981: Louisiana Downs Handicap (Goldiko)
1982: Hollywood Starlet Stakes (Fabulous Notion)
1983: Santa Susana Stakes (Fabulous Notion)

NEWBOLD PIERSON
1946: Arlington Matron Handicap (Good Blood)
1948: Blue Grass Stakes (Coaltown)
Jerome Handicap (Coaltown)
Dixie Handicap (Fervent)
Washington Park Handicap (Fervent)

LESTER PIGGOTT
1968: Washington D.C. International (Sir Ivor)
1969: Washington D.C. International (Karabas)
1974: Canadian International Championship (Dahlia)
1980: Washington D.C. International (Argument)
1990: Breeders' Cup Mile (Royal Academy)

LAFFIT PINCAY JR.
1964: Display Handicap (Primordial II)
1966: Alcibiades Stakes (Teacher's Art)
1967: Cowdin Stakes (Iron Ruler)
Arlington-Washington Lassie Stakes (Shenow)
Santa Margarita Handicap (Miss Moona)
San Felipe Handicap (Rising Market)
Jerome Handicap (High Tribute)
Arlington Handicap (Stupendous)
Charles H. Strub Stakes (Drin)
1968: Santa Susana Stakes (Allie's Serenade)
Beldame Stakes (Gamely)
Santa Barbara Handicap (Princessnesian)

Santa Anita Derby (Alley Fighter)
San Antonio Handicap (Rising Market)
Sunset Handicap (Fort Marcy)
1969: Hollywood Juvenile Championship (Insubordination)
Vanity Handicap (Desert Law)
Beldame Stakes (Gamely)
American Derby (Fast Hilarious)
Cinema Handicap (Noholme Jr.)
1970: Alcibiades Stakes (Patelin)
Selima Stakes (Patelin)
Brooklyn Handicap (Dewan)
San Antonio Stakes (Dewan)
Acorn Stakes (Cathy Honey)
Cinema Handicap (D'Artagnan)
Hollywood Gold Cup (Pleasure Seeker)
Charles H. Strub Stakes (Snow Sporting)
Sunset Handicap (One For All)
1971: Santa Margarita Handicap (Manta)
Beverly Hills Handicap (Manta)
Santa Barbara Handicap (Manta)
Hollywood Derby (Bold Reason)
Travers Stakes (Bold Reason)
American Derby (Bold Reason)
San Felipe Handicap (Unconscious)
California Derby (Unconscious)
Breeders' Futurity (Windjammer)
Hawthorne Gold Cup (Twice Worthy)
1972: Gazelle Handicap (Susan's Girl)
Beldame Stakes (Susan's Girl)
San Felipe Handicap (Solar Salute)
Santa Anita Derby (Solar Salute)
Spinster Stakes (Numbered Account)
Cinema Handicap (Finalista)
Vosburgh Handicap (Triple Bend)
San Juan Capistrano Handicap (Practicante)
1973: Delaware Handicap (Susan's Girl)
Santa Maria Handicap (Susan's Girl)
Santa Margarita Handicap (Susan's Girl)
Santa Barbara Handicap (Susan's Girl)
Selima Stakes (Dancealot)
Santa Anita Derby (Sham)
Santa Anita Handicap (Cougar II)
Hollywood Invitational Handicap (Life Cycle)
Manhattan Handicap (London Company)
1974: Vanity Handicap (Tallahto)
Santa Barbara Handicap (Tallahto)
Oak Tree Invitational Stakes (Tallahto)
Florida Derby (Judger)
Blue Grass Stakes (Judger)
San Fernando Stakes (Ancient Title)
Charles H. Strub Stakes (Ancient Title)
Hollywood Juvenile Championship (DiMaggio)
Frizette Stakes (Molly Ballentine)
Hollywood Oaks (Miss Musket)
Beldame Stakes (Desert Vixen)
Santa Maria Handicap (Convenience)
Whitney Stakes (Tri Jet)
San Antonio Stakes (Prince Dantan)
American Handicap (Plunk)
1975: Californian Stakes (Ancient Title)
Hollywood Gold Cup (Ancient Title)
Remsen Stakes (Hang Ten)
Demoiselle Stakes (Free Journey)
Maskette Handicap (Let Me Linger)
Spinster Stakes (Susan's Girl)
California Derby (Diabolo)
1976: Del Mar Futurity (Visible)
Del Mar Debutante Stakes (Telferner)
Beverly Hills Handicap (Bastonera II)
Santa Anita Derby (An Act)
San Luis Rey Stakes (Avatar)
1977: Californian Stakes (Crystal Water)
Hollywood Gold Cup (Crystal Water)
Santa Anita Handicap (Crystal Water)
Hollywood Juvenile Championship (Affirmed)
Cinema Handicap (Bad 'n Big)
San Fernando Stakes (Kirby Lane)
Century Handicap (Anne's Pretender)
1978: Santa Barbara Handicap (Kittyluck)
Santa Anita Derby (Affirmed)
American Handicap (Effervescing)
1979: Californian Stakes (Affirmed)
Hollywood Gold Cup (Affirmed)
Woodward Stakes (Affirmed)
Jockey Club Gold Cup (Affirmed)
Charles H. Strub Stakes (Affirmed)
Santa Anita Handicap (Affirmed)
Ramona Handicap (Country Queen)
Yellow Ribbon Stakes (Country Queen)
Ruffian Handicap (It's In the Air)
Swaps Stakes (Valdez)
1980: Frizette Stakes (Heavenly Cause)
Selima Stakes (Heavenly Cause)
Hollywood Juvenile Championship (Loma Malad)
Arlington-Washington Futurity (Well Decorated)
Vanity Handicap (It's In the Air)
Santa Barbara Handicap (Sisterhood)
Metropolitan Handicap (Czaravich)
Oak Tree Invitational Stakes (John Henry)
1981: Fantasy Stakes (Heavenly Cause)
Kentucky Oaks (Heavenly Cause)
Acorn Stakes (Heavenly Cause)
Santa Anita Handicap (John Henry)
Hollywood Invitational Handicap (John Henry)
San Luis Rey Stakes (John Henry)
Santa Margarita Handicap (Princess Karenda)
Matriarch Stakes (Kilijaro)
Swaps Stakes (Noble Nashua)
Super Derby (Island Whirl)
Bay Meadows Handicap (Super Moment)
1982: Hollywood Gold Cup (Perrault)
Budweiser Million (Perrault)
San Luis Rey Stakes (Perrault)
Del Mar Debutante Stakes (Landaluce)
Oak Leaf Stakes (Landaluce)
Santa Barbara Handicap (Ack's Secret)
Santa Margarita Handicap (Ack's Secret)
Santa Anita Derby (Muttering)
Belmont Stakes (Conquistador Cielo)
Californian Stakes (Erins Isle)
Hollywood Invitational Handicap (Exploded)
1983: Del Mar Futurity (Althea)
Del Mar Debutante Stakes (Althea)
Hollywood Starlet Stakes (Althea)
Hollywood Invitational Handicap (Erins Isle)
San Luis Rey Stakes (Erins Isle)
San Juan Capistrano Handicap (Erins Isle)
Ruffian Handicap (Heartlight No. One)
Belmont Stakes (Caveat)
Super Derby (Sunny's Halo)
1984: Florida Derby (Swale)
Kentucky Derby (Swale)
Belmont Stakes (Swale)
Futurity Stakes (Spectacular Love)
Matron Stakes (Fiesta Lady)
Oak Leaf Stakes (Folk Art)
Travers Stakes (Carr de Naskra)
Super Derby (Gate Dancer)
Santa Susana Stakes (Althea)
Delaware Handicap (Adored)
Century Handicap (Interco)
Rothmans International Stakes (Majesty's Prince)
San Juan Capistrano Handicap (Load the Cannons)
1985: Jersey Derby (Spend A Buck)
Monmouth Handicap (Spend A Buck)
Californian Stakes (Greinton)
Hollywood Gold Cup (Greinton)
Dwyer Stakes (Stephan's Odyssey)
Jim Dandy Stakes (Stephan's Odyssey)
Frizette Stakes (Family Style)
Arlington-Washington Lassie Stakes (Family Style)
Breeders' Futurity (Tasso)
Breeders' Cup Juvenile (Tasso)
San Felipe Handicap (Image of Greatness)
Santa Anita Derby (Skywalker)
Spinster Stakes (Dontstop Themusic)
1986: Norfolk Stakes (Capote)
Breeders' Cup Juvenile (Capote)
San Antonio Handicap (Hatim)
Santa Anita Handicap (Greinton)
Hollywood Gold Cup (Super Diamond)
Breeders' Cup Classic (Skywalker)
1987: Jockey Club Gold Cup (Creme Fraiche)
Meadowlands Cup (Creme Fraiche)
San Fernando Stakes (Variety Road)
San Juan Capistrano Handicap (Rosedale)
Del Mar Futurity (Lost Kitty)
Budweiser International Stakes (Le Glorieux)
Hollywood Futurity (Tejano)
1988: La Canada Stakes (Hollywood Glitter)
California Derby (All Thee Power)
Haskell Invitational Handicap (Forty Niner)
Frizette Stakes (Some Romance)
Breeders' Cup Juvenile (Is It True)
1989: Santa Margarita Handicap (Bayakoa)
Apple Blossom Handicap (Bayakoa)
Vanity Handicap (Bayakoa)
Ruffian Handicap (Bayakoa)
Spinster Stakes (Bayakoa)
Breeders' Cup Distaff (Bayakoa)
San Antonio Handicap (Super Diamond)
1990: Spinster Stakes (Bayakoa)
Breeders' Cup Distaff (Bayakoa)
Hollywood Turf Handicap (Steinlen)
Budweiser International Stakes (Fly Till Dawn)
1991: Eddie Read Handicap (Tight Spot)
Arlington Million (Tight Spot)
Gamely Handicap (Miss Josh)
1992: San Luis Rey Stakes (Fly Till Dawn)
NYRA Mile Handicap (Ibero)
Hollywood Futurity (River Special)
1993: Oak Leaf Stakes (Phone Chatter)
Breeders' Cup Juvenile Fillies (Phone Chatter)
Santa Barbara Handicap (Exchange)
Metropolitan Handicap (Ibero)
Swaps Stakes (Devoted Brass)
Pegasus Handicap (Diazo)
Hollywood Futurity (Valiant Nature)
1994: Strub Stakes (Diazo)
Matriarch Stakes (Exchange)
1995: Oak Leaf Stakes (Tipically Irish)
1998: Hollywood Futurity (Tactical Cat)
1999: Beverly Hills Handicap (Virginie)
Hollywood Turf Cup (Lazy Lode)
2001: Toyota Blue Grass Stakes (Millennium Wind)
Hollywood Gold Cup (Aptitude)

ALVARO PINEDA

1967: San Juan Capistrano Handicap (Niarkos)
1968: Hollywood Juvenile Championship (Fleet Kirsch)
Hollywood Oaks (Hooplah)
San Juan Capistrano Handicap (Niarkos)
1969: Hollywood Gold Cup (Figonero)
1970: Gulfstream Park Handicap (Snow Sporting)
1973: Arlington-Washington Lassie Stakes (Special Team)

ROBIN PLATTS

1968: Canadian International Championship (Frenetico)
1976: Arlington Handicap (Victorian Prince)
1979: Bowling Green Handicap (Overskate)
1981: Spinster Stakes (Glorious Song)
1985: Hialeah Turf Cup (Selous Scout)
1991: Donn Handicap (Jolie's Halo)
Gulfstream Park Handicap (Jolie's Halo)

AL POPARA

1952: Louisiana Derby (Gushing Oil)
1953: Alcibiades Stakes (Oil Painting)
Florida Derby (Money Broker)

GERALD PORCH

1950: Princess Pat Stakes (Flyamanita)
Hawthorne Gold Cup (Dr. Ole Nelson)
1952: Metropolitan Handicap (Mameluke)
1953: New Orleans Handicap (Smoke Screen)

EDGAR PRADO

1991: Budweiser International Stakes (Leariva)
1992: Philip H. Iselin Handicap (Jolie's Halo)
1994: Pegasus Handicap (Brass Scale)
2000: Brooklyn Handicap (Lemon Drop Kid)
Suburban Handicap (Lemon Drop Kid)
Whitney Handicap (Lemon Drop Kid)
Woodward Stakes (Lemon Drop Kid)
2001: Fountain of Youth Stakes (Songandaprayer)
Test Stakes (Victory Ride)
Go for Wand Handicap (Serra Lake)
Alabama Stakes (Flute)
Turf Classic (Timboroa)
Frizette Stakes (You)
2002: Florida Derby (Harlan's Holiday)
Toyota Blue Grass Stakes (Harlan's Holiday)
Hopeful Stakes (Sky Mesa)
Lane's End Breeders' Futurity (Sky Mesa)
Donn Handicap (Mongoose)
Belmont Stakes (Sarava)
Garden City Breeders' Cup Handicap (Wonder Again)
Futurity Stakes (Whywhywhy)
Turf Classic (Denon)
Shadwell Keeneland Turf Mile (Landseer)
Overbrook Spinster Stakes (Take Charge Lady)
2003: Kentucky Oaks (Bird Town)
Acorn Stakes (Bird Town)
Toyota Blue Grass Stakes (Peace Rules)
Haskell Invitational Handicap (Peace Rules)
Santa Anita Handicap (Milwaukee Brew)
Gulfstream Park Handicap (Hero's Tribute)
Spinaway Stakes (Ashado)
Matron Stakes (Marylebone)
Shadwell Turf Mile (Perfect Soul)
Overbrook Spinster Stakes (Take Charge Lady)
Queen Elizabeth II Challenge Cup (Film Maker)

HENRY PRATT

1946: San Vicente Handicap (Air Rate)
1947: Gazelle Stakes (Cosmic Missile)

BELOIN PULIDO

1956: Vanity Handicap (Mary Machree)

WILLIAM PYERS

1973: Washington D.C. International (Dahlia)

RICHARD QUINN

1992: Rothmans International Stakes (Snurge)

CHARLIE RALLS

1947: Longacres Mile (Hank H.)

JOHN RAMIREZ

1973: Oak Tree Invitational Stakes (Portentous)

RAUL RAMIREZ

1977: California Derby (Cuzwuzwrong)

WIGBERTO RAMOS

1993: Florida Derby (Bull Inthe Heather)

JOE RENICK

1946: McLennan Handicap (Concordian)
1949: Massachusetts Handicap (First Nighter)

W.W. RICE

1978: Sorority Stakes (Mongo Queen)

DOUG RICHARD

1967: Kentucky Jockey Club Stakes (Mr. Brogann)

NOEL RICHARDSON

1946: Longacres Mile (Amble In)
1947: Hollywood Derby (Yankee Valor)
Cinema Handicap (Yankee Valor)
1948: Longacres Mile (Amble In)

TONY RINI

1972: Illinois Derby (Fame and Power)
1973: Ohio Derby (Our Native)

ANGEL RIVERA

1949: Hawthorne Gold Cup (Volcanic)
1950: Arlington Futurity (To Market)
Washington Park Futurity (To Market)
Arlington Lassie Stakes (Shawnee Squaw)

MIGUEL RIVERA

1973: Monmouth Invitational Handicap (Our Native)
1974: Preakness Stakes (Little Current)
Belmont Stakes (Little Current)
Hialeah Turf Cup (Big Whippendeal)
Century Handicap (Big Whippendeal)
Acorn Stakes (Special Team)
Wood Memorial Stakes (Rube the Great)
Ohio Derby (Stonewalk)
Amory L. Haskell Handicap (True Knight)
1976: Jersey Derby (Life's Hope)
1977: Monmouth Invitational Handicap (Affiliate)
Hialeah Turf Cup (Improviser)

PORTER ROBERTS

1946: Bougainvillea Handicap (Cat Bridge)
1948: McLennan Handicap (El Mono)
Widener Handicap (El Mono)
Monmouth Handicap (Tide Rips)
1952: Molly Pitcher Handicap (Dixie Flyer)

S. ROBERTS

1946: Princess Pat Stakes (Say Blue)

JACK ROBERTSON

1950: Vosburgh Handicap (Tea-Maker)

CHRIS ROGERS

1950: Widener Handicap (Royal Governor)
1951: Garden State Stakes (Candle Wood)
1954: Bougainvillea Turf Handicap (Parnassus)
1956: Dixie Handicap (Chevation)
1959: Flamingo Stakes (Troilus)

KAREN ROGERS

1983: Top Flight Handicap (Adept)

RAUL ROJAS

1990: Ruffian Handicap (Quick Mischief)

RANDY ROMERO

1979: Louisiana Downs Handicap (Incredible Ease)
1982: Haskell Invitational Handicap (Wavering Monarch)
1984: Ruffian Handicap (Heatherten)
Ladies Handicap (Heatherten)
1986: Cowdin Stakes (Polish Navy)
Champagne Stakes (Polish Navy)
Gulfstream Park Handicap (Skip Trial)
Coaching Club American Oaks (Valley Victory)
Arlington Classic (Sumptious)
Frizette Stakes (Personal Ensign)
Jockey Club Gold Cup (Creme Fraiche)
Ladies Handicap (Life at the Top)
1987: Spinster Stakes (Sacahuista)
Breeders' Cup Distaff (Sacahuista)
Gulfstream Park Handicap (Skip Trial)
Hopeful Stakes (Crusader Sword)
Woodward Stakes (Polish Navy)
Beldame Stakes (Personal Ensign)
1988: Whitney Handicap (Personal Ensign)
Maskette Stakes (Personal Ensign)
Beldame Stakes (Personal Ensign)
Breeders' Cup Distaff (Personal Ensign)
Florida Derby (Brian's Time)
Vosburgh Stakes (Mining)
1989: Fountain of Youth Stakes (Dixieland Brass)
Blue Grass Stakes (Western Playboy)
Vosburgh Stakes (Sewickley)
Breeders' Cup Juvenile Fillies (Go for Wand)
1990: Ashland Stakes (Go for Wand)
Mother Goose Stakes (Go for Wand)
Alabama Stakes (Go for Wand)
Maskette Stakes (Go for Wand)
Beldame Stakes (Go for Wand)
1992: Brooklyn Handicap (Chief Honcho)
1995: Blue Grass Stakes (Wild Syn)

SHANE ROMERO

1988: Ohio Derby (Jim's Orbit)

RUDY ROSALES

1969: Oak Leaf Stakes (Opening Bid)
1971: Century Handicap (Big Shot II)
1973: San Juan Capistrano Handicap (Queen's Hustler)

JOHN ROTZ

1959: Breeders' Futurity (Toby's Brother)
Kentucky Oaks (Wedlock)
1960: Princess Pat Stakes (Rose Bower)
Matron Stakes (Rose Bower)
Spinster Stakes (Rash Statement)
1961: Wood Memorial Stakes (Globemaster)
Arlington Classic (Globemaster)
Bougainvillea Turf Handicap (Wolfram)
Hialeah Turf Cup (Wolfram)
Aqueduct Handicap (Tompion)
Remsen Stakes (Figaro Bob)
1962: Metropolitan Handicap (Carry Back)
Monmouth Handicap (Carry Back)
Remsen Stakes (Rocky Link)
Preakness Stakes (Greek Money)
1963: Canadian Championship Stakes (The Axe II)
Man o' War Stakes (The Axe II)
Champagne Stakes (Roman Brother)
Ladies Handicap (Goofed)
Wood Memorial Stakes (No Robbery)
Grey Lag Handicap (Sunrise County)
1964: Acorn Stakes (Castle Forbes)
Black Helen Handicap (Princess Arle)
Jerome Handicap (Irvkup)
John B. Campbell Handicap (Mongo)
Los Angeles Handicap (Cyrano)
1965: Alabama Stakes (What A Treat)
Gazelle Handicap (What A Treat)
Beldame Stakes (What A Treat)
Flamingo Stakes (Native Charger)
Florida Derby (Native Charger)
1966: Hopeful Stakes (Bold Hour)
Futurity Stakes (Bold Hour)
Sanford Stakes (Yorkville)
Pimlico Futurity (In Reality)
Spinaway Stakes (Silver True)
Matron Stakes (Swiss Cheese)
Black Helen Handicap (What A Treat)
Withers Stakes (Indulto)
Gallant Fox Handicap (Munden Point)
1968: Gardenia Stakes (Gallant Bloom)
Alabama Stakes (Gay Matelda)
Gotham Stakes (Verbatim)
Grey Lag Handicap (Bold Hour)
Metropolitan Handicap (In Reality)
Massachusetts Handicap (Out of the Way)
1969: Arlington-Washington Futurity (Silent Screen)
Cowdin Stakes (Silent Screen)
Champagne Stakes (Silent Screen)
Gazelle Handicap (Gallant Bloom)
Spinster Stakes (Gallant Bloom)
Futurity Stakes (High Echelon)
Delaware Handicap (Obeah)
Vosburgh Handicap (Ta Wee)
1970: Hopeful Stakes (Proudest Roman)
Futurity Stakes (Salem)
Garden State Stakes (Run the Gantlet)
Santa Margarita Handicap (Gallant Bloom)
Belmont Stakes (High Echelon)
1971: Acorn Stakes (Deceit)
Mother Goose Stakes (Deceit)
Carter Handicap (Native Royalty)
Woodward Stakes (West Coast Scout)
1972: Champagne Stakes (Stop the Music)
Amory L. Haskell Handicap (West Coast Scout)
1973: Vanity Handicap (Convenience)

JOHN RUANE

1958: Brooklyn Handicap (Cohoes)
Whitney Stakes (Cohoes)
Remsen Stakes (Atoll)
Hialeah Turf Handicap (Meeting)
1959: Carter Handicap (Jimmer)
1960: Man o' War Stakes (Harmonizing)
1964: Ladies Handicap (Steeple Jill)
1965: Delaware Handicap (Steeple Jill)
Vineland Handicap (Steeple Jill)
1970: Monmouth Invitational Handicap (Twice Worthy)
1971: Metropolitan Handicap (Tunex)
Suburban Handicap (Twice Worthy)
Vosburgh Handicap (Duck Dance)
1973: Widener Handicap (Vertee)
John B. Campbell Handicap (Vertee)

PHIL RUBBICCO

1970: New Orleans Handicap (Etony)
1972: Louisiana Derby (No Le Hace)
Arkansas Derby (No Le Hace)
1975: Illinois Derby (Colonel Power)
1982: Louisiana Downs Handicap (Rich and Ready)

MARY RUSS

1982: Widener Handicap (Lord Darnley)
Gulfstream Park Handicap (Lord Darnley)

GENE ST. LEON

1972: New Orleans Handicap (Urgent Message)
1975: Donn Handicap (Proud and Bold)
1986: Delaware Handicap (Shocker T.)
1987: Illinois Derby (Lost Code)
Ohio Derby (Lost Code)
Arlington Classic (Lost Code)

YVES ST. MARTIN

1962: Washington D.C. International (Match II)
1984: Breeders' Cup Turf (Lashkari)
1985: Hollywood Derby (Charming Duke)
1986: Breeders' Cup Mile (Last Tycoon)

JEAN-LUC SAMYN

1978: American Derby (Nasty and Bold)
Brooklyn Handicap (Nasty and Bold)
Carter Handicap (Jaipur's Gem)
1982: United Nations Handicap (Naskra's Breeze)
Man o' War Stakes (Naskra's Breeze)
Pegasus Handicap (Fast Gold)
1983: Coaching Club American Oaks (High Schemes)
Pan American Handicap (Field Cat)
1984: Withers Stakes (Play On)
1985: Ohio Derby (Skip Trial)
Haskell Invitational Handicap (Skip Trial)
Pennsylvania Derby (Skip Trial)
Top Flight Handicap (Flip's Pleasure)
Rothmans International Stakes (Nassipour)
1986: Brooklyn Handicap (Little Missouri)
1988: Hutcheson Stakes (Perfect Spy)
1991: Sword Dancer Handicap (Dr. Root)
1992: Flower Bowl Handicap (Christiecat)
1993: Nassau County Handicap (West by West)
Flower Bowl Handicap (Far Out Beast)
1994: Carter Handicap (Virginia Rapids)
1997: Caesars International Handicap (Influent)
1998: Frank J. De Francis Memorial Dash (Kelly Kip)
Jerome Handicap (Limit Out)
1999: Champagne Stakes (Greenwood Lake)
Remsen Stakes (Greenwood Lake)
2000: Sword Dancer Invitational Handicap (John's Call)
Turf Classic (John's Call)
Flower Bowl Invitational Handicap (Colstar)
2001: Ballerina Handicap (Shine Again)
2002: Ballerina Handicap (Shine Again)
2003: Sword Dancer Inv. Handicap (Whitmore's Conn)

J. SANCHEZ

1956: Canadian Championship Stakes (Eugenia II)
1957: Canadian Championship Stakes (Spinney)

NICK SANTAGATA

1985: Vosburgh Stakes (Another Reef)
1990: Young America Stakes (Southern Sign)

ANGEL SANTIAGO

1973: Champagne Stakes (Protagonist)
Laurel Futurity (Protagonist)
1974: Withers Stakes (Accipiter)
Secretariat Stakes (Glossary)
1975: Vosburgh Handicap (No Bias)
San Antonio Stakes (Cheriepe)
1978: Ladies Handicap (Ida Delia)
1982: Acorn Stakes (Cupecoy's Joy)
Mother Goose Stakes (Cupecoy's Joy)
1983: Illinois Derby (General Practitioner)

JOSE SANTOS

1985: Tropical Park Derby (Irish Sur)
1986: United Nations Handicap (Manila)
Turf Classic (Manila)
Breeders' Cup Turf (Manila)
Secretariat Stakes (Southjet)
Rothmans International Stakes (Southjet)
Fountain of Youth Stakes (My Prince Charming)
Mother Goose Stakes (Life at the Top)
Vosburgh Stakes (King's Swan)
1987: Everglades Stakes (Cryptoclearance)
Florida Derby (Cryptoclearance)
Wood Memorial Stakes (Gulch)
Kentucky Oaks (Buryyourbelief)
Peter Pan Stakes (Leo Castelli)
Remsen Stakes (Batty)
Yellow Ribbon Stakes (Carotene)
Breeders' Cup Juvenile (Success Express)
1988: Brooklyn Handicap (Waquoit)
Jockey Club Gold Cup (Waquoit)
San Fernando Stakes (On the Line)
Top Flight Handicap (Clabber Girl)
Metropolitan Handicap (Gulch)
United Nations Handicap (Equalize)
Laurel Futurity (Luge II)
1989: Arlington Million (Steinlen)
Breeders' Cup Mile (Steinlen)
Man o' War Stakes (Yankee Affair)
Turf Classic (Yankee Affair)
Widener Handicap (Cryptoclearance)
Jim Dandy Stakes (Is It True)
Futurity Stakes (Senor Pete)
Meadowlands Cup (Mi Selecto)
Young America Stakes (Roanoke)
Ladies Handicap (Dance Teacher)
1990: Matron Stakes (Meadow Star)
Spinaway Stakes (Meadow Star)
Frizette Stakes (Meadow Star)
Breeders' Cup Juvenile Fillies (Meadow Star)
Pimlico Special (Criminal Type)
Metropolitan Handicap (Criminal Type)
Hollywood Gold Cup (Criminal Type)
Peter Pan Stakes (Profit Key)
Dwyer Stakes (Profit Key)
Champagne Stakes (Fly So Free)
Breeders' Cup Juvenile (Fly So Free)
Caesars International Handicap (Steinlen)
Ladies Handicap (Colonial Waters)
Hollywood Futurity (Best Pal)
1991: Florida Derby (Fly So Free)
Jim Dandy Stakes (Fly So Free)
Jerome Handicap (Scan)
Pegasus Handicap (Scan)
Charles H. Strub Stakes (Defensive Play)
NYRA Mile Handicap (Rubiano)
1992: Carter Handicap (Rubiano)
1993: Caesars International Handicap (Star of Cozzene)
Arlington Million (Star of Cozzene)
Man o' War Stakes (Star of Cozzene)
Spinaway Stakes (Strategic Maneuver)
Matron Stakes (Strategic Maneuver)
Haskell Invitational Handicap (Kissin Kris)
1994: Whitney Handicap (Colonial Affair)
Jockey Club Gold Cup (Colonial Affair)
Peter Pan Stakes (Twining)
Coaching Club American Oaks (Two Altazano)
Jim Dandy Stakes (Unaccounted For)
Futurity Stakes (Montreal Red)
1995: Shuvee Handicap (Inside Information)
Coaching Club American Oaks (Golden Bri)
1996: Ohio Derby (Skip Away)
Buick Haskell Invitational Handicap (Skip Away)
Whitney Handicap (Mahogany Hall)
1997: Canadian Int. Championship (Chief Bearhart)
Breeders' Cup Turf (Chief Bearhart)
1998: Manhattan Handicap (Chief Bearhart)
Spinaway Stakes (Things Change)
1999: Belmont Stakes (Lemon Drop Kid)
Travers Stakes (Lemon Drop Kid)
Sword Dancer Invitational Handicap (Honor Glide)
2002: Gazelle Handicap (Imperial Gesture)
Ruffian Handicap (Mandy's Gold)
Breeders' Cup Classic (Volponi)
2003: Kentucky Derby (Funny Cide)
Preakness Stakes (Funny Cide)
Prioress Stakes (House Party)
Personal Ensign Handicap (Passing Shot)

LARRY SAUMELL

1976: Sapling Stakes (Ali Oop)
1977: Donn Handicap (Legion)
1988: Pennsylvania Derby (Cefis)

SMOKEY SAUNDERS

1948: Louisiana Derby (Bovard)

KENNETH SCAWTHORN

1946: Black Helen Handicap (Adroit)

RANDY SCHACHT

1976: Oak Leaf Stakes (Any Time Girl)

ALBERT SCHMIDT

1949: Astoria Stakes (Baby Comet)
1952: Westchester Handicap (Battlefield)

DON SCURLOCK

1949: Kentucky Jockey Club Stakes (Roman Bath)
1953: Trenton Handicap (Olympic)

OVIE SCURLOCK

1946: Arlington Handicap (Historian)
Sunset Handicap (Historian)
1947: Discovery Handicap (Cosmic Bomb)
Lawrence Realization Stakes (Cosmic Bomb)
Roamer Handicap (Cosmic Bomb)
Trenton Handicap (Cosmic Bomb)
Fall Highweight Handicap (Rippey)
Carter Handicap (Rippey)
Vineland Handicap (Miss Kimo)
1948: Vosburgh Handicap (Colosal)
1949: Washington Park Futurity (Curtice)
Remsen Handicap (Lights Up)
Gulfstream Park Handicap (Coaltown)
Grey Lag Handicap (Royal Governor)
1950: Dwyer Stakes (Greek Song)
Arlington Classic (Greek Song)
Cowdin Stakes (Away Away)
Astoria Stakes (Sungari)
Black Helen Handicap (Bewitch)
Comely Handicap (Siama)
1951: Discovery Handicap (Alerted)
Jerome Handicap (Alerted)
Grey Lag Handicap (Cochise)
Arlington Handicap (Cochise)
Westchester Handicap (Bryan G.)
Pimlico Special (Bryan G.)
Queens County Handicap (Sheilas Reward)
Marguerite Stakes (No Score)
1953: Spinaway Stakes (Evening Out)
Matron Stakes (Evening Out)
1954: Gallant Fox Handicap (Social Outcast)
1956: Molly Pitcher Handicap (Blue Sparkler)

ANDREA SEEFELDT

1991: Pennsylvania Derby (Valley Crossing)

JOHNNY SELLERS

1958: Washington Park Handicap (Clem)
Canadian Championship Stakes (Jack Ketch)
1960: Arlington Classic (T.V. Lark)
American Derby (T.V. Lark)
Washington Park Handicap (T.V. Lark)
United Nations Handicap (T.V. Lark)
Garden State Stakes (Carry Back)
Remsen Stakes (Carry Back)
Everglades Stakes (Moslem Chief)
1961: Everglades Stakes (Carry Back)
Flamingo Stakes (Carry Back)
Florida Derby (Carry Back)
Kentucky Derby (Carry Back)
Preakness Stakes (Carry Back)
Jerome Handicap (Carry Back)
Trenton Handicap (Carry Back)
McLennan Handicap (Yorky)
Widener Handicap (Yorky)
Selima Stakes (Tamarona)
1962: Monmouth Oaks (Firm Policy)
Alabama Stakes (Firm Policy)
Saratoga Special (Mr. Cold Storage)
Selima Stakes (Fool's Play)
Carter Handicap (Merry Ruler)
Whitney Stakes (Carry Back)
Hialeah Turf Cup (El Loco)
1963: Spinaway Stakes (Petite Rouge)
Trenton Handicap (Carry Back)
1965: Jersey Derby (Hail to All)
Belmont Stakes (Hail to All)
Travers Stakes (Hail to All)
Hollywood Oaks (Straight Deal)
Ladies Handicap (Straight Deal)
Suburban Handicap (Pia Star)
Brooklyn Handicap (Pia Star)
1966: Arkansas Derby (Better Sea)
Widener Handicap (Pia Star)
Grey Lag Handicap (Selari)
1967: Kentucky Oaks (Nancy Jr.)
Blue Grass Stakes (Diplomat Way)
Hollywood Derby (Tumble Wind)
Gulfstream Park Handicap (Pretense)
1968: San Felipe Handicap (Prince Pablo)
California Derby (Proper Proof)
1969: Sunset Handicap (Petrone)
San Juan Capistrano Handicap (Petrone)
1970: Del Mar Handicap (Daryl's Joy)
Oak Tree Stakes (Daryl's Joy)
1971: Charles H. Strub Stakes (War Heim)
1972: Sunset Handicap (Typecast)
1973: Charles H. Strub Stakes (Royal Owl)

MARK SELLERS

1979: Delaware Handicap (Likely Exchange)

SHANE SELLERS

1991: Ashland Stakes (Do It With Style)
1993: Ashland Stakes (Lunar Spook)
American Derby (Explosive Red)
1994: American Derby (Overbury)
1995: Wood Memorial Stakes (Talkin Man)
1996: Blue Grass Stakes (Skip Away)
Woodbine Million (Skip Away)
Jockey Club Gold Cup (Skip Away)
Secretariat Stakes (Marlin)
Spinaway Stakes (Oath)
1997: Fountain of Youth Stakes (Pulpit)
Toyota Blue Grass Stakes (Pulpit)
Spinaway Stakes (Countess Diana)
Breeders' Cup Juvenile Fillies (Countess Diana)
Oaklawn Handicap (Atticus)
Suburban Handicap (Skip Away)
Jerome Handicap (Richter Scale)
1998: Turf Classic (Buck's Boy)
Breeders' Cup Turf (Buck's Boy)
Florida Derby (Cape Town)
Ohio Derby (Classic Cat)
Ballerina Handicap (Stop Traffic)
Matron Stakes (Oh What a Windfall)
1999: Fountain of Youth Stakes (Vicar)
Florida Derby (Vicar)
Gallery Furniture.com Stakes (Stephen Got Even)
Early Times Turf Classic (Wild Event)
Brooklyn Handicap (Running Stag)
2000: Apple Blossom Handicap (Heritage of Gold)
Go for Wand Handicap (Heritage of Gold)
Donn Handicap (Stephen Got Even)
Ashland Stakes (Rings a Chime)
Travers Stakes (Unshaded)
Hopeful Stakes (City Zip)
Lane's End Breeders' Futurity (Arabian Light)
Queen Elizabeth II Challenge Cup (Collect the Cash)

BILL SHOEMAKER

1950: Hollywood Oaks (Mrs. Fuddy)
Del Mar Handicap (Frankly)
1951: Westerner Stakes (Grantor)
Del Mar Derby (Grantor)
Champagne Stakes (Armageddon)
Santa Margarita Handicap (Special Touch)
Beldame Handicap (Thelma Berger)
Will Rogers Handicap (Gold Note)
Vosburgh Handicap (War King)
San Antonio Handicap (All Blue)
Golden Gate Handicap (Palestinian)
Santa Anita Maturity (Great Circle)
1952: Santa Margarita Handicap (Bed o' Roses)
1953: Del Mar Debutante Stakes (Lady Cover Up)

BILL SHOEMAKER *(Continued)*
Cinema Handicap (Ali's Gem)
San Antonio Handicap (Trusting)
Del Mar Handicap (Goose Khal)
1954: Wood Memorial Stakes (Correlation)
Florida Derby (Correlation)
Santa Anita Handicap (Rejected)
American Handicap (Rejected)
Del Mar Futurity (Blue Ruler)
Del Mar Debutante Stakes (Fair Molly)
Santa Margarita Handicap (Cerise Reine)
Del Mar Handicap (Stranglehold)
1955: Kentucky Derby (Swaps)
Westerner Stakes (Swaps)
American Derby (Swaps)
Santa Anita Handicap (Poona II)
Washington Park Handicap (Jet Action)
William P. Kyne Handicap (Mister Gus)
1956: Inglewood Handicap (Swaps)
American Handicap (Swaps)
Hollywood Gold Cup (Swaps)
Sunset Handicap (Swaps)
Washington Park Handicap (Swaps)
Ladies Handicap (Flower Bowl)
Santa Anita Derby (Terrang)
San Luis Rey Handicap (Blue Volt)
1957: Cinema Handicap (Round Table)
Westerner Stakes (Round Table)
American Derby (Round Table)
Hollywood Gold Cup (Round Table)
United Nations Handicap (Round Table)
Arlington Matron Handicap (Pucker Up)
Beldame Handicap (Pucker Up)
Washington Park Handicap (Pucker Up)
Belmont Stakes (Gallant Man)
Travers Stakes (Gallant Man)
Jockey Club Gold Cup (Gallant Man)
Champagne Stakes (Jewel's Reward)
Pimlico Futurity (Jewel's Reward)
Californian Stakes (Social Climber)
San Luis Rey Handicap (Posadas)
1958: San Antonio Handicap (Round Table)
Santa Anita Handicap (Round Table)
Gulfstream Park Handicap (Round Table)
Hawthorne Gold Cup (Round Table)
Arlington Handicap (Round Table)
Metropolitan Handicap (Gallant Man)
Hollywood Gold Cup (Gallant Man)
Sunset Handicap (Gallant Man)
Starlet Stakes (Tomy Lee)
Del Mar Futurity (Tomy Lee)
Arlington Futurity (Restless Wind)
Washington Park Futurity (Restless Wind)
Futurity Stakes (Intentionally)
Pimlico Futurity (Intentionally)
Woodward Stakes (Clem)
United Nations Handicap (Clem)
Santa Anita Derby (Silky Sullivan)
Cinema Handicap (The Shoe)
Lawrence Realization Stakes (Martins Rullah)
1959: Washington Park Handicap (Round Table)
Manhattan Handicap (Round Table)
Stars and Stripes Handicap (Round Table)
Arlington Handicap (Round Table)
United Nations Handicap (Round Table)
Belmont Stakes (Sword Dancer)
Metropolitan Handicap (Sword Dancer)
Monmouth Handicap (Sword Dancer)
Blue Grass Stakes (Tomy Lee)
Kentucky Derby (Tomy Lee)
Hopeful Stakes (Tompion)
Top Flight Handicap (Big Effort)
Vanity Handicap (Tender Size)
Vanity Handicap (Zev's Joy)
Hollywood Derby (Bagdad)
1960: Santa Anita Derby (Tompion)
Blue Grass Stakes (Tompion)
San Antonio Handicap (Bagdad)
Inglewood Handicap (Bagdad)
Wood Memorial Stakes (Francis S.)
Gardenia Stakes (Bowl of Flowers)
Cinema Handicap (New Policy)
Roamer Handicap (Divine Comedy)
1961: Matron Stakes (Cicada)
Frizette Stakes (Cicada)
Gardenia Stakes (Cicada)
Santa Anita Handicap (Prove It)
San Fernando Stakes (Prove It)
Santa Anita Maturity (Prove It)
Garden State Stakes (Crimson Satan)
Pimlico Futurity (Crimson Satan)
Delaware Oaks (Primonetta)
Alabama Stakes (Primonetta)
Roamer Handicap (Sherluck)
San Juan Capistrano Handicap (Don't Alibi)
1962: Kentucky Oaks (Cicada)
Acorn Stakes (Cicada)
Mother Goose Stakes (Cicada)
Beldame Stakes (Cicada)
Gotham Stakes (Jaipur)
Withers Stakes (Jaipur)
Belmont Stakes (Jaipur)
Travers Stakes (Jaipur)
Sunset Handicap (Prove It)
Washington Park Handicap (Prove It)
Arlington-Washington Futurity (Candy Spots)
Futurity Stakes (Never Bend)
Garden State Stakes (Crewman)
Arlington Matron Handicap (Kootenai)
Spinster Stakes (Primonetta)
San Juan Capistrano Handicap (Olden Times)
1963: Santa Anita Derby (Candy Spots)
Florida Derby (Candy Spots)
Preakness Stakes (Candy Spots)
Jersey Derby (Candy Spots)
American Derby (Candy Spots)
Arlington Classic (Candy Spots)
Arlington-Washington Lassie Stakes (Sari's Song)
Hollywood Oaks (Delhi Maid)
Vanity Handicap (Table Mate)
American Handicap (Dr. Kacy)
Donn Handicap (Tutankhamen)
1964: Gulfstream Park Handicap (Gun Bow)
San Fernando Stakes (Gun Bow)
Charles H. Strub Stakes (Gun Bow)
San Antonio Handicap (Gun Bow)
Frizette Stakes (Queen Empress)
Gardenia Stakes (Queen Empress)
Santa Susana Stakes (Blue Norther)
Kentucky Oaks (Blue Norther)
Flamingo Stakes (Northern Dancer)
Florida Derby (Northern Dancer)
Arlington-Washington Futurity (Sadair)
Vanity Handicap (Star Maggie)
Cinema Handicap (Close By)
Sunset Handicap (Colorado King)
1965: Santa Anita Derby (Lucky Debonair)
Blue Grass Stakes (Lucky Debonair)
Kentucky Derby (Lucky Debonair)
Arlington Classic (Tom Rolfe)
American Derby (Tom Rolfe)
Hollywood Juvenile Championship (Port Wine)
Arlington Handicap (Chieftan)
1966: Monmouth Oaks (Natashka)
Alabama Stakes (Natashka)
Santa Margarita Handicap (Straight Deal)
Santa Barbara Handicap (Straight Deal)
Everglades Stakes (Buckpasser)
Flamingo Stakes (Buckpasser)
Sapling Stakes (Great Power)
Arlington-Washington Futurity (Diplomat Way)
Cowdin Stakes (Dr. Fager)
Acorn Stakes (Marking Time)
San Felipe Handicap (Saber Mountain)
Blue Grass Stakes (Abe's Hope)
Cinema Handicap (Drin)
Santa Anita Handicap (Lucky Debonair)
Aqueduct Handicap (Tom Rolfe)
Charles H. Strub Stakes (Bold Bidder)
San Luis Rey Handicap (Cedar Key)
1967: Wood Memorial Stakes (Damascus)
Preakness Stakes (Damascus)
Belmont Stakes (Damascus)
Dwyer Handicap (Damascus)
American Derby (Damascus)
Travers Stakes (Damascus)
Aqueduct Stakes (Damascus)
Woodward Stakes (Damascus)
Jockey Club Gold Cup (Damascus)
Santa Anita Handicap (Pretense)
San Antonio Handicap (Pretense)
Arlington-Washington Futurity (Vitriolic)
Futurity Stakes (Captain's Gig)
Santa Susana Stakes (Fish House)
Alabama Stakes (Gamely)
Santa Barbara Handicap (April Dawn)
Sunset Handicap (Hill Clown)
San Luis Rey Handicap (Niarkos)
San Luis Rey Handicap (Fleet Host)
1968: Malibu Stakes (Damascus)
San Fernando Stakes (Damascus)
1969: Arlington-Washington Lassie Stakes (Clover Lane)
Santa Susana Stakes (Dumptys Lady)
Blue Grass Stakes (Arts and Letters)
Century Handicap (Pinjara)
1970: Hollywood Park Inv. Turf Handicap (Fiddle Isle)
American Handicap (Fiddle Isle)
San Luis Rey Handicap (Fiddle Isle)
San Juan Capistrano Handicap (Fiddle Isle)
San Felipe Handicap (Terlago)
Santa Anita Derby (Terlago)
Beverly Hills Handicap (Pattee Canyon)
1971: Hollywood Gold Cup (Ack Ack)
San Antonio Stakes (Ack Ack)
Santa Anita Handicap (Ack Ack)
American Handicap (Ack Ack)
Californian Stakes (Cougar II)
Ford Pinto Invitational Turf Handicap (Cougar II)
Oak Tree Invitational Stakes (Cougar II)
San Juan Capistrano Handicap (Cougar II)
Norfolk Stakes (MacArthur Park)
Del Mar Futurity (MacArthur Park)
Santa Susana Stakes (Turkish Trousers)
Hollywood Oaks (Turkish Trousers)
Hollywood Juvenile Championship (Royal Owl)
Inglewood Handicap (Advance Guard)
Del Mar Handicap (Pinjara)
1972: Californian Stakes (Cougar II)
Century Handicap (Cougar II)
Oak Tree Invitational Stakes (Cougar II)
Norfolk Stakes (Groshawk)
Del Mar Futurity (Groshawk)
Santa Maria Handicap (Turkish Trousers)
Santa Margarita Handicap (Turkish Trousers)
Beverly Hills Handicap (Hill Circus)
Del Mar Debutante Stakes (Windy's Daughter)
Hollywood Oaks (Pallisima)
California Derby (Quack)
Malibu Stakes (Wing Out)
Charles H. Strub Stakes (Unconscious)
American Handicap (Buzkashi)
1973: Century Handicap (Cougar II)
Sunset Handicap (Cougar II)
Del Mar Futurity (Such a Rush)
Beverly Hills Handicap (Le Cle)
Hollywood Gold Cup (Kennedy Road)
1974: California Derby (Agitate)
Swaps Stakes (Agitate)
Hollywood Derby (Agitate)
Del Mar Futurity (Diabolo)
Del Mar Debutante Stakes (Bubblewin)
Fantasy Stakes (Miss Musket)
Ramona Handicap (Tizna)
Hollywood Gold Cup (Tree of Knowledge)
Sunset Handicap (Greco II)
1975: Vanity Handicap (Dulcia)
Ramona Handicap (Dulcia)
National Championship Inv. Handicap (Dulcia)
San Fernando Stakes (Stardust Mel)
Charles H. Strub Stakes (Stardust Mel)
Santa Anita Handicap (Stardust Mel)
Hollywood Oaks (Nicosia)
Santa Barbara Handicap (Gay Style)
Withers Stakes (Sarsar)
Belmont Stakes (Avatar)
Cinema Handicap (Terete)
Sunset Handicap (Barclay Joy)
Oak Tree Invitational Stakes (Top Command)
1976: Champions Invitational Handicap (King Pellinore)
American Handicap (King Pellinore)
Oak Tree Invitational Stakes (King Pellinore)
San Felipe Handicap (Crystal Water)
Hollywood Derby (Crystal Water)
Woodward Handicap (Forego)
Marlboro Cup Handicap (Forego)
Norfolk Stakes (Habitony)
La Canada Stakes (Raise Your Skirts)
Santa Barbara Handicap (Stravina)
Fall Highweight Handicap (Honorable Miss)
Del Mar Handicap (Riot in Paris)
Hollywood Invitational Handicap (Dahlia)
1977: Metropolitan Handicap (Forego)
Woodward Handicap (Forego)
Norfolk Stakes (Balzac)
Hollywood Oaks (Glenaris)
La Canada Stakes (Lucie Manet)
Santa Anita Derby (Habitony)
Swaps Stakes (J.O. Tobin)
Sunset Handicap (Today'n Tomorrow)
Oak Tree Invitational Stakes (Crystal Water)
1978: Hollywood Gold Cup (Exceller)
Jockey Club Gold Cup (Exceller)
Hollywood Invitational Handicap (Exceller)
Sunset Handicap (Exceller)
Oak Tree Invitational Stakes (Exceller)
San Juan Capistrano Handicap (Exceller)

Vanity Handicap (Afifa)
Yellow Ribbon Stakes (Amazer)
Longacres Mile (Bad 'n Big)
1979: Marlboro Cup Handicap (Spectacular Bid)
Meadowlands Cup (Spectacular Bid)
Hollywood Juvenile Championship (Parsec)
Del Mar Debutante Stakes (Table Hands)
Santa Susana Stakes (Caline)
Vanity Handicap (It's In the Air)
Santa Margarita Handicap (Sanedtki)
Flower Bowl Handicap (Pearl Necklace)
Amory L. Haskell Handicap (Text)
1980: Californian Stakes (Spectacular Bid)
Amory L. Haskell Handicap (Spectacular Bid)
Woodward Stakes (Spectacular Bid)
San Fernando Stakes (Spectacular Bid)
Charles H. Strub Stakes (Spectacular Bid)
Santa Anita Handicap (Spectacular Bid)
Arlington-Washington Lassie Stakes (Truly Bound)
Ramona Handicap (Queen to Conquer)
San Felipe Handicap (Raise A Man)
Century Handicap (Go West Young Man)
Sunset Handicap (Inkerman)
1981: Jockey Club Gold Cup (John Henry)
Sword Dancer Stakes (John Henry)
Arlington Million (John Henry)
Oak Tree Invitational Stakes (John Henry)
Sunset Handicap (Galaxy Libra)
Man o' War Stakes (Galaxy Libra)
Alcibiades Stakes (Apalachee Honey)
Santa Susana Stakes (Nell's Briquette)
Beldame Stakes (Love Sign)
1982: Santa Susana Stakes (Blush With Pride)
Kentucky Oaks (Blush With Pride)
Golden Harvest Handicap (Blush With Pride)
Santa Anita Handicap (John Henry)
Oak Tree Invitational Stakes (John Henry)
Vanity Handicap (Sangue)
Golden Harvest Handicap (Miss Huntington)
Blue Grass Stakes (Linkage)
Hollywood Derby (Racing Is Fun)
1983: Ramona Handicap (Sangue)
Golden Harvest Handicap (Sangue)
Yellow Ribbon Stakes (Sangue)
Matriarch Stakes (Sangue)
Californian Stakes (The Wonder)
Century Handicap (The Wonder)
Arlington Handicap (Palikaraki)
1985: San Antonio Handicap (Lord at War)
Santa Anita Handicap (Lord at War)
Yellow Ribbon Stakes (Estrapade)
1986: Santa Anita Oaks (Hidden Light)
Hollywood Oaks (Hidden Light)
Kentucky Derby (Ferdinand)
John Henry Handicap (Palace Music)
Philip H. Iselin Handicap (Roo Art)
Hollywood Derby (Thrill Show)
Hollywood Turf Cup (Alphabatim)
Hollywood Futurity (Temperate Sil)
1987: Santa Anita Derby (Temperate Sil)
Swaps Stakes (Temperate Sil)
Hollywood Gold Cup (Ferdinand)
Breeders' Cup Classic (Ferdinand)
Santa Barbara Handicap (Reloy)
Sunset Handicap (Swink)
1988: Fantasy Stakes (Jeanne Jones)
Swaps Stakes (Lively One)
1989: John Henry Handicap (Peace)

NICK SHUK

1951: Pimlico Futurity (Cajun)
1952: Champagne Stakes (Laffango)
Garden State Stakes (Laffango)
Delaware Oaks (Big Mo)
Ladies Handicap (How)
1953: Monmouth Oaks (Grecian Queen)
Gotham Stakes (Laffango)
Jerome Handicap (Navy Page)
1954: Spinaway Stakes (Gandharva)
1955: Saranac Handicap (Saratoga)
1957: Sapling Stakes (Plion)

RAY SIBILLE

1981: Arlington-Washington Lassie Stakes (Milingo)
American Derby (Pocket Zipper)
1982: Yellow Ribbon Stakes (Castilla)
Matriarch Stakes (Castilla)
Fantasy Stakes (Flying Partner)
Matriarch Stakes (Pale Purple)
Illinois Derby (Star Gallant)
1984: La Canada Stakes (Sweet Diane)
1985: Fantasy Stakes (Rascal Lass)

1986: Gamely Handicap (La Khoumia)
Hollywood Derby (Spellbound)
1987: Hollywood Oaks (Perchance to Dream)
1988: San Juan Capistrano 'Cap (Great Communicator)
Breeders' Cup Turf (Great Communicator)
Hollywood Turf Cup (Great Communicator)
1989: Hollywood Turf Handicap (Great Communicator)

EUGENE SIPUS

1988: Jim Beam Stakes (Kingpost)

ROCCO SISTO

1952: Dixie Handicap (Alerted)

JACK SKELLY

1954: Sapling Stakes (Royal Coinage)
1957: Arlington Futurity (Leather Button)
Monmouth Oaks (Romanita)

TONY SKORONSKI

1946: Inglewood Handicap (Quick Reward)
American Handicap (Quick Reward)
1948: Washington Park Futurity (Model Cadet)
Spinaway Stakes (Myrtle Charm)
San Carlos Handicap (Autocrat)

WILLIE SKUSE

1957: Vanity Handicap (Annie-Lu-San)
1958: Vanity Handicap (Annie-Lu-San)

STANLEY SMALL

1954: Maskette Handicap (Ballerina)
Ladies Handicap (Lavender Hill)
Jerome Handicap (Martyr)

C. SMIRKE

1953: Washington D.C. International (Worden II)

FRED SMITH

1947: Kentucky Jockey Club Stakes (Bold Gallant)
1948: Princess Pat Stakes (Sequence)
1949: Arlington Matron Handicap (Lithe)
1951: San Pasqual Handicap (Moonrush)
1954: Vineland Handicap (Spinning Top)

GREG SMITH

1984: Laurel Futurity (Mighty Appealing)
Remsen Stakes (Mighty Appealing)

MIKE SMITH

1990: Gotham Stakes (Thirty Six Red)
Wood Memorial Stakes (Thirty Six Red)
Jim Dandy Stakes (Chief Honcho)
1991: Jersey Derby (Greek Costume)
Hempstead Handicap (A Wild Ride)
Hopeful Stakes (Salt Lake)
Beldame Stakes (Sharp Dance)
1992: Gotham Stakes (Lure)
Breeders' Cup Mile (Lure)
Wood Memorial Stakes (Devil His Due)
Ruffian Handicap (Versailles Treaty)
1993: Acorn Stakes (Sky Beauty)
Mother Goose Stakes (Sky Beauty)
Coaching Club American Oaks (Sky Beauty)
Alabama Stakes (Sky Beauty)
Blue Grass Stakes (Prairie Bayou)
Preakness Stakes (Prairie Bayou)
Fantasy Stakes (Aztec Hill)
Whitney Handicap (Brunswick)
Futurity Stakes (Holy Bull)
Turf Classic (Apple Tree)
Vosburgh Stakes (Birdonthewire)
Frizette Stakes (Heavenly Prize)
Breeders' Cup Mile (Lure)
1994: Florida Derby (Holy Bull)
Blue Grass Stakes (Holy Bull)
Metropolitan Handicap (Holy Bull)
Dwyer Stakes (Holy Bull)
Haskell Invitational Handicap (Holy Bull)
Travers Stakes (Holy Bull)
Woodward Stakes (Holy Bull)
Shuvee Handicap (Sky Beauty)
Hempstead Handicap (Sky Beauty)
Go for Wand Stakes (Sky Beauty)
Ruffian Handicap (Sky Beauty)
Ashland Stakes (Inside Information)
Acorn Stakes (Inside Information)
Brooklyn Handicap (Devil His Due)
Suburban Handicap (Devil His Due)
Alabama Stakes (Heavenly Prize)
Gazelle Handicap (Heavenly Prize)
Apple Blossom Handicap (Nine Keys)

Caesars International Handicap (Lure)
Meadowlands Cup (Conveyor)
Breeders' Cup Sprint (Cherokee Run)
Breeders' Cup Turf (Tikkanen)
Top Flight Handicap (Educated Risk)
1995: Ruffian Handicap (Inside Information)
Spinster Stakes (Inside Information)
Breeders' Cup Distaff (Inside Information)
Florida Derby (Thunder Gulch)
Gotham Stakes (Talkin Man)
San Juan Capistrano Handicap (Red Bishop)
Californian Stakes (Concern)
Alabama Stakes (Pretty Discreet)
Breeders' Cup Juvenile (Unbridled's Song)
Top Flight Handicap (Twist Afleet)
1996: Florida Derby (Unbridled's Song)
Wood Memorial Stakes (Unbridled's Song)
Brooklyn Handicap (Wekiva Springs)
Suburban Handicap (Wekiva Springs)
Jim Beam Stakes (Roar)
Acorn Stakes (Star de Lady Ann)
Sword Dancer Invitational Handicap (Broadway Flyer)
Delta Air Lines Top Flight Handicap (Flat Fleet Feet)
NYRA Mile Handicap (Gold Fever)
1997: Mother Goose Stakes (Ajina)
Coaching Club American Oaks (Ajina)
Breeders' Cup Distaff (Ajina)
Ashland Stakes (Glitter Woman)
Jim Dandy Stakes (Awesome Again)
John A. Morris Handicap (Clear Mandate)
Turf Classic (Val's Prince)
Breeders' Cup Classic (Skip Away)
Remsen Stakes (Coronado's Quest)
1998: Acorn Stakes (Jersey Girl)
Mother Goose Stakes (Jersey Girl)
Test Stakes (Jersey Girl)
Buick Haskell Inv. Handicap (Coronado's Quest)
Travers Stakes (Coronado's Quest)
Go for Wand Handicap (Aldiza)
1999: Ballerina Handicap (Furlough)
2000: Coaching Club American Oaks (Jostle)
Alabama Stakes (Jostle)
Gazelle Handicap (Critical Eye)
2002: Santa Margarita Handicap (Azeri)
Apple Blossom Handicap (Azeri)
Milady Breeders' Cup Handicap (Azeri)
Vanity Handicap (Azeri)
Breeders' Cup Distaff (Azeri)
Swaps Stakes (Came Home)
Pacific Classic (Came Home)
San Carlos Handicap (Snow Ridge)
Clement L. Hirsch Mem. Turf Champ. (The Tin Man)
Bessemer Trust Breeders' Cup Juvenile (Vindication)
2003: Apple Blossom Handicap (Azeri)
Milady Breeders' Cup Handicap (Azeri)
Vanity Handicap (Azeri)
Hollywood Futurity (Lion Heart)

PAT SMULLEN

2002: Matriarch Stakes (Dress To Thrill)

ALBERT SNIDER

1947: Futurity Stakes (Citation)
Flamingo Stakes (Faultless)
Pimlico Special (Fervent)
1948: Flamingo Stakes (Citation)

LARRY SNYDER

1970: Oaklawn Handicap (Charlie Jr.)
1974: Arlington Handicap (Buffalo Lark)
1975: Pan American Handicap (Buffalo Lark)
1977: Ohio Derby (Silver Series)
American Derby (Silver Series)
1980: Sorority Stakes (Fancy Naskra)
1989: Arkansas Derby (Dansil)

ALEX SOLIS

1983: Flamingo Stakes (Current Hope)
1985: Norfolk Stakes (Snow Chief)
Hollywood Futurity (Snow Chief)
1986: Florida Derby (Snow Chief)
Santa Anita Derby (Snow Chief)
Preakness Stakes (Snow Chief)
Jersey Derby (Snow Chief)
San Luis Rey Stakes (Dahar)
San Juan Capistrano Handicap (Dahar)
1988: Hollywood Starlet Stakes (Stocks Up)
1989: Hollywood Derby (Live the Dream)
Hollywood Starlet Stakes (Cheval Volant)
1990: San Antonio Handicap (Criminal Type)
San Felipe Handicap (Real Cash)
1991: Del Mar Futurity (Bertrando)

ALEX SOLIS *(Continued)*
Norfolk Stakes (Bertrando)
1992: Donn Handicap (Sea Cadet)
Gulfstream Park Handicap (Sea Cadet)
Meadowlands Cup (Sea Cadet)
San Antonio Handicap (Ibero)
San Felipe Stakes (Bertrando)
1994: Vanity Handicap (Potridee)
Del Mar Futurity (On Target)
1995: Strub Stakes (Dare and Go)
Hollywood Turf Cup (Royal Chariot)
Hollywood Futurity (Matty G)
1996: San Juan Capistrano Handicap (Raintrap)
Pacific Classic (Dare and Go)
John A. Morris Handicap (Urbane)
Hollywood Futurity (Swiss Yodeler)
1997: Queen Elizabeth II Challenge Cup (Ryafan)
Yellow Ribbon Stakes (Ryafan)
Matriarch Stakes (Ryafan)
Florida Derby (Captain Bodgit)
Wood Memorial Stakes (Captain Bodgit)
Hollywood Turf Handicap (Rainbow Dancer)
Oak Tree Turf Championship (Rainbow Dancer)
Milady Breeders' Cup Handicap (Listening)
Hollywood Oaks (Sharp Cat)
Hollywood Turf Cup (River Bay)
1998: Santa Anita Handicap (Malek)
Arkansas Derby (Victory Gallop)
Matriarch Stakes (Squeak)
1999: Jim Dandy Stakes (Ecton Park)
Super Derby (Ecton Park)
Charles Whittingham Handicap (River Bay)
Norfolk Stakes (Dixie Union)
Early Times Hollywood Derby (Super Quercus)
2000: Haskell Invitational Handicap (Dixie Union)
Malibu Stakes (Dixie Union)
Breeders' Cup Sprint (Kona Gold)
Hollywood Starlet Stakes (I Believe in You)
2001: San Carlos Handicap (Kona Gold)
Eddie Read Handicap (Redattore)
Secretariat Stakes (Startac)
Clement L. Hirsch Mem. Turf Championship (Senure)
Hollywood Turf Cup (Super Quercus)
2002: Woodford Reserve Turf Classic (Beat Hollow)
Manhattan Handicap (Beat Hollow)
Santa Monica Handicap (Kalookan Queen)
Ancient Title BC Handicap (Kalookan Queen)
Hollywood Derby (Johar)
La Brea Stakes (Got Koko)
2003: Santa Monica Handicap (Affluent)
Shoemaker Breeders' Cup Mile (Redattore)
John C. Mabee Handicap (Megahertz)
John Deere Breeders' Cup Turf (Johar)
BC Classic—Powered/Dodge (Pleasantly Perfect)
Hollywood Turf Cup (Continuously)

MICKEY SOLOMONE
1963: Hawthorne Gold Cup (Admiral Vic)
1964: Seminole Handicap (Admiral Vic)
1971: Washington Park Handicap (Well Mannered)
1972: Donn Handicap (Going Straight)
1975: Fantasy Stakes (Hoso)
1987: Jersey Derby (Avies Copy)

BENNY SORENSEN
1958: Michigan Mile (Nearctic)

MIKE SORRENTINO
1960: Whitney Handicap (Warhead)
1963: Alabama Stakes (Tona)

SANTIAGO SOTO
1986: Hollywood Invitational Handicap (Flying Pidgeon)

LOUIS SPINDLER
1972: Oaklawn Handicap (Gage Line)

LARRY SPRAKER
1965: Arkansas Derby (Swift Ruler)
1966: Oaklawn Handicap (Swift Ruler)

GARY STAHLBAUM
1987: Jerome Handicap (Afleet)
Pennsylvania Derby (Afleet)

JOE STEINER
1987: Norfolk Stakes (Saratoga Passage)

GARY STEVENS
1985: Santa Barbara Handicap (Fact Finder)
Arkansas Derby (Tank's Prospect)
Sapling Stakes (Hilco Scamper)
1986: Fantasy Stakes (Tiffany Lass)
Kentucky Oaks (Tiffany Lass)
Ohio Derby (Broad Brush)
Arlington-Washington Lassie Stakes (Delicate Vine)
Del Mar Futurity (Qualify)
Marlboro Cup Handicap (Turkoman)
1987: La Canada Stakes (Family Style)
San Antonio Handicap (Bedside Promise)
Santa Anita Oaks (Timely Assertion)
Gamely Handicap (Northern Aspen)
1988: Santa Anita Oaks (Winning Colors)
Santa Anita Derby (Winning Colors)
Kentucky Derby (Winning Colors)
Hollywood Gold Cup (Cutlass Reality)
Matron Stakes (Some Romance)
Oak Tree Invitational Stakes (Nasr El Arab)
Alcibiades Stakes (Wonders Delight)
Hollywood Derby (Silver Circus)
1989: Santa Anita Oaks (Imaginary Lady)
Carter Handicap (On the Line)
Illinois Derby (Music Merci)
1990: Santa Anita Handicap (Ruhlmann)
Santa Anita Oaks (Hail Atlantis)
Santa Anita Derby (Mister Frisky)
Arkansas Derby (Silver Ending)
Hollywood Oaks (Patches)
Swaps Stakes (Jovial)
Whitney Handicap (Criminal Type)
Hopeful Stakes (Deposit Ticket)
Arlington Million (Golden Pheasant)
Breeders' Cup Turf (In the Wings)
Hollywood Starlet Stakes (Cuddles)
1991: San Fernando Stakes (In Excess)
Suburban Handicap (In Excess)
Whitney Handicap (In Excess)
Woodward Stakes (In Excess)
San Antonio Handicap (Farma Way)
Santa Anita Handicap (Farma Way)
Pimlico Special (Farma Way)
San Luis Rey Stakes (Pleasant Variety)
Hollywood Turf Handicap (Exbourne)
Hollywood Starlet Stakes (Magical Maiden)
1992: Hollywood Turf Handicap (Quest for Fame)
Gamely Handicap (Metamorphose)
Jockey Club Gold Cup (Pleasant Tap)
1993: Pacific Classic (Bertrando)
Woodward Stakes (Bertrando)
Santa Anita Derby (Personal Hope)
Californian Stakes (Latin American)
Breeders' Cup Juvenile (Brocco)
1994: Santa Anita Derby (Brocco)
Wood Memorial Stakes (Irgun)
Hollywood Turf Handicap (Grand Flotilla)
Hollywood Gold Cup (Slew of Damascus)
Secretariat Stakes (Vaudeville)
Norfolk Stakes (Supremo)
Breeders' Cup Distaff (One Dreamer)
Remsen Stakes (Thunder Gulch)
1995: Kentucky Derby (Thunder Gulch)
Belmont Stakes (Thunder Gulch)
Swaps Stakes (Thunder Gulch)
Travers Stakes (Thunder Gulch)
Mother Goose Stakes (Serena's Song)
Haskell Invitational Handicap (Serena's Song)
Gazelle Handicap (Serena's Song)
Beldame Stakes (Serena's Song)
Spinaway Stakes (Golden Attraction)
Matron Stakes (Golden Attraction)
Frizette Stakes (Golden Attraction)
Santa Anita Handicap (Urgent Request)
Santa Anita Derby (Larry the Legend)
Vanity Handicap (Private Persuasion)
Eddie Read Handicap (Fastness)
Hopeful Stakes (Hennessy)
Jerome Handicap (French Deputy)
Man o' War Stakes (Millkom)
1996: Santa Maria Handicap (Serena's Song)
Isle of Capri Casino Super Derby (Editor's Note)
Canadian International Championship (Singspiel)
Breeders' Cup Mile (Da Hoss)
Yellow Ribbon Stakes (Donna Viola)
1997: San Antonio Handicap (Gentlemen)
Pimlico Special (Gentlemen)
Hollywood Gold Cup (Gentlemen)
Pacific Classic (Gentlemen)
Kentucky Derby (Silver Charm)
Preakness Stakes (Silver Charm)
Futurity Stakes (Grand Slam)
Moet Champagne Stakes (Grand Slam)
Acorn Stakes (Sharp Cat)
Gamely Handicap (Donna Viola)
Arlington Million (Marlin)
Norfolk Stakes (Souvenir Copy)
1998: Walmac Int. Alcibiades Stakes (Silverbulletday)
Breeders' Cup Juvenile Fillies (Silverbulletday)
Strub Stakes (Silver Charm)
San Antonio Handicap (Gentlemen)
Santa Anita Derby (Indian Charlie)
Toyota Blue Grass Stakes (Halory Hunter)
Belmont Stakes (Victory Gallop)
Beverly Hills Handicap (Squeak)
Hollywood Oaks (Manistique)
Canadian Int. Championship (Royal Anthem)
Breeders' Cup Distaff (Escena)
La Brea Stakes (Magical Allure)
1999: Santa Margarita Handicap (Manistique)
Santa Anita Derby (General Challenge)
Kentucky Oaks (Silverbulletday)
Pimlico Special (Real Quiet)
Breeders' Cup Juvenile (Anees)
2000: Breeders' Cup Mile (War Chant)
Hollywood Futurity (Point Given)
2001: San Felipe Stakes (Point Given)
Santa Anita Derby (Point Given)
Preakness Stakes (Point Given)
Belmont Stakes (Point Given)
Haskell Invitational Handicap (Point Given)
Travers Stakes (Point Given)
Santa Maria Handicap (Lovellon)
Woodford Reserve Turf Classic (White Heart)
Shoemaker Breeders' Cup Mile (Irish Prize)
Vanity Handicap (Gourmet Girl)
Swaps Stakes (Congaree)
2002: Santa Maria Handicap (Favorite Funtime)
Del Mar Debutante Stakes (Miss Houdini)
2003: Charles Whittingham Handicap (Storming Home)
Clement L. Hirsch Mem. Turf Champ. (Storming Home)
Santa Anita Derby (Buddy Gil)
Carter Handicap (Congaree)

ROBERT STEVENSON
1960: New Orleans Handicap (Tudor Era)
1966: Florida Derby (Williamston Kid)

CALVIN STONE
1965: Oaklawn Handicap (Gay Revoke)
1966: Carter Handicap (Davis II)
1967: Illinois Derby (Royal Malabar)

JIMMY STOUT
1946: Delaware Oaks (Bonnie Beryl)
Trenton Handicap (Turbine)
1947: Miami Beach Handicap (Tel O'Sullivan)
1950: Vineland Handicap (Almahmoud)
1951: Sapling Stakes (Landseair)
Gulfstream Park Handicap (Ennobled)
1952: McLennan Handicap (Spartan Valor)
Widener Handicap (Spartan Valor)
Excelsior Handicap (Spartan Valor)
Gallant Fox Handicap (Spartan Valor)
1953: Sapling Stakes (Artismo)
Tropical Park Handicap (Spartan Valor)
1954: Roseben Handicap (White Skies)
Carter Handicap (White Skies)

BENJAMIN STRANGE
1946: Gulfstream Handicap (Do-Reigh-Me)
1949: Garden State Stakes (Cornwall)
Trenton Handicap (Sky Miracle)

KEITH STUART
1950: Grey Lag Handicap (Lotowhite)
1951: Suburban Handicap (Busanda)
1954: Gulfstream Park Handicap (Wise Margin)
Massachusetts Handicap (Wise Margin)

ANDREAS SUBORICS
2001: Arlington Million (Silvano)

BRIAN SWATUK
1979: Arlington Classic (Steady Growth)

WALTER SWINBURN
1983: Turf Classic (All Along)
Washington D.C. International (All Along)
Rothmans International Stakes (All Along)
1994: Beverly D. Stakes (Hatoof)
1996: Breeders' Cup Turf (Pilsudski)

GEORGE TANIGUCHI
1956: San Juan Capistrano Handicap (Bobby Brocato)
1958: San Felipe Handicap (Carrier X.)
1960: Hollywood Juvenile Championship (Pappa's All)
Arlington Futurity (Pappa's All)
1962: Santa Margarita Handicap (Queen America)

VICTOR TEJADA

1972: Santa Susana Stakes (Susan's Girl)
Kentucky Oaks (Susan's Girl)
Acorn Stakes (Susan's Girl)
Miller High Life Inglewood Handicap (War Heim)

JORGE TEJEIRA

1969: Kentucky Jockey Club Stakes (Evasive Action)
1970: Metropolitan Handicap (Nodouble)
Stars and Stripes Handicap (Mr. Leader)
1971: Manhattan Handicap (Big Shot II)
1972: Hollywood Juvenile Championship (Bold Liz)
Arlington-Washington Lassie Stakes (Natural Sound)
1975: Arlington Handicap (Royal Glint)
Hawthorne Gold Cup (Royal Glint)
United Nations Handicap (Royal Glint)
Santa Anita Derby (Avatar)
San Luis Rey Stakes (Trojan Bronze)
1976: Santa Anita Handicap (Royal Glint)
1979: Sorority Stakes (Love Street)

ROBERT THIBEAU

1984: Top Flight Handicap (Sweet Missus)

TERRY THOMPSON

2003: Arkansas Derby (Sir Cherokee)

BUCK THORNBURG

1963: Selima Stakes (My Card)
1964: Delaware Handicap (Old Hat)
1969: Gardenia Stakes (Fast Attack)
1975: Sapling Stakes (Full Out)
1977: Florida Derby (Coined Silver)
1979: Laurel Futurity (Plugged Nickle)
Remsen Stakes (Plugged Nickle)
1980: Florida Derby (Plugged Nickle)
Wood Memorial Stakes (Plugged Nickle)

THIERRY THULLIEZ

2002: NetJets Breeders' Cup Mile (Domedriver)

DENIS TIERNEY

1970: Hollywood Juvenile Championship (Fast Fellow)
Del Mar Debutante Stakes (Generous Portion)

ABDIEL TORIBIO

1993: Flamingo Stakes (Forever Whirl)
Ohio Derby (Forever Whirl)

FERNANDO TORO

1966: Pan American Handicap (Pillanlebun)
1969: Widener Handicap (Yumbel)
1971: Del Mar Futurity (D.B. Carm)
Vanity Handicap (Hi Q.)
Cinema Handicap (Niagara)
1972: Del Mar Handicap (Hill Circus)
1974: Malibu Stakes (Ancient Title)
Oak Leaf Stakes (Cut Class)
Santa Margarita Handicap (Tizna)
Del Mar Handicap (Redtop III)
1975: San Felipe Handicap (Fleet Velvet)
American Handicap (Pass the Glass)
American Handicap (Montmartre)
1976: Sunset Handicap (Caucasus)
Manhattan Handicap (Caucasus)
Vanity Handicap (Miss Toshiba)
Santa Margarita Handicap (Fascinating Girl)
Charles H. Strub Stakes (George Navonod)
1977: Ashland Stakes (Sound of Summer)
San Luis Rey Stakes (Caucasus)
1978: San Fernando Stakes (Text)
Bay Meadows Handicap (Bywayofchicago)
1979: Gamely Handicap (Sisterhood)
1980: Gamely Handicap (Wishing Well)
Bay Meadows Handicap (Super Moment)
1981: San Felipe Handicap (Stancharry)
Charles H. Strub Stakes (Super Moment)
Century Handicap (Spence Bay)
1982: Hollywood Turf Cup (The Hague)
1983: Swaps Stakes (Hyperborean)
Hollywood Derby (Royal Heroine)
Hollywood Derby (Ginger Brink)
1984: Santa Margarita Handicap (Adored)
Breeders' Cup Mile (Royal Heroine)
1985: Sunset Handicap (Kings Island)
1986: Budweiser-Arlington Million (Estrapade)
Oak Tree Invitational Stakes (Estrapade)
Charles H. Strub Stakes (Nostalgia's Star)
Yellow Ribbon Stakes (Bonne Ile)
1988: Apple Blossom Handicap (By Land By Sea)
Sunset Handicap (Roi Normand)

FRANCISCO TORRES

2000: Turfway Spiral Stakes (Globalize)

ROGELIO TREJOS

1956: Del Mar Debutante Stakes (Blue Vic)

HUBERT TRENT

1948: Starlet Stakes (Star Fiddle)

SENON TREVINO

1966: Vanity Handicap (Khal Ireland)

ANGELO TROSCLAIR

1977: New Orleans Handicap (Tudor Tambourine)

RON TURCOTTE

1964: Canadian Championship Stakes (Will I Rule)
Dixie Handicap (Will I Rule)
Cowdin Stakes (Tom Rolfe)
1965: Kentucky Oaks (Amerivan)
Preakness Stakes (Tom Rolfe)
1966: Suburban Handicap (Buffle)
1968: Selima Stakes (Shuvee)
1969: Canadian International Championship (Vent du Nord)
1970: Beldame Stakes (Shuvee)
Jockey Club Gold Cup (Shuvee)
Alabama Stakes (Fanfreluche)
Withers Stakes (Hagley)
Hawthorne Gold Cup (Gladwin)
Hialeah Turf Cup (Vent du Nord)
1971: Futurity Stakes (Riva Ridge)
Champagne Stakes (Riva Ridge)
Pimlico-Laurel Futurity (Riva Ridge)
Garden State Stakes (Riva Ridge)
Top Flight Handicap (Shuvee)
Gotham Stakes (Good Behaving)
Grey Lag Handicap (Judgable)
Canadian International Championship (One For All)
1972: Hopeful Stakes (Secretariat)
Futurity Stakes (Secretariat)
Laurel Futurity (Secretariat)
Garden State Stakes (Secretariat)
Blue Grass Stakes (Riva Ridge)
Kentucky Derby (Riva Ridge)
Belmont Stakes (Riva Ridge)
Hollywood Derby (Riva Ridge)
Coaching Club American Oaks (Summer Guest)
Alabama Stakes (Summer Guest)
Florida Derby (Upper Case)
Wood Memorial Stakes (Upper Case)
Manhattan Handicap (Ruritania)
1973: Gotham Stakes (Secretariat)
Kentucky Derby (Secretariat)
Preakness Stakes (Secretariat)
Belmont Stakes (Secretariat)
Marlboro Cup Handicap (Secretariat)
Man o' War Stakes (Secretariat)
Spinaway Stakes (Talking Picture)
Matron Stakes (Talking Picture)
Massachusetts Handicap (Riva Ridge)
Brooklyn Handicap (Riva Ridge)
Travers Stakes (Annihilate 'Em)
1974: Dwyer Handicap (Hatchet Man)
Santa Anita Handicap (Prince Dantan)
Bowling Green Handicap (Take Off)
Man o' War Stakes (Dahlia)
1976: American Derby (Fifth Marine)
Bowling Green Handicap (Erwin Boy)
1977: Sorority Stakes (Stub)
Arlington-Washington Lassie Stakes (Stub)
Alcibiades Stakes (L'Alezane)

RUDY TURCOTTE

1979: Hawthorne Gold Cup (Young Bob)
1980: Laurel Futurity (Cure the Blues)

BOBBY USSERY

1955: Canadian Championship Stakes (Park Dandy)
Bougainvillea Turf Handicap (Cascanuez)
1956: McLennan Handicap (Switch On)
1957: Acorn Stakes (Bayou)
Maskette Handicap (Bayou)
Grey Lag Handicap (Kingmaker)
Whitney Stakes (Kingmaker)
Spinaway Stakes (Sequoia)
Manhattan Handicap (Reneged)
Display Handicap (Oh Johnny)
1958: Alabama Stakes (Tempted)
Maskette Handicap (Tempted)
Cowdin Stakes (Crafty Skipper)
Travers Stakes (Piano Jim)
1959: Acorn Stakes (Quill)
Bowling Green Handicap (Bell Hop)
1960: Flamingo Stakes (Bally Ache)
Florida Derby (Bally Ache)
Preakness Stakes (Bally Ache)
Jersey Derby (Bally Ache)
Sapling Stakes (Hail to Reason)
Hopeful Stakes (Hail to Reason)
Delaware Handicap (Quill)
1961: Gotham Stakes (Ambiopoise)
Jersey Derby (Ambiopoise)
Mother Goose Stakes (Funloving)
Black Helen Handicap (Be Cautious)
Tropical Park Handicap (Bourbon Prince)
1962: Matron Stakes (Smart Deb)
Coaching Club American Oaks (Bramalea)
Grey Lag Handicap (Ambiopoise)
1963: Lawrence Realization Stakes (Dean Carl)
Roamer Handicap (Dean Carl)
Display Handicap (Deal Carl)
Metropolitan Handicap (Cyrano)
Brooklyn Handicap (Cyrano)
Dwyer Handicap (Outing Class)
Hialeah Turf Cup (Intercepted)
1964: Sorority Stakes (Bold Experience)
Matron Stakes (Candalita)
Withers Stakes (Mr. Brick)
1965: Gotham Stakes (Flag Raiser)
Wood Memorial Stakes (Flag Raiser)
Withers Stakes (Flag Raiser)
Sanford Stakes (Flame Tree)
Dwyer Handicap (Staunchness)
New Orleans Handicap (Valiant Man)
Aqueduct Stakes (Malicious)
1966: Saratoga Special (Favorable Turn)
Gardenia Stakes (Pepperwood)
1967: Gardenia Stakes (Gay Matelda)
Delaware Handicap (Straight Deal)
Everglades Stakes (Reflected Glory)
Kentucky Derby (Proud Clarion)
Manhattan Handicap (Munden Point)
1968: Wood Memorial Stakes (Dancer's Image)
1969: Selima Stakes (Predictable)
Carter Handicap (Promise)
1970: Carter Handicap (Tyrant)
1971: Brooklyn Handicap (Never Bow)
1973: Arlington-Washington Futurity (Lover John)

STEVE VALDEZ

1973: Oak Leaf Stakes (Divine Grace)

JOSE VALDIVIA JR.

2001: Oak Leaf Stakes (Tali'sluckybusride)
Breeders' Cup Mile (Val Royal)
2003: San Carlos Handicap (Aldebaran)
Beverly D. Stakes (Heat Haze)

HERIBERTO VALDIVIESO

1982: California Derby (Rockwall)

JOSE VALDIVIESO

1984: Widener Handicap (Mat Boy)
Gulfstream Park Handicap (Mat Boy)

FERNANDO VALDIZAN

1971: New Orleans Handicap (Rio Bravo)
Oaklawn Handicap (Rio Bravo)

ANGEL VALENZUELA

1955: Gazelle Stakes (Manotick)
Ladies Handicap (Manotick)
Garden State Stakes (Prince John)
Aqueduct Handicap (Icarian)
1956: Gazelle Handicap (Scampering)
Jerome Handicap (Reneged)
Roamer Handicap (Third Brother)
1959: Santa Margarita Handicap (Bug Brush)
San Antonio Handicap (Bug Brush)
Inglewood Handicap (Bug Brush)
1960: San Fernando Stakes (King o' Turf)
1961: Inglewood Handicap (Sea Orbit)

A.R. VALENZUELA

1967: Hollywood Oaks (Amerigo Lady)

ISMAEL VALENZUELA

1954: Cinema Handicap (Miz Clementine)
1955: Cinema Handicap (Guilton Madero)
1956: Woodward Stakes (Mister Gus)
Arlington Handicap (Mister Gus)
Cinema Handicap (Social Climber)
Californian Stakes (Porterhouse)
1957: Vineland Handicap (Dotted Line)

ISMAEL VALENZUELA *(Continued)*

Roamer Handicap (Promised Land)
San Antonio Handicap (Terrang)
Gallant Fox Handicap (Eddie Schmidt)
1958: Coaching Club American Oaks (A Glitter)
Monmouth Oaks (A Glitter)
Kentucky Derby (Tim Tam)
Preakness Stakes (Tim Tam)
John B. Campbell Mem. Handicap (Promised Land)
San Juan Capistrano Handicap (Promised Land)
1959: Cowdin Stakes (Warfare)
Champagne Stakes (Warfare)
Garden State Stakes (Warfare)
1960: California Derby (Noble Noor)
Brooklyn Handicap (On-and-On)
Pimlico Futurity (Garwol)
1961: Sapling Stakes (Sir Gaylord)
Spinaway Stakes (Cicada)
Manhattan Handicap (Nickel Boy)
1962: Sorority Stakes (Affectionately)
Spinaway Stakes (Affectionately)
Woodward Stakes (Kelso)
Jockey Club Gold Cup (Kelso)
Everglades Stakes (Sir Gaylord)
1963: Seminole Handicap (Kelso)
Gulfstream Park Handicap (Kelso)
John B. Campbell Handicap (Kelso)
Suburban Handicap (Kelso)
Aqueduct Stakes (Kelso)
Woodward Stakes (Kelso)
Jockey Club Gold Cup (Kelso)
Whitney Stakes (Kelso)
Hollywood Juvenile Championship (Malicious)
Gardenia Stakes (Castle Forbes)
San Juan Capistrano Handicap (Pardao)
1964: Aqueduct Stakes (Kelso)
Jockey Club Gold Cup (Kelso)
Washington D.C. International (Kelso)
Demoiselle Stakes (Discipline)
1965: Grey Lag Handicap (Quita Dude)
Whitney Stakes (Kelso)
1966: Arlington-Washington Lassie Stakes (Mira Femme)
Canadian International Championship (George Royal)
1967: Alcibiades Stakes (Lady Tramp)
Santa Barbara Handicap (Ormea)
1968: Blue Grass Stakes (Forward Pass)
Kentucky Derby (Forward Pass)
Preakness Stakes (Forward Pass)
American Derby (Forward Pass)
Arlington Classic (Exclusive Native)
1974: Santa Anita Derby (Destroyer)
Oaklawn Handicap (Royal Knight)

PAT VALENZUELA

1980: Santa Anita Derby (Codex)
1981: Vanity Handicap (Track Robbery)
San Juan Capistrano Handicap (Obraztsovy)
1982: Spinster Stakes (Track Robbery)
San Antonio Stakes (Score Twenty Four)
1983: Charles H. Strub Stakes (Swing Till Dawn)
1984: San Fernando Stakes (Interco)
Santa Anita Handicap (Interco)
San Luis Rey Stakes (Interco)
Sorority Stakes (Tiltalating)
Arkansas Derby (Althea)
1985: Santa Susana Stakes (Fran's Valentine)
Kentucky Oaks (Fran's Valentine)
Swaps Stakes (Padua)
Oak Leaf Stakes (Arewehavingfunyet)
1986: Breeders' Cup Juvenile Fillies (Brave Raj)
1987: Charles H. Strub Stakes (Snow Chief)
John Henry Handicap (Al Mamoon)
Breeders' Cup Sprint (Very Subtle)
1988: Norfolk Stakes (Hawkster)
1989: San Felipe Handicap (Sunday Silence)
Santa Anita Derby (Sunday Silence)
Kentucky Derby (Sunday Silence)
Preakness Stakes (Sunday Silence)
Super Derby (Sunday Silence)
Charles H. Strub Stakes (Nasr El Arab)
San Juan Capistrano Handicap (Nasr El Arab)
Sunset Handicap (Pranke)
1990: Del Mar Futurity (Best Pal)
Norfolk Stakes (Best Pal)
Californian Stakes (Sunday Silence)
American Derby (Real Cash)
1991: Milady Handicap (Brought to Mind)
Vanity Handicap (Brought to Mind)
Swaps Stakes (Best Pal)
Pacific Classic (Best Pal)
Metropolitan Handicap (In Excess)
Oak Tree Invitational Stakes (Filago)
Breeders' Cup Mile (Opening Verse)
Breeders' Cup Juvenile (Arazi)
1992: Arlington-Washington Lassie Stakes (Eliza)
Breeders' Cup Juvenile Fillies (Eliza)
San Juan Capistrano Handicap (Fly Till Dawn)
Spinster Stakes (Fowda)
Oak Tree Invitational Stakes (Navarone)
Breeders' Cup Turf (Fraise)
1993: Santa Anita Handicap (Sir Beaufort)
Santa Anita Oaks (Eliza)
1994: Sword Dancer Invitational Handicap (Alex the Great)
2002: Beverly D. Stakes (Golden Apples)
Yellow Ribbon Stakes (Golden Apples)
Shoemaker Breeders' Cup Mile (Ladies Din)
Hollywood Starlet Stakes (Elloluv)
2003: Santa Maria Handicap (Starrer)
Santa Margarita Handicap (Starrer)
Gamely Breeders' Cup Handicap (Tates Creek)
Yellow Ribbon Stakes (Tates Creek)
Triple Bend Breeders' Cup Handicap (Joey Franco)
Breeders' Cup Distaff (Adoration)
Hollywood Starlet Stakes (Hollywood Story)

JACINTO VASQUEZ

1963: Everglades Stakes (B. Major)
1967: Acorn Stakes (Furl Sail)
Mother Goose Stakes (Furl Sail)
Amory L. Haskell Handicap (Handsome Boy)
1969: Sorority Stakes (Box the Compass)
1970: Sanford Stakes (Executioner)
Travers Stakes (Loud)
1971: Withers Stakes (Bold Reasoning)
Jersey Derby (Bold Reasoning)
Hopeful Stakes (Rest Your Case)
Delaware Handicap (Blessing Angelica)
Flamingo Stakes (Executioner)
1972: American Derby (Dubassoff)
1973: Grey Lag Handicap (Summer Guest)
Bowling Green Handicap (Summer Guest)
Futurity Stakes (Wedge Shot)
Frizette Stakes (Bundler)
Flamingo Stakes (Our Native)
Wood Memorial Stakes (Angle Light)
Whitney Stakes (Onion)
Arlington Handicap (Dubassoff)
1974: Sapling Stakes (Foolish Pleasure)
Champagne Stakes (Foolish Pleasure)
San Luis Rey Stakes (Astray)
San Juan Capistrano Handicap (Astray)
Sorority Stakes (Ruffian)
Demoiselle Stakes (Land Girl)
Maskette Handicap (Ponte Vecchio)
1975: Acorn Stakes (Ruffian)
Mother Goose Stakes (Ruffian)
Coaching Club American Oaks (Ruffian)
Flamingo Stakes (Foolish Pleasure)
Wood Memorial Stakes (Foolish Pleasure)
Kentucky Derby (Foolish Pleasure)
Futurity Stakes (Soy Numero Uno)
Gazelle Handicap (Land Girl)
Fall Highweight Handicap (Honorable Miss)
San Fernando Stakes (First Back)
Century Handicap (Astray)
1976: Coaching Club American Oaks (Revidere)
Ruffian Stakes (Revidere)
1977: Maskette Handicap (What a Summer)
Marlboro Cup Handicap (Proud Birdie)
1978: Jerome Handicap (Sensitive Prince)
1979: Pan American Handicap (Noble Dancer II)
United Nations Handicap (Noble Dancer II)
San Luis Rey Stakes (Noble Dancer II)
Travers Stakes (General Assembly)
Vosburgh Stakes (General Assembly)
Gulfstream Park Handicap (Sensitive Prince)
1980: Ruffian Handicap (Genuine Risk)
Kentucky Derby (Genuine Risk)
Meadowlands Cup (Tunerup)
Hawthorne Gold Cup (Tunerup)
Flamingo Stakes (Superbity)
Man o' War Stakes (French Colonial)
1981: Maskette Stakes (Jameela)
1982: Coaching Club American Oaks (Christmas Past)
Ruffian Handicap (Christmas Past)
Pennsylvania Derby (Spanish Drums)
Marlboro Cup Handicap (Lemhi Gold)
1983: Brooklyn Handicap (Highland Blade)
Marlboro Cup Handicap (Highland Blade)
Pan American Handicap (Highland Blade)
Alcibiades Stakes (Lucky Lucky Lucky)
Kentucky Oaks (Princess Rooney)
Delaware Handicap (May Day Eighty)
Bowling Green Handicap (Tantalizing)
1985: Everglades Stakes (Rhoman Rule)
Louisiana Derby (Violado)
Withers Stakes (El Basco)
Arlington Classic (Smile)
1986: Gotham Stakes (Mogambo)
Breeders' Cup Sprint (Smile)
1987: Arlington-Washington Futurity (Tejano)
Cowdin Stakes (Tejano)
Hutcheson Stakes (Well Selected)
United Nations Handicap (Manila)
Hollywood Derby (Stately Don)
1988: Blue Grass Stakes (Granacus)
Ruffian Handicap (Sham Say)
Spinster Stakes (Hail a Cab)
1989: Cowdin Stakes (Adjudicating)
Champagne Stakes (Adjudicating)
Tropical Park Derby (Big Stanley)
Brooklyn Handicap (Forever Silver)
1990: Ohio Derby (Private School)
Brooklyn Handicap (Montubio)
1992: Blue Grass Stakes (Pistols and Roses)
Remsen Stakes (Silver of Silver)

CORNELIO VELASQUEZ

2002: Gulfstream Park Breeders' Cup Handicap (Cetewayo)
2003: Fountain of Youth Stakes (Trust N Luck)
Darley Alcibiades Stakes (Be Gentle)
Breeders' Cup Sprint (Cajun Beat)

DANNY VELASQUEZ

1971: Malibu Stakes (King of Cricket)
1972: San Luis Rey Handicap (Nor II)

JORGE VELASQUEZ

1966: Sorority Stakes (Like A Charm)
1967: Flamingo Stakes (Reflected Glory)
Seminole Handicap (Advocator)
1968: Top Flight Handicap (Amerigo Lady)
Jerome Handicap (Iron Ruler)
Carter Handicap (In Reality)
Display Handicap (Fast Count)
Man o' War Stakes (Czar Alexander)
1969: Gotham Stakes (Dike)
Wood Memorial Stakes (Dike)
United Nations Handicap (Hawaii)
Man o' War Stakes (Hawaii)
Matron Stakes (Cold Comfort)
Jerome Handicap (Mr. Leader)
Bowling Green Handicap (Czar Alexander)
1970: Dixie Handicap (Fort Marcy)
Bowling Green Handicap (Fort Marcy)
United Nations Handicap (Fort Marcy)
Man o' War Stakes (Fort Marcy)
Washington D.C. International (Fort Marcy)
Champagne Stakes (Limit to Reason)
Frizette Stakes (Forward Gal)
1971: Cowdin Stakes (Loquacious Don)
Whitney Stakes (Protanto)
Jockey Club Gold Cup (Shuvee)
Massachusetts Handicap (Chompion)
1972: Mother Goose Stakes (Wanda)
Manhattan Handicap (Star Envoy)
1973: Alabama Stakes (Desert Vixen)
Gazelle Handicap (Desert Vixen)
Beldame Stakes (Desert Vixen)
Woodward Stakes (Prove Out)
Jockey Club Gold Cup (Prove Out)
Metropolitan Handicap (Tentam)
United Nations Handicap (Tentam)
Arkansas Derby (Impecunious)
Withers Stakes (Linda's Chief)
1974: Acorn Stakes (Chris Evert)
Mother Goose Stakes (Chris Evert)
Coaching Club American Oaks (Chris Evert)
Hempstead Handicap (Poker Night)
Grey Lag Handicap (Prove Out)
Hawthorne Gold Cup (Group Plan)
United Nations Handicap (Halo)
1975: Man o' War Stakes (Snow Knight)
Canadian International Championship (Snow Knight)
Jockey Club Gold Cup (Group Plan)
1976: Top Flight Handicap (Proud Delta)
Hempstead Handicap (Proud Delta)
Beldame Stakes (Proud Delta)
Frizette Stakes (Sensational)
Selima Stakes (Sensational)
Acorn Stakes (Dearly Precious)
1977: Coaching Club American Oaks (Our Mims)
Alabama Stakes (Our Mims)
Delaware Handicap (Our Mims)
Champagne Stakes (Alydar)
1978: Flamingo Stakes (Alydar)

Florida Derby (Alydar)
Blue Grass Stakes (Alydar)
Travers Stakes (Alydar)
Whitney Stakes (Alydar)
Delaware Handicap (Late Bloomer)
Ruffian Handicap (Late Bloomer)
Beldame Stakes (Late Bloomer)
Sheepshead Bay Handicap (Late Bloomer)
Champagne Stakes (Spectacular Bid)
Young America Stakes (Spectacular Bid)
Acorn Stakes (Tempest Queen)
Spinster Stakes (Tempest Queen)
Gulfstream Park Handicap (Bowl Game)
Pan American Handicap (Bowl Game)
Suburban Handicap (Upper Nile)
1979: Fantasy Stakes (Davona Dale)
Kentucky Oaks (Davona Dale)
Acorn Stakes (Davona Dale)
Mother Goose Stakes (Davona Dale)
Coaching Club American Oaks (Davona Dale)
Hialeah Turf Cup (Bowl Game)
Arlington Handicap (Bowl Game)
Man o' War Stakes (Bowl Game)
Turf Classic (Bowl Game)
Washington D.C. International (Bowl Game)
Young America Stakes (Koluctoo Bay)
Suburban Handicap (State Dinner)
1980: Champagne Stakes (Lord Avie)
Young America Stakes (Lord Avie)
Alcibiades Stakes (Sweet Revenge)
Top Flight Handicap (Glorious Song)
Oaklawn Handicap (Uncool)
1981: Kentucky Derby (Pleasant Colony)
Preakness Stakes (Pleasant Colony)
Futurity Stakes (Irish Martini)
Matron Stakes (Before Dawn)
Santa Barbara Handicap (The Very One)
Louisiana Derby (Woodchopper)
Rothmans International Stakes (Open Call)
1982: Laurel Futurity (Cast Party)
Top Flight Handicap (Andover Way)
Super Derby (Reinvested)
Pan American Handicap (Robsphere)
Bowling Green Handicap (Open Call)
1983: Santa Anita Derby (Marfa)
Jim Beam Spiral Stakes (Marfa)
Remsen Stakes (Dr. Carter)
Apple Blossom Handicap (Miss Huntington)
Flower Bowl Handicap (First Approach)
Louisiana Derby (Balboa Native)
Gulfstream Park Handicap (Christmas Past)
Metropolitan Handicap (Star Choice)
1984: Mother Goose Stakes (Life's Magic)
Alabama Stakes (Life's Magic)
Beldame Stakes (Life's Magic)
1985: Maskette Stakes (Lady's Secret)
Ruffian Handicap (Lady's Secret)
Beldame Stakes (Lady's Secret)
Fountain of Youth Stakes (Proud Truth)
Florida Derby (Proud Truth)
Breeders' Cup Classic (Proud Truth)
Gulfstream Park Handicap (Dr. Carter)
Breeders' Cup Juvenile Fillies (Twilight Ridge)
Hollywood Derby (Slew the Dragon)
1986: Everglades Stakes (Badger Land)
Flamingo Stakes (Badger Land)
Santa Margarita Handicap (Lady's Secret)
Withers Stakes (Clear Choice)
1987: Widener Handicap (Launch a Pegasus)
Alabama Stakes (Up the Apalachee)
Young America Stakes (Firery Ensign)
1988: Mother Goose Stakes (Goodbye Halo)
Coaching Club American Oaks (Goodbye Halo)
Flamingo Stakes (Cherokee Colony)
1991: Arlington Classic (Whadjathink)
1993: Secretariat Stakes (Awad)

JOHN VELAZQUEZ

1991: Ohio Derby (Private Man)
1995: Turf Classic (Turk Passer)
1996: Mother Goose Stakes (Yanks Music)
Alabama Stakes (Yanks Music)
Ruffian Handicap (Yanks Music)
Beldame Stakes (Yanks Music)
Metropolitan Handicap (Honour and Glory)
Futurity Stakes (Traitor)
Moet Champagne Stakes (Ordway)
Crown Royal Hollywood Derby (Marlin)
1997: Gotham Stakes (Smokin Mel)
1998: Sword Dancer Invitational Handicap (Cetewayo)
Futurity Stakes (Lemon Drop Kid)
Flower Bowl Invitational Handicap (Auntie Mame)
Buick Meadowlands Cup Handicap (K.J.'s Appeal)
Breeders' Cup Mile (Da Hoss)
Early Times Hollywood Derby (Vergennes)
1999: Metropolitan Handicap (Sir Bear)
Test Stakes (Marley Vale)
Spinaway Stakes (Circle of Life)
2000: Acorn Stakes (Finder's Fee)
Breeders' Cup Juvenile Fillies (Caressing)
2001: Ashland Stakes (Fleet Renee)
Mother Goose Stakes (Fleet Renee)
Vosburgh Stakes (Left Bank)
Cigar Mile Handicap (Left Bank)
Coaching Club American Oaks (Tweedside)
Matriarch Stakes (Starine)
2002: Matron Stakes (Storm Flag Flying)
Frizette Stakes (Storm Flag Flying)
Long John Silver's BC Juv. Fillies (Storm Flag Flying)
Ogden Phipps Handicap (Raging Fever)
Prioress Stakes (Carson Hollow)
Suburban Handicap (E Dubai)
Whitney Handicap (Left Bank)
Personal Ensign Handicap (Summer Colony)
King's Bishop Stakes (Gygistar)
Breeders' Cup Filly and Mare Turf (Starine)
2003: Donn Handicap (Harlan's Holiday)
Jim Dandy Stakes (Strong Hope)
Alabama Stakes (Island Fashion)
Matriarch Stakes (Heat Haze)

JOSE VELEZ JR.

1983: Hialeah Turf Cup (Nijinsky's Secret)
1984: Hialeah Turf Cup (Nijinsky's Secret)
2002: Philip H. Iselin Handicap (Cat's at Home)
2003: United Nations Handicap (Balto Star)

ROGER VELEZ

1976: Whitney Handicap (Dancing Gun)
Hialeah Turf Cup (Lord Henham)
1978: Matron Stakes (Fall Aspen)
2000: Florida Derby (Hal's Hope)
2002: Gulfstream Park Handicap (Hal's Hope)

MIKE VENEZIA

1965: Everglades Stakes (Sparkling Johnny)
Gallant Fox Handicap (Choker)
1966: Massachusetts Handicap (Fast Count)
1972: Ladies Handicap (Grafitti)
Carter Handicap (Leematt)
1974: Remsen Stakes (El Pitirre)
1977: Top Flight Handicap (Shawi)
Ladies Handicap (Sensational)
1978: Alabama Stakes (White Star Line)
1980: Canadian International Championship (Great Neck)
1981: Secretariat Stakes (Sing Sing)
Hialeah Turf Cup (Lobsang II)
1984: Fountain of Youth Stakes (Darn That Alarm)
Arlington Handicap (Who's For Dinner)

OCTAVIO VERGARA

1976: Century Handicap (Winds of Thought)

MERLIN VOLZKE

1954: Santa Anita Maturity (Apple Valley)
1970: Hollywood Derby (Hanalei Bay)

B.J. WALKER JR.

1980: Golden Harvest Handicap (War Fame)

B. WALL

1967: Ohio Derby (Out the Window)

NICK WALL

1950: Demoiselle Stakes (Aunt Jinny)
Selima Stakes (Aunt Jinny)
1952: Saranac Handicap (Golden Gloves)

E. WALSH

1968: Monmouth Invitational Handicap (Balustrade)

BERNARD WALT

1976: Fantasy Stakes (T.V. Vixen)

PAUL WARD

1954: Ohio Derby (Timely Tip)

OWEN WEBSTER

1948: Cinema Handicap (Drumbeat)

JACK WESTROPE

1946: Hollywood Oaks (Honeymoon)
Cinema Handicap (Honeymoon)
Hollywood Derby (Honeymoon)
Vanity Handicap (Be Faithful)
1947: Frizette Stakes (Slumber Song)
Vanity Handicap (Honeymoon)
Vosburgh Handicap (With Pleasure)
1948: Inglewood Handicap (With Pleasure)
Del Mar Handicap (Frankly)
Golden Gate Handicap (Shannon II)
Santa Anita Maturity (Flashco)
1949: Will Rogers Handicap (Blue Dart)
Del Mar Derby (Bolero)
San Antonio Handicap (Dinner Gong)
1950: Westerner Stakes (Valquest)
Inglewood Handicap (Miche)
1951: Sunset Handicap (Alderman)
1953: Gallant Fox Handicap (Royal Vale)
Dixie Handicap (Royal Vale)
Massachusetts Handicap (Royal Vale)
Sunset Handicap (Lights Up)
1954: Delaware Oaks (Parlo)

DAVID WHITED

1969: Alcibiades Stakes (Belle Noire)
New Orleans Handicap (Miracle Hill)
Washington Park Handicap (Night Invader)
1970: Sapling Stakes (Staunch Avenger)
Kentucky Oaks (Lady Vi-E)
Washington Park Handicap (Doc's T.V.)
1973: Oaklawn Handicap (Prince Astro)
1975: Arkansas Derby (Promised City)

T. WILLIAMS

1948: Sunset Handicap (Drumbeat)

H.B. WILSON

1953: Black Helen Handicap (Atalanta)
Beldame Handicap (Atalanta)

RICK WILSON

1993: Wood Memorial Stakes (Storm Tower)
2000: Futurity Stakes (Burning Roma)
2001: Prioress Stakes (Xtra Heat)

DANNY WINICK

1981: Hollywood Derby (Silveyville)

BOBBY WOODHOUSE

1970: Dwyer Handicap (Judgable)
Whitney Stakes (Judgable)
Matron Stakes (Bonnie and Gay)
Manhattan Handicap (Shelter Bay)
1971: United Nations Handicap (Run the Gantlet)
Man o' War Stakes (Run the Gantlet)
Washington D.C. International (Run the Gantlet)
Sorority Stakes (Brenda Beauty)
Ohio Derby (Twist the Axe)
Widener Handicap (True North)
1972: Bowling Green Handicap (Run the Gantlet)
1973: Top Flight Handicap (Poker Night)

HEDLEY WOODHOUSE

1946: Astarita Stakes (Keynote)
Comely Handicap (Bonnie Beryl)
Grey Lag Handicap (Stymie)
1948: Gallant Fox Handicap (Faultless)
1949: Monmouth Handicap (Three Rings)
Westchester Handicap (Three Rings)
Metropolitan Handicap (Loser Weeper)
Roseben Handicap (Up Beat)
1950: Spinaway Stakes (Atalanta)
Matron Stakes (Atalanta)
McLennan Handicap (Three Rings)
Queens County Handicap (Three Rings)
Gulfstream Park Handicap (Chicle II)
Bougainvillea Handicap (Chicle II)
Champagne Stakes (Uncle Miltie)
Metropolitan Handicap (Greek Ship)
1951: Matron Stakes (Rose Jet)
Demoiselle Stakes (Rose Jet)
Bougainvillea Handicap (Chicle II)
1952: Roamer Handicap (Quiet Step)
1953: Cowdin Stakes (Fisherman)
Champagne Stakes (Fisherman)
Westchester Handicap (Cold Command)
1954: Gotham Stakes (Fisherman)
Travers Stakes (Fisherman)
Lawrence Realization Stakes (Fisherman)
Hialeah Turf Handicap (Picador)
1955: Pimlico Futurity (Nail)
Remsen Stakes (Nail)
Futurity Stakes (Nail)
Roamer Handicap (Sailor)
Fall Highweight Handicap (Sailor)

HEDLEY WOODHOUSE *(Continued)*

Pimlico Special (Sailor)
Maskette Handicap (Oil Painting)
Excelsior Handicap (Fisherman)
Whitney Stakes (First Aid)
1956: Coaching Club American Oaks (Levee)
Monmouth Oaks (Levee)
Withers Stakes (Oh Johnny)
Travers Stakes (Oh Johnny)
Cowdin Stakes (Mister Jive)
Gardenia Stakes (Magic Forest)
1957: Diana Handicap (Pardala)
Gotham Stakes (Mister Jive)
Lawrence Realization Stakes (Promised Land)
1959: Pimlico Futurity (Progressing)
1960: Acorn Stakes (Irish Jay)
Withers Stakes (John William)
1961: Withers Stakes (Hitting Away)
Dwyer Handicap (Hitting Away)
Sorority Stakes (Batter Up)
1965: Monmouth Handicap (Repeating)
1967: United Nations Handicap (Flit-to)

CHARLES WOODS JR.

1998: Ashland Stakes (Well Chosen)

DANNY WRIGHT

1977: Demoiselle Stakes (Caesar's Wish)
Jersey Derby (Cormorant)
1978: Mother Goose Stakes (Caesar's Wish)

WAYNE WRIGHT

1946: Roseben Handicap (Polynesian)
1948: Garden State Stakes (Blue Peter)

ROY YAKA

1962: Del Mar Futurity (Slipped Disc)

MIGUEL YANEZ

1968: Santa Anita Handicap (Mr. Right)
1969: San Antonio Stakes (Praise Jay)

ROBERT YANEZ

1961: Hollywood Juvenile Championship (Rattle Dancer)
Del Mar Debutante Stakes (Spark Plug)

MANNY YCAZA

1958: Santa Margarita Handicap (Born Rich)
Westerner Stakes (Strong Bay)
American Derby (Nadir)
1959: Suburban Handicap (Bald Eagle)
Gallant Fox Handicap (Bald Eagle)
Washington D.C. International (Bald Eagle)
Princess Pat Stakes (Heavenly Body)
Matron Stakes (Heavenly Body)
Coaching Club American Oaks (Resaca)
Delaware Oaks (Resaca)
Withers Stakes (Intentionally)
Jerome Handicap (Intentionally)
Kentucky Oaks (Hidden Talent)
Travers Stakes (Sword Dancer)
Whitney Stakes (Plion)
1960: Widener Handicap (Bald Eagle)
Gulfstream Park Handicap (Bald Eagle)
Metropolitan Handicap (Bald Eagle)
Aqueduct Handicap (Bald Eagle)
Washington D.C. International (Bald Eagle)
Kentucky Oaks (Make Sail)
Alabama Stakes (Make Sail)
San Carlos Handicap (Clandestine)
Display Handicap (Nickel Boy)
Arlington Handicap (One-Eyed King)
1961: Saratoga Special (Battle Joined)
Futurity Stakes (Cyane)
Champagne Stakes (Donut King)
Top Flight Handicap (Make Sail)
Sunset Handicap (Whodunit)
San Carlos Handicap (First Balcony)
1962: Cowdin Stakes (Never Bend)
Champagne Stakes (Never Bend)
Florida Derby (Ridan)
Blue Grass Stakes (Ridan)
Gallant Fox Handicap (Sensitivo)
Display Handicap (Sensitivo)
Arlington Lassie Stakes (Smart Deb)
Frizette Stakes (Pams Ego)
Lawrence Realization Stakes (Battle Joined)
Seminole Handicap (Intentionally)
1963: Hopeful Stakes (Traffic)
Kentucky Oaks (Sally Ship)
Top Flight Handicap (Firm Policy)
Beldame Stakes (Oil Royalty)
Spinster Stakes (Lamb Chop)
Flamingo Stakes (Never Bend)
Monmouth Handicap (Decidedly)
1964: Belmont Stakes (Quadrangle)
Dwyer Handicap (Quadrangle)
Travers Stakes (Quadrangle)
Lawrence Realization Stakes (Quadrangle)
Saratoga Special (Sadair)
Garden State Stakes (Sadair)
Pimlico Futurity (Sadair)
San Juan Capistrano Handicap (Cedar Key)
Donn Handicap (Cedar Key)
Santa Margarita Handicap (Batteur)
Everglades Stakes (Roman Brother)
Grey Lag Handicap (Saidam)
Suburban Handicap (Iron Peg)
San Fernando Stakes (Nevada Battler)
1965: Sorority Stakes (Native Street)
San Felipe Handicap (Jacinto)
Charles H. Strub Stakes (Duel)
San Antonio Handicap (Gun Bow)
Man o' War Stakes (Hill Rise)
San Luis Rey Handicap (Cedar Key)
1966: Frizette Stakes (Regal Gleam)
Selima Stakes (Regal Gleam)
Gazelle Handicap (Prides Profile)
Illinois Derby (Michigan Avenue)
Display Handicap (Damelo II)
San Antonio Handicap (Hill Rise)
1967: Breeders' Futurity (T.V. Commercial)
Gotham Stakes (Dr. Fager)
Washington D.C. International (Fort Marcy)
1968: Kentucky Oaks (Dark Mirage)
Acorn Stakes (Dark Mirage)
Mother Goose Stakes (Dark Mirage)
Coaching Club American Oaks (Dark Mirage)
Monmouth Oaks (Dark Mirage)
Hopeful Stakes (Top Knight)
Futurity Stakes (Top Knight)
Champagne Stakes (Top Knight)
Santa Margarita Handicap (Gamely)
Brooklyn Handicap (Damascus)
Century Handicap (Model Fool)
1969: Black Helen Handicap (Amerigo Lady)
Top Flight Handicap (Amerigo Lady)
Flamingo Stakes (Top Knight)
Florida Derby (Top Knight)
Pimlico-Laurel Futurity (High Echelon)
Spinaway Stakes (Meritus)
California Derby (Jay Ray)
Withers Stakes (Ack Ack)
Hollywood Park Inv. Turf Handicap (Fort Marcy)
Stars and Stripes Handicap (Hawaii)
1971: Sanford Stakes (Cohasset Tribe)

RAY YORK

1951: San Felipe Stakes (Phil D.)
1952: Gazelle Stakes (Hushaby Baby)
Withers Stakes (Armageddon)
San Antonio Handicap (Phil D.)
1954: San Felipe Handicap (Determine)
Santa Anita Derby (Determine)
Kentucky Derby (Determine)
Vanity Handicap (Bubbley)
San Juan Capistrano Handicap (By Zeus)
1955: Starlet Stakes (Bold Bazooka)
Del Mar Futurity (Blen Host)
Del Mar Debutante Stakes (Miss Todd)
Santa Anita Maturity (Determine)
1957: William P. Kyne Memorial Handicap (Pibe Carlitos)
1958: Del Mar Debutante Stakes (Khalita)
1959: Santa Anita Derby (Silver Spoon)
Sunset Handicap (Whodunit)
1960: Saratoga Special (Bronzerullah)
1961: Del Mar Futurity (Weldy)
1963: Hollywood Juvenile Championship (Nevada Bin)
1964: American Handicap (Colorado King)
Hollywood Gold Cup (Colorado King)
Del Mar Debutante Stakes (Admirably)
1965: Kentucky Jockey Club Stakes (War Censor)

JACK YOTHER

1961: Bowling Green Handicap (Dead Center)

FERRILL ZUFELT

1948: Excelsior Handicap (Knockdown)
Queens County Handicap (Knockdown)
Arlington Futurity (Mr. Busher)
1949: Inglewood Handicap (Ace Admiral)

MARCEL ZUNIGA

1984: Champagne Stakes (For Certain Doc)

Photo courtesy of Santa Anita Park

Charlie Whittingham, the Bald Eagle of the Sierra Madre, inspects the bust that was erected in the legendary trainer's honor at Santa Anita Park.

Trainers

IV: Trainers

Bald Eagle vs. Cool Hand Luke

In most sports, their equivalents are called coaches. In the case of baseball, the terminology is manager.

In thoroughbred racing, they're called trainers, and their decisions—good and bad—from what exercises to provide for their charges, what races to enter, and which jockeys to select for their prized animals are among the key ingredients in a horse's success or failure.

And, with few exceptions, a trainer's premier objective is to win. The higher the stakes, the better.

"Whenever you win a stakes, you feel that, after all the hard work you've done, you've really accomplished something," said Tony Foyt, who trained for, among others, Calumet Farm and his father, four-time Indianapolis 500 winner A.J. Foyt.

The *best* trainer of the modern era possibly could be someone who never won a major race, who labored at Backwater Park for decades, claiming horses for $5,000 in six-furlong races and turning them into winners in mile-and-one-eighth events for a $15,000 claiming tag without getting the opportunity to make his dreams come true.

"This is what every trainer dreams about," the late Eddie Gregson said after winning the 1982 Kentucky Derby with Gato Del Sol. "It's a dream that every trainer has. It's a beautiful thing."

While arguing the *best* of anything is often pointless, determining the most successful trainer of the modern era—based on winning major races—is a more reasonable proposition.

Photo courtesy of Churchill Downs

Jockey Gary Stevens (right) and trainer Wayne Lukas (left) hoisted the trophy after Thunder Gulch's victory in the 1995 Kentucky Derby, one of Lukas's 13 classic triumphs.

Even that is debatable, but rest assured that there are only two legitimate candidates for such acclaim.

While the likes of Nate Thurmond and Walt Bellamy, for instance, enjoyed marvelous National Basketball Association careers in the '60s, any debate about the best centers of that era always will boil down to Bill Russell vs. Wilt Chamberlain.

Similarly, Charlie Whittingham and Wayne Lukas have been the Affirmed and Alydar of modern trainers. Their magnificent accomplishments are just a nose apart, while the rest of their rivals can fight gamely for third place.

In Whittingham's Favor

"I consider Charlie Whittingham one of the great trainers in my time, and I go back quite a ways with the likes of Ben Jones, Max Hirsch, Sunny Jim Fitzsimmons, and many other great trainers," said the late Eddie Arcaro, one of history's premier jockeys. "I put Charlie right there with all of them."

In a career that began in 1953 and didn't end until his death in 1998, Whittingham captured 208 major races, a figure exceeded only by Lukas.

Whittingham finished atop the trainers' standings for major victories on six occasions, in 1971, '72, '74, '75, '81, and '82, a total exceeded only by Lukas. For 26 consecutive years, from 1969-94, Whittingham won at least one major race, and that streak is eight years longer than any other trainer has managed. He won three or more races and finished among the top nine trainers 15 years in a row (1969-83), both records. Among the other records held by the Bald Eagle of the Sierra Madre are the most top-three (17), top-four (18), top-five (21), top-six (23), top-eight (25), and top-nine seasons (27).

After Whittingham left the Marine Corps, he learned the ropes as an assistant to Hall of Fame trainer Horatio Luro, whom he said "taught me patience with horses."

Whittingham called patience the key to his success, and it didn't apply only to horses. He earned his first classic victory with Ferdinand in the 1986 Kentucky Derby, when, at 73, he became the oldest trainer to win the Run for the Roses. Whittingham broke that record three years later when he won both the Derby and the Preakness Stakes with Sunday Silence.

"Patience is the main thing when you're training," he said. "You get patience with age. You learn a little more. You are constantly learning in the horse business. Usually, if you go slower, you've got a better chance at having a good horse down the line. As you go along, a little rubs off on you from everyone, and every day you learn something new."

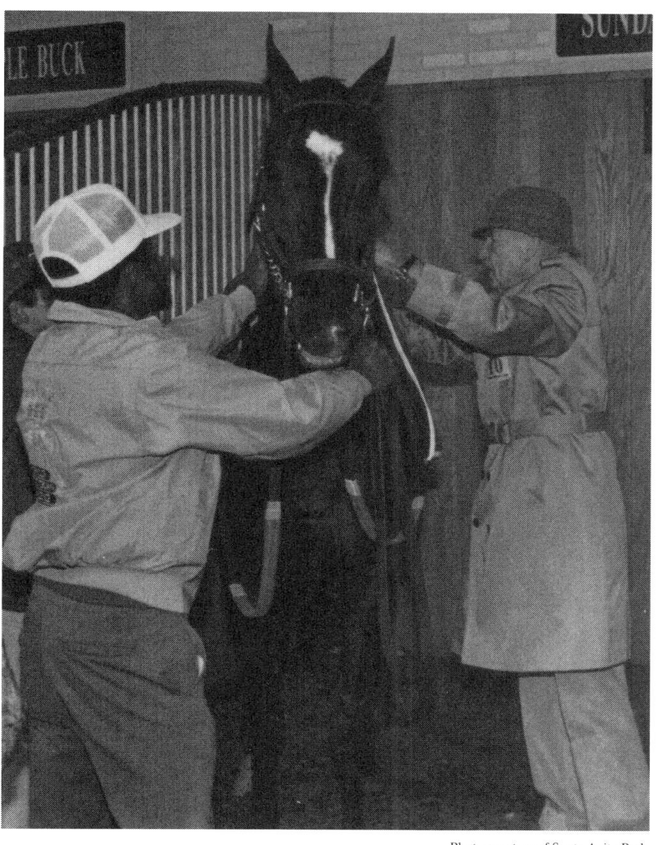

Photo courtesy of Santa Anita Park

Charlie Whittingham dressed appropriately for one of the most unseasonable Kentucky Derbies on record—a post-time temperature of 51 degrees and a track rendered muddy by nearly an inch of rain—when he saddled Sunday Silence before the 1989 Kentucky Derby. Sunday Silence romped home two-and-one-half lengths in front to make Whittingham, at 76, the oldest trainer to win the Derby, breaking the record he had set three years earlier with Ferdinand.

Patience is the key reason it took so long for Whittingham to taste classic success. Owners who were seeking a quick return on their investments with two- and three-year-olds generally knew Whittingham was not necessarily the trainer for them: His major victories include only nine with two-year-olds and 39 in races for three-year-olds.

"I take plenty of time with the younger horses," Whittingham said in 1989. "My philosophy is to wait on the two-year-olds. If you don't rest your two-year-olds, you won't have four- or five-year-olds, and if you have no older horses, you have nothing for the handicap division. Don't ever let your owner tell you how to run the show. Set your goals, and stick to them."

The Bald Eagle earned five or more victories with five different runners—Cougar II, Erins Isle, Exceller, Flawlessly, and Sunday Silence. Instructively, Sunday Silence was the only member of that quintet who was a major winner at three, and neither of Whittingham's Derby winners won at two.

Whittingham's 208 victories were earned by 104 different horses, and only six other trainers earned more total major victories in the modern era than the 93 he garnered in grass races.

"I think Charlie's the best trainer this country ever saw," added another legendary jockey, the late Bill Shoemaker.

"Racing couldn't find a more dedicated ambassador," Arthur B. Hancock III, who co-owned Sunday Silence, said of Whittingham. "His discipline has been an inspiration to me."

Stating the Case For Lukas

Before he turned his attention to training horses, first quarter-horses and then thoroughbreds, Lukas was a high school basketball coach and an assistant at his alma mater, the University of Wisconsin.

Had he pursued that path, those who know him have little doubt he would have carved a legacy on the hardwood that would have rivaled the achievements of Dean Smith at North Carolina, Mike Krzyzewski at Duke, or what Lukas's close friend, Bobby Knight, managed at Indiana before he turned Texas Tech into a nationally ranked powerhouse. That's because Lukas certainly has carved a legacy in thoroughbred racing at least equal—if not vastly superior to—the marks those aforementioned legends made in college basketball.

"If Wayne Lukas keeps going, he'll pass me, break all my records," Whittingham said nearly a decade before his death. "I think the world of Wayne—never saw a fellow so organized."

Lukas, who turned 69 in 2004, has won 222 major races, more than any trainer in the modern era. He has finished atop the standings for major victories a record 11 times, including a record six years in a row (1985-90). The only other time a trainer finished No. 1 more than three years in a row was from 1994-97. That trainer was Lukas.

Even before Lukas began a record streak of 12 consecutive top-eight seasons in 1980, he had taken the initial steps of revolutionizing training by seeking major—and lesser—stakes races far from his home base in Southern California. No other

Four Footed Fotos, Inc., courtesy of Churchill Downs

The late Chris Antley, aboard Charismatic (11), signaled to jockey Pat Day, riding Menifee (13), that he crossed the wire a neck in front in the 1999 Kentucky Derby. The victory by Charismatic, who had competed in a $62,500 claiming race 11 weeks earlier, was the fourth in the Run for the Roses for trainer Wayne Lukas.

trainer before him had been so likely to compete in a $1 million race on his home track one day, then ship another couple of horses thousands of miles away to compete with the best the locals had to offer for $50,000 the next.

"We're aggressive. We've got a better organization. The bottom line is that, in order to utilize and get the most out of every horse, we needed to set up a network or system that takes advantage of what it takes to win," said Lukas, who later established stables at numerous tracks around the country. "It's very expensive to go on the road. If you go on the road and don't win, it'll take all the juice out of your program. You must win when you go on the road."

Lukas has ranked among the top two trainers a record 16 times, including 10 years in a row from 1982-91—double the longest span of his nearest rival. In fact, the closest assault on that kind of consistent brilliance came when Woody Stephens finished among the top five trainers eight consecutive years from 1981-88. In each of those 10 seasons, Lukas won at least eight races. Other than Lukas, only Jimmy Jones (1947-54) and Stephens (1981-88) managed eight-year streaks of at least four victories.

During that incredible 10-year run, Lukas was voted the Eclipse Award as the nation's outstanding trainer on just three occasions.

"The voting goes funny at times. You just don't know what to make of it," Stephens once said. "Sometimes I wondered, 'What do you have to do?' "

Among the things that Lukas did was win at least 15 races in five consecutive seasons (1986-90). The only other times a modern-era trainer won 11 or more races more than two years in a row were—drum roll, please—Lukas, who won 12 or more three years in a row from 1994-96 and another 11 in 1997, and Bobby Frankel from 2001-03. Only twice has a trainer won 17 or more races in back-to-back campaigns. On both occasions, that trainer was Lukas. He accomplished that feat in both 1986 and '87—when he became the only trainer with back-to-back seasons with 18 or more victories—and again in 1989 and '90.

Further, when the sports world's spotlight shines on thoroughbred racing for the Triple Crown campaign and the Breeders' Cup, no other trainer has approached Lukas's impact.

Lukas has posted 13 classic victories and trained 10 different classic winners, both records, and he is one of only two modern trainers who has saddled as many as three dual classic winners—Tabasco Cat in 1994, Thunder Gulch in '95, and Charismatic in '99—and dual classic winners in back-to-back campaigns. In both 1995, when Timber Country won the Preakness Stakes to give Lukas a sweep of the classics, and in 1996, when Grindstone won the Kentucky Derby and Editor's Note captured the Belmont Stakes, Lukas won classics with two different horses. The only other modern trainer to accomplish that feat was John Jacobs, who won the Preakness with Personality and the Belmont with High Echelon in 1970.

If anything, Lukas has been even more dominant in the

Breeders' Cup. He won at least one Breeders' Cup race five years in a row (1985-89), and Aidan O'Brien is the only other trainer to post even a three-year streak (2001-03). Lukas has won two or more Breeders' Cup races on six different occasions, including four years in a row from 1985-88. No one else has managed multiple Breeders' Cup victories in back-to-back seasons. And Lukas not only has won a record 17 Breeders' Cup races, but he has done it with 17 different horses.

Lukas has trained 107 major winners, including eight who won five or more races under his command, more than any other trainer. Six of those eight—Life's Magic, Althea, Lady's Secret, Open Mind, Serena's Song, and Sharp Cat—are fillies, and he is one of only three trainers in history to win the Kentucky Derby with a distaffer, which he managed in 1988 with Winning Colors.

Lukas not only has demonstrated a special touch with fillies, but with young horses. He has earned 75 major triumphs with two-year-olds and another 82 in three-year-old races, including five with Thunder Gulch.

"You develop an eye for what you think will be an athlete," Lukas once said when asked his key to success.

Interestingly, the other horse Lukas guided to five victories was Criminal Type, who accomplished all of those triumphs during his 1990 Horse of the Year campaign as a five-year-old.

When Lukas was asked more than a decade ago if he was indeed the nation's best trainer, he replied, "I don't think so. But if statistics mean anything, yes."

The Best of the Rest

While Whittingham parlayed his patience and Lukas "his eye" for equine athleticism into peerless careers in the modern era, other trainers have employed their own secrets with legendary results.

Stephens once said that his secret to success was learning that horses "will tell you what they need, not the other way around."

According to Lee Snell, a trainer based in the Midwest who has never won a major race, every conditioner has different secrets.

"If you get 10 trainers in a room and ask them a question, you'll get 10 different answers. And they may all be right," she said. "There's no *right* way to do everything."

The following 28 trainers, however, are the first you'd ask, because their methods, like those of Whittingham and Lukas, obviously proved to be the right ones.

Another Scintillating Six

In addition to Lukas and Whittingham, six other Hall of Fame trainers enjoyed multiple No. 1 seasons, earned 66 or more victories, and captured at least one classic triumph. Those six trained as many as 68 (Frankel) and as few as 15 different major winners (Elliott Burch).

Listed in the order they rank in the modern-era standings for major victories, with their "big horses," as they're known in track vernacular—in this case defined as thoroughbreds who won five or more major races under their direction:

Woody Stephens won multiple major races 16 consecutive seasons (1974-89) and finished among the top seven trainers 11 campaigns in a row (1978-88), both records, and his five consecutive victories in the Belmont Stakes from 1982-86 make him the only modern trainer to capture a classic five years in succession. Stephens, the No. 1-ranked trainer in both 1960 and 1984, conditioned such "big horses" as Bald Eagle, Swale, Miss Oceana, Heavenly Cause, Creme Fraiche, and Forty Niner.

Photo courtesy of Santa Anita Park

Jockey Laffit Pincay Jr. was already a legend when he posed aboard Extra Hand in the winner's circle after the 1973 San Gorgonio Claiming Stakes at Santa Anita. The trainer who saddled Extra Hand had yet to achieve such status, but Bobby Frankel (third from left) certainly is now. The obscure San Gorgonio was Frankel's first stakes score at the Great Race Place, but in the 21st Century he has been America's dominant trainer: 61 major victories and three consecutive No. 1 seasons from 2001-03, including a record 27 major stakes in 2003.

Bobby Frankel, trainer of Possibly Perfect, You, and Medaglia d'Oro, has unquestionably been the 21st Century's most successful trainer. In 2003, he became only the sixth modern trainer to post a third consecutive No. 1 season and captured his first classic when Empire Maker won the Belmont Stakes. Frankel posted a single-season record 27 major triumphs in 2003, his unprecedented third consecutive season with 16 or more major stakes scores.

Only Lukas and Whittingham exceeded the five No. 1 seasons, including three in a row from 1947-49, posted by **Jimmy Jones.** Only Lukas and Stephens trained more different classic winners than Jones's five, and the stars of his stable included Armed, Citation, Coaltown, Ponder, Bewitch, Tim Tam, and Bardstown.

Bill Winfrey, who trained Bed o' Roses, Next Move, Native Dancer, Social Outcast, and Find, enjoyed No. 1 seasons in both 1950 and '53 and finished among the top two six times, which is bettered by only three other trainers.

Laz Barrera, trainer of 1978 Triple Crown winner Affirmed and It's In the Air, posted three straight No. 1 seasons (1977-79).

In guiding the careers of Sword Dancer, Bowl of Flowers, Quadrangle, Fort Marcy, Arts and Letters, Key to the Mint, Summer Guest, and Run the Gantlet, **Elliott Burch** posted three No. 1 seasons, including back-to-back campaigns in 1969 and '70.

Eight More Elite

Eight other Hall of Famers earned classic victories, won at least 44 major races, and had a No. 1 season. They trained between 30 (John Gaver) and 17 (Lucien Laurin and Bert Mulholland) major winners. Only LeRoy Jolley and Neil Drysdale are still active among these elite eight, and some, notably Sunny Jim Fitzsimmons, who trained Triple Crown winners Gallant Fox and Omaha in the '30s, had considerable accomplishments before the modern era. Listed in the order they rank in the modern-era standings for major victories—and their "big horses":

LeRoy Jolley trained Ridan, Foolish Pleasure, Optimistic Gal, Honest Pleasure, Manila, and Meadow Star. . . . **Max Hirsch's** stable stars included 1946 Triple Crown winner Assault, But Why Not, and High Gun. . . . **John Gaver** conditioned Capot, One Hitter, and Tom Fool. . . . **Jim Fitzsimmons** won at least one major race in 15 consecutive seasons (1948-62), a streak bettered by only three others, and trained Nashua, High Voltage, and Bold Ruler. . . . **Neil Drysdale,** whose six different Breeders' Cup winners rank third on the all-time list, trained Bold 'n Determined, Gorgeous, and A.P. Indy. . . . Under the direction of **Bill Molter,** Round Table retired in 1959 as the world's leading money-earner. . . . The stars of **Lucien Laurin's** stable included 1973 Triple Crown winner Secretariat, Quill, and Riva Ridge. . . . **Bert Mulholland** trained both Battlefield and Jaipur.

Yet Another Fab Four

Four Hall of Fame trainers have won 51 or more races and posted at least one No. 1 season, yet failed to win a classic, although two of them, Ron McAnally and Allen Jerkens, were still actively seeking that distinction entering 2004. They accomplished those feats training as many as 44 (McAnally) and as few as 20 (Hirsch Jacobs) different major winners. Listed in the order they rank in the modern-era standings for major victories—and their "big horses":

Keeneland-Cook photo courtesy of Keeneland Association

Sunny Jim Fitzsimmons, in his familiar straw hat and bow tie, was a familiar figure in winners' circles after major races for decades. Fitzsimmons captured the Triple Crown with Gallant Fox in 1930 and with Omaha in 1935, then earned two classic victories with Nashua in 1955 and another with Bold Ruler two years later.

Ron McAnally, conditioner of John Henry, Bayakoa, and Paseana, was the top-ranked trainer in both 1991 and '92 and, with 105 major triumphs, is one of only six modern trainers who has reached the century mark. . . . **Allen Jerkens,** who conditioned Beau Purple, Sky Beauty, and Devil His Due, earned the nickname "Giant Killer" for Beau Purple's conquests of Kelso, triumphs by Onion and Prove Out over Secretariat, and Wagon Limit's upset of Skip Away in the 1998 Jockey Club Gold Cup. . . . **Eddie Neloy,** trainer of Gun Bow and Buckpasser, posted four No. 1 seasons, including three in a row from 1966-68. He won 16 or more races in both 1966 and '67 and is one of only three trainers who has won 14 or more in back-to-back campaigns. . . . **Hirsch Jacobs,** whose career began before the modern era, trained post-war standouts Stymie, Promised Land, and Searching.

Four More Classic Hall of Famers

Four other Hall of Fame trainers won 43 or more races and enjoyed at least one classic victory, yet never attained a No. 1 season. They trained between 27 (Scotty Schulhofer) and 21 (Jimmy Conway) different major winners. Listed in the order they rank in the modern-era standings for major victories—and their "big horses":

Scotty Schulhofer trained two Belmont Stakes winners, including Lemon Drop Kid. . . . **Syl Veitch,** trainer of Fisherman, Phalanx, and Counterpoint, won the Belmont Stakes with the latter two. . . . **Jimmy Conway,** whose stable stars included My Request and Grecian Queen, also trained dual classic winner Chateaugay. . . . **Harry Trotsek's** top charges were Oil Capitol and Preakness winner Hasty Road.

Two More Standouts

Active Hall of Fame trainers **Bill Mott** and **Richard Mandella** have conditioned 28 and 32 different major winners, respectively, and won 58 or more races. Neither has won a classic nor enjoyed a No. 1 season, although only four trainers have saddled more than the five Breeders' Cup winners Mott has. Those include his best performer, Cigar, the sport's all-time leading money-winner. Only three trainers have longer streaks of seasons with four or more victories than the seven in a row posted from 1993-99 by Mandella, whose standouts have included Kotashaan, Sandpit, and Gentlemen, and his six Breeders' Cup victories include a single-day record four in 2003.

In a Class by Himself

Hall of Fame trainer **Mack Miller** saddled 26 major winners who captured 44 races, including Sea Hero in the 1993 Kentucky Derby, but he never enjoyed a No. 1 season or conditioned a winner of five major races.

Two Who Are Worthy of Induction

Only three modern trainers have won as many as 40 major races without earning a ticket to the Hall of Fame, and one hasn't completed the mandatory 25 years since he became a licensed trainer to earn eligibility for enshrinement. So among eligible trainers, none can make a more compelling argument to join the sport's elite in Saratoga Springs, N.Y., than these two:

Only six trainers in the modern era have exceeded the 99 victories **Shug McGaughey** has posted. Only one trainer has bettered his 12 consecutive seasons with three or more victories and a top-10 ranking (1985-96), his 18 consecutive seasons with at least one major victory (1985-2002), or his eight Breeders' Cup triumphs. McGaughey has trained 42 major winners, including 1989 Belmont Stakes winner Easy Goer, Inside Information, Heavenly Prize, and Personal Ensign—who retired unbeaten in 13 career starts. McGaughey has a No. 1 season and ranks in the top five in top-two (5) and top-10 (15) campaigns.

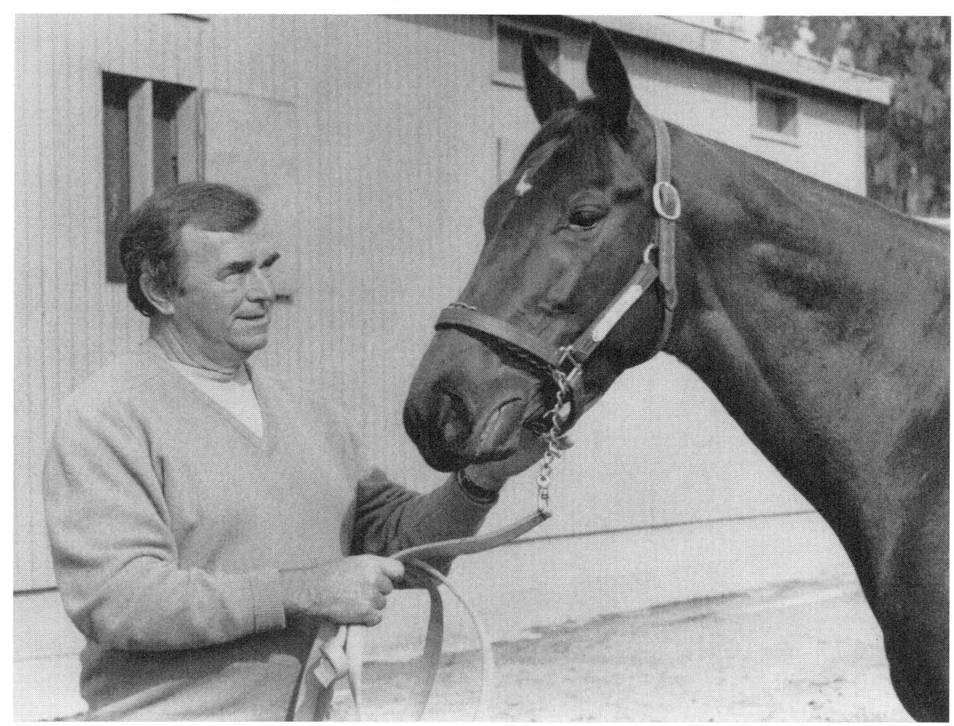

Photo courtesy of Santa Anita Park

Ron McAnally has saddled the winners of more than 100 major races. Nine of those victories were earned by Bayakoa, who captured the Breeders' Cup Distaff in 1989 and '90 and is the only two-time winner of that event.

While McGaughey no doubt ranks as the most accomplished eligible modern trainer who isn't in the Hall of Fame, **Casey Hayes** also has the credentials for induction. Hayes, who trained 15 horses to 42 major victories, conditioned 1950 Preakness victor Hill Prince, Cicada, and First Landing, each a winner of five or more major stakes under his watch.

Best Bet for the Future

Like Lukas, **Bob Baffert** abandoned quarter-horses to train thoroughbreds. And, like Lukas, it didn't take Baffert, who turned his attention to thoroughbreds in 1991, long to succeed.

His first major victory came in the 1992 Breeders' Cup Sprint with Thirty Slews, and 36 other horses have given him an additional 77 major victories since. Baffert posted three consecutive No. 1 seasons from 1998-2000, and only Lukas has a longer streak of top-two seasons than the five in a row Baffert posted from 1997-2001. Only Lukas has a longer streak of consecutive seasons with 10 or more victories than Baffert's four in a row from 1998-2001, and Lukas is the only other trainer to saddle dual classic winners in consecutive seasons in the modern era. Baffert turned that trick twice. He won the Kentucky Derby and Preakness with Silver Charm in 1997 and the same two races with Real Quiet a year later. Baffert failed to win a classic in 1999, but he did manage 23 major victories, a total exceeded in the modern era only by Frankel's 27 in 2003. In 2001, Point Given, who, along with Real Quiet, Silverbulletday, and Congaree, won five or more races under Baffert's care, captured the Preakness and Belmont. War Emblem's triumphs in the 2002 Kentucky Derby and Preakness not only allowed Baffert to saddle back-to-back dual classic winners for a second time, but enabled him to become the only conditioner to train four dual classic winners.

Photo courtesy of Santa Anita Park

Bob Baffert is the only modern trainer who has saddled four dual classic winners. His first charge to accomplish that feat was Silver Charm, who won the Kentucky Derby and Preakness Stakes in 1997.

Upon Further Examination

While 27 of the 29 eligible trainers with 40 or more modern-era major victories have been enshrined in the Hall of Fame, winning 20—or even 30—major races has been no guarantee of selection. Seven of the 12 who have exceeded 30 victories, but fallen short of 40, have been inducted, while just four of the nine with between 25 and 29 triumphs and only six of the 14 with 20 to 24 wins have been selected, although two members of the latter group, Juan Gonzalez and Todd Pletcher, are not yet eligible.

This is not meant to suggest that any of the 17 trainers with at least 20 and fewer than 40 modern-era triumphs who have been inducted into the Hall of Fame haven't been worthy of selection. "Plain" Ben Jones, for example, conditioned 1941 Triple Crown winner Whirlaway before the advent of the modern era. Rather, it is to suggest that the 18 who have accomplished that feat and haven't been selected should rank among the leading contenders for immortality.

Two of those 18, Jimmy Smith and Carl Hanford, had No. 1 seasons—nearly equaling the number of the Hall of Famers on the chart on the following page who enjoyed that distinction (Ben Jones, Mesh Tenney, and Bud Delp). And since Smith's No. 1 season came in 1946, he is among those who may have impressive credentials before the advent of the modern era.

Neither is this meant to suggest that these 18 trainers necessarily should have their tickets to Saratoga punched without further examination. Hanford's credentials, for example, no doubt are boosted by the fact that he is the only modern trainer to direct five consecutive Horse of the Year campaigns, which he managed with Kelso from 1960-64. Likewise, Hanford's case obviously isn't helped by the fact that he trained only one major winner other than Kelso. And, interestingly, four of those 18 who are waiting in the wings are sons of Hall of Fame trainers, and another on the list, Moody Jolley, is the father of one. Are John Veitch, Roger Laurin, David Whiteley, and Jimmy Smith, for example, being punished by the electorate for failing to meet the standards set by their fathers? Or have they simply failed to merit inclusion?

The charts below list the highlights of the careers of the 35 trainers who reached 20 victories yet failed to reach 40 during the modern era, with active trainers through 2003 denoted by an asterisk:

Hall of Fame

Trainer	Major Wins	Major Winners	Classic Wins	Winners of 5-Plus Major Races
Frank Whiteley Jr.	37	9	3	Tom Rolfe, Damascus, Ruffian, Forego
Jim Maloney	36	23	0	Gamely
Mesh Tenney	36	10	2	Swaps, Prove It, Candy Spots
Preston Burch	35	22	1	Sailor
Tommy Kelly	33	14	0	Droll Role, Noble Dancer II, Plugged Nickle
Jimmy Croll	31	12	1	Forward Gal, Bet Twice, Holy Bull
Horatio Luro	31	15	3	Northern Dancer
Angel Penna	29	19	0	
John Nerud	27	9	1	Gallant Man, Dr. Fager
Sherrill Ward	27	6	0	Summer Tan, Idun, Forego
Buddy Hirsch	25	15	0	
Sonny Hine	24	5	0	Skip Trial, Skip Away
Burley Parke	24	12	0	Noor, Roman Brother
Ben Jones	23	13	3	Real Delight
* Jack Van Berg	23	14	3	Alysheba
Henry Clark	22	9	0	Tempted
* Bud Delp	20	5	2	Spectacular Bid

Waiting in the Wings

Trainer	Major Wins	Major Winners	Classic Wins	Winners of 5-Plus Major Races
Bob Wheeler	37	23	0	
* John Veitch	33	14	0	Alydar, Davona Dale
* Nick Zito	33	20	3	
Gary Jones	31	18	0	Best Pal
Roger Laurin	30	12	0	Numbered Account, Chief's Crown
David Whiteley	28	16	1	
Tommy Doyle	27	20	1	
Carl Hanford	27	2	0	Kelso
John Russell	26	12	0	Susan's Girl, Majestic Light
Moody Jolley	25	13	0	
Oscar White	23	13	1	Kiss Me Kate
Johnny Campo	21	14	2	
Steven DiMauro	21	13	0	
* Juan Gonzalez	21	6	0	Bien Bien, Free House
* Todd Pletcher	21	14	0	
Jimmy Smith	21	13	0	
Ivan Parke	20	7	0	Olympia
* Wally Dollase	20	12	0	

Special Mention

Two other trainers have enjoyed No. 1 seasons in the modern era. **Jack Price** earned that acclaim in 1961, when he won seven races with Carry Back. Price captured 14 major races, all of them with Carry Back. **Martin Fallon** earned his first seven major victories with Hillsdale on his way to a No. 1 season in 1959, but he scored only two subsequent major triumphs, both with American Comet two years later.

Nine More Immortals

Winning major races is the best way to judge a trainer's success. But it obviously isn't the only way. Nine men who trained in the modern era have been inducted into the Hall of Fame with 17 or fewer major victories: Pancho Martin (17), Phil Johnson (17), Frank Childs (10), Jonathan Sheppard (9), Carey Winfrey (7), Hollie Hughes (4), Tom Smith (4), Dolly Byers (3), and Marion Van Berg (2).

Both Martin (13) and Johnson (12) reached double figures in major winners. Smith and Childs won modern classics, Smith saddling 1947 Kentucky Derby winner Jet Pilot and Childs winning the 1959 Run for the Roses with Tomy Lee.

Smith also trained the legendary Seabiscuit in the '30s and, like Hughes, Winfrey, and Byers, among others, predated the modern era. Hughes also trained steeplechase horses, and Sheppard is the all-time leader among steeplechase trainers and obviously was selected for that reason. Van Berg may have been the most successful claiming trainer in history. He led all owners in total races won 14 times, including 11 years in a row (1960-70), and trained most of those winners himself.

The following chart shows trainers' victories in the 6,461 major races held in North America from 1946-2003. Following that chart are charts that give the same information for the 174 classic races held from 1946-2003, the 145 Breeders' Cup races staged from 1984-2003, and the annual leaders, which are followed by an alphabetical listing of victories in major North American races for all trainers from 1946-2003, with the horses they trained in those events in parenthesis.

Standings for Trainers' Victories In Major North American Races From 1946-2003

1. Wayne Lukas (222)
2. Charlie Whittingham (208)
3. Woody Stephens (129)
4. Bobby Frankel (125)
5. Jimmy Jones (108)
6. Ron McAnally (105)
7. Shug McGaughey (99)
8. Bob Baffert (78)
9. LeRoy Jolley (76)
10. Bill Winfrey (74)
11. Allen Jerkens (73)
12. Laz Barrera (71)
13. Max Hirsch (70)
14. Elliott Burch, John Gaver (66)
16. Eddie Neloy (65)
17. Neil Drysdale, Jim Fitzsimmons (62)
19. Bill Mott (60)
20. Richard Mandella (58)
21. Syl Veitch (54)
22. Hirsch Jacobs, Scotty Schulhofer (51)
24. Bill Molter (46)
25. Lucien Laurin, Mack Miller (44)
27. Jimmy Conway, Harry Trotsek (43)
29. Casey Hayes (42)
30. Bert Mulholland (41)
31. Bob Wheeler, Frank Whiteley Jr. (37)
33. Jim Maloney, Mesh Tenney (36)
35. Preston Burch (35)
36. Tommy Kelly, John Veitch, Nick Zito (33)
39. Jimmy Croll, Gary Jones, Horatio Luro (31)
42. Roger Laurin (30)
43. Angel Penna (29)
44. David Whiteley (28)
45. Tommy Doyle, Carl Hanford, John Nerud, Sherrill Ward (27)
49. John Russell (26)
50. Buddy Hirsch, Moody Jolley (25)
52. Sonny Hine, Burley Parke (24)
54. Ben Jones, Jack Van Berg, Oscar White (23)
57. Henry Clark (22)
58. Johnny Campo, Steven DiMauro, Juan Gonzalez, Todd Pletcher, Jimmy Smith (21)
63. Bud Delp, Wally Dollase, Ivan Parke (20)
66. Bill Finnegan, Mike Freeman, Jack Gaver, Neil Howard, Jose Martin, Henry Moreno, George Odom, Mel Stute (18)
74. Phil Johnson, Pancho Martin, Buster Millerick, George Poole (17)
78. Joe Cantey, John Gosden, Dick Handlen, Lou Rondinello, Richard Small (16)
83. Frank Bonsal, Willie Booth, David Hofmans, Carl Nafzger, James Picou, Howard Tesher (15)
89. Frank Catrone, J.S. Dunn, Jerry Fanning, John Jacobs, Jack Price, Bert Sonnier, Warren Stute, Saeed bin Suroor, John Ward Jr., Sid Watters Jr., Eddie Yowell (14)
100. James Bond, Del Carroll, Reggie Cornell, Ross Fenstermaker, Mark Hennig, Norman McLeod, Clyde Troutt, Arnold Winick (13)
108. Gordon Campbell, Eugene Jacobs, John Kimmel, Vance Longden, Jan Nerud, Lefty Nickerson, Homer Pardue, Slim Roles, James Ryan (12)
117. Smiley Adams, Rusty Arnold, Tom Bohannan, Laura de Seroux, Pat Kelly, Chuck Parke, John Theall, Billy Turner, Elliott Walden (11)
126. Johnny Adams, Joe Bollero, Frank Brothers, Melvin Calvert, Julio Canani, John Canty, Frank Childs, Edward Christmas, Loyd Gentry Jr., Eddie Gregson, Bruce Headley, Jack Hodgins, Evan Jackson, Kay Jensen, John Meaux, Gordon Potter, Willard Proctor, Buddy Raines, Jenine Sahadi, Darrell Vienna (10)
146. Tony Basile, Bowes Bond, Francois Boutin, Ron Ellis, Martin Fallon, Hugh Fontaine, Jerry Hollendorfer, Edward Kelly, James Nazworthy, Paul Parker, Slim Pierce, Loren Rettele, Jay Robbins, Jonathan Sheppard, Wayne Stucki, J.E. Tinsley Jr., Harvey Vanier, Lynn Whiting, Maurice Zilber (9)
165. William Badgett, Roger Clapp, Jim Day, Michael Dickinson, Bobby Dotter, Wally Dunn, Andre Fabre, Henry Forrest, Everett King, Kenny McPeek, Ray Metcalf, Robert Odom, Joe Orseno, Angel Penna Jr., Richard Schosberg, Bill Stephens, Noble Threewitt, Jim Toner, Clyde Turk, Thomas Waller, Michael Whittingham, Randy Winick (8)
187. Frank Alexander, Roger Attfield, James Bentley, Patrick Byrne, Ben Cecil, Mark Frostad, George Gianos, Lou Glauburg, Phil Hauswald, Eduardo Inda, Bruce Jackson, Paul Kelley, Johnny Longden, Richard Lundy, Joe Manzi, Charles Norman, James Pierce Jr., William Post, Tommy Root, John Shirreffs, Yonnie Starr, John Sullivan, Ralph West, Ted West, Carey Winfrey (7)
212. Willie Alvarado, Frank Barnett, William Canney, Harry Daniels, Allen Drumheller, Dick Dutrow, Howard Hausner, Eddie Hayward, John Hertler, Robert Holthus, Steve Ippolito, Walter Kelley, Les Lear, Butch Lenzini, Mark Mergler, Leo O'Brien, Charlie Peoples, Graceton Philpot, Tom Pratt, Hack Ross, Randy Sechrest, Andy Schuttinger, Christopher Speckert, William Stucki, Red Terrill, Lex Wilson, Harold Young (6)
239. Edward Allard, Steve Asmussen, Ivan Balding, Luis Barrera, Thomas Barry, Patrick Biancone, Jess Byrd, Henry Carroll, Christophe Clement, Gene Cleveland, Vincent Clyne, Don Combs, Craig Dollase, David Donk, Phil England, Woody Fitzgerald, Lou Goldfine, Alex Hassinger Jr., Robert Hess, Dominic Imprescia, James Jimenez, Cecil Jolly, Farrell Jones, James Jordan, Tom Kelley, Willie Knapp, Craig Lewis, Mervin Marks, Brian Mayberry, Don McCoy, Ike Mourar, Aidan O'Brien, Bryant Ott, Monte Parke, Jonathan Pease, Ben Perkins Jr., Bill Perry, Joseph Piarulli, Anthony Pupino, William Resseguet Jr., Stanley Rieser, Frankie Sanders, Jerome Sarner Jr., Dewey Smith, Herb Stevens, Barclay Tagg, John Tammaro, Babe Wells, Bert Williams, Robert Wingfield, Tennessee Wright, Ralph Ziadie (5)
291. Thad Ackel, Bill Boniface, Randy Bradshaw, Merritt Buxton, Nick Combest, David Cross, Oscar Dishman Jr., John Fulton, Cam Gambolati, Woods Garth, Phil Gleaves, Ira Hanford, Thomas Heard Jr., Howard Hoffman, Stanley Hough, Hollie Hughes, Sid Jacobs, Charles Kerr, Charlie Leavitt, Jack Long, Duke McCue, Red McDaniel, Frank McManus, James Murphy, Herbert Nadler, Joseph Nash, Reynaldo Nobles, Pico Perdomo, Bill Peterson, Joseph Pierce Jr., Hurst Philpot, Jimmy Pitt, Ray Priddy, Mike Puype, Robert Reinacher, Linda Rice, Alcee Richard, Donald Richardson, Gil Rowntree, Lydell Ruff, Barry Ryan, Ted Saladin, Gary Sciacca, Al Scotti, Woody Sedlacek, A.F. Skelton, Tom Smith, Michael Stoute, Jack Weipert, Dermot Weld, Frank Wright (4)
342. Louis Albertrani, George Baker, Pascal Bary, Pete Battle, Bobby Barnett, Gerald Belanger Jr., David Bernstein, Simon Bray, Ross Brinson, John Bucalo, William Burch, Dolly Byers, Don Cameron, Robert Collet, Gin Collins, Luca Cumani, Doug Davis Jr., Richard DeStasio, Ray De Stefano, Morris Dixon, Bill Donovan, Oleg Dubassoff, Bob Durso, Rex Ellsworth, David Erb, Guido Federico, Peter Gacicia, Frank Gomez, John Milton Goode, Beau Greely, John Greely Jr., Mitchell Griffin, Thomas Grimes, Guy Harwood, Noel Hickey, Lester Holt, Peter Howe, Allen Hultz, Leonard Hunt, Whitey Jansen, Ian Jory, Frank Kearns, Michael Keogh, Preston King, Chay Knight, Joseph Kulina, Dale Landers, Budd Lepman, Charles Marikian, H.C. McBride, Frank Merrill, Tim Muckler, R. Nixon, Kenny Noe, Niall O'Callaghan, Richard O'Connell, John Oxley, John Partridge, Danny Perlswig, Rodney Rash, William Raymond, Willis Reavis, Maton Rieser, Bob Roberts, Larry Rose, James Rowe, Anthony Rupelt, Sol Rutchick, James Ryerson, David Sazer, Stanley Shapoff, A.E. Silver, Harold Simmons, Ben Slasky, Graves Sparks, Larry Sterling, Harold Tinker, Emanuel Tortora, Joe Trovato, Mary Lou Tuck, Jaime Villagomez, Ronnie Warren, Charles Werstler, Harold Williams, William Wilmot, John Winans, Marty Wolfson, William Wright, Steven Young (3)
431. George Adams, Paul Adwell, Happy Alter, Tom Amoss, Eddie Anspach, Juan Arias, Leo Azpurua Jr., Sallie Bailie, Armando Bani, Bobby Barbara, Anthony Baroni, Warren Beasley, Gerald Bennett, Leon Blusiewicz, Lynn Boice, Bernie Bond, Paul Bongarzone, Arthur Breasley, Lane Bridgford, L.J. Brooks, Harris Brown, Alfredo Callejas, Charles Calvin, Gary Capuano, Lou Carno, Dianne Carpenter, Frank Carr, Jack Carrara, Del Carroll II, W.E. Carroll, Louis Cavalaris Jr., Henry Cecil, Riley Cofer, Paul Cole, Lee Cotton, W.S. Cotton, Richard Cross, Pete Dispenza, Doug Dodson, H.C. Dodson, John Dolan, Carl Domino, Matthew Dragna, Samuel Edmundson, Eugene Euster, Floreano Fernandez, Fordell Fierce, Arnold Fink, Dick Fischer, Paul Fout, Dean Gaudet, George Getz, Roy Gillem, Vincent Glorioso, Nicholas Gonzales, Strother Griffin, Mel Gross, Charles Hadry, George Handy, Mike Harrington, Clarence Hartwick, James Hastie, Norman Haymaker, Duval Headley, Jim Healey, William Hightower, Leonard Imperio, Gerald Jabalee, Buddy Jacobson, Chuck Jenda, Larry Jennings, Albert Jensen, Tom Jolley, Elmer Kalensky, Dave Kassen, Mike Kay, Pete Keiser, D.W. Kerns, James King, Buddy Leavitt, Santiago Ledwith, John Lee, O'Donnell Lee, R.W. Lilly, Paulo Lobo, Daniel Lopez, Donn Luby, Paul Lycan, Anthony Margotta Jr., Sidney Martin, G.E. Mayberry, Edward McCann, Robert McGarvey, Paul McGee, R.W. McIlvaine, Donald McKellar, Kiaran McLaughlin, Freeman McMillan, Thomas Miles, F.A. Miquelez, Graham Motion, Richard Mulhall, Roderick Myers, Vincent O'Brien, Doug O'Neill, John Oxx, Hector Palma, C.W. Parish, D. Peregoy, Doug Peterson, Clyde Phillips, Clarence Picou, Tim Poole, Ernie Poulous, R.D. Prewitt, Vivian Pulliam, Hyman Ravich, C.V. Reynolds, A.G. Robertson, Hugh Robertson, Larry Robideaux, Thomas Rodrock, Harold Rose, Louie Roussel III, Mitri Saliba, Charlie Sanborn, John Scanlan, Scott Schwartz, John Servis, Charles W. Shaw Jr., Mitch Shirota, Bill Shoemaker, M. Sidell, Monti Sims, Sidney Smith, Victor Sovinski, Bill Spawr, Lionel Sternberger, Dallas Stewart, Kent Stirling, George Strate, Walter Taylor, Lawrence Thompson, R.C. Troxler, Marion Van Berg, David Vance, Daniel Vella, Richard Violette Jr., Donnie Von Hemel, Tom Voss, Lin Wheeler, Barney Willis, Neal Winick (2)
584. Barry Abrams, Robert Adams, Leroy Adcock, Laurie Anderson, Malcolm Anderson, George Arcenaux, Antonio Arcodia, Reed Armstrong, Thomas Arnemann, Lonnie Arterburn, N. Atchison, George Auerbach, Eduardo Azpurua, J.D. Bailey, James Baker, Michael Ball, Mike Bao, Edgar Barnes, James Bartlett, D. Bates, Jake Battles, Olen Battles, David Bell, Kaye Bell, George Berthold, C.A. Bidencope, Vincent Blengs, Billy Borders, Gordon Bowsher, Donald Bradley, John Bradley, Pat

Bert Morgan photo courtesy of Keeneland Association

Jimmy Jones had plenty of reasons to smile: He led America's trainers in major victories five times from 1947-58, including three consecutive years from 1947-49, the period when this photo was believed to have been taken.

Brady, Bill Breashear, M.W. Breshnen, F.W. Brewster, Dennis Brida, G. Bridgeland, Max Britt, Clive Brittain, D. Brooks, Joseph Broussard, L.A. Brusie, William Buck, J.W. Burton, C. Butler, N.L. Byer, John Cairns, Jerry Calvin, Bob Camac, E.L. Campbell, L. Campion, Nick Canani, Darrell Cannon, Charles Carlesimo, E.B. Carpenter, George Washington Carroll, R.B. Carroll, Bud Carter, C.J. Casey, Mark Casse, Wayne Catalano, Vladimir Cerin, Mike Chambers, B.F. Christmas, A. Cleff, Odie Clelland, William Cocks, Andrew Colando, Frank Colcord, William Cole, Pat Collins, Charlie Comiskey, Joseph Considine, Gary Contessa, Edgar Cox, Robert Craft, J. Creevy, Willie Crump, Frank Cundall, J. Cunnington Jr., William Curtis Jr., Van Cutsem, Oliver Cutshaw, Juan d'Agostino, Sam David Jr., John Davis, Thomas DeBonis, Jack Delzell, William Dennis, John DeStefano Jr., Pat Devereux, Peter Devito, J.A. Dewitt, Joseph DiAngelo, Charlie Dickens, John Dillard, John DiMario, Don Divine, Hepburn Dixon, E.C. Dobson, R. Donnell, Leonard Dorfman, Frank Dougherty, Francois Douman, John Dowd, Leonard Duncan, Robert Duncan, Bob Dunham, Edward Dunlop, Jean-Pierre Dupuis, Dick Dutrow Jr., Tony Dutrow, James Eckrosh, Mary Edens, Larry Edwards, J.T. Engle, Mary Eppler, Manny Estevez, Gomer Evans, David Fawkes, John Fellows, Charles Feltner, W. Fenwick, Michael Ferraro, Peter Ferriola, Richard Ferris, Kenneth Field, Bert Fields, Alex Fiore, Larry Flakes, Thomas Fleming, Bernard Flint, K. Force Jr., Mitchell Friedman, A. Funger, A. Gaal, Ned Gaines, Juan Garcia, Gilbert Gay, G. Geier, Rodger Gill, Frank Gilpin, Orin Glass Jr., Alan Goldberg, R.D. Goldsberry, Clint Goodrich, George Goodwin, H.H. Goodwin, P.S. Goodwin, Michael Gorham, Akiko Gothard, Nicholas Graffaginni, Newcomb Green, Robert Green, C.B. Greene, Walter Greenman, C.V. Gribbin, Hal Griffitt, Ray Grundy, Roger Guerini, Irv Guiney, Donald Habeeb, C.J. Hall, R.R. Hall, Stuart Hamblen, John Hammond, John Hanover, James Hardy, Don Harper, Mickey Harrison, Eoin Harty, William Hastings, J.C. Hauer, Richard Hazelton, Christiane Head, B. Heap, Dan Hendricks, William Hicks, R.H. Highley, Max Hirsch Jr., Harold Hodosh, Bill Holmes, Edward Holton, Dean Howell, Robert Irwin, Monty Jackson, Jeff Jacobs, Suzanne Jenkins, Jim Jerkens, Steve Jerkens, L.G. Joffrion, H.E. Johnson, Murray Johnson, Bucky Jolin, Herbert Jones, Martin Jones, W.L. Jones Jr., Harold Jordan Jr., Kenneth Jumps, Max Kahlbaum, Michael Katz, Rod Kaufman, J.P. Keezek, Mary Keim, F. Keller, Timothy Kelly, Michael Kerr, Burk Kessinger Jr., Allen King Jr., Terry Knight, J.I. Labelle, Frank LaBoccetta, J.F. Laboyne, David LaCroix, M. Lacy, Pete Laidley, Robert Lake, W.A. Larue, Raymond Lawrence Jr., King Leatherbury, John Leavitt, R. Lentini, Robert Leonard, D.C. LeVine, James Levitch, J. Lieux, Morton Lipton, David Loder, Mary Jo Lohmeier, Anthony Lombardi, Howard Long, Jack Ludwig, Frank Lyons, Brad MacDonald, Michael Machowsky, Red Mahoney, Dennis Manning, Stephen Margolis, Alfredo Marquez, Robert Marshall, Pedro Marti, Carlos Martin, Robert L. Martin, Francois Mathet, T.G. May, John Mazza, Pete McCann, Ted McClain, Chick McClellan, Conn McCreary, Wayne McDonnell, Jimmy McGee, Britt McGehee, M. McGonigle, Gerard McGrath, George McIvor, T. McMahon, Brian Meehan, Derek Meredith, Paul Meredith, Joseph Mergler, Jerome Meyer, Norman Miller III, P.F. Miller, Robert Miller, Barbara Minshall, Earl Mitchell, Mike Mitchell, Philip Mitchell, William Mitchell, Steven Miyadi, S.J. Molay, Marvin Moncrief, Joseph Moos, Carlos Morales, Jim Morgan, J.L. Mosbacher, Gasper Moschera, Peter Mosconi, Jeff Mullins, Eddie Mulrenan, Paul Murphy, Gene Navarro, James O'Bryant, Duane Offield, Francis Ogden, Luis Oliveras, Victor Oppegard, James Padgett, Herb Paley, John Pappalardo, John Parisella, Leon Parker Jr., Warren Pascuma, W.L. Passmore, G. Pelat, Alfio Pepino, Ben Perkins, W.R. Pickett, Edward Plesa Jr., Jake Pletcher, J.F. Plett, Norman Pointer, Marcelo Polanco, Dick Posey, R.E. Potts, Guadalupe Preciado, Mitchell Preger, James Price, W.C. Prickett, Thomas Proctor, J.D. Puckett, A. Puglisi, R.H. Raines, Michael Reavis, George Reeves, Robert Reid Jr., Phil Reilly, Milt Resseguet, Patrick Reynolds, Clyde Rice, W.U. Ridenour, G. Riola, Craig Roberts, Jorge Romero, Richard Root, C.W. Rose, J.B. Rosen, Chester Ross, Jean-Claude Rouget, Jimmy Rowan, Stephan Rowan, Dupre a de Royer, Anthony Russo, John Sadler, J.P. Sallee, Peter Salmen Jr., John Salzman, Greg Sanders, Bud Sarner, J.W. Sceusa, D.J. Schneider, W.J. Schmidt, Randy Schulhofer, Alex Scott, George Scott, T.R. Scott, Arnold Scruton Jr., Sam Sechrest, Mike Sedlacek, Julian Serna Jr., Philip Serpe, M. Shapoff, Paul Shawhan, Harry Shillick, Leo Sierra, Juan Pablo Silva, James Simpson, William Simpson, Phillip Simms, Tom Skiffington, James Skinner, David Smaga, Jere Smith, Sammy Smith, Thomas V. Smith, Earl Sorrell, Michael Soto, Larry Spraker, Albert Stall Jr., John Starr, Robert Steele, Roger Stein, M. Stewart, Michael Stidham, Bud Stotler, Charles Stutts, Clyde Sutphin, Bret Thomas, Gary Thomas, William Thomas, Willard Thompson, Vincent Timphony, Mike Tomlinson, George Towne, Steve Towne, Chuck Turco, H.C. Vandervoort, Judson Van Worp, Ralph Verderosa, Peter Vestal, F. Veysey, Katharine Voss, Dick Waggoner, Christian Wall, James Wallace, Kathy Walsh, G. Watson, John Watts, P.D.L. Watts, Richard Watts, John Waugh, Joseph Waunsch, J. Webber, George Weckerle Jr., M.M. Weil, Harry Wells, Ted H. West, T.F. White, W.R. White, J. Williams, Donald Winfree, Glenn Wismer, Andreas Wohler, R.C. Wood Jr., E.H. Wright, William Wyndle, Tom Young, Dave Zakoor Jr., John Zarthar, Eugene Zeren, John Zitnik, F. Zitto (1)

Classic-Winning Trainers 1946-2003

1. Wayne Lukas (13)
2. Bob Baffert, Woody Stephens (8)
4. Jimmy Jones (7)
5. Max Hirsch, Lucien Laurin (6)
7. Laz Barrera (5)
8. Henry Forrest (4)
9. Elliott Burch, Jim Fitzsimmons, John Gaver, Ben Jones, Horatio Luro, Billy Turner, Jack Van Berg, Frank Whiteley Jr., Charlie Whittingham, Nick Zito (3)
19. Juan Arias, Thomas Barry, Tom Bohannan, Frank Brothers, Johnny Campo, Jimmy Conway, Bud Delp, Neil Drysdale, Hugh Fontaine, John Jacobs, LeRoy Jolley, Johnny Longden, Jack Price, Lou Rondinello, Louie Roussel III, Scotty Schulhofer, Barclay Tagg, Mesh Tenney, Syl Veitch, Bill Winfrey, Eddie Yowell (2)
40. Smiley Adams, Paul Adwell, Luis Barrera, Bill Boniface, Preston Burch, Joe Cantey, Del Carroll, Frank Catrone, Frank Childs, Don Combs, Reggie Cornell, Jimmy Croll, David Cross, Tommy Doyle, Bobby Frankel, Cam Gambolati, Loyd Gentry Jr., Eddie Gregson, Casey Hayes, Eddie Hayward, David Hofmans, Neil Howard, Butch Lenzini, Shug McGaughey, Kenny McPeek, Mack Miller, Bill Molter, Bert Mulholland, Carl Nafzger, John Nerud, Joe Orseno, Jimmy Pitt, Buddy Raines, Sol Rutchick, Tom Smith, Victor Sovinski, Mel Stute, Harry Trotsek, Elliott Walden, John Ward Jr., Dermot Weld, Oscar White, David Whiteley, Lynn Whiting, Harold Young (1)

Breeders' Cup-Winning Trainers 1984-2003

1. Wayne Lukas (17)
2. Shug McGaughey (8)
3. Neil Drysdale, Richard Mandella (6)
5. Bill Mott (5)
6. Ron McAnally (4)
7. Bob Baffert, Pascal Bary, Francois Boutin, Patrick Byrne, Andre Fabre, Aidan O'Brien, Michael Stoute (3)
14. Julio Canani, Michael Dickinson, Bobby Frankel, Alex Hassinger Jr., David Hofmans, LeRoy Jolley, Joe Orseno, Jonathan Pease, Jay Robbins, Jenine Sahadi, Scotty Schulhofer, Mel Stute, Saeed bin Suroor, Charlie Whittingham (2)
28. Thad Ackel, Louis Albertrani, Frank Alexander, William Badgett, Bobby Barnett, Clive Brittain, Robert Collet, Luca Cumani, Jim Day, Laura de Seroux, Craig Dollase, Wally Dollase, Ross Fenstermaker, Mark Frostad, Alan Goldberg, John Gosden, Eoin Harty, Phil Hauswald, Bruce Headley, Noel Hickey, Sonny Hine, Phil Johnson, Roger Laurin, Budd Lepman, Richard Lundy, Frank Lyons, Stephen Margolis, Pancho Martin, Derek Meredith, Carl Nafzger, Jan Nerud, Vincent O'Brien, John Oxx, Ernie Poulous, Thomas Proctor, Dupre a de Royer, James Ryerson, Alex Scott, Richard Small, Christopher Speckert, Dallas Stewart, Vincent Timphony, Jim Toner, David Vance, Jack Van Berg, John Veitch, Darrell Vienna, John Ward Jr., Michael Whittingham, Randy Winick, Nick Zito (1)

1946

1. Jimmy Smith (9)
2. Max Hirsch (8)
3. Hirsch Jacobs (6)
4. Jim Fitzsimmons (5)
5. Preston Burch, Graceton Philpot, Syl Veitch, Oscar White (4)
9. Edward Christmas, John Gaver, Ben Jones, Jimmy Jones (3)

1947

1. Jimmy Jones (18)
2. Max Hirsch (12)
3. George Odom, Syl Veitch (7)
5. Willie Booth (6)
6. Hirsch Jacobs, Horatio Luro, A.F. Skelton (4)
9. Preston Burch, Bill Molter, Mesh Tenney (3)

1948

1. Jimmy Jones (10)
2. Jimmy Smith (7)
3. Jimmy Conway, Max Hirsch, William Post (5)
6. Horatio Luro, Andy Schuttinger (4)
8. Willie Booth, Woody Fitzgerald, Ben Jones, Bill Molter, Syl Veitch (3)

1949

1. Jimmy Jones (16)
2. John Gaver, Bill Molter (7)
4. Bill Winfrey (6)
5. Max Hirsch (5)
6. Ivan Parke (4)
7. Jimmy Conway, Willie Knapp (3)
9. Frank Barnett, Preston Burch, Don Cameron, Frank Childs, Dick Handlen, Ben Jones, George Odom, John Partridge, Slim Roles, James Ryan, M. Sidell, Harry Trotsek (2)

1950

1. Bill Winfrey (9)
2. Casey Hayes, Preston Burch (7)
4. John Gaver, Bert Mulholland (6)
6. Burley Parke (5)
7. Jimmy Jones (4)
8. Max Hirsch, Moody Jolley, Slim Pierce, Buddy Raines, Harry Trotsek (3)

1951

1. John Gaver (7)
2. Jimmy Jones, Bert Mulholland, Syl Veitch, Oscar White (5)
6. Preston Burch, Jim Fitzsimmons, Casey Hayes, James Ryan, Bill Winfrey (4)

1952

1. Ben Jones (10)
2. John Gaver, Bill Winfrey (7)
4. Jimmy Jones (6)
5. Max Hirsch, Oscar White (5)
7. Frank Catrone, Buddy Hirsch (4)
9. Merritt Buxton, Jim Fitzsimmons, Whitey Jansen, Robert Odom, Woody Stephens, Syl Veitch (3)

1953

1. Bill Winfrey (15)
2. Harry Trotsek (9)
3. John Gaver (7)
4. Jimmy Jones (5)
5. Jimmy Conway, James Ryan, Syl Veitch (4)
8. Bobby Dotter, Robert Odom (3)
10. Preston Burch, W.S. Cotton, J.S. Dunn, Carl Hanford, Eddie Hayward, Buddy Hirsch, Max Hirsch, Ben Jones, Jack Long, Vance Longden, Bert Mulholland, Harold Williams (2)

1954

1. Max Hirsch (8)
2. Bill Winfrey (6)
3. Jim Fitzsimmons, Jimmy Jones, Bill Molter (5)
6. Dick Handlen, Syl Veitch (4)
8. Preston Burch, Eddie Hayward, Buddy Hirsch, Tommy Kelly, Ike Mourar, Eddie Neloy, Noble Threewitt, Harry Trotsek (3)

1955

1. Jim Fitzsimmons (15)
2. Harry Trotsek (6)
3. Mesh Tenney, Bill Winfrey (5)
5. Preston Burch, Woody Stephens (4)
7. Loyd Gentry Jr., Howard Hausner, Max Hirsch, Vance Longden, George Odom (3)

1956

1. Jimmy Jones (7)
2. Jim Fitzsimmons, Mesh Tenney, Charlie Whittingham (6)
5. Norman McLeod, Syl Veitch (5)
7. Preston Burch, Hugh Fontaine, Bill Molter (4)
10. Reggie Cornell, Hirsch Jacobs, Moody Jolley, Mack Miller, Thomas Waller, Carey Winfrey (3)

1957

1. Bill Molter (9)
2. Jimmy Jones (8)
3. Jim Fitzsimmons, Moody Jolley (7)
5. Sherrill Ward, Charlie Whittingham (5)
7. Hirsch Jacobs, Jim Maloney, John Nerud, Ivan Parke, Bill Winfrey, Carey Winfrey, Frank Wright (3)

1958

1. Jimmy Jones (8)
2. Bill Molter (6)
3. Casey Hayes, Hirsch Jacobs (5)
5. Henry Clark, Bill Stephens (4)
7. Elliott Burch, Jim Fitzsimmons, Kay Jensen, Lucien Laurin, John Nerud (3)

1959

1. Elliott Burch, Martin Fallon (7)
3. Woody Stephens, Bob Wheeler (6)
5. Max Hirsch, Bill Molter (5)
7. Henry Clark, Jim Fitzsimmons (4)
9. Moody Jolley, Jimmy Jones, Joseph Piarulli, Hack Ross (3)

1960

1. Woody Stephens (8)
2. Bob Wheeler (6)
3. Elliott Burch (5)
4. Dick Handlen, Carl Hanford, Burley Parke, Paul Parker, Jimmy Pitt (4)
9. J.S. Dunn, Peter Gacicia, Jimmy Jones, Jack Price (3)

1961

1. Jack Price (7)
2. Carl Hanford (6)
3. Casey Hayes (5)
4. Jim Fitzsimmons, Jimmy Jones, Mesh Tenney, Harold Young (4)
8. Elliott Burch, LeRoy Jolley, James Nazworthy, Paul Parker (3)

1962

1. Bert Mulholland, Mesh Tenney (8)
3. Casey Hayes, Woody Stephens (5)
5. Jimmy Conway, Allen Jerkens, Chuck Parke, Arnold Winick (4)
9. LeRoy Jolley, Vance Longden, Jack Price (3)

1963

1. Carl Hanford (8)
2. John Gaver (7)
3. Mesh Tenney (6)
4. Jimmy Conway (4)
5. Jess Byrd, Charles Kerr, Jim Maloney, J.E. Tinsley Jr., Bob Wheeler, Charlie Whittingham (3)

1964

1. Eddie Neloy (9)
2. Bill Winfrey (8)
3. Frank Bonsal, Elliott Burch, Wally Dunn, Horatio Luro, Burley Parke (5)
8. Les Lear (4)
9. Carl Hanford, Roger Laurin, Mark Mergler, James Pierce Jr. (3)

1965

1. Hirsch Jacobs (7)
2. Bill Winfrey (5)
3. Eddie Neloy, Burley Parke, Harry Trotsek, Frank Whiteley Jr. (4)
7. Frank Catrone, Bill Finnegan, Jim Maloney, Charles Norman, William Stucki, Clyde Troutt, Syl Veitch, Eddie Yowell (3)

1966

1. Eddie Neloy (17)
2. Hirsch Jacobs (4)
3. Ivan Balding, Bill Peterson, Randy Sechrest, Woody Stephens, Arnold Winick (3)
8. Del Carroll, Steven DiMauro, Henry Forrest, Woods Garth, Ira Hanford, Casey Hayes, Max Hirsch, Lucien Laurin, Mark Mergler, Mack Miller, Bert Mulholland, Buddy Raines, Donald Richardson, Syl Veitch, Charlie Whittingham (2)

1967

1. Eddie Neloy (16)
2. Frank Whiteley Jr. (9)
3. John Nerud (6)
4. Allen Jerkens, Charlie Whittingham (5)
6. Johnny Adams, Hirsch Jacobs, John Jacobs, Bryant Ott (3)
10. Tony Basile, Melvin Calvert, John Gaver, Casey Hayes, Johnny Longden, Jim Maloney, Buster Millerick, James Picou, Bob Wheeler, John Winans (2)

1968

1. Eddie Neloy (9)
2. Jim Maloney (7)
3. Henry Forrest, Everett King, John Nerud (6)
6. Max Hirsch (5)
7. Frank Whiteley Jr. (4)
8. Melvin Calvert, Ray Metcalf, Bert Sonnier (3)

1969

1. Elliott Burch (10)
2. Mike Freeman (6)
3. Mack Miller (5)
4. Lucien Laurin, Jim Maloney, Eddie Neloy, Angel Penna, Bert Sonnier (4)
9. Bowes Bond, Jimmy Conway, Buddy Hirsch, Johnny Longden, Buster Millerick, Charlie Whittingham (3)

1970

1. Elliott Burch (7)
2. Charlie Whittingham (6)
3. John Jacobs, Warren Stute (5)
5. Evan Jackson, Tommy Kelly (4)
7. Jimmy Croll, Mike Freeman, Allen Jerkens, Jim Maloney, Woody Stephens (3)

1971

1. Charlie Whittingham (12)
2. Roger Laurin (7)
3. Johnny Campo, John Canty, Lucien Laurin, George Poole (4)
7. Elliott Burch, Del Carroll, Allen Jerkens, Farrell Jones, Joseph Kulina, Pancho Martin, Mack Miller, Angel Penna (3)

1972

1. Charlie Whittingham (12)
2. Lucien Laurin (10)
3. Elliott Burch, Tommy Kelly (8)
5. John Russell, Yonnie Starr (5)
7. Tommy Doyle (4)
8. John Canty, Pancho Martin, William Raymond (3)

1973

1. Lucien Laurin (10)
2. Allen Jerkens (9)
3. Charlie Whittingham (7)
4. John Russell (5)
5. Johnny Campo (4)
6. Laz Barrera, Elliott Burch, Bobby Frankel, William Resseguet Jr., Tommy Root (3)

1974

1. Charlie Whittingham (9)
2. Sherrill Ward (8)
3. Lou Rondinello (6)
4. LeRoy Jolley, Pancho Martin (4)
6. Allen Jerkens, James Jimenez, Woody Stephens, Wayne Stucki, Joe Trovato, David Whiteley (3)

1975

1. Charlie Whittingham (12)
2. LeRoy Jolley (10)
3. Steven DiMauro (6)
4. Sherrill Ward (5)
5. Tommy Doyle, Ron McAnally, Gordon Potter, John Russell, Frank Whiteley Jr. (4)
10. Smiley Adams, Wayne Stucki, William Wilmot (3)

1976

1. LeRoy Jolley (12)
2. Charlie Whittingham (9)
3. Laz Barrera (7)
4. John Russell (6)
5. Frank Whiteley Jr. (5)
6. Smiley Adams, Tommy Doyle, Woody Stephens (4)
9. Steven DiMauro, Jack Gaver, Peter Howe (3)

1977

1. Laz Barrera (9)
2. John Veitch (6)
3. Roger Clapp, Homer Pardue, Billy Turner (5)
6. Tommy Doyle, Jose Martin (4)
8. LeRoy Jolley, Lou Rondinello, John Russell, Jaime Villagomez, Charlie Whittingham (3)

1978

1. Laz Barrera (11)
2. John Veitch (7)
3. Jack Gaver, Charlie Whittingham (6)
5. Bud Delp, Phil Johnson, Tommy Kelly, Wayne Lukas, Jose Martin, Loren Rettele, Scotty Schulhofer, Woody Stephens, Bob Wheeler, David Whiteley (3)

1979

1. Laz Barrera (11)
2. David Whiteley (9)
3. Woody Stephens (8)
4. Bud Delp (7)
5. Jack Gaver (6)
6. Tommy Kelly, John Veitch (5)
8. Loren Rettele (4)
9. Willard Proctor, Herb Stevens, Charlie Whittingham (3)

1980

1. Bud Delp, Neil Drysdale (7)
3. Ron McAnally (6)
4. Joe Cantey (5)
5. Angel Penna, Charlie Whittingham (4)
7. Smiley Adams, Laz Barrera, Gerald Belanger Jr., Tommy Kelly, Wayne Lukas, Mack Miller, Woody Stephens, Howard Tesher, Mary Lou Tuck, David Whiteley (3)

1981

1. Charlie Whittingham (8)
2. Ron McAnally (7)
3. Jose Martin (6)
4. Johnny Campo (5)
5. Luis Barrera, Lefty Nickerson, Woody Stephens (4)
8. Wayne Lukas (3)
9. Joe Cantey, Ross Fenstermaker, Bobby Frankel, Jack Gaver, Sonny Hine, Dominic Imprescia, Mack Miller, Tim Muckler, Jan Nerud, Angel Penna, John Tammaro, Jack Van Berg (2)

1982

1. Charlie Whittingham (9)
2. Wayne Lukas (8)
3. Laz Barrera (7)
4. Woody Stephens, Howard Tesher (4)
6. Bobby Frankel, Mitchell Griffin, Joe Manzi, Ron McAnally (3)
10. Francois Boutin, Elliott Burch, Alfredo Callejas, Joe Cantey, Ross Fenstermaker, Dominic Imprescia, Phil Johnson, James Jordan, Roger Laurin, Jim Maloney, Angel Penna Jr., Robert Reinacher, John Sullivan, Bob Wheeler, Michael Whittingham (2)

1983

1. Wayne Lukas (10)
2. Woody Stephens (9)
3. Charlie Whittingham (7)
4. Laz Barrera, John Gosden, Henry Moreno, Harvey Vanier, Sid Watters Jr., David Whiteley (4)
10. Patrick Biancone, David Cross, Jerry Fanning, Angel Penna Jr. (3)

1984

1. Woody Stephens (10)
2. Wayne Lukas (8)
3. Neil Drysdale, Bill Mott, Lynn Whiting (5)
6. Laz Barrera, John Hertler, Roger Laurin, Ron McAnally, Mack Miller, Ted West (4)

1985

1. Wayne Lukas (11)
2. Charlie Whittingham (9)
3. Woody Stephens (6)
4. LeRoy Jolley (5)
5. Edward Allard, Roger Laurin, Shug McGaughey (4)
8. Neil Drysdale, Ross Fenstermaker, Cam Gambolati, Sonny Hine, Joe Manzi, John Veitch, Randy Winick (3)

1986

1. Wayne Lukas (18)
2. Charlie Whittingham (11)
3. LeRoy Jolley, Mel Stute (6)
5. John Gosden, Richard Small, Woody Stephens (5)
8. Shug McGaughey (4)
9. Laz Barrera, Phil Gleaves, Scotty Schulhofer, Howard Tesher (3)

1987

1. Wayne Lukas (19)
2. Charlie Whittingham (10)
3. Woody Stephens (7)
4. LeRoy Jolley (6)
5. Mack Miller, Bill Mott, Jack Van Berg (4)
8. Jimmy Croll, Bill Donovan, Shug McGaughey, Mel Stute (3)

1988

1. Wayne Lukas (15)
2. Shug McGaughey (13)
3. Charlie Whittingham (9)
4. Jack Van Berg (7)
5. Woody Stephens, John Veitch (5)
7. Thad Ackel, Craig Lewis (3)
9. Neil Drysdale, Guido Federico, Charles Hadry, Phil Hauswald, Robert Holthus, Gary Jones, Hector Palma, Louie Roussel III (2)

1989

1. Wayne Lukas (17)
2. Shug McGaughey, Charlie Whittingham (14)
4. Ron McAnally (7)
5. Neil Drysdale (6)
6. Henry Carroll, Scotty Schulhofer, Harvey Vanier (3)
9. William Badgett, Laz Barrera, Eddie Gregson, Jerry Hollendorfer, Robert Holthus, Woody Stephens, William Wright (2)

1990

1. Wayne Lukas (17)
2. William Badgett, LeRoy Jolley, Ron McAnally, Scotty Schulhofer (5)
6. Neil Drysdale, Neil Howard, Carl Nafzger, Charlie Whittingham (4)
10. Ian Jory, Shug McGaughey, Jay Robbins (3)

1991

1. Ron McAnally (11)
2. Wayne Lukas (8)
3. Bobby Frankel, Scotty Schulhofer (6)
5. Bruce Jackson, Shug McGaughey (5)
7. Tom Bohannan, Gary Jones (4)
9. Frank Brothers, Jimmy Croll, Jim Day, Neil Drysdale, Jerry Hollendorfer, LeRoy Jolley, Richard Lundy, Nick Zito (3)

1992

1. Ron McAnally (12)
2. Shug McGaughey (7)
3. Allen Jerkens (6)
4. Bobby Frankel, Gary Jones, Pat Kelly (5)
7. Neil Drysdale, Bill Mott, Darrell Vienna (4)
10. Juan Gonzalez, Alex Hassinger Jr., Robert Hess, Scotty Schulhofer, Christopher Speckert, Nick Zito (3)

1993

1. Allen Jerkens, Shug McGaughey (8)
3. Richard Mandella, Ron McAnally (7)
5. Bobby Frankel (6)
6. Tom Bohannan, Mark Hennig, Scotty Schulhofer, Charlie Whittingham (4)
10. Mack Miller, Red Terrill (3)

1994

1. Wayne Lukas (12)
2. Shug McGaughey (8)
3. Jimmy Croll, Allen Jerkens (7)
5. Bill Mott (6)
6. Scotty Schulhofer (5)
7. Gary Jones, Richard Mandella (4)
9. David Bernstein, David Hofmans, Ron McAnally (3)

1995

1. Wayne Lukas (19)
2. Bill Mott (12)
3. Ron McAnally (9)
4. Bobby Frankel, Shug McGaughey (8)
6. Richard Mandella (6)
7. John Kimmel (3)
8. Roger Attfield, Jim Day, David Donk, Neil Drysdale, Dick Dutrow, Richard Schosberg, Scotty Schulhofer, Jim Toner (2)

1996

1. Wayne Lukas (13)
2. Bill Mott (7)
3. Ron McAnally, Nick Zito (6)
5. Wally Dollase, Sonny Hine, Richard Mandella, Shug McGaughey (5)
9. Ron Ellis, Leo O'Brien (4)

1997

1. Wayne Lukas (11)
2. Bob Baffert, Richard Mandella (6)
4. Patrick Byrne, Wally Dollase, Bill Mott (5)
7. Mark Frostad, John Kimmel, Bill Perry (4)
10. James Bond, Bobby Frankel, Juan Gonzalez, Sonny Hine, David Hofmans, Jenine Sahadi (3)

1998

1. Bob Baffert (10)
2. Sonny Hine (6)
3. Richard Mandella, Shug McGaughey, Bill Mott (5)
6. Wally Dollase, Neil Drysdale, Wayne Lukas (4)
9. Ron Ellis, Bobby Frankel, Allen Jerkens, Ron McAnally, Carl Nafzger, Todd Pletcher (3)

1999

1. Bob Baffert (23)
2. Wayne Lukas (9)
3. James Bond, Bobby Frankel, Richard Mandella (6)
6. Elliott Walden (5)
7. Carl Nafzger, Nick Zito (4)
9. Louis Albertrani, John Ward Jr. (3)

2000

1. Bob Baffert (10)
2. Wayne Lukas (8)
3. Neil Drysdale (7)
4. Bobby Frankel, Eduardo Inda, Joe Orseno (5)
7. Bill Mott, Todd Pletcher, Scotty Schulhofer (4)
10. Julio Canani, Nick Zito (3)

2001

1. Bobby Frankel (18)
2. Bob Baffert (14)
3. Todd Pletcher (5)
4. Christophe Clement, Juan Gonzalez, David Hofmans, Ron McAnally, John Ward Jr. (3)
9. Simon Bray, Michael Dickinson, John Dolan, Neil Drysdale, John Kimmel, Shug McGaughey, Pico Perdoma, Ben Perkins Jr., Jay Robbins, Jenine Sahadi, Scotty Schulhofer, Jonathan Sheppard, Darrell Vienna, Nick Zito (2)

2002

1. Bobby Frankel (16)
2. Laura de Seroux (8)
3. Bob Baffert, Saeed bin Suroor (7)
5. Kenny McPeek (5)
6. Mark Hennig (4)
7. Juan Gonzalez, Bruce Headley, Wayne Lukas, Richard Mandella, Shug McGaughey, Jonathan Sheppard, John Ward Jr. (3)

2003

1. Bobby Frankel (27)
2. Richard Mandella (8)
3. Todd Pletcher (6)
4. Bob Baffert (5)
5. Neil Howard, Nick Zito (4)
7. Allen Jerkens, Ron McAnally, Laura de Seroux, John Shirreffs, Barclay Tagg (3)

Trainers' Victories In Major North American Races 1946-2003

BARRY ABRAMS
1997: Del Mar Oaks (Famous Digger)

THAD ACKEL
1988: San Juan Capistrano 'Cap (Great Communicator)
Breeders' Cup Turf (Great Communicator)
Hollywood Turf Cup (Great Communicator)
1989: Hollywood Turf Handicap (Great Communicator)

GEORGE ADAMS
1963: Del Mar Debutante Stakes (Leisurely Kin)
1964: San Fernando Stakes (Nevada Battler)

JOHNNY ADAMS
1960: Cinema Handicap (New Policy)
1962: Hollywood Derby (Drill Site)
1967: Gallant Fox Handicap (Niarkos)
San Juan Capistrano Handicap (Niarkos)
San Luis Rey Handicap (Niarkos)
1968: San Juan Capistrano Handicap (Niarkos)
1972: Beverly Hills Handicap (Hill Circus)
Del Mar Handicap (Hill Circus)
1977: Swaps Stakes (J.O. Tobin)
1979: Hollywood Oaks (Prize Spot)

ROBERT ADAMS
1975: John B. Campbell Handicap (Jolly Johu)

SMILEY ADAMS
1975: Louisiana Derby (Master Derby)
Blue Grass Stakes (Master Derby)
Preakness Stakes (Master Derby)
1976: Breeders' Futurity (Run Dusty Run)
Arlington-Washington Futurity (Run Dusty Run)
New Orleans Handicap (Master Derby)
Oaklawn Handicap (Master Derby)
1980: Arlington Classic (Spruce Needles)
Secretariat Stakes (Spruce Needles)
Illinois Derby (Ray's Word)
1981: Arlington Handicap (Spruce Needles)

LEROY ADCOCK
1981: Louisiana Downs Handicap (Shishkabob)

PAUL ADWELL
1976: Arkansas Derby (Elocutionist)
Preakness Stakes (Elocutionist)

LOUIS ALBERTRANI
1999: Carter Handicap (Artax)
Vosburgh Stakes (Artax)
Breeders' Cup Sprint (Artax)

FRANK ALEXANDER
1993: Dwyer Stakes (Cherokee Run)
Super Derby (Wallenda)
1994: Breeders' Cup Sprint (Cherokee Run)
1998: Hopeful Stakes (Lucky Roberto)
Buick Meadowlands Cup Handicap (K.J.'s Appeal)
2000: Remsen Stakes (Windsor Castle)
2002: Mother Goose Stakes (Nonsuch Bay)

EDWARD ALLARD
1984: Selima Stakes (Mom's Command)
1985: Acorn Stakes (Mom's Command)
Mother Goose Stakes (Mom's Command)
Coaching Club American Oaks (Mom's Command)
Alabama Stakes (Mom's Command)

HAPPY ALTER
1991: Donn Handicap (Jolie's Halo)
Gulfstream Park Handicap (Jolie's Halo)

WILLIE ALVARADO
1951: San Pasqual Handicap (Moonrush)
Santa Anita Handicap (Moonrush)
1952: San Felipe Handicap (Windy City II)
American Handicap (Admiral Drake)
1953: Del Mar Handicap (Goose Khal)
1957: San Luis Rey Handicap (Posadas)

TOM AMOSS
2000: Apple Blossom Handicap (Heritage of Gold)
Go for Wand Handicap (Heritage of Gold)

LAURIE ANDERSON
1984: Hollywood Derby (Foscarini)

MALCOLM ANDERSON
1958: Del Mar Debutante Stakes (Khalita)

EDDIE ANSPACH
1946: Arlington Handicap (Historian)
Sunset Handicap (Historian)

GEORGE ARCENAUX
1987: Alabama Stakes (Up the Apalachee)

ANTONIO ARCODIA
1982: Pennsylvania Derby (Spanish Drums)

JUAN ARIAS
1971: Kentucky Derby (Canonero II)
Preakness Stakes (Canonero II)

REED ARMSTRONG
1954: Ohio Derby (Timely Tip)

THOMAS ARNEMANN
1995: Blue Grass Stakes (Wild Syn)

RUSTY ARNOLD
1982: Haskell Invitational Handicap (Wavering Monarch)
1986: Brooklyn Handicap (Little Missouri)
1987: Futurity Stakes (Trapp Mountain)
1989: Demoiselle Stakes (Rootentootenwooten)
1992: Top Flight Handicap (Dreamy Mimi)
Arlington Classic (Sound of Cannons)
1993: Nassau County Handicap (West by West)
1996: Shuvee Handicap (Clear Mandate)
1997: John A. Morris Handicap (Clear Mandate)
Three Chimneys Spinster Stakes (Clear Mandate)
2001: Test Stakes (Victory Ride)

LONNIE ARTERBURN
2000: Ashland Stakes (Rings a Chime)

STEVE ASMUSSEN
1999: Mother Goose Stakes (Dreams Gallore)
2001: Spinaway Stakes (Cashier's Dream)
2002: Arkansas Derby (Private Emblem)
2003: Test Stakes (Lady Tak)
Futurity Stakes (Cuvee)

N. ATCHISON
1961: Washington Park Handicap (Chief of Chiefs)

ROGER ATTFIELD
1985: Hialeah Turf Cup (Selous Scout)
1987: Yellow Ribbon Stakes (Carotene)
1993: Carter Handicap (Alydeed)
Molson Export Million (Peteski)
1995: Gotham Stakes (Talkin Man)
Wood Memorial Stakes (Talkin Man)
2003: Shadwell Turf Mile (Perfect Soul)

GEORGE AUERBACH
1960: Gotham Stakes (John William)

EDUARDO AZPURUA
1989: Budweiser International Stakes (Caltech)

LEO AZPURUA JR.
1986: Fountain of Youth Stakes (Ensign Rhythm)
1999: Arkansas Derby (Certain)

WILLIAM BADGETT
1989: Withers Stakes (Fire Maker)
Breeders' Cup Juvenile Fillies (Go for Wand)
1990: Ashland Stakes (Go for Wand)
Mother Goose Stakes (Go for Wand)
Alabama Stakes (Go for Wand)

Photo courtesy of Santa Anita Park

Wayne Lukas (far right) and his son and assistant trainer, Jeff, joined with the late Gene Klein (far left), one of thoroughbred racing's most successful owners, to give pre-race instructions to jockey Chris McCarron at Santa Anita. Klein's blue-and-yellow silks were adorned with the same lightning bolt sported by the San Diego Chargers, the National Football League franchise Klein owned before he turned his attention to thoroughbred racing.

Trainers' Resumes

WILLIAM BADGETT *(Continued)*

Maskette Stakes (Go for Wand)
Beldame Stakes (Go for Wand)
1999: Futurity Stakes (Bevo)

BOB BAFFERT

1992: Breeders' Cup Sprint (Thirty Slews)
1996: Santa Anita Derby (Cavonnier)
Del Mar Futurity (Silver Charm)
1997: Kentucky Derby (Silver Charm)
Preakness Stakes (Silver Charm)
Del Mar Futurity (Souvenir Copy)
Norfolk Stakes (Souvenir Copy)
Oak Leaf Stakes (Vivid Angel)
Hollywood Futurity (Real Quiet)
1998: Kentucky Derby (Real Quiet)
Preakness Stakes (Real Quiet)
Walmac Int. Alcibiades Stakes (Silverbulletday)
Breeders' Cup Juvenile Fillies (Silverbulletday)
Oak Leaf Stakes (Excellent Meeting)
Hollywood Starlet Stakes (Excellent Meeting)
Strub Stakes (Silver Charm)
Santa Anita Derby (Indian Charlie)
Del Mar Futurity (Worldly Manner)
La Brea Stakes (Magical Allure)
1999: Ashland Stakes (Silverbulletday)
Kentucky Oaks (Silverbulletday)
Alabama Stakes (Silverbulletday)
Gazelle Handicap (Silverbulletday)
Las Virgenes Stakes (Excellent Meeting)
Santa Anita Oaks (Excellent Meeting)
Pimlico Special (Real Quiet)
Sempra Energy Hollywood Gold Cup (Real Quiet)
Santa Anita Derby (General Challenge)
Pacific Classic (General Challenge)
Woodward Stakes (River Keen)
Jockey Club Gold Cup (River Keen)
Vinery Del Mar Debutante Stakes (Chilukki)
Oak Leaf Stakes (Chilukki)
Lane's End Breeders' Futurity (Captain Steve)
Hollywood Futurity (Captain Steve)
San Felipe Stakes (Prime Timber)
Eddie Read Handicap (Joe Who)
Del Mar Oaks (Tout Charmant)
King's Bishop Stakes (Forestry)
Ramona Handicap (Tuzla)
Del Mar Futurity (Forest Camp)
La Brea Stakes (Hookedonthefeelin)
2000: Strub Stakes (General Challenge)
Santa Anita Handicap (General Challenge)
Del Mar Futurity (Flame Thrower)
Norfolk Stakes (Flame Thrower)
Swaps Stakes (Captain Steve)
Ramona Handicap (Caffe Latte)
Lane's End Breeders' Futurity (Arabian Light)
Oak Leaf Stakes (Notable Career)
Cigar Mile Handicap (El Corredor)
Hollywood Futurity (Point Given)
2001: San Felipe Stakes (Point Given)
Santa Anita Derby (Point Given)
Preakness Stakes (Point Given)
Belmont Stakes (Point Given)
Haskell Invitational Handicap (Point Given)
Travers Stakes (Point Given)
Wood Memorial Stakes (Congaree)
Swaps Stakes (Congaree)
Del Mar Futurity (Officer)
Champagne Stakes (Officer)
Del Mar Debutante Stakes (Habibti)
Hollywood Starlet Stakes (Habibti)
Donn Handicap (Captain Steve)
Strub Stakes (Wooden Phone)
2002: Kentucky Derby (War Emblem)
Preakness Stakes (War Emblem)
Haskell Invitational Handicap (War Emblem)
Santa Maria Handicap (Favorite Funtime)
Del Mar Futurity (Icecoldbeeratreds)
Bessemer Trust Breeders' Cup Juvenile (Vindication)
Cigar Mile Handicap (Congaree)
2003: Carter Handicap (Congaree)
Hollywood Gold Cup (Congaree)
Cigar Mile Handicap (Congaree)
Las Virgenes Stakes (Composure)
Santa Anita Oaks (Composure)

J.D. BAILEY

1954: New Orleans Handicap (Grover B.)

SALLIE BAILIE

1982: Pegasus Handicap (Fast Gold)
1985: Man o' War Stakes (Win)

GEORGE BAKER

1967: Molly Pitcher Handicap (Politely)
1968: Delaware Handicap (Politely)
Ladies Handicap (Politely)

JAMES BAKER

1996: Whitney Handicap (Mahogany Hall)

IVAN BALDING

1966: Spinaway Stakes (Silver True)
Matron Stakes (Swiss Cheese)
Massachusetts Handicap (Fast Count)
1967: Garden State Stakes (Bugged)
1968: Travers Stakes (Chompion)

MICHAEL BALL

1982: Hawthorne Gold Cup (Recusant)

ARMANDO BANI

1984: Widener Handicap (Mat Boy)
Gulfstream Park Handicap (Mat Boy)

MIKE BAO

1963: California Derby (On My Honor)

BOBBY BARBARA

1998: Remsen Stakes (Comeonmom)
2003: Garden City BC Handicap (Indy Five Hundred)

EDGAR BARNES

1950: Molly Pitcher Handicap (Danger Ahead)

BOBBY BARNETT

1997: Apple Blossom Handicap (Halo America)
1998: Oaklawn Handicap (Precocity)
Breeders' Cup Juvenile (Answer Lively)

FRANK BARNETT

1948: Demoiselle Stakes (Lithe)
1949: Arlington Matron Handicap (Lithe)
Comely Handicap (Lithe)
1950: Arlington Matron Handicap (Lithe)
Grey Lag Handicap (Lotowhite)
1951: Pimlico Futurity (Cajun)

ANTHONY BARONI

1948: San Carlos Handicap (Autocrat)
1949: San Carlos Handicap (Autocrat)

LAZ BARRERA

1966: Display Handicap (Damelo II)
1971: Jerome Handicap (Tinajero)
1973: Acorn Stakes (Windy's Daughter)
Mother Goose Stakes (Windy's Daughter)
Vosburgh Handicap (Aljamin)
1974: Remsen Stakes (El Pitirre)
1975: Hempstead Handicap (Raisela)
1976: Wood Memorial Stakes (Bold Forbes)
Kentucky Derby (Bold Forbes)
Belmont Stakes (Bold Forbes)
Illinois Derby (Life's Hope)
Jersey Derby (Life's Hope)
Carter Handicap (Due Diligence)
Whitney Handicap (Dancing Gun)
1977: Hollywood Juvenile Championship (Affirmed)
Hopeful Stakes (Affirmed)
Futurity Stakes (Affirmed)
Laurel Futurity (Affirmed)
Monmouth Invitational Handicap (Affiliate)
Vosburgh Handicap (Affiliate)
San Fernando Stakes (Kirby Lane)
Charles H. Strub Stakes (Kirby Lane)
Santa Barbara Handicap (Desiree)
1978: San Felipe Handicap (Affirmed)
Santa Anita Derby (Affirmed)
Hollywood Derby (Affirmed)
Kentucky Derby (Affirmed)
Preakness Stakes (Affirmed)
Belmont Stakes (Affirmed)
New Orleans Handicap (Life's Hope)
Amory L. Haskell Handicap (Life's Hope)
Oak Leaf Stakes (It's In the Air)
Ladies Handicap (Ida Delia)
Californian Stakes (J.O. Tobin)
1979: Californian Stakes (Affirmed)
Hollywood Gold Cup (Affirmed)
Woodward Stakes (Affirmed)
Jockey Club Gold Cup (Affirmed)
Charles H. Strub Stakes (Affirmed)
Santa Anita Handicap (Affirmed)
Alabama Stakes (It's In the Air)
Vanity Handicap (It's In the Air)
Ruffian Handicap (It's In the Air)
Gamely Handicap (Sisterhood)
Swaps Stakes (Valdez)
1980: Vanity Handicap (It's In the Air)
Santa Barbara Handicap (Sisterhood)
Swaps Stakes (First Albert)
1982: Marlboro Cup Handicap (Lemhi Gold)
Jockey Club Gold Cup (Lemhi Gold)
Sword Dancer Stakes (Lemhi Gold)
San Juan Capistrano Handicap (Lemhi Gold)
New Orleans Handicap (It's the One)
San Fernando Stakes (It's the One)
Charles H. Strub Stakes (It's the One)
1983: Hollywood Gold Cup (Island Whirl)
Whitney Handicap (Island Whirl)
California Derby (Paris Prince)
San Fernando Stakes (Wavering Monarch)
1984: Delaware Handicap (Adored)
Santa Margarita Handicap (Adored)
Futurity Stakes (Spectacular Love)
Fantasy Stakes (My Darling One)
1986: Fantasy Stakes (Tiffany Lass)
Kentucky Oaks (Tiffany Lass)
Del Mar Futurity (Qualify)
1987: Kentucky Oaks (Buryyourbelief)
1988: San Felipe Handicap (Mi Preferido)
1989: San Fernando Stakes (Mi Preferido)
California Derby (Endow)
1990: Santa Anita Derby (Mister Frisky)

LUIS BARRERA

1981: Pennsylvania Derby (Summing)
Belmont Stakes (Summing)
Pegasus Handicap (Summing)
Alabama Stakes (Prismatical)
1982: Louisiana Downs Handicap (Pair of Deuces)

THOMAS BARRY

1953: Pimlico Futurity (Errard King)
1954: Arlington Classic (Errard King)
American Derby (Errard King)
1958: Belmont Stakes (Cavan)
1960: Belmont Stakes (Celtic Ash)

JAMES BARTLETT

1966: Florida Derby (Williamston Kid)

PASCAL BARY

1991: Breeders' Cup Turf (Miss Alleged)
2002: NetJets Breeders' Cup Mile (Domedriver)
2003: NetJets Breeders' Cup Mile (Six Perfections)

TONY BASILE

1967: Arlington-Washington Futurity (T.V. Commercial)
Breeders' Futurity (T.V. Commercial)
1971: Washington Park Handicap (Well Mannered)
1972: Alcibiades Stakes (Coraggioso)
1973: Frizette Stakes (Bundler)
1974: Ladies Handicap (Coraggioso)
1981: Arlington-Washington Futurity (Lets Dont Fight)
1982: Breeders' Futurity (Highland Park)
1983: Secretariat Stakes (Fortnightly)

D. BATES

1966: Ohio Derby (War Censor)

PETE BATTLE

1947: Hawthorne Gold Cup (Be Faithful)
1952: Frizette Stakes (Sweet Patootie)
Alcibiades Stakes (Sweet Patootie)

JAKE BATTLES

1976: Oak Leaf Stakes (Any Time Girl)

OLEN BATTLES

1984: Hollywood Oaks (Moment to Buy)

WARREN BEASLEY

1967: Canadian Int. Championship (He's a Smoothie)
1968: Hialeah Turf Cup (He's a Smoothie)

GERALD BELANGER JR.

1980: Top Flight Handicap (Glorious Song)
La Canada Stakes (Glorious Song)
Santa Margarita Handicap (Glorious Song)

DAVID BELL

1993: Haskell Invitational Handicap (Kissin Kris)

KAYE BELL

1975: Michigan Mile and One-Eighth (Mr. Lucky Phoenix)

GERALD BENNETT
1990: Arlington Invitational Challenge Cup (Beau Genius)
Philip H. Iselin Handicap (Beau Genius)

JAMES BENTLEY
1949: Travers Stakes (Arise)
1950: Fall Highweight Handicap (Arise)
Excelsior Handicap (Arise)
1951: Carter Handicap (Arise)
Monmouth Handicap (Arise)
1971: Alabama Stakes (Lauries Dancer)
1980: Ohio Derby (Stone Manor)

DAVID BERNSTEIN
1994: San Antonio Stakes (The Wicked North)
Oaklawn Handicap (The Wicked North)
Californian Stakes (The Wicked North)

GEORGE BERTHOLD
1968: Ohio Derby (Te Vega)

PATRICK BIANCONE
1983: Turf Classic (All Along)
Washington D.C. International (All Along)
Rothmans International Stakes (All Along)
2002: Futurity Stakes (Whywhywhy)
2003: Hollywood Futurity (Lion Heart)

C.A. BIDENCOPE
1946: Kentucky Oaks (First Page)

VINCENT BLENGS
1991: Sword Dancer Handicap (Dr. Root)

LEON BLUSIEWICZ
1981: Selima Stakes (Snow Plow)
1988: Ashland Stakes (Willa on the Move)

TOM BOHANNAN
1989: Jerome Handicap (De Roche)
1991: Peter Pan Stakes (Lost Mountain)
Dwyer Stakes (Lost Mountain)
Haskell Invitational Handicap (Lost Mountain)
Remsen Stakes (Pine Bluff)
1992: Arkansas Derby (Pine Bluff)
Preakness Stakes (Pine Bluff)
1993: Jim Beam Stakes (Prairie Bayou)
Blue Grass Stakes (Prairie Bayou)
Preakness Stakes (Prairie Bayou)
Fantasy Stakes (Aztec Hill)

LYNN BOICE
1962: Santa Anita Handicap (Physician)
1963: San Antonio Handicap (Physician)

JOE BOLLERO
1963: Cowdin Stakes (Dunfee)
1969: American Derby (Fast Hilarious)
1970: Michigan Mile and One-Eighth (Fast Hilarious)
1971: Gulfstream Park Handicap (Fast Hilarious)
1973: Donn Handicap (Triumphant)
1974: Arlington Handicap (Buffalo Lark)
1975: Pan American Handicap (Buffalo Lark)
1978: Arlington Handicap (Romeo)
1979: Spinster Stakes (Safe)
1980: American Derby (Hurry Up Blue)

BERNIE BOND
1980: Laurel Futurity (Cure the Blues)
1982: Sorority Stakes (Singing Susan)

BOWES BOND
1951: Sapling Stakes (Landseair)
1958: Washington D.C. International (Sailor's Guide)
1964: Carter Handicap (Ahoy)
1965: Pimlico Futurity (Spring Double)
1968: Arlington-Washington Lassie Stakes (Process Shot)
1969: Arlington-Washington Futurity (Silent Screen)
Cowdin Stakes (Silent Screen)
Champagne Stakes (Silent Screen)
1980: Sapling Stakes (Travelling Music)

JAMES BOND
1996: Travers Stakes (Will's Way)
1997: Whitney Handicap (Will's Way)
Buick Pegasus Handicap (Behrens)
Cigar Mile Handicap (Devious Course)
1999: Gulfstream Park Handicap (Behrens)
Oaklawn Handicap (Behrens)
Suburban Handicap (Behrens)
Man o' War Stakes (Val's Prince)
Turf Classic (Val's Prince)
Meadowlands Cup Handicap (Pleasant Breeze)
2000: Gulfstream Park Handicap (Behrens)
2002: Donn Handicap (Mongoose)
Wood Memorial Stakes (Buddha)

PAUL BONGARZONE
1963: Roamer Handicap (Dean Carl)
Display Handicap (Dean Carl)

BILL BONIFACE
1969: Ohio Derby (Berkley Prince)
1983: Preakness Stakes (Deputed Testamony)
Haskell Invitational Handicap (Deputed Testamony)
1997: Manhattan Handicap (Ops Smile)

FRANK BONSAL
1950: New York Handicap (Pilaster)
1955: Saranac Handicap (Saratoga)
1962: Trenton Handicap (Mongo)
United Nations Handicap (Mongo)
1963: Washington D.C. International (Mongo)
United Nations Handicap (Mongo)
1964: Widener Handicap (Mongo)
John B. Campbell Handicap (Mongo)
Monmouth Handicap (Mongo)
Vineland Handicap (Tona)
Man o' War Stakes (Turbo Jet II)
1969: Withers Stakes (Ack Ack)
Arlington Classic (Ack Ack)
1970: John B. Campbell Handicap (Best Turn)
1974: Flamingo Stakes (Bushongo)

WILLIE BOOTH
1946: Arlington Futurity (Cosmic Bomb)
Cowdin Stakes (Cosmic Bomb)
1947: Discovery Handicap (Cosmic Bomb)
Lawrence Realization Stakes (Cosmic Bomb)
Roamer Handicap (Cosmic Bomb)
Trenton Handicap (Cosmic Bomb)
Fall Highweight Handicap (Rippey)
Carter Handicap (Rippey)
1948: San Vicente Handicap (Salmagundi)
Santa Anita Derby (Salmagundi)
Roseben Handicap (Rippey)
1950: Vineland Handicap (Almahmoud)
1951: Matron Stakes (Rose Jet)
Selima Stakes (Rose Jet)
Demoiselle Stakes (Rose Jet)

BILLY BORDERS
1979: Louisiana Downs Handicap (Incredible Ease)

FRANCOIS BOUTIN
1981: Turf Classic (April Run)
1982: Turf Classic (April Run)
Washington D.C. International (April Run)
1984: Hollywood Derby (Procida)
Washington D.C. International (Seattle Song)
1987: Selima Stakes (Minstrel's Lassie)
Breeders' Cup Mile (Miesque)
1988: Breeders' Cup Mile (Miesque)
1991: Breeders' Cup Juvenile (Arazi)

GORDON BOWSHER
1967: Hollywood Juvenile Championship (Jim White)

DONALD BRADLEY
1969: John B. Campbell Handicap (Juvenile John)

JOHN BRADLEY
1966: New Orleans Handicap (Just About)

RANDY BRADSHAW
1995: Ohio Derby (Petionville)
1996: John A. Morris Handicap (Urbane)
1998: Santa Anita Oaks (Hedonist)
San Felipe Stakes (Artax)

PAT BRADY
1955: Canadian Championship Stakes (Park Dandy)

SIMON BRAY
2000: Gamely Breeders' Cup Handicap (Astra)
2001: Beverly Hills Handicap (Astra)
Secretariat Stakes (Startac)

BILL BREASHEAR
1981: Golden Harvest Handicap (Mean Martha)

ARTHUR BREASLEY
1977: Bowling Green Handicap (Hunza Dancer)
American Handicap (Hunza Dancer)

M.W. BRESHNEN
1949: San Pasqual Handicap (Shim Malone)

F.W. BREWSTER
1950: Longacres Mile (Two and Twenty)

DENNIS BRIDA
1992: Metropolitan Handicap (Dixie Brass)

G. BRIDGELAND
1953: Washington D.C. International (Worden II)

LANE BRIDGFORD
1951: Inglewood Handicap (Sturdy One)
1952: Inglewood Handicap (Sturdy One)

ROSS BRINSON
1947: Hollywood Gold Cup (Cover Up)
Sunset Handicap (Cover Up)
1952: Starlet Stakes (Little Request)

MAX BRITT
1962: Del Mar Futurity (Slipped Disc)

CLIVE BRITTAIN
1985: Breeders' Cup Turf (Pebbles)

D. BROOKS
1954: Washington Park Futurity (Georgian)

L.J. BROOKS
1968: San Felipe Handicap (Prince Pablo)
1972: Cinema Handicap (Finalista)

FRANK BROTHERS
1980: Golden Harvest Handicap (War Fame)
1989: Arkansas Derby (Dansil)
1990: Arlington-Washington Futurity (Hansel)
1991: Jim Beam Stakes (Hansel)
Preakness Stakes (Hansel)
Belmont Stakes (Hansel)
1996: Spinaway Stakes (Oath)
1997: Fountain of Youth Stakes (Pulpit)
Toyota Blue Grass Stakes (Pulpit)
1998: Super Derby (Arch)

JOSEPH BROUSSARD
1977: New Orleans Handicap (Tudor Tambourine)

HARRIS BROWN
1960: Hialeah Turf Cup (Amerigo)
San Juan Capistrano Handicap (Amerigo)

L.A. BRUSIE
1951: Garden State Stakes (Candle Wood)

JOHN BUCALO
1975: American Handicap (Montmartre)
1977: Hollywood Juvenile Championship (Noble Bronze)
1978: California Derby (Noble Bronze)

WILLIAM BUCK
1946: California Derby (War Spun)

ELLIOTT BURCH
1958: Acorn Stakes (Big Effort)
Delaware Oaks (Big Effort)
Widener Handicap (Oligarchy)
1959: Belmont Stakes (Sword Dancer)
Travers Stakes (Sword Dancer)
Metropolitan Handicap (Sword Dancer)
Monmouth Handicap (Sword Dancer)
Woodward Stakes (Sword Dancer)
Jockey Club Gold Cup (Sword Dancer)
Top Flight Handicap (Big Effort)
1960: Grey Lag Handicap (Sword Dancer)
Suburban Handicap (Sword Dancer)
Woodward Stakes (Sword Dancer)
Gardenia Stakes (Bowl of Flowers)
Frizette Stakes (Bowl of Flowers)
1961: Acorn Stakes (Bowl of Flowers)
Coaching Club American Oaks (Bowl of Flowers)
Spinster Stakes (Bowl of Flowers)
1963: Pimlico Futurity (Quadrangle)
1964: Wood Memorial Stakes (Quadrangle)
Belmont Stakes (Quadrangle)
Dwyer Handicap (Quadrangle)
Travers Stakes (Quadrangle)
Lawrence Realization Stakes (Quadrangle)
1966: Gazelle Handicap (Prides Profile)
1967: Washington D.C. International (Fort Marcy)
1968: Top Flight Handicap (Amerigo Lady)

ELLIOTT BURCH *(Continued)*
Sunset Handicap (Fort Marcy)
1969: Everglades Stakes (Arts and Letters)
Blue Grass Stakes (Arts and Letters)
Belmont Stakes (Arts and Letters)
Travers Stakes (Arts and Letters)
Metropolitan Handicap (Arts and Letters)
Woodward Stakes (Arts and Letters)
Jockey Club Gold Cup (Arts and Letters)
Black Helen Handicap (Amerigo Lady)
Top Flight Handicap (Amerigo Lady)
Hollywood Park Inv. Turf Handicap (Fort Marcy)
1970: Dixie Handicap (Fort Marcy)
Bowling Green Handicap (Fort Marcy)
United Nations Handicap (Fort Marcy)
Man o' War Stakes (Fort Marcy)
Washington D.C. International (Fort Marcy)
Garden State Stakes (Run the Gantlet)
Grey Lag Handicap (Arts and Letters)
1971: United Nations Handicap (Run the Gantlet)
Man o' War Stakes (Run the Gantlet)
Washington D.C. International (Run the Gantlet)
1972: Withers Stakes (Key to the Mint)
Travers Stakes (Key to the Mint)
Brooklyn Handicap (Key to the Mint)
Whitney Stakes (Key to the Mint)
Woodward Stakes (Key to the Mint)
Coaching Club American Oaks (Summer Guest)
Alabama Stakes (Summer Guest)
Bowling Green Handicap (Run the Gantlet)
1973: Grey Lag Handicap (Summer Guest)
Bowling Green Handicap (Summer Guest)
Suburban Handicap (Key to the Mint)
1974: Spinster Stakes (Summer Guest)
1976: San Juan Capistrano Handicap (One On the Aisle)
1979: Metropolitan Handicap (State Dinner)
Century Handicap (State Dinner)
1980: Whitney Stakes (State Dinner)
1982: Suburban Handicap (Silver Buck)
Whitney Handicap (Silver Buck)

PRESTON BURCH
1946: Sapling Stakes (Donor)
Champagne Stakes (Donor)
Swift Stakes (Master Bid)
Fall Highweight Handicap (Cassis)
1947: Tremont Stakes (Inseparable)
Matron Stakes (Inheritance)
Frizette Stakes (Slumber Song)
1949: Saratoga Special (More Sun)
Dixie Handicap (Chains)
1950: Louisiana Derby (Greek Ship)
Metropolitan Handicap (Greek Ship)
Monmouth Handicap (Greek Ship)
Spinaway Stakes (Atalanta)
Matron Stakes (Atalanta)
Saranac Handicap (Sunglow)
Discovery Handicap (Sunglow)
1951: Preakness Stakes (Bold)
Saranac Handicap (Bold)
Vosburgh Handicap (War King)
Widener Handicap (Sunglow)
1952: Selima Stakes (Tritium)
Florida Derby (Sky Ship)
1953: Saranac Handicap (First Aid)
Aqueduct Handicap (First Aid)
1954: Spinaway Stakes (Gandharva)
Tropical Handicap (Capeador)
Hialeah Turf Handicap (Picador)
1955: Roamer Handicap (Sailor)
Fall Highweight Handicap (Sailor)
Pimlico Special (Sailor)
Whitney Stakes (First Aid)
1956: Delaware Handicap (Flower Bowl)
Ladies Handicap (Flower Bowl)
Gulfstream Park Handicap (Sailor)
John B. Campbell Memorial Handicap (Sailor)

WILLIAM BURCH
1979: Suburban Handicap (State Dinner)
1983: Pan American Handicap (Field Cat)
1985: Louisiana Derby (Violado)

J.W. BURTON
1950: Princess Pat Stakes (Flyamanita)

C. BUTLER
1972: Sapling Stakes (Assagai Jr.)

MERRITT BUXTON
1952: Sapling Stakes (Laffango)
Champagne Stakes (Laffango)
Garden State Stakes (Laffango)
1953: Gotham Stakes (Laffango)

N.L. BYER
1954: Molly Pitcher Handicap (Shady Tune)

DOLLY BYERS
1950: Vosburgh Handicap (Tea-Maker)
1961: Man o' War Handicap (Wise Ship)
1962: Dixie Handicap (Wise Ship)

JESS BYRD
1962: Hollywood Juvenile Championship (Y Flash)
Hollywood Juvenile Championship (Noti)
1963: Cinema Handicap (Y Flash)
Hollywood Derby (Y Flash)
Arlington-Washington Lassie Stakes (Sari's Song)

PATRICK BYRNE
1997: Spinaway Stakes (Countess Diana)
Breeders' Cup Juvenile Fillies (Countess Diana)
Hopeful Stakes (Favorite Trick)
Breeders' Cup Juvenile (Favorite Trick)
Jerome Handicap (Richter Scale)
1998: Whitney Handicap (Awesome Again)
Breeders' Cup Classic (Awesome Again)

JOHN CAIRNS
1981: Spinster Stakes (Glorious Song)

ALFREDO CALLEJAS
1982: Acorn Stakes (Cupecoy's Joy)
Mother Goose Stakes (Cupecoy's Joy)

MELVIN CALVERT
1951: Santa Anita Derby (Rough'n Tumble)
1959: Gardenia Stakes (My Dear Girl)
Frizette Stakes (My Dear Girl)
1966: Pimlico Futurity (In Reality)
1967: Florida Derby (In Reality)
Jersey Derby (In Reality)
1968: John B. Campbell Handicap (In Reality)
Carter Handicap (In Reality)
Metropolitan Handicap (In Reality)
1980: Flamingo Stakes (Superbity)

CHARLES CALVIN
1958: Kentucky Jockey Club Stakes (Winsome Winner)
1959: Arlington Matron Handicap (Wiggle II)

JERRY CALVIN
1980: Sorority Stakes (Fancy Naskra)

BOB CAMAC
1992: Philip H. Iselin Handicap (Jolie's Halo)

DON CAMERON
1949: Santa Anita Handicap (Vulcan's Forge)
Suburban Handicap (Vulcan's Forge)
1952: Santa Anita Handicap (Miche)

E.L. CAMPBELL
1981: Hollywood Derby (Silveyville)

GORDON CAMPBELL
1965: Del Mar Debutante Stakes (Century)
1971: Sunset Handicap (Over the Counter)
1972: Oak Leaf Stakes (Fresh Pepper)
1974: Norfolk Stakes (George Navonod)
1976: San Fernando Stakes (Messenger of Song)
Charles H. Strub Stakes (George Navonod)
1977: Vanity Handicap (Cascapedia)
1978: Del Mar Futurity (Flying Paster)
Norfolk Stakes (Flying Paster)
1979: Santa Anita Derby (Flying Paster)
Hollywood Derby (Flying Paster)
1981: San Antonio Stakes (Flying Paster)

L. CAMPION
1947: Golden Gate Handicap (Triplicate)

JOHNNY CAMPO
1969: Dwyer Handicap (Gleaming Light)
1971: Gotham Stakes (Good Behaving)
Wood Memorial Stakes (Good Behaving)
Santa Anita Derby (Jim French)
Dwyer Handicap (Jim French)
1973: Champagne Stakes (Protagonist)
Laurel Futurity (Protagonist)
Spinaway Stakes (Talking Picture)
Matron Stakes (Talking Picture)
1974: Futurity Stakes (Just the Time)
1975: Hopeful Stakes (Jackknife)
Demoiselle Stakes (Free Journey)
1976: Mother Goose Stakes (Girl in Love)
1977: Mother Goose Stakes (Road Princess)
1979: Hopeful Stakes (J.P. Brother)
1981: Wood Memorial Stakes (Pleasant Colony)
Kentucky Derby (Pleasant Colony)
Preakness Stakes (Pleasant Colony)
Woodward Stakes (Pleasant Colony)
Meadowlands Cup (Princelet)
1988: Flamingo Stakes (Cherokee Colony)

JULIO CANANI
1988: Hollywood Derby (Silver Circus)
1989: Santa Anita Handicap (Martial Law)
1999: Gamely Breeders' Cup Handicap (Tranquility Lake)
Breeders' Cup Mile (Silic)
2000: Shoemaker Breeders' Cup Mile (Silic)
Eddie Read Handicap (Ladies Din)
Yellow Ribbon Stakes (Tranquility Lake)
2001: Breeders' Cup Mile (Val Royal)
2002: Shoemaker Breeders' Cup Mile (Ladies Din)
2003: Eddie Read Handicap (Special Ring)

NICK CANANI
1998: Del Mar Oaks (Sicy D'Alsace)

WILLIAM CANNEY
1967: Display Handicap (Quicken Tree)
1968: Manhattan Handicap (Quicken Tree)
Jockey Club Gold Cup (Quicken Tree)
1970: Santa Anita Handicap (Quicken Tree)
San Juan Capistrano Handicap (Quicken Tree)
1971: Oak Leaf Stakes (Sporting Lass)

DARRELL CANNON
1949: Santa Margarita Handicap (Lurline B.)

JOE CANTEY
1978: Metropolitan Handicap (Cox's Ridge)
Oaklawn Handicap (Cox's Ridge)
1979: Apple Blossom Handicap (Miss Baja)
1980: Arkansas Derby (Temperence Hill)
Belmont Stakes (Temperence Hill)
Travers Stakes (Temperence Hill)
Super Derby (Temperence Hill)
Jockey Club Gold Cup (Temperence Hill)
1981: Suburban Handicap (Temperence Hill)
Oaklawn Handicap (Temperence Hill)
1982: Oaklawn Handicap (Eminency)
Rothmans International Stakes (Majesty's Prince)
1983: Sword Dancer Handicap (Majesty's Prince)
Man o' War Stakes (Majesty's Prince)
1984: Man o' War Stakes (Majesty's Prince)
Rothmans International Stakes (Majesty's Prince)

JOHN CANTY
1962: California Derby (Doc Jocoy)
1971: San Felipe Handicap (Unconscious)
Santa Anita Derby (Unconscious)
Hollywood Juvenile Championship (Royal Owl)
Del Mar Futurity (D.B. Carm)
1972: Charles H. Strub Stakes (Unconscious)
San Antonio Stakes (Unconscious)
San Luis Rey Handicap (Nor II)
1973: Charles H. Strub Stakes (Royal Owl)
1979: Santa Susana Stakes (Caline)

GARY CAPUANO
1997: Florida Derby (Captain Bodgit)
Wood Memorial Stakes (Captain Bodgit)

CHARLES CARLESIMO
1990: Ruffian Handicap (Quick Mischief)

LOU CARNO
1964: Hollywood Juvenile Championship (Charger's Kin)
1981: La Canada Stakes (Summer Siren)

DIANNE CARPENTER
1981: New Orleans Handicap (Sun Catcher)
1988: Jim Beam Stakes (Kingpost)

E.B. CARPENTER
1958: Arlington Lassie Stakes (Dark Vintage)

FRANK CARR
1958: Inglewood Handicap (Eddie Schmidt)
1962: Californian Stakes (Cadiz)

JACK CARRARA
1955: Bougainvillea Turf Handicap (Cascanuez)
1958: Fall Highweight Handicap (Bull Strength)

DEL CARROLL

1966: Breeders' Futurity (Gentleman James)
Blue Grass Stakes (Abe's Hope)
1967: Donn Handicap (Francis U.)
1968: Illinois Derby (Bold Favorite)
Gulfstream Park Handicap (Gentleman James)
1971: Acorn Stakes (Deceit)
Mother Goose Stakes (Deceit)
John B. Campbell Handicap (Bushido)
1972: Preakness Stakes (Bee Bee Bee)
1974: Jersey Derby (Better Arbitor)
1977: Young America Stakes (Forever Casting)
1978: Breeders' Futurity (Strike Your Colors)
1980: Alcibiades Stakes (Sweet Revenge)

DEL CARROLL II

1984: Frizette Stakes (Charleston Rag)
1992: Secretariat Stakes (Ghazi)

GEORGE WASHINGTON CARROLL

1947: Miami Beach Handicap (Tel O'Sullivan)

HENRY CARROLL

1989: United Nations Handicap (Yankee Affair)
Man o' War Stakes (Yankee Affair)
Turf Classic (Yankee Affair)
1996: Hopeful Stakes (Smoke Glacken)
1997: Frank J. De Francis Memorial Dash (Smoke Glacken)

R.B. CARROLL

1946: Gulfstream Handicap (Do-Reigh-Me)

W.E. CARROLL

1954: Black Helen Handicap (Gainsboro Girl)
New Castle Handicap (Gainsboro Girl)

BUD CARTER

1957: Gotham Stakes (Mister Jive)

C.J. CASEY

1948: Sunset Handicap (Drumbeat)

MARK CASSE

2001: Metropolitan Handicap (Exciting Story)

WAYNE CATALANO

1997: Arkansas Derby (Crypto Star)

FRANK CATRONE

1948: Remsen Stakes (Eternal World)
Astoria Stakes (Eternal Flag)
1951: Gulfstream Park Handicap (Ennobled)
1952: McLennan Handicap (Spartan Valor)
Widener Handicap (Spartan Valor)
Excelsior Handicap (Spartan Valor)
Gallant Fox Handicap (Spartan Valor)
1965: Santa Anita Derby (Lucky Debonair)
Blue Grass Stakes (Lucky Debonair)
Kentucky Derby (Lucky Debonair)
1966: Santa Anita Handicap (Lucky Debonair)
1973: Alcibiades Stakes (City Girl)
1974: Top Flight Handicap (Lady Love)
Bowling Green Handicap (Take Off)

LOUIS CAVALARIS JR.

1968: Wood Memorial Stakes (Dancer's Image)
Canadian International Championship (Frenetico)

BEN CECIL

1997: Gamely Handicap (Donna Viola)
1998: Beverly Hills Handicap (Squeak)
Matriarch Stakes (Squeak)
2001: Del Mar Oaks (Golden Apples)
2002: Beverly D. Stakes (Golden Apples)
Yellow Ribbon Stakes (Golden Apples)
2003: San Juan Capistrano Handicap (Passinetti)

HENRY CECIL

1997: Flower Bowl Invitational Handicap (Yashmak)
1998: Canadian Int. Championship (Royal Anthem)

VLADIMIR CERIN

2000: Sempra Energy Hollywood Gold Cup (Early Pioneer)

MIKE CHAMBERS

1985: Sapling Stakes (Hilco Scamper)

FRANK CHILDS

1948: Hollywood Oaks (Flying Rhythm)
1949: Del Mar Derby (Bolero)
San Antonio Handicap (Dinner Gong)
1951: San Carlos Handicap (Bolero)

1958: Starlet Stakes (Tomy Lee)
Del Mar Futurity (Tomy Lee)
1959: Blue Grass Stakes (Tomy Lee)
Kentucky Derby (Tomy Lee)
1961: Del Mar Futurity (Weldy)
1965: Cinema Handicap (Arksroni)

B.F. CHRISTMAS

1949: Garden State Stakes (Cornwall)

EDWARD CHRISTMAS

1946: Beldame Handicap (Gallorette)
Metropolitan Handicap (Gallorette)
Brooklyn Handicap (Gallorette)
1947: Queens County Handicap (Gallorette)
1948: Carter Handicap (Gallorette)
Whitney Stakes (Gallorette)
1954: Maskette Handicap (Ballerina)
1955: Gardenia Stakes (Nasrina)
Frizette Stakes (Nasrina)
1965: Mother Goose Stakes (Cordially)

ROGER CLAPP

1976: San Felipe Handicap (Crystal Water)
Hollywood Derby (Crystal Water)
1977: Californian Stakes (Crystal Water)
Hollywood Gold Cup (Crystal Water)
Santa Anita Handicap (Crystal Water)
Oak Tree Invitational Stakes (Crystal Water)
Sunset Handicap (Today'n Tomorrow)
1982: Hollywood Derby (Racing Is Fun)

HENRY CLARK

1948: Molly Pitcher Handicap (Camargo)
1955: Travers Stakes (Thinking Cap)
Lawrence Realization Stakes (Thinking Cap)
1958: Alabama Stakes (Tempted)
Maskette Handicap (Tempted)
Delaware Handicap (Endine)
Ladies Handicap (Endine)
1959: Diana Handicap (Tempted)
Beldame Handicap (Tempted)
Ladies Handicap (Tempted)
Delaware Handicap (Endine)
1961: Futurity Stakes (Cyane)
1962: Dwyer Handicap (Cyane)
1963: Manhattan Handicap (Smart)
1964: Massachusetts Handicap (Smart)
Gallant Fox Handicap (Smart)
1965: Massachusetts Handicap (Smart)
1969: Delaware Handicap (Obeah)
1970: Delaware Handicap (Obeah)
1972: Hempstead Handicap (Light Hearted)
Maskette Handicap (Light Hearted)
1982: Blue Grass Stakes (Linkage)

A. CLEFF

1971: Amory L. Haskell Handicap (Jontilla)

ODIE CLELLAND

1956: Alabama Stakes (Tournure)

CHRISTOPHE CLEMENT

1999: Sword Dancer Invitational Handicap (Honor Glide)
2001: Manhattan Handicap (Forbidden Apple)
Beverly D. Stakes (England's Legend)
Garden City BC Handicap (Voodoo Dancer)
2003: Diana Handicap (Voodoo Dancer)

GENE CLEVELAND

1968: Charles H. Strub Stakes (Most Host)
1970: San Felipe Handicap (Cool Hand)
1973: San Juan Capistrano Handicap (Queen's Hustler)
1978: Vanity Handicap (Afifa)
1981: Santa Margarita Handicap (Princess Karenda)

VINCENT CLYNE

1976: Del Mar Futurity (Visible)
1977: Secretariat Stakes (Text)
1978: San Fernando Stakes (Text)
1979: Amory L. Haskell Handicap (Text)
1982: California Derby (Rockwall)

WILLIAM COCKS

1988: Ruffian Handicap (Sham Say)

RILEY COFER

1980: California Derby (Jaklin Klugman)
Jerome Handicap (Jaklin Klugman)

ANDREW COLANDO

1950: Champagne Stakes (Uncle Miltie)

FRANK COLCORD

1964: Hollywood Oaks (Loukahi)

PAUL COLE

1992: Budweiser International Stakes (Zoman)
Rothmans International Stakes (Snurge)

WILLIAM COLE

1977: Travers Stakes (Jatski)

ROBERT COLLET

1986: Breeders' Cup Mile (Last Tycoon)
1987: Rothmans International Stakes (River Memories)
Budweiser International Stakes (Le Glorieux)

GIN COLLINS

1965: Arkansas Derby (Swift Ruler)
1966: Oaklawn Handicap (Swift Ruler)
1970: Sapling Stakes (Staunch Avenger)

PAT COLLINS

1988: Blue Grass Stakes (Granacus)

NICK COMBEST

1961: Vineland Handicap (Frimanaha)
1964: Gotham Stakes (Mr. Moonlight)
Roamer Handicap (Point du Jour)
1971: Manhattan Handicap (Happy Way)

DON COMBS

1970: Blue Grass Stakes (Dust Commander)
Kentucky Derby (Dust Commander)
1975: Oaklawn Handicap (Warbucks)
1980: Arlington Handicap (Yvonand)
Louisiana Downs Handicap (Yvonand)

CHARLIE COMISKEY

1970: Santa Barbara Handicap (Sallarina)

JOSEPH CONSIDINE

1972: Carter Handicap (Leematt)

GARY CONTESSA

1991: Ashland Stakes (Do It With Style)

JIMMY CONWAY

1947: Cowdin Stakes (My Request)
Louisiana Derby (Carolyn A.)
1948: Delaware Oaks (Miss Request)
Ladies Handicap (Miss Request)
Wood Memorial Stakes (My Request)
Dwyer Stakes (My Request)
Firenze Handicap (Carolyn A.)
1949: New Orleans Handicap (My Request)
Excelsior Handicap (My Request)
Beldame Handicap (Miss Request)
1950: Brooklyn Handicap (My Request)
1952: Demoiselle Stakes (Grecian Queen)
Fall Highweight Handicap (Hitex)
1953: Coaching Club American Oaks (Grecian Queen)
Gazelle Handicap (Grecian Queen)
Monmouth Oaks (Grecian Queen)
New Castle Handicap (Grecian Queen)
1957: Beldame Handicap (Pucker Up)
Washington Park Handicap (Pucker Up)
1958: Top Flight Handicap (Plucky Roman)
1961: Delaware Oaks (Primonetta)
Alabama Stakes (Primonetta)
1962: Breeders' Futurity (Ornamento)
Coaching Club American Oaks (Bramalea)
Spinster Stakes (Primonetta)
Jerome Handicap (Black Beard)
1963: Blue Grass Stakes (Chateaugay)
Kentucky Derby (Chateaugay)
Belmont Stakes (Chateaugay)
Jerome Handicap (Chateaugay)
1964: Spinaway Stakes (Candalita)
Matron Stakes (Candalita)
1967: United Nations Handicap (Flit-to)
1968: Widener Handicap (Sette Bello)
1969: Amory L. Haskell Handicap (Verbatim)
Whitney Stakes (Verbatim)
Lawrence Realization Stakes (Oil Power)
1970: Monmouth Invitational Handicap (Twice Worthy)
1971: Suburban Handicap (Twice Worthy)
Hawthorne Gold Cup (Twice Worthy)
1972: Mother Goose Stakes (Wanda)
1974: Louisiana Derby (Sellout)
1976: Bowling Green Handicap (Erwin Boy)

REGGIE CORNELL

1955: Del Mar Handicap (Arrogate)
1956: Del Mar Futurity (Swirling Abbey)

REGGIE CORNELL *(Continued)*
Del Mar Debutante Stakes (Blue Vic)
Del Mar Handicap (Arrogate)
1957: Santa Anita Maturity (Spinney)
1958: Santa Anita Derby (Silky Sullivan)
1959: Preakness Stakes (Royal Orbit)
1963: Sunset Handicap (Arbitrage)
1970: Vosburgh Handicap (Best Turn)
1971: Florida Derby (Eastern Fleet)
Pontiac Grand Prix Stakes (Son Ange)
1972: Hialeah Turf Cup (Gleaming)
1973: Hialeah Turf Cup (Gleaming)

LEE COTTON
1946: Ladies Handicap (Athenia)
Louisiana Derby (Pellicle)

W.S. COTTON
1953: Molly Pitcher Handicap (My Celeste)
Monmouth Handicap (My Celeste)

EDGAR COX
1956: San Luis Rey Handicap (Blue Volt)

ROBERT CRAFT
1969: Hollywood Oaks (Tipping Time)

J. CREEVY
1950: Sapling Stakes (Battlefield)

JIMMY CROLL
1955: Tropical Handicap (Scimitar)
1965: United Nations Handicap (Parka)
1966: Sorority Stakes (Like A Charm)
1967: Sapling Stakes (Subpet)
1969: Jersey Derby (Al Hattab)
Monmouth Invitational Handicap (Al Hattab)
1970: Sorority Stakes (Forward Gal)
Spinaway Stakes (Forward Gal)
Frizette Stakes (Forward Gal)
1971: Monmouth Oaks (Forward Gal)
Gazelle Handicap (Forward Gal)
1973: Florida Derby (Royal and Regal)
1976: Sapling Stakes (Ali Oop)
1986: Arlington-Washington Futurity (Bet Twice)
Laurel Futurity (Bet Twice)
1987: Fountain of Youth Stakes (Bet Twice)
Belmont Stakes (Bet Twice)
Haskell Invitational Handicap (Bet Twice)
1990: Withers Stakes (Housebuster)
Jerome Handicap (Housebuster)
1991: Carter Handicap (Housebuster)
Vosburgh Stakes (Housebuster)
Jersey Derby (Greek Costume)
1993: Futurity Stakes (Holy Bull)
1994: Florida Derby (Holy Bull)
Blue Grass Stakes (Holy Bull)
Metropolitan Handicap (Holy Bull)
Dwyer Stakes (Holy Bull)
Haskell Invitational Handicap (Holy Bull)
Travers Stakes (Holy Bull)
Woodward Stakes (Holy Bull)

DAVID CROSS
1983: Arkansas Derby (Sunny's Halo)
Kentucky Derby (Sunny's Halo)
Super Derby (Sunny's Halo)
1998: Ohio Derby (Classic Cat)

RICHARD CROSS
1994: Eddie Read Handicap (Approach the Bench)
1995: Hollywood Turf Handicap (Earl of Barking)

WILLIE CRUMP
1947: Kentucky Oaks (Blue Grass)

LUCA CUMANI
1983: Budweiser Million (Tolomeo)
1988: Rothmans International Stakes (Infamy)
1994: Breeders' Cup Mile (Barathea)

FRANK CUNDALL
1959: Carter Handicap (Jimmer)

J. CUNNINGTON JR.
1974: Washington D.C. International (Admetus)

WILLIAM CURTIS JR.
1979: Breeders' Futurity (Gold Stage)

VAN CUTSEM
1969: Washington D.C. International (Karabas)

OLIVER CUTSHAW
1969: Louisiana Derby (King of the Castle)

JUAN d'AGOSTINO
1961: Gulfstream Park Handicap (Tudor Way)

HARRY DANIELS
1949: Del Mar Futurity (Your Host)
1950: San Felipe Stakes (Your Host)
Santa Anita Derby (Your Host)
1951: Westerner Stakes (Grantor)
Del Mar Derby (Grantor)
Will Rogers Handicap (Gold Note)

SAM DAVID JR.
1997: Kentucky Oaks (Blushing K.D.)

DOUG DAVIS JR.
1964: Arkansas Derby (Prince Davelle)
1972: Breeders' Futurity (Annihilate 'Em)
1973: Travers Stakes (Annihilate 'Em)

JOHN DAVIS
1970: Gotham Stakes (Native Royalty)

JIM DAY
1991: Spinster Stakes (Wilderness Song)
Rothmans International Stakes (Sky Classic)
Breeders' Cup Distaff (Dance Smartly)
1992: Caesars International Handicap (Sky Classic)
Turf Classic (Sky Classic)
1995: Molson Export Million (Peaks and Valleys)
Meadowlands Cup (Peaks and Valleys)
1997: Secretariat Stakes (Honor Glide)

THOMAS DeBONIS
1984: Champagne Stakes (For Certain Doc)

BUD DELP
1977: Kentucky Oaks (Sweet Alliance)
1978: Champagne Stakes (Spectacular Bid)
Young America Stakes (Spectacular Bid)
Laurel Futurity (Spectacular Bid)
1979: Florida Derby (Spectacular Bid)
Flamingo Stakes (Spectacular Bid)
Blue Grass Stakes (Spectacular Bid)
Kentucky Derby (Spectacular Bid)
Preakness Stakes (Spectacular Bid)
Marlboro Cup Handicap (Spectacular Bid)
Meadowlands Cup (Spectacular Bid)
1980: Californian Stakes (Spectacular Bid)
Amory L. Haskell Handicap (Spectacular Bid)
Woodward Stakes (Spectacular Bid)
San Fernando Stakes (Spectacular Bid)
Charles H. Strub Stakes (Spectacular Bid)
Santa Anita Handicap (Spectacular Bid)
Arlington-Washington Lassie Stakes (Truly Bound)
1990: Woodward Handicap (Dispersal)
2001: Pimlico Special (Include)

JACK DELZELL
1973: Del Mar Handicap (Red Reality)

WILLIAM DENNIS
1951: Sunset Handicap (Alderman)

LAURA de SEROUX
2002: Santa Margarita Handicap (Azeri)
Apple Blossom Handicap (Azeri)
Milady Breeders' Cup Handicap (Azeri)
Vanity Handicap (Azeri)
Breeders' Cup Distaff (Azeri)
Gamely Breeders' Cup Handicap (Astra)
Beverly Hills Handicap (Astra)
Del Mar Oaks (Dublino)
2003: Apple Blossom Handicap (Azeri)
Milady Breeders' Cup Handicap (Azeri)
Vanity Handicap (Azeri)

RICHARD DeSTASIO
1980: Bowling Green Handicap (Sten)
1981: Futurity Stakes (Irish Martini)
1982: Brooklyn Handicap (Silver Supreme)

JOHN DeSTEFANO JR.
1997: Gotham Stakes (Smokin Mel)

RAY De STEFANO
1951: Discovery Handicap (Alerted)
Jerome Handicap (Alerted)
1952: Dixie Handicap (Alerted)

PAT DEVEREUX
1955: Michigan Mile (Greatest)

PETER DEVITO
1963: Arlington Park Handicap (Bounding Main)

J.A. DEWITT
1948: Suburban Handicap (Harmonica)

JOSEPH DiANGELO
1974: Illinois Derby (Sharp Gary)

CHARLIE DICKENS
1957: Del Mar Debutante Stakes (Sally Lee)

MICHAEL DICKINSON
1990: Delaware Handicap (Seattle Dawn)
1996: Breeders' Cup Mile (Da Hoss)
1998: Sword Dancer Invitational Handicap (Cetewayo)
Breeders' Cup Mile (Da Hoss)
2001: Ashland Stakes (Fleet Renee)
Mother Goose Stakes (Fleet Renee)
2002: Gulfstream Park Breeders' Cup Handicap (Cetewayo)
2003: Frank J. De Francis Memorial Dash (A Huevo)

JOHN DILLARD
1973: Oaklawn Handicap (Prince Astro)

JOHN DiMARIO
1982: Travers Stakes (Runaway Groom)

STEVEN DiMAURO
1962: Remsen Stakes (Rocky Link)
1966: Mother Goose Stakes (Lady Pitt)
Coaching Club American Oaks (Lady Pitt)
1970: Acorn Stakes (Royal Signal)
1974: Delaware Handicap (Krislin)
Wood Memorial Stakes (Flip Sal)
1975: Sorority Stakes (Dearly Precious)
Spinaway Stakes (Dearly Precious)
Arlington-Washington Lassie Stakes (Dearly Precious)
Monmouth Invitational Handicap (Wajima)
Travers Stakes (Wajima)
Marlboro Cup Handicap (Wajima)
1976: Acorn Stakes (Dearly Precious)
Withers Stakes (Sonkisser)
Hialeah Turf Cup (Lord Henham)
1981: Santa Barbara Handicap (The Very One)
1983: Florida Derby (Croeso)
1985: Rothmans International Stakes (Nassipour)
1987: Ladies Handicap (Nastique)
1988: Delaware Handicap (Nastique)
1989: Delaware Handicap (Nastique)

OSCAR DISHMAN JR.
1973: Michigan Mile and One-Eighth (Golden Don)
1977: Ohio Derby (Silver Series)
American Derby (Silver Series)
1978: Widener Handicap (Silver Series)

PETE DISPENZA
1963: Hawthorne Gold Cup (Admiral Vic)
1964: Seminole Handicap (Admiral Vic)

DON DIVINE
1966: Kentucky Jockey Club Stakes (Lightning Orphan)

HEPBURN DIXON
1970: John B. Campbell Handicap (Mitey Prince)

MORRIS DIXON
1946: Roseben Handicap (Polynesian)
1953: Fall Highweight Handicap (Kaster)
1968: Monmouth Invitational Handicap (Balustrade)

E.C. DOBSON
1949: Arlington Futurity (Wisconsin Boy)

DOUG DODSON
1965: Gulfstream Park Handicap (Ampose)
1974: Breeders' Futurity (Packer Captain)

H.C. DODSON
1946: Princess Pat Stakes (Say Blue)
1948: Marguerite Stakes (Alsab's Day)

JOHN DOLAN
2001: Santa Margarita Handicap (Lazy Slusan)
Milady Breeders' Cup Handicap (Lazy Slusan)

CRAIG DOLLASE
1998: Breeders' Cup Sprint (Reraise)
2001: Ancient Title BC Handicap (Swept Overboard)

2002: Metropolitan Handicap (Swept Overboard)
Hollywood Starlet Stakes (Elloluv)
2003: Ashland Stakes (Elloluv)

WALLY DOLLASE

1990: Hollywood Derby (Itsallgreektome)
Hollywood Turf Cup (Itsallgreektome)
1994: Santa Maria Handicap (Supah Gem)
Swaps Stakes (Silver Music)
1996: Vanity Handicap (Jewel Princess)
Breeders' Cup Distaff (Jewel Princess)
Strub Stakes (Helmsman)
San Luis Rey Stakes (Windsharp)
Malibu Stakes (King of the Heap)
1997: Santa Maria Handicap (Jewel Princess)
Santa Margarita Handicap (Jewel Princess)
Travers Stakes (Deputy Commander)
Super Derby (Deputy Commander)
Beverly Hills Handicap (Windsharp)
1998: Ruffian Handicap (Sharp Cat)
Beldame Stakes (Sharp Cat)
Oak Tree Turf Championship (Military)
Hollywood Turf Cup (Lazy Lode)
2003: Travers Stakes (Ten Most Wanted)
Super Derby (Ten Most Wanted)

CARL DOMINO

1985: Arlington Handicap (Pass the Line)
1991: Champagne Stakes (Tri to Watch)

DAVID DONK

1993: Secretariat Stakes (Awad)
1995: Early Times Manhattan Handicap (Awad)
Arlington Million (Awad)
1996: Moet Champagne Stakes (Ordway)
1997: Sword Dancer Invitational Handicap (Awad)

R. DONNELL

1949: Longacres Mile (Blue Tiger)

BILL DONOVAN

1987: Illinois Derby (Lost Code)
Ohio Derby (Lost Code)
Arlington Classic (Lost Code)

LEONARD DORFMAN

1966: Californian Stakes (Travel Orb)

BOBBY DOTTER

1951: Metropolitan Handicap (Casemate)
1952: Sapling Stakes (Landlocked)
1953: Sapling Stakes (Artismo)
Hopeful Stakes (Artismo)
Acorn Stakes (Secret Meeting)
1954: Widener Handicap (Landlocked)
1960: Manhattan Handicap (Don Poggio)
Gallant Fox Handicap (Don Poggio)

FRANK DOUGHERTY

1956: Gazelle Handicap (Scampering)

FRANCOIS DOUMAN

1988: Hialeah Turf Cup (Double Bed)

JOHN DOWD

2001: Fountain of Youth Stakes (Songandaprayer)

TOMMY DOYLE

1959: Del Mar Debutante Stakes (Darling June)
1966: Del Mar Debutante Stakes (Native Honey)
1968: Del Mar Debutante Stakes (Fourth Round)
1971: Norfolk Stakes (MacArthur Park)
Del Mar Futurity (MacArthur Park)
1972: Hollywood Invitational Handicap (Typecast)
Sunset Handicap (Typecast)
Man o' War Stakes (Typecast)
Del Mar Debutante Stakes (Windy's Daughter)
1973: Del Mar Debutante Stakes (Fleet Peach)
Hollywood Oaks (Sandy Blue)
1975: Santa Anita Derby (Avatar)
Belmont Stakes (Avatar)
Hollywood Invitational Handicap (Barclay Joy)
Sunset Handicap (Barclay Joy)
1976: Norfolk Stakes (Habitony)
Del Mar Debutante Stakes (Telferner)
Santa Margarita Handicap (Fascinating Girl)
San Luis Rey Stakes (Avatar)
1977: Ramona Handicap (Dancing Femme)
Santa Anita Derby (Habitony)
Century Handicap (Anne's Pretender)
San Juan Capistrano Handicap (Properantes)
1978: Charles H. Strub Stakes (Mr. Redoy)
1980: Del Mar Debutante Stakes (Raja's Delight)
1983: Acorn Stakes (Ski Goggle)
1984: Santa Anita Derby (Mighty Adversary)

MATTHEW DRAGNA

1960: Hollywood Derby (Tempestuous)
1961: San Juan Capistrano Handicap (Don't Alibi)

ALLEN DRUMHELLER

1947: Longacres Mile (Hank H.)
1948: Longacres Mile (Amble In)
1949: San Carlos Handicap (Manyunk)
1951: Santa Margarita Handicap (Special Touch)
1953: Santa Margarita Handicap (Spanish Cream)
1955: Starlet Stakes (Bold Bazooka)

NEIL DRYSDALE

1975: Swaps Stakes (Forceten)
1977: Apple Blossom Handicap (Hail Hilarious)
1979: Oak Leaf Stakes (Bold 'n Determined)
1980: Santa Susana Stakes (Bold 'n Determined)
Fantasy Stakes (Bold 'n Determined)
Kentucky Oaks (Bold 'n Determined)
Acorn Stakes (Bold 'n Determined)
Coaching Club American Oaks (Bold 'n Determined)
Maskette Stakes (Bold 'n Determined)
Spinster Stakes (Bold 'n Determined)
1981: Apple Blossom Handicap (Bold 'n Determined)
1984: Vanity Handicap (Princess Rooney)
Spinster Stakes (Princess Rooney)
Breeders' Cup Distaff (Princess Rooney)
Oak Leaf Stakes (Folk Art)
Oak Tree Invitational Stakes (Both Ends Burning)
1985: Breeders' Futurity (Tasso)
Breeders' Cup Juvenile (Tasso)
Hollywood Inv. Handicap (Both Ends Burning)
1986: Vanity Handicap (Magnificent Lindy)
1987: Hollywood Derby (Political Ambition)
1988: John Henry Handicap (Deputy Governor)
Hollywood Invitational Handicap (Political Ambition)
1989: Ashland Stakes (Gorgeous)
Hollywood Oaks (Gorgeous)
Swaps Stakes (Prized)
Breeders' Cup Turf (Prized)
Californian Stakes (Sabona)
Maskette Stakes (Miss Brio)
1990: La Canada Stakes (Gorgeous)
Apple Blossom Handicap (Gorgeous)
Vanity Handicap (Gorgeous)
San Luis Rey Stakes (Prized)
1991: Santa Barbara Handicap (Bequest)
Californian Stakes (Roanoke)
Hollywood Futurity (A.P. Indy)
1992: Santa Anita Derby (A.P. Indy)
Peter Pan Stakes (A.P. Indy)
Belmont Stakes (A.P. Indy)
Breeders' Cup Classic (A.P. Indy)
1993: Hollywood Oaks (Hollywood Wildcat)
Breeders' Cup Distaff (Hollywood Wildcat)
1994: Gamely Handicap (Hollywood Wildcat)
1995: Jerome Handicap (French Deputy)
Crown Royal Hollywood Derby (Labeeb)
1998: Gamely Breeders' Cup Handicap (Fiji)
Yellow Ribbon Stakes (Fiji)
Hollywood Turf Handicap (Storm Trooper)
Woodbine Mile (Labeeb)
1999: San Juan Capistrano Handicap (Single Empire)
2000: San Felipe Stakes (Fusaichi Pegasus)
Wood Memorial Stakes (Fusaichi Pegasus)
Kentucky Derby (Fusaichi Pegasus)
San Juan Capistrano Handicap (Sunshine Street)
Charles Whittingham Handicap (White Heart)
Del Mar Oaks (No Matter What)
Breeders' Cup Mile (War Chant)
2001: Woodford Reserve Turf Classic (White Heart)
Shoemaker Breeders' Cup Mile (Irish Prize)
2002: Eddie Read Handicap (Sarafan)
2003: Charles Whittingham Handicap (Storming Home)
Clement L. Hirsch Mem. Turf Champ. (Storming Home)

OLEG DUBASSOFF

1959: Bowling Green Handicap (Bell Hop)
1961: Canadian Championship Stakes (Our Jeep)
1963: Ladies Handicap (Goofed)

LEONARD DUNCAN

1999: Malibu Stakes (Love That Red)

ROBERT DUNCAN

1953: Demoiselle Stakes (O'Alison)

BOB DUNHAM

1971: Spinster Stakes (Chou Croute)

EDWARD DUNLOP

2001: Flower Bowl Invitational Handicap (Lailani)

J.S. DUNN

1953: Cinema Handicap (Ali's Gem)
San Antonio Handicap (Trusting)
1959: Hollywood Derby (Bagdad)
1960: San Antonio Handicap (Bagdad)
Inglewood Handicap (Bagdad)
Del Mar Debutante Stakes (Amri-An)
1962: Hollywood Oaks (Dingle Bay)
1963: Santa Margarita Handicap (Pixie Erin)
1964: Hollywood Juvenile Championship (Neke)
Vanity Handicap (Star Maggie)
1968: Hollywood Derby (Poleax)
1970: Hollywood Oaks (Last of the Line)
1974: Oak Leaf Stakes (Cut Class)
1975: Hollywood Oaks (Nicosia)

WALLY DUNN

1953: Blue Grass Stakes (Correspondent)
1954: Hollywood Gold Cup (Correspondent)
1958: California Derby (Nice Guy)
1964: American Handicap (Colorado King)
Hollywood Gold Cup (Colorado King)
Sunset Handicap (Colorado King)
Santa Susana Stakes (Blue Norther)
Kentucky Oaks (Blue Norther)

JEAN-PIERRE DUPUIS

1985: Hollywood Derby (Charming Duke)

BOB DURSO

1997: Ohio Derby (Frisk Me Now)
1998: Suburban Handicap (Frisk Me Now)
1999: Philip H. Iselin Handicap (Frisk Me Now)

DICK DUTROW

1986: Vosburgh Stakes (King's Swan)
1995: Carter Handicap (Lite the Fuse)
Frank J. De Francis Memorial Dash (Lite the Fuse)
1996: Carter Handicap (Lite the Fuse)
Frank J. De Francis Memorial Dash (Lite the Fuse)
Gotham Stakes (Romano Gucci)

DICK DUTROW JR.

2002: Prioress Stakes (Carson Hollow)

TONY DUTROW

2000: Futurity Stakes (Burning Roma)

JAMES ECKROSH

1970: Louisiana Derby (Jim's Alibhi)

MARY EDENS

1980: Delaware Handicap (Heavenly Ade)

SAMUEL EDMUNDSON

1954: Gulfstream Park Handicap (Wise Margin)
Massachusetts Handicap (Wise Margin)

LARRY EDWARDS

1990: Arlington-Washington Lassie Stakes (Through Flight)

RON ELLIS

1995: Milady Handicap (Pirate's Revenge)
1996: Santa Margarita Handicap (Twice the Vice)
Apple Blossom Handicap (Twice the Vice)
Milady Breeders' Cup Handicap (Twice the Vice)
Go for Wand Stakes (Exotic Wood)
1997: Vanity Handicap (Twice the Vice)
1998: Santa Monica Handicap (Exotic Wood)
Santa Maria Handicap (Exotic Wood)
Milady Breeders' Cup Handicap (I Ain't Bluffing)

REX ELLSWORTH

1963: Hollywood Oaks (Delhi Maid)
American Handicap (Dr. Kacy)
1964: Cinema Handicap (Close By)

PHIL ENGLAND

1987: Jerome Handicap (Afleet)
Pennsylvania Derby (Afleet)
1992: Molson Export Million (Benburb)
1993: Jerome Handicap (Schossberg)
1995: Philip H. Iselin Handicap (Schossberg)

J.T. ENGLE

1948: Cinema Handicap (Drumbeat)

MARY EPPLER
1996: Futurity Stakes (Traitor)

DAVID ERB
1963: Garden State Stakes (Hurry to Market)
1965: Vosburgh Handicap (R. Thomas)
1973: New Orleans Handicap (Combat Ready)

MANNY ESTEVEZ
1987: Tropical Park Derby (Baldski's Star)

EUGENE EUSTER
1976: Vosburgh Handicap (My Juliet)
1977: Michigan Mile and One-Eighth (My Juliet)

GOMER EVANS
1965: Oaklawn Handicap (Gay Revoke)

ANDRE FABRE
1983: Oak Tree Invitational Stakes (Zalataia)
1988: Budweiser Million (Mill Native)
1990: Rothmans International Stakes (French Glory)
Breeders' Cup Turf (In the Wings)
1993: Turf Classic (Apple Tree)
Breeders' Cup Classic (Arcangues)
1994: Rothmans International Stakes (Raintrap)
2001: Breeders' Cup Filly and Mare Turf (Banks Hill)

MARTIN FALLON
1959: San Carlos Handicap (Hillsdale)
Los Angeles Handicap (Hillsdale)
Californian Stakes (Hillsdale)
American Handicap (Hillsdale)
Hollywood Gold Cup (Hillsdale)
Aqueduct Handicap (Hillsdale)
Santa Anita Maturity (Hillsdale)
1961: San Antonio Handicap (American Comet)
Michigan Mile and One-Sixteenth (American Comet)

JERRY FANNING
1970: San Felipe Handicap (Terlago)
Santa Anita Derby (Terlago)
1972: Malibu Stakes (Kfar Tov)
1977: Breeders' Futurity (Gonquin)
1980: Oak Leaf Stakes (Astrious)
1983: Vanity Handicap (A Kiss For Luck)
San Felipe Handicap (Desert Wine)
Swaps Stakes (Hyperborean)
1984: Californian Stakes (Desert Wine)
Hollywood Gold Cup (Desert Wine)
Charles H. Strub Stakes (Desert Wine)
1985: Sunset Handicap (Kings Island)
1986: Spinster Stakes (Top Corsage)
1991: San Luis Rey Stakes (Pleasant Variety)

DAVID FAWKES
1999: Pegasus Handicap (Forty One Carats)

GUIDO FEDERICO
1987: Brooklyn Handicap (Waquoit)
1988: Brooklyn Handicap (Waquoit)
Jockey Club Gold Cup (Waquoit)

JOHN FELLOWS
1993: Rothmans International Stakes (Husband)

CHARLES FELTNER
1948: Trenton Handicap (Double Jay)

ROSS FENSTERMAKER
1975: Delaware Handicap (Susan's Girl)
Beldame Stakes (Susan's Girl)
1978: Futurity Stakes (Crest of the Wave)
1981: Del Mar Debutante Stakes (Skillful Joy)
Hollywood Starlet Stakes (Skillful Joy)
1982: San Felipe Handicap (Advance Man)
Swaps Stakes (Journey at Sea)
1984: Swaps Stakes (Precisionist)
1985: San Fernando Stakes (Precisionist)
Charles H. Strub Stakes (Precisionist)
Breeders' Cup Sprint (Precisionist)
1986: Californian Stakes (Precisionist)
Woodward Stakes (Precisionist)

W. FENWICK
1950: Santa Susana Stakes (Special Touch)

FLOREANO FERNANDEZ
1980: Meadowlands Cup (Tunerup)
Hawthorne Gold Cup (Tunerup)

MICHAEL FERRARO
1981: Whitney Handicap (Fio Rito)

PETER FERRIOLA
1979: Young America Stakes (Koluctoo Bay)

RICHARD FERRIS
1979: Whitney Stakes (Star de Naskra)

KENNETH FIELD
1966: Dixie Handicap (Knightly Manner)

BERT FIELDS
1960: Withers Stakes (John William)

FORDELL FIERCE
1994: American Derby (Vaudeville)
Secretariat Stakes (Vaudeville)

ARNOLD FINK
1988: Hopeful Stakes (Mercedes Won)
1989: Florida Derby (Mercedes Won)

BILL FINNEGAN
1952: Del Mar Handicap (Grantor)
1954: Starlet Stakes (Blue Ruler)
Del Mar Futurity (Blue Ruler)
1955: San Felipe Handicap (Jean's Joe)
1956: Vanity Handicap (Mary Machree)
1958: San Carlos Handicap (Seaneen)
Californian Stakes (Seaneen)
1959: San Felipe Handicap (Finnegan)
California Derby (Finnegan)
1960: Los Angeles Handicap (Finnegan)
1964: San Felipe Handicap (Hill Rise)
Santa Anita Derby (Hill Rise)
1965: Santa Anita Handicap (Hill Rise)
San Fernando Stakes (Hill Rise)
Man o' War Stakes (Hill Rise)
1966: San Antonio Handicap (Hill Rise)
1967: Sunset Handicap (Hill Clown)
1968: Hollywood Oaks (Hooplah)

ALEX FIORE
1969: San Luis Rey Handicap (Taneb)

DICK FISCHER
1967: Alcibiades Stakes (Lady Tramp)
1971: Kentucky Oaks (Silent Beauty)

WOODY FITZGERALD
1946: Inglewood Handicap (Quick Reward)
American Handicap (Quick Reward)
1948: California Derby (May Reward)
San Felipe Stakes (May Reward)
Will Rogers Handicap (Speculation)

JIM FITZSIMMONS
1946: Coaching Club American Oaks (Hypnotic)
Alabama Stakes (Hypnotic)
Delaware Oaks (Bonnie Beryl)
Comely Handicap (Bonnie Beryl)
Astarita Stakes (Keynote)
1948: Tremont Stakes (The Admiral)
1949: Dwyer Stakes (Shackleton)
1950: Alabama Stakes (Busanda)
1951: Top Flight Handicap (Busanda)
New Castle Handicap (Busanda)
Suburban Handicap (Busanda)
Black Helen Handicap (Antagonism)
1952: Spinaway Stakes (Flirtatious)
Saranac Handicap (Golden Gloves)
Discovery Handicap (Ancestor)
1953: Alabama Stakes (Sabette)
1954: Hopeful Stakes (Nashua)
Futurity Stakes (Nashua)
Selima Stakes (High Voltage)
Matron Stakes (High Voltage)
Monmouth Handicap (Bassanio)
1955: Flamingo Stakes (Nashua)
Florida Derby (Nashua)
Wood Memorial Stakes (Nashua)
Preakness Stakes (Nashua)
Belmont Stakes (Nashua)
Dwyer Stakes (Nashua)
Arlington Classic (Nashua)
Jockey Club Gold Cup (Nashua)
Acorn Stakes (High Voltage)
Coaching Club American Oaks (High Voltage)
Delaware Oaks (High Voltage)
Vineland Handicap (High Voltage)
Monmouth Oaks (Misty Morn)
Molly Pitcher Handicap (Misty Morn)
Gallant Fox Handicap (Misty Morn)
1956: Widener Handicap (Nashua)
Grey Lag Handicap (Nashua)
Suburban Handicap (Nashua)
Monmouth Handicap (Nashua)
Jockey Club Gold Cup (Nashua)
Futurity Stakes (Bold Ruler)
1957: Flamingo Stakes (Bold Ruler)
Wood Memorial Stakes (Bold Ruler)
Preakness Stakes (Bold Ruler)
Jerome Handicap (Bold Ruler)
Trenton Handicap (Bold Ruler)
Remsen Stakes (Misty Flight)
Dwyer Handicap (Bureaucracy)
1958: Carter Handicap (Bold Ruler)
Suburban Handicap (Bold Ruler)
Monmouth Handicap (Bold Ruler)
1959: Alabama Stakes (High Bid)
Vineland Handicap (High Bid)
Pimlico Futurity (Progressing)
Spinaway Stakes (Irish Jay)
1960: Acorn Stakes (Irish Jay)
1961: Withers Stakes (Hitting Away)
Dwyer Handicap (Hitting Away)
Sorority Stakes (Batter Up)
Mother Goose Stakes (Funloving)
1962: Selima Stakes (Fool's Play)

LARRY FLAKES
1976: Arlington-Washington Lassie Stakes (Special Warmth)

THOMAS FLEMING
1947: Vosburgh Handicap (With Pleasure)

BERNARD FLINT
2001: Super Derby (Outofthebox)

HUGH FONTAINE
1951: Cowdin Stakes (Eternal Moon)
1955: Sapling Stakes (Needles)
Hopeful Stakes (Needles)
1956: Flamingo Stakes (Needles)
Florida Derby (Needles)
Kentucky Derby (Needles)
Belmont Stakes (Needles)
1957: Diana Handicap (Pardala)
1958: Black Helen Handicap (Pardala)

K. FORCE JR.
1946: New Orleans Handicap (Hillyer Court)

HENRY FORREST
1966: Kentucky Derby (Kauai King)
Preakness Stakes (Kauai King)
1968: Everglades Stakes (Forward Pass)
Florida Derby (Forward Pass)
Blue Grass Stakes (Forward Pass)
Kentucky Derby (Forward Pass)
Preakness Stakes (Forward Pass)
American Derby (Forward Pass)

PAUL FOUT
1972: Del Mar Handicap (Chrisaway)
2000: Flower Bowl Invitational Handicap (Colstar)

BOBBY FRANKEL
1970: Suburban Handicap (Barometer)
1973: San Felipe Handicap (Linda's Chief)
Santa Anita Derby (Linda's Chief)
Hollywood Invitational Handicap (Life Cycle)
1979: Hollywood Invitational Handicap (Johnny's Image)
1981: Eddie Read Handicap (Wickerr)
Louisiana Downs Handicap (Goldiko)
1982: Monmouth Handicap (Mehmet)
Meadowlands Cup (Mehmet)
Eddie Read Handicap (Wickerr)
1983: Hawthorne Gold Cup (Water Bank)
1984: La Canada Stakes (Sweet Diane)
1986: Metropolitan Handicap (Garthorn)
Arlington-Washington Lassie Stakes (Delicate Vine)
1987: John Henry Handicap (Al Mamoon)
1988: Sunset Handicap (Roi Normand)
1990: Gamely Handicap (Double Wedge)
1991: Hollywood Turf Handicap (Exbourne)
Caesars International Handicap (Exbourne)
San Juan Capistrano Handicap (Mashkour)
Hollywood Gold Cup (Marquetry)
Oak Tree Invitational Stakes (Filago)
Hollywood Derby (Eternity Star)
1992: Hollywood Turf Handicap (Quest for Fame)
Gamely Handicap (Metamorphose)
Eddie Read Handicap (Marquetry)
Pacific Classic (Missionary Ridge)
Hollywood Starlet Stakes (Creaking Board)

1993: San Antonio Handicap (Marquetry)
Meadowlands Cup (Marquetry)
Pacific Classic (Bertrando)
Woodward Stakes (Bertrando)
Gamely Handicap (Toussaud)
Yellow Ribbon Stakes (Possibly Perfect)
1994: Santa Barbara Handicap (Possibly Perfect)
Pacific Classic (Tinners Way)
1995: Gamely Handicap (Possibly Perfect)
Ramona Handicap (Possibly Perfect)
Beverly D. Stakes (Possibly Perfect)
Metropolitan Handicap (You and I)
Brooklyn Handicap (You and I)
Santa Barbara Handicap (Wandesta)
Hollywood Oaks (Sleep Easy)
Pacific Classic (Tinners Way)
1996: San Juan Capistrano Handicap (Raintrap)
Californian Stakes (Tinners Way)
Matriarch Stakes (Wandesta)
1997: Eddie Read Handicap (Expelled)
Matriarch Stakes (Ryafan)
Hollywood Turf Cup (River Bay)
1998: Las Virgenes Stakes (Keeper Hill)
Kentucky Oaks (Keeper Hill)
Ramona Handicap (See You Soon)
1999: Charles Whittingham Handicap (River Bay)
Yellow Ribbon Stakes (Spanish Fern)
Oak Tree Turf Championship (Mash One)
Three Chimneys Spinster Stakes (Keeper Hill)
Early Times Hollywood Derby (Super Quercus)
Matriarch Stakes (Happyanunoit)
2000: Santa Monica Handicap (Honest Lady)
Beverly Hills Handicap (Happyanunoit)
Arlington Million (Chester House)
Pacific Classic (Skimming)
Clement L. Hirsch Mem. Turf Champ. (Mash One)
2001: Kentucky Oaks (Flute)
Alabama Stakes (Flute)
Whitney Handicap (Lido Palace)
Woodward Stakes (Lido Palace)
United Nations Handicap (Senure)
Clement L. Hirsch Memorial Turf Champ. (Senure)
Hollywood Gold Cup (Aptitude)
Jockey Club Gold Cup (Aptitude)
King's Bishop Stakes (Squirtle Squirt)
Penske Auto Center BC Sprint (Squirtle Squirt)
Gamely Breeders' Cup Handicap (Happyanunoit)
Pacific Classic (Skimming)
Turf Classic (Timboroa)
Frizette Stakes (You)
Matriarch Stakes (Starine)
Hollywood Derby (Denon)
Hollywood Turf Cup (Super Quercus)
Malibu Stakes (Mizzen Mast)
2002: Las Virgenes Stakes (You)
Santa Anita Oaks (You)
Acorn Stakes (You)
Test Stakes (You)
Woodford Reserve Turf Classic (Beat Hollow)
Manhattan Handicap (Beat Hollow)
Arlington Million (Beat Hollow)
Jim Dandy Stakes (Medaglia d'Oro)
Travers Stakes (Medaglia d'Oro)
Charles Whittingham Handicap (Denon)
Turf Classic (Denon)
Strub Stakes (Mizzen Mast)
Santa Anita Handicap (Milwaukee Brew)
Secretariat Stakes (Chiselling)
Woodward Stakes (Lido Palace)
Breeders' Cup Filly and Mare Turf (Starine)
2003: Humana Distaff Handicap (Sightseek)
Ogden Phipps Handicap (Sightseek)
Go for Wand Handicap (Sightseek)
Beldame Stakes (Sightseek)
Florida Derby (Empire Maker)
Wood Memorial Stakes (Empire Maker)
Belmont Stakes (Empire Maker)
Strub Stakes (Medaglia d'Oro)
Oaklawn Handicap (Medaglia d'Oro)
Whitney Handicap (Medaglia d'Oro)
San Carlos Handicap (Aldebaran)
Metropolitan Handicap (Aldebaran)
Forego Handicap (Aldebaran)
Mother Goose Stakes (Spoken Fur)
Coaching Club American Oaks (Spoken Fur)
Toyota Blue Grass Stakes (Peace Rules)
Haskell Invitational Handicap (Peace Rules)
Gamely Breeders' Cup Handicap (Tates Creek)
Yellow Ribbon Stakes (Tates Creek)
Beverly D. Stakes (Heat Haze)
Matriarch Stakes (Heat Haze)
Santa Anita Handicap (Milwaukee Brew)
Manhattan Handicap (Denon)
John C. Mabee Handicap (Megahertz)
Ruffian Handicap (Wild Spirit)
Vosburgh Stakes (Ghostzapper)
Hollywood Turf Cup (Continuously)

MIKE FREEMAN

1954: Bougainvillea Turf Handicap (Parnassus)
1968: Frizette Stakes (Shuvee)
Selima Stakes (Shuvee)
1969: Acorn Stakes (Shuvee)
Mother Goose Stakes (Shuvee)
Coaching Club American Oaks (Shuvee)
Alabama Stakes (Shuvee)
Ladies Handicap (Shuvee)
Matron Stakes (Cold Comfort)
1970: Top Flight Handicap (Shuvee)
Beldame Stakes (Shuvee)
Jockey Club Gold Cup (Shuvee)
1971: Top Flight Handicap (Shuvee)
Jockey Club Gold Cup (Shuvee)
1982: Arkansas Derby (Hostage)
1989: Rothmans International Stakes (Hodges Bay)
1993: Budweiser International Stakes (Buckhar)
1995: Dwyer Stakes (Hoolie)

MITCHELL FRIEDMAN

2000: Carter Handicap (Brutally Frank)

MARK FROSTAD

1996: Philip H. Iselin Handicap (Smart Strike)
1997: Canadian Int. Championship (Chief Bearhart)
Breeders' Cup Turf (Chief Bearhart)
Early Times Turf Classic (Always a Classic)
Vosburgh Stakes (Victor Cooley)
1998: Manhattan Handicap (Chief Bearhart)
2002: Go for Wand Handicap (Dancethruthedawn)

JOHN FULTON

1973: Illinois Derby (Big Whippendeal)
1974: Hialeah Turf Cup (Big Whippendeal)
Century Handicap (Big Whippendeal)
1977: Hollywood Derby (Steve's Friend)

A. FUNGER

1963: Lawrence Realization Stakes (Dean Carl)

A. GAAL

1946: Arlington Classic (The Dude)

PETER GACICIA

1960: Top Flight Handicap (Royal Native)
Arlington Matron Handicap (Royal Native)
Vineland Handicap (Royal Native)

NED GAINES

1950: Marguerite Stakes (Carolina Queen)

CAM GAMBOLATI

1984: Arlington-Washington Futurity (Spend A Buck)
1985: Kentucky Derby (Spend A Buck)
Jersey Derby (Spend A Buck)
Monmouth Handicap (Spend A Buck)

JUAN GARCIA

2002: San Juan Capistrano Handicap (Ringaskiddy)

WOODS GARTH

1965: Monmouth Oaks (Summer Scandal)
1966: Top Flight Handicap (Summer Scandal)
Beldame Stakes (Summer Scandal)
1970: Withers Stakes (Hagley)

DEAN GAUDET

1984: Laurel Futurity (Mighty Appealing)
Remsen Stakes (Mighty Appealing)

JACK GAVER

1976: Widener Handicap (Hatchet Man)
Amory L. Haskell Handicap (Hatchet Man)
Louisiana Derby (Johnny Appleseed)
1978: Delaware Handicap (Late Bloomer)
Ruffian Handicap (Late Bloomer)
Beldame Stakes (Late Bloomer)
Sheepshead Bay Handicap (Late Bloomer)
Gulfstream Park Handicap (Bowl Game)
Pan American Handicap (Bowl Game)
1979: Hialeah Turf Cup (Bowl Game)
Arlington Handicap (Bowl Game)
Man o' War Stakes (Bowl Game)
Turf Classic (Bowl Game)
Washington D.C. International (Bowl Game)
Oaklawn Handicap (San Juan Hill)
1980: Louisiana Derby (Prince Valiant)
1981: Louisiana Derby (Woodchopper)
Rothmans International Stakes (Open Call)

JOHN GAVER

1946: Vosburgh Handicap (Coincidence)
Aqueduct Handicap (Coincidence)
Lawrence Realization Stakes (School Tie)
1947: Excelsior Handicap (Coincidence)
1948: Champagne Stakes (Capot)
Pimlico Futurity (Capot)
1949: Preakness Stakes (Capot)
Belmont Stakes (Capot)
Jerome Handicap (Capot)
Pimlico Special (Capot)
Futurity Stakes (Guillotine)
Spinaway Stakes (Sunday Evening)
Aqueduct Handicap (Wine List)
1950: Breeders' Futurity (Big Stretch)
Pimlico Futurity (Big Stretch)
Manhattan Handicap (One Hitter)
Pimlico Special (One Hitter)
Carter Handicap (Guillotine)
Aqueduct Handicap (Wine List)
1951: Arlington Classic (Hall of Fame)
American Derby (Hall of Fame)
Massachusetts Handicap (One Hitter)
Whitney Stakes (One Hitter)
Futurity Stakes (Tom Fool)
Monmouth Oaks (Ruddy)
Fall Highweight Handicap (Guillotine)
1952: Breeders' Futurity (Straight Face)
Kentucky Jockey Club Stakes (Straight Face)
Suburban Handicap (One Hitter)
Monmouth Handicap (One Hitter)
Jerome Handicap (Tom Fool)
Grey Lag Handicap (Tom Fool)
Carter Handicap (Northern Star)
1953: Metropolitan Handicap (Tom Fool)
Suburban Handicap (Tom Fool)
Carter Handicap (Tom Fool)
Brooklyn Handicap (Tom Fool)
Whitney Stakes (Tom Fool)
Pimlico Special (Tom Fool)
Frizette Stakes (Indian Legend)
1954: Dixie Handicap (Straight Face)
Suburban Handicap (Straight Face)
1955: Spinaway Stakes (Register)
1956: Dwyer Handicap (Riley)
Lawrence Realization Stakes (Riley)
1958: Brooklyn Handicap (Cohoes)
Whitney Stakes (Cohoes)
1959: Futurity Stakes (Weatherwise)
1962: Hopeful Stakes (Outing Class)
Manhattan Handicap (Tutankhamen)
1963: Metropolitan Handicap (Cyrano)
Brooklyn Handicap (Cyrano)
Canadian Championship Stakes (The Axe II)
Man o' War Stakes (The Axe II)
Sanford Stakes (Delirium)
Wood Memorial Stakes (No Robbery)
Dwyer Handicap (Outing Class)
1965: Aqueduct Stakes (Malicious)
1967: Gazelle Handicap (Sweet Folly)
Ladies Handicap (Sweet Folly)
1968: Belmont Stakes (Stage Door Johnny)
Dwyer Handicap (Stage Door Johnny)
1972: Champagne Stakes (Stop the Music)
Manhattan Handicap (Ruritania)
1973: Dwyer Handicap (Stop the Music)
1974: Dwyer Handicap (Hatchet Man)

GILBERT GAY

1955: Gotham Stakes (Go Lightly)

G. GEIER

1970: New Orleans Handicap (Etony)

LOYD GENTRY JR.

1955: Kentucky Oaks (Lalun)
Beldame Handicap (Lalun)
Blue Grass Stakes (Racing Fool)
1956: Manhattan Handicap (Flying Fury)
1960: Princess Pat Stakes (Rose Bower)
Matron Stakes (Rose Bower)
1964: Breeders' Futurity (Umbrella Fella)
Kentucky Jockey Club Stakes (Umbrella Fella)
1967: Kentucky Derby (Proud Clarion)
1969: Kentucky Oaks (Hail to Patsy)

GEORGE GETZ
1977: Illinois Derby (Flag Officer)
1981: Arlington-Washington Lassie Stakes (Milingo)

GEORGE GIANOS
1984: Fountain of Youth Stakes (Darn That Alarm)
1986: Delaware Handicap (Shocker T.)
1989: Tropical Park Derby (Big Stanley)
1992: Flamingo Stakes (Pistols and Roses)
Blue Grass Stakes (Pistols and Roses)
1993: Donn Handicap (Pistols and Roses)
1994: Donn Handicap (Pistols and Roses)

RODGER GILL
1973: John B. Campbell Handicap (Delay)

ROY GILLEM
1970: Arkansas Derby (Herbalist)
1971: Oaklawn Handicap (Rio Bravo)

FRANK GILPIN
1954: Arlington Futurity (Royal Note)

ORIN GLASS JR.
1993: Arkansas Derby (Rockamundo)

LOU GLAUBURG
1964: Del Mar Debutante Stakes (Admirably)
1969: Oak Leaf Stakes (Opening Bid)
1970: Santa Susana Stakes (Opening Bid)
1972: San Felipe Handicap (Solar Salute)
Santa Anita Derby (Solar Salute)
1973: Hollywood Juvenile Championship (Century's Envoy)
1974: Del Mar Debutante Stakes (Bubblewin)

PHIL GLEAVES
1986: Haskell Invitational Handicap (Wise Times)
Travers Stakes (Wise Times)
Super Derby (Wise Times)
1988: Jerome Handicap (Evening Kris)

VINCENT GLORIOSO
1961: Cinema Handicap (Four-and-Twenty)
Hollywood Derby (Four-and-Twenty)

ALAN GOLDBERG
1990: Breeders' Cup Sprint (Safely Kept)

LOU GOLDFINE
1972: Arlington-Washington Futurity (Shecky Greene)
1973: Fountain of Youth Stakes (Shecky Greene)
Blue Grass Stakes (My Gallant)
1978: Arlington-Washington Lassie Stakes (It's In the Air)
1999: Early Times Turf Classic (Wild Event)

R.D. GOLDSBERRY
1967: Ohio Derby (Out the Window)

FRANK GOMEZ
1982: Frizette Stakes (Princess Rooney)
1983: Kentucky Oaks (Princess Rooney)
1985: Arlington Classic (Smile)

NICHOLAS GONZALES
1971: Withers Stakes (Bold Reasoning)
Jersey Derby (Bold Reasoning)

JUAN GONZALEZ
1992: Swaps Stakes (Bien Bien)
Hollywood Turf Cup (Bien Bien)
Hollywood Oaks (Pacific Squall)
1993: Hollywood Turf Handicap (Bien Bien)
1994: San Luis Rey Stakes (Bien Bien)
San Juan Capistrano Handicap (Bien Bien)
1996: San Felipe Stakes (Odyle)
Norfolk Stakes (Free House)
1997: San Felipe Stakes (Free House)
Santa Anita Derby (Free House)
Swaps Stakes (Free House)
1998: Pacific Classic (Free House)
1999: San Antonio Handicap (Free House)
Santa Anita Handicap (Free House)
2000: Hollywood Turf Cup (Bienamado)
2001: San Juan Capistrano Handicap (Bienamado)
Charles Whittingham Handicap (Bienamado)
Hopeful Stakes (Came Home)
2002: Santa Anita Derby (Came Home)
Swaps Stakes (Came Home)
Pacific Classic (Came Home)

JOHN MILTON GOODE
1946: Hawthorne Gold Cup (Jack's Jill)
1948: Princess Pat Stakes (Sequence)
Arlington Classic (Papa Redbird)

CLINT GOODRICH
1992: Arlington Classic (Saint Ballado)

GEORGE GOODWIN
1979: San Felipe Handicap (Pole Position)

H.H. GOODWIN
1970: Monmouth Oaks (Kilts N Kapers)

P.S. GOODWIN
1957: Hialeah Turf Handicap (Jabneh)

MICHAEL GORHAM
2002: Ruffian Handicap (Mandy's Gold)

JOHN GOSDEN
1983: Monmouth Handicap (Bates Motel)
San Antonio Stakes (Bates Motel)
Santa Anita Handicap (Bates Motel)
Hollywood Derby (Royal Heroine)
1984: Breeders' Cup Mile (Royal Heroine)
1985: Hollywood Turf Cup (Zoffany)
1986: San Antonio Handicap (Hatim)
Gamely Handicap (La Khoumia)
Sunset Handicap (Zoffany)
Yellow Ribbon Stakes (Bonne Ile)
Hollywood Turf Cup (Alphabatim)
1987: San Luis Rey Stakes (Zoffany)
Oak Tree Invitational Stakes (Allez Milord)
1988: Vanity Handicap (Annoconnor)
1997: Queen Elizabeth II Challenge Cup (Ryafan)
Yellow Ribbon Stakes (Ryafan)

AKIKO GOTHARD
2000: Oaklawn Handicap (K One King)

NICHOLAS GRAFFAGINNI
1960: Louisiana Derby (Tony Graff)

BEAU GREELY
2000: Woodford Reserve Turf Classic (Manndar)
Manhattan Handicap (Manndar)
2002: Hollywood Turf Cup (Sligo Bay)

JOHN GREELY JR.
1955: Hawthorne Gold Cup (Hasseyampa)
1960: Travers Stakes (Tompion)
1961: Aqueduct Handicap (Tompion)

NEWCOMB GREEN
1986: Fountain of Youth Stakes (My Prince Charming)

ROBERT GREEN
1954: Top Flight Handicap (Sunshine Nell)

C.B. GREENE
1974: Hollywood Juvenile Championship (DiMaggio)

WALTER GREENMAN
1996: Oak Tree Turf Championship (Admise)

EDDIE GREGSON
1978: Santa Barbara Handicap (Kittyluck)
1979: Del Mar Handicap (Ardiente)
1981: Del Mar Futurity (Gato Del Sol)
1982: Kentucky Derby (Gato Del Sol)
1986: Apple Blossom Handicap (Love Smitten)
Hollywood Gold Cup (Super Diamond)
1989: San Antonio Handicap (Super Diamond)
Sunset Handicap (Pranke)
1990: Sunset Handicap (Petite Ile)
1995: Hollywood Turf Cup (Royal Chariot)

C.V. GRIBBIN
1949: Vanity Handicap (Silver Drift)

MITCHELL GRIFFIN
1982: Hopeful Stakes (Copelan)
Futurity Stakes (Copelan)
Champagne Stakes (Copelan)

STROTHER GRIFFIN
1955: Breeders' Futurity (Jovial Jove)
Arlington Lassie Stakes (Judy Rullah)

HAL GRIFFITT
1984: Breeders' Futurity (Crater Fire)

THOMAS GRIMES
1947: Swift Stakes (Owners Choice)
San Felipe Stakes (Owners Choice)
1948: Frizette Stakes (Our Fleet)

MEL GROSS
1977: Jockey Club Gold Cup (On the Sly)
Hawthorne Gold Cup (On the Sly)

RAY GRUNDY
1957: Michigan Mile and One-Sixteenth (My Night Out)

ROGER GUERINI
1966: Pan American Handicap (Pillanlebun)

IRV GUINEY
1966: Arlington-Washington Lassie Stakes (Mira Femme)

DONALD HABEEB
1990: Ohio Derby (Private School)

CHARLES HADRY
1988: Gotham Stakes (Private Terms)
Wood Memorial Stakes (Private Terms)

C.J. HALL
1946: American Derby (Eternal Reward)

R.R. HALL
1948: Santa Susana Stakes (Mrs. Rabbit)

STUART HAMBLEN
1947: San Antonio Handicap (El Lobo)

JOHN HAMMOND
1992: Arlington Million (Dear Doctor)

DICK HANDLEN
1946: Withers Stakes (Hampden)
1948: Selima Stakes (Gaffery)
1949: Santa Susana Stakes (Gaffery)
Ladies Handicap (Gaffery)
1954: Delaware Oaks (Parlo)
Alabama Stakes (Parlo)
Beldame Handicap (Parlo)
Firenze Handicap (Parlo)
1955: Top Flight Handicap (Parlo)
Delaware Handicap (Parlo)
1956: Dixie Handicap (Chevation)
1957: Hopeful Stakes (Rose Trellis)
1960: Mother Goose Stakes (Berlo)
Coaching Club American Oaks (Berlo)
Beldame Stakes (Berlo)
Ladies Handicap (Berlo)

GEORGE HANDY
1973: Arkansas Derby (Impecunious)
1981: Illinois Derby (Paristo)

CARL HANFORD
1952: Monmouth Oaks (La Corredora)
1953: Ladies Handicap (La Corredora)
Comely Handicap (La Corredora)
1960: Jerome Handicap (Kelso)
Lawrence Realization Stakes (Kelso)
Hawthorne Gold Cup (Kelso)
Jockey Club Gold Cup (Kelso)
1961: Metropolitan Handicap (Kelso)
Suburban Handicap (Kelso)
Brooklyn Handicap (Kelso)
Woodward Stakes (Kelso)
Jockey Club Gold Cup (Kelso)
Whitney Handicap (Kelso)
1962: Woodward Stakes (Kelso)
Jockey Club Gold Cup (Kelso)
1963: Seminole Handicap (Kelso)
Gulfstream Park Handicap (Kelso)
John B. Campbell Handicap (Kelso)
Suburban Handicap (Kelso)
Aqueduct Stakes (Kelso)
Woodward Stakes (Kelso)
Jockey Club Gold Cup (Kelso)
Whitney Stakes (Kelso)
1964: Aqueduct Stakes (Kelso)
Jockey Club Gold Cup (Kelso)
Washington D.C. International (Kelso)
1965: Whitney Stakes (Kelso)

IRA HANFORD
1965: Lawrence Realization Stakes (Munden Point)
1966: Jersey Derby (Creme dela Creme)
Gallant Fox Handicap (Munden Point)
1967: Manhattan Handicap (Munden Point)

JOHN HANOVER
1952: Black Helen Handicap (Roman Miss)

JAMES HARDY
1981: Frizette Stakes (Proud Lou)

DON HARPER
1989: Oak Leaf Stakes (Dominant Dancer)

MIKE HARRINGTON
1996: Hollywood Futurity (Swiss Yodeler)
1998: Norfolk Stakes (Buck Trout)

MICKEY HARRISON
1947: Starlet Stakes (Zenoda)

CLARENCE HARTWICK
1951: Arlington Matron Handicap (Sickle's Image)
1953: Washington Park Handicap (Sickle's Image)

EOIN HARTY
2001: Breeders' Cup Juvenile Fillies (Tempera)

GUY HARWOOD
1984: Hollywood Turf Cup (Alphabatim)
1990: Man o' War Stakes (Defensive Play)
Turf Classic (Cacoethes)

ALEX HASSINGER JR.
1992: Arlington-Washington Lassie Stakes (Eliza)
Breeders' Cup Juvenile Fillies (Eliza)
Spinster Stakes (Fowda)
1993: Santa Anita Oaks (Eliza)
1999: Breeders' Cup Juvenile (Anees)

JAMES HASTIE
1959: Bougainvillea Turf Handicap (General Arthur)
1960: Bowling Green Handicap (Amber Morn)

WILLIAM HASTINGS
1988: Laurel Futurity (Luge II)

J.C. HAUER
1950: Kentucky Oaks (Ari's Mona)

HOWARD HAUSNER
1954: Pimlico Special (Helioscope)
Trenton Handicap (Helioscope)
1955: Massachusetts Handicap (Helioscope)
Suburban Handicap (Helioscope)
Monmouth Handicap (Helioscope)
1959: Sapling Stakes (Sky Clipper)

PHIL HAUSWALD
1986: Blue Grass Stakes (Bachelor Beau)
Arlington Classic (Sumptious)
1987: Arkansas Derby (Demons Begone)
Breeders' Cup Juvenile Fillies (Epitome)
1988: Spinster Stakes (Hail a Cab)
Ladies Handicap (Banker's Lady)
1989: Top Flight Handicap (Banker's Lady)

CASEY HAYES
1949: Cowdin Stakes (Hill Prince)
1950: Wood Memorial Stakes (Hill Prince)
Withers Stakes (Hill Prince)
Preakness Stakes (Hill Prince)
American Derby (Hill Prince)
Jerome Handicap (Hill Prince)
Jockey Club Gold Cup (Hill Prince)
Sunset Handicap (Hill Prince)
1951: Aqueduct Handicap (Bryan G.)
Westchester Handicap (Bryan G.)
Pimlico Special (Bryan G.)
New York Handicap (Hill Prince)
1955: Gazelle Stakes (Manotick)
Ladies Handicap (Manotick)
1956: Roamer Handicap (Third Brother)
1957: Molly Pitcher Handicap (Manotick)
1958: Hopeful Stakes (First Landing)
Champagne Stakes (First Landing)
Garden State Stakes (First Landing)
Spinaway Stakes (Rich Tradition)
Selima Stakes (Rich Tradition)
1959: Everglades Stakes (First Landing)
1960: Monmouth Handicap (First Landing)
Santa Anita Maturity (First Landing)
1961: Spinaway Stakes (Cicada)
Matron Stakes (Cicada)
Frizette Stakes (Cicada)
Gardenia Stakes (Cicada)
Sapling Stakes (Sir Gaylord)
1962: Kentucky Oaks (Cicada)
Acorn Stakes (Cicada)
Mother Goose Stakes (Cicada)
Beldame Stakes (Cicada)
Everglades Stakes (Sir Gaylord)
1963: Matron Stakes (Hasty Matelda)
1964: Sorority Stakes (Bold Experience)
1966: Gardenia Stakes (Pepperwood)
Gulfstream Park Handicap (First Family)
1967: Selima Stakes (Syrian Sea)
Gardenia Stakes (Gay Matelda)
1968: Spinaway Stakes (Queen's Double)
Alabama Stakes (Gay Matelda)

NORMAN HAYMAKER
1958: Arlington Classic (A Dragon Killer)
1960: Everglades Stakes (Moslem Chief)

EDDIE HAYWARD
1950: Inglewood Handicap (Miche)
1953: Garden State Stakes (Turn-to)
Kentucky Derby (Dark Star)
1954: Champagne Stakes (Flying Fury)
Coaching Club American Oaks (Cherokee Rose)
Flamingo Stakes (Turn-to)

RICHARD HAZELTON
1981: American Derby (Pocket Zipper)

CHRISTIANE HEAD
1994: Beverly D. Stakes (Hatoof)

BRUCE HEADLEY
1986: San Felipe Handicap (Variety Road)
1987: San Fernando Stakes (Variety Road)
1991: Del Mar Futurity (Bertrando)
Norfolk Stakes (Bertrando)
1992: San Felipe Stakes (Bertrando)
2000: Breeders' Cup Sprint (Kona Gold)
2001: San Carlos Handicap (Kona Gold)
2002: Santa Monica Handicap (Kalookan Queen)
Ancient Title BC Handicap (Kalookan Queen)
La Brea Stakes (Got Koko)

DUVAL HEADLEY
1950: Demoiselle Stakes (Aunt Jinny)
Selima Stakes (Aunt Jinny)

JIM HEALEY
1947: Delaware Oaks (Camargo)
1949: Tremont Stakes (Fox Time)

B. HEAP
1966: Arkansas Derby (Better Sea)

THOMAS HEARD JR.
1971: Sapling Stakes (Chevron Flight)
1973: Arlington-Washington Futurity (Lover John)
1975: Jerome Handicap (Guards Up)
1996: Fountain of Youth Stakes (Built for Pleasure)

DAN HENDRICKS
1985: Vanity Handicap (Private Persuasion)

MARK HENNIG
1993: Caesars International Handicap (Star of Cozzene)
Arlington Million (Star of Cozzene)
Man o' War Stakes (Star of Cozzene)
Santa Anita Derby (Personal Hope)
1994: Jerome Handicap (Prenup)
1998: Buick Pegasus Handicap (Tomorrows Cat)
Early Times Hollywood Derby (Vergennes)
2000: Matron Stakes (Raging Fever)
Frizette Stakes (Raging Fever)
2002: Ogden Phipps Handicap (Raging Fever)
Philip H. Iselin Handicap (Cat's at Home)
Personal Ensign Handicap (Summer Colony)
King's Bishop Stakes (Gygistar)

JOHN HERTLER
1984: Whitney Handicap (Slew O' Gold)
Woodward Stakes (Slew O' Gold)
Marlboro Cup Handicap (Slew O' Gold)
Jockey Club Gold Cup (Slew O' Gold)
1985: Hollywood Derby (Slew the Dragon)
1991: Ohio Derby (Private Man)

ROBERT HESS
1992: Del Mar Futurity (River Special)
Norfolk Stakes (River Special)
Hollywood Futurity (River Special)
1997: Californian Stakes (River Keen)
2002: Frank J. De Francis Memorial Dash (D'Wildcat)

NOEL HICKEY
1991: Flower Bowl Handicap (Lady Shirl)
1998: Turf Classic (Buck's Boy)
Breeders' Cup Turf (Buck's Boy)

WILLIAM HICKS
1955: Champagne Stakes (Beau Fond)

R.H. HIGHLEY
1959: Vanity Handicap (Zev's Joy)

WILLIAM HIGHTOWER
1974: Selima Stakes (Aunt Jin)
1975: New Orleans Handicap (Lord Rebeau)

SONNY HINE
1980: Dwyer Stakes (Amber Pass)
1981: Monmouth Handicap (Amber Pass)
Vosburgh Stakes (Guilty Conscience)
1985: Ohio Derby (Skip Trial)
Haskell Invitational Handicap (Skip Trial)
Pennsylvania Derby (Skip Trial)
1986: Gulfstream Park Handicap (Skip Trial)
1987: Gulfstream Park Handicap (Skip Trial)
1992: Florida Derby (Technology)
Haskell Invitational Handicap (Technology)
1996: Blue Grass Stakes (Skip Away)
Ohio Derby (Skip Away)
Buick Haskell Invitational Handicap (Skip Away)
Woodbine Million (Skip Away)
Jockey Club Gold Cup (Skip Away)
1997: Suburban Handicap (Skip Away)
Jockey Club Gold Cup (Skip Away)
Breeders' Cup Classic (Skip Away)
1998: Donn Handicap (Skip Away)
Gulfstream Park Handicap (Skip Away)
Pimlico Special (Skip Away)
Hollywood Gold Cup (Skip Away)
Philip H. Iselin Handicap (Skip Away)
Woodward Stakes (Skip Away)

BUDDY HIRSCH
1947: Sapling Stakes (Task)
1949: Discovery Handicap (Prophets Thumb)
1950: Arlington Futurity (To Market)
Washington Park Futurity (To Market)
1951: Washington Park Handicap (Curandero)
1952: San Juan Capistrano Handicap (Intent)
Santa Anita Maturity (Intent)
San Carlos Handicap (To Market)
Will Rogers Stakes (Forelock)
1953: Westerner Stakes (Rejected)
San Juan Capistrano Handicap (Intent)
1954: Santa Anita Handicap (Rejected)
American Handicap (Rejected)
San Juan Capistrano Handicap (By Zeus)
1955: Hollywood Gold Cup (Rejected)
1962: Santa Anita Derby (Royal Attack)
1963: San Juan Capistrano Handicap (Pardao)
1964: Los Angeles Handicap (Cyrano)
1966: Sunset Handicap (O'Hara)
1968: Santa Susana Stakes (Allie's Serenade)
1969: Monmouth Oaks (Gallant Bloom)
Gazelle Handicap (Gallant Bloom)
Spinster Stakes (Gallant Bloom)
1970: Santa Margarita Handicap (Gallant Bloom)
1972: Vosburgh Handicap (Triple Bend)

MAX HIRSCH
1946: Wood Memorial Stakes (Assault)
Kentucky Derby (Assault)
Preakness Stakes (Assault)
Belmont Stakes (Assault)
Dwyer Stakes (Assault)
Pimlico Special (Assault)
Westchester Handicap (Assault)
Carter Handicap (Flood Town)
1947: Pimlico Oaks (But Why Not)
Acorn Stakes (But Why Not)
Alabama Stakes (But Why Not)
Arlington Matron Handicap (But Why Not)
Beldame Handicap (But Why Not)
Arlington Classic (But Why Not)
Grey Lag Handicap (Assault)
Dixie Handicap (Assault)
Suburban Handicap (Assault)
Brooklyn Handicap (Assault)
Saratoga Special (Better Self)
Westchester Handicap (Bridal Flower)
1948: Pimlico Oaks (Scattered)
Coaching Club American Oaks (Scattered)
Discovery Handicap (Better Self)

MAX HIRSCH *(Continued)*

Westchester Handicap (Better Self)
Arlington Lassie Stakes (Pail of Water)
1949: Firenze Handicap (But Why Not)
Top Flight Handicap (But Why Not)
Hopeful Stakes (Middleground)
Carter Handicap (Better Self)
Brooklyn Handicap (Assault)
1950: Kentucky Derby (Middleground)
Belmont Stakes (Middleground)
Gallant Fox Handicap (Better Self)
1951: Firenze Handicap (Renew)
1952: Massachusetts Handicap (To Market)
Arlington Handicap (To Market)
Hawthorne Gold Cup (To Market)
Top Flight Handicap (Renew)
Comely Handicap (Devilkin)
1953: Discovery Handicap (Level Lea)
Jockey Club Gold Cup (Level Lea)
1954: Belmont Stakes (High Gun)
Dwyer Stakes (High Gun)
Jockey Club Gold Cup (High Gun)
Manhattan Handicap (High Gun)
Acorn Stakes (Riverina)
Gazelle Handicap (On Your Own)
Vineland Handicap (Spinning Top)
Hawthorne Gold Cup (Rejected)
1955: Metropolitan Handicap (High Gun)
Brooklyn Handicap (High Gun)
Alabama Stakes (Rico Reta)
1956: Delaware Oaks (Dotted Line)
1957: Alabama Stakes (Here and There)
Vineland Handicap (Dotted Line)
1959: Coaching Club American Oaks (Resaca)
Delaware Oaks (Resaca)
Selima Stakes (La Fuerza)
Dwyer Handicap (Waltz)
Man o' War Handicap (Dotted Line)
1961: Selima Stakes (Tamarona)
1962: Vineland Handicap (Tamarona)
1964: Grey Lag Handicap (Saidam)
1966: Withers Stakes (Indulto)
Suburban Handicap (Buffle)
1968: Matron Stakes (Gallant Bloom)
Gardenia Stakes (Gallant Bloom)
Jersey Derby (Out of the Way)
Massachusetts Handicap (Out of the Way)
Withers Stakes (Call Me Prince)

MAX HIRSCH JR.

1947: Coaching Club American Oaks (Harmonica)

JACK HODGINS

1946: Arlington Lassie Stakes (Four Winds)
1947: Breeders' Futurity (Shy Guy)
1948: Arlington Matron Handicap (Four Winds)
New Orleans Handicap (Star Reward)
1949: Princess Pat Stakes (Here's Hoping)
1951: Kentucky Jockey Club Stakes (Sub Fleet)
1952: Arlington Lassie Stakes (Fulvous)
Princess Pat Stakes (Fulvous)
1953: Hawthorne Gold Cup (Sub Fleet)
1957: Breeders' Futurity (Fulcrum)

HAROLD HODOSH

1975: Vosburgh Handicap (No Bias)

HOWARD HOFFMAN

1949: Kentucky Jockey Club Stakes (Roman Bath)
1952: Washington Park Futurity (Mr. Paradise)
1953: Delaware Oaks (Cerise Reine)
1957: Ohio Derby (Manteau)

DAVID HOFMANS

1994: Milady Handicap (Andestine)
Molson Export Million (Dramatic Gold)
Hollywood Derby (River Flyer)
1995: Acorn Stakes (Cat's Cradle)
1996: San Antonio Handicap (Alphabet Soup)
Breeders' Cup Classic (Alphabet Soup)
Buick Meadowlands Cup Handicap (Dramatic Gold)
1997: Belmont Stakes (Touch Gold)
Buick Haskell Invitational Handicap (Touch Gold)
Jim Dandy Stakes (Awesome Again)
2000: Vinery Del Mar Debutante Stakes (Cindy's Hero)
2001: Lane's End Breeders' Futurity (Siphonic)
Hollywood Futurity (Siphonic)
Toyota Blue Grass Stakes (Millennium Wind)
2003: Breeders' Cup Distaff (Adoration)

JERRY HOLLENDORFER

1988: Hollywood Futurity (King Glorious)
1989: Ohio Derby (King Glorious)
Haskell Invitational Handicap (King Glorious)
1991: Fantasy Stakes (Lite Light)
Kentucky Oaks (Lite Light)
Coaching Club American Oaks (Lite Light)
1996: Kentucky Oaks (Pike Place Dancer)
1998: Jim Beam Stakes (Event of the Year)
2000: Turfway Spiral Stakes (Globalize)

BILL HOLMES

1969: San Antonio Stakes (Praise Jay)

LESTER HOLT

1966: California Derby (Tragniew)
1982: Hollywood Turf Cup (Prince Spellbound)
1983: Eddie Read Handicap (Prince Spellbound)

ROBERT HOLTHUS

1962: Massachusetts Handicap (Air Pilot)
1965: Ohio Derby (Terri Hi)
1988: Arkansas Derby (Proper Reality)
Illinois Derby (Proper Reality)
1989: Metropolitan Handicap (Proper Reality)
Philip H. Iselin Handicap (Proper Reality)

EDWARD HOLTON

1970: Futurity Stakes (Salem)

STANLEY HOUGH

1981: Blue Grass Stakes (Proud Appeal)
1982: Secretariat Stakes (Half Iced)
1991: Arlington-Washington Futurity (Caller I.D.)
1993: Sword Dancer Handicap (Spectacular Tide)

NEIL HOWARD

1989: Hopeful Stakes (Summer Squall)
1990: Jim Beam Stakes (Summer Squall)
Blue Grass Stakes (Summer Squall)
Preakness Stakes (Summer Squall)
Pennsylvania Derby (Summer Squall)
1991: Arlington-Washington Lassie Stakes (Speed Dialer)
1992: Ashland Stakes (Prospectors Delite)
Acorn Stakes (Prospectors Delite)
1997: Alabama Stakes (Runup the Colors)
Ruffian Handicap (Tomisue's Delight)
1998: Fountain of Youth Stakes (Lil's Lad)
Personal Ensign Handicap (Tomisue's Delight)
2000: Kentucky Oaks (Secret Status)
Mother Goose Stakes (Secret Status)
2003: Pimlico Special (Mineshaft)
Suburban Handicap (Mineshaft)
Woodward Stakes (Mineshaft)
Jockey Club Gold Cup (Mineshaft)

PETER HOWE

1976: Top Flight Handicap (Proud Delta)
Hempstead Handicap (Proud Delta)
Beldame Stakes (Proud Delta)

DEAN HOWELL

1959: Arkansas Derby (Al Davelle)

HOLLIE HUGHES

1946: Flamingo Stakes (Round View)
1947: Monmouth Handicap (Round View)
1949: Whitney Stakes (Round View)
1958: Bowling Green Handicap (Rafty)

ALLEN HULTZ

1955: Princess Pat Stakes (Supple)
1960: Delaware Oaks (Rash Statement)
Spinster Stakes (Rash Statement)

LEONARD HUNT

1953: Vineland Handicap (Mi-Marigold)
1956: Sapling Stakes (King Hairan)
Hopeful Stakes (King Hairan)

LEONARD IMPERIO

1975: Bowling Green Handicap (Barcas)
1982: Illinois Derby (Star Gallant)

DOMINIC IMPRESCIA

1981: Hopeful Stakes (Timely Writer)
Champagne Stakes (Timely Writer)
1982: Flamingo Stakes (Timely Writer)
Florida Derby (Timely Writer)
1991: Secretariat Stakes (Jackie Wackie)

EDUARDO INDA

1997: Santa Monica Handicap (Toga Toga Toga)
1999: Santa Maria Handicap (India Divina)
2000: Santa Margarita Handicap (Riboletta)
Milady Breeders' Cup Handicap (Riboletta)
Vanity Handicap (Riboletta)
Ruffian Handicap (Riboletta)
Beldame Stakes (Riboletta)

STEVE IPPOLITO

1961: Arkansas Derby (Light Talk)
United Nations Handicap (Oink)
1967: Santa Margarita Handicap (Miss Moona)
1969: San Felipe Handicap (Elect the Ruler)
1970: Century Handicap (Quilche)
San Luis Rey Handicap (Quilche)

ROBERT IRWIN

1967: Oaklawn Handicap (Mike's Red)

GERALD JABALEE

1976: Hialeah Turf Cup (Legion)
1977: Donn Handicap (Legion)

BRUCE JACKSON

1990: Swaps Stakes (Jovial)
1991: San Fernando Stakes (In Excess)
Metropolitan Handicap (In Excess)
Suburban Handicap (In Excess)
Whitney Handicap (In Excess)
Woodward Stakes (In Excess)
1993: Oaklawn Handicap (Jovial)

EVAN JACKSON

1968: Santa Anita Handicap (Mr. Right)
Woodward Stakes (Mr. Right)
1969: Suburban Handicap (Mr. Right)
1970: Acorn Stakes (Cathy Honey)
Ladies Handicap (Cathy Honey)
Amory L. Haskell Handicap (Gladwin)
Hawthorne Gold Cup (Gladwin)
1973: Oak Tree Invitational Stakes (Portentous)
1974: Del Mar Handicap (Redtop III)
1976: Century Handicap (Winds of Thought)

MONTY JACKSON

1985: California Derby (Hajji's Treasure)

EUGENE JACOBS

1951: Queens County Handicap (Sheilas Reward)
1958: Lawrence Realization Stakes (Martins Rullah)
1961: Remsen Stakes (Figaro Bob)
1966: Saratoga Special (Favorable Turn)
1968: Donn Handicap (Favorable Turn)
1969: Garden State Stakes (Forum)
1974: American Derby (Determined King)
1977: Florida Derby (Ruthie's Native)
1979: Champagne Stakes (Joanie's Chief)
1980: Arlington-Washington Futurity (Well Decorated)
1986: Tropical Park Derby (Strong Performance)
1987: Hutcheson Stakes (Well Selected)

HIRSCH JACOBS

1946: Grey Lag Handicap (Stymie)
Whitney Stakes (Stymie)
Manhattan Handicap (Stymie)
New York Handicap (Stymie)
Gallant Fox Handicap (Stymie)
Molly Pitcher Handicap (Mahmoudess)
1947: Metropolitan Handicap (Stymie)
Massachusetts Handicap (Stymie)
Aqueduct Handicap (Stymie)
Gallant Fox Handicap (Stymie)
1948: Metropolitan Handicap (Stymie)
Aqueduct Handicap (Stymie)
1949: Roseben Handicap (Up Beat)
1950: Westchester Handicap (Palestinian)
1951: Brooklyn Handicap (Palestinian)
Golden Gate Handicap (Palestinian)
Acorn Stakes (Nothirdchance)
1954: John B. Campbell Memorial Handicap (Joe Jones)
1956: Top Flight Handicap (Searching)
Diana Handicap (Searching)
Maskette Handicap (Searching)
1957: Lawrence Realization Stakes (Promised Land)
Roamer Handicap (Promised Land)
Pimlico Special (Promised Land)
1958: John B. Campbell Mem. Handicap (Promised Land)
Massachusetts Handicap (Promised Land)
San Juan Capistrano Handicap (Promised Land)
Molly Pitcher Handicap (Searching)
Diana Handicap (Searching)
1960: Sapling Stakes (Hail to Reason)
Hopeful Stakes (Hail to Reason)
1961: Santa Margarita Handicap (Sister Antoine)
1962: Sorority Stakes (Affectionately)

Spinaway Stakes (Affectionately)
1964: Arlington-Washington Lassie Stakes (Admiring)
1965: Gotham Stakes (Flag Raiser)
Wood Memorial Stakes (Flag Raiser)
Withers Stakes (Flag Raiser)
Futurity Stakes (Priceless Gem)
Frizette Stakes (Priceless Gem)
Top Flight Handicap (Affectionately)
Ladies Handicap (Straight Deal)
1966: Santa Margarita Handicap (Straight Deal)
Santa Barbara Handicap (Straight Deal)
Frizette Stakes (Regal Gleam)
San Fernando Stakes (Isle of Greece)
1967: Everglades Stakes (Reflected Glory)
Flamingo Stakes (Reflected Glory)
Top Flight Handicap (Straight Deal)
1968: Flamingo Stakes (Wise Exchange)
1969: Futurity Stakes (High Echelon)

JEFF JACOBS

1999: Hempstead Handicap (Sister Act)

JOHN JACOBS

1965: Hollywood Oaks (Straight Deal)
1966: Selima Stakes (Regal Gleam)
1967: Delaware Handicap (Straight Deal)
Spinster Stakes (Straight Deal)
California Derby (Reason to Hail)
1969: Pimlico-Laurel Futurity (High Echelon)
1970: Wood Memorial Stakes (Personality)
Preakness Stakes (Personality)
Jersey Derby (Personality)
Woodward Stakes (Personality)
Belmont Stakes (High Echelon)
1971: Cowdin Stakes (Loquacious Don)
1972: United Nations Handicap (Acclimatization)
1974: Fountain of Youth Stakes (Green Gambados)

SID JACOBS

1954: United Nations Handicap (Closed Door)
1957: Bougainvillea Turf Handicap (Espea)
1959: Hialeah Turf Cup (Tudor Era)
1962: Saratoga Special (Mr. Cold Storage)

BUDDY JACOBSON

1963: Futurity Stakes (Bupers)
1965: Sanford Stakes (Flame Tree)

WHITEY JANSEN

1952: Louisiana Derby (Gushing Oil)
Blue Grass Stakes (Gushing Oil)
Stars and Stripes Handicap (Royal Mustang)

CHUCK JENDA

1989: Yellow Ribbon Stakes (Brown Bess)
1990: Santa Barbara Handicap (Brown Bess)

SUZANNE JENKINS

1987: Remsen Stakes (Batty)

LARRY JENNINGS

1978: Monmouth Invitational Handicap (Delta Flag)
1987: Widener Handicap (Launch a Pegasus)

ALBERT JENSEN

1950: Remsen Handicap (Repetoire)
1951: Wood Memorial Stakes (Repetoire)

KAY JENSEN

1952: Roamer Handicap (Quiet Step)
Manhattan Handicap (Lone Eagle)
1955: Aqueduct Handicap (Icarian)
1958: Jerome Handicap (Warhead)
Roamer Handicap (Warhead)
Manhattan Handicap (Warhead)
1960: Whitney Handicap (Warhead)
1968: Dixie Handicap (High Hat)
Bowling Green Handicap (High Hat)
1974: Manhattan Handicap (Golden Don)

ALLEN JERKENS

1957: Gallant Fox Handicap (Eddie Schmidt)
1958: Gallant Fox Handicap (Admiral Vee)
1962: Suburban Handicap (Beau Purple)
Brooklyn Handicap (Beau Purple)
Hawthorne Gold Cup (Beau Purple)
Man o' War Stakes (Beau Purple)
1963: Black Helen Handicap (Pocosaba)
Widener Handicap (Beau Purple)
1965: Seminole Handicap (Sunstruck)
Gallant Fox Handicap (Choker)
1967: Amory L. Haskell Handicap (Handsome Boy)
Brooklyn Handicap (Handsome Boy)
Washington Park Handicap (Handsome Boy)
Black Helen Handicap (Mac's Sparkler)
Beldame Stakes (Mac's Sparkler)
1969: Manhattan Handicap (Harem Lady)
1970: Black Helen Handicap (Taken Aback)
Spinster Stakes (Taken Aback)
Widener Handicap (Never Bow)
1971: Delaware Handicap (Blessing Angelica)
Metropolitan Handicap (Tunex)
Vosburgh Handicap (Duck Dance)
1972: Delaware Handicap (Blessing Angelica)
1973: Widener Handicap (Vertee)
John B. Campbell Handicap (Vertee)
Woodward Stakes (Prove Out)
Jockey Club Gold Cup (Prove Out)
Top Flight Handicap (Poker Night)
Ladies Handicap (Wakefield Miss)
Jerome Handicap (Step Nicely)
Carter Handicap (King's Bishop)
Whitney Stakes (Onion)
1974: Hempstead Handicap (Poker Night)
Grey Lag Handicap (Prove Out)
Hawthorne Gold Cup (Group Plan)
1975: Jockey Club Gold Cup (Group Plan)
1978: Jerome Handicap (Sensitive Prince)
1979: Gulfstream Park Handicap (Sensitive Prince)
1981: Brooklyn Handicap (Hechizado)
1982: Hollywood Derby (Victory Zone)
1984: Monmouth Handicap (Believe the Queen)
1985: Top Flight Handicap (Flip's Pleasure)
1988: Acorn Stakes (Aptostar)
1992: Gotham Stakes (Devil His Due)
Wood Memorial Stakes (Devil His Due)
Shuvee Handicap (Missy's Mirage)
Hempstead Handicap (Missy's Mirage)
Alabama Stakes (November Snow)
Matron Stakes (Sky Beauty)
1993: Acorn Stakes (Sky Beauty)
Mother Goose Stakes (Sky Beauty)
Coaching Club American Oaks (Sky Beauty)
Alabama Stakes (Sky Beauty)
Gulfstream Park Handicap (Devil His Due)
Pimlico Special (Devil His Due)
Suburban Handicap (Devil His Due)
Peter Pan Stakes (Virginia Rapids)
1994: Shuvee Handicap (Sky Beauty)
Hempstead Handicap (Sky Beauty)
Go for Wand Stakes (Sky Beauty)
Ruffian Handicap (Sky Beauty)
Brooklyn Handicap (Devil His Due)
Suburban Handicap (Devil His Due)
Carter Handicap (Virginia Rapids)
1997: Gazelle Handicap (Royal Indy)
1998: Frank J. De Francis Memorial Dash (Kelly Kip)
Jerome Handicap (Limit Out)
Jockey Club Gold Cup (Wagon Limit)
2001: Ballerina Handicap (Shine Again)
2002: Ballerina Handicap (Shine Again)
2003: Prioress Stakes (House Party)
Personal Ensign Handicap (Passing Shot)
Frizette Stakes (Society Selection)

JIM JERKENS

2002: Humana Distaff Handicap (Celtic Melody)

STEVE JERKENS

1982: Remsen Stakes (Pax in Bello)

JAMES JIMENEZ

1970: Cinema Handicap (D'Artagnan)
1974: California Derby (Agitate)
Swaps Stakes (Agitate)
Hollywood Derby (Agitate)
1977: Del Mar Debutante Stakes (Extravagant)

L.G. JOFFRION

1959: Kentucky Jockey Club Stakes (Oil Wick)

H.E. JOHNSON

1973: Hopeful Stakes (Gusty O'Shay)

MURRAY JOHNSON

2003: Stephen Foster Handicap (Perfect Drift)

PHIL JOHNSON

1973: Cinema Handicap (Amen II)
Hollywood Derby (Amen II)
1976: Dwyer Handicap (Quiet Little Table)
1977: Carter Handicap (Quiet Little Table)
Suburban Handicap (Quiet Little Table)
1978: American Derby (Nasty and Bold)
Brooklyn Handicap (Nasty and Bold)
Carter Handicap (Jaipur's Gem)
1982: United Nations Handicap (Naskra's Breeze)
Man o' War Stakes (Naskra's Breeze)
1983: Coaching Club American Oaks (High Schemes)
1987: Top Flight Handicap (Ms. Eloise)
1988: Alabama Stakes (Maplejinsky)
1989: Ladies Handicap (Dance Teacher)
1993: Flower Bowl Handicap (Far Out Beast)
1995: Sword Dancer Invitational Handicap (Kiri's Clown)
2002: Breeders' Cup Classic (Volponi)

BUCKY JOLIN

1990: Young America Stakes (Southern Sign)

LeROY JOLLEY

1961: Arlington Futurity (Ridan)
Washington Park Futurity (Ridan)
Arlington Lassie Stakes (Rudoma)
1962: Florida Derby (Ridan)
Blue Grass Stakes (Ridan)
Arlington Classic (Ridan)
1963: Saratoga Special (Duel)
Breeders' Futurity (Duel)
1972: Sorority Stakes (Sparkalark)
1973: Manhattan Handicap (London Company)
1974: Sapling Stakes (Foolish Pleasure)
Hopeful Stakes (Foolish Pleasure)
Champagne Stakes (Foolish Pleasure)
Pan American Handicap (London Company)
1975: Matron Stakes (Optimistic Gal)
Frizette Stakes (Optimistic Gal)
Alcibiades Stakes (Optimistic Gal)
Selima Stakes (Optimistic Gal)
Champagne Stakes (Honest Pleasure)
Laurel Futurity (Honest Pleasure)
Arlington-Washington Futurity (Honest Pleasure)
Flamingo Stakes (Foolish Pleasure)
Wood Memorial Stakes (Foolish Pleasure)
Kentucky Derby (Foolish Pleasure)
1976: Ashland Stakes (Optimistic Gal)
Kentucky Oaks (Optimistic Gal)
Alabama Stakes (Optimistic Gal)
Delaware Handicap (Optimistic Gal)
Spinster Stakes (Optimistic Gal)
Flamingo Stakes (Honest Pleasure)
Florida Derby (Honest Pleasure)
Blue Grass Stakes (Honest Pleasure)
Travers Stakes (Honest Pleasure)
Donn Handicap (Foolish Pleasure)
Suburban Handicap (Foolish Pleasure)
Futurity Stakes (For the Moment)
1977: Maskette Handicap (What a Summer)
Blue Grass Stakes (For the Moment)
Whitney Handicap (Nearly On Time)
1978: Hopeful Stakes (General Assembly)
1979: Travers Stakes (General Assembly)
Vosburgh Stakes (General Assembly)
1980: Ruffian Handicap (Genuine Risk)
Kentucky Derby (Genuine Risk)
1981: Breeders' Futurity (D'Accord)
1983: Sorority Stakes (Officer's Ball)
Alabama Stakes (Spit Curl)
1984: Dwyer Stakes (Track Barron)
Vosburgh Stakes (Track Barron)
Coaching Club American Oaks (Class Play)
1985: Woodward Stakes (Track Barron)
Whitney Handicap (Track Barron)
Illinois Derby (Important Business)
Champagne Stakes (Mogambo)
Remsen Stakes (Pillaster)
1986: United Nations Handicap (Manila)
Turf Classic (Manila)
Breeders' Cup Turf (Manila)
Hopeful Stakes (Gulch)
Futurity Stakes (Gulch)
Gotham Stakes (Mogambo)
1987: Wood Memorial Stakes (Gulch)
Metropolitan Handicap (Gulch)
United Nations Handicap (Manila)
Budweiser-Arlington Million (Manila)
Peter Pan Stakes (Leo Castelli)
Hollywood Derby (Stately Don)
1988: Young America Stakes (Irish Actor)
1990: Matron Stakes (Meadow Star)
Spinaway Stakes (Meadow Star)
Frizette Stakes (Meadow Star)
Breeders' Cup Juvenile Fillies (Meadow Star)
Ladies Handicap (Colonial Waters)
1991: Acorn Stakes (Meadow Star)
Mother Goose Stakes (Meadow Star)
Matron Stakes (Anh Duong)

MOODY JOLLEY

1950: Acorn Stakes (Siama)
Monmouth Oaks (Siama)
Comely Handicap (Siama)
1951: Champagne Stakes (Armageddon)
1952: Gazelle Stakes (Hushaby Baby)
Withers Stakes (Armageddon)
1954: Arlington Lassie Stakes (Delta)
Princess Pat Stakes (Delta)
1955: Matron Stakes (Doubledogdare)
Alcibiades Stakes (Doubledogdare)
1956: Breeders' Futurity (Round Table)
Arlington Matron Handicap (Delta)
Spinster Stakes (Doubledogdare)
1957: Acorn Stakes (Bayou)
Delaware Oaks (Bayou)
Gazelle Handicap (Bayou)
Maskette Handicap (Bayou)
Sapling Stakes (Plion)
Garden State Stakes (Nadir)
Spinaway Stakes (Sequoia)
1958: American Derby (Nadir)
1959: Arlington Classic (Dunce)
American Derby (Dunce)
Arlington Lassie Stakes (Monarchy)
1967: Kentucky Jockey Club Stakes (Mr. Brogann)

TOM JOLLEY

1958: Blue Grass Stakes (Plion)
1959: Whitney Stakes (Plion)

CECIL JOLLY

1957: Santa Anita Derby (Sir William)
1958: Los Angeles Handicap (How Now)
American Handicap (How Now)
1966: Hollywood Oaks (Spearfish)
1974: San Felipe Handicap (Aloha Mood)

BEN JONES

1946: Widener Handicap (Armed)
Washington Park Handicap (Armed)
Arlington Matron Handicap (Good Blood)
1947: Blue Grass Stakes (Faultless)
1948: Blue Grass Stakes (Coaltown)
Kentucky Derby (Citation)
Dixie Handicap (Fervent)
1949: Kentucky Oaks (Wistful)
Kentucky Derby (Ponder)
1950: Black Helen Handicap (Bewitch)
1951: Arlington Futurity (Hill Gail)
1952: Kentucky Oaks (Real Delight)
Black-Eyed Susan Stakes (Real Delight)
Coaching Club American Oaks (Real Delight)
Arlington Matron Stakes (Real Delight)
Beldame Handicap (Real Delight)
Arlington Classic (Mark-Ye-Well)
American Derby (Mark-Ye-Well)
Lawrence Realization Stakes (Mark-Ye-Well)
Santa Anita Derby (Hill Gail)
Kentucky Derby (Hill Gail)
1953: Kentucky Oaks (Bubbley)
Arlington Matron Handicap (Real Delight)

FARRELL JONES

1967: Californian Stakes (Biggs)
1968: San Luis Rey Handicap (Biggs)
1971: Santa Margarita Handicap (Manta)
Beverly Hills Handicap (Manta)
Santa Barbara Handicap (Manta)

GARY JONES

1976: San Antonio Stakes (Lightning Mandate)
1978: Swaps Stakes (Radar Ahead)
1979: San Fernando Stakes (Radar Ahead)
1980: Gamely Handicap (Wishing Well)
1981: Californian Stakes (Eleven Stitches)
1983: Norfolk Stakes (Fali Time)
Hollywood Futurity (Fali Time)
1984: San Felipe Handicap (Fali Time)
Santa Barbara Handicap (Comedy Act)
1985: Swaps Stakes (Padua)
1986: Widener Handicap (Turkoman)
Marlboro Cup Handicap (Turkoman)
1988: La Canada Stakes (Hollywood Glitter)
Apple Blossom Handicap (By Land By Sea)
1989: Fantasy Stakes (Fantastic Look)
1990: NYRA Mile Handicap (Quiet American)
1991: Swaps Stakes (Best Pal)
Pacific Classic (Best Pal)
Sunset Handicap (Black Monday)
Yellow Ribbon Stakes (Kostroma)
1992: Charles H. Strub Stakes (Best Pal)
Santa Anita Handicap (Best Pal)
Oaklawn Handicap (Best Pal)
Santa Barbara Handicap (Kostroma)
Beverly D. Stakes (Kostroma)
1993: Hollywood Gold Cup (Best Pal)
Del Mar Futurity (Winning Pact)
1994: Santa Anita Oaks (Lakeway)
Mother Goose Stakes (Lakeway)
Hollywood Oaks (Lakeway)
Santa Anita Handicap (Stuka)

HERBERT JONES

1971: Ladies Handicap (Sea Saga)

JIMMY JONES

1946: Dixie Handicap (Armed)
Suburban Handicap (Armed)
Vineland Handicap (Good Blood)
1947: McLennan Handicap (Armed)
Widener Handicap (Armed)
Gulfstream Park Handicap (Armed)
Stars and Stripes Handicap (Armed)
Arlington Handicap (Armed)
Washington Park Handicap (Armed)
Washington Park Futurity (Bewitch)
Arlington Lassie Stakes (Bewitch)
Princess Pat Stakes (Bewitch)
Withers Stakes (Faultless)
Flamingo Stakes (Faultless)
Preakness Stakes (Faultless)
Pimlico Futurity (Citation)
Futurity Stakes (Citation)
Selima Stakes (Whirl Some)
Marguerite Stakes (Whirl Some)
American Derby (Fervent)
Pimlico Special (Fervent)
1948: Flamingo Stakes (Citation)
Preakness Stakes (Citation)
Belmont Stakes (Citation)
American Derby (Citation)
Jockey Club Gold Cup (Citation)
Stars and Stripes Handicap (Citation)
Pimlico Special (Citation)
Jerome Handicap (Coaltown)
Gallant Fox Handicap (Faultless)
Washington Park Handicap (Fervent)
1949: McLennan Handicap (Coaltown)
Widener Handicap (Coaltown)
Gulfstream Park Handicap (Coaltown)
Gallant Fox Handicap (Coaltown)
Stars and Stripes Handicap (Coaltown)
Arlington Handicap (Coaltown)
Washington Park Handicap (Coaltown)
Arlington Classic (Ponder)
American Derby (Ponder)
Lawrence Realization Stakes (Ponder)
Jockey Club Gold Cup (Ponder)
Pimlico Oaks (Wistful)
Coaching Club American Oaks (Wistful)
Champagne Stakes (Theory)
Arlington Lassie Stakes (Dutchess Peg)
Vineland Handicap (Bewitch)
1950: San Antonio Handicap (Ponder)
Arlington Handicap (Ponder)
Santa Anita Maturity (Ponder)
Santa Margarita Handicap (Two Lea)
1951: American Handicap (Citation)
Hollywood Gold Cup (Citation)
Princess Pat Stakes (A Gleam)
Vanity Handicap (Bewitch)
San Antonio Handicap (All Blue)
1952: Hollywood Oaks (A Gleam)
Cinema Handicap (A Gleam)
Westerner Stakes (A Gleam)
Vanity Handicap (Two Lea)
Hollywood Gold Cup (Two Lea)
Del Mar Debutante Stakes (Lap Full)
1953: Santa Anita Handicap (Mark-Ye-Well)
Santa Anita Maturity (Mark-Ye-Well)
Starlet Stakes (Arrogate)
Santa Anita Derby (Chanlea)
Golden Gate Handicap (Fleet Bird)
1954: Cinema Handicap (Miz Clementine)
California Derby (Miz Clementine)
San Antonio Handicap (Mark-Ye-Well)
Sunset Handicap (Fleet Bird)
Vanity Handicap (Bubbley)
1956: Kentucky Oaks (Princess Turia)
Acorn Stakes (Princess Turia)
Acorn Stakes (Beyond)
Garden State Stakes (Barbizon)
Everglades Stakes (Liberty Sun)
Preakness Stakes (Fabius)
Trenton Handicap (Bardstown)
1957: Tropical Handicap (Bardstown)
Widener Handicap (Bardstown)
Gulfstream Park Handicap (Bardstown)
Everglades Stakes (Gen. Duke)
Florida Derby (Gen. Duke)
Black Helen Handicap (Amoret)
Delaware Handicap (Princess Turia)
Kentucky Derby (Iron Liege)
1958: Everglades Stakes (Tim Tam)
Flamingo Stakes (Tim Tam)
Florida Derby (Tim Tam)
Kentucky Derby (Tim Tam)
Preakness Stakes (Tim Tam)
Coaching Club American Oaks (A Glitter)
Monmouth Oaks (A Glitter)
McLennan Handicap (Iron Liege)
1959: Tropical Park Handicap (Bardstown)
Widener Handicap (Bardstown)
Black Helen Handicap (Rosewood)
1960: Tropical Park Handicap (On-and-On)
McLennan Handicap (On-and-On)
Brooklyn Handicap (On-and-On)
1961: American Derby (Beau Prince)
Travers Stakes (Beau Prince)
McLennan Handicap (Yorky)
Widener Handicap (Yorky)
1962: Widener Handicap (Yorky)
Michigan Mile and One-Sixteenth (Beau Prince)
1964: Black Helen Handicap (Princess Arle)

MARTIN JONES

1996: Gamely Handicap (Auriette)

W.L. JONES JR.

1947: Vineland Handicap (Miss Kimo)

HAROLD JORDAN JR.

1984: Illinois Derby (Delta Trace)

JAMES JORDAN

1951: San Felipe Stakes (Phil D.)
1952: San Antonio Handicap (Phil D.)
1982: Hollywood Starlet Stakes (Fabulous Notion)
San Antonio Stakes (Score Twenty Four)
1983: Santa Susana Stakes (Fabulous Notion)

IAN JORY

1990: Del Mar Futurity (Best Pal)
Norfolk Stakes (Best Pal)
Hollywood Futurity (Best Pal)

KENNETH JUMPS

1989: Hollywood Starlet Stakes (Cheval Volant)

MAX KAHLBAUM

1953: Manhattan Handicap (Jampol)

ELMER KALENSKY

1954: Michigan Mile (Spur On)
1959: Louisiana Derby (Master Palynch)

DAVE KASSEN

1981: Oak Leaf Stakes (Header Card)
1987: Jersey Derby (Avies Copy)

MICHAEL KATZ

2003: Secretariat Stakes (Kicken Kris)

ROD KAUFMAN

1972: Hollywood Juvenile Championship (Bold Liz)

MIKE KAY

1977: Washington D.C. International (Johnny D.)
Turf Classic (Johnny D.)

FRANK KEARNS

1946: Acorn Stakes (Earshot)
1949: Astoria Stakes (Baby Comet)
1950: Whitney Stakes (Piet)

J.P. KEEZEK

1953: Stars and Stripes Handicap (Abbe Sting)

MARY KEIM

1965: Kentucky Oaks (Amerivan)

PETE KEISER

1963: Ohio Derby (Lemon Twist)
1964: Louisiana Derby (Grecian Princess)

F. KELLER
1946: Longacres Mile (Amble In)

PAUL KELLEY
1948: Arlington Handicap (Stud Poker)
Miami Beach Handicap (Stud Poker)
1951: McLennan Handicap (Gangway)
1959: Florida Derby (Easy Spur)
1960: Canadian Championship Stakes (Rocky Royale)
1961: Arlington Handicap (Tudorich)
1968: Gazelle Handicap (Another Nell)

TOM KELLEY
1954: Arlington Matron Handicap (Lavender Hill)
Ladies Handicap (Lavender Hill)
1973: Hawthorne Gold Cup (Tri Jet)
1974: Kentucky Oaks (Quaze Quilt)
1975: Spinster Stakes (Susan's Girl)

WALTER KELLEY
1955: Garden State Stakes (Prince John)
1959: Hawthorne Gold Cup (Day Court)
1960: Display Handicap (Nickel Boy)
1961: Manhattan Handicap (Nickel Boy)
1963: Everglades Stakes (B. Major)
Gallant Fox Handicap (Sunrise Flight)

EDWARD KELLY
1952: Pimlico Futurity (Isasmoothie)
Matron Stakes (Is Proud)
1956: Fall Highweight Handicap (Impromptu)
1957: Fall Highweight Handicap (Itobe)
1958: Futurity Stakes (Intentionally)
Pimlico Futurity (Intentionally)
1959: Withers Stakes (Intentionally)
Jerome Handicap (Intentionally)
1984: Jerome Handicap (Is Your Pleasure)

PAT KELLY
1978: Dwyer Handicap (Junction)
1981: Remsen Stakes (Laser Light)
1991: Man o' War Stakes (Solar Splendor)
Turf Classic (Solar Splendor)
1992: Hollywood Gold Cup (Sultry Song)
Whitney Handicap (Sultry Song)
Woodward Stakes (Sultry Song)
Flower Bowl Handicap (Christiecat)
Man o' War Stakes (Solar Splendor)
2002: Jockey Club Gold Cup (Evening Attire)
Queen Elizabeth II Challenge Cup (Riskaverse)

TIMOTHY KELLY
1989: Peter Pan Stakes (Imbibe)

TOMMY KELLY
1954: Fall Highweight Handicap (Pet Bully)
Washington Park Handicap (Pet Bully)
Woodward Stakes (Pet Bully)
1961: Wood Memorial Stakes (Globemaster)
Arlington Classic (Globemaster)
1963: Grey Lag Handicap (Sunrise County)
1964: Michigan Mile and One-Sixteenth (Tibaldo)
1969: Sorority Stakes (Box the Compass)
1970: Champagne Stakes (Limit to Reason)
Pimlico-Laurel Futurity (Limit to Reason)
Ohio Derby (Climber)
Lawrence Realization Stakes (Kling Kling)
1972: Grey Lag Handicap (Droll Role)
Hawthorne Gold Cup (Droll Role)
Massachusetts Handicap (Droll Role)
Canadian International Championship (Droll Role)
Washington D.C. International (Droll Role)
Pontiac Grand Prix Stakes (King's Bishop)
Michigan Mile and One-Eighth (King's Bishop)
American Derby (Dubassoff)
1973: Arlington Handicap (Dubassoff)
1977: Arlington-Washington Futurity (Sauce Boat)
1978: Hialeah Turf Cup (Noble Dancer II)
United Nations Handicap (Noble Dancer II)
San Luis Rey Stakes (Noble Dancer II)
1979: Pan American Handicap (Noble Dancer II)
United Nations Handicap (Noble Dancer II)
San Luis Rey Stakes (Noble Dancer II)
Laurel Futurity (Plugged Nickle)
Remsen Stakes (Plugged Nickle)
1980: Florida Derby (Plugged Nickle)
Wood Memorial Stakes (Plugged Nickle)
Vosburgh Stakes (Plugged Nickle)

MICHAEL KEOGH
1996: Vosburgh Stakes (Langfuhr)
1997: Carter Handicap (Langfuhr)
Metropolitan Handicap (Langfuhr)

D.W. KERNS
1947: Garden State Stakes (Itsabet)
1950: Garden State Stakes (Iswas)

CHARLES KERR
1959: Michigan Mile and One-Sixteenth (Total Traffic)
1963: Massachusetts Handicap (Crimson Satan)
Michigan Mile and One-Sixteenth (Crimson Satan)
Washington Park Handicap (Crimson Satan)

MICHAEL KERR
1966: Michigan Mile and One-Eighth (Stanislas)

BURK KESSINGER JR.
1991: Apple Blossom Handicap (Degenerate Gal)

JOHN KIMMEL
1994: Test Stakes (Twist Afleet)
1995: Coaching Club American Oaks (Golden Bri)
Top Flight Handicap (Twist Afleet)
Remsen Stakes (Tropicool)
1996: Delta Air Lines Top Flight Handicap (Flat Fleet Feet)
1997: Hempstead Handicap (Hidden Lake)
Go for Wand Stakes (Hidden Lake)
Beldame Stakes (Hidden Lake)
Test Stakes (Fabulously Fast)
1999: Ruffian Handicap (Catinca)
2001: Personal Ensign Handicap (Pompeii)
Overbrook Spinster Stakes (Miss Linda)

ALLEN KING JR.
1978: Selima Stakes (Candy Eclair)

EVERETT KING
1960: Man o' War Stakes (Harmonizing)
1968: Kentucky Oaks (Dark Mirage)
Acorn Stakes (Dark Mirage)
Mother Goose Stakes (Dark Mirage)
Coaching Club American Oaks (Dark Mirage)
Monmouth Oaks (Dark Mirage)
Display Handicap (Fast Count)
1972: Manhattan Handicap (Star Envoy)

JAMES KING
1963: San Fernando Stakes (Crimson Satan)
Charles H. Strub Stakes (Crimson Satan)

PRESTON KING
1974: Hollywood Invitational Handicap (Court Ruling)
1975: San Antonio Stakes (Cheriepe)
1977: Carter Handicap (Gentle King)

WILLIE KNAPP
1949: Queens County Handicap (Three Rings)
Monmouth Handicap (Three Rings)
Westchester Handicap (Three Rings)
1950: McLennan Handicap (Three Rings)
Queens County Handicap (Three Rings)

CHAY KNIGHT
1979: Hollywood Juvenile Championship (Parsec)
1980: San Felipe Handicap (Raise A Man)
1981: Santa Anita Derby (Splendid Spruce)

TERRY KNIGHT
1994: Hollywood Turf Cup (Frenchpark)

JOSEPH KULINA
1971: Pan American Handicap (Chompion)
Dixie Handicap (Chompion)
Massachusetts Handicap (Chompion)

J.I. LABELLE
1955: Washington D.C. International (El Chama)

FRANK LaBOCCETTA
1982: Wood Memorial Stakes (Air Forbes Won)

J.F. LABOYNE
1955: San Antonio Handicap (Gigantic)

DAVID LaCROIX
1979: Longacres Mile (Always Gallant)

M. LACY
1961: Kentucky Jockey Club Stakes (Su Ka Wa)

PETE LAIDLEY
1963: Hollywood Juvenile Championship (Nevada Bin)

ROBERT LAKE
1971: Sorority Stakes (Brenda Beauty)

DALE LANDERS
1971: Charles H. Strub Stakes (War Heim)
1972: Miller High Life Inglewood Handicap (War Heim)
1973: Del Mar Futurity (Such a Rush)

W.A. LARUE
1965: Pan American Handicap (Cool Prince)

LUCIEN LAURIN
1956: Frizette Stakes (Capelet)
1958: Matron Stakes (Quill)
Gardenia Stakes (Quill)
Cowdin Stakes (Crafty Skipper)
1959: Acorn Stakes (Quill)
Mother Goose Stakes (Quill)
1960: Saratoga Special (Bronzerullah)
Delaware Handicap (Quill)
1963: Hopeful Stakes (Traffic)
1964: Ohio Derby (National)
1965: Monmouth Handicap (Repeating)
1966: Wood Memorial Stakes (Amberoid)
Belmont Stakes (Amberoid)
1967: Carter Handicap (Tumiga)
1968: Breeders' Futurity (Dike)
1969: Gotham Stakes (Dike)
Wood Memorial Stakes (Dike)
California Derby (Jay Ray)
Massachusetts Handicap (Beau Marker)
1971: Futurity Stakes (Riva Ridge)
Champagne Stakes (Riva Ridge)
Pimlico-Laurel Futurity (Riva Ridge)
Garden State Stakes (Riva Ridge)
1972: Hopeful Stakes (Secretariat)
Futurity Stakes (Secretariat)
Laurel Futurity (Secretariat)
Garden State Stakes (Secretariat)
Blue Grass Stakes (Riva Ridge)
Kentucky Derby (Riva Ridge)
Belmont Stakes (Riva Ridge)
Hollywood Derby (Riva Ridge)
Florida Derby (Upper Case)
Wood Memorial Stakes (Upper Case)
1973: Gotham Stakes (Secretariat)
Kentucky Derby (Secretariat)
Preakness Stakes (Secretariat)
Belmont Stakes (Secretariat)
Marlboro Cup Handicap (Secretariat)
Man o' War Stakes (Secretariat)
Canadian International Championship (Secretariat)
Massachusetts Handicap (Riva Ridge)
Brooklyn Handicap (Riva Ridge)
Wood Memorial Stakes (Angle Light)
1976: Maskette Handicap (Artfully)

ROGER LAURIN
1964: Coaching Club American Oaks (Miss Cavandish)
Monmouth Oaks (Miss Cavandish)
Alabama Stakes (Miss Cavandish)
1967: Futurity Stakes (Captain's Gig)
1970: Canadian International Championship (Drumtop)
1971: Spinaway Stakes (Numbered Account)
Matron Stakes (Numbered Account)
Frizette Stakes (Numbered Account)
Selima Stakes (Numbered Account)
Gardenia Stakes (Numbered Account)
Hialeah Turf Cup (Drumtop)
Bowling Green Handicap (Drumtop)
1972: Spinster Stakes (Numbered Account)
1976: Jockey Club Gold Cup (Great Contractor)
1977: Hempstead Handicap (Pacific Princess)
Brooklyn Handicap (Great Contractor)
1978: Demoiselle Stakes (Plankton)
Maskette Handicap (Pearl Necklace)
1979: Flower Bowl Handicap (Pearl Necklace)
1982: Widener Handicap (Lord Darnley)
Gulfstream Park Handicap (Lord Darnley)
1983: Flamingo Stakes (Current Hope)
1984: Hopeful Stakes (Chief's Crown)
Norfolk Stakes (Chief's Crown)
Breeders' Cup Juvenile (Chief's Crown)
Gotham Stakes (Bear Hunt)
1985: Flamingo Stakes (Chief's Crown)
Blue Grass Stakes (Chief's Crown)
Travers Stakes (Chief's Crown)
Marlboro Cup Handicap (Chief's Crown)

RAYMOND LAWRENCE JR.
1978: Alcibiades Stakes (Angel Island)

LES LEAR
1964: Saratoga Special (Sadair)
Arlington-Washington Futurity (Sadair)

LES LEAR *(Continued)*
Garden State Stakes (Sadair)
Pimlico Futurity (Sadair)
1965: Sorority Stakes (Native Street)
1966: Kentucky Oaks (Native Street)

KING LEATHERBURY
1994: Philip H. Iselin Handicap (Taking Risks)

BUDDY LEAVITT
1960: Hollywood Juvenile Championship (Pappa's All)
Arlington Futurity (Pappa's All)

CHARLIE LEAVITT
1946: Santa Anita Handicap (War Knight)
1947: Del Mar Handicap (Iron Maiden)
1951: Santa Susana Stakes (Ruth Lily)
Hollywood Oaks (Ruth Lily)

JOHN LEAVITT
1961: Inglewood Handicap (Sea Orbit)

SANTIAGO LEDWITH
1964: Display Handicap (Primordial II)
1965: Widener Handicap (Primordial II)

JOHN LEE
1953: Tropical Park Handicap (Spartan Valor)
1956: Remsen Stakes (Ambehaving)

O'DONNELL LEE
1975: Sapling Stakes (Full Out)
1980: Remsen Stakes (Pleasant Colony)

R. LENTINI
1946: San Vicente Handicap (Air Rate)

BUTCH LENZINI
1976: Laurel Futurity (Royal Ski)
Remsen Stakes (Royal Ski)
1982: Preakness Stakes (Aloma's Ruler)
1985: Gotham Stakes (Eternal Prince)
Wood Memorial Stakes (Eternal Prince)
1988: Withers Stakes (Once Wild)

ROBERT LEONARD
1987: Norfolk Stakes (Saratoga Passage)

BUDD LEPMAN
1970: Mother Goose Stakes (Office Queen)
1973: Sorority Stakes (Irish Sonnet)
1984: Breeders' Cup Sprint (Eillo)

D.C. LeVINE
1969: Sapling Stakes (Ring For Nurse)

JAMES LEVITCH
1984: American Derby (High Alexander)

CRAIG LEWIS
1988: Californian Stakes (Cutlass Reality)
Hollywood Gold Cup (Cutlass Reality)
Del Mar Futurity (Music Merci)
1989: Illinois Derby (Music Merci)
1995: Santa Anita Derby (Larry the Legend)

J. LIEUX
1966: Washington D.C. International (Behistoun)

R.W. LILLY
1955: United Nations Handicap (Blue Choir)
1967: Illinois Derby (Royal Malabar)

MORTON LIPTON
1966: Vanity Handicap (Khal Ireland)

PAULO LOBO
2002: Kentucky Oaks (Farda Amiga)
Alabama Stakes (Farda Amiga)

DAVID LODER
1994: American Derby (Overbury)

MARY JO LOHMEIER
2000: Frank J. De Francis Memorial Dash (Richter Scale)

ANTHONY LOMBARDI
1969: Grey Lag Handicap (Bushido)

HOWARD LONG
1948: Inglewood Handicap (With Pleasure)

JACK LONG
1953: Black Helen Handicap (Atalanta)
Beldame Handicap (Atalanta)
1956: Black Helen Handicap (Clear Dawn)
1970: Breeders' Futurity (Man of the Moment)

JOHNNY LONGDEN
1967: Del Mar Futurity (Baffle)
Santa Barbara Handicap (Ormea)
1969: Santa Anita Derby (Majestic Prince)
Kentucky Derby (Majestic Prince)
Preakness Stakes (Majestic Prince)
1970: Californian Stakes (Baffle)
1973: Norfolk Stakes (Money Lender)

VANCE LONGDEN
1953: American Handicap (Royal Serenade)
Hollywood Gold Cup (Royal Serenade)
1955: San Juan Capistrano Handicap (St. Vincent)
Dixie Handicap (St. Vincent)
Santa Margarita Handicap (Blue Butterfly)
1961: San Felipe Handicap (Flutterby)
Santa Anita Derby (Four-and-Twenty)
1962: San Fernando Stakes (Four-and-Twenty)
Santa Anita Maturity (Four-and-Twenty)
San Carlos Handicap (Four-and-Twenty)
1972: San Fernando Stakes (Triple Bend)
Santa Anita Handicap (Triple Bend)

DANIEL LOPEZ
1974: Ohio Derby (Stonewalk)
Jerome Handicap (Stonewalk)

DONN LUBY
1981: Hollywood Gold Cup (Eleven Stitches)
1988: Santa Margarita Handicap (Flying Julia)

JACK LUDWIG
1985: Vosburgh Stakes (Another Reef)

WAYNE LUKAS
1978: Hollywood Juvenile Championship (Terlingua)
Del Mar Debutante Stakes (Terlingua)
American Handicap (Effervescing)
1979: Bay Meadows Handicap (Leonotis)
1980: Santa Anita Derby (Codex)
Hollywood Derby (Codex)
Preakness Stakes (Codex)
1981: Norfolk Stakes (Stalwart)
Hollywood Futurity (Stalwart)
Super Derby (Island Whirl)
1982: Santa Susana Stakes (Blush With Pride)
Kentucky Oaks (Blush With Pride)
Golden Harvest Handicap (Blush With Pride)
Del Mar Debutante Stakes (Landaluce)
Oak Leaf Stakes (Landaluce)
Golden Harvest Handicap (Miss Huntington)
Santa Anita Derby (Muttering)
Woodward Stakes (Island Whirl)
1983: Del Mar Futurity (Althea)
Del Mar Debutante Stakes (Althea)
Hollywood Starlet Stakes (Althea)
Matron Stakes (Lucky Lucky Lucky)
Alcibiades Stakes (Lucky Lucky Lucky)
Santa Anita Derby (Marfa)
Jim Beam Spiral Stakes (Marfa)
Oak Leaf Stakes (Life's Magic)
Apple Blossom Handicap (Miss Huntington)
Louisiana Derby (Balboa Native)
1984: Mother Goose Stakes (Life's Magic)
Alabama Stakes (Life's Magic)
Beldame Stakes (Life's Magic)
Santa Susana Stakes (Althea)
Arkansas Derby (Althea)
Kentucky Oaks (Lucky Lucky Lucky)
Sorority Stakes (Tiltalating)
Matron Stakes (Fiesta Lady)
1985: Maskette Stakes (Lady's Secret)
Ruffian Handicap (Lady's Secret)
Beldame Stakes (Lady's Secret)
Arkansas Derby (Tank's Prospect)
Preakness Stakes (Tank's Prospect)
Arlington-Washington Lassie Stakes (Family Style)
Frizette Stakes (Family Style)
San Felipe Handicap (Image of Greatness)
Oak Leaf Stakes (Arewehavingfunyet)
Breeders' Cup Juvenile Fillies (Twilight Ridge)
Breeders' Cup Distaff (Life's Magic)
1986: La Canada Stakes (Lady's Secret)
Santa Margarita Handicap (Lady's Secret)
Whitney Handicap (Lady's Secret)
Maskette Stakes (Lady's Secret)
Ruffian Handicap (Lady's Secret)
Beldame Stakes (Lady's Secret)
Breeders' Cup Distaff (Lady's Secret)
Everglades Stakes (Badger Land)
Flamingo Stakes (Badger Land)
Withers Stakes (Clear Choice)
Swaps Stakes (Clear Choice)
Mother Goose Stakes (Life at the Top)
Ladies Handicap (Life at the Top)
Suburban Handicap (Roo Art)
Philip H. Iselin Handicap (Roo Art)
Norfolk Stakes (Capote)
Breeders' Cup Juvenile (Capote)
Oak Leaf Stakes (Sacahuista)
1987: Arlington-Washington Futurity (Tejano)
Cowdin Stakes (Tejano)
Hollywood Futurity (Tejano)
Santa Margarita Handicap (North Sider)
Apple Blossom Handicap (North Sider)
Maskette Stakes (North Sider)
Spinster Stakes (Sacahuista)
Breeders' Cup Distaff (Sacahuista)
Mother Goose Stakes (Fiesta Gal)
Coaching Club American Oaks (Fiesta Gal)
La Canada Stakes (Family Style)
Flamingo Stakes (Talinum)
Blue Grass Stakes (War)
Philip H. Iselin Handicap (Bordeaux Bob)
Del Mar Futurity (Lost Kitty)
Matron Stakes (Over All)
Frizette Stakes (Classic Crown)
Oak Leaf Stakes (Dream Team)
Breeders' Cup Juvenile (Success Express)
1988: Santa Anita Oaks (Winning Colors)
Santa Anita Derby (Winning Colors)
Kentucky Derby (Winning Colors)
Metropolitan Handicap (Gulch)
Breeders' Cup Sprint (Gulch)
Matron Stakes (Some Romance)
Frizette Stakes (Some Romance)
Breeders' Cup Juvenile Fillies (Open Mind)
Demoiselle Stakes (Open Mind)
San Fernando Stakes (On the Line)
Jersey Derby (Dynaformer)
Oak Leaf Stakes (One of a Klein)
Alcibiades Stakes (Wonders Delight)
Breeders' Cup Juvenile (Is It True)
Top Flight Handicap (Clabber Girl)
1989: Kentucky Oaks (Open Mind)
Acorn Stakes (Open Mind)
Mother Goose Stakes (Open Mind)
Coaching Club American Oaks (Open Mind)
Alabama Stakes (Open Mind)
Gulfstream Park Handicap (Slew City Slew)
Oaklawn Handicap (Slew City Slew)
Arlington Million (Steinlen)
Breeders' Cup Mile (Steinlen)
Matron Stakes (Stella Madrid)
Frizette Stakes (Stella Madrid)
Norfolk Stakes (Grand Canyon)
Hollywood Futurity (Grand Canyon)
Santa Anita Oaks (Imaginary Lady)
Carter Handicap (On the Line)
Jim Dandy Stakes (Is It True)
Flower Bowl Handicap (River Memories)
1990: San Antonio Handicap (Criminal Type)
Pimlico Special (Criminal Type)
Metropolitan Handicap (Criminal Type)
Hollywood Gold Cup (Criminal Type)
Whitney Handicap (Criminal Type)
San Felipe Handicap (Real Cash)
American Derby (Real Cash)
Peter Pan Stakes (Profit Key)
Dwyer Stakes (Profit Key)
Hollywood Turf Handicap (Steinlen)
Caesars International Handicap (Steinlen)
Santa Anita Oaks (Hail Atlantis)
Kentucky Oaks (Seaside Attraction)
Acorn Stakes (Stella Madrid)
Hollywood Oaks (Patches)
Hopeful Stakes (Deposit Ticket)
Hollywood Starlet Stakes (Cuddles)
1991: San Antonio Handicap (Farma Way)
Santa Anita Handicap (Farma Way)
Pimlico Special (Farma Way)
Hempstead Handicap (A Wild Ride)
Travers Stakes (Corporate Report)
Hopeful Stakes (Salt Lake)
Beldame Stakes (Sharp Dance)
Meadowlands Cup (Twilight Agenda)
1994: Spinaway Stakes (Flanders)
Matron Stakes (Flanders)

Frizette Stakes (Flanders)
Breeders' Cup Juvenile Fillies (Flanders)
Preakness Stakes (Tabasco Cat)
Belmont Stakes (Tabasco Cat)
Champagne Stakes (Timber Country)
Breeders' Cup Juvenile (Timber Country)
Oak Leaf Stakes (Serena's Song)
Hollywood Starlet Stakes (Serena's Song)
Vosburgh Stakes (Harlan)
Remsen Stakes (Thunder Gulch)
1995: Las Virgenes Stakes (Serena's Song)
Santa Anita Oaks (Serena's Song)
Jim Beam Stakes (Serena's Song)
Mother Goose Stakes (Serena's Song)
Haskell Invitational Handicap (Serena's Song)
Gazelle Handicap (Serena's Song)
Beldame Stakes (Serena's Song)
Florida Derby (Thunder Gulch)
Kentucky Derby (Thunder Gulch)
Belmont Stakes (Thunder Gulch)
Swaps Stakes (Thunder Gulch)
Travers Stakes (Thunder Gulch)
Spinaway Stakes (Golden Attraction)
Matron Stakes (Golden Attraction)
Frizette Stakes (Golden Attraction)
Preakness Stakes (Timber Country)
Hopeful Stakes (Hennessy)
Oak Leaf Stakes (Tipically Irish)
Hollywood Starlet Stakes (Cara Rafaela)
1996: Santa Maria Handicap (Serena's Song)
Hempstead Handicap (Serena's Song)
Belmont Stakes (Editor's Note)
Isle of Capri Casino Super Derby (Editor's Note)
Secretariat Stakes (Marlin)
Crown Royal Hollywood Derby (Marlin)
Matron Stakes (Sharp Cat)
Hollywood Starlet Stakes (Sharp Cat)
Kentucky Derby (Grindstone)
Metropolitan Handicap (Honour and Glory)
Swaps Stakes (Victory Speech)
Oak Leaf Stakes (City Band)
Breeders' Cup Juvenile (Boston Harbor)
1997: Las Virgenes Stakes (Sharp Cat)
Santa Anita Oaks (Sharp Cat)
Acorn Stakes (Sharp Cat)
Hollywood Oaks (Sharp Cat)
San Juan Capistrano Handicap (Marlin)
Arlington Million (Marlin)
Futurity Stakes (Grand Slam)
Moet Champagne Stakes (Grand Slam)
Strub Stakes (Victory Speech)
Ballerina Stakes (Pearl City)
Hollywood Starlet Stakes (Love Lock)
1998: Florida Derby (Cape Town)
Ashland Stakes (Well Chosen)
Lane's End Breeders' Futurity (Cat Thief)
Hollywood Futurity (Tactical Cat)
1999: Kentucky Derby (Charismatic)
Preakness Stakes (Charismatic)
Swaps Stakes (Cat Thief)
Breeders' Cup Classic (Cat Thief)
Frizette Stakes (Surfside)
Hollywood Starlet Stakes (Surfside)
Frank J. De Francis Memorial Dash (Yes It's True)
Hopeful Stakes (High Yield)
Breeders' Cup Juvenile Fillies (Cash Run)
2000: Las Virgenes Stakes (Surfside)
Santa Anita Oaks (Surfside)
Fountain of Youth Stakes (High Yield)
Toyota Blue Grass Stakes (High Yield)
Breeders' Cup Distaff (Spain)
La Brea Stakes (Spain)
Belmont Stakes (Commendable)
Hopeful Stakes (Yonaguska)
2001: Jim Dandy Stakes (Scorpion)
2002: Forego Handicap (Orientate)
NAPA Breeders' Cup Sprint (Orientate)
San Carlos Handicap (Snow Ridge)
2003: Darley Alcibiades Stakes (Be Gentle)

RICHARD LUNDY

1986: Jim Dandy Stakes (Lac Ouimet)
1988: Gulfstream Park Handicap (Jade Hunter)
1989: Hollywood Gold Cup (Blushing John)
1990: Oaklawn Handicap (Opening Verse)
1991: Santa Anita Derby (Dinard)
Hollywood Oaks (Fowda)
Breeders' Cup Mile (Opening Verse)

HORATIO LURO

1947: Whitney Stakes (Rico Monte)
Manhattan Handicap (Rico Monte)
New York Handicap (Rico Monte)
Black Helen Handicap (Miss Grillo)
1948: New Castle Handicap (Miss Grillo)
New York Handicap (Miss Grillo)
San Antonio Handicap (Talon)
Santa Anita Handicap (Talon)
1949: San Juan Capistrano Handicap (Miss Grillo)
1951: Kentucky Oaks (How)
Coaching Club American Oaks (How)
1952: Ladies Handicap (How)
1953: United Nations Handicap (Iceberg II)
1956: Canadian Championship Stakes (Eugenia II)
1957: Canadian Championship Stakes (Spinney)
1959: Remsen Stakes (Victoria Park)
1962: Kentucky Derby (Decidedly)
1963: Monmouth Handicap (Decidedly)
1964: Flamingo Stakes (Northern Dancer)
Florida Derby (Northern Dancer)
Blue Grass Stakes (Northern Dancer)
Kentucky Derby (Northern Dancer)
Preakness Stakes (Northern Dancer)
1970: Pan American Handicap (One For All)
Sunset Handicap (One For All)
1971: Canadian International Championship (One For All)
1972: Ladies Handicap (Grafitti)
1973: Black Helen Handicap (Grafitti)
1976: Gulfstream Park Handicap (Hail the Pirates)
1979: Widener Handicap (Jumping Hill)
1981: Flamingo Stakes (Tap Shoes)

PAUL LYCAN

1947: Hollywood Derby (Yankee Valor)
Cinema Handicap (Yankee Valor)

FRANK LYONS

1995: Breeders' Cup Sprint (Desert Stormer)

BRAD MacDONALD

1993: Norfolk Stakes (Shepherd's Field)

MICHAEL MACHOWSKY

2003: Malibu Stakes (Southern Image)

RED MAHONEY

1963: Arkansas Derby (Cosmic Tip)

JIM MALONEY

1947: Remsen Handicap (Big If)
1956: Spinaway Stakes (Alanesian)
1957: Metropolitan Handicap (Traffic Judge)
Suburban Handicap (Traffic Judge)
Mother Goose Stakes (Outer Space)
1958: Beldame Handicap (Outer Space)
1963: Coaching Club American Oaks (Lamb Chop)
Monmouth Oaks (Lamb Chop)
Spinster Stakes (Lamb Chop)
1964: Santa Margarita Handicap (Batteur)
1965: Santa Susana Stakes (Desert Love)
San Felipe Handicap (Jacinto)
Charles H. Strub Stakes (Duel)
1966: Santa Anita Derby (Boldnesian)
1967: Alabama Stakes (Gamely)
Vanity Handicap (Desert Love)
1968: Vanity Handicap (Gamely)
Beldame Stakes (Gamely)
Santa Margarita Handicap (Gamely)
Santa Barbara Handicap (Princessnesian)
Hollywood Gold Cup (Princessnesian)
San Felipe Handicap (Dewan)
Santa Anita Derby (Alley Fighter)
1969: Vanity Handicap (Desert Law)
Beldame Stakes (Gamely)
Santa Margarita Handicap (Princessnesian)
Charles H. Strub Stakes (Dignitas)
1970: Brooklyn Handicap (Dewan)
San Antonio Stakes (Dewan)
Travers Stakes (Loud)
1976: Jerome Handicap (Dance Spell)
1977: Marlboro Cup Handicap (Proud Birdie)
1981: Top Flight Handicap (Chain Bracelet)
1982: Alabama Stakes (Broom Dance)
Maskette Stakes (Too Chic)
1983: Dwyer Stakes (Au Point)

RICHARD MANDELLA

1977: Cinema Handicap (Bad 'n Big)
1978: Longacres Mile (Bad 'n Big)
1982: Hollywood Turf Cup (The Hague)
1984: San Antonio Handicap (Poley)
1992: Santa Anita Oaks (Golden Treat)
1993: San Luis Rey Stakes (Kotashaan)
San Juan Capistrano Handicap (Kotashaan)
Eddie Read Handicap (Kotashaan)
Oak Tree Invitational Stakes (Kotashaan)
Breeders' Cup Turf (Kotashaan)
Oak Leaf Stakes (Phone Chatter)
Breeders' Cup Juvenile Fillies (Phone Chatter)
1994: San Felipe Stakes (Soul of the Matter)
Super Derby (Soul of the Matter)
Oak Tree Invitational Stakes (Sandpit)
Hollywood Futurity (Afternoon Deelites)
1995: San Luis Rey Stakes (Sandpit)
Caesars International Handicap (Sandpit)
San Felipe Stakes (Afternoon Deelites)
Malibu Stakes (Afternoon Deelites)
Strub Stakes (Dare and Go)
San Antonio Handicap (Best Pal)
1996: Hollywood Turf Handicap (Sandpit)
Caesars International Handicap (Sandpit)
Hollywood Gold Cup (Siphon)
Ramona Handicap (Matiara)
Pacific Classic (Dare and Go)
1997: San Antonio Handicap (Gentlemen)
Pimlico Special (Gentlemen)
Hollywood Gold Cup (Gentlemen)
Pacific Classic (Gentlemen)
Santa Anita Handicap (Siphon)
Oaklawn Handicap (Atticus)
1998: Carter Handicap (Wild Rush)
Metropolitan Handicap (Wild Rush)
San Antonio Handicap (Gentlemen)
Santa Anita Handicap (Malek)
Ballerina Handicap (Stop Traffic)
1999: Donn Handicap (Puerto Madero)
Santa Monica Handicap (Stop Traffic)
Strub Stakes (Event of the Year)
Beverly Hills Handicap (Virginie)
Norfolk Stakes (Dixie Union)
Hollywood Turf Cup (Lazy Lode)
2000: Haskell Invitational Handicap (Dixie Union)
Malibu Stakes (Dixie Union)
2001: Eddie Read Handicap (Redattore)
2002: Oaklawn Handicap (Kudos)
Clement L. Hirsch Mem. Turf Champ. (The Tin Man)
Hollywood Derby (Johar)
2003: Del Mar Debutante Stakes (Halfbridled)
Breeders' Cup Juvenile Fillies (Halfbridled)
Shoemaker Breeders' Cup Mile (Redattore)
Del Mar Oaks (Dessert)
Del Mar Futurity (Siphonizer)
Bessemer Trust BC Juvenile (Action This Day)
John Deere Breeders' Cup Turf (Johar)
Breeders' Cup Classic/Dodge (Pleasantly Perfect)

DENNIS MANNING

2003: King's Bishop Stakes (Valid Video)

JOE MANZI

1971: San Fernando Stakes (Willowick)
1982: Del Mar Futurity (Roving Boy)
Norfolk Stakes (Roving Boy)
Hollywood Futurity (Roving Boy)
1985: Santa Susana Stakes (Fran's Valentine)
Kentucky Oaks (Fran's Valentine)
Hollywood Oaks (Fran's Valentine)

STEPHEN MARGOLIS

2003: Breeders' Cup Sprint (Cajun Beat)

ANTHONY MARGOTTA JR.

1993: Whitney Handicap (Brunswick)
1998: Malibu Stakes (Run Man Run)

CHARLES MARIKIAN

1980: Norfolk Stakes (Sir Dancer)
1983: Widener Handicap (Swing Till Dawn)
Charles H. Strub Stakes (Swing Till Dawn)

MERVIN MARKS

1971: Monmouth Invitational Handicap (West Coast Scout)
Woodward Stakes (West Coast Scout)
1972: Amory L. Haskell Handicap (West Coast Scout)
1973: Gulfstream Park Handicap (West Coast Scout)
Amory L. Haskell Handicap (West Coast Scout)

ALFREDO MARQUEZ

2001: Oak Leaf Stakes (Tali'sluckybusride)

ROBERT MARSHALL

1993: Californian Stakes (Latin American)

PEDRO MARTI

1983: Ruffian Handicap (Heartlight No. One)

CARLOS MARTIN

1991: Top Flight Handicap (Buy the Firm)

JOSE MARTIN

1972: New Orleans Handicap (Urgent Message)
1974: Frizette Stakes (Molly Ballentine)
1977: Matron Stakes (Lakeville Miss)
Frizette Stakes (Lakeville Miss)
Selima Stakes (Lakeville Miss)
Top Flight Handicap (Shawi)
1978: Arlington-Washington Futurity (Jose Binn)
Frizette Stakes (Golferette)
Coaching Club American Oaks (Lakeville Miss)
1981: Dwyer Stakes (Noble Nashua)
Swaps Stakes (Noble Nashua)
Jerome Handicap (Noble Nashua)
Marlboro Cup Handicap (Noble Nashua)
Mother Goose Stakes (Wayward Lass)
Coaching Club American Oaks (Wayward Lass)
1987: Vosburgh Stakes (Groovy)
Young America Stakes (Firery Ensign)
1995: Suburban Handicap (Key Contender)

PANCHO MARTIN

1959: Wood Memorial Stakes (Manassa Mauler)
1960: Trenton Handicap (Manassa Mauler)
1961: Monmouth Handicap (Don Poggio)
1963: Gotham Stakes (Debbysman)
1971: Century Handicap (Big Shot II)
Manhattan Handicap (Big Shot II)
Brooklyn Handicap (Never Bow)
1972: Jockey Club Gold Cup (Autobiography)
San Fernando Stakes (Autobiography)
Suburban Handicap (Hitchcock)
1973: Santa Anita Derby (Sham)
Jersey Derby (Knightly Dawn)
1974: San Antonio Stakes (Prince Dantan)
San Juan Capistrano Handicap (Prince Dantan)
Wood Memorial Stakes (Rube the Great)
Withers Stakes (Accipiter)
1984: Breeders' Cup Juvenile Fillies (Outstandingly)

ROBERT L. MARTIN

1987: San Antonio Handicap (Bedside Promise)

SIDNEY MARTIN

1974: Del Mar Futurity (Diabolo)
1975: California Derby (Diabolo)

FRANCOIS MATHET

1962: Washington D.C. International (Match II)

T.G. MAY

1951: Louisiana Derby (Whirling Bat)

BRIAN MAYBERRY

1991: Spinaway Stakes (Miss Iron Smoke)
1992: Oak Leaf Stakes (Zoonaqua)
1993: Hollywood Starlet Stakes (Sardula)
1994: Kentucky Oaks (Sardula)
1995: Ashland Stakes (Urbane)

G.E. MAYBERRY

1950: Westerner Stakes (Valquest)
1951: San Juan Capistrano Handicap (Be Fleet)

JOHN MAZZA

1992: Hopeful Stakes (Great Navigator)

RON McANALLY

1960: San Fernando Stakes (King o' Turf)
1961: Champagne Stakes (Donut King)
1975: Sunset Handicap (Cruiser II)
Del Mar Handicap (Cruiser II)
Del Mar Debutante Stakes (Queen to Be)
San Fernando Stakes (First Back)
1976: Santa Anita Derby (An Act)
Hollywood Gold Cup (Pay Tribute)
1977: Meadowlands Cup (Pay Tribute)
San Fernando Stakes (Pocket Park)
1978: Ramona Handicap (Drama Critic)
1980: Hialeah Turf Cup (John Henry)
Hollywood Invitational Handicap (John Henry)
Oak Tree Invitational Stakes (John Henry)
San Luis Rey Stakes (John Henry)
San Juan Capistrano Handicap (John Henry)
Bay Meadows Handicap (Super Moment)
1981: Santa Anita Handicap (John Henry)
Hollywood Invitational Handicap (John Henry)
Arlington Million (John Henry)
Oak Tree Invitational Stakes (John Henry)
San Luis Rey Stakes (John Henry)
Charles H. Strub Stakes (Super Moment)
Bay Meadows Handicap (Super Moment)
1982: Santa Anita Handicap (John Henry)
Oak Tree Invitational Stakes (John Henry)
Bay Meadows Handicap (Super Moment)
1983: Hollywood Turf Cup (John Henry)
1984: Hollywood Invitational Handicap (John Henry)
Sunset Handicap (John Henry)
Budweiser-Arlington Million (John Henry)
Turf Classic (John Henry)
1988: Norfolk Stakes (Hawkster)
1989: Santa Margarita Handicap (Bayakoa)
Apple Blossom Handicap (Bayakoa)
Vanity Handicap (Bayakoa)
Ruffian Handicap (Bayakoa)
Spinster Stakes (Bayakoa)
Breeders' Cup Distaff (Bayakoa)
Oak Tree Invitational Stakes (Hawkster)
1990: Santa Margarita Handicap (Bayakoa)
Spinster Stakes (Bayakoa)
Breeders' Cup Distaff (Bayakoa)
Arkansas Derby (Silver Ending)
Pegasus Handicap (Silver Ending)
1991: Oaklawn Handicap (Festin)
Nassau County Handicap (Festin)
Jockey Club Gold Cup (Festin)
Arkansas Derby (Olympio)
American Derby (Olympio)
Hollywood Derby (Olympio)
Milady Handicap (Brought to Mind)
Vanity Handicap (Brought to Mind)
Eddie Read Handicap (Tight Spot)
Arlington Million (Tight Spot)
San Felipe Stakes (Sea Cadet)
1992: Santa Margarita Handicap (Paseana)
Apple Blossom Handicap (Paseana)
Milady Handicap (Paseana)
Vanity Handicap (Paseana)
Breeders' Cup Distaff (Paseana)
Donn Handicap (Sea Cadet)
Gulfstream Park Handicap (Sea Cadet)
Meadowlands Cup (Sea Cadet)
San Antonio Stakes (Ibero)
NYRA Mile Handicap (Ibero)
Fantasy Stakes (Race the Wild Wind)
Yellow Ribbon Stakes (Super Staff)
1993: Apple Blossom Handicap (Paseana)
Milady Handicap (Paseana)
Spinster Stakes (Paseana)
Santa Maria Handicap (Race the Wild Wind)
Charles H. Strub Stakes (Siberian Summer)
Metropolitan Handicap (Ibero)
Hollywood Futurity (Valiant Nature)
1994: Santa Margarita Handicap (Paseana)
Vanity Handicap (Potridee)
Del Mar Futurity (On Target)
1995: Santa Maria Handicap (Queens Court Queen)
Santa Margarita Handicap (Queens Court Queen)
Del Mar Futurity (Future Quest)
Norfolk Stakes (Future Quest)
Oak Tree Invitational Stakes (Northern Spur)
Breeders' Cup Turf (Northern Spur)
Beverly Hills Handicap (Alpride)
Yellow Ribbon Stakes (Alpride)
Hollywood Futurity (Matty G)
1996: Las Virgenes Stakes (Antespend)
Santa Anita Oaks (Antespend)
Beverly Hills Handicap (Different)
Three Chimneys Spinster Stakes (Different)
Santa Anita Handicap (Mr. Purple)
Hollywood Oaks (Listening)
1997: Milady Breeders' Cup Handicap (Listening)
1998: Santa Margarita Handicap (Toda Una Dama)
San Juan Capistrano Handicap (Amerique)
Californian Stakes (Mud Route)
2000: Matriarch Stakes (Tout Charmant)
2001: Queen Elizabeth II Challenge Cup (Affluent)
La Brea Stakes (Affluent)
Santa Maria Handicap (Lovellon)
2002: John C. Mabee Ramona Handicap (Affluent)
2003: Santa Monica Handicap (Affluent)
Pacific Classic (Candy Ride)
Hollywood Derby (Sweet Return)

H.C. McBRIDE

1960: Santa Anita Handicap (Linmold)
1967: Santa Barbara Handicap (April Dawn)
1968: Del Mar Futurity (Fleet Allied)

EDWARD McCANN

1972: Donn Handicap (Going Straight)
1978: Ohio Derby (Special Honor)

PETE McCANN

1958: Michigan Mile (Nearctic)

TED McCLAIN

1979: Golden Harvest Handicap (Flaunter)

CHICK McCLELLAN

1954: Westerner Stakes (Fault Free)

DON McCOY

1963: Dixie Handicap (Cedar Key)
1964: San Juan Capistrano Handicap (Cedar Key)
Donn Handicap (Cedar Key)
1965: San Luis Rey Handicap (Cedar Key)
1966: San Luis Rey Handicap (Cedar Key)

CONN McCREARY

1968: Pan American Handicap (Irish Rebellion)

DUKE McCUE

1946: Garden State Stakes (Double Jay)
Kentucky Jockey Club Stakes (Double Jay)
1949: American Handicap (Double Jay)
1957: Washington Park Futurity (Jewel's Reward)

RED McDANIEL

1951: Del Mar Handicap (Blue Reading)
1954: Del Mar Handicap (Stranglehold)
Santa Anita Maturity (Apple Valley)
1955: Santa Anita Handicap (Poona II)

WAYNE McDONNELL

1981: California Derby (Always a Cinch)

ROBERT McGARVEY

1949: Washington Park Futurity (Curtice)
1951: Blue Grass Stakes (Ruhe)

SHUG McGAUGHEY

1978: Apple Blossom Handicap (Northernette)
1983: Spinster Stakes (Try Something New)
1985: Suburban Handicap (Vanlandingham)
Jockey Club Gold Cup (Vanlandingham)
Washington D.C. International (Vanlandingham)
Widener Handicap (Pine Circle)
1986: Cowdin Stakes (Polish Navy)
Champagne Stakes (Polish Navy)
Alabama Stakes (Classy Cathy)
Frizette Stakes (Personal Ensign)
1987: Jim Dandy Stakes (Polish Navy)
Woodward Stakes (Polish Navy)
Beldame Stakes (Personal Ensign)
1988: Whitney Handicap (Personal Ensign)
Maskette Stakes (Personal Ensign)
Beldame Stakes (Personal Ensign)
Breeders' Cup Distaff (Personal Ensign)
Peter Pan Stakes (Seeking the Gold)
Dwyer Stakes (Seeking the Gold)
Super Derby (Seeking the Gold)
Cowdin Stakes (Easy Goer)
Champagne Stakes (Easy Goer)
Breeders' Futurity (Fast Play)
Remsen Stakes (Fast Play)
Suburban Handicap (Personal Flag)
Vosburgh Stakes (Mining)
1989: Gotham Stakes (Easy Goer)
Wood Memorial Stakes (Easy Goer)
Belmont Stakes (Easy Goer)
Whitney Handicap (Easy Goer)
Travers Stakes (Easy Goer)
Woodward Handicap (Easy Goer)
Jockey Club Gold Cup (Easy Goer)
Flamingo Stakes (Awe Inspiring)
Jersey Derby (Awe Inspiring)
Suburban Handicap (Dancing Spree)
Breeders' Cup Sprint (Dancing Spree)
Champagne Stakes (Adjudicating)
Cowdin Stakes (Adjudicating)
Breeders' Cup Juvenile (Rhythm)
1990: Carter Handicap (Dancing Spree)
Suburban Handicap (Easy Goer)
Travers Stakes (Rhythm)
1991: Maskette Stakes (Queena)
Ruffian Handicap (Queena)
Charles H. Strub Stakes (Defensive Play)
Alabama Stakes (Versailles Treaty)
Frizette Stakes (Preach)
1992: Gotham Stakes (Lure)
Breeders' Cup Mile (Lure)
Go for Wand Stakes (Easy Now)
Jerome Handicap (Furiously)
Futurity Stakes (Strolling Along)

Ruffian Handicap (Versailles Treaty)
Frizette Stakes (Educated Risk)
1993: Kentucky Oaks (Dispute)
Gazelle Handicap (Dispute)
Beldame Stakes (Dispute)
Jim Dandy Stakes (Miner's Mark)
Jockey Club Gold Cup (Miner's Mark)
Frizette Stakes (Heavenly Prize)
Breeders' Cup Mile (Lure)
Brooklyn Handicap (Living Vicariously)
1994: Alabama Stakes (Heavenly Prize)
Gazelle Handicap (Heavenly Prize)
Beldame Stakes (Heavenly Prize)
Ashland Stakes (Inside Information)
Acorn Stakes (Inside Information)
Caesars International Handicap (Lure)
Spinster Stakes (Dispute)
Top Flight Handicap (Educated Risk)
1995: Shuvee Handicap (Inside Information)
Ruffian Handicap (Inside Information)
Spinster Stakes (Inside Information)
Breeders' Cup Distaff (Inside Information)
Apple Blossom Handicap (Heavenly Prize)
Hempstead Handicap (Heavenly Prize)
Go for Wand Stakes (Heavenly Prize)
Breeders' Cup Juvenile Fillies (My Flag)
1996: Ashland Stakes (My Flag)
Coaching Club American Oaks (My Flag)
Gazelle Handicap (My Flag)
Jim Beam Stakes (Roar)
NYRA Mile Handicap (Gold Fever)
1997: Ashland Stakes (Glitter Woman)
Remsen Stakes (Coronado's Quest)
1998: Wood Memorial Stakes (Coronado's Quest)
Buick Haskell Inv. Handicap (Coronado's Quest)
Travers Stakes (Coronado's Quest)
Go for Wand Handicap (Aldiza)
Matron Stakes (Oh What a Windfall)
1999: Ballerina Handicap (Furlough)
Matron Stakes (Finder's Fee)
2000: Acorn Stakes (Finder's Fee)
2001: Oaklawn Handicap (Traditionally)
Go for Wand Handicap (Serra Lake)
2002: Matron Stakes (Storm Flag Flying)
Frizette Stakes (Storm Flag Flying)
Long John Silver's BC Juv. Fillies (Storm Flag Flying)

JIMMY McGEE
1952: Pimlico Special (General Staff)

PAUL McGEE
2000: Hollywood Starlet Stakes (I Believe in You)
2003: Woodford Reserve Turf Classic (Honor in War)

BRITT McGEHEE
1997: Frizette Stakes (Silver Maiden)

M. McGONIGLE
1946: Miami Beach Handicap (Frere Jacques)

GERARD McGRATH
1979: Hawthorne Gold Cup (Young Bob)

R.W. McILVAINE
1946: Demoiselle Stakes (Carolyn A.)
1972: Jersey Derby (Smiling Jack)

GEORGE McIVOR
1964: San Luis Rey Handicap (Inclusive)

DONALD McKELLAR
1974: Alcibiades Stakes (Hope of Glory)
1976: Alcibiades Stakes (Sans Supplement)

KIARAN McLAUGHLIN
1996: Pegasus Breeders' Cup Handicap (Allied Forces)
2003: Man o' War Stakes (Lunar Sovereign)

NORMAN McLEOD
1952: Cowdin Stakes (Invigorator)
1955: Selima Stakes (Levee)
1956: Coaching Club American Oaks (Levee)
Monmouth Oaks (Levee)
Beldame Handicap (Levee)
Withers Stakes (Oh Johnny)
Travers Stakes (Oh Johnny)
1957: Display Handicap (Oh Johnny)
1958: Grey Lag Handicap (Oh Johnny)
1959: Saratoga Special (Irish Lancer)
1963: Alabama Stakes (Tona)
1964: Selima Stakes (Marshua)
1965: Coaching Club American Oaks (Marshua)

T. McMAHON
1958: Display Handicap (Civet)

FRANK McMANUS
1962: Bougainvillea Handicap (Eurasia)
1963: Donn Handicap (Tutankhamen)
1970: Flamingo Stakes (My Dad George)
Florida Derby (My Dad George)

FREEMAN McMILLAN
1956: Cowdin Stakes (Mister Jive)
1964: Mother Goose Stakes (Sceree)

KENNY McPEEK
2000: Walmac Int. Alcibiades Stakes (She's a Devil Due)
2001: Walmac Int. Alcibiades Stakes (Take Charge Lady)
2002: Florida Derby (Harlan's Holiday)
Toyota Blue Grass Stakes (Harlan's Holiday)
Ashland Stakes (Take Charge Lady)
Overbrook Spinster Stakes (Take Charge Lady)
Belmont Stakes (Sarava)
2003: Overbrook Spinster Stakes (Take Charge Lady)

JOHN MEAUX
1963: Louisiana Derby (City Line)
1966: Arlington-Washington Futurity (Diplomat Way)
1967: Blue Grass Stakes (Diplomat Way)
1968: New Orleans Handicap (Diplomat Way)
Oaklawn Handicap (Diplomat Way)
1969: Oaklawn Handicap (Listado)
1970: Washington Park Handicap (Doc's T.V.)
1972: Illinois Derby (Fame and Power)
1974: New Orleans Handicap (Smooth Dancer)
1975: Illinois Derby (Colonel Power)

BRIAN MEEHAN
2003: Gazelle Handicap (Buy the Sport)

DEREK MEREDITH
1993: Breeders' Cup Sprint (Cardmania)

PAUL MEREDITH
1959: Del Mar Futurity (Azure's Orphan)

JOSEPH MERGLER
1946: Black Helen Handicap (Adroit)

MARK MERGLER
1963: Frizette Stakes (Tosmah)
1964: Matron Handicap (Tosmah)
Beldame Stakes (Tosmah)
Arlington Classic (Tosmah)
1966: Seminole Handicap (Convex)
John B. Campbell Handicap (Tosmah)

FRANK MERRILL
1973: Pan American Handicap (Lord Vancouver)
1974: Arlington-Washington Futurity (Greek Answer)
1975: Fantasy Stakes (Hoso)

RAY METCALF
1959: Gotham Stakes (Atoll)
1965: Flamingo Stakes (Native Charger)
Florida Derby (Native Charger)
1968: Hopeful Stakes (Top Knight)
Futurity Stakes (Top Knight)
Champagne Stakes (Top Knight)
1969: Flamingo Stakes (Top Knight)
Florida Derby (Top Knight)

JEROME MEYER
1968: Gotham Stakes (Verbatim)

THOMAS MILES
1961: Massachusetts Handicap (Polylad)
Gallant Fox Handicap (Polylad)

MACK MILLER
1955: Maskette Handicap (Oil Painting)
1956: Arlington Lassie Stakes (Leallah)
Alcibiades Stakes (Leallah)
Selima Stakes (Lebkuchen)
1966: United Nations Handicap (Assagai)
Man o' War Stakes (Assagai)
1969: Stars and Stripes Handicap (Hawaii)
United Nations Handicap (Hawaii)
Man o' War Stakes (Hawaii)
Kentucky Jockey Club Stakes (Evasive Action)
Jerome Handicap (Mr. Leader)
1970: Stars and Stripes Handicap (Mr. Leader)
1971: Hopeful Stakes (Rest Your Case)
Breeders' Futurity (Windjammer)

Whitney Stakes (Protanto)
1973: Metropolitan Handicap (Tentam)
United Nations Handicap (Tentam)
1974: United Nations Handicap (Halo)
1975: Man o' War Stakes (Snow Knight)
Canadian International Championship (Snow Knight)
1978: Suburban Handicap (Upper Nile)
1979: Ladies Handicap (Spark of Life)
1980: Suburban Handicap (Winter's Tale)
Brooklyn Handicap (Winter's Tale)
Marlboro Cup Handicap (Winter's Tale)
1981: Flower Bowl Handicap (Rokeby Rose)
United Nations Handicap (Key To Content)
1982: Jerome Handicap (Fit to Fight)
1983: Suburban Handicap (Winter's Tale)
1984: Metropolitan Handicap (Fit to Fight)
Suburban Handicap (Fit to Fight)
Brooklyn Handicap (Fit to Fight)
United Nations Handicap (Hero's Honor)
1986: Man o' War Stakes (Dance of Life)
Remsen Stakes (Java Gold)
1987: Whitney Handicap (Java Gold)
Travers Stakes (Java Gold)
Marlboro Cup Handicap (Java Gold)
Hopeful Stakes (Crusader Sword)
1990: Futurity Stakes (Eastern Echo)
1992: Champagne Stakes (Sea Hero)
1993: Kentucky Derby (Sea Hero)
Travers Stakes (Sea Hero)
Top Flight Handicap (You'd Be Surprised)

NORMAN MILLER III
2002: Vosburgh Stakes (Bonapaw)

P.F. MILLER
1959: Arlington Futurity (T.V. Lark)

ROBERT MILLER
1970: Hollywood Derby (Hanalei Bay)

BUSTER MILLERICK
1948: Vanity Handicap (Hemet Squaw)
Del Mar Handicap (Frankly)
1950: Del Mar Handicap (Frankly)
1955: Vanity Handicap (Countess Fleet)
1956: Westerner Stakes (Count of Honor)
1963: Inglewood Handicap (Native Diver)
1964: Inglewood Handicap (Native Diver)
1965: American Handicap (Native Diver)
Hollywood Gold Cup (Native Diver)
1966: Hollywood Gold Cup (Native Diver)
1967: Del Mar Debutante Stakes (Fast Dish)
Hollywood Gold Cup (Native Diver)
1969: Del Mar Futurity (George Lewis)
Malibu Stakes (First Mate)
San Fernando Stakes (Cavamore)
1970: California Derby (George Lewis)
1974: American Handicap (Plunk)

BARBARA MINSHALL
1997: Gulfstream Park Handicap (Mt. Sassafras)

F.A. MIQUELEZ
1970: Del Mar Debutante Stakes (Generous Portion)
1971: Del Mar Debutante Stakes (Impressive Style)

EARL MITCHELL
1970: Hollywood Juvenile Championship (Fast Fellow)

MIKE MITCHELL
1984: California Derby (Distant Ryder)

PHILIP MITCHELL
1999: Brooklyn Handicap (Running Stag)

WILLIAM MITCHELL
1960: Futurity Stakes (Little Tumbler)

STEVEN MIYADI
1989: Del Mar Futurity (Drag Race)

S.J. MOLAY
1965: Hawthorne Gold Cup (Moss Vale)

BILL MOLTER
1947: Santa Anita Derby (On Trust)
Will Rogers Handicap (On Trust)
American Handicap (Burning Dream)
1948: Hollywood Gold Cup (Shannon II)
Golden Gate Handicap (Shannon II)
Westerner Handicap (Solidarity)
1949: Inglewood Handicap (Ace Admiral)

BILL MOLTER *(Continued)*

Sunset Handicap (Ace Admiral)
Santa Anita Maturity (Ace Admiral)
Westerner Stakes (Pedigree)
Cinema Handicap (Pedigree)
Hollywood Oaks (June Bride)
Del Mar Handicap (Top's Boy)
1951: Starlet Stakes (Prudy's Boy)
1953: San Felipe Handicap (Decorated)
1954: San Felipe Handicap (Determine)
Santa Anita Derby (Determine)
Kentucky Derby (Determine)
William P. Kyne Handicap (Imbros)
Californian Stakes (Imbros)
1955: American Handicap (Alidon)
Santa Anita Maturity (Determine)
1956: Santa Anita Handicap (Bobby Brocato)
San Juan Capistrano Handicap (Bobby Brocato)
Starlet Stakes (Lucky Mel)
Santa Margarita Handicap (Our Betters)
1957: Blue Grass Stakes (Round Table)
Cinema Handicap (Round Table)
Westerner Stakes (Round Table)
American Derby (Round Table)
Hollywood Gold Cup (Round Table)
Hawthorne Gold Cup (Round Table)
United Nations Handicap (Round Table)
Santa Margarita Handicap (Our Betters)
San Felipe Handicap (Joe Price)
1958: San Antonio Handicap (Round Table)
Santa Anita Handicap (Round Table)
Gulfstream Park Handicap (Round Table)
Hawthorne Gold Cup (Round Table)
Santa Anita Maturity (Round Table)
Arlington Handicap (Round Table)
1959: Washington Park Handicap (Round Table)
Manhattan Handicap (Round Table)
Stars and Stripes Handicap (Round Table)
Arlington Handicap (Round Table)
United Nations Handicap (Round Table)

MARVIN MONCRIEF

1985: Laurel Futurity (Southern Appeal)

JOSEPH MOOS

1971: Coaching Club American Oaks (Our Cheri Amour)

CARLOS MORALES

2000: Metropolitan Handicap (Yankee Victor)

HENRY MORENO

1965: Vanity Handicap (Jalousie II)
1974: Santa Margarita Handicap (Tizna)
Ramona Handicap (Tizna)
1975: Ladies Handicap (Tizna)
Santa Margarita Handicap (Tizna)
1976: Ladies Handicap (Bastonera II)
Beverly Hills Handicap (Bastonera II)
1978: Fantasy Stakes (Equanimity)
Del Mar Handicap (Palton)
1982: Vanity Handicap (Sangue)
1983: Ramona Handicap (Sangue)
Golden Harvest Handicap (Sangue)
Yellow Ribbon Stakes (Sangue)
Matriarch Stakes (Sangue)
1987: Santa Anita Oaks (Timely Assertion)
1990: Oak Leaf Stakes (Lite Light)
1991: Santa Anita Oaks (Lite Light)
1993: Vanity Handicap (Re Toss)

JIM MORGAN

1975: Ohio Derby (Brent's Prince)

J.L. MOSBACHER

1968: California Derby (Proper Proof)

GASPER MOSCHERA

1985: Ladies Handicap (Videogenic)

PETER MOSCONI

1965: Dwyer Handicap (Staunchness)

GRAHAM MOTION

2001: Philip H. Iselin Handicap (Broken Vow)
2003: Queen Elizabeth II Challenge Cup (Film Maker)

BILL MOTT

1984: Ruffian Handicap (Heatherten)
Ladies Handicap (Heatherten)
Apple Blossom Handicap (Heatherten)
Louisiana Derby (Taylor's Special)
Blue Grass Stakes (Taylor's Special)
1985: Apple Blossom Handicap (Sefa's Beauty)
1987: Hialeah Turf Cup (Theatrical)
Turf Classic (Theatrical)
Man o' War Stakes (Theatrical)
Breeders' Cup Turf (Theatrical)
1988: Flower Bowl Handicap (Gaily Gaily)
1989: Selima Stakes (Sweet Roberta)
1990: Jim Dandy Stakes (Chief Honcho)
1992: Sword Dancer Handicap (Fraise)
Breeders' Cup Turf (Fraise)
Hollywood Derby (Paradise Creek)
Brooklyn Handicap (Chief Honcho)
1993: Hollywood Turf Cup (Fraise)
1994: Early Times Manhattan Handicap (Paradise Creek)
Arlington Million (Paradise Creek)
Washington D.C. International (Paradise Creek)
Gulfstream Park Handicap (Scuffleberg)
Flower Bowl Inv. Handicap (Dahlia's Dreamer)
NYRA Mile Handicap (Cigar)
1995: Donn Handicap (Cigar)
Gulfstream Park Handicap (Cigar)
Oaklawn Handicap (Cigar)
Pimlico Special (Cigar)
Hollywood Gold Cup (Cigar)
Woodward Stakes (Cigar)
Jockey Club Gold Cup (Cigar)
Breeders' Cup Classic (Cigar)
Jim Dandy Stakes (Composer)
Flower Bowl Inv. Handicap (Northern Emerald)
Rothmans International Stakes (Lassigny)
Matriarch Stakes (Duda)
1996: Gulfstream Park Handicap (Wekiva Springs)
Brooklyn Handicap (Wekiva Springs)
Suburban Handicap (Wekiva Springs)
Donn Handicap (Cigar)
Woodward Stakes (Cigar)
Oaklawn Handicap (Geri)
Sword Dancer Invitational Handicap (Broadway Flyer)
1997: Mother Goose Stakes (Ajina)
Coaching Club American Oaks (Ajina)
Breeders' Cup Distaff (Ajina)
Ramona Handicap (Escena)
Woodbine Mile (Geri)
1998: Apple Blossom Handicap (Escena)
Vanity Handicap (Escena)
Breeders' Cup Distaff (Escena)
Jim Dandy Stakes (Favorite Trick)
Frizette Stakes (Confessional)
1999: Gulfstream Park Breeders' Cup Handicap (Yagli)
Manhattan Handicap (Yagli)
2000: Test Stakes (Dream Supreme)
Ballerina Handicap (Dream Supreme)
Gulfstream Park BC Handicap (Royal Anthem)
Beverly D. Stakes (Snow Polina)
2001: Gulfstream Park BC Handicap (Subtle Power)

IKE MOURAR

1954: Alcibiades Stakes (Myrtle's Jet)
Frizette Stakes (Myrtle's Jet)
Roamer Handicap (Jet Action)
1955: Washington Park Handicap (Jet Action)
1973: Fantasy Stakes (Knitted Gloves)

TIM MUCKLER

1981: Sorority Stakes (Apalachee Honey)
Alcibiades Stakes (Apalachee Honey)
1983: Arlington-Washington Futurity (All Fired Up)

RICHARD MULHALL

1987: San Felipe Handicap (Chart the Stars)
1994: Norfolk Stakes (Supremo)

BERT MULHOLLAND

1946: Monmouth Handicap (Lucky Draw)
1948: Acorn Stakes (Watermill)
Black Helen Handicap (Shotsilk)
1949: Remsen Handicap (Lights Up)
1950: Saratoga Special (Battlefield)
Hopeful Stakes (Battlefield)
Tremont Stakes (Battlefield)
Futurity Stakes (Battlefield)
Astoria Stakes (Sungari)
Travers Stakes (Lights Up)
1951: Withers Stakes (Battlefield)
Dwyer Stakes (Battlefield)
Travers Stakes (Battlefield)
Marguerite Stakes (No Score)
Black-Eyed Susan Stakes (Discreet)
1952: New York Handicap (Battlefield)
Westchester Handicap (Battlefield)
1953: Spinaway Stakes (Evening Out)
Matron Stakes (Evening Out)
1954: Monmouth Oaks (Evening Out)
1955: Firenze Handicap (Rare Treat)
1956: Vineland Handicap (Rare Treat)
1957: Futurity Stakes (Jester)
Ladies Handicap (Rare Treat)
1961: Hopeful Stakes (Jaipur)
Cowdin Stakes (Jaipur)
1962: Gotham Stakes (Jaipur)
Withers Stakes (Jaipur)
Jersey Derby (Jaipur)
Belmont Stakes (Jaipur)
Travers Stakes (Jaipur)
Black Helen Handicap (Seven Thirty)
Delaware Handicap (Seven Thirty)
Garden State Stakes (Crewman)
1963: Travers Stakes (Crewman)
1964: Ladies Handicap (Steeple Jill)
1965: Delaware Handicap (Steeple Jill)
Vineland Handicap (Steeple Jill)
1966: Hopeful Stakes (Bold Hour)
Futurity Stakes (Bold Hour)
1967: Widener Handicap (Ring Twice)

JEFF MULLINS

2003: Santa Anita Derby (Buddy Gil)

EDDIE MULRENAN

1946: San Antonio Handicap (First Fiddle)

JAMES MURPHY

1973: American Derby (Bemo)
1976: Demoiselle Stakes (Bring Out the Band)
1977: Acorn Stakes (Bring Out the Band)
United Nations Handicap (Bemo)

PAUL MURPHY

1986: Hollywood Derby (Spellbound)

RODERICK MYERS

1960: John B. Campbell Handicap (Yes You Will)
Carter Handicap (Yes You Will)

HERBERT NADLER

1970: Dwyer Handicap (Judgable)
Whitney Stakes (Judgable)
1971: Donn Handicap (Judgable)
Grey Lag Handicap (Judgable)

CARL NAFZGER

1980: Breeders' Futurity (Fairway Phantom)
1981: Arlington Classic (Fairway Phantom)
1990: Florida Derby (Unbridled)
Kentucky Derby (Unbridled)
Breeders' Cup Classic (Unbridled)
Super Derby (Home at Last)
1998: Coaching Club American Oaks (Banshee Breeze)
Alabama Stakes (Banshee Breeze)
Three Chimneys Spinster Stakes (Banshee Breeze)
1999: Fountain of Youth Stakes (Vicar)
Florida Derby (Vicar)
Apple Blossom Handicap (Banshee Breeze)
Go for Wand Handicap (Banshee Breeze)
2000: Travers Stakes (Unshaded)
2002: Walmac Int. Alcibiades Stakes (Westerly Breeze)

JOSEPH NASH

1964: Canadian Championship Stakes (Will I Rule)
Dixie Handicap (Will I Rule)
1965: Display Handicap (Brave Lad)
1981: Widener Handicap (Land of Eire)

GENE NAVARRO

1990: Coaching Club American Oaks (Charon)

JAMES NAZWORTHY

1960: Californian Stakes (Fleet Nasrullah)
1961: American Handicap (Prince Blessed)
Hollywood Gold Cup (Prince Blessed)
California Derby (Mr. Consistency)
1964: Santa Anita Handicap (Mr. Consistency)
San Juan Capistrano Handicap (Mr. Consistency)
1965: Carter Handicap (Viking Spirit)
Californian Stakes (Viking Spirit)
1969: Del Mar Debutante Stakes (Atomic Wings)

EDDIE NELOY

1954: Kentucky Oaks (Fascinator)
Withers Stakes (Jet Action)
Brooklyn Handicap (Invigorator)
1961: Ladies Handicap (Mighty Fair)
Display Handicap (Hillsborough)
1964: Gulfstream Park Handicap (Gun Bow)

Brooklyn Handicap (Gun Bow)
Washington Park Handicap (Gun Bow)
Woodward Stakes (Gun Bow)
San Fernando Stakes (Gun Bow)
Charles H. Strub Stakes (Gun Bow)
San Antonio Handicap (Gun Bow)
Whitney Stakes (Gun Bow)
Top Flight Handicap (Oil Royalty)
1965: Donn Handicap (Gun Bow)
Metropolitan Handicap (Gun Bow)
San Antonio Handicap (Gun Bow)
Acorn Stakes (Ground Control)
1966: Everglades Stakes (Buckpasser)
Flamingo Stakes (Buckpasser)
Arlington Classic (Buckpasser)
American Derby (Buckpasser)
Travers Stakes (Buckpasser)
Lawrence Realization Stakes (Buckpasser)
Brooklyn Handicap (Buckpasser)
Woodward Stakes (Buckpasser)
Jockey Club Gold Cup (Buckpasser)
Champagne Stakes (Successor)
Garden State Stakes (Successor)
Sapling Stakes (Great Power)
Acorn Stakes (Marking Time)
Ladies Handicap (Destro)
Gotham Stakes (Stupendous)
Jerome Handicap (Bold and Brave)
Metropolitan Handicap (Bold Lad)
1967: Saratoga Special (Vitriolic)
Arlington-Washington Futurity (Vitriolic)
Champagne Stakes (Vitriolic)
Pimlico-Laurel Futurity (Vitriolic)
Sorority Stakes (Queen of the Stage)
Spinaway Stakes (Queen of the Stage)
Matron Stakes (Queen of the Stage)
Frizette Stakes (Queen of the Stage)
Metropolitan Handicap (Buckpasser)
Suburban Handicap (Buckpasser)
San Fernando Stakes (Buckpasser)
Arlington Handicap (Stupendous)
Whitney Stakes (Stupendous)
Hopeful Stakes (What a Pleasure)
Lawrence Realization Stakes (Successor)
Bowling Green Handicap (Poker)
1968: Sanford Stakes (King Emperor)
Cowdin Stakes (King Emperor)
Pimlico-Laurel Futurity (King Emperor)
Sapling Stakes (Reviewer)
Saratoga Special (Reviewer)
Lawrence Realization Stakes (Funny Fellow)
Gallant Fox Handicap (Funny Fellow)
Garden State Stakes (Beau Brummel)
Sorority Stakes (Big Advance)
1969: Hopeful Stakes (Irish Castle)
Selima Stakes (Predictable)
Illinois Derby (King of the Castle)
Donn Handicap (Funny Fellow)
1970: American Derby (The Pruner)

JAN NERUD

1980: Canadian International Championship (Great Neck)
1981: Metropolitan Handicap (Fappiano)
Bowling Green Handicap (Great Neck)
1983: United Nations Handicap (Acaroid)
1984: Wood Memorial Stakes (Leroy S.)
Arlington Handicap (Who's For Dinner)
1985: Futurity Stakes (Ogygian)
Breeders' Cup Mile (Cozzene)
1986: Dwyer Stakes (Ogygian)
Jerome Handicap (Ogygian)
1987: Delaware Handicap (Coup de Fusil)
Ruffian Handicap (Coup de Fusil)

JOHN NERUD

1956: McLennan Handicap (Switch On)
1957: Belmont Stakes (Gallant Man)
Travers Stakes (Gallant Man)
Jockey Club Gold Cup (Gallant Man)
1958: Metropolitan Handicap (Gallant Man)
Hollywood Gold Cup (Gallant Man)
Sunset Handicap (Gallant Man)
1961: Black Helen Handicap (Be Cautious)
1962: Seminole Handicap (Intentionally)
1964: United Nations Handicap (Western Warrior)
1966: Cowdin Stakes (Dr. Fager)
1967: Gotham Stakes (Dr. Fager)
Withers Stakes (Dr. Fager)
Arlington Classic (Dr. Fager)
Hawthorne Gold Cup (Dr. Fager)
Vosburgh Handicap (Dr. Fager)
Man o' War Stakes (Ruffled Feathers)
1968: Californian Stakes (Dr. Fager)
Suburban Handicap (Dr. Fager)
Washington Park Handicap (Dr. Fager)
Vosburgh Handicap (Dr. Fager)
Whitney Stakes (Dr. Fager)
United Nations Handicap (Dr. Fager)
1974: Demoiselle Stakes (Land Girl)
1975: Gazelle Handicap (Land Girl)
1978: Vosburgh Handicap (Dr. Patches)
Meadowlands Cup (Dr. Patches)

LEFTY NICKERSON

1966: Whitney Stakes (Staunchness)
1967: Jerome Handicap (High Tribute)
1973: Coaching Club American Oaks (Magazine)
San Luis Rey Handicap (Big Spruce)
1974: Secretariat Stakes (Glossary)
Marlboro Cup Handicap (Big Spruce)
1975: Alabama Stakes (Spout)
1981: Jockey Club Gold Cup (John Henry)
Sword Dancer Stakes (John Henry)
Secretariat Stakes (Sing Sing)
Hialeah Turf Cup (Lobsang II)
1982: Super Derby (Reinvested)

R. NIXON

1946: Bougainvillea Handicap (Cat Bridge)
1948: Black Helen Handicap (Rampart)
Gulfstream Park Handicap (Rampart)

REYNALDO NOBLES

1980: Monmouth Invitational Handicap (Thanks to Tony)
1981: Gulfstream Park Handicap (Hurry Up Blue)
1993: Hopeful Stakes (Dehere)
Champagne Stakes (Dehere)

KENNY NOE

1959: Monmouth Oaks (Royal Native)
Spinster Stakes (Royal Native)
1960: Black Helen Handicap (Royal Native)

CHARLES NORMAN

1946: Excelsior Handicap (Fighting Step)
1958: Princess Pat Stakes (Battle Heart)
1964: Delaware Handicap (Old Hat)
Spinster Stakes (Old Hat)
1965: Black Helen Handicap (Old Hat)
Matron Handicap (Old Hat)
Michigan Mile and One-Eighth (Old Hat)

AIDAN O'BRIEN

2000: Secretariat Stakes (Ciro)
2001: Bessemer Trust BC Juvenile (Johannesburg)
2002: Shadwell Keeneland Turf Mile (Landseer)
John Deere Breeders' Cup Turf (High Chaparral)
2003: John Deere Breeders' Cup Turf (High Chaparral)

LEO O'BRIEN

1986: Coaching Club American Oaks (Valley Victory)
1994: Hopeful Stakes (Wild Escapade)
1996: Mother Goose Stakes (Yanks Music)
Alabama Stakes (Yanks Music)
Ruffian Handicap (Yanks Music)
Beldame Stakes (Yanks Music)

VINCENT O'BRIEN

1968: Washington D.C. International (Sir Ivor)
1990: Breeders' Cup Mile (Royal Academy)

JAMES O'BRYANT

1973: Sapling Stakes (Tisab)

NIALL O'CALLAGHAN

1992: Jersey Derby (American Chance)
1999: Coaching Club American Oaks (On a Soapbox)
2001: San Antonio Handicap (Guided Tour)

RICHARD O'CONNELL

1988: Selima Stakes (Capades)
1992: Jim Dandy Stakes (Thunder Rumble)
Travers Stakes (Thunder Rumble)

GEORGE ODOM

1946: Spinaway Stakes (Pipette)
1947: Spinaway Stakes (Bellesoeur)
Astarita Stakes (Bellesoeur)
Top Flight Handicap (Rytina)
Wood Memorial Stakes (I Will)
Travers Stakes (Young Peter)
Jerome Handicap (Donor)
Roseben Handicap (Inroc)
1949: Manhattan Handicap (Donor)
New York Handicap (Donor)
1952: Delaware Oaks (Big Mo)
1955: Pimlico Futurity (Nail)
Remsen Stakes (Nail)
Futurity Stakes (Nail)
1956: Hialeah Turf Handicap (Guardian II)
1957: Arlington Lassie Stakes (Poly Hi)
1958: Remsen Stakes (Atoll)
1959: Display Handicap (Beau Diable)

ROBERT ODOM

1946: McLennan Handicap (Concordian)
1948: Massachusetts Handicap (Beauchef)
1952: Gulfstream Park Handicap (Crafty Admiral)
Brooklyn Handicap (Crafty Admiral)
Washington Park Handicap (Crafty Admiral)
1953: McLennan Handicap (Crafty Admiral)
Gulfstream Park Handicap (Crafty Admiral)
New York Handicap (Crafty Admiral)

DUANE OFFIELD

1990: Haskell Invitational Handicap (Right Con)

FRANCIS OGDEN

1967: John B. Campbell Handicap (Quinta)

LUIS OLIVERAS

1986: Hollywood Invitational Handicap (Flying Pidgeon)

DOUG O'NEILL

2002: Hollywood Gold Cup (Sky Jack)
2003: Ancient Title Breeders' Cup Handicap (Avanzado)

VICTOR OPPEGARD

1987: Hollywood Oaks (Perchance to Dream)

JOE ORSENO

1998: Gazelle Handicap (Tap to Music)
1999: Garden City Breeders' Cup Handicap (Perfect Sting)
Queen Elizabeth II Challenge Cup (Perfect Sting)
2000: Pimlico Special (Golden Missile)
Preakness Stakes (Red Bullet)
Queen Elizabeth II Challenge Cup (Collect the Cash)
Breeders' Cup Juvenile (Macho Uno)
Breeders' Cup Filly and Mare Turf (Perfect Sting)

BRYANT OTT

1963: Kentucky Jockey Club Stakes (Journalist)
1965: Kentucky Jockey Club Stakes (War Censor)
1967: Hialeah Turf Cup (War Censor)
Pan American Handicap (War Censor)
Dixie Handicap (War Censor)

JOHN OXLEY

1970: Kentucky Oaks (Lady Vi-E)
1978: Michigan Mile and One-Eighth (A Letter to Harry)
1979: New Orleans Handicap (A Letter to Harry)

JOHN OXX

1995: Breeders' Cup Mile (Ridgewood Pearl)
1996: Beverly D. Stakes (Timarida)

JAMES PADGETT

1966: Louisiana Derby (Blue Skyer)

HERB PALEY

1973: Louisiana Derby (Leo's Pisces)

HECTOR PALMA

1988: Santa Barbara Handicap (Pen Bal Lady)
Gamely Handicap (Pen Bal Lady)

JOHN PAPPALARDO

1974: Hopeful Stakes (The Bagel Prince)

HOMER PARDUE

1955: Roseben Handicap (Red Hannigan)
1956: Jerome Handicap (Reneged)
Carter Handicap (Red Hannigan)
1957: Manhattan Handicap (Reneged)
1972: Louisiana Derby (No Le Hace)
Arkansas Derby (No Le Hace)
1975: Futurity Stakes (Soy Numero Uno)
1977: Louisiana Derby (Clev Er Tell)
Arkansas Derby (Clev Er Tell)
Carter Handicap (Soy Numero Uno)
Oaklawn Handicap (Soy Numero Uno)
Jerome Handicap (Broadway Forli)

JOHN PARISELLA

1987: California Derby (Simply Majestic)

C.W. PARISH
1957: Coaching Club American Oaks (Willamette)
1958: Sapling Stakes (Watch Your Step)

BURLEY PARKE
1946: Discovery Handicap (Mighty Story)
1949: Will Rogers Handicap (Blue Dart)
1950: Santa Anita Handicap (Noor)
San Juan Capistrano Handicap (Noor)
Golden Gate Handicap (Noor)
American Handicap (Noor)
Hollywood Gold Cup (Noor)
1960: Wood Memorial Stakes (Francis S.)
Dwyer Handicap (Francis S.)
Champagne Stakes (Roving Minstrel)
Pimlico Futurity (Garwol)
1961: Bougainvillea Turf Handicap (Wolfram)
Hialeah Turf Cup (Wolfram)
1962: Ladies Handicap (Royal Patrice)
1963: Champagne Stakes (Roman Brother)
1964: Everglades Stakes (Roman Brother)
Jersey Derby (Roman Brother)
American Derby (Roman Brother)
Jerome Handicap (Irvkup)
Arlington Handicap (Master Dennis)
1965: Woodward Stakes (Roman Brother)
Manhattan Handicap (Roman Brother)
Jockey Club Gold Cup (Roman Brother)
Everglades Stakes (Sparkling Johnny)

CHUCK PARKE
1960: Washington Park Futurity (Crozier)
Monmouth Oaks (Teacation)
1961: Kentucky Oaks (My Portrait)
1962: Louisiana Derby (Admiral's Voyage)
Wood Memorial Stakes (Admiral's Voyage)
Gardenia Stakes (Main Swap)
Aqueduct Stakes (Crozier)
1963: Carter Handicap (Admiral's Voyage)
1973: Futurity Stakes (Wedge Shot)
Spinster Stakes (Susan's Girl)
1974: Alabama Stakes (Quaze Quilt)

IVAN PARKE
1946: Washington Park Futurity (Education)
Breeders' Futurity (Education)
1948: Breeders' Futurity (Olympia)
Vosburgh Handicap (Colosal)
1949: Flamingo Stakes (Olympia)
San Felipe Stakes (Olympia)
Wood Memorial Stakes (Olympia)
Withers Stakes (Olympia)
1950: Roseben Handicap (Olympia)
1953: Trenton Handicap (Olympic)
1956: Arlington Futurity (Greek Game)
Washington Park Futurity (Greek Game)
1957: Cowdin Stakes (Jewel's Reward)
Champagne Stakes (Jewel's Reward)
Pimlico Futurity (Jewel's Reward)
1958: Wood Memorial Stakes (Jewel's Reward)
1967: Sanford Stakes (Exclusive Native)
1968: Arlington Classic (Exclusive Native)
1971: Carter Handicap (Native Royalty)
Michigan Mile and One-Eighth (Native Royalty)

MONTE PARKE
1948: Kentucky Jockey Club Stakes (Johns Joy)
1953: Del Mar Futurity (Double Speed)
1954: Acorn Stakes (Happy Mood)
1960: Arkansas Derby (Persian Gold)
1966: Hollywood Juvenile Champ. (Forgotten Dreams)

LEON PARKER JR.
1980: Pennsylvania Derby (Lively King)

PAUL PARKER
1960: Arlington Classic (T.V. Lark)
American Derby (T.V. Lark)
Washington Park Handicap (T.V. Lark)
United Nations Handicap (T.V. Lark)
1961: Los Angeles Handicap (T.V. Lark)
Hawthorne Gold Cup (T.V. Lark)
Washington D.C. International (T.V. Lark)
1969: Santa Barbara Handicap (Pink Pigeon)
1973: American Handicap (Kentuckian)

JOHN PARTRIDGE
1949: Acorn Stakes (Nell K.)
Gazelle Stakes (Nell K.)
1950: Top Flight Handicap (Nell K.)

WARREN PASCUMA
1963: Demoiselle Stakes (Windsor Lady)

W.L. PASSMORE
1948: Monmouth Handicap (Tide Rips)

JONATHAN PEASE
1987: Laurel Futurity (Antiqua)
1988: Yellow Ribbon Stakes (Delighter)
1994: Turf Classic (Tikkanen)
Breeders' Cup Turf (Tikkanen)
1997: Breeders' Cup Mile (Spinning World)

G. PELAT
1956: Washington D.C. International (Master Boing)

ANGEL PENNA
1968: Man o' War Stakes (Czar Alexander)
1969: Dixie Handicap (Czar Alexander)
Bowling Green Handicap (Czar Alexander)
Oak Tree Stakes (Czar Alexander)
Hialeah Turf Cup (Blanquette II)
1970: Massachusetts Handicap (Semillant)
1971: Hollywood Derby (Bold Reason)
Travers Stakes (Bold Reason)
American Derby (Bold Reason)
1978: Man o' War Stakes (Waya)
Turf Classic (Waya)
1979: Maskette Stakes (Blitey)
Brooklyn Handicap (The Liberal Member)
1980: Widener Handicap (Private Account)
Gulfstream Park Handicap (Private Account)
Pan American Handicap (Flitalong)
United Nations Handicap (Lyphard's Wish)
1981: Delaware Handicap (Relaxing)
Ruffian Handicap (Relaxing)
1983: Beldame Stakes (Dance Number)
Bowling Green Handicap (Tantalizing)
1984: Everglades Stakes (Time for a Change)
Flamingo Stakes (Time for a Change)
1985: Everglades Stakes (Rhoman Rule)
1986: Secretariat Stakes (Southjet)
Rothmans International Stakes (Southjet)
1988: United Nations Handicap (Equalize)
1990: Jersey Derby (Yonder)
Brooklyn Handicap (Montubio)

ANGEL PENNA JR.
1982: Coaching Club American Oaks (Christmas Past)
Ruffian Handicap (Christmas Past)
1983: Jerome Handicap (A Phenomenon)
Vosburgh Stakes (A Phenomenon)
Gulfstream Park Handicap (Christmas Past)
1990: Flower Bowl Handicap (Laugh and Be Merry)
1994: Apple Blossom Handicap (Nine Keys)
1998: Flower Bowl Invitational Handicap (Auntie Mame)

CHARLIE PEOPLES
1959: Flamingo Stakes (Troilus)
1983: Pennsylvania Derby (Dixieland Band)
1985: Hopeful Stakes (Papal Power)
1986: Hutcheson Stakes (Papal Power)
1989: Fountain of Youth Stakes (Dixieland Brass)
1994: Pegasus Handicap (Brass Scale)

ALFIO PEPINO
1965: Garden State Stakes (Prince Saim)

PICO PERDOMO
1990: Oak Tree Invitational Stakes (Rial)
1999: Milady Breeders' Cup Handicap (Gourmet Girl)
2001: Apple Blossom Handicap (Gourmet Girl)
Vanity Handicap (Gourmet Girl)

D. PEREGOY
1948: Vineland Handicap (Honeymoon)
Top Flight Handicap (Honeymoon)

BEN PERKINS
1981: Haskell Invitational Handicap (Five Star Flight)

BEN PERKINS JR.
1993: Wood Memorial Stakes (Storm Tower)
1994: Meadowlands Cup (Conveyor)
2000: Spinaway Stakes (Stormy Pick)
2001: Forego Handicap (Delaware Township)
Frank J. De Francis Mem. Dash (Delaware Township)

DANNY PERLSWIG
1980: Champagne Stakes (Lord Avie)
Young America Stakes (Lord Avie)
1981: Florida Derby (Lord Avie)

BILL PERRY
1996: Acorn Stakes (Star de Lady Ann)
1997: Donn Handicap (Formal Gold)
Brooklyn Handicap (Formal Gold)
Philip H. Iselin Handicap (Formal Gold)
Woodward Stakes (Formal Gold)

BILL PETERSON
1964: Californian Stakes (Mustard Plaster)
1966: Monmouth Oaks (Natashka)
Alabama Stakes (Natashka)
Santa Susana Stakes (Spearfish)

DOUG PETERSON
1978: Marlboro Cup Handicap (Seattle Slew)
Woodward Stakes (Seattle Slew)

CLYDE PHILLIPS
1946: San Juan Capistrano Handicap (Triplicate)
Hollywood Gold Cup (Triplicate)

GRACETON PHILPOT
1946: Hollywood Oaks (Honeymoon)
Cinema Handicap (Honeymoon)
Hollywood Derby (Honeymoon)
Vanity Handicap (Be Faithful)
1947: Vanity Handicap (Honeymoon)
1957: William P. Kyne Memorial Handicap (Pibe Carlitos)

HURST PHILPOT
1948: Santa Margarita Handicap (Miss Doreen)
1960: Del Mar Futurity (Short Jacket)
1968: Hollywood Juvenile Championship (Fleet Kirsch)
1971: Vanity Handicap (Hi Q.)

JOSEPH PIARULLI
1958: Pimlico Special (Vertex)
Trenton Handicap (Vertex)
1959: Gulfstream Park Handicap (Vertex)
John B. Campbell Handicap (Vertex)
Grey Lag Handicap (Vertex)

W.R. PICKETT
1976: Ohio Derby (Return of a Native)

CLARENCE PICOU
1988: Ohio Derby (Jim's Orbit)
1991: Super Derby (Free Spirit's Joy)

JAMES PICOU
1963: Sapling Stakes (Mr. Brick)
1964: Withers Stakes (Mr. Brick)
1967: Coaching Club American Oaks (Quillo Queen)
Monmouth Oaks (Quillo Queen)
1970: Matron Stakes (Bonnie and Gay)
1974: Acorn Stakes (Special Team)
1975: Oak Leaf Stakes (Answer)
1977: Sorority Stakes (Stub)
Arlington-Washington Lassie Stakes (Stub)
1978: Matron Stakes (Fall Aspen)
1981: Travers Stakes (Willow Hour)
1996: Early Times Manhattan Handicap (Diplomatic Jet)
Man o' War Stakes (Diplomatic Jet)
Turf Classic (Diplomatic Jet)
1997: Turf Classic (Val's Prince)

JAMES PIERCE JR.
1964: Michigan Mile and One-Sixteenth (Going Abroad)
Manhattan Handicap (Going Abroad)
Hawthorne Gold Cup (Going Abroad)
1965: New Orleans Handicap (Valiant Man)
1969: Arlington-Washington Lassie Stakes (Clover Lane)
Washington Park Handicap (Night Invader)
1972: Arlington-Washington Lassie Stakes (Natural Sound)

JOSEPH PIERCE JR.
1987: Acorn Stakes (Grecian Flight)
1991: Young America Stakes (Maston)
1992: Spinaway Stakes (Family Enterprize)
1996: Jerome Handicap (Why Change)

SLIM PIERCE
1950: Gulfstream Park Handicap (Chicle II)
Trenton Handicap (Chicle II)
Bougainvillea Handicap (Chicle II)
1951: Bougainvillea Handicap (Chicle II)
1954: Remsen Stakes (Roman Patrol)
1955: Louisiana Derby (Roman Patrol)
1962: Arlington Handicap (El Bandido)
Canadian Championship Stakes (El Bandido)
1963: Hialeah Turf Cup (Intercepted)

JIMMY PITT
1960: Flamingo Stakes (Bally Ache)
Florida Derby (Bally Ache)

Preakness Stakes (Bally Ache)
Jersey Derby (Bally Ache)

EDWARD PLESA JR.
1999: Acorn Stakes (Three Ring)

JAKE PLETCHER
1980: Oaklawn Handicap (Uncool)

TODD PLETCHER
1998: Acorn Stakes (Jersey Girl)
Mother Goose Stakes (Jersey Girl)
Test Stakes (Jersey Girl)
1999: Test Stakes (Marley Vale)
Spinaway Stakes (Circle of Life)
2000: Arkansas Derby (Graeme Hall)
Jim Dandy Stakes (Graeme Hall)
King's Bishop Stakes (More Than Ready)
Vosburgh Stakes (Trippi)
2001: Turfway Spiral Stakes (Balto Star)
Arkansas Derby (Balto Star)
Vosburgh Stakes (Left Bank)
Cigar Mile Handicap (Left Bank)
Coaching Club American Oaks (Tweedside)
2002: Whitney Handicap (Left Bank)
2003: Donn Handicap (Harlan's Holiday)
United Nations Handicap (Balto Star)
Jim Dandy Stakes (Strong Hope)
Ballerina Handicap (Harmony Lodge)
Spinaway Stakes (Ashado)
Matron Stakes (Marylebone)

J.F. PLETT
1969: Michigan Mile and One-Eighth (Calandrito)

NORMAN POINTER
2000: Philip H. Iselin Handicap (Rize)

MARCELO POLANCO
2003: La Brea Stakes (Island Fashion)

GEORGE POOLE
1953: Flamingo Stakes (Straight Face)
1954: Everglades Stakes (Maharajah)
1955: Tropical Handicap (Illusionist)
1960: Spinaway Stakes (Good Move)
Selima Stakes (Good Move)
1963: Withers Stakes (Get Around)
1966: Hialeah Turf Cup (Kentucky Jug)
1969: Gulfstream Park Handicap (Court Recess)
1971: Arkansas Derby (Twist the Axe)
Ohio Derby (Twist the Axe)
Blue Grass Stakes (Impetuosity)
Widener Handicap (True North)
1972: Top Flight Handicap (Inca Queen)
1973: Kentucky Oaks (Bag of Tunes)
1975: Ashland Stakes (Sun and Snow)
Kentucky Oaks (Sun and Snow)
1976: Hopeful Stakes (Banquet Table)

TIM POOLE
1977: Florida Derby (Coined Silver)
Widener Handicap (Yamanin)

DICK POSEY
1967: Arlington-Washington Lassie Stakes (Shenow)

WILLIAM POST
1946: Top Flight Handicap (Sicily)
1948: Vagrancy Handicap (Conniver)
Beldame Handicap (Conniver)
Comely Handicap (Conniver)
Brooklyn Handicap (Conniver)
Cowdin Stakes (Algasir)
1957: Top Flight Handicap (Plotter)

GORDON POTTER
1960: Kentucky Jockey Club Stakes (Crimson Fury)
1961: Garden State Stakes (Crimson Satan)
Pimlico Futurity (Crimson Satan)
1974: Arlington-Washington Lassie Stakes (Hot n Nasty)
1975: Amory L. Haskell Handicap (Royal Glint)
Arlington Handicap (Royal Glint)
Hawthorne Gold Cup (Royal Glint)
United Nations Handicap (Royal Glint)
1976: Santa Anita Handicap (Royal Glint)
1979: Sorority Stakes (Love Street)

R.E. POTTS
1947: Arlington Futurity (Piet)

ERNIE POULOUS
1991: Philip H. Iselin Handicap (Black Tie Affair)
Breeders' Cup Classic (Black Tie Affair)

TOM PRATT
1971: Cinema Handicap (Niagara)
1975: San Felipe Handicap (Fleet Velvet)
American Handicap (Pass the Glass)
1976: Vanity Handicap (Miss Toshiba)
1977: Ashland Stakes (Sound of Summer)
1978: Bay Meadows Handicap (Bywayofchicago)

GUADALUPE PRECIADO
1990: Demoiselle Stakes (Debutant's Halo)

MITCHELL PREGER
1983: Maskette Stakes (Ambassador of Luck)

R.D. PREWITT
1958: Ohio Derby (Terra Firma)
Stars and Stripes Handicap (Terra Firma)

JACK PRICE
1960: Cowdin Stakes (Carry Back)
Garden State Stakes (Carry Back)
Remsen Stakes (Carry Back)
1961: Everglades Stakes (Carry Back)
Flamingo Stakes (Carry Back)
Florida Derby (Carry Back)
Kentucky Derby (Carry Back)
Preakness Stakes (Carry Back)
Jerome Handicap (Carry Back)
Trenton Handicap (Carry Back)
1962: Metropolitan Handicap (Carry Back)
Monmouth Handicap (Carry Back)
Whitney Stakes (Carry Back)
1963: Trenton Handicap (Carry Back)

JAMES PRICE
1976: Michigan Mile and One-Eighth (Sharp Gary)

W.C. PRICKETT
1962: Delaware Oaks (North South Gal)

RAY PRIDDY
1949: Starlet Stakes (Thanks Again)
1966: Hollywood Derby (Fleet Host)
1967: San Luis Rey Handicap (Fleet Host)
1978: Cinema Handicap (Kamehameha)

THOMAS PROCTOR
1994: Breeders' Cup Distaff (One Dreamer)

WILLARD PROCTOR
1966: Vosburgh Handicap (Gallant Romeo)
1972: Vanity Handicap (Convenience)
Santa Barbara Handicap (Hail the Grey)
1973: Vanity Handicap (Convenience)
1974: Santa Maria Handicap (Convenience)
1975: Century Handicap (Astray)
1979: Del Mar Futurity (The Carpenter)
Norfolk Stakes (The Carpenter)
Del Mar Debutante Stakes (Table Hands)
1985: Santa Margarita Handicap (Lovlier Linda)

J.D. PUCKETT
1960: Breeders' Futurity (He's a Pistol)

A. PUGLISI
1959: McLennan Handicap (Sharpsburg)

VIVIAN PULLIAM
1983: La Canada Stakes (Avigaition)
Santa Barbara Handicap (Avigaition)

ANTHONY PUPINO
1951: Breeders' Futurity (Alladier)
1954: Sapling Stakes (Royal Coinage)
1957: Carter Handicap (Portersville)
Brooklyn Handicap (Portersville)
1961: Bowling Green Handicap (Dead Center)

MIKE PUYPE
1996: Hollywood Turf Cup (Running Flame)
1997: Malibu Stakes (Lord Grillo)
1998: Swaps Stakes (Old Trieste)
1999: Californian Stakes (Old Trieste)

BUDDY RAINES
1950: Dwyer Stakes (Greek Song)
Arlington Classic (Greek Song)
Massachusetts Handicap (Cochise)
1951: Grey Lag Handicap (Cochise)
Arlington Handicap (Cochise)
Astarita Stakes (Place Card)
1962: Preakness Stakes (Greek Money)
1966: Delaware Handicap (Open Fire)
Spinster Stakes (Open Fire)
1991: Brooklyn Handicap (Timely Warning)

R.H. RAINES
1955: Arlington Matron Handicap (Arab Actress)

RODNEY RASH
1992: Oak Tree Invitational Stakes (Navarone)
1994: Sword Dancer Invitational Handicap (Alex the Great)
1995: Santa Anita Handicap (Urgent Request)

HYMAN RAVICH
1981: Maskette Stakes (Jameela)
1982: Delaware Handicap (Jameela)

WILLIAM RAYMOND
1972: Gotham Stakes (Freetex)
Ohio Derby (Freetex)
Monmouth Invitational Handicap (Freetex)

MICHAEL REAVIS
1994: Arlington-Washington Lassie Stakes (Shining Light)

WILLIS REAVIS
1963: Cinema Handicap (Quita Dude)
1965: Grey Lag Handicap (Quita Dude)
1980: Del Mar Futurity (Bold And Gold)

GEORGE REEVES
1948: Santa Anita Maturity (Flashco)

ROBERT REID JR.
1992: Ohio Derby (Majestic Sweep)

PHIL REILLY
1947: Kentucky Jockey Club Stakes (Bold Gallant)

ROBERT REINACHER
1982: Laurel Futurity (Cast Party)
Bowling Green Handicap (Open Call)
1983: Louisiana Downs Handicap (Late Act)
1985: United Nations Handicap (Ends Well)

MILT RESSEGUET
1951: Washington Park Futurity (Oh Leo)

WILLIAM RESSEGUET JR.
1968: Arlington-Washington Futurity (Strong Strong)
1969: Hollywood Juvenile Championship (Insubordination)
1973: Flamingo Stakes (Our Native)
Ohio Derby (Our Native)
Monmouth Invitational Handicap (Our Native)

LOREN RETTELE
1976: Hollywood Juvenile Championship (Fleet Dragoon)
1977: Del Mar Futurity (Go West Young Man)
1978: Louisiana Derby (Esops Foibles)
Arkansas Derby (Esops Foibles)
Santa Susana Stakes (Grenzen)
1979: Louisiana Derby (Golden Act)
Arkansas Derby (Golden Act)
Secretariat Stakes (Golden Act)
Canadian International Championship (Golden Act)

C.V. REYNOLDS
1959: Trenton Handicap (Greek Star)
1961: New Orleans Handicap (Greek Star)

PATRICK REYNOLDS
2001: Carter Handicap (Peeping Tom)

CLYDE RICE
1978: Sorority Stakes (Mongo Queen)

LINDA RICE
1996: Remsen Stakes (The Silver Move)
1998: Spinaway Stakes (Things Change)
Queen Elizabeth II Challenge Cup (Tenski)
2000: Hopeful Stakes (City Zip)

ALCEE RICHARD
1964: New Orleans Handicap (Green Hornet)
1965: Louisiana Derby (Dapper Delegate)
1967: New Orleans Handicap (Cabildo)
1968: Louisiana Derby (Kentucky Sherry)

DONALD RICHARDSON
1965: San Juan Capistrano Handicap (George Royal)
Canadian Championship Stakes (George Royal)
1966: San Juan Capistrano Handicap (George Royal)
Canadian International Championship (George Royal)

W.U. RIDENOUR
1948: Kentucky Oaks (Challe Anne)

MATON RIESER
1949: Bougainvillea Handicap (Frere Jacques)
1956: Kentucky Jockey Club Stakes (Federal Hill)
1957: Louisiana Derby (Federal Hill)

STANLEY RIESER
1962: Arlington Matron Handicap (Kootenai)
1967: Kentucky Oaks (Nancy Jr.)
1969: Alcibiades Stakes (Belle Noire)
1970: Beverly Hills Handicap (Pattee Canyon)
1971: Beldame Stakes (Double Delta)

G. RIOLA
1949: Trenton Handicap (Sky Miracle)

JAY ROBBINS
1977: San Felipe Handicap (Smasher)
1986: Charles H. Strub Stakes (Nostalgia's Star)
1990: San Fernando Stakes (Flying Continental)
Charles H. Strub Stakes (Flying Continental)
Jockey Club Gold Cup (Flying Continental)
2000: Super Derby (Tiznow)
Breeders' Cup Classic (Tiznow)
2001: Santa Anita Handicap (Tiznow)
Breeders' Cup Classic (Tiznow)

BOB ROBERTS
1946: Santa Margarita Handicap (Canina)
1953: Del Mar Debutante Stakes (Lady Cover Up)
1955: Del Mar Futurity (Blen Host)

CRAIG ROBERTS
1994: Hollywood Gold Cup (Slew of Damascus)

A.G. ROBERTSON
1952: Flamingo Stakes (Charlie McAdam)
1957: Arlington Matron Handicap (Pucker Up)

HUGH ROBERTSON
1993: Arlington-Washington Futurity (Polar Expedition)
1994: Jim Beam Stakes (Polar Expedition)

LARRY ROBIDEAUX
1972: Arlington-Washington Lassie St. (Double Your Fun)
1975: American Derby (Honey Mark)

THOMAS RODROCK
1946: Pimlico Oaks (Red Shoes)
1949: Saranac Handicap (Sun Bahram)

SLIM ROLES
1946: San Carlos Handicap (Sirde)
1949: Golden Gate Handicap (Solidarity)
Hollywood Gold Cup (Solidarity)
1950: Starlet Stakes (Gold Capitol)
San Pasqual Handicap (Solidarity)
1957: San Antonio Handicap (Terrang)
1958: Santa Margarita Handicap (Born Rich)
1959: Santa Anita Handicap (Terrang)
1963: Del Mar Futurity (Perris)
1964: Del Mar Futurity (Terry's Secret)
1965: Hollywood Derby (Terry's Secret)
Sunset Handicap (Terry's Secret)

JORGE ROMERO
1990: Meadowlands Cup (Great Normand)

LOU RONDINELLO
1972: Jerome Handicap (True Knight)
Widener Handicap (Good Counsel)
1974: John B. Campbell Handicap (True Knight)
Amory L. Haskell Handicap (True Knight)
Suburban Handicap (True Knight)
Preakness Stakes (Little Current)
Belmont Stakes (Little Current)
Gazelle Handicap (Maud Muller)
1975: Florida Derby (Prince Thou Art)
1977: Ruffian Handicap (Cum Laude Laurie)
Beldame Stakes (Cum Laude Laurie)
Spinster Stakes (Cum Laude Laurie)
1978: Acorn Stakes (Tempest Queen)
Spinster Stakes (Tempest Queen)
1980: Matron Stakes (Prayers'n Promises)
1983: Hopeful Stakes (Capitol South)

RICHARD ROOT
1982: Pan American Handicap (Robsphere)

TOMMY ROOT
1954: Roseben Handicap (White Skies)
Carter Handicap (White Skies)
1973: Alabama Stakes (Desert Vixen)
Gazelle Handicap (Desert Vixen)
Beldame Stakes (Desert Vixen)
1974: Beldame Stakes (Desert Vixen)
1975: Dwyer Handicap (Valid Appeal)

C.W. ROSE
1975: Hopeful Stakes (Eustace)

HAROLD ROSE
2000: Florida Derby (Hal's Hope)
2002: Gulfstream Park Handicap (Hal's Hope)

LARRY ROSE
1969: Santa Susana Stakes (Dumptys Lady)
1979: California Derby (Beau's Eagle)
1980: San Antonio Stakes (Beau's Eagle)

J.B. ROSEN
1947: San Pasqual Handicap (Lets Dance)

CHESTER ROSS
1962: Tropical Park Handicap (Trans-Way)

HACK ROSS
1951: Del Mar Futurity (Big Noise)
1952: Golden Gate Handicap (Lights Up)
1953: Sunset Handicap (Lights Up)
1959: Cowdin Stakes (Warfare)
Champagne Stakes (Warfare)
Garden State Stakes (Warfare)

JEAN-CLAUDE ROUGET
1995: Man o' War Stakes (Millkom)

LOUIE ROUSSEL III
1988: Preakness Stakes (Risen Star)
Belmont Stakes (Risen Star)

JIMMY ROWAN
1948: Louisiana Derby (Bovard)

STEPHAN ROWAN
1984: Sapling Stakes (Doubly Clear)

JAMES ROWE
1959: Roamer Handicap (Polylad)
1963: Acorn Stakes (Spicy Living)
Mother Goose Stakes (Spicy Living)

GIL ROWNTREE
1969: Frizette Stakes (Tudor Queen)
1979: Bowling Green Handicap (Overskate)
1989: Meadowlands Cup (Mi Selecto)
1990: Gulfstream Park Handicap (Mi Selecto)

DUPRE a de ROYER
1984: Breeders' Cup Turf (Lashkari)

LYDELL RUFF
1946: Santa Susana Stakes (Enfilade)
Will Rogers Handicap (Burra Sahib)
1947: Santa Margarita Handicap (Monsoon)
1951: Excelsior Handicap (Lotowhite)

ANTHONY RUPELT
1952: Arlington Futurity (Mr. Good)
1953: Alcibiades Stakes (Oil Painting)
1961: Louisiana Derby (Bass Clef)

JOHN RUSSELL
1972: Santa Susana Stakes (Susan's Girl)
Kentucky Oaks (Susan's Girl)
Acorn Stakes (Susan's Girl)
Gazelle Handicap (Susan's Girl)
Beldame Stakes (Susan's Girl)
1973: Delaware Handicap (Susan's Girl)
Santa Maria Handicap (Susan's Girl)
Santa Margarita Handicap (Susan's Girl)
Santa Barbara Handicap (Susan's Girl)
Arlington-Washington Lassie Stakes (Special Team)
1974: Matron Stakes (Alpine Lass)
Whitney Stakes (Tri Jet)
1975: Hollywood Derby (Intrepid Hero)
Secretariat Stakes (Intrepid Hero)
Jersey Derby (Singh)
Hialeah Turf Cup (Outdoors)
1976: Swaps Stakes (Majestic Light)
Monmouth Invitational Handicap (Majestic Light)
Cinema Handicap (Majestic Light)
Sorority Stakes (Squander)
Maskette Handicap (Sugar Plum Time)
United Nations Handicap (Intrepid Hero)
1977: Amory L. Haskell Handicap (Majestic Light)
Man o' War Stakes (Majestic Light)
Arlington Handicap (Cunning Trick)
1982: Spinster Stakes (Track Robbery)

ANTHONY RUSSO
1983: Mother Goose Stakes (Able Money)

SOL RUTCHICK
1951: Kentucky Derby (Count Turf)
1952: Wood Memorial Stakes (Master Fiddle)
1962: Top Flight Handicap (Pepper Patch)

BARRY RYAN
1959: Lawrence Realization Stakes (Middle Brother)
1962: Monmouth Oaks (Firm Policy)
Alabama Stakes (Firm Policy)
1963: Top Flight Handicap (Firm Policy)

JAMES RYAN
1949: Fall Highweight Handicap (Royal Governor)
Grey Lag Handicap (Royal Governor)
1950: Widener Handicap (Royal Governor)
1951: Dixie Handicap (County Delight)
Gallant Fox Handicap (County Delight)
Manhattan Handicap (County Delight)
Stars and Stripes Handicap (Royal Governor)
1952: Queens County Handicap (County Delight)
1953: Gallant Fox Handicap (Royal Vale)
Dixie Handicap (Royal Vale)
Massachusetts Handicap (Royal Vale)
Miami Beach Handicap (Royal Vale)

JAMES RYERSON
1995: Breeders' Cup Juvenile (Unbridled's Song)
1996: Florida Derby (Unbridled's Song)
Wood Memorial Stakes (Unbridled's Song)

JOHN SADLER
1993: San Felipe Stakes (Corby)

JENINE SAHADI
1994: Hollywood Turf Handicap (Grand Flotilla)
1995: Eddie Read Handicap (Fastness)
1996: Eddie Read Handicap (Fastness)
Breeders' Cup Sprint (Lit de Justice)
1997: Hollywood Turf Handicap (Rainbow Dancer)
Oak Tree Turf Championship (Rainbow Dancer)
Breeders' Cup Sprint (Elmhurst)
2000: Santa Anita Derby (The Deputy)
2001: Las Virgenes Stakes (Golden Ballet)
Santa Anita Oaks (Golden Ballet)

TED SALADIN
1955: California Derby (Trackmaster)
1956: Santa Anita Maturity (Trackmaster)
1967: San Felipe Handicap (Rising Market)
1968: San Antonio Handicap (Rising Market)

MITRI SALIBA
1980: Turf Classic (Anifa)
1985: Turf Classic (Noble Fighter)

J.P. SALLEE
1957: Kentucky Jockey Club Stakes (Hill Country)

PETER SALMEN JR.
1976: Fantasy Stakes (T.V. Vixen)

JOHN SALZMAN
2001: Prioress Stakes (Xtra Heat)

CHARLIE SANBORN
1965: John B. Campbell Handicap (Lt. Stevens)
1982: Matron Stakes (Wings of Jove)

FRANKIE SANDERS
1953: New Orleans Handicap (Smoke Screen)
1955: Kentucky Jockey Club Stakes (Royal Sting)
1956: Matron Stakes (Romanita)
1957: Monmouth Oaks (Romanita)
1958: Louisiana Derby (Royal Union)

GREG SANDERS
1977: Arlington Classic Inv. Handicap (Private Thoughts)

BUD SARNER
1957: Arlington Futurity (Leather Button)

JEROME SARNER JR.
1973: Champagne Stakes (Holding Pattern)
1974: Monmouth Invitational Handicap (Holding Pattern)
Travers Stakes (Holding Pattern)
1985: Hutcheson Stakes (Banner Bob)
Jim Beam Stakes (Banner Bob)

DAVID SAZER
1967: Michigan Mile and One-Eighth (Estreno II)
1968: Pan American Handicap (Estreno II)
1972: Fountain of Youth Stakes (Gentle Smoke)

JOHN SCANLAN
2002: Champagne Stakes (Toccet)
Hollywood Futurity (Toccet)

J.W. SCEUSA
1958: Hialeah Turf Handicap (Meeting)

W.J. SCHMIDT
1960: Arlington Lassie Stakes (Colfax Maid)

D.J. SCHNEIDER
1954: McLennan Handicap (Elixir)

RICHARD SCHOSBERG
1993: Gotham Stakes (As Indicated)
1994: Pimlico Special (As Indicated)
1995: Futurity Stakes (Maria's Mon)
Champagne Stakes (Maria's Mon)
1998: Hempstead Handicap (Mossflower)
Vosburgh Stakes (Affirmed Success)
1999: Cigar Mile Handicap (Affirmed Success)
2002: Carter Handicap (Affirmed Success)

RANDY SCHULHOFER
2003: Sword Dancer Inv. Handicap (Whitmore's Conn)

SCOTTY SCHULHOFER
1969: Vosburgh Handicap (Ta Wee)
1970: Manhattan Handicap (Shelter Bay)
1978: Secretariat Stakes (Mac Diarmida)
Canadian Int. Championship (Mac Diarmida)
Washington D.C. International (Mac Diarmida)
1982: Ramona Handicap (Honey Fox)
1983: Pegasus Handicap (World Appeal)
1985: Gulfstream Park Handicap (Dr. Carter)
Delaware Handicap (Basie)
1986: Matron Stakes (Tappiano)
Breeders' Cup Sprint (Smile)
Selima Stakes (Collins)
1987: Everglades Stakes (Cryptoclearance)
Florida Derby (Cryptoclearance)
1988: Widener Handicap (Cryptoclearance)
Futurity Stakes (Senor Pete)
Vosburgh Stakes (Sewickley)
1990: Champagne Stakes (Fly So Free)
Breeders' Cup Juvenile (Fly So Free)
Cowdin Stakes (Scan)
Remsen Stakes (Scan)
Vosburgh Stakes (Sewickley)
1991: Florida Derby (Fly So Free)
Jim Dandy Stakes (Fly So Free)
Jerome Handicap (Scan)
Pegasus Handicap (Scan)
Wood Memorial Stakes (Cahill Road)
NYRA Mile Handicap (Rubiano)
1992: Carter Handicap (Rubiano)
Vosburgh Stakes (Rubiano)
Pegasus Handicap (Scuffleburg)
1993: Spinaway Stakes (Strategic Maneuver)
Matron Stakes (Strategic Maneuver)
Belmont Stakes (Colonial Affair)
Ruffian Handicap (Shared Interest)
1994: Whitney Handicap (Colonial Affair)
Jockey Club Gold Cup (Colonial Affair)
Peter Pan Stakes (Twining)
Jim Dandy Stakes (Unaccounted For)
Futurity Stakes (Montreal Red)
1995: Whitney Handicap (Unaccounted For)
Turf Classic (Turk Passer)
1998: Futurity Stakes (Lemon Drop Kid)
1999: Belmont Stakes (Lemon Drop Kid)
Travers Stakes (Lemon Drop Kid)
2000: Brooklyn Handicap (Lemon Drop Kid)
Suburban Handicap (Lemon Drop Kid)
Whitney Handicap (Lemon Drop Kid)
Woodward Stakes (Lemon Drop Kid)
2001: Gazelle Handicap (Exogenous)
Beldame Stakes (Exogenous)

ANDY SCHUTTINGER
1948: Garden State Stakes (Blue Peter)
Saratoga Special (Blue Peter)
Hopeful Stakes (Blue Peter)
Futurity Stakes (Blue Peter)
1950: Swift Stakes (Ferd)
1951: Spinaway Stakes (Blue Case)

SCOTT SCHWARTZ
2000: Gazelle Handicap (Critical Eye)
2001: Hempstead Handicap (Critical Eye)

GARY SCIACCA
1992: Beldame Stakes (Saratoga Dew)
1997: Crown Royal Hollywood Derby (Subordination)
1998: Brooklyn Handicap (Subordination)
Eddie Read Handicap (Subordination)

ALEX SCOTT
1991: Breeders' Cup Sprint (Sheikh Albadou)

GEORGE SCOTT
1987: Gamely Handicap (Northern Aspen)

T.R. SCOTT
1964: Hollywood Derby (Real Good Deal)

AL SCOTTI
1969: Canadian International Championship (Vent du Nord)
1970: Hialeah Turf Cup (Vent du Nord)
1973: Withers Stakes (Linda's Chief)
Pontiac Grand Prix Stakes (Linda's Chief)

ARNOLD SCRUTON JR.
1967: Massachusetts Handicap (Good Knight)

RANDY SECHREST
1965: Jerome Handicap (Bold Bidder)
1966: Manhattan Handicap (Moontrip)
Bowling Green Handicap (Moontrip)
Charles H. Strub Stakes (Bold Bidder)
1967: Grey Lag Handicap (Moontrip)
1973: Oak Leaf Stakes (Divine Grace)

SAM SECHREST
1951: Cinema Handicap (Mucho Hosso)

MIKE SEDLACEK
1984: Top Flight Handicap (Sweet Missus)

WOODY SEDLACEK
1963: Spinaway Stakes (Petite Rouge)
1983: Wood Memorial Stakes (Bounding Basque)
1985: Withers Stakes (El Basco)
Brooklyn Handicap (Bounding Basque)

JULIAN SERNA JR.
1969: Widener Handicap (Yumbel)

PHILIP SERPE
1993: Vosburgh Stakes (Birdonthewire)

JOHN SERVIS
2000: Coaching Club American Oaks (Jostle)
Alabama Stakes (Jostle)

M. SHAPOFF
1955: Black Helen Handicap (Rosemary B.)

STANLEY SHAPOFF
1988: Hutcheson Stakes (Perfect Spy)
1989: Brooklyn Handicap (Forever Silver)
1992: Remsen Stakes (Silver of Silver)

CHARLES W. SHAW JR.
1953: Jerome Handicap (Navy Page)
1954: Vagrancy Handicap (Canadiana)

PAUL SHAWHAN
1959: Kentucky Oaks (Wedlock)

JONATHAN SHEPPARD
1978: John B. Campbell Handicap (Ripon)
1982: Flower Bowl Handicap (Trevita)
1983: Flower Bowl Handicap (First Approach)
1985: Young America Stakes (Storm Cat)
2001: Sword Dancer Inv. Handicap (With Anticipation)
Man o' War Stakes (With Anticipation)
2002: United Nations Handicap (With Anticipation)
Sword Dancer Inv. Handicap (With Anticipation)
Man o' War Stakes (With Anticipation)

HARRY SHILLICK
1971: Alcibiades Stakes (Mrs. Cornwallis)

MITCH SHIROTA
1980: Apple Blossom Handicap (Billy Jane)
1992: Top Flight Handicap (Firm Stance)

JOHN SHIRREFFS
1998: Hollywood Oaks (Manistique)
1999: Santa Margarita Handicap (Manistique)
Vanity Handicap (Manistique)
2000: Santa Maria Handicap (Manistique)
2003: Santa Maria Handicap (Starrer)
Santa Margarita Handicap (Starrer)
Hollywood Starlet Stakes (Hollywood Story)

BILL SHOEMAKER
1993: Pegasus Handicap (Diazo)
1994: Strub Stakes (Diazo)

M. SIDELL
1949: New Castle Handicap (Allie's Pal)
Molly Pitcher Handicap (Allie's Pal)

LEO SIERRA
1983: Illinois Derby (General Practitioner)

JUAN PABLO SILVA
2002: Malibu Stakes (Debonair Joe)

A.E. SILVER
1946: Del Mar Handicap (Olhaverry)
1947: Santa Anita Handicap (Olhaverry)
1948: San Pasqual Handicap (Olhaverry)

HAROLD SIMMONS
1949: Massachusetts Handicap (First Nighter)
1952: Molly Pitcher Handicap (Dixie Flyer)
Vineland Handicap (Sickle's Image)

PHILLIP SIMMS
1985: Tropical Park Derby (Irish Sur)

JAMES SIMPSON
1977: Jersey Derby (Cormorant)

WILLIAM SIMPSON
1960: American Handicap (Prize Host)

MONTI SIMS
1974: Santa Anita Derby (Destroyer)
Oaklawn Handicap (Royal Knight)

A.F. SKELTON
1947: New Castle Handicap (Elpis)
Comely Handicap (Elpis)
Molly Pitcher Handicap (Elpis)
New Orleans Handicap (Earshot)

TOM SKIFFINGTON
1988: Sword Dancer Handicap (Anka Germania)

JAMES SKINNER
1956: Firenze Handicap (Blue Banner)

BEN SLASKY
1954: Del Mar Debutante Stakes (Fair Molly)
1959: Hollywood Juvenile Championship (Noble Noor)
1960: California Derby (Noble Noor)

DAVID SMAGA
1991: Budweiser International Stakes (Leariva)

RICHARD SMALL
1976: John B. Campbell Handicap (Festive Mood)
1977: Demoiselle Stakes (Caesar's Wish)
1978: Mother Goose Stakes (Caesar's Wish)
1986: Jim Beam Stakes (Broad Brush)
Wood Memorial Stakes (Broad Brush)
Ohio Derby (Broad Brush)
Pennsylvania Derby (Broad Brush)
Meadowlands Cup (Broad Brush)
1987: Santa Anita Handicap (Broad Brush)
Suburban Handicap (Broad Brush)
1989: Beldame Stakes (Tactile)
1991: Pennsylvania Derby (Valley Crossing)
1993: Philip H. Iselin Handicap (Valley Crossing)
1994: Arkansas Derby (Concern)
Breeders' Cup Classic (Concern)
1995: Californian Stakes (Concern)

DEWEY SMITH

1969: New Orleans Handicap (Miracle Hill)
1970: Oaklawn Handicap (Charlie Jr.)
1971: New Orleans Handicap (Rio Bravo)
1982: Louisiana Derby (El Baba)
1990: Fantasy Stakes (Silvered)

JERE SMITH

1974: Michigan Mile and One-Eighth (Tom Tulle)

JIMMY SMITH

1946: Gazelle Stakes (Bridal Flower)
New Castle Handicap (Bridal Flower)
Beldame Handicap (Bridal Flower)
Roamer Handicap (Bridal Flower)
Hopeful Stakes (Blue Border)
Frizette Stakes (Bimlette)
Selima Stakes (Bee Ann Mac)
Santa Anita Derby (Knockdown)
Blue Grass Stakes (Lord Boswell)
1948: Spinaway Stakes (Myrtle Charm)
Matron Stakes (Myrtle Charm)
Travers Stakes (Ace Admiral)
Lawrence Realization Stakes (Ace Admiral)
Excelsior Handicap (Knockdown)
Queens County Handicap (Knockdown)
Arlington Futurity (Mr. Busher)
1961: Arlington Matron Handicap (Shirley Jones)
Donn Handicap (General Arthur)
1962: Gulfstream Park Handicap (Jay Fox)
Donn Handicap (Jay Fox)
1967: Louisiana Derby (Ask the Fare)

SAMMY SMITH

1962: Frizette Stakes (Pams Ego)

SIDNEY SMITH

1958: Withers Stakes (Sir Robby)
1965: Hialeah Turf Cup (Hot Dust)

THOMAS V. SMITH

1982: Arlington-Washington Lassie St. (For Once'n My Life)

TOM SMITH

1946: Pimlico Futurity (Jet Pilot)
Tremont Stakes (Jet Pilot)
1947: Kentucky Derby (Jet Pilot)
1948: Washington Park Futurity (Model Cadet)

BERT SONNIER

1968: Arkansas Derby (Nodouble)
Michigan Mile and One-Eighth (Nodouble)
Hawthorne Gold Cup (Nodouble)
1969: Californian Stakes (Nodouble)
Brooklyn Handicap (Nodouble)
Hawthorne Gold Cup (Nodouble)
Santa Anita Handicap (Nodouble)
1970: Metropolitan Handicap (Nodouble)
1979: Arlington-Washington Futurity (Execution's Reason)
Arlington-Washington Lassie Stakes (Sissy's Time)
1981: Pan American Handicap (Little Bonny)
1982: Arlington-Washington Futurity (Total Departure)
1985: Arlington-Washington Futurity (Meadowlake)
1993: Ashland Stakes (Lunar Spook)

EARL SORRELL

1947: San Carlos Handicap (Texas Sandman)

MICHAEL SOTO

1957: Kentucky Oaks (Lori-El)

VICTOR SOVINSKI

1959: Washington Park Futurity (Venetian Way)
1960: Kentucky Derby (Venetian Way)

GRAVES SPARKS

1957: Spinster Stakes (Bornastar)
1958: Vineland Handicap (Bornastar)
Spinster Stakes (Bornastar)

BILL SPAWR

1993: Santa Barbara Handicap (Exchange)
1994: Matriarch Stakes (Exchange)

CHRISTOPHER SPECKERT

1989: Santa Barbara Handicap (No Review)
1991: Oak Leaf Stakes (Pleasant Stage)
Breeders' Cup Juvenile Fillies (Pleasant Stage)
1992: Suburban Handicap (Pleasant Tap)
Jockey Club Gold Cup (Pleasant Tap)
Californian Stakes (Another Review)

LARRY SPRAKER

1975: Arkansas Derby (Promised City)

ALBERT STALL JR.

1998: Early Times Turf Classic (Joyeaux Danseur)

JOHN STARR

1977: Alcibiades Stakes (L'Alezane)

YONNIE STARR

1970: Alabama Stakes (Fanfreluche)
1972: Spinaway Stakes (La Prevoyante)
Matron Stakes (La Prevoyante)
Frizette Stakes (La Prevoyante)
Selima Stakes (La Prevoyante)
Gardenia Stakes (La Prevoyante)
1974: Laurel Futurity (L'Enjoleur)

ROBERT STEELE

1960: Michigan Mile and One-Sixteenth (Little Fitz)

ROGER STEIN

1993: Santa Margarita Handicap (Southern Truce)

BILL STEPHENS

1957: Withers Stakes (Clem)
Arlington Classic (Clem)
1958: Washington Park Handicap (Clem)
Woodward Stakes (Clem)
United Nations Handicap (Clem)
Tropical Handicap (St. Amour II)
1961: Tropical Park Handicap (Bourbon Prince)
1966: Illinois Derby (Michigan Avenue)

WOODY STEPHENS

1949: Blue Grass Stakes (Halt)
1950: Cowdin Stakes (Away Away)
1951: Molly Pitcher Handicap (Marta)
Ladies Handicap (Marta)
1952: Flamingo Stakes (Blue Man)
Preakness Stakes (Blue Man)
Dwyer Stakes (Blue Man)
1953: Top Flight Handicap (Marta)
1954: Breeders' Futurity (Brother Tex)
Blue Grass Stakes (Goyamo)
1955: Withers Stakes (Traffic Judge)
Ohio Derby (Traffic Judge)
Jerome Handicap (Traffic Judge)
Woodward Stakes (Traffic Judge)
1956: Pimlico Futurity (Missile)
1958: Frizette Stakes (Merry Hill)
Dwyer Handicap (Victory Morn)
1959: Suburban Handicap (Bald Eagle)
Gallant Fox Handicap (Bald Eagle)
Washington D.C. International (Bald Eagle)
Princess Pat Stakes (Heavenly Body)
Matron Stakes (Heavenly Body)
Kentucky Oaks (Hidden Talent)
1960: Widener Handicap (Bald Eagle)
Gulfstream Park Handicap (Bald Eagle)
Metropolitan Handicap (Bald Eagle)
Aqueduct Handicap (Bald Eagle)
Washington D.C. International (Bald Eagle)
Kentucky Oaks (Make Sail)
Alabama Stakes (Make Sail)
Arlington Handicap (One-Eyed King)
1961: Saratoga Special (Battle Joined)
Top Flight Handicap (Make Sail)
1962: Futurity Stakes (Never Bend)
Cowdin Stakes (Never Bend)
Champagne Stakes (Never Bend)
Lawrence Realization Stakes (Battle Joined)
Roamer Handicap (Dead Ahead)
1963: Kentucky Oaks (Sally Ship)
Flamingo Stakes (Never Bend)
1964: Suburban Handicap (Iron Peg)
1966: Monmouth Handicap (Bold Bidder)
Washington Park Handicap (Bold Bidder)
Hawthorne Gold Cup (Bold Bidder)
1969: Spinaway Stakes (Meritus)
Pan American Handicap (Hibernian)
1970: Coaching Club American Oaks (Missile Belle)
Gazelle Handicap (Missile Belle)
Hopeful Stakes (Proudest Roman)
1971: Sanford Stakes (Cohasset Tribe)
Louisiana Derby (Northfields)
1973: Selima Stakes (Dancealot)
1974: Florida Derby (Judger)
Blue Grass Stakes (Judger)
Kentucky Derby (Cannonade)
1975: Breeders' Futurity (Harbor Springs)
Remsen Stakes (Hang Ten)
1976: Spinaway Stakes (Mrs. Warren)
Matron Stakes (Mrs. Warren)
Frizette Stakes (Sensational)
Selima Stakes (Sensational)
1977: Remsen Stakes (Believe It)
Ladies Handicap (Sensational)
1978: Kentucky Oaks (White Star Line)
Alabama Stakes (White Star Line)
Wood Memorial Stakes (Believe It)
1979: Illinois Derby (Smarten)
Pennsylvania Derby (Smarten)
Ohio Derby (Smarten)
American Derby (Smarten)
Matron Stakes (Smart Angle)
Frizette Stakes (Smart Angle)
Selima Stakes (Smart Angle)
Sheepshead Bay Handicap (Terpsichorist)
1980: Frizette Stakes (Heavenly Cause)
Selima Stakes (Heavenly Cause)
Louisiana Downs Handicap (It's True)
1981: Fantasy Stakes (Heavenly Cause)
Kentucky Oaks (Heavenly Cause)
Acorn Stakes (Heavenly Cause)
Hollywood Derby (De La Rose)
1982: Belmont Stakes (Conquistador Cielo)
Dwyer Stakes (Conquistador Cielo)
Metropolitan Handicap (Conquistador Cielo)
Selima Stakes (Bemissed)
1983: Futurity Stakes (Swale)
Young America Stakes (Swale)
Breeders' Futurity (Swale)
Arlington-Washington Lassie Stakes (Miss Oceana)
Selima Stakes (Miss Oceana)
Frizette Stakes (Miss Oceana)
Laurel Futurity (Devil's Bag)
Champagne Stakes (Devil's Bag)
Belmont Stakes (Caveat)
1984: Hutcheson Stakes (Swale)
Florida Derby (Swale)
Kentucky Derby (Swale)
Belmont Stakes (Swale)
Acorn Stakes (Miss Oceana)
Maskette Stakes (Miss Oceana)
Hollywood Futurity (Stephan's Odyssey)
Arlington-Washington Lassie Stakes (Contredance)
Tropical Park Derby (Morning Bob)
Yellow Ribbon Stakes (Sabin)
1985: Belmont Stakes (Creme Fraiche)
American Derby (Creme Fraiche)
Jerome Handicap (Creme Fraiche)
Super Derby (Creme Fraiche)
Dwyer Stakes (Stephan's Odyssey)
Jim Dandy Stakes (Stephan's Odyssey)
1986: Peter Pan Stakes (Danzig Connection)
Belmont Stakes (Danzig Connection)
Acorn Stakes (Lotka)
Jockey Club Gold Cup (Creme Fraiche)
Young America Stakes (Conquistarose)
1987: Gotham Stakes (Gone West)
Withers Stakes (Gone West)
Dwyer Stakes (Gone West)
Futurity Stakes (Forty Niner)
Champagne Stakes (Forty Niner)
Jockey Club Gold Cup (Creme Fraiche)
Meadowlands Cup (Creme Fraiche)
1988: Fountain of Youth Stakes (Forty Niner)
Haskell Invitational Handicap (Forty Niner)
Travers Stakes (Forty Niner)
Tropical Park Derby (Digress)
Pennsylvania Derby (Cefis)
1989: Dwyer Stakes (Roi Danzig)
Remsen Stakes (Yonder)

LARRY STERLING

1977: Hollywood Invitational Handicap (Vigors)
1978: San Antonio Stakes (Vigors)
Santa Anita Handicap (Vigors)

LIONEL STERNBERGER

1962: San Felipe Handicap (Doc Jocoy)
1963: Los Angeles Handicap (Doc Jocoy)

HERB STEVENS

1979: Sapling Stakes (Rockhill Native)
Futurity Stakes (Rockhill Native)
Delaware Handicap (Likely Exchange)
1980: Blue Grass Stakes (Rockhill Native)
1982: Alcibiades Stakes (Jelly Bean Holiday)

DALLAS STEWART

1999: Louisiana Derby (Kimberlite Pipe)
2001: Breeders' Cup Distaff (Unbridled Elaine)

M. STEWART
1965: Washington Park Handicap (Take Over)

MICHAEL STIDHAM
1994: Coaching Club American Oaks (Two Altazano)

KENT STIRLING
1983: Hialeah Turf Cup (Nijinsky's Secret)
1984: Hialeah Turf Cup (Nijinsky's Secret)

BUD STOTLER
1946: San Pasqual Handicap (Lou-Bre)

MICHAEL STOUTE
1996: Canadian International Championship (Singspiel)
Breeders' Cup Turf (Pilsudski)
2000: Breeders' Cup Turf (Kalanisi)
2003: Breeders' Cup Filly and Mare Turf (Islington)

GEORGE STRATE
1948: Alabama Stakes (Compliance)
1951: Astoria Stakes (Star-Enfin)

WAYNE STUCKI
1974: Malibu Stakes (Ancient Title)
San Fernando Stakes (Ancient Title)
Charles H. Strub Stakes (Ancient Title)
1975: Californian Stakes (Ancient Title)
Hollywood Gold Cup (Ancient Title)
Whitney Handicap (Ancient Title)
1976: Californian Stakes (Ancient Title)
1977: Del Mar Handicap (Ancient Title)
San Antonio Stakes (Ancient Title)

WILLIAM STUCKI
1948: American Handicap (Stepfather)
1965: Bowling Green Handicap (Or et Argent)
Dixie Handicap (Or et Argent)
Dixie Handicap (Flag)
1968: Century Handicap (Model Fool)
1976: Hollywood Oaks (Answer)

MEL STUTE
1961: Californian Stakes (First Balcony)
San Carlos Handicap (First Balcony)
1970: Vanity Handicap (Commissary)
1975: Del Mar Futurity (Telly's Pop)
Norfolk Stakes (Telly's Pop)
1976: California Derby (Telly's Pop)
1981: San Felipe Handicap (Stancharry)
1985: Norfolk Stakes (Snow Chief)
Hollywood Futurity (Snow Chief)
1986: Florida Derby (Snow Chief)
Santa Anita Derby (Snow Chief)
Preakness Stakes (Snow Chief)
Jersey Derby (Snow Chief)
San Fernando Stakes (Right Con)
Breeders' Cup Juvenile Fillies (Brave Raj)
1987: Fantasy Stakes (Very Subtle)
Breeders' Cup Sprint (Very Subtle)
Charles H. Strub Stakes (Snow Chief)

WARREN STUTE
1950: Cinema Handicap (Great Circle)
Del Mar Derby (Great Circle)
1951: Del Mar Debutante Stakes (Tonga)
Santa Anita Maturity (Great Circle)
1952: Sunset Handicap (Great Circle)
1963: Vanity Handicap (Table Mate)
1969: Hollywood Gold Cup (Figonero)
1970: Del Mar Futurity (June Darling)
Norfolk Stakes (June Darling)
Oak Leaf Stakes (June Darling)
Gulfstream Park Handicap (Snow Sporting)
Charles H. Strub Stakes (Snow Sporting)
1991: Hollywood Starlet Stakes (Magical Maiden)
2002: Del Mar Debutante Stakes (Miss Houdini)

CHARLES STUTTS
1992: American Derby (The Name's Jimmy)

JOHN SULLIVAN
1966: San Luis Rey Handicap (Polar Sea)
1972: Malibu Stakes (Wing Out)
1982: Hialeah Turf Cup (The Bart)
Century Handicap (The Bart)
1985: Metropolitan Handicap (Forzando II)
Oak Tree Invitational Stakes (Yashgan)
1986: California Derby (Vernon Castle)

SAEED BIN SUROOR
1995: San Juan Capistrano Handicap (Red Bishop)
1998: Man o' War Stakes (Daylami)
1999: Breeders' Cup Turf (Daylami)
2000: Man o' War Stakes (Fantastic Light)
2001: Breeders' Cup Turf (Fantastic Light)
2002: Gazelle Handicap (Imperial Gesture)
Beldame Stakes (Imperial Gesture)
Stephen Foster Handicap (Street Cry)
Suburban Handicap (E Dubai)
Coaching Club American Oaks (Jilbab)
Super Derby (Essence of Dubai)
Flower Bowl Invitational Stakes (Kazzia)
2003: Arlington Million (Sulamani)
Turf Classic (Sulamani)

CLYDE SUTPHIN
1957: Dixie Handicap (Akbar Khan)

BARCLAY TAGG
1991: Gamely Handicap (Miss Josh)
1994: Man o' War Stakes (Royal Mountain Inn)
2003: Kentucky Derby (Funny Cide)
Preakness Stakes (Funny Cide)
Alabama Stakes (Island Fashion)

JOHN TAMMARO
1970: Molly Pitcher Handicap (Double Ripple)
1979: Arlington Classic (Steady Growth)
1981: Laurel Futurity (Deputy Minister)
Young America Stakes (Deputy Minister)
1997: Jim Beam Stakes (Concerto)

WALTER TAYLOR
1950: Del Mar Futurity (Patch)
1952: Aqueduct Handicap (Bryan G.)

MESH TENNEY
1946: Starlet Stakes (U Time)
1947: Santa Susana Stakes (Hubble Bubble)
San Vicente Handicap (Hubble Bubble)
Hollywood Oaks (U Time)
1953: Vanity Handicap (Fleet Khal)
1955: Santa Anita Derby (Swaps)
Kentucky Derby (Swaps)
Westerner Stakes (Swaps)
American Derby (Swaps)
Californian Stakes (Swaps)
1956: Inglewood Handicap (Swaps)
American Handicap (Swaps)
Hollywood Gold Cup (Swaps)
Sunset Handicap (Swaps)
Washington Park Handicap (Swaps)
Santa Anita Derby (Terrang)
1958: Cinema Handicap (The Shoe)
1961: Santa Anita Handicap (Prove It)
San Fernando Stakes (Prove It)
Santa Anita Maturity (Prove It)
Cinema Handicap (Bushel-n-Peck)
1962: Inglewood Handicap (Prove It)
American Handicap (Prove It)
Hollywood Gold Cup (Prove It)
Sunset Handicap (Prove It)
Washington Park Handicap (Prove It)
San Antonio Handicap (Olden Times)
San Juan Capistrano Handicap (Olden Times)
Arlington-Washington Futurity (Candy Spots)
1963: Santa Anita Derby (Candy Spots)
Florida Derby (Candy Spots)
Preakness Stakes (Candy Spots)
Jersey Derby (Candy Spots)
American Derby (Candy Spots)
Arlington Classic (Candy Spots)
1964: Metropolitan Handicap (Olden Times)

RED TERRILL
1992: Mother Goose Stakes (Turnback the Alarm)
Coaching Club American Oaks (Turnback the Alarm)
1993: Shuvee Handicap (Turnback the Alarm)
Hempstead Handicap (Turnback the Alarm)
Go for Wand Stakes (Turnback the Alarm)
1995: Alabama Stakes (Pretty Discreet)

HOWARD TESHER
1971: Arlington-Washington Futurity (Governor Max)
1978: Carter Handicap (Pumpkin Moonshine)
1980: Hopeful Stakes (Tap Shoes)
Futurity Stakes (Tap Shoes)
Ladies Handicap (Plankton)
1982: Arlington Classic (Wolfie's Rascal)
American Derby (Wolfie's Rascal)
Top Flight Handicap (Andover Way)
Beldame Stakes (Weber City Miss)
1986: Hialeah Turf Cup (Sondrio)
Illinois Derby (Bolshoi Boy)
Washington D.C. International (Lieutenant's Lark)
1993: Florida Derby (Bull Inthe Heather)
1997: Caesars International Handicap (Influent)
Man o' War Stakes (Influent)

JOHN THEALL
1949: Louisiana Derby (Rookwood)
1950: Firenze Handicap (Red Camelia)
New Orleans Handicap (Red Camelia)
1951: Beldame Handicap (Thelma Berger)
1952: Acorn Stakes (Parading Lady)
Vosburgh Handicap (Parading Lady)
1953: Louisiana Derby (Matagorda)
1954: Louisiana Derby (Gigantic)
1955: Carter Handicap (Bobby Brocato)
1958: New Orleans Handicap (Tenacious)
1959: New Orleans Handicap (Tenacious)

BRET THOMAS
1996: Arkansas Derby (Zarb's Magic)

GARY THOMAS
1986: Arkansas Derby (Rampage)

WILLIAM THOMAS
1979: Alcibiades Stakes (Salud)

LAWRENCE THOMPSON
1956: Princess Pat Stakes (Splendored)
1961: Grey Lag Handicap (Mail Order)

WILLARD THOMPSON
1989: Young America Stakes (Roanoke)

NOBLE THREEWITT
1954: Wood Memorial Stakes (Correlation)
Florida Derby (Correlation)
Santa Margarita Handicap (Cerise Reine)
1961: Vanity Handicap (Perizade)
1971: Malibu Stakes (King of Cricket)
San Luis Rey Handicap (Try Sheep)
1977: California Derby (Cuzwuzwrong)
1993: Swaps Stakes (Devoted Brass)

VINCENT TIMPHONY
1984: Breeders' Cup Classic (Wild Again)

HAROLD TINKER
1962: Arkansas Derby (Aeropolis)
1970: Kentucky Jockey Club Stakes (Line City)
1974: Arkansas Derby (J.R.'s Pet)

J.E. TINSLEY JR.
1961: Monmouth Oaks (My Portrait)
1962: Kentucky Jockey Club Stakes (Sky Gem)
Los Angeles Handicap (Winonly)
1963: Santa Anita Handicap (Crozier)
San Carlos Handicap (Crozier)
Californian Stakes (Winonly)
1964: San Carlos Handicap (Admiral's Voyage)
1965: Breeders' Futurity (Tinsley)
1966: Alcibiades Stakes (Teacher's Art)

MIKE TOMLINSON
2003: Arkansas Derby (Sir Cherokee)

JIM TONER
1985: Selima Stakes (I'm Splendid)
1995: Pegasus Handicap (Flying Chevron)
NYRA Mile Handicap (Flying Chevron)
1996: Queen Elizabeth II Chal. Cup (Memories of Silver)
1997: Beverly D. Stakes (Memories of Silver)
1999: Flower Bowl Invitational Handicap (Soaring Softly)
Breeders' Cup Filly and Mare Turf (Soaring Softly)
2002: Garden City Breeders' Cup Handicap (Wonder Again)

EMANUEL TORTORA
1995: Super Derby (Mecke)
1996: Early Times Turf Classic (Mecke)
Arlington Million (Mecke)

GEORGE TOWNE
1971: Black Helen Handicap (Swoon's Flower)

STEVE TOWNE
1994: Ohio Derby (Exclusive Praline)

HARRY TROTSEK
1949: Breeders' Futurity (Oil Capitol)
Pimlico Futurity (Oil Capitol)
1950: Washington Park Handicap (Inseparable)
Stars and Stripes Handicap (Inseparable)

HARRY TROTSEK *(Continued)*

Flamingo Stakes (Oil Capitol)
1951: Arlington Lassie Stakes (Princess Lygia)
Hawthorne Gold Cup (Seaward)
1952: New Orleans Handicap (Oil Capitol)
1953: Arlington Futurity (Hasty Road)
Washington Park Futurity (Hasty Road)
Breeders' Futurity (Hasty Road)
Kentucky Jockey Club Stakes (Hasty Road)
Arlington Lassie Stakes (Queen Hopeful)
Princess Pat Stakes (Queen Hopeful)
Widener Handicap (Oil Capitol)
Arlington Handicap (Oil Capitol)
Lawrence Realization Stakes (Platan)
1954: Kentucky Jockey Club Stakes (Prince Noor)
Preakness Stakes (Hasty Road)
Arlington Handicap (Stan)
1955: Everglades Stakes (Prince Noor)
Widener Handicap (Hasty Road)
New Orleans Handicap (Sea O Erin)
Gulfstream Park Handicap (Mister Black)
Hialeah Turf Handicap (Stan)
Arlington Handicap (Platan)
1956: Bougainvillea Turf Handicap (Summer Solstice)
1957: Princess Pat Stakes (Hasty Doll)
Washington D.C. International (Mahan)
1958: Bougainvillea Turf Handicap (Stephanotis)
Canadian Championship Stakes (Jack Ketch)
1959: Canadian Championship Stakes (Martini II)
1962: Hialeah Turf Cup (El Loco)
1964: Hialeah Turf Cup (Carteret)
1965: Spinaway Stakes (Moccasin)
Matron Stakes (Moccasin)
Selima Stakes (Moccasin)
Gardenia Stakes (Moccasin)
1967: Arkansas Derby (Monitor)
1972: Pan American Handicap (Unanime)
1978: Illinois Derby (Batonnier)
1980: Golden Harvest Handicap (Ribbon)
New Orleans Handicap (Pool Court)

CLYDE TROUTT

1953: Everglades Stakes (Royal Bay Gem)
1959: Massachusetts Handicap (Air Pilot)
1960: Sorority Stakes (Apatontheback)
Massachusetts Handicap (Talent Show)
1961: Carter Handicap (Chief of Chiefs)
1962: Sapling Stakes (Delta Judge)
Pimlico Futurity (Right Proud)
1965: Suburban Handicap (Pia Star)
Brooklyn Handicap (Pia Star)
Cowdin Stakes (Advocator)
1966: Widener Handicap (Pia Star)
1967: Seminole Handicap (Advocator)
1970: Donn Handicap (Twogundan)

JOE TROVATO

1974: Acorn Stakes (Chris Evert)
Mother Goose Stakes (Chris Evert)
Coaching Club American Oaks (Chris Evert)

R.C. TROXLER

1948: McLennan Handicap (El Mono)
Widener Handicap (El Mono)

MARY LOU TUCK

1980: Hollywood Gold Cup (Go West Young Man)
Del Mar Handicap (Go West Young Man)
Century Handicap (Go West Young Man)

CHUCK TURCO

1995: Arkansas Derby (Dazzling Falls)

CLYDE TURK

1962: Vanity Handicap (Linita)
Santa Margarita Handicap (Queen America)
1964: Santa Margarita Handicap (Curious Clover)
1965: Del Mar Futurity (Coursing)
Santa Margarita Handicap (Curious Clover)
1966: Del Mar Futurity (Ruken)
1967: Santa Anita Derby (Ruken)
1968: San Luis Rey Handicap (Quicken Tree)

BILLY TURNER

1976: Champagne Stakes (Seattle Slew)
1977: Flamingo Stakes (Seattle Slew)
Wood Memorial Stakes (Seattle Slew)
Kentucky Derby (Seattle Slew)
Preakness Stakes (Seattle Slew)
Belmont Stakes (Seattle Slew)
1979: Jerome Handicap (Czaravich)
1980: Metropolitan Handicap (Czaravich)

Photo courtesy of Santa Anita Park

Jack Van Berg first led the nation's trainers in total races won in 1972 and accomplished that feat for the ninth time in 1984, when Gate Dancer won the Preakness Stakes to give Van Berg his first classic triumph. The Hall of Fame trainer finally got his Hall of Fame horse not long afterward in Alysheba, who won the Kentucky Derby and Preakness in 1987 and earned Horse of the Year acclaim in 1988.

1984: Withers Stakes (Play On)
1998: Fall Highweight Handicap (Punch Line)
2000: Garden City Breeders' Cup Handicap (Gaviola)

JACK VAN BERG

1976: Secretariat Stakes (Joachim)
Hawthorne Gold Cup (Almost Grown)
1978: Century Handicap (Landscaper)
1981: Santa Susana Stakes (Nell's Briquette)
Arkansas Derby (Bold Ego)
1982: Louisiana Downs Handicap (Rich and Ready)
1983: Fantasy Stakes (Brindy Brindy)
Oaklawn Handicap (Bold Style)
1984: Preakness Stakes (Gate Dancer)
Super Derby (Gate Dancer)
1987: Kentucky Derby (Alysheba)
Preakness Stakes (Alysheba)
Super Derby (Alysheba)
Hollywood Turf Cup (Vilzak)
1988: Charles H. Strub Stakes (Alysheba)
Santa Anita Handicap (Alysheba)
Philip H. Iselin Handicap (Alysheba)
Woodward Handicap (Alysheba)
Meadowlands Cup (Alysheba)
Breeders' Cup Classic (Alysheba)
California Derby (All Thee Power)
1991: La Canada Stakes (Fit to Scout)
Santa Margarita Handicap (Little Brianne)

MARION VAN BERG

1958: Arlington Matron Handicap (Estacion)
1960: Arkansas Derby (Spring Broker)

DAVID VANCE

1972: Oaklawn Handicap (Gage Line)
2000: Breeders' Cup Juvenile Fillies (Caressing)

H.C. VANDERVOORT

1970: Hollywood Gold Cup (Pleasure Seeker)

HARVEY VANIER

1982: La Canada Stakes (Safe Play)
1983: Blue Grass Stakes (Play Fellow)
Arlington Classic (Play Fellow)
American Derby (Play Fellow)
Travers Stakes (Play Fellow)
1987: American Derby (Fortunate Moment)
1989: Jim Beam Stakes (Western Playboy)
Blue Grass Stakes (Western Playboy)
Pennsylvania Derby (Western Playboy)

JUDSON VAN WORP

1995: Vosburgh Stakes (Not Surprising)

JOHN VEITCH

1977: Fantasy Stakes (Our Mims)
Coaching Club American Oaks (Our Mims)
Alabama Stakes (Our Mims)
Delaware Handicap (Our Mims)
Sapling Stakes (Alydar)
Champagne Stakes (Alydar)
1978: Flamingo Stakes (Alydar)
Florida Derby (Alydar)
Blue Grass Stakes (Alydar)
Arlington Classic (Alydar)

Travers Stakes (Alydar)
Whitney Stakes (Alydar)
Sapling Stakes (Tim the Tiger)
1979: Fantasy Stakes (Davona Dale)
Kentucky Oaks (Davona Dale)
Acorn Stakes (Davona Dale)
Mother Goose Stakes (Davona Dale)
Coaching Club American Oaks (Davona Dale)
1980: Mother Goose Stakes (Sugar and Spice)
1981: Matron Stakes (Before Dawn)
1983: Remsen Stakes (Dr. Carter)
Metropolitan Handicap (Star Choice)
1984: Young America Stakes (Script Ohio)
1985: Fountain of Youth Stakes (Proud Truth)
Florida Derby (Proud Truth)
Breeders' Cup Classic (Proud Truth)
1988: Man o' War Stakes (Sunshine Forever)
Turf Classic (Sunshine Forever)
Budweiser International Stakes (Sunshine Forever)
Florida Derby (Brian's Time)
Jim Dandy Stakes (Brian's Time)
1990: Yellow Ribbon Stakes (Plenty of Grace)
1991: Gotham Stakes (Kyle's Our Man)

SYL VEITCH

1946: Futurity Stakes (First Flight)
Astoria Stakes (First Flight)
Matron Stakes (First Flight)
Remsen Handicap (Phalanx)
1947: Wood Memorial Stakes (Phalanx)
Belmont Stakes (Phalanx)
Dwyer Stakes (Phalanx)
Jockey Club Gold Cup (Phalanx)
Champagne Stakes (Vulcan's Forge)
Astoria Stakes (Mackinaw)
Demoiselle Stakes (Ghost Run)
1948: Withers Stakes (Vulcan's Forge)
Saranac Handicap (Mount Marcy)
Fall Highweight Handicap (First Flight)
1949: Delaware Oaks (Nasophar)
1950: Blue Grass Stakes (Mr. Trouble)
1951: Belmont Stakes (Counterpoint)
Lawrence Realization Stakes (Counterpoint)
Jockey Club Gold Cup (Counterpoint)
Blue Grass Stakes (Mameluke)
New Orleans Handicap (Mount Marcy)
1952: Whitney Stakes (Counterpoint)
San Fernando Stakes (Counterpoint)
Metropolitan Handicap (Mameluke)
1953: Cowdin Stakes (Fisherman)
Champagne Stakes (Fisherman)
Selima Stakes (Small Favor)
Westchester Handicap (Cold Command)
1954: Gotham Stakes (Fisherman)
Travers Stakes (Fisherman)
Lawrence Realization Stakes (Fisherman)
Washington D.C. International (Fisherman)
1955: Excelsior Handicap (Fisherman)
1956: Gotham Stakes (Career Boy)
United Nations Handicap (Career Boy)
Gardenia Stakes (Magic Forest)
Wood Memorial Stakes (Head Man)
Ohio Derby (Born Mighty)
1958: Kentucky Oaks (Bug Brush)
1962: New Orleans Handicap (Yorktown)
John B. Campbell Handicap (Yorktown)
1963: New Orleans Handicap (Endymion)
1964: Sanford Stakes (Cornish Prince)
Seminole Handicap (Top Gallant)
1965: Alabama Stakes (What A Treat)
Gazelle Handicap (What A Treat)
Beldame Stakes (What A Treat)
1966: Sanford Stakes (Yorkville)
Black Helen Handicap (What A Treat)
1968: Grey Lag Handicap (Bold Hour)
Amory L. Haskell Handicap (Bold Hour)
1970: Alcibiades Stakes (Patelin)
Selima Stakes (Patelin)
1982: Vosburgh Stakes (Engine One)

DANIEL VELLA

1993: American Derby (Explosive Red)
Hollywood Derby (Explosive Red)

RALPH VERDEROSA

1972: John B. Campbell Handicap (Boone the Great)

PETER VESTAL

1992: Super Derby (Senor Tomas)

F. VEYSEY

1946: San Felipe Stakes (Galla Damion)

DARRELL VIENNA

1986: Santa Barbara Handicap (Mountain Bear)
1987: Arlington-Washington Lassie Stakes (Joe's Tammie)
1990: Budweiser International Stakes (Fly Till Dawn)
1992: San Luis Rey Stakes (Fly Till Dawn)
San Juan Capistrano Handicap (Fly Till Dawn)
Arlington-Washington Futurity (Gilded Time)
Breeders' Cup Juvenile (Gilded Time)
2001: Ramona Handicap (Janet)
Yellow Ribbon Stakes (Janet)
2003: Triple Bend Breeders' Cup Handicap (Joey Franco)

JAIME VILLAGOMEZ

1977: La Canada Stakes (Lucie Manet)
Santa Margarita Handicap (Lucie Manet)
Yellow Ribbon Stakes (Star Ball)

RICHARD VIOLETTE JR.

1995: Peter Pan Stakes (Citadeed)
2003: Gulfstream Park BC 'Cap (Man From Wicklow)

DONNIE VON HEMEL

1993: Arlington-Washington Lassie Stakes (Mariah's Storm)
1994: Arlington-Washington Futurity (Evansville Slew)

KATHARINE VOSS

1975: Top Flight Handicap (Twixt)

TOM VOSS

2000: Sword Dancer Invitational Handicap (John's Call)
Turf Classic (John's Call)

DICK WAGGONER

1956: California Derby (No Regrets)

ELLIOTT WALDEN

1995: Secretariat Stakes (Hawk Attack)
1998: Arkansas Derby (Victory Gallop)
Belmont Stakes (Victory Gallop)
1999: Toyota Blue Grass Stakes (Menifee)
Haskell Invitational Handicap (Menifee)
Jim Dandy Stakes (Ecton Park)
Super Derby (Ecton Park)
Whitney Handicap (Victory Gallop)
2000: Three Chimneys Spinster Stakes (Plenty of Light)
Early Times Hollywood Derby (Brahms)
2002: Spinaway Stakes (Awesome Humor)

CHRISTIAN WALL

1996: Yellow Ribbon Stakes (Donna Viola)

JAMES WALLACE

1964: California Derby (Real Good Deal)

THOMAS WALLER

1956: Metropolitan Handicap (Midafternoon)
Massachusetts Handicap (Midafternoon)
Display Handicap (Midafternoon)
1961: Gotham Stakes (Ambiopoise)
Jersey Derby (Ambiopoise)
1962: Flamingo Stakes (Prego)
Grey Lag Handicap (Ambiopoise)
1966: Dwyer Handicap (Mr. Right)

KATHY WALSH

2001: Santa Monica Handicap (Nany's Sweep)

JOHN WARD JR.

1995: Kentucky Oaks (Gal in a Ruckus)
1997: Matron Stakes (Beautiful Pleasure)
1999: Personal Ensign Handicap (Beautiful Pleasure)
Beldame Stakes (Beautiful Pleasure)
Breeders' Cup Distaff (Beautiful Pleasure)
2000: Hempstead Handicap (Beautiful Pleasure)
Personal Ensign Handicap (Beautiful Pleasure)
2001: Florida Derby (Monarchos)
Kentucky Derby (Monarchos)
Acorn Stakes (Forest Secrets)
2002: Hopeful Stakes (Sky Mesa)
Lane's End Breeders' Futurity (Sky Mesa)
Fountain of Youth Stakes (Booklet)
2003: Gulfstream Park Handicap (Hero's Tribute)

SHERRILL WARD

1954: Cowdin Stakes (Summer Tan)
Garden State Stakes (Summer Tan)
1955: Cowdin Stakes (Noorsaga)
1956: Gallant Fox Handicap (Summer Tan)
Pimlico Special (Summer Tan)
1957: Matron Stakes (Idun)
Gardenia Stakes (Idun)
Frizette Stakes (Idun)
McLennan Handicap (Summer Tan)
Massachusetts Handicap (Greek Spy)
1958: Mother Goose Stakes (Idun)
Gazelle Handicap (Idun)
1959: Maskette Handicap (Idun)
1968: Black Helen Handicap (Treacherous)
1974: Donn Handicap (Forego)
Gulfstream Park Handicap (Forego)
Widener Handicap (Forego)
Carter Handicap (Forego)
Brooklyn Handicap (Forego)
Woodward Stakes (Forego)
Vosburgh Handicap (Forego)
Jockey Club Gold Cup (Forego)
1975: Widener Handicap (Forego)
Carter Handicap (Forego)
Brooklyn Handicap (Forego)
Suburban Handicap (Forego)
Woodward Stakes (Forego)

RONNIE WARREN

1968: Kentucky Jockey Club Stakes (Traffic Mark)
Alcibiades Stakes (Lil's Bag)
1969: Arkansas Derby (Traffic Mark)

G. WATSON

1965: Washington D.C. International (Diatome)

SID WATTERS JR.

1970: Cowdin Stakes (Hoist the Flag)
1972: John B. Campbell Handicap (Favorecidian)
Michigan Mile and One-Eighth (Favorecidian)
1976: American Derby (Fifth Marine)
Fall Highweight Handicap (Relent)
1980: Alabama Stakes (Love Sign)
Beldame Stakes (Love Sign)
1981: Beldame Stakes (Love Sign)
1982: Young America Stakes (Slewpy)
1983: Wood Memorial Stakes (Slew O' Gold)
Woodward Stakes (Slew O' Gold)
Jockey Club Gold Cup (Slew O' Gold)
Meadowlands Cup (Slewpy)
1985: Matron Stakes (Musical Lark)

JOHN WATTS

1985: Budweiser-Arlington Million (Teleprompter)

P.D.L. WATTS

1946: Trenton Handicap (Turbine)

RICHARD WATTS

1949: Santa Anita Derby (Old Rockport)

JOHN WAUGH

1952: Washington D.C. International (Wilwyn)

JOSEPH WAUNSCH

1999: Walmac International Alcibiades Stakes (Scratch Pad)

J. WEBBER

1949: Black Helen Handicap (Roman Candle)

GEORGE WECKERLE JR.

1974: Metropolitan Handicap (Arbees Boy)

M.M. WEIL

1952: Trenton Handicap (Ken)

JACK WEIPERT

1958: Jockey Club Gold Cup (Inside Tract)
1959: Brooklyn Handicap (Babu)
1976: Pan American Handicap (Improviser)
1977: Hialeah Turf Cup (Improviser)

DERMOT WELD

1989: Laurel Futurity (Go and Go)
1990: Belmont Stakes (Go and Go)
2002: Matriarch Stakes (Dress To Thrill)
2003: Flower Bowl Invitational Stakes (Dimitrova)

BABE WELLS

1948: Hawthorne Gold Cup (Billings)
1949: Hawthorne Gold Cup (Volcanic)
1950: Arlington Lassie Stakes (Shawnee Squaw)
Hawthorne Gold Cup (Dr. Ole Nelson)
1969: Gardenia Stakes (Fast Attack)

HARRY WELLS

1956: Molly Pitcher Handicap (Blue Sparkler)

CHARLES WERSTLER

1963: Arlington-Washington Futurity (Golden Ruler)
1969: Breeders' Futurity (Hard Work)
1982: Arlington Handicap (Flying Target)

RALPH WEST

1947: Inglewood Handicap (Artillery)
1950: Hollywood Oaks (Mrs. Fuddy)
1952: Del Mar Futurity (Hour Regards)
1955: Cinema Handicap (Guilton Madero)
1957: Vanity Handicap (Annie-Lu-San)
1958: Vanity Handicap (Annie-Lu-San)
1968: Santa Barbara Handicap (Amerigo's Fancy)

TED WEST

1983: Hollywood Derby (Ginger Brink)
Bay Meadows Handicap (Interco)
1984: Century Handicap (Interco)
San Fernando Stakes (Interco)
Santa Anita Handicap (Interco)
San Luis Rey Stakes (Interco)
1988: Hollywood Starlet Stakes (Stocks Up)

TED H. WEST

2000: San Antonio Handicap (Budroyale)

BOB WHEELER

1955: Del Mar Debutante Stakes (Miss Todd)
1957: Starlet Stakes (Old Pueblo)
Del Mar Futurity (Old Pueblo)
1958: San Felipe Handicap (Carrier X.)
1959: Santa Margarita Handicap (Bug Brush)
San Antonio Handicap (Bug Brush)
Inglewood Handicap (Bug Brush)
Santa Anita Derby (Silver Spoon)
Cinema Handicap (Silver Spoon)
Hopeful Stakes (Tompion)
1960: Vanity Handicap (Silver Spoon)
Santa Margarita Handicap (Silver Spoon)
Santa Anita Derby (Tompion)
Blue Grass Stakes (Tompion)
Hollywood Gold Cup (Dotted Swiss)
Sunset Handicap (Dotted Swiss)
1961: Hollywood Juvenile Championship (Rattle Dancer)
Del Mar Debutante Stakes (Spark Plug)
1962: Del Mar Debutante Stakes (Brown Berry)
1963: Hollywood Juvenile Championship (Malicious)
Hollywood Gold Cup (Cadiz)
San Luis Rey Handicap (The Axe II)
1965: Hollywood Juvenile Championship (Port Wine)
Arlington-Washington Lassie Stakes (Silver Bright)
1967: Santa Susana Stakes (Fish House)
Hollywood Oaks (Amerigo Lady)
1969: Sunset Handicap (Petrone)
San Juan Capistrano Handicap (Petrone)
1975: Hollywood Juvenile Championship (Restless Restless)
1977: Oak Leaf Stakes (B. Thoughtful)
1978: La Canada Stakes (Taisez Vous)
Santa Margarita Handicap (Taisez Vous)
Hollywood Oaks (B. Thoughtful)
1979: La Canada Stakes (B. Thoughtful)
1981: Vanity Handicap (Track Robbery)
1982: Apple Blossom Handicap (Track Robbery)
Matriarch Stakes (Pale Purple)

LIN WHEELER

1980: Hollywood Juvenile Championship (Loma Malad)
1985: Fantasy Stakes (Rascal Lass)

OSCAR WHITE

1946: Jockey Club Gold Cup (Pavot)
Massachusetts Handicap (Pavot)
Travers Stakes (Natchez)
Jerome Handicap (Mahout)
1947: Beldame Handicap (Snow Goose)
Ladies Handicap (Snow Goose)
1948: Manhattan Handicap (Loyal Legion)
1949: Alabama Stakes (Adile)
1950: New Castle Handicap (Adile)
1951: Acorn Stakes (Kiss Me Kate)
Delaware Oaks (Kiss Me Kate)
Gazelle Stakes (Kiss Me Kate)
Alabama Stakes (Kiss Me Kate)
Flamingo Stakes (Yildiz)
1952: Belmont Stakes (One Count)
Travers Stakes (One Count)
Jockey Club Gold Cup (One Count)
Alabama Stakes (Lily White)
New Castle Handicap (Kiss Me Kate)
1953: Firenze Handicap (Kiss Me Kate)
1958: Travers Stakes (Piano Jim)
1963: Selima Stakes (My Card)
1970: Gardenia Stakes (Eggy)

T.F. WHITE

1963: Delaware Handicap (Waltz Song)

W.R. WHITE

1960: Bougainvillea Turf Handicap (Noble Sel)

DAVID WHITELEY

1974: San Luis Rey Stakes (Astray)
San Juan Capistrano Handicap (Astray)
Maskette Handicap (Ponte Vecchio)
1975: Withers Stakes (Sarsar)
1976: Coaching Club American Oaks (Revidere)
Ruffian Stakes (Revidere)
1977: Dwyer Handicap (Bailjumper)
1978: Remsen Stakes (Instrument Landing)
Top Flight Handicap (Northernette)
Bowling Green Handicap (Tiller)
1979: Top Flight Handicap (Waya)
Beldame Stakes (Waya)
Santa Barbara Handicap (Waya)
Belmont Stakes (Coastal)
Dwyer Stakes (Coastal)
Monmouth Invitational Handicap (Coastal)
San Antonio Stakes (Tiller)
San Juan Capistrano Handicap (Tiller)
Wood Memorial Stakes (Instrument Landing)
1980: Flower Bowl Handicap (Just A Game II)
Sword Dancer Stakes (Tiller)
Man o' War Stakes (French Colonial)
1983: Brooklyn Handicap (Highland Blade)
Marlboro Cup Handicap (Highland Blade)
Pan American Handicap (Highland Blade)
Delaware Handicap (May Day Eighty)
1984: Jim Dandy Stakes (Carr de Naskra)
Travers Stakes (Carr de Naskra)

FRANK WHITELEY JR.

1963: Cowdin Stakes (Chieftan)
1964: Cowdin Stakes (Tom Rolfe)
1965: Preakness Stakes (Tom Rolfe)
Arlington Classic (Tom Rolfe)
American Derby (Tom Rolfe)
Arlington Handicap (Chieftan)
1966: Aqueduct Handicap (Tom Rolfe)
1967: Wood Memorial Stakes (Damascus)
Preakness Stakes (Damascus)
Belmont Stakes (Damascus)
Dwyer Handicap (Damascus)
American Derby (Damascus)
Travers Stakes (Damascus)
Aqueduct Stakes (Damascus)
Woodward Stakes (Damascus)
Jockey Club Gold Cup (Damascus)
1968: Brooklyn Handicap (Damascus)
Aqueduct Stakes (Damascus)
Malibu Stakes (Damascus)
San Fernando Stakes (Damascus)
1969: Carter Handicap (Promise)
1970: Carter Handicap (Tyrant)
1972: Dwyer Handicap (Cloudy Dawn)
Arlington Park Handicap (Cloudy Dawn)
1974: Sorority Stakes (Ruffian)
Spinaway Stakes (Ruffian)
1975: Acorn Stakes (Ruffian)
Mother Goose Stakes (Ruffian)
Coaching Club American Oaks (Ruffian)
Fall Highweight Handicap (Honorable Miss)
1976: Metropolitan Handicap (Forego)
Brooklyn Handicap (Forego)
Woodward Handicap (Forego)
Marlboro Cup Handicap (Forego)
Fall Highweight Handicap (Honorable Miss)
1977: Metropolitan Handicap (Forego)
Woodward Handicap (Forego)

LYNN WHITING

1970: Jerome Handicap (Great Mystery)
1984: Jim Beam Stakes (At the Threshold)
Arlington Classic (At the Threshold)
Ohio Derby (At the Threshold)
American Derby (At the Threshold)
Haskell Invitational Handicap (Big Pistol)
1987: Jim Beam Stakes (J.T.'s Pet)
1992: Jim Beam Stakes (Lil E. Tee)
Kentucky Derby (Lil E. Tee)

CHARLIE WHITTINGHAM

1953: Futurity Stakes (Porterhouse)
1955: William P. Kyne Handicap (Mister Gus)
1956: San Antonio Handicap (Mister Gus)
Woodward Stakes (Mister Gus)
Arlington Handicap (Mister Gus)
San Felipe Handicap (Social Climber)
Cinema Handicap (Social Climber)
Californian Stakes (Porterhouse)
1957: Santa Anita Handicap (Corn Husker)
San Juan Capistrano Handicap (Corn Husker)
Selima Stakes (Guide Line)
Los Angeles Handicap (Porterhouse)
Californian Stakes (Social Climber)
1958: Arlington Futurity (Restless Wind)
Washington Park Futurity (Restless Wind)
1959: Vanity Handicap (Tender Size)
San Juan Capistrano Handicap (Royal Living)
1960: Roamer Handicap (Divine Comedy)
San Carlos Handicap (Clandestine)
1962: Cinema Handicap (Black Sheep)
American Derby (Black Sheep)
1963: Beldame Stakes (Oil Royalty)
Vineland Handicap (Oil Royalty)
San Felipe Handicap (Denodado)
1965: California Derby (Perfect Sky)
1966: San Felipe Handicap (Saber Mountain)
Cinema Handicap (Drin)
1967: Santa Anita Handicap (Pretense)
Gulfstream Park Handicap (Pretense)
San Antonio Handicap (Pretense)
Hollywood Derby (Tumble Wind)
Charles H. Strub Stakes (Drin)
1969: Hollywood Derby (Tell)
Cinema Handicap (Noholme Jr.)
Century Handicap (Pinjara)
1970: Hollywood Park Inv. Turf Handicap (Fiddle Isle)
American Handicap (Fiddle Isle)
San Luis Rey Handicap (Fiddle Isle)
San Juan Capistrano Handicap (Fiddle Isle)
Del Mar Handicap (Daryl's Joy)
Oak Tree Stakes (Daryl's Joy)
1971: Californian Stakes (Cougar II)
Ford Pinto Invitational Turf Handicap (Cougar II)
Oak Tree Invitational Stakes (Cougar II)
San Juan Capistrano Handicap (Cougar II)
Hollywood Gold Cup (Ack Ack)
San Antonio Stakes (Ack Ack)
Santa Anita Handicap (Ack Ack)
American Handicap (Ack Ack)
Santa Susana Stakes (Turkish Trousers)
Hollywood Oaks (Turkish Trousers)
Inglewood Handicap (Advance Guard)
Del Mar Handicap (Pinjara)
1972: Californian Stakes (Cougar II)
Century Handicap (Cougar II)
Oak Tree Invitational Stakes (Cougar II)
Norfolk Stakes (Groshawk)
Del Mar Futurity (Groshawk)
Santa Maria Handicap (Turkish Trousers)
Santa Margarita Handicap (Turkish Trousers)
California Derby (Quack)
Hollywood Gold Cup (Quack)
Hollywood Oaks (Pallisima)
American Handicap (Buzkashi)
San Juan Capistrano Handicap (Practicante)
1973: Santa Anita Handicap (Cougar II)
Century Handicap (Cougar II)
Sunset Handicap (Cougar II)
Hollywood Gold Cup (Kennedy Road)
San Antonio Stakes (Kennedy Road)
Beverly Hills Handicap (Le Cle)
Californian Stakes (Quack)
1974: Vanity Handicap (Tallahto)
Santa Barbara Handicap (Tallahto)
Oak Tree Invitational Stakes (Tallahto)
Fantasy Stakes (Miss Musket)
Hollywood Oaks (Miss Musket)
Beverly Hills Handicap (La Zanzara)
Californian Stakes (Quack)
Hollywood Gold Cup (Tree of Knowledge)
Sunset Handicap (Greco II)
1975: Vanity Handicap (Dulcia)
Ramona Handicap (Dulcia)
National Championship Inv. Handicap (Dulcia)
San Fernando Stakes (Stardust Mel)
Charles H. Strub Stakes (Stardust Mel)
Santa Anita Handicap (Stardust Mel)
Beverly Hills Handicap (La Zanzara)
San Juan Capistrano Handicap (La Zanzara)
Santa Barbara Handicap (Gay Style)
Cinema Handicap (Terete)
San Luis Rey Stakes (Trojan Bronze)
Oak Tree Invitational Stakes (Top Command)
1976: Champions Invitational Handicap (King Pellinore)
American Handicap (King Pellinore)
Oak Tree Invitational Stakes (King Pellinore)
Sunset Handicap (Caucasus)
Manhattan Handicap (Caucasus)
Ramona Handicap (Vagabonda)
Santa Barbara Handicap (Stravina)

Del Mar Handicap (Riot in Paris)
Hollywood Invitational Handicap (Dahlia)
1977: Norfolk Stakes (Balzac)
Hollywood Oaks (Glenaris)
San Luis Rey Stakes (Caucasus)
1978: Hollywood Gold Cup (Exceller)
Jockey Club Gold Cup (Exceller)
Hollywood Invitational Handicap (Exceller)
Sunset Handicap (Exceller)
Oak Tree Invitational Stakes (Exceller)
San Juan Capistrano Handicap (Exceller)
1979: Santa Margarita Handicap (Sanedtki)
Sunset Handicap (Sirlad)
Oak Tree Invitational Stakes (Balzac)
1980: Norfolk Stakes (High Counsel)
Ramona Handicap (Queen to Conquer)
Yellow Ribbon Stakes (Kilijaro)
Sunset Handicap (Inkerman)
1981: Ramona Handicap (Queen to Conquer)
Yellow Ribbon Stakes (Queen to Conquer)
Sunset Handicap (Galaxy Libra)
Man o' War Stakes (Galaxy Libra)
Washington D.C. International (Providential II)
Hollywood Turf Cup (Providential II)
Matriarch Stakes (Kilijaro)
San Juan Capistrano Handicap (Obraztsovy)
1982: Hollywood Gold Cup (Perrault)
Budweiser Million (Perrault)
San Luis Rey Stakes (Perrault)
Fantasy Stakes (Flying Partner)
Yellow Ribbon Stakes (Castilla)
Matriarch Stakes (Castilla)
Californian Stakes (Erins Isle)
Sunset Handicap (Erins Isle)
Hollywood Invitational Handicap (Exploded)
1983: Hollywood Invitational Handicap (Erins Isle)
San Luis Rey Stakes (Erins Isle)
San Juan Capistrano Handicap (Erins Isle)
Californian Stakes (The Wonder)
Century Handicap (The Wonder)
Sunset Handicap (Craelius)
Arlington Handicap (Palikaraki)
1984: San Juan Capistrano Handicap (Load the Cannons)
1985: San Antonio Handicap (Lord at War)
Santa Anita Handicap (Lord at War)
Californian Stakes (Greinton)
Hollywood Gold Cup (Greinton)
San Luis Rey Stakes (Prince True)
San Juan Capistrano Handicap (Prince True)
Santa Barbara Handicap (Fact Finder)
Century Handicap (Dahar)
Yellow Ribbon Stakes (Estrapade)
1986: San Luis Rey Stakes (Dahar)
San Juan Capistrano Handicap (Dahar)
Budweiser-Arlington Million (Estrapade)
Oak Tree Invitational Stakes (Estrapade)
Santa Anita Oaks (Hidden Light)
Hollywood Oaks (Hidden Light)
Santa Anita Handicap (Greinton)
Kentucky Derby (Ferdinand)
John Henry Handicap (Palace Music)
Hollywood Derby (Thrill Show)
Hollywood Futurity (Temperate Sil)
1987: Santa Anita Derby (Temperate Sil)
Swaps Stakes (Temperate Sil)
Hollywood Gold Cup (Ferdinand)
Breeders' Cup Classic (Ferdinand)
Santa Barbara Handicap (Reloy)
San Juan Capistrano Handicap (Rosedale)
Californian Stakes (Judge Angelucci)
Hollywood Invitational Handicap (Rivlia)
Vanity Handicap (Infinidad)
Sunset Handicap (Swink)
1988: Kentucky Oaks (Goodbye Halo)
Mother Goose Stakes (Goodbye Halo)
Coaching Club American Oaks (Goodbye Halo)
San Antonio Handicap (Judge Angelucci)
San Luis Rey Stakes (Rivlia)
Fantasy Stakes (Jeanne Jones)
Hollywood Oaks (Pattern Step)
Swaps Stakes (Lively One)
Oak Tree Invitational Stakes (Nasr El Arab)
1989: San Felipe Handicap (Sunday Silence)
Santa Anita Derby (Sunday Silence)
Kentucky Derby (Sunday Silence)
Preakness Stakes (Sunday Silence)
Super Derby (Sunday Silence)
Breeders' Cup Classic (Sunday Silence)
Charles H. Strub Stakes (Nasr El Arab)
San Juan Capistrano Handicap (Nasr El Arab)
San Luis Rey Stakes (Frankly Perfect)
Hollywood Turf Cup (Frankly Perfect)
La Canada Stakes (Goodbye Halo)
John Henry Handicap (Peace)
Gamely Handicap (Fitzwilliam Place)
Hollywood Derby (Live the Dream)
1990: John Henry Handicap (Golden Pheasant)
Arlington Million (Golden Pheasant)
Santa Anita Handicap (Ruhlmann)
Californian Stakes (Sunday Silence)
1991: Hollywood Turf Cup (Miss Alleged)
1992: Matriarch Stakes (Flawlessly)
1993: Ramona Handicap (Flawlessly)
Beverly D. Stakes (Flawlessly)
Matriarch Stakes (Flawlessly)
Santa Anita Handicap (Sir Beaufort)
1994: Ramona Handicap (Flawlessly)
Yellow Ribbon Stakes (Aube Indienne)

MICHAEL WHITTINGHAM

1976: Arlington Handicap (Victorian Prince)
1982: Santa Barbara Handicap (Ack's Secret)
Santa Margarita Handicap (Ack's Secret)
1983: Santa Margarita Handicap (Marimbula)
1985: Santa Anita Derby (Skywalker)
1986: Breeders' Cup Classic (Skywalker)
1990: San Juan Capistrano Handicap (Delegant)
1991: Arlington Classic (Whadjathink)

BERT WILLIAMS

1946: Marguerite Stakes (Cosmic Missile)
1947: Hopeful Stakes (Relic)
Gazelle Stakes (Cosmic Missile)
1961: Delaware Handicap (Airmans Guide)
Beldame Stakes (Airmans Guide)

HAROLD WILLIAMS

1953: Remsen Handicap (Galdar)
Queens County Handicap (Flaunt)
1954: Canadian Championship Stakes (Resilient)

J. WILLIAMS

1958: Westerner Stakes (Strong Bay)

BARNEY WILLIS

1976: La Canada Stakes (Raise Your Skirts)
1981: San Fernando Stakes (Doonesbury)

WILLIAM WILMOT

1975: Gulfstream Park Handicap (Gold and Myrrh)
Grey Lag Handicap (Gold and Myrrh)
Metropolitan Handicap (Gold and Myrrh)

LEX WILSON

1946: Stars and Stripes Handicap (Witch Sir)
1953: Michigan Mile (Second Avenue)
1955: Arlington Futurity (Swoon's Son)
Washington Park Futurity (Swoon's Son)
1956: Arlington Classic (Swoon's Son)
American Derby (Swoon's Son)

JOHN WINANS

1967: Acorn Stakes (Furl Sail)
Mother Goose Stakes (Furl Sail)
1968: Spinster Stakes (Sale Day)

DONALD WINFREE

1985: Sorority Stakes (Lazer Show)

BILL WINFREY

1948: Gazelle Stakes (Sweet Dream)
1949: Matron Stakes (Bed o' Roses)
Selima Stakes (Bed o' Roses)
Marguerite Stakes (Bed o' Roses)
Demoiselle Stakes (Bed o' Roses)
Vosburgh Handicap (Loser Weeper)
Metropolitan Handicap (Loser Weeper)
1950: Coaching Club American Oaks (Next Move)
Delaware Oaks (Next Move)
Gazelle Stakes (Next Move)
Beldame Handicap (Next Move)
Ladies Handicap (Next Move)
Vanity Handicap (Next Move)
Dixie Handicap (Loser Weeper)
Suburban Handicap (Loser Weeper)
Lawrence Realization Stakes (Bed o' Roses)
1951: Saratoga Special (Cousin)
Hopeful Stakes (Cousin)
Vineland Handicap (Bed o' Roses)
Comely Handicap (Bed o' Roses)
1952: Hopeful Stakes (Native Dancer)
Futurity Stakes (Native Dancer)
Firenze Handicap (Next Move)
Beldame Handicap (Next Move)
Remsen Handicap (Social Outcast)
Astoria Stakes (Home-Made)
Santa Margarita Handicap (Bed o' Roses)
1953: Gotham Stakes (Native Dancer)
Wood Memorial Stakes (Native Dancer)
Withers Stakes (Native Dancer)
Preakness Stakes (Native Dancer)
Belmont Stakes (Native Dancer)
Dwyer Stakes (Native Dancer)
Arlington Classic (Native Dancer)
Travers Stakes (Native Dancer)
American Derby (Native Dancer)
Vagrancy Handicap (Home-Made)
Comely Handicap (Home-Made)
Ohio Derby (Find)
Grey Lag Handicap (Find)
Vosburgh Handicap (Indian Land)
Excelsior Handicap (First Glance)
1954: Excelsior Handicap (Find)
Queens County Handicap (Find)
Whitney Handicap (Social Outcast)
Gallant Fox Handicap (Social Outcast)
Metropolitan Handicap (Native Dancer)
Aqueduct Handicap (Crash Dive)
1955: McLennan Handicap (Social Outcast)
John B. Campbell Mem. Handicap (Social Outcast)
Sunset Handicap (Social Outcast)
Manhattan Handicap (Social Outcast)
Trenton Handicap (Social Outcast)
1956: New Orleans Handicap (Find)
1957: Inglewood Handicap (Find)
American Handicap (Find)
Sunset Handicap (Find)
1959: Sunset Handicap (Whodunit)
1961: Sunset Handicap (Whodunit)
1963: Sorority Stakes (Castle Forbes)
Gardenia Stakes (Castle Forbes)
1964: Sapling Stakes (Bold Lad)
Hopeful Stakes (Bold Lad)
Futurity Stakes (Bold Lad)
Champagne Stakes (Bold Lad)
Frizette Stakes (Queen Empress)
Gardenia Stakes (Queen Empress)
Demoiselle Stakes (Discipline)
Acorn Stakes (Castle Forbes)
1965: Sapling Stakes (Buckpasser)
Hopeful Stakes (Buckpasser)
Arlington-Washington Futurity (Buckpasser)
Champagne Stakes (Buckpasser)
Saratoga Special (Impressive)

CAREY WINFREY

1954: Jerome Handicap (Martyr)
1956: Brooklyn Handicap (Dedicate)
Whitney Stakes (Dedicate)
Hawthorne Gold Cup (Dedicate)
1957: John B. Campbell Memorial Handicap (Dedicate)
Monmouth Handicap (Dedicate)
Woodward Stakes (Dedicate)

ROBERT WINGFIELD

1956: Blue Grass Stakes (Toby B.)
1959: Breeders' Futurity (Toby's Brother)
1965: Spinster Stakes (Star Maggie)
1973: Malibu Stakes (Bicker)
San Fernando Stakes (Bicker)

ARNOLD WINICK

1959: Man o' War Handicap (Tudor Era)
1960: New Orleans Handicap (Tudor Era)
1962: Arlington Lassie Stakes (Smart Deb)
Matron Stakes (Smart Deb)
Gallant Fox Handicap (Sensitivo)
Display Handicap (Sensitivo)
1963: Arlington Matron Handicap (Smart Deb)
1966: Donn Handicap (Tronado)
Arlington Handicap (Tronado)
Carter Handicap (Davis II)
1970: Arlington Classic (Corn off the Cob)
1971: Arlington-Washington Futurity (Hold Your Peace)
1972: Flamingo Stakes (Hold Your Peace)

NEAL WINICK

1977: Gulfstream Park Handicap (Strike Me Lucky)
Pan American Handicap (Gravelines)

RANDY WINICK

1979: Ramona Handicap (Country Queen)
Yellow Ribbon Stakes (Country Queen)
1981: Century Handicap (Spence Bay)
1985: Vanity Handicap (Dontstop Themusic)
Spinster Stakes (Dontstop Themusic)

RANDY WINICK *(Continued)*
La Canada Stakes (Mitterand)
1993: Breeders' Cup Juvenile (Brocco)
1994: Santa Anita Derby (Brocco)

GLENN WISMER
1992: Kentucky Oaks (Luv Me Luv Me Not)

ANDREAS WOHLER
2001: Arlington Million (Silvano)

MARTY WOLFSON
1993: Flamingo Stakes (Forever Whirl)
Ohio Derby (Forever Whirl)
1995: Test Stakes (Chaposa Springs)

R.C. WOOD JR.
1981: Hawthorne Gold Cup (Spruce Bouquet)

E.H. WRIGHT
1948: Starlet Stakes (Star Fiddle)

FRANK WRIGHT
1957: New Orleans Handicap (Kingmaker)
Grey Lag Handicap (Kingmaker)
Whitney Stakes (Kingmaker)
1983: Top Flight Handicap (Adept)

TENNESSEE WRIGHT
1953: Florida Derby (Money Broker)
1956: Louisiana Derby (Reaping Right)
Michigan Mile (Nonnie Jo)
1958: Breeders' Futurity (Namon)
1961: Breeders' Futurity (Roman Line)

WILLIAM WRIGHT
1989: Hialeah Turf Cup (El Senor)
Sword Dancer Handicap (El Senor)
1990: Sword Dancer Handicap (El Senor)

WILLIAM WYNDLE
1960: San Felipe Handicap (Flow Line)

HAROLD YOUNG
1954: Pimlico Futurity (Thinking Cap)
1961: Blue Grass Stakes (Sherluck)
Belmont Stakes (Sherluck)
Lawrence Realization Stakes (Sherluck)
Roamer Handicap (Sherluck)
1966: Grey Lag Handicap (Selari)

STEVEN YOUNG
1984: Jersey Derby (Birdie's Legend)
1994: Gotham Stakes (Irgun)
Wood Memorial Stakes (Irgun)

TOM YOUNG
1950: Kentucky Jockey Club Stakes (Pur Sang)

EDDIE YOWELL
1951: Trenton Handicap (Call Over)
1961: John B. Campbell Handicap (Conestoga)
1962: Carter Handicap (Merry Ruler)
1965: Jersey Derby (Hail to All)
Belmont Stakes (Hail to All)
Travers Stakes (Hail to All)
1967: Cowdin Stakes (Iron Ruler)
1968: Jerome Handicap (Iron Ruler)
1970: Sanford Stakes (Executioner)
1971: Flamingo Stakes (Executioner)
Belmont Stakes (Pass Catcher)
1972: Gulfstream Park Handicap (Executioner)
Metropolitan Handicap (Executioner)
1975: Maskette Handicap (Let Me Linger)

DAVE ZAKOOR JR.
1973: Breeders' Futurity (Provante)

JOHN ZARTHAR
1975: Donn Handicap (Proud and Bold)

EUGENE ZEREN
1980: Longacres Mile (Trooper Seven)

RALPH ZIADIE
1998: Cigar Mile Handicap (Sir Bear)
1999: Metropolitan Handicap (Sir Bear)
2001: Gulfstream Park Handicap (Sir Bear)
2003: Fountain of Youth Stakes (Trust N Luck)
Hopeful Stakes (Silver Wagon)

MAURICE ZILBER
1973: Washington D.C. International (Dahlia)
1974: Man o' War Stakes (Dahlia)
Canadian International Championship (Dahlia)
1975: Washington D.C. International (Nobiliary)
1976: Canadian International Championship (Youth)
Washington D.C. International (Youth)
1977: Canadian International Championship (Exceller)
1978: Yellow Ribbon Stakes (Amazer)
1980: Washington D.C. International (Argument)

JOHN ZITNIK
1957: Arlington Handicap (Manassas)

NICK ZITO
1984: Pennsylvania Derby (Morning Bob)
1986: Top Flight Handicap (Ride Sally)
1990: Gotham Stakes (Thirty Six Red)
Wood Memorial Stakes (Thirty Six Red)
1991: Blue Grass Stakes (Strike the Gold)
Kentucky Derby (Strike the Gold)
Futurity Stakes (Agincourt)
1992: Pimlico Special (Strike the Gold)
Nassau County Handicap (Strike the Gold)
Dwyer Stakes (Agincourt)
1993: Remsen Stakes (Go for Gin)
1994: Kentucky Derby (Go for Gin)
1996: Preakness Stakes (Louis Quatorze)
Jim Dandy Stakes (Louis Quatorze)
Frizette Stakes (Storm Song)
Breeders' Cup Juvenile Fillies (Storm Song)
Pimlico Special (Star Standard)
Flower Bowl Invitational Handicap (Chelsey Flower)
1998: Toyota Blue Grass Stakes (Halory Hunter)
Moet Champagne Stakes (The Groom Is Red)
1999: Champagne Stakes (Greenwood Lake)
Remsen Stakes (Greenwood Lake)
Gallery Furniture.com Stakes (Stephen Got Even)
Wood Memorial Stakes (Adonis)
2000: Donn Handicap (Stephen Got Even)
Champagne Stakes (A.P. Valentine)
Jockey Club Gold Cup (Albert the Great)
2001: Brooklyn Handicap (Albert the Great)
Suburban Handicap (Albert the Great)
2003: Kentucky Oaks (Bird Town)
Acorn Stakes (Bird Town)
Lane's End Breeders' Futurity (Eurosilver)
Champagne Stakes (Birdstone)

F. ZITTO
1972: Black Helen Handicap (Alma North)

Photo courtesy of Santa Anita Park

John Mabee (left), who with his wife, Betty, established Golden Eagle Farm, one of California's premier thoroughbred racing and breeding operations, was delighted to congratulate an equally happy Kent Desormeaux after a victory by a Golden Eagle Farm runner.

Owners

V: Owners

Calumet's Unchallenged Legacy

Being a successful thoroughbred owner is a little like being a good poker player: To quote Kenny Rogers, you've got to know when to hold 'em and when to fold 'em.

Although many successful race horses—including such standouts as Round Table, Nashua, and Traffic Judge—have been sold after they earned major victories and subsequently captured significant triumphs for their new owners, most owners prefer to keep their stars in their barns.

For breeders who both sell a portion of their yearlings and two-year-olds and keep others to race, the best of all worlds obviously would be to see their best youngsters eventually become major winners in their silks and those they don't believe will pan out bring high prices at yearling sales. If breeders consistently followed that pattern, however, they quickly would gain a reputation for sending only their substandard stock to the sales ring, which soon would discourage buyers and eventually put the breeder out of business.

And there are countless illustrations that prove that even well-heeled owners who can afford to purchase the most fashionably bred and regally built yearlings can't necessarily buy a future champion. Take the case of Snaafi Dancer, whose sale price of $10.2 million as a yearling in 1983 trails only the $13.1 million that Seattle Dancer brought. Snaafi Dancer never made it to the races. Canadian Bound, from the first crop of 1973 Triple Crown winner Secretariat, brought $1.5 million as a yearling, then a world record. Canadian Bound did make it to the races—where he earned a paltry $4,770 in a winless career.

Just one year before Canadian Bound entered the sales ring, savvy buyers purchased Seattle Slew as a yearling for $17,500, and the 1977 Triple Crown winner is hardly the only bargain-basement purchase to win a classic. Spectacular Bid, the 1979 Kentucky Derby and Preakness Stakes winner, sold for $37,000; 1985 Kentucky Derby winner Spend A Buck for $12,000, and Real Quiet—who in 1998 won the first two legs of the Triple Crown and lost the Belmont Stakes by a mere nose—for $17,000.

In the vast majority of all races held in North America, the entire field is for sale to any licensed owner or trainer for a predetermined claiming price. Successful owners must determine whether their horses—and those of their rivals—which are being entered for, say, a $25,000 claiming price, actually are worth more.

John Henry, who sold for a mere $1,100 as a yearling, could have been purchased for as little as $20,000 during his five starts as a claimer. By the time he was retired after his second Horse of the Year campaign in 1984, John Henry had earned $6,597,704, then a world record, and the undying respect of thousands of owners who regretted that they didn't seize the opportunity to purchase a potential legend for petty cash. And those owners who failed to claim Charismatic for $62,500 on February 11, 1999, at Santa Anita obviously didn't anticipate that he'd win the Kentucky Derby, Preakness Stakes, and $2,007,404 in the next four months.

This chapter examines those who best knew when to hold 'em and when to sell 'em, those who made lasting marks as owners by winning major North American races since World War II.

Photo courtesy of the National Thoroughbred Racing Association

Two of thoroughbred racing's most successful current owners, Dogwood Stable managing partner Cot Campbell and Robert Lewis (right), confer.

Photo courtesy of Santa Anita Park

In one of the most dramatic finishes since World War II, Johnny Longden drove Noor (No. 3 on the outside) home a nose in front of Citation, under Steve Brooks, to capture the 1950 San Juan Capistrano Handicap. Although Calumet Farm's Citation, who carried 130 pounds—13 more than his rival—lost the battle of America's two best handicap horses, the 1948 Triple Crown winner is widely considered the best of the Calumet runners who have captured a record 171 major North American stakes since World War II.

In order to ensure proper credit, each ownership entity is listed separately. Timber Country, for example, was the champion two-year-old colt in 1994 by virtue of his victories in the Champagne Stakes and Breeders' Cup Juvenile and also won the 1995 Preakness. Timber Country was owned by a partnership that consisted of Gainesway Farm, Beverly and Robert Lewis, and Overbrook Farm—and that partnership is listed as such. It unfairly would boost the victory totals of Gainesway, Overbrook, or the Lewises to add three wins to *each* of their individual totals, which would represent nine major triumphs for Timber Country instead of three.

Further, many ownership entities are listed simply as Dogwood Stable or Claiborne Farm, for example. Many stables and farms are simply racing aliases for owners who obviously prefer to run their horses in the stable name. In many other cases, however, it may be easier to unravel the Dead Sea Scrolls than to determine the actual names of all the owners. In the case of Dogwood Stable, Cot Campbell serves as the managing partner and may have as many as 40 different investors in each horse owned by Dogwood. Claiborne was founded by A.B. "Bull" Hancock Jr. and now is owned by his widow and three of his children, one of whom, Seth, serves as the farm's president, proudly carrying on the legacy of the farm's famed orange silks.

Greentree Stable, one of the most heralded ownership entities in thoroughbred history, offers an excellent illustration of why it's necessary to look at accomplishments of the ownership entity instead of attempting to list the individuals involved.

Greentree was founded by Payne Whitney, who upon his death in 1927 left his $179 million estate—at that time the largest ever inventoried in the United States—to his widow, Helen Hay Whitney, the "First Lady of the Turf." Upon her death in 1944, Greentree was inherited by her son, John Hay Whitney, and daughter, Joan Payson, who later owned baseball's New York Mets. Upon Payson's death, John Hay Whitney acquired his sister's share of Greentree from her widower. Upon John Hay Whitney's death in 1982, the stable became the property of his widow, Betsy Cushing Roosevelt Whitney. Yet, for most of a century, their horses ran in the name of Greentree Stable, which hasn't won a major race since 1985.

So it's best to consider thoroughbred ownership entities in the same manner that baseball fans do. The New York Yankees have won 39 American League pennants and 26 World Series, although certainly not all have come under the stewardship of current owner George Steinbrenner, whose horses, by the way, have won major races in his name and in both that of Kinship Stable and Kinsman Stable. And the Boston Celtics are credited with 15 National Basketball Association championships, not merely those that belong to former owner Harry Mangurian Jr., whose horses have won seven major races.

Steinbrenner and Mangurian aren't the only significant figures from other sports whose horses have won major races in the modern era. So have the likes of Wayne Gretzky, Jack Kent Cooke, and Bobby Hurley, an All-American who helped lead Duke University to two NCAA basketball titles and whose

Photo courtesy of Santa Anita Park

Nine times after major races in the early '90s, the combination of trainer Ron McAnally (far right on front row); jockey Chris McCarron (second from right on front row); owner Sidney Craig (second from left on front row), and Craig's wife, diet guru Jenny (third from right on front row), gathered in winners' circles after major triumphs by Paseana. Among the friends who joined them on this occasion was screenwriter, actor, and producer Mel Brooks (far left on back row) and his wife, actress Anne Bancroft.

stock races in the name of Devil Eleven Stable, a tribute to his alma mater's nickname and his jersey number. Even more conspicuous in thoroughbred racing winners' circles have been entertainment personalities, including producers Louis B. Mayer and Albert Broccoli; actors Sylvester Stallone, Fred Astaire, and Jack Klugman; composer Burt Bacharach; rapper M.C. Hammer, whose charges campaigned in the name of Oaktown Stable, and many more. In certain cases, there are celebrities among the list of victorious owners whose names don't necessarily appear in the ownership entities, such as Mr. and Mrs. Desi Arnez or Mr. and Mrs. Harry James. Arnez and James were married to Lucille Ball and Betty Grable, respectively, when those ownership entities captured major races. And few entertainers were as successful in thoroughbred racing as Academy Award-winning actress Greer Garson, who, along with husband E.E. "Buddy" Fogelson, campaigned 1971 Horse of the Year Ack Ack in the name of their Forked Lightning Ranch.

Yet none of those rank as the most successful modern owners—the 22 who have made an indelible mark on the sport by capturing 40 or more major races.

Thoroughbred Racing's Answer to the Yankees

The saga of Calumet Farm reads like a Greek tragedy, yet its stature as the leading owner of the modern era is unchallenged.

The pristine Lexington, Ky., nursery was founded in 1924 by William Wright, who named the farm in honor of the baking powder company he owned. After Wright died in 1931, his son, Warren, transformed Calumet from a standardbred to a thoroughbred operation. And by the time he died in 1950, Warren Wright had seen Calumet emerge as the most powerful force in thoroughbred racing.

Before the dawn of the modern era, Whirlaway captured the 1941 Triple Crown in Calumet's fabled devil's-red-and-blue silks.

From 1947-49, Calumet won 13 or more races each season, including at least one classic, thanks to such legends of the turf as Armed, Faultless, Coaltown, Bewitch, Ponder, and 1948 Triple Crown winner Citation. No other modern ownership entity has won eight or more races in three consecutive seasons or at least 12 races in back-to-back campaigns. Naturally, Calumet was ranked No. 1 among owners in each of those three seasons, including a single-season modern record of 20 victories in 1947, but that was merely the beginning.

Warren Wright's widow, Lucille, inherited Calumet upon his death, and under the leadership of Lucille and her second husband, Admiral Gene Markey, Calumet remained the New York Yankees of thoroughbred racing. Calumet won five or more major races and finished among the top six owners nine years in a row from 1946-54. No other modern owner has managed nine consecutive years of even three victories or top-nine seasons. Calumet was ranked No. 1 again in 1952 and for another three years in a row from 1956-58, when it became the only modern owner to win at least seven races in three consecutive seasons and capture a classic in three straight campaigns more than once.

Through 1983, one year after the death of Lucille Wright Markey and three years after the death of her second husband, such storied runners as Real Delight, Mark-Ye-Well, Bardstown, Tim Tam, Forward Pass, Alydar, and Davona Dale had helped Calumet accumulate an astounding 166 major victories since World War II.

But the dynasty's best days were behind it. J.T. Lundy, who married a granddaughter of Warren and Lucille Wright, took over management of the farm, and by 1989 Calumet was some $44 million in debt. Criminal Type brightened the outlook a year later by winning five races in the devil's red and blue on his way to Horse of the Year acclaim, but a year later Lundy resigned, and Calumet was sold at auction in 1992 to Henryk de Kwiatkowski, who died in 2003.

In 2000, Lundy and Gary Matthews, Calumet's former chief financial officer, were convicted of bank fraud and conspiracy. Lundy was sentenced to four-and-a-half years in prison and ordered to pay nearly $21 million in restitution charges, and Matthews received 21 months behind bars. And Calumet hasn't added a major victory to its modern-era record of 171 since Criminal Type's 1990 Horse of the Year campaign.

But Calumet remains a beacon in the record books. Included among its untouched feats are the most No. 1 (10), top-two (12), top-three (16), top-five (17), top-six (18), and top-eight (20) seasons. And, in many cases, Calumet's dominance is virtually unchallenged. Its 17 top-five seasons equal the number of top-nine campaigns any other modern owner can claim, and its 12 classic triumphs are double those of its nearest rival—as are its eight different classic winners.

A Clear Second

Ogden Phipps, who died in 2002, ranks second only to Calumet Farm among modern owners. His five No. 1 seasons and 114 total victories both rank second, and only Calumet and Phipps have earned 11 or more victories in back-to-back seasons. Phipps's runners accomplished that in both 1966 and '67 and again in 1988 and '89, when Easy Goer won the Belmont Stakes to give Phipps his only classic victory.

In addition to Easy Goer, Phipps's cherry-red-and-black silks were carried to the winner's circle in major races five or more times by Buckpasser, Numbered Account, Personal Ensign, and Heavenly Prize.

An Unmatched Four No. 1 Seasons in a Row

With 44 victories, not including those he earned in partnerships, the late Gene Klein ranks in a 17th-place tie among modern-era owners in major triumphs. But that doesn't begin to describe the impact he had on thoroughbred racing once he sold the National Football League's San Diego Chargers to concentrate on a sport in which his athletes never asked to renegotiate contracts.

Only two owners have more than the four No. 1 seasons Klein posted from 1985-88. But those two owners can't match Klein's four consecutive No. 1 seasons, and his streak of five consecutive top-two seasons (1985-89) is also a record.

Klein owned a record-tying five Breeders' Cup winners, a record-equaling seven if those owned in partnership are included, and is one of only three owners to earn a Breeders' Cup victory three years in a row (1986-88), a streak that actually began a year earlier if partnerships are included. The brightest stars to run in Klein's yellow-and-blue silks, which were adorned with the same lightning bolt the Chargers sport, were fillies Lady's Secret and Open Mind. But he also won the 1985 Preakness Stakes with Tank's Prospect, and another filly, Winning Colors, in 1988 made him only the third owner to win the Kentucky Derby with a distaffer.

Photo courtesy of Santa Anita Park

Harbor View Farm owners Louis (left) and Patrice Wolfson saw 1978 Triple Crown winner Affirmed, trained by Laz Barrera (right), help the Florida powerhouse earn three consecutive No. 1 seasons in major victories by owners from 1977-79.

Affirming Its Place in History

Louis and Patrice Wolfson's Harbor View Farm ranks fourth with three No. 1 seasons—and all were consecutive (1977-79). Not coincidentally, those were the three seasons that 1978 Triple Crown winner Affirmed raced for Harbor View. Such standouts as Roman Brother, It's In the Air, and Flawlessly also have helped the Florida farm's pink-and-black silks cross the wire first in 61 major races.

Seven More Superstar Owners

Seven other owners earned two No. 1 seasons, garnered one or more classic victories, and won at least 54 major races in the modern era. Six of them rank among the top 11 owners in modern major victories. The seventh, Meadow Stable, which earned its first of 44 major victories in 1959, would rank in the top 11 if its 23 triumphs from 1949-58—when its horses ran in the name of Meadow Stable founder C.T. Chenery—also are included. Listed in the order they rank in the modern-era standings for major victories, with the horses who won five or more major races under their stewardship:

Photo courtesy of Santa Anita Park

Greer Garson, who captured the Academy Award for best actress in 1942 for *Mrs. Miniver,* completed an unprecedented double in 1971, when Ack Ack, owned by Forked Lightning Ranch, earned Horse of the Year acclaim. Forked Lightning Ranch—and Ack Ack—were the property of Garson and her husband, E.E. "Buddy" Fogelson.

Greentree Stable, owner of Capot, One Hitter, Tom Fool, Straight Face, Bowl Game, Run the Gantlet, Key to the Mint, and Summer Guest, led the owners' standings in both 1951 and 1963. Greentree is the only owner to post five consecutive years with six or more victories (1949-53) and one of two to earn seven or more triumphs three years in a row (1951-53).

Rokeby Stable, owned by the late Paul Mellon, campaigned Quadrangle and, buoyed by standouts Arts and Letters and Fort Marcy, led the owners' standings in 1969 and '70.

King Ranch, which enjoyed its greatest success under the stewardship of Robert Kleberg Jr., owned 1946 Triple Crown winner Assault, But Why Not, Better Self, High Gun, Rejected, and Gallant Bloom. King Ranch, which enjoyed No. 1 seasons in 1946 and '54, also earned six modern-era classic victories, second only to Calumet Farm.

The late **Alfred G. Vanderbilt,** who finished among the top five owners a record seven years in a row (1949-55) and recorded No. 1 seasons in both 1950 and '53, campaigned Native Dancer, Bed o' Roses, Next Move, Find, and Social Outcast.

Wheatley Stable, owned by the late Mrs. Henry Carnegie Phipps, campaigned Bold Ruler, High Voltage, and Bold Lad and earned No. 1 seasons in both 1964 and 1968.

Juddmonte Farms enjoyed a No. 1 season in 1997 and another in 2003, when Empire Maker's Belmont Stakes victory gave Saudi Arabian Prince Khalid Abdullah his first classic victory. The 2003 campaign marked the fourth consecutive season Juddmonte's pink-and-green adorned runners had ranked among the top five, a total exceeded only by Vanderbilt, Greentree, and Klein.

Meadow Stable ranks third among modern ownership entities with five classic victories. C.T. Chenery earned 23 major modern victories racing in his name through 1958 before adopting the name Meadow Stable, which was operated by his daughter, Penny, after his death. Secretariat, winner of the 1973 Triple Crown, Riva Ridge, and Cicada each earned five or more major victories for Meadow Stable. Hill Prince also managed that feat, including capturing the 1950 Preakness, in Chenery's name and First Landing under a combination of both entities.

Classic No. 1 Success Stories

Four other owners captured from 42 to 53 major modern races, secured a No. 1 season, and tasted classic success. Listed in the order they rank in the modern-era standings for major victories, with the horses who won five or more major races under their stewardship:

Brookmeade Stable, owned by the late Isabel Dodge Sloane, campaigned the likes of Sword Dancer, Sailor, and Bowl of Flowers to 53 major victories and is the only member of this quartet with two classic scores. . . . The late **George Widener,** owner of Battlefield and Jaipur, posted 52 victories. . . . **Cain Hoy Stable,** the racing nom de plume for the late Captain Harry Guggenheim, earned 43 triumphs and campaigned Bald Eagle. . . . The most accomplished star owned by **William Haggin Perry,** winner of 42 races, was Gamely, for whom he named the breeding arm of his organization, The Gamely Corporation.

A Paragon of Success Without a Classic Victory

From the time Allen Paulson sold Gulfstream Aerospace and showed up at the Keeneland Selected Yearling Sale—then the world's most prestigious horse auction—in July of 1983 and began making expensive purchases, about the only thing he failed to accomplish before his death in 2000 was a classic victory.

Paulson earned 40 victories—not including those he won in partnership—and won a record-tying five Breeders' Cup races. Paulson also won two more Breeders' Cup races in partnership and is one of only three owners who can claim seven such victories, including those they captured as members of partnerships.

Paulson, whose top campaigner was Cigar, recorded two No. 1 seasons, and for nine consecutive years (1991-99) he posted multiple victories and finished among the top 10 owners, distinctions only Calumet Farm can match.

An Immediate Success

The late Fred W. Hooper actually did win a classic. In fact, no owner ever captured one faster. Hoop Jr., the first horse Hooper owned, won the 1945 Kentucky Derby. Because of government-mandated restrictions that had shut down thoroughbred racing, that 71st Run for the Roses was delayed until June 9, marking the last time America's favorite horse race wasn't contested on the first Saturday in May. Winning rider Eddie Arcaro told Hooper that the victory could be the worst thing that ever happened to him because he wouldn't realize just how difficult a feat he had accomplished.

Indeed, Hooper, perhaps the most influential figure in the Florida breeding industry's ascent to prominence, never tasted classic success in the post-war era. But bolstered by such stars as Olympia, Susan's Girl, and Precisionist, he won 65 major races in the modern era and enjoyed a No. 1 season in 1982.

Like Avis . . .

Four owners have garnered 40 or more victories and a pair of classic triumphs, yet failed to earn a No. 1 season. Listed in the order they rank in the modern-era standings for major victories and their "big horses":

With 82 victories, the late **C.V. Whitney,** who owned such standouts as Phalanx, Counterpoint, Fisherman, and Tompion, unquestionably ranks as the most successful modern owner who never enjoyed a No. 1 season. . . . **Claiborne Farm,** which has two second-place seasons, has posted 51 victories, and its two most accomplished runners, Swale and Forty Niner, both competed in the '80s. . . . The late **Ethel Jacobs,** who owned Stymie, Searching, Promised Land, and Straight Deal (1962), also had two second-place seasons and just one fewer victory than Claiborne. . . . **Rex Ellsworth,** the late California cowboy whose best campaigners were Swaps, Prove It, and Candy Spots, recorded 40 victories and three second-place seasons.

In a Class by Itself

In discussing the great ownership entities of the modern era, it's easy to overlook Elmendorf Farm, which never won a classic, enjoyed a No. 1 season, or had a horse win five major races in its colors. But Elmendorf, which enjoyed its greatest success under the stewardship of Max Gluck, won 46 major races, twice finished second in the owners' standings, and won a major race a record 15 consecutive years from 1971-85.

Special Mention

Only two owners with fewer than 40 victories have had more than one No. 1 season, and both earned that acclaim on the shoulders of a legend. Lazy F Ranch, owned by Mrs. E.H. Gerry, captured the No. 1 ranking in both 1974 and '75 on the back of Horse of the Year Forego. Carolyn Hine was the leading owner in 1996 and again in 1998, when Skip Away earned Horse of the Year honors. But 19 of Lazy F Ranch's 23 major victories were earned by Forego, and all 14 of Hine's were the property of Skip Away.

Knocking on the Door

Don Quixote may have a better chance of realizing the impossible dream than any active owner who dares to fantasize about exceeding Calumet Farm's 171 major victories. But joining the elite group of owners, including current powerhouses Juddmonte Farms, Claiborne Farm, and Perry, with 40 or more victories is a realistic goal for many current owners. The most likely to achieve that feat seemingly would be the following 16, whose impressive credentials include at least 15 major victories—including those earned in partnerships, which are far more popular now than in the early part of the modern era—and a major triumph as recently as 1998. The status of Golden Eagle Farm, The Thoroughbred Corporation, and Overbrook Farm as major campaigners could be in jeopardy because of the deaths of John C. Mabee and Prince Ahmed Salman in 2002 and of William T. Young in 2004, and other owners may have accumulated more impressive credentials than these 16. But based on recent performances, these are the 16 best bets to continue to enhance their resumes:

The Sweetest 16 Candidates to Join the Scions of the Turf

Owner (Principal Partner or Partners)	Major Wins	First Major Win	Last Major Win	Classic Wins	Breeders' Cup Wins	No. 1 Seasons	Winners of 5-Plus Major Races
(a) Golden Eagle Farm (Betty & John Mabee)	37	1976	2002	0	0	1992	Best Pal
(b) The Thoroughbred Corp. (Saudi Prince Ahmed Salman)	36	1994	2003	4	3	2001	Point Given, Sharp Cat
Hobeau Farm (Jack Dreyfus Jr.)	34	1962	1998	0	0		Beau Purple
Bohemia Stable (Mrs. Richard C. duPont)	33	1956	2002	0	0	1961	Kelso
Ogden Mills Phipps	31	1968	2002	0	3	1976	Inside Information, Majestic Light
(c) Overbrook Farm (William T. Young)	29	1985	2002	2	3	1996	
(d) Beverly & Robert Lewis	23	1994	2003	5	1	1995	Serena's Song
(e) Frank Stronach	22	1980	2003	1	3		
(f) Edmund Gann	20	1981	2003	0	0		Medaglia d'Oro, You
(g) Michael Tabor	19	1994	2003	2	0		Thunder Gulch
Dogwood Stable (Cot Campbell)	17	1971	2000	1	1	1990	Summer Squall
(h) Mike Pegram	17	1997	2002	2	1	1999	Real Quiet, Silverbulletday
(i) Gary Tanaka	16	1995	2003	0	0		
(j) Godolphin Stable (Sheikh Mohammad al Maktoum of Dubai)	15	1995	2003	0	3	2002	
(k) Trudy McCaffery & John Toffan	14	1992	2001	0	0		Bien Bien, Free House
(l) Stoneside Stable (Robert & Janice McNair)	11	1999	2003	0	0		Congaree

(a) Betty & John Mabee have an additional victory in their names in 1970.
(b) The Thoroughbred Corporation has four additional victories in partnership.
(c) Overbrook Farm has 11 additional victories in partnership, including three in classics and one in the Breeders' Cup.
(d) Beverly & Robert Lewis have six additional victories in partnership, including one classic and one Breeders' Cup triumph.
(e) Frank Stronach has five additional victories in partnership, including one in a classic.
(f) Edmund Gann has seven additional victories in partnership, including one in 1979.
(g) Michael Tabor has 11 additional victories in partnership, including three in the Breeders' Cup.
(h) Mike Pegram's additional victory in partnership came in the 1992 Breeders' Cup.
(i) Gary Tanaka has an additional victory in partnership.
(j) Sheikh Mohammad al Maktoum has nine additional victories since 1985, including two in the Breeders' Cup, in his name and another three, including two in the Breeders' Cup, in partnership.
(k) Trudy McCaffery & John Toffan have seven more victories in partnership with additional owners, including three in 2002.
(l) Stonerside Stable has four additional victories in partnership, including a 1997 classic.

The following chart shows owners' victories in the 6,461 major races held in North America from 1946-2003. Following that chart are charts that give the same information for the 174 classic races held from 1946-2003, the 145 Breeders' Cup races staged from 1984-2003, and the annual leaders, which are followed by an alphabetical listing of victories in major North American races for all owners from 1946-2003, with the horses they owned in those events in parenthesis.

Standings for Owners' Victories In Major North American Races From 1946-2003

1. Calumet Farm (171)
2. Ogden Phipps (114)
3. Greentree Stable (98)
4. C.V. Whitney (82)
5. Rokeby Stable (72)
6. King Ranch (69)
7. Fred W. Hooper (65)
8. Harbor View Farm (61)
9. Alfred G. Vanderbilt (60)
10. Wheatley Stable (57)
11. Juddmonte Farms (54)
12. Brookmeade Stable (53)
13. George Widener (52)
14. Claiborne Farm (51)
15. Ethel Jacobs (50)
16. Elmendorf Farm (46)
17. Gene Klein; Meadow Stable (44)
19. Cain Hoy Stable (43)
20. William Haggin Perry (42)
21. Rex Ellsworth; Allen Paulson (40)
23. Golden Eagle Farm (37)
24. The Thoroughbred Corporation (36)
25. Tartan Stable (35)
26. Darby Dan Farm; Hobeau Farm (34)
28. Bohemia Stable (33)
29. Hasty House Farm; Ada Rice (32)
31. Ogden Mills Phipps (31)
32. Maine Chance Farm (30)
33. Peter Brant; Overbrook Farm (29)
35. Christiana Stable (28)
36. Loblolly Stable (27)
37. Kerr Stable (26)
38. Nelson Bunker Hunt (24)
39. C.T. Chenery; Lazy F Ranch; Beverly & Robert Lewis (23)
42. Frances Genter; Llangollen Farm; Frank Stronach (22)
45. Edmund Gann; Mrs. Howard B. Keck (20)
47. Dotsam Stable; Michael Tabor (19)
49. Ryehill Farm; VHW Stable (18)
51. Belair Stud; Dogwood Stable; Bert Firestone; Diana Firestone; Foxcatcher Farm; William Helis; Hickory Tree Stable; Mike Pegram; John M. Schiff (17)
60. Buckland Farm; Bwamazon Farm; Hawksworth Farm; Gary Tanaka; Windfields Farm (16)
65. Sidney Craig; Henryk de Kwiatkowski; Godolphin Stable; Howard B. Keck (15)
69. Brookfield Farm; El Peco Ranch; Gedney Farm; Carolyn Hine; Trudy McCaffery & John Toffan; Robert Meyerhoff (14)
75. Edith Bancroft; Joe W. Brown; Cragwood Stable; William Helis Jr.; John Oxley; Saron Stable; Reginald Webster (13)
82. Mary Jones Bradley; Walter M. Jeffords; Aaron Jones; Montpelier Stable; Allen Paulson Living Trust; Louis Rowan; Sigmund Sommer; Mrs. Whitney Stone (12)
90. Amerman Racing Stable; Augustin Stables; Hal Price Headley; Georgia Hoffman; Frank McMahon; W.C. Partee; Gustav Ring; Sam-Son Farm; Stoneside Stable; Daniel Wildenstein (11)
100. Alberta Ranches Ltd.; Barry Beal & Lloyd R. French Jr.; Evergreen Farm; Golden Chance Farm; Mrs. Walter M. Jeffords; Robert Lehman; Pen-Y-Bryn Farm; Martin & Pam Wygod (10)
108. Aisco Stable; Isidore Bieber; Brandywine Stable; Brushwood Stable; Cardiff Stud Farm; Leslie Combs II; Andy Crevolin; Crimson King Farm; Dixiana; Equusequity Stable; Aaron & Marie Jones; Locust Hill Farm; Harvey Peltier; Dorothy & Pamela Scharbauer; Sheikh Mohammad al Maktoum; C.W. Smith Enterprises Inc.; Summa Stable; Ben F. Whitaker; Mrs. Ben F. Whitaker; Mr. and Mrs. Frank Whitham (9)
128. Joseph Allen; John A. Bell III; James Cox Brady; Brae Burn Farm; Jan Burke; Charfran Stable; Mrs. Ben Cohen; D&H Stable; James Elkins, Will Farish III & Temple Webber Jr.; Edward Evans; John Franks; Mrs. Wallace Gilroy; John Greer; Arnold Hanger; J.K. Houssels; La Presle Farm; Dan Lasater; Jean-Louis Levesque; Live Oak Plantation; Ralph Lowe; C.R. Mac Stable; Sheikh Maktoum al Maktoum; Neil McCarthy; Paraneck Stable; Cynthia Phipps; Katherine Price; Connie Ring; Star Crown Stable; Mrs. Arthur Stollery; James Tafel; Verna Lea Farm; Ethel duPont Weir; Janis Whitham (8)
161. Herbert Allen; Arthur Appleton; Mrs. C. Ulrick Bay; J.R. Bradley; Burt Bacharach; Centennial Farms; William Clifton Jr. & Rudlein Stable; Jimmy Croll; Flying Zee Stable; Peter Fuller; John R. Gaines; Dr. Ernest Gaillard, Arthur B. Hancock III & Charlie Whittingham; Glen Hill Farm; Carl Grinstead & Ben Rochelle; William R. Hawn; Neil Hellman; Clement L. Hirsch; Carl Icahn; Jaclyn Stable; Clifford H. Jones & Sons; Lion Crest Stable; Susan Magnier & Michael Tabor; Harry Mangurian Jr.; Louis B. Mayer; October House Farm; Powhatan Stable; Prestonwood Farm; Adele Rand; Reverie Knoll Farm; Ben Ridder; Joseph Roebling; Arthur Seeligson Jr.; Edward Seltzer; Mr. and Mrs. Louis Shapiro; Karen Taylor; Jeanne Vance (7)
197. Belair Stud Ltd. & Nelson Bunker Hunt; William L. Brann; Briardale Farm; Buckram Oak Farm; Circle M Farm; Irving & Marjorie Cowan; Dorchester Farm Stable; Will Farish III; Fourth Estate Stable; William Goetz; Mr. and Mrs. Ellwood Johnston; Ethel Kirkland; Harry LaMontagne; Wayne Lukas & Overbrook Farm; Lloyd I. Miller; Mill House Stable; Clifford Mooers; Jack Munari; Pin Oak Stable; Izzie Proler & Joseph Strauss Jr.; Russell Reineman; Marcia Whitney Schott; Bradley Shannon; Jacob Sher; Jan, Mace & Samantha Siegel; David Sofro; Spring Hill Farm; Paula Tucker; Woodvale Farm (6)

226. Addison Stable; Helen Alexander, David Aykroyd & Helen Groves; Jerry Basta; Blue Vista; Graham Brown; Mrs. Joe W. Brown; Alex Campbell Jr.; Norman Church; Robert Clay; Clover Racing Stable; William Condren & Joseph Cornacchia; Stanley Conrad; Jack Kent Cooke; Due Process Stable; Elcee-H Stable; Mr. and Mrs. John Elmore; Marjorie Everett; Forked Lightning Ranch; Serge Fradkoff; Haakon Fretheim; Dan Galbreath; Mrs. John Galbreath; Mrs. Nat Goldstone; Green Thumb Farm; Mrs. John D. Hertz; Robert Hibbert; Abe Hirschberg; Elizabeth Hopkins; Charles S. Howard; R.D. Hubbard, Gilberto Montagna, Aldo Soprano & Juan Jose Varsi; Howell Jackson; Patrice Jacobs; Mrs. Moody Jolley; Robert Levy; John Marsh; Meadowhill; Eugene & Laura Melnyk; Middletown Stable; Mooring Stable; Mr. and Mrs. Jerome Moss; John Murphy; Newstead Farm; Oak Cliff Stable; Oxford Stable; Charlene Parks; Madeleine Paulson; Joan & John Phillips; Poltex Stable; Louis Rowan & C.V. Whitney; Robert Sangster; Bayard Sharp; Sierra Thoroughbreds; Brian Sweeney; Team Valor; Phil Teinowitz; Tomonori Tsurumaki; Mr. and Mrs. Fred Turner Jr.; Valley View Farm; W-L Ranch; Yolo Stable (5)

286. Ackerley Brothers Farm; Richard Bailey; Mrs. Anson Bigelow; Joseph Brunetti & F.A. Piarulli; Alex Campbell Jr. & Arthur B. Hancock III; Cardiff Stud Farm & T-90 Ranch; Mrs. Vernon Cardy; Brandon & Marianne Chase; Stephen Clark Jr.; Class Act Stable; Charlton Clay; Cobra Farm; Fitz Dixon Jr.; Dr. A.R. Donaldson; Gay Drake; Dick Dutrow; Elberon Farm; Elobee Farm; Michael Fennessy; Bert Firestone & Allen Paulson; Mary Fisher; 505 Farms; Flaxman Holdings, Ltd.; Flaxman Holdings, Ltd. & Edmund Gann; Ford Stable; Jerry Frankel; Dolly Green; Alie Grissom; Alie & James Grissom; Perne Grissom; Hall & Hammond; Happy Valley Farm; Harborvale Stable; Hastings Harcourt; Mel Hatley & Gene Klein; Stephen Hilbert; Deering Howe; Hunter Farm; Kinsman Stable; Carl Lauer, Nancy Vanier & Robert Victor; Lazy Lane Farms; Preston Madden; Silas A. Mason II; Mill River Stable; Moyglare Stud Farm; Sol Nadler; John Nerud; Stavros Niarchos; Nitram Stable; Oaktown Stable; Ken Opstein; Palatine Stable; Pelican Stable; Leone J. Peters; John S. Phipps; Michael Phipps; John Paul Reddam; Ridgewood Stable; Mr. and Mrs. Robert F. Roberts; Mike Rutherford; Sanford Stud Farm; Mabel Scholtz; Select Stable; Joseph Shields Jr.; Martha (Perez) & Richard Stephen; Sunny Blue Farm; Dr. Jerome Torsney; Trio Stable; Thomas Valando; Randolph Weinsier; Westerly Stud Farm; Wild Plum Farm; Sheldon Willis; Steven Wilson; Jacques Wimpfheimer; Mrs. James Winn; Woodley Lane Farm (4)

363. Mrs. John Payson Adams; Aga Khan; Anstu Stables, Inc.; Fred Astaire; Pan de Azucar; Robert Baker, David Cornstein & William Mack; Barclay Stable; Bellehurst Stable; M.T. Berry; Mrs. Paul Blackman; Maribel Blum; Anthony & John Bodie & Anthony Speelman; Roland Bond, Keith Freeman, William R. Hawn & Poltex Stable; Paul Bongarzone; Mary Jones Bradley, Charlie Whittingham & Howell Wynne; Dana Bray Jr.; William Breliant; T.D. Buhl; George Bunn; Eugene Cashman; Celtic Pride Stable; Dr. and Mrs. John Chandler, Shug McGaughey & Autrey Otto; Chaus Stable; Cisley Stable & Blanche Levy; Robert Clay & Tracy Farmer; Clearwater Stable; Colonial Farm; Brownell Combs II; Edward A. Cox Jr.; Daybreak Farm; William de Burgh, Prestonwood Farm & Robert Sangster; Herman Delman; Carol Dender; Diamond A Racing Corporation; Diamond A Racing Corporation & Herman Sarkowsky; Donald Dizney & James English; Mrs. Peter Duchin; East-West Stable; Robert Evans; Everest Stables; Will Farish III, John Goodman, Trudy McCaffery & John Toffan; Tracy Farmer; Joseph Federico; Jack Finley; D.J. Foster Racing Stable; Serge Fradkoff & Baron Thierry von Zuylen; Frank Frankel; Frankfurt Stable & Charlie Whittingham; Albert Fried Jr.; Gainesway Farm, Beverly & Robert Lewis & Overbrook Farm; Gary Garber; Joseph Gavegnano; Olin Gentry; John Gerbas Jr.; Sally Gibson; Josephine Gleis; Tom Gray; L.P. Guy; Louis Lee Haggin II; Emory Hamilton; Hampton Stable; Arthur B. Hancock III & Leone J. Peters; Happy Hill Farm; Clarence Hartwick; Hasty House Farm & Cora Mae Trotsek; Gus Headley; Heiligbrodt Racing Stable & Team Valor; Mrs. H. Herff; Philip Hersh; Estate of Charles S. Howard; Wayne Hughes; Watts Humphrey Jr.; Nelson Bunker Hunt & Frank Stronach; Jacnot Stable; Ju Ju Gen Stable; Ewing Kauffman; Caesar Kimmel; Burt Kinerk; Kinghaven Farm; Kinship Stable; Klaravich Stables; Howard Koch & Telly Savalas; George Krikorian; Joseph La Combe; Mrs. Edward Lasker; William Levin; David Levinson; Beverly & Robert Lewis, Susan Magnier & Michael Tabor; James Lewis Jr.; Wayne Lukas & Paul Paternostro; Frances W. Luro; Jim Mamakos & Marc Stubrin; Trudy McCaffery, Robert Sangster & John Toffan; Mrs. Quincy Adams Shaw McKean; Donald McKellar; Meeken Stable; John A. Morris; James Moseley; Muckler Stables; Murcain Stable; New Farm; Harry Nichols; Nile Financial Corporation; Masayuki Nishiyama; North Forty Stable; Harry Oak; Marian O'Connor; W.J. Oldknow & R.W. Phipps; Padua Stables; Dr. Ignacio Pavlovsky & Frank Whitham; Jacqueline Getty Phillips & Michael Riordan; Pin Oak Farm; Sidney Port; Edward Potter Jr.; Elizabeth Pritchard, William Resseguet Jr. & Dr. Edwin Thomas; Kjell Qvale; Red Oak Stable; Mrs. Russell Reineman; Ridder Thoroughbred Stable; Dorothy Rigney; Mrs. Edward Robbins; Carl Rosen; Barry Ryan; Saddle Rock Farm; Prince Fahd bin Salman; Herman Sarkowsky; Gustav Schickedanz; Barry Schwartz; Fusao Sekiguchi; Mrs. Dale Shaffer; Craig Singer; Dr. and Mrs. J.R. Smith; Barbara Smollin; Starlight Stable; Martha (Perez) & Richard Stephen & The Thoroughbred Corporation; Stonereath Farm; Joseph Strauss Jr.; Roy Sturgis; Rodriguez Tizol; Sal Tufano; Don & John Valpredo; Walmac Farm; Walnut Hill Farm; Gary & Mary West; White Oak Stable; Marylou Whitney Stable; Mrs. George Widener; J.P. & William Wilmot; Charles T. Wilson Jr.; Sam Wilson Jr.; Wimborne Farm (3)

514. Z.T. Addington; Mr. and Mrs. Samuel Agnew; Alberta Ranches Ltd. & George Gardiner; Helen Alexander; Earl Allen; Joseph Allen & Tayhill Stable; Amerman Racing Stable & Roberto Palumbo Ossa; M. Andersen; Apheim Stable; John Applebaum; Louis Asistio; R. Ballis; Balmak Stable; Anthony Baroni & Battilana; Laz Barrera & Amin Saiden; S.M. Barton; Barry Beal, Lloyd R. French Jr. & Gene Klein; Barry Beal, Lloyd R. French Jr. & Wayne Lukas; Michael Becker & Richard Kumble; Robert Bensinger; Thomas Benson; Blum, Sarant & Randy Winick; Lynn Boice; Daniel Borislow; W.E. Britt; Mrs. Thomas Brittingham; Broadmoor Stable; Albert Broccoli; Mr. and Mrs. Albert Broccoli; Giles Brophy; Giles Brophy, William Condren & Joseph Cornacchia; Martin Burdette-Coutts & James Nelson; Edgar Caibett; Frank Calabrese; Frank Caldwell; Mr. and Mrs. Ray Camp; Colin Campbell; Henry Carroll, Alex Karkenny, Robert Levy & William Roberts; Cee's Stable; Charles Cella; Centaur Farms; Ecurie Chalhoub; Chance Hill Farm; Dr. John Chandler; R.E. Chapman; Gerry Cheevers; Chevalier Stable; James Chisholm, Horizon Stable, Michael Jarvis & John Paul Reddam; Mrs. Tilyou Christopher; Claiborne Farm & Adele Dilschneider; Mrs. Ambrose Clark; James Cody III; Israel Cohen; Ike Collins; Columbine Stable, Jay Jones Jr. & Tom Nichols; Leslie Combs II & Equites Stable; William Condren, Joseph Cornacchia & Georgia Hoffman; Lucille Conover; Edward Constantine & Flag Is Up Farm; Contreras, Jim Mamakos & Marc Stubrin; Dolores Conway, Joseph Cornacchia & Fred DeMattias; Michael Cooper & Cecilia Straub-Rubens; Angelo Costanza & Ron McAnally; Howard Crash & Jim Hankoff; Paul Cresci; A.J. Crevolin Company Inc.; Ron Crockett; J.N. Crofton; Crown Stable; C.F. Cullinan Jr.; Raymond Curtis; Louisa d'A Carpenter; Brian Davidson; Peter DeCarlo, Robert LaTorre, Harold & Ralph Rubenstein; Dee-Bob Stable; DeMarco, McClure, Paniolo Ranch & Prim; O.S. Deming & Gene Van Deren; Mrs. Emil Denemark; Mrs. Magruder Dent; Lou Doherty; John Dolan & Sam Longo; Emil Dolce; John Dominguez & Jack Klugman; Double Eagle Stable; Matthew Dragna & Son & Santoro; Anthony Drakas; Alain du Breil; Ann & Vernon Eachus; Edgehill Farm; Leo Edwards & Massey; Elkcam Stable; Irving Ellis & Alan Reskin; Dale & Morley Engelson & Bobby Frankel; Entremont; Stanley Ersoff; Fares Farm; Fifty-Fifty Stable; Matt Firestone; Mrs. Russell A. Firestone; Susan Fisher; William Floyd; Four M Stables Inc. & Halo Farms; Fox Hill Farms; Fox Ridge Farm; Bobby Frankel; Marion Frankel; Lloyd R. French Jr.; Jack Garey; Georgica Stable; George F. Getty II; W.P. Gilbride; Glencrest Farm; Robert Goh; Golden Triangle Stable; Joe Goodwin; Mrs. Joe Goodwin; Ed Gould; Hugh Grant; Green Hills Farm; John Greer, Mrs. Moody Jolley & Ernest Woods; Wayne Gretzky & Summa Stable; Mr. and Mrs. Dick Griegorian; Franklin Groves; Mrs. Gordon Guiberson; Mrs. Walter Haefner; Mrs. H.K. Haggerty; Arthur B. Hancock III & Jimmy Stone; Seth Hancock; Mrs. Taylor Hardin; Mel Hatley & Jeff Lukas; J.C. Hauer; Mrs. William R. Hawn; Bruce Headley, High Tech Stable & Andrew & Irwin Molasky; Duval Headley; Heatherwood Farm; Herff & La Croix; Abram Hewitt; Dr. and Mrs. Jim Hill, Ogden Phipps & Mr. and Mrs. Mickey Taylor; Barbara Holleran; Mrs. Fred W. Hooper; Horizon Stable; Tadahiro Hotehama; Mrs. Deering Howe; Hazel Huffman; Mrs. T.P. Hull Jr. & Ralph Wilson; Nelson Bunker Hunt & Allen Paulson; Nelson Bunker Hunt, Allen Paulson & Summa Stable; Barbara Hunter; Brian Hurst; Stuart Janney III; Stuart Janney III & Stonerside Stable; Jayeff B. Stable; Rukin Jelks & Peter McBean; Jockey Club Stable; James Jones; Mr. and Mrs. Vincent Kanowsky; Richard Kaster; Joe Kellman; Richard Kennedy; Kimran Stable; Mr. and Mrs. Grover King; King & Petite Luellwitz; Kinghaven Farm & Helen Stollery; Kinsey Ranch; Kirkland Stable; Phil Klipstein & Tom Ross; Knob Hill Stables; Kosgrove Stable; D. Lamont; Terrance Lanni, Kenneth Poslosky & Bernard Schiappa; Terrance Lanni & Bernard Schiappa; David Lanzman; Ron Larmarque & Louie Roussel III; Edward Lasker; Mrs. Lucien Laurin; Mrs. Laudy Lawrence; Santiago Ledwith; Gerald Leigh; Blanche Levy; M.A. Levy; Mr. and Mrs. George Lewis Stable; William F. Lucas; Richard Lundy & Virginia Kraft Payson; Clifford Lussky; Robert Lytle; W.B. MacDonald Jr.; Earle Mack; Alan Magerman; P.A. Markey; Mark Three Stable; John Marsch; Mr. and Mrs. Bert Martin; Mr. and Mrs. Quinn Martin; Randy Martin & Steve Weiner; Mrs. J.A. McDougald; Meadowbrook Stable; Shelton Meredith; Merrick Stable; Middletown Stable & William Stavola; Mrs. N.A. Mikell; David Milch; David Milch & Jack & Mark Silverman; Mill Ridge Farm; Claudia Mirkin; E. Mittman; C. Morabito; Edward Nahem & 505 Farms; Navonod Stable; George Newell; Newstead Farm Trust; Niarchos Family; T.S. Nichols; Mrs. Henry Obre; Old English Rancho; John M. Olin; Overbrook Farm & David Reynolds; Charles & Suzanne Pashayan; Pastorale Stable; Adele Paxson; William Pease; Anthony Pejsa; Lawrence Pendleton & Royal T. Stable; Ann Peppers; Robert Perez; Peter Perkins; Mr. and Mrs. F.N. Phelps; Jacqueline Getty Phillips; Mr. and Mrs. James Phillips; Pine Meadow Thoroughbreds; Pine Tree Stable; Post Time Stable; Edith Price; C.N. Pulliam; Quarter B Farm; Frank Rand Jr.; Red Baron's Barn; Jheri Redding; Relatively Stable; Hugo Reynolds; William Reynolds; Ri-Ma-Ro Stable; Rio Claro Thoroughbreds; Milton Ritzenberg; George Robb; Gerald Robins; Gerald Robins, Timothy Sams & Waldemar Farms; Jill Robinson; Paul Robsham; Ben Rochelle; Mr. and Mrs. Jack Rogers; Rogers Red Top Farm; Rolling Hills Farm; Raymond Roncari & Nancy Vanier; Harold Rose; Mrs. Morton Rosenthal; Roslyn Farm; Mrs. A.W. Ryan; R.N. Ryan; Mrs. Al Sabath; Sackatoga Stable; Amin Saiden; Estate of R.F. Salmen; Leonard Sasso; Scott Savin; Saxon Stable; Carol & Herb Schwartz; Daniel Schwartz; Eleanora Sears; C.J. Sebastian; Mr. and Mrs. Hal Seley; Shawmut Stable; S.D. Sidell; Michael Silver; Silver Star Stable; Mrs. Charles Silvers; Allen T. Simmons; SKS Stable; Mrs. Gerard Smith; Harold Snyder; Christopher Spencer; J.H. Stafford; Mark Stanley; Steve Stavro; Beverly Steinman; Heinz Steinmann; Lionel Sternberger Stable Inc.; Earl O. Stice & Sons; Stonerside Stable & Frank Stronach; Jeff Sullivan; Prince Sultan Mohammed al Kabeer; Swift Sure Stable; Luiz Alfredo Taunay; Tayhill Stable; E.P. Taylor; Mrs. E.K. Thomas; 3 Plus U Stable; Ravi Tikkoo; Timberland Stable; Trillium Stable; Turfland; Sidney Vail; Marion Van Berg; Thomas VanMeter II; Robert Van Worp; Vicgray Farm; E.E. Voynow; Peter Wall; Sharon Walsh; Robert Walter Family Trust; Warner Stable; George Weasel Jr.; Wertheimer Farm; Walter Wickham; Howard P. Wilson; Woolford Farm; Dr. and Mrs. Buck Wynne Jr.; Felty Yoder; Zenya Yoshida (2)

833. Steve Abrams, George Hicker & Michael Lima; Leroy Adcock; Dan Agnew & Chuck Baumbach; Stewart Aitken; AJB-PC Stable; F.O. Akin Estate & James Eckrosh; A. Akman; Alamode Farm; Albert & Stoke; Emory Alexander; Frank Alexander; Helen Alexander, Helen Groves & Sheikh Mohammad al Maktoum; Robert Alick; Al-Jo Stable; Joseph Allen & Peter Brant; Martin & Eileen Alpert; Alpha Stable & T. Taub; Greg Alsdorf, Bobby Frankel & Jerome Moss; Altandor Stable & Edgar Cox; Ambush Stable; Amherst Stable & Spruce Pond Stable; Jack Amiel; Edward & Judith Anchel; Edward Anderson; Anderson, Ray Priddy & Walters; Andes Stable; Ronald & Susie Anson; Arakelian Farms Inc.; Martyn Arbib; Gerald Armstrong; Mr. and Mrs. Herb Armstrong; Jurgen Arnemann; Mr. and Mrs. Desi Arnez; Jack Arnold; Ted Aroney; Aronow Stable; Eslie Asbury; Sonny Atkins; Audley Farm; Augustus & Nahm; Austad & Deeb; A.M. Badgett; Brown Badgett; Dr. Jerry Bailey & Kenneth Ellenberg; Sally Bailie, Paul Cornman & Fred Ephraim; Gary Baker & Team Valor; Robert Baker & Howard Kaskel; D. Ball; John Ball; Mrs. E.E. Bankhead; Peter Barberino; Marc Barge; Richard Barnes & Prestonwood Farm; Bar O Stable; Carmen Barrera; James Bartlett & Paul Ternes; Joanne Batchelor; Elizabeth & Tom Baxter; Bill Beasley; Warren Beasley; W.J. Beattie; Beaty & Dorney; Bedford Stable; Bradford Beilly & David Rominik; Art Belford & John Greathouse; Ray Bell; Stanley Bell; Michael Bello; August Belmont IV; Belmont Farms; Howard Bender; Mr. and Mrs. Robert Bensinger; Dario Bentavegna; Alex Berke & Michael Soto; Cal Bernstein & Tony Busching; C.T. Berry Jr.; Patrick Biancone & Faben Quaki; F. Bienstock & Prince Sultan Mohammed al Kabeer; Big I Farm; Billrick Stable; Billrick Stable & Hemacinto; Moreton Binn; Moreton Binn & Enllomar Stable; A.L. Birch; Birchfield Farm; Mrs. Frank Bishop; Black Chip Stable; Black Gold Stable; Blahut Stables; W.E. Blair Jr.; Warren Blasland, Sonya Brooks, Joan Desadora & Anthony Margotta Jr.; Patricia Blass; Mr. and Mrs. T.F. Bledsoe; Bloodstock Services Management & DeHaven; Blue Stone Farm; Maribel Blum & Harpeneau; Peter Blum; Joanne Blusiewicz; Enrique Carlos Boekcke; Mrs. J.A. Bohannon; W.R. Bohm & Bob Wheeler; C.B. Bohn & P.A. Markey; Richard Bokum II; Richard Bomze & Michael Spielman; Roland Bond & Poltex Stable; Bonnie Heath Farm & Robert Schaedle III; Frank Bonsal; Frank Bonsal Jr.; Cary Boshamer; G.H. Bostwick; Robert Boucher; R.L. Bowen & Arthur B. Hancock III; Carl Bowling, Lakland Farm & Charles Thompson; Dr. and Mrs. Thomas Bowman & Victor Ives; Gordon Bowsher, Marsh & Micklewood; Bradley, Bradley & Chandler; Mary Jones Bradley, Chandler & Charlie Whittingham; Mary Jones Bradley, Richard Duchossois & Charlie Whittingham; Bradley & Prizilas; Mary Jones Bradley & Charlie Whittingham; William Brady, Joseph Daniero, Suzanne Jenkins & John Ray; Vera Bragg; Mrs. Joseph Branham; O.E. Breault; Breel Stable; Breezy Hill Farm Inc.; Edward Brennan; Bretzfield & Oliver; Mrs. D. Brewster; Ron

Brimacombe, Trudy McCaffery & John Toffan; Elizabeth Brisbine; Baird Brittingham; Brokaw Inc., Johnson & H.C. Vandervoort; Brolite Farm; Maurice Bronfman; Harry Brown; Brown & King; Dr. and Mrs. T.M. Brown; Brun, Katz & Roberts; Joseph Brunetti; Brunswick Farm; Brushwood Stable & Derry Meeting Farm; Brynalan Stable; B.T. Energy & Wanaja Farm; Budget Stable; Buena Suerte Stable; Judy Bujnicki; Ruth Bunn; Mrs. Joseph O. Burgwin; W.P. Burke & Sheila Pierce; James & Sue Burns; Leroy Burns; Mr. and Mrs. Mel Burns; Victoria Calantoni; Steven Calder; Peter Callahan; Charles Calvin & Kaim; Julio Camargo, Santa Escolastica Stable & Marcos Simon; Camijo Stable; Mrs. H.J. Camm; Bruce Campbell; Johnny Campo; Camptown Stable; Canadiana Farms; Canam East Stable; R. Cano; John Canty & Castlebrook Farm; Thomas Capehart, Sherwood Chillingworth & Jack Liebau; Robert Caporella; Thomisina Caporella; Cardiff Stud Farm & Anderson Fowler; Thomas Carey; Buddy Carlesimo Jr. & Gregory Modas; Carlisle & Sheridan; Carolyn K Stable; Jaime Carrion; Del Carroll; R.B. Carroll; Carter, Will Farish III & Edward Hudson; Mr. and Mrs. Douglas Carver; Camilia Casby & Donald & Mary Zuckerman; James Cassels & Bob Zollers; J. Castle; Cavalier Stable; Mr. and Mrs. Thomas Cavanagh; Centennial Farms, Lillian Durst & Will Farish III; B.D. Chait; Henry Chalhoub; J.R. Chapman; Char-Mari Stable & Anthony Tornetta; Chateau Ridge Farm; Cherry Oca Stable; Cherry Valley Farm; Cheveley Park Stud & The Thoroughbred Corporation; Sherwood Chillingworth; Chinn & Marr; Suresh Chintamaneni; Dr. A.J. Chlad & Sam Mevorach; Dr. A.J. Chlad, Sam Mevorach & Elizabeth Vallone; Choctaw Racing & Duncan Taylor; V. Christopher & P.S. Heisler; P.C. Chuck; Circle C Ranch & Witt; Circle TWP Stable; Claiborne Farm & Howard B. Keck; J.C. Clark; Mr. and Mrs. Ross Clark II; Mr. and Mrs. Stephen Clark Jr.; Mary Classen; Classic Ire Stable; Robert Clay & Winter Farm; Clear Springs Stable; Louise Clements; William Clifton Jr.; Allan Clore; Charles Clore; Clover Racing Stable & Meadowbrook Farm; Cobbleview Stable & Sullimar Stable; Cobbleview Stable & Mary Sullivan; Cobra Farm & Gary Vandeweghe; Cockfield Stable; C. Cohen & Ruth Fertel; Lauren Cohen; Richard Cohen; Roy Cohen; Seymour Cohen; Joseph Colando; G.S. Colella; Collins & Foster; H.W. Collins Stable; Colts Ltd., James Karp & Kennard Warfield Jr.; Columbine Stable; Brownell Combs; Brownell Combs II, El Peco Ranch & Nelson Bunker Hunt; E. Constanin Jr.; Michael Cooper & Cecilia Straub-Rubens Revocable Trust; Albert Coppola; L. Cornell; Corradini & Dorney; Corradini & Nuccio; James Cottrell; Anne Coughlan; Courtlandt Farms; Jean Couvercelle; Covert Ranch; Jenny & Sidney Craig; Richard Craigo; C. Mark Crawford Jr.; Mrs. Jimmy Croll; George Cross, John Roche & Larry Wright; Jacqueline Crotty; Thomas J. Curnes; Custom Tailored Stables; Juan d'Agostino; C. D'Alessio; Daley & Ann Elmore; Dandar Stables; Dansar Stable; Constance Daparma & Armand Marcantony; Lord Darby; Darley Stable; Albert Davis; Rosalee Davison; D&B Enterprises; de Benedetti, O'Shea, Bob Roberts & Wilson; Jose de Camargo, Old Friends Inc. & Winner Silk Inc.; December Hill Farm; Dee Dee Stable; Edith DeGil; Mitch Degroot, Dutch Masters III & Mike Pegram; Delaplaine, Schaffer & Woolsey; Marvin Delfiner; Gus Demarinis & Carol Rocca; Jerry Denker; James & Richard Dennis; Emmanuel de Seroux & Summa Stable; Desperado Stables, Donnie McFadden, Merrill Stables, Tom Schriber & Roger Severson; James Devaney; Roger Devenport; T.F. Devereux; Devil Eleven Stable & D.J. Stable; Diamond Peg Stable; A.C. & K. Dibb; H.F. Dick; Richard Dick; Philip Dileo; Dimick & Hughes; Dinwiddie Farm; D&M Stable; Hajime Doi; Craig Dollase, Barry Fey, Moon Han & Frank Sinatra; Domino Stud; Dr. A.R. Donaldson & Dr. J.H. Goldcamp; Donamire Farm; Faith Donnelly; Dor-Mar Pat Inc.; Double B Ranch & Dr. Joseph Kidd; Double J Farm; Mrs. Gerry Dreier; Allen Drumheller; Ira Drymon; Richard Duchossois; Fred Duckett, Mary Jane Hinds & Margaret Robbins; J.H. Dunn; Duntreath Farm; Francis Dupre; Tom Durant & Jim & Marilyn Helzer; J.G. Dushock; Raymond Dweck; Mr. and Mrs. Peter Dye; Eagle Mountain Farm; Hal Earnhardt; Hal Earnhardt & John R. Gaines; East Acres; Tom Eazor; Mrs. E.H. Ellison Jr.; Eldorado Stables; Ann Elmore; John Elmore; Mr. and Mrs. Steven Elmore; El Rio Stud; Edward Elzemeyer; Emerald Hill Stable; Charles Engel; Charles Engelhard & Mack Miller; Dale & Morley Engelson; Morley Engelson, Bobby Frankel & Juddmonte Farms; Envoy Stable; Mrs. M. Erlander; R. Escudero; Gomer Evans; Evergreen Farm & Jenine Sahadi; Sidney Factor; Stiftung Gestut Fahrhof; Fairlawn Farm; Farfellow Farm; Will Farish III, Edward Hudson & Edward Hudson Jr.; Will Farish III & Watts Humphrey; Will Farish III & Jones; Will Farish III & Bayard Sharp; Yale Farrar & David Schloss; Paul Faulkenstein; Mac Fehsenfeld; Mrs. R.L. Feinberg; Fence Post Farm; B.F. Ferguson II; Fernwood Stables; H.W. Fincher; Morton Fink; Morton Fink & Roy Gottlieb; Charles Fipke; Pamela Firman; Pamela Firman & Watts Humphrey Jr.; Mrs. Montgomery Fisher; Five Star Stable; F.L. Flanders; Flash III Stable; Flatbird Stable; D. Flaxbeard, R. Oliphant & Bayard Sharp; Bill Fluor & Sidney Port; Flying Horse Stable & Amin Saiden; Flying M Stable; Fog City Stable; Buddy Fogelson; Folsom Farm; Fomon & George McIvor; Forgnone, Franklin & Levy; Forus Stable; Four-Way Ranch; Fourwyn Stable; Anderson Fowler; Nathan Fox & Nancy & Richard Kaster; Foxwood Plantation; Mr. and Mrs. Bill Foy; Serge Fradkoff & Edward Seltzer; Frankfurt Stable; Mrs. J.M. Franklin; Frazee & Frazee Inc.; Freeman-Cole & Gold; Free Spirit's Stable; H.O.H. Frelinghuysen; Lloyd R. French Jr. & Wayne Lukas; Friedman & Reader; Ed & Natalie Friendly; Mrs. A. Gaal; Gabrielle Farm, Sanford Goldfarb, Hemlock Hills Farm & Justine Zimmerman; Gailyndel Farms; Gainesway Farm; Gallagher Farm; Mrs. James Gallagher; Gallaher & Williams; Tom Gamel, Gino Roncelli & Sigband; Mr. and Mrs. Edmund Gann; Edmund Gann, Ritt & Ritt; Edmund Gann & Mark & Merly Ann Tanz; Juan Garcia & L.L. Scofield; Gardenia Stable; Gardiner Farm; Pat Garvey; Linda Gaston & A.D. Haynes; Andrew & Dan Gehl; Gem State Stable; Gentilly Stable; Tom Gentry; Syl George Stable; Robert Geringer, Michael Klein, Liberty Road Stables & San Gabriel Investments; Mrs. Robert L. Gerry; Getty & Barry Richards; Roxie Gian; M.R. Giberga; A.J. Giordano; G-K Stable; Philip Godfrey; Mike Goetz & Brian Griggs; S. Goldband; Oliver Goldsmith; Harold Goodman; Clint Goodrich, Herold & Lothenbach; M.N. Goodwin; Berry Gordy; Berry Gordy & Summa Stable; Anthony Graffaginni; William Graham; Grand Prix Stable; Hugh Grant & James Padgett; Mr. and Mrs. Joseph Grant & Tommy Kelly; S. Gray & S. Schmiedeskamp; Gray Willows Farm; Green Dunes Farm; Leonard Green; Greenville Farm Inc.; Mrs. John Greer; Wayne Gretzky, Sylvester Stallone & Summa Stable; Leslie Grimm; Leslie Grimm & Gene Voss; Margaret Grimm; Perne Grissom & Edward Grosfield; A.G. Groleau; Grovetree Stable; Raymond Guest; Mrs. W. Guest & Wacker; John Gunther & Hugh Harlington; John Gunther & Prairie Star Racing; Walter Haefner; Hajji Farm; Sarah Hall; Stuart Hamblen; J.T. Hammer & W.L. New; Arthur B. Hancock III; Bull Hancock; Mrs. John W. Hanes; R.C. Hanna; Alice Hansbrough; Har-Bar Ranch; Edris Harbeston, George Losh & Victor Naccarato; Harbor View Farm & Ethel Jacobs; Mr. and Mrs. Hastings Harcourt; Harris Farms Inc.; H.M. Harris; Sir Ernest Harrison; Lady Jane Harrison; Mr. and Mrs. Harry Hart; Mel Hatley; Mel Hatley & Yank; Hatskin & Sair; Havahome Stable; Alec Head; Aase Headley & Paul Leung; Thomas Heard Jr.; Heardsdale; Mrs. Henry Hecht; Mary Hecht; David & Jill Heerensperger; Mrs. Robert W. Heighe; Heiligbrodt Racing Stable; Helbush Farm; Estate of William Helis; O. Helman; Helmore Farm; Jim Helzer; John Hersberger; Mrs. Paul Hexter; Hidden Valley Farm; Joseph Higgins; High Ground Stable; High Tide Stable; Alice Hill; Ethel Hill; Dr. Jim Hill & Mickey Taylor; S.D. Hinkle; Bo Hirsch; Mr. and Mrs. Clement L. Hirsch; Henry Hirschman; Harold Hodosh; Holiday Stable; Jerry Hollendorfer & George Todaro; Jerry Hollendorfer, George Todaro & Temple Webber Jr.; George Holtsinger; Mrs. G.T. Hopkins; Mark Hopkins; Lynn Howard; Horizon Stable, Mike Jarvis & Lloyd Taber; Stanley Hough, John Pastorek & Roger Patton; R.D. Hubbard & Rio Claro Thoroughbreds; R.D. Hubbard & Dwight Sutherland; Edward Hudson; John Hudspeth; Louise & Watts Humphrey; W.L. Huntley; Phillip Hurley; Hurlock & Jack Van Berg; Bruce Hutson; John & Joseph Iracane & Padua Stables; Irish Acres Farm; Jimmy Iselin & Robert Kaufman; Allan Ivan; Lord Iveagh; Bruce Jackson & John Swift; Dr. Manuel Jacobs & Martin & Pam Wygod; Mr. and Mrs. Harry James; L. Jameson; Jawl Brothers; Dr. Kalarikkal Jayaraman; Jayeff B. Stable & Brereton C. Jones; Walter M. Jeffords Jr.; Rukin Jelks; A.T. Jergins; J.K. Stable & Royal Oaks Farm; J.E. Johnson; Ellwood Johnston; Fletcher Jones; Gary Jones & Estate of McLeod; H.G. Jones; Marie Jones; Jones, Roffe & Barney Willis; Mrs. Troy Jones; Jones & Tuckahoe Farm; Harold Jordan; Don Jordens; Kenneth Jumps, Steve Shapiro, David Stark & William Stratton; Max Kahlbaum; Morris Kaplan; Raymond Karlinsky; Susan Kaskel; Nancy & Richard Kaster; Mrs. J.P. Keezek; Mary Keim; Paul Kelley; Bob & Nancy Kelly & Sabine Stable; Mrs. W.R. Kelly; Charles Kenis; Ken-Love Farm; Michael Kerr; Keswick Stables; Saud bin Khaled; Roy Kidder; Killian Farms; Caesar Kimmel & Leonard & Phillip Solondz; Caesar Kimmel & Phillip Solondz; J.A. Kinard Jr.; Sadie King; Ethel Kirkland Estate; Walter Kitchen; Arthur Klein; Bertram, Elaine & Richard Klein; Gene Klein & Wayne Lukas; Dahana Klerer & Running R Stable; C. Mahlon Kline; K&L Stable; Mrs. Lawrence Knapp Jr.; E.D. Kohr; Joe Kowal; Kratz & Thayer; H.F. Krimendhal; Joseph Kroese; Herbert Kushner; William H. LaBoyteaux; S.W. Labrot Jr.; Joseph LaCroix; C.M. Lagrosa; Laguna Seca & Ward; Carlyle Lancaster; B.W. Landy; Lakeville Stables; Glenn Lane; Elizabeth La Tourrette & Middle Ranch; Carl Lauer & Nancy Vanier; Mrs. Roger Laurin; Laudy Lawrence; Louise Lazare; L.C. Ranch; Thomas Leachman; Richard Leahy & John Meriwether; Mrs. H. Lebowitz; R. LeCesse; T. LeClair; Samuel Lefrak; Mr. and Mrs. Robert Lehman; Gerald Leigh & Sheikh Mohammad al Maktoum; Lester Manor Stable; Let It Ride Stable; Leonard Leveen, Mike Shanley & Steve Weiss; Mrs. I.J. Levine; Al Levinson; Mr. and Mrs. J.B. Lewin; Craig Lewis; Debi & Lee Lewis; George Lewis; Lightning Stable; Michael Lima; Henry Lindh; Little M Farm; Llangollen Farm & Rock Springs Farm; Barney Lobel; W.A. Lofton; J.A. Logan; Andre Lombard; Greg Long, Uri Nemet & Dominic Sabatino Jr.; Mrs. Johnny Longden; Everett Lowrance; Mrs. Petite Luellwitz; Luke & Sneed; Lyons & Templeman; Lusarasion Inc.; Lushland Farm; Philip Maas; Mr. and Mrs. John Mabee; Mac-Conn Farm; Macon, Henry Moreno & Sawyer; Larry MacPhail; Jean-Francois Malle; Mrs. Jim Maloney; Mrs. R.J. Maloney; Manhasset Stable; Annette Mann; Thomas Mara; Marablue Farm; Gary Marano; Marant & Sessa; Marino Beach Stable; James Marino; Robert Marshall; Jose Martin; Martin & McKinney; Johns Martin, Paul Saylor & Starlight Stable; Mr. and Mrs. Quinn Martin & Murty Farm; Townsend Martin; W.C. Martin; Mr. and Mrs. W.C. Martin; Nicholas Martini; Mashek & Murty Farm; Joan Masterson; Sam Matar; T.G. May; Len Mayer; A.F. McClellan; Ron McDonald; Mrs. L.J. McMahan; Eugene Melnyk; A. Menditaguy; Mereworth Farm; John Meriwether; Merrill Stables; E.P. Metz; Tom Meyerhoff; J.D. Michaels; Middle Ranch; Steven Miles; Miles & Tauber; H.J. Miller; Robert Miller; Betty & Leon Millsap; Minshall Farms; Edward Mizrahi; Bill Modglin; Jack Mondel; T.P. Morgan; Edna Brokaw Morris; J.O. Morrisey Jr.; Mr. and Mrs. Frazer Morrison; Morven Stud Farm; V. Mosca; Jerome Moss; Moulder, Oldham & Smith; Mount Joy Stables; August Muckler; John Mulhern; Mrs. Eddie Mulrenan; Murlogg Farm; B.A. Murphy; William H. Murray; Myhelyn Stable; Narvick International Stable; Mrs. Joseph Nash; Nasty Stable; Mrs. H.L. Nathenson; Neddeff & Sundance Stable; Nedlaw Stable; Mr. and Mrs. Lin Nelson; New Phoenix Stable & Susan Roy; Niblick Stable; Nickels and Dimes Stable; V.J. Nickerson; No Limit Farm; Howard Noonan; Joanne Nor; B.A. Norris; North Star Ranch; Northwest Farms; Oak Crest Stable; Oatlands Stable; Edward O'Brien; Joseph O'Connell; Duane Offield; H.E. Olson; H.E. Olson & R.D. Prewitt; Sandra Oppegard; A.J. Ostriker; Otly Stable; Debby Oxley; John Oxley & Marvin Warner; Henry Pabst; J. Paddock; Paul Painter; Palev Stable; J. Palmisano; Jean Pancoast; William T. Pascoe III & Brian Sweeney; Josephine Paul; Allen & Madeleine Paulson; Allen Paulson & Sheikh Mohammad al Maktoum; Allen Paulson & Summa Stable; Virginia Kraft Payson; John Peace; W.M. Peavey; Pebblebrook Farm; Pegasus Stables; Alfio & J. Pepino; Ruth Perlmutter; L.E. Peterson; Mr. and Mrs. N.G. Phillips; Sheila Pierce; Jerry Pinkley; Pinwheel Farm; Joseph Platt Jr.; Helen Polinger; Milton Polinger; Hiram Polk & David Richardson; Carl Pollard; Jack Pollard; Poma Stable; Sidney Port, Annabelle Stute & Edwin Wachtel; Pratt & Jack Van Berg; William Punk Jr.; Anthony Pupino; Purner Jr. & Score Stable; Harold Queen; J.R. Querbes III; Lorraine Quinichett; Robert Quinichett; Mrs. L. Rabinowitz; F.J. Recio; Red Brick Stable; John & Nancy Reed; Ronald Reeves; Regal Rose Stable; Releib Stable; Ren-Mar Thoroughbreds; Victor Resk; William Resseguet Jr. & Robins; William Resseguet Jr. & Steiner III; Ted Rexius; Althea Richards; B.J. Richards; Arthur & Larry Risdon; Lynne Ristad; Rayleen Rittenberry; River Divide Farm; Jack Robbins & Jack Rogers; Jack Robbins, Jack Rogers & Ralph West; Corbin Robertson; Lyle Robey & Bruce Wilkinson; Mack Robinson; G. Roboski; Rockmore Farm; Adrian Roks; Rolling Ridge Farm; W.D. Rorex; Roron Stable; S. Rose; Harry Rosenblum; Wendell Rosso; Baron Guy de Rothschild; Edouard De Rothschild; George Rowand & Bonner Young; Royal Line Stable; Royal Oaks Farm & Owl Stable; Running Horse Farm Inc.; Mrs. Barry Ryan; Ted Sabarese; Helene Sadacca; M.A. & R. Saffir; Ramona & Roland Sahm; Roland Sahm; Hilal Salem; Hector Sanchez; Sandbar Farm; Sandera Farm; Grady Sanders; Greg Sanders; R.L. Sanford; Robert Sangster & Gary Tanaka; Saratoga I Stable; Mr. and Mrs. L.F. Saunders & Son; A.A. Savill; Joseph Scardino; James Scatuorchio; Robert Schaedle III; H.V. Schaff; Clarence Scharbauer Jr.; Edward Scharps; Arno Schefler; Nathan Scherr; L. Schlosser; Chuck Schmidt Jr.; Hilmer Schmidt; W.J. Schmidt & Trimble; D.J. Schneider; Mr. and Mrs. Robert Schulze; Mrs. Andy Schuttinger; Mrs. J. Schwartz; Scottdale Farm; Nina Scruton; Jim Scully; Sea High Stable; Francis Sears; Randy Sechrest; Farid Sefa; E. Seinfeld; Edward & Harry Seltzer; Mimi Selz & Smerker; Jeffrey Sengara; Serendipty Farm; B. Seroy; E. Shamle; Lyn & Michael Shanley; Milton Shapiro; Mrs. Bayard Sharp; Paul Shawhan; H.T. Sheridan; F.A. Sherman; Hassan Shoaib; Jan Siegel; John Sikura Jr.; Earl Silver; Mr. and Mrs. S.N. Simmons; D.A. Simon; Milos Simon; A. Skjeveland; Sledge Stable; Mike Sloan; Derrick Smith & Michael Tabor; Vera Smith; Archie Sneed; Robert Snell; Snowberry Farm; Max Sobell; Solymar Stud; Lockhart Spears; Spendthrift Farm; Spendthrift Farm & Ron Winchell; Robert Spreen; Spring Brook Farm Inc.; Springhill Stable; Dr. Ted Sprinkle; Mr. and Mrs. Wilbur Stadelman; A.H. Stall; A.H. & Albert M. Stall; Steadfast Stable & Joyce Young; Steeplechase Farm; Steifler, Tannyhill, Weinstein & Wells; George Steinbrenner; Woody Stephens; Mr. and Mrs. Lionel Sternberger; L.T. Stevens; M. Stewart; Mrs. Plunkett Stewart; Stonecrest Farm; Robert Strassburger; Richard Strauss; Stud Panter; Sugartown Stable; Sui Generis Stable; Albert Sultan; Sumaya Us Stables; Sundance Stable; Sunningdale Farm; Sunny Meadow Farm; Sunshine Stable; Surf and Turf Stable; Jack Tafel & Richard Waterford; Mr. and Mrs. H.R. Talmage;

Joseph Taub; Ahmed al Tayer; J.T. Taylor; Kenneth Taylor; Taylor Purchase Farm; Shirley Taylor; T-Bird Stable III; F.K. Tesher; The Hat Ranch; 3rd Turn Stables; J. Thomas; J.R.H. Thouron; Three G. Stable; Thunderhead Farms; TNT Stud; Aury & Ralph Todd; Top of the Marc Stable; Triad Stable; Triple C Stable; Triple L Stable; Cora Mae Trotsek; E. Trotta; T.R. Trout; Turf Side Stables; Twilite Farms; Two Sisters Stable; E. Ubarri; Universal Stable; Valley Farm; John Valpredo; Marion Van Berg Stable Inc.; Joan Van De Maele; Nancy Vanier; Vendome Stables; Vinery Stables; Richard Violette Jr.; Vistas Stable; Helen Vizzi; Baron von Zuylen de Nyervelt; A.G. Wagner; Waldemar Farms; Charles Warner; Mark Warner; Marvin Warner; Rea Warner; G.R. Watkins; Michael Watral; J.J. Watts; Robert Waxman; Mr. and Mrs. P.S. Weakly; F. Webster Jr. & W.S. Woodside; Mrs. E.K. Weil; Steve Weiner; Mrs. Randolph Weinsier; Lord Arnold Weinstock; Estate of Lord Arnold Weinstock; A. Weisweiller; Welcome Farm; D.H. Wells; Terry Wells; Mr. and Mrs. David Werblin; Mr. and Mrs. Ralph West; White Cliff Farm; White Star Stable; T.F. White; Edwin Whittaker; Wichita Equine Stable; Mrs. Peter A.B. Widener; Peter A.B. Widener III; Mr. and Mrs. Arnold Wilcox; Mrs. Arnold Wilcox; Bush & Jo Williams; David & Holly Wilson; L.C. Wilson; Roger Wilson; Estate of Steven Wilson; Wilton Stable; Mrs. Vernon H. Winchell Jr.; Winding Way Farm; Windways Farm; Malcolm Winfield; WinStar Farm; Horace Wise; Werner Wolf; D.O. Wolfe; Wonder Y Ranch; Woodland Farm; Woodlynn Farm; Ernest Woods; Mrs. Richard Worthington; Mrs. William C. Wright; Fred Wyse; Kazumasa Yano; Darrell & Evelyn Yates; Mrs. G. Zauderer; V. Zemborain; Eugene Zeren; John Zitnik (1)

Classic-Winning Owners 1946-2003

1. Calumet Farm (12)
2. King Ranch (6)
3. Darby Dan Farm; Beverly & Robert Lewis; Meadow Stable (5)
6. The Thoroughbred Corporation (4)
7. Greentree Stable; Harbor View Farm; Loblolly Stable; Rokeby Stable; Karen Taylor (3)
12. Edith Bancroft; Belair Stud; Brookmeade Stable; Buckland Farm; Edgar Caibett; Claiborne Farm; Henryk de Kwiatkowski; D&H Stable; Rex Ellsworth; Ford Stable; Dr. Ernest Gaillard, Arthur B. Hancock III & Charlie Whittingham; Hawksworth Farm; Ethel Jacobs; Gene Klein; Ron Larmarque & Louie Roussel III; Lazy Lane Farms; Frank McMahon; Overbrook Farm; Overbrook Farm & David Reynolds; Mike Pegram; Katherine Price; Sackatoga Stable; Dorothy & Pamela Scharbauer; Michael Tabor; Rodriguez Tizol; Alfred G. Vanderbilt; C.V. Whitney; Windfields Farm (2)
40. Jack Amiel; August Belmont IV; Brandywine Stable; Giles Brophy, William Condren & Joseph Cornacchia; Brushwood Stable; Cain Hoy Stable; Eugene Cashman; Centennial Farms; C.T. Chenery; Cisley Stable & Blanche Levy; Mrs. Ben Cohen; William Condren & Joseph Cornacchia; William Condren, Joseph Cornacchia & Georgia Hoffman; Andy Crevolin; Dogwood Stable; El Peco Ranch; Will Farish III; Diana Firestone; D.J. Foster Racing Stable; Gainesway Farm, Beverly & Robert Lewis & Overbrook Farm; Frances Genter; Golden Chance Farm; Green Dunes Farm; John Greer; Carl Grinstead & Ben Rochelle; Arthur B. Hancock III & Leone J. Peters; Hasty House Farm; Hunter Farm; Mrs. Walter M. Jeffords; Juddmonte Farms; Mrs. Howard B. Keck; Robert Lehman; Ralph Lowe; Maine Chance Farm; Louis B. Mayer; Moyglare Stud Farm; New Phoenix Stable & Susan Roy; Joseph O'Connell; October House Farm; John M. Olin; Ken Opstein; John Oxley; W.C. Partee; William Haggin Perry; Ogden Phipps; Powhatan Stable; Prestonwood Farm; Ada Rice; Arthur Seeligson Jr.; Nathan Scherr; Francis Sears; Fusao Sekiguchi; Jacob Sher; Stonerside Stable & Frank Stronach; Frank Stronach; Sunny Blue Farm; Tartan Stable; Tomonori Tsurumaki; Turfland; Mr. and Mrs. Fred Turner Jr.; Jeanne Vance; Reginald Webster; Wheatley Stable; White Oak Stable; George Widener; Charles T. Wilson Jr. (1)

Breeders' Cup-Winning Owners 1984-2003

1. Gene Klein; Allen Paulson (5)
3. Godolphin Stable; Susan Magnier & Michael Tabor; Overbrook Farm; Ogden Phipps; Ogden Mills Phipps; Frank Stronach; The Thoroughbred Corporation (3)
10. Aga Khan; Claiborne Farm; Irving & Marjorie Cowan; Frances Genter; Stavros Niarchos; Paraneck Stable; Prestonwood Farm; Sam-Son Farm; Sheikh Mohammad al Maktoum; Niarchos Family; Padua Stables; Mr. and Mrs. Frank Whitham; Daniel Wildenstein (2)
23. Amerman Racing Stable; Amherst Stable & Spruce Pond Stable; Augustin Stables; Barry Beal & Lloyd R. French Jr.; Barry Beal, Lloyd R. French Jr. & Gene Klein; John A. Bell III; Black Chip Stable; Peter Brant; Mr. and Mrs. Albert Broccoli; Buckland Farm; Cee's Stable; Charles Cella; Christiana Stable; Class Act Stable; Classic Ire Stable; Clover Racing Stable; Michael Cooper & Cecilia Straub-Rubens; Anne Coughlan; Jean Couvercelle; Sidney Craig; Crown Stable; Darby Dan Farm; Mitch Degroot, Dutch Masters III & Mike Pegram; Roger Devenport; Diamond A Racing Corporation; Dogwood Stable; Craig Dollase, Barry Fey, Moon Han & Frank Sinatra; Evergreen Farm; Evergreen Farm & Jenine Sahadi; Fares Farm; Bert Firestone & Allen Paulson; Flaxman Holdings, Ltd.; Bobby Frankel; John Franks; Dr. Ernest Gaillard, Arthur B. Hancock III & Charlie Whittingham; Gainesway Farm, Beverly & Robert Lewis & Overbrook Farm; Glen Hill Farm; Dolly Green; Harbor View Farm; Mel Hatley & Gene Klein; Bruce Headley, High Tech Stable & Andrew & Irwin Molasky; Carolyn Hine; Fred W. Hooper; Wayne Hughes; Carl Icahn; John & Joseph Iracane & Padua Stables; Jayeff B. Stable; Juddmonte Farms; Richard Kaster; Mrs. Howard B. Keck; Joseph La Combe; Terrance Lanni, Kenneth Poslosky & Bernard Schiappa; David Lanzman; La Presle Farm; Gerald Leigh & Sheikh Mohammad al Maktoum; Beverly & Robert Lewis; Robert Meyerhoff; David Milch; David Milch & Jack & Mark Silverman; John Nerud; Joanne Nor; Oak Cliff Stable; John Oxley; Allen Paulson & Sheikh Mohammad al Maktoum; Allen Paulson Living Trust; Madeleine Paulson; Mike Pegram; Joan & John Phillips; Carl Pollard; Quarter B Farm; Ridder Thoroughbred Stable; Gerald Robins, Timothy Sams & Waldemar Farms; Jill Robinson; Ben Rochelle; Hilal Salem; Robert Sangster; Herman Sarkowsky; Dorothy & Pamela Scharbauer; Bradley Shannon; Star Crown Stable; Martha (Perez) & Richard Stephen; Richard Strauss; Jeff Sullivan; Tomonori Tsurumaki; Paula Tucker; Thomas Valando; Lord Arnold Weinstock; Estate of Lord Arnold Weinstock; Wertheimer Farm (1)

1946

1. J.R. Bradley; King Ranch (7)
3. Calumet Farm; C.V. Whitney (6)
5. Ethel Jacobs (5)
6. Belair Stud; Maine Chance Farm; Louis B. Mayer (4)
9. William L. Brann; Greentree Stable; William Helis; Deering Howe (3)

1947

1. Calumet Farm (20)
2. King Ranch (13)
3. William Helis (11)
4. C.V. Whitney (8)
5. Ethel Jacobs (4)
6. Rex Ellsworth; Arnold Hanger (3)
8. Z.T. Addington; Brookmeade Stable; Circle M Farm; Elobee Farm; Mrs. John D. Hertz; Jaclyn Stable; Walter M. Jeffords; Mrs. Laudy Lawrence; Earl O. Stice & Sons; Ben F. Whitaker (2)

1948

1. Calumet Farm (13)
2. Maine Chance Farm (7)
3. King Ranch; Harry LaMontagne; Joseph Roebling (4)
6. Norman Church; William Helis; Ben F. Whitaker; C.V. Whitney; W-L Ranch (3)

1949

1. Calumet Farm (18)
2. Greentree Stable (7)
3. King Ranch; Alfred G. Vanderbilt (6)
5. Fred W. Hooper (4)
6. Elizabeth Hopkins; Clifford H. Jones & Sons; Maine Chance Farm (3)
9. Brookmeade Stable; Ike Collins; Foxcatcher Farm; Mrs. Nat Goldstone; Tom Gray; Hal Price Headley; Abe Hirschberg; Mrs. Deering Howe; S.D. Sidell; Spring Hill Farm; Ethel duPont Weir; Ben F. Whitaker (2)

1950

1. Alfred G. Vanderbilt (9)
2. Brookmeade Stable; C.T. Chenery; George Widener (7)
5. Greentree Stable (6)
6. Calumet Farm (5)
7. Brandywine Stable; Cain Hoy Stable; Estate of Charles S. Howard; King Ranch; Palatine Stable (3)

1951

1. Greentree Stable (7)
2. Calumet Farm (6)
3. C.V. Whitney; George Widener (5)
5. Brookmeade Stable; C.T. Chenery; Walter M. Jeffords; Alfred G. Vanderbilt (4)
9. Isidore Bieber; Brandywine Stable; William Goetz; Maine Chance Farm; Ogden Phipps; Rokeby Stable (3)

1952

1. Calumet Farm (16)
2. Greentree Stable; Alfred G. Vanderbilt (7)
4. Brookfield Farm; William Helis Jr.; Mrs. Walter M. Jeffords (4)
7. Charfran Stable; King Ranch; Trio Stable; White Oak Stable; C.V. Whitney; Sam Wilson Jr. (3)

1953

1. Alfred G. Vanderbilt (15)
2. Greentree Stable (8)
3. Calumet Farm; Hasty House Farm (7)
5. Ethel duPont Weir; Mrs. Ben F. Whitaker; C.V. Whitney (4)
8. James Cox Brady; Charfran Stable (3)
10. Alberta Ranches Ltd.; Brookmeade Stable; Cain Hoy Stable; Darby Dan Farm; Hasty House Farm & Cora Mae Trotsek; C. Morabito; Marian O'Connor; John S. Phipps; Mrs. George Widener (2)

1954

1. King Ranch (9)
2. Alfred G. Vanderbilt (6)
3. Calumet Farm; Maine Chance Farm (5)
5. Foxcatcher Farm; Ada Rice; C.V. Whitney (4)
8. Brookmeade Stable; Cain Hoy Stable; Andy Crevolin; Greentree Stable; Hasty House Farm (3)

1955

1. Belair Stud (8)
2. Wheatley Stable (7)
3. Hasty House Farm (6)
4. Rex Ellsworth; Alfred G. Vanderbilt (5)
6. Brookmeade Stable; Clifford Mooers (4)
8. Mrs. Anson Bigelow; Cain Hoy Stable; William Helis Jr.; King Ranch (3)

1956

1. Calumet Farm (7)
2. Rex Ellsworth; Llangollen Farm (6)
4. Leslie Combs II; C.V. Whitney (5)
6. Brookmeade Stable; D&H Stable (4)
8. Jan Burke; Mrs. Vernon Cardy; Claiborne Farm; Greentree Stable; Ethel Jacobs; Mrs. Edward Robbins (3)

1957

1. Calumet Farm (8)
2. Kerr Stable (7)
3. Claiborne Farm; Wheatley Stable (6)
5. Llangollen Farm (5)
6. Mrs. C. Ulrick Bay; Maine Chance Farm (4)
8. Jan Burke; Happy Hill Farm; Ethel Jacobs; Ralph Lowe; Ada Rice; Alfred G. Vanderbilt (3)

1958

1. Calumet Farm (8)
2. Kerr Stable (6)
3. C.T. Chenery; Ethel Jacobs (5)
5. Brookmeade Stable; Ralph Lowe; Adele Rand; Mabel Scholtz; Wheatley Stable (3)
10. Mrs. C. Ulrick Bay; Brookfield Farm; Graham Brown; Joe W. Brown; Christiana Stable; Greentree Stable; Hasty House Farm; Llangollen Farm; Neil McCarthy; Mooring Stable; George Newell; Mr. and Mrs. Fred Turner Jr.; Reginald Webster (2)

1959

1. Brookmeade Stable; C.W. Smith Enterprises Inc. (7)
3. Cain Hoy Stable; C.V. Whitney (6)
5. Kerr Stable (5)
6. King Ranch; Wheatley Stable (4)
8. Bellehurst Stable; Joseph Brunetti & F.A. Piarulli; Calumet Farm; Claiborne Farm; Mooring Stable (3)

1960

1. Cain Hoy Stable (8)
2. C.V. Whitney (7)
3. Brookmeade Stable (5)
4. Bohemia Stable; Foxcatcher Farm; Harbor View Farm; C.R. Mac Stable (4)
8. Calumet Farm (3)
9. Charlton Clay; Mrs. Tilyou Christopher; Edgehill Farm; Perne Grissom; Hal Price Headley; Fred W. Hooper; Patrice Jacobs; Howard B. Keck; Mr. and Mrs. Grover King; W.B. MacDonald Jr.; Meadow Stable; Merrick Stable; Edith Price; Katherine Price; Ada Rice; Gustav Ring; Turfland; Alfred G. Vanderbilt (2)

1961

1. Bohemia Stable (6)
2. Meadow Stable (5)
3. Alberta Ranches Ltd.; Calumet Farm; Dorchester Farm Stable; Rex Ellsworth; Jacob Sher (4)
8. Brookmeade Stable; Mrs. Moody Jolley; Kerr Stable; Ogden Phipps; Katherine Price; C.V. Whitney (3)

1962

1. George Widener (10)
2. Rex Ellsworth (8)
3. Fred W. Hooper (6)
4. Cain Hoy Stable; Meadow Stable (5)
6. Darby Dan Farm; Hobeau Farm (4)
8. Alberta Ranches Ltd.; Greentree Stable; Katherine Price (3)

1963

1. Greentree Stable (10)
2. Bohemia Stable; Rex Ellsworth (8)
4. Crimson King Farm; J.K. Houssels (5)
6. Darby Dan Farm; Fred W. Hooper (4)
8. Paul Bongarzone; William Haggin Perry (3)
10. Cain Hoy Stable; Claiborne Farm; John R. Gaines; Montpelier Stable; Eleanora Sears; Wheatley Stable; George Widener (2)

1964

1. Gedney Farm; Wheatley Stable (8)
3. Harbor View Farm; Rokeby Stable; Windfields Farm (5)
6. Bohemia Stable; Roland Bond, Keith Freeman, William R. Hawn & Poltex Stable; Briardale Farm; Montpelier Stable; Harry Nichols; North Forty Stable; Edward Seltzer; George Widener (3)

1965

1. Ada Rice (6)
2. Claiborne Farm; Ethel Jacobs; Ogden Phipps; George Widener (5)
6. Harbor View Farm; Powhatan Stable (4)
8. Isidore Bieber; Mrs. Ben Cohen; Stanley Conrad; El Peco Ranch; Gedney Farm (3)

1966

1. Ogden Phipps (11)
2. Wheatley Stable (6)
3. John R. Gaines; George Widener (4)
5. Ethel Jacobs; C.V. Whitney (3)
7. Brandywine Stable; Briardale Farm; Cragwood Stable; Ford Stable; George F. Getty II; Hall & Hammond; Harborvale Stable; Herff & La Croix; Patrice Jacobs; Ewing Kauffman; Howard B. Keck; Meadow Stable; Ada Rice; Michael Silver; Reginald Webster (2)

1967

1. Ogden Phipps (12)
2. Edith Bancroft (9)
3. Tartan Stable (6)
4. Hobeau Farm; Ethel Jacobs (5)
6. Wheatley Stable (4)
7. Fourth Estate Stable; Hasty House Farm; Llangollen Farm (3)
10. M. Andersen; Bwamazon Farm; Frances Genter; Greentree Stable; Frank McMahon; Meadow Stable; William Haggin Perry; Louis Rowan; Mr. and Mrs. Louis Shapiro; Mrs. E.K. Thomas; C.V. Whitney (2)

1968

1. Calumet Farm; William Haggin Perry; Tartan Stable; Wheatley Stable (6)
5. Lloyd I. Miller (5)
6. Edith Bancroft; King Ranch (4)
8. Frances Genter; Louis Rowan & C.V. Whitney; Verna Lea Farm; Steven Wilson (3)

1969

1. Rokeby Stable (10)
2. Mrs. Whitney Stone (5)
3. Cragwood Stable; William Haggin Perry; Gustav Ring; Verna Lea Farm (4)
7. Claiborne Farm; Elberon Farm; Elmendorf Farm; King Ranch; Frank McMahon; Wheatley Stable (3)

1970

1. Rokeby Stable (7)
2. Clement L. Hirsch; Ethel Jacobs (5)
4. Hastings Harcourt; Howard B. Keck (4)
6. Aisco Stable; Brookmeade Stable; Hobeau Farm; William Haggin Perry; Mrs. Whitney Stone (3)

1971

1. Ogden Phipps (5)
2. Forked Lightning Ranch; Mary Jones (Bradley); Meadow Stable (4)
5. Colonial Farm; Cragwood Stable; Elmendorf Farm; Hobeau Farm; William Levin; Rokeby Stable; Sigmund Sommer (3)

1972

1. Meadow Stable (10)
2. Rokeby Stable (8)
3. John M. Schiff (6)
4. Fred W. Hooper; Jean-Louis Levesque (5)
6. Mary Jones (Bradley); Bwamazon Farm; Mrs. Howard B. Keck; Frank McMahon; Middletown Stable; Sigmund Sommer; Westerly Stud Farm (3)

1973

1. Meadow Stable (9)
2. Hobeau Farm; Fred W. Hooper (8)
4. Elmendorf Farm (6)
5. Neil Hellman (4)
6. Mary Jones (Bradley); Harry Mangurian Jr.; Elizabeth Pritchard, William Resseguet Jr. & Dr. Edwin Thomas; Rokeby Stable (3)
10. Mrs. Paul Blackman; Bwamazon Farm; Christiana Stable; Cragwood Stable; Dee-Bob Stable; Green Thumb Farm; Oxford Stable; Sigmund Sommer; Mrs. Arthur Stollery (2)

1974

1. Lazy F Ranch (8)
2. Darby Dan Farm (6)
3. Fred W. Hooper; Sigmund Sommer (4)
5. John Greer; Hobeau Farm; Aaron Jones; Mrs. Howard B. Keck; Ethel Kirkland; Meeken Stable; William Haggin Perry; Carl Rosen (3)

1975

1. Lazy F Ranch (5)
2. Elmendorf Farm; Marjorie Everett; Diana Firestone; Dan Lasater (4)
6. Richard Bailey; East-West Stable; Bert Firestone; Golden Chance Farm; John Greer; Fred W. Hooper; Ethel Kirkland; Locust Hill Farm; Mrs. Arthur Stollery; J.P. & William Wilmot (3)

1976

1. Cardiff Stud Farm; Diana Firestone; Ogden Mills Phipps (5)
4. Elmendorf Farm; Bert Firestone; Golden Chance Farm; Lazy F Ranch (4)
8. Greentree Stable; Harbor View Farm; Nelson Bunker Hunt; Montpelier Stable; Rodriguez Tizol (3)

1977

1. Calumet Farm; Harbor View Farm (6)
3. Elmendorf Farm; Izzie Proler & Joseph Strauss Jr.; Connie Ring; Karen Taylor (5)
7. Dan Galbreath; Hickory Tree Stable; Don & John Valpredo; Randolph Weinsier (3)

1978

1. Harbor View Farm (9)
2. Calumet Farm (7)
3. Belair Stud Ltd. & Nelson Bunker Hunt; Greentree Stable (6)
5. Jerry Frankel; Haakon Fretheim; Hawksworth Farm; Dr. Jerome Torsney (3)
9. Barry Beal & Lloyd R. French Jr.; Peter Brant; Ann & Vernon Eachus; Elmendorf Farm; Mrs. John Galbreath; William R. Hawn; Loblolly Stable; Meadowhill; Newstead Farm; Pine Tree Stable; Ben Ridder; Tartan Stable; Tayhill Stable; Daniel Wildenstein (2)

1979

1. Harbor View Farm (10)
2. Hawksworth Farm; Ryehill Farm (7)
4. Greentree Stable (6)
5. Calumet Farm; William Haggin Perry (5)
7. Peter Brant; W.J. Oldknow & R.W. Phipps; C.V. Whitney (3)
10. Blum, Sarant & Randy Winick; Cardiff Stud Farm; Bert Firestone; Haakon Fretheim; Harry Oak; Ogden Phipps; Ben Ridder; John M. Schiff (2)

1980

1. Saron Stable (7)
2. Hawksworth Farm (6)
3. Dotsam Stable; Loblolly Stable (5)
5. Tartan Stable (4)
6. Ogden Phipps; Rokeby Stable; John M. Schiff; Wild Plum Farm (3)
10. Stephen Clark Jr.; Daybreak Farm; John Dominguez & Jack Klugman; Diana Firestone; Golden Chance Farm; Nelson Bunker Hunt & Frank Stronach; Leone J. Peters; Ryehill Farm; Summa Stable (2)

1981

1. Dotsam Stable (7)
2. Flying Zee Stable (6)
3. Buckland Farm (4)
4. Ryehill Farm; Charles T. Wilson Jr. (3)
6. Elmendorf Farm; Serge Fradkoff; Greentree Stable; Fred W. Hooper; M.A. Levy; Loblolly Stable; Claudia Mirkin; Muckler Stables; Nitram Stable; Ogden Phipps; Rokeby Stable; Louis Rowan; Wimborne Farm (2)

1982

1. Fred W. Hooper (5)
2. Aaron Jones (4)
3. Serge Fradkoff & Baron Thierry von Zuylen; Henryk de Kwiatkowski; Robert Hibbert; Stonereath Farm (3)
7. Joseph Allen; Barry Beal & Lloyd R. French Jr.; Mary Jones Bradley; Broadmoor Stable; Christiana Stable; Dotsam Stable; Elmendorf Farm; Diana Firestone; Greentree Stable; Franklin Groves; Happy Valley Farm; Nitram Stable; Oak Cliff Stable; Jacqueline Getty Phillips; Cynthia Phipps; Sidney Port; Ri-Ma-Ro Stable; Amin Saiden; Summa Stable; Brian Sweeney; C.V. Whitney (2)

Photo courtesy of Santa Anita Park

After they won the 1970 San Felipe Handicap with Cool Hand, John (right) and Betty Mabee established Golden Eagle Farm, which became such a powerful Southern California breeding entity in winning 37 major races from 1976-2002, that after John's death in 2002, Del Mar renamed the Ramona Handicap in his honor.

1983

1. Equusequity Stable; Carl Lauer, Nancy Vanier & Robert Victor; Charlene Parks (4)
4. Helen Alexander, David Aykroyd & Helen Groves; Claiborne Farm; D.J. Foster Racing Stable; Newstead Farm; Pen-Y-Bryn Farm; Jacqueline Getty Phillips & Michael Riordan; Brian Sweeney; Daniel Wildenstein (3)

1984

1. W.C. Partee (5)
2. Claiborne Farm; Dotsam Stable; Equusequity Stable; Rokeby Stable; David Sofro (4)
7. Peter Brant; Cardiff Stud Farm & T-90 Ranch; Henryk de Kwiatkowski; John Franks; Mel Hatley & Gene Klein; Star Crown Stable; Paula Tucker (3)

1985

1. Gene Klein (8)
2. Peter Brant; Brushwood Stable; Peter Fuller; Loblolly Stable; Star Crown Stable (4)
7. Mrs. Ben Cohen; Darby Dan Farm; Frances Genter; Green Thumb Farm; Fred W. Hooper; Hunter Farm (3)

1986

1. Gene Klein (9)
2. Robert Meyerhoff (5)
3. Henryk de Kwiatkowski; Carl Grinstead & Ben Rochelle (4)
5. Peter Brant; Frances Genter; Mrs. Howard B. Keck; Ogden Phipps; Russell Reineman; Bradley Shannon (3)

1987

1. Nelson Bunker Hunt; Gene Klein (6)
3. Barry Beal & Lloyd R. French Jr. (5)
4. Bert Firestone & Allen Paulson; Rokeby Stable (4)
6. Peter Brant; Cisley Stable & Blanche Levy; Hickory Tree Stable; David Levinson; Wayne Lukas & Paul Paternostro; Ogden Phipps; Dorothy & Pamela Scharbauer; Bradley Shannon (3)

1988

1. Gene Klein; Ogden Phipps (11)
3. Dorothy & Pamela Scharbauer (6)
4. Claiborne Farm; Evergreen Farm (4)
6. Alex Campbell Jr. & Arthur B. Hancock III; Class Act Stable; Darby Dan Farm (3)
9. Peter Brant; Howard Crash & Jim Hankoff; Peter DeCarlo, Robert LaTorre, Harold & Ralph Rubenstein; Joseph Federico; Dr. and Mrs. Jim Hill, Ogden Phipps & Mr. and Mrs. Mickey Taylor; Ron Larmarque & Louie Roussel III; Locust Hill Farm; Mr. and Mrs. James Phillips; Mrs. James Winn (2)

1989

1. Ogden Phipps (11)
2. Gene Klein (7)
3. Dr. Ernest Gaillard, Arthur B. Hancock III & Charlie Whittingham; Mr. and Mrs. Frank Whitham (6)
5. Peter Brant; Clover Racing Stable; Ju Ju Gen Stable; Ogden Mills Phipps (3)
9. Joseph Allen & Tayhill Stable; Robert Clay; Four M Stables Inc. & Halo Farms; Wayne Lukas & Overbrook Farm; Frances W. Luro; Raymond Roncari & Nancy Vanier; Sheikh Mohammad al Maktoum; Daniel Wildenstein; Mrs. James Winn (2)

1990

1. Calumet Farm; Christiana Stable; Dogwood Stable; Carl Icahn (5)
5. Overbrook Farm (4)
6. Robert Clay; Jack Kent Cooke; Frances Genter; Golden Eagle Farm; Mr. and Mrs. Frank Whitham (3)

1991

1. VHW Stable (6)
2. Jack Munari (5)
3. Juddmonte Farms; Loblolly Stable; Oaktown Stable (4)
6. George Bunn; Burt Kinerk; Lazy Lane Farms; Robert Levy; Allen Paulson; Sam-Son Farm (3)

1992

1. Golden Eagle Farm (7)
2. Sidney Craig (5)
3. Live Oak Plantation; Tomonori Tsurumaki (4)
5. Buckland Farm; Trudy McCaffery & John Toffan; Allen Paulson; VHW Stable (3)
9. Brae Burn Farm; Centennial Farms; Claiborne Farm; William Condren & Joseph Cornacchia; William de Burgh, Prestonwood Farm & Robert Sangster; James Elkins, Will Farish III & Temple Webber Jr.; Josephine Gleis; Juddmonte Farms; Lion Crest Stable; Loblolly Stable; Middletown Stable; David Milch & Jack & Mark Silverman; W.C. Partee; Madeleine Paulson; Dr. Ignacio Pavlovsky & Frank Whitham; Ogden Phipps; Sam-Son Farm; Scott Savin; Valley View Farm; Sheldon Willis (2)

1993

1. La Presle Farm (5)
2. Sidney Craig; Georgia Hoffman; Loblolly Stable; Ogden Mills Phipps (4)
6. Harbor View Farm; Lion Crest Stable; Allen Paulson; Ogden Phipps; Rokeby Stable; Team Valor; Valley View Farm (3)

1994

1. Jimmy Croll (7)
2. Overbrook Farm (5)
3. Georgia Hoffman; Ogden Mills Phipps (4)
5. Burt Bacharach; Philip Hersh; Masayuki Nishiyama; Allen Paulson; Ogden Phipps; Mike Rutherford (3)

1995

1. Beverly & Robert Lewis; Allen Paulson (8)
3. Michael Tabor (6)
4. Ogden Phipps; Ogden Mills Phipps (4)
6. Blue Vista; Juddmonte Farms; Overbrook Farm (3)
9. Burt Bacharach; Alex Campbell Jr.; Charles Cella; Sidney Craig; Dick Dutrow; Edmund Gann; Kimran Stable; Kinghaven Farm & Helen Stollery; Pin Oak Stable; Mrs. Morton Rosenthal; Ryehill Farm; Sierra Thoroughbreds; VHW Stable (2)

1996

1. Carolyn Hine; Overbrook Farm (5)
3. Michael Fennessy; Martin & Pam Wygod (4)
5. Donald Dizney & James English; Fred W. Hooper; Juddmonte Farms; Beverly & Robert Lewis; Allen Paulson; Ogden Phipps; Martha (Perez) & Richard Stephen; Michael Tabor (3)

1997

1. Juddmonte Farms; Allen Paulson (5)
3. R.D. Hubbard, Gilberto Montagna, Aldo Soprano & Juan Jose Varsi; John Murphy; The Thoroughbred Corporation (4)
6. Robert Clay & Tracy Farmer; Carolyn Hine; Trudy McCaffery & John Toffan; Sam-Son Farm; Martha (Perez) & Richard Stephen & The Thoroughbred Corporation; Michael Tabor (3)

1998

1. Carolyn Hine (6)
2. Golden Eagle Farm; Frank Stronach; The Thoroughbred Corporation (5)
5. Mike Pegram (4)
6. Ackerley Brothers Farm; Overbrook Farm; Allen Paulson; Prestonwood Farm; James Tafel (3)

1999

1. Mike Pegram (9)
2. Golden Eagle Farm (5)
3. Overbrook Farm; Paraneck Stable; James Tafel (4)
6. William Clifton Jr. & Rudlein Stable; Aaron & Marie Jones; John Oxley; Stonerside Stable (3)
10. Dolores Conway, Joseph Cornacchia & Fred DeMattias; 505 Farms; Arthur B. Hancock III & Jimmy Stone; Beverly & Robert Lewis; Randy Martin & Steve Weiner; Trudy McCaffery & John Toffan; Padua Stables; Allen Paulson; Joan & John Phillips; Ogden Phipps; Hugo Reynolds; Barry Schwartz; Mark Stanley; Frank Stronach; Gary Tanaka; The Thoroughbred Corporation; Jeanne Vance (2)

2000

1. Aaron & Marie Jones (6)
2. Frank Stronach; The Thoroughbred Corporation (5)
4. Jeanne Vance (4)
5. Golden Eagle Farm; Juddmonte Farms; Fusao Sekiguchi (3)
8. Columbine Stable, Jay Jones Jr. & Tom Nichols; Michael Cooper & Cecilia Straub-Rubens; Diamond A Racing Corporation & Herman Sarkowsky; James Elkins, Will Farish III & Temple Webber Jr.; Edward Evans; Fox Hill Farms; Gary Garber; Jack Garey; Kinsman Stable; Beverly & Robert Lewis, Susan Magnier & Michael Tabor; Eugene & Laura Melnyk; Overbrook Farm; John Oxley; Stonerside Stable; Trillium Stable (2)

2001

1. The Thoroughbred Corporation (11)
2. Juddmonte Farms (9)
3. Amerman Racing Stable (5)
4. Gary Tanaka (4)
5. Heiligbrodt Racing Stable & Team Valor; Sheikh Maktoum al Maktoum (3)
7. Anstu Stables, Inc.; Augustin Stables; Centaur Farms; John Dolan & Sam Longo; Tracy Farmer; Edmund Gann; Godolphin Stable; David Lanzman; Trudy McCaffery, Robert Sangster & John Toffan; New Farm; John Oxley; Allen Paulson Living Trust; Red Baron's Barn; Stonerside Stable; Michael Tabor; VHW Stable; Janis Whitham (2)

2002

1. Godolphin Stable; Allen Paulson Living Trust (7)
3. Edmund Gann (6)
4. Juddmonte Farms (5)
5. Edward Evans; The Thoroughbred Corporation (4)
7. Augustin Stables; Will Farish III, John Goodman, Trudy McCaffery & John Toffan; John Oxley; Ogden Mills Phipps; Gary Tanaka (3)

2003

1. Juddmonte Farms (11)
2. Edmund Gann (5)
3. James Elkins, Will Farish III & Temple Webber Jr.; Flaxman Holdings, Ltd. (4)
5. Amerman Racing Stable; George Krikorian; Marylou Whitney Stable; Allen Paulson Living Trust; Stonerside Stable (3)
10. Buckram Oak Farm; James Chisholm, Horizon Stable, Michael Jarvis & John Paul Reddam; Everest Stables; Georgica Stable; Godolphin Stable; Wayne Hughes; Beverly & Robert Lewis; Sheikh Maktoum al Maktoum; Eugene & Laura Melnyk; Sackatoga Stable; Joseph Shields Jr.; Frank Stronach; The Thoroughbred Corporation; Wertheimer Farm (2)

New York Racing Association photography/property of and courtesy of Keeneland Association

Movie audiences of the 21st Century were introduced to Alfred G. Vanderbilt as the diplomatic Pimlico promoter who made the match race between Seabiscuit and War Admiral a reality. Racing fans already were quite familiar with Vanderbilt, who campaigned such standouts as Bed o' Roses, Find, Social Outcast, Next Move, and Native Dancer.

Owners' Resumes

Owners With Victories In Major North American Races 1946-2003

STEVE ABRAMS, GEORGE HICKER & MICHAEL LIMA
1991: Sunset Handicap (Black Monday)

ACKERLEY BROTHERS FARM
1998: Acorn Stakes (Jersey Girl)
Mother Goose Stakes (Jersey Girl)
Test Stakes (Jersey Girl)
2001: Overbrook Spinster Stakes (Miss Linda)

MRS. JOHN PAYSON ADAMS
1947: American Handicap (Burning Dream)
1950: Inglewood Handicap (Miche)
1952: Santa Anita Handicap (Miche)

LEROY ADCOCK
1981: Louisiana Downs Handicap (Shishkabob)

Z.T. ADDINGTON
1947: Hollywood Gold Cup (Cover Up)
Sunset Handicap (Cover Up)

ADDISON STABLE
1949: Travers Stakes (Arise)
1950: Fall Highweight Handicap (Arise)
Excelsior Handicap (Arise)
1951: Carter Handicap (Arise)
Monmouth Handicap (Arise)

AGA KHAN
1984: Breeders' Cup Turf (Lashkari)
1996: Beverly D. Stakes (Timarida)
2000: Breeders' Cup Turf (Kalanisi)

DAN AGNEW & CHUCK BAUMBACH
1985: Sunset Handicap (Kings Island)

MR. and MRS. SAMUEL AGNEW
1970: San Felipe Handicap (Terlago)
Santa Anita Derby (Terlago)

AISCO STABLE
1965: Sorority Stakes (Native Street)
1966: Kentucky Oaks (Native Street)
1970: Sorority Stakes (Forward Gal)
Spinaway Stakes (Forward Gal)
Frizette Stakes (Forward Gal)
1971: Monmouth Oaks (Forward Gal)
Gazelle Handicap (Forward Gal)
1973: Florida Derby (Royal and Regal)
1982: Pegasus Handicap (Fast Gold)

STEWART AITKEN
1995: Santa Anita Handicap (Urgent Request)

AJB-PC STABLE
1992: Hollywood Starlet Stakes (Creaking Board)

F.O. AKIN ESTATE & JAMES ECKROSH
1970: Louisiana Derby (Jim's Alibhi)

A. AKMAN
1986: Vosburgh Stakes (King's Swan)

ALAMODE FARM
1961: Grey Lag Handicap (Mail Order)

ALBERT & STOKE
1971: Cinema Handicap (Niagara)

ALBERTA RANCHES LTD.
1953: American Handicap (Royal Serenade)
Hollywood Gold Cup (Royal Serenade)
1955: Santa Margarita Handicap (Blue Butterfly)
1961: Santa Anita Derby (Four-and-Twenty)
Cinema Handicap (Four-and-Twenty)
Hollywood Derby (Four-and-Twenty)
San Felipe Handicap (Flutterby)
1962: San Fernando Stakes (Four-and-Twenty)
Santa Anita Maturity (Four-and-Twenty)
San Carlos Handicap (Four-and-Twenty)

ALBERTA RANCHES LTD. & GEORGE GARDINER
1955: San Juan Capistrano Handicap (St. Vincent)
Dixie Handicap (St. Vincent)

EMORY ALEXANDER
1982: Maskette Stakes (Too Chic)

FRANK ALEXANDER
2000: Remsen Stakes (Windsor Castle)

HELEN ALEXANDER
1964: Grey Lag Handicap (Saidam)
1998: Go for Wand Handicap (Aldiza)

HELEN ALEXANDER, DAVID AYKROYD & HELEN GROVES
1983: Del Mar Futurity (Althea)
Del Mar Debutante Stakes (Althea)
Hollywood Starlet Stakes (Althea)
1984: Santa Susana Stakes (Althea)
Arkansas Derby (Althea)

H. ALEXANDER, H. GROVES & MOHAMMAD al MAKTOUM
1994: Peter Pan Stakes (Twining)

ROBERT ALICK
1991: Santa Margarita Handicap (Little Brianne)

AL-JO STABLE
1972: John B. Campbell Handicap (Boone the Great)

EARL ALLEN
1965: Arkansas Derby (Swift Ruler)
1966: Oaklawn Handicap (Swift Ruler)

HERBERT ALLEN
1966: Saratoga Special (Favorable Turn)
1968: Donn Handicap (Favorable Turn)
1969: Garden State Stakes (Forum)
1974: American Derby (Determined King)
1980: Arlington-Washington Futurity (Well Decorated)
1986: Tropical Park Derby (Strong Performance)
1987: Hutcheson Stakes (Well Selected)

JOSEPH ALLEN
1978: Carter Handicap (Pumpkin Moonshine)
1982: Top Flight Handicap (Andover Way)
Beldame Stakes (Weber City Miss)
1988: Jersey Derby (Dynaformer)
1990: Peter Pan Stakes (Profit Key)
Dwyer Stakes (Profit Key)
1991: Beldame Stakes (Sharp Dance)
1997: Ashland Stakes (Glitter Woman)

JOSEPH ALLEN & PETER BRANT
1979: Del Mar Debutante Stakes (Table Hands)

JOSEPH ALLEN & TAYHILL STABLE
1989: Gulfstream Park Handicap (Slew City Slew)
Oaklawn Handicap (Slew City Slew)

EILEEN & MARTIN ALPERT
1991: San Luis Rey Stakes (Pleasant Variety)

ALPHA STABLE & T. TAUB
1973: Louisiana Derby (Leo's Pisces)

GREG ALSDORF, BOBBY FRANKEL & JEROME MOSS
1986: Arlington-Washington Lassie Stakes (Delicate Vine)

ALTANDOR STABLE & EDGAR COX
1956: San Luis Rey Handicap (Blue Volt)

AMBUSH STABLE
1963: California Derby (On My Honor)

AMERMAN RACING STABLE
1999: Matriarch Stakes (Happyanunoit)
2000: Beverly Hills Handicap (Happyanunoit)
2001: Whitney Handicap (Lido Palace)
Woodward Stakes (Lido Palace)
Lane's End Breeders' Futurity (Siphonic)
Hollywood Futurity (Siphonic)
Gamely Breeders' Cup Handicap (Happyanunoit)
2002: Woodward Stakes (Lido Palace)
2003: Mother Goose Stakes (Spoken Fur)
Coaching Club American Oaks (Spoken Fur)
Breeders' Cup Distaff (Adoration)

AMERMAN RACING STABLE & ROBERTO PALUMBO OSSA
1999: Oak Tree Turf Championship (Mash One)
2000: Clement L. Hirsch Mem. Turf Champ. (Mash One)

AMHERST STABLE & SPRUCE POND STABLE
2002: Breeders' Cup Classic (Volponi)

JACK AMIEL
1951: Kentucky Derby (Count Turf)

EDWARD & JUDITH ANCHEL
1982: Wood Memorial Stakes (Air Forbes Won)

M. ANDERSEN
1967: Coaching Club American Oaks (Quillo Queen)
Monmouth Oaks (Quillo Queen)

EDWARD ANDERSON
1964: Del Mar Debutante Stakes (Admirably)

ANDERSON, RAY PRIDDY & WALTERS
1978: Cinema Handicap (Kamehameha)

ANDES STABLE
1948: Massachusetts Handicap (Beauchef)

RONALD & SUSIE ANSON
2001: Oak Leaf Stakes (Tali'sluckybusride)

ANSTU STABLES, INC.
2001: Turfway Spiral Stakes (Balto Star)
Arkansas Derby (Balto Star)
2003: United Nations Handicap (Balto Star)

APHEIM STABLE
1952: Roamer Handicap (Quiet Step)
1955: Aqueduct Handicap (Icarian)

JOHN APPLEBAUM
1956: Cowdin Stakes (Mister Jive)
1957: Gotham Stakes (Mister Jive)

ARTHUR APPLETON
1973: Blue Grass Stakes (My Gallant)
1989: Withers Stakes (Fire Maker)
1991: Donn Handicap (Jolie's Halo)
Gulfstream Park Handicap (Jolie's Halo)
1992: Philip H. Iselin Handicap (Jolie's Halo)
1999: Early Times Turf Classic (Wild Event)
2001: Manhattan Handicap (Forbidden Apple)

ARAKELIAN FARMS INC.
1980: Norfolk Stakes (Sir Dancer)

MARTYN ARBIB
1992: Rothmans International Stakes (Snurge)

GERALD ARMSTRONG
1980: Ohio Derby (Stone Manor)

MR. and MRS. HERB ARMSTRONG
1957: Santa Anita Derby (Sir William)

JURGEN ARNEMANN
1995: Blue Grass Stakes (Wild Syn)

MR. and MRS. DESI ARNEZ
1968: Santa Barbara Handicap (Amerigo's Fancy)

JACK ARNOLD
1987: San Felipe Handicap (Chart the Stars)

TED ARONEY
1988: Hollywood Futurity (King Glorious)

ARONOW STABLE
1986: Fountain of Youth Stakes (My Prince Charming)

ESLIE ASBURY
1956: Selima Stakes (Lebkuchen)

LOUIS ASISTIO
2002: Santa Monica Handicap (Kalookan Queen)
Ancient Title BC Handicap (Kalookan Queen)

FRED ASTAIRE
1946: San Juan Capistrano Handicap (Triplicate)
Hollywood Gold Cup (Triplicate)
1947: Golden Gate Handicap (Triplicate)

SONNY ATKINS
1990: Young America Stakes (Southern Sign)

AUDLEY FARM
1958: Fall Highweight Handicap (Bull Strength)

AUGUSTIN STABLES
1978: John B. Campbell Handicap (Ripon)
1982: Flower Bowl Handicap (Trevita)
1983: Flower Bowl Handicap (First Approach)
1994: Turf Classic (Tikkanen)
Breeders' Cup Turf (Tikkanen)
2000: Del Mar Oaks (No Matter What)
2001: Sword Dancer Inv. Handicap (With Anticipation)
Man o' War Stakes (With Anticipation)
2002: United Nations Handicap (With Anticipation)
Sword Dancer Inv. Handicap (With Anticipation)
Man o' War Stakes (With Anticipation)

AUGUSTUS & NAHM
1946: American Derby (Eternal Reward)

AUSTAD & DEEB
1977: Del Mar Debutante Stakes (Extravagant)

PAN de AZUCAR
1946: Del Mar Handicap (Olhaverry)
1947: Santa Anita Handicap (Olhaverry)
1948: San Pasqual Handicap (Olhaverry)

BURT BACHARACH
1971: Inglewood Handicap (Advance Guard)
1983: Ruffian Handicap (Heartlight No. One)
1994: San Felipe Stakes (Soul of the Matter)
Super Derby (Soul of the Matter)
Hollywood Futurity (Afternoon Deelites)
1995: San Felipe Stakes (Afternoon Deelites)
Malibu Stakes (Afternoon Deelites)

A.M. BADGETT
1986: Yellow Ribbon Stakes (Bonne Ile)

BROWN BADGETT
1987: Jersey Derby (Avies Copy)

DR. JERRY BAILEY & KENNETH ELLENBERG
1995: Remsen Stakes (Tropicool)

RICHARD BAILEY
1975: Sorority Stakes (Dearly Precious)
Spinaway Stakes (Dearly Precious)
Arlington-Washington Lassie Stakes (Dearly Precious)
1976: Acorn Stakes (Dearly Precious)

SALLY BAILIE, PAUL CORNMAN & FRED EPHRAIM
1985: Man o' War Stakes (Win)

GARY BAKER & TEAM VALOR
2000: Santa Anita Derby (The Deputy)

ROBERT BAKER, DAVID CORNSTEIN & WILLIAM MACK
1997: Belmont Futurity (Grand Slam)
Moet Champagne Stakes (Grand Slam)
2001: Jim Dandy Stakes (Scorpion)

ROBERT BAKER & HOWARD KASKEL
1983: Flamingo Stakes (Current Hope)

D. BALL
1972: Donn Handicap (Going Straight)

JOHN BALL
1998: Spinaway Stakes (Things Change)

R. BALLIS
1967: Michigan Mile and One-Eighth (Estreno II)
1968: Pan American Handicap (Estreno II)

BALMAK STABLE
1977: Jockey Club Gold Cup (On the Sly)
Hawthorne Gold Cup (On the Sly)

EDITH BANCROFT
1967: Wood Memorial Stakes (Damascus)
Preakness Stakes (Damascus)
Belmont Stakes (Damascus)
Dwyer Handicap (Damascus)
American Derby (Damascus)
Travers Stakes (Damascus)
Aqueduct Stakes (Damascus)
Woodward Stakes (Damascus)
Jockey Club Gold Cup (Damascus)
1968: Brooklyn Handicap (Damascus)
Aqueduct Stakes (Damascus)
Malibu Stakes (Damascus)
San Fernando Stakes (Damascus)

MRS. E.E. BANKHEAD
1957: Hialeah Turf Handicap (Jabneh)

PETER BARBERINO
1979: Champagne Stakes (Joanie's Chief)

BARCLAY STABLE
1964: Man o' War Stakes (Turbo Jet II)
1975: Hollywood Invitational Handicap (Barclay Joy)
Sunset Handicap (Barclay Joy)

MARC BARGE
1987: Philip H. Iselin Handicap (Bordeaux Bob)

RICHARD BARNES & PRESTONWOOD FARM
1996: Gamely Handicap (Auriette)

ANTHONY BARONI & BATTILANA
1948: San Carlos Handicap (Autocrat)
1949: San Carlos Handicap (Autocrat)

BAR O STABLE
1965: Ohio Derby (Terri Hi)

CARMEN BARRERA
1980: Swaps Stakes (First Albert)

LAZ BARRERA & AMIN SAIDEN
1988: San Felipe Handicap (Mi Preferido)
1989: San Fernando Stakes (Mi Preferido)

JAMES BARTLETT & PAUL TERNES
1966: Florida Derby (Williamston Kid)

S.M. BARTON
1959: Trenton Handicap (Greek Star)
1961: New Orleans Handicap (Greek Star)

JERRY BASTA
1963: Dixie Handicap (Cedar Key)
1964: San Juan Capistrano Handicap (Cedar Key)
Donn Handicap (Cedar Key)
1965: San Luis Rey Handicap (Cedar Key)
1966: San Luis Rey Handicap (Cedar Key)

JOANNE BATCHELOR
1988: La Canada Stakes (Hollywood Glitter)

ELIZABETH & TOM BAXTER
2000: Vinery Del Mar Debutante Stakes (Cindy's Hero)

MRS. C. ULRICK BAY
1955: Cowdin Stakes (Noorsaga)
1957: Matron Stakes (Idun)
Gardenia Stakes (Idun)
Frizette Stakes (Idun)
Massachusetts Handicap (Greek Spy)
1958: Mother Goose Stakes (Idun)
Gazelle Handicap (Idun)

BARRY BEAL & LLOYD R. FRENCH JR.
1978: Hollywood Juvenile Championship (Terlingua)
Del Mar Debutante Stakes (Terlingua)
1982: Del Mar Debutante Stakes (Landaluce)
Oak Leaf Stakes (Landaluce)
1986: Oak Leaf Stakes (Sacahuista)
1987: Arlington-Washington Futurity (Tejano)
Cowdin Stakes (Tejano)
Hollywood Futurity (Tejano)
Spinster Stakes (Sacahuista)
Breeders' Cup Distaff (Sacahuista)

BARRY BEAL, LLOYD R. FRENCH JR. & GENE KLEIN
1986: Norfolk Stakes (Capote)
Breeders' Cup Juvenile (Capote)

BARRY BEAL, LLOYD R. FRENCH JR. & WAYNE LUKAS
1983: Santa Anita Derby (Marfa)
Jim Beam Spiral Stakes (Marfa)

BILL BEASLEY
1967: Canadian Int. Championship (He's a Smoothie)

WARREN BEASLEY
1968: Hialeah Turf Cup (He's a Smoothie)

W.J. BEATTIE
1955: Canadian Championship Stakes (Park Dandy)

BEATY & DORNEY
1962: Santa Margarita Handicap (Queen America)

MICHAEL BECKER & RICHARD KUMBLE
1997: Caesars International Handicap (Influent)
Man o' War Stakes (Influent)

BEDFORD STABLE
1951: Trenton Handicap (Call Over)

BRADFORD BEILLY & DAVID ROMINIK
1989: Budweiser International Stakes (Caltech)

BELAIR STUD
1946: Coaching Club American Oaks (Hypnotic)
Alabama Stakes (Hypnotic)
Delaware Oaks (Bonnie Beryl)
Comely Handicap (Bonnie Beryl)
1949: Dwyer Stakes (Shackleton)
1952: Saranac Handicap (Golden Gloves)
1953: Alabama Stakes (Sabette)
1954: Hopeful Stakes (Nashua)
Futurity Stakes (Nashua)
1955: Flamingo Stakes (Nashua)
Florida Derby (Nashua)
Wood Memorial Stakes (Nashua)
Preakness Stakes (Nashua)
Belmont Stakes (Nashua)
Dwyer Stakes (Nashua)
Arlington Classic (Nashua)
Jockey Club Gold Cup (Nashua)

BELAIR STUD LTD. & NELSON BUNKER HUNT
1978: Hollywood Gold Cup (Exceller)
Jockey Club Gold Cup (Exceller)
Hollywood Invitational Handicap (Exceller)
Sunset Handicap (Exceller)
Oak Tree Invitational Stakes (Exceller)
San Juan Capistrano Handicap (Exceller)

ART BELFORD & JOHN GREATHOUSE
1986: Illinois Derby (Bolshoi Boy)

JOHN A. BELL III
1970: Pan American Handicap (One For All)
Sunset Handicap (One For All)
1971: Canadian International Championship (One For All)
1976: Gulfstream Park Handicap (Hail the Pirates)
1983: Spinster Stakes (Try Something New)
1986: Arlington Classic (Sumptious)
1987: Breeders' Cup Juvenile Fillies (Epitome)
1988: Spinster Stakes (Hail a Cab)

RAY BELL
1963: San Juan Capistrano Handicap (Pardao)

STANLEY BELL
1997: Santa Monica Handicap (Toga Toga Toga)

BELLEHURST STABLE
1959: Cowdin Stakes (Warfare)
Champagne Stakes (Warfare)
Garden State Stakes (Warfare)

MICHAEL BELLO
2003: John C. Mabee Handicap (Megahertz)

AUGUST BELMONT IV
1983: Belmont Stakes (Caveat)

BELMONT FARMS
1981: Illinois Derby (Paristo)

HOWARD BENDER
1985: Laurel Futurity (Southern Appeal)

ROBERT BENSINGER
1962: Gallant Fox Handicap (Sensitivo)
Display Handicap (Sensitivo)

MR. and MRS. ROBERT BENSINGER
1981: American Derby (Pocket Zipper)

THOMAS BENSON
1950: Grey Lag Handicap (Lotowhite)
1951: Excelsior Handicap (Lotowhite)

DARIO BENTAVEGNA
1970: Jerome Handicap (Great Mystery)

ALEX BERKE & MICHAEL SOTO
1957: Kentucky Oaks (Lori-El)

CAL BERNSTEIN & TONY BUSCHING
1977: Ashland Stakes (Sound of Summer)

C.T. BERRY JR.
1977: Jersey Derby (Cormorant)

M.T. BERRY
1969: Michigan Mile and One-Eighth (Calandrito)
1980: Bowling Green Handicap (Sten)
1982: Brooklyn Handicap (Silver Supreme)

PATRICK BIANCONE & FABEN QUAKI
2002: Futurity Stakes (Whywhywhy)

ISIDORE BIEBER
1949: Roseben Handicap (Up Beat)
1950: Westchester Handicap (Palestinian)
1951: Brooklyn Handicap (Palestinian)
Golden Gate Handicap (Palestinian)
Acorn Stakes (Nothirdchance)
1965: Gotham Stakes (Flag Raiser)
Wood Memorial Stakes (Flag Raiser)
Withers Stakes (Flag Raiser)
1968: Flamingo Stakes (Wise Exchange)

F. BIENSTOCK & PRINCE SULTAN MOHAMMED al KABEER
1996: Sword Dancer Invitational Handicap (Broadway Flyer)

MRS. ANSON BIGELOW
1955: Pimlico Futurity (Nail)
Remsen Stakes (Nail)
Futurity Stakes (Nail)
1956: Hialeah Turf Handicap (Guardian II)

BIG I FARM
1975: Arkansas Derby (Promised City)

BILLRICK STABLE
1972: Malibu Stakes (Kfar Tov)

BILLRICK STABLE & HEMACINTO
1967: Santa Barbara Handicap (April Dawn)

MORETON BINN
1978: Arlington-Washington Futurity (Jose Binn)

MORETON BINN & ENLLOMAR STABLE
2000: Metropolitan Handicap (Yankee Victor)

A.L. BIRCH
1954: Ohio Derby (Timely Tip)

BIRCHFIELD FARM
1971: Sorority Stakes (Brenda Beauty)

MRS. FRANK BISHOP
1968: Charles H. Strub Stakes (Most Host)

BLACK CHIP STABLE
1984: Breeders' Cup Classic (Wild Again)

BLACK GOLD STABLE
1953: Del Mar Debutante Stakes (Lady Cover Up)

MRS. PAUL BLACKMAN
1972: Del Mar Debutante Stakes (Windy's Daughter)
1973: Acorn Stakes (Windy's Daughter)
Mother Goose Stakes (Windy's Daughter)

BLAHUT STABLES
2003: Malibu Stakes (Southern Image)

W.E. BLAIR JR.
1983: Illinois Derby (General Practitioner)

W. BLASLAND, S. BROOKS, J. DESADORA, A. MARGOTTA
1998: Malibu Stakes (Run Man Run)

PATRICIA BLASS
1972: Breeders' Futurity (Annihilate 'Em)

MR. and MRS. T.F. BLEDSOE
1951: Cinema Handicap (Mucho Hosso)

BLOODSTOCK SERVICES MANAGEMENT & DeHAVEN
1998: Del Mar Oaks (Sicy D'Alsace)

BLUE STONE FARM
1955: Tropical Handicap (Scimitar)

BLUE VISTA
1993: Yellow Ribbon Stakes (Possibly Perfect)
1994: Santa Barbara Handicap (Possibly Perfect)
1995: Gamely Handicap (Possibly Perfect)
Ramona Handicap (Possibly Perfect)
Beverly D. Stakes (Possibly Perfect)

MARIBEL BLUM
1971: Arlington-Washington Futurity (Hold Your Peace)
1972: Flamingo Stakes (Hold Your Peace)
1977: Gulfstream Park Handicap (Strike Me Lucky)

MARIBEL BLUM & HARPENEAU
1977: Pan American Handicap (Gravelines)

PETER BLUM
1973: Hollywood Invitational Handicap (Life Cycle)

BLUM, SARANT & RANDY WINICK
1979: Ramona Handicap (Country Queen)
Yellow Ribbon Stakes (Country Queen)

JOANNE BLUSIEWICZ
1981: Selima Stakes (Snow Plow)

ANTHONY & JOHN BODIE & ANTHONY SPEELMAN
1985: Hollywood Turf Cup (Zoffany)
1986: Sunset Handicap (Zoffany)
1987: San Luis Rey Stakes (Zoffany)

ENRIQUE CARLOS BOEKCKE
1990: Oak Tree Invitational Stakes (Rial)

MRS. J.A. BOHANNON
1960: Everglades Stakes (Moslem Chief)

BOHEMIA STABLE
1956: Remsen Stakes (Ambehaving)
1960: Jerome Handicap (Kelso)
Lawrence Realization Stakes (Kelso)
Hawthorne Gold Cup (Kelso)
Jockey Club Gold Cup (Kelso)
1961: Metropolitan Handicap (Kelso)
Suburban Handicap (Kelso)
Brooklyn Handicap (Kelso)
Woodward Stakes (Kelso)
Jockey Club Gold Cup (Kelso)
Whitney Handicap (Kelso)
1962: Woodward Stakes (Kelso)
Jockey Club Gold Cup (Kelso)
1963: Seminole Handicap (Kelso)
Gulfstream Park Handicap (Kelso)
John B. Campbell Handicap (Kelso)
Suburban Handicap (Kelso)
Aqueduct Stakes (Kelso)
Woodward Stakes (Kelso)
Jockey Club Gold Cup (Kelso)
Whitney Stakes (Kelso)
1964: Aqueduct Stakes (Kelso)
Jockey Club Gold Cup (Kelso)
Washington D.C. International (Kelso)
1965: Whitney Stakes (Kelso)
1967: Molly Pitcher Handicap (Politely)
1968: Delaware Handicap (Politely)
Ladies Handicap (Politely)
1973: Carter Handicap (King's Bishop)
1982: Hollywood Derby (Victory Zone)
1984: Monmouth Handicap (Believe the Queen)
2001: Ballerina Handicap (Shine Again)
2002: Ballerina Handicap (Shine Again)

W.R. BOHM & BOB WHEELER
1977: Oak Leaf Stakes (B. Thoughtful)

C.B. BOHN & P.A. MARKEY
1947: Arlington Futurity (Piet)

LYNN BOICE
1962: Santa Anita Handicap (Physician)
1963: San Antonio Handicap (Physician)

RICHARD BOKUM II
1967: John B. Campbell Handicap (Quinta)

RICHARD BOMZE & MICHAEL SPIELMAN
1984: Pennsylvania Derby (Morning Bob)

ROLAND BOND & POLTEX STABLE
1959: Santa Anita Handicap (Terrang)

R. BOND, KEITH FREEMAN, W.R. HAWN & POLTEX STABLE
1964: American Handicap (Colorado King)
Hollywood Gold Cup (Colorado King)
Sunset Handicap (Colorado King)

PAUL BONGARZONE
1963: Lawrence Realization Stakes (Dean Carl)
Roamer Handicap (Dean Carl)
Display Handicap (Dean Carl)

BONNIE HEATH FARM & ROBERT SCHAEDLE III
1999: Sword Dancer Invitational Handicap (Honor Glide)

FRANK BONSAL
1950: New York Handicap (Pilaster)

FRANK BONSAL JR.
1980: Pennsylvania Derby (Lively King)

DANIEL BORISLOW
2002: Champagne Stakes (Toccet)
Hollywood Futurity (Toccet)

CARY BOSHAMER
1950: Marguerite Stakes (Carolina Queen)

G.H. BOSTWICK
1963: Black Helen Handicap (Pocosaba)

ROBERT BOUCHER
1952: Washington D.C. International (Wilwyn)

R.L. BOWEN & ARTHUR B. HANCOCK III
1990: Fantasy Stakes (Silvered)

CARL BOWLING, LAKLAND FARM & CHARLES THOMPSON
2000: Hopeful Stakes (City Zip)

DR. and MRS. THOMAS BOWMAN & VICTOR IVES
1998: Queen Elizabeth II Challenge Cup (Tenski)

GORDON BOWSHER, MARSH & MICKLEWOOD
1967: Hollywood Juvenile Championship (Jim White)

J.R. BRADLEY
1946: Gazelle Stakes (Bridal Flower)
New Castle Handicap (Bridal Flower)
Beldame Handicap (Bridal Flower)
Roamer Handicap (Bridal Flower)
Hopeful Stakes (Blue Border)
Frizette Stakes (Bimlette)
Selima Stakes (Bee Ann Mac)

MARY (JONES) BRADLEY
1971: Californian Stakes (Cougar II)
Ford Pinto Invitational Turf Handicap (Cougar II)
Oak Tree Invitational Stakes (Cougar II)
San Juan Capistrano Handicap (Cougar II)
1972: Californian Stakes (Cougar II)
Century Handicap (Cougar II)
Oak Tree Invitational Stakes (Cougar II)
1973: Santa Anita Handicap (Cougar II)
Century Handicap (Cougar II)
Sunset Handicap (Cougar II)
1982: Yellow Ribbon Stakes (Castilla)
Matriarch Stakes (Castilla)

BRADLEY, BRADLEY & CHANDLER
1989: Hollywood Derby (Live the Dream)

M.J. BRADLEY, CHANDLER & CHARLIE WHITTINGHAM
1982: Hollywood Invitational Handicap (Exploded)

M.J. BRADLEY, R. DUCHOSSOIS & C. WHITTINGHAM
1986: Hollywood Derby (Thrill Show)

BRADLEY & PRIZILAS
1980: Oaklawn Handicap (Uncool)

MARY JONES BRADLEY & CHARLIE WHITTINGHAM
1976: Del Mar Handicap (Riot in Paris)

MARY J. BRADLEY, C. WHITTINGHAM & HOWELL WYNNE
1985: Californian Stakes (Greinton)
Hollywood Gold Cup (Greinton)
1986: Santa Anita Handicap (Greinton)

JAMES COX BRADY
1951: Metropolitan Handicap (Casemate)
1952: Sapling Stakes (Landlocked)
1953: Sapling Stakes (Artismo)
Hopeful Stakes (Artismo)

	Acorn Stakes (Secret Meeting)
1954:	Widener Handicap (Landlocked)
1969:	Spinaway Stakes (Meritus)
	Pan American Handicap (Hibernian)

WM. BRADY, JOS. DANIERO, SUZANNE JENKINS & J. RAY

1987: Remsen Stakes (Batty)

BRAE BURN FARM

1951:	Astoria Stakes (Star-Enfin)
1959:	Bougainvillea Turf Handicap (General Arthur)
1961:	Arlington Matron Handicap (Shirley Jones)
	Donn Handicap (General Arthur)
1962:	Gulfstream Park Handicap (Jay Fox)
	Donn Handicap (Jay Fox)
1992:	Jim Dandy Stakes (Thunder Rumble)
	Travers Stakes (Thunder Rumble)

VERA BRAGG

1949: Tremont Stakes (Fox Time)

BRANDYWINE STABLE

1950:	Dwyer Stakes (Greek Song)
	Arlington Classic (Greek Song)
	Massachusetts Handicap (Cochise)
1951:	Grey Lag Handicap (Cochise)
	Arlington Handicap (Cochise)
	Astarita Stakes (Place Card)
1962:	Preakness Stakes (Greek Money)
1966:	Delaware Handicap (Open Fire)
	Spinster Stakes (Open Fire)

MRS. JOSEPH BRANHAM

1956: Alabama Stakes (Tournure)

WILLIAM L. BRANN

1946:	Beldame Handicap (Gallorette)
	Metropolitan Handicap (Gallorette)
	Brooklyn Handicap (Gallorette)
1947:	Queens County Handicap (Gallorette)
1948:	Carter Handicap (Gallorette)
	Whitney Stakes (Gallorette)

PETER BRANT

1978:	Top Flight Handicap (Northernette)
	Apple Blossom Handicap (Northernette)
1979:	Top Flight Handicap (Waya)
	Beldame Stakes (Waya)
	Santa Barbara Handicap (Waya)
1980:	Flower Bowl Handicap (Just A Game II)
1982:	Delaware Handicap (Jameela)
1983:	Sorority Stakes (Officer's Ball)
	Alabama Stakes (Spit Curl)
1984:	Dwyer Stakes (Track Barron)
	Vosburgh Stakes (Track Barron)
	Coaching Club American Oaks (Class Play)
1985:	Whitney Handicap (Track Barron)
	Woodward Stakes (Track Barron)
	Champagne Stakes (Mogambo)
	Remsen Stakes (Pillaster)
1986:	Hopeful Stakes (Gulch)
	Futurity Stakes (Gulch)
	Gotham Stakes (Mogambo)
1987:	Wood Memorial Stakes (Gulch)
	Metropolitan Handicap (Gulch)
	Peter Pan Stakes (Leo Castelli)
1988:	Metropolitan Handicap (Gulch)
	Breeders' Cup Sprint (Gulch)
1989:	Matron Stakes (Stella Madrid)
	Frizette Stakes (Stella Madrid)
	Flower Bowl Handicap (River Memories)
1990:	Acorn Stakes (Stella Madrid)
1991:	Matron Stakes (Anh Duong)

DANA BRAY JR.

1977:	Washington D.C. International (Johnny D.)
	Turf Classic (Johnny D.)
1987:	Kentucky Oaks (Buryyourbelief)

O.E. BREAULT

1947: Vosburgh Handicap (With Pleasure)

BREEL STABLE

1951: Sunset Handicap (Alderman)

BREEZY HILL FARM INC.

1976: Michigan Mile and One-Eighth (Sharp Gary)

WILLIAM BRELIANT

1975:	American Handicap (Montmartre)
1977:	Hollywood Juvenile Championship (Noble Bronze)
1978:	California Derby (Noble Bronze)

EDWARD BRENNAN

1986: Hollywood Derby (Spellbound)

BRETZFIELD & OLIVER

1984: San Antonio Stakes (Poley)

MRS. D. BREWSTER

1950: Longacres Mile (Two and Twenty)

BRIARDALE FARM

1963:	Frizette Stakes (Tosmah)
1964:	Matron Handicap (Tosmah)
	Beldame Stakes (Tosmah)
	Arlington Classic (Tosmah)
1966:	Seminole Handicap (Convex)
	John B. Campbell Handicap (Tosmah)

RON BRIMACOMBE, TRUDY McCAFFERY & JOHN TOFFAN

1996: San Felipe Stakes (Odyle)

ELIZABETH BRISBINE

1979: Spinster Stakes (Safe)

W.E. BRITT

1956:	California Derby (No Regrets)
1962:	Del Mar Futurity (Slipped Disc)

BAIRD BRITTINGHAM

1970: John B. Campbell Handicap (Mitey Prince)

MRS. THOMAS BRITTINGHAM

1965:	Carter Handicap (Viking Spirit)
	Californian Stakes (Viking Spirit)

BROADMOOR STABLE

1982:	United Nations Handicap (Naskra's Breeze)
	Man o' War Stakes (Naskra's Breeze)

ALBERT BROCCOLI

1985:	Vanity Handicap (Dontstop Themusic)
	Spinster Stakes (Dontstop Themusic)

MR. and MRS. ALBERT BROCCOLI

1993:	Breeders' Cup Juvenile (Brocco)
1994:	Santa Anita Derby (Brocco)

BROKAW INC., JOHNSON & H.C. VANDERVOORT

1970: Hollywood Gold Cup (Pleasure Seeker)

BROLITE FARM

1948: Inglewood Handicap (With Pleasure)

MAURICE BRONFMAN

1985: Tropical Park Derby (Irish Sur)

BROOKFIELD FARM

1947:	Garden State Stakes (Itsabet)
1950:	Garden State Stakes (Iswas)
1952:	San Juan Capistrano Handicap (Intent)
	Santa Anita Maturity (Intent)
	Pimlico Futurity (Isasmoothie)
	Matron Stakes (Is Proud)
1953:	San Juan Capistrano Handicap (Intent)
1956:	Fall Highweight Handicap (Impromptu)
1957:	Fall Highweight Handicap (Itobe)
1958:	Futurity Stakes (Intentionally)
	Pimlico Futurity (Intentionally)
1959:	Withers Stakes (Intentionally)
	Jerome Handicap (Intentionally)
1984:	Jerome Handicap (Is Your Pleasure)

BROOKMEADE STABLE

1946:	Swift Stakes (Master Bid)
1947:	Tremont Stakes (Inseparable)
	Frizette Stakes (Slumber Song)
1949:	Saratoga Special (More Sun)
	Dixie Handicap (Chains)
1950:	Louisiana Derby (Greek Ship)
	Metropolitan Handicap (Greek Ship)
	Monmouth Handicap (Greek Ship)
	Spinaway Stakes (Atalanta)
	Matron Stakes (Atalanta)
	Saranac Handicap (Sunglow)
	Discovery Handicap (Sunglow)
1951:	Preakness Stakes (Bold)
	Saranac Handicap (Bold)
	Vosburgh Handicap (War King)
	Widener Handicap (Sunglow)
1952:	Selima Stakes (Tritium)
	Florida Derby (Sky Ship)
1953:	Saranac Handicap (First Aid)
	Aqueduct Handicap (First Aid)
1954:	Spinaway Stakes (Gandharva)
	Tropical Handicap (Capeador)
	Hialeah Turf Handicap (Picador)
1955:	Roamer Handicap (Sailor)
	Fall Highweight Handicap (Sailor)
	Pimlico Special (Sailor)
	Whitney Stakes (First Aid)
1956:	Delaware Handicap (Flower Bowl)
	Ladies Handicap (Flower Bowl)
	Gulfstream Park Handicap (Sailor)
	John B. Campbell Memorial Handicap (Sailor)
1958:	Acorn Stakes (Big Effort)
	Delaware Oaks (Big Effort)
	Widener Handicap (Oligarchy)
1959:	Belmont Stakes (Sword Dancer)
	Travers Stakes (Sword Dancer)
	Metropolitan Handicap (Sword Dancer)
	Monmouth Handicap (Sword Dancer)
	Woodward Stakes (Sword Dancer)
	Jockey Club Gold Cup (Sword Dancer)
	Top Flight Handicap (Big Effort)
1960:	Grey Lag Handicap (Sword Dancer)
	Suburban Handicap (Sword Dancer)
	Woodward Stakes (Sword Dancer)
	Gardenia Stakes (Bowl of Flowers)
	Frizette Stakes (Bowl of Flowers)
1961:	Acorn Stakes (Bowl of Flowers)
	Coaching Club American Oaks (Bowl of Flowers)
	Spinster Stakes (Bowl of Flowers)
1969:	Sorority Stakes (Box the Compass)
1970:	Champagne Stakes (Limit to Reason)
	Pimlico-Laurel Futurity (Limit to Reason)
	Ohio Derby (Climber)

GILES BROPHY

1990:	Gotham Stakes (Thirty Six Red)
	Wood Memorial Stakes (Thirty Six Red)

G. BROPHY, WILLIAM CONDREN & JOSEPH CORNACCHIA

1991:	Blue Grass Stakes (Strike the Gold)
	Kentucky Derby (Strike the Gold)

GRAHAM BROWN

1957:	Spinster Stakes (Bornastar)
1958:	Vineland Handicap (Bornastar)
	Spinster Stakes (Bornastar)
1960:	Breeders' Futurity (He's a Pistol)
1966:	Vosburgh Handicap (Gallant Romeo)

HARRY BROWN

1953: Del Mar Handicap (Goose Khal)

JOE W. BROWN

1949:	Louisiana Derby (Rookwood)
1950:	Firenze Handicap (Red Camelia)
	New Orleans Handicap (Red Camelia)
1951:	Beldame Handicap (Thelma Berger)
1952:	Acorn Stakes (Parading Lady)
	Vosburgh Handicap (Parading Lady)
1953:	Louisiana Derby (Matagorda)
1954:	Louisiana Derby (Gigantic)
1955:	San Antonio Handicap (Gigantic)
	Carter Handicap (Bobby Brocato)
1958:	California Derby (Nice Guy)
	New Orleans Handicap (Tenacious)
1959:	New Orleans Handicap (Tenacious)

MRS. JOE W. BROWN

1964:	New Orleans Handicap (Green Hornet)
1965:	Louisiana Derby (Dapper Delegate)
1967:	New Orleans Handicap (Cabildo)
1968:	Louisiana Derby (Kentucky Sherry)
1982:	Louisiana Derby (El Baba)

BROWN & KING

1957: San Luis Rey Handicap (Posadas)

DR. and MRS. T.M. BROWN

1961: Vanity Handicap (Perizade)

BRUN, KATZ & ROBERTS

1976: Santa Anita Derby (An Act)

JOSEPH BRUNETTI

1958: Pimlico Special (Vertex)

JOSEPH BRUNETTI & F.A. PIARULLI

1958:	Trenton Handicap (Vertex)
1959:	Gulfstream Park Handicap (Vertex)
	John B. Campbell Handicap (Vertex)
	Grey Lag Handicap (Vertex)

BRUNSWICK FARM
1968: Ohio Derby (Te Vega)

BRUSHWOOD STABLE
1984: Tropical Park Derby (Morning Bob)
1985: Belmont Stakes (Creme Fraiche)
American Derby (Creme Fraiche)
Jerome Handicap (Creme Fraiche)
Super Derby (Creme Fraiche)
1986: Jockey Club Gold Cup (Creme Fraiche)
1987: Jockey Club Gold Cup (Creme Fraiche)
Meadowlands Cup (Creme Fraiche)
2003: Secretariat Stakes (Kicken Kris)

BRUSHWOOD STABLE & DERRY MEETING FARM
1994: Jim Dandy Stakes (Unaccounted For)

BRYNALAN STABLE
1958: Display Handicap (Civet)

B.T. ENERGY & WANAJA FARM
1983: Fantasy Stakes (Brindy Brindy)

BUCKLAND FARM
1971: Ladies Handicap (Sea Saga)
1974: Futurity Stakes (Just the Time)
1975: Sapling Stakes (Full Out)
1980: Remsen Stakes (Pleasant Colony)
1981: Wood Memorial Stakes (Pleasant Colony)
Kentucky Derby (Pleasant Colony)
Preakness Stakes (Pleasant Colony)
Woodward Stakes (Pleasant Colony)
1982: Fantasy Stakes (Flying Partner)
1988: Flamingo Stakes (Cherokee Colony)
1989: Santa Barbara Handicap (No Review)
1991: Oak Leaf Stakes (Pleasant Stage)
Breeders' Cup Juvenile Fillies (Pleasant Stage)
1992: Suburban Handicap (Pleasant Tap)
Jockey Club Gold Cup (Pleasant Tap)
Californian Stakes (Another Review)

BUCKRAM OAK FARM
1980: Turf Classic (Anifa)
1982: Illinois Derby (Star Gallant)
1985: Turf Classic (Noble Fighter)
1993: Charles H. Strub Stakes (Siberian Summer)
2003: Hopeful Stakes (Silver Wagon)
Lane's End Breeders' Futurity (Eurosilver)

BUDGET STABLE
2001: Santa Monica Handicap (Nany's Sweep)

BUENA SUERTE STABLE
1968: Del Mar Debutante Stakes (Fourth Round)

T.D. BUHL
1953: Michigan Mile (Second Avenue)
1963: Ohio Derby (Lemon Twist)
1964: Louisiana Derby (Grecian Princess)

JUDY BUJNICKI
1984: Sapling Stakes (Doubly Clear)

GEORGE BUNN
1991: San Antonio Handicap (Farma Way)
Santa Anita Handicap (Farma Way)
Pimlico Special (Farma Way)

RUTH BUNN
1982: Golden Harvest Handicap (Miss Huntington)

MARTIN BURDETTE-COUTTS & JAMES NELSON
1984: Oak Tree Invitational Stakes (Both Ends Burning)
1985: Hollywood Inv. Handicap (Both Ends Burning)

MRS. JOSEPH O. BURGWIN
1970: Matron Stakes (Bonnie and Gay)

JAN BURKE
1954: Jerome Handicap (Martyr)
1956: Brooklyn Handicap (Dedicate)
Whitney Stakes (Dedicate)
Hawthorne Gold Cup (Dedicate)
1957: John B. Campbell Memorial Handicap (Dedicate)
Monmouth Handicap (Dedicate)
Woodward Stakes (Dedicate)
1959: Sunset Handicap (Whodunit)

W.P. BURKE & SHEILA PIERCE
1972: Arlington-Washington Lassie Stakes (Natural Sound)

JAMES & SUE BURNS
1997: Kentucky Oaks (Blushing K.D.)

LEROY BURNS
1957: Gallant Fox Handicap (Eddie Schmidt)

MR. and MRS. MEL BURNS
1963: Del Mar Futurity (Perris)

BWAMAZON FARM
1955: Breeders' Futurity (Jovial Jove)
Arlington Lassie Stakes (Judy Rullah)
1966: Jersey Derby (Creme dela Creme)
1967: Arlington-Washington Futurity (T.V. Commercial)
Breeders' Futurity (T.V. Commercial)
1971: Washington Park Handicap (Well Mannered)
1972: California Derby (Quack)
Hollywood Gold Cup (Quack)
Alcibiades Stakes (Coraggioso)
1973: Frizette Stakes (Bundler)
Californian Stakes (Quack)
1974: Ladies Handicap (Coraggioso)
Californian Stakes (Quack)
1981: Arlington-Washington Futurity (Lets Dont Fight)
1982: Breeders' Futurity (Highland Park)
1983: Secretariat Stakes (Fortnightly)

EDGAR CAIBETT
1971: Kentucky Derby (Canonero II)
Preakness Stakes (Canonero II)

CAIN HOY STABLE
1950: Acorn Stakes (Siama)
Monmouth Oaks (Siama)
Comely Handicap (Siama)
1951: Champagne Stakes (Armageddon)
1952: Gazelle Stakes (Hushaby Baby)
Withers Stakes (Armageddon)
1953: Garden State Stakes (Turn-to)
Kentucky Derby (Dark Star)
1954: Champagne Stakes (Flying Fury)
Coaching Club American Oaks (Cherokee Rose)
Flamingo Stakes (Turn-to)
1955: Kentucky Oaks (Lalun)
Beldame Handicap (Lalun)
Blue Grass Stakes (Racing Fool)
1956: Manhattan Handicap (Flying Fury)
1958: Dwyer Handicap (Victory Morn)
1959: Suburban Handicap (Bald Eagle)
Gallant Fox Handicap (Bald Eagle)
Washington D.C. International (Bald Eagle)
Princess Pat Stakes (Heavenly Body)
Matron Stakes (Heavenly Body)
Kentucky Oaks (Hidden Talent)
1960: Widener Handicap (Bald Eagle)
Gulfstream Park Handicap (Bald Eagle)
Metropolitan Handicap (Bald Eagle)
Aqueduct Handicap (Bald Eagle)
Washington D.C. International (Bald Eagle)
Kentucky Oaks (Make Sail)
Alabama Stakes (Make Sail)
Arlington Handicap (One-Eyed King)
1961: Saratoga Special (Battle Joined)
Top Flight Handicap (Make Sail)
1962: Futurity Stakes (Never Bend)
Cowdin Stakes (Never Bend)
Champagne Stakes (Never Bend)
Lawrence Realization Stakes (Battle Joined)
Roamer Handicap (Dead Ahead)
1963: Kentucky Oaks (Sally Ship)
Flamingo Stakes (Never Bend)
1964: Suburban Handicap (Iron Peg)
1967: Futurity Stakes (Captain's Gig)
1969: Withers Stakes (Ack Ack)
Arlington Classic (Ack Ack)

FRANK CALABRESE
1994: Ohio Derby (Exclusive Praline)
1997: Frizette Stakes (Silver Maiden)

VICTORIA CALANTONI
1993: Santa Anita Handicap (Sir Beaufort)

STEVEN CALDER
1970: Mother Goose Stakes (Office Queen)

FRANK CALDWELL
1971: Santa Anita Derby (Jim French)
Dwyer Handicap (Jim French)

PETER CALLAHAN
1999: Futurity Stakes (Bevo)

CALUMET FARM
1946: Widener Handicap (Armed)
Dixie Handicap (Armed)
Suburban Handicap (Armed)
Washington Park Handicap (Armed)
Arlington Matron Handicap (Good Blood)
Vineland Handicap (Good Blood)
1947: McLennan Handicap (Armed)
Widener Handicap (Armed)
Gulfstream Park Handicap (Armed)
Stars and Stripes Handicap (Armed)
Arlington Handicap (Armed)
Washington Park Handicap (Armed)
Withers Stakes (Faultless)
Flamingo Stakes (Faultless)
Blue Grass Stakes (Faultless)
Preakness Stakes (Faultless)
Washington Park Futurity (Bewitch)
Arlington Lassie Stakes (Bewitch)
Princess Pat Stakes (Bewitch)
Pimlico Futurity (Citation)
Futurity Stakes (Citation)
Selima Stakes (Whirl Some)
Marguerite Stakes (Whirl Some)
American Derby (Fervent)
Pimlico Special (Fervent)
Matron Stakes (Inheritance)
1948: Flamingo Stakes (Citation)
Kentucky Derby (Citation)
Preakness Stakes (Citation)
Belmont Stakes (Citation)
American Derby (Citation)
Jockey Club Gold Cup (Citation)
Stars and Stripes Handicap (Citation)
Pimlico Special (Citation)
Blue Grass Stakes (Coaltown)
Jerome Handicap (Coaltown)
Dixie Handicap (Fervent)
Washington Park Handicap (Fervent)
Gallant Fox Handicap (Faultless)
1949: McLennan Handicap (Coaltown)
Widener Handicap (Coaltown)
Gulfstream Park Handicap (Coaltown)
Gallant Fox Handicap (Coaltown)
Arlington Handicap (Coaltown)
Stars and Stripes Handicap (Coaltown)
Washington Park Handicap (Coaltown)
Kentucky Derby (Ponder)
Arlington Classic (Ponder)
American Derby (Ponder)
Lawrence Realization Stakes (Ponder)
Jockey Club Gold Cup (Ponder)
Kentucky Oaks (Wistful)
Pimlico Oaks (Wistful)
Coaching Club American Oaks (Wistful)
Champagne Stakes (Theory)
Arlington Lassie Stakes (Dutchess Peg)
Vineland Handicap (Bewitch)
1950: San Antonio Handicap (Ponder)
Arlington Handicap (Ponder)
Santa Anita Maturity (Ponder)
Santa Margarita Handicap (Two Lea)
Black Helen Handicap (Bewitch)
1951: American Handicap (Citation)
Hollywood Gold Cup (Citation)
Arlington Futurity (Hill Gail)
Princess Pat Stakes (A Gleam)
Vanity Handicap (Bewitch)
San Antonio Handicap (All Blue)
1952: Kentucky Oaks (Real Delight)
Black-Eyed Susan Stakes (Real Delight)
Coaching Club American Oaks (Real Delight)
Arlington Matron Stakes (Real Delight)
Beldame Handicap (Real Delight)
Hollywood Oaks (A Gleam)
Cinema Handicap (A Gleam)
Westerner Stakes (A Gleam)
Arlington Classic (Mark-Ye-Well)
American Derby (Mark-Ye-Well)
Lawrence Realization Stakes (Mark-Ye-Well)
Vanity Handicap (Two Lea)
Hollywood Gold Cup (Two Lea)
Santa Anita Derby (Hill Gail)
Kentucky Derby (Hill Gail)
Del Mar Debutante Stakes (Lap Full)
1953: Santa Anita Handicap (Mark-Ye-Well)
Santa Anita Maturity (Mark-Ye-Well)
Starlet Stakes (Arrogate)
Kentucky Oaks (Bubbley)
Arlington Matron Handicap (Real Delight)
Santa Anita Derby (Chanlea)
Golden Gate Handicap (Fleet Bird)

1954: Cinema Handicap (Miz Clementine)
California Derby (Miz Clementine)
San Antonio Handicap (Mark-Ye-Well)
Sunset Handicap (Fleet Bird)
Vanity Handicap (Bubbley)
1956: Kentucky Oaks (Princess Turia)
Acorn Stakes (Princess Turia)
Garden State Stakes (Barbizon)
Acorn Stakes (Beyond)
Everglades Stakes (Liberty Sun)
Preakness Stakes (Fabius)
Trenton Handicap (Bardstown)
1957: Tropical Handicap (Bardstown)
Widener Handicap (Bardstown)
Gulfstream Park Handicap (Bardstown)
Everglades Stakes (Gen. Duke)
Florida Derby (Gen. Duke)
Black Helen Handicap (Amoret)
Delaware Handicap (Princess Turia)
Kentucky Derby (Iron Liege)
1958: Everglades Stakes (Tim Tam)
Flamingo Stakes (Tim Tam)
Florida Derby (Tim Tam)
Kentucky Derby (Tim Tam)
Preakness Stakes (Tim Tam)
Coaching Club American Oaks (A Glitter)
Monmouth Oaks (A Glitter)
McLennan Handicap (Iron Liege)
1959: Tropical Park Handicap (Bardstown)
Widener Handicap (Bardstown)
Black Helen Handicap (Rosewood)
1960: Tropical Park Handicap (On-and-On)
McLennan Handicap (On-and-On)
Brooklyn Handicap (On-and-On)
1961: American Derby (Beau Prince)
Travers Stakes (Beau Prince)
McLennan Handicap (Yorky)
Widener Handicap (Yorky)
1962: Widener Handicap (Yorky)
Michigan Mile and One-Sixteenth (Beau Prince)
1964: Black Helen Handicap (Princess Arle)
1966: Hialeah Turf Cup (Kentucky Jug)
1968: Everglades Stakes (Forward Pass)
Florida Derby (Forward Pass)
Blue Grass Stakes (Forward Pass)
Kentucky Derby (Forward Pass)
Preakness Stakes (Forward Pass)
American Derby (Forward Pass)
1970: John B. Campbell Handicap (Best Turn)
Vosburgh Handicap (Best Turn)
1971: Florida Derby (Eastern Fleet)
Pontiac Grand Prix Stakes (Son Ange)
1972: Hialeah Turf Cup (Gleaming)
1973: Hialeah Turf Cup (Gleaming)
1977: Fantasy Stakes (Our Mims)
Coaching Club American Oaks (Our Mims)
Alabama Stakes (Our Mims)
Delaware Handicap (Our Mims)
Sapling Stakes (Alydar)
Champagne Stakes (Alydar)
1978: Flamingo Stakes (Alydar)
Florida Derby (Alydar)
Blue Grass Stakes (Alydar)
Arlington Classic (Alydar)
Travers Stakes (Alydar)
Whitney Stakes (Alydar)
Sapling Stakes (Tim the Tiger)
1979: Fantasy Stakes (Davona Dale)
Kentucky Oaks (Davona Dale)
Acorn Stakes (Davona Dale)
Mother Goose Stakes (Davona Dale)
Coaching Club American Oaks (Davona Dale)
1980: Mother Goose Stakes (Sugar and Spice)
1981: Matron Stakes (Before Dawn)
1983: Delaware Handicap (May Day Eighty)
1990: San Antonio Handicap (Criminal Type)
Pimlico Special (Criminal Type)
Metropolitan Handicap (Criminal Type)
Hollywood Gold Cup (Criminal Type)
Whitney Handicap (Criminal Type)

CHARLES CALVIN & KAIM
1959: Arlington Matron Handicap (Wiggle II)

JULIO CAMARGO, SANTA ESCOLASTICA STABLE, M. SIMON
2002: Alabama Stakes (Farda Amiga)

CAMIJO STABLE
1975: San Antonio Stakes (Cheriepe)

MRS. H.J. CAMM
1955: Arlington Matron Handicap (Arab Actress)

MR. and MRS. RAY CAMP
1957: William P. Kyne Memorial Handicap (Pibe Carlitos)
1958: Westerner Stakes (Strong Bay)

ALEX CAMPBELL JR.
1989: Demoiselle Stakes (Rootentootenwooten)
1990: Top Flight Handicap (Dreamy Mimi)
1995: Santa Maria Handicap (Queens Court Queen)
Santa Margarita Handicap (Queens Court Queen)
1996: Santa Anita Handicap (Mr. Purple)

ALEX CAMPBELL JR. & ARTHUR B. HANCOCK III
1988: Kentucky Oaks (Goodbye Halo)
Mother Goose Stakes (Goodbye Halo)
Coaching Club American Oaks (Goodbye Halo)
1989: La Canada Stakes (Goodbye Halo)

BRUCE CAMPBELL
1961: John B. Campbell Handicap (Conestoga)

COLIN CAMPBELL
1965: Bowling Green Handicap (Or et Argent)
Dixie Handicap (Or et Argent)

JOHNNY CAMPO
1981: Meadowlands Cup (Princelet)

CAMPTOWN STABLE
1993: Norfolk Stakes (Shepherd's Field)

CANADIANA FARMS
1973: Del Mar Debutante Stakes (Fleet Peach)

CANAM EAST STABLE
1977: Carter Handicap (Gentle King)

R. CANO
1973: Vosburgh Handicap (Aljamin)

JOHN CANTY & CASTLEBROOK FARM
1972: San Luis Rey Handicap (Nor II)

THOMAS CAPEHART, S. CHILLINGWORTH & JACK LIEBAU
1985: Oak Tree Invitational (Yashgan)

ROBERT CAPORELLA
1984: Fountain of Youth Stakes (Darn That Alarm)

THOMISINA CAPORELLA
1986: Delaware Handicap (Shocker T.)

CARDIFF STUD FARM
1976: Champions Invitational Handicap (King Pellinore)
American Handicap (King Pellinore)
Oak Tree Invitational Stakes (King Pellinore)
Sunset Handicap (Caucasus)
Manhattan Handicap (Caucasus)
1977: San Luis Rey Stakes (Caucasus)
1979: Del Mar Futurity (The Carpenter)
Norfolk Stakes (The Carpenter)
1982: Matriarch Stakes (Pale Purple)

CARDIFF STUD FARM & ANDERSON FOWLER
1983: Florida Derby (Croeso)

CARDIFF STUD FARM & T-90 RANCH
1983: San Felipe Handicap (Desert Wine)
1984: Californian Stakes (Desert Wine)
Hollywood Gold Cup (Desert Wine)
Charles H. Strub Stakes (Desert Wine)

MRS. VERNON CARDY
1955: Selima Stakes (Levee)
1956: Coaching Club American Oaks (Levee)
Monmouth Oaks (Levee)
Beldame Handicap (Levee)

THOMAS CAREY
1992: Super Derby (Senor Tomas)

BUDDY CARLESIMO JR. & GREGORY MODAS
1990: Ruffian Handicap (Quick Mischief)

CARLISLE & SHERIDAN
1984: Hollywood Derby (Foscarini)

CAROLYN K STABLE
1954: Molly Pitcher Handicap (Shady Tune)

JAIME CARRION
1999: Walmac International Alcibiades Stakes (Scratch Pad)

DEL CARROLL
1974: Jersey Derby (Better Arbitor)

H. CARROLL, ALEX KARKENNY, R. LEVY & WM. ROBERTS
1996: Hopeful Stakes (Smoke Glacken)
1997: Frank J. De Francis Memorial Dash (Smoke Glacken)

R.B. CARROLL
1946: Gulfstream Handicap (Do-Reigh-Me)

CARTER, WILL FARISH III & EDWARD HUDSON
1984: Oak Leaf Stakes (Folk Art)

MR. and MRS. DOUGLAS CARVER
1974: Oak Leaf Stakes (Cut Class)

CAMILIA CASBY & DONALD & MARY ZUCKERMAN
1998: Buick Pegasus Handicap (Tomorrows Cat)

EUGENE CASHMAN
1975: Hopeful Stakes (Eustace)
1976: Arkansas Derby (Elocutionist)
Preakness Stakes (Elocutionist)

JAMES CASSELS & BOB ZOLLERS
2002: Arkansas Derby (Private Emblem)

J. CASTLE
1974: Frizette Stakes (Molly Ballentine)

CAVALIER STABLE
1995: Secretariat Stakes (Hawk Attack)

MR. and MRS. THOMAS CAVANAGH
1981: La Canada Stakes (Summer Siren)

CEE'S STABLE
2001: Breeders' Cup Classic (Tiznow)
2003: Ancient Title Breeders' Cup Handicap (Avanzado)

CHARLES CELLA
1995: Oak Tree Invitational Stakes (Northern Spur)
Breeders' Cup Turf (Northern Spur)

CELTIC PRIDE STABLE
1998: Toyota Blue Grass Stakes (Halory Hunter)
Moet Champagne Stakes (The Groom Is Red)
2000: Champagne Stakes (A.P. Valentine)

CENTAUR FARMS
2001: Gazelle Handicap (Exogenous)
Beldame Stakes (Exogenous)

CENTENNIAL FARMS
1988: Acorn Stakes (Aptostar)
1991: NYRA Mile Handicap (Rubiano)
1992: Carter Handicap (Rubiano)
Vosburgh Stakes (Rubiano)
1993: Belmont Stakes (Colonial Affair)
1994: Whitney Handicap (Colonial Affair)
Jockey Club Gold Cup (Colonial Affair)

CENTENNIAL FARMS, LILLIAN DURST & WILL FARISH III
1998: Fountain of Youth Stakes (Lil's Lad)

B.D. CHAIT
1949: Trenton Handicap (Sky Miracle)

ECURIE CHALHOUB
1997: Hollywood Turf Cup (River Bay)
1999: Charles Whittingham Handicap (River Bay)

HENRY CHALHOUB
1992: Arlington Million (Dear Doctor)

CHANCE HILL FARM
1972: Sorority Stakes (Sparkalark)
1973: Manhattan Handicap (London Company)

DR. JOHN CHANDLER
1998: Sword Dancer Invitational Handicap (Cetewayo)
2002: Gulfstream Park Breeders' Cup Handicap (Cetewayo)

DR. and MRS. J. CHANDLER, S. McGAUGHEY, AUTREY OTTO
1998: Las Virgenes Stakes (Keeper Hill)
Kentucky Oaks (Keeper Hill)
1999: Three Chimneys Spinster Stakes (Keeper Hill)

J.R. CHAPMAN
1967: Ohio Derby (Out the Window)

R.E. CHAPMAN
1976: Hialeah Turf Cup (Legion)
1977: Donn Handicap (Legion)

CHARFRAN STABLE
1952: Gulfstream Park Handicap (Crafty Admiral)
Brooklyn Handicap (Crafty Admiral)
Washington Park Handicap (Crafty Admiral)
1953: McLennan Handicap (Crafty Admiral)
Gulfstream Park Handicap (Crafty Admiral)
New York Handicap (Crafty Admiral)
1955: Bougainvillea Turf Handicap (Cascanuez)
1958: Cowdin Stakes (Crafty Skipper)

CHAR-MARI STABLE & ANTHONY TORNETTA
1993: Wood Memorial Stakes (Storm Tower)

BRANDON & MARIANNE CHASE
1992: Fantasy Stakes (Race the Wild Wind)
1993: Santa Maria Handicap (Race the Wild Wind)
1994: Gotham Stakes (Irgun)
Wood Memorial Stakes (Irgun)

CHATEAU RIDGE FARM
1995: Arkansas Derby (Dazzling Falls)

CHAUS STABLE
1987: Ladies Handicap (Nastique)
1988: Delaware Handicap (Nastique)
1989: Delaware Handicap (Nastique)

GERRY CHEEVERS
1976: Laurel Futurity (Royal Ski)
Remsen Stakes (Royal Ski)

C.T. CHENERY
1949: Cowdin Stakes (Hill Prince)
1950: Wood Memorial Stakes (Hill Prince)
Withers Stakes (Hill Prince)
Preakness Stakes (Hill Prince)
American Derby (Hill Prince)
Jerome Handicap (Hill Prince)
Jockey Club Gold Cup (Hill Prince)
Sunset Handicap (Hill Prince)
1951: Aqueduct Handicap (Bryan G.)
Westchester Handicap (Bryan G.)
Pimlico Special (Bryan G.)
New York Handicap (Hill Prince)
1952: Aqueduct Handicap (Bryan G.)
1955: Gazelle Stakes (Manotick)
Ladies Handicap (Manotick)
1956: Roamer Handicap (Third Brother)
1957: Coaching Club American Oaks (Willamette)
Molly Pitcher Handicap (Manotick)
1958: Hopeful Stakes (First Landing)
Champagne Stakes (First Landing)
Garden State Stakes (First Landing)
Spinaway Stakes (Rich Tradition)
Selima Stakes (Rich Tradition)

CHERRY OCA STABLE
1949: Massachusetts Handicap (First Nighter)

CHERRY VALLEY FARM
1996: Spinaway Stakes (Oath)

CHEVALIER STABLE
1989: Brooklyn Handicap (Forever Silver)
1992: Remsen Stakes (Silver of Silver)

CHEVELEY PARK STUD & THE THOROUGHBRED CORP.
1998: Hollywood Turf Handicap (Storm Trooper)

SHERWOOD CHILLINGWORTH
1985: Metropolitan Handicap (Forzando II)

CHINN & MARR
1981: California Derby (Always a Cinch)

SURESH CHINTAMANENI
1995: Test Stakes (Chaposa Springs)

J. CHISHOLM, HORIZON STABLE, M. JARVIS & J.P. REDDAM
2003: Travers Stakes (Ten Most Wanted)
Super Derby (Ten Most Wanted)

DR. A.J. CHLAD & SAM MEVORACH
1982: Monmouth Handicap (Mehmet)

DR. A.J. CHLAD, SAM MEVORACH & ELIZABETH VALLONE
1982: Meadowlands Cup (Mehmet)

CHOCKTAW RACING & DUNCAN TAYLOR
1999: Hempstead Handicap (Sister Act)

CHRISTIANA STABLE
1947: Delaware Oaks (Camargo)
1948: Molly Pitcher Handicap (Camargo)
1954: Pimlico Futurity (Thinking Cap)
1955: Travers Stakes (Thinking Cap)
Lawrence Realization Stakes (Thinking Cap)
1958: Delaware Handicap (Endine)
Ladies Handicap (Endine)
1959: Delaware Handicap (Endine)
1961: Futurity Stakes (Cyane)
1962: Dwyer Handicap (Cyane)
1963: Manhattan Handicap (Smart)
1964: Massachusetts Handicap (Smart)
Gallant Fox Handicap (Smart)
1965: Massachusetts Handicap (Smart)
1969: Delaware Handicap (Obeah)
1970: Futurity Stakes (Salem)
Delaware Handicap (Obeah)
1973: Hempstead Handicap (Light Hearted)
Maskette Handicap (Light Hearted)
1976: Jerome Handicap (Dance Spell)
1982: Alabama Stakes (Broom Dance)
Blue Grass Stakes (Linkage)
1989: Breeders' Cup Juvenile Fillies (Go for Wand)
1990: Ashland Stakes (Go for Wand)
Mother Goose Stakes (Go for Wand)
Alabama Stakes (Go for Wand)
Maskette Stakes (Go for Wand)
Beldame Stakes (Go for Wand)

MRS. TILYOU CHRISTOPHER
1960: Hialeah Turf Cup (Amerigo)
San Juan Capistrano Handicap (Amerigo)

V. CHRISTOPHER & P.S. HEISLER
1969: Ohio Derby (Berkley Prince)

P.C. CHUCK
1984: Champagne Stakes (For Certain Doc)

NORMAN CHURCH
1946: Inglewood Handicap (Quick Reward)
American Handicap (Quick Reward)
1948: California Derby (May Reward)
San Felipe Stakes (May Reward)
Will Rogers Handicap (Speculation)

CIRCLE C RANCH & WITT
1973: Hollywood Oaks (Sandy Blue)

CIRCLE M FARM
1946: Marguerite Stakes (Cosmic Missile)
1947: Hopeful Stakes (Relic)
Gazelle Stakes (Cosmic Missile)
1952: Delaware Oaks (Big Mo)
1958: Sapling Stakes (Watch Your Step)
1970: Breeders' Futurity (Man of the Moment)

CIRCLE TWP STABLE
1960: American Handicap (Prize Host)

CISLEY STABLE & BLANCHE LEVY
1987: Fountain of Youth Stakes (Bet Twice)
Belmont Stakes (Bet Twice)
Haskell Invitational Handicap (Bet Twice)

CLAIBORNE FARM
1954: Arlington Lassie Stakes (Delta)
Princess Pat Stakes (Delta)
1955: Matron Stakes (Doubledogdare)
Alcibiades Stakes (Doubledogdare)
1956: Breeders' Futurity (Round Table)
Arlington Matron Handicap (Delta)
Spinster Stakes (Doubledogdare)
1957: Acorn Stakes (Bayou)
Delaware Oaks (Bayou)
Gazelle Handicap (Bayou)
Maskette Handicap (Bayou)
Garden State Stakes (Nadir)
Spinaway Stakes (Sequoia)
1958: American Derby (Nadir)
1959: Arlington Lassie Stakes (Monarchy)
Arlington Classic (Dunce)
American Derby (Dunce)
1963: Saratoga Special (Duel)
Breeders' Futurity (Duel)
1965: Spinaway Stakes (Moccasin)
Matron Stakes (Moccasin)
Selima Stakes (Moccasin)
Gardenia Stakes (Moccasin)
Charles H. Strub Stakes (Duel)
1967: Arkansas Derby (Monitor)
1968: Breeders' Futurity (Dike)
1969: Gotham Stakes (Dike)
Wood Memorial Stakes (Dike)
California Derby (Jay Ray)
1972: San Juan Capistrano Handicap (Practicante)
1983: Futurity Stakes (Swale)
Young America Stakes (Swale)
Breeders' Futurity (Swale)
1984: Hutcheson Stakes (Swale)
Florida Derby (Swale)
Kentucky Derby (Swale)
Belmont Stakes (Swale)
1987: Futurity Stakes (Forty Niner)
Champagne Stakes (Forty Niner)
1988: Fountain of Youth Stakes (Forty Niner)
Haskell Invitational Handicap (Forty Niner)
Travers Stakes (Forty Niner)
Tropical Park Derby (Digress)
1989: Remsen Stakes (Yonder)
1991: Frizette Stakes (Preach)
1992: Gotham Stakes (Lure)
Breeders' Cup Mile (Lure)
1993: Breeders' Cup Mile (Lure)
1994: Caesars International Handicap (Lure)
1997: Fountain of Youth Stakes (Pulpit)
Toyota Blue Grass Stakes (Pulpit)

CLAIBORNE FARM & ADELE DILSCHNEIDER
1996: Jim Beam Stakes (Roar)
1998: Super Derby (Arch)

CLAIBORNE FARM & HOWARD B. KECK
1960: Inglewood Handicap (Bagdad)

MRS. AMBROSE CLARK
1948: Cowdin Stakes (Algasir)
1950: Vosburgh Handicap (Tea-Maker)

J.C. CLARK
1952: Flamingo Stakes (Charlie McAdam)

MR. and MRS. ROSS CLARK II
1960: San Fernando Stakes (King o' Turf)

STEPHEN CLARK JR.
1976: Fall Highweight Handicap (Relent)
1980: Alabama Stakes (Love Sign)
Beldame Stakes (Love Sign)
1981: Beldame Stakes (Love Sign)

MR. and MRS. STEPHEN CLARK JR.
1970: Cowdin Stakes (Hoist the Flag)

CLASS ACT STABLE
1988: San Juan Capistrano 'Cap (Great Communicator)
Breeders' Cup Turf (Great Communicator)
Hollywood Turf Cup (Great Communicator)
1989: Hollywood Turf Handicap (Great Communicator)

MARY CLASSEN
1975: Ohio Derby (Brent's Prince)

CLASSIC IRE STABLE
1990: Breeders' Cup Mile (Royal Academy)

CHARLTON CLAY
1956: Arlington Lassie Stakes (Leallah)
Alcibiades Stakes (Leallah)
1960: Princess Pat Stakes (Rose Bower)
Matron Stakes (Rose Bower)

ROBERT CLAY
1989: Ashland Stakes (Gorgeous)
Hollywood Oaks (Gorgeous)
1990: La Canada Stakes (Gorgeous)
Apple Blossom Handicap (Gorgeous)
Vanity Handicap (Gorgeous)

ROBERT CLAY & TRACY FARMER
1997: Hempstead Handicap (Hidden Lake)
Go for Wand Stakes (Hidden Lake)
Beldame Stakes (Hidden Lake)

ROBERT CLAY & WINTER FARM
2001: Personal Ensign Handicap (Pompeii)

CLEAR SPRINGS STABLE
1962: Frizette Stakes (Pams Ego)

CLEARWATER STABLE
1954: Sapling Stakes (Royal Coinage)
1957: Carter Handicap (Portersville)
Brooklyn Handicap (Portersville)

LOUISE CLEMENTS
1968: Spinster Stakes (Sale Day)

WILLIAM CLIFTON JR.
1999: Meadowlands Cup Handicap (Pleasant Breeze)

WILLIAM CLIFTON JR. & RUDLEIN STABLE
1996: Travers Stakes (Will's Way)
1997: Whitney Handicap (Will's Way)
Buick Pegasus Handicap (Behrens)
1999: Gulfstream Park Handicap (Behrens)
Oaklawn Handicap (Behrens)
Suburban Handicap (Behrens)
2000: Gulfstream Park Handicap (Behrens)

ALLAN CLORE
1987: Rothmans International Stakes (River Memories)

CHARLES CLORE
1977: Century Handicap (Anne's Pretender)

CLOVER RACING STABLE
1987: Hollywood Derby (Political Ambition)
1988: Hollywood Invitational Handicap (Political Ambition)
1989: Swaps Stakes (Prized)
Breeders' Cup Turf (Prized)
Santa Anita Handicap (Martial Law)

CLOVER RACING STABLE & MEADOWBROOK FARM
1990: San Luis Rey Stakes (Prized)

COBBLEVIEW STABLE & SULLIMAR STABLE
1995: Sword Dancer Invitational Handicap (Kiri's Clown)

COBBLEVIEW STABLE & MARY SULLIVAN
1993: Flower Bowl Handicap (Far Out Beast)

COBRA FARM
1996: Hollywood Turf Cup (Running Flame)
1997: Malibu Stakes (Lord Grillo)
1998: Swaps Stakes (Old Trieste)
1999: Californian Stakes (Old Trieste)

COBRA FARM & GARY VANDEWEGHE
1996: Oak Tree Turf Championship (Admise)

COCKFIELD STABLE
1957: Dixie Handicap (Akbar Khan)

JAMES CODY III
1993: Arlington-Washington Futurity (Polar Expedition)
1994: Jim Beam Stakes (Polar Expedition)

MRS. BEN COHEN
1965: Jersey Derby (Hail to All)
Belmont Stakes (Hail to All)
Travers Stakes (Hail to All)
1985: Ohio Derby (Skip Trial)
Haskell Invitational Handicap (Skip Trial)
Pennsylvania Derby (Skip Trial)
1986: Gulfstream Park Handicap (Skip Trial)
1987: Gulfstream Park Handicap (Skip Trial)

C. COHEN & RUTH FERTEL
1977: New Orleans Handicap (Tudor Tambourine)

ISRAEL COHEN
1984: Laurel Futurity (Mighty Appealing)
Remsen Stakes (Mighty Appealing)

LAUREN COHEN
1994: Swaps Stakes (Silver Music)

RICHARD COHEN
1999: Brooklyn Handicap (Running Stag)

ROY COHEN
1988: Hutcheson Stakes (Perfect Spy)

SEYMOUR COHEN
1981: Futurity Stakes (Irish Martini)

JOSEPH COLANDO
1950: Champagne Stakes (Uncle Miltie)

G.S. COLELLA
1956: McLennan Handicap (Switch On)

COLLINS & FOSTER
1949: San Carlos Handicap (Manyunk)

H.W. COLLINS STABLE
1953: Santa Margarita Handicap (Spanish Cream)

IKE COLLINS
1949: Santa Anita Handicap (Vulcan's Forge)
Suburban Handicap (Vulcan's Forge)

COLONIAL FARM
1971: Pan American Handicap (Chompion)
Dixie Handicap (Chompion)
Massachusetts Handicap (Chompion)

COLTS LTD., JAMES KARP & KENNARD WARFIELD JR.
1997: Manhattan Handicap (Ops Smile)

COLUMBINE STABLE
2002: Hollywood Turf Cup (Sligo Bay)

COLUMBINE STABLE, JAY JONES JR. & TOM NICHOLS
2000: Woodford Reserve Turf Classic (Manndar)
Manhattan Handicap (Manndar)

BROWNELL COMBS
1948: Princess Pat Stakes (Sequence)

BROWNELL COMBS II
1983: Jerome Handicap (A Phenomenon)
Vosburgh Stakes (A Phenomenon)
1985: Everglades Stakes (Rhoman Rule)

BROWNELL COMBS II, EL PECO RANCH & NELSON B. HUNT
1978: Californian Stakes (J.O. Tobin)

LESLIE COMBS II
1956: Widener Handicap (Nashua)
Grey Lag Handicap (Nashua)
Suburban Handicap (Nashua)
Monmouth Handicap (Nashua)
Jockey Club Gold Cup (Nashua)
1967: Alcibiades Stakes (Lady Tramp)
1971: Kentucky Oaks (Silent Beauty)
1978: Alcibiades Stakes (Angel Island)
1983: Matron Stakes (Lucky Lucky Lucky)

LESLIE COMBS II & EQUITES STABLE
1983: Alcibiades Stakes (Lucky Lucky Lucky)
1984: Kentucky Oaks (Lucky Lucky Lucky)

WILLIAM CONDREN & JOSEPH CORNACCHIA
1992: Pimlico Special (Strike the Gold)
Nassau County Handicap (Strike the Gold)
1993: Remsen Stakes (Go for Gin)
1994: Kentucky Derby (Go for Gin)
1996: Pimlico Special (Star Standard)

WM. CONDREN, J. CORNACCHIA & GEORGIA HOFFMAN
1996: Preakness Stakes (Louis Quatorze)
Jim Dandy Stakes (Louis Quatorze)

LUCILLE CONOVER
1994: Test Stakes (Twist Afleet)
1995: Top Flight Handicap (Twist Afleet)

STANLEY CONRAD
1964: Delaware Handicap (Old Hat)
Spinster Stakes (Old Hat)
1965: Black Helen Handicap (Old Hat)
Matron Handicap (Old Hat)
Michigan Mile and One-Eighth (Old Hat)

E. CONSTANIN JR.
1953: Everglades Stakes (Royal Bay Gem)

EDWARD CONSTANTINE & FLAG IS UP FARM
1969: Sunset Handicap (Petrone)
San Juan Capistrano Handicap (Petrone)

CONTRERAS, JIM MAMAKOS & MARC STUBRIN
1975: Sunset Handicap (Cruiser II)
Del Mar Handicap (Cruiser II)

DOLORES CONWAY, J. CORNACCHIA & FRED DeMATTIAS
1999: Champagne Stakes (Greenwood Lake)
Remsen Stakes (Greenwood Lake)

JACK KENT COOKE
1990: San Fernando Stakes (Flying Continental)
Charles H. Strub Stakes (Flying Continental)
Jockey Club Gold Cup (Flying Continental)

1996: Las Virgenes Stakes (Antespend)
Santa Anita Oaks (Antespend)

MICHAEL COOPER & CECILLIA STRAUB-RUBENS
2000: Super Derby (Tiznow)
Breeders' Cup Classic (Tiznow)

M. COOPER & C. STRAUB-RUBENS REVOKABLE TRUST
2001: Santa Anita Handicap (Tiznow)

ALBERT COPPOLA
1982: Travers Stakes (Runaway Groom)

L. CORNELL
1963: Sunset Handicap (Arbitrage)

CORRADINI & DORNEY
1962: Vanity Handicap (Linita)

CORRADINI & NUCCIO
1971: Malibu Stakes (King of Cricket)

ANGELO COSTANZA & RON McANALLY
1990: Arkansas Derby (Silver Ending)
Pegasus Handicap (Silver Ending)

JAMES COTTRELL
1988: Ohio Derby (Jim's Orbit)

ANNE COUGHLAN
1995: Breeders' Cup Mile (Ridgewood Pearl)

COURTLANDT FARMS
2003: Queen Elizabeth II Challenge Cup (Film Maker)

JEAN COUVERCELLE
1993: Breeders' Cup Sprint (Cardmania)

COVERT RANCH
1957: Del Mar Debutante Stakes (Sally Lee)

IRVING & MARJORIE COWAN
1993: Hollywood Oaks (Hollywood Wildcat)
Breeders' Cup Distaff (Hollywood Wildcat)
1994: Gamely Handicap (Hollywood Wildcat)
1995: Jerome Handicap (French Deputy)
2000: Breeders' Cup Mile (War Chant)
2003: Frizette Stakes (Society Selection)

EDWARD A. COX JR.
1986: Alabama Stakes (Classy Cathy)
1988: Ladies Handicap (Banker's Lady)
1989: Top Flight Handicap (Banker's Lady)

CRAGWOOD STABLE
1966: United Nations Handicap (Assagai)
Man o' War Stakes (Assagai)
1968: Santa Anita Derby (Alley Fighter)
1969: Stars and Stripes Handicap (Hawaii)
United Nations Handicap (Hawaii)
Man o' War Stakes (Hawaii)
Kentucky Jockey Club Stakes (Evasive Action)
1970: Stars and Stripes Handicap (Mr. Leader)
1971: Hopeful Stakes (Rest Your Case)
Breeders' Futurity (Windjammer)
Whitney Stakes (Protanto)
1973: Metropolitan Handicap (Tentam)
Del Mar Handicap (Red Reality)

JENNY & SIDNEY CRAIG
2003: Pacific Classic (Candy Ride)

SIDNEY CRAIG
1992: Santa Margarita Handicap (Paseana)
Apple Blossom Handicap (Paseana)
Milady Handicap (Paseana)
Vanity Handicap (Paseana)
Breeders' Cup Distaff (Paseana)
1993: Apple Blossom Handicap (Paseana)
Milady Handicap (Paseana)
Spinster Stakes (Paseana)
Santa Barbara Handicap (Exchange)
1994: Santa Margarita Handicap (Paseana)
Matriarch Stakes (Exchange)
1995: Beverly Hills Handicap (Alpride)
Yellow Ribbon Stakes (Alpride)
1996: Beverly Hills Handicap (Different)
Three Chimneys Spinster Stakes (Different)

RICHARD CRAIGO
1974: American Handicap (Plunk)

HOWARD CRASH & JIM HANKOFF
1988: Californian Stakes (Cutlass Reality)
Hollywood Gold Cup (Cutlass Reality)

C. MARK CRAWFORD JR.
1960: San Felipe Handicap (Flow Line)

PAUL CRESCI
1974: Selima Stakes (Aunt Jin)
1975: New Orleans Handicap (Lord Rebeau)

A.J. CREVOLIN COMPANY INC.
1954: William P. Kyne Handicap (Imbros)
Californian Stakes (Imbros)

ANDY CREVOLIN
1948: Hollywood Oaks (Flying Rhythm)
1950: Westerner Stakes (Valquest)
1951: San Juan Capistrano Handicap (Be Fleet)
1953: San Felipe Handicap (Decorated)
1954: San Felipe Handicap (Determine)
Santa Anita Derby (Determine)
Kentucky Derby (Determine)
1955: Santa Anita Maturity (Determine)
1961: Ladies Handicap (Mighty Fair)

CRIMSON KING FARM
1960: Kentucky Jockey Club Stakes (Crimson Fury)
1961: Garden State Stakes (Crimson Satan)
Pimlico Futurity (Crimson Satan)
1963: Massachusetts Handicap (Crimson Satan)
Michigan Mile and One-Sixteenth (Crimson Satan)
Washington Park Handicap (Crimson Satan)
San Fernando Stakes (Crimson Satan)
Charles H. Strub Stakes (Crimson Satan)
1976: Fantasy Stakes (T.V. Vixen)

RON CROCKETT
1994: American Derby (Vaudeville)
Secretariat Stakes (Vaudeville)

J.N. CROFTON
1950: Santa Susana Stakes (Special Touch)
1951: Santa Margarita Handicap (Special Touch)

JIMMY CROLL
1994: Florida Derby (Holy Bull)
Blue Grass Stakes (Holy Bull)
Metropolitan Handicap (Holy Bull)
Dwyer Stakes (Holy Bull)
Haskell Invitational Handicap (Holy Bull)
Travers Stakes (Holy Bull)
Woodward Stakes (Holy Bull)

MRS. JIMMY CROLL
1966: Sorority Stakes (Like A Charm)

GEORGE CROSS, JOHN ROCHE & LARRY WRIGHT
1985: Sapling Stakes (Hilco Scamper)

JACQUELINE CROTTY
1978: Carter Handicap (Jaipur's Gem)

CROWN STABLE
1973: Sorority Stakes (Irish Sonnet)
1984: Breeders' Cup Sprint (Eillo)

C.F. CULLINAN JR.
1972: Pontiac Grand Prix Stakes (King's Bishop)
Michigan Mile and One-Eighth (King's Bishop)

THOMAS J. CURNES
1988: Swaps Stakes (Lively One)

RAYMOND CURTIS
1970: Flamingo Stakes (My Dad George)
Florida Derby (My Dad George)

CUSTOM TAILORED STABLES
1985: Illinois Derby (Important Business)

LOUISA d'A CARPENTER
1972: Ladies Handicap (Grafitti)
1973: Black Helen Handicap (Grafitti)

JUAN d'AGOSTINO
1961: Gulfstream Park Handicap (Tudor Way)

C. D'ALESSIO
1983: Budweiser Million (Tolomeo)

DALEY & ANN ELMORE
1976: Beverly Hills Handicap (Bastonera II)

DANDAR STABLES
1986: Spinster Stakes (Top Corsage)

DANSAR STABLE
1969: Suburban Handicap (Mr. Right)

CONSTANCE DAPARMA & ARMAND MARCANTONY
1986: Hollywood Invitational Handicap (Flying Pidgeon)

DARBY DAN FARM
1953: Black Helen Handicap (Atalanta)
Beldame Handicap (Atalanta)
1956: Black Helen Handicap (Clear Dawn)
1961: Delaware Oaks (Primonetta)
Alabama Stakes (Primonetta)
1962: Breeders' Futurity (Ornamento)
Coaching Club American Oaks (Bramalea)
Spinster Stakes (Primonetta)
Jerome Handicap (Black Beard)
1963: Blue Grass Stakes (Chateaugay)
Kentucky Derby (Chateaugay)
Belmont Stakes (Chateaugay)
Jerome Handicap (Chateaugay)
1964: Spinaway Stakes (Candalita)
Matron Stakes (Candalita)
1967: Kentucky Derby (Proud Clarion)
1972: Jerome Handicap (True Knight)
Widener Handicap (Good Counsel)
1974: John B. Campbell Handicap (True Knight)
Amory L. Haskell Handicap (True Knight)
Suburban Handicap (True Knight)
Preakness Stakes (Little Current)
Belmont Stakes (Little Current)
Gazelle Handicap (Maud Muller)
1975: Florida Derby (Prince Thou Art)
1983: Hopeful Stakes (Capitol South)
1985: Fountain of Youth Stakes (Proud Truth)
Florida Derby (Proud Truth)
Breeders' Cup Classic (Proud Truth)
1988: Man o' War Stakes (Sunshine Forever)
Turf Classic (Sunshine Forever)
Budweiser International Stakes (Sunshine Forever)
1990: Yellow Ribbon Stakes (Plenty of Grace)
1991: Gotham Stakes (Kyle's Our Man)

LORD DARBY
1985: Budweiser-Arlington Million (Teleprompter)

DARLEY STABLE
2003: Man o' War Stakes (Lunar Sovereign)

BRIAN DAVIDSON
1990: Arlington Invitational Challenge Cup (Beau Genius)
Philip H. Iselin Handicap (Beau Genius)

ALBERT DAVIS
1985: Ladies Handicap (Videogenic)

ROSALEE DAVISON
1981: Vosburgh Stakes (Guilty Conscience)

DAYBREAK FARM
1972: Malibu Stakes (Wing Out)
1980: Meadowlands Cup (Tunerup)
Hawthorne Gold Cup (Tunerup)

D&B ENTERPRISES
1995: Hollywood Turf Cup (Royal Chariot)

de BENEDETTI, O'SHEA, BOB ROBERTS & WILSON
1955: Del Mar Futurity (Blen Host)

WM. de BURGH, PRESTONWOOD FARM & R. SANGSTER
1991: Yellow Ribbon Stakes (Kostroma)
1992: Santa Barbara Handicap (Kostroma)
Beverly D. Stakes (Kostroma)

JOSE de CAMARGO, OLD FRIENDS INC. & WINNER SILK INC.
2002: Kentucky Oaks (Farda Amiga)

P. DeCARLO, R. LaTORRE & HAROLD & R. RUBENSTEIN
1988: Santa Barbara Handicap (Pen Bal Lady)
Gamely Handicap (Pen Bal Lady)

DECEMBER HILL FARM
1998: Early Times Hollywood Derby (Vergennes)

DEE-BOB STABLE
1973: Cinema Handicap (Amen II)
Hollywood Derby (Amen II)

DEE DEE STABLE
1963: Cinema Handicap (Quita Dude)

EDITH DeGIL
1983: Oak Tree Invitational Stakes (Zalataia)

MITCH DEGROOT, DUTCH MASTERS III & MIKE PEGRAM
1992: Breeders' Cup Sprint (Thirty Slews)

HENRYK de KWIATKOWSKI
1981: Hollywood Derby (De La Rose)
1982: Belmont Stakes (Conquistador Cielo)
Dwyer Stakes (Conquistador Cielo)
Metropolitan Handicap (Conquistador Cielo)
1984: Hollywood Futurity (Stephan's Odyssey)
Arlington-Washington Lassie Stakes (Contredance)
Yellow Ribbon Stakes (Sabin)
1985: Dwyer Stakes (Stephan's Odyssey)
Jim Dandy Stakes (Stephan's Odyssey)
1986: Peter Pan Stakes (Danzig Connection)
Belmont Stakes (Danzig Connection)
Acorn Stakes (Lotka)
Young America Stakes (Conquistarose)
1989: Dwyer Stakes (Roi Danzig)
1995: Jim Dandy Stakes (Composer)

DELAPLAINE, SCHAFFER & WOOLSEY
1978: Santa Susana Stakes (Grenzen)

MARVIN DELFINER
1996: Jerome Handicap (Why Change)

HERMAN DELMAN
1951: Kentucky Oaks (How)
Coaching Club American Oaks (How)
1952: Ladies Handicap (How)

DeMARCO, McCLURE, PANIOLO RANCH & PRIM
1983: Widener Handicap (Swing Till Dawn)
Charles H. Strub Stakes (Swing Till Dawn)

GUS DEMARINIS & CAROL ROCCA
1991: Secretariat Stakes (Jackie Wackie)

O.S. DEMING & GENE VAN DEREN
1956: Blue Grass Stakes (Toby B.)
1959: Breeders' Futurity (Toby's Brother)

CAROL DENDER
1997: Ohio Derby (Frisk Me Now)
1998: Suburban Handicap (Frisk Me Now)
1999: Philip H. Iselin Handicap (Frisk Me Now)

MRS. EMIL DENEMARK
1949: Washington Park Futurity (Curtice)
1951: Blue Grass Stakes (Ruhe)

JERRY DENKER
1993: Whitney Handicap (Brunswick)

JAMES & RICHARD DENNIS
2002: Vosburgh Stakes (Bonapaw)

MRS. MAGRUDER DENT
1964: Gotham Stakes (Mr. Moonlight)
Roamer Handicap (Point du Jour)

EMMANEUL de SEROUX & SUMMA STABLE
1989: Gamely Handicap (Fitzwilliam Place)

DESPERADO STABLES, D. McFADDEN, MERRILL STABLES, T. SCHRIBER & R. SEVERSON
2003: Santa Anita Derby (Buddy Gil)

JAMES DEVANEY
1985: Sorority Stakes (Lazer Show)

ROGER DEVENPORT
2001: Breeders' Cup Distaff (Unbridled Elaine)

T.F. DEVEREUX
1955: Michigan Mile (Greatest)

DEVIL ELEVEN STABLE & D.J. STABLE
2001: Fountain of Youth Stakes (Songandaprayer)

D&H STABLE
1955: Sapling Stakes (Needles)
Hopeful Stakes (Needles)
1956: Flamingo Stakes (Needles)
Florida Derby (Needles)
Kentucky Derby (Needles)
Belmont Stakes (Needles)
1957: Diana Handicap (Pardala)
1958: Black Helen Handicap (Pardala)

DIAMOND A RACING CORPORATION
1998: Ballerina Handicap (Stop Traffic)
1999: Santa Monica Handicap (Stop Traffic)
2003: Breeders' Cup Classic/Dodge (Pleasantly Perfect)

DIAMOND A RACING CORP. & HERMAN SARKOWSKY
1999: Norfolk Stakes (Dixie Union)
2000: Haskell Invitational Handicap (Dixie Union)
Malibu Stakes (Dixie Union)

DIAMOND PEG STABLE
1979: Hopeful Stakes (J.P. Brother)

A.C. & K. DIBB
1958: Washington D.C. International (Sailor's Guide)

H.F. DICK
1959: Vanity Handicap (Zev's Joy)

RICHARD DICK
1986: Coaching Club American Oaks (Valley Victory)

PHILIP DILEO
1991: Ohio Derby (Private Man)

DIMICK & HUGHES
1966: Californian Stakes (Travel Orb)

DINWIDDIE FARM
1990: Delaware Handicap (Seattle Dawn)

DIXIANA
1946: Arlington Lassie Stakes (Four Winds)
1947: Breeders' Futurity (Shy Guy)
1948: Arlington Matron Handicap (Four Winds)
New Orleans Handicap (Star Reward)
1949: Princess Pat Stakes (Here's Hoping)
1951: Kentucky Jockey Club Stakes (Sub Fleet)
1953: Hawthorne Gold Cup (Sub Fleet)
1969: Breeders' Futurity (Hard Work)
1982: Arlington Handicap (Flying Target)

FITZ DIXON JR.
1948: Black Helen Handicap (Shotsilk)
1964: Canadian Championship Stakes (Will I Rule)
Dixie Handicap (Will I Rule)
1965: Display Handicap (Brave Lad)

DONALD DIZNEY & JAMES ENGLISH
1996: Gulfstream Park Handicap (Wekiva Springs)
Brooklyn Handicap (Wekiva Springs)
Suburban Handicap (Wekiva Springs)

D&M STABLE
1958: Jockey Club Gold Cup (Inside Tract)

DOGWOOD STABLE
1971: Alcibiades Stakes (Mrs. Cornwallis)
1978: Monmouth Invitational Handicap (Delta Flag)
1985: Rothmans International Stakes (Nassipour)
1986: Secretariat Stakes (Southjet)
Rothmans International Stakes (Southjet)
1988: Laurel Futurity (Luge II)
1989: Hopeful Stakes (Summer Squall)
1990: Jim Beam Stakes (Summer Squall)
Blue Grass Stakes (Summer Squall)
Preakness Stakes (Summer Squall)
Pennsylvania Derby (Summer Squall)
Brooklyn Handicap (Montubio)
1993: Super Derby (Wallenda)
1994: Hopeful Stakes (Wild Escapade)
1996: Frizette Stakes (Storm Song)
Breeders' Cup Juvenile Fillies (Storm Song)
2000: Vosburgh Stakes (Trippi)

LOU DOHERTY
1957: Metropolitan Handicap (Traffic Judge)
Suburban Handicap (Traffic Judge)

HAJIME DOI
1977: Widener Handicap (Yamanin)

JOHN DOLAN & SAM LONGO
2001: Santa Margarita Handicap (Lazy Slusan)
Milady Breeders' Cup Handicap (Lazy Slusan)

EMIL DOLCE
1959: Wood Memorial Stakes (Manassa Mauler)
1960: Trenton Handicap (Manassa Mauler)

C. DOLLASE, BARRY FEY, MOON HAN & FRANK SINATRA
1998: Breeders' Cup Sprint (Reraise)

JOHN DOMINGUEZ & JACK KLUGMAN
1980: California Derby (Jaklin Klugman)
Jerome Handicap (Jaklin Klugman)

DOMINO STUD
2003: Arkansas Derby (Sir Cherokee)

DR. A.R. DONALDSON
1974: Manhattan Handicap (Golden Don)
1977: Ohio Derby (Silver Series)
American Derby (Silver Series)
1978: Widener Handicap (Silver Series)

DR. A.R. DONALDSON & DR. J.H. GOLDCAMP
1973: Michigan Mile and One-Eighth (Golden Don)

DONAMIRE FARM
1982: Hawthorne Gold Cup (Recusant)

FAITH DONNELLY
1983: Mother Goose Stakes (Able Money)

DORCHESTER FARM STABLE
1960: Garden State Stakes (Carry Back)
1961: Everglades Stakes (Carry Back)
Flamingo Stakes (Carry Back)
Florida Derby (Carry Back)
Trenton Handicap (Carry Back)
1963: Trenton Handicap (Carry Back)

DOR-MAR PAT INC.
1971: Gulfstream Park Handicap (Fast Hilarious)

DOTSAM STABLE
1980: Hialeah Turf Cup (John Henry)
Hollywood Invitational Handicap (John Henry)
Oak Tree Invitational Stakes (John Henry)
San Luis Rey Stakes (John Henry)
San Juan Capistrano Handicap (John Henry)
1981: Jockey Club Gold Cup (John Henry)
Santa Anita Handicap (John Henry)
Hollywood Invitational Handicap (John Henry)
Sword Dancer Stakes (John Henry)
Arlington Million (John Henry)
Oak Tree Invitational Stakes (John Henry)
San Luis Rey Stakes (John Henry)
1982: Santa Anita Handicap (John Henry)
Oak Tree Invitational Stakes (John Henry)
1983: Hollywood Turf Cup (John Henry)
1984: Hollywood Invitational Handicap (John Henry)
Sunset Handicap (John Henry)
Budweiser-Arlington Million (John Henry)
Turf Classic (John Henry)

DOUBLE B RANCH & DR. JOSEPH KIDD
1981: Arkansas Derby (Bold Ego)

DOUBLE EAGLE STABLE
1980: Arlington Handicap (Yvonand)
1985: Hialeah Turf Cup (Selous Scout)

DOUBLE J FARM
1995: Hollywood Futurity (Matty G)

MATTHEW DRAGNA & SON & SANTORO
1960: Hollywood Derby (Tempestuous)
1961: San Juan Capistrano Handicap (Don't Alibi)

ANTHONY DRAKAS
1982: Pennsylvania Derby (Spanish Drums)
1987: Young America Stakes (Firery Ensign)

GAY DRAKE
1955: Arlington Futurity (Swoon's Son)
Washington Park Futurity (Swoon's Son)
1956: Arlington Classic (Swoon's Son)
American Derby (Swoon's Son)

MRS. GERRY DREIER
1969: San Felipe Handicap (Elect the Ruler)

ALLEN DRUMHELLER
1947: Longacres Mile (Hank H.)

IRA DRYMON
1971: Beldame Stakes (Double Delta)

ALAIN du BREIL
1983: Californian Stakes (The Wonder)
Century Handicap (The Wonder)

MRS. PETER DUCHIN
1966: Dwyer Handicap (Mr. Right)
1968: Santa Anita Handicap (Mr. Right)
Woodward Stakes (Mr. Right)

RICHARD DUCHOSSOIS
1991: Arlington Classic (Whadjathink)

FRED DUCKETT, MARY J. HINDS & MARGARET ROBBINS
1986: Charles H. Strub Stakes (Nostalgia's Star)

DUE PROCESS STABLE
1981: Gulfstream Park Handicap (Hurry Up Blue)
1985: Louisiana Derby (Violado)
1988: Jerome Handicap (Evening Kris)
1993: Hopeful Stakes (Dehere)
Champagne Stakes (Dehere)

J.H. DUNN
1951: Washington Park Futurity (Oh Leo)

DUNTREATH FARM
1952: Molly Pitcher Handicap (Dixie Flyer)

FRANCIS DUPRE
1962: Washington D.C. International (Match II)

TOM DURANT & JIM & MARILYN HELZER
2001: Strub Stakes (Wooden Phone)

J.G. DUSHOCK
1946: Molly Pitcher Handicap (Mahmoudess)

DICK DUTROW
1995: Carter Handicap (Lite the Fuse)
Frank J. De Francis Memorial Dash (Lite the Fuse)
1996: Carter Handicap (Lite the Fuse)
Frank J. De Francis Memorial Dash (Lite the Fuse)

RAYMOND DWECK
2000: Spinaway Stakes (Stormy Pick)

MR. and MRS. PETER DYE
1966: Del Mar Debutante Stakes (Native Honey)

ANN & VERNON EACHUS
1978: La Canada Stakes (Taisez Vous)
Santa Margarita Handicap (Taisez Vous)

EAGLE MOUNTAIN FARM
1974: Breeders' Futurity (Packer Captain)

HAL EARNHARDT
2000: Cigar Mile Handicap (El Corredor)

HAL EARNHARDT & JOHN R. GAINES
1998: Santa Anita Derby (Indian Charlie)

EAST ACRES
1972: Black Helen Handicap (Alma North)

EAST-WEST STABLE
1975: Monmouth Invitational Handicap (Wajima)
Travers Stakes (Wajima)
Marlboro Cup Handicap (Wajima)

TOM EAZOR
1966: Mother Goose Stakes (Lady Pitt)

EDGEHILL FARM
1960: Flamingo Stakes (Bally Ache)
Florida Derby (Bally Ache)

LEO EDWARDS & MASSEY
1956: Sapling Stakes (King Hairan)
Hopeful Stakes (King Hairan)

ELBERON FARM
1969: Arlington-Washington Futurity (Silent Screen)
Cowdin Stakes (Silent Screen)
Champagne Stakes (Silent Screen)
1980: Sapling Stakes (Travelling Music)

ELCEE-H STABLE
1972: Jersey Derby (Smiling Jack)
1981: Super Derby (Island Whirl)
1982: Woodward Stakes (Island Whirl)
1983: Hollywood Gold Cup (Island Whirl)
Whitney Handicap (Island Whirl)

ELDORADO STABLES
1979: San Felipe Handicap (Pole Position)

ELKCAM STABLE
1959: Gotham Stakes (Atoll)
1967: Illinois Derby (Royal Malabar)

JAMES ELKINS, WILL FARISH III & TEMPLE WEBBER JR.
1992: Ashland Stakes (Prospectors Delite)
Acorn Stakes (Prospectors Delite)
2000: Kentucky Oaks (Secret Status)
Mother Goose Stakes (Secret Status)
2003: Pimlico Special (Mineshaft)
Suburban Handicap (Mineshaft)
Woodward Stakes (Mineshaft)
Jockey Club Gold Cup (Mineshaft)

IRVING ELLIS & ALAN RESKIN
1993: Flamingo Stakes (Forever Whirl)
Ohio Derby (Forever Whirl)

MRS. E.H. ELLISON JR.
1949: Saranac Handicap (Sun Bahram)

REX ELLSWORTH
1946: Starlet Stakes (U Time)
1947: Santa Susana Stakes (Hubble Bubble)
San Vicente Handicap (Hubble Bubble)
Hollywood Oaks (U Time)
1953: Vanity Handicap (Fleet Khal)
1955: Santa Anita Derby (Swaps)
Kentucky Derby (Swaps)
Westerner Stakes (Swaps)
American Derby (Swaps)
Californian Stakes (Swaps)
1956: Inglewood Handicap (Swaps)
American Handicap (Swaps)
Hollywood Gold Cup (Swaps)
Sunset Handicap (Swaps)
Washington Park Handicap (Swaps)
Santa Anita Derby (Terrang)
1958: Cinema Handicap (The Shoe)
1961: Santa Anita Handicap (Prove It)
San Fernando Stakes (Prove It)
Santa Anita Maturity (Prove It)
Cinema Handicap (Bushel-n-Peck)
1962: Inglewood Handicap (Prove It)
American Handicap (Prove It)
Hollywood Gold Cup (Prove It)
Sunset Handicap (Prove It)
Washington Park Handicap (Prove It)
San Antonio Handicap (Olden Times)
San Juan Capistrano Handicap (Olden Times)
Arlington-Washington Futurity (Candy Spots)
1963: Santa Anita Derby (Candy Spots)
Florida Derby (Candy Spots)
Preakness Stakes (Candy Spots)
Jersey Derby (Candy Spots)
American Derby (Candy Spots)
Arlington Classic (Candy Spots)
Hollywood Oaks (Delhi Maid)
American Handicap (Dr. Kacy)
1964: Cinema Handicap (Close By)
Metropolitan Handicap (Olden Times)
1969: Hollywood Oaks (Tipping Time)

ELMENDORF FARM
1955: Garden State Stakes (Prince John)
1959: Hawthorne Gold Cup (Day Court)
1960: Display Handicap (Nickel Boy)
1961: Manhattan Handicap (Nickel Boy)
1963: Everglades Stakes (B. Major)
1967: Jerome Handicap (High Tribute)
1968: Gotham Stakes (Verbatim)
1969: Amory L. Haskell Handicap (Verbatim)
Whitney Stakes (Verbatim)
Lawrence Realization Stakes (Oil Power)
1971: Santa Margarita Handicap (Manta)
Beverly Hills Handicap (Manta)
Santa Barbara Handicap (Manta)
1972: Oak Leaf Stakes (Fresh Pepper)
1973: Champagne Stakes (Protagonist)
Laurel Futurity (Protagonist)
Spinaway Stakes (Talking Picture)
Matron Stakes (Talking Picture)
Coaching Club American Oaks (Magazine)
San Luis Rey Handicap (Big Spruce)
1974: Secretariat Stakes (Glossary)
Marlboro Cup Handicap (Big Spruce)
1975: Hopeful Stakes (Jackknife)
Del Mar Debutante Stakes (Queen to Be)
Demoiselle Stakes (Free Journey)
Alabama Stakes (Spout)
1976: Del Mar Futurity (Visible)
Mother Goose Stakes (Girl in Love)
Hollywood Gold Cup (Pay Tribute)
Pan American Handicap (Improviser)
1977: Mother Goose Stakes (Road Princess)
Secretariat Stakes (Text)
Meadowlands Cup (Pay Tribute)
San Fernando Stakes (Pocket Park)
Hialeah Turf Cup (Improviser)
1978: Ramona Handicap (Drama Critic)
San Fernando Stakes (Text)
1979: Amory L. Haskell Handicap (Text)
1980: Bay Meadows Handicap (Super Moment)
1981: Charles H. Strub Stakes (Super Moment)
Bay Meadows Handicap (Super Moment)
1982: Hollywood Turf Cup (The Hague)
Bay Meadows Handicap (Super Moment)
1983: Hawthorne Gold Cup (Water Bank)
1984: Santa Barbara Handicap (Comedy Act)
1985: Swaps Stakes (Padua)

ANN ELMORE
1976: Ladies Handicap (Bastonera II)

JOHN ELMORE
1956: Del Mar Debutante Stakes (Blue Vic)

MR. and MRS. JOHN ELMORE
1965: Del Mar Debutante Stakes (Century)
1970: Santa Susana Stakes (Opening Bid)
1972: San Felipe Handicap (Solar Salute)
Santa Anita Derby (Solar Salute)
1973: Hollywood Juvenile Championship (Century's Envoy)

MR. and MRS. STEVEN ELMORE
1969: Oak Leaf Stakes (Opening Bid)

ELOBEE FARM
1947: Hollywood Derby (Yankee Valor)
Cinema Handicap (Yankee Valor)
1949: Santa Margarita Handicap (Lurline B.)
1958: Inglewood Handicap (Eddie Schmidt)

EL PECO RANCH
1956: Vanity Handicap (Mary Machree)
1962: Kentucky Derby (Decidedly)
1963: Monmouth Handicap (Decidedly)
1964: San Felipe Handicap (Hill Rise)
Santa Anita Derby (Hill Rise)
1965: Santa Anita Handicap (Hill Rise)
San Fernando Stakes (Hill Rise)
Man o' War Stakes (Hill Rise)
1966: San Antonio Handicap (Hill Rise)
1967: Sunset Handicap (Hill Clown)
1972: Beverly Hills Handicap (Hill Circus)
Del Mar Handicap (Hill Circus)
1977: Swaps Stakes (J.O. Tobin)
1979: Widener Handicap (Jumping Hill)

EL RIO STUD
1955: Washington D.C. International (El Chama)

EDWARD ELZEMEYER
1975: Oaklawn Handicap (Warbucks)

EMERALD HILL STABLE
1951: Cowdin Stakes (Eternal Moon)

CHARLES ENGEL
1992: Beldame Stakes (Saratoga Dew)

CHARLES ENGELHARD & MACK MILLER
1969: Jerome Handicap (Mr. Leader)

DALE & MORLEY ENGELSON
1991: San Juan Capistrano Handicap (Mashkour)

DALE & MORLEY ENGELSON & BOBBY FRANKEL
1993: San Antonio Handicap (Marquetry)
Meadowlands Cup (Marquetry)

MORLEY ENGELSON, B. FRANKEL & JUDDMONTE FARMS
1992: Eddie Read Handicap (Marquetry)

ENTREMONT
1980: Dwyer Stakes (Amber Pass)
1981: Monmouth Handicap (Amber Pass)

ENVOY STABLE
1983: Maskette Stakes (Ambassador of Luck)

EQUUSEQUITY STABLE
1982: Young America Stakes (Slewpy)
1983: Wood Memorial Stakes (Slew O' Gold)
Woodward Stakes (Slew O' Gold)
Jockey Club Gold Cup (Slew O' Gold)
Meadowlands Cup (Slewpy)
1984: Whitney Handicap (Slew O' Gold)
Woodward Stakes (Slew O' Gold)
Marlboro Cup Handicap (Slew O' Gold)
Jockey Club Gold Cup (Slew O' Gold)

MRS. M. ERLANDER
1965: Pimlico Futurity (Spring Double)

STANLEY ERSOFF
1985: Arlington Handicap (Pass the Line)
1990: Coaching Club American Oaks (Charon)

R. ESCUDERO
1971: Jerome Handicap (Tinajero)

EDWARD EVANS
1989: Ladies Handicap (Dance Teacher)
1994: Jerome Handicap (Prenup)
2000: Matron Stakes (Raging Fever)
Frizette Stakes (Raging Fever)
2002: Ogden Phipps Handicap (Raging Fever)
Philip H. Iselin Handicap (Cat's at Home)
Personal Ensign Handicap (Summer Colony)
King's Bishop Stakes (Gygistar)

GOMER EVANS
1965: Oaklawn Handicap (Gay Revoke)

ROBERT EVANS
1989: Vosburgh Stakes (Sewickley)
1990: Vosburgh Stakes (Sewickley)
1993: Ruffian Handicap (Shared Interest)

EVEREST STABLES
1995: Ohio Derby (Petionville)
2003: Alabama Stakes (Island Fashion)
La Brea Stakes (Island Fashion)

MARJORIE EVERETT
1972: American Handicap (Buzkashi)
1975: San Fernando Stakes (Stardust Mel)
Charles H. Strub Stakes (Stardust Mel)
Santa Anita Handicap (Stardust Mel)
Cinema Handicap (Terete)

EVERGREEN FARM
1988: Hollywood Oaks (Pattern Step)
Budweiser-Arlington Million (Mill Native)
Ruffian Handicap (Sham Say)
Yellow Ribbon Stakes (Delighter)
1990: San Juan Capistrano Handicap (Delegant)
1995: Eddie Read Handicap (Fastness)
1996: Eddie Read Handicap (Fastness)
Breeders' Cup Sprint (Lit de Justice)
1997: Hollywood Turf Handicap (Rainbow Dancer)
Oak Tree Turf Championship (Rainbow Dancer)

EVERGREEN FARM & JENINE SAHADI
1997: Breeders' Cup Sprint (Elmhurst)

SIDNEY FACTOR
1965: Grey Lag Handicap (Quita Dude)

STIFTUNG GESTUT FAHRHOF
2001: Arlington Million (Silvano)

FAIRLAWN FARM
1959: McLennan Handicap (Sharpsburg)

FARES FARM
1991: Breeders' Cup Turf (Miss Alleged)
Hollywood Turf Cup (Miss Alleged)

FARFELLOW FARM
1996: Flower Bowl Invitational Handicap (Chelsey Flower)

WILL FARISH III
1972: Preakness Stakes (Bee Bee Bee)
1978: Breeders' Futurity (Strike Your Colors)
1980: Alcibiades Stakes (Sweet Revenge)
1984: Frizette Stakes (Charleston Rag)
1989: Maskette Stakes (Miss Brio)
1997: Alabama Stakes (Runup the Colors)

W. FARISH III, J. GOODMAN, T. McCAFFERY, J. TOFFAN
2002: Santa Anita Derby (Came Home)
Swaps Stakes (Came Home)
Pacific Classic (Came Home)

W. FARISH III, EDWARD HUDSON & EDWARD HUDSON JR.
1991: Arlington-Washington Lassie Stakes (Speed Dialer)

WILL FARISH III & WATTS HUMPHREY
1977: Young America Stakes (Forever Casting)

WILL FARISH III & JONES
1981: Santa Margarita Handicap (Princess Karenda)

WILL FARISH III & BAYARD SHARP
1989: Fountain of Youth Stakes (Dixieland Brass)

TRACY FARMER
2000: Jockey Club Gold Cup (Albert the Great)
2001: Brooklyn Handicap (Albert the Great)
Suburban Handicap (Albert the Great)

YALE FARRAR & DAVID SCHLOSS
1989: Oak Leaf Stakes (Dominant Dancer)

PAUL FAULKENSTEIN
1965: Jerome Handicap (Bold Bidder)

JOSEPH FEDERICO
1987: Brooklyn Handicap (Waquoit)
1988: Brooklyn Handicap (Waquoit)
Jockey Club Gold Cup (Waquoit)

MAC FEHSENFELD
2003: King's Bishop Stakes (Valid Video)

MRS. R.L. FEINBERG
1973: Arkansas Derby (Impecunious)

FENCE POST FARM
1970: Arlington Classic (Corn off the Cob)

MICHAEL FENNESSY
1996: Mother Goose Stakes (Yanks Music)
Alabama Stakes (Yanks Music)
Ruffian Handicap (Yanks Music)
Beldame Stakes (Yanks Music)

B.F. FERGUSON II
1982: Vosburgh Stakes (Engine One)

FERNWOOD STABLES
1988: Sword Dancer Handicap (Anka Germania)

FIFTY-FIFTY STABLE
1948: Cinema Handicap (Drumbeat)
Sunset Handicap (Drumbeat)

H.W. FINCHER
1950: Molly Pitcher Handicap (Danger Ahead)

MORTON FINK
2001: San Antonio Handicap (Guided Tour)

MORTON FINK & ROY GOTTLIEB
1988: Vanity Handicap (Annoconnor)

JACK FINLEY
1977: Ramona Handicap (Dancing Femme)
1980: Del Mar Debutante Stakes (Raja's Delight)
1990: Oak Leaf Stakes (Lite Light)

CHARLES FIPKE
2003: Shadwell Turf Mile (Perfect Soul)

BERT FIRESTONE
1974: Pan American Handicap (London Company)
1975: Champagne Stakes (Honest Pleasure)
Laurel Futurity (Honest Pleasure)
Arlington-Washington Futurity (Honest Pleasure)
1976: Flamingo Stakes (Honest Pleasure)
Florida Derby (Honest Pleasure)
Blue Grass Stakes (Honest Pleasure)
Travers Stakes (Honest Pleasure)
1978: Hopeful Stakes (General Assembly)
1979: Travers Stakes (General Assembly)
Vosburgh Stakes (General Assembly)
1980: Laurel Futurity (Cure the Blues)
1981: Breeders' Futurity (D'Accord)
1982: Secretariat Stakes (Half Iced)
1989: Selima Stakes (Sweet Roberta)
1990: Jim Dandy Stakes (Chief Honcho)
1992: Hollywood Derby (Paradise Creek)

BERT FIRESTONE & ALLEN PAULSON
1987: Hialeah Turf Cup (Theatrical)
Turf Classic (Theatrical)
Man o' War Stakes (Theatrical)
Breeders' Cup Turf (Theatrical)

DIANA FIRESTONE
1975: Matron Stakes (Optimistic Gal)
Frizette Stakes (Optimistic Gal)
Alcibiades Stakes (Optimistic Gal)
Selima Stakes (Optimistic Gal)
1976: Ashland Stakes (Optimistic Gal)
Kentucky Oaks (Optimistic Gal)
Alabama Stakes (Optimistic Gal)
Delaware Handicap (Optimistic Gal)
Spinster Stakes (Optimistic Gal)
1977: Maskette Handicap (What a Summer)
1980: Ruffian Handicap (Genuine Risk)
Kentucky Derby (Genuine Risk)
1981: Turf Classic (April Run)
1982: Turf Classic (April Run)
Washington D.C. International (April Run)
1985: Matron Stakes (Musical Lark)
1988: Flower Bowl Handicap (Gaily Gaily)

MATT FIRESTONE
1992: Brooklyn Handicap (Chief Honcho)
1994: Gulfstream Park Handicap (Scuffleburg)

MRS. RUSSELL A. FIRESTONE
1954: Cowdin Stakes (Summer Tan)
Garden State Stakes (Summer Tan)

PAMELA FIRMAN
1976: American Derby (Fifth Marine)

PAMELA FIRMAN & WATTS HUMPHREY JR.
1996: Shuvee Handicap (Clear Mandate)

MARY FISHER
1952: Arlington Lassie Stakes (Fulvous)
Princess Pat Stakes (Fulvous)
1957: Breeders' Futurity (Fulcrum)
1963: Arlington-Washington Futurity (Golden Ruler)

MRS. MONTGOMERY FISHER
1968: California Derby (Proper Proof)

SUSAN FISHER
1969: Grey Lag Handicap (Bushido)
1971: John B. Campbell Handicap (Bushido)

505 FARMS
1998: Hollywood Oaks (Manistique)
1999: Santa Margarita Handicap (Manistique)
Vanity Handicap (Manistique)
2000: Santa Maria Handicap (Manistique)

FIVE STAR STABLE
1987: Tropical Park Derby (Baldski's Star)

F.L. FLANDERS
1948: Kentucky Oaks (Challe Anne)

FLASH III STABLE
1976: Hawthorne Gold Cup (Almost Grown)

FLATBIRD STABLE
2001: Carter Handicap (Peeping Tom)

D. FLAXBEARD, R. OLIPHANT & BAYARD SHARP
1994: Arlington-Washington Lassie Stakes (Shining Light)

FLAXMAN HOLDINGS, LTD.
2003: San Carlos Handicap (Aldebaran)
Metropolitan Handicap (Aldebaran)
Forego Handicap (Aldebaran)
NetJets Breeders' Cup Mile (Six Perfections)

FLAXMAN HOLDINGS, LTD. & EDMUND GANN
2001: Hollywood Derby (Denon)
2002: Charles Whittingham Handicap (Denon)
Turf Classic (Denon)
2003: Manhattan Handicap (Denon)

WILLIAM FLOYD
1980: Breeders' Futurity (Fairway Phantom)
1981: Arlington Classic (Fairway Phantom)

BILL FLUOR & SIDNEY PORT
1978: Bay Meadows Handicap (Bywayofchicago)

FLYING HORSE STABLE & AMIN SAIDEN
1982: New Orleans Handicap (It's the One)

FLYING M STABLE
1963: San Felipe Handicap (Denodado)

FLYING ZEE STABLE
1981: Dwyer Stakes (Noble Nashua)
Swaps Stakes (Noble Nashua)
Jerome Handicap (Noble Nashua)
Marlboro Cup Handicap (Noble Nashua)
Mother Goose Stakes (Wayward Lass)
Coaching Club American Oaks (Wayward Lass)
1995: Suburban Handicap (Key Contender)

FOG CITY STABLE
2002: Frank J. De Francis Memorial Dash (D'Wildcat)

BUDDY FOGELSON
1974: Sunset Handicap (Greco II)

FOLSOM FARM
1971: Spinster Stakes (Chou Croute)

FOMON & GEORGE McIVOR
1964: San Luis Rey Handicap (Inclusive)

FORD STABLE
1964: Breeders' Futurity (Umbrella Fella)
Kentucky Jockey Club Stakes (Umbrella Fella)
1966: Kentucky Derby (Kauai King)
Preakness Stakes (Kauai King)

FORGNONE, FRANKLIN & LEVY
1986: Santa Barbara Handicap (Mountain Bear)

FORKED LIGHTNING RANCH
1969: Cinema Handicap (Noholme Jr.)
1971: Hollywood Gold Cup (Ack Ack)
San Antonio Stakes (Ack Ack)
Santa Anita Handicap (Ack Ack)
American Handicap (Ack Ack)

FORUS STABLE
1972: Fountain of Youth Stakes (Gentle Smoke)

D.J. FOSTER RACING STABLE
1983: Arkansas Derby (Sunny's Halo)
Kentucky Derby (Sunny's Halo)
Super Derby (Sunny's Halo)

FOUR M STABLES INC. & HALO FARMS
1989: Ohio Derby (King Glorious)
Haskell Invitational Handicap (King Glorious)

FOURTH ESTATE STABLE
1963: Kentucky Jockey Club Stakes (Journalist)
1965: Kentucky Jockey Club Stakes (War Censor)
1966: Ohio Derby (War Censor)
1967: Hialeah Turf Cup (War Censor)
Pan American Handicap (War Censor)
Dixie Handicap (War Censor)

FOUR-WAY RANCH
1958: Remsen Stakes (Atoll)

FOURWYN STABLE
1980: Illinois Derby (Ray's Word)

ANDERSON FOWLER
1991: Brooklyn Handicap (Timely Warning)

FOXCATCHER FARM
1946: Withers Stakes (Hampden)
1948: Selima Stakes (Gaffery)
1949: Santa Susana Stakes (Gaffery)
Ladies Handicap (Gaffery)
1954: Delaware Oaks (Parlo)
Alabama Stakes (Parlo)
Beldame Handicap (Parlo)
Firenze Handicap (Parlo)
1955: Top Flight Handicap (Parlo)
Delaware Handicap (Parlo)
1956: Dixie Handicap (Chevation)
1957: Hopeful Stakes (Rose Trellis)
1960: Mother Goose Stakes (Berlo)
Coaching Club American Oaks (Berlo)
Beldame Stakes (Berlo)
Ladies Handicap (Berlo)
1965: California Derby (Perfect Sky)

FOX HILL FARMS
2000: Coaching Club American Oaks (Jostle)
Alabama Stakes (Jostle)

NATHAN FOX & NANCY & RICHARD KASTER
2000: Frank J. De Francis Memorial Dash (Richter Scale)

FOX RIDGE FARM
1992: Flower Bowl Handicap (Christiecat)
2002: Queen Elizabeth II Challenge Cup (Riskaverse)

FOXWOOD PLANTATION
1996: Arkansas Derby (Zarb's Magic)

MR. and MRS. BILL FOY
1971: Vanity Handicap (Hi Q.)

SERGE FRADKOFF
1979: Santa Margarita Handicap (Sanedtki)
1980: Yellow Ribbon Stakes (Kilijaro)
1981: Washington D.C. International (Providential II)
Hollywood Turf Cup (Providential II)
1992: Gamely Handicap (Metamorphose)

SERGE FRADKOFF & EDWARD SELTZER
1981: Matriarch Stakes (Kilijaro)

SERGE FRADKOFF & BARON THIERRY von ZUYLEN
1982: Hollywood Gold Cup (Perrault)
Budweiser Million (Perrault)
San Luis Rey Stakes (Perrault)

BOBBY FRANKEL
2001: Matriarch Stakes (Starine)
2002: Breeders' Cup Filly and Mare Turf (Starine)

FRANK FRANKEL
1948: Del Mar Handicap (Frankly)
Santa Anita Maturity (Flashco)
1950: Del Mar Handicap (Frankly)

JERRY FRANKEL
1978: Louisiana Derby (Esops Foibles)
Arkansas Derby (Esops Foibles)
Arlington-Washington Lassie Stakes (It's In the Air)
2003: Triple Bend Breeders' Cup Handicap (Joey Franco)

MARION FRANKEL
1963: Futurity Stakes (Bupers)
1970: Suburban Handicap (Barometer)

FRANKFURT STABLE
1994: Yellow Ribbon Stakes (Aube Indienne)

FRANKFURT STABLE & CHARLIE WHITTINGHAM
1986: Hollywood Futurity (Temperate Sil)
1987: Santa Anita Derby (Temperate Sil)
Swaps Stakes (Temperate Sil)

MRS. J.M. FRANKLIN
1975: Top Flight Handicap (Twixt)

JOHN FRANKS
1984: Ruffian Handicap (Heatherten)
Ladies Handicap (Heatherten)
Apple Blossom Handicap (Heatherten)
1989: Arkansas Derby (Dansil)
1993: Haskell Invitational Handicap (Kissin Kris)
1997: Apple Blossom Handicap (Halo America)
1998: Oaklawn Handicap (Precocity)
Breeders' Cup Juvenile (Answer Lively)

FRAZEE & FRAZEE INC.
1972: Cinema Handicap (Finalista)

FREEMAN-COLE & GOLD
1981: San Felipe Handicap (Stancharry)

FREE SPIRIT'S STABLE
1991: Super Derby (Free Spirit's Joy)

H.O.H. FRELINGHUYSEN
1962: Carter Handicap (Merry Ruler)

LLOYD R. FRENCH JR.
1986: Mother Goose Stakes (Life at the Top)
Ladies Handicap (Life at the Top)

LLOYD R. FRENCH JR. & WAYNE LUKAS
1989: Santa Anita Oaks (Imaginary Lady)

HAAKON FRETHEIM
1978: Hialeah Turf Cup (Noble Dancer II)
United Nations Handicap (Noble Dancer II)
San Luis Rey Stakes (Noble Dancer II)
1979: Pan American Handicap (Noble Dancer II)
San Luis Rey Stakes (Noble Dancer II)

ALBERT FRIED JR.
1998: Vosburgh Stakes (Affirmed Success)
1999: Cigar Mile Handicap (Affirmed Success)
2002: Carter Handicap (Affirmed Success)

FRIEDMAN & READER
1980: Golden Harvest Handicap (War Fame)

ED & NATALIE FRIENDLY
1997: Oak Leaf Stakes (Vivid Angel)

PETER FULLER
1961: Display Handicap (Hillsborough)
1968: Wood Memorial Stakes (Dancer's Image)
1984: Selima Stakes (Mom's Command)
1985: Acorn Stakes (Mom's Command)
Mother Goose Stakes (Mom's Command)
Coaching Club American Oaks (Mom's Command)
Alabama Stakes (Mom's Command)

MRS. A. GAAL
1946: Arlington Classic (The Dude)

GABRIELLE, GOLDFARB, HEMLOCK HILLS, ZIMMERMAN
2002: Prioress Stakes (Carson Hollow)

DR. E. GAILLARD, A.B. HANCOCK III & C. WHITTINGHAM
1989: San Felipe Handicap (Sunday Silence)
Santa Anita Derby (Sunday Silence)
Kentucky Derby (Sunday Silence)
Preakness Stakes (Sunday Silence)
Super Derby (Sunday Silence)
Breeders' Cup Classic (Sunday Silence)
1990: Californian Stakes (Sunday Silence)

GAILYNDEL FARMS
1986: Apple Blossom Handicap (Love Smitten)

JOHN R. GAINES
1963: Beldame Stakes (Oil Royalty)
Vineland Handicap (Oil Royalty)
1964: Top Flight Handicap (Oil Royalty)
1966: Monmouth Handicap (Bold Bidder)
Washington Park Handicap (Bold Bidder)
Hawthorne Gold Cup (Bold Bidder)
Charles H. Strub Stakes (Bold Bidder)

GAINESWAY FARM
1992: Top Flight Handicap (Firm Stance)

GAINESWAY FARM, B. & R. LEWIS & OVERBROOK FARM
1994: Champagne Stakes (Timber Country)
Breeders' Cup Juvenile (Timber Country)
1995: Preakness Stakes (Timber Country)

DAN GALBREATH
1977: Ruffian Handicap (Cum Laude Laurie)
Beldame Stakes (Cum Laude Laurie)
Spinster Stakes (Cum Laude Laurie)
1980: Matron Stakes (Prayers'n Promises)
1984: Young America Stakes (Script Ohio)

MRS. JOHN GALBREATH
1956: Gallant Fox Handicap (Summer Tan)
Pimlico Special (Summer Tan)
1957: McLennan Handicap (Summer Tan)
1978: Acorn Stakes (Tempest Queen)
Spinster Stakes (Tempest Queen)

GALLAGHER FARM
1987: Oak Tree Invitational Stakes (Allez Milord)

MRS. JAMES GALLAGHER
1982: Alcibiades Stakes (Jelly Bean Holiday)

GALLAHER & WILLIAMS
1953: Vineland Handicap (Mi-Marigold)

TOM GAMEL, GINO RONCELLI & SIGBAND
1997: Californian Stakes (River Keen)

EDMUND GANN
1981: Eddie Read Handicap (Wickerr)
1982: Eddie Read Handicap (Wickerr)
1987: John Henry Handicap (Al Mamoon)
1990: Gamely Handicap (Double Wedge)
1991: Oak Tree Invitational Stakes (Filago)
1995: Metropolitan Handicap (You and I)
Brooklyn Handicap (You and I)
2001: Turf Classic (Timboroa)
Frizette Stakes (You)
2002: Las Virgenes Stakes (You)
Santa Anita Oaks (You)
Acorn Stakes (You)
Test Stakes (You)
Jim Dandy Stakes (Medaglia d'Oro)
Travers Stakes (Medaglia d'Oro)
2003: Strub Stakes (Medaglia d'Oro)
Oaklawn Handicap (Medaglia d'Oro)
Whitney Handicap (Medaglia d'Oro)
Toyota Blue Grass Stakes (Peace Rules)
Haskell Invitational Handicap (Peace Rules)

MR. and MRS. EDMUND GANN
1988: Sunset Handicap (Roi Normand)

EDMUND GANN, RITT & RITT
1981: Louisiana Downs Handicap (Goldiko)

EDMUND GANN & MARK & MERLY ANN TANZ
1979: Hollywood Invitational Handicap (Johnny's Image)

GARY GARBER
1998: Ohio Derby (Classic Cat)
2000: Del Mar Futurity (Flame Thrower)
Norfolk Stakes (Flame Thrower)

JUAN GARCIA & L.L. SCOFIELD
2002: San Juan Capistrano Handicap (Ringaskiddy)

GARDENIA STABLE
1949: Black Helen Handicap (Roman Candle)

GARDINER FARM
1968: Canadian International Championship (Frenetico)

JACK GAREY
2000: Apple Blossom Handicap (Heritage of Gold)
Go for Wand Handicap (Heritage of Gold)

PAT GARVEY
2000: San Juan Capistrano Handicap (Sunshine Street)

LINDA GASTON & A.D. HAYNES
1978: Ohio Derby (Special Honor)

JOSEPH GAVEGNANO
1953: Pimlico Futurity (Errard King)
1954: Arlington Classic (Errard King)
American Derby (Errard King)

GEDNEY FARM
1964: Gulfstream Park Handicap (Gun Bow)
Brooklyn Handicap (Gun Bow)
Washington Park Handicap (Gun Bow)
Woodward Stakes (Gun Bow)
San Fernando Stakes (Gun Bow)
Charles H. Strub Stakes (Gun Bow)
San Antonio Handicap (Gun Bow)
Whitney Stakes (Gun Bow)
1965: Donn Handicap (Gun Bow)
Metropolitan Handicap (Gun Bow)
San Antonio Handicap (Gun Bow)
1976: Whitney Handicap (Dancing Gun)
1977: San Fernando Stakes (Kirby Lane)
Charles H. Strub Stakes (Kirby Lane)

ANDREW & DAN GEHL
1969: Alcibiades Stakes (Belle Noire)

GEM STATE STABLE
1970: Hollywood Juvenile Championship (Fast Fellow)

FRANCES GENTER
1951: Santa Anita Derby (Rough'n Tumble)
1959: Gardenia Stakes (My Dear Girl)
Frizette Stakes (My Dear Girl)
1966: Pimlico Futurity (In Reality)
1967: Florida Derby (In Reality)
Jersey Derby (In Reality)
1968: John B. Campbell Handicap (In Reality)
Carter Handicap (In Reality)
Metropolitan Handicap (In Reality)
1980: Flamingo Stakes (Superbity)
1983: Remsen Stakes (Dr. Carter)
Metropolitan Handicap (Star Choice)
1985: Gulfstream Park Handicap (Dr. Carter)
Arlington Classic (Smile)
Delaware Handicap (Basie)
1986: Matron Stakes (Tappiano)
Selima Stakes (Collins)
Breeders' Cup Sprint (Smile)
1990: Florida Derby (Unbridled)
Kentucky Derby (Unbridled)

Breeders' Cup Classic (Unbridled)
1991: Wood Memorial Stakes (Cahill Road)

GENTILLY STABLE
1965: Hawthorne Gold Cup (Moss Vale)

OLIN GENTRY
1987: Californian Stakes (Judge Angelucci)
1988: San Antonio Handicap (Judge Angelucci)
1989: John Henry Handicap (Peace)

TOM GENTRY
1987: Blue Grass Stakes (War)

SYL GEORGE STABLE
1968: Display Handicap (Fast Count)

GEORGICA STABLE
2003: Gazelle Handicap (Buy the Sport)
Garden City BC Handicap (Indy Five Hundred)

JOHN GERBAS JR.
1973: Champagne Stakes (Holding Pattern)
1974: Monmouth Invitational Handicap (Holding Pattern)
Travers Stakes (Holding Pattern)

GERINGER, KLEIN, LIBERTY RD. & SAN GABRIEL
2002: Del Mar Oaks (Dublino)

MRS. ROBERT L. GERRY
1947: Travers Stakes (Young Peter)

GEORGE F. GETTY II
1966: Monmouth Oaks (Natashka)
Alabama Stakes (Natashka)

GETTY & BARRY RICHARDS
1977: San Juan Capistrano Handicap (Properantes)

ROXIE GIAN
1975: Fantasy Stakes (Hoso)

M.R. GIBERGA
1966: Display Handicap (Damelo II)

SALLY GIBSON
1976: John B. Campbell Handicap (Festive Mood)
1977: Demoiselle Stakes (Caesar's Wish)
1978: Mother Goose Stakes (Caesar's Wish)

W.P. GILBRIDE
1973: Pan American Handicap (Lord Vancouver)
1974: Arlington-Washington Futurity (Greek Answer)

MRS. WALLACE GILROY
1956: Withers Stakes (Oh Johnny)
Travers Stakes (Oh Johnny)
1957: Display Handicap (Oh Johnny)
1958: Grey Lag Handicap (Oh Johnny)
1964: Selima Stakes (Marshua)
1965: Coaching Club American Oaks (Marshua)
1968: Dixie Handicap (High Hat)
Bowling Green Handicap (High Hat)

A.J. GIORDANO
1965: Hialeah Turf Cup (Hot Dust)

G-K STABLE
1959: Michigan Mile and One-Sixteenth (Total Traffic)

JOSEPHINE GLEIS
1990: Budweiser International Stakes (Fly Till Dawn)
1992: San Luis Rey Stakes (Fly Till Dawn)
San Juan Capistrano Handicap (Fly Till Dawn)

GLENCREST FARM
1982: Haskell Invitational Handicap (Wavering Monarch)
1983: San Fernando Stakes (Wavering Monarch)

GLEN HILL FARM
1972: Vanity Handicap (Convenience)
Santa Barbara Handicap (Hail the Grey)
1973: Vanity Handicap (Convenience)
1974: Santa Maria Handicap (Convenience)
1979: Hollywood Oaks (Prize Spot)
1981: Oak Leaf Stakes (Header Card)
1994: Breeders' Cup Distaff (One Dreamer)

PHILIP GODFREY
1953: Demoiselle Stakes (O'Alison)

GODOLPHIN STABLE
1995: San Juan Capistrano Handicap (Red Bishop)
1998: Man o' War Stakes (Daylami)
1999: Breeders' Cup Turf (Daylami)
2000: Man o' War Stakes (Fantastic Light)
2001: Breeders' Cup Juvenile Fillies (Tempera)
Breeders' Cup Turf (Fantastic Light)
2002: Gazelle Handicap (Imperial Gesture)
Beldame Stakes (Imperial Gesture)
Stephen Foster Handicap (Street Cry)
Suburban Handicap (E Dubai)
Coaching Club American Oaks (Jilbab)
Super Derby (Essence of Dubai)
Flower Bowl Invitational Stakes (Kazzia)
2003: Arlington Million (Sulamani)
Turf Classic (Sulamani)

MIKE GOETZ & BRIAN GRIGGS
2000: Walmac Int. Alcibiades Stakes (She's a Devil Due)

WILLIAM GOETZ
1949: Del Mar Futurity (Your Host)
1950: San Felipe Stakes (Your Host)
Santa Anita Derby (Your Host)
1951: Westerner Stakes (Grantor)
Del Mar Derby (Grantor)
Will Rogers Handicap (Gold Note)

ROBERT GOH
1970: Del Mar Handicap (Daryl's Joy)
Oak Tree Stakes (Daryl's Joy)

S. GOLDBAND
1949: Starlet Stakes (Thanks Again)

GOLDEN CHANCE FARM
1975: Louisiana Derby (Master Derby)
Blue Grass Stakes (Master Derby)
Preakness Stakes (Master Derby)
1976: Breeders' Futurity (Run Dusty Run)
Arlington-Washington Futurity (Run Dusty Run)
New Orleans Handicap (Master Derby)
Oaklawn Handicap (Master Derby)
1980: Arlington Classic (Spruce Needles)
Secretariat Stakes (Spruce Needles)
1981: Arlington Handicap (Spruce Needles)

GOLDEN EAGLE FARM
1976: Santa Margarita Handicap (Fascinating Girl)
1988: Fantasy Stakes (Jeanne Jones)
1989: Fantasy Stakes (Fantastic Look)
1990: Del Mar Futurity (Best Pal)
Norfolk Stakes (Best Pal)
Hollywood Futurity (Best Pal)
1991: Swaps Stakes (Best Pal)
Pacific Classic (Best Pal)
1992: Charles H. Strub Stakes (Best Pal)
Santa Anita Handicap (Best Pal)
Oaklawn Handicap (Best Pal)
Del Mar Futurity (River Special)
Norfolk Stakes (River Special)
Hollywood Futurity (River Special)
Santa Anita Oaks (Golden Treat)
1993: Hollywood Gold Cup (Best Pal)
Del Mar Futurity (Winning Pact)
1994: Molson Export Million (Dramatic Gold)
Hollywood Derby (River Flyer)
1995: San Antonio Handicap (Best Pal)
1996: Buick Meadowlands Cup Handicap (Dramatic Gold)
1997: Del Mar Futurity (Souvenir Copy)
Norfolk Stakes (Souvenir Copy)
1998: Oak Leaf Stakes (Excellent Meeting)
Hollywood Starlet Stakes (Excellent Meeting)
Jim Beam Stakes (Event of the Year)
Del Mar Futurity (Worldly Manner)
La Brea Stakes (Magical Allure)
1999: Las Virgenes Stakes (Excellent Meeting)
Santa Anita Oaks (Excellent Meeting)
Santa Anita Derby (General Challenge)
Pacific Classic (General Challenge)
Strub Stakes (Event of the Year)
2000: Strub Stakes (General Challenge)
Santa Anita Handicap (General Challenge)
Oak Leaf Stakes (Notable Career)
2002: Santa Maria Handicap (Favorite Funtime)

GOLDEN TRIANGLE STABLE
1962: Remsen Stakes (Rocky Link)
1966: Coaching Club American Oaks (Lady Pitt)

OLIVER GOLDSMITH
1972: Carter Handicap (Leematt)

MRS. NAT GOLDSTONE
1948: Westerner Handicap (Solidarity)
1949: Golden Gate Handicap (Solidarity)
Hollywood Gold Cup (Solidarity)
1950: Starlet Stakes (Gold Capitol)
San Pasqual Handicap (Solidarity)

HAROLD GOODMAN
1994: Coaching Club American Oaks (Two Altazano)

CLINT GOODRICH, HEROLD & LOTHENBACH
1992: Arlington Classic (Saint Ballado)

JOE GOODWIN
1946: Hawthorne Gold Cup (Jack's Jill)
1948: Arlington Classic (Papa Redbird)

MRS. JOE GOODWIN
1953: Alcibiades Stakes (Oil Painting)
1955: Maskette Handicap (Oil Painting)

M.N. GOODWIN
1959: Carter Handicap (Jimmer)

BERRY GORDY
1985: Fantasy Stakes (Rascal Lass)

BERRY GORDY & SUMMA STABLE
1980: Washington D.C. International (Argument)

ED GOULD
1967: Californian Stakes (Biggs)
1968: San Luis Rey Handicap (Biggs)

ANTHONY GRAFFAGINNI
1960: Louisiana Derby (Tony Graff)

WILLIAM GRAHAM
1981: Frizette Stakes (Proud Lou)

GRAND PRIX STABLE
1966: Blue Grass Stakes (Abe's Hope)

HUGH GRANT
1961: Delaware Handicap (Airmans Guide)
Beldame Stakes (Airmans Guide)

HUGH GRANT & JAMES PADGETT
1966: Louisiana Derby (Blue Skyer)

MR. and MRS. JOSEPH GRANT & TOMMY KELLY
2002: Jockey Club Gold Cup (Evening Attire)

S. GRAY & S. SCHMIEDESKAMP
1970: New Orleans Handicap (Etony)

TOM GRAY
1949: Breeders' Futurity (Oil Capitol)
Pimlico Futurity (Oil Capitol)
1950: Flamingo Stakes (Oil Capitol)

GRAY WILLOWS FARM
1965: Gulfstream Park Handicap (Ampose)

DOLLY GREEN
1983: California Derby (Paris Prince)
1984: Futurity Stakes (Spectacular Love)
Fantasy Stakes (My Darling One)
1986: Breeders' Cup Juvenile Fillies (Brave Raj)

GREEN DUNES FARM
1960: Belmont Stakes (Celtic Ash)

GREEN HILLS FARM
2001: Garden City BC Handicap (Voodoo Dancer)
2003: Diana Handicap (Voodoo Dancer)

LEONARD GREEN
1991: Ashland Stakes (Do It With Style)

GREEN THUMB FARM
1973: Malibu Stakes (Bicker)
San Fernando Stakes (Bicker)
1985: Santa Susana Stakes (Fran's Valentine)
Kentucky Oaks (Fran's Valentine)
Hollywood Oaks (Fran's Valentine)

GREENTREE STABLE
1946: Vosburgh Handicap (Coincidence)
Aqueduct Handicap (Coincidence)
Lawrence Realization Stakes (School Tie)

GREENTREE STABLE *(Continued)*
1947: Excelsior Handicap (Coincidence)
1948: Champagne Stakes (Capot)
Pimlico Futurity (Capot)
1949: Preakness Stakes (Capot)
Belmont Stakes (Capot)
Jerome Handicap (Capot)
Pimlico Special (Capot)
Futurity Stakes (Guillotine)
Spinaway Stakes (Sunday Evening)
Aqueduct Handicap (Wine List)
1950: Breeders' Futurity (Big Stretch)
Pimlico Futurity (Big Stretch)
Manhattan Handicap (One Hitter)
Pimlico Special (One Hitter)
Carter Handicap (Guillotine)
Aqueduct Handicap (Wine List)
1951: Arlington Classic (Hall of Fame)
American Derby (Hall of Fame)
Massachusetts Handicap (One Hitter)
Whitney Stakes (One Hitter)
Futurity Stakes (Tom Fool)
Monmouth Oaks (Ruddy)
Fall Highweight Handicap (Guillotine)
1952: Breeders' Futurity (Straight Face)
Kentucky Jockey Club Stakes (Straight Face)
Suburban Handicap (One Hitter)
Monmouth Handicap (One Hitter)
Jerome Handicap (Tom Fool)
Grey Lag Handicap (Tom Fool)
Carter Handicap (Northern Star)
1953: Metropolitan Handicap (Tom Fool)
Suburban Handicap (Tom Fool)
Carter Handicap (Tom Fool)
Brooklyn Handicap (Tom Fool)
Whitney Stakes (Tom Fool)
Pimlico Special (Tom Fool)
Frizette Stakes (Indian Legend)
Flamingo Stakes (Straight Face)
1954: Dixie Handicap (Straight Face)
Suburban Handicap (Straight Face)
Everglades Stakes (Maharajah)
1955: Spinaway Stakes (Register)
1956: Dwyer Handicap (Riley)
Lawrence Realization Stakes (Riley)
Tropical Handicap (Illusionist)
1958: Brooklyn Handicap (Cohoes)
Whitney Stakes (Cohoes)
1959: Futurity Stakes (Weatherwise)
1962: Hopeful Stakes (Outing Class)
Manhattan Handicap (Tutankhamen)
Bougainvillea Handicap (Eurasia)
1963: Canadian Championship Stakes (The Axe II)
Man o' War Stakes (The Axe II)
San Luis Rey Stakes (The Axe II)
Metropolitan Handicap (Cyrano)
Brooklyn Handicap (Cyrano)
Hollywood Juvenile Championship (Malicious)
Sanford Stakes (Delirium)
Wood Memorial Stakes (No Robbery)
Dwyer Handicap (Outing Class)
Donn Handicap (Tutankhamen)
1964: Los Angeles Handicap (Cyrano)
1965: Aqueduct Stakes (Malicious)
1966: Sunset Handicap (O'Hara)
1967: Gazelle Handicap (Sweet Folly)
Ladies Handicap (Sweet Folly)
1968: Belmont Stakes (Stage Door Johnny)
Dwyer Handicap (Stage Door Johnny)
1970: Arkansas Derby (Herbalist)
1972: Champagne Stakes (Stop the Music)
Manhattan Handicap (Ruritania)
1973: Dwyer Handicap (Stop the Music)
1974: Dwyer Handicap (Hatchet Man)
1976: Widener Handicap (Hatchet Man)
Amory L. Haskell Handicap (Hatchet Man)
Louisiana Derby (Johnny Appleseed)
1978: Delaware Handicap (Late Bloomer)
Ruffian Handicap (Late Bloomer)
Beldame Stakes (Late Bloomer)
Sheepshead Bay Handicap (Late Bloomer)
Gulfstream Park Handicap (Bowl Game)
Pan American Handicap (Bowl Game)
1979: Hialeah Turf Cup (Bowl Game)
Arlington Handicap (Bowl Game)
Man o' War Stakes (Bowl Game)
Turf Classic (Bowl Game)
Washington D.C. International (Bowl Game)
Oaklawn Handicap (San Juan Hill)
1980: Louisiana Derby (Prince Valiant)
1981: Louisiana Derby (Woodchopper)
Rothmans International Stakes (Open Call)
1982: Laurel Futurity (Cast Party)
Bowling Green Handicap (Open Call)
1983: Louisiana Downs Handicap (Late Act)
1985: United Nations Handicap (Ends Well)

GREENVILLE FARM INC.
1961: Californian Stakes (First Balcony)

JOHN GREER
1974: Sapling Stakes (Foolish Pleasure)
Hopeful Stakes (Foolish Pleasure)
Champagne Stakes (Foolish Pleasure)
1975: Flamingo Stakes (Foolish Pleasure)
Wood Memorial Stakes (Foolish Pleasure)
Kentucky Derby (Foolish Pleasure)
1976: Donn Handicap (Foolish Pleasure)
Suburban Handicap (Foolish Pleasure)

MRS. JOHN GREER
1967: Kentucky Jockey Club Stakes (Mr. Brogann)

JOHN GREER, MRS. MOODY JOLLEY & ERNEST WOODS
1962: Blue Grass Stakes (Ridan)
Arlington Classic (Ridan)

W. GRETZKY, SYLVESTER STALLONE & SUMMA STABLE
1989: Hollywood Turf Cup (Frankly Perfect)

WAYNE GRETZKY & SUMMA STABLE
1990: John Henry Handicap (Golden Pheasant)
Arlington Million (Golden Pheasant)

MR. and MRS. DICK GRIEGORIAN
1955: Del Mar Handicap (Arrogate)
1956: Del Mar Handicap (Arrogate)

LESLIE GRIMM
1994: Vanity Handicap (Potridee)

LESLIE GRIMM & GENE VOSS
1999: Coaching Club American Oaks (On a Soapbox)

MARGARET GRIMM
1987: Top Flight Handicap (Ms. Eloise)

CARL GRINSTEAD & BEN ROCHELLE
1985: Norfolk Stakes (Snow Chief)
Hollywood Futurity (Snow Chief)
1986: Florida Derby (Snow Chief)
Santa Anita Derby (Snow Chief)
Preakness Stakes (Snow Chief)
Jersey Derby (Snow Chief)
1987: Charles H. Strub Stakes (Snow Chief)

ALIE GRISSOM
1956: Louisiana Derby (Reaping Right)
1958: Breeders' Futurity (Namon)
1961: Breeders' Futurity (Roman Line)
1963: Louisiana Derby (City Line)

ALIE & JAMES GRISSOM
1969: New Orleans Handicap (Miracle Hill)
1970: Oaklawn Handicap (Charlie Jr.)
1971: New Orleans Handicap (Rio Bravo)
Oaklawn Handicap (Rio Bravo)

PERNE GRISSOM
1959: Monmouth Oaks (Royal Native)
Spinster Stakes (Royal Native)
1960: Black Helen Handicap (Royal Native)
Top Flight Handicap (Royal Native)

PERNE GRISSOM & EDWARD GROSFIELD
1953: Florida Derby (Money Broker)

A.G. GROLEAU
1962: Delaware Oaks (North South Gal)

FRANKLIN GROVES
1982: Hialeah Turf Cup (The Bart)
Century Handicap (The Bart)

GROVETREE STABLE
1976: Arlington Handicap (Victorian Prince)

RAYMOND GUEST
1968: Washington D.C. International (Sir Ivor)

MRS. W. GUEST & WACKER
1960: San Carlos Handicap (Clandestine)

MRS. GORDON GUIBERSON
1953: Blue Grass Stakes (Correspondent)
1954: Hollywood Gold Cup (Correspondent)

JOHN GUNTHER & HUGH HARLINGTON
1992: Jersey Derby (American Chance)

JOHN GUNTHER & PRAIRIE STAR RACING
1999: Louisiana Derby (Kimberlite Pipe)

L.P. GUY
1965: Lawrence Realization Stakes (Munden Point)
1966: Gallant Fox Handicap (Munden Point)
1967: Manhattan Handicap (Munden Point)

WALTER HAEFNER
1981: Hialeah Turf Cup (Lobsang II)

MRS. WALTER HAEFNER
1978: Hollywood Oaks (B. Thoughtful)
1979: La Canada Stakes (B. Thoughtful)

MRS. H.K. HAGGERTY
1948: Black Helen Handicap (Rampart)
Gulfstream Park Handicap (Rampart)

LOUIS LEE HAGGIN II
1957: Ohio Derby (Manteau)
1971: Sanford Stakes (Cohasset Tribe)
1975: Breeders' Futurity (Harbor Springs)

HAJJI FARM
1985: California Derby (Hajji's Treasure)

SARAH HALL
1970: Massachusetts Handicap (Semillant)

HALL & HAMMOND
1965: San Juan Capistrano Handicap (George Royal)
Canadian Championship Stakes (George Royal)
1966: San Juan Capistrano Handicap (George Royal)
Canadian International Championship (George Royal)

STUART HAMBLEN
1947: San Antonio Handicap (El Lobo)

EMORY HAMILTON
1991: Maskette Stakes (Queena)
Ruffian Handicap (Queena)
2001: Go for Wand Handicap (Serra Lake)

J.T. HAMMER & W.L. NEW
1999: Pegasus Handicap (Forty One Carats)

HAMPTON STABLE
1951: Discovery Handicap (Alerted)
Jerome Handicap (Alerted)
1952: Dixie Handicap (Alerted)

ARTHUR B. HANCOCK III
1987: Vanity Handicap (Infinidad)

ARTHUR B. HANCOCK III & LEONE J. PETERS
1980: Golden Harvest Handicap (Ribbon)
1981: Del Mar Futurity (Gato Del Sol)
1982: Kentucky Derby (Gato Del Sol)

ARTHUR B. HANCOCK III & JIMMY STONE
1999: Toyota Blue Grass Stakes (Menifee)
Haskell Invitational Handicap (Menifee)

BULL HANCOCK
1947: Kentucky Oaks (Blue Grass)

SETH HANCOCK
1974: Florida Derby (Judger)
Blue Grass Stakes (Judger)

MRS. JOHN W. HANES
1952: Comely Handicap (Devilkin)

ARNOLD HANGER
1947: Whitney Stakes (Rico Monte)
Manhattan Handicap (Rico Monte)
New York Handicap (Rico Monte)
1948: Suburban Handicap (Harmonica)
1953: United Nations Handicap (Iceberg II)
1955: Alabama Stakes (Rico Reta)
1956: Canadian Championship Stakes (Eugenia II)
1959: Dwyer Handicap (Waltz)

R.C. HANNA
1951: Garden State Stakes (Candle Wood)

ALICE HANSBROUGH
1946: California Derby (War Spun)

HAPPY HILL FARM
1957: New Orleans Handicap (Kingmaker)
Grey Lag Handicap (Kingmaker)
Whitney Stakes (Kingmaker)

HAPPY VALLEY FARM
1970: Gotham Stakes (Native Royalty)
1981: Alabama Stakes (Prismatical)
1982: Oaklawn Handicap (Eminency)
Louisiana Downs Handicap (Pair of Deuces)

HAR-BAR RANCH
1969: Gardenia Stakes (Fast Attack)

EDRIS HARBESTON, GEO. LOSH & VICTOR NACCARATO
1994: Hollywood Gold Cup (Slew of Damascus)

HARBORVALE STABLE
1951: Breeders' Futurity (Alladier)
1965: Monmouth Oaks (Summer Scandal)
1966: Top Flight Handicap (Summer Scandal)
Beldame Stakes (Summer Scandal)

HARBOR VIEW FARM
1960: Wood Memorial Stakes (Francis S.)
Dwyer Handicap (Francis S.)
Champagne Stakes (Roving Minstrel)
Pimlico Futurity (Garwol)
1961: Bougainvillea Turf Handicap (Wolfram)
Hialeah Turf Cup (Wolfram)
1962: Ladies Handicap (Royal Patrice)
1963: Champagne Stakes (Roman Brother)
1964: Everglades Stakes (Roman Brother)
Jersey Derby (Roman Brother)
American Derby (Roman Brother)
Jerome Handicap (Irvkup)
Arlington Handicap (Master Dennis)
1965: Woodward Stakes (Roman Brother)
Manhattan Handicap (Roman Brother)
Jockey Club Gold Cup (Roman Brother)
Everglades Stakes (Sparkling Johnny)
1966: Hollywood Juvenile Champ. (Forgotten Dreams)
1967: Sanford Stakes (Exclusive Native)
1968: Arlington Classic (Exclusive Native)
1971: Carter Handicap (Native Royalty)
Michigan Mile and One-Eighth (Native Royalty)
1974: Fountain of Youth Stakes (Green Gambados)
1975: Hempstead Handicap (Raisela)
1976: Illinois Derby (Life's Hope)
Jersey Derby (Life's Hope)
Carter Handicap (Due Diligence)
1977: Hollywood Juvenile Championship (Affirmed)
Hopeful Stakes (Affirmed)
Futurity Stakes (Affirmed)
Laurel Futurity (Affirmed)
Monmouth Invitational Handicap (Affiliate)
Vosburgh Handicap (Affiliate)
1978: San Felipe Handicap (Affirmed)
Santa Anita Derby (Affirmed)
Hollywood Derby (Affirmed)
Kentucky Derby (Affirmed)
Preakness Stakes (Affirmed)
Belmont Stakes (Affirmed)
New Orleans Handicap (Life's Hope)
Amory L. Haskell Handicap (Life's Hope)
Oak Leaf Stakes (It's In the Air)
1979: Californian Stakes (Affirmed)
Hollywood Gold Cup (Affirmed)
Woodward Stakes (Affirmed)
Jockey Club Gold Cup (Affirmed)
Charles H. Strub Stakes (Affirmed)
Santa Anita Handicap (Affirmed)
Alabama Stakes (It's In the Air)
Vanity Handicap (It's In the Air)
Ruffian Handicap (It's In the Air)
Gamely Handicap (Sisterhood)
1980: Vanity Handicap (It's In the Air)
1982: Super Derby (Reinvested)
1984: Breeders' Cup Juvenile Fillies (Outstandingly)
1989: California Derby (Endow)
1992: Matriarch Stakes (Flawlessly)
1993: Ramona Handicap (Flawlessly)
Beverly D. Stakes (Flawlessly)
Matriarch Stakes (Flawlessly)
1994: Ramona Handicap (Flawlessly)

HARBOR VIEW FARM & ETHEL JACOBS
1977: Santa Barbara Handicap (Desiree)

HASTINGS HARCOURT
1970: Amory L. Haskell Handicap (Gladwin)
Hawthorne Gold Cup (Gladwin)
Acorn Stakes (Cathy Honey)
Ladies Handicap (Cathy Honey)

MR. and MRS. HASTINGS HARCOURT
1978: Santa Barbara Handicap (Kittyluck)

MRS. TAYLOR HARDIN
1976: Spinaway Stakes (Mrs. Warren)
Matron Stakes (Mrs. Warren)

HARRIS FARMS INC.
1976: La Canada Stakes (Raise Your Skirts)

H.M. HARRIS
1966: Carter Handicap (Davis II)

SIR ERNEST HARRISON
1989: Californian Stakes (Sabona)

LADY JANE HARRISON
1990: Turf Classic (Cacoethes)

MR. and MRS. HARRY HART
1965: Cinema Handicap (Arksroni)

CLARENCE HARTWICK
1951: Arlington Matron Handicap (Sickle's Image)
1952: Vineland Handicap (Sickle's Image)
1953: Washington Park Handicap (Sickle's Image)

HASTY HOUSE FARM
1950: Washington Park Handicap (Inseparable)
Stars and Stripes Handicap (Inseparable)
1951: Hawthorne Gold Cup (Seaward)
1953: Arlington Futurity (Hasty Road)
Washington Park Futurity (Hasty Road)
Breeders' Futurity (Hasty Road)
Kentucky Jockey Club Stakes (Hasty Road)
Arlington Lassie Stakes (Queen Hopeful)
Princess Pat Stakes (Queen Hopeful)
Lawrence Realization Stakes (Platan)
1954: Kentucky Jockey Club Stakes (Prince Noor)
Preakness Stakes (Hasty Road)
Arlington Handicap (Stan)
1955: Everglades Stakes (Prince Noor)
Widener Handicap (Hasty Road)
New Orleans Handicap (Sea O Erin)
Gulfstream Park Handicap (Mister Black)
Hialeah Turf Handicap (Stan)
Arlington Handicap (Platan)
1956: Bougainvillea Turf Handicap (Summer Solstice)
1957: Princess Pat Stakes (Hasty Doll)
Washington D.C. International (Mahan)
1958: Bougainvillea Turf Handicap (Stephanotis)
Canadian Championship Stakes (Jack Ketch)
1959: Canadian Championship Stakes (Martini II)
1962: Hialeah Turf Cup (El Loco)
1964: Hialeah Turf Cup (Carteret)
1967: Gallant Fox Handicap (Niarkos)
San Juan Capistrano Handicap (Niarkos)
San Luis Rey Handicap (Niarkos)
1968: San Juan Capistrano Handicap (Niarkos)
1972: Pan American Handicap (Unanime)

HASTY HOUSE FARM & CORA MAE TROTSEK
1952: New Orleans Handicap (Oil Capitol)
1953: Widener Handicap (Oil Capitol)
Arlington Handicap (Oil Capitol)

MEL HATLEY
1983: Oak Leaf Stakes (Life's Magic)

MEL HATLEY & GENE KLEIN
1984: Mother Goose Stakes (Life's Magic)
Alabama Stakes (Life's Magic)
Beldame Stakes (Life's Magic)
1985: Breeders' Cup Distaff (Life's Magic)

MEL HATLEY & JEFF LUKAS
1986: Everglades Stakes (Badger Land)
Flamingo Stakes (Badger Land)

MEL HATLEY & YANK
1978: American Handicap (Effervescing)

HATSKIN & SAIR
1959: Louisiana Derby (Master Palynch)

J.C. HAUER
1950: Kentucky Oaks (Ari's Mona)
1960: Michigan Mile and One-Sixteenth (Little Fitz)

HAVAHOME STABLE
1948: Gazelle Stakes (Sweet Dream)

HAWKSWORTH FARM
1978: Champagne Stakes (Spectacular Bid)
Young America Stakes (Spectacular Bid)
Laurel Futurity (Spectacular Bid)
1979: Florida Derby (Spectacular Bid)
Flamingo Stakes (Spectacular Bid)
Blue Grass Stakes (Spectacular Bid)
Kentucky Derby (Spectacular Bid)
Preakness Stakes (Spectacular Bid)
Marlboro Cup Handicap (Spectacular Bid)
Meadowlands Cup (Spectacular Bid)
1980: Californian Stakes (Spectacular Bid)
Amory L. Haskell Handicap (Spectacular Bid)
Woodward Stakes (Spectacular Bid)
San Fernando Stakes (Spectacular Bid)
Charles H. Strub Stakes (Spectacular Bid)
Santa Anita Handicap (Spectacular Bid)

WILLIAM R. HAWN
1968: Hollywood Derby (Poleax)
1970: Hollywood Oaks (Last of the Line)
1977: Hollywood Invitational Handicap (Vigors)
1978: San Antonio Stakes (Vigors)
Santa Anita Handicap (Vigors)
1985: Santa Margarita Handicap (Lovlier Linda)
1986: San Fernando Stakes (Right Con)

MRS. WILLIAM R. HAWN
1964: Santa Susana Stakes (Blue Norther)
Kentucky Oaks (Blue Norther)

ALEC HEAD
1996: Ramona Handicap (Matiara)

AASE HEADLEY & PAUL LEUNG
2002: La Brea Stakes (Got Koko)

B. HEADLEY, HIGH TECH ST. & ANDREW & I. MOLASKY
2000: Breeders' Cup Sprint (Kona Gold)
2001: San Carlos Handicap (Kona Gold)

DUVAL HEADLEY
1950: Demoiselle Stakes (Aunt Jinny)
Selima Stakes (Aunt Jinny)

GUS HEADLEY
1991: Del Mar Futurity (Bertrando)
Norfolk Stakes (Bertrando)
1992: San Felipe Stakes (Bertrando)

HAL PRICE HEADLEY
1946: Ladies Handicap (Athenia)
Louisiana Derby (Pellicle)
1948: Demoiselle Stakes (Lithe)
1949: Arlington Matron Handicap (Lithe)
Comely Handicap (Lithe)
1950: Arlington Matron Handicap (Lithe)
1951: Pimlico Futurity (Cajun)
1954: Washington Park Futurity (Georgian)
1955: Princess Pat Stakes (Supple)
1960: Delaware Oaks (Rash Statement)
Spinster Stakes (Rash Statement)

THOMAS HEARD JR.
1996: Fountain of Youth Stakes (Built for Pleasure)

HEARDSDALE
1975: Jerome Handicap (Guards Up)

HEATHERWOOD FARM
1993: Gotham Stakes (As Indicated)
1994: Pimlico Special (As Indicated)

MRS. HENRY HECHT
1955: Champagne Stakes (Beau Fond)

MARY HECHT
1964: Saratoga Special (Sadair)

DAVID & JILL HEERENSPERGER
2001: Toyota Blue Grass Stakes (Millennium Wind)

MRS. ROBERT W. HEIGHE
1946: Black Helen Handicap (Adroit)

HEILIGBRODT RACING STABLE
2003: Test Stakes (Lady Tak)

HEILIGBRODT RACING STABLE & TEAM VALOR
2001: Las Virgenes Stakes (Golden Ballet)
Santa Anita Oaks (Golden Ballet)
Spinaway Stakes (Cashier's Dream)

HELBUSH FARM
1955: Santa Anita Handicap (Poona II)

ESTATE OF WILLIAM HELIS
1950: Vineland Handicap (Almahmoud)

WILLIAM HELIS
1946: Arlington Futurity (Cosmic Bomb)
Cowdin Stakes (Cosmic Bomb)
Acorn Stakes (Earshot)
1947: Discovery Handicap (Cosmic Bomb)
Lawrence Realization Stakes (Cosmic Bomb)
Roamer Handicap (Cosmic Bomb)
Trenton Handicap (Cosmic Bomb)
New Castle Handicap (Elpis)
Comely Handicap (Elpis)
Molly Pitcher Handicap (Elpis)
Fall Highweight Handicap (Rippey)
Carter Handicap (Rippey)
Vineland Handicap (Miss Kimo)
New Orleans Handicap (Earshot)
1948: San Vicente Handicap (Salmagundi)
Santa Anita Derby (Salmagundi)
Roseben Handicap (Rippey)

WILLIAM HELIS JR.
1951: Gulfstream Park Handicap (Ennobled)
1952: McLennan Handicap (Spartan Valor)
Widener Handicap (Spartan Valor)
Excelsior Handicap (Spartan Valor)
Gallant Fox Handicap (Spartan Valor)
1953: Tropical Park Handicap (Spartan Valor)
1954: Pimlico Special (Helioscope)
Trenton Handicap (Helioscope)
1955: Massachusetts Handicap (Helioscope)
Suburban Handicap (Helioscope)
Monmouth Handicap (Helioscope)
1959: Sapling Stakes (Sky Clipper)
1965: Pan American Handicap (Cool Prince)

NEIL HELLMAN
1969: Dwyer Handicap (Gleaming Light)
1971: Gotham Stakes (Good Behaving)
Wood Memorial Stakes (Good Behaving)
1973: San Felipe Handicap (Linda's Chief)
California Derby (Linda's Chief)
Withers Stakes (Linda's Chief)
Pontiac Grand Prix Stakes (Linda's Chief)

O. HELMAN
1981: Pan American Handicap (Little Bonny)

HELMORE FARM
1982: Matron Stakes (Wings of Jove)

JIM HELZER
1999: Eddie Read Handicap (Joe Who)

MRS. H. HERFF
1959: Hialeah Turf Cup (Tudor Era)
Man o' War Handicap (Tudor Era)
1960: New Orleans Handicap (Tudor Era)

HERFF & LA CROIX
1966: Donn Handicap (Tronado)
Arlington Handicap (Tronado)

JOHN HERSBERGER
1969: John B. Campbell Handicap (Juvenile John)

PHILIP HERSH
1994: San Antonio Handicap (The Wicked North)
Oaklawn Handicap (The Wicked North)
Californian Stakes (The Wicked North)

MRS. JOHN D. HERTZ
1947: Swift Stakes (Owners Choice)
San Felipe Stakes (Owners Choice)
1948: Frizette Stakes (Our Fleet)
1953: Del Mar Futurity (Double Speed)
1954: Acorn Stakes (Happy Mood)

ABRAM HEWITT
1949: Garden State Stakes (Cornwall)
1979: Sunset Handicap (Sirlad)

MRS. PAUL HEXTER
1982: Arkansas Derby (Hostage)

ROBERT HIBBERT
1971: San Fernando Stakes (Willowick)
1982: Del Mar Futurity (Roving Boy)
Norfolk Stakes (Roving Boy)
Hollywood Futurity (Roving Boy)
1992: Oak Tree Invitational Stakes (Navarone)

HICKORY TREE STABLE
1964: Mother Goose Stakes (Sceree)
1970: Withers Stakes (Hagley)
1972: John B. Campbell Handicap (Favorecidian)
Michigan Mile and One-Eighth (Favorecidian)
1973: American Derby (Bemo)
1976: Demoiselle Stakes (Bring Out the Band)
1977: Remsen Stakes (Believe It)
Acorn Stakes (Bring Out the Band)
United Nations Handicap (Bemo)
1978: Wood Memorial Stakes (Believe It)
1979: Sheepshead Bay Handicap (Terpsichorist)
1980: Louisiana Downs Handicap (It's True)
1983: Laurel Futurity (Devil's Bag)
Champagne Stakes (Devil's Bag)
1987: Gotham Stakes (Gone West)
Withers Stakes (Gone West)
Dwyer Stakes (Gone West)

HIDDEN VALLEY FARM
1967: Kentucky Oaks (Nancy Jr.)

JOSEPH HIGGINS
2003: Flower Bowl Invitational Stakes (Dimitrova)

HIGH GROUND STABLE
1951: Sapling Stakes (Landseair)

HIGH TIDE STABLE
1961: Sunset Handicap (Whodunit)

STEPHEN HILBERT
1997: Ruffian Handicap (Tomisue's Delight)
1998: Personal Ensign Handicap (Tomisue's Delight)
1999: Gallery Furniture.com Stakes (Stephen Got Even)
2000: Donn Handicap (Stephen Got Even)

ALICE HILL
1966: New Orleans Handicap (Just About)

ETHEL HILL
1946: Santa Anita Handicap (War Knight)

DR. JIM HILL & MICKEY TAYLOR
1985: Hollywood Derby (Slew the Dragon)

DR. and MRS. J. HILL, O. PHIPPS, MR. and MRS. M. TAYLOR
1988: Breeders' Futurity (Fast Play)
Remsen Stakes (Fast Play)

CAROLYN HINE
1996: Blue Grass Stakes (Skip Away)
Ohio Derby (Skip Away)
Buick Haskell Invitational Handicap (Skip Away)
Woodbine Million (Skip Away)
Jockey Club Gold Cup (Skip Away)
1997: Suburban Handicap (Skip Away)
Jockey Club Gold Cup (Skip Away)
Breeders' Cup Classic (Skip Away)
1998: Donn Handicap (Skip Away)
Gulfstream Park Handicap (Skip Away)
Pimlico Special (Skip Away)
Hollywood Gold Cup (Skip Away)
Philip H. Iselin Handicap (Skip Away)
Woodward Stakes (Skip Away)

S.D. HINKLE
1984: Breeders' Futurity (Crater Fire)

BO HIRSCH
2002: Del Mar Debutante Stakes (Miss Houdini)

CLEMENT L. HIRSCH
1969: Hollywood Gold Cup (Figonero)
1970: Del Mar Futurity (June Darling)
Norfolk Stakes (June Darling)
Oak Leaf Stakes (June Darling)
Gulfstream Park Handicap (Snow Sporting)
Charles H. Strub Stakes (Snow Sporting)
1991: Hollywood Starlet Stakes (Magical Maiden)

MR. and MRS. CLEMENT L. HIRSCH
1951: Del Mar Handicap (Blue Reading)

ABE HIRSCHBERG
1946: Santa Margarita Handicap (Canina)
1949: Del Mar Derby (Bolero)
San Antonio Handicap (Dinner Gong)
1951: San Carlos Handicap (Bolero)
1952: American Handicap (Admiral Drake)

HENRY HIRSCHMAN
1979: Bay Meadows Handicap (Leonotis)

HOBEAU FARM
1962: Suburban Handicap (Beau Purple)
Brooklyn Handicap (Beau Purple)
Hawthorne Gold Cup (Beau Purple)
Man o' War Stakes (Beau Purple)
1963: Widener Handicap (Beau Purple)
1965: Seminole Handicap (Sunstruck)
Gallant Fox Handicap (Choker)
1967: Amory L. Haskell Handicap (Handsome Boy)
Brooklyn Handicap (Handsome Boy)
Washington Park Handicap (Handsome Boy)
Black Helen Handicap (Mac's Sparkler)
Beldame Stakes (Mac's Sparkler)
1969: Manhattan Handicap (Harem Lady)
1970: Black Helen Handicap (Taken Aback)
Spinster Stakes (Taken Aback)
Widener Handicap (Never Bow)
1971: Delaware Handicap (Blessing Angelica)
Metropolitan Handicap (Tunex)
Vosburgh Handicap (Duck Dance)
1972: Delaware Handicap (Blessing Angelica)
1973: Widener Handicap (Vertee)
John B. Campbell Handicap (Vertee)
Woodward Stakes (Prove Out)
Jockey Club Gold Cup (Prove Out)
Top Flight Handicap (Poker Night)
Ladies Handicap (Wakefield Miss)
Jerome Handicap (Step Nicely)
Whitney Stakes (Onion)
1974: Hempstead Handicap (Poker Night)
Grey Lag Handicap (Prove Out)
Hawthorne Gold Cup (Group Plan)
1975: Jockey Club Gold Cup (Group Plan)
1985: Top Flight Handicap (Flip's Pleasure)
1998: Frank J. De Francis Memorial Dash (Kelly Kip)

HAROLD HODOSH
1975: Vosburgh Handicap (No Bias)

GEORGIA HOFFMAN
1979: Breeders' Futurity (Gold Stage)
1992: Matron Stakes (Sky Beauty)
1993: Acorn Stakes (Sky Beauty)
Mother Goose Stakes (Sky Beauty)
Coaching Club American Oaks (Sky Beauty)
Alabama Stakes (Sky Beauty)
1994: Shuvee Handicap (Sky Beauty)
Hempstead Handicap (Sky Beauty)
Go for Wand Stakes (Sky Beauty)
Ruffian Handicap (Sky Beauty)
1997: Gazelle Handicap (Royal Indy)

HOLIDAY STABLE
1967: Louisiana Derby (Ask the Fare)

JERRY HOLLENDORFER & GEORGE TODARO
1996: Kentucky Oaks (Pike Place Dancer)

J. HOLLENDORFER, G. TODARO & TEMPLE WEBBER JR.
2000: Turfway Spiral Stakes (Globalize)

BARBARA HOLLERAN
1986: Suburban Handicap (Roo Art)
Philip H. Iselin Handicap (Roo Art)

GEORGE HOLTSINGER
1964: Arkansas Derby (Prince Davelle)

FRED W. HOOPER
1948: Breeders' Futurity (Olympia)
Vosburgh Handicap (Colosal)
1949: San Felipe Stakes (Olympia)
Flamingo Stakes (Olympia)
Wood Memorial Stakes (Olympia)
Withers Stakes (Olympia)
1950: Roseben Handicap (Olympia)
1953: Trenton Handicap (Olympic)
1956: Arlington Futurity (Greek Game)
Washington Park Futurity (Greek Game)
1960: Washington Park Futurity (Crozier)
Monmouth Oaks (Teacation)
1961: Kentucky Oaks (My Portrait)

Monmouth Oaks (My Portrait)
1962: Louisiana Derby (Admiral's Voyage)
Wood Memorial Stakes (Admiral's Voyage)
Kentucky Jockey Club Stakes (Sky Gem)
Gardenia Stakes (Main Swap)
Los Angeles Handicap (Winonly)
Aqueduct Stakes (Crozier)
1963: Santa Anita Handicap (Crozier)
San Carlos Handicap (Crozier)
Carter Handicap (Admiral's Voyage)
Californian Stakes (Winonly)
1964: San Carlos Handicap (Admiral's Voyage)
1965: Breeders' Futurity (Tinsley)
1966: Alcibiades Stakes (Teacher's Art)
1972: Santa Susana Stakes (Susan's Girl)
Kentucky Oaks (Susan's Girl)
Acorn Stakes (Susan's Girl)
Gazelle Handicap (Susan's Girl)
Beldame Stakes (Susan's Girl)
1973: Delaware Handicap (Susan's Girl)
Spinster Stakes (Susan's Girl)
Santa Maria Handicap (Susan's Girl)
Santa Margarita Handicap (Susan's Girl)
Santa Barbara Handicap (Susan's Girl)
Futurity Stakes (Wedge Shot)
Arlington-Washington Lassie Stakes (Special Team)
Hawthorne Gold Cup (Tri Jet)
1974: Kentucky Oaks (Quaze Quilt)
Alabama Stakes (Quaze Quilt)
Acorn Stakes (Special Team)
Whitney Stakes (Tri Jet)
1975: Delaware Handicap (Susan's Girl)
Beldame Stakes (Susan's Girl)
Spinster Stakes (Susan's Girl)
1978: Futurity Stakes (Crest of the Wave)
1981: Del Mar Debutante Stakes (Skillful Joy)
Hollywood Starlet Stakes (Skillful Joy)
1982: Hopeful Stakes (Copelan)
Futurity Stakes (Copelan)
Champagne Stakes (Copelan)
San Felipe Handicap (Advance Man)
Swaps Stakes (Journey at Sea)
1984: Swaps Stakes (Precisionist)
1985: San Fernando Stakes (Precisionist)
Charles H. Strub Stakes (Precisionist)
Breeders' Cup Sprint (Precisionist)
1986: Californian Stakes (Precisionist)
Woodward Stakes (Precisionist)
1991: Champagne Stakes (Tri to Watch)
1996: Early Times Manhattan Handicap (Diplomatic Jet)
Man o' War Stakes (Diplomatic Jet)
Turf Classic (Diplomatic Jet)

MRS. FRED W. HOOPER
1946: Washington Park Futurity (Education)
Breeders' Futurity (Education)

ELIZABETH HOPKINS
1949: Queens County Handicap (Three Rings)
Monmouth Handicap (Three Rings)
Westchester Handicap (Three Rings)
1950: McLennan Handicap (Three Rings)
Queens County Handicap (Three Rings)

MRS. G.T. HOPKINS
1973: Hopeful Stakes (Gusty O'Shay)

MARK HOPKINS
2003: Frank J. De Francis Memorial Dash (A Huevo)

HORIZON STABLE
1997: Travers Stakes (Deputy Commander)
Super Derby (Deputy Commander)

HORIZON STABLE, MIKE JARVIS & LLOYD TABER
1996: Strub Stakes (Helmsman)

TADAHIRO HOTEHAMA
1991: Milady Handicap (Brought to Mind)
Vanity Handicap (Brought to Mind)

STANLEY HOUGH, JOHN PASTOREK & ROGER PATTON
1991: Arlington-Washington Futurity (Caller I.D.)

J.K. HOUSSELS
1962: Hollywood Juvenile Championship (Y Flash)
Hollywood Juvenile Championship (Noti)
1963: Cinema Handicap (Y Flash)
Hollywood Derby (Y Flash)
Hollywood Juvenile Championship (Nevada Bin)
Arlington-Washington Lassie Stakes (Sari's Song)
Del Mar Debutante Stakes (Leisurely Kin)
1964: San Fernando Stakes (Nevada Battler)

ESTATE OF CHARLES S. HOWARD
1950: Golden Gate Handicap (Noor)
American Handicap (Noor)
Hollywood Gold Cup (Noor)

CHARLES S. HOWARD
1946: San Pasqual Handicap (Lou-Bre)
1948: Santa Margarita Handicap (Miss Doreen)
1949: Will Rogers Handicap (Blue Dart)
1950: Santa Anita Handicap (Noor)
San Juan Capistrano Handicap (Noor)

LYNN HOWARD
1963: Arlington Park Handicap (Bounding Main)

DEERING HOWE
1946: Sapling Stakes (Donor)
Champagne Stakes (Donor)
Fall Highweight Handicap (Cassis)
1947: Jerome Handicap (Donor)

MRS. DEERING HOWE
1949: Manhattan Handicap (Donor)
New York Handicap (Donor)

R.D. HUBBARD, G. MONTAGNA, A. SOPRANO, J.J. VARSI
1997: San Antonio Handicap (Gentlemen)
Pimlico Special (Gentlemen)
Hollywood Gold Cup (Gentlemen)
Pacific Classic (Gentlemen)
1998: San Antonio Handicap (Gentlemen)

R.D. HUBBARD & RIO CLARO THOROUGHBREDS
1999: Beverly Hills Handicap (Virginie)

R.D. HUBBARD & DWIGHT SUTHERLAND
1999: Donn Handicap (Puerto Madero)

EDWARD HUDSON
1980: Sunset Handicap (Inkerman)

JOHN HUDSPETH
1969: San Antonio Stakes (Praise Jay)

HAZEL HUFFMAN
1971: Charles H. Strub Stakes (War Heim)
1972: Miller High Life Inglewood Handicap (War Heim)

WAYNE HUGHES
1998: Early Times Turf Classic (Joyeaux Danseur)
2003: Del Mar Futurity (Siphonizer)
Bessemer Trust BC Juvenile (Action This Day)

MRS. T.P. HULL JR. & RALPH WILSON
1957: Kentucky Jockey Club Stakes (Hill Country)
1963: Garden State Stakes (Hurry to Market)

LOUISE & WATTS HUMPHREY JR.
2001: Test Stakes (Victory Ride)

WATTS HUMPHREY JR.
1979: Delaware Handicap (Likely Exchange)
1997: John A. Morris Handicap (Clear Mandate)
Three Chimneys Spinster Stakes (Clear Mandate)

NELSON BUNKER HUNT
1967: Hollywood Oaks (Amerigo Lady)
1971: Cowdin Stakes (Loquacious Don)
1972: United Nations Handicap (Acclimatization)
1973: Washington D.C. International (Dahlia)
1974: Man o' War Stakes (Dahlia)
Canadian International Championship (Dahlia)
1975: Bowling Green Handicap (Barcas)
Washington D.C. International (Nobiliary)
1976: Canadian International Championship (Youth)
Washington D.C. International (Youth)
Hollywood Invitational Handicap (Dahlia)
1977: Canadian International Championship (Exceller)
1978: Yellow Ribbon Stakes (Amazer)
1979: Golden Harvest Handicap (Flaunter)
1980: Norfolk Stakes (High Counsel)
1982: California Derby (Rockwall)
1983: Top Flight Handicap (Adept)
1985: Santa Barbara Handicap (Fact Finder)
1987: Flamingo Stakes (Talinum)
Santa Barbara Handicap (Reloy)
San Juan Capistrano Handicap (Rosedale)
Hollywood Invitational Handicap (Rivlia)
Sunset Handicap (Swink)
Laurel Futurity (Antiqua)

NELSON BUNKER HUNT & ALLEN PAULSON
1986: California Derby (Vernon Castle)
John Henry Handicap (Palace Music)

NELSON B. HUNT, ALLEN PAULSON & SUMMA STABLE
1986: San Luis Rey Stakes (Dahar)
San Juan Capistrano Handicap (Dahar)

NELSON BUNKER HUNT & FRANK STRONACH
1980: Top Flight Handicap (Glorious Song)
Santa Margarita Handicap (Glorious Song)
1981: Spinster Stakes (Glorious Song)

BARBARA HUNTER
1962: Arlington Matron Handicap (Kootenai)
1970: Beverly Hills Handicap (Pattee Canyon)

HUNTER FARM
1984: Arlington-Washington Futurity (Spend A Buck)
1985: Kentucky Derby (Spend A Buck)
Jersey Derby (Spend A Buck)
Monmouth Handicap (Spend A Buck)

W.L. HUNTLEY
1955: Black Helen Handicap (Rosemary B.)

PHILLIP HURLEY
1979: Alcibiades Stakes (Salud)

HURLOCK & JACK VAN BERG
1982: Louisiana Downs Handicap (Rich and Ready)

BRIAN HURST
1985: Gotham Stakes (Eternal Prince)
Wood Memorial Stakes (Eternal Prince)

BRUCE HUTSON
1990: Ohio Derby (Private School)

CARL ICAHN
1990: Spinaway Stakes (Meadow Star)
Matron Stakes (Meadow Star)
Frizette Stakes (Meadow Star)
Breeders' Cup Juvenile Fillies (Meadow Star)
Ladies Handicap (Colonial Waters)
1991: Acorn Stakes (Meadow Star)
Mother Goose Stakes (Meadow Star)

JOHN & JOSEPH IRACANE & PADUA STABLES
2003: Breeders' Cup Sprint (Cajun Beat)

IRISH ACRES FARM
1991: Flower Bowl Handicap (Lady Shirl)

JIMMY ISELIN & ROBERT KAUFMAN
1993: Vosburgh Stakes (Birdonthewire)

ALLAN IVAN
1995: Peter Pan Stakes (Citadeed)

LORD IVEAGH
1969: Washington D.C. International (Karabas)

BRUCE JACKSON & JOHN SWIFT
1993: Oaklawn Handicap (Jovial)

HOWELL JACKSON
1946: Pimlico Oaks (Red Shoes)
1954: Maskette Handicap (Ballerina)
1955: Gardenia Stakes (Nasrina)
Frizette Stakes (Nasrina)
1965: Mother Goose Stakes (Cordially)

JACLYN STABLE
1947: Wood Memorial Stakes (I Will)
Roseben Handicap (Inroc)
1954: United Nations Handicap (Closed Door)
1957: Bougainvillea Turf Handicap (Espea)
1964: Carter Handicap (Ahoy)
1968: Century Handicap (Model Fool)
1976: Sapling Stakes (Ali Oop)

JACNOT STABLE
1961: Arkansas Derby (Light Talk)
United Nations Handicap (Oink)
1967: Santa Margarita Handicap (Miss Moona)

ETHEL JACOBS
1946: Grey Lag Handicap (Stymie)
Whitney Stakes (Stymie)
Manhattan Handicap (Stymie)
New York Handicap (Stymie)

ETHEL JACOBS *(Continued)*
Gallant Fox Handicap (Stymie)
1947: Metropolitan Handicap (Stymie)
Massachusetts Handicap (Stymie)
Aqueduct Handicap (Stymie)
Gallant Fox Handicap (Stymie)
1948: Metropolitan Handicap (Stymie)
Aqueduct Handicap (Stymie)
1954: John B. Campbell Memorial Handicap (Joe Jones)
1956: Top Flight Handicap (Searching)
Diana Handicap (Searching)
Maskette Handicap (Searching)
1957: Lawrence Realization Stakes (Promised Land)
Roamer Handicap (Promised Land)
Pimlico Special (Promised Land)
1958: John B. Campbell Mem. Handicap (Promised Land)
Massachusetts Handicap (Promised Land)
San Juan Capistrano Handicap (Promised Land)
Molly Pitcher Handicap (Searching)
Diana Handicap (Searching)
1961: Santa Margarita Handicap (Sister Antoine)
1962: Sorority Stakes (Affectionately)
Spinaway Stakes (Affectionately)
1964: Arlington-Washington Lassie Stakes (Admiring)
1965: Futurity Stakes (Priceless Gem)
Frizette Stakes (Priceless Gem)
Hollywood Oaks (Straight Deal)
Ladies Handicap (Straight Deal)
Top Flight Handicap (Affectionately)
1966: Santa Margarita Handicap (Straight Deal)
Santa Barbara Handicap (Straight Deal)
San Fernando Stakes (Isle of Greece)
1967: Top Flight Handicap (Straight Deal)
Delaware Handicap (Straight Deal)
Spinster Stakes (Straight Deal)
Everglades Stakes (Reflected Glory)
Flamingo Stakes (Reflected Glory)
1969: Futurity Stakes (High Echelon)
Pimlico-Laurel Futurity (High Echelon)
1970: Wood Memorial Stakes (Personality)
Preakness Stakes (Personality)
Jersey Derby (Personality)
Woodward Stakes (Personality)
Belmont Stakes (High Echelon)
1984: Delaware Handicap (Adored)
Santa Margarita Handicap (Adored)
1986: Del Mar Futurity (Qualify)

DR. MANUEL JACOBS & MARTIN & PAM WYGOD
1995: Vanity Handicap (Private Persuasion)

PATRICE JACOBS
1960: Sapling Stakes (Hail to Reason)
Hopeful Stakes (Hail to Reason)
1966: Frizette Stakes (Regal Gleam)
Selima Stakes (Regal Gleam)
1967: California Derby (Reason to Hail)

MR. and MRS. HARRY JAMES
1951: Del Mar Futurity (Big Noise)

L. JAMESON
1979: Hollywood Juvenile Championship (Parsec)

STUART JANNEY III
1997: Remsen Stakes (Coronado's Quest)
1998: Wood Memorial Stakes (Coronado's Quest)

STUART JANNEY III & STONERSIDE STABLE
1998: Buick Haskell Inv. Handicap (Coronado's Quest)
Travers Stakes (Coronado's Quest)

JAWL BROTHERS
1987: San Antonio Handicap (Bedside Promise)

DR. KALARIKKAL JAYARAMAN
1988: Young America Stakes (Irish Actor)

JAYEFF B. STABLE
1990: Breeders' Cup Sprint (Safely Kept)
Secretariat Stakes (Ciro)

JAYEFF B. STABLE & BRERETON C. JONES
1988: Apple Blossom Handicap (By Land By Sea)

WALTER M. JEFFORDS
1946: Jockey Club Gold Cup (Pavot)
Massachusetts Handicap (Pavot)
1947: Beldame Handicap (Snow Goose)
Ladies Handicap (Snow Goose)
1948: Manhattan Handicap (Loyal Legion)
1951: Acorn Stakes (Kiss Me Kate)
Delaware Oaks (Kiss Me Kate)
Gazelle Stakes (Kiss Me Kate)
Alabama Stakes (Kiss Me Kate)
1952: New Castle Handicap (Kiss Me Kate)
1953: Firenze Handicap (Kiss Me Kate)
1958: Travers Stakes (Piano Jim)

MRS. WALTER M. JEFFORDS
1946: Travers Stakes (Natchez)
Jerome Handicap (Mahout)
1949: Alabama Stakes (Adile)
1950: New Castle Handicap (Adile)
1951: Flamingo Stakes (Yildiz)
1952: Belmont Stakes (One Count)
Travers Stakes (One Count)
Jockey Club Gold Cup (One Count)
Alabama Stakes (Lily White)
1963: Selima Stakes (My Card)

WALTER M. JEFFORDS JR.
1970: Gardenia Stakes (Eggy)

RUKIN JELKS
1955: Del Mar Debutante Stakes (Miss Todd)

RUKIN JELKS & PETER McBEAN
1957: Starlet Stakes (Old Pueblo)
Del Mar Futurity (Old Pueblo)

A.T. JERGINS
1947: Starlet Stakes (Zenoda)

J.K. STABLE & ROYAL OAKS FARM
1971: Hollywood Juvenile Championship (Royal Owl)

JOCKEY CLUB STABLE
1984: Widener Handicap (Mat Boy)
Gulfstream Park Handicap (Mat Boy)

J.E. JOHNSON
1978: Arlington Handicap (Romeo)

ELLWOOD JOHNSTON
1947: Del Mar Handicap (Iron Maiden)

MR. and MRS. ELLWOOD JOHNSTON
1959: Del Mar Debutante Stakes (Darling June)
1960: Californian Stakes (Fleet Nasrullah)
1964: California Derby (Real Good Deal)
Hollywood Derby (Real Good Deal)
1970: Del Mar Debutante Stakes (Generous Portion)
1971: Del Mar Debutante Stakes (Impressive Style)

MRS. MOODY JOLLEY
1961: Arlington Futurity (Ridan)
Washington Park Futurity (Ridan)
Arlington Lassie Stakes (Rudoma)
1962: Florida Derby (Ridan)
1977: Whitney Handicap (Nearly On Time)

AARON JONES
1974: Fantasy Stakes (Miss Musket)
Hollywood Oaks (Miss Musket)
Beverly Hills Handicap (La Zanzara)
1975: Beverly Hills Handicap (La Zanzara)
San Juan Capistrano Handicap (La Zanzara)
1978: Ladies Handicap (Ida Delia)
1982: Marlboro Cup Handicap (Lemhi Gold)
Jockey Club Gold Cup (Lemhi Gold)
Sword Dancer Stakes (Lemhi Gold)
San Juan Capistrano Handicap (Lemhi Gold)
1986: Fantasy Stakes (Tiffany Lass)
Kentucky Oaks (Tiffany Lass)

AARON & MARIE JONES
1999: San Felipe Stakes (Prime Timber)
King's Bishop Stakes (Forestry)
Del Mar Futurity (Forest Camp)
2000: Santa Margarita Handicap (Riboletta)
Milady Breeders' Cup Handicap (Riboletta)
Vanity Handicap (Riboletta)
Ruffian Handicap (Riboletta)
Beldame Stakes (Riboletta)
Three Chimneys Spinster Stakes (Plenty of Light)

CLIFFORD H. JONES & SONS
1949: Westerner Stakes (Pedigree)
Cinema Handicap (Pedigree)
Hollywood Oaks (June Bride)
1952: Golden Gate Handicap (Lights Up)
1953: Sunset Handicap (Lights Up)
1956: Santa Margarita Handicap (Our Betters)
1957: Santa Margarita Handicap (Our Betters)

FLETCHER JONES
1966: Hollywood Derby (Fleet Host)

GARY JONES & ESTATE OF McLEOD
1976: San Antonio Stakes (Lightning Mandate)

H.G. JONES
1946: Kentucky Oaks (First Page)

JAMES JONES
1964: Vanity Handicap (Star Maggie)
1965: Spinster Stakes (Star Maggie)

MARIE JONES
1979: Swaps Stakes (Valdez)

JONES, ROFFE & BARNEY WILLIS
1981: San Fernando Stakes (Doonesbury)

MRS. TROY JONES
1969: San Fernando Stakes (Cavamore)

JONES & TUCKAHOE FARM
1960: Arkansas Derby (Persian Gold)

HAROLD JORDAN
1984: Illinois Derby (Delta Trace)

DON JORDENS
1993: Swaps Stakes (Devoted Brass)

JUDDMONTE FARMS
1984: Hollywood Turf Cup (Alphabatim)
1986: San Antonio Handicap (Hatim)
Hollywood Turf Cup (Alphabatim)
1990: Man o' War Stakes (Defensive Play)
Rothmans International Stakes (French Glory)
1991: Hollywood Turf Handicap (Exbourne)
Caesars International Handicap (Exbourne)
Charles H. Strub Stakes (Defensive Play)
Hollywood Gold Cup (Marquetry)
1992: Hollywood Turf Handicap (Quest for Fame)
Yellow Ribbon Stakes (Super Staff)
1993: Gamely Handicap (Toussaud)
1994: Pacific Classic (Tinners Way)
Rothmans International Stakes (Raintrap)
1995: Santa Barbara Handicap (Wandesta)
Hollywood Oaks (Sleep Easy)
Pacific Classic (Tinners Way)
1996: San Juan Capistrano Handicap (Raintrap)
Californian Stakes (Tinners Way)
Matriarch Stakes (Wandesta)
1997: Queen Elizabeth II Challenge Cup (Ryafan)
Yellow Ribbon Stakes (Ryafan)
Matriarch Stakes (Ryafan)
Eddie Read Handicap (Expelled)
Flower Bowl Invitational Handicap (Yashmak)
1999: Yellow Ribbon Stakes (Spanish Fern)
2000: Santa Monica Handicap (Honest Lady)
Arlington Million (Chester House)
Pacific Classic (Skimming)
2001: Kentucky Oaks (Flute)
Alabama Stakes (Flute)
Hollywood Gold Cup (Aptitude)
Jockey Club Gold Cup (Aptitude)
Pacific Classic (Skimming)
United Nations Handicap (Senure)
Clement L. Hirsch Mem. Turf Championship (Senure)
Breeders' Cup Filly and Mare Turf (Banks Hill)
Malibu Stakes (Mizzen Mast)
2002: Woodford Reserve Turf Classic (Beat Hollow)
Manhattan Handicap (Beat Hollow)
Arlington Million (Beat Hollow)
Strub Stakes (Mizzen Mast)
Secretariat Stakes (Chiselling)
2003: Humana Distaff Handicap (Sightseek)
Ogden Phipps Handicap (Sightseek)
Go for Wand Handicap (Sightseek)
Beldame Stakes (Sightseek)
Florida Derby (Empire Maker)
Wood Memorial Stakes (Empire Maker)
Belmont Stakes (Empire Maker)
Gamely Breeders' Cup Handicap (Tates Creek)
Yellow Ribbon Stakes (Tates Creek)
Beverly D. Stakes (Heat Haze)
Matriarch Stakes (Heat Haze)

JU JU GEN STABLE
1989: United Nations Handicap (Yankee Affair)
Man o' War Stakes (Yankee Affair)
Turf Classic (Yankee Affair)

K. JUMPS, S. SHAPIRO, D. STARK & WM. STRATTON
1989: Hollywood Starlet Stakes (Cheval Volant)

PRINCE SULTAN MOHAMMED al KABEER
1993: Turf Classic (Apple Tree)
1995: Rothmans International Stakes (Lassigny)

MAX KAHLBAUM
1953: Manhattan Handicap (Jampol)

MR. and MRS. VINCENT KANOWSKY
1964: Hollywood Juvenile Championship (Charger's Kin)
1968: Del Mar Futurity (Fleet Allied)

MORRIS KAPLAN
1954: Top Flight Handicap (Sunshine Nell)

RAYMOND KARLINSKY
1963: Demoiselle Stakes (Windsor Lady)

SUSAN KASKEL
1988: Alabama Stakes (Maplejinsky)

NANCY & RICHARD KASTER
1997: Jerome Handicap (Richter Scale)

RICHARD KASTER
1997: Spinaway Stakes (Countess Diana)
Breeders' Cup Juvenile Fillies (Countess Diana)

EWING KAUFFMAN
1966: Manhattan Handicap (Moontrip)
Bowling Green Handicap (Moontrip)
1967: Grey Lag Handicap (Moontrip)

HOWARD B. KECK
1959: Hollywood Derby (Bagdad)
1960: Del Mar Debutante Stakes (Amri-An)
San Antonio Handicap (Bagdad)
1962: Hollywood Oaks (Dingle Bay)
1963: Santa Margarita Handicap (Pixie Erin)
1964: Hollywood Juvenile Championship (Neke)
1966: San Felipe Handicap (Saber Mountain)
Cinema Handicap (Drin)
1967: Charles H. Strub Stakes (Drin)
1969: Century Handicap (Pinjara)
1970: Hollywood Park Inv. Turf Handicap (Fiddle Isle)
American Handicap (Fiddle Isle)
San Luis Rey Handicap (Fiddle Isle)
San Juan Capistrano Handicap (Fiddle Isle)
1971: Del Mar Handicap (Pinjara)

MRS. HOWARD B. KECK
1969: Hollywood Derby (Tell)
1971: Santa Susana Stakes (Turkish Trousers)
Hollywood Oaks (Turkish Trousers)
1972: Santa Maria Handicap (Turkish Trousers)
Santa Margarita Handicap (Turkish Trousers)
Hollywood Oaks (Pallisima)
1973: Beverly Hills Handicap (Le Cle)
1974: Vanity Handicap (Tallahto)
Santa Barbara Handicap (Tallahto)
Oak Tree Invitational Stakes (Tallahto)
1977: Norfolk Stakes (Balzac)
1979: Oak Tree Invitational Stakes (Balzac)
1983: Sunset Handicap (Craelius)
1985: San Luis Rey Stakes (Prince True)
San Juan Capistrano Handicap (Prince True)
1986: Santa Anita Oaks (Hidden Light)
Hollywood Oaks (Hidden Light)
Kentucky Derby (Ferdinand)
1987: Hollywood Gold Cup (Ferdinand)
Breeders' Cup Classic (Ferdinand)

MRS. J.P. KEEZEK
1953: Stars and Stripes Handicap (Abbe Sting)

MARY KEIM
1965: Kentucky Oaks (Amerivan)

PAUL KELLEY
1951: McLennan Handicap (Gangway)

JOE KELLMAN
1972: Arlington-Washington Futurity (Shecky Greene)
1973: Fountain of Youth Stakes (Shecky Greene)

BOB & NANCY KELLY & SABINE STABLE
1998: Remsen Stakes (Comeonmom)

MRS. W.R. KELLY
1971: Amory L. Haskell Handicap (Jontilla)

CHARLES KENIS
1998: Ramona Handicap (See You Soon)

KEN-LOVE FARM
1960: Bowling Green Handicap (Amber Morn)

RICHARD KENNEDY
1987: Jerome Handicap (Afleet)
Pennsylvania Derby (Afleet)

MICHAEL KERR
1966: Michigan Mile and One-Eighth (Stanislas)

KERR STABLE
1956: Santa Anita Handicap (Bobby Brocato)
San Juan Capistrano Handicap (Bobby Brocato)
1957: Blue Grass Stakes (Round Table)
Cinema Handicap (Round Table)
Westerner Stakes (Round Table)
American Derby (Round Table)
Hollywood Gold Cup (Round Table)
Hawthorne Gold Cup (Round Table)
United Nations Handicap (Round Table)
1958: San Antonio Handicap (Round Table)
Santa Anita Handicap (Round Table)
Gulfstream Park Handicap (Round Table)
Hawthorne Gold Cup (Round Table)
Santa Anita Maturity (Round Table)
Arlington Handicap (Round Table)
1959: Washington Park Handicap (Round Table)
Manhattan Handicap (Round Table)
Stars and Stripes Handicap (Round Table)
Arlington Handicap (Round Table)
United Nations Handicap (Round Table)
1961: American Handicap (Prince Blessed)
Hollywood Gold Cup (Prince Blessed)
California Derby (Mr. Consistency)
1963: Vanity Handicap (Table Mate)
1970: Century Handicap (Quilche)
San Luis Rey Handicap (Quilche)

KESWICK STABLES
1993: Rothmans International Stakes (Husband)

SAUD BIN KHALED
2003: Hollywood Turf Cup (Continuously)

ROY KIDDER
1965: Dixie Handicap (Flag)

KILLIAN FARMS
1954: Canadian Championship Stakes (Resilient)

CAESAR KIMMEL
1971: Sapling Stakes (Chevron Flight)
1973: Arlington-Washington Futurity (Lover John)
1985: Selima Stakes (I'm Splendid)

CAESAR KIMMEL & LEONARD & PHILLIP SOLONDZ
1996: Delta Air Lines Top Flight Handicap (Flat Fleet Feet)

CAESAR KIMMEL & PHILLIP SOLONDZ
1997: Test Stakes (Fabulously Fast)

KIMRAN STABLE
1995: Pegasus Handicap (Flying Chevron)
NYRA Mile Handicap (Flying Chevron)

J.A. KINARD JR.
1948: Kentucky Jockey Club Stakes (Johns Joy)

BURT KINERK
1991: Oaklawn Handicap (Festin)
Nassau County Handicap (Festin)
Jockey Club Gold Cup (Festin)

MR. and MRS. GROVER KING
1960: Hollywood Juvenile Championship (Pappa's All)
Arlington Futurity (Pappa's All)

KING & PETITE LUELLWITZ
1951: San Pasqual Handicap (Moonrush)
Santa Anita Handicap (Moonrush)

KING RANCH
1946: Wood Memorial Stakes (Assault)
Kentucky Derby (Assault)
Preakness Stakes (Assault)
Belmont Stakes (Assault)
Dwyer Stakes (Assault)
Pimlico Special (Assault)
Westchester Handicap (Assault)
1947: Pimlico Oaks (But Why Not)
Acorn Stakes (But Why Not)
Alabama Stakes (But Why Not)
Arlington Matron Stakes (But Why Not)
Beldame Handicap (But Why Not)
Arlington Classic (But Why Not)
Grey Lag Handicap (Assault)
Dixie Handicap (Assault)
Suburban Handicap (Assault)
Brooklyn Handicap (Assault)
Sapling Stakes (Task)
Saratoga Special (Better Self)
Westchester Handicap (Bridal Flower)
1948: Pimlico Oaks (Scattered)
Coaching Club American Oaks (Scattered)
Discovery Handicap (Better Self)
Westchester Handicap (Better Self)
1949: Firenze Handicap (But Why Not)
Top Flight Handicap (But Why Not)
Hopeful Stakes (Middleground)
Discovery Handicap (Prophets Thumb)
Carter Handicap (Better Self)
Brooklyn Handicap (Assault)
1950: Kentucky Derby (Middleground)
Belmont Stakes (Middleground)
Gallant Fox Handicap (Better Self)
1951: Firenze Handicap (Renew)
Washington Park Handicap (Curandero)
1952: Arlington Handicap (To Market)
Hawthorne Gold Cup (To Market)
Top Flight Handicap (Renew)
1953: Westerner Stakes (Rejected)
1954: Belmont Stakes (High Gun)
Dwyer Stakes (High Gun)
Jockey Club Gold Cup (High Gun)
Manhattan Handicap (High Gun)
Santa Anita Handicap (Rejected)
American Handicap (Rejected)
Hawthorne Gold Cup (Rejected)
Acorn Stakes (Riverina)
Gazelle Handicap (On Your Own)
1955: Metropolitan Handicap (High Gun)
Brooklyn Handicap (High Gun)
Hawthorne Gold Cup (Rejected)
1956: Delaware Oaks (Dotted Line)
1957: Alabama Stakes (Here and There)
Vineland Handicap (Dotted Line)
1959: Coaching Club American Oaks (Resaca)
Delaware Oaks (Resaca)
Man o' War Handicap (Dotted Line)
Selima Stakes (La Fuerza)
1961: Selima Stakes (Tamarona)
1962: Vineland Handicap (Tamarona)
1966: Suburban Handicap (Buffle)
1968: Matron Stakes (Gallant Bloom)
Gardenia Stakes (Gallant Bloom)
Jersey Derby (Out of the Way)
Massachusetts Handicap (Out of the Way)
1969: Monmouth Oaks (Gallant Bloom)
Gazelle Handicap (Gallant Bloom)
Spinster Stakes (Gallant Bloom)
1970: Santa Margarita Handicap (Gallant Bloom)

SADIE KING
1960: Man o' War Stakes (Harmonizing)

KINGHAVEN FARM
1979: Arlington Classic (Steady Growth)
1987: Yellow Ribbon Stakes (Carotene)
1993: Carter Handicap (Alydeed)

KINGHAVEN FARM & HELEN STOLLERY
1995: Gotham Stakes (Talkin Man)
Wood Memorial Stakes (Talkin Man)

KINSEY RANCH
1949: Del Mar Handicap (Top's Boy)
1951: Starlet Stakes (Prudy's Boy)

KINSHIP STABLE
1973: Illinois Derby (Big Whippendeal)
1974: Hialeah Turf Cup (Big Whippendeal)
Century Handicap (Big Whippendeal)

KINSMAN STABLE
1985: San Felipe Handicap (Image of Greatness)
1997: Jim Beam Stakes (Concerto)
2000: Test Stakes (Dream Supreme)
Ballerina Handicap (Dream Supreme)

ETHEL KIRKLAND
1974: Malibu Stakes (Ancient Title)
San Fernando Stakes (Ancient Title)

ETHEL KIRKLAND *(Continued)*
Charles H. Strub Stakes (Ancient Title)
1975: Californian Stakes (Ancient Title)
Hollywood Gold Cup (Ancient Title)
Whitney Handicap (Ancient Title)

ETHEL KIRKLAND ESTATE
1976: Californian Stakes (Ancient Title)

KIRKLAND STABLE
1977: Del Mar Handicap (Ancient Title)
San Antonio Stakes (Ancient Title)

WALTER KITCHEN
1969: Kentucky Oaks (Hail to Patsy)

KLARAVICH STABLES
1997: Crown Royal Hollywood Derby (Subordination)
1998: Brooklyn Handicap (Subordination)
Eddie Read Handicap (Subordination)

ARTHUR KLEIN
1993: Florida Derby (Bull Inthe Heather)

BERTRAM, ELAINE & RICHARD KLEIN
2001: Super Derby (Outofthebox)

GENE KLEIN
1983: Apple Blossom Handicap (Miss Huntington)
1984: Sorority Stakes (Tiltalating)
Matron Stakes (Fiesta Lady)
1985: Maskette Stakes (Lady's Secret)
Ruffian Handicap (Lady's Secret)
Beldame Stakes (Lady's Secret)
Arkansas Derby (Tank's Prospect)
Preakness Stakes (Tank's Prospect)
Arlington-Washington Lassie Stakes (Family Style)
Frizette Stakes (Family Style)
Breeders' Cup Juvenile Fillies (Twilight Ridge)
1986: La Canada Stakes (Lady's Secret)
Santa Margarita Handicap (Lady's Secret)
Whitney Handicap (Lady's Secret)
Maskette Stakes (Lady's Secret)
Ruffian Handicap (Lady's Secret)
Beldame Stakes (Lady's Secret)
Breeders' Cup Distaff (Lady's Secret)
Withers Stakes (Clear Choice)
Swaps Stakes (Clear Choice)
1987: Mother Goose Stakes (Fiesta Gal)
Coaching Club American Oaks (Fiesta Gal)
La Canada Stakes (Family Style)
Matron Stakes (Over All)
Oak Leaf Stakes (Dream Team)
Breeders' Cup Juvenile (Success Express)
1988: Santa Anita Oaks (Winning Colors)
Santa Anita Derby (Winning Colors)
Kentucky Derby (Winning Colors)
Matron Stakes (Some Romance)
Frizette Stakes (Some Romance)
Breeders' Cup Juvenile Fillies (Open Mind)
Demoiselle Stakes (Open Mind)
San Fernando Stakes (On the Line)
Oak Leaf Stakes (One of a Klein)
Alcibiades Stakes (Wonders Delight)
Breeders' Cup Juvenile (Is It True)
1989: Kentucky Oaks (Open Mind)
Acorn Stakes (Open Mind)
Mother Goose Stakes (Open Mind)
Coaching Club American Oaks (Open Mind)
Alabama Stakes (Open Mind)
Carter Handicap (On the Line)
Jim Dandy Stakes (Is It True)

GENE KLEIN & WAYNE LUKAS
1987: Del Mar Futurity (Lost Kitty)

DAHANA KLERER & RUNNING R STABLE
1994: Milady Handicap (Andestine)

C. MAHLON KLINE
1953: Fall Highweight Handicap (Kaster)

PHIL KLIPSTEIN & TOM ROSS
1956: Del Mar Futurity (Swirling Abbey)
1958: Santa Anita Derby (Silky Sullivan)

K&L STABLE
1946: Longacres Mile (Amble In)

MRS. LAWRENCE KNAPP JR.
1970: Acorn Stakes (Royal Signal)

KNOB HILL STABLES
1988: Blue Grass Stakes (Granacus)
1992: Molson Export Million (Benburb)

HOWARD KOCH & TELLY SAVALAS
1975: Del Mar Futurity (Telly's Pop)
Norfolk Stakes (Telly's Pop)
1976: California Derby (Telly's Pop)

E.D. KOHR
1983: Pegasus Handicap (World Appeal)

KOSGROVE STABLE
1971: Withers Stakes (Bold Reasoning)
Jersey Derby (Bold Reasoning)

JOE KOWAL
1994: Hollywood Turf Cup (Frenchpark)

KRATZ & THAYER
1968: San Felipe Handicap (Prince Pablo)

GEORGE KRIKORIAN
2003: Santa Maria Handicap (Starrer)
Santa Margarita Handicap (Starrer)
Hollywood Starlet Stakes (Hollywood Story)

H.F. KRIMENDHAL
1952: Black Helen Handicap (Roman Miss)

JOSEPH KROESE
1958: Withers Stakes (Sir Robby)

HERBERT KUSHNER
1996: Gotham Stakes (Romano Gucci)

WILLIAM H. LaBOYTEAUX
1946: Spinaway Stakes (Pipette)

S.W. LABROT JR.
1948: Louisiana Derby (Bovard)

JOSEPH La COMBE
1997: Hopeful Stakes (Favorite Trick)
Breeders' Cup Juvenile (Favorite Trick)
1998: Jim Dandy Stakes (Favorite Trick)

JOSEPH LaCROIX
1979: Longacres Mile (Always Gallant)

C.M. LAGROSA
1971: Manhattan Handicap (Happy Way)

LAGUNA SECA & WARD
1973: San Juan Capistrano Handicap (Queen's Hustler)

LAKEVILLE STABLES
1994: Philip H. Iselin Handicap (Taking Risks)

D. LAMONT
1948: McLennan Handicap (El Mono)
Widener Handicap (El Mono)

HARRY LaMONTAGNE
1946: Top Flight Handicap (Sicily)
1948: Vagrancy Handicap (Conniver)
Beldame Handicap (Conniver)
Comely Handicap (Conniver)
Brooklyn Handicap (Conniver)
1957: Top Flight Handicap (Plotter)

CARLYLE LANCASTER
1979: Whitney Stakes (Star de Naskra)

B.W. LANDY
1954: Michigan Mile (Spur On)

GLENN LANE
1984: Top Flight Handicap (Sweet Missus)

T. LANNI, KENNETH POSLOSKY & BERNARD SCHIAPPA
1999: Breeders' Cup Mile (Silic)
2000: Shoemaker Breeders' Cup Mile (Silic)

TERRANCE LANNI & BERNARD SCHIAPPA
2000: Eddie Read Handicap (Ladies Din)
2002: Shoemaker Breeders' Cup Mile (Ladies Din)

DAVID LANZMAN
2001: King's Bishop Stakes (Squirtle Squirt)
Penske Auto Center BC Sprint (Squirtle Squirt)

LA PRESLE FARM
1993: San Luis Rey Stakes (Kotashaan)
San Juan Capistrano Handicap (Kotashaan)
Eddie Read Handicap (Kotashaan)
Oak Tree Invitational Stakes (Kotashaan)
Breeders' Cup Turf (Kotashaan)
1995: Strub Stakes (Dare and Go)
1996: Pacific Classic (Dare and Go)
1997: Oaklawn Handicap (Atticus)

RON LARMARQUE & LOUIE ROUSSEL III
1988: Preakness Stakes (Risen Star)
Belmont Stakes (Risen Star)

DAN LASATER
1972: Oaklawn Handicap (Gage Line)
1974: Arlington-Washington Lassie Stakes (Hot n Nasty)
1975: Amory L. Haskell Handicap (Royal Glint)
Arlington Handicap (Royal Glint)
Hawthorne Gold Cup (Royal Glint)
United Nations Handicap (Royal Glint)
1976: Santa Anita Handicap (Royal Glint)
1979: Sorority Stakes (Love Street)

EDWARD LASKER
1946: Carter Handicap (Flood Town)
1948: Arlington Lassie Stakes (Pail of Water)

MRS. EDWARD LASKER
1952: Will Rogers Stakes (Forelock)
1954: San Juan Capistrano Handicap (By Zeus)
1966: Withers Stakes (Indulto)

ELIZABETH LA TOURRETTE & MIDDLE RANCH
1971: San Luis Rey Handicap (Try Sheep)

CARL LAUER & NANCY VANIER
1982: La Canada Stakes (Safe Play)

CARL LAUER, NANCY VANIER & ROBERT VICTOR
1983: Blue Grass Stakes (Play Fellow)
Arlington Classic (Play Fellow)
American Derby (Play Fellow)
Travers Stakes (Play Fellow)

MRS. LUCIEN LAURIN
1965: Monmouth Handicap (Repeating)
1969: Massachusetts Handicap (Beau Marker)

MRS. ROGER LAURIN
1978: Demoiselle Stakes (Plankton)

LAUDY LAWRENCE
1959: Display Handicap (Beau Diable)

MRS. LAUDY LAWRENCE
1947: Spinaway Stakes (Bellesoeur)
Astarita Stakes (Bellesoeur)

LOUISE LAZARE
1951: Queens County Handicap (Sheilas Reward)

LAZY F RANCH
1968: Black Helen Handicap (Treacherous)
1974: Donn Handicap (Forego)
Gulfstream Park Handicap (Forego)
Widener Handicap (Forego)
Carter Handicap (Forego)
Brooklyn Handicap (Forego)
Woodward Stakes (Forego)
Vosburgh Handicap (Forego)
Jockey Club Gold Cup (Forego)
1975: Widener Handicap (Forego)
Carter Handicap (Forego)
Brooklyn Handicap (Forego)
Suburban Handicap (Forego)
Woodward Stakes (Forego)
1976: Metropolitan Handicap (Forego)
Brooklyn Handicap (Forego)
Woodward Handicap (Forego)
Marlboro Cup Handicap (Forego)
1977: Metropolitan Handicap (Forego)
Woodward Handicap (Forego)
1980: Man o' War Stakes (French Colonial)
1994: Apple Blossom Handicap (Nine Keys)
1998: Flower Bowl Invitational Handicap (Auntie Mame)

LAZY LANE FARMS
1990: Arlington-Washington Futurity (Hansel)
1991: Jim Beam Stakes (Hansel)
Preakness Stakes (Hansel)
Belmont Stakes (Hansel)

L.C. RANCH
1955: Starlet Stakes (Bold Bazooka)

THOMAS LEACHMAN
1985: Vosburgh Stakes (Another Reef)

RICHARD LEAHY & JOHN MERIWETHER
1995: Dwyer Stakes (Hoolie)

MRS. H. LEBOWITZ
1946: Trenton Handicap (Turbine)

R. LeCESSE
1981: Whitney Handicap (Fio Rito)

T. LeCLAIR
1967: Sapling Stakes (Subpet)

SANTIAGO LEDWITH
1964: Display Handicap (Primordial II)
1965: Widener Handicap (Primordial II)

SAMUEL LEFRAK
1965: Sanford Stakes (Flame Tree)

ROBERT LEHMAN
1955: Vanity Handicap (Countess Fleet)
1961: Gotham Stakes (Ambiopoise)
Jersey Derby (Ambiopoise)
1962: Flamingo Stakes (Prego)
Grey Lag Handicap (Ambiopoise)
1967: United Nations Handicap (Flit-to)
1968: Widener Handicap (Sette Bello)
1970: Blue Grass Stakes (Dust Commander)
Kentucky Derby (Dust Commander)
1973: Fantasy Stakes (Knitted Gloves)

MR. and MRS. ROBERT LEHMAN
1956: Westerner Stakes (Count of Honor)

GERALD LEIGH
1988: Rothmans International Stakes (Infamy)
1991: Santa Barbara Handicap (Bequest)

GERALD LEIGH & SHEIKH MOHAMMAD al MAKTOUM
1994: Breeders' Cup Mile (Barathea)

LESTER MANOR STABLE
1948: Alabama Stakes (Compliance)

LET IT RIDE STABLE
1997: Del Mar Oaks (Famous Digger)

LEONARD LEVEEN, MIKE SHANLEY & STEVE WEISS
1995: Turf Classic (Turk Passer)

JEAN-LOUIS LEVESQUE
1970: Alabama Stakes (Fanfreluche)
1972: Spinaway Stakes (La Prevoyante)
Matron Stakes (La Prevoyante)
Frizette Stakes (La Prevoyante)
Selima Stakes (La Prevoyante)
Gardenia Stakes (La Prevoyante)
1974: Laurel Futurity (L'Enjoleur)
1977: Alcibiades Stakes (L'Alezane)

WILLIAM LEVIN
1971: Hollywood Derby (Bold Reason)
Travers Stakes (Bold Reason)
American Derby (Bold Reason)

MRS. I.J. LEVINE
1948: Longacres Mile (Amble In)

AL LEVINSON
1975: Michigan Mile and One-Eighth (Mr. Lucky Phoenix)

DAVID LEVINSON
1987: Illinois Derby (Lost Code)
Ohio Derby (Lost Code)
Arlington Classic (Lost Code)

BLANCHE LEVY
1986: Arlington-Washington Futurity (Bet Twice)
Laurel Futurity (Bet Twice)

M.A. LEVY
1981: Laurel Futurity (Deputy Minister)
Young America Stakes (Deputy Minister)

ROBERT LEVY
1990: Withers Stakes (Housebuster)
Jerome Handicap (Housebuster)
1991: Carter Handicap (Housebuster)
Vosburgh Stakes (Housebuster)
Jersey Derby (Greek Costume)

MR. and MRS. J.B. LEWIN
1969: Santa Susana Stakes (Dumptys Lady)

BEVERLY & ROBERT LEWIS
1994: Oak Leaf Stakes (Serena's Song)
Hollywood Starlet Stakes (Serena's Song)
1995: Las Virgenes Stakes (Serena's Song)
Santa Anita Oaks (Serena's Song)
Jim Beam Stakes (Serena's Song)
Mother Goose Stakes (Serena's Song)
Haskell Invitational Handicap (Serena's Song)
Gazelle Handicap (Serena's Song)
Beldame Stakes (Serena's Song)
Hopeful Stakes (Hennessy)
1996: Santa Maria Handicap (Serena's Song)
Hempstead Handicap (Serena's Song)
Del Mar Futurity (Silver Charm)
1997: Kentucky Derby (Silver Charm)
Preakness Stakes (Silver Charm)
1998: Strub Stakes (Silver Charm)
1999: Kentucky Derby (Charismatic)
Preakness Stakes (Charismatic)
2000: Belmont Stakes (Commendable)
2002: Forego Handicap (Orientate)
NAPA Breeders' Cup Sprint (Orientate)
2003: Las Virgenes Stakes (Composure)
Santa Anita Oaks (Composure)

BEVERLY & R. LEWIS, SUSAN MAGNIER & M. TABOR
1999: Hopeful Stakes (High Yield)
2000: Fountain of Youth Stakes (High Yield)
Toyota Blue Grass Stakes (High Yield)

CRAIG LEWIS
1995: Santa Anita Derby (Larry the Legend)

DEBI & LEE LEWIS
1993: Santa Anita Derby (Personal Hope)

GEORGE LEWIS
1958: Lawrence Realization Stakes (Martins Rullah)

MR. and MRS. GEORGE LEWIS STABLE
1956: Starlet Stakes (Lucky Mel)
1957: San Felipe Handicap (Joe Price)

JAMES LEWIS JR.
1995: Super Derby (Mecke)
1996: Early Times Turf Classic (Mecke)
Arlington Million (Mecke)

LIGHTNING STABLE
1979: Young America Stakes (Koluctoo Bay)

MICHAEL LIMA
1980: Gamely Handicap (Wishing Well)

HENRY LINDH
1987: Acorn Stakes (Grecian Flight)

LION CREST STABLE
1992: Gotham Stakes (Devil His Due)
Wood Memorial Stakes (Devil His Due)
1993: Gulfstream Park Handicap (Devil His Due)
Pimlico Special (Devil His Due)
Suburban Handicap (Devil His Due)
1994: Brooklyn Handicap (Devil His Due)
Suburban Handicap (Devil His Due)

LITTLE M FARM
1963: Gallant Fox Handicap (Sunrise Flight)

LIVE OAK PLANTATION
1978: Dwyer Handicap (Junction)
1981: Remsen Stakes (Laser Light)
1991: Man o' War Stakes (Solar Splendor)
Turf Classic (Solar Splendor)
1992: Hollywood Gold Cup (Sultry Song)
Whitney Handicap (Sultry Song)
Woodward Stakes (Sultry Song)
Man o' War Stakes (Solar Splendor)

LLANGOLLEN FARM
1953: Futurity Stakes (Porterhouse)
1955: William P. Kyne Handicap (Mister Gus)
1956: San Antonio Handicap (Mister Gus)
Woodward Stakes (Mister Gus)
Arlington Handicap (Mister Gus)
San Felipe Handicap (Social Climber)
Cinema Handicap (Social Climber)
Californian Stakes (Porterhouse)
1957: Santa Anita Handicap (Corn Husker)
San Juan Capistrano Handicap (Corn Husker)
Selima Stakes (Guide Line)
Los Angeles Handicap (Porterhouse)
Californian Stakes (Social Climber)
1958: Arlington Futurity (Restless Wind)
Washington Park Futurity (Restless Wind)
1959: Vanity Handicap (Tender Size)
San Juan Capistrano Handicap (Royal Living)
1960: Roamer Handicap (Divine Comedy)
1967: Santa Anita Handicap (Pretense)
Gulfstream Park Handicap (Pretense)
San Antonio Handicap (Pretense)
1975: Hollywood Juvenile Championship (Restless Restless)

LLANGOLLEN FARM & ROCK SPRINGS FARM
1967: Hollywood Derby (Tumble Wind)

BARNEY LOBEL
1969: San Luis Rey Handicap (Taneb)

LOBLOLLY STABLE
1978: Metropolitan Handicap (Cox's Ridge)
Oaklawn Handicap (Cox's Ridge)
1980: Arkansas Derby (Temperence Hill)
Belmont Stakes (Temperence Hill)
Travers Stakes (Temperence Hill)
Super Derby (Temperence Hill)
Jockey Club Gold Cup (Temperence Hill)
1981: Suburban Handicap (Temperence Hill)
Oaklawn Handicap (Temperence Hill)
1985: Suburban Handicap (Vanlandingham)
Jockey Club Gold Cup (Vanlandingham)
Washington D.C. International (Vanlandingham)
Widener Handicap (Pine Circle)
1986: Brooklyn Handicap (Little Missouri)
1987: Arkansas Derby (Demons Begone)
1988: Futurity Stakes (Trapp Mountain)
1989: Jerome Handicap (De Roche)
1991: Peter Pan Stakes (Lost Mountain)
Dwyer Stakes (Lost Mountain)
Haskell Invitational Handicap (Lost Mountain)
Remsen Stakes (Pine Bluff)
1992: Arkansas Derby (Pine Bluff)
Preakness Stakes (Pine Bluff)
1993: Jim Beam Stakes (Prairie Bayou)
Blue Grass Stakes (Prairie Bayou)
Preakness Stakes (Prairie Bayou)
Fantasy Stakes (Aztec Hill)

LOCUST HILL FARM
1969: Carter Handicap (Promise)
1970: Carter Handicap (Tyrant)
1974: Sorority Stakes (Ruffian)
Spinaway Stakes (Ruffian)
1975: Acorn Stakes (Ruffian)
Mother Goose Stakes (Ruffian)
Coaching Club American Oaks (Ruffian)
1988: Gotham Stakes (Private Terms)
Wood Memorial Stakes (Private Terms)

W.A. LOFTON
1974: Michigan Mile and One-Eighth (Tom Tulle)

J.A. LOGAN
1979: Hawthorne Gold Cup (Young Bob)

ANDRE LOMBARD
1956: Washington D.C. International (Master Boing)

GREG LONG, URI NEMET & DOMINIC SABATINO JR.
1996: Malibu Stakes (King of the Heap)

MRS. JOHNNY LONGDEN
1973: Norfolk Stakes (Money Lender)

RALPH LOWE
1957: Belmont Stakes (Gallant Man)
Travers Stakes (Gallant Man)
Jockey Club Gold Cup (Gallant Man)
1958: Metropolitan Handicap (Gallant Man)
Hollywood Gold Cup (Gallant Man)
Sunset Handicap (Gallant Man)
1960: Cinema Handicap (New Policy)
1962: Hollywood Derby (Drill Site)

EVERETT LOWRANCE
1967: Arlington-Washington Lassie Stakes (Shenow)

WILLIAM F. LUCAS
1984: Louisiana Derby (Taylor's Special)
Blue Grass Stakes (Taylor's Special)

MRS. PETITE LUELLWITZ
1952: San Felipe Handicap (Windy City II)

WAYNE LUKAS & OVERBROOK FARM
1989: Norfolk Stakes (Grand Canyon)
Hollywood Futurity (Grand Canyon)
1990: San Felipe Handicap (Real Cash)
American Derby (Real Cash)
1991: Travers Stakes (Corporate Report)
Hopeful Stakes (Salt Lake)

WAYNE LUKAS & PAUL PATERNOSTRO
1987: Santa Margarita Handicap (North Sider)
Apple Blossom Handicap (North Sider)
Maskette Stakes (North Sider)

LUKE & SNEED
1948: Vanity Handicap (Hemet Squaw)

RICHARD LUNDY & VIRGINIA KRAFT PAYSON
1984: Jim Dandy Stakes (Carr de Naskra)
Travers Stakes (Carr de Naskra)

FRANCES W. LURO
1989: Hialeah Turf Cup (El Senor)
Sword Dancer Handicap (El Senor)
1990: Sword Dancer Handicap (El Senor)

LUSARASION INC.
1989: Tropical Park Derby (Big Stanley)

LUSHLAND FARM
1986: Fountain of Youth Stakes (Ensign Rhythm)

CLIFFORD LUSSKY
1956: Kentucky Jockey Club Stakes (Federal Hill)
1957: Louisiana Derby (Federal Hill)

LYONS & TEMPLEMAN
1982: Arlington-Washington Futurity (Total Departure)

ROBERT LYTLE
1954: Wood Memorial Stakes (Correlation)
Florida Derby (Correlation)

PHILIP MAAS
1992: Kentucky Oaks (Luv Me Luv Me Not)

MR. and MRS. JOHN MABEE
1970: San Felipe Handicap (Cool Hand)

MAC-CONN FARM
1968: Pan American Handicap (Irish Rebellion)

C.R. MAC STABLE
1959: Arlington Futurity (T.V. Lark)
1960: Arlington Classic (T.V. Lark)
American Derby (T.V. Lark)
Washington Park Handicap (T.V. Lark)
United Nations Handicap (T.V. Lark)
1961: Los Angeles Handicap (T.V. Lark)
1962: Cinema Handicap (Black Sheep)
American Derby (Black Sheep)

W.B. MacDONALD JR.
1960: Arlington Matron Handicap (Royal Native)
Vineland Handicap (Royal Native)

EARLE MACK
1992: Alabama Stakes (November Snow)
1993: Molson Export Million (Peteski)

MACON, HENRY MORENO & SAWYER
1965: Vanity Handicap (Jalousie II)

LARRY MacPHAIL
1952: Pimlico Special (General Staff)

PRESTON MADDEN
1961: Hawthorne Gold Cup (T.V. Lark)
Washington D.C. International (T.V. Lark)
1969: Santa Barbara Handicap (Pink Pigeon)
1973: American Handicap (Kentuckian)

ALAN MAGERMAN
1969: Del Mar Futurity (George Lewis)
1970: California Derby (George Lewis)

SUSAN MAGNIER & MICHAEL TABOR
1996: Swaps Stakes (Victory Speech)
1997: Strub Stakes (Victory Speech)
1998: Ashland Stakes (Well Chosen)
2001: Bessemer Trust BC Juvenile (Johannesburg)
2002: Shadwell Keeneland Turf Mile (Landseer)
John Deere Breeders' Cup Turf (High Chaparral)
2003: John Deere Breeders' Cup Turf (High Chaparral)

MAINE CHANCE FARM
1946: Pimlico Futurity (Jet Pilot)
Tremont Stakes (Jet Pilot)
Santa Anita Derby (Knockdown)
Blue Grass Stakes (Lord Boswell)
1947: Kentucky Derby (Jet Pilot)
1948: Spinaway Stakes (Myrtle Charm)
Matron Stakes (Myrtle Charm)
Travers Stakes (Ace Admiral)
Lawrence Realization Stakes (Ace Admiral)
Excelsior Handicap (Knockdown)
Queens County Handicap (Knockdown)
Arlington Futurity (Mr. Busher)
1949: Inglewood Handicap (Ace Admiral)
Sunset Handicap (Ace Admiral)
Santa Anita Maturity (Ace Admiral)
1951: Matron Stakes (Rose Jet)
Selima Stakes (Rose Jet)
Demoiselle Stakes (Rose Jet)
1954: Alcibiades Stakes (Myrtle's Jet)
Frizette Stakes (Myrtle's Jet)
Withers Stakes (Jet Action)
Roamer Handicap (Jet Action)
Kentucky Oaks (Fascinator)
1955: Washington Park Handicap (Jet Action)
1957: Washington Park Futurity (Jewel's Reward)
Cowdin Stakes (Jewel's Reward)
Champagne Stakes (Jewel's Reward)
Pimlico Futurity (Jewel's Reward)
1958: Wood Memorial Stakes (Jewel's Reward)
1963: Withers Stakes (Get Around)

SHEIKH MAKTOUM al MAKTOUM
1995: Crown Royal Hollywood Derby (Labeeb)
1998: Woodbine Mile (Labeeb)
2000: Charles Whittingham Handicap (White Heart)
2001: Woodford Reserve Turf Classic (White Heart)
Shoemaker Breeders' Cup Mile (Irish Prize)
Flower Bowl Invitational Handicap (Lailani)
2003: Charles Whittingham Handicap (Storming Home)
C.L. Hirsch Mem. Turf Champ. (Storming Home)

SHEIKH MOHAMMAD al MAKTOUM
1985: Breeders' Cup Turf (Pebbles)
1988: Oak Tree Invitational Stakes (Nasr El Arab)
1989: Charles H. Strub Stakes (Nasr El Arab)
San Juan Capistrano Handicap (Nasr El Arab)
1990: Breeders' Cup Turf (In the Wings)
NYRA Mile Handicap (Quiet American)
1994: American Derby (Overbury)
Beverly D. Stakes (Hatoof)
1996: Canadian International Championship (Singspiel)

JEAN-FRANCOIS MALLE
1990: Sunset Handicap (Petite Ile)

MRS. JIM MALONEY
1947: Remsen Handicap (Big If)

MRS. R.J. MALONEY
1949: Vanity Handicap (Silver Drift)

JIM MAMAKOS & MARC STUBRIN
1983: Norfolk Stakes (Fali Time)
Hollywood Futurity (Fali Time)
1984: San Felipe Handicap (Fali Time)

HARRY MANGURIAN JR.
1973: Alabama Stakes (Desert Vixen)
Gazelle Handicap (Desert Vixen)
Beldame Stakes (Desert Vixen)
1974: Beldame Stakes (Desert Vixen)
1975: Dwyer Handicap (Valid Appeal)
1982: Pan American Handicap (Robsphere)
2001: Metropolitan Handicap (Exciting Story)

MANHASSET STABLE
1986: Top Flight Handicap (Ride Sally)

ANNETTE MANN
1970: Sapling Stakes (Staunch Avenger)

THOMAS MARA
1991: Top Flight Handicap (Buy the Firm)

MARABLUE FARM
1977: Marlboro Cup Handicap (Proud Birdie)

GARY MARANO
1988: Withers Stakes (Once Wild)

MARANT & SESSA
1972: Sapling Stakes (Assagai Jr.)

MARINO BEACH STABLE
1979: Canadian International Championship (Golden Act)

JAMES MARINO
1988: Santa Margarita Handicap (Flying Julia)

P.A. MARKEY
1949: Astoria Stakes (Baby Comet)
1950: Whitney Stakes (Piet)

MARK THREE STABLE
1971: Norfolk Stakes (MacArthur Park)
Del Mar Futurity (MacArthur Park)

JOHN MARSCH
1946: Discovery Handicap (Mighty Story)
1949: Kentucky Jockey Club Stakes (Roman Bath)

JOHN MARSH
1982: Rothmans International Stakes (Majesty's Prince)
1983: Sword Dancer Handicap (Majesty's Prince)
Man o' War Stakes (Majesty's Prince)
1984: Man o' War Stakes (Majesty's Prince)
Rothmans International Stakes (Majesty's Prince)

ROBERT MARSHALL
1993: Californian Stakes (Latin American)

MR. and MRS. BERT MARTIN
1967: San Felipe Handicap (Rising Market)
1968: San Antonio Handicap (Rising Market)

JOHNS MARTIN, PAUL SAYLOR & STARLIGHT STABLE
2003: Spinaway Stakes (Ashado)

JOSE MARTIN
1978: Frizette Stakes (Golferette)

MR. and MRS. QUINN MARTIN
1972: Norfolk Stakes (Groshawk)
Del Mar Futurity (Groshawk)

MARTIN & McKINNEY
1952: Arlington Futurity (Mr. Good)

MR. and MRS. QUINN MARTIN & MURTY FARM
1975: Oak Tree Invitational Stakes (Top Command)

RANDY MARTIN & STEVE WEINER
1999: Man o' War Stakes (Val's Prince)
Turf Classic (Val's Prince)

TOWNSEND MARTIN
1963: Grey Lag Handicap (Sunrise County)

W.C. MARTIN
1951: San Felipe Stakes (Phil D.)

MR. and MRS. W.C. MARTIN
1952: San Antonio Handicap (Phil D.)

NICHOLAS MARTINI
1962: Top Flight Handicap (Pepper Patch)

MASHEK & MURTY FARM
1978: Century Handicap (Landscaper)

SILAS A. MASON II
1950: Arlington Futurity (To Market)
Washington Park Futurity (To Market)
1952: San Carlos Handicap (To Market)
Massachusetts Handicap (To Market)

JOAN MASTERSON
1982: Arlington-Washington Lassie St. (For Once'n My Life)

SAM MATAR
1988: California Derby (All Thee Power)

T.G. MAY
1951: Louisiana Derby (Whirling Bat)

LEN MAYER
1983: Oaklawn Handicap (Bold Style)

LOUIS B. MAYER
1946: Hollywood Oaks (Honeymoon)
Cinema Handicap (Honeymoon)
Hollywood Derby (Honeymoon)
Vanity Handicap (Be Faithful)
1952: Del Mar Handicap (Grantor)
1955: American Handicap (Alidon)
1959: Preakness Stakes (Royal Orbit)

TRUDY McCAFFERY, ROBERT SANGSTER & JOHN TOFFAN
2000: Hollywood Turf Cup (Bienamado)
2001: San Juan Capistrano Handicap (Bienamado)
Charles Whittingham Handicap (Bienamado)

TRUDY McCAFFERY & JOHN TOFFAN
1992: Swaps Stakes (Bien Bien)
Hollywood Turf Cup (Bien Bien)
Hollywood Oaks (Pacific Squall)
1993: Hollywood Turf Handicap (Bien Bien)
1994: San Luis Rey Stakes (Bien Bien)
San Juan Capistrano Handicap (Bien Bien)
1996: Norfolk Stakes (Free House)
1997: San Felipe Stakes (Free House)
Santa Anita Derby (Free House)
Swaps Stakes (Free House)
1998: Pacific Classic (Free House)
1999: San Antonio Handicap (Free House)
Santa Anita Handicap (Free House)
2001: Hopeful Stakes (Came Home)

NEIL McCARTHY
1948: Hollywood Gold Cup (Shannon II)
Golden Gate Handicap (Shannon II)
1958: San Carlos Handicap (Seaneen)
Californian Stakes (Seaneen)
1959: San Felipe Handicap (Finnegan)
California Derby (Finnegan)
1960: Los Angeles Handicap (Finnegan)
1962: Santa Anita Derby (Royal Attack)

A.F. McCLELLAN
1968: Hollywood Juvenile Championship (Fleet Kirsch)

RON McDONALD
1991: Apple Blossom Handicap (Degenerate Gal)

MRS. J.A. McDOUGALD
1983: Hialeah Turf Cup (Nijinsky's Secret)
1984: Hialeah Turf Cup (Nijinsky's Secret)

MRS. QUINCY ADAMS SHAW McKEAN
1959: Roamer Handicap (Polylad)
1961: Massachusetts Handicap (Polylad)
Gallant Fox Handicap (Polylad)

DONALD McKELLAR
1956: Princess Pat Stakes (Splendored)
1974: Alcibiades Stakes (Hope of Glory)
1976: Alcibiades Stakes (Sans Supplement)

L.J. McMAHAN
1958: San Felipe Handicap (Carrier X.)

FRANK McMAHON
1967: Del Mar Futurity (Baffle)
Santa Barbara Handicap (Ormea)
1969: Santa Anita Derby (Majestic Prince)
Kentucky Derby (Majestic Prince)
Preakness Stakes (Majestic Prince)
1970: Californian Stakes (Baffle)
1972: Vosburgh Handicap (Triple Bend)
San Fernando Stakes (Triple Bend)
Santa Anita Handicap (Triple Bend)
1974: Del Mar Futurity (Diabolo)
1975: California Derby (Diabolo)

MEADOW STABLE
1959: Everglades Stakes (First Landing)
1960: Monmouth Handicap (First Landing)
Santa Anita Maturity (First Landing)
1961: Spinaway Stakes (Cicada)
Matron Stakes (Cicada)
Frizette Stakes (Cicada)
Gardenia Stakes (Cicada)
Sapling Stakes (Sir Gaylord)
1962: Kentucky Oaks (Cicada)
Acorn Stakes (Cicada)
Mother Goose Stakes (Cicada)
Beldame Stakes (Cicada)
Everglades Stakes (Sir Gaylord)
1963: Matron Stakes (Hasty Matelda)
1964: Sorority Stakes (Bold Experience)
1966: Gardenia Stakes (Pepperwood)
Gulfstream Park Handicap (First Family)
1967: Selima Stakes (Syrian Sea)
Gardenia Stakes (Gay Matelda)
1968: Spinaway Stakes (Queen's Double)
Alabama Stakes (Gay Matelda)
1971: Futurity Stakes (Riva Ridge)
Champagne Stakes (Riva Ridge)
Pimlico-Laurel Futurity (Riva Ridge)
Garden State Stakes (Riva Ridge)
1972: Hopeful Stakes (Secretariat)
Futurity Stakes (Secretariat)
Laurel Futurity (Secretariat)
Garden State Stakes (Secretariat)
Blue Grass Stakes (Riva Ridge)
Kentucky Derby (Riva Ridge)
Belmont Stakes (Riva Ridge)
Hollywood Derby (Riva Ridge)
Florida Derby (Upper Case)
Wood Memorial Stakes (Upper Case)
1973: Gotham Stakes (Secretariat)
Kentucky Derby (Secretariat)
Preakness Stakes (Secretariat)
Belmont Stakes (Secretariat)
Marlboro Cup Handicap (Secretariat)
Man o' War Stakes (Secretariat)
Canadian International Championship (Secretariat)
Massachusetts Handicap (Riva Ridge)
Brooklyn Handicap (Riva Ridge)

MEADOWBROOK STABLE
1960: Futurity Stakes (Little Tumbler)
1961: Vineland Handicap (Frimanaha)

MEADOWHILL
1976: Dwyer Handicap (Quiet Little Table)
1977: Carter Handicap (Quiet Little Table)
Suburban Handicap (Quiet Little Table)
1978: American Derby (Nasty and Bold)
Brooklyn Handicap (Nasty and Bold)

MEEKEN STABLE
1974: California Derby (Agitate)
Swaps Stakes (Agitate)
Hollywood Derby (Agitate)

EUGENE MELNYK
1999: Test Stakes (Marley Vale)

EUGENE & LAURA MELNYK
2000: Arkansas Derby (Graeme Hall)
Jim Dandy Stakes (Graeme Hall)
2001: Coaching Club American Oaks (Tweedside)
2003: Jim Dandy Stakes (Strong Hope)
Ballerina Handicap (Harmony Lodge)

A. MENDITAGUY
1988: United Nations Handicap (Equalize)

SHELTON MEREDITH
1988: Norfolk Stakes (Hawkster)
1989: Oak Tree Invitational Stakes (Hawkster)

MEREWORTH FARM
1968: Santa Susana Stakes (Allie's Serenade)

JOHN MERIWETHER
1993: Budweiser International Stakes (Buckhar)

MERRICK STABLE
1960: Gotham Stakes (John William)
Withers Stakes (John William)

MERRILL STABLES
1988: Hollywood Starlet Stakes (Stocks Up)

E.P. METZ
1958: Princess Pat Stakes (Battle Heart)

ROBERT MEYERHOFF
1986: Jim Beam Stakes (Broad Brush)
Wood Memorial Stakes (Broad Brush)
Ohio Derby (Broad Brush)
Pennsylvania Derby (Broad Brush)
Meadowlands Cup (Broad Brush)
1987: Santa Anita Handicap (Broad Brush)
Suburban Handicap (Broad Brush)
1989: Beldame Stakes (Tactile)
1991: Pennsylvania Derby (Valley Crossing)
1993: Philip H. Iselin Handicap (Valley Crossing)
1994: Arkansas Derby (Concern)
Breeders' Cup Classic (Concern)
1995: Californian Stakes (Concern)
2001: Pimlico Special (Include)

TOM MEYERHOFF
1990: Woodward Handicap (Dispersal)

J.D. MICHAELS
1965: Acorn Stakes (Ground Control)

MIDDLE RANCH
1960: Del Mar Futurity (Short Jacket)

MIDDLETOWN STABLE
1972: Gotham Stakes (Freetex)
Ohio Derby (Freetex)
Monmouth Invitational Handicap (Freetex)
1992: Shuvee Handicap (Missy's Mirage)
Hempstead Handicap (Missy's Mirage)

MIDDLETOWN STABLE & WILLIAM STAVOLA
1993: Peter Pan Stakes (Virginia Rapids)
1994: Carter Handicap (Virginia Rapids)

MRS. N.A. MIKELL
1950: Remsen Handicap (Repetoire)
1951: Wood Memorial Stakes (Repetoire)

DAVID MILCH
1987: Arlington-Washington Lassie Stakes (Joe's Tammie)
2001: Breeders' Cup Mile (Val Royal)

DAVID MILCH & JACK & MARK SILVERMAN
1992: Arlington-Washington Futurity (Gilded Time)
Breeders' Cup Juvenile (Gilded Time)

STEVEN MILES
2002: Walmac Int. Alcibiades Stakes (Westerly Breeze)

MILES & TAUBER
1970: Cinema Handicap (D'Artagnan)

H.J. MILLER
1973: Del Mar Futurity (Such a Rush)

LLOYD I. MILLER
1968: Kentucky Oaks (Dark Mirage)
Acorn Stakes (Dark Mirage)
Mother Goose Stakes (Dark Mirage)
Coaching Club American Oaks (Dark Mirage)
Monmouth Oaks (Dark Mirage)
1972: Manhattan Handicap (Star Envoy)

ROBERT MILLER
1970: Hollywood Derby (Hanalei Bay)

MILL HOUSE STABLE
1973: Selima Stakes (Dancealot)
1975: Remsen Stakes (Hang Ten)
1976: Frizette Stakes (Sensational)
Selima Stakes (Sensational)
1977: Ladies Handicap (Sensational)
1992: Jerome Handicap (Furiously)

MILL RIDGE FARM
1973: Sapling Stakes (Tisab)
1975: Hollywood Oaks (Nicosia)

MILL RIVER STABLE
1947: Black Helen Handicap (Miss Grillo)
1948: New Castle Handicap (Miss Grillo)
New York Handicap (Miss Grillo)
1949: San Juan Capistrano Handicap (Miss Grillo)

BETTY & LEON MILLSAP
1990: Arlington-Washington Lassie Stakes (Through Flight)

MINSHALL FARMS
1997: Gulfstream Park Handicap (Mt. Sassafras)

CLAUDIA MIRKIN
1981: Californian Stakes (Eleven Stitches)
Hollywood Gold Cup (Eleven Stitches)

E. MITTMAN
1969: Canadian International Championship (Vent du Nord)
1970: Hialeah Turf Cup (Vent du Nord)

EDWARD MIZRAHI
1976: Hollywood Juvenile Championship (Fleet Dragoon)

BILL MODGLIN
1958: Del Mar Debutante Stakes (Khalita)

JACK MONDEL
1990: Demoiselle Stakes (Debutant's Halo)

MONTPELIER STABLE
1955: Saranac Handicap (Saratoga)
1962: Trenton Handicap (Mongo)
United Nations Handicap (Mongo)
1963: Washington D.C. International (Mongo)
United Nations Handicap (Mongo)
1964: Widener Handicap (Mongo)
John B. Campbell Handicap (Mongo)
Monmouth Handicap (Mongo)
1974: Flamingo Stakes (Bushongo)
1976: Top Flight Handicap (Proud Delta)
Hempstead Handicap (Proud Delta)
Beldame Stakes (Proud Delta)

CLIFFORD MOOERS
1947: Kentucky Jockey Club Stakes (Bold Gallant)
1949: Santa Anita Derby (Old Rockport)
1955: Withers Stakes (Traffic Judge)
Ohio Derby (Traffic Judge)
Jerome Handicap (Traffic Judge)
Woodward Stakes (Traffic Judge)

MOORING STABLE
1958: Alabama Stakes (Tempted)
Maskette Handicap (Tempted)
1959: Diana Handicap (Tempted)
Beldame Handicap (Tempted)
Ladies Handicap (Tempted)

C. MORABITO
1953: Molly Pitcher Handicap (My Celeste)
Monmouth Handicap (My Celeste)

T.P. MORGAN
1954: New Orleans Handicap (Grover B.)

EDNA BROKAW MORRIS
1970: Hopeful Stakes (Proudest Roman)

JOHN A. MORRIS
1956: Pimlico Futurity (Missile)
1970: Coaching Club American Oaks (Missile Belle)
Gazelle Handicap (Missile Belle)

J.O. MORRISEY JR.
1983: Coaching Club American Oaks (High Schemes)

MR. and MRS. FRAZER MORRISON
1964: Californian Stakes (Mustard Plaster)

MORVEN STUD FARM
1995: Whitney Handicap (Unaccounted For)

V. MOSCA
1970: Molly Pitcher Handicap (Double Ripple)

JAMES MOSELEY
1970: Canadian International Championship (Drumtop)
1971: Hialeah Turf Cup (Drumtop)
Bowling Green Handicap (Drumtop)

JEROME MOSS
1986: Metropolitan Handicap (Garthorn)

MR. and MRS. JEROME MOSS
1990: Santa Anita Handicap (Ruhlmann)
1992: Oak Leaf Stakes (Zoonaqua)
1993: Hollywood Starlet Stakes (Sardula)
1994: Kentucky Oaks (Sardula)
2002: Oaklawn Handicap (Kudos)

MOULDER, OLDHAM & SMITH
1959: Arkansas Derby (Al Davelle)

MOUNT JOY STABLES
1992: American Derby (The Name's Jimmy)

MOYGLARE STUD FARM
1989: Laurel Futurity (Go and Go)
1990: Belmont Stakes (Go and Go)
1991: Meadowlands Cup (Twilight Agenda)
2002: Matriarch Stakes (Dress To Thrill)

AUGUST MUCKLER
1962: Arkansas Derby (Aeropolis)

MUCKLER STABLES
1981: Sorority Stakes (Apalachee Honey)
Alcibiades Stakes (Apalachee Honey)
1983: Arlington-Washington Futurity (All Fired Up)

JOHN MULHERN
1994: Eddie Read Handicap (Approach the Bench)

MRS. EDDIE MULRENAN
1946: San Antonio Handicap (First Fiddle)

JACK MUNARI
1990: Swaps Stakes (Jovial)
1991: San Fernando Stakes (In Excess)
Metropolitan Handicap (In Excess)
Suburban Handicap (In Excess)
Whitney Handicap (In Excess)
Woodward Stakes (In Excess)

MURCAIN STABLE
1954: Starlet Stakes (Blue Ruler)
Del Mar Futurity (Blue Ruler)
1955: San Felipe Handicap (Jean's Joe)

MURLOGG FARM
1946: Excelsior Handicap (Fighting Step)

B.A. MURPHY
1946: McLennan Handicap (Concordian)

JOHN MURPHY
1996: Acorn Stakes (Star de Lady Ann)
1997: Donn Handicap (Formal Gold)
Brooklyn Handicap (Formal Gold)
Philip H. Iselin Handicap (Formal Gold)
Woodward Stakes (Formal Gold)

WILLIAM H. MURRAY
1977: Travers Stakes (Jatski)

MYHELYN STABLE
1952: Wood Memorial Stakes (Master Fiddle)

SOL NADLER
1970: Dwyer Handicap (Judgable)
Whitney Stakes (Judgable)
1971: Donn Handicap (Judgable)
Grey Lag Handicap (Judgable)

EDWARD NAHEM & 505 FARMS
1993: Pacific Classic (Bertrando)
Woodward Stakes (Bertrando)

NARVICK INTERNATIONAL STABLE
1988: San Luis Rey Stakes (Rivlia)

MRS. JOSEPH NASH
1981: Widener Handicap (Land of Eire)

NASTY STABLE
1977: Illinois Derby (Flag Officer)

MRS. H.L. NATHENSON
1955: United Nations Handicap (Blue Choir)

NAVONOD STABLE
1974: Norfolk Stakes (George Navonod)
1976: Charles H. Strub Stakes (George Navonod)

NEDDEFF & SUNDANCE STABLE
1981: New Orleans Handicap (Sun Catcher)

NEDLAW STABLE
1989: Young America Stakes (Roanoke)

MR. and MRS. LIN NELSON
1960: Santa Anita Handicap (Linmold)

JOHN NERUD
1981: Metropolitan Handicap (Fappiano)
1984: Wood Memorial Stakes (Leroy S.)
1985: Breeders' Cup Mile (Cozzene)
1988: Top Flight Handicap (Clabber Girl)

GEORGE NEWELL
1958: Los Angeles Handicap (How Now)
American Handicap (How Now)

NEW FARM
1994: Meadowlands Cup (Conveyor)
2001: Forego Handicap (Delaware Township)
Frank J. De Francis Mem. Dash (Delaware Township)

NEW PHOENIX STABLE & SUSAN ROY
2002: Belmont Stakes (Sarava)

NEWSTEAD FARM
1978: Kentucky Oaks (White Star Line)
Alabama Stakes (White Star Line)
1983: Arlington-Washington Lassie Stakes (Miss Oceana)
Selima Stakes (Miss Oceana)
Frizette Stakes (Miss Oceana)

NEWSTEAD FARM TRUST
1984: Acorn Stakes (Miss Oceana)
Maskette Stakes (Miss Oceana)

NIARCHOS FAMILY
1997: Breeders' Cup Mile (Spinning World)
2002: NetJets Breeders' Cup Mile (Domedriver)

STAVROS NIARCHOS
1984: Hollywood Derby (Procida)
Washington D.C. International (Seattle Song)
1987: Breeders' Cup Mile (Miesque)
1988: Breeders' Cup Mile (Miesque)

NIBLICK STABLE
1972: Mother Goose Stakes (Wanda)

HARRY NICHOLS
1964: Coaching Club American Oaks (Miss Cavandish)
Monmouth Oaks (Miss Cavandish)
Alabama Stakes (Miss Cavandish)

T.S. NICHOLS
1963: Alabama Stakes (Tona)
1964: Vineland Handicap (Tona)

NICKELS AND DIMES STABLE
1981: Arlington-Washington Lassie Stakes (Milingo)

V.J. NICKERSON
1956: Gazelle Handicap (Scampering)

NILE FINANCIAL CORPORATION
1974: Santa Margarita Handicap (Tizna)
Ramona Handicap (Tizna)
1975: Santa Margarita Handicap (Tizna)

MASAYUKI NISHIYAMA
1994: Early Times Manhattan Handicap (Paradise Creek)
Arlington Million (Paradise Creek)
Washington D.C. International (Paradise Creek)

NITRAM STABLE
1981: Hopeful Stakes (Timely Writer)
Champagne Stakes (Timely Writer)
1982: Flamingo Stakes (Timely Writer)
Florida Derby (Timely Writer)

NO LIMIT FARM
1984: American Derby (High Alexander)

HOWARD NOONAN
1979: Arlington-Washington Futurity (Execution's Reason)

JOANNE NOR
1995: Breeders' Cup Sprint (Desert Stormer)

B.A. NORRIS
1968: Gazelle Handicap (Another Nell)

NORTH FORTY STABLE
1964: Arlington-Washington Futurity (Sadair)
Garden State Stakes (Sadair)
Pimlico Futurity (Sadair)

NORTH STAR RANCH
1958: Arlington Lassie Stakes (Dark Vintage)

NORTHWEST FARMS
1980: San Felipe Handicap (Raise A Man)

OAK CLIFF STABLE
1982: Santa Barbara Handicap (Ack's Secret)
Santa Margarita Handicap (Ack's Secret)
1983: Santa Margarita Handicap (Marimbula)
1985: Santa Anita Derby (Skywalker)
1986: Breeders' Cup Classic (Skywalker)

OAK CREST STABLE
1975: Maskette Handicap (Let Me Linger)

HARRY OAK
1979: Sapling Stakes (Rockhill Native)
Futurity Stakes (Rockhill Native)
1980: Blue Grass Stakes (Rockhill Native)

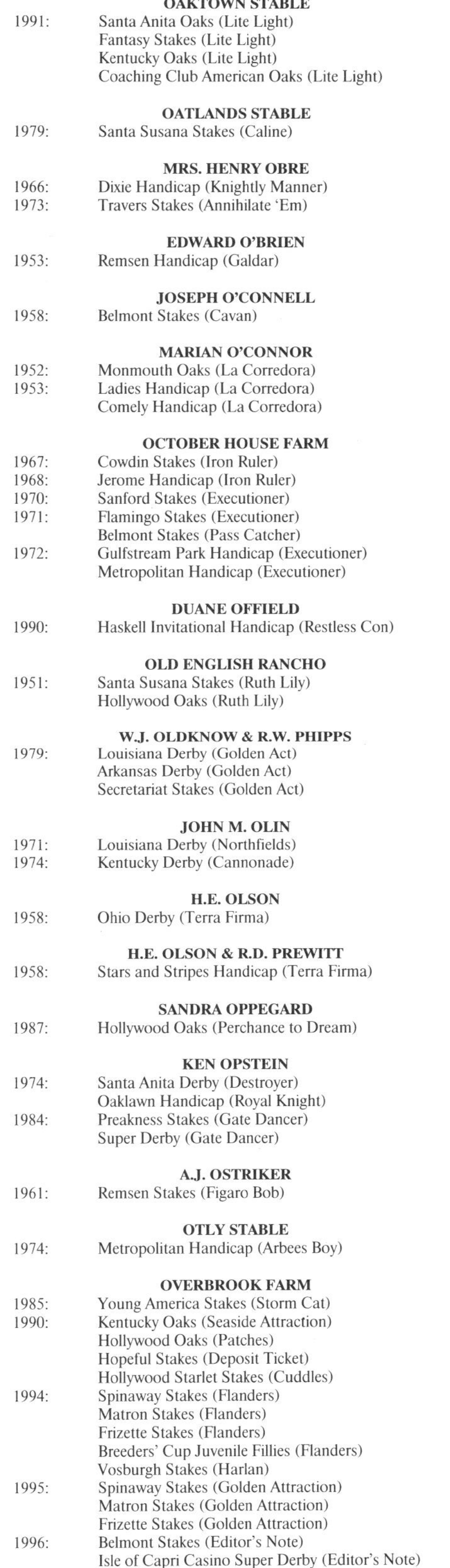

OAKTOWN STABLE
1991: Santa Anita Oaks (Lite Light)
Fantasy Stakes (Lite Light)
Kentucky Oaks (Lite Light)
Coaching Club American Oaks (Lite Light)

OATLANDS STABLE
1979: Santa Susana Stakes (Caline)

MRS. HENRY OBRE
1966: Dixie Handicap (Knightly Manner)
1973: Travers Stakes (Annihilate 'Em)

EDWARD O'BRIEN
1953: Remsen Handicap (Galdar)

JOSEPH O'CONNELL
1958: Belmont Stakes (Cavan)

MARIAN O'CONNOR
1952: Monmouth Oaks (La Corredora)
1953: Ladies Handicap (La Corredora)
Comely Handicap (La Corredora)

OCTOBER HOUSE FARM
1967: Cowdin Stakes (Iron Ruler)
1968: Jerome Handicap (Iron Ruler)
1970: Sanford Stakes (Executioner)
1971: Flamingo Stakes (Executioner)
Belmont Stakes (Pass Catcher)
1972: Gulfstream Park Handicap (Executioner)
Metropolitan Handicap (Executioner)

DUANE OFFIELD
1990: Haskell Invitational Handicap (Restless Con)

OLD ENGLISH RANCHO
1951: Santa Susana Stakes (Ruth Lily)
Hollywood Oaks (Ruth Lily)

W.J. OLDKNOW & R.W. PHIPPS
1979: Louisiana Derby (Golden Act)
Arkansas Derby (Golden Act)
Secretariat Stakes (Golden Act)

JOHN M. OLIN
1971: Louisiana Derby (Northfields)
1974: Kentucky Derby (Cannonade)

H.E. OLSON
1958: Ohio Derby (Terra Firma)

H.E. OLSON & R.D. PREWITT
1958: Stars and Stripes Handicap (Terra Firma)

SANDRA OPPEGARD
1987: Hollywood Oaks (Perchance to Dream)

KEN OPSTEIN
1974: Santa Anita Derby (Destroyer)
Oaklawn Handicap (Royal Knight)
1984: Preakness Stakes (Gate Dancer)
Super Derby (Gate Dancer)

A.J. OSTRIKER
1961: Remsen Stakes (Figaro Bob)

OTLY STABLE
1974: Metropolitan Handicap (Arbees Boy)

OVERBROOK FARM
1985: Young America Stakes (Storm Cat)
1990: Kentucky Oaks (Seaside Attraction)
Hollywood Oaks (Patches)
Hopeful Stakes (Deposit Ticket)
Hollywood Starlet Stakes (Cuddles)
1994: Spinaway Stakes (Flanders)
Matron Stakes (Flanders)
Frizette Stakes (Flanders)
Breeders' Cup Juvenile Fillies (Flanders)
Vosburgh Stakes (Harlan)
1995: Spinaway Stakes (Golden Attraction)
Matron Stakes (Golden Attraction)
Frizette Stakes (Golden Attraction)
1996: Belmont Stakes (Editor's Note)
Isle of Capri Casino Super Derby (Editor's Note)
Kentucky Derby (Grindstone)
Oak Leaf Stakes (City Band)
Breeders' Cup Juvenile (Boston Harbor)
1997: Ballerina Stakes (Pearl City)
1998: Florida Derby (Cape Town)
Lane's End Breeders' Futurity (Cat Thief)

Four Footed Fotos, Inc., courtesy of Churchill Downs

Few owners have been as successful since the mid-1980s as Overbrook Farm, which experienced perhaps its proudest moment when Grindstone (4) overtook Cavonnier (3) in the final strides to win the 1996 Kentucky Derby by a nose.

Hollywood Futurity (Tactical Cat)
1999: Swaps Stakes (Cat Thief)
Breeders' Cup Classic (Cat Thief)
Frizette Stakes (Surfside)
Hollywood Starlet Stakes (Surfside)
2000: Las Virgenes Stakes (Surfside)
Santa Anita Oaks (Surfside)
2002: San Carlos Handicap (Snow Ridge)

OVERBROOK FARM & DAVID REYNOLDS
1994: Preakness Stakes (Tabasco Cat)
Belmont Stakes (Tabasco Cat)

OXFORD STABLE
1971: Monmouth Invitational Handicap (West Coast Scout)
Woodward Stakes (West Coast Scout)
1972: Amory L. Haskell Handicap (West Coast Scout)
1973: Gulfstream Park Handicap (West Coast Scout)
Amory L. Haskell Handicap (West Coast Scout)

DEBBY OXLEY
2001: Acorn Stakes (Forest Secrets)

JOHN OXLEY
1995: Kentucky Oaks (Gal in a Ruckus)
1997: Matron Stakes (Beautiful Pleasure)
1999: Personal Ensign Handicap (Beautiful Pleasure)
Beldame Stakes (Beautiful Pleasure)
Breeders' Cup Distaff (Beautiful Pleasure)
2000: Hempstead Handicap (Beautiful Pleasure)
Personal Ensign Handicap (Beautiful Pleasure)
2001: Florida Derby (Monarchos)
Kentucky Derby (Monarchos)
2002: Fountain of Youth Stakes (Booklet)
Hopeful Stakes (Sky Mesa)
2003: Gulfstream Park Handicap (Hero's Tribute)

JOHN OXLEY & MARVIN WARNER
1981: Hollywood Futurity (Stalwart)

HENRY PABST
1995: Hollywood Turf Handicap (Earl of Barking)

J. PADDOCK
1956: Michigan Mile (Nonnie Jo)

PADUA STABLES
1999: Frank J. De Francis Memorial Dash (Yes It's True)
Breeders' Cup Juvenile Fillies (Cash Run)
2002: Bessemer Trust Breeders' Cup Juvenile (Vindication)

PAUL PAINTER
1984: Hollywood Oaks (Moment to Buy)

PALATINE STABLE
1950: Gulfstream Park Handicap (Chicle II)
Trenton Handicap (Chicle II)
Bougainvillea Handicap (Chicle II)
1951: Bougainvillea Handicap (Chicle II)

PALEV STABLE
1983: Haskell Invitational Handicap (Deputed Testamony)

J. PALMISANO
1952: Starlet Stakes (Little Request)

JEAN PANCOAST
1974: Louisiana Derby (Sellout)

PARANECK STABLE
1995: Breeders' Cup Juvenile (Unbridled's Song)
1996: Florida Derby (Unbridled's Song)
Wood Memorial Stakes (Unbridled's Song)
1998: San Felipe Stakes (Artax)
1999: Carter Handicap (Artax)
Vosburgh Stakes (Artax)
Breeders' Cup Sprint (Artax)
Wood Memorial Stakes (Adonis)

CHARLENE PARKS
1982: Vanity Handicap (Sangue)
1983: Ramona Handicap (Sangue)
Golden Harvest Handicap (Sangue)
Yellow Ribbon Stakes (Sangue)
Matriarch Stakes (Sangue)

W.C. PARTEE
1959: Brooklyn Handicap (Babu)
1970: Kentucky Jockey Club Stakes (Line City)
1974: Arkansas Derby (J.R.'s Pet)
1984: Jim Beam Stakes (At the Threshold)
Arlington Classic (At the Threshold)
Ohio Derby (At the Threshold)
American Derby (At the Threshold)
Haskell Invitational Handicap (Big Pistol)
1987: Jim Beam Stakes (J.T.'s Pet)
1992: Jim Beam Stakes (Lil E. Tee)
Kentucky Derby (Lil E. Tee)

WILLIAM T. PASCOE III & BRIAN SWEENEY
1981: San Juan Capistrano Handicap (Obraztsovy)

CHARLES & SUZANNE PASHAYAN
1989: Yellow Ribbon Stakes (Brown Bess)
1990: Santa Barbara Handicap (Brown Bess)

PASTORALE STABLE
1971: Arkansas Derby (Twist the Axe)
Ohio Derby (Twist the Axe)

JOSEPHINE PAUL
1959: Maskette Handicap (Idun)

ALLEN PAULSON
1986: Budweiser-Arlington Million (Estrapade)
Oak Tree Invitational Stakes (Estrapade)
1987: Gamely Handicap (Northern Aspen)
Selima Stakes (Minstrel's Lassie)
1989: Hollywood Gold Cup (Blushing John)
1990: Oaklawn Handicap (Opening Verse)
1991: Santa Anita Derby (Dinard)
Hollywood Oaks (Fowda)
Breeders' Cup Mile (Opening Verse)
1992: Arlington-Washington Lassie Stakes (Eliza)
Breeders' Cup Juvenile Fillies (Eliza)
Spinster Stakes (Fowda)
1993: Santa Anita Oaks (Eliza)
San Felipe Stakes (Corby)
Pegasus Handicap (Diazo)
1994: Strub Stakes (Diazo)
Santa Anita Handicap (Stuka)
NYRA Mile Handicap (Cigar)
1995: Donn Handicap (Cigar)
Gulfstream Park Handicap (Cigar)
Oaklawn Handicap (Cigar)
Pimlico Special (Cigar)
Hollywood Gold Cup (Cigar)
Woodward Stakes (Cigar)
Jockey Club Gold Cup (Cigar)

ALLEN PAULSON *(Continued)*
Breeders' Cup Classic (Cigar)
1996: Donn Handicap (Cigar)
Woodward Stakes (Cigar)
Oaklawn Handicap (Geri)
1997: Mother Goose Stakes (Ajina)
Coaching Club American Oaks (Ajina)
Breeders' Cup Distaff (Ajina)
Ramona Handicap (Escena)
Woodbine Mile (Geri)
1998: Apple Blossom Handicap (Escena)
Vanity Handicap (Escena)
Breeders' Cup Distaff (Escena)
1999: Gulfstream Park Breeders' Cup Handicap (Yagli)
Manhattan Handicap (Yagli)
2000: Gamely Breeders' Cup Handicap (Astra)

ALLEN PAULSON LIVING TRUST
2001: Beverly Hills Handicap (Astra)
Secretariat Stakes (Startac)
2002: Santa Margarita Handicap (Azeri)
Apple Blossom Handicap (Azeri)
Milady Breeders' Cup Handicap (Azeri)
Vanity Handicap (Azeri)
Breeders' Cup Distaff (Azeri)
Gamely Breeders' Cup Handicap (Astra)
Beverly Hills Handicap (Astra)
2003: Apple Blossom Handicap (Azeri)
Milady Breeders' Cup Handicap (Azeri)
Vanity Handicap (Azeri)

ALLEN & MADELEINE PAULSON
2000: Oaklawn Handicap (K One King)

MADELEINE PAULSON
1992: Sword Dancer Handicap (Fraise)
Breeders' Cup Turf (Fraise)
1993: Hollywood Turf Cup (Fraise)
1994: Flower Bowl Inv. Handicap (Dahlia's Dreamer)
1995: Matriarch Stakes (Duda)

ALLEN PAULSON & SHEIKH MOHAMMAD al MAKTOUM
1991: Breeders' Cup Juvenile (Arazi)

ALLEN PAULSON & SUMMA STABLE
1988: Gulfstream Park Handicap (Jade Hunter)

DR. IGNACIO PAVLOVSKY & FRANK WHITHAM
1992: San Antonio Handicap (Ibero)
NYRA Mile Handicap (Ibero)
1993: Metropolitan Handicap (Ibero)

ADELE PAXSON
1978: Selima Stakes (Candy Eclair)
1980: Delaware Handicap (Heavenly Ade)

VIRGINIA KRAFT PAYSON
1986: Jim Dandy Stakes (Lac Ouimet)

JOHN PEACE
1993: Nassau County Handicap (West by West)

WILLIAM PEASE
1982: Hollywood Turf Cup (Prince Spellbound)
1983: Eddie Read Handicap (Prince Spellbound)

W.M. PEAVEY
1949: Arlington Futurity (Wisconsin Boy)

PEBBLEBROOK FARM
1959: Saratoga Special (Irish Lancer)

PEGASUS STABLES
1987: Widener Handicap (Launch a Pegasus)

MIKE PEGRAM
1997: Hollywood Futurity (Real Quiet)
1998: Kentucky Derby (Real Quiet)
Preakness Stakes (Real Quiet)
Walmac Int. Alcibiades Stakes (Silverbulletday)
Breeders' Cup Juvenile Fillies (Silverbulletday)
1999: Ashland Stakes (Silverbulletday)
Kentucky Oaks (Silverbulletday)
Alabama Stakes (Silverbulletday)
Gazelle Handicap (Silverbulletday)
Pimlico Special (Real Quiet)
Sempra Energy Hollywood Gold Cup (Real Quiet)
Lane's End Breeders' Futurity (Captain Steve)
Hollywood Futurity (Captain Steve)
La Brea Stakes (Hookedonthefeelin)
2000: Swaps Stakes (Captain Steve)
2001: Donn Handicap (Captain Steve)
2002: Del Mar Futurity (Icecoldbeeratreds)

ANTHONY PEJSA
1976: Norfolk Stakes (Habitony)
1977: Santa Anita Derby (Habitony)

PELICAN STABLE
1965: United Nations Handicap (Parka)
1969: Jersey Derby (Al Hattab)
Monmouth Invitational Handicap (Al Hattab)
1993: Futurity Stakes (Holy Bull)

HARVEY PELTIER
1966: Arlington-Washington Futurity (Diplomat Way)
1967: Blue Grass Stakes (Diplomat Way)
1968: New Orleans Handicap (Diplomat Way)
Oaklawn Handicap (Diplomat Way)
1969: Oaklawn Handicap (Listado)
1970: Washington Park Handicap (Doc's T.V.)
1972: Illinois Derby (Fame and Power)
1974: New Orleans Handicap (Smooth Dancer)
1975: Illinois Derby (Colonel Power)

LAWRENCE PENDLETON & ROYAL T. STABLE
1988: Del Mar Futurity (Music Merci)
1989: Illinois Derby (Music Merci)

PEN-Y-BRYN FARM
1972: Dwyer Handicap (Cloudy Dawn)
Arlington Park Handicap (Cloudy Dawn)
1975: Fall Highweight Handicap (Honorable Miss)
1976: Fall Highweight Handicap (Honorable Miss)
1977: Dwyer Handicap (Bailjumper)
1978: Remsen Stakes (Instrument Landing)
1979: Wood Memorial Stakes (Instrument Landing)
1983: Brooklyn Handicap (Highland Blade)
Marlboro Cup Handicap (Highland Blade)
Pan American Handicap (Highland Blade)

ALFIO & J. PEPINO
1965: Garden State Stakes (Prince Saim)

ANN PEPPERS
1964: Santa Anita Handicap (Mr. Consistency)
San Juan Capistrano Handicap (Mr. Consistency)

ROBERT PEREZ
1991: Futurity Stakes (Agincourt)
1992: Dwyer Stakes (Agincourt)

PETER PERKINS
1985: San Antonio Handicap (Lord at War)
Santa Anita Handicap (Lord at War)

RUTH PERLMUTTER
1977: Florida Derby (Ruthie's Native)

WILLIAM HAGGIN PERRY
1956: Spinaway Stakes (Alanesian)
1963: Coaching Club American Oaks (Lamb Chop)
Monmouth Oaks (Lamb Chop)
Spinster Stakes (Lamb Chop)
1964: Santa Margarita Handicap (Batteur)
1965: Santa Susana Stakes (Desert Love)
San Felipe Handicap (Jacinto)
1966: Santa Anita Derby (Boldnesian)
1967: Alabama Stakes (Gamely)
Vanity Handicap (Desert Love)
1968: Vanity Handicap (Gamely)
Beldame Stakes (Gamely)
Santa Margarita Handicap (Gamely)
San Felipe Handicap (Dewan)
Santa Barbara Handicap (Princessnesian)
Hollywood Gold Cup (Princessnesian)
1969: Vanity Handicap (Desert Law)
Beldame Stakes (Gamely)
Santa Margarita Handicap (Princessnesian)
Charles H. Strub Stakes (Dignitas)
1970: Brooklyn Handicap (Dewan)
San Antonio Stakes (Dewan)
Travers Stakes (Loud)
1974: San Luis Rey Stakes (Astray)
San Juan Capistrano Handicap (Astray)
Maskette Handicap (Ponte Vecchio)
1975: Withers Stakes (Sarsar)
Century Handicap (Astray)
1976: Coaching Club American Oaks (Revidere)
Ruffian Stakes (Revidere)
1978: Bowling Green Handicap (Tiller)
1979: Belmont Stakes (Coastal)
Dwyer Stakes (Coastal)
Monmouth Invitational Handicap (Coastal)
San Antonio Stakes (Tiller)
San Juan Capistrano Handicap (Tiller)
1980: Sword Dancer Stakes (Tiller)
1990: Cowdin Stakes (Scan)
Remsen Stakes (Scan)
1991: Jerome Handicap (Scan)
Pegasus Handicap (Scan)
1992: Pegasus Handicap (Scuffleburg)

LEONE J. PETERS
1975: San Felipe Handicap (Fleet Velvet)
1980: Hopeful Stakes (Tap Shoes)
Futurity Stakes (Tap Shoes)
1981: Flamingo Stakes (Tap Shoes)

L.E. PETERSON
1970: Santa Barbara Handicap (Sallarina)

MR. and MRS. F.N. PHELPS
1951: Inglewood Handicap (Sturdy One)
1952: Inglewood Handicap (Sturdy One)

JACQUELINE GETTY PHILLIPS
1982: Widener Handicap (Lord Darnley)
Gulfstream Park Handicap (Lord Darnley)

JACQUELINE GETTY PHILLIPS & MICHAEL RIORDAN
1983: Monmouth Handicap (Bates Motel)
San Antonio Stakes (Bates Motel)
Santa Anita Handicap (Bates Motel)

MR. and MRS. JAMES PHILLIPS
1988: Florida Derby (Brian's Time)
Jim Dandy Stakes (Brian's Time)

JOAN & JOHN PHILLIPS
1996: Queen Elizabeth II Chal. Cup (Memories of Silver)
1997: Beverly D. Stakes (Memories of Silver)
1999: Flower Bowl Invitational Handicap (Soaring Softly)
Breeders' Cup Filly and Mare Turf (Soaring Softly)
2002: Garden City Breeders' Cup Handicap (Wonder Again)

MR. and MRS. N.G. PHILLIPS
1954: Del Mar Handicap (Stranglehold)

CYNTHIA PHIPPS
1975: Jersey Derby (Singh)
1976: Maskette Handicap (Sugar Plum Time)
1982: Coaching Club American Oaks (Christmas Past)
Ruffian Handicap (Christmas Past)
1983: Gulfstream Park Handicap (Christmas Past)
1991: Alabama Stakes (Versailles Treaty)
1992: Ruffian Handicap (Versailles Treaty)
1996: NYRA Mile Handicap (Gold Fever)

JOHN S. PHIPPS
1953: Discovery Handicap (Level Lea)
Jockey Club Gold Cup (Level Lea)
1954: Vineland Handicap (Spinning Top)
Bougainvillea Turf Handicap (Parnassus)

MICHAEL PHIPPS
1966: Breeders' Futurity (Gentleman James)
1967: Donn Handicap (Francis U.)
1968: Illinois Derby (Bold Favorite)
Gulfstream Park Handicap (Gentleman James)

OGDEN PHIPPS
1948: Tremont Stakes (The Admiral)
1950: Alabama Stakes (Busanda)
1951: Top Flight Handicap (Busanda)
New Castle Handicap (Busanda)
Suburban Handicap (Busanda)
1952: Spinaway Stakes (Flirtatious)
Discovery Handicap (Ancestor)
1954: Monmouth Handicap (Bassanio)
1957: Dwyer Handicap (Bureaucracy)
1961: Withers Stakes (Hitting Away)
Dwyer Handicap (Hitting Away)
Mother Goose Stakes (Funloving)
1965: Sapling Stakes (Buckpasser)
Hopeful Stakes (Buckpasser)
Arlington-Washington Futurity (Buckpasser)
Champagne Stakes (Buckpasser)
Saratoga Special (Impressive)
1966: Everglades Stakes (Buckpasser)
Flamingo Stakes (Buckpasser)
Arlington Classic (Buckpasser)
American Derby (Buckpasser)
Travers Stakes (Buckpasser)
Lawrence Realization Stakes (Buckpasser)
Brooklyn Handicap (Buckpasser)
Woodward Stakes (Buckpasser)
Jockey Club Gold Cup (Buckpasser)

	Acorn Stakes (Marking Time)
	Ladies Handicap (Destro)
1967:	Saratoga Special (Vitriolic)
	Arlington-Washington Futurity (Vitriolic)
	Champagne Stakes (Vitriolic)
	Pimlico-Laurel Futurity (Vitriolic)
	Sorority Stakes (Queen of the Stage)
	Spinaway Stakes (Queen of the Stage)
	Matron Stakes (Queen of the Stage)
	Frizette Stakes (Queen of the Stage)
	Metropolitan Handicap (Buckpasser)
	Suburban Handicap (Buckpasser)
	San Fernando Stakes (Buckpasser)
	Bowling Green Handicap (Poker)
1968:	Sapling Stakes (Reviewer)
	Saratoga Special (Reviewer)
1969:	Louisiana Derby (King of the Castle)
	Illinois Derby (King of the Castle)
1970:	American Derby (The Pruner)
1971:	Spinaway Stakes (Numbered Account)
	Matron Stakes (Numbered Account)
	Frizette Stakes (Numbered Account)
	Selima Stakes (Numbered Account)
	Gardenia Stakes (Numbered Account)
1972:	Spinster Stakes (Numbered Account)
1974:	Matron Stakes (Alpine Lass)
1975:	Hialeah Turf Cup (Outdoors)
1977:	Arlington Handicap (Cunning Trick)
1979:	Maskette Stakes (Blitey)
	Brooklyn Handicap (The Liberal Member)
1980:	Widener Handicap (Private Account)
	Gulfstream Park Handicap (Private Account)
	Pan American Handicap (Flitalong)
1981:	Delaware Handicap (Relaxing)
	Ruffian Handicap (Relaxing)
1983:	Beldame Stakes (Dance Number)
1984:	Everglades Stakes (Time for a Change)
	Flamingo Stakes (Time for a Change)
1986:	Cowdin Stakes (Polish Navy)
	Champagne Stakes (Polish Navy)
	Frizette Stakes (Personal Ensign)
1987:	Jim Dandy Stakes (Polish Navy)
	Woodward Stakes (Polish Navy)
	Beldame Stakes (Personal Ensign)
1988:	Whitney Handicap (Personal Ensign)
	Maskette Stakes (Personal Ensign)
	Beldame Stakes (Personal Ensign)
	Breeders' Cup Distaff (Personal Ensign)
	Peter Pan Stakes (Seeking the Gold)
	Dwyer Stakes (Seeking the Gold)
	Super Derby (Seeking the Gold)
	Cowdin Stakes (Easy Goer)
	Champagne Stakes (Easy Goer)
	Suburban Handicap (Personal Flag)
	Vosburgh Stakes (Mining)
1989:	Gotham Stakes (Easy Goer)
	Wood Memorial Stakes (Easy Goer)
	Belmont Stakes (Easy Goer)
	Whitney Handicap (Easy Goer)
	Travers Stakes (Easy Goer)
	Woodward Handicap (Easy Goer)
	Jockey Club Gold Cup (Easy Goer)
	Suburban Handicap (Dancing Spree)
	Breeders' Cup Sprint (Dancing Spree)
	Cowdin Stakes (Adjudicating)
	Champagne Stakes (Adjudicating)
1990:	Carter Handicap (Dancing Spree)
	Suburban Handicap (Easy Goer)
1992:	Go for Wand Stakes (Easy Now)
	Futurity Stakes (Strolling Along)
1993:	Jim Dandy Stakes (Miner's Mark)
	Jockey Club Gold Cup (Miner's Mark)
	Frizette Stakes (Heavenly Prize)
1994:	Alabama Stakes (Heavenly Prize)
	Gazelle Handicap (Heavenly Prize)
	Beldame Stakes (Heavenly Prize)
1995:	Apple Blossom Handicap (Heavenly Prize)
	Hempstead Handicap (Heavenly Prize)
	Go for Wand Stakes (Heavenly Prize)
	Breeders' Cup Juvenile Fillies (My Flag)
1996:	Ashland Stakes (My Flag)
	Coaching Club American Oaks (My Flag)
	Gazelle Handicap (My Flag)
1998:	Matron Stakes (Oh What a Windfall)
1999:	Ballerina Handicap (Furlough)
	Matron Stakes (Finder's Fee)
2000:	Acorn Stakes (Finder's Fee)
2001:	Oaklawn Handicap (Traditionally)

OGDEN MILLS PHIPPS

1968:	Garden State Stakes (Beau Brummel)
1975:	Hollywood Derby (Intrepid Hero)
	Secretariat Stakes (Intrepid Hero)
1976:	Swaps Stakes (Majestic Light)
	Monmouth Invitational Handicap (Majestic Light)
	Cinema Handicap (Majestic Light)
	Sorority Stakes (Squander)
	United Nations Handicap (Intrepid Hero)
1977:	Amory L. Haskell Handicap (Majestic Light)
	Man o' War Stakes (Majestic Light)
1983:	Bowling Green Handicap (Tantalizing)
1989:	Flamingo Stakes (Awe Inspiring)
	Jersey Derby (Awe Inspiring)
	Breeders' Cup Juvenile (Rhythm)
1990:	Travers Stakes (Rhythm)
1992:	Frizette Stakes (Educated Risk)
1993:	Kentucky Oaks (Dispute)
	Gazelle Handicap (Dispute)
	Beldame Stakes (Dispute)
	Brooklyn Handicap (Living Vicariously)
1994:	Ashland Stakes (Inside Information)
	Acorn Stakes (Inside Information)
	Spinster Stakes (Dispute)
	Top Flight Handicap (Educated Risk)
1995:	Shuvee Handicap (Inside Information)
	Ruffian Handicap (Inside Information)
	Spinster Stakes (Inside Information)
	Breeders' Cup Distaff (Inside Information)
2002:	Matron Stakes (Storm Flag Flying)
	Frizette Stakes (Storm Flag Flying)
	Long John Silver's BC Juv. Fillies (Storm Flag Flying)

SHEILA PIERCE

1969:	Washington Park Handicap (Night Invader)

PINE MEADOW THOROUGHBREDS

1982:	Hollywood Starlet Stakes (Fabulous Notion)
1983:	Santa Susana Stakes (Fabulous Notion)

PINE TREE STABLE

1978:	Fantasy Stakes (Equanimity)
	Del Mar Handicap (Palton)

JERRY PINKLEY

1987:	American Derby (Fortunate Moment)

PIN OAK FARM

1954:	Remsen Stakes (Roman Patrol)
1955:	Louisiana Derby (Roman Patrol)
1963:	Hialeah Turf Cup (Intercepted)

PIN OAK STABLE

1974:	Hollywood Gold Cup (Tree of Knowledge)
1990:	Flower Bowl Handicap (Laugh and Be Merry)
1995:	Molson Export Million (Peaks and Valleys)
	Meadowlands Cup (Peaks and Valleys)
1998:	Frizette Stakes (Confessional)
2001:	Philip H. Iselin Handicap (Broken Vow)

PINWHEEL FARM

1984:	La Canada Stakes (Sweet Diane)

JOSEPH PLATT JR.

2002:	Mother Goose Stakes (Nonsuch Bay)

HELEN POLINGER

1981:	Santa Barbara Handicap (The Very One)

MILTON POLINGER

1974:	Hollywood Invitational Handicap (Court Ruling)

HIRAM POLK & DAVID RICHARDSON

1995:	Flower Bowl Inv. Handicap (Northern Emerald)

CARL POLLARD

2000:	Breeders' Cup Juvenile Fillies (Caressing)

JACK POLLARD

1976:	Del Mar Debutante Stakes (Telferner)

POLTEX STABLE

1957:	San Antonio Handicap (Terrang)
1958:	Santa Margarita Handicap (Born Rich)
1964:	Del Mar Futurity (Terry's Secret)
1965:	Hollywood Derby (Terry's Secret)
	Sunset Handicap (Terry's Secret)

POMA STABLE

1988:	Selima Stakes (Capades)

SIDNEY PORT

1982:	Arlington Classic (Wolfie's Rascal)
	American Derby (Wolfie's Rascal)
1983:	Arlington Handicap (Palikaraki)

SIDNEY PORT, ANNABELLE STUTE & EDWIN WACHTEL

1997:	Gotham Stakes (Smokin Mel)

POST TIME STABLE

1975:	San Fernando Stakes (First Back)
1991:	Young America Stakes (Maston)

EDWARD POTTER JR.

1957:	Sapling Stakes (Plion)
1958:	Blue Grass Stakes (Plion)
1959:	Whitney Stakes (Plion)

POWHATAN STABLE

1963:	Cowdin Stakes (Chieftan)
1964:	Cowdin Stakes (Tom Rolfe)
1965:	Preakness Stakes (Tom Rolfe)
	Arlington Classic (Tom Rolfe)
	American Derby (Tom Rolfe)
	Arlington Handicap (Chieftan)
1966:	Aqueduct Handicap (Tom Rolfe)

PRATT & JACK VAN BERG

1976:	Secretariat Stakes (Joachim)

PRESTONWOOD FARM

1987:	Vosburgh Stakes (Groovy)
1996:	Breeders' Cup Mile (Da Hoss)
1998:	Arkansas Derby (Victory Gallop)
	Belmont Stakes (Victory Gallop)
	Breeders' Cup Mile (Da Hoss)
1999:	Whitney Handicap (Victory Gallop)
2003:	Eddie Read Handicap (Special Ring)

EDITH PRICE

1960:	John B. Campbell Handicap (Yes You Will)
	Carter Handicap (Yes You Will)

KATHERINE PRICE

1960:	Cowdin Stakes (Carry Back)
	Remsen Stakes (Carry Back)
1961:	Kentucky Derby (Carry Back)
	Preakness Stakes (Carry Back)
	Jerome Handicap (Carry Back)
1962:	Metropolitan Handicap (Carry Back)
	Monmouth Handicap (Carry Back)
	Whitney Stakes (Carry Back)

E. PRITCHARD, WM. RESSEGUET JR. & DR. E. THOMAS

1973:	Flamingo Stakes (Our Native)
	Ohio Derby (Our Native)
	Monmouth Invitational Handicap (Our Native)

IZZIE PROLER & JOSEPH STRAUSS JR.

1977:	Louisiana Derby (Clev Er Tell)
	Arkansas Derby (Clev Er Tell)
	Oaklawn Handicap (Soy Numero Uno)
	Carter Handicap (Soy Numero Uno)
	Jerome Handicap (Broadway Forli)
1979:	Louisiana Downs Handicap (Incredible Ease)

C.N. PULLIAM

1983:	La Canada Stakes (Avigaition)
	Santa Barbara Handicap (Avigaition)

WILLIAM PUNK JR.

1996:	Moet Champagne Stakes (Ordway)

ANTHONY PUPINO

1961:	Bowling Green Handicap (Dead Center)

PURNER JR. & SCORE STABLE

1982:	San Antonio Stakes (Score Twenty Four)

QUARTER B FARM

1998:	Turf Classic (Buck's Boy)
	Breeders' Cup Turf (Buck's Boy)

HAROLD QUEEN

2000:	Futurity Stakes (Burning Roma)

J.R. QUERBES III

1985:	Hollywood Derby (Charming Duke)

LORRAINE QUINICHETT

1988:	Ashland Stakes (Willa on the Move)

ROBERT QUINICHETT

1982:	Sorority Stakes (Singing Susan)

KJELL QVALE

1981:	Hollywood Derby (Silveyville)
1986:	San Felipe Handicap (Variety Road)
1987:	San Fernando Stakes (Variety Road)

MRS. L. RABINOWITZ
1947: Miami Beach Handicap (Tel O'Sullivan)

ADELE RAND
1957: Withers Stakes (Clem)
Arlington Classic (Clem)
1958: Washington Park Handicap (Clem)
Woodward Stakes (Clem)
United Nations Handicap (Clem)
1961: Tropical Park Handicap (Bourbon Prince)
1968: Withers Stakes (Call Me Prince)

FRANK RAND JR.
1958: Tropical Handicap (St. Amour II)
1966: Illinois Derby (Michigan Avenue)

F.J. RECIO
1960: Bougainvillea Turf Handicap (Noble Sel)

RED BARON'S BARN
2001: Ramona Handicap (Janet)
Yellow Ribbon Stakes (Janet)

RED BRICK STABLE
1969: Sapling Stakes (Ring For Nurse)

JOHN PAUL REDDAM
2001: Ancient Title BC Handicap (Swept Overboard)
2002: Metropolitan Handicap (Swept Overboard)
Hollywood Starlet Stakes (Elloluv)
2003: Ashland Stakes (Elloluv)

JHERI REDDING
1990: Hollywood Derby (Itsallgreektome)
Hollywood Turf Cup (Itsallgreektome)

RED OAK STABLE
1965: Dwyer Handicap (Staunchness)
1966: Whitney Stakes (Staunchness)
2003: Hollywood Derby (Sweet Return)

JOHN & NANCY REED
1986: Arkansas Derby (Rampage)

RONALD REEVES
1988: Hialeah Turf Cup (Double Bed)

REGAL ROSE STABLE
1993: Santa Margarita Handicap (Southern Truce)

RUSSELL REINEMAN
1973: Donn Handicap (Triumphant)
1980: American Derby (Hurry Up Blue)
1986: Haskell Invitational Handicap (Wise Times)
Travers Stakes (Wise Times)
Super Derby (Wise Times)
1990: Super Derby (Home at Last)

MRS. RUSSELL REINEMAN
1962: Arlington Lassie Stakes (Smart Deb)
Matron Stakes (Smart Deb)
1963: Arlington Matron Handicap (Smart Deb)

RELATIVELY STABLE
1979: California Derby (Beau's Eagle)
1980: San Antonio Stakes (Beau's Eagle)

RELEIB STABLE
1998: Buick Meadowlands Cup Handicap (K.J.'s Appeal)

REN-MAR THOROUGHBREDS
2002: Hollywood Gold Cup (Sky Jack)

VICTOR RESK
1990: Meadowlands Cup (Great Normand)

WILLIAM RESSEGUET JR. & ROBINS
1969: Hollywood Juvenile Championship (Insubordination)

WILLIAM RESSEGUET JR. & STEINER III
1968: Arlington-Washington Futurity (Strong Strong)

REVERIE KNOLL FARM
1950: Princess Pat Stakes (Flyamanita)
1953: New Orleans Handicap (Smoke Screen)
1955: Kentucky Jockey Club Stakes (Royal Sting)
1956: Matron Stakes (Romanita)
1957: Monmouth Oaks (Romanita)
1958: Louisiana Derby (Royal Union)
1966: Kentucky Jockey Club Stakes (Lightning Orphan)

TED REXIUS
1980: Del Mar Futurity (Bold And Gold)

HUGO REYNOLDS
1999: Woodward Stakes (River Keen)
Jockey Club Gold Cup (River Keen)

WILLIAM REYNOLDS
1979: Jerome Handicap (Czaravich)
1980: Metropolitan Handicap (Czaravich)

ADA RICE
1946: San Carlos Handicap (Sirde)
1948: Washington Park Futurity (Model Cadet)
1952: Washington Park Futurity (Mr. Paradise)
1953: Delaware Oaks (Cerise Reine)
1954: Fall Highweight Handicap (Pet Bully)
Washington Park Handicap (Pet Bully)
Woodward Stakes (Pet Bully)
Santa Margarita Handicap (Cerise Reine)
1957: Arlington Matron Handicap (Pucker Up)
Beldame Handicap (Pucker Up)
Washington Park Handicap (Pucker Up)
1958: Top Flight Handicap (Plucky Roman)
1959: Massachusetts Handicap (Air Pilot)
1960: Sorority Stakes (Apatontheback)
Massachusetts Handicap (Talent Show)
1961: Carter Handicap (Chief of Chiefs)
Washington Park Handicap (Chief of Chiefs)
1962: Sapling Stakes (Delta Judge)
Pimlico Futurity (Right Proud)
1965: Santa Anita Derby (Lucky Debonair)
Blue Grass Stakes (Lucky Debonair)
Kentucky Derby (Lucky Debonair)
Suburban Handicap (Pia Star)
Brooklyn Handicap (Pia Star)
Cowdin Stakes (Advocator)
1966: Widener Handicap (Pia Star)
Santa Anita Handicap (Lucky Debonair)
1967: Seminole Handicap (Advocator)
1970: Donn Handicap (Twogundan)
1973: Alcibiades Stakes (City Girl)
1974: Top Flight Handicap (Lady Love)
Bowling Green Handicap (Take Off)

ALTHEA RICHARDS
1998: Fall Highweight Handicap (Punch Line)

B.J. RICHARDS
1966: California Derby (Tragniew)

BEN RIDDER
1976: San Fernando Stakes (Messenger of Song)
1977: Vanity Handicap (Cascapedia)
1978: Del Mar Futurity (Flying Paster)
Norfolk Stakes (Flying Paster)
1979: Santa Anita Derby (Flying Paster)
Hollywood Derby (Flying Paster)
1981: San Antonio Stakes (Flying Paster)

RIDDER THOROUGHBRED STABLE
1995: Acorn Stakes (Cat's Cradle)
1996: San Antonio Handicap (Alphabet Soup)
Breeders' Cup Classic (Alphabet Soup)

RIDGEWOOD STABLE
1946: Garden State Stakes (Double Jay)
Kentucky Jockey Club Stakes (Double Jay)
1948: Trenton Handicap (Double Jay)
1949: American Handicap (Double Jay)

DOROTHY RIGNEY
1963: Cowdin Stakes (Dunfee)
1969: American Derby (Fast Hilarious)
1970: Michigan Mile and One-Eighth (Fast Hilarious)

RI-MA-RO STABLE
1982: Acorn Stakes (Cupecoy's Joy)
Mother Goose Stakes (Cupecoy's Joy)

CONNIE RING
1976: San Felipe Handicap (Crystal Water)
Hollywood Derby (Crystal Water)
1977: Californian Stakes (Crystal Water)
Hollywood Gold Cup (Crystal Water)
Santa Anita Handicap (Crystal Water)
Oak Tree Invitational Stakes (Crystal Water)
Sunset Handicap (Today'n Tomorrow)
1982: Hollywood Derby (Racing Is Fun)

GUSTAV RING
1952: Manhattan Handicap (Lone Eagle)
1960: Manhattan Handicap (Don Poggio)
Gallant Fox Handicap (Don Poggio)
1961: Monmouth Handicap (Don Poggio)

1963: Gotham Stakes (Debbysman)
1968: Man o' War Stakes (Czar Alexander)
1969: Dixie Handicap (Czar Alexander)
Bowling Green Handicap (Czar Alexander)
Oak Tree Stakes (Czar Alexander)
Hialeah Turf Cup (Blanquette II)
1972: New Orleans Handicap (Urgent Message)

RIO CLARO THOROUGHBREDS
1996: Hollywood Gold Cup (Siphon)
1997: Santa Anita Handicap (Siphon)

ARTHUR & LARRY RISDON
1993: Vanity Handicap (Re Toss)

LYNNE RISTAD
2002: Malibu Stakes (Debonair Joe)

RAYLEEN RITTENBERRY
1980: Louisiana Downs Handicap (Yvonand)

MILTON RITZENBERG
1961: Man o' War Handicap (Wise Ship)
1962: Dixie Handicap (Wise Ship)

RIVER DIVIDE FARM
1963: Arkansas Derby (Cosmic Tip)

GEORGE ROBB
1967: Carter Handicap (Tumiga)
1989: Rothmans International Stakes (Hodges Bay)

MRS. EDWARD ROBBINS
1956: Metropolitan Handicap (Midafternoon)
Massachusetts Handicap (Midafternoon)
Display Handicap (Midafternoon)

JACK ROBBINS & JACK ROGERS
1977: San Felipe Handicap (Smasher)

JACK ROBBINS, JACK ROGERS & RALPH WEST
1955: Cinema Handicap (Guilton Madero)

MR. and MRS. ROBERT F. ROBERTS
1968: Alcibiades Stakes (Lil's Bag)
Kentucky Jockey Club Stakes (Traffic Mark)
1969: Arkansas Derby (Traffic Mark)
1975: American Derby (Honey Mark)

CORBIN ROBERTSON
1985: Arlington-Washington Futurity (Meadowlake)

LYLE ROBEY & BRUCE WILKINSON
1990: Arlington Classic (Sound of Cannons)

GERALD ROBINS
1976: Futurity Stakes (For the Moment)
1977: Blue Grass Stakes (For the Moment)

GERALD ROBINS, TIMOTHY SAMS & WALDEMAR FARMS
1985: Breeders' Futurity (Tasso)
Breeders' Cup Juvenile (Tasso)

JILL ROBINSON
1993: Dwyer Stakes (Cherokee Run)
1994: Breeders' Cup Sprint (Cherokee Run)

MACK ROBINSON
1998: Hopeful Stakes (Lucky Roberto)

G. ROBOSKI
1978: Sorority Stakes (Mongo Queen)

PAUL ROBSHAM
1995: Alabama Stakes (Pretty Discreet)
2003: Fountain of Youth Stakes (Trust N Luck)

BEN ROCHELLE
1987: Fantasy Stakes (Very Subtle)
Breeders' Cup Sprint (Very Subtle)

ROCKMORE FARM
1957: Arlington Futurity (Leather Button)

JOSEPH ROEBLING
1948: Garden State Stakes (Blue Peter)
Saratoga Special (Blue Peter)
Hopeful Stakes (Blue Peter)
Futurity Stakes (Blue Peter)
1951: Spinaway Stakes (Blue Case)
1961: Black Helen Handicap (Be Cautious)
1978: Matron Stakes (Fall Aspen)

MR. and MRS. JACK ROGERS
1957: Vanity Handicap (Annie-Lu-San)
1958: Vanity Handicap (Annie-Lu-San)

ROGERS RED TOP FARM
1974: Arlington Handicap (Buffalo Lark)
1975: Pan American Handicap (Buffalo Lark)

ROKEBY STABLE
1951: Dixie Handicap (County Delight)
Gallant Fox Handicap (County Delight)
Manhattan Handicap (County Delight)
1952: Queens County Handicap (County Delight)
1956: Firenze Handicap (Blue Banner)
1963: Pimlico Futurity (Quadrangle)
1964: Wood Memorial Stakes (Quadrangle)
Belmont Stakes (Quadrangle)
Dwyer Handicap (Quadrangle)
Travers Stakes (Quadrangle)
Lawrence Realization Stakes (Quadrangle)
1966: Gazelle Handicap (Prides Profile)
1967: Washington D.C. International (Fort Marcy)
1968: Top Flight Handicap (Amerigo Lady)
Sunset Handicap (Fort Marcy)
1969: Everglades Stakes (Arts and Letters)
Blue Grass Stakes (Arts and Letters)
Belmont Stakes (Arts and Letters)
Travers Stakes (Arts and Letters)
Metropolitan Handicap (Arts and Letters)
Woodward Stakes (Arts and Letters)
Jockey Club Gold Cup (Arts and Letters)
Black Helen Handicap (Amerigo Lady)
Top Flight Handicap (Amerigo Lady)
Hollywood Park Inv. Turf Handicap (Fort Marcy)
1970: Dixie Handicap (Fort Marcy)
Bowling Green Handicap (Fort Marcy)
United Nations Handicap (Fort Marcy)
Man o' War Stakes (Fort Marcy)
Washington D.C. International (Fort Marcy)
Garden State Stakes (Run the Gantlet)
Grey Lag Handicap (Arts and Letters)
1971: United Nations Handicap (Run the Gantlet)
Man o' War Stakes (Run the Gantlet)
Washington D.C. International (Run the Gantlet)
1972: Withers Stakes (Key to the Mint)
Travers Stakes (Key to the Mint)
Brooklyn Handicap (Key to the Mint)
Whitney Stakes (Key to the Mint)
Woodward Stakes (Key to the Mint)
Coaching Club American Oaks (Summer Guest)
Alabama Stakes (Summer Guest)
Bowling Green Handicap (Run the Gantlet)
1973: Grey Lag Handicap (Summer Guest)
Bowling Green Handicap (Summer Guest)
Suburban Handicap (Key to the Mint)
1974: Spinster Stakes (Summer Guest)
1976: San Juan Capistrano Handicap (One On the Aisle)
1978: Suburban Handicap (Upper Nile)
1979: Ladies Handicap (Spark of Life)
1980: Suburban Handicap (Winter's Tale)
Brooklyn Handicap (Winter's Tale)
Marlboro Cup Handicap (Winter's Tale)
1981: Flower Bowl Handicap (Rokeby Rose)
United Nations Handicap (Key To Content)
1982: Jerome Handicap (Fit to Fight)
1983: Suburban Handicap (Winter's Tale)
1984: Metropolitan Handicap (Fit to Fight)
Suburban Handicap (Fit to Fight)
Brooklyn Handicap (Fit to Fight)
United Nations Handicap (Hero's Honor)
1986: Man o' War Stakes (Dance of Life)
Remsen Stakes (Java Gold)
1987: Whitney Handicap (Java Gold)
Travers Stakes (Java Gold)
Marlboro Cup Handicap (Java Gold)
Hopeful Stakes (Crusader Sword)
1990: Futurity Stakes (Eastern Echo)
1992: Champagne Stakes (Sea Hero)
1993: Kentucky Derby (Sea Hero)
Travers Stakes (Sea Hero)
Top Flight Handicap (You'd Be Surprised)

ADRIAN ROKS
1975: San Luis Rey Stakes (Trojan Bronze)

ROLLING HILLS FARM
1947: Inglewood Handicap (Artillery)
1949: San Pasqual Handicap (Shim Malone)

ROLLING RIDGE FARM
1975: John B. Campbell Handicap (Jolly Johu)

RAYMOND RONCARI & NANCY VANIER
1989: Blue Grass Stakes (Western Playboy)
Pennsylvania Derby (Western Playboy)

W.D. ROREX
1947: San Carlos Handicap (Texas Sandman)

RORON STABLE
1992: Hopeful Stakes (Great Navigator)

HAROLD ROSE
2000: Florida Derby (Hal's Hope)
2002: Gulfstream Park Handicap (Hal's Hope)

S. ROSE
1969: Arlington-Washington Lassie Stakes (Clover Lane)

CARL ROSEN
1974: Acorn Stakes (Chris Evert)
Mother Goose Stakes (Chris Evert)
Coaching Club American Oaks (Chris Evert)

HARRY ROSENBLUM
1987: Hollywood Turf Cup (Vilzak)

MRS. MORTON ROSENTHAL
1995: Futurity Stakes (Maria's Mon)
Champagne Stakes (Maria's Mon)

ROSLYN FARM
1955: Gotham Stakes (Go Lightly)
1989: Peter Pan Stakes (Imbibe)

WENDELL ROSSO
1971: Blue Grass Stakes (Impetuosity)

BARON GUY de ROTHSCHILD
1965: Washington D.C. International (Diatome)

EDOUDARD DE ROTHSCHILD
2001: Beverly D. Stakes (England's Legend)

LOUIS ROWAN
1948: Santa Susana Stakes (Mrs. Rabbit)
1957: Canadian Championship Stakes (Spinney)
Santa Anita Maturity (Spinney)
1964: Santa Margarita Handicap (Curious Clover)
1965: Del Mar Futurity (Coursing)
Santa Margarita Handicap (Curious Clover)
1966: Del Mar Futurity (Ruken)
1967: Santa Anita Derby (Ruken)
Display Handicap (Quicken Tree)
1971: Oak Leaf Stakes (Sporting Lass)
1981: Sunset Handicap (Galaxy Libra)
Man o' War Stakes (Galaxy Libra)

LOUIS ROWAN & C.V. WHITNEY
1968: Manhattan Handicap (Quicken Tree)
Jockey Club Gold Cup (Quicken Tree)
San Luis Rey Handicap (Quicken Tree)
1970: Santa Anita Handicap (Quicken Tree)
San Juan Capistrano Handicap (Quicken Tree)

GEORGE ROWAND & BONNER YOUNG
1991: Gamely Handicap (Miss Josh)

ROYAL LINE STABLE
1993: Sword Dancer Handicap (Spectacular Tide)

ROYAL OAKS FARM & OWL STABLE
1973: Charles H. Strub Stakes (Royal Owl)

RUNNING HORSE FARM INC.
2000: Philip H. Iselin Handicap (Rize)

MIKE RUTHERFORD
1989: Futurity Stakes (Senor Pete)
1994: Santa Anita Oaks (Lakeway)
Mother Goose Stakes (Lakeway)
Hollywood Oaks (Lakeway)

MRS. A.W. RYAN
1954: Westerner Stakes (Fault Free)
Santa Anita Maturity (Apple Valley)

BARRY RYAN
1962: Monmouth Oaks (Firm Policy)
Alabama Stakes (Firm Policy)
1963: Top Flight Handicap (Firm Policy)

MRS. BARRY RYAN
1959: Lawrence Realization Stakes (Middle Brother)

R.N. RYAN
1948: San Antonio Handicap (Talon)
Santa Anita Handicap (Talon)

RYEHILL FARM
1979: Illinois Derby (Smarten)
Pennsylvania Derby (Smarten)
Ohio Derby (Smarten)
American Derby (Smarten)
Matron Stakes (Smart Angle)
Frizette Stakes (Smart Angle)
Selima Stakes (Smart Angle)
1980: Frizette Stakes (Heavenly Cause)
Selima Stakes (Heavenly Cause)
1981: Fantasy Stakes (Heavenly Cause)
Kentucky Oaks (Heavenly Cause)
Acorn Stakes (Heavenly Cause)
1982: Selima Stakes (Bemissed)
1988: Pennsylvania Derby (Cefis)
1993: Secretariat Stakes (Awad)
1995: Early Times Manhattan Handicap (Awad)
Arlington Million (Awad)
1997: Sword Dancer Invitational Handicap (Awad)

TED SABARESE
1987: California Derby (Simply Majestic)

MRS. AL SABATH
1946: Princess Pat Stakes (Say Blue)
1948: Marguerite Stakes (Alsab's Day)

SACKATOGA STABLE
2003: Kentucky Derby (Funny Cide)
Preakness Stakes (Funny Cide)

HELENE SADACCA
1958: Arlington Classic (A Dragon Killer)

SADDLE ROCK FARM
1970: Monmouth Invitational Handicap (Twice Worthy)
1971: Suburban Handicap (Twice Worthy)
Hawthorne Gold Cup (Twice Worthy)

M.A. & R. SAFFIR
1950: Hawthorne Gold Cup (Dr. Ole Nelson)

RAMONA & ROLAND SAHM
1989: San Antonio Handicap (Super Diamond)

ROLAND SAHM
1986: Hollywood Gold Cup (Super Diamond)

AMIN SAIDEN
1982: San Fernando Stakes (It's the One)
Charles H. Strub Stakes (It's the One)

HILAL SALEM
1991: Breeders' Cup Sprint (Sheikh Albadou)

PRINCE FAHD bin SALMAN
1992: Budweiser International Stakes (Zoman)
1998: Gamely Breeders' Cup Handicap (Fiji)
Yellow Ribbon Stakes (Fiji)

ESTATE OF R.F. SALMEN
1978: Michigan Mile and One-Eighth (A Letter to Harry)
1979: New Orleans Handicap (A Letter to Harry)

SAM-SON FARM
1991: Spinster Stakes (Wilderness Song)
Rothmans International Stakes (Sky Classic)
Breeders' Cup Distaff (Dance Smartly)
1992: Caesars International Handicap (Sky Classic)
Turf Classic (Sky Classic)
1996: Philip H. Iselin Handicap (Smart Strike)
1997: Canadian Int. Championship (Chief Bearhart)
Breeders' Cup Turf (Chief Bearhart)
Early Times Turf Classic (Always a Classic)
1998: Manhattan Handicap (Chief Bearhart)
2002: Go for Wand Handicap (Dancethruthedawn)

HECTOR SANCHEZ
1989: Sunset Handicap (Pranke)

SANDBAR FARM
1993: Ashland Stakes (Lunar Spook)

SANDERA FARM
1977: Arlington Classic Inv. Handicap (Private Thoughts)

GRADY SANDERS
1984: California Derby (Distant Ryder)

GREG SANDERS
1973: Breeders' Futurity (Provante)

R.L. SANFORD
1994: Arlington-Washington Futurity (Evansville Slew)

SANFORD STUD FARM
1946: Flamingo Stakes (Round View)
1947: Monmouth Handicap (Round View)
1949: Whitney Stakes (Round View)
1958: Bowling Green Handicap (Rafty)

ROBERT SANGSTER
1976: Vanity Handicap (Miss Toshiba)
Hialeah Turf Cup (Lord Henham)
1983: Hollywood Derby (Royal Heroine)
1984: Breeders' Cup Mile (Royal Heroine)
1986: Gamely Handicap (La Khoumia)

ROBERT SANGSTER & GARY TANAKA
1999: San Juan Capistrano Handicap (Single Empire)

SARATOGA I STABLE
1987: Norfolk Stakes (Saratoga Passage)

HERMAN SARKOWSKY
1975: American Handicap (Pass the Glass)
1993: Oak Leaf Stakes (Phone Chatter)
Breeders' Cup Juvenile Fillies (Phone Chatter)

SARON STABLE
1975: Swaps Stakes (Forceten)
1977: Apple Blossom Handicap (Hail Hilarious)
1979: Oak Leaf Stakes (Bold 'n Determined)
1980: Santa Susana Stakes (Bold 'n Determined)
Fantasy Stakes (Bold 'n Determined)
Kentucky Oaks (Bold 'n Determined)
Acorn Stakes (Bold 'n Determined)
Coaching Club American Oaks (Bold 'n Determined)
Maskette Stakes (Bold 'n Determined)
Spinster Stakes (Bold 'n Determined)
1981: Apple Blossom Handicap (Bold 'n Determined)
1986: Widener Handicap (Turkoman)
Marlboro Cup Handicap (Turkoman)

LEONARD SASSO
1961: Wood Memorial Stakes (Globemaster)
Arlington Classic (Globemaster)

MR. and MRS. L.F. SAUNDERS & SON
1959: Del Mar Futurity (Azure's Orphan)

A.A. SAVILL
1980: Apple Blossom Handicap (Billy Jane)

SCOTT SAVIN
1992: Florida Derby (Technology)
Haskell Invitational Handicap (Technology)

SAXON STABLE
1952: Cowdin Stakes (Invigorator)
1954: Brooklyn Handicap (Invigorator)

JOSEPH SCARDINO
1988: Hollywood Derby (Silver Circus)

JAMES SCATUORCHIO
2000: King's Bishop Stakes (More Than Ready)

ROBERT SCHAEDLE III
1997: Secretariat Stakes (Honor Glide)

H.V. SCHAFF
1981: Golden Harvest Handicap (Mean Martha)

CLARENCE SCHARBAUER JR.
1997: Cigar Mile Handicap (Devious Course)

DOROTHY & PAMELA SCHARBAUER
1987: Kentucky Derby (Alysheba)
Preakness Stakes (Alysheba)
Super Derby (Alysheba)
1988: Charles H. Strub Stakes (Alysheba)
Santa Anita Handicap (Alysheba)
Philip H. Iselin Handicap (Alysheba)
Woodward Handicap (Alysheba)
Meadowlands Cup (Alysheba)
Breeders' Cup Classic (Alysheba)

EDWARD SCHARPS
1974: Illinois Derby (Sharp Gary)

ARNO SCHEFLER
1976: Ramona Handicap (Vagabonda)

NATHAN SCHERR
1982: Preakness Stakes (Aloma's Ruler)

GUSTAV SCHICKEDANZ
1996: Vosburgh Stakes (Langfuhr)
1997: Carter Handicap (Langfuhr)
Metropolitan Handicap (Langfuhr)

JOHN M. SCHIFF
1959: Bowling Green Handicap (Bell Hop)
1961: Canadian Championship Stakes (Our Jeep)
1963: Ladies Handicap (Goofed)
1970: Lawrence Realization Stakes (Kling Kling)
1972: Grey Lag Handicap (Droll Role)
Hawthorne Gold Cup (Droll Role)
Massachusetts Handicap (Droll Role)
Canadian International Championship (Droll Role)
Washington D.C. International (Droll Role)
American Derby (Dubassoff)
1973: Arlington Handicap (Dubassoff)
1977: Arlington-Washington Futurity (Sauce Boat)
1979: Laurel Futurity (Plugged Nickle)
Remsen Stakes (Plugged Nickle)
1980: Florida Derby (Plugged Nickle)
Wood Memorial Stakes (Plugged Nickle)
Vosburgh Stakes (Plugged Nickle)

L. SCHLOSSER
1946: Stars and Stripes Handicap (Witch Sir)

CHUCK SCHMIDT JR.
1981: Brooklyn Handicap (Hechizado)

HILMER SCHMIDT
1995: Coaching Club American Oaks (Golden Bri)

W.J. SCHMIDT & TRIMBLE
1960: Arlington Lassie Stakes (Colfax Maid)

D.J. SCHNEIDER
1954: McLennan Handicap (Elixir)

MABEL SCHOLTZ
1958: Jerome Handicap (Warhead)
Roamer Handicap (Warhead)
Manhattan Handicap (Warhead)
1960: Whitney Handicap (Warhead)

MARCIA WHITNEY SCHOTT
1970: Monmouth Oaks (Kilts N Kapers)
1975: Oak Leaf Stakes (Answer)
1976: Hollywood Oaks (Answer)
1977: Sorority Stakes (Stub)
Arlington-Washington Lassie Stakes (Stub)
1981: Travers Stakes (Willow Hour)

MR. and MRS. ROBERT SCHULZE
1961: San Carlos Handicap (First Balcony)

MRS. ANDY SCHUTTINGER
1950: Swift Stakes (Ferd)

BARRY SCHWARTZ
1991: Sword Dancer Handicap (Dr. Root)
1999: Santa Maria Handicap (India Divina)
Acorn Stakes (Three Ring)

CAROL & HERB SCHWARTZ
2000: Gazelle Handicap (Critical Eye)
2001: Hempstead Handicap (Critical Eye)

DANIEL SCHWARTZ
1973: Oak Tree Invitational Stakes (Portentous)
1974: Del Mar Handicap (Redtop III)

MRS. J. SCHWARTZ
1962: Tropical Park Handicap (Trans-Way)

SCOTTDALE FARM
1966: Arkansas Derby (Better Sea)

NINA SCRUTON
1967: Massachusetts Handicap (Good Knight)

JIM SCULLY
1977: Breeders' Futurity (Gonquin)

SEA HIGH STABLE
1976: Bowling Green Handicap (Erwin Boy)

ELEANORA SEARS
1963: Acorn Stakes (Spicy Living)
Mother Goose Stakes (Spicy Living)

FRANCIS SEARS
1983: Preakness Stakes (Deputed Testamony)

C.J. SEBASTIAN
1946: San Felipe Stakes (Galla Damion)
1949: Longacres Mile (Blue Tiger)

RANDY SECHREST
1973: Oak Leaf Stakes (Divine Grace)

ARTHUR SEELIGSON JR.
1971: San Felipe Handicap (Unconscious)
California Derby (Unconscious)
1972: Charles H. Strub Stakes (Unconscious)
San Antonio Stakes (Unconscious)
1975: Santa Anita Derby (Avatar)
Belmont Stakes (Avatar)
1976: San Luis Rey Stakes (Avatar)

FARID SEFA
1985: Apple Blossom Handicap (Sefa's Beauty)

E. SEINFELD
1958: Gallant Fox Handicap (Admiral Vee)

FUSAO SEKIGUCHI
2000: San Felipe Stakes (Fusaichi Pegasus)
Wood Memorial Stakes (Fusaichi Pegasus)
Kentucky Derby (Fusaichi Pegasus)

SELECT STABLE
2001: Walmac Int. Alcibiades Stakes (Take Charge Lady)
2002: Ashland Stakes (Take Charge Lady)
Overbrook Spinster Stakes (Take Charge Lady)
2003: Overbrook Spinster Stakes (Take Charge Lady)

MR. and MRS. HAL SELEY
1955: California Derby (Trackmaster)
1956: Santa Anita Maturity (Trackmaster)

EDWARD SELTZER
1962: Arlington Handicap (El Bandido)
Canadian Championship Stakes (El Bandido)
1964: Michigan Mile and One-Sixteenth (Going Abroad)
Manhattan Handicap (Going Abroad)
Hawthorne Gold Cup (Going Abroad)
1966: San Luis Rey Handicap (Polar Sea)
1978: Illinois Derby (Batonnier)

EDWARD & HARRY SELTZER
1965: New Orleans Handicap (Valiant Man)

MIMI SELZ & SMERKER
1979: Arlington-Washington Lassie Stakes (Sissy's Time)

JEFFREY SENGARA
2000: San Antonio Handicap (Budroyale)

SERENDIPTY FARM
1971: Arlington-Washington Futurity (Governor Max)

B. SEROY
1946: New Orleans Handicap (Hillyer Court)

MRS. DALE SHAFFER
1947: Hawthorne Gold Cup (Be Faithful)
1952: Frizette Stakes (Sweet Patootie)
Alcibiades Stakes (Sweet Patootie)

E. SHAMLE
1974: Hopeful Stakes (The Bagel Prince)

LYN & MIKE SHANLEY
2003: Sword Dancer Inv. Handicap (Whitmore's Conn)

BRADLEY SHANNON
1986: United Nations Handicap (Manila)
Turf Classic (Manila)
Breeders' Cup Turf (Manila)
1987: United Nations Handicap (Manila)
Budweiser-Arlington Million (Manila)
Hollywood Derby (Stately Don)

MR. and MRS. LOUIS SHAPIRO
1963: Inglewood Handicap (Native Diver)
1964: Inglewood Handicap (Native Diver)
1965: American Handicap (Native Diver)
Hollywood Gold Cup (Native Diver)

1966: Hollywood Gold Cup (Native Diver)
1967: Del Mar Debutante Stakes (Fast Dish)
Hollywood Gold Cup (Native Diver)

MILTON SHAPIRO
1974: Del Mar Debutante Stakes (Bubblewin)

BAYARD SHARP
1948: Monmouth Handicap (Tide Rips)
1959: Flamingo Stakes (Troilus)
1985: Hopeful Stakes (Papal Power)
1986: Hutcheson Stakes (Papal Power)
1994: Pegasus Handicap (Brass Scale)

MRS. BAYARD SHARP
1983: Pennsylvania Derby (Dixieland Band)

PAUL SHAWHAN
1959: Kentucky Oaks (Wedlock)

SHAWMUT STABLE
1954: Black Helen Handicap (Gainsboro Girl)
New Castle Handicap (Gainsboro Girl)

JACOB SHER
1946: Miami Beach Handicap (Frere Jacques)
1949: Bougainvillea Handicap (Frere Jacques)
1961: Blue Grass Stakes (Sherluck)
Belmont Stakes (Sherluck)
Lawrence Realization Stakes (Sherluck)
Roamer Handicap (Sherluck)

H.T. SHERIDAN
1971: Sunset Handicap (Over the Counter)

F.A. SHERMAN
1960: Saratoga Special (Bronzerullah)

JOSEPH SHIELDS JR.
1998: Jerome Handicap (Limit Out)
Jockey Club Gold Cup (Wagon Limit)
2003: Prioress Stakes (House Party)
Personal Ensign Handicap (Passing Shot)

HASSAN SHOAIB
1992: Secretariat Stakes (Ghazi)

S.D. SIDELL
1949: New Castle Handicap (Allie's Pal)
Molly Pitcher Handicap (Allie's Pal)

JAN SIEGEL
1979: Del Mar Handicap (Ardiente)

JAN, MACE & SAMANTHA SIEGEL
1991: Spinaway Stakes (Miss Iron Smoke)
1995: Ashland Stakes (Urbane)
1996: John A. Morris Handicap (Urbane)
1998: Santa Anita Oaks (Hedonist)
Milady Breeders' Cup Handicap (I Ain't Bluffing)
2000: Hollywood Starlet Stakes (I Believe in You)

SIERRA THOROUGHBREDS
1994: Oak Tree Invitational Stakes (Sandpit)
1995: San Luis Rey Stakes (Sandpit)
Caesars International Handicap (Sandpit)
1996: Hollywood Turf Handicap (Sandpit)
Caesars International Handicap (Sandpit)

JOHN SIKURA JR.
1975: Santa Barbara Handicap (Gay Style)

EARL SILVER
1996: Remsen Stakes (The Silver Move)

MICHAEL SILVER
1966: Santa Susana Stakes (Spearfish)
Hollywood Oaks (Spearfish)

MRS. CHARLES SILVERS
1954: Arlington Matron Handicap (Lavender Hill)
Ladies Handicap (Lavender Hill)

SILVER STAR STABLE
1976: Century Handicap (Winds of Thought)
1985: La Canada Stakes (Mitterand)

ALLEN T. SIMMONS
1948: Remsen Stakes (Eternal World)
Astoria Stakes (Eternal Flag)

MR. and MRS. S.N. SIMMONS
1971: Del Mar Futurity (D.B. Carm)

D.A. SIMON
1980: Champagne Stakes (Lord Avie)

MILOS SIMON
1987: Alabama Stakes (Up the Apalachee)

CRAIG SINGER
1983: Vanity Handicap (A Kiss For Luck)
Swaps Stakes (Hyperborean)
1986: Hialeah Turf Cup (Sondrio)

A. SKJEVELAND
1953: Queens County Handicap (Flaunt)

SKS STABLE
1980: Young America Stakes (Lord Avie)
1981: Florida Derby (Lord Avie)

SLEDGE STABLE
1969: Del Mar Debutante Stakes (Atomic Wings)

MIKE SLOAN
1994: Hollywood Turf Handicap (Grand Flotilla)

C.W. SMITH ENTERPRISES INC.
1959: San Carlos Handicap (Hillsdale)
Los Angeles Handicap (Hillsdale)
Californian Stakes (Hillsdale)
American Handicap (Hillsdale)
Hollywood Gold Cup (Hillsdale)
Aqueduct Handicap (Hillsdale)
Santa Anita Maturity (Hillsdale)
1961: San Antonio Handicap (American Comet)
Michigan Mile and One-Sixteenth (American Comet)

DERRICK SMITH & MICHAEL TABOR
2003: Hollywood Futurity (Lion Heart)

MRS. GERARD SMITH
1957: Mother Goose Stakes (Outer Space)
1958: Beldame Handicap (Outer Space)

DR. and MRS. J.R. SMITH
1954: Del Mar Debutante Stakes (Fair Molly)
1959: Hollywood Juvenile Championship (Noble Noor)
1960: California Derby (Noble Noor)

VERA SMITH
1961: Louisiana Derby (Bass Clef)

BARBARA SMOLLIN
1998: Cigar Mile Handicap (Sir Bear)
1999: Metropolitan Handicap (Sir Bear)
2001: Gulfstream Park Handicap (Sir Bear)

ARCHIE SNEED
1952: Del Mar Futurity (Hour Regards)

ROBERT SNELL
1991: La Canada Stakes (Fit to Scout)

SNOWBERRY FARM
1983: Dwyer Stakes (Au Point)

HAROLD SNYDER
1974: Delaware Handicap (Krislin)
1976: Withers Stakes (Sonkisser)

MAX SOBELL
1974: Washington D.C. International (Admetus)

DAVID SOFRO
1983: Hollywood Derby (Ginger Brink)
Bay Meadows Handicap (Interco)
1984: Century Handicap (Interco)
San Fernando Stakes (Interco)
Santa Anita Handicap (Interco)
San Luis Rey Stakes (Interco)

SOLYMAR STUD
1990: Santa Anita Derby (Mister Frisky)

SIGMUND SOMMER
1971: Century Handicap (Big Shot II)
Manhattan Handicap (Big Shot II)
Brooklyn Handicap (Never Bow)
1972: Jockey Club Gold Cup (Autobiography)
San Fernando Stakes (Autobiography)
Suburban Handicap (Hitchcock)
1973: Santa Anita Derby (Sham)
Jersey Derby (Knightly Dawn)
1974: San Antonio Stakes (Prince Dantan)
Santa Anita Handicap (Prince Dantan)
Withers Stakes (Accipiter)
Wood Memorial Stakes (Rube the Great)

LOCKHART SPEARS
1979: Apple Blossom Handicap (Miss Baja)

CHRISTOPHER SPENCER
1988: Hopeful Stakes (Mercedes Won)
1989: Florida Derby (Mercedes Won)

SPENDTHRIFT FARM
1985: Oak Leaf Stakes (Arewehavingfunyet)

SPENDTHRIFT FARM & RON WINCHELL
2003: Futurity Stakes (Cuvee)

ROBERT SPREEN
1983: Louisiana Derby (Balboa Native)

SPRING BROOK FARM INC.
1950: Kentucky Jockey Club Stakes (Pur Sang)

SPRING HILL FARM
1949: Acorn Stakes (Nell K.)
Gazelle Stakes (Nell K.)
1950: Top Flight Handicap (Nell K.)
1959: Florida Derby (Easy Spur)
1960: Canadian Championship Stakes (Rocky Royale)
1961: Arlington Handicap (Tudorich)

SPRINGHILL STABLE
1979: United Nations Handicap (Noble Dancer II)

DR. TED SPRINKLE
1991: Californian Stakes (Roanoke)

MR. and MRS. WILBUR STADELMAN
1976: Oak Leaf Stakes (Any Time Girl)

J.H. STAFFORD
1969: Frizette Stakes (Tudor Queen)
1979: Bowling Green Handicap (Overskate)

A.H. STALL
1973: New Orleans Handicap (Combat Ready)

A.H. & ALBERT M. STALL
1970: Kentucky Oaks (Lady Vi-E)

MARK STANLEY
1999: Jim Dandy Stakes (Ecton Park)
Super Derby (Ecton Park)

STAR CROWN STABLE
1984: Hopeful Stakes (Chief's Crown)
Norfolk Stakes (Chief's Crown)
Breeders' Cup Juvenile (Chief's Crown)
1985: Flamingo Stakes (Chief's Crown)
Blue Grass Stakes (Chief's Crown)
Travers Stakes (Chief's Crown)
Marlboro Cup Handicap (Chief's Crown)
1987: Frizette Stakes (Classic Crown)

STARLIGHT STABLE
2002: Florida Derby (Harlan's Holiday)
Toyota Blue Grass Stakes (Harlan's Holiday)
2003: Donn Handicap (Harlan's Holiday)

STEVE STAVRO
1993: Jerome Handicap (Schossberg)
1995: Philip H. Iselin Handicap (Schossberg)

STEADFAST STABLE & JOYCE YOUNG
1994: Man o' War Stakes (Royal Mountain Inn)

STEEPLECHASE FARM
2002: Ruffian Handicap (Mandy's Gold)

STEIFLER, TANNYHILL, WEINSTEIN & WELLS
1980: Oak Leaf Stakes (Astrious)

GEORGE STEINBRENNER
1977: Hollywood Derby (Steve's Friend)

BEVERLY STEINMAN
1972: Del Mar Handicap (Chrisaway)
2000: Flower Bowl Invitational Handicap (Colstar)

HEINZ STEINMANN
1996: Hollywood Futurity (Swiss Yodeler)
1998: Norfolk Stakes (Buck Trout)

MARTHA (PEREZ) & RICHARD STEPHEN
1994: Santa Maria Handicap (Supah Gem)
1996: Vanity Handicap (Jewel Princess)
Breeders' Cup Distaff (Jewel Princess)
San Luis Rey Stakes (Windsharp)

M. (PEREZ) & R. STEPHEN & THE THOROUGHBRED CORP.
1997: Santa Maria Handicap (Jewel Princess)
Santa Margarita Handicap (Jewel Princess)
Beverly Hills Handicap (Windsharp)

WOODY STEPHENS
1954: Breeders' Futurity (Brother Tex)

LIONEL STERNBERGER STABLE INC.
1962: California Derby (Doc Jocoy)
1963: Los Angeles Handicap (Doc Jocoy)

MR. and MRS. LIONEL STERNBERGER
1962: San Felipe Handicap (Doc Jocoy)

L.T. STEVENS
1986: Washington D.C. International (Lieutenant's Lark)

M. STEWART
1965: Washington Park Handicap (Take Over)

MRS. PLUNKETT STEWART
1947: Top Flight Handicap (Rytina)

EARL O. STICE & SONS
1947: Santa Anita Derby (On Trust)
Will Rogers Handicap (On Trust)

MRS. ARTHUR STOLLERY
1971: Alabama Stakes (Lauries Dancer)
1973: Hollywood Gold Cup (Kennedy Road)
San Antonio Stakes (Kennedy Road)
1975: Vanity Handicap (Dulcia)
Ramona Handicap (Dulcia)
National Championship Inv. Handicap (Dulcia)
1976: Santa Barbara Handicap (Stravina)
1977: Hollywood Oaks (Glenaris)

MRS. WHITNEY STONE
1968: Frizette Stakes (Shuvee)
Selima Stakes (Shuvee)
1969: Acorn Stakes (Shuvee)
Mother Goose Stakes (Shuvee)
Coaching Club American Oaks (Shuvee)
Alabama Stakes (Shuvee)
Ladies Handicap (Shuvee)
1970: Top Flight Handicap (Shuvee)
Beldame Stakes (Shuvee)
Jockey Club Gold Cup (Shuvee)
1971: Top Flight Handicap (Shuvee)
Jockey Club Gold Cup (Shuvee)

STONECREST FARM
2003: Stephen Foster Handicap (Perfect Drift)

STONEREATH FARM
1982: Santa Susana Stakes (Blush With Pride)
Kentucky Oaks (Blush With Pride)
Golden Harvest Handicap (Blush With Pride)

STONERSIDE STABLE
1999: Vinery Del Mar Debutante Stakes (Chilukki)
Oak Leaf Stakes (Chilukki)
Ramona Handicap (Tuzla)
2000: Ramona Handicap (Caffe Latte)
Matriarch Stakes (Tout Charmant)
2001: Wood Memorial Stakes (Congaree)
Swaps Stakes (Congaree)
2002: Cigar Mile Handicap (Congaree)
2003: Carter Handicap (Congaree)
Hollywood Gold Cup (Congaree)
Cigar Mile Handicap (Congaree)

STONERSIDE STABLE & FRANK STRONACH
1997: Belmont Stakes (Touch Gold)
Buick Haskell Invitational Handicap (Touch Gold)

ROBERT STRASSBURGER
1953: Washington D.C. International (Worden II)

JOSEPH STRAUSS JR.
1972: Louisiana Derby (No Le Hace)
Arkansas Derby (No Le Hace)
1975: Futurity Stakes (Soy Numero Uno)

RICHARD STRAUSS
1986: Breeders' Cup Mile (Last Tycoon)

FRANK STRONACH
1980: La Canada Stakes (Glorious Song)
1989: Meadowlands Cup (Mi Selecto)
1990: Gulfstream Park Handicap (Mi Selecto)
Jersey Derby (Yonder)
1993: American Derby (Explosive Red)
Hollywood Derby (Explosive Red)
1997: Jim Dandy Stakes (Awesome Again)
1998: Carter Handicap (Wild Rush)
Metropolitan Handicap (Wild Rush)
Whitney Handicap (Awesome Again)
Breeders' Cup Classic (Awesome Again)
Gazelle Handicap (Tap to Music)
1999: Garden City Breeders' Cup Handicap (Perfect Sting)
Queen Elizabeth II Challenge Cup (Perfect Sting)
2000: Pimlico Special (Golden Missile)
Preakness Stakes (Red Bullet)
Queen Elizabeth II Challenge Cup (Collect the Cash)
Breeders' Cup Filly and Mare Turf (Perfect Sting)
Breeders' Cup Juvenile (Macho Uno)
2002: Santa Anita Handicap (Milwaukee Brew)
2003: Santa Anita Handicap (Milwaukee Brew)
Vosburgh Stakes (Ghostzapper)

STUD PANTER
1998: Santa Anita Handicap (Malek)

ROY STURGIS
1963: Sapling Stakes (Mr. Brick)
1964: Withers Stakes (Mr. Brick)
1977: California Derby (Cuzwuzwrong)

SUGARTOWN STABLE
1981: Secretariat Stakes (Sing Sing)

SUI GENERIS STABLE
1980: Monmouth Invitational Handicap (Thanks to Tony)

JEFF SULLIVAN
1991: Philip H. Iselin Handicap (Black Tie Affair)
Breeders' Cup Classic (Black Tie Affair)

ALBERT SULTAN
1969: Malibu Stakes (First Mate)

SUMAYA US STABLES
2003: Ruffian Handicap (Wild Spirit)

SUMMA STABLE
1980: Hollywood Juvenile Championship (Loma Malad)
Santa Barbara Handicap (Sisterhood)
1981: Vanity Handicap (Track Robbery)
1982: Spinster Stakes (Track Robbery)
Apple Blossom Handicap (Track Robbery)
1984: San Juan Capistrano Handicap (Load the Cannons)
1985: Century Handicap (Dahar)
Yellow Ribbon Stakes (Estrapade)
1989: San Luis Rey Stakes (Frankly Perfect)

SUNDANCE STABLE
1976: Ohio Derby (Return of a Native)

SUNNINGDALE FARM
1950: Arlington Lassie Stakes (Shawnee Squaw)

SUNNY BLUE FARM
1959: Washington Park Futurity (Venetian Way)
1960: Kentucky Derby (Venetian Way)
1963: Hawthorne Gold Cup (Admiral Vic)
1964: Seminole Handicap (Admiral Vic)

SUNNY MEADOW FARM
2000: Carter Handicap (Brutally Frank)

SUNSHINE STABLE
1947: San Pasqual Handicap (Lets Dance)

SURF AND TURF STABLE
1981: Santa Anita Derby (Splendid Spruce)

BRIAN SWEENEY
1982: Californian Stakes (Erins Isle)
Sunset Handicap (Erins Isle)
1983: Hollywood Invitational Handicap (Erins Isle)
San Luis Rey Stakes (Erins Isle)
San Juan Capistrano Handicap (Erins Isle)

SWIFT SURE STABLE
1968: Hollywood Oaks (Hooplah)
1978: Vanity Handicap (Afifa)

MICHAEL TABOR
1994: Remsen Stakes (Thunder Gulch)
1995: Florida Derby (Thunder Gulch)
Kentucky Derby (Thunder Gulch)
Belmont Stakes (Thunder Gulch)
Swaps Stakes (Thunder Gulch)
Travers Stakes (Thunder Gulch)
Oak Leaf Stakes (Tipically Irish)
1996: Secretariat Stakes (Marlin)
Crown Royal Hollywood Derby (Marlin)
Metropolitan Handicap (Honour and Glory)
1997: San Juan Capistrano Handicap (Marlin)
Arlington Million (Marlin)
Hollywood Starlet Stakes (Love Lock)
1999: Spinaway Stakes (Circle of Life)
2000: Hopeful Stakes (Yonaguska)
2001: Vosburgh Stakes (Left Bank)
Cigar Mile Handicap (Left Bank)
2002: Whitney Handicap (Left Bank)
2003: Matron Stakes (Marylebone)

JACK TAFEL & RICHARD WATERFORD
1986: Blue Grass Stakes (Bachelor Beau)

JAMES TAFEL
1998: Coaching Club American Oaks (Banshee Breeze)
Alabama Stakes (Banshee Breeze)
Three Chimneys Spinster Stakes (Banshee Breeze)
1999: Fountain of Youth Stakes (Vicar)
Florida Derby (Vicar)
Apple Blossom Handicap (Banshee Breeze)
Go for Wand Handicap (Banshee Breeze)
2000: Travers Stakes (Unshaded)

MR. and MRS. H.R. TALMAGE
1964: Hollywood Oaks (Loukahi)

GARY TANAKA
1995: Man o' War Stakes (Millkom)
1996: Yellow Ribbon Stakes (Donna Viola)
1997: Gamely Handicap (Donna Viola)
1998: Beverly Hills Handicap (Squeak)
Matriarch Stakes (Squeak)
1999: Milady Breeders' Cup Handicap (Gourmet Girl)
Mother Goose Stakes (Dreams Gallore)
2000: Beverly D. Stakes (Snow Polina)
2001: Apple Blossom Handicap (Gourmet Girl)
Vanity Handicap (Gourmet Girl)
Santa Maria Handicap (Lovellon)
Del Mar Oaks (Golden Apples)
2002: Beverly D. Stakes (Golden Apples)
Yellow Ribbon Stakes (Golden Apples)
Eddie Read Handicap (Sarafan)
2003: San Juan Capistrano Handicap (Passinetti)

TARTAN STABLE
1958: Hialeah Turf Handicap (Meeting)
1962: Seminole Handicap (Intentionally)
1964: United Nations Handicap (Western Warrior)
1966: Cowdin Stakes (Dr. Fager)
1967: Gotham Stakes (Dr. Fager)
Withers Stakes (Dr. Fager)
Arlington Classic (Dr. Fager)
Hawthorne Gold Cup (Dr. Fager)
Vosburgh Handicap (Dr. Fager)
Man o' War Stakes (Ruffled Feathers)
1968: Californian Stakes (Dr. Fager)
Suburban Handicap (Dr. Fager)
Washington Park Handicap (Dr. Fager)
Vosburgh Handicap (Dr. Fager)
Whitney Stakes (Dr. Fager)
United Nations Handicap (Dr. Fager)
1969: Vosburgh Handicap (Ta Wee)
1970: Manhattan Handicap (Shelter Bay)
1974: Demoiselle Stakes (Land Girl)
1975: Gazelle Handicap (Land Girl)
1978: Vosburgh Handicap (Dr. Patches)
Meadowlands Cup (Dr. Patches)
1980: Santa Anita Derby (Codex)
Hollywood Derby (Codex)
Preakness Stakes (Codex)
Canadian International Championship (Great Neck)
1981: Bowling Green Handicap (Great Neck)
1982: Santa Anita Derby (Muttering)
1983: United Nations Handicap (Acaroid)
1984: Arlington Handicap (Who's For Dinner)
1985: Futurity Stakes (Ogygian)
1986: Dwyer Stakes (Ogygian)
Jerome Handicap (Ogygian)
1987: Delaware Handicap (Coup de Fusil)
Ruffian Handicap (Coup de Fusil)

JOSEPH TAUB
1979: Gulfstream Park Handicap (Sensitive Prince)

LUIZ ALFREDO TAUNAY
2001: Eddie Read Handicap (Redattore)
2003: Shoemaker Breeders' Cup Mile (Redattore)

AHMED al TAYER
1996: Pegasus Breeders' Cup Handicap (Allied Forces)

TAYHILL STABLE
1978: Marlboro Cup Handicap (Seattle Slew)
Woodward Stakes (Seattle Slew)

E.P. TAYLOR
1953: Jerome Handicap (Navy Page)
1954: Vagrancy Handicap (Canadiana)

J.T. TAYLOR
1950: Del Mar Futurity (Patch)

KAREN TAYLOR
1976: Champagne Stakes (Seattle Slew)
1977: Flamingo Stakes (Seattle Slew)
Wood Memorial Stakes (Seattle Slew)
Kentucky Derby (Seattle Slew)
Preakness Stakes (Seattle Slew)
Belmont Stakes (Seattle Slew)
1990: Santa Anita Oaks (Hail Atlantis)

KENNETH TAYLOR
2001: Prioress Stakes (Xtra Heat)

TAYLOR PURCHASE FARM
1984: Gotham Stakes (Bear Hunt)

SHIRLEY TAYLOR
1981: Top Flight Handicap (Chain Bracelet)

T-BIRD STABLE III
1984: Jersey Derby (Birdie's Legend)

TEAM VALOR
1993: Caesars International Handicap (Star of Cozzene)
Arlington Million (Star of Cozzene)
Man o' War Stakes (Star of Cozzene)
1997: Florida Derby (Captain Bodgit)
Wood Memorial Stakes (Captain Bodgit)

PHIL TEINOWITZ
1987: Everglades Stakes (Cryptoclearance)
Florida Derby (Cryptoclearance)
1989: Widener Handicap (Cryptoclearance)
1993: Spinaway Stakes (Strategic Maneuver)
Matron Stakes (Strategic Maneuver)

F.K. TESHER
1980: Ladies Handicap (Plankton)

THE HAT RANCH
1970: Vanity Handicap (Commissary)

THE THOROUGHBRED CORPORATION
1994: Norfolk Stakes (Supremo)
1996: Matron Stakes (Sharp Cat)
Hollywood Starlet Stakes (Sharp Cat)
1997: Las Virgenes Stakes (Sharp Cat)
Santa Anita Oaks (Sharp Cat)
Acorn Stakes (Sharp Cat)
Hollywood Oaks (Sharp Cat)
1998: Ruffian Handicap (Sharp Cat)
Beldame Stakes (Sharp Cat)
Oak Tree Turf Championship (Military)
Canadian Int. Championship (Royal Anthem)
Hollywood Turf Cup (Lazy Lode)
1999: Breeders' Cup Juvenile (Anees)
Hollywood Turf Cup (Lazy Lode)
2000: Breeders' Cup Distaff (Spain)
La Brea Stakes (Spain)
Gulfstream Park BC Handicap (Royal Anthem)
Lane's End Breeders' Futurity (Arabian Light)
Hollywood Futurity (Point Given)
2001: San Felipe Stakes (Point Given)
Santa Anita Derby (Point Given)
Preakness Stakes (Point Given)
Belmont Stakes (Point Given)
Haskell Invitational Handicap (Point Given)
Travers Stakes (Point Given)
Del Mar Futurity (Officer)
Champagne Stakes (Officer)
Del Mar Debutante Stakes (Habibti)
Hollywood Starlet Stakes (Habibti)
Gulfstream Park BC Handicap (Subtle Power)
2002: Kentucky Derby (War Emblem)
Preakness Stakes (War Emblem)
Haskell Invitational Handicap (War Emblem)
Hollywood Derby (Johar)
2003: Del Mar Oaks (Dessert)
John Deere Breeders' Cup Turf (Johar)

3RD TURN STABLES
2003: Woodford Reserve Turf Classic (Honor in War)

MRS. E.K. THOMAS
1967: Acorn Stakes (Furl Sail)
Mother Goose Stakes (Furl Sail)

J. THOMAS
1980: Sorority Stakes (Fancy Naskra)

J.R.H. THOURON
1964: Michigan Mile and One-Sixteenth (Tibaldo)

THREE G. STABLE
1992: Ohio Derby (Majestic Sweep)

3 PLUS U STABLE
1999: Early Times Hollywood Derby (Super Quercus)
2001: Hollywood Turf Cup (Super Quercus)

THUNDERHEAD FARMS
1993: Arlington-Washington Lassie Stakes (Mariah's Storm)

RAVI TIKKOO
1977: Bowling Green Handicap (Hunza Dancer)
American Handicap (Hunza Dancer)

TIMBERLAND STABLE
1974: Ohio Derby (Stonewalk)
Jerome Handicap (Stonewalk)

RODRIGUEZ TIZOL
1976: Wood Memorial Stakes (Bold Forbes)
Kentucky Derby (Bold Forbes)
Belmont Stakes (Bold Forbes)

TNT STUD
1995: Hollywood Starlet Stakes (Cara Rafaela)

AURY & RALPH TODD
2002: Clement L. Hirsch Mem. Turf Champ. (The Tin Man)

TOP OF THE MARC STABLE
1978: Jerome Handicap (Sensitive Prince)

DR. JEROME TORSNEY
1978: Secretariat Stakes (Mac Diarmida)
Canadian Int. Championship (Mac Diarmida)
Washington D.C. International (Mac Diarmida)
1982: Ramona Handicap (Honey Fox)

TRIAD STABLE
1966: Vanity Handicap (Khal Ireland)

TRILLIUM STABLE
2000: Sword Dancer Invitational Handicap (John's Call)
Turf Classic (John's Call)

TRIO STABLE
1952: Sapling Stakes (Laffango)
Champagne Stakes (Laffango)
Garden State Stakes (Laffango)
1953: Gotham Stakes (Laffango)

TRIPLE C STABLE
1958: Kentucky Jockey Club Stakes (Winsome Winner)

TRIPLE L STABLE
1981: Santa Susana Stakes (Nell's Briquette)

CORA MAE TROTSEK
1951: Arlington Lassie Stakes (Princess Lygia)

E. TROTTA
1981: Century Handicap (Spence Bay)

T.R. TROUT
1968: Monmouth Invitational Handicap (Balustrade)

TOMONORI TSURUMAKI
1991: Hollywood Futurity (A.P. Indy)
1992: Santa Anita Derby (A.P. Indy)
Peter Pan Stakes (A.P. Indy)
Belmont Stakes (A.P. Indy)
Breeders' Cup Classic (A.P. Indy)

PAULA TUCKER
1982: Frizette Stakes (Princess Rooney)
1983: Kentucky Oaks (Princess Rooney)
1984: Vanity Handicap (Princess Rooney)
Spinster Stakes (Princess Rooney)
Breeders' Cup Distaff (Princess Rooney)
1986: Vanity Handicap (Magnificent Lindy)

SAL TUFANO
1954: Gulfstream Park Handicap (Wise Margin)
Massachusetts Handicap (Wise Margin)
1974: Wood Memorial Stakes (Flip Sal)

TURFLAND
1960: Preakness Stakes (Bally Ache)
Jersey Derby (Bally Ache)

TURF SIDE STABLES
2000: Ashland Stakes (Rings a Chime)

MR. and MRS. FRED TURNER JR.
1958: Starlet Stakes (Tomy Lee)
Del Mar Futurity (Tomy Lee)
1959: Blue Grass Stakes (Tomy Lee)
Kentucky Derby (Tomy Lee)
1961: Del Mar Futurity (Weldy)

TWILITE FARMS
2000: Garden City Breeders' Cup Handicap (Gaviola)

TWO SISTERS STABLE
1992: Spinaway Stakes (Family Enterprize)

E. UBARRI
1974: Remsen Stakes (El Pitirre)

UNIVERSAL STABLE
1988: John Henry Handicap (Deputy Governor)

SIDNEY VAIL
1978: Swaps Stakes (Radar Ahead)
1979: San Fernando Stakes (Radar Ahead)

THOMAS VALANDO
1990: Champagne Stakes (Fly So Free)
Breeders' Cup Juvenile (Fly So Free)
1991: Florida Derby (Fly So Free)
Jim Dandy Stakes (Fly So Free)

VALLEY FARM
1966: Grey Lag Handicap (Selari)

VALLEY VIEW FARM
1992: Mother Goose Stakes (Turnback the Alarm)
Coaching Club American Oaks (Turnback the Alarm)
1993: Shuvee Handicap (Turnback the Alarm)
Hempstead Handicap (Turnback the Alarm)
Go for Wand Stakes (Turnback the Alarm)

DON & JOHN VALPREDO
1977: La Canada Stakes (Lucie Manet)
Santa Margarita Handicap (Lucie Manet)
Yellow Ribbon Stakes (Star Ball)

JOHN VALPREDO
1974: Hollywood Juvenile Championship (DiMaggio)

MARION VAN BERG
1958: Arlington Matron Handicap (Estacion)
1960: Arkansas Derby (Spring Broker)

MARION VAN BERG STABLE INC.
1967: Oaklawn Handicap (Mike's Red)

JEANNE VANCE
1998: Futurity Stakes (Lemon Drop Kid)
1999: Belmont Stakes (Lemon Drop Kid)
Travers Stakes (Lemon Drop Kid)
2000: Brooklyn Handicap (Lemon Drop Kid)
Suburban Handicap (Lemon Drop Kid)
Whitney Handicap (Lemon Drop Kid)
Woodward Stakes (Lemon Drop Kid)

JOAN VAN DE MAELE
1958: Frizette Stakes (Merry Hill)

ALFRED G. VANDERBILT
1949: Matron Stakes (Bed o' Roses)
Selima Stakes (Bed o' Roses)
Marguerite Stakes (Bed o' Roses)
Demoiselle Stakes (Bed o' Roses)
Vosburgh Handicap (Loser Weeper)

ALFRED G. VANDERBILT *(Continued)*

Metropolitan Handicap (Loser Weeper)
1950: Coaching Club American Oaks (Next Move)
Delaware Oaks (Next Move)
Gazelle Stakes (Next Move)
Beldame Handicap (Next Move)
Ladies Handicap (Next Move)
Vanity Handicap (Next Move)
Dixie Handicap (Loser Weeper)
Suburban Handicap (Loser Weeper)
Lawrence Realization Stakes (Bed o' Roses)
1951: Saratoga Special (Cousin)
Hopeful Stakes (Cousin)
Vineland Handicap (Bed o' Roses)
Comely Handicap (Bed o' Roses)
1952: Hopeful Stakes (Native Dancer)
Futurity Stakes (Native Dancer)
Firenze Handicap (Next Move)
Beldame Handicap (Next Move)
Remsen Handicap (Social Outcast)
Astoria Stakes (Home-Made)
Santa Margarita Handicap (Bed o' Roses)
1953: Gotham Stakes (Native Dancer)
Wood Memorial Stakes (Native Dancer)
Preakness Stakes (Native Dancer)
Withers Stakes (Native Dancer)
Belmont Stakes (Native Dancer)
Dwyer Stakes (Native Dancer)
Arlington Classic (Native Dancer)
Travers Stakes (Native Dancer)
American Derby (Native Dancer)
Vagrancy Handicap (Home-Made)
Comely Handicap (Home-Made)
Ohio Derby (Find)
Grey Lag Handicap (Find)
Vosburgh Handicap (Indian Land)
Excelsior Handicap (First Glance)
1954: Excelsior Handicap (Find)
Queens County Handicap (Find)
Whitney Handicap (Social Outcast)
Gallant Fox Handicap (Social Outcast)
Metropolitan Handicap (Native Dancer)
Aqueduct Handicap (Crash Dive)
1955: McLennan Handicap (Social Outcast)
John B. Campbell Mem. Handicap (Social Outcast)
Sunset Handicap (Social Outcast)
Manhattan Handicap (Social Outcast)
Trenton Handicap (Social Outcast)
1956: New Orleans Handicap (Find)
1957: Inglewood Handicap (Find)
American Handicap (Find)
Sunset Handicap (Find)
1960: Spinaway Stakes (Good Move)
Selima Stakes (Good Move)
1969: Matron Stakes (Cold Comfort)
1996: Futurity Stakes (Traitor)

NANCY VANIER

1989: Jim Beam Stakes (Western Playboy)

THOMAS VANMETER II

2000: Early Times Hollywood Derby (Brahms)
2003: Darley Alcibiades Stakes (Be Gentle)

ROBERT VAN WORP

1975: Donn Handicap (Proud and Bold)
1995: Vosburgh Stakes (Not Surprising)

VENDOME STABLES

1994: Futurity Stakes (Montreal Red)

VERNA LEA FARM

1968: Arkansas Derby (Nodouble)
Michigan Mile and One-Eighth (Nodouble)
Hawthorne Gold Cup (Nodouble)
1969: Californian Stakes (Nodouble)
Brooklyn Handicap (Nodouble)
Hawthorne Gold Cup (Nodouble)
Santa Anita Handicap (Nodouble)
1970: Metropolitan Handicap (Nodouble)

VHW STABLE

1961: Champagne Stakes (Donut King)
1966: Arlington-Washington Lassie Stakes (Mira Femme)
1991: Arkansas Derby (Olympio)
American Derby (Olympio)
Hollywood Derby (Olympio)
Eddie Read Handicap (Tight Spot)
Arlington Million (Tight Spot)
San Felipe Stakes (Sea Cadet)
1992: Donn Handicap (Sea Cadet)
Gulfstream Park Handicap (Sea Cadet)
Meadowlands Cup (Sea Cadet)
1993: Hollywood Futurity (Valiant Nature)
1994: Del Mar Futurity (On Target)
1995: Del Mar Futurity (Future Quest)
Norfolk Stakes (Future Quest)
1998: San Juan Capistrano Handicap (Amerique)
2001: Ashland Stakes (Fleet Renee)
Mother Goose Stakes (Fleet Renee)

VICGRAY FARM

1962: Californian Stakes (Cadiz)
1963: Hollywood Gold Cup (Cadiz)

VINERY STABLES

2002: Humana Distaff Handicap (Celtic Melody)

RICHARD VIOLETTE JR.

2003: Gulfstream Park BC Handicap (Man From Wicklow)

VISTAS STABLE

1994: Sword Dancer Invitational Handicap (Alex the Great)

HELEN VIZZI

1971: Coaching Club American Oaks (Our Cheri Amour)

BARON von ZUYLEN de NYERVELT

1991: Budweiser International Stakes (Leariva)

E.E. VOYNOW

1948: Arlington Handicap (Stud Poker)
Miami Beach Handicap (Stud Poker)

A.G. WAGNER

1980: New Orleans Handicap (Pool Court)

WALDEMAR FARMS

1971: Black Helen Handicap (Swoon's Flower)

PETER WALL

1991: Hollywood Derby (Eternity Star)
1992: Pacific Classic (Missionary Ridge)

WALMAC FARM

1948: Hawthorne Gold Cup (Billings)
1949: Hawthorne Gold Cup (Volcanic)
1955: Hawthorne Gold Cup (Hasseyampa)

WALNUT HILL FARM

1961: Kentucky Jockey Club Stakes (Su Ka Wa)
1966: Pan American Handicap (Pillanlebun)
1969: Widener Handicap (Yumbel)

SHARON WALSH

1985: Hutcheson Stakes (Banner Bob)
Jim Beam Stakes (Banner Bob)

ROBERT WALTER FAMILY TRUST

1996: Santa Anita Derby (Cavonnier)
1999: Del Mar Oaks (Tout Charmant)

CHARLES WARNER

1973: Oaklawn Handicap (Prince Astro)

MARK WARNER

1988: Jim Beam Stakes (Kingpost)

MARVIN WARNER

1981: Norfolk Stakes (Stalwart)

REA WARNER

1953: San Antonio Handicap (Trusting)

WARNER STABLE

1965: Flamingo Stakes (Native Charger)
Florida Derby (Native Charger)

G.R. WATKINS

1946: Bougainvillea Handicap (Cat Bridge)

MICHAEL WATRAL

1992: Metropolitan Handicap (Dixie Brass)

J.J. WATTS

1947: Coaching Club American Oaks (Harmonica)

ROBERT WAXMAN

1999: Ruffian Handicap (Catinca)

MR. and MRS. P.S. WEAKLY

1972: Hollywood Juvenile Championship (Bold Liz)

GEORGE WEASEL JR.

1976: Vosburgh Handicap (My Juliet)
1977: Michigan Mile and One-Eighth (My Juliet)

F. WEBSTER JR. & W.S. WOODSIDE

1972: Arlington-Washington Lassie St. (Double Your Fun)

REGINALD WEBSTER

1956: Frizette Stakes (Capelet)
1958: Matron Stakes (Quill)
Gardenia Stakes (Quill)
1959: Acorn Stakes (Quill)
Mother Goose Stakes (Quill)
1960: Delaware Handicap (Quill)
1963: Hopeful Stakes (Traffic)
1964: Ohio Derby (National)
1966: Wood Memorial Stakes (Amberoid)
Belmont Stakes (Amberoid)
1976: Maskette Handicap (Artfully)
1978: Maskette Handicap (Pearl Necklace)
1979: Flower Bowl Handicap (Pearl Necklace)

MRS. E.K. WEIL

1952: Trenton Handicap (Ken)

STEVE WEINER

1997: Turf Classic (Val's Prince)

RANDOLPH WEINSIER

1977: Matron Stakes (Lakeville Miss)
Frizette Stakes (Lakeville Miss)
Selima Stakes (Lakeville Miss)
1978: Coaching Club American Oaks (Lakeville Miss)

MRS. RANDOLPH WEINSIER

1977: Top Flight Handicap (Shawi)

ESTATE OF LORD ARNOLD WEINSTOCK

2003: Breeders' Cup Filly and Mare Turf (Islington)

LORD ARNOLD WEINSTOCK

1996: Breeders' Cup Turf (Pilsudski)

ETHEL duPONT WEIR

1949: Fall Highweight Handicap (Royal Governor)
Grey Lag Handicap (Royal Governor)
1950: Widener Handicap (Royal Governor)
1951: Stars and Stripes Handicap (Royal Governor)
1953: Gallant Fox Handicap (Royal Vale)
Dixie Handicap (Royal Vale)
Massachusetts Handicap (Royal Vale)
Miami Beach Handicap (Royal Vale)

A. WEISWEILLER

1966: Washington D.C. International (Behistoun)

WELCOME FARM

1984: Withers Stakes (Play On)

D.H. WELLS

1957: Michigan Mile and One-Sixteenth (My Night Out)

TERRY WELLS

1999: Malibu Stakes (Love That Red)

MR. and MRS. DAVID WERBLIN

1968: Arlington-Washington Lassie Stakes (Process Shot)

WERTHEIMER FARM

2003: Del Mar Debutante Stakes (Halfbridled)
Breeders' Cup Juvenile Fillies (Halfbridled)

GARY & MARY WEST

1993: Arkansas Derby (Rockamundo)
2002: Donn Handicap (Mongoose)
Wood Memorial Stakes (Mongoose)

MR. and MRS. RALPH WEST

1950: Hollywood Oaks (Mrs. Fuddy)

WESTERLY STUD FARM

1967: San Luis Rey Handicap (Fleet Host)
1972: Hollywood Invitational Handicap (Typecast)
Sunset Handicap (Typecast)
Man o' War Stakes (Typecast)

WHEATLEY STABLE

1946: Astarita Stakes (Keynote)
1951: Black Helen Handicap (Antagonism)
1954: Selima Stakes (High Voltage)
Matron Stakes (High Voltage)
1955: Acorn Stakes (High Voltage)

	Coaching Club American Oaks (High Voltage)
	Delaware Oaks (High Voltage)
	Vineland Handicap (High Voltage)
	Monmouth Oaks (Misty Morn)
	Molly Pitcher Handicap (Misty Morn)
	Gallant Fox Handicap (Misty Morn)
1956:	Futurity Stakes (Bold Ruler)
1957:	Flamingo Stakes (Bold Ruler)
	Wood Memorial Stakes (Bold Ruler)
	Preakness Stakes (Bold Ruler)
	Jerome Handicap (Bold Ruler)
	Trenton Handicap (Bold Ruler)
	Remsen Stakes (Misty Flight)
1958:	Carter Handicap (Bold Ruler)
	Suburban Handicap (Bold Ruler)
	Monmouth Handicap (Bold Ruler)
1959:	Alabama Stakes (High Bid)
	Vineland Handicap (High Bid)
	Pimlico Futurity (Progressing)
	Spinaway Stakes (Irish Jay)
1960:	Acorn Stakes (Irish Jay)
1961:	Sorority Stakes (Batter Up)
1962:	Selima Stakes (Fool's Play)
1963:	Sorority Stakes (Castle Forbes)
	Gardenia Stakes (Castle Forbes)
1964:	Sapling Stakes (Bold Lad)
	Hopeful Stakes (Bold Lad)
	Futurity Stakes (Bold Lad)
	Champagne Stakes (Bold Lad)
	Frizette Stakes (Queen Empress)
	Gardenia Stakes (Queen Empress)
	Demoiselle Stakes (Discipline)
	Acorn Stakes (Castle Forbes)
1966:	Champagne Stakes (Successor)
	Garden State Stakes (Successor)
	Sapling Stakes (Great Power)
	Gotham Stakes (Stupendous)
	Jerome Handicap (Bold and Brave)
	Metropolitan Handicap (Bold Lad)
1967:	Arlington Handicap (Stupendous)
	Whitney Stakes (Stupendous)
	Hopeful Stakes (What a Pleasure)
	Lawrence Realization Stakes (Successor)
1968:	Sanford Stakes (King Emperor)
	Cowdin Stakes (King Emperor)
	Pimlico-Laurel Futurity (King Emperor)
	Lawrence Realization Stakes (Funny Fellow)
	Gallant Fox Handicap (Funny Fellow)
	Sorority Stakes (Big Advance)
1969:	Hopeful Stakes (Irish Castle)
	Selima Stakes (Predictable)
	Donn Handicap (Funny Fellow)

BEN F. WHITAKER

1946:	Demoiselle Stakes (Carolyn A.)
1947:	Cowdin Stakes (My Request)
	Louisiana Derby (Carolyn A.)
1948:	Wood Memorial Stakes (My Request)
	Dwyer Stakes (My Request)
	Firenze Handicap (Carolyn A.)
1949:	New Orleans Handicap (My Request)
	Excelsior Handicap (My Request)
1950:	Brooklyn Handicap (My Request)

MRS. BEN F. WHITAKER

1948:	Delaware Oaks (Miss Request)
	Ladies Handicap (Miss Request)
1949:	Beldame Handicap (Miss Request)
1952:	Demoiselle Stakes (Grecian Queen)
	Fall Highweight Handicap (Hitex)
1953:	Coaching Club American Oaks (Grecian Queen)
	Gazelle Handicap (Grecian Queen)
	Monmouth Oaks (Grecian Queen)
	New Castle Handicap (Grecian Queen)

WHITE CLIFF FARM

1998:	Hempstead Handicap (Mossflower)

WHITE OAK STABLE

1952:	Flamingo Stakes (Blue Man)
	Preakness Stakes (Blue Man)
	Dwyer Stakes (Blue Man)

WHITE STAR STABLE

1948:	Starlet Stakes (Star Fiddle)

T.F. WHITE

1963:	Delaware Handicap (Waltz Song)

MR. and MRS. FRANK WHITHAM

1989:	Santa Margarita Handicap (Bayakoa)
	Apple Blossom Handicap (Bayakoa)
	Vanity Handicap (Bayakoa)
	Ruffian Handicap (Bayakoa)
	Spinster Stakes (Bayakoa)
	Breeders' Cup Distaff (Bayakoa)
1990:	Santa Margarita Handicap (Bayakoa)
	Spinster Stakes (Bayakoa)
	Breeders' Cup Distaff (Bayakoa)

JANIS WHITHAM

1996:	Hollywood Oaks (Listening)
1997:	Milady Breeders' Cup Handicap (Listening)
1998:	Santa Margarita Handicap (Toda Una Dama)
	Californian Stakes (Mud Route)
2001:	Queen Elizabeth II Challenge Cup (Affluent)
	La Brea Stakes (Affluent)
2002:	John C. Mabee Ramona Handicap (Affluent)
2003:	Santa Monica Handicap (Affluent)

C.V. WHITNEY

1946:	Futurity Stakes (First Flight)
	Astoria Stakes (First Flight)
	Matron Stakes (First Flight)
	Remsen Handicap (Phalanx)
	Santa Susana Stakes (Enfilade)
	Will Rogers Handicap (Burra Sahib)
1947:	Wood Memorial Stakes (Phalanx)
	Belmont Stakes (Phalanx)
	Dwyer Stakes (Phalanx)
	Jockey Club Gold Cup (Phalanx)
	Champagne Stakes (Vulcan's Forge)
	Astoria Stakes (Mackinaw)
	Demoiselle Stakes (Ghost Run)
	Santa Margarita Handicap (Monsoon)
1948:	Withers Stakes (Vulcan's Forge)
	Saranac Handicap (Mount Marcy)
	Fall Highweight Handicap (First Flight)
1949:	Delaware Oaks (Nasophar)
1950:	Blue Grass Stakes (Mr. Trouble)
1951:	Belmont Stakes (Counterpoint)
	Lawrence Realization Stakes (Counterpoint)
	Jockey Club Gold Cup (Counterpoint)
	Blue Grass Stakes (Mameluke)
	New Orleans Handicap (Mount Marcy)
1952:	Whitney Stakes (Counterpoint)
	San Fernando Stakes (Counterpoint)
	Metropolitan Handicap (Mameluke)
1953:	Cowdin Stakes (Fisherman)
	Champagne Stakes (Fisherman)
	Selima Stakes (Small Favor)
	Westchester Handicap (Cold Command)
1954:	Gotham Stakes (Fisherman)
	Travers Stakes (Fisherman)
	Lawrence Realization Stakes (Fisherman)
	Washington D.C. International (Fisherman)
1955:	Excelsior Handicap (Fisherman)
1956:	Gotham Stakes (Career Boy)
	United Nations Handicap (Career Boy)
	Gardenia Stakes (Magic Forest)
	Wood Memorial Stakes (Head Man)
	Ohio Derby (Born Mighty)
1958:	Kentucky Oaks (Bug Brush)
1959:	Santa Margarita Handicap (Bug Brush)
	San Antonio Handicap (Bug Brush)
	Inglewood Handicap (Bug Brush)
	Santa Anita Derby (Silver Spoon)
	Cinema Handicap (Silver Spoon)
	Hopeful Stakes (Tompion)
1960:	Santa Anita Derby (Tompion)
	Blue Grass Stakes (Tompion)
	Travers Stakes (Tompion)
	Vanity Handicap (Silver Spoon)
	Santa Margarita Handicap (Silver Spoon)
	Hollywood Gold Cup (Dotted Swiss)
	Sunset Handicap (Dotted Swiss)
1961:	Hollywood Juvenile Championship (Rattle Dancer)
	Del Mar Debutante Stakes (Spark Plug)
	Aqueduct Handicap (Tompion)
1962:	Del Mar Debutante Stakes (Brown Berry)
1965:	Hollywood Juvenile Championship (Port Wine)
	Arlington-Washington Lassie Stakes (Silver Bright)
1966:	Spinaway Stakes (Silver True)
	Matron Stakes (Swiss Cheese)
	Massachusetts Handicap (Fast Count)
1967:	Garden State Stakes (Bugged)
	Santa Susana Stakes (Fish House)
1968:	Travers Stakes (Chompion)
1969:	Gulfstream Park Handicap (Court Recess)
1971:	Widener Handicap (True North)
1972:	Top Flight Handicap (Inca Queen)
1973:	Kentucky Oaks (Bag of Tunes)
1975:	Ashland Stakes (Sun and Snow)
	Kentucky Oaks (Sun and Snow)
1976:	Hopeful Stakes (Banquet Table)
1977:	Florida Derby (Coined Silver)
1979:	Metropolitan Handicap (State Dinner)
	Suburban Handicap (State Dinner)
	Century Handicap (State Dinner)
1980:	Whitney Stakes (State Dinner)
1982:	Suburban Handicap (Silver Buck)
	Whitney Handicap (Silver Buck)
1983:	Pan American Handicap (Field Cat)

MARYLOU WHITNEY STABLE

2003:	Kentucky Oaks (Bird Town)
	Acorn Stakes (Bird Town)
	Champagne Stakes (Birdstone)

EDWIN WHITTAKER

1973:	Wood Memorial Stakes (Angle Light)

WICHITA EQUINE STABLE

1987:	Santa Anita Oaks (Timely Assertion)

WALTER WICKHAM

1954:	Roseben Handicap (White Skies)
	Carter Handicap (White Skies)

GEORGE WIDENER

1946:	Monmouth Handicap (Lucky Draw)
1948:	Acorn Stakes (Watermill)
1949:	Remsen Handicap (Lights Up)
1950:	Sapling Stakes (Battlefield)
	Saratoga Special (Battlefield)
	Hopeful Stakes (Battlefield)
	Tremont Stakes (Battlefield)
	Futurity Stakes (Battlefield)
	Astoria Stakes (Sungari)
	Travers Stakes (Lights Up)
1951:	Withers Stakes (Battlefield)
	Dwyer Stakes (Battlefield)
	Travers Stakes (Battlefield)
	Marguerite Stakes (No Score)
	Black-Eyed Susan Stakes (Discreet)
1952:	New York Handicap (Battlefield)
	Westchester Handicap (Battlefield)
1955:	Firenze Handicap (Rare Treat)
1956:	Vineland Handicap (Rare Treat)
1957:	Futurity Stakes (Jester)
	Ladies Handicap (Rare Treat)
1961:	Hopeful Stakes (Jaipur)
	Cowdin Stakes (Jaipur)
1962:	Gotham Stakes (Jaipur)
	Withers Stakes (Jaipur)
	Jersey Derby (Jaipur)
	Belmont Stakes (Jaipur)
	Travers Stakes (Jaipur)
	Black Helen Handicap (Seven Thirty)
	Delaware Handicap (Seven Thirty)
	New Orleans Handicap (Yorktown)
	John B. Campbell Handicap (Yorktown)
	Garden State Stakes (Crewman)
1963:	Travers Stakes (Crewman)
	New Orleans Handicap (Endymion)
1964:	Sanford Stakes (Cornish Prince)
	Ladies Handicap (Steeple Jill)
	Seminole Handicap (Top Gallant)
1965:	Alabama Stakes (What A Treat)
	Gazelle Handicap (What A Treat)
	Beldame Stakes (What A Treat)
	Delaware Handicap (Steeple Jill)
	Vineland Handicap (Steeple Jill)
1966:	Hopeful Stakes (Bold Hour)
	Futurity Stakes (Bold Hour)
	Sanford Stakes (Yorkville)
	Black Helen Handicap (What A Treat)
1967:	Widener Handicap (Ring Twice)
1968:	Grey Lag Handicap (Bold Hour)
	Amory L. Haskell Handicap (Bold Hour)
1970:	Alcibiades Stakes (Patelin)
	Selima Stakes (Patelin)

MRS. GEORGE WIDENER

1953:	Spinaway Stakes (Evening Out)
	Matron Stakes (Evening Out)
1954:	Monmouth Oaks (Evening Out)

MRS. PETER A.B. WIDENER

1946:	Roseben Handicap (Polynesian)

PETER A.B. WIDENER III

1959:	Kentucky Jockey Club Stakes (Oil Wick)

MR. and MRS. ARNOLD WILCOX

1981:	Haskell Invitational Handicap (Five Star Flight)

MRS. ARNOLD WILCOX
1982: Remsen Stakes (Pax in Bello)

DANIEL WILDENSTEIN
1978: Man o' War Stakes (Waya)
Turf Classic (Waya)
1980: United Nations Handicap (Lyphard's Wish)
1983: Turf Classic (All Along)
Washington D.C. International (All Along)
Rothmans International Stakes (All Along)
1989: Arlington Million (Steinlen)
Breeders' Cup Mile (Steinlen)
1990: Hollywood Turf Handicap (Steinlen)
Caesars International Handicap (Steinlen)
1993: Breeders' Cup Classic (Arcangues)

WILD PLUM FARM
1977: Del Mar Futurity (Go West Young Man)
1980: Hollywood Gold Cup (Go West Young Man)
Del Mar Handicap (Go West Young Man)
Century Handicap (Go West Young Man)

BUSH & JO WILLIAMS
1999: Arkansas Derby (Certain)

SHELDON WILLIS
1992: Flamingo Stakes (Pistols and Roses)
Blue Grass Stakes (Pistols and Roses)
1993: Donn Handicap (Pistols and Roses)
1994: Donn Handicap (Pistols and Roses)

J.P. & WILLIAM WILMOT
1975: Gulfstream Park Handicap (Gold and Myrrh)
Grey Lag Handicap (Gold and Myrrh)
Metropolitan Handicap (Gold and Myrrh)

CHARLES T. WILSON JR.
1981: Pennsylvania Derby (Summing)
Belmont Stakes (Summing)
Pegasus Handicap (Summing)

DAVID & HOLLY WILSON
2000: Sempra Energy Hollywood Gold Cup (Early Pioneer)

HOWARD P. WILSON
1976: Jockey Club Gold Cup (Great Contractor)
1977: Brooklyn Handicap (Great Contractor)

L.C. WILSON
1976: Arlington-Washington Lassie Stakes (Special Warmth)

ROGER WILSON
1965: Vosburgh Handicap (R. Thomas)

SAM WILSON JR.
1952: Louisiana Derby (Gushing Oil)
Blue Grass Stakes (Gushing Oil)
Stars and Stripes Handicap (Royal Mustang)

ESTATE OF STEVEN WILSON
1969: Florida Derby (Top Knight)

STEVEN WILSON
1968: Hopeful Stakes (Top Knight)
Futurity Stakes (Top Knight)
Champagne Stakes (Top Knight)
1969: Flamingo Stakes (Top Knight)

WILTON STABLE
1954: Arlington Futurity (Royal Note)

WIMBORNE FARM
1980: Ramona Handicap (Queen to Conquer)
1981: Ramona Handicap (Queen to Conquer)
Yellow Ribbon Stakes (Queen to Conquer)

JACQUES WIMPFHEIMER
1963: Spinaway Stakes (Petite Rouge)
1983: Wood Memorial Stakes (Bounding Basque)
1985: Withers Stakes (El Basco)
Brooklyn Handicap (Bounding Basque)

MRS. VERNON H. WINCHELL JR.
1974: San Felipe Handicap (Aloha Mood)

WINDFIELDS FARM
1958: Michigan Mile (Nearctic)
1959: Remsen Stakes (Victoria Park)
1964: Flamingo Stakes (Northern Dancer)
Florida Derby (Northern Dancer)
Blue Grass Stakes (Northern Dancer)
Kentucky Derby (Northern Dancer)
Preakness Stakes (Northern Dancer)
1971: Acorn Stakes (Deceit)
Mother Goose Stakes (Deceit)
1973: United Nations Handicap (Tentam)
1974: United Nations Handicap (Halo)
1975: Man o' War Stakes (Snow Knight)
Canadian International Championship (Snow Knight)
1977: Kentucky Oaks (Sweet Alliance)
Hempstead Handicap (Pacific Princess)
1980: Arlington-Washington Lassie Stakes (Truly Bound)

WINDING WAY FARM
1962: Saratoga Special (Mr. Cold Storage)

WINDWAYS FARM
1997: Vosburgh Stakes (Victor Cooley)

MALCOLM WINFIELD
1981: Blue Grass Stakes (Proud Appeal)

MRS. JAMES WINN
1988: Arkansas Derby (Proper Reality)
Illinois Derby (Proper Reality)
1989: Metropolitan Handicap (Proper Reality)
Philip H. Iselin Handicap (Proper Reality)

WINSTAR FARM
2002: Spinaway Stakes (Awesome Humor)

HORACE WISE
1962: Massachusetts Handicap (Air Pilot)

W-L RANCH
1947: Vanity Handicap (Honeymoon)
1948: Vineland Handicap (Honeymoon)
Top Flight Handicap (Honeymoon)
American Handicap (Stepfather)
1953: Cinema Handicap (Ali's Gem)

WERNER WOLF
1987: Budweiser International Stakes (Le Glorieux)

D.O. WOLFE
1981: Hawthorne Gold Cup (Spruce Bouquet)

WONDER Y RANCH
1961: Inglewood Handicap (Sea Orbit)

WOODLAND FARM
1956: Molly Pitcher Handicap (Blue Sparkler)

WOODLEY LANE FARM
1955: Roseben Handicap (Red Hannigan)
1956: Jerome Handicap (Reneged)
Carter Handicap (Red Hannigan)
1957: Manhattan Handicap (Reneged)

WOODLYNN FARM
1996: Whitney Handicap (Mahogany Hall)

ERNEST WOODS
1965: John B. Campbell Handicap (Lt. Stevens)

WOODVALE FARM
1949: Blue Grass Stakes (Halt)
1950: Cowdin Stakes (Away Away)
1951: Molly Pitcher Handicap (Marta)
Ladies Handicap (Marta)
1952: Top Flight Handicap (Marta)
1954: Blue Grass Stakes (Goyamo)

WOOLFORD FARM
1946: Arlington Handicap (Historian)
Sunset Handicap (Historian)

MRS. RICHARD WORTHINGTON
1981: Maskette Stakes (Jameela)

MRS. WILLIAM C. WRIGHT
1973: John B. Campbell Handicap (Delay)

MARTIN & PAM WYGOD
1995: Milady Handicap (Pirate's Revenge)
1996: Santa Margarita Handicap (Twice the Vice)
Apple Blossom Handicap (Twice the Vice)
Milady Breeders' Cup Handicap (Twice the Vice)
Go for Wand Stakes (Exotic Wood)
1997: Vanity Handicap (Twice the Vice)
1998: Santa Monica Handicap (Exotic Wood)
Santa Maria Handicap (Exotic Wood)
1999: Gamely Breeders' Cup Handicap (Tranquility Lake)
2000: Yellow Ribbon Stakes (Tranquility Lake)

DR. and MRS. BUCK WYNNE JR.
1977: Cinema Handicap (Bad 'n Big)
1978: Longacres Mile (Bad 'n Big)

FRED WYSE
1946: San Vicente Handicap (Air Rate)

KAZUMASA YANO
1989: Del Mar Futurity (Drag Race)

DARRELL & EVELYN YATES
1997: Arkansas Derby (Crypto Star)

FELTY YODER
1978: Charles H. Strub Stakes (Mr. Redoy)
1984: Santa Anita Derby (Mighty Adversary)

YOLO STABLE
1950: Cinema Handicap (Great Circle)
Del Mar Derby (Great Circle)
1951: Del Mar Debutante Stakes (Tonga)
Santa Anita Maturity (Great Circle)
1952: Sunset Handicap (Great Circle)

ZENYA YOSHIDA
1983: Acorn Stakes (Ski Goggle)
1991: Hempstead Handicap (A Wild Ride)

MRS. G. ZAUDERER
1957: Arlington Lassie Stakes (Poly Hi)

V. ZEMBORAIN
1975: Ladies Handicap (Tizna)

EUGENE ZEREN
1980: Longacres Mile (Trooper Seven)

JOHN ZITNIK
1957: Arlington Handicap (Manassas)

Photo courtesy of Churchill Downs

Pleasant Colony (4), with Jorge Velasquez in the saddle, held off a furious charge by Woodchopper (left under Eddie Delahoussaye) to capture the 1981 Kentucky Derby. Pleasant Colony subsequently has seen his offspring capture 26 major North American stakes. The offspring of only two winners of the Kentucky Derby, 1977 Triple Crown winner Seattle Slew and 1943 Triple Crown winner Count Fleet, can claim more victories in major North American stakes since World War II.

Stallions

VI: Stallions

Bullish on Calumet

The conventional wisdom of breeders long has been that the most important ingredient for a successful sire is his ability to transmit speed to his offspring.

Visit virtually any North American race track for a week, and that logic is quickly confirmed because of the overwhelming number of sprint races offered. So a stallion who can pass speed through his genes to his prodigy no doubt offers a higher rate of return to those who are seeking a sound, if not spectacular, investment.

Because this book's rating of sires is based solely on their offspring's victory totals in major North American races, most of which are contested at longer distances, many stallions who rank among the leaders in stakes victories or are noted for their ability to sire standout two-year-olds—whose races generally are contested at shorter distances and who provide quicker returns on their owners' investments—may not necessarily be the same as those who lead the list for major North American victories.

Further, measuring only the major victories earned by a stallion's prodigy is by no means a reliable yardstick in indicating whether a stallion has demonstrated a proclivity for passing on the ability to succeed as a sprinter, a miler, at one-and-one-quarter miles, at longer distances, to win on grass, or on wet tracks. It simply measures a stallion's ability to produce runners who can win against major North American competition—regardless of whether the stallion was based in North America or abroad.

More than a dozen sires have produced in excess of 100 different stakes winners, all in the modern era, but only one has had his offspring reach the century mark—or even 90—major victories. It is this treatise's contention that Bill Shoemaker's 357 major triumphs in the saddle rank as a more significant benchmark than his 8,833 total victories. Likewise, the number of victories by a stallion's offspring in major North American races is a more meaningful measure of success because it rightfully rewards multiple major winners and ignores, among other things, a son or daughter whose only stakes triumph came at Podunk Downs in a race one-tenth as lucrative as most major races—and perhaps restricted to horses bred in a particular state.

So forget that more than a dozen stallions have sired 100 or more stakes winners. The prodigy of only five modern-era stallions have reached even 70 major victories, and those of only three others have totaled 50.

Invinci-Bull

There is no question that Calumet Farm began the modern era as thoroughbred racing's reigning dynasty and established a legacy that is unequaled in the annals of the sport.

And if a single act can be deemed responsible for Calumet's remarkable success, it was Warren Wright's decision in 1936 to spend $14,000 for a yearling son of Bull Dog whom he named Bull Lea.

In each of the first nine years of the modern era, 1946-54, offspring of Bull Lea won at least six major stakes. No other modern-era sire enjoyed a string of nine consecutive years with even three major victories. Offspring of Bull Lea won at least seven races eight years in a row (1947-54) and earned eight or more triumphs four consecutive seasons (1947-50), both records. Bull Lea led the sires' list for major victories three years in a row from 1947-49, with his offspring earning at least nine wins each year, records since tied but never bettered.

When Bull Lea recorded his fourth No. 1 season in 1952, when he sired 16 winners—a record later tied but never broken—it marked his record sixth consecutive top-two season. By the conclusion of the 1954 campaign, he had posted eight consecutive top-two and nine straight top-four seasons. Not only are those records, but no other modern sire has managed to finish in the top 10 in nine consecutive campaigns.

Bull Lea holds the records for top-two (8) and top-four seasons (10), and he finished in the top 10 on 11 occasions, just one short of the record. And, in each of those 11 seasons, he was among the top five.

No modern owner was such a direct beneficiary of a stallion's success as Calumet was to Bull Lea's. Bull Lea's prodigy crossed the wire first a record 100 times in the modern era, and 83 of those victories were earned in the devil's-red-and-blue silks of Calumet Farm. In fact, of the 96 major races won by Calumet from 1946-54, 71 were captured by sons or daughters of Bull Lea.

Bull Lea's offspring included a modern-record four different classic winners who won six classics, more than any sire in the modern era. All of those classic winners—1948 Triple Crown winner Citation, Faultless, Hill Gail, and Iron Liege—were owned by Calumet. In fact, only Next Move among the eight Bull Lea offspring who captured five or more major races was not owned by Calumet. Citation, Faultless, Armed, Coaltown, Bewitch, Mark-Ye-Well, and Real Delight all helped build not only the legacy of their sire, but of Calumet as well.

The Top Four Challengers

Only one sire has managed three consecutive seasons in which his offspring reached double figures in major victories, and the sons and daughters of **Bold Ruler** actually managed at least 13 triumphs in his three consecutive No. 1 campaigns from 1966-68, including an unmatched 14 or more in each of those first two seasons. Bold Ruler shares the record for top-five seasons (11) and, although he had sired such standouts as Bold Bidder and Gamely, he put to rest the criticism that he couldn't produce a classic winner when Secretariat captured the 1973 Triple Crown to spearhead Bold Ruler's modern-record fifth No. 1 campaign.

Four Footed Fotos, Inc., courtesy of Churchill Downs

When David Flores drove Keeper Hill (4) to a neck victory over Banshee Breeze (on rail) in the 1998 Kentucky Oaks, her victory helped cement the growing reputation of her sire, Deputy Minister, as one of the top stallions since World War II. Five subsequent major victories by Banshee Breeze quickly helped establish her sire, 1990 Kentucky Derby winner Unbridled, as one of the finest to emerge in the '90s.

Nasrullah is one of only three modern sires who can claim four or more No. 1 seasons, and his 84 triumphs barely trail the 86 posted by his son, Bold Ruler, on the modern-era victory list. All five of Nasrullah's "big horses," those who captured five or more major races, were males: Noor, Bald Eagle, Nashua, Bold Ruler, and Jaipur. The latter three compiled four classic victories, making Nasrullah one of only five modern-era sires who can claim that many.

Princequillo long has enjoyed a well-deserved reputation as a great sire of broodmares. But he's often inexplicably overlooked as one of the elite sires of race horses. Princequillo's first major winner, Hill Prince, captured the 1950 Preakness Stakes and had earned acclaim as a "big horse" before his sire began a record string of 12 consecutive campaigns in which he sired multiple winners (1954-65), including the likes of Round Table, Dedicate, and Quill. Princequillo's offspring won a record-tying 16 races in 1957, the first of three consecutive No. 1 campaigns, and earned 80 major North American stakes victories.

Mr. Prospector, whose offspring had earned 73 victories through 2003, enjoyed back-to-back No. 1 seasons in 1987 and '88, is tied for first with 11 top-six campaigns, and ranks first in top-seven through top-10 seasons (12 of each). His best prodigy include It's In the Air, Gulch, and Forty Niner, and he sired different winners of each of the three classics—Conquistador Cielo in the 1982 Belmont Stakes, Tank's Prospect in the 1985 Preakness Stakes, and Fusaichi Pegasus in the 2000 Kentucky Derby.

Next in Line

Two other modern stallions posted 58 or more victories, two No. 1 seasons, and sired classic winners.

Seattle Slew, whose offspring include dual classic winner Swale, Belmont Stakes victor A.P. Indy, and Slew O' Gold, is tied for second in top-eight through top-10 seasons (11 of each) and earned consecutive No. 1 seasons in 1983 and '84.

Heliopolis, the sire of Ace Admiral, Olympia, Summer Tan, Parlo, Grecian Queen, and High Gun, was the top-ranked sire in both 1950 and again in '54, when High Gun captured the Belmont Stakes.

Completing the Dandiest Baker's Dozen

The offspring of six additional modern-era stallions have compiled multiple classic victories and either 50 or more victories or 30 or more triumphs and at least two No. 1 seasons.

Churchill Downs Incorporated/Kinetic Corporation photo courtesy of Churchill Downs

Since his two-and-one-quarter-length victory under Gary Stevens in the 1995 Kentucky Derby, Thunder Gulch has emerged as one of the world's most promising stallions, thanks to the performances of 2001 Preakness and Belmont Stakes winner Point Given and 2000 Breeders' Cup Distaff victor Spain.

Listed in the order of their ranking on the modern-era list of victories for a sire's offspring and including their "big horses":

Perhaps because **Alibhai** never enjoyed a No. 1, or even a top-two season, he is among the most overlooked of the great modern-era stallions. Yet the sire of Traffic Judge and Bardstown demonstrated amazing consistency: a record 16 consecutive years (1946-61) with a major winner, 11 top-eight finishes, and 57 victories. . . . **Alydar** ranks in a third-place tie with four modern-era classic victories, including two by Alysheba and one by Easy Goer. Alydar, who enjoyed consecutive No. 1 seasons in 1989 and '90—the year of his death in a controversial paddock accident—also sired Criminal Type, Althea, and Miss Oceana. . . . **Danzig** parlayed the success of Chief's Crown into a No. 1 season in 1985, then enjoyed another in 1992, the second of an unprecedented three consecutive years when he sired the winner of a Breeders' Cup race. . . . **Hail to Reason's** first No. 1 season came when he sired his first classic winner in 1965, and his last came in 1970, when, like, Mr. Prospector, he attained the last of his three classic victories produced by three different colts in three different classics. But his biggest winner was a filly, Straight Deal (1962), whose success was sandwiched between those classic triumphs. . . . **Exclusive Native** parlayed the success of his best runner, 1978 Triple Crown winner Affirmed, into back-to-back No. 1 seasons in 1978 and '79. . . . Although **Storm Cat's** 36 victories rank no higher than a 17th-place tie on the modern list, the sire of Sharp Cat posted a record-tying three consecutive No. 1 seasons from 1998-2000 and is the only sire who hadn't yet reached his 22nd birthday by January 1, 2004, who had reached 25 triumphs.

Rounding Out the Top 21

Five other modern-era stallions recorded a No. 1 season and saw their offspring earn 30 or more victories, while three others had two No. 1 campaigns and at least 20 victories. Listed in the order they appear on the modern-era list of sires' victories and including their "big horses":

Mahmoud, who began his career at stud before the modern era, posted a No. 1 season in 1946, the first of six consecutive top-seven campaigns for the sire of Oil Capitol. That streak is bettered only by Bull Lea, Bold Ruler, and Nasrullah. . . . **Count Fleet,** sire of Counterpoint, Kiss Me Kate, and Straight Face, is the only modern-era stallion other than Bull Lea who sired classic winners in back-to-back campaigns (1951-52). . . . **Deputy Minister's** best offspring have been fillies Open Mind and Go for Wand, but neither contributed to his No. 1 season in 1997, when his offspring recorded 10 major wins—the only double-figure total since 1988. . . . **Herbager** ranked among the top seven sires on four occasions, including a No. 1 season in 1977. . . . **Your Host** parlayed the success of his best runner, Kelso, into a No. 1 season in 1963. . . . Thanks to Forego, **Forli** posted consecutive No. 1 campaigns in 1974 and '75. . . **A.P. Indy,** who earned his second No. 1 season in four years in 2003, is the youngest stallion among this august group. The 1992 Horse of the Year's 15 major winners have posted a total of 24 major victories, including Tempera's triumph in the 2001 Breeders' Cup Juvenile Fillies. . . . **Blushing Groom** earned the No. 1 ranking in 1982 and again in 1993, the latter time with considerable help from Sky Beauty, his most successful offspring.

High Honorable Mention

Other stallions certainly could be lauded for special achievements. Nureyev, Sadler's Wells, Kris S., and Cox's Ridge, for example, are the only stallions to sire two Breeders' Cup winners in the same year, and the five Breeders' Cup victories posted by the offspring of Kris S. equal Danzig's as second only to the six posted by runners sired by Sadler's Wells. Bold

Venture, the 1936 Kentucky Derby and Preakness winner whose career at stud predates the modern era, is the only stallion who has had two multiple classic winners since World War II—1946 Triple Crown winner Assault and 1950 Kentucky Derby and Belmont Stakes victor Middleground. Skip Trial is one of only 16 modern-era stallions to earn two No. 1 seasons (including ties), but the 14 victories posted by his offspring all were compiled by Skip Away. The following chart includes the other 16 modern-era stallions who either sired offspring who totaled 30 or more major victories or earned or shared a No. 1 season and sired offspring that earned 20 or more major victories.

Stallion	Major Wins	Classic Wins	No. 1 Seasons	Winners of 5-Plus Major Races
Khaled	39	1		Swaps
Tom Fool	39	2		Buckpasser, Tim Tam, Tompion
Round Table	36	0		Royal Glint
Royal Charger	35	1		Idun, Mongo, Royal Native
Damascus	33	0		
Nashua	33	0		Shuvee
Graustark	28	1	1972	Key to the Mint
Buckpasser	26	0	1971	La Prevoyante, Numbered Account
Secretariat	24	2	1986	Lady's Secret
Vaguely Noble	24	0	1982	Exceller
Cox's Ridge	23	0	1985	Life's Magic
His Majesty	24	2	1982	Majesty's Prince, Pleasant Colony
Polynesian	22	2	1953	Native Dancer
Gummo	21	0	1979	Ancient Title, Flying Paster
Majestic Light	21	0	1991	Lite Light
What a Pleasure	20	1	1976	Foolish Pleasure, Honest Pleasure

Five to Watch

Perhaps in 2004 a stallion will begin a decade in which his offspring post double-figure victory totals every year and equal or exceed Bull Lea's total. Far more likely is that one or more will equal the achievements of some of the other great stallions in the modern era and join the ranks of the finest since World War II.

Based on their accomplishments at stud through 2003—and their impeccable bloodlines—the five best bets among those stallions who were born in 1985 or later to join the ranks of the best of the modern era, other than A.P. Indy, whose two No. 1 seasons and 24 major victories already have earned him that status, or to leave enduring legacies through their sons and daughters are:

Forty Niner's offspring had posted only three major victories when he was exported to Japan in 1995. But the 1988 Travers Stakes winner left behind six additional offspring, including 1996 Belmont Stakes winner Editor's Note, who posted 11 more victories, and seven of the Mr. Prospector stallion's sons—including four in 2003—already have sired major North American winners. . . . **Rahy's** seven major winners, including standout filly Serena's Song, have posted 22 victories. The most notable victory posted by the son of Blushing Groom's offspring is Fantastic Light's triumph in the 2001 Breeders' Cup Turf. . . . **Seeking the Gold,** a son of Mr. Prospector who earned a No. 1 season in 1994, has sired nine major winners who have combined for 19 victories, including Heavenly Prize and a pair of Breeders' Cup Juvenile Fillies winners: Flanders (1994) and Cash Run (1999). . . . **Thunder Gulch,** winner of the 1995 Kentucky Derby and Belmont Stakes, has sired only three major winners who have compiled 10 victories. But those include Spain's win in the 2000 Breeders' Cup Distaff, and Point Given's triumphs in the 2001 Preakness and Belmont helped Thunder Gulch, a son of the Mr. Prospector stallion Gulch, attain a No. 1 season. . . . **Unbridled,** the 1990 Kentucky Derby and Breeders' Cup Classic winner, died late in 2001, and his last crop to race will try to duplicate his Derby triumph in 2005. But Unbridled's 11 major winners, including standout filly Banshee Breeze, have combined for 24 victories, including two Breeders' Cup Juvenile triumphs (Unbridled's Song in 1995 and Anees in 1999), a Breeders' Cup Juvenile Fillies victory (Halfbridled in 2003), and three classic wins (Grindstone in the 1996 Kentucky Derby, Red Bullet in the 2000 Preakness, and Empire Maker in the 2003 Belmont Stakes). So the son of the Mr. Prospector stallion Fappiano still ranks among the best bets to join the ranks of the top modern sires.

The following chart shows stallions' victories in the 6,461 major races held in North America from 1946-2003. Following that chart are charts that give the same information for the 174 classic races held from 1946-2003, the 145 Breeders' Cup races staged from 1984-2003, and the annual leaders, which are followed by an alphabetical listing of victories in major North American races for all stallions from 1946-2003, with the horses they sired in those events in parenthesis.

Standings for Stallions' Victories In Major North American Races From 1946-2003

1. Bull Lea (100)
2. Bold Ruler (86)
3. Nasrullah (84)
4. Princequillo (80)
5. Mr. Prospector (73)
6. Heliopolis (66)
7. Seattle Slew (58)
8. Alibhai (57)
9. Alydar (49)
10. Danzig, Mahmoud (47)
12. Hail to Reason (44)
13. Count Fleet (42)
14. Khaled, Tom Fool (39)
16. Deputy Minister (37)
17. Exclusive Native, Round Table, Storm Cat (36)
20. Royal Charger (35)
21. Damascus, Nashua (33)
23. Herbager, Your Host (30)
25. Graustark, Nijinsky II (28)
27. Double Jay (27)
28. Buckpasser, Eight Thirty, Forli, Halo, Pleasant Colony, Tom Rolfe, War Admiral (26)
35. Olympia, Roman (25)
37. Ambiorix, A.P. Indy, Gallant Man, Grey Dawn II, His Majesty, Private Account, Raise a Native, Secretariat, Unbridled, Vaguely Noble (24)
47. Cox's Ridge, Rough'n Tumble (23)
49. In Reality, Kris S., Polynesian, Rahy (22)
53. Beau Pere, Blue Larkspur, Fappiano, Gummo, Majestic Light, Shut Out, Turn-to (21)
60. Blushing Groom, Discovery, Lyphard, What a Pleasure (20)
64. Amerigo, Endeavor II, Ole Bob Bowers, Seeking the Gold, Vertex (19)
69. Affirmed, Blenheim II, Bold Bidder, Key to the Mint, Menow, Northern Dancer, Nureyev, Prince John, Quadrangle, Sir Ivor, Theatrical (18)
80. Ack Ack, Bimelech, Naskra, Stop the Music, T.V. Lark (17)
85. Bold Venture, Hill Prince, Mt. Livermore, Native Charger, Rosemont, Saggy, Stage Door Johnny, Windy Sands (16)
93. Bagdad, Chieftan, First Landing, Gone West, Relaunch, Requested, Ribot, Strawberry Road II, Swaps, Sword Dancer, War Relic, Wild Again (15)
105. Caro, Forty Niner, Hoist the Flag, Jade Hunter, Nantallah, Never Bend, Sadler's Wells, Skip Trial, Slew O' Gold, Sun Again, The Axe II, Verbatim (14)
117. Challedon, Fleet Nasrullah, Intentionally, Riverman (13)
121. Beau Gar, Delta Judge, Fighting Fox, Habitony, Majestic Prince, Mr. Leader, Noholme II, Pharamond II, Pilate, Raja Baba, Roberto, Speak John, Spy Song (12)
134. Big Spruce, Buckaroo, Challenger II, Cozzene, Equestrian, Explodent, Gun Shot, Hillary, Irish River, Native Dancer, Palace Music, Questionnaire, Revoked, Silver Hawk, To Market, Tudor Minstrel (11)
150. Arts and Letters, Broad Brush, Citation, Crozier, Cyane, Johns Joy, My Babu, Nigromante, Northern Baby, Phalanx, Reaping Reward, Reflected Glory, Sailor, Tale of Two Cities, Thunder Gulch, Woodman (10)
166. Ahmad, Alsab, Blue Prince, Bold and Brave, Consultant's Bid, Counterpoint, Cryptoclearance, Darn That Alarm, Devil's Bag, Dr. Fager, Dynaformer, General Meeting, Indian Hemp, Jet Pilot, Kingmambo, Lear Fan, Maudlin, Pensive, Quiet American, Sunglow, Windy City II (9)
187. Advocator, Balladier, Bernborough, Bold Reasoning, Bryan G., Cee's Tizzy, Codex, Crafty Admiral, Devil Diver, Easy Goer, Errard, Fair Ruler, Great Above, Greek Song, Gulch, He Did, Imbros, Market Wise, Meadowlake, Noor, Our Native, Rainbow Quest, Reviewer, Silver Buck, Sovereign Dancer, Storm Bird, Time for a Change, Traffic Judge, Unbreakable, Whirlaway (8)
217. Air Forbes Won, Best Turn, Blue Swords, Boswell, Carson City, Caveat, Cohoes, Cornish Prince, Determine, Dust Commander, Free America, Gallant Romeo, Green Dancer, Jacinto, Jester, Nodouble, Notebook, Phone Trick, Ponder, Rich Cream, Roi Normand, Saint Ballado, Sir Gaylord, Smokester, Take Away, Third Brother, Tim Tam, Top Command (7)
245. Apalachee, Arazi, Battle Joined, Belong to Me, Busted, Caerleon, Chief's Crown, Conquistador Cielo, Cure the Blues, Dark Star, Dehere, Dixieland Band, Drone, Faraway Son, Flying Paster, Goya II, Habitat, Half Crown, Kingsway II, Lypheor, Marquetry, Migoli, Nearctic, Olden Times, On-and-On, Palestinian, Petare, Petrose, Pretense, Priam II, Prince de Galles, Royal Orbit, Runaway Groom, Sensitivo, Shannon II, Siberian Express, Silver Deputy, Star de Naskra, Summer Squall, Sunny's Halo, Valid Appeal, Vice Regent (6)
287. Again II, Alleged, Ambiopoise, Assagai, Attention, Bailjumper, Ballydam, Baynoun, Black Tie Affair, Boldnesian, Boston Doge, Brown King, Cougar II, Darshaan, Dedicate, Djakao, Doyoun, Easy Mon, El Gran Senor, El Prado, Envoy, Fly So Free, Foolish Pleasure, Green Desert, Harlan, Hawaii, Hold Your Peace, Intent, Intrepid Hero, Jet Jewel, Key to the Kingdom, Manila, Minnesota Mac, Miswaki, Norcliffe, No Robbery, Northern Jove, Pago Pago, Persian Road II, Private Terms, Proud Clarion, Robin des Bois, Run the Gantlet, Sea-Bird, Skywalker, Slewvescent, Sportin' Life, Staff Writer, Stymie, Summer Tan, Tentam, Terrang, The Doge, The Rhymer, Tiger, Topsider, Tri Jet, Tulyar, Unbridled's Song, You and I (5)
347. Ambehaving, Arctic Prince, Auditing, Bahram, Battle Morn, Believe It, Better Bee, Bold Forbes, Bold Lad, Bolger, Buckfinder, Bull Dog, Cannonade, Capote, Carry Back, Case Ace, Cavan, Chateaugay, Cherokee Run, Cormorant, Correspondent, Crowfoot, Dark Hawk, Dewan, Diesis, Distant View, Domingo, El Drag, End Sweep, Fairy Manhurst, Flushing II, Foxglove, Francis S., French Deputy, Glitterman, Hail the Pirates, Haital, Hash, Hilarious, Honest Pleasure, Irish Castle, Island Whirl, Jack High, King's Bishop, Madison, Marfa, Middleground, Mr. Greeley, Mr. Music, Nirgal, Northern Fling, One Count, On the Sly, Our Emblem, Pampered King II, Pivotal, Polish Navy, Porterhouse, Prince Royal II, Quibu, Rainy Lake, Reigh Count, Restless Wind, Rico Monte, Riva Ridge, Rolando, Royal Coinage, Royal Serenade, Silver Ghost, Sir Damion, Some Chance, Specialmante, Swoon's Son, Sword Dance, Tabasco Cat, Teddy's Comet, Tehran, Temperence Hill, The Irishman, The Minstrel, Thinking Cap, Timeless Moment, Tompion, Trevieres, Two Punch, Vigors, War Dog, Warfare, War Jeep, Windsor Ruler (4)
437. Afleet, Al Nasr, Ariel, Assert, Awesome Again, Baldski, Barbizon, Battlefield, Be My Guest, Ben Lomond, Bien Bien, Billings, Bold Combatant, Bold Commander, Bold Reason, Bold Ruckus, Bold Tactics, Bolero, Brookfield, By Jimminy, Carlemont, Cinco Grande, Citidancer, Cosmic Bomb, Count Speed, County Delight, Court Martial, Cover Up, Crimson Satan, Cutlass, Danehill, Distinctive, Distorted Humor, Don B., Eternal Bull, Eternal Prince, Faliraki, Far North, First Balcony, Flash o' Night, Forceten, Gilded Time, Go for Gin, Golden Eagle II, Gran Atleta, Grand Rapids II, Greek Ship, Grey Sovereign, Grounded II, Head Play, Heather Broom, Honor Grades, Icecapade, Jolie's Halo, Keen, King's Abbey, Le Fabuleux, Le Levanstell, Little Beans, Little Missouri, Lord at War, Lord Avie, Lord Gaylord, Los Curros, Lt. Stevens, Lucky Debonair, Machiavellian, Maribeau, Mat Boy, Mister Frisky, Montparnasse II, Moscow Ballet, My Host, Naevus, Nashville, Natchez, Nearco, Night Shift, Occupy, Old Bag, One For All, Owen Tudor, Papa Redbird, Pappa Fourway, Pardal, Petrone, Pia Star, Pirate's Bounty, Play Fellow, Pleasant Tap, Pompey, Prince Khaled, Promised Land, Pulpit, Quack, Red Ransom, Rejected, Relic, Restless Native, Rich Man's Gold, Ridan, Roman Diplomat, Roman Line, Royal Gem II, Saint Patrick, Salerno, Saros, Scelto, Sea Hawk II, Seaneen, Selari, Sickletoy, Siphon, Sir Leon, Sky High II, Spanish Riddle, State Dinner, Swing Till Dawn, Targowice, Tatan, Tell, Tobin Bronze, Tudor Grey, Utrillo II, Valdez, Vitriolic, Wallet Lifter, What Luck, Windy Sea, Yachtie (3)
567. African Sky, Alcibiades II, Al Hattab, Alquest, Alzao, Amarullah, Ambernash, Ardan, Argur, Arigotal, Armageddon, Ascot Knight, At the Threshold, Avenue of Flags, Batonnier, Beau Max, Be My Chief, Berseem, Bertrando, Better Self, Binary, Blue Ensign, Bold Hour, Bonnard, Boojum, Brick, Brocco, Bucksplasher, Buisson d'Or, Burg-El-Arab, Candy Spots, Candy Stripes, Cape Town, Chance Play, Chop Chop, Cipayo, Clem, Cochise, Con Brio, Condiment, Count Amber, Count Flame, Count Turf, Coursing, Crazy Kid, Creme dela Creme, Czaravich, Dahar, Dance Spell, Decathlon, Decidedly, Deerhound, Degage, Deputy Commander, Desert Wine, Dictus, DiMaggio, Din's Dancer, Distinctive Pro, Djeddah, Dogpatch, Dumpty Humpty, Eastern Echo, Easton, Eiffel Tower, Emperor Jones, Equifox, Fast Fox, Faultless, Firestreak, Fit to Fight, Forest Wildcat, General, Gold Legend, Grand Slam (1933), Grand Slam (1995), Gunflint, Happy Argo, Hatchet Man, Hawkin's Special, Heelfly, Helioscope, Hempen, Hennessy, Herculean, Hernando, Hero's Honor, High Echelon, High Tribute, His Nickel, Hoist the Silver, Holy Bull, Hunter's Moon IV, Hurry to Market, Hypnotist II, Ile de Bourbon, Indian Ridge, In Excess, Inverness Drive, Isolater, Itajara, Java Gold, Jig Time, Joey Bob, Johnstown, Jules, Kaldoun, Kennedy Road, King of the Tudors, King's Stride, Kirtling, Knightly Manner, Knights Choice, Kodiack, Ky. Colonel, Langfuhr, Lawrin, Li'l Fella, Liloy, Little Current, Lode, London Company, Lost Code, Magesterial, Mamboreta, Maria's Mon, Mashkour, Matun, McLellan, Mehmet, Mendocino, Metfield, Michel, Midstream, Milkman, Minera II, Mironton, Missile, Misty Flight, Mongo, Montbrook, Moondust II, Mr. Trouble, Mummy's Game, Nalees Man, Nashwan, Nasty and Bold, Native Royalty, Neddie, Never Say Die, Northerly, Northjet, Ocean Swell, Oh Johnny, Olympiad King, Only One, On Trust, Orbit Ruler, Palestine, Pantalon, Pass Catcher, Pass the Glass, Perrault, Petionville, Pine Bluff, Platter, Poker, Poona II, Pretendre, Prince Taj, Pronto, Proud Birdie, Proudest Roman, Prove It, Raise a Cup, Rambunctious, Ramsinga, Repicado II, Roi Dagobert, Rousillon, Royal Note, Royal Ski, Rustom Sirdar, Ruthie's Native, Ruysdael II, Saidam, Sea Hero, Search for Gold, Seattle Dancer, Selkirk, Shadeed, Sham, Sharpen Up, Sicambre, Sideral, Silent Screen, Sillery, Slipped Disc, Sir Ruler, Sky Ship, Smarten, Snark, Snow Cat, Somethingfabulous, Souepi, Southern Halo, Spectacular Bid, Spend A Buck, Stalwart, Stevward, Stunning, Summing, Sweep All, Table Run, Tale of the Cat, Tank's Prospect, Targui, The Battler, The Pie King, The Pruner, The Yuvaraj, Thunder Puddles, Top Row, Torsion, Touch Gold, Trace Call, Traffic Cop, Turkoman, Unconscious, Vandale, Victoria Park, Waquoit, Wavering Monarch, Welsh Pageant, Wig Out, Wise Exchange, With Approval, Wittgenstein, Wolver Hollow, Yorktown, Zacaweista (2)
808. Aaron's Concorde, Abadan, Abbe Pierre, Accipiter, Ace Admiral, Admiral Drake, Admiral Lea, Aethelstan II, Aferd, Afghan II, Ahoy, All Blue, Allen's Prospect, All Hands, Alydeed, Ambrose Light, Anyoldtime, Arkansas II, Assemblyman, Atomic, Aurelius II, Avatar, Avenger II, Bairn, Balconaje, Ballymoss, Barachois, Bates Motel, Battleship, Bazooka, Beau Buck, Beau Gem, Bering, Berkley Prince, Big Game, Bikala, Bit of Ireland, Black Forest, Bless Me, Bleu d'Or, Bluebird, Blue Flyer, Blue Gay, Blue Train, Blue Water, Blushing John, B. Major, Bold Hitter, Bold Joey, Bolinas Boy, Bonne Noel, Bow Wow, Boxthorn, Brambles, Brazado, Brevity, Briartic, Brinkmanship, British Empire, Brother Machree, Bull Dandy, Bull Run, Burning Star, Cadmus, California Kid, Cambremont, Canthare, Carr de Naskra, Carrier Pigeon, Casanova, Catalan, Caucasus, Celtic Swing, Challenge Me, Chance Shot, Charlevoix, Charlie McAdam, Chrysler II, City Line, Claim Staker, Claro, Coastal, Coastal Traffic, Cobra King, Colony Light, Come On Red, Comico, Commanding II, Common Grounds, Cool Hand, Cool Joe, Cool Victor, Coronado's Quest, Coulee Man, Count of Honor, Court Ruling, Crafty Prospector, Cravat, Criminal Type, Crystal Glitters, Curandero, Cyrano de Bergerac, Cyrus the Great, D'Accord, Dancer's Image, Dancing Czar, Dancing Dervish, Danzatore, Darby Creek Road, Daumier, Decorated, Degenerate Jon, Deliberator, Delineator, Delta Oil, Determined Man, Devil His Due, Dewan Keys, Diablo, Diplomat Way, Dixieland Brass, Dixieland Heat, Doc Sylvester, Donatello II, Donut King, Doswell, Dotted Swiss, Draft Card, Drawby, Dr. Carter, Dreaming Native, Eagle Eyed, Ecliptical, Effervescing, Egg Toss, Ela-Mana-Mou, Elevation, Elmaamul, Elocutionist, Encino, Engrillado, Erins Isle, Espadin, Eternal Bim, Eternal Reward, Etonian, Eudaemon, Executioner, Explosive Bid, Fair Truckle, Family Crest, Farewell Party, Far Out East, Fast Hilarious, Ferdinand, Fiddle Isle, Fire Dancer, Firethorn, First Fiddle, Fleet Allied, Fleet Host, Flip Sal, Florin, Flying Fury, Fools Holme, For the Moment, Frankie's Nod, Free For All, Full Pocket, Full Sail, Gaelic Dancer, Gallant Duke, Gallant Fox, Gallantsky, General Assembly, Gentle Art, George Royal, Get

Around, Gold Alert, Golden Act, Golden Ruler, Gold Meridian, Gold Note, Grand Revival, Graphic, Great Circle, Great Nephew, Greek Answer, Grenfall, Grindstone, Groovy, Groshawk, Groton, Guilo Cesere, Gun Bow, Halcyon, Halo's Image, Handsome Boy, Hansel, Hasty Road, Hesiod, Hethersett, Highest Honor, Highland Park, High Quest, High Strung, Hillsborough, Hillsdale, Hollyrood, Homebuilder, Honey Jay, Honour and Glory, Horatius, Hostage, Hot Grove, Hussonet, Idle Hour, I'm For More, Indian Emerald, In the Wings, Irish Ruler, Irish Tower, Iron Constitution, Iron Duke, Iron Ruler, Is It True, Islam, It's Freezing, Jaipur, Jaklin Klugman, Jamestown, Jatullah, Jaybil, Jean Valjean, Jet Action, Jig Dancer, Jolly Quick, Judge Smells, Kalaglow, Kaskaskia, Kautokeino, Kentucky Pride, King Cole, Kingly, King's Blue, Kipper Kelly, Knave High, Known Fact, Kris, Landing, Lanyon, Law Society, Legal Case, Leisure Time, Le Tyrol, Lighthouse II, Limelight, Lines of Power, Lively One, Local Talent, Lochinvar, Lomitas, Loom, Lord Carson, Lovely Night, Lucky Mel, Lucky Mike, Luhuk, Lure, Lyphard's Special, Lyphard's Wish, Majestic Venture, Malinowski, Mandate, Manzotti, Marsayas, Mastadon, Master Willie, Medieval Man, Medium, Menace, Menetrier, Menocal, Mi Cielo, Mill Reef, Mincio, Mio d'Arezzo, Mirza II, Mocito Guapo, Mo Exception, Mogambo, Money Broker, Monteverdi, Moonlight Run, More Sun, Mossborough, Mountain Cat, Mountdrago, Mount Marcy, Mr. Busher, Mr. Long, Mr. Mustard, Mr. Randy, Mr. Redoy, Mutakddim, My Gallant, My Lark, Nadir, Nahar II, National, Native Prospector, Nebbiolo, Near Man, Needles, New Policy, Noble Hero, Northern Answer, Northern Flagship, Nostalgia, Oceanus II, O'Grady, Oh Say, Oil Capitol, Ole, Opening Verse, Orbit II, Orbit Dancer, Our Michael, Out of Place, Overskate, Pancho Villa, Panoramic, Parbury, Partab, Pas Seul, Pavot, Peanuts, Perambulator, Persian Bold, Petardia, Petingo, Petition, Phar Mon, Phone Order, Pirateer, Piaster, Pick Up the Phone, Pied d'Or, Piet, Pink Flower, Piping Rock, Plum Bold, Poaching, Polish Numbers, Polish Precedent, Polly's Jet, Pollux, Poster, Potrillazo, Potrillon, Practitioner, Pretexto, Princely Pleasure, Prince Tenderfoot, Prospectors Gamble, Prospector's Music, Protanto, Proud Truth, Prove Out, Psychic Bid, Quadratic, Quest for Fame, Raised Socially, Rajab, Rash Prince, Reading II, Ready Say Go, Red Ryder, Reform, Rego, Rheingold, Rhodes Scholar, Ribocco, Ride the Rails, Risen Star, Rockefella, Rock Talk, Rocky Royale, Rollicking, Roman Sandal, Roman Sword, Romeo, Rose Argent, Rover, Roy, Royal Academy, Royal Dorimar, Royal Minstrel, Royal Union, Royal Vale, Rubiano, Run For Nurse, Rusticaro, Sabona, Sagace, Saim, Sallust, Salmagundi, Salse, Salt Lake, Saratoga Six, Sassafras, Sauce Boat, Scottish Meridian, Sculptor, Seattle Song, Semenenko, Semi-Pro, Septieme Ciel, Service Stripe, Sharivari, Shecky Greene, Shifting Sands II, Shirley Heights, Sickle, Sicyos, Side Boy, Signal Tap, Silver Horde, Simply Majestic, Sir Gallahad III, Sir Ribot, Sir Wimborne, Slewacide, Slew City Slew, Slewpy, Social Climber, Solo Landing, Solonaway, Snow Ball, Speak Up, Spectrum II, Spring Double, Stardust, Star Pilot, Staunchness, Sterling Bay, St. Jovite, Stonewalk, Storm Creek, Straight Die, Stronghold, Subpet, Sullivan, Sun Bahram, Sunny Boy, Sunny North, Sunshine Forever, Super Concorde, Surreal, Sultry Song, Swain, Sweet Candy, Tactical Advantage, Take Me Out, Tambourine, Tantieme, Tapioca, Tarboosh, Taylor's Falls, Terra Firma, Terresto, Terrible Tiger, Thatching, That's a Nice, The Irish Lord, The Porter, The Sultan, Third Martini, Thumbs Up, Tiger II, Tilt Up, Tintagel, Tipoquill, To B. or Not, Top Gallant II, Toulouse Lautrec, Towson, Traffic Mark, Transworld, Trempolino, Truce Maker, Try My Best, Tsunami Slew, Tudor Castle, Tudor Way, Turn to Reason, Two a Day, Tyrant, Understanding, Unfuwain, Upper Case, Val de L'Orne, Valid Wager, Venturon, Vertee, Victorian Era, Victory Morn, Villamor, Wagon Limit, Waidmannshell, War Glory, Watchmitick, Watch Your Step, Water Prince, Well Decorated, Well Mannered, Welsh Chanter, Western Sky II, White Gloves II, Wild Risk, Wild Rush, Wine List, Wing Out, With Regards, Wolfram, Worden II, Wrack of Gold, Wyndham, Your Alibhai, Zarbyev, Zen, Zenith, Zinaad, Zoning (1)

Stallions' Classic Victories 1946-2003

1. Bull Lea (6)
2. Bold Venture (5)
3. Alydar, Exclusive Native, Nasrullah (4)
6. Bold Bidder, Bold Reasoning, Bold Ruler, Count Fleet, Hail to Reason, Halo, Mr. Prospector, Seattle Slew, Unbridled, Woodman (3)
16. Danzig, Distorted Humor, First Landing, Gulch, His Majesty, Irish Castle, Menow, Native Dancer, Nearctic, On-and-On, Our Emblem, Polynesian, Ponder, Pretendre, Quiet American, Raise a Native, Ribot, Saggy, Sea-Bird, Secretariat, Silver Buck, Sovereign Dancer, Storm Cat, Summer Squall, Swaps, Sword Dancer, Thunder Gulch, Tom Fool (2)
44. Alibhai, All Hands, Arts and Letters, At the Threshold, Ballydam, Be My Guest, Better Bee, Blenheim II, Blue Swords, Bold Commander, Buckaroo, By Jimminy, Cannonade, Caro, Citation, Cohoes, Cormorant, Correspondent, Cougar II, Count Amber, Cryptoclearance, Deputy Minister, Determine, Dust Commander, Fappiano, Forty Niner, Gallant Romeo, Gone West, Graustark, Greek Song, Heliopolis, Iron Ruler, Khaled, Kingmambo, Little Missouri, Majestic Prince, Maria's Mon, Migoli, Mossborough, Native Charger, Nigromante, Nijinsky II, Pensive, Pilate, Pleasant Colony, Polish Navy, Prince John, Princequillo, Reflected Glory, Rich Cream, Roman, Royal Charger, Royal Coinage, Royal Gem II, Sicambre, Sportin' Life, Stop the Music, Storm Bird, Sunglow, Traffic Cop, Tudor Minstrel, Verbatim, Vertex, What a Pleasure, Wild Again (1)

Stallions' Breeders' Cup Victories 1984-2003

1. Sadler's Wells (6)
2. Danzig, Kris S. (5)
4. Nureyev (4)
5. Cox's Ridge, Deputy Minister, Gone West, Mr. Prospector, Nijinsky II, Seattle Slew, Storm Cat, Strawberry Road II, Unbridled (3)
14. Cee's Tizzy, Consultant's Bid, Cozzene, Doyoun, Fappiano, Indian Ridge, Marquetry, Mt. Livermore, Phone Trick, Pleasant Colony, Private Account, Raja Baba, Relaunch, Seeking the Gold (2)
28. Ahmad, Alleged, Alydar, A.P. Indy, Blushing Groom, Broad Brush, Bucksplasher, Capote, Caro, Celtic Swing, Chief's Crown, Crozier, Cryptoclearance, Danehill, Danzatore, Darshaan, Deerhound, Easy Goer, El Gran Senor, Exclusive Native, Grand Slam (1995), Graustark, Green Desert, Habitat, Halo, Hennessy, Hoist the Silver, Hold Your Peace, Holy Bull, Honor Grades, Honour and Glory, Horatius, Icecapade, In Reality, Jade Hunter, Java Gold, Key to the Kingdom, Key to the Mint, Lively One, Lyphard, Lypheor, Maudlin, Meadowlake, Mendocino, Mill Reef, Miswaki, Palace Music, Polish Precedent, Rahy, Rajab, Red Ransom, Royal Academy, Runaway Groom, Sagace, Secretariat, Sharpen Up, Sillery, Silver Deputy, Skip Trial, Slewpy, Summer Squall, Summing, The Minstrel, Thunder Gulch, Time for a Change, Timeless Moment, Try My Best, Unbridled's Song, Verbatim, Wild Again, Woodman (1)

Four Footed Fotos, Inc., courtesy of Churchill Downs

In one of the most dramatic finishes in Breeders' Cup history, Flanders (No. 1 on the inside with Pat Day in the irons) held off Serena's Song (No. 11 on the outside under Corey Nakatani) to win the 1994 Juvenile Fillies by a head at Churchill Downs. Flanders suffered a career-ending injury shortly after she crossed the finish line, while Serena's Song, who already had captured Santa Anita's Oak Leaf Stakes, rebounded to earn 10 more major stakes triumphs. Both Flanders, a daughter of Seeking the Gold, and Serena's Song, a daughter of Rahy, were major factors in helping their sires earn acclaim as two of the best to emerge in the past two decades.

1946

1. Mahmoud (8)
2. Bold Venture, Challenger II (7)
4. Bull Lea (6)
5. Equestrian (5)
6. Beau Pere, Fighting Fox, Reaping Reward (4)
9. Ariel, Bimelech, Jack High, Pharamond II, Questionnaire, Reigh Count, Sir Damion (3)

1947

1. Bull Lea (15)
2. Blue Larkspur (10)
3. Alibhai (6)
4. Blenheim II, Mahmoud (5)
6. Beau Pere, Bold Venture, Equestrian, Pharamond II, Pilate (4)

1948

1. Bull Lea (11)
2. Discovery, Requested, War Admiral (6)
5. Heliopolis, Mahmoud (5)
7. Beau Pere (4)
8. Alsab, Bahram, Hash, Reaping Reward (3)

1949

1. Bull Lea (9)
2. Heliopolis (7)
3. Eight Thirty, Mahmoud, Pensive (6)
6. Blue Larkspur (5)
7. Alibhai, Menow, Rosemont, Sun Again (4)

1950

1. Heliopolis (9)
2. Bull Lea (8)
3. Princequillo (7)
4. Alibhai, Nasrullah, War Relic (5)
7. Eight Thirty, Mahmoud (4)
9. Foxglove, Pensive, Sun Again, Tiger (3)

1951

1. Count Fleet (14)
2. Bull Lea (7)
3. Shut Out (5)
4. Blenheim II, Eight Thirty, War Admiral (4)
7. Alibhai, Beau Pere, Devil Diver, Jet Pilot, Mahmoud, Menow, Princequillo, Sun Again, War Relic (3)

1952

1. Bull Lea (16)
2. Count Fleet (9)
3. Attention, Blenheim II, Easy Mon, Errard, Fighting Fox, Market Wise, War Relic (4)
10. Blue Swords, Mahmoud, Menow, Shut Out (3)

1953

1. Polynesian (9)
2. Bull Lea (8)
3. Menow, Roman (6)
5. Count Fleet (5)
6. Heliopolis, Kingsway II (4)
8. Alibhai, Discovery, Fighting Fox, Goya II, Khaled, Royal Charger (3)

1954

1. Heliopolis (12)
2. Bull Lea (8)
3. Nasrullah (7)
4. Jet Pilot, Phalanx, Revoked, Shut Out (4)
8. Alibhai, Count Fleet, Petrose, Polynesian, Sun Again (3)

1955

1. Nasrullah (13)
2. Heliopolis (8)
3. Alibhai (7)
4. Khaled, Shut Out (5)
6. Ambiorix, Double Jay, Princequillo (4)
9. Eight Thirty, Nirgal (3)

1956

1. Nasrullah (13)
2. Heliopolis, Hill Prince, Khaled, Princequillo (6)
6. Alibhai, Ponder, War Admiral (4)
9. Billings, Eight Thirty, Olympia (3)

1957

1. Princequillo (16)
2. Nasrullah (7)
3. Alibhai (6)
4. Bull Lea, Heliopolis, Hill Prince, Jet Jewel, Olympia (4)
9. Discovery, Endeavor II, Migoli, Palestinian, Royal Charger (3)

1958

1. Princequillo (8)
2. Nasrullah (7)
3. Khaled, Tom Fool (5)
5. Royal Charger (4)
6. Alibhai, Battle Morn, Migoli, Palestinian, Shannon II, Turn-to, War Admiral (3)

1959

1. Princequillo (10)
2. Royal Charger, Take Away (7)
4. Nasrullah, Sunglow (6)
6. Tom Fool (4)
7. Alibhai, Citation, Dark Star, Determine, Half Crown, Rough'n Tumble, The Rhymer (3)

1960

1. Nasrullah (10)
2. Royal Charger (7)
3. Ambiorix (6)
4. Your Host (5)
5. Ballydam, Double Jay, Heliopolis, Indian Hemp, Khaled, Turn-to (4)

1961

1. Saggy (7)
2. Your Host (6)
3. Ambiorix, Princequillo (5)
5. Bryan G., Bull Lea, Correspondent (4)
8. Blue Prince, Endeavor II, Indian Hemp, Nantallah, One Count, Roman, Sailor, Tom Fool (3)

1962

1. Nasrullah (10)
2. Endeavor II, Swaps (5)
4. Beau Gar, Bryan G., Royal Charger (4)
7. Blue Prince, Nantallah, Nigromante, Olympia, Saggy, Turn-to (3)

1963

1. Your Host (8)
2. Nigromante (7)
3. Spy Song (6)
4. Swaps (5)
5. Bold Ruler, Nasrullah (4)
7. County Delight, Greek Song, Mahmoud, My Babu, Royal Charger, Tulyar (3)

1964

1. Bold Ruler (10)
2. Gun Shot (8)
3. Cohoes, Nearctic (5)
5. Petare (4)
6. Cavan, Grand Rapids II, Khaled, Nashua, Royal Charger, Third Brother, Tim Tam, Your Host (3)

1965

1. Hail to Reason (7)
2. Nantallah (5)
3. Bold Ruler, Tom Fool (4)
5. Boston Doge, Double Jay, Gun Shot, Hillary, Native Dancer, Ribot, Rough'n Tumble, Third Brother, Tudor Minstrel, Vertex (3)

1966

1. Bold Ruler (14)
2. Tom Fool (9)
3. Hail to Reason (5)
4. Bagdad, Madison, Native Dancer (3)
7. Better Bee, Cochise, Count Amber, Counterpoint, Dark Hawk, Dedicate, Fleet Nasrullah, Gallant Man, Olympia, Ribot, Summer Tan, Sword Dancer, The Yuvaraj, Vertex, Warfare (2)

1967

1. Bold Ruler (14)
2. Sword Dancer (9)
3. Rough'n Tumble (6)
4. Gallant Man, Hail to Reason, Round Table, Tom Fool (5)
8. Again II, Amerigo (4)
10. Beau Gar, Endeavor II (3)

1968

1. Bold Ruler (13)
2. Rough'n Tumble (7)
3. On-and-On (6)
4. Amerigo, Persian Road II (5)
6. Nashua, Sword Dancer (4)
8. Intentionally, Noholme II, Princequillo, Royal Orbit, Vertex (3)

1969

1. Ribot (7)
2. Bold Ruler, Nashua, Noholme II (5)
5. Amerigo, Gallant Man, Pampered King II, Prince John, Raise a Native, Utrillo II (3)

1970

1. Hail to Reason (7)
2. Amerigo (5)
3. Bagdad, Native Charger (4)
5. Bold Ruler, Delta Judge, Gallant Man, Herbager, Nashua, Northern Dancer, Windy Sands (3)

1971

1. Buckpasser (5)
2. Battle Joined, First Landing, Northern Dancer, Tale of Two Cities (4)
6. Ben Lomond, Delta Judge, Hail to Reason, Raise a Native, Round Table, The Axe II, Tompion, Tom Rolfe (3)

1972

1. Graustark (9)
2. Buckpasser, Tom Rolfe (6)
4. Quadrangle (5)
5. Bold Ruler, First Landing, Hail to Reason, Round Table (4)
9. Never Bend, Prince John, Tale of Two Cities, Vertex (3)

1973

1. Bold Ruler (7)
2. Quadrangle (6)
3. Chieftan, Graustark, Round Table (4)
6. Exclusive Native, Herbager, In Reality, Intentionally, Prince John, Tale of Two Cities, T.V. Lark (3)

1974

1. Forli (8)
2. Advocator, Damascus, Graustark (4)
5. Chateaugay, Gummo, Nantallah, Specialmante, Swoon's Son, T.V. Lark, What a Pleasure (3)

1975

1. Forli (8)
2. Damascus, What a Pleasure (7)
4. Bold Ruler, Sir Ivor (5)
6. Round Table (4)
7. Dr. Fager, Dust Commander, Gran Atleta, Gummo, Jacinto, Quadrangle, Reviewer, Wallet Lifter (3)

1976

1. Sir Ivor, What a Pleasure (7)
3. Forli, Round Table (5)
5. Dust Commander, Hail to Reason (4)
7. Delta Judge, Exclusive Native, Gallant Romeo, Hoist the Flag, Irish Castle, Majestic Prince (3)

1977

1. Herbager (6)
2. Bold Reasoning (5)
3. Damascus, Exclusive Native, Windy Sands (4)
6. Chieftan, Forli, Hail to Reason, Hoist the Flag, In Reality, Rainy Lake, Raise a Native (3)

1978

1. Exclusive Native (8)
2. Raise a Native, Vaguely Noble (6)
4. Grey Dawn II, Northern Dancer, Stage Door Johnny (4)
7. Bold Bidder, Graustark, Minnesota Mac, Nashua, Prince de Galles, Secretariat (3)

1979

1. Exclusive Native, Gummo (8)
3. Bold Bidder (7)
4. Best Turn, Tom Rolfe (5)
6. Buckpasser, Cyane, Majestic Prince, Mr. Prospector (4)
10. Faraway Son, Key to the Mint, Prince de Galles, Quadrangle (3)

1980

1. Bold and Brave (7)
2. Arts and Letters, Bold Bidder, Stop the Music (6)
5. Ole Bob Bowers (5)
6. Key to the Mint (4)
7. Advocator, Big Spruce, Exclusive Native, Halo, Herbager, Raja Baba (3)

1981

1. Ole Bob Bowers (7)
2. Big Spruce, His Majesty, Nashua (5)
5. Buckpasser, Grey Dawn II, Run the Gantlet, Stop the Music, Verbatim, Windy Sands (3)

1982

1. Blushing Groom, His Majesty, Vaguely Noble (5)
4. Mr. Prospector (4)
5. Ack Ack, Dewan, Djakao, Olden Times, Seattle Slew, Tri Jet (3)

1983

1. Seattle Slew (7)
2. Alydar (6)
3. Grey Dawn II, Halo, Lyphard (5)
6. Damascus, On the Sly (4)
8. Busted, Northern Dancer, Sir Ivor, Targowice (3)

1984

1. Seattle Slew (11)
2. Damascus, Danzig (5)
4. Alydar, Chieftan, Intrepid Hero, Norcliffe, Ole Bob Bowers, Verbatim (4)
10. Cox's Ridge, Forceten (3)

1985

1. Cox's Ridge, Danzig (6)
3. Rich Cream, Secretariat, Top Command (4)
6. Bailjumper, Buckaroo, Caro, Crozier, Graustark, Mr. Prospector, Saros, Stop the Music (3)

1986

1. Secretariat (7)
2. Danzig (6)
3. Ack Ack, Lyphard, Seattle Slew (5)
6. Reflected Glory (4)
7. Majestic Light, Mr. Leader, Mr. Prospector (3)
10. Alydar, Bold Forbes, Buckaroo, Codex, Crozier, Damascus, Key to the Mint, Nijinsky II, Nodouble, Northern Baby, Northjet, Private Account, Raise a Native, Raja Baba, Sportin' Life, Vaguely Noble (2)

1987

1. Mr. Prospector (11)
2. Nureyev (6)
3. Codex (5)
4. Alydar (4)
5. Caro, Key to the Mint, Sportin' Life, Topsider (3)
9. Ack Ack, Alleged, Believe It, Danzig, Fappiano, Hoist the Silver, Honest Pleasure, Liloy, Lyphard, Magesterial, Majestic Light, Nijinsky II, Raja Baba, Relaunch, Rich Cream, Riverman, Temperence Hill (2)

1988

1. Mr. Prospector (10)
2. Alydar (9)
3. Private Account (7)
4. Roberto (6)
5. Halo (4)
6. Caro, Fappiano, Key to the Kingdom, Nijinsky II, Nureyev (3)

1989

1. Alydar (9)
2. Halo (7)
3. Consultant's Bid, Deputy Minister (6)
5. Slew O' Gold (5)
6. Danzig, Fappiano, Kris S., Nijinsky II, Northern Fling, Play Fellow, Seattle Slew (3)

1990

1. Alydar (8)
2. Deputy Minister, Fappiano, Slew O' Gold (5)
5. Meadowlake, Mr. Prospector, Storm Bird (4)
8. Consultant's Bid, Flying Paster, Habitony, Seattle Slew (3)

1991

1. Majestic Light (7)
2. Mr. Prospector, Siberian Express (5)
4. Pleasant Colony (4)
5. Cox's Ridge, Danzig, Fappiano, Marfa, Mat Boy, Mt. Livermore, Naskra, Private Account, Woodman (3)

1992

1. Danzig (8)
2. Ahmad (5)
3. Cox's Ridge, Darn That Alarm, Seattle Slew (4)
6. Affirmed, Bolger, Caerleon, Habitony, Mr. Prospector, Riverman, Strawberry Road II (3)

1993

1. Blushing Groom, Darshaan (5)
3. Affirmed, Danzig, Darn That Alarm, Kris S. (4)
7. Ahmad, Cozzene, Devil's Bag, Explodent, Little Missouri, Pleasant Colony (3)

1994

1. Great Above, Seeking the Gold (7)
3. Blushing Groom, Irish River, Storm Cat (4)
6. Far North, Forty Niner, Private Account, Private Terms, Seattle Slew, Theatrical (3)

1995

1. Palace Music (8)
2. Rahy (7)
3. Private Account (6)
4. Gulch (5)
5. Seeking the Gold (4)
6. Mr. Prospector, Northern Baby (3)
8. Alzao, Baynoun, Broad Brush, Buckaroo, Carson City, Caveat, Easy Goer, Kris S., Lyphard, Mt. Livermore, Pirate's Bounty, Private Terms, Relaunch, Sadler's Wells, Silver Hawk, Storm Cat, Wavering Monarch, With Approval (2)

1996

1. Skip Trial (5)
2. Air Forbes Won, Easy Goer, Forty Niner (4)
5. Deputy Minister, Rahy, Roman Diplomat, Runaway Groom, Unbridled, Vice Regent (3)

1997

1. Deputy Minister (10)
2. A.P. Indy (5)
3. Black Tie Affair, Lear Fan, Quiet American, Robin des Bois, Storm Cat, Strawberry Road II (4)
9. Chief's Crown, Danzig, Silver Buck, Skip Trial, Smokester (3)

1998

1. Skip Trial, Storm Cat (6)
3. Deputy Minister (5)
4. Belong to Me, Strawberry Road II, Unbridled (4)
7. Forty Niner, General Meeting, Theatrical (3)
10. Affirmed, A.P. Indy, Bucksplasher, Cryptoclearance, Mt. Livermore, Pine Bluff, Quiet American, Rahy, Rainbow Quest, Seeking the Gold, Selkirk, Silver Deputy, Wild Again (2)

1999

1. Storm Cat (6)
2. Unbridled (5)
3. General Meeting, Silver Deputy (4)
5. Forty Niner, Kris S., Marquetry, Maudlin, Pleasant Colony, Seattle Slew, Wild Again (3)

2000

1. A.P. Indy, Roi Normand, Storm Cat (5)
4. Kingmambo, Mr. Prospector (4)
6. Cee's Tizzy, Doyoun, Rahy, Saint Ballado, Seattle Slew, Theatrical, Thunder Gulch, Unbridled (3)

2001

1. Thunder Gulch (7)
2. Seattle Slew (6)
3. Cee's Tizzy (4)
4. A.P. Indy, Nureyev, Unbridled (3)
7. Affirmed, Arazi, Bertrando, Bien Bien, Broad Brush, Emperor Jones, End Sweep, French Deputy, Glitterman, Go for Gin, Maria's Mon, Marquetry, Moscow Ballet, Notebook, Pleasant Colony, Relaunch, Rich Man's Gold, Siphon, Slewvescent, Tabasco Cat, Theatrical, Unbridled's Song (2)

2002

1. Gone West, Jade Hunter, Sadler's Wells (5)
4. Our Emblem, Storm Cat, You and I (4)
7. Affirmed, Broad Brush, Mr. Greeley, Pulpit, Relaunch, Wild Again (3)

2003

1. A.P. Indy (6)
2. Unbridled (5)
3. Distant View, Dynaformer (4)
5. Arazi, El Prado, Jade Hunter, Kris S., Mr. Prospector, Sadler's Wells (3)

Keeneland-Bert Morgan photo courtesy of Keeneland Association

Fresh off a victory in the Preakness Stakes, Bold Ruler neared the finish line in a workout under jockey Eddie Arcaro four days before the 1957 Belmont Stakes. Although Bold Ruler finished third behind victorious Gallant Man in the Belmont, he rebounded to earn Horse of the Year acclaim and stake his claim as one of the truly elite stallions in history.

Stallions' RESUMES

Stallions With Victories In Major North American Races 1946-2003

AARON'S CONCORDE
1996: Gotham Stakes (Romano Gucci)

ABADAN
1958: Canadian Championship Stakes (Jack Ketch)

ABBE PIERRE
1953: Stars and Stripes Handicap (Abbe Sting)

ACCIPITER
1984: Jerome Handicap (Is Your Pleasure)

ACE ADMIRAL
1958: Jockey Club Gold Cup (Inside Tract)

ACK ACK
1976: Canadian International Championship (Youth)
Washington D.C. International (Youth)
1979: Champagne Stakes (Joanie's Chief)
Santa Susana Stakes (Caline)
1980: Bowling Green Handicap (Sten)
1982: Santa Barbara Handicap (Ack's Secret)
Santa Margarita Handicap (Ack's Secret)
Arlington Handicap (Flying Target)
1985: Fantasy Stakes (Rascal Lass)
Louisiana Derby (Violado)
1986: Jim Beam Stakes (Broad Brush)
Wood Memorial Stakes (Broad Brush)
Ohio Derby (Broad Brush)
Pennsylvania Derby (Broad Brush)
Meadowlands Cup (Broad Brush)
1987: Santa Anita Handicap (Broad Brush)
Suburban Handicap (Broad Brush)

ADMIRAL DRAKE
1958: Bowling Green Handicap (Rafty)

ADMIRAL LEA
1958: Westerner Stakes (Strong Bay)

ADVOCATOR
1974: California Derby (Agitate)
Swaps Stakes (Agitate)
Hollywood Derby (Agitate)
Futurity Stakes (Just the Time)
1977: Del Mar Futurity (Go West Young Man)
1980: Hollywood Gold Cup (Go West Young Man)
Del Mar Handicap (Go West Young Man)
Century Handicap (Go West Young Man)

AETHELSTAN II
1946: Black Helen Handicap (Adroit)

AFERD
1998: Oaklawn Handicap (Precocity)

AFFIRMED
1991: Top Flight Handicap (Buy the Firm)
1992: Top Flight Handicap (Firm Stance)
Budweiser International Stakes (Zoman)
Matriarch Stakes (Flawlessly)
1993: Ramona Handicap (Flawlessly)
Beverly D. Stakes (Flawlessly)
Matriarch Stakes (Flawlessly)
Molson Export Million (Peteski)
1994: Ramona Handicap (Flawlessly)
1998: Hempstead Handicap (Mossflower)
Vosburgh Stakes (Affirmed Success)
1999: Cigar Mile Handicap (Affirmed Success)
2001: Queen Elizabeth II Challenge Cup (Affluent)
La Brea Stakes (Affluent)
2002: Carter Handicap (Affirmed Success)
John C. Mabee Ramona Handicap (Affluent)
Clement L. Hirsch Mem. Turf Champ. (The Tin Man)
2003: Santa Monica Handicap (Affluent)

AFGHAN II
1948: Massachusetts Handicap (Beauchef)

AFLEET
1994: Test Stakes (Twist Afleet)
1995: Top Flight Handicap (Twist Afleet)
1996: Delta Air Lines Top Flight Handicap (Flat Fleet Feet)

AFRICAN SKY
1980: Yellow Ribbon Stakes (Kilijaro)
1981: Matriarch Stakes (Kilijaro)

AGAIN II
1967: Gallant Fox Handicap (Niarkos)
San Juan Capistrano Handicap (Niarkos)
San Luis Rey Handicap (Niarkos)
Santa Barbara Handicap (Ormea)
1968: San Juan Capistrano Handicap (Niarkos)

AHMAD
1992: Santa Margarita Handicap (Paseana)
Apple Blossom Handicap (Paseana)
Milady Handicap (Paseana)
Vanity Handicap (Paseana)
Breeders' Cup Distaff (Paseana)
1993: Apple Blossom Handicap (Paseana)
Milady Handicap (Paseana)
Spinster Stakes (Paseana)
1994: Santa Margarita Handicap (Paseana)

AHOY
1970: Acorn Stakes (Royal Signal)

AIR FORBES WON
1988: Hopeful Stakes (Mercedes Won)
1989: Florida Derby (Mercedes Won)
1990: Arlington-Washington Lassie Stakes (Through Flight)
1996: Mother Goose Stakes (Yanks Music)
Alabama Stakes (Yanks Music)
Ruffian Handicap (Yanks Music)
Beldame Stakes (Yanks Music)

ALCIBIADES II
1964: Jerome Handicap (Irvkup)
Arlington Handicap (Master Dennis)

AL HATTAB
1976: Sapling Stakes (Ali Oop)
1982: Brooklyn Handicap (Silver Supreme)

ALIBHAI
1946: Arlington Classic (The Dude)
1947: Santa Anita Derby (On Trust)
Will Rogers Handicap (On Trust)
Hollywood Gold Cup (Cover Up)
Sunset Handicap (Cover Up)
Starlet Stakes (Zenoda)
Inglewood Handicap (Artillery)
1948: Westerner Handicap (Solidarity)
1949: Golden Gate Handicap (Solidarity)
Hollywood Gold Cup (Solidarity)
Del Mar Futurity (Your Host)
Santa Margarita Handicap (Lurline B.)
1950: San Felipe Stakes (Your Host)
Santa Anita Derby (Your Host)
Starlet Stakes (Gold Capitol)
Santa Susana Stakes (Special Touch)
San Pasqual Handicap (Solidarity)
1951: Westerner Stakes (Grantor)
Del Mar Derby (Grantor)
Santa Margarita Handicap (Special Touch)
1952: Will Rogers Stakes (Forelock)
Del Mar Handicap (Grantor)
1953: Acorn Stakes (Secret Meeting)
Cinema Handicap (Ali's Gem)
San Antonio Handicap (Trusting)
1954: San Felipe Handicap (Determine)
Santa Anita Derby (Determine)
Kentucky Derby (Determine)
1955: Withers Stakes (Traffic Judge)
Ohio Derby (Traffic Judge)
Jerome Handicap (Traffic Judge)
Woodward Stakes (Traffic Judge)
American Handicap (Alidon)
Hawthorne Gold Cup (Hasseyampa)
Santa Anita Maturity (Determine)
1956: Delaware Handicap (Flower Bowl)
Ladies Handicap (Flower Bowl)
Trenton Handicap (Bardstown)
Dixie Handicap (Chevation)
1957: Tropical Handicap (Bardstown)
Widener Handicap (Bardstown)
Gulfstream Park Handicap (Bardstown)
Metropolitan Handicap (Traffic Judge)
Suburban Handicap (Traffic Judge)
Spinster Stakes (Bornastar)
1958: Vineland Handicap (Bornastar)
Spinster Stakes (Bornastar)
Widener Handicap (Oligarchy)
1959: Tropical Park Handicap (Bardstown)
Widener Handicap (Bardstown)
McLennan Handicap (Sharpsburg)
1960: Everglades Stakes (Moslem Chief)
1961: California Derby (Mr. Consistency)
San Juan Capistrano Handicap (Don't Alibi)
1964: Santa Anita Handicap (Mr. Consistency)
San Juan Capistrano Handicap (Mr. Consistency)
1968: Hialeah Turf Cup (Kentucky Jug)

ALL BLUE
1956: Del Mar Debutante Stakes (Blue Vic)

ALLEGED
1987: Mother Goose Stakes (Fiesta Gal)
Coaching Club American Oaks (Fiesta Gal)
1991: Breeders' Cup Turf (Miss Alleged)
Hollywood Turf Cup (Miss Alleged)
1996: San Felipe Stakes (Odyle)

ALLEN'S PROSPECT
1996: Malibu Stakes (King of the Heap)

ALL HANDS
1971: Belmont Stakes (Pass Catcher)

AL NASR
1988: Oak Tree Invitational Stakes (Nasr El Arab)
1989: Charles H. Strub Stakes (Nasr El Arab)
San Juan Capistrano Handicap (Nasr El Arab)

ALQUEST
1952: Frizette Stakes (Sweet Patootie)
Alcibiades Stakes (Sweet Patootie)

ALSAB
1948: Spinaway Stakes (Myrtle Charm)
Matron Stakes (Myrtle Charm)
Marguerite Stakes (Alsab's Day)
1951: Champagne Stakes (Armageddon)
1952: Withers Stakes (Armageddon)
1953: Alabama Stakes (Sabette)
1956: Blue Grass Stakes (Toby B.)
1957: Breeders' Futurity (Toby's Brother)
Arkansas Derby (Al Davelle)

ALYDAR
1983: Del Mar Futurity (Althea)
Del Mar Debutante Stakes (Althea)
Hollywood Starlet Stakes (Althea)
Arlington-Washington Lassie Stakes (Miss Oceana)
Selima Stakes (Miss Oceana)
Frizette Stakes (Miss Oceana)
1984: Santa Susana Stakes (Althea)
Arkansas Derby (Althea)
Acorn Stakes (Miss Oceana)
Maskette Stakes (Miss Oceana)
1986: Widener Handicap (Turkoman)
Marlboro Cup Handicap (Turkoman)
1987: Kentucky Derby (Alysheba)
Preakness Stakes (Alysheba)
Super Derby (Alysheba)
Flamingo Stakes (Talinum)
1988: Charles H. Strub Stakes (Alysheba)
Santa Anita Handicap (Alysheba)
Philip H. Iselin Handicap (Alysheba)
Woodward Handicap (Alysheba)
Meadowlands Cup (Alysheba)
Breeders' Cup Classic (Alysheba)
Cowdin Stakes (Easy Goer)
Champagne Stakes (Easy Goer)
Top Flight Handicap (Clabber Girl)
1989: Gotham Stakes (Easy Goer)
Wood Memorial Stakes (Easy Goer)
Belmont Stakes (Easy Goer)
Whitney Handicap (Easy Goer)
Travers Stakes (Easy Goer)

ALYDAR *(Continued)*
Woodward Handicap (Easy Goer)
Jockey Club Gold Cup (Easy Goer)
Matron Stakes (Stella Madrid)
Frizette Stakes (Stella Madrid)
1990: San Antonio Handicap (Criminal Type)
Pimlico Special (Criminal Type)
Metropolitan Handicap (Criminal Type)
Hollywood Gold Cup (Criminal Type)
Whitney Handicap (Criminal Type)
Suburban Handicap (Easy Goer)
Acorn Stakes (Stella Madrid)
Turf Classic (Cacoethes)
1991: Blue Grass Stakes (Strike the Gold)
Kentucky Derby (Strike the Gold)
1992: Pimlico Special (Strike the Gold)
Nassau County Handicap (Strike the Gold)
1993: Del Mar Futurity (Winning Pact)
1995: Strub Stakes (Dare and Go)
1996: Pacific Classic (Dare and Go)

ALYDEED
1998: Santa Anita Oaks (Hedonist)

ALZAO
1995: Beverly Hills Handicap (Alpride)
Yellow Ribbon Stakes (Alpride)

AMARULLAH
1964: Canadian Championship Stakes (Will I Rule)
Dixie Handicap (Will I Rule)

AMBEHAVING
1965: Gulfstream Park Handicap (Ampose)
1968: Black Helen Handicap (Treacherous)
1971: Gotham Stakes (Good Behaving)
Wood Memorial Stakes (Good Behaving)

AMBERNASH
1978: Maskette Handicap (Pearl Necklace)
1979: Flower Bowl Handicap (Pearl Necklace)

AMBIOPOISE
1970: Ohio Derby (Climber)
Monmouth Invitational Handicap (Twice Worthy)
1971: Suburban Handicap (Twice Worthy)
Hawthorne Gold Cup (Twice Worthy)
1972: New Orleans Handicap (Urgent Message)

AMBIORIX
1954: Selima Stakes (High Voltage)
Matron Stakes (High Voltage)
1955: Acorn Stakes (High Voltage)
Coaching Club American Oaks (High Voltage)
Delaware Oaks (High Voltage)
Vineland Handicap (High Voltage)
1956: Remsen Stakes (Ambehaving)
1960: Kentucky Oaks (Make Sail)
Alabama Stakes (Make Sail)
Delaware Oaks (Rash Statement)
Spinster Stakes (Rash Statement)
Del Mar Debutante Stakes (Amri-An)
Bowling Green Handicap (Amber Morn)
1961: Gotham Stakes (Ambiopoise)
Jersey Derby (Ambiopoise)
Withers Stakes (Hitting Away)
Dwyer Handicap (Hitting Away)
Top Flight Handicap (Make Sail)
1962: Flamingo Stakes (Prego)
Grey Lag Handicap (Ambiopoise)
1965: Mother Goose Stakes (Cordially)
1969: Century Handicap (Pinjara)
1970: Hollywood Gold Cup (Pleasure Seeker)
1971: Del Mar Handicap (Pinjara)

AMBROSE LIGHT
1949: Hawthorne Gold Cup (Volcanic)

AMERIGO
1965: Santa Susana Stakes (Desert Love)
Kentucky Oaks (Amerivan)
1967: Hollywood Oaks (Amerigo Lady)
Molly Pitcher Handicap (Politely)
Vanity Handicap (Desert Love)
Washington D.C. International (Fort Marcy)
1968: Delaware Handicap (Politely)
Ladies Handicap (Politely)
Top Flight Handicap (Amerigo Lady)
Santa Barbara Handicap (Amerigo's Fancy)
Sunset Handicap (Fort Marcy)
1969: Black Helen Handicap (Amerigo Lady)
Top Flight Handicap (Amerigo Lady)
Hollywood Park Inv. Turf Handicap (Fort Marcy)
1970: Dixie Handicap (Fort Marcy)
Bowling Green Handicap (Fort Marcy)
United Nations Handicap (Fort Marcy)
Man o' War Stakes (Fort Marcy)
Washington D.C. International (Fort Marcy)

ANYOLDTIME
1957: Del Mar Debutante Stakes (Sally Lee)

APALACHEE
1980: Norfolk Stakes (High Counsel)
1981: Sorority Stakes (Apalachee Honey)
Alcibiades Stakes (Apalachee Honey)
1985: Sorority Stakes (Lazer Show)
1987: Alabama Stakes (Up the Apalachee)
2000: Oaklawn Handicap (K One King)

A.P. INDY
1997: Fountain of Youth Stakes (Pulpit)
Toyota Blue Grass Stakes (Pulpit)
Alabama Stakes (Runup the Colors)
Gazelle Handicap (Royal Indy)
Ruffian Handicap (Tomisue's Delight)
1998: Swaps Stakes (Old Trieste)
Personal Ensign Handicap (Tomisue's Delight)
1999: Gallery Furniture.com Stakes (Stephen Got Even)
Californian Stakes (Old Trieste)
2000: Kentucky Oaks (Secret Status)
Mother Goose Stakes (Secret Status)
Donn Handicap (Stephen Got Even)
Pimlico Special (Golden Missile)
Champagne Stakes (A.P. Valentine)
2001: Hollywood Gold Cup (Aptitude)
Jockey Club Gold Cup (Aptitude)
Breeders' Cup Juvenile Fillies (Tempera)
2002: Coaching Club American Oaks (Jilbab)
2003: Pimlico Special (Mineshaft)
Suburban Handicap (Mineshaft)
Woodward Stakes (Mineshaft)
Jockey Club Gold Cup (Mineshaft)
Personal Ensign Handicap (Passing Shot)
Garden City BC Handicap (Indy Five Hundred)

ARAZI
2001: Wood Memorial Stakes (Congaree)
Swaps Stakes (Congaree)
2002: Cigar Mile Handicap (Congaree)
2003: Carter Handicap (Congaree)
Hollywood Gold Cup (Congaree)
Cigar Mile Handicap (Congaree)

ARCTIC PRINCE
1962: Saratoga Special (Mr. Cold Storage)
1965: Pan American Handicap (Cool Prince)
United Nations Handicap (Parka)
1966: San Luis Rey Handicap (Polar Sea)

ARDAN
1953: Frizette Stakes (Indian Legend)
1956: Hialeah Turf Handicap (Guardian II)

ARGUR
1967: Michigan Mile and One-Eighth (Estreno II)
1968: Pan American Handicap (Estreno II)

ARIEL
1946: Washington Park Futurity (Education)
Breeders' Futurity (Education)
1947: New Orleans Handicap (Hillyer Court)

ARIGOTAL
1947: Santa Susana Stakes (Hubble Bubble)
San Vicente Handicap (Hubble Bubble)

ARKANSAS II
1965: Cinema Handicap (Arksroni)

ARMAGEDDON
1961: Saratoga Special (Battle Joined)
1962: Lawrence Realization Stakes (Battle Joined)

ARTS AND LETTERS
1974: Oak Leaf Stakes (Cut Class)
1980: Santa Anita Derby (Codex)
Hollywood Derby (Codex)
Preakness Stakes (Codex)
Suburban Handicap (Winter's Tale)
Brooklyn Handicap (Winter's Tale)
Marlboro Cup Handicap (Winter's Tale)
1982: Widener Handicap (Lord Darnley)
Gulfstream Park Handicap (Lord Darnley)
1983: Suburban Handicap (Winter's Tale)

ASCOT KNIGHT
1997: Caesars International Handicap (Influent)
Man o' War Stakes (Influent)

ASSAGAI
1972: Sapling Stakes (Assagai Jr.)
1973: Illinois Derby (Big Whippendeal)
1974: Hialeah Turf Cup (Big Whippendeal)
Century Handicap (Big Whippendeal)
1976: Hawthorne Gold Cup (Almost Grown)

ASSEMBLYMAN
1969: John B. Campbell Handicap (Juvenile John)

ASSERT
1987: Santa Anita Oaks (Timely Assertion)
1988: Ashland Stakes (Willa on the Move)
1996: Hollywood Turf Cup (Running Flame)

ATOMIC
1969: Del Mar Debutante Stakes (Atomic Wings)

ATTENTION
1952: McLennan Handicap (Spartan Valor)
Widener Handicap (Spartan Valor)
Excelsior Handicap (Spartan Valor)
Gallant Fox Handicap (Spartan Valor)
1953: Tropical Park Handicap (Spartan Valor)

AT THE THRESHOLD
1992: Jim Beam Stakes (Lil E. Tee)
Kentucky Derby (Lil E. Tee)

AUDITING
1966: Dwyer Handicap (Mr. Right)
1968: Santa Anita Handicap (Mr. Right)
Woodward Stakes (Mr. Right)
1969: Suburban Handicap (Mr. Right)

AURELIUS II
1976: Oak Leaf Stakes (Any Time Girl)

AVATAR
1983: Sunset Handicap (Craelius)

AVENGER II
1957: Washington D.C. International (Mahan)

AVENUE OF FLAGS
2000: Oak Leaf Stakes (Notable Career)
2003: Triple Bend Breeders' Cup Handicap (Joey Franco)

AWESOME AGAIN
2002: Champagne Stakes (Toccet)
Hollywood Futurity (Toccet)
2003: Vosburgh Stakes (Ghostzapper)

BAGDAD
1966: Breeders' Futurity (Gentleman James)
San Felipe Handicap (Saber Mountain)
Cinema Handicap (Drin)
1967: Charles H. Strub Stakes (Drin)
1968: Alcibiades Stakes (Lil's Bag)
Gulfstream Park Handicap (Gentleman James)
1969: Manhattan Handicap (Harem Lady)
1970: Hollywood Park Inv. Turf Handicap (Fiddle Isle)
American Handicap (Fiddle Isle)
San Luis Rey Handicap (Fiddle Isle)
San Juan Capistrano Handicap (Fiddle Isle)
1971: Santa Susana Stakes (Turkish Trousers)
Hollywood Oaks (Turkish Trousers)
1972: Santa Maria Handicap (Turkish Trousers)
Santa Margarita Handicap (Turkish Trousers)

BAHRAM
1948: Arlington Handicap (Stud Poker)
Miami Beach Handicap (Stud Poker)
Louisiana Derby (Bovard)
1949: Saranac Handicap (Sun Bahram)

BAILJUMPER
1985: Pennsylvania Derby (Skip Trial)
Ohio Derby (Skip Trial)
Haskell Invitational Handicap (Skip Trial)
1986: Gulfstream Park Handicap (Skip Trial)
1987: Gulfstream Park Handicap (Skip Trial)

BAIRN
1994: Sword Dancer Invitational Handicap (Alex the Great)

BALCONAJE
1983: Santa Margarita Handicap (Marimbula)

BALDSKI
1987: Tropical Park Derby (Baldski's Star)
1988: Withers Stakes (Once Wild)
1995: Test Stakes (Chaposa Springs)

BALLADIER
1946: Garden State Stakes (Double Jay)
Kentucky Jockey Club Stakes (Double Jay)
1948: Arlington Classic (Papa Redbird)
Trenton Handicap (Double Jay)
1949: American Handicap (Double Jay)
1951: Sapling Stakes (Landseair)
Breeders' Futurity (Alladier)
1953: San Felipe Handicap (Decorated)

BALLYDAM
1960: Flamingo Stakes (Bally Ache)
Florida Derby (Bally Ache)
Preakness Stakes (Bally Ache)
Jersey Derby (Bally Ache)
1963: Spinaway Stakes (Petite Rouge)

BALLYMOSS
1966: Sunset Handicap (O'Hara)

BARACHOIS
1985: Man o' War Stakes (Win)

BARBIZON
1961: Kentucky Jockey Club Stakes (Su Ka Wa)
1962: Frizette Stakes (Pams Ego)
1965: Arlington-Washington Lassie Stakes (Silver Bright)

BATES MOTEL
1990: Ohio Derby (Private School)

BATONNIER
1987: Remsen Stakes (Batty)
1996: Santa Anita Derby (Cavonnier)

BATTLEFIELD
1958: Princess Pat Stakes (Battle Heart)
1962: New Orleans Handicap (Yorktown)
John B. Campbell Handicap (Yorktown)

BATTLE JOINED
1969: Withers Stakes (Ack Ack)
Arlington Classic (Ack Ack)
1971: Hollywood Gold Cup (Ack Ack)
San Antonio Stakes (Ack Ack)
Santa Anita Handicap (Ack Ack)
American Handicap (Ack Ack)

BATTLE MORN
1958: Jerome Handicap (Warhead)
Roamer Handicap (Warhead)
Manhattan Handicap (Warhead)
1960: Whitney Handicap (Warhead)

BATTLESHIP
1948: Monmouth Handicap (Tide Rips)

BAYNOUN
1994: Oak Tree Invitational Stakes (Sandpit)
1995: Caesars International Handicap (Sandpit)
San Luis Rey Stakes (Sandpit)
1996: Hollywood Turf Handicap (Sandpit)
Caesars International Handicap (Sandpit)

BAZOOKA
1955: Starlet Stakes (Bold Bazooka)

BEAU BUCK
1986: San Fernando Stakes (Right Con)

BEAU GAR
1962: Suburban Handicap (Beau Purple)
Brooklyn Handicap (Beau Purple)
Hawthorne Gold Cup (Beau Purple)
Man o' War Stakes (Beau Purple)
1963: Widener Handicap (Beau Purple)
1967: Amory L. Haskell Handicap (Handsome Boy)
Brooklyn Handicap (Handsome Boy)
Washington Park Handicap (Handsome Boy)
1969: Massachusetts Handicap (Beau Marker)
1971: Delaware Handicap (Blessing Angelica)
1972: Delaware Handicap (Blessing Angelica)
Jersey Derby (Smiling Jack)

BEAU GEM
1955: Champagne Stakes (Beau Fond)

BEAU MAX
1958: Los Angeles Handicap (How Now)
American Handicap (How Now)

BEAU PERE
1946: Hollywood Oaks (Honeymoon)
Cinema Handicap (Honeymoon)
Hollywood Derby (Honeymoon)
Starlet Stakes (U Time)
1947: Spinaway Stakes (Bellesoeur)
Astarita Stakes (Bellesoeur)
Hollywood Oaks (U Time)
Vanity Handicap (Honeymoon)
1948: Vineland Handicap (Honeymoon)
Top Flight Handicap (Honeymoon)
Hollywood Oaks (Flying Rhythm)
American Handicap (Stepfather)
1949: Westerner Stakes (Pedigree)
Cinema Handicap (Pedigree)
Hollywood Oaks (June Bride)
1950: Cinema Handicap (Great Circle)
Del Mar Derby (Great Circle)
1951: Will Rogers Handicap (Gold Note)
Sunset Handicap (Alderman)
Santa Anita Maturity (Great Circle)
1952: Sunset Handicap (Great Circle)

BELIEVE IT
1984: Monmouth Handicap (Believe the Queen)
1986: Metropolitan Handicap (Garthorn)
1987: Kentucky Oaks (Buryyourbelief)
John Henry Handicap (Al Mamoon)

BELONG TO ME
1998: Acorn Stakes (Jersey Girl)
Mother Goose Stakes (Jersey Girl)
Test Stakes (Jersey Girl)
Hopeful Stakes (Lucky Roberto)
1999: Spinaway Stakes (Circle of Life)
2002: Del Mar Debutante Stakes (Belong to Me)

BE MY CHIEF
1996: Yellow Ribbon Stakes (Donna Viola)
1997: Gamely Handicap (Donna Viola)

BE MY GUEST
1988: Hialeah Turf Cup (Double Bed)
1989: Laurel Futurity (Go and Go)
1990: Belmont Stakes (Go and Go)

BEN LOMOND
1971: Santa Margarita Handicap (Manta)
Beverly Hills Handicap (Manta)
Santa Barbara Handicap (Manta)

BERING
1996: Ramona Handicap (Matiara)

BERKLEY PRINCE
1982: Beldame Stakes (Weber City Miss)

BERNBOROUGH
1952: Acorn Stakes (Parading Lady)
Vosburgh Handicap (Parading Lady)
1953: Saranac Handicap (First Aid)
Aqueduct Handicap (First Aid)
1954: Black Helen Handicap (Gainsboro Girl)
New Castle Handicap (Gainsboro Girl)
1955: Whitney Stakes (First Aid)
1958: Travers Stakes (Piano Jim)

BERSEEM
1964: Santa Margarita Handicap (Curious Clover)
1965: Santa Margarita Handicap (Curious Clover)

BERTRANDO
2001: Del Mar Futurity (Officer)
Champagne Stakes (Officer)

BEST TURN
1978: Metropolitan Handicap (Cox's Ridge)
Oaklawn Handicap (Cox's Ridge)
1979: Fantasy Stakes (Davona Dale)
Kentucky Oaks (Davona Dale)
Acorn Stakes (Davona Dale)
Mother Goose Stakes (Davona Dale)
Coaching Club American Oaks (Davona Dale)

BETTER BEE
1966: Arkansas Derby (Better Sea)
Blue Grass Stakes (Abe's Hope)
1972: Preakness Stakes (Bee Bee Bee)
1974: Jersey Derby (Better Arbitor)

BETTER SELF
1961: Selima Stakes (Tamarona)
1962: Vineland Handicap (Tamarona)

BIEN BIEN
2000: Hollywood Turf Cup (Bienamado)
2001: San Juan Capistrano Handicap (Bienamado)
Charles Whittingham Handicap (Bienamado)

BIG GAME
1953: Trenton Handicap (Olympic)

BIG SPRUCE
1980: Arlington Classic (Spruce Needles)
Secretariat Stakes (Spruce Needles)
Bay Meadows Handicap (Super Moment)
1981: Charles H. Strub Stakes (Super Moment)
Bay Meadows Handicap (Super Moment)
Santa Anita Derby (Splendid Spruce)
Hawthorne Gold Cup (Spruce Bouquet)
Arlington Handicap (Spruce Needles)
1982: Bay Meadows Handicap (Super Moment)
1983: United Nations Handicap (Acaroid)
1984: La Canada Stakes (Sweet Diane)

BIKALA
1994: Turf Classic (Apple Tree)

BILLINGS
1956: Metropolitan Handicap (Midafternoon)
Massachusetts Handicap (Midafternoon)
Display Handicap (Midafternoon)

BIMELECH
1946: Hopeful Stakes (Blue Border)
Frizette Stakes (Bimlette)
Vanity Handicap (Be Faithful)
1947: Saratoga Special (Better Self)
American Handicap (Burning Dream)
Hawthorne Gold Cup (Be Faithful)
1948: Discovery Handicap (Better Self)
Westchester Handicap (Better Self)
1949: Futurity Stakes (Guillotine)
Carter Handicap (Better Self)
1950: Gallant Fox Handicap (Better Self)
Carter Handicap (Guillotine)
1951: Fall Highweight Handicap (Guillotine)
1954: Monmouth Handicap (Bassanio)
1955: Spinaway Stakes (Register)
1957: Hialeah Turf Handicap (Jabneh)
1959: Pimlico Futurity (Progressing)

BINARY
1963: Hollywood Juvenile Championship (Nevada Bin)
1968: San Felipe Handicap (Prince Pablo)

BIT OF IRELAND
1966: Vanity Handicap (Khal Ireland)

BLACK FOREST
1947: Longacres Mile (Hank H.)

BLACK TIE AFFAIR
1997: Donn Handicap (Formal Gold)
Brooklyn Handicap (Formal Gold)
Philip H. Iselin Handicap (Formal Gold)
Woodward Stakes (Formal Gold)
2002: Jockey Club Gold Cup (Evening Attire)

BLENHEIM II
1946: Pimlico Futurity (Jet Pilot)
Tremont Stakes (Jet Pilot)
1947: American Derby (Fervent)
Pimlico Special (Fervent)
Swift Stakes (Owners Choice)
San Felipe Stakes (Owners Choice)
Kentucky Derby (Jet Pilot)
1948: Dixie Handicap (Fervent)
Washington Park Handicap (Fervent)
1951: Aqueduct Handicap (Bryan G.)
Westchester Handicap (Bryan G.)
Pimlico Special (Bryan G.)
Princess Pat Stakes (A Gleam)
1952: Hollywood Oaks (A Gleam)
Cinema Handicap (A Gleam)
Westerner Stakes (A Gleam)
Aqueduct Handicap (Bryan G.)
1955: Saranac Handicap (Saratoga)

BLESS ME
1952: Fall Highweight Handicap (Hitex)

BLEU D'OR
1954: McLennan Handicap (Elixir)

BLUEBIRD
1994: Yellow Ribbon Stakes (Aube Indienne)

BLUE ENSIGN
1986: Fountain of Youth Stakes (Ensign Rhythm)
1987: Young America Stakes (Firery Ensign)

BLUE FLYER
1952: Molly Pitcher Handicap (Dixie Flyer)

BLUE GAY
1965: Oaklawn Handicap (Gay Revoke)

BLUE LARKSPUR
1946: Princess Pat Stakes (Say Blue)
Selima Stakes (Bee Ann Mac)
1947: Pimlico Oaks (But Why Not)
Acorn Stakes (But Why Not)
Alabama Stakes (But Why Not)
Arlington Matron Handicap (But Why Not)
Beldame Handicap (But Why Not)
Arlington Classic (But Why Not)
New Castle Handicap (Elpis)
Comely Handicap (Elpis)
Molly Pitcher Handicap (Elpis)
Kentucky Oaks (Blue Grass)
1949: Queens County Handicap (Three Rings)
Monmouth Handicap (Three Rings)
Westchester Handicap (Three Rings)
Firenze Handicap (But Why Not)
Top Flight Handicap (But Why Not)
1950: McLennan Handicap (Three Rings)
Queens County Handicap (Three Rings)
1951: Firenze Handicap (Renew)
1952: Top Flight Handicap (Renew)

BLUE PRINCE
1961: Santa Anita Derby (Four-and-Twenty)
Cinema Handicap (Four-and-Twenty)
Hollywood Derby (Four-and-Twenty)
1962: San Fernando Stakes (Four-and-Twenty)
Santa Anita Maturity (Four-and-Twenty)
San Carlos Handicap (Four-and-Twenty)
1964: Arkansas Derby (Prince Davelle)
1970: Lawrence Realization Stakes (Kling Kling)
John B. Campbell Handicap (Mitey Prince)

BLUE SWORDS
1949: Will Rogers Handicap (Blue Dart)
1951: Acorn Stakes (Nothirdchance)
1952: Flamingo Stakes (Blue Man)
Preakness Stakes (Blue Man)
Dwyer Stakes (Blue Man)
1954: New Orleans Handicap (Grover B.)
1956: San Luis Rey Handicap (Blue Volt)

BLUE TRAIN
1955: Santa Margarita Handicap (Blue Butterfly)

BLUE WATER
1957: William P. Kyne Memorial Handicap (Pibe Carlitos)

BLUSHING GROOM
1982: Santa Susana Stakes (Blush With Pride)
Kentucky Oaks (Blush With Pride)
Golden Harvest Handicap (Blush With Pride)
Maskette Stakes (Too Chic)
Travers Stakes (Runaway Groom)
1984: Tropical Park Derby (Morning Bob)
Pennsylvania Derby (Morning Bob)
1985: Rothmans International Stakes (Nassipour)
1989: Hollywood Gold Cup (Blushing John)
1991: Breeders' Cup Juvenile (Arazi)
1992: Matron Stakes (Sky Beauty)
1993: Acorn Stakes (Sky Beauty)
Mother Goose Stakes (Sky Beauty)
Coaching Club American Oaks (Sky Beauty)
Alabama Stakes (Sky Beauty)
Top Flight Handicap (You'd Be Surprised)
1994: Shuvee Handicap (Sky Beauty)
Hempstead Handicap (Sky Beauty)
Go for Wand Stakes (Sky Beauty)
Ruffian Handicap (Sky Beauty)

BLUSHING JOHN
1997: Kentucky Oaks (Blushing K.D.)

B. MAJOR
1972: Oak Leaf Stakes (Fresh Pepper)

BOLD AND BRAVE
1979: Oak Leaf Stakes (Bold 'n Determined)
1980: Santa Susana Stakes (Bold 'n Determined)
Fantasy Stakes (Bold 'n Determined)
Kentucky Oaks (Bold 'n Determined)
Acorn Stakes (Bold 'n Determined)
Coaching Club American Oaks (Bold 'n Determined)
Maskette Stakes (Bold 'n Determined)
Spinster Stakes (Bold 'n Determined)
1981: Apple Blossom Handicap (Bold 'n Determined)

BOLD BIDDER
1974: Kentucky Derby (Cannonade)
1977: Breeders' Futurity (Gonquin)
1978: Champagne Stakes (Spectacular Bid)
Young America Stakes (Spectacular Bid)
Laurel Futurity (Spectacular Bid)
1979: Florida Derby (Spectacular Bid)
Flamingo Stakes (Spectacular Bid)
Blue Grass Stakes (Spectacular Bid)
Kentucky Derby (Spectacular Bid)
Preakness Stakes (Spectacular Bid)
Marlboro Cup Handicap (Spectacular Bid)
Meadowlands Cup (Spectacular Bid)
1980: Californian Stakes (Spectacular Bid)
Amory L. Haskell Handicap (Spectacular Bid)
Woodward Stakes (Spectacular Bid)
San Fernando Stakes (Spectacular Bid)
Charles H. Strub Stakes (Spectacular Bid)
Santa Anita Handicap (Spectacular Bid)

BOLD COMBATANT
1975: Del Mar Futurity (Telly's Pop)
Norfolk Stakes (Telly's Pop)
1976: California Derby (Telly's Pop)

BOLD COMMANDER
1970: Blue Grass Stakes (Dust Commander)
Kentucky Derby (Dust Commander)
1983: Oaklawn Handicap (Bold Style)

BOLD FORBES
1982: Wood Memorial Stakes (Air Forbes Won)
1986: Fantasy Stakes (Tiffany Lass)
Kentucky Oaks (Tiffany Lass)
1988: Young America Stakes (Irish Actor)

BOLD HITTER
1974: Hollywood Juvenile Championship (DiMaggio)

BOLD HOUR
1976: Del Mar Futurity (Visible)
1981: Travers Stakes (Willow Hour)

BOLD JOEY
1980: Del Mar Futurity (Bold And Gold)

BOLD LAD
1971: Cinema Handicap (Niagara)
1974: Wood Memorial Stakes (Rube the Great)
Oaklawn Handicap (Royal Knight)
1979: Sunset Handicap (Sirlad)

BOLDNESIAN
1971: Withers Stakes (Bold Reasoning)
Jersey Derby (Bold Reasoning)
1972: Malibu Stakes (Wing Out)
1975: Cinema Handicap (Terete)
San Antonio Stakes (Cheriepe)

BOLD REASON
1979: Brooklyn Handicap (The Liberal Member)
1982: Yellow Ribbon Stakes (Castilla)
Matriarch Stakes (Castilla)

BOLD REASONING
1976: Champagne Stakes (Seattle Slew)
1977: Flamingo Stakes (Seattle Slew)
Wood Memorial Stakes (Seattle Slew)
Kentucky Derby (Seattle Slew)
Preakness Stakes (Seattle Slew)
Belmont Stakes (Seattle Slew)
1978: Marlboro Cup Handicap (Seattle Slew)
Woodward Stakes (Seattle Slew)

BOLD RUCKUS
1990: Arlington Invitational Challenge Cup (Beau Genius)
Philip H. Iselin Handicap (Beau Genius)
1995: Kentucky Oaks (Gal in a Ruckus)

BOLD RULER
1962: Breeders' Futurity (Ornamento)
1963: Coaching Club American Oaks (Lamb Chop)
Monmouth Oaks (Lamb Chop)
Spinster Stakes (Lamb Chop)
Cowdin Stakes (Chieftan)
1964: Sapling Stakes (Bold Lad)
Hopeful Stakes (Bold Lad)
Futurity Stakes (Bold Lad)
Champagne Stakes (Bold Lad)
Frizette Stakes (Queen Empress)
Gardenia Stakes (Queen Empress)
Hollywood Juvenile Championship (Neke)
Sanford Stakes (Cornish Prince)
Sorority Stakes (Bold Experience)
Santa Margarita Handicap (Batteur)
1965: San Felipe Handicap (Jacinto)
Dwyer Handicap (Staunchness)
Jerome Handicap (Bold Bidder)
Arlington Handicap (Chieftan)
1966: Monmouth Handicap (Bold Bidder)
Washington Park Handicap (Bold Bidder)
Hawthorne Gold Cup (Bold Bidder)
Charles H. Strub Stakes (Bold Bidder)
Hopeful Stakes (Bold Hour)
Futurity Stakes (Bold Hour)
Champagne Stakes (Successor)
Garden State Stakes (Successor)
Sapling Stakes (Great Power)
Santa Anita Derby (Boldnesian)
Gotham Stakes (Stupendous)
Jerome Handicap (Bold and Brave)
Metropolitan Handicap (Bold Lad)
Whitney Stakes (Staunchness)
1967: Saratoga Special (Vitriolic)
Arlington-Washington Futurity (Vitriolic)
Champagne Stakes (Vitriolic)
Pimlico-Laurel Futurity (Vitriolic)
Sorority Stakes (Queen of the Stage)
Spinaway Stakes (Queen of the Stage)
Matron Stakes (Queen of the Stage)
Frizette Stakes (Queen of the Stage)
Arlington Handicap (Stupendous)
Whitney Stakes (Stupendous)
Hopeful Stakes (What a Pleasure)
Selima Stakes (Syrian Sea)
Alabama Stakes (Gamely)
Lawrence Realization Stakes (Successor)
1968: Sanford Stakes (King Emperor)
Cowdin Stakes (King Emperor)
Pimlico-Laurel Futurity (King Emperor)
Vanity Handicap (Gamely)
Beldame Stakes (Gamely)
Santa Margarita Handicap (Gamely)
Sapling Stakes (Reviewer)
Saratoga Special (Reviewer)
Grey Lag Handicap (Bold Hour)
Amory L. Haskell Handicap (Bold Hour)
Sorority Stakes (Big Advance)
San Felipe Handicap (Dewan)
Illinois Derby (Bold Favorite)
1969: Louisiana Derby (King of the Castle)
Illinois Derby (King of the Castle)
Hopeful Stakes (Irish Castle)
Spinaway Stakes (Meritus)
Beldame Stakes (Gamely)
1970: Brooklyn Handicap (Dewan)
San Antonio Stakes (Dewan)
Carter Handicap (Tyrant)
1972: Hopeful Stakes (Secretariat)
Futurity Stakes (Secretariat)
Laurel Futurity (Secretariat)
Garden State Stakes (Secretariat)
1973: Gotham Stakes (Secretariat)
Kentucky Derby (Secretariat)
Preakness Stakes (Secretariat)
Belmont Stakes (Secretariat)
Marlboro Cup Handicap (Secretariat)
Man o' War Stakes (Secretariat)
Canadian International Championship (Secretariat)
1974: Matron Stakes (Alpine Lass)
1975: Monmouth Invitational Handicap (Wajima)
Travers Stakes (Wajima)
Marlboro Cup Handicap (Wajima)
Jersey Derby (Singh)
Oak Tree Invitational Stakes (Top Command)
1976: Maskette Handicap (Sugar Plum Time)

BOLD TACTICS
1974: Norfolk Stakes (George Navonod)
1976: Charles H. Strub Stakes (George Navonod)
1981: Arkansas Derby (Bold Ego)

BOLD VENTURE

1946: Wood Memorial Stakes (Assault)
Kentucky Derby (Assault)
Preakness Stakes (Assault)
Belmont Stakes (Assault)
Dwyer Stakes (Assault)
Pimlico Special (Assault)
Westchester Handicap (Assault)
1947: Grey Lag Handicap (Assault)
Dixie Handicap (Assault)
Suburban Handicap (Assault)
Brooklyn Handicap (Assault)
1949: Hopeful Stakes (Middleground)
Brooklyn Handicap (Assault)
1950: Kentucky Derby (Middleground)
Belmont Stakes (Middleground)
1954: Gazelle Handicap (On Your Own)

BOLERO

1956: Frizette Stakes (Capelet)
1959: Carter Handicap (Jimmer)
1960: Del Mar Futurity (Short Jacket)

BOLGER

1991: San Felipe Stakes (Sea Cadet)
1992: Donn Handicap (Sea Cadet)
Gulfstream Park Handicap (Sea Cadet)
Meadowlands Cup (Sea Cadet)

BOLINAS BOY

1972: Illinois Derby (Fame and Power)

BONNARD

1975: Sunset Handicap (Cruiser II)
Del Mar Handicap (Cruiser II)

BONNE NOEL

1981: Pan American Handicap (Little Bonny)

BOOJUM

1946: Santa Susana Stakes (Enfilade)
1947: Demoiselle Stakes (Ghost Run)

BOSTON DOGE

1964: Delaware Handicap (Old Hat)
Spinster Stakes (Old Hat)
1965: Black Helen Handicap (Old Hat)
Matron Handicap (Old Hat)
Michigan Mile and One-Eighth (Old Hat)

BOSWELL

1946: Flamingo Stakes (Round View)
Blue Grass Stakes (Lord Boswell)
1947: Monmouth Handicap (Round View)
1949: Whitney Stakes (Round View)
1950: Massachusetts Handicap (Cochise)
1951: Grey Lag Handicap (Cochise)
Arlington Handicap (Cochise)

BOW WOW

1949: San Pasqual Handicap (Shim Malone)

BOXTHORN

1947: San Antonio Handicap (El Lobo)

BRAMBLES

1973: Oak Tree Invitational Stakes (Portentous)

BRAZADO

1951: Washington Park Handicap (Curandero)

BREVITY

1946: San Pasqual Handicap (Lou-Bre)

BRIARTIC

1979: Arlington Classic (Steady Growth)

BRICK

1956: Canadian Championship Stakes (Eugenia II)
1958: Hialeah Turf Handicap (Meeting)

BRINKMANSHIP

1983: Hollywood Derby (Ginger Brink)

BRITISH EMPIRE

1958: Arlington Matron Handicap (Estacion)

BROAD BRUSH

1993: Jerome Handicap (Schossberg)
1994: Arkansas Derby (Concern)
Breeders' Cup Classic (Concern)
1995: Californian Stakes (Concern)
Philip H. Iselin Handicap (Schossberg)
2001: Pimlico Special (Include)
Personal Ensign Handicap (Pompeii)
2002: Kentucky Oaks (Farda Amiga)
Alabama Stakes (Farda Amiga)
Donn Handicap (Mongoose)

BROCCO

2000: Coaching Club American Oaks (Jostle)
Alabama Stakes (Jostle)

BROOKFIELD

1952: Cowdin Stakes (Invigorator)
1954: Brooklyn Handicap (Invigorator)
1957: Fall Highweight Handicap (Itobe)

BROTHER MACHREE

1980: Golden Harvest Handicap (War Fame)

BROWN KING

1950: Firenze Handicap (Red Camelia)
New Orleans Handicap (Red Camelia)
1951: Beldame Handicap (Thelma Berger)
1953: Santa Margarita Handicap (Spanish Cream)
Louisiana Derby (Matagorda)

BRYAN G.

1961: Spinaway Stakes (Cicada)
Matron Stakes (Cicada)
Frizette Stakes (Cicada)
Gardenia Stakes (Cicada)
1962: Kentucky Oaks (Cicada)
Acorn Stakes (Cicada)
Mother Goose Stakes (Cicada)
Beldame Stakes (Cicada)

BUCKAROO

1984: Arlington-Washington Futurity (Spend A Buck)
1985: Kentucky Derby (Spend A Buck)
Jersey Derby (Spend A Buck)
Monmouth Handicap (Spend A Buck)
1986: Suburban Handicap (Roo Art)
Philip H. Iselin Handicap (Roo Art)
1992: Californian Stakes (Another Review)
1995: Carter Handicap (Lite the Fuse)
Frank J. De Francis Memorial Dash (Lite the Fuse)
1996: Carter Handicap (Lite the Fuse)
Frank J. De Francis Memorial Dash (Lite the Fuse)

BUCKFINDER

1985: Dwyer Stakes (Track Barron)
Vosburgh Stakes (Track Barron)
1986: Whitney Handicap (Track Barron)
Woodward Stakes (Track Barron)

BUCKPASSER

1971: Spinaway Stakes (Numbered Account)
Matron Stakes (Numbered Account)
Frizette Stakes (Numbered Account)
Selima Stakes (Numbered Account)
Gardenia Stakes (Numbered Account)
1972: Spinaway Stakes (La Prevoyante)
Matron Stakes (La Prevoyante)
Frizette Stakes (La Prevoyante)
Selima Stakes (La Prevoyante)
Gardenia Stakes (La Prevoyante)
Spinster Stakes (Numbered Account)
1974: Laurel Futurity (L'Enjoleur)
1975: American Handicap (Pass the Glass)
1976: Sorority Stakes (Squander)
1977: Norfolk Stakes (Balzac)
Arlington Handicap (Cunning Trick)
1979: Metropolitan Handicap (State Dinner)
Suburban Handicap (State Dinner)
Century Handicap (State Dinner)
Oak Tree Invitational Stakes (Balzac)
1980: Whitney Stakes (State Dinner)
1981: Delaware Handicap (Relaxing)
Ruffian Handicap (Relaxing)
Illinois Derby (Paristo)
1982: Suburban Handicap (Silver Buck)
Whitney Handicap (Silver Buck)

BUCKSPLASHER

1998: Turf Classic (Buck's Boy)
Breeders' Cup Turf (Buck's Boy)

BUISSON D'OR

1965: Bowling Green Handicap (Or et Argent)
Dixie Handicap (Or et Argent)

BULL DANDY

1955: Canadian Championship Stakes (Park Dandy)

BULL DOG

1946: Santa Margarita Handicap (Canina)
Fall Highweight Handicap (Cassis)
1948: Kentucky Jockey Club Stakes (Johns Joy)
1950: Marguerite Stakes (Carolina Queen)

BULL LEA

1946: Widener Handicap (Armed)
Dixie Handicap (Armed)
Suburban Handicap (Armed)
Washington Park Handicap (Armed)
Arlington Matron Handicap (Good Blood)
Vineland Handicap (Good Blood)
1947: McLennan Handicap (Armed)
Widener Handicap (Armed)
Gulfstream Park Handicap (Armed)
Stars and Stripes Handicap (Armed)
Arlington Handicap (Armed)
Washington Park Handicap (Armed)
Withers Stakes (Faultless)
Flamingo Stakes (Faultless)
Blue Grass Stakes (Faultless)
Preakness Stakes (Faultless)
Washington Park Futurity (Bewitch)
Arlington Lassie Stakes (Bewitch)
Princess Pat Stakes (Bewitch)
Pimlico Futurity (Citation)
Futurity Stakes (Citation)
1948: Flamingo Stakes (Citation)
Kentucky Derby (Citation)
Preakness Stakes (Citation)
Belmont Stakes (Citation)
American Derby (Citation)
Jockey Club Gold Cup (Citation)
Stars and Stripes Handicap (Citation)
Pimlico Special (Citation)
Blue Grass Stakes (Coaltown)
Jerome Handicap (Coaltown)
Gallant Fox Handicap (Faultless)
1949: McLennan Handicap (Coaltown)
Widener Handicap (Coaltown)
Gulfstream Park Handicap (Coaltown)
Gallant Fox Handicap (Coaltown)
Stars and Stripes Handicap (Coaltown)
Arlington Handicap (Coaltown)
Washington Park Handicap (Coaltown)
Vineland Handicap (Bewitch)
Discovery Handicap (Prophets Thumb)
1950: Coaching Club American Oaks (Next Move)
Delaware Oaks (Next Move)
Gazelle Stakes (Next Move)
Beldame Handicap (Next Move)
Ladies Handicap (Next Move)
Vanity Handicap (Next Move)
Santa Margarita Handicap (Two Lea)
Black Helen Handicap (Bewitch)
1951: American Handicap (Citation)
Hollywood Gold Cup (Citation)
Discovery Handicap (Alerted)
Jerome Handicap (Alerted)
Arlington Futurity (Hill Gail)
Vanity Handicap (Bewitch)
San Antonio Handicap (All Blue)
1952: Kentucky Oaks (Real Delight)
Black-Eyed Susan Stakes (Real Delight)
Coaching Club American Oaks (Real Delight)
Arlington Matron Stakes (Real Delight)
Beldame Handicap (Real Delight)
Arlington Classic (Mark-Ye-Well)
American Derby (Mark-Ye-Well)
Lawrence Realization Stakes (Mark-Ye-Well)
Firenze Handicap (Next Move)
Beldame Handicap (Next Move)
Vanity Handicap (Two Lea)
Hollywood Gold Cup (Two Lea)
Santa Anita Derby (Hill Gail)
Kentucky Derby (Hill Gail)
Del Mar Debutante Stakes (Lap Full)
Dixie Handicap (Alerted)
1953: Discovery Handicap (Level Lea)
Jockey Club Gold Cup (Level Lea)
Santa Anita Handicap (Mark-Ye-Well)
Santa Anita Maturity (Mark-Ye-Well)
Kentucky Oaks (Bubbley)
Arlington Matron Handicap (Real Delight)
Santa Anita Derby (Chanlea)
Golden Gate Handicap (Fleet Bird)
1954: Cinema Handicap (Miz Clementine)
California Derby (Miz Clementine)
Vanity Handicap (Bubbley)
Vineland Handicap (Spinning Top)
Tropical Handicap (Capeador)

BULL LEA *(Continued)*
San Antonio Handicap (Mark-Ye-Well)
Sunset Handicap (Fleet Bird)
Hialeah Turf Handicap (Picador)
1957: Everglades Stakes (Gen. Duke)
Florida Derby (Gen. Duke)
Black Helen Handicap (Amoret)
Kentucky Derby (Iron Liege)
1958: McLennan Handicap (Iron Liege)
1959: Black Helen Handicap (Rosewood)
1961: American Derby (Beau Prince)
Travers Stakes (Beau Prince)
McLennan Handicap (Yorky)
Widener Handicap (Yorky)
1962: Widener Handicap (Yorky)
Michigan Mile and One-Sixteenth (Beau Prince)

BULL RUN
1957: Arlington Handicap (Manassas)

BURG-EL-ARAB
1950: Arlington Lassie Stakes (Shawnee Squaw)
1955: Arlington Matron Handicap (Arab Actress)

BURNING STAR
1946: Trenton Handicap (Turbine)

BUSTED
1982: Californian Stakes (Erins Isle)
Sunset Handicap (Erins Isle)
1983: Hollywood Invitational Handicap (Erins Isle)
San Luis Rey Stakes (Erins Isle)
San Juan Capistrano Handicap (Erins Isle)
1991: Sunset Handicap (Black Monday)

BY JIMMINY
1951: Preakness Stakes (Bold)
Saranac Handicap (Bold)
1954: Jerome Handicap (Martyr)

CADMUS
1977: Pan American Handicap (Gravelines)

CAERLEON
1991: Yellow Ribbon Stakes (Kostroma)
1992: Beverly D. Stakes (Kostroma)
Santa Barbara Handicap (Kostroma)
Pacific Classic (Missionary Ridge)
1994: American Derby (Overbury)
1996: Gamely Handicap (Auriette)

CALIFORNIA KID
1970: Del Mar Debutante Stakes (Generous Portion)

CAMBREMONT
1981: Brooklyn Handicap (Hechizado)

CANDY SPOTS
1972: Louisiana Derby (No Le Hace)
Arkansas Derby (No Le Hace)

CANDY STRIPES
1996: Beverly Hills Handicap (Different)
Three Chimneys Spinster Stakes (Different)

CANNONADE
1980: Delaware Handicap (Heavenly Ade)
1982: California Derby (Rockwall)
1983: Belmont Stakes (Caveat)
1984: San Juan Capistrano Handicap (Load the Cannons)

CANTHARE
1969: Oaklawn Handicap (Listado)

CAPE TOWN
2003: Kentucky Oaks (Bird Town)
Acorn Stakes (Bird Town)

CAPOTE
1991: Futurity Stakes (Agincourt)
1993: Dwyer Stakes (Agincourt)
1995: Hollywood Futurity (Matty G.)
1996: Breeders' Cup Juvenile (Boston Harbor)

CARLEMONT
1974: San Luis Rey Stakes (Astray)
San Juan Capistrano Handicap (Astray)
1975: Century Handicap (Astray)

CARO
1982: Laurel Futurity (Cast Party)
1983: Remsen Stakes (Dr. Carter)
1985: Swaps Stakes (Padua)
Gulfstream Park Handicap (Dr. Carter)
Breeders' Cup Mile (Cozzene)
1987: Arlington-Washington Futurity (Tejano)
Cowdin Stakes (Tejano)
Hollywood Futurity (Tejano)
1988: Santa Anita Oaks (Winning Colors)
Santa Anita Derby (Winning Colors)
Kentucky Derby (Winning Colors)
1990: John Henry Handicap (Golden Pheasant)
Arlington Million (Golden Pheasant)
1994: Hollywood Turf Handicap (Grand Flotilla)

CARR DE NASKRA
1995: Remsen Stakes (Tropicool)

CARRIER PIGEON
1949: Santa Anita Derby (Old Rockport)

CARRY BACK
1970: Black Helen Handicap (Taken Aback)
Spinster Stakes (Taken Aback)
1974: Illinois Derby (Sharp Gary)
1976: Michigan Mile and One-Eighth (Sharp Gary)

CARSON CITY
1995: Pegasus Handicap (Flying Chevron)
NYRA Mile Handicap (Flying Chevron)
1996: Oak Leaf Stakes (City Band)
1997: Ballerina Stakes (Pearl City)
2000: Hopeful Stakes (City Zip)
2002: Prioress Stakes (Carson Hollow)
2003: Futurity Stakes (Cuvee)

CASANOVA
1968: Canadian International Championship (Frenetico)

CASE ACE
1946: Jockey Club Gold Cup (Pavot)
Massachusetts Handicap (Pavot)
1951: Spinaway Stakes (Blue Case)
Metropolitan Handicap (Casemate)

CATALAN
1946: Bougainvillea Handicap (Cat Bridge)

CAUCASUS
1985: Ladies Handicap (Videogenic)

CAVAN
1964: Coaching Club American Oaks (Miss Cavandish)
Monmouth Oaks (Miss Cavandish)
Alabama Stakes (Miss Cavandish)
1969: San Fernando Stakes (Cavamore)

CAVEAT
1988: Pennsylvania Derby (Cefis)
1991: Brooklyn Handicap (Timely Warning)
1993: Secretariat Stakes (Awad)
1995: Early Times Manhattan Handicap (Awad)
Arlington Million (Awad)
1997: Manhattan Handicap (Ops Smile)
Sword Dancer Invitational Handicap (Awad)

CEE'S TIZZY
1999: Milady Breeders' Cup Handicap (Gourmet Girl)
2000: Super Derby (Tiznow)
Breeders' Cup Classic (Tiznow)
San Antonio Handicap (Budroyale)
2001: Apple Blossom Handicap (Gourmet Girl)
Vanity Handicap (Gourmet Girl)
Santa Anita Handicap (Tiznow)
Breeders' Cup Classic (Tiznow)

CELTIC SWING
2003: NetJets Breeders' Cup Mile (Six Perfections)

CHALLEDON
1946: Sapling Stakes (Donor)
Champagne Stakes (Donor)
1947: Breeders' Futurity (Shy Guy)
Jerome Handicap (Donor)
1948: Kentucky Oaks (Challe Anne)
1949: Manhattan Handicap (Donor)
New York Handicap (Donor)
1950: Hollywood Oaks (Mrs. Fuddy)
1952: Discovery Handicap (Ancestor)
1954: Louisiana Derby (Gigantic)
1955: San Antonio Handicap (Gigantic)
1958: New Orleans Handicap (Tenacious)
1959: New Orleans Handicap (Tenacious)

CHALLENGE ME
1953: Queens County Handicap (Flaunt)

CHALLENGER II
1946: Gazelle Stakes (Bridal Flower)
New Castle Handicap (Bridal Flower)
Beldame Handicap (Bridal Flower)
Roamer Handicap (Bridal Flower)
Beldame Handicap (Gallorette)
Metropolitan Handicap (Gallorette)
Brooklyn Handicap (Gallorette)
1947: Queens County Handicap (Gallorette)
Westchester Handicap (Bridal Flower)
1948: Carter Handicap (Gallorette)
Whitney Stakes (Gallorette)

CHANCE PLAY
1947: Miami Beach Handicap (Tel O'Sullivan)
1948: Arlington Lassie Stakes (Pail of Water)

CHANCE SHOT
1948: Black Helen Handicap (Shotsilk)

CHARLEVOIX
1970: Oaklawn Handicap (Charlie Jr.)

CHARLIE MCADAM
1958: Kentucky Jockey Club Stakes (Winsome Winner)

CHATEAUGAY
1972: Jerome Handicap (True Knight)
1974: John B. Campbell Handicap (True Knight)
Amory L. Haskell Handicap (True Knight)
Suburban Handicap (True Knight)

CHEROKEE RUN
1999: Vinery Del Mar Debutante Stakes (Chilukki)
Oak Leaf Stakes (Chilukki)
2000: Hopeful Stakes (Yonaguska)
2003: Arkansas Derby (Sir Cherokee)

CHIEF'S CROWN
1990: Jim Dandy Stakes (Chief Honcho)
1992: Brooklyn Handicap (Chief Honcho)
1997: Canadian Int. Championship (Chief Bearhart)
Breeders' Cup Turf (Chief Bearhart)
Jim Beam Stakes (Concerto)
1998: Manhattan Handicap (Chief Bearhart)

CHIEFTAN
1973: San Felipe Handicap (Linda's Chief)
California Derby (Linda's Chief)
Withers Stakes (Linda's Chief)
Pontiac Grand Prix Stakes (Linda's Chief)
1977: Ohio Derby (Silver Series)
American Derby (Silver Series)
Vanity Handicap (Cascapedia)
1978: Widener Handicap (Silver Series)
1982: Jerome Handicap (Fit to Fight)
1983: Matron Stakes (Lucky Lucky Lucky)
Alcibiades Stakes (Lucky Lucky Lucky)
1984: Metropolitan Handicap (Fit to Fight)
Suburban Handicap (Fit to Fight)
Brooklyn Handicap (Fit to Fight)
Kentucky Oaks (Lucky Lucky Lucky)

CHOP CHOP
1954: Vagrancy Handicap (Canadiana)
1959: Remsen Stakes (Victoria Park)

CHRYSLER II
1947: San Pasqual Handicap (Lets Dance)

CINCO GRANDE
1992: San Antonio Handicap (Ibero)
NYRA Mile Handicap (Ibero)
1993: Metropolitan Handicap (Ibero)

CIPAYO
1989: Sunset Handicap (Pranke)
1998: Santa Margarita Handicap (Toda Una Dama)

CITATION
1956: Acorn Stakes (Beyond)
Preakness Stakes (Fabius)
1957: Ohio Derby (Manteau)
1958: Sapling Stakes (Watch Your Step)
1959: Santa Anita Derby (Silver Spoon)
Cinema Handicap (Silver Spoon)
Sapling Stakes (Sky Clipper)
1960: Vanity Handicap (Silver Spoon)
Santa Margarita Handicap (Silver Spoon)
1963: Withers Stakes (Get Around)

CITIDANCER
1995: Ashland Stakes (Urbane)
1996: John A. Morris Handicap (Urbane)
1999: La Brea Stakes (Hookedonthefeelin)

CITY LINE
1970: Kentucky Jockey Club Stakes (Line City)

CLAIM STAKER
1977: Gulfstream Park Handicap (Strike Me Lucky)

CLARO
1955: Washington D.C. International (El Chama)

CLEM
1967: Ohio Derby (Out the Window)
1972: United Nations Handicap (Acclimatization)

COASTAL
1991: Santa Margarita Handicap (Little Brianne)

COASTAL TRAFFIC
1959: Michigan Mile and One-Sixteenth (Total Traffic)

COBRA KING
2003: Man o' War Stakes (Lunar Sovereign)

COCHISE
1966: Delaware Handicap (Open Fire)
Spinster Stakes (Open Fire)

CODEX
1985: Illinois Derby (Important Business)
1986: Everglades Stakes (Badger Land)
Flamingo Stakes (Badger Land)
1987: Illinois Derby (Lost Code)
Ohio Derby (Lost Code)
Arlington Classic (Lost Code)
Delaware Handicap (Coup de Fusil)
Ruffian Handicap (Coup de Fusil)

COHOES
1963: Sanford Stakes (Delirium)
Pimlico Futurity (Quadrangle)
1964: Wood Memorial Stakes (Quadrangle)
Belmont Stakes (Quadrangle)
Dwyer Handicap (Quadrangle)
Travers Stakes (Quadrangle)
Lawrence Realization Stakes (Quadrangle)

COLONY LIGHT
2000: Three Chimneys Spinster Stakes (Plenty of Light)

COME ON RED
1967: Oaklawn Handicap (Mike's Red)

COMICO
1948: Vosburgh Handicap (Colosal)

COMMANDING II
1969: Hollywood Oaks (Tipping Time)

COMMON GROUNDS
1995: Hollywood Turf Handicap (Earl of Barking)

CON BRIO
1976: Ladies Handicap (Bastonero II)
Beverly Hills Handicap (Bastonero II)

CONDIMENT
1956: Alabama Stakes (Tournure)
McLennan Handicap (Switch On)

CONQUISTADOR CIELO
1986: Young America Stakes (Conquistarose)
1991: Hollywood Gold Cup (Marquetry)
1992: Eddie Read Handicap (Marquetry)
1993: Meadowlands Cup (Marquetry)
San Antonio Handicap (Marquetry)
1998: Jockey Club Gold Cup (Wagon Limit)

CONSULTANT'S BID
1989: Santa Margarita Handicap (Bayakoa)
Apple Blossom Handicap (Bayakoa)
Vanity Handicap (Bayakoa)
Ruffian Handicap (Bayakoa)
Spinster Stakes (Bayakoa)
Breeders' Cup Distaff (Bayakoa)
1990: Santa Margarita Handicap (Bayakoa)
Spinster Stakes (Bayakoa)
Breeders' Cup Distaff (Bayakoa)

COOL HAND
1980: Oaklawn Handicap (Uncool)

COOL JOE
2003: Frank J. De Francis Memorial Dash (A Huevo)

COOL VICTOR
1997: Vosburgh Stakes (Victor Cooley)

CORMORANT
1987: Acorn Stakes (Grecian Flight)
1992: Beldame Stakes (Saratoga Dew)
1993: Remsen Stakes (Go for Gin)
1994: Kentucky Derby (Go for Gin)

CORNISH PRINCE
1970: Alcibiades Stakes (Patelin)
Selima Stakes (Patelin)
1971: Sorority Stakes (Brenda Beauty)
1972: Sorority Stakes (Sparkalark)
Mother Goose Stakes (Wanda)
1975: Del Mar Debutante Stakes (Queen to Be)
Jerome Handicap (Guards Up)

CORONADO'S QUEST
2003: Frizette Stakes (Society Selection)

CORRESPONDENT
1961: Blue Grass Stakes (Sherluck)
Belmont Stakes (Sherluck)
Lawrence Realization Stakes (Sherluck)
Roamer Handicap (Sherluck)

COSMIC BOMB
1952: Selima Stakes (Tritium)
1956: Kentucky Jockey Club Stakes (Federal Hill)
1957: Louisiana Derby (Federal Hill)

COUGAR II
1978: Alcibiades Stakes (Angel Island)
1981: Del Mar Futurity (Gato Del Sol)
Arlington-Washington Lassie Stakes (Milingo)
1982: Kentucky Derby (Gato Del Sol)
Hollywood Invitational Handicap (Exploded)

COULEE MAN
1981: California Derby (Always a Cinch)

COUNT AMBER
1966: Wood Memorial Stakes (Amberoid)
Belmont Stakes (Amberoid)

COUNTERPOINT
1960: Hollywood Gold Cup (Dotted Swiss)
Sunset Handicap (Dotted Swiss)
Man o' War Stakes (Harmonizing)
1965: Lawrence Realization Stakes (Munden Point)
1966: Massachusetts Handicap (Fast Count)
Gallant Fox Handicap (Munden Point)
1967: Manhattan Handicap (Munden Point)
1968: Display Handicap (Fast Count)
1971: Sunset Handicap (Over the Counter)

COUNT FLAME
1960: Champagne Stakes (Roving Minstrel)
1965: Sanford Stakes (Flame Tree)

COUNT FLEET
1948: Frizette Stakes (Our Fleet)
Princess Pat Stakes (Sequence)
1950: Spinaway Stakes (Atalanta)
Matron Stakes (Atalanta)
1951: Acorn Stakes (Kiss Me Kate)
Delaware Oaks (Kiss Me Kate)
Gazelle Stakes (Kiss Me Kate)
Alabama Stakes (Kiss Me Kate)
Belmont Stakes (Counterpoint)
Lawrence Realization Stakes (Counterpoint)
Jockey Club Gold Cup (Counterpoint)
Dixie Handicap (County Delight)
Gallant Fox Handicap (County Delight)
Manhattan Handicap (County Delight)
Kentucky Jockey Club Stakes (Sub Fleet)
Kentucky Derby (Count Turf)
San Juan Capistrano Handicap (Be Fleet)
Gulfstream Park Handicap (Ennobled)
1952: Belmont Stakes (One Count)
Travers Stakes (One Count)
Jockey Club Gold Cup (One Count)
Breeders' Futurity (Straight Face)
Kentucky Jockey Club Stakes (Straight Face)
Whitney Stakes (Counterpoint)
San Fernando Stakes (Counterpoint)
New Castle Handicap (Kiss Me Kate)
Queens County Handicap (County Delight)
1953: Black Helen Handicap (Atalanta)
Beldame Handicap (Atalanta)
Firenze Handicap (Kiss Me Kate)
Flamingo Stakes (Straight Face)
Hawthorne Gold Cup (Sub Fleet)
1954: Dixie Handicap (Straight Face)
Suburban Handicap (Straight Face)
San Juan Capistrano Handicap (By Zeus)
1955: Vanity Handicap (Countess Fleet)
1956: Westerner Stakes (Count of Honor)
1957: Carter Handicap (Portersville)
Brooklyn Handicap (Portersville)
1958: San Felipe Handicap (Carrier X.)
1959: Bougainvillea Turf Handicap (General Arthur)
1961: Donn Handicap (General Arthur)

COUNT OF HONOR
1972: Cinema Handicap (Finalista)

COUNT SPEED
1953: Del Mar Futurity (Double Speed)
1957: Gallant Fox Handicap (Eddie Schmidt)
1958: Inglewood Handicap (Eddie Schmidt)

COUNT TURF
1959: Wood Memorial Stakes (Manassa Mauler)
1960: Trenton Handicap (Manassa Mauler)

COUNTY DELIGHT
1963: Lawrence Realization Stakes (Dean Carl)
Roamer Handicap (Dean Carl)
Display Handicap (Dean Carl)

COURSING
1971: Oak Leaf Stakes (Sporting Lass)
Malibu Stakes (King of Cricket)

COURT MARTIAL
1963: Ladies Handicap (Goofed)
1965: Saratoga Special (Impressive)
1969: Vanity Handicap (Desert Law)

COURT RULING
1981: Vosburgh Stakes (Guilty Conscience)

COVER UP
1953: Del Mar Debutante Stakes (Lady Cover Up)
1957: Canadian Championship Stakes (Spinney)
Santa Anita Maturity (Spinney)

COX'S RIDGE
1983: Oak Leaf Stakes (Life's Magic)
1984: Mother Goose Stakes (Life's Magic)
Alabama Stakes (Life's Magic)
Beldame Stakes (Life's Magic)
1985: Suburban Handicap (Vanlandingham)
Jockey Club Gold Cup (Vanlandingham)
Washington D.C. International (Vanlandingham)
Widener Handicap (Pine Circle)
Breeders' Cup Juvenile Fillies (Twilight Ridge)
Breeders' Cup Distaff (Life's Magic)
1986: Brooklyn Handicap (Little Missouri)
1987: Oak Leaf Stakes (Dream Team)
1988: Futurity Stakes (Trapp Mountain)
1989: Jerome Handicap (De Roche)
1991: Peter Pan Stakes (Lost Mountain)
Dwyer Stakes (Lost Mountain)
Haskell Invitational Handicap (Lost Mountain)
1992: Hollywood Gold Cup (Sultry Song)
Whitney Handicap (Sultry Song)
Woodward Stakes (Sultry Song)
Pegasus Handicap (Scuffleburg)
1993: Breeders' Cup Sprint (Cardmania)
1994: Gulfstream Park Handicap (Scuffleburg)

COZZENE
1993: Caesars International Handicap (Star of Cozzene)
Arlington Million (Star of Cozzene)
Man o' War Stakes (Star of Cozzene)
1994: Turf Classic (Tikkanen)
Breeders' Cup Turf (Tikkanen)
1996: San Antonio Handicap (Alphabet Soup)
Breeders' Cup Classic (Alphabet Soup)
1999: Brooklyn Handicap (Running Stag)
2000: Garden City Breeders' Cup Handicap (Gaviola)
2001: Malibu Stakes (Mizzen Mast)
2002: Strub Stakes (Mizzen Mast)

CRAFTY ADMIRAL

1958: Cowdin Stakes (Crafty Skipper)
1959: Louisiana Derby (Master Palynch)
1960: Michigan Mile and One-Sixteenth (Little Fitz)
1961: Vineland Handicap (Frimanaha)
1962: Louisiana Derby (Admiral's Voyage)
Wood Memorial Stakes (Admiral's Voyage)
1963: Carter Handicap (Admiral's Voyage)
1964: San Carlos Handicap (Admiral's Voyage)

CRAFTY PROSPECTOR

1997: Cigar Mile Handicap (Devious Course)

CRAVAT

1950: Hawthorne Gold Cup (Dr. Ole Nelson)

CRAZY KID

1971: Hollywood Juvenile Championship (Royal Owl)
1973: Charles H. Strub Stakes (Royal Owl)

CREME DELA CREME

1971: Kentucky Oaks (Silent Beauty)
1979: Young America Stakes (Koluctoo Bay)

CRIMINAL TYPE

1995: Dwyer Stakes (Hoolie)

CRIMSON SATAN

1969: Lawrence Realization Stakes (Oil Power)
1974: Delaware Handicap (Krislin)
1976: Fall Highweight Handicap (Relent)

CROWFOOT

1949: Acorn Stakes (Nell K.)
Gazelle Stakes (Nell K.)
1950: Top Flight Handicap (Nell K.)
1959: Florida Derby (Easy Spur)

CROZIER

1973: Futurity Stakes (Wedge Shot)
1978: Futurity Stakes (Crest of the Wave)
1982: San Felipe Handicap (Advance Man)
Swaps Stakes (Journey at Sea)
1984: Swaps Stakes (Precisionist)
1985: San Fernando Stakes (Precisionist)
Charles H. Strub Stakes (Precisionist)
Breeders' Cup Sprint (Precisionist)
1986: Californian Stakes (Precisionist)
Woodward Stakes (Precisionist)

CRYPTOCLEARANCE

1993: Spinaway Stakes (Strategic Maneuver)
Matron Stakes (Strategic Maneuver)
1996: Futurity Stakes (Traitor)
1997: Arkansas Derby (Crypto Star)
1998: Arkansas Derby (Victory Gallop)
Belmont Stakes (Victory Gallop)
1999: Whitney Handicap (Victory Gallop)
2001: Toyota Blue Grass Stakes (Millennium Wind)
2002: Breeders' Cup Classic (Volponi)

CRYSTAL GLITTERS

1992: Arlington Million (Dear Doctor)

CURANDERO

1964: San Luis Rey Handicap (Inclusive)

CURE THE BLUES

1985: Matron Stakes (Musical Lark)
1987: Budweiser International Stakes (Le Glorieux)
1988: Flower Bowl Handicap (Gaily Gaily)
1992: Jersey Derby (American Chance)
1998: Ballerina Handicap (Stop Traffic)
1999: Santa Monica Handicap (Stop Traffic)

CUTLASS

1979: Sorority Stakes (Love Street)
1988: Californian Stakes (Cutlass Reality)
Hollywood Gold Cup (Cutlass Reality)

CYANE

1969: Delaware Handicap (Obeah)
1970: Futurity Stakes (Salem)
Delaware Handicap (Obeah)
1973: Hempstead Handicap (Light Hearted)
Maskette Handicap (Light Hearted)
1978: Carter Handicap (Pumpkin Moonshine)
1979: Illinois Derby (Smarten)
Pennsylvania Derby (Smarten)
Ohio Derby (Smarten)
American Derby (Smarten)

CYRANO DE BERGERAC

1995: Man o' War Stakes (Millkom)

CYRUS THE GREAT

1962: Hialeah Turf Cup (El Loco)

CZARAVICH

1993: Gotham Stakes (As Indicated)
1994: Pimlico Special (As Indicated)

D'ACCORD

1994: Futurity Stakes (Montreal Red)

DAHAR

1993: San Felipe Stakes (Corby)
Budweiser International Stakes (Buckhar)

DAMASCUS

1973: Arlington-Washington Futurity (Lover John)
1974: Florida Derby (Judger)
Blue Grass Stakes (Judger)
Del Mar Futurity (Diabolo)
Withers Stakes (Accipiter)
1975: Gulfstream Park Handicap (Gold and Myrrh)
Grey Lag Handicap (Gold and Myrrh)
Metropolitan Handicap (Gold and Myrrh)
Futurity Stakes (Soy Numero Uno)
California Derby (Diabolo)
Withers Stakes (Sarsar)
Fall Highweight Handicap (Honorable Miss)
1976: Fall Highweight Handicap (Honorable Miss)
1977: Carter Handicap (Soy Numero Uno)
Oaklawn Handicap (Soy Numero Uno)
Hempstead Handicap (Pacific Princess)
Dwyer Handicap (Bailjumper)
1980: Widener Handicap (Private Account)
Gulfstream Park Handicap (Private Account)
1983: Brooklyn Handicap (Highland Blade)
Marlboro Cup Handicap (Highland Blade)
Pan American Handicap (Highland Blade)
San Felipe Handicap (Desert Wine)
1984: Charles H. Strub Stakes (Desert Wine)
Californian Stakes (Desert Wine)
Hollywood Gold Cup (Desert Wine)
Everglades Stakes (Time for a Change)
Flamingo Stakes (Time for a Change)
1985: Futurity Stakes (Ogygian)
1986: Dwyer Stakes (Ogygian)
Jerome Handicap (Ogygian)
1987: Hopeful Stakes (Crusader Sword)
1990: Futurity Stakes (Eastern Echo)

DANCER'S IMAGE

1974: New Orleans Handicap (Smooth Dancer)

DANCE SPELL

1982: Alabama Stakes (Broom Dance)
1983: Secretariat Stakes (Fortnightly)

DANCING CZAR

1991: Beldame Stakes (Sharp Dance)

DANCING DERVISH

1973: Oaklawn Handicap (Prince Astro)

DANEHILL

2001: Breeders' Cup Filly and Mare Turf (Banks Hill)
2002: Shadwell Keeneland Turf Mile (Landseer)
Matriarch Stakes (Dress To Thrill)

DANZATORE

1998: Breeders' Cup Sprint (Reraise)

DANZIG

1984: Hopeful Stakes (Chief's Crown)
Norfolk Stakes (Chief's Crown)
Breeders' Cup Juvenile (Chief's Crown)
Arlington-Washington Lassie Stakes (Contredance)
Hollywood Futurity (Stephan's Odyssey)
1985: Flamingo Stakes (Chief's Crown)
Blue Grass Stakes (Chief's Crown)
Travers Stakes (Chief's Crown)
Marlboro Cup Handicap (Chief's Crown)
Dwyer Stakes (Stephan's Odyssey)
Jim Dandy Stakes (Stephan's Odyssey)
1986: Peter Pan Stakes (Danzig Connection)
Belmont Stakes (Danzig Connection)
Cowdin Stakes (Polish Navy)
Champagne Stakes (Polish Navy)
Acorn Stakes (Lotka)
Del Mar Futurity (Qualify)
1987: Jim Dandy Stakes (Polish Navy)
Woodward Stakes (Polish Navy)
1988: Oak Leaf Stakes (One of a Klein)
1989: Cowdin Stakes (Adjudicating)
Champagne Stakes (Adjudicating)
Dwyer Stakes (Roi Danzig)
1991: Alabama Stakes (Versailles Treaty)
Breeders' Cup Distaff (Dance Smartly)
Remsen Stakes (Pine Bluff)
1992: Gotham Stakes (Lure)
Breeders' Cup Mile (Lure)
Arkansas Derby (Pine Bluff)
Preakness Stakes (Pine Bluff)
Go for Wand Stakes (Easy Now)
Jerome Handicap (Furiously)
Ruffian Handicap (Versailles Treaty)
Futurity Stakes (Strolling Along)
1993: Kentucky Oaks (Dispute)
Gazelle Handicap (Dispute)
Beldame Stakes (Dispute)
Breeders' Cup Mile (Lure)
1994: Spinster Stakes (Dispute)
Caesars International Handicap (Lure)
1996: Vosburgh Stakes (Langfuhr)
1997: Carter Handicap (Langfuhr)
Metropolitan Handicap (Langfuhr)
Flower Bowl Invitational Handicap (Yashmak)
1998: Oak Tree Turf Championship (Military)
2000: Breeders' Cup Mile (War Chant)
Early Times Hollywood Derby (Brahms)

DARBY CREEK ROAD

1989: Del Mar Futurity (Drag Race)

DARK HAWK

1965: San Juan Capistrano Handicap (George Royal)
Canadian Championship Stakes (George Royal)
1966: San Juan Capistrano Handicap (George Royal)
Canadian International Championship (George Royal)

DARK STAR

1959: Princess Pat Stakes (Heavenly Body)
Matron Stakes (Heavenly Body)
Kentucky Oaks (Hidden Talent)
1964: Suburban Handicap (Iron Peg)
1970: Flamingo Stakes (My Dad George)
Florida Derby (My Dad George)

DARN THAT ALARM

1992: Mother Goose Stakes (Turnback the Alarm)
Coaching Club American Oaks (Turnback the Alarm)
Flamingo Stakes (Pistols and Roses)
Blue Grass Stakes (Pistols and Roses)
1993: Shuvee Handicap (Turnback the Alarm)
Hempstead Handicap (Turnback the Alarm)
Go for Wand Stakes (Turnback the Alarm)
Donn Handicap (Pistols and Roses)
1994: Donn Handicap (Pistols and Roses)

DARSHAAN

1993: San Luis Rey Stakes (Kotashaan)
San Juan Capistrano Handicap (Kotashaan)
Eddie Read Handicap (Kotashaan)
Oak Tree Invitational Stakes (Kotashaan)
Breeders' Cup Turf (Kotashaan)

DAUMIER

1963: Black Helen Handicap (Pocosaba)

DECATHLON

1962: Del Mar Futurity (Slipped Disc)
1964: United Nations Handicap (Western Warrior)

DECIDEDLY

1971: Jerome Handicap (Tinajero)
1973: John B. Campbell Handicap (Delay)

DECORATED

1961: Ladies Handicap (Mighty Fair)

DEDICATE

1962: Arlington Lassie Stakes (Smart Deb)
Matron Stakes (Smart Deb)
1963: Arlington Matron Handicap (Smart Deb)
1966: Monmouth Oaks (Natashka)
Alabama Stakes (Natashka)

DEERHOUND

1997: Spinaway Stakes (Countess Diana)
Breeders' Cup Juvenile Fillies (Countess Diana)

DEGAGE

1964: Breeders' Futurity (Umbrella Fella)
Kentucky Jockey Club Stakes (Umbrella Fella)

DEGENERATE JON
1991: Apple Blossom Handicap (Degenerate Gal)

DEHERE
2000: Arkansas Derby (Graeme Hall)
Jim Dandy Stakes (Graeme Hall)
2001: Walmac Int. Alcibiades Stakes (Take Charge Lady)
2002: Ashland Stakes (Take Charge Lady)
Overbrook Spinster Stakes (Take Charge Lady)
2003: Overbrook Spinster Stakes (Take Charge Lady)

DELIBERATOR
1946: San Vicente Handicap (Air Rate)

DELINEATOR
2001: Oak Leaf Stakes (Tali'sluckybusride)

DELTA JUDGE
1970: Dwyer Handicap (Judgable)
Whitney Stakes (Judgable)
Gardenia Stakes (Eggy)
1971: Donn Handicap (Judgable)
Grey Lag Handicap (Judgable)
Beldame Stakes (Double Delta)
1973: Vosburgh Handicap (Aljamin)
1975: Hopeful Stakes (Eustace)
Alabama Stakes (Spout)
1976: Top Flight Handicap (Proud Delta)
Hempstead Handicap (Proud Delta)
Beldame Stakes (Proud Delta)

DELTA OIL
1984: Illinois Derby (Delta Trace)

DEPUTY COMMANDER
2003: Travers Stakes (Ten Most Wanted)
Super Derby (Ten Most Wanted)

DEPUTY MINISTER
1988: Breeders' Cup Juvenile Fillies (Open Mind)
Demoiselle Stakes (Open Mind)
1989: Kentucky Oaks (Open Mind)
Acorn Stakes (Open Mind)
Mother Goose Stakes (Open Mind)
Coaching Club American Oaks (Open Mind)
Alabama Stakes (Open Mind)
Breeders' Cup Juvenile Fillies (Go for Wand)
1990: Ashland Stakes (Go for Wand)
Mother Goose Stakes (Go for Wand)
Alabama Stakes (Go for Wand)
Maskette Stakes (Go for Wand)
Beldame Stakes (Go for Wand)
1991: Hopeful Stakes (Salt Lake)
1993: Hopeful Stakes (Dehere)
Champagne Stakes (Dehere)
1995: Jerome Handicap (French Deputy)
1996: Santa Anita Handicap (Mr. Purple)
Shuvee Handicap (Clear Mandate)
Swaps Stakes (Victory Speech)
1997: Belmont Stakes (Touch Gold)
Buick Haskell Invitational Handicap (Touch Gold)
John A. Morris Handicap (Clear Mandate)
Three Chimneys Spinster Stakes (Clear Mandate)
Travers Stakes (Deputy Commander)
Super Derby (Deputy Commander)
Strub Stakes (Victory Speech)
Early Times Turf Classic (Always a Classic)
Test Stakes (Fabulously Fast)
Jim Dandy Stakes (Awesome Again)
1998: Las Virgenes Stakes (Keeper Hill)
Kentucky Oaks (Keeper Hill)
Whitney Handicap (Awesome Again)
Breeders' Cup Classic (Awesome Again)
Ashland Stakes (Well Chosen)
1999: Del Mar Futurity (Forest Camp)
Three Chimneys Spinster Stakes (Keeper Hill)

DESERT WINE
1990: Peter Pan Stakes (Profit Key)
Dwyer Stakes (Profit Key)

DETERMINE
1959: Cowdin Stakes (Warfare)
Champagne Stakes (Warfare)
Garden State Stakes (Warfare)
1961: Champagne Stakes (Donut King)
1962: Kentucky Derby (Decidedly)
1963: Monmouth Handicap (Decidedly)
1971: San Luis Rey Handicap (Try Sheep)

DETERMINED MAN
1974: American Derby (Determined King)

DEVIL DIVER
1950: Grey Lag Handicap (Lotowhite)
1951: Monmouth Oaks (Ruddy)
Excelsior Handicap (Lotowhite)
Trenton Handicap (Call Over)
1952: Comely Handicap (Devilkin)
1954: Aqueduct Handicap (Crash Dive)
1956: Tropical Handicap (Illusionist)
1959: Display Handicap (Beau Diable)

DEVIL HIS DUE
2000: Walmac Int. Alcibiades Stakes (She's a Devil Due)

DEVIL'S BAG
1991: Meadowlands Cup (Twilight Agenda)
1992: Gotham Stakes (Devil His Due)
Wood Memorial Stakes (Devil His Due)
1993: Gulfstream Park Handicap (Devil His Due)
Pimlico Special (Devil His Due)
Suburban Handicap (Devil His Due)
1994: Brooklyn Handicap (Devil His Due)
Suburban Handicap (Devil His Due)
2003: Gazelle Handicap (Buy the Sport)

DEWAN
1978: Vanity Handicap (Afifa)
1982: New Orleans Handicap (It's the One)
San Fernando Stakes (It's the One)
Charles H. Strub Stakes (It's the One)

DEWAN KEYS
1987: Philip H. Iselin Handicap (Bordeaux Bob)

DIABLO
2001: Metropolitan Handicap (Exciting Story)

DICTUS
1983: Arlington Handicap (Palikaraki)
Oak Tree Invitational Stakes (Zalataia)

DIESIS
1989: Demoiselle Stakes (Rootentootenwooten)
1993: Rothmans International Stakes (Husband)
1998: Hollywood Turf Handicap (Storm Trooper)
2003: Hollywood Turf Cup (Continuously)

DIMAGGIO
1982: Hollywood Turf Cup (Prince Spellbound)
1983: Eddie Read Handicap (Prince Spellbound)

DIN'S DANCER
2000: Eddie Read Handicap (Ladies Din)
2002: Shoemaker Breeders' Cup Mile (Ladies Din)

DIPLOMAT WAY
1975: Illinois Derby (Colonel Power)

DISCOVERY
1946: Santa Anita Derby (Knockdown)
1948: Vagrancy Handicap (Conniver)
Beldame Handicap (Conniver)
Comely Handicap (Conniver)
Brooklyn Handicap (Conniver)
Excelsior Handicap (Knockdown)
Queens County Handicap (Knockdown)
1949: Vosburgh Handicap (Loser Weeper)
Metropolitan Handicap (Loser Weeper)
1950: Dixie Handicap (Loser Weeper)
Suburban Handicap (Loser Weeper)
1953: Ohio Derby (Find)
Grey Lag Handicap (Find)
Excelsior Handicap (First Glance)
1954: Excelsior Handicap (Find)
Queens County Handicap (Find)
1956: New Orleans Handicap (Find)
1957: Inglewood Handicap (Find)
American Handicap (Find)
Sunset Handicap (Find)

DISTANT VIEW
2003: Humana Distaff Handicap (Sightseek)
Ogden Phipps Handicap (Sightseek)
Go for Wand Handicap (Sightseek)
Beldame Stakes (Sightseek)

DISTINCTIVE
1978: Ohio Derby (Special Honor)
1981: Alabama Stakes (Prismatical)
1983: Mother Goose Stakes (Able Money)

DISTINCTIVE PRO
1989: Tropical Park Derby (Big Stanley)
1990: Ruffian Handicap (Quick Mischief)

DISTORTED HUMOR
2002: Spinaway Stakes (Awesome Humor)
2003: Kentucky Derby (Funny Cide)
Preakness Stakes (Funny Cide)

DIXIELAND BAND
1989: Fountain of Youth Stakes (Dixieland Brass)
1992: Metropolitan Handicap (Dixie Brass)
1993: Swaps Stakes (Devoted Brass)
1999: Norfolk Stakes (Dixie Union)
2000: Haskell Invitational Handicap (Dixie Union)
Malibu Stakes (Dixie Union)

DIXIELAND BRASS
1994: Pegasus Handicap (Brass Scale)

DIXIELAND HEAT
2001: Prioress Stakes (Xtra Heat)

DJAKAO
1980: Arlington Handicap (Yvonand)
Louisiana Downs Handicap (Yvonand)
1982: Hollywood Gold Cup (Perrault)
Budweiser Million (Perrault)
San Luis Rey Stakes (Perrault)

DJEDDAH
1955: Kentucky Oaks (Lalun)
Beldame Handicap (Lalun)

DOC SYLVESTER
1984: Champagne Stakes (For Certain Doc)

DOGPATCH
1950: Del Mar Futurity (Patch)
1951: Cinema Handicap (Mucho Hosso)

DOMINGO
1948: Cinema Handicap (Drumbeat)
Sunset Handicap (Drumbeat)
1967: Californian Stakes (Biggs)
1968: San Luis Rey Handicap (Biggs)

DONATELLO II
1959: Canadian Championship Stakes (Martini II)

DON B.
1977: Oak Leaf Stakes (B. Thoughtful)
1978: Hollywood Oaks (B. Thoughtful)
1979: La Canada Stakes (B. Thoughtful)

DONUT KING
1970: San Felipe Handicap (Cool Hand)

DOSWELL
1957: Coaching Club American Oaks (Willamette)

DOTTED SWISS
1966: Matron Stakes (Swiss Cheese)

DOUBLE JAY
1955: Matron Stakes (Doubledogdare)
Alcibiades Stakes (Doubledogdare)
Gazelle Stakes (Manotick)
Ladies Handicap (Manotick)
1956: Princess Pat Stakes (Splendored)
Spinster Stakes (Doubledogdare)
1957: Molly Pitcher Handicap (Manotick)
Top Flight Handicap (Plotter)
1959: Spinaway Stakes (Irish Jay)
Hollywood Derby (Bagdad)
1960: San Antonio Handicap (Bagdad)
Inglewood Handicap (Bagdad)
Acorn Stakes (Irish Jay)
San Carlos Handicap (Clandestine)
1961: Arlington Matron Handicap (Shirley Jones)
1962: Gulfstream Park Handicap (Jay Fox)
Donn Handicap (Jay Fox)
1963: Futurity Stakes (Bupers)
Gallant Fox Handicap (Sunrise Flight)
1965: Pimlico Futurity (Spring Double)
Monmouth Handicap (Repeating)
Gallant Fox Handicap (Choker)
1966: New Orleans Handicap (Just About)
1968: Spinaway Stakes (Queen's Double)
1969: California Derby (Jay Ray)
1970: Molly Pitcher Handicap (Double Ripple)
1972: Arlington-Washington Lassie St. (Double Your Fun)

DOYOUN
1998: Man o' War Stakes (Daylami)
1999: Breeders' Cup Turf (Daylami)

DOYOUN *(Continued)*
2000: Woodford Reserve Turf Classic (Manndar)
Manhattan Handicap (Manndar)
Breeders' Cup Turf (Kalanisi)

DRAFT CARD
1979: San Felipe Handicap (Pole Position)

DRAWBY
1953: New Orleans Handicap (Smoke Screen)

DR. CARTER
1992: Molson Export Million (Benburb)

DREAMING NATIVE
1981: Whitney Handicap (Fio Rito)

DR. FAGER
1974: Top Flight Handicap (Lady Love)
Hollywood Gold Cup (Tree of Knowledge)
1975: Sorority Stakes (Dearly Precious)
Spinaway Stakes (Dearly Precious)
Arlington-Washington Lassie Stakes (Dearly Precious)
1976: Acorn Stakes (Dearly Precious)
1977: Alcibiades Stakes (L'Alezane)
1978: Vosburgh Handicap (Dr. Patches)
Meadowlands Cup (Dr. Patches)

DRONE
1974: Wood Memorial Stakes (Flip Sal)
1976: Withers Stakes (Sonkisser)
1977: Ashland Stakes (Sound of Summer)
1981: Arlington-Washington Futurity (Lets Dont Fight)
1982: Alcibiades Stakes (Jelly Bean Holiday)
Santa Anita Derby (Muttering)

DUMPTY HUMPTY
1966: Arlington-Washington Lassie Stakes (Mira Femme)
1969: Santa Susana Stakes (Dumptys Lady)

DUST COMMANDER
1975: Louisiana Derby (Master Derby)
Blue Grass Stakes (Master Derby)
Preakness Stakes (Master Derby)
1976: Breeders' Futurity (Run Dusty Run)
Arlington-Washington Futurity (Run Dusty Run)
New Orleans Handicap (Master Derby)
Oaklawn Handicap (Master Derby)

DYNAFORMER
1998: Early Times Hollywood Derby (Vergennes)
2000: Gazelle Handicap (Critical Eye)
Queen Elizabeth II Challenge Cup (Collect the Cash)
2001: Hempstead Handicap (Critical Eye)
2002: Queen Elizabeth II Challenge Cup (Riskaverse)
2003: Santa Maria Handicap (Starrer)
Santa Margarita Handicap (Starrer)
Stephen Foster Handicap (Perfect Drift)
Queen Elizabeth II Challenge Cup (Film Maker)

EAGLE EYED
2001: Carter Handicap (Peeping Tom)

EASTERN ECHO
1996: Hollywood Futurity (Swiss Yodeler)
2003: Santa Anita Derby (Buddy Gil)

EASTON
1946: Pimlico Oaks (Red Shoes)
1952: Alabama Stakes (Lily White)

EASY GOER
1995: Breeders' Cup Juvenile Fillies (My Flag)
Jim Dandy Stakes (Composer)
1996: Ashland Stakes (My Flag)
Coaching Club American Oaks (My Flag)
Gazelle Handicap (My Flag)
Travers Stakes (Will's Way)
1997: Whitney Handicap (Will's Way)
1999: Ballerina Handicap (Furlough)

EASY MON
1951: Garden State Stakes (Candle Wood)
1952: Louisiana Derby (Gushing Oil)
Blue Grass Stakes (Gushing Oil)
Arlington Futurity (Mr. Good)
Stars and Stripes Handicap (Royal Mustang)

ECLIPTICAL
1994: Ohio Derby (Exclusive Praline)

EFFERVESCING
1985: Hialeah Turf Cup (Selous Scout)

EGG TOSS
1993: Vanity Handicap (Re Toss)

EIFFEL TOWER
1954: Santa Anita Maturity (Apple Valley)
1964: Hollywood Juvenile Championship (Charger's Kin)

EIGHT THIRTY
1947: Sapling Stakes (Task)
Frizette Stakes (Slumber Song)
1948: Acorn Stakes (Watermill)
1949: Remsen Handicap (Lights Up)
Spinaway Stakes (Sunday Evening)
Princess Pat Stakes (Here's Hoping)
Del Mar Derby (Bolero)
San Antonio Handicap (Dinner Gong)
Massachusetts Handicap (First Nighter)
1950: Breeders' Futurity (Big Stretch)
Pimlico Futurity (Big Stretch)
Astoria Stakes (Sungari)
Travers Stakes (Lights Up)
1951: Astarita Stakes (Place Card)
Black-Eyed Susan Stakes (Discreet)
Black Helen Handicap (Antagonism)
San Carlos Handicap (Bolero)
1952: Golden Gate Handicap (Lights Up)
1953: Sunset Handicap (Lights Up)
1954: Sapling Stakes (Royal Coinage)
1955: Roamer Handicap (Sailor)
Fall Highweight Handicap (Sailor)
Pimlico Special (Sailor)
1956: Gulfstream Park Handicap (Sailor)
John B. Campbell Memorial Handicap (Sailor)
Wood Memorial Stakes (Head Man)

ELA-MANA-MOU
1992: Rothmans International Stakes (Snurge)

EL DRAG
1962: San Felipe Handicap (Doc Jocoy)
California Derby (Doc Jocoy)
1963: California Derby (On My Honor)
Los Angeles Handicap (Doc Jocoy)

ELEVATION
1976: La Canada Stakes (Raise Your Skirts)

EL GRAN SENOR
1992: Super Derby (Senor Tomas)
1993: Gamely Handicap (Toussaud)
1996: Strub Stakes (Helmsman)
Breeders' Cup Sprint (Lit de Justice)
1999: Yellow Ribbon Stakes (Spanish Fern)

ELMAAMUL
2003: Hollywood Derby (Sweet Return)

ELOCUTIONIST
1987: Arkansas Derby (Demons Begone)

EL PRADO
2002: Jim Dandy Stakes (Medaglia d'Oro)
Travers Stakes (Medaglia d'Oro)
2003: Strub Stakes (Medaglia d'Oro)
Oaklawn Handicap (Medaglia d'Oro)
Whitney Handicap (Medaglia d'Oro)

EMPEROR JONES
2001: Ramona Handicap (Janet)
Yellow Ribbon Stakes (Janet)

ENCINO
1992: American Derby (The Name's Jimmy)

ENDEAVOR II
1953: Futurity Stakes (Porterhouse)
1956: Californian Stakes (Porterhouse)
1957: Santa Anita Handicap (Corn Husker)
San Juan Capistrano Handicap (Corn Husker)
Los Angeles Handicap (Porterhouse)
1958: Acorn Stakes (Big Effort)
Delaware Oaks (Big Effort)
1959: Top Flight Handicap (Big Effort)
1961: Santa Anita Handicap (Prove It)
San Fernando Stakes (Prove It)
Santa Anita Maturity (Prove It)
1962: Inglewood Handicap (Prove It)
American Handicap (Prove It)
Hollywood Gold Cup (Prove It)
Sunset Handicap (Prove It)
Washington Park Handicap (Prove It)
1967: Santa Anita Handicap (Pretense)
Gulfstream Park Handicap (Pretense)
San Antonio Handicap (Pretense)

END SWEEP
2000: Vosburgh Stakes (Trippi)
2001: Santa Monica Handicap (Nany's Sweep)
Ancient Title BC Handicap (Swept Overboard)
2002: Metropolitan Handicap (Swept Overboard)

ENGRILLADO
1997: Malibu Stakes (Lord Grillo)

ENVOY
1969: Del Mar Futurity (George Lewis)
1970: California Derby (George Lewis)
1973: Hollywood Juvenile Championship (Century's Envoy)
1974: Del Mar Debutante Stakes (Bubblewin)
1976: San Fernando Stakes (Messenger of Song)

EQUESTRIAN
1946: Grey Lag Handicap (Stymie)
Whitney Stakes (Stymie)
Manhattan Handicap (Stymie)
New York Handicap (Stymie)
Gallant Fox Handicap (Stymie)
1947: Metropolitan Handicap (Stymie)
Massachusetts Handicap (Stymie)
Aqueduct Handicap (Stymie)
Gallant Fox Handicap (Stymie)
1948: Metropolitan Handicap (Stymie)
Aqueduct Handicap (Stymie)

EQUIFOX
1949: Tremont Stakes (Fox Time)
1955: Michigan Mile (Greatest)

ERINS ISLE
1990: Flower Bowl Handicap (Laugh and Be Merry)

ERRARD
1952: Sapling Stakes (Laffango)
Champagne Stakes (Laffango)
Garden State Stakes (Laffango)
Washington Park Futurity (Mr. Paradise)
1953: Pimlico Futurity (Errard King)
Gotham Stakes (Laffango)
1954: Arlington Classic (Errard King)
American Derby (Errard King)

ESPADIN
1953: Washington D.C. International (Iceberg II)

ETERNAL BIM
1967: Arlington-Washington Lassie Stakes (Shenow)

ETERNAL BULL
1948: Remsen Stakes (Eternal World)
Astoria Stakes (Eternal Flag)
1951: Cowdin Stakes (Eternal Moon)

ETERNAL PRINCE
1997: Turf Classic (Val's Prince)
1999: Man o' War Stakes (Val's Prince)
Turf Classic (Val's Prince)

ETERNAL REWARD
1957: Kentucky Oaks (Lori-El)

ETONIAN
1970: New Orleans Handicap (Etony)

EUDAEMON
1963: New Orleans Handicap (Endymion)

EXCLUSIVE NATIVE
1973: Flamingo Stakes (Our Native)
Ohio Derby (Our Native)
Monmouth Invitational Handicap (Our Native)
1976: Illinois Derby (Life's Hope)
Jersey Derby (Life's Hope)
Bowling Green Handicap (Erwin Boy)
1977: Hollywood Juvenile Championship (Affirmed)
Hopeful Stakes (Affirmed)
Futurity Stakes (Affirmed)
Laurel Futurity (Affirmed)
1978: San Felipe Handicap (Affirmed)
Santa Anita Derby (Affirmed)
Hollywood Derby (Affirmed)
Kentucky Derby (Affirmed)
Preakness Stakes (Affirmed)
Belmont Stakes (Affirmed)
New Orleans Handicap (Life's Hope)

Amory L. Haskell Handicap (Life's Hope)
1979: Californian Stakes (Affirmed)
Hollywood Gold Cup (Affirmed)
Woodward Stakes (Affirmed)
Jockey Club Gold Cup (Affirmed)
Charles H. Strub Stakes (Affirmed)
Santa Anita Handicap (Affirmed)
Gamely Handicap (Sisterhood)
Swaps Stakes (Valdez)
1980: Ruffian Handicap (Genuine Risk)
Kentucky Derby (Genuine Risk)
Santa Barbara Handicap (Sisterhood)
1983: California Derby (Paris Prince)
1984: Breeders' Cup Juvenile Fillies (Outstandingly)
Fantasy Stakes (My Darling One)
1986: San Antonio Handicap (Hatim)
1988: Sunset Handicap (Roi Normand)
Arlington Million (Mill Native)
1989: Californian Stakes (Sabona)

EXECUTIONER
1979: Arlington-Washington Futurity (Execution's Reason)

EXPLODENT
1979: Ramona Handicap (Country Queen)
Yellow Ribbon Stakes (Country Queen)
1989: Meadowlands Cup (Mi Selecto)
1990: Gulfstream Park Handicap (Mi Selecto)
1991: Hollywood Turf Handicap (Exbourne)
Caesars International Handicap (Exbourne)
1993: American Derby (Explosive Red)
Hollywood Derby (Explosive Red)
Santa Barbara Handicap (Exchange)
1994: Matriarch Stakes (Exchange)
1997: Eddie Read Handicap (Expelled)

EXPLOSIVE BID
1989: Budweiser International Stakes (Caltech)

FAIR RULER
1960: Saratoga Special (Bronzerullah)
1963: Dixie Handicap (Cedar Key)
1964: San Juan Capistrano Handicap (Cedar Key)
Donn Handicap (Cedar Key)
1965: San Luis Rey Handicap (Cedar Key)
1966: San Luis Rey Handicap (Cedar Key)
1969: San Felipe Handicap (Elect the Ruler)
1970: Mother Goose Stakes (Office Queen)

FAIR TRUCKLE
1954: Del Mar Debutante Stakes (Fair Molly)

FAIRY MANHURST
1948: Selima Stakes (Gaffery)
1949: Santa Susana Stakes (Gaffery)
Ladies Handicap (Gaffery)
1952: Matron Stakes (Is Proud)

FALIRAKI
1983: Norfolk Stakes (Fali Time)
Hollywood Futurity (Fali Time)
1984: San Felipe Handicap (Fali Time)

FAMILY CREST
1990: Oak Tree Invitational Stakes (Rial)

FAPPIANO
1985: Breeders' Futurity (Tasso)
Breeders' Cup Juvenile (Tasso)
1986: Matron Stakes (Tappiano)
1987: Everglades Stakes (Cryptoclearance)
Florida Derby (Cryptoclearance)
1988: Matron Stakes (Some Romance)
Frizette Stakes (Some Romance)
Acorn Stakes (Aptostar)
1989: Norfolk Stakes (Grand Canyon)
Hollywood Futurity (Grand Canyon)
Widener Handicap (Cryptoclearance)
1990: Florida Derby (Unbridled)
Kentucky Derby (Unbridled)
Breeders' Cup Classic (Unbridled)
Man o' War Stakes (Defensive Play)
NYRA Mile Handicap (Quiet American)
1991: Charles H. Strub Stakes (Defensive Play)
Wood Memorial Stakes (Cahill Road)
NYRA Mile Handicap (Rubiano)
1992: Carter Handicap (Rubiano)
Vosburgh Stakes (Rubiano)

FARAWAY SON
1978: Man o' War Stakes (Waya)
Turf Classic (Waya)
1979: Top Flight Handicap (Waya)
Beldame Stakes (Waya)
Santa Barbara Handicap (Waya)
1983: Sorority Stakes (Officer's Ball)

FAREWELL PARTY
1977: San Felipe Handicap (Smasher)

FAR NORTH
1994: San Antonio Handicap (The Wicked North)
Oaklawn Handicap (The Wicked North)
Californian Stakes (The Wicked North)

FAR OUT EAST
1993: Flower Bowl Handicap (Far Out Beast)

FAST FOX
1961: Bougainvillea Turf Handicap (Wolfram)
Hialeah Turf Cup (Wolfram)

FAST HILARIOUS
1977: Apple Blossom Handicap (Hail Hilarious)

FAULTLESS
1954: Westerner Stakes (Fault Free)
1955: Gotham Stakes (Go Lightly)

FERDINAND
1993: Florida Derby (Bull Inthe Heather)

FIDDLE ISLE
1979: Del Mar Handicap (Ardiente)

FIGHTING FOX
1946: Delaware Oaks (Bonnie Beryl)
Comely Handicap (Bonnie Beryl)
Excelsior Handicap (Fighting Step)
Longacres Mile (Amble In)
1948: Longacres Mile (Amble In)
1952: Gulfstream Park Handicap (Crafty Admiral)
Brooklyn Handicap (Crafty Admiral)
Washington Park Handicap (Crafty Admiral)
Delaware Oaks (Big Mo)
1953: McLennan Handicap (Crafty Admiral)
Gulfstream Park Handicap (Crafty Admiral)
New York Handicap (Crafty Admiral)

FIRE DANCER
1989: Withers Stakes (Fire Maker)

FIRESTREAK
1975: Man o' War Stakes (Snow Knight)
Canadian International Championship (Snow Knight)

FIRETHORN
1949: Dixie Handicap (Chains)

FIRST BALCONY
1970: Santa Barbara Handicap (Sallarina)
1971: Norfolk Stakes (MacArthur Park)
Del Mar Futurity (MacArthur Park)

FIRST FIDDLE
1952: Wood Memorial Stakes (Master Fiddle)

FIRST LANDING
1966: Gulfstream Park Handicap (First Family)
1968: Monmouth Invitational Handicap (Balustrade)
1970: Amory L. Haskell Handicap (Gladwin)
Hawthorne Gold Cup (Gladwin)
1971: Futurity Stakes (Riva Ridge)
Champagne Stakes (Riva Ridge)
Pimlico-Laurel Futurity (Riva Ridge)
Garden State Stakes (Riva Ridge)
1972: Blue Grass Stakes (Riva Ridge)
Kentucky Derby (Riva Ridge)
Belmont Stakes (Riva Ridge)
Hollywood Derby (Riva Ridge)
1973: Massachusetts Handicap (Riva Ridge)
Brooklyn Handicap (Riva Ridge)
1976: Maskette Handicap (Artfully)

FIT TO FIGHT
1991: La Canada Stakes (Fit to Scout)
1995: Suburban Handicap (Key Contender)

FLASH O' NIGHT
1962: Hollywood Juvenile Championship (Y Flash)
1963: Cinema Handicap (Y Flash)
Hollywood Derby (Y Flash)

FLEET ALLIED
1976: Hollywood Juvenile Championship (Fleet Dragoon)

FLEET HOST
1973: San Juan Capistrano Handicap (Queen's Hustler)

FLEET NASRULLAH
1965: Del Mar Futurity (Coursing)
Del Mar Debutante Stakes (Century)
1966: Santa Susana Stakes (Spearfish)
Hollywood Oaks (Spearfish)
1967: Del Mar Debutante Stakes (Fast Dish)
1968: Hollywood Juvenile Championship (Fleet Kirsch)
Del Mar Futurity (Fleet Allied)
1971: Florida Derby (Eastern Fleet)
1972: Vanity Handicap (Convenience)
1973: Del Mar Debutante Stakes (Fleet Peach)
Vanity Handicap (Convenience)
1974: Santa Maria Handicap (Convenience)
1975: San Felipe Handicap (Fleet Velvet)

FLIP SAL
1985: Top Flight Handicap (Flip's Pleasure)

FLORIN
1970: Massachusetts Handicap (Semillant)

FLUSHING II
1954: Arlington Matron Handicap (Lavender Hill)
Ladies Handicap (Lavender Hill)
1958: Remsen Stakes (Atoll)
1959: Gotham Stakes (Atoll)

FLYING FURY
1960: Kentucky Jockey Club Stakes (Crimson Fury)

FLYING PASTER
1988: Santa Margarita Handicap (Flying Julia)
1989: California Derby (Endow)
1990: San Fernando Stakes (Flying Continental)
Charles H. Strub Stakes (Flying Continental)
Jockey Club Gold Cup (Flying Continental)
1995: Acorn Stakes (Cat's Cradle)

FLY SO FREE
1999: Lane's End Breeders' Futurity (Captain Steve)
Hollywood Futurity (Captain Steve)
2000: Swaps Stakes (Captain Steve)
Lane's End Breeders' Futurity (Arabian Light)
2001: Donn Handicap (Captain Steve)

FOOLISH PLEASURE
1980: Matron Stakes (Prayers'n Promises)
1983: Santa Anita Derby (Marfa)
Jim Beam Spiral Stakes (Marfa)
1991: Oak Tree Invitational Stakes (Filago)
1995: Sword Dancer Invitational Handicap (Kiri's Clown)

FOOLS HOLME
1994: Hollywood Turf Cup (Frenchpark)

FORCETEN
1984: Apple Blossom Handicap (Heatherten)
Ladies Handicap (Heatherten)
Ruffian Handicap (Heatherten)

FOREST WILDCAT
2001: Acorn Stakes (Forest Secrets)
2002: Frank J. De Francis Memorial Dash (D'Wildcat)

FORLI
1974: Donn Handicap (Forego)
Gulfstream Park Handicap (Forego)
Widener Handicap (Forego)
Carter Handicap (Forego)
Brooklyn Handicap (Forego)
Woodward Handicap (Forego)
Vosburgh Handicap (Forego)
Jockey Club Gold Cup (Forego)
1975: Widener Handicap (Forego)
Carter Handicap (Forego)
Brooklyn Handicap (Forego)
Suburban Handicap (Forego)
Woodward Stakes (Forego)
Hollywood Derby (Intrepid Hero)
Secretariat Stakes (Intrepid Hero)
Swaps Stakes (Forceten)
1976: Metropolitan Handicap (Forego)
Brooklyn Handicap (Forego)
Woodward Handicap (Forego)
Marlboro Cup Handicap (Forego)
United Nations Handicap (Intrepid Hero)
1977: Metropolitan Handicap (Forego)
Woodward Handicap (Forego)
Jerome Handicap (Broadway Forli)

FORLI *(Continued)*
1981: United Nations Handicap (Key To Content)
1985: Metropolitan Handicap (Forzando II)

FOR THE MOMENT
1987: American Derby (Fortunate Moment)

FORTY NINER
1994: Apple Blossom Handicap (Nine Keys)
Peter Pan Stakes (Twining)
Del Mar Futurity (On Target)
1996: Belmont Stakes (Editor's Note)
Isle of Capri Casino Super Derby (Editor's Note)
Jim Beam Stakes (Roar)
NYRA Mile Handicap (Gold Fever)
1997: Remsen Stakes (Coronado's Quest)
1998: Wood Memorial Stakes (Coronado's Quest)
Buick Haskell Inv. Handicap (Coronado's Quest)
Travers Stakes (Coronado's Quest)
1999: Jim Dandy Stakes (Ecton Park)
Super Derby (Ecton Park)
Test Stakes (Marley Vale)

FOXGLOVE
1950: Gulfstream Park Handicap (Chicle II)
Trenton Handicap (Chicle II)
Bougainvillea Handicap (Chicle II)
1951: Bougainvillea Handicap (Chicle II)

FRANCIS S.
1967: Donn Handicap (Francis U.)
1970: Acorn Stakes (Cathy Honey)
Ladies Handicap (Cathy Honey)
1973: New Orleans Handicap (Combat Ready)

FRANKIE'S NOD
1972: John B. Campbell Handicap (Boone the Great)

FREE AMERICA
1954: Wood Memorial Stakes (Correlation)
Florida Derby (Correlation)
1959: Del Mar Debutante Stakes (Darling June)
1961: San Antonio Handicap (American Comet)
Michigan Mile and One-Sixteenth (American Comet)
1962: Santa Margarita Handicap (Queen America)
1966: Gazelle Handicap (Prides Profile)

FREE FOR ALL
1951: Santa Anita Derby (Rough'n Tumble)

FRENCH DEPUTY
2001: Vosburgh Stakes (Left Bank)
Cigar Mile Handicap (Left Bank)
2002: Whitney Handicap (Left Bank)
2003: Prioress Stakes (House Party)

FULL POCKET
1981: American Derby (Pocket Zipper)

FULL SAIL
1955: Gulfstream Park Handicap (Mister Black)

GAELIC DANCER
1977: Ramona Handicap (Dancing Femme)

GALLANT DUKE
1950: Longacres Mile (Two and Twenty)

GALLANT FOX
1951: McLennan Handicap (Gangway)

GALLANT MAN
1963: Acorn Stakes (Spicy Living)
Mother Goose Stakes (Spicy Living)
1964: Seminole Handicap (Top Gallant)
1965: Kentucky Jockey Club Stakes (War Censor)
Hawthorne Gold Cup (Moss Vale)
1966: Ohio Derby (War Censor)
Vosburgh Handicap (Gallant Romeo)
1967: Hialeah Turf Cup (War Censor)
Pan American Handicap (War Censor)
Dixie Handicap (War Censor)
Santa Barbara Handicap (April Dawn)
Widener Handicap (Ring Twice)
1968: Matron Stakes (Gallant Bloom)
Gardenia Stakes (Gallant Bloom)
1969: Monmouth Oaks (Gallant Bloom)
Gazelle Handicap (Gallant Bloom)
Spinster Stakes (Gallant Bloom)
1970: Breeders' Futurity (Man of the Moment)
Santa Margarita Handicap (Gallant Bloom)
Beverly Hills Handicap (Pattee Canyon)
1972: Alcibiades Stakes (Coraggioso)
1973: Blue Grass Stakes (My Gallant)
1974: Ladies Handicap (Coraggioso)
1977: Mother Goose Stakes (Road Princess)

GALLANT ROMEO
1974: Remsen Stakes (El Pitirre)
1975: Hollywood Oaks (Nicosia)
1976: Arkansas Derby (Elocutionist)
Preakness Stakes (Elocutionist)
Vosburgh Handicap (My Juliet)
1977: Michigan Mile and One-Eighth (My Juliet)
1979: Longacres Mile (Always Gallant)

GALLANTSKY
1999: Donn Handicap (Puerto Madero)

GENERAL
1985: San Antonio Handicap (Lord at War)
Santa Anita Handicap (Lord at War)

GENERAL ASSEMBLY
1984: Frizette Stakes (Charleston Rag)

GENERAL MEETING
1998: Oak Leaf Stakes (Excellent Meeting)
Hollywood Starlet Stakes (Excellent Meeting)
La Brea Stakes (Magical Allure)
1999: Las Virgenes Stakes (Excellent Meeting)
Santa Anita Oaks (Excellent Meeting)
Santa Anita Derby (General Challenge)
Pacific Classic (General Challenge)
2000: Charles H. Strub Stakes (General Challenge)
Santa Anita Handicap (General Challenge)

GENTLE ART
1972: Fountain of Youth Stakes (Gentle Smoke)

GEORGE ROYAL
1973: Pan American Handicap (Lord Vancouver)

GET AROUND
1969: Kentucky Jockey Club Stakes (Evasive Action)

GILDED TIME
2002: Ruffian Handicap (Mandy's Gold)
Hollywood Starlet Stakes (Elloluv)
2003: Ashland Stakes (Elloluv)

GLITTERMAN
1997: Ashland Stakes (Glitter Woman)
2001: Turfway Spiral Stakes (Balto Star)
Arkansas Derby (Balto Star)
2003: United Nations Handicap (Balto Star)

GO FOR GIN
2000: Jockey Club Gold Cup (Albert the Great)
2001: Brooklyn Handicap (Albert the Great)
Suburban Handicap (Albert the Great)

GOLD ALERT
1995: Coaching Club American Oaks (Golden Bri)

GOLDEN ACT
1988: Hollywood Derby (Silver Circus)

GOLDEN EAGLE II
1979: California Derby (Beau's Eagle)
1980: San Antonio Stakes (Beau's Eagle)
1982: San Antonio Stakes (Score Twenty Four)

GOLDEN RULER
1969: Breeders' Futurity (Hard Work)

GOLD LEGEND
2000: Apple Blossom Handicap (Heritage of Gold)
Go for Wand Handicap (Heritage of Gold)

GOLD MERIDIAN
1994: Santa Maria Handicap (Supah Gem)

GOLD NOTE
1961: Louisiana Derby (Bass Clef)

GONE WEST
1993: Nassau County Handicap (West by West)
1994: Norfolk Stakes (Supremo)
1995: Rothmans International Stakes (Lassigny)
1996: Breeders' Cup Mile (Da Hoss)
1997: Futurity Stakes (Grand Slam)
Moet Champagne Stakes (Grand Slam)
1998: Breeders' Cup Mile (Da Hoss)
2000: Belmont Stakes (Commendable)
2001: Hopeful Stakes (Came Home)
2002: Santa Anita Derby (Came Home)
Swaps Stakes (Came Home)
Pacific Classic (Came Home)
Walmac Int. Alcibiades Stakes (Westerly Breeze)
Hollywood Derby (Johar)
2003: John Deere Breeders' Cup Turf (Johar)

GOYA II
1953: Sapling Stakes (Artismo)
Hopeful Stakes (Artismo)
Starlet Stakes (Arrogate)
1954: Blue Grass Stakes (Goyamo)
1955: Del Mar Handicap (Arrogate)
1956: Del Mar Handicap (Arrogate)

GRAN ATLETA
1975: Vanity Handicap (Dulcia)
Ramona Handicap (Dulcia)
National Championship Inv. Handicap (Dulcia)

GRAND RAPIDS II
1964: American Handicap (Colorado King)
Hollywood Gold Cup (Colorado King)
Sunset Handicap (Colorado King)

GRAND REVIVAL
1983: Fantasy Stakes (Brindy Brindy)

GRAND SLAM (1933)
1947: Arlington Futurity (Piet)
1950: Whitney Stakes (Piet)

GRAND SLAM (1995)
2003: Jim Dandy Stakes (Strong Hope)
Breeders' Cup Sprint (Cajun Beat)

GRAPHIC
1960: Louisiana Derby (Tony Graff)

GRAUSTARK
1971: Santa Anita Derby (Jim French)
Dwyer Handicap (Jim French)
1972: Withers Stakes (Key to the Mint)
Travers Stakes (Key to the Mint)
Brooklyn Handicap (Key to the Mint)
Whitney Stakes (Key to the Mint)
Woodward Stakes (Key to the Mint)
Norfolk Stakes (Groshawk)
Del Mar Futurity (Groshawk)
Ladies Handicap (Grafitti)
Manhattan Handicap (Ruritania)
1973: Woodward Stakes (Prove Out)
Jockey Club Gold Cup (Prove Out)
Black Helen Handicap (Grafitti)
Suburban Handicap (Key to the Mint)
1974: San Antonio Stakes (Prince Dantan)
Santa Anita Handicap (Prince Dantan)
Gazelle Handicap (Maud Muller)
Grey Lag Handicap (Prove Out)
1975: Santa Anita Derby (Avatar)
Belmont Stakes (Avatar)
1976: San Luis Rey Stakes (Avatar)
1978: Acorn Stakes (Tempest Queen)
Spinster Stakes (Tempest Queen)
Ladies Handicap (Ida Delia)
1985: Fountain of Youth Stakes (Proud Truth)
Florida Derby (Proud Truth)
Breeders' Cup Classic (Proud Truth)

GREAT ABOVE
1993: Futurity Stakes (Holy Bull)
1994: Florida Derby (Holy Bull)
Blue Grass Stakes (Holy Bull)
Metropolitan Handicap (Holy Bull)
Dwyer Stakes (Holy Bull)
Haskell Invitational Handicap (Holy Bull)
Travers Stakes (Holy Bull)
Woodward Stakes (Holy Bull)

GREAT CIRCLE
1961: Bowling Green Handicap (Dead Center)

GREAT NEPHEW
1987: Yellow Ribbon Stakes (Carotene)

GREEK ANSWER
1982: Arlington-Washington Futurity (Total Departure)

GREEK SHIP
1957: Sapling Stakes (Plion)
1958: Blue Grass Stakes (Plion)
1959: Whitney Stakes (Plion)

GREEK SONG

1957: Massachusetts Handicap (Greek Spy)
1961: Californian Stakes (First Balcony)
San Carlos Handicap (First Balcony)
1962: Preakness Stakes (Greek Money)
1963: Beldame Stakes (Oil Royalty)
Vineland Handicap (Oil Royalty)
Delaware Handicap (Waltz Song)
1964: Top Flight Handicap (Oil Royalty)

GREEN DANCER

1985: Californian Stakes (Greinton)
Hollywood Gold Cup (Greinton)
1986: Santa Anita Handicap (Greinton)
1987: Hollywood Turf Cup (Vilzak)
1989: Futurity Stakes (Senor Pete)
Fantasy Stakes (Fantastic Look)
1995: Flower Bowl Inv. Handicap (Northern Emerald)

GREEN DESERT

1991: Breeders' Cup Sprint (Sheikh Albadou)
2000: Charles Whittingham Handicap (White Heart)
2001: Woodford Reserve Turf Classic (White Heart)
2003: Beverly D. Stakes (Heat Haze)
Matriarch Stakes (Heat Haze)

GRENFALL

1978: Santa Susana Stakes (Grenzen)

GREY DAWN II

1972: Dwyer Handicap (Cloudy Dawn)
Arlington Park Handicap (Cloudy Dawn)
1976: Alcibiades Stakes (Sans Supplement)
1977: Hollywood Invitational Handicap (Vigors)
1978: San Antonio Stakes (Vigors)
Santa Anita Handicap (Vigors)
Remsen Stakes (Instrument Landing)
Charles H. Strub Stakes (Mr. Redoy)
1979: Wood Memorial Stakes (Instrument Landing)
1980: Frizette Stakes (Heavenly Cause)
Selima Stakes (Heavenly Cause)
1981: Fantasy Stakes (Heavenly Cause)
Kentucky Oaks (Heavenly Cause)
Acorn Stakes (Heavenly Cause)
1982: Coaching Club American Oaks (Christmas Past)
Ruffian Handicap (Christmas Past)
1983: Widener Handicap (Swing Till Dawn)
Charles H. Strub Stakes (Swing Till Dawn)
Top Flight Handicap (Adept)
Wood Memorial Stakes (Bounding Basque)
Gulfstream Park Handicap (Christmas Past)
1985: Brooklyn Handicap (Bounding Basque)
1990: Delaware Handicap (Seattle Dawn)
San Juan Capistrano Handicap (Delegant)

GREY SOVEREIGN

1961: Black Helen Handicap (Be Cautious)
1962: Carter Handicap (Merry Ruler)
1971: San Fernando Stakes (Willowick)

GRINDSTONE

2003: Champagne Stakes (Birdstone)

GROOVY

2000: Carter Handicap (Brutally Frank)

GROSHAWK

1980: Flamingo Stakes (Superbity)

GROTON

1971: Washington Park Handicap (Well Mannered)

GROUNDED II

1966: California Derby (Tragniew)
1970: Hollywood Derby (Hanalei Bay)
1974: Hopeful Stakes (The Bagel Prince)

GUILO CESERE

1970: Jerome Handicap (Great Mystery)

GULCH

1992: Hopeful Stakes (Great Navigator)
1993: Super Derby (Wallenda)
1994: Remsen Stakes (Thunder Gulch)
1995: Florida Derby (Thunder Gulch)
Kentucky Derby (Thunder Gulch)
Belmont Stakes (Thunder Gulch)
Swaps Stakes (Thunder Gulch)
Travers Stakes (Thunder Gulch)

GUMMO

1974: Malibu Stakes (Ancient Title)
San Fernando Stakes (Ancient Title)
Charles H. Strub Stakes (Ancient Title)
1975: Californian Stakes (Ancient Title)
Hollywood Gold Cup (Ancient Title)
Whitney Handicap (Ancient Title)
1976: Californian Stakes (Ancient Title)
1977: Del Mar Handicap (Ancient Title)
San Antonio Stakes (Ancient Title)
1978: Del Mar Futurity (Flying Paster)
Norfolk Stakes (Flying Paster)
1979: Louisiana Derby (Golden Act)
Arkansas Derby (Golden Act)
Secretariat Stakes (Golden Act)
Canadian International Championship (Golden Act)
Santa Anita Derby (Flying Paster)
Hollywood Derby (Flying Paster)
Del Mar Futurity (The Carpenter)
Norfolk Stakes (The Carpenter)
1981: Santa Margarita Handicap (Princess Karenda)
San Antonio Stakes (Flying Paster)

GUN BOW

1976: Whitney Handicap (Dancing Gun)

GUNFLINT

1974: Fantasy Stakes (Miss Musket)
Hollywood Oaks (Miss Musket)

GUN SHOT

1964: Gulfstream Park Handicap (Gun Bow)
Brooklyn Handicap (Gun Bow)
Washington Park Handicap (Gun Bow)
Woodward Stakes (Gun Bow)
San Fernando Stakes (Gun Bow)
Charles H. Strub Stakes (Gun Bow)
San Antonio Handicap (Gun Bow)
Whitney Stakes (Gun Bow)
1965: Donn Handicap (Gun Bow)
Metropolitan Handicap (Gun Bow)
San Antonio Handicap (Gun Bow)

HABITAT

1976: Norfolk Stakes (Habitony)
1977: Santa Anita Derby (Habitony)
1989: Arlington Million (Steinlen)
Breeders' Cup Mile (Steinlen)
1990: Hollywood Turf Handicap (Steinlen)
Caesars International Handicap (Steinlen)

HABITONY

1990: Del Mar Futurity (Best Pal)
Norfolk Stakes (Best Pal)
Hollywood Futurity (Best Pal)
1991: Swaps Stakes (Best Pal)
Pacific Classic (Best Pal)
1992: Charles H. Strub Stakes (Best Pal)
Santa Anita Handicap (Best Pal)
Oaklawn Handicap (Best Pal)
1993: Hollywood Gold Cup (Best Pal)
1995: San Antonio Handicap (Best Pal)
1997: Jerome Handicap (Richter Scale)
2000: Frank J. De Francis Memorial Dash (Richter Scale)

HAIL THE PIRATES

1981: Mother Goose Stakes (Wayward Lass)
Coaching Club American Oaks (Wayward Lass)
1983: Spinster Stakes (Try Something New)
1988: Spinster Stakes (Hail a Cab)

HAIL TO REASON

1964: Arlington-Washington Lassie Stakes (Admiring)
1965: Jersey Derby (Hail to All)
Belmont Stakes (Hail to All)
Travers Stakes (Hail to All)
Futurity Stakes (Priceless Gem)
Frizette Stakes (Priceless Gem)
Hollywood Oaks (Straight Deal)
Ladies Handicap (Straight Deal)
1966: Frizette Stakes (Regal Gleam)
Selima Stakes (Regal Gleam)
Santa Margarita Handicap (Straight Deal)
Santa Barbara Handicap (Straight Deal)
Spinaway Stakes (Silver True)
1967: Top Flight Handicap (Straight Deal)
Delaware Handicap (Straight Deal)
Spinster Stakes (Straight Deal)
California Derby (Reason to Hail)
Kentucky Derby (Proud Clarion)
1969: Kentucky Oaks (Hail to Patsy)
Jerome Handicap (Mr. Leader)
1970: Wood Memorial Stakes (Personality)
Preakness Stakes (Personality)
Jersey Derby (Personality)
Woodward Stakes (Personality)
Champagne Stakes (Limit to Reason)
Pimlico-Laurel Futurity (Limit to Reason)
Stars and Stripes Handicap (Mr. Leader)
1971: Hollywood Derby (Bold Reason)
Travers Stakes (Bold Reason)
American Derby (Bold Reason)
1972: Champagne Stakes (Stop the Music)
Top Flight Handicap (Inca Queen)
Santa Barbara Handicap (Hail the Grey)
Widener Handicap (Good Counsel)
1973: Dwyer Handicap (Stop the Music)
1974: United Nations Handicap (Halo)
1975: Florida Derby (Prince Thou Art)
1976: Spinaway Stakes (Mrs. Warren)
Matron Stakes (Mrs. Warren)
Gulfstream Park Handicap (Hail the Pirates)
Century Handicap (Winds of Thought)
1977: Ruffian Handicap (Cum Laude Laurie)
Beldame Stakes (Cum Laude Laurie)
Spinster Stakes (Cum Laude Laurie)

HAITAL

1949: Blue Grass Stakes (Halt)
1951: Molly Pitcher Handicap (Marta)
Ladies Handicap (Marta)
1953: Top Flight Handicap (Marta)

HALCYON

1948: Manhattan Handicap (Loyal Legion)

HALF CROWN

1953: Florida Derby (Money Broker)
1958: Alabama Stakes (Tempted)
Maskette Handicap (Tempted)
1959: Diana Handicap (Tempted)
Beldame Handicap (Tempted)
Ladies Handicap (Tempted)

HALO

1980: Top Flight Handicap (Glorious Song)
La Canada Stakes (Glorious Song)
Santa Margarita Handicap (Glorious Song)
1981: Spinster Stakes (Glorious Song)
1983: Arkansas Derby (Sunny's Halo)
Kentucky Derby (Sunny's Halo)
Super Derby (Sunny's Halo)
Laurel Futurity (Devil's Bag)
Champagne Stakes (Devil's Bag)
1988: Kentucky Oaks (Goodbye Halo)
Mother Goose Stakes (Goodbye Halo)
Coaching Club American Oaks (Goodbye Halo)
Swaps Stakes (Lively One)
1989: San Felipe Handicap (Sunday Silence)
Santa Anita Derby (Sunday Silence)
Kentucky Derby (Sunday Silence)
Preakness Stakes (Sunday Silence)
Super Derby (Sunday Silence)
Breeders' Cup Classic (Sunday Silence)
La Canada Stakes (Goodbye Halo)
1990: Fantasy Stakes (Silvered)
Californian Stakes (Sunday Silence)
1991: Donn Handicap (Jolie's Halo)
Gulfstream Park Handicap (Jolie's Halo)
1992: Arlington Classic (Saint Ballado)
Philip H. Iselin Handicap (Jolie's Halo)

HALO'S IMAGE

2003: Malibu Stakes (Southern Image)

HANDSOME BOY

1974: Metropolitan Handicap (Arbees Boy)

HANSEL

2001: San Antonio Handicap (Guided Tour)

HAPPY ARGO

1950: Remsen Handicap (Repetoire)
1951: Wood Memorial Stakes (Repetoire)

HARLAN

1999: Toyota Blue Grass Stakes (Menifee)
Haskell Invitational Handicap (Menifee)
2002: Florida Derby (Harlan's Holiday)
Toyota Blue Grass Stakes (Harlan's Holiday)
2003: Donn Handicap (Harlan's Holiday)

HASH

1947: Vineland Handicap (Miss Kimo)
1948: San Vicente Handicap (Salmagundi)
Santa Anita Derby (Salmagundi)
Santa Anita Maturity (Flashco)

HASTY ROAD

1963: Matron Stakes (Hasty Matelda)

HATCHET MAN

1981: Louisiana Derby (Woodchopper)
1982: Secretariat Stakes (Half Iced)

HAWAII

1975: Ashland Stakes (Sun and Snow)
Kentucky Oaks (Sun and Snow)
1977: Bowling Green Handicap (Hunza Dancer)
American Handicap (Hunza Dancer)
1978: Cinema Handicap (Kamehameha)

HAWKIN'S SPECIAL

1984: Louisiana Derby (Taylor's Special)
Blue Grass Stakes (Taylor's Special)

HEAD PLAY

1948: McLennan Handicap (El Mono)
Widener Handicap (El Mono)
1950: Molly Pitcher Handicap (Danger Ahead)

HEATHER BROOM

1950: Champagne Stakes (Uncle Miltie)
1959: Trenton Handicap (Greek Star)
1961: New Orleans Handicap (Greek Star)

HE DID

1947: Vosburgh Handicap (With Pleasure)
1948: Inglewood Handicap (With Pleasure)
1949: Travers Stakes (Arise)
1950: Fall Highweight Handicap (Arise)
Excelsior Handicap (Arise)
1951: Carter Handicap (Arise)
Monmouth Handicap (Arise)
1955: Cinema Handicap (Guilton Madero)

HEELFLY

1947: Hollywood Derby (Yankee Valor)
Cinema Handicap (Yankee Valor)

HELIOPOLIS

1946: Withers Stakes (Hampden)
1947: Delaware Oaks (Camargo)
Garden State Stakes (Itsabet)
1948: Travers Stakes (Ace Admiral)
Lawrence Realization Stakes (Ace Admiral)
Breeders' Futurity (Olympia)
Molly Pitcher Handicap (Camargo)
Del Mar Handicap (Frankly)
1949: Flamingo Stakes (Olympia)
San Felipe Stakes (Olympia)
Wood Memorial Stakes (Olympia)
Withers Stakes (Olympia)
Inglewood Handicap (Ace Admiral)
Sunset Handicap (Ace Admiral)
Santa Anita Maturity (Ace Admiral)
1950: Louisiana Derby (Greek Ship)
Metropolitan Handicap (Greek Ship)
Monmouth Handicap (Greek Ship)
Demoiselle Stakes (Aunt Jinny)
Selima Stakes (Aunt Jinny)
Dwyer Stakes (Greek Song)
Arlington Classic (Greek Song)
Roseben Handicap (Olympia)
Del Mar Handicap (Frankly)
1952: Demoiselle Stakes (Grecian Queen)
Flamingo Stakes (Charlie McAdam)
1953: Coaching Club American Oaks (Grecian Queen)
Gazelle Handicap (Grecian Queen)
Monmouth Oaks (Grecian Queen)
New Castle Handicap (Grecian Queen)
1954: Delaware Oaks (Parlo)
Alabama Stakes (Parlo)
Beldame Handicap (Parlo)
Firenze Handicap (Parlo)
Belmont Stakes (High Gun)
Dwyer Stakes (High Gun)
Jockey Club Gold Cup (High Gun)
Manhattan Handicap (High Gun)
Cowdin Stakes (Summer Tan)
Garden State Stakes (Summer Tan)
Pimlico Special (Helioscope)
Trenton Handicap (Helioscope)
1955: Massachusetts Handicap (Helioscope)
Suburban Handicap (Helioscope)
Monmouth Handicap (Helioscope)
Top Flight Handicap (Parlo)
Delaware Handicap (Parlo)
Metropolitan Handicap (High Gun)
Brooklyn Handicap (High Gun)
Roseben Handicap (Red Hannigan)
1956: Kentucky Oaks (Princess Turia)
Acorn Stakes (Princess Turia)
Gallant Fox Handicap (Summer Tan)
Pimlico Special (Summer Tan)
Black Helen Handicap (Clear Dawn)
Carter Handicap (Red Hannigan)
1957: Hopeful Stakes (Rose Trellis)
Kentucky Jockey Club Stakes (Hill Country)
Delaware Handicap (Princess Turia)
McLennan Handicap (Summer Tan)
1960: Mother Goose Stakes (Berlo)
Coaching Club American Oaks (Berlo)
Beldame Stakes (Berlo)
Ladies Handicap (Berlo)
1961: Wood Memorial Stakes (Globemaster)
Arlington Classic (Globemaster)

HELIOSCOPE

1963: Hollywood Juvenile Championship (Malicious)
1965: Aqueduct Stakes (Malicious)

HEMPEN

1972: Breeders' Futurity (Annihilate 'Em)
1973: Travers Stakes (Annihilate 'Em)

HENNESSY

2001: Bessemer Trust BC Juvenile (Johannesburg)
2003: Ballerina Handicap (Harmony Lodge)

HERBAGER

1964: Roamer Handicap (Point du Jour)
1968: Breeders' Futurity (Dike)
1969: Gotham Stakes (Dike)
Wood Memorial Stakes (Dike)
1970: Arkansas Derby (Herbalist)
Travers Stakes (Loud)
American Derby (The Pruner)
1971: Manhattan Handicap (Happy Way)
1972: Hialeah Turf Cup (Gleaming)
Del Mar Handicap (Chrisaway)
1973: Kentucky Oaks (Bag of Tunes)
Hialeah Turf Cup (Gleaming)
San Luis Rey Handicap (Big Spruce)
1974: Marlboro Cup Handicap (Big Spruce)
1975: Hialeah Turf Cup (Outdoors)
1977: Fantasy Stakes (Our Mims)
Coaching Club American Oaks (Our Mims)
Alabama Stakes (Our Mims)
Delaware Handicap (Our Mims)
Florida Derby (Coined Silver)
Widener Handicap (Yamanin)
1978: Century Handicap (Landscaper)
Bowling Green Handicap (Tiller)
1979: San Antonio Stakes (Tiller)
San Juan Capistrano Handicap (Tiller)
1980: Pan American Handicap (Flitalong)
Sword Dancer Stakes (Tiller)
Turf Classic (Anifa)
1981: Widener Handicap (Land of Eire)
1983: Pan American Handicap (Field Cat)

HERCULEAN

1985: Hutcheson Stakes (Banner Bob)
Jim Beam Stakes (Banner Bob)

HERNANDO

2003: Arlington Million (Sulamani)
Turf Classic (Sulamani)

HERO'S HONOR

1999: Early Times Hollywood Derby (Super Quercus)
2001: Hollywood Turf Cup (Super Quercus)

HESIOD

1964: Louisiana Derby (Grecian Princess)

HETHERSETT

1969: Pan American Handicap (Hibernian)

HIGH ECHELON

1979: Golden Harvest Handicap (Flaunter)
1983: Coaching Club American Oaks (High Schemes)

HIGHEST HONOR

1996: Oak Tree Turf Championship (Admise)

HIGHLAND PARK

1999: Malibu Stakes (Love That Red)

HIGH QUEST

1946: Santa Anita Handicap (War Knight)

HIGH STRUNG

1948: Starlet Stakes (Star Fiddle)

HIGH TRIBUTE

1976: Hollywood Gold Cup (Pay Tribute)
1977: Meadowlands Cup (Pay Tribute)

HILARIOUS

1963: Cowdin Stakes (Dunfee)
1969: American Derby (Fast Hilarious)
1970: Michigan Mile and One-Eighth (Fast Hilarious)
1971: Gulfstream Park Handicap (Fast Hilarious)

HILLARY

1964: San Felipe Handicap (Hill Rise)
Santa Anita Derby (Hill Rise)
1965: Santa Anita Handicap (Hill Rise)
San Fernando Stakes (Hill Rise)
Man o' War Stakes (Hill Rise)
1966: San Antonio Handicap (Hill Rise)
1967: Sunset Handicap (Hill Clown)
1968: Hollywood Oaks (Hooplah)
1972: Beverly Hills Handicap (Hill Circus)
Del Mar Handicap (Hill Circus)
1979: Widener Handicap (Jumping Hill)

HILL PRINCE

1955: Selima Stakes (Levee)
1956: Coaching Club American Oaks (Levee)
Monmouth Oaks (Levee)
Beldame Handicap (Levee)
Dwyer Handicap (Riley)
Lawrence Realization Stakes (Riley)
Selima Stakes (Lebkuchen)
1957: Acorn Stakes (Bayou)
Delaware Oaks (Bayou)
Gazelle Handicap (Bayou)
Maskette Handicap (Bayou)
1958: Frizette Stakes (Merry Hill)
Louisiana Derby (Royal Union)
1959: Lawrence Realization Stakes (Middle Brother)
San Juan Capistrano Handicap (Royal Living)
1966: Gardenia Stakes (Pepperwood)

HILLSBOROUGH

1969: New Orleans Handicap (Miracle Hill)

HILLSDALE

1971: Vanity Handicap (Hi Q.)

HIS MAJESTY

1977: Jersey Derby (Cormorant)
1978: Illinois Derby (Batonnier)
1980: Remsen Stakes (Pleasant Colony)
Golden Harvest Handicap (Ribbon)
1981: Wood Memorial Stakes (Pleasant Colony)
Kentucky Derby (Pleasant Colony)
Preakness Stakes (Pleasant Colony)
Woodward Stakes (Pleasant Colony)
San Juan Capistrano Handicap (Obraztsovy)
1982: Monmouth Handicap (Mehmet)
Meadowlands Cup (Mehmet)
Top Flight Handicap (Andover Way)
Hawthorne Gold Cup (Recusant)
Rothmans International Stakes (Majesty's Prince)
1983: Sword Dancer Handicap (Majesty's Prince)
Man o' War Stakes (Majesty's Prince)
1984: Man o' War Stakes (Majesty's Prince)
Rothmans International Stakes (Majesty's Prince)
1991: Eddie Read Handicap (Tight Spot)
Arlington Million (Tight Spot)
1993: Hollywood Futurity (Valiant Nature)
1996: Flower Bowl Invitational Handicap (Chelsey Flower)
1998: Sword Dancer Invitational Handicap (Cetewayo)
2002: Gulfstream Park Breeders' Cup Handicap (Cetewayo)

HIS NICKEL

1960: Display Handicap (Nickel Boy)
1961: Manhattan Handicap (Nickel Boy)

HOIST THE FLAG

1976: Frizette Stakes (Sensational)
Selima Stakes (Sensational)
American Derby (Fifth Marine)
1977: Ladies Handicap (Sensational)
California Derby (Cuzwuzwrong)
Illinois Derby (Flag Officer)
1978: Breeders' Futurity (Strike Your Colors)
Monmouth Invitational Handicap (Delta Flag)
1979: Oaklawn Handicap (San Juan Hill)
1981: Norfolk Stakes (Stalwart)
Hollywood Futurity (Stalwart)

1982: Fantasy Stakes (Flying Partner)
Blue Grass Stakes (Linkage)
1983: Delaware Handicap (May Day Eighty)

HOIST THE SILVER
1987: Fantasy Stakes (Very Subtle)
Breeders' Cup Sprint (Very Subtle)

HOLD YOUR PEACE
1982: Remsen Stakes (Pax in Bello)
1985: Arlington-Washington Futurity (Meadowlake)
La Canada Stakes (Mitterand)
1987: Breeders' Cup Juvenile (Success Express)
1991: Young America Stakes (Maston)

HOLLYROOD
1948: Vanity Handicap (Hemet Squaw)

HOLY BULL
1998: Frizette Stakes (Confessional)
2000: Breeders' Cup Juvenile (Macho Uno)

HOMEBUILDER
1996: Fountain of Youth Stakes (Built for Pleasure)

HONEST PLEASURE
1984: Wood Memorial Stakes (Leroy S.)
1987: San Antonio Handicap (Bedside Promise)
Californian Stakes (Judge Angelucci)
1988: San Antonio Handicap (Judge Angelucci)

HONEY JAY
1984: Top Flight Handicap (Sweet Missus)

HONOR GRADES
1997: Secretariat Stakes (Honor Glide)
1999: Sword Dancer Invitational Handicap (Honor Glide)
2003: Breeders' Cup Distaff (Adoration)

HONOUR AND GLORY
2000: Breeders' Cup Juvenile Fillies (Caressing)

HORATIUS
1990: Breeders' Cup Sprint (Safely Kept)

HOSTAGE
1991: Secretariat Stakes (Jackie Wackie)

HOT GROVE
1985: Oak Tree Invitational Stakes (Yashgan)

HUNTER'S MOON IV
1951: San Pasqual Handicap (Moonrush)
Santa Anita Handicap (Moonrush)

HURRY TO MARKET
1978: Michigan Mile and One-Eighth (A Letter to Harry)
1979: New Orleans Handicap (A Letter to Harry)

HUSSONET
2003: Ruffian Handicap (Wild Spirit)

HYPNOTIST II
1946: Coaching Club American Oaks (Hypnotic)
Alabama Stakes (Hypnotic)

ICECAPADE
1983: Swaps Stakes (Hyperborean)
1984: Breeders' Cup Classic (Wild Again)
1988: Alcibiades Stakes (Wonders Delight)

IDLE HOUR
1969: Hollywood Gold Cup (Figonero)

ILE DE BOURBON
1986: Yellow Ribbon Stakes (Bonne Ile)
1990: Sunset Handicap (Petite Ile)

IMBROS
1962: Hollywood Derby (Drill Site)
1963: Inglewood Handicap (Native Diver)
1964: Inglewood Handicap (Native Diver)
1965: American Handicap (Native Diver)
Hollywood Gold Cup (Native Diver)
1966: Hollywood Gold Cup (Native Diver)
1967: Hollywood Gold Cup (Native Diver)
1970: Hollywood Juvenile Championship (Fast Fellow)

I'M FOR MORE
1971: Sapling Stakes (Chevron Flight)

INDIAN EMERALD
1978: Carter Handicap (Jaipur's Gem)

INDIAN HEMP
1959: Arlington Futurity (T.V. Lark)
1960: Arlington Classic (T.V. Lark)
American Derby (T.V. Lark)
Washington Park Handicap (T.V. Lark)
United Nations Handicap (T.V. Lark)
1961: Los Angeles Handicap (T.V. Lark)
Hawthorne Gold Cup (T.V. Lark)
Washington D.C. International (T.V. Lark)
1962: Vanity Handicap (Linita)

INDIAN RIDGE
1995: Breeders' Cup Mile (Ridgewood Pearl)
2002: NetJets Breeders' Cup Mile (Domedriver)

IN EXCESS
1998: Santa Anita Derby (Indian Charlie)
2002: Del Mar Futurity (Icecoldbeeratreds)

IN REALITY
1973: Alabama Stakes (Desert Vixen)
Gazelle Handicap (Desert Vixen)
Beldame Stakes (Desert Vixen)
1974: Beldame Stakes (Desert Vixen)
1975: Oak Leaf Stakes (Answer)
Dwyer Handicap (Valid Appeal)
1976: Hollywood Oaks (Answer)
1977: Sorority Stakes (Stub)
Arlington-Washington Lassie Stakes (Stub)
Remsen Stakes (Believe It)
1978: Wood Memorial Stakes (Believe It)
1980: Arlington-Washington Lassie Stakes (Truly Bound)
Louisiana Downs Handicap (It's True)
1983: Metropolitan Handicap (Star Choice)
1985: Delaware Handicap (Basie)
Arlington Classic (Smile)
1986: Breeders' Cup Sprint (Smile)
1988: Arkansas Derby (Proper Reality)
Illinois Derby (Proper Reality)
1989: Metropolitan Handicap (Proper Reality)
Philip H. Iselin Handicap (Proper Reality)
1991: Gotham Stakes (Kyle's Our Man)

INTENT
1958: Futurity Stakes (Intentionally)
Pimlico Futurity (Intentionally)
1959: Withers Stakes (Intentionally)
Jerome Handicap (Intentionally)
1962: Seminole Handicap (Intentionally)

INTENTIONALLY
1966: Pimlico Futurity (In Reality)
1967: Florida Derby (In Reality)
Jersey Derby (In Reality)
1968: John B. Campbell Handicap (In Reality)
Carter Handicap (In Reality)
Metropolitan Handicap (In Reality)
1969: Vosburgh Handicap (Ta Wee)
1970: Manhattan Handicap (Shelter Bay)
1973: Metropolitan Handicap (Tentam)
United Nations Handicap (Tentam)
Del Mar Handicap (Red Reality)
1974: Hawthorne Gold Cup (Group Plan)
1975: Jockey Club Gold Cup (Group Plan)

IN THE WINGS
1996: Canadian International Championship (Singspiel)

INTREPID HERO
1983: Bay Meadows Handicap (Interco)
1984: San Fernando Stakes (Interco)
Santa Anita Handicap (Interco)
San Luis Rey Stakes (Interco)
Century Handicap (Interco)

INVERNESS DRIVE
1977: Cinema Handicap (Bad 'n Big)
1978: Longacres Mile (Bad 'n Big)

IRISH CASTLE
1976: Wood Memorial Stakes (Bold Forbes)
Kentucky Derby (Bold Forbes)
Belmont Stakes (Bold Forbes)
1982: Super Derby (Reinvested)

IRISH RIVER
1991: San Juan Capistrano Handicap (Mashkour)
Budweiser International Stakes (Leariva)
1992: Hollywood Derby (Paradise Creek)
Oak Tree Invitational Stakes (Navarone)
1994: Early Times Manhattan Handicap (Paradise Creek)
Arlington Million (Paradise Creek)
Washington D.C. International (Paradise Creek)
Beverly D. Stakes (Hatoof)
1997: Hollywood Turf Cup (River Bay)
1999: Charles Whittingham Handicap (River Bay)
2001: Shoemaker Breeders' Cup Mile (Irish Prize)

IRISH RULER
1973: Sorority Stakes (Irish Sonnet)

IRISH TOWER
1993: Wood Memorial Stakes (Storm Tower)

IRON CONSTITUTION
1991: Spinaway Stakes (Miss Iron Smoke)

IRON DUKE
1985: Hollywood Derby (Charming Duke)

IRON RULER
1982: Preakness Stakes (Aloma's Ruler)

IS IT TRUE
1999: Frank J. De Francis Memorial Dash (Yes It's True)

ISLAM
1949: Louisiana Derby (Rookwood)

ISLAND WHIRL
1988: San Felipe Handicap (Mi Preferido)
1989: San Fernando Stakes (Mi Preferido)
1993: Flamingo Stakes (Forever Whirl)
Ohio Derby (Forever Whirl)

ISOLATER
1952: Saranac Handicap (Golden Gloves)
Manhattan Handicap (Lone Eagle)

ITAJARA
1996: Hollywood Gold Cup (Siphon)
1997: Santa Anita Handicap (Siphon)

IT'S FREEZING
1992: Kentucky Oaks (Luv Me Luv Me Not)

JACINTO
1971: Sanford Stakes (Cohasset Tribe)
1972: Hollywood Juvenile Championship (Bold Liz)
American Handicap (Buzkashi)
1975: Hopeful Stakes (Jackknife)
Breeders' Futurity (Harbor Springs)
Vosburgh Handicap (No Bias)
1979: Louisiana Downs Handicap (Incredible Ease)

JACK HIGH
1946: Monmouth Handicap (Lucky Draw)
Hawthorne Gold Cup (Jack's Jill)
Miami Beach Handicap (Frere Jacques)
1949: Bougainvillea Handicap (Frere Jacques)

JADE HUNTER
1993: Pegasus Handicap (Diazo)
1994: Strub Stakes (Diazo)
Santa Anita Handicap (Stuka)
1998: Toyota Blue Grass Stakes (Halory Hunter)
1999: Gulfstream Park Breeders' Cup Handicap (Yagli)
Manhattan Handicap (Yagli)
2002: Santa Margarita Handicap (Azeri)
Apple Blossom Handicap (Azeri)
Milady Breeders' Cup Handicap (Azeri)
Vanity Handicap (Azeri)
Breeders' Cup Distaff (Azeri)
2003: Apple Blossom Handicap (Azeri)
Milady Breeders' Cup Handicap (Azeri)
Vanity Handicap (Azeri)

JAIPUR
1969: Garden State Stakes (Forum)

JAKLIN KLUGMAN
2002: Hollywood Gold Cup (Sky Jack)

JAMESTOWN
1946: Travers Stakes (Natchez)

JATULLAH
1977: Travers Stakes (Jatski)

JAVA GOLD
2000: Breeders' Cup Sprint (Kona Gold)
2001: San Carlos Handicap (Kona Gold)

JAYBIL
1969: San Antonio Stakes (Praise Jay)

JEAN VALJEAN
1951: Washington Park Futurity (Oh Leo)

JESTER
1964: Ladies Handicap (Steeple Jill)
1965: Delaware Handicap (Steeple Jill)
Vineland Handicap (Steeple Jill)
1967: Everglades Stakes (Reflected Glory)
Flamingo Stakes (Reflected Glory)
1973: Hawthorne Gold Cup (Tri Jet)
1974: Whitney Stakes (Tri Jet)

JET ACTION
1965: Hialeah Turf Cup (Hot Dust)

JET JEWEL
1957: Washington Park Futurity (Jewel's Reward)
Cowdin Stakes (Jewel's Reward)
Champagne Stakes (Jewel's Reward)
Pimlico Futurity (Jewel's Reward)
1958: Wood Memorial Stakes (Jewel's Reward)

JET PILOT
1951: Matron Stakes (Rose Jet)
Selima Stakes (Rose Jet)
Demoiselle Stakes (Rose Jet)
1954: Alcibiades Stakes (Myrtle's Jet)
Frizette Stakes (Myrtle's Jet)
Withers Stakes (Jet Action)
Roamer Handicap (Jet Action)
1955: Blue Grass Stakes (Racing Fool)
Washington Park Handicap (Jet Action)

JIG DANCER
1980: Norfolk Stakes (Sir Dancer)

JIG TIME
1984: Fountain of Youth Stakes (Darn That Alarm)
1986: Tropical Park Derby (Strong Performance)

JOEY BOB
1981: Louisiana Downs Handicap (Shishkabob)
1991: Super Derby (Free Spirit's Joy)

JOHNS JOY
1956: Withers Stakes (Oh Johnny)
Travers Stakes (Oh Johnny)
1957: Display Handicap (Oh Johnny)
1958: Grey Lag Handicap (Oh Johnny)
1960: Gotham Stakes (John William)
Withers Stakes (John William)
1963: Sapling Stakes (Mr. Brick)
1964: Withers Stakes (Mr. Brick)
1966: Michigan Mile and One-Eighth (Stanislas)
1976: John B. Campbell Handicap (Festive Mood)

JOHNSTOWN
1946: Kentucky Oaks (First Page)
Carter Handicap (Flood Town)

JOLIE'S HALO
1998: Remsen Stakes (Comeonmom)
2000: Florida Derby (Hal's Hope)
2002: Gulfstream Park Handicap (Hal's Hope)

JOLLY QUICK
1999: Eddie Read Handicap (Joe Who)

JUDGE SMELLS
1990: Arlington Classic (Sound of Cannons)

JULES
2003: Toyota Blue Grass Stakes (Peace Rules)
Haskell Invitational Handicap (Peace Rules)

KALAGLOW
1996: Beverly D. Stakes (Timarida)

KALDOUN
1986: Gamely Handicap (La Koumia)
1998: Ramona Handicap (See You Soon)

KASKASKIA
1977: Young America Stakes (Forever Casting)

KAUTOKEINO
1980: Washington D.C. International (Argument)

KEEN
1997: Californian Stakes (River Keen)
1999: Woodward Stakes (River Keen)
Jockey Club Gold Cup (River Keen)

KENNEDY ROAD
1986: San Felipe Handicap (Variety Road)
1987: San Fernando Stakes (Variety Road)

KENTUCKY PRIDE
1968: Louisiana Derby (Kentucky Sherry)

KEY TO THE KINGDOM
1982: Arlington-Washington Lassie St. (For Once'n My Life)
1988: San Juan Capistrano 'Cap (Great Communicator)
Breeders' Cup Turf (Great Communicator)
Hollywood Turf Cup (Great Communicator)
1989: Hollywood Turf Handicap (Great Communicator)

KEY TO THE MINT
1977: Arlington-Washington Futurity (Sauce Boat)
1979: Laurel Futurity (Plugged Nickle)
Remsen Stakes (Plugged Nickle)
Ladies Handicap (Spark of Life)
1980: Florida Derby (Plugged Nickle)
Wood Memorial Stakes (Plugged Nickle)
Vosburgh Stakes (Plugged Nickle)
Mother Goose Stakes (Sugar and Spice)
1986: Apple Blossom Handicap (Love Smitten)
Remsen Stakes (Java Gold)
1987: Travers Stakes (Java Gold)
Whitney Handicap (Java Gold)
Marlboro Cup Handicap (Java Gold)
1993: Arkansas Derby (Rockamundo)
1996: Vanity Handicap (Jewel Princess)
Breeders' Cup Distaff (Jewel Princess)
1997: Santa Maria Handicap (Jewel Princess)
Santa Margarita Handicap (Jewel Princess)

KHALED
1951: Del Mar Futurity (Big Noise)
1953: Vanity Handicap (Fleet Khal)
Blue Grass Stakes (Correspondent)
Del Mar Handicap (Goose Khal)
1954: Hollywood Gold Cup (Correspondent)
1955: Santa Anita Derby (Swaps)
Kentucky Derby (Swaps)
Westerner Stakes (Swaps)
American Derby (Swaps)
Californian Stakes (Swaps)
1956: Inglewood Handicap (Swaps)
American Handicap (Swaps)
Hollywood Gold Cup (Swaps)
Sunset Handicap (Swaps)
Washington Park Handicap (Swaps)
Santa Anita Derby (Terrang)
1957: Vanity Handicap (Annie-Lu-San)
San Antonio Handicap (Terrang)
1958: Coaching Club American Oaks (A Glitter)
Monmouth Oaks (A Glitter)
Del Mar Debutante Stakes (Khalita)
Vanity Handicap (Annie-Lu-San)
Cinema Handicap (The Shoe)
1959: Santa Anita Handicap (Terrang)
1960: San Felipe Handicap (Flow Line)
Cinema Handicap (New Policy)
Roamer Handicap (Divine Comedy)
Santa Anita Handicap (Linmold)
1961: Arkansas Derby (Light Talk)
Cinema Handicap (Bushel-n-Peck)
1962: Santa Anita Handicap (Physician)
1963: Hollywood Oaks (Delhi Maid)
San Antonio Handicap (Physician)
1964: Michigan Mile and One-Sixteenth (Going Abroad)
Manhattan Handicap (Going Abroad)
Hawthorne Gold Cup (Going Abroad)
1965: New Orleans Handicap (Valiant Man)
Washington Park Handicap (Take Over)
1970: Arlington Classic (Corn off the Cob)

KING COLE
1947: Remsen Handicap (Big If)

KINGLY
1963: Del Mar Debutante Stakes (Leisurely Kin)

KINGMAMBO
1998: Futurity Stakes (Lemon Drop Kid)
1999: Belmont Stakes (Lemon Drop Kid)
Travers Stakes (Lemon Drop Kid)
2000: Brooklyn Handicap (Lemon Drop Kid)
Suburban Handicap (Lemon Drop Kid)
Whitney Handicap (Lemon Drop Kid)
Woodward Stakes (Lemon Drop Kid)
2001: Garden City BC Handicap (Voodoo Dancer)
2003: Diana Handicap (Voodoo Dancer)

KING OF THE TUDORS
1963: Arlington-Washington Futurity (Golden Ruler)
1969: Frizette Stakes (Tudor Queen)

KING'S ABBEY
1951: Santa Susana Stakes (Ruth Lily)
Hollywood Oaks (Ruth Lily)
1956: Del Mar Futurity (Swirling Abbey)

KING'S BISHOP
1980: Ramona Handicap (Queen to Conquer)
1981: Ramona Handicap (Queen to Conquer)
Yellow Ribbon Stakes (Queen to Conquer)
1986: Vosburgh Stakes (King's Swan)

KING'S BLUE
1950: Kentucky Oaks (Ari's Mona)

KING'S STRIDE
1956: Sapling Stakes (King Hairan)
Hopeful Stakes (King Hairan)

KINGSWAY II
1953: Gallant Fox Handicap (Royal Vale)
Dixie Handicap (Royal Vale)
Massachusetts Handicap (Royal Vale)
Miami Beach Handicap (Royal Vale)
1954: Arlington Handicap (Stan)
1955: Hialeah Turf Handicap (Stan)

KIPPER KELLY
1998: Frank J. De Francis Memorial Dash (Kelly Kip)

KIRTLING
1987: Hollywood Derby (Political Ambition)
1988: Hollywood Invitational Handicap (Political Ambition)

KNAVE HIGH
1956: Molly Pitcher Handicap (Blue Sparkler)

KNIGHTLY MANNER
1974: Ohio Derby (Stonewalk)
Jerome Handicap (Stonewalk)

KNIGHTS CHOICE
1985: Sapling Stakes (Hilco Scamper)
1986: Arlington-Washington Lassie Stakes (Delicate Vine)

KNOWN FACT
1996: Spinaway Stakes (Oath)

KODIACK
1993: Arlington-Washington Futurity (Polar Expedition)
1994: Jim Beam Stakes (Polar Expedition)

KRIS
1999: San Juan Capistrano Handicap (Single Empire)

KRIS S.
1988: Jerome Handicap (Evening Kris)
Hollywood Starlet Stakes (Stocks Up)
1989: Swaps Stakes (Prized)
Breeders' Cup Turf (Prized)
Hollywood Starlet Stakes (Cheval Volant)
1990: San Luis Rey Stakes (Prized)
1993: Hollywood Oaks (Hollywood Wildcat)
Breeders' Cup Distaff (Hollywood Wildcat)
Haskell Invitational Handicap (Kissin Kris)
Breeders' Cup Juvenile (Brocco)
1994: Santa Anita Derby (Brocco)
Gamely Handicap (Hollywood Wildcat)
1995: Metropolitan Handicap (You and I)
Brooklyn Handicap (You and I)
1998: Super Derby (Arch)
1999: Flower Bowl Invitational Handicap (Soaring Softly)
Breeders' Cup Filly and Mare Turf (Soaring Softly)
Wood Memorial Stakes (Adonis)
2002: Oaklawn Handicap (Kudos)
2003: Sword Dancer Inv. Handicap (Whitmore's Conn)
Secretariat Stakes (Kicken Kris)
Bessemer Trust BC Juvenile (Action This Day)

KY. COLONEL
1958: Ohio Derby (Terra Firma)
Stars and Stripes Handicap (Terra Firma)

LANDING
1970: Louisiana Derby (Jim's Alibhi)

LANGFUHR
2002: Gazelle Handicap (Imperial Gesture)
Beldame Stakes (Imperial Gesture)

LANYON
1981: Santa Susana Stakes (Nell's Briquette)

LAWRIN
1946: Arlington Handicap (Historian)
Sunset Handicap (Historian)

LAW SOCIETY
1994: Eddie Read Handicap (Approach the Bench)

LEAR FAN
1995: Crown Royal Hollywood Derby (Labeeb)
1996: San Luis Rey Stakes (Windsharp)
1997: Queen Elizabeth II Challenge Cup (Ryafan)
Yellow Ribbon Stakes (Ryafan)
Matriarch Stakes (Ryafan)
Beverly Hills Handicap (Windsharp)
1998: Woodbine Mile (Labeeb)
2002: Eddie Read Handicap (Sarafan)
Del Mar Oaks (Dublino)

LE FABULEUX
1978: American Handicap (Effervescing)
1982: Hialeah Turf Cup (The Bart)
Century Handicap (The Bart)

LEGAL CASE
1999: Beverly Hills Handicap (Virginie)

LEISURE TIME
1962: Hollywood Juvenile Championship (Noti)

LE LEVANSTELL
1969: Hialeah Turf Cup (Blanquette II)
1975: Hollywood Invitational Handicap (Barclay Joy)
Sunset Handicap (Barclay Joy)

LE TYROL
1964: Hialeah Turf Cup (Carteret)

LIGHTHOUSE II
1958: Washington D.C. International (Sailor's Guide)

LI'L FELLA
1967: Del Mar Futurity (Baffle)
1970: Californian Stakes (Baffle)

LILOY
1987: Santa Barbara Handicap (Reloy)
Sunset Handicap (Swink)

LIMELIGHT
1969: Malibu Stakes (First Mate)

LINES OF POWER
1988: California Derby (All Thee Power)

LITTLE BEANS
1952: Monmouth Oaks (La Corredora)
1953: Ladies Handicap (La Corredora)
Comely Handicap (La Corredora)

LITTLE CURRENT
1979: Hollywood Oaks (Prize Spot)
1983: Flamingo Stakes (Current Hope)

LITTLE MISSOURI
1993: Jim Beam Stakes (Prairie Bayou)
Blue Grass Stakes (Prairie Bayou)
Preakness Stakes (Prairie Bayou)

LIVELY ONE
1998: Breeders' Cup Juvenile (Answer Lively)

LOCAL TALENT
1995: Santa Anita Derby (Larry the Legend)

LOCHINVAR
1950: Swift Stakes (Ferd)

LODE
1998: Hollywood Turf Cup (Lazy Lode)
1999: Hollywood Turf Cup (Lazy Lode)

LOMITAS
2001: Arlington Million (Silvano)

LONDON COMPANY
1982: Arlington Classic (Wolfie's Rascal)
American Derby (Wolfie's Rascal)

LOOM
1973: Sapling Stakes (Tisab)

LORD AT WAR
2000: Sword Dancer Invitational Handicap (John's Call)
Turf Classic (John's Call)
2003: Woodford Reserve Turf Classic (Honor in War)

LORD AVIE
1987: Jersey Derby (Avies Copy)
1991: Hollywood Starlet Stakes (Magical Maiden)
1992: Gamely Handicap (Metamorphose)

LORD CARSON
2000: Remsen Stakes (Windsor Castle)

LORD GAYLORD
1980: Champagne Stakes (Lord Avie)
Young America Stakes (Lord Avie)
1981: Florida Derby (Lord Avie)

LOS CURROS
1960: Manhattan Handicap (Don Poggio)
Gallant Fox Handicap (Don Poggio)
1961: Monmouth Handicap (Don Poggio)

LOST CODE
2002: Santa Monica Handicap (Kalookan Queen)
Ancient Title BC Handicap (Kalookan Queen)

LOVELY NIGHT
1948: Gazelle Stakes (Sweet Dream)

LT. STEVENS
1971: Spinster Stakes (Chou Croute)
1985: Apple Blossom Handicap (Sefa's Beauty)
1986: Washington D.C. International (Lieutenant's Lark)

LUCKY DEBONAIR
1973: Alcibiades Stakes (City Girl)
1975: Michigan Mile and One-Eighth (Mr. Lucky Phoenix)
1976: Mother Goose Stakes (Girl in Love)

LUCKY MEL
1968: Del Mar Debutante Stakes (Fourth Round)

LUCKY MIKE
1976: Arlington-Washington Lassie Stakes (Special Warmth)

LUHUK
2003: Ancient Title Breeders' Cup Handicap (Avanzado)

LURE
2001: Beverly D. Stakes (England's Legend)

LYPHARD
1980: United Nations Handicap (Lyphard's Wish)
1981: Top Flight Handicap (Chain Bracelet)
1982: Vanity Handicap (Sangue)
1983: Ramona Handicap (Sangue)
Golden Harvest Handicap (Sangue)
Yellow Ribbon Stakes (Sangue)
Matriarch Stakes (Sangue)
Dwyer Stakes (Au Point)
1984: Yellow Ribbon Stakes (Sabin)
1985: Century Handicap (Dahar)
United Nations Handicap (Ends Well)
1986: United Nations Handicap (Manila)
Turf Classic (Manila)
Breeders' Cup Turf (Manila)
San Luis Rey Stakes (Dahar)
San Juan Capistrano Handicap (Dahar)
1987: United Nations Handicap (Manila)
Budweiser-Arlington Million (Manila)
1995: Santa Maria Handicap (Queens Court Queen)
Santa Margarita Handicap (Queens Court Queen)

LYPHARD'S SPECIAL
1988: Laurel Futurity (Luge II)

LYPHARD'S WISH
1986: Hollywood Derby (Spellbound)

LYPHEOR
1983: Hollywood Derby (Royal Heroine)
Budweiser Million (Tolomeo)
1984: Breeders' Cup Mile (Royal Heroine)
1987: Laurel Futurity (Antiqua)
1988: Yellow Ribbon Stakes (Delighter)
1991: Santa Barbara Handicap (Bequest)

MACHIAVELLIAN
2002: Stephen Foster Handicap (Street Cry)
2003: Charles Whittingham Handicap (Storming Home)
C.L. Hirsch Mem. Turf Champ. (Storming Home)

MADISON
1966: Manhattan Handicap (Moontrip)
Bowling Green Handicap (Moontrip)
Carter Handicap (Davis II)
1967: Grey Lag Handicap (Moontrip)

MAGESTERIAL
1987: Jim Beam Stakes (J.T.'s Pet)
Del Mar Futurity (Lost Kitty)

MAHMOUD
1946: Futurity Stakes (First Flight)
Astoria Stakes (First Flight)
Matron Stakes (First Flight)
Astarita Stakes (Keynote)
Molly Pitcher Handicap (Mahmoudess)
Will Rogers Handicap (Burra Sahib)
Discovery Handicap (Mighty Story)
Jerome Handicap (Mahout)
1947: Beldame Handicap (Snow Goose)
Ladies Handicap (Snow Goose)
Champagne Stakes (Vulcan's Forge)
Astoria Stakes (Mackinaw)
Santa Margarita Handicap (Monsoon)
1948: Withers Stakes (Vulcan's Forge)
Will Rogers Handicap (Speculation)
Saranac Handicap (Mount Marcy)
Fall Highweight Handicap (First Flight)
Hawthorne Gold Cup (Billings)
1949: Breeders' Futurity (Oil Capitol)
Pimlico Futurity (Oil Capitol)
Santa Anita Handicap (Vulcan's Forge)
Suburban Handicap (Vulcan's Forge)
Delaware Oaks (Nasophar)
Alabama Stakes (Adile)
1950: New Castle Handicap (Adile)
Vineland Handicap (Almahmoud)
Flamingo Stakes (Oil Capitol)
Blue Grass Stakes (Mr. Trouble)
1951: Flamingo Stakes (Yildiz)
Blue Grass Stakes (Mameluke)
New Orleans Handicap (Mount Marcy)
1952: New Orleans Handicap (Oil Capitol)
Metropolitan Handicap (Mameluke)
Pimlico Special (General Staff)
1953: Widener Handicap (Oil Capitol)
Arlington Handicap (Oil Capitol)
1954: Acorn Stakes (Happy Mood)
Everglades Stakes (Maharajah)
1956: Gardenia Stakes (Magic Forest)
Ohio Derby (Born Mighty)
1958: Brooklyn Handicap (Cohoes)
Whitney Stakes (Cohoes)
1961: Del Mar Debutante Stakes (Spark Plug)
1962: Bougainvillea Handicap (Eurasia)
1963: Canadian Championship Stakes (The Axe II)
Man o' War Stakes (The Axe II)
San Luis Rey Handicap (The Axe II)

MAJESTIC LIGHT
1981: Remsen Stakes (Laser Light)
1982: Haskell Invitational Handicap (Wavering Monarch)
1983: San Fernando Stakes (Wavering Monarch)
1985: San Luis Rey Stakes (Prince True)
San Juan Capistrano Handicap (Prince True)
1986: Santa Anita Oaks (Hidden Light)
Hollywood Oaks (Hidden Light)
Selima Stakes (Collins)
1987: California Derby (Simply Majestic)
Blue Grass Stakes (War)
1990: Oak Leaf Stakes (Lite Light)
Hollywood Oaks (Patches)
1991: Santa Anita Oaks (Lite Light)
Fantasy Stakes (Lite Light)
Kentucky Oaks (Lite Light)
Coaching Club American Oaks (Lite Light)
Man o' War Stakes (Solar Splendor)
Turf Classic (Solar Splendor)
Hollywood Derby (Eternity Star)
1992: Flower Bowl Handicap (Christiecat)
Man o' War Stakes (Solar Splendor)

MAJESTIC PRINCE
1976: Swaps Stakes (Majestic Light)
Monmouth Invitational Handicap (Majestic Light)
Cinema Handicap (Majestic Light)
1977: Amory L. Haskell Handicap (Majestic Light)
Man o' War Stakes (Majestic Light)
1978: Jerome Handicap (Sensitive Prince)
1979: Belmont Stakes (Coastal)
Dwyer Stakes (Coastal)
Monmouth Invitational Handicap (Coastal)

MAJESTIC PRINCE *(Continued)*
Gulfstream Park Handicap (Sensitive Prince)
1985: Gotham Stakes (Eternal Prince)
Wood Memorial Stakes (Eternal Prince)

MAJESTIC VENTURE
1992: Ohio Derby (Majestic Sweep)

MALINOWSKI
1988: Sword Dancer Handicap (Anka Germania)

MAMBORETA
1968: Jersey Derby (Out of the Way)
Massachusetts Handicap (Out of the Way)

MANDATE
1976: San Antonio Stakes (Lightning Mandate)

MANILA
1992: Swaps Stakes (Bien Bien)
Hollywood Turf Cup (Bien Bien)
1993: Hollywood Turf Handicap (Bien Bien)
1994: San Luis Rey Stakes (Bien Bien)
San Juan Capistrano Handicap (Bien Bien)

MANZOTTI
1994: Coaching Club American Oaks (Two Altazano)

MARFA
1989: Santa Anita Oaks (Imaginary Lady)
1991: San Antonio Handicap (Farma Way)
Santa Anita Handicap (Farma Way)
Pimlico Special (Farma Way)

MARIA'S MON
2001: Florida Derby (Monarchos)
Kentucky Derby (Monarchos)

MARIBEAU
1973: American Derby (Bemo)
1975: New Orleans Handicap (Lord Rebeau)
1977: United Nations Handicap (Bemo)

MARKET WISE
1950: Arlington Futurity (To Market)
Washington Park Futurity (To Market)
1952: San Carlos Handicap (To Market)
Massachusetts Handicap (To Market)
Arlington Handicap (To Market)
Hawthorne Gold Cup (To Market)
1954: Gulfstream Park Handicap (Wise Margin)
Massachusetts Handicap (Wise Margin)

MARQUETRY
1998: San Felipe Stakes (Artax)
1999: Carter Handicap (Artax)
Vosburgh Stakes (Artax)
Breeders' Cup Sprint (Artax)
2001: King's Bishop Stakes (Squirtle Squirt)
Penske Auto Center BC Sprint (Squirtle Squirt)

MARSAYAS
1990: Santa Anita Derby (Mister Frisky)

MASHKOUR
1999: Oak Tree Turf Championship (Mash One)
2000: Clement L. Hirsch Mem. Turf Champ. (Mash One)

MASTADON
1981: San Fernando Stakes (Doonesbury)

MASTER WILLIE
1988: John Henry Handicap (Deputy Governor)

MAT BOY
1991: Oaklawn Handicap (Festin)
Nassau County Handicap (Festin)
Jockey Club Gold Cup (Festin)

MATUN
1984: Widener Handicap (Mat Boy)
Gulfstream Park Handicap (Mat Boy)

MAUDLIN
1995: Super Derby (Mecke)
1996: Early Times Turf Classic (Mecke)
Arlington Million (Mecke)
1997: Matron Stakes (Beautiful Pleasure)
1999: Personal Ensign Handicap (Beautiful Pleasure)
Beldame Stakes (Beautiful Pleasure)
Breeders' Cup Distaff (Beautiful Pleasure)
2000: Hempstead Handicap (Beautiful Pleasure)
Personal Ensign Handicap (Beautiful Pleasure)

MCLELLAN
1967: Black Helen Handicap (Mac's Sparkler)
Beldame Stakes (Mac's Sparkler)

MEADOWLAKE
1990: Spinaway Stakes (Meadow Star)
Matron Stakes (Meadow Star)
Frizette Stakes (Meadow Star)
Breeders' Cup Juvenile Fillies (Meadow Star)
1991: Acorn Stakes (Meadow Star)
Mother Goose Stakes (Meadow Star)
1999: Champagne Stakes (Greenwood Lake)
Remsen Stakes (Greenwood Lake)

MEDIEVAL MAN
1995: Vosburgh Stakes (Not Surprising)

MEDIUM
1956: Washington D.C. International (Master Boing)

MEHMET
1988: San Fernando Stakes (On the Line)
1989: Carter Handicap (On the Line)

MENACE
1975: Donn Handicap (Proud and Bold)

MENDOCINO
2001: Matriarch Stakes (Starine)
2002: Breeders' Cup Filly and Mare Turf (Starine)

MENETRIER
1955: United Nations Handicap (Blue Choir)

MENOCAL
1981: Golden Harvest Handicap (Mean Martha)

MENOW
1948: Champagne Stakes (Capot)
Pimlico Futurity (Capot)
1949: Preakness Stakes (Capot)
Belmont Stakes (Capot)
Jerome Handicap (Capot)
Pimlico Special (Capot)
1951: Pimlico Futurity (Cajun)
Futurity Stakes (Tom Fool)
Blue Grass Stakes (Ruhe)
1952: Jerome Handicap (Tom Fool)
Grey Lag Handicap (Tom Fool)
Spinaway Stakes (Flirtatious)
1953: Metropolitan Handicap (Tom Fool)
Suburban Handicap (Tom Fool)
Carter Handicap (Tom Fool)
Brooklyn Handicap (Tom Fool)
Whitney Stakes (Tom Fool)
Pimlico Special (Tom Fool)

METFIELD
1995: Oak Leaf Stakes (Tipically Irish)
2000: Ashland Stakes (Rings a Chime)

MICHEL
1950: Inglewood Handicap (Miche)
1952: Santa Anita Handicap (Miche)

MI CIELO
1999: Coaching Club American Oaks (On a Soapbox)

MIDDLEGROUND
1957: Alabama Stakes (Here and There)
1959: Coaching Club American Oaks (Resaca)
Delaware Oaks (Resaca)
1965: Acorn Stakes (Ground Control)

MIDSTREAM
1948: Hollywood Gold Cup (Shannon II)
Golden Gate Handicap (Shannon II)

MIGOLI
1957: Belmont Stakes (Gallant Man)
Travers Stakes (Gallant Man)
Jockey Club Gold Cup (Gallant Man)
1958: Metropolitan Handicap (Gallant Man)
Hollywood Gold Cup (Gallant Man)
Sunset Handicap (Gallant Man)

MILKMAN
1947: Top Flight Handicap (Rytina)
1948: Santa Susana Stakes (Mrs. Rabbit)

MILL REEF
1984: Breeders' Cup Turf (Lashkari)

MINCIO
1978: Yellow Ribbon Stakes (Amazer)

MINERA II
1977: La Canada Stakes (Lucie Manet)
Santa Margarita Handicap (Lucie Manet)

MINNESOTA MAC
1971: Arlington-Washington Futurity (Governor Max)
1978: Secretariat Stakes (Mac Diarmida)
Canadian Int. Championship (Mac Diarmida)
Washington D.C. International (Mac Diarmida)
1982: Ramona Handicap (Honey Fox)

MIO D'AREZZO
1946: San Carlos Handicap (Sirde)

MIRONTON
1964: Display Handicap (Primordial II)
1965: Widener Handicap (Primordial II)

MIRZA II
1952: Carter Handicap (Northern Star)

MISSILE
1970: Coaching Club American Oaks (Missile Belle)
Gazelle Handicap (Missile Belle)

MISTER FRISKY
1997: Ohio Derby (Frisk Me Now)
1998: Suburban Handicap (Frisk Me Now)
1999: Philip H. Iselin Handicap (Frisk Me Now)

MISTY FLIGHT
1965: Everglades Stakes (Sparkling Johnny)
1969: Washington Park Handicap (Night Invader)

MISWAKI
1985: Hopeful Stakes (Papal Power)
1986: Hutcheson Stakes (Papal Power)
1991: Philip H. Iselin Handicap (Black Tie Affair)
Breeders' Cup Classic (Black Tie Affair)
1996: Pegasus Breeders' Cup Handicap (Allied Forces)

MOCITO GUAPO
1998: Santa Anita Handicap (Malek)

MO EXCEPTION
1990: Coaching Club American Oaks (Charon)

MOGAMBO
1991: Matron Stakes (Anh Duong)

MONEY BROKER
1960: Arkansas Derby (Spring Broker)

MONGO
1974: Flamingo Stakes (Bushongo)
1978: Sorority Stakes (Mongo Queen)

MONTBROOK
2001: Super Derby (Outofthebox)
2003: Fountain of Youth Stakes (Trust N Luck)

MONTEVERDI
1990: Meadowlands Cup (Great Normand)

MONTPARNASSE II
1971: Century Handicap (Big Shot II)
Manhattan Handicap (Big Shot II)
1975: American Handicap (Montmartre)

MOONDUST II
1964: Gotham Stakes (Mr. Moonlight)
1967: Santa Margarita Handicap (Miss Moona)

MOONLIGHT RUN
1956: Vanity Handicap (Mary Machree)

MORE SUN
1960: Hollywood Derby (Tempestuous)

MOSCOW BALLET
1989: Oak Leaf Stakes (Dominant Dancer)
2001: Las Virgenes Stakes (Golden Ballet)
Santa Anita Oaks (Golden Ballet)

MOSSBOROUGH
1958: Belmont Stakes (Cavan)

MOUNTAIN CAT
1998: Ohio Derby (Classic Cat)

MOUNTDRAGO
1990: Brooklyn Handicap (Montubio)

MOUNT MARCY
1962: Del Mar Debutante Stakes (Brown Berry)

MR. BUSHER
1962: Top Flight Handicap (Pepper Patch)

MR. GREELEY
2000: Cigar Mile Handicap (El Corredor)
2002: Humana Distaff Handicap (Celtic Melody)
Mother Goose Stakes (Nonsuch Bay)
Futurity Stakes (Whywhywhy)

MR. LEADER
1974: Alcibiades Stakes (Hope of Glory)
1976: Dwyer Handicap (Quiet Little Table)
1977: Carter Handicap (Quiet Little Table)
Suburban Handicap (Quiet Little Table)
1979: Apple Blossom Handicap (Miss Baja)
1980: American Derby (Hurry Up Blue)
1981: Gulfstream Park Handicap (Hurry Up Blue)
1986: Haskell Invitational Handicap (Wise Times)
Travers Stakes (Wise Times)
Super Derby (Wise Times)
1989: Santa Anita Handicap (Martial Law)
1990: Santa Anita Handicap (Ruhlmann)

MR. LONG
1987: Vanity Handicap (Infinidad)

MR. MUSIC
1956: Cowdin Stakes (Mister Jive)
1957: Gotham Stakes (Mister Jive)
1962: Black Helen Handicap (Seven Thirty)
Delaware Handicap (Seven Thirty)

MR. MUSTARD
1964: Californian Stakes (Mustard Plaster)

MR. PROSPECTOR
1978: Arlington-Washington Lassie Stakes (It's In the Air)
Oak Leaf Stakes (It's In the Air)
1979: Alabama Stakes (It's In the Air)
Vanity Handicap (It's In the Air)
Ruffian Handicap (It's In the Air)
Breeders' Futurity (Gold Stage)
1980: Vanity Handicap (It's In the Air)
1981: Metropolitan Handicap (Fappiano)
1982: Belmont Stakes (Conquistador Cielo)
Dwyer Stakes (Conquistador Cielo)
Metropolitan Handicap (Conquistador Cielo)
Pegasus Handicap (Fast Gold)
1984: Breeders' Cup Sprint (Eillo)
Hollywood Derby (Procida)
1985: Arkansas Derby (Tank's Prospect)
Preakness Stakes (Tank's Prospect)
Champagne Stakes (Mogambo)
1986: Hopeful Stakes (Gulch)
Futurity Stakes (Gulch)
Gotham Stakes (Mogambo)
1987: Gotham Stakes (Gone West)
Withers Stakes (Gone West)
Dwyer Stakes (Gone West)
Wood Memorial Stakes (Gulch)
Metropolitan Handicap (Gulch)
Jerome Handicap (Afleet)
Pennsylvania Derby (Afleet)
Futurity Stakes (Forty Niner)
Champagne Stakes (Forty Niner)
Matron Stakes (Over All)
Frizette Stakes (Classic Crown)
1988: Fountain of Youth Stakes (Forty Niner)
Haskell Invitational Handicap (Forty Niner)
Travers Stakes (Forty Niner)
Peter Pan Stakes (Seeking the Gold)
Dwyer Stakes (Seeking the Gold)
Super Derby (Seeking the Gold)
Metropolitan Handicap (Gulch)
Breeders' Cup Sprint (Gulch)
Gulfstream Park Handicap (Jade Hunter)
Vosburgh Stakes (Mining)
1989: Breeders' Cup Juvenile (Rhythm)
1990: Cowdin Stakes (Scan)
Remsen Stakes (Scan)
Travers Stakes (Rhythm)
Hollywood Starlet Stakes (Cuddles)
1991: Maskette Stakes (Queena)
Ruffian Handicap (Queena)
Jerome Handicap (Scan)
Pegasus Handicap (Scan)
Frizette Stakes (Preach)
1992: Ashland Stakes (Prospectors Delite)
Acorn Stakes (Prospectors Delite)
Frizette Stakes (Educated Risk)
1993: Jim Dandy Stakes (Miner's Mark)
Jockey Club Gold Cup (Miner's Mark)
1994: Top Flight Handicap (Educated Risk)
1995: Spinaway Stakes (Golden Attraction)
Matron Stakes (Golden Attraction)
Frizette Stakes (Golden Attraction)
1996: Philip H. Iselin Handicap (Smart Strike)
1997: Del Mar Futurity (Souvenir Copy)
Norfolk Stakes (Souvenir Copy)
2000: San Felipe Stakes (Fusaichi Pegasus)
Wood Memorial Stakes (Fusaichi Pegasus)
Kentucky Derby (Fusaichi Pegasus)
Arlington Million (Chester House)
2001: Oaklawn Handicap (Traditionally)
2002: Suburban Handicap (E Dubai)
Go for Wand Handicap (Dancethruthedawn)
2003: San Carlos Handicap (Aldebaran)
Metropolitan Handicap (Aldebaran)
Forego Handicap (Aldebaran)

MR. RANDY
1978: Frizette Stakes (Golferette)

MR. REDOY
1984: Santa Anita Derby (Mighty Adversary)

MR. TROUBLE
1955: Princess Pat Stakes (Supple)
1958: Display Handicap (Civet)

MT. LIVERMORE
1990: Withers Stakes (Housebuster)
Jerome Handicap (Housebuster)
1991: Carter Handicap (Housebuster)
Vosburgh Stakes (Housebuster)
Jersey Derby (Greek Costume)
1992: Arlington-Washington Lassie Stakes (Eliza)
Breeders' Cup Juvenile Fillies (Eliza)
1993: Santa Anita Oaks (Eliza)
1995: Molson Export Million (Peaks and Valleys)
Meadowlands Cup (Peaks and Valleys)
1997: Crown Royal Hollywood Derby (Subordination)
Gulfstream Park Handicap (Mt. Sassafras)
1998: Brooklyn Handicap (Subordination)
Eddie Read Handicap (Subordination)
2002: Forego Handicap (Orientate)
NAPA Breeders' Cup Sprint (Orientate)

MUMMY'S GAME
1988: Gamely Handicap (Pen Bal Lady)
Santa Barbara Handicap (Pen Bal Lady)

MUTAKDDIM
2003: Test Stakes (Lady Tak)

MY BABU
1956: Santa Margarita Handicap (Our Betters)
1957: Santa Margarita Handicap (Our Betters)
1960: Washington Park Futurity (Crozier)
Pimlico Futurity (Garwol)
Arlington Lassie Stakes (Colfax Maid)
1962: Aqueduct Stakes (Crozier)
1963: Santa Anita Handicap (Crozier)
San Carlos Handicap (Crozier)
Selima Stakes (My Card)
1964: New Orleans Handicap (Green Hornet)

MY GALLANT
1982: Illinois Derby (Star Gallant)

MY HOST
1966: Hollywood Derby (Fleet Host)
1967: San Luis Rey Handicap (Fleet Host)
1968: Charles H. Strub Stakes (Most Host)

MY LARK
1973: Del Mar Futurity (Such a Rush)

NADIR
1965: Vosburgh Handicap (R. Thomas)

NAEVUS
1988: Hollywood Futurity (King Glorious)
1989: Ohio Derby (King Glorious)
Haskell Invitational Handicap (King Glorious)

NAHAR II
1958: Breeders' Futurity (Namon)

NALEES MAN
1984: Oak Tree Invitational Stakes (Both Ends Burning)
1985: Hollywood Inv. Handicap (Both Ends Burning)

NANTALLAH
1961: Arlington Futurity (Ridan)
Washington Park Futurity (Ridan)
Arlington Lassie Stakes (Rudoma)
1962: Florida Derby (Ridan)
Blue Grass Stakes (Ridan)
Arlington Classic (Ridan)
1965: Spinaway Stakes (Moccasin)
Matron Stakes (Moccasin)
Selima Stakes (Moccasin)
Gardenia Stakes (Moccasin)
John B. Campbell Handicap (Lt. Stevens)
1974: Vanity Handicap (Tallahto)
Santa Barbara Handicap (Tallahto)
Oak Tree Invitational Stakes (Tallahto)

NASHUA
1962: Coaching Club American Oaks (Bramalea)
1963: Kentucky Jockey Club Stakes (Journalist)
Alabama Stakes (Tona)
1964: Selima Stakes (Marshua)
Vineland Handicap (Tona)
Ohio Derby (National)
1965: Coaching Club American Oaks (Marshua)
1966: Arlington-Washington Futurity (Diplomat Way)
1967: Garden State Stakes (Bugged)
Blue Grass Stakes (Diplomat Way)
1968: Frizette Stakes (Shuvee)
Selima Stakes (Shuvee)
New Orleans Handicap (Diplomat Way)
Oaklawn Handicap (Diplomat Way)
1969: Acorn Stakes (Shuvee)
Mother Goose Stakes (Shuvee)
Coaching Club American Oaks (Shuvee)
Alabama Stakes (Shuvee)
Ladies Handicap (Shuvee)
1970: Top Flight Handicap (Shuvee)
Beldame Stakes (Shuvee)
Jockey Club Gold Cup (Shuvee)
1971: Top Flight Handicap (Shuvee)
Jockey Club Gold Cup (Shuvee)
1978: Louisiana Derby (Esops Foibles)
Arkansas Derby (Esops Foibles)
Sapling Stakes (Tim the Tiger)
1981: Dwyer Stakes (Noble Nashua)
Swaps Stakes (Noble Nashua)
Jerome Handicap (Noble Nashua)
Marlboro Cup Handicap (Noble Nashua)
Eddie Read Handicap (Wickerr)
1982: Eddie Read Handicap (Wickerr)

NASHVILLE
1966: Del Mar Futurity (Ruken)
1967: Santa Anita Derby (Ruken)
1973: Norfolk Stakes (Money Lender)

NASHWAN
1995: Santa Barbara Handicap (Wandesta)
1996: Matriarch Stakes (Wandesta)

NASKRA
1978: American Derby (Nasty and Bold)
Brooklyn Handicap (Nasty and Bold)
1979: Whitney Stakes (Star de Naskra)
1980: Sorority Stakes (Fancy Naskra)
Monmouth Invitational Handicap (Thanks to Tony)
1982: United Nations Handicap (Naskra's Breeze)
Man o' War Stakes (Naskra's Breeze)
1983: Hawthorne Gold Cup (Water Bank)
1984: Gotham Stakes (Bear Hunt)
1987: Ladies Handicap (Nastique)
1988: Delaware Handicap (Nastique)
1989: Delaware Handicap (Nastique)
John Henry Handicap (Peace)
1990: Top Flight Handicap (Dreamy Mimi)
1991: Arkansas Derby (Olympio)
American Derby (Olympio)
Hollywood Derby (Olympio)

NASRULLAH
1950: Santa Anita Handicap (Noor)
San Juan Capistrano Handicap (Noor)
Golden Gate Handicap (Noor)
American Handicap (Noor)
Hollywood Gold Cup (Noor)
1954: Starlet Stakes (Blue Ruler)
Del Mar Futurity (Blue Ruler)
Hopeful Stakes (Nashua)

NASRULLAH *(Continued)*

Futurity Stakes (Nashua)
Arlington Lassie Stakes (Delta)
Princess Pat Stakes (Delta)
Champagne Stakes (Flying Fury)
1955: Flamingo Stakes (Nashua)
Florida Derby (Nashua)
Wood Memorial Stakes (Nashua)
Preakness Stakes (Nashua)
Belmont Stakes (Nashua)
Dwyer Stakes (Nashua)
Arlington Classic (Nashua)
Jockey Club Gold Cup (Nashua)
Gardenia Stakes (Nasrina)
Frizette Stakes (Nasrina)
Arlington Lassie Stakes (Judy Rullah)
San Felipe Handicap (Jean's Joe)
William P. Kyne Handicap (Mister Gus)
1956: Widener Handicap (Nashua)
Grey Lag Handicap (Nashua)
Suburban Handicap (Nashua)
Monmouth Handicap (Nashua)
Jockey Club Gold Cup (Nashua)
San Antonio Handicap (Mister Gus)
Woodward Stakes (Mister Gus)
Arlington Handicap (Mister Gus)
Arlington Lassie Stakes (Leallah)
Alcibiades Stakes (Leallah)
Futurity Stakes (Bold Ruler)
Arlington Matron Stakes (Delta)
Manhattan Handicap (Flying Fury)
1957: Flamingo Stakes (Bold Ruler)
Wood Memorial Stakes (Bold Ruler)
Preakness Stakes (Bold Ruler)
Jerome Handicap (Bold Ruler)
Trenton Handicap (Bold Ruler)
Garden State Stakes (Nadir)
Selima Stakes (Guide Line)
1958: Carter Handicap (Bold Ruler)
Suburban Handicap (Bold Ruler)
Monmouth Handicap (Bold Ruler)
Kentucky Oaks (Bug Brush)
Dwyer Handicap (Victory Morn)
American Derby (Nadir)
Lawrence Realization Stakes (Martins Rullah)
1959: Santa Margarita Handicap (Bug Brush)
San Antonio Handicap (Bug Brush)
Inglewood Handicap (Bug Brush)
Suburban Handicap (Bald Eagle)
Gallant Fox Handicap (Bald Eagle)
Washington D.C. International (Bald Eagle)
1960: Widener Handicap (Bald Eagle)
Gulfstream Park Handicap (Bald Eagle)
Metropolitan Handicap (Bald Eagle)
Aqueduct Handicap (Bald Eagle)
Washington D.C. International (Bald Eagle)
Tropical Park Handicap (On-and-On)
McLennan Handicap (On-and-On)
Brooklyn Handicap (On-and-On)
Californian Stakes (Fleet Nasrullah)
Arlington Handicap (One-Eyed King)
1961: Hopeful Stakes (Jaipur)
Cowdin Stakes (Jaipur)
1962: Gotham Stakes (Jaipur)
Withers Stakes (Jaipur)
Jersey Derby (Jaipur)
Belmont Stakes (Jaipur)
Travers Stakes (Jaipur)
Futurity Stakes (Never Bend)
Cowdin Stakes (Never Bend)
Champagne Stakes (Never Bend)
Hopeful Stakes (Outing Class)
Manhattan Handicap (Tutankhamen)
1963: Flamingo Stakes (Never Bend)
Dwyer Handicap (Outing Class)
Hialeah Turf Cup (Intercepted)
Donn Handicap (Tutankhamen)

NASTY AND BOLD

1987: Top Flight Handicap (Ms. Eloise)
1991: Gamely Handicap (Miss Josh)

NATCHEZ

1955: Carter Handicap (Bobby Brocato)
1956: Santa Anita Handicap (Bobby Brocato)
San Juan Capistrano Handicap (Bobby Brocato)

NATIONAL

1970: Monmouth Oaks (Kilts N Kapers)

NATIVE CHARGER

1969: Futurity Stakes (High Echelon)
Pimlico-Laurel Futurity (High Echelon)
1970: Sorority Stakes (Forward Gal)
Spinaway Stakes (Forward Gal)
Frizette Stakes (Forward Gal)
Belmont Stakes (High Echelon)
1971: Monmouth Oaks (Forward Gal)
Gazelle Handicap (Forward Gal)
1972: Coaching Club American Oaks (Summer Guest)
Alabama Stakes (Summer Guest)
1973: Grey Lag Handicap (Summer Guest)
Bowling Green Handicap (Summer Guest)
1974: Spinster Stakes (Summer Guest)
1977: San Fernando Stakes (Kirby Lane)
Charles H. Strub Stakes (Kirby Lane)
1984: Arlington Handicap (Who's For Dinner)

NATIVE DANCER

1960: Spinaway Stakes (Good Move)
Selima Stakes (Good Move)
1961: Hollywood Juvenile Championship (Rattle Dancer)
1965: Flamingo Stakes (Native Charger)
Florida Derby (Native Charger)
Sorority Stakes (Native Street)
1966: Kentucky Derby (Kauai King)
Preakness Stakes (Kauai King)
Kentucky Oaks (Native Street)
1968: Wood Memorial Stakes (Dancer's Image)
1971: Whitney Stakes (Protanto)

NATIVE PROSPECTOR

1994: Milady Handicap (Andestine)

NATIVE ROYALTY

1977: Florida Derby (Ruthie's Native)
1983: Louisiana Derby (Balboa Native)

NEARCO

1958: Michigan Mile (Nearctic)
1960: Hialeah Turf Cup (Amerigo)
San Juan Capistrano Handicap (Amerigo)

NEARCTIC

1964: Flamingo Stakes (Northern Dancer)
Florida Derby (Northern Dancer)
Blue Grass Stakes (Northern Dancer)
Kentucky Derby (Northern Dancer)
Preakness Stakes (Northern Dancer)
1969: Matron Stakes (Cold Comfort)

NEAR MAN

1973: Louisiana Derby (Leo's Pisces)

NEBBIOLO

1986: Hialeah Turf Cup (Sondrio)

NEDDIE

1953: Molly Pitcher Handicap (My Celeste)
Monmouth Handicap (My Celeste)

NEEDLES

1968: Pan American Handicap (Irish Rebellion)

NEVER BEND

1967: Cowdin Stakes (Iron Ruler)
1968: Jerome Handicap (Iron Ruler)
1969: Dwyer Handicap (Gleaming Light)
1970: Hopeful Stakes (Proudest Roman)
Widener Handicap (Never Bow)
1971: Cowdin Stakes (Loquacious Don)
Brooklyn Handicap (Never Bow)
1972: Vosburgh Handicap (Triple Bend)
San Fernando Stakes (Triple Bend)
Santa Anita Handicap (Triple Bend)
1975: Sapling Stakes (Full Out)
1977: Swaps Stakes (J.O. Tobin)
1978: Dwyer Handicap (Junction)
Californian Stakes (J.O. Tobin)

NEVER SAY DIE

1959: Selima Stakes (La Fuerza)
1964: Grey Lag Handicap (Saidam)

NEW POLICY

1972: Malibu Stakes (Kfar Tov)

NIGHT SHIFT

1992: Hollywood Starlet Stakes (Creaking Board)
1996: Hollywood Oaks (Listening)
1997: Milady Breeders' Cup Handicap (Listening)

NIGROMANTE

1962: Cinema Handicap (Black Sheep)
American Derby (Black Sheep)
Arlington-Washington Futurity (Candy Spots)
1963: Santa Anita Derby (Candy Spots)
Florida Derby (Candy Spots)
Preakness Stakes (Candy Spots)
Jersey Derby (Candy Spots)
American Derby (Candy Spots)
Arlington Classic (Candy Spots)
American Handicap (Dr. Kacy)

NIJINSKY II

1976: Sunset Handicap (Caucasus)
Manhattan Handicap (Caucasus)
1977: San Luis Rey Stakes (Caucasus)
1978: Suburban Handicap (Upper Nile)
1979: Sheepshead Bay Handicap (Terpsichorist)
Jerome Handicap (Czaravich)
1980: Metropolitan Handicap (Czaravich)
1981: Hollywood Derby (De La Rose)
1982: Selima Stakes (Bemissed)
Arkansas Derby (Hostage)
1983: Hialeah Turf Cup (Nijinsky's Secret)
1984: Hialeah Turf Cup (Nijinsky's Secret)
Oak Leaf Stakes (Folk Art)
1986: Kentucky Derby (Ferdinand)
Man o' War Stakes (Dance of Life)
1987: Hollywood Gold Cup (Ferdinand)
Breeders' Cup Classic (Ferdinand)
1988: Fantasy Stakes (Jeanne Jones)
Alabama Stakes (Maplejinsky)
Ladies Handicap (Banker's Lady)
1989: Suburban Handicap (Dancing Spree)
Breeders' Cup Sprint (Dancing Spree)
Top Flight Handicap (Banker's Lady)
1990: Carter Handicap (Dancing Spree)
Breeders' Cup Mile (Royal Academy)
1991: Rothmans International Stakes (Sky Classic)
1992: Caesars International Handicap (Sky Classic)
Turf Classic (Sky Classic)

NIRGAL

1955: Pimlico Futurity (Nail)
Remsen Stakes (Nail)
Futurity Stakes (Nail)
1962: Delaware Oaks (North South Gal)

NOBLE HERO

1960: Bougainvillea Turf Handicap (Noble Sel)

NODOUBLE

1979: Bowling Green Handicap (Overskate)
1981: Del Mar Debutante Stakes (Skillful Joy)
Hollywood Starlet Stakes (Skillful Joy)
1982: Louisiana Downs Handicap (Pair of Deuces)
1986: Vanity Handicap (Magnificent Lindy)
Delaware Handicap (Shocker T.)
1989: Santa Barbara Handicap (No Review)

NOHOLME II

1968: Arkansas Derby (Nodouble)
Michigan Mile and One-Eighth (Nodouble)
Hawthorne Gold Cup (Nodouble)
1969: Californian Stakes (Nodouble)
Brooklyn Handicap (Nodouble)
Hawthorne Gold Cup (Nodouble)
Santa Anita Handicap (Nodouble)
Cinema Handicap (Noholme Jr.)
1970: Metropolitan Handicap (Nodouble)
1972: Arlington-Washington Futurity (Shecky Greene)
1973: Fountain of Youth Stakes (Shecky Greene)
1976: Ramona Handicap (Vagabonda)

NOOR

1954: Kentucky Jockey Club Stakes (Prince Noor)
1955: Cowdin Stakes (Noorsaga)
Everglades Stakes (Prince Noor)
1957: San Felipe Handicap (Joe Price)
1959: Hollywood Juvenile Championship (Noble Noor)
1960: California Derby (Noble Noor)
1961: San Felipe Handicap (Flutterby)
1963: Arlington Park Handicap (Bounding Main)

NORCLIFFE

1984: Jim Beam Stakes (At the Threshold)
Arlington Classic (At the Threshold)
Ohio Derby (At the Threshold)
American Derby (At the Threshold)
1987: Vosburgh Stakes (Groovy)

NO ROBBERY

1972: Donn Handicap (Going Straight)
1979: Spinster Stakes (Safe)
1981: Vanity Handicap (Track Robbery)
1982: Spinster Stakes (Track Robbery)
Apple Blossom Handicap (Track Robbery)

NORTHERLY

1982: Acorn Stakes (Cupecoy's Joy)
Mother Goose Stakes (Cupecoy's Joy)

NORTHERN ANSWER

1974: Arlington-Washington Futurity (Greek Answer)

NORTHERN BABY

1986: Arkansas Derby (Rampage)
Hollywood Derby (Thrill Show)
1989: Hollywood Derby (Live the Dream)
1990: Hopeful Stakes (Deposit Ticket)
Gamely Handicap (Double Wedge)
1993: Yellow Ribbon Stakes (Possibly Perfect)
1994: Santa Barbara Handicap (Possibly Perfect)
1995: Gamely Handicap (Possibly Perfect)
Ramona Handicap (Possibly Perfect)
Beverly D. Stakes (Possibly Perfect)

NORTHERN DANCER

1970: Pan American Handicap (One For All)
Sunset Handicap (One For All)
Alabama Stakes (Fanfreluche)
1971: Alabama Stakes (Lauries Dancer)
Louisiana Derby (Northfields)
Widener Handicap (True North)
Canadian International Championship (One For All)
1972: Black Helen Handicap (Alma North)
1976: Jerome Handicap (Dance Spell)
1978: Kentucky Oaks (White Star Line)
Alabama Stakes (White Star Line)
Top Flight Handicap (Northernette)
Apple Blossom Handicap (Northernette)
1983: Alabama Stakes (Spit Curl)
Beldame Stakes (Dance Number)
Pennsylvania Derby (Dixieland Band)
1984: United Nations Handicap (Hero's Honor)
1987: Gamely Handicap (Northern Aspen)

NORTHERN FLAGSHIP

1998: Jerome Handicap (Limit Out)

NORTHERN FLING

1983: Flower Bowl Handicap (First Approach)
1989: United Nations Handicap (Yankee Affair)
Man o' War Stakes (Yankee Affair)
Turf Classic (Yankee Affair)

NORTHERN JOVE

1978: Selima Stakes (Candy Eclair)
1982: Matron Stakes (Wings of Jove)
1988: United Nations Handicap (Equalize)
1990: Swaps Stakes (Jovial)
1993: Oaklawn Handicap (Jovial)

NORTHJET

1986: Secretariat Stakes (Southjet)
Rothmans International Stakes (Southjet)

NOSTALGIA

1986: Charles H. Strub Stakes (Nostalgia's Star)

NOTEBOOK

1999: Walmac International Alcibiades Stakes (Scratch Pad)
Acorn Stakes (Three Ring)
2001: Forego Handicap (Delaware Township)
Frank J. De Francis Mem. Dash (Delaware Township)
2002: Fountain of Youth Stakes (Booklet)
2003: Mother Goose Stakes (Spoken Fur)
Coaching Club American Oaks (Spoken Fur)

NUREYEV

1987: Hialeah Turf Cup (Theatrical)
Turf Classic (Theatrical)
Man o' War Stakes (Theatrical)
Breeders' Cup Turf (Theatrical)
Breeders' Cup Mile (Miesque)
Hollywood Derby (Stately Don)
1988: Hollywood Oaks (Pattern Step)
Vanity Handicap (Annoconnor)
Breeders' Cup Mile (Miesque)
1997: Oaklawn Handicap (Atticus)
Breeders' Cup Mile (Spinning World)
1998: Early Times Turf Classic (Joyeaux Danseur)
2000: Pacific Classic (Skimming)
Del Mar Oaks (No Matter What)
2001: United Nations Handicap (Senure)
Clement L. Hirsch Mem. Turf Championship (Senure)
Pacific Classic (Skimming)
2003: Eddie Read Handicap (Special Ring)

OCCUPY

1952: Astoria Stakes (Home-Made)
1953: Vagrancy Handicap (Home-Made)
Comely Handicap (Home-Made)

OCEAN SWELL

1955: San Juan Capistrano Handicap (St. Vincent)
Dixie Handicap (St. Vincent)

OCEANUS II

1964: Del Mar Debutante Stakes (Admirably)

O'GRADY

1966: Washington D.C. International (Behistoun)

OH JOHNNY

1968: Dixie Handicap (High Hat)
Bowling Green Handicap (High Hat)

OH SAY

1988: Ruffian Handicap (Sham Say)

OIL CAPITOL

1959: Kentucky Jockey Club Stakes (Oil Wick)

OLD BAG

1973: Champagne Stakes (Holding Pattern)
1974: Monmouth Invitational Handicap (Holding Pattern)
Travers Stakes (Holding Pattern)

OLDEN TIMES

1969: Alcibiades Stakes (Belle Noire)
1970: Withers Stakes (Hagley)
1972: Arlington-Washington Lassie Stakes (Natural Sound)
1982: Del Mar Futurity (Roving Boy)
Norfolk Stakes (Roving Boy)
Hollywood Futurity (Roving Boy)

OLE

2002: Malibu Stakes (Debonair Joe)

OLE BOB BOWERS

1980: Hialeah Turf Cup (John Henry)
Hollywood Invitational Handicap (John Henry)
Oak Tree Invitational Stakes (John Henry)
San Luis Rey Stakes (John Henry)
San Juan Capistrano Handicap (John Henry)
1981: Jockey Club Gold Cup (John Henry)
Santa Anita Handicap (John Henry)
Hollywood Invitational Handicap (John Henry)
Sword Dancer Stakes (John Henry)
Arlington Million (John Henry)
Oak Tree Invitational Stakes (John Henry)
San Luis Rey Stakes (John Henry)
1982: Santa Anita Handicap (John Henry)
Oak Tree Invitational Stakes (John Henry)
1983: Hollywood Turf Cup (John Henry)
1984: Hollywood Invitational Handicap (John Henry)
Sunset Handicap (John Henry)
Budweiser-Arlington Million (John Henry)
Turf Classic (John Henry)

OLYMPIA

1954: Spinaway Stakes (Gandharva)
1955: Breeders' Futurity (Jovial Jove)
1956: Arlington Futurity (Greek Game)
Washington Park Futurity (Greek Game)
Starlet Stakes (Lucky Mel)
1957: Arlington Matron Handicap (Pucker Up)
Beldame Handicap (Pucker Up)
Washington Park Handicap (Pucker Up)
Bougainvillea Turf Handicap (Espea)
1958: Fall Highweight Handicap (Bull Strength)
1959: Massachusetts Handicap (Air Pilot)
1960: Sorority Stakes (Apatontheback)
Massachusetts Handicap (Talent Show)
1961: Kentucky Oaks (My Portrait)
Monmouth Oaks (My Portrait)
1962: Pimlico Futurity (Right Proud)
Los Angeles Handicap (Winonly)
Massachusetts Handicap (Air Pilot)
1963: Californian Stakes (Winonly)
1964: Spinaway Stakes (Candalita)
Matron Stakes (Candalita)
1965: Suburban Handicap (Pia Star)
Brooklyn Handicap (Pia Star)
1966: Jersey Derby (Creme dela Creme)
Widener Handicap (Pia Star)

OLYMPIAD KING

1977: Sunset Handicap (Today'n Tomorrow)
1982: Hollywood Derby (Racing Is Fun)

ON-AND-ON

1968: Everglades Stakes (Forward Pass)
Florida Derby (Forward Pass)
Blue Grass Stakes (Forward Pass)
Kentucky Derby (Forward Pass)
Preakness Stakes (Forward Pass)
American Derby (Forward Pass)

ONE COUNT

1961: Delaware Handicap (Airmans Guide)
Beldame Stakes (Airmans Guide)
Grey Lag Handicap (Mail Order)
1964: Mother Goose Stakes (Sceree)

ONE FOR ALL

1976: Demoiselle Stakes (Bring Out the Band)
1977: Acorn Stakes (Bring Out the Band)
1981: Santa Barbara Handicap (The Very One)

ONLY ONE

1947: Roseben Handicap (Inroc)
1950: Vosburgh Handicap (Tea-Maker)

ON THE SLY

1984: Blue Grass Stakes (Play Fellow)
Arlington Classic (Play Fellow)
American Derby (Play Fellow)
Travers Stakes (Play Fellow)

ON TRUST

1955: California Derby (Trackmaster)
1956: Santa Anita Maturity (Trackmaster)

OPENING VERSE

2000: Flower Bowl Invitational Handicap (Colstar)

ORBIT II

1961: Inglewood Handicap (Sea Orbit)

ORBIT DANCER

1988: Ohio Derby (Jim's Orbit)

ORBIT RULER

1980: California Derby (Jaklin Klugman)
Jerome Handicap (Jaklin Klugman)

OUR EMBLEM

2002: Kentucky Derby (War Emblem)
Preakness Stakes (War Emblem)
Haskell Invitational Handicap (War Emblem)
Arkansas Derby (Private Emblem)

OUR MICHAEL

1982: Vosburgh Stakes (Engine One)

OUR NATIVE

1979: Sapling Stakes (Rockhill Native)
Futurity Stakes (Rockhill Native)
1980: Blue Grass Stakes (Rockhill Native)
1984: Breeders' Futurity (Crater Fire)
1985: Selima Stakes (I'm Splendid)
Hollywood Turf Cup (Zoffany)
1986: Sunset Handicap (Zoffany)
1987: San Luis Rey Stakes (Zoffany)

OUT OF PLACE

1999: Arkansas Derby (Certain)

OVERSKATE

1988: Selima Stakes (Capades)

OWEN TUDOR

1959: Hialeah Turf Cup (Tudor Era)
Man o' War Handicap (Tudor Era)
1960: New Orleans Handicap (Tudor Era)

PAGO PAGO

1974: San Felipe Handicap (Aloha Mood)
1981: Super Derby (Island Whirl)
1982: Woodward Stakes (Island Whirl)
1983: Hollywood Gold Cup (Island Whirl)
Whitney Handicap (Island Whirl)

PALACE MUSIC

1994: NYRA Mile Handicap (Cigar)
1995: Donn Handicap (Cigar)

PALACE MUSIC *(Continued)*
Gulfstream Park Handicap (Cigar)
Oaklawn Handicap (Cigar)
Pimlico Special (Cigar)
Hollywood Gold Cup (Cigar)
Woodward Stakes (Cigar)
Jockey Club Gold Cup (Cigar)
Breeders' Cup Classic (Cigar)
1996: Donn Handicap (Cigar)
Woodward Stakes (Cigar)

PALESTINE
1958: Tropical Handicap (St. Amour II)
1966: Arkansas Derby (Aeropolis)

PALESTINIAN
1957: Lawrence Realization Stakes (Promised Land)
Roamer Handicap (Promised Land)
Pimlico Special (Promised Land)
1958: John B. Campbell Mem. Handicap (Promised Land)
Massachusetts Handicap (Promised Land)
San Juan Capistrano Handicap (Promised Land)

PAMPERED KING II
1968: Man o' War Stakes (Czar Alexander)
1969: Dixie Handicap (Czar Alexander)
Bowling Green Handicap (Czar Alexander)
Oak Tree Stakes (Czar Alexander)

PANCHO VILLA
1991: Ashland Stakes (Do It With Style)

PANORAMIC
1999: Ramona Handicap (Tuzla)

PANTALON
1948: San Antonio Handicap (Talon)
Santa Anita Handicap (Talon)

PAPA REDBIRD
1953: Alcibiades Stakes (Oil Painting)
1955: Maskette Handicap (Oil Painting)
1958: Withers Stakes (Sir Robby)

PAPPA FOURWAY
1960: Hollywood Juvenile Championship (Pappa's All)
Arlington Futurity (Pappa's All)
1961: Del Mar Futurity (Weldy)

PARBURY
1978: Del Mar Handicap (Palton)

PARDAL
1957: Diana Handicap (Pardala)
1958: Black Helen Handicap (Pardala)
1963: San Juan Capistrano Handicap (Pardao)

PARTAB
1955: Bougainvillea Turf Handicap (Cascanuez)

PASS CATCHER
1980: Dwyer Stakes (Amber Pass)
1981: Monmouth Handicap (Amber Pass)

PAS SEUL
1985: Arlington Handicap (Pass the Line)

PASS THE GLASS
1986: Hollywood Gold Cup (Super Diamond)
1989: San Antonio Handicap (Super Diamond)

PAVOT
1956: Fall Highweight Handicap (Impromptu)

PEANUTS
1947: Travers Stakes (Young Peter)

PENSIVE
1949: Kentucky Derby (Ponder)
Arlington Classic (Ponder)
American Derby (Ponder)
Lawrence Realization Stakes (Ponder)
Jockey Club Gold Cup (Ponder)
Champagne Stakes (Theory)
1950: San Antonio Handicap (Ponder)
Arlington Handicap (Ponder)
Santa Anita Maturity (Ponder)

PERAMBULATOR
1966: Californian Stakes (Travel Orb)

PERRAULT
1989: San Luis Rey Stakes (Frankly Perfect)
Hollywood Turf Cup (Frankly Perfect)

PERSIAN BOLD
1985: Sunset Handicap (Kings Island)

PERSIAN ROAD II
1968: Kentucky Oaks (Dark Mirage)
Acorn Stakes (Dark Mirage)
Mother Goose Stakes (Dark Mirage)
Coaching Club American Oaks (Dark Mirage)
Monmouth Oaks (Dark Mirage)

PETARDIA
2000: Santa Anita Derby (The Deputy)

PETARE
1964: Saratoga Special (Sadair)
Arlington-Washington Futurity (Sadair)
Garden State Stakes (Sadair)
Pimlico Futurity (Sadair)
1967: Sapling Stakes (Subpet)
1970: Suburban Handicap (Barometer)

PETINGO
1981: Hollywood Turf Cup (Lobsang II)

PETIONVILLE
2003: Alabama Stakes (Island Fashion)
La Brea Stakes (Island Fashion)

PETITION
1959: Hawthorne Gold Cup (Day Court)

PETRONE
1981: Hollywood Derby (Silveyville)
1989: Yellow Ribbon Stakes (Brown Bess)
1990: Santa Barbara Handicap (Brown Bess)

PETROSE
1946: Acorn Stakes (Earshot)
1947: New Orleans Handicap (Earshot)
1950: Princess Pat Stakes (Flyamanita)
1954: Fall Highweight Handicap (Pet Bully)
Washington Park Handicap (Pet Bully)
Woodward Stakes (Pet Bully)

PHALANX
1953: Cowdin Stakes (Fisherman)
Champagne Stakes (Fisherman)
1954: Gotham Stakes (Fisherman)
Travers Stakes (Fisherman)
Lawrence Realization Stakes (Fisherman)
Washington D.C. International (Fisherman)
1955: Excelsior Handicap (Fisherman)
1956: Gotham Stakes (Career Boy)
United Nations Handicap (Career Boy)
1957: Michigan Mile and One-Sixteenth (My Night Out)

PHARAMOND II
1946: Arlington Futurity (Cosmic Bomb)
Cowdin Stakes (Cosmic Bomb)
Ladies Handicap (Athenia)
1947: Discovery Handicap (Cosmic Bomb)
Lawrence Realization Stakes (Cosmic Bomb)
Roamer Handicap (Cosmic Bomb)
Trenton Handicap (Cosmic Bomb)
1948: Demoiselle Stakes (Lithe)
1949: Arlington Matron Handicap (Lithe)
Comely Handicap (Lithe)
Roseben Handicap (Up Beat)
1950: Arlington Matron Handicap (Lithe)

PHAR MON
1957: Arlington Futurity (Leather Button)

PHONE ORDER
1997: Gotham Stakes (Smokin Mel)

PHONE TRICK
1991: Arlington-Washington Futurity (Caller I.D.)
Arlington-Washington Lassie Stakes (Speed Dialer)
1993: Oak Leaf Stakes (Phone Chatter)
Breeders' Cup Juvenile Fillies (Phone Chatter)
1997: Hopeful Stakes (Favorite Trick)
Breeders' Cup Juvenile (Favorite Trick)
1998: Jim Dandy Stakes (Favorite Trick)

PIA STAR
1972: Manhattan Handicap (Star Envoy)
1973: Arkansas Derby (Impecunious)
1984: San Antonio Handicap (Poley)

PIASTER
1980: Oak Leaf Stakes (Astrious)

PICK UP THE PHONE
2001: Strub Stakes (Wooden Phone)

PIED D'OR
1966: Sorority Stakes (Like A Charm)

PIET
1966: Florida Derby (Williamston Kid)

PILATE
1946: Remsen Handicap (Phalanx)
1947: Wood Memorial Stakes (Phalanx)
Belmont Stakes (Phalanx)
Dwyer Stakes (Phalanx)
Jockey Club Gold Cup (Phalanx)
1948: Santa Margarita Handicap (Miss Doreen)
1949: Fall Highweight Handicap (Royal Governor)
Grey Lag Handicap (Royal Governor)
1950: Widener Handicap (Royal Governor)
New York Handicap (Pilaster)
1951: Hawthorne Gold Cup (Seaward)
Stars and Stripes Handicap (Royal Governor)

PINE BLUFF
1998: Milady Breeders' Cup Handicap (I Ain't Bluffing)
Fountain of Youth Stakes (Lil's Lad)

PINK FLOWER
1952: Washington D.C. International (Wilwyn)

PIPING ROCK
1946: Spinaway Stakes (Pipette)

PIRATEER
1987: Norfolk Stakes (Saratoga Passage)

PIRATE'S BOUNTY
1985: California Derby (Hajji's Treasure)
1995: Milady Handicap (Pirate's Revenge)
Vanity Handicap (Private Persuasion)

PIVOTAL
2001: Del Mar Oaks (Golden Apples)
2002: Beverly D. Stakes (Golden Apples)
Yellow Ribbon Stakes (Golden Apples)
2003: John C. Mabee Handicap (Megahertz)

PLATTER
1953: Lawrence Realization Stakes (Platan)
1955: Arlington Handicap (Platan)

PLAY FELLOW
1989: Jim Beam Stakes (Western Playboy)
Blue Grass Stakes (Western Playboy)
Pennsylvania Derby (Western Playboy)

PLEASANT COLONY
1986: Jim Dandy Stakes (Lac Ouimet)
1988: Flamingo Stakes (Cherokee Colony)
1989: Young America Stakes (Roanoke)
1990: Ladies Handicap (Colonial Waters)
1991: Oak Leaf Stakes (Pleasant Stage)
Breeders' Cup Juvenile Fillies (Pleasant Stage)
San Luis Rey Stakes (Pleasant Variety)
Californian Stakes (Roanoke)
1992: Suburban Handicap (Pleasant Tap)
Jockey Club Gold Cup (Pleasant Tap)
1993: Santa Anita Handicap (Sir Beaufort)
Belmont Stakes (Colonial Affair)
Ruffian Handicap (Shared Interest)
1994: Whitney Handicap (Colonial Affair)
Jockey Club Gold Cup (Colonial Affair)
1997: Buick Pegasus Handicap (Behrens)
1999: Gulfstream Park Handicap (Behrens)
Oaklawn Handicap (Behrens)
Suburban Handicap (Behrens)
2000: Gulfstream Park Handicap (Behrens)
2001: Manhattan Handicap (Forbidden Apple)
Hollywood Derby (Denon)
2002: Charles Whittingham Handicap (Denon)
Turf Classic (Denon)
2003: Manhattan Handicap (Denon)
Breeders' Cup Classic/Dodge (Pleasantly Perfect)

PLEASANT TAP
1998: Gazelle Handicap (Tap to Music)
1999: Meadowlands Cup Handicap (Pleasant Breeze)
2000: Hollywood Starlet Stakes (I Believe in You)

PLUM BOLD
1985: Vosburgh Stakes (Another Reef)

POACHING
1967: Hollywood Juvenile Championship (Jim White)

POKER
1973: Top Flight Handicap (Poker Night)
1974: Hempstead Handicap (Poker Night)

POLISH NAVY
1992: Champagne Stakes (Sea Hero)
Secretariat Stakes (Ghazi)
1993: Kentucky Derby (Sea Hero)
Travers Stakes (Sea Hero)

POLISH NUMBERS
1998: Queen Elizabeth II Challenge Cup (Tenski)

POLISH PRECEDENT
1996: Breeders' Cup Turf (Pilsudski)

POLLUX
1977: Whitney Handicap (Nearly On Time)

POLLY'S JET
1964: Man o' War Stakes (Turbo Jet II)

POLYNESIAN
1951: Del Mar Debutante Stakes (Tonga)
1952: Hopeful Stakes (Native Dancer)
Futurity Stakes (Native Dancer)
1953: Gotham Stakes (Native Dancer)
Wood Memorial Stakes (Native Dancer)
Withers Stakes (Native Dancer)
Preakness Stakes (Native Dancer)
Belmont Stakes (Native Dancer)
Dwyer Stakes (Native Dancer)
Arlington Classic (Native Dancer)
Travers Stakes (Native Dancer)
American Derby (Native Dancer)
1954: William P. Kyne Handicap (Imbros)
Californian Stakes (Imbros)
Metropolitan Handicap (Native Dancer)
1956: Garden State Stakes (Barbizon)
Spinaway Stakes (Alanesian)
1957: Arlington Lassie Stakes (Poly Hi)
Dwyer Handicap (Bureaucracy)
1959: Roamer Handicap (Polylad)
1961: Massachusetts Handicap (Polylad)
Gallant Fox Handicap (Polylad)

POMPEY
1947: Fall Highweight Handicap (Rippey)
Carter Handicap (Rippey)
1948: Roseben Handicap (Rippey)

PONDER
1955: Sapling Stakes (Needles)
Hopeful Stakes (Needles)
1956: Flamingo Stakes (Needles)
Florida Derby (Needles)
Kentucky Derby (Needles)
Belmont Stakes (Needles)
1961: Display Handicap (Hillsborough)

POONA II
1964: Vanity Handicap (Star Maggie)
1965: Spinster Stakes (Star Maggie)

PORTERHOUSE
1965: Hollywood Juvenile Championship (Port Wine)
Louisiana Derby (Dapper Delegate)
1966: San Fernando Stakes (Isle of Greece)
1967: Santa Susana Stakes (Fish House)

POSTER
1957: San Luis Rey Handicap (Posadas)

POTRILLAZO
1994: Vanity Handicap (Potridee)

POTRILLON
2001: Santa Maria Handicap (Lovellon)

PRACTITIONER
1983: Illinois Derby (General Practitioner)

PRETENDRE
1971: Kentucky Derby (Canonero II)
Preakness Stakes (Canonero II)

PRETENSE
1973: Santa Anita Derby (Sham)
1974: Frizette Stakes (Molly Ballentine)
1976: Santa Anita Derby (An Act)
1977: Arlington Classic Inv. Handicap (Private Thoughts)
Century Handicap (Anne's Pretender)
1978: Matron Stakes (Fall Aspen)

PRETEXTO
1972: Pan American Handicap (Unanime)

PRIAM II
1951: Saratoga Special (Cousin)
Hopeful Stakes (Cousin)
1952: Sapling Stakes (Landlocked)
1953: Selima Stakes (Small Favor)
1954: Widener Handicap (Landlocked)
1959: Flamingo Stakes (Troilus)

PRINCE DE GALLES
1978: Hialeah Turf Cup (Noble Dancer II)
United Nations Handicap (Noble Dancer II)
San Luis Rey Stakes (Noble Dancer II)
1979: Pan American Handicap (Noble Dancer II)
United Nations Handicap (Noble Dancer II)
San Luis Rey Stakes (Noble Dancer II)

PRINCE JOHN
1963: Demoiselle Stakes (Windsor Lady)
Sunset Handicap (Arbitrage)
1966: Grey Lag Handicap (Selari)
1967: Jerome Handicap (High Tribute)
1968: Belmont Stakes (Stage Door Johnny)
Dwyer Handicap (Stage Door Johnny)
1969: Arlington-Washington Futurity (Silent Screen)
Cowdin Stakes (Silent Screen)
Champagne Stakes (Silent Screen)
1971: Acorn Stakes (Deceit)
Mother Goose Stakes (Deceit)
1972: Hollywood Invitational Handicap (Typecast)
Sunset Handicap (Typecast)
Man o' War Stakes (Typecast)
1973: Champagne Stakes (Protagonist)
Laurel Futurity (Protagonist)
Coaching Club American Oaks (Magazine)
1974: Secretariat Stakes (Glossary)

PRINCE KHALED
1963: Cinema Handicap (Quita Dude)
1964: Hollywood Oaks (Loukahi)
1965: Grey Lag Handicap (Quita Dude)

PRINCELY PLEASURE
1981: Futurity Stakes (Irish Martini)

PRINCEQUILLO
1949: Cowdin Stakes (Hill Prince)
1950: Wood Memorial Stakes (Hill Prince)
Withers Stakes (Hill Prince)
Preakness Stakes (Hill Prince)
American Derby (Hill Prince)
Jerome Handicap (Hill Prince)
Jockey Club Gold Cup (Hill Prince)
Sunset Handicap (Hill Prince)
1951: Kentucky Oaks (How)
Coaching Club American Oaks (How)
New York Handicap (Hill Prince)
1952: Ladies Handicap (How)
1954: Acorn Stakes (Riverina)
Coaching Club American Oaks (Cherokee Rose)
1955: Monmouth Oaks (Misty Morn)
Molly Pitcher Handicap (Misty Morn)
Gallant Fox Handicap (Misty Morn)
Garden State Stakes (Prince John)
1956: Brooklyn Handicap (Dedicate)
Whitney Stakes (Dedicate)
Hawthorne Gold Cup (Dedicate)
Breeders' Futurity (Round Table)
Delaware Oaks (Dotted Line)
Roamer Handicap (Third Brother)
1957: Blue Grass Stakes (Round Table)
Cinema Handicap (Round Table)
Westerner Stakes (Round Table)
American Derby (Round Table)
Hollywood Gold Cup (Round Table)
Hawthorne Gold Cup (Round Table)
United Nations Handicap (Round Table)
New Orleans Handicap (Kingmaker)
Grey Lag Handicap (Kingmaker)
Whitney Stakes (Kingmaker)
John B. Campbell Memorial Handicap (Dedicate)
Monmouth Handicap (Dedicate)
Woodward Stakes (Dedicate)
Remsen Stakes (Misty Flight)
Spinaway Stakes (Sequoia)
Vineland Handicap (Dotted Line)
1958: San Antonio Handicap (Round Table)
Santa Anita Handicap (Round Table)
Gulfstream Park Handicap (Round Table)
Hawthorne Gold Cup (Round Table)
Santa Anita Maturity (Round Table)
Arlington Handicap (Round Table)
Matron Stakes (Quill)
Gardenia Stakes (Quill)
1959: Washington Park Handicap (Round Table)
Manhattan Handicap (Round Table)
Stars and Stripes Handicap (Round Table)
Arlington Handicap (Round Table)
United Nations Handicap (Round Table)
Acorn Stakes (Quill)
Mother Goose Stakes (Quill)
Arlington Lassie Stakes (Monarchy)
Sunset Handicap (Whodunit)
Man o' War Handicap (Dotted Line)
1960: Princess Pat Stakes (Rose Bower)
Matron Stakes (Rose Bower)
Delaware Handicap (Quill)
1961: American Handicap (Prince Blessed)
Hollywood Gold Cup (Prince Blessed)
Vanity Handicap (Perizade)
Tropical Park Handicap (Bourbon Prince)
Sunset Handicap (Whodunit)
1962: Monmouth Oaks (Firm Policy)
Alabama Stakes (Firm Policy)
1963: Top Flight Handicap (Firm Policy)
Gotham Stakes (Debbysman)
1964: Demoiselle Stakes (Discipline)
Black Helen Handicap (Princess Arle)
1965: Display Handicap (Brave Lad)
Dixie Handicap (Flag)
1967: Coaching Club American Oaks (Quillo Queen)
Monmouth Oaks (Quillo Queen)
1968: Santa Barbara Handicap (Princessnesian)
Hollywood Gold Cup (Princessnesian)
Withers Stakes (Call Me Prince)
1969: Santa Margarita Handicap (Princessnesian)

PRINCE ROYAL II
1971: San Felipe Handicap (Unconscious)
Santa Anita Derby (Unconscious)
1972: Charles H. Strub Stakes (Unconscious)
San Antonio Stakes (Unconscious)

PRINCE TAJ
1969: Sunset Handicap (Petrone)
San Juan Capistrano Handicap (Petrone)

PRINCE TENDERFOOT
1976: Hialeah Turf Cup (Lord Henham)

PRIVATE ACCOUNT
1986: Frizette Stakes (Personal Ensign)
Alabama Stakes (Classy Cathy)
1987: Beldame Stakes (Personal Ensign)
1988: Whitney Handicap (Personal Ensign)
Maskette Stakes (Personal Ensign)
Beldame Stakes (Personal Ensign)
Breeders' Cup Distaff (Personal Ensign)
Gotham Stakes (Private Terms)
Wood Memorial Stakes (Private Terms)
Suburban Handicap (Personal Flag)
1991: Ohio Derby (Private Man)
Travers Stakes (Corporate Report)
Pennsylvania Derby (Valley Crossing)
1993: Philip H. Iselin Handicap (Valley Crossing)
Whitney Handicap (Brunswick)
1994: Ashland Stakes (Inside Information)
Acorn Stakes (Inside Information)
Jim Dandy Stakes (Unaccounted For)
1995: Shuvee Handicap (Inside Information)
Ruffian Handicap (Inside Information)
Spinster Stakes (Inside Information)
Breeders' Cup Distaff (Inside Information)
Whitney Handicap (Unaccounted For)
Alabama Stakes (Pretty Discreet)

PRIVATE TERMS
1994: San Felipe Stakes (Soul of the Matter)
Super Derby (Soul of the Matter)
Hollywood Futurity (Afternoon Deelites)
1995: San Felipe Stakes (Afternoon Deelites)
Malibu Stakes (Afternoon Deelites)

PROMISED LAND
1966: Louisiana Derby (Blue Skyer)
1968: Flamingo Stakes (Wise Exchange)
1975: Arkansas Derby (Promised City)

PRONTO
1972: San Juan Capistrano Handicap (Practicante)
1974: Del Mar Handicap (Redtop III)

PROSPECTORS GAMBLE
1999: Futurity Stakes (Bevo)

PROSPECTOR'S MUSIC
2002: King's Bishop Stakes (Gygistar)

PROTANTO
1977: San Juan Capistrano Handicap (Properantes)

PROUD BIRDIE
1984: Jersey Derby (Birdie's Legend)
1993: Vosburgh Stakes (Birdonthewire)

PROUD CLARION
1974: Breeders' Futurity (Packer Captain)
1975: Ohio Derby (Brent's Prince)
1976: Secretariat Stakes (Joachim)
1977: Marlboro Cup Handicap (Proud Birdie)
1981: Frizette Stakes (Proud Lou)

PROUDEST ROMAN
1977: Demoiselle Stakes (Caesar's Wish)
1978: Mother Goose Stakes (Caesar's Wish)

PROUD TRUTH
1993: Fantasy Stakes (Aztec Hill)

PROVE IT
1968: California Derby (Proper Proof)
1973: Breeders' Futurity (Provante)

PROVE OUT
1980: Ohio Derby (Stone Manor)

PSYCHIC BID
1946: Swift Stakes (Master Bid)

PULPIT
2002: Hopeful Stakes (Sky Mesa)
Lane's End Breeders' Futurity (Sky Mesa)
Super Derby (Essence of Dubai)

QUACK
1978: Demoiselle Stakes (Plankton)
1980: Ladies Handicap (Plankton)
1981: Oak Leaf Stakes (Header Card)

QUADRANGLE
1969: Sorority Stakes (Box the Compass)
1972: Santa Susana Stakes (Susan's Girl)
Kentucky Oaks (Susan's Girl)
Acorn Stakes (Susan's Girl)
Gazelle Handicap (Susan's Girl)
Beldame Stakes (Susan's Girl)
1973: Delaware Handicap (Susan's Girl)
Spinster Stakes (Susan's Girl)
Santa Maria Handicap (Susan's Girl)
Santa Margarita Handicap (Susan's Girl)
Santa Barbara Handicap (Susan's Girl)
Wood Memorial Stakes (Angle Light)
1975: Delaware Handicap (Susan's Girl)
Beldame Stakes (Susan's Girl)
Spinster Stakes (Susan's Girl)
1979: Matron Stakes (Smart Angle)
Frizette Stakes (Smart Angle)
Selima Stakes (Smart Angle)

QUADRATIC
1990: Super Derby (Home at Last)

QUEST FOR FAME
1997: Del Mar Oaks (Famous Digger)

QUESTIONNAIRE
1946: Vosburgh Handicap (Coincidence)
Aqueduct Handicap (Coincidence)
Demoiselle Stakes (Carolyn A.)
1947: Kentucky Jockey Club Stakes (Bold Gallant)
Louisiana Derby (Carolyn A.)
Excelsior Handicap (Coincidence)
1948: Firenze Handicap (Carolyn A.)
1949: Aqueduct Handicap (Wine List)
1950: Aqueduct Handicap (Wine List)
1952: Gazelle Stakes (Hushaby Baby)
1954: Molly Pitcher Handicap (Shady Tune)

QUIBU
1960: Monmouth Oaks (Teacation)
1962: Kentucky Jockey Club Stakes (Sky Gem)
1965: Breeders' Futurity (Tinsley)
1966: Alcibiades Stakes (Teacher's Pet)

QUIET AMERICAN
1995: Hollywood Starlet Stakes (Cara Rafaela)
1997: Hollywood Futurity (Real Quiet)
Hempstead Handicap (Hidden Lake)
Go for Wand Stakes (Hidden Lake)
Beldame Stakes (Hidden Lake)
1998: Kentucky Derby (Real Quiet)
Preakness Stakes (Real Quiet)
1999: Pimlico Special (Real Quiet)
Sempra Energy Hollywood Gold Cup (Real Quiet)

RAHY
1993: Arlington-Washington Lassie Stakes (Mariah's Storm)
1994: Oak Leaf Stakes (Serena's Song)
Hollywood Starlet Stakes (Serena's Song)
1995: Las Virgenes Stakes (Serena's Song)
Santa Anita Oaks (Serena's Song)
Jim Beam Stakes (Serena's Song)
Mother Goose Stakes (Serena's Song)
Haskell Invitational Handicap (Serena's Song)
Gazelle Handicap (Serena's Song)
Beldame Stakes (Serena's Song)
1996: Santa Maria Handicap (Serena's Song)
Hempstead Handicap (Serena's Song)
Go for Wand Stakes (Exotic Wood)
1998: Santa Monica Handicap (Exotic Wood)
Santa Maria Handicap (Exotic Wood)
1999: Gamely Breeders' Cup Handicap (Tranquility Lake)
2000: Sempra Energy Hollywood Gold Cup (Early Pioneer)
Man o' War Stakes (Fantastic Light)
Yellow Ribbon Stakes (Tranquility Lake)
2001: Breeders' Cup Turf (Fantastic Light)
2003: Gamely Breeders' Cup Handicap (Tates Creek)
Yellow Ribbon Stakes (Tates Creek)

RAINBOW QUEST
1992: Hollywood Turf Handicap (Quest for Fame)
1994: Rothmans International Stakes (Raintrap)
1995: Santa Anita Handicap (Urgent Request)
1996: San Juan Capistrano Handicap (Raintrap)
1997: Oak Tree Turf Championship (Rainbow Dancer)
Hollywood Turf Handicap (Rainbow Dancer)
1998: Gamely Breeders' Cup Handicap (Fiji)
Yellow Ribbon Stakes (Fiji)

RAINY LAKE
1977: Matron Stakes (Lakeville Miss)
Frizette Stakes (Lakeville Miss)
Selima Stakes (Lakeville Miss)
1978: Coaching Club American Oaks (Lakeville Miss)

RAISE A CUP
1979: Alcibiades Stakes (Salud)
1981: Matron Stakes (Before Dawn)

RAISE A NATIVE
1967: Sanford Stakes (Exclusive Native)
1968: Arlington Classic (Exclusive Native)
1969: Santa Anita Derby (Majestic Prince)
Kentucky Derby (Majestic Prince)
Preakness Stakes (Majestic Prince)
1970: Gotham Stakes (Native Royalty)
1971: Carter Handicap (Native Royalty)
Michigan Mile and One-Eighth (Native Royalty)
Pontiac Grand Prix Stakes (Son Ange)
1973: Frizette Stakes (Bundler)
1975: Hempstead Handicap (Raisela)
1977: Sapling Stakes (Alydar)
Champagne Stakes (Alydar)
Santa Barbara Handicap (Desiree)
1978: Flamingo Stakes (Alydar)
Florida Derby (Alydar)
Blue Grass Stakes (Alydar)
Arlington Classic (Alydar)
Travers Stakes (Alydar)
Whitney Stakes (Alydar)
1980: San Felipe Handicap (Raise A Man)
1982: Breeders' Futurity (Highland Park)
1986: Withers Stakes (Clear Choice)
Swaps Stakes (Clear Choice)

RAISED SOCIALLY
1986: Blue Grass Stakes (Bachelor Beau)

RAJAB
1986: Breeders' Cup Juvenile Fillies (Brave Raj)

RAJA BABA
1976: Laurel Futurity (Royal Ski)
Remsen Stakes (Royal Ski)
1980: Arlington-Washington Futurity (Well Decorated)
Del Mar Debutante Stakes (Raja's Delight)
Alcibiades Stakes (Sweet Revenge)
1982: Louisiana Derby (El Baba)
1986: Oak Leaf Stakes (Sacahuista)
Top Flight Handicap (Ride Sally)
1987: Spinster Stakes (Sacahuista)
Breeders' Cup Distaff (Sacahuista)
1988: Breeders' Cup Juvenile (Is It True)
1989: Jim Dandy Stakes (Is It True)

RAMBUNCTIOUS
1981: Maskette Stakes (Jameela)
1982: Delaware Handicap (Jameela)

RAMSINGA
1975: San Fernando Stakes (First Back)
1978: Santa Barbara Handicap (Kittyluck)

RASH PRINCE
1969: Ohio Derby (Berkley Prince)

READING II
1951: Del Mar Handicap (Blue Reading)

READY SAY GO
1971: Del Mar Debutante Stakes (Impressive Style)

REAPING REWARD
1946: Inglewood Handicap (Quick Reward)
American Handicap (Quick Reward)
Top Flight Handicap (Sicily)
American Derby (Eternal Reward)
1948: California Derby (May Reward)
San Felipe Stakes (May Reward)
New Orleans Handicap (Star Reward)
1951: Queens County Handicap (Sheilas Reward)
1956: Louisiana Derby (Reaping Right)
Michigan Mile (Nonnie Jo)

RED RANSOM
1999: Garden City Breeders' Cup Handicap (Perfect Sting)
Queen Elizabeth II Challenge Cup (Perfect Sting)
2000: Breeders' Cup Filly and Mare Turf (Perfect Sting)

RED RYDER
1984: California Derby (Distant Ryder)

REFLECTED GLORY
1974: Arlington-Washington Lassie Stakes (Hot n Nasty)
1981: La Canada Stakes (Summer Siren)
1983: Vanity Handicap (A Kiss For Luck)
1985: Norfolk Stakes (Snow Chief)
Hollywood Futurity (Snow Chief)
1986: Florida Derby (Snow Chief)
Santa Anita Derby (Snow Chief)
Preakness Stakes (Snow Chief)
Jersey Derby (Snow Chief)
1987: Charles H. Strub Stakes (Snow Chief)

REFORM
1974: Washington D.C. International (Admetus)

REGO
1959: Arlington Matron Handicap (Wiggle II)

REIGH COUNT
1946: San Juan Capistrano Handicap (Triplicate)
Hollywood Gold Cup (Triplicate)
Gulfstream Handicap (Do-Reigh-Me)
1947: Golden Gate Handicap (Triplicate)

REJECTED
1963: Ohio Derby (Lemon Twist)
Hawthorne Gold Cup (Admiral Vic)
1964: Seminole Handicap (Admiral Vic)

RELAUNCH
1985: Santa Anita Derby (Skywalker)
1986: Breeders' Cup Classic (Skywalker)
1987: Widener Handicap (Launch a Pegasus)
Brooklyn Handicap (Waquoit)
1988: Brooklyn Handicap (Waquoit)
Jockey Club Gold Cup (Waquoit)
1994: Breeders' Cup Distaff (One Dreamer)
1995: Del Mar Futurity (Future Quest)

Norfolk Stakes (Future Quest)
1996: Metropolitan Handicap (Honour and Glory)
2001: Sword Dancer Inv. Handicap (With Anticipation)
Man o' War Stakes (With Anticipation)
2002: United Nations Handicap (With Anticipation)
Sword Dancer Inv. Handicap (With Anticipation)
Man o' War Stakes (With Anticipation)

RELIC

1962: San Antonio Handicap (Olden Times)
San Juan Capistrano Handicap (Olden Times)
1964: Metropolitan Handicap (Olden Times)

REPICADO II

1978: Swaps Stakes (Radar Ahead)
1979: San Fernando Stakes (Radar Ahead)

REQUESTED

1947: Cowdin Stakes (My Request)
1948: Delaware Oaks (Miss Request)
Ladies Handicap (Miss Request)
Wood Memorial Stakes (My Request)
Dwyer Stakes (My Request)
Washington Park Futurity (Model Cadet)
Alabama Stakes (Compliance)
1949: New Orleans Handicap (My Request)
Excelsior Handicap (My Request)
Beldame Handicap (Miss Request)
1950: Westerner Stakes (Valquest)
Brooklyn Handicap (My Request)
1952: Starlet Stakes (Little Request)
1953: Delaware Oaks (Cerise Reine)
1954: Santa Margarita Handicap (Cerise Reine)

RESTLESS NATIVE

1975: Top Flight Handicap (Twixt)
John B. Campbell Handicap (Jolly Johu)
1990: Haskell Invitational Handicap (Restless Con)

RESTLESS WIND

1967: Hollywood Derby (Tumble Wind)
1968: Arlington-Washington Lassie Stakes (Process Shot)
1971: Breeders' Futurity (Windjammer)
1975: Hollywood Juvenile Championship (Restless Restless)

REVIEWER

1974: Sorority Stakes (Ruffian)
Spinaway Stakes (Ruffian)
1975: Acorn Stakes (Ruffian)
Mother Goose Stakes (Ruffian)
Coaching Club American Oaks (Ruffian)
1976: Coaching Club American Oaks (Revidere)
Ruffian Stakes (Revidere)
1978: Ramona Handicap (Drama Critic)

REVOKED

1953: Westerner Stakes (Rejected)
1954: Santa Anita Handicap (Rejected)
American Handicap (Rejected)
Hawthorne Gold Cup (Rejected)
Washington Park Futurity (Georgian)
1955: Hollywood Gold Cup (Rejected)
1956: California Derby (No Regrets)
Jerome Handicap (Reneged)
1957: Manhattan Handicap (Reneged)
1967: Acorn Stakes (Furl Sail)
Mother Goose Stakes (Furl Sail)

RHEINGOLD

1981: Louisiana Downs Handicap (Goldiko)

RHODES SCHOLAR

1949: Dwyer Stakes (Shackleton)

RIBOCCO

1978: John B. Campbell Handicap (Ripon)

RIBOT

1964: Cowdin Stakes (Tom Rolfe)
1965: Preakness Stakes (Tom Rolfe)
Arlington Classic (Tom Rolfe)
American Derby (Tom Rolfe)
1966: Ladies Handicap (Destro)
Aqueduct Handicap (Tom Rolfe)
1968: Widener Handicap (Sette Bello)
1969: Everglades Stakes (Arts and Letters)
Blue Grass Stakes (Arts and Letters)
Belmont Stakes (Arts and Letters)
Travers Stakes (Arts and Letters)
Metropolitan Handicap (Arts and Letters)
Woodward Stakes (Arts and Letters)
Jockey Club Gold Cup (Arts and Letters)
1970: Grey Lag Handicap (Arts and Letters)

RICH CREAM

1985: Belmont Stakes (Creme Fraiche)
American Derby (Creme Fraiche)
Jerome Handicap (Creme Fraiche)
Super Derby (Creme Fraiche)
1986: Jockey Club Gold Cup (Creme Fraiche)
1987: Jockey Club Gold Cup (Creme Fraiche)
Meadowlands Cup (Creme Fraiche)

RICH MAN'S GOLD

2001: Whitney Handicap (Lido Palace)
Woodward Stakes (Lido Palace)
2002: Woodward Stakes (Lido Palace)

RICO MONTE

1955: Alabama Stakes (Rico Reta)
1958: Delaware Handicap (Endine)
Ladies Handicap (Endine)
1959: Delaware Handicap (Endine)

RIDAN

1967: Kentucky Jockey Club Stakes (Mr. Brogann)
1972: John B. Campbell Handicap (Favorecidian)
Michigan Mile and One-Eighth (Favorecidian)

RIDE THE RAILS

2003: Pacific Classic (Candy Ride)

RISEN STAR

1996: Pimlico Special (Star Standard)

RIVA RIDGE

1979: Maskette Stakes (Blitey)
1980: Hopeful Stakes (Tap Shoes)
Futurity Stakes (Tap Shoes)
1981: Flamingo Stakes (Tap Shoes)

RIVERMAN

1985: Remsen Stakes (Pillaster)
1987: Hollywood Invitational Handicap (Rivlia)
Rothmans International Stakes (River Memories)
1988: San Luis Rey Stakes (Rivlia)
1989: Flower Bowl Handicap (River Memories)
1992: Del Mar Futurity (River Special)
Norfolk Stakes (River Special)
Hollywood Futurity (River Special)
1993: Peter Pan Stakes (Virginia Rapids)
Californian Stakes (Latin American)
1994: Carter Handicap (Virginia Rapids)
Hollywood Derby (River Flyer)
1998: Del Mar Futurity (Worldly Manner)

ROBERTO

1979: Hawthorne Gold Cup (Young Bob)
1982: Pan American Handicap (Robsphere)
1983: Hopeful Stakes (Capitol South)
1984: Young America Stakes (Script Ohio)
1988: Man o' War Stakes (Sunshine Forever)
Turf Classic (Sunshine Forever)
Budweiser International Stakes (Sunshine Forever)
Florida Derby (Brian's Time)
Jim Dandy Stakes (Brian's Time)
Jersey Derby (Dynaformer)
1989: Selima Stakes (Sweet Roberta)
1990: Yellow Ribbon Stakes (Plenty of Grace)

ROBIN DES BOIS

1997: San Antonio Handicap (Gentlemen)
Pimlico Special (Gentlemen)
Hollywood Gold Cup (Gentlemen)
Pacific Classic (Gentlemen)
1998: San Antonio Handicap (Gentlemen)

ROCKEFELLA

1960: Canadian Championship Stakes (Rocky Royale)

ROCK TALK

1983: Ruffian Handicap (Heartlight No. One)

ROCKY ROYALE

1968: Gazelle Handicap (Another Nell)

ROI DAGOBERT

1977: Jockey Club Gold Cup (On the Sly)
Hawthorne Gold Cup (On the Sly)

ROI NORMAND

2000: Milady Breeders' Cup Handicap (Riboletta)
Santa Margarita Handicap (Riboletta)
Vanity Handicap (Riboletta)
Ruffian Handicap (Riboletta)
Beldame Stakes (Riboletta)

2001: Eddie Read Handicap (Redattore)
2003: Shoemaker Breeders' Cup Mile (Redattore)

ROLANDO

1947: Black Helen Handicap (Miss Grillo)
1948: New Castle Handicap (Miss Grillo)
New York Handicap (Miss Grillo)
1949: San Juan Capistrano Handicap (Miss Grillo)

ROLLICKING

1982: Sorority Stakes (Singing Susan)

ROMAN

1946: Marguerite Stakes (Cosmic Missile)
1947: Wood Memorial Stakes (I Will)
Gazelle Stakes (Cosmic Missile)
1949: Washington Park Futurity (Curtice)
Kentucky Jockey Club Stakes (Roman Bath)
Black Helen Handicap (Roman Candle)
1951: Arlington Lassie Stakes (Princess Lygia)
1952: Black Helen Handicap (Roman Miss)
1953: Arlington Futurity (Hasty Road)
Washington Park Futurity (Hasty Road)
Breeders' Futurity (Hasty Road)
Kentucky Jockey Club Stakes (Hasty Road)
Arlington Lassie Stakes (Queen Hopeful)
Princess Pat Stakes (Queen Hopeful)
1954: Remsen Stakes (Roman Patrol)
Preakness Stakes (Hasty Road)
1955: Louisiana Derby (Roman Patrol)
Widener Handicap (Hasty Road)
1956: Matron Stakes (Romanita)
1957: Princess Pat Stakes (Hasty Doll)
Monmouth Oaks (Romanita)
1958: Top Flight Handicap (Plucky Roman)
1961: Carter Handicap (Chief of Chiefs)
Washington Park Handicap (Chief of Chiefs)
Breeders' Futurity (Roman Line)

ROMAN DIPLOMAT

1996: Early Times Manhattan Handicap (Diplomatic Jet)
Man o' War Stakes (Diplomatic Jet)
Turf Classic (Diplomatic Jet)

ROMAN LINE

1972: Oaklawn Handicap (Gage Line)
1976: Hialeah Turf Cup (Legion)
1977: Donn Handicap (Legion)

ROMAN SANDAL

1958: Arlington Classic (A Dragon Killer)

ROMAN SWORD

1967: John B. Campbell Handicap (Quinta)

ROMEO

1984: Haskell Invitational Handicap (Big Pistol)

ROSE ARGENT

1973: Hopeful Stakes (Gusty O'Shay)

ROSEMONT

1949: Matron Stakes (Bed o' Roses)
Selima Stakes (Bed o' Roses)
Marguerite Stakes (Bed o' Roses)
Demoiselle Stakes (Bed o' Roses)
1950: Lawrence Realization Stakes (Bed o' Roses)
1951: Vineland Handicap (Bed o' Roses)
Comely Handicap (Bed o' Roses)
1952: Pimlico Futurity (Isasmoothie)
Santa Margarita Handicap (Bed o' Roses)
1953: Demoiselle Stakes (O'Alison)
1954: Pimlico Futurity (Thinking Cap)
Maskette Handicap (Ballerina)
1955: Travers Stakes (Thinking Cap)
Lawrence Realization Stakes (Thinking Cap)
1958: Spinaway Stakes (Rich Tradition)
Selima Stakes (Rich Tradition)

ROUGH'N TUMBLE

1959: Gardenia Stakes (My Dear Girl)
Frizette Stakes (My Dear Girl)
Kentucky Oaks (Wedlock)
1960: John B. Campbell Handicap (Yes You Will)
Carter Handicap (Yes You Will)
1961: John B. Campbell Handicap (Conestoga)
1965: Gotham Stakes (Flag Raiser)
Wood Memorial Stakes (Flag Raiser)
Withers Stakes (Flag Raiser)
1966: Cowdin Stakes (Dr. Fager)
1967: Gotham Stakes (Dr. Fager)
Withers Stakes (Dr. Fager)

ROUGH'N TUMBLE *(Continued)*
Arlington Classic (Dr. Fager)
Hawthorne Gold Cup (Dr. Fager)
Vosburgh Handicap (Dr. Fager)
Man o' War Stakes (Ruffled Feathers)
1968: Californian Stakes (Dr. Fager)
Suburban Handicap (Dr. Fager)
Washington Park Handicap (Dr. Fager)
Vosburgh Handicap (Dr. Fager)
Whitney Stakes (Dr. Fager)
United Nations Handicap (Dr. Fager)
Santa Anita Derby (Alley Fighter)

ROUND TABLE
1963: Saratoga Special (Duel)
Breeders' Futurity (Duel)
1965: Cowdin Stakes (Advocator)
Charles H. Strub Stakes (Duel)
1966: Dixie Handicap (Knightly Manner)
1967: Arkansas Derby (Monitor)
Seminole Handicap (Advocator)
New Orleans Handicap (Cabildo)
Bowling Green Handicap (Poker)
Canadian Int. Championship (He's a Smoothie)
1968: Garden State Stakes (Beau Brummel)
Hialeah Turf Cup (He's a Smoothie)
1969: Hollywood Derby (Tell)
Charles H. Strub Stakes (Dignitas)
1970: Canadian International Championship (Drumtop)
1971: Hialeah Turf Cup (Drumtop)
Bowling Green Handicap (Drumtop)
Inglewood Handicap (Advance Guard)
1972: Florida Derby (Upper Case)
Wood Memorial Stakes (Upper Case)
Pontiac Grand Prix Stakes (King's Bishop)
Michigan Mile and One-Eighth (King's Bishop)
1973: Malibu Stakes (Bicker)
San Fernando Stakes (Bicker)
Selima Stakes (Dancealot)
Carter Handicap (King's Bishop)
1974: Maskette Handicap (Ponte Vecchio)
1975: Amory L. Haskell Handicap (Royal Glint)
Arlington Handicap (Royal Glint)
Hawthorne Gold Cup (Royal Glint)
United Nations Handicap (Royal Glint)
1976: Champions Invitational Handicap (King Pellinore)
American Handicap (King Pellinore)
Oak Tree Invitational Stakes (King Pellinore)
Hopeful Stakes (Banquet Table)
Santa Anita Handicap (Royal Glint)

ROUSILLON
1995: Eddie Read Handicap (Fastness)
1996: Eddie Read Handicap (Fastness)

ROVER
1957: Santa Anita Derby (Sir William)

ROY
1999: Santa Maria Handicap (India Divina)

ROYAL ACADEMY
2001: Breeders' Cup Mile (Val Royal)

ROYAL CHARGER
1953: American Handicap (Royal Serenade)
Hollywood Gold Cup (Royal Serenade)
Garden State Stakes (Turn-to)
1954: Flamingo Stakes (Turn-to)
1957: Matron Stakes (Idun)
Gardenia Stakes (Idun)
Frizette Stakes (Idun)
1958: Mother Goose Stakes (Idun)
Gazelle Handicap (Idun)
San Carlos Handicap (Seaneen)
Californian Stakes (Seaneen)
1959: Monmouth Oaks (Royal Native)
Spinster Stakes (Royal Native)
San Felipe Handicap (Finnegan)
California Derby (Finnegan)
Saratoga Special (Irish Lancer)
Maskette Handicap (Idun)
Preakness Stakes (Royal Orbit)
1960: Black Helen Handicap (Royal Native)
Top Flight Handicap (Royal Native)
Arlington Matron Handicap (Royal Native)
Vineland Handicap (Royal Native)
Wood Memorial Stakes (Francis S.)
Dwyer Handicap (Francis S.)
Los Angeles Handicap (Finnegan)
1962: Trenton Handicap (Mongo)
United Nations Handicap (Mongo)
Ladies Handicap (Royal Patrice)
Santa Anita Derby (Royal Attack)
1963: Washington D.C. International (Mongo)
United Nations Handicap (Mongo)
Vanity Handicap (Table Mate)
1964: Widener Handicap (Mongo)
John B. Campbell Handicap (Mongo)
Monmouth Handicap (Mongo)

ROYAL COINAGE
1959: Washington Park Futurity (Venetian Way)
1960: Breeders' Futurity (He's a Pistol)
Kentucky Derby (Venetian Way)
1966: Withers Stakes (Indulto)

ROYAL DORIMAR
1971: Amory L. Haskell Handicap (Jontilla)

ROYAL GEM II
1953: Everglades Stakes (Royal Bay Gem)
Kentucky Derby (Dark Star)
1955: Kentucky Jockey Club Stakes (Royal Sting)

ROYAL MINSTREL
1946: San Antonio Handicap (First Fiddle)

ROYAL NOTE
1960: Futurity Stakes (Little Tumbler)
1966: Hollywood Juvenile Champ. (Forgotten Dreams)

ROYAL ORBIT
1967: Display Handicap (Quicken Tree)
1968: Manhattan Handicap (Quicken Tree)
Jockey Club Gold Cup (Quicken Tree)
San Luis Rey Handicap (Quicken Tree)
1970: Santa Anita Handicap (Quicken Tree)
San Juan Capistrano Handicap (Quicken Tree)

ROYAL SERENADE
1959: Vanity Handicap (Tender Size)
1961: Santa Margarita Handicap (Sister Antoine)
1967: Illinois Derby (Royal Malabar)
1968: Santa Susana Stakes (Allie's Serenade)

ROYAL SKI
1981: Selima Stakes (Snow Plow)
1983: Acorn Stakes (Ski Goggle)

ROYAL UNION
1966: Kentucky Jockey Club Stakes (Lightning Orphan)

ROYAL VALE
1962: Arlington Matron Handicap (Kootenai)

RUBIANO
2000: Futurity Stakes (Burning Roma)

RUNAWAY GROOM
1993: Dwyer Stakes (Cherokee Run)
1994: Breeders' Cup Sprint (Cherokee Run)
1996: Gulfstream Park Handicap (Wekiva Springs)
Brooklyn Handicap (Wekiva Springs)
Suburban Handicap (Wekiva Springs)
1998: Moet Champagne Stakes (The Groom Is Red)

RUN FOR NURSE
1969: Sapling Stakes (Ring For Nurse)

RUN THE GANTLET
1981: Washington D.C. International (Providential II)
Hollywood Turf Cup (Providential II)
Turf Classic (April Run)
1982: Turf Classic (April Run)
Washington D.C. International (April Run)

RUSTICARO
1984: Hollywood Derby (Foscarini)

RUSTOM SIRDAR
1953: Remsen Handicap (Galdar)
1956: Gazelle Handicap (Scampering)

RUTHIE'S NATIVE
1991: Milady Handicap (Brought to Mind)
Vanity Handicap (Brought to Mind)

RUYSDAEL II
1973: Cinema Handicap (Amen II)
Hollywood Derby (Amen II)

SABONA
2002: Vosburgh Stakes (Bonapaw)

SADLER'S WELLS
1990: Rothmans International Stakes (French Glory)
Breeders' Cup Turf (In the Wings)
1994: Breeders' Cup Mile (Barathea)
1995: Oak Tree Invitational Stakes (Northern Spur)
Breeders' Cup Turf (Northern Spur)
2001: Gulfstream Park BC Handicap (Subtle Power)
2002: Woodford Reserve Turf Classic (Beat Hollow)
Manhattan Handicap (Beat Hollow)
Arlington Million (Beat Hollow)
John Deere Breeders' Cup Turf (High Chaparral)
Hollywood Turf Cup (Sligo Bay)
2003: Shadwell Turf Mile (Perfect Soul)
Breeders' Cup Filly and Mare Turf (Islington)
John Deere Breeders' Cup Turf (High Chaparral)

SAGACE
1993: Breeders' Cup Classic (Arcangues)

SAGGY
1957: Mother Goose Stakes (Outer Space)
1958: Beldame Handicap (Outer Space)
1960: Cowdin Stakes (Carry Back)
Garden State Stakes (Carry Back)
Remsen Stakes (Carry Back)
1961: Everglades Stakes (Carry Back)
Flamingo Stakes (Carry Back)
Florida Derby (Carry Back)
Kentucky Derby (Carry Back)
Preakness Stakes (Carry Back)
Jerome Handicap (Carry Back)
Trenton Handicap (Carry Back)
1962: Metropolitan Handicap (Carry Back)
Monmouth Handicap (Carry Back)
Whitney Stakes (Carry Back)
1963: Trenton Handicap (Carry Back)

SAIDAM
1971: New Orleans Handicap (Rio Bravo)
Oaklawn Handicap (Rio Bravo)

SAILOR
1960: Gardenia Stakes (Bowl of Flowers)
Frizette Stakes (Bowl of Flowers)
1961: Acorn Stakes (Bowl of Flowers)
Coaching Club American Oaks (Bowl of Flowers)
Spinster Stakes (Bowl of Flowers)
1962: Garden State Stakes (Crewman)
Remsen Stakes (Rocky Link)
1963: Travers Stakes (Crewman)
1964: Carter Handicap (Ahoy)
1975: Bowling Green Handicap (Barcas)

SAIM
1965: Garden State Stakes (Prince Saim)

SAINT BALLADO
1997: Florida Derby (Captain Bodgit)
Wood Memorial Stakes (Captain Bodgit)
1999: Hempstead Handicap (Sister Act)
2000: Del Mar Futurity (Flame Thrower)
Norfolk Stakes (Flame Thrower)
Metropolitan Handicap (Yankee Victor)
2003: Spinaway Stakes (Ashado)

SAINT PATRICK
1947: Whitney Stakes (Rico Monte)
Manhattan Handicap (Rico Monte)
New York Handicap (Rico Monte)

SALERNO
1946: Del Mar Handicap (Olhaverry)
1947: Santa Anita Handicap (Olhaverry)
1948: San Pasqual Handicap (Olhaverry)

SALLUST
1979: Santa Margarita Handicap (Sanedtki)

SALMAGUNDI
1960: San Fernando Stakes (King o' Turf)

SALSE
2001: Turf Classic (Timboroa)

SALT LAKE
1996: Moet Champagne Stakes (Ordway)

SARATOGA SIX
1997: Santa Monica Handicap (Toga Toga Toga)

SAROS
1985: Santa Susana Stakes (Fran's Valentine)
Kentucky Oaks (Fran's Valentine)
Hollywood Oaks (Fran's Valentine)

SASSAFRAS
1977: Hollywood Oaks (Glenaris)

SAUCE BOAT
1988: Apple Blossom Handicap (By Land By Sea)

SCELTO
1970: Century Handicap (Quilche)
San Luis Rey Handicap (Quilche)
1974: Sunset Handicap (Greco II)

SCOTTISH MERIDIAN
1959: Brooklyn Handicap (Babu)

SCULPTOR
1966: Display Handicap (Damelo II)

SEA-BIRD
1971: Ladies Handicap (Sea Saga)
1972: American Derby (Dubassoff)
1973: Arlington Handicap (Dubassoff)
1974: Preakness Stakes (Little Current)
Belmont Stakes (Little Current)

SEA HAWK II
1974: Beverly Hills Handicap (La Zanzara)
1975: Beverly Hills Handicap (La Zanzara)
San Juan Capistrano Handicap (La Zanzara)

SEA HERO
2000: Vinery Del Mar Debutante Stakes (Cindy's Hero)
2003: Gulfstream Park Handicap (Hero's Tribute)

SEANEEN
1971: Coaching Club American Oaks (Our Cheri Amour)
1974: American Handicap (Plunk)
1975: Oaklawn Handicap (Warbucks)

SEARCH FOR GOLD
1976: Ohio Derby (Return of a Native)
1981: New Orleans Handicap (Sun Catcher)

SEATTLE DANCER
1996: Kentucky Oaks (Pike Place Dancer)
2000: Ramona Handicap (Caffe Latte)

SEATTLE SLEW
1982: Del Mar Debutante Stakes (Landaluce)
Oak Leaf Stakes (Landaluce)
Young America Stakes (Slewpy)
1983: Futurity Stakes (Swale)
Young America Stakes (Swale)
Breeders' Futurity (Swale)
Wood Memorial Stakes (Slew O' Gold)
Woodward Stakes (Slew O' Gold)
Jockey Club Gold Cup (Slew O' Gold)
Meadowlands Cup (Slewpy)
1984: Hutcheson Stakes (Swale)
Florida Derby (Swale)
Kentucky Derby (Swale)
Belmont Stakes (Swale)
Whitney Handicap (Slew O' Gold)
Woodward Stakes (Slew O' Gold)
Marlboro Cup Handicap (Slew O' Gold)
Jockey Club Gold Cup (Slew O' Gold)
Santa Margarita Handicap (Adored)
Delaware Handicap (Adored)
Washington D.C. International (Seattle Song)
1985: Hollywood Derby (Slew the Dragon)
1986: Mother Goose Stakes (Life at the Top)
Ladies Handicap (Life at the Top)
Norfolk Stakes (Capote)
Breeders' Cup Juvenile (Capote)
California Derby (Vernon Castle)
1988: Breeders' Futurity (Fast Play)
Remsen Stakes (Fast Play)
1989: Gulfstream Park Handicap (Slew City Slew)
Oaklawn Handicap (Slew City Slew)
Remsen Stakes (Yonder)
1990: Santa Anita Oaks (Hail Atlantis)
Kentucky Oaks (Seaside Attraction)
Jersey Derby (Yonder)
1991: Hollywood Futurity (A.P. Indy)
1992: Santa Anita Derby (A.P. Indy)
Peter Pan Stakes (A.P. Indy)
Belmont Stakes (A.P. Indy)
Breeders' Cup Classic (A.P. Indy)
1994: Santa Anita Oaks (Lakeway)
Mother Goose Stakes (Lakeway)
Hollywood Oaks (Lakeway)
1995: Hollywood Oaks (Sleep Easy)
1998: Jim Beam Stakes (Event of the Year)
1999: Frizette Stakes (Surfside)
Hollywood Starlet Stakes (Surfside)
Strub Stakes (Event of the Year)
2000: Las Virgenes Stakes (Surfside)
Santa Anita Oaks (Surfside)
Santa Monica Handicap (Honest Lady)
2001: Ashland Stakes (Fleet Renee)
Mother Goose Stakes (Fleet Renee)
Kentucky Oaks (Flute)
Alabama Stakes (Flute)
Go for Wand Handicap (Serra Lake)
Jim Dandy Stakes (Scorpion)
2002: Bessemer Trust Breeders' Cup Juvenile (Vindication)

SEATTLE SONG
1991: Arlington Classic (Whadjathink)

SECRETARIAT
1978: Hollywood Juvenile Championship (Terlingua)
Del Mar Debutante Stakes (Terlingua)
Hopeful Stakes (General Assembly)
1979: Travers Stakes (General Assembly)
Vosburgh Stakes (General Assembly)
1981: Breeders' Futurity (D'Accord)
1984: Matron Stakes (Fiesta Lady)
1985: Ruffian Handicap (Lady's Secret)
Maskette Stakes (Lady's Secret)
Beldame Stakes (Lady's Secret)
San Felipe Handicap (Image of Greatness)
1986: La Canada Stakes (Lady's Secret)
Santa Margarita Handicap (Lady's Secret)
Whitney Handicap (Lady's Secret)
Maskette Stakes (Lady's Secret)
Ruffian Handicap (Lady's Secret)
Beldame Stakes (Lady's Secret)
Breeders' Cup Distaff (Lady's Secret)
1988: Preakness Stakes (Risen Star)
Belmont Stakes (Risen Star)
1992: Yellow Ribbon Stakes (Super Staff)
1994: Pacific Classic (Tinners Way)
1995: Pacific Classic (Tinners Way)
1996: Californian Stakes (Tinners Way)

SEEKING THE GOLD
1993: Frizette Stakes (Heavenly Prize)
1994: Spinaway Stakes (Flanders)
Matron Stakes (Flanders)
Frizette Stakes (Flanders)
Breeders' Cup Juvenile Fillies (Flanders)
Alabama Stakes (Heavenly Prize)
Gazelle Handicap (Heavenly Prize)
Beldame Stakes (Heavenly Prize)
1995: Apple Blossom Handicap (Heavenly Prize)
Hempstead Handicap (Heavenly Prize)
Go for Wand Stakes (Heavenly Prize)
Ohio Derby (Petionville)
1998: Matron Stakes (Oh What a Windfall)
Florida Derby (Cape Town)
1999: Breeders' Cup Juvenile Fillies (Cash Run)
2000: Test Stakes (Dream Supreme)
Ballerina Handicap (Dream Supreme)
2001: Test Stakes (Victory Ride)
2002: Santa Maria Handicap (Favorite Funtime)

SELARI
1974: Louisiana Derby (Sellout)
1976: Jockey Club Gold Cup (Great Contractor)
1977: Brooklyn Handicap (Great Contractor)

SELKIRK
1998: Beverly Hills Handicap (Squeak)
Matriarch Stakes (Squeak)

SEMENENKO
1989: Maskette Stakes (Miss Brio)

SEMI-PRO
1969: Hollywood Juvenile Championship (Insubordination)

SENSITIVO
1967: Alcibiades Stakes (Lady Tramp)
1971: Monmouth Invitational Handicap (West Coast Scout)
Woodward Stakes (West Coast Scout)
1972: Amory L. Haskell Handicap (West Coast Scout)
1973: Gulfstream Park Handicap (West Coast Scout)
Amory L. Haskell Handicap (West Coast Scout)

SEPTIEME CIEL
1997: Oak Leaf Stakes (Vivid Angel)

SERVICE STRIPE
2001: Spinaway Stakes (Cashier's Dream)

SHADEED
1993: Carter Handicap (Alydeed)
1995: Peter Pan Stakes (Citadeed)

SHAM
1982: La Canada Stakes (Safe Play)
1985: Oak Leaf Stakes (Arewehavingfunyet)

SHANNON II
1955: New Orleans Handicap (Sea O Erin)
1957: Withers Stakes (Clem)
Arlington Classic (Clem)
1958: Washington Park Handicap (Clem)
Woodward Stakes (Clem)
United Nations Handicap (Clem)

SHARIVARI
1979: Bay Meadows Handicap (Leonotis)

SHARPEN UP
1985: Breeders' Cup Turf (Pebbles)
1994: Meadowlands Cup (Conveyor)

SHECKY GREENE
1984: Santa Barbara Handicap (Comedy Act)

SHIFTING SANDS II
1947: San Carlos Handicap (Texas Sandman)

SHIRLEY HEIGHTS
1988: Rothmans International Stakes (Infamy)

SHUT OUT
1950: Manhattan Handicap (One Hitter)
Pimlico Special (One Hitter)
1951: Arlington Classic (Hall of Fame)
American Derby (Hall of Fame)
Massachusetts Handicap (One Hitter)
Whitney Stakes (One Hitter)
Marguerite Stakes (No Score)
1952: Suburban Handicap (One Hitter)
Monmouth Handicap (One Hitter)
Remsen Handicap (Social Outcast)
1953: Spinaway Stakes (Evening Out)
Matron Stakes (Evening Out)
1954: Whitney Handicap (Social Outcast)
Gallant Fox Handicap (Social Outcast)
Monmouth Oaks (Evening Out)
United Nations Handicap (Closed Door)
1955: McLennan Handicap (Social Outcast)
John B. Campbell Handicap (Social Outcast)
Sunset Handicap (Social Outcast)
Manhattan Handicap (Social Outcast)
Trenton Handicap (Social Outcast)

SIBERIAN EXPRESS
1991: San Fernando Stakes (In Excess)
Metropolitan Handicap (In Excess)
Suburban Handicap (In Excess)
Whitney Handicap (In Excess)
Woodward Stakes (In Excess)
1993: Charles H. Strub Stakes (Siberian Summer)

SICAMBRE
1960: Arkansas Derby (Celtic Ash)
1965: Washington D.C. International (Diatome)

SICKLE
1946: McLennan Handicap (Concordian)

SICKLETOY
1951: Arlington Matron Handicap (Sickle's Image)
1952: Vineland Handicap (Sickle's Image)
1953: Washington Park Handicap (Sickle's Image)

SICYOS
1998: Del Mar Oaks (Sicy D'Alsace)

SIDE BOY
1950: Kentucky Jockey Club Stakes (Pur Sang)

SIDERAL
1962: Gallant Fox Handicap (Sensitivo)
Display Handicap (Sensitivo)

SIGNAL TAP
2002: La Brea Stakes (Got Koko)

SILENT SCREEN
1978: La Canada Stakes (Taisez Vous)
Santa Margarita Handicap (Taisez Vous)

SILLERY
1999: Breeders' Cup Mile (Silic)
2000: Shoemaker Breeders' Cup Mile (Silic)

SILVER BUCK
1989: Brooklyn Handicap (Forever Silver)
1992: Remsen Stakes (Silver of Silver)
1996: Del Mar Futurity (Silver Charm)
Remsen Stakes (The Silver Move)
1997: Kentucky Derby (Silver Charm)
Preakness Stakes (Silver Charm)
Frizette Stakes (Silver Maiden)
1998: Strub Stakes (Silver Charm)

SILVER DEPUTY
1998: Walmac Int. Alcibiades Stakes (Silverbulletday)
Breeders' Cup Juvenile Fillies (Silverbulletday)
1999: Ashland Stakes (Silverbulletday)
Kentucky Oaks (Silverbulletday)
Alabama Stakes (Silverbulletday)
Gazelle Handicap (Silverbulletday)

SILVER GHOST
1993: Ashland Stakes (Lunar Spook)
1994: Swaps Stakes (Silver Music)
1997: Hollywood Starlet Stakes (Love Lock)
1999: Mother Goose Stakes (Dreams Gallore)

SILVER HAWK
1988: Norfolk Stakes (Hawkster)
1989: Arkansas Derby (Dansil)
Oak Tree Invitational Stakes (Hawkster)
1990: Arkansas Derby (Silver Ending)
Pegasus Handicap (Silver Ending)
1992: Oak Leaf Stakes (Zoonaqua)
1995: San Juan Capistrano Handicap (Red Bishop)
Secretariat Stakes (Hawk Attack)
1996: Queen Elizabeth II Chal. Cup (Memories of Silver)
1997: Beverly D. Stakes (Memories of Silver)
2002: Garden City Breeders' Cup Handicap (Wonder Again)

SILVER HORDE
1949: Vanity Handicap (Silver Drift)

SIMPLY MAJESTIC
1994: Arlington-Washington Lassie Stakes (Shining Light)

SIPHON
2001: Lane's End Breeders' Futurity (Siphonic)
Hollywood Futurity (Siphonic)
2003: Del Mar Futurity (Siphonizer)

SIR DAMION
1946: Louisiana Derby (Pellicle)
San Felipe Stakes (Galla Damion)
Stars and Stripes Handicap (Witch Sir)
1954: Canadian Championship Stakes (Resilient)

SIR GALLAHAD III
1948: Cowdin Stakes (Algasir)

SIR GAYLORD
1967: Gardenia Stakes (Gay Matelda)
1968: Alabama Stakes (Gay Matelda)
Washington D.C. International (Sir Ivor)
1970: Matron Stakes (Bonnie and Gay)
1972: Hollywood Oaks (Pallisima)
1973: Jersey Derby (Knightly Dawn)
1975: Santa Barbara Handicap (Gay Style)

SIR IVOR
1974: Demoiselle Stakes (Land Girl)
1975: Matron Stakes (Optimistic Gal)
Frizette Stakes (Optimistic Gal)
Alcibiades Stakes (Optimistic Gal)
Selima Stakes (Optimistic Gal)
Gazelle Handicap (Land Girl)
1976: Ashland Stakes (Optimistic Gal)
Kentucky Oaks (Optimistic Gal)
Alabama Stakes (Optimistic Gal)
Delaware Handicap (Optimistic Gal)
Spinster Stakes (Optimistic Gal)
Vanity Handicap (Miss Toshiba)
Santa Margarita Handicap (Fascinating Girl)
1977: Kentucky Oaks (Sweet Alliance)
1978: Fantasy Stakes (Equanimity)
1983: Monmouth Handicap (Bates Motel)
San Antonio Stakes (Bates Motel)
Santa Anita Handicap (Bates Motel)

SIR LEON
1998: Cigar Mile Handicap (Sir Bear)
1999: Metropolitan Handicap (Sir Bear)
2001: Gulfstream Park Handicap (Sir Bear)

SIR RIBOT
1976: Del Mar Handicap (Riot in Paris)

SIR RULER
1965: Arkansas Derby (Swift Ruler)
1966: Oaklawn Handicap (Swift Ruler)

SIR WIMBORNE
1986: Fountain of Youth Stakes (My Prince Charming)

SKIP TRIAL
1996: Blue Grass Stakes (Skip Away)
Ohio Derby (Skip Away)
Buick Haskell Invitational Handicap (Skip Away)
Woodbine Million (Skip Away)
Jockey Club Gold Cup (Skip Away)
1997: Suburban Handicap (Skip Away)
Jockey Club Gold Cup (Skip Away)
Breeders' Cup Classic (Skip Away)
1998: Donn Handicap (Skip Away)
Gulfstream Park Handicap (Skip Away)
Pimlico Special (Skip Away)
Hollywood Gold Cup (Skip Away)
Philip H. Iselin Handicap (Skip Away)
Woodward Stakes (Skip Away)

SKY HIGH II
1972: Jockey Club Gold Cup (Autobiography)
San Fernando Stakes (Autobiography)
1974: Bowling Green Handicap (Take Off)

SKY SHIP
1961: Man o' War Handicap (Wise Ship)
1962: Dixie Handicap (Wise Ship)

SKYWALKER
1991: Del Mar Futurity (Bertrando)
Norfolk Stakes (Bertrando)
1992: San Felipe Stakes (Bertrando)
1993: Pacific Classic (Bertrando)
Woodward Stakes (Bertrando)

SLEWACIDE
1994: Hollywood Gold Cup (Slew of Damascus)

SLEW CITY SLEW
1994: Arlington-Washington Futurity (Evansville Slew)

SLEW O' GOLD
1989: Flamingo Stakes (Awe Inspiring)
Jersey Derby (Awe Inspiring)
Ashland Stakes (Gorgeous)
Hollywood Oaks (Gorgeous)
Beldame Stakes (Tactile)
1990: La Canada Stakes (Gorgeous)
Apple Blossom Handicap (Gorgeous)
Vanity Handicap (Gorgeous)
Gotham Stakes (Thirty Six Red)
Wood Memorial Stakes (Thirty Six Red)
1991: Sword Dancer Handicap (Dr. Root)
1994: Molson Export Million (Dramatic Gold)
1996: Buick Meadowlands Cup Handicap (Dramatic Gold)
2003: San Juan Capistrano Handicap (Passinetti)

SLEWPY
1992: Breeders' Cup Sprint (Thirty Slews)

SLEWVESCENT
1999: Del Mar Oaks (Tout Charmant)
2000: Matriarch Stakes (Tout Charmant)
2001: Milady Breeders' Cup Handicap (Lazy Slusan)
Santa Margarita Handicap (Lazy Slusan)
2002: San Juan Capistrano Handicap (Ringaskiddy)

SLIPPED DISC
1971: Charles H. Strub Stakes (War Heim)
1972: Miller High Life Inglewood Handicap (War Heim)

SMARTEN
1989: Ladies Handicap (Dance Teacher)
1994: Jerome Handicap (Prenup)

SMOKESTER
1996: Norfolk Stakes (Free House)
1997: San Felipe Stakes (Free House)
Santa Anita Derby (Free House)
Swaps Stakes (Free House)
1998: Pacific Classic (Free House)
1999: San Antonio Handicap (Free House)
Santa Anita Handicap (Free House)

SNARK
1947: Coaching Club American Oaks (Harmonica)
1948: Suburban Handicap (Harmonica)

SNOW BALL
1977: Yellow Ribbon Stakes (Star Ball)

SNOW CAT
1970: Gulfstream Park Handicap (Snow Sporting)
Charles H. Strub Stakes (Snow Sporting)

SOCIAL CLIMBER
1963: Del Mar Futurity (Perris)

SOLO LANDING
1975: Fantasy Stakes (Hoso)

SOLONAWAY
1956: Bougainvillea Turf Handicap (Summer Solstice)

SOME CHANCE
1949: Garden State Stakes (Cornwall)
1952: Roamer Handicap (Quiet Step)
Trenton Handicap (Ken)
1961: Remsen Stakes (Figaro Bob)

SOMETHINGFABULOUS
1982: Hollywood Starlet Stakes (Fabulous Notion)
1983: Santa Susana Stakes (Fabulous Notion)

SOUEPI
1966: Pan American Handicap (Pillanlebun)
1969: Widener Handicap (Yumbel)

SOUTHERN HALO
2000: King's Bishop Stakes (More Than Ready)
2001: Overbrook Spinster Stakes (Miss Linda)

SOVEREIGN DANCER
1984: Preakness Stakes (Gate Dancer)
Super Derby (Gate Dancer)
1986: Illinois Derby (Bolshoi Boy)
1987: Peter Pan Stakes (Leo Castelli)
1990: Hollywood Derby (Itsallgreektome)
Hollywood Turf Cup (Itsallgreektome)
1996: Preakness Stakes (Louis Quatorze)
Jim Dandy Stakes (Louis Quatorze)

SPANISH RIDDLE
1980: Alabama Stakes (Love Sign)
Beldame Stakes (Love Sign)
1981: Beldame Stakes (Love Sign)

SPEAK JOHN
1968: Gotham Stakes (Verbatim)
1969: Amory L. Haskell Handicap (Verbatim)
Whitney Stakes (Verbatim)
1971: Arlington-Washington Futurity (Hold Your Peace)
1972: Flamingo Stakes (Hold Your Peace)
1973: Spinaway Stakes (Talking Picture)
Matron Stakes (Talking Picture)
1976: Pan American Handicap (Improviser)
1977: Secretariat Stakes (Text)
Hialeah Turf Cup (Improviser)
1978: San Fernando Stakes (Text)
1979: Amory L. Haskell Handicap (Text)

SPEAK UP
1959: Vanity Handicap (Zev's Joy)

SPECIALMANTE
1973: Arlington-Washington Lassie Stakes (Special Team)
1974: Kentucky Oaks (Quaze Quilt)
Alabama Stakes (Quaze Quilt)
Acorn Stakes (Special Team)

SPECTACULAR BID
1984: Futurity Stakes (Spectacular Love)
1993: Norfolk Stakes (Shepherd's Field)

SPECTRUM II
1959: Del Mar Futurity (Azure's Orphan)

SPEND A BUCK
1996: Las Virgenes Stakes (Antespend)
Santa Anita Oaks (Antespend)

SPORTIN' LIFE

1986: Arlington-Washington Futurity (Bet Twice)
Laurel Futurity (Bet Twice)
1987: Fountain of Youth Stakes (Bet Twice)
Belmont Stakes (Bet Twice)
Haskell Invitational Handicap (Bet Twice)

SPRING DOUBLE

1980: Sapling Stakes (Travelling Music)

SPY SONG

1952: Arlington Lassie Stakes (Fulvous)
Princess Pat Stakes (Fulvous)
1954: Arlington Futurity (Royal Note)
1957: Breeders' Futurity (Fulcrum)
1961: Garden State Stakes (Crimson Satan)
Pimlico Futurity (Crimson Satan)
1963: Massachusetts Handicap (Crimson Satan)
Michigan Mile and One-Sixteenth (Crimson Satan)
Washington Park Handicap (Crimson Satan)
San Fernando Stakes (Crimson Satan)
Charles H. Strub Stakes (Crimson Satan)
Arlington-Washington Lassie Stakes (Sari's Song)

STAFF WRITER

1981: Hopeful Stakes (Timely Writer)
Champagne Stakes (Timely Writer)
1982: Flamingo Stakes (Timely Writer)
Florida Derby (Timely Writer)
1985: Santa Barbara Handicap (Fact Finder)

STAGE DOOR JOHNNY

1976: Louisiana Derby (Johnny Appleseed)
San Juan Capistrano Handicap (One On the Aisle)
1977: Washington D.C. International (Johnny D.)
Turf Classic (Johnny D.)
1978: Delaware Handicap (Late Bloomer)
Ruffian Handicap (Late Bloomer)
Beldame Stakes (Late Bloomer)
Sheepshead Bay Handicap (Late Bloomer)
1979: Hollywood Invitational Handicap (Johnny's Image)
1980: Louisiana Derby (Prince Valiant)
1981: Meadowlands Cup (Princelet)
Rothmans International Stakes (Open Call)
1982: Bowling Green Handicap (Open Call)
Louisiana Downs Handicap (Rich and Ready)
1983: Louisiana Downs Handicap (Late Act)
1984: Coaching Club American Oaks (Class Play)

STALWART

1988: Jim Beam Stakes (Kingpost)
1998: Spinaway Stakes (Things Change)

STAR DE NASKRA

1984: Jim Dandy Stakes (Carr de Naskra)
Travers Stakes (Carr de Naskra)
1987: San Felipe Handicap (Chart the Stars)
1989: Vosburgh Stakes (Sewickley)
1990: Vosburgh Stakes (Sewickley)
1996: Acorn Stakes (Star de Lady Ann)

STARDUST

1958: Bougainvillea Turf Handicap (Stephanotis)

STAR PILOT

1951: Astoria Stakes (Star-Enfin)

STATE DINNER

1985: Arlington-Washington Lassie Stakes (Family Style)
Frizette Stakes (Family Style)
1987: La Canada Stakes (Family Style)

STAUNCHNESS

1970: Sapling Stakes (Staunch Avenger)

STERLING BAY

1981: Century Handicap (Spence Bay)

STEVWARD

1976: Carter Handicap (Due Diligence)
1977: Hollywood Derby (Steve's Friend)

ST. JOVITE

1998: San Juan Capistrano Handicap (Amerique)

STONEWALK

1988: Hutcheson Stakes (Perfect Spy)

STOP THE MUSIC

1980: Arkansas Derby (Temperence Hill)
Belmont Stakes (Temperence Hill)
Travers Stakes (Temperence Hill)
Super Derby (Temperence Hill)
Jockey Club Gold Cup (Temperence Hill)
Laurel Futurity (Cure the Blues)
1981: Suburban Handicap (Temperence Hill)
Oaklawn Handicap (Temperence Hill)
Secretariat Stakes (Sing Sing)
1984: Withers Stakes (Play On)
1985: Vanity Handicap (Dontstop Themusic)
Spinster Stakes (Dontstop Themusic)
Everglades Stakes (Rhoman Rule)
1988: Del Mar Futurity (Music Merci)
1989: Illinois Derby (Music Merci)
1992: Shuvee Handicap (Missy's Mirage)
Hempstead Handicap (Missy's Mirage)

STORM BIRD

1985: Young America Stakes (Storm Cat)
1989: Hopeful Stakes (Summer Squall)
1990: Jim Beam Stakes (Summer Squall)
Blue Grass Stakes (Summer Squall)
Preakness Stakes (Summer Squall)
Pennsylvania Derby (Summer Squall)
1992: Hollywood Oaks (Pacific Squall)
1993: Santa Anita Derby (Personal Hope)

STORM CAT

1992: Alabama Stakes (November Snow)
1993: Hollywood Starlet Stakes (Sardula)
1994: Preakness Stakes (Tabasco Cat)
Belmont Stakes (Tabasco Cat)
Kentucky Oaks (Sardula)
Vosburgh Stakes (Harlan)
1995: Hopeful Stakes (Hennessy)
Breeders' Cup Sprint (Desert Stormer)
1996: Matron Stakes (Sharp Cat)
Hollywood Starlet Stakes (Sharp Cat)
1997: Las Virgenes Stakes (Sharp Cat)
Santa Anita Oaks (Sharp Cat)
Acorn Stakes (Sharp Cat)
Hollywood Oaks (Sharp Cat)
1998: Ruffian Handicap (Sharp Cat)
Beldame Stakes (Sharp Cat)
Go for Wand Handicap (Aldiza)
Buick Pegasus Handicap (Tomorrows Cat)
Lane's End Breeders' Futurity (Cat Thief)
Hollywood Futurity (Tactical Cat)
1999: Swaps Stakes (Cat Thief)
Breeders' Cup Classic (Cat Thief)
King's Bishop Stakes (Forestry)
Hopeful Stakes (High Yield)
Ruffian Handicap (Catinca)
Matron Stakes (Finder's Fee)
2000: Fountain of Youth Stakes (High Yield)
Toyota Blue Grass Stakes (High Yield)
Matron Stakes (Raging Fever)
Frizette Stakes (Raging Fever)
Acorn Stakes (Finder's Fee)
2002: Matron Stakes (Storm Flag Flying)
Frizette Stakes (Storm Flag Flying)
Long John Silver's BC Juv. Fillies (Storm Flag Flying)
Ogden Phipps Handicap (Raging Fever)
2003: Del Mar Oaks (Dessert)

STORM CREEK

2000: Spinaway Stakes (Stormy Pick)

STRAIGHT DIE

1976: Santa Barbara Handicap (Stravina)

STRAWBERRY ROAD II

1991: Santa Anita Derby (Dinard)
Hollywood Oaks (Fowda)
1992: Sword Dancer Handicap (Fraise)
Breeders' Cup Turf (Fraise)
Spinster Stakes (Fowda)
1993: Hollywood Turf Cup (Fraise)
1995: Hollywood Turf Cup (Royal Chariot)
1997: Mother Goose Stakes (Ajina)
Coaching Club American Oaks (Ajina)
Breeders' Cup Distaff (Ajina)
Ramona Handicap (Escena)
1998: Apple Blossom Handicap (Escena)
Vanity Handicap (Escena)
Breeders' Cup Distaff (Escena)
Californian Stakes (Mud Route)

STRONGHOLD

1954: Del Mar Handicap (Stranglehold)

STUNNING

1970: Del Mar Handicap (Daryl's Joy)
Oak Tree Stakes (Daryl's Joy)

STYMIE

1954: John B. Campbell Memorial Handicap (Joe Jones)
1955: Firenze Handicap (Rare Treat)
1956: Vineland Handicap (Rare Treat)
1957: Ladies Handicap (Rare Treat)
1958: Santa Margarita Handicap (Born Rich)

SUBPET

1974: Arkansas Derby (J.R.'s Pet)

SULLIVAN

1958: Santa Anita Derby (Silky Sullivan)

SULTRY SONG

1999: San Felipe Stakes (Prime Timber)

SUMMER SQUALL

1996: Frizette Stakes (Storm Song)
Breeders' Cup Juvenile Fillies (Storm Song)
1999: Kentucky Derby (Charismatic)
Preakness Stakes (Charismatic)
2000: Turfway Spiral Stakes (Globalize)
2002: Personal Ensign Handicap (Summer Colony)

SUMMER TAN

1963: Everglades Stakes (B. Major)
Grey Lag Handicap (Sunrise County)
1965: Monmouth Oaks (Summer Scandal)
1966: Top Flight Handicap (Summer Scandal)
Beldame Stakes (Summer Scandal)

SUMMING

1986: Arlington Classic (Sumptious)
1987: Breeders' Cup Juvenile Fillies (Epitome)

SUN AGAIN

1949: Kentucky Oaks (Wistful)
Pimlico Oaks (Wistful)
Coaching Club American Oaks (Wistful)
Saratoga Special (More Sun)
1950: Saranac Handicap (Sunglow)
Discovery Handicap (Sunglow)
Westchester Handicap (Palestinian)
1951: Brooklyn Handicap (Palestinian)
Golden Gate Handicap (Palestinian)
Widener Handicap (Sunglow)
1954: Roseben Handicap (White Skies)
Carter Handicap (White Skies)
Top Flight Handicap (Sunshine Nell)
1956: Everglades Stakes (Liberty Sun)

SUN BAHRAM

1962: Tropical Park Handicap (Trans-Way)

SUNGLOW

1959: Belmont Stakes (Sword Dancer)
Travers Stakes (Sword Dancer)
Metropolitan Handicap (Sword Dancer)
Monmouth Handicap (Sword Dancer)
Woodward Stakes (Sword Dancer)
Jockey Club Gold Cup (Sword Dancer)
1960: Grey Lag Handicap (Sword Dancer)
Suburban Handicap (Sword Dancer)
Woodward Stakes (Sword Dancer)

SUNNY BOY

1959: Bowling Green Handicap (Bell Hop)

SUNNY NORTH

1990: Young America Stakes (Southern Sign)

SUNNY'S HALO

1990: Demoiselle Stakes (Debutant's Halo)
Woodward Stakes (Dispersal)
1992: Fantasy Stakes (Race the Wild Wind)
1993: Santa Maria Handicap (Race the Wild Wind)
1994: Gotham Stakes (Irgun)
Wood Memorial Stakes (Irgun)

SUNSHINE FOREVER

2000: San Juan Capistrano Handicap (Sunshine Street)

SUPER CONCORDE

1983: Florida Derby (Croeso)

SURREAL

1985: Tropical Park Derby (Irish Sur)

SWAIN

2003: Flower Bowl Invitational Stakes (Dimitrova)

SWAPS

1961: Delaware Oaks (Primonetta)
Alabama Stakes (Primonetta)
1962: Sorority Stakes (Affectionately)
Spinaway Stakes (Affectionately)
Gardenia Stakes (Main Swap)
Spinster Stakes (Primonetta)
Jerome Handicap (Black Beard)
1963: Blue Grass Stakes (Chateaugay)
Kentucky Derby (Chateaugay)
Belmont Stakes (Chateaugay)
Jerome Handicap (Chateaugay)
Wood Memorial Stakes (No Robbery)
1965: Top Flight Handicap (Affectionately)
1970: Kentucky Oaks (Lady Vi-E)
1974: Swaps Stakes (Green Gambados)

SWEEP ALL

1946: Arlington Lassie Stakes (Four Winds)
1948: Arlington Matron Handicap (Four Winds)

SWEET CANDY

1988: Blue Grass Stakes (Granacus)

SWING TILL DAWN

1990: Budweiser International Stakes (Fly Till Dawn)
1992: San Luis Rey Stakes (Fly Till Dawn)
San Juan Capistrano Handicap (Fly Till Dawn)

SWOON'S SON

1971: Black Helen Handicap (Swoon's Flower)
1974: Acorn Stakes (Chris Evert)
Mother Goose Stakes (Chris Evert)
Coaching Club American Oaks (Chris Evert)

SWORD DANCE

1996: Secretariat Stakes (Marlin)
Crown Royal Hollywood Derby (Marlin)
1997: San Juan Capistrano Handicap (Marlin)
Arlington Million (Marlin)

SWORD DANCER

1966: Mother Goose Stakes (Lady Pitt)
Coaching Club American Oaks (Lady Pitt)
1967: Wood Memorial Stakes (Damascus)
Preakness Stakes (Damascus)
Belmont Stakes (Damascus)
Dwyer Handicap (Damascus)
American Derby (Damascus)
Travers Stakes (Damascus)
Aqueduct Stakes (Damascus)
Woodward Stakes (Damascus)
Jockey Club Gold Cup (Damascus)
1968: Brooklyn Handicap (Damascus)
Aqueduct Stakes (Damascus)
Malibu Stakes (Damascus)
San Fernando Stakes (Damascus)

TABASCO CAT

2001: Del Mar Debutante Stakes (Habibti)
Hollywood Starlet Stakes (Habibti)
2002: San Carlos Handicap (Snow Ridge)
Philip H. Iselin Handicap (Cat's at Home)

TABLE RUN

1979: Del Mar Debutante Stakes (Table Hands)
1980: Longacres Mile (Trooper Seven)

TACTICAL ADVANTAGE

1999: Pegasus Handicap (Forty One Carats)

TAKE AWAY

1959: San Carlos Handicap (Hillsdale)
Los Angeles Handicap (Hillsdale)
Californian Stakes (Hillsdale)
American Handicap (Hillsdale)
Hollywood Gold Cup (Hillsdale)
Aqueduct Handicap (Hillsdale)
Santa Anita Maturity (Hillsdale)

TAKE ME OUT

1999: Louisiana Derby (Kimberlite Pipe)

TALE OF THE CAT

2003: Darley Alcibiades Stakes (Be Gentle)
Hollywood Futurity (Lion Heart)

TALE OF TWO CITIES

1971: Californian Stakes (Cougar II)
Ford Pinto Invitational Turf Handicap (Cougar II)
Oak Tree Invitational Stakes (Cougar II)
San Juan Capistrano Handicap (Cougar II)
1972: Californian Stakes (Cougar II)
Century Handicap (Cougar II)
Oak Tree Invitational Stakes (Cougar II)
1973: Santa Anita Handicap (Cougar II)
Century Handicap (Cougar II)
Sunset Handicap (Cougar II)

TAMBOURINE

1977: New Orleans Handicap (Tudor Tambourine)

TANK'S PROSPECT

1990: San Felipe Handicap (Real Cash)
American Derby (Real Cash)

TANTIEME

1962: Washington D.C. International (Match II)

TAPIOCA

1969: San Luis Rey Handicap (Taneb)

TARBOOSH

1980: Flower Bowl Handicap (Just A Game II)

TARGOWICE

1983: Turf Classic (All Along)
Washington D.C. International (All Along)
Rothmans International Stakes (All Along)

TARGUI

1962: Californian Stakes (Cadiz)
1963: Hollywood Gold Cup (Cadiz)

TATAN

1964: Michigan Mile and One-Sixteenth (Tibaldo)
1965: Vanity Handicap (Jalousie II)
1969: Selima Stakes (Predictable)

TAYLOR'S FALLS

1995: Arkansas Derby (Dazzling Falls)

TEDDY'S COMET

1949: Arlington Futurity (Wisconsin Boy)
Astoria Stakes (Baby Comet)
Trenton Handicap (Sky Miracle)
1952: Florida Derby (Sky Ship)

TEHRAN

1957: Dixie Handicap (Akbar Khan)
1960: Arkansas Derby (Persian Gold)
1962: Arlington Handicap (El Bandido)
Canadian Championship Stakes (El Bandido)

TELL

1976: Del Mar Debutante Stakes (Telferner)
1977: Louisiana Derby (Clev Er Tell)
Arkansas Derby (Clev Er Tell)

TEMPERENCE HILL

1986: Hollywood Futurity (Temperate Sil)
1987: Santa Anita Derby (Temperate Sil)
Swaps Stakes (Temperate Sil)
1989: Peter Pan Stakes (Imbibe)

TENTAM

1980: Pennsylvania Derby (Lively King)
Canadian International Championship (Great Neck)
1981: Bowling Green Handicap (Great Neck)
1983: Jerome Handicap (A Phenomenon)
Vosburgh Stakes (A Phenomenon)

TERRA FIRMA

1965: Ohio Derby (Terri Hi)

TERRANG

1964: Del Mar Futurity (Terry's Secret)
1965: Hollywood Derby (Terry's Secret)
Sunset Handicap (Terry's Secret)
1970: San Felipe Handicap (Terlago)
Santa Anita Derby (Terlago)

TERRESTO

1980: Hollywood Juvenile Championship (Loma Malad)

TERRIBLE TIGER

1979: Delaware Handicap (Likely Exchange)

THATCHING

1989: Gamely Handicap (Fitzwilliam Place)

THAT'S A NICE

1991: Flower Bowl Handicap (Lady Shirl)

THEATRICAL

1992: Santa Anita Oaks (Golden Treat)
1994: American Derby (Vaudeville)
Secretariat Stakes (Vaudeville)
Flower Bowl Inv. Handicap (Dahlia's Dreamer)
1995: Matriarch Stakes (Duda)
1996: Oaklawn Handicap (Geri)
Sword Dancer Invitational Handicap (Broadway Flyer)
1997: Woodbine Mile (Geri)
1998: Flower Bowl Invitational Handicap (Auntie Mame)
Canadian Int. Championship (Royal Anthem)
Malibu Stakes (Run Man Run)
2000: Gulfstream Park BC Handicap (Royal Anthem)
Gamely Breeders' Cup Handicap (Astra)
Philip H. Iselin Handicap (Rize)
2001: Beverly Hills Handicap (Astra)
Secretariat Stakes (Startac)
2002: Gamely Breeders' Cup Handicap (Astra)
Beverly Hills Handicap (Astra)

THE AXE II

1968: Hollywood Derby (Poleax)
1969: Jersey Derby (Al Hattab)
Monmouth Invitational Handicap (Al Hattab)
1970: Sanford Stakes (Executioner)
Hollywood Oaks (Last of the Line)
1971: Arkansas Derby (Twist the Axe)
Ohio Derby (Twist the Axe)
Flamingo Stakes (Executioner)
1972: Gulfstream Park Handicap (Executioner)
Metropolitan Handicap (Executioner)
1974: Dwyer Handicap (Hatchet Man)
1975: Remsen Stakes (Hang Ten)
1976: Widener Handicap (Hatchet Man)
Amory L. Haskell Handicap (Hatchet Man)

THE BATTLER

1958: California Derby (Nice Guy)
1964: San Fernando Stakes (Nevada Battler)

THE DOGE

1954: Ohio Derby (Timely Tip)
1955: Arlington Futurity (Swoon's Son)
Washington Park Futurity (Swoon's Son)
1956: Arlington Classic (Swoon's Son)
American Derby (Swoon's Son)

THE IRISH LORD

1988: La Canada Stakes (Hollywood Glitter)

THE IRISHMAN

1968: Lawrence Realization Stakes (Funny Fellow)
Gallant Fox Handicap (Funny Fellow)
1969: Donn Handicap (Funny Fellow)
Carter Handicap (Promise)

THE MINSTREL

1986: John Henry Handicap (Palace Music)
1987: Selima Stakes (Minstrel's Lassie)
1990: Oaklawn Handicap (Opening Verse)
1991: Breeders' Cup Mile (Opening Verse)

THE PIE KING

1964: California Derby (Real Good Deal)
Hollywood Derby (Real Good Deal)

THE PORTER

1946: Lawrence Realization Stakes (School Tie)

THE PRUNER

1980: Meadowlands Cup (Tunerup)
Hawthorne Gold Cup (Tunerup)

THE RHYMER

1958: Pimlico Special (Vertex)
Trenton Handicap (Vertex)
1959: Gulfstream Park Handicap (Vertex)
John B. Campbell Handicap (Vertex)
Grey Lag Handicap (Vertex)

THE SULTAN

1955: Tropical Handicap (Scimitar)

THE YUVARAJ

1966: Donn Handicap (Tronado)
Arlington Handicap (Tronado)

THINKING CAP

1963: Manhattan Handicap (Smart)
1964: Massachusetts Handicap (Smart)
Gallant Fox Handicap (Smart)
1965: Massachusetts Handicap (Smart)

THIRD BROTHER

1963: Champagne Stakes (Roman Brother)
1964: Everglades Stakes (Roman Brother)
Jersey Derby (Roman Brother)
American Derby (Roman Brother)
1965: Woodward Stakes (Roman Brother)
Manhattan Handicap (Roman Brother)
Jockey Club Gold Cup (Roman Brother)

THIRD MARTINI

1973: Whitney Stakes (Onion)

THUMBS UP

1953: Manhattan Handicap (Jampol)

THUNDER GULCH

2000: Breeders' Cup Distaff (Spain)
La Brea Stakes (Spain)
Hollywood Futurity (Point Given)
2001: San Felipe Stakes (Point Given)
Santa Anita Derby (Point Given)
Preakness Stakes (Point Given)
Belmont Stakes (Point Given)
Haskell Invitational Handicap (Point Given)
Travers Stakes (Point Given)
Coaching Club American Oaks (Tweedside)

THUNDER PUDDLES

1992: Jim Dandy Stakes (Thunder Rumble)
Travers Stakes (Thunder Rumble)

TIGER

1949: Longacres Mile (Blue Tiger)
1950: Acorn Stakes (Siama)
Monmouth Oaks (Siama)
Comely Handicap (Siama)
1955: Black Helen Handicap (Rosemary B.)

TIGER II

1972: San Luis Rey Handicap (Nor II)

TILT UP

1984: Sorority Stakes (Tiltalating)

TIME FOR A CHANGE

1990: Champagne Stakes (Fly So Free)
Breeders' Cup Juvenile (Fly So Free)
1991: Florida Derby (Fly So Free)
Jim Dandy Stakes (Fly So Free)
1992: Florida Derby (Technology)
Haskell Invitational Handicap (Technology)
1993: Brooklyn Handicap (Living Vicariously)
1996: Jerome Handicap (Why Change)

TIMELESS MOMENT

1983: Arlington-Washington Futurity (All Fired Up)
1984: Hollywood Oaks (Moment to Buy)
1992: Arlington-Washington Futurity (Gilded Time)
Breeders' Cup Juvenile (Gilded Time)

TIM TAM

1963: Frizette Stakes (Tosmah)
1964: Matron Handicap (Tosmah)
Beldame Stakes (Tosmah)
Arlington Classic (Tosmah)
1965: Seminole Handicap (Sunstruck)
1966: John B. Campbell Handicap (Tosmah)
1967: Kentucky Oaks (Nancy Jr.)

TINTAGEL

1953: Vosburgh Handicap (Indian Land)

TIPOQUILL

1963: Arkansas Derby (Cosmic Tip)

TOBIN BRONZE

1975: San Luis Rey Stakes (Trojan Bronze)
1977: Hollywood Juvenile Championship (Noble Bronze)
1978: California Derby (Noble Bronze)

TO B. OR NOT

1987: Hollywood Oaks (Perchance to Dream)

TO MARKET

1959: Alabama Stakes (High Bid)
Vineland Handicap (High Bid)
1961: United Nations Handicap (Oink)
1963: Garden State Stakes (Hurry to Market)
1965: Carter Handicap (Viking Spirit)
Californian Stakes (Viking Spirit)
1966: Acorn Stakes (Marking Time)
1967: San Felipe Handicap (Rising Market)
1968: Spinster Stakes (Sale Day)
San Antonio Handicap (Rising Market)
1970: Vanity Handicap (Commissary)

TOM FOOL

1957: Futurity Stakes (Jester)
1958: Everglades Stakes (Tim Tam)
Flamingo Stakes (Tim Tam)
Florida Derby (Tim Tam)
Kentucky Derby (Tim Tam)
Preakness Stakes (Tim Tam)
1959: Arlington Classic (Dunce)
American Derby (Dunce)
Hopeful Stakes (Tompion)
Futurity Stakes (Weatherwise)
1960: Santa Anita Derby (Tompion)
Blue Grass Stakes (Tompion)
Travers Stakes (Tompion)
1961: Sorority Stakes (Batter Up)
Mother Goose Stakes (Funloving)
Aqueduct Handicap (Tompion)
1962: Selima Stakes (Fool's Play)
1963: Metropolitan Handicap (Cyrano)
Brooklyn Handicap (Cyrano)
1964: Los Angeles Handicap (Cyrano)
1965: Sapling Stakes (Buckpasser)
Hopeful Stakes (Buckpasser)
Arlington-Washington Futurity (Buckpasser)
Champagne Stakes (Buckpasser)
1966: Everglades Stakes (Buckpasser)
Flamingo Stakes (Buckpasser)
Arlington Classic (Buckpasser)
American Derby (Buckpasser)
Travers Stakes (Buckpasser)
Lawrence Realization Stakes (Buckpasser)
Brooklyn Handicap (Buckpasser)
Woodward Stakes (Buckpasser)
Jockey Club Gold Cup (Buckpasser)
1967: Metropolitan Handicap (Buckpasser)
Suburban Handicap (Buckpasser)
San Fernando Stakes (Buckpasser)
Gazelle Handicap (Sweet Folly)
Ladies Handicap (Sweet Folly)
1968: Century Handicap (Model Fool)

TOMPION

1968: Travers Stakes (Chompion)
1971: Pan American Handicap (Chompion)
Dixie Handicap (Chompion)
Massachusetts Handicap (Chompion)

TOM ROLFE

1970: Cowdin Stakes (Hoist the Flag)
Garden State Stakes (Run the Gantlet)
1971: United Nations Handicap (Run the Gantlet)
Man o' War Stakes (Run the Gantlet)
Washington D.C. International (Run the Gantlet)
1972: Grey Lag Handicap (Droll Role)
Hawthorne Gold Cup (Droll Role)
Massachusetts Handicap (Droll Role)
Canadian International Championship (Droll Role)
Washington D.C. International (Droll Role)
Bowling Green Handicap (Run the Gantlet)
1973: Beverly Hills Handicap (Le Cle)
Manhattan Handicap (London Company)
1974: Michigan Mile and One-Eighth (Tom Tulle)
Pan American Handicap (London Company)
1978: Gulfstream Park Handicap (Bowl Game)
Pan American Handicap (Bowl Game)
1979: Hialeah Turf Cup (Bowl Game)
Arlington Handicap (Bowl Game)
Man o' War Stakes (Bowl Game)
Turf Classic (Bowl Game)
Washington D.C. International (Bowl Game)
1980: Man o' War Stakes (French Colonial)
1981: Flower Bowl Handicap (Rokeby Rose)
1983: Bowling Green Handicap (Tantalizing)
1987: Oak Tree Invitational Stakes (Allez Milord)

TOP COMMAND

1981: Haskell Invitational Handicap (Five Star Flight)
1982: Pennsylvania Derby (Spanish Drums)
1984: Selima Stakes (Mom's Command)
1985: Acorn Stakes (Mom's Command)
Mother Goose Stakes (Mom's Command)
Coaching Club American Oaks (Mom's Command)
Alabama Stakes (Mom's Command)

TOP GALLANT II

1971: Del Mar Futurity (D.B. Carm)

TOP ROW

1949: Starlet Stakes (Thanks Again)
Del Mar Handicap (Top's Boy)

TOPSIDER

1986: Spinster Stakes (Top Corsage)
1987: Santa Margarita Handicap (North Sider)
Apple Blossom Handicap (North Sider)
Maskette Stakes (North Sider)
1988: Tropical Park Derby (Digress)

TORSION

1982: Golden Harvest Handicap (Miss Huntington)
1983: Apple Blossom Handicap (Miss Huntington)

TOUCH GOLD

2003: Las Virgenes Stakes (Composure)
Santa Anita Oaks (Composure)

TOULOUSE LAUTREC

1964: Cinema Handicap (Close By)

TOWSON

1973: Ladies Handicap (Wakefield Miss)

TRACE CALL

1948: Black Helen Handicap (Rampart)
Gulfstream Park Handicap (Rampart)

TRAFFIC COP

1983: Preakness Stakes (Deputed Testamony)
Haskell Invitational Handicap (Deputed Testamony)

TRAFFIC JUDGE

1962: Sapling Stakes (Delta Judge)
1963: Hopeful Stakes (Traffic)
1968: Arlington-Washington Futurity (Strong Strong)
Kentucky Jockey Club Stakes (Traffic Mark)
1969: Arkansas Derby (Traffic Mark)
Gulfstream Park Handicap (Court Recess)
1971: Hopeful Stakes (Rest Your Case)
1974: Hollywood Invitational Handicap (Court Ruling)

TRAFFIC MARK

1975: American Derby (Honey Mark)

TRANSWORLD

1982: Hollywood Turf Cup (The Hague)

TREMPOLINO

2000: Beverly D. Stakes (Snow Polina)

TREVIERES

1974: Santa Margarita Handicap (Tizna)
Ramona Handicap (Tizna)
1975: Ladies Handicap (Tizna)
Santa Margarita Handicap (Tizna)

TRI JET

1982: Hopeful Stakes (Copelan)
Futurity Stakes (Copelan)
Champagne Stakes (Copelan)
1991: Champagne Stakes (Tri to Watch)
1992: Spinaway Stakes (Family Enterprize)

TRUCE MAKER

1993: Santa Margarita Handicap (Southern Truce)

TRY MY BEST

1986: Breeders' Cup Mile (Last Tycoon)

TSUNAMI SLEW

1993: Sword Dancer Handicap (Spectacular Tide)

TUDOR CASTLE

1961: Gulfstream Park Handicap (Tudor Way)

TUDOR GREY

1969: Grey Lag Handicap (Bushido)
1971: John B. Campbell Handicap (Bushido)
1980: Swaps Stakes (First Albert)

TUDOR MINSTREL

1955: Santa Anita Handicap (Poona II)
1958: Starlet Stakes (Tomy Lee)
Del Mar Futurity (Tomy Lee)
1959: Blue Grass Stakes (Tomy Lee)
Kentucky Derby (Tomy Lee)
1961: Arlington Handicap (Tudorich)
1965: Alabama Stakes (What A Treat)
Gazelle Handicap (What A Treat)
Beldame Stakes (What A Treat)

TUDOR MINSTREL *(Continued)*
1966: Black Helen Handicap (What A Treat)
1967: Carter Handicap (Tumiga)

TUDOR WAY
1969: Arlington-Washington Lassie Stakes (Clover Lane)

TULYAR
1962: Hollywood Oaks (Dingle Bay)
1963: Sorority Stakes (Castle Forbes)
Gardenia Stakes (Castle Forbes)
Santa Margarita Handicap (Pixie Erin)
1964: Acorn Stakes (Castle Forbes)

TURKOMAN
1995: Turf Classic (Turk Passer)
2003: Gulfstream Park BC 'Cap (Man From Wicklow)

TURN-TO
1958: Hopeful Stakes (First Landing)
Champagne Stakes (First Landing)
Garden State Stakes (First Landing)
1959: Everglades Stakes (First Landing)
Dwyer Handicap (Waltz)
1960: Sapling Stakes (Hail to Reason)
Hopeful Stakes (Hail to Reason)
Monmouth Handicap (First Landing)
Santa Anita Maturity (First Landing)
1961: Sapling Stakes (Sir Gaylord)
Futurity Stakes (Cyane)
1962: Everglades Stakes (Sir Gaylord)
Dwyer Handicap (Cyane)
Roamer Handicap (Dead Ahead)
1963: Kentucky Oaks (Sally Ship)
1966: Saratoga Special (Favorable Turn)
1967: Futurity Stakes (Captain's Gig)
United Nations Handicap (Flit-to)
1968: Donn Handicap (Favorable Turn)
1970: John B. Campbell Handicap (Best Turn)
Vosburgh Handicap (Best Turn)

TURN TO REASON
1972: Carter Handicap (Leematt)

T.V. LARK
1967: Arlington-Washington Futurity (T.V. Commercial)
Breeders' Futurity (T.V. Commercial)
1968: Ohio Derby (Te Vega)
1969: Santa Barbara Handicap (Pink Pigeon)
1970: Washington Park Handicap (Doc's T.V.)
1972: California Derby (Quack)
Hollywood Gold Cup (Quack)
1973: Californian Stakes (Quack)
Michigan Mile and One-Eighth (Golden Don)
American Handicap (Kentuckian)
1974: Californian Stakes (Quack)
Arlington Handicap (Buffalo Lark)
Manhattan Handicap (Golden Don)
1975: Pan American Handicap (Buffalo Lark)
1976: Fantasy Stakes (T.V. Vixen)
1978: Arlington Handicap (Romeo)
1980: New Orleans Handicap (Pool Court)

TWO A DAY
1984: Sapling Stakes (Doubly Clear)

TWO PUNCH
1994: Philip H. Iselin Handicap (Taking Risks)
1996: Hopeful Stakes (Smoke Glacken)
1997: Frank J. De Francis Memorial Dash (Smoke Glacken)
1998: Fall Highweight Handicap (Punch Line)

TYRANT
1982: Flower Bowl Handicap (Trevita)

UNBREAKABLE
1946: Roseben Handicap (Polynesian)
1947: Tremont Stakes (Inseparable)
1949: San Carlos Handicap (Manyunk)
1950: Washington Park Handicap (Inseparable)
Stars and Stripes Handicap (Inseparable)
1951: Inglewood Handicap (Sturdy One)
1952: Inglewood Handicap (Sturdy One)
1953: Fall Highweight Handicap (Kaster)

UNBRIDLED
1995: Breeders' Cup Juvenile (Unbridled's Song)
1996: Florida Derby (Unbridled's Song)
Wood Memorial Stakes (Unbridled's Song)
Kentucky Derby (Grindstone)
1998: Coaching Club American Oaks (Banshee Breeze)
Alabama Stakes (Banshee Breeze)
Three Chimneys Spinster Stakes (Banshee Breeze)
Hollywood Oaks (Manistique)
1999: Santa Margarita Handicap (Manistique)
Vanity Handicap (Manistique)
Apple Blossom Handicap (Banshee Breeze)
Go for Wand Handicap (Banshee Breeze)
Breeders' Cup Juvenile (Anees)
2000: Santa Maria Handicap (Manistique)
Preakness Stakes (Red Bullet)
Travers Stakes (Unshaded)
2001: Gazelle Handicap (Exogenous)
Beldame Stakes (Exogenous)
Philip H. Iselin Handicap (Broken Vow)
2003: Florida Derby (Empire Maker)
Wood Memorial Stakes (Empire Maker)
Belmont Stakes (Empire Maker)
Del Mar Debutante Stakes (Halfbridled)
Breeders' Cup Juvenile Fillies (Halfbridled)

UNBRIDLED'S SONG
2001: Fountain of Youth Stakes (Songandaprayer)
Breeders' Cup Distaff (Unbridled Elaine)
2002: Wood Memorial Stakes (Buddha)
2003: Matron Stakes (Marylebone)
Lane's End Breeders' Futurity (Eurosilver)

UNCONSCIOUS
1977: Monmouth Invitational Handicap (Affiliate)
Vosburgh Handicap (Affiliate)

UNDERSTANDING
1980: Gamely Handicap (Wishing Well)

UNFUWAIN
2001: Flower Bowl Invitational Handicap (Lailani)

UPPER CASE
1986: Hollywood Invitational Handicap (Flying Pidgeon)

UTRILLO II
1969: Stars and Stripes Handicap (Hawaii)
United Nations Handicap (Hawaii)
Man o' War Stakes (Hawaii)

VAGUELY NOBLE
1973: Florida Derby (Royal and Regal)
Washington D.C. International (Dahlia)
1974: Man o' War Stakes (Dahlia)
Canadian International Championship (Dahlia)
1975: Washington D.C. International (Nobiliary)
1976: Hollywood Invitational Handicap (Dahlia)
1977: Canadian International Championship (Exceller)
1978: Hollywood Gold Cup (Exceller)
Jockey Club Gold Cup (Exceller)
Hollywood Invitational Handicap (Exceller)
Sunset Handicap (Exceller)
Oak Tree Invitational Stakes (Exceller)
San Juan Capistrano Handicap (Exceller)
1980: Sunset Handicap (Inkerman)
1982: Marlboro Cup Handicap (Lemhi Gold)
Jockey Club Gold Cup (Lemhi Gold)
Sword Dancer Stakes (Lemhi Gold)
San Juan Capistrano Handicap (Lemhi Gold)
Oaklawn Handicap (Eminency)
1985: Yellow Ribbon Stakes (Estrapade)
Turf Classic (Noble Fighter)
1986: Budweiser-Arlington Million (Estrapade)
Oak Tree Invitational Stakes (Estrapade)
1987: San Juan Capistrano Handicap (Rosedale)

VAL DE L'ORNE
1982: Hollywood Derby (Victory Zone)

VALDEZ
1989: Hialeah Turf Cup (El Senor)
Sword Dancer Handicap (El Senor)
1990: Sword Dancer Handicap (El Senor)

VALID APPEAL
1981: Blue Grass Stakes (Proud Appeal)
1983: Pegasus Handicap (World Appeal)
1984: Laurel Futurity (Mighty Appealing)
Remsen Stakes (Mighty Appealing)
1985: Laurel Futurity (Southern Appeal)
1998: Buick Meadowlands Cup Handicap (K.J.'s Appeal)

VALID WAGER
2003: King's Bishop Stakes (Valid Video)

VANDALE
1969: Canadian International Championship (Vent du Nord)
1970: Hialeah Turf Cup (Vent du Nord)

VENTURON
1969: Michigan Mile and One-Eighth (Calandrito)

VERBATIM
1975: Demoiselle Stakes (Free Journey)
1977: San Fernando Stakes (Pocket Park)
1980: Illinois Derby (Ray's Word)
1981: Pennsylvania Derby (Summing)
Belmont Stakes (Summing)
Pegasus Handicap (Summing)
1982: Frizette Stakes (Princess Rooney)
Matriarch Stakes (Pale Purple)
1983: Kentucky Oaks (Princess Rooney)
1984: Vanity Handicap (Princess Rooney)
Spinster Stakes (Princess Rooney)
Breeders' Cup Distaff (Princess Rooney)
Hollywood Turf Cup (Alphabatim)
1986: Hollywood Turf Cup (Alphabatim)

VERTEE
1978: Arlington-Washington Futurity (Jose Binn)

VERTEX
1965: Santa Anita Derby (Lucky Debonair)
Blue Grass Stakes (Lucky Debonair)
Kentucky Derby (Lucky Debonair)
1966: Seminole Handicap (Convex)
Santa Anita Handicap (Lucky Debonair)
1968: Hopeful Stakes (Top Knight)
Futurity Stakes (Top Knight)
Champagne Stakes (Top Knight)
1969: Flamingo Stakes (Top Knight)
Florida Derby (Top Knight)
1970: Cinema Handicap (D'Artagnan)
Donn Handicap (Twogundan)
1971: Blue Grass Stakes (Impetuosity)
Metropolitan Handicap (Tunex)
1972: Gotham Stakes (Freetex)
Ohio Derby (Freetex)
Monmouth Invitational Handicap (Freetex)
1973: Widener Handicap (Vertee)
John B. Campbell Handicap (Vertee)

VICE REGENT
1981: Laurel Futurity (Deputy Minister)
Young America Stakes (Deputy Minister)
1996: Santa Margarita Handicap (Twice the Vice)
Apple Blossom Handicap (Twice the Vice)
Milady Breeders' Cup Handicap (Twice the Vice)
1997: Vanity Handicap (Twice the Vice)

VICTORIAN ERA
1976: Arlington Handicap (Victorian Prince)

VICTORIA PARK
1973: Hollywood Gold Cup (Kennedy Road)
San Antonio Stakes (Kennedy Road)

VICTORY MORN
1967: Massachusetts Handicap (Good Knight)

VIGORS
1985: Santa Margarita Handicap (Lovlier Linda)
Withers Stakes (El Basco)
1989: Rothmans International Stakes (Hodges Bay)
1994: Man o' War Stakes (Royal Mountain Inn)

VILLAMOR
1979: Arlington-Washington Lassie Stakes (Sissy's Time)

VITRIOLIC
1974: Selima Stakes (Aunt Jin)
Santa Anita Derby (Destroyer)
1977: Del Mar Debutante Stakes (Extravagant)

WAGON LIMIT
2003: Hopeful Stakes (Silver Wagon)

WAIDMANNSHELL
1972: Suburban Handicap (Hitchcock)

WALLET LIFTER
1975: San Fernando Stakes (Stardust Mel)
Charles H. Strub Stakes (Stardust Mel)
Santa Anita Handicap (Stardust Mel)

WAQUOIT
1997: Apple Blossom Handicap (Halo America)
1998: Norfolk Stakes (Buck Trout)

WAR ADMIRAL

1947: Matron Stakes (Inheritance)
Del Mar Handicap (Iron Maiden)
1948: Garden State Stakes (Blue Peter)
Saratoga Special (Blue Peter)
Hopeful Stakes (Blue Peter)
Futurity Stakes (Blue Peter)
Arlington Futurity (Mr. Busher)
Tremont Stakes (The Admiral)
1950: Alabama Stakes (Busanda)
1951: Top Flight Handicap (Busanda)
New Castle Handicap (Busanda)
Suburban Handicap (Busanda)
Vosburgh Handicap (War King)
1952: American Handicap (Admiral Drake)
1953: Jerome Handicap (Navy Page)
Westchester Handicap (Cold Command)
1954: Breeders' Futurity (Brother Tex)
Bougainvillea Turf Handicap (Parnassus)
1955: Aqueduct Handicap (Icarian)
1956: Top Flight Handicap (Searching)
Diana Handicap (Searching)
Maskette Handicap (Searching)
Firenze Handicap (Blue Banner)
1958: Molly Pitcher Handicap (Searching)
Diana Handicap (Searching)
Gallant Fox Handicap (Admiral Vee)

WAR DOG

1949: New Castle Handicap (Allie's Pal)
Molly Pitcher Handicap (Allie's Pal)
1951: San Felipe Stakes (Phil D.)
1952: San Antonio Handicap (Phil D.)

WARFARE

1966: United Nations Handicap (Assagai)
Man o' War Stakes (Assagai)
1967: Louisiana Derby (Ask the Fare)
1973: Donn Handicap (Triumphant)

WAR GLORY

1946: California Derby (War Spun)

WAR JEEP

1950: Garden State Stakes (Iswas)
1953: Michigan Mile (Second Avenue)
1954: Kentucky Oaks (Fascinator)
1961: Canadian Championship Stakes (Our Jeep)

WAR RELIC

1947: Hopeful Stakes (Relic)
1950: Sapling Stakes (Battlefield)
Saratoga Special (Battlefield)
Hopeful Stakes (Battlefield)
Tremont Stakes (Battlefield)
Futurity Stakes (Battlefield)
1951: Withers Stakes (Battlefield)
Dwyer Stakes (Battlefield)
Travers Stakes (Battlefield)
1952: San Juan Capistrano Handicap (Intent)
Santa Anita Maturity (Intent)
New York Handicap (Battlefield)
Westchester Handicap (Battlefield)
1953: San Juan Capistrano Handicap (Intent)
1956: Pimlico Futurity (Missile)

WATCHMITICK

1951: Starlet Stakes (Prudy's Boy)

WATCH YOUR STEP

1973: Jerome Handicap (Step Nicely)

WATER PRINCE

1971: Vosburgh Handicap (Duck Dance)

WAVERING MONARCH

1995: Futurity Stakes (Maria's Mon)
Champagne Stakes (Maria's Mon)

WELL DECORATED

1987: Hutcheson Stakes (Well Selected)

WELL MANNERED

1978: Bay Meadows Handicap (Bywayofchicago)

WELSH CHANTER

1986: Coaching Club American Oaks (Valley Victory)

WELSH PAGEANT

1985: Budweiser-Arlington Million (Teleprompter)
1986: Santa Barbara Handicap (Mountain Bear)

WESTERN SKY II

1965: California Derby (Perfect Sky)

WHAT A PLEASURE

1974: Sapling Stakes (Foolish Pleasure)
Hopeful Stakes (Foolish Pleasure)
Champagne Stakes (Foolish Pleasure)
1975: Champagne Stakes (Honest Pleasure)
Laurel Futurity (Honest Pleasure)
Arlington-Washington Futurity (Honest Pleasure)
Flamingo Stakes (Foolish Pleasure)
Wood Memorial Stakes (Foolish Pleasure)
Kentucky Derby (Foolish Pleasure)
Maskette Handicap (Let Me Linger)
1976: Flamingo Stakes (Honest Pleasure)
Florida Derby (Honest Pleasure)
Blue Grass Stakes (Honest Pleasure)
Travers Stakes (Honest Pleasure)
Donn Handicap (Foolish Pleasure)
Suburban Handicap (Foolish Pleasure)
Futurity Stakes (For the Moment)
1977: Blue Grass Stakes (For the Moment)
1980: Breeders' Futurity (Fairway Phantom)
1981: Arlington Classic (Fairway Phantom)

WHAT LUCK

1977: Maskette Handicap (What a Summer)
Carter Handicap (Gentle King)
1983: Maskette Stakes (Ambassador of Luck)

WHIRLAWAY

1947: Selima Stakes (Whirl Some)
Marguerite Stakes (Whirl Some)
1948: Pimlico Oaks (Scattered)
Coaching Club American Oaks (Scattered)
1949: Arlington Lassie Stakes (Dutchess Peg)
1950: Cowdin Stakes (Away Away)
1951: Louisiana Derby (Whirling Bat)
1954: Michigan Mile (Spur On)

WHITE GLOVES II

1973: Fantasy Stakes (Knitted Gloves)

WIG OUT

1979: Hopeful Stakes (J.P. Brother)
1980: Apple Blossom Handicap (Billy Jane)

WILD AGAIN

1991: Hempstead Handicap (A Wild Ride)
Spinster Stakes (Wilderness Song)
1994: Hopeful Stakes (Wild Escapade)
1995: Blue Grass Stakes (Wild Syn)
1997: Breeders' Cup Sprint (Elmhurst)
1998: Carter Handicap (Wild Rush)
Metropolitan Handicap (Wild Rush)
1999: Fountain of Youth Stakes (Vicar)
Florida Derby (Vicar)
Early Times Turf Classic (Wild Event)
2001: Ballerina Handicap (Shine Again)
2002: Santa Anita Handicap (Milwaukee Brew)
Belmont Stakes (Sarava)
Ballerina Handicap (Shine Again)
2003: Santa Anita Handicap (Milwaukee Brew)

WILD RISK

1953: Washington D.C. International (Worden II)

WILD RUSH

2003: Hollywood Starlet Stakes (Hollywood Story)

WINDSOR RULER

1969: Oak Leaf Stakes (Opening Bid)
1970: Santa Susana Stakes (Opening Bid)
1972: San Felipe Handicap (Solar Salute)
Santa Anita Derby (Solar Salute)

WINDY CITY II

1957: Starlet Stakes (Old Pueblo)
Del Mar Futurity (Old Pueblo)
1958: Arlington Futurity (Restless Wind)
Washington Park Futurity (Restless Wind)
1963: San Felipe Handicap (Denodado)
Louisiana Derby (City Line)
1964: Santa Susana Stakes (Blue Norther)
Kentucky Oaks (Blue Norther)
1966: Illinois Derby (Michigan Avenue)

WINDY SANDS

1966: Del Mar Debutante Stakes (Native Honey)
1970: Del Mar Futurity (June Darling)
Norfolk Stakes (June Darling)
Oak Leaf Stakes (June Darling)

1973: Hollywood Oaks (Sandy Blue)
1976: San Felipe Handicap (Crystal Water)
Hollywood Derby (Crystal Water)
1977: Californian Stakes (Crystal Water)
Hollywood Gold Cup (Crystal Water)
Santa Anita Handicap (Crystal Water)
Oak Tree Invitational Stakes (Crystal Water)
1981: Californian Stakes (Eleven Stitches)
Hollywood Gold Cup (Eleven Stitches)
San Felipe Handicap (Stancharry)
1983: La Canada Stakes (Avigaition)
Santa Barbara Handicap (Avigaition)

WINDY SEA

1972: Del Mar Debutante Stakes (Windy's Daughter)
1973: Acorn Stakes (Windy's Daughter)
Mother Goose Stakes (Windy's Daughter)

WINE LIST

1958: Arlington Lassie Stakes (Dark Vintage)

WING OUT

1979: Hollywood Juvenile Championship (Parsec)

WISE EXCHANGE

1973: Oak Leaf Stakes (Divine Grace)
1977: Top Flight Handicap (Shawi)

WITH APPROVAL

1995: Gotham Stakes (Talkin Man)
Wood Memorial Stakes (Talkin Man)

WITH REGARDS

1952: Del Mar Futurity (Hour Regards)

WITTGENSTEIN

1983: Californian Stakes (The Wonder)
Century Handicap (The Wonder)

WOLFRAM

1973: Hollywood Invitational Handicap (Life Cycle)

WOLVER HOLLOW

1981: Sunset Handicap (Galaxy Libra)
Man o' War Stakes (Galaxy Libra)

WOODMAN

1990: Arlington-Washington Futurity (Hansel)
1991: Jim Beam Stakes (Hansel)
Preakness Stakes (Hansel)
Belmont Stakes (Hansel)
1994: Champagne Stakes (Timber Country)
Breeders' Cup Juvenile (Timber Country)
1995: Preakness Stakes (Timber Country)
1996: Whitney Handicap (Mahogany Hall)
2000: Secretariat Stakes (Ciro)
2002: Secretariat Stakes (Chiselling)

WORDEN II

1969: Washington D.C. International (Karabas)

WRACK OF GOLD

1953: Vineland Handicap (Mi-Marigold)

WYNDHAM

1952: San Felipe Handicap (Windy City II)

YACHTIE

1999: Matriarch Stakes (Happyanunoit)
2000: Beverly Hills Handicap (Happyanunoit)
2001: Gamely Breeders' Cup Handicap (Happyanunoit)

YORKTOWN

1966: Sanford Stakes (Yorkville)
1971: Alcibiades Stakes (Mrs. Cornwallis)

YOU AND I

2001: Frizette Stakes (You)
2002: Las Virgenes Stakes (You)
Santa Anita Oaks (You)
Acorn Stakes (You)
Test Stakes (You)

YOUR ALIBHAI

1969: Gardenia Stakes (Fast Attack)

YOUR HOST

1955: Del Mar Futurity (Blen Host)
Del Mar Debutante Stakes (Miss Todd)
1956: San Felipe Handicap (Social Climber)
Cinema Handicap (Social Climber)
1957: Californian Stakes (Social Climber)

YOUR HOST *(Continued)*

1960: Jerome Handicap (Kelso)
Lawrence Realization Stakes (Kelso)
Hawthorne Gold Cup (Kelso)
Jockey Club Gold Cup (Kelso)
American Handicap (Prize Host)
1961: Metropolitan Handicap (Kelso)
Suburban Handicap (Kelso)
Brooklyn Handicap (Kelso)
Woodward Stakes (Kelso)
Jockey Club Gold Cup (Kelso)
Whitney Handicap (Kelso)
1962: Woodward Stakes (Kelso)
Jockey Club Gold Cup (Kelso)
1963: Seminole Handicap (Kelso)
Gulfstream Park Handicap (Kelso)
John B. Campbell Handicap (Kelso)
Suburban Handicap (Kelso)
Aqueduct Stakes (Kelso)
Woodward Stakes (Kelso)
Jockey Club Gold Cup (Kelso)
Whitney Stakes (Kelso)
1964: Aqueduct Stakes (Kelso)
Jockey Club Gold Cup (Kelso)
Washington D.C. International (Kelso)
1965: Whitney Stakes (Kelso)

ZACAWEISTA

1948: San Carlos Handicap (Autocrat)
1949: San Carlos Handicap (Autocrat)

ZARBYEV

1996: Arkansas Derby (Zarb's Magic)

ZEN

1984: American Derby (High Alexander)

ZENITH

1966: Suburban Handicap (Buffle)

ZINAAD

2002: Flower Bowl Invitational Stakes (Kazzia)

ZONING

1987: Arlington-Washington Lassie Stakes (Joe's Tammie)

Bill Straus photo courtesy of Keeneland Association

It's little wonder that the late Tom Caldwell (center on platform at left) dropped the gavel to announce that Hip No. 195 had sold for a sale-topping $3 million at the 1999 Keeneland July Selected Yearling Sale, which reigned as the world's most prestigious horse auction for decades. The colt, by standout stallion Storm Cat, is out of the Secretariat mare Weekend Surprise, who, as the dam of both Summer Squall and A.P. Indy, is the only mare since World War II to foal two North American classic winners. Lane's End Farm consigned the colt as agent, and he was purchased by Demi O'Byrne, Michael Tabor, and John Magnier.

Dams

VII: Dams

Some Royal Bloodlines

Unlike their male counterparts, virtually all female thoroughbreds are broodmare prospects. Even ignoring the fact that many less-promising males are gelded at early ages, during most of the modern era stallions were bred to some 40 mares per year, a figure that has crept well above the century mark for many in the past decade.

So there are dozens, perhaps as many as 50 or more, broodmares for every horse who embarks on a career at stud.

And unlike stallions who now may produce in excess of 100 offspring annually, because of an 11-month gestation period that limits mares to one foal per year, it would be foolish to judge a mare's success based on total major victories. Otherwise, Maid of Flight clearly would reign as the best mare of the modern era, because her offspring produced 24 major triumphs. All of them, however, were recorded by the Count Fleet mare's only major winner, Kelso.

Kinetic Corporation photo courtesy of Churchill Downs

Unbridled, who captured the 1990 Kentucky Derby under Craig Perret, followed that victory with a triumph in the Breeders' Cup Classic later that season. Those victories make his dam, the Le Fabuleux mare Gana Facil, also the dam of 1991 Wood Memorial Stakes winner Cahill Road, one of only three mares since World War II to foal multiple major North American stakes winners whose triumphs include both a classic and a Breeders' Cup victory.

Mares with superior race records obviously are going to be in great demand, but that is by no means a prerequisite for success as a broodmare.

There have been 302 dams who gave birth to more than one modern-era North American major stakes winner, but only 28 of those 302 were multiple major North American winners. Further, 85 percent of those dams who foaled more than one major winner failed to win a major race themselves, and 78 percent never even finished in the money in major North American competition during the modern era.

Of those 302 mares who have had more than one foal cross the wire first in major competition, only nine won four or more races and clearly can be considered the most successful modern distaffers both on the track and as producers: High Voltage, Numbered Account, and Personal Ensign with six victories; Quill and Searching with five, and A Gleam, Busanda, Conniver, and Dahlia with four.

Dahlia is one of only five mares who foaled four different major North American winners since World War II, and Personal Ensign, and the War Admiral mares Busanda and Searching are among the 41 others who foaled three different winners.

The Fab Five

While Dahlia enjoyed a Hall of Fame career on the track and Toussaud earned a major triumph in the 1993 Gamely Handicap, the other three mares who foaled four major winners—Blue Delight, Stepping Stone, and Somethingroyal—never posted an in-the-money finish in a major race during the modern era.

Dahlia's four winners were sired by four different stallions. Dahlia, a daughter of Vaguely Noble, produced Dahar (by

Lyphard), Dahlia's Dreamer (Theatrical), Delegant (Grey Dawn II), and Rivlia (Riverman). Likewise, Stepping Stone, who was sired by Princequillo, produced winners by four different sires: Big Advance (Bold Ruler), Moss Vale (Gallant Man), High Bid (To Market), and Progressing (Bimelech). Toussaud, a daughter of El Gran Senor and the only member of this august group who was still an active broodmare when the 2004 breeding season opened, also produced major winners by four different stallions: Empire Maker (Unbridled), Chester House (Mr. Prospector), Chiselling (Woodman), and Honest Lady (Seattle Slew). Somethingroyal, by Princequillo, produced First Family (First Landing) and Sir Gaylord (Turn-to) as well as Syrian Sea and Secretariat, full siblings by Bold Ruler. Blue Delight, a daughter of Blue Larkspur, produced Princess Turia (Heliopolis) and three full siblings by Bull Lea: All Blue, Bubbley, and Real Delight.

Somethingroyal and Toussaud are the only modern broodmares whose four major winners include a classic winner. Not only did Secretariat sweep the 1973 Triple Crown, but First Family finished third in the 1965 Belmont Stakes, while Empire Maker captured the 2003 Belmont Stakes.

Best of the Rest

Bubbley, Princess Turia, and Real Delight were multiple major winners, making Blue Delight one of only three dams to produce three multiple major winners during the modern era. Resolver, a daughter of Reviewer, is the dam of Adjudicating, Dispute (1990), and Time for a Change. Bourtai, by Stimulus, foaled Bayou, Delta, and Levee, and all three of Bourtai's major winners captured three or more major races, making her the only modern mare who can stake that claim.

Just three mares produced two foals who eventually claimed six or more major victories. Hildene, a daughter of Bubbling Over, produced Hill Prince and First Landing. Key Bridge, by Princequillo, foaled Fort Marcy and Key to the Mint. Traffic Court, a Discovery mare, is the dam of both Hasty Road and Traffic Judge. Three others produced two foals who won at least five races. The Black Toney mare Big Hurry foaled Bridal Flower and Searching; War Flower, by Man o' War, produced Ace Admiral and Helioscope, and Weekend Surprise, a daughter of Secretariat, is the dam of Summer Squall and A.P. Indy.

Only two of the 41 dams who have foaled three different major winners in the modern era, Ace Card and Golden Dust, can count a classic winner among their offspring. Ace Card, a Case Ace mare who also foaled My Card and Yildiz, was represented by 1952 Belmont Stakes winner One Count. Golden Dust, a daughter of Dusty Canyon, produced Bold And Gold and Golden Treat in addition to 1987 Belmont winner Bet Twice.

Personal Ensign, a daughter of Private Account, is the only dam whose three major winners include a Breeders' Cup winner. Personal Ensign is the dam of major winners Miner's Mark, Traditionally, and My Flag, who captured the 1995 Breeders' Cup Juvenile Fillies.

While 31 dams have produced a classic winner and at least one additional major winner in the modern era and 24 can count a Breeders' Cup winner among their multiple major winners, only one has produced two modern classic winners and just one has foaled two Breeders' Cup winners. Summer Squall and A.P. Indy, both out of Weekend Surprise, captured the 1990 Preakness Stakes and the 1992 Belmont Stakes, respectively. Primal Force, by Blushing Groom, is the dam of both 1998 Breeders' Cup Classic winner Awesome Again and 2000 Breeders' Cup Juvenile hero Macho Uno.

Those who have come closest to duplicating Weekend Surprise's feat, in addition to Somethingroyal, are Alluvial, Hildene, and Traffic Court. Alluvial, a daughter of Buckpasser, is the dam of both 1979 Belmont Stakes winner Coastal and '83 Belmont runner-up Slew O' Gold. Hildene was represented by 1950 Preakness winner Hill Prince, and First Landing finished third in the 1959 Kentucky Derby. Traffic Court's two standout offspring nearly won the Preakness in consecutive years, with Hasty Road winning the Run for the Black-Eyed Susans in 1954 and Traffic Judge finishing third a year later. Although she never foaled a classic winner, special mention must go to the Never Bend mare Anne Campbell, who produced multiple major winners Desert Wine and Menifee. The former finished second in both the Kentucky Derby and Preakness in 1983, and Menifee duplicated that feat 16 years later.

Although Primal Force is the only dam with two Breeders' Cup winners, Cee's Song might have a more impressive record in the Breeders' Cup. The daughter of Seattle Song has foaled major winners Tiznow, winner of the Breeders' Cup Classic in both 2000 and 2001, and Budroyale, runner-up in the '99 Classic. While only one of the two major winners out of the Key to the Mint mare Pure Profit, 1995 Distaff victor Inside Information, has a Breeders' Cup victory, her other major winner, Educated Risk, was the runner-up in the 1992 Juvenile Fillies. And while North of Eden has yet to produce a Breeders' Cup winner, two of the three major winners foaled by the daughter of Northfields, Paradise Creek and Forbidden Apple, finished second in the Mile, in 1992 and in 2001, respectively.

Only three dams who have foaled more than one major winner have produced foals who captured both classic and Breeders' Cup races. A.P. Indy added the 1992 Classic to his Belmont Stakes victory for Weekend Surprise. Gana Facil, a Le Fabuleux mare who produced major winner Cahill Road, is also the dam of Unbridled, winner of both the Kentucky Derby and the Classic in 1990. Fall Aspen, a daughter of Pretense, produced Northern Aspen in addition to Timber Country, who captured the 1994 Juvenile and the 1995 Preakness.

Full Siblings

In human terminology, any two people who share the same father but have different mothers are considered half-siblings. While, technically, that's also true for horses, because successful stallions sire hundreds of offspring in their careers, only those who share the same dam are considered half-brothers or half-sisters.

Since success breeds success—or so it would seem—it is quite common after a broodmare produces a major winner to return her to the court of that same sire for subsequent matings. Surprisingly enough, however, only 83 such matings have produced multiple major winners in the modern era, and just five of those have clicked to produce major winners on three occasions.

The Squaw II, a daughter of Sickle, produced Cherokee Rose, How, and Sequoia, all sired by Princequillo. Matings of the Gold Bridge mare Rough Shod II to Nantallah produced Lt. Stevens, Moccasin, and Ridan. The Tom Fool mare Dunce Cap II foaled Johnny Appleseed, Late Act, and Late Bloomer, each sired by Stage Door Johnny. Ballade, a daughter of Herbager, produced Devil's Bag, Glorious Song, and Saint Ballado, all by Halo.

It's not surprising that matings of Bull Lea and the Blue Larkspur mare Blue Delight were one of five that produced three full siblings who won major races. Bull Lea is the only stallion who sired six sets of full siblings who became major winners, and only three others sired more than two—Bold Ruler (5), Princequillo (5), and Danzig (3). Further, Blue Larkspur is the only broodmare sire who sired four daughters who produced full siblings who were major winners, one more than Nasrullah, Princequillo, and Sickle.

And only three combinations of the same sire and broodmare sire produced two sets of full siblings who were major winners: Bull Lea when matched with mares by Blue Larkspur and Blenheim II and Bold Ruler when matched with mares by Princequillo.

In addition to his successful matings with Blue Delight, Bull Lea sired Capeador and Picador, both out of the Blue Larkspur mare Bonnet Ann. Bull Lea's matings with Blenheim II mares that produced full siblings who became major winners were with Easy Lass (Coaltown and Rosewood) and Mar-Kell (Amoret and Mark-Ye-Well). In addition to his success with Somethingroyal, Bold Ruler also sired major winners Bold Lad and Successor, both out of Misty Morn, who, like Somethingroyal, was a daughter of Princequillo.

The following chart shows the complete list of full siblings who won major North American races during the modern era:

Full Siblings Who Won Major North American Races From 1946-2003

Sire—Dam by Dam's Sire	Full Siblings
Alibhai—Torch Rose by Torchilla	On Trust, Trusting
Alsab—Best Yet by The Rhymer	Toby B., Toby's Brother
Ambiorix—Banri-an Or by Royal Charger	Amri-An, Pinjara
A.P. Indy—Prospectors Delite by Mr. Prospector	Mineshaft, Tomisue's Delight
Beau Gar—Marullah by Nasrullah	Blessing Angelica, Handsome Boy
Beau Pere—Panoramic by Chance Shot	Honeymoon, Pedigree
Better Bee—Paula by Nizami II	Abe's Hope, Bee Bee Bee
Bimelech—Blade of Time by Sickle	Blue Border, Guillotine
Bimelech—Bloodroot by Blue Larkspur	Be Faithful, Bimlette
Blue Larkspur—Be Like Mom by Sickle	But Why Not, Renew
Bold Ruler—Broadway by Hasty Road	Queen of the Stage, Reviewer
Bold Ruler—Castle Forbes by Tulyar	Alpine Lass, Irish Castle
Bold Ruler—Irish Jay by Double Jay	King Emperor, Queen Empress
Bold Ruler—Misty Morn by Princequillo	Bold Lad, Successor
Bold Ruler—Somethingroyal by Princequillo	Secretariat, Syrian Sea
Bold Venture—Igual by Equipoise	Assault, On Your Own
Brick—Eos by Strip the Willow	Eugenia II, Meeting
Buckpasser—Intriguing by Swaps	Cunning Trick, Numbered Account
Bull Dog—My Auntie by Busy American	Carolina Queen, Johns Joy
Bull Lea—Armful by Chance Shot	Armed, Lap Full
Bull Lea—Blue Delight by Blue Larkspur	All Blue, Bubbley, Real Delight
Bull Lea—Bonnet Ann by Blue Larkspur	Capeador, Picador
Bull Lea—Easy Lass by Blenheim II	Coaltown, Rosewood
Bull Lea—Mar-Kell by Blenheim II	Amoret, Mark-Ye-Well
Bull Lea—Two Bob by The Porter	Miz Clementine, Two Lea
Cee's Tizzy—Cee's Song by Seattle Song	Budroyale, Tiznow
Challedon—Dorothy B. Jr. by Brown King	Gigantic, Tenacious
Counterpoint—Dawn Fleet by Noor	Fast Count, Over the Counter
Count Fleet—Honor Bound by Bull Dog	Countess Fleet, Count of Honor
Crafty Admiral—Adjournment by Court Martial	Frimanaha, Master Palynch
Cyane—Witching Hour by Thinking Cap	Pumpkin Moonshine, Salem
Damascus—Court Circuit by Royal Vale	Bailjumper, Honorable Miss
Danzig—Gydnia by Sir Ivor	Danzig Connection, Roi Danzig
Danzig—Kennelot by Gallant Man	Lotka, Stephan's Odyssey
Danzig—Resolver by Reviewer	Adjudicating, Dispute (1990)
Dark Star—Dangerous Dame by Nasrullah	Heavenly Body, Hidden Talent
Discovery—Bride Elect by High Time	First Glance, Knockdown
Double Jay—Conniver by Discovery	Clandestine, Plotter
Explodent—Social Lesson by Forum	Exbourne, Expelled
Fappiano—Gana Facil by Le Fabuleux	Cahill Road, Unbridled
Hail to Reason—Primonetta by Swaps	Cum Laude Laurie, Prince Thou Art
Hail to Reason—Searching by War Admiral	Admiring, Priceless Gem
Halo—Ballade by Herbager	Devil's Bag, Glorious Song, Saint Ballado
Heliopolis—War Flower by Man o' War	Ace Admiral, Helioscope
Hillary—Mary Machree by Moonlight Run	Hill Circus, Hill Clown
Hill Prince—Bourtai by Stimulus	Bayou, Levee
Hill Prince—Easy Living by Heliopolis	Riley, Royal Living
His Majesty—Premium Win by Lyphard	Tight Spot, Valiant Nature
Irish River—Cadeaux d'Amie by Lyphard	Hatoof, Irish Prize
In Reality—Breakfast Bell by Buckpasser	Believe It, It's True
In Reality—Desert Trial by Moslem Chief	Desert Vixen, Valid Appeal
Jack High—Tatanne by St. James	Frere Jacques, Lucky Draw
Jig Time—Extra Alarm by Blazing Count	Darn That Alarm, Strong Performance
Khaled—Iron Reward by Beau Pere	Swaps, The Shoe
Mahmoud—Arbitrator by Peace Chance	Almahmoud, Burra Sahib
Mahmoud—Maud Muller by Pennant	Monsoon, Mount Marcy
Majestic Light—Tallahto by Nantallah	Hidden Light, Prince True
Maudlin—Beautiful Bid by Baldski	Beautiful Pleasure, Mecke
Mr. Prospector—Personal Ensign by Private Account	Miner's Mark, Traditionally
Nantallah—Rough Shod II by Gold Bridge	Lt. Stevens, Moccasin, Ridan
Nasrullah—Siama by Tiger	Bald Eagle, One-Eyed King
Nasrullah—Track Medal by Khaled	Outing Class, Tutankhamen
Nijinsky II—Rosetta Stone by Round Table	De La Rose, Upper Nile
Princequillo—Grey Flight by Mahmoud	Misty Flight, Misty Morn
Princequillo—Hildene by Bubbling Over	Hill Prince, Third Brother
Princequillo—Knight's Daughter by Sir Cosmo	Monarchy, Round Table
Princequillo—Not Afraid by Count Fleet	Brave Lad, Prince John
Princequillo—The Squaw II by Sickle	Cherokee Rose, How, Sequoia
Private Account—Grecian Banner by Hoist the Flag	Personal Ensign, Personal Flag
Quibu—Haze by Olympia	Sky Gem, Tinsley
Round Table—Courtesy by Nasrullah	Dignitas, Knightly Manner
Royal Charger—Tige O'Myheart by Bull Lea	Idun, Irish Lancer
Royal Coinage—Firefly by Papa Redbird	He's a Pistol, Venetian Way
Seeking the Gold—Oh What a Dance by Nijinsky II	Heavenly Prize, Oh What a Windfall
Spy Song—Fulmar by Hairan	Fulcrum, Fulvous
Stage Door Johnny—Dunce Cap II by Tom Fool	Johnny Appleseed, Late Act, Late Bloomer
Swaps—Banquet Bell by Polynesian	Chateaugay, Primonetta
The Battler—Wonderful You by Brown King	Nevada Battler, Nice Guy
To Market—Hasty Girl by Princequillo	Hurry to Market, Sale Day
T.V. Lark—Chance Gauge by Degage	Buffalo Lark, Kentuckian
War Admiral—Big Hurry by Black Toney	Searching, The Admiral
War Admiral—Our Page by Blue Larkspur	Brother Tex, Navy Page
What a Pleasure—Tularia by Tulyar	For the Moment, Honest Pleasure

Family Trees

One of the ultimate measuring sticks for dams not only has been their ability to produce major winners, but to foal daughters who produce major winners.

Only once in the modern era has a dam produced multiple major winners that included a daughter who produced multiple winners who successfully extended that family tree to three generations by also producing a daughter who foaled multiple major winners.

Rock Drill, a daughter of 1941 Triple Crown winner Whirlaway, began that string by producing both Lady Pitt and Rocky Link. Lady Pitt, a daughter of Sword Dancer, subsequently foaled major winners Blitey and The Liberal Member. Finally, Blitey stretched that family's string to three generations when the daughter of Riva Ridge produced both Dancing Spree and Furlough.

Nineteen other dams who produced two or major winners in the modern era foaled a daughter who also produced multiple major winners: Those standout families, with the dam who began the string listed first: Alablue (Alanesian), Big Hurry (Searching), Bloodroot (Bimlette), Bourtai (Delta), Donatrice (Bellesoeur), Forever Yours (Mahmoudess), Grey Flight (Misty Morn), Grecian Banner (Personal Ensign), Intriguing (Numbered Account), Kamar (Seaside Attraction), Legato (Tallahto), Maud Muller (Monsoon), Quick Touch (Quill), Rare Perfume (Rare Treat), Silver Fog (Silver Bright), Surgery (Shared Interest), Twilight Tear (A Gleam), Two Bob (Two Lea), and Up the Flagpole (Prospectors Delite).

Breeding the Best to the Best

While countless major winners indeed have been produced from matches made in heaven, and numerous others from less-heralded stock, what indeed does happen when the standard adage of breeding—breed the best to the best, and hope for the best—is applied?

Only one major winner in the modern era is the product of a mating that included:

- A stallion who ranks second on the list for major victories;
- One of only five dams who foaled four major winners;
- A broodmare sire who heads the list of major victories;
- One of only three crosses of a sire and broodmare sire to produce more than one set of full siblings who won major races;
- A dam who had three offspring who already were major winners at the time of the mating.

When the best is bred to the best, expectations are understandably high, as they were when that regally bred chestnut colt, a product of the 1969 mating of Bold Ruler with the Princequillo mare Somethingroyal, was born on March 30, 1970. Suffice it to say that Secretariat exceeded even the loftiest of expectations.

The following chart shows every dam who produced more than one major North American winner from 1946-2003, including the dam's record in major North American races from 1946-2003 if she had an in-the-money finish, the dam's sire, the major winners she produced, and the records in major races from 1946-2003 of those major winners:

Dams Who Foaled Multiple Major North American Winners From 1946-2003

Dam	Record	Dam's Sire	Major Winner	Record
Ace Card		Case Ace	My Card	1-0-0/4
			One Count	3-2-2/18
			Yildiz	1-1-0/6
Adjournment		Court Martial	Frimanaha	1-0-1/5
			Master Palynch	1-0-2/6
A Gleam	4-2-3/23	Blenheim II	A Glitter	2-1-4/14
			Gleaming	2-2-2/14
Alablue	0-2-1/5	Blue Larkspur	Alanesian	1-1-0/6
			Middle Brother	1-2-1/9
Alanesian	1-1-0/6	Polynesian	Boldnesian	1-0-0/4
			Princessnesian	3-2-1/17
Alluvial		Buckpasser	Coastal	3-1-2/16
			Slew O' Gold	7-4-0/36
Amelia Bearhart		Bold Hour	Chief Bearhart	3-2-0/16
			Explosive Red	2-1-1/11
Amiga	0-0-1/1	Mahmoud	Carrier X.	1-0-0/4
			Tumiga	1-2-1/9
Anchors Aweigh		Devil Diver	Make Sail	3-1-2/16
			Never Bow	2-4-0/16
Anne Campbell		Never Bend	Desert Wine	4-8-0/32
			Menifee	2-3-1/15
Aplenstock III		Apelle	Alladier	1-1-0/6
			Ruhe	1-3-4/14
			Sturdy One	2-3-4/18
Arbitrator		Peace Chance	Almahmoud	1-0-0/4
			Burra Sahib	1-0-0/4
Armful		Chance Shot	Armed	10-5-4/54
			Lap Full	1-0-1/5
Aspidistra		Better Self	Dr. Fager	12-2-1/53
			Ta Wee	1-0-0/4
Au Printempts		Dancing Champ	Greenwood Lake	2-1-0/10
			Success Express	1-0-1/5
Avie		Gallant Man	Jolly Johu	1-1-1/7
			Lord Avie	3-4-1/21
Baby League		Bubbling Over	Harmonizing	1-2-1/9
			Mr. Busher	1-0-0/4
Baby Zip		Relaunch	City Zip	1-1-2/8
			Ghostzapper	1-0-1/5
Bali Babe		Drone	Charismatic	2-0-1/9
			Millennium Wind	1-1-0/6
Ballade		Herbager	Devil's Bag	2-0-0/8
			Glorious Song	4-5-0/26
			Saint Ballado	1-0-0/4
Banquet Bell		Polynesian	Chateaugay	4-1-2/20
			Primonetta	3-2-1/17
Banri-an Or		Royal Charger	Amri-An	1-0-0/4
			Pinjara	2-0-2/10
Beaming Bride		King Emperor	Husband	1-0-0/4
			Simply Majestic	1-0-2/6
Beautiful Bid		Baldski	Beautiful Pleasure	6-5-0/34
			Mecke	3-3-4/22
Bebopper		Tom Fool	Hatchet Man	3-1-0/14
			Stop the Music	2-7-3/25
Bee Mac		War Admiral	Better Self	5-5-2/32
			Prophets Thumb	1-0-1/5
			Riverina	1-1-2/8
Be Like Mom		Sickle	But Why Not	8-4-2/42
			Renew	2-2-1/13
Belle Jeep		War Jeep	Evasive Action	1-0-0/4
			Jewel's Reward	5-1-1/23
Bellerine		Sir Damion	Sunrise County	1-4-4/16
			Terra Firma	2-1-0/10
Bellesoeur	2-1-0/10	Beau Pere	Beau Diable	1-1-1/7
			Jabneh	1-2-0/8
Best Yet		The Rhymer	Toby B.	1-0-2/6
			Toby's Brother	1-0-0/4
Big Hurry		Black Toney	Bridal Flower	5-3-3/29
			Searching	5-2-2/26
			The Admiral	1-0-0/4
Bimlette	1-0-0/4	Bimelech	Maharajah	1-0-5/9
			No Robbery	1-0-0/4
Blackball		Shut Out	Malicious	2-2-2/14
			The Axe II	3-0-2/14
Blade of Time		Sickle	Blue Border	1-0-1/5
			Guillotine	3-0-0/12
			Ruddy	1-1-0/6
Blitey	1-1-2/8	Riva Ridge	Dancing Spree	3-2-1/17
			Furlough	1-2-0/8
Bloodroot		Blue Larkspur	Ancestor	1-0-0/4
			Be Faithful	2-0-3/11
			Bimlette	1-0-0/4
Blue Alibi		Alibhai	Apple Valley	1-0-0/4
			Blue Reading	1-0-3/7
Blue Delight		Blue Larkspur	All Blue	1-2-0/8
			Bubbley	2-0-0/8
			Princess Turia	3-1-1/15
			Real Delight	6-0-0/24
Boat		Man o' War	Greek Ship	3-5-2/24
			Rampart	2-1-2/12
			Sky Ship	1-0-0/4
Bold Princess		Bold Ruler	Intrepid Hero	3-2-0/16
			Predictable	1-1-0/6
Bonnet Ann		Blue Larkspur	Capeador	1-2-3/11
			Picador	1-2-0/8
Bourtai		Stimulus	Bayou	4-1-0/18
			Delta	3-1-0/14
			Levee	4-1-2/20
Bravura		Niccolo Dell'Arca	Candalita	2-0-0/8
			Hail the Pirates	1-0-1/5
Breakfast Bell		Buckpasser	Believe It	2-2-2/14
			It's True	1-0-0/4
Breath O'Morn		Djeddah	Knightly Dawn	1-0-0/4
			Proud Clarion	1-1-1/7
Bride Elect		High Time	First Glance	1-0-2/6
			Knockdown	3-0-0/12
Broadway	0-1-0/2	Hasty Road	Queen of the Stage	4-0-0/16
			Reviewer	2-3-1/15
Brown Berry	1-0-0/4	Mount Marcy	Avatar	3-4-0/20
			Unconscious	4-2-1/21
Brown Biscuit		Sir Andrew	Espea	1-0-0/4
			Lebkuchen	1-0-0/4
Busanda	4-1-3/21	War Admiral	Buckpasser	16-3-1/71
			Bupers	1-1-2/8
			Bureaucracy	1-2-0/8
By the Hand		Intentionally	Buy the Firm	1-1-2/8
			Image of Greatness	1-1-0/6
Cadeaux d'Amie		Lyphard	Hatoof	1-1-0/6
			Irish Prize	1-0-0/4
Careless Notion		Jester	Cacoethes	1-0-0/4
			Fabulous Notion	2-0-0/8
Carols Folly		Taylor's Falls	Glitter Woman	1-2-0/8
			Unbridled Elaine	1-0-0/4
Cascade II		Precipitation	Jacinto	1-1-0/6
			Niagara	1-0-0/4
Castle Forbes	3-2-4/20	Tulyar	Alpine Lass	1-1-0/6
			Irish Castle	1-0-1/5
Cee's Song		Seattle Song	Budroyale	1-4-0/12
			Tiznow	4-3-1/23
Cequillo		Princequillo	Hot Dust	1-3-1/11
			Ruffled Feathers	1-1-1/7
Chance Gauge		Degage	Buffalo Lark	2-2-5/17
			Kentuckian	1-1-1/7
Chantress		Hyperion	Gainsboro Girl	2-1-0/10
			Sea O Erin	1-0-5/9
Chappaquidick		Relic	Digress	1-0-1/5
			Tiller	4-5-1/27
Classy 'n Smart		Smarten	Dance Smartly	1-0-2/6
			Smart Strike	1-0-0/4
Clear Road	0-1-0/2	Hasty Road	Going Straight	1-0-0/4
			San Juan Hill	1-0-0/4
Con Game		Buckpasser	Fast Play	2-3-1/15
			Seeking the Gold	3-6-0/24
Conniver	4-2-1/21	Discovery	Clandestine	1-2-0/8
			Plotter	1-1-0/6
Cosmah	0-2-1/5	Cosmic Bomb	Halo	1-0-2/6
			Tosmah	5-1-2/24

Dam	Record	Dam's Sire	Major Winner	Record
Court Circuit		Royal Vale	Bailjumper	1-0-0/4
			Honorable Miss	2-2-0/12
Courtesy		Nasrullah	Dignitas	1-1-1/7
			Knightly Manner	1-4-6/18
Courtly Dee		Never Bend	Ali Oop	1-0-0/4
			Althea	5-2-0/24
			Twining	1-1-0/6
Crimson Saint		Crimson Satan	Royal Academy	1-0-0/4
			Terlingua	2-2-1/13
Dahlia	4-0-2/18	Vaguely Noble	Dahar	3-4-1/21
			Dahlia's Dreamer	1-1-0/6
			Delegant	1-0-0/4
			Rivlia	2-0-3/11
Dance Review		Northern Dancer	Another Review	1-0-2/6
			No Review	1-0-2/6
Dancing Puppet		Northern Dancer	Dancing Gun	1-0-3/7
			Kirby Lane	2-1-0/10
Dangerous Dame		Nasrullah	Heavenly Body	2-0-2/10
			Hidden Talent	1-0-0/4
Darby Dunedin		Blenheim II	Black Beard	1-0-0/4
			Clear Dawn	1-5-6/20
Darien Miss		Mr. Leader	Fleet Renee	2-0-1/9
			Future Quest	2-0-0/8
Daring Bidder		Bold Bidder	Dinard	1-1-0/6
			Eliza	3-1-1/15
Davelle		Shannon II	Al Davelle	1-0-0/4
			Prince Davelle	1-0-0/4
Dawn Fleet		Noor	Fast Count	2-0-0/8
			Over the Counter	1-1-1/7
Dear Birdie		Storm Bird	Birdstone	1-0-0/4
			Bird Town	2-2-0/12
Decor II		Court Martial	Forum	1-0-0/4
			High Counsel	1-1-1/7
Delta	3-1-0/14	Nasrullah	Cabildo	1-2-0/8
			Dike	3-3-4/22
Desert Trial		Moslem Chief	Desert Vixen	4-2-0/20
			Valid Appeal	1-1-1/7
Desert Vision		Roman	Astray	3-1-2/16
			Desert Law	1-1-1/7
			Desert Love	2-0-1/9
Dokki		Northern Dancer	Aptitude	2-2-1/13
			Sleep Easy	1-1-0/6
Donatrice		Donatello II	Bellesoeur	2-1-0/10
			The Dude	1-0-1/5
Dona Ysidra		Le Fabuleux	Manila	5-0-0/20
			Stately Don	1-0-0/4
Dorothy B. Jr.		Brown King	Gigantic	2-0-1/9
			Tenacious	2-0-2/10
Dunce Cap II		Tom Fool	Johnny Appleseed	1-0-1/5
			Late Act	1-0-1/5
			Late Bloomer	4-1-0/18
Durga		Tatan	An Act	1-0-0/4
			Sarsar	1-0-1/5
Dutchess Anita		Count Gallahad	Call Over	1-0-1/5
			Our Fleet	1-0-0/4
Easy Lass		Blenheim II	Coaltown	9-3-1/43
			Rosewood	1-0-1/5
			Wistful (1946)	3-2-4/20
Easy Living		Heliopolis	Riley	2-2-0/12
			Royal Living	1-1-1/7
Enchanted Eve	0-2-1/5	Lovely Night	Smart	4-4-1/25
			Tempted	5-1-4/26
Eos		Strip the Willow	Eugenia II	1-0-0/4
			Meeting	1-1-0/6
Equal Venture		Bold Venture	Prove Out	3-0-0/12
			Saidam	1-2-3/11
Excellent Lady		Smarten	General Challenge	4-2-0/20
			Notable Career	1-1-0/6
Exclusive		Shut Out	Exclusive Native	2-2-2/14
			Irvkup	1-1-0/6
Expectancy		Intentionally	Dr. Patches	2-4-0/16
			Who's For Dinner	1-1-1/7
Expression		The Porter	Register	1-0-0/4
			Straight Face	5-2-1/25
Extra Alarm		Blazing Count	Darn That Alarm	1-2-2/10
			Strong Performance	1-0-0/4
Face the Facts	0-2-1/5	Court Martial	Bicker	2-1-1/11
			Judger	2-1-2/12
Fairday		Fair Play	Inseparable	3-1-1/15
			Triplicate	3-0-1/13
Fairy Palace		Pilate	Parlo	6-2-0/28
			Perfect Sky	1-0-0/4
Fall Aspen	1-0-0/4	Pretense	Northern Aspen	1-1-0/6
			Timber Country	3-1-2/16
Fanfreluche	1-1-1/7	Northern Dancer	D'Accord	1-0-0/4
			L'Enjoleur	1-0-0/4
Favorecida II		Embrujo	Bold Favorite	1-0-0/4
			Favorecidian	2-0-2/10
Firefly		Papa Redbird	He's a Pistol	1-1-0/6
			Venetian Way	2-2-1/13
Flitabout	0-1-0/2	Challedon	Flirtatious	1-0-0/4
			Funloving	1-1-2/8
Flota		Jack High	Sailor	5-0-1/21
			Seaward	1-2-0/8
Flying Buttress		Exclusive Native	Class Play	1-0-1/5
			Pillaster	1-0-1/5
Foolish One		Tom Fool	Funny Fellow	3-3-2/20
			Protanto	1-3-0/10
Forever Yours		Toro	Eternal Reward	1-3-1/11
			Mahmoudess	1-0-1/5
Fresh as Fresh		Count Fleet	Lady Love	1-1-1/7
			Lucky Debonair	4-1-0/18
Fulmar		Hairan	Fulcrum	1-0-0/4
			Fulvous	2-1-0/10
Gaga		Bull Dog	Aunt Jinny	2-2-1/13
			Tom Fool	9-4-1/45
Gana Facil		Le Fabuleux	Cahill Road	1-0-0/4
			Unbridled	3-2-3/19
Glowing Tribute		Graustark	Hero's Honor	1-0-0/4
			Sea Hero	3-0-2/14
Golden Dust		Dusty Canyon	Bet Twice	5-3-3/29
			Bold And Gold	1-0-0/4
			Golden Treat	1-1-0/6
Good Blood	2-0-0/8	Bull Lea	Barbizon	1-0-0/4
			Hillsborough	1-3-0/10
Goofed	1-0-0/4	Court Martial	Barcas	1-1-0/6
			Nobiliary	1-0-0/4
Grecian Banner		Hoist the Flag	Personal Ensign	6-0-0/24
			Personal Flag	1-3-3/13
Grey Flight	0-2-2/6	Mahmoud	Misty Flight	1-2-1/9
			Misty Morn	3-2-1/17
			What a Pleasure	1-1-1/7
Gydnia		Sir Ivor	Danzig Connection	2-2-2/14
			Roi Danzig	1-2-1/9
Hadepine		Hadagal	Hushaby Baby	1-0-0/4
			Model Cadet	1-0-0/4
Harmonica	2-5-0/18	Snark	Rico Reta	1-2-1/9
			Waltz	1-0-2/6
Hasili		Kahyasi	Banks Hill	1-1-1/7
			Heat Haze	2-1-1/11
Hasty Girl		Princequillo	Hurry to Market	1-0-0/4
			Sale Day	1-0-1/5
Hattab Girl		Al Hattab	On Target	1-0-2/6
			Sea Cadet	4-2-2/22
Haze		Olympia	Sky Gem	1-2-0/8
			Tinsley	1-1-0/6
			Tri Jet	2-1-3/13
Heather Road		The Axe II	Bull Inthe Heather	1-1-0/6
			Heatherten	3-2-1/17
Heather Time		Time Maker	Correspondent	2-0-2/10
			U Time	2-0-0/8
Her Honor		Count Fleet	Loquacious Don	1-0-1/5
			Prego	1-0-1/5
Highland Mills		Pia Star	Miss Josh	1-0-0/4
			Royal Mountain Inn	1-0-0/4
High Voltage	6-0-3/27	Ambiorix	Great Power	1-1-0/6
			Impressive	1-2-2/10
Hildene		Bubbling Over	First Landing	6-8-2/42
			Hill Prince	9-3-2/44
			Third Brother	1-6-5/21
Hold Hands		Anyoldtime	Any Time Girl	1-0-0/4
			Table Hands	1-0-1/5
Homewrecker		Buckaroo	Cat's at Home	1-0-0/4
			Prenup	1-0-1/5
Honor an Offer		Hoist the Flag	Imperial Gesture	2-2-1/13
			Sardula	2-3-0/14
Honor Bound		Bull Dog	Countess Fleet	1-0-2/6
			Count of Honor	1-0-0/4
			Sette Bello	1-0-1/5
Hug Again		Stimulus	Arrogate	3-0-1/13
			Fervent	4-4-1/25
Igual		Equipoise	Assault	12-1-3/53
			On Your Own	1-0-0/4
In Neon		Ack Ack	Royal Anthem	2-1-0/10
			Sharp Cat	8-3-0/38
Intriguing		Swaps	Cunning Trick	1-0-0/4
			Numbered Account	6-0-1/25
Irish Jay	2-2-0/12	Double Jay	King Emperor	3-1-2/16
			Land of Eire	1-0-0/4
			Queen Empress	2-1-2/12
Iron Reward		Beau Pere	Swaps	10-1-0/42
			The Shoe	1-1-0/6
Island Kitty	0-0-1/1	Hawaii	Hennessy	1-1-0/6
			Pearl City	1-1-2/8
Kamar		Key to the Mint	Gorgeous	5-4-0/28
			Seaside Attraction	1-0-1/5
Kennelot		Gallant Man	Lotka	1-1-1/7
			Stephan's Odyssey	3-3-1/19
Key Bridge		Princequillo	Fort Marcy	8-8-7/55
			Key To Content	1-1-0/6
			Key to the Mint	6-3-2/32

Dam	Record	Dam's Sire	Major Winner	Record
Key Witness		Key to the Mint	Key Contender	1-1-0/6
			You'd Be Surprised	1-1-1/7
Klepto		No Robbery	Criminal Type	5-1-0/22
			Estrapade	3-3-3/21
Knight's Daughter		Sir Cosmo	Monarchy	1-0-0/4
			Round Table	19-6-4/92
Ky. Flash		Sun Teddy	Artismo	2-4-3/19
			Casemate	1-1-0/6
La Basque		Jean-Pierre	Bounding Basque	2-0-3/11
			El Basco	1-1-3/9
La Chaposa		Ups	Chaposa Springs	1-1-0/6
			You and I	2-1-1/11
Lady Beware		Bull Dog	Danger Ahead	1-0-1/5
			Trackmaster	2-0-0/8
Lady Pitt	2-5-2/20	Sword Dancer	Blitey	1-1-2/8
			The Liberal Member	1-1-2/8
Lady Vixen		Sir Ivor	Auntie Mame	1-1-0/6
			Star de Lady Ann	1-0-0/4
Lalun	2-1-1/11	Djeddah	Bold Reason	3-0-2/14
			Never Bend	4-4-3/27
Legato		Dark Star	Le Cle	1-0-0/4
			Tallahto	3-0-2/14
Legend Bearer		The Porter	Icarian	1-0-1/5
			Pepper Patch	1-0-0/4
Legendra		Challenger II	Hasty Doll	1-0-2/6
			Rich Tradition	2-1-2/12
			Sky Clipper	1-0-0/4
Little Saint		St. Germans	Born Mighty	1-0-0/4
			Small Favor	1-0-1/5
L'Omelette		Alibhai	Crimson Fury	1-0-0/4
			Shirley Jones	1-4-0/12
Loving Sister		Olympia	City Girl	1-0-0/4
			Proud Delta	3-2-0/16
Lucy Lufton		Nimbus	Greek Money	1-0-1/5
			Open Fire	2-0-0/8
Luiana		My Babu	Little Current	2-2-0/12
			Prayers'n Promises	1-0-1/5
Lurline B.	1-0-0/4	Alibhai	City Line	1-0-0/4
			Guide Line	1-0-0/4
			Roman Line	1-2-2/10
Lysistrata		Palestinian	Isle of Greece	1-1-1/7
			Reflected Glory	2-0-0/8
Mahmoudess	1-0-1/5	Mahmoud	Born Rich	1-0-1/5
			Promised Land	6-1-6/32
Many Waters		Johnstown	Bounding Main	1-0-0/4
			Swirling Abbey	1-1-0/6
Mar-Kell		Blenheim II	Amoret	1-4-0/12
			Mark-Ye-Well	6-1-2/28
Marullah		Nasrullah	Blessing Angelica	2-0-2/10
			Handsome Boy	3-1-3/17
Mary Machree	1-0-0/4	Moonlight Run	Hill Circus	2-0-2/10
			Hill Clown	1-0-2/6
Maud Muller		Pennant	Monsoon	1-0-0/4
			Mount Marcy	2-6-1/21
Me Sooner		Menow	Fair Molly	1-0-0/4
			Noble Noor	2-0-0/8
Misty Morn	3-2-1/17	Princequillo	Bold Lad	5-0-1/21
			Successor	3-2-2/18
			Sunrise Flight	1-4-3/15
Moment of Truth II		Matador	Convenience	3-5-1/23
			Indulto	1-1-3/9
Monsoon	1-0-0/4	Mahmoud	Cold Command	1-4-4/16
			Rattle Dancer	1-0-0/4
Mrs. Rabbit	1-0-0/4	Milkman	Coursing	1-0-0/4
			Spinney	2-1-1/11
My Auntie		Busy American	Carolina Queen	1-0-0/4
			Cousin	2-0-0/8
			Johns Joy	1-2-1/9
My Dear Girl	2-1-0/10	Rough'n Tumble	In Reality	6-6-0/36
			Superbity	1-1-0/6
Nanticious		Nantallah	Cut Class	1-0-1/5
			Group Plan	2-1-4/14
Nas-Mahal		Nasrullah	Craelius	1-1-0/6
			Tell	1-1-0/6
			Turkish Trousers	4-0-0/16
Native Gal		Sir Gallahad III	Billings	1-1-0/6
			Royal Native	6-3-1/31
Never Knock		Stage Door Johnny	Go for Gin	2-3-0/14
			Pleasant Tap	2-5-2/20
Nicoma		Nashua	Nicosia	1-0-0/4
			Tisab	1-0-0/4
No Class		Nodouble	Always a Classic	1-0-1/5
			Sky Classic	3-3-0/18
North of Eden		Northfields	Forbidden Apple	1-2-1/9
			Paradise Creek	4-2-1/21
			Wild Event	1-1-0/6
No Strings		Occupation	Globemaster	2-6-1/21
			Nail	3-0-2/14
Not Afraid		Count Fleet	Brave Lad	1-2-1/9
			Prince John	1-2-0/8

Dam	Record	Dam's Sire	Major Winner	Record
Numbered Account	6-0-1/25	Buckpasser	Dance Number	1-1-1/7
			Private Account	2-2-1/13
Obeah	2-1-2/12	Cyane	Dance Spell	1-3-3/13
			Go for Wand	6-2-0/28
Obedient		Mahmoud	Don't Alibi	1-0-0/4
			Iron Ruler	2-7-3/25
Oh What a Dance		Nijinsky II	Heavenly Prize	7-3-3/37
			Oh What a Windfall	1-1-0/6
One Lane		Prince John	Provante	1-0-0/4
			Road Princess	1-1-1/7
On to Royalty	0-1-0/2	On to Glory	Louis Quatorze	2-5-1/19
			Royal Indy	1-0-0/4
Our Cricket		Stymie	King of Cricket	1-0-0/4
			Linita	1-0-0/4
Our Page		Blue Larkspur	Brother Tex	1-0-0/4
			Navy Page	1-2-0/8
Panoramic		Chance Shot	Honeymoon	6-5-3/37
			Pedigree	2-0-0/8
Paula		Nizami II	Abe's Hope	1-2-1/9
			Bee Bee Bee	1-0-0/4
Peaceful Union		Royal Union	Junction	1-0-1/5
			Laser Light (1979)	1-3-1/11
Penroyal		Royal Minstrel	Royal Mustang	1-3-0/10
			Royal Note	1-1-0/6
Personal Ensign	6-0-0/24	Private Account	Miner's Mark	2-1-2/12
			My Flag	4-1-3/21
			Traditionally	1-0-0/4
Petite Diable		Sham	Dixie Brass	1-1-1/7
			Odyle	1-2-0/8
Piece of Pie		The Pie King	Generous Portion	1-1-0/6
			Special Warmth	1-0-0/4
Plum Cake		Ponder	Sugar and Spice	1-1-2/8
			Sugar Plum Time	1-0-1/5
Pocahontas		Roman	Chieftan	2-3-2/16
			Tom Rolfe	5-3-2/28
Pocket Edition		Roman	Double Speed	1-0-0/4
			Gold Capitol	1-1-3/9
			Jean's Joe	1-2-1/9
Polylady	0-1-0/2	Polynesian	Capitol South	1-0-0/4
			Good Counsel	1-1-3/9
Pradella		Preciptic	Droll Role	5-3-2/28
			Just About	1-2-0/8
Premium Win		Lyphard	Tight Spot	2-0-0/8
			Valiant Nature	1-1-2/8
Primal Force		Blushing Groom	Awesome Again	3-0-1/13
			Macho Uno	1-0-1/5
Primonetta	3-2-1/17	Swaps	Cum Laude Laurie	3-0-6/18
			Maud Muller (1971)	1-1-1/7
			Prince Thou Art	1-1-2/8
Prospectors Delite	2-0-1/9	Mr. Prospector	Mineshaft	4-1-0/18
			Tomisue's Delight	2-3-3/17
Pure Profit		Key to the Mint	Educated Risk	2-4-1/17
			Inside Information	6-0-1/25
Qbania		Questionnaire	Grecian Queen	5-3-3/29
			Hitex	1-2-0/8
Quaze	0-1-0/2	Quibu	Quaze Quilt	2-0-1/9
			Susan's Girl	13-5-6/68
Quick Touch		Count Fleet	Capelet	1-0-0/4
			Quill	5-2-1/25
Quill	5-2-1/25	Princequillo	Caucasus	3-2-3/19
			One For All	3-1-1/15
Rare Bouquet		Prince John	Fresh Pepper	1-0-0/4
			Slewpy	2-0-1/9
Rare Perfume	0-0-1/1	Eight Thirty	Jaipur	7-5-0/38
			Rare Treat	3-4-2/22
Rare Treat	3-4-2/22	Stymie	Ring Twice	1-4-1/13
			What A Treat	4-2-0/20
Red Shoes	1-2-2/10	Easton	Ballerina	1-1-0/6
			Nasrina	2-0-1/9
Relaxing	2-0-2/10	Buckpasser	Easy Goer	10-4-1/49
			Easy Now	1-2-0/8
Resolver	0-0-2/2	Reviewer	Adjudicating	2-2-1/13
			Dispute (1990)	4-3-0/22
			Time for a Change	2-0-0/8
Retama		Brazado	Resaca	2-1-0/10
			Tamarona	2-2-2/14
Rock Drill		Whirlaway	Lady Pitt	2-5-2/20
			Rocky Link	1-1-1/7
Rosetta Stone		Round Table	De La Rose	1-2-0/8
			Upper Nile	1-1-0/6
Rough Shod II		Gold Bridge	Lt. Stevens	1-3-2/12
			Moccasin	4-0-1/17
			Ridan	5-5-2/32
Royal Puzzler		Royal Charger	Charger's Kin	1-0-2/6
			Fleet Allied	1-1-1/7
Rowdy Angel		Halo	Demons Begone	1-2-0/8
			Pine Bluff	3-0-3/15
Sailor's Hunch		Sailor	Box the Compass	1-0-0/4
			Limit to Reason	2-2-0/12
Sally Stark		Graustark	Tiffany Lass	2-0-0/8
			Valdez	1-1-2/8

Dam	Record	Dam's Sire	Major Winner	Record
Sans Supplement	1-0-0/4	Grey Dawn II	Big Stanley	1-0-1/5
			Itsallgreektome	2-4-1/17
Sans Tares		Sind	Mahan	1-2-2/10
			Worden II	1-0-0/4
Searching	5-2-2/26	War Admiral	Admiring	1-1-1/7
			Affectionately	3-0-3/15
			Priceless Gem	2-0-0/8
Seaside Attraction	1-0-1/5	Seattle Slew	Cape Town	1-0-1/5
			Golden Attraction	3-0-1/13
Segula		Johnstown	Nashua	15-3-0/66
			Sabette	2-1-1/11
Shared Interest	1-2-1/9	Pleasant Colony	Cash Run	1-0-1/5
			Forestry	1-0-1/5
Siama	3-0-0/12	Tiger	Bald Eagle	8-4-3/43
			Dead Ahead	1-0-0/4
			One-Eyed King	1-3-0/10
Silver Bright	1-0-0/4	Barbizon	Banquet Table	1-2-0/8
			State Dinner	4-3-1/23
Silver Fog		Mahmoud	Silver Bright	1-0-0/4
			Silver Spoon	4-1-2/20
			Silver True	1-0-0/4
Silver Sari		Prince John	Big Spruce	2-7-4/26
			Manta	3-5-2/24
Six Crowns	0-0-1/1	Secretariat	Chief's Crown	7-2-3/35
			Classic Crown	1-2-0/8
Smartaire		Quibu	Smart Angle	3-0-0/12
			Smarten	4-4-0/24
Social Lesson		Forum	Exbourne	2-0-0/8
			Expelled	1-0-0/4
Some Pep		Stimulus	Whirl Some	2-0-0/8
			Winsome Winner	1-1-0/6
Somethingroyal		Princequillo	First Family	1-0-1/5
			Secretariat	11-3-1/51
			Sir Gaylord	2-0-4/12
			Syrian Sea	1-0-2/6
Sophist		Acropolis	Drama Critic (1974)	1-3-1/11
			Glossary	1-0-0/4
Star Gem		Pia Star	Matty G	1-0-0/4
			Star of Cozzene	3-0-2/14
Stepping Stone		Princequillo	Big Advance	1-0-1/5
			High Bid	2-1-1/11
			Moss Vale	1-0-0/4
			Progressing	1-1-0/6
Stepwisely		Wise Counsellor	Bolero	2-0-0/8
			Watch Your Step	1-0-0/4
Strike Oil		Prince John	Oil Power	1-1-0/6
			Spout	1-1-0/6
Striking	0-3-2/8	War Admiral	Batter Up	1-0-0/4
			Hitting Away	2-2-0/12
Sultry Sun		Buckfinder	Solar Splendor	3-2-1/17
			Sultry Song	3-1-3/19
Sunday Purchase		T.V. Lark	Bates Motel	3-1-1/15
			Hatim	1-0-1/5
Surgery		Dr. Fager	Sewickley	2-0-2/10
			Shared Interest	1-2-1/9
Suspicious Native		Raise a Native	Leo Castelli	1-1-1/7
			Meadowlake	1-0-0/4
Sweet Tooth	0-1-0/2	On-and-On	Alydar	8-8-1/49
			Our Mims	4-2-1/21
Swinging Lizzie		The Axe II	Lively One	1-1-2/8
			Swing Till Dawn	2-0-0/8
Tallahto	3-0-2/14	Nantallah	Hidden Light	2-0-0/8
			Prince True	2-1-1/11
Tamarette		Tim Tam	Tentam	2-4-1/17
			Terete	1-1-0/6
Tasma		Crafty Admiral	No Le Hace	2-2-2/14
			Soy Numero Uno	3-1-2/16
Tatanne		St. James	Frere Jacques	2-1-1/11
			Lucky Draw	1-1-0/6
			Platan	2-0-4/12
Tea Leaves		Pharamond II	Sweet Dream	1-0-0/4
			Tea-Maker	1-2-1/9
The Squaw II		Sickle	Cherokee Rose	1-0-0/4
			How	3-2-2/18
			Sequoia	1-0-0/4

Dam	Record	Dam's Sire	Major Winner	Record
Tige O'Myheart		Bull Lea	Idun	6-2-1/29
			Irish Lancer	1-1-0/6
Timely Roman		Sette Bello	Timely Assertion	1-0-0/4
			Timely Writer	4-0-1/17
Tir an Oir		Tehran	Endymion	1-0-1/5
			Seaneen	2-3-2/16
Toll Booth		Buckpasser	Christiecat	1-0-1/5
			Plugged Nickle	5-0-1/21
Too Bald		Bald Eagle	Capote	2-0-0/8
			Exceller	7-3-3/37
Torch Rose		Torchilla	On Trust	2-8-5/29
			Trusting	1-1-3/9
Toussaud	1-1-0/6	El Gran Senor	Chester House	1-1-0/6
			Chiselling	1-0-0/4
			Empire Maker	3-2-0/16
			Honest Lady	1-2-0/8
Track Medal		Khaled	O'Hara	1-2-3/11
			Outing Class	2-1-2/12
			Tutankhamen	2-0-0/8
Traffic Court		Discovery	Hasty Road	6-1-1/27
			Traffic Judge	6-5-1/35
Tularia		Tulyar	For the Moment	2-4-0/16
			Honest Pleasure	7-2-2/34
Turk O Witz		Stop the Music	Mr. Purple	1-0-3/7
			Queens Court Queen	2-0-1/9
Twilight Tear		Bull Lea	A Gleam	4-2-3/23
			Bardstown	6-2-0/28
Two Bob		The Porter	Miz Clementine	2-3-0/14
			Two Lea	3-1-1/15
Two Lea	3-1-1/15	Bull Lea	On-and-On	3-2-2/18
			Tim Tam	5-1-0/22
Up the Flagpole		Hoist the Flag	Prospectors Delite	2-0-1/9
			Runup the Colors	1-2-0/8
Up the Hill		Jacopo	Moslem Chief	1-0-0/4
			Pail of Water	1-1-0/6
Uvira II		Umidwar	Francis U.	1-1-0/6
			General Staff	1-1-2/8
			Parnassus	1-0-1/5
Vana Turns		Wavering Monarch	Petionville	1-0-1/5
			Pike Place Dancer	1-0-0/4
Victorian Queen		Victoria Park	Judge Angelucci	2-1-2/12
			Peace	1-0-0/4
			War	1-0-0/4
Viviana		Nureyev	Sightseek	4-2-0/20
			Tates Creek	2-1-0/10
War Flower		Man o' War	Ace Admiral	5-1-3/25
			Helioscope	5-2-2/26
Weekend Surprise	0-1-4/6	Secretariat	A.P. Indy	5-0-1/21
			Summer Squall	5-2-0/24
Wild Applause	0-0-1/1	Northern Dancer	Eastern Echo	1-0-0/4
			Roar	1-0-0/4
Willamae		Tentam	Willa on the Move ('85)	1-1-2/8
			Will's Way	2-2-1/13
Win Crafty Lady		Crafty Prospector	Graeme Hall	2-2-0/12
			Harmony Lodge	1-0-0/4
Windsharp	2-2-0/12	Lear Fan	Dessert	1-0-0/4
			Johar	2-1-0/10
Wings of Grace		Key to the Mint	Plenty of Grace	1-0-1/5
			Soaring Softly	2-0-0/8
Witching Hour		Thinking Cap	Broom Dance	1-1-1/7
			Pumpkin Moonshine	1-0-0/4
			Salem	1-0-1/5
Wonderful You		Brown King	Nevada Battler	1-0-0/4
			Nice Guy	1-0-0/4
Words of War		Lord at War	E. Dubai	1-2-0/8
			No Matter What	1-0-0/4
Young Flyer		Flying Paster	River Flyer	1-0-0/4
			Victory Ride	1-1-0/6
Your Hostess		Alibhai	Coraggioso	2-0-4/12
			T.V. Commercial	2-2-3/15
Zippy Do		Hilarious	Some Romance	2-1-1/11
			Vilzak	1-0-0/4

Broodmare

Sires

Photo courtesy of Bob Coglianese Photo's, Inc.

In one of the most famous photographs in thoroughbred racing history, Ron Turcotte sneaked a peak over his left shoulder to view the "competition" as he neared the finish line aboard Secretariat in the 1973 Belmont Stakes. Secretariat's 31-length victory—the largest in a major North American race since World War II—completed a sweep of the Triple Crown. Secretariat recorded an outstanding record at stud, including 34 victories as a broodmare sire, and is the only stallion since World War II to lead the single-season list for major victories for a sire (1986) after he already had led the single-season list for major victories as a broodmare sire (1985).

VIII: Broodmare Sires

Prince or an Admiral?

Successful race horses enter stud amid considerable fanfare and, based on the confirmation and sale prices of their yearlings, often are judged as successes or failures before their first crop sets foot on the track.

By the time many have established their credentials as broodmare sires, however, they are in the twilight—or beyond—of their stud careers.

If the ability to transfer speed to the next generation is considered the most important attribute of a sire, what traits do breeders consider significant for a top broodmare sire? Conventional wisdom contends that successful thoroughbreds inherit stamina through their dams and, of course, through the sires of their dams. But evidence suggests there is an even better indicator to determine which sires later will distinguish themselves as broodmare sires: Those who succeed as sires quite likely also will become capable, if not elite, broodmare sires.

Eighty-one of the 165 sires whose offspring have reached double figures in major victories during the modern era also rank among the 163 who have attained double-figure totals as broodmare sires, and 30 of the 63 stallions whose offspring have garnered 20 or more victories also rank among the 60 who have earned 20 or more triumphs as broodmare sires.

While both his sons and daughters have the potential to enhance a stallion's success as a sire, only his daughters—who eventually can become dams—can contribute to a stallion's accomplishments as a broodmare sire. Even a stallion who sires nearly 1,000 offspring, however, potentially can have an even larger number of maternal grandchildren produced by his daughters.

So it would seem logical to say that any stallion whose victory total as a sire is more than double his total as a broodmare sire is a failure as a broodmare sire. Twelve modern-era stallions who have reached 30 or more victories as sires have at least twice as many victories in that category as they do as broodmare sires: Alibhai, Bold Ruler, Danzig, Deputy Minister, Exclusive Native, Hail to Reason, Herbager, Mr. Prospector, Nashua, Royal Charger, Storm Cat, and Your Host.

Further examination of their records, however, reveals that such logic isn't necessarily so.

Three of those 12 stallions—Bold Ruler, Alibhai, and Mr. Prospector—are among the 47 who have reached 23 or more victories as broodmare sires and, although their totals may not compare with what they accomplished as sires, they still rank as outstanding broodmare sires. Your Host posted 30 victories as a sire and just seven as a broodmare sire, but his 30 victories as a sire are somewhat distorted by the fact that 80 percent of them were achieved by one runner: Kelso.

It does seem reasonably safe to state that Hail to Reason (44 victories as a sire and 17 as a broodmare sire), Exclusive Native (36/10), Royal Charger (35/15), Nashua (33/8), and Herbager (30/13) were far more successful as sires than as broodmare sires. But other stallions' legacies as broodmare sires well could be a work in progress. Danzig, who has 47 victories as a sire, didn't achieve his first triumph as a broodmare sire until 1994, and 12 of his 16 came from 1998-2003. Mr. Prospector, who has 73 victories as a sire, earned 21 of his 28 as a broodmare sire from 1996-2003 and enjoyed a No. 1 season in 1997. Deputy Minister and Storm Cat have earned 37 and 36 victories as sires, respectively. Deputy Minister finally earned his first triumph as a broodmare sire in 2001, added another a year later, then demonstrated that he eventually could prove to be as formidable a broodmare sire as a sire by adding four more in 2003. Storm Cat gave a similar indication when he earned his first three major victories as a broodmare sire in 2002.

A further illustration that those highly successful stallions' careers as broodmare sires are probably works in progress is the litany of broodmare sires who have added to their major victory totals 40 years or more after their births, including Blenheim II, Bold Venture, Bull Dog, Bull Lea, Challenger II, Chance Play, Court Martial, Double Jay, John P. Grier, Khaled, Man o' War, Nasrullah, Northern Dancer, Pennant, Peter Pan, Polynesian, Princequillo, Round Table, Sickle, Sir Gallahad III, Teddy, The Porter, and War Admiral.

Conversely, 13 stallions who have earned 30 or more victories as broodmare sires in the modern era have at least twice as many victories than their total on the modern-era sire list: Blenheim II, Blue Larkspur, Bull Dog, Discovery, Double Jay, Hyperion, Johnstown, Man o' War, Sickle, Sir Gallahad III, Stimulus, Swaps, and War Admiral. Ten of those 13, however, were born between 1917 (Man o' War) and 1931 (Discovery) and another in 1936 (Johnstown)—with Double Jay and Swaps the lone exceptions—and it's reasonable to assume that they were as proficient as sires prior to the modern era as they were as broodmare sires after World War II.

Further, Double Jay's 27 victories as a sire rank 27th on the modern-era list, so it's difficult to criticize his record, although it pales compared to his 56 triumphs as a broodmare sire.

So only Swaps, with 15 victories as a sire and 31 as a broodmare sire, among that baker's dozen truly might be considered a smashing success at passing his successful qualities on to his grandchildren through his daughters compared to his ability to sire outstanding race horses. Better examples of those who have distinguished themselves as broodmare sires after failing to do as sires include the likes of Summer Tan (five victories as a sire and 22 as a broodmare sire) and Northfields, who never sired a major North American winner but has accumulated 26 victories—and counting—as a broodmare sire.

Eight stallions have enjoyed No. 1 seasons as both sires and broodmare sires during the modern era. Three of those have multiple No. 1 seasons as both—Princequillo (three as a sire and four as a broodmare sire), Bull Lea (four as a sire and two as a broodmare sire), and Seattle Slew (two of each). Nasrullah led the sire list four times and the broodmare sire list once, Mr. Prospector led the sire list twice and the broodmare sire list once, and Buckpasser and Count Fleet each added three No. 1 seasons as a broodmare sire to a No. 1 season as a sire. No modern-era stallion has led both lists in the same year, and Secretariat, who led the broodmare list in 1985 and was the No. 1-ranked sire in 1986, is the only stallion who has led the sire list after enjoying a No. 1 season as a broodmare sire.

The Cream of the Crop

Princequillo's inclusion among the elite handful of the best sires of race horses in the modern era may come as a surprise, primarily because that aspect of his legacy has been overshadowed by his well-deserved reputation as a broodmare sire.

Princequillo is the only broodmare sire to record four No. 1 seasons in the modern era, and he also holds the records for top-three (7), top-four (8), top-six (10), and top-eight (11) campaigns and shares the record for top-two seasons (5). Buoyed by his first classic winner as a broodmare sire, Belmont Stakes victor High Echelon, Princequillo recorded his first No. 1 season in 1970. Offspring of the daughters of Princequillo—who was bred in Ireland and imported to the United States as a four-year-old—earned a record-tying 10 or more victories in his back-to-back No. 1 seasons in 1972 and 1973, including Secretariat's sweep of the 1973 Triple Crown. The 1973 campaign also concluded an unmatched streak of eight consecutive top-seven seasons for Princequillo, whose offspring as a broodmare sire also include Bold Lad, Fort Marcy, and Key to the Mint.

Photo courtesy of Bob Coglianese Photo's, Inc.

Lemon Drop Kid (No. 6 with Jose Santos in the saddle) held off Vision and Verse (on rail) to win the 1999 Belmont Stakes by a head and end the Triple Crown bid of Charismatic (third on the outside). Lemon Drop Kid subsequently added a victory in the Travers Stakes, then earned four major triumphs a year later to help Seattle Slew reign as the leader in major North American victories by a broodmare sire in 2000. That enabled Seattle Slew to become only the third stallion—joining Bull Lea and Princequillo—to lead both sires and broodmare sires in major North American victories on more than one occasion.

Princequillo's 88 major victories as a broodmare sire are a modern record, and he is the only stallion to reach 80 triumphs as both a sire and as a broodmare sire.

Despite the success of the offspring of daughters of Princequillo, his claim as the best broodmare sire of the modern era is by no means unchallenged.

War Admiral, the 1937 Triple Crown winner, recorded an

astonishing 24 consecutive seasons (1947-70) with at least one major winner as a broodmare sire and a record 12 in a row (1957-68) with multiple victories. In each of his record-equaling three consecutive No. 1 seasons (1964-66) as a broodmare sire, War Admiral recorded at least nine victories, and no other broodmare sire has had a three-year string of eight.

War Admiral finished among the top nine broodmare sires 12 times and among the top 10 on 14 occasions, both records, and was the broodmare sire of two classic winners: Iron Liege (1957 Kentucky Derby) and Royal Orbit (1959 Preakness Stakes). War Admiral's 81 victories include five or more by Better Self, Crafty Admiral, Gun Bow, and Buckpasser.

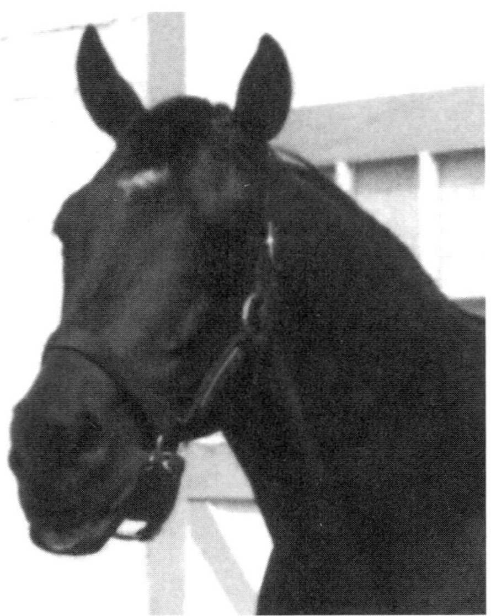

Photo courtesy of Galerie Graphics

Nijinsky II, the 1970 English Triple Crown winner, is the only thoroughbred born since World War II who has reached as many as 50 major North American triumphs as a broodmare sire.

Another Fabulous Five

Five other stallions earned 50 or more victories, enjoyed multiple No. 1 seasons, and recorded classic triumphs as broodmare sires during the modern era. Listed in the order they rank in the modern-era standings for major victories, with their maternal grandchildren who won five or more major races:

Bull Lea is the only broodmare sire to record six consecutive seasons with at least five triumphs (1957-62) or seven in succession (1956-62) with four or more wins during the modern era and is one of only two with four straight years with six or more victories (1957-60). Bull Lea was the top-ranked broodmare sire in 1957 and again in '58, when Tim Tam captured Bull Lea's first two classic victories as a broodmare sire. Bull Lea, who is also the broodmare sire of Bardstown, Idun, and 1964 Belmont Stakes winner Quadrangle, earned his final classic score as a broodmare sire when Gate Dancer captured the 1984 Preakness Stakes. Bull Lea not only shares the records for top-two (5) and top-five seasons (8), but his 65 victories make him one of only two stallions to produce at least 60 victories as both a sire and a broodmare sire during the modern era.

Count Fleet is the only broodmare sire who recorded nine consecutive years (1959-67) with at least three victories. In each of those seasons, he finished among the top 10, equaling another record. That nine-year stretch included No. 1 seasons in 1960, '61, and '63 and Count Fleet's only classic victory as a broodmare sire (Lucky Debonair's triumph in the 1965 Kentucky Derby). The 1943 Triple Crown winner's 63 victories as a broodmare sire include five or more by Kelso, Tompion, and Quill.

No broodmare sire has enjoyed a better campaign since World War II than **Blenheim II** did in 1949. The winner of the 1930 Epsom Derby—England's most important race for three-year-olds—saw two of his most distinguished maternal grandsons, Ponder and Coaltown, capture the Kentucky Derby and Horse of the Year acclaim, respectively, on their way to giving Blenheim II a single-season record of 15 victories. Blenheim II attained the No. 1 ranking again in 1952, when Hill Gail captured the Kentucky Derby, and boosted his record as a broodmare sire to four classic triumphs when Kauai King won the 1966 Kentucky Derby and Preakness. Mark-Ye-Well and Rejected were among the other standouts who helped Blenheim II record 60 modern-era victories as a broodmare sire.

The English-bred **Sickle** recorded No. 1 seasons in both 1947 and '51, and only two broodmare sires can claim more top-two (3) or top-four (6) seasons. Among those who contributed mightily to Sickle's 53 victories were But Why Not, My Request, Social Outcast, and 1951 Belmont Stakes hero Counterpoint.

Nijinsky II swept the English Triple Crown in 1970 to become the only thoroughbred to accomplish that feat since 1935, and his 53 victories as a broodmare sire also make him the only stallion who was born since World War II to reach 50. Nijinsky II posted three consecutive seasons as the No. 1 broodmare sire from 1992-94, earning a record-equaling seven or more victories in each and a record-tying 10 or more in each of the latter two. Colonial Affair's victory in the 1993 Belmont Stakes is the only classic score for Nijinsky II as a broodmare sire, and the most successful broodmare sire since the advent of the Breeders' Cup in 1984 earned his first victory as a broodmare sire in that event when Fantastic Light won the 2001 Turf. But all three of Nijinsky II's maternal grandchildren who have earned five or more victories—Flawlessly, Heavenly Prize, and Sky Beauty—are fillies, auguring a strong possibility that his legacy will continue to grow.

Another Magnificent Seven

Seven other broodmare sires have 48 or more victories and either a No. 1 season, a classic victory, or both during the modern era. Listed in the order they rank in the modern-era standings for major victories, with their maternal grandchildren who won at least five major races:

Double Jay, broodmare sire of John Henry, Nodouble, and Old Hat, attained the No. 1 ranking in 1981, and only one modern-era rival can claim more top-seven (9), top-eight (10), or top-nine (11) seasons. Ferdinand's victories in the 1986 Kentucky Derby and the 1987 Breeders' Cup Classic gave Double Jay his only classic and Breeders' Cup scores among his 56 major wins as a broodmare sire. . . . The French-bred **Bull Dog,** who holds the record of nine consecutive top-nine seasons (1948-56), earned the No. 1 ranking in 1952 and his only classic victory as a broodmare sire when Dark Star captured the Kentucky Derby a year later. Tom Fool, Three Rings, and Spartan Valor each contributed five or more triumphs to Bull Dog's total of 55. . . . Only one broodmare sire has exceeded the string of five consecutive years (1955-59) with four or more victories recorded by **Mahmoud,** the French-bred winner of the 1936 Epsom Derby. Mahmoud's 54 wins include Determine's triumph in the 1954 Kentucky Derby and Gallant Man's victory in the 1957 Belmont Stakes, and both Promised Land and Gallant Man contributed five or more of Mahmoud's victories as a broodmare sire. . . . **Discovery's** 50 triumphs as a broodmare sire encompass those of six runners who earned five or more major triumphs, including Bed o' Roses, Traffic Judge, and Intentionally. Remarkably, the other three—Native Dancer, Hasty Road, and Bold Ruler—all captured the Preakness in a five-year stretch from 1953-57. Native Dancer, who also won the Belmont Stakes, helped Discovery to a No. 1 season in 1953, and a year later Hasty Road made Discovery the only broodmare sire to earn classic victories in consecutive campaigns during the modern era. . . . **Blue Larkspur** enjoyed a record-tying stretch of four consecutive years (1951-54) with six or more victories, including No. 1 seasons in both 1952 and '54. Blue Larkspur's 50 triumphs include five or more by both Cosmic Bomb and Real Delight, but he is one of only two broodmare sires to attain 50 modern-era victories without a classic triumph. . . . Sharing that distinction with Blue Larkspur is **Nasrullah,** who earned the No. 1 ranking in 1971, posted 50 victories, and recorded nine top-seven seasons, a total bettered only by Princequillo. . . . **Buckpasser,** the broodmare sire of Plugged Nickle, Slew O' Gold, and Easy Goer, has amassed 48 victories and ranks second only to Nijinsky II among stallions born in the modern era. Buckpasser earned No. 1 seasons in 1983, '88, and '89, and all three of his classic winners—Coastal in 1979, Easy Goer in 1989, and Touch Gold in 1997—captured the Belmont Stakes.

Rounding Out the Top 20

Six other stallions have earned at least 40 victories or 30 or more triumphs and both a No. 1 season and classic success as broodmare sires in the modern era. Listed in the order they rank in the modern-era standings for major victories, with their maternal grandchildren who won five or more major races:

Sir Gallahad III, who was bred in France, is the broodmare sire of both Gallorette and Royal Native, and another of his maternal grandchildren, Jet Pilot, captured the 1947 Kentucky Derby. . . . **Heliopolis,** who posted three consecutive top-three seasons from 1971-73, is one of only three broodmare sires who has been represented by dual classic winners in the modern era. Forward Pass won the Kentucky Derby and the Preakness in 1968, and Riva Ridge captured the Derby and Belmont in 1972 and, along with Summer Guest, they rank as Heliopolis's most success maternal grandchildren. . . . **Johnstown,** a dual classic winner in 1939, was the broodmare sire of a dual classic winner, Preakness and Belmont winner Nashua, during his No. 1 season in 1955. To Market, Hillsdale, and Beau Purple were among the other standouts to represent Johnstown as a broodmare sire. . . . Cigar and Lemon Drop Kid are among the standouts to represent 1977 Triple Crown winner **Seattle Slew** as a broodmare sire. Cigar gave Seattle Slew his first Breeders' Cup victory when he won the Classic in 1995, the first of Seattle Slew's two No. 1 seasons, and Escena added his second Breeders' Cup triumph as a broodmare sire in the 1998 Distaff. Lemon Drop Kid gave Seattle Slew his only classic victory as a broodmare sire when he won the 1999

Four Footed Fotos, Inc., courtesy of Churchill Downs

Gary Stevens drove Silver Charm (6) to the wire a head in front of Captain Bodgit (5 under Alex Solis) to capture the 1997 Kentucky Derby. Silver Charm's subsequent triumph in the Preakness Stakes enabled his broodmare sire, Poker, to become the only stallion with five classic victories as a broodmare sire since World War II. Poker previously had been represented as a classic-winning broodmare sire by 1977 Triple Crown winner Seattle Slew.

Belmont Stakes, then was the leading contributor to his second No. 1 season a year later. . . . **Secretariat,** the 1973 Triple Crown winner, is the broodmare sire of Chief's Crown, Summer Squall, and A.P. Indy, each of whom helped Secretariat further enhance his resume. Chief's Crown won the Breeders' Cup Juvenile in 1984, then helped Secretariat enjoy a No. 1 season in 1985. Summer Squall captured the Preakness in 1990, and A.P. Indy won both the Belmont Stakes and the Breeders' Cup Classic in 1992. . . . **Hyperion** earned the No. 1 ranking when his best runner, Citation, swept the Triple Crown in 1948.

High Honorable Mention

Other stallions certainly have distinguished themselves as broodmare sires during the modern era. No other broodmare sire in the modern era has as many classic victories as Poker, but 12 of his 13 major triumphs as a broodmare sire were recorded by Seattle Slew and Silver Charm, who combined for all five of Poker's classic scores. On-and-On posted consecutive No. 1 seasons in 1977 and '78, but Alydar and Our Mims combined for 12 of On-and-On's 14 victories as a broodmare sire. Boldnesian is one of only four broodmare sires who has been represented by three different Breeders' Cup winners, but he has only nine major victories. The following 22 stallions are the only others in the modern era whose maternal grandchildren posted as many as 30 victories; won 25 or more races and posted either a No. 1 season (including ties), a classic victory, or three or more Breeders' Cup triumphs, or earned 20 victories and recorded both a No. 1 season and a classic triumph.

Stallion	Major Wins	Classic Wins	Breeders' Cup Wins	No. 1 Seasons	Winners of Five-Plus Major Races
Man o' War	39	0	0		Ace Admiral, Helioscope
Tom Fool	39	1	0		Foolish Pleasure, Majesty's Prince
Hasty Road	37	0	0	1974, 1975	Forego
Stimulus	33	0	0		Olympia
Roman	32	1	0		Roman Brother, Tom Rolfe
Prince John	31	0	1		
Swaps	31	1	0		Numbered Account
My Babu	29	4	0	1967, 1968	Damascus, Gamely
Crafty Admiral	28	3	0	1977, 1978, 1979	Affirmed
Mr. Prospector	28	0	2	1997	
Graustark	27	1	0		Bien Bien
Pharamond II	27	0	0	1951	Kiss Me Kate
Hoist the Flag	26	0	2	1986, 1987	Broad Brush, Personal Ensign
Key to the Mint	26	0	3		Gorgeous, Inside Information
Alydar	25	0	5		
Native Dancer	25	2	0		Northern Dancer, Ruffian
Northern Dancer	25	0	3		
Beau Pere	24	1	0	1956	Swaps
Khaled	24	1	1	1962	Candy Spots, Prove It
Promised Land	24	2	0	1979, 1980	Skip Trial, Spectacular Bid
Equipoise	22	3	0	1946	Assault
In Reality	20	1	1	1991	Lite Light, Meadow Star

The following chart shows stallions' victories as broodmare sires in the 6,461 major races held in North America from 1946-2003. Following that chart are charts that give the same information for the 174 classic races held from 1946-2003, the 145 Breeders' Cup races staged from 1984-2003, and the annual leaders, which are followed by an alphabetical listing of victories in major North American races for all broodmare sires from 1946-2003, with the horses foaled by their daughters in those events in parenthesis.

Standings for Broodmare Sires' Victories In Major North American Races From 1946-2003

1. Princequillo (88)
2. War Admiral (81)
3. Bull Lea (65)
4. Count Fleet (63)
5. Blenheim II (60)
6. Double Jay (56)
7. Bull Dog (55)
8. Mahmoud (54)
9. Nijinsky II, Sickle (53)
11. Blue Larkspur, Discovery, Nasrullah (50)
14. Buckpasser (48)
15. Sir Gallahad III (43)
16. Heliopolis (41)
17. Johnstown, Man o' War, Tom Fool (39)
20. Hasty Road (37)
21. Seattle Slew (35)
22. Secretariat (34)
23. Stimulus (33)
24. Roman (32)
25. Prince John, Swaps (31)
27. Hyperion (30)
28. My Babu (29)
29. Crafty Admiral, Graustark, Hoist the Flag, Mr. Prospector, Olympia (28)
34. Bold Ruler, Pharamond II, Round Table (27)
37. Key to the Mint, Northfields (26)
39. Alydar, Native Dancer, Northern Dancer (25)
42. Beau Pere, Khaled, Promised Land, Quibu (24)
46. Alibhai, Eight Thirty (23)
48. Equipoise, Summer Tan, Tom Rolfe (22)
51. Bimelech, Bubbling Over, Chance Shot, Never Bend (21)
55. Better Self, Grey Dawn II, In Reality, Sir Cosmo, Stage Door Johnny, Vaguely Noble (20)
61. Ack Ack, Ambiorix, Damascus, Hill Prince, Raise a Native (19)
66. Chance Play, Diplomat Way, Nantallah, Pilate, Sir Ivor, Tim Tam, T.V. Lark (18)
73. Al Hattab, Case Ace, Challenger II, Hail to Reason, John P. Grier, Le Fabuleux, Menow, Traffic Judge (17)
81. Battlefield, Court Martial, Danzig, Dr. Fager, Forli, Gallant Man, Jack High, Lyphard, Polynesian, Storm Bird, The Porter (16)
92. Bold Venture, Display, Green Dancer, Halcyon, Nureyev, Pompey, Ribot, Royal Charger (15)
100. Determine, Devil Diver, Icecapade, On-and-On, Pia Star, Star Blen, Vice Regent (14)
107. Blue Prince, Brazado, Herbager, Jacopo, Nearctic, Nodouble, Poker, Questionnaire, Revoked, St. Germans, Supremus, Valid Appeal (13)
119. Black Toney, Caro, Chieftan, Djeddah, Drone, Fleet Nasrullah, Mari's Book, No Robbery, On Watch, Royal Minstrel, Shut Out, Tehran, Tulyar, War Relic (12)
133. Ariel, Blushing Groom, Bold Bidder, First Landing, Gold Bridge, Halo, Private Account, Riva Ridge, Roberto, Rough'n Tumble, Sir Gaylord, Stymie, The Axe II (11)
146. Bahram, Baldski, Brown King, By Jimminy, Cyane, Dixieland Band, El Gran Senor, Exclusive Native, Flying Heels, Francis S., King Pellinore, Madara, Omaha, Reviewer, Stop the Music, Tiger, To Market, Turn-to (10)
164. Bald Eagle, Bar Le Duc, Blue Swords, Boldnesian, Cox's Ridge, Etonian, Flintham, Good Manners, Heelfly, Lovely Night, Lt. Stevens, Majestic Prince, Raise a Cup, Sailor, Sea-Bird, Shantung, Sun Again, Teddy, Vigors, What a Pleasure, Whirlaway (9)
185. Ahonoora, Annapolis, Bold Hour, Bossuet, Counterpoint, Dusty Canyon, Fappiano, Hard Tack, Hawaii, His Majesty, Insco, Intentionally, King Cole, Mount Marcy, Mr. Leader, Nashua, Pretense, Riverman, Run For Nurse, Snow Sporting, Speak John, Tri Jet, Turkoman, Windy Sands (8)
209. Alleged, Birikil, Cornish Prince, Cosmic Bomb, Dante, Diesis, Donatello II, Easton, Elocutionist, Gallant Fox, Gallant Romeo, Gun Shot, Hairan, Hatchet Man, High Time, Jet Action, Mr. Music, Pharos, Pleasant Colony, Relic, Requiebro, Royal Coinage, Smarten, Sun Briar, Tatan, Tentam, Terrible Tiger, Toro, Understanding, Wavering Monarch, War Jeep, Wise Counsellor, Your Host (7)
242. Affirmed, Arctic Prince, Ballyogan, Barbizon, Beau Max, Believe It, Blue Peter, Bold Commander, Briartic, Buckfinder, Candy Spots, Chief's Crown, Citation, Clever Trick, Con Brio, Dark Star, Deputy Minister, Dis Donc, Embrujo, Errard, Fair Play, Fighting Fox, Goya II, Groton, Isolater, Jacinto, Jamestown, Jester, Johns Joy, Lord at War, Mad Hatter, Miswaki, Noor, One Count, Olden Times, Pennant, Preciptic, Psychic Bid, Quadrangle, Rambunctious, Relaunch, Requested, Russia II, Sham, Sharpen Up, Sing Sing, Spy Song, Sunrise Flight, Swoon's Son, The Minstrel, Tudor Minstrel, Whichone, Whiskaway, Wildair, Your Alibhai (6)
297. Abernant, Acroterion, Apalachee, Apprehension, Avatar, Bailjumper, Beau Gar, Bolero, Buffalo Lark, Bull Dandy, Burgoo King, Caerleon, Colombo, Dancing Count, Dr. Blum, Droll Role, Figonero, Ghadeer, Great Above, Grey Sovereign, High Top, Hillary, Hold Your Peace, Homebuilder, Kaldoun, Known Fact, Loose Cannon, Majestic Light, Milkman, Moslem Chief, Mr. Busher, Nearco, Needles, Nimbus, Occupation, One-Eyed King, Our Boots, Pavot, Peace Chance, Prominer, Proudest Roman, Purchase, Rosemont, Royal Vale, Saros, Sassafras, Saulingo, Seattle Song, Seeking the Gold, Sette Bello, Slew O' Gold, Spectacular Bid, Stevward, St. James, Strawberry Road II, Sun Teddy, Topsider, T.V. Commercial, Vertex, Victoria Park, War Glory, Welsh Pageant (5)
359. Admiral Drake, Ambehaving, Anwar, Apelle, Arts and Letters, Balladier, Beekeeper, Big Game, Blade, Blue Pair, Bois Roussel, Bold Lad, Brantome, Broadside, Brookfield, Busted, Busy American, Cavan, Centime, Challedon, Chicle, Conquistador Cielo, Coronach, Count of Honor, Count Rendered, Crafty Prospector, Crimson Satan, Dancing Champ, Darby Creek Road, Degage, Delta Judge, Desert Wine, Empire Builder, Eurasian, Explodent, Flying Paster, Free America, Good Behaving, Hilarious, Honeys Alibi, Ipe, Jim French, King Emperor, La Brige, Licencioso, Lucky Debonair, Matador, Melyno, Minnesota Mac, Native Charger, Never Say Die, Niccolo Dell'Arca, Noble Dancer II, One For All, Papa Redbird, Pasha, Picacero, Precipitation, Princely Pleasure, Prince Tenderfoot, Reaping Reward, Restless Wind, Resurgent, Roman Line, Royal Gem II, Rubiano, Screen King, Silnet, Sir Damion, Solarium II, Sovereign Path, Sweep, Sweep Like, Swift and Sure, Sword Dancer, The Satrap, Time Maker, Transworld, Troy, Umidwar, Viceregal, Vito, Whisk Broom II, Whitesburg, Zacaweista (4)
444. Acropolis, All Blue, Alsab, Artillery, Bagdad, Baluarte, Bernborough, Berseem, Besomer, Bet Big, Bicker, Biribi, Bolinas Boy, Bright Knight, Bymeabond, Capote, Caruso, Carwhite, Caveat, Chancery, Chanteur II, Chicaro, Commodore M., Constant, Correspondent, Count Gallahad, Count Speed, Cutlass, Dancing Brave, Daniel Boone, Darshaan, Debbysman, Dedicate, Devil's Bag, Dictus, Djebel, Dogpatch, Easy Goer, El Relicario, Fairthorn, Fair Trial, Fair Truckle, Flaneur II, Forty Niner, Forum, Gino, Grand Admiral, Gulf Stream, He's a Pistol, His Highness, Hornbeam, Identify, I'ma Hell Raiser, Irish Tower, Iron Ruler, Jean-Pierre, Jean Valjean, Jock II, Kahyasi, Kris S., Lear Fan, Le Haar, Lypheor, Magesterial, Maribeau, Medaille d'Or, Medieval Man, Mehrali, Misty Flight, Moonlight Run, Mowlee, Mr. Trouble, My Dad George, My Host, Naskra, New Policy, No Argument, On to Glory, On Trust, Palestinian, Pass the Glass, Phalanx, Pharly, Practicante, Prince Royal II, Prove It, Quick Decision, Rajah, Rare Performer, Reflected Glory, Reigh Count, Rico, Rocky Royale, Rodosto, Royal Union, Run the Gantlet, Ruken, Sardanapale, Sensitivo, Shannon II, Shirley Heights, Snark, Star Envoy, Stefan the Great, Storm Cat, Sub Fleet, Sunny, Tantieme, Thinking Cap, Thumbs Up, Timor, Torchilla, To the Quick, Trevligio, Tropical Breeze, Tsunami Slew, Tunerup, Ups, Vandale, Vieux Manoir, Vitiges, Warfare, Watling Street, Welsh Saint, White Gloves II, Windy City II, Worden II (3)
571. Abe's Hope, Adrar, Airway, Al Nasr, Alsina, American Flag, A Native Danzig, Anyoldtime, Art Market, Asterus, Aurelius II, Babas Fables, Ballydonnell, Ballymoss, Balzac, Batonnier, Baybrook, Behave Yourself, Bel Bolide, Be My Guest, Berkley Prince, Blazing Count, Bold Discovery, Bold Irishman, Brigadier Gerard, Brig o' Doon, British Empire, Brumeaux, Buckaroo, Bull Reigh, Bunty's Flight, Bupers, Caldarium, Call the Witness, Caracolero, Challenge Me, Cherokee Colony, Claro, Coastal Traffic, Cocles, Cohoes, Cohort, Commanche Run, Conjure, Correlation, Court Harwell, Cozzene, Creme dela Creme, Criminal Type, Crozier, Cryptoclearance, Cure the Blues, Curragh King, D'Accord, Dan Cupid, Dark Ruler, Daryl's Joy, Decidedly, Destino, Diadogue, Diavolo, Disciplinarian, Donut King, Dumpty Humpty, Duplicator, Easy Mon, Education, Espea, Exbury, Exceller, Filibustero, Fit to Fight, Flushing II, Flush Royal, Forever Sparkle, For the Moment, Fulcrum, Gaelic Dancer, Gainsborough, Gallant Sir, Good Counsel, Greek Answer, Greek Game, Greek Song, Guerrero, Gun Bow, Habitat, Hadagal, Hagley, Haste, Hephaistos, High Hat, Hilal, Honeyway, Hunter's Moon IV, Hypnotist II, Imbros, Indian Chief, Indian Hemp, Intent, Involvement, Irish Stronghold, Kauai King, Knave High, Kublai Khan, Ky. Colonel, Lanark, Last Tycoon, Legend of France, L'Enjoleur, Limelight, Linacre, Little Current, Lost Code, Lucullite, Luthier, MacArthur Park, Magpie, Malinowski, Mandamus, Manna, Maron, Marshua's Dancer, Martins Rullah, Messenger, Metrogrand, Mieuxce, Mill Reef, Model Cadet, Mongo, Montparnasse II, My Play, Nashville, National, Nativo, New Providence, Nigromante, Nizami II, Noble Commander, Noble Decree, Northern Baby, North Star III, Occupy, Ogygian, Oh Johnny, Oil Capitol, Our Michael, Pago Pago, Pappa's All, Pardal, Pasch, Pastiche, Penny Post, Petition, Phone Trick, Pillory, Plugged Nickle, Ponder, Primera, Prince Chevalier, Propicio, Prove Out, Quack, Racing Room, Rainy Lake, Ramazon, Reading II, Reform, Regal and Royal, Relko, Rexson's Hope, Rheingold, Rico Monte, Rippey, Risen Star, Roi Dagobert, Roidore, Rolled Stocking, Royal Gunner, Royal Note, Royal Serenade, Ruthless, Sadair, Sadler's Wells, Saint Crispin, Sauce Boat, Septieme Ciel, Seven Corners, Shareef Dancer, Shifting Sands II, Siberian Express, Silly Season, Silver Saber, Sind, Sir Andrew, Sir Barton, Sky Raider, Skytracer, Slewacide, Solario, Somerset, Spartan Valor, Spend A Buck, Star de Naskra, Star Rover, Straight Deal, Stratmat, Strip the Willow, Strolling Player, Sunny North, Super Concorde, Table Play, Tale of Two Cities, Talon, Tanerko, Tapioca, Targowice, Taylor's Falls, Teddy's Comet, Temperence Hill, The Clan, The Doge, The Pie King, The Rabbi, The Rhymer, Third Martini, Tompion, Trimdon, Truculent, Twink, Two Punch, Tyrant, Unbelievable, Val de Loir, Venetian Jester, Verbatim, Vicinity, Wallet Lifter, War Cloud, War Eagle, Warrior, Wild Risk, Windfields, Wing Out, Wolf Power, Woodman (2)
817. Abdos, Aberion, Accipiter, Accordant, Agrarian, Akarad, Ali's Gem, Allen's Prospect, Aloma's Ruler, Always Gallant, Alycidon, Alysheba, Ambrose Light, Amerigo, Amphitheatre, Angle Light, Arctic Tern, Ariel John, Aspinwall, Assagai, Assert, Aureole, Baillamont, Ballydam, Bambure, Banner Sport, Barachois, Barbs Delight, Bar El Ghazal, Baronius, Barre Granite, Barrydown, Battle Joined, Bayou Bourg, Beau Genius, Beau Port, Beau Purple, Beau Repaire, Beau's Eagle, Bel Aethel, Belfonds, Belville Wood, Bering, Big Lark, Big Spruce, Bikala, Billings, Bistouri, Bit of Ireland, Black Peter, Black Servant, Bless Me, Blue Train, Boatswain, Bob's Dusty, Bold Gallant, Bold Hitter, Bold Reason, Bold Reasoning, Booz, Boston Doge, Bozzetto, Brave Shot, Bravo, Brochazo, Brooms, Bryan G., Bull Brier, Bullin, Bullreighzac, Bull Vic, Bully Boy, Bunting, Bustino, Busy Ridge, Busy Wire, Buy and Sell, Calgary Brook, Campfire, Candy Stripes, Cannonade, Canot, Can't Wait, Canyonero, Caracalla, Carral, Carrier Pigeon, Carry Back, Carvin II, Castel Fusano, Caucasus, Cavalcade, Chairman Walker, Chamossaire, Charlie's Song, Charlottesville, Chatterton, Cherokee, Chop Chop, Cientifico, Circle Home, Clandestine, Clarion, Claude Monet, Clem, Coastal, Combat, Commanding II, Connaught, Constant Son, Copelan, Corot, Corronation, Crasher, Crepello, Crewman, Crystal Glitters, Cyclotron, Czaravich, Dahar, Damister, Darn That Alarm, Dart Board, Dastur, Day Court, Dead Ahead, Debenture, Debonair Roger, Depth Charge, Deputed Testamony, Deux pour Cent, Dhoti, Dike, Distinctive, Djebe, Don B., Double Hitch, Drawby, Drums of Time, Durbar II, Dynaformer, Eddie Schmidt, El Drag, Elisathe, El Tigre Grande, Emerson, Endeavor II, Epinard, Equestrian, Escadru, Fabuleux Dancer, Fairy Manhurst, Falcon, Fante, Faraway Son, Fascinator, Fast Fox, Fast Gold, Fast Hilarious, Fast Play,

Fathers Image, Faubourg, Fightin' Guyton, Fil Rouge, Fire Dancer, Firmament, First Cabin, First Fiddle, Fitzcarraldo, Flag Pole, Flaming Fleet, Flares, Flash o' Night, Fleet Host, Flip Sal, Floribunda, Flying Ebony, Formidable, Formor, For Really, Fortino, Fort Salonga, Fox Cub, Free France, Friar Rock, Full Out, Gamin, Gato Del Sol, Golden Eagle II, Gold Favorite, Gold Stage, Good Ending, Good Goods, Grand Slam (1933), Great Nephew, Great Sun, Green Forest, Green Ticket, Grenfall, Grey Monarch, Guillotine, Gummo, Gun Magic, Hafiz, Hail to All, Harbor Prince, Hard to Beat, Hard Work, Hash, Helioptic, Heroic, Highest Tide, High Honors, High Tribute, Hildur, Hindostan, Holandes II, Homing, Honest Pleasure, Husar, I Appeal, Idle Minds, Impressive, I'm For More, Incantation, Infatuation, Infinite, Inverness Drive, Irish Dude, Irish River, Iron Warrior, It's Freezing, I Will, Jade Hunter, Jamaica Inn, Jan Ekels, Jardiniere, Jeep, Jet Pilot, Jig Time, Jimmer, Johnny Appleseed, John's Gold, John William, Jolly Warren, Jontilla, J.O. Tobin, Jungle Road, Karabas, Kashmir II, Kautokeino, Kenmare, King of the Tudors, King Salmon, King's Bishop, King's Blue, King's Troop, Knightly Dawn, Knightly Manner, Kris, Lagunas, Lancegaye, Laomedonte, Laser Light, Leisure Time, Le Levanstell, Lend Lease, Leo Castelli, Light Brigade, Light Idea, Liloy, Linkage, Linmold, Littletown, Loaningdale, Longstone, Lord Avie, Lord Gayle, Lord Gaylord, Loser Weeper, Lucky North, Luxemburgo, Machiavellian, Majority Blue, Malicious, Manifesto, Man o' Night, Market Wise, Martini II, Masetto, Master Gunner, Match The Hatch, Mate, Mel Hash, Meneval, Metric Mile, Mickey McGuire, Mighty Appealing, Migoli, Misstep, Mister Gus, Misti, Model Fool, Mokatam, Monetary Gift, Moolah Bux, Morston, Mr. Clinch, Mr. Jinks, Mr. Randy, Mummy's Game, Mustang, My Request, Nadir, Nalees Man, Nalur, Nasty and Bold, Native Heritage, Native Prospector, Native Royalty, Nedayr, Neddie, Nepenthe, Night Invader, Nilo, Nirgal, Noirmoutiers, Nonoalco, Nordlicht, Northern Jove, Northern Prospect, Northrup, Notebook, Oak Dancer, Oceanic, Olympiad King, Opera Hat, Orestes III, Ormont, Orsenigo, Orsini II, Orvieto II, Osiris II, Our Babu, Our Native, Overskate, Pan, Panorama, Pappa Fourway, Parral, Pass the Tab, Penalo, Pet Bully, Petee Wrack, Peter Hastings, Peterhof, Peter Pan, Peter Peter, Petingo, Pharis, Piercer, Piet, Pocket Ruler, Policeman, Polymelian, Pont l'Evveque, Poona II, Portcodine, Pot au Feu, Poughatchev, Premiership, Priam II, Prince Astro, Prince Bio, Prince Blessed, Prince Pal, Prince Taj, Pronto, Prophets Thumb, Quarter Deck, Queen City Lad, Quick Wink, Quiet American, Radiotherapy, Rahy, Raja Baba, Ramahorn, Ramsinga, Rash Prince, Red Hannigan, Red Ryder, Reneged, Restless Native, Rhodes Scholar, Ridan, Right Royal, Rio Bravo, Rise 'n Shine, Rising Market, River River, River War, Rockefella, Rolls Royce, Romantic, Rosolio, Royal Dorimar, Royal Ford, Royal Tip, Ruffinal, Rustom Pasha, Rustom Sirdar, Safety Zone, Sailor's Guide, Sails Pride, Salem, Saltville, Salvo, Sanctus, Saratoga Game, Saratoga Six, Seabiscuit, Sea Charger, Seductor, Selalbeda, Serio, Shadeed, Shredder, Sicambre, Sideral, Silent Screen, Silver Deputy, Silver Ghost, Silver Horde, Sir Blenheim, Sir Harry Lewis, Sir Wiggle, Skeeter II, Skywalker, Slave Ship, Slewpy, Snob, Snow Cat, Solidarity, Some Chance, Somethingfabulous, Son-in-Law, Son of John, Soon Over, Sortie, Sovereign Dancer, Spanish Prince II, Spring Double, Stallwood, Star Beacon, Statuto, Staunch Avenger, Star Gallant, St. Brideaux, Steady Growth, Stepfather, Sting, Successor, Summing, Sunglow, Sunny's Halo, Sweeping Light, Tacitus, Tap on Wood, Tejon, Teleferique, Tell, Tempest II, Terry, Te Vega, Tex Courage, Theatrical, The Pincher, The Scoundrel, Third Brother, Tick On, Tiger Wander, Tilt Up, Time for a Change, Tip-Toe, Tirreno, Tobin Bronze, Tom Cat, Tornado, Torsion, Toulouse Lautrec, Tourbillon, Tourist II, Trace Call, Track Spare, Trempolino, Trevieres, Trollius, Tudor Melody, Tudor Music, Tuleg, Turkhan, Tuscany, Two's a Plenty, Unconscious, Under Fire, Upper Nile, Vacarme, Valdina Way, Vanlandingham, Vatellor, Vent du Nord, Venture, Vic Day, Victorian, Victory Morn, Vigorous, Vitelio, Vox Pop, Wajima, War Dog, West Coast Scout, What Luck, Wheatly Hall, Wild Again, Windsor Lad, Winning Hit, Yatasto, Young Generation, Youth, Yrrah Jr., Zeddaan, Zenith, Zev (1)

Broodmare Sires' Classic Victories 1946-2003

1. Poker (5)
2. Blenheim II, Bull Lea, Discovery, Heliopolis, My Babu, Princequillo (4)
8. Buckpasser, Crafty Admiral, Drone, Equipoise, Hyperion (3)
13. Believe It, Chicaro, Commodore M., Dancing Count, Forli, His Majesty, Jack High, Johnstown, Lord at War, Lt. Stevens, Mahmoud, Nantallah, Native Dancer, Polynesian, Pretense, Promised Land, Royal Charger, Sauce Boat, Secretariat, Slewacide, Star Blen, St. Germans, Storm Bird, Sunrise Flight, Turkoman, Understanding, War Admiral (2)
40. Alleged, Ballymoss, Battlefield, Beau Pere, Bold Commander, Bold Hour, Brantome, Brazado, Bubbling Over, Bull Dog, By Jimminy, Caro, Case Ace, Caveat, Count Fleet, Dante, Danzig, Deputy Minister, Destino, Dixieland Band, Djeddah, Double Jay, Dusty Canyon, Eight Thirty, El Gran Senor, Etonian, Flaneur II, Fleet Nasrullah, For the Moment, Gallant Man, Graustark, Groton, Halo, Hatchet Man, Identify, In Reality, Insco, Jacinto, Jacopo, John P. Grier, Khaled, Le Fabuleux, Minnesota Mac, Mount Marcy, Native Charger, Nepenthe, Nijinsky II, Nimbus, Nizami II, On to Glory, Papa Redbird, Pompey, Prove It, Ribot, Roman, Royal Coinage, Royal Minstrel, Seattle Slew, Sickle, Sir Gallahad III, Sir Ivor, Solario, Speak John, Snow Sporting, Stage Door Johnny, Sunny, Supremus, Swaps, Terrible Tiger, The Axe II, Tom Fool, Vice Regent, Wavering Monarch, War Glory, War Relic, Windy City II (1)

Broodmare Sires' Breeders' Cup Victories 1984-2003

1. Alydar (5)
2. Boldnesian, Darshaan, Key to the Mint, Northern Dancer (3)
6. Blushing Groom, Good Manners, Hoist the Flag, Le Fabuleux, Mr. Prospector, Pretense, Prove Out, Riverman, Seattle Slew, Seattle Song, Secretariat, Stage Door Johnny, Tom Rolfe, Welsh Saint, What a Pleasure (2)
21. Affirmed, Ahonoora, Al Hattab, Apalachee, Arts and Letters, Aurelius II, Baillamont, Bald Eagle, Baldski, Beekeeper, Bikala, Bold Bidder, Bold Hour, Bravo, Caro, Connaught, Cox's Ridge, Crimson Satan, Cure the Blues, Cyane, Damascus, Dancing Champ, Deputy Minister, Dictus, Diplomat Way, Double Jay, Drone, Easy Goer, Elocutionist, Fappiano, Flintham, Forli, Grey Dawn II, Green Dancer, Habitat, Hatchet Man, Icecapade, In Reality, Irish River, Jim French, J.O. Tobin, Kahyasi, Kaldoun, Kenmare, Khaled, Kris S., Lear Fan, Lost Code, Lt. Stevens, Majestic Prince, Medieval Man, Melyno, Mill Reef, Miswaki, Mr. Leader, My Dad George, Never Bend, Nijinsky II, Ogygian, Pass the Glass, Pleasant Colony, Policeman, Prince John, Private Account, Proudest Roman, Quibu, Raise a Native, Rambunctious, Regal and Royal, Relko, Rheingold, Right Royal, Riva Ridge, Round Table, Sadler's Wells, Sassafras, Shirley Heights, Silver Saber, Sir Harry Lewis, Slew O' Gold, Smarten, Stevward, Storm Bird, Strawberry Road II, Summer Tan, Tap on Wood, Targowice, Taylor's Falls, Trempolino, Troy, Tunerup, T.V. Commercial, Two's a Plenty, Understanding, Valid Appeal, Verbatim, Vice Regent, Welsh Pageant, Winning Hit (1)

1946
1. Chance Shot, Equipoise (7)
3. Man o' War, Sir Gallahad III (6)
5. On Watch (5)
6. Black Toney, Blue Larkspur, Dis Donc, Pharamond II (4)
10. Bull Dog, Sickle, Toro (3)

1947
1. Sickle (8)
2. Chance Shot (7)
3. Blue Larkspur, Stimulus (6)
5. Equipoise, Insco (5)
7. Jacopo, On Watch, Sir Gallahad III (4)
10. Man o' War, Reigh Count, Rico, Sardanapale, Wildair (3)

1948
1. Hyperion (8)
2. Man o' War (6)
3. Case Ace, Challenger II, Flying Heels, Sir Gallahad III, Stimulus (4)
8. Equipoise, Sickle (3)
10. Blenheim II, Bull Dog, Caruso, Chance Shot, Gainsborough, High Time, Insco, Magpie, Maron, On Watch, Pharamond II, Picacero, St. Germans, Strolling Player, The Satrap, Trimdon, Twink, War Admiral (2)

1949
1. Blenheim II (15)
2. Sickle (7)
3. Man o' War (6)
4. Stimulus (5)
5. Discovery, St. Germans (4)
7. Bull Dog, Pharos, Pompey, Whichone (3)

1950
1. Display (8)
2. Bubbling Over (7)
3. Blenheim II, Chance Play, Man o' War (6)
6. Bahram, Bull Dog (5)
8. Sir Gallahad III (4)
9. La Brige, Mad Hatter, Royal Minstrel (3)

1951
1. Pharamond II, Sickle (8)
3. Sir Gallahad III (7)
4. Blue Larkspur (6)
5. John P. Grier, Pompey (5)
7. Apelle, Bull Dog, Display, Hyperion, War Admiral (3)

1952
1. Blenheim II, Blue Larkspur, Bull Dog (6)
4. Sickle (5)
5. Bull Lea, Johnstown, Sir Gallahad III, The Porter (4)
9. Case Ace, Discovery, Hairan, Identify, Teddy, Vito, War Admiral (3)

1953
1. Discovery (13)
2. Bull Dog (8)
3. Blue Larkspur (6)
4. Blenheim II, Coronach, Questionnaire (4)
7. Ariel, Bimelech, Chance Play, Pilate, War Admiral (3)

1954
1. Blue Larkspur (8)
2. Bull Dog (7)
3. Pilate (5)
4. Blenheim II, Brazado, Halcyon, Sickle, The Porter, War Admiral (4)
10. Bimelech, Discovery, Mahmoud, Menow (3)

1955
1. Johnstown (8)
2. Beau Pere, Jack High (6)
4. Discovery, Man o' War, Menow, Sickle (5)
8. Mahmoud (4)
9. Bull Dog, Hyperion, Occupation, Pilate (3)

1956
1. Beau Pere (7)
2. Jack High, Johnstown, Stimulus (6)
5. Bull Dog (5)
6. Blue Larkspur, Bull Lea, Mahmoud (4)
9. Black Toney, Colombo, Heliopolis, John P. Grier, Omaha, Pilate, Questionnaire (3)

1957
1. Bull Lea (9)
2. Discovery (8)
3. Mahmoud, Sir Cosmo (7)
5. Bimelech, Blenheim II, Stimulus, War Jeep (4)
9. Ariel, Case Ace, John P. Grier, Omaha, Questionnaire (3)

1958
1. Bull Lea (9)
2. Mahmoud (8)
3. Blue Larkspur, Sir Cosmo (6)
5. Discovery (5)
6. Blenheim II, Challenger II (4)
8. Bubbling Over, Eurasian, Supremus, War Admiral (3)

1959
1. Johnstown (7)
2. Bull Lea, By Jimminy, Sir Cosmo (6)
5. Mahmoud (4)
6. Brazado, Case Ace, Count Fleet, Fighting Fox, Lovely Night, Nasrullah, Princequillo, Sir Gallahad III, Tiger, War Glory (3)

1960
1. Count Fleet (9)
2. Bull Lea (7)
3. Tiger (6)
4. Sir Gallahad III (5)
5. Heelfly, Rosemont, Supremus (4)
8. Alibhai, Blenheim II, Bubbling Over, By Jimminy, Star Blen (3)

1961
1. Count Fleet, Star Blen (7)
3. War Admiral (6)
4. Alibhai, Bull Lea, Dante (5)
7. Bossuet, Bull Dog, Eight Thirty (4)
10. Ballyogan, Heelfly, Khaled, Mahmoud, Our Boots (3)

1962
1. Khaled (8)
2. Eight Thirty (6)
3. Bull Lea, Revoked (5)
5. Bossuet, Johnstown, Olympia, War Admiral (4)
9. Ballyogan, Count Fleet, Djeddah, Gold Bridge, Star Blen (3)

1963
1. Count Fleet (12)
2. Khaled (8)
3. Requiebro (5)
4. Nasrullah, Polynesian, Shut Out (4)
7. Brookfield, Menow, Olympia (3)
10. Annapolis, Bolero, Bymeabond, Cosmic Bomb, Devil Diver, Errard, Johnstown, Nearco, Princequillo, Revoked, Rodosto, Roman, War Admiral (2)

1964
1. War Admiral (9)
2. Bull Lea, Princequillo, Roman (6)
5. Native Dancer (5)
6. Blue Pair, Bold Venture, Double Jay, Tehran (4)
10. Annapolis, Cosmic Bomb, Count Fleet, Fairthorn (3)

1965
1. War Admiral (10)
2. Roman (9)
3. Count Fleet (8)
4. War Relic (6)
5. Gold Bridge (5)
6. Battlefield, Double Jay, Heliopolis, Mahmoud, Russia II, Stymie (3)

1966
1. War Admiral (10)
2. Nasrullah (6)
3. Princequillo (5)
4. Ambiorix, To Market (4)
6. Count Fleet, Stymie (3)
8. Blenheim II, Chancery, Destino, Determine, Diadogue, Khaled, King Cole, Mahmoud, Mr. Music, Nimbus, Pasha, Petition, Roman, Watling Street, Whirlaway (2)

1967
1. My Babu (11)
2. Ambiorix (7)
3. Nasrullah, Princequillo (6)
5. Better Self, Count Fleet, Hasty Road (5)
8. Mahmoud, War Admiral (4)
10. Birikil, Blue Swords, Hyperion, King Cole, Shut Out (3)

1968
1. Hill Prince, My Babu (7)
3. Better Self, Double Jay, Heliopolis (6)
6. Princequillo (5)
7. Counterpoint, Hasty Road, Nasrullah, Rough'n Tumble, Summer Tan, Sun Again (3)

1969
1. Battlefield (7)
2. Hill Prince, Royal Charger (5)
4. Better Self, Double Jay, Nasrullah, Princequillo (4)
8. Anwar, Beau Max, Mehrali (3)

1970
1. Princequillo (14)
2. Nasrullah, Swaps (6)
4. Jet Action (4)
5. Battlefield, Free America, Hill Prince, Johns Joy (3)
9. Better Self, Blue Peter, Claro, Counterpoint, Mr. Music, One-Eyed King, Ruthless, Sailor, Shut Out, Skytracer, Sun Again, Vicinity, War Admiral, Windy City II, Your Host (2)

1971
1. Nasrullah (7)
2. Swaps (5)
3. Heliopolis, Madara, Tom Fool, Turn-to (4)
7. Djeddah, Double Jay, First Landing, Hail to Reason, Mahmoud, Prince John, Princequillo, Swoon's Son (3)

1972
1. Princequillo (12)
2. Heliopolis (6)
3. Nearctic, Preciptic, Quibu (5)
6. Bold Ruler (4)
7. Fleet Nasrullah, Gun Shot, Madara, Mount Marcy, Nasrullah, Needles, Summer Tan (3)

1973
1. Princequillo (10)
2. Quibu (5)
3. Ambehaving, Fleet Nasrullah, Heliopolis, Tim Tam (4)
7. Crafty Admiral, Madara, Moslem Chief, Nashua, Olympia, Prince John (3)

1974
1. Hasty Road (9)
2. Olympia (5)
3. Bold Ruler, Prince John, Swaps, Tom Fool (4)
7. Bar Le Duc, Dark Star, Double Jay, Native Dancer, Roman, T.V. Lark (3)

1975
1. Hasty Road (7)
2. Traffic Judge (5)
3. Hail to Reason (4)
4. Bar Le Duc, Berseem, Bold Ruler, Chieftan, Court Martial, Heliopolis, Le Haar, Native Dancer, Prince John, Quibu, Royal Coinage, Timor, Tom Fool, Tulyar (3)

1976
1. Princequillo (7)
2. Tom Fool, Traffic Judge, Tulyar (5)
5. Hasty Road, Nantallah, Native Dancer (4)
8. Bold Ruler, Commodore M., Double Jay, Olympia, Ribot, T.V. Lark (3)

1977
1. Crafty Admiral, On-and-On (6)
3. Poker, Summer Tan, T.V. Lark (5)
6. Blue Prince, Swaps (4)
8. Northern Dancer, Prince John, Ribot (3)

1978
1. Bald Eagle, Crafty Admiral, On-and-On (6)
4. Tim Tam (5)
5. Blue Prince, Tom Fool (4)
7. Boldnesian, Promised Land, Round Table, Sing Sing, Summer Tan (3)

1979

1. Crafty Admiral, Promised Land, Quibu (7)
4. Buckpasser, Round Table, Tim Tam (5)
7. Francis S., Windy Sands (4)
9. Barbizon, Blue Prince, Sing Sing (3)

1980

1. Promised Land (9)
2. Determine (7)
3. Buckpasser, Etonian (6)
5. Double Jay (5)
6. Gallant Man (4)
7. Dr. Fager, Herbager, Lucky Debonair, Minnesota Mac, Nearctic (3)

1981

1. Double Jay (8)
2. Vaguely Noble (5)
3. Sunrise Flight (4)
4. Groton, Nantallah (3)
6. Abe's Hope, Bunty's Flight, Daryl's Joy, Dr. Fager, Etonian, Exbury, Gallant Man, Herbager, Iron Ruler, My Host, Primera, Raise a Native, Sette Bello, Shantung, Silnet, Sir Gaylord, Third Martini, To Market (2)

1982

1. Candy Spots, Hawaii, Quadrangle, Traffic Judge (4)
5. Bold Commander, Court Martial, Prince Royal II, Shantung (3)
9. Ack Ack, Alsina, Birikil, Bold Bidder, Bold Discovery, Bold Ruler, Double Jay, Dr. Fager, Drone, Hail to Reason, Herbager, No Argument, Olden Times, Raise a Native, Royal Gunner, Run For Nurse, Saint Crispin, Sette Bello, Swaps, Tale of Two Cities, Tropical Breeze, Your Alibhai (2)

1983

1. Buckpasser (5)
2. Never Bend, Prominer, Run For Nurse (4)
5. First Landing, Forli, Misty Flight, Northern Dancer, Raise a Native, Sea-Bird, Shantung, Sunny, The Axe II, Tom Fool, T.V. Lark, Vieux Manoir (3)

1984

1. Never Bend (6)
2. Forli, Raise a Native, The Axe II (5)
5. Buckpasser, Double Jay, Majestic Prince, Vertex (4)
9. Drone, One Count, Secretariat, Tom Rolfe (3)

1985

1. Pia Star, Secretariat (5)
3. Terrible Tiger (4)
4. Bicker, Forli, Gallant Man, Icecapade, Promised Land, Snow Sporting, Speak John, Star Envoy, Summer Tan, What a Pleasure (3)

1986

1. Hoist the Flag, Icecapade (7)
3. Prince John, Snow Sporting (4)
5. Graustark, He's a Pistol, High Top, Le Fabuleux, Vaguely Noble (3)
10. Bald Eagle, Boldnesian, Dusty Canyon, First Landing, Forli, Francis S., Grey Dawn II, In Reality, Nantallah, Nashua, Nijinsky II, No Robbery, Racing Room, Rambunctious, Ribot, Riva Ridge, Sir Ivor, Table Play, Tatan (2)

1987

1. Hoist the Flag (7)
2. Ack Ack (6)
3. Le Fabuleux, Secretariat (5)
5. Nijinsky II, Sassafras, Tom Rolfe (4)
8. Dusty Canyon, Exclusive Native, Lt. Stevens, Vaguely Noble (3)

1988

1. Buckpasser (8)
2. Graustark (7)
3. Lt. Stevens (6)
4. Hoist the Flag (5)
5. Beekeeper, Bold Hour, His Majesty, Sir Ivor, Stage Door Johnny, Tom Rolfe (3)

1989

1. Buckpasser (7)
2. Good Manners, Understanding (6)
4. Gallant Romeo, Stage Door Johnny (5)
6. Daniel Boone, Debbysman, Grey Dawn II, Key to the Mint, Riva Ridge (3)

1990

1. Grey Dawn II (6)
2. Cyane, In Reality, Key to the Mint, No Robbery (5)
6. Secretariat (4)
7. Good Manners, King Pellinore, Le Fabuleux, Round Table, Transworld (3)

1991

1. In Reality (6)
2. Saulingo (5)
3. Lyphard (4)
4. Al Hattab, Con Brio, Dancing Count, Diplomat Way, Nijinsky II, To the Quick, Whitesburg (3)

1992

1. Nijinsky II (7)
2. Flintham (5)
3. Alydar, Buckfinder, Secretariat (4)
6. Al Hattab, Buckpasser, Graustark, Hatchet Man, King Pellinore, Riva Ridge (3)

1993

1. Nijinsky II (10)
2. Elocutionist (5)
3. Alydar, Mr. Prospector (4)
5. Figonero, Flintham, Graustark, Pia Star, Raise a Cup, Reviewer, Wavering Monarch (3)

1994

1. Nijinsky II (10)
2. Al Hattab (8)
3. Northfields, Storm Bird (5)
5. Alydar, Key to the Mint (4)
7. Good Behaving, Pretense (3)
9. Danzig, Graustark, Green Dancer, Raise a Cup, Riverman, Sauce Boat, Secretariat, Targowice, The Minstrel, Tunerup, T.V. Commercial, Vaguely Noble (2)

1995

1. Seattle Slew (11)
2. Northfields (7)
3. Key to the Mint (6)
4. Storm Bird (5)
5. Caro, Green Dancer, Nijinsky II (4)
8. Avatar, Ups (3)
10. Droll Role, Herbager, Medaille d'Or, Miswaki, Mr. Leader, Noble Dancer II, Rheingold, Roberto, Stop the Music, The Minstrel (2)

1996

1. Tri Jet (6)
2. Diplomat Way (5)
3. Darby Creek Road (4)
4. Caveat, Fappiano, Majestic Light, Private Account, Resurgent, Sharpen Up (3)
10. Ack Ack, Arts and Letters, Baldski, Caro, Damascus, Droll Role, Green Dancer, Melyno, Mr. Prospector, Northfields, On to Glory, Practicante, Propicio, Seattle Slew, Secretariat, Troy (2)

1997

1. Mr. Prospector (5)
2. Ack Ack, Alydar, Loose Cannon, Screen King (4)
6. Damascus, Diplomat Way, Northern Dancer, Riverman, Round Table, Sharpen Up, Vigors (3)

1998

1. Diplomat Way (6)
2. Seattle Slew (5)
3. Ack Ack, Damascus, Known Fact, Sir Ivor, Valid Appeal (3)
8. Alydar, Believe It, Blushing Groom, Chief's Crown, Desert Wine, Dixieland Band, Explodent, Green Dancer, Lypheor, Miswaki, Mr. Prospector, Nureyev, Plugged Nickle, Roberto, Tom Rolfe, Verbatim, Vice Regent, Vigors (2)

1999

1. Tom Rolfe, Valid Appeal (4)
3. Alydar, Apalachee, Baldski, Danzig, Mari's Book, Vice Regent, Vigors (3)
10. Believe It, Caerleon, Chief's Crown, Damascus, Dancing Champ, Drone, El Gran Senor, Key to the Mint, Known Fact, Mr. Prospector, Never Bend, Nijinsky II, Northfields, Nureyev, Pleasant Colony, Seattle Slew, Seeking the Gold, Smarten (2)

2000

1. Seattle Slew (7)
2. Ghadeer (5)
3. Danzig (4)
4. Alydar, Lyphard, Seattle Song, Smarten, Valid Appeal (3)
9. Baldski, Be My Guest, Blushing Groom, Capote, Caro, Crafty Prospector, Diesis, Dixieland Band, Drone, El Gran Senor, Fappiano, Forty Niner, Kris S., Metrogrand, Mr. Prospector, Nijinsky II, Regal and Royal, Seeking the Gold, Slew O' Gold (2)

2001

1. Turkoman (6)
2. Blushing Groom, Dr. Blum, Lyphard, Mr. Prospector, Slew O' Gold, Topsider (3)
8. Cherokee Colony, Devil's Bag, Diesis, Dixieland Band, Fappiano, Kaldoun, Lost Code, Mari's Book, Mr. Leader, Nijinsky II, Northern Dancer, Northfields, Phone Trick, Private Account, Quick Decision, Saros, Seattle Song, Septieme Ciel, Spectacular Bid, Strawberry Road II, Sunny North, Temperence Hill, Valid Appeal, Vitiges, Welsh Pageant (2)

2002

1. Ahonoora (5)
2. Cox's Ridge, Homebuilder, Lord at War (4)
5. Affirmed, Clever Trick, Dancing Brave, Easy Goer, Halo, Kaldoun, Pleasant Colony, Saros, Seattle Slew, Storm Cat (3)

2003

1. Nureyev (6)
2. Mr. Prospector, Relaunch (5)
4. Alleged, Deputy Minister, Mari's Book, Storm Bird (4)
8. Ahonoora, Bailjumper, El Gran Senor, Private Account (3)

Photo courtesy of Santa Anita Park

No colt or horse has earned more major North American victories since World War II than Round Table, whose 19 prestigious triumphs included a two-and-a-half-length score in the 1958 Santa Anita Handicap under Bill Shoemaker. Round Table's sire, Princequillo, is the only stallion with more than 80 major North American stakes triumphs since World War II as both a sire and a broodmare sire. Round Table subsequently became not only the best runner sired by Princequillo, but the best stallion as well, earning 36 major victories as a sire and 27 more as a broodmare sire.

Broodmare Sires Resumes

Broodmare Sires With Victories In Major North American Races 1946-2003

ABDOS
1982: Hollywood Invitational Handicap (Exploded)

ABERION
1979: Hollywood Juvenile Championship (Parsec)

ABERNANT
1969: Jersey Derby (Al Hattab)
Monmouth Invitational Handicap (Al Hattab)
1972: Ladies Handicap (Grafitti)
1973: Black Helen Handicap (Grafitti)
1974: Oaklawn Handicap (Royal Knight)

ABE'S HOPE
1981: Sorority Stakes (Apalachee Honey)
Alcibiades Stakes (Apalachee Honey)

ACCIPITER
1994: Hollywood Gold Cup (Slew of Damascus)

ACCORDANT
1976: Fall Highweight Handicap (Relent)

ACK ACK
1982: Alcibiades Stakes (Jelly Bean Holiday)
Pegasus Handicap (Fast Gold)
1987: Santa Margarita Handicap (North Sider)
Apple Blossom Handicap (North Sider)
Maskette Stakes (North Sider)
Illinois Derby (Lost Code)
Ohio Derby (Lost Code)
Arlington Classic (Lost Code)
1990: Super Derby (Home at Last)
1996: Matron Stakes (Sharp Cat)
Hollywood Starlet Stakes (Sharp Cat)
1997: Las Virgenes Stakes (Sharp Cat)
Santa Anita Oaks (Sharp Cat)
Acorn Stakes (Sharp Cat)
Hollywood Oaks (Sharp Cat)
1998: Ruffian Handicap (Sharp Cat)
Beldame Stakes (Sharp Cat)
Canadian Int. Championship (Royal Anthem)
2000: Gulfstream Park BC Handicap (Royal Anthem)

ACROPOLIS
1974: Secretariat Stakes (Glossary)
1977: Hempstead Handicap (Pacific Princess)
1978: Ramona Handicap (Drama Critic)

ACROTERION
1978: Del Mar Futurity (Flying Paster)
Norfolk Stakes (Flying Paster)
1979: Santa Anita Derby (Flying Paster)
Hollywood Derby (Flying Paster)
1981: San Antonio Stakes (Flying Paster)

ADMIRAL DRAKE
1953: Garden State Stakes (Turn-to)
1954: Flamingo Stakes (Turn-to)
1963: Del Mar Futurity (Perris)
1967: California Derby (Reason to Hail)

ADRAR
1961: Bougainvillea Turf Handicap (Wolfram)
Hialeah Turf Cup (Wolfram)

AFFIRMED
1996: Flower Bowl Invitational Handicap (Chelsey Flower)
2002: Florida Derby (Harlan's Holiday)
Toyota Blue Grass Stakes (Harlan's Holiday)
Matriarch Stakes (Dress To Thrill)
2003: Donn Handicap (Harlan's Holiday)
Breeders' Cup Classic/Dodge (Pleasantly Perfect)

AGRARIAN
1955: Canadian Championship Stakes (Park Dandy)

AHONOORA
2002: Santa Margarita Handicap (Azeri)
Apple Blossom Handicap (Azeri)
Milady Breeders' Cup Handicap (Azeri)
Vanity Handicap (Azeri)
Breeders' Cup Distaff (Azeri)
2003: Apple Blossom Handicap (Azeri)
Milady Breeders' Cup Handicap (Azeri)
Vanity Handicap (Azeri)

AIRWAY
1962: Californian Stakes (Cadiz)
1963: Hollywood Gold Cup (Cadiz)

AKARAD
1998: Ramona Handicap (See You Soon)

AL HATTAB
1986: Arlington Classic (Sumptious)
1988: California Derby (All Thee Power)
1991: Philip H. Iselin Handicap (Black Tie Affair)
Breeders' Cup Classic (Black Tie Affair)
San Felipe Stakes (Sea Cadet)
1992: Donn Handicap (Sea Cadet)
Gulfstream Park Handicap (Sea Cadet)
Meadowlands Cup (Sea Cadet)
1993: Futurity Stakes (Holy Bull)
1994: Florida Derby (Holy Bull)
Blue Grass Stakes (Holy Bull)
Metropolitan Handicap (Holy Bull)
Dwyer Stakes (Holy Bull)
Haskell Invitational Handicap (Holy Bull)
Travers Stakes (Holy Bull)
Woodward Stakes (Holy Bull)
Del Mar Futurity (On Target)

ALIBHAI
1951: Del Mar Handicap (Blue Reading)
1954: Santa Anita Maturity (Apple Valley)
1957: Selima Stakes (Guide Line)
Gallant Fox Handicap (Eddie Schmidt)
1958: Inglewood Handicap (Eddie Schmidt)
1960: Gardenia Stakes (Bowl of Flowers)
Frizette Stakes (Bowl of Flowers)
Kentucky Jockey Club Stakes (Crimson Fury)
1961: Acorn Stakes (Bowl of Flowers)
Coaching Club American Oaks (Bowl of Flowers)
Spinster Stakes (Bowl of Flowers)
Arlington Matron Handicap (Shirley Jones)
Breeders' Futurity (Roman Line)
1963: Louisiana Derby (City Line)
1967: Arlington-Washington Futurity (T.V. Commercial)
Breeders' Futurity (T.V. Commercial)
1968: Jersey Derby (Out of the Way)
Massachusetts Handicap (Out of the Way)
1972: Alcibiades Stakes (Coraggioso)
1973: Del Mar Debutante Stakes (Fleet Peach)
Michigan Mile and One-Eighth (Golden Don)
1974: Ladies Handicap (Coraggioso)
Manhattan Handicap (Golden Don)

ALI'S GEM
1970: Hollywood Derby (Hanalei Bay)

ALL BLUE
1973: Champagne Stakes (Holding Pattern)
1974: Monmouth Invitational Handicap (Holding Pattern)
Travers Stakes (Holding Pattern)

ALLEGED
1989: Laurel Futurity (Go and Go)
1990: Belmont Stakes (Go and Go)
2000: Vinery Del Mar Debutante Stakes (Cindy's Hero)
2003: Las Virgenes Stakes (Composure)
Santa Anita Oaks (Composure)
Arlington Million (Sulamani)
Turf Classic (Sulamani)

ALLEN'S PROSPECT
1999: La Brea Stakes (Hookedonthefeelin)

AL NASR
1996: Metropolitan Handicap (Honour and Glory)
1998: Buick Pegasus Handicap (Tomorrows Cat)

ALOMA'S RULER
2002: Ruffian Handicap (Mandy's Gold)

ALSAB
1954: Alcibiades Stakes (Myrtle's Jet)
Frizette Stakes (Myrtle's Jet)
1970: Monmouth Oaks (Kilts N Kapers)

ALSINA
1982: Acorn Stakes (Cupecoy's Joy)
Mother Goose Stakes (Cupecoy's Joy)

ALWAYS GALLANT
1995: Vosburgh Stakes (Not Surprising)

ALYCIDON
1962: Arkansas Derby (Aeropolis)

ALYDAR
1992: Gotham Stakes (Lure)
Breeders' Cup Mile (Lure)
Alabama Stakes (November Snow)
Futurity Stakes (Strolling Along)
1993: Santa Anita Derby (Personal Hope)
Carter Handicap (Alydeed)
Brooklyn Handicap (Living Vicariously)
Breeders' Cup Mile (Lure)
1994: Santa Anita Oaks (Lakeway)
Mother Goose Stakes (Lakeway)
Hollywood Oaks (Lakeway)
Caesars International Handicap (Lure)
1996: Swaps Stakes (Victory Speech)
1997: Mother Goose Stakes (Ajina)
Coaching Club American Oaks (Ajina)
Breeders' Cup Distaff (Ajina)
Strub Stakes (Victory Speech)
1998: Lane's End Breeders' Futurity (Cat Thief)
Go for Wand Handicap (Aldiza)
1999: Swaps Stakes (Cat Thief)
Breeders' Cup Classic (Cat Thief)
Breeders' Cup Juvenile (Anees)
2000: Kentucky Oaks (Secret Status)
Mother Goose Stakes (Secret Status)
Champagne Stakes (A.P. Valentine)

ALYSHEBA
1999: Pegasus Handicap (Forty One Carats)

AMBEHAVING
1973: San Felipe Handicap (Linda's Chief)
California Derby (Linda's Chief)
Withers Stakes (Linda's Chief)
Pontiac Grand Prix Stakes (Linda's Chief)

AMBIORIX
1962: Gardenia Stakes (Main Swap)
1965: Saratoga Special (Impressive)
1966: Sapling Stakes (Great Power)
Gotham Stakes (Stupendous)
Jerome Handicap (Bold and Brave)
Grey Lag Handicap (Selari)
1967: Saratoga Special (Vitriolic)
Arlington-Washington Futurity (Vitriolic)
Champagne Stakes (Vitriolic)
Pimlico-Laurel Futurity (Vitriolic)
Arlington Handicap (Stupendous)
Whitney Stakes (Stupendous)
Futurity Stakes (Captain's Gig)
1968: Hollywood Derby (Poleax)
1969: Louisiana Derby (King of the Castle)
Illinois Derby (King of the Castle)
1972: Del Mar Handicap (Chrisaway)
1975: San Luis Rey Stakes (Trojan Bronze)
1977: Young America Stakes (Forever Casting)

AMBROSE LIGHT
1958: Santa Anita Derby (Silky Sullivan)

AMERICAN FLAG
1948: Astoria Stakes (Eternal Flag)
1954: Top Flight Handicap (Sunshine Nell)

AMERIGO
1975: American Handicap (Pass the Glass)

AMPHITHEATRE
1958: Princess Pat Stakes (Battle Heart)

A NATIVE DANZIG
2003: Alabama Stakes (Island Fashion)
La Brea Stakes (Island Fashion)

ANGLE LIGHT
1983: Arlington-Washington Futurity (All Fired Up)

ANNAPOLIS
1962: Trenton Handicap (Mongo)
United Nations Handicap (Mongo)
1963: Washington D.C. International (Mongo)
United Nations Handicap (Mongo)
1964: Widener Handicap (Mongo)
John B. Campbell Handicap (Mongo)
Monmouth Handicap (Mongo)
1966: San Luis Rey Handicap (Polar Sea)

ANWAR
1968: Man o' War Stakes (Czar Alexander)
1969: Dixie Handicap (Czar Alexander)
Bowling Green Handicap (Czar Alexander)
Oak Tree Stakes (Czar Alexander)

ANYOLDTIME
1976: Oak Leaf Stakes (Any Time Girl)
1979: Del Mar Debutante Stakes (Table Hands)

APALACHEE
1998: San Felipe Stakes (Artax)
1999: Carter Handicap (Artax)
Vosburgh Stakes (Artax)
Breeders' Cup Sprint (Artax)
2003: Man o' War Stakes (Lunar Sovereign)

APELLE
1951: Breeders' Futurity (Alladier)
Blue Grass Stakes (Ruhe)
Inglewood Handicap (Sturdy One)
1952: Inglewood Handicap (Sturdy One)

APPREHENSION
1949: Travers Stakes (Arise)
1950: Fall Highweight Handicap (Arise)
Excelsior Handicap (Arise)
1951: Carter Handicap (Arise)
Monmouth Handicap (Arise)

ARCTIC PRINCE
1973: American Derby (Bemo)
1975: Hollywood Invitational Handicap (Barclay Joy)
Sunset Handicap (Barclay Joy)
1977: United Nations Handicap (Bemo)
1982: Hollywood Turf Cup (Prince Spellbound)
1983: Eddie Read Handicap (Prince Spellbound)

ARCTIC TERN
2000: Ramona Handicap (Caffe Latte)

ARIEL
1946: San Vicente Handicap (Air Rate)
1951: Arlington Matron Handicap (Sickle's Image)
1952: Astoria Stakes (Home-Made)
Vineland Handicap (Sickle's Image)
1953: Vagrancy Handicap (Home-Made)
Comely Handicap (Home-Made)
Washington Park Handicap (Sickle's Image)
1956: Kentucky Jockey Club Stakes (Federal Hill)
1957: Starlet Stakes (Old Pueblo)
Del Mar Futurity (Old Pueblo)
Louisiana Derby (Federal Hill)

ARIEL JOHN
1974: San Felipe Handicap (Aloha Mood)

ARTILLERY
1963: San Felipe Handicap (Denodado)
1967: Californian Stakes (Biggs)
1968: San Luis Rey Handicap (Biggs)

ART MARKET
1977: Demoiselle Stakes (Caesar's Wish)
1978: Mother Goose Stakes (Caesar's Wish)

ARTS AND LETTERS
1986: Blue Grass Stakes (Bachelor Beau)
1995: Dwyer Stakes (Hoolie)
1996: San Antonio Handicap (Alphabet Soup)
Breeders' Cup Classic (Alphabet Soup)

ASPINWALL
1949: Del Mar Handicap (Top's Boy)

ASSAGAI
1947: San Carlos Handicap (Texas Sandman)

ASSERT
1998: Hollywood Turf Handicap (Storm Trooper)

ASTERUS
1952: Trenton Handicap (Ken)
1953: Fall Highweight Handicap (Kaster)

AURELIUS II
1993: Breeders' Cup Juvenile (Brocco)
1994: Santa Anita Derby (Brocco)

AUREOLE
1985: Rothmans International Stakes (Nassipour)

AVATAR
1993: Yellow Ribbon Stakes (Possibly Perfect)
1994: Santa Barbara Handicap (Possibly Perfect)
1995: Gamely Handicap (Possibly Perfect)
Ramona Handicap (Possibly Perfect)
Beverly D. Stakes (Possibly Perfect)

BABAS FABLES
1998: Hollywood Turf Cup (Lazy Lode)
1999: Hollywood Turf Cup (Lazy Lode)

BAGDAD
1977: Arlington Classic Inv. Handicap (Private Thoughts)
1980: Turf Classic (Anifa)
1981: Alabama Stakes (Prismatical)

BAHRAM
1950: Santa Anita Handicap (Noor)
San Juan Capistrano Handicap (Noor)
Golden Gate Handicap (Noor)
American Handicap (Noor)
Hollywood Gold Cup (Noor)
1954: Blue Grass Stakes (Goyamo)
1955: Santa Anita Handicap (Poona II)
1961: Grey Lag Handicap (Mail Order)
1967: Canadian Int. Championship (He's a Smoothie)
1968: Hialeah Turf Cup (He's a Smoothie)

BAILJUMPER
2002: Jim Dandy Stakes (Medaglia d'Oro)
Travers Stakes (Medaglia d'Oro)
2003: Strub Stakes (Medaglia d'Oro)
Oaklawn Handicap (Medaglia d'Oro)
Whitney Handicap (Medaglia d'Oro)

BAILLAMONT
2002: NetJets Breeders' Cup Mile (Domedriver)

BALD EAGLE
1977: Canadian International Championship (Exceller)
1978: Hollywood Gold Cup (Exceller)
Jockey Club Gold Cup (Exceller)
Hollywood Invitational Handicap (Exceller)
Sunset Handicap (Exceller)
Oak Tree Invitational Stakes (Exceller)
San Juan Capistrano Handicap (Exceller)
1986: Norfolk Stakes (Capote)
Breeders' Cup Juvenile (Capote)

BALDSKI
1995: Super Derby (Mecke)
1996: Early Times Turf Classic (Mecke)
Arlington Million (Mecke)
1997: Matron Stakes (Beautiful Pleasure)
1999: Personal Ensign Handicap (Beautiful Pleasure)
Beldame Stakes (Beautiful Pleasure)
Breeders' Cup Distaff (Beautiful Pleasure)
2000: Hempstead Handicap (Beautiful Pleasure)
Personal Ensign Handicap (Beautiful Pleasure)
2003: Frank J. De Francis Memorial Dash (A Huevo)

BALLADIER
1951: Kentucky Jockey Club Stakes (Sub Fleet)
1952: Matron Stakes (Is Proud)
1953: Hawthorne Gold Cup (Sub Fleet)
1959: Kentucky Jockey Club Stakes (Oil Wick)

BALLYDAM
1968: Ohio Derby (Te Vega)

BALLYDONNELL
1978: Metropolitan Handicap (Cox's Ridge)
Oaklawn Handicap (Cox's Ridge)

BALLYMOSS
1968: Belmont Stakes (Stage Door Johnny)
Dwyer Handicap (Stage Door Johnny)

BALLYOGAN
1961: Santa Anita Derby (Four-and-Twenty)
Cinema Handicap (Four-and-Twenty)
Hollywood Derby (Four-and-Twenty)
1962: San Fernando Stakes (Four-and-Twenty)
Santa Anita Maturity (Four-and-Twenty)
San Carlos Handicap (Four-and-Twenty)

BALUARTE
1960: Manhattan Handicap (Don Poggio)
Gallant Fox Handicap (Don Poggio)
1961: Monmouth Handicap (Don Poggio)

BALZAC
1993: Jerome Handicap (Schossberg)
1995: Philip H. Iselin Handicap (Schossberg)

BAMBURE
1983: Santa Margarita Handicap (Marimbula)

BANNER SPORT
1994: Vanity Handicap (Potridee)

BARACHOIS
1989: Hollywood Starlet Stakes (Cheval Volant)

BARBIZON
1976: Hopeful Stakes (Banquet Table)
1977: Del Mar Debutante Stakes (Extravagant)
1979: Metropolitan Handicap (State Dinner)
Suburban Handicap (State Dinner)
Century Handicap (State Dinner)
1980: Whitney Stakes (State Dinner)

BARBS DELIGHT
1985: Apple Blossom Handicap (Sefa's Beauty)

BAR EL GHAZAL
1959: Brooklyn Handicap (Babu)

BAR LE DUC
1974: Malibu Stakes (Ancient Title)
San Fernando Stakes (Ancient Title)
Charles H. Strub Stakes (Ancient Title)
1975: Californian Stakes (Ancient Title)
Hollywood Gold Cup (Ancient Title)
Whitney Handicap (Ancient Title)
1976: Californian Stakes (Ancient Title)
1977: Del Mar Handicap (Ancient Title)
San Antonio Stakes (Ancient Title)

BARONIUS
1999: Beverly Hills Handicap (Virginie)

BARRE GRANITE
1955: Kentucky Jockey Club Stakes (Royal Sting)

BARRYDOWN
1987: Norfolk Stakes (Saratoga Passage)

BATONNIER
1999: Del Mar Oaks (Tout Charmant)
2000: Matriarch Stakes (Tout Charmant)

BATTLEFIELD
1964: Ladies Handicap (Steeple Jill)
1965: Delaware Handicap (Steeple Jill)
Vineland Handicap (Steeple Jill)
Lawrence Realization Stakes (Munden Point)
1966: Gallant Fox Handicap (Munden Point)
1967: Manhattan Handicap (Munden Point)
1969: Everglades Stakes (Arts and Letters)
Blue Grass Stakes (Arts and Letters)
Belmont Stakes (Arts and Letters)
Travers Stakes (Arts and Letters)
Metropolitan Handicap (Arts and Letters)
Woodward Stakes (Arts and Letters)
Jockey Club Gold Cup (Arts and Letters)
1970: Alcibiades Stakes (Patelin)
Selima Stakes (Patelin)
Grey Lag Handicap (Arts and Letters)

BATTLE JOINED
1976: Mother Goose Stakes (Girl in Love)

BAYBROOK
1974: Del Mar Futurity (Diabolo)
1975: California Derby (Diabolo)

BAYOU BOURG
1985: Santa Barbara Handicap (Fact Finder)

BEAU GAR
1969: American Derby (Fast Hilarious)
1970: Michigan Mile and One-Eighth (Fast Hilarious)

BEAU GAR *(Continued)*
1971: Gulfstream Park Handicap (Fast Hilarious)
1973: Jerome Handicap (Step Nicely)
Whitney Stakes (Onion)

BEAU GENIUS
1999: Arkansas Derby (Certain)

BEAU MAX
1968: Matron Stakes (Gallant Bloom)
Gardenia Stakes (Gallant Bloom)
1969: Monmouth Oaks (Gallant Bloom)
Gazelle Handicap (Gallant Bloom)
Spinster Stakes (Gallant Bloom)
1970: Santa Margarita Handicap (Gallant Bloom)

BEAU PERE
1947: Hollywood Gold Cup (Cover Up)
Sunset Handicap (Cover Up)
1949: Santa Margarita Handicap (Lurline B.)
1951: Westerner Stakes (Grantor)
Del Mar Derby (Grantor)
1952: Del Mar Handicap (Grantor)
1955: Santa Anita Derby (Swaps)
Kentucky Derby (Swaps)
Westerner Stakes (Swaps)
American Derby (Swaps)
Californian Stakes (Swaps)
Arlington Lassie Stakes (Judy Rullah)
1956: Inglewood Handicap (Swaps)
American Handicap (Swaps)
Hollywood Gold Cup (Swaps)
Sunset Handicap (Swaps)
Washington Park Handicap (Swaps)
Delaware Handicap (Flower Bowl)
Ladies Handicap (Flower Bowl)
1957: Hialeah Turf Handicap (Jabneh)
1958: Cinema Handicap (The Shoe)
1959: Display Handicap (Beau Diable)
1961: Futurity Stakes (Cyane)
1962: Dwyer Handicap (Cyane)

BEAU PORT
1959: Arlington Matron Handicap (Wiggle II)

BEAU PURPLE
1981: Meadowlands Cup (Princelet)

BEAU REPAIRE
1979: Bay Meadows Handicap (Leonotis)

BEAU'S EAGLE
2001: Arlington Million (Silvano)

BEEKEEPER
1988: San Juan Capistrano 'Cap (Great Communicator)
Breeders' Cup Turf (Great Communicator)
Hollywood Turf Cup (Great Communicator)
1989: Hollywood Turf Handicap (Great Communicator)

BEHAVE YOURSELF
1950: Firenze Handicap (Red Camelia)
New Orleans Handicap (Red Camelia)

BEL AETHEL
1954: Ohio Derby (Timely Tip)

BEL BOLIDE
1997: Jerome Handicap (Richter Scale)
2000: Frank J. De Francis Memorial Dash (Richter Scale)

BELFONDS
1955: Champagne Stakes (Beau Fond)

BELIEVE IT
1995: Alabama Stakes (Pretty Discreet)
1997: Hollywood Futurity (Real Quiet)
1998: Kentucky Derby (Real Quiet)
Preakness Stakes (Real Quiet)
1999: Pimlico Special (Real Quiet)
Sempra Energy Hollywood Gold Cup (Real Quiet)

BELVILLE WOOD
1969: Cinema Handicap (Noholme Jr.)

BE MY GUEST
2000: Sword Dancer Invitational Handicap (John's Call)
Turf Classic (John's Call)

BERING
2003: Eddie Read Handicap (Special Ring)

BERKLEY PRINCE
1989: Gulfstream Park Handicap (Slew City Slew)
Oaklawn Handicap (Slew City Slew)

BERNBOROUGH
1962: Ladies Handicap (Royal Patrice)
1966: Illinois Derby (Michigan Avenue)
1968: Monmouth Invitational Handicap (Balustrade)

BERSEEM
1975: San Fernando Stakes (Stardust Mel)
Charles H. Strub Stakes (Stardust Mel)
Santa Anita Handicap (Stardust Mel)

BESOMER
1974: Ohio Derby (Stonewalk)
Jerome Handicap (Stonewalk)
1985: California Derby (Hajji's Treasure)

BET BIG
1998: Cigar Mile Handicap (Sir Bear)
1999: Metropolitan Handicap (Sir Bear)
2001: Gulfstream Park Handicap (Sir Bear)

BETTER SELF
1964: Demoiselle Stakes (Discipline)
1965: Acorn Stakes (Ground Control)
1966: Cowdin Stakes (Dr. Fager)
1967: Gotham Stakes (Dr. Fager)
Withers Stakes (Dr. Fager)
Arlington Classic (Dr. Fager)
Hawthorne Gold Cup (Dr. Fager)
Vosburgh Handicap (Dr. Fager)
1968: Californian Stakes (Dr. Fager)
Suburban Handicap (Dr. Fager)
Washington Park Handicap (Dr. Fager)
Vosburgh Handicap (Dr. Fager)
Whitney Stakes (Dr. Fager)
United Nations Handicap (Dr. Fager)
1969: Arlington-Washington Futurity (Silent Screen)
Cowdin Stakes (Silent Screen)
Champagne Stakes (Silent Screen)
Vosburgh Handicap (Ta Wee)
1970: Matron Stakes (Bonnie and Gay)
American Derby (The Pruner)

BICKER
1985: Santa Susana Stakes (Fran's Valentine)
Kentucky Oaks (Fran's Valentine)
Hollywood Oaks (Fran's Valentine)

BIG GAME
1959: Hialeah Turf Cup (Tudor Era)
Man o' War Handicap (Tudor Era)
1960: New Orleans Handicap (Tudor Era)
1963: San Juan Capistrano Handicap (Pardao)

BIG LARK
1999: Eddie Read Handicap (Joe Who)

BIG SPRUCE
1986: Charles H. Strub Stakes (Nostalgia's Star)

BIKALA
2001: Breeders' Cup Mile (Val Royal)

BILLINGS
1984: Illinois Derby (Delta Trace)

BIMELECH
1953: Ohio Derby (Find)
Grey Lag Handicap (Find)
Futurity Stakes (Porterhouse)
1954: Excelsior Handicap (Find)
Queens County Handicap (Find)
Everglades Stakes (Maharajah)
1955: Kentucky Oaks (Lalun)
Beldame Handicap (Lalun)
1956: New Orleans Handicap (Find)
Californian Stakes (Porterhouse)
1957: Inglewood Handicap (Find)
American Handicap (Find)
Sunset Handicap (Find)
Los Angeles Handicap (Porterhouse)
1961: Man o' War Handicap (Wise Ship)
1962: Breeders' Futurity (Ornamento)
Dixie Handicap (Wise Ship)
1963: Wood Memorial Stakes (No Robbery)
1965: New Orleans Handicap (Valiant Man)
Gulfstream Park Handicap (Ampose)
1970: Suburban Handicap (Barometer)

BIRIBI
1955: Gazelle Stakes (Manotick)
Ladies Handicap (Manotick)
1957: Molly Pitcher Handicap (Manotick)

BIRIKIL
1967: Gallant Fox Handicap (Niarkos)
San Juan Capistrano Handicap (Niarkos)
San Luis Rey Handicap (Niarkos)
1968: San Juan Capistrano Handicap (Niarkos)
1972: United Nations Handicap (Acclimatization)
1982: Santa Barbara Handicap (Ack's Secret)
Santa Margarita Handicap (Ack's Secret)

BISTOURI
1954: Del Mar Handicap (Stranglehold)

BIT OF IRELAND
1971: Oak Leaf Stakes (Sporting Lass)

BLACK PETER
1966: Display Handicap (Damelo II)

BLACK SERVANT
1949: Princess Pat Stakes (Here's Hoping)

BLACK TONEY
1946: Gazelle Stakes (Bridal Flower)
New Castle Handicap (Bridal Flower)
Beldame Handicap (Bridal Flower)
Roamer Handicap (Bridal Flower)
1947: Hopeful Stakes (Relic)
Westchester Handicap (Bridal Flower)
1948: Tremont Stakes (The Admiral)
1956: Top Flight Handicap (Searching)
Diana Handicap (Searching)
Maskette Handicap (Searching)
1958: Molly Pitcher Handicap (Searching)
Diana Handicap (Searching)

BLADE
1985: Arlington-Washington Lassie Stakes (Family Style)
Frizette Stakes (Family Style)
1987: Del Mar Futurity (Lost Kitty)
La Canada Stakes (Family Style)

BLAZING COUNT
1984: Fountain of Youth Stakes (Darn That Alarm)
1986: Tropical Park Derby (Strong Performance)

BLENHEIM II
1948: Blue Grass Stakes (Coaltown)
Jerome Handicap (Coaltown)
1949: McLennan Handicap (Coaltown)
Widener Handicap (Coaltown)
Gulfstream Park Handicap (Coaltown)
Gallant Fox Handicap (Coaltown)
Stars and Stripes Handicap (Coaltown)
Arlington Handicap (Coaltown)
Washington Park Handicap (Coaltown)
Kentucky Derby (Ponder)
Arlington Classic (Ponder)
American Derby (Ponder)
Lawrence Realization Stakes (Ponder)
Jockey Club Gold Cup (Ponder)
Kentucky Oaks (Wistful)
Pimlico Oaks (Wistful)
Coaching Club American Oaks (Wistful)
1950: San Antonio Handicap (Ponder)
Arlington Handicap (Ponder)
Santa Anita Maturity (Ponder)
Cinema Handicap (Great Circle)
Del Mar Derby (Great Circle)
Astoria Stakes (Sungari)
1951: Arlington Futurity (Hill Gail)
Santa Anita Maturity (Great Circle)
1952: Arlington Classic (Mark-Ye-Well)
American Derby (Mark-Ye-Well)
Lawrence Realization Stakes (Mark-Ye-Well)
Santa Anita Derby (Hill Gail)
Kentucky Derby (Hill Gail)
Sunset Handicap (Great Circle)
1953: Santa Anita Handicap (Mark-Ye-Well)
Santa Anita Maturity (Mark-Ye-Well)
Santa Margarita Handicap (Spanish Cream)
Westerner Stakes (Rejected)
1954: Santa Anita Handicap (Rejected)
American Handicap (Rejected)
Hawthorne Gold Cup (Rejected)
San Antonio Handicap (Mark-Ye-Well)
1955: Hollywood Gold Cup (Rejected)
1956: Matron Stakes (Romanita)

1957: Black Helen Handicap (Clear Dawn)
Coaching Club American Oaks (Willamette)
Monmouth Oaks (Romanita)
Black Helen Handicap (Amoret)
Ohio Derby (Manteau)
1958: Coaching Club American Oaks (A Glitter)
Monmouth Oaks (A Glitter)
Tropical Handicap (St. Amour II)
Gallant Fox Handicap (Admiral Vee)
1959: Black Helen Handicap (Rosewood)
1960: Futurity Stakes (Little Tumbler)
Arkansas Derby (Spring Broker)
Santa Anita Handicap (Linmold)
1962: Jerome Handicap (Black Beard)
1965: United Nations Handicap (Parka)
1966: Kentucky Derby (Kauai King)
Preakness Stakes (Kauai King)
1972: Hialeah Turf Cup (Gleaming)
1973: Hialeah Turf Cup (Gleaming)

BLESS ME

1958: Arlington Lassie Stakes (Dark Vintage)

BLUE LARKSPUR

1946: Arlington Futurity (Cosmic Bomb)
Cowdin Stakes (Cosmic Bomb)
Frizette Stakes (Bimlette)
Vanity Handicap (Be Faithful)
1947: Discovery Handicap (Cosmic Bomb)
Lawrence Realization Stakes (Cosmic Bomb)
Roamer Handicap (Cosmic Bomb)
Trenton Handicap (Cosmic Bomb)
Arlington Futurity (Piet)
Hawthorne Gold Cup (Be Faithful)
1950: Alabama Stakes (Busanda)
Whitney Stakes (Piet)
1951: Top Flight Handicap (Busanda)
New Castle Handicap (Busanda)
Suburban Handicap (Busanda)
Arlington Classic (Hall of Fame)
American Derby (Hall of Fame)
San Antonio Handicap (All Blue)
1952: Kentucky Oaks (Real Delight)
Black-Eyed Susan Stakes (Real Delight)
Coaching Club American Oaks (Real Delight)
Arlington Matron Stakes (Real Delight)
Beldame Handicap (Real Delight)
Discovery Handicap (Ancestor)
1953: Kentucky Oaks (Bubbley)
Arlington Matron Handicap (Real Delight)
Santa Anita Derby (Chanlea)
Cinema Handicap (Ali's Gem)
Jerome Handicap (Navy Page)
Golden Gate Handicap (Fleet Bird)
1954: Starlet Stakes (Blue Ruler)
Del Mar Futurity (Blue Ruler)
Breeders' Futurity (Brother Tex)
Vanity Handicap (Bubbley)
Tropical Handicap (Capeador)
Michigan Mile (Spur On)
Sunset Handicap (Fleet Bird)
Hialeah Turf Handicap (Picador)
1956: Kentucky Oaks (Princess Turia)
Acorn Stakes (Princess Turia)
Spinaway Stakes (Alanesian)
Firenze Handicap (Blue Banner)
1957: Delaware Handicap (Princess Turia)
1958: Los Angeles Handicap (How Now)
American Handicap (How Now)
Brooklyn Handicap (Cohoes)
Whitney Stakes (Cohoes)
Travers Stakes (Piano Jim)
Widener Handicap (Oligarchy)
1959: Lawrence Realization Stakes (Middle Brother)

BLUE PAIR

1964: Saratoga Special (Sadair)
Arlington-Washington Futurity (Sadair)
Garden State Stakes (Sadair)
Pimlico Futurity (Sadair)

BLUE PETER

1955: Saranac Handicap (Saratoga)
1959: Hollywood Derby (Bagdad)
1960: San Antonio Handicap (Bagdad)
Inglewood Handicap (Bagdad)
1970: Acorn Stakes (Cathy Honey)
Ladies Handicap (Cathy Honey)

BLUE PRINCE

1970: Gardenia Stakes (Eggy)
1977: Matron Stakes (Lakeville Miss)
Frizette Stakes (Lakeville Miss)
Selima Stakes (Lakeville Miss)
Hollywood Oaks (Steve's Friend)
1978: Man o' War Stakes (Waya)
Turf Classic (Waya)
Coaching Club American Oaks (Lakeville Miss)
Santa Barbara Handicap (Kittyluck)
1979: Top Flight Handicap (Waya)
Beldame Stakes (Waya)
Santa Barbara Handicap (Waya)
1980: Alcibiades Stakes (Sweet Revenge)

BLUE SWORDS

1960: Sapling Stakes (Hail to Reason)
Hopeful Stakes (Hail to Reason)
1964: Canadian Championship Stakes (Will I Rule)
Dixie Handicap (Will I Rule)
1965: Kentucky Jockey Club Stakes (War Censor)
1966: Ohio Derby (War Censor)
1967: Hialeah Turf Cup (War Censor)
Pan American Handicap (War Censor)
Dixie Handicap (War Censor)

BLUE TRAIN

1961: San Felipe Handicap (Flutterby)

BLUSHING GROOM

1991: Maskette Stakes (Queena)
Ruffian Handicap (Queena)
1997: Jim Dandy Stakes (Awesome Again)
1998: Whitney Handicap (Awesome Again)
Breeders' Cup Classic (Awesome Again)
1999: Yellow Ribbon Stakes (Spanish Fern)
2000: Charles Whittingham Handicap (White Heart)
Breeders' Cup Juvenile (Macho Uno)
2001: Kentucky Oaks (Flute)
Alabama Stakes (Flute)
Woodford Reserve Turf Classic (White Heart)

BOATSWAIN

1955: Cinema Handicap (Guilton Madero)

BOB'S DUSTY

2002: Fountain of Youth Stakes (Booklet)

BOIS ROUSSEL

1959: Hawthorne Gold Cup (Day Court)
1963: Hollywood Oaks (Delhi Maid)
1966: Cinema Handicap (Drin)
1967: Charles H. Strub Stakes (Drin)

BOLD BIDDER

1980: Hopeful Stakes (Tap Shoes)
Futurity Stakes (Tap Shoes)
1981: Flamingo Stakes (Tap Shoes)
1982: Del Mar Debutante Stakes (Landaluce)
Oak Leaf Stakes (Landaluce)
1983: Top Flight Handicap (Adept)
1985: Sorority Stakes (Lazer Show)
1991: Santa Anita Derby (Dinard)
1992: Arlington-Washington Lassie Stakes (Eliza)
Breeders' Cup Juvenile Fillies (Eliza)
1993: Santa Anita Oaks (Eliza)

BOLD COMMANDER

1976: Demoiselle Stakes (Bring Out the Band)
1977: Acorn Stakes (Bring Out the Band)
1982: Belmont Stakes (Conquistador Cielo)
Dwyer Stakes (Conquistador Cielo)
Metropolitan Handicap (Conquistador Cielo)
1991: Matron Stakes (Anh Duong)

BOLD DISCOVERY

1982: Arlington Classic (Wolfie's Rascal)
American Derby (Wolfie's Rascal)

BOLD GALLANT

1963: Hollywood Juvenile Championship (Nevada Bin)

BOLD HITTER

1982: Illinois Derby (Star Gallant)

BOLD HOUR

1988: Santa Anita Oaks (Winning Colors)
Santa Anita Derby (Winning Colors)
Kentucky Derby (Winning Colors)
1993: American Derby (Explosive Red)
Hollywood Derby (Explosive Red)
1997: Canadian Int. Championship (Chief Bearhart)
Breeders' Cup Turf (Chief Bearhart)
1998: Manhattan Handicap (Chief Bearhart)

BOLD IRISHMAN

1959: Spinaway Stakes (Irish Jay)
1960: Acorn Stakes (Irish Jay)

BOLD LAD

1978: Remsen Stakes (Instrument Landing)
1979: Wood Memorial Stakes (Instrument Landing)
1980: American Derby (Hurry Up Blue)
1981: Gulfstream Park Handicap (Hurry Up Blue)

BOLDNESIAN

1978: American Derby (Nasty and Bold)
Brooklyn Handicap (Nasty and Bold)
Breeders' Futurity (Strike Your Colors)
1985: Santa Anita Derby (Skywalker)
Arlington Classic (Smile)
1986: Breeders' Cup Sprint (Smile)
Breeders' Cup Classic (Skywalker)
1991: Breeders' Cup Turf (Miss Alleged)
Hollywood Turf Cup (Miss Alleged)

BOLD REASON

1992: Kentucky Oaks (Luv Me Luv Me Not)

BOLD REASONING

1987: Oak Tree Invitational Stakes (Allez Milord)

BOLD RULER

1969: Selima Stakes (Predictable)
1971: Ladies Handicap (Sea Saga)
1972: Florida Derby (Upper Case)
Wood Memorial Stakes (Upper Case)
Jockey Club Gold Cup (Autobiography)
San Fernando Stakes (Autobiography)
1974: San Antonio Stakes (Prince Dantan)
Santa Anita Handicap (Prince Dantan)
Maskette Handicap (Ponte Vecchio)
Withers Stakes (Accipiter)
1975: Hollywood Derby (Intrepid Hero)
Secretariat Stakes (Intrepid Hero)
Remsen Stakes (Hang Ten)
1976: Frizette Stakes (Sensational)
Selima Stakes (Sensational)
United Nations Handicap (Intrepid Hero)
1977: Ladies Handicap (Sensational)
Illinois Derby (Flag Officer)
1978: Century Handicap (Landscaper)
American Handicap (Effervescing)
1980: Pan American Handicap (Flitalong)
1982: Coaching Club American Oaks (Christmas Past)
Ruffian Handicap (Christmas Past)
1983: Gulfstream Park Handicap (Christmas Past)
1985: La Canada Stakes (Mitterand)
1988: Gotham Stakes (Private Terms)
Wood Memorial Stakes (Private Terms)

BOLD VENTURE

1950: Manhattan Handicap (One Hitter)
Pimlico Special (One Hitter)
1951: Massachusetts Handicap (One Hitter)
Whitney Stakes (One Hitter)
1952: Suburban Handicap (One Hitter)
Monmouth Handicap (One Hitter)
1954: Westerner Stakes (Fault Free)
1964: Coaching Club American Oaks (Miss Cavandish)
Monmouth Oaks (Miss Cavandish)
Alabama Stakes (Miss Cavandish)
Grey Lag Handicap (Saidam)
1966: Suburban Handicap (Buffle)
1973: Woodward Stakes (Prove Out)
Jockey Club Gold Cup (Prove Out)
1974: Grey Lag Handicap (Prove Out)

BOLERO

1963: Hopeful Stakes (Traffic)
Spinaway Stakes (Petite Rouge)
1973: Manhattan Handicap (London Company)
1974: Pan American Handicap (London Company)
1977: Marlboro Cup Handicap (Proud Birdie)

BOLINAS BOY

1984: Matron Stakes (Fiesta Lady)
1985: Hutcheson Stakes (Banner Bob)
Jim Beam Stakes (Banner Bob)

BOOZ

1990: Oak Tree Invitational Stakes (Rial)

BOSSUET

1961: Spinaway Stakes (Cicada)
Matron Stakes (Cicada)
Frizette Stakes (Cicada)

BOSSUET *(Continued)*
Gardenia Stakes (Cicada)
1962: Kentucky Oaks (Cicada)
Acorn Stakes (Cicada)
Mother Goose Stakes (Cicada)
Beldame Stakes (Cicada)

BOSTON DOGE
1971: Sanford Stakes (Cohasset Tribe)

BOZZETTO
1970: Lawrence Realization Stakes (Kling Kling)

BRANTOME
1958: Starlet Stakes (Tomy Lee)
Del Mar Futurity (Tomy Lee)
1959: Blue Grass Stakes (Tomy Lee)
Kentucky Derby (Tomy Lee)

BRAVE SHOT
1993: San Felipe Stakes (Corby)

BRAVO
1986: Breeders' Cup Juvenile Fillies (Brave Raj)

BRAZADO
1954: Belmont Stakes (High Gun)
Dwyer Stakes (High Gun)
Jockey Club Gold Cup (High Gun)
Manhattan Handicap (High Gun)
1955: Metropolitan Handicap (High Gun)
Brooklyn Handicap (High Gun)
1956: Delaware Oaks (Dotted Line)
1957: Vineland Handicap (Dotted Line)
1959: Coaching Club American Oaks (Resaca)
Delaware Oaks (Resaca)
Man o' War Handicap (Dotted Line)
1961: Selima Stakes (Tamarona)
1962: Vineland Handicap (Tamarona)

BRIARTIC
1988: Ladies Handicap (Banker's Lady)
1989: Top Flight Handicap (Banker's Lady)
1995: Coaching Club American Oaks (Golden Bri)
1996: Vosburgh Stakes (Langfuhr)
1997: Carter Handicap (Langfuhr)
Metropolitan Handicap (Langfuhr)

BRIGADIER GERARD
1985: Sunset Handicap (Kings Island)
1987: Laurel Futurity (Antiqua)

BRIGHT KNIGHT
1946: Fall Highweight Handicap (Cassis)
1948: Louisiana Derby (Bovard)
1953: Remsen Handicap (Galdar)

BRIG O' DOON
1947: Longacres Mile (Hank H.)
1956: Vanity Handicap (Mary Machree)

BRITISH EMPIRE
1967: Michigan Mile and One-Eighth (Estreno II)
1968: Pan American Handicap (Estreno II)

BROADSIDE
1952: Black Helen Handicap (Roman Miss)
1953: Saranac Handicap (First Aid)
Aqueduct Handicap (First Aid)
1955: Whitney Stakes (First Aid)

BROCHAZO
1961: Gulfstream Park Handicap (Tudor Way)

BROOKFIELD
1963: Lawrence Realization Stakes (Dean Carl)
Roamer Handicap (Dean Carl)
Display Handicap (Dean Carl)
1969: Massachusetts Handicap (Beau Marker)

BROOMS
1948: Santa Anita Maturity (Flashco)

BROWN KING
1954: Louisiana Derby (Gigantic)
1955: San Antonio Handicap (Gigantic)
Carter Handicap (Bobby Brocato)
1956: Santa Anita Handicap (Bobby Brocato)
San Juan Capistrano Handicap (Bobby Brocato)
1958: California Derby (Nice Guy)
New Orleans Handicap (Tenacious)
1959: Del Mar Futurity (Azure's Orphan)
New Orleans Handicap (Tenacious)
1964: San Fernando Stakes (Nevada Battler)

BRUMEAUX
1954: Arlington Handicap (Stan)
Hialeah Turf Handicap (Stan)

BRYAN G.
1973: Ladies Handicap (Wakefield Miss)

BUBBLING OVER
1948: Arlington Futurity (Mr. Busher)
1949: Cowdin Stakes (Hill Prince)
1950: Wood Memorial Stakes (Hill Prince)
Withers Stakes (Hill Prince)
Preakness Stakes (Hill Prince)
American Derby (Hill Prince)
Jerome Handicap (Hill Prince)
Jockey Club Gold Cup (Hill Prince)
Sunset Handicap (Hill Prince)
1951: New York Handicap (Hill Prince)
1952: San Juan Capistrano Handicap (Intent)
Santa Anita Maturity (Intent)
1953: San Juan Capistrano Handicap (Intent)
1956: Roamer Handicap (Third Brother)
1958: Hopeful Stakes (First Landing)
Champagne Stakes (First Landing)
Garden State Stakes (First Landing)
1959: Everglades Stakes (First Landing)
1960: Monmouth Handicap (First Landing)
Santa Anita Maturity (First Landing)
Man o' War Stakes (Harmonizing)

BUCKAROO
1994: Jerome Handicap (Prenup)
2002: Philip H. Iselin Handicap (Cat's at Home)

BUCKFINDER
1991: Man o' War Stakes (Solar Splendor)
Turf Classic (Solar Splendor)
1992: Hollywood Gold Cup (Sultry Song)
Whitney Handicap (Sultry Song)
Woodward Stakes (Sultry Song)
Man o' War Stakes (Solar Splendor)

BUCKPASSER
1977: Remsen Stakes (Believe It)
1978: Wood Memorial Stakes (Believe It)
1979: Belmont Stakes (Coastal)
Dwyer Stakes (Coastal)
Monmouth Invitational Handicap (Coastal)
Laurel Futurity (Plugged Nickle)
Remsen Stakes (Plugged Nickle)
1980: Florida Derby (Plugged Nickle)
Wood Memorial Stakes (Plugged Nickle)
Vosburgh Stakes (Plugged Nickle)
Widener Handicap (Private Account)
Gulfstream Park Handicap (Private Account)
Louisiana Downs Handicap (It's True)
1982: Haskell Invitational Handicap (Wavering Monarch)
1983: Wood Memorial Stakes (Slew O' Gold)
Woodward Stakes (Slew O'Gold)
Jockey Club Gold Cup (Slew O' Gold)
Beldame Stakes (Dance Number)
San Fernando Stakes (Wavering Monarch)
1984: Whitney Handicap (Slew O' Gold)
Woodward Stakes (Slew O' Gold)
Marlboro Cup Handicap (Slew O' Gold)
Jockey Club Gold Cup (Slew O' Gold)
1985: Man o' War Stakes (Win)
1988: Peter Pan Stakes (Seeking the Gold)
Dwyer Stakes (Seeking the Gold)
Super Derby (Seeking the Gold)
Cowdin Stakes (Easy Goer)
Champagne Stakes (Easy Goer)
Breeders' Futurity (Fast Play)
Remsen Stakes (Fast Play)
Vosburgh Stakes (Mining)
1989: Gotham Stakes (Easy Goer)
Wood Memorial Stakes (Easy Goer)
Belmont Stakes (Easy Goer)
Whitney Handicap (Easy Goer)
Travers Stakes (Easy Goer)
Woodward Handicap (Easy Goer)
Jockey Club Gold Cup (Easy Goer)
1990: Hollywood Oaks (Patches)
Suburban Handicap (Easy Goer)
1991: Alabama Stakes (Versailles Treaty)
1992: Go for Wand Stakes (Easy Now)
Ruffian Handicap (Versailles Treaty)
Flower Bowl Handicap (Christiecat)
1995: Turf Classic (Turk Passer)
1997: Belmont Stakes (Touch Gold)
Haskell Invitational Handicap (Touch Gold)

BUFFALO LARK
1991: Del Mar Futurity (Bertrando)
Norfolk Stakes (Bertrando)
1992: San Felipe Stakes (Bertrando)
1993: Pacific Classic (Bertrando)
Woodward Stakes (Bertrando)

BULL BRIER
1972: Carter Handicap (Leematt)

BULL DANDY
1971: Monmouth Invitational Handicap (West Coast Scout)
Woodward Stakes (West Coast Scout)
1972: Amory L. Haskell Handicap (West Coast Scout)
1973: Gulfstream Park Handicap (West Coast Scout)
Amory L. Haskell Handicap (West Coast Scout)

BULL DOG
1946: Demoiselle Stakes (Carolyn A.)
Acorn Stakes (Earshot)
Withers Stakes (Hampden)
1947: Louisiana Derby (Carolyn A.)
New Orleans Handicap (Earshot)
1948: Princess Pat Stakes (Sequence)
Firenze Handicap (Carolyn A.)
1949: Queens County Handicap (Three Rings)
Monmouth Handicap (Three Rings)
Westchester Handicap (Three Rings)
1950: Demoiselle Stakes (Aunt Jinny)
Selima Stakes (Aunt Jinny)
McLennan Handicap (Three Rings)
Queens County Handicap (Three Rings)
Molly Pitcher Handicap (Danger Ahead)
1951: Sapling Stakes (Landesair)
Futurity Stakes (Tom Fool)
Santa Anita Derby (Rough'n Tumble)
1952: McLennan Handicap (Spartan Valor)
Widener Handicap (Spartan Valor)
Excelsior Handicap (Spartan Valor)
Gallant Fox Handicap (Spartan Valor)
Jerome Handicap (Tom Fool)
Grey Lag Handicap (Tom Fool)
1953: Metropolitan Handicap (Tom Fool)
Suburban Handicap (Tom Fool)
Carter Handicap (Tom Fool)
Brooklyn Handicap (Tom Fool)
Whitney Stakes (Tom Fool)
Pimlico Special (Tom Fool)
Kentucky Derby (Dark Star)
Tropical Park Handicap (Spartan Valor)
1954: Fall Highweight Handicap (Pet Bully)
Washington Park Handicap (Pet Bully)
Woodward Stakes (Pet Bully)
William P. Kyne Handicap (Imbros)
Californian Stakes (Imbros)
Sapling Stakes (Royal Coinage)
Kentucky Oaks (Fascinator)
1955: Vanity Handicap (Countess Fleet)
Arlington Matron Handicap (Arab Actress)
California Derby (Trackmaster)
1956: Metropolitan Handicap (Midafternoon)
Massachusetts Handicap (Midafternoon)
Display Handicap (Midafternoon)
Westerner Stakes (Count of Honor)
Santa Anita Maturity (Trackmaster)
1958: Fall Highweight Handicap (Bull Strength)
1960: Massachusetts Handicap (Talent Show)
1961: American Handicap (Prince Blessed)
Hollywood Gold Cup (Prince Blessed)
Champagne Stakes (Donut King)
Bowling Green Handicap (Dead Center)
1965: Pan American Handicap (Cool Prince)
1968: Widener Handicap (Sette Bello)

BULLIN
1981: Arkansas Derby (Bold Ego)

BULL LEA
1949: Champagne Stakes (Theory)
1951: Princess Pat Stakes (A Gleam)
1952: Hollywood Oaks (A Gleam)
Cinema Handicap (A Gleam)
Westerner Stakes (A Gleam)
Selima Stakes (Tritium)
1956: Arlington Lassie Stakes (Leallah)
Alcibiades Stakes (Leallah)
Trenton Handicap (Bardstown)
Garden State Stakes (Barbizon)

1957: Matron Stakes (Idun)
Gardenia Stakes (Idun)
Frizette Stakes (Idun)
Arlington Matron Handicap (Pucker Up)
Beldame Handicap (Pucker Up)
Washington Park Handicap (Pucker Up)
Tropical Handicap (Bardstown)
Widener Handicap (Bardstown)
Gulfstream Park Handicap (Bardstown)
1958: Everglades Stakes (Tim Tam)
Flamingo Stakes (Tim Tam)
Florida Derby (Tim Tam)
Kentucky Derby (Tim Tam)
Preakness Stakes (Tim Tam)
Arlington Futurity (Restless Wind)
Washington Park Futurity (Restless Wind)
Mother Goose Stakes (Idun)
Gazelle Handicap (Idun)
1959: San Felipe Handicap (Finnegan)
California Derby (Finnegan)
Tropical Park Handicap (Bardstown)
Widener Handicap (Bardstown)
Saratoga Special (Irish Lancer)
Maskette Handicap (Idun)
1960: Tropical Park Handicap (On-and-On)
McLennan Handicap (On-and-On)
Brooklyn Handicap (On-and-On)
Spinaway Stakes (Good Move)
Selima Stakes (Good Move)
Sorority Stakes (Apatontheback)
Los Angeles Handicap (Finnegan)
1961: Gotham Stakes (Ambiopoise)
Jersey Derby (Ambiopoise)
Santa Margarita Handicap (Sister Antoine)
Tropical Park Handicap (Bourbon Prince)
Display Handicap (Hillsborough)
1962: Pimlico Futurity (Right Proud)
Coaching Club American Oaks (Bramalea)
Santa Anita Derby (Royal Attack)
Grey Lag Handicap (Ambiopoise)
Bougainvillea Handicap (Eurasia)
1963: Pimlico Futurity (Quadrangle)
1964: Wood Memorial Stakes (Quadrangle)
Belmont Stakes (Quadrangle)
Dwyer Handicap (Quadrangle)
Travers Stakes (Quadrangle)
Lawrence Realization Stakes (Quadrangle)
Black Helen Handicap (Princess Arle)
1965: Cowdin Stakes (Advocator)
1966: Hialeah Turf Cup (Kentucky Jug)
1967: Seminole Handicap (Advocator)
1971: Florida Derby (Eastern Fleet)
Manhattan Handicap (Happy Way)
1984: Preakness Stakes (Gate Dancer)
Super Derby (Gate Dancer)

BULL REIGH
1964: Vanity Handicap (Star Maggie)
1965: Spinster Stakes (Star Maggie)

BULLREIGHZAC
1968: Del Mar Debutante Stakes (Fourth Round)

BULL VIC
1983: Fantasy Stakes (Brindy Brindy)

BULLY BOY
1970: Arlington Classic (Corn off the Cob)

BUNTING
1949: Louisiana Derby (Rookwood)

BUNTY'S FLIGHT
1981: Laurel Futurity (Deputy Minister)
Young America Stakes (Deputy Minister)

BUPERS
1976: Vosburgh Handicap (My Juliet)
1977: Michigan Mile and One-Eighth (My Juliet)

BURGOO KING
1952: Pimlico Futurity (Isasmoothie)
1953: Pimlico Futurity (Errard King)
Acorn Stakes (Secret Meeting)
1954: Arlington Classic (Errard King)
American Derby (Errard King)

BUSTED
1984: Hollywood Derby (Foscarini)
1991: Yellow Ribbon Stakes (Kostroma)
1992: Beverly D. Stakes (Kostroma)
Santa Barbara Handicap (Kostroma)

BUSTINO
1994: American Derby (Overbury)

BUSY AMERICAN
1948: Kentucky Jockey Club Stakes (Johns Joy)
1950: Marguerite Stakes (Carolina Queen)
1951: Saratoga Special (Cousin)
Hopeful Stakes (Cousin)

BUSY RIDGE
1969: New Orleans Handicap (Miracle Hill)

BUSY WIRE
1960: Champagne Stakes (Roving Minstrel)

BUY AND SELL
1964: Del Mar Debutante Stakes (Admirably)

BY JIMMINY
1959: Belmont Stakes (Sword Dancer)
Travers Stakes (Sword Dancer)
Metropolitan Handicap (Sword Dancer)
Monmouth Handicap (Sword Dancer)
Woodward Stakes (Sword Dancer)
Jockey Club Gold Cup (Sword Dancer)
1960: Grey Lag Handicap (Sword Dancer)
Suburban Handicap (Sword Dancer)
Woodward Stakes (Sword Dancer)
1970: Louisiana Derby (Jim's Alibhi)

BYMEABOND
1962: Hollywood Juvenile Championship (Y Flash)
1963: Cinema Handicap (Y Flash)
Hollywood Derby (Y Flash)

CAERLEON
1994: Santa Anita Handicap (Stuka)
1997: Californian Stakes (River Keen)
1999: Woodward Stakes (River Keen)
Jockey Club Gold Cup (River Keen)
2003: Flower Bowl Invitational Stakes (Dimitrova)

CALDARIUM
1967: Gazelle Handicap (Sweet Folly)
Ladies Handicap (Sweet Folly)

CALGARY BROOK
1974: Hopeful Stakes (The Bagel Prince)

CALL THE WITNESS
1974: Wood Memorial Stakes (Flip Sal)
1982: Travers Stakes (Runaway Groom)

CAMPFIRE
1954: Aqueduct Handicap (Crash Dive)

CANDY SPOTS
1978: Selima Stakes (Candy Eclair)
1981: California Derby (Always a Cinch)
1982: Marlboro Cup Handicap (Lemhi Gold)
Jockey Club Gold Cup (Lemhi Gold)
Sword Dancer Stakes (Lemhi Gold)
San Juan Capistrano Handicap (Lemhi Gold)

CANDY STRIPES
2003: Pacific Classic (Candy Ride)

CANNONADE
1984: Breeders' Futurity (Crater Fire)

CANOT
1959: Bowling Green Handicap (Bell Hop)

CAN'T WAIT
1950: Del Mar Futurity (Patch)

CANYONERO
1966: Pan American Handicap (Pillanlebun)

CAPOTE
1999: Norfolk Stakes (Dixie Union)
2000: Haskell Invitational Handicap (Dixie Union)
Malibu Stakes (Dixie Union)

CARACALLA
1964: Roamer Handicap (Point du Jour)

CARACOLERO
1986: Gamely Handicap (La Koumia)
1999: Walmac International Alcibiades Stakes (Scratch Pad)

CARO
1990: Meadowlands Cup (Great Normand)
1993: Santa Anita Handicap (Sir Beaufort)
1995: Futurity Stakes (Maria's Mon)
Champagne Stakes (Maria's Mon)
Santa Anita Handicap (Urgent Request)
Breeders' Cup Juvenile (Unbridled's Song)
1996: Florida Derby (Unbridled's Song)
Wood Memorial Stakes (Unbridled's Song)
1998: Hollywood Futurity (Tactical Cat)
2000: Preakness Stakes (Red Bullet)
Metropolitan Handicap (Yankee Victor)
2002: Eddie Read Handicap (Sarafan)

CARRAL
1999: Santa Maria Handicap (India Divina)

CARRIER PIGEON
1956: Gardenia Stakes (Magic Forest)

CARRY BACK
1979: Apple Blossom Handicap (Miss Baja)

CARUSO
1948: Pimlico Oaks (Scattered)
Coaching Club American Oaks (Scattered)
1958: Westerner Stakes (Strong Bay)

CARVIN II
1993: Turf Classic (Apple Tree)

CARWHITE
1990: Budweiser International Stakes (Fly Till Dawn)
1992: San Luis Rey Stakes (Fly Till Dawn)
San Juan Capistrano Handicap (Fly Till Dawn)

CASE ACE
1948: Garden State Stakes (Blue Peter)
Saratoga Special (Blue Peter)
Hopeful Stakes (Blue Peter)
Futurity Stakes (Blue Peter)
1951: Flamingo Stakes (Yildiz)
1952: Belmont Stakes (One Count)
Travers Stakes (One Count)
Jockey Club Gold Cup (One Count)
1957: New Orleans Handicap (Kingmaker)
Grey Lag Handicap (Kingmaker)
Whitney Stakes (Kingmaker)
1958: Pimlico Special (Vertex)
Trenton Handicap (Vertex)
1959: Gulfstream Park Handicap (Vertex)
John B. Campbell Handicap (Vertex)
Grey Lag Handicap (Vertex)
1963: Selima Stakes (My Card)

CASTEL FUSANO
1959: Vanity Handicap (Zev's Joy)

CAUCASUS
2000: Travers Stakes (Unshaded)

CAVALCADE
1951: Starlet Stakes (Prudy's Boy)

CAVAN
1975: Vosburgh Handicap (No Bias)
1979: Sapling Stakes (Rockhill Native)
Futurity Stakes (Rockhill Native)
1980: Blue Grass Stakes (Rockhill Native)

CAVEAT
1996: Belmont Stakes (Editor's Note)
Isle of Capri Casino Super Derby (Editor's Note)
Santa Anita Derby (Cavonnier)

CENTIME
1970: Sanford Stakes (Executioner)
1971: Flamingo Stakes (Executioner)
1972: Gulfstream Park Handicap (Executioner)
Metropolitan Handicap (Executioner)

CHAIRMAN WALKER
1998: Santa Anita Handicap (Malek)

CHALLEDON
1952: Spinaway Stakes (Flirtatious)
1955: Michigan Mile (Greatest)
1957: Arlington Futurity (Leather Button)
1961: Mother Goose Stakes (Funloving)

CHALLENGE ME
1961: Kentucky Oaks (My Portrait)
Monmouth Oaks (My Portrait)

CHALLENGER II

1948: Vagrancy Handicap (Conniver)
Beldame Handicap (Conniver)
Comely Handicap (Conniver)
Brooklyn Handicap (Conniver)
1949: Vanity Handicap (Silver Drift)
1952: Louisiana Derby (Gushing Oil)
Blue Grass Stakes (Gushing Oil)
1954: Jerome Handicap (Martyr)
John B. Campbell Memorial Handicap (Joe Jones)
1957: Garden State Stakes (Nadir)
Princess Pat Stakes (Hasty Doll)
1958: Spinaway Stakes (Rich Tradition)
Selima Stakes (Rich Tradition)
Louisiana Derby (Royal Union)
American Derby (Nadir)
1959: Sapling Stakes (Sky Clipper)
1967: John B. Campbell Handicap (Quinta)

CHAMOSSAIRE

1961: Black Helen Handicap (Be Cautious)

CHANCE PLAY

1946: San Carlos Handicap (Sirde)
1948: Santa Susana Stakes (Mrs. Rabbit)
1949: Massachusetts Handicap (First Nighter)
1950: Coaching Club American Oaks (Next Move)
Delaware Oaks (Next Move)
Gazelle Stakes (Next Move)
Beldame Handicap (Next Move)
Ladies Handicap (Next Move)
Vanity Handicap (Next Move)
1952: Firenze Handicap (Next Move)
Beldame Handicap (Next Move)
1953: Arlington Lassie Stakes (Queen Hopeful)
Princess Pat Stakes (Queen Hopeful)
Everglades Stakes (Royal Bay Gem)
1960: Display Handicap (Nickel Boy)
1961: Manhattan Handicap (Nickel Boy)
1965: Carter Handicap (Viking Spirit)
Californian Stakes (Viking Spirit)

CHANCERY

1966: Manhattan Handicap (Moontrip)
Bowling Green Handicap (Moontrip)
1967: Grey Lag Handicap (Moontrip)

CHANCE SHOT

1946: Widener Handicap (Armed)
Dixie Handicap (Armed)
Suburban Handicap (Armed)
Washington Park Handicap (Armed)
Hollywood Oaks (Honeymoon)
Cinema Handicap (Honeymoon)
Hollywood Derby (Honeymoon)
1947: McLennan Handicap (Armed)
Widener Handicap (Armed)
Gulfstream Park Handicap (Armed)
Stars and Stripes Handicap (Armed)
Arlington Handicap (Armed)
Washington Park Handicap (Armed)
Vanity Handicap (Honeymoon)
1948: Vineland Handicap (Honeymoon)
Top Flight Handicap (Honeymoon)
1949: Westerner Stakes (Pedigree)
Cinema Handicap (Pedigree)
1952: Del Mar Debutante Stakes (Lap Full)
1956: Fall Highweight Handicap (Impromptu)
Dixie Handicap (Chevation)

CHANTEUR II

1963: American Handicap (Dr. Kacy)
1976: Pan American Handicap (Improviser)
1977: Hialeah Turf Cup (Improviser)

CHARLIE'S SONG

1973: Sorority Stakes (Irish Sonnet)

CHARLOTTESVILLE

1984: Frizette Stakes (Charleston Rag)

CHATTERTON

1948: Starlet Stakes (Star Fiddle)

CHEROKEE

1953: Vosburgh Handicap (Indian Land)

CHEROKEE COLONY

2001: Lane's End Breeders' Futurity (Siphonic)
Hollywood Futurity (Siphonic)

CHICARO

1949: Hopeful Stakes (Middleground)
1950: Kentucky Derby (Middleground)
Belmont Stakes (Middleground)

CHICLE

1946: Astarita Stakes (Keynote)
California Derby (War Spun)
1947: Miami Beach Handicap (Tel O'Sullivan)
1953: Queens County Handicap (Flaunt)

CHIEF'S CROWN

1998: Oak Leaf Stakes (Excellent Meeting)
Hollywood Starlet Stakes (Excellent Meeting)
1999: Las Virgenes Stakes (Excellent Meeting)
Santa Anita Oaks (Excellent Meeting)
2000: San Juan Capistrano Handicap (Sunshine Street)
2001: Jim Dandy Stakes (Scorpion)

CHIEFTAN

1975: Sorority Stakes (Dearly Precious)
Spinaway Stakes (Dearly Precious)
Arlington-Washington Lassie Stakes (Dearly Precious)
1976: Acorn Stakes (Dearly Precious)
1982: Oaklawn Handicap (Eminency)
1983: Remsen Stakes (Dr. Carter)
1985: Gulfstream Park Handicap (Dr. Carter)
1988: Santa Margarita Handicap (Flying Julia)
Norfolk Stakes (Hawkster)
1989: Oak Tree Invitational Stakes (Hawkster)
1990: Santa Anita Handicap (Ruhlmann)
1993: Santa Margarita Handicap (Southern Truce)

CHOP CHOP

1970: Alabama Stakes (Fanfreluche)

CIENTIFICO

1960: Arlington Lassie Stakes (Colfax Maid)

CIRCLE HOME

1999: Malibu Stakes (Love That Red)

CITATION

1963: Vanity Handicap (Table Mate)
1964: California Derby (Real Good Deal)
Hollywood Derby (Real Good Deal)
1966: Matron Stakes (Swiss Cheese)
1972: Top Flight Handicap (Inca Queen)
1977: Florida Derby (Ruthie's Native)

CLANDESTINE

1979: Whitney Stakes (Star de Naskra)

CLARION

1964: Hialeah Turf Cup (Carteret)

CLARO

1970: Gulfstream Park Handicap (Snow Sporting)
Charles H. Strub Stakes (Snow Sporting)

CLAUDE MONET

2003: Hollywood Derby (Sweet Return)

CLEM

1975: Jerome Handicap (Guards Up)

CLEVER TRICK

1996: Futurity Stakes (Traitor)
1999: Frank J. De Francis Memorial Dash (Yes It's True)
2001: Hopeful Stakes (Came Home)
2002: Santa Anita Derby (Came Home)
Swaps Stakes (Came Home)
Pacific Classic (Came Home)

COASTAL

1990: Santa Anita Oaks (Hail Atlantis)

COASTAL TRAFFIC

1966: Arkansas Derby (Better Sea)
1968: Flamingo Stakes (Wise Exchange)

COCLES

1950: Inglewood Handicap (Miche)
1952: Santa Anita Handicap (Miche)

COHOES

1973: Hempstead Handicap (Light Hearted)
Maskette Handicap (Light Hearted)

COHORT

1951: Washington Park Handicap (Curandero)
1953: Louisiana Derby (Matagorda)

COLOMBO

1955: William P. Kyne Handicap (Mister Gus)
1956: San Antonio Handicap (Mister Gus)
Woodward Stakes (Mister Gus)
Arlington Handicap (Mister Gus)
1959: Canadian Championship Stakes (Martini II)

COMBAT

1965: Seminole Handicap (Sunstruck)

COMMANCHE RUN

1996: Hollywood Turf Cup (Running Flame)
2001: Beverly D. Stakes (England's Legend)

COMMANDING II

1988: Hollywood Oaks (Pattern Step)

COMMODORE M.

1976: Wood Memorial Stakes (Bold Forbes)
Kentucky Derby (Bold Forbes)
Belmont Stakes (Bold Forbes)

CON BRIO

1985: San Antonio Handicap (Lord at War)
Santa Anita Handicap (Lord at War)
1989: Maskette Stakes (Miss Brio)
1991: Oaklawn Handicap (Festin)
Nassau County Handicap (Festin)
Jockey Club Gold Cup (Festin)

CONJURE

1971: Norfolk Stakes (MacArthur Park)
Del Mar Futurity (MacArthur Park)

CONNAUGHT

1985: Breeders' Cup Mile (Pebbles)

CONQUISTADOR CIELO

1991: Futurity Stakes (Agincourt)
1992: Dwyer Stakes (Agincourt)
1993: Spinaway Stakes (Strategic Maneuver)
Matron Stakes (Strategic Maneuver)

CONSTANT

1946: Del Mar Handicap (Olhaverry)
1947: Santa Anita Handicap (Olhaverry)
1948: San Pasqual Handicap (Olhaverry)

CONSTANT SON

1947: Starlet Stakes (Zenoda)

COPELAN

2000: Hollywood Starlet Stakes (I Believe in You)

CORNISH PRINCE

1979: Breeders' Futurity (Gold Stage)
Ladies Handicap (Spark of Life)
1982: Hawthorne Gold Cup (Recusant)
1984: Jim Dandy Stakes (Carr de Naskra)
Travers Stakes (Carr de Naskra)
1985: Matron Stakes (Musical Lark)
1991: Santa Margarita Handicap (Little Brianne)

CORONACH

1953: Gallant Fox Handicap (Royal Vale)
Dixie Handicap (Royal Vale)
Massachusetts Handicap (Royal Vale)
Miami Beach Handicap (Royal Vale)

COROT

1948: Vosburgh Handicap (Colosal)

CORRELATION

1971: Gotham Stakes (Good Behaving)
Wood Memorial Stakes (Good Behaving)

CORRESPONDENT

1973: Hollywood Invitational Handicap (Life Cycle)
1978: Michigan Mile and One-Eighth (A Letter to Harry)
1979: New Orleans Handicap (A Letter to Harry)

CORRONATION

1989: Brooklyn Handicap (Forever Silver)

COSMIC BOMB

1963: Frizette Stakes (Tosmah)
Arkansas Derby (Cosmic Tip)
1964: Matron Handicap (Tosmah)
Beldame Stakes (Tosmah)
Arlington Classic (Tosmah)
1966: John B. Campbell Handicap (Tosmah)
1974: United Nations Handicap (Halo)

COUNTERPOINT
1966: Acorn Stakes (Marking Time)
1967: Santa Susana Stakes (Fish House)
Display Handicap (Quicken Tree)
1968: Manhattan Handicap (Quicken Tree)
Jockey Club Gold Cup (Quicken Tree)
San Luis Rey Handicap (Quicken Tree)
1970: Santa Anita Handicap (Quicken Tree)
San Juan Capistrano Handicap (Quicken Tree)

COUNT FLEET
1955: Cowdin Stakes (Noorsaga)
Garden State Stakes (Prince John)
1956: Frizette Stakes (Capelet)
1958: Matron Stakes (Quill)
Gardenia Stakes (Quill)
1959: Acorn Stakes (Quill)
Mother Goose Stakes (Quill)
Hopeful Stakes (Tompion)
1960: Jerome Handicap (Kelso)
Lawrence Realization Stakes (Kelso)
Hawthorne Gold Cup (Kelso)
Jockey Club Gold Cup (Kelso)
Santa Anita Derby (Tompion)
Blue Grass Stakes (Tompion)
Travers Stakes (Tompion)
Delaware Handicap (Quill)
Californian Stakes (Fleet Nasrullah)
1961: Metropolitan Handicap (Kelso)
Suburban Handicap (Kelso)
Brooklyn Handicap (Kelso)
Woodward Stakes (Kelso)
Jockey Club Gold Cup (Kelso)
Whitney Handicap (Kelso)
Aqueduct Handicap (Tompion)
1962: Woodward Stakes (Kelso)
Jockey Club Gold Cup (Kelso)
Flamingo Stakes (Prego)
1963: Seminole Handicap (Kelso)
Gulfstream Park Handicap (Kelso)
John B. Campbell Handicap (Kelso)
Suburban Handicap (Kelso)
Aqueduct Stakes (Kelso)
Woodward Stakes (Kelso)
Jockey Club Gold Cup (Kelso)
Whitney Stakes (Kelso)
Coaching Club American Oaks (Lamb Chop)
Monmouth Oaks (Lamb Chop)
Spinster Stakes (Lamb Chop)
Gotham Stakes (Debbysman)
1964: Aqueduct Stakes (Kelso)
Jockey Club Gold Cup (Kelso)
Washington D.C. International (Kelso)
1965: Santa Anita Derby (Lucky Debonair)
Blue Grass Stakes (Lucky Debonair)
Kentucky Derby (Lucky Debonair)
Everglades Stakes (Sparkling Johnny)
Vosburgh Handicap (R. Thomas)
Gallant Fox Handicap (Choker)
Display Handicap (Brave Lad)
Whitney Stakes (Kelso)
1966: Hollywood Derby (Fleet Host)
Santa Anita Handicap (Lucky Debonair)
Vosburgh Handicap (Gallant Romeo)
1967: Acorn Stakes (Furl Sail)
Mother Goose Stakes (Furl Sail)
Kentucky Jockey Club Stakes (Mr. Brogann)
United Nations Handicap (Flit-to)
San Luis Rey Handicap (Fleet Host)
1969: California Derby (Jay Ray)
Gulfstream Park Handicap (Court Recess)
1970: Vanity Handicap (Commissary)
1971: Cowdin Stakes (Loquacious Don)
1974: Top Flight Handicap (Lady Love)

COUNT GALLAHAD
1948: Frizette Stakes (Our Fleet)
1951: Trenton Handicap (Call Over)
1954: Acorn Stakes (Happy Mood)

COUNT OF HONOR
1971: Hopeful Stakes (Rest Your Case)
1975: Del Mar Futurity (Telly's Pop)
Norfolk Stakes (Telly's Pop)
1976: California Derby (Telly's Pop)

COUNT RENDERED
1967: Hollywood Oaks (Amerigo Lady)
1968: Top Flight Handicap (Amerigo Lady)
1969: Black Helen Handicap (Amerigo Lady)
Top Flight Handicap (Amerigo Lady)

COUNT SPEED
1964: Santa Margarita Handicap (Curious Clover)
Californian Stakes (Mustard Plaster)
1965: Santa Margarita Handicap (Curious Clover)

COURT HARWELL
1979: Gamely Handicap (Sisterhood)
1980: Santa Barbara Handicap (Sisterhood)

COURT MARTIAL
1959: Louisiana Derby (Master Palynch)
1961: Vineland Handicap (Frimanaha)
1969: Garden State Stakes (Forum)
1972: American Handicap (Buzkashi)
1973: Malibu Stakes (Bicker)
San Fernando Stakes (Bicker)
1974: Florida Derby (Judger)
Blue Grass Stakes (Judger)
1975: Hialeah Turf Cup (Outdoors)
Bowling Green Handicap (Barcas)
Washington D.C. International (Nobiliary)
1978: Sapling Stakes (Tim the Tiger)
1980: Norfolk Stakes (High Counsel)
1982: Hollywood Gold Cup (Perrault)
Budweiser Million (Perrault)
San Luis Rey Stakes (Perrault)

COX'S RIDGE
1993: Fantasy Stakes (Aztec Hill)
Nassau County Handicap (West by West)
1998: Jockey Club Gold Cup (Wagon Limit)
1999: Gallery Furniture.com Stakes (Stephen Got Even)
2000: Donn Handicap (Stephen Got Even)
2002: Forego Handicap (Orientate)
NAPA Breeders' Cup Sprint (Orientate)
Donn Handicap (Mongoose)
Walmac Int. Alcibiades Stakes (Westerly Breeze)

COZZENE
2002: Champagne Stakes (Toccet)
Hollywood Futurity (Toccet)

CRAFTY ADMIRAL
1968: Santa Anita Derby (Alley Fighter)
1971: Metropolitan Handicap (Tunex)
1972: Louisiana Derby (No Le Hace)
Arkansas Derby (No Le Hace)
1973: Flamingo Stakes (Our Native)
Ohio Derby (Our Native)
Monmouth Invitational Handicap (Our Native)
1975: Futurity Stakes (Soy Numero Uno)
1977: Hollywood Juvenile Championship (Affirmed)
Hopeful Stakes (Affirmed)
Futurity Stakes (Affirmed)
Laurel Futurity (Affirmed)
Carter Handicap (Soy Numero Uno)
Oaklawn Handicap (Soy Numero Uno)
1978: San Felipe Handicap (Affirmed)
Santa Anita Derby (Affirmed)
Hollywood Derby (Affirmed)
Kentucky Derby (Affirmed)
Preakness Stakes (Affirmed)
Belmont Stakes (Affirmed)
1979: Californian Stakes (Affirmed)
Hollywood Gold Cup (Affirmed)
Woodward Stakes (Affirmed)
Jockey Club Gold Cup (Affirmed)
Charles H. Strub Stakes (Affirmed)
Santa Anita Handicap (Affirmed)
Alcibiades Stakes (Salud)
1982: Super Derby (Reinvested)

CRAFTY PROSPECTOR
2000: Arkansas Derby (Graeme Hall)
Jim Dandy Stakes (Graeme Hall)
2002: Del Mar Futurity (Icecoldbeeratreds)
2003: Ballerina Handicap (Harmony Lodge)

CRASHER
1976: Ohio Derby (Return of a Native)

CREME DELA CREME
1983: Coaching Club American Oaks (High Schemes)
1988: Oak Leaf Stakes (One of a Klein)

CREPELLO
1979: Arlington Classic (Steady Growth)

CREWMAN
1983: Hawthorne Gold Cup (Water Bank)

CRIMINAL TYPE
2003: Travers Stakes (Ten Most Wanted)
Super Derby (Ten Most Wanted)

CRIMSON SATAN
1976: Fantasy Stakes (T.V. Vixen)
1978: Hollywood Juvenile Championship (Terlingua)
Del Mar Debutante Stakes (Terlingua)
1990: Breeders' Cup Mile (Royal Academy)

CROZIER
1975: Ohio Derby (Brent's Prince)
1985: Santa Margarita Handicap (Lovlier Linda)

CRYPTOCLEARANCE
2002: Hollywood Starlet Stakes (Elloluv)
2003: Ashland Stakes (Elloluv)

CRYSTAL GLITTERS
1996: Gamely Handicap (Auriette)

CURE THE BLUES
2000: Pimlico Special (Golden Missile)
2003: Breeders' Cup Sprint (Cajun Beat)

CURRAGH KING
1973: San Juan Capistrano Handicap (Queen's Hustler)
1980: Hollywood Juvenile Championship (Loma Malad)

CUTLASS
1999: Acorn Stakes (Three Ring)
2001: Ancient Title BC Handicap (Swept Overboard)
2002: Metropolitan Handicap (Swept Overboard)

CYANE
1976: Jerome Handicap (Dance Spell)
1982: Blue Grass Stakes (Linkage)
1984: Arlington-Washington Lassie Stakes (Contredance)
1986: Metropolitan Handicap (Garthorn)
1989: Breeders' Cup Juvenile Fillies (Go for Wand)
1990: Ashland Stakes (Go for Wand)
Mother Goose Stakes (Go for Wand)
Alabama Stakes (Go for Wand)
Maskette Stakes (Go for Wand)
Beldame Stakes (Go for Wand)

CYCLOTRON
1978: Santa Susana Stakes (Grenzen)

CZARAVICH
1996: Delta Air Lines Top Flight Handicap (Flat Fleet Feet)

D'ACCORD
2002: Frank J. De Francis Memorial Dash (D'Wildcat)
2003: Gazelle Handicap (Buy the Sport)

DAHAR
2003: Fountain of Youth Stakes (Trust N Luck)

DAMASCUS
1981: Santa Anita Derby (Splendid Spruce)
1982: Arlington-Washington Lassie St. (For Once'n My Life)
1983: Sorority Stakes (Officer's Ball)
1987: Selima Stakes (Minstrel's Lassie)
1988: Selima Stakes (Capades)
1992: Secretariat Stakes (Ghazi)
1995: Breeders' Cup Sprint (Desert Stormer)
1996: Secretariat Stakes (Marlin)
Crown Royal Hollywood Derby (Marlin)
1997: San Juan Capistrano Handicap (Marlin)
Arlington Million (Marlin)
Remsen Stakes (Coronado's Quest)
1998: Wood Memorial Stakes (Coronado's Quest)
Buick Haskell Inv. Handicap (Coronado's Quest)
Travers Stakes (Coronado's Quest)
1999: Vinery Del Mar Debutante Stakes (Chilukki)
Oak Leaf Stakes (Chilukki)
2002: Oaklawn Handicap (Kudos)
2003: Gulfstream Park Handicap (Hero's Tribute)

DAMISTER
2001: Turf Classic (Timboroa)

DANCING BRAVE
2002: Woodford Reserve Turf Classic (Beat Hollow)
Manhattan Handicap (Beat Hollow)
Arlington Million (Beat Hollow)

DANCING CHAMP
1987: Breeders' Cup Juvenile (Success Express)
1988: Pennsylvania Derby (Cefis)
1999: Champagne Stakes (Greenwood Lake)
Remsen Stakes (Greenwood Lake)

DANCING COUNT
1990: Arlington-Washington Futurity (Hansel)
1991: Jim Beam Stakes (Hansel)
Preakness Stakes (Hansel)
Belmont Stakes (Hansel)
1996: Gotham Stakes (Romano Gucci)

DAN CUPID
1980: Arlington Handicap (Yvonand)
Louisiana Downs Handicap (Yvonand)

DANIEL BOONE
1989: Jim Beam Stakes (Western Playboy)
Blue Grass Stakes (Western Playboy)
Pennsylvania Derby (Western Playboy)

DANTE
1961: Blue Grass Stakes (Sherluck)
Belmont Stakes (Sherluck)
Lawrence Realization Stakes (Sherluck)
Roamer Handicap (Sherluck)
Cinema Handicap (Bushel-n-Peck)
1963: Matron Stakes (Hasty Matelda)
1965: Washington Park Handicap (Take Over)

DANZIG
1994: Norfolk Stakes (Supremo)
Molson Export Million (Dramatic Gold)
1995: Jim Dandy Stakes (Composer)
1996: Buick Meadowlands Cup Handicap (Dramatic Gold)
1998: Super Derby (Arch)
1999: Jim Dandy Stakes (Ecton Park)
Super Derby (Ecton Park)
Gamely Breeders' Cup Handicap (Tranquility Lake)
2000: San Felipe Stakes (Fusaichi Pegasus)
Wood Memorial Stakes (Fusaichi Pegasus)
Kentucky Derby (Fusaichi Pegasus)
Yellow Ribbon Stakes (Tranquility Lake)
2001: Garden City BC Handicap (Voodoo Dancer)
2002: Go for Wand Handicap (Dancethruthedawn)
Garden City Breeders' Cup Handicap (Wonder Again)
2003: Diana Handicap (Voodoo Dancer)

DARBY CREEK ROAD
1996: Mother Goose Stakes (Yanks Music)
Alabama Stakes (Yanks Music)
Ruffian Handicap (Yanks Music)
Beldame Stakes (Yanks Music)

DARK RULER
1971: Sapling Stakes (Chevron Flight)
1983: Maskette Stakes (Ambassador of Luck)

DARK STAR
1973: Beverly Hills Handicap (Le Cle)
1974: Vanity Handicap (Tallahto)
Santa Barbara Handicap (Tallahto)
Oak Tree Invitational Stakes (Tallahto)
1976: Canadian International Championship (Youth)
Washington D.C. International (Youth)

DARN THAT ALARM
2003: Hopeful Stakes (Silver Wagon)

DARSHAAN
2002: John Deere Breeders' Cup Turf (High Chaparral)
2003: Breeders' Cup Filly and Mare Turf (Islington)
John Deere Breeders' Cup Turf (High Chaparral)

DART BOARD
1989: Sunset Handicap (Pranke)

DARYL'S JOY
1981: Del Mar Debutante Stakes (Skillful Joy)
Hollywood Starlet Stakes (Skillful Joy)

DASTUR
1957: Del Mar Debutante Stakes (Sally Lee)

DAY COURT
1973: Coaching Club American Oaks (Magazine)

DEAD AHEAD
1982: Sorority Stakes (Singing Susan)

DEBBYSMAN
1989: United Nations Handicap (Yankee Affair)
Man o' War Stakes (Yankee Affair)
Turf Classic (Yankee Affair)

DEBENTURE
1961: Del Mar Futurity (Weldy)

DEBONAIR ROGER
2002: Malibu Stakes (Debonair Joe)

DECIDEDLY
1979: Widener Handicap (Jumping Hill)
1985: Fantasy Stakes (Rascal Lass)

DEDICATE
1969: Carter Handicap (Promise)
1973: Vosburgh Handicap (Aljamin)
1980: Arlington-Washington Lassie Stakes (Truly Bound)

DEGAGE
1972: Oaklawn Handicap (Gage Line)
1973: American Handicap (Kentuckian)
1974: Arlington Handicap (Buffalo Lark)
1975: Pan American Handicap (Buffalo Lark)

DELTA JUDGE
1978: Monmouth Invitational Handicap (Delta Flag)
1980: San Felipe Handicap (Raise A Man)
1983: Acorn Stakes (Ski Goggle)
Pennsylvania Derby (Dixieland Band)

DEPTH CHARGE
1969: Hollywood Juvenile Championship (Insubordination)

DEPUTED TESTAMONY
2003: Sword Dancer Inv. Handicap (Whitmore's Conn)

DEPUTY MINISTER
2001: Eddie Read Handicap (Redattore)
2002: Belmont Stakes (Sarava)
2003: Del Mar Debutante Stakes (Halfbridled)
Breeders' Cup Juvenile Fillies (Halfbridled)
Shoemaker Breeders' Cup Mile (Redattore)
Jim Dandy Stakes (Strong Hope)

DESERT WINE
1997: Crown Royal Hollywood Derby (Subordination)
1998: Brooklyn Handicap (Subordination)
Eddie Read Handicap (Subordination)
2002: Humana Distaff Handicap (Celtic Melody)

DESTINO
1966: Wood Memorial Stakes (Amberoid)
Belmont Stakes (Amberoid)

DETERMINE
1966: Santa Susana Stakes (Spearfish)
Hollywood Oaks (Spearfish)
1968: Arlington-Washington Lassie Stakes (Process Shot)
1970: Mother Goose Stakes (Office Queen)
1974: New Orleans Handicap (Smooth Dancer)
1979: Oak Leaf Stakes (Bold 'n Determined)
1980: Santa Susana Stakes (Bold 'n Determined)
Fantasy Stakes (Bold 'n Determined)
Kentucky Oaks (Bold 'n Determined)
Acorn Stakes (Bold 'n Determined)
Coaching Club American Oaks (Bold 'n Determined)
Maskette Stakes (Bold 'n Determined)
Spinster Stakes (Bold 'n Determined)
1981: Apple Blossom Handicap (Bold 'n Determined)

DEUX POUR CENT
1955: United Nations Handicap (Blue Choir)

DEVIL DIVER
1957: Mother Goose Stakes (Outer Space)
1958: Beldame Handicap (Outer Space)
1960: Kentucky Oaks (Make Sail)
Alabama Stakes (Make Sail)
1961: Top Flight Handicap (Make Sail)
1963: Sanford Stakes (Delirium)
Inglewood Handicap (Native Diver)
1964: Inglewood Handicap (Native Diver)
1965: American Handicap (Native Diver)
Hollywood Gold Cup (Native Diver)
1966: Hollywood Gold Cup (Native Diver)
1967: Hollywood Gold Cup (Native Diver)
1970: Widener Handicap (Never Bow)
1971: Brooklyn Handicap (Never Bow)

DEVIL'S BAG
2001: Turfway Spiral Stakes (Balto Star)
Arkansas Derby (Balto Star)
2003: United Nations Handicap (Balto Star)

DHOTI
1962: Hollywood Oaks (Dingle Bay)

DIADOGUE
1966: Donn Handicap (Tronado)
Arlington Handicap (Tronado)

DIAVOLO
1949: Will Rogers Handicap (Blue Dart)
1956: San Luis Rey Handicap (Blue Volt)

DICTUS
1992: Sword Dancer Handicap (Fraise)
Breeders' Cup Turf (Fraise)
1993: Hollywood Turf Cup (Fraise)

DIESIS
1998: Sword Dancer Invitational Handicap (Cetewayo)
2000: Woodford Reserve Turf Classic (Manndar)
Manhattan Handicap (Manndar)
2001: United Nations Handicap (Senure)
Clement L. Hirsch Mem. Turf Championship (Senure)
2002: Gulfstream Park Breeders' Cup Handicap (Cetewayo)
2003: Woodford Reserve Turf Classic (Honor in War)

DIKE
1983: Budweiser Million (Tolomeo)

DIPLOMAT WAY
1983: Illinois Derby (General Practitioner)
1991: San Antonio Handicap (Farma Way)
Santa Anita Handicap (Farma Way)
Pimlico Special (Farma Way)
1996: Blue Grass Stakes (Skip Away)
Ohio Derby (Skip Away)
Buick Haskell Invitational Handicap (Skip Away)
Woodbine Million (Skip Away)
Jockey Club Gold Cup (Skip Away)
1997: Suburban Handicap (Skip Away)
Jockey Club Gold Cup (Skip Away)
Breeders' Cup Classic (Skip Away)
1998: Donn Handicap (Skip Away)
Gulfstream Park Handicap (Skip Away)
Pimlico Special (Skip Away)
Hollywood Gold Cup (Skip Away)
Philip H. Iselin Handicap (Skip Away)
Woodward Stakes (Skip Away)

DISCIPLINARIAN
1988: San Felipe Handicap (Mi Preferido)
1989: San Fernando Stakes (Mi Preferido)

DISCOVERY
1949: Matron Stakes (Bed o' Roses)
Selima Stakes (Bed o' Roses)
Marguerite Stakes (Bed o' Roses)
Demoiselle Stakes (Bed o' Roses)
1950: Lawrence Realization Stakes (Bed o' Roses)
1951: Vineland Handicap (Bed o' Roses)
Comely Handicap (Bed o' Roses)
1952: Hopeful Stakes (Native Dancer)
Futurity Stakes (Native Dancer)
Santa Margarita Handicap (Bed o' Roses)
1953: Gotham Stakes (Native Dancer)
Wood Memorial Stakes (Native Dancer)
Withers Stakes (Native Dancer)
Preakness Stakes (Native Dancer)
Belmont Stakes (Native Dancer)
Dwyer Stakes (Native Dancer)
Arlington Classic (Native Dancer)
Travers Stakes (Native Dancer)
American Derby (Native Dancer)
Arlington Futurity (Hasty Road)
Washington Park Futurity (Hasty Road)
Breeders' Futurity (Hasty Road)
Kentucky Jockey Club Stakes (Hasty Road)
1954: Preakness Stakes (Hasty Road)
New Orleans Handicap (Grover B.)
Metropolitan Handicap (Native Dancer)
1955: Withers Stakes (Traffic Judge)
Ohio Derby (Traffic Judge)
Jerome Handicap (Traffic Judge)
Woodward Stakes (Traffic Judge)
Widener Handicap (Hasty Road)
1956: Futurity Stakes (Bold Ruler)
1957: Flamingo Stakes (Bold Ruler)
Wood Memorial Stakes (Bold Ruler)
Preakness Stakes (Bold Ruler)
Jerome Handicap (Bold Ruler)
Trenton Handicap (Bold Ruler)
Metropolitan Handicap (Traffic Judge)
Suburban Handicap (Traffic Judge)
Top Flight Handicap (Plotter)
1958: Carter Handicap (Bold Ruler)
Suburban Handicap (Bold Ruler)

Monmouth Handicap (Bold Ruler)
Futurity Stakes (Intentionally)
Pimlico Futurity (Intentionally)
1959: Withers Stakes (Intentionally)
Jerome Handicap (Intentionally)
1960: San Carlos Handicap (Clandestine)
1962: Seminole Handicap (Intentionally)
1965: Mother Goose Stakes (Cordially)

DIS DONC
1946: Futurity Stakes (First Flight)
Astoria Stakes (First Flight)
Matron Stakes (First Flight)
Princess Pat Stakes (Say Blue)
1948: Fall Highweight Handicap (First Flight)
1949: Blue Grass Stakes (Halt)

DISPLAY
1946: Inglewood Handicap (Quick Reward)
American Handicap (Quick Reward)
1950: Sapling Stakes (Battlefield)
Saratoga Special (Battlefield)
Hopeful Stakes (Battlefield)
Tremont Stakes (Battlefield)
Futurity Stakes (Battlefield)
Acorn Stakes (Siama)
Monmouth Oaks (Siama)
Comely Handicap (Siama)
1951: Withers Stakes (Battlefield)
Dwyer Stakes (Battlefield)
Travers Stakes (Battlefield)
1952: New York Handicap (Battlefield)
Westchester Handicap (Battlefield)

DISTINCTIVE
1984: Hollywood Derby (Procida)

DIXIELAND BAND
1996: Go for Wand Stakes (Exotic Wood)
1998: Santa Monica Handicap (Exotic Wood)
Santa Maria Handicap (Exotic Wood)
1999: Wood Memorial Stakes (Adonis)
2000: Test Stakes (Dream Supreme)
Ballerina Handicap (Dream Supreme)
2001: Florida Derby (Monarchos)
Kentucky Derby (Monarchos)
2003: Frizette Stakes (Society Selection)
Malibu Stakes (Southern Image)

DJEBE
1972: Manhattan Handicap (Ruritania)

DJEBEL
1962: San Antonio Handicap (Olden Times)
San Juan Capistrano Handicap (Olden Times)
1964: Metropolitan Handicap (Olden Times)

DJEDDAH
1962: Futurity Stakes (Never Bend)
Cowdin Stakes (Never Bend)
Champagne Stakes (Never Bend)
1963: Flamingo Stakes (Never Bend)
1967: Kentucky Derby (Proud Clarion)
1968: Hollywood Oaks (Hooplah)
1969: Jerome Handicap (Mr. Leader)
1970: Stars and Stripes Handicap (Mr. Leader)
1971: Hollywood Derby (Bold Reason)
Travers Stakes (Bold Reason)
American Derby (Bold Reason)
1973: Jersey Derby (Knightly Dawn)

DOGPATCH
1959: Del Mar Debutante Stakes (Darling June)
1961: Arkansas Derby (Light Talk)
1966: Del Mar Debutante Stakes (Native Honey)

DONATELLO II
1946: Arlington Classic (The Dude)
1947: Spinaway Stakes (Bellesoeur)
Astarita Stakes (Bellesoeur)
1948: American Handicap (Stepfather)
1952: Washington D.C. International (Wilwyn)
1955: American Handicap (Alidon)
1958: Bougainvillea Turf Handicap (Stephanotis)

DON B.
1994: Milady Handicap (Andestine)

DONUT KING
1978: Sorority Stakes (Mongo Queen)
1988: La Canada Stakes (Hollywood Glitter)

DOUBLE HITCH
1988: Jerome Handicap (Evening Kris)

DOUBLE JAY
1964: Frizette Stakes (Queen Empress)
Gardenia Stakes (Queen Empress)
Delaware Handicap (Old Hat)
Spinster Stakes (Old Hat)
1965: Black Helen Handicap (Old Hat)
Matron Handicap (Old Hat)
Michigan Mile and One-Eighth (Old Hat)
1968: Sanford Stakes (King Emperor)
Cowdin Stakes (King Emperor)
Pimlico-Laurel Futurity (King Emperor)
Arkansas Derby (Nodouble)
Michigan Mile and One-Eighth (Nodouble)
Hawthorne Gold Cup (Nodouble)
1969: Californian Stakes (Nodouble)
Brooklyn Handicap (Nodouble)
Hawthorne Gold Cup (Nodouble)
Santa Anita Handicap (Nodouble)
1970: Metropolitan Handicap (Nodouble)
1971: Acorn Stakes (Deceit)
Mother Goose Stakes (Deceit)
Beldame Stakes (Double Delta)
1972: Dwyer Handicap (Cloudy Dawn)
Arlington Park Handicap (Cloudy Dawn)
1974: Fantasy Stakes (Miss Musket)
Hollywood Oaks (Miss Musket)
Frizette Stakes (Molly Ballentine)
1976: Breeders' Futurity (Run Dusty Run)
Arlington-Washington Futurity (Run Dusty Run)
John B. Campbell Handicap (Festive Mood)
1977: Norfolk Stakes (Balzac)
Widener Handicap (Yamanin)
1979: Young America Stakes (Koluctoo Bay)
Oak Tree Invitational Stakes (Balzac)
1980: Hialeah Turf Cup (John Henry)
Hollywood Invitational Handicap (John Henry)
Oak Tree Invitational Stakes (John Henry)
San Luis Rey Stakes (John Henry)
San Juan Capistrano Handicap (John Henry)
1981: Jockey Club Gold Cup (John Henry)
Santa Anita Handicap (John Henry)
Hollywood Invitational Handicap (John Henry)
Sword Dancer Stakes (John Henry)
Arlington Million (John Henry)
Oak Tree Invitational Stakes (John Henry)
San Luis Rey Stakes (John Henry)
Widener Handicap (Land of Eire)
1982: Santa Anita Handicap (John Henry)
Oak Tree Invitational Stakes (John Henry)
1983: Hollywood Turf Cup (John Henry)
1984: Hollywood Invitational Handicap (John Henry)
Sunset Handicap (John Henry)
Budweiser-Arlington Million (John Henry)
Turf Classic (John Henry)
1986: Kentucky Derby (Ferdinand)
1987: Hollywood Gold Cup (Ferdinand)
Breeders' Cup Classic (Ferdinand)

DRAWBY
1972: Fountain of Youth Stakes (Gentle Smoke)

DR. BLUM
2000: Gazelle Handicap (Critical Eye)
2001: Vosburgh Stakes (Left Bank)
Cigar Mile Handicap (Left Bank)
Hempstead Handicap (Critical Eye)
2002: Whitney Handicap (Left Bank)

DR. FAGER
1980: Laurel Futurity (Cure the Blues)
Del Mar Debutante Stakes (Raja's Delight)
Canadian International Championship (Great Neck)
1981: Metropolitan Handicap (Fappiano)
Bowling Green Handicap (Great Neck)
1982: Matron Stakes (Wings of Jove)
Maskette Stakes (Too Chic)
1983: Bowling Green Handicap (Tantalizing)
1984: Wood Memorial Stakes (Leroy S.)
1987: Delaware Handicap (Coup de Fusil)
Ruffian Handicap (Coup de Fusil)
1988: United Nations Handicap (Equalize)
1989: Vosburgh Stakes (Sewickley)
1990: Vosburgh Stakes (Sewickley)
NYRA Mile Handicap (Quiet American)
1993: Ruffian Handicap (Shared Interest)

DROLL ROLE
1981: Illinois Derby (Paristo)
1995: Carter Handicap (Lite the Fuse)
Frank J. De Francis Memorial Dash (Lite the Fuse)
1996: Carter Handicap (Lite the Fuse)
Frank J. De Francis Memorial Dash (Lite the Fuse)

DRONE
1982: Frizette Stakes (Princess Rooney)
Pennsylvania Derby (Spanish Drums)
1983: Kentucky Oaks (Princess Rooney)
1984: Vanity Handicap (Princess Rooney)
Spinster Stakes (Princess Rooney)
Breeders' Cup Distaff (Princess Rooney)
1996: Kentucky Derby (Grindstone)
1999: Kentucky Derby (Charismatic)
Preakness Stakes (Charismatic)
2000: Coaching Club American Oaks (Jostle)
Alabama Stakes (Jostle)
2001: Toyota Blue Grass Stakes (Millennium Wind)

DRUMS OF TIME
1995: Matriarch Stakes (Duda)

DUMPTY HUMPTY
1977: Ramona Handicap (Dancing Femme)
1978: Illinois Derby (Batonnier)

DUPLICATOR
1971: Hollywood Juvenile Championship (Royal Owl)
1973: Charles H. Strub Stakes (Royal Owl)

DURBAR II
1946: Black Helen Handicap (Adroit)

DUSTY CANYON
1980: Del Mar Futurity (Bold And Gold)
1983: Vanity Handicap (A Kiss For Luck)
1986: Arlington-Washington Futurity (Bet Twice)
Laurel Futurity (Bet Twice)
1987: Fountain of Youth Stakes (Bet Twice)
Belmont Stakes (Bet Twice)
Haskell Invitational Handicap (Bet Twice)
1992: Santa Anita Oaks (Golden Treat)

DYNAFORMER
2003: Hollywood Starlet Stakes (Hollywood Story)

EASTON
1951: Cowdin Stakes (Eternal Moon)
1954: Maskette Handicap (Ballerina)
1955: Gardenia Stakes (Nasrina)
Frizette Stakes (Nasrina)
1956: San Felipe Handicap (Social Climber)
Cinema Handicap (Social Climber)
1957: Californian Stakes (Social Climber)

EASY GOER
2002: Matron Stakes (Storm Flag Flying)
Frizette Stakes (Storm Flag Flying)
Long John Silver's BC Juv. Fillies (Storm Flag Flying)

EASY MON
1958: Breeders' Futurity (Namon)
1959: Florida Derby (Easy Spur)

EDDIE SCHMIDT
1981: Haskell Invitational Handicap (Five Star Flight)

EDUCATION
1960: Monmouth Oaks (Teacation)
1963: Ohio Derby (Lemon Twist)

EIGHT THIRTY
1952: Saranac Handicap (Golden Gloves)
1953: Spinaway Stakes (Evening Out)
Matron Stakes (Evening Out)
1954: Monmouth Oaks (Evening Out)
1955: Firenze Handicap (Rare Treat)
1956: Vineland Handicap (Rare Treat)
1957: Futurity Stakes (Jester)
Ladies Handicap (Rare Treat)
1960: Bowling Green Handicap (Amber Morn)
1961: Hopeful Stakes (Jaipur)
Cowdin Stakes (Jaipur)
Californian Stakes (First Balcony)
San Carlos Handicap (First Balcony)
1962: Gotham Stakes (Jaipur)
Withers Stakes (Jaipur)
Jersey Derby (Jaipur)
Belmont Stakes (Jaipur)
Travers Stakes (Jaipur)
Selima Stakes (Fool's Play)
1964: Sanford Stakes (Cornish Prince)
1966: Sanford Stakes (Yorkville)

EIGHT THIRTY *(Continued)*
1971: Arlington-Washington Futurity (Hold Your Peace)
1972: Flamingo Stakes (Hold Your Peace)

EL DRAG
1976: Hollywood Juvenile Championship (Fleet Dragoon)

EL GRAN SENOR
1997: Futurity Stakes (Grand Slam)
Moet Champagne Stakes (Grand Slam)
1999: Fountain of Youth Stakes (Vicar)
Florida Derby (Vicar)
2000: Santa Monica Handicap (Honest Lady)
Arlington Million (Chester House)
2002: Secretariat Stakes (Chiselling)
2003: Florida Derby (Empire Maker)
Wood Memorial Stakes (Empire Maker)
Belmont Stakes (Empire Maker)

ELISATHE
1965: Vanity Handicap (Jalousie II)

ELOCUTIONIST
1986: Hollywood Derby (Spellbound)
1993: San Luis Rey Stakes (Kotashaan)
San Juan Capistrano Handicap (Kotashaan)
Eddie Read Handicap (Kotashaan)
Oak Tree Invitational Stakes (Kotashaan)
Breeders' Cup Turf (Kotashaan)
1995: Secretariat Stakes (Hawk Attack)

EL RELICARIO
1977: Hollywood Invitational Handicap (Vigors)
1978: San Antonio Stakes (Vigors)
Santa Anita Handicap (Vigors)

EL TIGRE GRANDE
1987: Matron Stakes (Over All)

EMBRUJO
1959: McLennan Handicap (Sharpsburg)
1962: Gallant Fox Handicap (Sensitivo)
Display Handicap (Sensitivo)
1968: Illinois Derby (Bold Favorite)
1972: John B. Campbell Handicap (Favorecidian)
Michigan Mile and One-Eighth (Favorecidian)

EMERSON
1987: Santa Barbara Handicap (Reloy)

EMPIRE BUILDER
1948: Westerner Stakes (Solidarity)
1949: Golden Gate Handicap (Solidarity)
Hollywood Gold Cup (Solidarity)
1950: San Pasqual Handicap (Solidarity)

ENDEAVOR II
1967: Hollywood Derby (Tumble Wind)

EPINARD
1946: Stars and Stripes Handicap (Witch Sir)

EQUESTRIAN
1964: San Luis Rey Handicap (Inclusive)

EQUIPOISE
1946: Wood Memorial Stakes (Assault)
Kentucky Derby (Assault)
Preakness Stakes (Assault)
Belmont Stakes (Assault)
Dwyer Stakes (Assault)
Pimlico Special (Assault)
Westchester Handicap (Assault)
1947: Grey Lag Handicap (Assault)
Dixie Handicap (Assault)
Suburban Handicap (Assault)
Brooklyn Handicap (Assault)
Astoria Stakes (Mackinaw)
1948: Spinaway Stakes (Myrtle Charm)
Matron Stakes (Myrtle Charm)
Cowdin Stakes (Algasir)
1949: San Antonio Handicap (Dinner Gong)
Brooklyn Handicap (Assault)
1950: Grey Lag Handicap (Lotowhite)
1951: Excelsior Handicap (Lotowhite)
1953: Discovery Handicap (Level Lea)
Jockey Club Gold Cup (Level Lea)
1954: Gazelle Handicap (On Your Own)

ERRARD
1958: Remsen Stakes (Atoll)
1959: Gotham Stakes (Atoll)
1961: John B. Campbell Handicap (Conestoga)
1963: Beldame Stakes (Oil Royalty)
Vineland Handicap (Oil Royalty)
1964: Top Flight Handicap (Oil Royalty)

ESCADRU
1977: Top Flight Handicap (Shawi)

ESPEA
1984: Louisiana Derby (Taylor's Special)
Blue Grass Stakes (Taylor's Special)

ETONIAN
1980: Arkansas Derby (Temperence Hill)
Belmont Stakes (Temperence Hill)
Travers Stakes (Temperence Hill)
Super Derby (Temperence Hill)
Jockey Club Gold Cup (Temperence Hill)
Illinois Derby (Ray's Word)
1981: Suburban Handicap (Temperence Hill)
Oaklawn Handicap (Temperence Hill)
1983: Secretariat Stakes (Fortnightly)

EURASIAN
1958: Jerome Handicap (Warhead)
Roamer Handicap (Warhead)
Manhattan Handicap (Warhead)
1960: Whitney Handicap (Warhead)

EXBURY
1981: Sunset Handicap (Galaxy Libra)
Man o' War Stakes (Galaxy Libra)

EXCELLER
1999: Oak Tree Turf Championship (Mash One)
2000: C.L. Hirsch Mem. Turf Championship (Mash One)

EXCLUSIVE NATIVE
1981: Frizette Stakes (Proud Lou)
1984: Coaching Club American Oaks (Class Play)
1985: Remsen Stakes (Pillaster)
Oak Leaf Stakes (Arewehavingfunyet)
1987: Arlington-Washington Futurity (Tejano)
Cowdin Stakes (Tejano)
Hollywood Futurity (Tejano)
1989: California Derby (Endow)
Futurity Stakes (Senor Pete)
1997: Oak Leaf Stakes (Vivid Angel)

EXPLODENT
1987: Hutcheson Stakes (Well Selected)
1992: Oak Leaf Stakes (Zoonaqua)
1998: Gamely Breeders' Cup Handicap (Fiji)
Yellow Ribbon Stakes (Fiji)

FABULEUX DANCER
1998: Early Times Hollywood Derby (Vergennes)

FAIR PLAY
1946: San Juan Capistrano Handicap (Triplicate)
Hollywood Gold Cup (Triplicate)
1947: Tremont Stakes (Inseparable)
Golden Gate Handicap (Triplicate)
1950: Washington Park Handicap (Inseparable)
Stars and Stripes Handicap (Inseparable)

FAIRTHORN
1964: American Handicap (Colorado King)
Hollywood Gold Cup (Colorado King)
Sunset Handicap (Colorado King)

FAIR TRIAL
1960: Cinema Handicap (New Policy)
1962: Cinema Handicap (Black Sheep)
American Derby (Black Sheep)

FAIR TRUCKLE
1977: Oak Leaf Stakes (B. Thoughtful)
1978: Hollywood Oaks (B. Thoughtful)
1979: La Canada Stakes (B. Thoughtful)

FAIRY MANHURST
1957: Hopeful Stakes (Rose Trellis)

FALCON
1980: Flower Bowl Handicap (Just A Game II)

FANTE
1972: Suburban Handicap (Hitchcock)

FAPPIANO
1994: Arlington-Washington Futurity (Evansville Slew)
1996: Frizette Stakes (Storm Song)
Breeders' Cup Juvenile Fillies (Storm Song)
Jerome Handicap (Why Change)
2000: Walmac Int. Alcibiades Stakes (She's a Devil Due)
Jockey Club Gold Cup (Albert the Great)
2001: Brooklyn Handicap (Albert the Great)
Suburban Handicap (Albert the Great)

FARAWAY SON
1992: Rothmans International Stakes (Snurge)

FASCINATOR
1966: Carter Handicap (Davis II)

FAST FOX
1970: Massachusetts Handicap (Semillant)

FAST GOLD
1998: Moet Champagne Stakes (The Groom Is Red)

FAST HILARIOUS
1998: Fall Highweight Handicap (Punch Line)

FAST PLAY
2003: Gulfstream Park BC 'Cap (Man From Wicklow)

FATHERS IMAGE
1979: Hollywood Invitational Handicap (Johnny's Image)

FAUBOURG
1968: Charles H. Strub Stakes (Most Host)

FIGHTING FOX
1958: Kentucky Oaks (Bug Brush)
1959: Santa Margarita Handicap (Bug Brush)
San Antonio Handicap (Bug Brush)
Inglewood Handicap (Bug Brush)
1960: San Felipe Handicap (Flow Line)
1963: Santa Margarita Handicap (Pixie Erin)

FIGHTIN' GUYTON
1981: Louisiana Downs Handicap (Shishkabob)

FIGONERO
1992: Mother Goose Stakes (Turnback the Alarm)
Coaching Club American Oaks (Turnback the Alarm)
1993: Shuvee Handicap (Turnback the Alarm)
Hempstead Handicap (Turnback the Alarm)
Go for Wand Stakes (Turnback the Alarm)

FILIBUSTERO
1969: Widener Handicap (Yumbel)
1974: Sunset Handicap (Greco II)

FIL ROUGE
1978: Del Mar Handicap (Palton)

FIRE DANCER
1990: Fantasy Stakes (Silvered)

FIRMAMENT
1948: Massachusetts Handicap (Beauchef)

FIRST CABIN
1971: Black Helen Handicap (Swoon's Flower)

FIRST FIDDLE
1974: American Handicap (Plunk)

FIRST LANDING
1970: Garden State Stakes (Run the Gantlet)
1971: United Nations Handicap (Run the Gantlet)
Man o' War Stakes (Run the Gantlet)
Washington D.C. International (Run the Gantlet)
1972: Bowling Green Handicap (Run the Gantlet)
1983: Norfolk Stakes (Fali Time)
Hollywood Futurity (Fali Time)
Flower Bowl Handicap (First Approach)
1984: San Felipe Handicap (Fali Time)
1986: Secretariat Stakes (Southjet)
Rothmans International Stakes (Southjet)

FIT TO FIGHT
1999: Mother Goose Stakes (Dreams Gallore)
2000: Turfway Spiral Stakes (Globalize)

FITZCARRALDO
2001: Overbrook Spinster Stakes (Miss Linda)

FLAG POLE
1949: Saratoga Special (More Sun)

FLAMING FLEET
1974: Metropolitan Handicap (Arbees Boy)

FLANEUR II
1971: Belmont Stakes (Pass Catcher)
1975: Maskette Handicap (Let Me Linger)
1984: Sapling Stakes (Doubly Clear)

FLARES
1959: Kentucky Oaks (Wedlock)

FLASH O' NIGHT
1962: Hollywood Juvenile Championship (Noti)

FLEET HOST
1979: Champagne Stakes (Joanie's Chief)

FLEET NASRULLAH
1972: Pontiac Grand Prix Stakes (King's Bishop)
Michigan Mile and One-Eighth (King's Bishop)
Del Mar Debutante Stakes (Windy's Daughter)
1973: Acorn Stakes (Windy's Daughter)
Mother Goose Stakes (Windy's Daughter)
Hollywood Juvenile Championship (Century's Envoy)
Carter Handicap (King's Bishop)
1976: Arkansas Derby (Elocutionist)
Preakness Stakes (Elocutionist)
1978: Alcibiades Stakes (Angel Island)
1985: Gotham Stakes (Eternal Prince)
Wood Memorial Stakes (Eternal Prince)

FLINTHAM
1992: Santa Margarita Handicap (Paseana)
Apple Blossom Handicap (Paseana)
Milady Handicap (Paseana)
Vanity Handicap (Paseana)
Breeders' Cup Distaff (Paseana)
1993: Milady Handicap (Paseana)
Spinster Stakes (Paseana)
Apple Blossom Handicap (Paseana)
1994: Santa Margarita Handicap (Paseana)

FLIP SAL
1991: Ashland Stakes (Do It With Style)

FLORIBUNDA
1976: Hialeah Turf Cup (Lord Henham)

FLUSHING II
1959: Carter Handicap (Jimmer)
1964: Sorority Stakes (Bold Experience)

FLUSH ROYAL
1975: Man o' War Stakes (Snow Knight)
Canadian International Championship (Snow Knight)

FLYING EBONY
1949: Starlet Stakes (Thanks Again)

FLYING HEELS
1948: Delaware Oaks (Miss Request)
Ladies Handicap (Miss Request)
Hollywood Oaks (Flying Rhythm)
Del Mar Handicap (Frankly)
1949: Beldame Handicap (Miss Request)
1950: Del Mar Handicap (Frankly)
1953: Vanity Handicap (Fleet Khal)
1956: Santa Anita Derby (Terrang)
1957: San Antonio Handicap (Terrang)
1959: Santa Anita Handicap (Terrang)

FLYING PASTER
1994: Hollywood Derby (River Flyer)
1995: Milady Handicap (Pirate's Revenge)
1998: Del Mar Futurity (Worldly Manner)
2001: Test Stakes (Victory Ride)

FOREVER SPARKLE
1993: Flamingo Stakes (Forever Whirl)
Ohio Derby (Forever Whirl)

FORLI
1983: Futurity Stakes (Swale)
Young America Stakes (Swale)
Breeders' Futurity (Swale)
1984: Hutcheson Stakes (Swale)
Florida Derby (Swale)
Kentucky Derby (Swale)
Belmont Stakes (Swale)
Swaps Stakes (Precisionist)
1985: San Fernando Stakes (Precisionist)
Charles H. Strub Stakes (Precisionist)
Breeders' Cup Sprint (Precisionist)
1986: Californian Stakes (Precisionist)
Woodward Stakes (Precisionist)
1989: Remsen Stakes (Yonder)
1990: Jersey Derby (Yonder)
1998: Ohio Derby (Classic Cat)

FORMIDABLE
1993: Flower Bowl Handicap (Far Out Beast)

FORMOR
1963: Ladies Handicap (Goofed)

FOR REALLY
2003: Santa Anita Derby (Buddy Gil)

FOR THE MOMENT
1992: Jim Beam Stakes (Lil E. Tee)
Kentucky Derby (Lil E. Tee)

FORTINO
1979: Santa Margarita Handicap (Sanedtki)

FORT SALONGA
1982: Ramona Handicap (Honey Fox)

FORTY NINER
1999: Hopeful Stakes (High Yield)
2000: Fountain of Youth Stakes (High Yield)
Florida Derby (High Yield)

FORUM
1991: Hollywood Turf Handicap (Exbourne)
Caesars International Handicap (Exbourne)
1997: Eddie Read Handicap (Expelled)

FOX CUB
1955: Gulfstream Park Handicap (Mister Black)

FRANCIS S.
1978: Arlington-Washington Lassie Stakes (It's In the Air)
Oak Leaf Stakes (It's In the Air)
1979: Alabama Stakes (It's In the Air)
Vanity Handicap (It's In the Air)
Ruffian Handicap (It's In the Air)
Sorority Stakes (Love Street)
1980: Vanity Handicap (It's In the Air)
1985: Futurity Stakes (Ogygian)
1986: Dwyer Stakes (Ogygian)
Jerome Handicap (Ogygian)

FREE AMERICA
1970: Del Mar Futurity (June Darling)
Norfolk Stakes (June Darling)
Oak Leaf Stakes (June Darling)
1976: Century Handicap (Winds of Thought)

FREE FRANCE
1969: San Antonio Stakes (Praise Jay)

FRIAR ROCK
1949: Delaware Oaks (Nasophar)

FULCRUM
1979: Del Mar Futurity (The Carpenter)
Norfolk Stakes (The Carpenter)

FULL OUT
1995: Oak Leaf Stakes (Tipically Irish)

GAELIC DANCER
1986: Hollywood Gold Cup (Super Diamond)
1989: San Antonio Handicap (Super Diamond)

GAINSBOROUGH
1948: Arlington Handicap (Stud Poker)
Miami Beach Handicap (Stud Poker)

GALLANT FOX
1946: San Pasqual Handicap (Lou-Bre)
1949: Hawthorne Gold Cup (Volcanic)
1956: Del Mar Debutante Stakes (Blue Vic)
Jerome Handicap (Reneged)
1957: Manhattan Handicap (Reneged)
1962: Gulfstream Park Handicap (Jay Fox)
Donn Handicap (Jay Fox)

GALLANT MAN
1972: Sorority Stakes (Sparkalark)
1975: John B. Campbell Handicap (Jolly Johu)
1976: Norfolk Stakes (Habitony)
1977: Santa Anita Derby (Habitony)
1980: Champagne Stakes (Lord Avie)
Young America Stakes (Lord Avie)
Ruffian Handicap (Genuine Risk)
Kentucky Derby (Genuine Risk)
1981: Florida Derby (Lord Avie)
Vosburgh Stakes (Guilty Conscience)
1984: Hollywood Futurity (Stephan's Odyssey)
1985: Dwyer Stakes (Stephan's Odyssey)
Jim Dandy Stakes (Stephan's Odyssey)
Widener Handicap (Pine Circle)
1986: Acorn Stakes (Lotka)
1988: Alcibiades Stakes (Wonders Delight)

GALLANT ROMEO
1989: Flamingo Stakes (Awe Inspiring)
Jersey Derby (Awe Inspiring)
Matron Stakes (Stella Madrid)
Frizette Stakes (Stella Madrid)
Fountain of Youth Stakes (Dixieland Brass)
1990: Acorn Stakes (Stella Madrid)
1991: Spinaway Stakes (Miss Iron Smoke)

GALLANT SIR
1947: Hollywood Derby (Yankee Valor)
Cinema Handicap (Yankee Valor)

GAMIN
1982: Santa Anita Derby (Muttering)

GATO DEL SOL
1998: Spinaway Stakes (Things Change)

GHADEER
2000: Santa Margarita Handicap (Riboletta)
Milady Breeders' Cup Handicap (Riboletta)
Vanity Handicap (Riboletta)
Ruffian Handicap (Riboletta)
Beldame Stakes (Riboletta)

GINO
1946: Top Flight Handicap (Sicily)
1951: Spinaway Stakes (Blue Case)
1954: United Nations Handicap (Closed Door)

GOLD BRIDGE
1952: Carter Handicap (Northern Star)
1961: Arlington Futurity (Ridan)
Washington Park Futurity (Ridan)
1962: Florida Derby (Ridan)
Blue Grass Stakes (Ridan)
Arlington Classic (Ridan)
1965: Spinaway Stakes (Moccasin)
Matron Stakes (Moccasin)
Selima Stakes (Moccasin)
Gardenia Stakes (Moccasin)
John B. Campbell Handicap (Lt. Stevens)

GOLDEN EAGLE II
1986: Hollywood Derby (Thrill Show)

GOLD FAVORITE
1989: Demoiselle Stakes (Rootentootenwooten)

GOLD STAGE
1992: Remsen Stakes (Silver of Silver)

GOOD BEHAVING
1983: Mother Goose Stakes (Able Money)
1994: San Antonio Handicap (The Wicked North)
Oaklawn Handicap (The Wicked North)
Californian Stakes (The Wicked North)

GOOD COUNSEL
1997: Hollywood Turf Cup (River Bay)
1999: Charles Whittingham Handicap (River Bay)

GOOD ENDING
1965: Del Mar Debutante Stakes (Century)

GOOD GOODS
1967: Oaklawn Handicap (Mike's Red)

GOOD MANNERS
1989: Santa Margarita Handicap (Bayakoa)
Apple Blossom Handicap (Bayakoa)
Vanity Handicap (Bayakoa)
Ruffian Handicap (Bayakoa)
Spinster Stakes (Bayakoa)
Breeders' Cup Distaff (Bayakoa)
1990: Santa Margarita Handicap (Bayakoa)
Spinster Stakes (Bayakoa)
Breeders' Cup Distaff (Bayakoa)

GOYA II
1956: Hialeah Turf Handicap (Guardian II)
1963: Dixie Handicap (Cedar Key)
1964: San Juan Capistrano Handicap (Cedar Key)
Donn Handicap (Cedar Key)
1965: San Luis Rey Handicap (Cedar Key)
1966: San Luis Rey Handicap (Cedar Key)

GRAND ADMIRAL
1957: Kentucky Oaks (Lori-El)
1963: Hawthorne Gold Cup (Admiral Vic)
1964: Seminole Handicap (Admiral Vic)

GRAND SLAM (1933)
1950: Kentucky Jockey Club Stakes (Pur Sang)

GRAUSTARK
1979: Swaps Stakes (Valdez)
1980: Alabama Stakes (Love Sign)
Beldame Stakes (Love Sign)
1981: Beldame Stakes (Love Sign)
1984: United Nations Handicap (Hero's Honor)
1985: Vanity Handicap (Dontstop Themusic)
Spinster Stakes (Dontstop Themusic)
1986: Fantasy Stakes (Tiffany Lass)
Kentucky Oaks (Tiffany Lass)
Vanity Handicap (Magnificent Lindy)
1988: Man o' War Stakes (Sunshine Forever)
Turf Classic (Sunshine Forever)
Budweiser International Stakes (Sunshine Forever)
Florida Derby (Brian's Time)
Jim Dandy Stakes (Brian's Time)
Jim Beam Stakes (Kingpost)
Acorn Stakes (Aptostar)
1991: Gotham Stakes (Kyle's Our Man)
1992: Swaps Stakes (Bien Bien)
Hollywood Turf Cup (Bien Bien)
Champagne Stakes (Sea Hero)
1993: Kentucky Derby (Sea Hero)
Travers Stakes (Sea Hero)
Hollywood Turf Handicap (Bien Bien)
1994: San Luis Rey Stakes (Bien Bien)
San Juan Capistrano Handicap (Bien Bien)
2001: Malibu Stakes (Mizzen Mast)
2002: Strub Stakes (Mizzen Mast)

GREAT ABOVE
1990: Withers Stakes (Housebuster)
Jerome Handicap (Housebuster)
1991: Carter Handicap (Housebuster)
Vosburgh Stakes (Housebuster)
1994: Santa Maria Handicap (Supah Gem)

GREAT NEPHEW
1991: Arlington Classic (Whadjathink)

GREAT SUN
1988: Apple Blossom Handicap (By Land By Sea)

GREEK ANSWER
1997: Florida Derby (Captain Bodgit)
Wood Memorial Stakes (Captain Bodgit)

GREEK GAME
1973: Futurity Stakes (Wedge Shot)
1977: Travers Stakes (Jatski)

GREEK SONG
1969: Spinaway Stakes (Meritus)
1972: New Orleans Handicap (Urgent Message)

GREEN DANCER
1988: Oak Tree Invitational Stakes (Nasr El Arab)
1989: Charles H. Strub Stakes (Nasr El Arab)
San Juan Capistrano Handicap (Nasr El Arab)
1992: Hollywood Turf Handicap (Quest for Fame)
1994: Philip H. Iselin Handicap (Taking Risks)
Oak Tree Invitational Stakes (Sandpit)
1995: Molson Export Million (Peaks and Valleys)
Meadowlands Cup (Peaks and Valleys)
San Luis Rey Stakes (Sandpit)
Caesars International Handicap (Sandpit)
1996: Hollywood Turf Handicap (Sandpit)
Caesars International Handicap (Sandpit)
1998: Frizette Stakes (Confessional)
Hempstead Handicap (Mossflower)
2000: Breeders' Cup Turf (Kalanisi)

GREEN FOREST
2000: Garden City Breeders' Cup Handicap (Gaviola)

GREEN TICKET
1987: Acorn Stakes (Grecian Flight)

GRENFALL
1991: Meadowlands Cup (Twilight Agenda)

GREY DAWN II
1975: Hopeful Stakes (Eustace)
1984: Hollywood Turf Cup (Alphabatim)
1985: Hollywood Turf Cup (Zoffany)
1986: Sunset Handicap (Zoffany)
Hollywood Turf Cup (Alphabatim)
1987: San Luis Rey Stakes (Zoffany)
Brooklyn Handicap (Waquoit)
1988: Brooklyn Handicap (Waquoit)
Jockey Club Gold Cup (Waquoit)
1989: Hialeah Turf Cup (El Senor)
Sword Dancer Handicap (El Senor)
Tropical Park Derby (Big Stanley)
1990: San Felipe Handicap (Real Cash)
American Derby (Real Cash)
Hollywood Derby (Itsallgreektome)
Hollywood Turf Cup (Itsallgreektome)
Oaklawn Handicap (Opening Verse)
Sword Dancer Handicap (El Senor)
1991: Breeders' Cup Mile (Opening Verse)
1992: American Derby (The Name's Jimmy)

GREY MONARCH
1977: Whitney Handicap (Nearly On Time)

GREY SOVEREIGN
1967: Hollywood Juvenile Championship (Jim White)
1972: Santa Barbara Handicap (Hail the Grey)
1976: Dwyer Handicap (Quiet Little Table)
1977: Carter Handicap (Quiet Little Table)
Suburban Handicap (Quiet Little Table)

GROTON
1980: Swaps Stakes (First Albert)
1981: Pennsylvania Derby (Summing)
Belmont Stakes (Summing)
Pegasus Handicap (Summing)
1984: San Antonio Handicap (Poley)
1994: Futurity Stakes (Montreal Red)

GUERRERO
1977: Cinema Handicap (Bad 'n Big)
1978: Longacres Mile (Bad 'n Big)

GUILLOTINE
1970: Jerome Handicap (Great Mystery)

GULF STREAM
1962: Hialeah Turf Cup (El Loco)
1975: Sunset Handicap (Cruiser II)
Del Mar Handicap (Cruiser II)

GUMMO
1995: Kentucky Oaks (Gal in a Ruckus)

GUN BOW
1980: Delaware Handicap (Heavenly Ade)
1984: Gotham Stakes (Bear Hunt)

GUN MAGIC
1975: American Derby (Honey Mark)

GUN SHOT
1972: Vosburgh Handicap (Triple Bend)
San Fernando Stakes (Triple Bend)
Santa Anita Handicap (Triple Bend)
1977: Secretariat Stakes (Text)
1978: San Fernando Stakes (Text)
1979: Amory L. Haskell Handicap (Text)
1987: Young America Stakes (Firery Ensign)

HABITAT
1985: Hollywood Derby (Charming Duke)
1994: Breeders' Cup Mile (Barathea)

HADAGAL
1948: Washington Park Futurity (Model Cadet)
1952: Gazelle Stakes (Hushaby Baby)

HAFIZ
1967: Alcibiades Stakes (Lady Tramp)

HAGLEY
1987: Jim Beam Stakes (J.T.'s Pet)
1999: Test Stakes (Marley Vale)

HAIL TO ALL
1982: Louisiana Derby (El Baba)

HAIL TO REASON
1971: Withers Stakes (Bold Reasoning)
Jersey Derby (Bold Reasoning)
Washington Park Handicap (Well Mannered)
1973: Oak Leaf Stakes (Divine Grace)
1975: Amory L. Haskell Handicap (Royal Glint)
Arlington Handicap (Royal Glint)
Hawthorne Gold Cup (Royal Glint)
United Nations Handicap (Royal Glint)
1976: Santa Anita Handicap (Royal Glint)
1977: Santa Barbara Handicap (Desiree)
Apple Blossom Handicap (Hail Hilarious)
1979: Arlington-Washington Futurity (Execution's Reason)
1980: Golden Harvest Handicap (Ribbon)
1982: Suburban Handicap (Silver Buck)
Whitney Handicap (Silver Buck)
1989: Californian Stakes (Sabona)
1990: Ladies Handicap (Colonial Waters)

HAIRAN
1952: Arlington Lassie Stakes (Fulvous)
Princess Pat Stakes (Fulvous)
Will Rogers Stakes (Forelock)
1956: Sapling Stakes (King Hairan)
Hopeful Stakes (King Hairan)
1957: Breeders' Futurity (Fulcrum)
1964: Gotham Stakes (Mr. Moonlight)

HALCYON
1946: Vosburgh Handicap (Coincidence)
Aqueduct Handicap (Coincidence)
1947: Excelsior Handicap (Coincidence)
1949: Acorn Stakes (Nell K.)
Gazelle Stakes (Nell K.)
1950: Top Flight Handicap (Nell K.)
1952: Alabama Stakes (Lily White)
1953: Cowdin Stakes (Fisherman)
Champagne Stakes (Fisherman)
1954: Gotham Stakes (Fisherman)
Travers Stakes (Fisherman)
Lawrence Realization Stakes (Fisherman)
Washington D.C. International (Fisherman)
1955: Excelsior Handicap (Fisherman)
1959: Vanity Handicap (Tender Size)

HALO
1987: Arkansas Derby (Demons Begone)
1991: Remsen Stakes (Pine Bluff)
1992: Arkansas Derby (Pine Bluff)
Preakness Stakes (Pine Bluff)
1994: Vosburgh Stakes (Harlan)
1996: Canadian International Championship (Singspiel)
1997: Apple Blossom Handicap (Halo America)
1998: Toyota Blue Grass Stakes (Halory Hunter)
2002: Arkansas Derby (Private Emblem)
San Juan Capistrano Handicap (Ringaskiddy)
Hollywood Turf Cup (Sligo Bay)

HARBOR PRINCE
1994: Hollywood Turf Handicap (Grand Flotilla)

HARD TACK
1946: Flamingo Stakes (Round View)
1947: Monmouth Handicap (Round View)
1949: Whitney Stakes (Round View)
1958: Delaware Handicap (Endine)
Ladies Handicap (Endine)
1959: Delaware Handicap (Endine)
1961: Delaware Handicap (Airmans Guide)
Beldame Stakes (Airmans Guide)

HARD TO BEAT
1990: Rothmans International Stakes (French Glory)

HARD WORK
1989: Santa Anita Oaks (Imaginary Lady)

HASH
1961: Louisiana Derby (Bass Clef)

HASTE
1947: Wood Memorial Stakes (I Will)
Black Helen Handicap (Shotsilk)

HASTY ROAD
1967: Sorority Stakes (Queen of the Stage)
Spinaway Stakes (Queen of the Stage)
Matron Stakes (Queen of the Stage)
Frizette Stakes (Queen of the Stage)
Gardenia Stakes (Gay Matelda)
1968: Sapling Stakes (Reviewer)
Saratoga Special (Reviewer)

Alabama Stakes (Gay Matelda)
1969: Dwyer Handicap (Gleaming Light)
1972: Donn Handicap (Going Straight)
1974: Donn Handicap (Forego)
Gulfstream Park Handicap (Forego)
Widener Handicap (Forego)
Carter Handicap (Forego)
Brooklyn Handicap (Forego)
Woodward Stakes (Forego)
Vosburgh Handicap (Forego)
Jockey Club Gold Cup (Forego)
Delaware Handicap (Krislin)
1975: Widener Handicap (Forego)
Carter Handicap (Forego)
Brooklyn Handicap (Forego)
Suburban Handicap (Forego)
Woodward Stakes (Forego)
Breeders' Futurity (Harbor Springs)
Demoiselle Stakes (Free Journey)
1976: Metropolitan Handicap (Forego)
Brooklyn Handicap (Forego)
Woodward Handicap (Forego)
Marlboro Cup Handicap (Forego)
1977: Metropolitan Handicap (Forego)
Woodward Handicap (Forego)
1978: Swaps Stakes (Radar Ahead)
1979: San Fernando Stakes (Radar Ahead)
Oaklawn Handicap (San Juan Hill)
1981: Selima Stakes (Snow Plow)
1990: Young America Stakes (Southern Sign)

HATCHET MAN

1991: Blue Grass Stakes (Strike the Gold)
Kentucky Derby (Strike the Gold)
1992: Pimlico Special (Strike the Gold)
Nassau County Handicap (Strike the Gold)
Breeders' Cup Sprint (Thirty Slews)
1998: Remsen Stakes (Comeonmom)
2001: Prioress Stakes (Xtra Heat)

HAWAII

1982: New Orleans Handicap (It's the One)
San Fernando Stakes (It's the One)
Charles H. Strub Stakes (It's the One)
Vosburgh Stakes (Engine One)
1990: Arkansas Derby (Silver Ending)
Pegasus Handicap (Silver Ending)
1995: Hopeful Stakes (Hennessy)
1997: Ballerina Stakes (Pearl City)

HEELFLY

1959: Arlington Futurity (T.V. Lark)
1960: Arlington Classic (T.V. Lark)
American Derby (T.V. Lark)
Washington Park Handicap (T.V. Lark)
United Nations Handicap (T.V. Lark)
1961: Los Angeles Handicap (T.V. Lark)
Hawthorne Gold Cup (T.V. Lark)
Washington D.C. International (T.V. Lark)
1964: Hollywood Oaks (Loukahi)

HELIOPOLIS

1954: Pimlico Futurity (Thinking Cap)
San Juan Capistrano Handicap (By Zeus)
1955: Travers Stakes (Thinking Cap)
Lawrence Realization Stakes (Thinking Cap)
1956: Dwyer Handicap (Riley)
Lawrence Realization Stakes (Riley)
Pimlico Futurity (Missile)
1959: Flamingo Stakes (Troilus)
San Juan Capistrano Handicap (Royal Living)
1962: Saratoga Special (Mr. Cold Storage)
1963: Sapling Stakes (Mr. Brick)
1964: Selima Stakes (Marshua)
Withers Stakes (Mr. Brick)
1965: Flamingo Stakes (Native Charger)
Florida Derby (Native Charger)
Coaching Club American Oaks (Marshua)
1968: Everglades Stakes (Forward Pass)
Florida Derby (Forward Pass)
Blue Grass Stakes (Forward Pass)
Kentucky Derby (Forward Pass)
Preakness Stakes (Forward Pass)
American Derby (Forward Pass)
1971: Futurity Stakes (Riva Ridge)
Champagne Stakes (Riva Ridge)
Pimlico-Laurel Futurity (Riva Ridge)
Garden State Stakes (Riva Ridge)
1972: Blue Grass Stakes (Riva Ridge)
Kentucky Derby (Riva Ridge)
Belmont Stakes (Riva Ridge)
Hollywood Derby (Riva Ridge)
Coaching Club American Oaks (Summer Guest)
Alabama Stakes (Summer Guest)
1973: Grey Lag Handicap (Summer Guest)
Bowling Green Handicap (Summer Guest)
Massachusetts Handicap (Riva Ridge)
Brooklyn Handicap (Riva Ridge)
1974: Spinster Stakes (Summer Guest)
Wood Memorial Stakes (Rube the Great)
1975: Gulfstream Park Handicap (Gold and Myrrh)
Grey Lag Handicap (Gold and Myrrh)
Metropolitan Handicap (Gold and Myrrh)

HELIOPTIC

1967: Arlington-Washington Lassie Stakes (Shenow)

HEPHAISTOS

1947: Santa Susana Stakes (Hubble Bubble)
San Vicente Handicap (Hubble Bubble)

HERBAGER

1980: Top Flight Handicap (Glorious Song)
La Canada Stakes (Glorious Song)
Santa Margarita Handicap (Glorious Song)
1981: Top Flight Handicap (Chain Bracelet)
Spinster Stakes (Glorious Song)
1982: Selima Stakes (Bemissed)
Louisiana Downs Handicap (Rich and Ready)
1983: Laurel Futurity (Devil's Bag)
Champagne Stakes (Devil's Bag)
1985: Delaware Handicap (Basie)
1992: Arlington Classic (Saint Ballado)
1995: Pegasus Handicap (Flying Chevron)
NYRA Mile Handicap (Flying Chevron)

HEROIC

1949: Hollywood Oaks (June Bride)

HE'S A PISTOL

1986: Haskell Invitational Handicap (Wise Times)
Travers Stakes (Wise Times)
Super Derby (Wise Times)

HIGHEST TIDE

1990: Santa Anita Derby (Mister Frisky)

HIGH HAT (1964)

1979: Sheepshead Bay Handicap (Terpsichorist)
1987: Yellow Ribbon Stakes (Carotene)

HIGH HONORS

2001: Strub Stakes (Wooden Phone)

HIGH TIME

1946: Kentucky Oaks (First Page)
Santa Anita Derby (Knockdown)
1947: Breeders' Futurity (Shy Guy)
1948: Excelsior Handicap (Knockdown)
Queens County Handicap (Knockdown)
1951: Washington Park Futurity (Oh Leo)
1953: Excelsior Handicap (First Glance)

HIGH TOP

1985: Californian Stakes (Greinton)
Hollywood Gold Cup (Greinton)
1986: Santa Barbara Handicap (Mountain Bear)
Santa Anita Handicap (Greinton)
Hialeah Turf Cup (Sondrio)

HIGH TRIBUTE

1983: Florida Derby (Croeso)

HILAL

1999: Early Times Hollywood Derby (Super Quercus)
2001: Hollywood Turf Cup (Super Quercus)

HILARIOUS

1981: Golden Harvest Handicap (Mean Martha)
1987: Hollywood Turf Cup (Vilzak)
1988: Matron Stakes (Some Romance)
Frizette Stakes (Some Romance)

HILDUR

1951: Astoria Stakes (Star-Enfin)

HILLARY

1975: American Handicap (Montmartre)
1977: Swaps Stakes (J.O. Tobin)
1978: Vanity Handicap (Afifa)
Californian Stakes (J.O. Tobin)
1979: Santa Susana Stakes (Caline)

HILL PRINCE

1964: Santa Margarita Handicap (Batteur)
1968: Kentucky Oaks (Dark Mirage)
Acorn Stakes (Dark Mirage)
Mother Goose Stakes (Dark Mirage)
Coaching Club American Oaks (Dark Mirage)
Monmouth Oaks (Dark Mirage)
Frizette Stakes (Shuvee)
Selima Stakes (Shuvee)
1969: Acorn Stakes (Shuvee)
Mother Goose Stakes (Shuvee)
Coaching Club American Oaks (Shuvee)
Alabama Stakes (Shuvee)
Ladies Handicap (Shuvee)
1970: Top Flight Handicap (Shuvee)
Beldame Stakes (Shuvee)
Jockey Club Gold Cup (Shuvee)
1971: Top Flight Handicap (Shuvee)
Jockey Club Gold Cup (Shuvee)
1976: Vanity Handicap (Miss Toshiba)

HINDOSTAN

1963: California Derby (On My Honor)

HIS HIGHNESS

1960: Hollywood Juvenile Championship (Pappa's All)
Arlington Futurity (Pappa's All)
1965: Garden State Stakes (Prince Saim)

HIS MAJESTY

1988: Preakness Stakes (Risen Star)
Belmont Stakes (Risen Star)
Jersey Derby (Dynaformer)
1991: Arlington-Washington Lassie Stakes (Speed Dialer)
Pennsylvania Derby (Valley Crossing)
1992: Spinaway Stakes (Family Enterprize)
1993: Swaps Stakes (Devoted Brass)
Philip H. Iselin Handicap (Valley Crossing)

HOIST THE FLAG

1986: Jim Beam Stakes (Broad Brush)
Wood Memorial Stakes (Broad Brush)
Ohio Derby (Broad Brush)
Pennsylvania Derby (Broad Brush)
Meadowlands Cup (Broad Brush)
Frizette Stakes (Personal Ensign)
Oak Leaf Stakes (Sacahuista)
1987: Everglades Stakes (Cryptoclearance)
Florida Derby (Cryptoclearance)
Santa Anita Handicap (Broad Brush)
Suburban Handicap (Broad Brush)
Spinster Stakes (Sacahuista)
Breeders' Cup Distaff (Sacahuista)
Beldame Stakes (Personal Ensign)
1988: Whitney Handicap (Personal Ensign)
Maskette Stakes (Personal Ensign)
Beldame Stakes (Personal Ensign)
Breeders' Cup Distaff (Personal Ensign)
Suburban Handicap (Personal Flag)
1989: Widener Handicap (Cryptoclearance)
1992: Ashland Stakes (Prospectors Delite)
Acorn Stakes (Prospectors Delite)
1993: Hollywood Starlet Stakes (Sardula)
1994: Kentucky Oaks (Sardula)
1996: Pimlico Special (Star Standard)
1997: Alabama Stakes (Runup the Colors)
2002: Gazelle Handicap (Imperial Gesture)
Beldame Stakes (Imperial Gesture)

HOLANDES II

1980: Longacres Mile (Trooper Seven)

HOLD YOUR PEACE

1995: Jerome Handicap (French Deputy)
1999: Del Mar Futurity (Forest Camp)
2002: Prioress Stakes (Carson Hollow)
2003: Toyota Blue Grass Stakes (Peace Rules)
Haskell Invitational Handicap (Peace Rules)

HOMEBUILDER

2001: Frizette Stakes (You)
2002: Las Virgenes Stakes (You)
Santa Anita Oaks (You)
Acorn Stakes (You)
Test Stakes (You)

HOMING

1992: Hollywood Starlet Stakes (Creaking Board)

HONEST PLEASURE

1991: Frizette Stakes (Preach)

HONEYS ALIBI
1973: Washington D.C. International (Dahlia)
1974: Man o' War Stakes (Dahlia)
Canadian International Championship (Dahlia)
1976: Hollywood Invitational Handicap (Dahlia)

HONEYWAY
1965: Washington D.C. International (Diatome)
1970: Hollywood Oaks (Last of the Line)

HORNBEAM
1973: Champagne Stakes (Protagonist)
Laurel Futurity (Protagonist)
1974: Washington D.C. International (Admetus)

HUNTER'S MOON IV
1953: Del Mar Handicap (Goose Khal)
1968: Spinaway Stakes (Queen's Double)

HUSAR
1997: Gotham Stakes (Smokin Mel)

HYPERION
1947: Pimlico Futurity (Citation)
Futurity Stakes (Citation)
1948: Flamingo Stakes (Citation)
Kentucky Derby (Citation)
Preakness Stakes (Citation)
Belmont Stakes (Citation)
American Derby (Citation)
Jockey Club Gold Cup (Citation)
Stars and Stripes Handicap (Citation)
Pimlico Special (Citation)
1951: American Handicap (Citation)
Hollywood Gold Cup (Citation)
McLennan Handicap (Gangway)
1954: Black Helen Handicap (Gainsboro Girl)
New Castle Handicap (Gainsboro Girl)
1955: San Juan Capistrano Handicap (St. Vincent)
Dixie Handicap (St. Vincent)
New Orleans Handicap (Sea O Erin)
1957: Dixie Handicap (Akbar Khan)
1958: Michigan Mile (Nearctic)
1959: Futurity Stakes (Weatherwise)
Selima Stakes (La Fuerza)
1962: Garden State Stakes (Crewman)
1963: Travers Stakes (Crewman)
1965: Pimlico Futurity (Spring Double)
Ohio Derby (Terri Hi)
1966: Seminole Handicap (Convex)
1967: Santa Anita Handicap (Pretense)
Gulfstream Park Handicap (Pretense)
San Antonio Handicap (Pretense)

HYPNOTIST II
1959: Sunset Handicap (Whodunit)
1961: Sunset Handicap (Whodunit)

I APPEAL
1968: Gazelle Handicap (Another Nell)

ICECAPADE
1985: Ruffian Handicap (Lady's Secret)
Maskette Stakes (Lady's Secret)
Beldame Stakes (Lady's Secret)
1986: La Canada Stakes (Lady's Secret)
Santa Margarita Handicap (Lady's Secret)
Whitney Handicap (Lady's Secret)
Maskette Stakes (Lady's Secret)
Ruffian Handicap (Lady's Secret)
Beldame Stakes (Lady's Secret)
Breeders' Cup Distaff (Lady's Secret)
1991: Milady Handicap (Brought to Mind)
Vanity Handicap (Brought to Mind)
1993: Charles H. Strub Stakes (Siberian Summer)
1999: Hempstead Handicap (Sister Act)

IDENTIFY
1952: Flamingo Stakes (Blue Man)
Preakness Stakes (Blue Man)
Dwyer Stakes (Blue Man)

IDLE MINDS
1993: Ashland Stakes (Lunar Spook)

I'MA HELL RAISER
1996: Fountain of Youth Stakes (Built for Pleasure)
1998: Ballerina Handicap (Stop Traffic)
1999: Santa Monica Handicap (Stop Traffic)

IMBROS
1966: California Derby (Tragniew)
1980: Ohio Derby (Stone Manor)

I'M FOR MORE
1985: Selima Stakes (I'm Splendid)

IMPRESSIVE
1984: Withers Stakes (Play On)

INCANTATION
1946: Trenton Handicap (Turbine)

INDIAN CHIEF
1992: Fantasy Stakes (Race the Wild Wind)
1993: Santa Maria Handicap (Race the Wild Wind)

INDIAN HEMP
1973: Pan American Handicap (Lord Vancouver)
1974: Hollywood Juvenile Championship (DiMaggio)

INFATUATION
1971: Inglewood Handicap (Advance Guard)

INFINITE
1956: California Derby (No Regrets)

IN REALITY
1984: Champagne Stakes (For Certain Doc)
1986: Man o' War Stakes (Dance of Life)
Matron Stakes (Tappiano)
1988: Californian Stakes (Cutlass Reality)
Hollywood Gold Cup (Cutlass Reality)
1990: Spinaway Stakes (Meadow Star)
Matron Stakes (Meadow Star)
Frizette Stakes (Meadow Star)
Breeders' Cup Juvenile Fillies (Meadow Star)
Oak Leaf Stakes (Lite Light)
1991: Santa Anita Oaks (Lite Light)
Fantasy Stakes (Lite Light)
Kentucky Oaks (Lite Light)
Coaching Club American Oaks (Lite Light)
Acorn Stakes (Meadow Star)
Mother Goose Stakes (Meadow Star)
1992: Beldame Stakes (Saratoga Dew)
1993: Gamely Handicap (Toussaud)
1997: Jim Beam Stakes (Concerto)
2000: Belmont Stakes (Commendable)

INSCO
1947: Flamingo Stakes (Faultless)
Blue Grass Stakes (Faultless)
Withers Stakes (Faultless)
Preakness Stakes (Faultless)
Vosburgh Handicap (With Pleasure)
1948: Gallant Fox Handicap (Faultless)
Inglewood Handicap (With Pleasure)
1954: McLennan Handicap (Elixir)

INTENT
1969: San Fernando Stakes (Cavamore)
1970: Breeders' Futurity (Man of the Moment)

INTENTIONALLY
1974: Demoiselle Stakes (Land Girl)
1975: Gazelle Handicap (Land Girl)
1978: Vosburgh Handicap (Dr. Patches)
Meadowlands Cup (Dr. Patches)
1983: United Nations Handicap (Acaroid)
1984: Arlington Handicap (Who's For Dinner)
1985: San Felipe Handicap (Image of Greatness)
1991: Top Flight Handicap (Buy the Firm)

INVERNESS DRIVE
1991: Hempstead Handicap (A Wild Ride)

INVOLVEMENT
1976: Laurel Futurity (Royal Ski)
Remsen Stakes (Royal Ski)

IPE
1955: Bougainvillea Turf Handicap (Cascanuez)
1957: William P. Kyne Memorial Handicap (Pibe Carlitos)
1971: Century Handicap (Big Shot II)
Manhattan Handicap (Big Shot II)

IRISH DUDE
1985: Tropical Park Derby (Irish Sur)

IRISH RIVER
1993: Breeders' Cup Classic (Arcangues)

IRISH STRONGHOLD
1993: Santa Barbara Handicap (Exchange)
1994: Matriarch Stakes (Exchange)

IRISH TOWER
1998: Vosburgh Stakes (Affirmed Success)
1999: Cigar Mile Handicap (Affirmed Success)
2002: Carter Handicap (Affirmed Success)

IRON RULER
1981: Norfolk Stakes (Stalwart)
Hollywood Futurity (Stalwart)
1987: Jersey Derby (Avies Copy)

IRON WARRIOR
1989: Del Mar Futurity (Drag Race)

ISOLATER
1954: Gulfstream Park Handicap (Wise Margin)
Massachusetts Handicap (Wise Margin)
1957: Sapling Stakes (Plion)
1958: Blue Grass Stakes (Plion)
1959: Whitney Stakes (Plion)
1963: Black Helen Handicap (Pocosaba)

IT'S FREEZING
2000: Remsen Stakes (Windsor Castle)

I WILL
1966: Gazelle Handicap (Prides Profile)

JACINTO
1981: Del Mar Futurity (Gato Del Sol)
1982: Kentucky Derby (Gato Del Sol)
1984: Santa Barbara Handicap (Comedy Act)
1986: Brooklyn Handicap (Little Missouri)
1988: Del Mar Futurity (Music Merci)
1989: Illinois Derby (Music Merci)

JACK HIGH
1946: Spinaway Stakes (Pipette)
1951: Beldame Handicap (Thelma Berger)
Hawthorne Gold Cup (Seaward)
1953: Alcibiades Stakes (Oil Painting)
1955: Roamer Handicap (Sailor)
Fall Highweight Handicap (Sailor)
Pimlico Special (Sailor)
Sapling Stakes (Needles)
Hopeful Stakes (Needles)
Maskette Handicap (Oil Painting)
1956: Flamingo Stakes (Needles)
Florida Derby (Needles)
Kentucky Derby (Needles)
Belmont Stakes (Needles)
Gulfstream Park Handicap (Sailor)
John B. Campbell Memorial Handicap (Sailor)

JACOPO
1946: Remsen Handicap (Phalanx)
Gulfstream Handicap (Do-Reigh-Me)
1947: Wood Memorial Stakes (Phalanx)
Belmont Stakes (Phalanx)
Dwyer Stakes (Phalanx)
Jockey Club Gold Cup (Phalanx)
1948: Arlington Lassie Stakes (Pail of Water)
1950: New York Handicap (Pilaster)
1953: San Felipe Handicap (Decorated)
1957: Arlington Lassie Stakes (Poly Hi)
1960: Everglades Stakes (Moslem Chief)
1961: United Nations Handicap (Oink)
1963: Cowdin Stakes (Dunfee)

JADE HUNTER
2003: Secretariat Stakes (Kicken Kris)

JAMAICA INN
1966: Sorority Stakes (Like A Charm)

JAMESTOWN
1948: Selima Stakes (Gaffery)
1949: Santa Susana Stakes (Gaffery)
Ladies Handicap (Gaffery)
1951: Queens County Handicap (Sheilas Reward)
1956: Black Helen Handicap (Seven Thirty)
Delaware Handicap (Seven Thirty)

JAN EKELS
1996: Sword Dancer Invitational Handicap (Broadway Flyer)

JARDINIERE
1976: Santa Barbara Handicap (Stravina)

JEAN-PIERRE
1983: Wood Memorial Stakes (Bounding Basque)
1985: Withers Stakes (El Basco)
Brooklyn Handicap (Bounding Basque)

JEAN VALJEAN
1948: Remsen Stakes (Eternal World)
1949: Astoria Stakes (Baby Comet)
1950: Westerner Stakes (Valquest)

JEEP
1963: Delaware Handicap (Waltz Song)

JESTER
1972: Norfolk Stakes (Groshawk)
Del Mar Futurity (Groshawk)
1977: San Felipe Handicap (Smasher)
1982: Hollywood Starlet Stakes (Fabulous Notion)
1983: Santa Susana Stakes (Fabulous Notion)
1990: Turf Classic (Cacoethes)

JET ACTION
1970: Sorority Stakes (Forward Gal)
Spinaway Stakes (Forward Gal)
Frizette Stakes (Forward Gal)
Withers Stakes (Hagley)
1971: Monmouth Oaks (Forward Gal)
Gazelle Handicap (Forward Gal)
1973: Wood Memorial Stakes (Angle Light)

JET PILOT
1977: San Fernando Stakes (Pocket Park)

JIG TIME
1985: Vosburgh Stakes (Another Reef)

JIM FRENCH
1989: Arlington Million (Steinlen)
Breeders' Cup Mile (Steinlen)
1990: Hollywood Turf Handicap (Steinlen)
Caesars International Handicap (Steinlen)

JIMMER
1982: California Derby (Rockwall)

JOCK II
1962: San Felipe Handicap (Doc Jocoy)
California Derby (Doc Jocoy)
1963: Los Angeles Handicap (Doc Jocoy)

JOHNNY APPLESEED
1990: Woodward Handicap (Dispersal)

JOHN P. GRIER
1946: Pimlico Oaks (Red Shoes)
1948: Acorn Stakes (Watermill)
1949: Fall Highweight Handicap (Royal Governor)
Grey Lag Handicap (Royal Governor)
1950: Widener Handicap (Royal Governor)
1951: Preakness Stakes (Bold)
Saranac Handicap (Bold)
Discovery Handicap (Alerted)
Jerome Handicap (Alerted)
Stars and Stripes Handicap (Royal Governor)
1952: Dixie Handicap (Alerted)
1956: Brooklyn Handicap (Dedicate)
Whitney Stakes (Dedicate)
Hawthorne Gold Cup (Dedicate)
1957: John B. Campbell Memorial Handicap (Dedicate)
Monmouth Handicap (Dedicate)
Woodward Stakes (Dedicate)

JOHN'S GOLD
1998: Frank J. De Francis Memorial Dash (Kelly Kip)

JOHNS JOY
1970: San Felipe Handicap (Terlago)
Santa Anita Derby (Terlago)
Beverly Hills Handicap (Pattee Canyon)
1976: Secretariat Stakes (Joachim)
1982: Golden Harvest Handicap (Miss Huntington)
1983: Apple Blossom Handicap (Miss Huntington)

JOHNSTOWN
1950: Arlington Futurity (To Market)
Washington Park Futurity (To Market)
1952: San Carlos Handicap (To Market)
Massachusetts Handicap (To Market)
Arlington Handicap (To Market)
Hawthorne Gold Cup (To Market)
1953: Alabama Stakes (Sabette)
1954: Hopeful Stakes (Nashua)
Futurity Stakes (Nashua)
1955: Flamingo Stakes (Nashua)
Florida Derby (Nashua)
Wood Memorial Stakes (Nashua)
Preakness Stakes (Nashua)
Belmont Stakes (Nashua)
Dwyer Stakes (Nashua)
Arlington Classic (Nashua)
Jockey Club Gold Cup (Nashua)
1956: Widener Handicap (Nashua)
Grey Lag Handicap (Nashua)
Suburban Handicap (Nashua)
Monmouth Handicap (Nashua)
Jockey Club Gold Cup (Nashua)
Del Mar Futurity (Swirling Abbey)
1959: San Carlos Handicap (Hillsdale)
Los Angeles Handicap (Hillsdale)
Californian Stakes (Hillsdale)
American Handicap (Hillsdale)
Hollywood Gold Cup (Hillsdale)
Aqueduct Handicap (Hillsdale)
Santa Anita Maturity (Hillsdale)
1960: San Fernando Stakes (King o' Turf)
1962: Suburban Handicap (Beau Purple)
Brooklyn Handicap (Beau Purple)
Hawthorne Gold Cup (Beau Purple)
Man o' War Stakes (Beau Purple)
1963: Widener Handicap (Beau Purple)
Arlington Park Handicap (Bounding Main)
1965: Arkansas Derby (Swift Ruler)
1966: Oaklawn Handicap (Swift Ruler)

JOHN WILLIAM
1979: Hopeful Stakes (J.P. Brother)

JOLLY WARREN
1984: Top Flight Handicap (Sweet Missus)

JONTILLA
1993: Vosburgh Stakes (Birdonthewire)

J.O. TOBIN
1993: Breeders' Cup Sprint (Cardmania)

JUNGLE ROAD
1981: American Derby (Pocket Zipper)

KAHYASI
2001: Breeders' Cup Filly and Mare Turf (Banks Hill)
2003: Beverly D. Stakes (Heat Haze)
Matriarch Stakes (Heat Haze)

KALDOUN
2001: Del Mar Oaks (Golden Apples)
Matriarch Stakes (Starine)
2002: Beverly D. Stakes (Golden Apples)
Yellow Ribbon Stakes (Golden Apples)
Breeders' Cup Filly and Mare Turf (Starine)

KARABAS
1991: San Juan Capistrano Handicap (Mashkour)

KASHMIR II
1996: Oak Tree Turf Championship (Admise)

KAUAI KING
1977: Hollywood Juvenile Championship (Noble Bronze)
1978: California Derby (Noble Bronze)

KAUTOKEINO
1999: Ramona Handicap (Tuzla)

KENMARE
1996: Breeders' Cup Sprint (Lit de Justice)

KEY TO THE MINT
1989: Ashland Stakes (Gorgeous)
Hollywood Oaks (Gorgeous)
Jerome Handicap (De Roche)
1990: La Canada Stakes (Gorgeous)
Apple Blossom Handicap (Gorgeous)
Vanity Handicap (Gorgeous)
Kentucky Oaks (Seaside Attraction)
Yellow Ribbon Stakes (Plenty of Grace)
1991: Travers Stakes (Corporate Report)
1992: Frizette Stakes (Educated Risk)
1993: Top Flight Handicap (You'd Be Surprised)
1994: Ashland Stakes (Inside Information)
Acorn Stakes (Inside Information)
Apple Blossom Handicap (Nine Keys)
Top Flight Handicap (Educated Risk)
1995: Shuvee Handicap (Inside Information)
Ruffian Handicap (Inside Information)
Spinster Stakes (Inside Information)
Breeders' Cup Distaff (Inside Information)
Suburban Handicap (Key Contender)
Hollywood Turf Cup (Royal Chariot)
1997: Caesars International Handicap (Influent)
Man o' War Stakes (Influent)
1999: Flower Bowl Invitational Handicap (Soaring Softly)
Breeders' Cup Filly and Mare Turf (Soaring Softly)
2003: Breeders' Cup Distaff (Adoration)

KHALED
1961: Santa Anita Handicap (Prove It)
San Fernando Stakes (Prove It)
Santa Anita Maturity (Prove It)
1962: Inglewood Handicap (Prove It)
American Handicap (Prove It)
Hollywood Gold Cup (Prove It)
Sunset Handicap (Prove It)
Washington Park Handicap (Prove It)
Hopeful Stakes (Outing Class)
Arlington-Washington Futurity (Candy Spots)
Manhattan Handicap (Tutankhamen)
1963: Santa Anita Derby (Candy Spots)
Florida Derby (Candy Spots)
Preakness Stakes (Candy Spots)
Jersey Derby (Candy Spots)
American Derby (Candy Spots)
Arlington Classic (Candy Spots)
Dwyer Handicap (Outing Class)
Donn Handicap (Tutankhamen)
1964: Cinema Handicap (Close By)
1966: Vanity Handicap (Khal Ireland)
Sunset Handicap (O'Hara)
1969: Hollywood Oaks (Tipping Time)
1984: Breeders' Cup Classic (Wild Again)

KING COLE
1964: Mother Goose Stakes (Sceree)
1965: Hollywood Oaks (Straight Deal)
Ladies Handicap (Straight Deal)
1966: Santa Margarita Handicap (Straight Deal)
Santa Barbara Handicap (Straight Deal)
1967: Top Flight Handicap (Straight Deal)
Delaware Handicap (Straight Deal)
Spinster Stakes (Straight Deal)

KING EMPEROR
1987: California Derby (Simply Majestic)
1990: Arlington Classic (Sound of Cannons)
1992: Budweiser International Stakes (Zoman)
1993: Rothmans International Stakes (Husband)

KING OF THE TUDORS
1977: New Orleans Handicap (Tudor Tambourine)

KING PELLINORE
1990: Del Mar Futurity (Best Pal)
Norfolk Stakes (Best Pal)
Hollywood Futurity (Best Pal)
1991: Swaps Stakes (Best Pal)
Pacific Classic (Best Pal)
1992: Charles H. Strub Stakes (Best Pal)
Santa Anita Handicap (Best Pal)
Oaklawn Handicap (Best Pal)
1993: Hollywood Gold Cup (Best Pal)
1995: San Antonio Handicap (Best Pal)

KING SALMON
1962: Carter Handicap (Merry Ruler)

KING'S BISHOP
1996: Strub Stakes (Helmsman)

KING'S BLUE
1960: Michigan Mile and One-Sixteenth (Little Fitz)

KING'S TROOP
1985: Metropolitan Handicap (Forzando II)

KNAVE HIGH
1967: Black Helen Handicap (Mac's Sparkler)
Beldame Stakes (Mac's Sparkler)

KNIGHTLY DAWN
1986: Washington D.C. International (Lieutenant's Lark)

KNIGHTLY MANNER
1991: Sword Dancer Handicap (Dr. Root)

KNOWN FACT
1998: Coaching Club American Oaks (Banshee Breeze)
Alabama Stakes (Banshee Breeze)
Three Chimneys Spinster Stakes (Banshee Breeze)
1999: Apple Blossom Handicap (Banshee Breeze)
Go for Wand Handicap (Banshee Breeze)

KRIS
1995: Sword Dancer Invitational Handicap (Kiri's Clown)

KRIS S.
2000: Eddie Read Handicap (Ladies Din)
Breeders' Cup Mile (War Chant)
2002: Shoemaker Breeders' Cup Mile (Ladies Din)

KUBLAI KHAN
1996: Hollywood Gold Cup (Siphon)
1997: Santa Anita Handicap (Siphon)

KY. COLONEL
1970: Kentucky Jockey Club Stakes (Line City)
1971: Spinster Stakes (Chou Croute)

LA BRIGE
1950: Gulfstream Park Handicap (Chicle II)
Trenton Handicap (Chicle II)
Bougainvillea Handicap (Chicle II)
1951: Bougainvillea Handicap (Chicle II)

LAGUNAS
2002: Flower Bowl Invitational Handicap (Kazzia)

LANARK
1983: Californian Stakes (The Wonder)
Century Handicap (The Wonder)

LANCEGAYE
1965: Monmouth Handicap (Repeating)

LAOMEDONTE
1992: Super Derby (Senor Tomas)

LASER LIGHT
1988: Blue Grass Stakes (Granacus)

LAST TYCOON
2000: Santa Anita Derby (The Deputy)
2003: Arkansas Derby (Sir Cherokee)

LEAR FAN
2002: Hollywood Derby (Johar)
2003: Del Mar Oaks (Dessert)
John Deere Breeders' Cup Turf (Johar)

LE FABULEUX
1983: Hollywood Derby (Ginger Brink)
1986: United Nations Handicap (Manila)
Turf Classic (Manila)
Breeders' Cup Turf (Manila)
1987: United Nations Handicap (Manila)
Budweiser-Arlington Million (Manila)
Budweiser International Stakes (Le Glorieux)
Ladies Handicap (Nastique)
Hollywood Derby (Stately Don)
1988: Delaware Handicap (Nastique)
1989: Delaware Handicap (Nastique)
1990: Florida Derby (Unbridled)
Kentucky Derby (Unbridled)
Breeders' Cup Classic (Unbridled)
1991: Wood Memorial Stakes (Cahill Road)
1995: Remsen Stakes (Tropicool)
1998: Early Times Turf Classic (Joyeaux Danseur)

LEGEND OF FRANCE
1958: Washington D.C. International (Sailor's Guide)
1964: Man o' War Stakes (Turbo Jet II)

LE HAAR
1975: Monmouth Invitational Handicap (Wajima)
Travers Stakes (Wajima)
Marlboro Cup Handicap (Wajima)

LEISURE TIME
1963: Del Mar Debutante Stakes (Leisurely Kin)

LE LEVANSTELL
1981: Century Handicap (Spence Bay)

LEND LEASE
1997: Vosburgh Stakes (Victor Cooley)

L'ENJOLEUR
1989: Norfolk Stakes (Grand Canyon)
Hollywood Futurity (Grand Canyon)

LEO CASTELLI
1998: Santa Anita Derby (Indian Charlie)

LICENCIOSO
1974: Santa Margarita Handicap (Tizna)
Ramona Handicap (Tizna)
1975: Ladies Handicap (Tizna)
Santa Margarita Handicap (Tizna)

LIGHT BRIGADE
1946: Bougainvillea Handicap (Cat Bridge)

LIGHT IDEA
2002: Mother Goose Stakes (Nonsuch Bay)

LILOY
1993: Super Derby (Wallenda)

LIMELIGHT
1973: Hollywood Oaks (Sandy Blue)
1976: San Antonio Stakes (Lightning Mandate)

LINACRE
1979: Jerome Handicap (Czaravich)
1980: Metropolitan Handicap (Czaravich)

LINKAGE
1995: Acorn Stakes (Cat's Cradle)

LINMOLD
1980: Norfolk Stakes (Sir Dancer)

LITTLE CURRENT
1996: Queen Elizabeth II Chal. Cup (Memories of Silver)
1997: Beverly D. Stakes (Memories of Silver)

LITTLETOWN
1967: Santa Margarita Handicap (Miss Moona)

LOANINGDALE
1953: Trenton Handicap (Olympic)

LONGSTONE
1972: Cinema Handicap (Finalista)

LOOSE CANNON
1997: San Antonio Handicap (Gentlemen)
Pimlico Special (Gentlemen)
Hollywood Gold Cup (Gentlemen)
Pacific Classic (Gentlemen)
1998: San Antonio Handicap (Gentlemen)

LORD AT WAR
2000: Del Mar Oaks (No Matter What)
2001: Oak Leaf Stakes (Tali'sluckybusride)
2002: Kentucky Derby (War Emblem)
Preakness Stakes (War Emblem)
Haskell Invitational Handicap (War Emblem)
Suburban Handicap (E. Dubai)

LORD AVIE
2002: Del Mar Debutante Stakes (Miss Houdini)

LORD GAYLE
1988: Flower Bowl Handicap (Gaily Gaily)

LORD GAYLORD
1998: Queen Elizabeth II Challenge Cup (Tenski)

LOSER WEEPER
1972: Arlington-Washington Lassie Stakes (Natural Sound)

LOST CODE
2001: King's Bishop Stakes (Squirtle Squirt)
Penske Auto Center BC Sprint (Squirtle Squirt)

LOVELY NIGHT
1958: Alabama Stakes (Tempted)
Maskette Handicap (Tempted)
1959: Diana Handicap (Tempted)
Beldame Handicap (Tempted)
Ladies Handicap (Tempted)
1963: Manhattan Handicap (Smart)
1964: Massachusetts Handicap (Smart)
Gallant Fox Handicap (Smart)
1965: Massachusetts Handicap (Smart)

LT. STEVENS
1987: Kentucky Derby (Alysheba)
Preakness Stakes (Alysheba)
Super Derby (Alysheba)
1988: Charles H. Strub Stakes (Alysheba)
Santa Anita Handicap (Alysheba)
Philip H. Iselin Handicap (Alysheba)
Woodward Handicap (Alysheba)
Meadowlands Cup (Alysheba)
Breeders' Cup Classic (Alysheba)

LUCKY DEBONAIR
1977: Del Mar Futurity (Go West Young Man)
1980: Hollywood Gold Cup (Go West Young Man)
Del Mar Handicap (Go West Young Man)
Century Handicap (Go West Young Man)

LUCKY NORTH
2003: Test Stakes (Lady Tak)

LUCULLITE
1952: Sapling Stakes (Landlocked)
1954: Widener Handicap (Landlocked)

LUTHIER
1988: Sunset Handicap (Roi Normand)
1991: Budweiser International Stakes (Leariva)

LUXEMBURGO
1969: Michigan Mile and One-Eighth (Calandrito)

LYPHARD
1991: Eddie Read Handicap (Tight Spot)
Arlington Million (Tight Spot)
Ohio Derby (Private Man)
Oak Tree Invitational Stakes (Filago)
1992: Jim Dandy Stakes (Thunder Rumble)
Travers Stakes (Thunder Rumble)
1993: Hollywood Futurity (Valiant Nature)
1994: Beverly D. Stakes (Hatoof)
2000: Apple Blossom Handicap (Heritage of Gold)
Go for Wand Handicap (Heritage of Gold)
Pacific Classic (Skimming)
2001: Shoemaker Breeders' Cup Mile (Irish Prize)
Go for Wand Handicap (Serra Lake)
Pacific Classic (Skimming)
2003: San Juan Capistrano Handicap (Passinetti)
Garden City BC Handicap (Indy Five Hundred)

LYPHEOR
1998: Las Virgenes Stakes (Keeper Hill)
Kentucky Oaks (Keeper Hill)
1999: Three Chimneys Spinster Stakes (Keeper Hill)

MACARTHUR PARK
1986: San Felipe Handicap (Variety Road)
1987: San Fernando Stakes (Variety Road)

MACHIAVELLIAN
2002: Coaching Club American Oaks (Jilbab)

MADARA
1971: Californian Stakes (Cougar II)
Ford Pinto Invitational Turf Handicap (Cougar II)
Oak Tree Invitational Stakes (Cougar II)
San Juan Capistrano Handicap (Cougar II)
1972: Californian Stakes (Cougar II)
Century Handicap (Cougar II)
Oak Tree Invitational Stakes (Cougar II)
1973: Santa Anita Handicap (Cougar II)
Century Handicap (Cougar II)
Sunset Handicap (Cougar II)

MAD HATTER
1946: New Orleans Handicap (Hillyer Court)
1950: Saranac Handicap (Sunglow)
Discovery Handicap (Sunglow)
Remsen Handicap (Repetoire)
1951: Wood Memorial Stakes (Repetoire)
Widener Handicap (Sunglow)

MAGESTERIAL
1991: Hollywood Starlet Stakes (Magical Maiden)
1996: Hopeful Stakes (Smoke Glacken)
1997: Frank J. De Francis Memorial Dash (Smoke Glacken)

MAGPIE
1948: Hollywood Gold Cup (Shannon II)
Golden Gate Handicap (Shannon II)

MAHMOUD
1949: Del Mar Futurity (Your Host)
1950: San Felipe Stakes (Your Host)
Santa Anita Derby (Your Host)
1951: Marguerite Stakes (No Score)
1953: Westchester Handicap (Cold Command)
1954: San Felipe Handicap (Determine)
Santa Anita Derby (Determine)
Kentucky Derby (Determine)
1955: Monmouth Oaks (Misty Morn)

Molly Pitcher Handicap (Misty Morn)
Gallant Fox Handicap (Misty Morn)
Santa Anita Maturity (Determine)
1956: Gotham Stakes (Career Boy)
United Nations Handicap (Career Boy)
Wood Memorial Stakes (Head Man)
Michigan Mile (Nonnie Jo)
1957: Belmont Stakes (Gallant Man)
Travers Stakes (Gallant Man)
Jockey Club Gold Cup (Gallant Man)
Lawrence Realization Stakes (Promised Land)
Roamer Handicap (Promised Land)
Pimlico Special (Promised Land)
Remsen Stakes (Misty Flight)
1958: Metropolitan Handicap (Gallant Man)
Hollywood Gold Cup (Gallant Man)
Sunset Handicap (Gallant Man)
John B. Campbell Mem. Handicap (Promised Land)
Massachusetts Handicap (Promised Land)
San Juan Capistrano Handicap (Promised Land)
Santa Margarita Handicap (Born Rich)
San Felipe Handicap (Carrier X.)
1959: Santa Anita Derby (Silver Spoon)
Cinema Handicap (Silver Spoon)
Arlington Classic (Dunce)
American Derby (Dunce)
1960: Vanity Handicap (Silver Spoon)
Santa Margarita Handicap (Silver Spoon)
1961: Hollywood Juvenile Championship (Rattle Dancer)
Vanity Handicap (Perizade)
San Juan Capistrano Handicap (Don't Alibi)
1965: Suburban Handicap (Pia Star)
Brooklyn Handicap (Pia Star)
Arlington-Washington Lassie Stakes (Silver Bright)
1966: Spinaway Stakes (Silver True)
Widener Handicap (Pia Star)
1967: Hopeful Stakes (What a Pleasure)
Cowdin Stakes (Iron Ruler)
Garden State Stakes (Bugged)
Carter Handicap (Tumiga)
1968: Travers Stakes (Chompion)
Jerome Handicap (Iron Ruler)
1971: Pan American Handicap (Chompion)
Dixie Handicap (Chompion)
Massachusetts Handicap (Chompion)

MAJESTIC LIGHT
1989: Selima Stakes (Sweet Roberta)
1996: Whitney Handicap (Mahogany Hall)
NYRA Mile Handicap (Gold Fever)
Remsen Stakes (The Silver Move)
2000: Lane's End Breeders' Futurity (Arabian Light)

MAJESTIC PRINCE
1980: Arlington-Washington Futurity (Well Decorated)
1983: Bay Meadows Handicap (Interco)
1984: San Fernando Stakes (Interco)
Santa Anita Handicap (Interco)
San Luis Rey Stakes (Interco)
Century Handicap (Interco)
2000: Breeders' Cup Juvenile Fillies (Caressing)
2002: Santa Monica Handicap (Kalookan Queen)
Ancient Title BC Handicap (Kalookan Queen)

MAJORITY BLUE
1986: Coaching Club American Oaks (Valley Victory)

MALICIOUS
1987: Alabama Stakes (Up the Apalachee)

MALINOWSKI
1997: Travers Stakes (Deputy Commander)
Super Derby (Deputy Commander)

MANDAMUS
1980: Yellow Ribbon Stakes (Kilijaro)
1981: Matriarch Stakes (Kilijaro)

MANIFESTO
1982: Arlington-Washington Futurity (Total Departure)

MANNA
1949: Aqueduct Handicap (Wine List)
1950: Aqueduct Handicap (Wine List)

MAN O' NIGHT
1951: Louisiana Derby (Whirling Bat)

MAN O' WAR
1946: Coaching Club American Oaks (Hypnotic)
Alabama Stakes (Hypnotic)
Jockey Club Gold Cup (Pavot)
Massachusetts Handicap (Pavot)
Ladies Handicap (Athenia)
Jerome Handicap (Mahout)
1947: Beldame Handicap (Snow Goose)
Ladies Handicap (Snow Goose)
Coaching Club American Oaks (Harmonica)
1948: Travers Stakes (Ace Admiral)
Lawrence Realization Stakes (Ace Admiral)
Black Helen Handicap (Rampart)
Gulfstream Park Handicap (Rampart)
Suburban Handicap (Harmonica)
Manhattan Handicap (Loyal Legion)
1949: Inglewood Handicap (Ace Admiral)
Sunset Handicap (Ace Admiral)
Santa Anita Maturity (Ace Admiral)
Kentucky Jockey Club Stakes (Roman Bath)
Alabama Stakes (Adile)
San Carlos Handicap (Manyunk)
1950: Louisiana Derby (Greek Ship)
Metropolitan Handicap (Greek Ship)
Monmouth Handicap (Greek Ship)
Cowdin Stakes (Away Away)
Hollywood Oaks (Mrs. Fuddy)
New Castle Handicap (Adile)
1951: Black Helen Handicap (Antagonism)
Sunset Handicap (Alderman)
1952: Florida Derby (Sky Ship)
1954: Pimlico Special (Helioscope)
Trenton Handicap (Helioscope)
1955: Massachusetts Handicap (Helioscope)
Suburban Handicap (Helioscope)
Monmouth Handicap (Helioscope)
Roseben Handicap (Red Hannigan)
Hawthorne Gold Cup (Hasseyampa)
1956: Carter Handicap (Red Hannigan)
1957: Kentucky Jockey Club Stakes (Hill Country)

MARIBEAU
1979: California Derby (Beau's Eagle)
1980: San Antonio Stakes (Beau's Eagle)
1982: San Felipe Handicap (Advance Man)

MARI'S BOOK
1997: Buick Pegasus Handicap (Behrens)
1999: Gulfstream Park Handicap (Behrens)
Oaklawn Handicap (Behrens)
Suburban Handicap (Behrens)
2000: Gulfstream Park Handicap (Behrens)
2001: Wood Memorial Stakes (Congaree)
Swaps Stakes (Congaree)
2002: Cigar Mile Handicap (Congaree)
2003: Carter Handicap (Congaree)
Hollywood Gold Cup (Congaree)
Cigar Mile Handicap (Congaree)
Spinaway Stakes (Ashado)

MARKET WISE
1958: Arlington Classic (A Dragon Killer)

MARON
1948: San Antonio Handicap (Talon)
Santa Anita Handicap (Talon)

MARSHUA'S DANCER
1988: Hollywood Starlet Stakes (Stocks Up)
1998: Malibu Stakes (Run Man Run)

MARTINI II
1981: Futurity Stakes (Irish Martini)

MARTINS RULLAH
1977: La Canada Stakes (Lucie Manet)
Santa Margarita Stakes (Lucie Manet)

MASETTO
1969: Pan American Handicap (Hibernian)

MASTER GUNNER
1973: Del Mar Futurity (Such a Rush)

MATADOR
1966: Withers Stakes (Indulto)
1972: Vanity Handicap (Convenience)
1973: Vanity Handicap (Convenience)
1974: Santa Maria Handicap (Convenience)

MATCH THE HATCH
1997: Malibu Stakes (Lord Grillo)

MATE
1947: Sapling Stakes (Task)

MEDAILLE D'OR
1994: Hollywood Futurity (Afternoon Deelites)
1995: San Felipe Stakes (Afternoon Deelites)
Malibu Stakes (Afternoon Deelites)

MEDIEVAL MAN
1997: Hopeful Stakes (Favorite Trick)
Breeders' Cup Juvenile (Favorite Trick)
1998: Jim Dandy Stakes (Favorite Trick)

MEHRALI
1969: Stars and Stripes Handicap (Hawaii)
United Nations Handicap (Hawaii)
Man o' War Stakes (Hawaii)

MEL HASH
1968: Black Helen Handicap (Treacherous)

MELYNO
1996: Vanity Handicap (Jewel Princess)
Breeders' Cup Distaff (Jewel Princess)
1997: Santa Maria Handicap (Jewel Princess)
Santa Margarita Handicap (Jewel Princess)

MENEVAL
1987: Hollywood Oaks (Perchance to Dream)

MENOW
1954: Selima Stakes (High Voltage)
Matron Stakes (High Voltage)
Del Mar Debutante Stakes (Fair Molly)
1955: Acorn Stakes (High Voltage)
Coaching Club American Oaks (High Voltage)
Delaware Oaks (High Voltage)
Vineland Handicap (High Voltage)
Blue Grass Stakes (Racing Fool)
1957: San Felipe Handicap (Joe Price)
1959: Hollywood Juvenile Championship (Noble Noor)
1960: California Derby (Noble Noor)
1961: Del Mar Debutante Stakes (Spark Plug)
1962: Frizette Stakes (Pams Ego)
1963: Sorority Stakes (Castle Forbes)
Gardenia Stakes (Castle Forbes)
Withers Stakes (Get Around)
1964: Acorn Stakes (Castle Forbes)

MESSENGER
1946: Arlington Handicap (Historian)
Sunset Handicap (Historian)

METRIC MILE
1984: American Derby (High Alexander)

METROGRAND
2000: Del Mar Futurity (Flame Thrower)
Norfolk Stakes (Flame Thrower)

MICKEY MCGUIRE
1991: Champagne Stakes (Tri to Watch)

MIEUXCE
1956: Santa Margarita Handicap (Our Betters)
1957: Santa Margarita Handicap (Our Betters)

MIGHTY APPEALING
1996: Oak Leaf Stakes (City Band)

MIGOLI
1970: Santa Barbara Handicap (Sallarina)

MILKMAN
1954: Roseben Handicap (White Skies)
Carter Handicap (White Skies)
1957: Canadian Championship Stakes (Spinney)
Santa Anita Maturity (Spinney)
1965: Del Mar Futurity (Coursing)

MILL REEF
1986: Breeders' Cup Mile (Last Tycoon)
1988: Arlington Million (Mill Native)

MINNESOTA MAC
1980: Santa Anita Derby (Codex)
Hollywood Derby (Codex)
Preakness Stakes (Codex)
1986: Hollywood Invitational Handicap (Flying Pidgeon)

MISSTEP
1946: Excelsior Handicap (Fighting Step)

MISTER GUS
1971: Breeders' Futurity (Windjammer)

MISTI
1979: Del Mar Handicap (Ardiente)

MISTY FLIGHT
1983: Brooklyn Handicap (Highland Blade)
Marlboro Cup Handicap (Highland Blade)
Pan American Handicap (Highland Blade)

MISWAKI
1995: Gotham Stakes (Talkin Man)
Wood Memorial Stakes (Talkin Man)
1998: Jerome Handicap (Limit Out)
Man o' War Stakes (Daylami)
1999: Breeders' Cup Turf (Daylami)
2002: Shadwell Keeneland Turf Mile (Landseer)

MODEL CADET
1972: Arlington-Washington Futurity (Shecky Greene)
1973: Fountain of Youth Stakes (Shecky Greene)

MODEL FOOL
1983: Louisiana Derby (Balboa Native)

MOKATAM
1950: Champagne Stakes (Uncle Miltie)

MONETARY GIFT
2001: Spinaway Stakes (Cashier's Dream)

MONGO
1977: California Derby (Cuzwuzwrong)
1984: Jersey Derby (Birdie's Legend)

MONTPARNASSE II
1980: Gamely Handicap (Wishing Well)
1992: Top Flight Handicap (Firm Stance)

MOOLAH BUX
1968: California Derby (Proper Proof)

MOONLIGHT RUN
1967: Sunset Handicap (Hill Clown)
1972: Beverly Hills Handicap (Hill Circus)
Del Mar Handicap (Hill Circus)

MORSTON
1995: Hollywood Turf Handicap (Earl of Barking)

MOSLEM CHIEF
1973: Alabama Stakes (Desert Vixen)
Gazelle Handicap (Desert Vixen)
Beldame Stakes (Desert Vixen)
1974: Beldame Stakes (Desert Vixen)
1975: Dwyer Handicap (Valid Appeal)

MOUNT MARCY
1971: San Felipe Handicap (Unconscious)
California Derby (Unconscious)
1972: Charles H. Strub Stakes (Unconscious)
San Antonio Stakes (Unconscious)
Mother Goose Stakes (Wanda)
1975: Santa Anita Derby (Avatar)
Belmont Stakes (Avatar)
1976: San Luis Rey Stakes (Avatar)

MOWLEE
1952: Monmouth Oaks (La Corredora)
1953: Ladies Handicap (La Corredora)
Comely Handicap (La Corredora)

MR. BUSHER
1963: Kentucky Jockey Club Stakes (Journalist)
1968: Alcibiades Stakes (Lil's Bag)
1972: Malibu Stakes (Kfar Tov)
1978: Kentucky Oaks (White Star Line)
Alabama Stakes (White Star Line)

MR. CLINCH
1991: Apple Blossom Handicap (Degenerate Gal)

MR. JINKS
1956: Bougainvillea Turf Handicap (Summer Solstice)

MR. LEADER
1987: Breeders' Cup Juvenile Fillies (Epitome)
1993: Norfolk Stakes (Shepherd's Field)
1995: Del Mar Futurity (Future Quest)
Norfolk Stakes (Future Quest)
1997: Cigar Mile Handicap (Devious Course)
2001: Ashland Stakes (Fleet Renee)
Mother Goose Stakes (Fleet Renee)
2003: Hollywood Futurity (Lion Heart)

MR. MUSIC
1966: Hopeful Stakes (Bold Hour)
Futurity Stakes (Bold Hour)
1968: Grey Lag Handicap (Bold Hour)
Amory L. Haskell Handicap (Bold Hour)
1970: Hollywood Juvenile Championship (Fast Fellow)
John B. Campbell Handicap (Mitey Prince)
1979: Spinster Stakes (Safe)

MR. PROSPECTOR
1988: Alabama Stakes (Maplejinsky)
1990: Hopeful Stakes (Deposit Ticket)
1993: Hollywood Oaks (Hollywood Wildcat)
Breeders' Cup Distaff (Hollywood Wildcat)
Californian Stakes (Latin American)
Whitney Handicap (Brunswick)
1994: Gamely Handicap (Hollywood Wildcat)
1996: Oaklawn Handicap (Geri)
Spinaway Stakes (Oath)
1997: Fountain of Youth Stakes (Pulpit)
Toyota Blue Grass Stakes (Pulpit)
Del Mar Oaks (Famous Digger)
Ruffian Handicap (Tomisue's Delight)
Woodbine Mile (Geri)
1998: Jim Beam Stakes (Event of the Year)
Personal Ensign Handicap (Tomisue's Delight)
1999: Strub Stakes (Event of the Year)
Matron Stakes (Finder's Fee)
2000: Acorn Stakes (Finder's Fee)
Early Times Hollywood Derby (Brahms)
2001: Secretariat Stakes (Startac)
Flower Bowl Invitational Handicap (Lailani)
Breeders' Cup Juvenile Fillies (Tempera)
2003: Pimlico Special (Mineshaft)
Suburban Handicap (Mineshaft)
Woodward Stakes (Mineshaft)
Jockey Club Gold Cup (Mineshaft)
Queen Elizabeth II Challenge Cup (Film Maker)

MR. RANDY
1978: Arlington-Washington Futurity (Jose Binn)

MR. TROUBLE
1966: Florida Derby (Williamston Kid)
1968: Washington D.C. International (Sir Ivor)
1970: Hollywood Gold Cup (Pleasure Seeker)

MUMMY'S GAME
1995: Man o' War Stakes (Millkom)

MUSTANG
1964: United Nations Handicap (Western Warrior)

MY BABU
1965: Sorority Stakes (Native Street)
1966: Kentucky Oaks (Native Street)
1967: Wood Memorial Stakes (Damascus)
Preakness Stakes (Damascus)
Belmont Stakes (Damascus)
Dwyer Handicap (Damascus)
American Derby (Damascus)
Travers Stakes (Damascus)
Aqueduct Stakes (Damascus)
Woodward Stakes (Damascus)
Jockey Club Gold Cup (Damascus)
Alabama Stakes (Gamely)
Santa Barbara Handicap (April Dawn)
1968: Brooklyn Handicap (Damascus)
Aqueduct Stakes (Damascus)
Malibu Stakes (Damascus)
San Fernando Stakes (Damascus)
Vanity Handicap (Gamely)
Beldame Stakes (Gamely)
Santa Margarita Handicap (Gamely)
1969: Beldame Stakes (Gamely)
1970: Carter Handicap (Tyrant)
1971: Kentucky Oaks (Silent Beauty)
1972: Hollywood Juvenile Championship (Bold Liz)
1974: Preakness Stakes (Little Current)
Belmont Stakes (Little Current)
1977: Arlington-Washington Futurity (Sauce Boat)
San Juan Capistrano Handicap (Properantes)
1980: Matron Stakes (Prayers'n Promises)

MY DAD GEORGE
1989: Swaps Stakes (Prized)
Breeders' Cup Turf (Prized)
1990: San Luis Rey Stakes (Prized)

MY HOST
1977: Breeders' Futurity (Gonquin)
1981: Californian Stakes (Eleven Stitches)
Hollywood Gold Cup (Eleven Stitches)

MY PLAY
1949: New Castle Handicap (Allie's Pal)
Molly Pitcher Handicap (Allie's Pal)

MY REQUEST
1966: Ladies Handicap (Destro)

NADIR
1973: Del Mar Handicap (Red Reality)

NALEES MAN
1991: Spinster Stakes (Wilderness Song)

NALUR
1973: Oaklawn Handicap (Prince Astro)

NANTALLAH
1971: Kentucky Derby (Canonero II)
Preakness Stakes (Canonero II)
1974: Oak Leaf Stakes (Cut Class)
Hawthorne Gold Cup (Group Plan)
1975: Jockey Club Gold Cup (Group Plan)
1976: Champions Invitational Handicap (King Pellinore)
American Handicap (King Pellinore)
Oak Tree Invitational Stakes (King Pellinore)
Hawthorne Gold Cup (Almost Grown)
1980: Frizette Stakes (Heavenly Cause)
Selima Stakes (Heavenly Cause)
1981: Fantasy Stakes (Heavenly Cause)
Kentucky Oaks (Heavenly Cause)
Acorn Stakes (Heavenly Cause)
1985: San Luis Rey Stakes (Prince True)
San Juan Capistrano Handicap (Prince True)
1986: Santa Anita Oaks (Hidden Light)
Hollywood Oaks (Hidden Light)

NASHUA
1973: Sapling Stakes (Tisab)
Arlington-Washington Futurity (Lover John)
Blue Grass Stakes (My Gallant)
1974: Santa Anita Derby (Destroyer)
1975: Hollywood Oaks (Nicosia)
1981: San Juan Capistrano Handicap (Obraztosvy)
1986: Withers Stakes (Clear Choice)
Swaps Stakes (Clear Choice)

NASHVILLE
1975: Arkansas Derby (Promised City)
1987: Tropical Park Derby (Baldski's Star)

NASKRA
1987: Philip H. Iselin Handicap (Bordeaux Bob)
1995: Flower Bowl Inv. Handicap (Northern Emerald)
2003: Stephen Foster Handicap (Perfect Drift)

NASRULLAH
1959: Princess Pat Stakes (Heavenly Body)
Matron Stakes (Heavenly Body)
Kentucky Oaks (Hidden Talent)
1960: Princess Pat Stakes (Rose Bower)
Matron Stakes (Rose Bower)
1963: Saratoga Special (Duel)
Breeders' Futurity (Duel)
Kentucky Oaks (Sally Ship)
Sunset Handicap (Arbitrage)
1965: Charles H. Strub Stakes (Duel)
1966: Monmouth Oaks (Natashka)
Alabama Stakes (Natashka)
Breeders' Futurity (Gentleman James)
San Felipe Handicap (Saber Mountain)
Jersey Derby (Creme dela Creme)
Dixie Handicap (Knightly Manner)
1967: Amory L. Haskell Handicap (Handsome Boy)
Brooklyn Handicap (Handsome Boy)
Washington Park Handicap (Handsome Boy)
Arkansas Derby (Monitor)
New Orleans Handicap (Cabildo)
Bowling Green Handicap (Poker)
1968: Breeders' Futurity (Dike)
Garden State Stakes (Beau Brummel)
Gulfstream Park Handicap (Gentleman James)
1969: Gotham Stakes (Dike)
Wood Memorial Stakes (Dike)
Hollywood Derby (Tell)
Charles H. Strub Stakes (Dignitas)
1970: Hollywood Park Inv. Turf Handicap (Fiddle Isle)
American Handicap (Fiddle Isle)
San Luis Rey Handicap (Fiddle Isle)
San Juan Capistrano Handicap (Fiddle Isle)
Gotham Stakes (Native Royalty)
Canadian International Championship (Drumtop)
1971: Santa Susana Stakes (Turkish Trousers)

Hollywood Oaks (Turkish Trousers)
Carter Handicap (Native Royalty)
Michigan Mile and One-Eighth (Native Royalty)
Hialeah Turf Cup (Drumtop)
Bowling Green Handicap (Drumtop)
Delaware Handicap (Blessing Angelica)
1972: Santa Maria Handicap (Turkish Trousers)
Santa Margarita Handicap (Turkish Trousers)
Delaware Handicap (Blessing Angelica)
1973: Spinaway Stakes (Talking Picture)
Matron Stakes (Talking Picture)
1974: Hollywood Gold Cup (Tree of Knowledge)
1977: Carter Handicap (Gentle King)
1983: Sunset Handicap (Craelius)

NASTY AND BOLD
2001: Carter Handicap (Peeping Tom)

NATIONAL
1977: Sorority Stakes (Stub)
Arlington-Washington Lassie Stakes (Stub)

NATIVE CHARGER
1982: Preakness Stakes (Aloma's Ruler)
1984: Santa Anita Derby (Mighty Adversary)
1987: San Antonio Handicap (Bedside Promise)
2000: Oaklawn Handicap (K One King)

NATIVE DANCER
1964: Flamingo Stakes (Northern Dancer)
Florida Derby (Northern Dancer)
Blue Grass Stakes (Northern Dancer)
Kentucky Derby (Northern Dancer)
Preakness Stakes (Northern Dancer)
1965: Hollywood Juvenile Championship (Port Wine)
1969: Matron Stakes (Cold Comfort)
1970: Travers Stakes (Loud)
1971: Coaching Club American Oaks (Our Cheri Amour)
1973: Florida Derby (Royal and Regal)
1974: Sorority Stakes (Ruffian)
Spinaway Stakes (Ruffian)
Norfolk Stakes (George Navonod)
1975: Acorn Stakes (Ruffian)
Mother Goose Stakes (Ruffian)
Coaching Club American Oaks (Ruffian)
1976: Spinaway Stakes (Mrs. Warren)
Matron Stakes (Mrs. Warren)
Charles H. Strub Stakes (George Navonod)
San Juan Capistrano Handicap (One On the Aisle)
1978: Hopeful Stakes (General Assembly)
1979: Travers Stakes (General Assembly)
Vosburgh Stakes (General Assembly)
1980: Breeders' Futurity (Fairway Phantom)
1981: Arlington Classic (Fairway Phantom)

NATIVE HERITAGE
1991: Flower Bowl Handicap (Lady Shirl)

NATIVE PROSPECTOR
2003: Triple Bend Breeders' Cup Handicap (Joey Franco)

NATIVE ROYALTY
1986: Spinster Stakes (Top Corsage)

NATIVO
1994: Test Stakes (Twist Afleet)
1995: Top Flight Handicap (Twist Afleet)

NEARCO
1958: Cowdin Stakes (Crafty Skipper)
1962: Arlington Handicap (El Bandido)
Canadian Championship Stakes (El Bandido)
1963: Acorn Stakes (Spicy Living)
Mother Goose Stakes (Spicy Living)

NEARCTIC
1972: Spinaway Stakes (La Prevoyante)
Matron Stakes (La Prevoyante)
Frizette Stakes (La Prevoyante)
Selima Stakes (La Prevoyante)
Gardenia Stakes (La Prevoyante)
1973: Hollywood Gold Cup (Kennedy Road)
San Antonio Stakes (Kennedy Road)
1974: Jersey Derby (Better Arbitor)
1977: Hollywood Oaks (Glenaris)
1980: Suburban Handicap (Winter's Tale)
Brooklyn Handicap (Winter's Tale)
Marlboro Cup Handicap (Winter's Tale)
1983: Suburban Handicap (Winter's Tale)

NEDAYR
1962: Tropical Park Handicap (Trans-Way)

NEDDIE
1947: Vineland Handicap (Miss Kimo)

NEEDLES
1972: Gotham Stakes (Freetex)
Ohio Derby (Freetex)
Monmouth Invitational Handicap (Freetex)
1973: Fantasy Stakes (Knitted Gloves)
1979: Arlington-Washington Lassie Stakes (Sissy's Time)

NEPENTHE
1960: Belmont Stakes (Celtic Ash)

NEVER BEND
1974: Futurity Stakes (Just the Time)
1976: Sapling Stakes (Ali Oop)
1977: Florida Derby (Coined Silver)
1978: Fantasy Stakes (Equanimity)
Ladies Handicap (Ida Delia)
1983: Del Mar Futurity (Althea)
Del Mar Debutante Stakes (Althea)
Hollywood Starlet Stakes (Althea)
San Felipe Handicap (Desert Wine)
1984: Charles H. Strub Stakes (Desert Wine)
Californian Stakes (Desert Wine)
Hollywood Gold Cup (Desert Wine)
Santa Susana Stakes (Althea)
Arkansas Derby (Althea)
Young America Stakes (Script Ohio)
1987: Fantasy Stakes (Very Subtle)
Breeders' Cup Sprint (Very Subtle)
1994: Peter Pan Stakes (Twining)
1998: La Brea Stakes (Magical Allure)
1999: Toyota Blue Grass Stakes (Menifee)
Haskell Invitational Handicap (Menifee)

NEVER SAY DIE
1968: Gotham Stakes (Verbatim)
1969: Amory L. Haskell Handicap (Verbatim)
Whitney Stakes (Verbatim)
1970: San Felipe Handicap (Cool Hand)

NEW POLICY
1989: Oak Leaf Stakes (Dominant Dancer)
1990: Peter Pan Stakes (Profit Key)
Dwyer Stakes (Profit Key)

NEW PROVIDENCE
1978: Top Flight Handicap (Northernette)
Apple Blossom Handicap (Northernette)

NICCOLO DELL'ARCA
1960: Canadian Championship Stakes (Rocky Royale)
1964: Spinaway Stakes (Candalita)
Matron Stakes (Candalita)
1976: Gulfstream Park Handicap (Hail the Pirates)

NIGHT INVADER
1991: Young America Stakes (Maston)

NIGROMANTE
1970: Cinema Handicap (D'Artagnan)
1982: Arlington Handicap (Flying Target)

NIJINSKY II
1986: Young America Stakes (Conquistarose)
Remsen Stakes (Java Gold)
1987: Travers Stakes (Java Gold)
Whitney Handicap (Java Gold)
Marlboro Cup Handicap (Java Gold)
Hopeful Stakes (Crusader Sword)
1988: Flamingo Stakes (Cherokee Colony)
1990: Cowdin Stakes (Scan)
Remsen Stakes (Scan)
1991: Jerome Handicap (Scan)
Pegasus Handicap (Scan)
NYRA Mile Handicap (Rubiano)
1992: Del Mar Futurity (River Special)
Norfolk Stakes (River Special)
Hollywood Futurity (River Special)
Carter Handicap (Rubiano)
Vosburgh Stakes (Rubiano)
Matron Stakes (Sky Beauty)
Matriarch Stakes (Flawlessly)
1993: Acorn Stakes (Sky Beauty)
Mother Goose Stakes (Sky Beauty)
Coaching Club American Oaks (Sky Beauty)
Alabama Stakes (Sky Beauty)
Ramona Handicap (Flawlessly)
Beverly D. Stakes (Flawlessly)
Matriarch Stakes (Flawlessly)
Arkansas Derby (Rockamundo)
Belmont Stakes (Colonial Affair)
Frizette Stakes (Heavenly Prize)
1994: Shuvee Handicap (Sky Beauty)
Hempstead Handicap (Sky Beauty)
Go for Wand Stakes (Sky Beauty)
Ruffian Handicap (Sky Beauty)
Alabama Stakes (Heavenly Prize)
Gazelle Handicap (Heavenly Prize)
Beldame Stakes (Heavenly Prize)
Whitney Handicap (Colonial Affair)
Jockey Club Gold Cup (Colonial Affair)
Ramona Handicap (Flawlessly)
1995: Apple Blossom Handicap (Heavenly Prize)
Hempstead Handicap (Heavenly Prize)
Go for Wand Stakes (Heavenly Prize)
Santa Barbara Handicap (Wandesta)
1996: Matriarch Stakes (Wandesta)
1998: Matron Stakes (Oh What a Windfall)
1999: Gulfstream Park Breeders' Cup Handicap (Yagli)
Manhattan Handicap (Yagli)
2000: Secretariat Stakes (Ciro)
Man o' War Stakes (Fantastic Light)
2001: Philip H. Iselin Handicap (Broken Vow)
Breeders' Cup Turf (Fantastic Light)
2002: Vosburgh Stakes (Bonapaw)
2003: Lane's End Breeders' Futurity (Eurosilver)

NILO
1970: Donn Handicap (Twogundan)

NIMBUS
1960: Arkansas Derby (Persian Gold)
1962: Preakness Stakes (Greek Money)
1965: Dixie Handicap (Flag)
1966: Delaware Handicap (Open Fire)
Spinster Stakes (Open Fire)

NIRGAL
1967: Sapling Stakes (Subpet)

NIZAMI II
1966: Blue Grass Stakes (Abe's Hope)
1972: Preakness Stakes (Bee Bee Bee)

NO ARGUMENT
1981: Turf Classic (April Run)
1982: Turf Classic (April Run)
Washington D.C. International (April Run)

NOBLE COMMANDER
1987: Mother Goose Stakes (Fiesta Gal)
Coaching Club American Oaks (Fiesta Gal)

NOBLE DANCER II
1993: Secretariat Stakes (Awad)
1995: Early Times Manhattan Handicap (Awad)
Arlington Million (Awad)
1997: Sword Dancer Invitational Handicap (Awad)

NOBLE DECREE
1985: Hopeful Stakes (Papal Power)
1986: Hutcheson Stakes (Papal Power)

NODOUBLE
1981: Santa Susana Stakes (Nell's Briquette)
1982: Matriarch Stakes (Pale Purple)
1985: Swaps Stakes (Padua)
1987: Oak Leaf Stakes (Dream Team)
1988: Arkansas Derby (Proper Reality)
Illinois Derby (Proper Reality)
1989: Metropolitan Handicap (Proper Reality)
Philip H. Iselin Handicap (Proper Reality)
1991: Rothmans International Stakes (Sky Classic)
1992: Caesars International Handicap (Sky Classic)
Turf Classic (Sky Classic)
1997: Early Times Turf Classic (Always a Classic)
1999: San Felipe Stakes (Prime Timber)

NOIRMOUTIERS
1957: San Luis Rey Handicap (Posadas)

NONOALCO
1992: Hopeful Stakes (Great Navigator)

NOOR
1962: Sapling Stakes (Delta Judge)
1966: Massachusetts Handicap (Fast Count)
1968: Wood Memorial Stakes (Dancer's Image)
Display Handicap (Fast Count)
1971: Sunset Handicap (Over the Counter)
1974: Arkansas Derby (J.R.'s Pet)

NORDLICHT
1966: Gardenia Stakes (Pepperwood)

NO ROBBERY
1976: Del Mar Debutante Stakes (Telferner)
1981: Secretariat Stakes (Sing Sing)
1985: Yellow Ribbon Stakes (Estrapade)
1986: Budweiser-Arlington Million (Estrapade)
Oak Tree Invitational Stakes (Estrapade)
1989: Peter Pan Stakes (Imbibe)
1990: San Antonio Handicap (Criminal Type)
Pimlico Special (Criminal Type)
Metropolitan Handicap (Criminal Type)
Hollywood Gold Cup (Criminal Type)
Whitney Handicap (Criminal Type)
1992: Ohio Derby (Majestic Sweep)

NORTHERN BABY
1997: Santa Monica Handicap (Toga Toga Toga)
2002: La Brea Stakes (Got Koko)

NORTHERN DANCER
1974: Laurel Futurity (L'Enjoleur)
1976: Whitney Handicap (Dancing Gun)
1977: San Fernando Stakes (Kirby Lane)
Charles H. Strub Stakes (Kirby Lane)
Alcibiades Stakes (L'Alezane)
1981: Breeders' Futurity (D'Accord)
1983: Jerome Handicap (A Phenomenon)
Vosburgh Stakes (A Phenomenon)
California Derby (Paris Prince)
1984: Breeders' Cup Sprint (Eillo)
1989: Santa Barbara Handicap (No Review)
Breeders' Cup Juvenile (Rhythm)
1990: Travers Stakes (Rhythm)
Futurity Stakes (Eastern Echo)
1991: Breeders' Cup Juvenile (Arazi)
Hollywood Derby (Eternity Star)
1992: Californian Stakes (Another Review)
1993: Del Mar Futurity (Winning Pact)
1995: Hollywood Oaks (Sleep Easy)
1996: Jim Beam Stakes (Roar)
1997: Queen Elizabeth II Challenge Cup (Ryafan)
Yellow Ribbon Stakes (Ryafan)
Matriarch Stakes (Ryafan)
2001: Hollywood Gold Cup (Aptitude)
Jockey Club Gold Cup (Aptitude)

NORTHERN JOVE
1997: Manhattan Handicap (Ops Smile)

NORTHERN PROSPECT
2003: Del Mar Futurity (Siphonizer)

NORTHFIELDS
1986: Jim Dandy Stakes (Lac Ouimet)
1988: Santa Barbara Handicap (Pen Bal Lady)
Gamely Handicap (Pen Bal Lady)
1992: Gamely Handicap (Metamorphose)
Hollywood Derby (Paradise Creek)
1994: Early Times Manhattan Handicap (Paradise Creek)
Arlington Million (Paradise Creek)
Washington D.C. International (Paradise Creek)
Oak Leaf Stakes (Serena's Song)
Hollywood Starlet Stakes (Serena's Song)
1995: Las Virgenes Stakes (Serena's Song)
Santa Anita Oaks (Serena's Song)
Jim Beam Stakes (Serena's Song)
Mother Goose Stakes (Serena's Song)
Haskell Invitational Handicap (Serena's Song)
Gazelle Handicap (Serena's Song)
Beldame Stakes (Serena's Song)
1996: Santa Maria Handicap (Serena's Song)
Hempstead Handicap (Serena's Song)
1999: San Juan Capistrano Handicap (Single Empire)
Early Times Turf Classic (Wild Event)
2001: Manhattan Handicap (Forbidden Apple)
Hollywood Derby (Denon)
2002: Charles Whittingham Handicap (Denon)
Turf Classic (Denon)
2003: Manhattan Handicap (Denon)

NORTHRUP
2000: Three Chimneys Spinster Stakes (Plenty of Light)

NORTH STAR III
1947: American Handicap (Burning Dream)
1948: New Orleans Handicap (Star Reward)

NOTEBOOK
2001: Super Derby (Outofthebox)

NUREYEV
1993: Molson Export Million (Peteski)
1996: Ramona Handicap (Matiara)
1997: Del Mar Futurity (Souvenir Copy)
Norfolk Stakes (Souvenir Copy)
1998: Hollywood Oaks (Manistique)
Gazelle Handicap (Tap to Music)
1999: Santa Margarita Handicap (Manistique)
Vanity Handicap (Manistique)
2000: Santa Maria Handicap (Manistique)
2003: Humana Distaff Handicap (Sightseek)
Ogden Phipps Handicap (Sightseek)
Go for Wand Handicap (Sightseek)
Beldame Stakes (Sightseek)
Gamely Breeders' Cup Handicap (Tates Creek)
Yellow Ribbon Stakes (Tates Creek)

OAK DANCER
2000: Philip H. Iselin Handicap (Rize)

OCCUPATION
1955: Pimlico Futurity (Nail)
Remsen Stakes (Nail)
Futurity Stakes (Nail)
1961: Wood Memorial Stakes (Globemaster)
Arlington Classic (Globemaster)

OCCUPY
1965: Kentucky Oaks (Amerivan)
1971: Louisiana Derby (Northfields)

OCEANIC
1953: Stars and Stripes Handicap (Abbe Sting)

OGYGIAN
2001: Bessemer Trust BC Juvenile (Johannesburg)
2002: King's Bishop Stakes (Gygistar)

OH JOHNNY
1976: Jockey Club Gold Cup (Great Contractor)
1977: Brooklyn Handicap (Great Contractor)

OIL CAPITOL
1966: Arlington-Washington Lassie Stakes (Mira Femme)
1969: Santa Barbara Handicap (Pink Pigeon)

OLDEN TIMES
1976: Withers Stakes (Sonkisser)
1977: Washington D.C. International (Johnny D.)
Turf Classic (Johnny D.)
1982: Breeders' Futurity (Highland Park)
Secretariat Stakes (Half Iced)
1986: Selima Stakes (Collins)

OLYMPIA
1960: Washington Park Futurity (Crozier)
1962: Louisiana Derby (Admiral's Voyage)
Wood Memorial Stakes (Admiral's Voyage)
Kentucky Jockey Club Stakes (Sky Gem)
Aqueduct Stakes (Crozier)
1963: Santa Anita Handicap (Crozier)
San Carlos Handicap (Crozier)
Carter Handicap (Admiral's Voyage)
1964: San Carlos Handicap (Admiral's Voyage)
1965: Breeders' Futurity (Tinsley)
1966: Alcibiades Stakes (Teacher's Art)
1969: Kentucky Oaks (Hail to Patsy)
1972: Jerome Handicap (True Knight)
1973: Arlington-Washington Lassie Stakes (Special Team)
Alcibiades Stakes (City Girl)
Hawthorne Gold Cup (Tri Jet)
1974: John B. Campbell Handicap (True Knight)
Amory L. Haskell Handicap (True Knight)
Suburban Handicap (True Knight)
Acorn Stakes (Special Team)
Whitney Stakes (Tri Jet)
1975: Ashland Stakes (Sun and Snow)
Kentucky Oaks (Sun and Snow)
1976: Top Flight Handicap (Proud Delta)
Hempstead Handicap (Proud Delta)
Beldame Stakes (Proud Delta)
1978: Carter Handicap (Jaipur's Gem)
1982: Top Flight Handicap (Andover Way)

OLYMPIAD KING
1988: Hollywood Derby (Silver Circus)

OMAHA
1954: Cowdin Stakes (Summer Tan)
Garden State Stakes (Summer Tan)
1955: Matron Stakes (Doubledogdare)
Alcibiades Stakes (Doubledogdare)
1956: Gallant Fox Handicap (Summer Tan)
Pimlico Special (Summer Tan)
Spinster Stakes (Doubledogdare)
1957: Santa Anita Handicap (Corn Husker)
San Juan Capistrano Handicap (Corn Husker)
McLennan Handicap (Summer Tan)

ON-AND-ON
1975: Swaps Stakes (Forceten)
1977: Fantasy Stakes (Our Mims)
Coaching Club American Oaks (Our Mims)
Alabama Stakes (Our Mims)
Delaware Handicap (Our Mims)
Sapling Stakes (Alydar)
Champagne Stakes (Alydar)
1978: Flamingo Stakes (Alydar)
Florida Derby (Alydar)
Blue Grass Stakes (Alydar)
Arlington Classic (Alydar)
Travers Stakes (Alydar)
Whitney Stakes (Alydar)
1981: San Felipe Handicap (Stancharry)

ONE COUNT
1969: Delaware Handicap (Obeah)
1970: Delaware Handicap (Obeah)
1982: Jerome Handicap (Fit to Fight)
1984: Metropolitan Handicap (Fit to Fight)
Suburban Handicap (Fit to Fight)
Brooklyn Handicap (Fit to Fight)

ONE-EYED KING
1970: Dwyer Handicap (Judgable)
Whitney Stakes (Judgable)
1971: Donn Handicap (Judgable)
Grey Lag Handicap (Judgable)
1973: Louisiana Derby (Leo's Pisces)

ONE FOR ALL
1983: Spinster Stakes (Try Something New)
1989: Rothmans International Stakes (Hodges Bay)
1992: Florida Derby (Technology)
Haskell Invitational Handicap (Technology)

ON TO GLORY
1996: Preakness Stakes (Louis Quatorze)
Jim Dandy Stakes (Louis Quatorze)
1997: Gazelle Handicap (Royal Indy)

ON TRUST
1972: Arlington-Washington Lassie St. (Double Your Fun)
1973: Top Flight Handicap (Poker Night)
1974: Hempstead Handicap (Poker Night)

ON WATCH
1946: Grey Lag Handicap (Stymie)
Whitney Stakes (Stymie)
Manhattan Handicap (Stymie)
New York Handicap (Stymie)
Gallant Fox Handicap (Stymie)
1947: Metropolitan Handicap (Stymie)
Massachusetts Handicap (Stymie)
Aqueduct Handicap (Stymie)
Gallant Fox Handicap (Stymie)
1948: Metropolitan Handicap (Stymie)
Aqueduct Handicap (Stymie)
1951: Vosburgh Handicap (War King)

OPERA HAT
1956: Molly Pitcher Handicap (Blue Sparkler)

ORESTES III
1963: Demoiselle Stakes (Windsor Lady)

ORMONT
1951: San Juan Capistrano Handicap (Be Fleet)

ORSENIGO
1967: Santa Barbara Handicap (Ormea)

ORSINI II
1999: Brooklyn Handicap (Running Stag)

ORVIETO II
1979: Sunset Handicap (Sirlad)

OSIRIS II
1954: Vagrancy Handicap (Canadiana)

OUR BABU
1969: Sapling Stakes (Ring For Nurse)

OUR BOOTS
1959: Roamer Handicap (Polylad)
1961: Massachusetts Handicap (Polylad)
Gallant Fox Handicap (Polylad)
Canadian Championship Stakes (Our Jeep)
1970: Oaklawn Handicap (Charlie Jr.)

OUR MICHAEL
1993: Gotham Stakes (As Indicated)
1994: Pimlico Special (As Indicated)

OUR NATIVE
2002: Jockey Club Gold Cup (Evening Attire)

OVERSKATE
2000: Futurity Stakes (Burning Roma)

PAGO PAGO
1983: Oaklawn Handicap (Bold Style)
1989: Widener Handicap (Launch a Pegasus)

PALESTINIAN
1966: San Fernando Stakes (Isle of Greece)
1967: Everglades Stakes (Reflected Glory)
Flamingo Stakes (Reflected Glory)

PAN
1989: Gamely Handicap (Fitzwilliam Place)

PANORAMA
1955: Santa Margarita Handicap (Blue Butterfly)

PAPA REDBIRD
1959: Washington Park Futurity (Venetian Way)
1960: Breeders' Futurity (He's a Pistol)
Kentucky Derby (Venetian Way)
1970: New Orleans Handicap (Etony)

PAPPA FOURWAY
1974: Del Mar Debutante Stakes (Bubblewin)

PAPPA'S ALL
1983: La Canada Stakes (Avigaition)
Santa Barbara Handicap (Avigaition)

PARDAL
1969: Hollywood Gold Cup (Figonero)
1974: American Derby (Determined King)

PARRAL
1977: Yellow Ribbon Stakes (Star Ball)

PASCH
1953: American Handicap (Royal Serenade)
Hollywood Gold Cup (Royal Serenade)

PASHA
1965: San Juan Capistrano Handicap (George Royal)
Canadian Championship Stakes (George Royal)
1966: San Juan Capistrano Handicap (George Royal)
Canadian International Championship (George Royal)

PASS THE GLASS
1988: Fantasy Stakes (Jeanne Jones)
1993: Oak Leaf Stakes (Phone Chatter)
Breeders' Cup Juvenile Fillies (Phone Chatter)

PASS THE TAB
2002: Spinaway Stakes (Awesome Humor)

PASTICHE
1984: Widener Handicap (Mat Boy)
Gulfstream Park Handicap (Mat Boy)

PAVOT
1959: Bougainvillea Turf Handicap (General Arthur)
1960: Hollywood Gold Cup (Dotted Swiss)
Sunset Handicap (Dotted Swiss)
1961: Arlington Lassie Stakes (Rudoma)
Donn Handicap (General Arthur)

PEACE CHANCE
1946: Will Rogers Handicap (Burra Sahib)
1950: Vineland Handicap (Almahmoud)
1954: Arlington Matron Handicap (Lavender Hill)
Ladies Handicap (Lavender Hill)
1957: Santa Anita Derby (Sir William)

PENALO
1953: Del Mar Debutante Stakes (Lady Cover Up)

PENNANT
1947: Santa Margarita Handicap (Monsoon)
Travers Stakes (Young Peter)
1948: Saranac Handicap (Mount Marcy)
1951: Blue Grass Stakes (Mameluke)
New Orleans Handicap (Mount Marcy)
1952: Metropolitan Handicap (Mameluke)

PENNY POST
1972: Pan American Handicap (Unanime)
San Juan Capistrano Handicap (Practicante)

PET BULLY
1966: Kentucky Jockey Club Stakes (Lightning Orphan)

PETEE WRACK
1946: San Felipe Stakes (Galla Damion)

PETER HASTINGS
1955: Tropical Handicap (Scimitar)

PETERHOF
2000: Spinaway Stakes (Stormy Pick)

PETER PAN
1947: Frizette Stakes (Slumber Song)

PETER PETER
1978: Bay Meadows Handicap (Bywayofchicago)

PETINGO
1988: Rothmans International Stakes (Infamy)

PETITION
1966: United Nations Handicap (Assagai)
Man o' War Stakes (Assagai)

PHALANX
1962: Del Mar Debutante Stakes (Brown Berry)
1969: Gardenia Stakes (Fast Attack)
1978: Frizette Stakes (Golferette)

PHARAMOND II
1946: Louisiana Derby (Pellicle)
Travers Stakes (Natchez)
Carter Handicap (Flood Town)
Longacres Mile (Amble In)
1947: Matron Stakes (Inheritance)
1948: Gazelle Stakes (Sweet Dream)
Longacres Mile (Amble In)
1950: Arlington Lassie Stakes (Shawnee Squaw)
Vosburgh Handicap (Tea-Maker)
1951: Acorn Stakes (Kiss Me Kate)
Delaware Oaks (Kiss Me Kate)
Gazelle Stakes (Kiss Me Kate)
Alabama Stakes (Kiss Me Kate)
Molly Pitcher Handicap (Marta)
Ladies Handicap (Marta)
San Pasqual Handicap (Moonrush)
Santa Anita Handicap (Moonrush)
1952: New Castle Handicap (Kiss Me Kate)
Flamingo Stakes (Charlie McAdam)
1953: Firenze Handicap (Kiss Me Kate)
Top Flight Handicap (Marta)
1954: Washington Park Futurity (Georgian)
1955: Princess Pat Stakes (Supple)
1956: Cowdin Stakes (Mister Jive)
1957: Gotham Stakes (Mister Jive)
1960: Delaware Oaks (Rash Statement)
Spinster Stakes (Rash Statement)

PHARIS
1964: Seminole Handicap (Top Gallant)

PHARLY
1988: Gulfstream Park Handicap (Jade Hunter)
1992: Yellow Ribbon Stakes (Super Staff)
1994: Eddie Read Handicap (Approach the Bench)

PHAROS
1949: Breeders' Futurity (Oil Capitol)
Pimlico Futurity (Oil Capitol)
Black Helen Handicap (Roman Candle)
1950: Flamingo Stakes (Oil Capitol)
1952: New Orleans Handicap (Oil Capitol)
1953: Widener Handicap (Oil Capitol)
Arlington Handicap (Oil Capitol)

PHONE TRICK
2001: Gazelle Handicap (Exogenous)
Beldame Stakes (Exogenous)

PIA STAR
1981: Travers Stakes (Willow Hour)
1984: Selima Stakes (Mom's Command)
Oak Tree Invitational Stakes (Both Ends Burning)
1985: Acorn Stakes (Mom's Command)
Mother Goose Stakes (Mom's Command)
Coaching Club American Oaks (Mom's Command)
Alabama Stakes (Mom's Command)
Hollywood Inv. Handicap (Both Ends Burning)
1991: Gamely Handicap (Miss Josh)
1993: Caesars International Handicap (Star of Cozzene)
Arlington Million (Star of Cozzene)
Man o' War Stakes (Star of Cozzene)
1994: Man o' War Stakes (Royal Mountain Inn)
1995: Hollywood Futurity (Matty G)

PICACERO
1947: Black Helen Handicap (Miss Grillo)
1948: New Castle Handicap (Miss Grillo)
New York Handicap (Miss Grillo)
1949: San Juan Capistrano Handicap (Miss Grillo)

PIERCER
1991: Beldame Stakes (Sharp Dance)

PIET
1971: Arlington-Washington Futurity (Governor Max)

PILATE
1953: Molly Pitcher Handicap (My Celeste)
Monmouth Handicap (My Celeste)
New Orleans Handicap (Smoke Screen)
1954: Delaware Oaks (Parlo)
Alabama Stakes (Parlo)
Beldame Handicap (Parlo)
Firenze Handicap (Parlo)
Kentucky Jockey Club Stakes (Prince Noor)
1955: Top Flight Handicap (Parlo)
Delaware Handicap (Parlo)
Everglades Stakes (Prince Noor)
1956: Withers Stakes (Oh Johnny)
Travers Stakes (Oh Johnny)
Gazelle Handicap (Scampering)
1957: Display Handicap (Oh Johnny)
1958: Grey Lag Handicap (Oh Johnny)
1960: Roamer Handicap (Divine Comedy)
1965: California Derby (Perfect Sky)

PILLORY
1948: San Carlos Handicap (Autocrat)
1949: San Carlos Handicap (Autocrat)

PLEASANT COLONY
1995: Ashland Stakes (Urbane)
1996: John A. Morris Handicap (Urbane)
1999: King's Bishop Stakes (Forestry)
Breeders' Cup Juvenile Fillies (Cash Run)
2002: Kentucky Oaks (Farda Amiga)
Alabama Stakes (Farda Amiga)
Personal Ensign Handicap (Summer Colony)

PLUGGED NICKLE
1998: Carter Handicap (Wild Rush)
Metropolitan Handicap (Wild Rush)

POCKET RULER
1978: Charles H. Strub Stakes (Mr. Redoy)

POKER
1976: Champagne Stakes (Seattle Slew)
1977: Flamingo Stakes (Seattle Slew)
Wood Memorial Stakes (Seattle Slew)
Kentucky Derby (Seattle Slew)
Preakness Stakes (Seattle Slew)
Belmont Stakes (Seattle Slew)
1978: Marlboro Cup Handicap (Seattle Slew)
Woodward Stakes (Seattle Slew)
1979: Louisiana Downs Handicap (Incredible Ease)
1996: Del Mar Futurity (Silver Charm)
1997: Kentucky Derby (Silver Charm)
Preakness Stakes (Silver Charm)
1998: Strub Stakes (Silver Charm)

POLICEMAN
1998: Breeders' Cup Sprint (Reraise)

POLYMELIAN
1946: Roseben Handicap (Polynesian)

POLYNESIAN
1960: Gotham Stakes (John William)
Withers Stakes (John William)

POLYNESIAN *(Continued)*
1961: Delaware Oaks (Primonetta)
Alabama Stakes (Primonetta)
1962: Spinster Stakes (Primonetta)
1963: Blue Grass Stakes (Chateaugay)
Kentucky Derby (Chateaugay)
Belmont Stakes (Chateaugay)
Jerome Handicap (Chateaugay)
1966: Santa Anita Derby (Boldnesian)
1968: Santa Barbara Handicap (Princessnesian)
Hollywood Gold Cup (Princessnesian)
1969: Arlington-Washington Lassie Stakes (Clover Lane)
Santa Margarita Handicap (Princessnesian)
1972: Widener Handicap (Good Counsel)
1983: Hopeful Stakes (Capitol South)

POMPEY
1946: Santa Susana Stakes (Enfilade)
1948: Vanity Handicap (Hemet Squaw)
1949: Vosburgh Handicap (Loser Weeper)
Metropolitan Handicap (Loser Weeper)
Arlington Lassie Stakes (Dutchess Peg)
1950: Dixie Handicap (Loser Weeper)
Suburban Handicap (Loser Weeper)
1951: Aqueduct Handicap (Bryan G.)
Westchester Handicap (Bryan G.)
Pimlico Special (Bryan G.)
Arlington Lassie Stakes (Princess Lygia)
Kentucky Derby (Count Turf)
1952: Comely Handicap (Devilkin)
Aqueduct Handicap (Bryan G.)
1954: Vineland Handicap (Spinning Top)

PONDER
1976: Maskette Handicap (Sugar Plum Time)
1980: Mother Goose Stakes (Sugar and Spice)

PONT L'EVVEQUE
1958: Arlington Matron Handicap (Estacion)

POONA II
1974: Arlington-Washington Lassie Stakes (Hot n Nasty)

PORTCODINE
1960: Saratoga Special (Bronzerullah)

POT AU FEU
1946: Santa Margarita Handicap (Canina)

POUGHATCHEV
1953: Florida Derby (Money Broker)

PRACTICANTE
1993: Vanity Handicap (Re Toss)
1996: Las Virgenes Stakes (Antespend)
Santa Anita Oaks (Antespend)

PRECIPITATION
1960: Hialeah Turf Cup (Amerigo)
San Juan Capistrano Handicap (Amerigo)
1965: San Felipe Handicap (Jacinto)
1971: Cinema Handicap (Niagara)

PRECIPTIC
1966: New Orleans Handicap (Just About)
1972: Grey Lag Handicap (Droll Role)
Hawthorne Gold Cup (Droll Role)
Massachusetts Handicap (Droll Role)
Canadian International Championship (Droll Role)
Washington D.C. International (Droll Role)

PREMIERSHIP
2001: Fountain of Youth Stakes (Songandaprayer)

PRETENSE
1982: Remsen Stakes (Pax in Bello)
1985: Arkansas Derby (Tank's Prospect)
Preakness Stakes (Tank's Prospect)
1987: Gamely Handicap (Northern Aspen)
1994: Champagne Stakes (Timber Country)
Breeders' Cup Juvenile (Timber Country)
Breeders' Cup Distaff (One Dreamer)
1995: Preakness Stakes (Timber Country)

PRIAM II
1973: Donn Handicap (Triumphant)

PRIMERA
1981: Washington D.C. International (Providential II)
Hollywood Turf Cup (Providential II)

PRINCE ASTRO
1995: Arkansas Derby (Dazzling Falls)

PRINCE BIO
1975: Oak Tree Invitational Stakes (Top Command)

PRINCE BLESSED
1984: Washington D.C. International (Seattle Song)

PRINCE CHEVALIER
1972: American Derby (Dubassoff)
1973: Arlington Handicap (Dubassoff)

PRINCE JOHN
1969: Santa Susana Stakes (Dumptys Lady)
Lawrence Realization Stakes (Oil Power)
1971: Santa Margarita Handicap (Manta)
Beverly Hills Handicap (Manta)
Santa Barbara Handicap (Manta)
1972: Oak Leaf Stakes (Fresh Pepper)
1973: Breeders' Futurity (Provante)
Illinois Derby (Big Whippendeal)
San Luis Rey Handicap (Big Spruce)
1974: Hialeah Turf Cup (Big Whippendeal)
Century Handicap (Big Whippendeal)
Illinois Derby (Sharp Gary)
Marlboro Cup Handicap (Big Spruce)
1975: Hopeful Stakes (Jackknife)
Del Mar Debutante Stakes (Queen to Be)
Alabama Stakes (Spout)
1976: Michigan Mile and One-Eighth (Sharp Gary)
1977: Jockey Club Gold Cup (On the Sly)
Hawthorne Gold Cup (On the Sly)
Mother Goose Stakes (Road Princess)
1982: Young America Stakes (Slewpy)
1983: Swaps Stakes (Hyperborean)
Meadowlands Cup (Slewpy)
1984: Fantasy Stakes (My Darling One)
1985: Hollywood Derby (Slew the Dragon)
Breeders' Cup Mile (Cozzene)
1986: Fountain of Youth Stakes (Ensign Rhythm)
California Derby (Vernon Castle)
Illinois Derby (Bolshoi Boy)
John Henry Handicap (Palace Music)
1989: Hollywood Gold Cup (Blushing John)

PRINCELY PLEASURE
1992: Flamingo Stakes (Pistols and Roses)
Blue Grass Stakes (Pistols and Roses)
1993: Donn Handicap (Pistols and Roses)
1994: Donn Handicap (Pistols and Roses)

PRINCE PAL
1947: San Antonio Handicap (El Lobo)

PRINCEQUILLO
1957: Arlington Handicap (Manassas)
1959: Alabama Stakes (High Bid)
Vineland Handicap (High Bid)
Pimlico Futurity (Progressing)
1961: Sapling Stakes (Sir Gaylord)
1962: Everglades Stakes (Sir Gaylord)
1963: Garden State Stakes (Hurry to Market)
Gallant Fox Handicap (Sunrise Flight)
1964: Sapling Stakes (Bold Lad)
Hopeful Stakes (Bold Lad)
Futurity Stakes (Bold Lad)
Champagne Stakes (Bold Lad)
Breeders' Futurity (Umbrella Fella)
Kentucky Jockey Club Stakes (Umbrella Fella)
1965: Hawthorne Gold Cup (Moss Vale)
Hialeah Turf Cup (Hot Dust)
1966: Champagne Stakes (Successor)
Garden State Stakes (Successor)
Arlington-Washington Futurity (Diplomat Way)
Gulfstream Park Handicap (First Family)
Metropolitan Handicap (Bold Lad)
1967: Selima Stakes (Syrian Sea)
Louisiana Derby (Ask the Fare)
Blue Grass Stakes (Diplomat Way)
Lawrence Realization Stakes (Successor)
Man o' War Stakes (Ruffled Feathers)
Washington D.C. International (Fort Marcy)
1968: New Orleans Handicap (Diplomat Way)
Oaklawn Handicap (Diplomat Way)
Sorority Stakes (Big Advance)
Spinster Stakes (Sale Day)
Sunset Handicap (Fort Marcy)
1969: Futurity Stakes (High Echelon)
Pimlico-Laurel Futurity (High Echelon)
Manhattan Handicap (Harem Lady)
Hollywood Park Inv. Turf Handicap (Fort Marcy)
1970: Dixie Handicap (Fort Marcy)
Bowling Green Handicap (Fort Marcy)
United Nations Handicap (Fort Marcy)
Man o' War Stakes (Fort Marcy)
Washington D.C. International (Fort Marcy)
Coaching Club American Oaks (Missile Belle)
Gazelle Handicap (Missile Belle)
Amory L. Haskell Handicap (Gladwin)
Hawthorne Gold Cup (Gladwin)
Pan American Handicap (One For All)
Sunset Handicap (One For All)
Kentucky Oaks (Lady Vi-E)
Molly Pitcher Handicap (Double Ripple)
Belmont Stakes (High Echelon)
1971: New Orleans Handicap (Rio Bravo)
Oaklawn Handicap (Rio Bravo)
Canadian International Championship (One For All)
1972: Withers Stakes (Key to the Mint)
Travers Stakes (Key to the Mint)
Brooklyn Handicap (Key to the Mint)
Whitney Stakes (Key to the Mint)
Woodward Stakes (Key to the Mint)
Hopeful Stakes (Secretariat)
Futurity Stakes (Secretariat)
Laurel Futurity (Secretariat)
Garden State Stakes (Secretariat)
California Derby (Quack)
Hollywood Gold Cup (Quack)
Illinois Derby (Fame and Power)
1973: Gotham Stakes (Secretariat)
Kentucky Derby (Secretariat)
Preakness Stakes (Secretariat)
Belmont Stakes (Secretariat)
Marlboro Cup Handicap (Secretariat)
Man o' War Stakes (Secretariat)
Canadian International Championship (Secretariat)
Santa Anita Derby (Sham)
Californian Stakes (Quack)
Suburban Handicap (Key to the Mint)
1974: Californian Stakes (Quack)
1975: Oak Leaf Stakes (Answer)
1976: Coaching Club American Oaks (Revidere)
Ruffian Stakes (Revidere)
Sunset Handicap (Caucasus)
Manhattan Handicap (Caucasus)
Sorority Stakes (Squander)
Hollywood Oaks (Answer)
American Derby (Fifth Marine)
1977: San Luis Rey Stakes (Caucasus)
1980: Sunset Handicap (Inkerman)
1981: United Nations Handicap (Key To Content)
1983: Dwyer Stakes (Au Point)

PRINCE ROYAL II
1982: Del Mar Futurity (Roving Boy)
Norfolk Stakes (Roving Boy)
Hollywood Starlet Stakes (Roving Boy)

PRINCE TAJ
1983: Arlington Handicap (Palikaraki)

PRINCE TENDERFOOT
1995: Crown Royal Hollywood Derby (Labeeb)
1996: Yellow Ribbon Stakes (Donna Viola)
1997: Gamely Handicap (Donna Viola)
1998: Woodbine Mile (Labeeb)

PRIVATE ACCOUNT
1993: Jim Dandy Stakes (Miner's Mark)
Jockey Club Gold Cup (Miner's Mark)
1995: Breeders' Cup Juvenile Fillies (My Flag)
1996: Ashland Stakes (My Flag)
Coaching Club American Oaks (My Flag)
Gazelle Handicap (My Flag)
2001: Oaklawn Handicap (Traditionally)
Personal Ensign Handicap (Pompeii)
2003: San Carlos Handicap (Aldebaran)
Metropolitan Handicap (Aldebaran)
Forego Handicap (Aldebaran)

PROMINER
1982: Vanity Handicap (Sangue)
1983: Ramona Handicap (Sangue)
Golden Harvest Handicap (Sangue)
Yellow Ribbon Stakes (Sangue)
Matriarch Stakes (Sangue)

PROMISED LAND
1978: Champagne Stakes (Spectacular Bid)
Young America Stakes (Spectacular Bid)
Laurel Futurity (Spectacular Bid)
1979: Florida Derby (Spectacular Bid)
Flamingo Stakes (Spectacular Bid)
Blue Grass Stakes (Spectacular Bid)
Kentucky Derby (Spectacular Bid)

Preakness Stakes (Spectacular Bid)
Marlboro Cup Handicap (Spectacular Bid)
Meadowlands Cup (Spectacular Bid)
1980: Californian Stakes (Spectacular Bid)
Amory L. Haskell Handicap (Spectacular Bid)
Woodward Stakes (Spectacular Bid)
San Fernando Stakes (Spectacular Bid)
Charles H. Strub Stakes (Spectacular Bid)
Santa Anita Handicap (Spectacular Bid)
California Derby (Jaklin Klugman)
Jerome Handicap (Jaklin Klugman)
Sorority Stakes (Fancy Naskra)
1985: Pennsylvania Derby (Skip Trial)
Ohio Derby (Skip Trial)
Haskell Invitational Handicap (Skip Trial)
1986: Gulfstream Park Handicap (Skip Trial)
1987: Gulfstream Park Handicap (Skip Trial)

PRONTO
1990: Ruffian Handicap (Quick Mischief)

PROPHETS THUMB
1964: Ohio Derby (National)

PROPICIO
1996: Beverly Hills Handicap (Different)
Three Chimneys Spinster Stakes (Different)

PROUDEST ROMAN
1981: Blue Grass Stakes (Proud Appeal)
1984: Sorority Stakes (Tiltalating)
1988: Breeders' Cup Juvenile (Is It True)
1989: Jim Dandy Stakes (Is It True)
1991: Jersey Derby (Greek Costume)

PROVE IT
1980: Oak Leaf Stakes (Astrious)
1983: Preakness Stakes (Deputed Testamony)
Haskell Invitational Handicap (Deputed Testamony)

PROVE OUT
1987: Breeders' Cup Mile (Miesque)
1988: Breeders' Cup Mile (Miesque)

PSYCHIC BID
1953: Vineland Handicap (Mi-Marigold)
1954: Remsen Stakes (Roman Patrol)
Spinaway Stakes (Gandharva)
1955: Louisiana Derby (Roman Patrol)
1960: American Handicap (Prize Host)
1962: Santa Margarita Handicap (Queen America)

PURCHASE
1946: Sapling Stakes (Donor)
Champagne Stakes (Donor)
1947: Jerome Handicap (Donor)
1949: Manhattan Handicap (Donor)
New York Handicap (Donor)

QUACK
1987: San Felipe Handicap (Chart the Stars)
1997: Frizette Stakes (Silver Maiden)

QUADRANGLE
1981: Flower Bowl Handicap (Rokeby Rose)
1982: Hopeful Stakes (Copelan)
Futurity Stakes (Copelan)
Champagne Stakes (Copelan)
La Canada Stakes (Safe Play)
1986: Apple Blossom Handicap (Love Smitten)

QUARTER DECK
1975: Top Flight Handicap (Twixt)

QUEEN CITY LAD
1991: Hopeful Stakes (Salt Lake)

QUESTIONNAIRE
1952: Demoiselle Stakes (Grecian Queen)
Fall Highweight Handicap (Hitex)
1953: Coaching Club American Oaks (Grecian Queen)
Gazelle Handicap (Grecian Queen)
Monmouth Oaks (Grecian Queen)
New Castle Handicap (Grecian Queen)
1956: Arlington Futurity (Greek Game)
Washington Park Futurity (Greek Game)
Tropical Handicap (Illusionist)
1957: Carter Handicap (Portersville)
Brooklyn Handicap (Portersville)
Vanity Handicap (Annie-Lu-San)
1958: Vanity Handicap (Annie-Lu-San)

QUIBU
1972: Santa Susana Stakes (Susan's Girl)
Kentucky Oaks (Susan's Girl)
Acorn Stakes (Susan's Girl)
Gazelle Handicap (Susan's Girl)
Beldame Stakes (Susan's Girl)
1973: Delaware Handicap (Susan's Girl)
Spinster Stakes (Susan's Girl)
Santa Maria Handicap (Susan's Girl)
Santa Margarita Handicap (Susan's Girl)
Santa Barbara Handicap (Susan's Girl)
1974: Kentucky Oaks (Quaze Quilt)
Alabama Stakes (Quaze Quilt)
1975: Delaware Handicap (Susan's Girl)
Beldame Stakes (Susan's Girl)
Spinster Stakes (Susan's Girl)
1978: Futurity Stakes (Crest of the Wave)
1979: Illinois Derby (Smarten)
Pennsylvania Derby (Smarten)
Ohio Derby (Smarten)
American Derby (Smarten)
Matron Stakes (Smart Angle)
Frizette Stakes (Smart Angle)
Selima Stakes (Smart Angle)
1985: Breeders' Cup Juvenile Fillies (Twilight Ridge)

QUICK DECISION
2001: Whitney Handicap (Lido Palace)
Woodward Stakes (Lido Palace)
2002: Woodward Stakes (Lido Palace)

QUICK WINK
1969: Del Mar Debutante Stakes (Atomic Wings)

QUIET AMERICAN
2002: Futurity Stakes (Whywhywhy)

RACING ROOM
1986: Everglades Stakes (Badger Land)
Flamingo Stakes (Badger Land)

RADIOTHERAPY
1971: Del Mar Futurity (D.B. Carm)

RAHY
2003: John C. Mabee Handicap (Megahertz)

RAINY LAKE
1985: Champagne Stakes (Mogambo)
1986: Gotham Stakes (Mogambo)

RAISE A CUP
1992: Gotham Stakes (Devil His Due)
Wood Memorial Stakes (Devil His Due)
1993: Gulfstream Park Handicap (Devil His Due)
Pimlico Special (Devil His Due)
Suburban Handicap (Devil His Due)
1994: Brooklyn Handicap (Devil His Due)
Suburban Handicap (Devil His Due)
1995: Peter Pan Stakes (Citadeed)
1998: Milady Breeders' Cup Handicap (I Ain't Bluffing)

RAISE A NATIVE
1977: Monmouth Invitational Handicap (Affiliate)
Vosburgh Handicap (Affiliate)
1981: Arlington-Washington Futurity (Lets Dont Fight)
Eddie Read Handicap (Wickerr)
1982: Fantasy Stakes (Flying Partner)
Eddie Read Handicap (Wickerr)
1983: Matron Stakes (Lucky Lucky Lucky)
Alcibiades Stakes (Lucky Lucky Lucky)
Hialeah Turf Cup (Nijinsky's Secret)
1984: Santa Margarita Handicap (Adored)
Delaware Handicap (Adored)
Hialeah Turf Cup (Nijinsky's Secret)
Kentucky Oaks (Lucky Lucky Lucky)
Monmouth Handicap (Believe the Queen)
1985: Arlington-Washington Futurity (Meadowlake)
1986: Del Mar Futurity (Qualify)
1987: Peter Pan Stakes (Leo Castelli)
1989: Withers Stakes (Fire Maker)
1997: Breeders' Cup Sprint (Elmhurst)

RAJA BABA
1996: Hollywood Futurity (Swiss Yodeler)

RAJAH
1999: Matriarch Stakes (Happyanunoit)
2000: Beverly Hills Handicap (Happyanunoit)
2001: Gamely Breeders' Cup Handicap (Happyanunoit)

RAMAHORN
1994: Hopeful Stakes (Wild Escapade)

RAMAZON
1964: Display Handicap (Primordial II)
1965: Widener Handicap (Primordial II)

RAMBUNCTIOUS
1986: Hopeful Stakes (Gulch)
Futurity Stakes (Gulch)
1987: Wood Memorial Stakes (Gulch)
Metropolitan Handicap (Gulch)
1988: Metropolitan Handicap (Gulch)
Breeders' Cup Sprint (Gulch)

RAMSINGA
1991: Arlington-Washington Futurity (Caller I.D.)

RARE PERFORMER
1991: Hollywood Oaks (Fowda)
1992: Spinster Stakes (Fowda)
2000: Carter Handicap (Brutally Frank)

RASH PRINCE
1980: Golden Harvest Handicap (War Fame)

READING II
1965: Cinema Handicap (Arksroni)
1971: San Luis Rey Handicap (Try Sheep)

REAPING REWARD
1956: Remsen Stakes (Ambehaving)
1960: John B. Campbell Handicap (Yes You Will)
Carter Handicap (Yes You Will)
1964: Arlington Handicap (Master Dennis)

RED HANNIGAN
1975: Michigan Mile and One-Eighth (Mr. Lucky Phoenix)

RED RYDER
2000: Ashland Stakes (Rings a Chime)

REFLECTED GLORY
1988: Hollywood Futurity (King Glorious)
1989: Ohio Derby (King Glorious)
Haskell Invitational Handicap (King Glorious)

REFORM
1982: Hollywood Turf Cup (The Hague)
1986: Yellow Ribbon Stakes (Bonne Ile)

REGAL AND ROYAL
2000: Breeders' Cup Distaff (Spain)
La Brea Stakes (Spain)

REIGH COUNT
1947: Swift Stakes (Owners Choice)
San Felipe Stakes (Owners Choice)
San Pasqual Handicap (Lets Dance)

RELAUNCH
2000: Hopeful Stakes (City Zip)
2003: Santa Maria Handicap (Starrer)
Santa Margarita Handicap (Starrer)
Prioress Stakes (House Party)
Personal Ensign Handicap (Passing Shot)
Vosburgh Stakes (Ghostzapper)

RELIC
1962: Washington D.C. International (Match II)
1974: Flamingo Stakes (Bushongo)
1978: Bowling Green Handicap (Tiller)
1979: San Antonio Stakes (Tiller)
San Juan Capistrano Handicap (Tiller)
1980: Sword Dancer Stakes (Tiller)
1988: Tropical Park Derby (Digress)

RELKO
1983: Hollywood Derby (Royal Heroine)
1984: Breeders' Cup Mile (Royal Heroine)

RENEGED
1975: Donn Handicap (Proud and Bold)

REQUESTED
1958: Top Flight Handicap (Plucky Roman)
1961: Carter Handicap (Chief of Chiefs)
Washington Park Handicap (Chief of Chiefs)
1962: Delaware Oaks (North South Gal)
1965: Dwyer Handicap (Staunchness)
1966: Whitney Stakes (Staunchness)

REQUIEBRO
1961: Garden State Stakes (Crimson Satan)
Pimlico Futurity (Crimson Satan)
1963: Massachusetts Handicap (Crimson Satan)
Michigan Mile and One-Sixteenth (Crimson Satan)
Washington Park Handicap (Crimson Satan)
San Fernando Stakes (Crimson Satan)
Charles H. Strub Stakes (Crimson Satan)

RESTLESS NATIVE
1986: Top Flight Handicap (Ride Sally)

RESTLESS WIND
1973: Hopeful Stakes (Gusty O'Shay)
1983: Pegasus Handicap (World Appeal)
1987: American Derby (Fortunate Moment)
Vosburgh Stakes (Groovy)

RESURGENT
1996: Santa Margarita Handicap (Twice the Vice)
Apple Blossom Handicap (Twice the Vice)
Milady Breeders' Cup Handicap (Twice the Vice)
1997: Vanity Handicap (Twice the Vice)

REVIEWER
1984: Everglades Stakes (Time for a Change)
Flamingo Stakes (Time for a Change)
1989: Cowdin Stakes (Adjudicating)
Champagne Stakes (Adjudicating)
1990: Top Flight Handicap (Dreamy Mimi)
Flower Bowl Handicap (Laugh and Be Merry)
1993: Kentucky Oaks (Dispute)
Gazelle Handicap (Dispute)
Beldame Stakes (Dispute)
1994: Spinster Stakes (Dispute)

REVOKED
1960: Pimlico Futurity (Garwol)
1961: Saratoga Special (Battle Joined)
1962: Arlington Lassie Stakes (Smart Deb)
Matron Stakes (Smart Deb)
Monmouth Oaks (Firm Policy)
Alabama Stakes (Firm Policy)
Lawrence Realization Stakes (Battle Joined)
1963: Top Flight Handicap (Firm Policy)
Arlington Matron Handicap (Smart Deb)
1964: Hollywood Juvenile Championship (Neke)
1965: Oaklawn Handicap (Gay Revoke)
1970: Sapling Stakes (Staunch Avenger)
1972: Sapling Stakes (Assagai Jr.)

REXSON'S HOPE
2000: Florida Derby (Hal's Hope)
2002: Gulfstream Park Handicap (Hal's Hope)

RHEINGOLD
1995: Oak Tree Invitational Stakes (Northern Spur)
Breeders' Cup Turf (Northern Spur)

RHODES SCHOLAR
1954: Monmouth Handicap (Bassanio)

RIBOT
1971: San Fernando Stakes (Willowick)
1974: Selima Stakes (Aunt Jin)
Kentucky Derby (Cannonade)
1976: Swaps Stakes (Majestic Light)
Monmouth Invitational Handicap (Majestic Light)
Cinema Handicap (Majestic Light)
1977: Amory L. Haskell Handicap (Majestic Light)
Man o' War Stakes (Majestic Light)
Vanity Handicap (Cascapedia)
1978: Louisiana Derby (Esops Foibles)
Arkansas Derby (Esops Foibles)
1986: Suburban Handicap (Roo Art)
Philip H. Iselin Handicap (Roo Art)
1989: Meadowlands Cup (Mi Selecto)
1990: Gulfstream Park Handicap (Mi Selecto)

RICO
1947: Whitney Stakes (Rico Monte)
Manhattan Handicap (Rico Monte)
New York Handicap (Rico Monte)

RICO MONTE
1961: Ladies Handicap (Mighty Fair)
1962: Hollywood Derby (Drill Site)

RIDAN
1983: Delaware Handicap (May Day Eighty)

RIGHT ROYAL
1984: Breeders' Cup Turf (Lashkari)

RIO BRAVO
1995: Rothmans International Stakes (Lassigny)

RIPPEY
1968: Dixie Handicap (High Hat)
Bowling Green Handicap (High Hat)

RISE 'N SHINE
1975: Hollywood Juvenile Championship (Restless Restless)

RISEN STAR
2000: Flower Bowl Invitational Handicap (Colstar)
2003: Darley Alcibiades Stakes (Be Gentle)

RISING MARKET
1988: Spinster Stakes (Hail a Cab)

RIVA RIDGE
1986: Mother Goose Stakes (Life at the Top)
Ladies Handicap (Life at the Top)
1989: Suburban Handicap (Dancing Spree)
Breeders' Cup Sprint (Dancing Spree)
Fantasy Stakes (Fantastic Look)
1990: Jim Dandy Stakes (Chief Honcho)
Carter Handicap (Dancing Spree)
1992: Shuvee Handicap (Missy's Mirage)
Hempstead Handicap (Missy's Mirage)
Brooklyn Handicap (Chief Honcho)
1999: Ballerina Handicap (Furlough)

RIVERMAN
1987: Flamingo Stakes (Talinum)
San Juan Capistrano Handicap (Rosedale)
1993: American Derby (Vaudeville)
Secretariat Stakes (Vaudeville)
1997: Hollywood Turf Handicap (Rainbow Dancer)
Oak Tree Turf Championship (Rainbow Dancer)
Breeders' Cup Mile (Spinning World)
2003: NetJets Breeders' Cup Mile (Six Perfections)

RIVER RIVER
1998: Del Mar Oaks (Sicy D'Alsace)

RIVER WAR
1968: Arlington-Washington Futurity (Strong Strong)

ROBERTO
1992: Jerome Handicap (Furiously)
1993: Arlington-Washington Lassie Stakes (Mariah's Storm)
1994: Rothmans International Stakes (Raintrap)
1995: Beverly Hills Handicap (Alpride)
Yellow Ribbon Stakes (Alpride)
1996: San Juan Capistrano Handicap (Raintrap)
1997: Kentucky Oaks (Blushing K.D.)
Flower Bowl Invitational Handicap (Yashmak)
1998: Hopeful Stakes (Lucky Roberto)
San Juan Capistrano Handicap (Amerique)
2001: Coaching Club American Oaks (Tweedside)

ROCKEFELLA
1971: Vanity Handicap (Hi Q.)

ROCKY ROYALE
1975: San Fernando Stakes (First Back)
1980: Meadowlands Cup (Tunerup)
Hawthorne Gold Cup (Tunerup)

RODOSTO
1963: Metropolitan Handicap (Cyrano)
Brooklyn Handicap (Cyrano)
1964: Los Angeles Handicap (Cyrano)

ROI DAGOBERT
1984: Laurel Futurity (Mighty Appealing)
Remsen Stakes (Mighty Appealing)

ROIDORE
1954: Wood Memorial Stakes (Correlation)
Florida Derby (Correlation)

ROLLED STOCKING
1947: Garden State Stakes (Itsabet)
1953: Michigan Mile (Second Avenue)

ROLLS ROYCE
1952: Molly Pitcher Handicap (Dixie Flyer)

ROMAN
1950: Starlet Stakes (Gold Capitol)
1952: Frizette Stakes (Sweet Patootie)
Alcibiades Stakes (Sweet Patootie)
1953: Del Mar Futurity (Double Speed)
1955: San Felipe Handicap (Jean's Joe)
1958: Lawrence Realization Stakes (Martins Rullah)
1963: Cowdin Stakes (Chieftan)
Champagne Stakes (Roman Brother)
1964: Everglades Stakes (Roman Brother)
Jersey Derby (Roman Brother)
American Derby (Roman Brother)
Cowdin Stakes (Tom Rolfe)
Louisiana Derby (Grecian Princess)
Suburban Handicap (Iron Peg)
1965: Preakness Stakes (Tom Rolfe)
Arlington Classic (Tom Rolfe)
American Derby (Tom Rolfe)
Woodward Stakes (Roman Brother)
Manhattan Handicap (Roman Brother)
Jockey Club Gold Cup (Roman Brother)
Sanford Stakes (Flame Tree)
Santa Susana Stakes (Desert Love)
Arlington Handicap (Chieftan)
1966: Hollywood Juvenile Champ. (Forgotten Dreams)
Aqueduct Handicap (Tom Rolfe)
1967: Vanity Handicap (Desert Love)
1969: Vanity Handicap (Desert Law)
1970: Hopeful Stakes (Proudest Roman)
1974: San Luis Rey Stakes (Astray)
San Juan Capistrano Handicap (Astray)
Bowling Green Handicap (Take Off)
1975: Century Handicap (Astray)

ROMAN LINE
1985: Hialeah Turf Cup (Selous Scout)
Arlington Handicap (Pass the Line)
1988: Hopeful Stakes (Mercedes Won)
1989: Florida Derby (Mercedes Won)

ROMANTIC
1968: Canadian International Championship (Frenetico)

ROSEMONT
1960: Mother Goose Stakes (Berlo)
Coaching Club American Oaks (Berlo)
Beldame Stakes (Berlo)
Ladies Handicap (Berlo)
1971: Widener Handicap (True North)

ROSOLIO
1947: Remsen Handicap (Big If)

ROUGH'N TUMBLE
1966: Pimlico Futurity (In Reality)
1967: Florida Derby (In Reality)
Jersey Derby (In Reality)
1968: John B. Campbell Handicap (In Reality)
Carter Handicap (In Reality)
Metropolitan Handicap (In Reality)
1969: San Felipe Handicap (Elect the Ruler)
1973: New Orleans Handicap (Combat Ready)
1979: Ramona Handicap (Country Queen)
Yellow Ribbon Stakes (Country Queen)
1980: Flamingo Stakes (Superbity)

ROUND TABLE
1975: Sapling Stakes (Full Out)
San Felipe Handicap (Fleet Velvet)
1978: Gulfstream Park Handicap (Bowl Game)
Pan American Handicap (Bowl Game)
Suburban Handicap (Upper Nile)
1979: Hialeah Turf Cup (Bowl Game)
Arlington Handicap (Bowl Game)
Man o' War Stakes (Bowl Game)
Turf Classic (Bowl Game)
Washington D.C. International (Bowl Game)
1981: Hollywood Derby (De La Rose)
1982: Hollywood Derby (Victory Zone)
1984: Oak Leaf Stakes (Folk Art)
Breeders' Cup Juvenile Fillies (Outstandingly)
1987: Hollywood Derby (Political Ambition)
1988: Futurity Stakes (Trapp Mountain)
Hollywood Invitational Handicap (Political Ambition)
1989: Santa Anita Handicap (Martial Law)
1990: John Henry Handicap (Golden Pheasant)
Arlington Million (Golden Pheasant)
Sunset Handicap (Petite Ile)
1992: Pegasus Handicap (Scuffleburg)
Oak Tree Invitational Stakes (Navarone)
1994: Gulfstream Park Handicap (Scuffleburg)
1997: Hempstead Handicap (Hidden Lake)
Go for Wand Stakes (Hidden Lake)
Beldame Stakes (Hidden Lake)

ROYAL CHARGER
1956: Starlet Stakes (Lucky Mel)
1958: Del Mar Debutante Stakes (Khalita)

1960: Del Mar Debutante Stakes (Amri-An)
1962: New Orleans Handicap (Yorktown)
John B. Campbell Handicap (Yorktown)
1964: Hollywood Juvenile Championship (Charger's Kin)
1967: Del Mar Debutante Stakes (Fast Dish)
1968: Hollywood Juvenile Championship (Fleet Kirsch)
Del Mar Futurity (Fleet Allied)
1969: Santa Anita Derby (Majestic Prince)
Kentucky Derby (Majestic Prince)
Preakness Stakes (Majestic Prince)
Frizette Stakes (Tudor Queen)
Century Handicap (Pinjara)
1971: Del Mar Handicap (Pinjara)

ROYAL COINAGE
1973: Norfolk Stakes (Money Lender)
Frizette Stakes (Bundler)
1975: Louisiana Derby (Master Derby)
Blue Grass Stakes (Master Derby)
Preakness Stakes (Master Derby)
1976: New Orleans Handicap (Master Derby)
Oaklawn Handicap (Master Derby)

ROYAL DORIMAR
1984: Futurity Stakes (Spectacular Love)

ROYAL FORD
1952: Starlet Stakes (Little Request)

ROYAL GEM II
1964: Santa Susana Stakes (Blue Norther)
Kentucky Oaks (Blue Norther)
1967: Massachusetts Handicap (Good Knight)
1971: Alabama Stakes (Lauries Dancer)

ROYAL GUNNER
1982: Widener Handicap (Lord Darnley)
Gulfstream Park Handicap (Lord Darnley)

ROYAL MINSTREL
1946: Hawthorne Gold Cup (Jack's Jill)
1949: Spinaway Stakes (Sunday Evening)
Roseben Handicap (Up Beat)
1950: Dwyer Stakes (Greek Song)
Arlington Classic (Greek Song)
Massachusetts Handicap (Cochise)
1951: Grey Lag Handicap (Cochise)
Arlington Handicap (Cochise)
1952: Stars and Stripes Handicap (Royal Mustang)
1953: Demoiselle Stakes (O'Alison)
1954: Arlington Futurity (Royal Note)
1956: Preakness Stakes (Fabius)

ROYAL NOTE
1969: John B. Campbell Handicap (Juvenile John)
1974: Breeders' Futurity (Packer Captain)

ROYAL SERENADE
1968: Louisiana Derby (Kentucky Sherry)
1974: Louisiana Derby (Sellout)

ROYAL TIP
1969: Oaklawn Handicap (Listado)

ROYAL UNION
1971: Jerome Handicap (Tinajero)
1978: Dwyer Handicap (Junction)
1981: Remsen Stakes (Laser Light)

ROYAL VALE
1970: Acorn Stakes (Royal Signal)
1975: Fall Highweight Handicap (Honorable Miss)
1976: Fall Highweight Handicap (Honorable Miss)
1977: Dwyer Handicap (Bailjumper)
1980: Bowling Green Handicap (Sten)

RUBIANO
2001: Walmac Int. Alcibiades Stakes (Take Charge Lady)
2002: Ashland Stakes (Take Charge Lady)
Overbrook Spinster Stakes (Take Charge Lady)
2003: Overbrook Spinster Stakes (Take Charge Lady)

RUFFINAL
1992: Hollywood Oaks (Pacific Squall)

RUKEN
1986: Hollywood Futurity (Temperate Sil)
1987: Santa Anita Derby (Temperate Sil)
Swaps Stakes (Temperate Sil)

RUN FOR NURSE
1980: Monmouth Invitational Handicap (Thanks to Tony)
1981: Vanity Handicap (Track Robbery)
1982: Spinster Stakes (Track Robbery)
Apple Blossom Handicap (Track Robbery)
1983: Blue Grass Stakes (Play Fellow)
Arlington Classic (Play Fellow)
American Derby (Play Fellow)
Travers Stakes (Play Fellow)

RUN THE GANTLET
1996: Arkansas Derby (Zarb's Magic)
1997: Secretariat Stakes (Honor Glide)
1999: Sword Dancer Invitational Handicap (Honor Glide)

RUSSIA II
1964: San Felipe Handicap (Hill Rise)
Santa Anita Derby (Hill Rise)
1965: Santa Anita Handicap (Hill Rise)
San Fernando Stakes (Hill Rise)
Man o' War Stakes (Hill Rise)
1966: San Antonio Handicap (Hill Rise)

RUSTOM PASHA
1953: Frizette Stakes (Indian Legend)

RUSTOM SIRDAR
1957: Fall Highweight Handicap (Itobe)

RUTHLESS
1970: Del Mar Handicap (Daryl's Joy)
Oak Tree Stakes (Daryl's Joy)

SADAIR
1979: Longacres Mile (Always Gallant)
1984: Hollywood Oaks (Moment to Buy)

SADLER'S WELLS
1999: Breeders' Cup Mile (Silic)
2000: Shoemaker Breeders' Cup Mile (Silic)

SAFETY ZONE
1981: Arlington-Washington Lassie Stakes (Milingo)

SAILOR
1967: Illinois Derby (Royal Malabar)
1968: Withers Stakes (Call Me Prince)
1969: Sorority Stakes (Box the Compass)
1970: Champagne Stakes (Limit to Reason)
Pimlico-Laurel Futurity (Limit to Reason)
1978: Demoiselle Stakes (Plankton)
1980: Ladies Handicap (Plankton)
1981: Hawthorne Gold Cup (Spruce Bouquet)
1982: Swaps Stakes (Journey at Sea)

SAILOR'S GUIDE
1971: Blue Grass Stakes (Impetuosity)

SAILS PRIDE
1995: Santa Anita Derby (Larry the Legend)

SAINT CRISPIN
1982: Hialeah Turf Cup (The Bart)
Century Handicap (The Bart)

SALEM
1995: Vanity Handicap (Private Persuasion)

SALTVILLE
1986: Arlington-Washington Lassie Stakes (Delicate Vine)

SALVO
1992: Pacific Classic (Missionary Ridge)

SANCTUS
1982: Brooklyn Handicap (Silver Supreme)

SARATOGA GAME
1999: Donn Handicap (Puerto Madero)

SARATOGA SIX
1999: Ruffian Handicap (Catinca)

SARDANAPALE
1947: New Castle Handicap (Elpis)
Comely Handicap (Elpis)
Molly Pitcher Handicap (Elpis)

SAROS
2001: Sword Dancer Inv. Handicap (With Anticipation)
Man o' War Stakes (With Anticipation)
2002: United Nations Handicap (With Anticipation)
Sword Dancer Inv. Handicap (With Anticipation)
Man o' War Stakes (With Anticipation)

SASSAFRAS
1987: Hialeah Turf Cup (Theatrical)
Turf Classic (Theatrical)
Man o' War Stakes (Theatrical)
Breeders' Cup Turf (Theatrical)
1997: Gulfstream Park Handicap (Mt. Sassafras)

SAUCE BOAT
1994: Preakness Stakes (Tabasco Cat)
Belmont Stakes (Tabasco Cat)

SAULINGO
1991: San Fernando Stakes (In Excess)
Metropolitan Handicap (In Excess)
Suburban Handicap (In Excess)
Whitney Handicap (In Excess)
Woodward Stakes (In Excess)

SCREEN KING
1997: Donn Handicap (Formal Gold)
Brooklyn Handicap (Formal Gold)
Philip H. Iselin Handicap (Formal Gold)
Woodward Stakes (Formal Gold)

SEA-BIRD
1983: Arlington-Washington Lassie Stakes (Miss Oceana)
Selima Stakes (Miss Oceana)
Frizette Stakes (Miss Oceana)
1984: Acorn Stakes (Miss Oceana)
Maskette Stakes (Miss Oceana)
1985: Turf Classic (Noble Fighter)
1986: Vosburgh Stakes (King's Swan)
1989: Young America Stakes (Roanoke)
1991: Californian Stakes (Roanoke)

SEABISCUIT
1961: Inglewood Handicap (Sea Orbit)

SEA CHARGER
1981: Whitney Handicap (Fio Rito)

SEATTLE SLEW
1990: Delaware Handicap (Seattle Dawn)
1992: Jersey Derby (American Chance)
1994: NYRA Mile Handicap (Cigar)
1995: Donn Handicap (Cigar)
Gulfstream Park Handicap (Cigar)
Oaklawn Handicap (Cigar)
Pimlico Special (Cigar)
Hollywood Gold Cup (Cigar)
Woodward Stakes (Cigar)
Jockey Club Gold Cup (Cigar)
Breeders' Cup Classic (Cigar)
Spinaway Stakes (Golden Attraction)
Matron Stakes (Golden Attraction)
Frizette Stakes (Golden Attraction)
1996: Donn Handicap (Cigar)
Woodward Stakes (Cigar)
1997: Ramona Handicap (Escena)
1998: Apple Blossom Handicap (Escena)
Vanity Handicap (Escena)
Breeders' Cup Distaff (Escena)
Florida Derby (Cape Town)
Futurity Stakes (Lemon Drop Kid)
1999: Belmont Stakes (Lemon Drop Kid)
Travers Stakes (Lemon Drop Kid)
2000: Brooklyn Handicap (Lemon Drop Kid)
Suburban Handicap (Lemon Drop Kid)
Whitney Handicap (Lemon Drop Kid)
Woodward Stakes (Lemon Drop Kid)
Matron Stakes (Raging Fever)
Frizette Stakes (Raging Fever)
Gamely Breeders' Cup Handicap (Astra)
2001: Beverly Hills Handicap (Astra)
2002: Gamely Breeders' Cup Handicap (Astra)
Beverly Hills Handicap (Astra)
Ogden Phipps Handicap (Raging Fever)

SEATTLE SONG
2000: Super Derby (Tiznow)
Breeders' Cup Classic (Tiznow)
San Antonio Handicap (Budroyale)
2001: Santa Anita Handicap (Tiznow)
Breeders' Cup Classic (Tiznow)

SECRETARIAT
1984: Hopeful Stakes (Chief's Crown)
Norfolk Stakes (Chief's Crown)
Breeders' Cup Juvenile (Chief's Crown)
1985: Flamingo Stakes (Chief's Crown)
Blue Grass Stakes (Chief's Crown)
Travers Stakes (Chief's Crown)

SECRETARIAT *(Continued)*
Marlboro Cup Handicap (Chief's Crown)
Young America Stakes (Storm Cat)
1987: Gotham Stakes (Gone West)
Withers Stakes (Gone West)
Dwyer Stakes (Gone West)
John Henry Handicap (Al Mamoon)
Frizette Stakes (Classic Crown)
1989: Hopeful Stakes (Summer Squall)
1990: Jim Beam Stakes (Summer Squall)
Blue Grass Stakes (Summer Squall)
Preakness Stakes (Summer Squall)
Pennsylvania Derby (Summer Squall)
1991: Hollywood Futurity (A.P. Indy)
1992: Santa Anita Derby (A.P. Indy)
Peter Pan Stakes (A.P. Indy)
Belmont Stakes (A.P. Indy)
Breeders' Cup Classic (A.P. Indy)
1993: Hopeful Stakes (Dehere)
Champagne Stakes (Dehere)
1994: Gotham Stakes (Irgun)
Wood Memorial Stakes (Irgun)
1995: Strub Stakes (Dare and Go)
1996: Hollywood Oaks (Listening)
Pacific Classic (Dare and Go)
1997: Oaklawn Handicap (Atticus)
Milady Breeders' Cup Handicap (Listening)
1998: Ashland Stakes (Well Chosen)
2003: Shadwell Turf Mile (Perfect Soul)

SEDUCTOR
1964: Michigan Mile and One-Sixteenth (Tibaldo)

SEEKING THE GOLD
1999: Frizette Stakes (Surfside)
Hollywood Starlet Stakes (Surfside)
2000: Las Virgenes Stakes (Surfside)
Santa Anita Oaks (Surfside)
2002: Queen Elizabeth II Challenge Cup (Riskaverse)

SELALBEDA
1960: Bougainvillea Turf Handicap (Noble Sel)

SENSITIVO
1978: Jerome Handicap (Sensitive Prince)
1979: Gulfstream Park Handicap (Sensitive Prince)
1980: United Nations Handicap (Lyphard's Wish)

SEPTIEME CIEL
2001: Del Mar Futurity (Officer)
Champagne Stakes (Officer)

SERIO
1955: Washington D.C. International (El Chama)

SETTE BELLO
1981: Hopeful Stakes (Timely Writer)
Champagne Stakes (Timely Writer)
1982: Flamingo Stakes (Timely Writer)
Florida Derby (Timely Writer)
1987: Santa Anita Oaks (Timely Assertion)

SEVEN CORNERS
1981: Maskette Stakes (Jameela)
1982: Delaware Handicap (Jameela)

SHADEED
1999: Spinaway Stakes (Circle of Life)

SHAM
1988: Ruffian Handicap (Sham Say)
1990: Man o' War Stakes (Defensive Play)
1991: Charles H. Strub Stakes (Defensive Play)
1992: Metropolitan Handicap (Dixie Brass)
1996: San Felipe Stakes (Odyle)
2001: Santa Maria Handicap (Lovellon)

SHANNON II
1959: Arkansas Derby (Al Davelle)
1964: Arkansas Derby (Prince Davelle)
1968: Pan American Handicap (Irish Rebellion)

SHANTUNG
1980: Bay Meadows Handicap (Super Moment)
1981: Charles H. Strub Stakes (Super Moment)
Bay Meadows Handicap (Super Moment)
1982: Californian Stakes (Erins Isle)
Sunset Handicap (Erins Isle)
Bay Meadows Handicap (Super Moment)
1983: Hollywood Invitational Handicap (Erins Isle)
San Luis Rey Stakes (Erins Isle)
San Juan Capistrano Handicap (Erins Isle)

SHAREEF DANCER
2003: Charles Whittingham Handicap (Storming Home)
C.L. Hirsch Mem. Turf Champ. (Storming Home)

SHARPEN UP
1996: San Luis Rey Stakes (Windsharp)
Shuvee Handicap (Clear Mandate)
Pegasus Breeders' Cup Handicap (Allied Forces)
1997: John A. Morris Handicap (Clear Mandate)
Three Chimneys Spinster Stakes (Clear Mandate)
Beverly Hills Handicap (Windsharp)

SHIFTING SANDS II
1967: Del Mar Futurity (Baffle)
1970: Californian Stakes (Baffle)

SHIRLEY HEIGHTS
1990: Breeders' Cup Turf (In the Wings)
1994: Hollywood Turf Cup (Frenchpark)
2001: Gulfstream Park BC Handicap (Subtle Power)

SHREDDER
1999: Budweiser International Stakes (Caltech)

SHUT OUT
1963: Canadian Championship Stakes (The Axe II)
Man o' War Stakes (The Axe II)
San Luis Rey Handicap (The Axe II)
Hollywood Juvenile Championship (Malicious)
1964: Jerome Handicap (Irvkup)
1965: Aqueduct Stakes (Malicious)
1967: Sanford Stakes (Exclusive Native)
Kentucky Oaks (Nancy Jr.)
Ohio Derby (Out the Window)
1968: Arlington Classic (Exclusive Native)
1970: Black Helen Handicap (Taken Aback)
Spinster Stakes (Taken Aback)

SIBERIAN EXPRESS
2003: Mother Goose Stakes (Spoken Fur)
Coaching Club American Oaks (Spoken Fur)

SICAMBRE
1979: Golden Harvest Handicap (Flaunter)

SICKLE
1946: Hopeful Stakes (Blue Border)
Marguerite Stakes (Cosmic Missile)
Discovery Handicap (Mighty Story)
1947: Pimlico Oaks (But Why Not)
Acorn Stakes (But Why Not)
Alabama Stakes (But Why Not)
Arlington Matron Handicap (But Why Not)
Beldame Handicap (But Why Not)
Arlington Classic (But Why Not)
Cowdin Stakes (My Request)
Gazelle Stakes (Cosmic Missile)
1948: Wood Memorial Stakes (My Request)
Dwyer Stakes (My Request)
Arlington Classic (Papa Redbird)
1949: New Orleans Handicap (My Request)
Excelsior Handicap (My Request)
Firenze Handicap (But Why Not)
Top Flight Handicap (But Why Not)
Arlington Futurity (Wisconsin Boy)
Washington Park Futurity (Curtice)
Futurity Stakes (Guillotine)
1950: Carter Handicap (Guillotine)
Brooklyn Handicap (My Request)
1951: Belmont Stakes (Counterpoint)
Lawrence Realization Stakes (Counterpoint)
Jockey Club Gold Cup (Counterpoint)
Kentucky Oaks (How)
Coaching Club American Oaks (How)
Monmouth Oaks (Ruddy)
Firenze Handicap (Renew)
Fall Highweight Handicap (Guillotine)
1952: Whitney Stakes (Counterpoint)
San Fernando Stakes (Counterpoint)
Remsen Handicap (Social Outcast)
Top Flight Handicap (Renew)
Ladies Handicap (How)
1954: Whitney Handicap (Social Outcast)
Gallant Fox Handicap (Social Outcast)
Champagne Stakes (Flying Fury)
Coaching Club American Oaks (Cherokee Rose)
1955: McLennan Handicap (Social Outcast)
John B. Campbell Handicap (Social Outcast)
Sunset Handicap (Social Outcast)
Manhattan Handicap (Social Outcast)
Trenton Handicap (Social Outcast)
1956: McLennan Handicap (Switch On)
Manhattan Handicap (Flying Fury)
1957: Spinaway Stakes (Sequoia)
Spinster Stakes (Bornastar)
1958: Vineland Handicap (Bornastar)
Spinster Stakes (Bornastar)
1962: Los Angeles Handicap (Winonly)
1963: Californian Stakes (Winonly)

SIDERAL
1981: Brooklyn Handicap (Hechizado)

SILENT SCREEN
1980: Sapling Stakes (Travelling Music)

SILLY SEASON
1985: Budweiser-Arlington Million (Teleprompter)
1995: San Juan Capistrano Handicap (Red Bishop)

SILNET
1977: Century Handicap (Anne's Pretender)
1980: Ramona Handicap (Queen to Conquer)
1981: Ramona Handicap (Queen to Conquer)
Yellow Ribbon Stakes (Queen to Conquer)

SILVER DEPUTY
2000: Cigar Mile Handicap (El Corredor)

SILVER GHOST
2000: Hopeful Stakes (Yonaguska)

SILVER HORDE
1955: Starlet Stakes (Bold Bazooka)

SILVER SABER
1993: Dwyer Stakes (Cherokee Run)
1994: Breeders' Cup Sprint (Cherokee Run)

SING SING
1978: Hialeah Turf Cup (Noble Dancer II)
United Nations Handicap (Noble Dancer II)
San Luis Rey Stakes (Noble Dancer II)
1979: Pan American Handicap (Noble Dancer II)
United Nations Handicap (Noble Dancer II)
San Luis Rey Stakes (Noble Dancer II)

SIND
1953: Washington D.C. International (Worden II)
1957: Washington D.C. International (Mahan)

SIR ANDREW
1956: Selima Stakes (Lebkuchen)
1957: Bougainvillea Turf Handicap (Espea)

SIR BARTON
1951: Santa Susana Stakes (Ruth Lily)
Hollywood Oaks (Ruth Lily)

SIR BLENHEIM
1955: Del Mar Futurity (Blen Host)

SIR COSMO
1956: Breeders' Futurity (Round Table)
1957: Blue Grass Stakes (Round Table)
Cinema Handicap (Round Table)
Westerner Stakes (Round Table)
American Derby (Round Table)
Hollywood Gold Cup (Round Table)
Hawthorne Gold Cup (Round Table)
United Nations Handicap (Round Table)
1958: San Antonio Handicap (Round Table)
Santa Anita Handicap (Round Table)
Gulfstream Park Handicap (Round Table)
Hawthorne Gold Cup (Round Table)
Santa Anita Maturity (Round Table)
Arlington Handicap (Round Table)
1959: Washington Park Handicap (Round Table)
Manhattan Handicap (Round Table)
Stars and Stripes Handicap (Round Table)
Arlington Handicap (Round Table)
United Nations Handicap (Round Table)
Arlington Lassie Stakes (Monarchy)

SIR DAMION
1952: Washington Park Futurity (Mr. Paradise)
1958: Ohio Derby (Terra Firma)
Stars and Stripes Handicap (Terra Firma)
1963: Grey Lag Handicap (Sunrise County)

SIR GALLAHAD III
1946: Beldame Handicap (Gallorette)
Metropolitan Handicap (Gallorette)
Brooklyn Handicap (Gallorette)

Pimlico Futurity (Jet Pilot)
Tremont Stakes (Jet Pilot)
Lawrence Realization Stakes (School Tie)
1947: Kentucky Oaks (Blue Grass)
Kentucky Derby (Jet Pilot)
Queens County Handicap (Gallorette)
Del Mar Handicap (Iron Maiden)
1948: Carter Handicap (Gallorette)
Whitney Stakes (Gallorette)
Will Rogers Handicap (Speculation)
Hawthorne Gold Cup (Billings)
1949: Dwyer Stakes (Shackleton)
1950: Spinaway Stakes (Atalanta)
Matron Stakes (Atalanta)
Princess Pat Stakes (Flyamanita)
Blue Grass Stakes (Mr. Trouble)
1951: Dixie Handicap (County Delight)
Gallant Fox Handicap (County Delight)
Manhattan Handicap (County Delight)
Champagne Stakes (Armageddon)
Black-Eyed Susan Stakes (Discreet)
Acorn Stakes (Nothirdchance)
Gulfstream Park Handicap (Ennobled)
1952: Withers Stakes (Armageddon)
Wood Memorial Stakes (Master Fiddle)
Queens County Handicap (County Delight)
Manhattan Handicap (Lone Eagle)
1953: Black Helen Handicap (Atalanta)
Beldame Handicap (Atalanta)
1958: Withers Stakes (Sir Robby)
Dwyer Handicap (Victory Morn)
1959: Monmouth Oaks (Royal Native)
Spinster Stakes (Royal Native)
Wood Memorial Stakes (Manassa Mauler)
1960: Black Helen Handicap (Royal Native)
Top Flight Handicap (Royal Native)
Arlington Matron Handicap (Royal Native)
Vineland Handicap (Royal Native)
Trenton Handicap (Manassa Mauler)
1963: Arlington-Washington Lassie Stakes (Sari's Song)

SIR GAYLORD
1978: La Canada Stakes (Taisez Vous)
Santa Margarita Handicap (Taisez Vous)
1980: Man o' War Stakes (French Colonial)
1981: New Orleans Handicap (Sun Catcher)
Rothmans International Stakes (Open Call)
1982: Bowling Green Handicap (Open Call)
1983: Alabama Stakes (Spit Curl)
1984: Dwyer Stakes (Track Barron)
Vosburgh Stakes (Track Barron)
1985: Whitney Handicap (Track Barron)
Woodward Stakes (Track Barron)

SIR HARRY LEWIS
2002: Breeders' Cup Classic (Volponi)

SIR IVOR
1981: Hialeah Turf Cup (Lobsang II)
1986: Peter Pan Stakes (Danzig Connection)
Belmont Stakes (Danzig Connection)
1988: Kentucky Oaks (Goodbye Halo)
Mother Goose Stakes (Goodbye Halo)
Coaching Club American Oaks (Goodbye Halo)
1989: La Canada Stakes (Goodbye Halo)
Dwyer Stakes (Roi Danzig)
1991: Donn Handicap (Jolie's Halo)
Gulfstream Park Handicap (Jolie's Halo)
1992: Philip H. Iselin Handicap (Jolie's Halo)
1993: Peter Pan Stakes (Virginia Rapids)
1994: Carter Handicap (Virginia Rapids)
1996: Acorn Stakes (Star de Lady Ann)
1997: Arkansas Derby (Crypto Star)
1998: Beverly Hills Handicap (Squeak)
Matriarch Stakes (Squeak)
Flower Bowl Invitational Handicap (Auntie Mame)

SIR WIGGLE
1990: Coaching Club American Oaks (Charon)

SKEETER II
1977: Gulfstream Park Handicap (Strike Me Lucky)

SKY RAIDER
1959: Massachusetts Handicap (Air Pilot)
1962: Massachusetts Handicap (Air Pilot)

SKYTRACER
1970: Flamingo Stakes (My Dad George)
Florida Derby (My Dad George)

SKYWALKER
2002: Hollywood Gold Cup (Sky Jack)

SLAVE SHIP
1957: Massachusetts Handicap (Greek Spy)

SLEWACIDE
2003: Kentucky Derby (Funny Cide)
Preakness Stakes (Funny Cide)

SLEW O' GOLD
2000: Sempra Energy Hollywood Gold Cup (Early Pioneer)
Breeders' Cup Sprint (Kona Gold)
2001: Las Virgenes Stakes (Golden Ballet)
Santa Anita Oaks (Golden Ballet)
San Carlos Handicap (Kona Gold)

SLEWPY
1998: Buick Meadowlands Cup Handicap (K.J.'s Appeal)

SMARTEN
1991: Breeders' Cup Distaff (Dance Smartly)
1996: Philip H. Iselin Handicap (Smart Strike)
1999: Santa Anita Derby (General Challenge)
Pacific Classic (General Challenge)
2000: Strub Stakes (General Challenge)
Santa Anita Handicap (General Challenge)
Oak Leaf Stakes (Notable Career)

SNARK
1951: Astarita Stakes (Place Card)
1955: Alabama Stakes (Rico Reta)
1959: Dwyer Handicap (Waltz)

SNOB
1974: Del Mar Handicap (Redtop III)

SNOW CAT
1990: Brooklyn Handicap (Montubio)

SNOW SPORTING
1985: Norfolk Stakes (Snow Chief)
Hollywood Futurity (Snow Chief)
Sapling Stakes (Hilco Scamper)
1986: Florida Derby (Snow Chief)
Santa Anita Derby (Snow Chief)
Preakness Stakes (Snow Chief)
Jersey Derby (Snow Chief)
1987: Charles H. Strub Stakes (Snow Chief)

SOLARIO
1951: Will Rogers Handicap (Gold Note)
1958: Belmont Stakes (Cavan)

SOLARIUM II
1969: Oak Leaf Stakes (Opening Bid)
1970: Santa Susana Stakes (Opening Bid)
1972: San Felipe Handicap (Solar Salute)
Santa Anita Derby (Solar Salute)

SOLIDARITY
1971: Del Mar Debutante Stakes (Impressive Style)

SOME CHANCE
1966: Louisiana Derby (Blue Skyer)

SOMERSET
1980: Dwyer Stakes (Amber Pass)
1981: Monmouth Handicap (Amber Pass)

SOMETHINGFABULOUS
1997: Test Stakes (Fabulously Fast)

SON-IN-LAW
1958: Canadian Championship Stakes (Jack Ketch)

SON OF JOHN
1949: Longacres Mile (Blue Tiger)

SOON OVER
1949: Tremont Stakes (Fox Time)

SORTIE
1951: Cinema Handicap (Mucho Hosso)

SOVEREIGN DANCER
1995: Blue Grass Stakes (Wild Syn)

SOVEREIGN PATH
1974: Beverly Hills Handicap (La Zanzara)
1975: Beverly Hills Handicap (La Zanzara)
San Juan Capistrano Handicap (La Zanzara)
1981: Pan American Handicap (Little Bonny)

SPANISH PRINCE II
1948: Santa Margarita Handicap (Miss Doreen)

SPARTAN VALOR
1967: Coaching Club American Oaks (Quillo Queen)
Monmouth Oaks (Quillo Queen)

SPEAK JOHN
1979: Bowling Green Handicap (Overskate)
1980: Apple Blossom Handicap (Billy Jane)
1984: Arlington-Washington Futurity (Spend A Buck)
1985: Kentucky Derby (Spend A Buck)
Jersey Derby (Spend A Buck)
Monmouth Handicap (Spend A Buck)
1988: San Fernando Stakes (On the Line)
1989: Carter Handicap (On the Line)

SPECTACULAR BID
1993: Sword Dancer Handicap (Spectacular Tide)
1994: Yellow Ribbon Stakes (Aube Indienne)
1995: Hollywood Starlet Stakes (Cara Rafaela)
2001: Ramona Handicap (Janet)
Yellow Ribbon Stakes (Janet)

SPEND A BUCK
1997: Hollywood Starlet Stakes (Love Lock)
1998: Norfolk Stakes (Buck Trout)

SPRING DOUBLE
1990: Gamely Handicap (Double Wedge)

SPY SONG
1963: Arlington-Washington Futurity (Golden Ruler)
1968: Kentucky Jockey Club Stakes (Traffic Mark)
1969: Arkansas Derby (Traffic Mark)
1972: Manhattan Handicap (Star Envoy)
1973: Selima Stakes (Dancealot)
1975: Jersey Derby (Singh)

STAGE DOOR JOHNNY
1982: Laurel Futurity (Cast Party)
1985: United Nations Handicap (Ends Well)
1986: Fountain of Youth Stakes (My Prince Charming)
1988: Breeders' Cup Juvenile Fillies (Open Mind)
Demoiselle Stakes (Open Mind)
Young America Stakes (Irish Actor)
1989: Kentucky Oaks (Open Mind)
Acorn Stakes (Open Mind)
Mother Goose Stakes (Open Mind)
Coaching Club American Oaks (Open Mind)
Alabama Stakes (Open Mind)
1990: Gotham Stakes (Thirty Six Red)
Wood Memorial Stakes (Thirty Six Red)
1991: Oak Leaf Stakes (Pleasant Stage)
Breeders' Cup Juvenile Fillies (Pleasant Stage)
1992: Suburban Handicap (Pleasant Tap)
Jockey Club Gold Cup (Pleasant Tap)
1993: Remsen Stakes (Go for Gin)
1994: Kentucky Derby (Go for Gin)
1999: Coaching Club American Oaks (On a Soapbox)

STALLWOOD
1998: Santa Margarita Handicap (Toda Una Dama)

STAR BEACON
1960: Del Mar Futurity (Short Jacket)

STAR BLEN
1960: Cowdin Stakes (Carry Back)
Garden State Stakes (Carry Back)
Remsen Stakes (Carry Back)
1961: Everglades Stakes (Carry Back)
Flamingo Stakes (Carry Back)
Florida Derby (Carry Back)
Kentucky Derby (Carry Back)
Preakness Stakes (Carry Back)
Jerome Handicap (Carry Back)
Trenton Handicap (Carry Back)
1962: Metropolitan Handicap (Carry Back)
Monmouth Handicap (Carry Back)
Whitney Stakes (Carry Back)
1963: Trenton Handicap (Carry Back)

STAR DE NASKRA
1994: Arlington-Washington Lassie Stakes (Shining Light)
2003: Futurity Stakes (Cuvee)

STAR ENVOY
1985: Suburban Handicap (Vanlandingham)
Jockey Club Gold Cup (Vanlandingham)
Washington D.C. International (Vanlandingham)

STAR GALLANT
2003: King's Bishop Stakes (Valid Video)

STAR ROVER
1972: Breeders' Futurity (Annihilate 'Em)
1973: Travers Stakes (Annihilate 'Em)

STATUTO
1953: United Nations Handicap (Iceberg II)

STAUNCH AVENGER
1991: Super Derby (Free Spirit's Joy)

ST. BRIDEAUX
1954: Canadian Championship Stakes (Resilient)

STEADY GROWTH
1998: Santa Anita Oaks (Hedonist)

STEFAN THE GREAT
1946: McLennan Handicap (Concordian)
1947: Kentucky Jockey Club Stakes (Bold Gallant)
Demoiselle Stakes (Ghost Run)

STEPFATHER
1980: Oaklawn Handicap (Uncool)

STEVWARD
1986: Delaware Handicap (Shocker T.)
1990: Champagne Stakes (Fly So Free)
Breeders' Cup Juvenile (Fly So Free)
1991: Florida Derby (Fly So Free)
Jim Dandy Stakes (Fly So Free)

ST. GERMANS
1946: San Antonio Handicap (First Fiddle)
1948: Champagne Stakes (Capot)
Pimlico Futurity (Capot)
1949: Preakness Stakes (Capot)
Belmont Stakes (Capot)
Jerome Handicap (Capot)
Pimlico Special (Capot)
1950: Breeders' Futurity (Big Stretch)
Pimlico Futurity (Big Stretch)
1951: Pimlico Futurity (Cajun)
1952: Delaware Oaks (Big Mo)
1953: Selima Stakes (Small Favor)
1956: Ohio Derby (Born Mighty)

STIMULUS
1946: Santa Anita Handicap (War Knight)
1947: Selima Stakes (Whirl Some)
Marguerite Stakes (Whirl Some)
American Derby (Fervent)
Pimlico Special (Fervent)
Fall Highweight Handicap (Rippey)
Carter Handicap (Rippey)
1948: Dixie Handicap (Fervent)
Washington Park Handicap (Fervent)
Breeders' Futurity (Olympia)
Roseben Handicap (Rippey)
1949: Withers Stakes (Olympia)
Flamingo Stakes (Olympia)
San Felipe Stakes (Olympia)
Wood Memorial Stakes (Olympia)
Santa Anita Derby (Old Rockport)
1950: Roseben Handicap (Olympia)
1953: Starlet Stakes (Arrogate)
1954: Arlington Lassie Stakes (Delta)
Princess Pat Stakes (Delta)
1955: Selima Stakes (Levee)
Del Mar Handicap (Arrogate)
1956: Coaching Club American Oaks (Levee)
Monmouth Oaks (Levee)
Arlington Matron Handicap (Delta)
Beldame Handicap (Levee)
Princess Pat Stakes (Splendored)
Del Mar Handicap (Arrogate)
1957: Acorn Stakes (Bayou)
Delaware Oaks (Bayou)
Gazelle Handicap (Bayou)
Maskette Handicap (Bayou)
1958: Kentucky Jockey Club Stakes (Winsome Winner)

STING
1950: Swift Stakes (Ferd)

ST. JAMES
1946: Monmouth Handicap (Lucky Draw)
Miami Beach Handicap (Frere Jacques)
1949: Bougainvillea Handicap (Frere Jacques)
1953: Lawrence Realization Stakes (Platan)
1955: Arlington Handicap (Platan)

STOP THE MUSIC
1990: Swaps Stakes (Jovial)
Arlington-Washington Lassie Stakes (Through Flight)
1991: Brooklyn Handicap (Timely Warning)
1993: Oaklawn Handicap (Jovial)
1994: Swaps Stakes (Silver Music)
1995: Santa Maria Handicap (Queens Court Queen)
Santa Margarita Handicap (Queens Court Queen)
1996: Santa Anita Handicap (Mr. Purple)
2001: Pimlico Special (Include)
2003: Hollywood Turf Cup (Continuously)

STORM BIRD
1993: Wood Memorial Stakes (Storm Tower)
1994: Spinaway Stakes (Flanders)
Matron Stakes (Flanders)
Frizette Stakes (Flanders)
Breeders' Cup Juvenile Fillies (Flanders)
Remsen Stakes (Thunder Gulch)
1995: Florida Derby (Thunder Gulch)
Kentucky Derby (Thunder Gulch)
Belmont Stakes (Thunder Gulch)
Swaps Stakes (Thunder Gulch)
Travers Stakes (Thunder Gulch)
1999: Louisiana Derby (Kimberlite Pipe)
2003: Kentucky Oaks (Bird Town)
Acorn Stakes (Bird Town)
Champagne Stakes (Birdstone)
Ancient Title Breeders' Cup Handicap (Avanzado)

STORM CAT
2002: Hopeful Stakes (Sky Mesa)
Lane's End Breeders' Futurity (Sky Mesa)
Wood Memorial Stakes (Buddha)

STRAIGHT DEAL
1957: Diana Handicap (Pardala)
1958: Black Helen Handicap (Pardala)

STRATMAT
1983: Santa Anita Derby (Marfa)
Jim Beam Spiral Stakes (Marfa)

STRAWBERRY ROAD II
2001: Queen Elizabeth II Challenge Cup (Affluent)
La Brea Stakes (Affluent)
2002: John C. Mabee Ramona Handicap (Affluent)
Bessemer Trust Breeders' Cup Juvenile (Vindication)
2003: Santa Monica Handicap (Affluent)

STRIP THE WILLOW
1956: Canadian Championship Stakes (Eugenia II)
1958: Hialeah Turf Handicap (Meeting)

STROLLING PLAYER
1948: McLennan Handicap (El Mono)
Widener Handicap (El Mono)

STYMIE
1961: Remsen Stakes (Figaro Bob)
1962: Vanity Handicap (Linita)
1963: Everglades Stakes (B. Major)
1965: Alabama Stakes (What A Treat)
Gazelle Handicap (What A Treat)
Beldame Stakes (What A Treat)
1966: Frizette Stakes (Regal Gleam)
Selima Stakes (Regal Gleam)
Black Helen Handicap (What A Treat)
1967: Widener Handicap (Ring Twice)
1971: Malibu Stakes (King of Cricket)

SUB FLEET
1969: Breeders' Futurity (Hard Work)
Grey Lag Handicap (Bushido)
1971: John B. Campbell Handicap (Bushido)

SUCCESSOR
1981: Hollywood Derby (Silveyville)

SUMMER TAN
1968: Hopeful Stakes (Top Knight)
Futurity Stakes (Top Knight)
Champagne Stakes (Top Knight)
1969: Flamingo Stakes (Top Knight)
Florida Derby (Top Knight)
1972: Hollywood Invitational Handicap (Typecast)
Sunset Handicap (Typecast)
Man o' War Stakes (Typecast)
1976: Hialeah Turf Cup (Legion)
1977: Ohio Derby (Silver Series)
American Derby (Silver Series)
Ashland Stakes (Sound of Summer)
Maskette Handicap (What a Summer)
Donn Handicap (Legion)
1978: Acorn Stakes (Tempest Queen)
Spinster Stakes (Tempest Queen)
Widener Handicap (Silver Series)
1979: Hawthorne Gold Cup (Young Bob)
1981: La Canada Stakes (Summer Siren)
1985: Fountain of Youth Stakes (Proud Truth)
Florida Derby (Proud Truth)
Breeders' Cup Classic (Proud Truth)

SUMMING
2002: Super Derby (Essence of Dubai)

SUN AGAIN
1957: Everglades Stakes (Gen. Duke)
Florida Derby (Gen. Duke)
1966: Michigan Mile and One-Eighth (Stanislas)
1967: Molly Pitcher Handicap (Politely)
1968: Delaware Handicap (Politely)
Ladies Handicap (Politely)
San Felipe Handicap (Dewan)
1970: Brooklyn Handicap (Dewan)
San Antonio Stakes (Dewan)

SUN BRIAR
1948: Monmouth Handicap (Tide Rips)
1949: Saranac Handicap (Sun Bahram)
1952: Acorn Stakes (Parading Lady)
Vosburgh Handicap (Parading Lady)
1958: Acorn Stakes (Big Effort)
Delaware Oaks (Big Effort)
1959: Top Flight Handicap (Big Effort)

SUNGLOW
1969: Washington Park Handicap (Night Invader)

SUNNY
1983: Arkansas Derby (Sunny's Halo)
Kentucky Derby (Sunny's Halo)
Super Derby (Sunny's Halo)

SUNNY NORTH
2001: Forego Handicap (Delaware Township)
Frank J. De Francis Mem. Dash (Delaware Township)

SUNNY'S HALO
1998: Californian Stakes (Mud Route)

SUNRISE FLIGHT
1980: Remsen Stakes (Pleasant Colony)
1981: Wood Memorial Stakes (Pleasant Colony)
Kentucky Derby (Pleasant Colony)
Preakness Stakes (Pleasant Colony)
Woodward Stakes (Pleasant Colony)
1982: Beldame Stakes (Weber City Miss)

SUN TEDDY
1950: Hawthorne Gold Cup (Dr. Ole Nelson)
1951: Metropolitan Handicap (Casemate)
1953: Sapling Stakes (Artismo)
Hopeful Stakes (Artismo)
1956: Acorn Stakes (Beyond)

SUPER CONCORDE
1991: Sunset Handicap (Black Monday)
1998: Oaklawn Handicap (Precocity)

SUPREMUS
1948: Demoiselle Stakes (Lithe)
1949: Arlington Matron Handicap (Lithe)
Comely Handicap (Lithe)
1950: Arlington Matron Handicap (Lithe)
1957: Withers Stakes (Clem)
Arlington Classic (Clem)
1958: Washington Park Handicap (Clem)
Woodward Stakes (Clem)
United Nations Handicap (Clem)
1960: Flamingo Stakes (Bally Ache)
Florida Derby (Bally Ache)
Preakness Stakes (Bally Ache)
Jersey Derby (Bally Ache)

SWAPS
1970: Wood Memorial Stakes (Personality)
Preakness Stakes (Personality)
Jersey Derby (Personality)
Woodward Stakes (Personality)
John B. Campbell Handicap (Best Turn)
Vosburgh Handicap (Best Turn)
1971: Spinaway Stakes (Numbered Account)
Matron Stakes (Numbered Account)

Frizette Stakes (Numbered Account)
Selima Stakes (Numbered Account)
Gardenia Stakes (Numbered Account)
1972: Black Helen Handicap (Alma North)
Spinster Stakes (Numbered Account)
1974: California Derby (Agitate)
Swaps Stakes (Agitate)
Hollywood Derby (Agitate)
Gazelle Handicap (Maud Muller)
1975: Florida Derby (Prince Thou Art)
San Antonio Stakes (Cheriepe)
1976: Maskette Handicap (Artfully)
1977: Ruffian Handicap (Cum Laude Laurie)
Beldame Stakes (Cum Laude Laurie)
Spinster Stakes (Cum Laude Laurie)
Arlington Handicap (Cunning Trick)
1978: Matron Stakes (Fall Aspen)
John B. Campbell Handicap (Ripon)
1979: Delaware Handicap (Likely Exchange)
1981: Louisiana Derby (Woodchopper)
1982: Monmouth Handicap (Mehmet)
Meadowlands Cup (Mehmet)
1985: Everglades Stakes (Rhoman Rule)

SWEEP
1946: Arlington Matron Handicap (Good Blood)
Vineland Handicap (Good Blood)
1947: Delaware Oaks (Camargo)
1948: Molly Pitcher Handicap (Camargo)

SWEEPING LIGHT
1960: Louisiana Derby (Tony Graff)

SWEEP LIKE
1955: Arlington Futurity (Swoon's Son)
Washington Park Futurity (Swoon's Son)
1956: Arlington Classic (Swoon's Son)
American Derby (Swoon's Son)

SWIFT AND SURE
1946: Washington Park Futurity (Education)
Breeders' Futurity (Education)
1949: Garden State Stakes (Cornwall)
1955: Black Helen Handicap (Rosemary B.)

SWOON'S SON
1971: Arkansas Derby (Twist the Axe)
Ohio Derby (Twist the Axe)
Vosburgh Handicap (Duck Dance)
1973: Kentucky Oaks (Bag of Tunes)
1977: Louisiana Derby (Clev Er Tell)
Arkansas Derby (Clev Er Tell)

SWORD DANCER
1977: Bowling Green Handicap (Hunza Dancer)
American Handicap (Hunza Dancer)
1979: Maskette Stakes (Blitey)
Brooklyn Handicap (The Liberal Member)

TABLE PLAY
1986: Widener Handicap (Turkoman)
Marlboro Cup Handicap (Turkoman)

TACITUS
1982: Flower Bowl Handicap (Trevita)

TALE OF TWO CITIES
1982: Yellow Ribbon Stakes (Castilla)
Matriarch Stakes (Castilla)

TALON
1962: Santa Anita Handicap (Physician)
1963: San Antonio Handicap (Physician)

TANERKO
1973: Cinema Handicap (Amen II)
Hollywood Derby (Amen II)

TANTIEME
1969: Washington D.C. International (Karabas)
1976: Alcibiades Stakes (Sans Supplement)
1981: Louisiana Downs Handicap (Goldiko)

TAPIOCA
1980: Washington D.C. International (Argument)
1983: Oak Tree Invitational Stakes (Zalataia)

TAP ON WOOD
1995: Breeders' Cup Mile (Ridgewood Pearl)

TARGOWICE
1994: Turf Classic (Tikkanen)
Breeders' Cup Turf (Tikkanen)

TATAN
1975: Withers Stakes (Sarsar)
1976: Santa Anita Derby (An Act)
1981: Oak Leaf Stakes (Header Card)
1986: Cowdin Stakes (Polish Navy)
Champagne Stakes (Polish Navy)
1987: Jim Dandy Stakes (Polish Navy)
Woodward Stakes (Polish Navy)

TAYLOR'S FALLS
1997: Ashland Stakes (Glitter Woman)
2001: Breeders' Cup Distaff (Unbridled Elaine)

TEDDY
1946: Selima Stakes (Bee Ann Mac)
1947: Inglewood Handicap (Artillery)
1949: Remsen Handicap (Lights Up)
1950: Travers Stakes (Lights Up)
1951: San Felipe Stakes (Phil D.)
1952: San Antonio Handicap (Phil D.)
Golden Gate Handicap (Lights Up)
American Handicap (Admiral Drake)
1953: Sunset Handicap (Lights Up)

TEDDY'S COMET
1961: San Antonio Handicap (American Comet)
Michigan Mile and One-Sixteenth (American Comet)

TEHRAN
1958: San Carlos Handicap (Seaneen)
Californian Stakes (Seaneen)
1961: Arlington Handicap (Tudorich)
1963: New Orleans Handicap (Endymion)
1964: Michigan Mile and One-Sixteenth (Going Abroad)
Manhattan Handicap (Going Abroad)
Hawthorne Gold Cup (Going Abroad)
New Orleans Handicap (Green Hornet)
1966: Dwyer Handicap (Mr. Right)
1968: Santa Anita Handicap (Mr. Right)
Woodward Stakes (Mr. Right)
1969: Suburban Handicap (Mr. Right)

TEJON
1971: Amory L. Haskell Handicap (Jontilla)

TELEFERIQUE
1969: San Luis Rey Handicap (Taneb)

TELL
1983: Ruffian Handicap (Heartlight No. One)

TEMPERENCE HILL
2001: Del Mar Debutante Stakes (Habibti)
Hollywood Starlet Stakes (Habibti)

TEMPEST II
1974: Alcibiades Stakes (Hope of Glory)

TENTAM
1985: Illinois Derby (Important Business)
1987: Arlington-Washington Lassie Stakes (Joe's Tammie)
1988: Ashland Stakes (Willa on the Move)
1989: Ladies Handicap (Dance Teacher)
1990: Hollywood Starlet Stakes (Cuddles)
1996: Travers Stakes (Will's Way)
1997: Whitney Handicap (Will's Way)

TERRIBLE TIGER
1985: Belmont Stakes (Creme Fraiche)
American Derby (Creme Fraiche)
Jerome Handicap (Creme Fraiche)
Super Derby (Creme Fraiche)
1986: Jockey Club Gold Cup (Creme Fraiche)
1987: Jockey Club Gold Cup (Creme Fraiche)
Meadowlands Cup (Creme Fraiche)

TERRY
1958: Jockey Club Gold Cup (Inside Tract)

TE VEGA
1988: Ohio Derby (Jim's Orbit)

TEX COURAGE
1984: California Derby (Distant Ryder)

THEATRICAL
2002: Del Mar Oaks (Dublino)

THE AXE II
1983: Widener Handicap (Swing Till Dawn)
Charles H. Strub Stakes (Swing Till Dawn)
Belmont Stakes (Caveat)

1984: Apple Blossom Handicap (Heatherten)
Ruffian Handicap (Heatherten)
Ladies Handicap (Heatherten)
Tropical Park Derby (Morning Bob)
Pennsylvania Derby (Morning Bob)
1988: Swaps Stakes (Lively One)
1993: Florida Derby (Bull Inthe Heather)
Budweiser International Stakes (Buckhar)

THE CLAN
1971: Charles H. Strub Stakes (War Heim)
1972: Miller High Life Inglewood Handicap (War Heim)

THE DOGE
1974: Hollywood Invitational Handicap (Court Ruling)
1980: New Orleans Handicap (Pool Court)

THE MINSTREL
1991: Santa Barbara Handicap (Bequest)
1994: Jim Dandy Stakes (Unaccounted For)
Pacific Classic (Tinners Way)
1995: Pacific Classic (Tinners Way)
Whitney Handicap (Unaccounted For)
1996: Californian Stakes (Tinners Way)

THE PIE KING
1970: Del Mar Debutante Stakes (Generous Portion)
1976: Arlington-Washington Lassie Stakes (Special Warmth)

THE PINCHER
1975: New Orleans Handicap (Lord Rebeau)

THE PORTER
1946: Swift Stakes (Master Bid)
1949: Trenton Handicap (Sky Miracle)
1950: Santa Margarita Handicap (Two Lea)
1952: Breeders' Futurity (Straight Face)
Kentucky Jockey Club Stakes (Straight Face)
Vanity Handicap (Two Lea)
Hollywood Gold Cup (Two Lea)
1953: Flamingo Stakes (Straight Face)
1954: Cinema Handicap (Miz Clementine)
California Derby (Miz Clementine)
Dixie Handicap (Straight Face)
Suburban Handicap (Straight Face)
1955: Spinaway Stakes (Register)
Aqueduct Handicap (Icarian)
1959: Michigan Mile and One-Sixteenth (Total Traffic)
1962: Top Flight Handicap (Pepper Patch)

THE RABBI
1976: Ladies Handicap (Bastonera II)
Beverly Hills Handicap (Bastonera II)

THE RHYMER
1956: Blue Grass Stakes (Toby B.)
1959: Breeders' Futurity (Toby's Brother)

THE SATRAP
1948: San Vicente Handicap (Salmagundi)
Santa Anita Derby (Salmagundi)
1951: Garden State Stakes (Candle Wood)
1952: San Felipe Handicap (Windy City II)

THE SCOUNDREL
1987: Remsen Stakes (Batty)

THINKING CAP
1970: Futurity Stakes (Salem)
1978: Carter Handicap (Pumpkin Moonshine)
1982: Alabama Stakes (Broom Dance)

THIRD BROTHER
1976: Carter Handicap (Due Diligence)

THIRD MARTINI
1981: Mother Goose Stakes (Wayward Lass)
Coaching Club American Oaks (Wayward Lass)

THUMBS UP
1961: California Derby (Mr. Consistency)
1964: Santa Anita Handicap (Mr. Consistency)
San Juan Capistrano Handicap (Mr. Consistency)

TICK ON
1951: Del Mar Debutante Stakes (Tonga)

TIGER
1959: Suburban Handicap (Bald Eagle)
Gallant Fox Handicap (Bald Eagle)
Washington D.C. International (Bald Eagle)
1960: Widener Handicap (Bald Eagle)

TIGER *(Continued)*
Gulfstream Park Handicap (Bald Eagle)
Metropolitan Handicap (Bald Eagle)
Aqueduct Handicap (Bald Eagle)
Washington D.C. International (Bald Eagle)
Arlington Handicap (One-Eyed King)
1962: Roamer Handicap (Dead Ahead)

TIGER WANDER
1978: Arlington Handicap (Romeo)

TILT UP
1991: Secretariat Stakes (Jackie Wackie)

TIME FOR A CHANGE
2001: Acorn Stakes (Forest Secrets)

TIME MAKER
1946: Starlet Stakes (U Time)
1947: Hollywood Oaks (U Time)
1953: Blue Grass Stakes (Correspondent)
1954: Hollywood Gold Cup (Correspondent)

TIMOR
1975: Vanity Handicap (Dulcia)
Ramona Handicap (Dulcia)
National Championship Inv. Handicap (Dulcia)

TIM TAM
1973: Widener Handicap (Vertee)
John B. Campbell Handicap (Vertee)
Metropolitan Handicap (Tentam)
United Nations Handicap (Tentam)
1975: Cinema Handicap (Terete)
1976: Illinois Derby (Life's Hope)
Jersey Derby (Life's Hope)
1978: Secretariat Stakes (Mac Diarmida)
Canadian Int. Championship (Mac Diarmida)
Washington D.C. International (Mac Diarmida)
New Orleans Handicap (Life's Hope)
Amory L. Haskell Handicap (Life's Hope)
1979: Fantasy Stakes (Davona Dale)
Kentucky Oaks (Davona Dale)
Acorn Stakes (Davona Dale)
Mother Goose Stakes (Davona Dale)
Coaching Club American Oaks (Davona Dale)
1981: Matron Stakes (Before Dawn)

TIP-TOE
1969: Ohio Derby (Berkley Prince)

TIRRENO
1983: Metropolitan Handicap (Star Choice)

TOBIN BRONZE
1982: Wood Memorial Stakes (Air Forbes Won)

TO MARKET
1965: Jerome Handicap (Bold Bidder)
1966: Monmouth Handicap (Bold Bidder)
Washington Park Handicap (Bold Bidder)
Hawthorne Gold Cup (Bold Bidder)
Charles H. Strub Stakes (Bold Bidder)
1971: Sorority Stakes (Brenda Beauty)
1976: Del Mar Futurity (Visible)
1978: Yellow Ribbon Stakes (Amazer)
1981: Delaware Handicap (Relaxing)
Ruffian Handicap (Relaxing)

TOM CAT
1983: Pan American Handicap (Field Cat)

TOM FOOL
1963: Alabama Stakes (Tona)
1964: Vineland Handicap (Tona)
1968: Lawrence Realization Stakes (Funny Fellow)
Gallant Fox Handicap (Funny Fellow)
1969: Alcibiades Stakes (Belle Noire)
Donn Handicap (Funny Fellow)
1970: Arkansas Derby (Herbalist)
1971: Santa Anita Derby (Jim French)
Dwyer Handicap (Jim French)
Pontiac Grand Prix Stakes (Son Ange)
Whitney Stakes (Protanto)
1972: Champagne Stakes (Stop the Music)
Jersey Derby (Smiling Jack)
1973: Arkansas Derby (Impecunious)
Dwyer Handicap (Stop the Music)
1974: Sapling Stakes (Foolish Pleasure)
Hopeful Stakes (Foolish Pleasure)
Champagne Stakes (Foolish Pleasure)
Dwyer Handicap (Hatchet Man)
1975: Flamingo Stakes (Foolish Pleasure)
Wood Memorial Stakes (Foolish Pleasure)
Kentucky Derby (Foolish Pleasure)
1976: Widener Handicap (Hatchet Man)
Amory L. Haskell Handicap (Hatchet Man)
Donn Handicap (Foolish Pleasure)
Suburban Handicap (Foolish Pleasure)
Louisiana Derby (Johnny Appleseed)
1977: Kentucky Oaks (Sweet Alliance)
1978: Delaware Handicap (Late Bloomer)
Ruffian Handicap (Late Bloomer)
Beldame Stakes (Late Bloomer)
Sheepshead Bay Handicap (Late Bloomer)
1980: Louisiana Derby (Prince Valiant)
1982: Rothmans International Stakes (Majesty's Prince)
1983: Sword Dancer Handicap (Majesty's Prince)
Man o' War Stakes (Majesty's Prince)
Louisiana Downs Handicap (Late Act)
1984: Man o' War Stakes (Majesty's Prince)
Rothmans International Stakes (Majesty's Prince)

TOMPION
1976: Hollywood Gold Cup (Pay Tribute)
1977: Meadowlands Cup (Pay Tribute)

TOM ROLFE
1978: Cinema Handicap (Kamehameha)
1983: Oak Leaf Stakes (Life's Magic)
1984: Mother Goose Stakes (Life's Magic)
Alabama Stakes (Life's Magic)
Beldame Stakes (Life's Magic)
1985: Breeders' Cup Distaff (Life's Magic)
Louisiana Derby (Violado)
1986: Alabama Stakes (Classy Cathy)
1987: Futurity Stakes (Forty Niner)
Champagne Stakes (Forty Niner)
Kentucky Oaks (Buryyourbelief)
Top Flight Handicap (Ms. Eloise)
1988: Fountain of Youth Stakes (Forty Niner)
Haskell Invitational Handicap (Forty Niner)
Travers Stakes (Forty Niner)
1998: Walmac Int. Alcibiades Stakes (Silverbulletday)
Breeders' Cup Juvenile Fillies (Silverbulletday)
1999: Ashland Stakes (Silverbulletday)
Kentucky Oaks (Silverbulletday)
Alabama Stakes (Silverbulletday)
Gazelle Handicap (Silverbulletday)
2002: Clement L. Hirsch Mem. Turf Champ. (The Tin Man)

TOPSIDER
1994: Coaching Club American Oaks (Two Altazano)
1996: Malibu Stakes (King of the Heap)
2001: Santa Margarita Handicap (Lazy Slusan)
Milady Breeders' Cup Handicap (Lazy Slusan)
San Antonio Handicap (Guided Tour)

TORCHILLA
1947: Santa Anita Derby (On Trust)
Will Rogers Handicap (On Trust)
1953: San Antonio Handicap (Trusting)

TORNADO
1957: Michigan Mile and One-Sixteenth (My Night Out)

TORO
1946: Arlington Lassie Stakes (Four Winds)
Molly Pitcher Handicap (Mahmoudess)
American Derby (Eternal Reward)
1947: Top Flight Handicap (Rytina)
Roseben Handicap (Inroc)
1948: Arlington Matron Handicap (Four Winds)
1950: Longacres Mile (Two and Twenty)

TORSION
1990: Ohio Derby (Private School)

TO THE QUICK
1991: Peter Pan Stakes (Lost Mountain)
Dwyer Stakes (Lost Mountain)
Haskell Invitational Handicap (Lost Mountain)

TOULOUSE LAUTREC
1972: Malibu Stakes (Wing Out)

TOURBILLON
1960: Hollywood Derby (Tempestuous)

TOURIST II
1956: Alabama Stakes (Tournure)

TRACE CALL
1951: Del Mar Futurity (Big Noise)

TRACK SPARE
1996: Beverly D. Stakes (Timarida)

TRAFFIC JUDGE
1974: Remsen Stakes (El Pitirre)
1975: Matron Stakes (Optimistic Gal)
Frizette Stakes (Optimistic Gal)
Alcibiades Stakes (Optimistic Gal)
Selima Stakes (Optimistic Gal)
Santa Barbara Handicap (Gay Style)
1976: Ashland Stakes (Optimistic Gal)
Kentucky Oaks (Optimistic Gal)
Alabama Stakes (Optimistic Gal)
Delaware Handicap (Optimistic Gal)
Spinster Stakes (Optimistic Gal)
1978: Maskette Handicap (Pearl Necklace)
1979: Flower Bowl Handicap (Pearl Necklace)
1982: Santa Susana Stakes (Blush With Pride)
Kentucky Oaks (Blush With Pride)
Golden Harvest Handicap (Blush With Pride)
San Antonio Stakes (Score Twenty Four)

TRANSWORLD
1989: Beldame Stakes (Tactile)
1990: San Fernando Stakes (Flying Continental)
Charles H. Strub Stakes (Flying Continental)
Jockey Club Gold Cup (Flying Continental)

TREMPOLINO
2003: Bessemer Trust BC Juvenile (Action This Day)

TREVIERES
1987: Vanity Handicap (Infinidad)

TREVLIGIO
1992: San Antonio Handicap (Ibero)
NYRA Mile Handicap (Ibero)
1993: Metropolitan Handicap (Ibero)

TRI JET
1990: Demoiselle Stakes (Debutant's Halo)
1994: Ohio Derby (Exclusive Praline)
1996: Gulfstream Park Handicap (Wekiva Springs)
Brooklyn Handicap (Wekiva Springs)
Suburban Handicap (Wekiva Springs)
Early Times Manhattan Handicap (Diplomatic Jet)
Man o' War Stakes (Diplomatic Jet)
Turf Classic (Diplomatic Jet)

TRIMDON
1948: Cinema Handicap (Drumbeat)
Sunset Handicap (Drumbeat)

TROLLIUS
1956: Washington D.C. International (Master Boing)

TROPICAL BREEZE
1982: United Nations Handicap (Naskra's Breeze)
Man o' War Stakes (Naskra's Breeze)
1985: Laurel Futurity (Southern Appeal)

TROY
1995: Eddie Read Handicap (Fastness)
1996: Eddie Read Handicap (Fastness)
Breeders' Cup Turf (Pilsudski)
2002: Stephen Foster Handicap (Street Cry)

TRUCULENT
1950: Santa Susana Stakes (Special Touch)
1951: Santa Margarita Handicap (Special Touch)

TSUNAMI SLEW
1997: Ohio Derby (Frisk Me Now)
1998: Suburban Handicap (Frisk Me Now)
1999: Philip H. Iselin Handicap (Frisk Me Now)

TUDOR MELODY
1977: Jerome Handicap (Broadway Forli)

TUDOR MINSTREL
1964: Carter Handicap (Ahoy)
1965: Louisiana Derby (Dapper Delegate)
1971: Alcibiades Stakes (Mrs. Cornwallis)
1976: La Canada Stakes (Raise Your Skirts)
San Fernando Stakes (Messenger of Song)
1977: Jersey Derby (Cormorant)

TUDOR MUSIC
1988: Sword Dancer Handicap (Anka Germania)

TULEG
1976: Del Mar Handicap (Riot in Paris)

TULYAR
1969: Hopeful Stakes (Irish Castle)
1972: Hollywood Oaks (Pallisima)
1974: Matron Stakes (Alpine Lass)
1975: Champagne Stakes (Honest Pleasure)
Laurel Futurity (Honest Pleasure)
Arlington-Washington Futurity (Honest Pleasure)
1976: Flamingo Stakes (Honest Pleasure)
Florida Derby (Honest Pleasure)
Blue Grass Stakes (Honest Pleasure)
Travers Stakes (Honest Pleasure)
Futurity Stakes (For the Moment)
1977: Blue Grass Stakes (For the Moment)

TUNERUP
1994: Arkansas Derby (Concern)
Breeders' Cup Classic (Concern)
1995: Californian Stakes (Concern)

TURKHAN
1961: Kentucky Jockey Club Stakes (Su Ka Wa)

TURKOMAN
1999: Meadowlands Cup Handicap (Pleasant Breeze)
2000: Hollywood Futurity (Point Given)
2001: San Felipe Stakes (Point Given)
Santa Anita Derby (Point Given)
Preakness Stakes (Point Given)
Belmont Stakes (Point Given)
Haskell Invitational Handicap (Point Given)
Travers Stakes (Point Given)

TURN-TO
1969: Withers Stakes (Ack Ack)
Arlington Classic (Ack Ack)
1971: Hollywood Gold Cup (Ack Ack)
San Antonio Stakes (Ack Ack)
Santa Anita Handicap (Ack Ack)
American Handicap (Ack Ack)
1973: John B. Campbell Handicap (Delay)
Oak Tree Invitational Stakes (Portentous)
1974: Fountain of Youth Stakes (Green Gambados)
1979: Hollywood Oaks (Prize Spot)

TUSCANY
1972: John B. Campbell Handicap (Boone the Great)

T.V. COMMERCIAL
1985: Ladies Handicap (Videogenic)
1994: San Felipe Stakes (Soul of the Matter)
Super Derby (Soul of the Matter)
1997: Spinaway Stakes (Countess Diana)
Breeders' Cup Juvenile Fillies (Countess Diana)

T.V. LARK
1974: Acorn Stakes (Chris Evert)
Mother Goose Stakes (Chris Evert)
Coaching Club American Oaks (Chris Evert)
1975: Oaklawn Handicap (Warbucks)
1976: San Felipe Handicap (Crystal Water)
Hollywood Derby (Crystal Water)
Ramona Handicap (Vagabonda)
1977: Californian Stakes (Crystal Water)
Hollywood Gold Cup (Crystal Water)
Santa Anita Handicap (Crystal Water)
Oak Tree Invitational Stakes (Crystal Water)
Pan American Handicap (Gravelines)
1983: Monmouth Handicap (Bates Motel)
San Antonio Stakes (Bates Motel)
Santa Anita Handicap (Bates Motel)
1986: San Antonio Handicap (Hatim)
1989: Hollywood Derby (Live the Dream)
1991: San Luis Rey Stakes (Pleasant Variety)

TWINK
1948: California Derby (May Reward)
San Felipe Stakes (May Reward)

TWO PUNCH
2001: Ballerina Handicap (Shine Again)
2002: Ballerina Handicap (Shine Again)

TWO'S A PLENTY
1998: Breeders' Cup Juvenile (Answer Lively)

TYRANT
1993: Pegasus Handicap (Diazo)
1994: Strub Stakes (Diazo)

UMIDWAR
1952: Pimlico Special (General Staff)
1954: Bougainvillea Turf Handicap (Parnassus)
1967: Donn Handicap (Francis U.)
1969: Hialeah Turf Cup (Blanquette II)

UNBELIEVABLE
1969: Del Mar Futurity (George Lewis)
1970: California Derby (George Lewis)

UNCONSCIOUS
1986: San Fernando Stakes (Right Con)

UNDER FIRE
1948: Alabama Stakes (Compliance)

UNDERSTANDING
1989: San Felipe Handicap (Sunday Silence)
Santa Anita Derby (Sunday Silence)
Kentucky Derby (Sunday Silence)
Preakness Stakes (Sunday Silence)
Super Derby (Sunday Silence)
Breeders' Cup Classic (Sunday Silence)
1990: Californian Stakes (Sunday Silence)

UPPER NILE
1989: Arkansas Derby (Dansil)

UPS
1995: Metropolitan Handicap (You and I)
Brooklyn Handicap (You and I)
Test Stakes (Chaposa Springs)

VACARME
2000: Beverly D. Stakes (Snow Polina)

VAGUELY NOBLE
1981: Dwyer Stakes (Noble Nashua)
Swaps Stakes (Noble Nashua)
Jerome Handicap (Noble Nashua)
Marlboro Cup Handicap (Noble Nashua)
San Fernando Stakes (Doonesbury)
1984: Yellow Ribbon Stakes (Sabin)
1985: Century Handicap (Dahar)
1986: San Luis Rey Stakes (Dahar)
San Juan Capistrano Handicap (Dahar)
Arkansas Derby (Rampage)
1987: Hollywood Invitational Handicap (Rivlia)
Sunset Handicap (Swink)
Rothmans International Stakes (River Memories)
1988: San Luis Rey Stakes (Rivlia)
Yellow Ribbon Stakes (Delighter)
1989: Flower Bowl Handicap (River Memories)
1990: San Juan Capistrano Handicap (Delegant)
1994: Flower Bowl Inv. Handicap (Dahlia's Dreamer)
Pegasus Handicap (Brass Scale)
1996: Moet Champagne Stakes (Ordway)

VAL DE LOIR
1982: Arkansas Derby (Hostage)
1985: Oak Tree Invitational Stakes (Yashgan)

VALDINA WAY
1966: Californian Stakes (Travel Orb)

VALID APPEAL
1997: Turf Classic (Val's Prince)
1998: Acorn Stakes (Jersey Girl)
Mother Goose Stakes (Jersey Girl)
Test Stakes (Jersey Girl)
1999: Garden City Breeders' Cup Handicap (Perfect Sting)
Queen Elizabeth II Challenge Cup (Perfect Sting)
Man o' War Stakes (Val's Prince)
Turf Classic (Val's Prince)
2000: Queen Elizabeth II Challenge Cup (Collect the Cash)
Vosburgh Stakes (Trippi)
Breeders' Cup Filly and Mare Turf (Perfect Sting)
2001: Santa Monica Handicap (Nany's Sweep)
Metropolitan Handicap (Exciting Story)

VANDALE
1970: Monmouth Invitational Handicap (Twice Worthy)
1971: Suburban Handicap (Twice Worthy)
Hawthorne Gold Cup (Twice Worthy)

VANLANDINGHAM
1998: Fountain of Youth Stakes (Lil's Lad)

VATELLOR
1958: Bowling Green Handicap (Rafty)

VENETIAN JESTER
1987: Jerome Handicap (Afleet)
Pennsylvania Derby (Afleet)

VENT DU NORD
1988: Vanity Handicap (Annoconnor)

VENTURE
1981: Santa Barbara Handicap (The Very One)

VERBATIM
1998: Turf Classic (Buck's Boy)
Breeders' Cup Turf (Buck's Boy)

VERTEX
1975: Illinois Derby (Colonel Power)
1984: Jim Beam Stakes (At the Threshold)
Arlington Classic (At the Threshold)
Ohio Derby (At the Threshold)
American Derby (At the Threshold)

VIC DAY
1972: San Luis Rey Handicap (Nor II)

VICEREGAL
1989: San Luis Rey Stakes (Frankly Perfect)
Hollywood Turf Cup (Frankly Perfect)
1990: Arlington Invitational Challenge Cup (Beau Genius)
Philip H. Iselin Handicap (Beau Genius)

VICE REGENT
1988: John Henry Handicap (Deputy Governor)
1991: Hollywood Gold Cup (Marquetry)
1992: Eddie Read Handicap (Marquetry)
Molson Export Million (Benburb)
1993: San Antonio Handicap (Marquetry)
Meadowlands Cup (Marquetry)
1996: Breeders' Cup Juvenile (Boston Harbor)
1998: Arkansas Derby (Victory Gallop)
Belmont Stakes (Victory Gallop)
1999: Lane's End Breeders' Futurity (Captain Steve)
Hollywood Futurity (Captain Steve)
Whitney Handicap (Victory Gallop)
2000: Swaps Stakes (Captain Steve)
2001: Donn Handicap (Captain Steve)

VICINITY
1970: Century Handicap (Quilche)
San Luis Rey Handicap (Quilche)

VICTORIAN
1948: Kentucky Oaks (Challe Anne)

VICTORIA PARK
1974: Arlington-Washington Futurity (Greek Answer)
1987: Blue Grass Stakes (War)
Californian Stakes (Judge Angelucci)
1988: San Antonio Handicap (Judge Angelucci)
1989: John Henry Handicap (Peace)

VICTORY MORN
1975: Fantasy Stakes (Hoso)

VIEUX MANOIR
1983: Turf Classic (All Along)
Washington D.C. International (All Along)
Rothmans International Stakes (All Along)

VIGOROUS
1968: San Felipe Handicap (Prince Pablo)

VIGORS
1996: Norfolk Stakes (Free House)
1997: San Felipe Stakes (Free House)
Santa Anita Derby (Free House)
Swaps Stakes (Free House)
1998: Swaps Stakes (Old Trieste)
Pacific Classic (Free House)
1999: San Antonio Handicap (Free House)
Santa Anita Handicap (Free House)
Californian Stakes (Old Trieste)

VITELIO
1980: Pennsylvania Derby (Lively King)

VITIGES
2000: Hollywood Turf Cup (Bienamado)
2001: San Juan Capistrano Handicap (Bienamado)
Charles Whittingham Handicap (Bienamado)

VITO
1952: Sapling Stakes (Laffango)
Champagne Stakes (Laffango)
Garden State Stakes (Laffango)
1953: Gotham Stakes (Laffango)

VOX POP

1978: Ohio Derby (Special Honor)

WAJIMA

1988: Hutcheson Stakes (Perfect Spy)

WALLET LIFTER

1979: San Felipe Handicap (Pole Position)
1990: Haskell Invitational Handicap (Restless Con)

WAR ADMIRAL

1947: Saratoga Special (Better Self)
1948: Discovery Handicap (Better Self)
Westchester Handicap (Better Self)
1949: Discovery Handicap (Prophets Thumb)
Carter Handicap (Better Self)
1950: Gallant Fox Handicap (Better Self)
1951: Matron Stakes (Rose Jet)
Selima Stakes (Rose Jet)
Demoiselle Stakes (Rose Jet)
1952: Gulfstream Park Handicap (Crafty Admiral)
Brooklyn Handicap (Crafty Admiral)
Washington Park Handicap (Crafty Admiral)
1953: McLennan Handicap (Crafty Admiral)
Gulfstream Park Handicap (Crafty Admiral)
New York Handicap (Crafty Admiral)
1954: Withers Stakes (Jet Action)
Roamer Handicap (Jet Action)
Acorn Stakes (Riverina)
Molly Pitcher Handicap (Shady Tune)
1955: Washington Park Handicap (Jet Action)
1956: Everglades Stakes (Liberty Sun)
1957: Kentucky Derby (Iron Liege)
Dwyer Handicap (Bureaucracy)
1958: Frizette Stakes (Merry Hill)
McLennan Handicap (Iron Liege)
Display Handicap (Civet)
1959: Preakness Stakes (Royal Orbit)
Trenton Handicap (Greek Star)
1960: Wood Memorial Stakes (Francis S.)
Dwyer Handicap (Francis S.)
1961: Withers Stakes (Hitting Away)
Dwyer Handicap (Hitting Away)
McLennan Handicap (Yorky)
Widener Handicap (Yorky)
Sorority Stakes (Batter Up)
New Orleans Handicap (Greek Star)
1962: Sorority Stakes (Affectionately)
Spinaway Stakes (Affectionately)
Del Mar Futurity (Slipped Disc)
Widener Handicap (Yorky)
1963: Futurity Stakes (Bupers)
Hialeah Turf Cup (Intercepted)
1964: Gulfstream Park Handicap (Gun Bow)
Brooklyn Handicap (Gun Bow)
Washington Park Handicap (Gun Bow)
Woodward Stakes (Gun Bow)
San Fernando Stakes (Gun Bow)
Charles H. Strub Stakes (Gun Bow)
San Antonio Handicap (Gun Bow)
Whitney Stakes (Gun Bow)
Arlington-Washington Lassie Stakes (Admiring)
1965: Sapling Stakes (Buckpasser)
Hopeful Stakes (Buckpasser)
Arlington-Washington Futurity (Buckpasser)
Champagne Stakes (Buckpasser)
Donn Handicap (Gun Bow)
Metropolitan Handicap (Gun Bow)
San Antonio Handicap (Gun Bow)
Futurity Stakes (Priceless Gem)
Frizette Stakes (Priceless Gem)
Top Flight Handicap (Affectionately)
1966: Everglades Stakes (Buckpasser)
Flamingo Stakes (Buckpasser)
Arlington Classic (Buckpasser)
American Derby (Buckpasser)
Travers Stakes (Buckpasser)
Lawrence Realization Stakes (Buckpasser)
Brooklyn Handicap (Buckpasser)
Woodward Stakes (Buckpasser)
Jockey Club Gold Cup (Buckpasser)
Saratoga Special (Favorable Turn)
1967: Metropolitan Handicap (Buckpasser)
Suburban Handicap (Buckpasser)
San Fernando Stakes (Buckpasser)
San Felipe Handicap (Rising Market)
1968: Donn Handicap (Favorable Turn)
San Antonio Handicap (Rising Market)
1969: Malibu Stakes (First Mate)
1970: Cowdin Stakes (Hoist the Flag)
Washington Park Handicap (Doc's T.V.)
1974: Michigan Mile and One-Eighth (Tom Tulle)

WAR CLOUD

1946: Delaware Oaks (Bonnie Beryl)
Comely Handicap (Bonnie Beryl)

WAR DOG

1968: Santa Susana Stakes (Allie's Serenade)

WAR EAGLE

1963: Cinema Handicap (Quita Dude)
1965: Grey Lag Handicap (Quita Dude)

WARFARE

1976: Bowling Green Handicap (Erwin Boy)
1981: Santa Margarita Handicap (Princess Karenda)
1983: Flamingo Stakes (Current Hope)

WAR GLORY

1959: Cowdin Stakes (Warfare)
Champagne Stakes (Warfare)
Garden State Stakes (Warfare)
1962: Kentucky Derby (Decidedly)
1963: Monmouth Handicap (Decidedly)

WAR JEEP

1957: Washington Park Futurity (Jewel's Reward)
Cowdin Stakes (Jewel's Reward)
Champagne Stakes (Jewel's Reward)
Pimlico Futurity (Jewel's Reward)
1958: Wood Memorial Stakes (Jewel's Reward)
1968: Century Handicap (Model Fool)
1969: Kentucky Jockey Club Stakes (Evasive Action)

WAR RELIC

1955: Del Mar Debutante Stakes (Miss Todd)
1959: Gardenia Stakes (My Dear Girl)
Frizette Stakes (My Dear Girl)
1962: Arlington Matron Handicap (Kootenai)
1965: Gotham Stakes (Flag Raiser)
Wood Memorial Stakes (Flag Raiser)
Withers Stakes (Flag Raiser)
Jersey Derby (Hail to All)
Belmont Stakes (Hail to All)
Travers Stakes (Hail to All)
1967: Jerome Handicap (High Tribute)
1968: Santa Barbara Handicap (Amerigo's Fancy)

WARRIOR

1965: Bowling Green Handicap (Or et Argent)
Dixie Handicap (Or et Argent)

WATLING STREET

1965: Monmouth Oaks (Summer Scandal)
1966: Top Flight Handicap (Summer Scandal)
Beldame Stakes (Summer Scandal)

WAVERING MONARCH

1993: Jim Beam Stakes (Prairie Bayou)
Blue Grass Stakes (Prairie Bayou)
Preakness Stakes (Prairie Bayou)
1995: Ohio Derby (Petionville)
1996: Kentucky Oaks (Pike Place Dancer)
1998: Oak Tree Turf Championship (Military)
2003: Matron Stakes (Marylebone)

WELSH PAGEANT

1991: Breeders' Cup Sprint (Sheikh Albadou)
1994: Sword Dancer Invitational Handicap (Alex the Great)
1999: Milady Breeders' Cup Handicap (Gourmet Girl)
2001: Vanity Handicap (Gourmet Girl)
Apple Blossom Handicap (Gourmet Girl)

WELSH SAINT

1988: Hialeah Turf Cup (Double Bed)
1996: Breeders' Cup Mile (Da Hoss)
1998: Breeders' Cup Mile (Da Hoss)

WEST COAST SCOUT

1991: La Canada Stakes (Fit to Scout)

WHAT A PLEASURE

1984: La Canada Stakes (Sweet Diane)
Jerome Handicap (Is Your Pleasure)
1985: Breeders' Futurity (Tasso)
Breeders' Cup Juvenile (Tasso)
Top Flight Handicap (Flip's Pleasure)
1988: Top Flight Handicap (Clabber Girl)
Withers Stakes (Once Wild)
1992: Arlington-Washington Futurity (Gilded Time)
Breeders' Cup Juvenile (Gilded Time)

WHAT LUCK

1994: Meadowlands Cup (Conveyor)

WHEATLY HALL

1999: Futurity Stakes (Bevo)

WHICHONE

1946: Blue Grass Stakes (Lord Boswell)
1947: Champagne Stakes (Vulcan's Forge)
1948: Withers Stakes (Vulcan's Forge)
1949: Santa Anita Handicap (Vulcan's Forge)
Suburban Handicap (Vulcan's Forge)
Dixie Handicap (Chains)

WHIRLAWAY

1955: Breeders' Futurity (Jovial Jove)
Gotham Stakes (Go Lightly)
1957: Alabama Stakes (Here and There)
1961: American Derby (Beau Prince)
Travers Stakes (Beau Prince)
1962: Remsen Stakes (Rocky Link)
Michigan Mile and One-Sixteenth (Beau Prince)
1966: Mother Goose Stakes (Lady Pitt)
Coaching Club American Oaks (Lady Pitt)

WHISKAWAY

1950: Kentucky Oaks (Ari's Mona)
Westchester Handicap (Palestinian)
1951: Brooklyn Handicap (Palestinian)
Golden Gate Handicap (Palestinian)
1953: Delaware Oaks (Cerise Reine)
1954: Santa Margarita Handicap (Cerise Reine)

WHISK BROOM II

1946: Garden State Stakes (Double Jay)
Kentucky Jockey Club Stakes (Double Jay)
1948: Trenton Handicap (Double Jay)
1949: American Handicap (Double Jay)

WHITE GLOVES II

1980: Arlington Classic (Spruce Needles)
Secretariat Stakes (Spruce Needles)
1981: Arlington Handicap (Spruce Needles)

WHITESBURG

1984: Haskell Invitational Handicap (Big Pistol)
1991: Arkansas Derby (Olympio)
American Derby (Olympio)
Hollywood Derby (Olympio)

WILD AGAIN

2003: Ruffian Handicap (Wild Spirit)

WILDAIR

1947: Washington Park Futurity (Bewitch)
Arlington Lassie Stakes (Bewitch)
Princess Pat Stakes (Bewitch)
1949: Vineland Handicap (Bewitch)
1950: Black Helen Handicap (Bewitch)
1951: Vanity Handicap (Bewitch)

WILD RISK

1969: Sunset Handicap (Petrone)
San Juan Capistrano Handicap (Petrone)

WINDFIELDS

1959: Remsen Stakes (Victoria Park)
1976: Arlington Handicap (Victorian Prince)

WINDSOR LAD

1953: Manhattan Handicap (Jampol)

WINDY CITY II

1970: Blue Grass Stakes (Dust Commander)
Kentucky Derby (Dust Commander)
1976: Santa Margarita Handicap (Fascinating Girl)

WINDY SANDS

1977: Sunset Handicap (Today'n Tomorrow)
1979: Louisiana Derby (Golden Act)
Arkansas Derby (Golden Act)
Secretariat Stakes (Golden Act)
Canadian International Championship (Golden Act)
1982: Hollywood Derby (Racing Is Fun)
1989: Yellow Ribbon Stakes (Brown Bess)
1990: Santa Barbara Handicap (Brown Bess)

WING OUT

1993: Arlington-Washington Futurity (Polar Expedition)
1994: Jim Beam Stakes (Polar Expedition)

WINNING HIT

1990: Breeders' Cup Sprint (Safely Kept)

WISE COUNSELLOR

1949: Del Mar Derby (Bolero)
1950: Garden State Stakes (Iswas)
1951: San Carlos Handicap (Bolero)
1952: Cowdin Stakes (Invigorator)
Roamer Handicap (Quiet Step)
1954: Brooklyn Handicap (Invigorator)
1958: Sapling Stakes (Watch Your Step)

WOLF POWER

2002: Santa Anita Handicap (Milwaukee Brew)
2003: Santa Anita Handicap (Milwaukee Brew)

WOODMAN

2000: King's Bishop Stakes (More Than Ready)
2002: San Carlos Handicap (Snow Ridge)

WORDEN II

1966: Washington D.C. International (Behistoun)
1969: Canadian International Championship (Vent du Nord)
1970: Hialeah Turf Cup (Vent du Nord)

YATASTO

1975: Hempstead Handicap (Raisela)

YOUNG GENERATION

1988: Laurel Futurity (Luge II)

YOUR ALIBHAI

1981: Super Derby (Island Whirl)
1982: Woodward Stakes (Island Whirl)
Louisiana Downs Handicap (Pair of Deuces)
1983: Hollywood Gold Cup (Island Whirl)
Whitney Handicap (Island Whirl)
1993: Haskell Invitational Handicap (Kissin Kris)

YOUR HOST

1964: Del Mar Futurity (Terry's Secret)
1965: Hollywood Derby (Terry's Secret)
Sunset Handicap (Terry's Secret)
1966: Del Mar Futurity (Ruken)
1967: Santa Anita Derby (Ruken)
1970: Ohio Derby (Climber)
Manhattan Handicap (Shelter Bay)

YOUTH

2002: Santa Maria Handicap (Favorite Funtime)

YRRAH JR.

1984: San Juan Capistrano Handicap (Load the Cannons)

ZACAWEISTA

1948: Marguerite Stakes (Alsab's Day)
1952: Arlington Futurity (Mr. Good)
Del Mar Futurity (Hour Regards)
1956: Louisiana Derby (Reaping Right)

ZEDDAAN

1992: Arlington Million (Dear Doctor)

ZENITH

1982: Pan American Handicap (Robsphere)

ZEV

1949: San Pasqual Handicap (Shim Malone)

Photo courtesy of Bob Coglianese Photo's, Inc.

No thoroughbred has come as close to winning the Triple Crown, yet failed, than Real Quiet (on rail), who won the Kentucky Derby and Preakness Stakes in 1998, but finished a nose behind Victory Gallop (No. 11 on the outside under Gary Stevens) in the Belmont Stakes. Both colts boosted the incredible record of the Raise a Native sire line in the classics, which has accounted for 36 North American classic victories, including 12 of the last 13 through 2003.

Sire Line INDEX

IX: Sire Line Index

A 'Rullah' for Generations

Astute observers of thoroughbred racing no doubt noticed the absence of such heralded stallions as Northern Dancer and Raise a Native in the chapter that discussed the elite sires of the modern era. True students of bloodlines—or those who have longer memories—also may have been puzzled as to why the equally significant Hyperion wasn't included.

Northern Dancer, Raise a Native, and Hyperion weren't included because those ratings were based solely on a stallion's record in siring winners of major North American races since World War II.

Although Northern Dancer, a North American-based sire whose best offspring raced in Europe, and Raise a Native excelled in that arena, they were not among the truly elite in producing major North American winners. Yet when the bloodstock market enjoyed its biggest boom in yearling prices in the early '80s, male-line descendants of Northern Dancer and Raise a Native were the highest-priced commodities, and that's still the case two decades later.

"The whole Northern Dancer line is the best in the world. That's the one we go for," Robert Sangster, one of the leading exporters of Northern Dancer's offspring to Europe, said in the early '80s.

"The Northern Dancers really started coming on four or five years ago. Why people are buying and have been buying is they realize his sons have really taken off and started winning everything in sight," Lane's End Farm owner Will Farish, now the Ambassador to the Court of St. James, said in 1982.

"If you can get a (son of) Raise a Native that's game and sound, I can't think of a better stud prospect," added owner and breeder Brereton C. Jones, who later became Governor of Kentucky.

Sons and daughters of Northern Dancer earned 18 major North American victories, but that doesn't begin to measure the true value of his impact as a stallion. A better yardstick is that Northern Dancer has sired 36 sons who have produced major winners, more than any modern stallion. Raise a Native's offspring captured 24 major races, and he is the only modern stallion to reach 20 victories who sired more than one stallion who exceeded his total. For good measure, Raise a Native sired three: Mr. Prospector (73), Alydar (49), and Exclusive Native (36).

The Sire Line Index clearly illustrates that Northern Dancer, Raise a Native, and Hyperion—not to mention Turn-to, Ribot, and others—rank among history's most influential sires.

The Sire Line Index measures a stallion's ability to sire major winners—and to produce stallions who also sire major winners and continue the legacy for generations. Eight points are awarded to the sire of the winner of a major North American race, with four points awarded to the paternal grandsire, two to the paternal great-grandsire, and one to the paternal great-great grandsire. The formula rates the contribution of each generation as being twice as significant as that of the previous generation, which, not coincidentally, corresponds with the fact that, like any other species, thoroughbreds have two parents, four grandparents, eight great-grandparents, and 16 great-great grandparents. And, although every thoroughbred has two grandsires, four great-grandsires, and eight great-great grandsires, only the paternal—or male-line—sire, grandsire, great-grandsire, and great-great grandsire are factors in the Sire Line Index.

For example, Point Given, the 2001 Horse of the Year, is a son of Thunder Gulch out of the Turkoman mare Turko's Turn. Turkoman, Point Given's broodmare sire, gets no credit in the Sire Line Index. Those who are awarded points in the Sire Line Index for each of Point Given's major victories—or *any* major triumphs by sons or daughters of Thunder Gulch—are Thunder Gulch (eight points); Thunder Gulch's sire, Gulch (four points); Gulch's sire, Mr. Prospector (two points), and Mr. Prospector's sire, Raise a Native (one point).

Some breeders contend that the influence of particular sires and dams can be seen in foals as many as six, seven, or eight generations later. That may be true, but the eighth generation would include 128 sets of great-great-great-great-great-great-grandparents, and even professional geneticists probably would render such influence negligible.

All thoroughbreds can be traced to three stallions—Byerly Turk, Darley Arabian, and Godolphin Barb—and virtually all of today's North American-based thoroughbreds trace in male lineage to Eclipse, who was born in 1764. So extending the Sire

Line Index further back than the first four generations of a race horse's pedigree would be a little like saying that all humans are descendants of Adam—or at least can trace their ancestry to Noah. While that information may be accurate, it's also worthless. It is considerably more significant, for example, to say that when George W. Bush was inaugurated as President of the United States in 2001, he became only the second President whose father also occupied the White House than the 42nd direct descendent of Noah to assume the presidency since the Ark landed on high ground.

A quick glance at the lists of sire lines that accompany this chapter may prompt the conclusion that more modern-era major winners descended from Cyllene—through his son Polymelus's son Phalaris—than any other stallion. While that conclusion is correct, it hardly tells the entire story.

Cyllene was sired by Bona Vista, who was by Bend Or, who was by Doncaster, who was by Stockwell, who was by The Baron, who was by Irish Birdcatcher, who was by Sir Hercules, who was by Whalebone, who was by Waxy, who was by Pot-8-O's, who was by Eclipse. Point Given is a direct descendant of Eclipse—if you put 20 greats and the word grandsire in front of Eclipse's name. But crediting Eclipse—or any of the other 4,194,303 ancestors who trace back exactly 22 generations—for Point Given's accomplishments would be foolish. It also would do little to explain the success of his sire line, because at least 99 percent of the horses Point Given beat also were probably direct descendants of Eclipse.

It isn't unusual to read about the Native Dancer sire line, the Raise a Native sire line, or the Mr. Prospector sire line, which seems somewhat mystifying because Native Dancer sired Raise a Native, who sired Mr. Prospector. So they all actually are the same *line* or branches of the same line. Instead of worrying about whether Mr. Prospector or Raise a Native actually has begun a new sire line, the Sire Line Index properly gives credit where it's due.

If the offspring of Gulch, for example, win 10 major races in 2004, he'll receive 80 points, while his sire, Mr. Prospector, will receive 40. Since Mr. Prospector's reputation as a stallion is significantly greater than Gulch's, it's an odds-on bet that from the moment Gulch's offspring cross the wire, horsemen, horseplayers, and the media will give significantly more credit to Mr. Prospector for being the paternal grandsire of the winners of those 10 races than to Gulch. Conversely, if 10 different sons of Mr. Prospector each sire one major winner in 2004, they'll receive eight points apiece, yet Mr. Prospector still will receive 40. And he will deserve the attention he'll receive from horsemen, horseplayers, and the media because he's the closest common denominator in all of those victories.

Photo courtesy of Galerie Graphics

Back-to-back No. 1 seasons in 2002 and 2003 marked the seventh and eighth times in 16 years that Mr. Prospector, who stood at Claiborne Farm before his death in 1999, ranked No. 1 in the Sire Line Index.

Seattle Slew offers an even better example of how the Sire Line Index gives proper credit where it's due. As the 1977 Triple Crown winner and one of the greatest stallions of the modern era, Seattle Slew appropriately has been lauded as the sire after each of the 58 major victories by his offspring. But it has been about as rare to hear those same winners heralded as grandchildren of Bold Reasoning or great-grandchildren of Boldnesian as it has been to hear Luciano Pavarotti warble, "Tiptoe Through the Tulips." Yet those same winners have been heralded as great-great grandsons or great-great granddaughters of Bold Ruler—a considerably more famous sire than Boldnesian or Bold Reasoning—nearly as often as they've been lauded as Seattle Slew's offspring. The Sire Line Index properly rewards not only the contributions of Seattle Slew to his offspring, but those of Bold Reasoning, Boldnesian, and Bold Ruler—and in that order.

Presenting the top 25 stallions in the modern Sire Line Index in order of rank:

The Line at the Top

No action has had a more significant impact on North American racing and breeding than the decision of a syndicate headed by Arthur B. "Bull" Hancock Jr. to pay the then-astonishing sum of $372,000 for the Irish-bred Nasrullah, who subsequently was imported to Hancock's Claiborne Farm in Paris, Ky., in 1950.

Nasrullah not only sired the winners of 84 major North American races, but he established a Sire Line that is unequaled in the modern era. Twenty-four sons, 64 paternal grandsons, and 71 paternal great-grandsons of Nasrullah also have sired major winners, and Nasrullah's Sire Line Index of 2,410 points makes him unquestionably the most influential sire of the modern era.

Nasrullah led the Sire Line Index on eight occasions: 1955, '56, '60, '62, '65, '68, '69, and '82, but that doesn't begin to measure his impact. In 1954, Nasrullah began streaks of 22 straight top-four, 25 consecutive top-five, 32 straight 30-point,

Photo courtesy of Bob Coglianese Photo's, Inc.

Ruffian was undefeated and fresh off a sweep of New York's Triple Tiara for three-year-old fillies, which then consisted of the Acorn Stakes, Mother Goose Stakes, and Coaching Club American Oaks, until the great filly lost her life in a match race with Kentucky Derby winner Foolish Pleasure in July of 1975. During her brief life, the ill-fated Ruffian further enhanced the considerable legacy of her male-line ancestors. The daughter of Reviewer's paternal grandsire is Bold Ruler, and her paternal great-grandsire is Nasrullah.

and 29 consecutive 40-point seasons. No other stallion has had more than fourteen 40-point seasons in a row, and during each of those 29 seasons, Nasrullah's Sire Line Index ranked among the top six. No other stallion has finished in the top 10 more than 22 years in a row.

Nasrullah holds the records for top-two (16), top-three (20), top-four (26), top-five (28), and top-10 (31) seasons, and in each of those 31 campaigns, he actually finished among the top six. In no decade was Nasrullah's influence stronger than the '60s, when he posted a record eight consecutive 60-point campaigns (1962-69). He is the only stallion who has reached 100 points five times, and he also holds the records for 70- (10), 60- (18), and 50-point (23) seasons. Nasrullah was the leading classic sire on three occasions, and his Sire Line Index ranks third in modern-era classic races.

Another Nifty Nine

Nearco, a son of Pharos, sired three of the top 15 stallions in the Sire Line Index—Nasrullah, Nearctic, and Royal Charger. He is tied with Nasrullah both for most consecutive seasons with double-figure point totals, an astonishing 45 in a row from 1953-97, and an equally impressive 36 straight 20-point campaigns (1954-89). Nearco, who led the Sire Line Index in both 1970 and '71, also is tied for fifth in classic influence and ranks 12th in Breeders' Cup influence.

Bold Ruler, the most accomplished son of Nasrullah at stud, is equally as famous as a sire of outstanding race horses—86 major victories—and as a sire of sires. He is one of only two stallions to produce 30 or more sons who sired major winners in the modern era. Bold Ruler had the No. 1 Sire Line Index six times and ranks as the fourth-leading classic influence. Bold Ruler's five 90-point seasons equal those of his sire as the most in the modern era, and his streak of three consecutive 100-point seasons (1966-68) is unequaled in the modern era.

Although **Northern Dancer's** Sire Line Index of 1,613 trails that of Nasrullah by nearly 800 points, only one stallion has as promising an opportunity to overtake Nasrullah as the Canadian-bred son of Nearctic. Northern Dancer posted his first No. 1 season in 1983, then added 10 more in 14 years from 1985-98, including a record seven consecutive top-two seasons from 1992-98. Northern Dancer's Sire Line Index has been the most influential in the Breeders' Cup and ranks ninth among classic sire lines. Northern Dancer ranks second to Nasrullah in numerous categories, including top-two (15), top-three (18), top-four (19), top-five (22), and top-six (23) seasons, and through 2003 he had finished in the top six 22 consecutive years, a streak bettered only by Nasrullah.

No sire has had more influence on modern-era classics than **Raise a Native.** Majestic Prince, who won both the Kentucky Derby and Preakness Stakes in 1969, was the only classic winner sired by Raise a Native. Since then, however, 25 additional thoroughbreds who trace in male line to Raise a Native have won a total of 34 more classics. Raise a Native led the Sire Line Index three consecutive seasons beginning in 1977 and again in 1988, and his sire line is as strong as ever. Through 2003, Raise a Native had finished in the top 10 for 22 consecutive years, equaling the second-longest such streak in history, and 20 of the last 27, 15 of the last 18, and 12 of the last 13 classics had been captured by male-line descendants of Raise a Native.

Considering that he was born nine years after Northern Dancer, the sire whose line probably has the best opportunity to overtake Nasrullah is that of **Mr. Prospector,** who recorded eight No. 1 seasons from 1988-2003. In 2002 and '03, Mr. Prospector's Sire Line Index ranked above 110 in both seasons, a feat previously accomplished only by Bold Ruler, and through 2003 had finished among the top three an unprecedented 14 consecutive times. Mr. Prospector also recorded his 10th consecutive 50-point campaign and eighth 80-point season in 2003, both records. Eighteen of the 26 classic winners who trace in male line to Raise a Native, Mr. Prospector's sire, are through Mr. Prospector, ranking his classic Sire Line Index second in the modern era. Mr. Prospector also ranks second on the Breeders' Cup Sire Line Index and already has sired 29 sons who have sired major winners.

Only two stallions have posted longer streaks of double-figure seasons than the 32 in a row **Hyperion** had from 1946-77, and he ranks among the top five in both 50-point (13) and 60-point seasons (11). But the influence of Hyperion, who led the Sire Line Index in 1961 and '64, has waned considerably and may be on the verge of dying. Only three male-line descendants of Hyperion have sired major winners since 1990. Two of those are sons of and the other a grandson of Noholme II, a great-grandson of Hyperion.

Princequillo is the only stallion other than Nasrullah to record four consecutive seasons with a Sire Line Index of 70 points or more (1956-59), and he held the No. 1 ranking in each of the last three of those seasons. But Princequillo's line is another in danger of extinction: His great-great grandson, Meadowlake, accounted for two major victories as a sire in 1999, the only triumphs for Princequillo-line stallions since 1992.

Only four stallions rank ahead of **Native Dancer,** the sire of Raise a Native, in classic influence, and he has the highest Sire Line Index among stallions who never enjoyed a No. 1 campaign.

In addition to being the sire of Northern Dancer, the Canadian-bred **Nearctic** sired Explodent (11 major victories) and Icecapade, who sired Wild Again (15 major victories), and only Northern Dancer and Mr. Prospector have higher Sire Line Indexes in the Breeders' Cup.

Four Footed Fotos, Inc., courtesy of Churchill Downs

War Chant (11 with Gary Stevens in the irons) held off North East Bound (10) to win the 2000 Breeders' Cup Mile at Churchill Downs by a neck. War Chant's sire, Danzig, has the fourth-highest Sire Line Index in the Breeders' Cup, a list headed by Danzig's sire, Northern Dancer.

Rounding Out the Top 25

Turn-to, who was bred in Ireland but raced in America, not only earned 21 victories as a sire, but he sired three sons, six grandsons, and three great-grandsons with double-figure victory totals. . . . No other Sire Line Index ranks as high with so little help beyond the stallion's contribution as a sire than that of **Bull Lea,** who sired a record 100 major winners and led the Sire Line Index three consecutive years from 1947-49. Bull Lea produced 11 sons who sired major winners. But the major winners sired by those sons produced only 25 victories, and just three grandsons of Bull Lea sired major winners—and none of them more than one. No great-grandson extended Bull Lea's sire line, which has not produced a major victory since 1973. . . . **Hail to Reason,** whose 44 victories as a sire make him the most successful stallion sired by Turn-to, also produced four sons and two grandsons who have reached double figures in major victories. . . . **Alibhai,** a son of Hyperion, was more successful as a sire (57 victories) than as a sire of sires, although he produced a son, Your Host, who had 30 victories as a sire, and a paternal grandson, Windy Sands, who earned 16. No male line descendant of Alibhai—even including those who trace back further than four generations—has won a major race since 1984. . . .

Royal Charger, sire of Turn-to, sired the winners of 35 major races. . . . Like Alibhai, **Heliopolis,** who led the Sire Line Index in 1950 and again in '54, was another son of Hyperion who was more successful as a sire of race horses than of stallions. Heliopolis's most successful son at stud was Olympia, with 25 major victories, but no male-line descendant of Heliopolis has won a major North American race since 1987. . . . **Seattle Slew,** the most influential sire in 1984 and 2001, has been a great sire of race horses—58 victories. As the sire of 15 stallions who have produced major winners, most of them still active, the legacy of the son of Bold Reasoning figures to continue to grow. . . . **Ribot,** generally considered Europe's greatest race horse of the 20th Century, was unbeaten in 16 races, including back-to-back victories in Europe's most prestigious race, the Prix de l'Arc de Triomphe, in 1955 and '56. Ribot, a son of Tenerani, produced four sons and three paternal grandsons who reached double figures in victories as sires. . . . French-bred **Bull Dog,** a son of Teddy whose greatest contribution was as the sire of Bull Lea, hasn't had a male-line descendant win a major North American race since 1976. . . . Although the most notable contribution of **Prince Rose** was as the sire of Princequillo, his great-great-great-great grandson Siphon has continued his legacy by siring Siphonic, the winner two races major races as a two-year-old in 2001, and Siphonizer, who earned a major victory as a juvenile in 2003. . . . **Gainsborough,** a son of Bayardo and the sire of Hyperion, has the highest Sire Line Index for any stallion who neither sired any winners nor sired any sons who sired winners during the modern era. Despite the considerable success of Gainsborough's grandsons and great-grandsons at stud, no major winner has traced in male line to Gainsborough since 1991. . . . As the sire of Nearco, who subsequently produced Nasrullah, Nearctic, and Royal Charger, winners who trace in male line to **Pharos** have continued to be plentiful. . . . **Tom Fool,** a son of Menow who posted 39 victories as a sire, has continued his influence primarily through his son Buckpasser. . . . The most notable contribution of **Blenheim II** was through his son, Mahmoud, sire of 47 major winners. No male-line descendant of Blenheim II, a son of Blandford, has captured a major race since 1991. . . . The 2003 campaign marked the 45th year in a row that a major winner traced in male line to **Polynesian.** The son of Unbreakable led the Sire Line Index in 1953, when his most notable son, Native Dancer, captured the Preakness and Belmont Stakes.

Preakness May Be Best Guideline

It's impossible to predict which race horses will become sires whose influence will last for decades. If a guideline does exist, however, it may be their ability to win a nine-and-a-half-furlong classic on the third Saturday in May. Thirteen winners of the Preakness Stakes rank among the top 100 in the Sire Line Index, two more than the Belmont Stakes has produced.

In addition to Triple Crown winners War Admiral, Count Fleet, Secretariat, and Seattle Slew, four others among the top 100 won both the Preakness and the Belmont—Man o' War, Native Dancer, Nashua, and Damascus. Northern Dancer and Pleasant Colony won both the Kentucky Derby and the Preakness, and Preakness winners Polynesian, Bold Ruler, and Tom Rolfe also rank among the top 100, as do Belmont victors Blue Larkspur, Gallant Man, and Sword Dancer. Reigh Count and Unbridled are the only members of the top 100 who won the Kentucky Derby without adding an additional classic victory.

A strong indication of the influence of great European race horses on the American turf in the modern era is that six Epsom Derby winners—Gainsborough, Hyperion, Blenheim II, Mahmoud, Nijinsky II, and Roberto—rank among the top 100. An indication that influence may be waning is that no Epsom Derby winner since Roberto, the 1972 victor, ranks among the top 246.

Sons of Top Sires Rarely Match Their Father's Feats

Certain stallions, notably Secretariat, have been criticized unfairly for their failure to reproduce themselves. Although Secretariat sired the likes of Lady's Secret, one of only two fillies to earn Horse of the Year acclaim since 1983, and dual classic winner Risen Star, he indeed failed to sire a Triple Crown winner. Of course, no other sire has managed that feat since Exclusive Native's 1974 mating to Won't Tell You produced Affirmed.

And, although there is precedent for outstanding sires of race horses to become outstanding sires of sires, it's rather unlikely that they'll produce stallions who will exceed their major victory totals. In fact, only the following 21 stallions whose offspring earned as many as 10 major victories in the modern era produced stallions who exceeded their totals.

Sire	Major Wins	Son(s) Who Exceeded Their Total
Nasrullah	84	Bold Ruler (86)
His Majesty	24	Pleasant Colony (26)
Raise a Native	24	Mr. Prospector (73), Alydar (49), Exclusive Native (36)
Fappiano	21	Unbridled (24)
Turn-to	21	Hail to Reason (44)
Blushing Groom	20	Rahy (22)
Blenheim II	18	Mahmoud (47)
Menow	18	Tom Fool (39)
Northern Dancer	18	Danzig (47), Nijinsky II (28), Lyphard (20)
Ribot	15	Graustark (28), Tom Rolfe (26), His Majesty (24)
Sword Dancer	15	Damascus (33)

Sire	Major Wins	Son(s) Who Exceeded Their Total
Fleet Nasrullah	13	Gummo (21)
Intentionally	13	In Reality (22)
Majestic Prince	12	Majestic Light (21)
Pharamond II	12	Menow (18)
Pilate	12	Eight Thirty (26)
Roberto	12	Kris S. (22)
Speak John	12	Verbatim (14)
Challenger II	11	Challedon (13)
Native Dancer	11	Raise a Native (24), Native Charger (16)
Questionnaire	11	Requested (15)

Best Bets for the Future

The Sire Line Indexes of many modern-era stallions remain a work in progress and will continue to be for decades.

"A sire sometimes doesn't take off immediately, even with a Bold Ruler," said Lane's End's Farish. "Sometimes it takes 12 or 15 years to see what a sire's sons do to find out if he's really a great sire."

Whose legacies will continue to grow? Among the logical candidates are the 19 stallions who have produced 10 or more sons who sired major winners in the modern era: Northern Dancer (36), Bold Ruler (30), Mr. Prospector (29), Nasrullah (24), Nijinsky II (18), Danzig (16), Seattle Slew (15), Hyperion (14), Damascus (13), Alibhai (12), Raise a Native (12), Bull Dog (11), Bull Lea (11), Khaled (11), Blushing Groom (10), Buckpasser (10), Native Dancer (10), Princequillo (10), and Royal Charger (10).

Danzig was the only active sire among that group when the 2004 breeding season began, while Seattle Slew remained an active stallion until his death in 2002 at age 28. Northern Dancer and Raise a Native were both born in 1961, and Buckpasser, Damascus, Nijinsky II, Mr. Prospector, and Blushing Groom were foaled from 1963-74, so it's likely their influence could continue for decades.

Indeed, 1918 English Triple Crown winner Gainsborough appeared in the male line of the first four generations of a major North American winner's pedigree as recently as 1985—70 years after his birth.

Those whose statures—and rankings on the Sire Line Index—are unlikely to continue to grow not only include Gainsborough and others of that era, but those whose rank on the list is far more attributable to their ability to sire outstanding race horses than sires.

If the points earned for victories as a sire are subtracted from the Sire Line Index totals, Nearco, Nasrullah's sire, replaces him at the top of the list with 1,854 points, 116 more than Nasrullah would have.

Bull Lea would tumble from 12th to a tie for 98th and Heliopolis from 16th to 43rd. Twenty-three others in the top 100 would fall more than 33 spots and out of the top 100, including dramatic free falls by Alydar (from a 35th-place tie to a tie for 168th) and the still-active Deputy Minister (from 42nd to a tie for 108th) and Storm Cat (from 46th to a deadlock for 135th). Six of those would drop more than 100 places and out of the top 200, including Forli from 84th to a tie for 202nd, Grey Dawn II and Private Account from a tie for 94th to a tie for 209th, Secretariat from 96th to a tie for 220th, and Unbridled—the youngest member of the top 100, who died at age 14 in 2001—from a tie for 99th to 245th.

No stallion would tumble further, however, than War Admiral, from 98th to a tie for 333rd. War Admiral was a very successful sire of major winners, producing 26 triumphs in the modern era, and the 81 victories produced by offspring of his daughters make him the second-ranked broodmare sire. But his sons sired only three major winners, two by The Battler and one by Mr. Busher. And no other male-line descendant of the 1937 Triple Crown winner continued his legacy beyond The Battler and Mr. Busher.

Perhaps worse are the cases of Shut Out and Discovery, who sired the winners of 21 and 20 major races, respectively. No male-line descendant by either stallion ever sired a major winner, a distinction also held by active stallion Rahy, who has 22 victories but has yet to produce a son with one.

Those who significantly move up the list if victories by a stallion's sons and daughters are subtracted from his Sire Line Index are primarily those stallions whose best runners predate the modern era and those who have been significantly more successful as sires of sires than of runners. Those in the top 100 who predate the modern era who would advance as many as 35 spots include Man o' War (to 37th), Ajax (to 42nd), Sir Gallahad III (to a tie for 44th), and Tourbillon (to 47th). Those in the latter category who would advance as many as 25 spots include Boldnesian (to 41st), Vandale (to 49th), Red God (to 44th), and Vice Regent (to 56th). Twenty-two others would rise more than 40 places and into the top 100, including eight who would improve their positions more than 85 places: Aristophanes (to 86th), Sting (to 91st), Polymelus (to 92nd), Fairway and The Porter (to a tie for 94th), Plassy (to 96th), Sun Teddy (to 98th), and Fortino (to a tie for 100th).

An illustration of just how rare it has been for stallions to continue their legacies through multiple sons who have outstanding careers at stud is that only the following 24 stallions have sired more than one son whose offspring reached double-figure victory totals in the modern era:

Sire	Sons With 10-Plus Major Wins as Stallions
Mr. Prospector	Fappiano (21), Seeking the Gold (19), Gone West (15), Forty Niner (14), Jade Hunter (14), Woodman (10)
Northern Dancer	Danzig (47), Nijinsky II (28), Lyphard (20), Nureyev (18), Sadler's Wells (14), Northern Baby (10)
Bold Ruler	Secretariat (24), What a Pleasure (20), Bold Bidder (18), Chieftan (15), Raja Baba (12)
Nasrullah	Bold Ruler (86), Nashua (33), Nantallah (14), Never Bend (14), Fleet Nasrullah (13)
Hail to Reason	Halo (26), Stop the Music (17), Mr. Leader (12), Roberto (12)
Hyperion	Heliopolis (66), Alibhai (57), Khaled (39), Gun Shot (11)
Raise a Native	Mr. Prospector (73), Alydar (49), Exclusive Native (36), Majestic Prince (12)
Ribot	Graustark (28), Tom Rolfe (26), His Majesty (24), Arts and Letters (10)
Nearco	Nasrullah (84), Royal Charger (35), Amerigo (19)
Princequillo	Round Table (36), Prince John (18), Hill Prince (16)
Turn-to	Hail to Reason (44), First Landing (15), Cyane (10)
Balladier	Double Jay (27), Spy Song (12)
Blushing Groom	Rahy (22), Mt. Livermore (16)
Bull Dog	Bull Lea (100), Johns Joy (10)
Equipoise	Shut Out (21), Equestrian (11)
Herbager	Grey Dawn II (24), Big Spruce (11)
Khaled	Swaps (15), Hillary (11)
Native Dancer	Raise a Native (24), Native Charger (16)
Nearctic	Northern Dancer (18), Explodent (11)
Pilate	Eight Thirty (26), Phalanx (10)
Prince John	Stage Door Johnny (16), Speak John (12)
Roberto	Kris S. (22), Silver Hawk (11)
Seattle Slew	A.P. Indy (24), Slew O' Gold (14)
Sir Gallahad III	Roman (25), Fighting Fox (12)

The following chart shows stallions' ranking on the Sire Line Index for the 6,461 major races held in North America from 1946-2003. Following that chart are charts that give the same information for the 174 classic races held from 1946-2003, the 145 Breeders' Cup races staged from 1984-2003, and the annual leaders from 1946-2003.

Sire Line Index 1946-2003

1. Nasrullah (2,410)
2. Nearco (1,878)
3. Bold Ruler (1,666)
4. Northern Dancer (1,613)
5. Raise a Native (1,508)
6. Mr. Prospector (1,457)
7. Hyperion (1,381)
8. Princequillo (1,233)
9. Native Dancer (953)
10. Nearctic (917)
11. Turn-to (911)
12. Bull Lea (906)
13. Hail to Reason (884)
14. Alibhai (799)
15. Royal Charger (783)
16. Heliopolis (750)
17. Seattle Slew (746)
18. Ribot (724)
19. Bull Dog (659)
20. Prince Rose (649)
21. Gainsborough (642)
22. Pharos (633)
23. Tom Fool (605)
24. Blenheim II (574)
25. Polynesian (567)
26. Mahmoud (559)
27. Damascus (558)
28. Danzig (552)
29. Teddy (532)
30. Khaled (530)
31. Count Fleet (490)
32. Phalaris (478)
33. Bold Reasoning, Menow (443)
35. Alydar, Exclusive Native (440)
37. Blushing Groom, Nijinsky II (438)
39. Herbager (416)
40. Round Table (414)
41. Sword Dancer (399)
42. Deputy Minister (396)
43. Buckpasser (374)
44. Fappiano (366)
45. Blandford (361)
46. Storm Cat (360)
47. Tenerani (359)
48. Prince John (352)
49. Roberto (350)
50. His Majesty (344)
51. Pharamond II (343)
52. Black Toney (339)
53. Halo, Tom Rolfe (328)
55. Graustark, In Reality (326)
56. Swynford (324)
58. Nashua (321)
59. Balladier (313)
60. Your Host (308)
61. Double Jay (298)
62. Reigh Count (297)
63. Eight Thirty, Pilate (296)
65. Intentionally (292)
66. Blue Larkspur (283)
67. Boldnesian (276)
68. Storm Bird (272)
69. Rose Prince (271)
70. Rough'n Tumble (270)
71. Never Bend (268)
72. Man o' War (263)
73. Olympia (256)
74. Sunglow (255)
75. Lyphard (254)
76. Nureyev (252)
77. Unbreakable (251)
78. Ambiorix (250)
79. Sun Again, War Relic (248)
81. Vice Regent (246)
82. Questionnaire (245)
83. Roman (244)
84. Forli (242)
85. Gallant Man (238)
86. Fleet Nasrullah (232)
87. Bold Bidder, What a Pleasure (230)
89. Sir Gallahad III (229)
90. Pleasant Colony, Vandale (228)
92. Ajax, Sir Gaylord (226)
94. Grey Dawn II, Private Account (224)
96. Secretariat (222)
97. Red God (221)
98. War Admiral (220)
99. Tourbillon, Unbridled (216)
101. Bayardo, Caro, Majestic Prince (208)
104. Endeavor II, Equipoise (206)
106. A.P. Indy, Cox's Ridge, Kris S. (204)
109. Speak John, Vaguely Noble (200)
111. Fair Play (199)
112. Gummo (196)
113. Peter Pan (190)
114. Beau Pere, Relaunch (188)
116. Hoist the Flag, Majestic Light (184)
118. Ack Ack (180)
119. Migoli (179)
120. Stop the Music (178)
121. Intent (177)
122. Challenger II, Rahy (176)
124. Bimelech, Sickle (174)
126. Forty Niner, Seeking the Gold (172)
128. Naskra (170)
129. Shut Out, Vertex (168)
131. St. Germans (166)
132. Indian Hemp (163)
133. Discovery, Riverman (160)
135. Best Turn, T.V. Lark (158)
137. Amerigo, Key to the Mint, Sir Ivor, Swaps (156)
141. Ole Bob Bowers, Theatrical (152)
143. Bois Roussel (150)
144. Quadrangle (148)
145. Sunreigh (147)
146. Friar Rock, Nantallah (146)
148. Black Servant (145)
149. Affirmed, Bold Venture, Gone West, Rosemont, Saggy (144)
154. Free For All (142)
155. Bagdad, First Landing, Native Charger, Noholme II (140)
159. Battle Joined (138)
160. Son-in-Law (137)
161. Sadler's Wells (136)
162. Bellini (135)
163. Hill Prince, The Axe II (132)
165. Cohoes, Raja Baba, Traffic Judge (130)
168. Tudor Minstrel (129)
169. Chieftan, Fighting Fox, Mt. Livermore, My Babu, Stage Door Johnny, Windy Sands (128)
175. Aristophanes (127)
176. Owen Tudor, The Rhymer, Wild Again (124)
179. Requested, Strawberry Road II, Verbatim (120)
182. The Porter (119)
183. Arts and Letters, Jester, Spy Song (116)
186. Sting (114)
187. Jade Hunter, Market Wise, Polymelus, Skip Trial, Slew O' Gold (112)
192. British Empire, Fairway (111)
194. Pensive, Plassy (110)
196. Alsab (109)
197. Equestrian (108)
198. Sun Teddy, Tehran (106)
200. Beau Gar, Buckaroo, Challedon, Fortino, Gulch, Nigromante, Windy City II (104)
207. Revoked (102)
208. Icecapade, John o' Gaunt, Pennant (101)
211. Delta Judge, Determine, Tale of Two Cities, Vienna (100)
215. Jet Pilot (98)
216. Bailjumper, Djebel, Habitat, Habitony, Irish River, Mr. Leader, To Market (96)
223. Ksar (95)
224. Foolish Pleasure (93)
225. Explodent, Gun Shot, Johns Joy (92)
228. Hastings (90)
229. Big Spruce, Citation, Cozzene, Crozier, Cyane, Hillary, Palace Music, Silver Hawk (88)
237. Armageddon, Grey Sovereign, Nasram (85)
240. Northern Baby, Reaping Reward, Sailor, Time for a Change, Woodman (84)
245. Blue Prince, Star Kingdom (82)
247. Ahmad, Broad Brush, Conquistador Cielo, Devil's Bag, Display, Dr. Fager, Phalanx, Prince Palatin, Reflected Glory, The Minstrel, Thunder Gulch (80)
258. Sweep (79)
259. The Doge (78)
260. Bold and Brave, Counterpoint, Cryptoclearance, Greek Song, Minnesota Mac, Prince Blessed (76)
266. Colombo (74)
267. Bernborough, Codex, Consultant's Bid, Darn That Alarm, Dynaformer, General Meeting, Great Above, Hold Your Peace, Kingmambo, Lear Fan, Maudlin, Quiet American, Rainbow Quest, Sovereign Dancer, Stardust, Swing and Sway (72)
283. Dark Ronald, Dixieland Band, Goya II, Reviewer (68)
287. Bosworth, Brantome, Vatout (67)
290. Irish Castle, Palestinian (66)
292. Rock Sand (65)
293. Advocator, Ambiopoise, Boswell, Bryan G., Cee's Tizzy, Crafty Admiral, Devil Diver, Easy Goer, Errard, Fair Ruler, He Did, Imbros, Meadowlake, Noor, Our Native, Ponder, Runaway Groom, Sharpen Up, Silver Buck, Whirlaway (64)
313. Pharis, Sundridge (62)
315. Congreve (61)
316. Bold Forbes, Cannonade, Carson City, Cornish Prince, Gallant Romeo, Miswaki, Nodouble, Phone Trick, Relic, Take Away, Whiskey Road, Wyndham (60)
328. Air Forbes Won, Bahram, Blue Swords, Brokers Tip, Caveat, Chief's Crown, Dust Commander, Free America, Green Dancer, Jacinto, Notebook, Olden Times, Pago Pago, Pretense, Rich Cream, Roi Normand, Saint Ballado, Shannon II, Siberian Express, Smokester, Third Brother, Tim Tam, Top Command, Valid Appeal (56)
352. Embrujo, Sea-Bird (54)
354. Bold Commander, Busted, Cure the Blues, Dewan, Drone, Half Crown, Jig Time, John P. Grier, Kingsway II, Manila, Norcliffe, Petare, Star de Naskra, Warfare (52)
368. Aureole (50)
369. Prince Chevalier, Sicambre (49)
371. Alleged, Apalachee, Arazi, Belong to Me, Caerleon, Chance Play, Dark Star, Dehere, Djakao, Faraway Son, Flying Paster, Lypheor, Marquetry, On-and-On, Petrose, Priam II, Prince de Galles, Proud Clarion, Royal Gem II, Royal Orbit, Sensitivo, Silver Deputy, Skywalker, Summer Squall, Summer Tan, Sunny's Halo (48)
397. Arctic Prince, Good Goods, Good Manners, Roi Dagobert (46)
401. Spur (45)
402. Cormorant, Creme dela Creme, Easy Mon, Foxhunter, Jet Jewel, Le Fabuleux, Midstream, Mill Reef, On the Sly, Tentam, Timeless Moment, Topsider, Utrillo II (44)
415. Fair Trial, Pardal (41)
417. Again II, Assagai, Attention, Ballydam, Baynoun, Black Tie Affair, Bold Lad, Boston Doge, Brown King, Case Ace, Commando, Cougar II, Darshaan, Dedicate, Doyoun, El Gran Senor, El Prado, Envoy, Fly So Free, Green Desert, Harlan, Hawaii, Intrepid Hero, Jack High, Key to the Kingdom, Nirgal, No Robbery, Northern Jove, Persian Road II, Polish Navy, Prince Bio, Prince Royal II, Private Terms, Robin des Bois, Run the Gantlet, Saint Patrick, Sassafras, Sideral, Slewvescent, Sportin' Life, Staff Writer, Stymie, Teddy's Comet, Terrang, Tiger, Tri Jet, Tulyar, Unbridled's Song, You and I (40)
466. Hash (38)
467. Ben Brush (37)
468. Be My Guest, Bolero, Dark Hawk, Diesis, Emborough, Fairy Manhurst, Hilarious, Lord Gaylord, Neddie, Porterhouse, Prince Taj, Promised Land, Ridan, Some Chance, Swoon's Son, Well Decorated (36)
484. Crepello, Donatello II, Marfa, Toulouse Lautrec, Wild Risk (34)
489. Ambehaving, Ariel, Atan, Auditing, Battlefield, Battle Morn, Believe It, Better Bee, Bolger, Boojum, Buckfinder, Capote, Carry Back, Cavan, Chateaugay, Cherokee Run, Correspondent, Crowfoot, Distant View, Domingo, El Drag, End Sweep, Flushing II, Foxglove, Francis S., French Deputy, Glitterman, Hail the Pirates, Haital, Honest Pleasure, Island Whirl, King's Bishop, Madison, Middleground, Mr. Greeley, Mr. Music, My Host, Never Say Die, Northern Fling, One Count, Our Emblem, Pampered King II, Persian Gulf, Pivotal, Quibu, Rainy Lake, Restless Wind, Rico Monte, Riva Ridge, Rolando, Royal Coinage, Royal Serenade, Scelto, Shirley Heights, Silver Ghost, Sir Damion, Specialmante, Sword Dance, Tabasco Cat, Temperence Hill, The Irishman, Thinking Cap, Tompion, Trevieres, Two Punch, Victorian, Vigors, War Dog, War Jeep, Windsor Ruler (32)
559. Manna (31)
560. Aneroid, Bruleur, Chop Chop, Clever Trick (30)

564. Bold Combatant, Don B., Eternal Bull, General, Itajara, Jamestown, Matrice, Matun, Mossborough, Never Tabled, The Yuvaraj, Victoria Park, Whisk Broom II (28)
577. Copyright, Dan Cupid (27)
579. Court Martial, Moslem, Tanerko (26)
582. Abernant, Afleet, Al Nasr, Assert, Awesome Again, Baldski, Barbizon, Bay Ronald, Ben Lomond, Bien Bien, Billings, Bold Reason, Bold Ruckus, Bold Tactics, Brookfield, By Jimminy, Carlemont, Cinco Grande, Citidancer, Cosmic Bomb, Count Speed, County Delight, Cover Up, Crimson Satan, Cutlass, Danehill, Decathlon, Dhoti, Distinctive, Distorted Humor, Eternal Prince, Faliraki, Far North, First Balcony, Flash o' Night, Forceten, Full Sail, Gilded Time, Go for Gin, Golden Eagle II, Gran Atleta, Grand Rapids II, Greek Ship, Grounded II, Head Play, Heather Broom, Honor Grades, Jolie's Halo, Keen, King's Abbey, Le Levanstell, Little Beans, Little Missouri, Lord at War, Lord Avie, Los Curros, Lt. Stevens, Lucky Debonair, Machiavellian, Maribeau, Mat Boy, Meadow, Mister Frisky, Montparnasse II, Moscow Ballet, Naevus, Nashville, Natchez, Native Royalty, Night Shift, Occupy, Old Bag, One For All, Papa Redbird, Pappa Fourway, Peter Hastings, Petrone, Pia Star, Pirate's Bounty, Play Fellow, Pleasant Tap, Pompey, Prince Khaled, Pulpit, Quack, Red Ransom, Rejected, Restless Native, Rich Man's Gold, Roman Diplomat, Roman Line, Salerno, Saros, Sea Hawk II, Seaneen, Seductor, Selari, Sickletoy, Siphon, Sir Leon, Sky High II, Spanish Riddle, State Dinner, Swing Till Dawn, Targowice, Tatan, Tell, Tobin Bronze, Tudor Grey, Valdez, Vitriolic, Wallet Lifter, Wavering Monarch, What Luck, Windy Sea, Yachtie (24)
698. Foxlaw (22)
699. Blue Peter, Colin, Jaipur, King of the Tudors, Tantieme (21)
704. Ballyogan, Beau Max, Fast Fox, Grand Slam (1933), Gulf Stream, Hasty Road, Knightly Manner, Ky. Colonel, Marsayas, Nashwan, Nid d'Or, Orbit Ruler, Palestine, Prince Tenderfoot, Pronto, Proudest Roman, Rambunctious, Right Royal, Shadeed, Sheshoon, Silent Screen, Welsh Pageant (20)
726. Alycidon, Cavaliere d'Arpino, Firestreak, High Time (18)
730. Dante, Rialto, Rustom Pasha (17)
733. African Sky, Alcibiades II, Al Hattab, All Hands, Alquest, Alzao, Amarullah, Ambernash, Ardan, Argur, Arigotal, Ascot Knight, At the Threshold, Avenue of Flags, Batonnier, Be My Chief, Berseem, Bertrando, Better Self, Binary, Blue Ensign, Bold Hitter, Bold Hour, Bonnard, Brick, Brocco, Bucksplasher, Buisson d'Or, Burg-El-Arab, Candy Spots, Candy Stripes, Cape Town, Cipayo, Clem, Coastal Traffic, Cochise, Con Brio, Condiment, Count Amber, Count Flame, Count Turf, Coursing, Crazy Kid, Czaravich, Dahar, Dance Spell, Decidedly, Deerhound, Degage, Deputy Commander, Desert Wine, Dictus, DiMaggio, Din's Dancer, Distinctive Pro, Djeddah, Dogpatch, Dumpty Humpty, Eastern Echo, Easton, Eiffel Tower, Emperor Jones, Equifox, Eternal, Faultless, Fit to Fight, Forest Wildcat, Gold Legend, Grand Slam (1995), Gunflint, Gusty, Happy Argo, Hatchet Man, Hawkin's Special, Heelfly, Helioscope, Hempen, Hennessy, Herculean, Hernando, Hero's Honor, High Echelon, High Tribute, His Nickel, Hoist the Silver, Holy Bull, Hunter's Moon IV, Hurry to Market, Hypnotist II, Ile de Bourbon, Indian Ridge, In Excess, Inverness Drive, Isolater, Java Gold, Joey Bob, Johnstown, Jules, Kaldoun, Kennedy Road, King's Stride, Kirtling, Knights Choice, Kodiack, Langfuhr, Lawrin, Li'l Fella, Liloy, Little Current, Lode, London Company, Lost Code, Magesterial, Mamboreta, Maria's Mon, Mashkour, Mehmet, Mendocino, McLellan, Metfield, Michel, Milkman, Minera II, Mironton, Missile, Misty Flight, Mongo, Montbrook, Moondust II, Mr. Trouble, Mummy's Game, Nalees Man, Nasty and Bold, Northerly, Northjet, Ocean Swell, Oh Johnny, Olympiad King, Only One, On Trust, Pantalon, Pass Catcher, Pass the Glass, Peanuts, Perrault, Petionville, Pine Bluff, Platter, Poker, Polar Falcon, Poona II, Pretendre, Proud Birdie, Prove It, Ramsinga, Raise a Cup, Repicado II, Rousillon, Royal Note, Royal Ski, Run For Nurse, Rustom Sirdar, Ruthie's Native, Ruysdael II, Saidam, Scratch, Sea Hero, Search for Gold, Seattle Dancer, Selkirk, Sham, Sillery, Sir Ruler, Sky Ship, Slipped Disc, Smarten, Snark, Snow Cat, Somethingfabulous, Souepi, Southern Halo, Spectacular Bid, Spend A Buck, Stalwart, Stevward, Stunning, Summing, Sun Briar, Sweep All, Table Run, Tale of the Cat, Tank's Prospect, Targui, The Battler, The Pie King, The Pruner, Thunder Puddles, Top Row, Torsion, Touch Gold, Trace Call, Traffic Cop, Tresiete, Triplicate, Turkoman, Unconscious, Waquoit, Wig Out, Wise Exchange, With Approval, Wittgenstein, Wolver Hollow, Yorktown, Zacaweista (16)
947. Alorter, Flares (15)
949. Beigler Bey, Brigadier Gerard, Felicio, Gallant Fox, Masthead, Rasper II, St. James (14)
956. Cyllene, Petition, Precipitation (13)
959. All Serene, Arctic Explorer, Atlas, Brazado, Broad Reach, Chance Shot, Charlottesville, Churrinche, Crafty Prospector, Dastur, Donut King, Great Nephew, Groton, Iron Ruler, Isabelino, Jean Valjean, King Cole, King Salmon, Kris, Le Lavandou, Lucky Mel, Macherio, Mirafel, My Play, Niniski, Northern Answer, Pappageno II, Rash Prince, Rockefella, Royal Minstrel, Sainfoin, Sing Sing, Super Concorde, Welsh Abbot (12)
993. Flying Fox, Isinglass, King James, Ultimus (11)
997. Fastnet, Faucheur, Golden Ruler, Kalamoun, Our Rulla, Panorama, Petingo, Prince Chimay, Prunus, Timor, Tudor Melody (10)
1,008. Aethelstan II, Deux Pour Cent, The Tetrarch (9)
1,011. Aaron's Concorde, Abadan, Abbe Pierre, Accipiter, Ace Admiral, Admiral Drake, Admiral Lea, Aferd, Afghan II, Ahonoora, Ahoy, Alan Breck, All Blue, Allen's Prospect, Alydeed, Ambassador IV, Ambrose Light, Amphion, Anyoldtime, Argosy, Arkansas II, Assemblyman, Atomic, Aurelius II, Avatar, Avenger II, Bairn, Balconaje, Ballymoss, Barachois, Bates Motel, Battleship, Bazooka, Beau Buck, Beau Gem, Bering, Berkley Prince, Big Game, Bikala, Bit of Ireland, Black Forest, Bless Me, Bleu d'Or, Bluebird, Blue Flyer, Blue Gay, Blue Train, Blue Water, Blushing John, B. Major, Bold Hemp, Bold Joey, Bolinas Boy, Bonne Noel, Bow Wow, Boxthorn, Brambles, Brevity, Briartic, Brinkmanship, Broomstick, Brother Machree, Bull Dandy, Bull Run, Burning Star, Cadmus, California Kid, Call Boy, Cambremont, Canthare, Carr de Naskra, Carrier Pigeon, Casanova, Catalan, Caucasus, Celtic Swing, Challenge Me, Charlevoix, Charlie McAdam, Chrysler II, City Line, Claim Staker, Claro, Coastal, Cobra King, Coldstream, Colony Light, Come On Red, Comico, Commanding II, Common Grounds, Cool Hand, Cool Joe, Cool Victor, Coronado's Quest, Coulee Man, Count of Honor, Court Ruling, Cravat, Criminal Type, Crystal Glitters, Cudgel, Curandero, Curragh King, Cyrano de Bergerac, Cyrus the Great, D'Accord, Dancer's Image, Dancing Czar, Dancing Dervish, Danzatore, Darby Creek Road, Dark Legend, Daumier, Decorated, Degenerate Jon, Deliberator, Delineator, Delta Oil, Determined Man, Devil His Due, Dewan Keys, Diablo, Diplomat Way, Dixieland Brass, Dixieland Heat, Doc Sylvester, Doswell, Dotted Swiss, Doutelle, Draft Card, Drawby, Dr. Carter, Dreaming Native, Drum Fire, Eagle Eyed, Ecliptical, Effervescing, Egg Toss, Ela-Mana-Mou, Elevation, Elmaamul, Elocutionist, Encino, Engrillado, Epigram, Erins Isle, Espadin, Eternal Bim, Eternal Reward, Etonian, Eudaemon, Executioner, Explosive Bid, Fair Truckle, Family Crest, Farewell Party, Far Out East, Fast Hilarious, Ferdinand, Fiddle Isle, Fire Dancer, Firethorn, First Fiddle, Fleet Allied, Fleet Host, Flip Sal, Florin, Flying Fury, Fools Holme, For the Moment, Frankie's Nod, Full Pocket, Gaelic Dancer, Gallant Duke, Gallantsky, General Assembly, Gentle Art, George Royal, Get Around, Gold Alert, Golden Act, Gold Meridian, Gold Note, Grand Revival, Graphic, Great Circle, Great Sun, Greek Answer, Grenfall, Grindstone, Groovy, Groshawk, Grundy, Guilo Cesere, Gun Bow, Halcyon, Halo's Image, Handsome Boy, Hansel, Hesiod, Hethersett, Highest Honor, Highland Park, High Quest, High Strung, Hillsborough, Hillsdale, His Grace, Hollyrood, Homebuilder, Honey Jay, Honour and Glory, Horatius, Hostage, Hot Grove, Hussonet, Idle Hour, I'm For More, Indian Emerald, Insco, In the Wings, Irish Ruler, Irish Tower, Iron Constitution, Iron Duke, Is It True, Islam, It's Freezing, Jaklin Klugman, Jatullah, Jaybil, Jet Action, Jig Dancer, Jolly Quick, Judge Smells, Kalaglow, Kaskaskia, Kautokeino, Kentucky Pride, Kingly, King's Blue, Kipper Kelly, Knave High, Known Fact, Krakatao, Lacydon, Landing, Lanyon, Law Society, Legal Case, Leisure Time, Le Tyrol, Lighthouse II, Limelight, Lines of Power, Lively One, Local Talent, Lochinvar, Lomitas, Loom, Lord Carson, Lovely Night, Lucillite, Lucky Mike, Luhuk, Lure, Lyphard's Special, Lyphard's Wish, Majestic Venture, Malinowski, Mandate, Manzotti, Mastadon, Master Willie, Medieval Man, Medium, Menace, Menetrier, Menocal, Mi Cielo, Mincio, Mio d'Arezzo, Mirza II, Mocito Guapo, Mo Exception, Mogambo, Money Broker, Monteverdi, Moonlight Run, More Sun, Mountain Cat, Mountdrago, Mount Marcy, Mr. Busher, Mr. Long, Mr. Mustard, Mr. Randy, Mr. Redoy, Mummy's Pet, Mutakddim, My Gallant, My Lark, Nadir, Nahar II, National, Native Prospector, Near Man, Nebbiolo, Needles, New Policy, Noble Hero, Northern Flagship, Northfields, Nostalgia, Oceanus II, O'Grady, Oh Say, Oil Capitol, Ole, On Watch, Opening Verse, Orbit II, Orbit Dancer, Our Michael, Out of Place, Overskate, Pall Mall, Pancho Villa, Panoramic, Parbury, Partab, Parwix, Pas Seul, Pavot, Perambulator, Persian Bold, Petardia, Phar Mon, Phone Order, Piaster, Pick Up the Phone, Pied d'Or, Piet, Pink Flower, Piping Rock, Pirateer, Plum Bold, Poaching, Polish Numbers, Polish Precedent, Pollux, Polly's Jet, Poster, Potrillazo, Potrillon, Practitioner, Pretexto, Princely Pleasure, Prospectors Gamble, Prospector's Music, Protanto, Proud Truth, Prove Out, Psychic Bid, Quadratic, Quest for Fame, Rabelais, Raised Socially, Rajab, Reading II, Ready Say Go, Red Ryder, Reform, Rego, Rheingold, Rhodes Scholar, Ribocco, Ride the Rails, Risen Star, Rock Talk, Rocky Royale, Rollicking, Roman Sandal, Roman Sword, Romeo, Rose Argent, Rover, Roy, Royal Academy, Royal Dorimar, Royal Ford, Royal Union, Royal Vale, Rubiano, Rusticaro, Sabona, Sagace, Saim, Sallust, Salmagundi, Salse, Salt Lake, Sanctus, Saratoga Six, Sauce Boat, Scaramouche, Scottish Meridian, Sculptor, Seattle Song, Semenenko, Semi-Pro, Septieme Ciel, Service Stripe, Sharivari, Shecky Greene, Shifting Sands II, Sicyos, Side Boy, Signal Tap, Silver Horde, Simply Majestic, Sir Ribot, Sir Wimborne, Slewacide, Slew City Slew, Slewpy, Snow Ball, Social Climber, Solo Landing, Solonaway, Sovereign Path, Speak Up, Spectrum II, Spring Double, Stalino, Star Pilot, Staunchness, Sterling Bay, St. Jovite, Stonewalk, Storm Creek, Straight Die, Stronghold, Subpet, Sullivan, Sultry Song, Sun Bahram, Sunny Boy, Sunny North, Sunshine Forever, Surreal, Swain, Sweet Candy, Tactical Advantage, Take Me Out, Tambourine, Tapioca, Tarboosh, Taylor's Falls, Terra Firma, Terresto, Terrible Tiger, Thatching, That's a Nice, The Irish Lord, The Solicitor II, The Sultan, Third Martini, Thumbs Up, Tiger II, Tilt Up, Tintagel, Tipoquill, To B. or Not, Top Gallant II, Towson, Traffic Mark, Transworld, Trempolino, Truce Maker, Try My Best, Tsunami Slew, Tudor Castle, Tudor Way, Turn to Reason, Two a Day, Tyrant, Understanding, Unfuwain, Upper Case, Val de L'Orne, Valid Wager, Venturon, Vertee, Victorian Era, Victory Morn, Villamor, Wagon Limit, Waidmannshell, War Glory, Watchmitick, Watch Your Step, Water Prince, Well Mannered, Welsh Chanter, Western Sky II, White Gloves II, Wild Rush, Wine List, Wing Out, With Regards, Wolfram, Worden II, Wrack of Gold, Your Alibhai, Zarbyev, Zen, Zenith, Zinaad, Zoning (8)
1,532. Bey, Hurry On, Queen's Hussar, Shantung (7)
1,536. El Tango, High Hat, Honeyway, Oleander, Ortello, Salmon-Trout, Stefan the Great, Sunstar, Tetratema, Zephyr Bay (6)
1,546. Bona Vista, Perth, Sir Cosmo, Solario, Zeddaan (5)
1,551. Arctic Tern, Asterios, Australian, Bachelor's Double, Bobsleigh, Bramble, Burning Blaze, Caduto, Catullus, Cloth o' Gold, Coaraze, Cold Reception, Cornwall, Craig an Eran, Damister, Diadochos, Diavolo, Durbar II, Faberge, Fair Copy, Falls of Clyde, Farma Way, Fine Top, Fontenay, Friul, Go Marching, Grass Court, Hard Tack, Hard Work, Helios, Hey Good Lookin, High Cloud, Hot Foot, High Line, His Highness, Hugh Lupus, Iron Warrior, Jock II, Kenmare, Klarion, Knight's Romance, Laland, Lorenzaccio, Luthier, Marconigram, Mel Hash, Meridien, Mid-day, Nathoo, Niccolo Dell'Arca, Nilad, Parlanchin, Petong, Phidias, Pitcairn, Primate, Relko, Reneged, Santa Claus, Sheet Anchor, Solferino, Supreme Court, Thatch, Tick On, Trap Rock, Tudor Era, T.V. Commercial, Val de Loir, Verso II, Victrix, What's Ahead, Whistler, White Horses, Wise Counsellor, Yellow God (4)
1,626. Biscay, Olascoaga (3)
1,628. Abbots Trace, Alcantara II, Asterus, Big Blaze, Chamossaire, Coronach, Deiri, Domino, Fels, Fine Art, Kantar, Macar, Mansingh, March Past, Marcovil, Maurepas, Mentor, Orby, Pinceau, Princely Gift, Roi Herode, Tanner, Tornado, Tredennis, Vieux Manoir (2)
1,653. Blackstock, Campfire, Clarion, Craganour, Hannibal, St. Simons, Tracery, Waldmeister (1)

Classic Sire Line Index 1946-2003

1. Raise a Native (96)
2. Mr. Prospector (88)
3. Nasrullah (78)
4. Bold Ruler (73)
5. Native Dancer, Nearco (67)
7. Bull Lea (52)
8. Polynesian (44)
9. Northern Dancer (42)
10. Bold Venture, Hail to Reason (40)
12. Nearctic (39)
13. Bold Reasoning, Ribot (36)
15. Hyperion (33)
16. Alydar, Exclusive Native, Fappiano (32)
19. Turn-to (29)
20. Bold Bidder, Menow (28)
22. Bull Dog, Royal Charger (26)
24. Tom Fool (25)
25. Count Fleet, Gulch, Halo, His Majesty, Seattle Slew, Storm Bird, Unbridled, Woodman (24)
33. Pharos, St. Germans (22)
35. Danzig, Khaled (20)
37. Boldnesian, Phalaris, Tenerani (18)
40. Distorted Humor, First Landing, Forty Niner, Gainsborough, Irish Castle, On-and-On, Our Emblem, Pensive, Pharamond II, Ponder, Pretendre, Quiet American, Saggy, Sea-Bird, Secretariat, Silver Buck, Sovereign Dancer, Storm Cat, Summer Squall, Sunglow, Swaps, Sword Dancer, Teddy, Thunder Gulch (16)
64. Unbreakable (15)
65. Alibhai, Buckpasser, Reigh Count (14)
68. Heliopolis, Princequillo, Swynford (13)
71. Bold Commander, Nijinsky II (12)
73. Migoli (11)
74. Blenheim II, Pilate, Prince John, Prince Rose (10)
78. Majestic Prince (9)
79. All Hands, Arts and Letters, At the Threshold, Ballydam, Bellini, Be My Guest, Better Bee, Blue Swords, Buckaroo, By Jimminy, Cannonade, Caro, Citation, Cohoes, Cormorant, Correspondent, Cougar II, Count Amber, Cryptoclearance, Dan Cupid, Deputy Minister, Determine, Doutelle, Dust Commander, Gallant Romeo, Gone West, Graustark, Greek Song, Iron Ruler, Kingmambo, Little Missouri, Maria's Mon, Mossborough, Native Charger, Nigromante, Pleasant Colony, Polish Navy, Reflected Glory, Rich Cream, Roman, Royal Coinage, Royal Gem II, Sicambre, Sportin' Life, Stop the Music, Sun Again, Swing and Sway, Traffic Cop, Tudor Minstrel, Verbatim, Vertex, What a Pleasure, Wild Again (8)
132. Ajax, Sunreigh (7)
134. John o' Gaunt, Sickle (6)
136. Blandford, Bois Roussel, Friar Rock (5)
139. Ambiorix, Ballyogan, Bayardo, Blue Larkspur, Cox's Ridge, Creme dela Creme, Dhoti, Eight Thirty, Embrujo, Equipoise, Fortino, Gallant Man, Icecapade, Jester, Mahmoud, Never Bend, Norcliffe, Owen Tudor, Prince Bio, Prince Chevalier, Rose Prince, Sir Gallahad III, Speak John, Sun Teddy, Tale of Two Cities, The Rhymer, Traffic Judge, Triplicate, Vice Regent, Wavering Monarch (4)
169. Polymelus, Sundridge (3)
171. Best Turn, Black Servant, Cavaliere d'Arpino, Congreve, Dastur, Fair Trial, Grey Sovereign, Majestic Light, Olympia, Pennant, Rock Sand, Tehran, Tourbillon, Vatout (2)
185. Black Toney, Copyright, Fairway, Ksar, Prince Chimay, Prince Palatin, Sainfoin, Solario (1)

Breeders' Cup Sire Line Index 1984-2003

1. Northern Dancer (130)
2. Mr. Prospector (83)
3. Nearctic (70)
4. Danzig (64)
5. Raise a Native (51)
6. Sadler's Wells (48)
7. Kris S. (40)
8. Seattle Slew (36)
9. Fappiano, Nijinsky II, Nureyev (34)
12. Nearco (33)
13. Blushing Groom, Deputy Minister, Gone West, Relaunch, Storm Cat, Unbridled (28)
19. Nasrullah (26)
20. Bold Ruler, Cox's Ridge, Roberto, Strawberry Road II (24)
24. Native Dancer (23)
25. In Reality (22)
26. Bold Reasoning, Damascus, Hail to Reason, Mill Reef, Storm Bird (18)
31. Turn-to (17)
32. Caro, Cee's Tizzy, Consultant's Bid, Cozzene, Doyoun, Icecapade, Indian Ridge, Marquetry, Mt. Livermore, Phone Trick, Pleasant Colony, Private Account, Raja Baba, Seeking the Gold (16)
46. Graustark, Red God, Vice Regent (14)
49. Ribot (13)
50. Alydar, Best Turn, Halo, Hold Your Peace, Key to the Mint, Lyphard, Speak John, The Minstrel, Verbatim, Whiskey Road (12)
60. Intentionally, Never Bend (11)
62. Boldnesian, Sword Dancer (9)
64. Ahmad, Ahonoora, Alleged, A.P. Indy, Bold Bidder, Broad Brush, Bucksplasher, Capote, Celtic Swing, Chief's Crown, Clever Trick, Conquistador Cielo, Crozier, Cryptoclearance, Danehill, Danzatore, Darshaan, Deerhound, Easy Goer, El Gran Senor, Exclusive Native, Fortino, Grand Slam (1995) Green Desert, Habitat, Hennessy, His Majesty, Hoist the Flag, Hoist the Silver, Holy Bull, Honor Grades, Honour and Glory, Horatius, Jade Hunter, Java Gold, Key to the Kingdom, Lively One, Lypheor, Maudlin, Meadowlake, Mendocino, Miswaki, Palace Music, Polish Precedent, Rahy, Rajab, Red Ransom, Royal Academy, Runaway Groom, Sagace, Secretariat, Sharpen Up, Sillery, Silver Deputy, Skip Trial, Slewpy, Summer Squall, Summing, Thunder Gulch, Time for a Change, Timeless Moment, Try My Best, Unbridled's Song, Wild Again, Woodman (8)
129. Polynesian, Prince John (6)
131. Royal Charger, Tenerani (5)
133. Ack Ack, Atan, Bailjumper, Buckpasser, Damister, Foolish Pleasure, Good Manners, Great Above, Grey Sovereign, Gulch, Intent, Jaipur, Klarion, Lorenzaccio, Luthier, My Babu, Proudest Roman, Shirley Heights, Sir Gaylord, Sunglow, Theatrical, Tom Rolfe (4)
155. Battle Joined, Djebel, Minnesota Mac, Nashua, Princequillo, Tom Fool, What a Pleasure (2)
162. Armageddon, Bellini, Clarion, Menow, Pharos, Rough'n Tumble, Tourbillon, War Relic (1)

1946

1. Challenger II, Mahmoud (64)
3. Swynford (58)
4. Bold Venture (56)
5. Teddy (52)
6. Blenheim II, Bull Lea (48)
8. Bull Dog, Equestrian, Sir Gallahad III (40)

1947

1. Bull Lea (120)
2. Blue Larkspur (84)
3. Blenheim II, Bull Dog (60)
5. Alibhai (48)
6. Black Servant (46)
7. Swynford (41)
8. Mahmoud, Pilate (40)
10. Teddy (38)

1948

1. Bull Lea (88)
2. Bull Dog (60)
3. Discovery, Requested, War Admiral (48)
6. Mahmoud, Questionnaire (44)
8. Blandford (43)
9. Fair Play, Heliopolis (40)

1949

1. Bull Lea (72)
2. Hyperion (68)
3. Bull Dog, Heliopolis (56)
5. Teddy (54)
6. Blue Larkspur (52)
7. Eight Thirty, Mahmoud, Pensive (48)
10. Pharamond II, Pilate (40)

1950

1. Heliopolis (72)
2. Hyperion (68)
3. Bull Lea (64)
4. Bull Dog, Princequillo (56)
6. Alibhai, Nasrullah, War Relic (40)
9. Teddy (36)
10. Gainsborough (34)

1951

1. Count Fleet (112)
2. Blenheim II, Bull Lea, Reigh Count (56)
5. Bull Dog, Shut Out (40)
7. Teddy (38)
8. Eight Thirty, Pilate, War Admiral (32)

1952

1. Bull Lea (128)
2. Bull Dog, Count Fleet (72)
4. Teddy (50)
5. Blenheim II (48)
6. Reigh Count (36)
7. Blandford (34)
8. Attention, Easy Mon, Errard, Fighting Fox, Market Wise, Pharamond II, War Relic (32)

1953

1. Polynesian (72)
2. Bull Lea (64)
3. Menow, Roman (48)
5. Hyperion (46)
6. Unbreakable (44)
7. Phalaris, Sir Gallahad III (42)
9. Teddy (41)
10. Bull Dog, Count Fleet (40)

1954

1. Heliopolis (100)
2. Bull Lea (68)
3. Hyperion (66)
4. Nasrullah (60)
5. Bull Dog (38)
6. Gainsborough (37)
7. Blenheim II (36)
8. Nearco (34)
9. Jet Pilot, Phalanx, Revoked, Shut Out (32)

1955

1. Nasrullah (112)
2. Hyperion (96)
3. Alibhai, Heliopolis (68)
5. Nearco (56)
6. Gainsborough (50)
7. Khaled, Shut Out (40)
9. Princequillo (36)
10. Ambiorix, Double Jay (32)

1956

1. Nasrullah (104)
2. Hyperion (84)
3. Princequillo (72)
4. Heliopolis (60)
5. Nearco (56)
6. Hill Prince, Khaled (48)
8. Alibhai, Gainsborough (44)
10. Eight Thirty, Prince Rose (36)

1957

1. Princequillo (144)
2. Prince Rose (72)
3. Hyperion (66)
4. Alibhai, Nasrullah (60)
6. Heliopolis (56)
7. Bull Lea (44)
8. Nearco (42)
9. Rose Prince (36)
10. Gainsborough (33)

1958

1. Princequillo (72)
2. Nearco (62)
3. Hyperion (58)
4. Nasrullah (56)
5. Royal Charger (44)
6. Khaled, Tom Fool (40)
8. Prince Rose (36)
9. Pharos (35)
10. Gainsborough (31)

1959

1. Princequillo (88)
2. Nasrullah, Nearco, Royal Charger (68)
5. Take Away (56)
6. Hyperion (54)
7. Sunglow (48)
8. Prince Rose (44)
9. Alibhai (36)
10. Pharos (34)

1960

1. Nasrullah (108)
2. Nearco (106)
3. Royal Charger (72)
4. Hyperion (62)
5. Pharos (53)
6. Ambiorix (48)
7. Heliopolis (44)
8. Your Host (40)
9. Alibhai, Ballydam, Double Jay, Indian Hemp, Khaled, Turn-to (32)

1961

1. Hyperion (68)
2. Saggy (56)
3. Princequillo (52)
4. Nasrullah, Your Host (48)
6. Alibhai (44)
7. Ambiorix, Khaled (40)
9. Gainsborough (34)
10. Bryan G., Bull Lea, Correspondent, Heliopolis (32)

1962

1. Nasrullah (108)
2. Nearco (76)
3. Royal Charger (44)
4. Endeavor II, Swaps (40)
6. Pharos (38)
7. Hyperion (37)
8. Khaled, Princequillo (36)
10. Beau Gar, Bryan G. (32)

1963

1. Your Host (68)
2. Nasrullah (64)
3. Hyperion (62)
4. Nigromante (56)
5. Khaled (52)
6. Spy Song (48)
7. Nearco (46)
8. Princequillo (44)
9. Alibhai (42)
10. Swaps (40)

1964

1. Hyperion (86)
2. Bold Ruler (80)
3. Nearco (77)
4. Nasrullah (72)
5. Gun Shot (64)
6. Gainsborough (43)
7. Cohoes, Khaled, Nearctic (40)
10. Pharos (38)

1965

1. Nasrullah (62)
2. Hyperion (61)
3. Hail to Reason (56)
4. Nearco (46)
5. Khaled, Tom Fool (44)
7. Nantallah, Princequillo (40)
9. Bold Ruler (32)
10. Gainsborough (31)

1966

1. Bold Ruler (112)
2. Nasrullah (84)
3. Tom Fool (76)
4. Nearco (54)
5. Hail to Reason (40)
6. Menow (38)
7. Turn-to (32)
8. Hyperion (30)
9. Alibhai (26)
10. Bagdad, Madison, Native Dancer, Pharos (24)

1967

1. Bold Ruler (112)
2. Nasrullah (86)
3. Nearco (75)
4. Sword Dancer (72)
5. Tom Fool (52)
6. Rough'n Tumble (48)
7. Gallant Man, Hail to Reason, Princequillo, Round Table, Turn-to (40)

1968

1. Nasrullah (114)
2. Bold Ruler (104)
3. Nearco (90)
4. Rough'n Tumble (56)
5. On-and-On (48)
6. Pharos (43)
7. Princequillo (42)
8. Amerigo, Persian Road II (40)
10. Nashua, Sword Dancer (32)

1969

1. Nasrullah (76)
2. Nearco (63)
3. Ribot (56)
4. Bold Ruler (48)
5. Nashua, Noholme II (40)
7. Princequillo (38)
8. Prince John (36)
9. Prince Rose (29)
10. Tenerani (28)

1970

1. Nearco (78)
2. Turn-to (64)
3. Hail to Reason, Nasrullah (56)
5. Bold Ruler, Royal Charger (48)
7. Amerigo (40)
8. Bagdad, Native Charger (32)
10. Hyperion, Pharos (29)

1971

1. Nearco (49)
2. Nasrullah (48)
3. Buckpasser (40)
4. Battle Joined, First Landing, Northern Dancer, Tale of Two Cities, Tom Fool (32)
9. Native Dancer (30)
10. Ribot, Turn-to (28)

1972

1. Graustark (72)
2. Ribot (68)
3. Nasrullah (62)
4. Bold Ruler (52)
5. Buckpasser, Tom Rolfe (48)
7. Nearco (42)
8. Quadrangle (40)
9. Turn-to (38)
10. Hail to Reason (36)

1973

1. Bold Ruler (80)
2. Nasrullah (60)
3. Quadrangle (48)
4. Nearco (40)
5. Intentionally, Round Table (36)
7. Princequillo (34)
8. Chieftan, Graustark, Prince John (32)

1974

1. Forli (64)
2. Bold Ruler (60)
3. Nasrullah (58)
4. Nearco, Round Table (36)
6. Advocator, Aristophanes, Damascus, Graustark (32)
10. Ribot (28)

1975

1. Bold Ruler (122)
2. Nasrullah (79)
3. Forli (64)
4. Damascus, What a Pleasure (56)
6. Nearco (42)
7. Sir Ivor (40)
8. Aristophanes (38)
9. Round Table (32)
10. Hyperion (31)

1976

1. Bold Ruler (90)
2. Sir Ivor, What a Pleasure (56)
4. Nasrullah (55)
5. Round Table (44)
6. Turn-to (42)
7. Forli, Hail to Reason (40)
9. Princequillo, Sir Gaylord (36)

1977

1. Herbager, Raise a Native (52)
3. Bold Ruler, Native Dancer (42)
5. Nasrullah (41)
6. Bold Reasoning (40)
7. Hail to Reason (36)
8. Damascus, Exclusive Native, Windy Sands (32)

1978

1. Raise a Native (92)
2. Exclusive Native (64)
3. Nasrullah (62)
4. Vaguely Noble (48)
5. Native Dancer, Nearco (46)
7. Bold Ruler, Northern Dancer (40)
9. Ribot (34)
10. Grey Dawn II, Herbager, Stage Door Johnny (32)

1979

1. Exclusive Native, Raise a Native (72)
3. Gummo (64)
4. Bold Bidder (56)
5. Bold Ruler (50)
6. Nasrullah (47)
7. Nearco, Tom Rolfe, Turn-to (44)
10. Native Dancer (43)

1980

1. Bold Ruler (74)
2. Bold and Brave (56)
3. Bold Bidder, Herbager (52)
5. Nasrullah (51)
6. Arts and Letters, Ribot, Stop the Music (48)
9. Hail to Reason, Ole Bob Bowers (40)

1981

1. Ole Bob Bowers (56)
2. Nasrullah (49)
3. Big Spruce, Herbager, His Majesty, Nashua (40)
7. Ribot (36)
8. Hail to Reason (32)
9. Bold Ruler (30)
10. Princequillo (29)

1982

1. Nasrullah (47)
2. Bold Ruler (45)
3. Northern Dancer (42)
4. Blushing Groom, His Majesty, Ribot, Vaguely Noble (40)
8. Mr. Prospector (32)
9. Nearco (30)
10. Raise a Native (26)

1983

1. Northern Dancer (64)
2. Seattle Slew (56)
3. Alydar, Lyphard (48)
5. Grey Dawn II, Halo (40)
7. Damascus, Nearctic (36)
9. Bold Ruler, Raise a Native (34)

1984

1. Seattle Slew (88)
2. Damascus (52)
3. Northern Dancer (50)
4. Bold Ruler (49)
5. Bold Reasoning (44)
6. Danzig (40)
7. Raise a Native (38)
8. Alydar, Chieftan, Intrepid Hero, Norcliffe, Ole Bob Bowers, Verbatim (32)

1985

1. Northern Dancer (54)
2. Bold Ruler (49)
3. Cox's Ridge, Danzig (48)
5. Mr. Prospector (36)
6. Nasrullah, Raise a Native (34)
8. Rich Cream, Secretariat, Top Command (32)

1986

1. Northern Dancer (90)
2. Raise a Native (58)
3. Secretariat (56)
4. Danzig (48)
5. Bold Ruler, Nearctic (45)
7. Lyphard (44)
8. Ack Ack, Seattle Slew (40)
10. Mr. Prospector (36)

1987

1. Northern Dancer (98)
2. Mr. Prospector (96)
3. Raise a Native (70)
4. Nearctic (49)
5. Nureyev (48)
6. Codex (40)
7. Native Dancer, Nijinsky II (36)
9. Alydar (32)
10. Ribot (30)

1988

1. Mr. Prospector, Raise a Native (96)
3. Alydar (72)
4. Roberto (60)
5. Northern Dancer (58)
6. Hail to Reason, Private Account (56)
8. Native Dancer (48)
9. Bold Ruler (38)
10. Damascus (36)

1989

1. Northern Dancer (78)
2. Alydar (72)
3. Raise a Native (60)
4. Halo (56)
5. Hail to Reason (54)
6. Consultant's Bid, Deputy Minister (48)
8. Nearctic (45)
9. Seattle Slew (44)
10. Slew O' Gold (40)

1990

1. Northern Dancer (80)
2. Raise a Native (72)
3. Mr. Prospector (68)
4. Alydar (64)
5. Nearctic, Seattle Slew (44)
7. Deputy Minister, Fappiano, Native Dancer, Slew O' Gold (40)

1991

1. Mr. Prospector (80)
2. Raise a Native (70)
3. Majestic Light (56)
4. Siberian Express (40)
5. Native Dancer (37)
6. Northern Dancer (34)
7. His Majesty, Majestic Prince, Pleasant Colony (32)
10. Nearctic (30)

1992

1. Northern Dancer (81)
2. Danzig (76)
3. Ahmad, Mr. Prospector, Raise a Native, Seattle Slew (40)
7. Nearctic (39)
8. Nijinsky II (38)
9. Cox's Ridge, Darn That Alarm, Riverman (32)

1993

1. Northern Dancer (59)
2. Blushing Groom (52)
3. Mr. Prospector (48)
4. Nearctic (43)
5. Danzig, Darshaan (40)
7. Raise a Native (36)
8. Affirmed, Darn That Alarm, Kris S. (32)

1994

1. Mr. Prospector (88)
2. Northern Dancer (60)
3. Great Above, Seeking the Gold (56)
5. Raise a Native (49)
6. Blushing Groom (48)
7. Seattle Slew (40)
8. Nearctic, Private Account (36)
10. Irish River, Riverman, Storm Cat (32)

1995

1. Mr. Prospector (88)
2. Northern Dancer (69)
3. Palace Music (64)
4. Raise a Native (58)
5. Private Account, Rahy (56)
7. Blushing Groom (44)
8. Gulch (40)
9. Nearctic (36)
10. Seeking the Gold, The Minstrel (32)

1996

1. Northern Dancer (78)
2. Mr. Prospector (64)
3. Raise a Native (44)
4. Blushing Groom, Skip Trial (40)
6. Nearctic, Vice Regent (38)
8. Air Forbes Won, Easy Goer, Forty Niner (32)

1997

1. Northern Dancer (91)
2. Deputy Minister (80)
3. Mr. Prospector (64)
4. Danzig (58)
5. Nearctic (51)
6. Vice Regent (48)
7. A.P. Indy (40)
8. Raise a Native (38)
9. Nureyev (36)
10. Black Tie Affair, Lear Fan, Quiet American, Robin des Bois, Storm Cat, Strawberry Road II (32)

1998

1. Northern Dancer (72)
2. Mr. Prospector (62)
3. Storm Cat (52)
4. Deputy Minister, Skip Trial (48)
6. Danzig (40)
7. Nearctic (37)
8. Raise a Native (35)
9. Belong to Me, Fappiano, Strawberry Road II, Unbridled (32)

1999

1. Mr. Prospector (70)
2. Storm Cat (56)
3. Seattle Slew (52)
4. Raise a Native (47)
5. Northern Dancer (46)
6. Unbridled (40)
7. Fappiano, Storm Bird (36)
9. Deputy Minister, General Meeting, Silver Deputy (32)

2000

1. Mr. Prospector (88)
2. Seattle Slew (72)
3. Northern Dancer (55)
4. Raise a Native (54)
5. Storm Cat (44)
6. A.P. Indy, Roi Normand (40)
8. Bold Reasoning (36)
9. Kingmambo (32)
10. Nureyev (28)

2001

1. Seattle Slew (68)
2. Northern Dancer (64)
3. Mr. Prospector (58)
4. Thunder Gulch (56)
5. Nureyev, Relaunch (36)
7. Bold Reasoning, Raise a Native (34)
9. Cee's Tizzy, Unbridled (32)

2002

1. Mr. Prospector (111)
2. Northern Dancer (65)
3. Raise a Native (63)
4. Gone West, Storm Cat (52)
6. Sadler's Wells (48)
7. Jade Hunter (40)
8. Nearctic, Our Emblem, You and I (32)

2003

1. Mr. Prospector (120)
2. Raise a Native (64)
3. Unbridled (52)
4. A.P. Indy (48)
5. Northern Dancer (45)
6. Sadler's Wells (36)
7. Distant View, Dynaformer, Seattle Slew (32)
10. Deputy Minister, Fappiano, Roberto (28)

The following tables represent all sire lines that have produced victories in the 6,461 major races held in North America from 1946-2003. The number of major victories by the offspring of each stallion are in parenthesis after that stallion's name. Each indention to the right represents a new, and younger, generation, and each sire line begins with the first, and oldest, generation that receives points in the Sire Line Index—the paternal great-great-grandsire of the first stallion from that sire line to produce major winners from 1946-2003. Each of those stallions' names is in bold all capitals. Stallions who are listed in bold italics are those (in addition to Cyllene and Bayardo, the first stallion listed in their respective lines) whose lineages include too many sires to fill one page and therefore are repeated—without any victories by their offspring listed in parenthesis in subsequent mentions—elsewhere in the section.

Sire Lines That Produced the Winners Of Major North American Races From 1946-2003

- **FLYING FOX**
    - ***Ajax***
        - ***Teddy***
            - Aethelstan II (1)
                - Maurepas
                    - Deux Pour Cent
                        - Tantieme (1)
                            - Tanerko
                                - Djakao (5)
                                    - Perrault (2)
                            - Relko
                                - Kautokeino (1)
            - Sun Teddy
                - Sun Again (14)
                    - More Sun (1)
                    - Palestinian (6)
                        - Promised Land (3)
                            - Understanding (1)
                            - Wise Exchange (2)
                    - Sunglow (9)
                        - Sword Dancer (15)
                            - Damascus (33)
                                - Accipiter (1)
                                - Bailjumper (5)
                                    - Skip Trial (14)
                                - Bolger (4)
                                - Cutlass (3)
                                - Desert Wine (2)
                                - Eastern Echo (2)
                                - Marsayas (1)
                                    - Mister Frisky (3)
                                - Mastadon (1)
                                - Piaster (1)
                                - Private Account (24)
                                    - Private Terms (5)
                                    - Sir Leon (3)
                                - Time for a Change (8)
                                    - Fly So Free (5)
                                - Timeless Moment (4)
                                    - Gilded Time (3)
                                - Zen (1)
                - Teddy's Comet (4)
                    - Sky Ship (2)

- **FLYING FOX**
  - *Ajax*
    - ***Teddy***
      - Asterus
        - Jock II
          - Sunny Boy (1)
      - Bull Dog (4)
        - Bow Wow (1)
        - Bull Lea (100)
          - Admiral Lea (1)
          - All Blue (1)
          - Beau Max (2)
            - Brambles (1)
          - Bull Dandy (1)
          - Bull Run (1)
          - Citation (10)
            - Get Around (1)
            - Watch Your Step (1)
          - Degage (2)
          - Doswell (1)
          - Faultless (2)
          - Flash o' Night (3)
          - Kentucky Pride (1)
        - Coldstream
          - King's Stride (2)
        - Dogpatch (2)
        - Eternal Bull (3)
          - Eternal Bim (1)
        - Johns Joy (10)
          - Frankie's Nod (1)
          - Oh Johnny (2)
        - Occupy (3)
        - Ortello
          - Macherio
            - Grand Rapids II (3)
        - Rover (1)
        - Silver Horde (1)
        - The Doge (5)
          - Boston Doge (5)
          - Swoon's Son (4)
            - Loom (1)
        - Tiger (5)
        - War Dog (4)
      - Case Ace (4)
        - Lochinvar (1)
        - Pavot (1)
      - Chrysler II (1)
      - Sir Gallahad III (1)
        - Cloth o' Gold
          - Wrack of Gold (1)
        - Fighting Fox (12)
          - Crafty Admiral (8)
        - Gallant Fox (1)
          - Flares
            - Chop Chop (2)
              - Victoria Park (2)
                - Kennedy Road (2)
                - Victorian Era (1)
        - High Quest (1)
        - Insco
          - Lawrin (2)
        - Roman (25)
          - Catullus
            - Kaskaskia (1)
          - Hasty Road (1)
            - Run For Nurse (1)
              - Kodiack (2)
            - Third Martini (1)
          - Kingly (1)
          - McLellan (2)
          - Roman Line (3)
          - Roman Sandal (1)
          - Roman Sword (1)
        - Sir Damion (4)
        - Tintagel (1)

- **CYLLENE**
  - ***Polymelus***
    - ***Phalaris***
      - Fairway
        - Blue Peter
          - Blue Train (1)
          - Blue Water (1)
          - Ocean Swell (2)
          - Masthead
            - Matrice
              - Pago Pago (5)
                - Island Whirl (4)
        - Fair Trial
          - Ballyogan
            - Ballydam (5)
          - Court Martial (3)
            - Grass Court
              - Aurelius II (1)
          - Fair Copy
            - Menetrier (1)
          - Fair Truckle (1)
          - Falls of Clyde
            - Florin (1)
          - Petition (1)
            - Petingo (1)
              - Pitcairn
                - Ela-Mana-Mou (1)
          - The Solicitor II
            - The Pie King (2)
        - Full Sail (1)
          - Espadin (1)
          - Seductor
            - Casanova (1)
            - Sideral (2)
              - Sensitivo (6)
        - Honeyway
          - Great Nephew (1)
            - Grundy
              - Kirtling (2)
        - Kingsway II (6)
          - Royal Vale (1)
        - Meadow
          - Mironton (2)
          - Quibu (4)
        - Palestine (2)
          - Pall Mall
            - Reform (1)
            - Sallust (1)
        - Piping Rock (1)
        - Shifting Sands II (1)
        - Solferino
          - Solonaway (1)
        - The Yuvaraj (2)
          - Tatan (3)
      - Manna
        - Colombo
          - British Empire (1)
            - Endeavor II (19)
              - Pretense (6)
                - Sham (2)
              - Porterhouse (4)
                - Farewell Party (1)
              - Prove It (2)
          - Claro (1)
          - Domingo (4)
      - Parwix
        - Michel (2)
      - Pharis
        - Ardan (2)
        - Pardal (3)
          - Eudaemon (1)
          - Firestreak (2)
            - Hot Foot
              - Hot Grove (1)
          - Parbury (1)
        - Phidias
          - Pretexto (1)
        - Priam II (6)
        - Scratch
          - Scelto (3)
            - Repicado II (2)

- **CYLLENE**
  - ***Polymelus***
    - ***Phalaris***
      - Pharamond II (12)
        - By Jimminy (3)
        - Cosmic Bomb (3)
        - King Cole (1)
          - Assemblyman (1)
        - Menow (18)
          - Tom Fool (39)
            - Buckpasser (26)
              - Beau Buck (1)
              - Buckaroo (11)
                - Montbrook (2)
                - Spend A Buck (2)
              - Buckfinder (4)
              - Bucksplasher (2)
              - Coulee Man (1)
              - Egg Toss (1)
              - Norcliffe (5)
                - At the Threshold (2)
                - Groovy (1)
              - Pass the Glass (2)
              - Silver Buck (8)
              - State Dinner (3)
            - Jester (7)
              - Reflected Glory (10)
              - Tri Jet (5)
            - Menace (1)
            - Tim Tam (7)
            - Tompion (4)
        - Easy Mon (5)
          - Phar Mon (1)
      - ***Pharos***
        - Ambrose Light (1)
        - Fastnet
          - Fast Fox (2)
            - Wolfram (1)
        - Lighthouse II (1)
        - Rhodes Scholar (1)
        - ***Nearco (3)***
          - Amerigo (19)
            - Terrible Tiger (1)
          - Dante
            - Toulouse Lautrec (1)
              - Claim Staker (1)
              - Utrillo II (3)
                - Hawaii (5)
          - Krakatao
            - Crazy Kid (2)
          - Mossborough (1)
            - Ballymoss (1)
            - Cavan (4)
          - Rustom Sirdar (2)
          - What's Ahead
            - Sharivari (1)
          - White Horses
            - Top Gallant II (1)

- **CYLLENE**
  - ***Polymelus***
    - ***Phalaris***
      - ***Pharos***
        - ***Nearco***
          - Royal Charger (35)
            - All Hands (1)
              - Pass Catcher (2)
            - Bit of Ireland (1)
            - Francis S. (4)
            - Knight's Romance
              - Commanding II (1)
            - Mongo (2)
            - Rainy Lake (4)
            - Royal Dorimar (1)
            - Royal Orbit (6)
            - Royal Serenade (4)
            - Seaneen (3)
            - Turn-to (21)
              - Best Turn (7)
                - Cox's Ridge (23)
                  - Little Missouri (3)
                  - Out of Place (1)
                  - Sultry Song (1)
              - Cyane (10)
                - Smarten (2)
              - First Landing (15)
                - Riva Ridge (4)
                - Solo Landing (1)
              - Hail to Reason (44)
                - Bold Reason (3)
                - Hail the Pirates (4)
                - Halo (26)
                  - Devil's Bag (9)
                    - Devil His Due (1)
                    - Diablo (1)
                  - Halo's Image (1)
                  - Jolie's Halo (3)
                  - Lively One (1)
                  - Saint Ballado (7)
                  - Southern Halo (2)
                  - Sunny's Halo (6)
                - Mr. Leader (12)
                - Proud Clarion (5)
                  - Proud Birdie (2)
                - Roberto (12)
                  - Darby Creek Road (1)
                  - Dynaformer (9)
                  - Kris S. (22)
                    - Brocco (2)
                    - You and I (5)
                  - Lear Fan (9)
                  - Pirateer (1)
                  - Red Ransom (3)
                  - Roman Diplomat (3)
                  - Silver Hawk (11)
                  - Sunshine Forever (1)
                - Stop the Music (17)
                  - Cure the Blues (6)
                    - Take Me Out (1)
                  - Temperence Hill (4)
                - Turn to Reason (1)
              - Sir Gaylord (7)
                - Drone (6)
                  - Flip Sal (1)
                - Habitat (6)
                  - Habitony (12)
                - Lord Gaylord (3)
                  - Lord Avie (3)
                - Sir Ivor (18)
                  - Bates Motel (1)
                  - Malinowski (1)
                  - Sir Wimborne (1)

- **CYLLENE**
  - ***Polymelus***
    - ***Phalaris***
      - ***Pharos***
        - ***Nearco***
          - ***Nasrullah (84)***
            - Amarullah (2)
            - Curragh King
              - Olympiad King (2)
            - Fair Ruler (8)
            - Fleet Nasrullah (13)
              - Coursing (2)
              - Don B. (3)
                - To B. or Not (1)
              - Fleet Allied (1)
              - Gummo (21)
                - Flying Paster (6)
                - Golden Act (1)
              - Ready Say Go (1)
            - Flying Fury (1)
            - Grey Sovereign (3)
              - Fortino
                - Caro (14)
                  - Cozzene (11)
                  - Dr. Carter (1)
                  - Kaldoun (2)
                  - Rusticaro (1)
                  - Siberian Express (6)
                    - In Excess (2)
                  - With Approval (2)
              - Sovereign Path
                - Wolver Hollow (2)
              - Sterling Bay (1)
              - Zeddaan
                - Kalamoun
                  - Bikala (1)
                  - Kalaglow (1)
                  - Kenmare
                    - Highest Honor (1)
            - Indian Hemp (9)
              - Bold Hemp
                - Joey Bob (2)
              - Hempen (2)
              - T.V. Lark (17)
                - Brother Machree (1)
                - Quack (3)
                - Romeo (1)
                - T.V. Commercial
                  - It's Freezing (1)
            - Jaipur (1)
              - Indian Emerald (1)
              - Jatullah (1)
              - Mansingh
                - Petong
                  - Petardia (1)
              - Rajab (1)
            - Limelight (1)
            - Nadir (1)
            - Nantallah (14)
              - Bolinas Boy (1)
              - Lt. Stevens (3)
              - Ridan (3)
                - Spanish Riddle (3)
            - Nashua (33)
              - Ambernash (2)
              - Diplomat Way (1)
              - Good Manners
                - Ahmad (9)
                  - Potrillazo (1)
                  - Potrillon (1)
                - Friul
                  - Engrillado (1)
                - Mocito Guapo (1)
              - Groton (1)
                - Well Mannered (1)
              - National (1)
              - Snow Ball (1)
              - Stevward (2)
            - Nashville (3)
            - Nathoo
              - Jaybil (1)

CYLLENE
- ***Polymelus***
  - ***Phalaris***
    - ***Pharos***
      - ***Nearco***
        - ***Nasrullah***
          - Nasram
            - Naskra (17)
              - Nasty and Bold (2)
              - Star de Naskra (6)
                - Carr de Naskra (1)
          - Never Bend (14)
            - Distinctive (3)
            - Drum Fire
              - Knights Choice (2)
            - Iron Ruler (1)
              - Iron Constitution (1)
            - Mill Reef (1)
              - Doyoun (5)
              - Shirley Heights (1)
                - Darshaan (5)
                - Zinaad (1)
            - Never Tabled
              - Smokester (7)
            - Proudest Roman (2)
              - Horatius (1)
            - Riverman (13)
              - Irish River (11)
                - Mashkour (2)
              - Rousillon (2)
            - Torsion (2)
          - Never Say Die (2)
            - Saidam (2)
            - Straight Die (1)
            - Western Sky II (1)
          - Noor (8)
          - On-and-On (6)
          - Our Rulla
            - Orbit Ruler (2)
              - Jaklin Klugman (1)
          - Pied d'Or (1)
          - Princely Gift
            - Faberge
              - Rheingold (1)
          - Red God
            - Blushing Groom (20)
              - Arazi (6)
              - Blushing John (1)
              - Candy Stripes (2)
              - Crystal Glitters (1)
              - Mt. Livermore (16)
              - Nashwan (2)
                - Swain (1)
              - Rahy (22)
              - Rainbow Quest (8)
                - Panoramic (1)
                - Quest for Fame (1)
              - Runaway Groom (6)
                - Cherokee Run (4)
              - Sillery (2)
            - Yellow God
              - Nebbiolo (1)
          - Rego (1)
          - Sir Ruler (2)
          - Spectrum II (1)
          - The Irishman (4)
          - Victory Morn (1)
          - Windsor Ruler (4)

- **CYLLENE**
  - ***Polymelus***
    - ***Phalaris***
      - ***Pharos***
        - ***Nearco***
          - ***Nasrullah***
            - ***Bold Ruler (86)***
              - Atomic (1)
              - Bold and Brave (9)
                - Sweet Candy (1)
              - Bold Bidder (18)
                - Cannonade (4)
                  - Caveat (7)
                - Consultant's Bid (9)
                - Liloy (2)
                - Spectacular Bid (2)
                - Two a Day (1)
              - Bold Combatant (3)
                - Bold Joey (1)
              - Bold Commander (3)
                - Dust Commander (7)
              - Bold Hitter (1)
                - DiMaggio (2)
              - Bold Hour (2)
              - Bold Lad (4)
                - Cyrano de Bergerac (1)
                - Persian Bold (1)
              - Bold Tactics (3)
              - Chieftan (15)
                - Fit to Fight (2)
              - Cornish Prince (7)
                - Lanyon (1)
              - Dewan (4)
                - Dewan Keys (1)
                - Glitterman (4)
              - Envoy (5)
              - Great Sun
                - Hawkin's Special (2)
              - Herculean (2)
              - Irish Castle (4)
                - Bold Forbes (4)
                  - Air Forbes Won (7)
                - Irish Tower (1)
              - Irish Ruler (1)
              - Jacinto (7)
              - Key to the Kingdom (5)
              - Plum Bold (1)
              - Raja Baba (12)
                - Far Out East (1)
                - Is It True (1)
                - Royal Ski (2)
                - Well Decorated (1)
                  - Notebook (7)
              - Reviewer (8)
                - Surreal (1)
              - Secretariat (24)
                - Cinco Grande (3)
                - Cold Reception
                  - Cool Joe (1)
                - D'Accord (1)
                - General Assembly (1)
                - Pancho Villa (1)
                - Risen Star (1)
              - Staunchness (1)
              - The Irish Lord (1)
              - Top Command (7)
              - Tyrant (1)
              - Vitriolic (3)
              - What a Pleasure (20)
                - Foolish Pleasure (5)
                  - Marfa (4)
                    - Farma Way
                      - Cobra King (1)
                  - Maudlin (9)
                - For the Moment (1)
                - Honest Pleasure (4)
                - Princely Pleasure (1)
              - What Luck (3)

CYLLENE
- ***Polymelus***
  - ***Phalaris***
    - ***Pharos***
      - ***Nearco***
        - ***Nasrullah***
          - ***Bold Ruler***
            - Boldnesian (5)
              - Bold Reasoning (8)
                - Super Concorde (1)
                  - Aaron's Concorde (1)
                - Seattle Slew (58)
                  - A.P. Indy (24)
                    - Pulpit (3)
                  - Avenue of Flags (2)
                  - Capote (4)
                  - General Meeting (9)
                  - Gold Legend (2)
                  - Gold Meridian (1)
                  - Metfield (2)
                  - Seattle Song (1)
                  - Septieme Ciel (1)
                  - Slewacide (1)
                  - Slew City Slew (1)
                  - Slew O' Gold (14)
                  - Slewpy (1)
                  - Slewvescent (5)
                  - Tsunami Slew (1)
              - Bold Ruckus (3)
              - Wing Out (1)

- **CYLLENE**
  - ***Polymelus***
    - ***Phalaris***
      - ***Pharos***
        - ***Nearco***
          - ***Nearctic (6)***
            - ***Northern Dancer (18)***
              - Barachois (1)
              - Be My Guest (3)
                - Assert (3)
              - Dance Spell (2)
              - Danzatore (1)
              - Danzig (47)
                - Ascot Knight (2)
                - Belong to Me (6)
                - Chief's Crown (6)
                  - Be My Chief (2)
                - Danehill (3)
                - Deerhound (2)
                - Eagle Eyed (1)
                - Emperor Jones (2)
                - Green Desert (5)
                - Honor Grades (3)
                - Langfuhr (2)
                - Lure (1)
                - Ole (1)
                - Pine Bluff (2)
                - Polish Navy (4)
                  - Sea Hero (2)
                - Polish Numbers (1)
                - Polish Precedent (1)
              - Dixieland Band (6)
                - Citidancer (3)
                - Dixieland Brass (1)
                - Dixieland Heat (1)
              - El Gran Senor (5)
              - Far North (3)
              - Fire Dancer (1)
              - Hero's Honor (2)
              - Local Talent (1)
              - Lyphard (20)
                - Al Nasr (3)
                - Alzao (2)
                - Dahar (2)
                - Lyphard's Special (1)
                - Lyphard's Wish (1)
                - Lypheor (6)
                - Manila (5)
                  - Bien Bien (3)
                - Monteverdi (1)
                - Sicyos (1)
              - Magesterial (2)
              - Night Shift (3)
              - Nijinsky II (28)
                - Baldski (3)
                - Caerleon (6)
                - Caucasus (1)
                - Czaravich (2)
                - Dancing Czar (1)
                - Encino (1)
                - Ferdinand (1)
                - Gallantsky (1)
                - Green Dancer (7)
                - Hostage (1)
                - Ile de Bourbon (2)
                - Manzotti (1)
                - Moscow Ballet (3)
                - Niniski
                  - Hernando (2)
                  - Lomitas (1)
                - Royal Academy (1)
                - Seattle Dancer (2)
                - Shadeed (2)
                  - Alydeed (1)
                - Sportin' Life (5)
                - Sword Dance (4)
                - Whiskey Road
                  - Strawberry Road II (15)
              - Northerly (2)
              - Northern Answer (1)
                - Greek Answer (1)

CYLLENE
- ***Polymelus***
  - ***Phalaris***
    - ***Pharos***
      - ***Nearco***
        - ***Nearctic***
          - ***Northern Dancer***
            - Northern Baby (10)
              - Bairn (1)
            - Northern Flagship (1)
            - Northern Fling (4)
            - Northern Jove (5)
            - Northfields
              - Northjet (2)
            - Nureyev (18)
              - Polar Falcon
                - Pivotal (4)
              - Robin des Bois (5)
              - Theatrical (18)
                - Mendocino (2)
              - Zarbyev (1)
            - One For All (3)
            - Orbit Dancer (1)
            - Pas Seul (1)
            - Sadler's Wells (14)
              - El Prado (5)
              - In the Wings (1)
            - Somethingfabulous (2)
            - Sovereign Dancer (8)
              - Din's Dancer (2)
            - Staff Writer (5)
            - Storm Bird (8)
              - Bluebird (1)
              - Storm Cat (36)
                - Delineator (1)
                - Forest Wildcat (2)
                - Harlan (5)
                - Hennessy (2)
                - Mountain Cat (1)
                - Storm Creek (1)
                - Tabasco Cat (4)
                - Tale of the Cat (2)
              - Summer Squall (6)
            - Sunny North (1)
            - The Minstrel (4)
              - Opening Verse (1)
              - Palace Music (11)
            - Topsider (5)
              - Salse (1)
            - Try My Best (1)
            - Unfuwain (1)
            - Vice Regent (6)
              - Deputy Minister (37)
                - Awesome Again (3)
                - Dehere (6)
                - Deputy Commander (2)
                - French Deputy (4)
                - Salt Lake (1)
                - Service Stripe (1)
                - Silver Deputy (6)
                - Touch Gold (2)
          - Briarctic (1)
          - Explodent (11)
            - Explosive Bid (1)
          - Icecapade (3)
            - Clever Trick
              - Phone Trick (7)
                - Pick Up the Phone (1)
            - Wild Again (15)
              - Wild Rush (1)

- **CYLLENE**
  - ***Polymelus***
    - ***Phalaris***
      - ***Sickle (1)***
        - Bless Me (1)
        - Cravat (1)
        - Reaping Reward (10)
          - Eternal Reward (1)
        - Sickletoy (3)
        - Star Pilot (1)
        - ***Unbreakable (8)***
          - Polly's Jet (1)
          - ***Polynesian (22)***
            - Barbizon (3)
            - Imbros (8)
            - ***Native Dancer (11)***
              - Atan
                - Sharpen Up (2)
                  - Diesis (4)
                    - Elmaamul (1)
                  - Keen (3)
                  - Kris (1)
                    - Common Grounds (1)
                  - Selkirk (2)
                  - Trempolino (1)
              - Dancer's Image (1)
              - Dancing Dervish (1)
              - Dan Cupid
                - Sea-Bird (5)
                  - Arctic Tern
                    - Bering (1)
                  - Little Current (2)
                  - Mr. Long (1)
              - Gaelic Dancer (1)
              - Grand Revival (1)
              - Iron Warrior
                - Degenerate Jon (1)
              - Jig Time (2)
                - Darn That Alarm (9)
              - Native Charger (16)
                - Dreaming Native (1)
                - High Echelon (2)
              - Protanto (1)
              - ***Raise a Native (24)***
                - Alydar (49)
                  - Criminal Type (1)
                  - Easy Goer (8)
                  - Saratoga Six (1)
                  - Turkoman (2)
                - Elevation (1)
                - Exclusive Native (36)
                  - Affirmed (18)
                  - Ecliptical (1)
                  - Our Native (8)
                  - Roi Normand (7)
                  - Sabona (1)
                  - Valdez (3)
                - Highland Park (1)
                - Lines of Power (1)
                - Majestic Prince (12)
                  - Coastal (1)
                  - Eternal Prince (3)
                  - Majestic Light (21)
                    - Simply Majestic (1)
                    - Wavering Monarch (2)
                      - Maria's Mon (2)
                  - Majestic Venture (1)
                - Native Royalty (2)
                  - Ruthie's Native (2)
                - Raise a Cup (2)
                - Raised Socially (1)
                - Red Ryder (1)
                - Search for Gold (2)
              - Restless Native (3)
              - Villamor (1)

CYLLENE
- ***Polymelus***
  - ***Phalaris***
    - ***Sickle***
      - ***Unbreakable***
        - ***Polynesian***
          - ***Native Dancer***
            - ***Raise a Native***
              - Mr. Prospector (73)
                - Afleet (3)
                - Allen's Prospect (1)
                - Carson City (7)
                  - Lord Carson (1)
                - Conquistador Cielo (6)
                  - Marquetry (6)
                  - Mi Cielo (1)
                  - Wagon Limit (1)
                - Crafty Prospector (1)
                  - Prospectors Gamble (1)
                - Damister
                  - Celtic Swing (1)
                - Distant View (4)
                - Distinctive Pro (2)
                - Fappiano (21)
                  - Cryptoclearance (9)
                    - Ride the Rails (1)
                  - Phone Order (1)
                  - Quiet American (9)
                  - Roy (1)
                  - Rubiano (1)
                  - Signal Tap (1)
                  - Unbridled (24)
                    - Grindstone (1)
                    - Unbridled's Song (5)
                - Forty Niner (14)
                  - Coronado's Quest (1)
                  - Distorted Humor (3)
                  - End Sweep (4)
                  - Jules (2)
                  - Luhuk (1)
                  - Rich Man's Gold (3)
                  - Tactical Advantage (1)
                - Gold Alert (1)
                - Gone West (15)
                  - Grand Slam (1995) (2)
                  - Mr. Greeley (4)
                - Gulch (8)
                  - Thunder Gulch (10)
                - Homebuilder (1)
                - Hussonet (1)
                - Jade Hunter (14)
                - Kingmambo (9)
                - Lode (2)
                - Machiavellian (3)
                - Miswaki (5)
                  - Black Tie Affair (5)
                - Mogambo (1)
                - Naevus (3)
                - Native Prospector (1)
                - Our Emblem (4)
                - Prospector's Music (1)
                - Seeking the Gold (19)
                  - Cape Town (2)
                  - Mutakddim (1)
                  - Petionville (2)
                - Silver Ghost (4)
                - Tank's Prospect (2)
                - Two Punch (4)
                - Woodman (10)
                  - Hansel (1)

- **BAYARDO**
  - ***Gainsborough***
    - Bobsleigh
      - Moonlight Run (1)
    - Emborough
      - Bernborough (8)
        - Berseem (2)
    - ***Hyperion***
      - Alibhai (57)
        - Cover Up (3)
        - Dark Hawk (4)
          - George Royal (1)
        - Determine (7)
          - Decidedly (2)
          - Determined Man (1)
          - Donut King (1)
            - Cool Hand (1)
          - Warfare (4)
            - Assagai (5)
        - Graphic (1)
        - Landing (1)
        - Leisure Time (1)
        - Mr. Mustard (1)
        - My Host (3)
          - Fleet Host (1)
          - My Lark (1)
        - On Trust (2)
        - Traffic Judge (8)
          - Court Ruling (1)
          - Delta Judge (12)
            - Delta Oil (1)
          - Traffic Cop (2)
          - Traffic Mark (1)
        - Your Alibhai (1)
        - Your Host (30)
          - Social Climber (1)
          - Windy Sands (16)
      - Aristophanes
        - Atlas
          - Gran Atleta (3)
        - Forli (26)
          - Forceten (3)
          - Intrepid Hero (5)
          - Thatch
            - Thatching (1)
      - Aureole
        - Vienna
          - Vaguely Noble (24)
            - Family Crest (1)
            - Semenenko (1)
      - Coastal Traffic (1)
        - Buisson d'Or (2)
      - Gulf Stream
        - Mamboreta (2)
        - Montparnasse II (3)
      - Gun Shot (11)
        - Gun Bow (1)
      - Half Crown (6)
        - Money Broker (1)
      - Heliopolis (66)
        - Ace Admiral (1)
        - Charlie McAdam (1)
        - Greek Ship (3)
        - Greek Song (8)
          - First Balcony (3)
        - Helioscope (2)
        - Noble Hero (1)
        - Olympia (25)
          - Creme dela Creme (2)
            - Rich Cream (7)
          - Decathlon (2)
            - Slipped Disc (2)
          - I'm For More (1)
          - Lucky Mel (1)
            - Lucky Mike (1)
          - Pia Star (3)
        - Summer Tan (5)
          - B. Major (1)
          - Jig Dancer (1)
      - Helios
        - Beau Gem (1)

- **BAYARDO**
  - ***Gainsborough***
    - Solario
      - Dastur
        - Dhoti
          - Royal Gem II (3)
              - Dark Star (6)
      - Mid-day
        - Scottish Meridian (1)

- **BAYARDO**
  - ***Gainsborough***
    - ***Hyperion***
      - Hesiod (1)
      - High Hat
        - High Line
          - Master Willie (1)
        - White Gloves II (1)
      - His Highness
        - Arkansas II (1)
      - Hypnotist II (2)
      - Khaled (39)
        - Binary (2)
        - California Kid (1)
        - Correspondent (4)
        - El Drag (4)
        - Hillary (11)
        - New Policy (1)
        - Prince Khaled (3)
        - Semi-Pro (1)
        - Swaps (15)
          - Chateaugay (4)
          - No Robbery (5)
        - Terrang (5)
        - Wallet Lifter (3)
      - Oceanus II (1)
      - Orbit II (1)
      - Owen Tudor (3)
        - Etonian (1)
        - Poaching (1)
        - Rasper II
          - Rambunctious (2)
            - Rollicking (1)
          - Rock Talk (1)
        - Right Royal
          - Golden Eagle II (3)
          - Ruysdael II (2)
        - Tudor Castle (1)
        - Tudor Era
          - Tudor Way (1)
        - Tudor Minstrel (11)
          - King of the Tudors (2)
            - Golden Ruler (1)
              - Hard Work
                - Mo Exception (1)
          - Poona II (2)
          - Sing Sing
            - African Sky (2)
            - Mummy's Pet
              - Mummy's Game (2)
          - Tudor Grey (3)
          - Tudor Melody
            - Welsh Pageant (2)
              - Welsh Chanter (1)
        - Welsh Abbot
          - Abernant
            - Prince de Galles (6)
      - Pensive (9)
        - Ponder (7)
          - Hillsborough (1)
          - Needles (1)
        - Rockefella (1)
          - Rocky Royale (1)
      - Stardust (1)
        - Moondust II (2)
        - Nahar II (1)
        - Stalino
          - Dumpty Humpty (2)
        - Star Kingdom
          - Noholme II (12)
            - Fools Holme (1)
            - Hey Good Lookin
              - That's a Nice (1)
            - Medieval Man (1)
            - Nodouble (7)
              - Overskate (1)
            - Shecky Greene (1)
          - Sky High II (3)
        - Stunning (2)
      - Zenith (1)

ISINGLASS

- John o' Gaunt
  - Swynford
    - Blandford
      - Bahram (4)
        - Big Game (1)
        - Persian Gulf
          - Abadan (1)
          - Idle Hour (1)
          - Persian Road II (5)
          - Tiger II (1)
        - Sun Bahram (1)
      - Blenheim II (18)
        - Battle Morn (4)
        - Bryan G. (8)
        - Donatello II (1)
          - Alycidon
            - Alcibiades II (2)
            - All Serene
              - Ben Lomond (3)
            - Lacydon
              - Cipayo (2)
          - Crepello
            - Busted (6)
              - Erins Isle (1)
            - Minera II (2)
        - Free America (7)
        - Gallant Duke (1)
        - Jet Pilot (9)
          - Jet Action (1)
          - Jet Jewel (5)
            - Pollux (1)
        - Mahmoud (47)
          - Afghan II (1)
          - Billings (3)
          - Cohoes (7)
            - Quadrangle (18)
              - Quadratic (1)
          - Flushing II (4)
          - Mount Marcy (1)
          - Mr. Trouble (2)
          - Oil Capitol (1)
          - The Axe II (14)
            - Al Hattab (2)
            - Executioner (1)
            - Hatchet Man (2)
          - The Sultan (1)
        - Mirza II (1)
        - Thumbs Up (1)
      - Brantome
        - Abbe Pierre (1)
        - Whirlaway (8)
        - Wyndham (1)
          - Windy City II (9)
            - City Line (1)
            - Restless Wind (4)
            - Windy Sea (3)
        - Vieux Manoir
          - Val de Loir
            - Val de L'Orne (1)
      - His Grace
        - His Nickel (2)
      - Isolater (2)
      - Midstream (2)
        - Shannon II (6)
          - Clem (2)
    - Challenger II (11)
      - Challedon (13)
      - Challenge Me (1)
      - Errard (8)
    - Royal Ford
      - Heelfly (2)
    - St. Germans
      - Bold Venture (16)
        - Middleground (4)
      - Devil Diver (8)
      - The Rhymer (5)
        - Vertex (19)
          - Lucky Debonair (3)
          - Vertee (1)

- **DOMINO**
  - Commando
    - Colin
      - Neddie (2)
        - Good Goods
          - Alsab (9)
            - Armageddon (2)
              - Battle Joined (6)
                - Ack Ack (17)
                  - Broad Brush (10)
                  - Truce Maker (1)
      - On Watch
        - Brazado (1)
          - Curandero (1)
        - Tick On
          - Watchmitick (1)
    - Peter Pan
      - Black Toney
        - Balladier (8)
          - Decorated (1)
          - Double Jay (27)
            - Bagdad (15)
              - Fiddle Isle (1)
              - Old Bag (3)
              - Tarboosh (1)
            - Honey Jay (1)
            - Rose Argent (1)
            - Spring Double (1)
          - Ky. Colonel (2)
            - Terra Firma (1)
          - Mr. Music (4)
          - Papa Redbird (3)
          - Spy Song (12)
            - Crimson Satan (3)
            - Royal Note (2)
        - Bimelech (17)
          - Better Self (2)
          - Brookfield (3)
          - Hilarious (4)
            - Fast Hilarious (1)
        - Black Servant
          - Black Forest (1)
          - Blue Larkspur (21)
            - Bleu d'Or (1)
            - Blue Flyer (1)
            - Blue Gay (1)
            - Blue Swords (7)
            - Boxthorn (1)
            - Crowfoot (4)
            - King's Blue (1)
            - Revoked (11)
              - Rejected (3)
              - Reneged
                - Mr. Randy (1)
        - Brokers Tip
          - Market Wise (8)
            - To Market (11)
              - Hurry to Market (2)
      - Pennant
        - Equipoise
          - Attention (5)
          - Carrier Pigeon (1)
          - Equestrian (11)
            - Stymie (5)
          - Equifox (2)
          - Shut Out (21)
          - Swing and Sway
            - Saggy (16)
              - Carry Back (4)
      - Peter Hastings
        - Petrose (6)
    - Ultimus
      - High Cloud
        - Hollyrood (1)
      - High Time
        - High Strung (1)
        - Mirafel
          - Little Beans (3)
        - Zacaweista (2)

- **PRINCE PALATIN**
  - Rose Prince
    - Prince Rose
      - Pappageno II
        - Pappa Fourway (3)
      - Prince Bio
        - Prince Taj (2)
          - Petrone (3)
          - Ramsinga (2)
        - Sicambre (2)
          - Cambremont (1)
          - Iron Duke (1)
          - Roi Dagobert (2)
            - On the Sly (4)
              - Play Fellow (3)
            - Wittgenstein (2)
          - Shantung
            - Felicio
              - Itajara (2)
                - Siphon (3)
      - Prince Chevalier
        - Arctic Prince (4)
          - Arctic Explorer
            - Tobin Bronze (3)
          - Snow Cat (2)
        - Charlottesville
          - Carlemont (3)
        - Doutelle
          - Pretendre (2)
        - Pampered King II (4)
      - Princequillo (80)
        - Blue Prince (9)
          - Prince Tenderfoot (1)
            - Faliraki (3)
        - Charlevoix (1)
        - Dedicate (5)
        - Go Marching
          - Brinkmanship (1)
        - Hill Prince (16)
          - Royal Union (1)
        - Misty Flight (2)
        - Prince Blessed
          - Ole Bob Bowers (19)
        - Prince John (18)
          - High Tribute (2)
          - Mandate (1)
          - Rash Prince (1)
            - Berkley Prince (1)
          - Selari (3)
          - Silent Screen (2)
            - Nostalgia (1)
          - Speak John (12)
            - Hold Your Peace (5)
              - Meadowlake (8)
            - Thunder Puddles (2)
            - Verbatim (14)
              - Summing (2)
          - Stage Door Johnny (16)
          - Transworld (1)
        - Round Table (36)
          - Advocator (8)
          - Apalachee (6)
          - King's Bishop (4)
          - Knightly Manner (2)
            - Stonewalk (1)
          - Poker (2)
          - Table Run (2)
          - Targowice (3)
          - Tell (3)
          - Upper Case (1)
        - Tambourine (1)
        - Third Brother (7)
        - Tipoquill (1)

AUSTRALIAN

- Hastings
  - Fair Play
    - Catalan (1)
    - Chance Play (2)
      - Grand Slam (1933) (2)
        - Piet (1)
      - Psychic Bid (1)
      - Some Chance (4)
        - Cornwall
          - Towson (1)
        - Primate
          - Near Man (1)
    - Chance Shot (1)
      - Brevity (1)
    - Display
      - Discovery (20)
    - Man o' War
      - Battleship (1)
      - Fairy Manhurst (4)
        - Come On Red (1)
      - Hard Tack
        - Stronghold (1)
      - War Admiral (26)
        - Mr. Busher (1)
        - The Battler (2)
      - War Glory (1)
      - War Jeep (4)
      - War Relic (15)
        - Battlefield (3)
          - Yorktown (2)
        - Intent (5)
          - Intentionally (13)
            - In Reality (22)
              - Believe It (4)
              - Judge Smells (1)
              - Known Fact (1)
              - Relaunch (15)
                - Cee's Tizzy (8)
                - Honour and Glory (1)
                - Skywalker (5)
                  - Bertrando (2)
                - Waquoit (2)
              - Taylor's Falls (1)
              - Valid Appeal (6)
                - Kipper Kelly (1)
                - Valid Wager (1)
            - Tentam (5)
              - Cool Victor (1)
            - Terresto (1)
        - Missile (2)
        - Relic (3)
          - Mincio (1)
          - O'Grady (1)
          - Olden Times (6)
            - Full Pocket (1)
            - Tilt Up (1)
    - My Play
      - Head Play (3)

KING JAMES

- Spur
  - Sting
    - Questionnaire (11)
      - Alquest (2)
      - Free For All (1)
        - Rough'n Tumble (23)
          - Dr. Fager (9)
            - Doc Sylvester (1)
            - Practitioner (1)
          - Gunflint (2)
          - Minnesota Mac (5)
            - Great Above (8)
              - Holy Bull (2)
      - Hash (4)
        - Mel Hash
          - Guilo Cesere (1)
        - Salmagundi (1)
      - Requested (15)
      - Wine List (1)

BAY RONALD

- Dark Ronald
  - Ambassador IV
    - Peanuts (1)
      - Top Row (2)
  - Dark Legend
    - Easton (2)
  - Prunus
    - Oleander
      - Asterios
        - Waidmannshell (1)
      - Pink Flower (1)
    - St. James
      - Jamestown (1)
        - Johnstown (2)
        - Natchez (3)
  - Son-in-Law
    - Beau Pere (21)
      - Eiffel Tower (2)
      - Gold Note (1)
      - Great Circle (1)
      - Speak Up (1)
    - Bosworth
      - Boswell (7)
        - Cochise (2)
      - Plassy
        - Vandale (2)
          - Herbager (30)
            - Big Spruce (11)
            - Grey Dawn II (24)
              - Mr. Redoy (1)
              - Swing Till Dawn (3)
              - Vigors (4)
            - Sea Hawk II (3)
            - The Pruner (2)
          - Tapioca (1)
    - Diadochos
      - Comico (1)
    - Epigram
      - Souepi (2)
    - Foxlaw
      - Foxhunter
        - Again II (5)
        - Foxglove (4)
        - Hunter's Moon IV (2)
    - Rustom Pasha
      - Moslem
        - Petare (6)
          - Subpet (1)
      - Partab (1)

AMPHION

- Sundridge
  - Sun Briar
    - Firethorn (1)
    - Pompey (3)
  - Sunreigh
    - Reigh Count (4)
      - Count Fleet (42)
        - Auditing (4)
        - Beau Gar (12)
          - Handsome Boy (1)
          - Water Prince (1)
        - Counterpoint (9)
          - Dotted Swiss (1)
        - Count Flame (2)
        - Count of Honor (1)
        - Count Turf (2)
        - County Delight (3)
        - One Count (4)
      - Count Speed (3)
      - Triplicate
        - Better Bee (4)
  - Sunstar
    - Alan Breck
      - Tresiete
        - Rolando (4)
    - Craig an Eran
      - Admiral Drake (1)

CAVALIERE D'ARPINO

- Bellini
  - Tenerani
    - Bonnard (2)
    - Ribot (15)
      - Arts and Letters (10)
        - Codex (8)
          - Lost Code (2)
      - Con Brio (2)
      - Graustark (28)
        - Avatar (1)
        - Grenfall (1)
        - Groshawk (1)
        - Key to the Mint (18)
          - Java Gold (2)
          - Sauce Boat (1)
        - Menocal (1)
        - Proud Truth (1)
        - Prove Out (1)
      - His Majesty (24)
        - Batonnier (2)
        - Cormorant (4)
          - Go for Gin (3)
        - Mehmet (2)
        - Pleasant Colony (26)
          - Colony Light (1)
          - Pleasant Tap (3)
          - St. Jovite (1)
      - Maribeau (3)
      - Prince Royal II (4)
        - Unconscious (2)
      - Ribocco (1)
      - Sir Ribot (1)
      - Tom Rolfe (26)
        - Hoist the Flag (14)
          - Aferd (1)
          - Alleged (5)
            - Law Society (1)
            - Legal Case (1)
          - Blue Ensign (2)
          - Hoist the Silver (2)
          - Oh Say (1)
          - Pirate's Bounty (3)
          - Stalwart (2)
          - Zoning (1)
        - London Company (2)
        - Run the Gantlet (5)
    - Sculptor (1)

PRINCE CHIMAY

- Vatout
  - Bois Roussel
    - Gusty
      - Madison (4)
    - Migoli (6)
      - Gallant Man (24)
        - Draft Card (1)
        - Gallant Romeo (7)
          - Elocutionist (1)
        - My Gallant (1)
        - Nalees Man (2)
      - Grounded II (3)
    - Tehran (4)
      - Cyrus the Great (1)
      - Tale of Two Cities (10)
        - Cougar II (5)
      - Tulyar (5)

ROI HERODE

- The Tetrarch
  - Salmon-Trout
    - King Salmon
      - King's Abbey (3)
  - Stefan the Great
    - Jean Valjean (1)
      - Side Boy (1)
  - Tetratema
    - Royal Minstrel (1)
      - First Fiddle (1)

BRULEUR
- Ksar
  - Tourbillon
    - Ambiorix (24)
      - Ambehaving (4)
      - Ambiopoise (5)
        - Faraway Son (6)
      - Count Amber (2)
      - Sheet Anchor
        - Mountdrago (1)
    - Coaraze
      - Canthare (1)
    - Djebel
      - Argur (2)
      - Djeddah (2)
      - Hugh Lupus
        - Hethersett (1)
      - Le Lavandou
        - Le Levanstell (3)
      - My Babu (10)
        - Crozier (10)
          - Inverness Drive (2)
        - Perambulator (1)
      - Targui (2)
    - Goya II (6)
      - Nirgal (4)
        - Li'l Fella (2)
    - Meridien
      - Medium (1)
    - Timor
      - Pronto (2)
        - Balconaje (1)
    - Tornado
      - Fontenay
        - Saim (1)

BRAMBLE
- Ben Brush
  - Broomstick
    - Cudgel
      - Milkman (2)
    - Halcyon (1)
  - Sweep
    - Eternal
      - Ariel (3)
        - Arigotal (2)
    - Sweep All (2)
    - The Porter (1)
      - Alorter
        - Aneroid
          - Take Away (7)
            - Hillsdale (1)
      - Haital (4)
      - Heather Broom (3)
      - Islam (1)
      - Rosemont (16)
        - Thinking Cap (4)
    - Whisk Broom II
      - Diavolo
        - Drawby (1)
      - John P. Grier
        - Boojum (2)
          - Burg-El-Arab (2)
          - Snark (2)
        - Jack High (4)
          - Knave High (1)
          - With Regards (1)
        - Victorian
        - He Did (8)

CLARION
- Klarion
  - Lorenzaccio
    - Ahonoora
      - Indian Ridge (2)
  - Luthier
    - Sagace (1)

SAINFOIN
- Rock Sand
  - Friar Rock
    - Pilate (12)
      - Eight Thirty (26)
        - Anyoldtime (1)
        - Bolero (3)
          - Our Michael (1)
          - Wig Out (2)
        - Condiment (2)
        - Royal Coinage (4)
        - Sailor (10)
          - Ahoy (1)
      - Lovely Night (1)
      - Phalanx (10)
      - Platter (2)
  - Trap Rock
    - Lucillite
      - Only One (2)

MARCOVIL
- Hurry On
  - Call Boy
    - Trace Call (2)
  - Coronach
    - Niccolo Dell'Arca
      - Daumier (1)
  - Precipitation
    - Chamossaire
      - Santa Claus
        - Bonne Noel (1)
    - Sheshoon
      - Sassafras (1)
        - Baynoun (5)
        - Saros (3)
    - Supreme Court
      - Cadmus (1)

BONA VISTA
- Copyright
  - Congreve
    - Brick (2)
    - Churrinche
      - Los Curros (3)
    - Embrujo
      - Nigromante (10)
        - Candy Spots (2)
        - Specialmante (4)
      - Nilad
        - Venturon (1)
    - Saint Patrick (3)
      - Rico Monte (4)

ST. SIMONS
- Rabelais
  - Durbar II
    - Scaramouche
      - Pantalon (2)
  - Rialto
    - Wild Risk (1)
      - Le Fabuleux (3)
        - Effervescing (1)
        - Trevieres (4)
      - Worden II (1)

WALDMEISTER
- Macar
  - Caduto
    - Jolly Quick (1)

ALCANTARA II
- Kantar
  - Victrix
    - Avenger II (1)
- Pinceau
  - Verso II
    - Le Tyrol (1)

BISCAY
- Zephyr Bay
  - Broad Reach
    - Yachtie (3)

BLACKSTOCK
- Mentor
  - Wise Counsellor
    - Deliberator (1)

CAMPFIRE
- Big Blaze
  - Burning Blaze
    - Burning Star (1)

CRAGANOUR
- Tanner
  - Parlinchin
    - Poster (1)

DEIRI
- Bey
  - Beigler Bay
    - Matun (2)
      - Mat Boy (3)

FINE ART
- Fine Top
  - Sanctus
    - Dictus (2)

HANNIBAL
- Fels
  - Laland
    - Mio d'Arezzo (1)

MARCH PAST
- Queen's Hussar
  - Brigadier Gerard
    - General (2)
      - Lord at War (3)

OLASCOAGA
- El Tango
  - Isabelino
    - Salerno (3)

ORBY
- Sir Cosmo
  - Panorama
    - Bazooka (1)
    - Sullivan (1)
    - Whistler
      - Gentle Art (1)

PERTH
- Faucher
  - Nid d'Or
    - Brown King (5)

TRACERY
- Abbots Trace
  - Marconigram
    - Reading II (1)

TREDENNIS
- Bachelor's Double
  - Argosy
    - Happy Argo (2)

Photo courtesy of Santa Anita Park

No foreign bred has compiled a better record in major North American races since World War II than Cougar II. Bred in Chile, Cougar II captured 10 victories and finished in the money on 27 occasions in major North American stakes, yet hasn't been selected for thoroughbred racing's Hall of Fame.

Birthplaces

X: Birthplaces

Blue-Chip Stock in Blue Grass

Perhaps it's the weather, far cooler in April and milder in October than one would expect. Maybe it's the blue grass, the tips of which, according to any native of Kentucky, actually are blue.

"This is the best place in the world for a horse," trainer Tony Basile said after shipping his Bwamazon Farm-owned stable, which included two colts, Highland Park and Freezing Rain, who were preparing for the Kentucky Derby, from a winter in Florida to the Blue Grass State in the spring of 1983.

Photo courtesy of Shadwell Farm

The exquisitely bred Elle Seule (by Exclusive Native out of the Pretense mare Fall Aspen) and her foal, a bay filly by Danzig, graze at Shadwell Farm in Kentucky, the state that produced the winners of more major North American races than any other every year from 1966-2003.

The facts certainly support Basile's claim—and that of a state that proudly featured a horse on its commemorative quarters—that Kentucky is indeed the birthplace of the winners of more major North American races than any other locale.

And while the distance between Kentucky and its nearest rival may not be quite as large a gap as the difference in the lineages of baseball's New York Yankees and Tampa Bay Devil Rays, it's certainly in the ball park.

While countless sources list where today's race horses are bred, that hasn't always been the case. The *Daily Racing Form,* for example, didn't begin listing where horses were bred in its entries or charts until the mid-'60s—unless they were bred outside of North America. When it began doing so, it did so only for those who were foaled in 1963 or later. For instance, 1966 entries and charts listed where two- and three-year-olds were bred, but not those who were four or older. The Jockey Club, which registers all North American thoroughbreds, didn't begin compiling that information until "sometime in the '60s."

So while this treatise can safely claim that 91.98 percent of all major winners in North America in the modern era have been bred on this continent, it may be easier for the average horseplayer to translate *War and Peace* from the original Russian into Chinese than to determine where all of the major winners who were born before 1963 were bred.

But the complete data for the 4,236 major races—and 4,245 winners of those races because of nine dead-heats for first place—held in North America from 1966-2003 demonstrates that Kentucky indeed has been the capital of thoroughbred breeding.

Not only has Kentucky led the list of major victories every year from 1966-2003, but a *majority* of the victories in major races during that 38-year period have been earned by Kentucky-breds on 34 occasions. That includes every campaign from 1980-2003, including a record 81 victories by Kentucky-breds in 1984 (72.32 percent). The fewest number of Kentucky-bred winners in any season came in 1973, when only 46 crossed the wire first, a mere 41.07 percent.

Because 56.44 percent of all major North American races have been won by Kentucky-breds during the past 38 years, the real race is for second, which Florida-breds hold by a comfortable margin with 13.62 percent of the victories during that span. California (6.2 percent), Virginia (4.52), and Maryland (2.92) round out the top five. Florida has finished second to

Kentucky 31 times during that 38-year period, and the 31 victories posted by Florida-breds in 1973 mark the highest total recorded by horses bred in a locale other than Kentucky. California, Virginia, and Ireland each finished second twice and Maryland once during that 38-year span.

Ireland (2.64 percent), Canada (2.07), Argentina (1.98), England (1.91), and France (1.3) not only are the five countries other than the United States that have produced the highest percentages of major winners in North America from 1966-2003, but they rank sixth through 10th among all locales during a period when foreign-breds won 11.33 percent of the major races in North America. Foreign-breds probably are gaining ground, because in the first 20 years of the modern era, thoroughbreds bred outside North America won only 7.79 percent of the major races in North America. Yet it's not possible to state with complete certainty that foreign-breds are gaining ground because the victories for foreign-breds from 1966-2003 include Canada's 2.07 percent of the total, while Canada's total for the first two decades of the modern era is grouped with those of horses bred in the United States.

The performance of Kentucky-breds in the classics and Breeders' Cup has been even more dominant. Kentucky-breds have won 113 of the 174 modern classics (64.94 percent), and 86 of the 146 thoroughbreds who have crossed the wire first in Breeders' Cup races (58.9 percent) since that event began in 1984 have been bred in Kentucky. Florida-breds rank second in the Breeders' Cup with 18 victories and share that distinction with Virginia-breds in the classics, each with 17 triumphs since World War II. Foreign-bred runners have been considerably more successful in the Breeders' Cup (21.23 percent of all winners), led by 13 triumphs by horses bred in Ireland, than in the classics (5.17 percent). Canada's four modern classic victories lead all countries outside the United States and are an indication that the Breeders' Cup—and classics in other countries—obviously are more compelling goals for many owners and trainers with standouts bred in Europe or South America.

The following chart shows states and countries other than the United States in which victorious horses were bred in the 4,236 major races held in North America from 1966-2003. Beside that is a chart that shows the number of victories for horses bred in each country—other than the United States and Canada, which are grouped together as North America—in the 6,461 major races held in North America from 1946-2003. Following those charts are charts that give the same information for the 174 classic races held from 1946-2003 and the 145 Breeders' Cup races staged from 1984-2003.

Victory Standings for Breeding States and Countries In Major North American Races From 1966-2003

1. Kentucky (2,396)
2. Florida (578)
3. California (263)
4. Virginia (192)
5. Maryland (124)
6. Ireland (112)
7. Canada (88)
8. Argentina (84)
9. England (81)
10. France (55)
11. Pennsylvania (43)
12. New York (40)
13. Chile (33)
14. New Jersey (26)
15. Illinois (19)
16. Brazil (16)
17. Washington (14)
18. Oklahoma (12)
19. Arkansas, Ohio (10)
21. Louisiana (9)
22. Texas (8)
23. West Virginia (7)
24. New Zealand (6)
25. Michigan (4)
26. Germany, South Africa, Tennessee (3)
29. Arizona (2)
30. Alabama, Nebraska, New Mexico, Oregon (1)

Victory Standings for North America And Countries Outside North America In Major North American Races From 1946-2003

1. North America (5,956)
2. Ireland (139)
3. Argentina, England (117)
5. France (68)
6. Chile (41)
7. Brazil (16)
8. New Zealand (8)
9. South Africa (6)
10. Australia (4)
11. Germany (3)

Victory Standings for Breeding States and Countries In Classic Races From 1946-2003

1. Kentucky (113)
2. Florida, Virginia (17)
4. Maryland, Texas (5)
6. California, Canada (4)
8. England (3)
9. Ireland, New York (2)
11. Illinois, Pennsylvania (1)

Victory Standings for Breeding States and Countries In the Breeders' Cup From 1984-2003

1. Kentucky (86)
2. Florida (18)
3. Ireland (13)
4. England (7)
5. France (5)
6. Argentina, Canada, Maryland, Pennsylvania (3)
10. California (2)
11. Illinois, New Jersey, Oklahoma (1)

Equine Heroes for 24 States and 11 Countries

No other state or country can boast that horses bred within its borders have enjoyed the success that Kentucky-breds have. But at least 24 states and 11 foreign countries can claim that they have produced major winners during the modern era. That figure possibly could be higher if ample evidence of where all thoroughbreds foaled before 1963 were born existed. And, of course, some of those standouts possibly could bump one or more of these equine heroes from the following list, which shows the most successful entire male, gelding, and distaffer bred in each state or foreign country—if it indeed can claim a major winner in each of those categories—during the modern era according to the standings for in-the-money finishes in major North American races from 1946-2003.

Four Footed Fotos, Inc., courtesy of Hawthorne Park

Mark Guidry raised his right arm in triumph after he won the 1997 Hawthorne Gold Cup aboard Buck's Boy, the most successful Illinois-bred gelding since World War II and the only thoroughbred bred in the Land of Lincoln to capture a Breeders' Cup race (the 1998 Turf).

Country/State	Colt/Horse	Record	Gelding	Record	Filly/Mare	Record
Alabama	Tinsley	1-1-0/6			Teacher's Art	1-1-0/6
Argentina	Gentlemen	5-3-2/28	Colosal	1-1-3/9	Paseana	9-9-1/55
Arizona	Radar Ahead	2-0-1/9				
Arkansas	Nodouble	8-7-2/48				
Australia	Shannon II	2-0-1/9			Wiggle II	1-0-1/5
Brazil	Sandpit	5-5-3/33			Riboletta	5-0-0/20
California	Swaps	10-1-0/42	Ancient Title	9-6-5/53	Honeymoon	6-5-3/37
Canada	Northern Dancer	5-0-1/21	Music Merci	2-2-2/14	La Prevoyante	5-1-0/22
Chile	Cougar II	10-5-12/62			Tizna	4-3-4/26
England	Gallant Man	6-4-1/33	St. Vincent	2-0-3/11	La Zanzara	3-2-3/17
Florida	Skip Away	14-8-4/76	Roman Brother	7-6-4/44	Susan's Girl	13-5-6/68
France	Kotashaan	5-0-0/20	Or et Argent	2-1-3/13	Waya	5-2-2/26
Germany	Hitchcock	1-3-3/13				
Illinois	Western Playboy	3-1-1/15	Buck's Boy	2-1-2/12	Lady Shirl	1-0-0/4
Indiana	Fighting Step	1-0-1/5				
Ireland	Erins Isle	5-3-2/28	Admetus, Summer Solstice	1-0-0/4	Sangue	5-2-2/26
Kentucky	Round Table	19-6-4/92	Kelso	24-10-1/117	Serena's Song	11-7-2/60
Louisiana	Crest of the Wave	1-0-2/6	Shishkabob	1-0-1/5	Fit to Scout	1-3-3/13
Maryland	Cigar	11-2-1/49	Nickel Boy	2-4-3/19	Gallorette	6-6-8/44
Michigan	Bushido	2-1-1/11			Cashier's Dream	1-1-0/6
Nebraska	Dazzling Falls	1-1-0/6				
New Jersey	Zoffany	3-0-0/12			Open Mind	7-1-2/32
New Mexico	Bold Ego	1-1-1/7				
New York	Mr. Right	4-2-2/22	Funny Cide	2-1-2/12	Cupecoy's Joy	2-1-0/10
New Zealand	Daryl's Joy	2-0-0/8	Cadiz	2-0-3/11	Happyanunoit	3-4-1/21
Ohio	Harlan's Holiday	3-3-1/19	Kingpost	1-1-1/7	Safe Play	1-1-1/7
Oklahoma					Lady's Secret	10-3-2/48
Oregon	Praise Jay	1-0-0/4				
Pennsylvania	High Yield	3-2-2/18	With Anticipation	5-3-1/27	Go for Wand	6-2-0/28
South Africa	Hawaii	3-1-0/14				
Tennessee			Slew of Damascus	1-1-1/7	Fancy Naskra	1-0-0/4
Texas	Stymie	11-12-5/73			Two Altazano	1-0-0/4
Virginia	Secretariat	11-3-1/51	Fort Marcy	8-8-7/55	Shuvee	12-2-3/55
Washington	Saratoga Passage, Smokin Mel	1-0-2/6	Biggs	2-1-1/11	Rings a Chime	1-1-1/7
West Virginia	Afternoon Deelites	3-3-0/18	A Huevo	1-0-0/4	Mongo Queen	1-0-0/4

HUMAN/OWNERSHIP ENTITY & EQUINE *Indexes*

Equi-Photo, Inc. courtesy of Gulfstream Park

Few thoroughbreds in the past quarter of a century have captivated the public quite like Cigar. Gulfstream Park erected a statue in honor of the 1995 and 1996 Horse of the Year.

HUMAN/OWNERSHIP ENTITY INDEX

EQUINE INDEX

Photo courtesy of Shadwell Farm

A familiar scene during the Kentucky breeding season: Icicles hang from the trees and snow covers the ground on Shadwell Farm.

ACKNOWLEDGEMENTS

The information in this book was compiled specifically for this project and presented in a unique manner, but I obviously was not fortunate enough to attend all of the 6,461 major races held in North America from 1946-2003.

I first embraced thoroughbred racing while watching Carry Back's memorable charge in the final quarter-mile of the 1961 Kentucky Derby on a black-and-white Zenith and first wrote a newspaper article about the sport in 1974. So it's virtually impossible to pinpoint where a lot of specific information was obtained, and I began compiling the results of major races—and pertinent information about them—more than 20 years ago.

On the all-too-numerous occasions I wasn't fortunate enough to be able to copy the results off the toteboard, information about those 6,461 major races—much of it pieced together bit by bit over decades—was obtained from a variety of sources. Among those are the TV networks that have televised racing: ABC, NBC, CBS, ESPN, ESPN2, Fox, and TVG. Other helpful reference sources include Equibase, The Associated Press, *The* (Louisville) *Courier-Journal,* and too many other newspapers to begin to name; *The Thoroughbred Record* and Thoroughbred Racing Communications, which no longer exist, and *Daily Racing Form.* Media guides, particularly those of Churchill Downs, Santa Anita, the Breeders' Cup, Keeneland, Gulfstream Park, the New York Racing Association, Del Mar, Oaklawn Park, Arlington Park, Hawthorne, the Maryland Jockey Club, Thistledown, Suffolk Downs, and Monmouth Park/Meadowlands also were particularly useful. Sales catalogues from the Keeneland Association and Fasig-Tipton, editions of the *Stallion Register,* published by *The Blood-Horse,* and *The Thoroughbred Record Sire Book* also proved invaluable. But perhaps the most valuable reference materials were *The Blood-Horse, American Racing Manual,* and *Daily Racing Form Chart Books,* including many that date to 1946.

I'd also like to thank *The Martinsville* (Va.) *Bulletin* and *The Gastonia* (N.C.) *Gazette* for giving me my first tastes of writing about thoroughbred racing—and particularly *The Courier-Journal* and *The Sporting News,* which allowed me to cover the sport extensively for more than a decade.

And I can't begin to thank those who helped me learn the ropes about the sport, including Keeneland Director of Communications Jim Williams, Churchill Downs Director of Publicity Tony Terry, and the now retired Edgar Allen of Churchill Downs. Especially helpful—as he has been to so many for more than half a century—was Joe Hirsch of the *Daily Racing Form,* and I dearly wish former *Louisville Times* writers Mike Barry and Jim Bolus, former *Courier-Journal* writer Bob Adair, and Bill Leggett of *Sports Illustrated* were still around to thank for their help and guidance.

I'd also like to give a heartfelt thanks to everyone who was quoted in this book—and every other horseman or official who was kind enough to give me a few minutes, few hours, or more of their time during my tenure covering thoroughbred racing—including Smiley Adams, Tony Basile, Don Brumfield, Angel Cordero, Bud Delp, Dennis Diaz, Will Farish, Bert Firestone, Tony Foyt, Bill Gavidia, Heliodoro Gustines, Arthur B. Hancock III, Seth Hancock, Brereton C. Jones, Frank LaBoccetta, Dr. Gary Lavin, Chris McCarron, Darrel McHargue, John Nerud, Stanley Rieser, Herson Sanchez, Lee Snell, Lynn Stone, Ron Turcotte, Jacinto Vasquez, John Veitch, and Ronnie Warren.

Particular thanks for so often giving so much of their valuable time whenever I seemed to ask, which was often, goes to Wayne Lukas and Pat Day.

I also wish others, including Eddie Arcaro, Keene Daingerfield, John Galbreath, Fred W. Hooper, Gene Klein, Robert Sangster, Bill Shoemaker, Woody Stephens, Charlie Whittingham, and two of the finest gentlemen I've ever encountered—Eddie Gregson and Lucien Laurin—were still around to thank.

This book wouldn't contain nearly the information it does without the help of those who were kind enough to track down so many missing bits and pieces, including Emma Dailey of Bloodstock Research; Joe Tanenbaum, Director of Communications at Gulfstream Park; Tom Ferrall, Publicity Manager for Golden Gate Fields and Bay Meadows; John Brokopp, Director of Publicity for the National Jockey Club (Sportsman's Park); Jim Miller, Director of Media Relations at Hawthorne; Heather McColloch, Media Relations Manager at Thistledown, and Keeneland's Williams. I'd be remiss if I didn't single out four who went above and beyond the call of duty to find so much missing information: Ryan Kelly of the Maryland Jockey Club; Terry Wallace, Media Relations Director and Track Announcer at Oaklawn Park; Dan Smith, Director of Marketing and Media at the Del Mar Thoroughbred Club, and Glen Mathes, Director of Public and Media Relations for the

New York Racing Association.

This book wouldn't be nearly as appealing had it not been for the generosity of those who loaned beautiful and historic photographs and allowed their use in the book. Those incredibly helpful people include Eric Wing, Media Relations Director of the National Thoroughbred Racing Association; Rick Nichols, the Vice President and General Manager, and Joy Padgett of Shadwell Farm LLC; Josephine Abercrombie, owner of Pin Oak Stud; Amy Oberhauser of The Bell Group LLC, and David Longinotti of CJRW Outmarketing. They also include the previously mentioned Dan Smith of Del Mar, Jim Miller of Hawthorne, Jim Williams of Keeneland, Heather McColloch of Thistledown, Joe Tanenbaum of Gulfstream Park, Terry Wallace of Oaklawn Park, and Glen Mathes of the New York Racing Association, with an additional tip of the hat to two of his colleagues, Assistant Director of Communications Francis LaBelle Jr. and photographer Bob Coglianese. And I'd like to express my heartfelt thanks for their incredible generosity in providing pictures to Tony Terry of Churchill Downs and to Stuart Zanville, Santa Anita's former Director of Publicity and Public Relations, and Norma Vermeer of his staff.

I'd also like to thank the Lexington (Ky.) Public Library, the University of Kentucky's William T. Young Library and its Agricultural Information Center, and Betty Stone Flynn and Charlie Little of the Thoroughbred Club of America for graciously allowing me to use their fine facilities. And I'm truly grateful for the hospitality and help provided by General Manager Richard Vimont and assistant stallion manager Jim Kirk of Hopewell Farm—and to Hopewell's pride and joy, Skip Away.

I'm especially grateful for the untiring help given by the world's best librarians—Cathy Schenck and Phyllis Rogers of the Keeneland Library. Not only are they incredibly good at their jobs, but their amazing willingness to come to the rescue on the countless occasions I needed help has been deeply appreciated. I'd particularly like to cite Phyllis's hospitality, which made the Keeneland Library seem like a home away from home, and for her encouragement, friendship, and unending willingness to go above and beyond the call of duty to help make this book a reality.

Of course, a heartfelt thank you goes to Old Sport Publishing for making this book a reality.

Finally, and most significantly, I'd like to thank Valerie for her love, encouragement, friendship, and support.

—Richard Sowers

To purchase *The Abstract Primer of Thoroughbred Racing: Separating Myth From Fact to Identify the Genuine Gems & Dandies 1946-2003,* visit your local bookstore, or order directly from:

Old Sport Publishing Company
P.O. Box 2757
Stockbridge, Ga. 30281
770-914-2237
www.oldsportpublishing.com